presented to

by

on

Your word is a lamp to my feet
and a light for my path.
PSALM 119:105

[illegible]

new international version

new Women's DEVOTIONAL BIBLE

ZONDERVAN®

GRAND RAPIDS, MICHIGAN 49530 USA

WWW.ZONDERVAN.COM

ZONDERVAN®

Published by Zondervan
Grand Rapids, Michigan 49530, U.S.A.

Produced with the assistance of the Livingstone Corporation (www.LivingstoneCorp.com)

ISBN: 978-0-310-93613-8

Printed in the United States of America

Table of Contents

THE OLD TESTAMENT

THE NEW TESTAMENT

WELCOME TO THE *New Women's Devotional Bible!*

We've designed this special Bible with you in mind. We know you're a busy woman who needs private time with God to stay spiritually strong. You want to keep God first in your heart, but you don't always have the time you'd like. So we've included some great features to help you as you pursue your relationship with God.

Why a Devotional Bible?

So you can be enveloped in God's transforming love. So you can know him better and trust him more. So you can find out how to share what you've learned with others. Let God use this Bible to change your life.

What Is a Devotional Bible?

The devotions in this Bible are designed to help you develop a daily time with God—to help you praise him, cultivate an intimate relationship with him and become more like him. Your devotional time will affect all areas of your life: heart, mind and spirit.

But these devotionals don't just benefit you; they allow you to help those around you with the wisdom you've gleaned from God's Word. Through your time spent with God each day, you'll be better equipped to meet the needs of those you come in contact with. You'll be challenged to apply what you have been taught so that you can share with others your knowledge and understanding of the loving and powerful God you serve.

How Do I Schedule My Time With God?

You have a busy schedule, and sometimes it seems impossible for you to cultivate a regular devotional habit. But you can have a meaningful daily devotional life. Here are some tips that may help you:

- Set aside a block of time each day to spend with God. Think of this as a scheduled appointment—something that can't be postponed or rescheduled. Guard your time with God. Set your alarm clock fifteen minutes earlier in the morning or go to bed fifteen minutes later in the evening. You can have your devotional during your lunch break, while waiting to pick up your kids or before you go to bed. Decide that spending time with God is the most important thing you can do for yourself and others. And remember, God is available anytime!
- Joyfully look forward to your time with God, as you would anticipate a luncheon with a friend or a date with your husband. Come prepared with your Bible, a notebook and a pen. Pray before you begin, asking God to give you wisdom and insight into his Word. Ponder and pray about the passages you don't quite understand. Mull over concepts that are new to you or that don't fit your preconceived ideas. Throughout the day call to mind what you've read so that it takes root in your heart. Ask your pastor or a mature believer any questions you may have.
- Devotions involve a variety of spiritual disciplines. As you spend time with God, try to develop any or all of the following devotional habits:
  - Memorize relevant Scripture passages.
  - Praise God for who he is and for what he has done and is doing.
  - Listen in silence for God's voice.
  - Sing songs of praise and thanksgiving.
  - Journal your thoughts, insights and answered prayers.

How Do I Get Started?

Are you ready to get started? Within the *New Women's Devotional Bible* you'll find features designed specifically to help you develop a devotional life that's just right for you.

• The New International Version of the Bible

The Bible text itself is the most important part of any Bible. Readable and accurate, the NIV is the most read, most trusted version of the Bible.

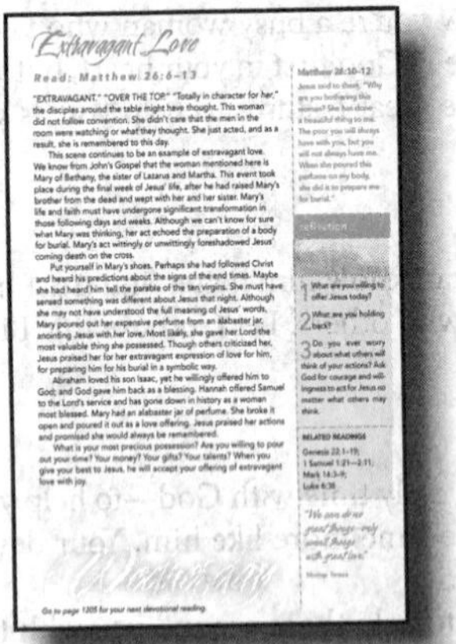

Extravagant Love

Read: Matthew 26:6–13

• 260 devotions, one for each weekday of the year

All of the daily devotions were written by godly women—women who have experienced the joys and struggles of living a Christian life in today's world. Some of them are names you'll recognize. Others will be new to you. But all of them have one thing in common: they love the Lord and want you to draw near to him in a fresh and exciting way. Each devotion also includes thought-provoking questions to help you personally apply what you've read. You'll also find links to related passages of Scripture for further study. Sometimes you'll find meaningful quotes to add depth to the day's devotion.

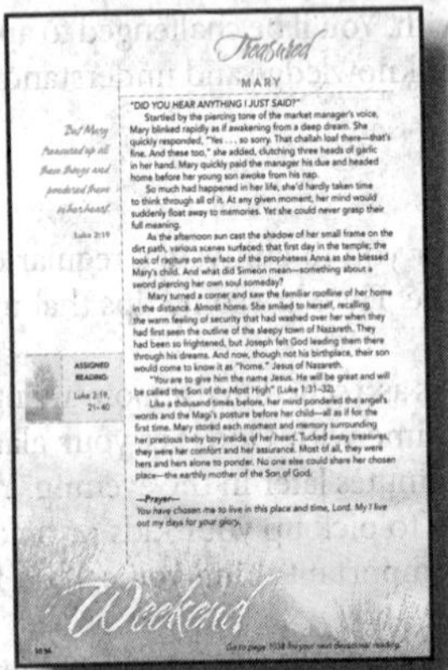

Treasured

MARY

Weekend

• 52 weekend devotions

Grounded in Scripture but incorporating some imaginative retelling, each weekend devotion profiles a woman in the Bible, offering insights into her character and helping you realize that she was a real woman who lived and breathed so many years ago. You may be surprised by the insights you'll find and the lessons you'll learn from her life. Each weekend devotion ends with a prayer of application to help you draw closer to God from your time spent in reading.

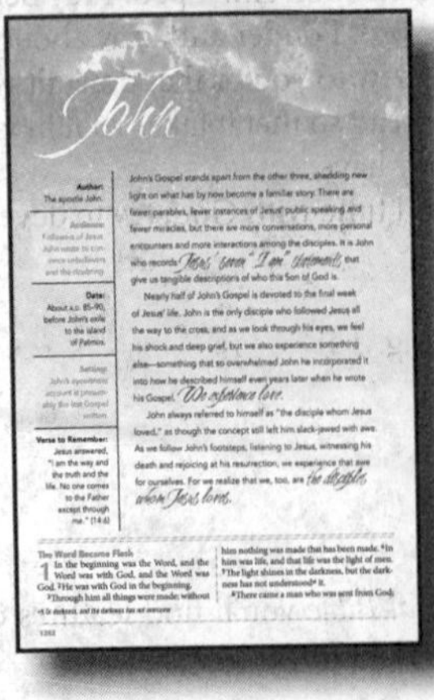

John

• Book introductions

Each book introduction gives information on the book of the Bible and its place in the canon of God's Word. A side-column section offers basic facts on each book.

• Reading plans

You'll be able to discover the devotional path that works best for you by exploring the reading plans included in the back of this book.

READING PLANS

One Year Through the Bible

DAY	PASSAGE	DAY	PASSAGE
January 1	Genesis 1—4	February 16	Numbers 22—24
January 2	Genesis 5—8	February 17	Numbers 25—26
January 3	Genesis 9—12	February 18	Numbers 27—29
January 4	Genesis 13—17	February 19	Numbers 30—32
January 5	Genesis 18—20	February 20	Numbers 33—36
January 6	Genesis 21—23	February 21	Deuteronomy 1—2
January 7	Genesis 24—25	February 22	Deuteronomy 3—4
January 8	Genesis 26—28	February 23	Deuteronomy 5—8
January 9	Genesis 29—31	February 24	Deuteronomy 9—11
January 10	Genesis 32—35	February 25	Deuteronomy 12—15
January 11	Genesis 36—38	February 26	Deuteronomy 16—19
January 12	Genesis 39—41	February 27	Deuteronomy 20—23
January 13	Genesis 42—43	February 28	Deuteronomy 24—27
January 14	Genesis 44—46	March 1	Deuteronomy 28—29
January 15	Genesis 47—50	March 2	Deuteronomy 30—32
January 16	Exodus 1—4	March 3	Deuteronomy 33—34
January 17	Exodus 5—7	March 4	Joshua 1—4
January 18	Exodus 8—10	March 5	Joshua 5—7
January 19	Exodus 11—13	March 6	Joshua 8—10
January 20	Exodus 14—16	March 7	Joshua 11—13
January 21	Exodus 17—20	March 8	Joshua 14—17
January 22	Exodus 21—23	March 9	Joshua 18—20
January 23	Exodus 24—27	March 10	Joshua 21—22
January 24	Exodus 28—30	March 11	Joshua 23—24
January 25	Exodus 31—34	March 12	Judges 1—3
January 26	Exodus 35—37	March 13	Judges 4—5
January 27	Exodus 38—40	March 14	Judges 6—8
January 28	Leviticus 1—4	March 15	Judges 9—10
January 29	Leviticus 5—7	March 16	Judges 11—13
January 30	Leviticus 8—10	March 17	Judges 14—16
January 31	Leviticus 11—13	March 18	Judges 17—19
February 1	Leviticus 14—15	March 19	Judges 20—21
February 2	Leviticus 16—18	March 20	Ruth 1—4
February 3	Leviticus 19—21	March 21	1 Samuel 1—3
February 4	Leviticus 22—23	March 22	1 Samuel 4—7
February 5	Leviticus 24—25	March 23	1 Samuel 8—12
February 6	Leviticus 26—27	March 24	1 Samuel 13—14
February 7	Numbers 1—2	March 25	1 Samuel 15—16
February 8	Numbers 3—4	March 26	1 Samuel 17—18
February 9	Numbers 5—6	March 27	1 Samuel 19—21
February 10	Numbers 7	March 28	1 Samuel 22—24
February 11	Numbers 8—10	March 29	1 Samuel 25—27
February 12	Numbers 11—13	March 30	1 Samuel 28—31
February 13	Numbers 14—15	March 31	2 Samuel 1—3
February 14	Numbers 16—18	April 1	2 Samuel 4—7
February 15	Numbers 19—21	April 2	2 Samuel 8—11

• Subject index

You can look up a wide variety of subjects in the index in the back of this Bible and can then turn to the listed page number for a devotion that fits your need.

Subject Index

There's no better time than *now* to devote yourself to God and his Word. Start to build a strong and intimate relationship with the One who created you and loved you before the foundation of the earth by beginning a devotional relationship with God. May God reveal himself to you in profound ways as you open the door to his Word and his heart!

A Library in Itself

The Bible is comprised of 66 individual books . . . written by different authors . . . with different writing styles . . . in different eras of history . . . with different purposes. What separates the Bible from other anthologies is the fact that God himself guided the writing of Scripture. The result is one amazingly cohesive book made up of disparate parts. Here's a quick look at the different genres you'll find as you explore the books of Scripture.

OLD TESTAMENT

Books of the Law

Genesis through Deuteronomy

The first five books of the Bible (the Pentateuch) detail God's interaction with his human creation. They offer vivid stories of God making himself known to individuals. Specifically, these books catalog God's dealings with the Israelites, his chosen people. They give us snapshots of his love, mercy, justice and holiness. We see how he rewards faithfulness and punishes disobedience. In these books, God establishes his rules for living and how he expects to govern the lives of his people.

Books of History

Joshua through Esther

These books record the history of the Israelites, including stories of women such as Rahab, Delilah, Bathsheba and Queen Esther. This time period establishes a familiar pattern in Israel's relationship with God: God instructs his people and desires to reward them with blessings and fellowship; they reject his instructions and disobey him; God reprimands the disobedient; they recognize their error and cry out in repentance; God forgives them and restores them to fellowship. This pattern of rejection-reprimand-repentance-restoration is repeated throughout the books of history.

Books of Poetry

Job through Song of Songs

These books record the thoughts, personal struggles and hard-earned wisdom of God's people. They address timeless topics such as why people suffer, what kind of worship is pleasing to God and how God's wisdom can be applied to our lives today.

Books of the Prophets

Isaiah through Malachi

The books of prophecy are God's way of speaking to his people, making his intentions and plans known to them, as well as giving them directives for their attitudes and behaviors. Not only do the prophets offer warnings to the people of Israel, they also point to the long-awaited Messiah, the One who would ultimately restore the relationship between God and humans and will come again to establish his eternal kingdom.

NEW TESTAMENT

Books of History

Matthew through Acts

The first four books of the New Testament—the Gospels—present four different yet complementary accounts of the life of Christ.

Before Jesus returned to heaven, he instructed his followers to spread his Good News throughout the world. The book of Acts details the efforts of early believers—including many women—to do just that. Here you'll see the beginning of the church, the body of Christ on earth.

Letters

Romans through Revelation

The Epistles, which were written to the early churches and church leaders, encouraged believers and addressed problems they faced. Through them, the Lord outlined the basic doctrines of faith and the responsibilities of believers. Since women were a vital part of the early church, you can see the impact they had in the churches and how their lives can inspire and encourage you today.

Preface to the New International Version

THE NEW INTERNATIONAL VERSION is a completely new translation of the Holy Bible made by over a hundred scholars working directly from the best available Hebrew, Aramaic and Greek texts. It had its beginning in 1965 when, after several years of exploratory study by committees from the Christian Reformed Church and the National Association of Evangelicals, a group of scholars met at Palos Heights, Illinois, and concurred in the need for a new translation of the Bible in contemporary English. This group, though not made up of official church representatives, was transdenominational. Its conclusion was endorsed by a large number of leaders from many denominations who met in Chicago in 1966.

Responsibility for the new version was delegated by the Palos Heights group to a self-governing body of fifteen, the Committee on Bible Translation, composed for the most part of biblical scholars from colleges, universities and seminaries. In 1967 the New York Bible Society (now the International Bible Society) generously undertook the financial sponsorship of the project—a sponsorship that made it possible to enlist the help of many distinguished scholars. The fact that participants from the United States, Great Britain, Canada, Australia and New Zealand worked together gave the project its international scope. That they were from many denominations—including Anglican, Assemblies of God, Baptist, Brethren, Christian Reformed, Church of Christ, Evangelical Free, Lutheran, Mennonite, Methodist, Nazarene, Presbyterian, Wesleyan and other churches—helped to safeguard the translation from sectarian bias.

How it was made helps to give the New International Version its distinctiveness. The translation of each book was assigned to a team of scholars. Next, one of the Intermediate Editorial Committees revised the initial translation, with constant reference to the Hebrew, Aramaic or Greek. Their work then went to one of the General Editorial Committees, which checked it in detail and made another thorough revision. This revision in turn was carefully reviewed by the Committee on Bible Translation, which made further changes and then released the final version for publication. In this way the entire Bible underwent three revisions, during each of which the translation was examined for its faithfulness to the original languages and for its English style.

All this involved many thousands of hours of research and discussion regarding the meaning of the texts and the precise way of putting them into English. It may well be that no other translation has been made by a more thorough process of review and revision from committee to committee than this one.

From the beginning of the project, the Committee on Bible Translation held to certain goals for the New International Version: that it would be an accurate translation and one that would have clarity and literary quality and so prove suitable for public and private reading, teaching, preaching, memorizing and liturgical use. The Committee also sought to preserve some measure of continuity with the long tradition of translating the Scriptures into English.

In working toward these goals, the translators were united in their commitment to the authority and infallibility of the Bible as God's Word in written form. They believe that it contains the divine answer to the deepest needs of humanity, that it sheds unique light on our path in a dark world, and that it sets forth the way to our eternal well-being.

The first concern of the translators has been the accuracy of the translation and its fidelity to the thought of the biblical writers. They have weighed the significance of the lexical and grammatical details of the Hebrew, Aramaic and Greek texts. At the same time, they have striven for more than a word-for-word translation. Because thought patterns and syntax differ from language to language, faithful communication of the meaning of the writers of the Bible demands frequent modifications in sentence structure and constant regard for the contextual meanings of words.

A sensitive feeling for style does not always accompany scholarship. Accordingly the Committee on Bible Translation submitted the developing version to a number of stylistic consultants. Two of them read every book of both Old and New Testaments twice—once before and once after the last major revision—and made invaluable suggestions. Samples of the translation were tested for clarity and ease of reading by various kinds of people—young and old, highly educated and less well educated, ministers and laymen.

Concern for clear and natural English—that the New International Version should be idiomatic but not idiosyncratic, contemporary but not dated—motivated the translators and consultants. At the same time, they tried to reflect the differing styles of the biblical writers. In view of the international use of English, the translators sought to avoid obvious Americanisms on the one hand and obvious Anglicisms on the other. A British edition reflects the comparatively few differences of significant idiom and of spelling.

As for the traditional pronouns "thou," "thee" and "thine" in reference to the Deity, the translators judged that to use these archaisms (along with the old verb forms such as "doest," wouldest" and "hadst") would violate accuracy in translation. Neither Hebrew, Aramaic nor Greek uses special pronouns for the persons of the Godhead. A present-day translation is not enhanced by forms that in the time of the King James Version were used in everyday speech, whether referring to God or man.

For the Old Testament the standard Hebrew text, the Masoretic Text as published in the latest editions of Biblia Hebraica, was used throughout. The Dead Sea Scrolls contain material bearing on an earlier stage of the Hebrew text. They were consulted, as were the Samaritan Pentateuch and the ancient scribal traditions relating to textual changes. Sometimes a variant Hebrew reading in the margin of the Masoretic Text was followed instead of the text itself. Such instances, being variants within the Masoretic tradition, are not specified by footnotes. In rare cases, words in the consonantal text were divided differently from the way they appear in the Masoretic Text. Footnotes indicate this. The translators also consulted the more important early versions—the Septuagint; Aquila, Symmachus and Theodotion; the Vulgate; the Syriac Peshitta; the Targums; and for the Psalms the Juxta Hebraica of Jerome. Readings from these versions were occasionally followed where the Masoretic Text seemed doubtful and where accepted principles of textual criticism showed that one or more of these textual witnesses appeared to provide the correct reading. Such instances are footnoted. Sometimes vowel letters and vowel signs did not, in the judgment of the translators, represent the correct vowels for the original consonantal text. Accordingly some words were read with a different set of vowels. These instances are usually not indicated by footnotes.

The Greek text used in translating the New Testament was an eclectic one. No other piece of ancient literature has such an abundance of manuscript witnesses as does the New Testament. Where existing manuscripts differ, the translators made their choice of readings according to accepted principles of New Testament textual criticism. Footnotes call attention to places where there was uncertainty about what the original text was. The best current printed texts of the Greek New Testament were used.

There is a sense in which the work of translation is never wholly finished. This applies to all great literature and uniquely so to the Bible. In 1973 the New Testament in the New International Version was published. Since then, suggestions for corrections and revisions have been received from various sources. The Committee on Bible Translation carefully considered the suggestions and adopted a number of them. These were incorporated in the first printing of the entire Bible in 1978. Additional revisions were made by the Committee on Bible Translation in 1983 and appear in printings after that date.

As in other ancient documents, the precise meaning of the biblical texts is sometimes uncertain. This is more often the case with the Hebrew and Aramaic texts than with the Greek text. Although archaeological and linguistic discoveries in this century aid in understanding difficult passages, some uncertainties remain. The more significant of these have been called to the reader's attention in the footnotes.

In regard to the divine name YHWH, commonly referred to as the Tetragrammaton, the translators adopted the device used in most English versions of rendering that name as "LORD" in capital letters to distinguish it from Adonai, another Hebrew word rendered "Lord," for which small letters are used. Wherever the two names stand together in the Old Testament as a compound name of God, they are rendered "Sovereign LORD."

Because for most readers today the phrases "the LORD of hosts" and "God of hosts" have little meaning, this version renders them "the LORD Almighty" and "God Almighty." These renderings convey the sense of the Hebrew, namely, "he who is sovereign over all the 'hosts' (powers) in heaven and on earth, especially over the 'hosts' (armies) of Israel." For readers unacquainted with Hebrew this does not make clear the distinction between Sabaoth ("hosts" or "Almighty") and Shaddai (which can also be translated "Almighty"), but the latter occurs infrequently and is always footnoted. When Adonai and YHWH Sabaoth occur together, they are rendered "the Lord, the LORD Almighty."

As for other proper nouns, the familiar spellings of the King James Version are generally retained. Names traditionally spelled with "ch," except where it is final, are usually spelled in this translation with "k" or "c," since the biblical languages do not have the sound that "ch" frequently indicates in English—for example, in chant. For well-known names such as Zechariah, however, the traditional spelling has been retained. Variation in the spelling of names in the original languages has usually not been indicated. Where a person or place has two or more different names in the Hebrew, Aramaic or Greek texts, the more familiar one has generally been used, with footnotes where needed.

To achieve clarity the translators sometimes supplied words not in the original texts but required by the context. If there was uncertainty about such material, it is enclosed in brackets. Also for the sake of clarity or style, nouns, including some proper nouns, are sometimes substituted for pronouns, and vice versa. And though the Hebrew writers often shifted back and forth between first, second and third personal pronouns without change of antecedent, this translation often makes them uniform, in accordance with English style and without the use of footnotes.

Poetical passages are printed as poetry, that is, with indentation of lines and with separate stanzas. These are generally designed to reflect the structure of Hebrew poetry. This poetry is normally characterized by parallelism in balanced lines. Most of the poetry in the Bible is in the Old Testament, and scholars differ regarding the scansion of Hebrew lines. The translators determined the stanza divisions for the most part by analysis of the subject matter. The stanzas therefore serve as poetic paragraphs.

As an aid to the reader, italicized sectional headings are inserted in most of the books. They are not to be regarded as part of the NIV text, are not for oral reading, and are not intended to dictate the interpretation of the sections they head.

The footnotes in this version are of several kinds, most of which need no explanation. Those giving alternative translations begin with "Or" and generally introduce the alternative with the last word preceding it in the text, except when it is a single-word alternative; in poetry quoted in a footnote a slant mark indicates a line division. Footnotes introduced by "Or" do not have uniform significance. In some cases two possible translations were considered to have about equal validity. In other cases, though the translators were convinced that the translation in the text was correct, they judged that another interpretation was possible and of sufficient importance to be represented in a footnote.

In the New Testament, footnotes that refer to uncertainty regarding the original text are introduced by "Some manuscripts" or similar expressions. In the Old Testament, evidence for the reading chosen is given first and evidence for the alternative is added after a semicolon (for example: Septuagint; Hebrew father). In such notes the term "Hebrew" refers to the Masoretic Text.

It should be noted that minerals, flora and fauna, architectural details, articles of clothing and jewelry, musical instruments and other articles cannot always be identified with precision. Also measures of capacity in the biblical period are particularly uncertain (see the table of weights and measures following the text).

Like all translations of the Bible, made as they are by imperfect man, this one undoubtedly falls short of its goals. Yet we are grateful to God for the extent to which he has enabled us to realize these goals and for the strength he has given us and our colleagues to complete our task. We offer this version of the Bible to him in whose name and for whose glory it has been made. We pray that it will lead many into a better understanding of the Holy Scriptures and a fuller knowledge of Jesus Christ the incarnate Word, of whom the Scriptures so faithfully testify.

The Committee on Bible Translation
June 1978
(Revised August 1983)

Names of the translators and editors may be secured
from the International Bible Society,
translation sponsors of the New International Version,
1820 Jet Stream Drive, Colorado Springs, CO 80921-3696 U.S.A

The Old Testament

Genesis

Every story has *a beginning*, a genesis. The beginning of God's story of his interactions with humanity is found in the very first words of the Bible. In the beginning God created. From the start God was present. He was at work.

However, in the freshness of *a new world* where the first man and woman walked and talked with God, sin slithered in, marring creation forever. But the God who hung every star in place and laid every grain of sand upon the shore had, from the beginning, a plan. The whole of Scripture, and indeed the whole of history, is unveiled within the seeds of Genesis. It will be many years before we see the fruit of those seeds, but they are not years of dormancy. Throughout the world and within individual lives, *God is actively working* to redeem his creation. In Genesis we see him form covenants, bestow blessings, test faithfulness and turn evil intentions into a greater good—all for the purpose of one day *redeeming the people* he created in his image. It's a work that will continue until the end of time, but the beginnings for all of it are found in Genesis.

Author:
Moses.

Audience:
The people of Israel.

Date:
Between 1446 and 1406 B.C.

Setting:
The area called the Middle East today.

Verse to Remember:
In the beginning God . . . (1:1)

The Beginning

1 In the beginning God created the heavens and the earth. 2Now the earth was[a]
formless and empty, darkness was over the
surface of the deep, and the Spirit of God
was hovering over the waters.

3And God said, "Let there be light," and there
was light. 4God saw that the light was
good, and he separated the light from the
darkness. 5God called the light "day," and
the darkness he called "night." And there
was evening, and there was morning—the
first day.

6And God said, "Let there be an expanse between the waters to separate water from
water." 7So God made the expanse and

[a]2 Or possibly *became*

separated the water under the expanse
from the water above it. And it was so.
8 God called the expanse "sky." And there
was evening, and there was morning—the
second day.
9 And God said, "Let the water under the
sky be gathered to one place, and let dry
ground appear." And it was so. 10 God
called the dry ground "land," and the gathered waters he called "seas." And God saw
that it was good.
11 Then God said, "Let the land produce
vegetation: seed-bearing plants and trees
on the land that bear fruit with seed in it, according to their various kinds." And it was
so. 12 The land produced vegetation: plants
bearing seed according to their kinds and
trees bearing fruit with seed in it according to their kinds. And God saw that it was
good. 13 And there was evening, and there
was morning—the third day.
14 And God said, "Let there be lights in the expanse of the sky to separate the day from
the night, and let them serve as signs to
mark seasons and days and years, 15 and
let them be lights in the expanse of the sky
to give light on the earth." And it was so.
16 God made two great lights—the greater
light to govern the day and the lesser light
to govern the night. He
also made the stars. 17 God
set them in the expanse of
the sky to give light on the
earth, 18 to govern the day
and the night, and to separate light from darkness.
And God saw that it was
good. 19 And there was evening, and there was morn-
ing—the fourth day.
20 And God said, "Let the water
teem with living creatures,
and let birds fly above the
earth across the expanse
of the sky." 21 So God created the great
creatures of the sea and every living and
moving thing with which the water teems,
according to their kinds, and every winged
bird according to its kind. And God saw
that it was good. 22 God blessed them and
said, "Be fruitful and increase in number
and fill the water in the seas, and let the
birds increase on the earth." 23 And there
was evening, and there was morning—the
fifth day.
24 And God said, "Let the land produce living creatures according to their kinds:
livestock, creatures that move along the
ground, and wild animals, each according
to its kind." And it was so. 25 God made the
wild animals according to their kinds, the
livestock according to their kinds, and all
the creatures that move along the ground
according to their kinds. And God saw that
it was good.
26 Then God said, "Let us make man in
our image, in our likeness, and let them
rule over the fish of the sea and the birds
of the air, over the livestock, over all the
earth,[a] and over all the creatures that move
along the ground."

27 So God created man in his own image,
in the image of God he created him;
male and female he created them.

28 God blessed them and said to them,
"Be fruitful and increase in number; fill
the earth and subdue it. Rule over the fish
of the sea and the birds of
the air and over every living creature that moves on
the ground."
29 Then God said, "I
give you every seed-bear-
ing plant on the face of
the whole earth and every
tree that has fruit with seed
in it. They will be yours
for food. 30 And to all the
beasts of the earth and all
the birds of the air and
all the creatures that move
on the ground—everything
that has the breath of life in it—I give every
green plant for food." And it was so.
31 God saw all that he had made, and it
was very good. And there was evening, and
there was morning—the sixth day.

Genesis 1:27

God Is Our Creator

So God created man
in his own image,
in the image of God
he created him;
male and female he
created them.

[a] 26 Hebrew; Syriac *all the wild animals*

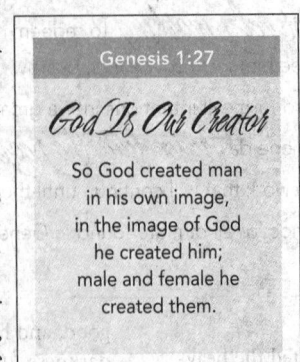

God's Image Bearers

Read: Genesis 1:27–31

IMAGINE THE SCENE. Holding her hair back with one hand, the woman kneels and leans forward to drink from the clear pool of water. As her cupped hand reaches for the clear liquid, she draws back, startled. Who is the long-haired stranger staring back at her?

Perhaps even since the time Eve first caught sight of her reflection in the Garden of Eden, women have dealt with the question of image. Polls consistently reveal that the majority of us are dissatisfied with our appearance. Confronted with a barrage of airbrushed photos of supermodels and celebrities adorning magazine covers, the average woman thinks she is too short, too fat, too unattractive, too imperfect. How can we ever measure up with the media's standards of perfection?

The first chapter of the Bible supplies the answer. We were created in the image of one paradigm of perfection: our Creator. Our height, weight and skin color may indicate our human origins, but our soul and spirit reflect our Sovereign God.

When a child is born, it's not unusual for someone to claim she's the very "image" of a relative. But what does it mean to be created in the image of our heavenly Father? An image is a likeness or resemblance—a reflection as seen in a mirror. Scripture teaches that Jesus Christ is the "image of the invisible God" (Colossians 1:15). As we grow in faith, we who believe are gradually "being transformed into [Christ's] likeness" (2 Corinthians 3:18). When we become like Jesus, we begin to look more and more like our heavenly Father.

God created us to convey the distinctive imprint of his divine nature to a world often blinded to his existence. Even our differences reflect the One who delighted in creating a world of dazzling diversity: peculiar penguins and majestic eagles; towering redwoods and dwarf pines; blondes, brunettes and redheads . . . every person created with the individual imprint of the Creator's hand to bear his image. So the next time you pass by a mirror, pause a moment to gaze in wonder at the designer original whom God loves so dearly—you!

Genesis 1:27
So God created man in his own image, in the image of God he created him; male and female he created them.

reflection

1 How do you see God's image reflected in the lives of others you admire?

2 What factors from the past have damaged your sense of self-worth?

3 Think of three ways in which you can beautifully reflect the characteristics of your Creator by imitating Christ.

RELATED READINGS
Psalm 139:14;
2 Corinthians 3:18;
Colossians 1:15;
Revelation 7:9

"A handful of the earth to make God's image!"
Elizabeth Barrett Browning

Monday

Go to page 9 for your next devotional reading.

2 Thus the heavens and the earth were completed in all their vast array.

[2]By the seventh day God had finished the work he had been doing; so on the seventh day he rested[a] from all his work. [3]And God blessed the seventh day and made it holy, because on it he rested from all the work of creating that he had done.

> **Genesis 2:24**
>
> ***God Ordains Marriage***
>
> For this reason a man will leave his father and mother and be united to his wife, and they will become one flesh.

Adam and Eve

[4]This is the account of the heavens and the earth when they were created.

When the LORD God made the earth and the heavens—[5]and no shrub of the field had yet appeared on the earth[b] and no plant of the field had yet sprung up, for the LORD God had not sent rain on the earth[b] and there was no man to work the ground, [6]but streams[c] came up from the earth and watered the whole surface of the ground— [7]the LORD God formed the man[d] from the dust of the ground and breathed into his nostrils the breath of life, and the man became a living being.

[8]Now the LORD God had planted a garden in the east, in Eden; and there he put the man he had formed. [9]And the LORD God made all kinds of trees grow out of the ground—trees that were pleasing to the eye and good for food. In the middle of the garden were the tree of life and the tree of the knowledge of good and evil.

[10]A river watering the garden flowed from Eden; from there it was separated into four headwaters. [11]The name of the first is the Pishon; it winds through the entire land of Havilah, where there is gold. [12](The gold of that land is good; aromatic resin[e] and onyx are also there.) [13]The name of the second river is the Gihon; it winds through the entire land of Cush.[f] [14]The name of the third river is the Tigris; it runs along the east side of Asshur. And the fourth river is the Euphrates.

[15]The LORD God took the man and put him in the Garden of Eden to work it and take care of it. [16]And the LORD God commanded the man, "You are free to eat from any tree in the garden; [17]but you must not eat from the tree of the knowledge of good and evil, for when you eat of it you will surely die."

[18]The LORD God said, "It is not good for the man to be alone. I will make a helper suitable for him."

[19]Now the LORD God had formed out of the ground all the beasts of the field and all the birds of the air. He brought them to the man to see what he would name them; and whatever the man called each living creature, that was its name. [20]So the man gave names to all the livestock, the birds of the air and all the beasts of the field.

But for Adam[g] no suitable helper was found. [21]So the LORD God caused the man to fall into a deep sleep; and while he was sleeping, he took one of the man's ribs[h] and closed up the place with flesh. [22]Then the LORD God made a woman from the rib[i] he had taken out of the man, and he brought her to the man.

[23]The man said,

"This is now bone of my bones
  and flesh of my flesh;
she shall be called 'woman,[j]'
  for she was taken out of man."

[24]For this reason a man will leave his father and mother and be united to his wife, and they will become one flesh.

[25]The man and his wife were both naked, and they felt no shame.

The Fall of Man

3 Now the serpent was more crafty than any of the wild animals the LORD God had made. He said to the woman, "Did God really say, 'You must not eat from any tree in the garden'?"

[a]2 Or *ceased*; also in verse 3 [b]5 Or *land*; also in verse 6 [c]6 Or *mist* [d]7 The Hebrew for *man (adam)* sounds like and may be related to the Hebrew for *ground (adamah)*; it is also the name *Adam* (see Gen. 2:20). [e]12 Or *good; pearls* [f]13 Possibly southeast Mesopotamia [g]20 Or *the man* [h]21 Or *took part of the man's side* [i]22 Or *part* [j]23 The Hebrew for *woman* sounds like the Hebrew for *man.*

2The woman said to the serpent, "We may
eat fruit from the trees in the garden, 3but God
did say, 'You must not eat fruit from the tree
that is in the middle of the garden, and you
must not touch it, or you will die.'"
4"You will not surely die," the serpent said to
the woman. 5"For God knows that when you
eat of it your eyes will be opened, and you will
be like God, knowing good and evil."
6When the woman saw that the fruit of the
tree was good for food and pleasing to the eye,
and also desirable for gaining wisdom, she
took some and ate it. She also gave some to
her husband, who was with her, and he ate it.
7Then the eyes of both of them were opened,
and they realized they were naked; so they
sewed fig leaves together and made coverings
for themselves.
8Then the man and his wife heard the sound
of the LORD God as he was walking in the garden in the cool of the day, and they hid from
the LORD God among the trees of the garden.
9But the LORD God called to the man, "Where
are you?"
10He answered, "I heard you in the garden, and I was afraid because I was naked; so
I hid."
11And he said, "Who told you that you were
naked? Have you eaten from
the tree that I commanded you
not to eat from?"
12The man said, "The
woman you put here with
me—she gave me some fruit
from the tree, and I ate it."
13Then the LORD God said
to the woman, "What is this
you have done?"
The woman said, "The ser-
pent deceived me, and I ate."
14So the LORD God said to
the serpent, "Because you have
done this,

"Cursed are you above all
the livestock
and all the wild animals!
You will crawl on your belly
and you will eat dust
all the days of your life.
15And I will put enmity
between you and the woman,
and between your offspring[a] and hers;
he will crush[b] your head,
and you will strike his heel."

16To the woman he said,

"I will greatly increase your pains in
childbearing;
with pain you will give birth to children.
Your desire will be for your husband,
and he will rule over you."

17To Adam he said, "Because you listened to
your wife and ate from the tree about which I
commanded you, 'You must not eat of it,'

"Cursed is the ground because of you;
through painful toil you will eat of it
all the days of your life.
18It will produce thorns and thistles for you,
and you will eat the plants of the field.
19By the sweat of your brow
you will eat your food
until you return to the ground,
since from it you were taken;
for dust you are
and to dust you will return."

20Adam[c] named his wife
Eve,[d] because she would become the mother of all the living.
21The LORD God made gar-
ments of skin for Adam and his
wife and clothed them. 22And
the LORD God said, "The man
has now become like one of
us, knowing good and evil.
He must not be allowed to
reach out his hand and take
also from the tree of life and
eat, and live forever." 23So the
LORD God banished him from
the Garden of Eden to work
the ground from which he had
been taken. 24After he drove
the man out, he placed on the east side[e] of the
Garden of Eden cherubim and a flaming sword

Genesis 3:15

God Overcomes Satan

"And I will put enmity
between you and
the woman,
and between your
offspring and hers;
he will crush your head,
and you will strike
his heel."

[a]15 Or *seed* [b]15 Or *strike* [c]20 Or *The man* [d]20 *Eve* probably means *living.* [e]24 Or *placed in front*

flashing back and forth to guard the way to the
tree of life.

Cain and Abel

4 Adam[a] lay with his wife Eve, and she became pregnant and gave birth to Cain.[b]
She said, "With the help of the LORD I have
brought forth[c] a man." 2Later she gave birth to
his brother Abel.

Now Abel kept flocks, and Cain worked
the soil. 3In the course of time Cain brought
some of the fruits of the soil as an offering to
the LORD. 4But Abel brought fat portions from
some of the firstborn of his flock. The LORD
looked with favor on Abel and his offering,
5but on Cain and his offering he did not look
with favor. So Cain was very angry, and his face
was downcast.

6Then the LORD said to Cain, "Why are you
angry? Why is your face downcast? 7If you do
what is right, will you not be accepted? But if
you do not do what is right, sin is crouching at
your door; it desires to have you, but you must
master it."

8Now Cain said to his brother Abel, "Let's
go out to the field."[d] And while they were in
the field, Cain attacked his brother Abel and
killed him.

9Then the LORD said to Cain, "Where is
your brother Abel?"

"I don't know," he replied. "Am I my brother's keeper?"

10The LORD said, "What have you done?
Listen! Your brother's blood cries out to me
from the ground. 11Now you are under a curse
and driven from the ground, which opened its
mouth to receive your brother's blood from
your hand. 12When you work the ground, it
will no longer yield its crops for you. You will
be a restless wanderer on the earth."

13Cain said to the LORD, "My punishment is
more than I can bear. 14Today you are driving
me from the land, and I will be hidden from
your presence; I will be a restless wanderer on
the earth, and whoever finds me will kill me."

15But the LORD said to him, "Not so[e]; if anyone kills Cain, he will suffer vengeance seven
times over." Then the LORD put a mark on Cain
so that no one who found him would kill him.
16So Cain went out from the LORD's presence
and lived in the land of Nod,[f] east of Eden.

17Cain lay with his wife, and she became
pregnant and gave birth to Enoch. Cain was
then building a city, and he named it after his
son Enoch. 18To Enoch was born Irad, and
Irad was the father of Mehujael, and Mehujael
was the father of Methushael, and Methushael
was the father of Lamech.

19Lamech married two women, one named
Adah and the other Zillah. 20Adah gave birth
to Jabal; he was the father of those who live in
tents and raise livestock. 21His brother's name
was Jubal; he was the father of all who play
the harp and flute. 22Zillah also had a son, Tubal-Cain, who forged all kinds of tools out of[g]
bronze and iron. Tubal-Cain's sister was Naamah.

23Lamech said to his wives,

"Adah and Zillah, listen to me;
  wives of Lamech, hear my words.
I have killed[h] a man for wounding me,
  a young man for injuring me.
24If Cain is avenged seven times,
  then Lamech seventy-seven times."

25Adam lay with his wife again, and she gave
birth to a son and named him Seth,[i] saying,
"God has granted me another child in place of
Abel, since Cain killed him." 26Seth also had a
son, and he named him Enosh.

At that time men began to call on[j] the name
of the LORD.

From Adam to Noah

5 This is the written account of Adam's
line.

When God created man, he made him in the
likeness of God. 2He created them male and female and blessed them. And when they were
created, he called them "man.[k]"

3When Adam had lived 130 years, he had
a son in his own likeness, in his own image;
and he named him Seth. 4After Seth was born,

[a]1 Or *The man* [b]1 *Cain* sounds like the Hebrew for *brought forth* or *acquired.* [c]1 Or *have acquired* [d]8 Samaritan Pentateuch, Septuagint, Vulgate and Syriac; Masoretic Text does not have *"Let's go out to the field."* [e]15 Septuagint, Vulgate and Syriac; Hebrew *Very well* [f]16 *Nod* means *wandering* (see verses 12 and 14). [g]22 Or *who instructed all who work in* [h]23 Or *I will kill* [i]25 *Seth* probably means *granted.* [j]26 Or *to proclaim* [k]2 Hebrew *adam*

Adam lived 800 years and had other sons and
daughters. 5Altogether, Adam lived 930 years,
and then he died.
6When Seth had lived 105 years, he became
the father[a] of Enosh. 7And after he became the
father of Enosh, Seth lived 807 years and had
other sons and daughters. 8Altogether, Seth
lived 912 years, and then he died.
9When Enosh had lived 90 years, he became
the father of Kenan. 10And after he became the
father of Kenan, Enosh lived
815 years and had other sons
and daughters. 11Altogether,
Enosh lived 905 years, and
then he died.
12When Kenan had lived
70 years, he became the father
of Mahalalel. 13And after he
became the father of Mahalalel, Kenan lived 840 years and
had other sons and daughters.
14Altogether, Kenan lived 910
years, and then he died.
15When Mahalalel had
lived 65 years, he became the
father of Jared. 16And after
he became the father of Jared, Mahalalel lived
830 years and had other sons and daughters.
17Altogether, Mahalalel lived 895 years, and
then he died.
18When Jared had lived 162 years, he became
the father of Enoch. 19And after he became the
father of Enoch, Jared lived 800 years and had
other sons and daughters. 20Altogether, Jared
lived 962 years, and then he died.
21When Enoch had lived 65 years, he became the father of Methuselah. 22And after
he became the father of Methuselah, Enoch
walked with God 300 years and had other sons
and daughters. 23Altogether, Enoch lived 365
years. 24Enoch walked with God; then he was
no more, because God took him away.
25When Methuselah had lived 187 years, he
became the father of Lamech. 26And after he
became the father of Lamech, Methuselah lived
782 years and had other sons and daughters.
27Altogether, Methuselah lived 969 years, and
then he died.
28When Lamech had lived 182 years, he had
a son. 29He named him Noah[b] and said, "He
will comfort us in the labor and painful toil of
our hands caused by the ground the LORD has
cursed." 30After Noah was born, Lamech lived
595 years and had other sons and daughters.
31Altogether, Lamech lived 777 years, and then
he died.
32After Noah was 500 years old, he became
the father of Shem, Ham and Japheth.

> **Genesis 5:24**
>
> *God Walks With His People*
>
> Enoch walked with God; then he was no more, because God took him away.

The Flood

6 When men began to in-
crease in number on the
earth and daughters were born
to them, 2the sons of God saw
that the daughters of men were
beautiful, and they married any
of them they chose. 3Then the
LORD said, "My Spirit will not
contend with[c] man forever, for
he is mortal[d]; his days will be a
hundred and twenty years."
4The Nephilim were on the
earth in those days—and also
afterward—when the sons of
God went to the daughters of men and had
children by them. They were the heroes of old,
men of renown.
5The LORD saw how great man's wickedness
on the earth had become, and that every inclination of the thoughts of his heart was only
evil all the time. 6The LORD was grieved that
he had made man on the earth, and his heart
was filled with pain. 7So the LORD said, "I will
wipe mankind, whom I have created, from the
face of the earth—men and animals, and creatures that move along the ground, and birds
of the air—for I am grieved that I have made
them." 8But Noah found favor in the eyes of
the LORD.

9This is the account of Noah.

Noah was a righteous man, blameless
among the people of his time, and he walked
with God. 10Noah had three sons: Shem, Ham
and Japheth.
11Now the earth was corrupt in God's sight

[a]6 *Father* may mean *ancestor*; also in verses 7–26. [b]29 *Noah* sounds like the Hebrew for *comfort*. [c]3 Or *My spirit will not remain in*
[d]3 Or *corrupt*

and was full of violence. 12God saw how corrupt the earth had become, for all the people
on earth had corrupted their ways. 13So God
said to Noah, "I am going to put an end to all
people, for the earth is filled with violence because of them. I am surely going to destroy
both them and the earth. 14So make yourself
an ark of cypress[a] wood; make rooms in it and
coat it with pitch inside and out. 15This is how
you are to build it: The ark is to be 450 feet long,
75 feet wide and 45 feet high.[b] 16Make a roof
for it and finish[c] the ark to within 18 inches[d]
of the top. Put a door in the side of the ark and
make lower, middle and upper decks. 17I am going to bring floodwaters on the earth to destroy
all life under the heavens, every creature that
has the breath of life in it. Everything on earth
will perish. 18But I will establish my covenant
with you, and you will enter the ark—you and
your sons and your wife and
your sons' wives with you.
19You are to bring into the ark
two of all living creatures, male
and female, to keep them alive
with you. 20Two of every kind
of bird, of every kind of animal
and of every kind of creature
that moves along the ground
will come to you to be kept
alive. 21You are to take every
kind of food that is to be eaten
and store it away as food for
you and for them."
22Noah did everything just
as God commanded him.

> **Genesis 6:17–18**
>
> ### *God Protects Us*
>
> "I am going to bring floodwaters on the earth . . . Everything on earth will perish. But I will establish my covenant with you, and you will enter the ark—you and your sons and your wife and your sons' wives with you."

7

The LORD then said to
Noah, "Go into the ark,
you and your whole family, be-
cause I have found you righteous in this generation. 2Take with you seven[e] of every kind
of clean animal, a male and its mate, and two
of every kind of unclean animal, a male and
its mate, 3and also seven of every kind of bird,
male and female, to keep their various kinds
alive throughout the earth. 4Seven days from
now I will send rain on the earth for forty days
and forty nights, and I will wipe from the face
of the earth every living creature I have made."
5And Noah did all that the LORD commanded him.
6Noah was six hundred years old when the
floodwaters came on the earth. 7And Noah and
his sons and his wife and his sons' wives entered
the ark to escape the waters of the flood. 8Pairs
of clean and unclean animals, of birds and of
all creatures that move along the ground, 9male
and female, came to Noah and entered the ark,
as God had commanded Noah. 10And after the
seven days the floodwaters came on the earth.
11In the six hundredth year of Noah's life, on
the seventeenth day of the second month—on
that day all the springs of the great deep burst
forth, and the floodgates of the heavens were
opened. 12And rain fell on the earth forty days
and forty nights.
13On that very day Noah and his sons, Shem,
Ham and Japheth, together
with his wife and the wives of
his three sons, entered the ark.
14They had with them every
wild animal according to its
kind, all livestock according to
their kinds, every creature that
moves along the ground according to its kind and every bird according to its kind, everything
with wings. 15Pairs of all creatures that have the breath of
life in them came to Noah and
entered the ark. 16The animals
going in were male and female
of every living thing, as God
had commanded Noah. Then
the LORD shut him in.
17For forty days the flood
kept coming on the earth, and as the waters increased they lifted the ark high above the earth.
18The waters rose and increased greatly on the
earth, and the ark floated on the surface of the
water. 19They rose greatly on the earth, and
all the high mountains under the entire heavens were covered. 20The waters rose and covered the mountains to a depth of more than
twenty feet.[f,g] 21Every living thing that moved

[a]14 The meaning of the Hebrew for this word is uncertain. [b]15 Hebrew *300 cubits long, 50 cubits wide and 30 cubits high* (about 140 meters long, 23 meters wide and 13.5 meters high) [c]16 Or *Make an opening for light by finishing* [d]16 Hebrew *a cubit* (about 0.5 meter) [e]2 Or *seven pairs*; also in verse 3 [f]20 Hebrew *fifteen cubits* (about 6.9 meters) [g]20 Or *rose more than twenty feet, and the mountains were covered*

When Floods Come

Read: Genesis 7:1–24

A NATURAL DISASTER hits a community, city or country, and the loss is mind-boggling. The media reports facts and figures to describe the devastation, but the tragedy doesn't hit home until we see the pictures and hear the stories. Tears. Faces etched in agony. Eyes roaming for lost loved ones. Families torn apart: A man who lost his son; a woman whose husband is missing; a child looking for a familiar face. The unbearable pain and sorrow become more personal.

Long ago there was a great flood. Noah and his family knew catastrophe was coming, so they built an ark at God's command. They followed instructions. They braced for impending crisis. They endured umpteen years of looking foolish. They faced criticism, ridicule, rejection. They plodded in the slow work of faith and love. Then the downpour came and the final command: "Go into the ark." So Noah and his family left everything and evacuated to the big boat. Noah led the eight members of his family into a floating zoo—out of harm's way. The devastation of the world they knew had to be heartbreaking. But they followed God, and his grace saved them from the disaster.

When storms come in your own life, they may not be a calamity on the scale of a flood. But they may bring just as much sorrow and pain—an illness, an accident, a betrayal. In the midst of the event, your decisions can help save you and your family. Let's face it; disaster can strike whether you're a saint or sinner. To survive requires spiritual preparation. When you build your home on the foundation of God's Word, you can find safety despite the downpour outside. You can help those you love to weather the storm. Begin now to prepare your house for the storms that are sure to come: Spend time in the Bible. Strengthen your relationship with God and with a godly community. Bring those you love before God in prayer. When (not *if*) the tempest strikes, you will have shelter.

Genesis 7:1

The LORD then said to Noah, "Go into the ark, you and your family, because I have found you righteous in this generation."

reflection

1 In the face of a flood, who would you take with you into the ark?

2 How are you preparing for the inevitable storms of life? How will your family benefit from your actions?

3 Has God commanded you to do things that may seem foolish to others? In what ways are you obeying him?

RELATED READINGS

Hebrews 11:1–16;
1 Peter 3:13–22;
2 Peter 3:11–18

"There are some things you learn best in calm, and some in storm."

Willa Cather

Go to page 13 for your next devotional reading.

on the earth perished—birds, livestock, wild
animals, all the creatures that swarm over the
earth, and all mankind. 22Everything on dry
land that had the breath of life in its nostrils
died. 23Every living thing on the face of the
earth was wiped out; men and animals and
the creatures that move along the ground and
the birds of the air were wiped from the earth.
Only Noah was left, and those with him in
the ark.
24The waters flooded the earth for a hundred and fifty days.

8 But God remembered Noah and all the
wild animals and the livestock that were with him in the
ark, and he sent a wind over the
earth, and the waters receded.
2Now the springs of the deep
and the floodgates of the heavens had been closed, and the
rain had stopped falling from
the sky. 3The water receded
steadily from the earth. At the
end of the hundred and fifty
days the water had gone down,
4and on the seventeenth day
of the seventh month the ark
came to rest on the mountains
of Ararat. 5The waters continued to recede until the tenth
month, and on the first day of
the tenth month the tops of the mountains became visible.

Genesis 8:1

God Remembers Us

But God remembered Noah and all the wild animals and the livestock that were with him in the ark, and he sent a wind over the earth, and the waters receded.

6After forty days Noah opened the window
he had made in the ark 7and sent out a raven,
and it kept flying back and forth until the water had dried up from the earth. 8Then he sent
out a dove to see if the water had receded from
the surface of the ground. 9But the dove could
find no place to set its feet because there was
water over all the surface of the earth; so it returned to Noah in the ark. He reached out his
hand and took the dove and brought it back
to himself in the ark. 10He waited seven more
days and again sent out the dove from the ark.
11When the dove returned to him in the evening, there in its beak was a freshly plucked
olive leaf! Then Noah knew that the water had
receded from the earth. 12He waited seven
more days and sent the dove out again, but this
time it did not return to him.
13By the first day of the first month of
Noah's six hundred and first year, the water had
dried up from the earth. Noah then removed
the covering from the ark and saw that the surface of the ground was dry. 14By the twenty-
seventh day of the second month the earth was
completely dry.
15Then God said to Noah, 16"Come out of
the ark, you and your wife and your sons and
their wives. 17Bring out every kind of living
creature that is with you—the birds, the animals, and all the creatures that
move along the ground—so
they can multiply on the earth
and be fruitful and increase in
number upon it."
18So Noah came out, to-
gether with his sons and his
wife and his sons' wives. 19All
the animals and all the creatures that move along the
ground and all the birds—
everything that moves on the
earth—came out of the ark,
one kind after another.
20Then Noah built an altar
to the LORD and, taking some
of all the clean animals and
clean birds, he sacrificed burnt
offerings on it. 21The LORD smelled the pleasing aroma and said in his heart: "Never again
will I curse the ground because of man, even
though[a] every inclination of his heart is evil
from childhood. And never again will I destroy
all living creatures, as I have done.

22"As long as the earth endures,
seedtime and harvest,
cold and heat,
summer and winter,
day and night
will never cease."

God's Covenant With Noah

9 Then God blessed Noah and his sons, saying to them, "Be fruitful and increase in
number and fill the earth. 2The fear and dread
of you will fall upon all the beasts of the earth

[a]21 Or *man, for*

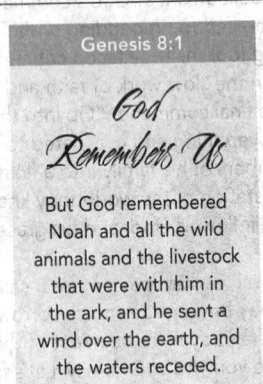

and all the birds of the air, upon every creature
that moves along the ground, and upon all the
fish of the sea; they are given into your hands.
3 Everything that lives and moves will be food
for you. Just as I gave you the green plants, I
now give you everything.
4 "But you must not eat meat that has its lifeblood still in it. 5 And for your lifeblood I will
surely demand an accounting. I will demand
an accounting from every animal. And from
each man, too, I will demand an accounting for
the life of his fellow man.

6 "Whoever sheds the blood
of man,
by man shall his blood be
shed;
for in the image of God
has God made man.

7 As for you, be fruitful and
increase in number; multiply
on the earth and increase upon it."
8 Then God said to Noah
and to his sons with him: 9 "I
now establish my covenant
with you and with your descendants after you 10 and with
every living creature that was
with you—the birds, the livestock and all the
wild animals, all those that came out of the ark
with you—every living creature on earth. 11 I
establish my covenant with you: Never again
will all life be cut off by the waters of a flood;
never again will there be a flood to destroy
the earth."
12 And God said, "This is the sign of the
covenant I am making between me and you
and every living creature with you, a covenant
for all generations to come: 13 I have set my
rainbow in the clouds, and it will be the sign
of the covenant between me and the earth.
14 Whenever I bring clouds over the earth and
the rainbow appears in the clouds, 15 I will remember my covenant between me and you
and all living creatures of every kind. Never
again will the waters become a flood to destroy
all life. 16 Whenever the rainbow appears in the
clouds, I will see it and remember the everlasting covenant between God and all living creatures of every kind on the earth."
17 So God said to Noah, "This is the sign of
the covenant I have established between me
and all life on the earth."

> **Genesis 9:15**
>
> *God Keeps His Promises*
>
> "I will remember my covenant between me and you and all living creatures of every kind. Never again will the waters become a flood to destroy all life."

The Sons of Noah

18 The sons of Noah who came out of the ark
were Shem, Ham and Japheth. (Ham was the
father of Canaan.) 19 These were the three sons
of Noah, and from them came the people who
were scattered over the earth.
20 Noah, a man of the soil,
proceeded[a] to plant a vineyard.
21 When he drank some of its
wine, he became drunk and
lay uncovered inside his tent.
22 Ham, the father of Canaan,
saw his father's nakedness and
told his two brothers outside.
23 But Shem and Japheth took a
garment and laid it across their
shoulders; then they walked in
backward and covered their
father's nakedness. Their faces
were turned the other way so
that they would not see their
father's nakedness.
24 When Noah awoke from
his wine and found out what
his youngest son had done to him, 25 he said,

"Cursed be Canaan!
The lowest of slaves
will he be to his brothers."

26 He also said,

"Blessed be the LORD, the God of Shem!
May Canaan be the slave of Shem.[b]
27 May God extend the territory of Japheth[c];
may Japheth live in the tents of Shem,
and may Canaan be his[d] slave."

28 After the flood Noah lived 350 years.
29 Altogether, Noah lived 950 years, and then
he died.

The Table of Nations

10 This is the account of Shem, Ham and
Japheth, Noah's sons, who themselves
had sons after the flood.

[a] 20 Or *soil, was the first* [b] 26 Or *be his slave* [c] 27 *Japheth* sounds like the Hebrew for *extend.* [d] 27 Or *their*

The Japhethites

2 The sons[a] of Japheth:
Gomer, Magog, Madai, Javan, Tubal,
Meshech and Tiras.
3 The sons of Gomer:
Ashkenaz, Riphath and Togarmah.
4 The sons of Javan:
Elishah, Tarshish, the Kittim and the
Rodanim.[b] 5 (From these the maritime
peoples spread out into their territories
by their clans within their nations, each
with its own language.)

The Hamites

6 The sons of Ham:
Cush, Mizraim,[c] Put and Canaan.
7 The sons of Cush:
Seba, Havilah, Sabtah, Raamah and
Sabteca.
The sons of Raamah:
Sheba and Dedan.

8 Cush was the father[d] of Nimrod, who grew
to be a mighty warrior on the earth. 9 He was a
mighty hunter before the LORD; that is why it
is said, "Like Nimrod, a mighty hunter before
the LORD." 10 The first centers of his kingdom
were Babylon, Erech, Akkad and Calneh, in[e]
Shinar.[f] 11 From that land he went to Assyria,
where he built Nineveh, Rehoboth Ir,[g] Calah
12 and Resen, which is between Nineveh and
Calah; that is the great city.

13 Mizraim was the father of
the Ludites, Anamites, Lehabites, Naphtuhites, 14 Pathrusites, Casluhites (from
whom the Philistines came) and Caphtorites.
15 Canaan was the father of
Sidon his firstborn,[h] and of the Hittites,
16 Jebusites, Amorites, Girgashites, 17 Hivites, Arkites, Sinites, 18 Arvadites, Zemarites and Hamathites.

Later the Canaanite clans scattered 19 and
the borders of Canaan reached from Sidon
toward Gerar as far as Gaza, and then toward
Sodom, Gomorrah, Admah and Zeboiim, as
far as Lasha.
20 These are the sons of Ham by their clans
and languages, in their territories and nations.

The Semites

21 Sons were also born to Shem, whose older
brother was[i] Japheth; Shem was the ancestor of
all the sons of Eber.

22 The sons of Shem:
Elam, Asshur, Arphaxad, Lud and
Aram.
23 The sons of Aram:
Uz, Hul, Gether and Meshech.[j]
24 Arphaxad was the father of[k] Shelah,
and Shelah the father of Eber.
25 Two sons were born to Eber:
One was named Peleg,[l] because in his
time the earth was divided; his brother
was named Joktan.
26 Joktan was the father of
Almodad, Sheleph, Hazarmaveth, Jerah, 27 Hadoram, Uzal, Diklah, 28 Obal,
Abimael, Sheba, 29 Ophir, Havilah and
Jobab. All these were sons of Joktan.

30 The region where they lived stretched from
Mesha toward Sephar, in the eastern hill country.
31 These are the sons of Shem by their clans
and languages, in their territories and nations.
32 These are the clans of Noah's sons, according to their lines of descent, within their
nations. From these the nations spread out
over the earth after the flood.

The Tower of Babel

11 Now the whole world had one language and a common speech. 2 As men
moved eastward,[m] they found a plain in Shinar[f] and settled there.
3 They said to each other, "Come, let's make
bricks and bake them thoroughly." They used
brick instead of stone, and tar for mortar. 4 Then
they said, "Come, let us build ourselves a city,
with a tower that reaches to the heavens, so that

[a] 2 *Sons* may mean *descendants* or *successors* or *nations*; also in verses 3, 4, 6, 7, 20–23, 29 and 31. [b] 4 Some manuscripts of the Masoretic Text and Samaritan Pentateuch (see also Septuagint and 1 Chron. 1:7); most manuscripts of the Masoretic Text *Dodanim* [c] 6 That is, Egypt; also in verse 13 [d] 8 *Father* may mean *ancestor* or *predecessor* or *founder*; also in verses 13, 15, 24 and 26. [e] 10 Or *Erech and Akkad—all of them in* [f] 10,2 That is, Babylonia [g] 11 Or *Nineveh with its city squares* [h] 15 Or *of the Sidonians, the foremost* [i] 21 Or *Shem, the older brother of* [j] 23 See Septuagint and 1 Chron. 1:17; Hebrew *Mash* [k] 24 Hebrew; Septuagint *father of Cainan, and Cainan was the father of* [l] 25 *Peleg* means *division.* [m] 2 Or *from the east*; or *in the east*

Reaching for the Heavens

Read: Genesis 11:1–9

LOUIS SULLIVAN, the inventor of the modern skyscraper, said, "The tall building . . . should be a proud and soaring thing that makes a powerful appeal to the architectural imagination." Today, many women embody the same spirit of pride and self-sufficiency that is represented in the lofty towers that make up our cities. We focus on personal perfection. Many women seek the pinnacle of age-defying beauty through creams, procedures or surgeries. Some become obsessed with fashion or feel that they must conform to some media-driven image. Over time, it becomes easier and easier to build monuments to ourselves. After all, as the famous ad says, "I'm worth it."

The builders of the tower of Babel shared a key aspect of Sullivan's vision of the tall building: pride. And they had one purpose: to build a name for themselves. They wanted to claim glory that rightly belonged to God—after all, they were worth it.

The longing to climb higher than God didn't begin in Babel. Before time began Lucifer said, "I will raise my throne above the stars of God" (Isaiah 14:13). It didn't end with Babel, either. The pyramids of Egypt proclaim the power of the rulers buried beneath them. Many lives were lost in the building of the pyramids, "collateral damage" to the princes who built them. Often Egyptian slaves were killed when their masters died and were buried alongside them. But just as the Egyptian kings sacrificed everything to their own legacy, women often sacrifice the good of those around them for fleeting recognition, not to mention the humble spirit God desires. The rulers of ancient Egypt were not all-powerful—they died the deaths of mere men. Don't be deceived, your soul will not be saved by flawless skin or the perfect career any more than the towering mountains of stone raised over the mummies of kings saved them.

What do you take pride in? What keeps you from glorifying God? Has your focus become self-absorbed? Have you become self-glorifying? The solution is simple: Whatever is keeping you from God, give it to him for his glory. Let your relationship with Jesus be the source of your significance. When you humble yourself before God, you'll be lifted up.

Wednesday

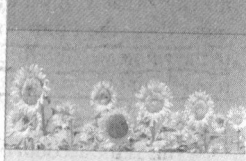

Go to page 18 for your next devotional reading.

Genesis 11:4

"Come, let us build ourselves a city, with a tower that reaches to the heavens, so that we may make a name for ourselves and not be scattered over the face of the whole earth."

reflection

1 Name some of the towers you see others building around you that take glory away from God. What kinds of towers have you built?

2 Have you ever taken credit for work when another person really deserved it, or has someone taken credit for work you have done? How did that feel?

3 How do you think God feels when we take the credit for his work in our lives?

RELATED READINGS

Psalm 86:8–10; Proverbs 18:10–12; Matthew 23:12

"The one sole thing in myself in which I glory is that I see in myself nothing in which I can glory."

Catherine of Genoa

we may make a name for ourselves and not be
scattered over the face of the whole earth."
5 But the LORD came down to see the city
and the tower that the men were building. 6 The
LORD said, "If as one people speaking the same
language they have begun to do this, then nothing they plan to do will be impossible for them.
7 Come, let us go down and confuse their language so they will not understand each other."
8 So the LORD scattered them from there
over all the earth, and they stopped building
the city. 9 That is why it was called Babel[a]—because there the LORD confused the language
of the whole world. From there the LORD scattered them over the face of the whole earth.

From Shem to Abram

10 This is the account of Shem.

Two years after the flood, when Shem
was 100 years old, he became the father[b] of
Arphaxad. 11 And after he became the father of
Arphaxad, Shem lived 500 years and had other
sons and daughters.
12 When Arphaxad had lived 35 years, he
became the father of Shelah. 13 And after he
became the father of Shelah,
Arphaxad lived 403 years and
had other sons and daugh-
ters.[c]
14 When Shelah had lived 30
years, he became the father of
Eber. 15 And after he became
the father of Eber, Shelah lived
403 years and had other sons
and daughters.
16 When Eber had lived 34
years, he became the father of
Peleg. 17 And after he became
the father of Peleg, Eber lived
430 years and had other sons
and daughters.
18 When Peleg had lived 30 years, he became
the father of Reu. 19 And after he became the father of Reu, Peleg lived 209 years and had other
sons and daughters.
20 When Reu had lived 32 years, he became
the father of Serug. 21 And after he became the
father of Serug, Reu lived 207 years and had
other sons and daughters.
22 When Serug had lived 30 years, he became
the father of Nahor. 23 And after he became the
father of Nahor, Serug lived 200 years and had
other sons and daughters.
24 When Nahor had lived 29 years, he became the father of Terah. 25 And after he became the father of Terah, Nahor lived 119 years
and had other sons and daughters.
26 After Terah had lived 70 years, he became
the father of Abram, Nahor and Haran.

27 This is the account of Terah.

Terah became the father of Abram, Nahor
and Haran. And Haran became the father of
Lot. 28 While his father Terah was still alive, Haran died in Ur of the Chaldeans, in the land of
his birth. 29 Abram and Nahor both married.
The name of Abram's wife was Sarai, and the
name of Nahor's wife was Milcah; she was the
daughter of Haran, the father of both Milcah
and Iscah. 30 Now Sarai was barren; she had
no children.
31 Terah took his son Abram, his grandson
Lot son of Haran, and his
daughter-in-law Sarai, the wife
of his son Abram, and together
they set out from Ur of the
Chaldeans to go to Canaan.
But when they came to Haran,
they settled there.
32 Terah lived 205 years, and
he died in Haran.

> Genesis 12:2
>
> **God Extends His Blessing**
>
> "I will make you into
> a great nation
> and I will bless you;
> I will make your
> name great,
> and you will be a blessing."

The Call of Abram

12 The LORD had said to
Abram, "Leave your
country, your people and your
father's household and go to
the land I will show you.

2 "I will make you into a great nation
and I will bless you;
I will make your name great,
and you will be a blessing.
3 I will bless those who bless you,
and whoever curses you I will curse;

[a] 9 That is, Babylon; *Babel* sounds like the Hebrew for *confused.* [b] 10 *Father* may mean *ancestor*; also in verses 11–25. [c] 12,13 Hebrew; Septuagint (see also Luke 3:35, 36 and note at Gen. 10:24) *35 years, he became the father of Cainan.* [13] *And after he became the father of Cainan, Arphaxad lived 430 years and had other sons and daughters, and then he died. When Cainan had lived 130 years, he became the father of Shelah. And after he became the father of Shelah, Cainan lived 330 years and had other sons and daughters*

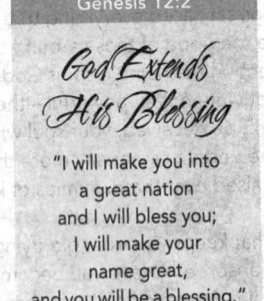

and all peoples on earth
will be blessed through you."

4So Abram left, as the LORD had told him;
and Lot went with him. Abram was seventy-
five years old when he set out from Haran.
5He took his wife Sarai, his nephew Lot, all
the possessions they had accumulated and
the people they had acquired in Haran, and
they set out for the land of Canaan, and they
arrived there.

6Abram traveled through the land as far as
the site of the great tree of Moreh at Shechem.
At that time the Canaanites were in the land.
7The LORD appeared to Abram and said, "To
your offspring[a] I will give this land." So he built
an altar there to the LORD, who had appeared
to him.

8From there he went on toward the hills east
of Bethel and pitched his tent, with Bethel on
the west and Ai on the east. There he built an
altar to the LORD and called on the name of
the LORD. 9Then Abram set out and continued
toward the Negev.

Abram in Egypt

10Now there was a famine in the land, and
Abram went down to Egypt to live there for a
while because the famine was severe. 11As he
was about to enter Egypt, he said to his wife
Sarai, "I know what a beautiful woman you are.
12When the Egyptians see you, they will say,
'This is his wife.' Then they will kill me but will
let you live. 13Say you are my sister, so that I
will be treated well for your sake and my life
will be spared because of you."

14When Abram came to Egypt, the Egyptians saw that she was a very beautiful woman.
15And when Pharaoh's officials saw her, they
praised her to Pharaoh, and she was taken into
his palace. 16He treated Abram well for her
sake, and Abram acquired sheep and cattle,
male and female donkeys, menservants and
maidservants, and camels.

17But the LORD inflicted serious diseases on
Pharaoh and his household because of Abram's
wife Sarai. 18So Pharaoh summoned Abram.
"What have you done to me?" he said. "Why
didn't you tell me she was your wife? 19Why
did you say, 'She is my sister,' so that I took her
to be my wife? Now then, here is your wife.
Take her and go!" 20Then Pharaoh gave orders
about Abram to his men, and they sent him on
his way, with his wife and everything he had.

Abram and Lot Separate

13 So Abram went up from Egypt to the
Negev, with his wife and everything
he had, and Lot went with him. 2Abram had
become very wealthy in livestock and in silver
and gold.

3From the Negev he went from place to
place until he came to Bethel, to the place between Bethel and Ai where his tent had been
earlier 4and where he had first built an altar.
There Abram called on the name of the LORD.

5Now Lot, who was moving about with
Abram, also had flocks and herds and tents.
6But the land could not support them while
they stayed together, for their possessions were
so great that they were not able to stay together.
7And quarreling arose between Abram's herdsmen and the herdsmen of Lot. The Canaanites
and Perizzites were also living in the land at
that time.

8So Abram said to Lot, "Let's not have any
quarreling between you and me, or between
your herdsmen and mine, for we are brothers.
9Is not the whole land before you? Let's part
company. If you go to the left, I'll go to the
right; if you go to the right, I'll go to the left."

10Lot looked up and saw that the whole
plain of the Jordan was well watered, like the
garden of the LORD, like the land of Egypt,
toward Zoar. (This was before the LORD destroyed Sodom and Gomorrah.) 11So Lot
chose for himself the whole plain of the Jordan and set out toward the east. The two men
parted company: 12Abram lived in the land of
Canaan, while Lot lived among the cities of the
plain and pitched his tents near Sodom. 13Now
the men of Sodom were wicked and were sinning greatly against the LORD.

14The LORD said to Abram after Lot had
parted from him, "Lift up your eyes from
where you are and look north and south, east
and west. 15All the land that you see I will give
to you and your offspring[b] forever. 16I will
make your offspring like the dust of the earth,

[a]7 Or *seed* [b]15 Or *seed*; also in verse 16

so that if anyone could count the dust, then
your offspring could be counted. [17]Go, walk
through the length and breadth of the land, for
I am giving it to you."

[18]So Abram moved his tents and went to live
near the great trees of Mamre at Hebron, where
he built an altar to the LORD.

Abram Rescues Lot

14 At this time Amraphel king of Shinar,[a]
Arioch king of Ellasar, Kedorlaomer
king of Elam and Tidal king of Goiim [2]went
to war against Bera king of Sodom, Birsha king
of Gomorrah, Shinab king of Admah, Sheme-
ber king of Zeboiim, and the king of Bela (that
is, Zoar). [3]All these latter kings joined forces
in the Valley of Siddim (the Salt Sea[b]). [4]For
twelve years they had been subject to Kedorlaomer, but in the thirteenth year they rebelled.

[5]In the fourteenth year, Kedorlaomer and the
kings allied with him went out and defeated the
Rephaites in Ashteroth Karnaim, the Zuzites
in Ham, the Emites in Shaveh Kiriathaim [6]and
the Horites in the hill country of Seir, as far as
El Paran near the desert. [7]Then they turned
back and went to En Mishpat (that is, Kadesh),
and they conquered the whole territory of the
Amalekites, as well as the Amorites who were
living in Hazazon Tamar.

[8]Then the king of Sodom, the king of Gomorrah, the king of Admah, the king of Zeboiim
and the king of Bela (that is, Zoar) marched
out and drew up their battle lines in the Valley
of Siddim [9]against Kedorlaomer king of Elam,
Tidal king of Goiim, Amraphel king of Shinar
and Arioch king of Ellasar—four kings against
five. [10]Now the Valley of Siddim was full of tar
pits, and when the kings of Sodom and Gomorrah fled, some of the men fell into them and
the rest fled to the hills. [11]The four kings seized
all the goods of Sodom and Gomorrah and all
their food; then they went away. [12]They also
carried off Abram's nephew Lot and his possessions, since he was living in Sodom.

[13]One who had escaped came and reported
this to Abram the Hebrew. Now Abram was living near the great trees of Mamre the Amorite,
a brother[c] of Eshcol and Aner, all of whom were
allied with Abram. [14]When Abram heard that
his relative had been taken captive, he called
out the 318 trained men born in his household
and went in pursuit as far as Dan. [15]During the
night Abram divided his men to attack them
and he routed them, pursuing them as far as
Hobah, north of Damascus. [16]He recovered all
the goods and brought back his relative Lot and
his possessions, together with the women and
the other people.

[17]After Abram returned from defeating Kedorlaomer and the kings allied with him, the
king of Sodom came out to meet him in the
Valley of Shaveh (that is, the King's Valley).

[18]Then Melchizedek king of Salem[d] brought
out bread and wine. He was priest of God Most
High, [19]and he blessed Abram, saying,

"Blessed be Abram by God Most High,
Creator[e] of heaven and earth.
[20]And blessed be[f] God Most High,
who delivered your enemies into your
hand."

Then Abram gave him a tenth of everything.

[21]The king of Sodom said to Abram, "Give
me the people and keep the goods for yourself."

[22]But Abram said to the king of Sodom, "I
have raised my hand to the LORD, God Most
High, Creator of heaven and earth, and have
taken an oath [23]that I will accept nothing belonging to you, not even a thread or the thong
of a sandal, so that you will never be able to say,
'I made Abram rich.' [24]I will accept nothing but
what my men have eaten and the share that belongs to the men who went with me—to Aner,
Eshcol and Mamre. Let them have their share."

God's Covenant With Abram

15 After this, the word of the LORD came
to Abram in a vision:

"Do not be afraid, Abram.
I am your shield,[g]
your very great reward.[h]"

[2]But Abram said, "O Sovereign LORD, what
can you give me since I remain childless and
the one who will inherit[i] my estate is Eliezer

[a]1 That is, Babylonia; also in verse 9 [b]3 That is, the Dead Sea [c]13 Or *a relative*; or *an ally* [d]18 That is, Jerusalem [e]19 Or *Possessor*; also in verse 22 [f]20 Or *And praise be to* [g]1 Or *sovereign* [h]1 Or *shield; / your reward will be very great* [i]2 The meaning of the Hebrew for this phrase is uncertain.

of Damascus?" 3And Abram said, "You have
given me no children; so a servant in my household will be my heir."
4Then the word of the LORD
came to him: "This man will
not be your heir, but a son coming from your own body will
be your heir." 5He took him
outside and said, "Look up
at the heavens and count the
stars—if indeed you can count
them." Then he said to him, "So
shall your offspring be."
6Abram believed the LORD,
and he credited it to him
as righteousness.

> **Genesis 15:1**
>
> *God Protects*
>
> "Do not be afraid,
> Abram.
> I am your shield,
> your very great reward."

7He also said to him, "I am the LORD, who
brought you out of Ur of the Chaldeans to give
you this land to take possession of it."
8But Abram said, "O Sovereign LORD, how
can I know that I will gain possession of it?"
9So the LORD said to him, "Bring me a heifer,
a goat and a ram, each three years old, along
with a dove and a young pigeon."
10Abram brought all these to him, cut them
in two and arranged the halves opposite each
other; the birds, however, he did not cut in
half. 11Then birds of prey came down on the
carcasses, but Abram drove them away.
12As the sun was setting, Abram fell into a
deep sleep, and a thick and dreadful darkness
came over him. 13Then the LORD said to him,
"Know for certain that your descendants will
be strangers in a country not their own, and
they will be enslaved and mistreated four hundred years. 14But I will punish the nation they
serve as slaves, and afterward they will come
out with great possessions. 15You, however,
will go to your fathers in peace and be buried
at a good old age. 16In the fourth generation
your descendants will come back here, for
the sin of the Amorites has not yet reached its
full measure."
17When the sun had set and darkness had
fallen, a smoking firepot with a blazing torch
appeared and passed between the pieces. 18On
that day the LORD made a covenant with Abram
and said, "To your descendants I give this land,
from the river[a] of Egypt to the great river, the
Euphrates— 19the land of the Kenites, Keniz-
zites, Kadmonites, 20Hittites, Perizzites, Rephaites, 21Amorites, Canaanites,
Girgashites and Jebusites."

Hagar and Ishmael

16 Now Sarai, Abram's
wife, had borne him
no children. But she had an
Egyptian maidservant named
Hagar; 2so she said to Abram,
"The LORD has kept me from
having children. Go, sleep with
my maidservant; perhaps I can
build a family through her."
Abram agreed to what Sarai said. 3So after
Abram had been living in Canaan ten years, Sarai his wife took her Egyptian maidservant Hagar and gave her to her husband to be his wife.
4He slept with Hagar, and she conceived.
When she knew she was pregnant, she began to despise her mistress. 5Then Sarai said
to Abram, "You are responsible for the wrong
I am suffering. I put my servant in your arms,
and now that she knows she is pregnant, she
despises me. May the LORD judge between you
and me."
6"Your servant is in your hands," Abram said.
"Do with her whatever you think best." Then Sarai mistreated Hagar; so she fled from her.
7The angel of the LORD found Hagar near
a spring in the desert; it was the spring that is
beside the road to Shur. 8And he said, "Hagar,
servant of Sarai, where have you come from,
and where are you going?"
"I'm running away from my mistress Sarai,"
she answered.
9Then the angel of the LORD told her, "Go
back to your mistress and submit to her."
10The angel added, "I will so increase your
descendants that they will be too numerous
to count."
11The angel of the LORD also said to her:

"You are now with child
    and you will have a son.
You shall name him Ishmael,[b]
    for the LORD has heard of your misery.
12He will be a wild donkey of a man;
    his hand will be against everyone

[a]18 Or *Wadi* [b]11 *Ishmael* means *God hears.*

Promises Worth Waiting For

Read: Genesis 16:1–16

Genesis 16:1–2

Now Sarai, Abram's wife, had borne him no children. But she had an Egyptian maidservant named Hagar; so she said to Abram, "The LORD has kept me from having children. Go, sleep with my maidservant; perhaps I can build a family through her."

WHAT ARE YOU WAITING FOR? Who or what do you believe will satisfy and complete you? You may be waiting for Mr. Right, your dream job, a precious baby or any number of things to fulfill your hopes and dreams.

Waiting is hard when you just *know* your life will be so much better if your hopes become reality. Waiting is hard . . . especially when years pass and there is no sign of your expectations being met. Often, the longer you wait, the more desperate you become.

Sarai was fed up with waiting for the baby God had promised. She grew older every day, and her body showed no sign of pregnancy. Perhaps she questioned that God's promise of children for Abram included her: *Why is God taking so long? What if I'm not the one to bear the promised child?* So Sarai took matters into her own hands. She gave her maidservant Hagar to Abram to bear a child to fulfill God's promise.

However, things didn't quite turn out the way Sarai expected. Hagar became pregnant as planned, but Hagar's pride and Sarai's jealousy caused a jagged rift between the two women. And Abram was caught in the middle. The consequences of Sarai's actions not only affected Sarai's family and household, but also generations of people who came after them. To this day, the children of Hagar and Sarai war against one another as the Arabs and Jews fight for control over the land of Israel.

But God had a plan. A plan to bless Abram and Sarai with their very own baby. A plan to bless the world through their offspring. Isaac would be the fulfillment of God's promise. That plan was worth waiting for.

God has plans for your life, too. Plans that will make you thrive and not be knocked down by life's setbacks (see Jeremiah 29:11–13). God's plans are well worth waiting for. You may be tempted to take matters into your own hands, thinking God is just a little bit late. But don't risk God's perfect intentions for you by relying on your own schemes. Waiting for God's perfect timing can save you years of heartbreak. Remember, God is faithful and always keeps his promises . . . even if you have to wait.

reflection

1. Is there something you're waiting for right now? What has God promised through his Word?
2. Describe a time when you took matters into your own hands. What were the results? Was it worth it?
3. How do you respond when your actions have unexpected consequences? Do you blame someone else, as Sarai blamed Abram, or do you go to God and ask for his help and forgiveness?

RELATED READINGS

1 Samuel 1:3–17; Romans 4:13–18; Galatians 4:21–23

Go to page 22 for your next devotional reading.

and everyone's hand against him,
and he will live in hostility
toward[a] all his brothers."

13 She gave this name to the LORD who spoke
to her: "You are the God who sees me," for she
said, "I have now seen[b] the One who sees me."
14 That is why the well was called Beer Lahai
Roi[c]; it is still there, between Kadesh and Bered.

15 So Hagar bore Abram a son, and Abram
gave the name Ishmael to the son she had
borne. 16 Abram was eighty-six years old when
Hagar bore him Ishmael.

The Covenant of Circumcision

17 When Abram was ninety-nine years
old, the LORD appeared to him and
said, "I am God Almighty[d]; walk before me
and be blameless. 2 I will confirm my covenant
between me and you and will greatly increase
your numbers."

3 Abram fell facedown, and God said to him,
4 "As for me, this is my covenant with you: You
will be the father of many nations. 5 No longer
will you be called Abram[e]; your name will be
Abraham,[f] for I have made you a father of
many nations. 6 I will make you very fruitful; I
will make nations of you, and kings will come
from you. 7 I will establish my covenant as an
everlasting covenant between me and you and
your descendants after you for the generations
to come, to be your God and the God of your
descendants after you. 8 The whole land of Canaan, where you are now an alien, I will give as
an everlasting possession to you and your descendants after you; and I will be their God."

9 Then God said to Abraham, "As for you,
you must keep my covenant, you and your
descendants after you for the generations to
come. 10 This is my covenant with you and
your descendants after you, the covenant you
are to keep: Every male among you shall be circumcised. 11 You are to undergo circumcision,
and it will be the sign of the covenant between
me and you. 12 For the generations to come
every male among you who is eight days old
must be circumcised, including those born in
your household or bought with money from a
foreigner—those who are not your offspring.
13 Whether born in your household or bought
with your money, they must be circumcised.
My covenant in your flesh is to be an everlasting covenant. 14 Any uncircumcised male, who
has not been circumcised in the flesh, will be
cut off from his people; he has broken my covenant."

15 God also said to Abraham, "As for Sarai
your wife, you are no longer to call her Sarai;
her name will be Sarah. 16 I will bless her and
will surely give you a son by her. I will bless her
so that she will be the mother of nations; kings
of peoples will come from her."

17 Abraham fell facedown; he laughed and
said to himself, "Will a son be born to a man
a hundred years old? Will Sarah bear a child
at the age of ninety?" 18 And Abraham said to
God, "If only Ishmael might live under your
blessing!"

19 Then God said, "Yes, but your wife Sarah
will bear you a son, and you will call him Isaac.[g]
I will establish my covenant with him as an
everlasting covenant for his descendants after
him. 20 And as for Ishmael, I have heard you:
I will surely bless him; I will make him fruitful
and will greatly increase his numbers. He will
be the father of twelve rulers, and I will make
him into a great nation. 21 But my covenant I
will establish with Isaac, whom Sarah will bear
to you by this time next year." 22 When he had
finished speaking with Abraham, God went up
from him.

23 On that very day Abraham took his son
Ishmael and all those born in his household or
bought with his money, every male in his household, and circumcised them, as God told him.
24 Abraham was ninety-nine years old when he
was circumcised, 25 and his son Ishmael was
thirteen; 26 Abraham and his son Ishmael were
both circumcised on that same day. 27 And
every male in Abraham's household, including
those born in his household or bought from a
foreigner, was circumcised with him.

The Three Visitors

18 The LORD appeared to Abraham near
the great trees of Mamre while he was
sitting at the entrance to his tent in the heat of

[a] 12 Or *live to the east / of* [b] 13 Or *seen the back of* [c] 14 *Beer Lahai Roi* means *well of the Living One who sees me.* [d] 1 Hebrew *El-Shaddai* [e] 5 *Abram* means *exalted father.* [f] 5 *Abraham* means *father of many.* [g] 19 *Isaac* means *he laughs.*

the day. [2]Abraham looked up and saw three men standing nearby. When he saw them, he hurried from the entrance of his tent to meet them and bowed low to the ground.

[3]He said, "If I have found favor in your eyes, my lord,[a] do not pass your servant by. [4]Let a little water be brought, and then you may all wash your feet and rest under this tree. [5]Let me get you something to eat, so you can be refreshed and then go on your way—now that you have come to your servant."

"Very well," they answered, "do as you say."

[6]So Abraham hurried into the tent to Sarah. "Quick," he said, "get three seahs[b] of fine flour and knead it and bake some bread."

[7]Then he ran to the herd and selected a choice, tender calf and gave it to a servant, who hurried to prepare it. [8]He then brought some curds and milk and the calf that had been prepared, and set these before them. While they ate, he stood near them under a tree.

[9]"Where is your wife Sarah?" they asked him.

"There, in the tent," he said.

[10]Then the LORD[c] said, "I will surely return to you about this time next year, and Sarah your wife will have a son."

Now Sarah was listening at the entrance to the tent, which was behind him. [11]Abraham and Sarah were already old and well advanced in years, and Sarah was past the age of childbearing. [12]So Sarah laughed to herself as she thought, "After I am worn out and my master[d] is old, will I now have this pleasure?"

[13]Then the LORD said to Abraham, "Why did Sarah laugh and say, 'Will I really have a child, now that I am old?' [14]Is anything too hard for the LORD? I will return to you at the appointed time next year and Sarah will have a son."

[15]Sarah was afraid, so she lied and said, "I did not laugh."

But he said, "Yes, you did laugh."

Abraham Pleads for Sodom

[16]When the men got up to leave, they looked down toward Sodom, and Abraham walked along with them to see them on their way. [17]Then the LORD said, "Shall I hide from Abraham what I am about to do? [18]Abraham will surely become a great and powerful nation, and all nations on earth will be blessed through him. [19]For I have chosen him, so that he will direct his children and his household after him to keep the way of the LORD by doing what is right and just, so that the LORD will bring about for Abraham what he has promised him."

[20]Then the LORD said, "The outcry against Sodom and Gomorrah is so great and their sin so grievous [21]that I will go down and see if what they have done is as bad as the outcry that has reached me. If not, I will know."

[22]The men turned away and went toward Sodom, but Abraham remained standing before the LORD.[e] [23]Then Abraham approached him and said: "Will you sweep away the righteous with the wicked? [24]What if there are fifty righteous people in the city? Will you really sweep it away and not spare[f] the place for the sake of the fifty righteous people in it? [25]Far be it from you to do such a thing—to kill the righteous with the wicked, treating the righteous and the wicked alike. Far be it from you! Will not the Judge[g] of all the earth do right?"

[26]The LORD said, "If I find fifty righteous people in the city of Sodom, I will spare the whole place for their sake."

[27]Then Abraham spoke up again: "Now that I have been so bold as to speak to the Lord, though I am nothing but dust and ashes, [28]what if the number of the righteous is five less than fifty? Will you destroy the whole city because of five people?"

"If I find forty-five there," he said, "I will not destroy it."

[29]Once again he spoke to him, "What if only forty are found there?"

> **Genesis 18:14**
>
> *God Does the Impossible*
>
> "Is anything too hard for the LORD? I will return to you at the appointed time next year and Sarah will have a son."

[a]3 Or *O Lord* [b]6 That is, probably about 20 quarts (about 22 liters) [c]10 Hebrew *Then he* [d]12 Or *husband* [e]22 Masoretic Text; an ancient Hebrew scribal tradition *but the LORD remained standing before Abraham* [f]24 Or *forgive*; also in verse 26 [g]25 Or *Ruler*

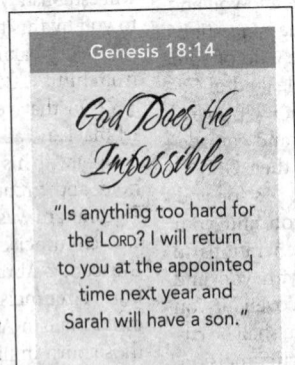

He said, "For the sake of forty, I will not
do it."
30 Then he said, "May the Lord not be angry,
but let me speak. What if only thirty can be
found there?"
He answered, "I will not do it if I find thirty
there."
31 Abraham said, "Now that I have been
so bold as to speak to the Lord, what if only
twenty can be found there?"
He said, "For the sake of twenty, I will not
destroy it."
32 Then he said, "May the Lord not be angry,
but let me speak just once more. What if only
ten can be found there?"
He answered, "For the sake of ten, I will not
destroy it."
33 When the LORD had finished speaking
with Abraham, he left, and Abraham returned
home.

Sodom and Gomorrah Destroyed

19 The two angels arrived at Sodom in the
evening, and Lot was sitting in the gateway of the city. When he saw them, he got up
to meet them and bowed down with his face to
the ground. 2 "My lords," he said, "please turn
aside to your servant's house. You can wash
your feet and spend the night and then go on
your way early in the morning."
"No," they answered, "we will spend the
night in the square."
3 But he insisted so strongly that they did go
with him and entered his house. He prepared
a meal for them, baking bread without yeast,
and they ate. 4 Before they had gone to bed, all
the men from every part of the city of Sodom—
both young and old—surrounded the house.
5 They called to Lot, "Where are the men who
came to you tonight? Bring them out to us so
that we can have sex with them."
6 Lot went outside to meet them and shut the
door behind him 7 and said, "No, my friends.
Don't do this wicked thing. 8 Look, I have two
daughters who have never slept with a man. Let
me bring them out to you, and you can do what
you like with them. But don't do anything to
these men, for they have come under the protection of my roof."
9 "Get out of our way," they replied. And
they said, "This fellow came here as an alien,
and now he wants to play the judge! We'll treat
you worse than them." They kept bringing pressure on Lot and moved forward to break down
the door.
10 But the men inside reached out and pulled
Lot back into the house and shut the door.
11 Then they struck the men who were at the
door of the house, young and old, with blindness so that they could not find the door.
12 The two men said to Lot, "Do you have
anyone else here—sons-in-law, sons or daughters, or anyone else in the city who belongs to
you? Get them out of here, 13 because we are
going to destroy this place. The outcry to the
LORD against its people is so great that he has
sent us to destroy it."
14 So Lot went out and spoke to his sons-in-
law, who were pledged to marry[a] his daughters. He said, "Hurry and get out of this place,
because the LORD is about to destroy the city!"
But his sons-in-law thought he was joking.
15 With the coming of dawn, the angels
urged Lot, saying, "Hurry! Take your wife and
your two daughters who are here, or you will be
swept away when the city is punished."
16 When he hesitated, the men grasped his
hand and the hands of his wife and of his two
daughters and led them safely out of the city,
for the LORD was merciful to them. 17 As soon
as they had brought them out, one of them
said, "Flee for your lives! Don't look back, and
don't stop anywhere in the plain! Flee to the
mountains or you will be swept away!"
18 But Lot said to them, "No, my lords,[b]
please! 19 Your[c] servant has found favor in
your[c] eyes, and you[c] have shown great kindness to me in sparing my life. But I can't flee
to the mountains; this disaster will overtake
me, and I'll die. 20 Look, here is a town near
enough to run to, and it is small. Let me flee
to it—it is very small, isn't it? Then my life will
be spared."
21 He said to him, "Very well, I will grant this
request too; I will not overthrow the town you
speak of. 22 But flee there quickly, because I cannot do anything until you reach it." (That is why
the town was called Zoar.[d])
23 By the time Lot reached Zoar, the sun

[a] 14 Or *were married to* [b] 18 Or *No, Lord;* or *No, my lord* [c] 19 The Hebrew is singular. [d] 22 *Zoar* means *small.*

Letting Go of the Familiar

Read: Genesis 19:1–26

Genesis 19:26

But Lot's wife looked back, and she became a pillar of salt.

reflection

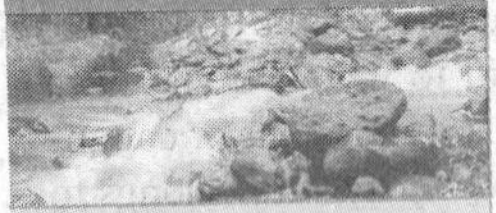

1 What does the passage in today's reading teach you about letting go in order to move forward?

2 Why is it so difficult sometimes to let go of the past?

3 What is one thing you think God may be asking you to let go of right now? Spend some time praying that God will help you let go of whatever is hindering you from moving forward in your spiritual journey.

RELATED READINGS

Genesis 12:1–7; Numbers 14:1–38; Philippians 3:13

LETTING GO OF THE FAMILIAR is tough. Changing careers or colleges or moving to a new city can take an emotional toll on us. It's even more difficult to leave behind old habits, attitudes and behaviors.

Lot's wife wasn't able to let go of her home in Sodom, even though God sent angels to warn her family to run for their lives because judgment was coming. In fact, the angels' warnings included such grave commands as "Don't look back" and "Don't stop." Why in the world did this woman choose to stop and look back? Could it be that she loved the life she was leaving too much? Though Sodom was full to overflowing with sin and vice, apparently the dark and oppressive city was comfortably familiar to Lot's wife.

It *is* difficult to leave the familiar behind. That fact is as true today as it was in the days of Sodom and Gomorrah's destruction—even when God himself is saying, "It's time to move on." If you've ever struggled with a destructive habit, you've felt the pull of the familiar—even as you've sensed God's nudge, "Move on now." You've experienced the temptation to turn back just one more time, for one last look, one last taste, one last "fix"—even as God has whispered, "Don't look back." Maybe you've agonized over a loved one's downward spiral, desperately attempting to rescue them time and time again—until finally God impressed upon you, "Stop. Let go."

Unlike Lot's wife, none of us has ever become a pillar of salt by turning back for one last peek. Yet we all struggle with the difficulties of letting go of the old in order to grasp the new. Take heart. God understands that letting go of the familiar is hard. Yet he has called us to move on to new life in Jesus Christ by letting go of our old worldly lives, our old habits, our old dreams—to boldly move forward without looking back. When you feel God's call to move, allow him to guide you. He will give you the grace to do whatever he has asked.

Go to page 26 for your next devotional reading.

had risen over the land. [24]Then the LORD rained down burning sulfur on Sodom and Gomorrah—from the LORD out of the heavens. [25]Thus he overthrew those cities and the entire plain, including all those living in the cities—and also the vegetation in the land. [26]But Lot's wife looked back, and she became a pillar of salt.

[27]Early the next morning Abraham got up and returned to the place where he had stood before the LORD. [28]He looked down toward Sodom and Gomorrah, toward all the land of the plain, and he saw dense smoke rising from the land, like smoke from a furnace.

[29]So when God destroyed the cities of the plain, he remembered Abraham, and he brought Lot out of the catastrophe that overthrew the cities where Lot had lived.

Lot and His Daughters

[30]Lot and his two daughters left Zoar and settled in the mountains, for he was afraid to stay in Zoar. He and his two daughters lived in a cave. [31]One day the older daughter said to the younger, "Our father is old, and there is no man around here to lie with us, as is the custom all over the earth. [32]Let's get our father to drink wine and then lie with him and preserve our family line through our father."

[33]That night they got their father to drink wine, and the older daughter went in and lay with him. He was not aware of it when she lay down or when she got up.

[34]The next day the older daughter said to the younger, "Last night I lay with my father. Let's get him to drink wine again tonight, and you go in and lie with him so we can preserve our family line through our father." [35]So they got their father to drink wine that night also, and the younger daughter went and lay with him. Again he was not aware of it when she lay down or when she got up.

[36]So both of Lot's daughters became pregnant by their father. [37]The older daughter had a son, and she named him Moab[a]; he is the father of the Moabites of today. [38]The younger daughter also had a son, and she named him Ben-Ammi[b]; he is the father of the Ammonites of today.

Abraham and Abimelech

20 Now Abraham moved on from there into the region of the Negev and lived between Kadesh and Shur. For a while he stayed in Gerar, [2]and there Abraham said of his wife Sarah, "She is my sister." Then Abimelech king of Gerar sent for Sarah and took her.

[3]But God came to Abimelech in a dream one night and said to him, "You are as good as dead because of the woman you have taken; she is a married woman."

[4]Now Abimelech had not gone near her, so he said, "Lord, will you destroy an innocent nation? [5]Did he not say to me, 'She is my sister,' and didn't she also say, 'He is my brother'? I have done this with a clear conscience and clean hands."

[6]Then God said to him in the dream, "Yes, I know you did this with a clear conscience, and so I have kept you from sinning against me. That is why I did not let you touch her. [7]Now return the man's wife, for he is a prophet, and he will pray for you and you will live. But if you do not return her, you may be sure that you and all yours will die."

[8]Early the next morning Abimelech summoned all his officials, and when he told them all that had happened, they were very much afraid. [9]Then Abimelech called Abraham in and said, "What have you done to us? How have I wronged you that you have brought such great guilt upon me and my kingdom? You have done things to me that should not be done." [10]And Abimelech asked Abraham, "What was your reason for doing this?"

[11]Abraham replied, "I said to myself, 'There is surely no fear of God in this place, and they will kill me because of my wife.' [12]Besides, she really is my sister, the daughter of my father though not of my mother; and she became my wife. [13]And when God had me wander from my father's household, I said to her, 'This is how you can show your love to me: Everywhere we go, say of me, "He is my brother."'"

[14]Then Abimelech brought sheep and cattle and male and female slaves and gave them to Abraham, and he returned Sarah his wife to him. [15]And Abimelech said, "My land is before you; live wherever you like."

[a]37 *Moab* sounds like the Hebrew for *from father.* [b]38 *Ben-Ammi* means *son of my people.*

16To Sarah he said, "I am giving your
brother a thousand shekels[a] of silver. This is to
cover the offense against you before all who are
with you; you are completely
vindicated."
17Then Abraham prayed to
God, and God healed Abim-
elech, his wife and his slave
girls so they could have children again, 18for the LORD had
closed up every womb in Abimelech's household because of
Abraham's wife Sarah.

> Genesis 20:17
>
> *God Heals*
>
> Then Abraham prayed to God, and God healed Abimelech, his wife and his slave girls so they could have children again.

The Birth of Isaac

21 Now the LORD was
gracious to Sarah as he
had said, and the LORD did for
Sarah what he had promised. 2Sarah became
pregnant and bore a son to Abraham in his old
age, at the very time God had promised him.
3Abraham gave the name Isaac[b] to the son
Sarah bore him. 4When his son Isaac was eight
days old, Abraham circumcised him, as God
commanded him. 5Abraham was a hundred
years old when his son Isaac was born to him.
6Sarah said, "God has brought me laughter, and everyone who hears about this will
laugh with me." 7And she added, "Who would
have said to Abraham that Sarah would nurse
children? Yet I have borne him a son in his
old age."

Hagar and Ishmael Sent Away

8The child grew and was weaned, and on the
day Isaac was weaned Abraham held a great
feast. 9But Sarah saw that the son whom Hagar the Egyptian had borne to Abraham was
mocking, 10and she said to Abraham, "Get rid
of that slave woman and her son, for that slave
woman's son will never share in the inheritance
with my son Isaac."
11The matter distressed Abraham greatly
because it concerned his son. 12But God said
to him, "Do not be so distressed about the
boy and your maidservant. Listen to whatever
Sarah tells you, because it is through Isaac that
your offspring[c] will be reckoned. 13I will make
the son of the maidservant into a nation also,
because he is your offspring."
14Early the next morning Abraham took
some food and a skin of water and gave them to
Hagar. He set them on her shoulders and then
sent her off with the boy. She
went on her way and wandered
in the desert of Beersheba.
15When the water in the
skin was gone, she put the
boy under one of the bushes.
16Then she went off and sat
down nearby, about a bowshot
away, for she thought, "I cannot watch the boy die." And as
she sat there nearby, she[d] began to sob.
17God heard the boy crying,
and the angel of God called to
Hagar from heaven and said
to her, "What is the matter, Hagar? Do not be
afraid; God has heard the boy crying as he lies
there. 18Lift the boy up and take him by the
hand, for I will make him into a great nation."
19Then God opened her eyes and she saw
a well of water. So she went and filled the skin
with water and gave the boy a drink.
20God was with the boy as he grew up.
He lived in the desert and became an archer.
21While he was living in the Desert of Paran,
his mother got a wife for him from Egypt.

The Treaty at Beersheba

22At that time Abimelech and Phicol the
commander of his forces said to Abraham,
"God is with you in everything you do. 23Now
swear to me here before God that you will not
deal falsely with me or my children or my descendants. Show to me and the country where
you are living as an alien the same kindness I
have shown to you."
24Abraham said, "I swear it."
25Then Abraham complained to Abimelech
about a well of water that Abimelech's servants
had seized. 26But Abimelech said, "I don't
know who has done this. You did not tell me,
and I heard about it only today."
27So Abraham brought sheep and cattle
and gave them to Abimelech, and the two
men made a treaty. 28Abraham set apart seven
ewe lambs from the flock, 29and Abimelech
asked Abraham, "What is the meaning of these

[a]16 That is, about 25 pounds (about 11.5 kilograms) [b]3 *Isaac* means *he laughs.* [c]12 Or *seed* [d]16 Hebrew; Septuagint *the child*

seven ewe lambs you have set apart by themselves?"
30He replied, "Accept these seven lambs from
my hand as a witness that I dug this well."
31So that place was called Beersheba,[a] because the two men swore an oath there.
32After the treaty had been made at Beersheba, Abimelech and Phicol the commander
of his forces returned to the land of the Philistines. 33Abraham planted
a tamarisk tree in Beersheba,
and there he called upon the
name of the LORD, the Eternal
God. 34And Abraham stayed
in the land of the Philistines
for a long time.

> **Genesis 21:33**
>
> *God Is Eternal*
>
> Abraham . . . called upon the name of the LORD, the Eternal God.

Abraham Tested

22 Some time later God
tested Abraham. He
said to him, "Abraham!"
"Here I am," he replied.
2Then God said, "Take your son, your only
son, Isaac, whom you love, and go to the region of Moriah. Sacrifice him there as a burnt
offering on one of the mountains I will tell
you about."
3Early the next morning Abraham got up
and saddled his donkey. He took with him two
of his servants and his son Isaac. When he had
cut enough wood for the burnt offering, he set
out for the place God had told him about. 4On
the third day Abraham looked up and saw the
place in the distance. 5He said to his servants,
"Stay here with the donkey while I and the boy
go over there. We will worship and then we will
come back to you."
6Abraham took the wood for the burnt offering and placed it on his son Isaac, and he himself carried the fire and the knife. As the two
of them went on together, 7Isaac spoke up and
said to his father Abraham, "Father?"
"Yes, my son?" Abraham replied.
"The fire and wood are here," Isaac said, "but
where is the lamb for the burnt offering?"
8Abraham answered, "God himself will provide the lamb for the burnt offering, my son."
And the two of them went on together.
9When they reached the place God had told
him about, Abraham built an altar there and arranged the wood on it. He bound his son Isaac
and laid him on the altar, on top of the wood.
10Then he reached out his hand and took the
knife to slay his son. 11But the angel of the
LORD called out to him from heaven, "Abraham! Abraham!"
"Here I am," he replied.
12"Do not lay a hand on the boy," he said.
"Do not do anything to him.
Now I know that you fear God,
because you have not withheld from me your son, your
only son."
13Abraham looked up and
there in a thicket he saw a ram[b]
caught by its horns. He went
over and took the ram and sacrificed it as a burnt offering instead of his son. 14So Abraham
called that place The LORD
Will Provide. And to this day it is said, "On the
mountain of the LORD it will be provided."
15The angel of the LORD called to Abraham
from heaven a second time 16and said, "I swear
by myself, declares the LORD, that because you
have done this and have not withheld your
son, your only son, 17I will surely bless you
and make your descendants as numerous as
the stars in the sky and as the sand on the seashore. Your descendants will take possession of
the cities of their enemies, 18and through your
offspring[c] all nations on earth will be blessed,
because you have obeyed me."
19Then Abraham returned to his servants,
and they set off together for Beersheba. And
Abraham stayed in Beersheba.

Nahor's Sons

20Some time later Abraham was told, "Milcah is also a mother; she has borne sons to
your brother Nahor: 21Uz the firstborn, Buz his
brother, Kemuel (the father of Aram), 22Kesed,
Hazo, Pildash, Jidlaph and Bethuel." 23Bethuel
became the father of Rebekah. Milcah bore
these eight sons to Abraham's brother Nahor.
24His concubine, whose name was Reumah,
also had sons: Tebah, Gaham, Tahash and Maacah.

[a]31 *Beersheba* can mean *well of seven* or *well of the oath.* [b]13 Many manuscripts of the Masoretic Text, Samaritan Pentateuch, Septuagint and Syriac; most manuscripts of the Masoretic Text *a ram behind* ⌊*him*⌋ [c]18 Or *seed*

The Heart of a Mother

EVE

[Eve] said, "With the help of the LORD I have brought forth a man."

Genesis 4:1

STRANGE CRAVINGS. That first flutter. Her body was changing, growing and stretching in unpredictable and unsettling ways. The first mother in history conceived a child, carried him to term and gave birth without ever knowing what to expect next.

She didn't have a girlfriend to confide in when Adam just didn't understand her moods. She had no one to assure the young mother that sudden clumsiness was normal or that the awful bloated feelings would pass. Her experience was the ultimate as natural childbirth goes—she made it without the benefit of an obstetrician, a midwife or a drop of morphine. She couldn't even run to her mother!

And that was just the pregnancy.

She recalled cradling Cain in her arms as a newborn and gently leading him to nurse for the first time. She remembered fingering his tiny hands and counting all his toes, one by one. She didn't know she could love someone so much.

How, oh how, would she ever be able to be what he needed her to be—his mother? Eve answered her own question when she spoke in the afterglow of giving birth. "With the help of the LORD I have brought forth a man."

No one was there to inform Eve about the significance of what had just transpired. They didn't have to. She got it. She instinctively knew what every mother knows in an instant: She had *not* brought forth this miracle by her own power. And almost simultaneously, she knew she would not be able to raise him in her own strength either. The very first mother in history would have to raise her child the very same way mothers throughout history have conceived and nurtured children—fully relying on God's help.

If that fact wasn't obvious then, it soon would be. Like when she had to steal away for a moment alone to cry because it was the first time she had to punish him. When he bickered with his brother. When his career choice went south. And whenever her own poor choices threatened to scar her children's future.

Eve was the first to experience joy and heartache as a mother. But no one could tell her then that she certainly wouldn't be the last.

ASSIGNED READING:
Genesis 4:1–26

—Prayer—

Thank you, Lord, for never leaving me alone. I take comfort in your guidance and care.

Weekend

Go to page 28 for your next devotional reading.

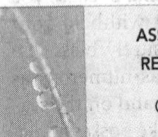

The Death of Sarah

23 Sarah lived to be a hundred and
twenty-seven years old. 2She died at
Kiriath Arba (that is, Hebron) in the land of Canaan, and Abraham went to mourn for Sarah
and to weep over her.
3Then Abraham rose from beside his dead
wife and spoke to the Hittites.[a] He said, 4"I
am an alien and a stranger among you. Sell me
some property for a burial site here so I can
bury my dead."
5The Hittites replied to Abraham, 6"Sir, listen to us. You are a mighty prince among us.
Bury your dead in the choicest of our tombs.
None of us will refuse you his tomb for burying
your dead."
7Then Abraham rose and bowed down before the people of the land, the Hittites. 8He
said to them, "If you are willing to let me bury
my dead, then listen to me and intercede with
Ephron son of Zohar on my behalf 9so he will
sell me the cave of Machpelah, which belongs
to him and is at the end of his field. Ask him
to sell it to me for the full price as a burial site
among you."
10Ephron the Hittite was sitting among his
people and he replied to Abraham in the hearing of all the Hittites who had come to the gate
of his city. 11"No, my lord," he said. "Listen to
me; I give[b] you the field, and I give[b] you the
cave that is in it. I give[b] it to you in the presence
of my people. Bury your dead."
12Again Abraham bowed down before the
people of the land 13and he said to Ephron in
their hearing, "Listen to me, if you will. I will
pay the price of the field. Accept it from me so
I can bury my dead there."
14Ephron answered Abraham, 15"Listen to
me, my lord; the land is worth four hundred
shekels[c] of silver, but what is that between me
and you? Bury your dead."
16Abraham agreed to Ephron's terms and
weighed out for him the price he had named in
the hearing of the Hittites: four hundred shekels of silver, according to the weight current
among the merchants.
17So Ephron's field in Machpelah near
Mamre—both the field and the cave in it, and
all the trees within the borders of the field—
was deeded 18to Abraham as his property in
the presence of all the Hittites who had come
to the gate of the city. 19Afterward Abraham
buried his wife Sarah in the cave in the field of
Machpelah near Mamre (which is at Hebron)
in the land of Canaan. 20So the field and the
cave in it were deeded to Abraham by the Hittites as a burial site.

Isaac and Rebekah

24 Abraham was now old and well advanced in years, and the LORD had
blessed him in every way. 2He said to the chief[d]
servant in his household, the one in charge of
all that he had, "Put your hand under my thigh.
3I want you to swear by the LORD, the God of
heaven and the God of earth, that you will not
get a wife for my son from the daughters of the
Canaanites, among whom I am living, 4but will
go to my country and my own relatives and get
a wife for my son Isaac."
5The servant asked him, "What if the woman
is unwilling to come back with me to this land?
Shall I then take your son back to the country
you came from?"
6"Make sure that you do not take my son
back there," Abraham said. 7"The LORD, the
God of heaven, who brought me out of my father's household and my native land and who
spoke to me and promised me on oath, saying,
'To your offspring[e] I will give this land'—he
will send his angel before you so that you can
get a wife for my son from there. 8If the woman
is unwilling to come back with you, then you
will be released from this oath of mine. Only
do not take my son back there." 9So the servant put his hand under the thigh of his master
Abraham and swore an oath to him concerning this matter.
10Then the servant took ten of his master's
camels and left, taking with him all kinds of
good things from his master. He set out for
Aram Naharaim[f] and made his way to the
town of Nahor. 11He had the camels kneel
down near the well outside the town; it was toward evening, the time the women go out to
draw water.

[a]3 Or *the sons of Heth*; also in verses 5, 7, 10, 16, 18 and 20 [b]11 Or *sell* [c]15 That is, about 10 pounds (about 4.5 kilograms)
[d]2 Or *oldest* [e]7 Or *seed* [f]10 That is, Northwest Mesopotamia

Making Hard Choices

Read: Genesis 24:1–67

Genesis 24:2–4

[Abraham] said to the chief servant in his household, the one in charge of all that he had, . . . "I want you to swear by the LORD, the God of heaven and the God of earth, that you will not get a wife for my son from the daughters of the Canaanites, among whom I am living, but will go to my country and my own relatives and get a wife for my son Isaac."

reflection

1 What hard choice is confronting you today?

2 What factors make your decision difficult?

3 How is God asking you to trust him in this situation? Will you obey him?

RELATED READINGS

Joshua 24:15; 1 Kings 8:57–58; Psalm 32:8–9

"HAVE IT YOUR WAY." Remember that popular advertising slogan? Our culture demands choice—the freedom to choose precisely what we want, exactly how we want it. One national coffee chain reportedly can serve your morning cup in as many as nineteen thousand different ways.[1] Some choices, such as *tall*, *grande* or *venti mocha*, are insignificant. Other choices can determine the course of a lifetime.

The story of Isaac and Rebekah is all about people making choices. Think about it. Wouldn't it have been infinitely easier for Abraham to choose a wife for his son from among local families he already knew? Next, consider the servant. He'd been assigned to find a matrimonial needle in a haystack. His job was to choose the perfect wife for his master's son. And then there was Rebekah. She was asked to choose to leave her home, family and everything familiar to travel to a distant country to marry a man she'd never met.

Choices. We all make them. Abraham chose to obey God's directive that his family not intermarry with the Canaanites. The servant chose to accept a complicated challenge from his employer, trusting God to lead him to the right woman. And Rebekah—Rebekah had to make a decision that would affect the rest of her life. She ultimately chose to trust her life and future to the servant of a distant relative whose God was her God. The story of the divinely arranged marriage between Isaac and Rebekah reminds us that nothing is too difficult for God.

Trust and obey—these two words go together like coffee and cream. Yet every day we face difficult situations that seem to defy simple solutions. As women, myriad difficult choices face us—the right course of care for a sick child, moving from everything familiar for a new opportunity, following God's leading even when the outcome is hazy, even when the right choice frightens us. You may toss and turn for nights without finding peace in your choice. The right choice is often the hard choice, but not always. How do we determine the right choice? *Obey* the guidance you find in God's Word, earnestly pray and seek trusted counsel, then *trust* God with the outcome. Will you have it your way or God's way? First trust God to have your best interest at heart, and then trust him to lead you to the right choice.

[1] Horovitz, Bruce. "You Want It Your Way." Posted March 5, 2004. USAToday.com. www.usatoday.com. (Accessed November 9, 2005.)

Go to page 34 for your next devotional reading.

12 Then he prayed, "O LORD, God of my master Abraham, give me success today, and show
kindness to my master Abraham. 13 See, I am
standing beside this spring, and the daughters
of the townspeople are coming out to draw water. 14 May it be that when I say to a girl, 'Please
let down your jar that I may
have a drink,' and she says,
'Drink, and I'll water your camels too'—let her be the one you
have chosen for your servant
Isaac. By this I will know that
you have shown kindness to
my master."
15 Before he had finished
praying, Rebekah came out
with her jar on her shoulder.
She was the daughter of Bethuel
son of Milcah, who was the
wife of Abraham's brother Nahor. 16 The girl was very beautiful, a virgin; no man had ever
lain with her. She went down
to the spring, filled her jar and
came up again.
17 The servant hurried to meet her and said,
"Please give me a little water from your jar."
18 "Drink, my lord," she said, and quickly
lowered the jar to her hands and gave him a
drink.
19 After she had given him a drink, she said,
"I'll draw water for your camels too, until they
have finished drinking." 20 So she quickly emptied her jar into the trough, ran back to the well
to draw more water, and drew enough for all
his camels. 21 Without saying a word, the man
watched her closely to learn whether or not the
LORD had made his journey successful.
22 When the camels had finished drinking,
the man took out a gold nose ring weighing
a beka[a] and two gold bracelets weighing ten
shekels.[b] 23 Then he asked, "Whose daughter
are you? Please tell me, is there room in your
father's house for us to spend the night?"
24 She answered him, "I am the daughter of
Bethuel, the son that Milcah bore to Nahor."
25 And she added, "We have plenty of straw
and fodder, as well as room for you to spend
the night."

Genesis 24:27

God Guides Our Paths

"Praise be to the LORD, the God of my master Abraham, who has not abandoned his kindness and faithfulness to my master. As for me, the LORD has led me on the journey."

26 Then the man bowed down and worshiped
the LORD, 27 saying, "Praise be to the LORD,
the God of my master Abraham, who has not
abandoned his kindness and faithfulness to my
master. As for me, the LORD has led me on the
journey to the house of my master's relatives."
28 The girl ran and told her
mother's household about
these things. 29 Now Rebekah
had a brother named Laban,
and he hurried out to the man
at the spring. 30 As soon as he
had seen the nose ring, and the
bracelets on his sister's arms,
and had heard Rebekah tell
what the man said to her, he
went out to the man and found
him standing by the camels
near the spring. 31 "Come, you
who are blessed by the LORD,"
he said. "Why are you standing out here? I have prepared
the house and a place for the
camels."
32 So the man went to the
house, and the camels were unloaded. Straw
and fodder were brought for the camels, and
water for him and his men to wash their feet.
33 Then food was set before him, but he said,
"I will not eat until I have told you what I have
to say."
"Then tell us," ⌞Laban⌟ said.
34 So he said, "I am Abraham's servant. 35 The
LORD has blessed my master abundantly, and
he has become wealthy. He has given him
sheep and cattle, silver and gold, menservants
and maidservants, and camels and donkeys.
36 My master's wife Sarah has borne him a son
in her[c] old age, and he has given him everything he owns. 37 And my master made me
swear an oath, and said, 'You must not get a
wife for my son from the daughters of the Canaanites, in whose land I live, 38 but go to my
father's family and to my own clan, and get a
wife for my son.'
39 "Then I asked my master, 'What if the
woman will not come back with me?'
40 "He replied, 'The LORD, before whom I
have walked, will send his angel with you and

[a]22 That is, about 1/5 ounce (about 5.5 grams) [b]22 That is, about 4 ounces (about 110 grams) [c]36 Or *his*

make your journey a success, so that you can get a wife for my son from my own clan and from my father's family. 41Then, when you go to my clan, you will be released from my oath even if they refuse to give her to you—you will be released from my oath.'

42"When I came to the spring today, I said, 'O LORD, God of my master Abraham, if you will, please grant success to the journey on which I have come. 43See, I am standing beside this spring; if a maiden comes out to draw water and I say to her, "Please let me drink a little water from your jar," 44and if she says to me, "Drink, and I'll draw water for your camels too," let her be the one the LORD has chosen for my master's son.'

45"Before I finished praying in my heart, Rebekah came out, with her jar on her shoulder. She went down to the spring and drew water, and I said to her, 'Please give me a drink.'

46"She quickly lowered her jar from her shoulder and said, 'Drink, and I'll water your camels too.' So I drank, and she watered the camels also.

47"I asked her, 'Whose daughter are you?'

"She said, 'The daughter of Bethuel son of Nahor, whom Milcah bore to him.'

"Then I put the ring in her nose and the bracelets on her arms, 48and I bowed down and worshiped the LORD. I praised the LORD, the God of my master Abraham, who had led me on the right road to get the granddaughter of my master's brother for his son. 49Now if you will show kindness and faithfulness to my master, tell me; and if not, tell me, so I may know which way to turn."

50Laban and Bethuel answered, "This is from the LORD; we can say nothing to you one way or the other. 51Here is Rebekah; take her and go, and let her become the wife of your master's son, as the LORD has directed."

52When Abraham's servant heard what they said, he bowed down to the ground before the LORD. 53Then the servant brought out gold and silver jewelry and articles of clothing and gave them to Rebekah; he also gave costly gifts to her brother and to her mother. 54Then he and the men who were with him ate and drank and spent the night there.

When they got up the next morning, he said, "Send me on my way to my master."

55But her brother and her mother replied, "Let the girl remain with us ten days or so; then you[a] may go."

56But he said to them, "Do not detain me, now that the LORD has granted success to my journey. Send me on my way so I may go to my master."

57Then they said, "Let's call the girl and ask her about it." 58So they called Rebekah and asked her, "Will you go with this man?"

"I will go," she said.

59So they sent their sister Rebekah on her way, along with her nurse and Abraham's servant and his men. 60And they blessed Rebekah and said to her,

"Our sister, may you increase
  to thousands upon thousands;
may your offspring possess
  the gates of their enemies."

61Then Rebekah and her maids got ready and mounted their camels and went back with the man. So the servant took Rebekah and left.

62Now Isaac had come from Beer Lahai Roi, for he was living in the Negev. 63He went out to the field one evening to meditate,[b] and as he looked up, he saw camels approaching. 64Rebekah also looked up and saw Isaac. She got down from her camel 65and asked the servant, "Who is that man in the field coming to meet us?"

"He is my master," the servant answered. So she took her veil and covered herself.

66Then the servant told Isaac all he had done. 67Isaac brought her into the tent of his mother Sarah, and he married Rebekah. So she became his wife, and he loved her; and Isaac was comforted after his mother's death.

The Death of Abraham

25 Abraham took[c] another wife, whose name was Keturah. 2She bore him Zimran, Jokshan, Medan, Midian, Ishbak and Shuah. 3Jokshan was the father of Sheba and Dedan; the descendants of Dedan were the Asshurites, the Letushites and the Leummites.

[a]55 Or *she* [b]63 The meaning of the Hebrew for this word is uncertain. [c]1 Or *had taken*

4The sons of Midian were Ephah, Epher, Hanoch, Abida and Eldaah. All these were descendants of Keturah.
5Abraham left everything he owned to Isaac.
6But while he was still living,
he gave gifts to the sons of
his concubines and sent them
away from his son Isaac to the
land of the east.
7Altogether, Abraham lived
a hundred and seventy-five
years. 8Then Abraham breathed
his last and died at a good old
age, an old man and full of
years; and he was gathered to
his people. 9His sons Isaac and
Ishmael buried him in the cave
of Machpelah near Mamre, in
the field of Ephron son of Zohar the Hittite, 10the field Abraham had bought from the
Hittites.[a] There Abraham was
buried with his wife Sarah. 11After Abraham's
death, God blessed his son Isaac, who then
lived near Beer Lahai Roi.

Ishmael's Sons

12This is the account of Abraham's son
Ishmael, whom Sarah's maidservant, Hagar the
Egyptian, bore to Abraham.

13These are the names of the sons of Ishmael,
listed in the order of their birth: Nebaioth the
firstborn of Ishmael, Kedar, Adbeel, Mibsam,
14Mishma, Dumah, Massa, 15Hadad, Tema,
Jetur, Naphish and Kedemah. 16These were
the sons of Ishmael, and these are the names
of the twelve tribal rulers according to their
settlements and camps. 17Altogether, Ishmael
lived a hundred and thirty-seven years. He
breathed his last and died, and he was gathered
to his people. 18His descendants settled in the
area from Havilah to Shur, near the border of
Egypt, as you go toward Asshur. And they lived
in hostility toward[b] all their brothers.

Jacob and Esau

19This is the account of Abraham's son
Isaac.

Abraham became the father of Isaac, 20and
Isaac was forty years old when he married
Rebekah daughter of Bethuel the Aramean
from Paddan Aram[c] and sister of Laban the
Aramean.
21Isaac prayed to the LORD
on behalf of his wife, because
she was barren. The LORD
answered his prayer, and his
wife Rebekah became preg-
nant. 22The babies jostled each
other within her, and she said,
"Why is this happening to
me?" So she went to inquire of
the LORD.
23The LORD said to her,

"Two nations are in your
womb,
and two peoples from
within you will be
separated;
one people will be stronger
than the other,
and the older will serve the younger."

24When the time came for her to give birth,
there were twin boys in her womb. 25The first
to come out was red, and his whole body was
like a hairy garment; so they named him Esau.[d]
26After this, his brother came out, with his
hand grasping Esau's heel; so he was named Jacob.[e] Isaac was sixty years old when Rebekah
gave birth to them.
27The boys grew up, and Esau became a skillful hunter, a man of the open country, while Jacob was a quiet man, staying among the tents.
28Isaac, who had a taste for wild game, loved
Esau, but Rebekah loved Jacob.
29Once when Jacob was cooking some stew,
Esau came in from the open country, famished.
30He said to Jacob, "Quick, let me have some of
that red stew! I'm famished!" (That is why he
was also called Edom.[f])
31Jacob replied, "First sell me your birthright."
32"Look, I am about to die," Esau said. "What
good is the birthright to me?"
33But Jacob said, "Swear to me first." So he

> **Genesis 25:21**
>
> *God Hears Prayers*
>
> Isaac prayed to the LORD on behalf of his wife, because she was barren. The LORD answered his prayer, and his wife Rebekah became pregnant.

[a]10 Or *the sons of Heth* [b]18 Or *lived to the east of* [c]20 That is, Northwest Mesopotamia [d]25 *Esau* may mean *hairy*; he was also called Edom, which means *red.* [e]26 *Jacob* means *he grasps the heel* (figuratively, *he deceives*). [f]30 *Edom* means *red.*

swore an oath to him, selling his birthright
to Jacob.
34Then Jacob gave Esau some bread and
some lentil stew. He ate and drank, and then
got up and left.
So Esau despised his birthright.

Isaac and Abimelech

26 Now there was a famine in the land—
besides the earlier famine of Abraham's
time—and Isaac went to Abimelech king of the
Philistines in Gerar. 2The LORD appeared to
Isaac and said, "Do not go down to Egypt; live
in the land where I tell you to live. 3Stay in this
land for a while, and I will be with you and will
bless you. For to you and your descendants I
will give all these lands and will confirm the
oath I swore to your father Abraham. 4I will
make your descendants as numerous as the
stars in the sky and will give them all these
lands, and through your offspring[a] all nations
on earth will be blessed, 5because Abraham
obeyed me and kept my requirements, my
commands, my decrees and my laws." 6So Isaac
stayed in Gerar.
7When the men of that place
asked him about his wife, he
said, "She is my sister," because
he was afraid to say, "She is my
wife." He thought, "The men of
this place might kill me on account of Rebekah, because she
is beautiful."
8When Isaac had been there
a long time, Abimelech king
of the Philistines looked down
from a window and saw Isaac
caressing his wife Rebekah. 9So
Abimelech summoned Isaac
and said, "She is really your
wife! Why did you say, 'She is
my sister'?"
Isaac answered him, "Be-
cause I thought I might lose my
life on account of her."
10Then Abimelech said, "What is this you
have done to us? One of the men might well
have slept with your wife, and you would have
brought guilt upon us."

> **Genesis 26:24**
>
> *God Keeps Promises*
>
> The LORD appeared to him and said, "I am the God of your father Abraham. Do not be afraid, for I am with you; I will bless you and will increase the number of your descendants for the sake of my servant Abraham."

11So Abimelech gave orders to all the people: "Anyone who molests this man or his wife
shall surely be put to death."
12Isaac planted crops in that land and the
same year reaped a hundredfold, because the
LORD blessed him. 13The man became rich,
and his wealth continued to grow until he became very wealthy. 14He had so many flocks
and herds and servants that the Philistines
envied him. 15So all the wells that his father's
servants had dug in the time of his father Abraham, the Philistines stopped up, filling them
with earth.
16Then Abimelech said to Isaac, "Move
away from us; you have become too powerful
for us."
17So Isaac moved away from there and encamped in the Valley of Gerar and settled
there. 18Isaac reopened the wells that had been
dug in the time of his father Abraham, which
the Philistines had stopped up after Abraham
died, and he gave them the same names his father had given them.
19Isaac's servants dug in the valley and discovered a well of fresh water
there. 20But the herdsmen of
Gerar quarreled with Isaac's
herdsmen and said, "The water
is ours!" So he named the well
Esek,[b] because they disputed
with him. 21Then they dug
another well, but they quarreled over that one also; so he
named it Sitnah.[c] 22He moved
on from there and dug another
well, and no one quarreled over
it. He named it Rehoboth,[d] saying, "Now the LORD has given
us room and we will flourish in
the land."
23From there he went up to
Beersheba. 24That night the
LORD appeared to him and
said, "I am the God of your
father Abraham. Do not be
afraid, for I am with you; I will bless you and
will increase the number of your descendants
for the sake of my servant Abraham."
25Isaac built an altar there and called on the

[a]4 Or *seed* [b]20 *Esek* means *dispute.* [c]21 *Sitnah* means *opposition.* [d]22 *Rehoboth* means *room.*

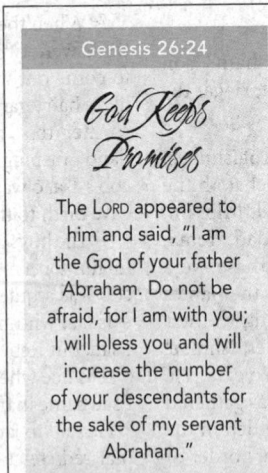

name of the LORD. There he pitched his tent,
and there his servants dug a well.
26 Meanwhile, Abimelech had come to him
from Gerar, with Ahuzzath his personal adviser
and Phicol the commander of his forces. 27 Isaac
asked them, "Why have you come to me, since
you were hostile to me and sent me away?"
28 They answered, "We saw clearly that the
LORD was with you; so we said, 'There ought
to be a sworn agreement between us'—between us and you. Let us make a treaty with
you 29 that you will do us no harm, just as we
did not molest you but always treated you well
and sent you away in peace. And now you are
blessed by the LORD."
30 Isaac then made a feast for them, and they
ate and drank. 31 Early the next morning the
men swore an oath to each other. Then Isaac
sent them on their way, and they left him
in peace.
32 That day Isaac's servants came and told
him about the well they had dug. They said,
"We've found water!" 33 He called it Shibah,[a]
and to this day the name of the town has been
Beersheba.[b]
34 When Esau was forty years old, he married Judith daughter of Beeri the Hittite, and
also Basemath daughter of Elon the Hittite.
35 They were a source of grief to Isaac and
Rebekah.

Jacob Gets Isaac's Blessing

27 When Isaac was old and his eyes were
so weak that he could no longer see, he
called for Esau his older son and said to him,
"My son."
"Here I am," he answered.
2 Isaac said, "I am now an old man and don't
know the day of my death. 3 Now then, get your
weapons—your quiver and bow—and go out
to the open country to hunt some wild game
for me. 4 Prepare me the kind of tasty food I like
and bring it to me to eat, so that I may give you
my blessing before I die."
5 Now Rebekah was listening as Isaac spoke to
his son Esau. When Esau left for the open country to hunt game and bring it back, 6 Rebekah
said to her son Jacob, "Look, I overheard your
father say to your brother Esau, 7 'Bring me
some game and prepare me some tasty food to
eat, so that I may give you my blessing in the
presence of the LORD before I die.' 8 Now, my
son, listen carefully and do what I tell you: 9 Go
out to the flock and bring me two choice young
goats, so I can prepare some tasty food for your
father, just the way he likes it. 10 Then take it to
your father to eat, so that he may give you his
blessing before he dies."
11 Jacob said to Rebekah his mother, "But
my brother Esau is a hairy man, and I'm a man
with smooth skin. 12 What if my father touches
me? I would appear to be tricking him and
would bring down a curse on myself rather
than a blessing."
13 His mother said to him, "My son, let the
curse fall on me. Just do what I say; go and get
them for me."
14 So he went and got them and brought
them to his mother, and she prepared some
tasty food, just the way his father liked it.
15 Then Rebekah took the best clothes of Esau
her older son, which she had in the house, and
put them on her younger son Jacob. 16 She also
covered his hands and the smooth part of his
neck with the goatskins. 17 Then she handed to
her son Jacob the tasty food and the bread she
had made.
18 He went to his father and said, "My father."
"Yes, my son," he answered. "Who is it?"
19 Jacob said to his father, "I am Esau your
firstborn. I have done as you told me. Please sit
up and eat some of my game so that you may
give me your blessing."
20 Isaac asked his son, "How did you find it
so quickly, my son?"
"The LORD your God gave me success," he
replied.
21 Then Isaac said to Jacob, "Come near so I
can touch you, my son, to know whether you
really are my son Esau or not."
22 Jacob went close to his father Isaac, who
touched him and said, "The voice is the voice
of Jacob, but the hands are the hands of Esau."
23 He did not recognize him, for his hands
were hairy like those of his brother Esau; so he
blessed him. 24 "Are you really my son Esau?"
he asked.
"I am," he replied.

[a] 33 *Shibah* can mean *oath* or *seven*. [b] 33 *Beersheba* can mean *well of the oath* or *well of seven.*

Meddling

Read: Genesis 27:1–40

Genesis 27:13–15

His mother said to him, "My son, let the curse fall on me. Just do what I say; go and get them for me." So he went and got them and brought them to his mother, and she prepared some tasty food, just the way his father liked it. Then Rebekah took the best clothes of Esau her older son, which she had in the house, and put them on her younger son Jacob.

OH, HOW WE LOVE TO MEDDLE. We may call it by other names, of course. Motherly concern. Friendly advice. A word to the wise. But when we boil it down and take a good look at what's left in the bottom of the pot, it's really just plain, old-fashioned meddling.

Rebekah thought she had good reason to meddle. (But then, don't we always *think* we have a good reason?) During her pregnancy, her twin baby boys had wrestled in her womb for position. That's when God told her that Esau, her older son, would serve Jacob, the younger. Now her husband was preparing to give the blessing and all of its benefits to Esau. She had to do something—fast! So she meddled.

You know, a funny thing happens when we meddle. We usually succeed: something changes. But succeeding can come with a high price tag—much higher than we ever expected to pay. The price Rebekah paid for meddling was painfully high. She turned her sons against one another. She sent Jacob away to escape Esau's wrath, never to see him again. She alienated herself from her husband and her firstborn son. But worst of all, she deprived herself of seeing how God would have fulfilled his promise to her.

If you search your Bible, you won't find any verses telling you to trust in your own ways or to interfere in other people's business because God can't handle it. You won't find God telling you to meddle so that his perfect will can be done. God doesn't encourage his people to scheme or to plan or to quick, come up with something—anything! If you are frantically trying to figure out what to do, it's a good clue that you need to slow down, take a deep breath and take a giant step back.

Instead of wasting your energy meddling, try pouring your energy into meditating. Meditate on God's goodness, his faithfulness, his character traits and his promises. When you begin turning your eyes to the Lord rather than sticking your nose into other people's business, you'll soon discover that he is always busy intervening on behalf of his people—including you and the people you love.

reflection

1 When have you meddled your way through a problem instead of waiting on God to solve it? What were the results?

2 When have you seen God solve a problem in a way that surprised you?

3 What are you waiting on God for now? What will you meditate *on* rather than meddle *in*?

RELATED READINGS

Genesis 25:19–28; Psalms 27:14; 77:10–14; Proverbs 19:2

Go to page 38 for your next devotional reading.

25Then he said, "My son, bring me some of
your game to eat, so that I may give you my
blessing."
Jacob brought it to him and he ate; and he
brought some wine and he drank. 26Then his
father Isaac said to him, "Come here, my son,
and kiss me."
27So he went to him and kissed him. When
Isaac caught the smell of his clothes, he blessed
him and said,

"Ah, the smell of my son
is like the smell of a field
that the LORD has blessed.
28May God give you of heaven's dew
and of earth's richness—
an abundance of grain and new
wine.
29May nations serve you
and peoples bow down to you.
Be lord over your brothers,
and may the sons of your mother bow
down to you.
May those who curse you be cursed
and those who bless you be blessed."

30After Isaac finished blessing him and Jacob had scarcely left his father's presence, his
brother Esau came in from hunting. 31He too
prepared some tasty food and brought it to his
father. Then he said to him, "My father, sit up
and eat some of my game, so that you may give
me your blessing."
32His father Isaac asked him, "Who are
you?"
"I am your son," he answered, "your firstborn, Esau."
33Isaac trembled violently and said, "Who
was it, then, that hunted game and brought it to
me? I ate it just before you came and I blessed
him—and indeed he will be blessed!"
34When Esau heard his father's words, he
burst out with a loud and bitter cry and said to
his father, "Bless me—me too, my father!"
35But he said, "Your brother came deceitfully
and took your blessing."
36Esau said, "Isn't he rightly named Jacob[a]?
He has deceived me these two times: He took
my birthright, and now he's taken my blessing!" Then he asked, "Haven't you reserved any
blessing for me?"
37Isaac answered Esau, "I have made him
lord over you and have made all his relatives his
servants, and I have sustained him with grain
and new wine. So what can I possibly do for
you, my son?"
38Esau said to his father, "Do you have only
one blessing, my father? Bless me too, my father!" Then Esau wept aloud.
39His father Isaac answered him,

"Your dwelling will be
away from the earth's richness,
away from the dew of heaven above.
40You will live by the sword
and you will serve your brother.
But when you grow restless,
you will throw his yoke
from off your neck."

Jacob Flees to Laban

41Esau held a grudge against Jacob because
of the blessing his father had given him. He said
to himself, "The days of mourning for my father
are near; then I will kill my brother Jacob."
42When Rebekah was told what her older
son Esau had said, she sent for her younger
son Jacob and said to him, "Your brother Esau
is consoling himself with the thought of killing
you. 43Now then, my son, do what I say: Flee
at once to my brother Laban in Haran. 44Stay
with him for a while until your brother's fury
subsides. 45When your brother is no longer angry with you and forgets what you did to him,
I'll send word for you to come back from there.
Why should I lose both of you in one day?"
46Then Rebekah said to Isaac, "I'm disgusted
with living because of these Hittite women. If
Jacob takes a wife from among the women of
this land, from Hittite women like these, my
life will not be worth living."

28 So Isaac called for Jacob and blessed[b]
him and commanded him: "Do not
marry a Canaanite woman. 2Go at once to
Paddan Aram,[c] to the house of your mother's
father Bethuel. Take a wife for yourself there,
from among the daughters of Laban, your
mother's brother. 3May God Almighty[d] bless

a36 *Jacob* means *he grasps the heel* (figuratively, *he deceives*). b1 Or *greeted* c2 That is, Northwest Mesopotamia; also in verses 5, 6 and 7 d3 Hebrew *El-Shaddai*

you and make you fruitful and increase your
numbers until you become a community of
peoples. 4May he give you and your descendants the blessing given to Abraham, so that
you may take possession of the land where you
now live as an alien, the land God gave to Abraham." 5Then Isaac sent Jacob on his way, and he
went to Paddan Aram, to Laban son of Bethuel
the Aramean, the brother of Rebekah, who was
the mother of Jacob and Esau.

6Now Esau learned that Isaac had blessed Jacob and had sent him to Paddan Aram to take
a wife from there, and that when he blessed
him he commanded him, "Do not marry a Canaanite woman," 7and that Jacob had obeyed
his father and mother and had gone to Paddan
Aram. 8Esau then realized how displeasing
the Canaanite women were to his father Isaac;
9so he went to Ishmael and married Mahalath,
the sister of Nebaioth and daughter of Ishmael
son of Abraham, in addition to the wives he
already had.

Jacob's Dream at Bethel

10Jacob left Beersheba and set out for Haran.
11When he reached a certain place, he stopped
for the night because the sun had set. Taking
one of the stones there, he put it under his head
and lay down to sleep. 12He
had a dream in which he saw a
stairway[a] resting on the earth,
with its top reaching to heaven,
and the angels of God were ascending and descending on
it. 13There above it[b] stood the
LORD, and he said: "I am the
LORD, the God of your father
Abraham and the God of Isaac.
I will give you and your descendants the land on which you
are lying. 14Your descendants
will be like the dust of the
earth, and you will spread out
to the west and to the east, to
the north and to the south. All
peoples on earth will be blessed
through you and your offspring. 15I am with
you and will watch over you wherever you go,
and I will bring you back to this land. I will not
leave you until I have done what I have promised
you."

16When Jacob awoke from his sleep, he
thought, "Surely the LORD is in this place, and
I was not aware of it." 17He was afraid and
said, "How awesome is this place! This is none
other than the house of God; this is the gate
of heaven."

18Early the next morning Jacob took the
stone he had placed under his head and set it
up as a pillar and poured oil on top of it. 19He
called that place Bethel,[c] though the city used
to be called Luz.

20Then Jacob made a vow, saying, "If God
will be with me and will watch over me on this
journey I am taking and will give me food to
eat and clothes to wear 21so that I return safely
to my father's house, then the LORD[d] will be
my God 22and[e] this stone that I have set up as
a pillar will be God's house, and of all that you
give me I will give you a tenth."

Jacob Arrives in Paddan Aram

29 Then Jacob continued on his journey
and came to the land of the eastern
peoples. 2There he saw a well in the field, with
three flocks of sheep lying near it because the
flocks were watered from that
well. The stone over the mouth
of the well was large. 3When
all the flocks were gathered
there, the shepherds would
roll the stone away from the
well's mouth and water the
sheep. Then they would return
the stone to its place over the
mouth of the well.

4Jacob asked the shepherds,
"My brothers, where are
you from?"

"We're from Haran," they replied.

5He said to them, "Do you
know Laban, Nahor's grandson?"

"Yes, we know him," they answered.

6Then Jacob asked them, "Is he well?"

Genesis 28:15

God Watches Over Us

"I am with you and will watch over you wherever you go, and I will bring you back to this land. I will not leave you until I have done what I have promised you."

[a]12 Or *ladder* [b]13 Or *There beside him* [c]19 *Bethel* means *house of God.* [d]20,21 Or *Since God . . . father's house, the LORD*
[e]21,22 Or *house, and the LORD will be my God, 22then*

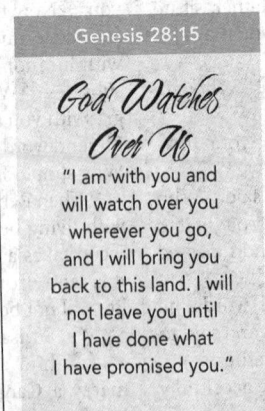

"Yes, he is," they said, "and here comes his
daughter Rachel with the sheep."
7"Look," he said, "the sun is still high; it is
not time for the flocks to be gathered. Water
the sheep and take them back to pasture."
8"We can't," they replied, "until all the flocks
are gathered and the stone has been rolled
away from the mouth of the well. Then we will
water the sheep."
9While he was still talking with them, Rachel came with her father's sheep, for she was a
shepherdess. 10When Jacob saw Rachel daughter of Laban, his mother's brother, and Laban's
sheep, he went over and rolled the stone away
from the mouth of the well and watered his
uncle's sheep. 11Then Jacob kissed Rachel and
began to weep aloud. 12He had told Rachel
that he was a relative of her father and a son of
Rebekah. So she ran and told her father.
13As soon as Laban heard the news about
Jacob, his sister's son, he hurried to meet him.
He embraced him and kissed him and brought
him to his home, and there Jacob told him all
these things. 14Then Laban said to him, "You
are my own flesh and blood."

Jacob Marries Leah and Rachel

After Jacob had stayed with him for a whole
month, 15Laban said to him, "Just because
you are a relative of mine, should you work
for me for nothing? Tell me what your wages
should be."
16Now Laban had two daughters; the name
of the older was Leah, and the name of the
younger was Rachel. 17Leah had weak[a] eyes,
but Rachel was lovely in form, and beautiful.
18Jacob was in love with Rachel and said, "I'll
work for you seven years in return for your
younger daughter Rachel."
19Laban said, "It's better that I give her to
you than to some other man. Stay here with
me." 20So Jacob served seven years to get Rachel, but they seemed like only a few days to
him because of his love for her.
21Then Jacob said to Laban, "Give me my
wife. My time is completed, and I want to lie
with her."
22So Laban brought together all the people
of the place and gave a feast. 23But when evening came, he took his daughter Leah and gave
her to Jacob, and Jacob lay with her. 24And Laban gave his servant girl Zilpah to his daughter
as her maidservant.
25When morning came, there was Leah! So
Jacob said to Laban, "What is this you have
done to me? I served you for Rachel, didn't I?
Why have you deceived me?"
26Laban replied, "It is not our custom here
to give the younger daughter in marriage before the older one. 27Finish this daughter's
bridal week; then we will give you the younger one also, in return for another seven years
of work."
28And Jacob did so. He finished the week
with Leah, and then Laban gave him his daughter Rachel to be his wife. 29Laban gave his servant girl Bilhah to his daughter Rachel as her
maidservant. 30Jacob lay with Rachel also,
and he loved Rachel more than Leah. And he
worked for Laban another seven years.

Jacob's Children

31When the LORD saw that Leah was not
loved, he opened her womb, but Rachel was barren. 32Leah became pregnant and gave birth to
a son. She named him Reuben,[b] for she said, "It
is because the LORD has seen my misery. Surely
my husband will love me now."
33She conceived again, and when she gave
birth to a son she said, "Because the LORD
heard that I am not loved, he gave me this one
too." So she named him Simeon.[c]
34Again she conceived, and when she gave
birth to a son she said, "Now at last my husband will become attached to me, because I
have borne him three sons." So he was named
Levi.[d]
35She conceived again, and when she gave
birth to a son she said, "This time I will praise
the LORD." So she named him Judah.[e] Then she
stopped having children.

30 When Rachel saw that she was not bearing Jacob any children, she became jealous of her sister. So she said to Jacob, "Give me
children, or I'll die!"
2Jacob became angry with her and said,

[a]17 Or *delicate* [b]32 *Reuben* sounds like the Hebrew for *he has seen my misery*; the name means *see, a son.* [c]33 *Simeon* probably means *one who hears.* [d]34 *Levi* sounds like and may be derived from the Hebrew for *attached.* [e]35 *Judah* sounds like and may be derived from the Hebrew for *praise.*

When Morning Comes

Read: Genesis 29:16–30

Genesis 29:23,25

But when evening came, he took his daughter Leah and gave her to Jacob . . . When morning came, there was Leah!

IMAGINE THE SINKING FEELING you might feel when a beautiful, intelligent, accomplished woman arrives on the scene. She may be the new hire who took a promotion you've worked years to attain. She may be the charming wife of a friend. She may be the mother whose children have impeccable manners and dress. Whoever she is, she shakes your confidence, and ugly feelings of envy and self-loathing rear their heads, if only for a moment.

Leah came to her wedding night cloaked under layers of bridal veils. But her cover didn't last long: Morning came and her true identity came to light. Jacob was shocked to find that he had been deceived into marrying his beloved Rachel's sister.

The Bible places the blame squarely on Laban's shoulders: "He took his daughter Leah and gave her to Jacob." But did Leah play any part in the deceit? Was she simply obeying a conniving father, was she making a last-ditch effort to win a lover, or—on some hidden level—was she seeking to spite a sister more beautiful than herself? We will never know what kept Leah quiet as she went to marry Jacob, disguised beneath veils and robes, bangles and jewels. But we do know that in the clear light of morning, the game was up for the whole family.

If Leah hid beneath her veil, Laban hid behind the status quo. He failed to take responsibility for the pain Jacob, Leah and Rachel were to endure for years. He shifted the blame to his country's customs. And he shamelessly drove a hard bargain to keep Jacob in bondage. Laban's greed overcame common decency. He inflicted permanent and painful scars on his family.

Do you feel you have to hide your true self to gain a relationship? Perhaps you are elaborately and even beautifully veiling yourself with another person's interests, hobbies or pursuits to win their affections. Does the equivalent of a beautiful sister and deceitful father make you feel pushed to the sidelines, forced to veil yourself because you are afraid you won't be accepted as you are?

It could be that, like Leah, you fear that you are unlovely compared to others. But God created you—you are both lovely and lovable just as you are. Today, ask God for the courage to remove the veils covering your heart and recognize the beauty of his image in you.

reflection

1 Take a look in the mirror and describe the things you like about yourself.

2 What don't you like about yourself? Describe some of the things you'd change if you could.

3 What parts of yourself have you been afraid to show your loved ones (spiritually, emotionally or physically), and why? Take a chance and expose one part you've hidden behind the mask. Ask God to give you the strength to take this step. And ask God to surprise you with how much your loved ones accept the real you.

RELATED READINGS

Psalm 139:23–24; 1 John 1:5–7

Wednesday

Go to page 43 for your next devotional reading.

"Am I in the place of God, who has kept you
from having children?"
3 Then she said, "Here is Bilhah, my maidservant. Sleep with her so that she can bear
children for me and that through her I too can
build a family."
4 So she gave him her servant Bilhah as a
wife. Jacob slept with her, 5 and she became
pregnant and bore him a son. 6 Then Rachel
said, "God has vindicated me; he has listened
to my plea and given me a son." Because of this
she named him Dan.[a]
7 Rachel's servant Bilhah conceived again and
bore Jacob a second son. 8 Then Rachel said, "I
have had a great struggle with my sister, and I
have won." So she named him Naphtali.[b]
9 When Leah saw that she had stopped having
children, she took her maidservant Zilpah and
gave her to Jacob as a wife. 10 Leah's servant Zilpah bore Jacob a son. 11 Then Leah said, "What
good fortune!"[c] So she named him Gad.[d]
12 Leah's servant Zilpah bore Jacob a second
son. 13 Then Leah said, "How happy I am! The
women will call me happy." So she named him
Asher.[e]
14 During wheat harvest, Reuben went out
into the fields and found some mandrake
plants, which he brought to his mother Leah.
Rachel said to Leah, "Please give me some of
your son's mandrakes."
15 But she said to her, "Wasn't it enough that
you took away my husband? Will you take my
son's mandrakes too?"
"Very well," Rachel said, "he can sleep with
you tonight in return for your son's mandrakes."
16 So when Jacob came in from the fields
that evening, Leah went out to meet him. "You
must sleep with me," she said. "I have hired you
with my son's mandrakes." So he slept with her
that night.
17 God listened to Leah, and she became
pregnant and bore Jacob a fifth son. 18 Then
Leah said, "God has rewarded me for giving
my maidservant to my husband." So she named
him Issachar.[f]
19 Leah conceived again and bore Jacob a
sixth son. 20 Then Leah said, "God has presented
me with a precious gift. This time my husband
will treat me with honor, because I have borne
him six sons." So she named him Zebulun.[g]
21 Some time later she gave birth to a daughter and named her Dinah.
22 Then God remembered Rachel; he listened to her and opened her womb. 23 She
became pregnant and gave birth to a son and
said, "God has taken away my disgrace." 24 She
named him Joseph,[h] and said, "May the LORD
add to me another son."

Jacob's Flocks Increase

25 After Rachel gave birth to Joseph, Jacob
said to Laban, "Send me on my way so I can
go back to my own homeland. 26 Give me my
wives and children, for whom I have served
you, and I will be on my way. You know how
much work I've done for you."
27 But Laban said to him, "If I have found
favor in your eyes, please stay. I have learned
by divination that[i] the LORD has blessed me because of you." 28 He added, "Name your wages,
and I will pay them."
29 Jacob said to him, "You know how I have
worked for you and how your livestock has
fared under my care. 30 The little you had before I came has increased greatly, and the LORD
has blessed you wherever I have been. But now,
when may I do something for my own household?"
31 "What shall I give you?" he asked.
"Don't give me anything," Jacob replied. "But
if you will do this one thing for me, I will go on
tending your flocks and watching over them:
32 Let me go through all your flocks today and
remove from them every speckled or spotted
sheep, every dark-colored lamb and every spotted or speckled goat. They will be my wages.
33 And my honesty will testify for me in the
future, whenever you check on the wages you
have paid me. Any goat in my possession that is
not speckled or spotted, or any lamb that is not
dark-colored, will be considered stolen."
34 "Agreed," said Laban. "Let it be as you have
said." 35 That same day he removed all the male
goats that were streaked or spotted, and all the
speckled or spotted female goats (all that had

[a]6 *Dan* here means *he has vindicated.* [b]8 *Naphtali* means *my struggle.* [c]11 Or *"A troop is coming!"* [d]11 *Gad* can mean *good fortune* or *a troop.* [e]13 *Asher* means *happy.* [f]18 *Issachar* sounds like the Hebrew for *reward.* [g]20 *Zebulun* probably means *honor.* [h]24 *Joseph* means *may he add.* [i]27 Or possibly *have become rich and*

white on them) and all the dark-colored lambs,
and he placed them in the care of his sons.
[36]Then he put a three-day journey between
himself and Jacob, while Jacob continued to
tend the rest of Laban's flocks.
[37]Jacob, however, took fresh-cut branches
from poplar, almond and plane
trees and made white stripes
on them by peeling the bark
and exposing the white inner
wood of the branches. [38]Then
he placed the peeled branches
in all the watering troughs, so
that they would be directly in
front of the flocks when they
came to drink. When the
flocks were in heat and came
to drink, [39]they mated in front
of the branches. And they
bore young that were streaked
or speckled or spotted. [40]Ja-
cob set apart the young of the
flock by themselves, but made
the rest face the streaked and
dark-colored animals that belonged to Laban. Thus he made separate flocks for himself
and did not put them with Laban's animals.
[41]Whenever the stronger females were in heat,
Jacob would place the branches in the troughs
in front of the animals so they would mate near
the branches, [42]but if the animals were weak,
he would not place them there. So the weak
animals went to Laban and the strong ones to
Jacob. [43]In this way the man grew exceedingly
prosperous and came to own large flocks, and
maidservants and menservants, and camels
and donkeys.

Jacob Flees From Laban

31 Jacob heard that Laban's sons were saying, "Jacob has taken everything our
father owned and has gained all this wealth
from what belonged to our father." [2]And Jacob
noticed that Laban's attitude toward him was
not what it had been.
[3]Then the LORD said to Jacob, "Go back to
the land of your fathers and to your relatives,
and I will be with you."
[4]So Jacob sent word to Rachel and Leah to
come out to the fields where his flocks were.
[5]He said to them, "I see that your father's attitude toward me is not what it was before, but
the God of my father has been with me. [6]You
know that I've worked for your father with all
my strength, [7]yet your father has cheated me by
changing my wages ten times.
However, God has not allowed
him to harm me. [8]If he said,
'The speckled ones will be your
wages,' then all the flocks gave
birth to speckled young; and
if he said, 'The streaked ones
will be your wages,' then all the
flocks bore streaked young.
[9]So God has taken away your
father's livestock and has given
them to me.
[10]"In breeding season I once
had a dream in which I looked
up and saw that the male goats
mating with the flock were
streaked, speckled or spotted.
[11]The angel of God said to me
in the dream, 'Jacob.' I answered, 'Here I am.'
[12]And he said, 'Look up and see that all the
male goats mating with the flock are streaked,
speckled or spotted, for I have seen all that Laban has been doing to you. [13]I am the God of
Bethel, where you anointed a pillar and where
you made a vow to me. Now leave this land at
once and go back to your native land.'"
[14]Then Rachel and Leah replied, "Do we still
have any share in the inheritance of our father's
estate? [15]Does he not regard us as foreigners?
Not only has he sold us, but he has used up
what was paid for us. [16]Surely all the wealth
that God took away from our father belongs to
us and our children. So do whatever God has
told you."
[17]Then Jacob put his children and his wives
on camels, [18]and he drove all his livestock
ahead of him, along with all the goods he had
accumulated in Paddan Aram,[a] to go to his father Isaac in the land of Canaan.
[19]When Laban had gone to shear his
sheep, Rachel stole her father's household
gods. [20]Moreover, Jacob deceived Laban the
Aramean by not telling him he was running

Genesis 31:6–7

God Defends the Disadvantaged

"You know that I've worked for your father with all my strength, yet your father has cheated me by changing my wages ten times. However, God has not allowed him to harm me."

[a]18 That is, Northwest Mesopotamia

away. 21So he fled with all he had, and crossing the River,[a] he headed for the hill country
of Gilead.

Laban Pursues Jacob

22On the third day Laban was told that Jacob had fled. 23Taking his relatives with him,
he pursued Jacob for seven days and caught up
with him in the hill country of Gilead. 24Then
God came to Laban the Aramean in a dream
at night and said to him, "Be careful not to say
anything to Jacob, either good or bad."

25Jacob had pitched his tent in the hill country of Gilead when Laban overtook him, and
Laban and his relatives camped there too.
26Then Laban said to Jacob, "What have you
done? You've deceived me, and you've carried
off my daughters like captives in war. 27Why
did you run off secretly and deceive me?
Why didn't you tell me, so I could send you
away with joy and singing to the music of tambourines and harps? 28You didn't even let me
kiss my grandchildren and my daughters good-
by. You have done a foolish thing. 29I have the
power to harm you; but last night the God of
your father said to me, 'Be careful not to say
anything to Jacob, either good or bad.' 30Now
you have gone off because you longed to return
to your father's house. But why did you steal
my gods?"

31Jacob answered Laban, "I was afraid, because I thought you would take your daughters away from me by force. 32But if you find
anyone who has your gods, he shall not live. In
the presence of our relatives, see for yourself
whether there is anything of yours here with
me; and if so, take it." Now Jacob did not know
that Rachel had stolen the gods.

33So Laban went into Jacob's tent and into
Leah's tent and into the tent of the two maidservants, but he found nothing. After he came
out of Leah's tent, he entered Rachel's tent.
34Now Rachel had taken the household gods
and put them inside her camel's saddle and was
sitting on them. Laban searched through everything in the tent but found nothing.

35Rachel said to her father, "Don't be angry,
my lord, that I cannot stand up in your presence; I'm having my period." So he searched
but could not find the household gods.

36Jacob was angry and took Laban to task.
"What is my crime?" he asked Laban. "What
sin have I committed that you hunt me down?
37Now that you have searched through all my
goods, what have you found that belongs to
your household? Put it here in front of your relatives and mine, and let them judge between
the two of us.

38"I have been with you for twenty years
now. Your sheep and goats have not miscarried,
nor have I eaten rams from your flocks. 39I did
not bring you animals torn by wild beasts; I
bore the loss myself. And you demanded payment from me for whatever was stolen by day
or night. 40This was my situation: The heat consumed me in the daytime and the cold at night,
and sleep fled from my eyes. 41It was like this
for the twenty years I was in your household.
I worked for you fourteen years for your two
daughters and six years for your flocks, and you
changed my wages ten times. 42If the God of
my father, the God of Abraham and the Fear of
Isaac, had not been with me, you would surely
have sent me away empty-handed. But God
has seen my hardship and the toil of my hands,
and last night he rebuked you."

43Laban answered Jacob, "The women are
my daughters, the children are my children,
and the flocks are my flocks. All you see is mine.
Yet what can I do today about these daughters
of mine, or about the children they have borne?
44Come now, let's make a covenant, you and I,
and let it serve as a witness between us."

45So Jacob took a stone and set it up as a
pillar. 46He said to his relatives, "Gather some
stones." So they took stones and piled them in
a heap, and they ate there by the heap. 47Laban
called it Jegar Sahadutha,[b] and Jacob called it
Galeed.[c]

48Laban said, "This heap is a witness between you and me today." That is why it was
called Galeed. 49It was also called Mizpah,[d]
because he said, "May the LORD keep watch
between you and me when we are away from
each other. 50If you mistreat my daughters or if
you take any wives besides my daughters, even

[a]21 That is, the Euphrates [b]47 The Aramaic *Jegar Sahadutha* means *witness heap.* [c]47 The Hebrew *Galeed* means *witness heap.*
[d]49 *Mizpah* means *watchtower.*

though no one is with us, remember that God
is a witness between you and me."
51Laban also said to Jacob, "Here is this
heap, and here is this pillar I have set up between you and me. 52This heap is a witness,
and this pillar is a witness, that I will not go
past this heap to your side to harm you and
that you will not go past this heap and pillar to
my side to harm me. 53May the God of Abraham and the God of Nahor, the God of their
father, judge between us."
So Jacob took an oath in the name of the
Fear of his father Isaac. 54He offered a sacrifice there in the hill country and invited his
relatives to a meal. After they had eaten, they
spent the night there.
55Early the next morning Laban kissed his
grandchildren and his daughters and blessed
them. Then he left and returned home.

Jacob Prepares to Meet Esau

32 Jacob also went on his way, and the angels of God met him. 2When Jacob saw
them, he said, "This is the camp of God!" So he
named that place Mahanaim.[a]
3Jacob sent messengers ahead of him to his
brother Esau in the land of Seir, the country
of Edom. 4He instructed them: "This is what
you are to say to my master Esau: 'Your servant
Jacob says, I have been staying with Laban and
have remained there till now. 5I have cattle
and donkeys, sheep and goats, menservants
and maidservants. Now I am sending this message to my lord, that I may find favor in your
eyes.'"
6When the messengers returned to Jacob,
they said, "We went to your brother Esau, and
now he is coming to meet you, and four hundred men are with him."
7In great fear and distress Jacob divided the
people who were with him into two groups,[b]
and the flocks and herds and camels as well.
8He thought, "If Esau comes and attacks one
group,[c] the group[c] that is left may escape."
9Then Jacob prayed, "O God of my father
Abraham, God of my father Isaac, O LORD,
who said to me, 'Go back to your country and
your relatives, and I will make you prosper,' 10I
am unworthy of all the kindness and faithfulness you have shown your servant. I had only
my staff when I crossed this Jordan, but now
I have become two groups. 11Save me, I pray,
from the hand of my brother Esau, for I am
afraid he will come and attack me, and also the
mothers with their children. 12But you have
said, 'I will surely make you prosper and will
make your descendants like the sand of the sea,
which cannot be counted.'"
13He spent the night there, and from what he
had with him he selected a gift for his brother
Esau: 14two hundred female goats and twenty
male goats, two hundred ewes and twenty
rams, 15thirty female camels with their young,
forty cows and ten bulls, and twenty female
donkeys and ten male donkeys. 16He put them
in the care of his servants, each herd by itself,
and said to his servants, "Go ahead of me, and
keep some space between the herds."
17He instructed the one in the lead: "When
my brother Esau meets you and asks, 'To whom
do you belong, and where are you going, and
who owns all these animals in front of you?'
18then you are to say, 'They belong to your servant Jacob. They are a gift sent to my lord Esau,
and he is coming behind us.'"
19He also instructed the second, the third
and all the others who followed the herds: "You
are to say the same thing to Esau when you
meet him. 20And be sure to say, 'Your servant
Jacob is coming behind us.'" For he thought,
"I will pacify him with these gifts I am sending on ahead; later, when I see him, perhaps
he will receive me." 21So Jacob's gifts went on
ahead of him, but he himself spent the night
in the camp.

Jacob Wrestles With God

22That night Jacob got up and took his two
wives, his two maidservants and his eleven
sons and crossed the ford of the Jabbok. 23Af-
ter he had sent them across the stream, he
sent over all his possessions. 24So Jacob was
left alone, and a man wrestled with him till
daybreak. 25When the man saw that he could
not overpower him, he touched the socket of
Jacob's hip so that his hip was wrenched as he
wrestled with the man. 26Then the man said,
"Let me go, for it is daybreak."

[a]2 *Mahanaim* means *two camps.* [b]7 Or *camps*; also in verse 10 [c]8 Or *camp*

He Breaks Us to Make Us

Read: Genesis 32:22–32

THERE'S A GOOD REASON God calls his people sheep. Sometimes they act ba-a-a-ad and wander away from the paths he has mapped out for them.

A good shepherd will relentlessly search for a wayward sheep. Sometimes, if the sheep refuses to follow his master, the shepherd takes drastic action. He breaks the sheep's leg, places it upon his shoulders and carries the sheep until it learns total dependence. This is tough love—the shepherd breaks the sheep to make sure the sheep always follows the shepherd.

Jacob had always been a wanderer. He fled his home in Beersheba to escape his brother's wrath and find a wife in Haran. On his journey, he encountered God at a place called Bethel and saw a stairway leading to heaven. Years later, Jacob left Haran along with his wives, children and property. One night he found himself at Jabbok, utterly alone. At this solitary place God, in the form of "a man," sought out Jacob. God wanted to make Jacob into a different person, so he took drastic action. He initiated a wrestling match that lasted from dusk till dawn. Jacob's willfulness would not allow him to give up. So the man "broke" Jacob, touching his hip so that he walked with a limp for the rest of his life. Many people might become bitter and turn away from God for breaking them. But Jacob had just the opposite response. He clung to God saying, "I will not let you go unless you bless me."

We may think that a God of love would never allow his children to feel any pain. But sometimes God breaks us to make us better. He may break our hearts so we will make room for him there. He may break our will so we can discover his will for us. He may break our physical strength so we discover that God's strength is made perfect in our weakness (see 2 Corinthians 12:9). Like Jacob, the best response to God's tough love is to cling to him and earnestly pray, "I will not let you go unless you bless me."

If you've been acting like ba-a-a-ad sheep and have wandered off the path, climb up on the shepherd's shoulders and let him carry you home to healing.

Genesis 32:24–26

So Jacob was left alone, and a man wrestled with him till daybreak. When the man saw that he could not overpower him, he touched the socket of Jacob's hip so that his hip was wrenched as he wrestled with the man. Then the man said, "Let me go, for it is daybreak." But Jacob replied, "I will not let you go unless you bless me."

reflection

1 Describe the times you have wandered from God and how you sensed him relentlessly seeking you.

2 How has God broken you physically, emotionally or spiritually? What was the result?

3 God is a good shepherd; thank him for his care for you even when you don't always understand his methods.

RELATED READINGS

Psalms 23; 51:15–17; James 1:2–5; 1 Peter 4:12–14

Go to page 46 for your next devotional reading.

But Jacob replied, "I will not let you go unless you bless me."
27The man asked him, "What is your
name?"
"Jacob," he answered.
28Then the man said, "Your name will
no longer be Jacob, but Israel,[a] because you
have struggled with God and with men and
have overcome."
29Jacob said, "Please tell me
your name."
But he replied, "Why do you
ask my name?" Then he blessed
him there.
30So Jacob called the place
Peniel,[b] saying, "It is because I
saw God face to face, and yet
my life was spared."
31The sun rose above him
as he passed Peniel,[c] and he
was limping because of his hip.
32Therefore to this day the Israelites do not eat the tendon
attached to the socket of the
hip, because the socket of Jacob's hip was touched near the
tendon.

Genesis 32:28

God Wrestles With His People

Then the man said, "Your name will no longer be Jacob, but Israel, because you have struggled with God and with men and have overcome."

Jacob Meets Esau

33 Jacob looked up and there was Esau,
coming with his four hundred men;
so he divided the children among Leah, Rachel and the two maidservants. 2He put the
maidservants and their children in front, Leah
and her children next, and Rachel and Joseph
in the rear. 3He himself went on ahead and
bowed down to the ground seven times as he
approached his brother.
4But Esau ran to meet Jacob and embraced
him; he threw his arms around his neck and
kissed him. And they wept. 5Then Esau looked
up and saw the women and children. "Who are
these with you?" he asked.
Jacob answered, "They are the children God
has graciously given your servant."
6Then the maidservants and their children
approached and bowed down. 7Next, Leah
and her children came and bowed down. Last
of all came Joseph and Rachel, and they too
bowed down.
8Esau asked, "What do you mean by all these
droves I met?"
"To find favor in your eyes, my lord,"
he said.
9But Esau said, "I already have plenty, my
brother. Keep what you have for yourself."
10"No, please!" said Jacob. "If I have found
favor in your eyes, accept this
gift from me. For to see your
face is like seeing the face of
God, now that you have received me favorably. 11Please
accept the present that was
brought to you, for God has
been gracious to me and I have
all I need." And because Jacob
insisted, Esau accepted it.
12Then Esau said, "Let us
be on our way; I'll accompany
you."
13But Jacob said to him, "My
lord knows that the children
are tender and that I must care
for the ewes and cows that are
nursing their young. If they are
driven hard just one day, all the
animals will die. 14So let my lord go on ahead
of his servant, while I move along slowly at the
pace of the droves before me and that of the
children, until I come to my lord in Seir."
15Esau said, "Then let me leave some of my
men with you."
"But why do that?" Jacob asked. "Just let me
find favor in the eyes of my lord."
16So that day Esau started on his way back
to Seir. 17Jacob, however, went to Succoth,
where he built a place for himself and made
shelters for his livestock. That is why the place
is called Succoth.[d]
18After Jacob came from Paddan Aram,[e]
he arrived safely at the[f] city of Shechem in Canaan and camped within sight of the city. 19For
a hundred pieces of silver,[g] he bought from the
sons of Hamor, the father of Shechem, the plot
of ground where he pitched his tent. 20There he
set up an altar and called it El Elohe Israel.[h]

[a]28 *Israel* means *he struggles with God.* [b]30 *Peniel* means *face of God.* [c]31 Hebrew *Penuel,* a variant of *Peniel* [d]17 *Succoth* means *shelters.* [e]18 That is, Northwest Mesopotamia [f]18 Or *arrived at Shalem, a* [g]19 Hebrew *hundred kesitahs*; a kesitah was a unit of money of unknown weight and value. [h]20 *El Elohe Israel* can mean *God, the God of Israel* or *mighty is the God of Israel.*

Dinah and the Shechemites

34 Now Dinah, the daughter Leah had
borne to Jacob, went out to visit the
women of the land. 2 When Shechem son of
Hamor the Hivite, the ruler of that area, saw
her, he took her and violated her. 3 His heart
was drawn to Dinah daughter of Jacob, and he
loved the girl and spoke tenderly to her. 4 And
Shechem said to his father Hamor, "Get me this
girl as my wife."
5 When Jacob heard that his daughter Dinah
had been defiled, his sons were in the fields
with his livestock; so he kept quiet about it until they came home.
6 Then Shechem's father Hamor went out to
talk with Jacob. 7 Now Jacob's sons had come in
from the fields as soon as they heard what had
happened. They were filled with grief and fury,
because Shechem had done a disgraceful thing
in[a] Israel by lying with Jacob's daughter—a
thing that should not be done.
8 But Hamor said to them, "My son Shechem
has his heart set on your daughter. Please give
her to him as his wife. 9 Intermarry with us;
give us your daughters and take our daughters
for yourselves. 10 You can settle among us; the
land is open to you. Live in it, trade[b] in it, and
acquire property in it."
11 Then Shechem said to Dinah's father and
brothers, "Let me find favor in your eyes, and
I will give you whatever you ask. 12 Make the
price for the bride and the gift I am to bring as
great as you like, and I'll pay whatever you ask
me. Only give me the girl as my wife."
13 Because their sister Dinah had been defiled, Jacob's sons replied deceitfully as they
spoke to Shechem and his father Hamor.
14 They said to them, "We can't do such a thing;
we can't give our sister to a man who is not circumcised. That would be a disgrace to us. 15 We
will give our consent to you on one condition
only: that you become like us by circumcising
all your males. 16 Then we will give you our
daughters and take your daughters for ourselves. We'll settle among you and become one
people with you. 17 But if you will not agree to
be circumcised, we'll take our sister[c] and go."
18 Their proposal seemed good to Hamor
and his son Shechem. 19 The young man, who
was the most honored of all his father's household, lost no time in doing what they said, because he was delighted with Jacob's daughter.
20 So Hamor and his son Shechem went to the
gate of their city to speak to their fellow townsmen. 21 "These men are friendly toward us,"
they said. "Let them live in our land and trade
in it; the land has plenty of room for them. We
can marry their daughters and they can marry
ours. 22 But the men will consent to live with
us as one people only on the condition that
our males be circumcised, as they themselves
are. 23 Won't their livestock, their property and
all their other animals become ours? So let us
give our consent to them, and they will settle
among us."
24 All the men who went out of the city gate
agreed with Hamor and his son Shechem, and
every male in the city was circumcised.
25 Three days later, while all of them were
still in pain, two of Jacob's sons, Simeon and
Levi, Dinah's brothers, took their swords and
attacked the unsuspecting city, killing every
male. 26 They put Hamor and his son Shechem
to the sword and took Dinah from Shechem's
house and left. 27 The sons of Jacob came upon
the dead bodies and looted the city where[d]
their sister had been defiled. 28 They seized
their flocks and herds and donkeys and everything else of theirs in the city and out in the
fields. 29 They carried off all their wealth and all
their women and children, taking as plunder
everything in the houses.
30 Then Jacob said to Simeon and Levi, "You
have brought trouble on me by making me a
stench to the Canaanites and Perizzites, the people living in this land. We are few in number,
and if they join forces against me and attack
me, I and my household will be destroyed."
31 But they replied, "Should he have treated
our sister like a prostitute?"

Jacob Returns to Bethel

35 Then God said to Jacob, "Go up to
Bethel and settle there, and build an
altar there to God, who appeared to you when
you were fleeing from your brother Esau."
2 So Jacob said to his household and to all
who were with him, "Get rid of the foreign

[a] 7 Or *against* [b] 10 Or *move about freely*; also in verse 21 [c] 17 Hebrew *daughter* [d] 27 Or *because*

Innocence Lost

Read: Genesis 34:1–31

DINAH WAS JACOB'S ONLY DAUGHTER. When she ventured from her family's home to visit with the local people, she was taken and raped by Shechem, the son of a local ruler. Because of his position of power, he may have been able to take her without anyone intervening. Or perhaps he was adept at verbal manipulation, and he smoothly talked Dinah into a compromising position. Imagine Dinah's terror, vulnerability and defenselessness as she realized what Shechem intended. Add to Dinah's anguish the fact that only pure women could marry in Hebraic culture. Not being married meant having no social standing, no identity and no hope for the future.

No one is the same after sin—not the victim, not the perpetrator and not those who love the victim or victimizer. In this story, Shechem was a powerful man who thought he could have whatever he wanted. So he took it. Ultimately, he paid the price with his life, and his men paid the price with their lives.

Then there was Dinah's family. They, too, suffered because of Shechem's sin. Dinah's brothers became vigilantes, seeking vengeance not just on Shechem but on his helpless men. Two of the brothers acted with such brutality that Jacob cursed them from his deathbed.

And what about Dinah? She was violated, attacked, abused. Her pain is barely mentioned in this account. What must she have felt when her father did nothing? Or when her brothers overreacted? And what of her future? What would she do now?

No one suffers or sins in a vacuum. We can see that in the results of sin all around us. But we can see it in our own lives too. Maybe you have been abused or taken advantage of. You may feel that you have no future or no hope. Maybe others you know are suffering because of the actions of one person. God can work through any situation. He cannot change the past, but he can work through your present to help you cope, change, grow and ultimately thrive. God was victorious over sin at the cross. No matter what happened to you, God knows. Turn to him for comfort. Turn to him with your pain. Ask him to heal your hurting heart and restore you. He is the only one who can restore your soul.

Genesis 34:7

Now Jacob's sons had come in from the fields as soon as they heard what had happened. They were filled with grief and fury, because Shechem had done a disgraceful thing in Israel by lying with Jacob's daughter—a thing that should not be done.

reflection

1 Describe a time when someone abused you either physically, mentally or emotionally.

2 How did it impact not just you but also those around you?

3 What are God's promises to you that he will forgive you and restore you? Write an exchange prayer, trading in your feelings of pain, sorrow or loss for the victory of being a believer (e.g., "I trade in my loss of innocence for the truth that I can regain purity through Christ's blood").

RELATED READINGS

Genesis 49:1,5–7; Psalm 147:3–6; Isaiah 43:18–19; Romans 12:19–21

Go to page 52 for your next devotional reading.

gods you have with you, and purify yourselves
and change your clothes. [3]Then come, let us
go up to Bethel, where I will
build an altar to God, who answered me in the day of my
distress and who has been with
me wherever I have gone." [4]So
they gave Jacob all the foreign
gods they had and the rings
in their ears, and Jacob buried
them under the oak at Shechem. [5]Then they set out, and
the terror of God fell upon the
towns all around them so that
no one pursued them.
[6]Jacob and all the people
with him came to Luz (that is,
Bethel) in the land of Canaan.
[7]There he built an altar, and he
called the place El Bethel,[a] because it was there that God revealed himself to
him when he was fleeing from his brother.
[8]Now Deborah, Rebekah's nurse, died and
was buried under the oak below Bethel. So it
was named Allon Bacuth.[b]
[9]After Jacob returned from Paddan Aram,[c]
God appeared to him again and blessed him.
[10]God said to him, "Your name is Jacob,[d] but
you will no longer be called Jacob; your name
will be Israel.[e]" So he named him Israel.
[11]And God said to him, "I am God Almighty[f]; be fruitful and increase in number. A
nation and a community of nations will come
from you, and kings will come from your body.
[12]The land I gave to Abraham and Isaac I also
give to you, and I will give this land to your
descendants after you." [13]Then God went up
from him at the place where he had talked
with him.
[14]Jacob set up a stone pillar at the place where
God had talked with him, and he poured out a
drink offering on it; he also poured oil on it.
[15]Jacob called the place where God had talked
with him Bethel.[g]

> Genesis 35:3
>
> **God Meets Our Distress**
>
> "Then come, let us go up to Bethel, where I will build an altar to God, who answered me in the day of my distress and who has been with me wherever I have gone."

The Deaths of Rachel and Isaac

[16]Then they moved on from Bethel. While
they were still some distance from Ephrath, Rachel began to give birth and had great difficulty.
[17]And as she was having great difficulty in
childbirth, the midwife said
to her, "Don't be afraid, for
you have another son." [18]As
she breathed her last—for she
was dying—she named her
son Ben-Oni.[h] But his father
named him Benjamin.[i]
[19]So Rachel died and was
buried on the way to Ephrath
(that is, Bethlehem). [20]Over
her tomb Jacob set up a pillar, and to this day that pillar
marks Rachel's tomb.
[21]Israel moved on again and
pitched his tent beyond Migdal
Eder. [22]While Israel was living
in that region, Reuben went in
and slept with his father's concubine Bilhah, and Israel heard of it.

Jacob had twelve sons:
[23]The sons of Leah:
Reuben the firstborn of Jacob,
Simeon, Levi, Judah, Issachar and Zebulun.
[24]The sons of Rachel:
Joseph and Benjamin.
[25]The sons of Rachel's maidservant Bilhah:
Dan and Naphtali.
[26]The sons of Leah's maidservant Zilpah:
Gad and Asher.
These were the sons of Jacob, who were born
to him in Paddan Aram.

[27]Jacob came home to his father Isaac in
Mamre, near Kiriath Arba (that is, Hebron),
where Abraham and Isaac had stayed. [28]Isaac
lived a hundred and eighty years. [29]Then he
breathed his last and died and was gathered to
his people, old and full of years. And his sons
Esau and Jacob buried him.

Esau's Descendants

36 This is the account of Esau (that is,
Edom).

[2]Esau took his wives from the women
of Canaan: Adah daughter of Elon the

[a]7 *El Bethel* means *God of Bethel.* [b]8 *Allon Bacuth* means *oak of weeping.* [c]9 That is, Northwest Mesopotamia; also in verse 26
[d]10 *Jacob* means *he grasps the heel* (figuratively, *he deceives*). [e]10 *Israel* means *he struggles with God.* [f]11 Hebrew *El-Shaddai*
[g]15 *Bethel* means *house of God.* [h]18 *Ben-Oni* means *son of my trouble.* [i]18 *Benjamin* means *son of my right hand.*

Hittite, and Oholibamah daughter of
Anah and granddaughter of Zibeon the
Hivite— 3also Basemath daughter of
Ishmael and sister of Nebaioth.
4Adah bore Eliphaz to Esau, Basemath
bore Reuel, 5and Oholibamah bore Jeush,
Jalam and Korah. These were the sons of
Esau, who were born to him in Canaan.
6Esau took his wives and sons and
daughters and all the members of his
household, as well as his livestock and
all his other animals and all the goods he
had acquired in Canaan, and moved to a
land some distance from his brother Jacob. 7Their possessions were too great for
them to remain together; the land where
they were staying could not support them
both because of their livestock. 8So Esau
(that is, Edom) settled in the hill country
of Seir.

9This is the account of Esau the father of the
Edomites in the hill country of Seir.

10 These are the names of Esau's sons:
Eliphaz, the son of Esau's wife Adah, and
Reuel, the son of Esau's wife Basemath.
11 The sons of Eliphaz:
Teman, Omar, Zepho, Gatam and Kenaz.
12 Esau's son Eliphaz also had a concubine named Timna, who bore him Amalek. These were grandsons of Esau's
wife Adah.
13 The sons of Reuel:
Nahath, Zerah, Shammah and Mizzah. These were grandsons of Esau's wife Basemath.
14 The sons of Esau's wife Oholibamah
daughter of Anah and granddaughter of
Zibeon, whom she bore to Esau:
Jeush, Jalam and Korah.

15These were the chiefs among Esau's descendants:

The sons of Eliphaz the firstborn of Esau:
Chiefs Teman, Omar, Zepho, Kenaz,
16Korah,[a] Gatam and Amalek. These
were the chiefs descended from Eliphaz in Edom; they were grandsons of Adah.
17 The sons of Esau's son Reuel:
Chiefs Nahath, Zerah, Shammah and Mizzah. These were the chiefs descended from Reuel in Edom; they were grandsons of Esau's wife Basemath.
18 The sons of Esau's wife Oholibamah:
Chiefs Jeush, Jalam and Korah. These were the chiefs descended from Esau's wife Oholibamah daughter of Anah.
19These were the sons of Esau (that is, Edom), and these were their chiefs.

20These were the sons of Seir the Horite, who were living in the region:
Lotan, Shobal, Zibeon, Anah, 21Di-
shon, Ezer and Dishan. These sons of Seir in Edom were Horite chiefs.
22 The sons of Lotan:
Hori and Homam.[b] Timna was Lotan's sister.
23 The sons of Shobal:
Alvan, Manahath, Ebal, Shepho and Onam.
24 The sons of Zibeon:
Aiah and Anah. This is the Anah who discovered the hot springs[c] in the desert while he was grazing the donkeys of his father Zibeon.
25 The children of Anah:
Dishon and Oholibamah daughter of Anah.
26 The sons of Dishon[d]:
Hemdan, Eshban, Ithran and Keran.
27 The sons of Ezer:
Bilhan, Zaavan and Akan.
28 The sons of Dishan:
Uz and Aran.
29 These were the Horite chiefs:
Lotan, Shobal, Zibeon, Anah, 30Di-
shon, Ezer and Dishan. These were the Horite chiefs, according to their divisions, in the land of Seir.

The Rulers of Edom

31These were the kings who reigned in Edom before any Israelite king reigned[e]:

[a]16 Masoretic Text; Samaritan Pentateuch (see also Gen. 36:11 and 1 Chron. 1:36) does not have *Korah.* [b]22 Hebrew *Hemam,* a variant of *Homam* (see 1 Chron. 1:39) [c]24 Vulgate; Syriac *discovered water;* the meaning of the Hebrew for this word is uncertain. [d]26 Hebrew *Dishan,* a variant of *Dishon* [e]31 Or *before an Israelite king reigned over them*

32 Bela son of Beor became king of Edom.
His city was named Dinhabah.
33 When Bela died, Jobab son of Zerah from
Bozrah succeeded him as king.
34 When Jobab died, Husham from the
land of the Temanites succeeded him
as king.
35 When Husham died, Hadad son of Bedad,
who defeated Midian in the country of
Moab, succeeded him as king. His city
was named Avith.
36 When Hadad died, Samlah from Masrekah succeeded him as king.
37 When Samlah died, Shaul from Rehoboth
on the river[a] succeeded him as king.
38 When Shaul died, Baal-Hanan son of Acbor succeeded him as king.
39 When Baal-Hanan son of Acbor died, Hadad[b] succeeded him as king. His city
was named Pau, and his wife's name
was Mehetabel daughter of Matred, the
daughter of Me-Zahab.

40 These were the chiefs descended from Esau,
by name, according to their clans and regions:
Timna, Alvah, Jetheth, 41 Oholibamah,
Elah, Pinon, 42 Kenaz, Teman, Mibzar,
43 Magdiel and Iram. These were the
chiefs of Edom, according to their settlements in the land they occupied.

This was Esau the father of the Edomites.

Joseph's Dreams

37 Jacob lived in the land where his father
had stayed, the land of Canaan.

2 This is the account of Jacob.

Joseph, a young man of seventeen, was
tending the flocks with his brothers, the sons
of Bilhah and the sons of Zilpah, his father's
wives, and he brought their father a bad report
about them.

3 Now Israel loved Joseph more than any
of his other sons, because he had been born
to him in his old age; and he made a richly
ornamented[c] robe for him. 4 When his brothers
saw that their father loved him more than any
of them, they hated him and could not speak a
kind word to him.

5 Joseph had a dream, and when he told it
to his brothers, they hated him all the more.
6 He said to them, "Listen to this dream I had:
7 We were binding sheaves of grain out in the
field when suddenly my sheaf rose and stood
upright, while your sheaves gathered around
mine and bowed down to it."

8 His brothers said to him, "Do you intend
to reign over us? Will you actually rule us?"
And they hated him all the more because of his
dream and what he had said.

9 Then he had another dream, and he told it
to his brothers. "Listen," he said, "I had another
dream, and this time the sun and moon and
eleven stars were bowing down to me."

10 When he told his father as well as his brothers, his father rebuked him and said, "What is
this dream you had? Will your mother and I
and your brothers actually come and bow
down to the ground before you?" 11 His brothers were jealous of him, but his father kept the
matter in mind.

Joseph Sold by His Brothers

12 Now his brothers had gone to graze their
father's flocks near Shechem, 13 and Israel said
to Joseph, "As you know, your brothers are grazing the flocks near Shechem. Come, I am going
to send you to them."

"Very well," he replied.

14 So he said to him, "Go and see if all is well
with your brothers and with the flocks, and
bring word back to me." Then he sent him off
from the Valley of Hebron.

When Joseph arrived at Shechem, 15 a man
found him wandering around in the fields and
asked him, "What are you looking for?"

16 He replied, "I'm looking for my brothers. Can you tell me where they are grazing
their flocks?"

17 "They have moved on from here," the man
answered. "I heard them say, 'Let's go to Dothan.'"

So Joseph went after his brothers and found
them near Dothan. 18 But they saw him in the
distance, and before he reached them, they plotted to kill him.

19 "Here comes that dreamer!" they said to
each other. 20 "Come now, let's kill him and

[a]37 Possibly the Euphrates [b]39 Many manuscripts of the Masoretic Text, Samaritan Pentateuch and Syriac (see also 1 Chron. 1:50); most manuscripts of the Masoretic Text *Hadar* [c]3 The meaning of the Hebrew for *richly ornamented* is uncertain; also in verses 23 and 32.

throw him into one of these cisterns and say
that a ferocious animal devoured him. Then
we'll see what comes of his dreams."
21When Reuben heard this, he tried to rescue him from their hands. "Let's not take his
life," he said. 22"Don't shed any blood. Throw
him into this cistern here in the desert, but
don't lay a hand on him." Reuben said this to
rescue him from them and take him back to
his father.
23So when Joseph came to his brothers, they
stripped him of his robe—the richly ornamented
robe he was wearing— 24and they took him
and threw him into the cistern. Now the cistern
was empty; there was no water in it.
25As they sat down to eat their meal, they
looked up and saw a caravan of Ishmaelites
coming from Gilead. Their camels were loaded
with spices, balm and myrrh, and they were on
their way to take them down to Egypt.
26Judah said to his brothers, "What will we
gain if we kill our brother and cover up his
blood? 27Come, let's sell him to the Ishmaelites and not lay our hands on
him; after all, he is our brother,
our own flesh and blood." His
brothers agreed.
28So when the Midianite
merchants came by, his brothers pulled Joseph up out of the
cistern and sold him for twenty
shekels[a] of silver to the Ishmaelites, who took him to Egypt.
29When Reuben returned
to the cistern and saw that Joseph was not there, he tore his
clothes. 30He went back to his
brothers and said, "The boy
isn't there! Where can I turn now?"
31Then they got Joseph's robe, slaughtered a
goat and dipped the robe in the blood. 32They
took the ornamented robe back to their father
and said, "We found this. Examine it to see
whether it is your son's robe."
33He recognized it and said, "It is my son's
robe! Some ferocious animal has devoured
him. Joseph has surely been torn to pieces."
34Then Jacob tore his clothes, put on sackcloth and mourned for his son many days.
35All his sons and daughters came to comfort
him, but he refused to be comforted. "No," he
said, "in mourning will I go down to the grave[b]
to my son." So his father wept for him.
36Meanwhile, the Midianites[c] sold Joseph
in Egypt to Potiphar, one of Pharaoh's officials,
the captain of the guard.

Judah and Tamar

38 At that time, Judah left his brothers
and went down to stay with a man of
Adullam named Hirah. 2There Judah met the
daughter of a Canaanite man named Shua. He
married her and lay with her; 3she became pregnant and gave birth to a son, who was named
Er. 4She conceived again and gave birth to a
son and named him Onan. 5She gave birth to
still another son and named him Shelah. It was
at Kezib that she gave birth to him.
6Judah got a wife for Er, his firstborn, and
her name was Tamar. 7But Er, Judah's firstborn,
was wicked in the LORD's sight; so the LORD
put him to death.
8Then Judah said to Onan,
"Lie with your brother's wife
and fulfill your duty to her as
a brother-in-law to produce offspring for your brother." 9But
Onan knew that the offspring
would not be his; so whenever
he lay with his brother's wife,
he spilled his semen on the
ground to keep from producing offspring for his brother.
10What he did was wicked in
the LORD's sight; so he put him
to death also.
11Judah then said to his daughter-in-law Tamar, "Live as a widow in your father's house
until my son Shelah grows up." For he thought,
"He may die too, just like his brothers." So Tamar went to live in her father's house.
12After a long time Judah's wife, the daughter
of Shua, died. When Judah had recovered from
his grief, he went up to Timnah, to the men
who were shearing his sheep, and his friend Hirah the Adullamite went with him.

Genesis 38:7

God Hates Sin

But Er, Judah's firstborn, was wicked in the LORD's sight; so the LORD put him to death.

[a]28 That is, about 8 ounces (about 0.2 kilogram) [b]35 Hebrew *Sheol* [c]36 Samaritan Pentateuch, Septuagint, Vulgate and Syriac (see also verse 28); Masoretic Text *Medanites*

13 When Tamar was told, "Your father-in-
law is on his way to Timnah to shear his sheep,"
14 she took off her widow's clothes, covered herself with a veil to disguise herself, and then sat
down at the entrance to Enaim, which is on the
road to Timnah. For she saw that, though Shelah had now grown up, she had not been given
to him as his wife.
15 When Judah saw her, he thought she was a
prostitute, for she had covered her face. 16 Not
realizing that she was his daughter-in-law,
he went over to her by the roadside and said,
"Come now, let me sleep with you."
"And what will you give me to sleep with
you?" she asked.
17 "I'll send you a young goat from my flock,"
he said.
"Will you give me something as a pledge until you send it?" she asked.
18 He said, "What pledge should I give
you?"
"Your seal and its cord, and the staff in your
hand," she answered. So he gave them to her
and slept with her, and she became pregnant by
him. 19 After she left, she took off her veil and
put on her widow's clothes again.
20 Meanwhile Judah sent the young goat by
his friend the Adullamite in order to get his
pledge back from the woman, but he did not
find her. 21 He asked the men who lived there,
"Where is the shrine prostitute who was beside
the road at Enaim?"
"There hasn't been any shrine prostitute
here," they said.
22 So he went back to Judah and said, "I didn't
find her. Besides, the men who lived there said,
'There hasn't been any shrine prostitute here.'"
23 Then Judah said, "Let her keep what she
has, or we will become a laughingstock. After
all, I did send her this young goat, but you
didn't find her."
24 About three months later Judah was told,
"Your daughter-in-law Tamar is guilty of prostitution, and as a result she is now pregnant."
Judah said, "Bring her out and have her
burned to death!"
25 As she was being brought out, she sent a
message to her father-in-law. "I am pregnant
by the man who owns these," she said. And she
added, "See if you recognize whose seal and
cord and staff these are."
26 Judah recognized them and said, "She is
more righteous than I, since I wouldn't give her
to my son Shelah." And he did not sleep with
her again.
27 When the time came for her to give birth,
there were twin boys in her womb. 28 As she
was giving birth, one of them put out his hand;
so the midwife took a scarlet thread and tied
it on his wrist and said, "This one came out
first." 29 But when he drew back his hand, his
brother came out, and she said, "So this is how
you have broken out!" And he was named Perez.[a] 30 Then his brother, who had the scarlet
thread on his wrist, came out and he was given
the name Zerah.[b]

Joseph and Potiphar's Wife

39 Now Joseph had been taken down to
Egypt. Potiphar, an Egyptian who was
one of Pharaoh's officials, the captain of the
guard, bought him from the Ishmaelites who
had taken him there.
2 The LORD was with Joseph and he prospered, and he lived in the house of his Egyptian
master. 3 When his master saw that the LORD
was with him and that the LORD gave him
success in everything he did, 4 Joseph found
favor in his eyes and became his attendant. Potiphar put him in charge of his household, and
he entrusted to his care everything he owned.
5 From the time he put him in charge of his
household and of all that he owned, the LORD
blessed the household of the Egyptian because
of Joseph. The blessing of the LORD was on everything Potiphar had, both in the house and
in the field. 6 So he left in Joseph's care everything he had; with Joseph in charge, he did not
concern himself with anything except the food
he ate.
Now Joseph was well-built and handsome,
7 and after a while his master's wife took notice
of Joseph and said, "Come to bed with me!"
8 But he refused. "With me in charge," he told
her, "my master does not concern himself with
anything in the house; everything he owns he
has entrusted to my care. 9 No one is greater in
this house than I am. My master has withheld

[a] 29 *Perez* means *breaking out.* [b] 30 *Zerah* can mean *scarlet* or *brightness.*

More Than a Promise

SARAH

"IT'S A BOY." Oh, the joy!

For her husband, this baby brought the prospect of being the father of a nation, of seeing his name carried throughout generations. For Abraham, the baby meant his lineage was now secure. He smiled in satisfaction as he contemplated the future.

But not Sarah. The idea of mothering an entire race of people was beyond her for the moment. She was content to just let herself be entirely dazzled by the innocence in her baby's eyes, the scent of his flawless skin, the softness of his tiny hands.

"I will bless her and will surely give you a son by her. I will bless her so that she will be the mother of nations."

Genesis 17:16

Sarah was caught up in the "now." All she had ever wanted in life she could now cradle in the crook of her arm. She was a new mother; she likely wasn't thinking of the next generation. Nor of next year. Nor of tomorrow or even the next minute. She'd experienced a lifetime of being the daughter, the friend, the wife, the mistress of her household. Now, today, she reveled in her new primary identity—mother.

If given a choice, maybe she would have held the promise to her and kept him small forever. However, the much-anticipated promise also came with much-needed perspective. You see, the promise would one day grow up and grow old. More than likely, this baby boy would outlive his mom and dad altogether and, if he lived near them at all, bury them both. Maybe Sarah had a motherly tendency to focus on the now, and Abraham envisioned several generations into the future, but God had eternity clearly in view. It wasn't about the promise as much as it was about the Promise Maker.

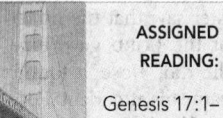

ASSIGNED READING:

Genesis 17:1–27; 21:1–6

Behind the promise Sarah could see the unseen Promise Maker. Far beyond the tiniest branch of the family tree that Abraham could envision, eternity stretched outward. The indescribable delight and pleasure of holding her son was meant to teach Sarah about the rapture of God cradling her in the palm of his hand. Beyond the joy of becoming a mother for the first time after 90 years and being in a unique relationship with another human being, there was a greater kind of happiness beyond measure: the joy of being in relationship with God.

—Prayer—

God, you know what my future holds. I can trust you no matter what I'm facing right now.

Weekend

Go to page 56 for your next devotional reading.

nothing from me except you, because you are
his wife. How then could I do such a wicked
thing and sin against God?" 10 And though she
spoke to Joseph day after day, he refused to go
to bed with her or even be with her.
11 One day he went into the house to attend
to his duties, and none of the household servants was inside. 12 She caught him by his cloak
and said, "Come to bed with me!" But he left his
cloak in her hand and ran out of the house.
13 When she saw that he had left his cloak in
her hand and had run out of the house, 14 she
called her household servants. "Look," she said
to them, "this Hebrew has been brought to us
to make sport of us! He came in here to sleep
with me, but I screamed. 15 When he heard me
scream for help, he left his cloak beside me and
ran out of the house."
16 She kept his cloak beside her until his
master came home. 17 Then she told him this
story: "That Hebrew slave you brought us came
to me to make sport of me. 18 But as soon as I
screamed for help, he left his cloak beside me
and ran out of the house."
19 When his master heard the story his wife
told him, saying, "This is how your slave treated
me," he burned with anger. 20 Jo-
seph's master took him and put
him in prison, the place where
the king's prisoners were confined.
But while Joseph was there
in the prison, 21 the LORD was
with him; he showed him kindness and granted him favor in
the eyes of the prison warden.
22 So the warden put Joseph in
charge of all those held in the
prison, and he was made responsible for all that was done
there. 23 The warden paid no
attention to anything under Jo-
seph's care, because the LORD was with Joseph
and gave him success in whatever he did.

> **Genesis 39:21**
>
> *God Remains Faithful*
>
> The LORD was with him; he showed him kindness and granted him favor in the eyes of the prison warden.

The Cupbearer and the Baker

40 Some time later, the cupbearer and the
baker of the king of Egypt offended
their master, the king of Egypt. 2 Pharaoh was
angry with his two officials, the chief cupbearer
and the chief baker, 3 and put them in custody
in the house of the captain of the guard, in the
same prison where Joseph was confined. 4 The
captain of the guard assigned them to Joseph,
and he attended them.
After they had been in custody for some
time, 5 each of the two men—the cupbearer and
the baker of the king of Egypt, who were being
held in prison—had a dream the same night,
and each dream had a meaning of its own.
6 When Joseph came to them the next morning, he saw that they were dejected. 7 So he
asked Pharaoh's officials who were in custody
with him in his master's house, "Why are your
faces so sad today?"
8 "We both had dreams," they answered, "but
there is no one to interpret them."
Then Joseph said to them, "Do not interpretations belong to God? Tell me your dreams."
9 So the chief cupbearer told Joseph his
dream. He said to him, "In my dream I saw
a vine in front of me, 10 and on the vine were
three branches. As soon as it budded, it blossomed, and its clusters ripened into grapes.
11 Pharaoh's cup was in my hand, and I took
the grapes, squeezed them into
Pharaoh's cup and put the cup
in his hand."
12 "This is what it means,"
Joseph said to him. "The
three branches are three days.
13 Within three days Pharaoh
will lift up your head and restore you to your position, and
you will put Pharaoh's cup in
his hand, just as you used to do
when you were his cupbearer.
14 But when all goes well with
you, remember me and show
me kindness; mention me to
Pharaoh and get me out of this
prison. 15 For I was forcibly carried off from the
land of the Hebrews, and even here I have done
nothing to deserve being put in a dungeon."
16 When the chief baker saw that Joseph had
given a favorable interpretation, he said to Joseph, "I too had a dream: On my head were
three baskets of bread.[a] 17 In the top basket

[a] 16 Or *three wicker baskets*

were all kinds of baked goods for Pharaoh, but
the birds were eating them out of the basket on
my head.”
18“This is what it means,” Joseph said. “The
three baskets are three days. 19Within three
days Pharaoh will lift off your head and hang
you on a tree.[a] And the birds will eat away
your flesh.”
20Now the third day was Pharaoh’s birthday,
and he gave a feast for all his officials. He lifted
up the heads of the chief cupbearer and the
chief baker in the presence of his officials: 21He
restored the chief cupbearer to his position, so
that he once again put the cup into Pharaoh’s
hand, 22but he hanged[b] the chief baker, just as
Joseph had said to them in his interpretation.
23The chief cupbearer, however, did not remember Joseph; he forgot him.

Pharaoh’s Dreams

41 When two full years had passed, Pharaoh had a dream: He was standing by
the Nile, 2when out of the river there came
up seven cows, sleek and fat, and they grazed
among the reeds. 3After them,
seven other cows, ugly and
gaunt, came up out of the Nile
and stood beside those on the
riverbank. 4And the cows that
were ugly and gaunt ate up the
seven sleek, fat cows. Then
Pharaoh woke up.
5He fell asleep again and
had a second dream: Seven
heads of grain, healthy and
good, were growing on a single
stalk. 6After them, seven other
heads of grain sprouted—thin
and scorched by the east wind. 7The thin heads
of grain swallowed up the seven healthy, full
heads. Then Pharaoh woke up; it had been
a dream.
8In the morning his mind was troubled, so
he sent for all the magicians and wise men of
Egypt. Pharaoh told them his dreams, but no
one could interpret them for him.
9Then the chief cupbearer said to Pharaoh,
“Today I am reminded of my shortcomings.
10Pharaoh was once angry with his servants,
and he imprisoned me and the chief baker in
the house of the captain of the guard. 11Each of
us had a dream the same night, and each dream
had a meaning of its own. 12Now a young Hebrew was there with us, a servant of the captain
of the guard. We told him our dreams, and he
interpreted them for us, giving each man the interpretation of his dream. 13And things turned
out exactly as he interpreted them to us: I was
restored to my position, and the other man
was hanged.[b]”
14So Pharaoh sent for Joseph, and he was
quickly brought from the dungeon. When he
had shaved and changed his clothes, he came
before Pharaoh.
15Pharaoh said to Joseph, “I had a dream,
and no one can interpret it. But I have heard
it said of you that when you hear a dream you
can interpret it.”
16“I cannot do it,” Joseph replied to Pharaoh,
“but God will give Pharaoh the answer he desires.”
17Then Pharaoh said to Joseph, “In my dream
I was standing on the bank of the Nile, 18when
out of the river there came up
seven cows, fat and sleek, and
they grazed among the reeds.
19After them, seven other cows
came up—scrawny and very
ugly and lean. I had never seen
such ugly cows in all the land
of Egypt. 20The lean, ugly cows
ate up the seven fat cows that
came up first. 21But even after
they ate them, no one could
tell that they had done so; they
looked just as ugly as before.
Then I woke up.
22“In my dreams I also saw seven heads of
grain, full and good, growing on a single stalk.
23After them, seven other heads sprouted—
withered and thin and scorched by the east
wind. 24The thin heads of grain swallowed up
the seven good heads. I told this to the magicians, but none could explain it to me.”
25Then Joseph said to Pharaoh, “The dreams
of Pharaoh are one and the same. God has revealed to Pharaoh what he is about to do. 26The
seven good cows are seven years, and the seven

Genesis 41:16

God Provides Answers

“I cannot do it,” Joseph replied to Pharaoh, “but God will give Pharaoh the answer he desires.”

[a]19 Or *and impale you on a pole* [b]22,13 Or *impaled*

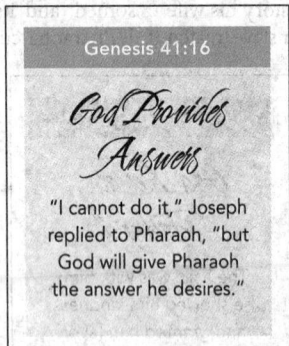

good heads of grain are seven years; it is one and the same dream. 27The seven lean, ugly cows that came up afterward are seven years, and so are the seven worthless heads of grain scorched by the east wind: They are seven years of famine.

28"It is just as I said to Pharaoh: God has shown Pharaoh what he is about to do. 29Seven years of great abundance are coming throughout the land of Egypt, 30but seven years of famine will follow them. Then all the abundance in Egypt will be forgotten, and the famine will ravage the land. 31The abundance in the land will not be remembered, because the famine that follows it will be so severe. 32The reason the dream was given to Pharaoh in two forms is that the matter has been firmly decided by God, and God will do it soon.

33"And now let Pharaoh look for a discerning and wise man and put him in charge of the land of Egypt. 34Let Pharaoh appoint commissioners over the land to take a fifth of the harvest of Egypt during the seven years of abundance. 35They should collect all the food of these good years that are coming and store up the grain under the authority of Pharaoh, to be kept in the cities for food. 36This food should be held in reserve for the country, to be used during the seven years of famine that will come upon Egypt, so that the country may not be ruined by the famine."

37The plan seemed good to Pharaoh and to all his officials. 38So Pharaoh asked them, "Can we find anyone like this man, one in whom is the spirit of God[a]?"

39Then Pharaoh said to Joseph, "Since God has made all this known to you, there is no one so discerning and wise as you. 40You shall be in charge of my palace, and all my people are to submit to your orders. Only with respect to the throne will I be greater than you."

Joseph in Charge of Egypt

41So Pharaoh said to Joseph, "I hereby put you in charge of the whole land of Egypt." 42Then Pharaoh took his signet ring from his finger and put it on Joseph's finger. He dressed him in robes of fine linen and put a gold chain around his neck. 43He had him ride in a chariot as his second-in-command,[b] and men shouted before him, "Make way[c]!" Thus he put him in charge of the whole land of Egypt.

44Then Pharaoh said to Joseph, "I am Pharaoh, but without your word no one will lift hand or foot in all Egypt." 45Pharaoh gave Joseph the name Zaphenath-Paneah and gave him Asenath daughter of Potiphera, priest of On,[d] to be his wife. And Joseph went throughout the land of Egypt.

46Joseph was thirty years old when he entered the service of Pharaoh king of Egypt. And Joseph went out from Pharaoh's presence and traveled throughout Egypt. 47During the seven years of abundance the land produced plentifully. 48Joseph collected all the food produced in those seven years of abundance in Egypt and stored it in the cities. In each city he put the food grown in the fields surrounding it. 49Joseph stored up huge quantities of grain, like the sand of the sea; it was so much that he stopped keeping records because it was beyond measure.

50Before the years of famine came, two sons were born to Joseph by Asenath daughter of Potiphera, priest of On. 51Joseph named his firstborn Manasseh[e] and said, "It is because God has made me forget all my trouble and all my father's household." 52The second son he named Ephraim[f] and said, "It is because God has made me fruitful in the land of my suffering."

53The seven years of abundance in Egypt came to an end, 54and the seven years of famine began, just as Joseph had said. There was famine in all the other lands, but in the whole land of Egypt there was food. 55When all Egypt began to feel the famine, the people cried to Pharaoh for food. Then Pharaoh told all the Egyptians, "Go to Joseph and do what he tells you."

56When the famine had spread over the whole country, Joseph opened the storehouses and sold grain to the Egyptians, for the famine was severe throughout Egypt. 57And all the countries came to Egypt to buy grain from Joseph, because the famine was severe in all the world.

[a]38 Or *of the gods* [b]43 Or *in the chariot of his second-in-command*; or *in his second chariot* [c]43 Or *Bow down* [d]45 That is, Heliopolis; also in verse 50 [e]51 *Manasseh* sounds like and may be derived from the Hebrew for *forget.* [f]52 *Ephraim* sounds like the Hebrew for *twice fruitful.*

Genesis 41:51–52

Joseph named his firstborn Manasseh and said, "It is because God has made me forget all my trouble and all my father's household." The second son he named Ephraim and said, "It is because God has made me fruitful in the land of my suffering."

God's Silent Work

Read: Genesis 41:41–57

IN MAY 1820 a six-week-old baby caught a cold. When her eyes became inflamed, a man posing as a doctor treated her with the wrong medication. Within days her eyesight was destroyed. But Fanny Crosby was not content to be a victim. She voraciously memorized five books of the Old Testament and most of the New Testament by the time she was ten years old. She attended the New York Institute for the Blind, where she became a teacher and gifted poet. After surviving the cholera epidemic in 1849, Fanny realized something was missing in her life and turned to Christ at the age of 30. God had been silently working in her heart. The poetry that formerly flowed from her heart turned into hymns of praise, many of which we still sing today. "To God Be the Glory," "Praise Him, Praise Him," "Tell Me the Story of Jesus" and many more songs speak of how Fanny loved God and the ways he worked in her life—even when she couldn't see it.

In Genesis 41 we see God silently working in Joseph's life. Joseph could have grown bitter and inflamed by the dreadful circumstances of his life. After all, he had been sold into slavery by his own brothers at the age of 17 and then sent to prison after refusing to sleep with his master's wife. Finally, after Joseph waited 13 long years, God transformed his wretched circumstances into something good. At the age of 30, Joseph experienced a new beginning. He rose to prominence within Pharaoh's court, saved the nation from famine and was blessed with a family of his own.

Joseph's sons' names poetically described his life story: *Manasseh*, "God has made me forget all my trouble"; and *Ephraim*, "God has made me fruitful in the land of my suffering." Amazingly, Joseph experienced God's silent work as much in slavery and in prison as he did when he rose to prominence.

Whatever your circumstances, you can trust that God is working behind the scenes. When you experience trouble—and you will—God can make you fruitful and full of praise, just as he did with Joseph and with Fanny Crosby.

reflection

1 What difficulties have you faced in the past? How did God use those times to shape you?

2 What situations are you currently facing that seem hopeless? How do you see God silently working to get you through them?

3 Sing Fanny Crosby's hymn "To God Be the Glory" as a way of thanking him for working behind the scenes in your life.

RELATED READINGS

Genesis 39:2–6,21–23; Romans 8:28–30

"Everything has its wonders, even darkness and silence, and I learn, whatever state I may be in, therein to be content."

Helen Adams Keller

Go to page 67 for your next devotional reading.

Joseph's Brothers Go to Egypt

42 When Jacob learned that there was
grain in Egypt, he said to his sons,
"Why do you just keep looking at each other?"
2He continued, "I have heard that there is grain
in Egypt. Go down there and buy some for us,
so that we may live and not die."

3Then ten of Joseph's brothers went down to
buy grain from Egypt. 4But Jacob did not send
Benjamin, Joseph's brother, with the others, because he was afraid that harm might come to
him. 5So Israel's sons were among those who
went to buy grain, for the famine was in the
land of Canaan also.

6Now Joseph was the governor of the land,
the one who sold grain to all its people. So when
Joseph's brothers arrived, they bowed down to
him with their faces to the ground. 7As soon as
Joseph saw his brothers, he recognized them,
but he pretended to be a stranger and spoke
harshly to them. "Where do you come from?"
he asked.

"From the land of Canaan," they replied, "to
buy food."

8Although Joseph recognized his brothers,
they did not recognize him. 9Then he remembered his dreams about them and said to them,
"You are spies! You have come to see where our
land is unprotected."

10"No, my lord," they answered. "Your servants have come to buy food. 11We are all the
sons of one man. Your servants are honest
men, not spies."

12"No!" he said to them. "You have come to
see where our land is unprotected."

13But they replied, "Your servants were
twelve brothers, the sons of one man, who lives
in the land of Canaan. The youngest is now
with our father, and one is no more."

14Joseph said to them, "It is just as I told
you: You are spies! 15And this is how you
will be tested: As surely as Pharaoh lives, you
will not leave this place unless your youngest
brother comes here. 16Send one of your number to get your brother; the rest of you will
be kept in prison, so that your words may be
tested to see if you are telling the truth. If you
are not, then as surely as Pharaoh lives, you
are spies!" 17And he put them all in custody
for three days.

18On the third day, Joseph said to them, "Do
this and you will live, for I fear God: 19If you
are honest men, let one of your brothers stay
here in prison, while the rest of you go and take
grain back for your starving households. 20But
you must bring your youngest brother to me,
so that your words may be verified and that you
may not die." This they proceeded to do.

21They said to one another, "Surely we are
being punished because of our brother. We saw
how distressed he was when he pleaded with us
for his life, but we would not listen; that's why
this distress has come upon us."

22Reuben replied, "Didn't I tell you not to
sin against the boy? But you wouldn't listen!
Now we must give an accounting for his blood."
23They did not realize that Joseph could understand them, since he was using an interpreter.

24He turned away from them and began to
weep, but then turned back and spoke to them
again. He had Simeon taken from them and
bound before their eyes.

25Joseph gave orders to fill their bags with
grain, to put each man's silver back in his sack,
and to give them provisions for their journey.
After this was done for them, 26they loaded
their grain on their donkeys and left.

27At the place where they stopped for the
night one of them opened his sack to get feed
for his donkey, and he saw his silver in the
mouth of his sack. 28"My silver has been returned," he said to his brothers. "Here it is in
my sack."

Their hearts sank and they turned to each
other trembling and said, "What is this that
God has done to us?"

29When they came to their father Jacob in
the land of Canaan, they told him all that had
happened to them. They said, 30"The man
who is lord over the land spoke harshly to us
and treated us as though we were spying on
the land. 31But we said to him, 'We are honest
men; we are not spies. 32We were twelve brothers, sons of one father. One is no more, and the
youngest is now with our father in Canaan.'

33"Then the man who is lord over the land
said to us, 'This is how I will know whether you
are honest men: Leave one of your brothers
here with me, and take food for your starving
households and go. 34But bring your youngest
brother to me so I will know that you are not
spies but honest men. Then I will give your

brother back to you, and you can trade[a] in
the land.' "
35 As they were emptying their sacks, there
in each man's sack was his pouch of silver!
When they and their father saw the money
pouches, they were frightened. 36 Their father
Jacob said to them, "You have deprived me of
my children. Joseph is no more and Simeon is
no more, and now you want to take Benjamin.
Everything is against me!"
37 Then Reuben said to his father, "You may
put both of my sons to death if I do not bring
him back to you. Entrust him to my care, and I
will bring him back."
38 But Jacob said, "My son will not go down
there with you; his brother is dead and he is
the only one left. If harm comes to him on the
journey you are taking, you will bring my gray
head down to the grave[b] in sorrow."

The Second Journey to Egypt

43 Now the famine was still severe in the
land. 2 So when they had eaten all the
grain they had brought from Egypt, their father said to them, "Go back and buy us a little
more food."
3 But Judah said to him, "The man warned
us solemnly, 'You will not see my face again unless your brother is with you.' 4 If you will send
our brother along with us, we will go down and
buy food for you. 5 But if you will not send him,
we will not go down, because the man said to
us, 'You will not see my face again unless your
brother is with you.' "
6 Israel asked, "Why did you bring this
trouble on me by telling the man you had
another brother?"
7 They replied, "The man questioned us
closely about ourselves and our family. 'Is your
father still living?' he asked us. 'Do you have
another brother?' We simply answered his
questions. How were we to know he would say,
'Bring your brother down here'?"
8 Then Judah said to Israel his father, "Send
the boy along with me and we will go at once, so
that we and you and our children may live and
not die. 9 I myself will guarantee his safety; you
can hold me personally responsible for him. If I
do not bring him back to you and set him here
before you, I will bear the blame before you
all my life. 10 As it is, if we had not delayed, we
could have gone and returned twice."
11 Then their father Israel said to them, "If
it must be, then do this: Put some of the best
products of the land in your bags and take
them down to the man as a gift—a little balm
and a little honey, some spices and myrrh,
some pistachio nuts and almonds. 12 Take
double the amount of silver with you, for you
must return the silver that was put back into
the mouths of your sacks. Perhaps it was a mistake. 13 Take your brother also and go back to
the man at once. 14 And may God Almighty[c]
grant you mercy before the man so that he will
let your other brother and Benjamin come
back with you. As for me, if I am bereaved, I
am bereaved."
15 So the men took the gifts and double the
amount of silver, and Benjamin also. They hurried down to Egypt and presented themselves
to Joseph. 16 When Joseph saw Benjamin with
them, he said to the steward of his house, "Take
these men to my house, slaughter an animal
and prepare dinner; they are to eat with me
at noon."
17 The man did as Joseph told him and took
the men to Joseph's house. 18 Now the men
were frightened when they were taken to his
house. They thought, "We were brought here
because of the silver that was put back into our
sacks the first time. He wants to attack us and
overpower us and seize us as slaves and take
our donkeys."
19 So they went up to Joseph's steward and
spoke to him at the entrance to the house.
20 "Please, sir," they said, "we came down here
the first time to buy food. 21 But at the place
where we stopped for the night we opened our
sacks and each of us found his silver—the exact
weight—in the mouth of his sack. So we have
brought it back with us. 22 We have also brought
additional silver with us to buy food. We don't
know who put our silver in our sacks."
23 "It's all right," he said. "Don't be afraid.
Your God, the God of your father, has given
you treasure in your sacks; I received your silver." Then he brought Simeon out to them.
24 The steward took the men into Joseph's
house, gave them water to wash their feet and

[a] 34 Or *move about freely* [b] 38 Hebrew *Sheol* [c] 14 Hebrew *El-Shaddai*

provided fodder for their donkeys. 25They prepared their gifts for Joseph's arrival at noon,
because they had heard that they were to
eat there.
26When Joseph came home, they presented
to him the gifts they had brought into the
house, and they bowed down before him to the
ground. 27He asked them how they were, and
then he said, "How is your aged father you told
me about? Is he still living?"
28They replied, "Your servant our father is
still alive and well." And they bowed low to pay
him honor.
29As he looked about and saw his brother
Benjamin, his own mother's son, he asked, "Is
this your youngest brother, the one you told
me about?" And he said, "God be gracious to
you, my son." 30Deeply moved at the sight of
his brother, Joseph hurried out and looked for
a place to weep. He went into his private room
and wept there.
31After he had washed his face, he came
out and, controlling himself, said, "Serve
the food."
32They served him by himself, the brothers
by themselves, and the Egyptians who ate with
him by themselves, because Egyptians could
not eat with Hebrews, for that is detestable to
Egyptians. 33The men had been seated before
him in the order of their ages, from the firstborn to the youngest; and they looked at each
other in astonishment. 34When portions were
served to them from Joseph's table, Benjamin's
portion was five times as much as anyone else's.
So they feasted and drank freely with him.

A Silver Cup in a Sack

44 Now Joseph gave these instructions to
the steward of his house: "Fill the men's
sacks with as much food as they can carry, and
put each man's silver in the mouth of his sack.
2Then put my cup, the silver one, in the mouth
of the youngest one's sack, along with the silver
for his grain." And he did as Joseph said.
3As morning dawned, the men were sent
on their way with their donkeys. 4They had
not gone far from the city when Joseph said to
his steward, "Go after those men at once, and
when you catch up with them, say to them,
'Why have you repaid good with evil? 5Isn't
this the cup my master drinks from and also
uses for divination? This is a wicked thing you
have done.'"
6When he caught up with them, he repeated
these words to them. 7But they said to him,
"Why does my lord say such things? Far be it
from your servants to do anything like that!
8We even brought back to you from the land of
Canaan the silver we found inside the mouths
of our sacks. So why would we steal silver or
gold from your master's house? 9If any of your
servants is found to have it, he will die; and the
rest of us will become my lord's slaves."
10"Very well, then," he said, "let it be as you
say. Whoever is found to have it will become my
slave; the rest of you will be free from blame."
11Each of them quickly lowered his sack to
the ground and opened it. 12Then the steward
proceeded to search, beginning with the oldest
and ending with the youngest. And the cup
was found in Benjamin's sack. 13At this, they
tore their clothes. Then they all loaded their
donkeys and returned to the city.
14Joseph was still in the house when Judah and his brothers came in, and they threw
themselves to the ground before him. 15Joseph
said to them, "What is this you have done?
Don't you know that a man like me can find
things out by divination?"
16"What can we say to my lord?" Judah replied. "What can we say? How can we prove
our innocence? God has uncovered your servants' guilt. We are now my lord's slaves—we
ourselves and the one who was found to have
the cup."
17But Joseph said, "Far be it from me to do
such a thing! Only the man who was found to
have the cup will become my slave. The rest of
you, go back to your father in peace."
18Then Judah went up to him and said:
"Please, my lord, let your servant speak a word
to my lord. Do not be angry with your servant,
though you are equal to Pharaoh himself. 19My
lord asked his servants, 'Do you have a father
or a brother?' 20And we answered, 'We have an
aged father, and there is a young son born to
him in his old age. His brother is dead, and he
is the only one of his mother's sons left, and his
father loves him.'
21"Then you said to your servants, 'Bring
him down to me so I can see him for myself.'

22 And we said to my lord, 'The boy cannot
leave his father; if he leaves him, his father will
die.' 23 But you told your servants, 'Unless your
youngest brother comes down with you, you
will not see my face again.' 24 When we went
back to your servant my father, we told him
what my lord had said.
25 "Then our father said, 'Go back and buy a
little more food.' 26 But we said, 'We cannot go
down. Only if our youngest brother is with us
will we go. We cannot see the
man's face unless our youngest
brother is with us.'
27 "Your servant my father
said to us, 'You know that my
wife bore me two sons. 28 One
of them went away from me,
and I said, "He has surely been
torn to pieces." And I have
not seen him since. 29 If you
take this one from me too and
harm comes to him, you will
bring my gray head down to
the grave[a] in misery.'
30 "So now, if the boy is not
with us when I go back to your servant my
father and if my father, whose life is closely
bound up with the boy's life, 31 sees that the boy
isn't there, he will die. Your servants will bring
the gray head of our father down to the grave
in sorrow. 32 Your servant guaranteed the boy's
safety to my father. I said, 'If I do not bring him
back to you, I will bear the blame before you,
my father, all my life!'
33 "Now then, please let your servant remain
here as my lord's slave in place of the boy, and
let the boy return with his brothers. 34 How can
I go back to my father if the boy is not with me?
No! Do not let me see the misery that would
come upon my father."

Joseph Makes Himself Known

45 Then Joseph could no longer control
himself before all his attendants, and he
cried out, "Have everyone leave my presence!"
So there was no one with Joseph when he made
himself known to his brothers. 2 And he wept
so loudly that the Egyptians heard him, and
Pharaoh's household heard about it.
3 Joseph said to his brothers, "I am Joseph!
Is my father still living?" But his brothers were
not able to answer him, because they were terrified at his presence.
4 Then Joseph said to his brothers, "Come
close to me." When they had done so, he said,
"I am your brother Joseph, the one you sold
into Egypt! 5 And now, do not be distressed
and do not be angry with yourselves for selling
me here, because it was to save lives that God
sent me ahead of you. 6 For
two years now there has been
famine in the land, and for the
next five years there will not
be plowing and reaping. 7 But
God sent me ahead of you to
preserve for you a remnant on
earth and to save your lives by
a great deliverance.[b]
8 "So then, it was not you
who sent me here, but God. He
made me father to Pharaoh,
lord of his entire household
and ruler of all Egypt. 9 Now
hurry back to my father and
say to him, 'This is what your son Joseph says:
God has made me lord of all Egypt. Come
down to me; don't delay. 10 You shall live in
the region of Goshen and be near me—you,
your children and grandchildren, your flocks
and herds, and all you have. 11 I will provide
for you there, because five years of famine are
still to come. Otherwise you and your household and all who belong to you will become
destitute.'
12 "You can see for yourselves, and so can
my brother Benjamin, that it is really I who
am speaking to you. 13 Tell my father about
all the honor accorded me in Egypt and about
everything you have seen. And bring my father
down here quickly."
14 Then he threw his arms around his brother
Benjamin and wept, and Benjamin embraced
him, weeping. 15 And he kissed all his brothers
and wept over them. Afterward his brothers
talked with him.
16 When the news reached Pharaoh's palace
that Joseph's brothers had come, Pharaoh and
all his officials were pleased. 17 Pharaoh said

> **Genesis 45:7**
>
> *God Plans Ahead*
>
> "But God sent me ahead of you to preserve for you a remnant on earth and to save your lives by a great deliverance."

[a]29 Hebrew *Sheol*; also in verse 31 [b]7 Or *save you as a great band of survivors*

to Joseph, "Tell your brothers, 'Do this: Load
your animals and return to the land of Canaan,
18and bring your father and your families back
to me. I will give you the best of the land of
Egypt and you can enjoy the fat of the land.'

19"You are also directed to tell them, 'Do
this: Take some carts from Egypt for your children and your wives, and get your father and
come. 20Never mind about your belongings,
because the best of all Egypt will be yours.'"

21So the sons of Israel did this. Joseph gave
them carts, as Pharaoh had commanded, and
he also gave them provisions for their journey.
22To each of them he gave new clothing, but
to Benjamin he gave three hundred shekels[a]
of silver and five sets of clothes. 23And this is
what he sent to his father: ten donkeys loaded
with the best things of Egypt, and ten female
donkeys loaded with grain and bread and other
provisions for his journey. 24Then he sent his
brothers away, and as they were leaving he said
to them, "Don't quarrel on the way!"

25So they went up out of Egypt and came
to their father Jacob in the land of Canaan.
26They told him, "Joseph is still alive! In fact,
he is ruler of all Egypt." Jacob was stunned; he
did not believe them. 27But when they told
him everything Joseph had said to them, and
when he saw the carts Joseph had sent to carry
him back, the spirit of their father Jacob revived. 28And Israel said, "I'm convinced! My
son Joseph is still alive. I will go and see him
before I die."

Jacob Goes to Egypt

46 So Israel set out with all that was his,
and when he reached Beersheba, he offered sacrifices to the God of his father Isaac.

2And God spoke to Israel in a vision at night
and said, "Jacob! Jacob!"

"Here I am," he replied.

3"I am God, the God of your father," he said.
"Do not be afraid to go down to Egypt, for I
will make you into a great nation there. 4I will
go down to Egypt with you, and I will surely
bring you back again. And Joseph's own hand
will close your eyes."

5Then Jacob left Beersheba, and Israel's sons
took their father Jacob and their children and
their wives in the carts that Pharaoh had sent to
transport him. 6They also took with them their
livestock and the possessions they had acquired
in Canaan, and Jacob and all his offspring went
to Egypt. 7He took with him to Egypt his sons
and grandsons and his daughters and granddaughters—all his offspring.

8These are the names of the sons of Israel
(Jacob and his descendants) who went to
Egypt:

Reuben the firstborn of Jacob.
9 The sons of Reuben:
  Hanoch, Pallu, Hezron and Carmi.
10 The sons of Simeon:
  Jemuel, Jamin, Ohad, Jakin, Zohar and
  Shaul the son of a Canaanite woman.
11 The sons of Levi:
  Gershon, Kohath and Merari.
12 The sons of Judah:
  Er, Onan, Shelah, Perez and Zerah (but
  Er and Onan had died in the land of
  Canaan).
  The sons of Perez:
    Hezron and Hamul.
13 The sons of Issachar:
  Tola, Puah,[b] Jashub[c] and Shimron.
14 The sons of Zebulun:
  Sered, Elon and Jahleel.

15These were the sons Leah bore to Jacob in
Paddan Aram,[d] besides his daughter Dinah.
These sons and daughters of his were thirty-
three in all.

16 The sons of Gad:
  Zephon,[e] Haggi, Shuni, Ezbon, Eri,
  Arodi and Areli.
17 The sons of Asher:
  Imnah, Ishvah, Ishvi and Beriah.
  Their sister was Serah.
  The sons of Beriah:
    Heber and Malkiel.

18These were the children born to Jacob by
Zilpah, whom Laban had given to his daughter
Leah—sixteen in all.

[a]22 That is, about 7 1/2 pounds (about 3.5 kilograms) [b]13 Samaritan Pentateuch and Syriac (see also 1 Chron. 7:1); Masoretic Text *Puvah* [c]13 Samaritan Pentateuch and some Septuagint manuscripts (see also Num. 26:24 and 1 Chron. 7:1); Masoretic Text *Iob* [d]15 That is, Northwest Mesopotamia [e]16 Samaritan Pentateuch and Septuagint (see also Num. 26:15); Masoretic Text *Ziphion*

19 The sons of Jacob's wife Rachel:
Joseph and Benjamin. 20 In Egypt, Manasseh and Ephraim were born to Joseph by Asenath daughter of Potiphera,
priest of On.[a]
21 The sons of Benjamin:
Bela, Beker, Ashbel, Gera, Naaman,
Ehi, Rosh, Muppim, Huppim and Ard.
22 These were the sons of Rachel who were
born to Jacob—fourteen in all.

23 The son of Dan:
Hushim.
24 The sons of Naphtali:
Jahziel, Guni, Jezer and Shillem.
25 These were the sons born to Jacob by Bilhah, whom Laban had given to his daughter
Rachel—seven in all.

26 All those who went to Egypt with Jacob—those who were his direct descendants,
not counting his sons' wives—numbered sixty-
six persons. 27 With the two sons[b] who had
been born to Joseph in Egypt, the members
of Jacob's family, which went to Egypt, were
seventy[c] in all.

28 Now Jacob sent Judah ahead of him to Joseph to get directions to Goshen. When they
arrived in the region of Goshen, 29 Joseph had
his chariot made ready and went to Goshen
to meet his father Israel. As soon as Joseph appeared before him, he threw his arms around
his father[d] and wept for a long time.
30 Israel said to Joseph, "Now I am ready to
die, since I have seen for myself that you are
still alive."
31 Then Joseph said to his brothers and to his
father's household, "I will go up and speak to
Pharaoh and will say to him, 'My brothers and
my father's household, who were living in the
land of Canaan, have come to me. 32 The men
are shepherds; they tend livestock, and they
have brought along their flocks and herds and
everything they own.' 33 When Pharaoh calls
you in and asks, 'What is your occupation?'
34 you should answer, 'Your servants have
tended livestock from our boyhood on, just as
our fathers did.' Then you will be allowed to settle in the region of Goshen, for all shepherds
are detestable to the Egyptians."

47 Joseph went and told Pharaoh, "My
father and brothers, with their flocks
and herds and everything they own, have
come from the land of Canaan and are now
in Goshen." 2 He chose five of his brothers and
presented them before Pharaoh.
3 Pharaoh asked the brothers, "What is
your occupation?"
"Your servants are shepherds," they replied
to Pharaoh, "just as our fathers were." 4 They
also said to him, "We have come to live here
awhile, because the famine is severe in Canaan
and your servants' flocks have no pasture. So
now, please let your servants settle in Goshen."
5 Pharaoh said to Joseph, "Your father and
your brothers have come to you, 6 and the land
of Egypt is before you; settle your father and
your brothers in the best part of the land. Let
them live in Goshen. And if you know of any
among them with special ability, put them in
charge of my own livestock."
7 Then Joseph brought his father Jacob in
and presented him before Pharaoh. After Jacob
blessed[e] Pharaoh, 8 Pharaoh asked him, "How
old are you?"
9 And Jacob said to Pharaoh, "The years of
my pilgrimage are a hundred and thirty. My
years have been few and difficult, and they do
not equal the years of the pilgrimage of my
fathers." 10 Then Jacob blessed[f] Pharaoh and
went out from his presence.
11 So Joseph settled his father and his brothers in Egypt and gave them property in the
best part of the land, the district of Rameses,
as Pharaoh directed. 12 Joseph also provided
his father and his brothers and all his father's
household with food, according to the number
of their children.

Joseph and the Famine

13 There was no food, however, in the whole
region because the famine was severe; both
Egypt and Canaan wasted away because of
the famine. 14 Joseph collected all the money
that was to be found in Egypt and Canaan in
payment for the grain they were buying, and

[a] 20 That is, Heliopolis [b] 27 Hebrew; Septuagint *the nine children* [c] 27 Hebrew (see also Exodus 1:5 and footnote); Septuagint (see also Acts 7:14) *seventy-five* [d] 29 Hebrew *around him* [e] 7 Or *greeted* [f] 10 Or *said farewell to*

he brought it to Pharaoh's palace. 15When the
money of the people of Egypt and Canaan was
gone, all Egypt came to Joseph and said, "Give
us food. Why should we die before your eyes?
Our money is used up."

16"Then bring your livestock," said Joseph.
"I will sell you food in exchange for your livestock, since your money is gone." 17So they
brought their livestock to Joseph, and he gave
them food in exchange for their horses, their
sheep and goats, their cattle and donkeys. And
he brought them through that year with food
in exchange for all their livestock.

18When that year was over, they came to him
the following year and said, "We cannot hide
from our lord the fact that since our money is
gone and our livestock belongs to you, there
is nothing left for our lord except our bodies
and our land. 19Why should we perish before
your eyes—we and our land as well? Buy us
and our land in exchange for food, and we with
our land will be in bondage to Pharaoh. Give us
seed so that we may live and not die, and that
the land may not become desolate."

20So Joseph bought all the land in Egypt
for Pharaoh. The Egyptians, one and all, sold
their fields, because the famine was too severe
for them. The land became Pharaoh's, 21and
Joseph reduced the people to servitude,[a] from
one end of Egypt to the other. 22However, he
did not buy the land of the priests, because
they received a regular allotment from Pharaoh and had food enough from the allotment
Pharaoh gave them. That is why they did not
sell their land.

23Joseph said to the people, "Now that I
have bought you and your land today for Pharaoh, here is seed for you so you can plant the
ground. 24But when the crop comes in, give a
fifth of it to Pharaoh. The other four-fifths you
may keep as seed for the fields and as food for
yourselves and your households and your children."

25"You have saved our lives," they said. "May
we find favor in the eyes of our lord; we will be
in bondage to Pharaoh."

26So Joseph established it as a law concerning land in Egypt—still in force today—that
a fifth of the produce belongs to Pharaoh. It
was only the land of the priests that did not become Pharaoh's.

27Now the Israelites settled in Egypt in the
region of Goshen. They acquired property
there and were fruitful and increased greatly
in number.

28Jacob lived in Egypt seventeen years, and
the years of his life were a hundred and forty-
seven. 29When the time drew near for Israel
to die, he called for his son Joseph and said to
him, "If I have found favor in your eyes, put
your hand under my thigh and promise that
you will show me kindness and faithfulness.
Do not bury me in Egypt, 30but when I rest
with my fathers, carry me out of Egypt and
bury me where they are buried."

"I will do as you say," he said.

31"Swear to me," he said. Then Joseph swore
to him, and Israel worshiped as he leaned on
the top of his staff.[b]

Manasseh and Ephraim

48 Some time later Joseph was told, "Your
father is ill." So he took his two sons Manasseh and Ephraim along with him. 2When
Jacob was told, "Your son Joseph has come to
you," Israel rallied his strength and sat up on
the bed.

3Jacob said to Joseph, "God Almighty[c] appeared to me at Luz in the land of Canaan, and
there he blessed me 4and said to me, 'I am going to make you fruitful and will increase your
numbers. I will make you a community of peoples, and I will give this land as an everlasting
possession to your descendants after you.'

5"Now then, your two sons born to you in
Egypt before I came to you here will be reckoned as mine; Ephraim and Manasseh will be
mine, just as Reuben and Simeon are mine.
6Any children born to you after them will
be yours; in the territory they inherit they will
be reckoned under the names of their brothers.
7As I was returning from Paddan,[d] to my sorrow Rachel died in the land of Canaan while
we were still on the way, a little distance from
Ephrath. So I buried her there beside the road
to Ephrath" (that is, Bethlehem).

[a]21 Samaritan Pentateuch and Septuagint (see also Vulgate); Masoretic Text *and he moved the people into the cities* [b]31 Or *Israel bowed down at the head of his bed* [c]3 Hebrew *El-Shaddai* [d]7 That is, Northwest Mesopotamia

8When Israel saw the sons of Joseph, he
asked, "Who are these?"
9"They are the sons God has given me here,"
Joseph said to his father.
Then Israel said, "Bring them to me so I may
bless them."
10Now Israel's eyes were failing because of
old age, and he could hardly see. So Joseph
brought his sons close to him, and his father
kissed them and embraced them.
11Israel said to Joseph, "I never expected to
see your face again, and now God has allowed
me to see your children too."
12Then Joseph removed them from Israel's
knees and bowed down with
his face to the ground. 13And
Joseph took both of them,
Ephraim on his right toward
Israel's left hand and Manasseh
on his left toward Israel's right
hand, and brought them close
to him. 14But Israel reached
out his right hand and put it on
Ephraim's head, though he was
the younger, and crossing his
arms, he put his left hand on
Manasseh's head, even though
Manasseh was the firstborn.
15Then he blessed Joseph
and said,

"May the God before whom
my fathers
Abraham and Isaac walked,
the God who has been my shepherd
all my life to this day,
16the Angel who has delivered me from all
harm
—may he bless these boys.
May they be called by my name
and the names of my fathers Abraham
and Isaac,
and may they increase greatly
upon the earth."

17When Joseph saw his father placing
his right hand on Ephraim's head he was displeased; so he took hold of his father's hand
to move it from Ephraim's head to Manasseh's
head. 18Joseph said to him, "No, my father,
this one is the firstborn; put your right hand
on his head."
19But his father refused and said, "I know,
my son, I know. He too will become a people,
and he too will become great. Nevertheless, his
younger brother will be greater than he, and his
descendants will become a group of nations."
20He blessed them that day and said,

"In your[a] name will Israel pronounce this
blessing:
'May God make you like Ephraim and
Manasseh.'"

So he put Ephraim ahead of
Manasseh.
21Then Israel said to Joseph,
"I am about to die, but God
will be with you[b] and take
you[b] back to the land of your[b]
fathers. 22And to you, as one
who is over your brothers, I
give the ridge of land[c] I took
from the Amorites with my
sword and my bow."

> **Genesis 48:15**
>
> *God Is Our Shepherd*
>
> "May the God before
> whom my fathers
> Abraham and Isaac
> walked,
> the God who has been
> my shepherd
> all my life to this day…"

Jacob Blesses His Sons

49 Then Jacob called
for his sons and said:
"Gather around so I can tell
you what will happen to you in
days to come.

2"Assemble and listen, sons of Jacob;
listen to your father Israel.

3"Reuben, you are my firstborn,
my might, the first sign of my strength,
excelling in honor, excelling in power.
4Turbulent as the waters, you will no longer
excel,
for you went up onto your father's bed,
onto my couch and defiled it.

5"Simeon and Levi are brothers—
their swords[d] are weapons of
violence.
6Let me not enter their council,
let me not join their assembly,
for they have killed men in their anger

[a]20 The Hebrew is singular. [b]21 The Hebrew is plural. [c]22 Or *And to you I give one portion more than to your brothers—the portion*
[d]5 The meaning of the Hebrew for this word is uncertain.

and hamstrung oxen as they pleased.
7 Cursed be their anger, so fierce,
and their fury, so cruel!
I will scatter them in Jacob
and disperse them in Israel.

8 "Judah,[a] your brothers will praise you;
your hand will be on the neck of your enemies;
your father's sons will bow down to you.
9 You are a lion's cub, O Judah;
you return from the prey, my son.
Like a lion he crouches and lies down,
like a lioness—who dares to rouse him?
10 The scepter will not depart from Judah,
nor the ruler's staff from between his feet,
until he comes to whom it belongs[b]
and the obedience of the nations is his.
11 He will tether his donkey to a vine,
his colt to the choicest branch;
he will wash his garments in wine,
his robes in the blood of grapes.
12 His eyes will be darker than wine,
his teeth whiter than milk.[c]

13 "Zebulun will live by the seashore
and become a haven for ships;
his border will extend toward Sidon.

14 "Issachar is a rawboned[d] donkey
lying down between two saddlebags.[e]
15 When he sees how good is his resting place
and how pleasant is his land,
he will bend his shoulder to the burden
and submit to forced labor.

16 "Dan[f] will provide justice for his people
as one of the tribes of Israel.
17 Dan will be a serpent by the roadside,
a viper along the path,
that bites the horse's heels
so that its rider tumbles backward.

18 "I look for your deliverance, O LORD.

19 "Gad[g] will be attacked by a band of raiders,
but he will attack them at their heels.

20 "Asher's food will be rich;
he will provide delicacies fit for a king.

21 "Naphtali is a doe set free
that bears beautiful fawns.[h]

22 "Joseph is a fruitful vine,
a fruitful vine near a spring,
whose branches climb over a wall.[i]
23 With bitterness archers attacked him;
they shot at him with hostility.
24 But his bow remained steady,
his strong arms stayed[j] limber,
because of the hand of the Mighty One of Jacob,
because of the Shepherd, the Rock of Israel,
25 because of your father's God, who helps you,
because of the Almighty,[k] who blesses you
with blessings of the heavens above,
blessings of the deep that lies below,
blessings of the breast and womb.
26 Your father's blessings are greater
than the blessings of the ancient mountains,
than[l] the bounty of the age-old hills.
Let all these rest on the head of Joseph,
on the brow of the prince among[m] his brothers.

27 "Benjamin is a ravenous wolf;
in the morning he devours the prey,
in the evening he divides the plunder."

28 All these are the twelve tribes of Israel, and this is what their father said to them when he blessed them, giving each the blessing appropriate to him.

The Death of Jacob

29 Then he gave them these instructions: "I am about to be gathered to my people. Bury me with my fathers in the cave in the field of Ephron

[a]8 *Judah* sounds like and may be derived from the Hebrew for *praise.* [b]10 Or *until Shiloh comes;* or *until he comes to whom tribute belongs* [c]12 Or *will be dull from wine, / his teeth white from milk* [d]14 Or *strong* [e]14 Or *campfires* [f]16 *Dan* here means *he provides justice.* [g]19 *Gad* can mean *attack* and *band of raiders.* [h]21 Or *free; / he utters beautiful words* [i]22 Or *Joseph is a wild colt, / a wild colt near a spring, / a wild donkey on a terraced hill* [j]23,24 Or *archers will attack... will shoot... will remain... will stay* [k]25 Hebrew *Shaddai* [l]26 Or *of my progenitors, / as great as* [m]26 Or *the one separated from*

the Hittite, 30the cave in the field of Machpelah, near Mamre in Canaan, which Abraham
bought as a burial place from Ephron the Hittite, along with the field. 31There Abraham and
his wife Sarah were buried, there Isaac and his
wife Rebekah were buried, and there I buried
Leah. 32The field and the cave in it were bought
from the Hittites.[a]"
33When Jacob had finished giving instructions to his sons, he drew his feet up into the
bed, breathed his last and was gathered to
his people.

50 Joseph threw himself upon his father
and wept over him and kissed him.
2Then Joseph directed the physicians in his
service to embalm his father Israel. So the
physicians embalmed him, 3taking a full forty
days, for that was the time required for em-
balming. And the Egyptians mourned for him
seventy days.
4When the days of mourning had passed, Joseph said to Pharaoh's court, "If I have found
favor in your eyes, speak to Pharaoh for me.
Tell him, 5'My father made me swear an oath
and said, "I am about to die; bury me in the
tomb I dug for myself in the land of Canaan."
Now let me go up and bury my father; then I
will return.'"
6Pharaoh said, "Go up and
bury your father, as he made
you swear to do."
7So Joseph went up to bury
his father. All Pharaoh's officials accompanied him—the
dignitaries of his court and
all the dignitaries of Egypt—
8besides all the members of
Joseph's household and his
brothers and those belonging
to his father's household. Only
their children and their flocks
and herds were left in Goshen.
9Chariots and horsemen[b] also went up with
him. It was a very large company.
10When they reached the threshing floor of
Atad, near the Jordan, they lamented loudly
and bitterly; and there Joseph observed a
seven-day period of mourning for his father.
11When the Canaanites who lived there saw
the mourning at the threshing floor of Atad,
they said, "The Egyptians are holding a solemn
ceremony of mourning." That is why that place
near the Jordan is called Abel Mizraim.[c]
12So Jacob's sons did as he had commanded
them: 13They carried him to the land of Canaan and buried him in the cave in the field
of Machpelah, near Mamre, which Abraham
had bought as a burial place from Ephron the
Hittite, along with the field. 14After burying his
father, Joseph returned to Egypt, together with
his brothers and all the others who had gone
with him to bury his father.

Joseph Reassures His Brothers

15When Joseph's brothers saw that their father was dead, they said, "What if Joseph holds
a grudge against us and pays us back for all the
wrongs we did to him?" 16So they sent word to
Joseph, saying, "Your father left these instructions before he died: 17'This is what you are to
say to Joseph: I ask you to forgive your brothers
the sins and the wrongs they committed in treating you so badly.' Now please forgive the sins of
the servants of the God of your father." When
their message came to him, Joseph wept.
18His brothers then came and threw themselves down before him. "We
are your slaves," they said.
19But Joseph said to them,
"Don't be afraid. Am I in the
place of God? 20You intended
to harm me, but God intended
it for good to accomplish what
is now being done, the saving
of many lives. 21So then, don't
be afraid. I will provide for you
and your children." And he reassured them and spoke kindly
to them.

The Death of Joseph

22Joseph stayed in Egypt, along with all his
father's family. He lived a hundred and ten
years 23and saw the third generation of Ephraim's children. Also the children of Makir son
of Manasseh were placed at birth on Joseph's
knees.[d]
24Then Joseph said to his brothers, "I am

> Genesis 50:20
>
> **God Overcomes Evil**
>
> "You intended to harm me, but God intended it for good to accomplish what is now being done, the saving of many lives."

[a]32 Or *the sons of Heth* [b]9 Or *charioteers* [c]11 *Abel Mizraim* means *mourning of the Egyptians.* [d]23 That is, were counted as his

A Good Gift from a Good God

Read: Genesis 50:15–21

Sometimes our worry is the thread by which we hang onto the belief that we can do something to change our situation and end our fear. As ridiculous as it is, we believe that our anxiety gives us some measure of control. Or we believe it keeps God mindful of our problem. We are afraid that without the pressure of our fear, He might forget what we want from Him. But our anxiety and demanding prayers accomplish nothing. We fear giving up our fear because if we don't worry, who will remember to care? If we don't worry, would God decide we really aren't concerned about the issue? If we don't worry, are we giving up hope of God involving Himself in our world?

Cutting across all our stubborn reasons for remaining in our fear, Paul wrote, "May the God of hope fill you with all joy and peace as you trust in him, so that you may overflow with hope by the power of the Holy Spirit" (Romans 15:13). God's joy and peace are available to us as we trust Him; they are not the result of absolute guarantees about the outcomes of our worries. We have a choice: will we trust Him and receive His joy and peace, or will we insist on seeking our joy and peace from resolved fears and changed circumstances?

The choice really is ours. We can hang onto our fears, insisting that until they are resolved, there is no way for us to enter into rest, or we can see those same fears as the door by which we can enter a rest far richer and sweeter than the rest that might arise from a tenuous arrangement of perfect circumstances. It is a rest that believes that a life without all the pieces in place, a life in which we do indeed suffer lack, is still a life to celebrate, a good gift from a good God.

—*Sally Breedlove*

Genesis 50:20–21

"You intended to harm me, but God intended it for good to accomplish what is now being done, the saving of many lives. So then, don't be afraid. I will provide for you and your children." And [Joseph] reassured them and spoke kindly to them.

reflection

1 Based on your knowledge of Joseph's life, how often might he have given into fear and worry over the course of his life?

2 What circumstances are causing you to feel fearful or worried?

3 Spend time with God asking him to use your fears as "the door" through which you can enter your rest, trusting that God will use your present circumstances for your good and his glory.

RELATED READINGS

Psalm 34;
Acts 7:9–17;
James 1:9–18

Go to page 71 for your next devotional reading.

about to die. But God will surely come to your
aid and take you up out of this land to the land
he promised on oath to Abraham, Isaac and
Jacob." 25 And Joseph made the sons of Israel
swear an oath and said, "God will surely come
to your aid, and then you must carry my bones
up from this place."

26 So Joseph died at the age of a hundred
and ten. And after they embalmed him, he was
placed in a coffin in Egypt.

Exodus

Four centuries pass from the time Jacob went to Egypt at the end of Genesis to the time the story picks up again in Exodus. The age of the patriarchs has ended, and we find the Israelites laboring as slaves under the Egyptian sun, *longing for a redeemer* to free them. God's promises to Abraham have become timeworn and faded. The Israelites are indeed numerous, as God promised, but their numbers seem to be not a blessing but a curse, the cause of their slavery. As for the land of promise—not one Israelite living has laid eyes on it. *And yet they hope.* Thin threads of promise can at least hold hope.

Exodus literally means *"exit,"* and that is precisely what the Israelites do, in a way that only God could orchestrate. God then sets about teaching them how to live in their newfound freedom. But knowing how to live it and actually living it are two very different things. With the Law comes the realization of *their need for another Redeemer,* one who could free the people from their bondage to sin.

Author:
Moses.

Audience:
The people of Israel.

Date:
Between 1450 and 1410 B.C.

Setting:
Opening scenes are in Egypt. The plot then moves to the region of the Sinai Peninsula.

Verse to Remember:
The LORD replied, "My Presence will go with you, and I will give you rest." (33:14)

The Israelites Oppressed

1 These are the names of the sons of Israel
who went to Egypt with Jacob, each with
his family: 2Reuben, Simeon, Levi and Judah;
3Issachar, Zebulun and Benjamin; 4Dan and
Naphtali; Gad and Asher. 5The descendants of
Jacob numbered seventy[a] in all; Joseph was already in Egypt.
6Now Joseph and all his brothers and all
that generation died, 7but the Israelites were
fruitful and multiplied greatly and became
exceedingly numerous, so that the land was
filled with them.
8Then a new king, who did not know about
Joseph, came to power in Egypt. 9"Look," he
said to his people, "the Israelites have become

[a]5 Masoretic Text (see also Gen. 46:27); Dead Sea Scrolls and Septuagint (see also Acts 7:14 and note at Gen. 46:27) *seventy-five*

much too numerous for us. [10]Come, we must
deal shrewdly with them or they will become
even more numerous and, if war breaks out,
will join our enemies, fight against us and leave
the country."

[11]So they put slave masters over them to
oppress them with forced labor, and they built
Pithom and Rameses as store cities for Pharaoh. [12]But the more they were oppressed, the
more they multiplied and spread; so the Egyptians came to dread the Israelites [13]and worked
them ruthlessly. [14]They made their lives bitter
with hard labor in brick and mortar and with
all kinds of work in the fields; in all their hard
labor the Egyptians used them ruthlessly.

[15]The king of Egypt said to the Hebrew midwives, whose names were Shiphrah and Puah,
[16]"When you help the Hebrew women in childbirth and observe them on the delivery stool, if
it is a boy, kill him; but if it is a girl, let her live."
[17]The midwives, however, feared God and did
not do what the king of Egypt had told them
to do; they let the boys live. [18]Then the king
of Egypt summoned the midwives and asked
them, "Why have you done this? Why have you
let the boys live?"

[19]The midwives answered Pharaoh, "Hebrew women are not like Egyptian women;
they are vigorous and give birth before the midwives arrive."

[20]So God was kind to the midwives and the
people increased and became even more numerous. [21]And because the midwives feared
God, he gave them families of their own.

[22]Then Pharaoh gave this order to all his people: "Every boy that is born[a] you must throw
into the Nile, but let every girl live."

The Birth of Moses

2 Now a man of the house of Levi married a
Levite woman, [2]and she became pregnant
and gave birth to a son. When she saw that he
was a fine child, she hid him for three months.
[3]But when she could hide him no longer, she
got a papyrus basket for him and coated it with
tar and pitch. Then she placed the child in it
and put it among the reeds along the bank of
the Nile. [4]His sister stood at a distance to see
what would happen to him.

[5]Then Pharaoh's daughter went down to the
Nile to bathe, and her attendants were walking
along the river bank. She saw the basket among
the reeds and sent her slave girl to get it. [6]She
opened it and saw the baby. He was crying, and
she felt sorry for him. "This is one of the Hebrew babies," she said.

[7]Then his sister asked Pharaoh's daughter,
"Shall I go and get one of the Hebrew women
to nurse the baby for you?"

[8]"Yes, go," she answered. And the girl went
and got the baby's mother. [9]Pharaoh's daughter said to her, "Take this baby and nurse him
for me, and I will pay you." So the woman
took the baby and nursed him. [10]When the
child grew older, she took him to Pharaoh's
daughter and he became her son. She named
him Moses,[b] saying, "I drew him out of the
water."

Moses Flees to Midian

[11]One day, after Moses had grown up, he
went out to where his own people were and
watched them at their hard labor. He saw an
Egyptian beating a Hebrew, one of his own people. [12]Glancing this way and that and seeing
no one, he killed the Egyptian and hid him in
the sand. [13]The next day he went out and saw
two Hebrews fighting. He asked the one in the
wrong, "Why are you hitting your fellow Hebrew?"

[14]The man said, "Who made you ruler and
judge over us? Are you thinking of killing me
as you killed the Egyptian?" Then Moses was
afraid and thought, "What I did must have become known."

[15]When Pharaoh heard of this, he tried to
kill Moses, but Moses fled from Pharaoh and
went to live in Midian, where he sat down by a
well. [16]Now a priest of Midian had seven daughters, and they came to draw water and fill the
troughs to water their father's flock. [17]Some
shepherds came along and drove them away,
but Moses got up and came to their rescue and
watered their flock.

[18]When the girls returned to Reuel their father, he asked them, "Why have you returned
so early today?"

[19]They answered, "An Egyptian rescued us

[a]22 Masoretic Text; Samaritan Pentateuch, Septuagint and Targums *born to the Hebrews* [b]10 *Moses* sounds like the Hebrew for *draw out.*

Wait and Watch

Read: Exodus 2:1–10

NOW THAT SHE WAS ALONE, the widow faced a decision: "Should I sell my house and move to a secure retirement community?" For years she had watched the changes in her neighborhood. Many things concerned her: unattended children, unkempt yards, unleashed pets and unwatched houses. But one personal tug kept her from moving. She observed one family and saw the unscrupulous behavior of the adults in the house: Strange cars would pull up, shady characters would come and go at all hours. She'd look out her window and see the young brother and sister who lived there climb into their tree house at odd times. Were they going there for shelter?

The widow wondered how she could leave these children. She had a mission . . . to keep a close eye on these two. The widow waited, watched and prayed for a chance to help. Though the children didn't know it, a neighbor became a part of their life story by keeping surveillance and interceding from the sidelines.

Before Moses was born, the pharaoh of Egypt issued a cruel edict: To keep the Hebrew people from becoming too powerful, every Hebrew baby boy must be killed. But the Hebrew women waited for the right opportunities to frustrate Pharaoh's genocidal plan. The midwives, mothers and sisters subverted the edict and saved some of the babies. Moses' mother put the baby Moses in a basket and placed it in the Nile. Moses' sister watched from the shore. Pharaoh's daughter joined in the cause by taking the baby Moses out of the reeds and into her heart. Even as Moses was saved from the fate of so many other children, Miriam "stood at a distance to see what would happen to him."

Every newborn baby enters the context of a human story, even though some of those stories are less than hopeful. You may see this and realize how unfair the world is. You want to do something to help but feel sidelined. You wait. You watch. You pray. You want to perform some act of practical compassion. The truth is, sometimes the best action is the sideline action: Wait, watch and pray. God will guide you to action when the time is right.

You're a part of others' stories. And they're a part of yours. Who needs your vigilant prayer protection? God may ask you to wait behind the scenes until he shows you how to step in.

Wednesday

Go to page 73 for your next devotional reading.

Exodus 2:4

[Moses'] sister stood at a distance to see what would happen to him.

reflection

1 Whom are you watching over right now?

2 How does prayer empower you as you wait?

3 How does this perspective of waiting and watching help you in your own life's story?

RELATED READINGS

Exodus 15:19–21; 1 Samuel 12:23

from the shepherds. He even drew water for us
and watered the flock."
20"And where is he?" he asked his daughters.
"Why did you leave him? Invite him to have
something to eat."
21Moses agreed to stay with the man, who
gave his daughter Zipporah to
Moses in marriage. 22Zipporah
gave birth to a son, and Moses
named him Gershom,[a] saying,
"I have become an alien in a foreign land."
23During that long period,
the king of Egypt died. The
Israelites groaned in their slavery and cried out, and their
cry for help because of their
slavery went up to God. 24God
heard their groaning and he remembered his covenant with
Abraham, with Isaac and with
Jacob. 25So God looked on the
Israelites and was concerned about them.

> **Exodus 2:24**
>
> *God Never Forgets Us*
>
> God heard their groaning and he remembered his covenant with Abraham, with Isaac and with Jacob.

Moses and the Burning Bush

3 Now Moses was tending the flock of
Jethro his father-in-law, the priest of Midian, and he led the flock to the far side of the
desert and came to Horeb, the mountain of
God. 2There the angel of the LORD appeared
to him in flames of fire from within a bush. Moses saw that though the bush was on fire it did
not burn up. 3So Moses thought, "I will go over
and see this strange sight—why the bush does
not burn up."
4When the LORD saw that he had gone over
to look, God called to him from within the
bush, "Moses! Moses!"
And Moses said, "Here I am."
5"Do not come any closer," God said. "Take
off your sandals, for the place where you are
standing is holy ground." 6Then he said, "I am
the God of your father, the God of Abraham,
the God of Isaac and the God of Jacob." At this,
Moses hid his face, because he was afraid to
look at God.
7The LORD said, "I have indeed seen the misery of my people in Egypt. I have heard them
crying out because of their slave drivers, and I
am concerned about their suffering. 8So I have
come down to rescue them from the hand of
the Egyptians and to bring them up out of that
land into a good and spacious land, a land flowing with milk and honey—the home of the
Canaanites, Hittites, Amorites,
Perizzites, Hivites and Jebusites. 9And now the cry of the
Israelites has reached me, and
I have seen the way the Egyptians are oppressing them.
10So now, go. I am sending you
to Pharaoh to bring my people
the Israelites out of Egypt."
11But Moses said to God,
"Who am I, that I should go to
Pharaoh and bring the Israelites out of Egypt?"
12And God said, "I will be
with you. And this will be the
sign to you that it is I who have
sent you: When you have brought the people
out of Egypt, you[b] will worship God on this
mountain."
13Moses said to God, "Suppose I go to the Israelites and say to them, 'The God of your fathers
has sent me to you,' and they ask me, 'What is
his name?' Then what shall I tell them?"
14God said to Moses, "I AM WHO I AM.[c] This
is what you are to say to the Israelites: 'I AM has
sent me to you.'"
15God also said to Moses, "Say to the Israelites, 'The LORD,[d] the God of your fathers—the
God of Abraham, the God of Isaac and the God
of Jacob—has sent me to you.' This is my name
forever, the name by which I am to be remembered from generation to generation.
16"Go, assemble the elders of Israel and say to
them, 'The LORD, the God of your fathers—the
God of Abraham, Isaac and Jacob—appeared
to me and said: I have watched over you and
have seen what has been done to you in Egypt.
17And I have promised to bring you up out of
your misery in Egypt into the land of the Canaanites, Hittites, Amorites, Perizzites, Hivites
and Jebusites—a land flowing with milk and
honey.'

[a]22 *Gershom* sounds like the Hebrew for *an alien there.* [b]12 The Hebrew is plural. [c]14 Or *I WILL BE WHAT I WILL BE* [d]15 The Hebrew for *LORD* sounds like and may be derived from the Hebrew for *I AM* in verse 14.

Availability Check

Read: Exodus 3:1–22

THE GOOD OFTEN cannibalizes the best. Think about it: How often do schedules, long to-do lists and our immediate line of sight trump the things we claim to love the most? A pile of laundry certainly seems insignificant the day a close friend wrecks her car or a parent falls ill. Certainly, life involves responsibility, but it also involves a need for *responsiveness* to urgent situations—a child struggling in school or a severely depressed coworker.

Moses was tending sheep—fulfilling a needed task—when God intervened with an urgent call. A bush burned without being consumed. God called Moses' name from within the fiery bush. Moses immediately answered. Moses was available and obedient. But then God told him what he wanted: Moses was to go back to Egypt to lead a rescue mission for the Hebrew people.

In the midst of our ordinary days—tending to our families, our jobs, our friends—how do we respond to the persistent pull of God's call? Regardless of how God makes his wishes known—a burning bush, a burning desire or a burning need—are we willing to have our tidy plans and schedules interrupted to listen to his voice? Or are we too busy or too distracted to answer? Bottom line: Are we willing to be recruited at God's bidding?

Like Moses, we may feel inadequate for the job: "I'm just a student, just a mother, just an hourly employee. I'm not equipped for this mission!" However, when God calls us to do something bigger than we think we can accomplish, he will equip us by working through us. We learn to rely on his strength, not on our own abilities. Simply put, God doesn't look for abilities; he looks for availabilities. That's how we can be confident of success: His great power trumps our lack of talent. We act in the power of the great "I AM" (3:14).

So when you hear the voice of God calling your name, answer without hesitation, "Here I am."

God's call. God's strength. Your availability.

Go to page 78 for your next devotional reading.

Exodus 3:4
When the LORD saw that he had gone over to look, God called to him from within the bush, "Moses! Moses!" And Moses said, "Here I am."

reflection

1 In what ways has God indicated he has something for you to do, and how have you responded?

2 Recount a time when you felt inadequate to do something you knew God wanted you to do. How did God equip you to accomplish it?

3 What interferes with your availability to answer God's call?

RELATED READINGS

1 Samuel 3:1–10; Isaiah 6:8; 50:2; 2 Corinthians 12:9–10

"In a very real sense, not one of us is qualified, but it seems that God continually chooses the most unqualified to do his work, to bear his glory."

Madeleine L'Engle

18"The elders of Israel will listen to you. Then you and the elders are to go to the king of Egypt and say to him, 'The LORD, the God of the Hebrews, has met with us. Let us take a three-day journey into the desert to offer sacrifices to the LORD our God.' 19But I know that the king of Egypt will not let you go unless a mighty hand compels him. 20So I will stretch out my hand and strike the Egyptians with all the wonders that I will perform among them. After that, he will let you go.

21"And I will make the Egyptians favorably disposed toward this people, so that when you leave you will not go empty-handed. 22Every woman is to ask her neighbor and any woman living in her house for articles of silver and gold and for clothing, which you will put on your sons and daughters. And so you will plunder the Egyptians."

Exodus 4:11

God Prepares Us

The LORD said to him, "Who gave man his mouth? Who makes him deaf or mute? Who gives him sight or makes him blind? Is it not I, the LORD?"

Signs for Moses

4 Moses answered, "What if they do not believe me or listen to me and say, 'The LORD did not appear to you'?"

2Then the LORD said to him, "What is that in your hand?"

"A staff," he replied.

3The LORD said, "Throw it on the ground."

Moses threw it on the ground and it became a snake, and he ran from it. 4Then the LORD said to him, "Reach out your hand and take it by the tail." So Moses reached out and took hold of the snake and it turned back into a staff in his hand. 5"This," said the LORD, "is so that they may believe that the LORD, the God of their fathers—the God of Abraham, the God of Isaac and the God of Jacob—has appeared to you."

6Then the LORD said, "Put your hand inside your cloak." So Moses put his hand into his cloak, and when he took it out, it was leprous,[a] like snow.

7"Now put it back into your cloak," he said. So Moses put his hand back into his cloak, and when he took it out, it was restored, like the rest of his flesh.

8Then the LORD said, "If they do not believe you or pay attention to the first miraculous sign, they may believe the second. 9But if they do not believe these two signs or listen to you, take some water from the Nile and pour it on the dry ground. The water you take from the river will become blood on the ground."

10Moses said to the LORD, "O Lord, I have never been eloquent, neither in the past nor since you have spoken to your servant. I am slow of speech and tongue."

11The LORD said to him, "Who gave man his mouth? Who makes him deaf or mute? Who gives him sight or makes him blind? Is it not I, the LORD? 12Now go; I will help you speak and will teach you what to say."

13But Moses said, "O Lord, please send someone else to do it."

14Then the LORD's anger burned against Moses and he said, "What about your brother, Aaron the Levite? I know he can speak well. He is already on his way to meet you, and his heart will be glad when he sees you. 15You shall speak to him and put words in his mouth; I will help both of you speak and will teach you what to do. 16He will speak to the people for you, and it will be as if he were your mouth and as if you were God to him. 17But take this staff in your hand so you can perform miraculous signs with it."

Moses Returns to Egypt

18Then Moses went back to Jethro his father-in-law and said to him, "Let me go back to my own people in Egypt to see if any of them are still alive."

Jethro said, "Go, and I wish you well."

19Now the LORD had said to Moses in Midian, "Go back to Egypt, for all the men who wanted to kill you are dead." 20So Moses took his wife and sons, put them on a donkey and started back to Egypt. And he took the staff of God in his hand.

21The LORD said to Moses, "When you re-

[a] 6 The Hebrew word was used for various diseases affecting the skin—not necessarily leprosy.

turn to Egypt, see that you perform before Pharaoh all the wonders I have given you the power to do. But I will harden his heart so that he will not let the people go. [22]Then say to Pharaoh, 'This is what the LORD says: Israel is my firstborn son, [23]and I told you, "Let my son go, so he may worship me." But you refused to let him go; so I will kill your firstborn son.' "

[24]At a lodging place on the way, the LORD met ⌞Moses⌟[a] and was about to kill him. [25]But Zipporah took a flint knife, cut off her son's foreskin and touched ⌞Moses'⌟ feet with it.[b] "Surely you are a bridegroom of blood to me," she said. [26]So the LORD let him alone. (At that time she said "bridegroom of blood," referring to circumcision.)

[27]The LORD said to Aaron, "Go into the desert to meet Moses." So he met Moses at the mountain of God and kissed him. [28]Then Moses told Aaron everything the LORD had sent him to say, and also about all the miraculous signs he had commanded him to perform.

[29]Moses and Aaron brought together all the elders of the Israelites, [30]and Aaron told them everything the LORD had said to Moses. He also performed the signs before the people, [31]and they believed. And when they heard that the LORD was concerned about them and had seen their misery, they bowed down and worshiped.

Bricks Without Straw

5 Afterward Moses and Aaron went to Pharaoh and said, "This is what the LORD, the God of Israel, says: 'Let my people go, so that they may hold a festival to me in the desert.' "

[2]Pharaoh said, "Who is the LORD, that I should obey him and let Israel go? I do not know the LORD and I will not let Israel go."

[3]Then they said, "The God of the Hebrews has met with us. Now let us take a three-day journey into the desert to offer sacrifices to the LORD our God, or he may strike us with plagues or with the sword."

[4]But the king of Egypt said, "Moses and Aaron, why are you taking the people away from their labor? Get back to your work!" [5]Then Pharaoh said, "Look, the people of the land are now numerous, and you are stopping them from working."

[6]That same day Pharaoh gave this order to the slave drivers and foremen in charge of the people: [7]"You are no longer to supply the people with straw for making bricks; let them go and gather their own straw. [8]But require them to make the same number of bricks as before; don't reduce the quota. They are lazy; that is why they are crying out, 'Let us go and sacrifice to our God.' [9]Make the work harder for the men so that they keep working and pay no attention to lies."

[10]Then the slave drivers and the foremen went out and said to the people, "This is what Pharaoh says: 'I will not give you any more straw. [11]Go and get your own straw wherever you can find it, but your work will not be reduced at all.' " [12]So the people scattered all over Egypt to gather stubble to use for straw. [13]The slave drivers kept pressing them, saying, "Complete the work required of you for each day, just as when you had straw." [14]The Israelite foremen appointed by Pharaoh's slave drivers were beaten and were asked, "Why didn't you meet your quota of bricks yesterday or today, as before?"

[15]Then the Israelite foremen went and appealed to Pharaoh: "Why have you treated your servants this way? [16]Your servants are given no straw, yet we are told, 'Make bricks!' Your servants are being beaten, but the fault is with your own people."

[17]Pharaoh said, "Lazy, that's what you are—lazy! That is why you keep saying, 'Let us go and sacrifice to the LORD.' [18]Now get to work. You will not be given any straw, yet you must produce your full quota of bricks."

[19]The Israelite foremen realized they were in trouble when they were told, "You are not to reduce the number of bricks required of you for each day." [20]When they left Pharaoh, they found Moses and Aaron waiting to meet them, [21]and they said, "May the LORD look upon you and judge you! You have made us a stench to Pharaoh and his officials and have put a sword in their hand to kill us."

God Promises Deliverance

[22]Moses returned to the LORD and said, "O Lord, why have you brought trouble upon this people? Is this why you sent me? [23]Ever

[a]24 Or ⌞*Moses' son*⌟; Hebrew *him* [b]25 Or *and drew near* ⌞*Moses'*⌟ *feet*

since I went to Pharaoh to speak in your name,
he has brought trouble upon this people, and
you have not rescued your people at all."

6 Then the LORD said to Moses, "Now you
will see what I will do to Pharaoh: Because
of my mighty hand he will let them go; because
of my mighty hand he will drive them out of
his country."
2 God also said to Moses, "I am the LORD. 3 I
appeared to Abraham, to Isaac and to Jacob as
God Almighty,[a] but by my name the LORD[b] I
did not make myself known to them.[c] 4 I also established my covenant with them to give them
the land of Canaan, where they lived as aliens.
5 Moreover, I have heard the groaning of the Israelites, whom the Egyptians are enslaving, and
I have remembered my covenant.
6 "Therefore, say to the Israelites: 'I am the
LORD, and I will bring you
out from under the yoke of
the Egyptians. I will free you
from being slaves to them, and
I will redeem you with an outstretched arm and with mighty
acts of judgment. 7 I will take
you as my own people, and
I will be your God. Then you
will know that I am the LORD
your God, who brought you
out from under the yoke of
the Egyptians. 8 And I will
bring you to the land I swore
with uplifted hand to give to
Abraham, to Isaac and to Ja-
cob. I will give it to you as a possession. I am
the LORD.'"
9 Moses reported this to the Israelites, but
they did not listen to him because of their discouragement and cruel bondage.
10 Then the LORD said to Moses, 11 "Go, tell
Pharaoh king of Egypt to let the Israelites go
out of his country."
12 But Moses said to the LORD, "If the Israelites will not listen to me, why would Pharaoh listen to me, since I speak with faltering lips[d]?"

Family Record of Moses and Aaron

13 Now the LORD spoke to Moses and Aaron
about the Israelites and Pharaoh king of Egypt,
and he commanded them to bring the Israelites out of Egypt.
14 These were the heads of their families[e]:

The sons of Reuben the firstborn son of
Israel were Hanoch and Pallu, Hezron and
Carmi. These were the clans of Reuben.
15 The sons of Simeon were Jemuel, Jamin, Ohad, Jakin, Zohar and Shaul the
son of a Canaanite woman. These were
the clans of Simeon.
16 These were the names of the sons of
Levi according to their records: Gershon,
Kohath and Merari. Levi lived 137 years.
17 The sons of Gershon, by clans, were
Libni and Shimei.
18 The sons of Kohath were Amram,
Izhar, Hebron and Uzziel. Kohath lived
133 years.
19 The sons of Merari were
Mahli and Mushi.
These were the clans of
Levi according to their records.
20 Amram married his fa-
ther's sister Jochebed, who
bore him Aaron and Moses.
Amram lived 137 years.
21 The sons of Izhar were
Korah, Nepheg and Zicri.
22 The sons of Uzziel were
Mishael, Elzaphan and
Sithri.
23 Aaron married Elishe-
ba, daughter of Amminadab and sister of
Nahshon, and she bore him Nadab and
Abihu, Eleazar and Ithamar.
24 The sons of Korah were Assir, Elkanah and Abiasaph. These were the Korahite clans.
25 Eleazar son of Aaron married one
of the daughters of Putiel, and she bore
him Phinehas.

These were the heads of the Levite families, clan by clan.

26 It was this same Aaron and Moses to
whom the LORD said, "Bring the Israelites

> **Exodus 6:6**
>
> *God Liberates His People*
>
> "I am the LORD, and I will bring you out from under the yoke of the Egyptians. I will free you from being slaves to them, and I will redeem you."

[a] 3 Hebrew *El-Shaddai* [b] 3 See note at Exodus 3:15. [c] 3 Or *Almighty, and by my name the LORD did I not let myself be known to them?*
[d] 12 Hebrew *I am uncircumcised of lips*; also in verse 30 [e] 14 The Hebrew for *families* here and in verse 25 refers to units larger than clans.

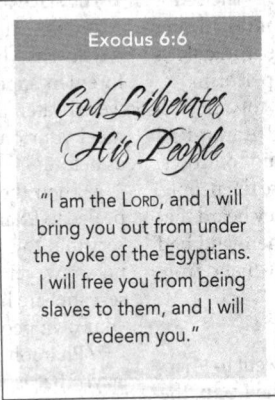

out of Egypt by their divisions." 27They were
the ones who spoke to Pharaoh king of Egypt
about bringing the Israelites out of Egypt. It
was the same Moses and Aaron.

Aaron to Speak for Moses

28Now when the LORD spoke to Moses in
Egypt, 29he said to him, "I am the LORD. Tell
Pharaoh king of Egypt everything I tell you."
30But Moses said to the LORD, "Since I speak
with faltering lips, why would Pharaoh listen
to me?"

7 Then the LORD said to Moses, "See, I have
made you like God to Pharaoh, and your
brother Aaron will be your prophet. 2You are
to say everything I command you, and your
brother Aaron is to tell Pharaoh to let the Israelites go out of his country. 3But I will harden
Pharaoh's heart, and though I multiply my miraculous signs and wonders in Egypt, 4he will
not listen to you. Then I will lay my hand on
Egypt and with mighty acts of judgment I will
bring out my divisions, my people the Israelites. 5And the Egyptians will know that I am
the LORD when I stretch out my hand against
Egypt and bring the Israelites out of it."
6Moses and Aaron did just as the LORD
commanded them. 7Moses was eighty years
old and Aaron eighty-three when they spoke
to Pharaoh.

Aaron's Staff Becomes a Snake

8The LORD said to Moses and Aaron, 9"When
Pharaoh says to you, 'Perform a miracle,' then
say to Aaron, 'Take your staff and throw it down
before Pharaoh,' and it will become a snake."
10So Moses and Aaron went to Pharaoh and
did just as the LORD commanded. Aaron threw
his staff down in front of Pharaoh and his officials, and it became a snake. 11Pharaoh then
summoned wise men and sorcerers, and the
Egyptian magicians also did the same things
by their secret arts: 12Each one threw down his
staff and it became a snake. But Aaron's staff
swallowed up their staffs. 13Yet Pharaoh's heart
became hard and he would not listen to them,
just as the LORD had said.

The Plague of Blood

14Then the LORD said to Moses, "Pharaoh's
heart is unyielding; he refuses to let the people
go. 15Go to Pharaoh in the morning as he goes
out to the water. Wait on the bank of the Nile to
meet him, and take in your hand the staff that
was changed into a snake. 16Then say to him,
'The LORD, the God of the Hebrews, has sent
me to say to you: Let my people go, so that they
may worship me in the desert. But until now
you have not listened. 17This is what the LORD
says: By this you will know that I am the LORD:
With the staff that is in my hand I will strike the
water of the Nile, and it will be changed into
blood. 18The fish in the Nile will die, and the
river will stink; the Egyptians will not be able
to drink its water.' "
19The LORD said to Moses, "Tell Aaron,
'Take your staff and stretch out your hand
over the waters of Egypt—over the streams
and canals, over the ponds and all the reservoirs'—and they will turn to blood. Blood will
be everywhere in Egypt, even in the wooden
buckets and stone jars."
20Moses and Aaron did just as the LORD had
commanded. He raised his staff in the presence
of Pharaoh and his officials and struck the water of the Nile, and all the water was changed
into blood. 21The fish in the Nile died, and the
river smelled so bad that the Egyptians could
not drink its water. Blood was everywhere
in Egypt.
22But the Egyptian magicians did the same
things by their secret arts, and Pharaoh's heart
became hard; he would not listen to Moses
and Aaron, just as the LORD had said. 23In-
stead, he turned and went into his palace, and
did not take even this to heart. 24And all the
Egyptians dug along the Nile to get drinking
water, because they could not drink the water
of the river.

The Plague of Frogs

25Seven days passed after the LORD struck
8 the Nile. 1Then the LORD said to Moses,
"Go to Pharaoh and say to him, 'This is
what the LORD says: Let my people go, so that
they may worship me. 2If you refuse to let them
go, I will plague your whole country with frogs.
3The Nile will teem with frogs. They will come
up into your palace and your bedroom and
onto your bed, into the houses of your officials
and on your people, and into your ovens and
kneading troughs. 4The frogs will go up on you
and your people and all your officials.' "

Let His People Go!

Read: Exodus 7:1–24

Exodus 7:5

"And the Egyptians will know that I am the LORD when I stretch out my hand against Egypt and bring the Israelites out of it."

reflection

1 How do you see God revealing himself to you as the one true God?

2 Whom do you look on as God's enemies?

3 How can you share God's power in your life with others?

RELATED READINGS

Psalm 46:8–10; Isaiah 10:33—11:10; 12:1–6; 2 Peter 3:9

IT WAS FAMILY MOVIE NIGHT, and Cecile B. DeMille's epic *The Ten Commandments* was playing on TV. Five-year-old Emily watched in fascination as Aaron's staff became a snake and swallowed the magically conjured snakes. She saw the river flowing blood and the plagues terrorize the Egyptians. But Yul Brenner as Pharaoh was unflinching when Charlton Heston as Moses demanded, "Let my people go!" The girl grew more and more agitated. Finally she cried out, "Why doesn't Moses just hit that bad guy?"

Reading about the plagues and Pharaoh's hard-hearted responses can leave us frustrated. Why did Moses and Aaron have to go through all of that hoopla? Why did the Egyptians have to suffer plague after plague? Why didn't God just "hit that bad guy" so the Hebrews could immediately leave Egypt? The answer is clear: "The Egyptians will know that I am the LORD when I stretch out my hand against Egypt and bring the Israelites out of it." God was just as concerned with the Egyptians as he was with the Israelites.

Yes, God wanted to free the Israelites from years of cruel bondage. But he wanted everyone—Egyptians and Israelites alike—to experience his power as the one true God. God used individual plagues to challenge the Egyptians' belief in their pagan gods. When God turned the Nile into blood, he proved that Re, their creator god, was powerless against his might. The sorcerers might turn water to blood, but Re couldn't turn blood back to water. Though the Egyptians believed the god Thoth brought frogs to life, God proved that Egyptian gods were defenseless against a plague of frogs.

Today, God still wants everyone to know that he is the only true God. And he shows his power through the events and circumstances of our lives. When we see the miracles of God, do we share those happenings with others? God still wants all people to know him. We usually think of the Egyptians as the "bad guys," and we wonder why God wasted his time on them. But unlike the black-and-white world portrayed in TV shows and movies, God goes beyond our expectations and spends some time showing the Egyptians and the Israelites about himself. The next time you see God reveal himself to you, don't hesitate to share your experiences with others—even those you might think don't have time for God.

Go to page 83 for your next devotional reading.

5 Then the LORD said to Moses, "Tell Aaron,
'Stretch out your hand with your staff over the
streams and canals and ponds, and make frogs
come up on the land of Egypt.'"
6 So Aaron stretched out his hand over the
waters of Egypt, and the frogs came up and covered the land. 7 But the magicians did the same
things by their secret arts; they also made frogs
come up on the land of Egypt.
8 Pharaoh summoned Moses and Aaron and
said, "Pray to the LORD to take the frogs away
from me and my people, and I will let your people go to offer sacrifices to the LORD."
9 Moses said to Pharaoh, "I leave to you the
honor of setting the time for me to pray for you
and your officials and your people that you and
your houses may be rid of the frogs, except for
those that remain in the Nile."
10 "Tomorrow," Pharaoh said.
Moses replied, "It will be as you say, so that
you may know there is no one like the LORD
our God. 11 The frogs will leave you and your
houses, your officials and your people; they will
remain only in the Nile."
12 After Moses and Aaron left Pharaoh, Moses cried out to the LORD about the frogs he
had brought on Pharaoh. 13 And the LORD
did what Moses asked. The frogs died in the
houses, in the courtyards and in the fields.
14 They were piled into heaps, and the land
reeked of them. 15 But when Pharaoh saw that
there was relief, he hardened his heart and
would not listen to Moses and Aaron, just as
the LORD had said.

The Plague of Gnats

16 Then the LORD said to Moses, "Tell
Aaron, 'Stretch out your staff and strike the
dust of the ground,' and throughout the land
of Egypt the dust will become gnats." 17 They
did this, and when Aaron stretched out his
hand with the staff and struck the dust of the
ground, gnats came upon men and animals.
All the dust throughout the land of Egypt became gnats. 18 But when the magicians tried
to produce gnats by their secret arts, they
could not. And the gnats were on men and animals.
19 The magicians said to Pharaoh, "This is
the finger of God." But Pharaoh's heart was
hard and he would not listen, just as the LORD
had said.

The Plague of Flies

20 Then the LORD said to Moses, "Get up
early in the morning and confront Pharaoh as
he goes to the water and say to him, 'This is
what the LORD says: Let my people go, so that
they may worship me. 21 If you do not let my
people go, I will send swarms of flies on you
and your officials, on your people and into your
houses. The houses of the Egyptians will be full
of flies, and even the ground where they are.
22 "'But on that day I will deal differently
with the land of Goshen, where my people live;
no swarms of flies will be there, so that you will
know that I, the LORD, am in this land. 23 I will
make a distinction[a] between my people and
your people. This miraculous sign will occur tomorrow.'"
24 And the LORD did this. Dense swarms of
flies poured into Pharaoh's palace and into the
houses of his officials, and throughout Egypt
the land was ruined by the flies.
25 Then Pharaoh summoned Moses and
Aaron and said, "Go, sacrifice to your God here
in the land."
26 But Moses said, "That would not be right.
The sacrifices we offer the LORD our God would
be detestable to the Egyptians. And if we offer
sacrifices that are detestable in their eyes, will
they not stone us? 27 We must take a three-day
journey into the desert to offer sacrifices to the
LORD our God, as he commands us."
28 Pharaoh said, "I will let you go to offer
sacrifices to the LORD your God in the desert, but you must not go very far. Now pray
for me."
29 Moses answered, "As soon as I leave you,
I will pray to the LORD, and tomorrow the flies
will leave Pharaoh and his officials and his people. Only be sure that Pharaoh does not act
deceitfully again by not letting the people go to
offer sacrifices to the LORD."
30 Then Moses left Pharaoh and prayed to the
LORD, 31 and the LORD did what Moses asked:
The flies left Pharaoh and his officials and his
people; not a fly remained. 32 But this time also
Pharaoh hardened his heart and would not let
the people go.

[a] 23 Septuagint and Vulgate; Hebrew *will put a deliverance*

The Plague on Livestock

9 Then the LORD said to Moses, "Go to
Pharaoh and say to him, 'This is what the
LORD, the God of the Hebrews, says: "Let my
people go, so that they may worship me." 2 If
you refuse to let them go and continue to hold
them back, 3 the hand of the LORD will bring a
terrible plague on your livestock in the field—
on your horses and donkeys
and camels and on your cattle
and sheep and goats. 4 But the
LORD will make a distinction
between the livestock of Israel
and that of Egypt, so that no animal belonging to the Israelites
will die.' "
5 The LORD set a time and
said, "Tomorrow the LORD will
do this in the land." 6 And the
next day the LORD did it: All
the livestock of the Egyptians
died, but not one animal belonging to the Israelites died.
7 Pharaoh sent men to investigate and found
that not even one of the animals of the Israelites had died. Yet his heart was unyielding and
he would not let the people go.

> **Exodus 9:1**
>
> *God Seeks Worshipers*
>
> This is what the LORD, the God of the Hebrews, says: "Let my people go, so that they may worship me."

The Plague of Boils

8 Then the LORD said to Moses and Aaron,
"Take handfuls of soot from a furnace and have
Moses toss it into the air in the presence of Pharaoh. 9 It will become fine dust over the whole
land of Egypt, and festering boils will break out
on men and animals throughout the land."
10 So they took soot from a furnace and
stood before Pharaoh. Moses tossed it into the
air, and festering boils broke out on men and
animals. 11 The magicians could not stand before Moses because of the boils that were on
them and on all the Egyptians. 12 But the LORD
hardened Pharaoh's heart and he would not listen to Moses and Aaron, just as the LORD had
said to Moses.

The Plague of Hail

13 Then the LORD said to Moses, "Get up
early in the morning, confront Pharaoh and
say to him, 'This is what the LORD, the God of
the Hebrews, says: Let my people go, so that
they may worship me, 14 or this time I will send
the full force of my plagues against you and
against your officials and your people, so you
may know that there is no one like me in all the
earth. 15 For by now I could have stretched out
my hand and struck you and your people with
a plague that would have wiped you off the
earth. 16 But I have raised you up[a] for this very
purpose, that I might show you
my power and that my name
might be proclaimed in all the
earth. 17 You still set yourself
against my people and will not
let them go. 18 Therefore, at this
time tomorrow I will send the
worst hailstorm that has ever
fallen on Egypt, from the day
it was founded till now. 19 Give
an order now to bring your livestock and everything you have
in the field to a place of shelter,
because the hail will fall on
every man and animal that has
not been brought in and is still out in the field,
and they will die.' "
20 Those officials of Pharaoh who feared the
word of the LORD hurried to bring their slaves
and their livestock inside. 21 But those who ignored the word of the LORD left their slaves and
livestock in the field.
22 Then the LORD said to Moses, "Stretch
out your hand toward the sky so that hail will
fall all over Egypt—on men and animals and
on everything growing in the fields of Egypt."
23 When Moses stretched out his staff toward
the sky, the LORD sent thunder and hail, and
lightning flashed down to the ground. So the
LORD rained hail on the land of Egypt; 24 hail
fell and lightning flashed back and forth. It was
the worst storm in all the land of Egypt since
it had become a nation. 25 Throughout Egypt
hail struck everything in the fields—both men
and animals; it beat down everything growing
in the fields and stripped every tree. 26 The only
place it did not hail was the land of Goshen,
where the Israelites were.
27 Then Pharaoh summoned Moses and
Aaron. "This time I have sinned," he said to
them. "The LORD is in the right, and I and my

[a] 16 Or *have spared you*

people are in the wrong. 28Pray to the LORD,
for we have had enough thunder and hail. I will
let you go; you don't have to stay any longer."
29Moses replied, "When I have gone out of
the city, I will spread out my hands in prayer
to the LORD. The thunder will stop and there
will be no more hail, so you may know that the
earth is the LORD's. 30But I know that you and
your officials still do not fear the LORD God."
31(The flax and barley were destroyed, since
the barley had headed and the flax was in
bloom. 32The wheat and spelt, however, were
not destroyed, because they ripen later.)
33Then Moses left Pharaoh and went out
of the city. He spread out his hands toward
the LORD; the thunder and hail stopped, and
the rain no longer poured down on the land.
34When Pharaoh saw that the rain and hail
and thunder had stopped, he sinned again: He
and his officials hardened their hearts. 35So
Pharaoh's heart was hard and he would not
let the Israelites go, just as the LORD had said
through Moses.

The Plague of Locusts

10 Then the LORD said to Moses, "Go
to Pharaoh, for I have hardened his
heart and the hearts of his officials so that I
may perform these miraculous signs of mine
among them 2that you may tell your children
and grandchildren how I dealt harshly with
the Egyptians and how I performed my signs
among them, and that you may know that I am
the LORD."
3So Moses and Aaron went to Pharaoh and
said to him, "This is what the LORD, the God of
the Hebrews, says: 'How long will you refuse
to humble yourself before me? Let my people
go, so that they may worship me. 4If you refuse
to let them go, I will bring locusts into your
country tomorrow. 5They will cover the face of
the ground so that it cannot be seen. They will
devour what little you have left after the hail, including every tree that is growing in your fields.
6They will fill your houses and those of all your
officials and all the Egyptians—something neither your fathers nor your forefathers have ever
seen from the day they settled in this land till
now.'" Then Moses turned and left Pharaoh.
7Pharaoh's officials said to him, "How long
will this man be a snare to us? Let the people
go, so that they may worship the LORD their
God. Do you not yet realize that Egypt is
ruined?"
8Then Moses and Aaron were brought back
to Pharaoh. "Go, worship the LORD your God,"
he said. "But just who will be going?"
9Moses answered, "We will go with our
young and old, with our sons and daughters,
and with our flocks and herds, because we are
to celebrate a festival to the LORD."
10Pharaoh said, "The LORD be with you—if I
let you go, along with your women and children!
Clearly you are bent on evil.[a] 11No! Have only
the men go; and worship the LORD, since that's
what you have been asking for." Then Moses and
Aaron were driven out of Pharaoh's presence.
12And the LORD said to Moses, "Stretch out
your hand over Egypt so that locusts will swarm
over the land and devour everything growing
in the fields, everything left by the hail."
13So Moses stretched out his staff over
Egypt, and the LORD made an east wind blow
across the land all that day and all that night.
By morning the wind had brought the locusts;
14they invaded all Egypt and settled down in
every area of the country in great numbers.
Never before had there been such a plague of
locusts, nor will there ever be again. 15They
covered all the ground until it was black. They
devoured all that was left after the hail—everything growing in the fields and the fruit on the
trees. Nothing green remained on tree or plant
in all the land of Egypt.
16Pharaoh quickly summoned Moses and
Aaron and said, "I have sinned against the LORD
your God and against you. 17Now forgive my
sin once more and pray to the LORD your God
to take this deadly plague away from me."
18Moses then left Pharaoh and prayed to the
LORD. 19And the LORD changed the wind to a
very strong west wind, which caught up the locusts and carried them into the Red Sea.[b] Not
a locust was left anywhere in Egypt. 20But the
LORD hardened Pharaoh's heart, and he would
not let the Israelites go.

The Plague of Darkness

21Then the LORD said to Moses, "Stretch out
your hand toward the sky so that darkness will

[a] 10 Or *Be careful, trouble is in store for you!* [b] 19 Hebrew *Yam Suph*; that is, Sea of Reeds

spread over Egypt—darkness that can be felt."
22So Moses stretched out his hand toward the
sky, and total darkness covered all Egypt for
three days. 23No one could see anyone else or
leave his place for three days. Yet all the Israelites had light in the places where they lived.

24Then Pharaoh summoned Moses and said,
"Go, worship the LORD. Even your women and
children may go with you; only leave your
flocks and herds behind."

25But Moses said, "You must allow us to
have sacrifices and burnt offerings to present
to the LORD our God. 26Our livestock too
must go with us; not a hoof is to be left behind.
We have to use some of them in worshiping
the LORD our God, and until we get there we
will not know what we are to use to worship
the LORD."

27But the LORD hardened Pharaoh's heart,
and he was not willing to let them go. 28Phar-
aoh said to Moses, "Get out of my sight! Make
sure you do not appear before me again! The
day you see my face you will die."

29"Just as you say," Moses replied, "I will
never appear before you again."

The Plague on the Firstborn

11 Now the LORD had said to Moses, "I
will bring one more plague on Pharaoh and on Egypt. After that, he will let you
go from here, and when he does, he will drive
you out completely. 2Tell the people that men
and women alike are to ask their neighbors for
articles of silver and gold." 3(The LORD made
the Egyptians favorably disposed toward the
people, and Moses himself was highly regarded
in Egypt by Pharaoh's officials and by the
people.)

4So Moses said, "This is what the LORD says:
'About midnight I will go throughout Egypt.
5Every firstborn son in Egypt will die, from
the firstborn son of Pharaoh, who sits on the
throne, to the firstborn son of the slave girl,
who is at her hand mill, and all the firstborn
of the cattle as well. 6There will be loud wailing
throughout Egypt—worse than there has ever
been or ever will be again. 7But among the Israelites not a dog will bark at any man or animal.'
Then you will know that the LORD makes a distinction between Egypt and Israel. 8All these officials of yours will come to me, bowing down
before me and saying, 'Go, you and all the people who follow you!' After that I will leave."
Then Moses, hot with anger, left Pharaoh.

9The LORD had said to Moses, "Pharaoh
will refuse to listen to you—so that my wonders may be multiplied in Egypt." 10Moses
and Aaron performed all these wonders before
Pharaoh, but the LORD hardened Pharaoh's
heart, and he would not let the Israelites go out
of his country.

The Passover

12 The LORD said to Moses and Aaron in
Egypt, 2"This month is to be for you
the first month, the first month of your year.
3Tell the whole community of Israel that on the
tenth day of this month each man is to take a
lamb[a] for his family, one for each household.
4If any household is too small for a whole
lamb, they must share one with their nearest
neighbor, having taken into account the number of people there are. You are to determine
the amount of lamb needed in accordance
with what each person will eat. 5The animals
you choose must be year-old males without defect, and you may take them from the sheep
or the goats. 6Take care of them until the fourteenth day of the month, when all the people
of the community of Israel must slaughter
them at twilight. 7Then they are to take some
of the blood and put it on the sides and tops of
the doorframes of the houses where they eat
the lambs. 8That same night they are to eat the
meat roasted over the fire, along with bitter
herbs, and bread made without yeast. 9Do not
eat the meat raw or cooked in water, but roast it
over the fire—head, legs and inner parts. 10Do
not leave any of it till morning; if some is left till
morning, you must burn it. 11This is how you
are to eat it: with your cloak tucked into your
belt, your sandals on your feet and your staff in
your hand. Eat it in haste; it is the LORD's Passover.

12"On that same night I will pass through
Egypt and strike down every firstborn—both
men and animals—and I will bring judgment
on all the gods of Egypt. I am the LORD. 13The
blood will be a sign for you on the houses
where you are; and when I see the blood, I will

[a]3 The Hebrew word can mean *lamb* or *kid*; also in verse 4.

Life at the Crossroads

HAGAR

WHERE HAVE YOU COME FROM and where are you going?

The question came to Hagar at the pinnacle of a crucial decision. She was torn between allegiance to her mistress, Sarai (known as Sarah later in the story), and the innate desire to be free to raise the baby now growing inside of her. As with most questions one faces when standing at one of life's many crossroads, it haunted her.

Where had she come from? Where was she going? It was painful for Hagar to reflect on her past, much less attempt to see through the gauze of an uncertain future, but the angel's question pierced her soul with its persistence.

Where have I come from . . .? Hagar thought to herself as she contemplated the events over the past few months. She concluded that she'd come from a place no woman should have to be.

I've come from the grasp of a woman who hates me. I've come from the burden of carrying a baby whose father loves someone else. I've come from a terrifying place of confusion, isolation and abandonment. *That's* where I have come from.

But that was only half of the equation. ". . . And where are you *going*?"

This question was even more painful than the previous one. She knew from where she'd come, but she had no idea where she was going. In fact, she was wandering the desert, considering her options at that very moment.

Could she make it? Would she die? As if the Lord's angel had traced her thoughts, he cut through her myriad of optional scenarios with a command. "Go back to your mistress and submit to her."

In truth, it was the last thing she felt like doing at the moment. *Go back? Had she heard the angel's message clearly?* Surely there was a misunderstanding.

However, there was no misunderstanding. The crossroads pointed to a path she did not want to take—had not planned to take. God had spoken, and Hagar must obey. She peered down the road that represented her future, but it looked suspiciously like the road that led to a painful past.

—Prayer—

Dear God, please help me accept your will for me even if it's not what I had planned for myself.

[The angel of the LORD] said, "Hagar, servant of Sarai, where have you come from, and where are you going?"

Genesis 16:8

ASSIGNED READING:

Genesis 16:1–16; 21:8–21

Weekend

Go to page 87 for your next devotional reading.

pass over you. No destructive plague will touch
you when I strike Egypt.
14“This is a day you are to commemorate;
for the generations to come you shall celebrate
it as a festival to the LORD—a lasting ordinance.
15For seven days you are to eat bread made
without yeast. On the first day remove the yeast
from your houses, for whoever eats anything
with yeast in it from the first day through the
seventh must be cut off from Israel. 16On the
first day hold a sacred assembly, and another
one on the seventh day. Do no work at all on
these days, except to prepare food for everyone
to eat—that is all you may do.
17“Celebrate the Feast of Unleavened Bread,
because it was on this very day that I brought
your divisions out of Egypt. Celebrate this day as
a lasting ordinance for the generations to come.
18In the first month you are to eat bread made
without yeast, from the evening of the fourteenth day until the evening of the twenty-first
day. 19For seven days no yeast is to be found in
your houses. And whoever eats anything with
yeast in it must be cut off from the community
of Israel, whether he is an alien or native-born.
20Eat nothing made with yeast. Wherever you
live, you must eat unleavened bread.”
21Then Moses summoned all the elders of
Israel and said to them, “Go at once and select
the animals for your families and slaughter the
Passover lamb. 22Take a bunch of hyssop, dip it
into the blood in the basin and put some of the
blood on the top and on both sides of the doorframe. Not one of you shall go out the door of
his house until morning. 23When the LORD
goes through the land to strike down the Egyptians, he will see the blood on the top and sides
of the doorframe and will pass over that doorway, and he will not permit the destroyer to enter your houses and strike you down.
24“Obey these instructions as a lasting ordinance for you and your descendants. 25When
you enter the land that the LORD will give you
as he promised, observe this ceremony. 26And
when your children ask you, ‘What does this
ceremony mean to you?’ 27then tell them, ‘It is
the Passover sacrifice to the LORD, who passed
over the houses of the Israelites in Egypt and
spared our homes when he struck down the
Egyptians.’” Then the people bowed down and
worshiped. 28The Israelites did just what the
LORD commanded Moses and Aaron.
29At midnight the LORD struck down all the
firstborn in Egypt, from the firstborn of Pharaoh, who sat on the throne, to the firstborn of
the prisoner, who was in the dungeon, and the
firstborn of all the livestock as well. 30Pharaoh
and all his officials and all the Egyptians got up
during the night, and there was loud wailing in
Egypt, for there was not a house without someone dead.

The Exodus

31During the night Pharaoh summoned Moses and Aaron and said, “Up! Leave my people,
you and the Israelites! Go, worship the LORD
as you have requested. 32Take your flocks
and herds, as you have said, and go. And also
bless me.”
33The Egyptians urged the people to hurry
and leave the country. “For otherwise,” they
said, “we will all die!” 34So the people took
their dough before the yeast was added, and carried it on their shoulders in kneading troughs
wrapped in clothing. 35The Israelites did as
Moses instructed and asked the Egyptians
for articles of silver and gold and for clothing.
36The LORD had made the Egyptians favorably
disposed toward the people, and they gave
them what they asked for; so they plundered
the Egyptians.
37The Israelites journeyed from Rameses to
Succoth. There were about six hundred thousand men on foot, besides women and children. 38Many other people went up with them,
as well as large droves of livestock, both flocks
and herds. 39With the dough they had brought
from Egypt, they baked cakes of unleavened
bread. The dough was without yeast because
they had been driven out of Egypt and did not
have time to prepare food for themselves.
40Now the length of time the Israelite people
lived in Egypt[a] was 430 years. 41At the end of
the 430 years, to the very day, all the LORD’s divisions left Egypt. 42Because the LORD kept vigil
that night to bring them out of Egypt, on this
night all the Israelites are to keep vigil to honor
the LORD for the generations to come.

[a]40 Masoretic Text; Samaritan Pentateuch and Septuagint *Egypt and Canaan*

Passover Restrictions

[43]The LORD said to Moses and Aaron,
"These are the regulations for the Passover:
"No foreigner is to eat of it.
[44]Any slave you have bought
may eat of it after you have
circumcised him, [45]but a temporary resident and a hired
worker may not eat of it.
[46]"It must be eaten inside
one house; take none of the
meat outside the house. Do not
break any of the bones. [47]The
whole community of Israel
must celebrate it.
[48]"An alien living among
you who wants to celebrate the
LORD's Passover must have all
the males in his household circumcised; then
he may take part like one born in the land. No
uncircumcised male may eat of it. [49]The same
law applies to the native-born and to the alien
living among you."

[50]All the Israelites did just what the LORD
had commanded Moses and Aaron. [51]And on
that very day the LORD brought the Israelites
out of Egypt by their divisions.

> **Exodus 12:41**
>
> *God Has Perfect Timing*
>
> At the end of the 430 years, to the very day, all the LORD's divisions left Egypt.

Consecration of the Firstborn

13 The LORD said to Moses, [2]"Consecrate
to me every firstborn male. The first
offspring of every womb among the Israelites
belongs to me, whether man or animal."
[3]Then Moses said to the people, "Commemorate this day, the day you came out of Egypt,
out of the land of slavery, because the LORD
brought you out of it with a mighty hand. Eat
nothing containing yeast. [4]Today, in the month
of Abib, you are leaving. [5]When the LORD
brings you into the land of the Canaanites, Hittites, Amorites, Hivites and Jebusites—the land
he swore to your forefathers to give you, a land
flowing with milk and honey—you are to observe this ceremony in this month: [6]For seven
days eat bread made without yeast and on the
seventh day hold a festival to the LORD. [7]Eat
unleavened bread during those seven days;
nothing with yeast in it is to be seen among
you, nor shall any yeast be seen anywhere
within your borders. [8]On that day tell your
son, 'I do this because of what the LORD did
for me when I came out of Egypt.' [9]This observance will be for you like a sign
on your hand and a reminder
on your forehead that the law
of the LORD is to be on your
lips. For the LORD brought you
out of Egypt with his mighty
hand. [10]You must keep this ordinance at the appointed time
year after year.
[11]"After the LORD brings
you into the land of the Canaanites and gives it to you,
as he promised on oath to you
and your forefathers, [12]you are
to give over to the LORD the
first offspring of every womb. All the firstborn
males of your livestock belong to the LORD.
[13]Redeem with a lamb every firstborn donkey,
but if you do not redeem it, break its neck. Redeem every firstborn among your sons.
[14]"In days to come, when your son asks
you, 'What does this mean?' say to him, 'With
a mighty hand the LORD brought us out of
Egypt, out of the land of slavery. [15]When Pharaoh stubbornly refused to let us go, the LORD
killed every firstborn in Egypt, both man and
animal. This is why I sacrifice to the LORD the
first male offspring of every womb and redeem
each of my firstborn sons.' [16]And it will be like
a sign on your hand and a symbol on your forehead that the LORD brought us out of Egypt
with his mighty hand."

Crossing the Sea

[17]When Pharaoh let the people go, God did
not lead them on the road through the Philistine country, though that was shorter. For God
said, "If they face war, they might change their
minds and return to Egypt." [18]So God led the
people around by the desert road toward the
Red Sea.[a] The Israelites went up out of Egypt
armed for battle.
[19]Moses took the bones of Joseph with him
because Joseph had made the sons of Israel
swear an oath. He had said, "God will surely
come to your aid, and then you must carry my
bones up with you from this place."[b]

[a]18 Hebrew *Yam Suph*; that is, Sea of Reeds [b]19 See Gen. 50:25.

20After leaving Succoth they camped at
Etham on the edge of the desert. 21By day the
LORD went ahead of them in a pillar of cloud
to guide them on their way and by night in a
pillar of fire to give them light,
so that they could travel by day
or night. 22Neither the pillar
of cloud by day nor the pillar
of fire by night left its place in
front of the people.

14 Then the LORD said to
Moses, 2"Tell the Isra-
elites to turn back and encamp
near Pi Hahiroth, between Migdol and the sea. They are to
encamp by the sea, directly opposite Baal Zephon. 3Pharaoh
will think, 'The Israelites are
wandering around the land in
confusion, hemmed in by the
desert.' 4And I will harden Pharaoh's heart, and he will pursue
them. But I will gain glory for
myself through Pharaoh and all his army, and
the Egyptians will know that I am the LORD."
So the Israelites did this.

5When the king of Egypt was told that the
people had fled, Pharaoh and his officials
changed their minds about them and said,
"What have we done? We have let the Israelites
go and have lost their services!" 6So he had his
chariot made ready and took his army with
him. 7He took six hundred of the best chariots,
along with all the other chariots of Egypt, with
officers over all of them. 8The LORD hardened
the heart of Pharaoh king of Egypt, so that he
pursued the Israelites, who were marching out
boldly. 9The Egyptians—all Pharaoh's horses
and chariots, horsemen[a] and troops—pursued the Israelites and overtook them as they
camped by the sea near Pi Hahiroth, opposite
Baal Zephon.

10As Pharaoh approached, the Israelites
looked up, and there were the Egyptians,
marching after them. They were terrified and
cried out to the LORD. 11They said to Moses,
"Was it because there were no graves in Egypt
that you brought us to the desert to die? What
have you done to us by bringing us out of
Egypt? 12Didn't we say to you in Egypt, 'Leave
us alone; let us serve the Egyptians'? It would
have been better for us to serve the Egyptians
than to die in the desert!"

13Moses answered the peo-
ple, "Do not be afraid. Stand
firm and you will see the deliverance the LORD will bring you
today. The Egyptians you see
today you will never see again.
14The LORD will fight for you;
you need only to be still."

15Then the LORD said to
Moses, "Why are you crying
out to me? Tell the Israelites
to move on. 16Raise your staff
and stretch out your hand
over the sea to divide the water so that the Israelites can go
through the sea on dry ground.
17I will harden the hearts of
the Egyptians so that they will
go in after them. And I will
gain glory through Pharaoh and all his army,
through his chariots and his horsemen. 18The
Egyptians will know that I am the LORD when
I gain glory through Pharaoh, his chariots and
his horsemen."

19Then the angel of God, who had been
traveling in front of Israel's army, withdrew
and went behind them. The pillar of cloud
also moved from in front and stood behind
them, 20coming between the armies of Egypt
and Israel. Throughout the night the cloud
brought darkness to the one side and light to
the other side; so neither went near the other
all night long.

21Then Moses stretched out his hand over
the sea, and all that night the LORD drove the
sea back with a strong east wind and turned it
into dry land. The waters were divided, 22and
the Israelites went through the sea on dry
ground, with a wall of water on their right and
on their left.

23The Egyptians pursued them, and all
Pharaoh's horses and chariots and horsemen
followed them into the sea. 24During the last
watch of the night the LORD looked down from
the pillar of fire and cloud at the Egyptian army

Exodus 13:21

God Lights Our Path

By day the LORD went ahead of them in a pillar of cloud to guide them on their way and by night in a pillar of fire to give them light, so that they could travel by day or night.

[a]9 Or *charioteers*; also in verses 17, 18, 23, 26 and 28

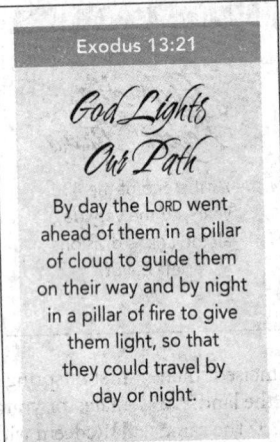

Be Still

Read: Exodus 14:1–31

IMAGINE THE FEAR. You've just escaped from the most powerful kingdom on earth to follow an 80-year-old shepherd. Now Pharaoh is coming after you with 600 of his best chariots and "all Pharaoh's horses and chariots, horsemen and troops" (Exodus 14:9). The best trained army in the world is pursuing a ragtag group of Hebrew slaves and camp followers. Now might be a good time to panic.

We find the Israelites at Pi Hahiroth in an open space with their backs to the sea . . . and escape seemed impossible. But this fear was not just in their minds. Pharaoh was coming, and they had every right to panic. Rather than telling them to take up arms or run for their lives, Moses gave a surprising command, "Do not be afraid . . . The LORD will fight for you; you need only to be still." We all know the end of the story. The waters parted, and the Israelites crossed the sea on dry land while the sea closed over the pursuing army.

So what can we learn from this well-known story as women living in the twenty-first century? Perhaps God wants us to recognize that we all harbor some kind of fear—real or imagined. For some it may be a fear of the future or a fear of failure. For others it may be the fear of rejection. Many fear the threat of terrorism. Some of us may even have a phobia, a fear that seems irrational to others, but is overwhelming and life-altering to us. No matter what our fear may be, God's Word still resounds, "Do not be afraid." Did you notice that God didn't make fearlessness a suggestion but a command?

So how do we overcome our fears? We can begin by taking the time to be still—not always an easy thing to do in our culture. But with practice and deliberation, we can make the time and cultivate a lifestyle in which we learn to draw our courage from our times of stillness, quietness and prayer.

Exodus 14:13–14

Moses answered the people, "Do not be afraid. Stand firm and you will see the deliverance the LORD will bring you today. The Egyptians you see today you will never see again. The LORD will fight for you; you need only to be still."

reflection

1 What do you most fear?

2 How has your fear caused you to fight or take flight rather than be still and trust God?

3 Take some time to "be still" before the Lord and ask him to deliver you from your fears.

RELATED READINGS

Psalms 37:1–7; 46:8–11; Mark 4:35–41

Monday

Go to page 90 for your next devotional reading.

and threw it into confusion. 25He made the
wheels of their chariots come off[a] so that they
had difficulty driving. And the Egyptians said,
"Let's get away from the Israelites! The LORD is
fighting for them against Egypt."
26Then the LORD said to Moses, "Stretch out
your hand over the sea so that the waters may
flow back over the Egyptians and their chariots and horsemen." 27Moses stretched out his
hand over the sea, and at daybreak the sea went
back to its place. The Egyptians were fleeing toward[b] it, and the LORD swept them into the sea.
28The water flowed back and covered the chariots and horsemen—the entire army of Pharaoh
that had followed the Israelites into the sea. Not
one of them survived.
29But the Israelites went through the sea
on dry ground, with a wall of water on their
right and on their left. 30That day the LORD
saved Israel from the hands of the Egyptians,
and Israel saw the Egyptians lying dead on the
shore. 31And when the Israelites saw the great
power the LORD displayed against the Egyptians, the people feared the LORD and put their
trust in him and in Moses his servant.

The Song of Moses and Miriam

15 Then Moses and the Israelites sang this song to the LORD:

"I will sing to the LORD,
for he is highly exalted.
The horse and its rider
he has hurled into the sea.
2 The LORD is my strength and my song;
he has become my salvation.
He is my God, and I will praise him,
my father's God, and I will exalt him.
3 The LORD is a warrior;
the LORD is his name.
4 Pharaoh's chariots and his army
he has hurled into the sea.
The best of Pharaoh's officers
are drowned in the Red Sea.[c]
5 The deep waters have covered them;
they sank to the depths like a stone.

6 "Your right hand, O LORD,
was majestic in power.
Your right hand, O LORD,
shattered the enemy.
7 In the greatness of your majesty
you threw down those who opposed
you.
You unleashed your burning anger;
it consumed them like stubble.
8 By the blast of your nostrils
the waters piled up.
The surging waters stood firm like a wall;
the deep waters congealed in the heart
of the sea.

9 "The enemy boasted,
'I will pursue, I will overtake them.
I will divide the spoils;
I will gorge myself on them.
I will draw my sword
and my hand will destroy them.'
10 But you blew with your breath,
and the sea covered them.
They sank like lead
in the mighty waters.

11 "Who among the gods is like you, O LORD?
Who is like you—
majestic in holiness,
awesome in glory,
working wonders?
12 You stretched out your right hand
and the earth swallowed them.

13 "In your unfailing love you will lead
the people you have redeemed.
In your strength you will guide them
to your holy dwelling.
14 The nations will hear and tremble;
anguish will grip the people of Philistia.
15 The chiefs of Edom will be terrified,
the leaders of Moab will be seized with
trembling,
the people[d] of Canaan will melt away;
16 terror and dread will fall upon them.
By the power of your arm
they will be as still as a stone—
until your people pass by, O LORD,
until the people you bought[e] pass by.
17 You will bring them in and plant them
on the mountain of your inheritance—
the place, O LORD, you made for your
dwelling,

[a]25 Or *He jammed the wheels of their chariots* (see Samaritan Pentateuch, Septuagint and Syriac) [b]27 Or *from* [c]4 Hebrew *Yam Suph*; that is, Sea of Reeds; also in verse 22 [d]15 Or *rulers* [e]16 Or *created*

the sanctuary, O Lord, your hands
established.
18 The LORD will reign
for ever and ever."

19 When Pharaoh's horses, chariots and
horsemen[a] went into the sea, the LORD brought
the waters of the sea back over them, but the Israelites walked through the sea on dry ground.
20 Then Miriam the prophetess, Aaron's sister,
took a tambourine in her hand, and all the
women followed her, with tambourines and
dancing. 21 Miriam sang to them:

"Sing to the LORD,
for he is highly exalted.
The horse and its rider
he has hurled into the sea."

The Waters of Marah and Elim

22 Then Moses led Israel from the Red Sea
and they went into the Desert of Shur. For three
days they traveled in the desert without finding
water. 23 When they came to Marah, they could
not drink its water because it was bitter. (That is
why the place is called Marah.[b]) 24 So the people grumbled against Moses, saying, "What are
we to drink?"

25 Then Moses cried out to the LORD, and the
LORD showed him a piece of wood. He threw it
into the water, and the water became sweet.

There the LORD made a de-
cree and a law for them, and
there he tested them. 26 He
said, "If you listen carefully
to the voice of the LORD your
God and do what is right in his
eyes, if you pay attention to his
commands and keep all his decrees, I will not bring on you
any of the diseases I brought
on the Egyptians, for I am the
LORD, who heals you."

> **Exodus 15:26**
>
> *God Heals Our Wounds*
>
> "I am the LORD, who heals you."

27 Then they came to Elim, where there were
twelve springs and seventy palm trees, and they
camped there near the water.

Manna and Quail

16 The whole Israelite community set out
from Elim and came to the Desert of
Sin, which is between Elim and Sinai, on the
fifteenth day of the second month after they
had come out of Egypt. 2 In the desert the
whole community grumbled against Moses
and Aaron. 3 The Israelites said to them, "If
only we had died by the LORD's hand in Egypt!
There we sat around pots of meat and ate all the
food we wanted, but you have brought us out
into this desert to starve this entire assembly
to death."

4 Then the LORD said to Moses, "I will rain
down bread from heaven for you. The people
are to go out each day and gather enough for
that day. In this way I will test them and see
whether they will follow my instructions. 5 On
the sixth day they are to prepare what they
bring in, and that is to be twice as much as they
gather on the other days."

6 So Moses and Aaron said to all the Israelites, "In the evening you will know that it was
the LORD who brought you out of Egypt, 7 and
in the morning you will see the glory of the
LORD, because he has heard your grumbling
against him. Who are we, that you should
grumble against us?" 8 Moses also said, "You
will know that it was the LORD when he gives
you meat to eat in the evening and all the bread
you want in the morning, because he has heard
your grumbling against him. Who are we?
You are not grumbling against us, but against
the LORD."

9 Then Moses told Aaron,
"Say to the entire Israelite
community, 'Come before the
LORD, for he has heard your
grumbling.'"

10 While Aaron was speak-
ing to the whole Israelite community, they looked toward
the desert, and there was the
glory of the LORD appearing in
the cloud.

11 The LORD said to Moses,
12 "I have heard the grumbling of the Israelites.
Tell them, 'At twilight you will eat meat, and
in the morning you will be filled with bread.
Then you will know that I am the LORD your
God.'"

13 That evening quail came and covered the
camp, and in the morning there was a layer of

[a] 19 Or *charioteers* [b] 23 *Marah* means *bitter.*

How Quickly We Forget

Exodus 16:4

Then the LORD said to Moses, "I will rain down bread from heaven for you. The people are to go out each day and gather enough for that day. In this way I will test them and see whether they will follow my instructions."

reflection

1 In what ways have you been brought "out of bondage"? What circumstances cause you to look back? What do you look back to?

2 How often do you blame others for circumstances God has allowed in your life?

3 How has God graciously provided for your needs despite your grumbling and complaining? Spend some time praising the bread of life, Jesus Christ, for feeding your soul.

RELATED READINGS

Deuteronomy 8:2–3;
John 6:32–35;
Philippians 4:6–7

Read: Exodus 16:1–36

FRIGID WEATHER ON THE CROSSING, a food shortage, a desperate need for shelter in a dark wilderness winter. Contrasted with the dire straits the Puritan pilgrims faced their first winter in America, religious persecution might have seemed downright appealing. At least in England they could have a hot meal while being ostracized. Their plight in the new world included death from sickness and starvation.

Suffering sears the human spirit so fully that we begin to believe lies about the past, and, even more dangerous, the future becomes a dead wasteland in our clouded vision. We tend to doubt God's goodness when we follow him through difficult experiences. Trapped by physical, emotional or spiritual pain, we long for happier times; we may even wish for death over pain before we acknowledge God's presence. God cares for us beyond imagination. Although we know that, how do we *feel* it when our guts tighten with fear and a sense of abandonment?

The moment the Israelites didn't get the food they craved, they began to blame Moses and Aaron. How quickly they forgot the God who had brought them out of Egypt. You might think God would react with anger: *Those ungrateful people. Grumbling after all I've done for them. I'll just let them starve.* But instead God chose to "rain down bread from heaven." Though the Israelites remembered Egypt fondly and blamed their deliverer, the Almighty still chose to provide what they needed.

Provision doesn't always arrive as tangibly as manna from heaven. Gut-wrenching starvation afflicted the Pilgrims in a very real way: many of them died that first winter. Sometimes we forget that the world groans under the weight of a curse, that God's love doesn't instantly remove all discomfort, the far-reaching effects of the fall, from our lives. But hidden in God's nature we find answers. When the world threatens to crush our hope, we must cling to the knowledge of God's goodness. Even when our *feelings* tell us otherwise, that we miss England or Egypt or another decade of our lives, *knowing* God's goodness will gradually restore our sight. Then we can see our situation clearly, as daughters of a heavenly Father who desires our good more than we possibly can imagine.

Go to page 93 for your next devotional reading.

dew around the camp. 14 When the dew was
gone, thin flakes like frost on the ground appeared on the desert floor. 15 When the Israelites saw it, they said to each other, "What is it?"
For they did not know what it was.
Moses said to them, "It is the bread the
LORD has given you to eat. 16 This is what the
LORD has commanded: 'Each one is to gather
as much as he needs. Take an omer[a] for each
person you have in your tent.'"
17 The Israelites did as they were told; some
gathered much, some little. 18 And when they
measured it by the omer, he who gathered
much did not have too much, and he who gathered little did not have too little. Each one gathered as much as he needed.
19 Then Moses said to them, "No one is to
keep any of it until morning."
20 However, some of them paid no attention
to Moses; they kept part of it until morning,
but it was full of maggots and began to smell.
So Moses was angry with them.
21 Each morning everyone gathered as much
as he needed, and when the sun grew hot, it
melted away. 22 On the sixth day, they gathered twice as much—two omers[b] for each person—and the leaders of the community came
and reported this to Moses. 23 He said to them,
"This is what the LORD commanded: 'Tomorrow is to be a day of rest, a holy Sabbath to the
LORD. So bake what you want to bake and boil
what you want to boil. Save whatever is left and
keep it until morning.'"
24 So they saved it until morning, as Moses
commanded, and it did not stink or get maggots in it. 25 "Eat it today," Moses said, "because
today is a Sabbath to the LORD. You will not
find any of it on the ground today. 26 Six days
you are to gather it, but on the seventh day, the
Sabbath, there will not be any."
27 Nevertheless, some of the people went out
on the seventh day to gather it, but they found
none. 28 Then the LORD said to Moses, "How
long will you[c] refuse to keep my commands
and my instructions? 29 Bear in mind that the
LORD has given you the Sabbath; that is why on
the sixth day he gives you bread for two days.
Everyone is to stay where he is on the seventh
day; no one is to go out." 30 So the people rested
on the seventh day.
31 The people of Israel called the bread
manna.[d] It was white like coriander seed and
tasted like wafers made with honey. 32 Moses
said, "This is what the LORD has commanded:
'Take an omer of manna and keep it for the generations to come, so they can see the bread I
gave you to eat in the desert when I brought
you out of Egypt.'"
33 So Moses said to Aaron, "Take a jar and
put an omer of manna in it. Then place it before the LORD to be kept for the generations
to come."
34 As the LORD commanded Moses, Aaron
put the manna in front of the Testimony, that it
might be kept. 35 The Israelites ate manna forty
years, until they came to a land that was settled;
they ate manna until they reached the border
of Canaan.
36 (An omer is one tenth of an ephah.)

Water From the Rock

17 The whole Israelite community set out
from the Desert of Sin, traveling from
place to place as the LORD commanded. They
camped at Rephidim, but there was no water
for the people to drink. 2 So they quarreled with
Moses and said, "Give us water to drink."
Moses replied, "Why do you quarrel with
me? Why do you put the LORD to the test?"
3 But the people were thirsty for water there,
and they grumbled against Moses. They said,
"Why did you bring us up out of Egypt to
make us and our children and livestock die
of thirst?"
4 Then Moses cried out to the LORD, "What
am I to do with these people? They are almost
ready to stone me."
5 The LORD answered Moses, "Walk on ahead
of the people. Take with you some of the elders
of Israel and take in your hand the staff with
which you struck the Nile, and go. 6 I will stand
there before you by the rock at Horeb. Strike
the rock, and water will come out of it for the
people to drink." So Moses did this in the sight
of the elders of Israel. 7 And he called the place
Massah[e] and Meribah[f] because the Israelites

[a] 16 That is, probably about 2 quarts (about 2 liters); also in verses 18, 32, 33 and 36 [b] 22 That is, probably about 4 quarts (about 4.5 liters) [c] 28 The Hebrew is plural. [d] 31 *Manna* means *What is it?* (see verse 15). [e] 7 *Massah* means *testing.* [f] 7 *Meribah* means *quarreling.*

quarreled and because they tested the LORD saying, "Is the LORD among us or not?"

The Amalekites Defeated

8The Amalekites came and attacked the Israelites at Rephidim. 9Moses said to Joshua, "Choose some of our men and go out to fight the Amalekites. Tomorrow I will stand on top of the hill with the staff of God in my hands."

10So Joshua fought the Amalekites as Moses had ordered, and Moses, Aaron and Hur went to the top of the hill. 11As long as Moses held up his hands, the Israelites were winning, but whenever he lowered his hands, the Amalekites were winning. 12When Moses' hands grew tired, they took a stone and put it under him and he sat on it. Aaron and Hur held his hands up—one on one side, one on the other—so that his hands remained steady till sunset. 13So Joshua overcame the Amalekite army with the sword.

14Then the LORD said to Moses, "Write this on a scroll as something to be remembered and make sure that Joshua hears it, because I will completely blot out the memory of Amalek from under heaven."

15Moses built an altar and called it The LORD is my Banner. 16He said, "For hands were lifted up to the throne of the LORD. The[a] LORD will be at war against the Amalekites from generation to generation."

Jethro Visits Moses

18 Now Jethro, the priest of Midian and father-in-law of Moses, heard of everything God had done for Moses and for his people Israel, and how the LORD had brought Israel out of Egypt.

2After Moses had sent away his wife Zipporah, his father-in-law Jethro received her 3and her two sons. One son was named Gershom,[b] for Moses said, "I have become an alien in a foreign land"; 4and the other was named Eliezer,[c] for he said, "My father's God was my helper; he saved me from the sword of Pharaoh."

5Jethro, Moses' father-in-law, together with Moses' sons and wife, came to him in the desert, where he was camped near the mountain of God. 6Jethro had sent word to him, "I, your father-in-law Jethro, am coming to you with your wife and her two sons."

7So Moses went out to meet his father-in-law and bowed down and kissed him. They greeted each other and then went into the tent. 8Moses told his father-in-law about everything the LORD had done to Pharaoh and the Egyptians for Israel's sake and about all the hardships they had met along the way and how the LORD had saved them.

9Jethro was delighted to hear about all the good things the LORD had done for Israel in rescuing them from the hand of the Egyptians. 10He said, "Praise be to the LORD, who rescued you from the hand of the Egyptians and of Pharaoh, and who rescued the people from the hand of the Egyptians. 11Now I know that the LORD is greater than all other gods, for he did this to those who had treated Israel arrogantly." 12Then Jethro, Moses' father-in-law, brought a burnt offering and other sacrifices to God, and Aaron came with all the elders of Israel to eat bread with Moses' father-in-law in the presence of God.

13The next day Moses took his seat to serve as judge for the people, and they stood around him from morning till evening. 14When his father-in-law saw all that Moses was doing for the people, he said, "What is this you are doing for the people? Why do you alone sit as judge, while all these people stand around you from morning till evening?"

15Moses answered him, "Because the people come to me to seek God's will. 16Whenever they have a dispute, it is brought to me, and I decide between the parties and inform them of God's decrees and laws."

17Moses' father-in-law replied, "What you are doing is not good. 18You and these people who come to you will only wear yourselves out. The work is too heavy for you; you cannot handle it alone. 19Listen now to me and I will give you some advice, and may God be with you. You must be the people's representative before God and bring their disputes to him. 20Teach them the decrees and laws, and show them the way to live and the duties they are to perform. 21But select capable men from all the people—

[a]16 Or *"Because a hand was against the throne of the LORD, the* [b]3 *Gershom* sounds like the Hebrew for *an alien there.* [c]4 *Eliezer* means *my God is helper.*

All Things to All People

Read: Exodus 18:1–27

AN ADVERTISEMENT in a colonial newspaper listed these qualifications for a housekeeper: "An affable, cheerful, and amiable Disposition; cleanly, industrious, perfectly qualified to direct and manage the female Concerns of country business, as raising small stock, dairying, marketing, combing, carding, spinning, knitting, sewing, pickling, preserving, etc., and occasionally to instruct two Young Ladies in those Branches of Economy." Whew! And we think we're busy!

Juggling a hectic life is not new or unique to women in our culture. However, our culture glorifies the multi-tasking woman. Many times we over-schedule our lives because we can't say no. Sometimes we don't want to miss out, so we try to do everything.

Moses could relate. He led Israel as a prophet, guide, intercessor, teacher, lawyer and judge. (Sound like good practice for motherhood?) In short, he was trying to be all things to the Israelites. But it was too much for him to handle by himself. Fortunately, his wise father-in-law saw that he was wearing himself out. Jethro made a great suggestion: You can't do it alone; share the burden with trusted friends. Moses recognized good advice when he heard it, and so he acted upon it, placing capable leaders over various groups of Israelites.

Many women struggle with the "need" to please everyone. But we simply can't be everywhere at once. We can't do everything everyone would like us to do. We can't even do everything *we* would like to do. Trying to be all things to all people puts us on the fast track to burnout. But when we delegate, we are freed up to focus on the things God has given us to do.

Delegating also creates the opportunity for another capable person to grow into a new role. The people around Moses might never have become leaders if he hadn't given them the opportunity. It's the same for us today. Sometimes we stay in a position because we think that we are irreplaceable. Sometimes we're afraid no one else will do it. Maybe there's some pride involved—we think no one else can do the work as well as we do. But failing to share the load may impede another person's God-given potential. Sometimes the best thing we can do, for others and ourselves, is to step aside so someone else can step up.

Go to page 96 for your next devotional reading.

Exodus 18:17–18

Moses' father-in-law replied, "What you are doing is not good. You and these people who come to you will only wear yourselves out. The work is too heavy for you; you cannot handle it alone."

reflection

1 What things do you feel God is showing you as your highest priorities? What things are distracting you from that calling?

2 Look at the capable women in your life. Can you release a responsibility to someone else and encourage her to grow in serving God?

3 What chores and responsibilities can you delegate to your children, so that they, too, may grow in learning skills and serving others?

RELATED READINGS

Galatians 6:2;
2 Timothy 2:1–3

men who fear God, trustworthy men who hate
dishonest gain—and appoint them as officials
over thousands, hundreds, fifties and tens.
22 Have them serve as judges for the people at
all times, but have them bring every difficult
case to you; the simple cases they can decide
themselves. That will make your load lighter,
because they will share it with you. 23 If you do
this and God so commands, you will be able
to stand the strain, and all these people will go
home satisfied."
24 Moses listened to his father-in-law and
did everything he said. 25 He chose capable
men from all Israel and made them leaders of
the people, officials over thousands, hundreds,
fifties and tens. 26 They served as judges for
the people at all times. The difficult cases they
brought to Moses, but the simple ones they
decided themselves.
27 Then Moses sent his father-in-law on his
way, and Jethro returned to his own country.

At Mount Sinai

19 In the third month after the Israelites
left Egypt—on the very day—they
came to the Desert of Sinai. 2 After they set out
from Rephidim, they entered the Desert of Sinai, and Israel camped there in the desert in
front of the mountain.
3 Then Moses went up to God, and the LORD
called to him from the moun-
tain and said, "This is what you
are to say to the house of Jacob
and what you are to tell the people of Israel: 4 'You yourselves
have seen what I did to Egypt,
and how I carried you on eagles' wings and brought you to
myself. 5 Now if you obey me
fully and keep my covenant,
then out of all nations you will
be my treasured possession.
Although the whole earth is
mine, 6 you[a] will be for me a
kingdom of priests and a holy nation.' These are
the words you are to speak to the Israelites."
7 So Moses went back and summoned the
elders of the people and set before them all
the words the LORD had commanded him to
speak. 8 The people all responded together, "We
will do everything the LORD has said." So Moses brought their answer back to the LORD.
9 The LORD said to Moses, "I am going to
come to you in a dense cloud, so that the people will hear me speaking with you and will always put their trust in you." Then Moses told
the LORD what the people had said.
10 And the LORD said to Moses, "Go to the
people and consecrate them today and tomorrow. Have them wash their clothes 11 and be
ready by the third day, because on that day
the LORD will come down on Mount Sinai in
the sight of all the people. 12 Put limits for the
people around the mountain and tell them, 'Be
careful that you do not go up the mountain
or touch the foot of it. Whoever touches the
mountain shall surely be put to death. 13 He
shall surely be stoned or shot with arrows; not
a hand is to be laid on him. Whether man or
animal, he shall not be permitted to live.' Only
when the ram's horn sounds a long blast may
they go up to the mountain."
14 After Moses had gone down the mountain
to the people, he consecrated them, and they
washed their clothes. 15 Then he said to the people, "Prepare yourselves for the third day. Abstain from sexual relations."
16 On the morning of the third day there was
thunder and lightning, with a
thick cloud over the mountain, and a very loud trumpet
blast. Everyone in the camp
trembled. 17 Then Moses led
the people out of the camp
to meet with God, and they
stood at the foot of the mountain. 18 Mount Sinai was covered with smoke, because the
LORD descended on it in fire.
The smoke billowed up from it
like smoke from a furnace, the
whole mountain[b] trembled
violently, 19 and the sound of the trumpet grew
louder and louder. Then Moses spoke and the
voice of God answered him.[c]
20 The LORD descended to the top of Mount

Exodus 19:4

God Carries Us

"You yourselves have seen what I did to Egypt, and how I carried you on eagles' wings and brought you to myself."

[a] 5,6 Or *possession, for the whole earth is mine.* [6] *You* [b] 18 Most Hebrew manuscripts; a few Hebrew manuscripts and Septuagint *all the people* [c] 19 Or *and God answered him with thunder*

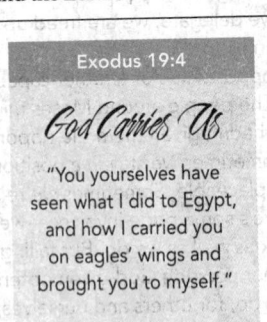

Sinai and called Moses to the top of the mountain. So Moses went up 21 and the LORD said
to him, "Go down and warn the people so
they do not force their way through to see the
LORD and many of them perish. 22 Even the
priests, who approach the LORD, must consecrate themselves, or the LORD will break out
against them."
23 Moses said to the LORD, "The people cannot come up Mount Sinai, because you yourself
warned us, 'Put limits around the mountain
and set it apart as holy.' "
24 The LORD replied, "Go down and bring
Aaron up with you. But the priests and the
people must not force their way through to
come up to the LORD, or he will break out
against them."
25 So Moses went down to the people and
told them.

The Ten Commandments

20 And God spoke all these words:

2 "I am the LORD your God, who
brought you out of Egypt, out of
the land of slavery.
3 "You shall have no other gods before[a] me.
4 "You shall not make for yourself an idol
in the form of anything in heaven
above or on the earth beneath or in
the waters below. 5 You shall not bow
down to them or worship them; for
I, the LORD your God, am a jealous
God, punishing the children for the
sin of the fathers to the third and
fourth generation of those who hate
me, 6 but showing love to a thousand
⌊generations⌋ of those who love me
and keep my commandments.
7 "You shall not misuse the name of the
LORD your God, for the LORD will
not hold anyone guiltless who mis-
uses his name.
8 "Remember the Sabbath day by keeping
it holy. 9 Six days you shall labor and
do all your work, 10 but the seventh
day is a Sabbath to the LORD your
God. On it you shall not do any
work, neither you, nor your son or
daughter, nor your manservant or
maidservant, nor your animals, nor
the alien within your gates. 11 For in
six days the LORD made the heavens
and the earth, the sea, and all that is
in them, but he rested on the seventh
day. Therefore the LORD blessed the
Sabbath day and made it holy.
12 "Honor your father and your mother, so
that you may live long in the land the
LORD your God is giving you.
13 "You shall not murder.
14 "You shall not commit adultery.
15 "You shall not steal.
16 "You shall not give false testimony against
your neighbor.
17 "You shall not covet your neighbor's
house. You shall not covet your
neighbor's wife, or his manservant
or maidservant, his ox or donkey, or
anything that belongs to your neighbor."

18 When the people saw the thunder and
lightning and heard the trumpet and saw the
mountain in smoke, they trembled with fear.
They stayed at a distance 19 and said to Moses,
"Speak to us yourself and we will listen. But do
not have God speak to us or we will die."
20 Moses said to the people, "Do not be
afraid. God has come to test you, so that
the fear of God will be with you to keep you
from sinning."
21 The people remained at a distance, while
Moses approached the thick darkness where
God was.

Idols and Altars

22 Then the LORD said to Moses, "Tell the Israelites this: 'You have seen for yourselves that
I have spoken to you from heaven: 23 Do not
make any gods to be alongside me; do not make
for yourselves gods of silver or gods of gold.
24 " 'Make an altar of earth for me and sacrifice on it your burnt offerings and fellowship
offerings,[b] your sheep and goats and your cattle. Wherever I cause my name to be honored,
I will come to you and bless you. 25 If you make
an altar of stones for me, do not build it with
dressed stones, for you will defile it if you use

[a] 3 Or *besides* [b] 24 Traditionally *peace offerings*

Heart Troublers

Read: Exodus 20:1–26

SO MANY THINGS can trouble our hearts. Unpaid bills. A frightening medical prognosis. Loss of a job. The death of a loved one. Upcoming surgery. An unexpected move. An argument with a close friend. A savage rumor. A church dispute.

The world is full of "heart troublers," and it always will be. Yet Jesus does not want our hearts to remain troubled. And he does not expect us to deal with those troubles so much by ignoring them as by turning toward him. As he said to his anxious disciples in John 14:1, "Trust in God, trust also in me."

When suffering and persecution and pain and difficulties do is not so much *make* us weak, as show us we *are* weak. Without them, we can deceive ourselves into believing we're prizefighters. With them, we're reminded that we're not constructed to function on our own power. The trick is to allow suffering to be used as a tool to help us depend on God and not on ourselves.

God didn't go halfway when he went to work on my behalf. He did it all. Even when I couldn't feel him, even when I couldn't sense him, even when I wasn't holding on to him anymore, God worked on my behalf. He didn't need me to do a thing!

When I faced far worse than my worst imaginings, something unexpected and wonderful happened. I realized that God is in control and God is good—even when bad things happen in our lives.

Even though I didn't know what I might have to go through next, I could rest and accept it. Because now I knew that when I let go, I would fall into the strong hands of God.

—Jan Dravecky

Exodus 20:18–20

When the people saw the thunder and lightning and heard the trumpet and saw the mountain in smoke, they trembled with fear. They stayed at a distance and said to Moses, "Speak to us yourself and we will listen. But do not have God speak to us or we will die." Moses said to the people, "Do not be afraid. God has come to test you, so that the fear of God will be with you to keep you from sinning."

reflection

1 Have you ever found yourself fearing God in the way the Israelites feared him at Mt. Sinai?

2 How does the fear of the Lord keep you from sinning, as God said to Moses?

3 What "heart troubler" are you experiencing right now? As Jan suggested, turn to God in trust and ask him to perform his good work on your behalf.

RELATED READINGS

Proverbs 1:1–7; Proverbs 3:5–6; Luke 18:18–27

Go to page 109 for your next devotional reading.

a tool on it. 26And do not go up to my altar on
steps, lest your nakedness be exposed on it.'

21 "These are the laws you are to set before them:

Hebrew Servants

2"If you buy a Hebrew servant, he is to serve
you for six years. But in the seventh year, he
shall go free, without paying anything. 3If he
comes alone, he is to go free alone; but if he has
a wife when he comes, she is to go with him. 4If
his master gives him a wife and she bears him
sons or daughters, the woman and her children
shall belong to her master, and only the man
shall go free.

5"But if the servant declares, 'I love my master and my wife and children and do not want
to go free,' 6then his master must take him before the judges.[a] He shall take him to the door
or the doorpost and pierce his ear with an awl.
Then he will be his servant for life.

7"If a man sells his daughter as a servant, she
is not to go free as menservants do. 8If she does
not please the master who has selected her for
himself,[b] he must let her be redeemed. He has
no right to sell her to foreigners, because he has
broken faith with her. 9If he selects her for his
son, he must grant her the rights of a daughter. 10If he marries another woman, he must
not deprive the first one of her food, clothing
and marital rights. 11If he does not provide her
with these three things, she is to go free, without any payment of money.

Personal Injuries

12"Anyone who strikes a man and kills him
shall surely be put to death. 13However, if he
does not do it intentionally, but God lets it
happen, he is to flee to a place I will designate.
14But if a man schemes and kills another man
deliberately, take him away from my altar and
put him to death.

15"Anyone who attacks[c] his father or his
mother must be put to death.

16"Anyone who kidnaps another and either
sells him or still has him when he is caught
must be put to death.

17"Anyone who curses his father or mother
must be put to death.

18"If men quarrel and one hits the other
with a stone or with his fist[d] and he does not
die but is confined to bed, 19the one who
struck the blow will not be held responsible
if the other gets up and walks around outside
with his staff; however, he must pay the injured
man for the loss of his time and see that he is
completely healed.

20"If a man beats his male or female slave
with a rod and the slave dies as a direct result,
he must be punished, 21but he is not to be punished if the slave gets up after a day or two,
since the slave is his property.

22"If men who are fighting hit a pregnant
woman and she gives birth prematurely[e] but
there is no serious injury, the offender must be
fined whatever the woman's husband demands
and the court allows. 23But if there is serious
injury, you are to take life for life, 24eye for eye,
tooth for tooth, hand for hand, foot for foot,
25burn for burn, wound for wound, bruise
for bruise.

26"If a man hits a manservant or maidservant
in the eye and destroys it, he must let the servant go free to compensate for the eye. 27And
if he knocks out the tooth of a manservant or
maidservant, he must let the servant go free to
compensate for the tooth.

28"If a bull gores a man or a woman to death,
the bull must be stoned to death, and its meat
must not be eaten. But the owner of the bull
will not be held responsible. 29If, however, the
bull has had the habit of goring and the owner
has been warned but has not kept it penned
up and it kills a man or woman, the bull must
be stoned and the owner also must be put to
death. 30However, if payment is demanded of
him, he may redeem his life by paying whatever
is demanded. 31This law also applies if the bull
gores a son or daughter. 32If the bull gores a
male or female slave, the owner must pay thirty
shekels[f] of silver to the master of the slave, and
the bull must be stoned.

33"If a man uncovers a pit or digs one and
fails to cover it and an ox or a donkey falls into
it, 34the owner of the pit must pay for the loss;

[a]6 Or *before God* [b]8 Or *master so that he does not choose her* [c]15 Or *kills* [d]18 Or *with a tool* [e]22 Or *she has a miscarriage*
[f]32 That is, about 12 ounces (about 0.3 kilogram)

he must pay its owner, and the dead animal will
be his.
35“If a man’s bull injures the bull of another
and it dies, they are to sell the live one and
divide both the money and the dead animal
equally. 36However, if it was known that the
bull had the habit of goring, yet the owner did
not keep it penned up, the owner must pay,
animal for animal, and the dead animal will
be his.

Protection of Property

22 “If a man steals an ox or a sheep and
slaughters it or sells it, he must pay
back five head of cattle for the ox and four
sheep for the sheep.
2“If a thief is caught breaking in and is struck
so that he dies, the defender is not guilty of
bloodshed; 3but if it happens[a] after sunrise, he
is guilty of bloodshed.
“A thief must certainly make restitution, but
if he has nothing, he must be sold to pay for
his theft.
4“If the stolen animal is found alive in his
possession—whether ox or donkey or sheep—
he must pay back double.
5“If a man grazes his livestock in a field or
vineyard and lets them stray and they graze in
another man’s field, he must make restitution
from the best of his own field or vineyard.
6“If a fire breaks out and spreads into
thornbushes so that it burns
shocks of grain or standing
grain or the whole field, the
one who started the fire must
make restitution.
7“If a man gives his neighbor silver or goods for safekeeping and they are stolen from
the neighbor’s house, the thief,
if he is caught, must pay back
double. 8But if the thief is not
found, the owner of the house
must appear before the judges[b]
to determine whether he has
laid his hands on the other man’s property. 9In
all cases of illegal possession of an ox, a donkey,
a sheep, a garment, or any other lost property
about which somebody says, ‘This is mine,’
both parties are to bring their cases before
the judges. The one whom the judges declare[c]
guilty must pay back double to his neighbor.
10“If a man gives a donkey, an ox, a sheep or
any other animal to his neighbor for safekeeping and it dies or is injured or is taken away
while no one is looking, 11the issue between
them will be settled by the taking of an oath
before the LORD that the neighbor did not
lay hands on the other person’s property. The
owner is to accept this, and no restitution is
required. 12But if the animal was stolen from
the neighbor, he must make restitution to the
owner. 13If it was torn to pieces by a wild animal, he shall bring in the remains as evidence
and he will not be required to pay for the
torn animal.
14“If a man borrows an animal from his neighbor and it is injured or dies while the owner is
not present, he must make restitution. 15But if
the owner is with the animal, the borrower will
not have to pay. If the animal was hired, the
money paid for the hire covers the loss.

Social Responsibility

16“If a man seduces a virgin who is not
pledged to be married and sleeps with her, he
must pay the bride-price, and she shall be his
wife. 17If her father absolutely refuses to give
her to him, he must still pay the bride-price
for virgins.
18“Do not allow a sorceress
to live.
19“Anyone who has sexual
relations with an animal must
be put to death.
20“Whoever sacrifices to any
god other than the LORD must
be destroyed.[d]
21“Do not mistreat an alien
or oppress him, for you were
aliens in Egypt.
22“Do not take advantage
of a widow or an orphan. 23If
you do and they cry out to me,
I will certainly hear their cry. 24My anger will
be aroused, and I will kill you with the sword;
your wives will become widows and your children fatherless.

> **Exodus 22:21**
>
> *God Cares for Outsiders*
>
> “Do not mistreat an alien or oppress him, for you were aliens in Egypt.”

[a]3 Or *if he strikes him* [b]8 Or *before God*; also in verse 9 [c]9 Or *whom God declares* [d]20 The Hebrew term refers to the irrevocable giving over of things or persons to the LORD, often by totally destroying them.

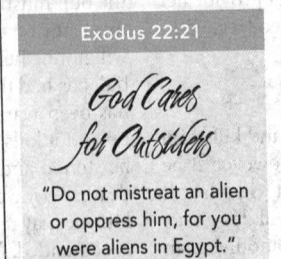

25"If you lend money to one of my people
among you who is needy, do not be like a
moneylender; charge him no interest.[a] 26If you
take your neighbor's cloak as a pledge, return
it to him by sunset, 27because his cloak is the
only covering he has for his body. What else
will he sleep in? When he cries out to me, I will
hear, for I am compassionate.
28"Do not blaspheme God[b] or curse the
ruler of your people.
29"Do not hold back offerings from your granaries or your vats.[c]
"You must give me the firstborn of your sons.
30Do the same with your cattle and your sheep.
Let them stay with their mothers for seven
days, but give them to me on the eighth day.
31"You are to be my holy people. So do not
eat the meat of an animal torn by wild beasts;
throw it to the dogs.

Laws of Justice and Mercy

23 "Do not spread false reports. Do not
help a wicked man by being a malicious witness.
2"Do not follow the crowd in doing wrong.
When you give testimony in a lawsuit, do not
pervert justice by siding with the crowd, 3and
do not show favoritism to a
poor man in his lawsuit.
4"If you come across your
enemy's ox or donkey wandering off, be sure to take it back to
him. 5If you see the donkey of
someone who hates you fallen
down under its load, do not
leave it there; be sure you help
him with it.
6"Do not deny justice to
your poor people in their lawsuits. 7Have nothing to do with
a false charge and do not put an
innocent or honest person to
death, for I will not acquit the guilty.
8"Do not accept a bribe, for a bribe blinds
those who see and twists the words of the righteous.
9"Do not oppress an alien; you yourselves
know how it feels to be aliens, because you
were aliens in Egypt.

Sabbath Laws

10"For six years you are to sow your fields
and harvest the crops, 11but during the seventh year let the land lie unplowed and un-
used. Then the poor among your people may
get food from it, and the wild animals may eat
what they leave. Do the same with your vineyard and your olive grove.
12"Six days do your work, but on the seventh
day do not work, so that your ox and your donkey may rest and the slave born in your household, and the alien as well, may be refreshed.
13"Be careful to do everything I have said to
you. Do not invoke the names of other gods; do
not let them be heard on your lips.

The Three Annual Festivals

14"Three times a year you are to celebrate a
festival to me.
15"Celebrate the Feast of Unleavened Bread;
for seven days eat bread made without yeast,
as I commanded you. Do this at the appointed
time in the month of Abib, for in that month
you came out of Egypt.
"No one is to appear before me empty-
handed.
16"Celebrate the Feast of Harvest with the
firstfruits of the crops you sow in your field.
"Celebrate the Feast of In-
gathering at the end of the year,
when you gather in your crops
from the field.
17"Three times a year all the
men are to appear before the
Sovereign LORD.
18"Do not offer the blood of
a sacrifice to me along with anything containing yeast.
"The fat of my festival offerings must not be kept until morning.
19"Bring the best of the firstfruits of your soil to the house
of the LORD your God.
"Do not cook a young goat in its mother's milk.

God's Angel to Prepare the Way

20"See, I am sending an angel ahead of you
to guard you along the way and to bring you

> **Exodus 23:20**
>
> *God Prepares Our Way*
>
> "See, I am sending an angel ahead of you to guard you along the way and to bring you to the place I have prepared."

[a]25 Or *excessive interest* [b]28 Or *Do not revile the judges* [c]29 The meaning of the Hebrew for this phrase is uncertain.

to the place I have prepared. 21Pay attention
to him and listen to what he says. Do not rebel against him; he will not forgive your rebellion, since my Name is in him. 22If you listen
carefully to what he says and do all that I say,
I will be an enemy to your enemies and will
oppose those who oppose you. 23My angel will
go ahead of you and bring you into the land of
the Amorites, Hittites, Perizzites, Canaanites,
Hivites and Jebusites, and I will wipe them out.
24Do not bow down before their gods or worship them or follow their practices. You must
demolish them and break their sacred stones
to pieces. 25Worship the LORD your God, and
his blessing will be on your food and water.
I will take away sickness from among you,
26and none will miscarry or be barren in your
land. I will give you a full life span.
27"I will send my terror ahead of you and
throw into confusion every nation you encounter. I will make all your enemies turn their backs
and run. 28I will send the hornet ahead of you
to drive the Hivites, Canaanites and Hittites out
of your way. 29But I will not drive them out in
a single year, because the land would become
desolate and the wild animals too numerous
for you. 30Little by little I will drive them out
before you, until you have increased enough to
take possession of the land.
31"I will establish your borders from the Red Sea[a] to the
Sea of the Philistines,[b] and
from the desert to the River.[c]
I will hand over to you the people who live in the land and
you will drive them out before
you. 32Do not make a covenant
with them or with their gods.
33Do not let them live in your
land, or they will cause you to
sin against me, because the worship of their gods will certainly
be a snare to you."

The Covenant Confirmed

24 Then he said to Moses, "Come up to
the LORD, you and Aaron, Nadab and
Abihu, and seventy of the elders of Israel. You
are to worship at a distance, 2but Moses alone
is to approach the LORD; the others must not
come near. And the people may not come up
with him."
3When Moses went and told the people all
the LORD's words and laws, they responded
with one voice, "Everything the LORD has said
we will do." 4Moses then wrote down everything the LORD had said.
He got up early the next morning and built
an altar at the foot of the mountain and set up
twelve stone pillars representing the twelve
tribes of Israel. 5Then he sent young Israelite
men, and they offered burnt offerings and sacrificed young bulls as fellowship offerings[d] to the
LORD. 6Moses took half of the blood and put it
in bowls, and the other half he sprinkled on the
altar. 7Then he took the Book of the Covenant
and read it to the people. They responded,
"We will do everything the LORD has said; we
will obey."
8Moses then took the blood, sprinkled it on
the people and said, "This is the blood of the
covenant that the LORD has made with you in
accordance with all these words."
9Moses and Aaron, Nadab and Abihu, and
the seventy elders of Israel went up 10and saw
the God of Israel. Under his feet was something like a pavement made
of sapphire,[e] clear as the sky
itself. 11But God did not raise
his hand against these leaders
of the Israelites; they saw God,
and they ate and drank.
12The LORD said to Moses,
"Come up to me on the mountain and stay here, and I will
give you the tablets of stone,
with the law and commands I
have written for their instruction."
13Then Moses set out with
Joshua his aide, and Moses
went up on the mountain of
God. 14He said to the elders,
"Wait here for us until we come back to you.
Aaron and Hur are with you, and anyone involved in a dispute can go to them."

Exodus 24:12

God Instructs Us

The LORD said to Moses, "Come up to me on the mountain and stay here, and I will give you the tablets of stone, with the law and commands I have written for their instruction."

[a]31 Hebrew *Yam Suph*; that is, Sea of Reeds [b]31 That is, the Mediterranean [c]31 That is, the Euphrates [d]5 Traditionally *peace offerings* [e]10 Or *lapis lazuli*

15When Moses went up on the mountain,
the cloud covered it, 16and the glory of the
LORD settled on Mount Sinai. For six days the
cloud covered the mountain, and on the seventh day the LORD called to Moses from within
the cloud. 17To the Israelites the glory of the
LORD looked like a consuming fire on top of
the mountain. 18Then Moses entered the cloud
as he went on up the mountain. And he stayed
on the mountain forty days and forty nights.

Offerings for the Tabernacle

25 The LORD said to Moses, 2"Tell the Israelites to bring me an offering. You
are to receive the offering for me from each
man whose heart prompts him to give. 3These
are the offerings you are to receive from them:
gold, silver and bronze; 4blue, purple and scarlet yarn and fine linen; goat hair; 5ram skins
dyed red and hides of sea cows[a]; acacia wood;
6olive oil for the light; spices for the anointing
oil and for the fragrant incense; 7and onyx
stones and other gems to be mounted on the
ephod and breastpiece.

8"Then have them make a sanctuary for me,
and I will dwell among them. 9Make this tabernacle and all its furnishings exactly like the
pattern I will show you.

The Ark

10"Have them make a chest of acacia
wood—two and a half cubits long, a cubit
and a half wide, and a cubit and a half high.[b]
11Overlay it with pure gold, both inside and
out, and make a gold molding around it.
12Cast four gold rings for it and fasten them
to its four feet, with two rings on one side and
two rings on the other. 13Then make poles
of acacia wood and overlay them with gold.
14Insert the poles into the rings on the sides
of the chest to carry it. 15The poles are to remain in the rings of this ark; they are not to be
removed. 16Then put in the ark the Testimony,
which I will give you.

17"Make an atonement cover[c] of pure
gold—two and a half cubits long and a cubit
and a half wide.[d] 18And make two cherubim
out of hammered gold at the ends of the cover.
19Make one cherub on one end and the second cherub on the other; make the cherubim
of one piece with the cover, at the two ends.
20The cherubim are to have their wings spread
upward, overshadowing the cover with them.
The cherubim are to face each other, looking toward the cover. 21Place the cover on top of the
ark and put in the ark the Testimony, which I
will give you. 22There, above the cover between
the two cherubim that are over the ark of the
Testimony, I will meet with you and give you
all my commands for the Israelites.

The Table

23"Make a table of acacia wood—two cubits long, a cubit wide and a cubit and a half
high.[e] 24Overlay it with pure gold and make a
gold molding around it. 25Also make around
it a rim a handbreadth[f] wide and put a gold
molding on the rim. 26Make four gold rings
for the table and fasten them to the four corners, where the four legs are. 27The rings are
to be close to the rim to hold the poles used in
carrying the table. 28Make the poles of acacia
wood, overlay them with gold and carry the
table with them. 29And make its plates and
dishes of pure gold, as well as its pitchers and
bowls for the pouring out of offerings. 30Put
the bread of the Presence on this table to be
before me at all times.

The Lampstand

31"Make a lampstand of pure gold and hammer it out, base and shaft; its flowerlike cups,
buds and blossoms shall be of one piece with
it. 32Six branches are to extend from the sides
of the lampstand—three on one side and three
on the other. 33Three cups shaped like almond
flowers with buds and blossoms are to be on
one branch, three on the next branch, and the
same for all six branches extending from the
lampstand. 34And on the lampstand there are
to be four cups shaped like almond flowers
with buds and blossoms. 35One bud shall be
under the first pair of branches extending from
the lampstand, a second bud under the second
pair, and a third bud under the third pair—six
branches in all. 36The buds and branches shall

[a] 5 That is, dugongs [b] 10 That is, about 3 3/4 feet (about 1.1 meters) long and 2 1/4 feet (about 0.7 meter) wide and high
[c] 17 Traditionally *a mercy seat* [d] 17 That is, about 3 3/4 feet (about 1.1 meters) long and 2 1/4 feet (about 0.7 meter) wide [e] 23 That is,
about 3 feet (about 0.9 meter) long and 1 1/2 feet (about 0.5 meter) wide and 2 1/4 feet (about 0.7 meter) high [f] 25 That is, about
3 inches (about 8 centimeters)

all be of one piece with the lampstand, hammered out of pure gold.
37“Then make its seven lamps and set them
up on it so that they light the space in front of it.
38Its wick trimmers and trays are to be of pure
gold. 39A talent[a] of pure gold is to be used for
the lampstand and all these accessories. 40See
that you make them according to the pattern
shown you on the mountain.

The Tabernacle

26 “Make the tabernacle with ten curtains
of finely twisted linen and blue, purple
and scarlet yarn, with cherubim worked into
them by a skilled craftsman. 2All the curtains
are to be the same size—twenty-eight cubits
long and four cubits wide.[b] 3Join five of the
curtains together, and do the same with the
other five. 4Make loops of blue material along
the edge of the end curtain in one set, and do
the same with the end curtain in the other set.
5Make fifty loops on one curtain and fifty loops
on the end curtain of the other set, with the
loops opposite each other. 6Then make fifty
gold clasps and use them to fasten the curtains
together so that the tabernacle is a unit.
7“Make curtains of goat hair for the tent
over the tabernacle—eleven altogether. 8All
eleven curtains are to be the same size—thirty
cubits long and four cubits wide.[c] 9Join five
of the curtains together into one set and the
other six into another set. Fold the sixth curtain double at the front of the tent. 10Make
fifty loops along the edge of the end curtain in
one set and also along the edge of the end curtain in the other set. 11Then make fifty bronze
clasps and put them in the loops to fasten the
tent together as a unit. 12As for the additional
length of the tent curtains, the half curtain
that is left over is to hang down at the rear of
the tabernacle. 13The tent curtains will be a cubit[d] longer on both sides; what is left will hang
over the sides of the tabernacle so as to cover
it. 14Make for the tent a covering of ram skins
dyed red, and over that a covering of hides of
sea cows.[e]
15“Make upright frames of acacia wood for
the tabernacle. 16Each frame is to be ten cubits
long and a cubit and a half wide,[f] 17with two
projections set parallel to each other. Make
all the frames of the tabernacle in this way.
18Make twenty frames for the south side of the
tabernacle 19and make forty silver bases to go
under them—two bases for each frame, one
under each projection. 20For the other side,
the north side of the tabernacle, make twenty
frames 21and forty silver bases—two under
each frame. 22Make six frames for the far end,
that is, the west end of the tabernacle, 23and
make two frames for the corners at the far end.
24At these two corners they must be double
from the bottom all the way to the top, and
fitted into a single ring; both shall be like that.
25So there will be eight frames and sixteen silver bases—two under each frame.
26“Also make crossbars of acacia wood: five
for the frames on one side of the tabernacle,
27five for those on the other side, and five for
the frames on the west, at the far end of the
tabernacle. 28The center crossbar is to extend
from end to end at the middle of the frames.
29Overlay the frames with gold and make gold
rings to hold the crossbars. Also overlay the
crossbars with gold.
30“Set up the tabernacle according to the
plan shown you on the mountain.
31“Make a curtain of blue, purple and scarlet yarn and finely twisted linen, with cherubim worked into it by a skilled craftsman.
32Hang it with gold hooks on four posts of
acacia wood overlaid with gold and standing
on four silver bases. 33Hang the curtain from
the clasps and place the ark of the Testimony
behind the curtain. The curtain will separate
the Holy Place from the Most Holy Place.
34Put the atonement cover on the ark of the
Testimony in the Most Holy Place. 35Place the
table outside the curtain on the north side of
the tabernacle and put the lampstand opposite
it on the south side.
36“For the entrance to the tent make a curtain of blue, purple and scarlet yarn and finely
twisted linen—the work of an embroiderer.
37Make gold hooks for this curtain and five
posts of acacia wood overlaid with gold. And
cast five bronze bases for them.

[a] 39 That is, about 75 pounds (about 34 kilograms) [b] 2 That is, about 42 feet (about 12.5 meters) long and 6 feet (about 1.8 meters) wide
[c] 8 That is, about 45 feet (about 13.5 meters) long and 6 feet (about 1.8 meters) wide [d] 13 That is, about 1 1/2 feet (about 0.5 meter)
[e] 14 That is, dugongs [f] 16 That is, about 15 feet (about 4.5 meters) long and 2 1/4 feet (about 0.7 meter) wide

The Altar of Burnt Offering

27 "Build an altar of acacia wood, three
cubits[a] high; it is to be square, five cubits long and five cubits wide.[b] 2Make a horn
at each of the four corners, so that the horns
and the altar are of one piece, and overlay the
altar with bronze. 3Make all its utensils of
bronze—its pots to remove the ashes, and its
shovels, sprinkling bowls, meat forks and firepans. 4Make a grating for it, a bronze network,
and make a bronze ring at each of the four corners of the network. 5Put it under the ledge of
the altar so that it is halfway up the altar. 6Make
poles of acacia wood for the altar and overlay
them with bronze. 7The poles are to be inserted
into the rings so they will be on two sides of the
altar when it is carried. 8Make the altar hollow,
out of boards. It is to be made just as you were
shown on the mountain.

The Courtyard

9"Make a courtyard for the tabernacle. The
south side shall be a hundred cubits[c] long
and is to have curtains of finely twisted linen,
10with twenty posts and twenty bronze bases
and with silver hooks and bands on the posts.
11The north side shall also be a hundred cubits
long and is to have curtains, with twenty posts
and twenty bronze bases and with silver hooks
and bands on the posts.

12"The west end of the courtyard shall be
fifty cubits[d] wide and have curtains, with ten
posts and ten bases. 13On the east end, toward
the sunrise, the courtyard shall also be fifty cubits wide. 14Curtains fifteen cubits[e] long are
to be on one side of the entrance, with three
posts and three bases, 15and curtains fifteen cubits long are to be on the other side, with three
posts and three bases.

16"For the entrance to the courtyard, provide a curtain twenty cubits[f] long, of blue,
purple and scarlet yarn and finely twisted
linen—the work of an embroiderer—with
four posts and four bases. 17All the posts
around the courtyard are to have silver bands
and hooks, and bronze bases. 18The courtyard
shall be a hundred cubits long and fifty cubits
wide,[g] with curtains of finely twisted linen five
cubits[h] high, and with bronze bases. 19All the
other articles used in the service of the tabernacle, whatever their function, including all the
tent pegs for it and those for the courtyard, are
to be of bronze.

Oil for the Lampstand

20"Command the Israelites to bring you
clear oil of pressed olives for the light so that
the lamps may be kept burning. 21In the Tent
of Meeting, outside the curtain that is in front
of the Testimony, Aaron and his sons are to
keep the lamps burning before the LORD from
evening till morning. This is to be a lasting ordinance among the Israelites for the generations
to come.

The Priestly Garments

28 "Have Aaron your brother brought to
you from among the Israelites, along
with his sons Nadab and Abihu, Eleazar and Ithamar, so they may serve me as priests. 2Make sacred garments for your brother Aaron, to give
him dignity and honor. 3Tell all the skilled men
to whom I have given wisdom in such matters
that they are to make garments for Aaron, for
his consecration, so he may serve me as priest.
4These are the garments they are to make: a
breastpiece, an ephod, a robe, a woven tunic,
a turban and a sash. They are to make these sacred garments for your brother Aaron and his
sons, so they may serve me as priests. 5Have
them use gold, and blue, purple and scarlet
yarn, and fine linen.

The Ephod

6"Make the ephod of gold, and of blue,
purple and scarlet yarn, and of finely twisted
linen—the work of a skilled craftsman. 7It is
to have two shoulder pieces attached to two of
its corners, so it can be fastened. 8Its skillfully
woven waistband is to be like it—of one piece
with the ephod and made with gold, and with
blue, purple and scarlet yarn, and with finely
twisted linen.

9"Take two onyx stones and engrave on
them the names of the sons of Israel 10in the

[a] 1 That is, about 4 1/2 feet (about 1.3 meters) [b] 1 That is, about 7 1/2 feet (about 2.3 meters) long and wide [c] 9 That is, about 150 feet (about 46 meters); also in verse 11 [d] 12 That is, about 75 feet (about 23 meters); also in verse 13 [e] 14 That is, about 22 1/2 feet (about 6.9 meters); also in verse 15 [f] 16 That is, about 30 feet (about 9 meters) [g] 18 That is, about 150 feet (about 46 meters) long and 75 feet (about 23 meters) wide [h] 18 That is, about 7 1/2 feet (about 2.3 meters)

order of their birth—six names on one stone
and the remaining six on the other. 11 Engrave
the names of the sons of Israel on the two
stones the way a gem cutter engraves a seal.
Then mount the stones in gold filigree settings
12 and fasten them on the shoulder pieces of
the ephod as memorial stones for the sons of
Israel. Aaron is to bear the names on his shoulders as a memorial before the LORD. 13 Make
gold filigree settings 14 and two braided chains
of pure gold, like a rope, and attach the chains
to the settings.

The Breastpiece

15 "Fashion a breastpiece for making decisions—the work of a skilled craftsman. Make it
like the ephod: of gold, and of blue, purple and
scarlet yarn, and of finely twisted linen. 16 It is
to be square—a span[a] long and a span wide—
and folded double. 17 Then mount four rows of
precious stones on it. In the first row there shall
be a ruby, a topaz and a beryl; 18 in the second
row a turquoise, a sapphire[b] and an emerald;
19 in the third row a jacinth, an agate and an
amethyst; 20 in the fourth row a chrysolite, an
onyx and a jasper.[c] Mount them in gold filigree
settings. 21 There are to be twelve stones, one
for each of the names of the sons of Israel, each
engraved like a seal with the name of one of the
twelve tribes.

22 "For the breastpiece make braided chains
of pure gold, like a rope. 23 Make two gold
rings for it and fasten them to two corners of
the breastpiece. 24 Fasten the two gold chains
to the rings at the corners of the breastpiece,
25 and the other ends of the chains to the two
settings, attaching them to the shoulder pieces
of the ephod at the front. 26 Make two gold
rings and attach them to the other two corners
of the breastpiece on the inside edge next to the
ephod. 27 Make two more gold rings and attach
them to the bottom of the shoulder pieces on
the front of the ephod, close to the seam just
above the waistband of the ephod. 28 The rings
of the breastpiece are to be tied to the rings
of the ephod with blue cord, connecting it to
the waistband, so that the breastpiece will not
swing out from the ephod.

29 "Whenever Aaron enters the Holy Place,
he will bear the names of the sons of Israel
over his heart on the breastpiece of decision
as a continuing memorial before the LORD.
30 Also put the Urim and the Thummim in the
breastpiece, so they may be over Aaron's heart
whenever he enters the presence of the LORD.
Thus Aaron will always bear the means of making decisions for the Israelites over his heart
before the LORD.

Other Priestly Garments

31 "Make the robe of the ephod entirely of
blue cloth, 32 with an opening for the head in
its center. There shall be a woven edge like a
collar[d] around this opening, so that it will not
tear. 33 Make pomegranates of blue, purple and
scarlet yarn around the hem of the robe, with
gold bells between them. 34 The gold bells and
the pomegranates are to alternate around the
hem of the robe. 35 Aaron must wear it when
he ministers. The sound of the bells will be
heard when he enters the Holy Place before the
LORD and when he comes out, so that he will
not die.

36 "Make a plate of pure gold and engrave on
it as on a seal: HOLY TO THE LORD. 37 Fasten
a blue cord to it to attach it to the turban; it
is to be on the front of the turban. 38 It will be
on Aaron's forehead, and he will bear the guilt
involved in the sacred gifts the Israelites consecrate, whatever their gifts may be. It will be on
Aaron's forehead continually so that they will
be acceptable to the LORD.

39 "Weave the tunic of fine linen and make
the turban of fine linen. The sash is to be the
work of an embroiderer. 40 Make tunics, sashes
and headbands for Aaron's sons, to give them
dignity and honor. 41 After you put these
clothes on your brother Aaron and his sons,
anoint and ordain them. Consecrate them so
they may serve me as priests.

42 "Make linen undergarments as a covering
for the body, reaching from the waist to the
thigh. 43 Aaron and his sons must wear them
whenever they enter the Tent of Meeting or approach the altar to minister in the Holy Place,
so that they will not incur guilt and die.

"This is to be a lasting ordinance for Aaron
and his descendants.

[a]16 That is, about 9 inches (about 22 centimeters) [b]18 Or *lapis lazuli* [c]20 The precise identification of some of these precious stones is uncertain. [d]32 The meaning of the Hebrew for this word is uncertain.

Consecration of the Priests

29 "This is what you are to do to consecrate them, so they may serve me as priests: Take a young bull and two rams without defect. 2 And from fine wheat flour, without yeast, make bread, and cakes mixed with oil, and wafers spread with oil. 3 Put them in a basket and present them in it—along with the bull and the two rams. 4 Then bring Aaron and his sons to the entrance to the Tent of Meeting and wash them with water. 5 Take the garments and dress Aaron with the tunic, the robe of the ephod, the ephod itself and the breastpiece. Fasten the ephod on him by its skillfully woven waistband. 6 Put the turban on his head and attach the sacred diadem to the turban. 7 Take the anointing oil and anoint him by pouring it on his head. 8 Bring his sons and dress them in tunics 9 and put headbands on them. Then tie sashes on Aaron and his sons.[a] The priesthood is theirs by a lasting ordinance. In this way you shall ordain Aaron and his sons.

10 "Bring the bull to the front of the Tent of Meeting, and Aaron and his sons shall lay their hands on its head. 11 Slaughter it in the LORD's presence at the entrance to the Tent of Meeting. 12 Take some of the bull's blood and put it on the horns of the altar with your finger, and pour out the rest of it at the base of the altar. 13 Then take all the fat around the inner parts, the covering of the liver, and both kidneys with the fat on them, and burn them on the altar. 14 But burn the bull's flesh and its hide and its offal outside the camp. It is a sin offering.

15 "Take one of the rams, and Aaron and his sons shall lay their hands on its head. 16 Slaughter it and take the blood and sprinkle it against the altar on all sides. 17 Cut the ram into pieces and wash the inner parts and the legs, putting them with the head and the other pieces. 18 Then burn the entire ram on the altar. It is a burnt offering to the LORD, a pleasing aroma, an offering made to the LORD by fire.

19 "Take the other ram, and Aaron and his sons shall lay their hands on its head. 20 Slaughter it, take some of its blood and put it on the lobes of the right ears of Aaron and his sons, on the thumbs of their right hands, and on the big toes of their right feet. Then sprinkle blood against the altar on all sides. 21 And take some of the blood on the altar and some of the anointing oil and sprinkle it on Aaron and his garments and on his sons and their garments. Then he and his sons and their garments will be consecrated.

22 "Take from this ram the fat, the fat tail, the fat around the inner parts, the covering of the liver, both kidneys with the fat on them, and the right thigh. (This is the ram for the ordination.) 23 From the basket of bread made without yeast, which is before the LORD, take a loaf, and a cake made with oil, and a wafer. 24 Put all these in the hands of Aaron and his sons and wave them before the LORD as a wave offering. 25 Then take them from their hands and burn them on the altar along with the burnt offering for a pleasing aroma to the LORD, an offering made to the LORD by fire. 26 After you take the breast of the ram for Aaron's ordination, wave it before the LORD as a wave offering, and it will be your share.

27 "Consecrate those parts of the ordination ram that belong to Aaron and his sons: the breast that was waved and the thigh that was presented. 28 This is always to be the regular share from the Israelites for Aaron and his sons. It is the contribution the Israelites are to make to the LORD from their fellowship offerings.[b]

29 "Aaron's sacred garments will belong to his descendants so that they can be anointed and ordained in them. 30 The son who succeeds him as priest and comes to the Tent of Meeting to minister in the Holy Place is to wear them seven days.

31 "Take the ram for the ordination and cook the meat in a sacred place. 32 At the entrance to the Tent of Meeting, Aaron and his sons are to eat the meat of the ram and the bread that is in the basket. 33 They are to eat these offerings by which atonement was made for their ordination and consecration. But no one else may eat them, because they are sacred. 34 And if any of the meat of the ordination ram or any bread is left over till morning, burn it up. It must not be eaten, because it is sacred.

35 "Do for Aaron and his sons everything I have commanded you, taking seven days to

[a] 9 Hebrew; Septuagint *on them* [b] 28 Traditionally *peace offerings*

ordain them. 36Sacrifice a bull each day as a sin
offering to make atonement. Purify the altar by
making atonement for it, and anoint it to consecrate it. 37For seven days make atonement
for the altar and consecrate it. Then the altar
will be most holy, and whatever touches it will
be holy.
38"This is what you are to offer on the altar regularly each day: two lambs a year old.
39Offer one in the morning and the other at
twilight. 40With the first lamb offer a tenth of
an ephah[a] of fine flour mixed with a quarter of
a hin[b] of oil from pressed olives, and a quarter
of a hin of wine as a drink offering. 41Sacrifice
the other lamb at twilight with the same grain
offering and its drink offering as in the morning—a pleasing aroma, an offering made to the
LORD by fire.
42"For the generations to come this burnt offering is to be made regularly at the entrance to
the Tent of Meeting before the LORD. There I
will meet you and speak to you;
43there also I will meet with the
Israelites, and the place will be
consecrated by my glory.
44"So I will consecrate the
Tent of Meeting and the altar
and will consecrate Aaron and
his sons to serve me as priests.
45Then I will dwell among the
Israelites and be their God.
46They will know that I am the
LORD their God, who brought
them out of Egypt so that I
might dwell among them. I am
the LORD their God.

The Altar of Incense

30 "Make an altar of acacia wood for
burning incense. 2It is to be square,
a cubit long and a cubit wide, and two cubits
high[c]—its horns of one piece with it. 3Overlay
the top and all the sides and the horns with
pure gold, and make a gold molding around it.
4Make two gold rings for the altar below the
molding—two on opposite sides—to hold the
poles used to carry it. 5Make the poles of acacia
wood and overlay them with gold. 6Put the altar in front of the curtain that is before the ark
of the Testimony—before the atonement cover
that is over the Testimony—where I will meet
with you.
7"Aaron must burn fragrant incense on the
altar every morning when he tends the lamps.
8He must burn incense again when he lights the
lamps at twilight so incense will burn regularly
before the LORD for the generations to come.
9Do not offer on this altar any other incense
or any burnt offering or grain offering, and
do not pour a drink offering on it. 10Once a
year Aaron shall make atonement on its horns.
This annual atonement must be made with the
blood of the atoning sin offering for the generations to come. It is most holy to the LORD."

Atonement Money

11Then the LORD said to Moses, 12"When
you take a census of the Israelites to count
them, each one must pay the LORD a ransom
for his life at the time he is counted. Then no
plague will come on them
when you number them.
13Each one who crosses over to
those already counted is to give
a half shekel,[d] according to the
sanctuary shekel, which weighs
twenty gerahs. This half shekel
is an offering to the LORD. 14All
who cross over, those twenty
years old or more, are to give
an offering to the LORD. 15The
rich are not to give more than
a half shekel and the poor are
not to give less when you make
the offering to the LORD to
atone for your lives. 16Receive
the atonement money from the Israelites and
use it for the service of the Tent of Meeting. It
will be a memorial for the Israelites before the
LORD, making atonement for your lives."

Basin for Washing

17Then the LORD said to Moses, 18"Make a
bronze basin, with its bronze stand, for washing. Place it between the Tent of Meeting and
the altar, and put water in it. 19Aaron and his
sons are to wash their hands and feet with water from it. 20Whenever they enter the Tent of

Exodus 29:46

God Dwells With Us

"They will know that
I am the LORD their God,
who brought them out
of Egypt so that I might
dwell among them. I am
the LORD their God."

[a]40 That is, probably about 2 quarts (about 2 liters) [b]40 That is, probably about 1 quart (about 1 liter) [c]2 That is, about 1 1/2 feet (about 0.5 meter) long and wide and about 3 feet (about 0.9 meter) high [d]13 That is, about 1/5 ounce (about 6 grams); also in verse 15

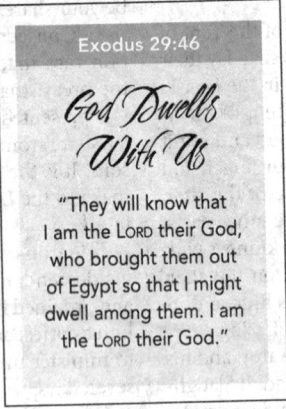

Meeting, they shall wash with water so that they will not die. Also, when they approach the altar to minister by presenting an offering made to the LORD by fire, 21they shall wash their hands and feet so that they will not die. This is to be a lasting ordinance for Aaron and his descendants for the generations to come."

Anointing Oil

22Then the LORD said to Moses, 23"Take the following fine spices: 500 shekels[a] of liquid myrrh, half as much (that is, 250 shekels) of fragrant cinnamon, 250 shekels of fragrant cane, 24500 shekels of cassia—all according to the sanctuary shekel—and a hin[b] of olive oil. 25Make these into a sacred anointing oil, a fragrant blend, the work of a perfumer. It will be the sacred anointing oil. 26Then use it to anoint the Tent of Meeting, the ark of the Testimony, 27the table and all its articles, the lampstand and its accessories, the altar of incense, 28the altar of burnt offering and all its utensils, and the basin with its stand. 29You shall consecrate them so they will be most holy, and whatever touches them will be holy.

30"Anoint Aaron and his sons and consecrate them so they may serve me as priests. 31Say to the Israelites, 'This is to be my sacred anointing oil for the generations to come. 32Do not pour it on men's bodies and do not make any oil with the same formula. It is sacred, and you are to consider it sacred. 33Whoever makes perfume like it and whoever puts it on anyone other than a priest must be cut off from his people.' "

Incense

34Then the LORD said to Moses, "Take fragrant spices—gum resin, onycha and galbanum—and pure frankincense, all in equal amounts, 35and make a fragrant blend of incense, the work of a perfumer. It is to be salted and pure and sacred. 36Grind some of it to powder and place it in front of the Testimony in the Tent of Meeting, where I will meet with you. It shall be most holy to you. 37Do not make any incense with this formula for yourselves; consider it holy to the LORD. 38Whoever makes any like it to enjoy its fragrance must be cut off from his people."

Bezalel and Oholiab

31 Then the LORD said to Moses, 2"See, I have chosen Bezalel son of Uri, the son of Hur, of the tribe of Judah, 3and I have filled him with the Spirit of God, with skill, ability and knowledge in all kinds of crafts— 4to make artistic designs for work in gold, silver and bronze, 5to cut and set stones, to work in wood, and to engage in all kinds of craftsmanship. 6Moreover, I have appointed Oholiab son of Ahisamach, of the tribe of Dan, to help him. Also I have given skill to all the craftsmen to make everything I have commanded you: 7the Tent of Meeting, the ark of the Testimony with the atonement cover on it, and all the other furnishings of the tent— 8the table and its articles, the pure gold lampstand and all its accessories, the altar of incense, 9the altar of burnt offering and all its utensils, the basin with its stand— 10and also the woven garments, both the sacred garments for Aaron the priest and the garments for his sons when they serve as priests, 11and the anointing oil and fragrant incense for the Holy Place. They are to make them just as I commanded you."

Exodus 31:2–3

God Assigns Our Talents

"See, I have chosen Bezalel son of Uri, the son of Hur, of the tribe of Judah, and I have filled him with the Spirit of God, with skill, ability and knowledge in all kinds of crafts."

The Sabbath

12Then the LORD said to Moses, 13"Say to the Israelites, 'You must observe my Sabbaths. This will be a sign between me and you for the generations to come, so you may know that I am the LORD, who makes you holy.[c]

14" 'Observe the Sabbath, because it is holy to you. Anyone who desecrates it must be put to death; whoever does any work on that day must be cut off from his people. 15For six days,

[a]23 That is, about 12 1/2 pounds (about 6 kilograms) [b]24 That is, probably about 4 quarts (about 4 liters) [c]13 Or *who sanctifies you;* or *who sets you apart as holy*

work is to be done, but the seventh day is a Sabbath of rest, holy to the LORD. Whoever does
any work on the Sabbath day must be put to
death. 16 The Israelites are to observe the Sabbath, celebrating it for the generations to come
as a lasting covenant. 17 It will be a sign between
me and the Israelites forever, for in six days the
LORD made the heavens and the earth, and on
the seventh day he abstained from work and
rested.' "
18 When the LORD finished speaking to Moses on Mount Sinai, he gave him the two tablets
of the Testimony, the tablets of stone inscribed
by the finger of God.

The Golden Calf

32 When the people saw that Moses was
so long in coming down from the
mountain, they gathered around Aaron and
said, "Come, make us gods[a] who will go before
us. As for this fellow Moses who brought us
up out of Egypt, we don't know what has happened to him."
2 Aaron answered them, "Take off the gold
earrings that your wives, your sons and your
daughters are wearing, and bring them to me."
3 So all the people took off their earrings and
brought them to Aaron. 4 He took what they
handed him and made it into an idol cast in the
shape of a calf, fashioning it with a tool. Then
they said, "These are your gods,[b] O Israel, who
brought you up out of Egypt."
5 When Aaron saw this, he built an altar in
front of the calf and announced, "Tomorrow
there will be a festival to the LORD." 6 So the
next day the people rose early and sacrificed
burnt offerings and presented fellowship offerings.[c] Afterward they sat down to eat and drink
and got up to indulge in revelry.
7 Then the LORD said to Moses, "Go down, because your people, whom you brought up out of
Egypt, have become corrupt. 8 They have been
quick to turn away from what I commanded
them and have made themselves an idol cast
in the shape of a calf. They have bowed down
to it and sacrificed to it and have said, 'These
are your gods, O Israel, who brought you up
out of Egypt.'
9 "I have seen these people," the LORD said
to Moses, "and they are a stiff-necked people.
10 Now leave me alone so that my anger may
burn against them and that I may destroy them.
Then I will make you into a great nation."
11 But Moses sought the favor of the LORD
his God. "O LORD," he said, "why should your
anger burn against your people, whom you
brought out of Egypt with great power and a
mighty hand? 12 Why should the Egyptians say,
'It was with evil intent that he brought them
out, to kill them in the mountains and to wipe
them off the face of the earth'? Turn from your
fierce anger; relent and do not bring disaster on
your people. 13 Remember your servants Abraham, Isaac and Israel, to whom you swore by
your own self: 'I will make your descendants
as numerous as the stars in the sky and I will
give your descendants all this land I promised
them, and it will be their inheritance forever.' "
14 Then the LORD relented and did not bring on
his people the disaster he had threatened.
15 Moses turned and went down the mountain with the two tablets of the Testimony in his
hands. They were inscribed on both sides, front
and back. 16 The tablets were the work of God;
the writing was the writing of God, engraved
on the tablets.
17 When Joshua heard the noise of the people shouting, he said to Moses, "There is the
sound of war in the camp."
18 Moses replied:

"It is not the sound of victory,
  it is not the sound of defeat;
  it is the sound of singing that I hear."

19 When Moses approached the camp and
saw the calf and the dancing, his anger burned
and he threw the tablets out of his hands, breaking them to pieces at the foot of the mountain.
20 And he took the calf they had made and
burned it in the fire; then he ground it to powder, scattered it on the water and made the Israelites drink it.
21 He said to Aaron, "What did these people
do to you, that you led them into such great
sin?"
22 "Do not be angry, my lord," Aaron answered. "You know how prone these people
are to evil. 23 They said to me, 'Make us gods

[a] 1 Or *a god*; also in verses 23 and 31 [b] 4 Or *This is your god*; also in verse 8 [c] 6 Traditionally *peace offerings*

Gold or God?

Read: Exodus 32:1–35

IDOLATRY IS ALIVE and well in the modern world. People worship at the temple of self. They bow down to the god of money. They make sacrifices to elusive dreams of perfection—the perfect husband, the perfect family, the perfect body, the perfect life. Perfection becomes a substitute for the gold and jewels the Israelites used to create idols. As women, we often find it easier to worship temporal dreams of earthly perfection than the eternal God. The resplendent life we have planned shimmers before us, but the mirage will fail to satisfy our thirst.

When the Israelites fled Egypt, they left a land steeped in idolatry. The Egyptians worshiped thousands of deities, ascribing god-like qualities to animals, birds and trees. They created temples and statues swathed in gold and jewels to elevate these false gods. When Moses, the Israelites' spiritual leader, left to meet with God on Mount Sinai, the people quickly returned to idol worship. The fickle Israelites, delivered from slavery by the unseen God, quickly exchanged worshiping God for worshiping a golden dream they could control, a deity they could manipulate.

You may not think you're guilty of idol worship. You wouldn't bow down to an animal figurine. You go to church every Sunday. You have a Bible sitting on your bedside table. But do you long for a golden dream you can fashion to your own whims? God's goodness, his justice and his holiness do not necessarily make him safe. Our golden dreams of earthly perfection encapsulate only what we allow; they stay as safe as we like them, as shimmering and domestic as we dare. God is wild, unsafe, unpredictable even. He does not fit into the neat fairy tale we sometimes prefer to him.

What do you return to when God feels untamed? What do you adore? Perhaps a relationship fills your every waking thought; perhaps you spend your time dreaming of ascending to greatness as an artist or breaking new ground in your field; perhaps you idolize your children. When something catches your thoughts, eventually it captures your heart. Idol worship is alive and well, but the golden dream will not soothe your soul. The illusion of perfection does not comfort you when you mourn. Gold will not go with you into eternity. But God can, and will, do all these things when you worship him "in spirit and in truth" (John 4:24).

Exodus 32:2–4

Aaron answered them, "Take off the gold earrings that your wives, your sons and your daughters are wearing, and bring them to me." So all the people took off their earrings and brought them to Aaron. He took what they handed him and made it into an idol cast in the shape of a calf, fashioning it with a tool. Then they said, "These are your gods, O Israel, who brought you up out of Egypt."

reflection

1 What types of idols have you noticed in the world around you?

2 In what subtle ways have you been guilty of putting things, people or ideas before God?

3 How will you show God that you love him more than any person, place or thing?

RELATED READINGS

Exodus 20:1–17; Micah 6:6–8; Matthew 6:19–21

Go to page 111 for your next devotional reading.

who will go before us. As for this fellow Moses
who brought us up out of Egypt, we don't know
what has happened to him.' 24 So I told them,
'Whoever has any gold jewelry, take it off.' Then
they gave me the gold, and I threw it into the
fire, and out came this calf!"

25 Moses saw that the people were running
wild and that Aaron had let them get out of control and so become a laughingstock to their enemies. 26 So he stood at the entrance to the camp
and said, "Whoever is for the LORD, come to
me." And all the Levites rallied to him.

27 Then he said to them, "This is what the
LORD, the God of Israel, says: 'Each man strap
a sword to his side. Go back and forth through
the camp from one end to the other, each killing his brother and friend and neighbor.'"
28 The Levites did as Moses commanded, and
that day about three thousand of the people
died. 29 Then Moses said, "You have been set
apart to the LORD today, for you were against
your own sons and brothers, and he has blessed
you this day."

30 The next day Moses said to the people,
"You have committed a great sin. But now I will
go up to the LORD; perhaps I can make atonement for your sin."

31 So Moses went back to the LORD and said,
"Oh, what a great sin these people have committed! They have made themselves gods of gold.
32 But now, please forgive their sin—but if not,
then blot me out of the book you have written."

33 The LORD replied to Moses, "Whoever has
sinned against me I will blot out of my book.
34 Now go, lead the people to the place I spoke
of, and my angel will go before you. However,
when the time comes for me to punish, I will
punish them for their sin."

35 And the LORD struck the people with a
plague because of what they did with the calf
Aaron had made.

33 Then the LORD said to Moses, "Leave
this place, you and the people you
brought up out of Egypt, and go up to the land
I promised on oath to Abraham, Isaac and Jacob, saying, 'I will give it to your descendants.'
2 I will send an angel before you and drive out
the Canaanites, Amorites, Hittites, Perizzites,
Hivites and Jebusites. 3 Go up to the land flowing with milk and honey. But I will not go with
you, because you are a stiff-necked people and
I might destroy you on the way."

4 When the people heard these distressing
words, they began to mourn and no one put
on any ornaments. 5 For the LORD had said
to Moses, "Tell the Israelites, 'You are a stiff-
necked people. If I were to go with you even
for a moment, I might destroy you. Now take
off your ornaments and I will decide what to do
with you.'" 6 So the Israelites stripped off their
ornaments at Mount Horeb.

The Tent of Meeting

7 Now Moses used to take a tent and pitch it
outside the camp some distance away, calling it
the "tent of meeting." Anyone inquiring of the
LORD would go to the tent of meeting outside
the camp. 8 And whenever Moses went out to
the tent, all the people rose and stood at the
entrances to their tents, watching Moses until
he entered the tent. 9 As Moses went into the
tent, the pillar of cloud would come down and
stay at the entrance, while the LORD spoke with
Moses. 10 Whenever the people saw the pillar
of cloud standing at the entrance to the tent,
they all stood and worshiped, each at the entrance to his tent. 11 The LORD would speak to
Moses face to face, as a man speaks with his
friend. Then Moses would return to the camp,
but his young aide Joshua son of Nun did not
leave the tent.

Moses and the Glory of the LORD

12 Moses said to the LORD, "You have been
telling me, 'Lead these people,' but you have not
let me know whom you will send with me. You
have said, 'I know you by name and you have
found favor with me.' 13 If you are pleased with
me, teach me your ways so I may know you
and continue to find favor with you. Remember that this nation is your people."

14 The LORD replied, "My Presence will go
with you, and I will give you rest."

15 Then Moses said to him, "If your Presence
does not go with us, do not send us up from
here. 16 How will anyone know that you are
pleased with me and with your people unless
you go with us? What else will distinguish me
and your people from all the other people on
the face of the earth?"

Sleepless in Sodom

LOT'S WIFE

SHE HEARD THE CROWD coming down the street, a discord of voices, echoes, shouts and drunken laughter. They stopped at the house she shared with her husband, Lot, and pressed their bodies up against the doorframe, jeering loudly.

"Another sleepless night in Sodom," she thought.

Earlier that evening, two strangers had entered her home, and she'd been on edge ever since. They looked like ordinary men. However, something told her there was nothing ordinary about them. The men certainly did not remind her of the flesh-and-blood world she was accustomed to. She had grown somewhat used to the sounds of Sodom—late night brawls and the like. But being in the same house as these unearthly, quiet men made her feel downright anxious. Uncomfortable. Almost as if they could somehow see right through her.

It reminded her of when her family first moved to Sodom long ago. Whatever lifestyle she'd known before seemed quaint amid the unnatural ways of the diverse crowd. Nevertheless, it took less time than one could have ever imagined to grow accustomed to life in Sodom. The frightening soon became familiar. And, looking back now, it felt strange to think of living anywhere else.

"Who in your family is still here?" The voice of the strangers interrupted her thoughts. "Get them out of here now!" At once, she battled an indescribable urge to obey them against the desire to stay where she was. If it was easy to ignore her intuition to flee those first nights in Sodom, how much easier would it be now to downplay the men's warnings?

She didn't have time to decide. Still in her bedclothes, the two men rushed her and her family out of the house. Her feet barely seemed to touch the streets or the sandy path as the men fled with them out of the city and toward the mountains. Ahead, she could see a thin slice of pomegranate red spreading east against the night sky. Behind, the noise from the jeering crowd grew fainter. But she could still feel the city pulling her back.

With the coming of dawn, the angels urged Lot, saying, "Hurry! Take your wife and your two daughters who are here, or you will be swept away when the city is punished."

Genesis 19:15

ASSIGNED READING:

Genesis 19:1–29

—Prayer—

Father, I pray that I will hold true to Jesus' words and always remember Lot's wife as an example for my own life.

Weekend

Go to page 125 for your next devotional reading.

17And the LORD said to Moses, "I will do
the very thing you have asked, because I am
pleased with you and I know you by name."
18Then Moses said, "Now show me your
glory."
19And the LORD said, "I
will cause all my goodness to
pass in front of you, and I will
proclaim my name, the LORD,
in your presence. I will have
mercy on whom I will have
mercy, and I will have compassion on whom I will have compassion. 20But," he said, "you
cannot see my face, for no one
may see me and live."
21Then the LORD said, "There
is a place near me where you
may stand on a rock. 22When
my glory passes by, I will put
you in a cleft in the rock and
cover you with my hand until I
have passed by. 23Then I will remove my hand and you will see
my back; but my face must not be seen."

> **Exodus 33:19**
>
> *God Is Compassionate*
>
> "I will cause all my goodness to pass in front of you, and I will proclaim my name, the LORD, in your presence. I will have mercy on whom I will have mercy, and I will have compassion on whom I will have compassion."

The New Stone Tablets

34 The LORD said to Moses, "Chisel out
two stone tablets like the first ones,
and I will write on them the words that were
on the first tablets, which you broke. 2Be ready
in the morning, and then come up on Mount
Sinai. Present yourself to me there on top of
the mountain. 3No one is to come with you
or be seen anywhere on the mountain; not
even the flocks and herds may graze in front
of the mountain."
4So Moses chiseled out two stone tablets like
the first ones and went up Mount Sinai early
in the morning, as the LORD had commanded
him; and he carried the two stone tablets in
his hands. 5Then the LORD came down in the
cloud and stood there with him and proclaimed
his name, the LORD. 6And he passed in front
of Moses, proclaiming, "The LORD, the LORD,
the compassionate and gracious God, slow
to anger, abounding in love and faithfulness,
7maintaining love to thousands, and forgiving
wickedness, rebellion and sin. Yet he does not
leave the guilty unpunished; he punishes the
children and their children for the sin of the
fathers to the third and fourth generation."
8Moses bowed to the ground at once and
worshiped. 9"O Lord, if I have
found favor in your eyes," he
said, "then let the Lord go with
us. Although this is a stiff-
necked people, forgive our
wickedness and our sin, and
take us as your inheritance."
10Then the LORD said: "I am
making a covenant with you.
Before all your people I will
do wonders never before done
in any nation in all the world.
The people you live among
will see how awesome is the
work that I, the LORD, will do
for you. 11Obey what I command you today. I will drive
out before you the Amorites,
Canaanites, Hittites, Perizzites,
Hivites and Jebusites. 12Be care-
ful not to make a treaty with those who live in
the land where you are going, or they will be
a snare among you. 13Break down their altars,
smash their sacred stones and cut down their
Asherah poles.[a] 14Do not worship any other
god, for the LORD, whose name is Jealous, is a
jealous God.
15"Be careful not to make a treaty with
those who live in the land; for when they prostitute themselves to their gods and sacrifice
to them, they will invite you and you will eat
their sacrifices. 16And when you choose some
of their daughters as wives for your sons and
those daughters prostitute themselves to their
gods, they will lead your sons to do the same.
17"Do not make cast idols.
18"Celebrate the Feast of Unleavened Bread.
For seven days eat bread made without yeast,
as I commanded you. Do this at the appointed
time in the month of Abib, for in that month
you came out of Egypt.
19"The first offspring of every womb belongs
to me, including all the firstborn males of your
livestock, whether from herd or flock. 20Re-
deem the firstborn donkey with a lamb, but if

[a]13 That is, symbols of the goddess Asherah

you do not redeem it, break its neck. Redeem
all your firstborn sons.
"No one is to appear before me empty-
handed.
21"Six days you shall labor, but on the seventh day you shall rest; even during the plowing season and harvest you must rest.
22"Celebrate the Feast of Weeks with the
firstfruits of the wheat harvest, and the Feast
of Ingathering at the turn of the year.[a] 23Three
times a year all your men are to appear before
the Sovereign LORD, the God of Israel. 24I will
drive out nations before you and enlarge your
territory, and no one will covet your land when
you go up three times each year to appear before the LORD your God.
25"Do not offer the blood of a sacrifice to me
along with anything containing yeast, and do
not let any of the sacrifice from the Passover
Feast remain until morning.
26"Bring the best of the firstfruits of your soil
to the house of the LORD your God.
"Do not cook a young goat in its mother's
milk."
27Then the LORD said to Moses, "Write
down these words, for in accordance with
these words I have made a covenant with you
and with Israel." 28Moses was there with the
LORD forty days and forty nights without eating bread or drinking water. And he wrote on
the tablets the words of the covenant—the Ten
Commandments.

The Radiant Face of Moses

29When Moses came down from Mount
Sinai with the two tablets of the Testimony in
his hands, he was not aware that his face was
radiant because he had spoken with the LORD.
30When Aaron and all the Israelites saw Moses, his face was radiant, and they were afraid
to come near him. 31But Moses called to them;
so Aaron and all the leaders of the community
came back to him, and he spoke to them. 32Af-
terward all the Israelites came near him, and
he gave them all the commands the LORD had
given him on Mount Sinai.
33When Moses finished speaking to them,
he put a veil over his face. 34But whenever he
entered the LORD's presence to speak with him,
he removed the veil until he came out. And
when he came out and told the Israelites what
he had been commanded, 35they saw that his
face was radiant. Then Moses would put the
veil back over his face until he went in to speak
with the LORD.

Sabbath Regulations

35 Moses assembled the whole Israelite
community and said to them, "These
are the things the LORD has commanded you
to do: 2For six days, work is to be done, but the
seventh day shall be your holy day, a Sabbath of
rest to the LORD. Whoever does any work on it
must be put to death. 3Do not light a fire in any
of your dwellings on the Sabbath day."

Materials for the Tabernacle

4Moses said to the whole Israelite community, "This is what the LORD has commanded:
5From what you have, take an offering for the
LORD. Everyone who is willing is to bring to
the LORD an offering of gold, silver and bronze;
6blue, purple and scarlet yarn and fine linen;
goat hair; 7ram skins dyed red and hides of
sea cows[b]; acacia wood; 8olive oil for the light;
spices for the anointing oil and for the fragrant
incense; 9and onyx stones and other gems to be
mounted on the ephod and breastpiece.
10"All who are skilled among you are to
come and make everything the LORD has
commanded: 11the tabernacle with its tent and
its covering, clasps, frames, crossbars, posts
and bases; 12the ark with its poles and the
atonement cover and the curtain that shields it;
13the table with its poles and all its articles and
the bread of the Presence; 14the lampstand that
is for light with its accessories, lamps and oil for
the light; 15the altar of incense with its poles,
the anointing oil and the fragrant incense; the
curtain for the doorway at the entrance to the
tabernacle; 16the altar of burnt offering with its
bronze grating, its poles and all its utensils; the
bronze basin with its stand; 17the curtains of
the courtyard with its posts and bases, and the
curtain for the entrance to the courtyard; 18the
tent pegs for the tabernacle and for the courtyard, and their ropes; 19the woven garments
worn for ministering in the sanctuary—both

[a]22 That is, in the fall [b]7 That is, dugongs; also in verse 23

the sacred garments for Aaron the priest and
the garments for his sons when they serve
as priests."
20 Then the whole Israelite community withdrew from Moses' presence, 21 and everyone
who was willing and whose heart moved him
came and brought an offering to the LORD for
the work on the Tent of Meeting, for all its service, and for the sacred garments. 22 All who
were willing, men and women alike, came and
brought gold jewelry of all kinds: brooches, earrings, rings and ornaments. They all presented
their gold as a wave offering to the LORD.
23 Everyone who had blue, purple or scarlet
yarn or fine linen, or goat hair, ram skins dyed
red or hides of sea cows brought them. 24 Those
presenting an offering of silver or bronze
brought it as an offering to the LORD, and
everyone who had acacia wood for any part
of the work brought it. 25 Every skilled woman
spun with her hands and brought what she
had spun—blue, purple or scarlet yarn or fine
linen. 26 And all the women who were willing
and had the skill spun the goat hair. 27 The leaders brought onyx stones and other gems to be
mounted on the ephod and breastpiece. 28 They
also brought spices and olive oil for the light
and for the anointing oil and for the fragrant incense. 29 All the Israelite men and women who
were willing brought to the LORD freewill offerings for all the work the LORD through Moses
had commanded them to do.

Bezalel and Oholiab

30 Then Moses said to the Israelites, "See, the
LORD has chosen Bezalel son of Uri, the son of
Hur, of the tribe of Judah, 31 and he has filled
him with the Spirit of God, with skill, ability
and knowledge in all kinds of crafts— 32 to
make artistic designs for work in gold, silver
and bronze, 33 to cut and set stones, to work
in wood and to engage in all kinds of artistic
craftsmanship. 34 And he has given both him
and Oholiab son of Ahisamach, of the tribe of
Dan, the ability to teach others. 35 He has filled
them with skill to do all kinds of work as craftsmen, designers, embroiderers in blue, purple
and scarlet yarn and fine linen, and weavers—
all of them master craftsmen and designers.

36 So Bezalel, Oholiab and every skilled
person to whom the LORD has given
skill and ability to know how to carry out all the
work of constructing the sanctuary are to do
the work just as the LORD has commanded."
2 Then Moses summoned Bezalel and
Oholiab and every skilled person to whom
the LORD had given ability and who was willing to come and do the work. 3 They received
from Moses all the offerings the Israelites had
brought to carry out the work of constructing
the sanctuary. And the people continued to
bring freewill offerings morning after morning. 4 So all the skilled craftsmen who were
doing all the work on the sanctuary left their
work 5 and said to Moses, "The people are bringing more than enough for doing the work the
LORD commanded to be done."
6 Then Moses gave an order and they sent
this word throughout the camp: "No man or
woman is to make anything else as an offering
for the sanctuary." And so the people were restrained from bringing more, 7 because what
they already had was more than enough to do
all the work.

The Tabernacle

8 All the skilled men among the workmen
made the tabernacle with ten curtains of finely
twisted linen and blue, purple and scarlet yarn,
with cherubim worked into them by a skilled
craftsman. 9 All the curtains were the same
size—twenty-eight cubits long and four cubits wide.[a] 10 They joined five of the curtains
together and did the same with the other five.
11 Then they made loops of blue material along
the edge of the end curtain in one set, and the
same was done with the end curtain in the
other set. 12 They also made fifty loops on one
curtain and fifty loops on the end curtain of the
other set, with the loops opposite each other.
13 Then they made fifty gold clasps and used
them to fasten the two sets of curtains together
so that the tabernacle was a unit.
14 They made curtains of goat hair for the tent
over the tabernacle—eleven altogether. 15 All
eleven curtains were the same size—thirty cubits
long and four cubits wide.[b] 16 They joined five of
the curtains into one set and the other six into

[a] 9 That is, about 42 feet (about 12.5 meters) long and 6 feet (about 1.8 meters) wide [b] 15 That is, about 45 feet (about 13.5 meters) long and 6 feet (about 1.8 meters) wide

another set. 17 Then they made fifty loops along
the edge of the end curtain in one set and also
along the edge of the end curtain in the other
set. 18 They made fifty bronze clasps to fasten
the tent together as a unit. 19 Then they made
for the tent a covering of ram skins dyed red,
and over that a covering of hides of sea cows.[a]

20 They made upright frames of acacia wood
for the tabernacle. 21 Each frame was ten cubits long and a cubit and a half wide,[b] 22 with
two projections set parallel to each other. They
made all the frames of the tabernacle in this
way. 23 They made twenty frames for the south
side of the tabernacle 24 and made forty silver
bases to go under them—two bases for each
frame, one under each projection. 25 For the
other side, the north side of the tabernacle,
they made twenty frames 26 and forty silver
bases—two under each frame. 27 They made
six frames for the far end, that is, the west end
of the tabernacle, 28 and two frames were made
for the corners of the tabernacle at the far end.
29 At these two corners the frames were double
from the bottom all the way to the top and fitted into a single ring; both were made alike.
30 So there were eight frames and sixteen silver
bases—two under each frame.

31 They also made crossbars of acacia wood:
five for the frames on one side of the tabernacle, 32 five for those on the other side, and five
for the frames on the west, at the far end of the
tabernacle. 33 They made the center crossbar so
that it extended from end to end at the middle
of the frames. 34 They overlaid the frames with
gold and made gold rings to hold the crossbars.
They also overlaid the crossbars with gold.

35 They made the curtain of blue, purple
and scarlet yarn and finely twisted linen, with
cherubim worked into it by a skilled craftsman.
36 They made four posts of acacia wood for it
and overlaid them with gold. They made gold
hooks for them and cast their four silver bases.
37 For the entrance to the tent they made a curtain of blue, purple and scarlet yarn and finely
twisted linen—the work of an embroiderer;
38 and they made five posts with hooks for
them. They overlaid the tops of the posts and
their bands with gold and made their five bases
of bronze.

The Ark

37 Bezalel made the ark of acacia wood—
two and a half cubits long, a cubit and
a half wide, and a cubit and a half high.[c] 2 He
overlaid it with pure gold, both inside and out,
and made a gold molding around it. 3 He cast
four gold rings for it and fastened them to its
four feet, with two rings on one side and two
rings on the other. 4 Then he made poles of acacia wood and overlaid them with gold. 5 And he
inserted the poles into the rings on the sides of
the ark to carry it.

6 He made the atonement cover of pure
gold—two and a half cubits long and a cubit
and a half wide.[d] 7 Then he made two cherubim
out of hammered gold at the ends of the cover.
8 He made one cherub on one end and the second cherub on the other; at the two ends he
made them of one piece with the cover. 9 The
cherubim had their wings spread upward, overshadowing the cover with them. The cherubim
faced each other, looking toward the cover.

The Table

10 They[e] made the table of acacia wood—two
cubits long, a cubit wide, and a cubit and a half
high.[f] 11 Then they overlaid it with pure gold
and made a gold molding around it. 12 They
also made around it a rim a handbreadth[g] wide
and put a gold molding on the rim. 13 They cast
four gold rings for the table and fastened them
to the four corners, where the four legs were.
14 The rings were put close to the rim to hold
the poles used in carrying the table. 15 The
poles for carrying the table were made of acacia wood and were overlaid with gold. 16 And
they made from pure gold the articles for the
table—its plates and dishes and bowls and its
pitchers for the pouring out of drink offerings.

The Lampstand

17 They made the lampstand of pure gold
and hammered it out, base and shaft; its flowerlike cups, buds and blossoms were of one piece
with it. 18 Six branches extended from the sides

a 19 That is, dugongs b 21 That is, about 15 feet (about 4.5 meters) long and 2 1/4 feet (about 0.7 meter) wide c 1 That is, about 3 3/4 feet (about 1.1 meters) long and 2 1/4 feet (about 0.7 meter) wide and high d 6 That is, about 3 3/4 feet (about 1.1 meters) long and 2 1/4 feet (about 0.7 meter) wide e 10 Or *He*; also in verses 11–29 f 10 That is, about 3 feet (about 0.9 meter) long, 1 1/2 feet (about 0.5 meter) wide, and 2 1/4 feet (about 0.7 meter) high g 12 That is, about 3 inches (about 8 centimeters)

of the lampstand—three on one side and three
on the other. 19Three cups shaped like almond
flowers with buds and blossoms were on one
branch, three on the next branch and the same
for all six branches extending from the lampstand. 20And on the lampstand were four cups
shaped like almond flowers with buds and
blossoms. 21One bud was under the first pair
of branches extending from the lampstand, a
second bud under the second pair, and a third
bud under the third pair—six branches in all.
22The buds and the branches were all of one
piece with the lampstand, hammered out of
pure gold.

23They made its seven lamps, as well as its
wick trimmers and trays, of pure gold. 24They
made the lampstand and all its accessories
from one talent[a] of pure gold.

The Altar of Incense

25They made the altar of incense out of acacia wood. It was square, a cubit long and a cubit
wide, and two cubits high[b]—its horns of one
piece with it. 26They overlaid the top and all
the sides and the horns with pure gold, and
made a gold molding around it. 27They made
two gold rings below the molding—two on opposite sides—to hold the poles used to carry
it. 28They made the poles of acacia wood and
overlaid them with gold.

29They also made the sacred anointing oil
and the pure, fragrant incense—the work of
a perfumer.

The Altar of Burnt Offering

38 They[c] built the altar of burnt offering
of acacia wood, three cubits[d] high;
it was square, five cubits long and five cubits
wide.[e] 2They made a horn at each of the four
corners, so that the horns and the altar were
of one piece, and they overlaid the altar with
bronze. 3They made all its utensils of bronze—
its pots, shovels, sprinkling bowls, meat forks
and firepans. 4They made a grating for the
altar, a bronze network, to be under its ledge,
halfway up the altar. 5They cast bronze rings
to hold the poles for the four corners of the
bronze grating. 6They made the poles of acacia
wood and overlaid them with bronze. 7They
inserted the poles into the rings so they would
be on the sides of the altar for carrying it. They
made it hollow, out of boards.

Basin for Washing

8They made the bronze basin and its bronze
stand from the mirrors of the women who
served at the entrance to the Tent of Meeting.

The Courtyard

9Next they made the courtyard. The south
side was a hundred cubits[f] long and had curtains of finely twisted linen, 10with twenty
posts and twenty bronze bases, and with silver
hooks and bands on the posts. 11The north
side was also a hundred cubits long and had
twenty posts and twenty bronze bases, with silver hooks and bands on the posts.

12The west end was fifty cubits[g] wide and
had curtains, with ten posts and ten bases, with
silver hooks and bands on the posts. 13The east
end, toward the sunrise, was also fifty cubits
wide. 14Curtains fifteen cubits[h] long were on
one side of the entrance, with three posts and
three bases, 15and curtains fifteen cubits long
were on the other side of the entrance to the
courtyard, with three posts and three bases.
16All the curtains around the courtyard were
of finely twisted linen. 17The bases for the posts
were bronze. The hooks and bands on the posts
were silver, and their tops were overlaid with
silver; so all the posts of the courtyard had silver bands.

18The curtain for the entrance to the courtyard was of blue, purple and scarlet yarn
and finely twisted linen—the work of an
embroiderer. It was twenty cubits[i] long and,
like the curtains of the courtyard, five cubits[j]
high, 19with four posts and four bronze bases.
Their hooks and bands were silver, and their
tops were overlaid with silver. 20All the tent
pegs of the tabernacle and of the surrounding
courtyard were bronze.

The Materials Used

21These are the amounts of the materials
used for the tabernacle, the tabernacle of the

[a] **24** That is, about 75 pounds (about 34 kilograms) [b] **25** That is, about 1 1/2 feet (about 0.5 meter) long and wide, and about 3 feet (about 0.9 meter) high [c] **1** Or *He;* also in verses 2–9 [d] **1** That is, about 4 1/2 feet (about 1.3 meters) [e] **1** That is, about 7 1/2 feet (about 2.3 meters) long and wide [f] **9** That is, about 150 feet (about 46 meters) [g] **12** That is, about 75 feet (about 23 meters) [h] **14** That is, about 22 1/2 feet (about 6.9 meters) [i] **18** That is, about 30 feet (about 9 meters) [j] **18** That is, about 7 1/2 feet (about 2.3 meters)

Testimony, which were recorded at Moses' command by the Levites under the direction of Ithamar son of Aaron, the priest. 22(Bezalel son of
Uri, the son of Hur, of the tribe of Judah, made
everything the LORD commanded Moses;
23with him was Oholiab son of Ahisamach,
of the tribe of Dan—a craftsman and designer,
and an embroiderer in blue, purple and scarlet
yarn and fine linen.) 24The total amount of the
gold from the wave offering used for all the
work on the sanctuary was 29 talents and 730
shekels,[a] according to the sanctuary shekel.

25The silver obtained from those of the
community who were counted in the census
was 100 talents and 1,775 shekels,[b] according
to the sanctuary shekel— 26one beka per person, that is, half a shekel,[c] according to the
sanctuary shekel, from everyone who had
crossed over to those counted, twenty years
old or more, a total of 603,550 men. 27The 100
talents[d] of silver were used to cast the bases for
the sanctuary and for the curtain—100 bases
from the 100 talents, one talent for each base.
28They used the 1,775 shekels[e] to make the
hooks for the posts, to overlay the tops of the
posts, and to make their bands.

29The bronze from the wave offering was
70 talents and 2,400 shekels.[f] 30They used it to
make the bases for the entrance to the Tent of
Meeting, the bronze altar with its bronze grating and all its utensils, 31the bases for the surrounding courtyard and those for its entrance
and all the tent pegs for the tabernacle and
those for the surrounding courtyard.

The Priestly Garments

39 From the blue, purple and scarlet
yarn they made woven garments for
ministering in the sanctuary. They also made
sacred garments for Aaron, as the LORD
commanded Moses.

The Ephod

2They[g] made the ephod of gold, and of blue,
purple and scarlet yarn, and of finely twisted
linen. 3They hammered out thin sheets of gold
and cut strands to be worked into the blue, purple and scarlet yarn and fine linen—the work of
a skilled craftsman. 4They made shoulder pieces
for the ephod, which were attached to two of its
corners, so it could be fastened. 5Its skillfully
woven waistband was like it—of one piece with
the ephod and made with gold, and with blue,
purple and scarlet yarn, and with finely twisted
linen, as the LORD commanded Moses.

6They mounted the onyx stones in gold filigree settings and engraved them like a seal with
the names of the sons of Israel. 7Then they fastened them on the shoulder pieces of the ephod
as memorial stones for the sons of Israel, as the
LORD commanded Moses.

The Breastpiece

8They fashioned the breastpiece—the work
of a skilled craftsman. They made it like the
ephod: of gold, and of blue, purple and scarlet yarn, and of finely twisted linen. 9It was
square—a span[h] long and a span wide—and
folded double. 10Then they mounted four rows
of precious stones on it. In the first row there
was a ruby, a topaz and a beryl; 11in the second
row a turquoise, a sapphire[i] and an emerald;
12in the third row a jacinth, an agate and an
amethyst; 13in the fourth row a chrysolite, an
onyx and a jasper.[j] They were mounted in gold
filigree settings. 14There were twelve stones,
one for each of the names of the sons of Israel,
each engraved like a seal with the name of one
of the twelve tribes.

15For the breastpiece they made braided
chains of pure gold, like a rope. 16They made
two gold filigree settings and two gold rings,
and fastened the rings to two of the corners of
the breastpiece. 17They fastened the two gold
chains to the rings at the corners of the breastpiece, 18and the other ends of the chains to the
two settings, attaching them to the shoulder
pieces of the ephod at the front. 19They made
two gold rings and attached them to the other
two corners of the breastpiece on the inside
edge next to the ephod. 20Then they made two
more gold rings and attached them to the bottom of the shoulder pieces on the front of the
ephod, close to the seam just above the waist-

[a] **24** The weight of the gold was a little over one ton (about 1 metric ton). [b] **25** The weight of the silver was a little over 3 3/4 tons (about 3.4 metric tons). [c] **26** That is, about 1/5 ounce (about 5.5 grams) [d] **27** That is, about 3 3/4 tons (about 3.4 metric tons) [e] **28** That is, about 45 pounds (about 20 kilograms) [f] **29** The weight of the bronze was about 2 1/2 tons (about 2.4 metric tons). [g] **2** Or *He*; also in verses 7, 8 and 22 [h] **9** That is, about 9 inches (about 22 centimeters) [i] **11** Or *lapis lazuli* [j] **13** The precise identification of some of these precious stones is uncertain.

band of the ephod. 21They tied the rings of the
breastpiece to the rings of the ephod with blue
cord, connecting it to the waistband so that
the breastpiece would not swing out from the
ephod—as the LORD commanded Moses.

Other Priestly Garments

22They made the robe of the ephod entirely
of blue cloth—the work of a weaver— 23with
an opening in the center of the robe like the
opening of a collar,[a] and a band around this
opening, so that it would not tear. 24They made
pomegranates of blue, purple and scarlet yarn
and finely twisted linen around the hem of
the robe. 25And they made bells of pure gold
and attached them around the hem between
the pomegranates. 26The bells and pomegranates alternated around the hem of the
robe to be worn for ministering, as the LORD
commanded Moses.

27For Aaron and his sons, they made tunics
of fine linen—the work of a weaver— 28and the
turban of fine linen, the linen headbands and
the undergarments of finely twisted linen. 29The
sash was of finely twisted linen and blue, purple
and scarlet yarn—the work of an embroiderer—
as the LORD commanded Moses.

30They made the plate, the sacred diadem,
out of pure gold and engraved on it, like an inscription on a seal: HOLY TO THE LORD. 31Then
they fastened a blue cord to it to attach it to the
turban, as the LORD commanded Moses.

Moses Inspects the Tabernacle

32So all the work on the tabernacle, the Tent
of Meeting, was completed. The Israelites did
everything just as the LORD commanded Moses. 33Then they brought the tabernacle to Moses: the tent and all its furnishings, its clasps,
frames, crossbars, posts and bases; 34the covering of ram skins dyed red, the covering of
hides of sea cows[b] and the shielding curtain;
35the ark of the Testimony with its poles and
the atonement cover; 36the table with all its articles and the bread of the Presence; 37the pure
gold lampstand with its row of lamps and all
its accessories, and the oil for the light; 38the
gold altar, the anointing oil, the fragrant incense, and the curtain for the entrance to the
tent; 39the bronze altar with its bronze grating,
its poles and all its utensils; the basin with its
stand; 40the curtains of the courtyard with
its posts and bases, and the curtain for the
entrance to the courtyard; the ropes and tent
pegs for the courtyard; all the furnishings for
the tabernacle, the Tent of Meeting; 41and the
woven garments worn for ministering in the
sanctuary, both the sacred garments for Aaron
the priest and the garments for his sons when
serving as priests.

42The Israelites had done all the work just
as the LORD had commanded Moses. 43Moses
inspected the work and saw that they had done
it just as the LORD had commanded. So Moses
blessed them.

Setting Up the Tabernacle

40 Then the LORD said to Moses: 2"Set up
the tabernacle, the Tent of Meeting, on
the first day of the first month. 3Place the ark
of the Testimony in it and shield the ark with
the curtain. 4Bring in the table and set out what
belongs on it. Then bring in the lampstand and
set up its lamps. 5Place the gold altar of incense
in front of the ark of the Testimony and put the
curtain at the entrance to the tabernacle.

6"Place the altar of burnt offering in front
of the entrance to the tabernacle, the Tent of
Meeting; 7place the basin between the Tent of
Meeting and the altar and put water in it. 8Set
up the courtyard around it and put the curtain
at the entrance to the courtyard.

9"Take the anointing oil and anoint the tabernacle and everything in it; consecrate it and
all its furnishings, and it will be holy. 10Then
anoint the altar of burnt offering and all its
utensils; consecrate the altar, and it will be most
holy. 11Anoint the basin and its stand and consecrate them.

12"Bring Aaron and his sons to the entrance
to the Tent of Meeting and wash them with
water. 13Then dress Aaron in the sacred garments, anoint him and consecrate him so he
may serve me as priest. 14Bring his sons and
dress them in tunics. 15Anoint them just as you
anointed their father, so they may serve me as
priests. Their anointing will be to a priesthood
that will continue for all generations to come."
16Moses did everything just as the LORD
commanded him.

[a]23 The meaning of the Hebrew for this word is uncertain. [b]34 That is, dugongs

17 So the tabernacle was set up on the first day of the first month in the second year. 18 When Moses set up the tabernacle, he put the bases in place, erected the frames, inserted the crossbars and set up the posts. 19 Then he spread the tent over the tabernacle and put the covering over the tent, as the LORD commanded him.

20 He took the Testimony and placed it in the ark, attached the poles to the ark and put the atonement cover over it. 21 Then he brought the ark into the tabernacle and hung the shielding curtain and shielded the ark of the Testimony, as the LORD commanded him.

22 Moses placed the table in the Tent of Meeting on the north side of the tabernacle outside the curtain 23 and set out the bread on it before the LORD, as the LORD commanded him.

24 He placed the lampstand in the Tent of Meeting opposite the table on the south side of the tabernacle 25 and set up the lamps before the LORD, as the LORD commanded him.

26 Moses placed the gold altar in the Tent of Meeting in front of the curtain 27 and burned fragrant incense on it, as the LORD commanded him. 28 Then he put up the curtain at the entrance to the tabernacle.

29 He set the altar of burnt offering near the entrance to the tabernacle, the Tent of Meeting, and offered on it burnt offerings and grain offerings, as the LORD commanded him.

30 He placed the basin between the Tent of Meeting and the altar and put water in it for washing, 31 and Moses and Aaron and his sons used it to wash their hands and feet. 32 They washed whenever they entered the Tent of Meeting or approached the altar, as the LORD commanded Moses.

33 Then Moses set up the courtyard around the tabernacle and altar and put up the curtain at the entrance to the courtyard. And so Moses finished the work.

Exodus 40:38

God Remains With Us

So the cloud of the LORD was over the tabernacle by day, and fire was in the cloud by night, in the sight of all the house of Israel during all their travels.

The Glory of the LORD

34 Then the cloud covered the Tent of Meeting, and the glory of the LORD filled the tabernacle. 35 Moses could not enter the Tent of Meeting because the cloud had settled upon it, and the glory of the LORD filled the tabernacle.

36 In all the travels of the Israelites, whenever the cloud lifted from above the tabernacle, they would set out; 37 but if the cloud did not lift, they did not set out—until the day it lifted. 38 So the cloud of the LORD was over the tabernacle by day, and fire was in the cloud by night, in the sight of all the house of Israel during all their travels.

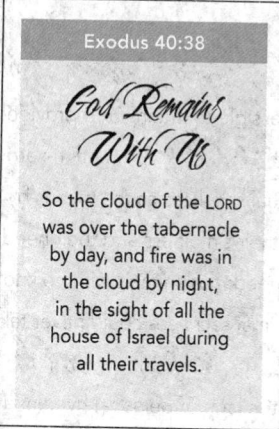

Leviticus

Author:
Moses.

Audience:
The people of Israel.

Date:
During the 1400s B.C., while the Israelites were traveling in the desert.

Setting:
At the foot of Mount Sinai, God introduces laws for living.

Verse to Remember:
"I am the LORD who brought you up out of Egypt to be your God; therefore be holy, because I am holy." (11:45)

God's holiness demands purity, yet human perfection is impossible to attain. God provided a perfect sacrifice for sin in *Jesus Christ*, but until he arrived, the Law demanded continual sacrifices as the means by which God's people recognized their sinfulness and their need for repentance. The Law demanded that animals with no known blemishes be sacrificed, but animal sacrifices could never take away sin.

Leviticus is a book focused on holiness.

From the laws of personal hygiene to the scapegoat that was allowed to live while a second goat was killed, the book highlights the need for personal and moral purity of God's people—and it describes the provisions to deal with the inevitable lack of purity. Notice how costly sin was and how seriously it was treated. But notice, too, that *God provides a way* for his people to come to him.

The Burnt Offering

1 The LORD called to Moses and spoke to
him from the Tent of Meeting. He said,
2"Speak to the Israelites and say to them:
'When any of you brings an offering to the
LORD, bring as your offering an animal from
either the herd or the flock.
3"'If the offering is a burnt offering from
the herd, he is to offer a male without defect.
He must present it at the entrance to the Tent
of Meeting so that it[a] will be acceptable to the
LORD. 4He is to lay his hand on the head of the
burnt offering, and it will be accepted on his
behalf to make atonement for him. 5He is to
slaughter the young bull before the LORD, and
then Aaron's sons the priests shall bring the

[a]3 Or *he*

blood and sprinkle it against the altar on all sides at the entrance to the Tent of Meeting. 6He is to skin the burnt offering and cut it into pieces. 7The sons of Aaron the priest are to put fire on the altar and arrange wood on the fire. 8Then Aaron's sons the priests shall arrange the pieces, including the head and the fat, on the burning wood that is on the altar. 9He is to wash the inner parts and the legs with water, and the priest is to burn all of it on the altar. It is a burnt offering, an offering made by fire, an aroma pleasing to the LORD.

> Leviticus 1:1
>
> *God Speaks*
>
> The LORD called to Moses and spoke to him from the Tent of Meeting.

10"'If the offering is a burnt offering from the flock, from either the sheep or the goats, he is to offer a male without defect. 11He is to slaughter it at the north side of the altar before the LORD, and Aaron's sons the priests shall sprinkle its blood against the altar on all sides. 12He is to cut it into pieces, and the priest shall arrange them, including the head and the fat, on the burning wood that is on the altar. 13He is to wash the inner parts and the legs with water, and the priest is to bring all of it and burn it on the altar. It is a burnt offering, an offering made by fire, an aroma pleasing to the LORD.

14"'If the offering to the LORD is a burnt offering of birds, he is to offer a dove or a young pigeon. 15The priest shall bring it to the altar, wring off the head and burn it on the altar; its blood shall be drained out on the side of the altar. 16He is to remove the crop with its contents[a] and throw it to the east side of the altar, where the ashes are. 17He shall tear it open by the wings, not severing it completely, and then the priest shall burn it on the wood that is on the fire on the altar. It is a burnt offering, an offering made by fire, an aroma pleasing to the LORD.

The Grain Offering

2 "'When someone brings a grain offering to the LORD, his offering is to be of fine flour. He is to pour oil on it, put incense on it 2and take it to Aaron's sons the priests. The priest shall take a handful of the fine flour and oil, together with all the incense, and burn this as a memorial portion on the altar, an offering made by fire, an aroma pleasing to the LORD. 3The rest of the grain offering belongs to Aaron and his sons; it is a most holy part of the offerings made to the LORD by fire.

4"'If you bring a grain offering baked in an oven, it is to consist of fine flour: cakes made without yeast and mixed with oil, or[b] wafers made without yeast and spread with oil. 5If your grain offering is prepared on a griddle, it is to be made of fine flour mixed with oil, and without yeast. 6Crumble it and pour oil on it; it is a grain offering. 7If your grain offering is cooked in a pan, it is to be made of fine flour and oil. 8Bring the grain offering made of these things to the LORD; present it to the priest, who shall take it to the altar. 9He shall take out the memorial portion from the grain offering and burn it on the altar as an offering made by fire, an aroma pleasing to the LORD. 10The rest of the grain offering belongs to Aaron and his sons; it is a most holy part of the offerings made to the LORD by fire.

11"'Every grain offering you bring to the LORD must be made without yeast, for you are not to burn any yeast or honey in an offering made to the LORD by fire. 12You may bring them to the LORD as an offering of the firstfruits, but they are not to be offered on the altar as a pleasing aroma. 13Season all your grain offerings with salt. Do not leave the salt of the covenant of your God out of your grain offerings; add salt to all your offerings.

14"'If you bring a grain offering of firstfruits to the LORD, offer crushed heads of new grain roasted in the fire. 15Put oil and incense on it; it is a grain offering. 16The priest shall burn the memorial portion of the crushed grain and the oil, together with all the incense, as an offering made to the LORD by fire.

The Fellowship Offering

3 "'If someone's offering is a fellowship offering,[c] and he offers an animal from the herd, whether male or female, he is to present

[a]16 Or *crop and the feathers*; the meaning of the Hebrew for this word is uncertain. [b]4 Or *and* [c]1 Traditionally *peace offering*; also in verses 3, 6 and 9

before the LORD an animal without defect. [2]He is to lay his hand on the head of his offering and slaughter it at the entrance to the Tent of Meeting. Then Aaron's sons the priests shall sprinkle the blood against the altar on all sides. [3]From the fellowship offering he is to bring a sacrifice made to the LORD by fire: all the fat that covers the inner parts or is connected to them, [4]both kidneys with the fat on them near the loins, and the covering of the liver, which he will remove with the kidneys. [5]Then Aaron's sons are to burn it on the altar on top of the burnt offering that is on the burning wood, as an offering made by fire, an aroma pleasing to the LORD.

[6]" 'If he offers an animal from the flock as a fellowship offering to the LORD, he is to offer a male or female without defect. [7]If he offers a lamb, he is to present it before the LORD. [8]He is to lay his hand on the head of his offering and slaughter it in front of the Tent of Meeting. Then Aaron's sons shall sprinkle its blood against the altar on all sides. [9]From the fellowship offering he is to bring a sacrifice made to the LORD by fire: its fat, the entire fat tail cut off close to the backbone, all the fat that covers the inner parts or is connected to them, [10]both kidneys with the fat on them near the loins, and the covering of the liver, which he will remove with the kidneys. [11]The priest shall burn them on the altar as food, an offering made to the LORD by fire.

[12]" 'If his offering is a goat, he is to present it before the LORD. [13]He is to lay his hand on its head and slaughter it in front of the Tent of Meeting. Then Aaron's sons shall sprinkle its blood against the altar on all sides. [14]From what he offers he is to make this offering to the LORD by fire: all the fat that covers the inner parts or is connected to them, [15]both kidneys with the fat on them near the loins, and the covering of the liver, which he will remove with the kidneys. [16]The priest shall burn them on the altar as food, an offering made by fire, a pleasing aroma. All the fat is the LORD's.

[17]" 'This is a lasting ordinance for the generations to come, wherever you live: You must not eat any fat or any blood.' "

> **Leviticus 3:6**
>
> *God Deserves Our Best*
>
> "If he offers an animal from the flock as a fellowship offering to the LORD, he is to offer a male or female without defect."

The Sin Offering

4 The LORD said to Moses, [2]"Say to the Israelites: 'When anyone sins unintentionally and does what is forbidden in any of the LORD's commands—

[3]" 'If the anointed priest sins, bringing guilt on the people, he must bring to the LORD a young bull without defect as a sin offering for the sin he has committed. [4]He is to present the bull at the entrance to the Tent of Meeting before the LORD. He is to lay his hand on its head and slaughter it before the LORD. [5]Then the anointed priest shall take some of the bull's blood and carry it into the Tent of Meeting. [6]He is to dip his finger into the blood and sprinkle some of it seven times before the LORD, in front of the curtain of the sanctuary. [7]The priest shall then put some of the blood on the horns of the altar of fragrant incense that is before the LORD in the Tent of Meeting. The rest of the bull's blood he shall pour out at the base of the altar of burnt offering at the entrance to the Tent of Meeting. [8]He shall remove all the fat from the bull of the sin offering—the fat that covers the inner parts or is connected to them, [9]both kidneys with the fat on them near the loins, and the covering of the liver, which he will remove with the kidneys— [10]just as the fat is removed from the ox[a] sacrificed as a fellowship offering.[b] Then the priest shall burn them on the altar of burnt offering. [11]But the hide of the bull and all its flesh, as well as the head and legs, the inner parts and offal— [12]that is, all the rest of the bull—he must take outside the camp to a place ceremonially clean, where the ashes are thrown, and burn it in a wood fire on the ash heap.

[a]10 The Hebrew word can include both male and female. [b]10 Traditionally *peace offering*; also in verses 26, 31 and 35

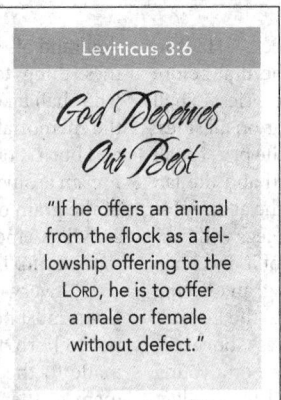

13 " 'If the whole Israelite community sins unintentionally and does what is forbidden in any of the LORD's commands, even though the community is unaware of the matter, they are guilty. 14 When they become aware of the sin they committed, the assembly must bring a young bull as a sin offering and present it before the Tent of Meeting. 15 The elders of the community are to lay their hands on the bull's head before the LORD, and the bull shall be slaughtered before the LORD. 16 Then the anointed priest is to take some of the bull's blood into the Tent of Meeting. 17 He shall dip his finger into the blood and sprinkle it before the LORD seven times in front of the curtain. 18 He is to put some of the blood on the horns of the altar that is before the LORD in the Tent of Meeting. The rest of the blood he shall pour out at the base of the altar of burnt offering at the entrance to the Tent of Meeting. 19 He shall remove all the fat from it and burn it on the altar, 20 and do with this bull just as he did with the bull for the sin offering. In this way the priest will make atonement for them, and they will be forgiven. 21 Then he shall take the bull outside the camp and burn it as he burned the first bull. This is the sin offering for the community.

22 " 'When a leader sins unintentionally and does what is forbidden in any of the commands of the LORD his God, he is guilty. 23 When he is made aware of the sin he committed, he must bring as his offering a male goat without defect. 24 He is to lay his hand on the goat's head and slaughter it at the place where the burnt offering is slaughtered before the LORD. It is a sin offering. 25 Then the priest shall take some of the blood of the sin offering with his finger and put it on the horns of the altar of burnt offering and pour out the rest of the blood at the base of the altar. 26 He shall burn all the fat on the altar as he burned the fat of the fellowship offering. In this way the priest will make atonement for the man's sin, and he will be forgiven.

Leviticus 4:35

God Offers Forgiveness

"In this way the priest will make atonement for him for the sin he has committed, and he will be forgiven."

27 " 'If a member of the community sins unintentionally and does what is forbidden in any of the LORD's commands, he is guilty. 28 When he is made aware of the sin he committed, he must bring as his offering for the sin he committed a female goat without defect. 29 He is to lay his hand on the head of the sin offering and slaughter it at the place of the burnt offering. 30 Then the priest is to take some of the blood with his finger and put it on the horns of the altar of burnt offering and pour out the rest of the blood at the base of the altar. 31 He shall remove all the fat, just as the fat is removed from the fellowship offering, and the priest shall burn it on the altar as an aroma pleasing to the LORD. In this way the priest will make atonement for him, and he will be forgiven.

32 " 'If he brings a lamb as his sin offering, he is to bring a female without defect. 33 He is to lay his hand on its head and slaughter it for a sin offering at the place where the burnt offering is slaughtered. 34 Then the priest shall take some of the blood of the sin offering with his finger and put it on the horns of the altar of burnt offering and pour out the rest of the blood at the base of the altar. 35 He shall remove all the fat, just as the fat is removed from the lamb of the fellowship offering, and the priest shall burn it on the altar on top of the offerings made to the LORD by fire. In this way the priest will make atonement for him for the sin he has committed, and he will be forgiven.

5 " 'If a person sins because he does not speak up when he hears a public charge to testify regarding something he has seen or learned about, he will be held responsible.

2 " 'Or if a person touches anything ceremonially unclean—whether the carcasses of unclean wild animals or of unclean livestock or of unclean creatures that move along the ground—even though he is unaware of it, he has become unclean and is guilty.

3 " 'Or if he touches human uncleanness—anything that would make him unclean—even

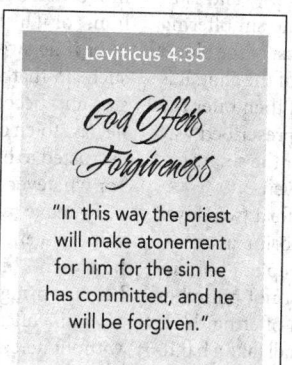

though he is unaware of it, when he learns of it
he will be guilty.
4“ ‘Or if a person thoughtlessly takes an oath
to do anything, whether good or evil—in any
matter one might carelessly swear about—even
though he is unaware of it, in any case when he
learns of it he will be guilty.
5“ ‘When anyone is guilty in any of these
ways, he must confess in what way he has
sinned 6and, as a penalty for the sin he has
committed, he must bring to the LORD a female
lamb or goat from the flock as a sin offering;
and the priest shall make atonement for him
for his sin.
7“ ‘If he cannot afford a lamb, he is to bring
two doves or two young pigeons to the LORD as
a penalty for his sin—one for a sin offering and
the other for a burnt offering. 8He is to bring
them to the priest, who shall first offer the one
for the sin offering. He is to wring its head from
its neck, not severing it completely, 9and is to
sprinkle some of the blood of the sin offering
against the side of the altar; the rest of the blood
must be drained out at the base of the altar. It is
a sin offering. 10The priest shall then offer the
other as a burnt offering in the prescribed way
and make atonement for him for the sin he has
committed, and he will be forgiven.
11“ ‘If, however, he cannot afford two doves
or two young pigeons, he is to bring as an offering for his sin a tenth of an ephah[a] of fine
flour for a sin offering. He must not put oil or
incense on it, because it is a sin offering. 12He
is to bring it to the priest, who shall take a handful of it as a memorial portion and burn it on
the altar on top of the offerings made to the
LORD by fire. It is a sin offering. 13In this way
the priest will make atonement for him for any
of these sins he has committed, and he will be
forgiven. The rest of the offering will belong to
the priest, as in the case of the grain offering.’ ”

The Guilt Offering

14The LORD said to Moses: 15“When a person
commits a violation and sins unintentionally in
regard to any of the LORD's holy things, he is
to bring to the LORD as a penalty a ram from
the flock, one without defect and of the proper
value in silver, according to the sanctuary
shekel.[b] It is a guilt offering. 16He must make
restitution for what he has failed to do in regard
to the holy things, add a fifth of the value to
that and give it all to the priest, who will make
atonement for him with the ram as a guilt offering, and he will be forgiven.
17“If a person sins and does what is forbidden in any of the LORD's commands, even
though he does not know it, he is guilty and
will be held responsible. 18He is to bring to
the priest as a guilt offering a ram from the
flock, one without defect and of the proper
value. In this way the priest will make atonement for him for the wrong he has committed
unintentionally, and he will be forgiven. 19It is
a guilt offering; he has been guilty of[c] wrongdoing against the LORD.”
6 The LORD said to Moses: 2“If anyone sins
and is unfaithful to the LORD by deceiving
his neighbor about something entrusted to
him or left in his care or stolen, or if he cheats
him, 3or if he finds lost property and lies about
it, or if he swears falsely, or if he commits any
such sin that people may do— 4when he thus
sins and becomes guilty, he must return what
he has stolen or taken by extortion, or what was
entrusted to him, or the lost property he found,
5or whatever it was he swore falsely about. He
must make restitution in full, add a fifth of the
value to it and give it all to the owner on the day
he presents his guilt offering. 6And as a penalty
he must bring to the priest, that is, to the LORD,
his guilt offering, a ram from the flock, one
without defect and of the proper value. 7In this
way the priest will make atonement for him before the LORD, and he will be forgiven for any
of these things he did that made him guilty.”

The Burnt Offering

8The LORD said to Moses: 9“Give Aaron and
his sons this command: ‘These are the regulations for the burnt offering: The burnt offering
is to remain on the altar hearth throughout the
night, till morning, and the fire must be kept
burning on the altar. 10The priest shall then put
on his linen clothes, with linen undergarments
next to his body, and shall remove the ashes of
the burnt offering that the fire has consumed
on the altar and place them beside the altar.

[a] 11 That is, probably about 2 quarts (about 2 liters) [b] 15 That is, about 2/5 ounce (about 11.5 grams) [c] 19 Or *has made full expiation for his*

Not Guilty

Read: Leviticus 5:14–19

ISN'T IT PAINFUL to harm others intentionally? Premeditated evils can be set right by our finite sense of justice, even if guilt then rests on our own head. But imagine the fear and frustration of being held accountable for hundreds of violations that you committed without knowing it. Nothing you ever did would be good enough; you would carry around the guilt of wrongs you never intended to commit. Talk about paranoia.

Yet in Old Testament times, you would certainly have been guilty of such unwitting sins, and they would have required blood sacrifice. The Law of God was clear: no one could be good enough, not even those who sinned without awareness, unintentionally. Few of us think of sin in these terms today, but God remains the same. His standard of perfection cannot be attained, even by the best of us on our best day.

The sacrifices of the Old Testament foreshadowed the ultimate sacrifice: Jesus Christ. When Jesus offered himself on the cross, he paid the debt of sin in full. He declared his followers "not guilty." The law was fulfilled. We no longer need the sacrifice of a ram to cleanse us from the sins we knowingly commit or the sins we unintentionally commit. No other blood sacrifice will ever be required.

Women today are often burdened by guilt. We are inundated with "shoulds" and "oughts." We feel guilty if we work; guilty if we don't; guilty for not spending enough time with our husband, kids and friends; and guilty for not taking time for God and ourselves. We have a hard time knowing when we're really guilty and when we suffer from false guilt. But Jesus' declaration from the cross that we are not guilty covers all of our sins—even the unintentional ones. Instead of blood sacrifice, we can make offerings of gratitude: repentance, praise and service.

We all both unintentionally and intentionally wrong God and others. But Jesus Christ bought our forgiveness on the cross. Offer him the sacrifice of confession, and you'll be covered for overlooking the things you should have done and the things you ought not have. Then pour out the sacrifice of praise. Present the sacrifice of service, helping others in God's name, for "love covers over a multitude of sins" (1 Peter 4:8). Despair has no place here; our advocate perfectly kept even the hidden laws.

Leviticus 5:18

"He is to bring to the priest as a guilt offering a ram from the flock, one without defect and of the proper value. In this way the priest will make atonement for him for the wrong he has committed unintentionally, and he will be forgiven."

reflection

1 What unintentional sins have you committed in the past few days? Spend some time asking God to reveal your sins to you.

2 Now offer God a sacrifice of repentance and of praise for declaring you not guilty.

3 Whom can you serve sacrificially? How will you go about this?

RELATED READINGS

Psalm 139:23–24; Proverbs 28:13; Isaiah 55:6–7; Hebrews 8:8–12

Monday

Go to page 130 for your next devotional reading.

11 Then he is to take off these clothes and put
on others, and carry the ashes outside the camp
to a place that is ceremonially clean. 12 The fire
on the altar must be kept burning; it must not
go out. Every morning the priest is to add firewood and arrange the burnt offering on the fire
and burn the fat of the fellowship offerings[a] on
it. 13 The fire must be kept burning on the altar
continuously; it must not go out.

The Grain Offering

14 " 'These are the regulations for the grain
offering: Aaron's sons are to bring it before the
LORD, in front of the altar. 15 The priest is to
take a handful of fine flour and oil, together
with all the incense on the grain offering, and
burn the memorial portion on the altar as an
aroma pleasing to the LORD. 16 Aaron and his
sons shall eat the rest of it, but it is to be eaten
without yeast in a holy place; they are to eat it in
the courtyard of the Tent of Meeting. 17 It must
not be baked with yeast; I have given it as their
share of the offerings made to me by fire. Like
the sin offering and the guilt offering, it is most
holy. 18 Any male descendant of Aaron may eat
it. It is his regular share of the offerings made
to the LORD by fire for the generations to come.
Whatever touches them will become holy.[b]' "

19 The LORD also said to Moses, 20 "This is
the offering Aaron and his sons are to bring to
the LORD on the day he[c] is anointed: a tenth
of an ephah[d] of fine flour as a regular grain
offering, half of it in the morning and half in
the evening. 21 Prepare it with oil on a griddle;
bring it well-mixed and present the grain offering broken[e] in pieces as an aroma pleasing to
the LORD. 22 The son who is to succeed him as
anointed priest shall prepare it. It is the LORD's
regular share and is to be burned completely.
23 Every grain offering of a priest shall be
burned completely; it must not be eaten."

The Sin Offering

24 The LORD said to Moses, 25 "Say to Aaron
and his sons: 'These are the regulations for the
sin offering: The sin offering is to be slaughtered before the LORD in the place the burnt
offering is slaughtered; it is most holy. 26 The
priest who offers it shall eat it; it is to be eaten
in a holy place, in the courtyard of the Tent of
Meeting. 27 Whatever touches any of the flesh
will become holy, and if any of the blood is
spattered on a garment, you must wash it in a
holy place. 28 The clay pot the meat is cooked in
must be broken; but if it is cooked in a bronze
pot, the pot is to be scoured and rinsed with
water. 29 Any male in a priest's family may eat
it; it is most holy. 30 But any sin offering whose
blood is brought into the Tent of Meeting to
make atonement in the Holy Place must not be
eaten; it must be burned.

The Guilt Offering

7 " 'These are the regulations for the guilt
offering, which is most holy: 2 The guilt offering is to be slaughtered in the place where
the burnt offering is slaughtered, and its blood
is to be sprinkled against the altar on all sides.
3 All its fat shall be offered: the fat tail and the
fat that covers the inner parts, 4 both kidneys
with the fat on them near the loins, and the covering of the liver, which is to be removed with
the kidneys. 5 The priest shall burn them on the
altar as an offering made to the LORD by fire. It
is a guilt offering. 6 Any male in a priest's family
may eat it, but it must be eaten in a holy place;
it is most holy.

7 " 'The same law applies to both the sin offering and the guilt offering: They belong to the
priest who makes atonement with them. 8 The
priest who offers a burnt offering for anyone
may keep its hide for himself. 9 Every grain offering baked in an oven or cooked in a pan or
on a griddle belongs to the priest who offers
it, 10 and every grain offering, whether mixed
with oil or dry, belongs equally to all the sons
of Aaron.

The Fellowship Offering

11 " 'These are the regulations for the fellowship offering[f] a person may present to
the LORD:

12 " 'If he offers it as an expression of thankfulness, then along with this thank offering he is
to offer cakes of bread made without yeast and
mixed with oil, wafers made without yeast and

[a] 12 Traditionally *peace offerings* [b] 18 Or *Whoever touches them must be holy*; similarly in verse 27 [c] 20 Or *each* [d] 20 That is, probably about 2 quarts (about 2 liters) [e] 21 The meaning of the Hebrew for this word is uncertain. [f] 11 Traditionally *peace offering*; also in verses 13–37

spread with oil, and cakes of fine flour well-kneaded and mixed with oil. 13Along with his fellowship offering of thanksgiving he is to present an offering with cakes of bread made with yeast. 14He is to bring one of each kind as an offering, a contribution to the LORD; it belongs to the priest who sprinkles the blood of the fellowship offerings. 15The meat of his fellowship offering of thanksgiving must be eaten on the day it is offered; he must leave none of it till morning.

16" 'If, however, his offering is the result of a vow or is a freewill offering, the sacrifice shall be eaten on the day he offers it, but anything left over may be eaten on the next day. 17Any meat of the sacrifice left over till the third day must be burned up. 18If any meat of the fellowship offering is eaten on the third day, it will not be accepted. It will not be credited to the one who offered it, for it is impure; the person who eats any of it will be held responsible.

19" 'Meat that touches anything ceremonially unclean must not be eaten; it must be burned up. As for other meat, anyone ceremonially clean may eat it. 20But if anyone who is unclean eats any meat of the fellowship offering belonging to the LORD, that person must be cut off from his people. 21If anyone touches something unclean—whether human uncleanness or an unclean animal or any unclean, detestable thing—and then eats any of the meat of the fellowship offering belonging to the LORD, that person must be cut off from his people.' "

Eating Fat and Blood Forbidden

22The LORD said to Moses, 23"Say to the Israelites: 'Do not eat any of the fat of cattle, sheep or goats. 24The fat of an animal found dead or torn by wild animals may be used for any other purpose, but you must not eat it. 25Anyone who eats the fat of an animal from which an offering by fire may be[a] made to the LORD must be cut off from his people. 26And wherever you live, you must not eat the blood of any bird or animal. 27If anyone eats blood, that person must be cut off from his people.' "

The Priests' Share

28The LORD said to Moses, 29"Say to the Israelites: 'Anyone who brings a fellowship offering to the LORD is to bring part of it as his sacrifice to the LORD. 30With his own hands he is to bring the offering made to the LORD by fire; he is to bring the fat, together with the breast, and wave the breast before the LORD as a wave offering. 31The priest shall burn the fat on the altar, but the breast belongs to Aaron and his sons. 32You are to give the right thigh of your fellowship offerings to the priest as a contribution. 33The son of Aaron who offers the blood and the fat of the fellowship offering shall have the right thigh as his share. 34From the fellowship offerings of the Israelites, I have taken the breast that is waved and the thigh that is presented and have given them to Aaron the priest and his sons as their regular share from the Israelites.' "

35This is the portion of the offerings made to the LORD by fire that were allotted to Aaron and his sons on the day they were presented to serve the LORD as priests. 36On the day they were anointed, the LORD commanded that the Israelites give this to them as their regular share for the generations to come.

37These, then, are the regulations for the burnt offering, the grain offering, the sin offering, the guilt offering, the ordination offering and the fellowship offering, 38which the LORD gave Moses on Mount Sinai on the day he commanded the Israelites to bring their offerings to the LORD, in the Desert of Sinai.

The Ordination of Aaron and His Sons

8 The LORD said to Moses, 2"Bring Aaron and his sons, their garments, the anointing oil, the bull for the sin offering, the two rams and the basket containing bread made without yeast, 3and gather the entire assembly at the entrance to the Tent of Meeting." 4Moses did as the LORD commanded him, and the assembly gathered at the entrance to the Tent of Meeting.

5Moses said to the assembly, "This is what the LORD has commanded to be done." 6Then Moses brought Aaron and his sons forward and washed them with water. 7He put the tunic on Aaron, tied the sash around him, clothed him with the robe and put the ephod on him. He also tied the ephod to him by its skillfully

[a]25 Or *fire is*

woven waistband; so it was fastened on him.
8He placed the breastpiece on him and put the
Urim and Thummim in the breastpiece. 9Then
he placed the turban on Aaron's head and set
the gold plate, the sacred diadem, on the front
of it, as the LORD commanded Moses.

10Then Moses took the anointing oil and
anointed the tabernacle and everything in it,
and so consecrated them. 11He sprinkled some
of the oil on the altar seven times, anointing the
altar and all its utensils and the basin with its
stand, to consecrate them. 12He poured some of
the anointing oil on Aaron's head and anointed
him to consecrate him. 13Then he brought
Aaron's sons forward, put tunics on them, tied
sashes around them and put headbands on
them, as the LORD commanded Moses.

14He then presented the bull for the sin offering, and Aaron and his sons laid their hands on
its head. 15Moses slaughtered the bull and took
some of the blood, and with his finger he put it
on all the horns of the altar to purify the altar.
He poured out the rest of the blood at the base
of the altar. So he consecrated it to make atonement for it. 16Moses also took all the fat around
the inner parts, the covering of the liver, and
both kidneys and their fat, and burned it on the
altar. 17But the bull with its hide and its flesh
and its offal he burned up outside the camp, as
the LORD commanded Moses.

18He then presented the ram for the burnt
offering, and Aaron and his sons laid their
hands on its head. 19Then Moses slaughtered
the ram and sprinkled the blood against the altar on all sides. 20He cut the ram into pieces
and burned the head, the pieces and the fat.
21He washed the inner parts and the legs with
water and burned the whole ram on the altar
as a burnt offering, a pleasing aroma, an offering made to the LORD by fire, as the LORD
commanded Moses.

22He then presented the other ram, the ram
for the ordination, and Aaron and his sons laid
their hands on its head. 23Moses slaughtered
the ram and took some of its blood and put it
on the lobe of Aaron's right ear, on the thumb
of his right hand and on the big toe of his right
foot. 24Moses also brought Aaron's sons forward and put some of the blood on the lobes
of their right ears, on the thumbs of their right
hands and on the big toes of their right feet.
Then he sprinkled blood against the altar on
all sides. 25He took the fat, the fat tail, all the
fat around the inner parts, the covering of the
liver, both kidneys and their fat and the right
thigh. 26Then from the basket of bread made
without yeast, which was before the LORD, he
took a cake of bread, and one made with oil,
and a wafer; he put these on the fat portions
and on the right thigh. 27He put all these in the
hands of Aaron and his sons and waved them
before the LORD as a wave offering. 28Then Moses took them from their hands and burned
them on the altar on top of the burnt offering
as an ordination offering, a pleasing aroma, an
offering made to the LORD by fire. 29He also
took the breast—Moses' share of the ordination
ram—and waved it before the LORD as a wave
offering, as the LORD commanded Moses.

30Then Moses took some of the anointing
oil and some of the blood from the altar and
sprinkled them on Aaron and his garments
and on his sons and their garments. So he
consecrated Aaron and his garments and his
sons and their garments.

31Moses then said to Aaron and his sons,
"Cook the meat at the entrance to the Tent
of Meeting and eat it there with the bread
from the basket of ordination offerings, as I
commanded, saying,[a] 'Aaron and his sons are
to eat it.' 32Then burn up the rest of the meat
and the bread. 33Do not leave the entrance to
the Tent of Meeting for seven days, until the
days of your ordination are completed, for
your ordination will last seven days. 34What
has been done today was commanded by the
LORD to make atonement for you. 35You must
stay at the entrance to the Tent of Meeting day
and night for seven days and do what the LORD
requires, so you will not die; for that is what
I have been commanded." 36So Aaron and his
sons did everything the LORD commanded
through Moses.

The Priests Begin Their Ministry

9 On the eighth day Moses summoned
Aaron and his sons and the elders of
Israel. 2He said to Aaron, "Take a bull calf for

[a]31 Or *I was commanded:*

your sin offering and a ram for your burnt offering, both without defect, and present them
before the LORD. 3Then say to the Israelites:
'Take a male goat for a sin offering, a calf and a
lamb—both a year old and without defect—for
a burnt offering, 4and an ox[a] and a ram for a fellowship offering[b] to sacrifice before the LORD,
together with a grain offering mixed with oil.
For today the LORD will appear to you.' "
5They took the things Moses commanded
to the front of the Tent of Meeting, and the
entire assembly came near and stood before
the LORD. 6Then Moses said, "This is what the
LORD has commanded you to do, so that the
glory of the LORD may appear to you."
7Moses said to Aaron, "Come to the altar
and sacrifice your sin offering
and your burnt offering and
make atonement for yourself
and the people; sacrifice the offering that is for the people and
make atonement for them, as
the LORD has commanded."
8So Aaron came to the altar
and slaughtered the calf as a sin
offering for himself. 9His sons
brought the blood to him, and
he dipped his finger into the
blood and put it on the horns
of the altar; the rest of the blood
he poured out at the base of the
altar. 10On the altar he burned
the fat, the kidneys and the cov-
ering of the liver from the sin offering, as the
LORD commanded Moses; 11the flesh and the
hide he burned up outside the camp.
12Then he slaughtered the burnt offering.
His sons handed him the blood, and he sprinkled it against the altar on all sides. 13They
handed him the burnt offering piece by piece,
including the head, and he burned them on the
altar. 14He washed the inner parts and the legs
and burned them on top of the burnt offering
on the altar.
15Aaron then brought the offering that was
for the people. He took the goat for the people's
sin offering and slaughtered it and offered it for
a sin offering as he did with the first one.
16He brought the burnt offering and offered
it in the prescribed way. 17He also brought the
grain offering, took a handful of it and burned
it on the altar in addition to the morning's
burnt offering.
18He slaughtered the ox and the ram as the
fellowship offering for the people. His sons
handed him the blood, and he sprinkled it
against the altar on all sides. 19But the fat portions of the ox and the ram—the fat tail, the
layer of fat, the kidneys and the covering of
the liver— 20these they laid on the breasts,
and then Aaron burned the fat on the altar.
21Aaron waved the breasts and the right thigh
before the LORD as a wave offering, as Moses
commanded.
22Then Aaron lifted his hands toward the
people and blessed them. And
having sacrificed the sin offering, the burnt offering and
the fellowship offering, he
stepped down.
23Moses and Aaron then
went into the Tent of Meeting.
When they came out, they
blessed the people; and the
glory of the LORD appeared to
all the people. 24Fire came out
from the presence of the LORD
and consumed the burnt offering and the fat portions on the
altar. And when all the people
saw it, they shouted for joy and
fell facedown.

Leviticus 9:24

God Inspires Awe

Fire came out from the presence of the LORD and consumed the burnt offering and the fat portions on the altar. And when all the people saw it, they shouted for joy and fell facedown.

The Death of Nadab and Abihu

10 Aaron's sons Nadab and Abihu took
their censers, put fire in them and
added incense; and they offered unauthorized
fire before the LORD, contrary to his command.
2So fire came out from the presence of the LORD
and consumed them, and they died before the
LORD. 3Moses then said to Aaron, "This is what
the LORD spoke of when he said:

" 'Among those who approach me
I will show myself holy;
in the sight of all the people
I will be honored.' "

Aaron remained silent.

[a]4 The Hebrew word can include both male and female; also in verses 18 and 19. [b]4 Traditionally *peace offering*; also in verses 18 and 22

Leviticus 10:2–3

So fire came out from the presence of the LORD and consumed them, and they died before the LORD. Moses then said to Aaron, "This is what the LORD spoke of when he said: 'Among those who approach me I will show myself holy; in the sight of all the people I will be honored.'" Aaron remained silent.

reflection

1 What was the last command God gave you through his Word?

2 Did you obey or disobey?

3 How did your actions honor or dishonor God? If you disobeyed, what can you do to set things right, right now?

RELATED READINGS

Isaiah 55:8–9; Hebrews 12:14; 1 Peter 2:4–9

"Holiness does not consist in doing extraordinary things. It consists in accepting, with a smile, what Jesus sends us. It consists in accepting and following the will of God."

Mother Teresa

Holy Fire

Read: Leviticus 10:1–3

YOU ARRIVE AT A DINNER PARTY, bottle of wine in hand, and your hostess meets you at the door with a scowl. You knew they didn't drink, but chalked it up to conservatism and thought a little loosening up was in order. You didn't know your friend's husband had struggled with a drinking problem for years. You had good intentions, but sometimes good intentions aren't good enough.

We can't always see the reasons for God's requirements, any more than we can divine the motivations of our friends. Nadab and Abihu might have assumed a good intention would find favor equal to obedience; perhaps God would even reward them for their ingenuity. As high priest, Aaron made the burnt offering decreed by God. Then, perhaps caught up in the enthusiasm of the moment, Nadab and Abihu offered their own "unauthorized fire." The sacrifice had already been offered. God's glory had appeared. Nadab and Abihu presumptuously tried to add to God's decree for sacrifice. The result? Instant death. Verse 3 takes us to the heart of the matter: The closer we come to God, the more we must honor his holiness by obeying his commands.

As women, we face numerous opportunities to second-guess God. We justify detours from God's will by believing we're following the spirit of the law in our own creative way. The double-edged sword of ingenuity gets us into trouble. In this age of grace, such an exacting standard may seem harsh. But God's ways are not our ways. His holiness surpasses our comprehension. He is just, while we only seek justice. He has intentions for us that we cannot, with our finite minds, grasp. That's why obedience to God and what his Word tells us is crucial. Obedience shows God we consider him holy and worthy of honor.

How can you honor God daily? When God says something to you in his Word, take it personally. Reading the passage on honoring your husband or taming the tongue doesn't fulfill your obligation; your actions reflect your heart toward God. Obedience honors God. Disobedience dishonors him. The practice of obedience will align your heart with God's own desire. For "just as he who called you is holy, so be holy in all you do; for it is written: 'Be holy, because I am holy'" (1 Peter 1:15–16).

Go to page 139 for your next devotional reading.

4Moses summoned Mishael and Elzaphan,
sons of Aaron's uncle Uzziel, and said to them,
"Come here; carry your cousins outside the
camp, away from the front of the sanctuary."
5So they came and carried them, still in their
tunics, outside the camp, as Moses ordered.
6Then Moses said to Aaron and his sons
Eleazar and Ithamar, "Do not let your hair become unkempt,[a] and do not tear your clothes,
or you will die and the LORD will be angry with
the whole community. But your relatives, all
the house of Israel, may mourn for those the
LORD has destroyed by fire. 7Do not leave the
entrance to the Tent of Meeting or you will die,
because the LORD's anointing oil is on you." So
they did as Moses said.
8Then the LORD said to Aaron, 9"You and
your sons are not to drink wine or other
fermented drink whenever you go into the
Tent of Meeting, or you will die. This is a lasting
ordinance for the generations to come. 10You
must distinguish between the holy and the common, between the unclean and the clean, 11and
you must teach the Israelites all the decrees the
LORD has given them through Moses."
12Moses said to Aaron and his remaining
sons, Eleazar and Ithamar, "Take the grain offering left over from the offerings made to the
LORD by fire and eat it prepared without yeast
beside the altar, for it is most holy. 13Eat it in
a holy place, because it is your share and your
sons' share of the offerings made to the LORD
by fire; for so I have been commanded. 14But
you and your sons and your daughters may eat
the breast that was waved and the thigh that
was presented. Eat them in a ceremonially
clean place; they have been given to you and
your children as your share of the Israelites'
fellowship offerings.[b] 15The thigh that was
presented and the breast that was waved must
be brought with the fat portions of the offerings
made by fire, to be waved before the LORD as
a wave offering. This will be the regular share
for you and your children, as the LORD has
commanded."
16When Moses inquired about the goat of
the sin offering and found that it had been
burned up, he was angry with Eleazar and
Ithamar, Aaron's remaining sons, and asked,
17"Why didn't you eat the sin offering in the
sanctuary area? It is most holy; it was given to
you to take away the guilt of the community by
making atonement for them before the LORD.
18Since its blood was not taken into the Holy
Place, you should have eaten the goat in the
sanctuary area, as I commanded."
19Aaron replied to Moses, "Today they sacrificed their sin offering and their burnt offering
before the LORD, but such things as this have
happened to me. Would the LORD have been
pleased if I had eaten the sin offering today?"
20When Moses heard this, he was satisfied.

Clean and Unclean Food

11 The LORD said to Moses and Aaron,
2"Say to the Israelites: 'Of all the animals that live on land, these are the ones you
may eat: 3You may eat any animal that has a
split hoof completely divided and that chews
the cud.
4" 'There are some that only chew the cud
or only have a split hoof, but you must not eat
them. The camel, though it chews the cud, does
not have a split hoof; it is ceremonially unclean
for you. 5The coney,[c] though it chews the cud,
does not have a split hoof; it is unclean for you.
6The rabbit, though it chews the cud, does not
have a split hoof; it is unclean for you. 7And
the pig, though it has a split hoof completely
divided, does not chew the cud; it is unclean
for you. 8You must not eat their meat or touch
their carcasses; they are unclean for you.
9" 'Of all the creatures living in the water
of the seas and the streams, you may eat any
that have fins and scales. 10But all creatures
in the seas or streams that do not have fins
and scales—whether among all the swarming
things or among all the other living creatures in
the water—you are to detest. 11And since you
are to detest them, you must not eat their meat
and you must detest their carcasses. 12Any-
thing living in the water that does not have fins
and scales is to be detestable to you.
13" 'These are the birds you are to detest and
not eat because they are detestable: the eagle,
the vulture, the black vulture, 14the red kite,
any kind of black kite, 15any kind of raven,
16the horned owl, the screech owl, the gull, any

[a]6 Or *Do not uncover your heads* [b]14 Traditionally *peace offerings* [c]5 That is, the hyrax or rock badger

kind of hawk, 17the little owl, the cormorant, the great owl, 18the white owl, the desert owl, the osprey, 19the stork, any kind of heron, the hoopoe and the bat.[a]

20" 'All flying insects that walk on all fours are to be detestable to you. 21There are, however, some winged creatures that walk on all fours that you may eat: those that have jointed legs for hopping on the ground. 22Of these you may eat any kind of locust, katydid, cricket or grasshopper. 23But all other winged creatures that have four legs you are to detest.

24" 'You will make yourselves unclean by these; whoever touches their carcasses will be unclean till evening. 25Whoever picks up one of their carcasses must wash his clothes, and he will be unclean till evening.

26" 'Every animal that has a split hoof not completely divided or that does not chew the cud is unclean for you; whoever touches ⌊the carcass of⌋ any of them will be unclean. 27Of all the animals that walk on all fours, those that walk on their paws are unclean for you; whoever touches their carcasses will be unclean till evening. 28Anyone who picks up their carcasses must wash his clothes, and he will be unclean till evening. They are unclean for you.

29" 'Of the animals that move about on the ground, these are unclean for you: the weasel, the rat, any kind of great lizard, 30the gecko, the monitor lizard, the wall lizard, the skink and the chameleon. 31Of all those that move along the ground, these are unclean for you. Whoever touches them when they are dead will be unclean till evening. 32When one of them dies and falls on something, that article, whatever its use, will be unclean, whether it is made of wood, cloth, hide or sackcloth. Put it in water; it will be unclean till evening, and then it will be clean. 33If one of them falls into a clay pot, everything in it will be unclean, and you must break the pot. 34Any food that could be eaten but has water on it from such a pot is unclean, and any liquid that could be drunk from it is unclean. 35Anything that one of their carcasses falls on becomes unclean; an oven or cooking pot must be broken up. They are unclean, and you are to regard them as unclean. 36A spring, however, or a cistern for collecting water remains clean, but anyone who touches one of these carcasses is unclean. 37If a carcass falls on any seeds that are to be planted, they remain clean. 38But if water has been put on the seed and a carcass falls on it, it is unclean for you.

39" 'If an animal that you are allowed to eat dies, anyone who touches the carcass will be unclean till evening. 40Anyone who eats some of the carcass must wash his clothes, and he will be unclean till evening. Anyone who picks up the carcass must wash his clothes, and he will be unclean till evening.

41" 'Every creature that moves about on the ground is detestable; it is not to be eaten. 42You are not to eat any creature that moves about on the ground, whether it moves on its belly or walks on all fours or on many feet; it is detestable. 43Do not defile yourselves by any of these creatures. Do not make yourselves unclean by means of them or be made unclean by them. 44I am the LORD your God; consecrate yourselves and be holy, because I am holy. Do not make yourselves unclean by any creature that moves about on the ground. 45I am the LORD who brought you up out of Egypt to be your God; therefore be holy, because I am holy.

46" 'These are the regulations concerning animals, birds, every living thing that moves in the water and every creature that moves about on the ground. 47You must distinguish between the unclean and the clean, between living creatures that may be eaten and those that may not be eaten.' "

Leviticus 11:45

God Is Holy

"I am the LORD who brought you up out of Egypt to be your God; therefore be holy, because I am holy."

Purification After Childbirth

12 The LORD said to Moses, 2"Say to the Israelites: 'A woman who becomes pregnant and gives birth to a son will be ceremonially unclean for seven days, just as she

[a]19 The precise identification of some of the birds, insects and animals in this chapter is uncertain.

is unclean during her monthly period. 3On the
eighth day the boy is to be circumcised. 4Then
the woman must wait thirty-three days to be
purified from her bleeding. She must not touch
anything sacred or go to the sanctuary until the
days of her purification are over. 5If she gives
birth to a daughter, for two weeks the woman
will be unclean, as during her period. Then she
must wait sixty-six days to be purified from
her bleeding.
6" 'When the days of her purification for a
son or daughter are over, she is to bring to the
priest at the entrance to the Tent of Meeting a
year-old lamb for a burnt offering and a young
pigeon or a dove for a sin offering. 7He shall offer them before the LORD to make atonement
for her, and then she will be ceremonially clean
from her flow of blood.
" 'These are the regulations for the woman
who gives birth to a boy or a girl. 8If she cannot afford a lamb, she is to bring two doves or
two young pigeons, one for a burnt offering
and the other for a sin offering. In this way the
priest will make atonement for her, and she will
be clean.' "

Regulations About Infectious Skin Diseases

13 The LORD said to Moses and Aaron,
2"When anyone has a swelling or a rash
or a bright spot on his skin that may become an
infectious skin disease,[a] he must be brought to
Aaron the priest or to one of his sons[b] who is
a priest. 3The priest is to examine the sore on
his skin, and if the hair in the sore has turned
white and the sore appears to be more than skin
deep,[c] it is an infectious skin disease. When the
priest examines him, he shall pronounce him
ceremonially unclean. 4If the spot on his skin is
white but does not appear to be more than skin
deep and the hair in it has not turned white, the
priest is to put the infected person in isolation
for seven days. 5On the seventh day the priest
is to examine him, and if he sees that the sore
is unchanged and has not spread in the skin, he
is to keep him in isolation another seven days.
6On the seventh day the priest is to examine
him again, and if the sore has faded and has not
spread in the skin, the priest shall pronounce
him clean; it is only a rash. The man must wash
his clothes, and he will be clean. 7But if the rash
does spread in his skin after he has shown himself to the priest to be pronounced clean, he
must appear before the priest again. 8The priest
is to examine him, and if the rash has spread in
the skin, he shall pronounce him unclean; it is
an infectious disease.
9"When anyone has an infectious skin disease, he must be brought to the priest. 10The
priest is to examine him, and if there is a white
swelling in the skin that has turned the hair
white and if there is raw flesh in the swelling,
11it is a chronic skin disease and the priest shall
pronounce him unclean. He is not to put him
in isolation, because he is already unclean.
12"If the disease breaks out all over his skin
and, so far as the priest can see, it covers all the
skin of the infected person from head to foot,
13the priest is to examine him, and if the disease
has covered his whole body, he shall pronounce
that person clean. Since it has all turned white,
he is clean. 14But whenever raw flesh appears
on him, he will be unclean. 15When the priest
sees the raw flesh, he shall pronounce him unclean. The raw flesh is unclean; he has an infectious disease. 16Should the raw flesh change
and turn white, he must go to the priest. 17The
priest is to examine him, and if the sores have
turned white, the priest shall pronounce the
infected person clean; then he will be clean.
18"When someone has a boil on his skin
and it heals, 19and in the place where the boil
was, a white swelling or reddish-white spot appears, he must present himself to the priest.
20The priest is to examine it, and if it appears
to be more than skin deep and the hair in it has
turned white, the priest shall pronounce him
unclean. It is an infectious skin disease that has
broken out where the boil was. 21But if, when
the priest examines it, there is no white hair in
it and it is not more than skin deep and has
faded, then the priest is to put him in isolation
for seven days. 22If it is spreading in the skin,
the priest shall pronounce him unclean; it is infectious. 23But if the spot is unchanged and has
not spread, it is only a scar from the boil, and
the priest shall pronounce him clean.
24"When someone has a burn on his skin

[a]2 Traditionally *leprosy*; the Hebrew word was used for various diseases affecting the skin—not necessarily leprosy; also elsewhere in this chapter. [b]2 Or *descendants* [c]3 Or *be lower than the rest of the skin*; also elsewhere in this chapter

and a reddish-white or white spot appears in
the raw flesh of the burn, 25the priest is to examine the spot, and if the hair in it has turned
white, and it appears to be more than skin deep,
it is an infectious disease that has broken out in
the burn. The priest shall pronounce him unclean; it is an infectious skin disease. 26But if
the priest examines it and there is no white hair
in the spot and if it is not more than skin deep
and has faded, then the priest is to put him in
isolation for seven days. 27On the seventh day
the priest is to examine him, and if it is spreading in the skin, the priest shall pronounce him
unclean; it is an infectious skin disease. 28If,
however, the spot is unchanged and has not
spread in the skin but has faded, it is a swelling
from the burn, and the priest shall pronounce
him clean; it is only a scar from the burn.

29"If a man or woman has a sore on the head
or on the chin, 30the priest is to examine the
sore, and if it appears to be more than skin
deep and the hair in it is yellow and thin, the
priest shall pronounce that person unclean; it
is an itch, an infectious disease of the head or
chin. 31But if, when the priest examines this
kind of sore, it does not seem to be more than
skin deep and there is no black hair in it, then
the priest is to put the infected person in isolation for seven days. 32On the seventh day the
priest is to examine the sore, and if the itch has
not spread and there is no yellow hair in it and
it does not appear to be more than skin deep,
33he must be shaved except for the diseased
area, and the priest is to keep him in isolation
another seven days. 34On the seventh day the
priest is to examine the itch, and if it has not
spread in the skin and appears to be no more
than skin deep, the priest shall pronounce him
clean. He must wash his clothes, and he will be
clean. 35But if the itch does spread in the skin
after he is pronounced clean, 36the priest is to
examine him, and if the itch has spread in the
skin, the priest does not need to look for yellow
hair; the person is unclean. 37If, however, in his
judgment it is unchanged and black hair has
grown in it, the itch is healed. He is clean, and
the priest shall pronounce him clean.

38"When a man or woman has white spots
on the skin, 39the priest is to examine them,
and if the spots are dull white, it is a harmless
rash that has broken out on the skin; that person is clean.

40"When a man has lost his hair and is bald,
he is clean. 41If he has lost his hair from the
front of his scalp and has a bald forehead, he
is clean. 42But if he has a reddish-white sore
on his bald head or forehead, it is an infectious
disease breaking out on his head or forehead.
43The priest is to examine him, and if the swollen sore on his head or forehead is reddish-
white like an infectious skin disease, 44the
man is diseased and is unclean. The priest shall
pronounce him unclean because of the sore on
his head.

45"The person with such an infectious disease must wear torn clothes, let his hair be unkempt,[a] cover the lower part of his face and cry
out, 'Unclean! Unclean!' 46As long as he has
the infection he remains unclean. He must live
alone; he must live outside the camp.

Regulations About Mildew

47"If any clothing is contaminated with mildew—any woolen or linen clothing, 48any woven or knitted material of linen or wool, any
leather or anything made of leather— 49and if
the contamination in the clothing, or leather,
or woven or knitted material, or any leather
article, is greenish or reddish, it is a spreading
mildew and must be shown to the priest. 50The
priest is to examine the mildew and isolate the
affected article for seven days. 51On the seventh day he is to examine it, and if the mildew
has spread in the clothing, or the woven or knitted material, or the leather, whatever its use, it
is a destructive mildew; the article is unclean.
52He must burn up the clothing, or the woven
or knitted material of wool or linen, or any
leather article that has the contamination in it,
because the mildew is destructive; the article
must be burned up.

53"But if, when the priest examines it, the
mildew has not spread in the clothing, or the
woven or knitted material, or the leather article, 54he shall order that the contaminated
article be washed. Then he is to isolate it for
another seven days. 55After the affected article has been washed, the priest is to examine

[a]45 Or *clothes, uncover his head*

it, and if the mildew has not changed its appearance, even though it has not spread, it is
unclean. Burn it with fire, whether the mildew
has affected one side or the other. 56If, when
the priest examines it, the mildew has faded after the article has been washed, he is to tear the
contaminated part out of the clothing, or the
leather, or the woven or knitted material. 57But
if it reappears in the clothing, or in the woven
or knitted material, or in the leather article, it is
spreading, and whatever has the mildew must
be burned with fire. 58The clothing, or the woven or knitted material, or any leather article
that has been washed and is rid of the mildew,
must be washed again, and it will be clean."

59These are the regulations concerning
contamination by mildew in woolen or linen
clothing, woven or knitted material, or any
leather article, for pronouncing them clean or
unclean.

Cleansing From Infectious Skin Diseases

14 The LORD said to Moses, 2"These are
the regulations for the diseased person
at the time of his ceremonial cleansing, when he
is brought to the priest: 3The priest is to go outside the camp and examine him. If the person
has been healed of his infectious skin disease,[a]
4the priest shall order that two live clean birds
and some cedar wood, scarlet yarn and hyssop
be brought for the one to be cleansed. 5Then
the priest shall order that one of the birds be
killed over fresh water in a clay pot. 6He is then
to take the live bird and dip it, together with the
cedar wood, the scarlet yarn and the hyssop,
into the blood of the bird that was killed over
the fresh water. 7Seven times he shall sprinkle
the one to be cleansed of the infectious disease
and pronounce him clean. Then he is to release
the live bird in the open fields.

8"The person to be cleansed must wash his
clothes, shave off all his hair and bathe with water; then he will be ceremonially clean. After
this he may come into the camp, but he must
stay outside his tent for seven days. 9On the
seventh day he must shave off all his hair; he
must shave his head, his beard, his eyebrows
and the rest of his hair. He must wash his
clothes and bathe himself with water, and he
will be clean.

10"On the eighth day he must bring two
male lambs and one ewe lamb a year old, each
without defect, along with three-tenths of an
ephah[b] of fine flour mixed with oil for a grain
offering, and one log[c] of oil. 11The priest who
pronounces him clean shall present both the
one to be cleansed and his offerings before the
LORD at the entrance to the Tent of Meeting.

12"Then the priest is to take one of the male
lambs and offer it as a guilt offering, along with
the log of oil; he shall wave them before the
LORD as a wave offering. 13He is to slaughter
the lamb in the holy place where the sin offering and the burnt offering are slaughtered.
Like the sin offering, the guilt offering belongs
to the priest; it is most holy. 14The priest is to
take some of the blood of the guilt offering and
put it on the lobe of the right ear of the one
to be cleansed, on the thumb of his right hand
and on the big toe of his right foot. 15The priest
shall then take some of the log of oil, pour it in
the palm of his own left hand, 16dip his right
forefinger into the oil in his palm, and with his
finger sprinkle some of it before the LORD seven
times. 17The priest is to put some of the oil remaining in his palm on the lobe of the right ear
of the one to be cleansed, on the thumb of his
right hand and on the big toe of his right foot,
on top of the blood of the guilt offering. 18The
rest of the oil in his palm the priest shall put on
the head of the one to be cleansed and make
atonement for him before the LORD.

19"Then the priest is to sacrifice the sin offering and make atonement for the one to be
cleansed from his uncleanness. After that, the
priest shall slaughter the burnt offering 20and
offer it on the altar, together with the grain offering, and make atonement for him, and he
will be clean.

21"If, however, he is poor and cannot afford
these, he must take one male lamb as a guilt
offering to be waved to make atonement for
him, together with a tenth of an ephah[d] of fine
flour mixed with oil for a grain offering, a log
of oil, 22and two doves or two young pigeons,

[a]3 Traditionally *leprosy*; the Hebrew word was used for various diseases affecting the skin—not necessarily leprosy; also elsewhere in this chapter. [b]10 That is, probably about 6 quarts (about 6.5 liters) [c]10 That is, probably about 2/3 pint (about 0.3 liter); also in verses 12, 15, 21 and 24 [d]21 That is, probably about 2 quarts (about 2 liters)

which he can afford, one for a sin offering and
the other for a burnt offering.
23“On the eighth day he must bring them
for his cleansing to the priest at the entrance
to the Tent of Meeting, before the LORD. 24The
priest is to take the lamb for the guilt offering,
together with the log of oil, and wave them
before the LORD as a wave offering. 25He shall
slaughter the lamb for the guilt offering and
take some of its blood and put it on the lobe
of the right ear of the one to be cleansed, on
the thumb of his right hand and on the big toe
of his right foot. 26The priest is to pour some
of the oil into the palm of his own left hand,
27and with his right forefinger sprinkle some
of the oil from his palm seven times before
the LORD. 28Some of the oil in his palm he
is to put on the same places he put the blood
of the guilt offering—on the lobe of the right
ear of the one to be cleansed, on the thumb
of his right hand and on the big toe of his
right foot. 29The rest of the oil in his palm the
priest shall put on the head of the one to be
cleansed, to make atonement for him before
the LORD. 30Then he shall sacrifice the doves
or the young pigeons, which the person can
afford, 31one[a] as a sin offering and the other
as a burnt offering, together with the grain offering. In this way the priest will make atonement before the LORD on behalf of the one to
be cleansed.”
32These are the regulations for anyone who
has an infectious skin disease and who cannot
afford the regular offerings for his cleansing.

Cleansing From Mildew

33The LORD said to Moses and Aaron,
34“When you enter the land of Canaan, which
I am giving you as your possession, and I put a
spreading mildew in a house in that land, 35the
owner of the house must go and tell the priest,
‘I have seen something that looks like mildew
in my house.’ 36The priest is to order the house
to be emptied before he goes in to examine the
mildew, so that nothing in the house will be
pronounced unclean. After this the priest is to
go in and inspect the house. 37He is to examine
the mildew on the walls, and if it has greenish
or reddish depressions that appear to be deeper
than the surface of the wall, 38the priest shall
go out the doorway of the house and close it
up for seven days. 39On the seventh day the
priest shall return to inspect the house. If the
mildew has spread on the walls, 40he is to order that the contaminated stones be torn out
and thrown into an unclean place outside the
town. 41He must have all the inside walls of the
house scraped and the material that is scraped
off dumped into an unclean place outside the
town. 42Then they are to take other stones to
replace these and take new clay and plaster
the house.
43“If the mildew reappears in the house after
the stones have been torn out and the house
scraped and plastered, 44the priest is to go and
examine it and, if the mildew has spread in the
house, it is a destructive mildew; the house is
unclean. 45It must be torn down—its stones,
timbers and all the plaster—and taken out of
the town to an unclean place.
46“Anyone who goes into the house while it
is closed up will be unclean till evening. 47Any-
one who sleeps or eats in the house must wash
his clothes.
48“But if the priest comes to examine it and
the mildew has not spread after the house has
been plastered, he shall pronounce the house
clean, because the mildew is gone. 49To purify
the house he is to take two birds and some cedar
wood, scarlet yarn and hyssop. 50He shall kill
one of the birds over fresh water in a clay pot.
51Then he is to take the cedar wood, the hyssop,
the scarlet yarn and the live bird, dip them into
the blood of the dead bird and the fresh water,
and sprinkle the house seven times. 52He shall
purify the house with the bird’s blood, the fresh
water, the live bird, the cedar wood, the hyssop
and the scarlet yarn. 53Then he is to release the
live bird in the open fields outside the town. In
this way he will make atonement for the house,
and it will be clean.”
54These are the regulations for any infectious
skin disease, for an itch, 55for mildew in clothing or in a house, 56and for a swelling, a rash or
a bright spot, 57to determine when something
is clean or unclean.
These are the regulations for infectious skin
diseases and mildew.

[a]31 Septuagint and Syriac; Hebrew 31 *such as the person can afford, one*

Discharges Causing Uncleanness

15 The LORD said to Moses and Aaron, 2“Speak to the Israelites and say to them: ‘When any man has a bodily discharge, the discharge is unclean. 3Whether it continues flowing from his body or is blocked, it will make him unclean. This is how his discharge will bring about uncleanness:

4“ ‘Any bed the man with a discharge lies on will be unclean, and anything he sits on will be unclean. 5Anyone who touches his bed must wash his clothes and bathe with water, and he will be unclean till evening. 6Whoever sits on anything that the man with a discharge sat on must wash his clothes and bathe with water, and he will be unclean till evening.

7“ ‘Whoever touches the man who has a discharge must wash his clothes and bathe with water, and he will be unclean till evening.

8“ ‘If the man with the discharge spits on someone who is clean, that person must wash his clothes and bathe with water, and he will be unclean till evening.

9“ ‘Everything the man sits on when riding will be unclean, 10and whoever touches any of the things that were under him will be unclean till evening; whoever picks up those things must wash his clothes and bathe with water, and he will be unclean till evening.

11“ ‘Anyone the man with a discharge touches without rinsing his hands with water must wash his clothes and bathe with water, and he will be unclean till evening.

12“ ‘A clay pot that the man touches must be broken, and any wooden article is to be rinsed with water.

13“ ‘When a man is cleansed from his discharge, he is to count off seven days for his ceremonial cleansing; he must wash his clothes and bathe himself with fresh water, and he will be clean. 14On the eighth day he must take two doves or two young pigeons and come before the LORD to the entrance to the Tent of Meeting and give them to the priest. 15The priest is to sacrifice them, the one for a sin offering and the other for a burnt offering. In this way he will make atonement before the LORD for the man because of his discharge.

16“ ‘When a man has an emission of semen, he must bathe his whole body with water, and he will be unclean till evening. 17Any clothing or leather that has semen on it must be washed with water, and it will be unclean till evening. 18When a man lies with a woman and there is an emission of semen, both must bathe with water, and they will be unclean till evening.

19“ ‘When a woman has her regular flow of blood, the impurity of her monthly period will last seven days, and anyone who touches her will be unclean till evening.

20“ ‘Anything she lies on during her period will be unclean, and anything she sits on will be unclean. 21Whoever touches her bed must wash his clothes and bathe with water, and he will be unclean till evening. 22Whoever touches anything she sits on must wash his clothes and bathe with water, and he will be unclean till evening. 23Whether it is the bed or anything she was sitting on, when anyone touches it, he will be unclean till evening.

24“ ‘If a man lies with her and her monthly flow touches him, he will be unclean for seven days; any bed he lies on will be unclean.

25“ ‘When a woman has a discharge of blood for many days at a time other than her monthly period or has a discharge that continues beyond her period, she will be unclean as long as she has the discharge, just as in the days of her period. 26Any bed she lies on while her discharge continues will be unclean, as is her bed during her monthly period, and anything she sits on will be unclean, as during her period. 27Whoever touches them will be unclean; he must wash his clothes and bathe with water, and he will be unclean till evening.

28“ ‘When she is cleansed from her discharge, she must count off seven days, and after that she will be ceremonially clean. 29On the eighth day she must take two doves or two young pigeons and bring them to the priest at the entrance to the Tent of Meeting. 30The priest is to sacrifice one for a sin offering and the other for a burnt offering. In this way he will make atonement for her before the LORD for the uncleanness of her discharge.

31“ ‘You must keep the Israelites separate from things that make them unclean, so they

will not die in their uncleanness for defiling my
dwelling place,[a] which is among them.' "
32These are the regulations for a man with a
discharge, for anyone made unclean by an emission of semen, 33for a woman in her monthly
period, for a man or a woman with a discharge,
and for a man who lies with a woman who is
ceremonially unclean.

The Day of Atonement

16 The LORD spoke to Moses after the
death of the two sons of Aaron who
died when they approached the LORD. 2The
LORD said to Moses: "Tell your brother Aaron
not to come whenever he chooses into the
Most Holy Place behind the curtain in front
of the atonement cover on the ark, or else he
will die, because I appear in the cloud over the
atonement cover.
3"This is how Aaron is to enter the sanctuary area: with a young bull for a sin offering
and a ram for a burnt offering. 4He is to put
on the sacred linen tunic, with linen undergarments next to his body; he is to tie the linen
sash around him and put on the linen turban.
These are sacred garments; so he must bathe
himself with water before he puts them on.
5From the Israelite community he is to take
two male goats for a sin offering and a ram for
a burnt offering.
6"Aaron is to offer the bull for his own sin
offering to make atonement for himself and his
household. 7Then he is to take the two goats
and present them before the LORD at the entrance to the Tent of Meeting. 8He is to cast lots
for the two goats—one lot for the LORD and the
other for the scapegoat.[b] 9Aaron shall bring the
goat whose lot falls to the LORD and sacrifice it
for a sin offering. 10But the goat chosen by lot
as the scapegoat shall be presented alive before
the LORD to be used for making atonement by
sending it into the desert as a scapegoat.
11"Aaron shall bring the bull for his own sin
offering to make atonement for himself and
his household, and he is to slaughter the bull
for his own sin offering. 12He is to take a censer full of burning coals from the altar before
the LORD and two handfuls of finely ground
fragrant incense and take them behind the
curtain. 13He is to put the incense on the fire
before the LORD, and the smoke of the incense
will conceal the atonement cover above the
Testimony, so that he will not die. 14He is to
take some of the bull's blood and with his finger
sprinkle it on the front of the atonement cover;
then he shall sprinkle some of it with his finger
seven times before the atonement cover.
15"He shall then slaughter the goat for the
sin offering for the people and take its blood
behind the curtain and do with it as he did with
the bull's blood: He shall sprinkle it on the atonement cover and in front of it. 16In this way he
will make atonement for the Most Holy Place
because of the uncleanness and rebellion of the
Israelites, whatever their sins have been. He is
to do the same for the Tent of Meeting, which is
among them in the midst of their uncleanness.
17No one is to be in the Tent of Meeting from
the time Aaron goes in to make atonement in
the Most Holy Place until he comes out, having made atonement for himself, his household
and the whole community of Israel.
18"Then he shall come out to the altar that is
before the LORD and make atonement for it. He
shall take some of the bull's blood and some of
the goat's blood and put it on all the horns of
the altar. 19He shall sprinkle some of the blood
on it with his finger seven times to cleanse it
and to consecrate it from the uncleanness of
the Israelites.
20"When Aaron has finished making atonement for the Most Holy Place, the Tent of Meeting and the altar, he shall bring forward the live
goat. 21He is to lay both hands on the head of
the live goat and confess over it all the wickedness and rebellion of the Israelites—all their
sins—and put them on the goat's head. He shall
send the goat away into the desert in the care
of a man appointed for the task. 22The goat will
carry on itself all their sins to a solitary place;
and the man shall release it in the desert.
23"Then Aaron is to go into the Tent of Meeting and take off the linen garments he put on
before he entered the Most Holy Place, and he
is to leave them there. 24He shall bathe himself
with water in a holy place and put on his regular garments. Then he shall come out and sacrifice the burnt offering for himself and the burnt
offering for the people, to make atonement for

[a]31 Or *my tabernacle* [b]8 That is, the goat of removal; Hebrew *azazel*; also in verses 10 and 26

Once and for All

Read: Leviticus 16:10,20–22

IN A DUSTY, DESERT WASTELAND, a man slowly unties a rope from the goat's neck. His fingers trace the dried blood on the goat's forehead, where a few hours before the priest had laid his hands. The transfer of sin is complete. All that remains is for it to be far removed from sight.

The man slaps the animal's rump and it jumps. It runs a few paces, then stops and looks back. "Go on," the man yells. "Run. Run away!" He claps his hands. He chases the goat. And it runs. But it keeps looking back, hesitating, waiting and wondering if the man will change his mind.

But the man doesn't change his mind—he can't. When he is sure the goat has gone far enough, he turns to leave. He makes the dusty journey back alone, without the sound of trotting hooves or bleating to keep him company. The sin of the Israelites has been temporarily atoned for, sent away on the head of the goat that was left in the desert.

The Day of Atonement was Israel's most solemn holy day. On that day, God made a way for his sinful people to set things right with him, the Holy One of Israel. But like the scapegoat that kept looking back, sin and guilt always returned. Year after year, goat after goat, the ritual was repeated: One goat slaughtered to atone for sin, the other sent far into the desert to remove the presence of guilt. But it wasn't enough. It merely symbolized what was to come.

When Jesus died on the cross and was banished to the tomb, he fulfilled the requirement for the two goats on the Day of Atonement. His sacrificial death on the cross atoned for our sin, finally making us one with God for all time. His journey to death removed our guilt for all time. He took our sins with him to the pit of hell, just as the scapegoat was banished into the solitary wasteland.

It was a high price to pay. The scapegoat didn't have a choice, but Jesus did. He chose to die because of his unfathomable love for us. "This is how we know what love is: Jesus Christ laid down his life for us" (1 John 3:16).

Go to page 144 for your next devotional reading.

Leviticus 16:22

"The goat will carry on itself all their sins to a solitary place; and the man shall release it in the desert."

reflection

1 What do the images of the sacrificial goat and scapegoat tell you about the high price of sin?

2 What does the image of the scapegoat reveal about how far Christ was willing to go for you?

3 What guilt are you holding onto? Speak it out loud to Jesus today and ask his forgiveness so he can carry it far away, never to be seen again.

RELATED READINGS

Psalm 103:11–12; Isaiah 53:3–6; Hebrews 10:1–18

himself and for the people. 25He shall also burn
the fat of the sin offering on the altar.
26"The man who releases the goat as a scapegoat must wash his clothes and bathe himself
with water; afterward he may come into the
camp. 27The bull and the goat for the sin offerings, whose blood was brought into the Most
Holy Place to make atonement, must be taken
outside the camp; their hides, flesh and offal are
to be burned up. 28The man who burns them
must wash his clothes and bathe himself with
water; afterward he may come into the camp.
29"This is to be a lasting ordinance for you:
On the tenth day of the seventh month you
must deny yourselves[a] and not do any work—
whether native-born or an alien living among
you— 30because on this day atonement will be
made for you, to cleanse you. Then, before the
LORD, you will be clean from all your sins. 31It
is a sabbath of rest, and you must deny yourselves; it is a lasting ordinance. 32The priest
who is anointed and ordained
to succeed his father as high
priest is to make atonement.
He is to put on the sacred linen
garments 33and make atonement for the Most Holy Place,
for the Tent of Meeting and the
altar, and for the priests and all
the people of the community.
34"This is to be a lasting ordinance for you: Atonement is to
be made once a year for all the
sins of the Israelites."
And it was done, as the LORD
commanded Moses.

Eating Blood Forbidden

17 The LORD said to Moses, 2"Speak to
Aaron and his sons and to all the Israelites and say to them: 'This is what the LORD
has commanded: 3Any Israelite who sacrifices
an ox,[b] a lamb or a goat in the camp or outside
of it 4instead of bringing it to the entrance to
the Tent of Meeting to present it as an offering
to the LORD in front of the tabernacle of the
LORD—that man shall be considered guilty of
bloodshed; he has shed blood and must be cut
off from his people. 5This is so the Israelites will
bring to the LORD the sacrifices they are now
making in the open fields. They must bring
them to the priest, that is, to the LORD, at the
entrance to the Tent of Meeting and sacrifice
them as fellowship offerings.[c] 6The priest is to
sprinkle the blood against the altar of the LORD
at the entrance to the Tent of Meeting and burn
the fat as an aroma pleasing to the LORD. 7They
must no longer offer any of their sacrifices to
the goat idols[d] to whom they prostitute themselves. This is to be a lasting ordinance for them
and for the generations to come.'
8"Say to them: 'Any Israelite or any alien
living among them who offers a burnt offering or sacrifice 9and does not bring it to the
entrance to the Tent of Meeting to sacrifice it
to the LORD—that man must be cut off from
his people.
10" 'Any Israelite or any alien living among
them who eats any blood—I will set my face
against that person who eats
blood and will cut him off
from his people. 11For the life
of a creature is in the blood,
and I have given it to you to
make atonement for yourselves
on the altar; it is the blood that
makes atonement for one's life.
12Therefore I say to the Israelites, "None of you may eat
blood, nor may an alien living
among you eat blood."
13" 'Any Israelite or any alien
living among you who hunts
any animal or bird that may be
eaten must drain out the blood
and cover it with earth, 14be-
cause the life of every creature is its blood. That
is why I have said to the Israelites, "You must
not eat the blood of any creature, because the
life of every creature is its blood; anyone who
eats it must be cut off."
15" 'Anyone, whether native-born or alien,
who eats anything found dead or torn by wild
animals must wash his clothes and bathe with
water, and he will be ceremonially unclean till
evening; then he will be clean. 16But if he does

Leviticus 17:11

God Requires Atonement

"For the life of a creature is in the blood, and I have given it to you to make atonement for yourselves on the altar; it is the blood that makes atonement for one's life."

[a]29 Or *must fast*; also in verse 31 [b]3 The Hebrew word can include both male and female. [c]5 Traditionally *peace offerings*
[d]7 Or *demons*

not wash his clothes and bathe himself, he will
be held responsible.’ ”

Unlawful Sexual Relations

18 The LORD said to Moses, 2“Speak to
the Israelites and say
to them: ‘I am the LORD your
God. 3You must not do as they
do in Egypt, where you used
to live, and you must not do as
they do in the land of Canaan,
where I am bringing you. Do
not follow their practices.
4You must obey my laws and
be careful to follow my decrees. I am the LORD your
God. 5Keep my decrees and
laws, for the man who obeys
them will live by them. I am
the LORD.

> **Leviticus 18:4**
>
> *God Expects Obedience*
>
> “You must obey my laws and be careful to follow my decrees. I am the LORD your God.”

6“ ‘No one is to approach any close relative to
have sexual relations. I am the LORD.
7“ ‘Do not dishonor your father by having
sexual relations with your mother. She is your
mother; do not have relations with her.
8“ ‘Do not have sexual relations with your father’s wife; that would dishonor your father.
9“ ‘Do not have sexual relations with your
sister, either your father’s daughter or your
mother’s daughter, whether she was born in
the same home or elsewhere.
10“ ‘Do not have sexual relations with your
son’s daughter or your daughter’s daughter;
that would dishonor you.
11“ ‘Do not have sexual relations with the
daughter of your father’s wife, born to your father; she is your sister.
12“ ‘Do not have sexual relations with your
father’s sister; she is your father’s close relative.
13“ ‘Do not have sexual relations with your
mother’s sister, because she is your mother’s
close relative.
14“ ‘Do not dishonor your father’s brother by
approaching his wife to have sexual relations;
she is your aunt.
15“ ‘Do not have sexual relations with your
daughter-in-law. She is your son’s wife; do not
have relations with her.
16“ ‘Do not have sexual relations with your
brother’s wife; that would dishonor your
brother.
17“ ‘Do not have sexual relations with both a
woman and her daughter. Do not have sexual
relations with either her son’s
daughter or her daughter’s
daughter; they are her close relatives. That is wickedness.
18“ ‘Do not take your wife’s
sister as a rival wife and have
sexual relations with her while
your wife is living.
19“ ‘Do not approach a
woman to have sexual relations
during the uncleanness of her
monthly period.
20“ ‘Do not have sexual relations with your neighbor’s wife
and defile yourself with her.
21“ ‘Do not give any of your children to be
sacrificed[a] to Molech, for you must not profane the name of your God. I am the LORD.
22“ ‘Do not lie with a man as one lies with a
woman; that is detestable.
23“ ‘Do not have sexual relations with an animal and defile yourself with it. A woman must
not present herself to an animal to have sexual
relations with it; that is a perversion.
24“ ‘Do not defile yourselves in any of these
ways, because this is how the nations that I am
going to drive out before you became defiled.
25Even the land was defiled; so I punished it for
its sin, and the land vomited out its inhabitants.
26But you must keep my decrees and my laws.
The native-born and the aliens living among
you must not do any of these detestable things,
27for all these things were done by the people
who lived in the land before you, and the land
became defiled. 28And if you defile the land, it
will vomit you out as it vomited out the nations
that were before you.
29“ ‘Everyone who does any of these detestable things—such persons must be cut off from
their people. 30Keep my requirements and do
not follow any of the detestable customs that
were practiced before you came and do not
defile yourselves with them. I am the LORD
your God.’ ”

[a]21 Or *to be passed through* ⌊*the fire*⌋

Various Laws

19 The LORD said to Moses, 2"Speak to the entire assembly of Israel and say to them: 'Be holy because I, the LORD your God, am holy.

3" 'Each of you must respect his mother and father, and you must observe my Sabbaths. I am the LORD your God.

4" 'Do not turn to idols or make gods of cast metal for yourselves. I am the LORD your God.

5" 'When you sacrifice a fellowship offering[a] to the LORD, sacrifice it in such a way that it will be accepted on your behalf. 6It shall be eaten on the day you sacrifice it or on the next day; anything left over until the third day must be burned up. 7If any of it is eaten on the third day, it is impure and will not be accepted. 8Whoever eats it will be held responsible because he has desecrated what is holy to the LORD; that person must be cut off from his people.

9" 'When you reap the harvest of your land, do not reap to the very edges of your field or gather the gleanings of your harvest. 10Do not go over your vineyard a second time or pick up the grapes that have fallen. Leave them for the poor and the alien. I am the LORD your God.

11" 'Do not steal.

" 'Do not lie.

" 'Do not deceive one another.

12" 'Do not swear falsely by my name and so profane the name of your God. I am the LORD.

13" 'Do not defraud your neighbor or rob him.

" 'Do not hold back the wages of a hired man overnight.

14" 'Do not curse the deaf or put a stumbling block in front of the blind, but fear your God. I am the LORD.

15" 'Do not pervert justice; do not show partiality to the poor or favoritism to the great, but judge your neighbor fairly.

16" 'Do not go about spreading slander among your people.

" 'Do not do anything that endangers your neighbor's life. I am the LORD.

17" 'Do not hate your brother in your heart. Rebuke your neighbor frankly so you will not share in his guilt.

18" 'Do not seek revenge or bear a grudge against one of your people, but love your neighbor as yourself. I am the LORD.

19" 'Keep my decrees.

" 'Do not mate different kinds of animals.

" 'Do not plant your field with two kinds of seed.

" 'Do not wear clothing woven of two kinds of material.

20" 'If a man sleeps with a woman who is a slave girl promised to another man but who has not been ransomed or given her freedom, there must be due punishment. Yet they are not to be put to death, because she had not been freed. 21The man, however, must bring a ram to the entrance to the Tent of Meeting for a guilt offering to the LORD. 22With the ram of the guilt offering the priest is to make atonement for him before the LORD for the sin he has committed, and his sin will be forgiven.

23" 'When you enter the land and plant any kind of fruit tree, regard its fruit as forbidden.[b] For three years you are to consider it forbidden[b]; it must not be eaten. 24In the fourth year all its fruit will be holy, an offering of praise to the LORD. 25But in the fifth year you may eat its fruit. In this way your harvest will be increased. I am the LORD your God.

26" 'Do not eat any meat with the blood still in it.

" 'Do not practice divination or sorcery.

27" 'Do not cut the hair at the sides of your head or clip off the edges of your beard.

28" 'Do not cut your bodies for the dead or put tattoo marks on yourselves. I am the LORD.

29" 'Do not degrade your daughter by making her a prostitute, or the land will turn to prostitution and be filled with wickedness.

30" 'Observe my Sabbaths and have reverence for my sanctuary. I am the LORD.

31" 'Do not turn to mediums or seek out

Leviticus 19:15

God Is Fair

"Do not pervert justice; do not show partiality to the poor or favoritism to the great, but judge your neighbor fairly."

[a]5 Traditionally *peace offering* [b]23 Hebrew *uncircumcised*

spiritists, for you will be defiled by them. I am
the LORD your God.
32 "'Rise in the presence of the aged, show
respect for the elderly and revere your God. I
am the LORD.
33 "'When an alien lives with you in your
land, do not mistreat him. 34 The alien living
with you must be treated as one of your native-
born. Love him as yourself, for you were aliens
in Egypt. I am the LORD your God.
35 "'Do not use dishonest standards when
measuring length, weight or quantity. 36 Use
honest scales and honest weights, an honest
ephah[a] and an honest hin.[b] I am the LORD
your God, who brought you out of Egypt.
37 "'Keep all my decrees and all my laws and
follow them. I am the LORD.'"

Punishments for Sin

20 The LORD said to Moses, 2 "Say to the
Israelites: 'Any Israelite or any alien living in Israel who gives[c] any of his children to
Molech must be put to death. The people of the
community are to stone him. 3 I will set my face
against that man and I will cut him off from his
people; for by giving his children to Molech,
he has defiled my sanctuary and profaned my
holy name. 4 If the people of the community
close their eyes when that
man gives one of his children
to Molech and they fail to put
him to death, 5 I will set my
face against that man and his
family and will cut off from
their people both him and all
who follow him in prostituting
themselves to Molech.
6 "'I will set my face against
the person who turns to mediums and spiritists to prostitute
himself by following them,
and I will cut him off from his
people.
7 "'Consecrate yourselves and be holy, because I am the LORD your God. 8 Keep my
decrees and follow them. I am the LORD, who
makes you holy.[d]
9 "'If anyone curses his father or mother, he
must be put to death. He has cursed his father
or his mother, and his blood will be on his
own head.
10 "'If a man commits adultery with another
man's wife—with the wife of his neighbor—
both the adulterer and the adulteress must be
put to death.
11 "'If a man sleeps with his father's wife, he
has dishonored his father. Both the man and
the woman must be put to death; their blood
will be on their own heads.
12 "'If a man sleeps with his daughter-in-law,
both of them must be put to death. What they
have done is a perversion; their blood will be
on their own heads.
13 "'If a man lies with a man as one lies with
a woman, both of them have done what is detestable. They must be put to death; their blood
will be on their own heads.
14 "'If a man marries both a woman and her
mother, it is wicked. Both he and they must be
burned in the fire, so that no wickedness will
be among you.
15 "'If a man has sexual relations with an animal, he must be put to death, and you must
kill the animal.
16 "'If a woman approaches an animal to have
sexual relations with it, kill both the woman
and the animal. They must be
put to death; their blood will be
on their own heads.
17 "'If a man marries his sister, the daughter of either his
father or his mother, and they
have sexual relations, it is a
disgrace. They must be cut off
before the eyes of their people.
He has dishonored his sister
and will be held responsible.
18 "'If a man lies with a
woman during her monthly
period and has sexual relations with her, he has exposed
the source of her flow, and she has also uncovered it. Both of them must be cut off from
their people.
19 "'Do not have sexual relations with the
sister of either your mother or your father, for

Leviticus 20:8

God Makes Us Holy

"Keep my decrees and follow them. I am the LORD, who makes you holy."

[a] 36 An ephah was a dry measure. [b] 36 A hin was a liquid measure. [c] 2 Or *sacrifices*; also in verses 3 and 4 [d] 8 Or *who sanctifies you*; or *who sets you apart as holy*

Loving the Alien

Leviticus 19:33–34

"When an alien lives with you in your land, do not mistreat him. The alien living with you must be treated as one of your native-born. Love him as yourself, for you were aliens in Egypt. I am the LORD your God."

reflection

1 Have you ever felt like an alien because of your faith in Christ?

2 Have you ever treated someone like an alien because they didn't look, dress or believe as you do? How has this devotional changed your mind and heart?

3 Who in your sphere of influence is alienated from God? How can you apply the Golden Rule to help them see God in a new light?

RELATED READINGS

Ephesians 2:11–22; Philippians 3:20–21; Hebrews 11:13–16; 1 Peter 2:11–12

Read: Leviticus 19:33–34

MILDRED HOYT, "MID" TO HER FRIENDS, left this world and went to rest in the arms of Jesus at the age of 97. She was born December 24, 1899. Imagine what her eyes saw, the changes that transformed this world of ours—it's staggering if you think about it.

If we were beamed to an alien world—to a galaxy far, far away, would we experience any greater change than Mid did during her lifetime? Two world wars, not to mention several smaller ones, the advent of cars, planes, electricity, radio, television and, yes, computers and the Net. The list could go on for more pages than a New York City phone book.

Spending time with Mid left one with a longing . . . a longing to return to a different time. A time of simplicity, a time for family and community. A time when doors were left unlocked and neighbors would drop everything and help you rebuild a barn. A time when family and faith reigned supreme.

Perhaps a similar longing prompted a group of so-called aliens to accompany the Israelites out of Egypt. These weren't little green men; they were non-Hebrews who followed the Hebrews' God. So when the Hebrews left Egypt, they weren't alone, as "many other people went up with them." These aliens just didn't fit in Egypt anymore. They longed for a life that honored God. They had seen God's power and wanted what he offered. They left families, homes, businesses and country.

God honored their determination by protecting them with this commandment, reminding the Israelites that they, too, had once been aliens in a foreign land. God reminded them of the harsh treatment they'd endured so they would treat the aliens as they would want to be treated—the Golden Rule in the desert.

Who are the aliens today? Perhaps the alien is a neighbor who admires your faith and with a little encouragement would come to church with you. Perhaps the alien is a store clerk who notices the little cross around your neck as well as your kindness and patience. Perhaps the alien is someone at work whose lifestyle you would not choose, but who might be drawn to God through your gracious attitude. The challenge is to live the Golden Rule in the desert of life. Don't treat the aliens as strangers, but treat them as you would one of your friends or family. Treat the aliens in your life to a taste of God's love.

Go to page 147 for your next devotional reading.

that would dishonor a close relative; both of
you would be held responsible.
20“‘If a man sleeps with his aunt, he has dishonored his uncle. They will be held responsible; they will die childless.
21“‘If a man marries his brother’s wife, it
is an act of impurity; he has dishonored his
brother. They will be childless.
22“‘Keep all my decrees and laws and follow
them, so that the land where I am bringing you
to live may not vomit you out. 23You must not
live according to the customs of the nations I
am going to drive out before you. Because they
did all these things, I abhorred them. 24But I
said to you, “You will possess their land; I will
give it to you as an inheritance, a land flowing
with milk and honey.” I am the LORD your
God, who has set you apart from the nations.
25“‘You must therefore make a distinction
between clean and unclean animals and between unclean and clean birds. Do not defile
yourselves by any animal or bird or anything
that moves along the ground—those which I
have set apart as unclean for you. 26You are to
be holy to me[a] because I, the LORD, am holy,
and I have set you apart from the nations to
be my own.
27“‘A man or woman who is a medium or
spiritist among you must be put to death. You
are to stone them; their blood will be on their
own heads.’”

Rules for Priests

21 The LORD said to Moses, “Speak to
the priests, the sons of Aaron, and
say to them: ‘A priest must not make himself
ceremonially unclean for any of his people
who die, 2except for a close relative, such as
his mother or father, his son or daughter, his
brother, 3or an unmarried sister who is dependent on him since she has no husband—for her
he may make himself unclean. 4He must not
make himself unclean for people related to him
by marriage,[b] and so defile himself.
5“‘Priests must not shave their heads or
shave off the edges of their beards or cut their
bodies. 6They must be holy to their God and
must not profane the name of their God. Because they present the offerings made to the
LORD by fire, the food of their God, they are
to be holy.
7“‘They must not marry women defiled by
prostitution or divorced from their husbands,
because priests are holy to their God. 8Regard
them as holy, because they offer up the food of
your God. Consider them holy, because I the
LORD am holy—I who make you holy.[c]
9“‘If a priest’s daughter defiles herself by becoming a prostitute, she disgraces her father;
she must be burned in the fire.
10“‘The high priest, the one among his brothers who has had the anointing oil poured on his
head and who has been ordained to wear the
priestly garments, must not let his hair become
unkempt[d] or tear his clothes. 11He must not enter a place where there is a dead body. He must
not make himself unclean, even for his father or
mother, 12nor leave the sanctuary of his God or
desecrate it, because he has been dedicated by
the anointing oil of his God. I am the LORD.
13“‘The woman he marries must be a virgin. 14He must not marry a widow, a divorced
woman, or a woman defiled by prostitution,
but only a virgin from his own people, 15so he
will not defile his offspring among his people. I
am the LORD, who makes him holy.[e]’”
16The LORD said to Moses, 17“Say to Aaron:
‘For the generations to come none of your descendants who has a defect may come near
to offer the food of his God. 18No man who
has any defect may come near: no man who
is blind or lame, disfigured or deformed; 19no
man with a crippled foot or hand, 20or who is
hunchbacked or dwarfed, or who has any eye
defect, or who has festering or running sores or
damaged testicles. 21No descendant of Aaron
the priest who has any defect is to come near
to present the offerings made to the LORD by
fire. He has a defect; he must not come near
to offer the food of his God. 22He may eat the
most holy food of his God, as well as the holy
food; 23yet because of his defect, he must not
go near the curtain or approach the altar, and
so desecrate my sanctuary. I am the LORD, who
makes them holy.[f]’”
24So Moses told this to Aaron and his sons
and to all the Israelites.

[a]26 Or *be my holy ones* [b]4 Or *unclean as a leader among his people* [c]8 Or *who sanctify you*; or *who set you apart as holy* [d]10 Or *not uncover his head* [e]15 Or *who sanctifies him*; or *who sets him apart as holy* [f]23 Or *who sanctifies them*; or *who sets them apart as holy*

22 The LORD said to Moses, 2"Tell Aaron and his sons to treat with respect the sacred offerings the Israelites consecrate to me, so they will not profane my holy name. I am the LORD.

3"Say to them: 'For the generations to come, if any of your descendants is ceremonially unclean and yet comes near the sacred offerings that the Israelites consecrate to the LORD, that person must be cut off from my presence. I am the LORD.

4" 'If a descendant of Aaron has an infectious skin disease[a] or a bodily discharge, he may not eat the sacred offerings until he is cleansed. He will also be unclean if he touches something defiled by a corpse or by anyone who has an emission of semen, 5or if he touches any crawling thing that makes him unclean, or any person who makes him unclean, whatever the uncleanness may be. 6The one who touches any such thing will be unclean till evening. He must not eat any of the sacred offerings unless he has bathed himself with water. 7When the sun goes down, he will be clean, and after that he may eat the sacred offerings, for they are his food. 8He must not eat anything found dead or torn by wild animals, and so become unclean through it. I am the LORD.

9" 'The priests are to keep my requirements so that they do not become guilty and die for treating them with contempt. I am the LORD, who makes them holy.[b]

10" 'No one outside a priest's family may eat the sacred offering, nor may the guest of a priest or his hired worker eat it. 11But if a priest buys a slave with money, or if a slave is born in his household, that slave may eat his food. 12If a priest's daughter marries anyone other than a priest, she may not eat any of the sacred contributions. 13But if a priest's daughter becomes a widow or is divorced, yet has no children, and she returns to live in her father's house as in her youth, she may eat of her father's food. No unauthorized person, however, may eat any of it.

14" 'If anyone eats a sacred offering by mistake, he must make restitution to the priest for the offering and add a fifth of the value to it. 15The priests must not desecrate the sacred offerings the Israelites present to the LORD 16by allowing them to eat the sacred offerings and so bring upon them guilt requiring payment. I am the LORD, who makes them holy.' "

Unacceptable Sacrifices

17The LORD said to Moses, 18"Speak to Aaron and his sons and to all the Israelites and say to them: 'If any of you—either an Israelite or an alien living in Israel—presents a gift for a burnt offering to the LORD, either to fulfill a vow or as a freewill offering, 19you must present a male without defect from the cattle, sheep or goats in order that it may be accepted on your behalf. 20Do not bring anything with a defect, because it will not be accepted on your behalf. 21When anyone brings from the herd or flock a fellowship offering[c] to the LORD to fulfill a special vow or as a freewill offering, it must be without defect or blemish to be acceptable. 22Do not offer to the LORD the blind, the injured or the maimed, or anything with warts or festering or running sores. Do not place any of these on the altar as an offering made to the LORD by fire. 23You may, however, present as a freewill offering an ox[d] or a sheep that is deformed or stunted, but it will not be accepted in fulfillment of a vow. 24You must not offer to the LORD an animal whose testicles are bruised, crushed, torn or cut. You must not do this in your own land, 25and you must not accept such animals from the hand of a foreigner and offer them as the food of your God. They will not be accepted on your behalf, because they are deformed and have defects.' "

26The LORD said to Moses, 27"When a calf, a lamb or a goat is born, it is to remain with its mother for seven days. From the eighth day on, it will be acceptable as an offering made to the LORD by fire. 28Do not slaughter a cow or a sheep and its young on the same day.

29"When you sacrifice a thank offering to the LORD, sacrifice it in such a way that it will be accepted on your behalf. 30It must be eaten that same day; leave none of it till morning. I am the LORD.

31"Keep my commands and follow them. I am the LORD. 32Do not profane my holy name.

[a]4 Traditionally *leprosy*; the Hebrew word was used for various diseases affecting the skin—not necessarily leprosy. [b]9 Or *who sanctifies them*; or *who sets them apart as holy*; also in verse 16 [c]21 Traditionally *peace offering* [d]23 The Hebrew word can include both male and female.

A Time Apart

Read Leviticus 23

TO ENTER INTO SOLITUDE and silence is to take the spiritual life seriously. It is to take seriously our need to quiet the noise of our lives, to cease the constant striving of human effort, to pull away from our absorption in human relationships for a time in order to give God our undivided attention. In solitude God begins to free us from our bondage to human expectations, for there we experience God as our ultimate reality—the One in whom we live and move and have our being. In solitude our thoughts and our mind, our will and our desires are reoriented Godward so we become less and less attracted by external forces and can be more deeply responsive to God's desire and prayer in us.

Silence deepens the experience of solitude. In silence we not only withdraw from the demands of life in the company of others but also allow the noise of our own thoughts, strivings and compulsions to settle down so we can hear a truer and more reliable Voice. Reliance on our own thoughts and words, even in our praying, can be one facet of a need to control things, to set the agenda, or at least to know what the agenda is even in our relationship with God. It is in silence that we habitually release our own agendas and our need to control and become more willing and able to give ourselves to God's loving initiative. In silence we create space for God's activity rather than filling every minute with our own . . .

Solitude and silence are not, in the end, about success and failure. They are about showing up and letting God do the rest. They are not an end in themselves; they are merely a *means* through which we regularly make ourselves available to God for the intimacy of relationship and for the work of transformation that only God can accomplish.

—*Ruth Haley Barton*

Leviticus 23:3
"There are six days when you may work, but the seventh day is a Sabbath of rest, a day of sacred assembly. You are not to do any work; wherever you live, it is a Sabbath to the LORD."

reflection

1 How often do you give God your undivided attention?

2 Picture in your mind a quiet place where you can "withdraw from the demands of life." When will you go there, so you can be alone with God?

3 No matter what day you chose to set apart to God, make sure that during that time you make yourself available to him for "the work of transformation" that he alone can accomplish in your life.

RELATED READINGS

Exodus 20:8–11;
Acts 17:24–28;
Romans 12:1–2

Go to page 152 for your next devotional reading.

I must be acknowledged as holy by the Israelites. I am the LORD, who makes[a] you holy[b]
33and who brought you out of Egypt to be your
God. I am the LORD."

23 The LORD said to Moses, 2"Speak to
the Israelites and say to them: 'These
are my appointed feasts, the appointed feasts
of the LORD, which you are to proclaim as sacred assemblies.

The Sabbath

3" 'There are six days when you may work,
but the seventh day is a Sabbath of rest, a day
of sacred assembly. You are not to do any
work; wherever you live, it is a Sabbath to the
LORD.

The Passover and Unleavened Bread

4" 'These are the LORD's appointed feasts, the
sacred assemblies you are to proclaim at their
appointed times: 5The LORD's Passover begins
at twilight on the fourteenth day of the first
month. 6On the fifteenth day of that month the
LORD's Feast of Unleavened Bread begins; for
seven days you must eat bread made without
yeast. 7On the first day hold a sacred assembly
and do no regular work. 8For seven days present an offering made to the LORD by fire. And
on the seventh day hold a sacred assembly and
do no regular work.' "

Firstfruits

9The LORD said to Moses, 10"Speak to the
Israelites and say to them: 'When you enter
the land I am going to give you and you reap
its harvest, bring to the priest a sheaf of the
first grain you harvest. 11He is to wave the
sheaf before the LORD so it will be accepted
on your behalf; the priest is to wave it on the
day after the Sabbath. 12On the day you wave
the sheaf, you must sacrifice as a burnt offering
to the LORD a lamb a year old without defect,
13together with its grain offering of two-tenths
of an ephah[c] of fine flour mixed with oil—an
offering made to the LORD by fire, a pleasing
aroma—and its drink offering of a quarter of
a hin[d] of wine. 14You must not eat any bread,
or roasted or new grain, until the very day you
bring this offering to your God. This is to be a
lasting ordinance for the generations to come,
wherever you live.

Feast of Weeks

15" 'From the day after the Sabbath, the day
you brought the sheaf of the wave offering,
count off seven full weeks. 16Count off fifty
days up to the day after the seventh Sabbath,
and then present an offering of new grain to
the LORD. 17From wherever you live, bring two
loaves made of two-tenths of an ephah of fine
flour, baked with yeast, as a wave offering of
firstfruits to the LORD. 18Present with this bread
seven male lambs, each a year old and without
defect, one young bull and two rams. They will
be a burnt offering to the LORD, together with
their grain offerings and drink offerings—an
offering made by fire, an aroma pleasing to the
LORD. 19Then sacrifice one male goat for a sin
offering and two lambs, each a year old, for a
fellowship offering.[e] 20The priest is to wave the
two lambs before the LORD as a wave offering,
together with the bread of the firstfruits. They
are a sacred offering to the LORD for the priest.
21On that same day you are to proclaim a sacred assembly and do no regular work. This is
to be a lasting ordinance for the generations to
come, wherever you live.

22" 'When you reap the harvest of your land,
do not reap to the very edges of your field or
gather the gleanings of your harvest. Leave
them for the poor and the alien. I am the LORD
your God.' "

Feast of Trumpets

23The LORD said to Moses, 24"Say to the Israelites: 'On the first day of the seventh month
you are to have a day of rest, a sacred assembly
commemorated with trumpet blasts. 25Do no
regular work, but present an offering made to
the LORD by fire.' "

Day of Atonement

26The LORD said to Moses, 27"The tenth day
of this seventh month is the Day of Atonement.
Hold a sacred assembly and deny yourselves,[f]
and present an offering made to the LORD by
fire. 28Do no work on that day, because it is the
Day of Atonement, when atonement is made
for you before the LORD your God. 29Anyone

[a]32 Or *made* [b]32 Or *who sanctifies you*; or *who sets you apart as holy* [c]13 That is, probably about 4 quarts (about 4.5 liters); also in verse 17 [d]13 That is, probably about 1 quart (about 1 liter) [e]19 Traditionally *peace offering* [f]27 Or *and fast*; also in verses 29 and 32

who does not deny himself on that day must be
cut off from his people. 30 I will destroy from
among his people anyone who does any work
on that day. 31 You shall do no work at all. This
is to be a lasting ordinance for the generations
to come, wherever you live. 32 It is a sabbath
of rest for you, and you must deny yourselves.
From the evening of the ninth day of the month
until the following evening you are to observe
your sabbath."

Feast of Tabernacles

33 The LORD said to Moses, 34 "Say to the
Israelites: 'On the fifteenth day of the seventh
month the LORD's Feast of Tabernacles begins,
and it lasts for seven days. 35 The first day is a
sacred assembly; do no regular work. 36 For
seven days present offerings made to the LORD
by fire, and on the eighth day hold a sacred assembly and present an offering made to the
LORD by fire. It is the closing assembly; do no
regular work.

37 (" 'These are the LORD's appointed feasts,
which you are to proclaim as sacred assemblies for bringing offerings made to the LORD
by fire—the burnt offerings and grain offerings, sacrifices and drink offerings required
for each day. 38 These offerings are in addition
to those for the LORD's Sabbaths and[a] in addition to your gifts and whatever you have
vowed and all the freewill offerings you give
to the LORD.)

39 " 'So beginning with the fifteenth day of
the seventh month, after you have gathered
the crops of the land, celebrate the festival to
the LORD for seven days; the first day is a day
of rest, and the eighth day also is a day of rest.
40 On the first day you are to take choice fruit
from the trees, and palm fronds, leafy branches
and poplars, and rejoice before the LORD your
God for seven days. 41 Celebrate this as a festival to the LORD for seven days each year. This is
to be a lasting ordinance for the generations to
come; celebrate it in the seventh month. 42 Live
in booths for seven days: All native-born Israelites are to live in booths 43 so your descendants
will know that I had the Israelites live in booths
when I brought them out of Egypt. I am the
LORD your God.' "

44 So Moses announced to the Israelites the
appointed feasts of the LORD.

Oil and Bread Set Before the LORD

24 The LORD said to Moses, 2 "Command
the Israelites to bring you clear oil of
pressed olives for the light so that the lamps
may be kept burning continually. 3 Outside the
curtain of the Testimony in the Tent of Meeting, Aaron is to tend the lamps before the LORD
from evening till morning, continually. This is
to be a lasting ordinance for the generations to
come. 4 The lamps on the pure gold lampstand
before the LORD must be tended continually.

5 "Take fine flour and bake twelve loaves of
bread, using two-tenths of an ephah[b] for each
loaf. 6 Set them in two rows, six in each row, on
the table of pure gold before the LORD. 7 Along
each row put some pure incense as a memorial
portion to represent the bread and to be an offering made to the LORD by fire. 8 This bread is
to be set out before the LORD regularly, Sabbath
after Sabbath, on behalf of the Israelites, as a
lasting covenant. 9 It belongs to Aaron and his
sons, who are to eat it in a holy place, because it
is a most holy part of their regular share of the
offerings made to the LORD by fire."

A Blasphemer Stoned

10 Now the son of an Israelite mother and
an Egyptian father went out among the Israelites, and a fight broke out in the camp between
him and an Israelite. 11 The son of the Israelite
woman blasphemed the Name with a curse; so
they brought him to Moses. (His mother's name
was Shelomith, the daughter of Dibri the Dan-
ite.) 12 They put him in custody until the will of
the LORD should be made clear to them.

13 Then the LORD said to Moses: 14 "Take the
blasphemer outside the camp. All those who
heard him are to lay their hands on his head,
and the entire assembly is to stone him. 15 Say
to the Israelites: 'If anyone curses his God, he
will be held responsible; 16 anyone who blasphemes the name of the LORD must be put to
death. The entire assembly must stone him.
Whether an alien or native-born, when he blasphemes the Name, he must be put to death.

17 " 'If anyone takes the life of a human being,
he must be put to death. 18 Anyone who takes

[a]38 Or *These feasts are in addition to the LORD's Sabbaths, and these offerings are*   [b]5 That is, probably about 4 quarts (about 4.5 liters)

the life of someone's animal must make restitution—life for life. 19 If anyone injures his neighbor, whatever he has done must be done to
him: 20 fracture for fracture, eye for eye, tooth
for tooth. As he has injured the other, so he is
to be injured. 21 Whoever kills an animal must
make restitution, but whoever kills a man must
be put to death. 22 You are to have the same law
for the alien and the native-born. I am the
LORD your God.'"

23 Then Moses spoke to the Israelites, and
they took the blasphemer outside the camp
and stoned him. The Israelites did as the LORD
commanded Moses.

The Sabbath Year

25 The LORD said to Moses on Mount Sinai, 2 "Speak to the Israelites and say to
them: 'When you enter the land I am going to
give you, the land itself must observe a sabbath
to the LORD. 3 For six years sow your fields, and
for six years prune your vineyards and gather
their crops. 4 But in the seventh year the land
is to have a sabbath of rest, a sabbath to the
LORD. Do not sow your fields or prune your
vineyards. 5 Do not reap what grows of itself
or harvest the grapes of your untended vines.
The land is to have a year of rest. 6 Whatever the
land yields during the sabbath
year will be food for you—for
yourself, your manservant and
maidservant, and the hired
worker and temporary resident who live among you, 7 as
well as for your livestock and
the wild animals in your land.
Whatever the land produces
may be eaten.

The Year of Jubilee

8 " 'Count off seven sabbaths
of years—seven times seven
years—so that the seven sabbaths of years amount to a
period of forty-nine years. 9 Then have the
trumpet sounded everywhere on the tenth
day of the seventh month; on the Day of Atonement sound the trumpet throughout your land.
10 Consecrate the fiftieth year and proclaim
liberty throughout the land to all its inhabitants. It shall be a jubilee for you; each one of
you is to return to his family property and each
to his own clan. 11 The fiftieth year shall be a jubilee for you; do not sow and do not reap what
grows of itself or harvest the untended vines.
12 For it is a jubilee and is to be holy for you; eat
only what is taken directly from the fields.

13 " 'In this Year of Jubilee everyone is to return to his own property.

14 " 'If you sell land to one of your countrymen or buy any from him, do not take advantage of each other. 15 You are to buy from your
countryman on the basis of the number of
years since the Jubilee. And he is to sell to you
on the basis of the number of years left for harvesting crops. 16 When the years are many, you
are to increase the price, and when the years
are few, you are to decrease the price, because
what he is really selling you is the number of
crops. 17 Do not take advantage of each other,
but fear your God. I am the LORD your God.

18 " 'Follow my decrees and be careful to obey
my laws, and you will live safely in the land.
19 Then the land will yield its fruit, and you will
eat your fill and live there in safety. 20 You may
ask, "What will we eat in the seventh year if
we do not plant or harvest our crops?" 21 I will
send you such a blessing in the sixth year that
the land will yield enough for
three years. 22 While you plant
during the eighth year, you will
eat from the old crop and will
continue to eat from it until
the harvest of the ninth year
comes in.

23 " 'The land must not be
sold permanently, because
the land is mine and you are
but aliens and my tenants.
24 Throughout the country that
you hold as a possession, you
must provide for the redemption of the land.

25 " 'If one of your coun-
trymen becomes poor and sells some of his
property, his nearest relative is to come and
redeem what his countryman has sold. 26 If,
however, a man has no one to redeem it for him
but he himself prospers and acquires sufficient
means to redeem it, 27 he is to determine the
value for the years since he sold it and refund

> **Leviticus 25:23**
>
> *God Owns Everything*
>
> "The land must not be sold permanently, because the land is mine and you are but aliens and my tenants."

the balance to the man to whom he sold it; he
can then go back to his own property. 28But if
he does not acquire the means to repay him,
what he sold will remain in the possession of
the buyer until the Year of Jubilee. It will be returned in the Jubilee, and he can then go back
to his property.
29" 'If a man sells a house in a walled city,
he retains the right of redemption a full year
after its sale. During that time he may redeem
it. 30If it is not redeemed before a full year has
passed, the house in the walled city shall belong
permanently to the buyer and his descendants.
It is not to be returned in the Jubilee. 31But
houses in villages without walls around them
are to be considered as open country. They can
be redeemed, and they are to be returned in
the Jubilee.
32" 'The Levites always have the right to
redeem their houses in the Levitical towns,
which they possess. 33So the property of the
Levites is redeemable—that is, a house sold in
any town they hold—and is to be returned in
the Jubilee, because the houses in the towns of
the Levites are their property among the Israelites. 34But the pastureland belonging to their
towns must not be sold; it is their permanent
possession.
35" 'If one of your countrymen becomes
poor and is unable to support himself among
you, help him as you would an alien or a temporary resident, so he can continue to live among
you. 36Do not take interest of any kind[a] from
him, but fear your God, so that your countryman may continue to live among you. 37You
must not lend him money at interest or sell
him food at a profit. 38I am the LORD your
God, who brought you out of Egypt to give you
the land of Canaan and to be your God.
39" 'If one of your countrymen becomes
poor among you and sells himself to you, do
not make him work as a slave. 40He is to be
treated as a hired worker or a temporary resident among you; he is to work for you until
the Year of Jubilee. 41Then he and his children
are to be released, and he will go back to his
own clan and to the property of his forefathers.
42Because the Israelites are my servants, whom
I brought out of Egypt, they must not be sold as
slaves. 43Do not rule over them ruthlessly, but
fear your God.
44" 'Your male and female slaves are to come
from the nations around you; from them you
may buy slaves. 45You may also buy some of
the temporary residents living among you and
members of their clans born in your country,
and they will become your property. 46You can
will them to your children as inherited property
and can make them slaves for life, but you must
not rule over your fellow Israelites ruthlessly.
47" 'If an alien or a temporary resident
among you becomes rich and one of your countrymen becomes poor and sells himself to the
alien living among you or to a member of the
alien's clan, 48he retains the right of redemption after he has sold himself. One of his relatives may redeem him: 49An uncle or a cousin
or any blood relative in his clan may redeem
him. Or if he prospers, he may redeem himself.
50He and his buyer are to count the time from
the year he sold himself up to the Year of Jubilee. The price for his release is to be based on
the rate paid to a hired man for that number of
years. 51If many years remain, he must pay for
his redemption a larger share of the price paid
for him. 52If only a few years remain until the
Year of Jubilee, he is to compute that and pay
for his redemption accordingly. 53He is to be
treated as a man hired from year to year; you
must see to it that his owner does not rule over
him ruthlessly.
54" 'Even if he is not redeemed in any of
these ways, he and his children are to be released in the Year of Jubilee, 55for the Israelites
belong to me as servants. They are my servants,
whom I brought out of Egypt. I am the LORD
your God.

Reward for Obedience

26 " 'Do not make idols or set up an image
or a sacred stone for yourselves, and do
not place a carved stone in your land to bow
down before it. I am the LORD your God.
2" 'Observe my Sabbaths and have reverence
for my sanctuary. I am the LORD.
3" 'If you follow my decrees and are careful
to obey my commands, 4I will send you rain in
its season, and the ground will yield its crops

[a]36 Or *take excessive interest*; similarly in verse 37

An Answer to Prayer

REBEKAH

> *Before he had finished praying, Rebekah came out with her jar on her shoulder.*
>
> Genesis 24:15

ONE MINUTE she was a single woman, going to fetch water—something she routinely did every day of her life—and the next minute she had a ring and a proposal of marriage to a man she had never met. One minute she was going about her normal routine, and then suddenly she was destined to be the answer to prayer.

Abraham was insistent that his son, his chosen son, Isaac, marry a woman from Abraham's own people. Abraham made his servant swear an oath that he would get the boy a bride. Both Abraham and the servant prayed that God would direct this marriage. The prayers had been specific. Certain. And entirely trusting. In response, and against all odds, the Lord intertwined the lives of a man and a woman many miles apart and drew a knot between their two hearts.

Upon meeting Abraham's servant, Rebekah didn't know she was an answer to prayer. She just saw a man who was thirsty and needing water. Because she was kind and hospitable, she quickly allowed the man water from her jar. And then she watered the man's camels too.

It wasn't until later that Rebekah realized that Isaac's family had *prayed* for someone like her. And here she was—voilà! Beautiful. Poised. Hospitable. A virgin. What an awesome feeling: to be someone's answer to prayer. Someone's "dream girl."

ASSIGNED READING:
Genesis 24–27

Armed with that knowledge, Rebekah was ready to take a radical step of faith. "Do you want to go right now with this servant or do you want to stay here for a few days to say goodbye to your friends, neighbors and family?" Rebekah's mom and brother asked, already feeling her loss. Rebekah looked at the man and took a deep breath. "I'm ready to go now."

—Prayer—

My Lord, thank you for the opportunities you give me every day to demonstrate my faith in you.

Weekend

Go to page 163 for your next devotional reading.

and the trees of the field their fruit. 5 Your
threshing will continue until grape harvest and
the grape harvest will continue until planting,
and you will eat all the food you want and live
in safety in your land.
6 " 'I will grant peace in the land, and you will
lie down and no one will make you afraid. I will
remove savage beasts from the land, and the
sword will not pass through your country. 7 You
will pursue your enemies, and they will fall by
the sword before you. 8 Five of you will chase a
hundred, and a hundred of you will chase ten
thousand, and your enemies will fall by the
sword before you.
9 " 'I will look on you with favor and make
you fruitful and increase your numbers, and
I will keep my covenant with
you. 10 You will still be eating
last year's harvest when you
will have to move it out to
make room for the new. 11 I will
put my dwelling place[a] among
you, and I will not abhor you.
12 I will walk among you and be
your God, and you will be my
people. 13 I am the LORD your
God, who brought you out of
Egypt so that you would no longer be slaves to the Egyptians; I
broke the bars of your yoke and enabled you to
walk with heads held high.

> **Leviticus 26:12**
>
> *God Identifies With Us*
>
> "I will walk among you and be your God, and you will be my people."

Punishment for Disobedience

14 " 'But if you will not listen to me and carry
out all these commands, 15 and if you reject my
decrees and abhor my laws and fail to carry out
all my commands and so violate my covenant,
16 then I will do this to you: I will bring upon
you sudden terror, wasting diseases and fever
that will destroy your sight and drain away your
life. You will plant seed in vain, because your enemies will eat it. 17 I will set my face against you
so that you will be defeated by your enemies;
those who hate you will rule over you, and you
will flee even when no one is pursuing you.
18 " 'If after all this you will not listen to me,
I will punish you for your sins seven times
over. 19 I will break down your stubborn pride
and make the sky above you like iron and
the ground beneath you like bronze. 20 Your
strength will be spent in vain, because your soil
will not yield its crops, nor will the trees of the
land yield their fruit.
21 " 'If you remain hostile toward me and
refuse to listen to me, I will multiply your afflictions seven times over, as your sins deserve.
22 I will send wild animals against you, and they
will rob you of your children, destroy your cattle and make you so few in number that your
roads will be deserted.
23 " 'If in spite of these things you do not accept my correction but continue to be hostile
toward me, 24 I myself will be hostile toward
you and will afflict you for your sins seven
times over. 25 And I will bring the sword upon
you to avenge the breaking of
the covenant. When you withdraw into your cities, I will
send a plague among you, and
you will be given into enemy
hands. 26 When I cut off your
supply of bread, ten women
will be able to bake your bread
in one oven, and they will dole
out the bread by weight. You
will eat, but you will not be satisfied.
27 " 'If in spite of this you still
do not listen to me but continue to be hostile
toward me, 28 then in my anger I will be hostile
toward you, and I myself will punish you for
your sins seven times over. 29 You will eat the
flesh of your sons and the flesh of your daughters. 30 I will destroy your high places, cut down
your incense altars and pile your dead bodies
on the lifeless forms of your idols, and I will abhor you. 31 I will turn your cities into ruins and
lay waste your sanctuaries, and I will take no
delight in the pleasing aroma of your offerings.
32 I will lay waste the land, so that your enemies
who live there will be appalled. 33 I will scatter
you among the nations and will draw out my
sword and pursue you. Your land will be laid
waste, and your cities will lie in ruins. 34 Then
the land will enjoy its sabbath years all the time
that it lies desolate and you are in the country
of your enemies; then the land will rest and
enjoy its sabbaths. 35 All the time that it lies

[a] 11 Or *my tabernacle*

desolate, the land will have the rest it did not
have during the sabbaths you lived in it.
36 "'As for those of you who are left, I will
make their hearts so fearful in the lands of their
enemies that the sound of a windblown leaf
will put them to flight. They will run as though
fleeing from the sword, and they will fall, even
though no one is pursuing them. 37 They will
stumble over one another as though fleeing
from the sword, even though no one is pursuing them. So you will not be able to stand before your enemies. 38 You will perish among the
nations; the land of your enemies will devour
you. 39 Those of you who are left will waste
away in the lands of their enemies because of
their sins; also because of their fathers' sins
they will waste away.
40 "'But if they will confess their sins and the
sins of their fathers—their treachery against me
and their hostility toward me, 41 which made
me hostile toward them so that I sent them into
the land of their enemies—then when their uncircumcised hearts are humbled and they pay
for their sin, 42 I will remember my covenant
with Jacob and my covenant with Isaac and
my covenant with Abraham, and I will remember the land. 43 For the land will be deserted by
them and will enjoy its sabbaths while it lies desolate without them. They will pay for their sins
because they rejected my laws and abhorred
my decrees. 44 Yet in spite of this, when they
are in the land of their enemies, I will not reject them or abhor them so as to destroy them
completely, breaking my covenant with them.
I am the LORD their God. 45 But for their sake
I will remember the covenant with their ancestors whom I brought out of Egypt in the sight of
the nations to be their God. I am the LORD.'"
46 These are the decrees, the laws and the regulations that the LORD established on Mount Sinai between himself and the Israelites through
Moses.

Redeeming What Is the LORD's

27 The LORD said to Moses, 2 "Speak to
the Israelites and say to them: 'If anyone makes a special vow to dedicate persons
to the LORD by giving equivalent values, 3 set
the value of a male between the ages of twenty
and sixty at fifty shekels[a] of silver, according to
the sanctuary shekel[b]; 4 and if it is a female, set
her value at thirty shekels.[c] 5 If it is a person between the ages of five and twenty, set the value
of a male at twenty shekels[d] and of a female
at ten shekels.[e] 6 If it is a person between one
month and five years, set the value of a male
at five shekels[f] of silver and that of a female at
three shekels[g] of silver. 7 If it is a person sixty
years old or more, set the value of a male at fifteen shekels[h] and of a female at ten shekels. 8 If
anyone making the vow is too poor to pay the
specified amount, he is to present the person
to the priest, who will set the value for him
according to what the man making the vow
can afford.
9 "'If what he vowed is an animal that is acceptable as an offering to the LORD, such an
animal given to the LORD becomes holy. 10 He
must not exchange it or substitute a good one
for a bad one, or a bad one for a good one; if he
should substitute one animal for another, both
it and the substitute become holy. 11 If what he
vowed is a ceremonially unclean animal—one
that is not acceptable as an offering to the
LORD—the animal must be presented to the
priest, 12 who will judge its quality as good or
bad. Whatever value the priest then sets, that is
what it will be. 13 If the owner wishes to redeem
the animal, he must add a fifth to its value.
14 "'If a man dedicates his house as something holy to the LORD, the priest will judge
its quality as good or bad. Whatever value the
priest then sets, so it will remain. 15 If the man
who dedicates his house redeems it, he must
add a fifth to its value, and the house will again
become his.
16 "'If a man dedicates to the LORD part of
his family land, its value is to be set according
to the amount of seed required for it—fifty
shekels of silver to a homer[i] of barley seed. 17 If
he dedicates his field during the Year of Jubilee,
the value that has been set remains. 18 But if he
dedicates his field after the Jubilee, the priest
will determine the value according to the num-

[a] 3 That is, about 1 1/4 pounds (about 0.6 kilogram); also in verse 16 [b] 3 That is, about 2/5 ounce (about 11.5 grams); also in verse 25 [c] 4 That is, about 12 ounces (about 0.3 kilogram) [d] 5 That is, about 8 ounces (about 0.2 kilogram) [e] 5 That is, about 4 ounces (about 110 grams); also in verse 7 [f] 6 That is, about 2 ounces (about 55 grams) [g] 6 That is, about 1 1/4 ounces (about 35 grams) [h] 7 That is, about 6 ounces (about 170 grams) [i] 16 That is, probably about 6 bushels (about 220 liters)

ber of years that remain until the next Year of Jubilee, and its set value will be reduced. 19 If the
man who dedicates the field wishes to redeem
it, he must add a fifth to its value, and the field
will again become his. 20 If, however, he does
not redeem the field, or if he has sold it to someone else, it can never be redeemed. 21 When the
field is released in the Jubilee, it will become
holy, like a field devoted to the LORD; it will become the property of the priests.[a]

22 "'If a man dedicates to the LORD a field he
has bought, which is not part of his family land,
23 the priest will determine its value up to the
Year of Jubilee, and the man must pay its value
on that day as something holy to the LORD.
24 In the Year of Jubilee the field will revert to
the person from whom he bought it, the one
whose land it was. 25 Every value is to be set according to the sanctuary shekel, twenty gerahs
to the shekel.

26 "'No one, however, may dedicate the firstborn of an animal, since the firstborn already
belongs to the LORD; whether an ox[b] or a sheep,
it is the LORD's. 27 If it is one of the unclean animals, he may buy it back at its set value, adding
a fifth of the value to it. If he does not redeem
it, it is to be sold at its set value.

28 "'But nothing that a man owns and de-
votes[c] to the LORD—whether man or animal
or family land—may be sold or redeemed; everything so devoted is most holy to the LORD.

29 "'No person devoted to destruction[d] may
be ransomed; he must be put to death.

30 "'A tithe of everything from the land,
whether grain from the soil or fruit from the
trees, belongs to the LORD; it is holy to the
LORD. 31 If a man redeems any of his tithe, he
must add a fifth of the value to it. 32 The entire
tithe of the herd and flock—every tenth animal
that passes under the shepherd's rod—will be
holy to the LORD. 33 He must not pick out the
good from the bad or make any substitution.
If he does make a substitution, both the animal and its substitute become holy and cannot
be redeemed.'"

34 These are the commands the LORD gave
Moses on Mount Sinai for the Israelites.

[a] 21 Or *priest* [b] 26 The Hebrew word can include both male and female. [c] 28 The Hebrew term refers to the irrevocable giving over of things or persons to the LORD. [d] 29 The Hebrew term refers to the irrevocable giving over of things or persons to the LORD, often by totally destroying them.

Numbers

Author:
Moses.

Audience:
The people of Israel.

Date:
Between 1446 and 1406 B.C.

Setting:
After a year in the Sinai Desert, a census is taken. Then the Israelites move onward to Canaan and spend 39 more years wandering in the desert.

Verses to Remember:
"We went into the land to which you sent us, and it does flow with milk and honey! Here is its fruit." . . . But the men who had gone up with him said, "We can't attack those people; they are stronger than we are." (13:27,31)

The book of Numbers is named for the two "numberings," or countings, of the Hebrew people that took place. The first census was taken to organize the camps by tribal clans (see Numbers 1–4). After this event, the people prepared to enter the land of promise. But when they *scouted out the promised land* preparing to enter, they balked in fear. Although they had seen God's provision over and over, they grumbled and disbelieved. So the *people journeyed* on a 40-year roller coaster of obedience and defiance.

The second census was taken of the next generation (see Numbers 26), a new faithful generation, as they stood poised by the Jordan River, *ready to cross over into Canaan.*

The Census

1 The LORD spoke to Moses in the Tent
of Meeting in the Desert of Sinai on the
first day of the second month of the second
year after the Israelites came out of Egypt. He
said: 2"Take a census of the whole Israelite
community by their clans and families, listing
every man by name, one by one. 3You and
Aaron are to number by their divisions all the
men in Israel twenty years old or more who are
able to serve in the army. 4One man from each
tribe, each the head of his family, is to help you.
5These are the names of the men who are to
assist you:

from Reuben, Elizur son of Shedeur;
6 from Simeon, Shelumiel son of Zurishaddai;
7 from Judah, Nahshon son of Amminadab;
8 from Issachar, Nethanel son of Zuar;
9 from Zebulun, Eliab son of Helon;
10 from the sons of Joseph:
from Ephraim, Elishama son of Ammihud;
from Manasseh, Gamaliel son of Pedahzur;
11 from Benjamin, Abidan son of Gideoni;
12 from Dan, Ahiezer son of Ammishaddai;
13 from Asher, Pagiel son of Ocran;
14 from Gad, Eliasaph son of Deuel;
15 from Naphtali, Ahira son of Enan."

16 These were the men appointed from the
community, the leaders of their ancestral tribes.
They were the heads of the clans of Israel.
17 Moses and Aaron took these men whose
names had been given, 18 and they called the
whole community together on the first day of
the second month. The people indicated their
ancestry by their clans and families, and the
men twenty years old or more were listed by
name, one by one, 19 as the LORD commanded
Moses. And so he counted them in the Desert
of Sinai:

20 From the descendants of Reuben the firstborn son of Israel:
All the men twenty years old or more
who were able to serve in the army
were listed by name, one by one, according to the records of their clans
and families. 21 The number from the
tribe of Reuben was 46,500.

22 From the descendants of Simeon:
All the men twenty years old or more
who were able to serve in the army
were counted and listed by name, one
by one, according to the records of their
clans and families. 23 The number from
the tribe of Simeon was 59,300.

Numbers 1:1

God Communicates

The LORD spoke to Moses in the Tent of Meeting in the Desert of Sinai on the first day of the second month of the second year after the Israelites came out of Egypt.

24 From the descendants of Gad:
All the men twenty years old or more
who were able to serve in the army
were listed by name, according to the
records of their clans and families.
25 The number from the tribe of Gad
was 45,650.

26 From the descendants of Judah:
All the men twenty years
old or more who were able
to serve in the army were
listed by name, according
to the records of their
clans and families. 27 The
number from the tribe of
Judah was 74,600.

28 From the descendants of Issachar:
All the men twenty years
old or more who were
able to serve in the army
were listed by name, according to the
records of their clans and families.
29 The number from the tribe of Issachar was 54,400.

30 From the descendants of Zebulun:
All the men twenty years old or more
who were able to serve in the army
were listed by name, according to the
records of their clans and families.
31 The number from the tribe of Zebulun was 57,400.

32 From the sons of Joseph:
From the descendants of Ephraim:
All the men twenty years old or more
who were able to serve in the army were
listed by name, according to the records of their clans and families. 33 The
number from the tribe of Ephraim
was 40,500.

34 From the descendants of Manasseh:
All the men twenty years old or more
who were able to serve in the army
were listed by name, according to the
records of their clans and families.
35 The number from the tribe of Manasseh was 32,200.

36From the descendants of Benjamin:
All the men twenty years old or more
who were able to serve in the army
were listed by name, according to the
records of their clans and families.
37The number from the tribe of Benjamin was 35,400.

38From the descendants of Dan:
All the men twenty years old or more
who were able to serve in the army
were listed by name, according to the
records of their clans and families.
39The number from the tribe of Dan
was 62,700.

40From the descendants of Asher:
All the men twenty years old or more
who were able to serve in the army
were listed by name, according to the
records of their clans and families.
41The number from the tribe of Asher
was 41,500.

42From the descendants of Naphtali:
All the men twenty years old or more
who were able to serve in the army were
listed by name, according to the records of their clans and families. 43The
number from the tribe of Naphtali
was 53,400.

44These were the men counted by Moses
and Aaron and the twelve leaders of Israel,
each one representing his family. 45All the
Israelites twenty years old or more who were
able to serve in Israel's army were counted according to their families. 46The total number
was 603,550.
47The families of the tribe of Levi, however,
were not counted along with the others. 48The
LORD had said to Moses: 49"You must not count
the tribe of Levi or include them in the census
of the other Israelites. 50Instead, appoint the
Levites to be in charge of the tabernacle of the
Testimony—over all its furnishings and everything belonging to it. They are to carry the tabernacle and all its furnishings; they are to take
care of it and encamp around it. 51Whenever
the tabernacle is to move, the Levites are to take
it down, and whenever the tabernacle is to be
set up, the Levites shall do it. Anyone else who
goes near it shall be put to death. 52The Israelites are to set up their tents by divisions, each
man in his own camp under his own standard.
53The Levites, however, are to set up their tents
around the tabernacle of the Testimony so that
wrath will not fall on the Israelite community.
The Levites are to be responsible for the care of
the tabernacle of the Testimony."
54The Israelites did all this just as the LORD
commanded Moses.

The Arrangement of the Tribal Camps

2 The LORD said to Moses and Aaron: 2"The
Israelites are to camp around the Tent of
Meeting some distance from it, each man under
his standard with the banners of his family."

3On the east, toward the sunrise, the
divisions of the camp of Judah are to encamp under their standard. The leader of
the people of Judah is Nahshon son of Amminadab. 4His division numbers 74,600.
5The tribe of Issachar will camp next to
them. The leader of the people of Issachar
is Nethanel son of Zuar. 6His division
numbers 54,400.
7The tribe of Zebulun will be next.
The leader of the people of Zebulun is
Eliab son of Helon. 8His division numbers 57,400.
9All the men assigned to the camp of
Judah, according to their divisions, number 186,400. They will set out first.

10On the south will be the divisions of
the camp of Reuben under their standard.
The leader of the people of Reuben is Elizur son of Shedeur. 11His division numbers 46,500.
12The tribe of Simeon will camp next to
them. The leader of the people of Simeon
is Shelumiel son of Zurishaddai. 13His division numbers 59,300.
14The tribe of Gad will be next. The
leader of the people of Gad is Eliasaph
son of Deuel.[a] 15His division numbers
45,650.
16All the men assigned to the camp of

[a]14 Many manuscripts of the Masoretic Text, Samaritan Pentateuch and Vulgate (see also Num. 1:14); most manuscripts of the Masoretic Text *Reuel*

Reuben, according to their divisions, number 151,450. They will set out second.

17 Then the Tent of Meeting and the camp of the Levites will set out in the middle of the camps. They will set out in the same order as they encamp, each in his own place under his standard.

18 On the west will be the divisions of the camp of Ephraim under their standard. The leader of the people of Ephraim is Elishama son of Ammihud. 19 His division numbers 40,500.

20 The tribe of Manasseh will be next to them. The leader of the people of Manasseh is Gamaliel son of Pedahzur. 21 His division numbers 32,200.

22 The tribe of Benjamin will be next. The leader of the people of Benjamin is Abidan son of Gideoni. 23 His division numbers 35,400.

24 All the men assigned to the camp of Ephraim, according to their divisions, number 108,100. They will set out third.

25 On the north will be the divisions of the camp of Dan, under their standard. The leader of the people of Dan is Ahiezer son of Ammishaddai. 26 His division numbers 62,700.

27 The tribe of Asher will camp next to them. The leader of the people of Asher is Pagiel son of Ocran. 28 His division numbers 41,500.

29 The tribe of Naphtali will be next. The leader of the people of Naphtali is Ahira son of Enan. 30 His division numbers 53,400.

31 All the men assigned to the camp of Dan number 157,600. They will set out last, under their standards.

32 These are the Israelites, counted according to their families. All those in the camps, by their divisions, number 603,550. 33 The Levites, however, were not counted along with the other Israelites, as the LORD commanded Moses.

34 So the Israelites did everything the LORD commanded Moses; that is the way they encamped under their standards, and that is the way they set out, each with his clan and family.

The Levites

3 This is the account of the family of Aaron and Moses at the time the LORD talked with Moses on Mount Sinai.

2 The names of the sons of Aaron were Nadab the firstborn and Abihu, Eleazar and Ithamar. 3 Those were the names of Aaron's sons, the anointed priests, who were ordained to serve as priests. 4 Nadab and Abihu, however, fell dead before the LORD when they made an offering with unauthorized fire before him in the Desert of Sinai. They had no sons; so only Eleazar and Ithamar served as priests during the lifetime of their father Aaron.

5 The LORD said to Moses, 6 "Bring the tribe of Levi and present them to Aaron the priest to assist him. 7 They are to perform duties for him and for the whole community at the Tent of Meeting by doing the work of the tabernacle. 8 They are to take care of all the furnishings of the Tent of Meeting, fulfilling the obligations of the Israelites by doing the work of the tabernacle. 9 Give the Levites to Aaron and his sons; they are the Israelites who are to be given wholly to him.[a] 10 Appoint Aaron and his sons to serve as priests; anyone else who approaches the sanctuary must be put to death."

11 The LORD also said to Moses, 12 "I have taken the Levites from among the Israelites in place of the first male offspring of every Israelite woman. The Levites are mine, 13 for all the firstborn are mine. When I struck down all the firstborn in Egypt, I set apart for myself every firstborn in Israel, whether man or animal. They are to be mine. I am the LORD."

14 The LORD said to Moses in the Desert of Sinai, 15 "Count the Levites by their families and clans. Count every male a month old or more." 16 So Moses counted them, as he was commanded by the word of the LORD.

17 These were the names of the sons of Levi:
Gershon, Kohath and Merari.

18 These were the names of the Gershonite clans:

[a]9 Most manuscripts of the Masoretic Text; some manuscripts of the Masoretic Text, Samaritan Pentateuch and Septuagint (see also Num. 8:16) *to me*

Libni and Shimei.
19 The Kohathite clans:
Amram, Izhar, Hebron and Uzziel.
20 The Merarite clans:
Mahli and Mushi.
These were the Levite clans, according to
their families.

21 To Gershon belonged the clans of the Lib-
nites and Shimeites; these were the Gershonite
clans. 22 The number of all the males a month
old or more who were counted was 7,500.
23 The Gershonite clans were to camp on the
west, behind the tabernacle. 24 The leader of the
families of the Gershonites was Eliasaph son of
Lael. 25 At the Tent of Meeting the Gershonites
were responsible for the care of the tabernacle
and tent, its coverings, the curtain at the entrance to the Tent of Meeting, 26 the curtains
of the courtyard, the curtain at the entrance to
the courtyard surrounding the tabernacle and
altar, and the ropes—and everything related to
their use.

27 To Kohath belonged the clans of the Amramites, Izharites, Hebronites and Uzzielites;
these were the Kohathite clans. 28 The number of all the males a month old or more was
8,600.[a] The Kohathites were responsible for the
care of the sanctuary. 29 The Kohathite clans
were to camp on the south side of the tabernacle. 30 The leader of the families of the Kohathite clans was Elizaphan son of Uzziel. 31 They
were responsible for the care of the ark, the
table, the lampstand, the altars, the articles of
the sanctuary used in ministering, the curtain,
and everything related to their use. 32 The chief
leader of the Levites was Eleazar son of Aaron,
the priest. He was appointed over those who
were responsible for the care of the sanctuary.

33 To Merari belonged the clans of the Mah-
lites and the Mushites; these were the Merarite
clans. 34 The number of all the males a month
old or more who were counted was 6,200. 35 The
leader of the families of the Merarite clans was
Zuriel son of Abihail; they were to camp on the
north side of the tabernacle. 36 The Merarites
were appointed to take care of the frames of
the tabernacle, its crossbars, posts, bases, all its
equipment, and everything related to their use,
37 as well as the posts of the surrounding courtyard with their bases, tent pegs and ropes.

38 Moses and Aaron and his sons were to
camp to the east of the tabernacle, toward
the sunrise, in front of the Tent of Meeting.
They were responsible for the care of the sanctuary on behalf of the Israelites. Anyone else
who approached the sanctuary was to be put
to death.

39 The total number of Levites counted at
the LORD's command by Moses and Aaron according to their clans, including every male a
month old or more, was 22,000.

40 The LORD said to Moses, "Count all the
firstborn Israelite males who are a month old
or more and make a list of their names. 41 Take
the Levites for me in place of all the firstborn
of the Israelites, and the livestock of the Levites
in place of all the firstborn of the livestock of
the Israelites. I am the LORD."
42 So Moses counted all the firstborn of the
Israelites, as the LORD commanded him. 43 The
total number of firstborn males a month old or
more, listed by name, was 22,273.
44 The LORD also said to Moses, 45 "Take the
Levites in place of all the firstborn of Israel,
and the livestock of the Levites in place of their
livestock. The Levites are to be mine. I am the
LORD. 46 To redeem the 273 firstborn Israelites
who exceed the number of the Levites, 47 collect five shekels[b] for each one, according to the
sanctuary shekel, which weighs twenty gerahs.
48 Give the money for the redemption of the
additional Israelites to Aaron and his sons."
49 So Moses collected the redemption
money from those who exceeded the number
redeemed by the Levites. 50 From the firstborn
of the Israelites he collected silver weighing
1,365 shekels,[c] according to the sanctuary
shekel. 51 Moses gave the redemption money
to Aaron and his sons, as he was commanded
by the word of the LORD.

[a] 28 Hebrew; some Septuagint manuscripts *8,300* [b] 47 That is, about 2 ounces (about 55 grams) [c] 50 That is, about 35 pounds (about 15.5 kilograms)

The Kohathites

4 The LORD said to Moses and Aaron: 2“Take
a census of the Kohathite branch of the Levites by their clans and families. 3Count all the
men from thirty to fifty years of age who come
to serve in the work in the Tent of Meeting.
4“This is the work of the Kohathites in the
Tent of Meeting: the care of the most holy
things. 5When the camp is to move, Aaron and
his sons are to go in and take down the shielding curtain and cover the ark of the Testimony
with it. 6Then they are to cover this with hides
of sea cows,[a] spread a cloth of solid blue over
that and put the poles in place.
7“Over the table of the Presence they are
to spread a blue cloth and put on it the plates,
dishes and bowls, and the jars for drink offerings; the bread that is continually there is to
remain on it. 8Over these they are to spread a
scarlet cloth, cover that with hides of sea cows
and put its poles in place.
9“They are to take a blue cloth and cover the
lampstand that is for light, together with its
lamps, its wick trimmers and trays, and all its
jars for the oil used to supply it. 10Then they
are to wrap it and all its accessories in a covering of hides of sea cows and put it on a carrying frame.
11“Over the gold altar they are to spread a
blue cloth and cover that with hides of sea cows
and put its poles in place.
12“They are to take all the articles used for
ministering in the sanctuary, wrap them in a
blue cloth, cover that with hides of sea cows
and put them on a carrying frame.
13“They are to remove the ashes from the
bronze altar and spread a purple cloth over it.
14Then they are to place on it all the utensils
used for ministering at the altar, including the
firepans, meat forks, shovels and sprinkling
bowls. Over it they are to spread a covering of
hides of sea cows and put its poles in place.
15“After Aaron and his sons have finished
covering the holy furnishings and all the holy
articles, and when the camp is ready to move,
the Kohathites are to come to do the carrying.
But they must not touch the holy things or
they will die. The Kohathites are to carry those
things that are in the Tent of Meeting.
16“Eleazar son of Aaron, the priest, is to
have charge of the oil for the light, the fragrant
incense, the regular grain offering and the
anointing oil. He is to be in charge of the entire
tabernacle and everything in it, including its
holy furnishings and articles.”
17The LORD said to Moses and Aaron, 18“See
that the Kohathite tribal clans are not cut off
from the Levites. 19So that they may live and
not die when they come near the most holy
things, do this for them: Aaron and his sons
are to go into the sanctuary and assign to each
man his work and what he is to carry. 20But the
Kohathites must not go in to look at the holy
things, even for a moment, or they will die.”

The Gershonites

21The LORD said to Moses, 22“Take a census
also of the Gershonites by their families and
clans. 23Count all the men from thirty to fifty
years of age who come to serve in the work at
the Tent of Meeting.
24“This is the service of the Gershonite clans
as they work and carry burdens: 25They are to
carry the curtains of the tabernacle, the Tent
of Meeting, its covering and the outer covering
of hides of sea cows, the curtains for the entrance to the Tent of Meeting, 26the curtains of
the courtyard surrounding the tabernacle and
altar, the curtain for the entrance, the ropes
and all the equipment used in its service. The
Gershonites are to do all that needs to be done
with these things. 27All their service, whether
carrying or doing other work, is to be done under the direction of Aaron and his sons. You
shall assign to them as their responsibility all
they are to carry. 28This is the service of the
Gershonite clans at the Tent of Meeting. Their
duties are to be under the direction of Ithamar
son of Aaron, the priest.

The Merarites

29“Count the Merarites by their clans and
families. 30Count all the men from thirty to
fifty years of age who come to serve in the work
at the Tent of Meeting. 31This is their duty as
they perform service at the Tent of Meeting:
to carry the frames of the tabernacle, its crossbars, posts and bases, 32as well as the posts of
the surrounding courtyard with their bases,

[a]6 That is, dugongs; also in verses 8, 10, 11, 12, 14 and 25

tent pegs, ropes, all their equipment and everything related to their use. Assign to each man the specific things he is to carry. [33]This is the service of the Merarite clans as they work at the Tent of Meeting under the direction of Ithamar son of Aaron, the priest."

The Numbering of the Levite Clans

[34]Moses, Aaron and the leaders of the community counted the Kohathites by their clans and families. [35]All the men from thirty to fifty years of age who came to serve in the work in the Tent of Meeting, [36]counted by clans, were 2,750. [37]This was the total of all those in the Kohathite clans who served in the Tent of Meeting. Moses and Aaron counted them according to the LORD's command through Moses.

[38]The Gershonites were counted by their clans and families. [39]All the men from thirty to fifty years of age who came to serve in the work at the Tent of Meeting, [40]counted by their clans and families, were 2,630. [41]This was the total of those in the Gershonite clans who served at the Tent of Meeting. Moses and Aaron counted them according to the LORD's command.

[42]The Merarites were counted by their clans and families. [43]All the men from thirty to fifty years of age who came to serve in the work at the Tent of Meeting, [44]counted by their clans, were 3,200. [45]This was the total of those in the Merarite clans. Moses and Aaron counted them according to the LORD's command through Moses.

[46]So Moses, Aaron and the leaders of Israel counted all the Levites by their clans and families. [47]All the men from thirty to fifty years of age who came to do the work of serving and carrying the Tent of Meeting [48]numbered 8,580. [49]At the LORD's command through Moses, each was assigned his work and told what to carry.

Thus they were counted, as the LORD commanded Moses.

The Purity of the Camp

5 The LORD said to Moses, [2]"Command the Israelites to send away from the camp anyone who has an infectious skin disease[a] or a discharge of any kind, or who is ceremonially unclean because of a dead body. [3]Send away male and female alike; send them outside the camp so they will not defile their camp, where I dwell among them." [4]The Israelites did this; they sent them outside the camp. They did just as the LORD had instructed Moses.

Restitution for Wrongs

[5]The LORD said to Moses, [6]"Say to the Israelites: 'When a man or woman wrongs another in any way[b] and so is unfaithful to the LORD, that person is guilty [7]and must confess the sin he has committed. He must make full restitution for his wrong, add one fifth to it and give it all to the person he has wronged. [8]But if that person has no close relative to whom restitution can be made for the wrong, the restitution belongs to the LORD and must be given to the priest, along with the ram with which atonement is made for him. [9]All the sacred contributions the Israelites bring to a priest will belong to him. [10]Each man's sacred gifts are his own, but what he gives to the priest will belong to the priest.' "

The Test for an Unfaithful Wife

[11]Then the LORD said to Moses, [12]"Speak to the Israelites and say to them: 'If a man's wife goes astray and is unfaithful to him [13]by sleeping with another man, and this is hidden from her husband and her impurity is undetected (since there is no witness against her and she has not been caught in the act), [14]and if feelings of jealousy come over her husband and he suspects his wife and she is impure—or if he is jealous and suspects her even though she is not impure— [15]then he is to take his wife to the priest. He must also take an offering of a tenth of an ephah[c] of barley flour on her behalf. He must not pour oil on it or put incense on it, because it is a grain offering for jealousy, a reminder offering to draw attention to guilt.

[16]" 'The priest shall bring her and have her stand before the LORD. [17]Then he shall take some holy water in a clay jar and put some dust from the tabernacle floor into the water. [18]After the priest has had the woman stand before the LORD, he shall loosen her hair and place in her hands the reminder offering, the grain

[a]2 Traditionally *leprosy*; the Hebrew word was used for various diseases affecting the skin—not necessarily leprosy. [b]6 Or *woman commits any wrong common to mankind* [c]15 That is, probably about 2 quarts (about 2 liters)

How to Restore Relationships

Read: Numbers 5:5–8

SUE *LOVED* HER NEW SWEATER. She couldn't wait to show it to her friend Leslie. The two decided to meet for dinner and a movie. Leslie loved the sweater too. She immediately said, "That sweater would be perfect for my office party. Can I borrow it?" Sue hesitated, but decided a friend was more valuable than an article of clothing, so she agreed. When she got the sweater back, there was a hole under the arm. Leslie apologized profusely, saying, "It must have unraveled. I'm so sorry." Sue nodded and said, "Oh, it's okay." But things were never the same between the two of them. Sue felt that Leslie had taken advantage of her. Leslie thought Sue had overreacted over a simple article of clothing. Over time, the friendship unraveled like the sweater. What would have happened if Leslie had offered to repair or replace the sweater . . . and maybe added a scarf to apologize?

When God gave Moses the Law, he instituted a system of restitution: Anyone who injured another paid the price for what was stolen or destroyed and added 20 percent to the value. We may think of restitution as justice for the wronged party and punishment for the offender. But restitution offers more: It builds a bridge between the two parties, paving the way for relationships to be restored. By confessing the sin and compensating for any loss, the offender no longer has to deal with guilt. Receiving restitution and more frees the injured party from feeling unfairly treated.

Forgiveness from God coupled with responsibility toward the other person are key to restoring relationships. In Jesus' eyes, those broken relationships are always our responsibility. If someone has something against us, he calls us to go and make it right (see Matthew 5:23–24). If we have something against another, we're responsible to take the initiative to settle our differences with them (see Matthew 18:15). It's not always comfortable. But it's always the right thing to do.

Do you feel taken advantage of? Maybe it's time to engage someone in conversation rather than detach from your relationship with them. Or maybe you've unintentionally mistreated a friend . . . you owe them money or lunch or a favor. Consider what needs to be done and take action: Repay the debt, replace the item and apologize for a wrong. Do whatever it takes to restore the relationship. Do it because it pleases God and because your relationships will be richer for it.

Numbers 5:5–7

The LORD said to Moses, "Say to the Israelites: 'When a man or woman wrongs another in any way and so is unfaithful to the LORD, that person is guilty and must confess the sin he has committed. He must make full restitution for his wrong, add one fifth to it and give it all to the person he has wronged.' "

reflection

1. Why is restitution necessary?
2. Think about a relationship that is unraveling. How can you make restitution?
3. What are some ways you can reconcile with God after you have sinned? What restitution can you offer?

RELATED READINGS

Leviticus 6:1–7;
Luke 19:8–10

Go to page 165 for your next devotional reading.

offering for jealousy, while he himself holds
the bitter water that brings a curse. 19Then the
priest shall put the woman under oath and say
to her, "If no other man has slept with you and
you have not gone astray and become impure
while married to your husband, may this bitter
water that brings a curse not harm you. 20But
if you have gone astray while married to your
husband and you have defiled yourself by sleeping with a man other than your husband"—
21here the priest is to put the woman under
this curse of the oath—"may the LORD cause
your people to curse and denounce you when
he causes your thigh to waste away and your abdomen to swell.[a] 22May this water that brings
a curse enter your body so that your abdomen
swells and your thigh wastes away.[b]"
"'Then the woman is to say, "Amen. So
be it."
23"'The priest is to write these curses on a
scroll and then wash them off into the bitter
water. 24He shall have the woman drink the
bitter water that brings a curse, and this water
will enter her and cause bitter suffering. 25The
priest is to take from her hands the grain offering for jealousy, wave it before the LORD and
bring it to the altar. 26The priest is then to take
a handful of the grain offering as a memorial
offering and burn it on the altar; after that, he
is to have the woman drink the water. 27If she
has defiled herself and been unfaithful to her
husband, then when she is made to drink the
water that brings a curse, it will go into her and
cause bitter suffering; her abdomen will swell
and her thigh waste away,[c] and she will become
accursed among her people. 28If, however, the
woman has not defiled herself and is free from
impurity, she will be cleared of guilt and will be
able to have children.
29"'This, then, is the law of jealousy when
a woman goes astray and defiles herself while
married to her husband, 30or when feelings
of jealousy come over a man because he suspects his wife. The priest is to have her stand
before the LORD and is to apply this entire
law to her. 31The husband will be innocent of
any wrongdoing, but the woman will bear the
consequences of her sin.'"

The Nazirite

6 The LORD said to Moses, 2"Speak to the
Israelites and say to them: 'If a man or
woman wants to make a special vow, a vow of
separation to the LORD as a Nazirite, 3he must
abstain from wine and other fermented drink
and must not drink vinegar made from wine
or from other fermented drink. He must not
drink grape juice or eat grapes or raisins. 4As
long as he is a Nazirite, he must not eat anything that comes from the grapevine, not even
the seeds or skins.
5"'During the entire period of his vow of
separation no razor may be used on his head.
He must be holy until the period of his separation to the LORD is over; he must let the
hair of his head grow long. 6Throughout the
period of his separation to the LORD he must
not go near a dead body. 7Even if his own father or mother or brother or sister dies, he
must not make himself ceremonially unclean
on account of them, because the symbol of his
separation to God is on his head. 8Throughout
the period of his separation he is consecrated
to the LORD.
9"'If someone dies suddenly in his presence,
thus defiling the hair he has dedicated, he must
shave his head on the day of his cleansing—the
seventh day. 10Then on the eighth day he must
bring two doves or two young pigeons to the
priest at the entrance to the Tent of Meeting.
11The priest is to offer one as a sin offering and
the other as a burnt offering to make atonement for him because he sinned by being in
the presence of the dead body. That same day
he is to consecrate his head. 12He must dedicate himself to the LORD for the period of his
separation and must bring a year-old male
lamb as a guilt offering. The previous days do
not count, because he became defiled during
his separation.
13"'Now this is the law for the Nazirite when
the period of his separation is over. He is to be
brought to the entrance to the Tent of Meeting.
14There he is to present his offerings to the
LORD: a year-old male lamb without defect for
a burnt offering, a year-old ewe lamb without
defect for a sin offering, a ram without defect

[a]21 Or *causes you to have a miscarrying womb and barrenness* [b]22 Or *body and cause you to be barren and have a miscarrying womb*
[c]27 Or *suffering; she will have barrenness and a miscarrying womb*

What's in a Name?

Read: Numbers 6:1–27

ONE POPULAR WEBSITE offers 970 books to help you name your baby. Titles like *Cool Names for Babies* and *75,000+ Baby Names for the 21st Century* reveal a truth most parents already know: Names mean something. We spend months agonizing over just the right name for the new baby coming into the world. Should we name the baby after the father or the mother's father? If we name the baby this will they call her that? What if we get it wrong—will she be scarred for life?

In the Old Testament, names were not chosen because they were cute or cool. They represented the parents' hopes, dreams and prayers for their child. Take Daniel the prophet, for example, held captive in Babylon. His name meant "God is my judge." Names sometimes represented the circumstances of the child's birth: Isaac's name reflected his mother's laughter; Esau's, his hairy appearance.

God's name is so revered to the Jews that, starting in the later Old Testament days, they would not say it out loud. Even today in synagogues, they won't say the sacred name YHWH (Jehovah). Instead they call him *Adonai*—the LORD.

When God instructed Aaron to bless the Israelites with his sacred name, he bestowed a great honor on the newborn nation. He was promising to bless them. He was setting them apart for his own special purpose. As the priests pronounced this blessing on the Israelites, they were, in effect, calling upon God to live in their midst and meet their needs as their heavenly provider. To be called by God's holy name meant that they would be expected to act as holy people. They would have to live up to the name they'd been given.

When we were born again, we received a new name: Christian. We now carry the name of our Savior. Just as the Israelites were expected to bear God's name with dignity, we are to honor Christ's name by reflecting his character with our words and actions. That also means not using his name in vain or allowing others to defame it.

Jesus' name is the name above all names. Wear it proudly. Defend it loudly. Make it mean something holy and wonderful to everyone you meet.

Numbers 6:27

"So they will put my name on the Israelites, and I will bless them."

reflection

1 Think about your own name. How does your name reflect who you are?

2 How do you feel when you hear someone use Christ's name in vain? How do you respond?

3 How did today's devotion affect your understanding of the importance of bearing God's name?

RELATED READINGS

Genesis 2:19–20; 4:1,25–26; Exodus 34:1–7; Revelation 2:17

Go to page 171 for your next devotional reading.

for a fellowship offering,[a] 15 together with their
grain offerings and drink offerings, and a basket of bread made without yeast—cakes made
of fine flour mixed with oil, and wafers spread
with oil.
16 " 'The priest is to present them before the
LORD and make the sin offering and the burnt
offering. 17 He is to present the basket of unleavened bread and is to sacrifice the ram as a fellowship offering to the LORD, together with its
grain offering and drink offering.
18 " 'Then at the entrance to the Tent of Meeting, the Nazirite must shave off the hair that he
dedicated. He is to take the hair and put it in
the fire that is under the sacrifice of the fellowship offering.
19 " 'After the Nazirite has shaved off the hair
of his dedication, the priest is to place in his
hands a boiled shoulder of the ram, and a cake
and a wafer from the basket, both made without yeast. 20 The priest shall then wave them
before the LORD as a wave offering; they are
holy and belong to the priest, together with the
breast that was waved and the thigh that was
presented. After that, the Nazirite may drink
wine.
21 " 'This is the law of the Nazirite who vows
his offering to the LORD in accordance with his
separation, in addition to whatever else he can
afford. He must fulfill the vow he has made, according to the law of the Nazirite.' "

The Priestly Blessing

22 The LORD said to Moses,
23 "Tell Aaron and his sons,
'This is how you are to bless the
Israelites. Say to them:

24 " ' "The LORD bless you
and keep you;
25 the LORD make his face
shine upon you
and be gracious to you;
26 the LORD turn his face
toward you
and give you peace." '

27 "So they will put my name on the Israelites, and I will bless them."

Numbers 6:25

God Blesses His People

"The LORD make his face
shine upon you
and be gracious to you."

Offerings at the Dedication of the Tabernacle

7 When Moses finished setting up the tabernacle, he anointed it and consecrated it
and all its furnishings. He also anointed and
consecrated the altar and all its utensils. 2 Then
the leaders of Israel, the heads of families who
were the tribal leaders in charge of those who
were counted, made offerings. 3 They brought
as their gifts before the LORD six covered carts
and twelve oxen—an ox from each leader and
a cart from every two. These they presented before the tabernacle.
4 The LORD said to Moses, 5 "Accept these
from them, that they may be used in the work
at the Tent of Meeting. Give them to the Levites
as each man's work requires."
6 So Moses took the carts and oxen and gave
them to the Levites. 7 He gave two carts and
four oxen to the Gershonites, as their work required, 8 and he gave four carts and eight oxen
to the Merarites, as their work required. They
were all under the direction of Ithamar son of
Aaron, the priest. 9 But Moses did not give any
to the Kohathites, because they were to carry
on their shoulders the holy things, for which
they were responsible.
10 When the altar was anointed, the leaders
brought their offerings for its dedication and
presented them before the altar. 11 For the
LORD had said to Moses, "Each day one leader
is to bring his offering for the dedication of the
altar."
12 The one who brought his offering on the first day was Nahshon son of Amminadab of the
tribe of Judah.
13 His offering was one silver plate weighing a hun-
dred and thirty shekels,[b]
and one silver sprinkling
bowl weighing seventy
shekels,[c] both according to
the sanctuary shekel, each
filled with fine flour mixed
with oil as a grain offering; 14 one gold dish
weighing ten shekels,[d] filled with incense;

[a]14 Traditionally *peace offering*; also in verses 17 and 18 [b]13 That is, about 3 1/4 pounds (about 1.5 kilograms); also elsewhere in this chapter [c]13 That is, about 1 3/4 pounds (about 0.8 kilogram); also elsewhere in this chapter [d]14 That is, about 4 ounces (about 110 grams); also elsewhere in this chapter

15 one young bull, one ram and one male
lamb a year old, for a burnt offering; 16 one
male goat for a sin offering; 17 and two
oxen, five rams, five male goats and five
male lambs a year old, to be sacrificed as a
fellowship offering.[a] This was the offering
of Nahshon son of Amminadab.

18 On the second day Nethanel son of Zuar, the
leader of Issachar, brought his offering.
19 The offering he brought was one silver
plate weighing a hundred and thirty shekels, and one silver sprinkling bowl weighing seventy shekels, both according to the
sanctuary shekel, each filled with fine flour
mixed with oil as a grain offering; 20 one
gold dish weighing ten shekels, filled with
incense; 21 one young bull, one ram and
one male lamb a year old, for a burnt offering; 22 one male goat for a sin offering;
23 and two oxen, five rams, five male goats
and five male lambs a year old, to be sacrificed as a fellowship offering. This was the
offering of Nethanel son of Zuar.

24 On the third day, Eliab son of Helon, the
leader of the people of Zebulun, brought his offering.
25 His offering was one silver plate weighing a hundred and thirty shekels, and one
silver sprinkling bowl weighing seventy
shekels, both according to the sanctuary
shekel, each filled with fine flour mixed
with oil as a grain offering; 26 one gold
dish weighing ten shekels, filled with incense; 27 one young bull, one ram and one
male lamb a year old, for a burnt offering;
28 one male goat for a sin offering; 29 and
two oxen, five rams, five male goats and
five male lambs a year old, to be sacrificed
as a fellowship offering. This was the offering of Eliab son of Helon.

30 On the fourth day Elizur son of Shedeur, the
leader of the people of Reuben, brought his offering.
31 His offering was one silver plate weighing a hundred and thirty shekels, and one
silver sprinkling bowl weighing seventy
shekels, both according to the sanctuary
shekel, each filled with fine flour mixed
with oil as a grain offering; 32 one gold
dish weighing ten shekels, filled with incense; 33 one young bull, one ram and one
male lamb a year old, for a burnt offering;
34 one male goat for a sin offering; 35 and
two oxen, five rams, five male goats and
five male lambs a year old, to be sacrificed
as a fellowship offering. This was the offering of Elizur son of Shedeur.

36 On the fifth day Shelumiel son of Zurishaddai, the leader of the people of Simeon, brought
his offering.
37 His offering was one silver plate weighing a hundred and thirty shekels, and one
silver sprinkling bowl weighing seventy
shekels, both according to the sanctuary
shekel, each filled with fine flour mixed
with oil as a grain offering; 38 one gold
dish weighing ten shekels, filled with incense; 39 one young bull, one ram and one
male lamb a year old, for a burnt offering;
40 one male goat for a sin offering; 41 and
two oxen, five rams, five male goats and
five male lambs a year old, to be sacrificed
as a fellowship offering. This was the offering of Shelumiel son of Zurishaddai.

42 On the sixth day Eliasaph son of Deuel, the
leader of the people of Gad, brought his offering.
43 His offering was one silver plate weighing a hundred and thirty shekels, and one
silver sprinkling bowl weighing seventy
shekels, both according to the sanctuary
shekel, each filled with fine flour mixed
with oil as a grain offering; 44 one gold
dish weighing ten shekels, filled with incense; 45 one young bull, one ram and one
male lamb a year old, for a burnt offering;
46 one male goat for a sin offering; 47 and
two oxen, five rams, five male goats and
five male lambs a year old, to be sacrificed
as a fellowship offering. This was the offering of Eliasaph son of Deuel.

48 On the seventh day Elishama son of Ammihud, the leader of the people of Ephraim,
brought his offering.

[a] 17 Traditionally *peace offering*; also elsewhere in this chapter

49His offering was one silver plate weighing a hundred and thirty shekels, and one
silver sprinkling bowl weighing seventy
shekels, both according to the sanctuary
shekel, each filled with fine flour mixed
with oil as a grain offering; 50one gold
dish weighing ten shekels, filled with incense; 51one young bull, one ram and
one male lamb a year old, for a burnt
offering; 52one male goat for a sin offering; 53and two oxen, five rams, five male
goats and five male lambs a year old, to
be sacrificed as a fellowship offering.
This was the offering of Elishama son of
Ammihud.

54On the eighth day Gamaliel son of Pedahzur,
the leader of the people of Manasseh, brought
his offering.

55His offering was one silver plate weighing a hundred and thirty shekels, and one
silver sprinkling bowl weighing seventy
shekels, both according to the sanctuary
shekel, each filled with fine flour mixed
with oil as a grain offering; 56one gold
dish weighing ten shekels, filled with incense; 57one young bull, one ram and one
male lamb a year old, for a burnt offering;
58one male goat for a sin offering; 59and
two oxen, five rams, five male goats and
five male lambs a year old, to be sacrificed
as a fellowship offering. This was the offering of Gamaliel son of Pedahzur.

60On the ninth day Abidan son of Gideoni,
the leader of the people of Benjamin, brought
his offering.

61His offering was one silver plate weighing a hundred and thirty shekels, and one
silver sprinkling bowl weighing seventy
shekels, both according to the sanctuary
shekel, each filled with fine flour mixed
with oil as a grain offering; 62one gold
dish weighing ten shekels, filled with incense; 63one young bull, one ram and one
male lamb a year old, for a burnt offering;
64one male goat for a sin offering; 65and
two oxen, five rams, five male goats and
five male lambs a year old, to be sacrificed
as a fellowship offering. This was the offering of Abidan son of Gideoni.

66On the tenth day Ahiezer son of Ammishaddai, the leader of the people of Dan, brought
his offering.

67His offering was one silver plate weighing a hundred and thirty shekels, and one
silver sprinkling bowl weighing seventy
shekels, both according to the sanctuary
shekel, each filled with fine flour mixed
with oil as a grain offering; 68one gold
dish weighing ten shekels, filled with incense; 69one young bull, one ram and one
male lamb a year old, for a burnt offering;
70one male goat for a sin offering; 71and
two oxen, five rams, five male goats and
five male lambs a year old, to be sacrificed
as a fellowship offering. This was the offering of Ahiezer son of Ammishaddai.

72On the eleventh day Pagiel son of Ocran,
the leader of the people of Asher, brought his offering.

73His offering was one silver plate weighing a hundred and thirty shekels, and one
silver sprinkling bowl weighing seventy
shekels, both according to the sanctuary
shekel, each filled with fine flour mixed
with oil as a grain offering; 74one gold
dish weighing ten shekels, filled with incense; 75one young bull, one ram and one
male lamb a year old, for a burnt offering;
76one male goat for a sin offering; 77and
two oxen, five rams, five male goats and
five male lambs a year old, to be sacrificed
as a fellowship offering. This was the offering of Pagiel son of Ocran.

78On the twelfth day Ahira son of Enan, the
leader of the people of Naphtali, brought his offering.

79His offering was one silver plate weighing a hundred and thirty shekels, and one
silver sprinkling bowl weighing seventy
shekels, both according to the sanctuary
shekel, each filled with fine flour mixed
with oil as a grain offering; 80one gold
dish weighing ten shekels, filled with incense; 81one young bull, one ram and one
male lamb a year old, for a burnt offering;
82one male goat for a sin offering; 83and
two oxen, five rams, five male goats and
five male lambs a year old, to be sacrificed

as a fellowship offering. This was the offering of Ahira son of Enan.

84These were the offerings of the Israelite
leaders for the dedication of the altar when it
was anointed: twelve silver plates, twelve silver
sprinkling bowls and twelve gold dishes. 85Each
silver plate weighed a hundred and thirty shekels, and each sprinkling bowl seventy shekels.
Altogether, the silver dishes weighed two thousand four hundred shekels,[a] according to the
sanctuary shekel. 86The twelve gold dishes
filled with incense weighed ten shekels each,
according to the sanctuary shekel. Altogether,
the gold dishes weighed a hundred and twenty
shekels.[b] 87The total number of animals for the
burnt offering came to twelve
young bulls, twelve rams and
twelve male lambs a year old,
together with their grain offering. Twelve male goats were
used for the sin offering. 88The
total number of animals for the
sacrifice of the fellowship offering came to twenty-four oxen,
sixty rams, sixty male goats
and sixty male lambs a year
old. These were the offerings
for the dedication of the altar
after it was anointed.

89When Moses entered the
Tent of Meeting to speak with
the LORD, he heard the voice
speaking to him from between
the two cherubim above the
atonement cover on the ark of
the Testimony. And he spoke with him.

> **Numbers 7:89**
>
> *God Can Be Known*
>
> When Moses entered the Tent of Meeting to speak with the LORD, he heard the voice speaking to him from between the two cherubim above the atonement cover on the ark of the Testimony. And he spoke with him.

Setting Up the Lamps

8 The LORD said to Moses, 2"Speak to Aaron
and say to him, 'When you set up the
seven lamps, they are to light the area in front
of the lampstand.' "

3Aaron did so; he set up the lamps so that
they faced forward on the lampstand, just as
the LORD commanded Moses. 4This is how
the lampstand was made: It was made of hammered gold—from its base to its blossoms. The
lampstand was made exactly like the pattern
the LORD had shown Moses.

The Setting Apart of the Levites

5The LORD said to Moses: 6"Take the Levites
from among the other Israelites and make them
ceremonially clean. 7To purify them, do this:
Sprinkle the water of cleansing on them; then
have them shave their whole bodies and wash
their clothes, and so purify themselves. 8Have
them take a young bull with its grain offering of
fine flour mixed with oil; then you are to take a
second young bull for a sin offering. 9Bring the
Levites to the front of the Tent of Meeting and
assemble the whole Israelite community. 10You
are to bring the Levites before the LORD, and
the Israelites are to lay their hands on them.
11Aaron is to present the Levites before the
LORD as a wave offering from the Israelites, so
that they may be ready to do
the work of the LORD.

12"After the Levites lay their
hands on the heads of the bulls,
use the one for a sin offering to
the LORD and the other for a
burnt offering, to make atonement for the Levites. 13Have
the Levites stand in front of
Aaron and his sons and then
present them as a wave offering
to the LORD. 14In this way you
are to set the Levites apart from
the other Israelites, and the Levites will be mine.

15"After you have purified
the Levites and presented them
as a wave offering, they are to
come to do their work at the
Tent of Meeting. 16They are the Israelites who
are to be given wholly to me. I have taken them
as my own in place of the firstborn, the first
male offspring from every Israelite woman.
17Every firstborn male in Israel, whether man
or animal, is mine. When I struck down all the
firstborn in Egypt, I set them apart for myself.
18And I have taken the Levites in place of all the
firstborn sons in Israel. 19Of all the Israelites, I
have given the Levites as gifts to Aaron and his
sons to do the work at the Tent of Meeting on
behalf of the Israelites and to make atonement
for them so that no plague will strike the Israelites when they go near the sanctuary."

[a]85 That is, about 60 pounds (about 28 kilograms) [b]86 That is, about 3 pounds (about 1.4 kilograms)

20Moses, Aaron and the whole Israelite community did with the Levites just as the LORD commanded Moses. 21The Levites purified themselves and washed their clothes. Then Aaron presented them as a wave offering before the LORD and made atonement for them to purify them. 22After that, the Levites came to do their work at the Tent of Meeting under the supervision of Aaron and his sons. They did with the Levites just as the LORD commanded Moses.

23The LORD said to Moses, 24"This applies to the Levites: Men twenty-five years old or more shall come to take part in the work at the Tent of Meeting, 25but at the age of fifty, they must retire from their regular service and work no longer. 26They may assist their brothers in performing their duties at the Tent of Meeting, but they themselves must not do the work. This, then, is how you are to assign the responsibilities of the Levites."

The Passover

9 The LORD spoke to Moses in the Desert of Sinai in the first month of the second year after they came out of Egypt. He said, 2"Have the Israelites celebrate the Passover at the appointed time. 3Celebrate it at the appointed time, at twilight on the fourteenth day of this month, in accordance with all its rules and regulations."

4So Moses told the Israelites to celebrate the Passover, 5and they did so in the Desert of Sinai at twilight on the fourteenth day of the first month. The Israelites did everything just as the LORD commanded Moses.

6But some of them could not celebrate the Passover on that day because they were ceremonially unclean on account of a dead body. So they came to Moses and Aaron that same day 7and said to Moses, "We have become unclean because of a dead body, but why should we be kept from presenting the LORD's offering with the other Israelites at the appointed time?"

8Moses answered them, "Wait until I find out what the LORD commands concerning you."

> **Numbers 9:17**
>
> *God Leads*
>
> Whenever the cloud lifted from above the Tent, the Israelites set out; wherever the cloud settled, the Israelites encamped.

9Then the LORD said to Moses, 10"Tell the Israelites: 'When any of you or your descendants are unclean because of a dead body or are away on a journey, they may still celebrate the LORD's Passover. 11They are to celebrate it on the fourteenth day of the second month at twilight. They are to eat the lamb, together with unleavened bread and bitter herbs. 12They must not leave any of it till morning or break any of its bones. When they celebrate the Passover, they must follow all the regulations. 13But if a man who is ceremonially clean and not on a journey fails to celebrate the Passover, that person must be cut off from his people because he did not present the LORD's offering at the appointed time. That man will bear the consequences of his sin.

14" 'An alien living among you who wants to celebrate the LORD's Passover must do so in accordance with its rules and regulations. You must have the same regulations for the alien and the native-born.' "

The Cloud Above the Tabernacle

15On the day the tabernacle, the Tent of the Testimony, was set up, the cloud covered it. From evening till morning the cloud above the tabernacle looked like fire. 16That is how it continued to be; the cloud covered it, and at night it looked like fire. 17Whenever the cloud lifted from above the Tent, the Israelites set out; wherever the cloud settled, the Israelites encamped. 18At the LORD's command the Israelites set out, and at his command they encamped. As long as the cloud stayed over the tabernacle, they remained in camp. 19When the cloud remained over the tabernacle a long time, the Israelites obeyed the LORD's order and did not set out. 20Sometimes the cloud was over the tabernacle only a few days; at the LORD's command they would encamp, and then at his command they would set out. 21Sometimes the cloud stayed only from evening till morning, and when it lifted in the morning, they set out. Whether by day or by night, whenever the cloud lifted, they

Life in the Fast Lane

Read: Numbers 9:15–23

JOANIE COULD SCARCELY BELIEVE her eyes. The woman speeding along the Los Angeles freeway next to her balanced a cup of coffee and a cigarette in one hand and ignored her three children bouncing around in the back seat. At that moment, Joanie longed to quit her job and move to the mountains. She prayed, *Lord, I'm tired of this fast-paced life. Can I get off this merry-go-round?*

Maybe life in the fast lane doesn't appeal to you anymore either. You're tired. You need a break. Maybe you're thinking of buying a nice little cabin with a fireplace, a cat and a rocking chair. *Anywhere but here, Lord,* you think. But what does God think?

Following her release from Ravensbruck concentration camp, Corrie ten Boom purchased a house called Schapendunien and turned it into a home for disabled people and ex-prisoners. She thought that was where God wanted her to settle down. But in late 1945, she began to sense that God wanted her to travel to the United States to tell her story. So she crossed the Atlantic and became what she described as a "tramp for the Lord." It wasn't until 1977, when she suffered a stroke, that she finally retired to a home in Orange, California. Choosing to follow God's leading rather than her own comfort-level, Corrie ten Boom maintained an itinerant lifestyle of travel for Christ.

You may be facing unbearable pressures in your daily life, pressures you think will get better if you settle down in a peaceful location of your choice. But God showed the Israelites that he chooses our paths. He gave them a visible reminder of his presence to guide them: a cloud by day and a fire by night. When the cloud lifted, they set out; when it stopped, they camped. God's sign in the sky marked their course and set the pace. By looking up, the Israelites discovered that the Lord ordained the movements of his people; God saying "no" was just as important as God saying "go." God alone knew the reasons for the journey, the unseen dangers ahead and the ultimate purpose beyond each move.

God ordered the lives of the Israelites. And he'll order yours if you will let him. If you need to know which way to turn, look up.

Numbers 9:17–18

Whenever the cloud lifted from above the Tent, the Israelites set out; wherever the cloud settled, the Israelites encamped. At the LORD's command the Israelites set out, and at his command they encamped. As long as the cloud stayed over the tabernacle, they remained in camp.

reflection

1 What changes are you considering in your life? Have you asked God about them?

2 What are the obstacles (if any) that you face in making your life-changing decisions? Could God be telling you "no" instead of "go"?

3 Is it difficult for you to be patient, or are you willing to wait for God's guidance? Take the time to look up and ask the Lord to show you what he wants you to do.

RELATED READINGS

Deuteronomy 4:1; 28:1; Psalm 43:3–4

Go to page 174 for your next devotional reading.

set out. 22 Whether the cloud stayed over the tabernacle for two days or a month or a year, the Israelites would remain in camp and not set out; but when it lifted, they would set out. 23 At the LORD's command they encamped, and at the LORD's command they set out. They obeyed the LORD's order, in accordance with his command through Moses.

The Silver Trumpets

10 The LORD said to Moses: 2 "Make two trumpets of hammered silver, and use them for calling the community together and for having the camps set out. 3 When both are sounded, the whole community is to assemble before you at the entrance to the Tent of Meeting. 4 If only one is sounded, the leaders—the heads of the clans of Israel—are to assemble before you. 5 When a trumpet blast is sounded, the tribes camping on the east are to set out. 6 At the sounding of a second blast, the camps on the south are to set out. The blast will be the signal for setting out. 7 To gather the assembly, blow the trumpets, but not with the same signal.

8 "The sons of Aaron, the priests, are to blow the trumpets. This is to be a lasting ordinance for you and the generations to come. 9 When you go into battle in your own land against an enemy who is oppressing you, sound a blast on the trumpets. Then you will be remembered by the LORD your God and rescued from your enemies. 10 Also at your times of rejoicing—your appointed feasts and New Moon festivals—you are to sound the trumpets over your burnt offerings and fellowship offerings,[a] and they will be a memorial for you before your God. I am the LORD your God."

The Israelites Leave Sinai

11 On the twentieth day of the second month of the second year, the cloud lifted from above the tabernacle of the Testimony. 12 Then the Israelites set out from the Desert of Sinai and traveled from place to place until the cloud came to rest in the Desert of Paran. 13 They set out, this first time, at the LORD's command through Moses.

14 The divisions of the camp of Judah went first, under their standard. Nahshon son of Amminadab was in command. 15 Nethanel son of Zuar was over the division of the tribe of Issachar, 16 and Eliab son of Helon was over the division of the tribe of Zebulun. 17 Then the tabernacle was taken down, and the Gershonites and Merarites, who carried it, set out.

18 The divisions of the camp of Reuben went next, under their standard. Elizur son of Shedeur was in command. 19 Shelumiel son of Zurishaddai was over the division of the tribe of Simeon, 20 and Eliasaph son of Deuel was over the division of the tribe of Gad. 21 Then the Kohathites set out, carrying the holy things. The tabernacle was to be set up before they arrived.

22 The divisions of the camp of Ephraim went next, under their standard. Elishama son of Ammihud was in command. 23 Gamaliel son of Pedahzur was over the division of the tribe of Manasseh, 24 and Abidan son of Gideoni was over the division of the tribe of Benjamin.

25 Finally, as the rear guard for all the units, the divisions of the camp of Dan set out, under their standard. Ahiezer son of Ammishaddai was in command. 26 Pagiel son of Ocran was over the division of the tribe of Asher, 27 and Ahira son of Enan was over the division of the tribe of Naphtali. 28 This was the order of march for the Israelite divisions as they set out.

29 Now Moses said to Hobab son of Reuel the Midianite, Moses' father-in-law, "We are setting out for the place about which the LORD said, 'I will give it to you.' Come with us and we will treat you well, for the LORD has promised good things to Israel."

30 He answered, "No, I will not go; I am going back to my own land and my own people."

31 But Moses said, "Please do not leave us. You know where we should camp in the desert, and you can be our eyes. 32 If you come with us, we will share with you whatever good things the LORD gives us."

33 So they set out from the mountain of the LORD and traveled for three days. The ark of the covenant of the LORD went before them during those three days to find them a place to rest. 34 The cloud of the LORD was over them by day when they set out from the camp.

35 Whenever the ark set out, Moses said,

[a] 10 Traditionally *peace offerings*

"Rise up, O LORD!
May your enemies be scattered;
may your foes flee before you."

36Whenever it came to rest, he said,

"Return, O LORD,
to the countless thousands of Israel."

Fire From the LORD

11 Now the people complained about
their hardships in the hearing of the
LORD, and when he heard them his anger
was aroused. Then fire from the LORD burned
among them and consumed some of the outskirts of the camp. 2When the people cried
out to Moses, he prayed to the LORD and the
fire died down. 3So that place was called Taberah,[a] because fire from the LORD had burned
among them.

Quail From the LORD

4The rabble with them began to crave other
food, and again the Israelites started wailing
and said, "If only we had meat to eat! 5We remember the fish we ate in Egypt at no cost—
also the cucumbers, melons, leeks, onions and
garlic. 6But now we have lost our appetite; we
never see anything but this manna!"
7The manna was like coriander seed and
looked like resin. 8The people went around
gathering it, and then ground it in a handmill
or crushed it in a mortar. They
cooked it in a pot or made it
into cakes. And it tasted like
something made with olive oil.
9When the dew settled on the
camp at night, the manna also
came down.
10Moses heard the people
of every family wailing, each
at the entrance to his tent. The
LORD became exceedingly angry, and Moses was troubled.
11He asked the LORD, "Why
have you brought this trouble
on your servant? What have I
done to displease you that you put the burden
of all these people on me? 12Did I conceive
all these people? Did I give them birth? Why
do you tell me to carry them in my arms, as a
nurse carries an infant, to the land you promised on oath to their forefathers? 13Where can I
get meat for all these people? They keep wailing
to me, 'Give us meat to eat!' 14I cannot carry all
these people by myself; the burden is too heavy
for me. 15If this is how you are going to treat
me, put me to death right now—if I have found
favor in your eyes—and do not let me face my
own ruin."
16The LORD said to Moses: "Bring me
seventy of Israel's elders who are known to you
as leaders and officials among the people. Have
them come to the Tent of Meeting, that they
may stand there with you. 17I will come down
and speak with you there, and I will take of the
Spirit that is on you and put the Spirit on them.
They will help you carry the burden of the people so that you will not have to carry it alone.
18"Tell the people: 'Consecrate yourselves in
preparation for tomorrow, when you will eat
meat. The LORD heard you when you wailed,
"If only we had meat to eat! We were better off
in Egypt!" Now the LORD will give you meat,
and you will eat it. 19You will not eat it for just
one day, or two days, or five, ten or twenty days,
20but for a whole month—until it comes out of
your nostrils and you loathe it—because you
have rejected the LORD, who is among you, and
have wailed before him, saying, "Why did we
ever leave Egypt?"'"
21But Moses said, "Here I
am among six hundred thousand men on foot, and you say,
'I will give them meat to eat for
a whole month!' 22Would they
have enough if flocks and herds
were slaughtered for them?
Would they have enough if all
the fish in the sea were caught
for them?"
23The LORD answered Mo-
ses, "Is the LORD's arm too
short? You will now see whether or not what I say will come
true for you."
24So Moses went out and told the people
what the LORD had said. He brought together
seventy of their elders and had them stand
around the Tent. 25Then the LORD came down

Numbers 11:23

God Is Powerful

The LORD answered Moses, "Is the LORD's arm too short? You will now see whether or not what I say will come true for you."

[a]3 *Taberah* means *burning.*

The Light of His Love

Numbers 11:4–6

The rabble with them began to crave other food, and again the Israelites started wailing and said, "If only we had meat to eat! We remember the fish we ate in Egypt at no cost—also the cucumbers, melons, leeks, onions and garlic. But now we have lost our appetite; we never see anything but this manna!"

Read: Numbers 11:1–35

I WANT TO BE YOUR ENCOURAGER, a voice that cheers you on to believe that God is who he says he is and that walking in his ways will prosper your soul. There's a lot at stake. Without personal encouragement we begin to lose sight of the goal. We get lost in the isolation of making so many choices. The days blend into one another and we slowly lose perspective. To complicate matters, the voices that offer false promises are too alluring to refuse.

No wonder God told us to whisper the truth in each other's ears, because sin is deceitful. It lies. It makes promises it can ever deliver in the long run. Initially sin feels good. An affair is exhilarating. Controlling others is empowering. Taking revenge feels therapeutic. Building a bigger house is an anesthetic to the pain. Gossip makes us feel better about ourselves. Fighting for our rights massages the pain of unfairness. The list goes on.

The longer I choose to believe (and act on) the false promises of sin, the harder my heart becomes. If I sin today, I will be more hardened tomorrow. I'll be even less likely to be affected by the truth. God's voice will be more unwelcome. The purity of his ways will seem more perverted.

Let's put our arms around someone who is struggling with critical choices today. Let's remind them that God's ways are worth it. He delivers what he promises: peace, confidence, eternal rewards and the joy of living in the light of his love.

— *Christine Wyrtzen*

reflection

1 How might things have been different for the Israelites if they had encouraged one another rather than listening to the grumbles of the "rabble"?

2 What situation is causing you to grumble and lose perspective concerning God's provision?

3 Who do you know that needs a word of encouragement? Follow Christine's advice and remind her that God's ways are worth it.

RELATED READINGS

Psalm 25:1–22;
1 Thessalonians 5:8–11;
Hebrews 6:16–20

Go to page 176 for your next devotional reading.

in the cloud and spoke with him, and he took
of the Spirit that was on him and put the Spirit
on the seventy elders. When the Spirit rested
on them, they prophesied, but they did not do
so again.[a]
26However, two men, whose names were
Eldad and Medad, had remained in the camp.
They were listed among the elders, but did not
go out to the Tent. Yet the Spirit also rested on
them, and they prophesied in the camp. 27A
young man ran and told Moses, "Eldad and Medad are prophesying in the camp."
28Joshua son of Nun, who had been Moses'
aide since youth, spoke up and said, "Moses,
my lord, stop them!"
29But Moses replied, "Are you jealous for
my sake? I wish that all the LORD's people were
prophets and that the LORD would put his
Spirit on them!" 30Then Moses and the elders
of Israel returned to the camp.
31Now a wind went out from the LORD and
drove quail in from the sea. It brought them[b]
down all around the camp to about three feet[c]
above the ground, as far as a day's walk in any
direction. 32All that day and night and all the
next day the people went out and gathered
quail. No one gathered less than ten homers.[d]
Then they spread them out all around the
camp. 33But while the meat was still between
their teeth and before it could be consumed,
the anger of the LORD burned against the people, and he struck them with a severe plague.
34Therefore the place was named Kibroth Hattaavah,[e] because there they buried the people
who had craved other food.
35From Kibroth Hattaavah the people traveled to Hazeroth and stayed there.

Miriam and Aaron Oppose Moses

12 Miriam and Aaron began to talk
against Moses because of his Cushite wife, for he had married a Cushite. 2"Has
the LORD spoken only through Moses?" they
asked. "Hasn't he also spoken through us?"
And the LORD heard this.
3(Now Moses was a very humble man, more
humble than anyone else on the face of the
earth.)
4At once the LORD said to Moses, Aaron and
Miriam, "Come out to the Tent of Meeting, all
three of you." So the three of them came out.
5Then the LORD came down in a pillar of
cloud; he stood at the entrance to the Tent and
summoned Aaron and Miriam. When both
of them stepped forward, 6he said, "Listen to
my words:

"When a prophet of the LORD is among
you,
I reveal myself to him in visions,
I speak to him in dreams.
7But this is not true of my servant Moses;
he is faithful in all my house.
8With him I speak face to face,
clearly and not in riddles;
he sees the form of the LORD.
Why then were you not afraid
to speak against my servant Moses?"

9The anger of the LORD burned against
them, and he left them.
10When the cloud lifted from above the
Tent, there stood Miriam—leprous,[f] like snow.
Aaron turned toward her and saw that she had
leprosy; 11and he said to Moses, "Please, my
lord, do not hold against us the sin we have so
foolishly committed. 12Do not let her be like
a stillborn infant coming from its mother's
womb with its flesh half eaten away."
13So Moses cried out to the LORD, "O God,
please heal her!"
14The LORD replied to Moses, "If her father
had spit in her face, would she not have been
in disgrace for seven days? Confine her outside
the camp for seven days; after that she can be
brought back." 15So Miriam was confined outside the camp for seven days, and the people
did not move on till she was brought back.
16After that, the people left Hazeroth and encamped in the Desert of Paran.

Exploring Canaan

13 The LORD said to Moses, 2"Send some
men to explore the land of Canaan,
which I am giving to the Israelites. From each
ancestral tribe send one of its leaders."
3So at the LORD's command Moses sent

[a]25 Or *prophesied and continued to do so* [b]31 Or *They flew* [c]31 Hebrew *two cubits* (about 1 meter) [d]32 That is, probably about 60 bushels (about 2.2 kiloliters) [e]34 *Kibroth Hattaavah* means *graves of craving.* [f]10 The Hebrew word was used for various diseases affecting the skin—not necessarily leprosy.

Boiling Over

Read: Numbers 12:1–15

Numbers 12:2

"Has the LORD spoken only through Moses?" they asked. "Hasn't he also spoken through us?" And the LORD heard this.

APPLAUDING OTHERS can be surprisingly difficult. It's easy enough to fake it, to smile approvingly and nod in agreement. But sometimes when others are recognized for achievements, it's hard to feel anything but that ugly burning twinge of jealousy. Outwardly we're clapping and congratulating, but inwardly we're slowly beginning to simmer. *Who does she think she is anyway? What's so special about her? Why all the fuss over one person?* And if we don't catch it in time, that simmer can turn into a hard boil that erupts in anger, harsh words and broken relationships.

The root of jealousy, when we dig down deep enough, is often insecurity. It's not so much a question of what's so special about someone else as it is a question of what's so un-special about me? What's wrong with me, we wonder, that God doesn't use me like that?

When Miriam and Aaron saw the way God was using Moses, they were jealous. They wanted to be what he was. And who wouldn't? God actually talked to Moses face-to-face. He had a unique role in history that no one else had ever played.

But Miriam and Aaron also had unique roles in history, roles that Moses couldn't fill, roles that they alone could fill. God had used them in wonderful ways. Miriam was a prophetess. Think of how rare in that day—a female prophet! Aaron was the high priest—the priest above all other priests. He was different from Moses but amazingly gifted. Miriam and Aaron both had gifts used by God, but their jealousy started to burn, and they allowed their negative feelings to affect their positions.

God has made a place for you in his kingdom that only you can fill. You may be a Moses, out front leading the way. Or you may be serving in more behind-the-scenes ways like Miriam and Aaron. Your job is not to compare your work to another's and attach value based on what you can see. Your job is to turn down the heat of jealousy and quietly go about the work God has given you to do: "Each one should test his own actions. Then he can take pride in himself, without comparing himself to somebody else, for each one should carry his own load" (Galatians 6:4–5). When it's God's work, it's valuable. When we allow jealousy to simmer up and boil over, our own bitterness will only burn us.

reflection

1 How do you respond when you see others receiving acclamation for their spiritual or natural gifts?

2 How do you act when you receive acclamation? How do you respond when others are jealous of you?

3 Jealousy is a sneaky sin. What do you do when you sense it starting to simmer?

RELATED READINGS
Exodus 15:20–21; 28:1–5; Proverbs 14:30; James 3:14–18

Go to page 178 for your next devotional reading.

5Then Moses and Aaron fell facedown in
front of the whole Israelite assembly gathered
there. 6Joshua son of Nun and Caleb son of
Jephunneh, who were among those who had
explored the land, tore their clothes 7and said
to the entire Israelite assembly, "The land we
passed through and explored is exceedingly
good. 8If the LORD is pleased with us, he will
lead us into that land, a land flowing with milk
and honey, and will give it to us. 9Only do not
rebel against the LORD. And do not be afraid
of the people of the land, because we will swallow them up. Their protection is gone, but the
LORD is with us. Do not be afraid of them."

10But the whole assembly talked about stoning them. Then the glory of the LORD appeared
at the Tent of Meeting to all the Israelites. 11The
LORD said to Moses, "How long will these people treat me with contempt? How long will they
refuse to believe in me, in spite of all the miraculous signs I have performed among them?
12I will strike them down with a plague and destroy them, but I will make you into a nation
greater and stronger than they."

13Moses said to the LORD, "Then the Egyptians will hear about it! By your power you
brought these people up from among them.
14And they will tell the inhabitants of this land
about it. They have already heard that you,
O LORD, are with these people and that you,
O LORD, have been seen face to face, that your
cloud stays over them, and that you go before
them in a pillar of cloud by day and a pillar of
fire by night. 15If you put these people to death
all at one time, the nations who
have heard this report about
you will say, 16'The LORD was
not able to bring these people into the land he promised
them on oath; so he slaughtered them in the desert.'

17"Now may the Lord's
strength be displayed, just
as you have declared: 18'The
LORD is slow to anger, abounding in love and forgiving sin
and rebellion. Yet he does not
leave the guilty unpunished; he punishes the
children for the sin of the fathers to the third
and fourth generation.' 19In accordance with
your great love, forgive the sin of these people,
just as you have pardoned them from the time
they left Egypt until now."

20The LORD replied, "I have forgiven them,
as you asked. 21Nevertheless, as surely as I live
and as surely as the glory of the LORD fills the
whole earth, 22not one of the men who saw my
glory and the miraculous signs I performed in
Egypt and in the desert but who disobeyed me
and tested me ten times— 23not one of them
will ever see the land I promised on oath to
their forefathers. No one who has treated me
with contempt will ever see it. 24But because
my servant Caleb has a different spirit and follows me wholeheartedly, I will bring him into
the land he went to, and his descendants will
inherit it. 25Since the Amalekites and Canaanites are living in the valleys, turn back tomorrow and set out toward the desert along the
route to the Red Sea.[a]"

26The LORD said to Moses and Aaron:
27"How long will this wicked community grumble against me? I have heard the complaints of
these grumbling Israelites. 28So tell them, 'As
surely as I live, declares the LORD, I will do to
you the very things I heard you say: 29In this
desert your bodies will fall—every one of you
twenty years old or more who was counted in
the census and who has grumbled against me.
30Not one of you will enter the land I swore
with uplifted hand to make your home, except
Caleb son of Jephunneh and Joshua son of Nun.
31As for your children that you said would be
taken as plunder, I will bring
them in to enjoy the land you
have rejected. 32But you—your
bodies will fall in this desert.
33Your children will be shepherds here for forty years, suffering for your unfaithfulness,
until the last of your bodies
lies in the desert. 34For forty
years—one year for each of
the forty days you explored the
land—you will suffer for your
sins and know what it is like to
have me against you.' 35I, the LORD, have spoken, and I will surely do these things to this

Numbers 14:18

God Forgives Sin

"The LORD is slow to anger, abounding in love and forgiving sin and rebellion."

[a]25 Hebrew *Yam Suph*; that is, Sea of Reeds

whole wicked community, which has banded
together against me. They will meet their end
in this desert; here they will die."
36So the men Moses had sent to explore
the land, who returned and made the whole
community grumble against him by spreading
a bad report about it— 37these men responsible for spreading the bad report about the land
were struck down and died of a plague before
the LORD. 38Of the men who went to explore
the land, only Joshua son of Nun and Caleb son
of Jephunneh survived.
39When Moses reported this to all the Israelites, they mourned bitterly. 40Early the next
morning they went up toward the high hill
country. "We have sinned," they said. "We will
go up to the place the LORD promised."
41But Moses said, "Why are you disobeying
the LORD's command? This will not succeed!
42Do not go up, because the LORD is not with
you. You will be defeated by your enemies,
43for the Amalekites and Canaanites will face
you there. Because you have turned away from
the LORD, he will not be with you and you will
fall by the sword."
44Nevertheless, in their presumption they
went up toward the high hill country, though
neither Moses nor the ark of the LORD's covenant moved from the camp. 45Then the Amalekites and Canaanites who lived in that hill
country came down and attacked them and
beat them down all the way to Hormah.

Supplementary Offerings

15 The LORD said to Moses, 2"Speak to
the Israelites and say to them: 'After
you enter the land I am giving you as a home
3and you present to the LORD offerings made
by fire, from the herd or the flock, as an aroma
pleasing to the LORD—whether burnt offerings
or sacrifices, for special vows or freewill offerings or festival offerings— 4then the one who
brings his offering shall present to the LORD a
grain offering of a tenth of an ephah[a] of fine
flour mixed with a quarter of a hin[b] of oil.
5With each lamb for the burnt offering or the
sacrifice, prepare a quarter of a hin of wine as
a drink offering.
6" 'With a ram prepare a grain offering of
two-tenths of an ephah[c] of fine flour mixed
with a third of a hin[d] of oil, 7and a third of a
hin of wine as a drink offering. Offer it as an
aroma pleasing to the LORD.
8" 'When you prepare a young bull as a
burnt offering or sacrifice, for a special vow or
a fellowship offering[e] to the LORD, 9bring with
the bull a grain offering of three-tenths of an
ephah[f] of fine flour mixed with half a hin[g] of
oil. 10Also bring half a hin of wine as a drink
offering. It will be an offering made by fire, an
aroma pleasing to the LORD. 11Each bull or
ram, each lamb or young goat, is to be prepared
in this manner. 12Do this for each one, for as
many as you prepare.
13" 'Everyone who is native-born must do
these things in this way when he brings an offering made by fire as an aroma pleasing to the
LORD. 14For the generations to come, whenever
an alien or anyone else living among you presents an offering made by fire as an aroma pleasing to the LORD, he must do exactly as you do.
15The community is to have the same rules
for you and for the alien living among you;
this is a lasting ordinance for the generations
to come. You and the alien shall be the same
before the LORD: 16The same laws and regulations will apply both to you and to the alien
living among you.' "
17The LORD said to Moses, 18"Speak to the
Israelites and say to them: 'When you enter the
land to which I am taking you 19and you eat
the food of the land, present a portion as an
offering to the LORD. 20Present a cake from the
first of your ground meal and present it as an
offering from the threshing floor. 21Through-
out the generations to come you are to give
this offering to the LORD from the first of your
ground meal.

Offerings for Unintentional Sins

22" 'Now if you unintentionally fail to keep
any of these commands the LORD gave Moses— 23any of the LORD's commands to you
through him, from the day the LORD gave
them and continuing through the generations
to come— 24and if this is done unintentionally

[a]4 That is, probably about 2 quarts (about 2 liters) [b]4 That is, probably about 1 quart (about 1 liter); also in verse 5 [c]6 That is, probably about 4 quarts (about 4.5 liters) [d]6 That is, probably about 1 1/4 quarts (about 1.2 liters); also in verse 7 [e]8 Traditionally *peace offering* [f]9 That is, probably about 6 quarts (about 6.5 liters) [g]9 That is, probably about 2 quarts (about 2 liters); also in verse 10

without the community being aware of it, then
the whole community is to offer a young bull
for a burnt offering as an aroma pleasing to the
LORD, along with its prescribed grain offering
and drink offering, and a male goat for a sin
offering. 25 The priest is to make atonement
for the whole Israelite community, and they
will be forgiven, for it was not intentional
and they have brought to the LORD for their
wrong an offering made by fire and a sin offering. 26 The whole Israelite community and
the aliens living among them will be forgiven,
because all the people were involved in the
unintentional wrong.

27 " 'But if just one person sins unintentionally, he must bring a year-old female goat for a
sin offering. 28 The priest is to make atonement
before the LORD for the one who erred by sinning unintentionally, and when atonement has
been made for him, he will be forgiven. 29 One
and the same law applies to everyone who sins
unintentionally, whether he is a native-born Israelite or an alien.

30 " 'But anyone who sins defiantly, whether
native-born or alien, blasphemes the LORD,
and that person must be cut off from his people. 31 Because he has despised the LORD's word
and broken his commands, that person must
surely be cut off; his guilt remains on him.' "

The Sabbath-Breaker Put to Death

32 While the Israelites were in the desert, a
man was found gathering wood on the Sabbath day. 33 Those who found him gathering
wood brought him to Moses and Aaron and
the whole assembly, 34 and they kept him in
custody, because it was not clear what should be
done to him. 35 Then the LORD said to Moses,
"The man must die. The whole assembly must
stone him outside the camp." 36 So the assembly
took him outside the camp and stoned him to
death, as the LORD commanded Moses.

Tassels on Garments

37 The LORD said to Moses, 38 "Speak to the
Israelites and say to them: 'Throughout the generations to come you are to make tassels on the
corners of your garments, with a blue cord on
each tassel. 39 You will have these tassels to look
at and so you will remember all the commands
of the LORD, that you may obey them and not
prostitute yourselves by going after the lusts
of your own hearts and eyes. 40 Then you will
remember to obey all my commands and will
be consecrated to your God. 41 I am the LORD
your God, who brought you out of Egypt to be
your God. I am the LORD your God.' "

Korah, Dathan and Abiram

16 Korah son of Izhar, the son of Kohath,
the son of Levi, and certain Reubenites—Dathan and Abiram, sons of Eliab, and
On son of Peleth—became insolent[a] 2 and rose
up against Moses. With them were 250 Israelite
men, well-known community leaders who had
been appointed members of the council. 3 They
came as a group to oppose Moses and Aaron
and said to them, "You have gone too far! The
whole community is holy, every one of them,
and the LORD is with them. Why then do you
set yourselves above the LORD's assembly?"

4 When Moses heard this, he fell facedown.
5 Then he said to Korah and all his followers: "In
the morning the LORD will show who belongs
to him and who is holy, and he will have that
person come near him. The man he chooses he
will cause to come near him. 6 You, Korah, and
all your followers are to do this: Take censers
7 and tomorrow put fire and incense in them
before the LORD. The man the LORD chooses
will be the one who is holy. You Levites have
gone too far!"

8 Moses also said to Korah, "Now listen, you
Levites! 9 Isn't it enough for you that the God
of Israel has separated you from the rest of the
Israelite community and brought you near himself to do the work at the LORD's tabernacle and
to stand before the community and minister to
them? 10 He has brought you and all your fellow
Levites near himself, but now you are trying to
get the priesthood too. 11 It is against the LORD
that you and all your followers have banded
together. Who is Aaron that you should grumble against him?"

12 Then Moses summoned Dathan and
Abiram, the sons of Eliab. But they said, "We
will not come! 13 Isn't it enough that you have
brought us up out of a land flowing with milk
and honey to kill us in the desert? And now

[a] 1 Or *Peleth—took* ⌊*men*⌋

A Grumbling Church

Read: Numbers 16:1–35

GAYLE WONDERED HOW she had gotten herself into this mess. She had agreed to oversee a women's Bible study this year, and while things started off great, somehow everything started going wrong. Her small group leaders were upset with curriculum; some of the women in the study were upset with the women's ministries leaders; and everyone seemed to be talking about everyone else. Gayle wondered if perhaps she should just resign and let someone else deal with the complaining, bickering and power struggles.

What would you do in this situation? Would you try to take control and fix the problems? Would you call five of your best friends to discuss it? Or would you pray and ask God to fix his ministry?

Clearly, Korah and the leaders didn't respect Aaron and Moses' positions, overlooking the fact that God had appointed the brothers to lead Israel. Today, we don't hear audible voices like Moses did, so it seems more difficult to perceive that God has appointed the leaders in our churches. But if we don't submit to and respect our leaders, in essence we are saying, "God, I don't believe you are in control." Often, we are part of the problems that we are complaining about. We point fingers at pastors and leaders instead of recognizing that our own actions or inactions might have been part of the problem. Dathan and Abiram blamed Aaron and Moses for their circumstances. They jeered, "Isn't it enough that you have brought us up out of a land flowing with milk and honey to kill us in the desert?" Their twisted thinking allowed them to remember Egypt as a paradise rather than a land of slavery. And they conveniently forgot their cowardly refusal to enter the promised land (see chapter 14), the true "land flowing with milk and honey."

Problems occur in every church and ministry. After all, God uses fallible human beings to accomplish his work. But it is God's church and he is in control. We may not always agree with all of our spiritual leaders' decisions, but we can pray that God will lead them and guard their hearts and minds. We can examine our own actions and attitudes to make sure we're not causing more problems. And we can trust God to finish the work he has started—especially the work he has called us to do.

Numbers 16:1–2

Korah son of Izhar, the son of Kohath, the son of Levi, and certain Reubenites—Dathan and Abiram, sons of Eliab, and On son of Peleth—became insolent and rose up against Moses. With them were 250 Israelite men, well-known community leaders who had been appointed members of the council.

reflection

1 What are some ways you can show respect to the leaders in your church?

2 Recount a time of conflict within a church. Looking back, can you see ways that God was in control?

3 How have your actions or inactions negatively or positively affected your church?

RELATED READINGS

Philippians 4:2–3; 1 Timothy 5:17–20; Titus 3:1–2

Go to page 187 for your next devotional reading.

you also want to lord it over us? 14Moreover,
you haven't brought us into a land flowing with
milk and honey or given us an inheritance of
fields and vineyards. Will you gouge out the
eyes of[a] these men? No, we will not come!"
15Then Moses became very angry and said
to the LORD, "Do not accept their offering. I
have not taken so much as a donkey from
them, nor have I wronged any of them."
16Moses said to Korah, "You and all your
followers are to appear before the LORD tomorrow—you and they and Aaron. 17Each man is
to take his censer and put incense in it—250
censers in all—and present it before the LORD.
You and Aaron are to present your censers
also." 18So each man took his
censer, put fire and incense
in it, and stood with Moses
and Aaron at the entrance to
the Tent of Meeting. 19When
Korah had gathered all his followers in opposition to them
at the entrance to the Tent of
Meeting, the glory of the LORD
appeared to the entire assembly. 20The LORD said to Moses
and Aaron, 21"Separate your-
selves from this assembly so I can put an end
to them at once."
22But Moses and Aaron fell facedown and
cried out, "O God, God of the spirits of all mankind, will you be angry with the entire assembly when only one man sins?"
23Then the LORD said to Moses, 24"Say to
the assembly, 'Move away from the tents of Korah, Dathan and Abiram.'"
25Moses got up and went to Dathan and
Abiram, and the elders of Israel followed him.
26He warned the assembly, "Move back from
the tents of these wicked men! Do not touch
anything belonging to them, or you will be
swept away because of all their sins." 27So they
moved away from the tents of Korah, Dathan
and Abiram. Dathan and Abiram had come out
and were standing with their wives, children
and little ones at the entrances to their tents.
28Then Moses said, "This is how you will
know that the LORD has sent me to do all these
things and that it was not my idea: 29If these
men die a natural death and experience only
what usually happens to men, then the LORD
has not sent me. 30But if the LORD brings about
something totally new, and the earth opens its
mouth and swallows them, with everything
that belongs to them, and they go down alive
into the grave,[b] then you will know that these
men have treated the LORD with contempt."
31As soon as he finished saying all this, the
ground under them split apart 32and the earth
opened its mouth and swallowed them, with
their households and all Korah's men and all
their possessions. 33They went down alive
into the grave, with everything they owned;
the earth closed over them, and they perished and were gone from the
community. 34At their cries, all
the Israelites around them fled,
shouting, "The earth is going to
swallow us too!"
35And fire came out from
the LORD and consumed the
250 men who were offering
the incense.
36The LORD said to Moses,
37"Tell Eleazar son of Aaron,
the priest, to take the censers
out of the smoldering remains and scatter the
coals some distance away, for the censers are
holy— 38the censers of the men who sinned
at the cost of their lives. Hammer the censers
into sheets to overlay the altar, for they were
presented before the LORD and have become
holy. Let them be a sign to the Israelites."
39So Eleazar the priest collected the bronze
censers brought by those who had been burned
up, and he had them hammered out to overlay
the altar, 40as the LORD directed him through
Moses. This was to remind the Israelites that no
one except a descendant of Aaron should come
to burn incense before the LORD, or he would
become like Korah and his followers.
41The next day the whole Israelite community
grumbled against Moses and Aaron. "You have
killed the LORD's people," they said.
42But when the assembly gathered in opposition to Moses and Aaron and turned toward
the Tent of Meeting, suddenly the cloud covered it and the glory of the LORD appeared.

Numbers 16:21

God Addresses Sin

"Separate yourselves from this assembly so I can put an end to them at once."

[a]14 Or *you make slaves of*; or *you deceive* [b]30 Hebrew *Sheol*; also in verse 33

43Then Moses and Aaron went to the front
of the Tent of Meeting, 44and the LORD said
to Moses, 45"Get away from this assembly so
I can put an end to them at once." And they
fell facedown.
46Then Moses said to Aaron, "Take your censer and put incense in it, along with fire from
the altar, and hurry to the assembly to make
atonement for them. Wrath has come out from
the LORD; the plague has started." 47So Aaron
did as Moses said, and ran into the midst of
the assembly. The plague had already started
among the people, but Aaron offered the incense and made atonement for them. 48He
stood between the living and the dead, and the
plague stopped. 49But 14,700 people died from
the plague, in addition to those who had died
because of Korah. 50Then Aaron returned to
Moses at the entrance to the Tent of Meeting,
for the plague had stopped.

The Budding of Aaron's Staff

17 The LORD said to Moses, 2"Speak to
the Israelites and get twelve staffs from
them, one from the leader of each of their ancestral tribes. Write the name of each man on
his staff. 3On the staff of Levi write Aaron's
name, for there must be one staff for the head
of each ancestral tribe. 4Place them in the Tent
of Meeting in front of the Testimony, where
I meet with you. 5The staff belonging to the
man I choose will sprout, and I will rid myself
of this constant grumbling against you by the
Israelites."
6So Moses spoke to the Israelites, and their
leaders gave him twelve staffs, one for the leader
of each of their ancestral tribes, and Aaron's
staff was among them. 7Moses placed the staffs
before the LORD in the Tent of the Testimony.
8The next day Moses entered the Tent of the
Testimony and saw that Aaron's staff, which
represented the house of Levi, had not only
sprouted but had budded, blossomed and produced almonds. 9Then Moses brought out all
the staffs from the LORD's presence to all the
Israelites. They looked at them, and each man
took his own staff.
10The LORD said to Moses, "Put back Aaron's staff in front of the Testimony, to be kept
as a sign to the rebellious. This will put an end
to their grumbling against me, so that they
will not die." 11Moses did just as the LORD
commanded him.
12The Israelites said to Moses, "We will die!
We are lost, we are all lost! 13Anyone who even
comes near the tabernacle of the LORD will die.
Are we all going to die?"

Duties of Priests and Levites

18 The LORD said to Aaron, "You, your
sons and your father's family are to
bear the responsibility for offenses against the
sanctuary, and you and your sons alone are to
bear the responsibility for offenses against the
priesthood. 2Bring your fellow Levites from
your ancestral tribe to join you and assist you
when you and your sons minister before the
Tent of the Testimony. 3They are to be responsible to you and are to perform all the duties
of the Tent, but they must not go near the furnishings of the sanctuary or the altar, or both
they and you will die. 4They are to join you and
be responsible for the care of the Tent of Meeting—all the work at the Tent—and no one else
may come near where you are.
5"You are to be responsible for the care of
the sanctuary and the altar, so that wrath will
not fall on the Israelites again. 6I myself have
selected your fellow Levites from among the Israelites as a gift to you, dedicated to the LORD
to do the work at the Tent of Meeting. 7But only
you and your sons may serve as priests in connection with everything at the altar and inside
the curtain. I am giving you the service of the
priesthood as a gift. Anyone else who comes
near the sanctuary must be put to death."

Offerings for Priests and Levites

8Then the LORD said to Aaron, "I myself have
put you in charge of the offerings presented to
me; all the holy offerings the Israelites give me
I give to you and your sons as your portion and
regular share. 9You are to have the part of the
most holy offerings that is kept from the fire.
From all the gifts they bring me as most holy offerings, whether grain or sin or guilt offerings,
that part belongs to you and your sons. 10Eat it
as something most holy; every male shall eat it.
You must regard it as holy.
11"This also is yours: whatever is set aside
from the gifts of all the wave offerings of the
Israelites. I give this to you and your sons and

daughters as your regular share. Everyone in
your household who is ceremonially clean may
eat it.
12“I give you all the finest olive oil and all the
finest new wine and grain they give the LORD
as the firstfruits of their harvest. 13All the land’s
firstfruits that they bring to the LORD will be
yours. Everyone in your household who is
ceremonially clean may eat it.
14“Everything in Israel that is devoted[a] to
the LORD is yours. 15The first offspring of every
womb, both man and animal, that is offered
to the LORD is yours. But you
must redeem every firstborn
son and every firstborn male
of unclean animals. 16When
they are a month old, you must
redeem them at the redemption price set at five shekels[b]
of silver, according to the sanctuary shekel, which weighs
twenty gerahs.
17“But you must not redeem
the firstborn of an ox, a sheep
or a goat; they are holy. Sprinkle their blood on the altar and
burn their fat as an offering
made by fire, an aroma pleasing to the LORD.
18Their meat is to be yours, just as the breast of
the wave offering and the right thigh are yours.
19Whatever is set aside from the holy offerings
the Israelites present to the LORD I give to you
and your sons and daughters as your regular
share. It is an everlasting covenant of salt before
the LORD for both you and your offspring.”
20The LORD said to Aaron, “You will have no
inheritance in their land, nor will you have any
share among them; I am your share and your
inheritance among the Israelites.
21“I give to the Levites all the tithes in Israel
as their inheritance in return for the work they
do while serving at the Tent of Meeting. 22From
now on the Israelites must not go near the Tent
of Meeting, or they will bear the consequences
of their sin and will die. 23It is the Levites who
are to do the work at the Tent of Meeting and
bear the responsibility for offenses against it.
This is a lasting ordinance for the generations
to come. They will receive no inheritance
among the Israelites. 24Instead, I give to the Levites as their inheritance the tithes that the Israelites present as an offering to the LORD. That is
why I said concerning them: ‘They will have no
inheritance among the Israelites.’ ”
25The LORD said to Moses, 26“Speak to the
Levites and say to them: ‘When you receive
from the Israelites the tithe I give you as your inheritance, you must present a tenth of that tithe
as the LORD’s offering. 27Your offering will be
reckoned to you as grain from the threshing
floor or juice from the winepress. 28In this
way you also will present an
offering to the LORD from all
the tithes you receive from the
Israelites. From these tithes
you must give the LORD’s portion to Aaron the priest. 29You
must present as the LORD’s portion the best and holiest part of
everything given to you.’
30“Say to the Levites: ‘When
you present the best part, it will
be reckoned to you as the product of the threshing floor or
the winepress. 31You and your
households may eat the rest of
it anywhere, for it is your wages for your work
at the Tent of Meeting. 32By presenting the best
part of it you will not be guilty in this matter;
then you will not defile the holy offerings of the
Israelites, and you will not die.’ ”

Numbers 18:29

God Deserves Our Best

“You must present as the LORD’s portion the best and holiest part of everything given to you.”

The Water of Cleansing

19 The LORD said to Moses and Aaron:
2“This is a requirement of the law
that the LORD has commanded: Tell the Israelites to bring you a red heifer without defect or
blemish and that has never been under a yoke.
3Give it to Eleazar the priest; it is to be taken
outside the camp and slaughtered in his presence. 4Then Eleazar the priest is to take some
of its blood on his finger and sprinkle it seven
times toward the front of the Tent of Meeting.
5While he watches, the heifer is to be burned—
its hide, flesh, blood and offal. 6The priest is to
take some cedar wood, hyssop and scarlet wool
and throw them onto the burning heifer. 7Af-
ter that, the priest must wash his clothes and

[a]14 The Hebrew term refers to the irrevocable giving over of things or persons to the LORD. [b]16 That is, about 2 ounces (about 55 grams)

bathe himself with water. He may then come
into the camp, but he will be ceremonially unclean till evening. 8The man who burns it must
also wash his clothes and bathe with water, and
he too will be unclean till evening.
9"A man who is clean shall gather up the ashes
of the heifer and put them in a ceremonially
clean place outside the camp. They shall be
kept by the Israelite community for use in the
water of cleansing; it is for purification from
sin. 10The man who gathers up the ashes of the
heifer must also wash his clothes, and he too
will be unclean till evening. This will be a lasting ordinance both for the Israelites and for the
aliens living among them.
11"Whoever touches the dead body of anyone will be unclean for seven days. 12He must
purify himself with the water on the third
day and on the seventh day; then he will be
clean. But if he does not purify himself on the
third and seventh days, he will not be clean.
13Whoever touches the dead body of anyone
and fails to purify himself defiles the LORD's
tabernacle. That person must be cut off from
Israel. Because the water of cleansing has not
been sprinkled on him, he is unclean; his uncleanness remains on him.
14"This is the law that applies when a person
dies in a tent: Anyone who enters the tent and
anyone who is in it will be unclean for seven
days, 15and every open container without a lid
fastened on it will be unclean.
16"Anyone out in the open who touches
someone who has been killed with a sword or
someone who has died a natural death, or anyone who touches a human bone or a grave, will
be unclean for seven days.
17"For the unclean person, put some ashes
from the burned purification offering into a jar
and pour fresh water over them. 18Then a man
who is ceremonially clean is to take some hyssop, dip it in the water and sprinkle the tent
and all the furnishings and the people who
were there. He must also sprinkle anyone who
has touched a human bone or a grave or someone who has been killed or someone who has
died a natural death. 19The man who is clean
is to sprinkle the unclean person on the third
and seventh days, and on the seventh day he is
to purify him. The person being cleansed must
wash his clothes and bathe with water, and that
evening he will be clean. 20But if a person who
is unclean does not purify himself, he must be
cut off from the community, because he has
defiled the sanctuary of the LORD. The water
of cleansing has not been sprinkled on him,
and he is unclean. 21This is a lasting ordinance
for them.
"The man who sprinkles the water of cleansing must also wash his clothes, and anyone
who touches the water of cleansing will be unclean till evening. 22Anything that an unclean
person touches becomes unclean, and anyone
who touches it becomes unclean till evening."

Water From the Rock

20 In the first month the whole Israelite
community arrived at the Desert of
Zin, and they stayed at Kadesh. There Miriam
died and was buried.
2Now there was no water for the community,
and the people gathered in opposition to Moses
and Aaron. 3They quarreled with Moses and
said, "If only we had died when our brothers fell
dead before the LORD! 4Why did you bring the
LORD's community into this desert, that we and
our livestock should die here? 5Why did you
bring us up out of Egypt to this terrible place?
It has no grain or figs, grapevines or pomegranates. And there is no water to drink!"
6Moses and Aaron went from the assembly
to the entrance to the Tent of Meeting and fell
facedown, and the glory of the LORD appeared
to them. 7The LORD said to Moses, 8"Take the
staff, and you and your brother Aaron gather
the assembly together. Speak to that rock before
their eyes and it will pour out its water. You will
bring water out of the rock for the community
so they and their livestock can drink."
9So Moses took the staff from the LORD's
presence, just as he commanded him. 10He
and Aaron gathered the assembly together in
front of the rock and Moses said to them, "Listen, you rebels, must we bring you water out
of this rock?" 11Then Moses raised his arm
and struck the rock twice with his staff. Water
gushed out, and the community and their livestock drank.
12But the LORD said to Moses and Aaron,
"Because you did not trust in me enough to
honor me as holy in the sight of the Israelites,

Credit Where Credit Is Due

Read: Numbers 20:2–13

SINCE SCHOOL DAYS, it's been drummed into our collective conscience to give credit where credit is due. If a person "borrows" a concept without properly giving recognition, they are guilty of plagiarizing—stealing ideas, words or creations. Oftentimes, the plagiarist pays the price by losing their reputation or career. The same is true spiritually. We must be willing to give God the credit for his work in our lives.

The Israelites had almost reached the end of their desert wanderings. The new generation was ready to enter the promised land. They had witnessed miracles and tasted manna. Yet they worried that God would not provide water. So they complained against Moses.

Moses went to the Lord and asked for guidance. God spelled out his instructions: Bring the staff and speak to the rock. God promised that water would pour forth to nourish the people and flocks. Then Moses made two big mistakes. First, he took credit for God's work by complaining about being forced to bring water out of the rock himself. Then he disobeyed God by overreacting. He struck the rock—WHAM! Then again—WHAM!

It's heartbreaking to realize that Moses, God's faithful servant, was left behind. He didn't get to go into the promised land. But God had his reasons: "You did not trust in me enough to honor me as holy in the sight of the Israelites" (Numbers 20:12). In other words, Moses did not give God credit where credit was due. He stole God's glory by striking the rock—twice. But in the end, God loved Moses so much he showed him the promised land from the top of Mount Nebo and then had him buried there.

But rather than being hard on Moses, perhaps we should look at our own attitudes and motives. When we accomplish God's work, do we take the credit and bask in our own sense of accomplishment? When we benefit from God's grace in our lives, do we take it for granted and think that we somehow deserve it? Take a moment each day to sort out who is doing what, and give God the credit—for the gifts and abilities he has given you and for everything he is able to do through you. In short, for everything.

Numbers 20:10–11

[Moses] and Aaron gathered the assembly together in front of the rock and Moses said to them, "Listen, you rebels, must we bring you water out of this rock?" Then Moses raised his arm and struck the rock twice with his staff. Water gushed out, and the community and their livestock drank.

reflection

1 Have you ever taken credit for another person's accomplishments?

2 When was the last time you didn't give God credit for his work in your life?

3 How will you honor God in the presence of those you encounter today?

RELATED READINGS

1 Chronicles 16:7–36;
Psalm 106:1–2,32–48;
1 Corinthians 10:1–5

Go to page 189 for your next devotional reading.

you will not bring this community into the
land I give them."
13 These were the waters of Meribah,[a] where
the Israelites quarreled with the LORD and
where he showed himself holy among them.

Edom Denies Israel Passage

14 Moses sent messengers from Kadesh to
the king of Edom, saying:

"This is what your brother Israel says:
You know about all the hardships that
have come upon us. 15 Our forefathers
went down into Egypt, and we lived there
many years. The Egyptians mistreated us
and our fathers, 16 but when we cried out
to the LORD, he heard our cry and sent an
angel and brought us out of Egypt.
"Now we are here at Kadesh, a town on
the edge of your territory. 17 Please let us
pass through your country. We will not go
through any field or vineyard, or drink water from any well. We will travel along the
king's highway and not turn to the right
or to the left until we have passed through
your territory."

18 But Edom answered:

"You may not pass through here; if you
try, we will march out and attack you with
the sword."

19 The Israelites replied:

"We will go along the main road, and if
we or our livestock drink any of your water, we will pay for it. We only want to pass
through on foot—nothing else."

20 Again they answered:

"You may not pass through."

Then Edom came out against them with a
large and powerful army. 21 Since Edom refused to let them go through their territory,
Israel turned away from them.

The Death of Aaron

22 The whole Israelite community set out
from Kadesh and came to Mount Hor. 23 At
Mount Hor, near the border of Edom, the
LORD said to Moses and Aaron, 24 "Aaron will
be gathered to his people. He will not enter the
land I give the Israelites, because both of you
rebelled against my command at the waters of
Meribah. 25 Get Aaron and his son Eleazar and
take them up Mount Hor. 26 Remove Aaron's
garments and put them on his son Eleazar, for
Aaron will be gathered to his people; he will
die there."
27 Moses did as the LORD commanded:
They went up Mount Hor in the sight of the
whole community. 28 Moses removed Aaron's
garments and put them on his son Eleazar.
And Aaron died there on top of the mountain.
Then Moses and Eleazar came down from the
mountain, 29 and when the whole community
learned that Aaron had died, the entire house
of Israel mourned for him thirty days.

Arad Destroyed

21 When the Canaanite king of Arad,
who lived in the Negev, heard that
Israel was coming along the road to Atharim,
he attacked the Israelites and captured some
of them. 2 Then Israel made this vow to the
LORD: "If you will deliver these people into
our hands, we will totally destroy[b] their cities."
3 The LORD listened to Israel's plea and gave the
Canaanites over to them. They completely destroyed them and their towns; so the place was
named Hormah.[c]

The Bronze Snake

4 They traveled from Mount Hor along the
route to the Red Sea,[d] to go around Edom. But
the people grew impatient on the way; 5 they
spoke against God and against Moses, and said,
"Why have you brought us up out of Egypt to
die in the desert? There is no bread! There is no
water! And we detest this miserable food!"
6 Then the LORD sent venomous snakes
among them; they bit the people and many
Israelites died. 7 The people came to Moses
and said, "We sinned when we spoke against
the LORD and against you. Pray that the LORD
will take the snakes away from us." So Moses
prayed for the people.
8 The LORD said to Moses, "Make a snake
and put it up on a pole; anyone who is

[a] 13 *Meribah* means *quarreling.* [b] 2 The Hebrew term refers to the irrevocable giving over of things or persons to the LORD, often by totally destroying them; also in verse 3. [c] 3 *Hormah* means *destruction.* [d] 4 Hebrew *Yam Suph*; that is, Sea of Reeds

Look Up and Live

Read: Numbers 21:4–9

WANDERING THROUGH OUR DAY, thirsting for evidence of God's presence, hungry for the blessings everyone else seems to enjoy . . . stumbling blindly in the same old drudgery. We, too, can begin to doubt whether God is really guiding us, whether he really has chosen us. And if he has, why is life so hard? And then we begin to doubt . . . just like the Israelites.

They tramped through a scorching desert, their feet dusty and sore. They faced yet another day of water rations and a menu of manna—the same as every other day. Sure, the Israelites had God's cloud to guide them by day and that fire to follow by night. Yes, he told them he had "chosen" them. The miracles to get them out of Egypt had been amazing. Yet the way was so rough, it was easy to forget all that. Looking out at the hot desert, it was easy to assume God had left them alone there.

Does this sound familiar as you tramp through your daily life?

If God really loved me, I'd get that promotion at work!

Mumble, mumble, mumble.

Why doesn't God heal me?

Grumble, grumble, grumble.

I pray and pray, but God never seems to answer.

Whine, whine, whine.

Eventually, the Israelites' grumbling exploded into venomous blasphemy against God. In retribution, God sent a plague of poisonous snakes to stop their poisonous treason. Sometimes God's rebuke might feel like one more reason to resent him. But God's compassion drives his punishments. When his people called out for help—wailing for the cure—he provided a remedy. The afflicted needed to look up at the picture of their sinful rebellion—the bronze serpent raised high on a pole. God raised their sin on a pole, and they were healed. And millennia later, he raised up a Savior on a cross so that humankind could look to him and be saved (see John 3:14–15).

Do frustration and discouragement sometimes drive you to mumble and complain? Have you begun to detest the things of God because they just aren't quite what you expected?

Stop. Look up to Jesus Christ. He took on your sin to heal your heart. He is the only way you can rid yourself of the venom of bitterness. Look up to him and live.

Numbers 21:8

The LORD said to Moses, "Make a snake and put it up on a pole; anyone who is bitten can look at it and live."

reflection

1 What "desert" experience has caused you to grumble?

2 What sin has poisoned your heart? Is it envy? Bitterness? Anger?

3 Today, lift your eyes up toward Jesus and ask him to take the poisonous thoughts from your heart.

RELATED READINGS

Psalm 121:1–2; John 8:27–28

Go to page 198 for your next devotional reading.

bitten can look at it and live." 9So Moses made
a bronze snake and put it up on a pole. Then
when anyone was bitten by a snake and looked
at the bronze snake, he lived.

The Journey to Moab

10The Israelites moved on and camped at
Oboth. 11Then they set out from Oboth and
camped in Iye Abarim, in the desert that faces
Moab toward the sunrise. 12From there they
moved on and camped in the Zered Valley.
13They set out from there and camped alongside the Arnon, which is in the desert extending into Amorite territory. The Arnon is the
border of Moab, between Moab and the Amorites. 14That is why the Book of the Wars of
the LORD says:

"... Waheb in Suphah[a] and the ravines,
the Arnon 15and[b] the slopes of the ravines
that lead to the site of Ar
and lie along the border of Moab."

16From there they continued on to Beer, the
well where the LORD said to Moses, "Gather the
people together and I will give them water."
17Then Israel sang this song:

"Spring up, O well!
Sing about it,
18about the well that the princes dug,
that the nobles of the people sank—
the nobles with scepters and staffs."

Then they went from the desert to Mattanah,
19from Mattanah to Nahaliel, from Nahaliel
to Bamoth, 20and from Bamoth to the valley
in Moab where the top of Pisgah overlooks
the wasteland.

Defeat of Sihon and Og

21Israel sent messengers to say to Sihon king
of the Amorites:

22"Let us pass through your country.
We will not turn aside into any field or
vineyard, or drink water from any well.
We will travel along the king's highway
until we have passed through your territory."

23But Sihon would not let Israel pass
through his territory. He mustered his entire
army and marched out into the desert against
Israel. When he reached Jahaz, he fought with
Israel. 24Israel, however, put him to the sword
and took over his land from the Arnon to the
Jabbok, but only as far as the Ammonites,
because their border was fortified. 25Israel
captured all the cities of the Amorites and occupied them, including Heshbon and all its
surrounding settlements. 26Heshbon was the
city of Sihon king of the Amorites, who had
fought against the former king of Moab and
had taken from him all his land as far as the
Arnon.
27That is why the poets say:

"Come to Heshbon and let it be rebuilt;
let Sihon's city be restored.

28"Fire went out from Heshbon,
a blaze from the city of Sihon.
It consumed Ar of Moab,
the citizens of Arnon's heights.
29Woe to you, O Moab!
You are destroyed, O people of
Chemosh!
He has given up his sons as fugitives
and his daughters as captives
to Sihon king of the Amorites.

30"But we have overthrown them;
Heshbon is destroyed all the way to
Dibon.
We have demolished them as far as
Nophah,
which extends to Medeba."

31So Israel settled in the land of the Amorites.
32After Moses had sent spies to Jazer, the Israelites captured its surrounding settlements
and drove out the Amorites who were there.
33Then they turned and went up along the
road toward Bashan, and Og king of Bashan
and his whole army marched out to meet them
in battle at Edrei.
34The LORD said to Moses, "Do not be afraid
of him, for I have handed him over to you, with
his whole army and his land. Do to him what
you did to Sihon king of the Amorites, who
reigned in Heshbon."
35So they struck him down, together with his

[a]14 The meaning of the Hebrew for this phrase is uncertain. [b]14,15 Or *"I have been given from Suphah and the ravines / of the Arnon 15to*

sons and his whole army, leaving them no survivors. And they took possession of his land.

Balak Summons Balaam

22 Then the Israelites traveled to the
plains of Moab and camped along the
Jordan across from Jericho.[a]
2Now Balak son of Zippor saw all that Israel
had done to the Amorites, 3and Moab was terrified because there were so many people. Indeed, Moab was filled with dread because of
the Israelites.
4The Moabites said to the elders of Midian,
"This horde is going to lick up everything
around us, as an ox licks up the grass of the
field."
So Balak son of Zippor, who was king of
Moab at that time, 5sent messengers to summon Balaam son of Beor, who was at Pethor,
near the River,[b] in his native land. Balak said:

> "A people has come out of Egypt; they
> cover the face of the land and have set-
> tled next to me. 6Now come and put a
> curse on these people, because they are
> too powerful for me. Perhaps then I will
> be able to defeat them and drive them
> out of the country. For I know that those
> you bless are blessed, and those you curse
> are cursed."

7The elders of Moab and Midian left, taking
with them the fee for divination. When they
came to Balaam, they told him what Balak
had said.
8"Spend the night here," Balaam said to
them, "and I will bring you back the answer the
LORD gives me." So the Moabite princes stayed
with him.
9God came to Balaam and asked, "Who are
these men with you?"
10Balaam said to God, "Balak son of Zippor,
king of Moab, sent me this message: 11'A people that has come out of Egypt covers the face
of the land. Now come and put a curse on them
for me. Perhaps then I will be able to fight them
and drive them away.'"
12But God said to Balaam, "Do not go with
them. You must not put a curse on those people, because they are blessed."
13The next morning Balaam got up and
said to Balak's princes, "Go back to your own
country, for the LORD has refused to let me go
with you."
14So the Moabite princes returned to Balak
and said, "Balaam refused to come with us."
15Then Balak sent other princes, more numerous and more distinguished than the first.
16They came to Balaam and said:

> "This is what Balak son of Zippor says:
> Do not let anything keep you from coming
> to me, 17because I will reward you hand-
> somely and do whatever you say. Come
> and put a curse on these people for me."

18But Balaam answered them, "Even if Balak gave me his palace filled with silver and
gold, I could not do anything great or small to
go beyond the command of the LORD my God.
19Now stay here tonight as the others did, and I
will find out what else the LORD will tell me."
20That night God came to Balaam and said,
"Since these men have come to summon you,
go with them, but do only what I tell you."

Balaam's Donkey

21Balaam got up in the morning, saddled
his donkey and went with the princes of Moab.
22But God was very angry when he went, and
the angel of the LORD stood in the road to oppose him. Balaam was riding on his donkey,
and his two servants were with him. 23When
the donkey saw the angel of the LORD standing
in the road with a drawn sword in his hand, she
turned off the road into a field. Balaam beat her
to get her back on the road.
24Then the angel of the LORD stood in a narrow path between two vineyards, with walls
on both sides. 25When the donkey saw the angel of the LORD, she pressed close to the wall,
crushing Balaam's foot against it. So he beat
her again.
26Then the angel of the LORD moved on
ahead and stood in a narrow place where there
was no room to turn, either to the right or to
the left. 27When the donkey saw the angel of
the LORD, she lay down under Balaam, and he
was angry and beat her with his staff. 28Then
the LORD opened the donkey's mouth, and she

[a]1 Hebrew *Jordan of Jericho*; possibly an ancient name for the Jordan River [b]5 That is, the Euphrates

said to Balaam, "What have I done to you to
make you beat me these three times?"
29 Balaam answered the donkey, "You have
made a fool of me! If I had a sword in my hand,
I would kill you right now."
30 The donkey said to Balaam, "Am I not
your own donkey, which you have always ridden, to this day? Have I been in the habit of
doing this to you?"
"No," he said.
31 Then the LORD opened Balaam's eyes, and
he saw the angel of the LORD standing in the
road with his sword drawn. So he bowed low
and fell facedown.
32 The angel of the LORD asked him, "Why
have you beaten your donkey these three times?
I have come here to oppose you because your
path is a reckless one before me.[a] 33 The donkey saw me and turned away from me these
three times. If she had not turned away, I would
certainly have killed you by now, but I would
have spared her."
34 Balaam said to the angel of the LORD, "I
have sinned. I did not realize you were standing in the road to oppose me. Now if you are
displeased, I will go back."
35 The angel of the LORD said to Balaam, "Go
with the men, but speak only what I tell you."
So Balaam went with the princes of Balak.
36 When Balak heard that Balaam was coming, he went out to meet him at the Moabite
town on the Arnon border, at the edge of his territory. 37 Balak said to Balaam, "Did I not send
you an urgent summons? Why didn't you come
to me? Am I really not able to reward you?"
38 "Well, I have come to you now," Balaam replied. "But can I say just anything? I must speak
only what God puts in my mouth."
39 Then Balaam went with Balak to Kiriath
Huzoth. 40 Balak sacrificed cattle and sheep,
and gave some to Balaam and the princes who
were with him. 41 The next morning Balak took
Balaam up to Bamoth Baal, and from there he
saw part of the people.

Balaam's First Oracle

23 Balaam said, "Build me seven altars
here, and prepare seven bulls and
seven rams for me." 2 Balak did as Balaam said,
and the two of them offered a bull and a ram
on each altar.
3 Then Balaam said to Balak, "Stay here beside your offering while I go aside. Perhaps the
LORD will come to meet with me. Whatever he
reveals to me I will tell you." Then he went off
to a barren height.
4 God met with him, and Balaam said, "I
have prepared seven altars, and on each altar I
have offered a bull and a ram."
5 The LORD put a message in Balaam's mouth
and said, "Go back to Balak and give him this
message."
6 So he went back to him and found him
standing beside his offering, with all the princes
of Moab. 7 Then Balaam uttered his oracle:

"Balak brought me from Aram,
the king of Moab from the eastern
mountains.
'Come,' he said, 'curse Jacob for me;
come, denounce Israel.'
8 How can I curse
those whom God has not cursed?
How can I denounce
those whom the LORD has not
denounced?
9 From the rocky peaks I see them,
from the heights I view them.
I see a people who live apart
and do not consider themselves one of
the nations.
10 Who can count the dust of Jacob
or number the fourth part of
Israel?
Let me die the death of the righteous,
and may my end be like theirs!"

11 Balak said to Balaam, "What have you
done to me? I brought you to curse my enemies,
but you have done nothing but bless them!"
12 He answered, "Must I not speak what the
LORD puts in my mouth?"

Balaam's Second Oracle

13 Then Balak said to him, "Come with me to
another place where you can see them; you will
see only a part but not all of them. And from
there, curse them for me." 14 So he took him to
the field of Zophim on the top of Pisgah, and

[a] 32 The meaning of the Hebrew for this clause is uncertain.

there he built seven altars and offered a bull
and a ram on each altar.
15 Balaam said to Balak, "Stay here beside your offering while I meet with him
over there."
16 The LORD met with Balaam and put a message in his mouth and said, "Go back to Balak
and give him this message."
17 So he went to him and found him standing
beside his offering, with the princes of Moab.
Balak asked him, "What did the LORD say?"
18 Then he uttered his oracle:

"Arise, Balak, and listen;
hear me, son of Zippor.
19 God is not a man, that he should lie,
nor a son of man, that he should change his mind.
Does he speak and then not act?
Does he promise and not fulfill?
20 I have received a command to bless;
he has blessed, and I cannot change it.

21 "No misfortune is seen in Jacob,
no misery observed in Israel.[a]
The LORD their God is with them;
the shout of the King is among them.
22 God brought them out of Egypt;
they have the strength of a wild ox.
23 There is no sorcery against Jacob,
no divination against Israel.
It will now be said of Jacob
and of Israel, 'See what God has done!'
24 The people rise like a lioness;
they rouse themselves like a lion
that does not rest till he devours his prey
and drinks the blood of his victims."

25 Then Balak said to Balaam, "Neither curse
them at all nor bless them at all!"
26 Balaam answered, "Did I not tell you I
must do whatever the LORD says?"

Numbers 23:19

God Is Truthful

"God is not a man,
that he should lie,
nor a son of man, that he
should change his mind.
Does he speak and
then not act?
Does he promise
and not fulfill?"

Balaam's Third Oracle

27 Then Balak said to Balaam, "Come, let me
take you to another place. Perhaps it will please
God to let you curse them for me from there."
28 And Balak took Balaam to the top of Peor,
overlooking the wasteland.
29 Balaam said, "Build me seven altars here,
and prepare seven bulls and seven rams for
me." 30 Balak did as Balaam had said, and offered a bull and a ram on each altar.

24 Now when Balaam saw that it pleased
the LORD to bless Israel, he did not resort to sorcery as at other times, but turned his
face toward the desert. 2 When Balaam looked
out and saw Israel encamped tribe by tribe, the
Spirit of God came upon him 3 and he uttered
his oracle:

"The oracle of Balaam son of Beor,
the oracle of one whose eye sees clearly,
4 the oracle of one who hears the words of God,
who sees a vision from the Almighty,[b]
who falls prostrate, and whose eyes are opened:
5 "How beautiful are your tents, O Jacob,
your dwelling places, O Israel!

6 "Like valleys they spread out,
like gardens beside a river,
like aloes planted by the LORD,
like cedars beside the waters.
7 Water will flow from their buckets;
their seed will have abundant water.

"Their king will be greater than Agag;
their kingdom will be exalted.

8 "God brought them out of Egypt;
they have the strength of a wild ox.
They devour hostile nations
and break their bones in pieces;
with their arrows they pierce them.
9 Like a lion they crouch and lie down,
like a lioness—who dares to rouse them?

[a] 21 Or *He has not looked on Jacob's offenses / or on the wrongs found in Israel.* [b] 4 Hebrew *Shaddai*; also in verse 16

"May those who bless you be blessed
and those who curse you be cursed!"

10 Then Balak's anger burned against Balaam. He struck his hands together and said to
him, "I summoned you to curse my enemies,
but you have blessed them these three times.
11 Now leave at once and go home! I said I
would reward you handsomely, but the LORD
has kept you from being rewarded."
12 Balaam answered Balak, "Did I not tell
the messengers you sent me, 13 'Even if Balak
gave me his palace filled with silver and gold,
I could not do anything of my own accord,
good or bad, to go beyond the command of
the LORD—and I must say only what the LORD
says'? 14 Now I am going back to my people, but
come, let me warn you of what this people will
do to your people in days to come."

Balaam's Fourth Oracle

15 Then he uttered his oracle:

"The oracle of Balaam son of Beor,
the oracle of one whose eye sees clearly,
16 the oracle of one who hears the words of God,
who has knowledge from the Most High,
who sees a vision from the Almighty,
who falls prostrate, and whose eyes are opened:

17 "I see him, but not now;
I behold him, but not near.
A star will come out of Jacob;
a scepter will rise out of Israel.
He will crush the foreheads of Moab,
the skulls[a] of[b] all the sons of Sheth.[c]
18 Edom will be conquered;
Seir, his enemy, will be conquered,
but Israel will grow strong.
19 A ruler will come out of Jacob
and destroy the survivors of the city."

Balaam's Final Oracles

20 Then Balaam saw Amalek and uttered
his oracle:

"Amalek was first among the nations,
but he will come to ruin at last."

21 Then he saw the Kenites and uttered his
oracle:

"Your dwelling place is secure,
your nest is set in a rock;
22 yet you Kenites will be destroyed
when Asshur takes you captive."

23 Then he uttered his oracle:

"Ah, who can live when God does this?[d]
24 Ships will come from the shores of Kittim;
they will subdue Asshur and Eber,
but they too will come to ruin."

25 Then Balaam got up and returned home
and Balak went his own way.

Moab Seduces Israel

25 While Israel was staying in Shittim,
the men began to indulge in sexual
immorality with Moabite women, 2 who invited
them to the sacrifices to their gods. The people
ate and bowed down before these gods. 3 So
Israel joined in worshiping the Baal of Peor.
And the LORD's anger burned against them.
4 The LORD said to Moses, "Take all the leaders of these people, kill them and expose them
in broad daylight before the LORD, so that
the LORD's fierce anger may turn away from
Israel."
5 So Moses said to Israel's judges, "Each of
you must put to death those of your men who
have joined in worshiping the Baal of Peor."
6 Then an Israelite man brought to his family
a Midianite woman right before the eyes of
Moses and the whole assembly of Israel while
they were weeping at the entrance to the Tent of
Meeting. 7 When Phinehas son of Eleazar, the
son of Aaron, the priest, saw this, he left the assembly, took a spear in his hand 8 and followed
the Israelite into the tent. He drove the spear
through both of them—through the Israelite
and into the woman's body. Then the plague
against the Israelites was stopped; 9 but those
who died in the plague numbered 24,000.
10 The LORD said to Moses, 11 "Phinehas son
of Eleazar, the son of Aaron, the priest, has
turned my anger away from the Israelites; for
he was as zealous as I am for my honor among

[a] 17 Samaritan Pentateuch (see also Jer. 48:45); the meaning of the word in the Masoretic Text is uncertain. [b] 17 Or possibly *Moab, / batter* [c] 17 Or *all the noisy boasters* [d] 23 Masoretic Text; with a different word division of the Hebrew *A people will gather from the north.*

them, so that in my zeal I did not put an end
to them. 12Therefore tell him I am making
my covenant of peace with him. 13He and his
descendants will have a covenant of a lasting
priesthood, because he was zealous for the
honor of his God and made
atonement for the Israelites."
14The name of the Israelite
who was killed with the Midianite woman was Zimri son of
Salu, the leader of a Simeonite
family. 15And the name of the
Midianite woman who was put
to death was Cozbi daughter of
Zur, a tribal chief of a Midianite family.
16The LORD said to Moses,
17"Treat the Midianites as enemies and kill them, 18because
they treated you as enemies
when they deceived you in the
affair of Peor and their sister
Cozbi, the daughter of a Midi-
anite leader, the woman who was killed when
the plague came as a result of Peor."

> Numbers 25:11
>
> *God Is Zealous*
>
> "Phinehas son of Eleazar, the son of Aaron, the priest, has turned my anger away from the Israelites; for he was as zealous as I am for my honor among them, so that in my zeal I did not put an end to them."

The Second Census

26 After the plague the LORD said to
Moses and Eleazar son of Aaron, the
priest, 2"Take a census of the whole Israelite
community by families—all those twenty years
old or more who are able to serve in the army
of Israel." 3So on the plains of Moab by the Jordan across from Jericho,[a] Moses and Eleazar
the priest spoke with them and said, 4"Take a
census of the men twenty years old or more, as
the LORD commanded Moses."

These were the Israelites who came out
of Egypt:

5The descendants of Reuben, the firstborn son
of Israel, were:
through Hanoch, the Hanochite clan;
through Pallu, the Palluite clan;
6through Hezron, the Hezronite clan;
through Carmi, the Carmite clan.
7These were the clans of Reuben; those numbered were 43,730.
8The son of Pallu was Eliab, 9and the sons of
Eliab were Nemuel, Dathan and Abiram. The
same Dathan and Abiram were the community
officials who rebelled against Moses and Aaron
and were among Korah's followers when they
rebelled against the LORD. 10The earth opened
its mouth and swallowed them
along with Korah, whose followers died when the fire devoured the 250 men. And they
served as a warning sign. 11The
line of Korah, however, did not
die out.

12The descendants of Simeon
by their clans were:
through Nemuel, the Nem-
uelite clan;
through Jamin, the Jamin-
ite clan;
through Jakin, the Jakinite
clan;
13through Zerah, the Zerahite clan;
through Shaul, the Shaulite clan.
14These were the clans of Simeon; there were
22,200 men.

15The descendants of Gad by their clans were:
through Zephon, the Zephonite clan;
through Haggi, the Haggite clan;
through Shuni, the Shunite clan;
16through Ozni, the Oznite clan;
through Eri, the Erite clan;
17through Arodi,[b] the Arodite clan;
through Areli, the Arelite clan.
18These were the clans of Gad; those numbered
were 40,500.

19Er and Onan were sons of Judah, but they
died in Canaan.
20The descendants of Judah by their clans
were:
through Shelah, the Shelanite clan;
through Perez, the Perezite clan;
through Zerah, the Zerahite clan.
21The descendants of Perez were:
through Hezron, the Hezronite clan;
through Hamul, the Hamulite clan.
22These were the clans of Judah; those numbered were 76,500.

[a]3 Hebrew *Jordan of Jericho*; possibly an ancient name for the Jordan River; also in verse 63 [b]17 Samaritan Pentateuch and Syriac (see also Gen. 46:16); Masoretic Text *Arod*

23 The descendants of Issachar by their clans were:
through Tola, the Tolaite clan;
through Puah, the Puite[a] clan;
24 through Jashub, the Jashubite clan;
through Shimron, the Shimronite clan.
25 These were the clans of Issachar; those numbered were 64,300.

26 The descendants of Zebulun by their clans were:
through Sered, the Seredite clan;
through Elon, the Elonite clan;
through Jahleel, the Jahleelite clan.
27 These were the clans of Zebulun; those numbered were 60,500.

28 The descendants of Joseph by their clans through Manasseh and Ephraim were:

29 The descendants of Manasseh:
through Makir, the Makirite clan (Makir was the father of Gilead);
through Gilead, the Gileadite clan.
30 These were the descendants of Gilead:
through Iezer, the Iezerite clan;
through Helek, the Helekite clan;
31 through Asriel, the Asrielite clan;
through Shechem, the Shechemite clan;
32 through Shemida, the Shemidaite clan;
through Hepher, the Hepherite clan.
33 (Zelophehad son of Hepher had no sons; he had only daughters, whose names were Mahlah, Noah, Hoglah, Milcah and Tirzah.)
34 These were the clans of Manasseh; those numbered were 52,700.

35 These were the descendants of Ephraim by their clans:
through Shuthelah, the Shuthelahite clan;
through Beker, the Bekerite clan;
through Tahan, the Tahanite clan.
36 These were the descendants of Shuthelah:
through Eran, the Eranite clan.
37 These were the clans of Ephraim; those numbered were 32,500.
These were the descendants of Joseph by their clans.

38 The descendants of Benjamin by their clans were:
through Bela, the Belaite clan;
through Ashbel, the Ashbelite clan;
through Ahiram, the Ahiramite clan;
39 through Shupham,[b] the Shuphamite clan;
through Hupham, the Huphamite clan.
40 The descendants of Bela through Ard and Naaman were:
through Ard,[c] the Ardite clan;
through Naaman, the Naamite clan.
41 These were the clans of Benjamin; those numbered were 45,600.

42 These were the descendants of Dan by their clans:
through Shuham, the Shuhamite clan.
These were the clans of Dan:
43 All of them were Shuhamite clans; and those numbered were 64,400.

44 The descendants of Asher by their clans were:
through Imnah, the Imnite clan;
through Ishvi, the Ishvite clan;
through Beriah, the Beriite clan;
45 and through the descendants of Beriah:
through Heber, the Heberite clan;
through Malkiel, the Malkielite clan.
46 (Asher had a daughter named Serah.)
47 These were the clans of Asher; those numbered were 53,400.

48 The descendants of Naphtali by their clans were:
through Jahzeel, the Jahzeelite clan;
through Guni, the Gunite clan;
49 through Jezer, the Jezerite clan;
through Shillem, the Shillemite clan.
50 These were the clans of Naphtali; those numbered were 45,400.

51 The total number of the men of Israel was 601,730.

52 The LORD said to Moses,
53 "The land is to be allotted to them as an inheritance based on

[a]23 Samaritan Pentateuch, Septuagint, Vulgate and Syriac (see also 1 Chron. 7:1); Masoretic Text *through Puvah, the Punite* [b]39 A few manuscripts of the Masoretic Text, Samaritan Pentateuch, Vulgate and Syriac (see also Septuagint); most manuscripts of the Masoretic Text *Shephupham* [c]40 Samaritan Pentateuch and Vulgate (see also Septuagint); Masoretic Text does not have *through Ard.*

the number of names. 54To a larger group give
a larger inheritance, and to a smaller group a
smaller one; each is to receive its inheritance according to the number of those listed. 55Be sure
that the land is distributed by lot. What each
group inherits will be according to the names
for its ancestral tribe. 56Each inheritance is
to be distributed by lot among the larger and
smaller groups."

57These were the Levites who were counted by
their clans:
through Gershon, the Gershonite clan;
through Kohath, the Kohathite clan;
through Merari, the Merarite clan.
58These also were Levite clans:
the Libnite clan,
the Hebronite clan,
the Mahlite clan,
the Mushite clan,
the Korahite clan.
(Kohath was the forefather of Amram;
59the name of Amram's wife was Jochebed, a descendant of Levi, who was born
to the Levites[a] in Egypt. To Amram
she bore Aaron, Moses and their sister
Miriam. 60Aaron was the father of Nadab
and Abihu, Eleazar and Ithamar. 61But
Nadab and Abihu died when they made
an offering before the LORD
with unauthorized fire.)

62All the male Levites a month
old or more numbered 23,000.
They were not counted along
with the other Israelites because they received no inheritance among them.

63These are the ones counted
by Moses and Eleazar the priest
when they counted the Israelites on the plains of Moab by
the Jordan across from Jericho.
64Not one of them was among
those counted by Moses and
Aaron the priest when they counted the Israelites in the Desert of Sinai. 65For the LORD had
told those Israelites they would surely die in the
desert, and not one of them was left except Caleb son of Jephunneh and Joshua son of Nun.

[a]59 Or *Jochebed, a daughter of Levi, who was born to Levi*

Zelophehad's Daughters

27 The daughters of Zelophehad son of
Hepher, the son of Gilead, the son of
Makir, the son of Manasseh, belonged to the
clans of Manasseh son of Joseph. The names
of the daughters were Mahlah, Noah, Hoglah,
Milcah and Tirzah. They approached 2the entrance to the Tent of Meeting and stood before
Moses, Eleazar the priest, the leaders and the
whole assembly, and said, 3"Our father died in
the desert. He was not among Korah's followers, who banded together against the LORD, but
he died for his own sin and left no sons. 4Why
should our father's name disappear from his
clan because he had no son? Give us property
among our father's relatives."
5So Moses brought their case before the
LORD 6and the LORD said to him, 7"What Zelophehad's daughters are saying is right. You
must certainly give them property as an inheritance among their father's relatives and turn
their father's inheritance over to them.
8"Say to the Israelites, 'If a man dies and
leaves no son, turn his inheritance over to his
daughter. 9If he has no daughter, give his inheritance to his brothers. 10If he has no brothers,
give his inheritance to his father's brothers. 11If
his father had no brothers, give his inheritance
to the nearest relative in his clan, that he may
possess it. This is to be a legal
requirement for the Israelites,
as the LORD commanded Mo-
ses.'"

> **Numbers 27:8**
>
> ***God Is Fair to All People***
>
> "Say to the Israelites, 'If a man dies and leaves no son, turn his inheritance over to his daughter.'"

Joshua to Succeed Moses

12Then the LORD said to
Moses, "Go up this mountain
in the Abarim range and see
the land I have given the Israelites. 13After you have seen
it, you too will be gathered to
your people, as your brother
Aaron was, 14for when the
community rebelled at the waters in the Desert of Zin, both
of you disobeyed my command to honor me as
holy before their eyes." (These were the waters
of Meribah Kadesh, in the Desert of Zin.)
15Moses said to the LORD, 16"May the LORD,
the God of the spirits of all mankind, appoint

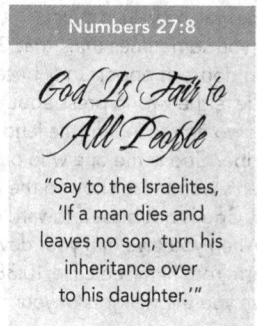

Devotion and Dignity

Read: Numbers 27:1–11

Numbers 27:5–7

So Moses brought their case before the LORD and the LORD said to him, "What Zelophehad's daughters are saying is right. You must certainly give them property as an inheritance among their father's relatives and turn their father's inheritance over to them."

SINCE THE NINETEENTH CENTURY, *Pride and Prejudice* has been one of the most beloved of all love stories. Jane Austen's tale of five sisters bound by the rigid rules of Victorian society has captivated readers, television audiences and movie buffs for years. We all want the beautiful elder sister Jane to marry Mr. Bingley. We so want Lizzie to overcome her pride and Mr. Darcy to conquer his prejudice and finally admit they love each other so they can live happily ever after. We want Mr. Wickham to be discovered for the cad he truly is. And really, the old-fashioned inheritance law of entailment which required that the family estate be passed on to the nearest male relative puzzles us. Why couldn't Mr. Bennet bequeath the family fortune to his daughters so they could marry well? Why were society's laws so male-dominated that women were prevented from keeping the family estate?

Zelophehad's five daughters had a similar problem. Their father died in the desert with no male offspring left to inherit the land. God had given the land to the tribes of Israel in perpetuity. If there was no male to inherit, what should be done? The daughters came to Moses and asked for a hearing. They wanted their portion of the inheritance. They wanted to be treated with dignity. Moses listened to the sisters make their case, and then he brought it to the Lord. God's immediate response: "Of course they should have the land."

God is not sexist, as some believe him to be. He created all of his children as equals. He pours out his Spirit on both genders equally (see Acts 2:17). He values females who are devoted to him the same way he values males.

Do you sometimes think that God is limiting you rather than opening doors of opportunity because you are a woman? Then you believe the wrong press about him. God is the one who allowed women to inherit the land so long as they married into the same tribe. God is the one who put the Savior of the world into a woman's womb. He showed the risen Lord to women first, not to men. God is not biased toward men; he's an equal-opportunity deity. When you give him your devotion, when you sit at his feet and learn from him (see Luke 10:38–42), he'll treat you with dignity and give you the delights of your heart.

reflection

1 Has this passage helped you rethink your view of God and his treatment of women?

2 How can you treat God with devotion each and every day?

3 If you feel you've been treated unfairly, how can taking your feelings to God help you deal with the experience?

RELATED READINGS

Joshua 17:3–4; Luke 24:1–10; Romans 16:12; Galatians 3:28

Go to page 206 for your next devotional reading.

a man over this community 17to go out and
come in before them, one who will lead them
out and bring them in, so the LORD's people
will not be like sheep without a shepherd."
18So the LORD said to Moses, "Take Joshua
son of Nun, a man in whom is the spirit,[a] and
lay your hand on him. 19Have him stand before
Eleazar the priest and the entire assembly and
commission him in their presence. 20Give him
some of your authority so the whole Israelite
community will obey him. 21He is to stand
before Eleazar the priest, who will obtain decisions for him by inquiring of the Urim before
the LORD. At his command he and the entire
community of the Israelites will go out, and at
his command they will come in."
22Moses did as the LORD commanded him.
He took Joshua and had him stand before
Eleazar the priest and the whole assembly.
23Then he laid his hands on him and commis-
sioned him, as the LORD instructed through
Moses.

Daily Offerings

28 The LORD said to Moses, 2"Give this
command to the Israelites and say
to them: 'See that you present to me at the
appointed time the food for my offerings made
by fire, as an aroma pleasing to me.' 3Say to
them: 'This is the offering made by fire that
you are to present to the LORD: two lambs a
year old without defect, as a regular burnt
offering each day. 4Prepare one lamb in the
morning and the other at twilight, 5together
with a grain offering of a tenth of an ephah[b] of
fine flour mixed with a quarter of a hin[c] of oil
from pressed olives. 6This is the regular burnt
offering instituted at Mount Sinai as a pleasing
aroma, an offering made to the LORD by fire.
7The accompanying drink offering is to be a
quarter of a hin of fermented drink with each
lamb. Pour out the drink offering to the LORD
at the sanctuary. 8Prepare the second lamb at
twilight, along with the same kind of grain offering and drink offering that you prepare in
the morning. This is an offering made by fire,
an aroma pleasing to the LORD.

Sabbath Offerings

9" 'On the Sabbath day, make an offering of
two lambs a year old without defect, together
with its drink offering and a grain offering of
two-tenths of an ephah[d] of fine flour mixed
with oil. 10This is the burnt offering for every
Sabbath, in addition to the regular burnt offering and its drink offering.

Monthly Offerings

11" 'On the first of every month, present to
the LORD a burnt offering of two young bulls,
one ram and seven male lambs a year old, all
without defect. 12With each bull there is to be
a grain offering of three-tenths of an ephah[e] of
fine flour mixed with oil; with the ram, a grain
offering of two-tenths of an ephah of fine flour
mixed with oil; 13and with each lamb, a grain
offering of a tenth of an ephah of fine flour
mixed with oil. This is for a burnt offering, a
pleasing aroma, an offering made to the LORD
by fire. 14With each bull there is to be a drink
offering of half a hin[f] of wine; with the ram, a
third of a hin[g]; and with each lamb, a quarter of
a hin. This is the monthly burnt offering to be
made at each new moon during the year. 15Be-
sides the regular burnt offering with its drink
offering, one male goat is to be presented to the
LORD as a sin offering.

The Passover

16" 'On the fourteenth day of the first month
the LORD's Passover is to be held. 17On the fifteenth day of this month there is to be a festival;
for seven days eat bread made without yeast.
18On the first day hold a sacred assembly and
do no regular work. 19Present to the LORD an
offering made by fire, a burnt offering of two
young bulls, one ram and seven male lambs a
year old, all without defect. 20With each bull
prepare a grain offering of three-tenths of an
ephah of fine flour mixed with oil; with the
ram, two-tenths; 21and with each of the seven
lambs, one-tenth. 22Include one male goat as a
sin offering to make atonement for you. 23Pre-
pare these in addition to the regular morning
burnt offering. 24In this way prepare the food
for the offering made by fire every day for

[a]18 Or *Spirit* [b]5 That is, probably about 2 quarts (about 2 liters); also in verses 13, 21 and 29 [c]5 That is, probably about 1 quart (about 1 liter); also in verses 7 and 14 [d]9 That is, probably about 4 quarts (about 4.5 liters); also in verses 12, 20 and 28 [e]12 That is, probably about 6 quarts (about 6.5 liters); also in verses 20 and 28 [f]14 That is, probably about 2 quarts (about 2 liters) [g]14 That is, probably about 1 1/4 quarts (about 1.2 liters)

seven days as an aroma pleasing to the LORD; it is to be prepared in addition to the regular burnt offering and its drink offering. 25On the seventh day hold a sacred assembly and do no regular work.

Feast of Weeks

26" 'On the day of firstfruits, when you present to the LORD an offering of new grain during the Feast of Weeks, hold a sacred assembly and do no regular work. 27Present a burnt offering of two young bulls, one ram and seven male lambs a year old as an aroma pleasing to the LORD. 28With each bull there is to be a grain offering of three-tenths of an ephah of fine flour mixed with oil; with the ram, two-tenths; 29and with each of the seven lambs, one-tenth. 30Include one male goat to make atonement for you. 31Prepare these together with their drink offerings, in addition to the regular burnt offering and its grain offering. Be sure the animals are without defect.

Feast of Trumpets

29 " 'On the first day of the seventh month hold a sacred assembly and do no regular work. It is a day for you to sound the trumpets. 2As an aroma pleasing to the LORD, prepare a burnt offering of one young bull, one ram and seven male lambs a year old, all without defect. 3With the bull prepare a grain offering of three-tenths of an ephah[a] of fine flour mixed with oil; with the ram, two-tenths[b]; 4and with each of the seven lambs, one-tenth.[c] 5Include one male goat as a sin offering to make atonement for you. 6These are in addition to the monthly and daily burnt offerings with their grain offerings and drink offerings as specified. They are offerings made to the LORD by fire—a pleasing aroma.

Day of Atonement

7" 'On the tenth day of this seventh month hold a sacred assembly. You must deny yourselves[d] and do no work. 8Present as an aroma pleasing to the LORD a burnt offering of one young bull, one ram and seven male lambs a year old, all without defect. 9With the bull prepare a grain offering of three-tenths of an ephah of fine flour mixed with oil; with the ram, two-tenths; 10and with each of the seven lambs, one-tenth. 11Include one male goat as a sin offering, in addition to the sin offering for atonement and the regular burnt offering with its grain offering, and their drink offerings.

Feast of Tabernacles

12" 'On the fifteenth day of the seventh month, hold a sacred assembly and do no regular work. Celebrate a festival to the LORD for seven days. 13Present an offering made by fire as an aroma pleasing to the LORD, a burnt offering of thirteen young bulls, two rams and fourteen male lambs a year old, all without defect. 14With each of the thirteen bulls prepare a grain offering of three-tenths of an ephah of fine flour mixed with oil; with each of the two rams, two-tenths; 15and with each of the fourteen lambs, one-tenth. 16Include one male goat as a sin offering, in addition to the regular burnt offering with its grain offering and drink offering.

17" 'On the second day prepare twelve young bulls, two rams and fourteen male lambs a year old, all without defect. 18With the bulls, rams and lambs, prepare their grain offerings and drink offerings according to the number specified. 19Include one male goat as a sin offering, in addition to the regular burnt offering with its grain offering, and their drink offerings.

20" 'On the third day prepare eleven bulls, two rams and fourteen male lambs a year old, all without defect. 21With the bulls, rams and lambs, prepare their grain offerings and drink offerings according to the number specified. 22Include one male goat as a sin offering, in addition to the regular burnt offering with its grain offering and drink offering.

23" 'On the fourth day prepare ten bulls, two rams and fourteen male lambs a year old, all without defect. 24With the bulls, rams and lambs, prepare their grain offerings and drink offerings according to the number specified. 25Include one male goat as a sin offering, in addition to the regular burnt offering with its grain offering and drink offering.

26" 'On the fifth day prepare nine bulls, two rams and fourteen male lambs a year old, all without defect. 27With the bulls, rams and

[a] 3 That is, probably about 6 quarts (about 6.5 liters); also in verses 9 and 14 [b] 3 That is, probably about 4 quarts (about 4.5 liters); also in verses 9 and 14 [c] 4 That is, probably about 2 quarts (about 2 liters); also in verses 10 and 15 [d] 7 Or *must fast*

lambs, prepare their grain offerings and drink
offerings according to the number specified.
28 Include one male goat as a sin offering, in
addition to the regular burnt offering with its
grain offering and drink offering.
29 " 'On the sixth day prepare eight bulls,
two rams and fourteen male lambs a year old,
all without defect. 30 With the bulls, rams and
lambs, prepare their grain offerings and drink
offerings according to the number specified.
31 Include one male goat as a sin offering, in
addition to the regular burnt offering with its
grain offering and drink offering.
32 " 'On the seventh day prepare seven bulls,
two rams and fourteen male lambs a year old,
all without defect. 33 With the bulls, rams and
lambs, prepare their grain offerings and drink
offerings according to the number specified.
34 Include one male goat as a sin offering, in
addition to the regular burnt offering with its
grain offering and drink offering.
35 " 'On the eighth day hold an assembly
and do no regular work. 36 Present an offering made by fire as an aroma pleasing to the
LORD, a burnt offering of one bull, one ram and
seven male lambs a year old, all without defect.
37 With the bull, the ram and the lambs, prepare their grain offerings and drink offerings
according to the number specified. 38 Include
one male goat as a sin offering, in addition to
the regular burnt offering with its grain offering and drink offering.
39 " 'In addition to what you vow and your
freewill offerings, prepare these for the LORD
at your appointed feasts: your burnt offerings,
grain offerings, drink offerings and fellowship offerings.[a]' "
40 Moses told the Israelites all that the LORD
commanded him.

Vows

30 Moses said to the heads of the tribes
of Israel: "This is what the LORD commands: 2 When a man makes a vow to the
LORD or takes an oath to obligate himself by
a pledge, he must not break his word but must
do everything he said.
3 "When a young woman still living in her
father's house makes a vow to the LORD or obligates herself by a pledge 4 and her father hears
about her vow or pledge but says nothing to
her, then all her vows and every pledge by
which she obligated herself will stand. 5 But if
her father forbids her when he hears about it,
none of her vows or the pledges by which she
obligated herself will stand; the LORD will release her because her father has forbidden her.
6 "If she marries after she makes a vow or after her lips utter a rash promise by which she
obligates herself 7 and her husband hears about
it but says nothing to her, then her vows or
the pledges by which she obligated herself will
stand. 8 But if her husband forbids her when
he hears about it, he nullifies the vow that obligates her or the rash promise by which she obligates herself, and the LORD will release her.
9 "Any vow or obligation taken by a widow or
divorced woman will be binding on her.
10 "If a woman living with her husband
makes a vow or obligates herself by a pledge
under oath 11 and her husband hears about it
but says nothing to her and does not forbid
her, then all her vows or the pledges by which
she obligated herself will stand. 12 But if her
husband nullifies them when he hears about
them, then none of the vows or pledges that
came from her lips will stand. Her husband
has nullified them, and the LORD will release
her. 13 Her husband may confirm or nullify any
vow she makes or any sworn pledge to deny
herself. 14 But if her husband says nothing to
her about it from day to day, then he confirms
all her vows or the pledges binding on her. He
confirms them by saying nothing to her when
he hears about them. 15 If, however, he nullifies
them some time after he hears about them,
then he is responsible for her guilt."
16 These are the regulations the LORD gave
Moses concerning relationships between a
man and his wife, and between a father and his
young daughter still living in his house.

Vengeance on the Midianites

31 The LORD said to Moses, 2 "Take vengeance on the Midianites for the Israelites. After that, you will be gathered to your
people."
3 So Moses said to the people, "Arm some of

[a]39 Traditionally *peace offerings*

your men to go to war against the Midianites
and to carry out the LORD's vengeance on them.
4Send into battle a thousand men from each of
the tribes of Israel." 5So twelve thousand men
armed for battle, a thousand from each tribe,
were supplied from the clans of Israel. 6Moses
sent them into battle, a thousand from each
tribe, along with Phinehas son of Eleazar, the
priest, who took with him articles from the
sanctuary and the trumpets for signaling.
7They fought against Midian, as the LORD
commanded Moses, and killed every man.
8Among their victims were Evi, Rekem, Zur,
Hur and Reba—the five kings of Midian. They
also killed Balaam son of Beor with the sword.
9The Israelites captured the Midianite women
and children and took all the Midianite herds,
flocks and goods as plunder. 10They burned
all the towns where the Midianites had settled,
as well as all their camps. 11They took all the
plunder and spoils, including the people and
animals, 12and brought the captives, spoils and
plunder to Moses and Eleazar the priest and the
Israelite assembly at their camp on the plains of
Moab, by the Jordan across from Jericho.[a]
13Moses, Eleazar the priest and all the leaders of the community went to meet them outside the camp. 14Moses was angry with the
officers of the army—the commanders of thousands and commanders of hundreds—who returned from the battle.
15"Have you allowed all the women to live?"
he asked them. 16"They were the ones who followed Balaam's advice and were the means of
turning the Israelites away from the LORD in
what happened at Peor, so that a plague struck
the LORD's people. 17Now kill all the boys. And
kill every woman who has slept with a man,
18but save for yourselves every girl who has
never slept with a man.
19"All of you who have killed anyone or
touched anyone who was killed must stay outside the camp seven days. On the third and seventh days you must purify yourselves and your
captives. 20Purify every garment as well as everything made of leather, goat hair or wood."
21Then Eleazar the priest said to the soldiers
who had gone into battle, "This is the requirement of the law that the LORD gave Moses:
22Gold, silver, bronze, iron, tin, lead 23and anything else that can withstand fire must be put
through the fire, and then it will be clean. But
it must also be purified with the water of cleansing. And whatever cannot withstand fire must
be put through that water. 24On the seventh
day wash your clothes and you will be clean.
Then you may come into the camp."

Dividing the Spoils

25The LORD said to Moses, 26"You and Eleazar the priest and the family heads of the
community are to count all the people and animals that were captured. 27Divide the spoils between the soldiers who took part in the battle
and the rest of the community. 28From the soldiers who fought in the battle, set apart as tribute for the LORD one out of every five hundred,
whether persons, cattle, donkeys, sheep or
goats. 29Take this tribute from their half share
and give it to Eleazar the priest as the LORD's
part. 30From the Israelites' half, select one out
of every fifty, whether persons, cattle, donkeys,
sheep, goats or other animals. Give them to
the Levites, who are responsible for the care of
the LORD's tabernacle." 31So Moses and Eleazar
the priest did as the LORD commanded Moses.
32The plunder remaining from the spoils that
the soldiers took was 675,000 sheep, 3372,000
cattle, 3461,000 donkeys 35and 32,000 women
who had never slept with a man.
36The half share of those who fought in the
battle was:

337,500 sheep, 37of which the tribute for
the LORD was 675;
38 36,000 cattle, of which the tribute for the
LORD was 72;
39 30,500 donkeys, of which the tribute for
the LORD was 61;
40 16,000 people, of which the tribute for the
LORD was 32.

41Moses gave the tribute to Eleazar the priest
as the LORD's part, as the LORD commanded
Moses.
42The half belonging to the Israelites, which
Moses set apart from that of the fighting
men— 43the community's half—was 337,500
sheep, 4436,000 cattle, 4530,500 donkeys 46and

[a] 12 Hebrew *Jordan of Jericho*; possibly an ancient name for the Jordan River

16,000 people. 47From the Israelites' half, Moses selected one out of every fifty persons and animals, as the LORD commanded him, and gave them to the Levites, who were responsible for the care of the LORD's tabernacle.

48Then the officers who were over the units of the army—the commanders of thousands and commanders of hundreds—went to Moses 49and said to him, "Your servants have counted the soldiers under our command, and not one is missing. 50So we have brought as an offering to the LORD the gold articles each of us acquired—armlets, bracelets, signet rings, earrings and necklaces—to make atonement for ourselves before the LORD."

51Moses and Eleazar the priest accepted from them the gold—all the crafted articles. 52All the gold from the commanders of thousands and commanders of hundreds that Moses and Eleazar presented as a gift to the LORD weighed 16,750 shekels.[a] 53Each soldier had taken plunder for himself. 54Moses and Eleazar the priest accepted the gold from the commanders of thousands and commanders of hundreds and brought it into the Tent of Meeting as a memorial for the Israelites before the LORD.

The Transjordan Tribes

32 The Reubenites and Gadites, who had very large herds and flocks, saw that the lands of Jazer and Gilead were suitable for livestock. 2So they came to Moses and Eleazar the priest and to the leaders of the community, and said, 3"Ataroth, Dibon, Jazer, Nimrah, Heshbon, Elealeh, Sebam, Nebo and Beon— 4the land the LORD subdued before the people of Israel—are suitable for livestock, and your servants have livestock. 5If we have found favor in your eyes," they said, "let this land be given to your servants as our possession. Do not make us cross the Jordan."

6Moses said to the Gadites and Reubenites, "Shall your countrymen go to war while you sit here? 7Why do you discourage the Israelites from going over into the land the LORD has given them? 8This is what your fathers did when I sent them from Kadesh Barnea to look over the land. 9After they went up to the Valley of Eshcol and viewed the land, they discouraged the Israelites from entering the land the LORD had given them. 10The LORD's anger was aroused that day and he swore this oath: 11'Because they have not followed me wholeheartedly, not one of the men twenty years old or more who came up out of Egypt will see the land I promised on oath to Abraham, Isaac and Jacob— 12not one except Caleb son of Jephunneh the Kenizzite and Joshua son of Nun, for they followed the LORD wholeheartedly.' 13The LORD's anger burned against Israel and he made them wander in the desert forty years, until the whole generation of those who had done evil in his sight was gone.

14"And here you are, a brood of sinners, standing in the place of your fathers and making the LORD even more angry with Israel. 15If you turn away from following him, he will again leave all this people in the desert, and you will be the cause of their destruction."

16Then they came up to him and said, "We would like to build pens here for our livestock and cities for our women and children. 17But we are ready to arm ourselves and go ahead of the Israelites until we have brought them to their place. Meanwhile our women and children will live in fortified cities, for protection from the inhabitants of the land. 18We will not return to our homes until every Israelite has received his inheritance. 19We will not receive any inheritance with them on the other side of the Jordan, because our inheritance has come to us on the east side of the Jordan."

20Then Moses said to them, "If you will do this—if you will arm yourselves before the LORD for battle, 21and if all of you will go armed over the Jordan before the LORD until he has driven his enemies out before him— 22then when the land is subdued before the LORD, you may return and be free from your obligation to the LORD and to Israel. And this land will be your possession before the LORD.

23"But if you fail to do this, you will be sinning against the LORD; and you may be sure that your sin will find you out. 24Build cities for your women and children, and pens for your flocks, but do what you have promised."

25The Gadites and Reubenites said to Moses,

[a]52 That is, about 420 pounds (about 190 kilograms)

"We your servants will do as our lord commands. 26Our children and wives, our flocks
and herds will remain here in
the cities of Gilead. 27But your
servants, every man armed for
battle, will cross over to fight
before the LORD, just as our
lord says."
28Then Moses gave orders
about them to Eleazar the
priest and Joshua son of Nun
and to the family heads of the
Israelite tribes. 29He said to
them, "If the Gadites and Reubenites, every man armed for
battle, cross over the Jordan
with you before the LORD, then
when the land is subdued before you, give them the land of
Gilead as their possession. 30But if they do not
cross over with you armed, they must accept
their possession with you in Canaan."
31The Gadites and Reubenites answered,
"Your servants will do what the LORD has said.
32We will cross over before the LORD into Canaan armed, but the property we inherit will be
on this side of the Jordan."
33Then Moses gave to the Gadites, the Reubenites and the half-tribe of Manasseh son of
Joseph the kingdom of Sihon king of the Amorites and the kingdom of Og king of Bashan—
the whole land with its cities and the territory
around them.
34The Gadites built up Dibon, Ataroth,
Aroer, 35Atroth Shophan, Jazer, Jogbehah,
36Beth Nimrah and Beth Haran as fortified
cities, and built pens for their flocks. 37And
the Reubenites rebuilt Heshbon, Elealeh and
Kiriathaim, 38as well as Nebo and Baal Meon
(these names were changed) and Sibmah. They
gave names to the cities they rebuilt.
39The descendants of Makir son of Manasseh went to Gilead, captured it and drove out
the Amorites who were there. 40So Moses gave
Gilead to the Makirites, the descendants of Manasseh, and they settled there. 41Jair, a descendant of Manasseh, captured their settlements
and called them Havvoth Jair.[a] 42And Nobah
captured Kenath and its surrounding settlements and called it Nobah after himself.

Numbers 32:23

God Sees Everything

"But if you fail to do this, you will be sinning against the LORD; and you may be sure that your sin will find you out."

Stages in Israel's Journey

33 Here are the stages in
the journey of the Is-
raelites when they came out
of Egypt by divisions under
the leadership of Moses and
Aaron. 2At the LORD's command Moses recorded the
stages in their journey. This is
their journey by stages:
3The Israelites set out
from Rameses on the
fifteenth day of the first
month, the day after the
Passover. They marched
out boldly in full view
of all the Egyptians, 4who were burying
all their firstborn, whom the LORD had
struck down among them; for the LORD
had brought judgment on their gods.
5The Israelites left Rameses and camped
at Succoth.
6They left Succoth and camped at
Etham, on the edge of the desert.
7They left Etham, turned back to Pi
Hahiroth, to the east of Baal Zephon, and
camped near Migdol.
8They left Pi Hahiroth[b] and passed
through the sea into the desert, and when
they had traveled for three days in the Desert of Etham, they camped at Marah.
9They left Marah and went to Elim,
where there were twelve springs and seventy palm trees, and they camped there.
10They left Elim and camped by the
Red Sea.[c]
11They left the Red Sea and camped in
the Desert of Sin.
12They left the Desert of Sin and
camped at Dophkah.
13They left Dophkah and camped at
Alush.
14They left Alush and camped at Rephidim, where there was no water for the
people to drink.

[a]41 Or *them the settlements of Jair* [b]8 Many manuscripts of the Masoretic Text, Samaritan Pentateuch and Vulgate; most manuscripts of the Masoretic Text *left from before Hahiroth* [c]10 Hebrew *Yam Suph*; that is, Sea of Reeds; also in verse 11

15 They left Rephidim and camped in
the Desert of Sinai.
16 They left the Desert of Sinai and
camped at Kibroth Hattaavah.
17 They left Kibroth Hattaavah and
camped at Hazeroth.
18 They left Hazeroth and camped at
Rithmah.
19 They left Rithmah and camped at
Rimmon Perez.
20 They left Rimmon Perez and camped
at Libnah.
21 They left Libnah and camped at Rissah.
22 They left Rissah and camped at Kehelathah.
23 They left Kehelathah and camped at
Mount Shepher.
24 They left Mount Shepher and camped
at Haradah.
25 They left Haradah and camped at
Makheloth.
26 They left Makheloth and camped
at Tahath.
27 They left Tahath and camped at Terah.
28 They left Terah and camped at Mithcah.
29 They left Mithcah and camped at
Hashmonah.
30 They left Hashmonah and camped
at Moseroth.
31 They left Moseroth and camped at
Bene Jaakan.
32 They left Bene Jaakan and camped at
Hor Haggidgad.
33 They left Hor Haggidgad and camped
at Jotbathah.
34 They left Jotbathah and camped at
Abronah.
35 They left Abronah and camped at
Ezion Geber.
36 They left Ezion Geber and camped at
Kadesh, in the Desert of Zin.
37 They left Kadesh and camped at
Mount Hor, on the border of Edom. 38 At
the LORD's command Aaron the priest
went up Mount Hor, where he died on
the first day of the fifth month of the fortieth year after the Israelites came out
of Egypt. 39 Aaron was a hundred and
twenty-three years old when he died on
Mount Hor.
40 The Canaanite king of Arad, who
lived in the Negev of Canaan, heard that
the Israelites were coming.
41 They left Mount Hor and camped
at Zalmonah.
42 They left Zalmonah and camped
at Punon.
43 They left Punon and camped
at Oboth.
44 They left Oboth and camped at Iye
Abarim, on the border of Moab.
45 They left Iyim[a] and camped at Dibon Gad.
46 They left Dibon Gad and camped at
Almon Diblathaim.
47 They left Almon Diblathaim and
camped in the mountains of Abarim,
near Nebo.
48 They left the mountains of Abarim
and camped on the plains of Moab by the
Jordan across from Jericho.[b] 49 There on
the plains of Moab they camped along
the Jordan from Beth Jeshimoth to Abel
Shittim.

50 On the plains of Moab by the Jordan across
from Jericho the LORD said to Moses, 51 "Speak
to the Israelites and say to them: 'When you
cross the Jordan into Canaan, 52 drive out all
the inhabitants of the land before you. Destroy
all their carved images and their cast idols,
and demolish all their high places. 53 Take possession of the land and settle in it, for I have
given you the land to possess. 54 Distribute
the land by lot, according to your clans. To a
larger group give a larger inheritance, and to a
smaller group a smaller one. Whatever falls to
them by lot will be theirs. Distribute it according to your ancestral tribes.
55 " 'But if you do not drive out the inhabitants of the land, those you allow to remain
will become barbs in your eyes and thorns in
your sides. They will give you trouble in the
land where you will live. 56 And then I will do
to you what I plan to do to them.' "

[a]45 That is, Iye Abarim [b]48 Hebrew *Jordan of Jericho*; possibly an ancient name for the Jordan River; also in verse 50

No Loopholes

Read: Numbers 33:50–56

Numbers 33:55–56

"But if you do not drive out the inhabitants of the land, those you allow to remain will become barbs in your eyes and thorns in your sides. They will give you trouble in the land where you will live. And then I will do to you what I plan to do to them."

SURE, DESTROY THE IDOLS. Can you hear the Israelites' thoughts as they finally entered the promised land? *Dividing up the land—that sounds good. After all, we want the land.* So far, they're liking what God tells them. Then comes the rub. God tells them to drive everyone from the land. Every single person living in the land has got to go. *Wait a minute! How could our good and loving God drive these folks from their homes? Even fragile women, helpless old people and innocent little children? That's just not fair!*

Sometimes we come to portions of the Bible we cannot reconcile with our notions of what is fair. But we can't avoid these difficult passages. God said, "Drive out everyone." And in our limited understanding we argue, question and challenge: "Surely 'everyone' doesn't mean *everyone*. You just mean a few—like the really bad guys. 'Cause you're loving and fair, right?"

But instead of responding to our demands, God points us back to his Word and reveals more of who he is: "'My thoughts are not your thoughts, neither are your ways my ways,' declares the LORD. 'As the heavens are higher than the earth, so are my ways higher than your ways and my thoughts than your thoughts' " (Isaiah 55:8–9). Yes, God is loving and fair. But God is also just. When he said "everyone," he meant every single person. He wasn't being cruel. He was being protective.

God recognized that the Canaanites were thoroughly infected with the highly contagious disease of idolatry. Allowing them to stay in the land would mean exposing the Israelites to their contamination. The moral illness would certainly destroy them.

Do you ever find yourself second-guessing God? Even when his instruction is clearly laid out in his Word? Do you bristle and say, "Wait! Surely 'all' doesn't mean *all*?" Yet when Paul wrote, "As we have opportunity, let us do good to *all* people" (Galatians 6:10, emphasis added), we don't find much wiggle room . . . "all people" means *all* people. We might try to say, "Surely 'every' doesn't mean *every*. I'm sure there are exceptions to your rules. Isn't there a loophole?" But God doesn't ask for our advice or our input—just our obedience, even when his ways don't seem to make sense. The truth is this: There is no better way than God's way. In every area, in all things, at all times, God is good and loving and just. And he always, in all ways, knows best.

reflection

1. When do you find it especially difficult to obey God?

2. Have you experienced "barbs and thorns" because you insisted on doing things your own way?

3. How does it comfort you to know that God's ways are far above your ways?

RELATED READINGS

2 Chronicles 31:20–21; Romans 8:28; 2 Timothy 3:16–17

Go to page 212 for your next devotional reading.

Boundaries of Canaan

34 The LORD said to Moses, 2"Command the Israelites and say to them: 'When you enter Canaan, the land that will be allotted to you as an inheritance will have these boundaries:

3"'Your southern side will include some of the Desert of Zin along the border of Edom. On the east, your southern boundary will start from the end of the Salt Sea,[a] 4cross south of Scorpion[b] Pass, continue on to Zin and go south of Kadesh Barnea. Then it will go to Hazar Addar and over to Azmon, 5where it will turn, join the Wadi of Egypt and end at the Sea.[c]

6"'Your western boundary will be the coast of the Great Sea. This will be your boundary on the west.

7"'For your northern boundary, run a line from the Great Sea to Mount Hor 8and from Mount Hor to Lebo[d] Hamath. Then the boundary will go to Zedad, 9continue to Ziphron and end at Hazar Enan. This will be your boundary on the north.

10"'For your eastern boundary, run a line from Hazar Enan to Shepham. 11The boundary will go down from Shepham to Riblah on the east side of Ain and continue along the slopes east of the Sea of Kinnereth.[e] 12Then the boundary will go down along the Jordan and end at the Salt Sea.

"'This will be your land, with its boundaries on every side.'"

13Moses commanded the Israelites: "Assign this land by lot as an inheritance. The LORD has ordered that it be given to the nine and a half tribes, 14because the families of the tribe of Reuben, the tribe of Gad and the half-tribe of Manasseh have received their inheritance. 15These two and a half tribes have received their inheritance on the east side of the Jordan of Jericho,[f] toward the sunrise."

16The LORD said to Moses, 17"These are the names of the men who are to assign the land for you as an inheritance: Eleazar the priest and Joshua son of Nun. 18And appoint one leader from each tribe to help assign the land. 19These are their names:

Caleb son of Jephunneh,
from the tribe of Judah;
20Shemuel son of Ammihud,
from the tribe of Simeon;
21Elidad son of Kislon,
from the tribe of Benjamin;
22Bukki son of Jogli,
the leader from the tribe of Dan;
23Hanniel son of Ephod,
the leader from the tribe of Manasseh son of Joseph;
24Kemuel son of Shiphtan,
the leader from the tribe of Ephraim son of Joseph;
25Elizaphan son of Parnach,
the leader from the tribe of Zebulun;
26Paltiel son of Azzan,
the leader from the tribe of Issachar;
27Ahihud son of Shelomi,
the leader from the tribe of Asher;
28Pedahel son of Ammihud,
the leader from the tribe of Naphtali."

29These are the men the LORD commanded to assign the inheritance to the Israelites in the land of Canaan.

Towns for the Levites

35 On the plains of Moab by the Jordan across from Jericho,[g] the LORD said to Moses, 2"Command the Israelites to give the Levites towns to live in from the inheritance the Israelites will possess. And give them pasturelands around the towns. 3Then they will have towns to live in and pasturelands for their cattle, flocks and all their other livestock.

4"The pasturelands around the towns that you give the Levites will extend out fifteen hundred feet[h] from the town wall. 5Outside the town, measure three thousand feet[i] on the east side, three thousand on the south side, three thousand on the west and three thousand on the north, with the town in the center. They will have this area as pastureland for the towns.

Cities of Refuge

6"Six of the towns you give the Levites will be cities of refuge, to which a person who has killed someone may flee. In addition, give them

[a]3 That is, the Dead Sea; also in verse 12 [b]4 Hebrew *Akrabbim* [c]5 That is, the Mediterranean; also in verses 6 and 7 [d]8 Or *to the entrance to* [e]11 That is, Galilee [f]15 *Jordan of Jericho* was possibly an ancient name for the Jordan River. [g]1 Hebrew *Jordan of Jericho*; possibly an ancient name for the Jordan River [h]4 Hebrew *a thousand cubits* (about 450 meters) [i]5 Hebrew *two thousand cubits* (about 900 meters)

forty-two other towns. 7In all you must give the Levites forty-eight towns, together with their pasturelands. 8The towns you give the Levites from the land the Israelites possess are to be given in proportion to the inheritance of each tribe: Take many towns from a tribe that has many, but few from one that has few."

9Then the LORD said to Moses: 10"Speak to the Israelites and say to them: 'When you cross the Jordan into Canaan, 11select some towns to be your cities of refuge, to which a person who has killed someone accidentally may flee. 12They will be places of refuge from the avenger, so that a person accused of murder may not die before he stands trial before the assembly. 13These six towns you give will be your cities of refuge. 14Give three on this side of the Jordan and three in Canaan as cities of refuge. 15These six towns will be a place of refuge for Israelites, aliens and any other people living among them, so that anyone who has killed another accidentally can flee there.

16" 'If a man strikes someone with an iron object so that he dies, he is a murderer; the murderer shall be put to death. 17Or if anyone has a stone in his hand that could kill, and he strikes someone so that he dies, he is a murderer; the murderer shall be put to death. 18Or if anyone has a wooden object in his hand that could kill, and he hits someone so that he dies, he is a murderer; the murderer shall be put to death. 19The avenger of blood shall put the murderer to death; when he meets him, he shall put him to death. 20If anyone with malice aforethought shoves another or throws something at him intentionally so that he dies 21or if in hostility he hits him with his fist so that he dies, that person shall be put to death; he is a murderer. The avenger of blood shall put the murderer to death when he meets him.

22" 'But if without hostility someone suddenly shoves another or throws something at him unintentionally 23or, without seeing him, drops a stone on him that could kill him, and he dies, then since he was not his enemy and he did not intend to harm him, 24the assembly must judge between him and the avenger of blood according to these regulations. 25The assembly must protect the one accused of murder from the avenger of blood and send him back to the city of refuge to which he fled. He must stay there until the death of the high priest, who was anointed with the holy oil.

26" 'But if the accused ever goes outside the limits of the city of refuge to which he has fled 27and the avenger of blood finds him outside the city, the avenger of blood may kill the accused without being guilty of murder. 28The accused must stay in his city of refuge until the death of the high priest; only after the death of the high priest may he return to his own property.

29" 'These are to be legal requirements for you throughout the generations to come, wherever you live.

30" 'Anyone who kills a person is to be put to death as a murderer only on the testimony of witnesses. But no one is to be put to death on the testimony of only one witness.

31" 'Do not accept a ransom for the life of a murderer, who deserves to die. He must surely be put to death.

32" 'Do not accept a ransom for anyone who has fled to a city of refuge and so allow him to go back and live on his own land before the death of the high priest.

33" 'Do not pollute the land where you are. Bloodshed pollutes the land, and atonement cannot be made for the land on which blood has been shed, except by the blood of the one who shed it. 34Do not defile the land where you live and where I dwell, for I, the LORD, dwell among the Israelites.' "

> **Numbers 35:34**
>
> *God Lives With Us*
>
> "Do not defile the land where you live and where I dwell, for I, the LORD, dwell among the Israelites."

Inheritance of Zelophehad's Daughters

36 The family heads of the clan of Gilead son of Makir, the son of Manasseh, who were from the clans of the descendants of Joseph, came and spoke before Moses and the leaders, the heads of the Israelite families. 2They

said, "When the LORD commanded my lord to give the land as an inheritance to the Israelites by lot, he ordered you to give the inheritance of our brother Zelophehad to his daughters.
[3]Now suppose they marry men from other Israelite tribes; then their inheritance will be taken from our ancestral inheritance and added to that of the tribe they marry into. And so part of the inheritance allotted to us will be taken
away. [4]When the Year of Jubilee for the Israelites comes, their inheritance will be added to that of the tribe into which they marry, and their property will be taken from the tribal inheritance of our forefathers."

[5]Then at the LORD's command Moses gave this order to the Israelites: "What the tribe of the descendants of Joseph is saying is right.
[6]This is what the LORD commands for Zelophehad's daughters: They may marry anyone they please as long as they marry within the tribal clan of their father.
[7]No inheritance in Israel is to pass from tribe to tribe, for every Israelite shall keep the tribal land inherited from his forefathers.
[8]Every daughter who inherits land in any Israelite tribe must marry someone in her father's tribal clan, so that every Israelite will possess the inheritance of his fathers.
[9]No inheritance may pass from tribe to tribe, for each Israelite tribe is to keep the land it inherits."

[10]So Zelophehad's daughters did as the LORD commanded Moses.
[11]Zelophehad's daughters—Mahlah, Tirzah, Hoglah, Milcah and Noah—married their cousins on their father's side.
[12]They married within the clans of the descendants of Manasseh son of Joseph, and their inheritance remained in their father's clan and tribe.

[13]These are the commands and regulations the LORD gave through Moses to the Israelites on the plains of Moab by the Jordan across from Jericho.[a]

[a]13 Hebrew *Jordan of Jericho*; possibly an ancient name for the Jordan River

Deuteronomy

Author:
Moses.

Audience:
The people of Israel.

Date:
About 1406 B.C.

Setting:
In the desert east of the Jordan River, preparing to enter the promised land.

Verse to Remember:
Love the LORD your God with all your heart and with all your soul and with all your strength. (6:5)

Deuteronomy reads like a farewell address given by a leader to his beloved people. *Moses is 120 years old now,* still strong, still clear of vision and still very much a leader. But *it is time for a change.* He has watched a generation of the Israelites die in the wilderness. He knows that he too will soon die. He will not be the one to cross the Jordan River and lead the Israelites into *the promised land.* Before he departs he wants to impress upon the people who God is and what God requires. Moses won't be going with them, but he wants to be sure the people go with God. They must know what *God's Law says,* and they must live it out. The only way for them to reach and secure the promised land is to love God and obey him.

The Command to Leave Horeb

1 These are the words Moses spoke to all
Israel in the desert east of the Jordan—that
is, in the Arabah—opposite Suph, between Paran and Tophel, Laban, Hazeroth and Dizahab.
2(It takes eleven days to go from Horeb to Kadesh Barnea by the Mount Seir road.)
3In the fortieth year, on the first day of the
eleventh month, Moses proclaimed to the Israelites all that the LORD had commanded him concerning them. 4This was after he had defeated
Sihon king of the Amorites, who reigned in
Heshbon, and at Edrei had defeated Og king of
Bashan, who reigned in Ashtaroth.
5East of the Jordan in the territory of Moab,
Moses began to expound this law, saying:

6The LORD our God said to us at Horeb,
"You have stayed long enough at this mountain. 7Break camp and advance into the hill
country of the Amorites; go to all the neighboring peoples in the Arabah, in the mountains,
in the western foothills, in the Negev and along
the coast, to the land of the Canaanites and to

Lebanon, as far as the great river, the Euphrates. 8See, I have given you this land. Go in and
take possession of the land that the LORD swore
he would give to your fathers—to Abraham,
Isaac and Jacob—and to their descendants after them."

The Appointment of Leaders

9At that time I said to you, "You are too
heavy a burden for me to carry alone. 10The
LORD your God has increased your numbers
so that today you are as many as the stars in
the sky. 11May the LORD, the God of your fathers, increase you a thousand times and bless
you as he has promised! 12But how can I bear
your problems and your burdens and your disputes all by myself? 13Choose some wise, understanding and respected men from each of
your tribes, and I will set them over you."

14You answered me, "What you propose to
do is good."

15So I took the leading men of your tribes,
wise and respected men, and appointed them
to have authority over you—as commanders of
thousands, of hundreds, of fifties and of tens
and as tribal officials. 16And I charged your
judges at that time: Hear the disputes between
your brothers and judge fairly, whether the
case is between brother Israelites or between
one of them and an alien. 17Do
not show partiality in judging;
hear both small and great alike.
Do not be afraid of any man,
for judgment belongs to God.
Bring me any case too hard for
you, and I will hear it. 18And at
that time I told you everything
you were to do.

Spies Sent Out

19Then, as the LORD our
God commanded us, we set
out from Horeb and went toward the hill country of the
Amorites through all that vast
and dreadful desert that you have seen, and so
we reached Kadesh Barnea. 20Then I said to
you, "You have reached the hill country of the
Amorites, which the LORD our God is giving
us. 21See, the LORD your God has given you
the land. Go up and take possession of it as the
LORD, the God of your fathers, told you. Do not
be afraid; do not be discouraged."

22Then all of you came to me and said, "Let
us send men ahead to spy out the land for us
and bring back a report about the route we are
to take and the towns we will come to."

23The idea seemed good to me; so I selected
twelve of you, one man from each tribe. 24They
left and went up into the hill country, and came
to the Valley of Eshcol and explored it. 25Tak-
ing with them some of the fruit of the land,
they brought it down to us and reported, "It
is a good land that the LORD our God is giving us."

Rebellion Against the LORD

26But you were unwilling to go up; you rebelled against the command of the LORD your
God. 27You grumbled in your tents and said,
"The LORD hates us; so he brought us out of
Egypt to deliver us into the hands of the Amorites to destroy us. 28Where can we go? Our
brothers have made us lose heart. They say,
'The people are stronger and taller than we are;
the cities are large, with walls up to the sky. We
even saw the Anakites there.'"

29Then I said to you, "Do not be terrified; do
not be afraid of them. 30The LORD your God,
who is going before you, will fight for you, as
he did for you in Egypt, before
your very eyes, 31and in the
desert. There you saw how the
LORD your God carried you,
as a father carries his son, all
the way you went until you
reached this place."

32In spite of this, you did not
trust in the LORD your God,
33who went ahead of you on
your journey, in fire by night
and in a cloud by day, to search
out places for you to camp
and to show you the way you
should go.

34When the LORD heard what you said,
he was angry and solemnly swore: 35"Not a
man of this evil generation shall see the good
land I swore to give your forefathers, 36except
Caleb son of Jephunneh. He will see it, and I
will give him and his descendants the land he

> **Deuteronomy 1:31**
>
> ***God Carries Us***
>
> "There you saw how the LORD your God carried you, as a father carries his son, all the way you went until you reached this place."

This Time . . .

LEAH

"This time my husband will treat me with honor, because I have borne him six sons."

Genesis 30:20

ASSIGNED READING:

Genesis 29–30

RACHEL, HER SISTER, had always had something she didn't. Rachel had beauty, Leah didn't. Rachel had Jacob's heart, Leah didn't. However, with the birth of her first child, she finally had something Rachel didn't: a son.

"Surely my husband will love me *now*," she recalled thinking after Reuben was born. What she desperately wanted would finally belong to her and her alone. She had bargaining power, and she planned to use it.

This is the way that Leah considered each of her children. They served as a strange sort of currency, each one "buying" her a certain level of emotional security and social standing. However, whatever dividends she gained depreciated all too quickly. She had to have another baby, and another, to keep her emotional security afloat.

Unsettled in her own skin for most of her life, Leah longed to feel comfortable around other women. She would never be the prettiest. Never the smartest. Not even the wealthiest. She knew that. But a baby gave women reason to envy. "The women will call me happy!" she recalled, fantasizing at the time of yet another son's birth. She thought every eye would be on her. The odds would finally be in her favor.

After five strapping sons and with one on the way, she imagined herself becoming a queen among her princes. As she contemplated the next birth, she thought that surely her husband would finally look at her with eyes of love. This time, her peers would approve of her. This time, she would earn everyone's respect.

The last time hadn't worked out like she'd hoped. And the time before that, well . . . the rewards had been short-lived at best. Every "last time" was, after all, *last* time. She needed something new in order to feel good about herself today. As she looked up and saw her husband coming in from the fields, she absently stroked her pregnant belly. This time . . .

—Prayer—

Lord, the next time I look to some person, thing or idea to complete me, draw my eyes to you instead.

Weekend

Go to page 219 for your next devotional reading.

set his feet on, because he followed the LORD
wholeheartedly."
37Because of you the LORD became angry
with me also and said, "You shall not enter it,
either. 38But your assistant, Joshua son of Nun,
will enter it. Encourage him, because he will
lead Israel to inherit it. 39And
the little ones that you said
would be taken captive, your
children who do not yet know
good from bad—they will enter the land. I will give it to
them and they will take possession of it. 40But as for you, turn
around and set out toward the
desert along the route to the
Red Sea.[a]"
41Then you replied, "We
have sinned against the LORD.
We will go up and fight, as the
LORD our God commanded
us." So every one of you put on
his weapons, thinking it easy to
go up into the hill country.
42But the LORD said to me, "Tell them, 'Do
not go up and fight, because I will not be with
you. You will be defeated by your enemies.' "
43So I told you, but you would not listen.
You rebelled against the LORD's command and
in your arrogance you marched up into the hill
country. 44The Amorites who lived in those
hills came out against you; they chased you like
a swarm of bees and beat you down from Seir
all the way to Hormah. 45You came back and
wept before the LORD, but he paid no attention
to your weeping and turned a deaf ear to you.
46And so you stayed in Kadesh many days—all
the time you spent there.

Wanderings in the Desert

2 Then we turned back and set out toward
the desert along the route to the Red Sea,[a]
as the LORD had directed me. For a long time
we made our way around the hill country
of Seir.
2Then the LORD said to me, 3"You have
made your way around this hill country long
enough; now turn north. 4Give the people
these orders: 'You are about to pass through
the territory of your brothers the descendants
of Esau, who live in Seir. They will be afraid of
you, but be very careful. 5Do not provoke them
to war, for I will not give you any of their land,
not even enough to put your foot on. I have
given Esau the hill country of Seir as his own.
6You are to pay them in silver
for the food you eat and the water you drink.' "
7The LORD your God has
blessed you in all the work of
your hands. He has watched
over your journey through this
vast desert. These forty years
the LORD your God has been
with you, and you have not
lacked anything.
8So we went on past our
brothers the descendants of
Esau, who live in Seir. We
turned from the Arabah road,
which comes up from Elath
and Ezion Geber, and traveled
along the desert road of Moab.
9Then the LORD said to me, "Do not harass
the Moabites or provoke them to war, for I will
not give you any part of their land. I have given
Ar to the descendants of Lot as a possession."
10(The Emites used to live there—a people
strong and numerous, and as tall as the Anakites. 11Like the Anakites, they too were considered Rephaites, but the Moabites called them
Emites. 12Horites used to live in Seir, but the
descendants of Esau drove them out. They destroyed the Horites from before them and settled in their place, just as Israel did in the land
the LORD gave them as their possession.)
13And the LORD said, "Now get up and cross
the Zered Valley." So we crossed the valley.
14Thirty-eight years passed from the time
we left Kadesh Barnea until we crossed the
Zered Valley. By then, that entire generation
of fighting men had perished from the camp,
as the LORD had sworn to them. 15The LORD's
hand was against them until he had completely
eliminated them from the camp.
16Now when the last of these fighting men
among the people had died, 17the LORD said
to me, 18"Today you are to pass by the region

Deuteronomy 2:7

God Watches Over Us

He has watched over your journey through this vast desert. These forty years the LORD your God has been with you, and you have not lacked anything.

[a]40,1 Hebrew *Yam Suph*; that is, Sea of Reeds

of Moab at Ar. 19When you come to the Ammonites, do not harass them or provoke them
to war, for I will not give you possession of any
land belonging to the Ammonites. I have given
it as a possession to the descendants of Lot."

20(That too was considered a land of the
Rephaites, who used to live there; but the Ammonites called them Zamzummites. 21They
were a people strong and numerous, and as
tall as the Anakites. The LORD destroyed them
from before the Ammonites, who drove them
out and settled in their place. 22The LORD had
done the same for the descendants of Esau, who
lived in Seir, when he destroyed the Horites
from before them. They drove them out and
have lived in their place to this day. 23And as for
the Avvites who lived in villages as far as Gaza,
the Caphtorites coming out from Caphtor[a] destroyed them and settled in their place.)

Defeat of Sihon King of Heshbon

24"Set out now and cross the Arnon Gorge.
See, I have given into your hand Sihon the Amorite, king of Heshbon, and his country. Begin
to take possession of it and engage him in battle. 25This very day I will begin to put the terror
and fear of you on all the nations under heaven.
They will hear reports of you and will tremble
and be in anguish because of you."

26From the desert of Kedemoth I sent messengers to Sihon king of Heshbon offering
peace and saying, 27"Let us pass through your
country. We will stay on the main road; we will
not turn aside to the right or to the left. 28Sell us
food to eat and water to drink for their price in
silver. Only let us pass through on foot— 29as
the descendants of Esau, who live in Seir, and
the Moabites, who live in Ar, did for us—until
we cross the Jordan into the land the LORD our
God is giving us." 30But Sihon king of Heshbon
refused to let us pass through. For the LORD
your God had made his spirit stubborn and his
heart obstinate in order to give him into your
hands, as he has now done.

31The LORD said to me, "See, I have begun to
deliver Sihon and his country over to you. Now
begin to conquer and possess his land."

32When Sihon and all his army came out to
meet us in battle at Jahaz, 33the LORD our God
delivered him over to us and we struck him
down, together with his sons and his whole
army. 34At that time we took all his towns and
completely destroyed[b] them—men, women
and children. We left no survivors. 35But the
livestock and the plunder from the towns we
had captured we carried off for ourselves.
36From Aroer on the rim of the Arnon Gorge,
and from the town in the gorge, even as far as
Gilead, not one town was too strong for us. The
LORD our God gave us all of them. 37But in accordance with the command of the LORD our
God, you did not encroach on any of the land
of the Ammonites, neither the land along the
course of the Jabbok nor that around the towns
in the hills.

Defeat of Og King of Bashan

3 Next we turned and went up along the
road toward Bashan, and Og king of Bashan with his whole army marched out to meet
us in battle at Edrei. 2The LORD said to me, "Do
not be afraid of him, for I have handed him
over to you with his whole army and his land.
Do to him what you did to Sihon king of the
Amorites, who reigned in Heshbon."

3So the LORD our God also gave into our
hands Og king of Bashan and all his army. We
struck them down, leaving no survivors. 4At
that time we took all his cities. There was not
one of the sixty cities that we did not take from
them—the whole region of Argob, Og's kingdom in Bashan. 5All these cities were fortified
with high walls and with gates and bars, and
there were also a great many unwalled villages.
6We completely destroyed[b] them, as we had
done with Sihon king of Heshbon, destroying[b]
every city—men, women and children. 7But all
the livestock and the plunder from their cities
we carried off for ourselves.

8So at that time we took from these two
kings of the Amorites the territory east of the
Jordan, from the Arnon Gorge as far as Mount
Hermon. 9(Hermon is called Sirion by the Sidonians; the Amorites call it Senir.) 10We took
all the towns on the plateau, and all Gilead, and
all Bashan as far as Salecah and Edrei, towns of
Og's kingdom in Bashan. 11(Only Og king of
Bashan was left of the remnant of the Repha-

[a]23 That is, Crete [b]34,6 The Hebrew term refers to the irrevocable giving over of things or persons to the LORD, often by totally destroying them.

ites. His bed[a] was made of iron and was more
than thirteen feet long and six feet wide.[b] It is
still in Rabbah of the Ammonites.)

Division of the Land

12Of the land that we took over at that
time, I gave the Reubenites and the Gadites
the territory north of Aroer by
the Arnon Gorge, including
half the hill country of Gilead,
together with its towns. 13The
rest of Gilead and also all of Bashan, the kingdom of Og, I gave
to the half-tribe of Manasseh.
(The whole region of Argob in
Bashan used to be known as a
land of the Rephaites. 14Jair, a
descendant of Manasseh, took
the whole region of Argob as
far as the border of the Geshurites and the Maacathites; it
was named after him, so that
to this day Bashan is called Havvoth Jair.[c]) 15And I gave Gilead
to Makir. 16But to the Reubenites and the Gadites I gave the
territory extending from Gilead down to the
Arnon Gorge (the middle of the gorge being
the border) and out to the Jabbok River, which
is the border of the Ammonites. 17Its western
border was the Jordan in the Arabah, from Kinnereth to the Sea of the Arabah (the Salt Sea[d]),
below the slopes of Pisgah.
18I commanded you at that time: "The LORD
your God has given you this land to take possession of it. But all your able-bodied men, armed
for battle, must cross over ahead of your brother
Israelites. 19However, your wives, your children
and your livestock (I know you have much livestock) may stay in the towns I have given you,
20until the LORD gives rest to your brothers as
he has to you, and they too have taken over the
land that the LORD your God is giving them,
across the Jordan. After that, each of you may
go back to the possession I have given you."

Moses Forbidden to Cross the Jordan

21At that time I commanded Joshua: "You
have seen with your own eyes all that the LORD
your God has done to these two kings. The
LORD will do the same to all the kingdoms over
there where you are going. 22Do not be afraid
of them; the LORD your God himself will fight
for you."
23At that time I pleaded with the LORD:
24"O Sovereign LORD, you have
begun to show to your servant
your greatness and your strong
hand. For what god is there in
heaven or on earth who can do
the deeds and mighty works
you do? 25Let me go over and
see the good land beyond the
Jordan—that fine hill country
and Lebanon."
26But because of you the
LORD was angry with me and
would not listen to me. "That
is enough," the LORD said.
"Do not speak to me anymore
about this matter. 27Go up to
the top of Pisgah and look west
and north and south and east.
Look at the land with your own
eyes, since you are not going to
cross this Jordan. 28But commission Joshua,
and encourage and strengthen him, for he will
lead this people across and will cause them
to inherit the land that you will see." 29So we
stayed in the valley near Beth Peor.

Deuteronomy 3:24

God Is Without Equal

"O Sovereign LORD, you have begun to show to your servant your greatness and your strong hand. For what god is there in heaven or on earth who can do the deeds and mighty works you do?"

Obedience Commanded

4 Hear now, O Israel, the decrees and laws
I am about to teach you. Follow them so
that you may live and may go in and take possession of the land that the LORD, the God of
your fathers, is giving you. 2Do not add to what
I command you and do not subtract from it,
but keep the commands of the LORD your God
that I give you.
3You saw with your own eyes what the LORD
did at Baal Peor. The LORD your God destroyed
from among you everyone who followed the
Baal of Peor, 4but all of you who held fast to
the LORD your God are still alive today.
5See, I have taught you decrees and laws as
the LORD my God commanded me, so that you

[a]11 Or *sarcophagus* [b]11 Hebrew *nine cubits long and four cubits wide* (about 4 meters long and 1.8 meters wide) [c]14 Or *called the settlements of Jair* [d]17 That is, the Dead Sea

may follow them in the land you are entering to
take possession of it. 6Observe them carefully,
for this will show your wisdom and understanding to the nations, who will hear about all these
decrees and say, "Surely this great nation is a
wise and understanding people." 7What other
nation is so great as to have their gods near
them the way the LORD our God is near us
whenever we pray to him? 8And what other nation is so great as to have such
righteous decrees and laws as
this body of laws I am setting
before you today?

9Only be careful, and watch
yourselves closely so that you
do not forget the things your
eyes have seen or let them
slip from your heart as long as
you live. Teach them to your
children and to their children
after them. 10Remember the
day you stood before the LORD
your God at Horeb, when he
said to me, "Assemble the peo-
ple before me to hear my words so that they
may learn to revere me as long as they live in
the land and may teach them to their children."
11You came near and stood at the foot of the
mountain while it blazed with fire to the very
heavens, with black clouds and deep darkness.
12Then the LORD spoke to you out of the fire.
You heard the sound of words but saw no form;
there was only a voice. 13He declared to you
his covenant, the Ten Commandments, which
he commanded you to follow and then wrote
them on two stone tablets. 14And the LORD
directed me at that time to teach you the decrees and laws you are to follow in the land that
you are crossing the Jordan to possess.

Deuteronomy 4:7

God Is Near

What other nation is so great as to have their gods near them the way the LORD our God is near us whenever we pray to him?

Idolatry Forbidden

15You saw no form of any kind the day the
LORD spoke to you at Horeb out of the fire.
Therefore watch yourselves very carefully, 16so
that you do not become corrupt and make
for yourselves an idol, an image of any shape,
whether formed like a man or a woman, 17or
like any animal on earth or any bird that flies in
the air, 18or like any creature that moves along
the ground or any fish in the waters below.
19And when you look up to the sky and see the
sun, the moon and the stars—all the heavenly
array—do not be enticed into bowing down
to them and worshiping things the LORD your
God has apportioned to all the nations under
heaven. 20But as for you, the LORD took you
and brought you out of the iron-smelting furnace, out of Egypt, to be the people of his inheritance, as you now are.

21The LORD was angry with
me because of you, and he solemnly swore that I would not
cross the Jordan and enter the
good land the LORD your God
is giving you as your inheritance. 22I will die in this land;
I will not cross the Jordan; but
you are about to cross over and
take possession of that good
land. 23Be careful not to forget
the covenant of the LORD your
God that he made with you;
do not make for yourselves an
idol in the form of anything the
LORD your God has forbidden. 24For the LORD
your God is a consuming fire, a jealous God.

25After you have had children and grandchildren and have lived in the land a long time—
if you then become corrupt and make any kind
of idol, doing evil in the eyes of the LORD your
God and provoking him to anger, 26I call
heaven and earth as witnesses against you this
day that you will quickly perish from the land
that you are crossing the Jordan to possess. You
will not live there long but will certainly be destroyed. 27The LORD will scatter you among
the peoples, and only a few of you will survive
among the nations to which the LORD will drive
you. 28There you will worship man-made gods
of wood and stone, which cannot see or hear
or eat or smell. 29But if from there you seek the
LORD your God, you will find him if you look
for him with all your heart and with all your
soul. 30When you are in distress and all these
things have happened to you, then in later days
you will return to the LORD your God and obey
him. 31For the LORD your God is a merciful
God; he will not abandon or destroy you or forget the covenant with your forefathers, which
he confirmed to them by oath.

The Lord Is God

32 Ask now about the former days, long before your time, from the day God created man
on the earth; ask from one end of the heavens
to the other. Has anything so great as this ever
happened, or has anything like it ever been
heard of? 33 Has any other people heard the
voice of God[a] speaking out of fire, as you have,
and lived? 34 Has any god ever tried to take for
himself one nation out of another nation, by
testings, by miraculous signs and wonders,
by war, by a mighty hand and an outstretched
arm, or by great and awesome deeds, like all
the things the LORD your God did for you in
Egypt before your very eyes?
35 You were shown these things so that you
might know that the LORD is God; besides him
there is no other. 36 From heaven he made you
hear his voice to discipline you. On earth he
showed you his great fire, and you heard his
words from out of the fire. 37 Because he loved
your forefathers and chose their descendants
after them, he brought you out of Egypt by his
Presence and his great strength, 38 to drive out
before you nations greater and stronger than
you and to bring you into their land to give it to
you for your inheritance, as it is today.
39 Acknowledge and take to heart this day
that the LORD is God in heaven above and on
the earth below. There is no other. 40 Keep his
decrees and commands, which I am giving you
today, so that it may go well with you and your
children after you and that you may live long
in the land the LORD your God gives you for
all time.

Cities of Refuge

41 Then Moses set aside three cities east of the
Jordan, 42 to which anyone who had killed a person could flee if he had unintentionally killed
his neighbor without malice aforethought. He
could flee into one of these cities and save his
life. 43 The cities were these: Bezer in the desert plateau, for the Reubenites; Ramoth in
Gilead, for the Gadites; and Golan in Bashan,
for the Manassites.

Introduction to the Law

44 This is the law Moses set before the Israelites. 45 These are the stipulations, decrees and
laws Moses gave them when they came out
of Egypt 46 and were in the valley near Beth
Peor east of the Jordan, in the land of Sihon
king of the Amorites, who reigned in Heshbon
and was defeated by Moses and the Israelites
as they came out of Egypt. 47 They took possession of his land and the land of Og king of Bashan, the two Amorite kings east of the Jordan.
48 This land extended from Aroer on the rim
of the Arnon Gorge to Mount Siyon[b] (that is,
Hermon), 49 and included all the Arabah east
of the Jordan, as far as the Sea of the Arabah,[c]
below the slopes of Pisgah.

The Ten Commandments

5 Moses summoned all Israel and said:
Hear, O Israel, the decrees and laws I declare in your hearing today. Learn them and be
sure to follow them. 2 The LORD our God made
a covenant with us at Horeb. 3 It was not with
our fathers that the LORD made this covenant,
but with us, with all of us who are alive here today. 4 The LORD spoke to you face to face out of
the fire on the mountain. 5 (At that time I stood
between the LORD and you to declare to you
the word of the LORD, because you were afraid
of the fire and did not go up the mountain.)
And he said:

6 "I am the LORD your God, who
brought you out of Egypt, out of the
land of slavery.
7 "You shall have no other gods before[d]
me.
8 "You shall not make for yourself an idol
in the form of anything in heaven
above or on the earth beneath or in
the waters below. 9 You shall not bow
down to them or worship them; for
I, the LORD your God, am a jealous
God, punishing the children for the
sin of the fathers to the third and
fourth generation of those who hate
me, 10 but showing love to a thousand ⌞generations⌟ of those who love
me and keep my commandments.
11 "You shall not misuse the name of the
LORD your God, for the LORD will
not hold anyone guiltless who mis-
uses his name.

[a] 33 Or *of a god* [b] 48 Hebrew; Syriac (see also Deut. 3:9) *Sirion* [c] 49 That is, the Dead Sea [d] 7 Or *besides*

12 “Observe the Sabbath day by keeping
it holy, as the LORD your God has
commanded you. 13 Six days you shall
labor and do all your work, 14 but the
seventh day is a Sabbath to the LORD
your God. On it you shall not do any
work, neither you, nor your son or
daughter, nor your manservant or
maidservant, nor your ox, your donkey or any of your animals, nor the
alien within your gates, so that your
manservant and maidservant may
rest, as you do. 15 Remember that
you were slaves in Egypt and that
the LORD your God brought you out
of there with a mighty
hand and an out-
stretched arm. There-
fore the LORD your
God has commanded
you to observe the Sab-
bath day.
16 “Honor your father and
your mother, as the
LORD your God has
commanded you, so
that you may live long
and that it may go well
with you in the land
the LORD your God is
giving you.
17 “You shall not murder.
18 “You shall not commit adultery.
19 “You shall not steal.
20 “You shall not give false testimony against
your neighbor.
21 “You shall not covet your neighbor’s wife.
You shall not set your desire on your
neighbor’s house or land, his manservant or maidservant, his ox or
donkey, or anything that belongs to
your neighbor.”

22 These are the commandments the LORD
proclaimed in a loud voice to your whole assembly there on the mountain from out of the
fire, the cloud and the deep darkness; and he
added nothing more. Then he wrote them on
two stone tablets and gave them to me.
23 When you heard the voice out of the
darkness, while the mountain was ablaze with
fire, all the leading men of your tribes and
your elders came to me. 24 And you said, “The
LORD our God has shown us his glory and his
majesty, and we have heard his voice from the
fire. Today we have seen that a man can live
even if God speaks with him. 25 But now, why
should we die? This great fire will consume
us, and we will die if we hear the voice of the
LORD our God any longer. 26 For what mortal
man has ever heard the voice of the living God
speaking out of fire, as we have, and survived?
27 Go near and listen to all that the LORD our
God says. Then tell us whatever the LORD our
God tells you. We will listen and obey.”
28 The LORD heard you when
you spoke to me and the LORD
said to me, “I have heard what
this people said to you. Everything they said was good. 29 Oh,
that their hearts would be inclined to fear me and keep all
my commands always, so that
it might go well with them and
their children forever!
30 “Go, tell them to return to
their tents. 31 But you stay here
with me so that I may give you
all the commands, decrees and
laws you are to teach them to
follow in the land I am giving
them to possess.”
32 So be careful to do what
the LORD your God has commanded you; do
not turn aside to the right or to the left. 33 Walk
in all the way that the LORD your God has
commanded you, so that you may live and prosper and prolong your days in the land that you
will possess.

> Deuteronomy 5:29
>
> *God Rewards the Faithful*
>
> “Oh, that their hearts would be inclined to fear me and keep all my commands always, so that it might go well with them and their children forever!”

Love the LORD Your God

6 These are the commands, decrees and
laws the LORD your God directed me to
teach you to observe in the land that you are
crossing the Jordan to possess, 2 so that you,
your children and their children after them
may fear the LORD your God as long as you
live by keeping all his decrees and commands
that I give you, and so that you may enjoy long
life. 3 Hear, O Israel, and be careful to obey so
that it may go well with you and that you may

Interior Designs

Read: Deuteronomy 6:1–9

"HE SEEMED LIKE SUCH A NICE BOY." How many times have we seen the neighbors of a convicted criminal interviewed on TV, shaking their heads in disbelief that an outwardly nice person could hide such evil intentions? Outer appearance can deceive, but the heart reveals itself eventually.

God provides a master guidebook to redesigning our spirits: the Bible. He directs us to tie his Word on our hands as we would tie a cord around a curtain, to bind his commandments to our foreheads as solidly as we would hang a valuable painting, to write his promises on our hearts as carefully as we would follow a blueprint. This is the ultimate form of home improvement.

Redesign must begin with our hearts. That is why God commanded the Israelites to pass on his holy commands, decrees and laws to their children and to allow them to permeate their lives and thought processes. Even today, Jewish families often fasten a small box called a mezuzah, containing Scriptures from Deuteronomy 6:4–9 and 11:13–21, to the doorposts of their homes to remind them that because "the LORD is one" they should "faithfully obey the commands . . . to love the LORD your God and to serve him with all your heart and with all your soul." Only God's Word can do the work of improving the lives of his people, generation to generation.

In Jesus' day, the Pharisees wore phylacteries, literally fastening Scripture to their foreheads. Some of the Pharisees wore their phylacteries pridefully to display how "religious" they were. Unfortunately, many failed to live out what the Scriptures inside their phylacteries said. Christ called them hypocrites. You may succeed in fooling the neighbors, but God is not deceived. He doesn't want his principles displayed outwardly if they don't impact us inwardly. When ingrained on our inmost being, his principles will change the way we think, act and live.

Would your neighbors be shocked to see inside your locked rooms? Would your own family? Perhaps you spend so much time on decorating your exterior that you've neglected what Teresa of Avila called your "interior castle," the cloistered rooms of your soul? Take the time to memorize Scripture, meditate on it and tell the children in your life about God. That kind of home improvement is eternal.

Deuteronomy 6:8–9

Tie them as symbols on your hands and bind them on your foreheads. Write them on the doorframes of your houses and on your gates.

reflection

1 What disconnects your spirit from your outer facade?

2 Who might God want you to "adopt" as a spiritual child so you can talk with them, teach them and train them to know and love him?

3 How much time do you spend redecorating the inner rooms of your soul through prayer and Bible reading? How can you deepen and nurture your faith?

RELATED READINGS

Exodus 13:1–16; Deuteronomy 11:13–21; Proverbs 7:1–4

Go to page 223 for your next devotional reading.

increase greatly in a land flowing with milk
and honey, just as the Lord, the God of your
fathers, promised you.
4Hear, O Israel: The Lord our God, the Lord
is one.[a] 5Love the Lord your God with all your
heart and with all your soul and with all your
strength. 6These commandments that I give
you today are to be upon your hearts. 7Impress
them on your children. Talk about them when
you sit at home and when you walk along the
road, when you lie down and when you get up.
8Tie them as symbols on your hands and bind
them on your foreheads. 9Write them on the
doorframes of your houses and on your gates.
10When the Lord your God brings you into
the land he swore to your fathers, to Abraham,
Isaac and Jacob, to give you—a land with large,
flourishing cities you did not build, 11houses
filled with all kinds of good things you did not
provide, wells you did not dig, and vineyards
and olive groves you did not plant—then when
you eat and are satisfied, 12be careful that you
do not forget the Lord, who brought you out
of Egypt, out of the land of slavery.
13Fear the Lord your God, serve him only
and take your oaths in his name. 14Do not follow other gods, the gods of the peoples around
you; 15for the Lord your God, who is among
you, is a jealous God and his anger will burn
against you, and he will destroy you from the
face of the land. 16Do not test the Lord your
God as you did at Massah. 17Be sure to keep the
commands of the Lord your God and the stipulations and decrees he has given you. 18Do what
is right and good in the Lord's sight, so that it
may go well with you and you may go in and
take over the good land that the Lord promised
on oath to your forefathers, 19thrusting out all
your enemies before you, as the Lord said.
20In the future, when your son asks you,
"What is the meaning of the stipulations,
decrees and laws the Lord our God has
commanded you?" 21tell him: "We were slaves
of Pharaoh in Egypt, but the Lord brought
us out of Egypt with a mighty hand. 22Before
our eyes the Lord sent miraculous signs and
wonders—great and terrible—upon Egypt and
Pharaoh and his whole household. 23But he
brought us out from there to bring us in and
give us the land that he promised on oath to
our forefathers. 24The Lord commanded us
to obey all these decrees and to fear the Lord
our God, so that we might always prosper and
be kept alive, as is the case today. 25And if we
are careful to obey all this law before the Lord
our God, as he has commanded us, that will be
our righteousness."

Driving Out the Nations

7 When the Lord your God brings you
into the land you are entering to possess
and drives out before you many nations—the
Hittites, Girgashites, Amorites, Canaanites,
Perizzites, Hivites and Jebusites, seven nations
larger and stronger than you— 2and when the
Lord your God has delivered them over to you
and you have defeated them, then you must destroy them totally.[b] Make no treaty with them,
and show them no mercy. 3Do not intermarry
with them. Do not give your daughters to their
sons or take their daughters for your sons, 4for
they will turn your sons away from following
me to serve other gods, and the Lord's anger
will burn against you and will quickly destroy
you. 5This is what you are to do to them: Break
down their altars, smash their sacred stones,
cut down their Asherah poles[c] and burn their
idols in the fire. 6For you are a people holy to
the Lord your God. The Lord your God has
chosen you out of all the peoples on the face
of the earth to be his people, his treasured possession.
7The Lord did not set his affection on
you and choose you because you were more
numerous than other peoples, for you were the
fewest of all peoples. 8But it was because the
Lord loved you and kept the oath he swore
to your forefathers that he brought you out
with a mighty hand and redeemed you from
the land of slavery, from the power of Pharaoh king of Egypt. 9Know therefore that the
Lord your God is God; he is the faithful God,
keeping his covenant of love to a thousand generations of those who love him and keep his
commands. 10But

[a]4 Or *The Lord our God is one Lord*; or *The Lord is our God, the Lord is one*; or *The Lord is our God, the Lord alone* [b]2 The Hebrew term refers to the irrevocable giving over of things or persons to the Lord, often by totally destroying them; also in verse 26. [c]5 That is, symbols of the goddess Asherah; here and elsewhere in Deuteronomy

those who hate him he will repay to their
face by destruction;
he will not be slow to repay to their face
those who hate him.

11Therefore, take care to follow
the commands, decrees and
laws I give you today.
12If you pay attention to
these laws and are careful to follow them, then the LORD your
God will keep his covenant of
love with you, as he swore to
your forefathers. 13He will love
you and bless you and increase
your numbers. He will bless the
fruit of your womb, the crops
of your land—your grain, new
wine and oil—the calves of
your herds and the lambs of
your flocks in the land that he
swore to your forefathers to
give you. 14You will be blessed more than any
other people; none of your men or women will
be childless, nor any of your livestock without
young. 15The LORD will keep you free from
every disease. He will not inflict on you the horrible diseases you knew in Egypt, but he will
inflict them on all who hate you. 16You must
destroy all the peoples the LORD your God
gives over to you. Do not look on them with
pity and do not serve their gods, for that will
be a snare to you.
17You may say to yourselves, "These nations
are stronger than we are. How can we drive
them out?" 18But do not be afraid of them;
remember well what the LORD your God did
to Pharaoh and to all Egypt. 19You saw with
your own eyes the great trials, the miraculous
signs and wonders, the mighty hand and outstretched arm, with which the LORD your God
brought you out. The LORD your God will
do the same to all the peoples you now fear.
20Moreover, the LORD your God will send the
hornet among them until even the survivors
who hide from you have perished. 21Do not be
terrified by them, for the LORD your God, who
is among you, is a great and awesome God.
22The LORD your God will drive out those nations before you, little by little. You will not be allowed to eliminate them all at once, or the wild
animals will multiply around you. 23But the
LORD your God will deliver them over to you,
throwing them into great confusion until they
are destroyed. 24He will give their kings into
your hand, and you will wipe
out their names from under
heaven. No one will be able to
stand up against you; you will
destroy them. 25The images of
their gods you are to burn in
the fire. Do not covet the silver
and gold on them, and do not
take it for yourselves, or you
will be ensnared by it, for it is
detestable to the LORD your
God. 26Do not bring a detestable thing into your house or
you, like it, will be set apart for
destruction. Utterly abhor and
detest it, for it is set apart for destruction.

Deuteronomy 7:9

God Is Faithful

Know therefore that the LORD your God is God; he is the faithful God, keeping his covenant of love to a thousand generations of those who love him and keep his commands.

Do Not Forget the LORD

8 Be careful to follow every command I am
giving you today, so that you may live and
increase and may enter and possess the land
that the LORD promised on oath to your forefathers. 2Remember how the LORD your God
led you all the way in the desert these forty
years, to humble you and to test you in order
to know what was in your heart, whether or
not you would keep his commands. 3He humbled you, causing you to hunger and then feeding you with manna, which neither you nor
your fathers had known, to teach you that man
does not live on bread alone but on every word
that comes from the mouth of the LORD. 4Your
clothes did not wear out and your feet did not
swell during these forty years. 5Know then in
your heart that as a man disciplines his son, so
the LORD your God disciplines you.
6Observe the commands of the LORD your
God, walking in his ways and revering him.
7For the LORD your God is bringing you into
a good land—a land with streams and pools of
water, with springs flowing in the valleys and
hills; 8a land with wheat and barley, vines and
fig trees, pomegranates, olive oil and honey; 9a
land where bread will not be scarce and you
will lack nothing; a land where the rocks are
iron and you can dig copper out of the hills.

10When you have eaten and are satisfied,
praise the LORD your God for the good land he
has given you. 11Be careful that you do not forget the LORD your God, failing to observe his
commands, his laws and his decrees that I am
giving you this day. 12Otherwise, when you eat
and are satisfied, when you build fine houses
and settle down, 13and when your herds and
flocks grow large and your silver and gold increase and all you have is multiplied, 14then
your heart will become proud and you will
forget the LORD your God, who brought you
out of Egypt, out of the land of slavery. 15He
led you through the vast and dreadful desert,
that thirsty and waterless land, with its venomous snakes and scorpions. He
brought you water out of hard
rock. 16He gave you manna to
eat in the desert, something
your fathers had never known,
to humble and to test you so
that in the end it might go
well with you. 17You may say
to yourself, "My power and
the strength of my hands have
produced this wealth for me."
18But remember the LORD
your God, for it is he who
gives you the ability to produce
wealth, and so confirms his covenant, which he swore to your
forefathers, as it is today.

> Deuteronomy 8:18
>
> *God Provides All*
>
> But remember the LORD your God, for it is he who gives you the ability to produce wealth, and so confirms his covenant, which he swore to your forefathers, as it is today.

19If you ever forget the LORD your God and
follow other gods and worship and bow down
to them, I testify against you today that you
will surely be destroyed. 20Like the nations the
LORD destroyed before you, so you will be destroyed for not obeying the LORD your God.

Not Because of Israel's Righteousness

9 Hear, O Israel. You are now about to cross
the Jordan to go in and dispossess nations
greater and stronger than you, with large cities
that have walls up to the sky. 2The people are
strong and tall—Anakites! You know about
them and have heard it said: "Who can stand
up against the Anakites?" 3But be assured today that the LORD your God is the one who
goes across ahead of you like a devouring fire.
He will destroy them; he will subdue them
before you. And you will drive them out and
annihilate them quickly, as the LORD has promised you.

4After the LORD your God has driven them
out before you, do not say to yourself, "The
LORD has brought me here to take possession
of this land because of my righteousness." No,
it is on account of the wickedness of these nations that the LORD is going to drive them out
before you. 5It is not because of your righteousness or your integrity that you are going in to
take possession of their land; but on account
of the wickedness of these nations, the LORD
your God will drive them out before you, to
accomplish what he swore to your fathers, to
Abraham, Isaac and Jacob. 6Understand, then,
that it is not because of your
righteousness that the LORD
your God is giving you this
good land to possess, for you
are a stiff-necked people.

The Golden Calf

7Remember this and never
forget how you provoked the
LORD your God to anger in
the desert. From the day you
left Egypt until you arrived
here, you have been rebellious
against the LORD. 8At Horeb
you aroused the LORD's wrath
so that he was angry enough to
destroy you. 9When I went up
on the mountain to receive the tablets of stone,
the tablets of the covenant that the LORD had
made with you, I stayed on the mountain forty
days and forty nights; I ate no bread and drank
no water. 10The LORD gave me two stone tablets
inscribed by the finger of God. On them were
all the commandments the LORD proclaimed
to you on the mountain out of the fire, on the
day of the assembly.

11At the end of the forty days and forty
nights, the LORD gave me the two stone tablets,
the tablets of the covenant. 12Then the LORD
told me, "Go down from here at once, because
your people whom you brought out of Egypt
have become corrupt. They have turned away
quickly from what I commanded them and
have made a cast idol for themselves."

13And the LORD said to me, "I have seen
this people, and they are a stiff-necked people

Who Can Stand?

Read: Deuteronomy 9:1–6

SHE STARES DOWN at us from the wide screen or up from the magazine. She's the "perfect" woman. She's tall. She's willowy. She always knows just the right thing to say . . . and when to say it. She's the picture of who the world says we should be. We feel like the Israelites felt about the Anakites: "Who can stand up against that?"

No doubt the Hebrew nation trembled in their sandals at the thought of facing the mighty Anakites. However, God promised to be more than an ally to his people. He didn't just say, "I will go with you to conquer the enemy." Instead, he promised to go ahead of them. He promised to lead the charge into battle. God would conquer and take the land on their behalf. Of course, God kept his word. The Anakites were destroyed.

As believers, we're not really at war with "perfect" women. When you put yourself in their high-heeled sandals, you realize they have their own insecurities: Do people like me for me? Am I a slave to my looks? Opposition and uncertainties loom in every woman's heart. Do we really have to squeeze into the culture's mold to fit in? To get the man? To get the job? To have the friends? So many times our internal struggles are the real giants we must conquer. Conquering the heart and mind are the front line of the battle of faith.

When uncertainties about who you are make you feel small, remember that God is more than just a friendly ally. He is a trusted warrior who will go out ahead and battle your giants. As you grow in your faith and in grace, he will conquer your insecurities about your looks and abilities as you grow to realize that you are "fearfully and wonderfully made" (Psalm 139:14). He will conquer your lack of confidence in conversation by giving you the proper words to say through his Holy Spirit. He will fill you with security by giving you his righteousness. Then, when you've walked through the challenge, you'll know it was God who won the war, and you can give him all the glory.

What personal battles are causing your stomach to tie up in knots? What giant challenges are stopping you dead in your tracks? Rest assured; God will go before you to devour your doubts.

Deuteronomy 9:2–3

The people are strong and tall—Anakites! You know about them and have heard it said: "Who can stand up against the Anakites?" But be assured today that the LORD your God is the one who goes across ahead of you like a devouring fire.

reflection

1 What personal battles seem huge and daunting?

2 What emotions are causing you to doubt your strength?

3 How has God shown you his love by fighting a battle for you? Recount a time in the past when God went ahead of you to conquer a situation.

RELATED READINGS

2 Chronicles 20:15–17; Psalm 28:6–7; Ephesians 6:10–18

"Let nothing disturb you, let nothing frighten you: everything passes away except God; God alone is sufficient."

Teresa of Avila

Go to page 225 for your next devotional reading.

indeed! 14Let me alone, so that I may destroy
them and blot out their name from under
heaven. And I will make you into a nation stronger and more numerous than they."

15So I turned and went down from the
mountain while it was ablaze with fire. And the
two tablets of the covenant were in my hands.[a]
16When I looked, I saw that you had sinned
against the LORD your God; you had made for
yourselves an idol cast in the shape of a calf.
You had turned aside quickly from the way that
the LORD had commanded you. 17So I took the
two tablets and threw them out of my hands,
breaking them to pieces before your eyes.

18Then once again I fell prostrate before the
LORD for forty days and forty nights; I ate no
bread and drank no water, because of all the sin
you had committed, doing what was evil in the
LORD's sight and so provoking him to anger.
19I feared the anger and wrath of the LORD, for
he was angry enough with you to destroy you.
But again the LORD listened to me. 20And the
LORD was angry enough with Aaron to destroy
him, but at that time I prayed for Aaron too.
21Also I took that sinful thing of yours, the calf
you had made, and burned it in the fire. Then
I crushed it and ground it to powder as fine
as dust and threw the dust into a stream that
flowed down the mountain.

22You also made the LORD angry at Taberah,
at Massah and at Kibroth Hattaavah.

23And when the LORD sent you out from
Kadesh Barnea, he said, "Go up and take possession of the land I have given you." But you
rebelled against the command of the LORD
your God. You did not trust him or obey him.
24You have been rebellious against the LORD
ever since I have known you.

25I lay prostrate before the LORD those forty
days and forty nights because the LORD had
said he would destroy you. 26I prayed to the
LORD and said, "O Sovereign LORD, do not destroy your people, your own inheritance that
you redeemed by your great power and brought
out of Egypt with a mighty hand. 27Remember
your servants Abraham, Isaac and Jacob. Overlook the stubbornness of this people, their wickedness and their sin. 28Otherwise, the country
from which you brought us will say, 'Because
the LORD was not able to take them into the
land he had promised them, and because he
hated them, he brought them out to put them
to death in the desert.' 29But they are your people, your inheritance that you brought out by
your great power and your outstretched arm."

Tablets Like the First Ones

10 At that time the LORD said to me,
"Chisel out two stone tablets like the
first ones and come up to me on the mountain. Also make a wooden chest.[b] 2I will write
on the tablets the words that were on the first
tablets, which you broke. Then you are to put
them in the chest."

3So I made the ark out of acacia wood and
chiseled out two stone tablets like the first ones,
and I went up on the mountain with the two
tablets in my hands. 4The LORD wrote on these
tablets what he had written before, the Ten
Commandments he had proclaimed to you
on the mountain, out of the fire, on the day of
the assembly. And the LORD gave them to me.
5Then I came back down the mountain and put
the tablets in the ark I had made, as the LORD
commanded me, and they are there now.

6(The Israelites traveled from the wells of the
Jaakanites to Moserah. There Aaron died and
was buried, and Eleazar his son succeeded him
as priest. 7From there they traveled to Gudgo-
dah and on to Jotbathah, a land with streams
of water. 8At that time the LORD set apart the
tribe of Levi to carry the ark of the covenant
of the LORD, to stand before the LORD to minister and to pronounce blessings in his name,
as they still do today. 9That is why the Levites
have no share or inheritance among their brothers; the LORD is their inheritance, as the LORD
your God told them.)

10Now I had stayed on the mountain forty
days and nights, as I did the first time, and the
LORD listened to me at this time also. It was
not his will to destroy you. 11"Go," the LORD
said to me, "and lead the people on their way,
so that they may enter and possess the land that
I swore to their fathers to give them."

Fear the LORD

12And now, O Israel, what does the LORD
your God ask of you but to fear the LORD your

[a]15 Or *And I had the two tablets of the covenant with me, one in each hand* [b]1 That is, an ark

Count the Ways

Read: Deuteronomy 10:12–22

MOTHERS UNCONDITIONALLY LOVE their children long before their child can return that love in tangible ways. Who can measure the power of the moment when a child first utters, "I love you, Mommy"?

Just as a mom longs to hear her child utter those four simple words, God, who loves us far more than any human mother, wants to hear us say that we love him. A simple, "I love you, God" will do.

But moms know that children must also show their love in tangible ways. Moms start by asking for obedience to simple commands like, "Hold Mommy's hand while we cross the street" and "Pick up your toys and put them away." These simple acts of obedience speak volumes.

It's much the same with God. He asks us to walk in his ways, to hold his hand as we walk through life. He wants us to take time to be with him, conversing or just sitting in silence with him. We show him we love him by living at peace with our brothers and sisters and by showing love to all his children. Simple acts of kindness show God that we love him as he loves us—sacrificially.

Children should also develop a healthy fear and respect for their moms. They know if they do something wrong, there will be consequences, such as a time-out. God's children should have a reverential awe of him too. He is the great and mighty Lord of lords. His presence makes kings and armies tremble. And he is loving enough to discipline those he loves. If God has told you to take a personal time-out to reflect and repent, it's important that you take time to sit at his feet and pour out your heart.

A good mother wouldn't feed her children junk food or put her children into dangerous situations. She wants her children to grow strong and healthy, so they'll live long lives. So, too, a child of God learns to discipline her spirit, mind and body, so as to become more Christlike. To avoid what he forbids so that she can stay strong. To eat what is good for her body and take in that which feeds her mind and spirit.

Loving God is a choice that grows through continued acts of obedience. Katherine Anne Porter observed, "Love must be learned again and again; there is no end to it." Choosing to love will please God, and it will bring joy to your life.

Wednesday

Go to page 231 for your next devotional reading.

Deuteronomy 10:12–13

And now, O Israel, what does the LORD your God ask of you but to fear the LORD your God, to walk in all his ways, to love him, to serve the LORD your God with all your heart and with all your soul, and to observe the LORD's commands and decrees that I am giving you today for your own good?

reflection

1 When was the last time you told God you love him?

2 When was the last time you served another out of love for God?

3 Can you think of a benefit you've enjoyed because you obeyed a specific command of God?

RELATED READINGS

Psalm 63:1–11;
Micah 6:6–8;
Mark 12:28–34

God, to walk in all his ways, to love him, to serve the LORD your God with all your heart and with all your soul, 13and to observe the LORD's commands and decrees that I am giving you today for your own good?

14To the LORD your God belong the heavens, even the highest heavens, the earth and everything in it. 15Yet the LORD set his affection on your forefathers and loved them, and he chose you, their descendants, above all the nations, as it is today. 16Circumcise your hearts, therefore, and do not be stiff-necked any longer. 17For the LORD your God is God of gods and Lord of lords, the great God, mighty and awesome, who shows no partiality and accepts no bribes. 18He defends the cause of the fatherless and the widow, and loves the alien, giving him food and clothing. 19And you are to love those who are aliens, for you yourselves were aliens in Egypt. 20Fear the LORD your God and serve him. Hold fast to him and take your oaths in his name. 21He is your praise; he is your God, who performed for you those great and awesome wonders you saw with your own eyes. 22Your forefathers who went down into Egypt were seventy in all, and now the LORD your God has made you as numerous as the stars in the sky.

> **Deuteronomy 10:17**
>
> *God Is Impartial*
>
> For the LORD your God is God of gods and Lord of lords, the great God, mighty and awesome, who shows no partiality and accepts no bribes.

Love and Obey the LORD

11 Love the LORD your God and keep his requirements, his decrees, his laws and his commands always. 2Remember today that your children were not the ones who saw and experienced the discipline of the LORD your God: his majesty, his mighty hand, his outstretched arm; 3the signs he performed and the things he did in the heart of Egypt, both to Pharaoh king of Egypt and to his whole country; 4what he did to the Egyptian army, to its horses and chariots, how he overwhelmed them with the waters of the Red Sea[a] as they were pursuing you, and how the LORD brought lasting ruin on them. 5It was not your children who saw what he did for you in the desert until you arrived at this place, 6and what he did to Dathan and Abiram, sons of Eliab the Reubenite, when the earth opened its mouth right in the middle of all Israel and swallowed them up with their households, their tents and every living thing that belonged to them. 7But it was your own eyes that saw all these great things the LORD has done.

8Observe therefore all the commands I am giving you today, so that you may have the strength to go in and take over the land that you are crossing the Jordan to possess, 9and so that you may live long in the land that the LORD swore to your forefathers to give to them and their descendants, a land flowing with milk and honey. 10The land you are entering to take over is not like the land of Egypt, from which you have come, where you planted your seed and irrigated it by foot as in a vegetable garden. 11But the land you are crossing the Jordan to take possession of is a land of mountains and valleys that drinks rain from heaven. 12It is a land the LORD your God cares for; the eyes of the LORD your God are continually on it from the beginning of the year to its end.

13So if you faithfully obey the commands I am giving you today—to love the LORD your God and to serve him with all your heart and with all your soul— 14then I will send rain on your land in its season, both autumn and spring rains, so that you may gather in your grain, new wine and oil. 15I will provide grass in the fields for your cattle, and you will eat and be satisfied.

16Be careful, or you will be enticed to turn away and worship other gods and bow down to them. 17Then the LORD's anger will burn against you, and he will shut the heavens so that it will not rain and the ground will yield no produce, and you will soon perish from the good land the LORD is giving you. 18Fix these words of mine in your hearts and minds; tie them as symbols on your hands and bind them

[a]4 Hebrew *Yam Suph*; that is, Sea of Reeds

on your foreheads. 19 Teach them to your children, talking about them when you sit at home
and when you walk along the road, when you
lie down and when you get up. 20 Write them
on the doorframes of your houses and on your
gates, 21 so that your days and the days of your
children may be many in the land that the LORD
swore to give your forefathers, as many as the
days that the heavens are above the earth.

22 If you carefully observe all these commands I am giving you to follow—to love the
LORD your God, to walk in all his ways and to
hold fast to him— 23 then the LORD will drive
out all these nations before you, and you will
dispossess nations larger and stronger than
you. 24 Every place where you set your foot
will be yours: Your territory will extend from
the desert to Lebanon, and from the Euphrates
River to the western sea.[a] 25 No man will be
able to stand against you. The LORD your God,
as he promised you, will put the terror and fear
of you on the whole land, wherever you go.

26 See, I am setting before you today a blessing and a curse— 27 the blessing if you obey the
commands of the LORD your God that I am giving you today; 28 the curse if you disobey the
commands of the LORD your God and turn
from the way that I command you today by following other gods, which you have not known.
29 When the LORD your God has brought you
into the land you are entering to possess, you
are to proclaim on Mount Gerizim the blessings, and on Mount Ebal the curses. 30 As you
know, these mountains are across the Jordan,
west of the road,[b] toward the setting sun, near
the great trees of Moreh, in the territory of
those Canaanites living in the Arabah in the
vicinity of Gilgal. 31 You are about to cross the
Jordan to enter and take possession of the land
the LORD your God is giving you. When you
have taken it over and are living there, 32 be
sure that you obey all the decrees and laws I
am setting before you today.

The One Place of Worship

12 These are the decrees and laws you
must be careful to follow in the land
that the LORD, the God of your fathers, has
given you to possess—as long as you live in the
land. 2 Destroy completely all the places on the
high mountains and on the hills and under every spreading tree where the nations you are
dispossessing worship their gods. 3 Break down
their altars, smash their sacred stones and burn
their Asherah poles in the fire; cut down the
idols of their gods and wipe out their names
from those places.

4 You must not worship the LORD your God
in their way. 5 But you are to seek the place the
LORD your God will choose from among all
your tribes to put his Name there for his dwelling. To that place you must go; 6 there bring
your burnt offerings and sacrifices, your tithes
and special gifts, what you have vowed to give
and your freewill offerings, and the firstborn of
your herds and flocks. 7 There, in the presence
of the LORD your God, you and your families
shall eat and shall rejoice in everything you
have put your hand to, because the LORD your
God has blessed you.

8 You are not to do as we do here today,
everyone as he sees fit, 9 since you have not yet
reached the resting place and the inheritance
the LORD your God is giving you. 10 But you
will cross the Jordan and settle in the land the
LORD your God is giving you as an inheritance,
and he will give you rest from all your enemies
around you so that you will live in safety. 11 Then
to the place the LORD your God will choose
as a dwelling for his Name—there you are to
bring everything I command you: your burnt
offerings and sacrifices, your tithes and special
gifts, and all the choice possessions you have
vowed to the LORD. 12 And there rejoice before
the LORD your God, you, your sons and daughters, your menservants and maidservants, and
the Levites from your towns, who have no allotment or inheritance of their own. 13 Be careful
not to sacrifice your burnt offerings anywhere
you please. 14 Offer them only at the place the
LORD will choose in one of your tribes, and
there observe everything I command you.

15 Nevertheless, you may slaughter your animals in any of your towns and eat as much of
the meat as you want, as if it were gazelle or
deer, according to the blessing the LORD your
God gives you. Both the ceremonially unclean
and the clean may eat it. 16 But you must not eat

[a]24 That is, the Mediterranean [b]30 Or *Jordan, westward*

the blood; pour it out on the ground like water.
17You must not eat in your own towns the tithe
of your grain and new wine and oil, or the firstborn of your herds and flocks, or whatever you
have vowed to give, or your freewill offerings
or special gifts. 18Instead, you are to eat them
in the presence of the LORD your God at the
place the LORD your God will choose—you,
your sons and daughters, your menservants
and maidservants, and the Levites from your
towns—and you are to rejoice before the LORD
your God in everything you put your hand to.
19Be careful not to neglect the Levites as long
as you live in your land.
20When the LORD your God has enlarged
your territory as he promised you, and you
crave meat and say, "I would like some meat,"
then you may eat as much of it as you want. 21If
the place where the LORD your God chooses to
put his Name is too far away from you, you may
slaughter animals from the herds and flocks the
LORD has given you, as I have commanded you,
and in your own towns you may eat as much of
them as you want. 22Eat them
as you would gazelle or deer.
Both the ceremonially unclean
and the clean may eat. 23But be
sure you do not eat the blood,
because the blood is the life,
and you must not eat the life
with the meat. 24You must not
eat the blood; pour it out on
the ground like water. 25Do
not eat it, so that it may go well
with you and your children after you, because you will be doing what is right in the eyes of
the LORD.
26But take your consecrated
things and whatever you have vowed to give,
and go to the place the LORD will choose. 27Pre-
sent your burnt offerings on the altar of the
LORD your God, both the meat and the blood.
The blood of your sacrifices must be poured beside the altar of the LORD your God, but you
may eat the meat. 28Be careful to obey all these
regulations I am giving you, so that it may always go well with you and your children after
you, because you will be doing what is good
and right in the eyes of the LORD your God.

Deuteronomy 13:3

God Tests Our Love

The LORD your God is testing you to find out whether you love him with all your heart and with all your soul.

29The LORD your God will cut off before you
the nations you are about to invade and dispossess. But when you have driven them out and
settled in their land, 30and after they have been
destroyed before you, be careful not to be ensnared by inquiring about their gods, saying,
"How do these nations serve their gods? We
will do the same." 31You must not worship the
LORD your God in their way, because in worshiping their gods, they do all kinds of detestable things the LORD hates. They even burn
their sons and daughters in the fire as sacrifices
to their gods.
32See that you do all I command you; do not
add to it or take away from it.

Worshiping Other Gods

13 If a prophet, or one who foretells by
dreams, appears among you and announces to you a miraculous sign or wonder,
2and if the sign or wonder of which he has
spoken takes place, and he says, "Let us follow
other gods" (gods you have not known) "and
let us worship them," 3you
must not listen to the words of
that prophet or dreamer. The
LORD your God is testing you
to find out whether you love
him with all your heart and
with all your soul. 4It is the
LORD your God you must follow, and him you must revere.
Keep his commands and obey
him; serve him and hold fast to
him. 5That prophet or dreamer
must be put to death, because
he preached rebellion against
the LORD your God, who
brought you out of Egypt and
redeemed you from the land of slavery; he has
tried to turn you from the way the LORD your
God commanded you to follow. You must
purge the evil from among you.
6If your very own brother, or your son or
daughter, or the wife you love, or your closest
friend secretly entices you, saying, "Let us go
and worship other gods" (gods that neither you
nor your fathers have known, 7gods of the peoples around you, whether near or far, from one
end of the land to the other), 8do not yield to

him or listen to him. Show him no pity. Do not spare him or shield him. 9You must certainly put him to death. Your hand must be the first in putting him to death, and then the hands of all the people. 10Stone him to death, because he tried to turn you away from the LORD your God, who brought you out of Egypt, out of the land of slavery. 11Then all Israel will hear and be afraid, and no one among you will do such an evil thing again.

12If you hear it said about one of the towns the LORD your God is giving you to live in 13that wicked men have arisen among you and have led the people of their town astray, saying, "Let us go and worship other gods" (gods you have not known), 14then you must inquire, probe and investigate it thoroughly. And if it is true and it has been proved that this detestable thing has been done among you, 15you must certainly put to the sword all who live in that town. Destroy it completely,[a] both its people and its livestock. 16Gather all the plunder of the town into the middle of the public square and completely burn the town and all its plunder as a whole burnt offering to the LORD your God. It is to remain a ruin forever, never to be rebuilt. 17None of those condemned things[a] shall be found in your hands, so that the LORD will turn from his fierce anger; he will show you mercy, have compassion on you, and increase your numbers, as he promised on oath to your forefathers, 18because you obey the LORD your God, keeping all his commands that I am giving you today and doing what is right in his eyes.

Clean and Unclean Food

14 You are the children of the LORD your God. Do not cut yourselves or shave the front of your heads for the dead, 2for you are a people holy to the LORD your God. Out of all the peoples on the face of the earth, the LORD has chosen you to be his treasured possession.

3Do not eat any detestable thing. 4These are the animals you may eat: the ox, the sheep, the goat, 5the deer, the gazelle, the roe deer, the wild goat, the ibex, the antelope and the mountain sheep.[b] 6You may eat any animal that has a split hoof divided in two and that chews the cud. 7However, of those that chew the cud or that have a split hoof completely divided you may not eat the camel, the rabbit or the coney.[c] Although they chew the cud, they do not have a split hoof; they are ceremonially unclean for you. 8The pig is also unclean; although it has a split hoof, it does not chew the cud. You are not to eat their meat or touch their carcasses.

9Of all the creatures living in the water, you may eat any that has fins and scales. 10But anything that does not have fins and scales you may not eat; for you it is unclean.

11You may eat any clean bird. 12But these you may not eat: the eagle, the vulture, the black vulture, 13the red kite, the black kite, any kind of falcon, 14any kind of raven, 15the horned owl, the screech owl, the gull, any kind of hawk, 16the little owl, the great owl, the white owl, 17the desert owl, the osprey, the cormorant, 18the stork, any kind of heron, the hoopoe and the bat.

19All flying insects that swarm are unclean to you; do not eat them. 20But any winged creature that is clean you may eat.

21Do not eat anything you find already dead. You may give it to an alien living in any of your towns, and he may eat it, or you may sell it to a foreigner. But you are a people holy to the LORD your God.

Do not cook a young goat in its mother's milk.

Tithes

22Be sure to set aside a tenth of all that your fields produce each year. 23Eat the tithe of your grain, new wine and oil, and the firstborn of your herds and flocks in the presence of the LORD your God at the place he will choose as a dwelling for his Name, so that you may learn to revere the LORD your God always. 24But if that place is too distant and you have been blessed by the LORD your God and cannot carry your tithe (because the place where the LORD will choose to put his Name is so far away), 25then exchange your tithe for silver, and take the silver with you and go to the place the LORD your God will choose. 26Use the silver to buy whatever you like: cattle, sheep, wine or other

[a]15,17 The Hebrew term refers to the irrevocable giving over of things or persons to the LORD, often by totally destroying them.
[b]5 The precise identification of some of the birds and animals in this chapter is uncertain. [c]7 That is, the hyrax or rock badger

fermented drink, or anything you wish. Then you and your household shall eat there in the presence of the LORD your God and rejoice. 27And do not neglect the Levites living in your towns, for they have no allotment or inheritance of their own.

28At the end of every three years, bring all the tithes of that year's produce and store it in your towns, 29so that the Levites (who have no allotment or inheritance of their own) and the aliens, the fatherless and the widows who live in your towns may come and eat and be satisfied, and so that the LORD your God may bless you in all the work of your hands.

> **Deuteronomy 15:10**
>
> *God Blesses Us*
>
> Give generously to him and do so without a grudging heart; then because of this the LORD your God will bless you in all your work and in everything you put your hand to.

The Year for Canceling Debts

15 At the end of every seven years you must cancel debts. 2This is how it is to be done: Every creditor shall cancel the loan he has made to his fellow Israelite. He shall not require payment from his fellow Israelite or brother, because the LORD's time for canceling debts has been proclaimed. 3You may require payment from a foreigner, but you must cancel any debt your brother owes you. 4However, there should be no poor among you, for in the land the LORD your God is giving you to possess as your inheritance, he will richly bless you, 5if only you fully obey the LORD your God and are careful to follow all these commands I am giving you today. 6For the LORD your God will bless you as he has promised, and you will lend to many nations but will borrow from none. You will rule over many nations but none will rule over you.

7If there is a poor man among your brothers in any of the towns of the land that the LORD your God is giving you, do not be hardhearted or tightfisted toward your poor brother. 8Rather be openhanded and freely lend him whatever he needs. 9Be careful not to harbor this wicked thought: "The seventh year, the year for canceling debts, is near," so that you do not show ill will toward your needy brother and give him nothing. He may then appeal to the LORD against you, and you will be found guilty of sin. 10Give generously to him and do so without a grudging heart; then because of this the LORD your God will bless you in all your work and in everything you put your hand to. 11There will always be poor people in the land. Therefore I command you to be openhanded toward your brothers and toward the poor and needy in your land.

Freeing Servants

12If a fellow Hebrew, a man or a woman, sells himself to you and serves you six years, in the seventh year you must let him go free. 13And when you release him, do not send him away empty-handed. 14Supply him liberally from your flock, your threshing floor and your winepress. Give to him as the LORD your God has blessed you. 15Remember that you were slaves in Egypt and the LORD your God redeemed you. That is why I give you this command today.

16But if your servant says to you, "I do not want to leave you," because he loves you and your family and is well off with you, 17then take an awl and push it through his ear lobe into the door, and he will become your servant for life. Do the same for your maidservant.

18Do not consider it a hardship to set your servant free, because his service to you these six years has been worth twice as much as that of a hired hand. And the LORD your God will bless you in everything you do.

The Firstborn Animals

19Set apart for the LORD your God every firstborn male of your herds and flocks. Do not put the firstborn of your oxen to work, and do not shear the firstborn of your sheep. 20Each year you and your family are to eat them in the presence of the LORD your God at the place he will choose. 21If an animal has a defect, is lame or blind, or has any serious flaw, you must not sacrifice it to the LORD your God. 22You are to eat it in your own towns. Both the ceremonially

Openhearted and Openhanded

Read: Deuteronomy 15:1–11

THERE IS MUCH SUFFERING in the world—very much. Material suffering is suffering from hunger, suffering from homelessness, from all kinds of disease, but I still think that the greatest suffering is being lonely, feeling unloved, just having no one. I have come more and more to realize that it is being unwanted that is the worst disease that any human being can ever experience. In these times of development, the whole world runs and is hurried. But there are some who fall down on the way and have no strength to go ahead. These are the ones we must care about.

Let us be very sincere in our dealings with each other and have the courage to accept each other as we are. Do not be surprised at or become preoccupied with each other's failure; rather see and find the good in each other, for each one of us is created in the image of God. Jesus has said it beautifully: "I am the vine, you are the branches." The life-giving sap that flows from the vine through each of the branches is the same.

Be kind in your actions. Do not think that you are the only one who can do efficient work, work worth showing. This makes you harsh in your judgment of others who may not have the same talents. Do your best and trust that others do their best. And be faithful in small things because it is in them that your strength lies.

In loving one another through our works we bring an increase of grace and a growth in divine love.

Be the living expression of God's kindness:
kindness in your face,
kindness in your eyes,
kindness in your smile,
kindness in your warm greeting.
— Mother Teresa

Deuteronomy 15:7–8

If there is a poor man among your brothers in any of the towns of the land that the LORD your God is giving you, do not be hardhearted or tightfisted toward your poor brother. Rather be openhanded and freely lend him whatever he needs.

reflection

1 Whom do you have trouble accepting? Are there people that you find yourself judging?

2 How have you shown that you care for the downtrodden?

3 List three practical ways you will follow Mother Teresa's example of loving others by being openhanded to those less fortunate than you.

RELATED READINGS

Psalm 72:12–14;
Isaiah 61:1–3;
Luke 6:37–38

Go to page 238 for your next devotional reading.

unclean and the clean may eat it, as if it were gazelle or deer. 23But you must not eat the blood;
pour it out on the ground like water.

Passover

16 Observe the month of Abib and celebrate the Passover of the LORD your
God, because in the month of Abib he brought
you out of Egypt by night. 2Sacrifice as the
Passover to the LORD your God an animal
from your flock or herd at the place the LORD
will choose as a dwelling for his Name. 3Do
not eat it with bread made with yeast, but for
seven days eat unleavened bread, the bread of
affliction, because you left Egypt in haste—so
that all the days of your life you may remember
the time of your departure from Egypt. 4Let no
yeast be found in your possession in all your
land for seven days. Do not let any of the meat
you sacrifice on the evening of the first day remain until morning.

5You must not sacrifice the Passover in any
town the LORD your God gives you 6except in
the place he will choose as a dwelling for his
Name. There you must sacrifice the Passover in
the evening, when the sun goes
down, on the anniversary[a] of
your departure from Egypt.
7Roast it and eat it at the
place the LORD your God will
choose. Then in the morning
return to your tents. 8For six
days eat unleavened bread and
on the seventh day hold an assembly to the LORD your God
and do no work.

Feast of Weeks

9Count off seven weeks
from the time you begin to
put the sickle to the standing grain. 10Then
celebrate the Feast of Weeks to the LORD your
God by giving a freewill offering in proportion
to the blessings the LORD your God has given
you. 11And rejoice before the LORD your God
at the place he will choose as a dwelling for his
Name—you, your sons and daughters, your
menservants and maidservants, the Levites
in your towns, and the aliens, the fatherless
and the widows living among you. 12Remem-
ber that you were slaves in Egypt, and follow
carefully these decrees.

Feast of Tabernacles

13Celebrate the Feast of Tabernacles for
seven days after you have gathered the produce
of your threshing floor and your winepress.
14Be joyful at your Feast—you, your sons and
daughters, your menservants and maidservants, and the Levites, the aliens, the fatherless
and the widows who live in your towns. 15For
seven days celebrate the Feast to the LORD your
God at the place the LORD will choose. For the
LORD your God will bless you in all your harvest and in all the work of your hands, and your
joy will be complete.

16Three times a year all your men must appear before the LORD your God at the place he
will choose: at the Feast of Unleavened Bread,
the Feast of Weeks and the Feast of Tabernacles. No man should appear before the LORD
empty-handed: 17Each of you must bring a gift
in proportion to the way the LORD your God
has blessed you.

> **Deuteronomy 16:20**
>
> *God Loves Justice*
>
> Follow justice and justice alone, so that you may live and possess the land the LORD your God is giving you.

Judges

18Appoint judges and officials for each of your tribes
in every town the LORD your
God is giving you, and they
shall judge the people fairly.
19Do not pervert justice or
show partiality. Do not accept
a bribe, for a bribe blinds the
eyes of the wise and twists the
words of the righteous. 20Fol-
low justice and justice alone, so
that you may live and possess
the land the LORD your God is
giving you.

Worshiping Other Gods

21Do not set up any wooden Asherah pole[b]
beside the altar you build to the LORD your
God, 22and do not erect a sacred stone, for
these the LORD your God hates.

17 Do not sacrifice to the LORD your God
an ox or a sheep that has any defect or
flaw in it, for that would be detestable to him.

2If a man or woman living among you in

[a]6 Or *down, at the time of day* [b]21 Or *Do not plant any tree dedicated to Asherah*

one of the towns the LORD gives you is found
doing evil in the eyes of the LORD your God in
violation of his covenant, 3and contrary to my
command has worshiped other gods, bowing
down to them or to the sun or the moon or
the stars of the sky, 4and this has been brought
to your attention, then you must investigate it
thoroughly. If it is true and it has been proved
that this detestable thing has been done in
Israel, 5take the man or woman who has done
this evil deed to your city gate and stone that
person to death. 6On the testimony of two or
three witnesses a man shall be put to death, but
no one shall be put to death on the testimony of
only one witness. 7The hands of the witnesses
must be the first in putting him to death, and
then the hands of all the people. You must
purge the evil from among you.

Law Courts

8If cases come before your courts that are too
difficult for you to judge—whether bloodshed,
lawsuits or assaults—take them to the place the
LORD your God will choose. 9Go to the priests,
who are Levites, and to the judge who is in office at that time. Inquire of them and they will
give you the verdict. 10You must act according
to the decisions they give you at the place the
LORD will choose. Be careful to do everything
they direct you to do. 11Act according to the
law they teach you and the decisions they give
you. Do not turn aside from what they tell you,
to the right or to the left. 12The man who shows
contempt for the judge or for the priest who
stands ministering there to the LORD your God
must be put to death. You must purge the evil
from Israel. 13All the people will hear and be
afraid, and will not be contemptuous again.

The King

14When you enter the land the LORD your
God is giving you and have taken possession of
it and settled in it, and you say, "Let us set a king
over us like all the nations around us," 15be sure
to appoint over you the king the LORD your
God chooses. He must be from among your
own brothers. Do not place a foreigner over
you, one who is not a brother Israelite. 16The
king, moreover, must not acquire great numbers of horses for himself or make the people
return to Egypt to get more of them, for the
LORD has told you, "You are not to go back that
way again." 17He must not take many wives, or
his heart will be led astray. He must not accumulate large amounts of silver and gold.

18When he takes the throne of his kingdom,
he is to write for himself on a scroll a copy of
this law, taken from that of the priests, who are
Levites. 19It is to be with him, and he is to read
it all the days of his life so that he may learn to
revere the LORD his God and follow carefully all
the words of this law and these decrees 20and
not consider himself better than his brothers
and turn from the law to the right or to the left.
Then he and his descendants will reign a long
time over his kingdom in Israel.

Offerings for Priests and Levites

18 The priests, who are Levites—indeed
the whole tribe of Levi—are to have no
allotment or inheritance with Israel. They shall
live on the offerings made to the LORD by fire,
for that is their inheritance. 2They shall have no
inheritance among their brothers; the LORD is
their inheritance, as he promised them.

3This is the share due the priests from the
people who sacrifice a bull or a sheep: the shoulder, the jowls and the inner parts. 4You are to
give them the firstfruits of your grain, new
wine and oil, and the first wool from the shearing of your sheep, 5for the LORD your God has
chosen them and their descendants out of all
your tribes to stand and minister in the LORD's
name always.

6If a Levite moves from one of your towns
anywhere in Israel where he is living, and
comes in all earnestness to the place the LORD
will choose, 7he may minister in the name of
the LORD his God like all his fellow Levites
who serve there in the presence of the LORD.
8He is to share equally in their benefits, even
though he has received money from the sale of
family possessions.

Detestable Practices

9When you enter the land the LORD your
God is giving you, do not learn to imitate the detestable ways of the nations there. 10Let no one
be found among you who sacrifices his son or
daughter in[a] the fire, who practices divination

[a] 10 Or *who makes his son or daughter pass through*

or sorcery, interprets omens, engages in witchcraft, 11or casts spells, or who is a medium or
spiritist or who consults the dead. 12Anyone
who does these things is detestable to the
LORD, and because of these detestable practices
the LORD your God will drive out those nations
before you. 13You must be blameless before the
LORD your God.

The Prophet

14The nations you will dispossess listen to
those who practice sorcery or divination. But
as for you, the LORD your God has not permitted you to do so. 15The LORD your God will
raise up for you a prophet like me from among
your own brothers. You must listen to him.
16For this is what you asked of the LORD your
God at Horeb on the day of the assembly when
you said, "Let us not hear the voice of the LORD
our God nor see this great fire anymore, or we
will die."

17The LORD said to me: "What they say is
good. 18I will raise up for them a prophet like
you from among their brothers; I will put my
words in his mouth, and he will tell them everything I command him. 19If anyone does not listen to my words that the prophet speaks in my
name, I myself will call him to account. 20But
a prophet who presumes to speak in my name
anything I have not commanded him to say,
or a prophet who speaks in the name of other
gods, must be put to death."

21You may say to yourselves, "How can we
know when a message has not been spoken by
the LORD?" 22If what a prophet proclaims in the
name of the LORD does not take place or come
true, that is a message the LORD has not spoken. That prophet has spoken presumptuously.
Do not be afraid of him.

Cities of Refuge

19 When the LORD your God has destroyed the nations whose land he is
giving you, and when you have driven them
out and settled in their towns and houses, 2then
set aside for yourselves three cities centrally
located in the land the LORD your God is giving you to possess. 3Build roads to them and
divide into three parts the land the LORD your
God is giving you as an inheritance, so that anyone who kills a man may flee there.

4This is the rule concerning the man who
kills another and flees there to save his life—
one who kills his neighbor unintentionally,
without malice aforethought. 5For instance, a
man may go into the forest with his neighbor
to cut wood, and as he swings his ax to fell a
tree, the head may fly off and hit his neighbor
and kill him. That man may flee to one of these
cities and save his life. 6Otherwise, the avenger
of blood might pursue him in a rage, overtake
him if the distance is too great, and kill him
even though he is not deserving of death, since
he did it to his neighbor without malice aforethought. 7This is why I command you to set
aside for yourselves three cities.

8If the LORD your God enlarges your
territory, as he promised on oath to your
forefathers, and gives you the whole land he
promised them, 9because you carefully follow
all these laws I command you today—to love
the LORD your God and to walk always in his
ways—then you are to set aside three more cities. 10Do this so that innocent blood will not be
shed in your land, which the LORD your God is
giving you as your inheritance, and so that you
will not be guilty of bloodshed.

11But if a man hates his neighbor and lies in
wait for him, assaults and kills him, and then
flees to one of these cities, 12the elders of his
town shall send for him, bring him back from
the city, and hand him over to the avenger of
blood to die. 13Show him no pity. You must
purge from Israel the guilt of shedding innocent blood, so that it may go well with you.

14Do not move your neighbor's boundary
stone set up by your predecessors in the inheritance you receive in the land the LORD your
God is giving you to possess.

Witnesses

15One witness is not enough to convict a
man accused of any crime or offense he may
have committed. A matter must be established
by the testimony of two or three witnesses.

16If a malicious witness takes the stand to accuse a man of a crime, 17the two men involved
in the dispute must stand in the presence of the
LORD before the priests and the judges who are
in office at the time. 18The judges must make
a thorough investigation, and if the witness
proves to be a liar, giving false testimony against

his brother, [19]then do to him as he intended to
do to his brother. You must purge the evil from
among you. [20]The rest of the people will hear
of this and be afraid, and never again will such
an evil thing be done among you. [21]Show no
pity: life for life, eye for eye, tooth for tooth,
hand for hand, foot for foot.

Going to War

20 When you go to war against your enemies and see horses and chariots and
an army greater than yours, do not be afraid
of them, because the Lord your God, who
brought you up out of Egypt, will be with you.
[2]When you are about to go into battle, the priest
shall come forward and address
the army. [3]He shall say: "Hear,
O Israel, today you are going
into battle against your enemies. Do not be fainthearted
or afraid; do not be terrified or
give way to panic before them.
[4]For the Lord your God is the
one who goes with you to fight
for you against your enemies to
give you victory."
[5]The officers shall say to the
army: "Has anyone built a new
house and not dedicated it? Let
him go home, or he may die in
battle and someone else may
dedicate it. [6]Has anyone planted a vineyard
and not begun to enjoy it? Let him go home,
or he may die in battle and someone else enjoy
it. [7]Has anyone become pledged to a woman
and not married her? Let him go home, or he
may die in battle and someone else marry her."
[8]Then the officers shall add, "Is any man afraid
or fainthearted? Let him go home so that his
brothers will not become disheartened too."
[9]When the officers have finished speaking
to the army, they shall appoint commanders
over it.
[10]When you march up to attack a city, make
its people an offer of peace. [11]If they accept and
open their gates, all the people in it shall be subject to forced labor and shall work for you. [12]If
they refuse to make peace and they engage you
in battle, lay siege to that city. [13]When the Lord
your God delivers it into your hand, put to the
sword all the men in it. [14]As for the women,
the children, the livestock and everything else
in the city, you may take these as plunder for
yourselves. And you may use the plunder the
Lord your God gives you from your enemies.
[15]This is how you are to treat all the cities that
are at a distance from you and do not belong to
the nations nearby.
[16]However, in the cities of the nations the
Lord your God is giving you as an inheritance,
do not leave alive anything that breathes.
[17]Completely destroy[a] them—the Hittites, Amorites, Canaanites, Perizzites, Hivites and Jebusites—as the Lord your God
has commanded you. [18]Otherwise, they will teach you to follow all the detestable things
they do in worshiping their
gods, and you will sin against
the Lord your God.
[19]When you lay siege to a
city for a long time, fighting
against it to capture it, do not
destroy its trees by putting an
ax to them, because you can
eat their fruit. Do not cut them
down. Are the trees of the field
people, that you should besiege
them?[b] [20]However, you may
cut down trees that you know are not fruit trees
and use them to build siege works until the city
at war with you falls.

> **Deuteronomy 20:4**
>
> *God Gives Victories*
>
> "For the Lord your God is the one who goes with you to fight for you against your enemies to give you victory."

Atonement for an Unsolved Murder

21 If a man is found slain, lying in a field
in the land the Lord your God is giving you to possess, and it is not known who
killed him, [2]your elders and judges shall go
out and measure the distance from the body to
the neighboring towns. [3]Then the elders of the
town nearest the body shall take a heifer that
has never been worked and has never worn a
yoke [4]and lead her down to a valley that has
not been plowed or planted and where there
is a flowing stream. There in the valley they
are to break the heifer's neck. [5]The priests, the
sons of Levi, shall step forward, for the Lord
your God has chosen them to minister and to

[a]17 The Hebrew term refers to the irrevocable giving over of things or persons to the Lord, often by totally destroying them. [b]19 Or *down to use in the siege, for the fruit trees are for the benefit of man.*

pronounce blessings in the name of the LORD
and to decide all cases of dispute and assault.
6Then all the elders of the town nearest the
body shall wash their hands over the heifer
whose neck was broken in the valley, 7and
they shall declare: "Our hands did not shed this
blood, nor did our eyes see it done. 8Accept
this atonement for your people Israel, whom
you have redeemed, O LORD, and do not hold
your people guilty of the blood of an innocent
man." And the bloodshed will be atoned for.
9So you will purge from yourselves the guilt of
shedding innocent blood, since you have done
what is right in the eyes of the LORD.

Marrying a Captive Woman

10When you go to war against your enemies
and the LORD your God delivers them into
your hands and you take captives, 11if you notice among the captives a beautiful woman and
are attracted to her, you may take her as your
wife. 12Bring her into your home and have her
shave her head, trim her nails 13and put aside
the clothes she was wearing when captured. After she has lived in your house and mourned
her father and mother for a full month, then
you may go to her and be her husband and she
shall be your wife. 14If you are not pleased with
her, let her go wherever she wishes. You must
not sell her or treat her as a slave, since you
have dishonored her.

The Right of the Firstborn

15If a man has two wives, and he loves one
but not the other, and both bear him sons but
the firstborn is the son of the wife he does not
love, 16when he wills his property to his sons,
he must not give the rights of the firstborn to
the son of the wife he loves in preference to his
actual firstborn, the son of the wife he does not
love. 17He must acknowledge the son of his
unloved wife as the firstborn by giving him a
double share of all he has. That son is the first
sign of his father's strength. The right of the
firstborn belongs to him.

A Rebellious Son

18If a man has a stubborn and rebellious son
who does not obey his father and mother and
will not listen to them when they discipline
him, 19his father and mother shall take hold of
him and bring him to the elders at the gate of
his town. 20They shall say to the elders, "This
son of ours is stubborn and rebellious. He will
not obey us. He is a profligate and a drunkard."
21Then all the men of his town shall stone him
to death. You must purge the evil from among
you. All Israel will hear of it and be afraid.

Various Laws

22If a man guilty of a capital offense is put
to death and his body is hung on a tree, 23you
must not leave his body on the tree overnight.
Be sure to bury him that same day, because anyone who is hung on a tree is under God's curse.
You must not desecrate the land the LORD your
God is giving you as an inheritance.

22 If you see your brother's ox or sheep
straying, do not ignore it but be sure to
take it back to him. 2If the brother does not live
near you or if you do not know who he is, take
it home with you and keep it until he comes
looking for it. Then give it back to him. 3Do the
same if you find your brother's donkey or his
cloak or anything he loses. Do not ignore it.

4If you see your brother's donkey or his ox
fallen on the road, do not ignore it. Help him
get it to its feet.

5A woman must not wear men's clothing,
nor a man wear women's clothing, for the LORD
your God detests anyone who does this.

6If you come across a bird's nest beside the
road, either in a tree or on the ground, and
the mother is sitting on the young or on the
eggs, do not take the mother with the young.
7You may take the young, but be sure to let the
mother go, so that it may go well with you and
you may have a long life.

8When you build a new house, make a parapet around your roof so that you may not bring
the guilt of bloodshed on your house if someone falls from the roof.

9Do not plant two kinds of seed in your vineyard; if you do, not only the crops you plant but
also the fruit of the vineyard will be defiled.[a]

10Do not plow with an ox and a donkey
yoked together.

11Do not wear clothes of wool and linen woven together.

[a]9 Or *be forfeited to the sanctuary*

12Make tassels on the four corners of the
cloak you wear.

Marriage Violations

13If a man takes a wife and, after lying with
her, dislikes her 14and slanders her and gives
her a bad name, saying, "I married this woman,
but when I approached her, I did not find
proof of her virginity," 15then the girl's father
and mother shall bring proof that she was a virgin to the town elders at the gate. 16The girl's
father will say to the elders, "I gave my daughter in marriage to this man, but he dislikes her.
17Now he has slandered her and said, 'I did
not find your daughter to be a virgin.' But here
is the proof of my daughter's virginity." Then
her parents shall display the cloth before the
elders of the town, 18and the elders shall take
the man and punish him. 19They shall fine him
a hundred shekels of silver[a] and give them to
the girl's father, because this man has given an
Israelite virgin a bad name. She shall continue
to be his wife; he must not divorce her as long
as he lives.

20If, however, the charge is true and no proof
of the girl's virginity can be found, 21she shall
be brought to the door of her father's house
and there the men of her town shall stone her
to death. She has done a disgraceful thing in
Israel by being promiscuous while still in her
father's house. You must purge the evil from
among you.

22If a man is found sleeping with another
man's wife, both the man who slept with her
and the woman must die. You must purge the
evil from Israel.

23If a man happens to meet in a town a virgin pledged to be married and he sleeps with
her, 24you shall take both of them to the gate
of that town and stone them to death—the girl
because she was in a town and did not scream
for help, and the man because he violated
another man's wife. You must purge the evil
from among you.

25But if out in the country a man happens to
meet a girl pledged to be married and rapes her,
only the man who has done this shall die. 26Do
nothing to the girl; she has committed no sin
deserving death. This case is like that of someone who attacks and murders his neighbor,
27for the man found the girl out in the country,
and though the betrothed girl screamed, there
was no one to rescue her.

28If a man happens to meet a virgin who is
not pledged to be married and rapes her and
they are discovered, 29he shall pay the girl's
father fifty shekels of silver.[b] He must marry
the girl, for he has violated her. He can never
divorce her as long as he lives.

30A man is not to marry his father's wife; he
must not dishonor his father's bed.

Exclusion From the Assembly

23 No one who has been emasculated by
crushing or cutting may enter the assembly of the LORD.

2No one born of a forbidden marriage[c] nor
any of his descendants may enter the assembly
of the LORD, even down to the tenth generation.

3No Ammonite or Moabite or any of his descendants may enter the assembly of the LORD,
even down to the tenth generation. 4For they
did not come to meet you with bread and water
on your way when you came out of Egypt, and
they hired Balaam son of Beor from Pethor in
Aram Naharaim[d] to pronounce a curse on you.
5However, the LORD your God would not listen
to Balaam but turned the curse into a blessing
for you, because the LORD your God loves you.
6Do not seek a treaty of friendship with them
as long as you live.

7Do not abhor an Edomite, for he is your
brother. Do not abhor an Egyptian, because
you lived as an alien in his country. 8The third
generation of children born to them may enter
the assembly of the LORD.

Uncleanness in the Camp

9When you are encamped against your enemies, keep away from everything impure. 10If
one of your men is unclean because of a noctur-
nal emission, he is to go outside the camp and
stay there. 11But as evening approaches he is
to wash himself, and at sunset he may return
to the camp.

12Designate a place outside the camp where
you can go to relieve yourself. 13As part of your

[a]19 That is, about 2 1/2 pounds (about 1 kilogram) [b]29 That is, about 1 1/4 pounds (about 0.6 kilogram) [c]2 Or *one of illegitimate birth*
[d]4 That is, Northwest Mesopotamia

Sexual Honor

Deuteronomy 22:22

If a man is found sleeping with another man's wife, both the man who slept with her and the woman must die. You must purge the evil from Israel.

reflection

1 In what ways do you think your views of sexuality and morality have been shaped by our culture?

2 What feelings come to mind when you think about your past and present sexual behavior? Have you asked Jesus to cleanse you of any dishonorable actions? Have you accepted his forgiveness?

3 How are you instilling and upholding God's principles of sexual honor in your children's lives?

RELATED READINGS

Matthew 5:27–28;
1 Corinthians 6:19–20;
1 Thessalonians 4:3–7;
Hebrews 13:4

Read: Deuteronomy 22:13–30

IN THE HELL OF DANTE'S *INFERNO*, the poet reserves the lowest pit for the traitors. There rests Judas Iscariot among other treacherous friends. Dante imagined that the worst of sins sent the perpetrators to the worst of punishment. Breach of trust, dishonoring intimate friendship, carried the harshest sentence: eternal freezing.

Though Dante rooted his poetry in allegory more than Scripture, God's severe punishment for betrayal can be seen throughout the book of Deuteronomy. And what human betrayal surpasses that of a wife against her husband or vice versa? God instituted a sexual union between man and woman from the beginning of time. Sex was integral to God's plan. Marriage would be a blessing, honorable in every way.

However, what God intended for honor, we often pervert into dishonorable, selfish acts. The enormous capacity for sex to bind two people together also carries an equal capacity to destroy lives when practiced outside God's purpose. The harsh penalties for sexual misconduct confirm the grave importance God placed on sexual intimacy.

Jesus did not abandon God's best intentions for human sexuality but brought forgiveness and grace, especially to those who were the most sexually powerless. In John's Gospel, we see Jesus respond practically and lovingly to two women. He did not join those condemning the adulterous woman to death by stoning (see John 8:3–11). Instead, he forgave her, instructing her not to sin again. To the woman at the well, married five times and living with a man, Jesus offered "living water" to wash her clean (see John 4:7–26). Without condoning her sexual history, Jesus graciously offered forgiveness and new life.

What many term as "sexual freedom" comes at a very high price; those who pursue it can reap consequences, such as sexually transmitted diseases, emotional wounds, guilt, broken relationships and more. But we can be free of a painful sexual history by asking Christ for forgiveness.

If past sexual sin still harrows your soul, accept the love and forgiveness he offers. If you feel guilty for a marital collapse, know that Jesus knows all about it and offers a clean slate. God created you as a beautifully sexual human being. Celebrate that fact, but honor him with it.

Go to page 243 for your next devotional reading.

equipment have something to dig with, and when you relieve yourself, dig a hole and cover up your excrement. 14For the LORD your God moves about in your camp to protect you and to deliver your enemies to you. Your camp must be holy, so that he will not see among you anything indecent and turn away from you.

> **Deuteronomy 23:14**
>
> *God Defends Us*
>
> For the LORD your God moves about in your camp to protect you and to deliver your enemies to you.

Miscellaneous Laws

15If a slave has taken refuge with you, do not hand him over to his master. 16Let him live among you wherever he likes and in whatever town he chooses. Do not oppress him.

17No Israelite man or woman is to become a shrine prostitute. 18You must not bring the earnings of a female prostitute or of a male prostitute[a] into the house of the LORD your God to pay any vow, because the LORD your God detests them both.

19Do not charge your brother interest, whether on money or food or anything else that may earn interest. 20You may charge a foreigner interest, but not a brother Israelite, so that the LORD your God may bless you in everything you put your hand to in the land you are entering to possess.

21If you make a vow to the LORD your God, do not be slow to pay it, for the LORD your God will certainly demand it of you and you will be guilty of sin. 22But if you refrain from making a vow, you will not be guilty. 23Whatever your lips utter you must be sure to do, because you made your vow freely to the LORD your God with your own mouth.

24If you enter your neighbor's vineyard, you may eat all the grapes you want, but do not put any in your basket. 25If you enter your neighbor's grainfield, you may pick kernels with your hands, but you must not put a sickle to his standing grain.

24 If a man marries a woman who becomes displeasing to him because he finds something indecent about her, and he writes her a certificate of divorce, gives it to her and sends her from his house, 2and if after she leaves his house she becomes the wife of another man, 3and her second husband dislikes her and writes her a certificate of divorce, gives it to her and sends her from his house, or if he dies, 4then her first husband, who divorced her, is not allowed to marry her again after she has been defiled. That would be detestable in the eyes of the LORD. Do not bring sin upon the land the LORD your God is giving you as an inheritance.

5If a man has recently married, he must not be sent to war or have any other duty laid on him. For one year he is to be free to stay at home and bring happiness to the wife he has married.

6Do not take a pair of millstones—not even the upper one—as security for a debt, because that would be taking a man's livelihood as security.

7If a man is caught kidnapping one of his brother Israelites and treats him as a slave or sells him, the kidnapper must die. You must purge the evil from among you.

8In cases of leprous[b] diseases be very careful to do exactly as the priests, who are Levites, instruct you. You must follow carefully what I have commanded them. 9Remember what the LORD your God did to Miriam along the way after you came out of Egypt.

10When you make a loan of any kind to your neighbor, do not go into his house to get what he is offering as a pledge. 11Stay outside and let the man to whom you are making the loan bring the pledge out to you. 12If the man is poor, do not go to sleep with his pledge in your possession. 13Return his cloak to him by sunset so that he may sleep in it. Then he will thank you, and it will be regarded as a righteous act in the sight of the LORD your God.

14Do not take advantage of a hired man who is poor and needy, whether he is a brother Israelite or an alien living in one of your towns. 15Pay him his wages each day before sunset, because he is poor and is counting on

[a]18 Hebrew *of a dog* [b]8 The Hebrew word was used for various diseases affecting the skin—not necessarily leprosy.

it. Otherwise he may cry to the LORD against
you, and you will be guilty of sin.
16 Fathers shall not be put to death for their
children, nor children put to death for their fathers; each is to die for his own sin.
17 Do not deprive the alien or the fatherless
of justice, or take the cloak of the widow as a
pledge. 18 Remember that you were slaves in
Egypt and the LORD your God redeemed you
from there. That is why I command you to do
this.
19 When you are harvesting in your field
and you overlook a sheaf, do not go back to
get it. Leave it for the alien, the
fatherless and the widow, so
that the LORD your God may
bless you in all the work of
your hands. 20 When you beat
the olives from your trees, do
not go over the branches a second time. Leave what remains
for the alien, the fatherless
and the widow. 21 When you
harvest the grapes in your vineyard, do not go over the vines
again. Leave what remains for
the alien, the fatherless and the
widow. 22 Remember that you
were slaves in Egypt. That is why I command
you to do this.

> Deuteronomy 24:19
>
> *God Is Generous*
>
> When you are harvesting in your field and you overlook a sheaf, do not go back to get it. Leave it for the alien, the fatherless and the widow.

25 When men have a dispute, they are to
take it to court and the judges will decide the case, acquitting the innocent and condemning the guilty. 2 If the guilty man deserves
to be beaten, the judge shall make him lie down
and have him flogged in his presence with the
number of lashes his crime deserves, 3 but he
must not give him more than forty lashes. If
he is flogged more than that, your brother will
be degraded in your eyes.
4 Do not muzzle an ox while it is treading out
the grain.
5 If brothers are living together and one
of them dies without a son, his widow must
not marry outside the family. Her husband's
brother shall take her and marry her and fulfill
the duty of a brother-in-law to her. 6 The first
son she bears shall carry on the name of the
dead brother so that his name will not be blotted out from Israel.
7 However, if a man does not want to marry
his brother's wife, she shall go to the elders at
the town gate and say, "My husband's brother
refuses to carry on his brother's name in Israel.
He will not fulfill the duty of a brother-in-law
to me." 8 Then the elders of his town shall summon him and talk to him. If he persists in saying, "I do not want to marry her," 9 his brother's
widow shall go up to him in the presence of
the elders, take off one of his sandals, spit in his
face and say, "This is what is done to the man
who will not build up his brother's family line."
10 That man's line shall be known in Israel as
The Family of the Unsandaled.
11 If two men are fighting and
the wife of one of them comes
to rescue her husband from his
assailant, and she reaches out
and seizes him by his private
parts, 12 you shall cut off her
hand. Show her no pity.
13 Do not have two differing weights in your bag—one
heavy, one light. 14 Do not have
two differing measures in your
house—one large, one small.
15 You must have accurate and
honest weights and measures,
so that you may live long in the land the LORD
your God is giving you. 16 For the LORD your
God detests anyone who does these things, anyone who deals dishonestly.
17 Remember what the Amalekites did to
you along the way when you came out of Egypt.
18 When you were weary and worn out, they
met you on your journey and cut off all who
were lagging behind; they had no fear of God.
19 When the LORD your God gives you rest
from all the enemies around you in the land
he is giving you to possess as an inheritance,
you shall blot out the memory of Amalek from
under heaven. Do not forget!

Firstfruits and Tithes

26 When you have entered the land the
LORD your God is giving you as an inheritance and have taken possession of it and
settled in it, 2 take some of the firstfruits of all
that you produce from the soil of the land the
LORD your God is giving you and put them in
a basket. Then go to the place the LORD your

God will choose as a dwelling for his Name
3and say to the priest in office at the time, "I
declare today to the LORD your God that I have
come to the land the LORD swore to our forefathers to give us." 4The priest shall take the basket from your hands and set it down in front
of the altar of the LORD your God. 5Then you
shall declare before the LORD your God: "My
father was a wandering Aramean, and he went
down into Egypt with a few people and lived
there and became a great nation, powerful and
numerous. 6But the Egyptians mistreated us
and made us suffer, putting us to hard labor.
7Then we cried out to the LORD, the God of our
fathers, and the LORD heard
our voice and saw our misery,
toil and oppression. 8So the
LORD brought us out of Egypt
with a mighty hand and an outstretched arm, with great terror and with miraculous signs
and wonders. 9He brought us
to this place and gave us this
land, a land flowing with milk
and honey; 10and now I bring
the firstfruits of the soil that
you, O LORD, have given me."
Place the basket before the
LORD your God and bow down
before him. 11And you and the
Levites and the aliens among you shall rejoice
in all the good things the LORD your God has
given to you and your household.
12When you have finished setting aside a
tenth of all your produce in the third year, the
year of the tithe, you shall give it to the Levite,
the alien, the fatherless and the widow, so that
they may eat in your towns and be satisfied.
13Then say to the LORD your God: "I have
removed from my house the sacred portion
and have given it to the Levite, the alien, the
fatherless and the widow, according to all you
commanded. I have not turned aside from
your commands nor have I forgotten any of
them. 14I have not eaten any of the sacred
portion while I was in mourning, nor have I
removed any of it while I was unclean, nor have
I offered any of it to the dead. I have obeyed
the LORD my God; I have done everything you
commanded me. 15Look down from heaven,
your holy dwelling place, and bless your people
Israel and the land you have given us as you
promised on oath to our forefathers, a land
flowing with milk and honey."

Deuteronomy 26:18

God Treasures Us

And the LORD has declared this day that you are his people, his treasured possession as he promised, and that you are to keep all his commands.

Follow the LORD's Commands

16The LORD your God commands you this
day to follow these decrees and laws; carefully
observe them with all your heart and with all
your soul. 17You have declared this day that
the LORD is your God and that you will walk
in his ways, that you will keep his decrees, commands and laws, and that you will obey him.
18And the LORD has declared this day that you
are his people, his treasured
possession as he promised, and
that you are to keep all his commands. 19He has declared that
he will set you in praise, fame
and honor high above all the
nations he has made and that
you will be a people holy to the
LORD your God, as he promised.

The Altar on Mount Ebal

27 Moses and the elders
of Israel commanded
the people: "Keep all these commands that I give you today.
2When you have crossed the Jordan into the
land the LORD your God is giving you, set up
some large stones and coat them with plaster.
3Write on them all the words of this law when
you have crossed over to enter the land the
LORD your God is giving you, a land flowing
with milk and honey, just as the LORD, the God
of your fathers, promised you. 4And when you
have crossed the Jordan, set up these stones on
Mount Ebal, as I command you today, and coat
them with plaster. 5Build there an altar to the
LORD your God, an altar of stones. Do not use
any iron tool upon them. 6Build the altar of the
LORD your God with fieldstones and offer burnt
offerings on it to the LORD your God. 7Sacrifice
fellowship offerings[a] there, eating them and
rejoicing in the presence of the LORD your God.
8And you shall write very clearly all the words
of this law on these stones you have set up."

[a]7 Traditionally *peace offerings*

Curses From Mount Ebal

9Then Moses and the priests, who are Levites, said to all Israel, "Be silent, O Israel, and
listen! You have now become the people of the
LORD your God. 10Obey the LORD your God
and follow his commands and decrees that I
give you today."

11On the same day Moses commanded
the people:

12When you have crossed the Jordan, these
tribes shall stand on Mount Gerizim to bless
the people: Simeon, Levi, Judah, Issachar,
Joseph and Benjamin. 13And these tribes
shall stand on Mount Ebal to pronounce
curses: Reuben, Gad, Asher, Zebulun, Dan
and Naphtali.

14The Levites shall recite to all the people of
Israel in a loud voice:

15"Cursed is the man who carves an
image or casts an idol—a thing detestable
to the LORD, the work of the craftsman's
hands—and sets it up in secret."

Then all the people shall say, "Amen!"

16"Cursed is the man who dishonors
his father or his mother."

Then all the people shall say, "Amen!"

17"Cursed is the man who moves his
neighbor's boundary stone."

Then all the people shall say, "Amen!"

18"Cursed is the man who leads the
blind astray on the road."

Then all the people shall say, "Amen!"

19"Cursed is the man who withholds
justice from the alien, the fatherless or
the widow."

Then all the people shall say, "Amen!"

20"Cursed is the man who sleeps with
his father's wife, for he dishonors his father's bed."

Then all the people shall say, "Amen!"

21"Cursed is the man who has sexual
relations with any animal."

Then all the people shall say, "Amen!"

22"Cursed is the man who sleeps with
his sister, the daughter of his father or the
daughter of his mother."

Then all the people shall say, "Amen!"

23"Cursed is the man who sleeps with
his mother-in-law."

Then all the people shall say, "Amen!"

24"Cursed is the man who kills his
neighbor secretly."

Then all the people shall say, "Amen!"

25"Cursed is the man who accepts a
bribe to kill an innocent person."

Then all the people shall say, "Amen!"

26"Cursed is the man who does not
uphold the words of this law by carrying
them out."

Then all the people shall say, "Amen!"

Blessings for Obedience

28 If you fully obey the LORD your God
and carefully follow all his commands I
give you today, the LORD your God will set you
high above all the nations on earth. 2All these
blessings will come upon you and accompany
you if you obey the LORD your God:

3You will be blessed in the city and
blessed in the country.

4The fruit of your womb will be blessed,
and the crops of your land and the young
of your livestock—the calves of your herds
and the lambs of your flocks.

5Your basket and your kneading trough
will be blessed.

6You will be blessed when you come in
and blessed when you go out.

7The LORD will grant that the enemies who
rise up against you will be defeated before you.
They will come at you from one direction but
flee from you in seven.

8The LORD will send a blessing on your
barns and on everything you put your hand to.
The LORD your God will bless you in the land
he is giving you.

9The LORD will establish you as his holy people, as he promised you on oath, if you keep the
commands of the LORD your God and walk in
his ways. 10Then all the peoples on earth will
see that you are called by the name of the LORD,
and they will fear you. 11The LORD will grant
you abundant prosperity—in the fruit of your
womb, the young of your livestock and the
crops of your ground—in the land he swore to
your forefathers to give you.

12The LORD will open the heavens, the storehouse of his bounty, to send rain on your land
in season and to bless all the work of your
hands. You will lend to many nations but will

Two

DINAH

DINAH REMEMBERED BEING LOVED by two men. One had tickled her ears with whispered words of affection. He made her heart flutter with his promises—she'd never heard a man be so vulnerable with a woman. She'd caught him staring at her when they talked, almost transfixed. And his boyish eyes seemed to ask, almost plead with her, to be his forever.

His words were tender and gentle, but not his touch.

No, his touch seemed to be that of another man altogether. A demanding, self-centered man who roughed her face with his beard; whose fingertips were more like talons, securing her so she could not get away. This man did not listen to her cries. He only thought about what he wanted.

But what did Dinah want? It hadn't seemed to matter. Her name floated among the tall grass in the fields in a discussion among the two families—as casually as if they were negotiating a business deal, not a marriage.

"My son Shechem has his heart set on your daughter," his father had told her father and brothers. The man who had violated her was now talking about his heart? Were we now back to the other man with the winsome words?

"I'll pay whatever you ask me . . . Only give me the girl as my wife."

Devoted and sacrificial, *this* man spoke the language of love fluently. *This* man said what every girl her age wanted to hear. She could have loved *that* man, she would often think to herself years later. The events from that summer traipsed across her mind at the oddest times. Washing clothes. Walking to market. Whenever her mind grew still enough to remember what her heart could not forget.

Did the man with the velvety words ever really exist? Perhaps she simply wanted to believe he existed to assuage her misplaced guilt. However, she could not deny the memory of the other man who haunted her dreams. Two men had loved Dinah. But they shared one name.

She had been sure time would heal her wounds. Yet here she was, years later, not yet over either one.

—Prayer—

"O Lord, hear my voice. Let your ears be attentive to my cry for mercy" (Psalm 130:2).

When Shechem . . . saw her, he took her and violated her. His heart was drawn to Dinah daughter of Jacob, and he loved the girl and spoke tenderly to her.

Genesis 34:2–3

ASSIGNED READING:

Genesis 34

Weekend

Go to page 248 for your next devotional reading.

borrow from none. 13The LORD will make you
the head, not the tail. If you pay attention to the
commands of the LORD your God that I give
you this day and carefully follow them, you will
always be at the top, never at the bottom. 14Do
not turn aside from any of the commands I
give you today, to the right or to the left, following other gods and serving them.

Curses for Disobedience

15However, if you do not obey the LORD
your God and do not carefully follow all his
commands and decrees I am giving you today,
all these curses will come upon you and overtake you:

16You will be cursed in the city and
cursed in the country.
17Your basket and your kneading
trough will be cursed.
18The fruit of your womb will be
cursed, and the crops of your land, and
the calves of your herds and the lambs of
your flocks.
19You will be cursed when you come in
and cursed when you go out.

20The LORD will send on you curses, confusion and rebuke in everything you put your
hand to, until you are destroyed and come to
sudden ruin because of the evil you have done
in forsaking him.[a] 21The LORD will plague you
with diseases until he has destroyed you from
the land you are entering to possess. 22The
LORD will strike you with wasting disease, with
fever and inflammation, with scorching heat
and drought, with blight and mildew, which
will plague you until you perish. 23The sky over
your head will be bronze, the ground beneath
you iron. 24The LORD will turn the rain of your
country into dust and powder; it will come
down from the skies until you are destroyed.
25The LORD will cause you to be defeated before your enemies. You will come at them from
one direction but flee from them in seven, and
you will become a thing of horror to all the
kingdoms on earth. 26Your carcasses will be
food for all the birds of the air and the beasts of
the earth, and there will be no one to frighten
them away. 27The LORD will afflict you with the
boils of Egypt and with tumors, festering sores
and the itch, from which you cannot be cured.
28The LORD will afflict you with madness, blindness and confusion of mind. 29At midday you
will grope about like a blind man in the dark.
You will be unsuccessful in everything you do;
day after day you will be oppressed and robbed,
with no one to rescue you.
30You will be pledged to be married to a
woman, but another will take her and ravish
her. You will build a house, but you will not live
in it. You will plant a vineyard, but you will not
even begin to enjoy its fruit. 31Your ox will be
slaughtered before your eyes, but you will eat
none of it. Your donkey will be forcibly taken
from you and will not be returned. Your sheep
will be given to your enemies, and no one will
rescue them. 32Your sons and daughters will
be given to another nation, and you will wear
out your eyes watching for them day after day,
powerless to lift a hand. 33A people that you
do not know will eat what your land and labor
produce, and you will have nothing but cruel
oppression all your days. 34The sights you see
will drive you mad. 35The LORD will afflict your
knees and legs with painful boils that cannot be
cured, spreading from the soles of your feet to
the top of your head.
36The LORD will drive you and the king
you set over you to a nation unknown to you
or your fathers. There you will worship other
gods, gods of wood and stone. 37You will become a thing of horror and an object of scorn
and ridicule to all the nations where the LORD
will drive you.
38You will sow much seed in the field but
you will harvest little, because locusts will devour it. 39You will plant vineyards and cultivate
them but you will not drink the wine or gather
the grapes, because worms will eat them. 40You
will have olive trees throughout your country
but you will not use the oil, because the olives
will drop off. 41You will have sons and daughters but you will not keep them, because they
will go into captivity. 42Swarms of locusts
will take over all your trees and the crops of
your land.
43The alien who lives among you will rise
above you higher and higher, but you will sink

[a]20 Hebrew *me*

lower and lower. 44He will lend to you, but you will not lend to him. He will be the head, but you will be the tail.

45All these curses will come upon you. They will pursue you and overtake you until you are destroyed, because you did not obey the LORD your God and observe the commands and decrees he gave you. 46They will be a sign and a wonder to you and your descendants forever. 47Because you did not serve the LORD your God joyfully and gladly in the time of prosperity, 48therefore in hunger and thirst, in nakedness and dire poverty, you will serve the enemies the LORD sends against you. He will put an iron yoke on your neck until he has destroyed you.

49The LORD will bring a nation against you from far away, from the ends of the earth, like an eagle swooping down, a nation whose language you will not understand, 50a fierce-looking nation without respect for the old or pity for the young. 51They will devour the young of your livestock and the crops of your land until you are destroyed. They will leave you no grain, new wine or oil, nor any calves of your herds or lambs of your flocks until you are ruined. 52They will lay siege to all the cities throughout your land until the high fortified walls in which you trust fall down. They will besiege all the cities throughout the land the LORD your God is giving you.

53Because of the suffering that your enemy will inflict on you during the siege, you will eat the fruit of the womb, the flesh of the sons and daughters the LORD your God has given you. 54Even the most gentle and sensitive man among you will have no compassion on his own brother or the wife he loves or his surviving children, 55and he will not give to one of them any of the flesh of his children that he is eating. It will be all he has left because of the suffering your enemy will inflict on you during the siege of all your cities. 56The most gentle and sensitive woman among you—so sensitive and gentle that she would not venture to touch the ground with the sole of her foot—will begrudge the husband she loves and her own son or daughter 57the afterbirth from her womb and the children she bears. For she intends to eat them secretly during the siege and in the distress that your enemy will inflict on you in your cities.

58If you do not carefully follow all the words of this law, which are written in this book, and do not revere this glorious and awesome name—the LORD your God— 59the LORD will send fearful plagues on you and your descendants, harsh and prolonged disasters, and severe and lingering illnesses. 60He will bring upon you all the diseases of Egypt that you dreaded, and they will cling to you. 61The LORD will also bring on you every kind of sickness and disaster not recorded in this Book of the Law, until you are destroyed. 62You who were as numerous as the stars in the sky will be left but few in number, because you did not obey the LORD your God. 63Just as it pleased the LORD to make you prosper and increase in number, so it will please him to ruin and destroy you. You will be uprooted from the land you are entering to possess.

64Then the LORD will scatter you among all nations, from one end of the earth to the other. There you will worship other gods—gods of wood and stone, which neither you nor your fathers have known. 65Among those nations you will find no repose, no resting place for the sole of your foot. There the LORD will give you an anxious mind, eyes weary with longing, and a despairing heart. 66You will live in constant suspense, filled with dread both night and day, never sure of your life. 67In the morning you will say, "If only it were evening!" and in the evening, "If only it were morning!"—because of the terror that will fill your hearts and the sights that your eyes will see. 68The LORD will send you back in ships to Egypt on a journey I said you should never make again. There you will offer yourselves for sale to your enemies as male and female slaves, but no one will buy you.

Renewal of the Covenant

29 These are the terms of the covenant the LORD commanded Moses to make with the Israelites in Moab, in addition to the covenant he had made with them at Horeb.

2Moses summoned all the Israelites and said to them:

Your eyes have seen all that the LORD did in Egypt to Pharaoh, to all his officials and to all

his land. [3]With your own eyes you saw those
great trials, those miraculous signs and great
wonders. [4]But to this day the LORD has not
given you a mind that understands or eyes that
see or ears that hear. [5]During the forty years
that I led you through the desert, your clothes
did not wear out, nor did the sandals on your
feet. [6]You ate no bread and drank no wine or
other fermented drink. I did this so that you
might know that I am the LORD your God.
[7]When you reached this place, Sihon king
of Heshbon and Og king of Bashan came out
to fight against us, but we defeated them. [8]We
took their land and gave it as an inheritance to
the Reubenites, the Gadites and the half-tribe
of Manasseh.
[9]Carefully follow the terms of this covenant,
so that you may prosper in everything you do.
[10]All of you are standing today in the presence
of the LORD your God—your leaders and chief
men, your elders and officials, and all the other
men of Israel, [11]together with your children and
your wives, and the aliens living in your camps
who chop your wood and carry your water.
[12]You are standing here in order to enter into a
covenant with the LORD your God, a covenant
the LORD is making with you this day and seal-
ing with an oath, [13]to confirm you this day as
his people, that he may be your
God as he promised you and as
he swore to your fathers, Abraham, Isaac and Jacob. [14]I am
making this covenant, with its
oath, not only with you [15]who
are standing here with us today
in the presence of the LORD our
God but also with those who
are not here today.
[16]You yourselves know how
we lived in Egypt and how we
passed through the countries
on the way here. [17]You saw
among them their detestable
images and idols of wood
and stone, of silver and gold.
[18]Make sure there is no man or
woman, clan or tribe among you today whose
heart turns away from the LORD our God to go
and worship the gods of those nations; make
sure there is no root among you that produces
such bitter poison.
[19]When such a person hears the words of
this oath, he invokes a blessing on himself and
therefore thinks, "I will be safe, even though I
persist in going my own way." This will bring
disaster on the watered land as well as the dry.[a]
[20]The LORD will never be willing to forgive
him; his wrath and zeal will burn against that
man. All the curses written in this book will
fall upon him, and the LORD will blot out his
name from under heaven. [21]The LORD will single him out from all the tribes of Israel for disaster, according to all the curses of the covenant
written in this Book of the Law.
[22]Your children who follow you in later generations and foreigners who come from distant
lands will see the calamities that have fallen on
the land and the diseases with which the LORD
has afflicted it. [23]The whole land will be a burning waste of salt and sulfur—nothing planted,
nothing sprouting, no vegetation growing on it.
It will be like the destruction of Sodom and Gomorrah, Admah and Zeboiim, which the LORD
overthrew in fierce anger. [24]All the nations will
ask: "Why has the LORD done this to this land?
Why this fierce, burning anger?"
[25]And the answer will be: "It is because this
people abandoned the cov-
enant of the LORD, the God
of their fathers, the covenant
he made with them when he
brought them out of Egypt.
[26]They went off and worshiped
other gods and bowed down to
them, gods they did not know,
gods he had not given them.
[27]Therefore the LORD's anger
burned against this land, so that
he brought on it all the curses
written in this book. [28]In furious anger and in great wrath
the LORD uprooted them from
their land and thrust them into
another land, as it is now."
[29]The secret things belong
to the LORD our God, but the things revealed
belong to us and to our children forever, that
we may follow all the words of this law.

Deuteronomy 29:29

God Is Mysterious

The secret things belong
to the LORD our God,
but the things revealed
belong to us and to our
children forever, that
we may follow all the
words of this law.

[a]19 Or *way, in order to add drunkenness to thirst."*

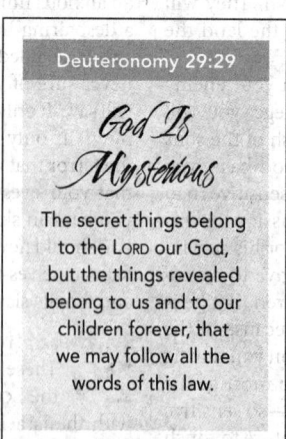

Prosperity After Turning to the Lord

30 When all these blessings and curses
I have set before you come upon you
and you take them to heart wherever the Lord
your God disperses you among the nations,
2 and when you and your children return to the
Lord your God and obey him with all your
heart and with all your soul according to everything I command you today, 3 then the Lord
your God will restore your fortunes[a] and have
compassion on you and gather you again from
all the nations where he scattered you. 4 Even
if you have been banished to the most distant
land under the heavens, from there the Lord
your God will gather you and bring you back.
5 He will bring you to the land that belonged to
your fathers, and you will take possession of it.
He will make you more prosper-
ous and numerous than your
fathers. 6 The Lord your God
will circumcise your hearts and
the hearts of your descendants,
so that you may love him with
all your heart and with all your
soul, and live. 7 The Lord your
God will put all these curses
on your enemies who hate and
persecute you. 8 You will again
obey the Lord and follow all
his commands I am giving you
today. 9 Then the Lord your
God will make you most prosperous in all the work of your
hands and in the fruit of your
womb, the young of your livestock and the crops of your
land. The Lord will again delight in you and
make you prosperous, just as he delighted in
your fathers, 10 if you obey the Lord your God
and keep his commands and decrees that are
written in this Book of the Law and turn to the
Lord your God with all your heart and with
all your soul.

The Offer of Life or Death

11 Now what I am commanding you today is
not too difficult for you or beyond your reach.
12 It is not up in heaven, so that you have to ask,
"Who will ascend into heaven to get it and proclaim it to us so we may obey it?" 13 Nor is it
beyond the sea, so that you have to ask, "Who
will cross the sea to get it and proclaim it to us
so we may obey it?" 14 No, the word is very near
you; it is in your mouth and in your heart so
you may obey it.
15 See, I set before you today life and prosperity, death and destruction. 16 For I command
you today to love the Lord your God, to walk
in his ways, and to keep his commands, decrees
and laws; then you will live and increase, and
the Lord your God will bless you in the land
you are entering to possess.
17 But if your heart turns away and you are
not obedient, and if you are drawn away to bow
down to other gods and worship them, 18 I declare to you this day that you will certainly be
destroyed. You will not live long in the land you
are crossing the Jordan to enter
and possess.
19 This day I call heaven
and earth as witnesses against
you that I have set before you
life and death, blessings and
curses. Now choose life, so that
you and your children may live
20 and that you may love the
Lord your God, listen to his
voice, and hold fast to him. For
the Lord is your life, and he
will give you many years in the
land he swore to give to your
fathers, Abraham, Isaac and
Jacob.

> **Deuteronomy 30:20**
>
> *God Is Life*
>
> And that you may love the Lord your God, listen to his voice, and hold fast to him. For the Lord is your life, and he will give you many years in the land he swore to give to your fathers, Abraham, Isaac and Jacob.

Joshua to Succeed Moses

31 Then Moses went
out and spoke these
words to all Israel: 2 "I am now a hundred
and twenty years old and I am no longer able
to lead you. The Lord has said to me, 'You
shall not cross the Jordan.' 3 The Lord your
God himself will cross over ahead of you. He
will destroy these nations before you, and
you will take possession of their land. Joshua
also will cross over ahead of you, as the Lord
said. 4 And the Lord will do to them what he
did to Sihon and Og, the kings of the Amorites,
whom he destroyed along with their land. 5 The
Lord will deliver them to you, and you must
do to them all that I have commanded you.

[a] 3 Or *will bring you back from captivity*

Who's the Boss?

Deuteronomy 30:11

Now what I am commanding you today is not too difficult for you or beyond your reach.

reflection

1 Do you ever find yourself offering excuses for failing to follow God's commandments?

2 In what ways have you benefited by obeying God's rules of conduct?

3 How quick are you to obey the voice of your Master—instantly, hesitantly, occasionally? What does this tell you about your relationship with him?

RELATED READINGS

Exodus 20:2–17; Philippians 2:12–13; 1 Thessalonians 5:24

Read: Deuteronomy 30:11–20

IN HIS AUTOBIOGRAPHY, *A Life in Our Times*, historian John Kenneth Galbraith wrote admiringly of his family's housekeeper, Emily Gloria Wilson. "It had been a wearying day, and I asked Emily to hold all telephone calls while I had a nap. Shortly thereafter the phone rang. Lyndon Johnson was calling from the White House."

"Get me Ken Galbraith. This is Lyndon Johnson."

"He is sleeping, Mr. President. He said not to disturb him."

"Well, wake him up. I want to talk to him."

"No, Mr. President," Emily replied firmly. "I work for him, not you." She refused to wake her employer.

When Ken returned the president's call later, he reported that LBJ could scarcely control his pleasure. "Tell that woman I want her here in the White House!"

Ken's instructions to his housekeeper had been clear, and Emily Wilson followed them faithfully. Another might have been tempted to cave in to the demands of the caller, but Emily had her orders and she followed them to the letter. She knew for whom she worked.

When God gave his commandments to the nation of Israel, he was very clear. He stipulated laws and rules of conduct for the well-being and prosperity of his beloved people. Their job was to simply obey.

In the book of Deuteronomy (often referred to as the book of the Law) God reminds the people of what he has done on their behalf. He also reassures them that obedience is not beyond their reach. His standards are not impossibly high or patronizingly low. Instead, God has clearly revealed his will through his Word. He has even written it on their hearts! Their response is to obey.

Do you find yourself offering excuses for breaking God's laws? Are you tempted to regard the Ten Commandments as the "Ten Suggestions"? Do the demands of others drown out the voice of your Creator?

Emily Wilson was able to say "no" to a president because her instructions from her master were clear. Do you listen to the voice of your Master?

Monday

Go to page 254 for your next devotional reading.

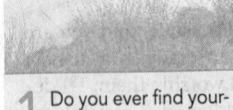

6Be strong and courageous. Do not be afraid
or terrified because of them, for the LORD your
God goes with you; he will never leave you nor
forsake you."
7Then Moses summoned Joshua and said
to him in the presence of all Israel, "Be strong
and courageous, for you must go with this people into the land that the LORD swore to their
forefathers to give them, and you must divide
it among them as their inheritance. 8The LORD
himself goes before you and will be with you;
he will never leave you nor forsake you. Do not
be afraid; do not be discouraged."

The Reading of the Law

9So Moses wrote down this law and gave
it to the priests, the sons of Levi, who carried
the ark of the covenant of the LORD, and to all
the elders of Israel. 10Then Moses commanded
them: "At the end of every seven years, in the
year for canceling debts, during the Feast of
Tabernacles, 11when all Israel comes to appear
before the LORD your God at the place he will
choose, you shall read this law before them in
their hearing. 12Assemble the people—men,
women and children, and the aliens living in
your towns—so they can listen and learn to
fear the LORD your God and follow carefully all
the words of this law. 13Their children, who do
not know this law, must hear it and learn to fear
the LORD your God as long as you live in the
land you are crossing the Jordan to possess."

Israel's Rebellion Predicted

14The LORD said to Moses, "Now the day
of your death is near. Call Joshua and present
yourselves at the Tent of Meeting, where I will
commission him." So Moses and Joshua came
and presented themselves at the Tent of Meeting.
15Then the LORD appeared at the Tent in a
pillar of cloud, and the cloud stood over the
entrance to the Tent. 16And the LORD said to
Moses: "You are going to rest with your fathers,
and these people will soon prostitute themselves
to the foreign gods of the land they are entering.
They will forsake me and break the covenant I
made with them. 17On that day I will become
angry with them and forsake them; I will hide
my face from them, and they will be destroyed.
Many disasters and difficulties will come upon
them, and on that day they will ask, 'Have not
these disasters come upon us because our God
is not with us?' 18And I will certainly hide my
face on that day because of all their wickedness
in turning to other gods.
19"Now write down for yourselves this song
and teach it to the Israelites and have them sing
it, so that it may be a witness for me against
them. 20When I have brought them into the
land flowing with milk and honey, the land
I promised on oath to their forefathers, and
when they eat their fill and thrive, they will turn
to other gods and worship them, rejecting me
and breaking my covenant. 21And when many
disasters and difficulties come upon them, this
song will testify against them, because it will
not be forgotten by their descendants. I know
what they are disposed to do, even before I
bring them into the land I promised them on
oath." 22So Moses wrote down this song that
day and taught it to the Israelites.
23The LORD gave this command to Joshua
son of Nun: "Be strong and courageous, for you
will bring the Israelites into the land I promised
them on oath, and I myself will be with you."
24After Moses finished writing in a book the
words of this law from beginning to end, 25he
gave this command to the Levites who carried
the ark of the covenant of the LORD: 26"Take
this Book of the Law and place it beside the ark
of the covenant of the LORD your God. There
it will remain as a witness against you. 27For I
know how rebellious and stiff-necked you are.
If you have been rebellious against the LORD
while I am still alive and with you, how much
more will you rebel after I die! 28Assemble
before me all the elders of your tribes and all
your officials, so that I can speak these words
in their hearing and call heaven and earth to
testify against them. 29For I know that after my
death you are sure to become utterly corrupt
and to turn from the way I have commanded
you. In days to come, disaster will fall upon
you because you will do evil in the sight of the
LORD and provoke him to anger by what your
hands have made."

The Song of Moses

30And Moses recited the words of this song
from beginning to end in the hearing of the
whole assembly of Israel:

32 Listen, O heavens, and I will speak;
hear, O earth, the words of my mouth.
2 Let my teaching fall like rain
and my words descend like dew,
like showers on new grass,
like abundant rain on tender plants.

3 I will proclaim the name of the LORD.
Oh, praise the greatness of our God!
4 He is the Rock, his works are perfect,
and all his ways are just.
A faithful God who does no wrong,
upright and just is he.
5 They have acted corruptly toward him;
to their shame they are no longer his children,
but a warped and crooked generation.[a]
6 Is this the way you repay the LORD,
O foolish and unwise people?
Is he not your Father, your Creator,[b]
who made you and formed you?

7 Remember the days of old;
consider the generations long past.
Ask your father and he will tell you,
your elders, and they will explain to you.
8 When the Most High gave the nations their inheritance,
when he divided all mankind,
he set up boundaries for the peoples
according to the number of the sons of Israel.[c]
9 For the LORD's portion is his people,
Jacob his allotted inheritance.

10 In a desert land he found him,
in a barren and howling waste.
He shielded him and cared for him;
he guarded him as the apple of his eye,
11 like an eagle that stirs up its nest
and hovers over its young,
that spreads its wings to catch them
and carries them on its pinions.
12 The LORD alone led him;
no foreign god was with him.
13 He made him ride on the heights of the land
and fed him with the fruit of the fields.
He nourished him with honey from the rock,
and with oil from the flinty crag,
14 with curds and milk from herd and flock
and with fattened lambs and goats,
with choice rams of Bashan
and the finest kernels of wheat.
You drank the foaming blood of the grape.
15 Jeshurun[d] grew fat and kicked;
filled with food, he became heavy and sleek.
He abandoned the God who made him
and rejected the Rock his Savior.
16 They made him jealous with their foreign gods
and angered him with their detestable idols.
17 They sacrificed to demons, which are not God—
gods they had not known,
gods that recently appeared,
gods your fathers did not fear.
18 You deserted the Rock, who fathered you;
you forgot the God who gave you birth.

19 The LORD saw this and rejected them
because he was angered by his sons and daughters.
20 "I will hide my face from them," he said,
"and see what their end will be;
for they are a perverse generation,
children who are unfaithful.
21 They made me jealous by what is no god
and angered me with their worthless idols.

Deuteronomy 32:4

God Is Resolute

He is the Rock,
his works are perfect,
and all his ways are just.
A faithful God who
does no wrong,
upright and just is he.

[a]5 Or *Corrupt are they and not his children, / a generation warped and twisted to their shame* [b]6 Or *Father, who bought you*
[c]8 Masoretic Text; Dead Sea Scrolls (see also Septuagint) *sons of God* [d]15 *Jeshurun* means *the upright one,* that is, Israel.

I will make them envious by those who are
not a people;
I will make them angry by a nation that
has no understanding.
22 For a fire has been kindled by my wrath,
one that burns to the realm of death[a]
below.
It will devour the earth and its harvests
and set afire the foundations of the
mountains.

23 "I will heap calamities upon them
and spend my arrows against them.
24 I will send wasting famine against them,
consuming pestilence and deadly
plague;
I will send against them the fangs of wild
beasts,
the venom of vipers that glide in the dust.
25 In the street the sword will make them
childless;
in their homes terror will reign.
Young men and young women will perish,
infants and gray-haired men.
26 I said I would scatter them
and blot out their memory from
mankind,
27 but I dreaded the taunt of the enemy,
lest the adversary misunderstand
and say, 'Our hand has triumphed;
the LORD has not done all this.'"

28 They are a nation without sense,
there is no discernment in them.
29 If only they were wise and would
understand this
and discern what their end will be!
30 How could one man chase a thousand,
or two put ten thousand to flight,
unless their Rock had sold them,
unless the LORD had given them up?
31 For their rock is not like our Rock,
as even our enemies concede.
32 Their vine comes from the vine of Sodom
and from the fields of Gomorrah.
Their grapes are filled with poison,
and their clusters with bitterness.
33 Their wine is the venom of serpents,
the deadly poison of cobras.

34 "Have I not kept this in reserve
and sealed it in my vaults?
35 It is mine to avenge; I will repay.
In due time their foot will slip;
their day of disaster is near
and their doom rushes upon them."

36 The LORD will judge his people
and have compassion on his servants
when he sees their strength is gone
and no one is left, slave or free.
37 He will say: "Now where are their gods,
the rock they took refuge in,
38 the gods who ate the fat of their sacrifices
and drank the wine of their drink
offerings?
Let them rise up to help you!
Let them give you shelter!

39 "See now that I myself am He!
There is no god besides me.
I put to death and I bring to life,
I have wounded and I will heal,
and no one can deliver out of my
hand.
40 I lift my hand to heaven and declare:
As surely as I live forever,
41 when I sharpen my flashing sword
and my hand grasps it in judgment,
I will take vengeance on my adversaries
and repay those who hate me.
42 I will make my arrows drunk with blood,
while my sword devours flesh:
the blood of the slain and the captives,
the heads of the enemy leaders."

43 Rejoice, O nations, with his people,[b,c]
for he will avenge the blood of his
servants;
he will take vengeance on his enemies
and make atonement for his land and
people.

44 Moses came with Joshua[d] son of Nun and
spoke all the words of this song in the hearing
of the people. 45 When Moses finished reciting
all these words to all Israel, 46 he said to them,
"Take to heart all the words I have solemnly
declared to you this day, so that you may command your children to obey carefully all the

[a] 22 Hebrew *to Sheol* [b] 43 Or *Make his people rejoice, O nations* [c] 43 Masoretic Text; Dead Sea Scrolls (see also Septuagint) *people, / and let all the angels worship him /* [d] 44 Hebrew *Hoshea,* a variant of *Joshua*

words of this law. 47They are not just idle words
for you—they are your life. By them you will
live long in the land you are crossing the Jordan
to possess."

Moses to Die on Mount Nebo

48On that same day the LORD told Moses,
49"Go up into the Abarim Range to Mount
Nebo in Moab, across from Jericho, and view
Canaan, the land I am giving the Israelites as
their own possession. 50There on the mountain that you have climbed you will die and be
gathered to your people, just as your brother
Aaron died on Mount Hor and was gathered
to his people. 51This is because both of you
broke faith with me in the presence of the Israelites at the waters of Meribah Kadesh in the
Desert of Zin and because you did not uphold
my holiness among the Israelites. 52Therefore,
you will see the land only from a distance; you
will not enter the land I am giving to the people
of Israel."

Moses Blesses the Tribes

33 This is the blessing that Moses the man of God pronounced on the Israelites before his death. 2He said:

"The LORD came from Sinai
and dawned over them from Seir;
he shone forth from Mount Paran.
He came with[a] myriads of holy ones
from the south, from his mountain slopes.[b]
3 Surely it is you who love the people;
all the holy ones are in your hand.
At your feet they all bow down,
and from you receive instruction,
4 the law that Moses gave us,
the possession of the assembly of Jacob.
5 He was king over Jeshurun[c]
when the leaders of the people assembled,
along with the tribes of Israel.

6 "Let Reuben live and not die,
nor[d] his men be few."

7 And this he said about Judah:

"Hear, O LORD, the cry of Judah;
bring him to his people.
With his own hands he defends his cause.
Oh, be his help against his foes!"

8 About Levi he said:

"Your Thummim and Urim belong
to the man you favored.
You tested him at Massah;
you contended with him at the waters of Meribah.
9 He said of his father and mother,
'I have no regard for them.'
He did not recognize his brothers
or acknowledge his own children,
but he watched over your word
and guarded your covenant.
10 He teaches your precepts to Jacob
and your law to Israel.
He offers incense before you
and whole burnt offerings on your altar.
11 Bless all his skills, O LORD,
and be pleased with the work of his hands.
Smite the loins of those who rise up against him;
strike his foes till they rise no more."

12 About Benjamin he said:

"Let the beloved of the LORD
rest secure in him,
for he shields him all day long,
and the one the LORD
loves rests between his shoulders."

13 About Joseph he said:

"May the LORD bless his land
with the precious dew from heaven above
and with the deep waters that lie below;

> Deuteronomy 33:12
>
> **God Shields Us**
>
> About Benjamin he said:
> "Let the beloved of the
> LORD rest secure in him,
> for he shields him
> all day long,
> and the one the LORD
> loves rests between
> his shoulders."

[a]2 Or *from* [b]2 The meaning of the Hebrew for this phrase is uncertain. [c]5 *Jeshurun* means *the upright one,* that is, Israel; also in verse 26. [d]6 Or *but let*

14 with the best the sun brings forth
and the finest the moon can yield;
15 with the choicest gifts of the ancient mountains
and the fruitfulness of the everlasting hills;
16 with the best gifts of the earth and its fullness
and the favor of him who dwelt in the burning bush.
Let all these rest on the head of Joseph,
on the brow of the prince among[a] his brothers.
17 In majesty he is like a firstborn bull;
his horns are the horns of a wild ox.
With them he will gore the nations,
even those at the ends of the earth.
Such are the ten thousands of Ephraim;
such are the thousands of Manasseh."

18 About Zebulun he said:

"Rejoice, Zebulun, in your going out,
and you, Issachar, in your tents.
19 They will summon peoples to the mountain
and there offer sacrifices of righteousness;
they will feast on the abundance of the seas,
on the treasures hidden in the sand."

20 About Gad he said:

"Blessed is he who enlarges Gad's domain!
Gad lives there like a lion,
tearing at arm or head.
21 He chose the best land for himself;
the leader's portion was kept for him.
When the heads of the people assembled,
he carried out the LORD's righteous will,
and his judgments concerning Israel."

22 About Dan he said:

"Dan is a lion's cub,
springing out of Bashan."

23 About Naphtali he said:

"Naphtali is abounding with the favor of the LORD
and is full of his blessing;
he will inherit southward to the lake."

24 About Asher he said:

"Most blessed of sons is Asher;
let him be favored by his brothers,
and let him bathe his feet in oil.
25 The bolts of your gates will be iron and bronze,
and your strength will equal your days.

26 "There is no one like the God of Jeshurun,
who rides on the heavens to help you
and on the clouds in his majesty.
27 The eternal God is your refuge,
and underneath are the everlasting arms.
He will drive out your enemy before you,
saying, 'Destroy him!'
28 So Israel will live in safety alone;
Jacob's spring is secure
in a land of grain and new wine,
where the heavens drop dew.
29 Blessed are you, O Israel!
Who is like you,
a people saved by the LORD?
He is your shield and helper
and your glorious sword.
Your enemies will cower before you,
and you will trample down their high places.[b]"

The Death of Moses

34 Then Moses climbed Mount Nebo
from the plains of Moab to the top of
Pisgah, across from Jericho. There the LORD
showed him the whole land—from Gilead to
Dan, 2 all of Naphtali, the territory of Ephraim
and Manasseh, all the land of Judah as far as the
western sea,[c] 3 the Negev and the whole region
from the Valley of Jericho, the City of Palms,
as far as Zoar. 4 Then the LORD said to him,
"This is the land I promised on oath to Abraham, Isaac and Jacob when I said, 'I will give it
to your descendants.' I have let you see it with
your eyes, but you will not cross over into it."
5 And Moses the servant of the LORD died
there in Moab, as the LORD had said. 6 He buried him[d] in Moab, in the valley opposite Beth

[a] 16 Or *of the one separated from* [b] 29 Or *will tread upon their bodies* [c] 2 That is, the Mediterranean [d] 6 Or *He was buried*

Legacies

Deuteronomy 34:4–5

Then the LORD said to him, "This is the land I promised on oath to Abraham, Isaac and Jacob when I said, 'I will give it to your descendants.' I have let you see it with your eyes, but you will not cross over into it." And Moses the servant of the LORD died there in Moab, as the LORD had said.

Read: Deuteronomy 34:1–12

ONE FEBRUARY DAY in Ireland in the 1800s, John D'Esterre was killed in a duel, leaving an 18-year-old widow named Jane. With little money and past due bills, the bailiffs came to seize their property and threatened to return to sell her husband's body to the mortuary. Jane took her husband's body and buried it in an unmarked grave. Then she fled to a village on the Scottish-English border.

One day, feeling despondent, Jane sat beside the river and contemplated suicide. Just then, Jane heard whistling. A young ploughman, known as a "hymn-whistler," had begun work in the fields. Jane was touched. She thought of her two small children who needed her. She was healthy and had her whole life before her. If a man plowing fields could whistle, she could keep going. So she returned to Dublin. Shortly afterward, she attended St. George's Church and trusted Jesus Christ as her Savior. God gave her an unusual burden: to pray earnestly for her children and the 12 generations to follow, desiring to leave a spiritual legacy.

Jane later married a wealthy man named Captain John Guinness and continued in prayer. Her son, Grattan, became a minister. His preaching helped trigger the 1859 Irish revival where up to 100,000 people came to Christ in one year. Generations later, Dr. Os Guinness, son of Chinese missionaries, gained worldwide acclaim as Christ's spokesman. Though she didn't live to see all the results of her many prayers, Jane left an incredible legacy.

For 40 years, Moses faithfully served God. He nurtured the promise planted centuries earlier that his people would live in their own land and worship the one true God. Though Moses had a moment of defiance when he struck the rock, he was still allowed to see the promised land. His legacy? He recorded God's laws for posterity; he led God's people to freedom—all the way to the brink of the promised land.

You may not be a Moses leading a nation out of bondage, but, like Jane Guinness, you can leave a spiritual heritage. The most powerful instrument at your disposal is prayer. No matter what your situation in life, no matter what your gifts or talents, you can pray for others. You can leave a beautiful legacy, asking God that those who follow after you will impact the world for Christ.

reflection

1 Put yourself in Moses' shoes. Do you think he was satisfied with his legacy? Why or why not?

2 Who are you responsible for leading at home, work or church?

3 Pray that you will leave a spiritual legacy in your wake—that those who follow after you will tell others about Jesus Christ.

RELATED READINGS

Genesis 12:1–2; Hebrews 10:39—12:2

Go to page 259 for your next devotional reading.

Peor, but to this day no one knows where his
grave is. 7Moses was a hundred and twenty
years old when he died, yet his eyes were not
weak nor his strength gone. 8The Israelites
grieved for Moses in the plains of Moab thirty
days, until the time of weeping and mourning
was over.

9Now Joshua son of Nun was filled with
the spirit[a] of wisdom because Moses had
laid his hands on him. So the Israelites listened to him and did what the LORD had
commanded Moses.

10Since then, no prophet has risen in Israel
like Moses, whom the LORD knew face to face,
11who did all those miraculous signs and wonders the LORD sent him to do in Egypt—to
Pharaoh and to all his officials and to his whole
land. 12For no one has ever shown the mighty
power or performed the awesome deeds that
Moses did in the sight of all Israel.

[a]9 Or *Spirit*

Joshua

Author:
Joshua.

Audience:
The Israelites who settled in the promised land.

Date:
Late 1300s B.C., with additions and edits at later dates, possibly during the early monarchy of Israel.

Setting:
Crossing the Jordan River and entering the promised land, also called Canaan.

Verse to Remember:
"Be strong and courageous, because you will lead these people to inherit the land I swore to their forefathers to give them." (1:6)

After 40 years of wandering, it was time for the children of Israel to conquer the promised land. The book of Joshua begins with several exhortations to their new leader, Joshua, to "be strong and courageous." *God was ready to fight for his people.* In some of the many battles they faced, the people disobeyed God or failed to trust him—with disastrous results. But when they obeyed God, *they experienced grand victories,* and the nations learned to fear them. The book of Joshua covers Israel's history from the crossing of the Jordan River to the successful division of the land by tribes, including cities of refuge and towns for the Levites.

The LORD Commands Joshua

1 After the death of Moses the servant of
the LORD, the LORD said to Joshua son of
Nun, Moses' aide: 2"Moses my servant is dead.
Now then, you and all these people, get ready
to cross the Jordan River into the land I am
about to give to them—to the Israelites. 3I will
give you every place where you set your foot, as
I promised Moses. 4Your territory will extend
from the desert to Lebanon, and from the great
river, the Euphrates—all the Hittite country—
to the Great Sea[a] on the west. 5No one will be
able to stand up against you all the days of your
life. As I was with Moses, so I will be with you;
I will never leave you nor forsake you.
6"Be strong and courageous, because you will
lead these people to inherit the land I swore to
their forefathers to give them. 7Be strong and

[a]4 That is, the Mediterranean

very courageous. Be careful to obey all the law
my servant Moses gave you; do not turn from
it to the right or to the left, that you may be successful wherever you go. [8]Do not let this Book
of the Law depart from your
mouth; meditate on it day and
night, so that you may be careful to do everything written in
it. Then you will be prosperous
and successful. [9]Have I not
commanded you? Be strong
and courageous. Do not be terrified; do not be discouraged,
for the LORD your God will be
with you wherever you go."
[10]So Joshua ordered the
officers of the people: [11]"Go
through the camp and tell
the people, 'Get your supplies
ready. Three days from now
you will cross the Jordan here
to go in and take possession of the land the
LORD your God is giving you for your own.' "
[12]But to the Reubenites, the Gadites and the
half-tribe of Manasseh, Joshua said, [13]"Remember the command that Moses the servant of the
LORD gave you: 'The LORD your God is giving
you rest and has granted you this land.' [14]Your
wives, your children and your livestock may
stay in the land that Moses gave you east of the
Jordan, but all your fighting men, fully armed,
must cross over ahead of your brothers. You are
to help your brothers [15]until the LORD gives
them rest, as he has done for you, and until
they too have taken possession of the land that
the LORD your God is giving them. After that,
you may go back and occupy your own land,
which Moses the servant of the LORD gave you
east of the Jordan toward the sunrise."
[16]Then they answered Joshua, "Whatever
you have commanded us we will do, and
wherever you send us we will go. [17]Just as we
fully obeyed Moses, so we will obey you. Only
may the LORD your God be with you as he was
with Moses. [18]Whoever rebels against your
word and does not obey your words, whatever
you may command them, will be put to death.
Only be strong and courageous!"

> **Joshua 1:9**
>
> *God Is With Us*
>
> "Have I not commanded you? Be strong and courageous. Do not be terrified; do not be discouraged, for the LORD your God will be with you wherever you go."

Rahab and the Spies

2 Then Joshua son of Nun secretly sent
two spies from Shittim. "Go, look over
the land," he said, "especially Jericho." So they
went and entered the house of
a prostitute[a] named Rahab and
stayed there.
[2]The king of Jericho was
told, "Look! Some of the Israelites have come here tonight to
spy out the land." [3]So the king
of Jericho sent this message to
Rahab: "Bring out the men who
came to you and entered your
house, because they have come
to spy out the whole land."
[4]But the woman had taken
the two men and hidden them.
She said, "Yes, the men came to
me, but I did not know where
they had come from. [5]At dusk,
when it was time to close the city gate, the men
left. I don't know which way they went. Go after them quickly. You may catch up with them."
[6](But she had taken them up to the roof and
hidden them under the stalks of flax she had
laid out on the roof.) [7]So the men set out in
pursuit of the spies on the road that leads to the
fords of the Jordan, and as soon as the pursuers
had gone out, the gate was shut.
[8]Before the spies lay down for the night,
she went up on the roof [9]and said to them,
"I know that the LORD has given this land to
you and that a great fear of you has fallen on
us, so that all who live in this country are melting in fear because of you. [10]We have heard
how the LORD dried up the water of the Red
Sea[b] for you when you came out of Egypt, and
what you did to Sihon and Og, the two kings
of the Amorites east of the Jordan, whom you
completely destroyed.[c] [11]When we heard of
it, our hearts melted and everyone's courage
failed because of you, for the LORD your God is
God in heaven above and on the earth below.
[12]Now then, please swear to me by the LORD
that you will show kindness to my family, because I have shown kindness to you. Give me
a sure sign [13]that you will spare the lives of my

[a]1 Or possibly *an innkeeper* [b]10 Hebrew *Yam Suph*; that is, Sea of Reeds [c]10 The Hebrew term refers to the irrevocable giving over of things or persons to the LORD, often by totally destroying them.

father and mother, my brothers and sisters, and
all who belong to them, and that you will save
us from death."
14"Our lives for your lives!" the men assured her. "If you don't tell what we are doing,
we will treat you kindly and
faithfully when the LORD gives
us the land."
15So she let them down by a
rope through the window, for
the house she lived in was part
of the city wall. 16Now she had
said to them, "Go to the hills so
the pursuers will not find you.
Hide yourselves there three
days until they return, and
then go on your way."
17The men said to her, "This
oath you made us swear will
not be binding on us 18unless, when we enter the land, you have tied this scarlet cord in
the window through which you let us down,
and unless you have brought your father and
mother, your brothers and all your family into
your house. 19If anyone goes outside your
house into the street, his blood will be on his
own head; we will not be responsible. As for
anyone who is in the house with you, his blood
will be on our head if a hand is laid on him.
20But if you tell what we are doing, we will be
released from the oath you made us swear."
21"Agreed," she replied. "Let it be as you say."
So she sent them away and they departed. And
she tied the scarlet cord in the window.
22When they left, they went into the hills
and stayed there three days, until the pursuers
had searched all along the road and returned
without finding them. 23Then the two men
started back. They went down out of the hills,
forded the river and came to Joshua son of Nun
and told him everything that had happened to
them. 24They said to Joshua, "The LORD has
surely given the whole land into our hands; all
the people are melting in fear because of us."

Crossing the Jordan

3 Early in the morning Joshua and all the
Israelites set out from Shittim and went
to the Jordan, where they camped before crossing over. 2After three days the officers went
throughout the camp, 3giving orders to the
people: "When you see the ark of the covenant
of the LORD your God, and the priests, who are
Levites, carrying it, you are to move out from
your positions and follow it.
4Then you will know which
way to go, since you have never
been this way before. But keep
a distance of about a thousand
yards[a] between you and the
ark; do not go near it."
5Joshua told the people,
"Consecrate yourselves, for tomorrow the LORD will do amazing things among you."
6Joshua said to the priests,
"Take up the ark of the covenant and pass on ahead of
the people." So they took it up and went ahead
of them.
7And the LORD said to Joshua, "Today I will
begin to exalt you in the eyes of all Israel, so
they may know that I am with you as I was with
Moses. 8Tell the priests who carry the ark of
the covenant: 'When you reach the edge of the
Jordan's waters, go and stand in the river.'"
9Joshua said to the Israelites, "Come here
and listen to the words of the LORD your God.
10This is how you will know that the living God
is among you and that he will certainly drive
out before you the Canaanites, Hittites, Hivites,
Perizzites, Girgashites, Amorites and Jebusites.
11See, the ark of the covenant of the Lord of all
the earth will go into the Jordan ahead of you.
12Now then, choose twelve men from the tribes
of Israel, one from each tribe. 13And as soon as
the priests who carry the ark of the LORD—the
Lord of all the earth—set foot in the Jordan, its
waters flowing downstream will be cut off and
stand up in a heap."
14So when the people broke camp to cross
the Jordan, the priests carrying the ark of the
covenant went ahead of them. 15Now the Jordan is at flood stage all during harvest. Yet as
soon as the priests who carried the ark reached
the Jordan and their feet touched the water's
edge, 16the water from upstream stopped flowing. It piled up in a heap a great distance away,

Joshua 3:5

God Is Amazing

Joshua told the people, "Consecrate yourselves, for tomorrow the LORD will do amazing things among you."

[a]4 Hebrew *about two thousand cubits* (about 900 meters)

Dry Ground

Read: Joshua 3:1–17

I BELIEVE THAT, in guiding us, God deals with us as He dealt with the Israelites as He led them out of Egypt.

The first crossing of the sea was made very easy.

The guidance could not have been simpler: The east wind blew and divided the sea before the people had to cross. Not so much as a foot was wet, except perhaps by a wind-driven spray. Moreover, it was impossible, as it were, to disobey, since they were pursued by Pharaoh's chariots and horsemen (Exodus 14).

But how different it was on the second occasion. The priests had to walk into the strong current of a flooded river and stand still there. What an order to scoff at, and what a sight it would pose to other men! But it was not until they obeyed—without a particle of visible proof that they were doing right—and carried the ark right into the river, that the water rolled back before them (Joshua 3).

So it may be for us, as we go on with God. You and I may be called again and again to walk right into our own "rivers," whatever they may be—to wet our feet in them. We may be called to do what nobody understands except those to whom the word of guidance is given—and with it, His promise too.

But understand this: The word must come first, and also His promise. You and I must be sure of what we are called to do, with an inward conviction that absolutely nothing can shake. In my own case, again and again, I have had to wet my feet in the water . . . Only God and those who have to walk in that path know how hard this kind of faith-life can be. But He does know.

If only the next step is clear, then the one thing to do is take it! Don't pledge your Lord or yourself to any steps beyond what you know. You don't see them yet.

Once when I was climbing at night, in a forest before there was a made path, I learned what was meant by the words of Psalm 119:105: Your word is a lamp to my feet, and a light for my path.

I had only a lantern, and had to hold it very low or I would certainly have slipped on those rough rocks.

We don't walk spiritually by electric light, but by a hand-held lantern. And a lantern shows only the next step—not several steps ahead.

—Amy Carmichael

Joshua 3:17

The priests who carried the ark of the covenant of the LORD stood firm on dry ground in the middle of the Jordan, while all Israel passed by until the whole nation had completed the crossing on dry ground.

reflection

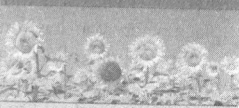

1 Why do you suppose God saw fit to repeat this miracle for a new generation?

2 Why did God direct the Israelites through such a difficult path?

3 When have you sensed God's guidance leading you in a difficult direction?

RELATED READINGS

Exodus 13:17—14:31; Psalm 106:1–12

Go to page 261 for your next devotional reading.

at a town called Adam in the vicinity of Zarethan, while the water flowing down to the Sea
of the Arabah (the Salt Sea[a]) was completely
cut off. So the people crossed over opposite
Jericho. 17The priests who carried the ark of
the covenant of the LORD stood firm on dry
ground in the middle of the Jordan, while all
Israel passed by until the whole nation had
completed the crossing on dry ground.

4 When the whole nation had finished crossing the Jordan, the LORD said to Joshua,
2"Choose twelve men from among the people,
one from each tribe, 3and tell them to take up
twelve stones from the middle of the Jordan
from right where the priests stood and to carry
them over with you and put them down at the
place where you stay tonight."

4So Joshua called together the twelve men
he had appointed from the Israelites, one from
each tribe, 5and said to them, "Go over before
the ark of the LORD your God into the middle
of the Jordan. Each of you is to take up a stone
on his shoulder, according to the number of
the tribes of the Israelites, 6to serve as a sign
among you. In the future, when your children
ask you, 'What do these stones mean?' 7tell
them that the flow of the Jor-
dan was cut off before the ark
of the covenant of the LORD.
When it crossed the Jordan,
the waters of the Jordan were
cut off. These stones are to be
a memorial to the people of
Israel forever."

8So the Israelites did as
Joshua commanded them.
They took twelve stones from
the middle of the Jordan, according to the number of the
tribes of the Israelites, as the
LORD had told Joshua; and
they carried them over with
them to their camp, where they
put them down. 9Joshua set up
the twelve stones that had been[b] in the middle
of the Jordan at the spot where the priests who
carried the ark of the covenant had stood. And
they are there to this day.

10Now the priests who carried the ark remained standing in the middle of the Jordan
until everything the LORD had commanded
Joshua was done by the people, just as Moses
had directed Joshua. The people hurried over,
11and as soon as all of them had crossed, the ark
of the LORD and the priests came to the other
side while the people watched. 12The men of
Reuben, Gad and the half-tribe of Manasseh
crossed over, armed, in front of the Israelites, as
Moses had directed them. 13About forty thousand armed for battle crossed over before the
LORD to the plains of Jericho for war.

14That day the LORD exalted Joshua in the
sight of all Israel; and they revered him all the
days of his life, just as they had revered Moses.

15Then the LORD said to Joshua, 16"Command the priests carrying the ark of the Testimony to come up out of the Jordan."

17So Joshua commanded the priests, "Come
up out of the Jordan."

18And the priests came up out of the river
carrying the ark of the covenant of the LORD.
No sooner had they set their feet on the dry
ground than the waters of the Jordan returned
to their place and ran at flood stage as before.

19On the tenth day of the first month the
people went up from the Jor-
dan and camped at Gilgal
on the eastern border of Jericho. 20And Joshua set up at
Gilgal the twelve stones they
had taken out of the Jordan.
21He said to the Israelites, "In
the future when your descendants ask their fathers, 'What
do these stones mean?' 22tell
them, 'Israel crossed the Jordan on dry ground.' 23For the
LORD your God dried up the
Jordan before you until you
had crossed over. The LORD
your God did to the Jordan
just what he had done to the
Red Sea[c] when he dried it up
before us until we had crossed over. 24He did
this so that all the peoples of the earth might
know that the hand of the LORD is powerful
and so that you might always fear the LORD
your God."

Joshua 4:24

God Is Remarkable

"He did this so that
all the peoples of the
earth might know that
the hand of the LORD is
powerful and so that you
might always fear the
LORD your God."

[a]16 That is, the Dead Sea [b]9 Or *Joshua also set up twelve stones* [c]23 Hebrew *Yam Suph*; that is, Sea of Reeds

Memorial Stones

Read: Joshua 4:1–7

FROM BIRTHSTONES TO GRAVESTONES, diamond rings to marble statues, humankind has used stones from time immemorial to mark significant life passages: births, deaths, engagements, victory in war, monuments to great people. What is it that makes stones such perfect material for the job? They're durable, slow to age, solid and often very beautiful. Stones symbolize a permanence reaching beyond our short human life spans.

God knows that we need tangible reminders of our encounters with him. No matter how life-changing an event may be, our memories cannot always retain the impact. We forget. And we forget to tell our children. A spiritual heritage can be washed away. This is why God instructed Joshua, Israel's leader, to build a memorial of stones when God piled up the waters of the Jordan so that the Israelites could walk across the dry riverbed, just as he had parted the waters of the Red Sea. The memorial was to be a visible reminder that he would lead their children across a sea of obstacles for generations to come.

Consider where God directed Joshua to get the stones from—not the river shallows or banks, but from the middle of the Jordan where the priests stood with the ark of the covenant. It was a picture of the presence of God in the depths, among his people. Once-submerged stones were brought to the riverbank and set up as a memorial.

What are you facing today? Whatever the challenge, do you believe that God can part the deep and flowing waters? Take a moment and ask God to reveal his presence and power. Then find some sort of "stone" (something concrete—a literal rock, a photograph, a note from a friend) to serve as a visual reminder of God's power to intervene in your journey. Build a monument in your yard or in your house or on your desk—and in your heart. Use this monument as a reminder of this moment, both for you and for generations to come. God cares deeply that you remember his goodness and pass those memories on to the next generation.

Go to page 263 for your next devotional reading.

Joshua 4:5–7

"Go over before the ark of the LORD your God into the middle of the Jordan. Each of you is to take up a stone on his shoulder, according to the number of the tribes of the Israelites, to serve as a sign among you. In the future, when your children ask you, 'What do these stones mean?' tell them that the flow of the Jordan was cut off before the ark of the covenant of the LORD."

reflection

1 Recall one instance in which God miraculously cleared the way for you.

2 What memory "stone" can you save to remind you of God's work?

3 Whether or not you are a mother, children probably live in your community or extended family. Choose a child in your life to tell this story to. Who will you share this memory with and how might it glorify God?

RELATED READINGS

Exodus 3:14–15; Psalms 77:11–12; 78:5–8; 145:4–5

Circumcision at Gilgal

5 Now when all the Amorite kings west of
the Jordan and all the Canaanite kings
along the coast heard how the LORD had dried
up the Jordan before the Israelites until we had
crossed over, their hearts melted and they no
longer had the courage to face the Israelites.
2At that time the LORD said to Joshua, "Make
flint knives and circumcise the Israelites again."
3So Joshua made flint knives and circumcised
the Israelites at Gibeath Haaraloth.[a]
4Now this is why he did so: All those who
came out of Egypt—all the men of military
age—died in the desert on the way after leaving Egypt. 5All the people that came out had
been circumcised, but all the people born in
the desert during the journey from Egypt had
not. 6The Israelites had moved about in the
desert forty years until all the men who were
of military age when they left Egypt had died,
since they had not obeyed the LORD. For the
LORD had sworn to them that they would not
see the land that he had solemnly promised
their fathers to give us, a land flowing with
milk and honey. 7So he raised up their sons
in their place, and these were the ones Joshua
circumcised. They were still uncircumcised because they had not been circumcised on the
way. 8And after the whole nation had been circumcised, they remained where they were in
camp until they were healed.
9Then the LORD said to Joshua, "Today I
have rolled away the reproach of Egypt from
you." So the place has been called Gilgal[b] to
this day.
10On the evening of the fourteenth day
of the month, while camped at Gilgal on the
plains of Jericho, the Israelites celebrated the
Passover. 11The day after the Passover, that
very day, they ate some of the produce of the
land: unleavened bread and roasted grain.
12The manna stopped the day after[c] they ate
this food from the land; there was no longer
any manna for the Israelites, but that year they
ate of the produce of Canaan.

The Fall of Jericho

13Now when Joshua was near Jericho, he
looked up and saw a man standing in front of
him with a drawn sword in his hand. Joshua
went up to him and asked, "Are you for us or
for our enemies?"
14"Neither," he replied, "but as commander
of the army of the LORD I have now come."
Then Joshua fell facedown to the ground in reverence, and asked him, "What message does
my Lord[d] have for his servant?"
15The commander of the LORD's army replied, "Take off your sandals, for the place
where you are standing is holy." And Joshua
did so.

6 Now Jericho was tightly shut up because
of the Israelites. No one went out and no
one came in.
2Then the LORD said to Joshua, "See, I have
delivered Jericho into your hands, along with its
king and its fighting men. 3March around the
city once with all the armed men. Do this for
six days. 4Have seven priests carry trumpets of
rams' horns in front of the ark. On the seventh
day, march around the city seven times, with
the priests blowing the trumpets. 5When you
hear them sound a long blast on the trumpets,
have all the people give a loud shout; then the
wall of the city will collapse and the people will
go up, every man straight in."
6So Joshua son of Nun called the priests
and said to them, "Take up the ark of the covenant of the LORD and have seven priests carry
trumpets in front of it." 7And he ordered the
people, "Advance! March around the city, with
the armed guard going ahead of the ark of
the LORD."
8When Joshua had spoken to the people,
the seven priests carrying the seven trumpets
before the LORD went forward, blowing their
trumpets, and the ark of the LORD's covenant
followed them. 9The armed guard marched
ahead of the priests who blew the trumpets, and
the rear guard followed the ark. All this time
the trumpets were sounding. 10But Joshua had
commanded the people, "Do not give a war cry,
do not raise your voices, do not say a word until the day I tell you to shout. Then shout!" 11So
he had the ark of the LORD carried around the
city, circling it once. Then the people returned
to camp and spent the night there.
12Joshua got up early the next morning and

[a] 3 *Gibeath Haaraloth* means *hill of foreskins.* [b] 9 *Gilgal* sounds like the Hebrew for *roll.* [c] 12 Or *the day* [d] 14 Or *lord*

Victory Cry

Read: Joshua 6:1–20

PICTURE YOURSELF at your niece's final soccer game of the season. If they win, they will be in the playoffs. The team has been behind the entire game, and they look exhausted. But just in the last few minutes they've tied the score. Now the seconds are ticking away. The game is almost over. The parents are white-knuckled. The fans are holding their breath. Your niece makes a great move and takes the ball down the field. You're shouting at the top of your lungs, "Go, go!" She makes a an incredible pass across the field. You know this is it . . . just one goal away from victory.

The Israelites had waited 40 years to shout the victory cry. Now they're at the goal. For six days they had followed God's commands and had marched silently around Jericho. Now it was the seventh day. Imagine the suspense . . . the eerie quiet building up for six long days. Would God himself appear to tear down the walls? Would the inhabitants of Jericho surrender without a fight? Would the Israelites make the right play? Then God gave the go-ahead: Sound the trumpets; shout for victory, and the walls of the city will collapse. Just as God promised, "the trumpets sounded, the people shouted," and victory was theirs. The Israelites conquered the city of Jericho, finally claiming their rightful place in the promised land.

The Israelites must have felt so relieved to claim a victory after so many years of waiting and preparing. Can you relate? Have you been feeling that you are in a holding pattern, that your circumstances are not changing? Do you long to have resolution, to have even a small victory? God is working even while you are waiting. Think of this time of waiting as a process that will eventually culminate in a victory. In the meantime, remain faithful and know that God is there with you, preparing you for the battles, goals and victories to come.

Joshua 6:20

When the trumpets sounded, the people shouted, and at the sound of the trumpet, when the people gave a loud shout, the wall collapsed; so every man charged straight in, and they took the city.

reflection

1 Is there an area in your life in which you are waiting for a change? What is God teaching you as you wait?

2 What is your attitude when you are forced into waiting for something? What can you learn from the Israelites' experiences in the desert and then in the promised land?

3 Have you recently experienced a victory in your life? Who can you encourage by sharing your story?

RELATED READINGS

Numbers 14:6–9;
Joshua 2:1–24;
2 Corinthians 4:16–18

Go to page 269 for your next devotional reading.

the priests took up the ark of the LORD. 13The
seven priests carrying the seven trumpets went
forward, marching before the ark of the LORD
and blowing the trumpets. The armed men
went ahead of them and the rear guard followed the ark of the LORD, while the trumpets
kept sounding. 14So on the second day they
marched around the city once and returned to
the camp. They did this for six days.

15On the seventh day, they got up at daybreak and marched around the city seven times
in the same manner, except that on that day
they circled the city seven times. 16The seventh
time around, when the priests sounded the
trumpet blast, Joshua commanded the people,
"Shout! For the LORD has given you the city!
17The city and all that is in it are to be devoted[a]
to the LORD. Only Rahab the prostitute[b] and all
who are with her in her house shall be spared,
because she hid the spies we sent. 18But keep
away from the devoted things, so that you will
not bring about your own destruction by taking any of them. Otherwise you will make the
camp of Israel liable to destruction and bring
trouble on it. 19All the silver and gold and the
articles of bronze and iron are sacred to the
LORD and must go into his treasury."

20When the trumpets sounded, the people shouted, and at the sound of the trumpet,
when the people gave a loud shout, the wall collapsed; so every man charged straight in, and
they took the city. 21They devoted the city to
the LORD and destroyed with the sword every
living thing in it—men and women, young and
old, cattle, sheep and donkeys.

22Joshua said to the two men who had spied
out the land, "Go into the prostitute's house
and bring her out and all who belong to her,
in accordance with your oath to her." 23So the
young men who had done the spying went in
and brought out Rahab, her father and mother
and brothers and all who belonged to her. They
brought out her entire family and put them in a
place outside the camp of Israel.

24Then they burned the whole city and everything in it, but they put the silver and gold
and the articles of bronze and iron into the treasury of the LORD's house. 25But Joshua spared
Rahab the prostitute, with her family and all
who belonged to her, because she hid the men
Joshua had sent as spies to Jericho—and she
lives among the Israelites to this day.

26At that time Joshua pronounced this solemn oath: "Cursed before the LORD is the man
who undertakes to rebuild this city, Jericho:

"At the cost of his firstborn son
    will he lay its foundations;
at the cost of his youngest
    will he set up its gates."

27So the LORD was with Joshua, and his
fame spread throughout the land.

Achan's Sin

7 But the Israelites acted unfaithfully in regard to the devoted things[c]; Achan son of
Carmi, the son of Zimri,[d] the son of Zerah, of
the tribe of Judah, took some of them. So the
LORD's anger burned against Israel.

2Now Joshua sent men from Jericho to Ai,
which is near Beth Aven to the east of Bethel,
and told them, "Go up and spy out the region."
So the men went up and spied out Ai.

3When they returned to Joshua, they said,
"Not all the people will have to go up against
Ai. Send two or three thousand men to take it
and do not weary all the people, for only a few
men are there." 4So about three thousand men
went up; but they were routed by the men of
Ai, 5who killed about thirty-six of them. They
chased the Israelites from the city gate as far
as the stone quarries[e] and struck them down
on the slopes. At this the hearts of the people
melted and became like water.

6Then Joshua tore his clothes and fell facedown to the ground before the ark of the LORD,
remaining there till evening. The elders of
Israel did the same, and sprinkled dust on their
heads. 7And Joshua said, "Ah, Sovereign LORD,
why did you ever bring this people across the
Jordan to deliver us into the hands of the Amorites to destroy us? If only we had been content to stay on the other side of the Jordan!
8O Lord, what can I say, now that Israel has

[a]17 The Hebrew term refers to the irrevocable giving over of things or persons to the LORD, often by totally destroying them; also in verses 18 and 21. [b]17 Or possibly *innkeeper*; also in verses 22 and 25 [c]1 The Hebrew term refers to the irrevocable giving over of things or persons to the LORD, often by totally destroying them; also in verses 11, 12, 13 and 15. [d]1 See Septuagint and 1 Chron. 2:6; Hebrew *Zabdi*; also in verses 17 and 18. [e]5 Or *as far as Shebarim*

been routed by its enemies? 9The Canaanites
and the other people of the country will hear
about this and they will surround us and wipe
out our name from the earth.
What then will you do for your
own great name?"
10The LORD said to Joshua,
"Stand up! What are you doing
down on your face? 11Israel has
sinned; they have violated my
covenant, which I commanded
them to keep. They have taken
some of the devoted things;
they have stolen, they have
lied, they have put them with
their own possessions. 12That
is why the Israelites cannot
stand against their enemies;
they turn their backs and run
because they have been made liable to destruction. I will not be with you anymore unless you
destroy whatever among you is devoted to destruction.
13"Go, consecrate the people. Tell them,
'Consecrate yourselves in preparation for tomorrow; for this is what the LORD, the God
of Israel, says: That which is devoted is among
you, O Israel. You cannot stand against your enemies until you remove it.
14" 'In the morning, present yourselves
tribe by tribe. The tribe that the LORD takes
shall come forward clan by clan; the clan that
the LORD takes shall come forward family by
family; and the family that the LORD takes
shall come forward man by man. 15He who
is caught with the devoted things shall be destroyed by fire, along with all that belongs to
him. He has violated the covenant of the LORD
and has done a disgraceful thing in Israel!' "
16Early the next morning Joshua had Israel
come forward by tribes, and Judah was taken.
17The clans of Judah came forward, and he
took the Zerahites. He had the clan of the Zerahites come forward by families, and Zimri was
taken. 18Joshua had his family come forward
man by man, and Achan son of Carmi, the son
of Zimri, the son of Zerah, of the tribe of Judah,
was taken.
19Then Joshua said to Achan, "My son, give
glory to the LORD,[a] the God of Israel, and give
him the praise.[b] Tell me what you have done;
do not hide it from me."
20Achan replied, "It is true! I
have sinned against the LORD,
the God of Israel. This is what
I have done: 21When I saw in
the plunder a beautiful robe
from Babylonia,[c] two hundred
shekels[d] of silver and a wedge
of gold weighing fifty shekels,[e]
I coveted them and took them.
They are hidden in the ground
inside my tent, with the silver underneath."
22So Joshua sent messengers, and they ran to the tent,
and there it was, hidden in his
tent, with the silver underneath. 23They took
the things from the tent, brought them to
Joshua and all the Israelites and spread them
out before the LORD.
24Then Joshua, together with all Israel, took
Achan son of Zerah, the silver, the robe, the
gold wedge, his sons and daughters, his cattle,
donkeys and sheep, his tent and all that he had,
to the Valley of Achor. 25Joshua said, "Why
have you brought this trouble on us? The LORD
will bring trouble on you today."
Then all Israel stoned him, and after they
had stoned the rest, they burned them. 26Over
Achan they heaped up a large pile of rocks,
which remains to this day. Then the LORD
turned from his fierce anger. Therefore that
place has been called the Valley of Achor[f]
ever since.

Ai Destroyed

8 Then the LORD said to Joshua, "Do not be
afraid; do not be discouraged. Take the
whole army with you, and go up and attack Ai.
For I have delivered into your hands the king
of Ai, his people, his city and his land. 2You
shall do to Ai and its king as you did to Jericho
and its king, except that you may carry off their
plunder and livestock for yourselves. Set an ambush behind the city."

Joshua 7:7

God Is Sovereign

And Joshua said, "Ah, Sovereign LORD, why did you ever bring this people across the Jordan to deliver us into the hands of the Amorites to destroy us?"

[a]19 A solemn charge to tell the truth [b]19 Or *and confess to him* [c]21 Hebrew *Shinar* [d]21 That is, about 5 pounds (about 2.3 kilograms) [e]21 That is, about 1 1/4 pounds (about 0.6 kilogram) [f]26 *Achor* means *trouble.*

3So Joshua and the whole army moved out
to attack Ai. He chose thirty thousand of his
best fighting men and sent them out at night
4with these orders: "Listen carefully. You are to
set an ambush behind the city. Don't go very
far from it. All of you be on
the alert. 5I and all those with
me will advance on the city,
and when the men come out
against us, as they did before,
we will flee from them. 6They
will pursue us until we have
lured them away from the city,
for they will say, 'They are running away from us as they did
before.' So when we flee from
them, 7you are to rise up from
ambush and take the city. The
LORD your God will give it into
your hand. 8When you have
taken the city, set it on fire. Do
what the LORD has commanded. See to it; you
have my orders."
9Then Joshua sent them off, and they went
to the place of ambush and lay in wait between
Bethel and Ai, to the west of Ai—but Joshua
spent that night with the people.
10Early the next morning Joshua mustered
his men, and he and the leaders of Israel
marched before them to Ai. 11The entire force
that was with him marched up and approached
the city and arrived in front of it. They set up
camp north of Ai, with the valley between them
and the city. 12Joshua had taken about five thousand men and set them in ambush between
Bethel and Ai, to the west of the city. 13They
had the soldiers take up their positions—all
those in the camp to the north of the city and
the ambush to the west of it. That night Joshua
went into the valley.
14When the king of Ai saw this, he and all
the men of the city hurried out early in the
morning to meet Israel in battle at a certain
place overlooking the Arabah. But he did not
know that an ambush had been set against
him behind the city. 15Joshua and all Israel let
themselves be driven back before them, and
they fled toward the desert. 16All the men of
Ai were called to pursue them, and they pursued Joshua and were lured away from the city.
17Not a man remained in Ai or Bethel who did
not go after Israel. They left the city open and
went in pursuit of Israel.
18Then the LORD said to Joshua, "Hold out
toward Ai the javelin that is in
your hand, for into your hand I
will deliver the city." So Joshua
held out his javelin toward
Ai. 19As soon as he did this,
the men in the ambush rose
quickly from their position
and rushed forward. They entered the city and captured it
and quickly set it on fire.
20The men of Ai looked
back and saw the smoke of the
city rising against the sky, but
they had no chance to escape
in any direction, for the Israelites who had been fleeing to-
ward the desert had turned back against their
pursuers. 21For when Joshua and all Israel saw
that the ambush had taken the city and that
smoke was going up from the city, they turned
around and attacked the men of Ai. 22The men
of the ambush also came out of the city against
them, so that they were caught in the middle,
with Israelites on both sides. Israel cut them
down, leaving them neither survivors nor fugitives. 23But they took the king of Ai alive and
brought him to Joshua.
24When Israel had finished killing all the
men of Ai in the fields and in the desert where
they had chased them, and when every one of
them had been put to the sword, all the Israelites returned to Ai and killed those who were
in it. 25Twelve thousand men and women fell
that day—all the people of Ai. 26For Joshua did
not draw back the hand that held out his javelin until he had destroyed[a] all who lived in Ai.
27But Israel did carry off for themselves the livestock and plunder of this city, as the LORD had
instructed Joshua.
28So Joshua burned Ai and made it a permanent heap of ruins, a desolate place to this day.
29He hung the king of Ai on a tree and left him
there until evening. At sunset, Joshua ordered
them to take his body from the tree and throw

Joshua 8:18

God Is a Deliverer

Then the LORD said to Joshua, "Hold out toward Ai the javelin that is in your hand, for into your hand I will deliver the city." So Joshua held out his javelin toward Ai.

[a]26 The Hebrew term refers to the irrevocable giving over of things or persons to the LORD, often by totally destroying them.

it down at the entrance of the city gate. And
they raised a large pile of rocks over it, which
remains to this day.

The Covenant Renewed at Mount Ebal

30Then Joshua built on Mount Ebal an altar
to the LORD, the God of Israel, 31as Moses the
servant of the LORD had commanded the Israelites. He built it according to what is written in
the Book of the Law of Moses—an altar of uncut stones, on which no iron tool had been used.
On it they offered to the LORD burnt offerings
and sacrificed fellowship offerings.[a] 32There,
in the presence of the Israelites, Joshua copied
on stones the law of Moses, which he had written. 33All Israel, aliens and citizens alike, with
their elders, officials and judges, were standing
on both sides of the ark of the covenant of the
LORD, facing those who carried it—the priests,
who were Levites. Half of the people stood in
front of Mount Gerizim and half of them in
front of Mount Ebal, as Moses the servant of
the LORD had formerly commanded when he
gave instructions to bless the people of Israel.
34Afterward, Joshua read all the words of the
law—the blessings and the curses—just as it is
written in the Book of the Law. 35There was not
a word of all that Moses had commanded that
Joshua did not read to the whole assembly of
Israel, including the women and children, and
the aliens who lived among them.

The Gibeonite Deception

9 Now when all the kings west of the Jordan
heard about these things—those in the hill
country, in the western foothills, and along the
entire coast of the Great Sea[b] as far as Lebanon
(the kings of the Hittites, Amorites, Canaanites, Perizzites, Hivites and Jebusites)— 2they
came together to make war against Joshua and
Israel.

3However, when the people of Gibeon heard
what Joshua had done to Jericho and Ai, 4they
resorted to a ruse: They went as a delegation
whose donkeys were loaded[c] with worn-out
sacks and old wineskins, cracked and mended.
5The men put worn and patched sandals on
their feet and wore old clothes. All the bread
of their food supply was dry and moldy. 6Then
they went to Joshua in the camp at Gilgal and
said to him and the men of Israel, "We have
come from a distant country; make a treaty
with us."

7The men of Israel said to the Hivites, "But
perhaps you live near us. How then can we
make a treaty with you?"

8"We are your servants," they said to
Joshua.

But Joshua asked, "Who are you and where
do you come from?"

9They answered: "Your servants have come
from a very distant country because of the
fame of the LORD your God. For we have heard
reports of him: all that he did in Egypt, 10and
all that he did to the two kings of the Amorites
east of the Jordan—Sihon king of Heshbon,
and Og king of Bashan, who reigned in Ashtaroth. 11And our elders and all those living
in our country said to us, 'Take provisions
for your journey; go and meet them and say
to them, "We are your servants; make a treaty
with us."' 12This bread of ours was warm when
we packed it at home on the day we left to come
to you. But now see how dry and moldy it is.
13And these wineskins that we filled were new,
but see how cracked they are. And our clothes
and sandals are worn out by the very long
journey."

14The men of Israel sampled their provisions
but did not inquire of the LORD. 15Then Joshua
made a treaty of peace with them to let them
live, and the leaders of the assembly ratified it
by oath.

16Three days after they made the treaty with
the Gibeonites, the Israelites heard that they
were neighbors, living near them. 17So the Israelites set out and on the third day came to
their cities: Gibeon, Kephirah, Beeroth and Kiriath Jearim. 18But the Israelites did not attack
them, because the leaders of the assembly had
sworn an oath to them by the LORD, the God
of Israel.

The whole assembly grumbled against the
leaders, 19but all the leaders answered, "We
have given them our oath by the LORD, the God
of Israel, and we cannot touch them now. 20This
is what we will do to them: We will let them

[a]31 Traditionally *peace offerings* [b]1 That is, the Mediterranean [c]4 Most Hebrew manuscripts; some Hebrew manuscripts, Vulgate and Syriac (see also Septuagint) *They prepared provisions and loaded their donkeys*

live, so that wrath will not fall on us for breaking
the oath we swore to them." 21 They continued,
"Let them live, but let them be woodcutters and
water carriers for the entire community." So the
leaders' promise to them was kept.
22 Then Joshua summoned the Gibeonites
and said, "Why did you deceive us by saying,
'We live a long way from you,' while actually
you live near us? 23 You are now under a curse:
You will never cease to serve as woodcutters
and water carriers for the house of my God."
24 They answered Joshua, "Your servants
were clearly told how the LORD your God had
commanded his servant Moses to give you the
whole land and to wipe out all its inhabitants
from before you. So we feared for our lives because of you, and that is why we did this. 25 We
are now in your hands. Do to us whatever
seems good and right to you."
26 So Joshua saved them from the Israelites,
and they did not kill them. 27 That day he made
the Gibeonites woodcutters and water carriers for the community and for the altar of the
LORD at the place the LORD would choose. And
that is what they are to this day.

The Sun Stands Still

10 Now Adoni-Zedek king of Jerusalem
heard that Joshua had taken Ai and
totally destroyed[a] it, doing to Ai and its king as
he had done to Jericho and its
king, and that the people of
Gibeon had made a treaty of
peace with Israel and were living near them. 2 He and his people were very much alarmed
at this, because Gibeon was an
important city, like one of the
royal cities; it was larger than
Ai, and all its men were good
fighters. 3 So Adoni-Zedek king
of Jerusalem appealed to Ho-
ham king of Hebron, Piram
king of Jarmuth, Japhia king of
Lachish and Debir king of Eg-
lon. 4 "Come up and help me attack Gibeon," he
said, "because it has made peace with Joshua
and the Israelites."

> Joshua 10:14
>
> *God Fights for Us*
>
> There has never been a day like it before or since, a day when the LORD listened to a man. Surely the LORD was fighting for Israel!

5 Then the five kings of the Amorites—the
kings of Jerusalem, Hebron, Jarmuth, Lachish
and Eglon—joined forces. They moved up with
all their troops and took up positions against
Gibeon and attacked it.
6 The Gibeonites then sent word to Joshua in
the camp at Gilgal: "Do not abandon your servants. Come up to us quickly and save us! Help
us, because all the Amorite kings from the hill
country have joined forces against us."
7 So Joshua marched up from Gilgal with his
entire army, including all the best fighting men.
8 The LORD said to Joshua, "Do not be afraid of
them; I have given them into your hand. Not
one of them will be able to withstand you."
9 After an all-night march from Gilgal,
Joshua took them by surprise. 10 The LORD
threw them into confusion before Israel, who
defeated them in a great victory at Gibeon.
Israel pursued them along the road going up
to Beth Horon and cut them down all the way
to Azekah and Makkedah. 11 As they fled before Israel on the road down from Beth Horon
to Azekah, the LORD hurled large hailstones
down on them from the sky, and more of them
died from the hailstones than were killed by the
swords of the Israelites.
12 On the day the LORD gave the Amorites
over to Israel, Joshua said to the LORD in the
presence of Israel:

"O sun, stand still over
Gibeon,
O moon, over the Valley
of Aijalon."
13 So the sun stood still,
and the moon stopped,
till the nation avenged
itself on[b] its
enemies,

as it is written in the Book of Jashar.
The sun stopped in the middle of the sky and delayed going
down about a full day. 14 There
has never been a day like it before or since, a
day when the LORD listened to a man. Surely
the LORD was fighting for Israel!

[a] 1 The Hebrew term refers to the irrevocable giving over of things or persons to the LORD, often by totally destroying them; also in verses 28, 35, 37, 39 and 40. [b] 13 Or *nation triumphed over*

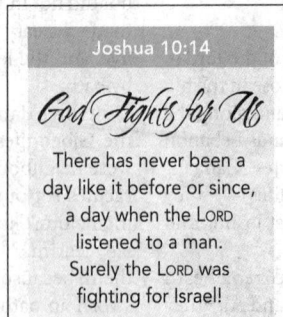

It's Time

SHIPHRAH AND PUAH

"COME QUICKLY! It's almost time."

Gathering the folds of her long robe in her well-worn hands, Shiphrah hurried through the door. Her eyes narrowed and adjusted to the relative darkness inside the home. Light from a small oil lantern cast the shadow of two women on the wall. One squatted in a corner, knees bent, as another woman hunched beside her.

"A fresh cloth, Shiphrah!" one of the shadows barked. "I can see the head."

Puah always was the bossier of the two women. They were midwives by training and friends by choice. Shiphrah obediently brought the strips of cloth to Puah.

It was an ordinary day. Women birthed babies into the world all the time. But today was different. This baby was different; it was a boy. The king of Egypt made his order clear: If it is a girl, let her live. If it is a boy, kill him. The strength of the Hebrews threatened Pharaoh and intimidated him. He would quell their numbers with his murderous plot and keep their supposed rebellion at bay. But if the women obeyed him, what would that make them? Murderers?

Shiphrah and Puah did not discuss Pharaoh's orders openly. Silently they worked alongside each other, except for the routine bedside manner required at each birth. However, every time, when it became clear they would have to make a decision, their minds raced through their options.

To disobey the highest authority meant certain death. Pharaoh was willing to slaughter innocent children; two midwives were nothing to him. If they did their job, someone would die, but they would live another day. The dilemma tugged at their hearts each time they pondered their duties. The God of the Hebrews had made himself real to them in ways they could not explain. They feared Pharaoh, but they revered God.

Just then, an agonized scream, followed by a loud sigh, snapped both women to attention. It was time.

"Push! Push!" they responded in unison.

—Prayer—

My awesome God, I serve you alone, not the world. Help me to be strong against outside influences and keep me focused on your commands.

The midwives, however, feared God and did not do what the king of Egypt had told them to do; they let the boys live.

Exodus 1:17

ASSIGNED READING:

Exodus 1:15–21

Weekend

Go to page 273 for your next devotional reading.

15Then Joshua returned with all Israel to the
camp at Gilgal.

Five Amorite Kings Killed

16Now the five kings had fled and hidden in
the cave at Makkedah. 17When Joshua was told
that the five kings had been found hiding in the
cave at Makkedah, 18he said, "Roll large rocks
up to the mouth of the cave, and post some
men there to guard it. 19But don't stop! Pursue
your enemies, attack them from the rear and
don't let them reach their cities, for the LORD
your God has given them into your hand."

20So Joshua and the Israelites destroyed
them completely—almost to a man—but the
few who were left reached their fortified cities. 21The whole army then returned safely to
Joshua in the camp at Makkedah, and no one
uttered a word against the Israelites.

22Joshua said, "Open the mouth of the cave
and bring those five kings out to me." 23So they
brought the five kings out of the cave—the
kings of Jerusalem, Hebron, Jarmuth, Lachish
and Eglon. 24When they had brought these
kings to Joshua, he summoned all the men of
Israel and said to the army commanders who
had come with him, "Come here and put your
feet on the necks of these kings." So they came
forward and placed their feet on their necks.

25Joshua said to them, "Do not be afraid; do
not be discouraged. Be strong and courageous.
This is what the LORD will do to all the enemies
you are going to fight." 26Then Joshua struck
and killed the kings and hung them on five
trees, and they were left hanging on the trees
until evening.

27At sunset Joshua gave the order and they
took them down from the trees and threw
them into the cave where they had been hiding. At the mouth of the cave they placed large
rocks, which are there to this day.

28That day Joshua took Makkedah. He put
the city and its king to the sword and totally
destroyed everyone in it. He left no survivors.
And he did to the king of Makkedah as he had
done to the king of Jericho.

Southern Cities Conquered

29Then Joshua and all Israel with him moved
on from Makkedah to Libnah and attacked it.
30The LORD also gave that city and its king
into Israel's hand. The city and everyone in it
Joshua put to the sword. He left no survivors
there. And he did to its king as he had done to
the king of Jericho.

31Then Joshua and all Israel with him
moved on from Libnah to Lachish; he took up
positions against it and attacked it. 32The LORD
handed Lachish over to Israel, and Joshua took
it on the second day. The city and everyone
in it he put to the sword, just as he had done
to Libnah. 33Meanwhile, Horam king of Gezer had come up to help Lachish, but Joshua
defeated him and his army—until no survivors
were left.

34Then Joshua and all Israel with him moved
on from Lachish to Eglon; they took up positions against it and attacked it. 35They captured
it that same day and put it to the sword and
totally destroyed everyone in it, just as they had
done to Lachish.

36Then Joshua and all Israel with him went
up from Eglon to Hebron and attacked it.
37They took the city and put it to the sword,
together with its king, its villages and everyone
in it. They left no survivors. Just as at Eglon,
they totally destroyed it and everyone in it.

38Then Joshua and all Israel with him
turned around and attacked Debir. 39They
took the city, its king and its villages, and put
them to the sword. Everyone in it they totally
destroyed. They left no survivors. They did to
Debir and its king as they had done to Libnah
and its king and to Hebron.

40So Joshua subdued the whole region, including the hill country, the Negev, the western foothills and the mountain slopes, together
with all their kings. He left no survivors. He
totally destroyed all who breathed, just as the
LORD, the God of Israel, had commanded.
41Joshua subdued them from Kadesh Barnea
to Gaza and from the whole region of Goshen
to Gibeon. 42All these kings and their lands
Joshua conquered in one campaign, because
the LORD, the God of Israel, fought for Israel.

43Then Joshua returned with all Israel to the
camp at Gilgal.

Northern Kings Defeated

11 When Jabin king of Hazor heard of
this, he sent word to Jobab king of
Madon, to the kings of Shimron and Acshaph,

2and to the northern kings who were in the
mountains, in the Arabah south of Kinnereth,
in the western foothills and in Naphoth Dor[a]
on the west; 3to the Canaanites in the east and
west; to the Amorites, Hittites, Perizzites and
Jebusites in the hill country; and to the Hivites
below Hermon in the region of Mizpah. 4They
came out with all their troops and a large number of horses and chariots—a huge army, as numerous as the sand on the seashore. 5All these
kings joined forces and made camp together at
the Waters of Merom, to fight against Israel.

6The LORD said to Joshua, "Do not be
afraid of them, because by this time tomorrow I will hand all of them over to Israel, slain.
You are to hamstring their horses and burn
their chariots."

7So Joshua and his whole army came against
them suddenly at the Waters of Merom and attacked them, 8and the LORD gave them into
the hand of Israel. They defeated them and pursued them all the way to Greater Sidon, to Misrephoth Maim, and to the Valley of Mizpah on
the east, until no survivors were left. 9Joshua
did to them as the LORD had directed: He hamstrung their horses and burned their chariots.

10At that time Joshua turned back and captured Hazor and put its king to the sword. (Hazor had been the head of all these kingdoms.)
11Everyone in it they put to the sword. They
totally destroyed[b] them, not sparing anything
that breathed, and he burned up Hazor itself.

12Joshua took all these royal cities and their
kings and put them to the sword. He totally destroyed them, as Moses the servant of the LORD
had commanded. 13Yet Israel did not burn any
of the cities built on their mounds—except
Hazor, which Joshua burned. 14The Israelites
carried off for themselves all the plunder and
livestock of these cities, but all the people
they put to the sword until they completely destroyed them, not sparing anyone that breathed.
15As the LORD commanded his servant Moses,
so Moses commanded Joshua, and Joshua did
it; he left nothing undone of all that the LORD
commanded Moses.

16So Joshua took this entire land: the hill
country, all the Negev, the whole region of Goshen, the western foothills, the Arabah and the
mountains of Israel with their foothills, 17from
Mount Halak, which rises toward Seir, to Baal
Gad in the Valley of Lebanon below Mount
Hermon. He captured all their kings and struck
them down, putting them to death. 18Joshua
waged war against all these kings for a long
time. 19Except for the Hivites living in Gibeon,
not one city made a treaty of peace with the Israelites, who took them all in battle. 20For it was
the LORD himself who hardened their hearts
to wage war against Israel, so that he might destroy them totally, exterminating them without
mercy, as the LORD had commanded Moses.

21At that time Joshua went and destroyed
the Anakites from the hill country: from Hebron, Debir and Anab, from all the hill country
of Judah, and from all the hill country of Israel.
Joshua totally destroyed them and their towns.
22No Anakites were left in Israelite territory;
only in Gaza, Gath and Ashdod did any survive. 23So Joshua took the entire land, just as
the LORD had directed Moses, and he gave it
as an inheritance to Israel according to their
tribal divisions.

Then the land had rest from war.

List of Defeated Kings

12 These are the kings of the land whom
the Israelites had defeated and whose
territory they took over east of the Jordan, from
the Arnon Gorge to Mount Hermon, including
all the eastern side of the Arabah:

2Sihon king of the Amorites,
who reigned in Heshbon. He ruled from
Aroer on the rim of the Arnon Gorge—
from the middle of the gorge—to the
Jabbok River, which is the border of the
Ammonites. This included half of Gilead.
3He also ruled over the eastern Arabah
from the Sea of Kinnereth[c] to the Sea of
the Arabah (the Salt Sea[d]), to Beth Jeshimoth, and then southward below the
slopes of Pisgah.

4And the territory of Og king of Bashan,
one of the last of the Rephaites, who
reigned in Ashtaroth and Edrei. 5He
ruled over Mount Hermon, Salecah, all

[a]2 Or *in the heights of Dor* [b]11 The Hebrew term refers to the irrevocable giving over of things or persons to the LORD, often by totally destroying them; also in verses 12, 20 and 21. [c]3 That is, Galilee [d]3 That is, the Dead Sea

of Bashan to the border of the people of
Geshur and Maacah, and half of Gilead to
the border of Sihon king of Heshbon.

6 Moses, the servant of the LORD, and the Israelites conquered them. And Moses the servant
of the LORD gave their land to the Reubenites,
the Gadites and the half-tribe of Manasseh to
be their possession.

7 These are the kings of the land that Joshua
and the Israelites conquered on the west side
of the Jordan, from Baal Gad in the Valley of
Lebanon to Mount Halak, which rises toward
Seir (their lands Joshua gave as an inheritance
to the tribes of Israel according to their tribal
divisions— 8 the hill country, the western foothills, the Arabah, the mountain slopes, the
desert and the Negev—the lands of the Hittites, Amorites, Canaanites, Perizzites, Hivites
and Jebusites):

9 the king of Jericho	one
the king of Ai (near Bethel)	one
10 the king of Jerusalem	one
the king of Hebron	one
11 the king of Jarmuth	one
the king of Lachish	one
12 the king of Eglon	one
the king of Gezer	one
13 the king of Debir	one
the king of Geder	one
14 the king of Hormah	one
the king of Arad	one
15 the king of Libnah	one
the king of Adullam	one
16 the king of Makkedah	one
the king of Bethel	one
17 the king of Tappuah	one
the king of Hepher	one
18 the king of Aphek	one
the king of Lasharon	one
19 the king of Madon	one
the king of Hazor	one
20 the king of Shimron Meron	one
the king of Acshaph	one
21 the king of Taanach	one
the king of Megiddo	one
22 the king of Kedesh	one
the king of Jokneam in Carmel	one
23 the king of Dor (in Naphoth Dor[a])	one
the king of Goyim in Gilgal	one
24 the king of Tirzah	one

thirty-one kings in all.

Land Still to Be Taken

13 When Joshua was old and well advanced in years, the LORD said to him,
"You are very old, and there are still very large
areas of land to be taken over.

2 "This is the land that remains: all the regions of the Philistines and Geshurites:
3 from the Shihor River on the east of Egypt
to the territory of Ekron on the north, all
of it counted as Canaanite (the territory of
the five Philistine rulers in Gaza, Ashdod,
Ashkelon, Gath and Ekron—that of the
Avvites); 4 from the south, all the land of
the Canaanites, from Arah of the Sidonians as far as Aphek, the region of the Amorites, 5 the area of the Gebalites[b]; and all
Lebanon to the east, from Baal Gad below
Mount Hermon to Lebo[c] Hamath.

6 "As for all the inhabitants of the mountain
regions from Lebanon to Misrephoth Maim,
that is, all the Sidonians, I myself will drive
them out before the Israelites. Be sure to allo-
cate this land to Israel for an inheritance, as I
have instructed you, 7 and divide it as an inheritance among the nine tribes and half of the
tribe of Manasseh."

Division of the Land East of the Jordan

8 The other half of Manasseh,[d] the Reubenites
and the Gadites had received the inheritance
that Moses had given them east of the Jordan,
as he, the servant of the LORD, had assigned it
to them.

9 It extended from Aroer on the rim of
the Arnon Gorge, and from the town in
the middle of the gorge, and included the
whole plateau of Medeba as far as Dibon,
10 and all the towns of Sihon king of the
Amorites, who ruled in Heshbon, out to
the border of the Ammonites. 11 It also
included Gilead, the territory of the people of Geshur and Maacah, all of Mount

[a] 23 Or *in the heights of Dor* [b] 5 That is, the area of Byblos [c] 5 Or *to the entrance to* [d] 8 Hebrew *With it* (that is, with the other half of Manasseh)

Never Too Old

Read: Joshua 13:1–7

IN THE EARLY 1900s, a desperate father prayed for his sick daughter: "God, spare her life and I'll serve you with mine." Miraculously, the girl recovered. The grateful father quit his job, packed his large family (along with a cow and some chickens) and moved to Texas for seminary. In his mid-30s, he became an evangelist who held tent revivals in Texas and Oklahoma.

For many years, the pastor faithfully preached the gospel. Even after reaching the century mark, he'd rise every day and don a three-piece suit. Despite shaky legs and cataract-clouded eyes, he'd wait for his son-in-law, married to the daughter who had nearly died so many years ago, to guide him downtown for coffee. A newcomer asked, "Why do you get so dressed up?" The aged pastor replied, "I never know when I'll lead someone to the Lord. By the way, son, do you know Jesus?" Reverend A. F. Whitlock understood a simple truth: You're never too old to serve God.

As a young man, Joshua was sent to spy out the promised land. Only he and Caleb believed the Israelites could conquer the enemies living there. So the people wandered 40 years until the exodus generation perished—save the two spies. Then, succeeding Moses, Joshua led Israel into the promised land. Though he was about 80, Joshua captained Israel to victory over six nations and 31 kings.

Fast-forward 20 years. Joshua 13:1 somewhat understates, "Joshua was old and well advanced in years." It is estimated he was around 100 years old. Joshua might have expected God to send him on vacation: go float atop the Dead Sea or fish in the Lake of Galilee. But God didn't offer Joshua a retirement plan. Instead he said, "There are still very large areas of land to be taken over." Joshua's next task was to divide the land.

Maybe you think you're too old to keep serving God. You've offered your tithes, taught Sunday school, led women's ministry and sung in the choir. What's left? There are always "lands" left to conquer. There are children to tell stories to, younger women who would love to hear about your history, sick people to visit, prayers to pray, people who have yet to hear the Good News. You're never too old to tell others about God's love.

Go to page 285 for your next devotional reading.

Joshua 13:1

When Joshua was old and well advanced in years, the LORD said to him, "You are very old, and there are still very large areas of land to be taken over."

reflection

1 How has your age affected your ability to serve God (perhaps people don't take you seriously because you're younger or overlook you due to advanced age)?

2 What areas has God placed before you to "conquer" (neighborhood, work, family, etc.)?

3 Explain how Joshua's story encourages you to continue serving God regardless of your age—young or old.

RELATED READINGS

Numbers 13:16—14:10; Psalm 71:18; Proverbs 16:31; 20:29; Isaiah 46:3–4

"I've discovered, to my delight, that spiritual gifts don't age."

Jill Briscoe

Hermon and all Bashan as far as Salecah— 12that is, the whole kingdom of Og
in Bashan, who had reigned in Ashtaroth
and Edrei and had survived as one of the
last of the Rephaites. Moses had defeated
them and taken over their land. 13But the
Israelites did not drive out the people of
Geshur and Maacah, so they continue to
live among the Israelites to this day.

14But to the tribe of Levi he gave no inheritance, since the offerings made by fire to the
LORD, the God of Israel, are their inheritance,
as he promised them.

15This is what Moses had given to the tribe of
Reuben, clan by clan:

16The territory from Aroer on the rim of
the Arnon Gorge, and from the town in
the middle of the gorge, and the whole
plateau past Medeba 17to Heshbon and
all its towns on the plateau, including Dibon, Bamoth Baal, Beth Baal Meon, 18Ja-
haz, Kedemoth, Mephaath, 19Kiriathaim,
Sibmah, Zereth Shahar on the hill in the
valley, 20Beth Peor, the slopes of Pisgah,
and Beth Jeshimoth— 21all the towns on
the plateau and the entire realm of Sihon
king of the Amorites, who ruled at Heshbon. Moses had defeated him and the
Midianite chiefs, Evi, Rekem, Zur, Hur
and Reba—princes allied with Sihon—
who lived in that country. 22In addition
to those slain in battle, the Israelites had
put to the sword Balaam son of Beor, who
practiced divination. 23The boundary of
the Reubenites was the bank of the Jordan. These towns and their villages were
the inheritance of the Reubenites, clan
by clan.

24This is what Moses had given to the tribe of
Gad, clan by clan:

25The territory of Jazer, all the towns of
Gilead and half the Ammonite country
as far as Aroer, near Rabbah; 26and from
Heshbon to Ramath Mizpah and Beto-
nim, and from Mahanaim to the territory
of Debir; 27and in the valley, Beth Haram,
Beth Nimrah, Succoth and Zaphon with
the rest of the realm of Sihon king of
Heshbon (the east side of the Jordan, the
territory up to the end of the Sea of Kinnereth[a]). 28These towns and their villages
were the inheritance of the Gadites, clan
by clan.

29This is what Moses had given to the half-
tribe of Manasseh, that is, to half the family of
the descendants of Manasseh, clan by clan:

30The territory extending from Mahanaim
and including all of Bashan, the entire
realm of Og king of Bashan—all the settlements of Jair in Bashan, sixty towns,
31half of Gilead, and Ashtaroth and Edrei
(the royal cities of Og in Bashan). This
was for the descendants of Makir son of
Manasseh—for half of the sons of Makir,
clan by clan.

32This is the inheritance Moses had given
when he was in the plains of Moab across the
Jordan east of Jericho. 33But to the tribe of Levi,
Moses had given no inheritance; the LORD, the
God of Israel, is their inheritance, as he prom-
ised them.

Division of the Land West of the Jordan

14 Now these are the areas the Israelites received as an inheritance in the land of
Canaan, which Eleazar the priest, Joshua son of
Nun and the heads of the tribal clans of Israel
allotted to them. 2Their inheritances were assigned by lot to the nine-and-a-half tribes, as
the LORD had commanded through Moses.
3Moses had granted the two-and-a-half tribes
their inheritance east of the Jordan but had not
granted the Levites an inheritance among the
rest, 4for the sons of Joseph had become two
tribes—Manasseh and Ephraim. The Levites received no share of the land but only towns to
live in, with pasturelands for their flocks and
herds. 5So the Israelites divided the land, just
as the LORD had commanded Moses.

Hebron Given to Caleb

6Now the men of Judah approached Joshua
at Gilgal, and Caleb son of Jephunneh the Kenizzite said to him, "You know what the LORD

[a]27 That is, Galilee

said to Moses the man of God at Kadesh Barnea about you and me. 7 I was forty years old
when Moses the servant of the LORD sent me
from Kadesh Barnea to explore the land. And
I brought him back a report according to my
convictions, 8 but my brothers who went up
with me made the hearts of the people melt
with fear. I, however, followed the LORD my
God wholeheartedly. 9 So on that day Moses
swore to me, 'The land on which your feet
have walked will be your inheritance and that
of your children forever, because you have followed the LORD my God wholeheartedly.'[a]

10 "Now then, just as the LORD promised, he
has kept me alive for forty-five years since the
time he said this to Moses, while Israel moved
about in the desert. So here I am today, eighty-
five years old! 11 I am still as strong today as the
day Moses sent me out; I'm just as vigorous to
go out to battle now as I was then. 12 Now give
me this hill country that the LORD promised
me that day. You yourself heard then that the
Anakites were there and their cities were large
and fortified, but, the LORD helping me, I will
drive them out just as he said."

13 Then Joshua blessed Caleb son of Jephunneh and gave him Hebron as his inheritance.
14 So Hebron has belonged to Caleb son of
Jephunneh the Kenizzite ever since, because
he followed the LORD, the God of Israel,
wholeheartedly. 15 (Hebron used to be called
Kiriath Arba after Arba, who was the greatest
man among the Anakites.)

Then the land had rest from war.

Allotment for Judah

15 The allotment for the tribe of Judah,
clan by clan, extended down to the
territory of Edom, to the Desert of Zin in the
extreme south.

2 Their southern boundary started
from the bay at the southern end of the
Salt Sea,[b] 3 crossed south of Scorpion[c]
Pass, continued on to Zin and went over
to the south of Kadesh Barnea. Then it
ran past Hezron up to Addar and curved
around to Karka. 4 It then passed along
to Azmon and joined the Wadi of Egypt,
ending at the sea. This is their[d] southern
boundary.

5 The eastern boundary is the Salt Sea as
far as the mouth of the Jordan.

The northern boundary started from
the bay of the sea at the mouth of the Jordan, 6 went up to Beth Hoglah and continued north of Beth Arabah to the Stone
of Bohan son of Reuben. 7 The boundary
then went up to Debir from the Valley of
Achor and turned north to Gilgal, which
faces the Pass of Adummim south of the
gorge. It continued along to the waters of
En Shemesh and came out at En Rogel.
8 Then it ran up the Valley of Ben Hinnom
along the southern slope of the Jebusite
city (that is, Jerusalem). From there it
climbed to the top of the hill west of the
Hinnom Valley at the northern end of
the Valley of Rephaim. 9 From the hilltop
the boundary headed toward the spring of
the waters of Nephtoah, came out at the
towns of Mount Ephron and went down
toward Baalah (that is, Kiriath Jearim).
10 Then it curved westward from Baalah to
Mount Seir, ran along the northern slope
of Mount Jearim (that is, Kesalon), continued down to Beth Shemesh and crossed to
Timnah. 11 It went to the northern slope of
Ekron, turned toward Shikkeron, passed
along to Mount Baalah and reached
Jabneel. The boundary ended at the sea.

12 The western boundary is the coastline of the Great Sea.[e]

These are the boundaries around the people of
Judah by their clans.

13 In accordance with the LORD's command
to him, Joshua gave to Caleb son of Jephunneh a portion in Judah—Kiriath Arba, that is,
Hebron. (Arba was the forefather of Anak.)
14 From Hebron Caleb drove out the three
Anakites—Sheshai, Ahiman and Talmai—descendants of Anak. 15 From there he marched
against the people living in Debir (formerly
called Kiriath Sepher). 16 And Caleb said, "I
will give my daughter Acsah in marriage to the
man who attacks and captures Kiriath Sepher."

[a] 9 Deut. 1:36 [b] 2 That is, the Dead Sea; also in verse 5 [c] 3 Hebrew *Akrabbim* [d] 4 Hebrew *your* [e] 12 That is, the Mediterranean; also in verse 47

17 Othniel son of Kenaz, Caleb's brother, took
it; so Caleb gave his daughter Acsah to him
in marriage.
18 One day when she came to Othniel, she
urged him[a] to ask her father for a field. When
she got off her donkey, Caleb asked her, "What
can I do for you?"
19 She replied, "Do me a special favor. Since
you have given me land in the Negev, give me
also springs of water." So Caleb gave her the upper and lower springs.

20 This is the inheritance of the tribe of Judah, clan by clan:

21 The southernmost towns of the tribe of
Judah in the Negev toward the boundary of
Edom were:

Kabzeel, Eder, Jagur, 22 Kinah, Dimo-
nah, Adadah, 23 Kedesh, Hazor, Ithnan,
24 Ziph, Telem, Bealoth, 25 Hazor Hadat-
tah, Kerioth Hezron (that is, Hazor),
26 Amam, Shema, Moladah, 27 Hazar Gad-
dah, Heshmon, Beth Pelet, 28 Hazar Shual,
Beersheba, Biziothiah, 29 Baalah, Iim,
Ezem, 30 Eltolad, Kesil, Hormah, 31 Ziklag, Madmannah, Sansannah, 32 Lebaoth,
Shilhim, Ain and Rimmon—a total of
twenty-nine towns and their villages.

33 In the western foothills:

Eshtaol, Zorah, Ashnah, 34 Zanoah,
En Gannim, Tappuah, Enam, 35 Jarmuth, Adullam, Socoh, Azekah,
36 Shaaraim, Adithaim and Gederah (or
Gederothaim)[b]—fourteen towns and
their villages.

37 Zenan, Hadashah, Migdal Gad,
38 Dilean, Mizpah, Joktheel, 39 Lachish,
Bozkath, Eglon, 40 Cabbon, Lahmas,
Kitlish, 41 Gederoth, Beth Dagon, Naamah and Makkedah—sixteen towns and
their villages.

42 Libnah, Ether, Ashan, 43 Iphtah, Ashnah, Nezib, 44 Keilah, Aczib and Mareshah—nine towns and their villages.

45 Ekron, with its surrounding settlements and villages; 46 west of Ekron,
all that were in the vicinity of Ashdod,
together with their villages; 47 Ashdod, its
surrounding settlements and villages; and
Gaza, its settlements and villages, as far as
the Wadi of Egypt and the coastline of the
Great Sea.

48 In the hill country:

Shamir, Jattir, Socoh, 49 Dannah, Kir-
iath Sannah (that is, Debir), 50 Anab,
Eshtemoh, Anim, 51 Goshen, Holon and
Giloh—eleven towns and their villages.

52 Arab, Dumah, Eshan, 53 Janim, Beth
Tappuah, Aphekah, 54 Humtah, Kiriath
Arba (that is, Hebron) and Zior—nine
towns and their villages.

55 Maon, Carmel, Ziph, Juttah, 56 Jezreel,
Jokdeam, Zanoah, 57 Kain, Gibeah and
Timnah—ten towns and their villages.

58 Halhul, Beth Zur, Gedor, 59 Maarath,
Beth Anoth and Eltekon—six towns and
their villages.

60 Kiriath Baal (that is, Kiriath Jearim) and Rabbah—two towns and their
villages.

61 In the desert:

Beth Arabah, Middin, Secacah, 62 Nib-
shan, the City of Salt and En Gedi—six
towns and their villages.

63 Judah could not dislodge the Jebusites,
who were living in Jerusalem; to this day the
Jebusites live there with the people of Judah.

Allotment for Ephraim and Manasseh

16 The allotment for Joseph began at
the Jordan of Jericho,[c] east of the
waters of Jericho, and went up from there
through the desert into the hill country of
Bethel. 2 It went on from Bethel (that is,
Luz),[d] crossed over to the territory of the
Arkites in Ataroth, 3 descended westward
to the territory of the Japhletites as far as
the region of Lower Beth Horon and on to
Gezer, ending at the sea.

4 So Manasseh and Ephraim, the descendants
of Joseph, received their inheritance.

5 This was the territory of Ephraim, clan by
clan:

[a] 18 Hebrew and some Septuagint manuscripts; other Septuagint manuscripts (see also note at Judges 1:14) *Othniel, he urged her*
[b] 36 Or *Gederah and Gederothaim* [c] 1 *Jordan of Jericho* was possibly an ancient name for the Jordan River. [d] 2 Septuagint; Hebrew *Bethel to Luz*

The boundary of their inheritance went
from Ataroth Addar in the east to Upper
Beth Horon 6and continued to the sea.
From Micmethath on the north it curved
eastward to Taanath Shiloh, passing by
it to Janoah on the east. 7Then it went
down from Janoah to Ataroth and Naarah, touched Jericho and came out at the
Jordan. 8From Tappuah the border went
west to the Kanah Ravine and ended at the
sea. This was the inheritance of the tribe
of the Ephraimites, clan by clan. 9It also
included all the towns and their villages
that were set aside for the Ephraimites
within the inheritance of the Manassites.
10They did not dislodge the Canaanites living
in Gezer; to this day the Canaanites live among
the people of Ephraim but are required to do
forced labor.

17 This was the allotment for the tribe of
Manasseh as Joseph's firstborn, that is,
for Makir, Manasseh's firstborn. Makir was the
ancestor of the Gileadites, who had received
Gilead and Bashan because the Makirites were
great soldiers. 2So this allotment was for the
rest of the people of Manasseh—the clans of
Abiezer, Helek, Asriel, Shechem, Hepher and
Shemida. These are the other male descendants
of Manasseh son of Joseph by their clans.
3Now Zelophehad son of Hepher, the son
of Gilead, the son of Makir, the son of Manasseh, had no sons but only
daughters, whose names were
Mahlah, Noah, Hoglah, Milcah and Tirzah. 4They went to
Eleazar the priest, Joshua son
of Nun, and the leaders and
said, "The LORD commanded
Moses to give us an inheritance among our brothers."
So Joshua gave them an inheritance along with the brothers
of their father, according to
the LORD's command. 5Ma-
nasseh's share consisted of ten
tracts of land besides Gilead
and Bashan east of the Jordan, 6because the
daughters of the tribe of Manasseh received
an inheritance among the sons. The land of
Gilead belonged to the rest of the descendants
of Manasseh.
7The territory of Manasseh extended
from Asher to Micmethath east of Shechem. The boundary ran southward
from there to include the people living
at En Tappuah. 8(Manasseh had the land
of Tappuah, but Tappuah itself, on the
boundary of Manasseh, belonged to the
Ephraimites.) 9Then the boundary continued south to the Kanah Ravine. There
were towns belonging to Ephraim lying
among the towns of Manasseh, but the
boundary of Manasseh was the northern side of the ravine and ended at the
sea. 10On the south the land belonged to
Ephraim, on the north to Manasseh. The
territory of Manasseh reached the sea and
bordered Asher on the north and Issachar
on the east.
11Within Issachar and Asher, Manasseh also had Beth Shan, Ibleam and
the people of Dor, Endor, Taanach and
Megiddo, together with their surrounding settlements (the third in the list is Naphoth[a]).
12Yet the Manassites were not able to occupy
these towns, for the Canaanites were determined to live in that region. 13However, when
the Israelites grew stronger, they subjected the
Canaanites to forced labor but did not drive
them out completely.
14The people of Joseph said
to Joshua, "Why have you
given us only one allotment
and one portion for an inheritance? We are a numerous people and the LORD has blessed
us abundantly."
15"If you are so numerous,"
Joshua answered, "and if the
hill country of Ephraim is
too small for you, go up into
the forest and clear land for
yourselves there in the land of
the Perizzites and Rephaites."
16The people of Joseph replied, "The
hill country is not enough for us, and all the
Canaanites who live in the plain have iron

Joshua 17:4

God Is Fair

So Joshua gave them an inheritance along with the brothers of their father, according to the LORD's command.

[a]11 That is, Naphoth Dor

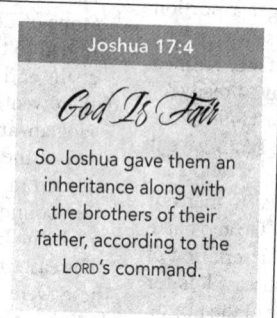

chariots, both those in Beth Shan and its settlements and those in the Valley of Jezreel."
17 But Joshua said to the house of Joseph—to
Ephraim and Manasseh—"You are numerous
and very powerful. You will have not only
one allotment 18 but the forested hill country
as well. Clear it, and its farthest limits will be
yours; though the Canaanites have iron chariots and though they are strong, you can drive
them out."

Division of the Rest of the Land

18 The whole assembly of the Israelites
gathered at Shiloh and set up the Tent
of Meeting there. The country was brought
under their control, 2 but there were still
seven Israelite tribes who had not yet received
their inheritance.
3 So Joshua said to the Israelites: "How long
will you wait before you begin to take possession of the land that the LORD, the God of your
fathers, has given you? 4 Appoint three men
from each tribe. I will send them out to make
a survey of the land and to write a description
of it, according to the inheritance of each. Then
they will return to me. 5 You are to divide the
land into seven parts. Judah is to remain in its
territory on the south and the house of Joseph
in its territory on the north. 6 After you have
written descriptions of the seven parts of the
land, bring them here to me and I will cast lots
for you in the presence of the LORD our God.
7 The Levites, however, do not get a portion
among you, because the priestly service of the
LORD is their inheritance. And Gad, Reuben
and the half-tribe of Manasseh have already received their inheritance on the east side of the
Jordan. Moses the servant of the LORD gave it
to them."
8 As the men started on their way to map out
the land, Joshua instructed them, "Go and make
a survey of the land and write a description of
it. Then return to me, and I will cast lots for
you here at Shiloh in the presence of the LORD."
9 So the men left and went through the land.
They wrote its description on a scroll, town by
town, in seven parts, and returned to Joshua
in the camp at Shiloh. 10 Joshua then cast lots
for them in Shiloh in the presence of the LORD,
and there he distributed the land to the Israelites according to their tribal divisions.

Allotment for Benjamin

11 The lot came up for the tribe of Benjamin,
clan by clan. Their allotted territory lay between the tribes of Judah and Joseph:
12 On the north side their boundary
began at the Jordan, passed the northern
slope of Jericho and headed west into the
hill country, coming out at the desert of
Beth Aven. 13 From there it crossed to the
south slope of Luz (that is, Bethel) and
went down to Ataroth Addar on the hill
south of Lower Beth Horon.
14 From the hill facing Beth Horon on
the south the boundary turned south
along the western side and came out at
Kiriath Baal (that is, Kiriath Jearim), a
town of the people of Judah. This was the
western side.
15 The southern side began at the outskirts of Kiriath Jearim on the west, and
the boundary came out at the spring of
the waters of Nephtoah. 16 The boundary
went down to the foot of the hill facing
the Valley of Ben Hinnom, north of the
Valley of Rephaim. It continued down the
Hinnom Valley along the southern slope
of the Jebusite city and so to En Rogel. 17 It
then curved north, went to En Shemesh,
continued to Geliloth, which faces the
Pass of Adummim, and ran down to the
Stone of Bohan son of Reuben. 18 It continued to the northern slope of Beth Arabah[a] and on down into the Arabah. 19 It
then went to the northern slope of Beth
Hoglah and came out at the northern
bay of the Salt Sea,[b] at the mouth of the
Jordan in the south. This was the southern boundary.
20 The Jordan formed the boundary on
the eastern side.
These were the boundaries that marked out
the inheritance of the clans of Benjamin on
all sides.
21 The tribe of Benjamin, clan by clan, had the
following cities:
Jericho, Beth Hoglah, Emek Keziz,

[a] 18 Septuagint; Hebrew *slope facing the Arabah* [b] 19 That is, the Dead Sea

[22]Beth Arabah, Zemaraim, Bethel, [23]Av-
vim, Parah, Ophrah, [24]Kephar Ammoni,
Ophni and Geba—twelve towns and
their villages.
[25]Gibeon, Ramah, Beeroth, [26]Mizpah,
Kephirah, Mozah, [27]Rekem, Irpeel, Tar-
alah, [28]Zelah, Haeleph, the Jebusite city
(that is, Jerusalem), Gibeah and Kiriath—
fourteen towns and their villages.
This was the inheritance of Benjamin for
its clans.

Allotment for Simeon

19 The second lot came out for the tribe
of Simeon, clan by clan. Their inheritance lay within the territory of Judah. [2]It
included:

Beersheba (or Sheba),[a] Moladah, [3]Ha-
zar Shual, Balah, Ezem, [4]Eltolad, Bethul,
Hormah, [5]Ziklag, Beth Marcaboth,
Hazar Susah, [6]Beth Lebaoth and Sharu-
hen—thirteen towns and their villages;
[7]Ain, Rimmon, Ether and Ashan—
four towns and their villages— [8]and all
the villages around these towns as far as
Baalath Beer (Ramah in the Negev).
This was the inheritance of the tribe of the Simeonites, clan by clan. [9]The inheritance of the
Simeonites was taken from the share of Judah,
because Judah's portion was more than they
needed. So the Simeonites received their inheritance within the territory of Judah.

Allotment for Zebulun

[10]The third lot came up for Zebulun, clan
by clan:

The boundary of their inheritance went
as far as Sarid. [11]Going west it ran to Mar-
alah, touched Dabbesheth, and extended
to the ravine near Jokneam. [12]It turned
east from Sarid toward the sunrise to the
territory of Kisloth Tabor and went on
to Daberath and up to Japhia. [13]Then it
continued eastward to Gath Hepher and
Eth Kazin; it came out at Rimmon and
turned toward Neah. [14]There the boundary went around on the north to Hanna-
thon and ended at the Valley of Iphtah El.
[15]Included were Kattath, Nahalal, Shimron, Idalah and Bethlehem. There were
twelve towns and their villages.
[16]These towns and their villages were the inheritance of Zebulun, clan by clan.

Allotment for Issachar

[17]The fourth lot came out for Issachar, clan by
clan. [18]Their territory included:

Jezreel, Kesulloth, Shunem, [19]Hapha-
raim, Shion, Anaharath, [20]Rabbith,
Kishion, Ebez, [21]Remeth, En Gannim, En
Haddah and Beth Pazzez. [22]The boundary touched Tabor, Shahazumah and
Beth Shemesh, and ended at the Jordan.
There were sixteen towns and their
villages.
[23]These towns and their villages were the inheritance of the tribe of Issachar, clan by clan.

Allotment for Asher

[24]The fifth lot came out for the tribe of Asher,
clan by clan. [25]Their territory included:

Helkath, Hali, Beten, Acshaph, [26]Al-
lammelech, Amad and Mishal. On the
west the boundary touched Carmel and
Shihor Libnath. [27]It then turned east toward Beth Dagon, touched Zebulun and
the Valley of Iphtah El, and went north
to Beth Emek and Neiel, passing Cabul
on the left. [28]It went to Abdon,[b] Rehob,
Hammon and Kanah, as far as Greater
Sidon. [29]The boundary then turned back
toward Ramah and went to the fortified
city of Tyre, turned toward Hosah and
came out at the sea in the region of Aczib,
[30]Ummah, Aphek and Rehob. There were
twenty-two towns and their villages.
[31]These towns and their villages were the inheritance of the tribe of Asher, clan by clan.

Allotment for Naphtali

[32]The sixth lot came out for Naphtali, clan
by clan:

[33]Their boundary went from Heleph
and the large tree in Zaanannim, passing
Adami Nekeb and Jabneel to Lakkum and
ending at the Jordan. [34]The boundary ran
west through Aznoth Tabor and came
out at Hukkok. It touched Zebulun on the
south, Asher on the west and the Jordan[c]

[a]2 Or *Beersheba, Sheba*; 1 Chron. 4:28 does not have *Sheba*. [b]28 Some Hebrew manuscripts (see also Joshua 21:30); most Hebrew manuscripts *Ebron* [c]34 Septuagint; Hebrew *west, and Judah, the Jordan,*

on the east. 35The fortified cities were Ziddim, Zer, Hammath, Rakkath, Kinnereth, 36Adamah, Ramah, Hazor, 37Kedesh, Edrei, En Hazor, 38Iron, Migdal El, Horem, Beth Anath and Beth Shemesh. There were nineteen towns and their villages.

39These towns and their villages were the inheritance of the tribe of Naphtali, clan by clan.

Allotment for Dan

40The seventh lot came out for the tribe of Dan, clan by clan. 41The territory of their inheritance included:

Zorah, Eshtaol, Ir Shemesh, 42Shaalabbin, Aijalon, Ithlah, 43Elon, Timnah, Ekron, 44Eltekeh, Gibbethon, Baalath, 45Jehud, Bene Berak, Gath Rimmon, 46Me Jarkon and Rakkon, with the area facing Joppa.

47(But the Danites had difficulty taking possession of their territory, so they went up and attacked Leshem, took it, put it to the sword and occupied it. They settled in Leshem and named it Dan after their forefather.)

48These towns and their villages were the inheritance of the tribe of Dan, clan by clan.

Allotment for Joshua

49When they had finished dividing the land into its allotted portions, the Israelites gave Joshua son of Nun an inheritance among them, 50as the LORD had commanded. They gave him the town he asked for—Timnath Serah[a] in the hill country of Ephraim. And he built up the town and settled there.

51These are the territories that Eleazar the priest, Joshua son of Nun and the heads of the tribal clans of Israel assigned by lot at Shiloh in the presence of the LORD at the entrance to the Tent of Meeting. And so they finished dividing the land.

Cities of Refuge

20 Then the LORD said to Joshua: 2"Tell the Israelites to designate the cities of refuge, as I instructed you through Moses, 3so that anyone who kills a person accidentally and unintentionally may flee there and find protection from the avenger of blood.

4"When he flees to one of these cities, he is to stand in the entrance of the city gate and state his case before the elders of that city. Then they are to admit him into their city and give him a place to live with them. 5If the avenger of blood pursues him, they must not surrender the one accused, because he killed his neighbor unintentionally and without malice aforethought. 6He is to stay in that city until he has stood trial before the assembly and until the death of the high priest who is serving at that time. Then he may go back to his own home in the town from which he fled."

7So they set apart Kedesh in Galilee in the hill country of Naphtali, Shechem in the hill country of Ephraim, and Kiriath Arba (that is, Hebron) in the hill country of Judah. 8On the east side of the Jordan of Jericho[b] they designated Bezer in the desert on the plateau in the tribe of Reuben, Ramoth in Gilead in the tribe of Gad, and Golan in Bashan in the tribe of Manasseh. 9Any of the Israelites or any alien living among them who killed someone accidentally could flee to these designated cities and not be killed by the avenger of blood prior to standing trial before the assembly.

Towns for the Levites

21 Now the family heads of the Levites approached Eleazar the priest, Joshua son of Nun, and the heads of the other tribal families of Israel 2at Shiloh in Canaan and said to them, "The LORD commanded through Moses that you give us towns to live in, with pasturelands for our livestock." 3So, as the LORD had commanded, the Israelites gave the Levites the following towns and pasturelands out of their own inheritance:

4The first lot came out for the Kohathites, clan by clan. The Levites who were descendants of Aaron the priest were allotted thirteen towns from the tribes of Judah, Simeon and Benjamin. 5The rest of Kohath's descendants were allotted ten towns from the clans of the tribes of Ephraim, Dan and half of Manasseh.

6The descendants of Gershon were allotted thirteen towns from the clans of the tribes of Issachar, Asher, Naphtali and the half-tribe of Manasseh in Bashan.

7The descendants of Merari, clan by clan, re-

[a]50 Also known as *Timnath Heres* (see Judges 2:9) [b]8 *Jordan of Jericho* was possibly an ancient name for the Jordan River.

ceived twelve towns from the tribes of Reuben, Gad and Zebulun.
8So the Israelites allotted to the Levites these
towns and their pasturelands, as the LORD had commanded through Moses.

9From the tribes of Judah and Simeon they allotted the following towns by name 10(these
towns were assigned to the descendants of Aaron who were from the Kohathite clans of the Levites, because the first lot fell to them):
11They gave them Kiriath Arba (that is, Hebron), with its surrounding pastureland, in the hill country of Judah. (Arba
was the forefather of Anak.) 12But the
fields and villages around the city they had given to Caleb son of Jephunneh as his possession.
13So to the descendants of Aaron the
priest they gave Hebron (a city of refuge
for one accused of murder), Libnah, 14Jat-
tir, Eshtemoa, 15Holon, Debir, 16Ain,
Juttah and Beth Shemesh, together with their pasturelands—nine towns from these two tribes.
17And from the tribe of Benjamin they
gave them Gibeon, Geba, 18Anathoth
and Almon, together with their pasturelands—four towns.
19All the towns for the priests, the descendants of Aaron, were thirteen, together with their pasturelands.

20The rest of the Kohathite clans of the Levites were allotted towns from the tribe of Ephraim:
21In the hill country of Ephraim they
were given Shechem (a city of refuge for one accused of murder) and Gezer,
22Kibzaim and Beth Horon, together with
their pasturelands—four towns.
23Also from the tribe of Dan they received Eltekeh, Gibbethon, 24Aijalon and
Gath Rimmon, together with their pasturelands—four towns.
25From half the tribe of Manasseh they
received Taanach and Gath Rimmon, together with their pasturelands—two towns.
26All these ten towns and their pasturelands
were given to the rest of the Kohathite clans.

27The Levite clans of the Gershonites were
given:
from the half-tribe of Manasseh,
Golan in Bashan (a city of refuge for one accused of murder) and Be Eshtarah, together with their pasturelands—two towns;
28from the tribe of Issachar,
Kishion, Daberath, 29Jarmuth and En
Gannim, together with their pasturelands—four towns;
30from the tribe of Asher,
Mishal, Abdon, 31Helkath and Rehob,
together with their pasturelands—four towns;
32from the tribe of Naphtali,
Kedesh in Galilee (a city of refuge for one accused of murder), Hammoth Dor and Kartan, together with their pasturelands—three towns.
33All the towns of the Gershonite clans were
thirteen, together with their pasturelands.

34The Merarite clans (the rest of the Levites)
were given:
from the tribe of Zebulun,
Jokneam, Kartah, 35Dimnah and Naha-
lal, together with their pasturelands—four towns;
36from the tribe of Reuben,
Bezer, Jahaz, 37Kedemoth and Mepha-
ath, together with their pasturelands—four towns;
38from the tribe of Gad,
Ramoth in Gilead (a city of refuge for one accused of murder), Mahanaim, 39Hesh-
bon and Jazer, together with their pasturelands—four towns in all.
40All the towns allotted to the Merarite clans,
who were the rest of the Levites, were twelve.
41The towns of the Levites in the territory
held by the Israelites were forty-eight in all,
together with their pasturelands. 42Each of
these towns had pasturelands surrounding it; this was true for all these towns.

43So the LORD gave Israel all the land he
had sworn to give their forefathers, and they
took possession of it and settled there. 44The
LORD gave them rest on every side, just as he had sworn to their forefathers. Not one of their

enemies withstood them; the LORD handed all
their enemies over to them. 45 Not one of all
the LORD's good promises to the house of Israel
failed; every one was fulfilled.

Eastern Tribes Return Home

22 Then Joshua sum-
moned the Reuben-
ites, the Gadites and the
half-tribe of Manasseh 2 and
said to them, "You have done
all that Moses the servant of
the LORD commanded, and
you have obeyed me in everything I commanded. 3 For a
long time now—to this very
day—you have not deserted
your brothers but have carried
out the mission the LORD your
God gave you. 4 Now that the LORD your God
has given your brothers rest as he promised,
return to your homes in the land that Moses
the servant of the LORD gave you on the other
side of the Jordan. 5 But be very careful to keep
the commandment and the law that Moses the
servant of the LORD gave you: to love the LORD
your God, to walk in all his ways, to obey his
commands, to hold fast to him and to serve
him with all your heart and all your soul."
6 Then Joshua blessed them and sent them
away, and they went to their homes. 7 (To the
half-tribe of Manasseh Moses had given land
in Bashan, and to the other half of the tribe
Joshua gave land on the west side of the Jordan
with their brothers.) When Joshua sent them
home, he blessed them, 8 saying, "Return to
your homes with your great wealth—with large
herds of livestock, with silver, gold, bronze and
iron, and a great quantity of clothing—and
divide with your brothers the plunder from
your enemies."
9 So the Reubenites, the Gadites and the half-
tribe of Manasseh left the Israelites at Shiloh
in Canaan to return to Gilead, their own land,
which they had acquired in accordance with
the command of the LORD through Moses.
10 When they came to Geliloth near the Jordan in the land of Canaan, the Reubenites, the
Gadites and the half-tribe of Manasseh built an
imposing altar there by the Jordan. 11 And when
the Israelites heard that they had built the altar
on the border of Canaan at Geliloth near the
Jordan on the Israelite side, 12 the whole assembly of Israel gathered at Shiloh
to go to war against them.
13 So the Israelites sent Phinehas son of Eleazar, the priest,
to the land of Gilead—to Reuben, Gad and the half-tribe of
Manasseh. 14 With him they
sent ten of the chief men, one
for each of the tribes of Israel,
each the head of a family division among the Israelite clans.
15 When they went to
Gilead—to Reuben, Gad and
the half-tribe of Manasseh—
they said to them: 16 "The
whole assembly of the LORD says: 'How could
you break faith with the God of Israel like this?
How could you turn away from the LORD and
build yourselves an altar in rebellion against
him now? 17 Was not the sin of Peor enough
for us? Up to this very day we have not cleansed
ourselves from that sin, even though a plague
fell on the community of the LORD! 18 And are
you now turning away from the LORD?
" 'If you rebel against the LORD today, tomorrow he will be angry with the whole community
of Israel. 19 If the land you possess is defiled,
come over to the LORD's land, where the LORD's
tabernacle stands, and share the land with us.
But do not rebel against the LORD or against us
by building an altar for yourselves, other than
the altar of the LORD our God. 20 When Achan
son of Zerah acted unfaithfully regarding the
devoted things,[a] did not wrath come upon
the whole community of Israel? He was not the
only one who died for his sin.' "
21 Then Reuben, Gad and the half-tribe of
Manasseh replied to the heads of the clans of
Israel: 22 "The Mighty One, God, the LORD! The
Mighty One, God, the LORD! He knows! And
let Israel know! If this has been in rebellion or
disobedience to the LORD, do not spare us this
day. 23 If we have built our own altar to turn
away from the LORD and to offer burnt offerings and grain offerings, or to sacrifice fellow-

> **Joshua 21:45**
>
> *God Delivers on His Promises*
>
> "Not one of all the LORD's good promises to the house of Israel failed; every one was fulfilled."

[a]20 The Hebrew term refers to the irrevocable giving over of things or persons to the LORD, often by totally destroying them.

ship offerings[a] on it, may the LORD himself call
us to account.
24“No! We did it for fear that some day your
descendants might say to ours, ‘What do you
have to do with the LORD, the
God of Israel? 25The LORD has
made the Jordan a boundary
between us and you—you Reubenites and Gadites! You have
no share in the LORD.’ So your
descendants might cause ours to
stop fearing the LORD.
26“That is why we said, ‘Let
us get ready and build an altar—but not for burnt offerings
or sacrifices.’ 27On the contrary,
it is to be a witness between us
and you and the generations that
follow, that we will worship the
LORD at his sanctuary with our
burnt offerings, sacrifices and fellowship offerings. Then in the future your descendants will not be able to say to ours, ‘You
have no share in the LORD.’
28“And we said, ‘If they ever say this to us, or
to our descendants, we will answer: Look at the
replica of the LORD’s altar, which our fathers
built, not for burnt offerings and sacrifices, but
as a witness between us and you.’
29“Far be it from us to rebel against the LORD
and turn away from him today by building an
altar for burnt offerings, grain offerings and
sacrifices, other than the altar of the LORD our
God that stands before his tabernacle.”
30When Phinehas the priest and the leaders
of the community—the heads of the clans of
the Israelites—heard what Reuben, Gad and
Manasseh had to say, they were pleased. 31And
Phinehas son of Eleazar, the priest, said to Reuben, Gad and Manasseh, “Today we know that
the LORD is with us, because you have not acted
unfaithfully toward the LORD in this matter.
Now you have rescued the Israelites from the
LORD’s hand.”
32Then Phinehas son of Eleazar, the priest,
and the leaders returned to Canaan from their
meeting with the Reubenites and Gadites in
Gilead and reported to the Israelites. 33They
were glad to hear the report and praised God.

Joshua 22:22

God Is Mighty

"The Mighty One, God, the LORD! The Mighty One, God, the LORD! He knows! And let Israel know! If this has been in rebellion or disobedience to the LORD, do not spare us this day."

And they talked no more about going to war
against them to devastate the country where
the Reubenites and the Gadites lived.
34And the Reubenites and the Gadites gave
the altar this name: A Wit-
ness Between Us that the
LORD is God.

Joshua’s Farewell to the Leaders

23 After a long time had
passed and the LORD
had given Israel rest from
all their enemies around
them, Joshua, by then old
and well advanced in years,
2summoned all Israel—their
elders, leaders, judges and
officials—and said to them:
“I am old and well advanced
in years. 3You yourselves
have seen everything the LORD your God has
done to all these nations for your sake; it was
the LORD your God who fought for you. 4Re-
member how I have allotted as an inheritance
for your tribes all the land of the nations that
remain—the nations I conquered—between
the Jordan and the Great Sea[b] in the west. 5The
LORD your God himself will drive them out of
your way. He will push them out before you,
and you will take possession of their land, as
the LORD your God promised you.
6“Be very strong; be careful to obey all that is
written in the Book of the Law of Moses, without turning aside to the right or to the left. 7Do
not associate with these nations that remain
among you; do not invoke the names of their
gods or swear by them. You must not serve
them or bow down to them. 8But you are to
hold fast to the LORD your God, as you have
until now.
9“The LORD has driven out before you great
and powerful nations; to this day no one has
been able to withstand you. 10One of you routs
a thousand, because the LORD your God fights
for you, just as he promised. 11So be very careful to love the LORD your God.
12“But if you turn away and ally yourselves
with the survivors of these nations that remain

[a]23 Traditionally *peace offerings*; also in verse 27 [b]4 That is, the Mediterranean

among you and if you intermarry with them
and associate with them, 13then you may be
sure that the LORD your God will no longer
drive out these nations before you. Instead,
they will become snares and
traps for you, whips on your
backs and thorns in your eyes,
until you perish from this good
land, which the LORD your
God has given you.
14"Now I am about to go
the way of all the earth. You
know with all your heart and
soul that not one of all the
good promises the LORD your
God gave you has failed. Every
promise has been fulfilled; not
one has failed. 15But just as every good promise of the LORD
your God has come true, so the LORD will bring
on you all the evil he has threatened, until he
has destroyed you from this good land he has
given you. 16If you violate the covenant of the
LORD your God, which he commanded you,
and go and serve other gods and bow down to
them, the LORD's anger will burn against you,
and you will quickly perish from the good land
he has given you."

> **Joshua 23:10**
>
> *God Brings Success*
>
> "One of you routs a thousand, because the LORD your God fights for you, just as he promised."

The Covenant Renewed at Shechem

24 Then Joshua assembled all the tribes of
Israel at Shechem. He summoned the
elders, leaders, judges and officials of Israel,
and they presented themselves before God.
2Joshua said to all the people, "This is what
the LORD, the God of Israel, says: 'Long ago
your forefathers, including Terah the father of
Abraham and Nahor, lived beyond the River[a]
and worshiped other gods. 3But I took your father Abraham from the land beyond the River
and led him throughout Canaan and gave him
many descendants. I gave him Isaac, 4and to
Isaac I gave Jacob and Esau. I assigned the hill
country of Seir to Esau, but Jacob and his sons
went down to Egypt.
5"'Then I sent Moses and Aaron, and I
afflicted the Egyptians by what I did there,
and I brought you out. 6When I brought your
fathers out of Egypt, you came to the sea, and
the Egyptians pursued them with chariots and
horsemen[b] as far as the Red Sea.[c] 7But they
cried to the LORD for help, and he put darkness
between you and the Egyptians; he brought
the sea over them and covered
them. You saw with your own
eyes what I did to the Egyptians. Then you lived in the desert for a long time.
8"'I brought you to the land
of the Amorites who lived east
of the Jordan. They fought
against you, but I gave them
into your hands. I destroyed
them from before you, and
you took possession of their
land. 9When Balak son of
Zippor, the king of Moab, prepared to fight against Israel, he
sent for Balaam son of Beor to put a curse on
you. 10But I would not listen to Balaam, so he
blessed you again and again, and I delivered
you out of his hand.
11"'Then you crossed the Jordan and came
to Jericho. The citizens of Jericho fought against
you, as did also the Amorites, Perizzites, Canaanites, Hittites, Girgashites, Hivites and Jebusites, but I gave them into your hands. 12I sent
the hornet ahead of you, which drove them out
before you—also the two Amorite kings. You
did not do it with your own sword and bow.
13So I gave you a land on which you did not
toil and cities you did not build; and you live in
them and eat from vineyards and olive groves
that you did not plant.'
14"Now fear the LORD and serve him with
all faithfulness. Throw away the gods your
forefathers worshiped beyond the River and in
Egypt, and serve the LORD. 15But if serving the
LORD seems undesirable to you, then choose
for yourselves this day whom you will serve,
whether the gods your forefathers served beyond the River, or the gods of the Amorites, in
whose land you are living. But as for me and
my household, we will serve the LORD."
16Then the people answered, "Far be it from
us to forsake the LORD to serve other gods! 17It
was the LORD our God himself who brought us
and our fathers up out of Egypt, from that land

[a]2 That is, the Euphrates; also in verses 3, 14 and 15 [b]6 Or *charioteers* [c]6 Hebrew *Yam Suph*; that is, Sea of Reeds

Choose Wisely

Read: Joshua 24:14–24

JOSHUA HAD FAITHFULLY led the Israelites into the promised land. Yet the time had come for the new nation to move forward. So he gave his farewell address, urging the people to choose wisely whom they would serve. He challenged them to make a conscious decision not to become entangled with the old gods but to serve the one true God. Knowing that the best leaders lead by example, he told the people that he and his household would "serve the LORD."

If you read the story of Susannah Wesley's life, you realize that her farewell address might have sounded very similar to Joshua's. Her son John Wesley, the eighteenth-century evangelist and co-founder of Methodism, wrote how she had wisely chosen to impact her household for the Lord. In *The Journal of John Wesley* he remembered, "The mother of the Wesleys was a remarkable woman, though cast in a mold not much to our minds nowadays. She had nineteen children and greatly prided herself on having taught them, one after another, by frequent chastisements to—what do you think? to cry softly. She had theories of education and strength of will, and of arm too, to carry them out . . . The mother of the Wesleys thought more of her children's souls than of their bodies . . . Coming . . . as he did of a theological stock, having a saint for a father and a notable devout woman for a mother, Wesley from his early days learned to regard religion as the business." Susannah Wesley's wise choice to train her children in the ways of the Lord helped pave the way for a spiritual revival in England.

It has been said that a choice repeated becomes a habit; a habit develops your character; and your character determines your destiny. Joshua's choices led to a destiny of faithful leadership and a family of faith. Susannah Wesley's wise choices led to a family of faith and a spiritual heritage that has stood the test of time. You are faced with the same choices today: to lead your household in serving the Lord or to serve the gods of the world. Will you choose wisely?

Joshua 24:15

"But if serving the LORD seems undesirable to you, then choose for yourselves this day whom you will serve, whether the gods your forefathers served beyond the River, or the gods of the Amorites, in whose land you are living. But as for me and my household, we will serve the LORD."

reflection

1 Who makes up your "house" (it could be extended family, friends, coworkers, etc.)?

2 How have you chosen to serve the Lord by serving them?

3 Pray that God will show you some creative ways to impact others for the Lord. Pray that you can choose wisely as you make decisions for those in your "household" of influence.

RELATED READINGS

Deuteronomy 30:15–19;
1 Kings 18:20–21;
2 Timothy 3:14–15

Tuesday

Go to page 292 for your next devotional reading.

of slavery, and performed those great signs before our eyes. He protected us on our entire
journey and among all the nations through
which we traveled. 18And the LORD drove out
before us all the nations, including the Amorites, who lived in the land. We too will serve
the LORD, because he is our God."
19Joshua said to the people, "You are not
able to serve the LORD. He is a holy God; he
is a jealous God. He will not forgive your rebellion and your sins. 20If you forsake the LORD
and serve foreign gods, he will turn and bring
disaster on you and make an end of you, after
he has been good to you."
21But the people said to Joshua, "No! We
will serve the LORD."
22Then Joshua said, "You are witnesses
against yourselves that you have chosen to
serve the LORD."
"Yes, we are witnesses," they replied.
23"Now then," said Joshua, "throw away the
foreign gods that are among you and yield your
hearts to the LORD, the God of Israel."
24And the people said to Joshua, "We will
serve the LORD our God and obey him."
25On that day Joshua made a covenant for
the people, and there at Shechem he drew
up for them decrees and laws. 26And Joshua
recorded these things in the Book of the Law
of God. Then he took a large stone and set it
up there under the oak near the holy place of
the LORD.
27"See!" he said to all the people. "This
stone will be a witness against us. It has heard
all the words the LORD has said to us. It will
be a witness against you if you are untrue to
your God."

Buried in the Promised Land

28Then Joshua sent the people away, each to
his own inheritance.
29After these things, Joshua son of Nun,
the servant of the LORD, died at the age of a
hundred and ten. 30And they buried him
in the land of his inheritance, at Timnath Serah[a] in the hill country of Ephraim, north of
Mount Gaash.
31Israel served the LORD throughout the lifetime of Joshua and of the elders who outlived
him and who had experienced everything the
LORD had done for Israel.
32And Joseph's bones, which the Israelites
had brought up from Egypt, were buried at Shechem in the tract of land that Jacob bought for
a hundred pieces of silver[b] from the sons of Hamor, the father of Shechem. This became the
inheritance of Joseph's descendants.
33And Eleazar son of Aaron died and was
buried at Gibeah, which had been allotted to his
son Phinehas in the hill country of Ephraim.

[a]30 Also known as *Timnath Heres* (see Judges 2:9) [b]32 Hebrew *hundred kesitahs*; a kesitah was a unit of money of unknown weight and value.

Judges

It never takes long to fall. In the generation following Joshua's spectacular conquest of Canaan, the people succumbed to *complacency and outright rebellion.* The people who were to worship only God strayed and began to worship the pagan deities of their neighbors. It was an affront that God could not ignore. He brought judgment by means of other nations that swept in and attacked Israel. But even in his judgment, God never lost his love for them. *He gave them judges,* people who would lead them and save them from their enemies. And so began the cycle: When the people were in distress, *they cried out to God.* When God helped them and all was well again, they slipped right back into their idol worship.

Author:
Likely Samuel.

Audience:
The Israelites living in the promised land.

Date:
Around 1000 B.C.

Setting:
Israel's ups and (mostly) downs after the time of Joshua.

Verse to Remember:
After that whole generation had been gathered to their fathers, another generation grew up, who knew neither the LORD nor what he had done for Israel. (2:10)

Israel Fights the Remaining Canaanites

1 After the death of Joshua, the Israelites
asked the LORD, "Who will be the first to
go up and fight for us against the Canaanites?"
2The LORD answered, "Judah is to go; I have
given the land into their hands."
3Then the men of Judah said to the Simeonites their brothers, "Come up with us into
the territory allotted to us, to fight against the
Canaanites. We in turn will go with you into
yours." So the Simeonites went with them.
4When Judah attacked, the LORD gave the
Canaanites and Perizzites into their hands and
they struck down ten thousand men at Bezek.
5It was there that they found Adoni-Bezek and
fought against him, putting to rout the Canaanites and Perizzites. 6Adoni-Bezek fled, but they
chased him and caught him, and cut off his
thumbs and big toes.
7Then Adoni-Bezek said, "Seventy kings
with their thumbs and big toes cut off have
picked up scraps under my table. Now God

has paid me back for what I did to them." They
brought him to Jerusalem, and he died there.
8 The men of Judah attacked Jerusalem also
and took it. They put the city to the sword and
set it on fire.
9 After that, the men of Judah went down to
fight against the Canaanites living in the hill
country, the Negev and the western foothills.
10 They advanced against the Canaanites living
in Hebron (formerly called Kiriath Arba) and
defeated Sheshai, Ahiman and Talmai.
11 From there they advanced against the
people living in Debir (formerly called Kiriath Sepher). 12 And Caleb said, "I will give my
daughter Acsah in marriage to the man who
attacks and captures Kiriath Sepher." 13 Othniel
son of Kenaz, Caleb's younger brother, took
it; so Caleb gave his daughter Acsah to him
in marriage.
14 One day when she came to Othniel, she
urged him[a] to ask her father for a field. When
she got off her donkey, Caleb asked her, "What
can I do for you?"
15 She replied, "Do me a special favor. Since
you have given me land in the Negev, give me
also springs of water." Then Caleb gave her the
upper and lower springs.
16 The descendants of Moses' father-in-law,
the Kenite, went up from the City of Palms[b]
with the men of Judah to live among the people
of the Desert of Judah in the Negev near Arad.
17 Then the men of Judah went with the
Simeonites their brothers and attacked the
Canaanites living in Zephath, and they totally
destroyed[c] the city. Therefore it was called
Hormah.[d] 18 The men of Judah also took[e]
Gaza, Ashkelon and Ekron—each city with its
territory.
19 The LORD was with the men of Judah.
They took possession of the hill country, but
they were unable to drive the people from the
plains, because they had iron chariots. 20 As
Moses had promised, Hebron was given to Caleb, who drove from it the three sons of Anak.
21 The Benjamites, however, failed to dislodge
the Jebusites, who were living in Jerusalem; to
this day the Jebusites live there with the Benjamites.
22 Now the house of Joseph attacked Bethel,
and the LORD was with them. 23 When they
sent men to spy out Bethel (formerly called
Luz), 24 the spies saw a man coming out of the
city and they said to him, "Show us how to get
into the city and we will see that you are treated
well." 25 So he showed them, and they put the
city to the sword but spared the man and his
whole family. 26 He then went to the land of the
Hittites, where he built a city and called it Luz,
which is its name to this day.
27 But Manasseh did not drive out the people
of Beth Shan or Taanach or Dor or Ibleam or
Megiddo and their surrounding settlements,
for the Canaanites were determined to live in
that land. 28 When Israel became strong, they
pressed the Canaanites into forced labor but
never drove them out completely. 29 Nor did
Ephraim drive out the Canaanites living in Gezer, but the Canaanites continued to live there
among them. 30 Neither did Zebulun drive out
the Canaanites living in Kitron or Nahalol,
who remained among them; but they did subject them to forced labor. 31 Nor did Asher drive
out those living in Acco or Sidon or Ahlab or
Aczib or Helbah or Aphek or Rehob, 32 and because of this the people of Asher lived among
the Canaanite inhabitants of the land. 33 Neither did Naphtali drive out those living in Beth
Shemesh or Beth Anath; but the Naphtalites
too lived among the Canaanite inhabitants of
the land, and those living in Beth Shemesh and
Beth Anath became forced laborers for them.
34 The Amorites confined the Danites to the
hill country, not allowing them to come down
into the plain. 35 And the Amorites were determined also to hold out in Mount Heres, Aijalon
and Shaalbim, but when the power of the house
of Joseph increased, they too were pressed into
forced labor. 36 The boundary of the Amorites
was from Scorpion[f] Pass to Sela and beyond.

The Angel of the LORD at Bokim

2 The angel of the LORD went up from Gilgal to Bokim and said, "I brought you up
out of Egypt and led you into the land that I
swore to give to your forefathers. I said, 'I will
never break my covenant with you, 2 and you

[a] 14 Hebrew; Septuagint and Vulgate *Othniel, he urged her* [b] 16 That is, Jericho [c] 17 The Hebrew term refers to the irrevocable giving over of things or persons to the LORD, often by totally destroying them. [d] 17 *Hormah* means *destruction.* [e] 18 Hebrew; Septuagint *Judah did not take* [f] 36 Hebrew *Akrabbim*

shall not make a covenant with the people of
this land, but you shall break down their altars.' Yet you have disobeyed me. Why have
you done this? 3Now therefore I tell you that I
will not drive them out before you; they will be
⌞thorns⌟ in your sides and their
gods will be a snare to you."
4When the angel of the
LORD had spoken these things
to all the Israelites, the people
wept aloud, 5and they called
that place Bokim.[a] There they
offered sacrifices to the LORD.

Judges 2:18

God Is Compassionate

Whenever the LORD raised up a judge for them, he was with the judge and saved them out of the hands of their enemies as long as the judge lived.

Disobedience and Defeat

6After Joshua had dismissed
the Israelites, they went to take
possession of the land, each to
his own inheritance. 7The people served the LORD throughout the lifetime of Joshua and
of the elders who outlived him
and who had seen all the great
things the LORD had done for Israel.
8Joshua son of Nun, the servant of the LORD,
died at the age of a hundred and ten. 9And they
buried him in the land of his inheritance, at
Timnath Heres[b] in the hill country of Ephraim,
north of Mount Gaash.
10After that whole generation had been gath-
red to their fathers, another generation grew
p, who knew neither the LORD nor what he
ad done for Israel. 11Then the Israelites did
vil in the eyes of the LORD and served the
aals. 12They forsook the LORD, the God of
heir fathers, who had brought them out of
gypt. They followed and worshiped various
ods of the peoples around them. They pro-
oked the LORD to anger 13because they for-
ook him and served Baal and the Ashtoreths.
In his anger against Israel the LORD handed
em over to raiders who plundered them. He
ld them to their enemies all around, whom
ey were no longer able to resist. 15Whenever
rael went out to fight, the hand of the LORD
as against them to defeat them, just as he had
orn to them. They were in great distress.
16Then the LORD raised up judges,[c] who
saved them out of the hands of these raiders.
17Yet they would not listen to their judges but
prostituted themselves to other gods and worshiped them. Unlike their fathers, they quickly
turned from the way in which their fathers
had walked, the way of obedi-
ence to the LORD's commands.
18Whenever the LORD raised
up a judge for them, he was
with the judge and saved them
out of the hands of their enemies as long as the judge lived;
for the LORD had compassion
on them as they groaned under those who oppressed and
afflicted them. 19But when the
judge died, the people returned
to ways even more corrupt
than those of their fathers, following other gods and serving
and worshiping them. They
refused to give up their evil
practices and stubborn ways.
20Therefore the LORD was very angry
with Israel and said, "Because this nation has
violated the covenant that I laid down for their
forefathers and has not listened to me, 21I will
no longer drive out before them any of the
nations Joshua left when he died. 22I will use
them to test Israel and see whether they will
keep the way of the LORD and walk in it as their
forefathers did." 23The LORD had allowed those
nations to remain; he did not drive them out at
once by giving them into the hands of Joshua.
3 These are the nations the LORD left to test
all those Israelites who had not experienced any of the wars in Canaan 2(he did this
only to teach warfare to the descendants of the
Israelites who had not had previous battle experience): 3the five rulers of the Philistines, all
the Canaanites, the Sidonians, and the Hivites
living in the Lebanon mountains from Mount
Baal Hermon to Lebo[d] Hamath. 4They were
left to test the Israelites to see whether they
would obey the LORD's commands, which he
had given their forefathers through Moses.
5The Israelites lived among the Canaanites, Hittites, Amorites, Perizzites, Hivites and

Bokim means *weepers*. [b]9 Also known as *Timnath Serah* (see Joshua 19:50 and 24:30) [c]16 Or *leaders*; similarly in verses 17–19
Or *to the entrance to*

Jebusites. 6 They took their daughters in marriage and gave their own daughters to their sons, and served their gods.

Othniel

7 The Israelites did evil in the eyes of the LORD; they forgot the LORD their God and served the Baals and the Asherahs. 8 The anger of the LORD burned against Israel so that he sold them into the hands of Cushan-Rishathaim king of Aram Naharaim,[a] to whom the Israelites were subject for eight years. 9 But when they cried out to the LORD, he raised up for them a deliverer, Othniel son of Kenaz, Caleb's younger brother, who saved them. 10 The Spirit of the LORD came upon him, so that he became Israel's judge[b] and went to war. The LORD gave Cushan-Rishathaim king of Aram into the hands of Othniel, who overpowered him. 11 So the land had peace for forty years, until Othniel son of Kenaz died.

> **Judges 3:8**
>
> *God Hates Sin*
>
> The anger of the LORD burned against Israel so that he sold them into the hands of Cushan-Rishathaim king of Aram Naharaim, to whom the Israelites were subject for eight years.

Ehud

12 Once again the Israelites did evil in the eyes of the LORD, and because they did this evil the LORD gave Eglon king of Moab power over Israel. 13 Getting the Ammonites and Amalekites to join him, Eglon came and attacked Israel, and they took possession of the City of Palms.[c] 14 The Israelites were subject to Eglon king of Moab for eighteen years.

15 Again the Israelites cried out to the LORD, and he gave them a deliverer—Ehud, a left-handed man, the son of Gera the Benjamite. The Israelites sent him with tribute to Eglon king of Moab. 16 Now Ehud had made a double-edged sword about a foot and a half[d] long, which he strapped to his right thigh under his clothing. 17 He presented the tribute to Eglon king of Moab, who was a very fat man. 18 After Ehud had presented the tribute, he sent on their way the men who had carried it. 19 At the idols[e] near Gilgal he himself turned back and said, "I have a secret message for you, O king."

The king said, "Quiet!" And all his attendants left him.

20 Ehud then approached him while he was sitting alone in the upper room of his summer palace[f] and said, "I have a message from God for you." As the king rose from his seat, 21 Ehud reached with his left hand, drew the sword from his right thigh and plunged it into the king's belly. 22 Even the handle sank in after the blade, which came out his back. Ehud did not pull the sword out, and the fat closed in over it. 23 Then Ehud went out to the porch[g]; he shut the doors of the upper room behind him and locked them.

24 After he had gone, the servants came and found the doors of the upper room locked. They said, "He must be relieving himself in the inner room of the house." 25 They waited to the point of embarrassment, but when he did not open the doors of the room, they took a key and unlocked them. There they saw their lord fallen to the floor, dead.

26 While they waited, Ehud got away. He passed by the idols and escaped to Seirah. 27 When he arrived there, he blew a trumpet in the hill country of Ephraim, and the Israelites went down with him from the hills, with him leading them.

28 "Follow me," he ordered, "for the LORD has given Moab, your enemy, into your hands." So they followed him down and, taking possession of the fords of the Jordan that led to Moab, they allowed no one to cross over. 29 At that time they struck down about ten thousand Moabites, all vigorous and strong; not a man escaped. 30 That day Moab was made subject to Israel, and the land had peace for eighty years.

Shamgar

31 After Ehud came Shamgar son of Anath, who struck down six hundred Philistines with an oxgoad. He too saved Israel.

[a] 8 That is, Northwest Mesopotamia [b] 10 Or *leader* [c] 13 That is, Jericho [d] 16 Hebrew *a cubit* (about 0.5 meter) [e] 19 Or *the stone quarries*; also in verse 26 [f] 20 The meaning of the Hebrew for this phrase is uncertain. [g] 23 The meaning of the Hebrew for this word is uncertain.

Deborah

4 After Ehud died, the Israelites once again
did evil in the eyes of the LORD. 2 So the
LORD sold them into the hands of Jabin, a
king of Canaan, who reigned in Hazor. The
commander of his army was Sisera, who lived
in Harosheth Haggoyim. 3 Because he had
nine hundred iron chariots and had cruelly
oppressed the Israelites for twenty years, they
cried to the LORD for help.
4 Deborah, a prophetess, the wife of Lappidoth, was leading[a] Israel at that time. 5 She held
court under the Palm of Deborah between Ramah and Bethel in the hill country of Ephraim,
and the Israelites came to her to have their
disputes decided. 6 She sent for Barak son of
Abinoam from Kedesh in Naphtali and said
to him, "The LORD, the God of Israel, commands you: 'Go, take with you ten thousand
men of Naphtali and Zebulun and lead the
way to Mount Tabor. 7 I will lure Sisera, the
commander of Jabin's army, with his chariots
and his troops to the Kishon River and give
him into your hands.'"
8 Barak said to her, "If you go with me, I will
go; but if you don't go with me, I won't go."
9 "Very well," Deborah said, "I will go with
you. But because of the way you are going
about this,[b] the honor will not be yours, for the
LORD will hand Sisera over to a woman." So
Deborah went with Barak to Kedesh, 10 where
he summoned Zebulun and Naphtali. Ten thousand men followed him, and Deborah also
went with him.
11 Now Heber the Kenite had left the other
Kenites, the descendants of Hobab, Moses'
brother-in-law,[c] and pitched his tent by the
great tree in Zaanannim near Kedesh.
12 When they told Sisera that Barak son of
Abinoam had gone up to Mount Tabor, 13 Sisera gathered together his nine hundred iron
chariots and all the men with him, from Harosheth Haggoyim to the Kishon River.
14 Then Deborah said to Barak, "Go! This
is the day the LORD has given Sisera into your
hands. Has not the LORD gone ahead of you?"
So Barak went down Mount Tabor, followed
by ten thousand men. 15 At Barak's advance,
the LORD routed Sisera and all his chariots
and army by the sword, and Sisera abandoned
his chariot and fled on foot. 16 But Barak pursued the chariots and army as far as Harosheth
Haggoyim. All the troops of Sisera fell by the
sword; not a man was left.
17 Sisera, however, fled on foot to the tent of
Jael, the wife of Heber the Kenite, because there
were friendly relations between Jabin king of
Hazor and the clan of Heber the Kenite.
18 Jael went out to meet Sisera and said to
him, "Come, my lord, come right in. Don't be
afraid." So he entered her tent, and she put a
covering over him.
19 "I'm thirsty," he said. "Please give me some
water." She opened a skin of milk, gave him a
drink, and covered him up.
20 "Stand in the doorway of the tent," he told
her. "If someone comes by and asks you, 'Is anyone here?' say 'No.'"
21 But Jael, Heber's wife, picked up a tent peg
and a hammer and went quietly to him while
he lay fast asleep, exhausted. She drove the
peg through his temple into the ground, and
he died.
22 Barak came by in pursuit of Sisera, and
Jael went out to meet him. "Come," she said, "I
will show you the man you're looking for." So
he went in with her, and there lay Sisera with
the tent peg through his temple—dead.
23 On that day God subdued Jabin, the Canaanite king, before the Israelites. 24 And the
hand of the Israelites grew stronger and stronger against Jabin, the Canaanite king, until they
destroyed him.

The Song of Deborah

5 On that day Deborah and Barak son of
Abinoam sang this song:

2 "When the princes in Israel take the lead,
when the people willingly offer
themselves—
praise the LORD!

3 "Hear this, you kings! Listen, you rulers!
I will sing to[d] the LORD, I will sing;
I will make music to[e] the LORD, the God
of Israel.

[a] 4 Traditionally *judging* [b] 9 Or *But on the expedition you are undertaking* [c] 11 Or *father-in-law* [d] 3 Or *of* [e] 3 Or *I with song I will praise*

Deborah the Sabra

Read: Judges 4–5

Judges 4:4–5
Deborah, a prophetess, the wife of Lappidoth, was leading Israel at that time. She held court under the Palm of Deborah between Ramah and Bethel in the hill country of Ephraim, and the Israelites came to her to have their disputes decided.

SOMETIMES LIFE ON EARTH can seem like a wilderness in which we must learn to thrive under sometimes harsh conditions. But walking in the world's wilderness, I've discovered some beautiful desert plants growing in my garden of friends.

One of my desert plant friends is a prickly pear cactus. Prickly pears are covered with spikes, but when they bloom their flowers are big and brilliant. Today in Israel, people born in the land are called *sabras*, because they are tough on the outside and sweet on the inside. That's like my friend Pia, who grew up in the tough streets of New York and learned to stick up for herself because she grew up in a single-parent household and her mother was at work all day, leaving Pia as the family protector . . . The first time we met, she slapped down one of my ideas for a women's retreat. Later, however, she called to give me a Scripture as encouragement. I've learned that I can bring Pia my troubles and she will blossom into a prayer warrior . . .

I think of Deborah as a prickly pear cactus. Though she was female, Deborah was given the responsibility of judging the wayward Israelites. Scripture tells us "[she held court under the Palm of Deborah between Ramah and Bethel in the hill country of Ephraim, and the Israelites came up to her to have their disputes decided]" (Judges 4:5). To understand her personality, you need to understand her name. Deborah literally means wasp and her story reveals that she was willing to sting if need be, even leading an army to war if the Lord led. She was uncompromising in her zeal for the Lord, singing, "[So may all your enemies perish, O LORD! But may they who love you be like the sun when it rises in its strength]" (Judges 5:31). This godly woman could be prickly, but she also blessed those who followed the Lord . . .

Perhaps you know someone who is as prickly as a cactus. The care of prickly pears is quite simple: Put them in the sun and don't overwater them. You can care for your prickly friends the same way. Make sure you place them in the Son by praying for them often. And don't saturate them with too much attention. That's when you might get stung.

— Penny Pierce Rose

reflection

1. Who among your friends is most like the prickly pear Penny described?
2. In what ways are you sometimes sharp on the outside yet sweet on the inside?
3. Spend some time praying that God would soften your edges. Pray for the friends in your life, asking God to strengthen them when necessary and sweeten them when needed.

RELATED READINGS

Exodus 15:20–21;
Isaiah 51:3;
Ephesians 6:18

Go to page 294 for your next devotional reading.

4 "O LORD, when you went out from Seir,
when you marched from the land of Edom,
the earth shook, the heavens poured,
the clouds poured down water.
5 The mountains quaked before the LORD, the One of Sinai,
before the LORD, the God of Israel.

6 "In the days of Shamgar son of Anath,
in the days of Jael, the roads were abandoned;
travelers took to winding paths.
7 Village life[a] in Israel ceased,
ceased until I,[b] Deborah, arose,
arose a mother in Israel.
8 When they chose new gods,
war came to the city gates,
and not a shield or spear was seen
among forty thousand in Israel.
9 My heart is with Israel's princes,
with the willing volunteers among the people.
Praise the LORD!

10 "You who ride on white donkeys,
sitting on your saddle blankets,
and you who walk along the road,
consider 11 the voice of the singers[c] at the watering places.
They recite the righteous acts of the LORD,
the righteous acts of his warriors[d] in Israel.

"Then the people of the LORD
went down to the city gates.
12 'Wake up, wake up, Deborah!
Wake up, wake up, break out in song!
Arise, O Barak!
Take captive your captives, O son of Abinoam.'

13 "Then the men who were left
came down to the nobles;
the people of the LORD
came to me with the mighty.
14 Some came from Ephraim, whose roots were in Amalek;
Benjamin was with the people who followed you.
From Makir captains came down,
from Zebulun those who bear a commander's staff.
15 The princes of Issachar were with Deborah;
yes, Issachar was with Barak,
rushing after him into the valley.
In the districts of Reuben
there was much searching of heart.
16 Why did you stay among the campfires[e]
to hear the whistling for the flocks?
In the districts of Reuben
there was much searching of heart.
17 Gilead stayed beyond the Jordan.
And Dan, why did he linger by the ships?
Asher remained on the coast
and stayed in his coves.
18 The people of Zebulun risked their very lives;
so did Naphtali on the heights of the field.

19 "Kings came, they fought;
the kings of Canaan fought
at Taanach by the waters of Megiddo,
but they carried off no silver, no plunder.
20 From the heavens the stars fought,
from their courses they fought against Sisera.
21 The river Kishon swept them away,
the age-old river, the river Kishon.
March on, my soul; be strong!
22 Then thundered the horses' hoofs—
galloping, galloping go his mighty steeds.
23 'Curse Meroz,' said the angel of the LORD.

Judges 5:3

God Deserves Praise

"Hear this, you kings!
Listen, you rulers!
I will sing to the LORD,
I will sing;
I will make music to the
LORD, the God of Israel."

[a]7 Or *Warriors* [b]7 Or *you* [c]11 Or *archers*; the meaning of the Hebrew for this word is uncertain. [d]11 Or *villagers* [e]16 Or *saddlebags*

Spiritual Motherhood

Read: Judges 4–5

Judges 5:7

Village life in Israel ceased, ceased until I, Deborah, arose, arose a mother in Israel.

reflection

1 What are some specific ways in which you can become a spiritual mother to someone else?

2 How does the story of Deborah encourage you in your various leadership roles?

3 Whom do you think God may have placed in your life to nurture or encourage?

RELATED READINGS

Proverbs 31:10–31; Titus 2:3–8

WHAT WOULD YOU CALL a woman who sits under a palm tree, mediates disputes, offers godly counsel and takes up weapons to go to war against a fierce enemy? A madwoman? A multitasker? How about a mother?

Deborah filled each of these roles. She was a prophetess, ruler, mediator and warrior. As one of only a handful of prophetesses mentioned in Scripture, Deborah exercised the divine ability to discern the commandments of God and declare them to others. As a ruler, she led Israel as the only female judge. As a mediator, Deborah conducted arbitration and settled disputes. As a warrior, she went to battle on behalf of her extended family, the children of Israel.

A woman this gifted at multitasking could be called many things, but Deborah designated one title for herself: mother. Although her husband is named in Scripture, there is no record that she had children. However, rather than referring to herself as a judge or prophetess she instead called herself "I, Deborah . . . a mother in Israel."

The Biblical record of this highly respected leader is a case study in spiritual motherhood. Deborah was leading Israel at a time when the country needed protection from the domination of the Canaanites, ruled by King Jabin and his military commander Sisera. God told her to instruct an Israelite warrior named Barak to take ten thousand troops into battle against Sisera. God promised victory if Barak followed his directions. Barak, however, refused to go unless Deborah went with him.

Although Deborah warned Barak that his honor would suffer as a result of his lack of faith, she agreed to accompany him into battle. Rather than holding his timidity against him, Deborah decided to do what was best for her nation: She fought the enemy like a mother bear.

We do not have to carry, adopt or raise children in order to qualify as spiritual mothers. Instead, we only need to display a willingness to use the gifts that God has entrusted to us in order to nurture others and strengthen others in their faith. Deborah was such a woman. Are you willing to let God use you?

Thursday

Go to page 298 for your next devotional reading.

'Curse its people bitterly,
because they did not come to help the
LORD,
to help the LORD against the mighty.'

24 "Most blessed of women be Jael,
the wife of Heber the Kenite,
most blessed of tent-dwelling women.
25 He asked for water, and she gave him milk;
in a bowl fit for nobles she brought him
curdled milk.
26 Her hand reached for the tent peg,
her right hand for the workman's
hammer.
She struck Sisera, she crushed his head,
she shattered and pierced his temple.
27 At her feet he sank,
he fell; there he lay.
At her feet he sank, he fell;
where he sank, there he fell—dead.

28 "Through the window peered Sisera's
mother;
behind the lattice she cried out,
'Why is his chariot so long in coming?
Why is the clatter of his chariots
delayed?'
29 The wisest of her ladies answer her;
indeed, she keeps saying to herself,
30 'Are they not finding and dividing the
spoils:
a girl or two for each man,
colorful garments as plunder for Sisera,
colorful garments embroidered,
highly embroidered garments for my
neck—
all this as plunder?'

31 "So may all your enemies perish, O LORD!
But may they who love you be like the
sun
when it rises in its strength."

Then the land had peace forty years.

Gideon

6 Again the Israelites did evil in the eyes
of the LORD, and for seven years he gave
them into the hands of the Midianites. 2 Because the power of Midian was so oppressive,
the Israelites prepared shelters for themselves
in mountain clefts, caves and strongholds.
3 Whenever the Israelites planted their crops,
the Midianites, Amalekites and other eastern
peoples invaded the country. 4 They camped
on the land and ruined the crops all the way to
Gaza and did not spare a living thing for Israel,
neither sheep nor cattle nor donkeys. 5 They
came up with their livestock and their tents
like swarms of locusts. It was impossible to
count the men and their camels; they invaded
the land to ravage it. 6 Midian so impoverished
the Israelites that they cried out to the LORD
for help.

7 When the Israelites cried to the LORD because of Midian, 8 he sent them a prophet, who
said, "This is what the LORD, the God of Israel,
says: I brought you up out of Egypt, out of the
land of slavery. 9 I snatched you from the power
of Egypt and from the hand of all your oppressors. I drove them from before you and gave
you their land. 10 I said to you, 'I am the LORD
your God; do not worship the gods of the Amorites, in whose land you live.' But you have not
listened to me."

11 The angel of the LORD came and sat down
under the oak in Ophrah that belonged to Joash the Abiezrite, where his son Gideon was
threshing wheat in a winepress to keep it from
the Midianites. 12 When the angel of the LORD
appeared to Gideon, he said, "The LORD is with
you, mighty warrior."

13 "But sir," Gideon replied, "if the LORD
is with us, why has all this happened to us?
Where are all his wonders that our fathers told
us about when they said, 'Did not the LORD
bring us up out of Egypt?' But now the LORD
has abandoned us and put us into the hand of
Midian."

14 The LORD turned to him and said, "Go
in the strength you have and save Israel out of
Midian's hand. Am I not sending you?"

15 "But Lord,[a]" Gideon asked, "how can I
save Israel? My clan is the weakest in Manasseh, and I am the least in my family."

16 The LORD answered, "I will be with you,
and you will strike down all the Midianites
together."

17 Gideon replied, "If now I have found favor

[a] 15 Or *sir*

in your eyes, give me a sign that it is really you
talking to me. 18Please do not go away until
I come back and bring my offering and set it
before you."
And the LORD said, "I will wait until you return."
19Gideon went in, prepared a young goat,
and from an ephah[a] of flour he made bread
without yeast. Putting the meat in a basket and
its broth in a pot, he brought them out and offered them to him under the oak.
20The angel of God said to him, "Take the
meat and the unleavened bread, place them
on this rock, and pour out the broth." And
Gideon did so. 21With the tip of the staff that
was in his hand, the angel of the LORD touched
the meat and the unleavened bread. Fire flared
from the rock, consuming the meat and the
bread. And the angel of the LORD disappeared.
22When Gideon realized that it was the angel
of the LORD, he exclaimed,
"Ah, Sovereign LORD! I have
seen the angel of the LORD face
to face!"
23But the LORD said to him,
"Peace! Do not be afraid. You
are not going to die."
24So Gideon built an altar
to the LORD there and called it
The LORD is Peace. To this day
it stands in Ophrah of the Abiezrites.
25That same night the LORD
said to him, "Take the second
bull from your father's herd,
the one seven years old.[b] Tear down your father's altar to Baal and cut down the Asherah
pole[c] beside it. 26Then build a proper kind of[d]
altar to the LORD your God on the top of this
height. Using the wood of the Asherah pole
that you cut down, offer the second[e] bull as a
burnt offering."
27So Gideon took ten of his servants and
did as the LORD told him. But because he was
afraid of his family and the men of the town, he
did it at night rather than in the daytime.
28In the morning when the men of the town
got up, there was Baal's altar, demolished, with
the Asherah pole beside it cut down and the second bull sacrificed on the newly built altar!
29They asked each other, "Who did this?"
When they carefully investigated, they were
told, "Gideon son of Joash did it."
30The men of the town demanded of Joash,
"Bring out your son. He must die, because he
has broken down Baal's altar and cut down the
Asherah pole beside it."
31But Joash replied to the hostile crowd
around him, "Are you going to plead Baal's
cause? Are you trying to save him? Whoever
fights for him shall be put to death by morning!
If Baal really is a god, he can defend himself
when someone breaks down his altar." 32So
that day they called Gideon "Jerub-Baal,[f]" saying, "Let Baal contend with him," because he
broke down Baal's altar.
33Now all the Midianites, Amalekites and
other eastern peoples joined forces and crossed
over the Jordan and camped in
the Valley of Jezreel. 34Then
the Spirit of the LORD came
upon Gideon, and he blew a
trumpet, summoning the Abiezrites to follow him. 35He sent
messengers throughout Manasseh, calling them to arms, and
also into Asher, Zebulun and
Naphtali, so that they too went
up to meet them.
36Gideon said to God, "If
you will save Israel by my hand
as you have promised— 37look,
I will place a wool fleece on the
threshing floor. If there is dew only on the fleece
and all the ground is dry, then I will know that
you will save Israel by my hand, as you said."
38And that is what happened. Gideon rose
early the next day; he squeezed the fleece and
wrung out the dew—a bowlful of water.
39Then Gideon said to God, "Do not be
angry with me. Let me make just one more request. Allow me one more test with the fleece.
This time make the fleece dry and the ground
covered with dew." 40That night God did so.
Only the fleece was dry; all the ground was covered with dew.

Judges 6:24

God Is Peace

So Gideon built an altar to the LORD there and called it The LORD is Peace. To this day it stands in Ophrah of the Abiezrites.

[a]19 That is, probably about 3/5 bushel (about 22 liters) [b]25 Or *Take a full-grown, mature bull from your father's herd* [c]25 That is, a symbol of the goddess Asherah; here and elsewhere in Judges [d]26 Or *build with layers of stone an* [e]26 Or *full-grown*; also in verse 28 [f]32 *Jerub-Baal* means *let Baal contend.*

Gideon Defeats the Midianites

7 Early in the morning, Jerub-Baal (that
is, Gideon) and all his men camped at
the spring of Harod. The camp of Midian was
north of them in the valley near the hill of
Moreh. 2The LORD said to Gideon, "You have
too many men for me to deliver Midian into
their hands. In order that Israel may not boast
against me that her own strength has saved her,
3announce now to the people, 'Anyone who
trembles with fear may turn back and leave
Mount Gilead.'" So twenty-two thousand men
left, while ten thousand remained.
4But the LORD said to Gideon, "There are
still too many men. Take them down to the water, and I will sift them for you there. If I say,
'This one shall go with you,' he shall go; but if
I say, 'This one shall not go with you,' he shall
not go."
5So Gideon took the men down to the water. There the LORD told him, "Separate those
who lap the water with their tongues like a dog
from those who kneel down to drink." 6Three
hundred men lapped with their hands to their
mouths. All the rest got down on their knees
to drink.
7The LORD said to Gideon, "With the three
hundred men that lapped I will save you and
give the Midianites into your hands. Let all
the other men go, each to his own place." 8So
Gideon sent the rest of the Israelites to their
tents but kept the three hundred, who took over
the provisions and trumpets of the others.
Now the camp of Midian lay below him in
the valley. 9During that night the LORD said to
Gideon, "Get up, go down against the camp, because I am going to give it into your hands. 10If
you are afraid to attack, go down to the camp
with your servant Purah 11and listen to what
they are saying. Afterward, you will be encouraged to attack the camp." So he and Purah his
servant went down to the outposts of the camp.
12The Midianites, the Amalekites and all the
other eastern peoples had settled in the valley,
thick as locusts. Their camels could no more be
counted than the sand on the seashore.
13Gideon arrived just as a man was telling a
friend his dream. "I had a dream," he was saying. "A round loaf of barley bread came tumbling into the Midianite camp. It struck the
tent with such force that the tent overturned
and collapsed."
14His friend responded, "This can be nothing other than the sword of Gideon son of Joash, the Israelite. God has given the Midianites
and the whole camp into his hands."
15When Gideon heard the dream and its interpretation, he worshiped God. He returned
to the camp of Israel and called out, "Get up!
The LORD has given the Midianite camp into
your hands." 16Dividing the three hundred
men into three companies, he placed trumpets
and empty jars in the hands of all of them, with
torches inside.
17"Watch me," he told them. "Follow my
lead. When I get to the edge of the camp, do
exactly as I do. 18When I and all who are with
me blow our trumpets, then from all around
the camp blow yours and shout, 'For the LORD
and for Gideon.'"
19Gideon and the hundred men with him
reached the edge of the camp at the beginning of the middle watch, just after they had
changed the guard. They blew their trumpets
and broke the jars that were in their hands.
20The three companies blew the trumpets and
smashed the jars. Grasping the torches in their
left hands and holding in their right hands the
trumpets they were to blow, they shouted, "A
sword for the LORD and for Gideon!" 21While
each man held his position around the camp,
all the Midianites ran, crying out as they fled.
22When the three hundred trumpets
sounded, the LORD caused the men throughout the camp to turn on each other with their
swords. The army fled to Beth Shittah toward
Zererah as far as the border of Abel Meholah
near Tabbath. 23Israelites from Naphtali, Asher
and all Manasseh were called out, and they pursued the Midianites. 24Gideon sent messengers
throughout the hill country of Ephraim, saying,
"Come down against the Midianites and seize
the waters of the Jordan ahead of them as far
as Beth Barah."
So all the men of Ephraim were called out
and they took the waters of the Jordan as far
as Beth Barah. 25They also captured two of the
Midianite leaders, Oreb and Zeeb. They killed
Oreb at the rock of Oreb, and Zeeb at the winepress of Zeeb. They pursued the Midianites and

Is the Battle Too Big?

Judges 7:9

During that night the LORD said to Gideon, "Get up, go down against the camp, because I am going to give it into your hands."

reflection

1 Describe the last battle you faced.

2 Did you rely on your own power or the power of God?

3 After reading this Scripture passage, how will you face your next battle?

RELATED READINGS

1 Samuel 17:32–50; 2 Chronicles 20:5–15; 1 Timothy 6:11–12

Read: Judges 7:1–22

HAVE YOU EVER TURNED AWAY from a battle you knew you should fight to its conclusion? Lynn desperately wanted to run from her battle. But she didn't.

When the phone rang at her house, she picked it up at the same time as her husband. She started to say something, but stopped when she overheard a female voice on the line. Lynn bit her quivering lip as she overheard evidence of her husband's affair. After a confrontation, her husband moved into the woman's house. Deeply depressed, she found herself unable to face her neighbors and friends.

One day Maggie, one of Lynn's friends, insisted on dropping by. Maggie took one look at Lynn's tear-streaked face and the defeated slump of her shoulders and sent Lynn to bed. That night Maggie stayed by her bedside, praying. Every time Lynn awoke from her restless sleep, she saw her friend's lips moving, pleading with God. The next morning, Maggie made Lynn get up, shower and dress. She helped her brush her hair, then prepared breakfast. Afterward, they prayed together about Lynn's situation.

Gideon was brave, but he knew the enemy was strong. So God came to Gideon and promised him victory. He instructed Gideon to battle the massive army of the Midianites with only 300 men. Imagine how Gideon felt. He faced a battle in which he was significantly outnumbered. But Gideon battled the enemy using the weapons God had chosen: blaring trumpets and glowing torches.

Through the help and support of many friends, God gave Lynn the spiritual strength and courage to talk to her husband. Regardless of the outcome of her heartbreaking situation, she knew that she had to face the battle head-on. She couldn't lock herself in her house and wish it all away. Lynn had to fight.

What do you do when you face a battle? Do you run away? Do you hope it will go away? Or do you stand and fight, leaning on God for support?

Perhaps for you it's the dawn of a battle: a difficult discussion with your spouse, a confrontation with a coworker, a meeting with a school principal. Take a few deep breaths and then ask God to go with you and give you *his* weapons for the battle. Though you may feel small and powerless, God will be mighty and powerful. He will equip you to do what is required of you.

Go to page 304 for your next devotional reading.

brought the heads of Oreb and Zeeb to Gideon,
who was by the Jordan.

Zebah and Zalmunna

8 Now the Ephraimites asked Gideon, "Why
have you treated us like this? Why didn't
you call us when you went to fight Midian?"
And they criticized him sharply.
2But he answered them, "What have I accomplished compared to you? Aren't the gleanings
of Ephraim's grapes better than the full grape
harvest of Abiezer? 3God gave Oreb and Zeeb,
the Midianite leaders, into your hands. What
was I able to do compared to you?" At this,
their resentment against him subsided.
4Gideon and his three hundred men,
exhausted yet keeping up the pursuit, came to
the Jordan and crossed it. 5He said to the men
of Succoth, "Give my troops some bread; they
are worn out, and I am still pursuing Zebah
and Zalmunna, the kings of Midian."
6But the officials of Succoth said, "Do you already have the hands of Zebah and Zalmunna
in your possession? Why should we give bread
to your troops?"
7Then Gideon replied, "Just for that, when
the LORD has given Zebah and Zalmunna
into my hand, I will tear your flesh with desert
thorns and briers."
8From there he went up to Peniel[a] and made
the same request of them, but they answered as
the men of Succoth had. 9So he said to the men
of Peniel, "When I return in triumph, I will tear
down this tower."
10Now Zebah and Zalmunna
were in Karkor with a force of
about fifteen thousand men, all
that were left of the armies of
the eastern peoples; a hundred
and twenty thousand swordsmen had fallen. 11Gideon went
up by the route of the nomads
east of Nobah and Jogbehah
and fell upon the unsuspecting
army. 12Zebah and Zalmunna,
the two kings of Midian, fled,
but he pursued them and captured them, routing their entire army.
13Gideon son of Joash then returned from
the battle by the Pass of Heres. 14He caught a
young man of Succoth and questioned him,
and the young man wrote down for him the
names of the seventy-seven officials of Succoth,
the elders of the town. 15Then Gideon came
and said to the men of Succoth, "Here are Zebah and Zalmunna, about whom you taunted
me by saying, 'Do you already have the hands
of Zebah and Zalmunna in your possession?
Why should we give bread to your exhausted
men?'" 16He took the elders of the town and
taught the men of Succoth a lesson by punishing them with desert thorns and briers. 17He
also pulled down the tower of Peniel and killed
the men of the town.
18Then he asked Zebah and Zalmunna,
"What kind of men did you kill at Tabor?"
"Men like you," they answered, "each one
with the bearing of a prince."
19Gideon replied, "Those were my brothers, the sons of my own mother. As surely as
the LORD lives, if you had spared their lives, I
would not kill you." 20Turning to Jether, his oldest son, he said, "Kill them!" But Jether did not
draw his sword, because he was only a boy and
was afraid.
21Zebah and Zalmunna said, "Come, do it
yourself. 'As is the man, so is his strength.'" So
Gideon stepped forward and killed them, and
took the ornaments off their camels' necks.

Gideon's Ephod

22The Israelites said to Gideon, "Rule over
us—you, your son and your grandson—because you have saved us out of
the hand of Midian."
23But Gideon told them,
"I will not rule over you, nor
will my son rule over you.
The LORD will rule over you."
24And he said, "I do have one
request, that each of you give
me an earring from your share
of the plunder." (It was the custom of the Ishmaelites to wear
gold earrings.)
25They answered, "We'll
be glad to give them." So they
spread out a garment, and each man threw a
ring from his plunder onto it. 26The weight of

Judges 8:23

God Is Our Ruler

But Gideon told them, "I will not rule over you, nor will my son rule over you. The LORD will rule over you."

[a]8 Hebrew *Penuel,* a variant of *Peniel;* also in verses 9 and 17

the gold rings he asked for came to seventeen
hundred shekels,[a] not counting the ornaments,
the pendants and the purple garments worn by
the kings of Midian or the chains that were on
their camels' necks. 27 Gideon made the gold
into an ephod, which he placed in Ophrah,
his town. All Israel prostituted themselves by
worshiping it there, and it became a snare to
Gideon and his family.

Gideon's Death

28 Thus Midian was subdued before the Israelites and did not raise its head again. During Gideon's lifetime, the land enjoyed peace
forty years.

29 Jerub-Baal son of Joash went back home
to live. 30 He had seventy sons of his own, for he
had many wives. 31 His concubine, who lived
in Shechem, also bore him a son, whom he
named Abimelech. 32 Gideon son of Joash died
at a good old age and was buried in the tomb of
his father Joash in Ophrah of the Abiezrites.

33 No sooner had Gideon died than the Israelites again prostituted themselves to the Baals.
They set up Baal-Berith as their god and 34 did
not remember the LORD their God, who had
rescued them from the hands of all their enemies on every side. 35 They also failed to show
kindness to the family of Jerub-Baal (that is,
Gideon) for all the good things he had done
for them.

Abimelech

9 Abimelech son of Jerub-Baal went to his
mother's brothers in Shechem and said to
them and to all his mother's clan, 2 "Ask all the
citizens of Shechem, 'Which is better for you:
to have all seventy of Jerub-Baal's sons rule
over you, or just one man?' Remember, I am
your flesh and blood."

3 When the brothers repeated all this to the citizens of Shechem, they were inclined to follow
Abimelech, for they said, "He is our brother."
4 They gave him seventy shekels[b] of silver from
the temple of Baal-Berith, and Abimelech used
it to hire reckless adventurers, who became his
followers. 5 He went to his father's home in Ophrah and on one stone murdered his seventy
brothers, the sons of Jerub-Baal. But Jotham,
the youngest son of Jerub-Baal, escaped by hiding. 6 Then all the citizens of Shechem and Beth
Millo gathered beside the great tree at the pillar
in Shechem to crown Abimelech king.

7 When Jotham was told about this, he
climbed up on the top of Mount Gerizim and
shouted to them, "Listen to me, citizens of Shechem, so that God may listen to you. 8 One day
the trees went out to anoint a king for themselves. They said to the olive tree, 'Be our king.'

9 "But the olive tree answered, 'Should I give
up my oil, by which both gods and men are honored, to hold sway over the trees?'

10 "Next, the trees said to the fig tree, 'Come
and be our king.'

11 "But the fig tree replied, 'Should I give up
my fruit, so good and sweet, to hold sway over
the trees?'

12 "Then the trees said to the vine, 'Come
and be our king.'

13 "But the vine answered, 'Should I give up
my wine, which cheers both gods and men, to
hold sway over the trees?'

14 "Finally all the trees said to the thornbush,
'Come and be our king.'

15 "The thornbush said to the trees, 'If you
really want to anoint me king over you, come
and take refuge in my shade; but if not, then let
fire come out of the thornbush and consume
the cedars of Lebanon!'

16 "Now if you have acted honorably and in
good faith when you made Abimelech king,
and if you have been fair to Jerub-Baal and his
family, and if you have treated him as he deserves— 17 and to think that my father fought
for you, risked his life to rescue you from the
hand of Midian 18 (but today you have revolted
against my father's family, murdered his seventy
sons on a single stone, and made Abimelech,
the son of his slave girl, king over the citizens
of Shechem because he is your brother)— 19 if
then you have acted honorably and in good
faith toward Jerub-Baal and his family today,
may Abimelech be your joy, and may you be
his, too! 20 But if you have not, let fire come out
from Abimelech and consume you, citizens of
Shechem and Beth Millo, and let fire come out
from you, citizens of Shechem and Beth Millo,
and consume Abimelech!"

21 Then Jotham fled, escaping to Beer, and

[a] 26 That is, about 43 pounds (about 19.5 kilograms) [b] 4 That is, about 1 3/4 pounds (about 0.8 kilogram)

lived there because he was afraid of his
ther Abimelech.
22 After Abimelech had governed Israel three
rs, 23 God sent an evil spirit between Abim-
ch and the citizens of Shechem, who acted
acherously against Abimelech. 24 God did
s in order that the crime against Jerub-Baal's
enty sons, the shedding of their blood, might
avenged on their brother Abimelech and on
citizens of Shechem, who had helped him
rder his brothers. 25 In opposition to him
se citizens of Shechem set men on the hill-
s to ambush and rob everyone who passed
and this was reported to Abimelech.
26 Now Gaal son of Ebed moved with his
thers into Shechem, and its citizens put
ir confidence in him. 27 After they had gone
into the fields and gathered the grapes and
dden them, they held a festival in the tem-
of their god. While they were eating and
nking, they cursed Abimelech. 28 Then Gaal
of Ebed said, "Who is Abimelech, and who
hechem, that we should be subject to him?
't he Jerub-Baal's son, and isn't Zebul his
uty? Serve the men of Hamor, Shechem's
ier! Why should we serve Abimelech? 29 If
y this people were under my command!
en I would get rid of him. I would say to
imelech, 'Call out your whole army!' "[a]
30 When Zebul the governor of the city heard
at Gaal son of Ebed said, he was very angry.
Jnder cover he sent messengers to Abime-
h, saying, "Gaal son of Ebed and his brothers
e come to Shechem and are stirring up the
against you. 32 Now then, during the night
and your men should come and lie in wait
the fields. 33 In the morning at sunrise, ad-
ce against the city. When Gaal and his men
ne out against you, do whatever your hand
ds to do."
34 So Abimelech and all his troops set out
night and took up concealed positions near
chem in four companies. 35 Now Gaal son
Ebed had gone out and was standing at the
rance to the city gate just as Abimelech and
soldiers came out from their hiding place.
36 When Gaal saw them, he said to Zebul,
ok, people are coming down from the tops
he mountains!"

Zebul replied, "You mistake the shadows of
the mountains for men."
37 But Gaal spoke up again: "Look, people
are coming down from the center of the land,
and a company is coming from the direction of
the soothsayers' tree."
38 Then Zebul said to him, "Where is your big
talk now, you who said, 'Who is Abimelech that
we should be subject to him?' Aren't these the
men you ridiculed? Go out and fight them!"
39 So Gaal led out[b] the citizens of Shechem
and fought Abimelech. 40 Abimelech chased
him, and many fell wounded in the flight—all
the way to the entrance to the gate. 41 Abimelech stayed in Arumah, and Zebul drove Gaal
and his brothers out of Shechem.
42 The next day the people of Shechem went
out to the fields, and this was reported to Abimelech. 43 So he took his men, divided them into
three companies and set an ambush in the
fields. When he saw the people coming out of
the city, he rose to attack them. 44 Abimelech
and the companies with him rushed forward to
a position at the entrance to the city gate. Then
two companies rushed upon those in the fields
and struck them down. 45 All that day Abimelech pressed his attack against the city until he
had captured it and killed its people. Then he
destroyed the city and scattered salt over it.
46 On hearing this, the citizens in the tower
of Shechem went into the stronghold of the
temple of El-Berith. 47 When Abimelech heard
that they had assembled there, 48 he and all his
men went up Mount Zalmon. He took an ax
and cut off some branches, which he lifted to
his shoulders. He ordered the men with him,
"Quick! Do what you have seen me do!" 49 So
all the men cut branches and followed Abimelech. They piled them against the stronghold
and set it on fire over the people inside. So all
the people in the tower of Shechem, about a
thousand men and women, also died.
50 Next Abimelech went to Thebez and besieged it and captured it. 51 Inside the city,
however, was a strong tower, to which all the
men and women—all the people of the city—
fled. They locked themselves in and climbed
up on the tower roof. 52 Abimelech went to the
tower and stormed it. But as he approached

Septuagint; Hebrew *him." Then he said to Abimelech, "Call out your whole army!"* [b]39 Or *Gaal went out in the sight of*

the entrance to the tower to set it on fire, 53a
woman dropped an upper millstone on his
head and cracked his skull.
54Hurriedly he called to his armor-bearer,
"Draw your sword and kill me, so that they
can't say, 'A woman killed him.'" So his servant
ran him through, and he died. 55When the
Israelites saw that Abimelech was dead, they
went home.
56Thus God repaid the wickedness that
Abimelech had done to his father by murdering his seventy brothers. 57God also made the
men of Shechem pay for all
their wickedness. The curse of
Jotham son of Jerub-Baal came
on them.

> **Judges 10:16**
>
> *God Is Merciful*
>
> Then they got rid of the foreign gods among them and served the LORD. And he could bear Israel's misery no longer.

Tola

10 After the time of
Abimelech a man of
Issachar, Tola son of Puah, the
son of Dodo, rose to save Israel.
He lived in Shamir, in the hill
country of Ephraim. 2He led[a]
Israel twenty-three years; then
he died, and was buried in Shamir.

Jair

3He was followed by Jair of Gilead, who led
Israel twenty-two years. 4He had thirty sons,
who rode thirty donkeys. They controlled
thirty towns in Gilead, which to this day are
called Havvoth Jair.[b] 5When Jair died, he was
buried in Kamon.

Jephthah

6Again the Israelites did evil in the eyes of
the LORD. They served the Baals and the Ashtoreths, and the gods of Aram, the gods of Sidon,
the gods of Moab, the gods of the Ammonites
and the gods of the Philistines. And because
the Israelites forsook the LORD and no longer
served him, 7he became angry with them. He
sold them into the hands of the Philistines
and the Ammonites, 8who that year shattered
and crushed them. For eighteen years they
oppressed all the Israelites on the east side of
the Jordan in Gilead, the land of the Amorites.
9The Ammonites also crossed the Jordan to
fight against Judah, Benjamin and the house
of Ephraim; and Israel was in great distress.
10Then the Israelites cried out to the LORD,
"We have sinned against you, forsaking our
God and serving the Baals."
11The LORD replied, "When the Egyptians,
the Amorites, the Ammonites, the Philistines,
12the Sidonians, the Amalekites and the Ma-
onites[c] oppressed you and you cried to me
for help, did I not save you from their hands?
13But you have forsaken me and served other
gods, so I will no longer save you. 14Go and cry
out to the gods you have cho-
sen. Let them save you when
you are in trouble!"
15But the Israelites said to
the LORD, "We have sinned.
Do with us whatever you think
best, but please rescue us now."
16Then they got rid of the foreign gods among them and
served the LORD. And he could
bear Israel's misery no longer.
17When the Ammonites
were called to arms and camped
in Gilead, the Israelites assembled and camped at Mizpah. 18The leaders of
the people of Gilead said to each other,
"Whoever will launch the attack against the
Ammonites will be the head of all those living
in Gilead."

11 Jephthah the Gileadite was a mighty
warrior. His father was Gilead; his
mother was a prostitute. 2Gilead's wife also
bore him sons, and when they were grown up,
they drove Jephthah away. "You are not going
to get any inheritance in our family," they said,
"because you are the son of another woman."
3So Jephthah fled from his brothers and settled
in the land of Tob, where a group of adventurers gathered around him and followed him.
4Some time later, when the Ammonites
made war on Israel, 5the elders of Gilead went
to get Jephthah from the land of Tob. 6"Come,"
they said, "be our commander, so we can fight
the Ammonites."
7Jephthah said to them, "Didn't you hate me
and drive me from my father's house? Why do
you come to me now, when you're in trouble?"

[a]2 Traditionally *judged*; also in verse 3 [b]4 Or *called the settlements of Jair* [c]12 Hebrew; some Septuagint manuscripts *Midianites*

8 The elders of Gilead said to him, "Nevertheless, we are turning to you now; come with us
to fight the Ammonites, and you will be our
head over all who live in Gilead."
9 Jephthah answered, "Suppose you take me
back to fight the Ammonites and the LORD
gives them to me—will I really be your head?"
10 The elders of Gilead replied, "The LORD
is our witness; we will certainly do as you
say." 11 So Jephthah went with the elders of
Gilead, and the people made him head and
commander over them. And he repeated all
his words before the LORD in Mizpah.
12 Then Jephthah sent messengers to the
Ammonite king with the question: "What do
you have against us that you have attacked
our country?"
13 The king of the Ammonites answered Jephthah's messengers, "When Israel came up out of
Egypt, they took away my land from the Arnon
to the Jabbok, all the way to the Jordan. Now
give it back peaceably."
14 Jephthah sent back messengers to the Ammonite king, 15 saying:

"This is what Jephthah says: Israel did
not take the land of Moab or the land of
the Ammonites. 16 But when they came
up out of Egypt, Israel went through the
desert to the Red Sea[a] and on to Kadesh.
17 Then Israel sent messengers to the king
of Edom, saying, 'Give us permission to
go through your country,' but the king of
Edom would not listen. They sent also
to the king of Moab, and he refused. So
Israel stayed at Kadesh.
18 "Next they traveled through the desert, skirted the lands of Edom and Moab,
passed along the eastern side of the country of Moab, and camped on the other
side of the Arnon. They did not enter
the territory of Moab, for the Arnon was
its border.
19 "Then Israel sent messengers to Sihon king of the Amorites, who ruled in
Heshbon, and said to him, 'Let us pass
through your country to our own place.'
20 Sihon, however, did not trust Israel[b] to
pass through his territory. He mustered
all his men and encamped at Jahaz and
fought with Israel.
21 "Then the LORD, the God of Israel,
gave Sihon and all his men into Israel's
hands, and they defeated them. Israel
took over all the land of the Amorites who
lived in that country, 22 capturing all of it
from the Arnon to the Jabbok and from
the desert to the Jordan.
23 "Now since the LORD, the God of
Israel, has driven the Amorites out before
his people Israel, what right have you to
take it over? 24 Will you not take what
your god Chemosh gives you? Likewise,
whatever the LORD our God has given
us, we will possess. 25 Are you better than
Balak son of Zippor, king of Moab? Did
he ever quarrel with Israel or fight with
them? 26 For three hundred years Israel occupied Heshbon, Aroer, the surrounding
settlements and all the towns along the
Arnon. Why didn't you retake them during that time? 27 I have not wronged you,
but you are doing me wrong by waging
war against me. Let the LORD, the Judge,[c]
decide the dispute this day between the Israelites and the Ammonites."

28 The king of Ammon, however, paid no attention to the message Jephthah sent him.
29 Then the Spirit of the LORD came upon
Jephthah. He crossed Gilead and Manasseh,
passed through Mizpah of Gilead, and from
there he advanced against the Ammonites.
30 And Jephthah made a vow to the LORD:
"If you give the Ammonites into my hands,
31 whatever comes out of the door of my house
to meet me when I return in triumph from the
Ammonites will be the LORD's, and I will sacrifice it as a burnt offering."
32 Then Jephthah went over to fight the Ammonites, and the LORD gave them into his
hands. 33 He devastated twenty towns from
Aroer to the vicinity of Minnith, as far as Abel
Keramim. Thus Israel subdued Ammon.
34 When Jephthah returned to his home in
Mizpah, who should come out to meet him
but his daughter, dancing to the sound of tambourines! She was an only child. Except for her

[a] 16 Hebrew *Yam Suph*; that is, Sea of Reeds [b] 20 Or *however, would not make an agreement for Israel* [c] 27 Or *Ruler*

Steps of Faith

MIRIAM

But the Israelites went through the sea on dry ground, with a wall of water on their right and on their left.

Exodus 14:29

"OUCH!" INSTINCTIVELY, SHE nursed her finger in her mouth.

The blade of a reed grass had grazed her finger as she hurriedly joined her mother near the riverbank.

"Shh, be quiet darling," her mother whispered. Although her mother spoke calmly, she'd never seen her look so preoccupied. Her face seemed heavy, almost stone-like, burdened with emotion that Miriam couldn't quite pinpoint.

What was it Mother felt . . . fear . . . worry . . . distress? Miriam decided that whatever it was, it frightened her.

Of course, Miriam had been scared before—hearing strange sounds at night or a sudden clap of thunder. But what she saw on her mother's face ushered in her first experience of cold-blooded fear. A strange, raw energy channeled like currents of lightning between them as they huddled together near the shore.

"What if the princess doesn't find my brother nestled in the curve of the shallow embankment? What if she becomes angry with me because he is a Hebrew boy? What if she wants to kill us?" Miriam's mind raced with anxiety.

She cast one last worried glance over her shoulder at her mother before stepping into the shallow water along the shoreline and making her way toward the princess. Moving forward in faith in the midst of fear, she began a strange dance step she would dance again later in her life.

ASSIGNED READING:

Exodus 2:1–10; 13:17—15:21

And now, years later as an adult woman, standing at the shore of the Red Sea after fleeing from slavery in Egypt, she felt that same fear in the core of her being—that same adrenaline-laced, metallic sensation in her mouth. The two days were like bookends in her mind, full of similarities: risk, uncertainty, limited options.

"What if Pharaoh's army reaches the shore before we all cross over? What if one of our carts breaks down or a child falls in the sea? What if . . ."

But something was different this time as an adult. She could call upon the same faith in the midst of fear that she'd practiced as a child. It would strengthen her to step forward and do what must be done once more. Miriam cast another glance over her shoulder at the approaching Egyptian army before confidently and resolutely striding into the shallow water.

—Prayer—

Savior, I can and will, with your help, overcome my fears.

Weekend

Go to page 309 for your next devotional reading.

had neither son nor daughter. 35 When he
v her, he tore his clothes and cried, "Oh! My
ighter! You have made me miserable and
etched, because I have made a vow to the
RD that I cannot break."
36 "My father," she replied, "you have given
ır word to the LORD. Do to me just as you
omised, now that the LORD has avenged you
your enemies, the Ammonites. 37 But grant
this one request," she said. "Give me two
nths to roam the hills and weep with my
nds, because I will never marry."
38 "You may go," he said. And he let her go
two months. She and the girls went into the
s and wept because she would never marry.
After the two months, she returned to her fa-
r and he did to her as he had vowed. And
was a virgin.
From this comes the Israelite custom 40 that
h year the young women of Israel go out
four days to commemorate the daughter of
hthah the Gileadite.

ohthah and Ephraim

2 The men of Ephraim called out their
forces, crossed over to Zaphon and
d to Jephthah, "Why did you go to fight the
ımonites without calling us to go with you?
're going to burn down your house over
ır head."
2 Jephthah answered, "I and my people were
gaged in a great struggle with the Ammon-
s, and although I called, you didn't save
out of their hands. 3 When I saw that you
uldn't help, I took my life in my hands and
ssed over to fight the Ammonites, and the
RD gave me the victory over them. Now why
ve you come up today to fight me?"
4 Jephthah then called together the men of
lead and fought against Ephraim. The Gil-
lites struck them down because the Ephra-
ites had said, "You Gileadites are renegades
m Ephraim and Manasseh." 5 The Gileadites
otured the fords of the Jordan leading to
hraim, and whenever a survivor of Ephraim
d, "Let me cross over," the men of Gilead
ted him, "Are you an Ephraimite?" If he reed, "No," 6 they said, "All right, say 'Shibbo-
h.'" If he said, "Sibboleth," because he could
not pronounce the word correctly, they seized
him and killed him at the fords of the Jordan.
Forty-two thousand Ephraimites were killed at
that time.
7 Jephthah led[a] Israel six years. Then Jephthah the Gileadite died, and was buried in a
town in Gilead.

Ibzan, Elon and Abdon

8 After him, Ibzan of Bethlehem led Israel.
9 He had thirty sons and thirty daughters. He
gave his daughters away in marriage to those
outside his clan, and for his sons he brought in
thirty young women as wives from outside his
clan. Ibzan led Israel seven years. 10 Then Ibzan
died, and was buried in Bethlehem.
11 After him, Elon the Zebulunite led Israel
ten years. 12 Then Elon died, and was buried in
Aijalon in the land of Zebulun.
13 After him, Abdon son of Hillel, from Pirathon, led Israel. 14 He had forty sons and thirty
grandsons, who rode on seventy donkeys. He
led Israel eight years. 15 Then Abdon son of Hillel died, and was buried at Pirathon in Ephraim,
in the hill country of the Amalekites.

The Birth of Samson

13 Again the Israelites did evil in the
eyes of the LORD, so the LORD delivered them into the hands of the Philistines for
forty years.
2 A certain man of Zorah, named Manoah,
from the clan of the Danites, had a wife who
was sterile and remained childless. 3 The angel
of the LORD appeared to her and said, "You are
sterile and childless, but you are going to conceive and have a son. 4 Now see to it that you
drink no wine or other fermented drink and
that you do not eat anything unclean, 5 because
you will conceive and give birth to a son. No
razor may be used on his head, because the boy
is to be a Nazirite, set apart to God from birth,
and he will begin the deliverance of Israel from
the hands of the Philistines."
6 Then the woman went to her husband
and told him, "A man of God came to me. He
looked like an angel of God, very awesome. I
didn't ask him where he came from, and he
didn't tell me his name. 7 But he said to me, 'You
will conceive and give birth to a son. Now then,

'raditionally *judged*; also in verses 8–14

drink no wine or other fermented drink and do
not eat anything unclean, because the boy will
be a Nazirite of God from birth until the day
of his death.’ ”
8 Then Manoah prayed to the LORD: “O Lord,
I beg you, let the man of God you sent to us
come again to teach us how to bring up the boy
who is to be born.”
9 God heard Manoah, and the angel of God
came again to the woman while she was out
in the field; but her husband Manoah was not
with her. 10 The woman hurried to tell her husband, “He’s here! The man who appeared to me
the other day!”
11 Manoah got up and followed his wife.
When he came to the man, he said, “Are you
the one who talked to my wife?”
“I am,” he said.
12 So Manoah asked him, “When your words
are fulfilled, what is to be the rule for the boy’s
life and work?”
13 The angel of the LORD answered, “Your
wife must do all that I have told her. 14 She must
not eat anything that comes from the grapevine, nor drink any wine or other fermented
drink nor eat anything unclean. She must do
everything I have commanded her.”
15 Manoah said to the angel of the LORD,
“We would like you to stay until we prepare a
young goat for you.”
16 The angel of the LORD replied, “Even though you detain
me, I will not eat any of your
food. But if you prepare a burnt
offering, offer it to the LORD.”
(Manoah did not realize that it
was the angel of the LORD.)
17 Then Manoah inquired of
the angel of the LORD, “What
is your name, so that we may
honor you when your word
comes true?”
18 He replied, “Why do you
ask my name? It is beyond understanding.[a]”
19 Then Manoah took a young goat, together
with the grain offering, and sacrificed it on a
rock to the LORD. And the LORD did an amazing thing while Manoah and his wife watched:
20 As the flame blazed up from the altar toward
heaven, the angel of the LORD ascended in the
flame. Seeing this, Manoah and his wife fell
with their faces to the ground. 21 When the angel of the LORD did not show himself again to
Manoah and his wife, Manoah realized that it
was the angel of the LORD.
22 “We are doomed to die!” he said to his
wife. “We have seen God!”
23 But his wife answered, “If the LORD had
meant to kill us, he would not have accepted
a burnt offering and grain offering from our
hands, nor shown us all these things or now
told us this.”
24 The woman gave birth to a boy and named
him Samson. He grew and the LORD blessed
him, 25 and the Spirit of the LORD began to stir
him while he was in Mahaneh Dan, between
Zorah and Eshtaol.

Samson’s Marriage

14 Samson went down to Timnah and
saw there a young Philistine woman.
2 When he returned, he said to his father and
mother, “I have seen a Philistine woman in
Timnah; now get her for me as my wife.”
3 His father and mother replied, “Isn’t there
an acceptable woman among your relatives or
among all our people? Must you go to the uncircumcised Philistines to get a wife?”
But Samson said to his father, “Get her for me. She’s the
right one for me.” 4 (His parents
did not know that this was from
the LORD, who was seeking an
occasion to confront the Philistines; for at that time they were
ruling over Israel.) 5 Samson
went down to Timnah together
with his father and mother. As
they approached the vineyards
of Timnah, suddenly a young
lion came roaring toward him.
6 The Spirit of the LORD came
upon him in power so that he tore the lion
apart with his bare hands as he might have
torn a young goat. But he told neither his father nor his mother what he had done. 7 Then
he went down and talked with the woman, and
he liked her.

Judges 13:18

God Is Beyond Comprehension

He replied, “Why do you ask my name? It is beyond understanding.”

[a] 18 Or *is wonderful*

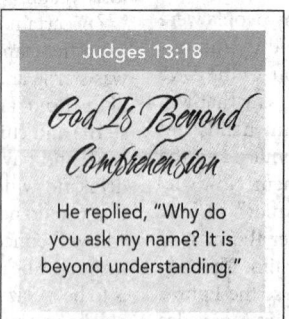

8 Some time later, when he went back to
marry her, he turned aside to look at the lion's
carcass. In it was a swarm of bees and some
honey, 9 which he scooped out with his hands
and ate as he went along. When he rejoined his
parents, he gave them some, and they too ate it.
But he did not tell them that he had taken the
honey from the lion's carcass.
10 Now his father went down to see the
woman. And Samson made a feast there, as
was customary for bridegrooms. 11 When he
appeared, he was given thirty companions.
12 "Let me tell you a riddle," Samson said to
them. "If you can give me the answer within the
seven days of the feast, I will give you thirty linen
garments and thirty sets of clothes. 13 If you
can't tell me the answer, you must give me thirty
linen garments and thirty sets of clothes."
"Tell us your riddle," they said. "Let's
hear it."
14 He replied,

"Out of the eater, something to eat;
out of the strong, something sweet."

For three days they could not give the answer.
15 On the fourth[a] day, they said to Samson's
wife, "Coax your husband into explaining the
riddle for us, or we will burn you and your father's household to death. Did you invite us
here to rob us?"
16 Then Samson's wife threw herself on him,
sobbing, "You hate me! You don't really love
me. You've given my people a riddle, but you
haven't told me the answer."
"I haven't even explained it to my father or
mother," he replied, "so why should I explain
it to you?" 17 She cried the whole seven days of
the feast. So on the seventh day he finally told
her, because she continued to press him. She in
turn explained the riddle to her people.
18 Before sunset on the seventh day the men
of the town said to him,

"What is sweeter than honey?
What is stronger than a lion?"

Samson said to them,

"If you had not plowed with my heifer,
you would not have solved my riddle."

19 Then the Spirit of the LORD came upon
him in power. He went down to Ashkelon,
struck down thirty of their men, stripped them
of their belongings and gave their clothes to
those who had explained the riddle. Burning
with anger, he went up to his father's house.
20 And Samson's wife was given to the friend
who had attended him at his wedding.

Samson's Vengeance on the Philistines

15 Later on, at the time of wheat harvest,
Samson took a young goat and went to
visit his wife. He said, "I'm going to my wife's
room." But her father would not let him go in.
2 "I was so sure you thoroughly hated her,"
he said, "that I gave her to your friend. Isn't
her younger sister more attractive? Take her
instead."
3 Samson said to them, "This time I have
a right to get even with the Philistines; I will
really harm them." 4 So he went out and caught
three hundred foxes and tied them tail to tail in
pairs. He then fastened a torch to every pair of
tails, 5 lit the torches and let the foxes loose in
the standing grain of the Philistines. He burned
up the shocks and standing grain, together with
the vineyards and olive groves.
6 When the Philistines asked, "Who did this?"
they were told, "Samson, the Timnite's son-in-
law, because his wife was given to his friend."
So the Philistines went up and burned her
and her father to death. 7 Samson said to them,
"Since you've acted like this, I won't stop until
I get my revenge on you." 8 He attacked them
viciously and slaughtered many of them. Then
he went down and stayed in a cave in the rock
of Etam.
9 The Philistines went up and camped in Judah, spreading out near Lehi. 10 The men of Judah asked, "Why have you come to fight us?"
"We have come to take Samson prisoner,"
they answered, "to do to him as he did to us."
11 Then three thousand men from Judah
went down to the cave in the rock of Etam and
said to Samson, "Don't you realize that the Philistines are rulers over us? What have you done
to us?"
He answered, "I merely did to them what
they did to me."

[a] 15 Some Septuagint manuscripts and Syriac; Hebrew *seventh*

12They said to him, "We've come to tie you
up and hand you over to the Philistines."
Samson said, "Swear to me that you won't
kill me yourselves."
13"Agreed," they answered. "We will only
tie you up and hand you over to them. We will
not kill you." So they bound him with two new
ropes and led him up from the rock. 14As he
approached Lehi, the Philistines came toward
him shouting. The Spirit of the LORD came
upon him in power. The ropes on his arms
became like charred flax, and the bindings
dropped from his hands. 15Finding a fresh
jawbone of a donkey, he grabbed it and struck
down a thousand men.
16Then Samson said,

"With a donkey's jawbone
I have made donkeys of them.[a]
With a donkey's jawbone
I have killed a thousand men."

17When he finished speaking, he threw away
the jawbone; and the place was called Ramath Lehi.[b]
18Because he was very thirsty, he cried out
to the LORD, "You have given your servant this
great victory. Must I now die of thirst and fall
into the hands of the uncircumcised?" 19Then
God opened up the hollow place in Lehi, and
water came out of it. When Samson drank,
his strength returned and he revived. So the
spring was called En Hakkore,[c] and it is still
there in Lehi.
20Samson led[d] Israel for twenty years in the
days of the Philistines.

Samson and Delilah

16 One day Samson went to Gaza, where
he saw a prostitute. He went in to spend
the night with her. 2The people of Gaza were
told, "Samson is here!" So they surrounded the
place and lay in wait for him all night at the city
gate. They made no move during the night, saying, "At dawn we'll kill him."
3But Samson lay there only until the middle
of the night. Then he got up and took hold of
the doors of the city gate, together with the
two posts, and tore them loose, bar and all. He
lifted them to his shoulders and carried them
to the top of the hill that faces Hebron.
4Some time later, he fell in love with a
woman in the Valley of Sorek whose name was
Delilah. 5The rulers of the Philistines went to
her and said, "See if you can lure him into showing you the secret of his great strength and how
we can overpower him so we may tie him up
and subdue him. Each one of us will give you
eleven hundred shekels[e] of silver."
6So Delilah said to Samson, "Tell me the secret of your great strength and how you can be
tied up and subdued."
7Samson answered her, "If anyone ties me
with seven fresh thongs[f] that have not been
dried, I'll become as weak as any other man."
8Then the rulers of the Philistines brought
her seven fresh thongs that had not been dried,
and she tied him with them. 9With men hidden in the room, she called to him, "Samson,
the Philistines are upon you!" But he snapped
the thongs as easily as a piece of string snaps
when it comes close to a flame. So the secret of
his strength was not discovered.
10Then Delilah said to Samson, "You have
made a fool of me; you lied to me. Come now,
tell me how you can be tied."
11He said, "If anyone ties me securely with
new ropes that have never been used, I'll become as weak as any other man."
12So Delilah took new ropes and tied him
with them. Then, with men hidden in the
room, she called to him, "Samson, the Philistines are upon you!" But he snapped the ropes
off his arms as if they were threads.
13Delilah then said to Samson, "Until now,
you have been making a fool of me and lying to
me. Tell me how you can be tied."
He replied, "If you weave the seven braids
of my head into the fabric ⌞on the loom⌟ and
tighten it with the pin, I'll become as weak as
any other man." So while he was sleeping, Delilah took the seven braids of his head, wove
them into the fabric 14and[g] tightened it with
the pin.
Again she called to him, "Samson, the Phi-

[a]16 Or *made a heap or two*; the Hebrew for *donkey* sounds like the Hebrew for *heap*. [b]17 *Ramath Lehi* means *jawbone hill*. [c]19 *En Hakkore* means *caller's spring*. [d]20 Traditionally *judged* [e]5 That is, about 28 pounds (about 13 kilograms) [f]7 Or *bowstrings*; also in verses 8 and 9 [g]13,14 Some Septuagint manuscripts; Hebrew *"⌞I can⌟ if you weave the seven braids of my head into the fabric ⌞on the loom⌟." 14So she*

Femme Fatales

Read: Judges 16:4–22

A FEMME FATALE IS A WOMAN who uses the powers of seduction to lure a man into a dangerous or compromising situation. One woman infamous for her influence was Mata Hari. At the turn of the twentieth century in Paris, Mata Hari created a fictitious persona and performed exotic Indian dance to great acclaim. Although her background was fabricated, Parisian society embraced her . . . and men were beguiled by her. Her sensuous dance seduced powerful men in influential positions. Many believe she used feminine guile to extract military secrets. Ultimately, the French tried Mata Hari and executed her as a double agent in World War I. At her trial she said, "Harlot, yes. But traitor? Never!"

In the Bible, we meet another woman who used her feminine allure to affect the destiny of a man. During the time of the judges, Delilah used her influence to discover the secrets of one of Israel's judges, Samson. Three different times Delilah begged him to give her information about the source of his strength. Three times he resisted. Each time Delilah proved herself false, calling for the Philistines to subdue the strong man. More stunning is that Delilah used the same method over and over again . . . and Samson allowed himself to be tricked each time. Ultimately, Delilah discovered the truth about Samson's strength and turned him over to her countrymen.

Delilah's story shows how men can be swayed by women's wiles and their own desires. Delilah used her sexual attraction and her cunning to bring a man down—for a price. She relentlessly manipulated Samson in order to get the information she needed. When he finally revealed the truth, she rushed to the Philistine rulers to gather her reward. In a heartbeat, Samson lost not just his strength, but the divine gift God had bestowed upon him.

We think it would be great to be able to get our husbands, boyfriends, coworkers, etc. to do what we want. And perhaps, sometimes, we *do* use feminine wiles, manipulation and nagging to get our way. But are such methods honest? Are they loving? Wouldn't it be better to be the kind of woman others can trust? How much better to employ honesty, kindness and patience to build up the men we love, rather than trample them in the pursuit of our selfish desires

Monday

Judges 16:15–16

Then she said to him, "How can you say, 'I love you,' when you won't confide in me? This is the third time you have made a fool of me and haven't told me the secret of your great strength." With such nagging she prodded him day after day until he was tired to death.

reflection

1 Have you ever nagged, manipulated or tricked a man in order to get your way?

2 How did it make you feel? How do you think it made him feel?

3 What words will you use to build up the men in your life?

RELATED READINGS

Proverbs 14:1; 19:13; 31:11–12;
1 Peter 3:1–6

Go to page 316 for your next devotional reading.

listines are upon you!" He awoke from his
sleep and pulled up the pin and the loom, with
the fabric.
15Then she said to him, "How can you say,
'I love you,' when you won't confide in me?
This is the third time you have made a fool
of me and haven't told me the secret of your
great strength." 16With such nagging she prodded him day after day until he was tired to
death.
17So he told her everything. "No razor has
ever been used on my head," he said, "because
I have been a Nazirite set apart to God since
birth. If my head were shaved, my strength
would leave me, and I would become as weak
as any other man."
18When Delilah saw that he had told her
everything, she sent word to the rulers of the
Philistines, "Come back once
more; he has told me everything." So the rulers of the
Philistines returned with the
silver in their hands. 19Having
put him to sleep on her lap, she
called a man to shave off the
seven braids of his hair, and so
began to subdue him.[a] And his
strength left him.
20Then she called, "Samson,
the Philistines are upon you!"
He awoke from his sleep and
thought, "I'll go out as before
and shake myself free." But he
did not know that the LORD
had left him.
21Then the Philistines seized
him, gouged out his eyes and
took him down to Gaza. Binding him with
bronze shackles, they set him to grinding in
the prison. 22But the hair on his head began to
grow again after it had been shaved.

The Death of Samson

23Now the rulers of the Philistines assembled to offer a great sacrifice to Dagon their god
and to celebrate, saying, "Our god has delivered
Samson, our enemy, into our hands."
24When the people saw him, they praised
their god, saying,

"Our god has delivered our enemy
into our hands,
the one who laid waste our land
and multiplied our slain."

25While they were in high spirits, they
shouted, "Bring out Samson to entertain us."
So they called Samson out of the prison, and
he performed for them.
When they stood him among the pillars,
26Samson said to the servant who held his
hand, "Put me where I can feel the pillars that
support the temple, so that I may lean against
them." 27Now the temple was crowded with
men and women; all the rulers of the Philistines
were there, and on the roof were about three
thousand men and women watching Samson
perform. 28Then Samson prayed to the LORD,
"O Sovereign LORD, remember
me. O God, please strengthen
me just once more, and let me
with one blow get revenge on
the Philistines for my two eyes."
29Then Samson reached to-
ward the two central pillars on
which the temple stood. Brac-
ing himself against them, his
right hand on the one and his
left hand on the other, 30Sam-
son said, "Let me die with the
Philistines!" Then he pushed
with all his might, and down
came the temple on the rulers
and all the people in it. Thus
he killed many more when he
died than while he lived.
31Then his brothers and his
father's whole family went down to get him.
They brought him back and buried him between
Zorah and Eshtaol in the tomb of Manoah his
father. He had led[b] Israel twenty years.

> **Judges 16:28**
>
> *God Remembers His Children*
>
> Then Samson prayed to the LORD, "O Sovereign LORD, remember me. O God, please strengthen me just once more, and let me with one blow get revenge on the Philistines for my two eyes."

Micah's Idols

17 Now a man named Micah from the
hill country of Ephraim 2said to his
mother, "The eleven hundred shekels[c] of silver
that were taken from you and about which I
heard you utter a curse—I have that silver with
me; I took it."

[a]19 Hebrew; some Septuagint manuscripts *and he began to weaken* [b]31 Traditionally *judged* [c]2 That is, about 28 pounds (about 13 kilograms)

Then his mother said, "The LORD bless you,
my son!"
3When he returned the eleven hundred shekels of silver to his mother, she said, "I solemnly
consecrate my silver to the LORD for my son to
make a carved image and a cast idol. I will give
it back to you."
4So he returned the silver to his mother, and
she took two hundred shekels[a] of silver and
gave them to a silversmith, who made them
into the image and the idol. And they were put
in Micah's house.
5Now this man Micah had a shrine, and he
made an ephod and some idols and installed
one of his sons as his priest. 6In those days
Israel had no king; everyone did as he saw fit.
7A young Levite from Bethlehem in Judah,
who had been living within the clan of Judah,
8left that town in search of some other place to
stay. On his way[b] he came to Micah's house in
the hill country of Ephraim.
9Micah asked him, "Where are you from?"
"I'm a Levite from Bethlehem in Judah," he
said, "and I'm looking for a place to stay."
10Then Micah said to him, "Live with me
and be my father and priest, and I'll give you
ten shekels[c] of silver a year, your clothes and
your food." 11So the Levite agreed to live with
him, and the young man was to him like one
of his sons. 12Then Micah installed the Levite,
and the young man became his priest and lived
in his house. 13And Micah said, "Now I know
that the LORD will be good to me, since this Levite has become my priest."

Danites Settle in Laish

18 In those days Israel had no king.
And in those days the tribe of the Danites was seeking a place of their own where they
might settle, because they had not yet come
into an inheritance among the tribes of Israel.
2So the Danites sent five warriors from Zorah
and Eshtaol to spy out the land and explore it.
These men represented all their clans. They
told them, "Go, explore the land."
The men entered the hill country of Ephraim
and came to the house of Micah, where they
spent the night. 3When they were near Micah's
house, they recognized the voice of the young
Levite; so they turned in there and asked him,
"Who brought you here? What are you doing
in this place? Why are you here?"
4He told them what Micah had done for
him, and said, "He has hired me and I am
his priest."
5Then they said to him, "Please inquire of
God to learn whether our journey will be successful."
6The priest answered them, "Go in peace.
Your journey has the LORD's approval."
7So the five men left and came to Laish,
where they saw that the people were living in
safety, like the Sidonians, unsuspecting and secure. And since their land lacked nothing, they
were prosperous.[d] Also, they lived a long way
from the Sidonians and had no relationship
with anyone else.[e]
8When they returned to Zorah and Eshtaol,
their brothers asked them, "How did you find
things?"
9They answered, "Come on, let's attack them!
We have seen that the land is very good. Aren't
you going to do something? Don't hesitate to
go there and take it over. 10When you get there,
you will find an unsuspecting people and a spacious land that God has put into your hands, a
land that lacks nothing whatever."
11Then six hundred men from the clan of
the Danites, armed for battle, set out from Zorah and Eshtaol. 12On their way they set up
camp near Kiriath Jearim in Judah. This is why
the place west of Kiriath Jearim is called Mahaneh Dan[f] to this day. 13From there they went
on to the hill country of Ephraim and came to
Micah's house.
14Then the five men who had spied out the
land of Laish said to their brothers, "Do you
know that one of these houses has an ephod,
other household gods, a carved image and
a cast idol? Now you know what to do." 15So
they turned in there and went to the house of
the young Levite at Micah's place and greeted
him. 16The six hundred Danites, armed for
battle, stood at the entrance to the gate. 17The
five men who had spied out the land went

[a]4 That is, about 5 pounds (about 2.3 kilograms) [b]8 Or *To carry on his profession* [c]10 That is, about 4 ounces (about 110 grams)
[d]7 The meaning of the Hebrew for this clause is uncertain. [e]7 Hebrew; some Septuagint manuscripts *with the Arameans*
[f]12 *Mahaneh Dan* means *Dan's camp.*

inside and took the carved image, the ephod,
the other household gods and the cast idol
while the priest and the six hundred armed
men stood at the entrance to the gate.
18When these men went into Micah's
house and took the carved image, the ephod,
the other household gods and the cast idol,
the priest said to them, "What are you doing?"
19They answered him, "Be quiet! Don't say
a word. Come with us, and be our father and
priest. Isn't it better that you serve a tribe and
clan in Israel as priest rather than just one
man's household?" 20Then the priest was glad.
He took the ephod, the other household gods
and the carved image and went along with the
people. 21Putting their little children, their livestock and their possessions in front of them,
they turned away and left.
22When they had gone some distance
from Micah's house, the men who lived near
Micah were called together and overtook the
Danites. 23As they shouted after them, the
Danites turned and said to Micah, "What's
the matter with you that you called out your
men to fight?"
24He replied, "You took the gods I made,
and my priest, and went away. What else do
I have? How can you ask, 'What's the matter
with you?'"
25The Danites answered, "Don't argue with
us, or some hot-tempered men will attack you,
and you and your family will lose your lives."
26So the Danites went their way, and Micah,
seeing that they were too strong for him, turned
around and went back home.
27Then they took what Micah had made,
and his priest, and went on to Laish, against
a peaceful and unsuspecting people. They attacked them with the sword and burned down
their city. 28There was no one to rescue them
because they lived a long way from Sidon and
had no relationship with anyone else. The city
was in a valley near Beth Rehob.
The Danites rebuilt the city and settled there.
29They named it Dan after their forefather
Dan, who was born to Israel—though the city
used to be called Laish. 30There the Danites set
up for themselves the idols, and Jonathan son
of Gershom, the son of Moses,[a] and his sons
were priests for the tribe of Dan until the time
of the captivity of the land. 31They continued
to use the idols Micah had made, all the time
the house of God was in Shiloh.

A Levite and His Concubine

19 In those days Israel had no king.
Now a Levite who lived in a remote
area in the hill country of Ephraim took a concubine from Bethlehem in Judah. 2But she was
unfaithful to him. She left him and went back
to her father's house in Bethlehem, Judah. After she had been there four months, 3her husband went to her to persuade her to return. He
had with him his servant and two donkeys. She
took him into her father's house, and when her
father saw him, he gladly welcomed him. 4His
father-in-law, the girl's father, prevailed upon
him to stay; so he remained with him three
days, eating and drinking, and sleeping there.
5On the fourth day they got up early and he
prepared to leave, but the girl's father said to his
son-in-law, "Refresh yourself with something
to eat; then you can go." 6So the two of them sat
down to eat and drink together. Afterward the
girl's father said, "Please stay tonight and enjoy
yourself." 7And when the man got up to go,
his father-in-law persuaded him, so he stayed
there that night. 8On the morning of the fifth
day, when he rose to go, the girl's father said,
"Refresh yourself. Wait till afternoon!" So the
two of them ate together.
9Then when the man, with his concubine
and his servant, got up to leave, his father-in-
law, the girl's father, said, "Now look, it's almost
evening. Spend the night here; the day is nearly
over. Stay and enjoy yourself. Early tomorrow
morning you can get up and be on your way
home." 10But, unwilling to stay another night,
the man left and went toward Jebus (that is, Jerusalem), with his two saddled donkeys and
his concubine.
11When they were near Jebus and the day
was almost gone, the servant said to his master,
"Come, let's stop at this city of the Jebusites and
spend the night."
12His master replied, "No. We won't go into
an alien city, whose people are not Israelites.
We will go on to Gibeah." 13He added, "Come,

[a]30 An ancient Hebrew scribal tradition, some Septuagint manuscripts and Vulgate; Masoretic Text *Manasseh*

let's try to reach Gibeah or Ramah and spend
the night in one of those places." 14 So they went
on, and the sun set as they neared Gibeah in
Benjamin. 15 There they stopped to spend the
night. They went and sat in the city square, but
no one took them into his home for the night.
16 That evening an old man from the hill
country of Ephraim, who was living in Gibeah
(the men of the place were Benjamites), came in
from his work in the fields. 17 When he looked
and saw the traveler in the city square, the old
man asked, "Where are you going? Where did
you come from?"
18 He answered, "We are on our way from
Bethlehem in Judah to a remote area in the hill
country of Ephraim where I live. I have been to
Bethlehem in Judah and now I am going to the
house of the LORD. No one has taken me into
his house. 19 We have both straw and fodder for
our donkeys and bread and wine for ourselves
your servants—me, your maidservant, and the
young man with us. We don't need anything."
20 "You are welcome at my house," the old
man said. "Let me supply whatever you need.
Only don't spend the night in the square." 21 So
he took him into his house and fed his donkeys. After they had washed their feet, they had
something to eat and drink.
22 While they were enjoying themselves,
some of the wicked men of the city surrounded
the house. Pounding on the door, they shouted
to the old man who owned the house, "Bring
out the man who came to your house so we can
have sex with him."
23 The owner of the house went outside and
said to them, "No, my friends, don't be so vile.
Since this man is my guest, don't do this disgraceful thing. 24 Look, here is my virgin daughter, and his concubine. I will bring them out to
you now, and you can use them and do to them
whatever you wish. But to this man, don't do
such a disgraceful thing."
25 But the men would not listen to him. So
the man took his concubine and sent her outside to them, and they raped her and abused
her throughout the night, and at dawn they let
her go. 26 At daybreak the woman went back
to the house where her master was staying, fell
down at the door and lay there until daylight.
27 When her master got up in the morning
and opened the door of the house and stepped
out to continue on his way, there lay his concubine, fallen in the doorway of the house,
with her hands on the threshold. 28 He said to
her, "Get up; let's go." But there was no answer.
Then the man put her on his donkey and set
out for home.
29 When he reached home, he took a knife
and cut up his concubine, limb by limb, into
twelve parts and sent them into all the areas
of Israel. 30 Everyone who saw it said, "Such a
thing has never been seen or done, not since the
day the Israelites came up out of Egypt. Think
about it! Consider it! Tell us what to do!"

Israelites Fight the Benjamites

20 Then all the Israelites from Dan to
Beersheba and from the land of Gilead
came out as one man and assembled before the
LORD in Mizpah. 2 The leaders of all the people
of the tribes of Israel took their places in the
assembly of the people of God, four hundred
thousand soldiers armed with swords. 3 (The
Benjamites heard that the Israelites had gone
up to Mizpah.) Then the Israelites said, "Tell us
how this awful thing happened."
4 So the Levite, the husband of the murdered
woman, said, "I and my concubine came to
Gibeah in Benjamin to spend the night. 5 During the night the men of Gibeah came after me
and surrounded the house, intending to kill
me. They raped my concubine, and she died.
6 I took my concubine, cut her into pieces and
sent one piece to each region of Israel's inheritance, because they committed this lewd and
disgraceful act in Israel. 7 Now, all you Israelites, speak up and give your verdict."
8 All the people rose as one man, saying,
"None of us will go home. No, not one of us
will return to his house. 9 But now this is what
we'll do to Gibeah: We'll go up against it as the
lot directs. 10 We'll take ten men out of every
hundred from all the tribes of Israel, and a hundred from a thousand, and a thousand from
ten thousand, to get provisions for the army.
Then, when the army arrives at Gibeah[a] in Benjamin, it can give them what they deserve for
all this vileness done in Israel." 11 So all the men

[a] 10 One Hebrew manuscript; most Hebrew manuscripts *Geba,* a variant of *Gibeah*

of Israel got together and united as one man
against the city.
12 The tribes of Israel sent men throughout
the tribe of Benjamin, saying, "What about
this awful crime that was committed among you? 13 Now
surrender those wicked men
of Gibeah so that we may put
them to death and purge the
evil from Israel."
But the Benjamites would
not listen to their fellow Israelites. 14 From their towns they
came together at Gibeah to
fight against the Israelites. 15 At
once the Benjamites mobilized
twenty-six thousand swordsmen from their towns, in addition to seven hundred chosen
men from those living in Gibeah. 16 Among all
these soldiers there were seven hundred chosen men who were left-handed, each of whom
could sling a stone at a hair and not miss.
17 Israel, apart from Benjamin, mustered
four hundred thousand swordsmen, all of
them fighting men.
18 The Israelites went up to Bethel[a] and inquired of God. They said, "Who of us shall go
first to fight against the Benjamites?"
The LORD replied, "Judah shall go first."
19 The next morning the Israelites got up
and pitched camp near Gibeah. 20 The men of
Israel went out to fight the Benjamites and took
up battle positions against them at Gibeah.
21 The Benjamites came out of Gibeah and cut
down twenty-two thousand Israelites on the
battlefield that day. 22 But the men of Israel
encouraged one another and again took up
their positions where they had stationed themselves the first day. 23 The Israelites went up
and wept before the LORD until evening, and
they inquired of the LORD. They said, "Shall we
go up again to battle against the Benjamites,
our brothers?"
The LORD answered, "Go up against them."
24 Then the Israelites drew near to Benjamin
the second day. 25 This time, when the Benjamites came out from Gibeah to oppose them,
they cut down another eighteen thousand Israelites, all of them armed with swords.
26 Then the Israelites, all the people, went up
to Bethel, and there they sat weeping before
the LORD. They fasted that day
until evening and presented
burnt offerings and fellowship
offerings[b] to the LORD. 27 And
the Israelites inquired of the
LORD. (In those days the ark of
the covenant of God was there,
28 with Phinehas son of Eleazar,
the son of Aaron, ministering
before it.) They asked, "Shall we
go up again to battle with Benjamin our brother, or not?"
The LORD responded, "Go,
for tomorrow I will give them
into your hands."
29 Then Israel set an ambush around Gibeah.
30 They went up against the Benjamites on the
third day and took up positions against Gibeah
as they had done before. 31 The Benjamites
came out to meet them and were drawn away
from the city. They began to inflict casualties on
the Israelites as before, so that about thirty men
fell in the open field and on the roads—the one
leading to Bethel and the other to Gibeah.
32 While the Benjamites were saying, "We
are defeating them as before," the Israelites
were saying, "Let's retreat and draw them away
from the city to the roads."
33 All the men of Israel moved from their
places and took up positions at Baal Tamar,
and the Israelite ambush charged out of its place
on the west[c] of Gibeah.[d] 34 Then ten thousand
of Israel's finest men made a frontal attack on
Gibeah. The fighting was so heavy that the Benjamites did not realize how near disaster was.
35 The LORD defeated Benjamin before Israel,
and on that day the Israelites struck down 25,100
Benjamites, all armed with swords. 36 Then the
Benjamites saw that they were beaten.
Now the men of Israel had given way before
Benjamin, because they relied on the ambush
they had set near Gibeah. 37 The men who
had been in ambush made a sudden dash into
Gibeah, spread out and put the whole city to

Judges 20:28

God Comes Through

The LORD responded, "Go, for tomorrow I will give them into your hands."

[a]18 Or *to the house of God*; also in verse 26 [b]26 Traditionally *peace offerings* [c]33 Some Septuagint manuscripts and Vulgate; the meaning of the Hebrew for this word is uncertain. [d]33 Hebrew *Geba*, a variant of *Gibeah*

the sword. 38The men of Israel had arranged with the ambush that they should send up a great cloud of smoke from the city, 39and then the men of Israel would turn in the battle.

The Benjamites had begun to inflict casualties on the men of Israel (about thirty), and they said, "We are defeating them as in the first battle." 40But when the column of smoke began to rise from the city, the Benjamites turned and saw the smoke of the whole city going up into the sky. 41Then the men of Israel turned on them, and the men of Benjamin were terrified, because they realized that disaster had come upon them. 42So they fled before the Israelites in the direction of the desert, but they could not escape the battle. And the men of Israel who came out of the towns cut them down there. 43They surrounded the Benjamites, chased them and easily[a] overran them in the vicinity of Gibeah on the east. 44Eighteen thousand Benjamites fell, all of them valiant fighters. 45As they turned and fled toward the desert to the rock of Rimmon, the Israelites cut down five thousand men along the roads. They kept pressing after the Benjamites as far as Gidom and struck down two thousand more.

46On that day twenty-five thousand Benjamite swordsmen fell, all of them valiant fighters. 47But six hundred men turned and fled into the desert to the rock of Rimmon, where they stayed four months. 48The men of Israel went back to Benjamin and put all the towns to the sword, including the animals and everything else they found. All the towns they came across they set on fire.

Wives for the Benjamites

21 The men of Israel had taken an oath at Mizpah: "Not one of us will give his daughter in marriage to a Benjamite."

2The people went to Bethel,[b] where they sat before God until evening, raising their voices and weeping bitterly. 3"O LORD, the God of Israel," they cried, "why has this happened to Israel? Why should one tribe be missing from Israel today?"

4Early the next day the people built an altar and presented burnt offerings and fellowship offerings.[c]

5Then the Israelites asked, "Who from all the tribes of Israel has failed to assemble before the LORD?" For they had taken a solemn oath that anyone who failed to assemble before the LORD at Mizpah should certainly be put to death.

6Now the Israelites grieved for their brothers, the Benjamites. "Today one tribe is cut off from Israel," they said. 7"How can we provide wives for those who are left, since we have taken an oath by the LORD not to give them any of our daughters in marriage?" 8Then they asked, "Which one of the tribes of Israel failed to assemble before the LORD at Mizpah?" They discovered that no one from Jabesh Gilead had come to the camp for the assembly. 9For when they counted the people, they found that none of the people of Jabesh Gilead were there.

10So the assembly sent twelve thousand fighting men with instructions to go to Jabesh Gilead and put to the sword those living there, including the women and children. 11"This is what you are to do," they said. "Kill every male and every woman who is not a virgin." 12They found among the people living in Jabesh Gilead four hundred young women who had never slept with a man, and they took them to the camp at Shiloh in Canaan.

13Then the whole assembly sent an offer of peace to the Benjamites at the rock of Rimmon. 14So the Benjamites returned at that time and were given the women of Jabesh Gilead who had been spared. But there were not enough for all of them.

15The people grieved for Benjamin, because the LORD had made a gap in the tribes of Israel. 16And the elders of the assembly said, "With the women of Benjamin destroyed, how shall we provide wives for the men who are left? 17The Benjamite survivors must have heirs," they said, "so that a tribe of Israel will not be wiped out. 18We can't give them our daughters as wives, since we Israelites have taken this oath: 'Cursed be anyone who gives a wife to a Benjamite.' 19But look, there is the annual festival of the LORD in Shiloh, to the north of Bethel, and east of the road that goes from Bethel to Shechem, and to the south of Lebonah."

20So they instructed the Benjamites, saying,

[a]43 The meaning of the Hebrew for this word is uncertain. [b]2 Or *to the house of God* [c]4 Traditionally *peace offerings*

God Is Faithful

Read: Judges 21:1–25

Judges 21:2–4

The people went to Bethel, where they sat before God until evening, raising their voices and weeping bitterly. "O Lord, the God of Israel," they cried, "why has this happened to Israel? Why should one tribe be missing from Israel today?" Early the next day the people built an altar and presented burnt offerings and fellowship offerings.

reflection

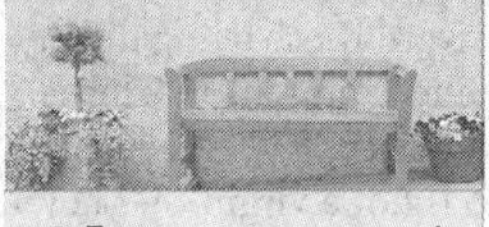

1 From your experiences in life, what do you know to be true about God?

2 How has God shown himself to be faithful in the past? How does this give you confidence for the future?

3 Follow Sheila's suggestion and spend some time turning your face in trust toward God, even if things seem dark right now. Ask God to turn you into a faithful woman serving a faithful God.

RELATED READINGS

Deuteronomy 7:7–9; Joshua 18:11–21; Acts 13:16–25

I USED TO HAVE AN ANSWER for most problems in life. I had a lot to say on almost any subject. I now have fewer answers, and might be reduced to the simple phrase, God is faithful. I don't say that lightly or without thought; I say it because I know it is true, and I have discovered that it is true no matter what is happening in my life. With confidence, I add these words to the end of the worst statements in the world: My child is sick and I don't know what to do . . . but God is faithful; I lost my job and I don't know how I will pay my bills . . . but God is faithful; my husband has left me and my heart is torn in two . . . but God is faithful.

I don't mean that he will wave a magic wand and everything will fall into place; far from it. What I mean is that if in the darkest times in our lives we will learn to keep turning our face toward him, he is faithful. Faithful to be with us, faithful to watch over us, faithful to work in us to make us the men and women we are called to be . . .

Think of your own life. Stop for a moment and reflect on any situation where it seemed as if you were on your own, that it was hopeless, that you were forgotten. Remember how you could never have anticipated God showing up, but he did, with flying colors—even if it seemed like he left you dangling just a little too long for comfort!

I don't know what the circumstances of your life are right now, or how fast you feel you're falling, or whether you're frozen on the bar, afraid to let go and grab hold of God's hands. What I can tell you is that he is here, right now, and he won't let you go. He will catch you in midair. The net of his faithful love will cushion you when you free-fall.

—*Sheila Walsh*

Go to page 320 for your next devotional reading.

"Go and hide in the vineyards 21and watch.
When the girls of Shiloh come out to join in
the dancing, then rush from the vineyards and
each of you seize a wife from the girls of Shiloh
and go to the land of Benjamin. 22When their
fathers or brothers complain to us, we will say
to them, 'Do us a kindness by helping them, because we did not get wives for them during the
war, and you are innocent, since you did not
give your daughters to them.'"

23So that is what the Benjamites did. While
the girls were dancing, each man caught one
and carried her off to be his wife. Then they
returned to their inheritance and rebuilt the
towns and settled in them.

24At that time the Israelites left that place
and went home to their tribes and clans, each
to his own inheritance.

25In those days Israel had no king; everyone
did as he saw fit.

Ruth

Author:
Unknown.

Audience:
The people of Israel.

Date:
Around 1000 B.C.

Setting:
The story is set sometime during the time of the judges when Israel and Moab were at peace.

Verse to Remember:
"Don't urge me to leave you or to turn back from you. Where you go I will go, and where you stay I will stay. Your people will be my people and your God my God." (1:16)

The book of Ruth is an ancient story that follows the journey of *one Jewish family's struggle* for survival. Escaping famine, Elimelech traveled to Moab with his wife, Naomi, and two sons. But ten years later, we find *Naomi in mourning* at the loss of both her husband and two sons. She is left alone in a foreign land with two Moabite daughters-in-law and no hope of future happiness . . . or so it seems. Naomi is a woman who forgot her dream, but *God had not forgotten her.* Through an unlikely chain of events, God restored her joy through her foreigner daughter-in-law and a kind, wealthy relative.

Naomi and Ruth

1 In the days when the judges ruled,[a] there
was a famine in the land, and a man from
Bethlehem in Judah, together with his wife and
two sons, went to live for a while in the country of Moab. 2The man's name was Elimelech,
his wife's name Naomi, and the names of his
two sons were Mahlon and Kilion. They were
Ephrathites from Bethlehem, Judah. And they
went to Moab and lived there.
3Now Elimelech, Naomi's husband, died,
and she was left with her two sons. 4They married Moabite women, one named Orpah and
the other Ruth. After they had lived there about
ten years, 5both Mahlon and Kilion also died,
and Naomi was left without her two sons and
her husband.
6When she heard in Moab that the LORD had
come to the aid of his people by providing food
for them, Naomi and her daughters-in-law pre-

[a]1 Traditionally *judged*

pared to return home from there. 7With her
two daughters-in-law she left the place where
she had been living and set out on the road that
would take them back to the land of Judah.
8Then Naomi said to her two daughters-in-
law, "Go back, each of you, to your mother's
home. May the LORD show kindness to you, as
you have shown to your dead and to me. 9May
the LORD grant that each of you will find rest in
the home of another husband."
Then she kissed them and they wept aloud
10and said to her, "We will go back with you to
your people."
11But Naomi said, "Return home, my daughters. Why would you come with me? Am I going to have any more sons, who could become
your husbands? 12Return home, my daughters;
I am too old to have another husband. Even if I
thought there was still hope for me—even if I
had a husband tonight and then gave birth to
sons— 13would you wait until they grew up?
Would you remain unmarried for them? No,
my daughters. It is more bitter for me than for
you, because the LORD's hand has gone out
against me!"
14At this they wept again.
Then Orpah kissed her mother-
in-law good-by, but Ruth clung
to her.
15"Look," said Naomi, "your
sister-in-law is going back to
her people and her gods. Go
back with her."
16But Ruth replied, "Don't
urge me to leave you or to turn
back from you. Where you go
I will go, and where you stay
I will stay. Your people will be
my people and your God my
God. 17Where you die I will
die, and there I will be buried.
May the LORD deal with me, be
it ever so severely, if anything
but death separates you and me." 18When
Naomi realized that Ruth was determined to
go with her, she stopped urging her.
19So the two women went on until they
came to Bethlehem. When they arrived in Bethlehem, the whole town was stirred because of
them, and the women exclaimed, "Can this be
Naomi?"
20"Don't call me Naomi,[a]" she told them.
"Call me Mara,[b] because the Almighty[c] has
made my life very bitter. 21I went away full, but
the LORD has brought me back empty. Why call
me Naomi? The LORD has afflicted[d] me; the
Almighty has brought misfortune upon me."
22So Naomi returned from Moab accompanied by Ruth the Moabitess, her daughter-in-
law, arriving in Bethlehem as the barley harvest
was beginning.

Ruth 1:16

God Adopts His Followers

But Ruth replied, "Don't urge me to leave you or to turn back from you. Where you go I will go, and where you stay I will stay. Your people will be my people and your God my God."

Ruth Meets Boaz

2 Now Naomi had a relative on her husband's side, from the clan of Elimelech, a
man of standing, whose name was Boaz.
2And Ruth the Moabitess said to Naomi,
"Let me go to the fields and pick up the left-
over grain behind anyone in whose eyes I find
favor."
Naomi said to her, "Go ahead, my daughter."
3So she went out and began to glean in the
fields behind the harvesters. As
it turned out, she found herself
working in a field belonging to
Boaz, who was from the clan
of Elimelech.
4Just then Boaz arrived
from Bethlehem and greeted
the harvesters, "The LORD be
with you!"
"The LORD bless you!" they
called back.
5Boaz asked the foreman of
his harvesters, "Whose young
woman is that?"
6The foreman replied, "She
is the Moabitess who came
back from Moab with Naomi.
7She said, 'Please let me glean
and gather among the sheaves
behind the harvesters.' She went into the field
and has worked steadily from morning till now,
except for a short rest in the shelter."
8So Boaz said to Ruth, "My daughter, listen
to me. Don't go and glean in another field and

[a]20 *Naomi* means *pleasant*; also in verse 21. [b]20 *Mara* means *bitter.* [c]20 Hebrew *Shaddai*; also in verse 21 [d]21 Or *has testified against*

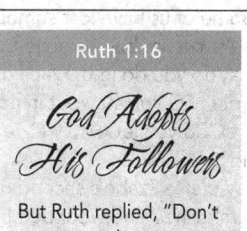

From Death to New Life

Read: Ruth 1:1–22

Ruth 1:16

But Ruth replied, "Don't urge me to leave you or to turn back from you. Where you go I will go, and where you stay I will stay. Your people will be my people and your God my God.

IN 1942, VIOLETTE SZABO'S HUSBAND, Lieutenant Etienne Szabo of the Free French Forces, died in action. Violette could easily have retired from sight. Their marriage had lasted barely two years. Etienne would never meet their daughter. But shortly after Etienne's death, 21-year-old Violette faced a choice: remain in the relative safety of England or go behind enemy lines as a spy in occupied France. She chose to venture courageously into her husband's country.

Ruth faced a similar decision when her husband died. Her mother-in-law, Naomi, had decided to return to Bethlehem. When Naomi urged Ruth and her sister-in-law to stay in Moab, Orpah chose to stay among her people and pagan gods. She disappeared into the land and from the Scriptural record. Ruth, however, chose to follow her mother-in-law to the land of Judah.

So, with Naomi, Ruth journeyed to the promised land, where she found new hope, a new husband and a place in the genealogy of the Messiah. Her story illustrates a paradox of faith: New life can come from the tragedy of death (see John 12:24).

Not all of us have experienced the death of a spouse as Violette or Ruth did, but we have all experienced death in some form. Some of us have lost someone dear, leaving emptiness in our hearts. We go on, but we ache for their presence.

What do you do in the face of death? Do you blame God, as Naomi did? Do you stay put in nowhere land, as Orpah stayed in Moab? Or do you let God weave your grief into a new story, as Ruth did?

On Violette Szabo's second mission in France, a German patrol ambushed and wounded her. She insisted her French guide save himself and escape, which he did. During her capture and imprisonment, her fellow prisoners would remember her incredible generosity and courage. In the winter of 1945, Madame Szabo gave her life aiding in the effort to free her husband's homeland.

Our faith promises new life. God knows the "deaths" you've experienced. His plans for you are good, though they may look different than you expected. Rest in the knowledge that God uses every circumstance to strengthen your faith in him. When you think that life as you knew it is over, remember the One who said "I am making everything new" (Revelation 21:5).

reflection

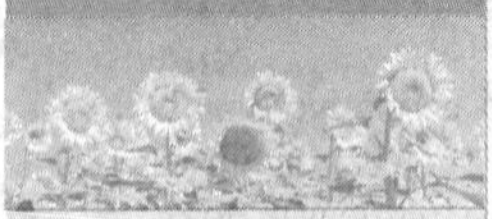

1 How has death touched your life?

2 How has God used death to resurrect your hope?

3 Can you help someone you know who is struggling with loss? Share your journey with her and encourage her from your own experiences.

RELATED READINGS

Jeremiah 29:11–14; Romans 6:4–10; Philippians 3:7–14; 1 Peter 1:3–7

"The ability to find joy in the world of sorrow and hope at the edge of despair is a woman's witness to courage and her gift of new life to all."

Miriam Theresa Winter

Wednesday

Go to page 326 for your next devotional reading.

don't go away from here. Stay here with my
servant girls. 9Watch the field where the men
are harvesting, and follow along after the girls.
I have told the men not to touch you. And
whenever you are thirsty, go and get a drink
from the water jars the men have filled."
10At this, she bowed down with her face to
the ground. She exclaimed, "Why have I found
such favor in your eyes that you notice me—a
foreigner?"
11Boaz replied, "I've been told all about what
you have done for your mother-in-law since
the death of your husband—how you left your
father and mother and your homeland and
came to live with a people you did not know
before. 12May the LORD repay you for what you
have done. May you be richly rewarded by the
LORD, the God of Israel, under whose wings
you have come to take refuge."
13"May I continue to find favor in your
eyes, my lord," she said. "You have given me
comfort and have spoken kindly to your servant—though I do not have the standing of one
of your servant girls."
14At mealtime Boaz said to her, "Come
over here. Have some bread and dip it in the
wine vinegar."
When she sat down with the harvesters, he
offered her some roasted grain. She ate all she
wanted and had some left over. 15As she got up
to glean, Boaz gave orders to his men, "Even if
she gathers among the sheaves, don't embarrass
her. 16Rather, pull out some stalks for her from
the bundles and leave them for her to pick up,
and don't rebuke her."
17So Ruth gleaned in the field until evening.
Then she threshed the barley she had gathered,
and it amounted to about an ephah.[a] 18She carried it back to town, and her mother-in-law saw
how much she had gathered. Ruth also brought
out and gave her what she had left over after
she had eaten enough.
19Her mother-in-law asked her, "Where did
you glean today? Where did you work? Blessed
be the man who took notice of you!"
Then Ruth told her mother-in-law about the
one at whose place she had been working. "The
name of the man I worked with today is Boaz,"
she said.
20"The LORD bless him!" Naomi said to her
daughter-in-law. "He has not stopped showing
his kindness to the living and the dead." She
added, "That man is our close relative; he is one
of our kinsman-redeemers."
21Then Ruth the Moabitess said, "He even
said to me, 'Stay with my workers until they finish harvesting all my grain.'"
22Naomi said to Ruth her daughter-in-law,
"It will be good for you, my daughter, to go
with his girls, because in someone else's field
you might be harmed."
23So Ruth stayed close to the servant girls
of Boaz to glean until the barley and wheat
harvests were finished. And she lived with her
mother-in-law.

Ruth and Boaz at the Threshing Floor

3 One day Naomi her mother-in-law said
to her, "My daughter, should I not try to
find a home[b] for you, where you will be well
provided for? 2Is not Boaz, with whose servant girls you have been, a kinsman of ours?
Tonight he will be winnowing barley on the
threshing floor. 3Wash and perfume yourself,
and put on your best clothes. Then go down to
the threshing floor, but don't let him know you
are there until he has finished eating and drinking. 4When he lies down, note the place where
he is lying. Then go and uncover his feet and lie
down. He will tell you what to do."
5"I will do whatever you say," Ruth answered.
6So she went down to the threshing floor and
did everything her mother-in-law told her
to do.
7When Boaz had finished eating and drinking and was in good spirits, he went over to
lie down at the far end of the grain pile. Ruth
approached quietly, uncovered his feet and lay
down. 8In the middle of the night something
startled the man, and he turned and discovered
a woman lying at his feet.
9"Who are you?" he asked.
"I am your servant Ruth," she said. "Spread
the corner of your garment over me, since you
are a kinsman-redeemer."
10"The LORD bless you, my daughter," he replied. "This kindness is greater than that which
you showed earlier: You have not run after the

[a]17 That is, probably about 3/5 bushel (about 22 liters) [b]1 Hebrew *find rest* (see Ruth 1:9)

younger men, whether rich or poor. 11 And
now, my daughter, don't be afraid. I will do for
you all you ask. All my fellow townsmen know
that you are a woman of noble character. 12 Although it is true that I am near of kin, there is a
kinsman-redeemer nearer than
I. 13 Stay here for the night, and
in the morning if he wants to
redeem, good; let him redeem.
But if he is not willing, as surely
as the LORD lives I will do it.
Lie here until morning."
14 So she lay at his feet until
morning, but got up before anyone could be recognized; and
he said, "Don't let it be known
that a woman came to the
threshing floor."
15 He also said, "Bring me
the shawl you are wearing and
hold it out." When she did so,
he poured into it six measures
of barley and put it on her.
Then he[a] went back to town.
16 When Ruth came to her mother-in-law,
Naomi asked, "How did it go, my daughter?"
Then she told her everything Boaz had done
for her 17 and added, "He gave me these six measures of barley, saying, 'Don't go back to your
mother-in-law empty-handed.'"
18 Then Naomi said, "Wait, my daughter, until you find out what happens. For the man will
not rest until the matter is settled today."

> **Ruth 4:14**
>
> ***God Meets Our Needs***
>
> The women said to Naomi: "Praise be to the LORD, who this day has not left you without a kinsman-redeemer. May he become famous throughout Israel!"

Boaz Marries Ruth

4 Meanwhile Boaz went up to the town
gate and sat there. When the kinsman-
redeemer he had mentioned came along,
Boaz said, "Come over here, my friend, and sit
down." So he went over and sat down.
2 Boaz took ten of the elders of the town and
said, "Sit here," and they did so. 3 Then he said
to the kinsman-redeemer, "Naomi, who has
come back from Moab, is selling the piece of
land that belonged to our brother Elimelech. 4 I
thought I should bring the matter to your attention and suggest that you buy it in the presence
of these seated here and in the presence of the
elders of my people. If you will redeem it, do so.
But if you[b] will not, tell me, so I will know. For
no one has the right to do it except you, and I
am next in line."
"I will redeem it," he said.
5 Then Boaz said, "On the day you buy the
land from Naomi and from
Ruth the Moabitess, you acquire[c] the dead man's widow,
in order to maintain the name
of the dead with his property."
6 At this, the kinsman-
redeemer said, "Then I cannot redeem it because I might
endanger my own estate. You
redeem it yourself. I cannot
do it."
7 (Now in earlier times in
Israel, for the redemption and
transfer of property to become
final, one party took off his
sandal and gave it to the other.
This was the method of legaliz-
ing transactions in Israel.)
8 So the kinsman-redeemer said to Boaz,
"Buy it yourself." And he removed his sandal.
9 Then Boaz announced to the elders and
all the people, "Today you are witnesses that
I have bought from Naomi all the property of
Elimelech, Kilion and Mahlon. 10 I have also acquired Ruth the Moabitess, Mahlon's widow, as
my wife, in order to maintain the name of the
dead with his property, so that his name will
not disappear from among his family or from
the town records. Today you are witnesses!"
11 Then the elders and all those at the gate
said, "We are witnesses. May the LORD make
the woman who is coming into your home like
Rachel and Leah, who together built up the
house of Israel. May you have standing in Ephrathah and be famous in Bethlehem. 12 Through
the offspring the LORD gives you by this young
woman, may your family be like that of Perez,
whom Tamar bore to Judah."

The Genealogy of David

13 So Boaz took Ruth and she became his
wife. Then he went to her, and the LORD enabled her to conceive, and she gave birth to a
son. 14 The women said to Naomi: "Praise be to

[a]15 Most Hebrew manuscripts; many Hebrew manuscripts, Vulgate and Syriac *she* [b]4 Many Hebrew manuscripts, Septuagint, Vulgate and Syriac; most Hebrew manuscripts *he* [c]5 Hebrew; Vulgate and Syriac *Naomi, you acquire Ruth the Moabitess,*

the LORD, who this day has not left you without
a kinsman-redeemer. May he become famous
throughout Israel! 15 He will renew your life and
sustain you in your old age. For your daughter-
in-law, who loves you and who is better to you
than seven sons, has given him birth."
16 Then Naomi took the child, laid him in
her lap and cared for him. 17 The women living
there said, "Naomi has a son." And they named
him Obed. He was the father of Jesse, the father
of David.

18 This, then, is the family line of Perez:

Perez was the father of Hezron,
19 Hezron the father of Ram,
Ram the father of Amminadab,
20 Amminadab the father of Nahshon,
Nahshon the father of Salmon,[a]
21 Salmon the father of Boaz,
Boaz the father of Obed,
22 Obed the father of Jesse,
and Jesse the father of David.

[a] **20** A few Hebrew manuscripts, some Septuagint manuscripts and Vulgate (see also verse 21 and Septuagint of 1 Chron. 2:11); most Hebrew manuscripts *Salma*

1 Samuel

Author:
Unknown.

Audience:
The people of Israel.

Date:
Sometime after the division of Israel into the northern and southern kingdoms, around 930 B.C.

Setting:
The people of Israel want to shift from a theocracy to a monarchy.

Verse to Remember:
"Does the LORD delight in burnt offerings and sacrifices as much as in obeying the voice of the LORD? To obey is better than sacrifice, and to heed is better than the fat of rams." (15:22)

First Samuel is one of the *most action-packed* books in the Bible. It marks a crucial turn in Israel's history when the people shifted from being ruled by theocracy (rule by God) and led by judges to a monarchy (rule by a king). This turn forever *alters the course of history*, and around the bend lie battles, allegiances, valor, cowardice, enemies and the truest of friends.

Samuel presided over Israel during this time of transition as both prophet and judge. He anointed two kings during his lifetime—*Saul and David.* He loved both men and believed in their abilities as leaders, and yet he watched one fail and the other flourish. Each man had choices to make, and each had consequences to live with as a result of those choices. They faced personal and national crises, and as we watch them work their way through those challenges, we see both what happens when we follow what seems best to our human reasoning and what happens when we entrust ourselves to *God's care and timing.*

The Birth of Samuel

1 There was a certain man from Ramathaim,
a Zuphite[a] from the hill country of Ephraim, whose name was Elkanah son of Jeroham,
the son of Elihu, the son of Tohu, the son of
Zuph, an Ephraimite. 2He had two wives; one
was called Hannah and the other Peninnah. Peninnah had children, but Hannah had none.

3Year after year this man went up from his
town to worship and sacrifice to the LORD Almighty at Shiloh, where Hophni and Phinehas,
the two sons of Eli, were priests of the LORD.
4Whenever the day came for Elkanah to sacrifice, he would give portions of the meat to his
wife Peninnah and to all her sons and daughters. 5But to Hannah he gave a double portion

[a]1 Or *from Ramathaim Zuphim*

because he loved her, and the LORD had closed her womb. 6 And because the LORD had closed her womb, her rival kept provoking her in order to irritate her. 7 This went on year after year. Whenever Hannah went up to the house of the LORD, her rival provoked her till she wept and would not eat. 8 Elkanah her husband would say to her, "Hannah, why are you weeping? Why don't you eat? Why are you downhearted? Don't I mean more to you than ten sons?"

9 Once when they had finished eating and drinking in Shiloh, Hannah stood up. Now Eli the priest was sitting on a chair by the doorpost of the LORD's temple.[a] 10 In bitterness of soul Hannah wept much and prayed to the LORD. 11 And she made a vow, saying, "O LORD Almighty, if you will only look upon your servant's misery and remember me, and not forget your servant but give her a son, then I will give him to the LORD for all the days of his life, and no razor will ever be used on his head."

12 As she kept on praying to the LORD, Eli observed her mouth. 13 Hannah was praying in her heart, and her lips were moving but her voice was not heard. Eli thought she was drunk 14 and said to her, "How long will you keep on getting drunk? Get rid of your wine."

15 "Not so, my lord," Hannah replied, "I am a woman who is deeply troubled. I have not been drinking wine or beer; I was pouring out my soul to the LORD. 16 Do not take your servant for a wicked woman; I have been praying here out of my great anguish and grief."

17 Eli answered, "Go in peace, and may the God of Israel grant you what you have asked of him."

18 She said, "May your servant find favor in your eyes." Then she went her way and ate something, and her face was no longer downcast.

19 Early the next morning they arose and worshiped before the LORD and then went back to their home at Ramah. Elkanah lay with Hannah his wife, and the LORD remembered her. 20 So in the course of time Hannah conceived and gave birth to a son. She named him Samuel,[b] saying, "Because I asked the LORD for him."

> **1 Samuel 1:20**
>
> *God Answers Prayer*
>
> So in the course of time Hannah conceived and gave birth to a son. She named him Samuel, saying, "Because I asked the LORD for him."

Hannah Dedicates Samuel

21 When the man Elkanah went up with all his family to offer the annual sacrifice to the LORD and to fulfill his vow, 22 Hannah did not go. She said to her husband, "After the boy is weaned, I will take him and present him before the LORD, and he will live there always."

23 "Do what seems best to you," Elkanah her husband told her. "Stay here until you have weaned him; only may the LORD make good his[c] word." So the woman stayed at home and nursed her son until she had weaned him.

24 After he was weaned, she took the boy with her, young as he was, along with a three-year-old bull,[d] an ephah[e] of flour and a skin of wine, and brought him to the house of the LORD at Shiloh. 25 When they had slaughtered the bull, they brought the boy to Eli, 26 and she said to him, "As surely as you live, my lord, I am the woman who stood here beside you praying to the LORD. 27 I prayed for this child, and the LORD has granted me what I asked of him. 28 So now I give him to the LORD. For his whole life he will be given over to the LORD." And he worshiped the LORD there.

Hannah's Prayer

2 Then Hannah prayed and said:

"My heart rejoices in the LORD;
in the LORD my horn[f] is lifted high.
My mouth boasts over my enemies,
for I delight in your deliverance.

2 "There is no one holy[g] like the LORD;
there is no one besides you;
there is no Rock like our God.

[a] 9 That is, tabernacle [b] 20 *Samuel* sounds like the Hebrew for *heard of God.* [c] 23 Masoretic Text; Dead Sea Scrolls, Septuagint and Syriac *your* [d] 24 Dead Sea Scrolls, Septuagint and Syriac; Masoretic Text *with three bulls* [e] 24 That is, probably about 3/5 bushel (about 22 liters) [f] 1 *Horn* here symbolizes strength; also in verse 10. [g] 2 Or *no Holy One*

Ultimate Surrender

Read: 1 Samuel 1:1–28

1 Samuel 1:28

"So now I give him to the LORD. For his whole life he will be given over to the LORD."

reflection

1 What one thing are you holding back from God?

2 What would happen if you released it?

3 Why does God insist we sometimes give up things that seem to bring us joy?

RELATED READINGS

Genesis 22:1–19; Matthew 6:19–34

PROBABLY THE HARDEST THING for me to surrender to God—and this may sound silly because you may be expecting me to say, "My children"—was the huge, five-bedroom home I purchased five years after my divorce. I knew that my home belonged to God and that I was simply a steward of what he had entrusted to me, but that didn't keep it from becoming an idol. My wonderful house in its expensive zip code supplied status. I couldn't imagine giving it up, especially if God wanted me to live somewhere I didn't like.

I eventually realized I was supposed to sell that house, but for a full year I dug in my heels and refused to do it. What a nightmare I lived trying to untangle God's best for my life while still continuing to weave in my stubborn wishes. But God was persistent. He kept reminding me of his desire through the wise counsel of my brother Paul and sister Cathy. He continued to impress on me the need to downsize and simplify my life.

I finally came to the point where I knew I simply needed to obey God and sell the house. When I moved into a smaller home, I suddenly had much more time and energy. I found that I could focus more earnestly on my writing, which was something I had not been able to do previously with all the repairs, chores and decorating.

As terrible as it sounds, it was easier for me to surrender my children to God than it was to trust him with my home. Sad, huh? But I knew in my heart that my children would be in better hands with God than with me. While it was still excruciatingly hard to turn my children's lives over to him, I released them to his loving care by saying a simple, heartfelt prayer to that effect. Actually, I had to say that prayer many times. It seemed to take me forever to be able to voice words that were not a lie. Though I did not drop off my kids at the local temple to be raised by a holy man, like Hannah did with her son Samuel, I did choose to trust that God would love them and guide their lives better than I could.

—Katie Brazelton

Go to page 329 for your next devotional reading.

3 "Do not keep talking so proudly
or let your mouth speak such arrogance,
for the LORD is a God who knows,
and by him deeds are weighed.

4 "The bows of the warriors
are broken,
but those who stumbled
are armed with
strength.
5 Those who were full hire
themselves out for
food,
but those who were
hungry hunger no
more.
She who was barren
has borne seven
children,
but she who has had
many sons pines away.

6 "The LORD brings death and makes alive;
he brings down to the grave[a] and raises
up.
7 The LORD sends poverty and wealth;
he humbles and he exalts.
8 He raises the poor from the dust
and lifts the needy from the ash heap;
he seats them with princes
and has them inherit a throne of honor.

"For the foundations of the earth are the
LORD's;
upon them he has set the world.
9 He will guard the feet of his saints,
but the wicked will be silenced in
darkness.

"It is not by strength that one prevails;
10 those who oppose the LORD will be
shattered.
He will thunder against them from heaven;
the LORD will judge the ends of the
earth.

"He will give strength to his king
and exalt the horn of his anointed."

11 Then Elkanah went home to Ramah, but
the boy ministered before the LORD under Eli
the priest.

1 Samuel 2:2

God Is Holy

"There is no one holy
like the LORD;
there is no one
besides you;
there is no Rock
like our God."

Eli's Wicked Sons

12 Eli's sons were wicked men; they had no
regard for the LORD. 13 Now it was the practice
of the priests with the people that whenever
anyone offered a sacrifice
and while the meat was being
boiled, the servant of the priest
would come with a three-
pronged fork in his hand. 14 He
would plunge it into the pan or
kettle or caldron or pot, and
the priest would take for himself whatever the fork brought
up. This is how they treated all
the Israelites who came to Shiloh. 15 But even before the fat
was burned, the servant of the
priest would come and say to
the man who was sacrificing,
"Give the priest some meat to roast; he won't
accept boiled meat from you, but only raw."

16 If the man said to him, "Let the fat be
burned up first, and then take whatever you
want," the servant would then answer, "No,
hand it over now; if you don't, I'll take it
by force."

17 This sin of the young men was very great
in the LORD's sight, for they[b] were treating the
LORD's offering with contempt.

18 But Samuel was ministering before the
LORD—a boy wearing a linen ephod. 19 Each
year his mother made him a little robe and took
it to him when she went up with her husband
to offer the annual sacrifice. 20 Eli would bless
Elkanah and his wife, saying, "May the LORD
give you children by this woman to take the
place of the one she prayed for and gave to the
LORD." Then they would go home. 21 And the
LORD was gracious to Hannah; she conceived
and gave birth to three sons and two daughters.
Meanwhile, the boy Samuel grew up in the presence of the LORD.

22 Now Eli, who was very old, heard about
everything his sons were doing to all Israel and
how they slept with the women who served at
the entrance to the Tent of Meeting. 23 So he
said to them, "Why do you do such things? I
hear from all the people about these wicked
deeds of yours. 24 No, my sons; it is not a good

[a] 6 Hebrew *Sheol* [b] 17 Or *men*

report that I hear spreading among the LORD's
people. 25 If a man sins against another man,
God[a] may mediate for him; but if a man sins
against the LORD, who will intercede for him?"
His sons, however, did not listen to their father's rebuke, for it was the LORD's will to put
them to death.

26 And the boy Samuel continued to grow
in stature and in favor with the LORD and
with men.

Prophecy Against the House of Eli

27 Now a man of God came to Eli and said
to him, "This is what the LORD says: 'Did I
not clearly reveal myself to your father's house
when they were in Egypt under Pharaoh? 28 I
chose your father out of all the tribes of Israel
to be my priest, to go up to my altar, to burn
incense, and to wear an ephod in my presence.
I also gave your father's house all the offerings
made with fire by the Israelites. 29 Why do you[b]
scorn my sacrifice and offering that I prescribed
for my dwelling? Why do you honor your sons
more than me by fattening yourselves on the
choice parts of every offering made by my people Israel?'

30 "Therefore the LORD, the God of Israel, declares: 'I promised that your house and your father's house would minister before me forever.'
But now the LORD declares: 'Far be it from me!
Those who honor me I will honor, but those
who despise me will be disdained. 31 The time
is coming when I will cut short your strength
and the strength of your father's house, so that
there will not be an old man in your family
line 32 and you will see distress in my dwelling.
Although good will be done to Israel, in your
family line there will never be an old man. 33 Every one of you that I do not cut off from my
altar will be spared only to blind your eyes with
tears and to grieve your heart, and all your descendants will die in the prime of life.

34 " 'And what happens to your two sons,
Hophni and Phinehas, will be a sign to you—
they will both die on the same day. 35 I will raise
up for myself a faithful priest, who will do according to what is in my heart and mind. I will
firmly establish his house, and he will minister
before my anointed one always. 36 Then everyone left in your family line will come and bow
down before him for a piece of silver and a
crust of bread and plead, "Appoint me to some
priestly office so I can have food to eat." ' "

The LORD Calls Samuel

3 The boy Samuel ministered before the
LORD under Eli. In those days the word
of the LORD was rare; there were not many visions.

2 One night Eli, whose eyes were becoming
so weak that he could barely see, was lying
down in his usual place. 3 The lamp of God had
not yet gone out, and Samuel was lying down
in the temple[c] of the LORD, where the ark of
God was. 4 Then the LORD called Samuel.

Samuel answered, "Here I am." 5 And he ran
to Eli and said, "Here I am; you called me."

But Eli said, "I did not call; go back and lie
down." So he went and lay down.

6 Again the LORD called, "Samuel!" And Samuel got up and went to Eli and said, "Here I am;
you called me."

"My son," Eli said, "I did not call; go back
and lie down."

7 Now Samuel did not yet know the LORD:
The word of the LORD had not yet been revealed to him.

8 The LORD called Samuel a third time, and
Samuel got up and went to Eli and said, "Here
I am; you called me."

Then Eli realized that the LORD was calling
the boy. 9 So Eli told Samuel, "Go and lie down,
and if he calls you, say, 'Speak, LORD, for your
servant is listening.' " So Samuel went and lay
down in his place.

10 The LORD came and stood there, calling as
at the other times, "Samuel! Samuel!"

Then Samuel said, "Speak, for your servant
is listening."

11 And the LORD said to Samuel: "See, I am
about to do something in Israel that will make
the ears of everyone who hears of it tingle.
12 At that time I will carry out against Eli everything I spoke against his family—from beginning to end. 13 For I told him that I would
judge his family forever because of the sin he
knew about; his sons made themselves contemptible,[d] and he failed to restrain them.

[a] 25 Or *the judges* [b] 29 The Hebrew is plural. [c] 3 That is, tabernacle [d] 13 Masoretic Text; an ancient Hebrew scribal tradition and Septuagint *sons blasphemed God*

Are You Listening?

Read: 1 Samuel 3:1–21

WHEN WAS THE LAST TIME you heard from God? Think about it. Has God's still, small voice been drowned out by the hum of too much noise from work, family, church and friends?

The adolescent boy Samuel was lying in the temple. It was still night because "the lamp of God had not yet gone out" (the lamp would not have been allowed to go out before morning). Samuel was probably lonely, having been separated from his family and dedicated by his mother Hannah to work for the old, blind priest Eli in the temple. It seems to have been a discouraging time to work there: "The word of the LORD was rare; there were not many visions." But as Samuel drowsed on his pallet, the sound of his name cut through the flickering dimness.

"Samuel!"

Naturally, Samuel thought Eli had called. "Here I am," replied the boy. Again, "Samuel!" Again, "Here I am." Samuel listened keenly, but the summons didn't come from Eli. God himself called Samuel that evening, and Eli taught the boy the right response: "Speak, for your servant is listening."

What made Samuel so ready to hear God's voice? For one thing, he was a faithful and obedient servant. He was ready to respond to his master, and his willingness made him ready to respond to God as well. He was being faithful in the small things of his everyday life and was therefore entrusted with a great thing, to be a prophet of God and to restore the priesthood's honor.

Samuel was also in the right place to listen. Are you? His posture *invited* God to speak to him: *faithful, obedient, humble, waiting, receptive.* His willingness to respond became instrumental in restoring holiness to the land: "[God] revealed himself to Samuel through his word. And Samuel's word came to all Israel."

If you want to hear God speak, do what you can to be ready. Be prepared when you're in a place of outward silence and sanctuary: as you lay awake in the early hours of the morning, while you wait in your car for your children to get out of school, when you walk the dog in the evening. Seek an inner silence and sanctuary also: Let go of mental noise and emotional confusion. Take deep breaths in and out until your heart and respiration rate slow. Humbly and receptively invite God to speak to you, and wait with faithful and obedient readiness. When God calls your name, respond, "Speak, Lord, for your servant is listening."

1 Samuel 3:10

The LORD came and stood there, calling as at the other times, "Samuel! Samuel!" Then Samuel said, "Speak, for your servant is listening."

reflection

1 What are some things that drown out God's voice for you? What makes it difficult for you to be still in God's presence?

2 Are personal sins blocking you from hearing God's voice? Take time to confess any wrongs you've committed and ask God to cleanse you.

3 Read Psalm 84 to prepare you to spend time in God's presence.

RELATED READINGS

Psalms 84:1–12; 86:1–17; Matthew 5:8; John 10:1–6

Go to page 334 for your next devotional reading.

14 Therefore, I swore to the house of Eli, 'The guilt of Eli's house will never be atoned for by sacrifice or offering.' "

15 Samuel lay down until morning and then opened the doors of the house of the LORD. He was afraid to tell Eli the vision, 16 but Eli called him and said, "Samuel, my son."

Samuel answered, "Here I am."

17 "What was it he said to you?" Eli asked. "Do not hide it from me. May God deal with you, be it ever so severely, if you hide from me anything he told you." 18 So Samuel told him everything, hiding nothing from him. Then Eli said, "He is the LORD; let him do what is good in his eyes."

19 The LORD was with Samuel as he grew up, and he let none of his words fall to the ground. 20 And all Israel from Dan to Beersheba recognized that Samuel was attested as a prophet of the LORD. 21 The LORD continued to appear at Shiloh, and there he revealed himself to Samuel through his word.

4 And Samuel's word came to all Israel.

The Philistines Capture the Ark

Now the Israelites went out to fight against the Philistines. The Israelites camped at Ebenezer, and the Philistines at Aphek. 2 The Philistines deployed their forces to meet Israel, and as the battle spread, Israel was defeated by the Philistines, who killed about four thousand of them on the battlefield. 3 When the soldiers returned to camp, the elders of Israel asked, "Why did the LORD bring defeat upon us today before the Philistines? Let us bring the ark of the LORD's covenant from Shiloh, so that it[a] may go with us and save us from the hand of our enemies."

4 So the people sent men to Shiloh, and they brought back the ark of the covenant of the LORD Almighty, who is enthroned between the cherubim. And Eli's two sons, Hophni and Phinehas, were there with the ark of the covenant of God.

5 When the ark of the LORD's covenant came into the camp, all Israel raised such a great shout that the ground shook. 6 Hearing the uproar, the Philistines asked, "What's all this shouting in the Hebrew camp?"

When they learned that the ark of the LORD had come into the camp, 7 the Philistines were afraid. "A god has come into the camp," they said. "We're in trouble! Nothing like this has happened before. 8 Woe to us! Who will deliver us from the hand of these mighty gods? They are the gods who struck the Egyptians with all kinds of plagues in the desert. 9 Be strong, Philistines! Be men, or you will be subject to the Hebrews, as they have been to you. Be men, and fight!"

10 So the Philistines fought, and the Israelites were defeated and every man fled to his tent. The slaughter was very great; Israel lost thirty thousand foot soldiers. 11 The ark of God was captured, and Eli's two sons, Hophni and Phinehas, died.

Death of Eli

12 That same day a Benjamite ran from the battle line and went to Shiloh, his clothes torn and dust on his head. 13 When he arrived, there was Eli sitting on his chair by the side of the road, watching, because his heart feared for the ark of God. When the man entered the town and told what had happened, the whole town sent up a cry.

14 Eli heard the outcry and asked, "What is the meaning of this uproar?"

The man hurried over to Eli, 15 who was ninety-eight years old and whose eyes were set so that he could not see. 16 He told Eli, "I have just come from the battle line; I fled from it this very day."

Eli asked, "What happened, my son?"

17 The man who brought the news replied, "Israel fled before the Philistines, and the army has suffered heavy losses. Also your two sons, Hophni and Phinehas, are dead, and the ark of God has been captured."

18 When he mentioned the ark of God, Eli fell backward off his chair by the side of the gate. His neck was broken and he died, for he was an old man and heavy. He had led[b] Israel forty years.

19 His daughter-in-law, the wife of Phinehas, was pregnant and near the time of delivery. When she heard the news that the ark of God had been captured and that her father-in-law

[a] 3 Or *he* [b] 18 Traditionally *judged*

and her husband were dead, she went into labor and gave birth, but was overcome by her
labor pains. 20As she was dying, the women
attending her said, “Don’t despair; you have
given birth to a son.” But she did not respond
or pay any attention.
21She named the boy Ichabod,[a] saying, “The
glory has departed from Israel”—because of
the capture of the ark of God and the deaths of
her father-in-law and her husband. 22She said,
“The glory has departed from Israel, for the ark
of God has been captured.”

The Ark in Ashdod and Ekron

5 After the Philistines had captured the ark
of God, they took it from Ebenezer to Ashdod. 2Then they carried the ark
into Dagon’s temple and set it
beside Dagon. 3When the people of Ashdod rose early the next
day, there was Dagon, fallen on
his face on the ground before
the ark of the LORD! They took
Dagon and put him back in his
place. 4But the following morning when they rose, there was
Dagon, fallen on his face on the
ground before the ark of the
LORD! His head and hands had
been broken off and were lying
on the threshold; only his body
remained. 5That is why to this
day neither the priests of Dagon nor any others who enter
Dagon’s temple at Ashdod step
on the threshold.
6The LORD’s hand was heavy upon the people of Ashdod and its vicinity; he brought devastation upon them and afflicted them with
tumors.[b] 7When the men of Ashdod saw what
was happening, they said, “The ark of the god
of Israel must not stay here with us, because his
hand is heavy upon us and upon Dagon our
god.” 8So they called together all the rulers of
the Philistines and asked them, “What shall we
do with the ark of the god of Israel?”
They answered, “Have the ark of the god of
Israel moved to Gath.” So they moved the ark
of the God of Israel.
9But after they had moved it, the LORD’s
hand was against that city, throwing it into a
great panic. He afflicted the people of the city,
both young and old, with an outbreak of tumors.[c] 10So they sent the ark of God to Ekron.
As the ark of God was entering Ekron, the
people of Ekron cried out, “They have brought
the ark of the god of Israel around to us to kill
us and our people.” 11So they called together all
the rulers of the Philistines and said, “Send the
ark of the god of Israel away; let it go back to
its own place, or it[d] will kill us and our people.”
For death had filled the city with panic; God’s
hand was very heavy upon it. 12Those who did
not die were afflicted with tumors, and the outcry of the city went up to heaven.

1 Samuel 5:4

God Is Supreme

But the following morning when they rose, there was Dagon, fallen on his face on the ground before the ark of the LORD! His head and hands had been broken off and were lying on the threshold; only his body remained.

The Ark Returned to Israel

6 When the ark of the
LORD had been in Philis-
tine territory seven months,
2the Philistines called for the
priests and the diviners and
said, “What shall we do with
the ark of the LORD? Tell us
how we should send it back to
its place.”
3They answered, “If you return the ark of the god of Israel,
do not send it away empty, but
by all means send a guilt offering to him. Then you will be
healed, and you will know why
his hand has not been lifted
from you.”
4The Philistines asked, “What guilt offering
should we send to him?”
They replied, “Five gold tumors and five gold
rats, according to the number of the Philistine
rulers, because the same plague has struck both
you and your rulers. 5Make models of the tumors and of the rats that are destroying the
country, and pay honor to Israel’s god. Perhaps
he will lift his hand from you and your gods and
your land. 6Why do you harden your hearts
as the Egyptians and Pharaoh did? When he[e]
treated them harshly, did they not send the Israelites out so they could go on their way?
7“Now then, get a new cart ready, with two

[a]21 *Ichabod* means *no glory.* [b]6 Hebrew; Septuagint and Vulgate *tumors. And rats appeared in their land, and death and destruction were throughout the city* [c]9 Or *with tumors in the groin* (see Septuagint) [d]11 Or *he* [e]6 That is, God

cows that have calved and have never been
yoked. Hitch the cows to the cart, but take
their calves away and pen them up. 8Take the
ark of the LORD and put it on the cart, and in
a chest beside it put the gold objects you are
sending back to him as a guilt offering. Send
it on its way, 9but keep watching it. If it goes
up to its own territory, toward
Beth Shemesh, then the LORD
has brought this great disaster
on us. But if it does not, then
we will know that it was not his
hand that struck us and that it
happened to us by chance."
10So they did this. They took
two such cows and hitched
them to the cart and penned
up their calves. 11They placed
the ark of the LORD on the cart
and along with it the chest containing the gold rats and the
models of the tumors. 12Then
the cows went straight up toward Beth Shemesh, keeping on the road and lowing all the
way; they did not turn to the right or to the left.
The rulers of the Philistines followed them as
far as the border of Beth Shemesh.
13Now the people of Beth Shemesh were harvesting their wheat in the valley, and when they
looked up and saw the ark, they rejoiced at the
sight. 14The cart came to the field of Joshua of
Beth Shemesh, and there it stopped beside a
large rock. The people chopped up the wood
of the cart and sacrificed the cows as a burnt
offering to the LORD. 15The Levites took down
the ark of the LORD, together with the chest containing the gold objects, and placed them on
the large rock. On that day the people of Beth
Shemesh offered burnt offerings and made
sacrifices to the LORD. 16The five rulers of the
Philistines saw all this and then returned that
same day to Ekron.
17These are the gold tumors the Philistines
sent as a guilt offering to the LORD—one each
for Ashdod, Gaza, Ashkelon, Gath and Ekron.
18And the number of the gold rats was according to the number of Philistine towns belonging
to the five rulers—the fortified towns with their
country villages. The large rock, on which[a]
they set the ark of the LORD, is a witness to this
day in the field of Joshua of Beth Shemesh.
19But God struck down some of the men
of Beth Shemesh, putting seventy[b] of them to
death because they had looked into the ark of
the LORD. The people mourned because of the
heavy blow the LORD had dealt
them, 20and the men of Beth
Shemesh asked, "Who can
stand in the presence of the
LORD, this holy God? To whom
will the ark go up from here?"
21Then they sent messen-
gers to the people of Kiriath Jearim, saying, "The Philistines
have returned the ark of the
LORD. Come down and
take it up to your place."

1 Samuel 6:20

God Is Holy

And the men of Beth Shemesh asked, "Who can stand in the presence of the LORD, this holy God? To whom will the ark go up from here?"

7
1So the men of Kiriath Jearim came and took up the ark
of the LORD. They took it to
Abinadab's house on the hill and consecrated
Eleazar his son to guard the ark of the LORD.

Samuel Subdues the Philistines at Mizpah

2It was a long time, twenty years in all, that
the ark remained at Kiriath Jearim, and all the
people of Israel mourned and sought after the
LORD. 3And Samuel said to the whole house
of Israel, "If you are returning to the LORD
with all your hearts, then rid yourselves of the
foreign gods and the Ashtoreths and commit
yourselves to the LORD and serve him only, and
he will deliver you out of the hand of the Philistines." 4So the Israelites put away their Baals
and Ashtoreths, and served the LORD only.
5Then Samuel said, "Assemble all Israel at
Mizpah and I will intercede with the LORD for
you." 6When they had assembled at Mizpah,
they drew water and poured it out before the
LORD. On that day they fasted and there they
confessed, "We have sinned against the LORD."
And Samuel was leader[c] of Israel at Mizpah.
7When the Philistines heard that Israel had
assembled at Mizpah, the rulers of the Philistines came up to attack them. And when the
Israelites heard of it, they were afraid because
of the Philistines. 8They said to Samuel, "Do

[a]18 A few Hebrew manuscripts (see also Septuagint); most Hebrew manuscripts *villages as far as Greater Abel, where* [b]19 A few Hebrew manuscripts; most Hebrew manuscripts and Septuagint *50,070* [c]6 Traditionally *judge*

not stop crying out to the LORD our God for us,
that he may rescue us from the hand of the Philistines." 9 Then Samuel took a suckling lamb
and offered it up as a whole burnt offering to
the LORD. He cried out to the LORD on Israel's
behalf, and the LORD answered him.
10 While Samuel was sacrificing the burnt offering, the Philistines drew near to engage
Israel in battle. But that day
the LORD thundered with loud
thunder against the Philistines
and threw them into such a
panic that they were routed before the Israelites. 11 The men
of Israel rushed out of Mizpah
and pursued the Philistines,
slaughtering them along the
way to a point below Beth Car.
12 Then Samuel took a stone
and set it up between Mizpah
and Shen. He named it Ebene-
zer,[a] saying, "Thus far has the LORD helped us."
13 So the Philistines were subdued and did not
invade Israelite territory again.
Throughout Samuel's lifetime, the hand of
the LORD was against the Philistines. 14 The
towns from Ekron to Gath that the Philistines
had captured from Israel were restored to her,
and Israel delivered the neighboring territory
from the power of the Philistines. And there
was peace between Israel and the Amorites.
15 Samuel continued as judge over Israel all
the days of his life. 16 From year to year he went
on a circuit from Bethel to Gilgal to Mizpah,
judging Israel in all those places. 17 But he always went back to Ramah, where his home
was, and there he also judged Israel. And he
built an altar there to the LORD.

1 Samuel 7:10

God Thunders

That day the LORD thundered with loud thunder against the Philistines and threw them into such a panic that they were routed before the Israelites.

Israel Asks for a King

8 When Samuel grew old, he appointed his
sons as judges for Israel. 2 The name of his
firstborn was Joel and the name of his second
was Abijah, and they served at Beersheba. 3 But
his sons did not walk in his ways. They turned
aside after dishonest gain and accepted bribes
and perverted justice.
4 So all the elders of Israel gathered together
and came to Samuel at Ramah. 5 They said to
him, "You are old, and your sons do not walk
in your ways; now appoint a king to lead[b] us,
such as all the other nations have."
6 But when they said, "Give us a king to lead
us," this displeased Samuel; so he prayed to
the LORD. 7 And the LORD told
him: "Listen to all that the people are saying to you; it is not
you they have rejected, but
they have rejected me as their
king. 8 As they have done from
the day I brought them up out
of Egypt until this day, forsaking me and serving other gods,
so they are doing to you. 9 Now
listen to them; but warn them
solemnly and let them know
what the king who will reign
over them will do."
10 Samuel told all the words
of the LORD to the people who
were asking him for a king. 11 He said, "This is
what the king who will reign over you will do:
He will take your sons and make them serve
with his chariots and horses, and they will run
in front of his chariots. 12 Some he will assign
to be commanders of thousands and commanders of fifties, and others to plow his ground
and reap his harvest, and still others to make
weapons of war and equipment for his chariots.
13 He will take your daughters to be perfumers
and cooks and bakers. 14 He will take the best
of your fields and vineyards and olive groves
and give them to his attendants. 15 He will take
a tenth of your grain and of your vintage and
give it to his officials and attendants. 16 Your
menservants and maidservants and the best
of your cattle[c] and donkeys he will take for his
own use. 17 He will take a tenth of your flocks,
and you yourselves will become his slaves.
18 When that day comes, you will cry out for
relief from the king you have chosen, and the
LORD will not answer you in that day."
19 But the people refused to listen to Samuel. "No!" they said. "We want a king over us.
20 Then we will be like all the other nations,
with a king to lead us and to go out before us
and fight our battles."

[a]12 *Ebenezer* means *stone of help.* [b]5 Traditionally *judge*; also in verses 6 and 20 [c]16 Septuagint; Hebrew *young men*

Seeing the Unseen

JOCHEBED

By faith Moses' parents hid him for three months after he was born, because they saw he was no ordinary child, and they were not afraid of the king's edict.

Hebrews 11:23

ASSIGNED READING:
Exodus 2:1–10; 6:1—7:6

"SO SORRY YOU CAN'T STAY LONGER," Jochebed said to her friend and stood pointedly by the door. The warmth of the afternoon sun streamed onto their timeworn faces.

A neighbor had dropped by for the afternoon. Jochebed liked her well enough, and she enjoyed the welcome break during the day's routine. But Jochebed carried a secret no one outside of her immediate family could know. And if the woman stayed much longer late in the day like this, her mystery would be found out.

Jochebed had been privy to many secrets herself over the years—things most anyone keeps secret: a friend's envy, a neighbor's indiscretion. However, those secrets were nothing like this; nothing like a matter of life and death. And so it was well worth it to appear rude to her neighbor, to be a little more reclusive than she'd been before, to find creative ways to time her trips to the market.

What she did, she did in faith. Simple faith.

Faith: The hope that what she was doing was for the right reason, at the right time. That God had bestowed her with a sense of timing that was beyond human reasoning. *Faith*: The knowledge that there was no guarantee for the future, but there was grace for the day. Each evening gave her strength to continue her mission the next day. *Faith*: A tiny seed that she nurtured faithfully; a seed that grew delicate tendrils of courage to keep going despite the risks. *Faith*: The assurance that the God-given hunch, the slightest suspicion and the dream burrowed deep within the heart are not one's own doing, but the very evidence of God at work

Jochebed pondered these thoughts and watched her neighbor amble down the street. Just then, her little secret awoke from his nap.

—Prayer—

Father in heaven, help me to live out my faith in tangible ways today and every day.

Weekend

Go to page 343 for your next devotional reading.

21When Samuel heard all that the people
said, he repeated it before the LORD. 22The
LORD answered, "Listen to them and give them
a king."

Then Samuel said to the men of Israel, "Everyone go back to his town."

Samuel Anoints Saul

9 There was a Benjamite, a man of standing, whose name was Kish son of Abiel,
the son of Zeror, the son of Becorath, the son
of Aphiah of Benjamin. 2He had a son named
Saul, an impressive young man without equal
among the Israelites—a head taller than any of
the others.

3Now the donkeys belonging to Saul's father
Kish were lost, and Kish said to his son Saul,
"Take one of the servants with you and go and
look for the donkeys." 4So he passed through
the hill country of Ephraim and through the
area around Shalisha, but they did not find
them. They went on into the district of Shaa-
lim, but the donkeys were not there. Then he
passed through the territory of Benjamin, but
they did not find them.

5When they reached the district of Zuph,
Saul said to the servant who was with him,
"Come, let's go back, or my father will stop
thinking about the donkeys and start worrying
about us."

6But the servant replied, "Look, in this town
there is a man of God; he is highly respected,
and everything he says comes true. Let's go
there now. Perhaps he will tell us what way
to take."

7Saul said to his servant, "If we go, what can
we give the man? The food in our sacks is gone.
We have no gift to take to the man of God.
What do we have?"

8The servant answered him again. "Look,"
he said, "I have a quarter of a shekel[a] of silver.
I will give it to the man of God so that he will
tell us what way to take." 9(Formerly in Israel,
if a man went to inquire of God, he would
say, "Come, let us go to the seer," because the
prophet of today used to be called a seer.)

10"Good," Saul said to his servant. "Come,
let's go." So they set out for the town where the
man of God was.

11As they were going up the hill to the town,
they met some girls coming out to draw water,
and they asked them, "Is the seer here?"

12"He is," they answered. "He's ahead of you.
Hurry now; he has just come to our town today, for the people have a sacrifice at the high
place. 13As soon as you enter the town, you will
find him before he goes up to the high place
to eat. The people will not begin eating until
he comes, because he must bless the sacrifice;
afterward, those who are invited will eat. Go up
now; you should find him about this time."

14They went up to the town, and as they
were entering it, there was Samuel, coming toward them on his way up to the high place.

15Now the day before Saul came, the LORD
had revealed this to Samuel: 16"About this time
tomorrow I will send you a man from the land
of Benjamin. Anoint him leader over my people Israel; he will deliver my people from the
hand of the Philistines. I have looked upon my
people, for their cry has reached me."

17When Samuel caught sight of Saul, the
LORD said to him, "This is the man I spoke to
you about; he will govern my people."

18Saul approached Samuel in the gateway
and asked, "Would you please tell me where
the seer's house is?"

19"I am the seer," Samuel replied. "Go up
ahead of me to the high place, for today you are
to eat with me, and in the morning I will let you
go and will tell you all that is in your heart. 20As
for the donkeys you lost three days ago, do not
worry about them; they have been found. And
to whom is all the desire of Israel turned, if not
to you and all your father's family?"

21Saul answered, "But am I not a Benjamite,
from the smallest tribe of Israel, and is not my
clan the least of all the clans of the tribe of Benjamin? Why do you say such a thing to me?"

22Then Samuel brought Saul and his servant into the hall and seated them at the head
of those who were invited—about thirty in
number. 23Samuel said to the cook, "Bring the
piece of meat I gave you, the one I told you to
lay aside."

24So the cook took up the leg with what
was on it and set it in front of Saul. Samuel
said, "Here is what has been kept for you. Eat,

[a]8 That is, about 1/10 ounce (about 3 grams)

because it was set aside for you for this occasion, from the time I said, 'I have invited
guests.'" And Saul dined with Samuel that day.
25After they came down from the high
place to the town, Samuel talked with Saul on
the roof of his house. 26They rose about daybreak and Samuel called to Saul on the roof,
"Get ready, and I will send you on your way."
When Saul got ready, he and Samuel went outside together. 27As they were going down to
the edge of the town, Samuel said to Saul, "Tell
the servant to go on ahead of us"—and the servant did so—"but you stay here awhile, so that
I may give you a message from God."
10 Then Samuel took a flask of oil and
poured it on Saul's head and kissed
him, saying, "Has not the LORD anointed you
leader over his inheritance?[a] 2When you leave
me today, you will meet two men near Rachel's
tomb, at Zelzah on the border of Benjamin.
They will say to you, 'The donkeys you set out
to look for have been found. And now your father has stopped thinking about them and is
worried about you. He is asking, "What shall I
do about my son?"'
3"Then you will go on from there until you
reach the great tree of Tabor.
Three men going up to God
at Bethel will meet you there.
One will be carrying three
young goats, another three
loaves of bread, and another a
skin of wine. 4They will greet
you and offer you two loaves
of bread, which you will accept
from them.
5"After that you will go to
Gibeah of God, where there is
a Philistine outpost. As you approach the town, you will meet
a procession of prophets coming down from the high place
with lyres, tambourines, flutes
and harps being played before them, and they
will be prophesying. 6The Spirit of the LORD
will come upon you in power, and you will
prophesy with them; and you will be changed
into a different person. 7Once these signs are
fulfilled, do whatever your hand finds to do,
for God is with you.
8"Go down ahead of me to Gilgal. I will
surely come down to you to sacrifice burnt offerings and fellowship offerings,[b] but you must
wait seven days until I come to you and tell you
what you are to do."

Saul Made King

9As Saul turned to leave Samuel, God
changed Saul's heart, and all these signs were
fulfilled that day. 10When they arrived at
Gibeah, a procession of prophets met him; the
Spirit of God came upon him in power, and he
joined in their prophesying. 11When all those
who had formerly known him saw him prophesying with the prophets, they asked each other,
"What is this that has happened to the son of
Kish? Is Saul also among the prophets?"
12A man who lived there answered, "And
who is their father?" So it became a saying: "Is
Saul also among the prophets?" 13After Saul
stopped prophesying, he went to the high
place.
14Now Saul's uncle asked him and his servant, "Where have you been?"
"Looking for the donkeys,"
he said. "But when we saw they
were not to be found, we went
to Samuel."
15Saul's uncle said, "Tell me
what Samuel said to you."
16Saul replied, "He assured
us that the donkeys had been
found." But he did not tell his
uncle what Samuel had said
about the kingship.
17Samuel summoned the
people of Israel to the LORD
at Mizpah 18and said to them,
"This is what the LORD, the
God of Israel, says: 'I brought
Israel up out of Egypt, and I
delivered you from the power of Egypt and all
the kingdoms that oppressed you.' 19But you
have now rejected your God, who saves you
out of all your calamities and distresses. And
you have said, 'No, set a king over us.' So now

1 Samuel 10:6

God Supplies Power

"The Spirit of the LORD will come upon you in power, and you will prophesy with them; and you will be changed into a different person."

[a]1 Hebrew; Septuagint and Vulgate *over his people Israel? You will reign over the LORD's people and save them from the power of their enemies round about. And this will be a sign to you that the LORD has anointed you leader over his inheritance:* [b]8 Traditionally *peace offerings*

present yourselves before the LORD by your
tribes and clans."
20When Samuel brought all the tribes of
Israel near, the tribe of Benjamin was chosen.
21Then he brought forward the tribe of Benjamin, clan by clan, and Matri's clan was chosen.
Finally Saul son of Kish was chosen. But when
they looked for him, he was not to be found.
22So they inquired further of the LORD, "Has
the man come here yet?"
And the LORD said, "Yes, he has hidden himself among the baggage."
23They ran and brought him out, and as he
stood among the people he was a head taller
than any of the others. 24Samuel said to all the
people, "Do you see the man the LORD has
chosen? There is no one like him among all
the people."
Then the people shouted, "Long live the
king!"
25Samuel explained to the people the regulations of the kingship. He wrote them down
on a scroll and deposited it before the LORD.
Then Samuel dismissed the people, each to his
own home.
26Saul also went to his home in Gibeah, accompanied by valiant men whose hearts God
had touched. 27But some troublemakers said,
"How can this fellow save us?" They despised
him and brought him no gifts. But Saul kept
silent.

Saul Rescues the City of Jabesh

11 Nahash the Ammonite went up and besieged Jabesh Gilead. And all the men
of Jabesh said to him, "Make a treaty with us,
and we will be subject to you."
2But Nahash the Ammonite replied, "I will
make a treaty with you only on the condition
that I gouge out the right eye of every one of
you and so bring disgrace on all Israel."
3The elders of Jabesh said to him, "Give us
seven days so we can send messengers throughout Israel; if no one comes to rescue us, we will
surrender to you."
4When the messengers came to Gibeah of
Saul and reported these terms to the people,
they all wept aloud. 5Just then Saul was returning from the fields, behind his oxen, and he
asked, "What is wrong with the people? Why
are they weeping?" Then they repeated to him
what the men of Jabesh had said.
6When Saul heard their words, the Spirit of
God came upon him in power, and he burned
with anger. 7He took a pair of oxen, cut them
into pieces, and sent the pieces by messengers
throughout Israel, proclaiming, "This is what
will be done to the oxen of anyone who does
not follow Saul and Samuel." Then the terror
of the LORD fell on the people, and they turned
out as one man. 8When Saul mustered them
at Bezek, the men of Israel numbered three
hundred thousand and the men of Judah
thirty thousand.
9They told the messengers who had come,
"Say to the men of Jabesh Gilead, 'By the time
the sun is hot tomorrow, you will be delivered.' "
When the messengers went and reported this
to the men of Jabesh, they were elated. 10They
said to the Ammonites, "Tomorrow we will surrender to you, and you can do to us whatever
seems good to you."
11The next day Saul separated his men into
three divisions; during the last watch of the
night they broke into the camp of the Ammonites and slaughtered them until the heat of the
day. Those who survived were scattered, so that
no two of them were left together.

Saul Confirmed as King

12The people then said to Samuel, "Who
was it that asked, 'Shall Saul reign over us?'
Bring these men to us and we will put them
to death."
13But Saul said, "No one shall be put to
death today, for this day the LORD has rescued
Israel."
14Then Samuel said to the people, "Come,
let us go to Gilgal and there reaffirm the kingship." 15So all the people went to Gilgal and
confirmed Saul as king in the presence of the
LORD. There they sacrificed fellowship offerings[a] before the LORD, and Saul and all the Israelites held a great celebration.

Samuel's Farewell Speech

12 Samuel said to all Israel, "I have listened
to everything you said to me and have
set a king over you. 2Now you have a king as

[a]15 Traditionally *peace offerings*

your leader. As for me, I am old and gray, and my sons are here with you. I have been your leader from my youth until this day. 3Here I stand. Testify against me in the presence of the LORD and his anointed. Whose ox have I taken? Whose donkey have I taken? Whom have I cheated? Whom have I oppressed? From whose hand have I accepted a bribe to make me shut my eyes? If I have done any of these, I will make it right."

4"You have not cheated or oppressed us," they replied. "You have not taken anything from anyone's hand."

5Samuel said to them, "The LORD is witness against you, and also his anointed is witness this day, that you have not found anything in my hand."

"He is witness," they said.

6Then Samuel said to the people, "It is the LORD who appointed Moses and Aaron and brought your forefathers up out of Egypt. 7Now then, stand here, because I am going to confront you with evidence before the LORD as to all the righteous acts performed by the LORD for you and your fathers.

8"After Jacob entered Egypt, they cried to the LORD for help, and the LORD sent Moses and Aaron, who brought your forefathers out of Egypt and settled them in this place.

9"But they forgot the LORD their God; so he sold them into the hand of Sisera, the commander of the army of Hazor, and into the hands of the Philistines and the king of Moab, who fought against them. 10They cried out to the LORD and said, 'We have sinned; we have forsaken the LORD and served the Baals and the Ashtoreths. But now deliver us from the hands of our enemies, and we will serve you.' 11Then the LORD sent Jerub-Baal,[a] Barak,[b] Jephthah and Samuel,[c] and he delivered you from the hands of your enemies on every side, so that you lived securely.

12"But when you saw that Nahash king of the Ammonites was moving against you, you said to me, 'No, we want a king to rule over us'—even though the LORD your God was your king. 13Now here is the king you have chosen, the one you asked for; see, the LORD has set a king over you. 14If you fear the LORD and serve and obey him and do not rebel against his commands, and if both you and the king who reigns over you follow the LORD your God—good! 15But if you do not obey the LORD, and if you rebel against his commands, his hand will be against you, as it was against your fathers.

16"Now then, stand still and see this great thing the LORD is about to do before your eyes! 17Is it not wheat harvest now? I will call upon the LORD to send thunder and rain. And you will realize what an evil thing you did in the eyes of the LORD when you asked for a king."

18Then Samuel called upon the LORD, and that same day the LORD sent thunder and rain. So all the people stood in awe of the LORD and of Samuel.

19The people all said to Samuel, "Pray to the LORD your God for your servants so that we will not die, for we have added to all our other sins the evil of asking for a king."

20"Do not be afraid," Samuel replied. "You have done all this evil; yet do not turn away from the LORD, but serve the LORD with all your heart. 21Do not turn away after useless idols. They can do you no good, nor can they rescue you, because they are useless. 22For the sake of his great name the LORD will not reject his people, because the LORD was pleased to make you his own. 23As for me, far be it from me that I should sin against the LORD by failing to pray for you. And I will teach you the way that is good and right. 24But be sure to fear the LORD and serve him faithfully with all your heart; consider what great things he has done for you. 25Yet if you persist in doing evil, both you and your king will be swept away."

1 Samuel 12:24

God Performs Great Deeds

"But be sure to fear the LORD and serve him faithfully with all your heart; consider what great things he has done for you."

[a]11 Also called *Gideon* [b]11 Some Septuagint manuscripts and Syriac; Hebrew *Bedan* [c]11 Hebrew; some Septuagint manuscripts and Syriac *Samson*

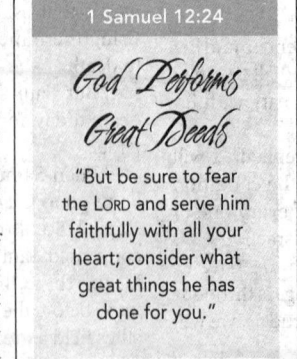

Samuel Rebukes Saul

13 Saul was ⌊thirty⌋[a] years old when he became king, and he reigned over Israel ⌊forty-⌋[b] two years.

2 Saul[c] chose three thousand men from Israel; two thousand were with him at Micmash and in the hill country of Bethel, and a thousand were with Jonathan at Gibeah in Benjamin. The rest of the men he sent back to their homes.

3 Jonathan attacked the Philistine outpost at Geba, and the Philistines heard about it. Then Saul had the trumpet blown throughout the land and said, "Let the Hebrews hear!" 4 So all Israel heard the news: "Saul has attacked the Philistine outpost, and now Israel has become a stench to the Philistines." And the people were summoned to join Saul at Gilgal.

5 The Philistines assembled to fight Israel, with three thousand[d] chariots, six thousand charioteers, and soldiers as numerous as the sand on the seashore. They went up and camped at Micmash, east of Beth Aven. 6 When the men of Israel saw that their situation was critical and that their army was hard pressed, they hid in caves and thickets, among the rocks, and in pits and cisterns. 7 Some Hebrews even crossed the Jordan to the land of Gad and Gilead.

Saul remained at Gilgal, and all the troops with him were quaking with fear. 8 He waited seven days, the time set by Samuel; but Samuel did not come to Gilgal, and Saul's men began to scatter. 9 So he said, "Bring me the burnt offering and the fellowship offerings.[e]" And Saul offered up the burnt offering. 10 Just as he finished making the offering, Samuel arrived, and Saul went out to greet him.

11 "What have you done?" asked Samuel.

Saul replied, "When I saw that the men were scattering, and that you did not come at the set time, and that the Philistines were assembling at Micmash, 12 I thought, 'Now the Philistines will come down against me at Gilgal, and I have not sought the LORD's favor.' So I felt compelled to offer the burnt offering."

13 "You acted foolishly," Samuel said. "You have not kept the command the LORD your God gave you; if you had, he would have established your kingdom over Israel for all time. 14 But now your kingdom will not endure; the LORD has sought out a man after his own heart and appointed him leader of his people, because you have not kept the LORD's command."

15 Then Samuel left Gilgal[f] and went up to Gibeah in Benjamin, and Saul counted the men who were with him. They numbered about six hundred.

Israel Without Weapons

16 Saul and his son Jonathan and the men with them were staying in Gibeah[g] in Benjamin, while the Philistines camped at Micmash. 17 Raiding parties went out from the Philistine camp in three detachments. One turned toward Ophrah in the vicinity of Shual, 18 another toward Beth Horon, and the third toward the borderland overlooking the Valley of Zeboim facing the desert.

19 Not a blacksmith could be found in the whole land of Israel, because the Philistines had said, "Otherwise the Hebrews will make swords or spears!" 20 So all Israel went down to the Philistines to have their plowshares, mattocks, axes and sickles[h] sharpened. 21 The price was two thirds of a shekel[i] for sharpening plowshares and mattocks, and a third of a shekel[j] for sharpening forks and axes and for repointing goads.

22 So on the day of the battle not a soldier with Saul and Jonathan had a sword or spear in his hand; only Saul and his son Jonathan had them.

Jonathan Attacks the Philistines

23 Now a detachment of Philistines had gone out to the pass at Micmash. **14** 1 One day Jonathan son of Saul said to the young man bearing his armor, "Come, let's go over to the Philistine outpost on the other side." But he did not tell his father.

2 Saul was staying on the outskirts of Gibeah under a pomegranate tree in Migron. With him were about six hundred men, 3 among

[a] 1 A few late manuscripts of the Septuagint; Hebrew does not have *thirty.* [b] 1 See the round number in Acts 13:21; Hebrew does not have *forty-.* [c] 1,2 Or *and when he had reigned over Israel two years,* 2 *he* [d] 5 Some Septuagint manuscripts and Syriac; Hebrew *thirty thousand* [e] 9 Traditionally *peace offerings* [f] 15 Hebrew; Septuagint *Gilgal and went his way; the rest of the people went after Saul to meet the army, and they went out of Gilgal* [g] 16 Two Hebrew manuscripts; most Hebrew manuscripts *Geba,* a variant of *Gibeah* [h] 20 Septuagint; Hebrew *plowshares* [i] 21 Hebrew *pim;* that is, about 1/4 ounce (about 8 grams) [j] 21 That is, about 1/8 ounce (about 4 grams)

whom was Ahijah, who was wearing an ephod.
He was a son of Ichabod's brother Ahitub son
of Phinehas, the son of Eli, the LORD's priest
in Shiloh. No one was aware that Jonathan
had left.
4On each side of the pass that Jonathan
intended to cross to reach the Philistine outpost
was a cliff; one was called Bozez, and the other
Seneh. 5One cliff stood to the north toward
Micmash, the other to the south toward Geba.
6Jonathan said to his young armor-bearer,
"Come, let's go over to the outpost of those uncircumcised fellows. Perhaps the LORD will act
in our behalf. Nothing can hinder the LORD
from saving, whether by many or by few."
7"Do all that you have in mind," his armor-
bearer said. "Go ahead; I am with you heart
and soul."
8Jonathan said, "Come, then; we will cross
over toward the men and let them see us. 9If
they say to us, 'Wait there until we come to
you,' we will stay where we are and not go up to
them. 10But if they say, 'Come up to us,' we will
climb up, because that will be our sign that the
LORD has given them into our hands."
11So both of them showed themselves to the
Philistine outpost. "Look!" said the Philistines.
"The Hebrews are crawling out of the holes
they were hiding in." 12The men of the outpost
shouted to Jonathan and his armor-bearer,
"Come up to us and we'll teach you a lesson."
So Jonathan said to his armor-bearer, "Climb
up after me; the LORD has given them into the
hand of Israel."
13Jonathan climbed up, using his hands and
feet, with his armor-bearer right behind him.
The Philistines fell before Jonathan, and his
armor-bearer followed and killed behind him.
14In that first attack Jonathan and his armor-
bearer killed some twenty men in an area of
about half an acre.[a]

Israel Routs the Philistines

15Then panic struck the whole army—those
in the camp and field, and those in the outposts
and raiding parties—and the ground shook. It
was a panic sent by God.[b]
16Saul's lookouts at Gibeah in Benjamin saw
the army melting away in all directions. 17Then
Saul said to the men who were with him, "Muster the forces and see who has left us." When
they did, it was Jonathan and his armor-bearer
who were not there.
18Saul said to Ahijah, "Bring the ark of
God." (At that time it was with the Israelites.)[c]
19While Saul was talking to the priest, the tumult in the Philistine camp increased more
and more. So Saul said to the priest, "Withdraw
your hand."
20Then Saul and all his men assembled and
went to the battle. They found the Philistines in
total confusion, striking each other with their
swords. 21Those Hebrews who had previously
been with the Philistines and had gone up with
them to their camp went over to the Israelites
who were with Saul and Jonathan. 22When all
the Israelites who had hidden in the hill country of Ephraim heard that the Philistines were
on the run, they joined the battle in hot pursuit.
23So the LORD rescued Israel that day, and the
battle moved on beyond Beth Aven.

Jonathan Eats Honey

24Now the men of Israel were in distress
that day, because Saul had bound the people
under an oath, saying, "Cursed be any man
who eats food before evening comes, before I
have avenged myself on my enemies!" So none
of the troops tasted food.
25The entire army[d] entered the woods, and
there was honey on the ground. 26When they
went into the woods, they saw the honey ooz-
ing out, yet no one put his hand to his mouth,
because they feared the oath. 27But Jonathan
had not heard that his father had bound the
people with the oath, so he reached out the end
of the staff that was in his hand and dipped it
into the honeycomb. He raised his hand to his
mouth, and his eyes brightened.[e] 28Then one
of the soldiers told him, "Your father bound the
army under a strict oath, saying, 'Cursed be any
man who eats food today!' That is why the men
are faint."
29Jonathan said, "My father has made trouble for the country. See how my eyes brightened[f] when I tasted a little of this honey.

[a]14 Hebrew *half a yoke*; a "yoke" was the land plowed by a yoke of oxen in one day. [b]15 Or *a terrible panic* [c]18 Hebrew; Septuagint *"Bring the ephod." (At that time he wore the ephod before the Israelites.)* [d]25 Or *Now all the people of the land* [e]27 Or *his strength was renewed* [f]29 Or *my strength was renewed*

[30]How much better it would have been if the
men had eaten today some of the plunder they
took from their enemies. Would not the slaughter of the Philistines have been even greater?"
[31]That day, after the Israelites had struck
down the Philistines from Micmash to Aijalon,
they were exhausted. [32]They pounced on the
plunder and, taking sheep, cattle and calves,
they butchered them on the ground and ate
them, together with the blood. [33]Then someone said to Saul, "Look, the men are sinning
against the LORD by eating meat that has blood
in it."

"You have broken faith," he said. "Roll a large
stone over here at once." [34]Then he said, "Go
out among the men and tell them, 'Each of you
bring me your cattle and sheep, and slaughter
them here and eat them. Do not sin against the
LORD by eating meat with blood still in it.' "

So everyone brought his ox that night and
slaughtered it there. [35]Then Saul built an altar to the LORD; it was the first time he had
done this.

[36]Saul said, "Let us go down after the Philistines by night and plunder them till dawn, and
let us not leave one of them alive."

"Do whatever seems best to you," they replied.

But the priest said, "Let us inquire of
God here."

[37]So Saul asked God, "Shall I go down after
the Philistines? Will you give them into Israel's
hand?" But God did not answer him that day.

[38]Saul therefore said, "Come here, all you
who are leaders of the army, and let us find out
what sin has been committed today. [39]As surely
as the LORD who rescues Israel lives, even if it
lies with my son Jonathan, he must die." But
not one of the men said a word.

[40]Saul then said to all the Israelites, "You
stand over there; I and Jonathan my son will
stand over here."

"Do what seems best to you," the men replied.

[41]Then Saul prayed to the LORD, the God of
Israel, "Give me the right answer."[a] And Jonathan and Saul were taken by lot, and the men
were cleared. [42]Saul said, "Cast the lot between
me and Jonathan my son." And Jonathan was
taken.

[43]Then Saul said to Jonathan, "Tell me what
you have done."

So Jonathan told him, "I merely tasted a little honey with the end of my staff. And now
must I die?"

[44]Saul said, "May God deal with me, be it
ever so severely, if you do not die, Jonathan."

[45]But the men said to Saul, "Should Jonathan die—he who has brought about this great
deliverance in Israel? Never! As surely as the
LORD lives, not a hair of his head will fall to the
ground, for he did this today with God's help."
So the men rescued Jonathan, and he was not
put to death.

[46]Then Saul stopped pursuing the Philistines, and they withdrew to their own land.

[47]After Saul had assumed rule over Israel,
he fought against their enemies on every side:
Moab, the Ammonites, Edom, the kings[b] of Zobah, and the Philistines. Wherever he turned,
he inflicted punishment on them.[c] [48]He fought
valiantly and defeated the Amalekites, delivering Israel from the hands of those who had
plundered them.

Saul's Family

[49]Saul's sons were Jonathan, Ishvi and
Malki-Shua. The name of his older daughter
was Merab, and that of the younger was Michal. [50]His wife's name was Ahinoam daughter
of Ahimaaz. The name of the commander of
Saul's army was Abner son of Ner, and Ner was
Saul's uncle. [51]Saul's father Kish and Abner's father Ner were sons of Abiel.

[52]All the days of Saul there was bitter war
with the Philistines, and whenever Saul saw a
mighty or brave man, he took him into his service.

The LORD Rejects Saul as King

15 Samuel said to Saul, "I am the one the
LORD sent to anoint you king over
his people Israel; so listen now to the message
from the LORD. [2]This is what the LORD Almighty says: 'I will punish the Amalekites for
what they did to Israel when they waylaid them
as they came up from Egypt. [3]Now go, attack

[a]41 Hebrew; Septuagint *"Why have you not answered your servant today? If the fault is in me or my son Jonathan, respond with Urim, but if the men of Israel are at fault, respond with Thummim."* [b]47 Masoretic Text; Dead Sea Scrolls and Septuagint *king* [c]47 Hebrew; Septuagint *he was victorious*

the Amalekites and totally destroy[a] everything
that belongs to them. Do not spare them; put to
death men and women, children and infants,
cattle and sheep, camels and donkeys.'"
4So Saul summoned the men and mustered
them at Telaim—two hundred thousand foot
soldiers and ten thousand men from Judah.
5Saul went to the city of Amalek and set an
ambush in the ravine. 6Then he said to the Kenites, "Go away, leave the Amalekites so that I
do not destroy you along with them; for you
showed kindness to all the Israelites when they
came up out of Egypt." So the Kenites moved
away from the Amalekites.
7Then Saul attacked the Amalekites all the
way from Havilah to Shur, to the east of Egypt.
8He took Agag king of the Amalekites alive,
and all his people he totally destroyed with the
sword. 9But Saul and the army spared Agag and
the best of the sheep and cattle, the fat calves[b]
and lambs—everything that was good. These
they were unwilling to destroy completely, but
everything that was despised and weak they
totally destroyed.
10Then the word of the LORD came to Samuel: 11"I am grieved that I have made Saul king,
because he has turned away from me and has
not carried out my instructions." Samuel was
troubled, and he cried out to the LORD all that
night.
12Early in the morning Samuel got up and
went to meet Saul, but he was told, "Saul has
gone to Carmel. There he has set up a monument in his own honor and has turned and
gone on down to Gilgal."
13When Samuel reached him, Saul said,
"The LORD bless you! I have carried out the
LORD's instructions."
14But Samuel said, "What then is this bleating of sheep in my ears? What is this lowing of
cattle that I hear?"
15Saul answered, "The soldiers brought
them from the Amalekites; they spared the best
of the sheep and cattle to sacrifice to the LORD
your God, but we totally destroyed the rest."
16"Stop!" Samuel said to Saul. "Let me tell
you what the LORD said to me last night."
"Tell me," Saul replied.
17Samuel said, "Although you were once
small in your own eyes, did you not become
the head of the tribes of Israel? The LORD
anointed you king over Israel. 18And he sent
you on a mission, saying, 'Go and completely
destroy those wicked people, the Amalekites;
make war on them until you have wiped them
out.' 19Why did you not obey the LORD? Why
did you pounce on the plunder and do evil in
the eyes of the LORD?"
20"But I did obey the LORD," Saul said. "I
went on the mission the LORD assigned me.
I completely destroyed the Amalekites and
brought back Agag their king. 21The soldiers
took sheep and cattle from the plunder, the best
of what was devoted to God, in order to sacrifice them to the LORD your God at Gilgal."
22But Samuel replied:

"Does the LORD delight in burnt offerings
and sacrifices
as much as in obeying the voice of the
LORD?
To obey is better than sacrifice,
and to heed is better than the fat of
rams.
23For rebellion is like the sin of divination,
and arrogance like the evil of
idolatry.
Because you have rejected the word of the
LORD,
he has rejected you as king."

24Then Saul said to Samuel, "I have sinned. I
violated the LORD's command and your instructions. I was afraid of the people and so I gave
in to them. 25Now I beg you, forgive my sin
and come back with me, so that I may worship
the LORD."
26But Samuel said to him, "I will not go back
with you. You have rejected the word of the
LORD, and the LORD has rejected you as king
over Israel!"
27As Samuel turned to leave, Saul caught
hold of the hem of his robe, and it tore. 28Sam-
uel said to him, "The LORD has torn the kingdom of Israel from you today and has given it
to one of your neighbors—to one better than
you. 29He who is the Glory of Israel does not

[a]3 The Hebrew term refers to the irrevocable giving over of things or persons to the LORD, often by totally destroying them; also in verses 8, 9, 15, 18, 20 and 21. [b]9 Or *the grown bulls*; the meaning of the Hebrew for this phrase is uncertain.

But, Lord!

Read: 1 Samuel 15:1–23

"YES, MOM, I HEAR YOU! I'll get my homework done and unload the dishwasher before I watch TV." Brent looked his mom straight in the eyes and repeated her instructions. Marlene had to work the third shift this week, and she wouldn't be around when Brent got home from school. Later, when she inspected her son's work, she realized he hadn't followed all of her directions. When she confronted him, Brent rolled his eyes and said, "But, Mom, I didn't think you meant all of it!" Walking away in disgust, she muttered, "Where did I go wrong?"

Marlene sounds a little like Samuel when he expressed God's grief over Saul's misbehavior: "I am grieved that I have made Saul king." Samuel, God's messenger on earth, had given Saul clear instructions: Wipe out all of the Amalekites and take no plunder. No exceptions.

But Saul's actions revealed his self-willed heart: "But, Lord, I didn't think you meant all of them!" God's commands didn't fit Saul's plans, so he tweaked them to fit his convenience.

We're all a little like Saul. We all fall into the "but, Lord" trap.

I know your grace is sufficient, but, Lord, I think I'll take the easy way out.

But, Lord, why can't I tell five of my best friends about what happened?

But, Lord, surely flirting isn't cheating.

But, Lord, this chat room helps me escape my boring life.

But, Lord, overeating isn't hurting anyone else, is it?

We dig ourselves in deeper when, instead of squelching temptation, we turn toward it. The turn starts when, like Saul, we respond to God's promptings within us with "*But, Lord . . .*" and "[reject] the word of the Lord." The more frequently we make that turn, the more we fool ourselves that we are innocent.

Our daily lives present us with ample opportunity to choose God's leading or to reject it. Saul chose to disobey, and it cost him the kingdom. Jesus chose to obey, and he gained the keys to the kingdom of heaven. The only "but" believers should utter is the one Christ taught us to pray, "Not as I will, *but* as you will" (Matthew 26:39, emphasis added).

Go to page 347 for your next devotional reading.

1 Samuel 15:11

"I am grieved that I have made Saul king, because he has turned away from me and has not carried out my instructions." Samuel was troubled, and he cried out to the Lord all that night.

reflection

1 How is "*but, Lord*" a phrase that creeps into your vocabulary?

2 In what ways have you tweaked God's instructions to suit your convenience?

3 What are some practical ways you can turn from a temptation in your life? Make a commitment today to take whatever steps you must to obey God with no *ifs, ands* or *buts*.

RELATED READINGS

Proverbs 4:20–27;
Matthew 26:36–46;
1 John 3:21–24

lie or change his mind; for he is not a man, that
he should change his mind."
30 Saul replied, "I have sinned. But please
honor me before the elders of my people and
before Israel; come back with
me, so that I may worship the
LORD your God." 31 So Samuel
went back with Saul, and Saul
worshiped the LORD.
32 Then Samuel said, "Bring
me Agag king of the Amalekites."
Agag came to him con-
fidently,[a] thinking, "Surely the
bitterness of death is past."
33 But Samuel said,

> "As your sword has made
> women childless,
> so will your mother be childless among
> women."

And Samuel put Agag to death before the LORD
at Gilgal.
34 Then Samuel left for Ramah, but Saul
went up to his home in Gibeah of Saul. 35 Until
the day Samuel died, he did not go to see Saul
again, though Samuel mourned for him. And
the LORD was grieved that he had made Saul
king over Israel.

1 Samuel 15:29

God Is Resolute

"He who is the Glory of Israel does not lie or change his mind; for he is not a man, that he should change his mind."

Samuel Anoints David

16 The LORD said to Samuel, "How long
will you mourn for Saul, since I have
rejected him as king over Israel? Fill your horn
with oil and be on your way; I am sending you
to Jesse of Bethlehem. I have chosen one of his
sons to be king."
2 But Samuel said, "How can I go? Saul will
hear about it and kill me."
The LORD said, "Take a heifer with you and
say, 'I have come to sacrifice to the LORD.' 3 Invite Jesse to the sacrifice, and I will show you
what to do. You are to anoint for me the one
I indicate."
4 Samuel did what the LORD said. When he
arrived at Bethlehem, the elders of the town
trembled when they met him. They asked, "Do
you come in peace?"
5 Samuel replied, "Yes, in peace; I have come
to sacrifice to the LORD. Consecrate yourselves
and come to the sacrifice with me." Then he
consecrated Jesse and his sons and invited
them to the sacrifice.
6 When they arrived, Samuel saw Eliab and
thought, "Surely the LORD's
anointed stands here before
the LORD."
7 But the LORD said to Samuel, "Do not consider his appearance or his height, for I
have rejected him. The LORD
does not look at the things
man looks at. Man looks at the
outward appearance, but the
LORD looks at the heart."
8 Then Jesse called Abinadab and had him pass in front
of Samuel. But Samuel said,
"The LORD has not chosen this one either."
9 Jesse then had Shammah pass by, but Samuel said, "Nor has the LORD chosen this one."
10 Jesse had seven of his sons pass before Samuel, but Samuel said to him, "The LORD has
not chosen these." 11 So he asked Jesse, "Are
these all the sons you have?"
"There is still the youngest," Jesse answered,
"but he is tending the sheep."
Samuel said, "Send for him; we will not sit
down[b] until he arrives."
12 So he sent and had him brought in. He
was ruddy, with a fine appearance and handsome features.
Then the LORD said, "Rise and anoint him;
he is the one."
13 So Samuel took the horn of oil and
anointed him in the presence of his brothers,
and from that day on the Spirit of the LORD
came upon David in power. Samuel then went
to Ramah.

David in Saul's Service

14 Now the Spirit of the LORD had departed
from Saul, and an evil[c] spirit from the LORD
tormented him.
15 Saul's attendants said to him, "See, an evil
spirit from God is tormenting you. 16 Let our
lord command his servants here to search for
someone who can play the harp. He will play
when the evil spirit from God comes upon you,
and you will feel better."

[a] 32 Or *him trembling, yet* [b] 11 Some Septuagint manuscripts; Hebrew *not gather around* [c] 14 Or *injurious;* also in verses 15, 16 and 23

17So Saul said to his attendants, "Find someone who plays well and bring him to me."
18One of the servants answered, "I have seen a son of Jesse of Bethlehem who knows how to play the harp. He is a brave man and a warrior. He speaks well and is a fine-looking man. And the LORD is with him."
19Then Saul sent messengers to Jesse and said, "Send me your son David, who is with the
sheep." 20So Jesse took a donkey loaded with bread, a skin of wine and a young goat and sent them with his son David to Saul.
21David came to Saul and entered his service. Saul liked him very much, and David became
one of his armor-bearers. 22Then Saul sent word to Jesse, saying, "Allow David to remain in my service, for I am pleased with him."
23Whenever the spirit from God came upon Saul, David would take his harp and play. Then relief would come to Saul; he would feel better, and the evil spirit would leave him.

David and Goliath

17 Now the Philistines gathered their forces for war and assembled at Socoh in Judah. They pitched camp at Ephes Dammim, between Socoh and Azekah. 2Saul and
the Israelites assembled and camped in the Valley of Elah and drew up their battle line to meet
the Philistines. 3The Philistines occupied one hill and the Israelites another, with the valley between them.
4A champion named Goliath, who was from Gath, came out of the Philistine camp. He was
over nine feet[a] tall. 5He had a bronze helmet on his head and wore a coat of scale armor of
bronze weighing five thousand shekels[b]; 6on his legs he wore bronze greaves, and a bronze jave-
lin was slung on his back. 7His spear shaft was like a weaver's rod, and its iron point weighed six hundred shekels.[c] His shield bearer went ahead of him.
8Goliath stood and shouted to the ranks of Israel, "Why do you come out and line up for battle? Am I not a Philistine, and are you not the servants of Saul? Choose a man and have him
come down to me. 9If he is able to fight and kill me, we will become your subjects; but if I overcome him and kill him, you will become our
subjects and serve us." 10Then the Philistine said, "This day I defy the ranks of Israel! Give
me a man and let us fight each other." 11On hearing the Philistine's words, Saul and all the Israelites were dismayed and terrified.
12Now David was the son of an Ephrathite named Jesse, who was from Bethlehem in Judah. Jesse had eight sons, and in Saul's time
he was old and well advanced in years. 13Jesse's three oldest sons had followed Saul to the war: The firstborn was Eliab; the second, Abinadab; and the third, Shammah. 14David was the
youngest. The three oldest followed Saul, 15but David went back and forth from Saul to tend his father's sheep at Bethlehem.
16For forty days the Philistine came forward every morning and evening and took his stand.
17Now Jesse said to his son David, "Take this ephah[d] of roasted grain and these ten loaves of bread for your brothers and hurry to their
camp. 18Take along these ten cheeses to the commander of their unit.[e] See how your brothers are and bring back some assurance[f] from
them. 19They are with Saul and all the men of Israel in the Valley of Elah, fighting against the Philistines."
20Early in the morning David left the flock with a shepherd, loaded up and set out, as Jesse had directed. He reached the camp as the army was going out to its battle positions, shouting
the war cry. 21Israel and the Philistines were
drawing up their lines facing each other. 22David left his things with the keeper of supplies, ran to the battle lines and greeted his brothers.
23As he was talking with them, Goliath, the Philistine champion from Gath, stepped out from his lines and shouted his usual defiance, and
David heard it. 24When the Israelites saw the man, they all ran from him in great fear.
25Now the Israelites had been saying, "Do you see how this man keeps coming out? He comes out to defy Israel. The king will give great wealth to the man who kills him. He will also give him his daughter in marriage and will exempt his father's family from taxes in Israel."
26David asked the men standing near

[a]4 Hebrew *was six cubits and a span* (about 3 meters) [b]5 That is, about 125 pounds (about 57 kilograms) [c]7 That is, about 15 pounds (about 7 kilograms) [d]17 That is, probably about 3/5 bushel (about 22 liters) [e]18 Hebrew *thousand* [f]18 Or *some token*; or *some pledge of spoils*

him, "What will be done for the man who
kills this Philistine and removes this disgrace
from Israel? Who is this uncircumcised Philistine that he should defy the armies of the living God?"
27 They repeated to him what they had been
saying and told him, "This is what will be done
for the man who kills him."
28 When Eliab, David's oldest brother, heard
him speaking with the men, he burned with
anger at him and asked, "Why have you come
down here? And with whom did you leave
those few sheep in the desert? I know how
conceited you are and how wicked your heart
is; you came down only to watch the battle."
29 "Now what have I done?" said David.
"Can't I even speak?" 30 He then turned away to
someone else and brought up the same matter,
and the men answered him as before. 31 What
David said was overheard and reported to Saul,
and Saul sent for him.
32 David said to Saul, "Let
no one lose heart on account
of this Philistine; your servant
will go and fight him."
33 Saul replied, "You are not
able to go out against this Philistine and fight him; you are only
a boy, and he has been a fighting man from his youth."
34 But David said to Saul,
"Your servant has been keeping his father's sheep. When a
lion or a bear came and carried
off a sheep from the flock, 35 I
went after it, struck it and rescued the sheep from its mouth.
When it turned on me, I seized
it by its hair, struck it and killed
it. 36 Your servant has killed both the lion and
the bear; this uncircumcised Philistine will be
like one of them, because he has defied the
armies of the living God. 37 The LORD who
delivered me from the paw of the lion and the
paw of the bear will deliver me from the hand
of this Philistine."
Saul said to David, "Go, and the LORD be
with you."
38 Then Saul dressed David in his own tunic.
He put a coat of armor on him and a bronze
helmet on his head. 39 David fastened on his
sword over the tunic and tried walking around,
because he was not used to them.
"I cannot go in these," he said to Saul, "because I am not used to them." So he took them
off. 40 Then he took his staff in his hand, chose
five smooth stones from the stream, put them
in the pouch of his shepherd's bag and, with
his sling in his hand, approached the Philistine.
41 Meanwhile, the Philistine, with his shield
bearer in front of him, kept coming closer to
David. 42 He looked David over and saw that
he was only a boy, ruddy and handsome, and
he despised him. 43 He said to David, "Am I a
dog, that you come at me with sticks?" And the
Philistine cursed David by his gods. 44 "Come
here," he said, "and I'll give your flesh to the
birds of the air and the beasts of the field!"
45 David said to the Philistine, "You come
against me with sword and spear and javelin,
but I come against you in the
name of the LORD Almighty,
the God of the armies of Israel,
whom you have defied. 46 This
day the LORD will hand you
over to me, and I'll strike you
down and cut off your head.
Today I will give the carcasses
of the Philistine army to the
birds of the air and the beasts
of the earth, and the whole
world will know that there is a
God in Israel. 47 All those gathered here will know that it is
not by sword or spear that the
LORD saves; for the battle is the
LORD's, and he will give all of
you into our hands."
48 As the Philistine moved closer to attack
him, David ran quickly toward the battle line to
meet him. 49 Reaching into his bag and taking
out a stone, he slung it and struck the Philistine
on the forehead. The stone sank into his forehead, and he fell facedown on the ground.
50 So David triumphed over the Philistine
with a sling and a stone; without a sword in
his hand he struck down the Philistine and
killed him.
51 David ran and stood over him. He took

> **1 Samuel 17:47**
>
> *God Saves His Own*
>
> "All those gathered here will know that it is not by sword or spear that the LORD saves; for the battle is the LORD's, and he will give all of you into our hands."

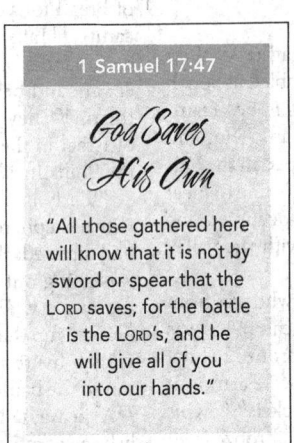

No Underdogs

Read: 1 Samuel 17:32–51

LONG REVILED AND FEARED by humans, due in part to their unearthly cackle, hyenas stand up to virtually any other animal. They are scrappy underdogs willing to fight enormous predators and staggering odds. The female hyena stays with and cares for her young longer than any other carnivore. Mothers will battle other bands of hyenas, and have even been known to face nearly certain death at the fangs of lions, when fighting for their young.

David, hardly more than a boy himself, defended something even more dear than an offspring: his people's God. God delights in calling those who are small and weak. It's a picture of God granting his people strength and power, equipping them to accomplish amazing things for his good purpose. We see the principle—God empowering the weak to conquer the strong—demonstrated throughout the Bible: The stories of Moses standing before Pharaoh, Elijah standing against the prophets of Baal, and Gideon fighting the Midianites all display the power of God working through weak human beings. And the principle doesn't stop there. When we look around in our churches, we see the same thing happening today on both large and small scales. Women pray together to battle for their families and marriages. Sunday school teachers work tirelessly to instill the knowledge of God in young hearts. Families provide food for those who have little. Missionary attorneys battle slavery and other injustices all over the world.

What hulking giant swaggers and struts through your territory, trying to keep you from moving forward? Do you have a monstrous fear of rejection? Do you harbor huge questions about your faith? Does the complexity of society's mammoth problems cause you to doubt God's strength?

Perhaps God is calling *you* to move from defense to offense, to count the importance of *who* you're defending before assessing the odds. For a female hyena, her young always trump physical danger, however big the predator. Perhaps, like David, God has called you to the battlefield. Before you go, carefully don the armor of God (see Ephesians 6:10–18). Then, when the giant tries to intimidate you, pick out your stone of faith and take aim. And cover your ears, because when you fight in the power of God through Jesus Christ, the crash will be deafening when the giant falls.

1 Samuel 17:45

David said to the Philistine, "You come against me with sword and spear and javelin, but I come against you in the name of the LORD Almighty, the God of the armies of Israel, whom you have defied."

reflection

1 Why do you think God used a shepherd boy rather than an entire army to bring down Goliath?

2 How does it encourage you to see how God empowers ordinary people to accomplish his purposes?

3 In which of your battles do you particularly need God's strength? Take the time to ask him to arm you head to toe. Ask him to transform your tiny pebble of faith into a powerful missile.

RELATED READINGS

1 Samuel 16:6–13;
Isaiah 41:10;
Ephesians 6:10–18

Go to page 351 for your next devotional reading.

hold of the Philistine's sword and drew it from
the scabbard. After he killed him, he cut off his
head with the sword.
When the Philistines saw that their hero was
dead, they turned and ran. 52 Then the men of
Israel and Judah surged forward with a shout
and pursued the Philistines to the entrance of
Gath[a] and to the gates of Ekron. Their dead
were strewn along the Shaaraim road to Gath
and Ekron. 53 When the Israelites returned
from chasing the Philistines, they plundered
their camp. 54 David took the Philistine's head
and brought it to Jerusalem, and he put the Philistine's weapons in his own tent.
55 As Saul watched David going out to meet
the Philistine, he said to Abner, commander
of the army, "Abner, whose son is that
young man?"
Abner replied, "As surely as you live, O king,
I don't know."
56 The king said, "Find out whose son this
young man is."
57 As soon as David returned from killing
the Philistine, Abner took him and brought
him before Saul, with David still holding the
Philistine's head.
58 "Whose son are you, young man?" Saul
asked him.
David said, "I am the son of your servant
Jesse of Bethlehem."

Saul's Jealousy of David

18 After David had finished talking with
Saul, Jonathan became one in spirit
with David, and he loved him as himself.
2 From that day Saul kept David with him and
did not let him return to his father's house.
3 And Jonathan made a covenant with David because he loved him as himself. 4 Jonathan took
off the robe he was wearing and gave it to David, along with his tunic, and even his sword,
his bow and his belt.
5 Whatever Saul sent him to do, David did it
so successfully[b] that Saul gave him a high rank
in the army. This pleased all the people, and
Saul's officers as well.
6 When the men were returning home after
David had killed the Philistine, the women
came out from all the towns of Israel to meet
King Saul with singing and dancing, with joyful songs and with tambourines and lutes. 7 As
they danced, they sang:

"Saul has slain his thousands,
and David his tens of thousands."

8 Saul was very angry; this refrain galled
him. "They have credited David with tens of
thousands," he thought, "but me with only
thousands. What more can he get but the kingdom?" 9 And from that time on Saul kept a jealous eye on David.
10 The next day an evil[c] spirit from God came
forcefully upon Saul. He was prophesying in his
house, while David was playing the harp, as he
usually did. Saul had a spear in his hand 11 and
he hurled it, saying to himself, "I'll pin David to
the wall." But David eluded him twice.
12 Saul was afraid of David, because the
LORD was with David but had left Saul. 13 So
he sent David away from him and gave him
command over a thousand men, and David
led the troops in their campaigns. 14 In everything he did he had great success,[d] because the
LORD was with him. 15 When Saul saw how successful[e] he was, he was afraid of him. 16 But all
Israel and Judah loved David, because he led
them in their campaigns.
17 Saul said to David, "Here is my older
daughter Merab. I will give her to you in marriage; only serve me bravely and fight the battles of the LORD." For Saul said to himself, "I
will not raise a hand against him. Let the Philistines do that!"
18 But David said to Saul, "Who am I, and
what is my family or my father's clan in Israel,
that I should become the king's son-in-law?"
19 So[f] when the time came for Merab, Saul's
daughter, to be given to David, she was given
in marriage to Adriel of Meholah.
20 Now Saul's daughter Michal was in love
with David, and when they told Saul about it,
he was pleased. 21 "I will give her to him," he
thought, "so that she may be a snare to him
and so that the hand of the Philistines may be
against him." So Saul said to David, "Now you
have a second opportunity to become my son-
in-law."

[a]52 Some Septuagint manuscripts; Hebrew *a valley* [b]5 Or *wisely* [c]10 Or *injurious* [d]14 Or *he was very wise* [e]15 Or *wise*
[f]19 Or *However,*

22Then Saul ordered his attendants: "Speak
to David privately and say, 'Look, the king is
pleased with you, and his attendants all like
you; now become his son-in-law.'"
23They repeated these words to David. But
David said, "Do you think it is a small matter to
become the king's son-in-law? I'm only a poor
man and little known."
24When Saul's servants told him what David
had said, 25Saul replied, "Say to David, 'The
king wants no other price for the bride than
a hundred Philistine foreskins, to take revenge
on his enemies.'" Saul's plan was to have David
fall by the hands of the Philistines.
26When the attendants told David these
things, he was pleased to become the king's
son-in-law. So before the allotted time elapsed,
27David and his men went out and killed two
hundred Philistines. He brought their foreskins
and presented the full number to the king so
that he might become the king's son-in-law.
Then Saul gave him his daughter Michal in
marriage.
28When Saul realized that the LORD was with
David and that his daughter Michal loved David, 29Saul became still more afraid of him, and
he remained his enemy the rest of his days.
30The Philistine commanders continued to
go out to battle, and as often as they did, David
met with more success[a] than the rest of Saul's
officers, and his name became well known.

Saul Tries to Kill David

19 Saul told his son Jonathan and all the
attendants to kill David. But Jonathan
was very fond of David 2and warned him, "My
father Saul is looking for a chance to kill you.
Be on your guard tomorrow morning; go into
hiding and stay there. 3I will go out and stand
with my father in the field where you are. I'll
speak to him about you and will tell you what
I find out."
4Jonathan spoke well of David to Saul his father and said to him, "Let not the king do wrong
to his servant David; he has not wronged you,
and what he has done has benefited you greatly.
5He took his life in his hands when he killed
the Philistine. The LORD won a great victory
for all Israel, and you saw it and were glad. Why
then would you do wrong to an innocent man
like David by killing him for no reason?"
6Saul listened to Jonathan and took this
oath: "As surely as the LORD lives, David will
not be put to death."
7So Jonathan called David and told him the
whole conversation. He brought him to Saul,
and David was with Saul as before.
8Once more war broke out, and David went
out and fought the Philistines. He struck them
with such force that they fled before him.
9But an evil[b] spirit from the LORD came
upon Saul as he was sitting in his house with
his spear in his hand. While David was playing
the harp, 10Saul tried to pin him to the wall
with his spear, but David eluded him as Saul
drove the spear into the wall. That night David
made good his escape.
11Saul sent men to David's house to watch
it and to kill him in the morning. But Michal,
David's wife, warned him, "If you don't run for
your life tonight, tomorrow you'll be killed."
12So Michal let David down through a window, and he fled and escaped. 13Then Michal
took an idol[c] and laid it on the bed, covering
it with a garment and putting some goats' hair
at the head.
14When Saul sent the men to capture David,
Michal said, "He is ill."
15Then Saul sent the men back to see David
and told them, "Bring him up to me in his bed
so that I may kill him." 16But when the men entered, there was the idol in the bed, and at the
head was some goats' hair.
17Saul said to Michal, "Why did you deceive
me like this and send my enemy away so that
he escaped?"
Michal told him, "He said to me, 'Let me get
away. Why should I kill you?'"
18When David had fled and made his escape,
he went to Samuel at Ramah and told him all
that Saul had done to him. Then he and Samuel
went to Naioth and stayed there. 19Word came
to Saul: "David is in Naioth at Ramah"; 20so he
sent men to capture him. But when they saw
a group of prophets prophesying, with Samuel
standing there as their leader, the Spirit of God
came upon Saul's men and they also prophesied. 21Saul was told about it, and he sent more

[a] 30 Or *David acted more wisely* [b] 9 Or *injurious* [c] 13 Hebrew *teraphim*; also in verse 16

men, and they prophesied too. Saul sent men a
third time, and they also prophesied. 22Finally,
he himself left for Ramah and went to the great
cistern at Secu. And he asked, "Where are Samuel and David?"
"Over in Naioth at Ramah," they said.
23So Saul went to Naioth at Ramah. But the
Spirit of God came even upon him, and he
walked along prophesying until he came to Naioth. 24He stripped off his robes and also prophesied in Samuel's presence. He lay that way all
that day and night. This is why people say, "Is
Saul also among the prophets?"

David and Jonathan

20 Then David fled from Naioth at Ramah and went to Jonathan and asked,
"What have I done? What is my crime? How
have I wronged your father, that he is trying to
take my life?"
2"Never!" Jonathan replied. "You are not going to die! Look, my father doesn't do anything,
great or small, without confiding in me. Why
would he hide this from me? It's not so!"
3But David took an oath and said, "Your father knows very well that I have found favor in
your eyes, and he has said to himself, 'Jonathan
must not know this or he will be grieved.' Yet as
surely as the LORD lives and as you live, there is
only a step between me and death."
4Jonathan said to David, "Whatever you
want me to do, I'll do for you."
5So David said, "Look, tomorrow is the New
Moon festival, and I am supposed to dine with
the king; but let me go and hide in the field until the evening of the day after tomorrow. 6If
your father misses me at all, tell him, 'David
earnestly asked my permission to hurry to
Bethlehem, his hometown, because an annual
sacrifice is being made there for his whole clan.'
7If he says, 'Very well,' then your servant is safe.
But if he loses his temper, you can be sure that
he is determined to harm me. 8As for you,
show kindness to your servant, for you have
brought him into a covenant with you before
the LORD. If I am guilty, then kill me yourself!
Why hand me over to your father?"
9"Never!" Jonathan said. "If I had the least
inkling that my father was determined to harm
you, wouldn't I tell you?"
10David asked, "Who will tell me if your father answers you harshly?"
11"Come," Jonathan said, "let's go out into
the field." So they went there together.
12Then Jonathan said to David: "By the
LORD, the God of Israel, I will surely sound out
my father by this time the day after tomorrow!
If he is favorably disposed toward you, will I not
send you word and let you know? 13But if my
father is inclined to harm you, may the LORD
deal with me, be it ever so severely, if I do not
let you know and send you away safely. May
the LORD be with you as he has been with my
father. 14But show me unfailing kindness like
that of the LORD as long as I live, so that I may
not be killed, 15and do not ever cut off your
kindness from my family—not even when the
LORD has cut off every one of David's enemies
from the face of the earth."
16So Jonathan made a covenant with the
house of David, saying, "May the LORD call David's enemies to account." 17And Jonathan had
David reaffirm his oath out of love for him, because he loved him as he loved himself.
18Then Jonathan said to David: "Tomorrow
is the New Moon festival. You will be missed,
because your seat will be empty. 19The day after tomorrow, toward evening, go to the place
where you hid when this trouble began, and
wait by the stone Ezel. 20I will shoot three arrows to the side of it, as though I were shooting
at a target. 21Then I will send a boy and say,
'Go, find the arrows.' If I say to him, 'Look, the
arrows are on this side of you; bring them here,'
then come, because, as surely as the LORD lives,
you are safe; there is no danger. 22But if I say
to the boy, 'Look, the arrows are beyond you,'
then you must go, because the LORD has sent
you away. 23And about the matter you and I
discussed—remember, the LORD is witness between you and me forever."
24So David hid in the field, and when the
New Moon festival came, the king sat down to
eat. 25He sat in his customary place by the wall,
opposite Jonathan,[a] and Abner sat next to Saul,
but David's place was empty. 26Saul said nothing
that day, for he thought, "Something must have
happened to David to make him ceremonially
unclean—surely he is unclean." 27But the next

[a]25 Septuagint; Hebrew *wall. Jonathan arose*

Friends

Read: 1 Samuel 20:1–42

A BRITISH PUBLICATION once offered a prize for the best definition of a friend. Among the thousands of answers mailed in, the top five were:

5) "One who multiplies joys, divides grief, and whose honesty is inviolable."
4 "One who understands our silence."
3) "A volume of sympathy bound in cloth."
2) "A watch that beats true for all time and never runs down."

The winning definition simply read:

1) "A friend is the one who comes in when the whole world has gone out."

David and Jonathan perfectly fit these definitions of a true friend. Jonathan had become "one in spirit with David, and he loved him as himself," and the two had made a covenant of friendship (1 Samuel 18:1,3). When Samuel anointed David to succeed Jonathan's father as king, Saul erupted in unbridled anger and forced David from the land. But Jonathan swore loyalty to God's chosen heir to the throne.

David and Jonathan's deep friendship was based not on family ties or warm, fuzzy feelings; they were bound by dedication to God and steadfast commitment to one another. Rather than being jealous of David for usurping his potential place as king, Jonathan accepted God's plan to make David king, sacrificially stepping down and supporting his friend.

And David reciprocated by remaining loyal to Jonathan and Jonathan's family. Even after Jonathan's death, David kept his vow of loyalty to his dear friend. He made sure that Jonathan and Saul were buried with royal honors. He invited Jonathan's disabled son, Mephibosheth, into his home and treated him like a prince.

In our culture, it seems more common to hear of women who have close friendships than men who do, so we're surprised that one of the most beautiful portraits of friendship in Scripture is the bond between these two warriors, who we might be inclined to think of as unemotional and detached. But we, as women, can model David and Jonathan's friendship. When our friendships are based on our common love for God and our desire for God's best for each other, then our friendships can be as tough and true and deep as the one between David and Jonathan.

1 Samuel 20:42

Jonathan said to David, "Go in peace, for we have sworn friendship with each other in the name of the LORD, saying, 'The LORD is witness between you and me, and between your descendants and my descendants forever.'" Then David left, and Jonathan went back to the town.

reflection

1 Which of your friends will "come in even if the world goes out"?

2 With whom do you share a covenant friendship, and how has this person shown herself to be a godly friend?

3 How has Jesus proved to be your *best* friend?

RELATED READINGS

Ruth 1:3–17; Proverbs 17:17; 18:24; Ecclesiastes 4:9–10; John 3:27–30

"The impulse of love that leads us to the doorway of a friend is the voice of God within and we need not be afraid to follow it."

Agnes Sanford

Go to page 356 for your next devotional reading.

day, the second day of the month, David's place
was empty again. Then Saul said to his son Jonathan, "Why hasn't the son of Jesse come to the
meal, either yesterday or today?"
28 Jonathan answered, "David earnestly
asked me for permission to go
to Bethlehem. 29 He said, 'Let
me go, because our family is observing a sacrifice in the town
and my brother has ordered
me to be there. If I have found
favor in your eyes, let me get
away to see my brothers.' That
is why he has not come to the
king's table."
30 Saul's anger flared up at
Jonathan and he said to him,
"You son of a perverse and rebellious woman! Don't I know
that you have sided with the
son of Jesse to your own shame and to the
shame of the mother who bore you? 31 As
long as the son of Jesse lives on this earth,
neither you nor your kingdom will be established. Now send and bring him to me, for he
must die!"
32 "Why should he be put to death? What has
he done?" Jonathan asked his father. 33 But Saul
hurled his spear at him to kill him. Then Jonathan knew that his father intended to kill David.
34 Jonathan got up from the table in fierce
anger; on that second day of the month he did
not eat, because he was grieved at his father's
shameful treatment of David.
35 In the morning Jonathan went out to the
field for his meeting with David. He had a
small boy with him, 36 and he said to the boy,
"Run and find the arrows I shoot." As the boy
ran, he shot an arrow beyond him. 37 When the
boy came to the place where Jonathan's arrow
had fallen, Jonathan called out after him, "Isn't
the arrow beyond you?" 38 Then he shouted,
"Hurry! Go quickly! Don't stop!" The boy
picked up the arrow and returned to his master. 39 (The boy knew nothing of all this; only
Jonathan and David knew.) 40 Then Jonathan
gave his weapons to the boy and said, "Go,
carry them back to town."
41 After the boy had gone, David got up from
the south side ⌞of the stone⌟ and bowed down
before Jonathan three times, with his face to
the ground. Then they kissed each other and
wept together—but David wept the most.
42 Jonathan said to David,
"Go in peace, for we have
sworn friendship with each
other in the name of the LORD,
saying, 'The LORD is witness
between you and me, and between your descendants and
my descendants forever.'" Then
David left, and Jonathan went
back to the town.

> **1 Samuel 20:42**
>
> ***God Cements Friendships***
>
> Jonathan said to David, "Go in peace, for we have sworn friendship with each other in the name of the LORD."

David at Nob

21 David went to Nob, to
Ahimelech the priest.
Ahimelech trembled when he
met him, and asked, "Why are
you alone? Why is no one with you?"
2 David answered Ahimelech the priest,
"The king charged me with a certain matter
and said to me, 'No one is to know anything
about your mission and your instructions.' As
for my men, I have told them to meet me at a
certain place. 3 Now then, what do you have on
hand? Give me five loaves of bread, or whatever you can find."
4 But the priest answered David, "I don't have
any ordinary bread on hand; however, there is
some consecrated bread here—provided the
men have kept themselves from women."
5 David replied, "Indeed women have been
kept from us, as usual whenever[a] I set out.
The men's things[b] are holy even on missions
that are not holy. How much more so today!"
6 So the priest gave him the consecrated bread,
since there was no bread there except the bread
of the Presence that had been removed from
before the LORD and replaced by hot bread on
the day it was taken away.
7 Now one of Saul's servants was there that
day, detained before the LORD; he was Doeg
the Edomite, Saul's head shepherd.
8 David asked Ahimelech, "Don't you have
a spear or a sword here? I haven't brought my
sword or any other weapon, because the king's
business was urgent."

[a] 5 Or *from us in the past few days since* [b] 5 Or *bodies*

9The priest replied, "The sword of Goliath
the Philistine, whom you killed in the Valley of
Elah, is here; it is wrapped in a cloth behind the
ephod. If you want it, take it; there is no sword
here but that one."
David said, "There is none like it; give it
to me."

David at Gath

10That day David fled from Saul and went
to Achish king of Gath. 11But the servants of
Achish said to him, "Isn't this David, the king
of the land? Isn't he the one they sing about in
their dances:

"'Saul has slain his thousands,
and David his tens of thousands'?"

12David took these words to heart and was
very much afraid of Achish king of Gath. 13So
he pretended to be insane in their presence;
and while he was in their hands he acted like
a madman, making marks on the doors of the
gate and letting saliva run down his beard.
14Achish said to his servants, "Look at the
man! He is insane! Why bring him to me? 15Am
I so short of madmen that you have to bring this
fellow here to carry on like this in front of me?
Must this man come into my house?"

David at Adullam and Mizpah

22 David left Gath and escaped to the
cave of Adullam. When his brothers
and his father's household heard about it, they
went down to him there. 2All those who were
in distress or in debt or discontented gathered
around him, and he became their leader. About
four hundred men were with him.
3From there David went to Mizpah in Moab
and said to the king of Moab, "Would you let
my father and mother come and stay with
you until I learn what God will do for me?"
4So he left them with the king of Moab, and
they stayed with him as long as David was in
the stronghold.
5But the prophet Gad said to David, "Do
not stay in the stronghold. Go into the land
of Judah." So David left and went to the forest
of Hereth.

Saul Kills the Priests of Nob

6Now Saul heard that David and his men
had been discovered. And Saul, spear in hand,
was seated under the tamarisk tree on the hill
at Gibeah, with all his officials standing around
him. 7Saul said to them, "Listen, men of Benjamin! Will the son of Jesse give all of you fields
and vineyards? Will he make all of you commanders of thousands and commanders of
hundreds? 8Is that why you have all conspired
against me? No one tells me when my son
makes a covenant with the son of Jesse. None
of you is concerned about me or tells me that
my son has incited my servant to lie in wait for
me, as he does today."
9But Doeg the Edomite, who was standing
with Saul's officials, said, "I saw the son of Jesse
come to Ahimelech son of Ahitub at Nob.
10Ahimelech inquired of the LORD for him; he
also gave him provisions and the sword of Goliath the Philistine."
11Then the king sent for the priest Ahimelech son of Ahitub and his father's whole
family, who were the priests at Nob, and they
all came to the king. 12Saul said, "Listen now,
son of Ahitub."
"Yes, my lord," he answered.
13Saul said to him, "Why have you conspired
against me, you and the son of Jesse, giving him
bread and a sword and inquiring of God for
him, so that he has rebelled against me and lies
in wait for me, as he does today?"
14Ahimelech answered the king, "Who of
all your servants is as loyal as David, the king's
son-in-law, captain of your bodyguard and
highly respected in your household? 15Was
that day the first time I inquired of God for
him? Of course not! Let not the king accuse
your servant or any of his father's family, for
your servant knows nothing at all about this
whole affair."
16But the king said, "You will surely die,
Ahimelech, you and your father's whole
family."
17Then the king ordered the guards at his
side: "Turn and kill the priests of the LORD,
because they too have sided with David. They
knew he was fleeing, yet they did not tell me."
But the king's officials were not willing to
raise a hand to strike the priests of the LORD.
18The king then ordered Doeg, "You turn
and strike down the priests." So Doeg the Edomite turned and struck them down. That day

he killed eighty-five men who wore the linen ephod. 19He also put to the sword Nob, the town of the priests, with its men and women, its children and infants, and its cattle, donkeys and sheep.

20But Abiathar, a son of Ahimelech son of Ahitub, escaped and fled to join David. 21He told David that Saul had killed the priests of the LORD. 22Then David said to Abiathar: "That day, when Doeg the Edomite was there, I knew he would be sure to tell Saul. I am responsible for the death of your father's whole family. 23Stay with me; don't be afraid; the man who is seeking your life is seeking mine also. You will be safe with me."

David Saves Keilah

23 When David was told, "Look, the Philistines are fighting against Keilah and are looting the threshing floors," 2he inquired of the LORD, saying, "Shall I go and attack these Philistines?"

The LORD answered him, "Go, attack the Philistines and save Keilah."

> 1 Samuel 23:16
>
> *God Gives Strength*
>
> And Saul's son Jonathan went to David at Horesh and helped him find strength in God.

3But David's men said to him, "Here in Judah we are afraid. How much more, then, if we go to Keilah against the Philistine forces!"

4Once again David inquired of the LORD, and the LORD answered him, "Go down to Keilah, for I am going to give the Philistines into your hand." 5So David and his men went to Keilah, fought the Philistines and carried off their livestock. He inflicted heavy losses on the Philistines and saved the people of Keilah. 6(Now Abiathar son of Ahimelech had brought the ephod down with him when he fled to David at Keilah.)

Saul Pursues David

7Saul was told that David had gone to Keilah, and he said, "God has handed him over to me, for David has imprisoned himself by entering a town with gates and bars." 8And Saul called up all his forces for battle, to go down to Keilah to besiege David and his men.

9When David learned that Saul was plotting against him, he said to Abiathar the priest, "Bring the ephod." 10David said, "O LORD, God of Israel, your servant has heard definitely that Saul plans to come to Keilah and destroy the town on account of me. 11Will the citizens of Keilah surrender me to him? Will Saul come down, as your servant has heard? O LORD, God of Israel, tell your servant."

And the LORD said, "He will."

12Again David asked, "Will the citizens of Keilah surrender me and my men to Saul?"

And the LORD said, "They will."

13So David and his men, about six hundred in number, left Keilah and kept moving from place to place. When Saul was told that David had escaped from Keilah, he did not go there.

14David stayed in the desert strongholds and in the hills of the Desert of Ziph. Day after day Saul searched for him, but God did not give David into his hands.

15While David was at Horesh in the Desert of Ziph, he learned that Saul had come out to take his life. 16And Saul's son Jonathan went to David at Horesh and helped him find strength in God. 17"Don't be afraid," he said. "My father Saul will not lay a hand on you. You will be king over Israel, and I will be second to you. Even my father Saul knows this." 18The two of them made a covenant before the LORD. Then Jonathan went home, but David remained at Horesh.

19The Ziphites went up to Saul at Gibeah and said, "Is not David hiding among us in the strongholds at Horesh, on the hill of Hakilah, south of Jeshimon? 20Now, O king, come down whenever it pleases you to do so, and we will be responsible for handing him over to the king."

21Saul replied, "The LORD bless you for your concern for me. 22Go and make further preparation. Find out where David usually goes and who has seen him there. They tell me he is very crafty. 23Find out about all the hiding places he uses and come back to me with definite information.[a] Then I will go with you; if he is in the area, I will track him down among all the clans of Judah."

[a]23 Or *me at Nacon*

24 So they set out and went to Ziph ahead
of Saul. Now David and his men were in the
Desert of Maon, in the Arabah south of Jeshimon. 25 Saul and his men began the search, and
when David was told about it, he went down
to the rock and stayed in the Desert of Maon.
When Saul heard this, he went into the Desert
of Maon in pursuit of David.
26 Saul was going along one side of the mountain, and David and his men were on the other
side, hurrying to get away from Saul. As Saul
and his forces were closing in on David and his
men to capture them, 27 a messenger came to
Saul, saying, "Come quickly! The Philistines
are raiding the land." 28 Then Saul broke off his
pursuit of David and went to meet the Philistines. That is why they call this place Sela Hammahlekoth.[a] 29 And David went up from there
and lived in the strongholds of En Gedi.

David Spares Saul's Life

24 After Saul returned from pursuing
the Philistines, he was told, "David is
in the Desert of En Gedi." 2 So Saul took three
thousand chosen men from all Israel and set
out to look for David and his men near the
Crags of the Wild Goats.
3 He came to the sheep pens along the way; a
cave was there, and Saul went in to relieve himself. David and his men were far back in the
cave. 4 The men said, "This is the day the LORD
spoke of when he said[b] to you, 'I will give your
enemy into your hands for you to deal with as
you wish.'" Then David crept up unnoticed and
cut off a corner of Saul's robe.
5 Afterward, David was conscience-stricken
for having cut off a corner of his robe. 6 He said
to his men, "The LORD forbid that I should
do such a thing to my master, the LORD's
anointed, or lift my hand against him; for he is
the anointed of the LORD." 7 With these words
David rebuked his men and did not allow them
to attack Saul. And Saul left the cave and went
his way.
8 Then David went out of the cave and called
out to Saul, "My lord the king!" When Saul
looked behind him, David bowed down and
prostrated himself with his face to the ground.
9 He said to Saul, "Why do you listen when men
say, 'David is bent on harming you'? 10 This
day you have seen with your own eyes how the
LORD delivered you into my hands in the cave.
Some urged me to kill you, but I spared you; I
said, 'I will not lift my hand against my master,
because he is the LORD's anointed.' 11 See, my father, look at this piece of your robe in my hand!
I cut off the corner of your robe but did not
kill you. Now understand and recognize that
I am not guilty of wrongdoing or rebellion. I
have not wronged you, but you are hunting me
down to take my life. 12 May the LORD judge between you and me. And may the LORD avenge
the wrongs you have done to me, but my hand
will not touch you. 13 As the old saying goes,
'From evildoers come evil deeds,' so my hand
will not touch you.
14 "Against whom has the king of Israel come
out? Whom are you pursuing? A dead dog? A
flea? 15 May the LORD be our judge and decide
between us. May he consider my cause and uphold it; may he vindicate me by delivering me
from your hand."
16 When David finished saying this, Saul
asked, "Is that your voice, David my son?" And
he wept aloud. 17 "You are more righteous than
I," he said. "You have treated me well, but I have
treated you badly. 18 You have just now told me
of the good you did to me; the LORD delivered
me into your hands, but you did not kill me.
19 When a man finds his enemy, does he let him
get away unharmed? May the LORD reward
you well for the way you treated me today. 20 I
know that you will surely be king and that the
kingdom of Israel will be established in your
hands. 21 Now swear to me by the LORD that
you will not cut off my descendants or wipe out
my name from my father's family."
22 So David gave his oath to Saul. Then Saul
returned home, but David and his men went
up to the stronghold.

David, Nabal and Abigail

25 Now Samuel died, and all Israel assembled and mourned for him; and they
buried him at his home in Ramah.
Then David moved down into the Desert
of Maon.[c] 2 A certain man in Maon, who had
property there at Carmel, was very wealthy.

[a] 28 *Sela Hammahlekoth* means *rock of parting.* [b] 4 Or *"Today the LORD is saying* [c] 1 Some Septuagint manuscripts; Hebrew *Paran*

1 Samuel 24:6

"The LORD forbid that I should do such a thing to my master, the LORD's anointed, or lift my hand against him; for he is the anointed of the LORD."

reflection

1 In what ways have you been mistreated or misunderstood for doing the right thing?

2 What opportunities have you had to retaliate? How can you respond with blessing instead?

3 Who are the people in your life that misunderstand or persecute you? Pray that you will learn to walk in the footsteps of David and Jesus, learning to forgive and bless others who hurt you.

RELATED READINGS

Proverbs 8:12–21; Matthew 5:38–48; Romans 12:17–21; 1 Timothy 2:1–8

"Snuggle in God's arms. When you are hurting, when you feel lonely, left out, let him cradle you, comfort you, reassure you of his all-sufficient power and love."

Kay Arthur

Being Misunderstood

Read: 1 Samuel 24:1–7

CLARA BARTON, dubbed "the angel of the battlefield," had a reputation for refusing to hold a grudge against anyone. As founder of the Red Cross, people labeled her leadership style as authoritarian and used Congress's charter as a lever against her to force her to resign from her own organization. Once, a friend tried to get her to recall a cruel thing that had happened to her years before, but Clara claimed to have forgotten the incident. "Don't you remember the wrong that was done you?" the friend hounded. Clara answered calmly, "No, I distinctly remember forgetting that."

We've all been misunderstood or mistreated. No matter how hard we work at doing things right, there may be someone who doesn't see things the way we do or like the way we do things. Maybe it's a husband, child, coworker, parent or friend. They may not hear what we're trying to tell them, see what we're trying to show them or appreciate the intentions behind our actions. The philosopher Goethe said, "So long as you live and work, you will be misunderstood." But Clara Barton's philosophy is helpful: Choose to forget the insults and wrongs.

David seemed to live by this philosophy too. He didn't deserve to be persecuted by King Saul. He had served the king well. Yet here we find the two men at odds in a desert oasis, meeting unexpectedly in the back of a cold, damp cave. With a single, well-placed thrust of his sword, David could have killed Saul. But he recognized that Saul was God's anointed, so David chose to forget Saul's wrongs and not lay a hand against him.

How do you respond when you've been misunderstood? Can you leave matters in God's hands and choose to forget? Or will you take a bit of vengeance here and a slice of repayment there? Can you be content to wait for God to set things right . . . on his timetable rather than yours?

The next time you feel misunderstood or mistreated, remember that you're following in some pretty big footsteps. King David was persecuted for doing God's bidding and did not retaliate when he was attacked. Jesus, the sinless God-man, was persecuted and died for our sins, yet he willingly forgave from the cross those who had tormented him. What will you do the next time you're wronged?

Thursday

Go to page 358 for your next devotional reading.

He had a thousand goats and three thousand
sheep, which he was shearing in Carmel. 3His
name was Nabal and his wife's name was Abigail. She was an intelligent and beautiful
woman, but her husband, a Calebite, was surly
and mean in his dealings.
4While David was in the desert, he heard
that Nabal was shearing sheep. 5So he sent ten
young men and said to them, "Go up to Nabal
at Carmel and greet him in my name. 6Say to
him: 'Long life to you! Good health to you and
your household! And good health to all that
is yours!
7"'Now I hear that it is sheep-shearing time.
When your shepherds were with us, we did not
mistreat them, and the whole time they were
at Carmel nothing of theirs was missing. 8Ask
your own servants and they will tell you. Therefore be favorable toward my young men, since
we come at a festive time. Please give your servants and your son David whatever you can
find for them.'"
9When David's men arrived, they gave Nabal this message in David's name. Then they
waited.
10Nabal answered David's servants, "Who
is this David? Who is this son of Jesse? Many
servants are breaking away from their masters
these days. 11Why should I take my bread and
water, and the meat I have slaughtered for my
shearers, and give it to men coming from who
knows where?"
12David's men turned around and went
back. When they arrived, they reported every
word. 13David said to his men, "Put on your
swords!" So they put on their swords, and David put on his. About four hundred men went
up with David, while two hundred stayed with
the supplies.
14One of the servants told Nabal's wife Abigail: "David sent messengers from the desert to
give our master his greetings, but he hurled insults at them. 15Yet these men were very good
to us. They did not mistreat us, and the whole
time we were out in the fields near them nothing was missing. 16Night and day they were a
wall around us all the time we were herding
our sheep near them. 17Now think it over and
see what you can do, because disaster is hanging over our master and his whole household.
He is such a wicked man that no one can talk
to him."
18Abigail lost no time. She took two hundred loaves of bread, two skins of wine, five
dressed sheep, five seahs[a] of roasted grain,
a hundred cakes of raisins and two hundred
cakes of pressed figs, and loaded them on donkeys. 19Then she told her servants, "Go on
ahead; I'll follow you." But she did not tell her
husband Nabal.
20As she came riding her donkey into a
mountain ravine, there were David and his
men descending toward her, and she met them.
21David had just said, "It's been useless—all my
watching over this fellow's property in the desert so that nothing of his was missing. He has
paid me back evil for good. 22May God deal
with David,[b] be it ever so severely, if by morning I leave alive one male of all who belong
to him!"
23When Abigail saw David, she quickly got
off her donkey and bowed down before David
with her face to the ground. 24She fell at his
feet and said: "My lord, let the blame be on
me alone. Please let your servant speak to you;
hear what your servant has to say. 25May my
lord pay no attention to that wicked man Nabal. He is just like his name—his name is Fool,
and folly goes with him. But as for me, your servant, I did not see the men my master sent.
26"Now since the LORD has kept you, my
master, from bloodshed and from avenging
yourself with your own hands, as surely as the
LORD lives and as you live, may your enemies
and all who intend to harm my master be like
Nabal. 27And let this gift, which your servant
has brought to my master, be given to the men
who follow you. 28Please forgive your servant's
offense, for the LORD will certainly make a lasting dynasty for my master, because he fights the
LORD's battles. Let no wrongdoing be found in
you as long as you live. 29Even though someone
is pursuing you to take your life, the life of my
master will be bound securely in the bundle of
the living by the LORD your God. But the lives
of your enemies he will hurl away as from the
pocket of a sling. 30When the LORD has done
for my master every good thing he promised

[a]18 That is, probably about a bushel (about 37 liters) [b]22 Some Septuagint manuscripts; Hebrew *with David's enemies*

A Woman of Discernment

Read: 1 Samuel 25:1–42

MANY ANCIENT SOCIETIES protected the guest-host relationship as a sacred covenant, with grave consequences should an individual choose to disregard it. The Greeks called this hospitality bond *xenia*, and fought one of the most famous wars of antiquity, the Trojan War, over a breech of *xenia*. Paris kidnapped King Menelaus' wife, Helen, while a guest in the king's household. He was transgressing the sacred obligations of the *xenos*, the guest-friend within their gates, and his entire nation would pay.

Failure to return hospitality carried serious implications in Biblical times. Foolish, alcohol-abusing Nabal had insulted David by refusing to offer him and his men the typical Eastern courtesy: a share in the bounty of his household at sheep-shearing time. In so doing, Nabal put his wife and entire household at risk of retaliation. When Abigail heard about the situation, she could have responded by criticizing her husband or cursing his stupidity. She did neither. Instead, Abigail carried courage in one hand and provisions in the other. She restored peace on behalf of her household. Her discernment and tact calmed David's anger and honored God.

Abigail offered hospitality in the face of hostility. David was grateful that her wise intervention stopped him from committing murder. Ultimately, Nabal died of "natural" causes, brought about when Abigail told him of the crisis that had been averted. His heart turned to stone—God dealt with this hard-hearted man in his own way.

Hannah Hurnard says an intercessor is "one who is in such vital contact with God and with his fellowmen that he is like a live wire closing the gap between the saving power of God and the sinful men who have been cut off from that power."

While your community may not punish rudeness or slander with actual warfare, you're probably very familiar with the damage that smoldering hostility or gossip can bring to a family, a workplace or a church. When you become aware of an escalating crisis, ask God to give you the discernment to think quickly and act decisively. Then intervene with kindness on your lips and grace in your heart. Be more concerned with what you *can* offer than with what you cannot. Like Abigail, use the resources that God has placed at your disposal to help find a peaceful solution to a possibly explosive situation.

1 Samuel 25:32–33

David said to Abigail, "Praise be to the LORD, the God of Israel, who has sent you today to meet me. May you be blessed for your good judgment and for keeping me from bloodshed this day and from avenging myself with my own hands."

reflection

1 Whom did David credit with Abigail's actions?

2 How have you seen a "gentle answer [turn] away wrath" (Proverbs 15:1)?

3 Whom could use your peaceful intervention right now? What situation calls for you to pray, offer gentle words or even invite warring parties to share a meal?

RELATED READINGS

1 Chronicles 3:1;
Psalm 141:3–4;
Proverbs 15:1–4;
Philemon 1–25

"The purpose of all prayer is to find God's will and to make that will our prayer."

Catherine Marshall

Go to page 366 for your next devotional reading.

concerning him and has appointed him leader
over Israel, 31 my master will not have on his
conscience the staggering burden of needless
bloodshed or of having avenged himself. And
when the LORD has brought my master success,
remember your servant."

32 David said to Abigail, "Praise be to the
LORD, the God of Israel, who has sent you today to meet me. 33 May you be blessed for your
good judgment and for keeping me from bloodshed this day and from avenging myself with
my own hands. 34 Otherwise, as surely as the
LORD, the God of Israel, lives, who has kept me
from harming you, if you had not come quickly
to meet me, not one male belonging to Nabal
would have been left alive by daybreak."

35 Then David accepted from her hand what
she had brought him and said, "Go home in
peace. I have heard your words and granted
your request."

36 When Abigail went to Nabal, he was in
the house holding a banquet like that of a king.
He was in high spirits and very drunk. So she
told him nothing until daybreak. 37 Then in the
morning, when Nabal was sober, his wife told
him all these things, and his heart failed him
and he became like a stone. 38 About ten days
later, the LORD struck Nabal and he died.

39 When David heard that Nabal was dead,
he said, "Praise be to the LORD, who has upheld
my cause against Nabal for treating me with
contempt. He has kept his servant from doing
wrong and has brought Nabal's wrongdoing
down on his own head."

Then David sent word to Abigail, asking her
to become his wife. 40 His servants went to Carmel and said to Abigail, "David has sent us to
you to take you to become his wife."

41 She bowed down with her face to the
ground and said, "Here is your maidservant,
ready to serve you and wash the feet of my master's servants." 42 Abigail quickly got on a donkey and, attended by her five maids, went with
David's messengers and became his wife. 43 David had also married Ahinoam of Jezreel, and
they both were his wives. 44 But Saul had given
his daughter Michal, David's wife, to Paltiel[a]
son of Laish, who was from Gallim.

David Again Spares Saul's Life

26 The Ziphites went to Saul at Gibeah
and said, "Is not David hiding on the
hill of Hakilah, which faces Jeshimon?"

2 So Saul went down to the Desert of Ziph,
with his three thousand chosen men of Israel,
to search there for David. 3 Saul made his camp
beside the road on the hill of Hakilah facing Jeshimon, but David stayed in the desert. When
he saw that Saul had followed him there, 4 he
sent out scouts and learned that Saul had
definitely arrived.[b]

5 Then David set out and went to the place
where Saul had camped. He saw where Saul
and Abner son of Ner, the commander of the
army, had lain down. Saul was lying inside the
camp, with the army encamped around him.

6 David then asked Ahimelech the Hittite and
Abishai son of Zeruiah, Joab's brother, "Who
will go down into the camp with me to Saul?"

"I'll go with you," said Abishai.

7 So David and Abishai went to the army by
night, and there was Saul, lying asleep inside
the camp with his spear stuck in the ground
near his head. Abner and the soldiers were lying around him.

8 Abishai said to David, "Today God has delivered your enemy into your hands. Now let
me pin him to the ground with one thrust of
my spear; I won't strike him twice."

9 But David said to Abishai, "Don't destroy
him! Who can lay a hand on the LORD's
anointed and be guiltless? 10 As surely as the
LORD lives," he said, "the LORD himself will
strike him; either his time will come and he will
die, or he will go into battle and perish. 11 But
the LORD forbid that I should lay a hand on the
LORD's anointed. Now get the spear and water
jug that are near his head, and let's go."

12 So David took the spear and water jug
near Saul's head, and they left. No one saw or
knew about it, nor did anyone wake up. They
were all sleeping, because the LORD had put
them into a deep sleep.

13 Then David crossed over to the other side
and stood on top of the hill some distance away;
there was a wide space between them. 14 He
called out to the army and to Abner son of Ner,
"Aren't you going to answer me, Abner?"

[a]44 Hebrew *Palti,* a variant of *Paltiel* [b]4 Or *had come to Nacon*

Abner replied, "Who are you who calls to
the king?"
15David said, "You're a man, aren't you? And
who is like you in Israel? Why didn't you guard
your lord the king? Someone came to destroy
your lord the king. 16What you have done is
not good. As surely as the LORD lives, you and
your men deserve to die, because you did not
guard your master, the LORD's anointed. Look
around you. Where are the king's spear and water jug that were near his head?"
17Saul recognized David's voice and said, "Is
that your voice, David my son?"
David replied, "Yes it is, my lord the king."
18And he added, "Why is my lord pursuing his
servant? What have I done, and what wrong
am I guilty of? 19Now let my lord the king
listen to his servant's words. If the LORD has
incited you against me, then may he accept an
offering. If, however, men have done it, may
they be cursed before the LORD! They have
now driven me from my share in the LORD's inheritance and have said, 'Go, serve other gods.'
20Now do not let my blood fall to the ground
far from the presence of the LORD. The king of
Israel has come out to look for a flea—as one
hunts a partridge in the mountains."
21Then Saul said, "I have sinned. Come back,
David my son. Because you
considered my life precious today, I will not try to harm you
again. Surely I have acted like a
fool and have erred greatly."
22"Here is the king's spear,"
David answered. "Let one of
your young men come over and
get it. 23The LORD rewards every man for his righteousness
and faithfulness. The LORD delivered you into my hands today,
but I would not lay a hand on
the LORD's anointed. 24As surely
as I valued your life today, so
may the LORD value my life and
deliver me from all trouble."
25Then Saul said to David,
"May you be blessed, my son David; you will
do great things and surely triumph."
So David went on his way, and Saul returned home.

1 Samuel 26:23

God Rewards Faithfulness

"The LORD rewards every man for his righteousness and faithfulness. The LORD delivered you into my hands today, but I would not lay a hand on the LORD's anointed."

David Among the Philistines

27 But David thought to himself, "One
of these days I will be destroyed by
the hand of Saul. The best thing I can do is
to escape to the land of the Philistines. Then
Saul will give up searching for me anywhere in
Israel, and I will slip out of his hand."
2So David and the six hundred men with him
left and went over to Achish son of Maoch king
of Gath. 3David and his men settled in Gath
with Achish. Each man had his family with
him, and David had his two wives: Ahinoam of
Jezreel and Abigail of Carmel, the widow of Nabal. 4When Saul was told that David had fled to
Gath, he no longer searched for him.
5Then David said to Achish, "If I have found
favor in your eyes, let a place be assigned to
me in one of the country towns, that I may
live there. Why should your servant live in the
royal city with you?"
6So on that day Achish gave him Ziklag, and
it has belonged to the kings of Judah ever since.
7David lived in Philistine territory a year and
four months.
8Now David and his men went up and
raided the Geshurites, the Girzites and the Amalekites. (From ancient times these peoples had
lived in the land extending to Shur and Egypt.)
9Whenever David attacked an
area, he did not leave a man or
woman alive, but took sheep
and cattle, donkeys and camels,
and clothes. Then he returned
to Achish.
10When Achish asked, "Where
did you go raiding today?" David would say, "Against the
Negev of Judah" or "Against
the Negev of Jerahmeel" or
"Against the Negev of the Kenites." 11He did not leave a man
or woman alive to be brought
to Gath, for he thought, "They
might inform on us and say,
'This is what David did.'" And
such was his practice as long as
he lived in Philistine territory. 12Achish trusted
David and said to himself, "He has become so
odious to his people, the Israelites, that he will
be my servant forever."

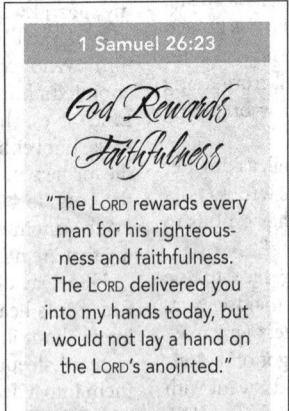

Saul and the Witch of Endor

28 In those days the Philistines gathered
their forces to fight against Israel.
Achish said to David, "You must understand
that you and your men will accompany me in
the army."
2David said, "Then you will see for yourself
what your servant can do."
Achish replied, "Very well, I will make you
my bodyguard for life."
3Now Samuel was dead, and all Israel had
mourned for him and buried him in his own
town of Ramah. Saul had expelled the mediums and spiritists from the land.
4The Philistines assembled and came and set
up camp at Shunem, while Saul gathered all the
Israelites and set up camp at Gilboa. 5When
Saul saw the Philistine army, he was afraid; terror filled his heart. 6He inquired of the LORD,
but the LORD did not answer him by dreams or
Urim or prophets. 7Saul then said to his attendants, "Find me a woman who is a medium, so
I may go and inquire of her."
"There is one in Endor," they said.
8So Saul disguised himself, putting on other
clothes, and at night he and two men went to
the woman. "Consult a spirit for me," he said,
"and bring up for me the one I name."
9But the woman said to him, "Surely you
know what Saul has done. He has cut off the
mediums and spiritists from the land. Why
have you set a trap for my life to bring about
my death?"
10Saul swore to her by the LORD, "As surely
as the LORD lives, you will not be punished
for this."
11Then the woman asked, "Whom shall I
bring up for you?"
"Bring up Samuel," he said.
12When the woman saw Samuel, she cried
out at the top of her voice and said to Saul,
"Why have you deceived me? You are Saul!"
13The king said to her, "Don't be afraid.
What do you see?"
The woman said, "I see a spirit[a] coming up
out of the ground."
14"What does he look like?" he asked.
"An old man wearing a robe is coming up,"
she said.
Then Saul knew it was Samuel, and he
bowed down and prostrated himself with his
face to the ground.
15Samuel said to Saul, "Why have you disturbed me by bringing me up?"
"I am in great distress," Saul said. "The Philistines are fighting against me, and God has
turned away from me. He no longer answers
me, either by prophets or by dreams. So I have
called on you to tell me what to do."
16Samuel said, "Why do you consult me,
now that the LORD has turned away from you
and become your enemy? 17The LORD has
done what he predicted through me. The LORD
has torn the kingdom out of your hands and
given it to one of your neighbors—to David.
18Because you did not obey the LORD or carry
out his fierce wrath against the Amalekites, the
LORD has done this to you today. 19The LORD
will hand over both Israel and you to the Philistines, and tomorrow you and your sons will
be with me. The LORD will also hand over the
army of Israel to the Philistines."
20Immediately Saul fell full length on the
ground, filled with fear because of Samuel's
words. His strength was gone, for he had eaten
nothing all that day and night.
21When the woman came to Saul and saw
that he was greatly shaken, she said, "Look,
your maidservant has obeyed you. I took my
life in my hands and did what you told me to
do. 22Now please listen to your servant and
let me give you some food so you may eat and
have the strength to go on your way."
23He refused and said, "I will not eat."
But his men joined the woman in urging
him, and he listened to them. He got up from
the ground and sat on the couch.
24The woman had a fattened calf at the
house, which she butchered at once. She took
some flour, kneaded it and baked bread without yeast. 25Then she set it before Saul and his
men, and they ate. That same night they got up
and left.

Achish Sends David Back to Ziklag

29 The Philistines gathered all their
forces at Aphek, and Israel camped
by the spring in Jezreel. 2As the Philistine rulers marched with their units of hundreds and

[a]13 Or *see spirits*; or *see gods*

thousands, David and his men were marching at the rear with Achish. 3The commanders of the Philistines asked, "What about these Hebrews?"

Achish replied, "Is this not David, who was an officer of Saul king of Israel? He has already been with me for over a year, and from the day he left Saul until now, I have found no fault in him."

4But the Philistine commanders were angry with him and said, "Send the man back, that he may return to the place you assigned him. He must not go with us into battle, or he will turn against us during the fighting. How better could he regain his master's favor than by taking the heads of our own men? 5Isn't this the David they sang about in their dances:

"'Saul has slain his
thousands,
and David his tens of
thousands'?"

6So Achish called David and said to him, "As surely as the LORD lives, you have been reliable, and I would be pleased to have you serve with me in the army. From the day you came to me until now, I have found no fault in you, but the rulers don't approve of you. 7Turn back and go in peace; do nothing to displease the Philistine rulers."

8"But what have I done?" asked David. "What have you found against your servant from the day I came to you until now? Why can't I go and fight against the enemies of my lord the king?"

9Achish answered, "I know that you have been as pleasing in my eyes as an angel of God; nevertheless, the Philistine commanders have said, 'He must not go up with us into battle.' 10Now get up early, along with your master's servants who have come with you, and leave in the morning as soon as it is light."

11So David and his men got up early in the morning to go back to the land of the Philistines, and the Philistines went up to Jezreel.

1 Samuel 30:6

God Provides Strength

David was greatly distressed because the men were talking of stoning him; each one was bitter in spirit because of his sons and daughters. But David found strength in the LORD his God.

David Destroys the Amalekites

30 David and his men reached Ziklag on the third day. Now the Amalekites had raided the Negev and Ziklag. They had attacked Ziklag and burned it, 2and had taken captive the women and all who were in it, both young and old. They killed none of them, but carried them off as they went on their way.

3When David and his men came to Ziklag, they found it destroyed by fire and their wives and sons and daughters taken captive. 4So David and his men wept aloud until they had no strength left to weep. 5David's two wives had been captured—Ahinoam of Jezreel and Abigail, the widow of Nabal of Carmel. 6David was greatly distressed because the men were talking of stoning him; each one was bitter in spirit because of his sons and daughters. But David found strength in the LORD his God.

7Then David said to Abiathar the priest, the son of Ahimelech, "Bring me the ephod." Abiathar brought it to him, 8and David inquired of the LORD, "Shall I pursue this raiding party? Will I overtake them?"

"Pursue them," he answered. "You will certainly overtake them and succeed in the rescue."

9David and the six hundred men with him came to the Besor Ravine, where some stayed behind, 10for two hundred men were too exhausted to cross the ravine. But David and four hundred men continued the pursuit.

11They found an Egyptian in a field and brought him to David. They gave him water to drink and food to eat— 12part of a cake of pressed figs and two cakes of raisins. He ate and was revived, for he had not eaten any food or drunk any water for three days and three nights.

13David asked him, "To whom do you belong, and where do you come from?"

He said, "I am an Egyptian, the slave of an Amalekite. My master abandoned me when I

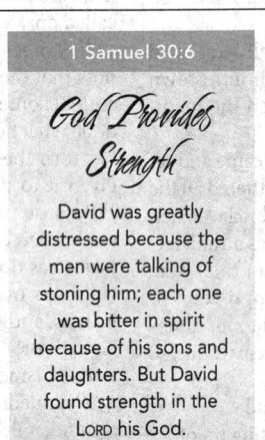

became ill three days ago. 14We raided the Negev of the Kerethites and the territory belonging to Judah and the Negev of Caleb. And we
burned Ziklag."
15David asked him, "Can you lead me down
to this raiding party?"
He answered, "Swear to me before God that
you will not kill me or hand me over to my master, and I will take you down to them."
16He led David down, and there they were,
scattered over the countryside, eating, drinking and reveling because of the great amount
of plunder they had taken from the land of the
Philistines and from Judah. 17David fought
them from dusk until the evening of the next
day, and none of them got away, except four
hundred young men who rode off on camels
and fled. 18David recovered everything the
Amalekites had taken, including his two wives.
19Nothing was missing: young or old, boy or
girl, plunder or anything else they had taken.
David brought everything back. 20He took all
the flocks and herds, and his men drove them
ahead of the other livestock, saying, "This is David's plunder."
21Then David came to the two hundred men
who had been too exhausted to follow him
and who were left behind at the Besor Ravine.
They came out to meet David and the people
with him. As David and his men approached,
he greeted them. 22But all the evil men and
troublemakers among David's followers said,
"Because they did not go out with us, we will
not share with them the plunder we recovered.
However, each man may take his wife and children and go."
23David replied, "No, my brothers, you must
not do that with what the LORD has given us.
He has protected us and handed over to us the
forces that came against us. 24Who will listen
to what you say? The share of the man who
stayed with the supplies is to be the same as
that of him who went down to the battle. All
will share alike." 25David made this a statute
and ordinance for Israel from that day to this.
26When David arrived in Ziklag, he sent
some of the plunder to the elders of Judah, who
were his friends, saying, "Here is a present for
you from the plunder of the LORD's enemies."
27He sent it to those who were in Bethel,
Ramoth Negev and Jattir; 28to those in Aroer,
Siphmoth, Eshtemoa 29and Racal; to those in
the towns of the Jerahmeelites and the Kenites;
30to those in Hormah, Bor Ashan, Athach
31and Hebron; and to those in all the other
places where David and his men had roamed.

Saul Takes His Life

31 Now the Philistines fought against
Israel; the Israelites fled before them,
and many fell slain on Mount Gilboa. 2The Philistines pressed hard after Saul and his sons,
and they killed his sons Jonathan, Abinadab
and Malki-Shua. 3The fighting grew fierce
around Saul, and when the archers overtook
him, they wounded him critically.
4Saul said to his armor-bearer, "Draw your
sword and run me through, or these uncircumcised fellows will come and run me through
and abuse me."
But his armor-bearer was terrified and
would not do it; so Saul took his own sword
and fell on it. 5When the armor-bearer saw
that Saul was dead, he too fell on his sword and
died with him. 6So Saul and his three sons and
his armor-bearer and all his men died together
that same day.
7When the Israelites along the valley and
those across the Jordan saw that the Israelite
army had fled and that Saul and his sons had
died, they abandoned their towns and fled.
And the Philistines came and occupied them.
8The next day, when the Philistines came to
strip the dead, they found Saul and his three
sons fallen on Mount Gilboa. 9They cut off his
head and stripped off his armor, and they sent
messengers throughout the land of the Philistines to proclaim the news in the temple of
their idols and among their people. 10They put
his armor in the temple of the Ashtoreths and
fastened his body to the wall of Beth Shan.
11When the people of Jabesh Gilead heard
of what the Philistines had done to Saul, 12all
their valiant men journeyed through the night
to Beth Shan. They took down the bodies of
Saul and his sons from the wall of Beth Shan
and went to Jabesh, where they burned them.
13Then they took their bones and buried them
under a tamarisk tree at Jabesh, and they fasted
seven days.

2 Samuel

Author:
Unknown.

Audience:
The people of Israel.

Date:
Sometime after the division of Israel into the northern and southern kingdoms, around 930 B.C.

Setting:
Saul has proven to be a bad king. David is poised to begin his reign.

Verse to Remember:
And David knew that the LORD had established him as king over Israel and had exalted his kingdom for the sake of his people Israel. (5:12)

Nothing in the *life of King David* was boring. Giant killer, psalm writer, vagabond, king, adulterer, murderer, warrior . . . and founder of the dynasty that led to the greatest King of all. David's life had great highs and great lows. *But his love for God was deep* and sincere. He was open to God's redirection. He was humble and repentant before his own King. His worship was heartfelt and selfless. The story of David is the story of how God can work through someone who loves him.

Scripture presents an untouched portrait of its greatest human king. The picture comes complete with human failure. But *David relied upon God,* trusted God, loved God and submitted to God—and those attitudes deepened his relationship and friendship with his God.

David Hears of Saul's Death

1 After the death of Saul, David returned
from defeating the Amalekites and stayed
in Ziklag two days. 2On the third day a man
arrived from Saul's camp, with his clothes torn
and with dust on his head. When he came to
David, he fell to the ground to pay him honor.
3"Where have you come from?" David
asked him.
He answered, "I have escaped from the Israelite camp."
4"What happened?" David asked. "Tell me."
He said, "The men fled from the battle.
Many of them fell and died. And Saul and his
son Jonathan are dead."
5Then David said to the young man who
brought him the report, "How do you know
that Saul and his son Jonathan are dead?"
6"I happened to be on Mount Gilboa," the
young man said, "and there was Saul, leaning
on his spear, with the chariots and riders almost upon him. 7When he turned around and

saw me, he called out to me, and I said, ‘What
can I do?’
8“He asked me, ‘Who are you?’
“ ‘An Amalekite,’ I answered.
9“Then he said to me, ‘Stand over me and
kill me! I am in the throes of death, but I'm
still alive.’
10“So I stood over him and killed him, because I knew that after he had fallen he could
not survive. And I took the crown that was on
his head and the band on his arm and have
brought them here to my lord.”
11Then David and all the men with him took
hold of their clothes and tore them. 12They
mourned and wept and fasted till evening for
Saul and his son Jonathan, and for the army of
the LORD and the house of Israel, because they
had fallen by the sword.
13David said to the young man who brought
him the report, “Where are you from?”
“I am the son of an alien, an Amalekite,”
he answered.
14David asked him, “Why were you not
afraid to lift your hand to destroy the LORD's
anointed?”
15Then David called one of his men and
said, “Go, strike him down!” So he struck him
down, and he died. 16For David had said to
him, “Your blood be on your own head. Your
own mouth testified against you when you
said, ‘I killed the LORD's anointed.’ ”

David's Lament for Saul and Jonathan

17David took up this lament concerning
Saul and his son Jonathan, 18and ordered that
the men of Judah be taught this lament of the
bow (it is written in the Book of Jashar):

19“Your glory, O Israel, lies slain on your
heights.
How the mighty have fallen!

20“Tell it not in Gath,
proclaim it not in the streets of
Ashkelon,
lest the daughters of the Philistines be
glad,
lest the daughters of the uncircumcised
rejoice.

21“O mountains of Gilboa,
may you have neither dew nor rain,
nor fields that yield offerings ⌞of grain⌟.
For there the shield of the mighty was
defiled,
the shield of Saul—no longer rubbed
with oil.
22From the blood of the slain,
from the flesh of the mighty,
the bow of Jonathan did not turn back,
the sword of Saul did not return
unsatisfied.

23“Saul and Jonathan—
in life they were loved and gracious,
and in death they were not parted.
They were swifter than eagles,
they were stronger than lions.

24“O daughters of Israel,
weep for Saul,
who clothed you in scarlet and finery,
who adorned your garments with
ornaments of gold.

25“How the mighty have fallen in battle!
Jonathan lies slain on your heights.
26I grieve for you, Jonathan my brother;
you were very dear to me.
Your love for me was wonderful,
more wonderful than that of women.

27“How the mighty have fallen!
The weapons of war have perished!”

David Anointed King Over Judah

2 In the course of time, David inquired
of the LORD. “Shall I go up to one of the
towns of Judah?” he asked.
The LORD said, “Go up.”
David asked, “Where shall I go?”
“To Hebron,” the LORD answered.
2So David went up there with his two wives,
Ahinoam of Jezreel and Abigail, the widow of
Nabal of Carmel. 3David also took the men
who were with him, each with his family, and
they settled in Hebron and its towns. 4Then the
men of Judah came to Hebron and there they
anointed David king over the house of Judah.
When David was told that it was the men of
Jabesh Gilead who had buried Saul, 5he sent
messengers to the men of Jabesh Gilead to say
to them, “The LORD bless you for showing this
kindness to Saul your master by burying him.
6May the LORD now show you kindness and

A Thread of Faith

RAHAB

But Joshua spared Rahab the prostitute, with her family and all who belonged to her, because she hid the men Joshua had sent as spies to Jericho—and she lives among the Israelites to this day.

Joshua 6:25

ASSIGNED READING:

Joshua 2:1–24; 5:13—6:27; Hebrews 11:31

ALL HER HOPES AND DREAMS were fluttering in the wind outside her window. A tattered cord of scarlet material was all that separated certain death and the possibility of new life. Cart-bearing oxen lazily trudged through the city gate amid sounds of clattering wheels and lively street chatter. Sheepherders prodded their lumbering animals on their daily trip to market. Children played games directly underneath her window, barely noticing the scarlet cord now flapping against the city wall in a gentle wind.

Rahab's modest home was built into the city wall—prominently positioned, but vulnerable to the skillful soldiers she knew would soon advance on her city. Days earlier, when two enemy spies had made a pact with her to protect her home, she'd hung a scarlet cord outside her window as a sign, identifying her address to would-be attackers.

It was an unspoken symbol of agreement between three strangers. More than that, it was a powerful statement of faith—a testament of trust in a God she barely knew. A pagan by birth, Rahab had nothing more than a fledgling belief that the stories she'd heard about the miraculous power of the God of the Hebrews were true.

In the tension-filled days that followed, did she question herself? "Is your faith enough for you? Enough to stake everything on?" But she'd made up her mind. And hanging from her house was her testament to her resolution. She was making her stand, issuing her statement, identifying herself with a group of God-followers she'd never encountered and committing her life to a God she'd never seen.

And yet now, just days before the battle, the significance of the scarlet emblem went largely unnoticed by the men and women traveling the dusty streets of the walled city of Jericho. Her neighbors were unaware. However, Rahab knew that her decision had changed everything.

Time crept slowly by. She didn't know when the battle would occur. In the meantime, she anxiously checked and rechecked to be sure the cord was still there. The solitary strand reminded her in no uncertain terms that faith was now all she had. And that turned out to be all she needed.

—Prayer—

God, you are my powerful protector. Thank you for your care in my life.

Weekend

Go to page 371 for your next devotional reading.

faithfulness, and I too will show you the same
favor because you have done this. 7 Now then,
be strong and brave, for Saul your master is
dead, and the house of Judah has anointed me
king over them."

War Between the Houses of David and Saul

8 Meanwhile, Abner son of Ner, the commander of Saul's army, had taken Ish-Bosheth
son of Saul and brought him over to Mahanaim.
9 He made him king over Gilead, Ashuri[a] and
Jezreel, and also over Ephraim, Benjamin and
all Israel.

10 Ish-Bosheth son of Saul was forty years
old when he became king over Israel, and
he reigned two years. The house of Judah,
however, followed David. 11 The length of time
David was king in Hebron over the house of
Judah was seven years and six months.

12 Abner son of Ner, together with the men
of Ish-Bosheth son of Saul, left Mahanaim and
went to Gibeon. 13 Joab son of Zeruiah and David's men went out and met them at the pool of
Gibeon. One group sat down on one side of the
pool and one group on the other side.

14 Then Abner said to Joab, "Let's have some
of the young men get up and fight hand to
hand in front of us."

"All right, let them do it," Joab said.

15 So they stood up and were counted off—
twelve men for Benjamin and Ish-Bosheth son
of Saul, and twelve for David. 16 Then each man
grabbed his opponent by the head and thrust
his dagger into his opponent's side, and they
fell down together. So that place in Gibeon was
called Helkath Hazzurim.[b]

17 The battle that day was very fierce, and
Abner and the men of Israel were defeated by
David's men.

18 The three sons of Zeruiah were there: Joab,
Abishai and Asahel. Now Asahel was as fleet-
footed as a wild gazelle. 19 He chased Abner,
turning neither to the right nor to the left as he
pursued him. 20 Abner looked behind him and
asked, "Is that you, Asahel?"

"It is," he answered.

21 Then Abner said to him, "Turn aside to
the right or to the left; take on one of the young
men and strip him of his weapons." But Asahel
would not stop chasing him.

22 Again Abner warned Asahel, "Stop chasing me! Why should I strike you down? How
could I look your brother Joab in the face?"

23 But Asahel refused to give up the pursuit;
so Abner thrust the butt of his spear into Asahel's stomach, and the spear came out through
his back. He fell there and died on the spot.
And every man stopped when he came to the
place where Asahel had fallen and died.

24 But Joab and Abishai pursued Abner, and
as the sun was setting, they came to the hill of
Ammah, near Giah on the way to the wasteland
of Gibeon. 25 Then the men of Benjamin rallied
behind Abner. They formed themselves into a
group and took their stand on top of a hill.

26 Abner called out to Joab, "Must the sword
devour forever? Don't you realize that this will
end in bitterness? How long before you order
your men to stop pursuing their brothers?"

27 Joab answered, "As surely as God lives, if
you had not spoken, the men would have continued the pursuit of their brothers until morning.[c]"

28 So Joab blew the trumpet, and all the men
came to a halt; they no longer pursued Israel,
nor did they fight anymore.

29 All that night Abner and his men marched
through the Arabah. They crossed the Jordan,
continued through the whole Bithron[d] and
came to Mahanaim.

30 Then Joab returned from pursuing Abner
and assembled all his men. Besides Asahel,
nineteen of David's men were found missing.
31 But David's men had killed three hundred
and sixty Benjamites who were with Abner.
32 They took Asahel and buried him in his father's tomb at Bethlehem. Then Joab and his
men marched all night and arrived at Hebron
by daybreak.

3 The war between the house of Saul and the
house of David lasted a long time. David
grew stronger and stronger, while the house of
Saul grew weaker and weaker.

2 Sons were born to David in Hebron:

[a] 9 Or *Asher* [b] 16 *Helkath Hazzurim* means *field of daggers* or *field of hostilities.* [c] 27 Or *spoken this morning, the men would not have taken up the pursuit of their brothers*; or *spoken, the men would have given up the pursuit of their brothers by morning* [d] 29 Or *morning*; or *ravine*; the meaning of the Hebrew for this word is uncertain.

His firstborn was Amnon the son of
Ahinoam of Jezreel;
3 his second, Kileab the son of Abigail
the widow of Nabal of Carmel;
the third, Absalom the son of Maacah
daughter of Talmai king of Geshur;
4 the fourth, Adonijah the son of Haggith;
the fifth, Shephatiah the son of Abital;
5 and the sixth, Ithream the son of David's wife Eglah.
These were born to David in Hebron.

Abner Goes Over to David

6 During the war between the house of
Saul and the house of David, Abner had been
strengthening his own position in the house of
Saul. 7 Now Saul had had a concubine named
Rizpah daughter of Aiah. And Ish-Bosheth
said to Abner, "Why did you sleep with my father's concubine?"
8 Abner was very angry because of what Ish-
Bosheth said and he answered, "Am I a dog's
head—on Judah's side? This very day I am
loyal to the house of your father Saul and to his
family and friends. I haven't handed you over
to David. Yet now you accuse me of an offense
involving this woman! 9 May God deal with
Abner, be it ever so severely, if I do not do for
David what the LORD promised him on oath
10 and transfer the kingdom from the house of
Saul and establish David's throne over Israel
and Judah from Dan to Beersheba." 11 Ish-Bosheth did not dare to say another word to Abner, because he was afraid of him.
12 Then Abner sent messengers on his behalf
to say to David, "Whose land is it? Make an
agreement with me, and I will help you bring
all Israel over to you."
13 "Good," said David. "I will make an agreement with you. But I demand one thing of you:
Do not come into my presence unless you bring
Michal daughter of Saul when you come to see
me." 14 Then David sent messengers to Ish-Bosheth son of Saul, demanding, "Give me my
wife Michal, whom I betrothed to myself for
the price of a hundred Philistine foreskins."
15 So Ish-Bosheth gave orders and had her
taken away from her husband Paltiel son of Laish. 16 Her husband, however, went with her,
weeping behind her all the way to Bahurim.
Then Abner said to him, "Go back home!" So
he went back.
17 Abner conferred with the elders of Israel
and said, "For some time you have wanted to
make David your king. 18 Now do it! For the
LORD promised David, 'By my servant David
I will rescue my people Israel from the hand
of the Philistines and from the hand of all
their enemies.'"
19 Abner also spoke to the Benjamites in
person. Then he went to Hebron to tell David
everything that Israel and the whole house of
Benjamin wanted to do. 20 When Abner, who
had twenty men with him, came to David at
Hebron, David prepared a feast for him and his
men. 21 Then Abner said to David, "Let me go
at once and assemble all Israel for my lord the
king, so that they may make a compact with
you, and that you may rule over all that your
heart desires." So David sent Abner away, and
he went in peace.

Joab Murders Abner

22 Just then David's men and Joab returned
from a raid and brought with them a great deal
of plunder. But Abner was no longer with David in Hebron, because David had sent him
away, and he had gone in peace. 23 When Joab
and all the soldiers with him arrived, he was
told that Abner son of Ner had come to the
king and that the king had sent him away and
that he had gone in peace.
24 So Joab went to the king and said, "What
have you done? Look, Abner came to you. Why
did you let him go? Now he is gone! 25 You
know Abner son of Ner; he came to deceive
you and observe your movements and find out
everything you are doing."
26 Joab then left David and sent messengers
after Abner, and they brought him back from
the well of Sirah. But David did not know it.
27 Now when Abner returned to Hebron, Joab
took him aside into the gateway, as though to
speak with him privately. And there, to avenge
the blood of his brother Asahel, Joab stabbed
him in the stomach, and he died.
28 Later, when David heard about this, he
said, "I and my kingdom are forever innocent
before the LORD concerning the blood of Abner son of Ner. 29 May his blood fall upon the
head of Joab and upon all his father's house!

May Joab's house never be without someone
who has a running sore or leprosy[a] or who
leans on a crutch or who falls by the sword or
who lacks food."
30 (Joab and his brother Abishai murdered
Abner because he had killed their brother Asahel in the battle at Gibeon.)
31 Then David said to Joab and all the people with him, "Tear your clothes and put on
sackcloth and walk in mourning in front of
Abner." King David himself walked behind the
bier. 32 They buried Abner in Hebron, and the
king wept aloud at Abner's tomb. All the people
wept also.
33 The king sang this lament for Abner:

"Should Abner have died as the lawless
die?
34 Your hands were not bound,
your feet were not fettered.
You fell as one falls before wicked men."

And all the people wept over him again.
35 Then they all came and urged David to
eat something while it was still day; but David
took an oath, saying, "May God deal with me,
be it ever so severely, if I taste bread or anything
else before the sun sets!"
36 All the people took note and were pleased;
indeed, everything the king did pleased them.
37 So on that day all the people and all Israel
knew that the king had no part in the murder
of Abner son of Ner.
38 Then the king said to his men, "Do you
not realize that a prince and a great man has
fallen in Israel this day? 39 And today, though
I am the anointed king, I am weak, and these
sons of Zeruiah are too strong for me. May
the LORD repay the evildoer according to his
evil deeds!"

Ish-Bosheth Murdered

4 When Ish-Bosheth son of Saul heard that
Abner had died in Hebron, he lost courage, and all Israel became alarmed. 2 Now Saul's
son had two men who were leaders of raiding
bands. One was named Baanah and the other
Recab; they were sons of Rimmon the Beerothite from the tribe of Benjamin—Beeroth is considered part of Benjamin, 3 because the people
of Beeroth fled to Gittaim and have lived there
as aliens to this day.
4 (Jonathan son of Saul had a son who was
lame in both feet. He was five years old when
the news about Saul and Jonathan came from
Jezreel. His nurse picked him up and fled, but
as she hurried to leave, he fell and became crippled. His name was Mephibosheth.)
5 Now Recab and Baanah, the sons of Rimmon the Beerothite, set out for the house of
Ish-Bosheth, and they arrived there in the heat
of the day while he was taking his noonday rest.
6 They went into the inner part of the house as
if to get some wheat, and they stabbed him in
the stomach. Then Recab and his brother Baanah slipped away.
7 They had gone into the house while he was
lying on the bed in his bedroom. After they
stabbed and killed him, they cut off his head.
Taking it with them, they traveled all night by
way of the Arabah. 8 They brought the head of
Ish-Bosheth to David at Hebron and said to the
king, "Here is the head of Ish-Bosheth son of
Saul, your enemy, who tried to take your life.
This day the LORD has avenged my lord the
king against Saul and his offspring."
9 David answered Recab and his brother Baanah, the sons of Rimmon the Beerothite, "As
surely as the LORD lives, who has delivered
me out of all trouble, 10 when a man told me,
'Saul is dead,' and thought he was bringing
good news, I seized him and put him to death
in Ziklag. That was the reward I gave him for
his news! 11 How much more—when wicked
men have killed an innocent man in his own
house and on his own bed—should I not now
demand his blood from your hand and rid the
earth of you!"
12 So David gave an order to his men, and
they killed them. They cut off their hands and
feet and hung the bodies by the pool in Hebron.
But they took the head of Ish-Bosheth and buried it in Abner's tomb at Hebron.

David Becomes King Over Israel

5 All the tribes of Israel came to David at Hebron and said, "We are your own flesh and
blood. 2 In the past, while Saul was king over
us, you were the one who led Israel on their

[a]29 The Hebrew word was used for various diseases affecting the skin—not necessarily leprosy.

military campaigns. And the LORD said to you,
'You will shepherd my people Israel, and you
will become their ruler.'"
3When all the elders of Israel had come to
King David at Hebron, the king made a compact with them at Hebron before the LORD, and
they anointed David king over Israel.
4David was thirty years old when he became
king, and he reigned forty years. 5In Hebron he
reigned over Judah seven years and six months,
and in Jerusalem he reigned over all Israel and
Judah thirty-three years.

David Conquers Jerusalem

6The king and his men marched to Jerusalem to attack the Jebusites, who lived there.
The Jebusites said to David, "You will not get in
here; even the blind and the lame can ward you
off." They thought, "David cannot get in here."
7Nevertheless, David captured the fortress of
Zion, the City of David.
8On that day, David said, "Anyone who con-
quers the Jebusites will have to use the water
shaft[a] to reach those 'lame and blind' who are
David's enemies.[b]" That is why they say, "The
'blind and lame' will not enter the palace."
9David then took up residence in the fortress
and called it the City of David. He built up the
area around it, from the supporting terraces[c]
inward. 10And he became more and more powerful, because the LORD God Almighty was
with him.
11Now Hiram king of Tyre
sent messengers to David,
along with cedar logs and carpenters and stonemasons, and
they built a palace for David.
12And David knew that the
LORD had established him as
king over Israel and had exalted
his kingdom for the sake of his
people Israel.
13After he left Hebron, David took more concubines and
wives in Jerusalem, and more
sons and daughters were born
to him. 14These are the names of the children
born to him there: Shammua, Shobab, Nathan,
Solomon, 15Ibhar, Elishua, Nepheg, Japhia,
16Elishama, Eliada and Eliphelet.

> **2 Samuel 5:12**
>
> ***God Is in Control***
>
> And David knew that the LORD had established him as king over Israel and had exalted his kingdom for the sake of his people Israel.

David Defeats the Philistines

17When the Philistines heard that David had
been anointed king over Israel, they went up in
full force to search for him, but David heard
about it and went down to the stronghold.
18Now the Philistines had come and spread out
in the Valley of Rephaim; 19so David inquired
of the LORD, "Shall I go and attack the Philistines? Will you hand them over to me?"
The LORD answered him, "Go, for I will
surely hand the Philistines over to you."
20So David went to Baal Perazim, and there
he defeated them. He said, "As waters break
out, the LORD has broken out against my enemies before me." So that place was called Baal
Perazim.[d] 21The Philistines abandoned their
idols there, and David and his men carried
them off.
22Once more the Philistines came up and
spread out in the Valley of Rephaim; 23so David inquired of the LORD, and he answered,
"Do not go straight up, but circle around behind them and attack them in front of the balsam trees. 24As soon as you hear the sound of
marching in the tops of the balsam trees, move
quickly, because that will mean the LORD has
gone out in front of you to strike the Philistine
army." 25So David did as the LORD commanded
him, and he struck down the Philistines all the
way from Gibeon[e] to Gezer.

The Ark Brought to Jerusalem

6 David again brought to-
gether out of Israel cho-
sen men, thirty thousand in
all. 2He and all his men set
out from Baalah of Judah[f] to
bring up from there the ark
of God, which is called by the
Name,[g] the name of the LORD
Almighty, who is enthroned
between the cherubim that
are on the ark. 3They set the
ark of God on a new cart and brought it from
the house of Abinadab, which was on the hill.

[a] 8 Or *use scaling hooks* [b] 8 Or *are hated by David* [c] 9 Or *the Millo* [d] 20 *Baal Perazim* means *the lord who breaks out.* [e] 25 Septuagint (see also 1 Chron. 14:16); Hebrew *Geba* [f] 2 That is, Kiriath Jearim; Hebrew *Baale Judah,* a variant of *Baalah of Judah* [g] 2 Hebrew; Septuagint and Vulgate do not have *the Name.*

Celebrate!

Read: 2 Samuel 6:1–23

IMAGINE THE QUEEN OF ENGLAND or the first lady of the United States leaping and dancing in her underclothes, shaking tambourines through the streets of London or Washington, crying, "Celebrate God!" Soon drums and cymbals join the merriment. Shocked bystanders raise their eyebrows; tongues wag and flashbulbs pop at such undignified decorum. The tabloids have a heyday.

Such would have been the scene if we today would have seen King David bringing the ark of the covenant back to Jerusalem. We might have been shocked that David and other dignitaries came into the city leaping, shouting and dancing through the streets. We read that at least one person was more than shocked; she was angry. Michal, David's wife, "despised him in her heart." David, however, didn't care what others thought, even if the disapproval came from one of his wives, Saul's daughter. He told her, "I will celebrate before the LORD. I will become even more undignified than this" (2 Samuel 6:21–22).

David rejoiced because the ark of the covenant, Israel's most sacred object of worship, had been reclaimed from the Philistines. David had every reason to dance for joy: The ark was back in Jerusalem, ready to regain its proper place in the Most Holy Place. David's exuberance spilled over in uninhibited public praise.

We all celebrate births and birthdays, weddings and anniversaries, graduations, promotions, holidays and winning seasons. But do we ever, like King David, celebrate God's blessings without concern for what others may think? Do we rejoice over the beauty of his creation or give him unrestrained praise for his loving-kindness and faithfulness?

We don't have to shake tambourines to exhibit hearts of worship. Our rejoicing may be outwardly exuberant or quietly subdued. Our praise may be either public or private. But when our hearts are filled with gratitude, outward expressions of praise will naturally overflow.

As women of God, we have every reason to dance with joy that the Lord is among us. If we choose to raise our hands or bend our knees in true worship, it's not undignified; it's a genuine expression of praise. Let's celebrate God by caring more about what God thinks than about what others think.

2 Samuel 6:14–15

David . . . danced before the LORD with all his might, while he and the entire house of Israel brought up the ark of the LORD with shouts and the sound of trumpets.

reflection

1 How does your personality affect the way you praise God?

2 How do you react to others' behavior during worship? Have you ever pursed your lips or raised your eyebrows when someone was overly exuberant? Based on the Related Readings, what do you think is a good balance in worship?

3 What are some recent blessings that God has given you? Make a list of those blessings and sing a song of praise to God . . . and dance if you feel like it!

RELATED READINGS

Psalms 68:3–4; 150:1–6; 1 Corinthians 14:39–40; James 5:13

Monday

Go to page 375 for your next devotional reading.

Uzzah and Ahio, sons of Abinadab, were guiding the new cart 4with the ark of God on it,[a] and Ahio was walking in front of it. 5David and the whole house of Israel were celebrating with all their might before the LORD, with songs[b] and with harps, lyres, tambourines, sistrums and cymbals.

6When they came to the threshing floor of Nacon, Uzzah reached out and took hold of the ark of God, because the oxen stumbled. 7The LORD's anger burned against Uzzah because of his irreverent act; therefore God struck him down and he died there beside the ark of God.

8Then David was angry because the LORD's wrath had broken out against Uzzah, and to this day that place is called Perez Uzzah.[c]

9David was afraid of the LORD that day and said, "How can the ark of the LORD ever come to me?" 10He was not willing to take the ark of the LORD to be with him in the City of David. Instead, he took it aside to the house of Obed-Edom the Gittite. 11The ark of the LORD remained in the house of Obed-Edom the Gittite for three months, and the LORD blessed him and his entire household.

12Now King David was told, "The LORD has blessed the household of Obed-Edom and everything he has, because of the ark of God." So David went down and brought up the ark of God from the house of Obed-Edom to the City of David with rejoicing. 13When those who were carrying the ark of the LORD had taken six steps, he sacrificed a bull and a fattened calf. 14David, wearing a linen ephod, danced before the LORD with all his might, 15while he and the entire house of Israel brought up the ark of the LORD with shouts and the sound of trumpets.

16As the ark of the LORD was entering the City of David, Michal daughter of Saul watched from a window. And when she saw King David leaping and dancing before the LORD, she despised him in her heart.

17They brought the ark of the LORD and set it in its place inside the tent that David had pitched for it, and David sacrificed burnt offerings and fellowship offerings[d] before the LORD. 18After he had finished sacrificing the burnt offerings and fellowship offerings, he blessed the people in the name of the LORD Almighty. 19Then he gave a loaf of bread, a cake of dates and a cake of raisins to each person in the whole crowd of Israelites, both men and women. And all the people went to their homes.

20When David returned home to bless his household, Michal daughter of Saul came out to meet him and said, "How the king of Israel has distinguished himself today, disrobing in the sight of the slave girls of his servants as any vulgar fellow would!"

21David said to Michal, "It was before the LORD, who chose me rather than your father or anyone from his house when he appointed me ruler over the LORD's people Israel—I will celebrate before the LORD. 22I will become even more undignified than this, and I will be humiliated in my own eyes. But by these slave girls you spoke of, I will be held in honor."

23And Michal daughter of Saul had no children to the day of her death.

God's Promise to David

7 After the king was settled in his palace and the LORD had given him rest from all his enemies around him, 2he said to Nathan the prophet, "Here I am, living in a palace of cedar, while the ark of God remains in a tent."

3Nathan replied to the king, "Whatever you have in mind, go ahead and do it, for the LORD is with you."

4That night the word of the LORD came to Nathan, saying:

5"Go and tell my servant David, 'This is what the LORD says: Are you the one to build me a house to dwell in? 6I have not dwelt in a house from the day I brought the Israelites up out of Egypt to this day. I have been moving from place to place with a tent as my dwelling. 7Wherever I have moved with all the Israelites, did I ever say to any of their rulers whom I commanded to shepherd my people Israel, "Why have you not built me a house of cedar?"'

8"Now then, tell my servant David, 'This is what the LORD Almighty says: I

[a]3,4 Dead Sea Scrolls and some Septuagint manuscripts; Masoretic Text *cart 4and they brought it with the ark of God from the house of Abinadab, which was on the hill* [b]5 See Dead Sea Scrolls, Septuagint and 1 Chronicles 13:8; Masoretic Text *celebrating before the LORD with all kinds of instruments made of pine.* [c]8 *Perez Uzzah* means *outbreak against Uzzah.* [d]17 Traditionally *peace offerings*; also in verse 18

took you from the pasture and from following the flock to be ruler over my people Israel. 9I have been with you wherever
you have gone, and I have cut off all your
enemies from before you. Now I will make
your name great, like the names of the
greatest men of the earth. 10And I will provide a place for my people Israel and will
plant them so that they can have a home
of their own and no longer be disturbed.
Wicked people will not oppress them anymore, as they did at the beginning 11and
have done ever since the time I appointed
leaders[a] over my people Israel. I will also
give you rest from all your enemies.

"'The LORD declares to you that the
LORD himself will establish a house for
you: 12When your days are over and you
rest with your fathers, I will raise up your
offspring to succeed you, who will come
from your own body, and I will establish
his kingdom. 13He is the one who will
build a house for my Name, and I will establish the throne of his kingdom forever.
14I will be his father, and he will be my
son. When he does wrong,
I will punish him with the
rod of men, with floggings
inflicted by men. 15But my
love will never be taken
away from him, as I took
it away from Saul, whom I
removed from before you.
16Your house and your kingdom will endure forever before me[b]; your throne will be
established forever.'"

17Nathan reported to David
all the words of this entire revelation.

David's Prayer

18Then King David went in and sat before
the LORD, and he said:

"Who am I, O Sovereign LORD, and
what is my family, that you have brought
me this far? 19And as if this were not
enough in your sight, O Sovereign LORD,
you have also spoken about the future of
the house of your servant. Is this your
usual way of dealing with man, O Sovereign LORD?

20"What more can David say to you?
For you know your servant, O Sovereign
LORD. 21For the sake of your word and according to your will, you have done this
great thing and made it known to your
servant.

22"How great you are, O Sovereign
LORD! There is no one like you, and there
is no God but you, as we have heard with
our own ears. 23And who is like your
people Israel—the one nation on earth
that God went out to redeem as a people
for himself, and to make a name for himself, and to perform great and awesome
wonders by driving out nations and their
gods from before your people, whom you
redeemed from Egypt?[c] 24You have established your people Israel as your very own
forever, and you, O LORD, have become
their God.

25"And now, LORD God,
keep forever the promise
you have made concerning
your servant and his house.
Do as you promised, 26so
that your name will be great
forever. Then men will say,
'The LORD Almighty is God
over Israel!' And the house
of your servant David will
be established before you.

27"O LORD Almighty, God
of Israel, you have revealed
this to your servant, saying, 'I will build a house for
you.' So your servant has
found courage to offer you
this prayer. 28O Sovereign LORD, you are
God! Your words are trustworthy, and
you have promised these good things to
your servant. 29Now be pleased to bless
the house of your servant, that it may
continue forever in your sight; for you,

2 Samuel 7:28

God Is Dependable

"O Sovereign LORD, you are God! Your words are trustworthy, and you have promised these good things to your servant."

[a]11 Traditionally *judges* [b]16 Some Hebrew manuscripts and Septuagint; most Hebrew manuscripts *you* [c]23 See Septuagint and 1 Chron. 17:21; Hebrew *wonders for your land and before your people, whom you redeemed from Egypt, from the nations and their gods.*

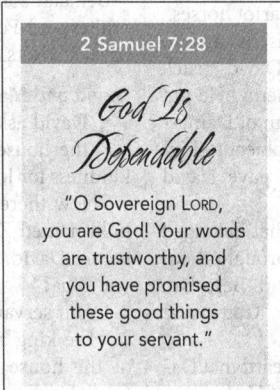

O Sovereign Lord, have spoken, and with
your blessing the house of your servant
will be blessed forever."

David's Victories

8 In the course of time, David defeated the
Philistines and subdued them, and he took
Metheg Ammah from the control of the Philistines.
2David also defeated the Moabites. He made them lie down
on the ground and measured
them off with a length of cord.
Every two lengths of them
were put to death, and the third
length was allowed to live. So
the Moabites became subject to
David and brought tribute.
3Moreover, David fought
Hadadezer son of Rehob, king
of Zobah, when he went to restore his control along the Euphrates River. 4David captured
a thousand of his chariots,
seven thousand charioteers[a]
and twenty thousand foot soldiers. He hamstrung all but a hundred of the chariot horses.
5When the Arameans of Damascus came to
help Hadadezer king of Zobah, David struck
down twenty-two thousand of them. 6He put
garrisons in the Aramean kingdom of Damascus, and the Arameans became subject to him
and brought tribute. The Lord gave David
victory wherever he went.
7David took the gold shields that belonged
to the officers of Hadadezer and brought them
to Jerusalem. 8From Tebah[b] and Berothai,
towns that belonged to Hadadezer, King David
took a great quantity of bronze.
9When Tou[c] king of Hamath heard that David had defeated the entire army of Hadadezer,
10he sent his son Joram[d] to King David to greet
him and congratulate him on his victory in battle over Hadadezer, who had been at war with
Tou. Joram brought with him articles of silver
and gold and bronze.
11King David dedicated these articles to the
Lord, as he had done with the silver and gold
from all the nations he had subdued: 12Edom[e]
and Moab, the Ammonites and the Philistines,
and Amalek. He also dedicated the plunder
taken from Hadadezer son of Rehob, king
of Zobah.
13And David became famous after he returned from striking down
eighteen thousand Edomites[f]
in the Valley of Salt.
14He put garrisons throughout Edom, and all the Edomites became subject to David.
The Lord gave David victory
wherever he went.

2 Samuel 8:14

God Gives Victories

He put garrisons throughout Edom, and all the Edomites became subject to David. The Lord gave David victory wherever he went.

David's Officials

15David reigned over all
Israel, doing what was just and
right for all his people. 16Joab
son of Zeruiah was over the
army; Jehoshaphat son of Ahilud was recorder; 17Zadok son
of Ahitub and Ahimelech son
of Abiathar were priests; Seraiah was secretary;
18Benaiah son of Jehoiada was over the Kerethites and Pelethites; and David's sons were
royal advisers.[g]

David and Mephibosheth

9 David asked, "Is there anyone still left of
the house of Saul to whom I can show
kindness for Jonathan's sake?"
2Now there was a servant of Saul's household named Ziba. They called him to appear
before David, and the king said to him, "Are
you Ziba?"
"Your servant," he replied.
3The king asked, "Is there no one still left
of the house of Saul to whom I can show
God's kindness?"
Ziba answered the king, "There is still a son
of Jonathan; he is crippled in both feet."
4"Where is he?" the king asked.
Ziba answered, "He is at the house of Makir
son of Ammiel in Lo Debar."

a4 Septuagint (see also Dead Sea Scrolls and 1 Chron. 18:4); Masoretic Text *captured seventeen hundred of his charioteers* b8 See some Septuagint manuscripts (see also 1 Chron. 18:8); Hebrew *Betah.* c9 Hebrew *Toi,* a variant of *Tou;* also in verse 10 d10 A variant of *Hadoram* e12 Some Hebrew manuscripts, Septuagint and Syriac (see also 1 Chron. 18:11); most Hebrew manuscripts *Aram* f13 A few Hebrew manuscripts, Septuagint and Syriac (see also 1 Chron. 18:12); most Hebrew manuscripts *Aram* (that is, Arameans) g18 Or *were priests*

Finding Sanctuary

Read: 2 Samuel 9:1–13

CLAIMING SANCTUARY IN A CHURCH dates to Britain in A.D. 600. Though the practice was formally abandoned in the seventeenth century, people seeking asylum still flee to churches today, clinging to the idea that into God's house no violence may enter. Do you long for a place of sanctuary when you sense imminent judgment? Maybe you've told a lie and stand before the wronged party. Perhaps you're innocent, but face a relative's creditors. We can all relate to the desire to crawl underground and disappear. Prince Mephibosheth certainly trembled at what King David would do to him.

After all, Mephibosheth was the last survivor in the line of his grandfather King Saul. In ancient Eastern culture, that position usually meant death, especially because Saul had repeatedly attempted to murder David. But David had no intention of handing down a death sentence. Instead he offered Mephibosheth sanctuary in his own palace. Because of Mephibosheth's relationship to David's dear friend Jonathan, the king welcomed him as an honored guest at his own table.

We all long for sanctuary. Crippled by sin, we enter God's presence with death hanging over our heads. But when we accept Jesus Christ's offer of eternal friendship, we receive eternal sanctuary at the King's table. At this feast, we will be given white robes to wear, and we will bow down in praise and adoration before the Prince of Peace.

Does an invitation to the King's palace fill you with fear or excitement? You may think that everything about you—your background, your body's condition, your emotional state, your past sins—should keep you away from the King's table. But none of that matters to God. Regardless of how unworthy you feel, you can know that you have been made worthy because you are a child of God.

Today, as you ponder the surprise of finding sanctuary instead of judgment, consider how you will live like a guest who carries an invitation to the King's table. Awake each day in anticipation of Christ's royal summons and walk tall, nurturing a longing for the day when you will sit before the King at the wedding supper of the Lamb.

2 Samuel 9:7–8

"Don't be afraid," David said to him, "for I will surely show you kindness for the sake of your father Jonathan. I will restore to you all the land that belonged to your grandfather Saul, and you will always eat at my table." Mephibosheth bowed down and said, "What is your servant, that you should notice a dead dog like me?"

reflection

1. Think about sitting at the King's table. What does this mean to you?
2. Read Matthew 22:1–14. What is the invitation? Is there anything that keeps you from fully accepting God's gift of grace? If so, what is it?
3. Read Revelation 7:9–17. What is your reaction to this passage?

RELATED READINGS

1 Samuel 20:12–17;
2 Samuel 4:4–6

Go to page 379 for your next devotional reading.

5So King David had him brought from Lo Debar, from the house of Makir son of Ammiel.
6When Mephibosheth son of Jonathan, the
son of Saul, came to David, he bowed down to
pay him honor.
David said, “Mephibosheth!”
“Your servant,” he replied.
7“Don’t be afraid,” David said to him, “for
I will surely show you kindness for the sake
of your father Jonathan. I will restore to you
all the land that belonged to your grandfather
Saul, and you will always eat at my table.”
8Mephibosheth bowed down and said,
“What is your servant, that you should notice a
dead dog like me?”
9Then the king summoned Ziba, Saul’s
servant, and said to him, “I have given your
master’s grandson everything that belonged
to Saul and his family. 10You and your sons
and your servants are to farm the land for him
and bring in the crops, so that your master’s
grandson may be provided for. And Mephibosheth, grandson of your master, will always eat
at my table.” (Now Ziba had fifteen sons and
twenty servants.)
11Then Ziba said to the king, “Your servant
will do whatever my lord the
king commands his servant
to do.” So Mephibosheth ate at
David’s[a] table like one of the
king’s sons.
12Mephibosheth had a young
son named Mica, and all the
members of Ziba’s household
were servants of Mephibosheth.
13And Mephibosheth lived in
Jerusalem, because he always
ate at the king’s table, and he
was crippled in both feet.

2 Samuel 10:12

God Is Good

“Be strong and let us fight bravely for our people and the cities of our God. The LORD will do what is good in his sight.”

David Defeats the Ammonites

10 In the course of time, the king of the
Ammonites died, and his son Hanun
succeeded him as king. 2David thought, “I will
show kindness to Hanun son of Nahash, just as
his father showed kindness to me.” So David
sent a delegation to express his sympathy to Hanun concerning his father.
When David’s men came to the land of
the Ammonites, 3the Ammonite nobles said
to Hanun their lord, “Do you think David is
honoring your father by sending men to you
to express sympathy? Hasn’t David sent them
to you to explore the city and spy it out and
overthrow it?” 4So Hanun seized David’s men,
shaved off half of each man’s beard, cut off their
garments in the middle at the buttocks, and
sent them away.
5When David was told about this, he sent
messengers to meet the men, for they were
greatly humiliated. The king said, “Stay at Jericho till your beards have grown, and then
come back.”
6When the Ammonites realized that they
had become a stench in David’s nostrils, they
hired twenty thousand Aramean foot soldiers
from Beth Rehob and Zobah, as well as the
king of Maacah with a thousand men, and also
twelve thousand men from Tob.
7On hearing this, David sent Joab out with
the entire army of fighting men. 8The Ammonites came out and drew up in battle formation
at the entrance to their city gate, while the Arameans of Zobah and Rehob and the men of
Tob and Maacah were by themselves in the
open country.
9Joab saw that there were battle lines in front of him and behind him; so he selected some
of the best troops in Israel and
deployed them against the Arameans. 10He put the rest of
the men under the command
of Abishai his brother and deployed them against the Ammonites. 11Joab said, “If the
Arameans are too strong for
me, then you are to come to
my rescue; but if the Ammon-
ites are too strong for you, then I will come to
rescue you. 12Be strong and let us fight bravely
for our people and the cities of our God. The
LORD will do what is good in his sight.”
13Then Joab and the troops with him advanced to fight the Arameans, and they fled
before him. 14When the Ammonites saw that
the Arameans were fleeing, they fled before
Abishai and went inside the city. So Joab re-

[a]11 Septuagint; Hebrew *my*

turned from fighting the Ammonites and came
to Jerusalem.
15After the Arameans saw that they had
been routed by Israel, they regrouped. 16Had-
adezer had Arameans brought from beyond
the River[a]; they went to Helam, with Shobach
the commander of Hadadezer's army leading them.
17When David was told of this, he gathered
all Israel, crossed the Jordan and went to Helam. The Arameans formed their battle lines to
meet David and fought against him. 18But they
fled before Israel, and David killed seven hundred of their charioteers and forty thousand
of their foot soldiers.[b] He also struck down
Shobach the commander of their army, and
he died there. 19When all the kings who were
vassals of Hadadezer saw that they had been
defeated by Israel, they made peace with the Israelites and became subject to them.
So the Arameans were afraid to help the Ammonites anymore.

David and Bathsheba

11 In the spring, at the time when kings
go off to war, David sent Joab out with
the king's men and the whole Israelite army.
They destroyed the Ammonites and besieged
Rabbah. But David remained in Jerusalem.
2One evening David got up from his bed and
walked around on the roof of the palace. From
the roof he saw a woman bathing. The woman
was very beautiful, 3and David sent someone
to find out about her. The man said, "Isn't this
Bathsheba, the daughter of Eliam and the wife
of Uriah the Hittite?" 4Then David sent messengers to get her. She came to him, and he slept
with her. (She had purified herself from her uncleanness.) Then[c] she went back home. 5The
woman conceived and sent word to David, saying, "I am pregnant."
6So David sent this word to Joab: "Send me
Uriah the Hittite." And Joab sent him to David.
7When Uriah came to him, David asked him
how Joab was, how the soldiers were and how
the war was going. 8Then David said to Uriah,
"Go down to your house and wash your feet."
So Uriah left the palace, and a gift from the
king was sent after him. 9But Uriah slept at the
entrance to the palace with all his master's servants and did not go down to his house.
10When David was told, "Uriah did not go
home," he asked him, "Haven't you just come
from a distance? Why didn't you go home?"
11Uriah said to David, "The ark and Israel
and Judah are staying in tents, and my master
Joab and my lord's men are camped in the open
fields. How could I go to my house to eat and
drink and lie with my wife? As surely as you
live, I will not do such a thing!"
12Then David said to him, "Stay here one
more day, and tomorrow I will send you back."
So Uriah remained in Jerusalem that day and
the next. 13At David's invitation, he ate and
drank with him, and David made him drunk.
But in the evening Uriah went out to sleep on
his mat among his master's servants; he did not
go home.
14In the morning David wrote a letter to
Joab and sent it with Uriah. 15In it he wrote,
"Put Uriah in the front line where the fighting
is fiercest. Then withdraw from him so he will
be struck down and die."
16So while Joab had the city under siege, he
put Uriah at a place where he knew the strongest defenders were. 17When the men of the
city came out and fought against Joab, some of
the men in David's army fell; moreover, Uriah
the Hittite died.
18Joab sent David a full account of the battle. 19He instructed the messenger: "When you
have finished giving the king this account of
the battle, 20the king's anger may flare up, and
he may ask you, 'Why did you get so close to
the city to fight? Didn't you know they would
shoot arrows from the wall? 21Who killed
Abimelech son of Jerub-Besheth[d]? Didn't a
woman throw an upper millstone on him from
the wall, so that he died in Thebez? Why did
you get so close to the wall?' If he asks you this,
then say to him, 'Also, your servant Uriah the
Hittite is dead.'"
22The messenger set out, and when he arrived
he told David everything Joab had sent him to
say. 23The messenger said to David, "The men
overpowered us and came out against us in the
open, but we drove them back to the entrance

[a]16 That is, the Euphrates [b]18 Some Septuagint manuscripts (see also 1 Chron. 19:18); Hebrew *horsemen* [c]4 Or *with her. When she purified herself from her uncleanness,* [d]21 Also known as *Jerub-Baal* (that is, Gideon)

to the city gate. 24Then the archers shot arrows at your servants from the wall, and some of the king's men died. Moreover, your servant Uriah the Hittite is dead."

25David told the messenger, "Say this to Joab: 'Don't let this upset you; the sword devours one as well as another. Press the attack against the city and destroy it.' Say this to encourage Joab."

26When Uriah's wife heard that her husband was dead, she mourned for him. 27After the time of mourning was over, David had her brought to his house, and she became his wife and bore him a son. But the thing David had done displeased the LORD.

Nathan Rebukes David

12 The LORD sent Nathan to David. When he came to him, he said, "There were two men in a certain town, one rich and the other poor. 2The rich man had a very large number of sheep and cattle, 3but the poor man had nothing except one little ewe lamb he had bought. He raised it, and it grew up with him and his children. It shared his food, drank from his cup and even slept in his arms. It was like a daughter to him.

4"Now a traveler came to the rich man, but the rich man refrained from taking one of his own sheep or cattle to prepare a meal for the traveler who had come to him. Instead, he took the ewe lamb that belonged to the poor man and prepared it for the one who had come to him."

5David burned with anger against the man and said to Nathan, "As surely as the LORD lives, the man who did this deserves to die! 6He must pay for that lamb four times over, because he did such a thing and had no pity."

7Then Nathan said to David, "You are the man! This is what the LORD, the God of Israel, says: 'I anointed you king over Israel, and I delivered you from the hand of Saul. 8I gave your master's house to you, and your master's wives into your arms. I gave you the house of Israel and Judah. And if all this had been too little, I would have given you even more. 9Why did you despise the word of the LORD by doing what is evil in his eyes? You struck down Uriah the Hittite with the sword and took his wife to be your own. You killed him with the sword of the Ammonites. 10Now, therefore, the sword will never depart from your house, because you despised me and took the wife of Uriah the Hittite to be your own.'

> **2 Samuel 12:13**
>
> *God Is Forgiving*
>
> Then David said to Nathan, "I have sinned against the LORD." Nathan replied, "The LORD has taken away your sin. You are not going to die."

11"This is what the LORD says: 'Out of your own household I am going to bring calamity upon you. Before your very eyes I will take your wives and give them to one who is close to you, and he will lie with your wives in broad daylight. 12You did it in secret, but I will do this thing in broad daylight before all Israel.'"

13Then David said to Nathan, "I have sinned against the LORD."

Nathan replied, "The LORD has taken away your sin. You are not going to die. 14But because by doing this you have made the enemies of the LORD show utter contempt,[a] the son born to you will die."

15After Nathan had gone home, the LORD struck the child that Uriah's wife had borne to David, and he became ill. 16David pleaded with God for the child. He fasted and went into his house and spent the nights lying on the ground. 17The elders of his household stood beside him to get him up from the ground, but he refused, and he would not eat any food with them.

18On the seventh day the child died. David's servants were afraid to tell him that the child was dead, for they thought, "While the child was still living, we spoke to David but he would not listen to us. How can we tell him the child is dead? He may do something desperate."

19David noticed that his servants were whispering among themselves and he realized the child was dead. "Is the child dead?" he asked.

"Yes," they replied, "he is dead."

[a]14 Masoretic Text; an ancient Hebrew scribal tradition *this you have shown utter contempt for the LORD*

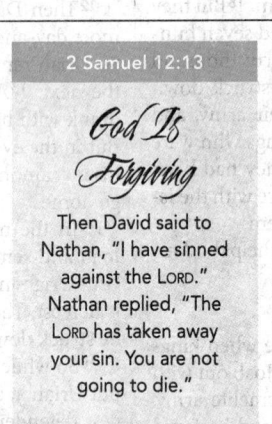

Cleansed by the Light

Read: 2 Samuel 12:1–15

WHERE DO YOU GO when you feel flawed? Where do you find healing when you know you are sick?

For me, the only place to go was to the feet of the only One who is perfect, the only One who fully understands how flawed I am and yet who loves me completely.

Jesus said, "Come to me, all you who are weary and burdened, and I will give you rest" (Matthew 11:28). When our Lord was being brutally executed, he was taking upon himself all the filth and decay of a diseased world. He knew that we could not make it on our own, so he took our place. Wherever he encountered darkness, he brought light. When he met people who were in hiding, he called them out. Whether it was a "scarlet woman" or a little man hiding up a tree, his words were words of healing and hope and freedom. Isaiah told us, "The people walking in darkness have seen a great light; on those living in the land of the shadow of death a light has dawned" (Isaiah 9:2).

I have a friend who is a missionary on the border between Thailand and Cambodia. One of his concerns is for people suffering from leprosy in the refugee camps. He and his colleagues began to spend time with those men and women, doing what they could to aid them physically and spiritually. Eventually a church was born, right there in the middle of a leper camp. During one of their services, a man who had been among the first to make a commitment to following Christ said, "One of the most wonderful things that has happened to me since I met Jesus is that now I can look you in the face. I was too ashamed before because of my disfigurement, but if Jesus loves me so much, then I think that I can hold my head up high."

That is how it is supposed to be for us all. Jesus has restored our dignity. What we sold so cheaply in Eden, he has bought back for us at a great price. We all struggle with our humanity, with our selfishness, but cleansing is not found in the shadows; it is found in the burning light.

—Sheila Walsh

2 Samuel 12:13

Then David said to Nathan, "I have sinned against the LORD." Nathan replied, "The LORD has taken away your sin. You are not going to die."

reflection

1 The man in the story felt ashamed before he met Jesus. Do you struggle with negative feelings?

2 How does it make you feel to know that you are completely loved?

3 Follow Sheila's advice (and David's example) and bring your sin into the burning light by offering a prayer of confession and repentance. Thank God for sending his Son to restore your dignity.

RELATED READINGS

Psalm 51:1–19;
John 8:12;
1 Corinthians 6:19–20

"As long as we are meddling with any part of sin, we shall never see clearly the blissful countenance of our Lord."

Julian of Norwich

Go to page 389 for your next devotional reading.

20Then David got up from the ground. After he had washed, put on lotions and changed his clothes, he went into the house of the LORD and worshiped. Then he went to his own house, and at his request they served him food, and he ate.

21His servants asked him, "Why are you acting this way? While the child was alive, you fasted and wept, but now that the child is dead, you get up and eat!"

22He answered, "While the child was still alive, I fasted and wept. I thought, 'Who knows? The LORD may be gracious to me and let the child live.' 23But now that he is dead, why should I fast? Can I bring him back again? I will go to him, but he will not return to me."

24Then David comforted his wife Bathsheba, and he went to her and lay with her. She gave birth to a son, and they named him Solomon. The LORD loved him; 25and because the LORD loved him, he sent word through Nathan the prophet to name him Jedidiah.[a]

26Meanwhile Joab fought against Rabbah of the Ammonites and captured the royal citadel. 27Joab then sent messengers to David, saying, "I have fought against Rabbah and taken its water supply. 28Now muster the rest of the troops and besiege the city and capture it. Otherwise I will take the city, and it will be named after me."

29So David mustered the entire army and went to Rabbah, and attacked and captured it. 30He took the crown from the head of their king[b]—its weight was a talent[c] of gold, and it was set with precious stones—and it was placed on David's head. He took a great quantity of plunder from the city 31and brought out the people who were there, consigning them to labor with saws and with iron picks and axes, and he made them work at brickmaking.[d] He did this to all the Ammonite towns. Then David and his entire army returned to Jerusalem.

Amnon and Tamar

13 In the course of time, Amnon son of David fell in love with Tamar, the beautiful sister of Absalom son of David.

2Amnon became frustrated to the point of illness on account of his sister Tamar, for she was a virgin, and it seemed impossible for him to do anything to her.

3Now Amnon had a friend named Jonadab son of Shimeah, David's brother. Jonadab was a very shrewd man. 4He asked Amnon, "Why do you, the king's son, look so haggard morning after morning? Won't you tell me?"

Amnon said to him, "I'm in love with Tamar, my brother Absalom's sister."

5"Go to bed and pretend to be ill," Jonadab said. "When your father comes to see you, say to him, 'I would like my sister Tamar to come and give me something to eat. Let her prepare the food in my sight so I may watch her and then eat it from her hand.' "

6So Amnon lay down and pretended to be ill. When the king came to see him, Amnon said to him, "I would like my sister Tamar to come and make some special bread in my sight, so I may eat from her hand."

7David sent word to Tamar at the palace: "Go to the house of your brother Amnon and prepare some food for him." 8So Tamar went to the house of her brother Amnon, who was lying down. She took some dough, kneaded it, made the bread in his sight and baked it. 9Then she took the pan and served him the bread, but he refused to eat.

"Send everyone out of here," Amnon said. So everyone left him. 10Then Amnon said to Tamar, "Bring the food here into my bedroom so I may eat from your hand." And Tamar took the bread she had prepared and brought it to her brother Amnon in his bedroom. 11But when she took it to him to eat, he grabbed her and said, "Come to bed with me, my sister."

12"Don't, my brother!" she said to him. "Don't force me. Such a thing should not be done in Israel! Don't do this wicked thing. 13What about me? Where could I get rid of my disgrace? And what about you? You would be like one of the wicked fools in Israel. Please speak to the king; he will not keep me from being married to you." 14But he refused to listen to her, and since he was stronger than she, he raped her.

15Then Amnon hated her with intense hatred. In fact, he hated her more than he had

[a]25 *Jedidiah* means *loved by the LORD.* [b]30 Or *of Milcom* (that is, Molech) [c]30 That is, about 75 pounds (about 34 kilograms)
[d]31 The meaning of the Hebrew for this clause is uncertain.

loved her. Amnon said to her, “Get up and
get out!”
16“No!” she said to him. “Sending me away
would be a greater wrong than what you have
already done to me.”
But he refused to listen to her. 17He called
his personal servant and said, “Get this woman
out of here and bolt the door after her.” 18So
his servant put her out and bolted the door after her. She was wearing a richly ornamented[a]
robe, for this was the kind of garment the virgin
daughters of the king wore. 19Tamar put ashes
on her head and tore the ornamented[b] robe she
was wearing. She put her hand on her head and
went away, weeping aloud as she went.
20Her brother Absalom said to her, “Has that
Amnon, your brother, been with you? Be quiet
now, my sister; he is your brother. Don’t take
this thing to heart.” And Tamar lived in her
brother Absalom’s house, a desolate woman.
21When King David heard all this, he was furious. 22Absalom never said a word to Amnon,
either good or bad; he hated Amnon because
he had disgraced his sister Tamar.

Absalom Kills Amnon

23Two years later, when Absalom’s sheep-
shearers were at Baal Hazor near the border of
Ephraim, he invited all the king’s sons to come
there. 24Absalom went to the king and said,
“Your servant has had shearers come. Will the
king and his officials please join me?”
25“No, my son,” the king replied. “All of us
should not go; we would only be a burden to
you.” Although Absalom urged him, he still refused to go, but gave him his blessing.
26Then Absalom said, “If not, please let my
brother Amnon come with us.”
The king asked him, “Why should he go
with you?” 27But Absalom urged him, so he
sent with him Amnon and the rest of the king’s
sons.
28Absalom ordered his men, “Listen! When
Amnon is in high spirits from drinking wine
and I say to you, ‘Strike Amnon down,’ then
kill him. Don’t be afraid. Have not I given you
this order? Be strong and brave.” 29So Absalom’s men did to Amnon what Absalom had ordered. Then all the king’s sons got up, mounted
their mules and fled.
30While they were on their way, the report
came to David: “Absalom has struck down all
the king’s sons; not one of them is left.” 31The
king stood up, tore his clothes and lay down on
the ground; and all his servants stood by with
their clothes torn.
32But Jonadab son of Shimeah, David’s
brother, said, “My lord should not think that
they killed all the princes; only Amnon is
dead. This has been Absalom’s expressed intention ever since the day Amnon raped his sister
Tamar. 33My lord the king should not be concerned about the report that all the king’s sons
are dead. Only Amnon is dead.”
34Meanwhile, Absalom had fled.
Now the man standing watch looked up and
saw many people on the road west of him, coming down the side of the hill. The watchman
went and told the king, “I see men in the direction of Horonaim, on the side of the hill.”[c]
35Jonadab said to the king, “See, the king’s
sons are here; it has happened just as your servant said.”
36As he finished speaking, the king’s sons
came in, wailing loudly. The king, too, and all
his servants wept very bitterly.
37Absalom fled and went to Talmai son of
Ammihud, the king of Geshur. But King David
mourned for his son every day.
38After Absalom fled and went to Geshur,
he stayed there three years. 39And the spirit of
the king[d] longed to go to Absalom, for he was
consoled concerning Amnon’s death.

Absalom Returns to Jerusalem

14 Joab son of Zeruiah knew that the
king’s heart longed for Absalom. 2So
Joab sent someone to Tekoa and had a wise
woman brought from there. He said to her,
“Pretend you are in mourning. Dress in mourning clothes, and don’t use any cosmetic lotions.
Act like a woman who has spent many days
grieving for the dead. 3Then go to the king and
speak these words to him.” And Joab put the
words in her mouth.
4When the woman from Tekoa went[e] to the

[a] 18 The meaning of the Hebrew for this phrase is uncertain. [b] 19 The meaning of the Hebrew for this word is uncertain. [c] 34 Septuagint; Hebrew does not have this sentence. [d] 39 Dead Sea Scrolls and some Septuagint manuscripts; Masoretic Text *But ⌊the spirit of⌋ David the king* [e] 4 Many Hebrew manuscripts, Septuagint, Vulgate and Syriac; most Hebrew manuscripts *spoke*

king, she fell with her face to the ground to pay
him honor, and she said, "Help me, O king!"
5The king asked her, "What is troubling
you?"
She said, "I am indeed a widow; my husband
is dead. 6I your servant had two sons. They got
into a fight with each other in the field, and no
one was there to separate them. One struck the
other and killed him. 7Now the whole clan has
risen up against your servant; they say, 'Hand
over the one who struck his brother down, so
that we may put him to death for the life of his
brother whom he killed; then we will get rid of
the heir as well.' They would put out the only
burning coal I have left, leaving my husband
neither name nor descendant on the face of
the earth."
8The king said to the woman, "Go home,
and I will issue an order in your behalf."
9But the woman from Tekoa said to him,
"My lord the king, let the blame rest on me and
on my father's family, and let the king and his
throne be without guilt."
10The king replied, "If anyone says anything
to you, bring him to me, and he will not bother
you again."
11She said, "Then let the king invoke the
LORD his God to prevent the avenger of blood
from adding to the destruction, so that my son
will not be destroyed."
"As surely as the LORD lives," he said, "not
one hair of your son's head will
fall to the ground."
12Then the woman said,
"Let your servant speak a word
to my lord the king."
"Speak," he replied.
13The woman said, "Why
then have you devised a thing
like this against the people of
God? When the king says this,
does he not convict himself,
for the king has not brought
back his banished son? 14Like
water spilled on the ground,
which cannot be recovered, so
we must die. But God does not
take away life; instead, he devises ways so that
a banished person may not remain estranged
from him.

> **2 Samuel 14:14**
>
> ***God Seeks Us***
>
> But God does not take away life; instead, he devises ways so that a banished person may not remain estranged from him.

15"And now I have come to say this to my
lord the king because the people have made
me afraid. Your servant thought, 'I will speak
to the king; perhaps he will do what his servant
asks. 16Perhaps the king will agree to deliver
his servant from the hand of the man who is
trying to cut off both me and my son from the
inheritance God gave us.'
17"And now your servant says, 'May the
word of my lord the king bring me rest, for my
lord the king is like an angel of God in discerning good and evil. May the LORD your God be
with you.'"
18Then the king said to the woman, "Do not
keep from me the answer to what I am going
to ask you."
"Let my lord the king speak," the woman
said.
19The king asked, "Isn't the hand of Joab
with you in all this?"
The woman answered, "As surely as you
live, my lord the king, no one can turn to the
right or to the left from anything my lord the
king says. Yes, it was your servant Joab who
instructed me to do this and who put all these
words into the mouth of your servant. 20Your
servant Joab did this to change the present situation. My lord has wisdom like that of an angel
of God—he knows everything that happens in
the land."
21The king said to Joab, "Very well, I will do
it. Go, bring back the young
man Absalom."
22Joab fell with his face to
the ground to pay him honor,
and he blessed the king. Joab
said, "Today your servant
knows that he has found favor
in your eyes, my lord the king,
because the king has granted
his servant's request."
23Then Joab went to Geshur
and brought Absalom back to
Jerusalem. 24But the king said,
"He must go to his own house;
he must not see my face." So Absalom went to his own house
and did not see the face of the king.
25In all Israel there was not a man so highly
praised for his handsome appearance as Absa-

lom. From the top of his head to the sole of his
foot there was no blemish in him. 26Whenever
he cut the hair of his head—he used to cut
his hair from time to time when it became
too heavy for him—he would weigh it, and
its weight was two hundred shekels[a] by the
royal standard.
27Three sons and a daughter were born to
Absalom. The daughter's name was Tamar, and
she became a beautiful woman.
28Absalom lived two years in Jerusalem without seeing the king's face. 29Then Absalom sent
for Joab in order to send him to the king, but
Joab refused to come to him. So he sent a second time, but he refused to come. 30Then he
said to his servants, "Look, Joab's field is next
to mine, and he has barley there. Go and set
it on fire." So Absalom's servants set the field
on fire.
31Then Joab did go to Absalom's house and
he said to him, "Why have your servants set my
field on fire?"
32Absalom said to Joab, "Look, I sent word
to you and said, 'Come here so I can send you
to the king to ask, "Why have I come from Geshur? It would be better for me if I were still
there!"' Now then, I want to see the king's face,
and if I am guilty of anything, let him put me
to death."
33So Joab went to the king and told him
this. Then the king summoned Absalom, and
he came in and bowed down with his face
to the ground before the king. And the king
kissed Absalom.

Absalom's Conspiracy

15 In the course of time, Absalom
provided himself with a chariot and
horses and with fifty men to run ahead of him.
2He would get up early and stand by the side of
the road leading to the city gate. Whenever anyone came with a complaint to be placed before
the king for a decision, Absalom would call out
to him, "What town are you from?" He would
answer, "Your servant is from one of the tribes
of Israel." 3Then Absalom would say to him,
"Look, your claims are valid and proper, but
there is no representative of the king to hear
you." 4And Absalom would add, "If only I were
appointed judge in the land! Then everyone
who has a complaint or case could come to me
and I would see that he gets justice."
5Also, whenever anyone approached him to
bow down before him, Absalom would reach
out his hand, take hold of him and kiss him.
6Absalom behaved in this way toward all the
Israelites who came to the king asking for justice, and so he stole the hearts of the men of
Israel.
7At the end of four[b] years, Absalom said to
the king, "Let me go to Hebron and fulfill a vow
I made to the LORD. 8While your servant was
living at Geshur in Aram, I made this vow: 'If
the LORD takes me back to Jerusalem, I will
worship the LORD in Hebron.[c]'"
9The king said to him, "Go in peace." So he
went to Hebron.
10Then Absalom sent secret messengers
throughout the tribes of Israel to say, "As soon
as you hear the sound of the trumpets, then
say, 'Absalom is king in Hebron.'" 11Two hundred men from Jerusalem had accompanied
Absalom. They had been invited as guests and
went quite innocently, knowing nothing about
the matter. 12While Absalom was offering
sacrifices, he also sent for Ahithophel the Gilonite, David's counselor, to come from Giloh,
his hometown. And so the conspiracy gained
strength, and Absalom's following kept on increasing.

David Flees

13A messenger came and told David, "The
hearts of the men of Israel are with Absalom."
14Then David said to all his officials who
were with him in Jerusalem, "Come! We must
flee, or none of us will escape from Absalom.
We must leave immediately, or he will move
quickly to overtake us and bring ruin upon us
and put the city to the sword."
15The king's officials answered him, "Your
servants are ready to do whatever our lord the
king chooses."
16The king set out, with his entire household
following him; but he left ten concubines to
take care of the palace. 17So the king set out,
with all the people following him, and they
halted at a place some distance away. 18All his

[a]26 That is, about 5 pounds (about 2.3 kilograms) [b]7 Some Septuagint manuscripts, Syriac and Josephus; Hebrew *forty* [c]8 Some Septuagint manuscripts; Hebrew does not have *in Hebron.*

men marched past him, along with all the Kerethites and Pelethites; and all the six hundred Gittites who had accompanied him from Gath marched before the king.

19The king said to Ittai the Gittite, "Why should you come along with us? Go back and stay with King Absalom. You are a foreigner, an exile from your homeland. 20You came only yesterday. And today shall I make you wander about with us, when I do not know where I am going? Go back, and take your countrymen. May kindness and faithfulness be with you."

21But Ittai replied to the king, "As surely as the LORD lives, and as my lord the king lives, wherever my lord the king may be, whether it means life or death, there will your servant be."

22David said to Ittai, "Go ahead, march on." So Ittai the Gittite marched on with all his men and the families that were with him.

23The whole countryside wept aloud as all the people passed by. The king also crossed the Kidron Valley, and all the people moved on toward the desert.

24Zadok was there, too, and all the Levites who were with him were carrying the ark of the covenant of God. They set down the ark of God, and Abiathar offered sacrifices[a] until all the people had finished leaving the city.

25Then the king said to Zadok, "Take the ark of God back into the city. If I find favor in the LORD's eyes, he will bring me back and let me see it and his dwelling place again. 26But if he says, 'I am not pleased with you,' then I am ready; let him do to me whatever seems good to him."

27The king also said to Zadok the priest, "Aren't you a seer? Go back to the city in peace, with your son Ahimaaz and Jonathan son of Abiathar. You and Abiathar take your two sons with you. 28I will wait at the fords in the desert until word comes from you to inform me." 29So Zadok and Abiathar took the ark of God back to Jerusalem and stayed there.

30But David continued up the Mount of Olives, weeping as he went; his head was covered and he was barefoot. All the people with him covered their heads too and were weeping as they went up. 31Now David had been told, "Ahithophel is among the conspirators with Absalom." So David prayed, "O LORD, turn Ahithophel's counsel into foolishness."

32When David arrived at the summit, where people used to worship God, Hushai the Arkite was there to meet him, his robe torn and dust on his head. 33David said to him, "If you go with me, you will be a burden to me. 34But if you return to the city and say to Absalom, 'I will be your servant, O king; I was your father's servant in the past, but now I will be your servant,' then you can help me by frustrating Ahithophel's advice. 35Won't the priests Zadok and Abiathar be there with you? Tell them anything you hear in the king's palace. 36Their two sons, Ahimaaz son of Zadok and Jonathan son of Abiathar, are there with them. Send them to me with anything you hear."

37So David's friend Hushai arrived at Jerusalem as Absalom was entering the city.

David and Ziba

16 When David had gone a short distance beyond the summit, there was Ziba, the steward of Mephibosheth, waiting to meet him. He had a string of donkeys saddled and loaded with two hundred loaves of bread, a hundred cakes of raisins, a hundred cakes of figs and a skin of wine.

2The king asked Ziba, "Why have you brought these?"

Ziba answered, "The donkeys are for the king's household to ride on, the bread and fruit are for the men to eat, and the wine is to refresh those who become exhausted in the desert."

3The king then asked, "Where is your master's grandson?"

Ziba said to him, "He is staying in Jerusalem, because he thinks, 'Today the house of Israel will give me back my grandfather's kingdom.'"

4Then the king said to Ziba, "All that belonged to Mephibosheth is now yours."

"I humbly bow," Ziba said. "May I find favor in your eyes, my lord the king."

Shimei Curses David

5As King David approached Bahurim, a man from the same clan as Saul's family came out from there. His name was Shimei son of Gera, and he cursed as he came out. 6He pelted

[a]24 Or *Abiathar went up*

David and all the king's officials with stones,
though all the troops and the special guard
were on David's right and left. 7As he cursed,
Shimei said, "Get out, get out, you man of
blood, you scoundrel! 8The LORD has repaid
you for all the blood you shed in the household
of Saul, in whose place you have reigned. The
LORD has handed the kingdom over to your
son Absalom. You have come to ruin because
you are a man of blood!"
9Then Abishai son of Zeruiah said to the
king, "Why should this dead dog curse my lord
the king? Let me go over and cut off his head."
10But the king said, "What do you and I
have in common, you sons of Zeruiah? If he is
cursing because the LORD said to him, 'Curse
David,' who can ask, 'Why do you do this?' "
11David then said to Abishai and all his officials, "My son, who is of my own flesh, is trying to take my life. How much more, then, this
Benjamite! Leave him alone; let him curse, for
the LORD has told him to. 12It may be that the
LORD will see my distress and repay me with
good for the cursing I am receiving today."
13So David and his men continued along the
road while Shimei was going along the hillside
opposite him, cursing as he went and throwing
stones at him and showering him with dirt.
14The king and all the people with him arrived
at their destination exhausted. And there he refreshed himself.

The Advice of Ahithophel and Hushai

15Meanwhile, Absalom and all the men
of Israel came to Jerusalem, and Ahithophel
was with him. 16Then Hushai the Arkite, David's friend, went to Absalom and said to him,
"Long live the king! Long live the king!"
17Absalom asked Hushai, "Is this the love
you show your friend? Why didn't you go with
your friend?"
18Hushai said to Absalom, "No, the one chosen by the LORD, by these people, and by all
the men of Israel—his I will be, and I will remain with him. 19Furthermore, whom should
I serve? Should I not serve the son? Just as I
served your father, so I will serve you."
20Absalom said to Ahithophel, "Give us
your advice. What should we do?"
21Ahithophel answered, "Lie with your father's concubines whom he left to take care of
the palace. Then all Israel will hear that you
have made yourself a stench in your father's
nostrils, and the hands of everyone with you
will be strengthened." 22So they pitched a tent
for Absalom on the roof, and he lay with his father's concubines in the sight of all Israel.
23Now in those days the advice Ahithophel gave was like that of one who inquires of
God. That was how both David and Absalom
regarded all of Ahithophel's advice.
17 Ahithophel said to Absalom, "I would[a]
choose twelve thousand men and set
out tonight in pursuit of David. 2I would[b] attack him while he is weary and weak. I would[b]
strike him with terror, and then all the people
with him will flee. I would[b] strike down only
the king 3and bring all the people back to you.
The death of the man you seek will mean the
return of all; all the people will be unharmed."
4This plan seemed good to Absalom and to all
the elders of Israel.
5But Absalom said, "Summon also Hushai
the Arkite, so we can hear what he has to say."
6When Hushai came to him, Absalom said,
"Ahithophel has given this advice. Should we
do what he says? If not, give us your opinion."
7Hushai replied to Absalom, "The advice
Ahithophel has given is not good this time.
8You know your father and his men; they are
fighters, and as fierce as a wild bear robbed
of her cubs. Besides, your father is an experienced fighter; he will not spend the night with
the troops. 9Even now, he is hidden in a cave
or some other place. If he should attack your
troops first,[c] whoever hears about it will say,
'There has been a slaughter among the troops
who follow Absalom.' 10Then even the bravest
soldier, whose heart is like the heart of a lion,
will melt with fear, for all Israel knows that
your father is a fighter and that those with him
are brave.
11"So I advise you: Let all Israel, from Dan
to Beersheba—as numerous as the sand on the
seashore—be gathered to you, with you yourself leading them into battle. 12Then we will
attack him wherever he may be found, and we
will fall on him as dew settles on the ground.

[a]1 Or *Let me* [b]2 Or *will* [c]9 Or *When some of the men fall at the first attack*

Neither he nor any of his men will be left alive.
13If he withdraws into a city, then all Israel
will bring ropes to that city, and we will drag it
down to the valley until not even a piece of it
can be found."

14Absalom and all the men of Israel said,
"The advice of Hushai the Arkite is better than
that of Ahithophel." For the LORD had determined to frustrate the good advice of Ahithophel in order to bring disaster on Absalom.

15Hushai told Zadok and Abiathar, the
priests, "Ahithophel has advised Absalom and
the elders of Israel to do such and such, but I
have advised them to do so and so. 16Now send
a message immediately and tell David, 'Do not
spend the night at the fords in the desert; cross
over without fail, or the king and all the people
with him will be swallowed up.' "

17Jonathan and Ahimaaz were staying at
En Rogel. A servant girl was to go and inform
them, and they were to go and tell King David, for they could not risk being seen entering
the city. 18But a young man saw them and told
Absalom. So the two of them left quickly and
went to the house of a man in Bahurim. He
had a well in his courtyard, and they climbed
down into it. 19His wife took a covering and
spread it out over the opening of the well and
scattered grain over it. No one knew anything
about it.

20When Absalom's men came to the woman
at the house, they asked, "Where are Ahimaaz
and Jonathan?"

The woman answered them, "They crossed
over the brook."[a] The men searched but found
no one, so they returned to Jerusalem.

21After the men had gone, the two climbed
out of the well and went to inform King David.
They said to him, "Set out and cross the river
at once; Ahithophel has advised such and such
against you." 22So David and all the people
with him set out and crossed the Jordan. By
daybreak, no one was left who had not crossed
the Jordan.

23When Ahithophel saw that his advice had
not been followed, he saddled his donkey and
set out for his house in his hometown. He put
his house in order and then hanged himself. So
he died and was buried in his father's tomb.

24David went to Mahanaim, and Absalom
crossed the Jordan with all the men of Israel.
25Absalom had appointed Amasa over the
army in place of Joab. Amasa was the son of a
man named Jether,[b] an Israelite[c] who had married Abigail,[d] the daughter of Nahash and sister
of Zeruiah the mother of Joab. 26The Israelites
and Absalom camped in the land of Gilead.

27When David came to Mahanaim, Shobi
son of Nahash from Rabbah of the Ammonites, and Makir son of Ammiel from Lo Debar, and Barzillai the Gileadite from Rogelim
28brought bedding and bowls and articles of
pottery. They also brought wheat and barley,
flour and roasted grain, beans and lentils,[e]
29honey and curds, sheep, and cheese from
cows' milk for David and his people to eat. For
they said, "The people have become hungry
and tired and thirsty in the desert."

Absalom's Death

18 David mustered the men who were
with him and appointed over them
commanders of thousands and commanders of
hundreds. 2David sent the troops out—a third
under the command of Joab, a third under Joab's brother Abishai son of Zeruiah, and a third
under Ittai the Gittite. The king told the troops,
"I myself will surely march out with you."

3But the men said, "You must not go out;
if we are forced to flee, they won't care about
us. Even if half of us die, they won't care; but
you are worth ten thousand of us.[f] It would be
better now for you to give us support from the
city."

4The king answered, "I will do whatever
seems best to you."

So the king stood beside the gate while all
the men marched out in units of hundreds and
of thousands. 5The king commanded Joab,
Abishai and Ittai, "Be gentle with the young
man Absalom for my sake." And all the troops
heard the king giving orders concerning Absalom to each of the commanders.

6The army marched into the field to fight

[a]20 Or *"They passed by the sheep pen toward the water."* [b]25 Hebrew *Ithra,* a variant of *Jether* [c]25 Hebrew and some Septuagint manuscripts; other Septuagint manuscripts (see also 1 Chron. 2:17) *Ishmaelite* or *Jezreelite* [d]25 Hebrew *Abigal,* a variant of *Abigail* [e]28 Most Septuagint manuscripts and Syriac; Hebrew *lentils, and roasted grain* [f]3 Two Hebrew manuscripts, some Septuagint manuscripts and Vulgate; most Hebrew manuscripts *care; for now there are ten thousand like us*

Israel, and the battle took place in the forest
of Ephraim. 7There the army of Israel was
defeated by David's men, and the casualties
that day were great—twenty thousand men.
8The battle spread out over the whole countryside, and the forest claimed more lives that day
than the sword.

9Now Absalom happened to meet David's
men. He was riding his mule, and as the mule
went under the thick branches of a large oak,
Absalom's head got caught in the tree. He was
left hanging in midair, while the mule he was
riding kept on going.

10When one of the men saw this, he told
Joab, "I just saw Absalom hanging in an
oak tree."

11Joab said to the man who had told him
this, "What! You saw him? Why didn't you
strike him to the ground right there? Then I
would have had to give you ten shekels[a] of silver and a warrior's belt."

12But the man replied, "Even if a thousand
shekels[b] were weighed out into my hands, I
would not lift my hand against the king's son.
In our hearing the king commanded you and
Abishai and Ittai, 'Protect the young man Absalom for my sake.[c]' 13And if I had put my life
in jeopardy[d]—and nothing is hidden from
the king—you would have kept your distance
from me."

14Joab said, "I'm not going to wait like this
for you." So he took three javelins in his hand
and plunged them into Absalom's heart while
Absalom was still alive in the oak tree. 15And
ten of Joab's armor-bearers surrounded Absalom, struck him and killed him.

16Then Joab sounded the trumpet, and the
troops stopped pursuing Israel, for Joab halted
them. 17They took Absalom, threw him into a
big pit in the forest and piled up a large heap
of rocks over him. Meanwhile, all the Israelites
fled to their homes.

18During his lifetime Absalom had taken
a pillar and erected it in the King's Valley as a
monument to himself, for he thought, "I have
no son to carry on the memory of my name."
He named the pillar after himself, and it is
called Absalom's Monument to this day.

David Mourns

19Now Ahimaaz son of Zadok said, "Let
me run and take the news to the king that
the LORD has delivered him from the hand of
his enemies."

20"You are not the one to take the news today," Joab told him. "You may take the news
another time, but you must not do so today, because the king's son is dead."

21Then Joab said to a Cushite, "Go, tell the
king what you have seen." The Cushite bowed
down before Joab and ran off.

22Ahimaaz son of Zadok again said to Joab,
"Come what may, please let me run behind
the Cushite."

But Joab replied, "My son, why do you want
to go? You don't have any news that will bring
you a reward."

23He said, "Come what may, I want to run."

So Joab said, "Run!" Then Ahimaaz ran by
way of the plain[e] and outran the Cushite.

24While David was sitting between the inner
and outer gates, the watchman went up to the
roof of the gateway by the wall. As he looked
out, he saw a man running alone. 25The watchman called out to the king and reported it.

The king said, "If he is alone, he must have
good news." And the man came closer and
closer.

26Then the watchman saw another man running, and he called down to the gatekeeper,
"Look, another man running alone!"

The king said, "He must be bringing good
news, too."

27The watchman said, "It seems to me that
the first one runs like Ahimaaz son of Zadok."

"He's a good man," the king said. "He comes
with good news."

28Then Ahimaaz called out to the king, "All
is well!" He bowed down before the king with
his face to the ground and said, "Praise be to
the LORD your God! He has delivered up the
men who lifted their hands against my lord the
king."

29The king asked, "Is the young man Absalom safe?"

Ahimaaz answered, "I saw great confusion
just as Joab was about to send the king's servant

[a]11 That is, about 4 ounces (about 115 grams) [b]12 That is, about 25 pounds (about 11 kilograms) [c]12 A few Hebrew manuscripts, Septuagint, Vulgate and Syriac; most Hebrew manuscripts may be translated *Absalom, whoever you may be.* [d]13 Or *Otherwise, if I had acted treacherously toward him* [e]23 That is, the plain of the Jordan

and me, your servant, but I don't know what
it was."
30 The king said, "Stand aside and wait here."
So he stepped aside and stood there.
31 Then the Cushite arrived and said, "My
lord the king, hear the good news! The LORD
has delivered you today from all who rose up
against you."
32 The king asked the Cushite, "Is the young
man Absalom safe?"

The Cushite replied, "May the enemies of my
lord the king and all who rise up to harm you
be like that young man."
33 The king was shaken. He went up to the
room over the gateway and wept. As he went,
he said: "O my son Absalom! My son, my son
Absalom! If only I had died instead of you—
O Absalom, my son, my son!"

19 Joab was told, "The king is weeping
and mourning for Absalom." 2 And for
the whole army the victory that day was turned
into mourning, because on that day the troops
heard it said, "The king is grieving for his son."
3 The men stole into the city that day as men
steal in who are ashamed when they flee from
battle. 4 The king covered his face and cried
aloud, "O my son Absalom! O Absalom, my
son, my son!"
5 Then Joab went into the house to the king
and said, "Today you have humiliated all your
men, who have just saved your life and the
lives of your sons and daughters and the lives
of your wives and concubines. 6 You love those
who hate you and hate those who love you. You
have made it clear today that the commanders
and their men mean nothing to you. I see that
you would be pleased if Absalom were alive today and all of us were dead. 7 Now go out and
encourage your men. I swear by the LORD that
if you don't go out, not a man will be left with
you by nightfall. This will be worse for you than
all the calamities that have come upon you
from your youth till now."
8 So the king got up and took his seat in
the gateway. When the men were told, "The
king is sitting in the gateway," they all came before him.

David Returns to Jerusalem

Meanwhile, the Israelites had fled to their
homes. 9 Throughout the tribes of Israel, the
people were all arguing with each other, saying,
"The king delivered us from the hand of our enemies; he is the one who rescued us from the
hand of the Philistines. But now he has fled the
country because of Absalom; 10 and Absalom,
whom we anointed to rule over us, has died in
battle. So why do you say nothing about bringing the king back?"
11 King David sent this message to Zadok
and Abiathar, the priests: "Ask the elders of Judah, 'Why should you be the last to bring the
king back to his palace, since what is being said
throughout Israel has reached the king at his
quarters? 12 You are my brothers, my own flesh
and blood. So why should you be the last to
bring back the king?' 13 And say to Amasa, 'Are
you not my own flesh and blood? May God
deal with me, be it ever so severely, if from now
on you are not the commander of my army in
place of Joab.' "
14 He won over the hearts of all the men of
Judah as though they were one man. They sent
word to the king, "Return, you and all your
men." 15 Then the king returned and went as
far as the Jordan.

Now the men of Judah had come to Gilgal to
go out and meet the king and bring him across
the Jordan. 16 Shimei son of Gera, the Benjamite from Bahurim, hurried down with the
men of Judah to meet King David. 17 With him
were a thousand Benjamites, along with Ziba,
the steward of Saul's household, and his fifteen
sons and twenty servants. They rushed to the
Jordan, where the king was. 18 They crossed at
the ford to take the king's household over and
to do whatever he wished.

When Shimei son of Gera crossed the Jordan, he fell prostrate before the king 19 and said
to him, "May my lord not hold me guilty. Do
not remember how your servant did wrong on
the day my lord the king left Jerusalem. May the
king put it out of his mind. 20 For I your servant
know that I have sinned, but today I have come
here as the first of the whole house of Joseph to
come down and meet my lord the king."
21 Then Abishai son of Zeruiah said,
"Shouldn't Shimei be put to death for this? He
cursed the LORD's anointed."
22 David replied, "What do you and I have in
common, you sons of Zeruiah? This day you

Overwhelmed With Grief

Read: 2 Samuel 19:1–8

HAVE YOU EVER TRIED to comfort someone who refused to be comforted? Or maybe you were the one whose sorrow was so deep that no words or actions could penetrate your grief. We've all seen or experienced the gut-wrenching sorrow that causes us to want to deny the pain and turn back the hands of time. Sometimes all we can do is utter the name of the person we've lost.

Such was David's grief when he heard of Absalom's death. He stopped everything and, in true Eastern fashion, wailed for his rebellious son, even though Absalom was killed in a coup to steal his father's kingdom. Nevertheless, David was so grief-stricken that he was unable to cope with the responsibilities of reclaiming the kingdom. In fact, his grief was so debilitating that his closest aides warned him that if he didn't pull himself together and rejoice that his armies had conquered his enemies (including his son), his subjects would grow disheartened. As a father, David had every right to feel grief. However, as the leader of a nation, King David had to rise above his grief and carry on for the sake of his people.

The death of a child is beyond tragic. It is the deepest grief and sorrow. And there are other losses worth grieving: the death of a marriage, the end of a friendship or the loss of your health. Then comes the anguish. You want to blank out the present and look to the past. You deeply want to turn back the clock and reverse what has happened. You can't eat, sleep or work. In the freshness of the pain, it might seem you can never again function.

Maybe you are overwhelmed by a devastating grief right now or are trying to encourage someone else in a similar situation. Maybe you need to think about what David did. Embrace your personal grief, but remember your responsibilities to others, even though it may be the hardest thing to do.

God has not promised immunity from sorrow, but he has promised that he will be present with us through it: "Blessed are those who mourn, for they will be comforted" (Matthew 5:4).

Thursday

2 Samuel 19:4

The king covered his face and cried aloud, "O my son Absalom! O Absalom, my son, my son!"

reflection

1 What event or events in your life have nearly overwhelmed you with grief? Describe what happened.

2 What responsibilities forced you to face your pain and function again?

3 How did God come alongside to comfort and strengthen you in your sorrow?

RELATED READINGS

Genesis 37:35; Psalms 116:1–19; 126:5–6

"The risk of love is loss, and the price of loss is grief."

Hilary Stanton Zunin

Go to page 393 for your next devotional reading.

have become my adversaries! Should anyone be put to death in Israel today? Do I not know that today I am king over Israel?" 23So the king said to Shimei, "You shall not die." And the king promised him on oath.

24Mephibosheth, Saul's grandson, also went down to meet the king. He had not taken care of his feet or trimmed his mustache or washed his clothes from the day the king left until the day he returned safely. 25When he came from Jerusalem to meet the king, the king asked him, "Why didn't you go with me, Mephibosheth?"

26He said, "My lord the king, since I your servant am lame, I said, 'I will have my donkey saddled and will ride on it, so I can go with the king.' But Ziba my servant betrayed me. 27And he has slandered your servant to my lord the king. My lord the king is like an angel of God; so do whatever pleases you. 28All my grandfather's descendants deserved nothing but death from my lord the king, but you gave your servant a place among those who eat at your table. So what right do I have to make any more appeals to the king?"

29The king said to him, "Why say more? I order you and Ziba to divide the fields."

30Mephibosheth said to the king, "Let him take everything, now that my lord the king has arrived home safely."

31Barzillai the Gileadite also came down from Rogelim to cross the Jordan with the king and to send him on his way from there. 32Now Barzillai was a very old man, eighty years of age. He had provided for the king during his stay in Mahanaim, for he was a very wealthy man. 33The king said to Barzillai, "Cross over with me and stay with me in Jerusalem, and I will provide for you."

34But Barzillai answered the king, "How many more years will I live, that I should go up to Jerusalem with the king? 35I am now eighty years old. Can I tell the difference between what is good and what is not? Can your servant taste what he eats and drinks? Can I still hear the voices of men and women singers? Why should your servant be an added burden to my lord the king? 36Your servant will cross over the Jordan with the king for a short distance, but why should the king reward me in this way? 37Let your servant return, that I may die in my own town near the tomb of my father and mother. But here is your servant Kimham. Let him cross over with my lord the king. Do for him whatever pleases you."

38The king said, "Kimham shall cross over with me, and I will do for him whatever pleases you. And anything you desire from me I will do for you."

39So all the people crossed the Jordan, and then the king crossed over. The king kissed Barzillai and gave him his blessing, and Barzillai returned to his home.

40When the king crossed over to Gilgal, Kimham crossed with him. All the troops of Judah and half the troops of Israel had taken the king over.

41Soon all the men of Israel were coming to the king and saying to him, "Why did our brothers, the men of Judah, steal the king away and bring him and his household across the Jordan, together with all his men?"

42All the men of Judah answered the men of Israel, "We did this because the king is closely related to us. Why are you angry about it? Have we eaten any of the king's provisions? Have we taken anything for ourselves?"

43Then the men of Israel answered the men of Judah, "We have ten shares in the king; and besides, we have a greater claim on David than you have. So why do you treat us with contempt? Were we not the first to speak of bringing back our king?"

But the men of Judah responded even more harshly than the men of Israel.

Sheba Rebels Against David

20 Now a troublemaker named Sheba son of Bicri, a Benjamite, happened to be there. He sounded the trumpet and shouted,

"We have no share in David,
  no part in Jesse's son!
Every man to his tent, O Israel!"

2So all the men of Israel deserted David to follow Sheba son of Bicri. But the men of Judah stayed by their king all the way from the Jordan to Jerusalem.

3When David returned to his palace in Jerusalem, he took the ten concubines he had left to take care of the palace and put them in a house under guard. He provided for them, but did not lie with them. They were kept in confinement till the day of their death, living as widows.

4Then the king said to Amasa, "Summon the men of Judah to come to me within three days, and be here yourself." 5But when Amasa went to summon Judah, he took longer than the time the king had set for him.

6David said to Abishai, "Now Sheba son of Bicri will do us more harm than Absalom did. Take your master's men and pursue him, or he will find fortified cities and escape from us." 7So Joab's men and the Kerethites and Pelethites and all the mighty warriors went out under the command of Abishai. They marched out from Jerusalem to pursue Sheba son of Bicri.

8While they were at the great rock in Gibeon, Amasa came to meet them. Joab was wearing his military tunic, and strapped over it at his waist was a belt with a dagger in its sheath. As he stepped forward, it dropped out of its sheath.

9Joab said to Amasa, "How are you, my brother?" Then Joab took Amasa by the beard with his right hand to kiss him. 10Amasa was not on his guard against the dagger in Joab's hand, and Joab plunged it into his belly, and his intestines spilled out on the ground. Without being stabbed again, Amasa died. Then Joab and his brother Abishai pursued Sheba son of Bicri.

11One of Joab's men stood beside Amasa and said, "Whoever favors Joab, and whoever is for David, let him follow Joab!" 12Amasa lay wallowing in his blood in the middle of the road, and the man saw that all the troops came to a halt there. When he realized that everyone who came up to Amasa stopped, he dragged him from the road into a field and threw a garment over him. 13After Amasa had been removed from the road, all the men went on with Joab to pursue Sheba son of Bicri.

14Sheba passed through all the tribes of Israel to Abel Beth Maacah[a] and through the entire region of the Berites, who gathered together and followed him. 15All the troops with Joab came and besieged Sheba in Abel Beth Maacah. They built a siege ramp up to the city, and it stood against the outer fortifications. While they were battering the wall to bring it down, 16a wise woman called from the city, "Listen! Listen! Tell Joab to come here so I can speak to him." 17He went toward her, and she asked, "Are you Joab?"

"I am," he answered.

She said, "Listen to what your servant has to say."

"I'm listening," he said.

18She continued, "Long ago they used to say, 'Get your answer at Abel,' and that settled it. 19We are the peaceful and faithful in Israel. You are trying to destroy a city that is a mother in Israel. Why do you want to swallow up the LORD's inheritance?"

20"Far be it from me!" Joab replied, "Far be it from me to swallow up or destroy! 21That is not the case. A man named Sheba son of Bicri, from the hill country of Ephraim, has lifted up his hand against the king, against David. Hand over this one man, and I'll withdraw from the city."

The woman said to Joab, "His head will be thrown to you from the wall."

22Then the woman went to all the people with her wise advice, and they cut off the head of Sheba son of Bicri and threw it to Joab. So he sounded the trumpet, and his men dispersed from the city, each returning to his home. And Joab went back to the king in Jerusalem.

23Joab was over Israel's entire army; Benaiah son of Jehoiada was over the Kerethites and Pelethites; 24Adoniram[b] was in charge of forced labor; Jehoshaphat son of Ahilud was recorder; 25Sheva was secretary; Zadok and Abiathar were priests; 26and Ira the Jairite was David's priest.

The Gibeonites Avenged

21 During the reign of David, there was a famine for three successive years; so David sought the face of the LORD. The LORD said, "It is on account of Saul and his blood-stained house; it is because he put the Gibeonites to death."

2The king summoned the Gibeonites and spoke to them. (Now the Gibeonites were not a part of Israel but were survivors of the Amorites; the Israelites had sworn to ⌞spare⌟ them, but Saul in his zeal for Israel and Judah had

[a]14 Or *Abel, even Beth Maacah*; also in verse 15 [b]24 Some Septuagint manuscripts (see also 1 Kings 4:6 and 5:14); Hebrew *Adoram*

tried to annihilate them.) 3David asked the
Gibeonites, "What shall I do for you? How
shall I make amends so that you will bless the
LORD's inheritance?"

4The Gibeonites answered him, "We have no
right to demand silver or gold from Saul or his
family, nor do we have the right to put anyone
in Israel to death."

"What do you want me to do for you?" David asked.

5They answered the king, "As for the man
who destroyed us and plotted against us so that
we have been decimated and have no place anywhere in Israel, 6let seven of his male descendants be given to us to be killed and exposed
before the LORD at Gibeah of Saul—the LORD's
chosen one."

So the king said, "I will give them to you."

7The king spared Mephibosheth son of Jonathan, the son of Saul, because of the oath before
the LORD between David and Jonathan son of
Saul. 8But the king took Armoni and Mephibosheth, the two sons of Aiah's daughter Rizpah,
whom she had borne to Saul, together with the
five sons of Saul's daughter Merab,[a] whom she
had borne to Adriel son of Barzillai the Mehola-
thite. 9He handed them over to the Gibeonites,
who killed and exposed them on a hill before
the LORD. All seven of them fell together; they
were put to death during the first days of the
harvest, just as the barley harvest was beginning.

10Rizpah daughter of Aiah took sackcloth
and spread it out for herself on a rock. From
the beginning of the harvest till the rain poured
down from the heavens on the bodies, she did
not let the birds of the air touch them by day
or the wild animals by night. 11When David
was told what Aiah's daughter Rizpah, Saul's
concubine, had done, 12he went and took the
bones of Saul and his son Jonathan from the citizens of Jabesh Gilead. (They had taken them
secretly from the public square at Beth Shan,
where the Philistines had hung them after they
struck Saul down on Gilboa.) 13David brought
the bones of Saul and his son Jonathan from
there, and the bones of those who had been
killed and exposed were gathered up.

14They buried the bones of Saul and his son
Jonathan in the tomb of Saul's father Kish, at
Zela in Benjamin, and did everything the king
commanded. After that, God answered prayer
in behalf of the land.

Wars Against the Philistines

15Once again there was a battle between the
Philistines and Israel. David went down with
his men to fight against the Philistines, and he
became exhausted. 16And Ishbi-Benob, one of
the descendants of Rapha, whose bronze spear-
head weighed three hundred shekels[b] and who
was armed with a new ⌞sword⌟, said he would
kill David. 17But Abishai son of Zeruiah came
to David's rescue; he struck the Philistine down
and killed him. Then David's men swore to
him, saying, "Never again will you go out with
us to battle, so that the lamp of Israel will not
be extinguished."

18In the course of time, there was another
battle with the Philistines, at Gob. At that time
Sibbecai the Hushathite killed Saph, one of the
descendants of Rapha.

19In another battle with the Philistines at
Gob, Elhanan son of Jaare-Oregim[c] the Beth-
lehemite killed Goliath[d] the Gittite, who had a
spear with a shaft like a weaver's rod.

20In still another battle, which took place at
Gath, there was a huge man with six fingers on
each hand and six toes on each foot—twenty-
four in all. He also was descended from Rapha.
21When he taunted Israel, Jonathan son of
Shimeah, David's brother, killed him.

22These four were descendants of Rapha in
Gath, and they fell at the hands of David and
his men.

David's Song of Praise

22 David sang to the LORD the words of
this song when the LORD delivered
him from the hand of all his enemies and from
the hand of Saul. 2He said:

"The LORD is my rock, my fortress and my
deliverer;
3 my God is my rock, in whom I take
refuge,
my shield and the horn[e] of my salvation.

[a]8 Two Hebrew manuscripts, some Septuagint manuscripts and Syriac (see also 1 Samuel 18:19); most Hebrew and Septuagint manuscripts *Michal* [b]16 That is, about 7 1/2 pounds (about 3.5 kilograms) [c]19 Or *son of Jair the weaver* [d]19 Hebrew and Septuagint; 1 Chron. 20:5 *son of Jair killed Lahmi the brother of Goliath* [e]3 *Horn* here symbolizes strength.

Lifted Up

Read: 2 Samuel 22:1–51

GERALDINE SINGLETON FACED an unusual enemy. Her body waged war against her. She survived breast cancer and a mastectomy. Less than a decade later, the insidious disease returned as a brain tumor that spread to her bones. USA Today reports: "She has since weathered a car accident; a house fire; three 'mini strokes'; and hardest of all, the death of a brother and two sisters." Amazingly, Singleton doesn't feel downcast. She reports, "God has chosen to 'lift her up.' " Singleton now educates other cancer victims and has joined a choir of other breast cancer survivors who "sing through our storm."

You may not have experienced the same type of tempest as Geraldine Singleton, but life sends all kinds of storms: Financial struggles. Wayward children. The death of a loved one. Broken relationships. These events whip through our lives with gale force winds and leave us feeling shattered, powerless and adrift like victims of a mighty tempest.

Engulfed by the floods of life and surrounded by his enemies, David was in a vulnerable place. But he remained strong because he knew the One who could bring triumph out of tragedy and victory from defeat. David trusted his mighty Savior because their relationship rested on a rock-solid, centuries-old covenant that could not be swayed. Like a small child enveloped by his parents' love, David expected God to intervene. Based on what he knew of God's character and his covenant promise to his people, David expected redemption. His hopes were not in vain. God reached down and pulled David up from the depths.

The One who rescued David still waits for his people to call on him during whatever trials they face. The God who lifted David to new heights and gave him a song to sing wants to reach down from on high to lift your spirits and help you rise above your circumstances.

What can you do when the storm breaks? Where do you turn when your world seems to crumble around you? You're not in this alone! Follow David's lead and run to God, who wants to be your strong tower. Look to God to regenerate your strength. Just as David did, and as cancer survivors and survivors of other catastrophes do, cry out to the Lord for help. Then sing his praises when he reaches down to lift you up.

2 Samuel 22:17

"He reached down from on high and took hold of me; he drew me out of deep waters."

reflection

1 What storm are you currently weathering?

2 In what ways have you seen God lift you up in the past? Sing a song of praise to the Lord for his mighty works in the past, trusting that he will continue to work in the present.

3 What have you learned in the midst of your own storm to help lift up others?

RELATED READINGS

Psalms 18:1–50; 59:16–17; Jonah 2:1–9

Go to page 398 for your next devotional reading.

He is my stronghold, my refuge and my savior—
from violent men you save me.
4 I call to the LORD, who is worthy of praise,
and I am saved from my enemies.

5 "The waves of death swirled about me;
the torrents of destruction overwhelmed me.
6 The cords of the grave[a] coiled around me;
the snares of death confronted me.
7 In my distress I called to the LORD;
I called out to my God.
From his temple he heard my voice;
my cry came to his ears.

8 "The earth trembled and quaked,
the foundations of the heavens[b] shook;
they trembled because he was angry.
9 Smoke rose from his nostrils;
consuming fire came from his mouth,
burning coals blazed out of it.
10 He parted the heavens and came down;
dark clouds were under his feet.
11 He mounted the cherubim and flew;
he soared[c] on the wings of the wind.
12 He made darkness his canopy around him—
the dark[d] rain clouds of the sky.
13 Out of the brightness of his presence
bolts of lightning blazed forth.
14 The LORD thundered from heaven;
the voice of the Most High resounded.
15 He shot arrows and scattered ⌊the enemies⌋,
bolts of lightning and routed them.
16 The valleys of the sea were exposed
and the foundations of the earth laid bare
at the rebuke of the LORD,
at the blast of breath from his nostrils.

17 "He reached down from on high and took hold of me;
he drew me out of deep waters.
18 He rescued me from my powerful enemy,
from my foes, who were too strong for me.
19 They confronted me in the day of my disaster,
but the LORD was my support.
20 He brought me out into a spacious place;
he rescued me because he delighted in me.

21 "The LORD has dealt with me according to my righteousness;
according to the cleanness of my hands he has rewarded me.
22 For I have kept the ways of the LORD;
I have not done evil by turning from my God.
23 All his laws are before me;
I have not turned away from his decrees.
24 I have been blameless before him
and have kept myself from sin.
25 The LORD has rewarded me according to my righteousness,
according to my cleanness[e] in his sight.

26 "To the faithful you show yourself faithful,
to the blameless you show yourself blameless,
27 to the pure you show yourself pure,
but to the crooked you show yourself shrewd.
28 You save the humble,
but your eyes are on the haughty to bring them low.
29 You are my lamp, O LORD;
the LORD turns my darkness into light.
30 With your help I can advance against a troop[f];
with my God I can scale a wall.

31 "As for God, his way is perfect;
the word of the LORD is flawless.
He is a shield
for all who take refuge in him.
32 For who is God besides the LORD?
And who is the Rock except our God?
33 It is God who arms me with strength[g]
and makes my way perfect.
34 He makes my feet like the feet of a deer;
he enables me to stand on the heights.
35 He trains my hands for battle;
my arms can bend a bow of bronze.

[a]6 Hebrew *Sheol* [b]8 Hebrew; Vulgate and Syriac (see also Psalm 18:7) *mountains* [c]11 Many Hebrew manuscripts (see also Psalm 18:10); most Hebrew manuscripts *appeared* [d]12 Septuagint and Vulgate (see also Psalm 18:11); Hebrew *massed* [e]25 Hebrew; Septuagint and Vulgate (see also Psalm 18:24) *to the cleanness of my hands* [f]30 Or *can run through a barricade* [g]33 Dead Sea Scrolls, some Septuagint manuscripts, Vulgate and Syriac (see also Psalm 18:32); Masoretic Text *who is my strong refuge*

36 You give me your shield of victory;
you stoop down to make me great.
37 You broaden the path beneath me,
so that my ankles do not turn.

38 "I pursued my enemies and crushed them;
I did not turn back till they were destroyed.
39 I crushed them completely, and they could not rise;
they fell beneath my feet.
40 You armed me with strength for battle;
you made my adversaries bow at my feet.
41 You made my enemies turn their backs in flight,
and I destroyed my foes.
42 They cried for help, but there was no one to save them—
to the LORD, but he did not answer.
43 I beat them as fine as the dust of the earth;
I pounded and trampled them like mud in the streets.

44 "You have delivered me from the attacks of my people;
you have preserved me as the head of nations.
People I did not know are subject to me,
45 and foreigners come cringing to me;
as soon as they hear me, they obey me.
46 They all lose heart;
they come trembling[a] from their strongholds.

47 "The LORD lives! Praise be to my Rock!
Exalted be God, the Rock, my Savior!
48 He is the God who avenges me,
who puts the nations under me,
49 who sets me free from my enemies.
You exalted me above my foes;
from violent men you rescued me.
50 Therefore I will praise you, O LORD,
among the nations;
I will sing praises to your name.
51 He gives his king great victories;
he shows unfailing kindness to his anointed,
to David and his descendants forever."

2 Samuel 23:4

God Is Light

"He is like the light of morning at sunrise on a cloudless morning, like the brightness after rain that brings the grass from the earth."

The Last Words of David

23 These are the last words of David:

"The oracle of David son of Jesse,
the oracle of the man exalted by the Most High,
the man anointed by the God of Jacob,
Israel's singer of songs[b]:

2 "The Spirit of the LORD spoke through me;
his word was on my tongue.
3 The God of Israel spoke,
the Rock of Israel said to me:
'When one rules over men in righteousness,
when he rules in the fear of God,
4 he is like the light of morning at sunrise
on a cloudless morning,
like the brightness after rain
that brings the grass from the earth.'
5 "Is not my house right with God?
Has he not made with me an everlasting covenant,
arranged and secured in every part?
Will he not bring to fruition my salvation
and grant me my every desire?
6 But evil men are all to be cast aside like thorns,
which are not gathered with the hand.
7 Whoever touches thorns
uses a tool of iron or the shaft of a spear;
they are burned up where they lie."

David's Mighty Men

8 These are the names of David's mighty men:

Josheb-Basshebeth,[c] a Tahkemonite,[d] was

[a]46 Some Septuagint manuscripts and Vulgate (see also Psalm 18:45); Masoretic Text *they arm themselves.* [b]1 Or *Israel's beloved singer*
[c]8 Hebrew; some Septuagint manuscripts suggest *Ish-Bosheth*, that is, *Esh-Baal* (see also 1 Chron. 11:11 *Jashobeam*). [d]8 Probably a variant of *Hacmonite* (see 1 Chron. 11:11)

chief of the Three; he raised his spear against
eight hundred men, whom he killed[a] in one encounter.
9 Next to him was Eleazar son of Dodai the
Ahohite. As one of the three mighty men, he
was with David when they taunted the Philistines gathered ⌊at Pas Dammim⌋[b] for battle.
Then the men of Israel retreated, 10 but he
stood his ground and struck down the Philistines till his hand grew tired and froze to the
sword. The LORD brought about a great victory
that day. The troops returned to Eleazar, but
only to strip the dead.
11 Next to him was Shammah son of Agee
the Hararite. When the Philistines banded
together at a place where there was a field
full of lentils, Israel's troops fled from them.
12 But Shammah took his stand in the middle
of the field. He defended it and struck the Philistines down, and the LORD brought about a
great victory.
13 During harvest time, three of the thirty
chief men came down to David at the cave of
Adullam, while a band of Philistines was encamped in the Valley of Rephaim. 14 At that
time David was in the stronghold, and the
Philistine garrison was at Bethlehem. 15 David
longed for water and said, "Oh, that someone
would get me a drink of water from the well
near the gate of Bethlehem!" 16 So the three
mighty men broke through the Philistine
lines, drew water from the well near the gate
of Bethlehem and carried it back to David. But
he refused to drink it; instead, he poured it out
before the LORD. 17 "Far be it from me, O LORD,
to do this!" he said. "Is it not the blood of men
who went at the risk of their lives?" And David
would not drink it.
Such were the exploits of the three mighty
men.
18 Abishai the brother of Joab son of Zeruiah
was chief of the Three.[c] He raised his spear
against three hundred men, whom he killed,
and so he became as famous as the Three.
19 Was he not held in greater honor than the
Three? He became their commander, even
though he was not included among them.
20 Benaiah son of Jehoiada was a valiant
fighter from Kabzeel, who performed great
exploits. He struck down two of Moab's best
men. He also went down into a pit on a snowy
day and killed a lion. 21 And he struck down a
huge Egyptian. Although the Egyptian had a
spear in his hand, Benaiah went against him
with a club. He snatched the spear from the
Egyptian's hand and killed him with his own
spear. 22 Such were the exploits of Benaiah son
of Jehoiada; he too was as famous as the three
mighty men. 23 He was held in greater honor
than any of the Thirty, but he was not included
among the Three. And David put him in charge
of his bodyguard.

24 Among the Thirty were:
Asahel the brother of Joab,
Elhanan son of Dodo from Bethlehem,
25 Shammah the Harodite,
Elika the Harodite,
26 Helez the Paltite,
Ira son of Ikkesh from Tekoa,
27 Abiezer from Anathoth,
Mebunnai[d] the Hushathite,
28 Zalmon the Ahohite,
Maharai the Netophathite,
29 Heled[e] son of Baanah the Netophathite,
Ithai son of Ribai from Gibeah in Benjamin,
30 Benaiah the Pirathonite,
Hiddai[f] from the ravines of Gaash,
31 Abi-Albon the Arbathite,
Azmaveth the Barhumite,
32 Eliahba the Shaalbonite,
the sons of Jashen,
Jonathan 33 son of[g] Shammah the Hararite,
Ahiam son of Sharar[h] the Hararite,
34 Eliphelet son of Ahasbai the Maacathite,
Eliam son of Ahithophel the Gilonite,
35 Hezro the Carmelite,

[a] 8 Some Septuagint manuscripts (see also 1 Chron. 11:11); Hebrew and other Septuagint manuscripts *Three; it was Adino the Eznite who killed eight hundred men* [b] 9 See 1 Chron. 11:13; Hebrew *gathered there.* [c] 18 Most Hebrew manuscripts (see also 1 Chron. 11:20); two Hebrew manuscripts and Syriac *Thirty* [d] 27 Hebrew; some Septuagint manuscripts (see also 1 Chron. 11:29) *Sibbecai* [e] 29 Some Hebrew manuscripts and Vulgate (see also 1 Chron. 11:30); most Hebrew manuscripts *Heleb* [f] 30 Hebrew; some Septuagint manuscripts (see also 1 Chron. 11:32) *Hurai* [g] 33 Some Septuagint manuscripts (see also 1 Chron. 11:34); Hebrew does not have *son of.* [h] 33 Hebrew; some Septuagint manuscripts (see also 1 Chron. 11:35) *Sacar*

Paarai the Arbite,
36 Igal son of Nathan from Zobah,
the son of Hagri,[a]
37 Zelek the Ammonite,
Naharai the Beerothite, the armor-
bearer of Joab son of Zeruiah,
38 Ira the Ithrite,
Gareb the Ithrite
39 and Uriah the Hittite.
There were thirty-seven in all.

avid Counts the Fighting Men

24 Again the anger of the LORD burned
against Israel, and he incited David
ainst them, saying, "Go and take a census of
rael and Judah."
2 So the king said to Joab and the army com-
anders[b] with him, "Go throughout the tribes
Israel from Dan to Beersheba and enroll the
hting men, so that I may know how many
ere are."
3 But Joab replied to the king, "May the LORD
ur God multiply the troops a hundred times
er, and may the eyes of my lord the king see
But why does my lord the king want to do
ch a thing?"
4 The king's word, however, overruled Joab
d the army commanders; so they left the
esence of the king to enroll the fighting men
Israel.
5 After crossing the Jordan, they camped
ar Aroer, south of the town in the gorge, and
en went through Gad and on to Jazer. 6 They
nt to Gilead and the region of Tahtim Hod-
i, and on to Dan Jaan and around toward
lon. 7 Then they went toward the fortress of
re and all the towns of the Hivites and Ca-
anites. Finally, they went on to Beersheba in
e Negev of Judah.
8 After they had gone through the entire
nd, they came back to Jerusalem at the end of
ne months and twenty days.
9 Joab reported the number of the fighting
en to the king: In Israel there were eight
ndred thousand able-bodied men who
uld handle a sword, and in Judah five hun-
ed thousand.
10 David was conscience-stricken after he
d counted the fighting men, and he said to
the LORD, "I have sinned greatly in what I have
done. Now, O LORD, I beg you, take away the
guilt of your servant. I have done a very foolish thing."
11 Before David got up the next morning,
the word of the LORD had come to Gad the
prophet, David's seer: 12 "Go and tell David,
'This is what the LORD says: I am giving you
three options. Choose one of them for me to
carry out against you.'"
13 So Gad went to David and said to him,
"Shall there come upon you three[c] years of famine in your land? Or three months of fleeing
from your enemies while they pursue you? Or
three days of plague in your land? Now then,
think it over and decide how I should answer
the one who sent me."
14 David said to Gad, "I am in deep distress.
Let us fall into the hands of the LORD, for his
mercy is great; but do not let me fall into the
hands of men."
15 So the LORD sent a plague on Israel
from that morning until the end of the time
designated, and seventy thousand of the people
from Dan to Beersheba died. 16 When the angel stretched out his hand to destroy Jerusalem,
the LORD was grieved because of the calamity
and said to the angel who was afflicting the people, "Enough! Withdraw your hand." The angel
of the LORD was then at the threshing floor of
Araunah the Jebusite.
17 When David saw the angel who was striking down the people, he said to the LORD, "I am
the one who has sinned and done wrong. These
are but sheep. What have they done? Let your
hand fall upon me and my family."

David Builds an Altar

18 On that day Gad went to David and said
to him, "Go up and build an altar to the LORD
on the threshing floor of Araunah the Jebusite." 19 So David went up, as the LORD had
commanded through Gad. 20 When Araunah
looked and saw the king and his men coming
toward him, he went out and bowed down before the king with his face to the ground.
21 Araunah said, "Why has my lord the king
come to his servant?"
"To buy your threshing floor," David

Some Septuagint manuscripts (see also 1 Chron. 11:38); Hebrew *Haggadi* [b]2 Septuagint (see also verse 4 and 1 Chron. 21:2); Hebrew
b the army commander [c]13 Septuagint (see also 1 Chron. 21:12); Hebrew *seven*

The Other Side of Decision

JAEL

Sisera, however, fled on foot to the tent of Jael, the wife of Heber the Kenite.

Judges 4:17

JAEL HAD HEARD THE RUMORS. There was talk about her husband, Heber. People said that he was the one who had most likely betrayed the Israelites to the commander of the Canaanite army, Sisera. Although they were Kenites, loyal descendants of Moses' brother-in-law, Jael knew more than most that one could never tell where Heber's loyalty lay. "He has a mind of his own," Jael had reminded herself many times when she didn't understand her husband's decisions.

She remembered the time Heber decided to take the family and split off from the rest of his tribespeople—the Kenites (who supported Israel)—in favor of a home closer to Kedesh. He had come home one day all excited, saying something about a gigantic tree he'd seen near Zaanannim that would make a great tent site. The next thing she knew, Jael was pacing the property line of her new home, nailing pegs in the ground and pitching the tent.

Jael, like many in her clan, had never had an occasion for testing her own decision-making abilities. They were nomads, and nomads were generally "go with the flow" folk who preferred to stay out of controversy. Taking a stand leads to putting down roots, which means making a decision. She remembered the times her leather-skinned grandmother had taken her face in her wrinkled hands and touted the family philosophy: "When times get tough, the tough get going." Somewhere. Anywhere. Wherever the problems couldn't follow you.

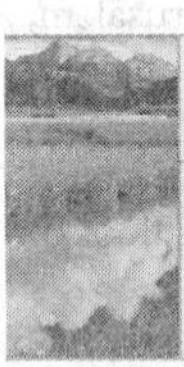

ASSIGNED READING: Judges 4:11—5:31

So, when the opportunity came to cast a decisive vote in favor of Israel, an unexpected chance to go her own way, Jael faced a dilemma on several fronts. On the other side of her decision lay a number of unanswerable questions. Her husband had made his intentions rather clear—and they were *not* pro-Israel. How would he react if she killed Israel's greatest enemy? Her tribespeople—all of the influential people in her life—had exemplified passivity to an extreme. Would she be remembered as a hero? A traitor? As a crazy, peg-wielding warrior?

She took a deep breath and made her decision. Later, whenever Deborah's song was sung in her presence, she always smiled and looked away in embarrassment at the lyrics, "Most blessed of women be Jael . . ."

—Prayer—

Jesus, give me the courage and resolution to stay true to what I know is right!

Weekend

Go to page 405 for your next devotional reading.

answered, "so I can build an
altar to the LORD, that the
plague on the people may
be stopped."
22 Araunah said to David,
"Let my lord the king take
whatever pleases him and offer it up. Here are oxen for the
burnt offering, and here are
threshing sledges and ox yokes
for the wood. 23 O king, Araunah gives all this to the king."
Araunah also said to him,
"May the LORD your God accept you."

> 2 Samuel 24:25
>
> *God Answers Prayer*
>
> Then the LORD answered prayer in behalf of the land, and the plague on Israel was stopped.

24 But the king replied to
Araunah, "No, I insist on paying you for it. I will not sacrifice
to the LORD my God burnt offerings that cost me nothing."
So David bought the threshing floor and the oxen and
paid fifty shekels[a] of silver for
them. 25 David built an altar to
the LORD there and sacrificed
burnt offerings and fellowship
offerings.[b] Then the LORD answered prayer in behalf of the
land, and the plague on Israel
was stopped.

[a]24 That is, about 1 1/4 pounds (about 0.6 kilogram) [b]25 Traditionally *peace offerings*

1 Kings

Author:
Unknown.

Audience:
The people of Israel.

Date:
Originally, 1 and 2 Kings were one book, probably written during the Israelites' Babylonian exile, sometime between 560 and 550 B.C.

Setting:
David's faithful rule is the model for Israel's future kings.

Verse to Remember:
"May he turn our hearts to him, to walk in all his ways and to keep the commands, decrees and regulations he gave our fathers." (8:58)

The record of Israel's kings reads not as a "who's who," but rather as a *"who did and who didn't."* The measure of these men who led God's people, first as one nation and then as a divided kingdom, is based on one thing only: whether or not they did what was right in the eyes of the Lord. *Their lives set the standard* for the nation, and when they set the bar high, the people rose to it. But more often than not, they set a low standard, and the people stooped to it.

When the standard seemed to be at its lowest, *an intriguing man stepped onto the scene.* Elijah traveled the sin-soaked land with a message condemning idolatry and the miracles to back it up. He had a stubborn audience, but *he found open hearts* in unlikely places. In the worst of times, there will always be those who seek to do what is right in the eyes of the Lord, and those are the very people whom God still seeks today.

Adonijah Sets Himself Up as King

1 When King David was old and well advanced in years, he could not keep warm
even when they put covers over him. 2So his
servants said to him, "Let us look for a young
virgin to attend the king and take care of him.
She can lie beside him so that our lord the king
may keep warm."
3Then they searched throughout Israel for
a beautiful girl and found Abishag, a Shunammite, and brought her to the king. 4The girl was
very beautiful; she took care of the king and
waited on him, but the king had no intimate
relations with her.
5Now Adonijah, whose mother was Haggith, put himself forward and said, "I will be
king." So he got chariots and horses[a] ready,
with fifty men to run ahead of him. 6(His fa-

[a]5 Or *charioteers*

ther had never interfered with him by asking,
"Why do you behave as you do?" He was also
very handsome and was born next after Absalom.)
7 Adonijah conferred with Joab son of
Zeruiah and with Abiathar the priest, and they
gave him their support. 8 But Zadok the priest,
Benaiah son of Jehoiada, Nathan the prophet,
Shimei and Rei[a] and David's special guard did
not join Adonijah.
9 Adonijah then sacrificed sheep, cattle and
fattened calves at the Stone of Zoheleth near
En Rogel. He invited all his brothers, the king's
sons, and all the men of Judah who were royal
officials, 10 but he did not invite Nathan the
prophet or Benaiah or the special guard or his
brother Solomon.
11 Then Nathan asked Bathsheba, Solomon's
mother, "Have you not heard that Adonijah,
the son of Haggith, has become king without
our lord David's knowing it? 12 Now then, let
me advise you how you can save your own life
and the life of your son Solomon. 13 Go in to
King David and say to him, 'My lord the king,
did you not swear to me your servant: "Surely
Solomon your son shall be king after me, and
he will sit on my throne"? Why then has Adonijah become king?' 14 While you are still there
talking to the king, I will come in and confirm
what you have said."
15 So Bathsheba went to see the aged king in
his room, where Abishag the Shunammite was
attending him. 16 Bathsheba bowed low and
knelt before the king.
"What is it you want?" the king asked.
17 She said to him, "My lord, you yourself
swore to me your servant by the LORD your
God: 'Solomon your son shall be king after
me, and he will sit on my throne.' 18 But now
Adonijah has become king, and you, my lord
the king, do not know about it. 19 He has sacrificed great numbers of cattle, fattened calves,
and sheep, and has invited all the king's sons,
Abiathar the priest and Joab the commander
of the army, but he has not invited Solomon
your servant. 20 My lord the king, the eyes of all
Israel are on you, to learn from you who will
sit on the throne of my lord the king after him.
21 Otherwise, as soon as my lord the king is laid
to rest with his fathers, I and my son Solomon
will be treated as criminals."
22 While she was still speaking with the king,
Nathan the prophet arrived. 23 And they told
the king, "Nathan the prophet is here." So he
went before the king and bowed with his face
to the ground.
24 Nathan said, "Have you, my lord the king,
declared that Adonijah shall be king after you,
and that he will sit on your throne? 25 Today he
has gone down and sacrificed great numbers
of cattle, fattened calves, and sheep. He has
invited all the king's sons, the commanders of
the army and Abiathar the priest. Right now
they are eating and drinking with him and
saying, 'Long live King Adonijah!' 26 But me
your servant, and Zadok the priest, and Benaiah son of Jehoiada, and your servant Solomon
he did not invite. 27 Is this something my lord
the king has done without letting his servants
know who should sit on the throne of my lord
the king after him?"

David Makes Solomon King

28 Then King David said, "Call in Bathsheba."
So she came into the king's presence and stood
before him.
29 The king then took an oath: "As surely as
the LORD lives, who has delivered me out of
every trouble, 30 I will surely carry out today
what I swore to you by the LORD, the God of
Israel: Solomon your son shall be king after me,
and he will sit on my throne in my place."
31 Then Bathsheba bowed low with her face
to the ground and, kneeling before the king,
said, "May my lord King David live forever!"
32 King David said, "Call in Zadok the
priest, Nathan the prophet and Benaiah son
of Jehoiada." When they came before the king,
33 he said to them: "Take your lord's servants
with you and set Solomon my son on my own
mule and take him down to Gihon. 34 There
have Zadok the priest and Nathan the prophet
anoint him king over Israel. Blow the trumpet
and shout, 'Long live King Solomon!' 35 Then
you are to go up with him, and he is to come
and sit on my throne and reign in my place.
I have appointed him ruler over Israel and
Judah."

[a] 8 Or *and his friends*

36 Benaiah son of Jehoiada answered the
king, "Amen! May the LORD, the God of my
lord the king, so declare it. 37 As the LORD was
with my lord the king, so may
he be with Solomon to make
his throne even greater than
the throne of my lord King
David!"
38 So Zadok the priest, Nathan the prophet, Benaiah son
of Jehoiada, the Kerethites and
the Pelethites went down and
put Solomon on King David's
mule and escorted him to Gihon. 39 Zadok the priest took
the horn of oil from the sacred
tent and anointed Solomon.
Then they sounded the trumpet and all the people shouted,
"Long live King Solomon!"
40 And all the people went up after him, playing
flutes and rejoicing greatly, so that the ground
shook with the sound.
41 Adonijah and all the guests who were with
him heard it as they were finishing their feast.
On hearing the sound of the trumpet, Joab
asked, "What's the meaning of all the noise in
the city?"
42 Even as he was speaking, Jonathan son
of Abiathar the priest arrived. Adonijah said,
"Come in. A worthy man like you must be
bringing good news."
43 "Not at all!" Jonathan answered. "Our lord
King David has made Solomon king. 44 The
king has sent with him Zadok the priest, Nathan the prophet, Benaiah son of Jehoiada, the
Kerethites and the Pelethites, and they have put
him on the king's mule, 45 and Zadok the priest
and Nathan the prophet have anointed him
king at Gihon. From there they have gone up
cheering, and the city resounds with it. That's
the noise you hear. 46 Moreover, Solomon has
taken his seat on the royal throne. 47 Also, the
royal officials have come to congratulate our
lord King David, saying, 'May your God make
Solomon's name more famous than yours
and his throne greater than yours!' And the
king bowed in worship on his bed 48 and said,
'Praise be to the LORD, the God of Israel, who
has allowed my eyes to see a successor on my
throne today.'"
49 At this, all Adonijah's guests rose in alarm
and dispersed. 50 But Adoni-
jah, in fear of Solomon, went
and took hold of the horns of
the altar. 51 Then Solomon was
told, "Adonijah is afraid of King
Solomon and is clinging to the
horns of the altar. He says, 'Let
King Solomon swear to me today that he will not put his servant to death with the sword.'"
52 Solomon replied, "If he
shows himself to be a worthy
man, not a hair of his head will
fall to the ground; but if evil
is found in him, he will die."
53 Then King Solomon sent
men, and they brought him
down from the altar. And Adonijah came and
bowed down to King Solomon, and Solomon
said, "Go to your home."

1 Kings 1:37

God Establishes Rulers

"As the LORD was with my lord the king, so may he be with Solomon to make his throne even greater than the throne of my lord King David!"

David's Charge to Solomon

2 When the time drew near for David to die,
he gave a charge to Solomon his son.
2 "I am about to go the way of all the earth,"
he said. "So be strong, show yourself a man,
3 and observe what the LORD your God requires: Walk in his ways, and keep his decrees
and commands, his laws and requirements, as
written in the Law of Moses, so that you may
prosper in all you do and wherever you go,
4 and that the LORD may keep his promise to
me: 'If your descendants watch how they live,
and if they walk faithfully before me with all
their heart and soul, you will never fail to have
a man on the throne of Israel.'
5 "Now you yourself know what Joab son
of Zeruiah did to me—what he did to the two
commanders of Israel's armies, Abner son of
Ner and Amasa son of Jether. He killed them,
shedding their blood in peacetime as if in battle, and with that blood stained the belt around
his waist and the sandals on his feet. 6 Deal with
him according to your wisdom, but do not let
his gray head go down to the grave[a] in peace.
7 "But show kindness to the sons of Barzillai
of Gilead and let them be among those who

[a]6 Hebrew *Sheol*; also in verse 9

eat at your table. They stood by me when I fled
from your brother Absalom.
8“And remember, you have with you Shimei
son of Gera, the Benjamite
from Bahurim, who called
down bitter curses on me the
day I went to Mahanaim. When
he came down to meet me at
the Jordan, I swore to him by
the LORD: ‘I will not put you to
death by the sword.’ 9But now,
do not consider him innocent.
You are a man of wisdom; you
will know what to do to him.
Bring his gray head down to
the grave in blood.”
10Then David rested with
his fathers and was buried
in the City of David. 11He
had reigned forty years over
Israel—seven years in Hebron
and thirty-three in Jerusalem. 12So Solomon sat on the
throne of his father David, and
his rule was firmly established.

> **1 Kings 2:3**
>
> *God Blesses Obedience*
>
> “And observe what the LORD your God requires: Walk in his ways, and keep his decrees and commands, his laws and requirements, as written in the Law of Moses, so that you may prosper in all you do and wherever you go.”

Solomon’s Throne Established

13Now Adonijah, the son of Haggith, went
to Bathsheba, Solomon’s mother. Bathsheba
asked him, “Do you come peacefully?”
He answered, “Yes, peacefully.” 14Then he
added, “I have something to say to you.”
“You may say it,” she replied.
15“As you know,” he said, “the kingdom was
mine. All Israel looked to me as their king. But
things changed, and the kingdom has gone to
my brother; for it has come to him from the
LORD. 16Now I have one request to make of
you. Do not refuse me.”
“You may make it,” she said.
17So he continued, “Please ask King Solomon—he will not refuse you—to give me Abishag the Shunammite as my wife.”
18“Very well,” Bathsheba replied, “I will
speak to the king for you.”
19When Bathsheba went to King Solomon
to speak to him for Adonijah, the king stood
up to meet her, bowed down to her and sat
down on his throne. He had a throne brought
for the king’s mother, and she sat down at his
right hand.
20“I have one small request to make of you,”
she said. “Do not refuse me.”
The king replied, “Make it, my mother; I will
not refuse you.”
21So she said, “Let Abishag
the Shunammite be given in
marriage to your brother Adonijah.”
22King Solomon answered
his mother, “Why do you request Abishag the Shunam-
mite for Adonijah? You might
as well request the kingdom for
him—after all, he is my older
brother—yes, for him and for
Abiathar the priest and Joab
son of Zeruiah!”
23Then King Solomon swore
by the LORD: “May God deal
with me, be it ever so severely,
if Adonijah does not pay with
his life for this request! 24And
now, as surely as the LORD
lives—he who has established
me securely on the throne of my father David
and has founded a dynasty for me as he promised—Adonijah shall be put to death today!”
25So King Solomon gave orders to Benaiah
son of Jehoiada, and he struck down Adonijah
and he died.
26To Abiathar the priest the king said, “Go
back to your fields in Anathoth. You deserve to
die, but I will not put you to death now, because
you carried the ark of the Sovereign LORD before my father David and shared all my father’s
hardships.” 27So Solomon removed Abiathar
from the priesthood of the LORD, fulfilling the
word the LORD had spoken at Shiloh about the
house of Eli.
28When the news reached Joab, who had
conspired with Adonijah though not with Absalom, he fled to the tent of the LORD and took
hold of the horns of the altar. 29King Solomon
was told that Joab had fled to the tent of the
LORD and was beside the altar. Then Solomon
ordered Benaiah son of Jehoiada, “Go, strike
him down!”
30So Benaiah entered the tent of the LORD
and said to Joab, “The king says, ‘Come out!’ ”
But he answered, “No, I will die here.”

Benaiah reported to the king, "This is how
Joab answered me."
31 Then the king commanded Benaiah, "Do
as he says. Strike him down and bury him, and
so clear me and my father's house of the guilt of
the innocent blood that Joab shed. 32 The LORD
will repay him for the blood he shed, because
without the knowledge of my father David
he attacked two men and killed them with
the sword. Both of them—Abner son of Ner,
commander of Israel's army, and Amasa son
of Jether, commander of Judah's army—were
better men and more upright than he. 33 May
the guilt of their blood rest on the head of Joab
and his descendants forever. But on David and
his descendants, his house and his throne, may
there be the LORD's peace forever."
34 So Benaiah son of Jehoiada went up and
struck down Joab and killed him, and he was
buried on his own land[a] in the desert. 35 The
king put Benaiah son of Jehoiada over the army
in Joab's position and replaced Abiathar with
Zadok the priest.
36 Then the king sent for Shimei and said to
him, "Build yourself a house in Jerusalem and
live there, but do not go anywhere else. 37 The
day you leave and cross the Kidron Valley, you
can be sure you will die; your blood will be on
your own head."
38 Shimei answered the king, "What you say
is good. Your servant will do as my lord the
king has said." And Shimei stayed in Jerusalem
for a long time.
39 But three years later, two of Shimei's slaves
ran off to Achish son of Maacah, king of Gath,
and Shimei was told, "Your slaves are in Gath."
40 At this, he saddled his donkey and went
to Achish at Gath in search of his slaves. So
Shimei went away and brought the slaves back
from Gath.
41 When Solomon was told that Shimei had
gone from Jerusalem to Gath and had returned,
42 the king summoned Shimei and said to him,
"Did I not make you swear by the LORD and
warn you, 'On the day you leave to go anywhere
else, you can be sure you will die'? At that time
you said to me, 'What you say is good. I will
obey.' 43 Why then did you not keep your oath to
the LORD and obey the command I gave you?"
44 The king also said to Shimei, "You know
in your heart all the wrong you did to my father David. Now the LORD will repay you for
your wrongdoing. 45 But King Solomon will be
blessed, and David's throne will remain secure
before the LORD forever."
46 Then the king gave the order to Benaiah
son of Jehoiada, and he went out and struck
Shimei down and killed him.
The kingdom was now firmly established in
Solomon's hands.

Solomon Asks for Wisdom

3 Solomon made an alliance with Pharaoh
king of Egypt and married his daughter.
He brought her to the City of David until he finished building his palace and the temple of the
LORD, and the wall around Jerusalem. 2 The people, however, were still sacrificing at the high
places, because a temple had not yet been built
for the Name of the LORD. 3 Solomon showed
his love for the LORD by walking according to
the statutes of his father David, except that he
offered sacrifices and burned incense on the
high places.
4 The king went to Gibeon to offer sacrifices,
for that was the most important high place, and
Solomon offered a thousand burnt offerings
on that altar. 5 At Gibeon the LORD appeared
to Solomon during the night in a dream, and
God said, "Ask for whatever you want me to
give you."
6 Solomon answered, "You have shown great
kindness to your servant, my father David, because he was faithful to you and righteous and
upright in heart. You have continued this great
kindness to him and have given him a son to sit
on his throne this very day.
7 "Now, O LORD my God, you have made
your servant king in place of my father David.
But I am only a little child and do not know
how to carry out my duties. 8 Your servant is
here among the people you have chosen, a
great people, too numerous to count or number. 9 So give your servant a discerning heart to
govern your people and to distinguish between
right and wrong. For who is able to govern this
great people of yours?"
10 The Lord was pleased that Solomon had

[a]34 Or *buried in his tomb*

Worship and Wisdom

Read: 1 Kings 3:4–15

DARK CLOUDS SLIP between the guardian mountain peaks and scurry across the empty skies above Death Valley in California. Heat waves tremble over the parched earth as cloud shadows nibble at the eroded badlands and salt pans. Thunder rumbles in the distance. By late afternoon, the rain-gorged sky swings low. Suddenly the heavens burst! Fat raindrops jump like marbles on the hard-packed earth. Gradually the thirsty brown clods drink in water, softening to soak in more. A curtain of silver rain hangs between the churning sky and muddy valley floor. In a few weeks, Death Valley will explode to life in an astonishing feast of wildflowers.

Upon ascending to the throne, young Solomon traveled ten miles northwest to the hills of Gibeon to offer an extravagant sacrifice—a thousand burnt offerings. This was the same place where the sun stood still for Joshua and where twelve of David's strong men defeated twelve of Saul's men (see Joshua 10:1–14; 2 Samuel 2:12–17). In the middle of the night, God burst through to Solomon in a dream. Solomon could have requested anything in all the earth. Through time spent in worship, Solomon realized that wisdom was the greatest of all God's gifts.

Worship is like the rains that prepare the earth for God's blessings. The story of the youthful Solomon preparing to take the throne is a beautiful reminder to us of the importance of worship. The story of God granting him the gift of wisdom opens with a swell of costly and reverent worship. For us, too, worship creates a context for us to encounter God; it sets our souls in motion in an upward spiral by which we pursue God, and he gladly responds.

Worship book-ended the exchange between the Sovereign God and the new sovereign of Israel. Solomon returned from his heavenly encounter and again made an offering to the God of Israel in Jerusalem before the ark of the covenant.

Like a gathering cloud, worship encircles and protects God's people. It softens the soil of our hearts like nourishing rain. When we've been in a dark place and long for colorful beauty to replace the hardness that has settled into our scorched souls, simple acts of worship can prepare the way for God's words of wisdom to permeate our hearts. If your life seems parched, won't you allow God to paint a palette of colorful joy by spending time worshiping your Lord?

Go to page 412 for your next devotional reading.

1 Kings 3:5,15

At Gibeon the LORD appeared to Solomon during the night in a dream, and God said, "Ask for whatever you want me to give you." . . . He returned to Jerusalem, stood before the ark of the Lord's covenant and sacrificed burnt offerings and fellowship offerings.

reflection

1 Why is worship so important to God?

2 What kinds of extravagant (or at least consistent) worship characterize your life?

3 If God offered you anything you wish, what would you ask for? Has it changed having read this passage?

RELATED READINGS

Psalms 29; 100;
Proverbs 3:13–24;
Isaiah 55:10–12

asked for this. 11So God said to him, "Since you have asked for this and not for long life or wealth for yourself, nor have asked for the death of your enemies but for discernment in administering justice, 12I will do what you have asked. I will give you a wise and discerning heart, so that there will never have been anyone like you, nor will there ever be. 13Moreover, I will give you what you have not asked for—both riches and honor—so that in your lifetime you will have no equal among kings. 14And if you walk in my ways and obey my statutes and commands as David your father did, I will give you a long life." 15Then Solomon awoke—and he realized it had been a dream.

He returned to Jerusalem, stood before the ark of the Lord's covenant and sacrificed burnt offerings and fellowship offerings.[a] Then he gave a feast for all his court.

A Wise Ruling

16Now two prostitutes came to the king and stood before him. 17One of them said, "My lord, this woman and I live in the same house. I had a baby while she was there with me. 18The third day after my child was born, this woman also had a baby. We were alone; there was no one in the house but the two of us.

19"During the night this woman's son died because she lay on him. 20So she got up in the middle of the night and took my son from my side while I your servant was asleep. She put him by her breast and put her dead son by my breast. 21The next morning, I got up to nurse my son—and he was dead! But when I looked at him closely in the morning light, I saw that it wasn't the son I had borne."

22The other woman said, "No! The living one is my son; the dead one is yours."

But the first one insisted, "No! The dead one is yours; the living one is mine." And so they argued before the king.

23The king said, "This one says, 'My son is alive and your son is dead,' while that one says, 'No! Your son is dead and mine is alive.'"

24Then the king said, "Bring me a sword." So they brought a sword for the king. 25He then gave an order: "Cut the living child in two and give half to one and half to the other."

26The woman whose son was alive was filled with compassion for her son and said to the king, "Please, my lord, give her the living baby! Don't kill him!"

But the other said, "Neither I nor you shall have him. Cut him in two!"

27Then the king gave his ruling: "Give the living baby to the first woman. Do not kill him; she is his mother."

28When all Israel heard the verdict the king had given, they held the king in awe, because they saw that he had wisdom from God to administer justice.

Solomon's Officials and Governors

4 So King Solomon ruled over all Israel. 2And these were his chief officials:

Azariah son of Zadok—the priest;
3 Elihoreph and Ahijah, sons of Shisha—secretaries;
Jehoshaphat son of Ahilud—recorder;
4 Benaiah son of Jehoiada—commander in chief;
Zadok and Abiathar—priests;
5 Azariah son of Nathan—in charge of the district officers;
Zabud son of Nathan—a priest and personal adviser to the king;
6 Ahishar—in charge of the palace;
Adoniram son of Abda—in charge of forced labor.

7Solomon also had twelve district governors over all Israel, who supplied provisions for the king and the royal household. Each one had to provide supplies for one month in the year. 8These are their names:

Ben-Hur—in the hill country of Ephraim;
9 Ben-Deker—in Makaz, Shaalbim, Beth Shemesh and Elon Bethhanan;
10 Ben-Hesed—in Arubboth (Socoh and all the land of Hepher were his);
11 Ben-Abinadab—in Naphoth Dor[b] (he was married to Taphath daughter of Solomon);
12 Baana son of Ahilud—in Taanach and Megiddo, and in all of Beth Shan next to Zarethan below Jezreel, from Beth Shan to Abel Meholah across to Jokmeam;

[a] 15 Traditionally *peace offerings* [b] 11 Or *in the heights of Dor*

13 Ben-Geber—in Ramoth Gilead (the settlements of Jair son of Manasseh in Gilead were his, as well as the district of Argob in Bashan and its sixty large walled cities with bronze gate bars);
14 Ahinadab son of Iddo—in Mahanaim;
15 Ahimaaz—in Naphtali (he had married Basemath daughter of Solomon);
16 Baana son of Hushai—in Asher and in Aloth;
17 Jehoshaphat son of Paruah—in Issachar;
18 Shimei son of Ela—in Benjamin;
19 Geber son of Uri—in Gilead (the country of Sihon king of the Amorites and the country of Og king of Bashan). He was the only governor over the district.

Solomon's Daily Provisions

20The people of Judah and Israel were as
numerous as the sand on the seashore; they
ate, they drank and they were happy. 21And
Solomon ruled over all the kingdoms from the
River[a] to the land of the Philistines, as far as
the border of Egypt. These countries brought
tribute and were Solomon's subjects all his life.
22Solomon's daily provisions were thirty
cors[b] of fine flour and sixty cors[c] of meal,
23ten head of stall-fed cattle, twenty of pasture-fed cattle and a hundred sheep and goats,
as well as deer, gazelles, roebucks and choice
fowl. 24For he ruled over all the kingdoms west
of the River, from Tiphsah to Gaza, and had
peace on all sides. 25During Solomon's lifetime
Judah and Israel, from Dan to Beersheba, lived
in safety, each man under his own vine and
fig tree.

26Solomon had four[d] thousand stalls for
chariot horses, and twelve thousand horses.[e]

27The district officers, each in his month,
supplied provisions for King Solomon and all
who came to the king's table. They saw to it that
nothing was lacking. 28They also brought to the
proper place their quotas of barley and straw
for the chariot horses and the other horses.

> **1 Kings 4:29**
>
> *God Gives Wisdom*
>
> God gave Solomon wisdom and very great insight, and a breadth of understanding as measureless as the sand on the seashore.

Solomon's Wisdom

29God gave Solomon wisdom and very
great insight, and a breadth of understanding
as measureless as the sand on the seashore.
30Solomon's wisdom was greater than the wisdom of all the men of the East, and greater than
all the wisdom of Egypt. 31He
was wiser than any other man,
including Ethan the Ezrahite—
wiser than Heman, Calcol and
Darda, the sons of Mahol. And
his fame spread to all the surrounding nations. 32He spoke
three thousand proverbs and
his songs numbered a thousand
and five. 33He described plant
life, from the cedar of Lebanon
to the hyssop that grows out
of walls. He also taught about
animals and birds, reptiles and
fish. 34Men of all nations came
to listen to Solomon's wisdom,
sent by all the kings of the
world, who had heard of his wisdom.

Preparations for Building the Temple

5 When Hiram king of Tyre heard that Solomon had been anointed king to succeed
his father David, he sent his envoys to Solomon,
because he had always been on friendly terms
with David. 2Solomon sent back this message
to Hiram:

3"You know that because of the wars
waged against my father David from all
sides, he could not build a temple for the
Name of the LORD his God until the LORD
put his enemies under his feet. 4But now
the LORD my God has given me rest on
every side, and there is no adversary or disaster. 5I intend, therefore, to build a temple for the Name of the LORD my God,
as the LORD told my father David, when
he said, 'Your son whom I will put on the
throne in your place will build the temple
for my Name.'

6"So give orders that cedars of Lebanon
be cut for me. My men will work with
yours, and I will pay you for your men

[a]21 That is, the Euphrates; also in verse 24 [b]22 That is, probably about 185 bushels (about 6.6 kiloliters) [c]22 That is, probably about 375 bushels (about 13.2 kiloliters) [d]26 Some Septuagint manuscripts (see also 2 Chron. 9:25); Hebrew *forty* [e]26 Or *charioteers*

whatever wages you set. You know that we have no one so skilled in felling timber as the Sidonians."

7 When Hiram heard Solomon's message, he was greatly pleased and said, "Praise be to the LORD today, for he has given David a wise son to rule over this great nation."

8 So Hiram sent word to Solomon:

"I have received the message you sent me and will do all you want in providing the cedar and pine logs. 9 My men will haul them down from Lebanon to the sea, and I will float them in rafts by sea to the place you specify. There I will separate them and you can take them away. And you are to grant my wish by providing food for my royal household."

10 In this way Hiram kept Solomon supplied with all the cedar and pine logs he wanted, 11 and Solomon gave Hiram twenty thousand cors[a] of wheat as food for his household, in addition to twenty thousand baths[b,c] of pressed olive oil. Solomon continued to do this for Hiram year after year. 12 The LORD gave Solomon wisdom, just as he had promised him. There were peaceful relations between Hiram and Solomon, and the two of them made a treaty.

13 King Solomon conscripted laborers from all Israel—thirty thousand men. 14 He sent them off to Lebanon in shifts of ten thousand a month, so that they spent one month in Lebanon and two months at home. Adoniram was in charge of the forced labor. 15 Solomon had seventy thousand carriers and eighty thousand stonecutters in the hills, 16 as well as thirty-three hundred[d] foremen who supervised the project and directed the workmen. 17 At the king's command they removed from the quarry large blocks of quality stone to provide a foundation of dressed stone for the temple. 18 The craftsmen of Solomon and Hiram and the men of Gebal[e] cut and prepared the timber and stone for the building of the temple.

Solomon Builds the Temple

6 In the four hundred and eightieth[f] year after the Israelites had come out of Egypt, in the fourth year of Solomon's reign over Israel, in the month of Ziv, the second month, he began to build the temple of the LORD.

2 The temple that King Solomon built for the LORD was sixty cubits long, twenty wide and thirty high.[g] 3 The portico at the front of the main hall of the temple extended the width of the temple, that is twenty cubits,[h] and projected ten cubits[i] from the front of the temple. 4 He made narrow clerestory windows in the temple. 5 Against the walls of the main hall and inner sanctuary he built a structure around the building, in which there were side rooms. 6 The lowest floor was five cubits[j] wide, the middle floor six cubits[k] and the third floor seven.[l] He made offset ledges around the outside of the temple so that nothing would be inserted into the temple walls.

7 In building the temple, only blocks dressed at the quarry were used, and no hammer, chisel or any other iron tool was heard at the temple site while it was being built.

8 The entrance to the lowest[m] floor was on the south side of the temple; a stairway led up to the middle level and from there to the third. 9 So he built the temple and completed it, roofing it with beams and cedar planks. 10 And he built the side rooms all along the temple. The height of each was five cubits, and they were attached to the temple by beams of cedar.

11 The word of the LORD came to Solomon: 12 "As for this temple you are building, if you follow my decrees, carry out my regulations and keep all my commands and obey them, I will fulfill through you the promise I gave to David your father. 13 And I will live among the Israelites and will not abandon my people Israel."

14 So Solomon built the temple and completed it. 15 He lined its interior walls with cedar boards, paneling them from the floor of the temple to the ceiling, and covered the floor of the temple with planks of pine. 16 He parti-

[a] 11 That is, probably about 125,000 bushels (about 4,400 kiloliters) [b] 11 Septuagint (see also 2 Chron. 2:10); Hebrew *twenty cors* [c] 11 That is, about 115,000 gallons (about 440 kiloliters) [d] 16 Hebrew; some Septuagint manuscripts (see also 2 Chron. 2:2,18) *thirty-six hundred* [e] 18 That is, Byblos [f] 1 Hebrew; Septuagint *four hundred and fortieth* [g] 2 That is, about 90 feet (about 27 meters) long and 30 feet (about 9 meters) wide and 45 feet (about 13.5 meters) high [h] 3 That is, about 30 feet (about 9 meters) [i] 3 That is, about 15 feet (about 4.5 meters) [j] 6 That is, about 7 1/2 feet (about 2.3 meters); also in verses 10 and 24 [k] 6 That is, about 9 feet (about 2.7 meters) [l] 6 That is, about 10 1/2 feet (about 3.1 meters) [m] 8 Septuagint; Hebrew *middle*

tioned off twenty cubits[a] at the rear of the temple with cedar boards from floor to ceiling to
form within the temple an inner sanctuary, the
Most Holy Place. 17The main hall in front of
this room was forty cubits[b] long. 18The inside
of the temple was cedar, carved with gourds
and open flowers. Everything was cedar; no
stone was to be seen.
19He prepared the inner sanctuary within the
temple to set the ark of the covenant of the LORD there. 20The
inner sanctuary was twenty
cubits long, twenty wide and
twenty high.[c] He overlaid the
inside with pure gold, and he
also overlaid the altar of cedar.
21Solomon covered the inside
of the temple with pure gold,
and he extended gold chains
across the front of the inner
sanctuary, which was overlaid
with gold. 22So he overlaid the
whole interior with gold. He
also overlaid with gold the altar that belonged
to the inner sanctuary.
23In the inner sanctuary he made a pair of
cherubim of olive wood, each ten cubits[d] high.
24One wing of the first cherub was five cubits
long, and the other wing five cubits—ten cubits
from wing tip to wing tip. 25The second cherub
also measured ten cubits, for the two cherubim
were identical in size and shape. 26The height
of each cherub was ten cubits. 27He placed the
cherubim inside the innermost room of the
temple, with their wings spread out. The wing
of one cherub touched one wall, while the wing
of the other touched the other wall, and their
wings touched each other in the middle of the
room. 28He overlaid the cherubim with gold.
29On the walls all around the temple, in
both the inner and outer rooms, he carved cherubim, palm trees and open flowers. 30He also
covered the floors of both the inner and outer
rooms of the temple with gold.
31For the entrance of the inner sanctuary
he made doors of olive wood with five-sided
jambs. 32And on the two olive wood doors he
carved cherubim, palm trees and open flowers,
and overlaid the cherubim and palm trees with
beaten gold. 33In the same way he made four-
sided jambs of olive wood for the entrance to
the main hall. 34He also made two pine doors,
each having two leaves that turned in sockets.
35He carved cherubim, palm trees and open
flowers on them and overlaid them with gold
hammered evenly over the carvings.
36And he built the inner
courtyard of three courses of
dressed stone and one course
of trimmed cedar beams.
37The foundation of the temple of the LORD was laid in the
fourth year, in the month of
Ziv. 38In the eleventh year in
the month of Bul, the eighth
month, the temple was finished
in all its details according to its
specifications. He had spent
seven years building it.

1 Kings 6:13

God Refuses to Abandon Us

"And I will live among the Israelites and will not abandon my people Israel."

Solomon Builds His Palace

7 It took Solomon thirteen years, however,
to complete the construction of his palace.
2He built the Palace of the Forest of Lebanon
a hundred cubits long, fifty wide and thirty
high,[e] with four rows of cedar columns supporting trimmed cedar beams. 3It was roofed
with cedar above the beams that rested on the
columns—forty-five beams, fifteen to a row.
4Its windows were placed high in sets of three,
facing each other. 5All the doorways had rectangular frames; they were in the front part in
sets of three, facing each other.[f]
6He made a colonnade fifty cubits long and
thirty wide.[g] In front of it was a portico, and
in front of that were pillars and an overhanging roof.
7He built the throne hall, the Hall of Justice,
where he was to judge, and he covered it with
cedar from floor to ceiling.[h] 8And the palace
in which he was to live, set farther back, was
similar in design. Solomon also made a palace
like this hall for Pharaoh's daughter, whom he
had married.

[a]16 That is, about 30 feet (about 9 meters) [b]17 That is, about 60 feet (about 18 meters) [c]20 That is, about 30 feet (about 9 meters) long, wide and high [d]23 That is, about 15 feet (about 4.5 meters) [e]2 That is, about 150 feet (about 46 meters) long, 75 feet (about 23 meters) wide and 45 feet (about 13.5 meters) high [f]5 The meaning of the Hebrew for this verse is uncertain. [g]6 That is, about 75 feet (about 23 meters) long and 45 feet (about 13.5 meters) wide [h]7 Vulgate and Syriac; Hebrew *floor*

9All these structures, from the outside to the
great courtyard and from foundation to eaves,
were made of blocks of high-grade stone cut
to size and trimmed with a saw on their inner
and outer faces. 10The foundations were laid
with large stones of good quality, some measuring ten cubits[a] and some eight.[b] 11Above
were high-grade stones, cut to size, and cedar
beams. 12The great courtyard was surrounded
by a wall of three courses of dressed stone and
one course of trimmed cedar beams, as was the
inner courtyard of the temple of the LORD with
its portico.

The Temple's Furnishings

13King Solomon sent to Tyre and brought
Huram,[c] 14whose mother was a widow from
the tribe of Naphtali and whose father was a
man of Tyre and a craftsman in bronze. Huram
was highly skilled and experienced in all kinds
of bronze work. He came to King Solomon and
did all the work assigned to him.

15He cast two bronze pillars, each eighteen
cubits high and twelve cubits around,[d] by line.
16He also made two capitals of cast bronze to
set on the tops of the pillars; each capital was
five cubits[e] high. 17A network of interwoven
chains festooned the capitals on top of the pillars, seven for each capital. 18He made pomegranates in two rows[f] encircling each network
to decorate the capitals on top of the pillars.[g]
He did the same for each capital. 19The capitals on top of the pillars in the portico were in
the shape of lilies, four cubits[h] high. 20On the
capitals of both pillars, above the bowl-shaped
part next to the network, were the two hundred
pomegranates in rows all around. 21He erected
the pillars at the portico of the temple. The pillar to the south he named Jakin[i] and the one
to the north Boaz.[j] 22The capitals on top were
in the shape of lilies. And so the work on the
pillars was completed.

23He made the Sea of cast metal, circular
in shape, measuring ten cubits[a] from rim to
rim and five cubits high. It took a line of thirty
cubits[k] to measure around it. 24Below the
rim, gourds encircled it—ten to a cubit. The
gourds were cast in two rows in one piece with
the Sea.

25The Sea stood on twelve bulls, three facing north, three facing west, three facing south
and three facing east. The Sea rested on top of
them, and their hindquarters were toward the
center. 26It was a handbreadth[l] in thickness,
and its rim was like the rim of a cup, like a lily
blossom. It held two thousand baths.[m]

27He also made ten movable stands of
bronze; each was four cubits long, four wide
and three high.[n] 28This is how the stands were
made: They had side panels attached to uprights. 29On the panels between the uprights
were lions, bulls and cherubim—and on the uprights as well. Above and below the lions and
bulls were wreaths of hammered work. 30Each
stand had four bronze wheels with bronze axles,
and each had a basin resting on four supports,
cast with wreaths on each side. 31On the inside
of the stand there was an opening that had a
circular frame one cubit[o] deep. This opening
was round, and with its basework it measured
a cubit and a half.[p] Around its opening there
was engraving. The panels of the stands were
square, not round. 32The four wheels were under the panels, and the axles of the wheels were
attached to the stand. The diameter of each
wheel was a cubit and a half. 33The wheels
were made like chariot wheels; the axles, rims,
spokes and hubs were all of cast metal.

34Each stand had four handles, one on each
corner, projecting from the stand. 35At the top
of the stand there was a circular band half a
cubit[q] deep. The supports and panels were attached to the top of the stand. 36He engraved
cherubim, lions and palm trees on the surfaces
of the supports and on the panels, in every available space, with wreaths all around. 37This is
the way he made the ten stands. They were all

[a]10,23 That is, about 15 feet (about 4.5 meters) [b]10 That is, about 12 feet (about 3.6 meters) [c]13 Hebrew *Hiram*, a variant of *Huram*; also in verses 40 and 45 [d]15 That is, about 27 feet (about 8.1 meters) high and 18 feet (about 5.4 meters) around [e]16 That is, about 7 1/2 feet (about 2.3 meters); also in verse 23 [f]18 Two Hebrew manuscripts and Septuagint; most Hebrew manuscripts *made the pillars, and there were two rows* [g]18 Many Hebrew manuscripts and Syriac; most Hebrew manuscripts *pomegranates* [h]19 That is, about 6 feet (about 1.8 meters); also in verse 38 [i]21 *Jakin* probably means *he establishes.* [j]21 *Boaz* probably means *in him is strength.* [k]23 That is, about 45 feet (about 13.5 meters) [l]26 That is, about 3 inches (about 8 centimeters) [m]26 That is, probably about 11,500 gallons (about 44 kiloliters); the Septuagint does not have this sentence. [n]27 That is, about 6 feet (about 1.8 meters) long and wide and about 4 1/2 feet (about 1.3 meters) high [o]31 That is, about 1 1/2 feet (about 0.5 meter) [p]31 That is, about 2 1/4 feet (about 0.7 meter); also in verse 32 [q]35 That is, about 3/4 foot (about 0.2 meter)

cast in the same molds and were identical in
size and shape.
38 He then made ten bronze basins, each
holding forty baths[a] and measuring four cubits
across, one basin to go on each of the ten stands.
39 He placed five of the stands on the south side
of the temple and five on the north. He placed
the Sea on the south side, at the southeast corner of the temple. 40 He also made the basins
and shovels and sprinkling bowls.
So Huram finished all the work he had
undertaken for King Solomon in the temple of
the LORD:

41 the two pillars;
the two bowl-shaped capitals on top of
the pillars;
the two sets of network decorating the
two bowl-shaped capitals on top of the
pillars;
42 the four hundred pomegranates for the
two sets of network (two rows of pomegranates for each network, decorating
the bowl-shaped capitals on top of
the pillars);
43 the ten stands with their ten basins;
44 the Sea and the twelve bulls under it;
45 the pots, shovels and sprinkling bowls.

All these objects that Huram made for King
Solomon for the temple of the LORD were of
burnished bronze. 46 The king had them cast
in clay molds in the plain of the Jordan between Succoth and Zarethan. 47 Solomon left
all these things unweighed, because there were
so many; the weight of the bronze was not determined.
48 Solomon also made all the furnishings
that were in the LORD's temple:

the golden altar;
the golden table on which was the bread
of the Presence;
49 the lampstands of pure gold (five on the
right and five on the left, in front of the
inner sanctuary);
the gold floral work and lamps and tongs;
50 the pure gold basins, wick trimmers, sprinkling bowls, dishes and censers;
and the gold sockets for the doors of the
innermost room, the Most Holy Place,
and also for the doors of the main hall
of the temple.

51 When all the work King Solomon had
done for the temple of the LORD was finished,
he brought in the things his father David had
dedicated—the silver and gold and the furnishings—and he placed them in the treasuries of
the LORD's temple.

The Ark Brought to the Temple

8 Then King Solomon summoned into his
presence at Jerusalem the elders of Israel,
all the heads of the tribes and the chiefs of the
Israelite families, to bring up the ark of the
LORD's covenant from Zion, the City of David. 2 All the men of Israel came together to
King Solomon at the time of the festival in the
month of Ethanim, the seventh month.
3 When all the elders of Israel had arrived,
the priests took up the ark, 4 and they brought
up the ark of the LORD and the Tent of Meeting and all the sacred furnishings in it. The
priests and Levites carried them up, 5 and King
Solomon and the entire assembly of Israel that
had gathered about him were before the ark,
sacrificing so many sheep and cattle that they
could not be recorded or counted.
6 The priests then brought the ark of the
LORD's covenant to its place in the inner sanctuary of the temple, the Most Holy Place, and
put it beneath the wings of the cherubim. 7 The
cherubim spread their wings over the place of
the ark and overshadowed the ark and its carrying poles. 8 These poles were so long that their
ends could be seen from the Holy Place in front
of the inner sanctuary, but not from outside
the Holy Place; and they are still there today.
9 There was nothing in the ark except the two
stone tablets that Moses had placed in it at Horeb, where the LORD made a covenant with the
Israelites after they came out of Egypt.
10 When the priests withdrew from the Holy
Place, the cloud filled the temple of the LORD.
11 And the priests could not perform their service because of the cloud, for the glory of the
LORD filled his temple.
12 Then Solomon said, "The LORD has said
that he would dwell in a dark cloud; 13 I have

[a] 38 That is, about 230 gallons (about 880 liters)

1 Kings 8:57–58

"May the LORD our God be with us as he was with our fathers; may he never leave us nor forsake us. May he turn our hearts to him, to walk in all his ways and to keep the commands, decrees and regulations he gave our fathers."

Fit for His Dwelling

Read: 1 Kings 8:1–66

THE GRANDEUR OF OUR CITIES, the comforts of our homes, the conveniences of modern life saturate our consciousness. Unlike the Israelites, most of us do not lead a nomadic life, worshiping God in a tent designed for transience, by nature impermanent. We take for granted that the Holy Spirit now calls us the temple in which he resides. But consider what the temple meant to a people who longed for a lasting dwelling place for their God, a place of beauty where his presence would rest. Imagine the excitement when Solomon's magnificent temple was finally complete. As God's Spirit entered the completed sanctuary, it's likely that a reverential awe fell over the crowd.

Thousands of years have passed since that unforgettable day, and Solomon's temple is gone. But God continues to reside among us. He lives among us through his Holy Spirit and in each of us within the temple of our bodies. The God who could not be contained by the heavens has chosen his followers as the vessel of his presence.

But if God lives in us, why does it sometimes seem like he's far away? Solomon's prayer and blessing provide the answer: We lose our sense of God when our lives are not completely oriented to him. Verse 61 states: "But your hearts must be fully committed to the LORD." J. Oswald Sanders notes: "We are at this moment as close to God as we really choose to be. True, there are times when we would like to know a deeper intimacy, but when it comes to the point, we are not prepared to pay the price involved."

Solomon also recognized that we can't *force* God to dwell within us. The good things we do are never enough. In the end we are completely dependent upon God to make us fit for his dwelling, but if we invite him in, he will live with us. Jesus promised us this Spirit of truth, this Counselor, "If you love me, you will obey what I command. And I will ask the Father, and he will give you another Counselor to be with you forever—the Spirit of truth" (John 14:15–17). And Paul tells us that if the Spirit dwells in us, we will bear its harvest: "The fruit of the Spirit is love, joy, peace, patience, kindness, goodness, faithfulness, gentleness and self-control" (Galatians 5:22–23).

reflection

1 What does it mean to you to know that God dwells in you?

2 What is your reaction to the quote by J. Oswald Sanders? How intimate with God do you choose to be? What price would you pay to be closer to God?

3 When was the last time you were in awe of God or felt overwhelmed by his presence?

RELATED READINGS

Ezekiel 11:16–20; Romans 6:12–14; Ephesians 4:30; Hebrews 8:8–12

"God is above, presiding; beneath, sustaining; within, filling."

Hildebert of Lavardin

Go to page 418 for your next devotional reading.

indeed built a magnificent temple for you, a
place for you to dwell forever."
14While the whole assembly of Israel was
standing there, the king turned around and
blessed them. 15Then he said:

"Praise be to the LORD, the God of
Israel, who with his own hand has fulfilled
what he promised with his own mouth to
my father David. For he said, 16'Since
the day I brought my people Israel out
of Egypt, I have not chosen a city in any
tribe of Israel to have a temple built for
my Name to be there, but I have chosen
David to rule my people Israel.'
17"My father David had it in his heart
to build a temple for the Name of the
LORD, the God of Israel. 18But the LORD
said to my father David, 'Because it was
in your heart to build a temple for my
Name, you did well to have this in your
heart. 19Nevertheless, you are not the one
to build the temple, but your son, who is
your own flesh and blood—he is the one
who will build the temple for my Name.'
20"The LORD has kept the promise he
made: I have succeeded David my father
and now I sit on the throne of Israel, just
as the LORD promised, and I have built the
temple for the Name of the LORD, the God
of Israel. 21I have provided a place there
for the ark, in which is the covenant of the
LORD that he made with our fathers when
he brought them out of Egypt."

Solomon's Prayer of Dedication

22Then Solomon stood before the altar of
the LORD in front of the whole assembly of
Israel, spread out his hands toward heaven
23and said:

"O LORD, God of Israel, there is no
God like you in heaven above or on earth
below—you who keep your covenant of
love with your servants who continue
wholeheartedly in your way. 24You have
kept your promise to your servant David
my father; with your mouth you have
promised and with your hand you have
fulfilled it—as it is today.
25"Now LORD, God of Israel, keep
for your servant David my father the
promises you made to him when you
said, 'You shall never fail to have a man
to sit before me on the throne of Israel, if
only your sons are careful in all they do to
walk before me as you have done.' 26And
now, O God of Israel, let your word that
you promised your servant David my father come true.
27"But will God really dwell on earth?
The heavens, even the highest heaven,
cannot contain you. How much less this
temple I have built! 28Yet give attention
to your servant's prayer and his plea for
mercy, O LORD my God. Hear the cry and
the prayer that your servant is praying in
your presence this day. 29May your eyes
be open toward this temple night and day,
this place of which you said, 'My Name
shall be there,' so that you will hear the
prayer your servant prays toward this
place. 30Hear the supplication of your
servant and of your people Israel when
they pray toward this place. Hear from
heaven, your dwelling place, and when
you hear, forgive.
31"When a man wrongs his neighbor
and is required to take an oath and he
comes and swears the oath before your
altar in this temple, 32then hear from
heaven and act. Judge between your servants, condemning the guilty and bringing down on his own head what he has
done. Declare the innocent not guilty, and
so establish his innocence.
33"When your people Israel have been
defeated by an enemy because they have
sinned against you, and when they turn
back to you and confess your name, praying and making supplication to you in
this temple, 34then hear from heaven and
forgive the sin of your people Israel and
bring them back to the land you gave to
their fathers.
35"When the heavens are shut up and
there is no rain because your people have
sinned against you, and when they pray
toward this place and confess your name
and turn from their sin because you have
afflicted them, 36then hear from heaven
and forgive the sin of your servants, your

people Israel. Teach them the right way to
live, and send rain on the land you gave
your people for an inheritance.
37 "When famine or plague comes to
the land, or blight or mildew, locusts or
grasshoppers, or when an enemy besieges
them in any of their cities, whatever disaster or disease may come, 38 and when
a prayer or plea is made by any of your
people Israel—each one aware of the afflictions of his own heart, and spreading out
his hands toward this temple— 39 then
hear from heaven, your dwelling place.
Forgive and act; deal with each man according to all he does, since you know his
heart (for you alone know the hearts of all
men), 40 so that they will fear you all the
time they live in the land you gave our fathers.
41 "As for the foreigner who does not
belong to your people Israel but has
come from a distant land because of your
name— 42 for men will hear of your great
name and your mighty hand and your
outstretched arm—when he comes and
prays toward this temple, 43 then hear
from heaven, your dwelling place, and
do whatever the foreigner asks of you, so
that all the peoples of the earth may know
your name and fear you, as do your own
people Israel, and may know
that this house I have built
bears your Name.
44 "When your people go
to war against their enemies,
wherever you send them,
and when they pray to the
LORD toward the city you
have chosen and the temple
I have built for your Name,
45 then hear from heaven
their prayer and their plea,
and uphold their cause.
46 "When they sin against
you—for there is no one
who does not sin—and you
become angry with them
and give them over to the enemy, who
takes them captive to his own land, far
away or near; 47 and if they have a change
of heart in the land where they are held
captive, and repent and plead with you
in the land of their conquerors and say,
'We have sinned, we have done wrong, we
have acted wickedly'; 48 and if they turn
back to you with all their heart and soul in
the land of their enemies who took them
captive, and pray to you toward the land
you gave their fathers, toward the city
you have chosen and the temple I have
built for your Name; 49 then from heaven,
your dwelling place, hear their prayer and
their plea, and uphold their cause. 50 And
forgive your people, who have sinned
against you; forgive all the offenses they
have committed against you, and cause
their conquerors to show them mercy;
51 for they are your people and your inheritance, whom you brought out of Egypt,
out of that iron-smelting furnace.
52 "May your eyes be open to your servant's plea and to the plea of your people Israel, and may you listen to them
whenever they cry out to you. 53 For you
singled them out from all the nations of
the world to be your own inheritance,
just as you declared through your servant
Moses when you, O Sovereign LORD,
brought our fathers out of Egypt."
54 When Solomon had fin-
ished all these prayers and
supplications to the LORD, he
rose from before the altar of
the LORD, where he had been
kneeling with his hands spread
out toward heaven. 55 He stood
and blessed the whole assembly of Israel in a loud voice,
saying:
56 "Praise be to the
LORD, who has given rest
to his people Israel just
as he promised. Not one
word has failed of all the
good promises he gave
through his servant Mo-
ses. 57 May the LORD our God be with us
as he was with our fathers; may he never
leave us nor forsake us. 58 May he turn our

1 Kings 8:56

God Gives Rest

"Praise be to the LORD, who has given rest to his people Israel just as he promised. Not one word has failed of all the good promises he gave through his servant Moses."

hearts to him, to walk in all his ways and
to keep the commands, decrees and regulations he gave our fathers. 59And may
these words of mine, which I have prayed
before the LORD, be near to the LORD our
God day and night, that he may uphold
the cause of his servant and the cause of
his people Israel according to each day's
need, 60so that all the peoples of the earth
may know that the LORD is God and that
there is no other. 61But your hearts must
be fully committed to the LORD our God,
to live by his decrees and obey his commands, as at this time."

The Dedication of the Temple

62Then the king and all Israel with him offered sacrifices before the LORD. 63Solomon
offered a sacrifice of fellowship offerings[a] to
the LORD: twenty-two thousand cattle and a
hundred and twenty thousand sheep and goats.
So the king and all the Israelites dedicated the
temple of the LORD.
64On that same day the king consecrated
the middle part of the courtyard in front of the
temple of the LORD, and there he offered burnt
offerings, grain offerings and the fat of the fellowship offerings, because the bronze altar before the LORD was too small to hold the burnt
offerings, the grain offerings and the fat of the
fellowship offerings.
65So Solomon observed the festival at that
time, and all Israel with him—a vast assembly, people from Lebo[b] Hamath to the Wadi
of Egypt. They celebrated it before the LORD
our God for seven days and seven days more,
fourteen days in all. 66On the following day he
sent the people away. They blessed the king and
then went home, joyful and glad in heart for
all the good things the LORD had done for his
servant David and his people Israel.

The LORD Appears to Solomon

9 When Solomon had finished building the
temple of the LORD and the royal palace,
and had achieved all he had desired to do, 2the
LORD appeared to him a second time, as he
had appeared to him at Gibeon. 3The LORD
said to him:
"I have heard the prayer and plea you
have made before me; I have consecrated
this temple, which you have built, by putting my Name there forever. My eyes and
my heart will always be there.
4"As for you, if you walk before me in
integrity of heart and uprightness, as David your father did, and do all I command
and observe my decrees and laws, 5I will
establish your royal throne over Israel
forever, as I promised David your father
when I said, 'You shall never fail to have a
man on the throne of Israel.'
6"But if you[c] or your sons turn away
from me and do not observe the commands and decrees I have given you[c] and
go off to serve other gods and worship
them, 7then I will cut off Israel from the
land I have given them and will reject this
temple I have consecrated for my Name.
Israel will then become a byword and an
object of ridicule among all peoples. 8And
though this temple is now imposing, all
who pass by will be appalled and will
scoff and say, 'Why has the LORD done
such a thing to this land and to this temple?' 9People will answer, 'Because they
have forsaken the LORD their God, who
brought their fathers out of Egypt, and
have embraced other gods, worshiping
and serving them—that is why the LORD
brought all this disaster on them.'"

Solomon's Other Activities

10At the end of twenty years, during which
Solomon built these two buildings—the temple
of the LORD and the royal palace— 11King Solomon gave twenty towns in Galilee to Hiram
king of Tyre, because Hiram had supplied him
with all the cedar and pine and gold he wanted.
12But when Hiram went from Tyre to see the
towns that Solomon had given him, he was
not pleased with them. 13"What kind of towns
are these you have given me, my brother?" he
asked. And he called them the Land of Cabul,[d]
a name they have to this day. 14Now Hiram
had sent to the king 120 talents[e] of gold.
15Here is the account of the forced labor
King Solomon conscripted to build the LORD's

[a]63 Traditionally *peace offerings*; also in verse 64 [b]65 Or *from the entrance to* [c]6 The Hebrew is plural. [d]13 *Cabul* sounds like the Hebrew for *good-for-nothing.* [e]14 That is, about 4 1/2 tons (about 4 metric tons)

temple, his own palace, the supporting
terraces,[a] the wall of Jerusalem, and Hazor,
Megiddo and Gezer. 16 (Pharaoh king of Egypt
had attacked and captured Gezer. He had set it
on fire. He killed its Canaanite inhabitants and
then gave it as a wedding gift to his daughter,
Solomon's wife. 17 And Solomon rebuilt Gezer.)
He built up Lower Beth Horon, 18 Baalath, and
Tadmor[b] in the desert, within his land, 19 as
well as all his store cities and the towns for his
chariots and for his horses[c]—whatever he desired to build in Jerusalem, in Lebanon and
throughout all the territory he ruled.

20 All the people left from the Amorites, Hittites, Perizzites, Hivites and Jebusites (these
peoples were not Israelites), 21 that is, their descendants remaining in the land, whom the Israelites could not exterminate[d]—these Solomon
conscripted for his slave labor force, as it is to
this day. 22 But Solomon did not make slaves of
any of the Israelites; they were his fighting men,
his government officials, his officers, his captains, and the commanders of his chariots and
charioteers. 23 They were also the chief officials
in charge of Solomon's projects—550 officials
supervising the men who did the work.

24 After Pharaoh's daughter had come up
from the City of David to the palace Solomon
had built for her, he constructed the supporting terraces.

25 Three times a year Solomon sacrificed
burnt offerings and fellowship offerings[e] on
the altar he had built for the LORD, burning incense before the LORD along with them, and so
fulfilled the temple obligations.

26 King Solomon also built ships at Ezion
Geber, which is near Elath in Edom, on the
shore of the Red Sea.[f] 27 And Hiram sent his
men—sailors who knew the sea—to serve in
the fleet with Solomon's men. 28 They sailed to
Ophir and brought back 420 talents[g] of gold,
which they delivered to King Solomon.

The Queen of Sheba Visits Solomon

10 When the queen of Sheba heard about
the fame of Solomon and his relation
to the name of the LORD, she came to test him
with hard questions. 2 Arriving at Jerusalem
with a very great caravan—with camels carrying spices, large quantities of gold, and precious
stones—she came to Solomon and talked with
him about all that she had on her mind. 3 Solomon answered all her questions; nothing was
too hard for the king to explain to her. 4 When
the queen of Sheba saw all the wisdom of Solomon and the palace he had built, 5 the food on
his table, the seating of his officials, the attending servants in their robes, his cupbearers, and
the burnt offerings he made at[h] the temple of
the LORD, she was overwhelmed.

6 She said to the king, "The report I heard in
my own country about your achievements and
your wisdom is true. 7 But I did not believe these
things until I came and saw with my own eyes.
Indeed, not even half was told me; in wisdom
and wealth you have far exceeded the report I
heard. 8 How happy your men must be! How
happy your officials, who continually stand before you and hear your wisdom! 9 Praise be to the
LORD your God, who has delighted in you and
placed you on the throne of Israel. Because of the
LORD's eternal love for Israel, he has made you
king, to maintain justice and righteousness."

10 And she gave the king 120 talents[i] of gold,
large quantities of spices, and precious stones.
Never again were so many spices brought in as
those the queen of Sheba gave to King Solomon.

11 (Hiram's ships brought gold from Ophir;
and from there they brought great cargoes of
almugwood[j] and precious stones. 12 The king
used the almugwood to make supports for the
temple of the LORD and for the royal palace,
and to make harps and lyres for the musicians.
So much almugwood has never been imported
or seen since that day.)

13 King Solomon gave the queen of Sheba
all she desired and asked for, besides what he
had given her out of his royal bounty. Then
she left and returned with her retinue to her
own country.

Solomon's Splendor

14 The weight of the gold that Solomon received yearly was 666 talents,[k] 15 not including

[a] 15 Or *the Millo*; also in verse 24 [b] 18 The Hebrew may also be read *Tamar.* [c] 19 Or *charioteers* [d] 21 The Hebrew term refers to the irrevocable giving over of things or persons to the LORD, often by totally destroying them. [e] 25 Traditionally *peace offerings* [f] 26 Hebrew *Yam Suph*; that is, Sea of Reeds [g] 28 That is, about 16 tons (about 14.5 metric tons) [h] 5 Or *the ascent by which he went up to* [i] 10 That is, about 4 1/2 tons (about 4 metric tons) [j] 11 Probably a variant of *algumwood*; also in verse 12 [k] 14 That is, about 25 tons (about 23 metric tons)

the revenues from merchants and traders and
from all the Arabian kings and the governors
of the land.
16 King Solomon made two hundred large
shields of hammered gold; six hundred bekas[a]
of gold went into each shield. 17 He also made
three hundred small shields of hammered gold,
with three minas[b] of gold in each shield. The
king put them in the Palace of the Forest of
Lebanon.
18 Then the king made a great throne inlaid with ivory and overlaid with fine gold.
19 The throne had six steps, and its back had
a rounded top. On both sides of the seat were
armrests, with a lion standing beside each of
them. 20 Twelve lions stood on the six steps,
one at either end of each step. Nothing like it
had ever been made for any other kingdom.
21 All King Solomon's goblets were gold, and
all the household articles in the Palace of the
Forest of Lebanon were pure gold. Nothing was
made of silver, because silver was considered
of little value in Solomon's days. 22 The king
had a fleet of trading ships[c] at sea along with
the ships of Hiram. Once every three years it
returned, carrying gold, silver and ivory, and
apes and baboons.
23 King Solomon was greater in riches and
wisdom than all the other kings of the earth.
24 The whole world sought audience with Solomon to hear the wisdom God had put in his
heart. 25 Year after year, everyone who came
brought a gift—articles of silver and gold, robes,
weapons and spices, and horses and mules.
26 Solomon accumulated chariots and horses;
he had fourteen hundred chariots and twelve
thousand horses,[d] which he kept in the chariot
cities and also with him in Jerusalem. 27 The
king made silver as common in Jerusalem as
stones, and cedar as plentiful as sycamore-fig
trees in the foothills. 28 Solomon's horses were
imported from Egypt[e] and from Kue[f]—the
royal merchants purchased them from Kue.
29 They imported a chariot from Egypt for six
hundred shekels[g] of silver, and a horse for a
hundred and fifty.[b] They also exported them
to all the kings of the Hittites and of the Arameans.

Solomon's Wives

11 King Solomon, however, loved many
foreign women besides Pharaoh's
daughter—Moabites, Ammonites, Edomites,
Sidonians and Hittites. 2 They were from nations about which the LORD had told the Israelites, "You must not intermarry with them,
because they will surely turn your hearts after
their gods." Nevertheless, Solomon held fast to
them in love. 3 He had seven hundred wives of
royal birth and three hundred concubines, and
his wives led him astray. 4 As Solomon grew
old, his wives turned his heart after other gods,
and his heart was not fully devoted to the LORD
his God, as the heart of David his father had
been. 5 He followed Ashtoreth the goddess of
the Sidonians, and Molech[h] the detestable god
of the Ammonites. 6 So Solomon did evil in the
eyes of the LORD; he did not follow the LORD
completely, as David his father had done.
7 On a hill east of Jerusalem, Solomon built
a high place for Chemosh the detestable god
of Moab, and for Molech the detestable god of
the Ammonites. 8 He did the same for all his
foreign wives, who burned incense and offered
sacrifices to their gods.
9 The LORD became angry with Solomon
because his heart had turned away from the
LORD, the God of Israel, who had appeared to
him twice. 10 Although he had forbidden Solomon to follow other gods, Solomon did not
keep the LORD's command. 11 So the LORD said
to Solomon, "Since this is your attitude and you
have not kept my covenant and my decrees,
which I commanded you, I will most certainly
tear the kingdom away from you and give it to
one of your subordinates. 12 Nevertheless, for
the sake of David your father, I will not do it
during your lifetime. I will tear it out of the
hand of your son. 13 Yet I will not tear the whole
kingdom from him, but will give him one tribe
for the sake of David my servant and for the
sake of Jerusalem, which I have chosen."

Solomon's Adversaries

14 Then the LORD raised up against Solomon
an adversary, Hadad the Edomite, from the
royal line of Edom. 15 Earlier when David was

[a] **16** That is, about 7 1/2 pounds (about 3.5 kilograms) [b] **17,29** That is, about 3 3/4 pounds (about 1.7 kilograms) [c] **22** Hebrew *of ships of Tarshish* [d] **26** Or *charioteers* [e] **28** Or possibly *Muzur*, a region in Cilicia; also in verse 29 [f] **28** Probably *Cilicia* [g] **29** That is, about 15 pounds (about 7 kilograms) [h] **5** Hebrew *Milcom*; also in verse 33

The Woman Who Had Everything

Read: 1 Kings 10:1–29

1 Kings 10:1
When the queen of Sheba heard about the fame of Solomon and his relation to the name of the LORD, she came to test him with hard questions.

WHAT DO YOU ASK FOR if you are a queen? New jewels, a bigger palace or more servants? Maybe you look for wisdom. Here in 1 Kings 10 we meet the exotic queen of Sheba who had heard of King Solomon and the wisdom he possessed. So this woman, the ruler of a great empire in southern Arabia, ordered her servants to pack up her belongings and caravanned by camel to see the king. But she didn't come empty-handed. Like the Magi visiting Jesus, she came bearing gifts: spices, gold and precious stones. As a politician, she could have come to Solomon seeking a new trade route or asking for a peace treaty. But her purpose in making the long, grueling journey was clear: "She came to test him with hard questions" (1 Kings 10:1). The queen was on a spiritual quest, wanting to learn about Solomon's God. So she "talked with him about all that she had on her mind" (verse 2).

Do you have questions for God that you think he cannot or will not answer? Maybe you wonder about the origins of the universe. Perhaps you have questions about the apparent contradictions found in Scripture. It could be you have reservations about whether God even exists . . . or if you believe in his existence, you question whether he cares about the circumstances of your life.

Rest assured that God is not offended when you come to him with your candid questions. He knows that wisdom is more valuable than any treasure on earth. You don't need to be the queen of a nation or travel to a distant land to seek the answers to your heartfelt questions; you simply need to open the pages of God's Word and go to him in prayer. Solomon wrote, "Choose [God's] instruction instead of silver, knowledge rather than choice gold, for wisdom is more precious than rubies, and nothing you desire can compare with her" (Proverbs 8:10–11).

The woman who seemingly had everything the world had to offer knew she needed God's wisdom and went out of her way to obtain it. What lengths will you go to obtain the wisdom more valuable than jewels?

reflection

1. List some of the "hard questions" you'd bring to the wisest man on earth.
2. As you've grown in your faith, have some of your hard questions or seeming contradictions grown less important to you? Why or why not?
3. Spend some time telling God all that you have on your mind. Then listen to what he has on his.

RELATED READINGS

Psalm 72:1–17; Matthew 12:39–42

Wednesday

Go to page 427 for your next devotional reading.

fighting with Edom, Joab the commander
of the army, who had gone up to bury the
dead, had struck down all the men in Edom.
16 Joab and all the Israelites stayed there for six
months, until they had destroyed all the men
in Edom. 17 But Hadad, still only a boy, fled to
Egypt with some Edomite officials who had
served his father. 18 They set out from Midian
and went to Paran. Then taking men from Paran with them, they went to Egypt, to Pharaoh
king of Egypt, who gave Hadad a house and
land and provided him with food.

19 Pharaoh was so pleased with Hadad that
he gave him a sister of his own wife, Queen
Tahpenes, in marriage. 20 The sister of Tahpe-
nes bore him a son named Genubath, whom
Tahpenes brought up in the royal palace. There
Genubath lived with Pharaoh's own children.

21 While he was in Egypt, Hadad heard that
David rested with his fathers and that Joab the
commander of the army was also dead. Then
Hadad said to Pharaoh, "Let me go, that I may
return to my own country."

22 "What have you lacked here that you
want to go back to your own country?" Pharaoh asked.

"Nothing," Hadad replied, "but do let me
go!"

23 And God raised up against Solomon
another adversary, Rezon son of Eliada, who
had fled from his master, Hadadezer king of
Zobah. 24 He gathered men around him and
became the leader of a band of rebels when David destroyed the forces[a] ⌞of Zobah⌟; the rebels
went to Damascus, where they settled and took
control. 25 Rezon was Israel's adversary as long
as Solomon lived, adding to the trouble caused
by Hadad. So Rezon ruled in Aram and was
hostile toward Israel.

Jeroboam Rebels Against Solomon

26 Also, Jeroboam son of Nebat rebelled
against the king. He was one of Solomon's officials, an Ephraimite from Zeredah, and his
mother was a widow named Zeruah.

27 Here is the account of how he rebelled
against the king: Solomon had built the supporting terraces[b] and had filled in the gap in
the wall of the city of David his father. 28 Now
Jeroboam was a man of standing, and when
Solomon saw how well the young man did his
work, he put him in charge of the whole labor
force of the house of Joseph.

29 About that time Jeroboam was going out
of Jerusalem, and Ahijah the prophet of Shiloh
met him on the way, wearing a new cloak. The
two of them were alone out in the country,
30 and Ahijah took hold of the new cloak he was
wearing and tore it into twelve pieces. 31 Then
he said to Jeroboam, "Take ten pieces for yourself, for this is what the Lord, the God of Israel,
says: 'See, I am going to tear the kingdom out of
Solomon's hand and give you ten tribes. 32 But
for the sake of my servant David and the city of
Jerusalem, which I have chosen out of all the
tribes of Israel, he will have one tribe. 33 I will
do this because they have[c] forsaken me and
worshiped Ashtoreth the goddess of the Sidonians, Chemosh the god of the Moabites, and
Molech the god of the Ammonites, and have
not walked in my ways, nor done what is right
in my eyes, nor kept my statutes and laws as
David, Solomon's father, did.

34 "'But I will not take the whole kingdom
out of Solomon's hand; I have made him ruler
all the days of his life for the sake of David my
servant, whom I chose and who observed my
commands and statutes. 35 I will take the kingdom from his son's hands and give you ten
tribes. 36 I will give one tribe to his son so that
David my servant may always have a lamp before me in Jerusalem, the city where I chose to
put my Name. 37 However, as for you, I will take
you, and you will rule over all that your heart
desires; you will be king over Israel. 38 If you do
whatever I command you and walk in my ways
and do what is right in my eyes by keeping my
statutes and commands, as David my servant
did, I will be with you. I will build you a dynasty
as enduring as the one I built for David and will
give Israel to you. 39 I will humble David's descendants because of this, but not forever.'"

40 Solomon tried to kill Jeroboam, but
Jeroboam fled to Egypt, to Shishak the king,
and stayed there until Solomon's death.

Solomon's Death

41 As for the other events of Solomon's
reign—all he did and the wisdom he displayed—are they not written in the book of

[a] 24 Hebrew *destroyed them* [b] 27 Or *the Millo* [c] 33 Hebrew; Septuagint, Vulgate and Syriac *because he has*

the annals of Solomon? [42]Solomon reigned in
Jerusalem over all Israel forty years. [43]Then he
rested with his fathers and was buried in the
city of David his father. And Rehoboam his son
succeeded him as king.

Israel Rebels Against Rehoboam

12 Rehoboam went to Shechem, for all the
Israelites had gone there to make him
king. [2]When Jeroboam son of Nebat heard this
(he was still in Egypt, where he had fled from
King Solomon), he returned from[a] Egypt. [3]So
they sent for Jeroboam, and he and the whole
assembly of Israel went to Rehoboam and said
to him: [4]"Your father put a heavy yoke on us,
but now lighten the harsh labor and the heavy
yoke he put on us, and we will serve you."

[5]Rehoboam answered, "Go away for three
days and then come back to me." So the people
went away.

[6]Then King Rehoboam consulted the elders
who had served his father Solomon during his
lifetime. "How would you advise me to answer
these people?" he asked.

[7]They replied, "If today you will be a servant
to these people and serve them and give them
a favorable answer, they will always be your servants."

[8]But Rehoboam rejected the advice the elders gave him and consulted the young men
who had grown up with him and were serving
him. [9]He asked them, "What is your advice?
How should we answer these people who say to
me, 'Lighten the yoke your father put on us'?"

[10]The young men who had grown up with
him replied, "Tell these people who have said
to you, 'Your father put a heavy yoke on us, but
make our yoke lighter'—tell them, 'My little
finger is thicker than my father's waist. [11]My
father laid on you a heavy yoke; I will make
it even heavier. My father scourged you with
whips; I will scourge you with scorpions.'"

[12]Three days later Jeroboam and all the people returned to Rehoboam, as the king had
said, "Come back to me in three days." [13]The
king answered the people harshly. Rejecting
the advice given him by the elders, [14]he followed the advice of the young men and said,
"My father made your yoke heavy; I will make
it even heavier. My father scourged you with
whips; I will scourge you with scorpions." [15]So
the king did not listen to the people, for this
turn of events was from the LORD, to fulfill the
word the LORD had spoken to Jeroboam son of
Nebat through Ahijah the Shilonite.

[16]When all Israel saw that the king refused
to listen to them, they answered the king:

"What share do we have in David,
  what part in Jesse's son?
To your tents, O Israel!
  Look after your own house, O David!"

So the Israelites went home. [17]But as for the Israelites who were living in the towns of Judah,
Rehoboam still ruled over them.

[18]King Rehoboam sent out Adoniram,[b]
who was in charge of forced labor, but all
Israel stoned him to death. King Rehoboam,
however, managed to get into his chariot and
escape to Jerusalem. [19]So Israel has been in rebellion against the house of David to this day.

[20]When all the Israelites heard that Jeroboam
had returned, they sent and called him to the
assembly and made him king over all Israel.
Only the tribe of Judah remained loyal to the
house of David.

[21]When Rehoboam arrived in Jerusalem,
he mustered the whole house of Judah and the
tribe of Benjamin—a hundred and eighty thousand fighting men—to make war against the
house of Israel and to regain the kingdom for
Rehoboam son of Solomon.

[22]But this word of God came to Shemaiah
the man of God: [23]"Say to Rehoboam son of
Solomon king of Judah, to the whole house of
Judah and Benjamin, and to the rest of the people, [24]'This is what the LORD says: Do not go up
to fight against your brothers, the Israelites. Go
home, every one of you, for this is my doing.'"
So they obeyed the word of the LORD and went
home again, as the LORD had ordered.

Golden Calves at Bethel and Dan

[25]Then Jeroboam fortified Shechem in the
hill country of Ephraim and lived there. From
there he went out and built up Peniel.[c]

[26]Jeroboam thought to himself, "The kingdom will now likely revert to the house of

[a]2 Or *he remained in* [b]18 Some Septuagint manuscripts and Syriac (see also 1 Kings 4:6 and 5:14); Hebrew *Adoram* [c]25 Hebrew *Penuel,* a variant of *Peniel*

David. 27If these people go up to offer sacrifices
at the temple of the LORD in Jerusalem, they
will again give their allegiance to their lord,
Rehoboam king of Judah. They will kill me and
return to King Rehoboam."
28After seeking advice, the
king made two golden calves.
He said to the people, "It is
too much for you to go up to
Jerusalem. Here are your gods,
O Israel, who brought you up
out of Egypt." 29One he set up
in Bethel, and the other in Dan.
30And this thing became a sin;
the people went even as far as
Dan to worship the one there.
31Jeroboam built shrines
on high places and appointed
priests from all sorts of people, even though they were
not Levites. 32He instituted a
festival on the fifteenth day of
the eighth month, like the festival held in Judah, and offered
sacrifices on the altar. This he
did in Bethel, sacrificing to the calves he had
made. And at Bethel he also installed priests
at the high places he had made. 33On the fifteenth day of the eighth month, a month of his
own choosing, he offered sacrifices on the altar
he had built at Bethel. So he instituted the festival for the Israelites and went up to the altar to
make offerings.

The Man of God From Judah

13 By the word of the LORD a man of
God came from Judah to Bethel, as
Jeroboam was standing by the altar to make
an offering. 2He cried out against the altar by
the word of the LORD: "O altar, altar! This is
what the LORD says: 'A son named Josiah will
be born to the house of David. On you he will
sacrifice the priests of the high places who now
make offerings here, and human bones will be
burned on you.'" 3That same day the man of
God gave a sign: "This is the sign the LORD has
declared: The altar will be split apart and the
ashes on it will be poured out."
4When King Jeroboam heard what the man
of God cried out against the altar at Bethel, he
stretched out his hand from the altar and said,
"Seize him!" But the hand he stretched out toward the man shriveled up, so that he could not
pull it back. 5Also, the altar was split apart and
its ashes poured out according to the sign given
by the man of God by the word
of the LORD.

> 1 Kings 13:6
>
> *God Answers Prayer*
>
> Then the king said . . . "Intercede with the LORD your God and pray for me that my hand may be restored." So the man of God interceded with the LORD, and the king's hand was restored and became as it was before.

6Then the king said to the
man of God, "Intercede with
the LORD your God and pray
for me that my hand may be
restored." So the man of God
interceded with the LORD, and
the king's hand was restored
and became as it was before.
7The king said to the man
of God, "Come home with me
and have something to eat, and
I will give you a gift."
8But the man of God an-
swered the king, "Even if you
were to give me half your possessions, I would not go with
you, nor would I eat bread or
drink water here. 9For I was
commanded by the word of the LORD: 'You
must not eat bread or drink water or return by
the way you came.'" 10So he took another road
and did not return by the way he had come to
Bethel.
11Now there was a certain old prophet living
in Bethel, whose sons came and told him all
that the man of God had done there that day.
They also told their father what he had said to
the king. 12Their father asked them, "Which
way did he go?" And his sons showed him
which road the man of God from Judah had
taken. 13So he said to his sons, "Saddle the donkey for me." And when they had saddled the
donkey for him, he mounted it 14and rode after
the man of God. He found him sitting under an
oak tree and asked, "Are you the man of God
who came from Judah?"
"I am," he replied.
15So the prophet said to him, "Come home
with me and eat."
16The man of God said, "I cannot turn back
and go with you, nor can I eat bread or drink
water with you in this place. 17I have been
told by the word of the LORD: 'You must not

eat bread or drink water there or return by the
way you came.'"
18The old prophet answered, "I too am a
prophet, as you are. And an angel said to me
by the word of the LORD: 'Bring him back with
you to your house so that he may eat bread and
drink water.'" (But he was lying to him.) 19So
the man of God returned with him and ate and
drank in his house.
20While they were sitting at the table, the
word of the LORD came to the old prophet
who had brought him back. 21He cried out to
the man of God who had come from Judah,
"This is what the LORD says: 'You have defied
the word of the LORD and have not kept the
command the LORD your God gave you. 22You
came back and ate bread and drank water in
the place where he told you not to eat or drink.
Therefore your body will not be buried in the
tomb of your fathers.'"
23When the man of God had finished eating
and drinking, the prophet who had brought
him back saddled his donkey for him. 24As he
went on his way, a lion met him on the road
and killed him, and his body was thrown down
on the road, with both the donkey and the lion
standing beside it. 25Some people who passed
by saw the body thrown down there, with
the lion standing beside the body, and they
went and reported it in the city where the old
prophet lived.
26When the prophet who had brought him
back from his journey heard of it, he said, "It
is the man of God who defied the word of the
LORD. The LORD has given him over to the lion,
which has mauled him and killed him, as the
word of the LORD had warned him."
27The prophet said to his sons, "Saddle the
donkey for me," and they did so. 28Then he
went out and found the body thrown down on
the road, with the donkey and the lion standing beside it. The lion had neither eaten the
body nor mauled the donkey. 29So the prophet
picked up the body of the man of God, laid it on
the donkey, and brought it back to his own city
to mourn for him and bury him. 30Then he laid
the body in his own tomb, and they mourned
over him and said, "Oh, my brother!"
31After burying him, he said to his sons,
"When I die, bury me in the grave where the
man of God is buried; lay my bones beside his
bones. 32For the message he declared by the
word of the LORD against the altar in Bethel and
against all the shrines on the high places in the
towns of Samaria will certainly come true."
33Even after this, Jeroboam did not change
his evil ways, but once more appointed priests
for the high places from all sorts of people.
Anyone who wanted to become a priest he
consecrated for the high places. 34This was
the sin of the house of Jeroboam that led to its
downfall and to its destruction from the face
of the earth.

Ahijah's Prophecy Against Jeroboam

14 At that time Abijah son of Jeroboam
became ill, 2and Jeroboam said to his
wife, "Go, disguise yourself, so you won't be recognized as the wife of Jeroboam. Then go to
Shiloh. Ahijah the prophet is there—the one
who told me I would be king over this people.
3Take ten loaves of bread with you, some cakes
and a jar of honey, and go to him. He will tell
you what will happen to the boy." 4So Jeroboam's wife did what he said and went to Ahijah's
house in Shiloh.
Now Ahijah could not see; his sight was
gone because of his age. 5But the LORD had
told Ahijah, "Jeroboam's wife is coming to ask
you about her son, for he is ill, and you are to
give her such and such an answer. When she arrives, she will pretend to be someone else."
6So when Ahijah heard the sound of her
footsteps at the door, he said, "Come in, wife
of Jeroboam. Why this pretense? I have been
sent to you with bad news. 7Go, tell Jeroboam
that this is what the LORD, the God of Israel,
says: 'I raised you up from among the people
and made you a leader over my people Israel.
8I tore the kingdom away from the house of
David and gave it to you, but you have not
been like my servant David, who kept my commands and followed me with all his heart, doing only what was right in my eyes. 9You have
done more evil than all who lived before you.
You have made for yourself other gods, idols
made of metal; you have provoked me to anger
and thrust me behind your back.
10"'Because of this, I am going to bring disaster on the house of Jeroboam. I will cut off

from Jeroboam every last male in Israel—slave or free. I will burn up the house of Jeroboam as one burns dung, until it is all gone. 11 Dogs will eat those belonging to Jeroboam who die in the city, and the birds of the air will feed on those who die in the country. The LORD has spoken!'

> 1 Kings 14:9
>
> **God Desires Worship**
>
> "You have done more evil than all who lived before you. You have made for yourself other gods, idols made of metal; you have provoked me to anger and thrust me behind your back."

12 "As for you, go back home. When you set foot in your city, the boy will die. 13 All Israel will mourn for him and bury him. He is the only one belonging to Jeroboam who will be buried, because he is the only one in the house of Jeroboam in whom the LORD, the God of Israel, has found anything good.

14 "The LORD will raise up for himself a king over Israel who will cut off the family of Jeroboam. This is the day! What? Yes, even now.[a] 15 And the LORD will strike Israel, so that it will be like a reed swaying in the water. He will uproot Israel from this good land that he gave to their forefathers and scatter them beyond the River,[b] because they provoked the LORD to anger by making Asherah poles.[c] 16 And he will give Israel up because of the sins Jeroboam has committed and has caused Israel to commit."

17 Then Jeroboam's wife got up and left and went to Tirzah. As soon as she stepped over the threshold of the house, the boy died. 18 They buried him, and all Israel mourned for him, as the LORD had said through his servant the prophet Ahijah.

19 The other events of Jeroboam's reign, his wars and how he ruled, are written in the book of the annals of the kings of Israel. 20 He reigned for twenty-two years and then rested with his fathers. And Nadab his son succeeded him as king.

Rehoboam King of Judah

21 Rehoboam son of Solomon was king in Judah. He was forty-one years old when he became king, and he reigned seventeen years in Jerusalem, the city the LORD had chosen out of all the tribes of Israel in which to put his Name. His mother's name was Naamah; she was an Ammonite.

22 Judah did evil in the eyes of the LORD. By the sins they committed they stirred up his jealous anger more than their fathers had done. 23 They also set up for themselves high places, sacred stones and Asherah poles on every high hill and under every spreading tree. 24 There were even male shrine prostitutes in the land; the people engaged in all the detestable practices of the nations the LORD had driven out before the Israelites.

25 In the fifth year of King Rehoboam, Shishak king of Egypt attacked Jerusalem. 26 He carried off the treasures of the temple of the LORD and the treasures of the royal palace. He took everything, including all the gold shields Solomon had made. 27 So King Rehoboam made bronze shields to replace them and assigned these to the commanders of the guard on duty at the entrance to the royal palace. 28 Whenever the king went to the LORD's temple, the guards bore the shields, and afterward they returned them to the guardroom.

29 As for the other events of Rehoboam's reign, and all he did, are they not written in the book of the annals of the kings of Judah? 30 There was continual warfare between Rehoboam and Jeroboam. 31 And Rehoboam rested with his fathers and was buried with them in the City of David. His mother's name was Naamah; she was an Ammonite. And Abijah[d] his son succeeded him as king.

Abijah King of Judah

15 In the eighteenth year of the reign of Jeroboam son of Nebat, Abijah[e] became king of Judah, 2 and he reigned in

[a] 14 The meaning of the Hebrew for this sentence is uncertain. [b] 15 That is, the Euphrates [c] 15 That is, symbols of the goddess Asherah; here and elsewhere in 1 Kings [d] 31 Some Hebrew manuscripts and Septuagint (see also 2 Chron. 12:16); most Hebrew manuscripts *Abijam* [e] 1 Some Hebrew manuscripts and Septuagint (see also 2 Chron. 12:16); most Hebrew manuscripts *Abijam*; also in verses 7 and 8

Jerusalem three years. His mother's name was
Maacah daughter of Abishalom.[a]
3He committed all the sins his father had
done before him; his heart was not fully devoted
to the LORD his God, as the heart of David his
forefather had been. 4Nevertheless, for David's
sake the LORD his God gave him a lamp in Jerusalem by raising up a son to succeed him and
by making Jerusalem strong. 5For David had
done what was right in the eyes of the LORD
and had not failed to keep any of the LORD's
commands all the days of his life—except in
the case of Uriah the Hittite.
6There was war between Rehoboam[b] and
Jeroboam throughout ⌞Abijah's⌟ lifetime. 7As
for the other events of Abijah's reign, and all
he did, are they not written in the book of the
annals of the kings of Judah? There was war
between Abijah and Jeroboam. 8And Abijah
rested with his fathers and was buried in the
City of David. And Asa his son succeeded him
as king.

Asa King of Judah

9In the twentieth year of Jeroboam king
of Israel, Asa became king of Judah, 10and
he reigned in Jerusalem forty-one years. His
grandmother's name was Maacah daughter
of Abishalom.
11Asa did what was right in the eyes of the
LORD, as his father David had done. 12He expelled the male shrine prostitutes from the land
and got rid of all the idols his fathers had made.
13He even deposed his grandmother Maacah
from her position as queen mother, because
she had made a repulsive Asherah pole. Asa
cut the pole down and burned it in the Kidron
Valley. 14Although he did not remove the high
places, Asa's heart was fully committed to the
LORD all his life. 15He brought into the temple
of the LORD the silver and gold and the articles
that he and his father had dedicated.
16There was war between Asa and Baasha
king of Israel throughout their reigns. 17Baasha
king of Israel went up against Judah and fortified Ramah to prevent anyone from leaving or
entering the territory of Asa king of Judah.
18Asa then took all the silver and gold that
was left in the treasuries of the LORD's temple
and of his own palace. He entrusted it to his officials and sent them to Ben-Hadad son of Tab-
rimmon, the son of Hezion, the king of Aram,
who was ruling in Damascus. 19"Let there be a
treaty between me and you," he said, "as there
was between my father and your father. See, I
am sending you a gift of silver and gold. Now
break your treaty with Baasha king of Israel so
he will withdraw from me."
20Ben-Hadad agreed with King Asa and
sent the commanders of his forces against
the towns of Israel. He conquered Ijon, Dan,
Abel Beth Maacah and all Kinnereth in addition to Naphtali. 21When Baasha heard this,
he stopped building Ramah and withdrew to
Tirzah. 22Then King Asa issued an order to all
Judah—no one was exempt—and they carried
away from Ramah the stones and timber Baasha had been using there. With them King Asa
built up Geba in Benjamin, and also Mizpah.
23As for all the other events of Asa's reign,
all his achievements, all he did and the cities
he built, are they not written in the book of the
annals of the kings of Judah? In his old age,
however, his feet became diseased. 24Then Asa
rested with his fathers and was buried with
them in the city of his father David. And Jehoshaphat his son succeeded him as king.

Nadab King of Israel

25Nadab son of Jeroboam became king of
Israel in the second year of Asa king of Judah,
and he reigned over Israel two years. 26He did
evil in the eyes of the LORD, walking in the
ways of his father and in his sin, which he had
caused Israel to commit.
27Baasha son of Ahijah of the house of Issachar plotted against him, and he struck him
down at Gibbethon, a Philistine town, while
Nadab and all Israel were besieging it. 28Baa-
sha killed Nadab in the third year of Asa king
of Judah and succeeded him as king.
29As soon as he began to reign, he killed
Jeroboam's whole family. He did not leave
Jeroboam anyone that breathed, but destroyed
them all, according to the word of the LORD
given through his servant Ahijah the Shilonite— 30because of the sins Jeroboam had
committed and had caused Israel to commit,

[a] 2 A variant of *Absalom*; also in verse 10 [b] 6 Most Hebrew manuscripts; some Hebrew manuscripts and Syriac *Abijam* (that is, Abijah)

and because he provoked the LORD, the God of
Israel, to anger.
31As for the other events of Nadab's reign,
and all he did, are they not written in the book
of the annals of the kings of Israel? 32There
was war between Asa and Baasha king of Israel
throughout their reigns.

Baasha King of Israel

33In the third year of Asa king of Judah, Baasha son of Ahijah became king of all Israel in
Tirzah, and he reigned twenty-four years. 34He
did evil in the eyes of the LORD, walking in the
ways of Jeroboam and in his sin, which he had
caused Israel to commit.

16 Then the word of the LORD came to
Jehu son of Hanani against Baasha:
2"I lifted you up from the dust and made you
leader of my people Israel, but you walked in
the ways of Jeroboam and caused my people
Israel to sin and to provoke me to anger by
their sins. 3So I am about to consume Baasha
and his house, and I will make your house like
that of Jeroboam son of Nebat. 4Dogs will eat
those belonging to Baasha who die in the city,
and the birds of the air will feed on those who
die in the country."
5As for the other events of Baasha's reign,
what he did and his achievements, are they not
written in the book of the annals of the kings of
Israel? 6Baasha rested with his fathers and was
buried in Tirzah. And Elah his son succeeded
him as king.
7Moreover, the word of the LORD came
through the prophet Jehu son of Hanani to Baasha and his house, because of all the evil he had
done in the eyes of the LORD, provoking him to
anger by the things he did, and becoming like
the house of Jeroboam—and also because he
destroyed it.

Elah King of Israel

8In the twenty-sixth year of Asa king of Judah, Elah son of Baasha became king of Israel,
and he reigned in Tirzah two years.
9Zimri, one of his officials, who had command of half his chariots, plotted against him.
Elah was in Tirzah at the time, getting drunk
in the home of Arza, the man in charge of the
palace at Tirzah. 10Zimri came in, struck him
down and killed him in the twenty-seventh
year of Asa king of Judah. Then he succeeded
him as king.
11As soon as he began to reign and was
seated on the throne, he killed off Baasha's
whole family. He did not spare a single male,
whether relative or friend. 12So Zimri destroyed
the whole family of Baasha, in accordance
with the word of the LORD spoken against Baasha through the prophet Jehu— 13because of
all the sins Baasha and his son Elah had committed and had caused Israel to commit, so that
they provoked the LORD, the God of Israel, to
anger by their worthless idols.
14As for the other events of Elah's reign, and
all he did, are they not written in the book of
the annals of the kings of Israel?

Zimri King of Israel

15In the twenty-seventh year of Asa king of
Judah, Zimri reigned in Tirzah seven days. The
army was encamped near Gibbethon, a Philistine town. 16When the Israelites in the camp
heard that Zimri had plotted against the king
and murdered him, they proclaimed Omri, the
commander of the army, king over Israel that
very day there in the camp. 17Then Omri and
all the Israelites with him withdrew from Gibbethon and laid siege to Tirzah. 18When Zimri
saw that the city was taken, he went into the
citadel of the royal palace and set the palace
on fire around him. So he died, 19because of
the sins he had committed, doing evil in the
eyes of the LORD and walking in the ways of
Jeroboam and in the sin he had committed and
had caused Israel to commit.
20As for the other events of Zimri's reign,
and the rebellion he carried out, are they not
written in the book of the annals of the kings
of Israel?

Omri King of Israel

21Then the people of Israel were split into
two factions; half supported Tibni son of Ginath for king, and the other half supported
Omri. 22But Omri's followers proved stronger
than those of Tibni son of Ginath. So Tibni
died and Omri became king.
23In the thirty-first year of Asa king of
Judah, Omri became king of Israel, and he
reigned twelve years, six of them in Tirzah.
24He bought the hill of Samaria from Shemer

for two talents[a] of silver and built a city on the
hill, calling it Samaria, after Shemer, the name
of the former owner of the hill.
25But Omri did evil in the eyes of the LORD
and sinned more than all those before him.
26He walked in all the ways of Jeroboam son
of Nebat and in his sin, which he had caused
Israel to commit, so that they provoked the
LORD, the God of Israel, to anger by their
worthless idols.
27As for the other events of Omri's reign,
what he did and the things he achieved, are
they not written in the book of the annals of the
kings of Israel? 28Omri rested with his fathers
and was buried in Samaria. And Ahab his son
succeeded him as king.

Ahab Becomes King of Israel

29In the thirty-eighth year of Asa king of Judah, Ahab son of Omri became king of Israel,
and he reigned in Samaria over Israel twenty-
two years. 30Ahab son of Omri did more evil in
the eyes of the LORD than any of those before
him. 31He not only considered it trivial to commit the sins of Jeroboam son of Nebat, but he
also married Jezebel daughter of Ethbaal king
of the Sidonians, and began to serve Baal and
worship him. 32He set up an altar for Baal in the
temple of Baal that he built in Samaria. 33Ahab
also made an Asherah pole and did more to provoke the LORD, the God of Israel, to anger than
did all the kings of Israel before him.
34In Ahab's time, Hiel of Bethel rebuilt Jericho. He laid its foundations at the cost of his
firstborn son Abiram, and he set up its gates
at the cost of his youngest son Segub, in accordance with the word of the LORD spoken by
Joshua son of Nun.

Elijah Fed by Ravens

17 Now Elijah the Tishbite, from Tishbe[b]
in Gilead, said to Ahab, "As the LORD,
the God of Israel, lives, whom I serve, there will
be neither dew nor rain in the next few years
except at my word."
2Then the word of the LORD came to Elijah:
3"Leave here, turn eastward and hide in the Kerith Ravine, east of the Jordan. 4You will drink
from the brook, and I have ordered the ravens
to feed you there."
5So he did what the LORD had told him. He
went to the Kerith Ravine, east of the Jordan,
and stayed there. 6The ravens brought him
bread and meat in the morning and bread
and meat in the evening, and he drank from
the brook.

The Widow at Zarephath

7Some time later the brook dried up because
there had been no rain in the land. 8Then the
word of the LORD came to him: 9"Go at once
to Zarephath of Sidon and stay there. I have
commanded a widow in that place to supply
you with food." 10So he went to Zarephath.
When he came to the town gate, a widow was
there gathering sticks. He called to her and
asked, "Would you bring me a little water in
a jar so I may have a drink?" 11As she was going to get it, he called, "And bring me, please, a
piece of bread."
12"As surely as the LORD your God lives," she
replied, "I don't have any bread—only a handful of flour in a jar and a little oil in a jug. I am
gathering a few sticks to take home and make
a meal for myself and my son, that we may eat
it—and die."
13Elijah said to her, "Don't be afraid. Go
home and do as you have said. But first make a
small cake of bread for me from what you have
and bring it to me, and then make something
for yourself and your son. 14For this is what
the LORD, the God of Israel, says: 'The jar of
flour will not be used up and the jug of oil will
not run dry until the day the LORD gives rain
on the land.'"
15She went away and did as Elijah had told
her. So there was food every day for Elijah and
for the woman and her family. 16For the jar of
flour was not used up and the jug of oil did not
run dry, in keeping with the word of the LORD
spoken by Elijah.
17Some time later the son of the woman who
owned the house became ill. He grew worse
and worse, and finally stopped breathing. 18She
said to Elijah, "What do you have against me,
man of God? Did you come to remind me of
my sin and kill my son?"
19"Give me your son," Elijah replied. He
took him from her arms, carried him to the

[a]24 That is, about 150 pounds (about 70 kilograms) [b]1 Or *Tishbite, of the settlers*

Nothing's Impossible

Read: 1 Kings 17:7–24

"FAITH SEES THE INVISIBLE, believes the unbelievable and receives the impossible." It may be easy to say these words when times are good and food is plenty. But these words were spoken by Corrie ten Boom, who, along with her sister Betsie, suffered horribly at the hands of Nazi guards at the Ravensbruck concentration camp. They were imprisoned for providing a hiding place for persecuted Jews from Hitler's murderous Nazis.

With Betsie sick, Corrie tried to hoard a tiny brown bottle of liquid vitamins, but other women burned with fever, their teeth chattered with chill. She wanted to save the small amount left for the weakest inmates—but the numbers grew, reaching as many as 25. Corrie knew that sharing the drops would mean she'd have none left for her sister, but Betsie was emphatic that God would provide.

Amazingly, every time Corrie tilted the bottle for a sick inmate, one drop would pour out. When there couldn't possibly be any more, another dose was dispensed. When a guard smuggled in some vitamins for the prisoners, Corrie was elated. But first she determined to finish the drops in the bottle. She tipped it over, but no matter how hard she shook, no more came out.

Elijah was not in a prison camp, but the land was suffering from God's judgment of drought and famine. When he was hiding from King Ahab and he found refuge with a widow and her son, their jar of flour and jug of oil never ran dry. God faithfully supplied for his prophet and the people who harbored him during their time of need.

It may seem impossible to you that God would supply you with such basic things as flour and vitamins, but these stories are about the Savior who is the same yesterday, today and forever. What do you need from God? Is the paycheck barely enough to cover the bills? Do the clothes seem as though they won't last another season? Do you feel you can't handle another day in your present circumstances? Ask God to provide everything you need to live. He will multiply his grace toward you in your times of trouble. He sees you in your hiding place and will find a way to meet your needs. Believe it. All things are possible with God.

1 Kings 17:16

For the jar of flour was not used up and the jug of oil did not run dry, in keeping with the word of the LORD spoken by Elijah.

reflection

1 Describe a time in your life when your faith was running dry and you needed God to come through.

2 How did God provide?

3 Are you in need of anything from God right now? If you are in want, ask God to multiply what you have to meet your needs.

RELATED READINGS

Psalm 37:23–26; John 6:1–13; Philippians 4:10–12

Go to page 429 for your next devotional reading.

upper room where he was staying, and laid him on his bed. 20Then he cried out to the LORD, "O LORD my God, have you brought tragedy also upon this widow I am staying with, by causing her son to die?" 21Then he stretched himself out on the boy three times and cried to the LORD, "O LORD my God, let this boy's life return to him!"

22The LORD heard Elijah's cry, and the boy's life returned to him, and he lived. 23Elijah picked up the child and carried him down from the room into the house. He gave him to his mother and said, "Look, your son is alive!"

24Then the woman said to Elijah, "Now I know that you are a man of God and that the word of the LORD from your mouth is the truth."

Elijah and Obadiah

18 After a long time, in the third year, the word of the LORD came to Elijah: "Go and present yourself to Ahab, and I will send rain on the land." 2So Elijah went to present himself to Ahab.

Now the famine was severe in Samaria, 3and Ahab had summoned Obadiah, who was in charge of his palace. (Obadiah was a devout believer in the LORD. 4While Jezebel was killing off the LORD's prophets, Obadiah had taken a hundred prophets and hidden them in two caves, fifty in each, and had supplied them with food and water.) 5Ahab had said to Obadiah, "Go through the land to all the springs and valleys. Maybe we can find some grass to keep the horses and mules alive so we will not have to kill any of our animals." 6So they divided the land they were to cover, Ahab going in one direction and Obadiah in another.

7As Obadiah was walking along, Elijah met him. Obadiah recognized him, bowed down to the ground, and said, "Is it really you, my lord Elijah?"

8"Yes," he replied. "Go tell your master, 'Elijah is here.'"

9"What have I done wrong," asked Obadiah, "that you are handing your servant over to Ahab to be put to death? 10As surely as the LORD your God lives, there is not a nation or kingdom where my master has not sent someone to look for you. And whenever a nation or kingdom claimed you were not there, he made them swear they could not find you. 11But now you tell me to go to my master and say, 'Elijah is here.' 12I don't know where the Spirit of the LORD may carry you when I leave you. If I go and tell Ahab and he doesn't find you, he will kill me. Yet I your servant have worshiped the LORD since my youth. 13Haven't you heard, my lord, what I did while Jezebel was killing the prophets of the LORD? I hid a hundred of the LORD's prophets in two caves, fifty in each, and supplied them with food and water. 14And now you tell me to go to my master and say, 'Elijah is here.' He will kill me!"

15Elijah said, "As the LORD Almighty lives, whom I serve, I will surely present myself to Ahab today."

Elijah on Mount Carmel

16So Obadiah went to meet Ahab and told him, and Ahab went to meet Elijah. 17When he saw Elijah, he said to him, "Is that you, you troubler of Israel?"

18"I have not made trouble for Israel," Elijah replied. "But you and your father's family have. You have abandoned the LORD's commands and have followed the Baals. 19Now summon the people from all over Israel to meet me on Mount Carmel. And bring the four hundred and fifty prophets of Baal and the four hundred prophets of Asherah, who eat at Jezebel's table."

20So Ahab sent word throughout all Israel and assembled the prophets on Mount Carmel. 21Elijah went before the people and said, "How long will you waver between two opinions? If the LORD is God, follow him; but if Baal is God, follow him."

But the people said nothing.

22Then Elijah said to them, "I am the only one of the LORD's prophets left, but Baal has four hundred and fifty prophets. 23Get two bulls for us. Let them choose one for themselves, and let them cut it into pieces and put it on the wood but not set fire to it. I will prepare the other bull and put it on the wood but not set fire to it. 24Then you call on the name of your god, and I will call on the name of the LORD. The god who answers by fire—he is God."

Then all the people said, "What you say is good."

25Elijah said to the prophets of Baal, "Choose

Caught in the Act

Read: 1 Kings 18:16–40

HAVE YOU EVER PRETENDED to think one thing while really believing something else? At one time or another most of us have tacitly agreed with a persuasive person simply by failing to disagree. Or we've looked the other way or nodded knowingly while a red flag went up in our minds. It's a difficult and even dangerous balancing act attempting to please people on both sides of a controversial fence. The only remedy for avoiding such a precarious position is to decide which side of the fence really matters and then get down from the fence and take a stand.

The prophet Elijah confronted the people of his day and demanded they choose whom they would serve—the true God of Israel or the false gods of the pagan nations surrounding them. He basically challenged them, "Get off the fence! You can't have it both ways. Either live your lives in a way that is pleasing to the one true God . . . or not."

Most of us have never been put in a position in which we had to choose between worshiping the true God or bowing down to statues made of wood or stone. Yet we often find ourselves tempted to try that balancing act while living in a spiritually and morally bankrupt culture. We may compromise our lifestyles, going to places or doing things we really know we shouldn't. We may even justify our behavior by saying we don't want to offend anyone. Or we neglect to say the things we know we should and then excuse ourselves by saying we will let our faith be seen in our actions rather than heard in our words. At times these may be legitimate claims, but at other times they may be nothing more than convenient excuses so we don't have to risk rejection.

Elijah wasn't concerned with rejection when he challenged the false prophets and called the people to serve the true God. He put it all on the line—even his life. The prophet refused to compromise or put himself in the precarious position of riding the fence; as a result, God vindicated him in the sight of his enemies. He was caught in the act of standing up for God. Can that be said of you?

1 Kings 18:21

Elijah went before the people and said, "How long will you waver between two opinions? If the LORD is God, follow him; but if Baal is God, follow him."

reflection

1 How have you been caught up in the balancing act of compromise?

2 Why do you sometimes compromise?

3 In what ways can you stand up for righteousness?

RELATED READINGS

Deuteronomy 30:15–20; Joshua 24:14–19; Matthew 10:32–39

Go to page 431 for your next devotional reading.

one of the bulls and prepare it first, since there
are so many of you. Call on the name of your
god, but do not light the fire." 26So they took
the bull given them and prepared it.
Then they called on the name of Baal from
morning till noon. "O Baal, answer us!" they
shouted. But there was no response; no one answered. And they danced around the altar they
had made.
27At noon Elijah began to taunt them. "Shout
louder!" he said. "Surely he is a god! Perhaps he
is deep in thought, or busy, or traveling. Maybe
he is sleeping and must be awakened." 28So
they shouted louder and slashed themselves
with swords and spears, as was their custom,
until their blood flowed. 29Midday passed, and
they continued their frantic prophesying until
the time for the evening sacrifice. But there was
no response, no one answered, no one paid attention.
30Then Elijah said to all the people, "Come
here to me." They came to him, and he repaired
the altar of the LORD, which was in ruins. 31Eli-
jah took twelve stones, one for
each of the tribes descended
from Jacob, to whom the word
of the LORD had come, saying,
"Your name shall be Israel."
32With the stones he built an
altar in the name of the LORD,
and he dug a trench around it
large enough to hold two seahs[a] of seed. 33He arranged the
wood, cut the bull into pieces
and laid it on the wood. Then
he said to them, "Fill four large
jars with water and pour it on
the offering and on the wood."
34"Do it again," he said, and they did it
again.
"Do it a third time," he ordered, and they did
it the third time. 35The water ran down around
the altar and even filled the trench.
36At the time of sacrifice, the prophet Elijah
stepped forward and prayed: "O LORD, God of
Abraham, Isaac and Israel, let it be known today that you are God in Israel and that I am
your servant and have done all these things
at your command. 37Answer me, O LORD, answer me, so these people will know that you,
O LORD, are God, and that you are turning
their hearts back again."
38Then the fire of the LORD fell and burned
up the sacrifice, the wood, the stones and the
soil, and also licked up the water in the trench.
39When all the people saw this, they fell prostrate and cried, "The LORD—he is God! The
LORD—he is God!"
40Then Elijah commanded them, "Seize
the prophets of Baal. Don't let anyone get
away!" They seized them, and Elijah had them
brought down to the Kishon Valley and slaughtered there.
41And Elijah said to Ahab, "Go, eat and
drink, for there is the sound of a heavy rain."
42So Ahab went off to eat and drink, but Elijah
climbed to the top of Carmel, bent down to the
ground and put his face between his knees.
43"Go and look toward the sea," he told his
servant. And he went up and looked.
"There is nothing there," he said.
Seven times Elijah said, "Go back."
44The seventh time the
servant reported, "A cloud as
small as a man's hand is rising
from the sea."
So Elijah said, "Go and tell
Ahab, 'Hitch up your chariot
and go down before the rain
stops you.'"
45Meanwhile, the sky grew
black with clouds, the wind
rose, a heavy rain came on and
Ahab rode off to Jezreel. 46The
power of the LORD came upon
Elijah and, tucking his cloak
into his belt, he ran ahead of
Ahab all the way to Jezreel.

> **1 Kings 18:46**
>
> *God Gives Energy*
>
> The power of the LORD came upon Elijah and, tucking his cloak into his belt, he ran ahead of Ahab all the way to Jezreel.

Elijah Flees to Horeb

19 Now Ahab told Jezebel everything Elijah had done and how he had killed all
the prophets with the sword. 2So Jezebel sent a
messenger to Elijah to say, "May the gods deal
with me, be it ever so severely, if by this time
tomorrow I do not make your life like that of
one of them."
3Elijah was afraid[b] and ran for his life. When

[a]32 That is, probably about 13 quarts (about 15 liters) [b]3 Or *Elijah saw*

Legendary Leadership
DEBORAH

EACH NIGHT IT WAS THE SAME ROUTINE: rinse teeth, change clothes and off to bed—but never to sleep without a story first. Her children especially loved to hear her tell "Deborah stories" about their hero. The family favorite? The story of Barak and Sisera.

"Sometimes," she whispered, as she tucked them in, "I even think I saw her smiling." It was a long time ago, but she remembered her hero as if it were yesterday. She grew up near the Palm of Deborah, during a time when her family lived in oppression and fear. Those were dark days . . . until Deborah. Now when she recounted the stories to her boys, she tried to remember everything just as it was: The slight curl at the corners of Judge Deborah's lips that formed whenever she was deep in thought. Deborah's serious concentration when Barak breathlessly announced Sisera's encroaching ironclad army. She remembered how Deborah got a faraway look in her eyes; it was almost as if her mind were somewhere else altogether—drawing perspective, honing her instincts, receiving a wise word.

"She was a prophet!" her youngest Reuben gasped and tugged at his blanket.

"A prophet*ess*," she corrected him kindly.

"What happened next?"

Of course, her boys knew what happened next—they could even tell the story themselves, like any Israelite child could do. They were enamored with the legendary heroism, battle, treachery and victory surrounding the story of Deborah, Barak, Sisera and Jael.

She smiled as she found her place in the story again. This was the most exciting story about Deborah, but she recalled the simple acts of leadership that Deborah had provided in those first days of turmoil after the death of Sisera. She had observed Her Honor up close. She respected her work ethic, admired her utter dependence on God for strength and marveled at her wisdom.

"Can we sing the song?" Reuben's voice interrupted and whispered in the darkness. "Just the last part?"

"Just once," she smiled. "You start . . ."

"So . . . may . . . all . . ." he started slowly.

"Your enemies perish, O LORD!" big brother joined in.

"But may they who love you be like the sun . . ."

Before they had finished the last verse together, both boys were asleep. She continued contentedly singing softly to herself, trimmed the lamp and tiptoed out of their room.

—Prayer—

Lord, as you provided wisdom for Deborah, give me wisdom in all my decisions and responsibilities.

"Village life in Israel ceased, ceased until I, Deborah, arose, arose a mother in Israel."

Judges 5:7

ASSIGNED READING:

Judges 4–5

Weekend

Go to page 437 for your next devotional reading.

he came to Beersheba in Judah, he left his servant there, 4while he himself went a day's journey into the desert. He came to a broom tree,
sat down under it and prayed that he might die.
"I have had enough, LORD," he said. "Take my
life; I am no better than my ancestors." 5Then
he lay down under the tree and fell asleep.

All at once an angel touched him and said,
"Get up and eat." 6He looked around, and there
by his head was a cake of bread baked over hot
coals, and a jar of water. He ate and drank and
then lay down again.

7The angel of the LORD came back a second
time and touched him and said, "Get up and
eat, for the journey is too much for you." 8So
he got up and ate and drank. Strengthened
by that food, he traveled forty days and forty
nights until he reached Horeb, the mountain
of God. 9There he went into a cave and spent
the night.

The LORD Appears to Elijah

And the word of the LORD came to him:
"What are you doing here, Elijah?"

10He replied, "I have been very zealous for
the LORD God Almighty. The Israelites have
rejected your covenant, broken down your altars, and put your prophets to death with the
sword. I am the only one left, and now they are
trying to kill me too."

11The LORD said, "Go out and stand on the
mountain in the presence of the LORD, for the
LORD is about to pass by."

Then a great and powerful
wind tore the mountains apart
and shattered the rocks before
the LORD, but the LORD was
not in the wind. After the wind
there was an earthquake, but
the LORD was not in the earthquake. 12After the earthquake
came a fire, but the LORD was
not in the fire. And after the
fire came a gentle whisper.
13When Elijah heard it, he
pulled his cloak over his face
and went out and stood at the
mouth of the cave.

Then a voice said to him, "What are you doing here, Elijah?"

14He replied, "I have been very zealous for
the LORD God Almighty. The Israelites have
rejected your covenant, broken down your altars, and put your prophets to death with the
sword. I am the only one left, and now they are
trying to kill me too."

15The LORD said to him, "Go back the way
you came, and go to the Desert of Damascus.
When you get there, anoint Hazael king over
Aram. 16Also, anoint Jehu son of Nimshi king
over Israel, and anoint Elisha son of Shaphat
from Abel Meholah to succeed you as prophet.
17Jehu will put to death any who escape the
sword of Hazael, and Elisha will put to death
any who escape the sword of Jehu. 18Yet I reserve seven thousand in Israel—all whose
knees have not bowed down to Baal and all
whose mouths have not kissed him."

1 Kings 19:11

God Is Near

The LORD said, "Go
out and stand on the
mountain in the presence
of the LORD, for the LORD
is about to pass by."

The Call of Elisha

19So Elijah went from there and found
Elisha son of Shaphat. He was plowing with
twelve yoke of oxen, and he himself was driving the twelfth pair. Elijah went up to him and
threw his cloak around him. 20Elisha then left
his oxen and ran after Elijah. "Let me kiss my
father and mother good-by," he said, "and then
I will come with you."

"Go back," Elijah replied. "What have I done
to you?"

21So Elisha left him and went back. He took
his yoke of oxen and slaughtered them. He
burned the plowing equipment to cook the
meat and gave it to the people, and they ate.
Then he set out to follow Elijah
and became his attendant.

Ben-Hadad Attacks Samaria

20 Now Ben-Hadad king
of Aram mustered his
entire army. Accompanied by
thirty-two kings with their
horses and chariots, he went
up and besieged Samaria and
attacked it. 2He sent messengers into the city to Ahab king
of Israel, saying, "This is what
Ben-Hadad says: 3'Your silver
and gold are mine, and the best of your wives
and children are mine.'"

4The king of Israel answered, "Just as you say,
my lord the king. I and all I have are yours."

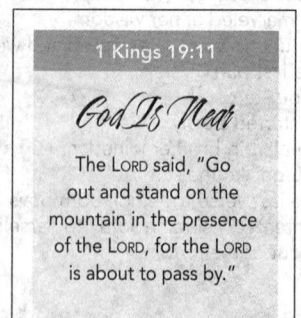

[5]The messengers came again and said, "This is what Ben-Hadad says: 'I sent to demand your silver and gold, your wives and your children.
[6]But about this time tomorrow I am going to send my officials to search your palace and the houses of your officials. They will seize everything you value and carry it away.'"
[7]The king of Israel summoned all the elders of the land and said to them, "See how this man is looking for trouble! When he sent for my wives and my children, my silver and my gold, I did not refuse him."
[8]The elders and the people all answered, "Don't listen to him or agree to his demands."
[9]So he replied to Ben-Hadad's messengers, "Tell my lord the king, 'Your servant will do all you demanded the first time, but this demand I cannot meet.'" They left and took the answer back to Ben-Hadad.
[10]Then Ben-Hadad sent another message to Ahab: "May the gods deal with me, be it ever so severely, if enough dust remains in Samaria to give each of my men a handful."
[11]The king of Israel answered, "Tell him: 'One who puts on his armor should not boast like one who takes it off.'"
[12]Ben-Hadad heard this message while he and the kings were drinking in their tents,[a] and he ordered his men: "Prepare to attack." So they prepared to attack the city.

Ahab Defeats Ben-Hadad

[13]Meanwhile a prophet came to Ahab king of Israel and announced, "This is what the LORD says: 'Do you see this vast army? I will give it into your hand today, and then you will know that I am the LORD.'"
[14]"But who will do this?" asked Ahab.

The prophet replied, "This is what the LORD says: 'The young officers of the provincial commanders will do it.'"

"And who will start the battle?" he asked.

The prophet answered, "You will."

[15]So Ahab summoned the young officers of the provincial commanders, 232 men. Then he assembled the rest of the Israelites, 7,000 in all.
[16]They set out at noon while Ben-Hadad and the 32 kings allied with him were in their tents getting drunk.
[17]The young officers of the provincial commanders went out first.

Now Ben-Hadad had dispatched scouts, who reported, "Men are advancing from Samaria."

[18]He said, "If they have come out for peace, take them alive; if they have come out for war, take them alive."

[19]The young officers of the provincial commanders marched out of the city with the army behind them
[20]and each one struck down his opponent. At that, the Arameans fled, with the Israelites in pursuit. But Ben-Hadad king of Aram escaped on horseback with some of his horsemen.
[21]The king of Israel advanced and overpowered the horses and chariots and inflicted heavy losses on the Arameans.
[22]Afterward, the prophet came to the king of Israel and said, "Strengthen your position and see what must be done, because next spring the king of Aram will attack you again."
[23]Meanwhile, the officials of the king of Aram advised him, "Their gods are gods of the hills. That is why they were too strong for us. But if we fight them on the plains, surely we will be stronger than they.
[24]Do this: Remove all the kings from their commands and replace them with other officers.
[25]You must also raise an army like the one you lost—horse for horse and chariot for chariot—so we can fight Israel on the plains. Then surely we will be stronger than they." He agreed with them and acted accordingly.
[26]The next spring Ben-Hadad mustered the Arameans and went up to Aphek to fight against Israel.
[27]When the Israelites were also mustered and given provisions, they marched out to meet them. The Israelites camped opposite them like two small flocks of goats, while the Arameans covered the countryside.
[28]The man of God came up and told the king of Israel, "This is what the LORD says: 'Because the Arameans think the LORD is a god of the hills and not a god of the valleys, I will deliver this vast army into your hands, and you will know that I am the LORD.'"
[29]For seven days they camped opposite each other, and on the seventh day the battle was joined. The Israelites inflicted a hundred thousand casualties on the Aramean foot soldiers in one day.
[30]The rest of them escaped to the city of Aphek, where the wall collapsed on

[a]12 Or *in Succoth*; also in verse 16

twenty-seven thousand of them. And Ben-
Hadad fled to the city and hid in an inner room.
31 His officials said to him, "Look, we have
heard that the kings of the house of Israel are
merciful. Let us go to the king of Israel with
sackcloth around our waists and ropes around
our heads. Perhaps he will spare your life."
32 Wearing sackcloth around their waists
and ropes around their heads, they went to
the king of Israel and said, "Your servant Ben-
Hadad says: 'Please let me live.'"
The king answered, "Is he still alive? He is
my brother."
33 The men took this as a good sign and were
quick to pick up his word. "Yes, your brother
Ben-Hadad!" they said.
"Go and get him," the king said. When Ben-
Hadad came out, Ahab had him come up into
his chariot.
34 "I will return the cities my father took
from your father," Ben-Hadad offered. "You
may set up your own market areas in Damascus, as my father did in Samaria."
⌊Ahab said,⌋ "On the basis of a treaty I will
set you free." So he made a treaty with him, and
let him go.

A Prophet Condemns Ahab

35 By the word of the LORD one of the sons of
the prophets said to his companion, "Strike me
with your weapon," but the man refused.
36 So the prophet said, "Because you have
not obeyed the LORD, as soon as you leave me
a lion will kill you." And after the man went
away, a lion found him and killed him.
37 The prophet found another man and said,
"Strike me, please." So the man struck him and
wounded him. 38 Then the prophet went and
stood by the road waiting for the king. He disguised himself with his headband down over his
eyes. 39 As the king passed by, the prophet called
out to him, "Your servant went into the thick of
the battle, and someone came to me with a captive and said, 'Guard this man. If he is missing,
it will be your life for his life, or you must pay a
talent[a] of silver.' 40 While your servant was busy
here and there, the man disappeared."
"That is your sentence," the king of Israel
said. "You have pronounced it yourself."
41 Then the prophet quickly removed the
headband from his eyes, and the king of Israel
recognized him as one of the prophets. 42 He
said to the king, "This is what the LORD says:
'You have set free a man I had determined
should die.[b] Therefore it is your life for his life,
your people for his people.'" 43 Sullen and angry,
the king of Israel went to his palace in Samaria.

Naboth's Vineyard

21 Some time later there was an incident
involving a vineyard belonging to Naboth the Jezreelite. The vineyard was in Jezreel,
close to the palace of Ahab king of Samaria.
2 Ahab said to Naboth, "Let me have your vineyard to use for a vegetable garden, since it is
close to my palace. In exchange I will give you
a better vineyard or, if you prefer, I will pay you
whatever it is worth."
3 But Naboth replied, "The LORD forbid that I
should give you the inheritance of my fathers."
4 So Ahab went home, sullen and angry because Naboth the Jezreelite had said, "I will not
give you the inheritance of my fathers." He lay
on his bed sulking and refused to eat.
5 His wife Jezebel came in and asked him,
"Why are you so sullen? Why won't you eat?"
6 He answered her, "Because I said to Naboth
the Jezreelite, 'Sell me your vineyard; or if you
prefer, I will give you another vineyard in its
place.' But he said, 'I will not give you my vineyard.'"
7 Jezebel his wife said, "Is this how you act as
king over Israel? Get up and eat! Cheer up. I'll
get you the vineyard of Naboth the Jezreelite."
8 So she wrote letters in Ahab's name, placed
his seal on them, and sent them to the elders
and nobles who lived in Naboth's city with him.
9 In those letters she wrote:

> "Proclaim a day of fasting and seat
> Naboth in a prominent place among the
> people. 10 But seat two scoundrels oppo-
> site him and have them testify that he has
> cursed both God and the king. Then take
> him out and stone him to death."

11 So the elders and nobles who lived in Naboth's city did as Jezebel directed in the letters
she had written to them. 12 They proclaimed

[a] 39 That is, about 75 pounds (about 34 kilograms) [b] 42 The Hebrew term refers to the irrevocable giving over of things or persons to the LORD, often by totally destroying them.

a fast and seated Naboth in a prominent
place among the people. 13 Then two scoundrels came and sat opposite him and brought
charges against Naboth before
the people, saying, "Naboth
has cursed both God and the
king." So they took him outside the city and stoned him to
death. 14 Then they sent word
to Jezebel: "Naboth has been
stoned and is dead."
15 As soon as Jezebel heard
that Naboth had been stoned
to death, she said to Ahab, "Get
up and take possession of the
vineyard of Naboth the Jezreelite that he refused to sell you.
He is no longer alive, but dead."
16 When Ahab heard that Naboth was dead, he got up and
went down to take possession
of Naboth's vineyard.
17 Then the word of the LORD came to Elijah
the Tishbite: 18 "Go down to meet Ahab king
of Israel, who rules in Samaria. He is now in
Naboth's vineyard, where he has gone to take
possession of it. 19 Say to him, 'This is what the
LORD says: Have you not murdered a man and
seized his property?' Then say to him, 'This is
what the LORD says: In the place where dogs
licked up Naboth's blood, dogs will lick up your
blood—yes, yours!'"
20 Ahab said to Elijah, "So you have found
me, my enemy!"
"I have found you," he answered, "because
you have sold yourself to do evil in the eyes of
the LORD. 21 'I am going to bring disaster on
you. I will consume your descendants and cut
off from Ahab every last male in Israel—slave
or free. 22 I will make your house like that of
Jeroboam son of Nebat and that of Baasha son
of Ahijah, because you have provoked me to
anger and have caused Israel to sin.'
23 "And also concerning Jezebel the LORD
says: 'Dogs will devour Jezebel by the wall of[a]
Jezreel.'
24 "Dogs will eat those belonging to Ahab
who die in the city, and the birds of the air will
feed on those who die in the country."

1 Kings 21:28–29

God Is Merciful

Then the word of the LORD came to Elijah the Tishbite: "Have you noticed how Ahab has humbled himself before me? Because he has humbled himself, I will not bring this disaster in his day."

25 (There was never a man like Ahab, who
sold himself to do evil in the eyes of the LORD,
urged on by Jezebel his wife. 26 He behaved in
the vilest manner by going af-
ter idols, like the Amorites the
LORD drove out before Israel.)
27 When Ahab heard these
words, he tore his clothes,
put on sackcloth and fasted.
He lay in sackcloth and went
around meekly.
28 Then the word of the
LORD came to Elijah the Tishbite: 29 "Have you noticed how
Ahab has humbled himself before me? Because he has humbled himself, I will not bring
this disaster in his day, but I
will bring it on his house in the
days of his son."

Micaiah Prophesies Against Ahab

22 For three years there was no war between Aram and Israel. 2 But in the
third year Jehoshaphat king of Judah went
down to see the king of Israel. 3 The king of
Israel had said to his officials, "Don't you know
that Ramoth Gilead belongs to us and yet we
are doing nothing to retake it from the king
of Aram?"
4 So he asked Jehoshaphat, "Will you go with
me to fight against Ramoth Gilead?"
Jehoshaphat replied to the king of Israel, "I
am as you are, my people as your people, my
horses as your horses." 5 But Jehoshaphat also
said to the king of Israel, "First seek the counsel
of the LORD."
6 So the king of Israel brought together the
prophets—about four hundred men—and
asked them, "Shall I go to war against Ramoth
Gilead, or shall I refrain?"
"Go," they answered, "for the Lord will give
it into the king's hand."
7 But Jehoshaphat asked, "Is there not a
prophet of the LORD here whom we can inquire of?"
8 The king of Israel answered Jehoshaphat,
"There is still one man through whom we can
inquire of the LORD, but I hate him because he

[a] 23 Most Hebrew manuscripts; a few Hebrew manuscripts, Vulgate and Syriac (see also 2 Kings 9:26) *the plot of ground at*

never prophesies anything good about me, but
always bad. He is Micaiah son of Imlah."
"The king should not say that," Jehoshaphat replied.
9 So the king of Israel called
one of his officials and said,
"Bring Micaiah son of Imlah
at once."
10 Dressed in their royal
robes, the king of Israel and Jehoshaphat king of Judah were
sitting on their thrones at the
threshing floor by the entrance
of the gate of Samaria, with
all the prophets prophesying
before them. 11 Now Zedekiah
son of Kenaanah had made
iron horns and he declared,
"This is what the LORD says:
'With these you will gore the
Arameans until they are destroyed.'"
12 All the other prophets
were prophesying the same thing. "Attack Ramoth Gilead and be victorious," they said, "for
the LORD will give it into the king's hand."
13 The messenger who had gone to summon
Micaiah said to him, "Look, as one man the
other prophets are predicting success for the
king. Let your word agree with theirs, and
speak favorably."
14 But Micaiah said, "As surely as the LORD
lives, I can tell him only what the LORD
tells me."
15 When he arrived, the king asked him,
"Micaiah, shall we go to war against Ramoth
Gilead, or shall I refrain?"
"Attack and be victorious," he answered, "for
the LORD will give it into the king's hand."
16 The king said to him, "How many times
must I make you swear to tell me nothing but
the truth in the name of the LORD?"
17 Then Micaiah answered, "I saw all Israel
scattered on the hills like sheep without a shepherd, and the LORD said, 'These people have no
master. Let each one go home in peace.'"
18 The king of Israel said to Jehoshaphat,
"Didn't I tell you that he never prophesies anything good about me, but only bad?"

1 Kings 22:19

God Is King of All

Micaiah continued, "Therefore hear the word of the LORD: I saw the LORD sitting on his throne with all the host of heaven standing around him on his right and on his left."

19 Micaiah continued, "Therefore hear the
word of the LORD: I saw the LORD sitting on
his throne with all the host of heaven standing
around him on his right and on his left. 20 And
the LORD said, 'Who will en-
tice Ahab into attacking Ramoth Gilead and going to his
death there?'
"One suggested this, and
another that. 21 Finally, a spirit
came forward, stood before
the LORD and said, 'I will entice him.'
22 "'By what means?' the
LORD asked.
"'I will go out and be a lying
spirit in the mouths of all his
prophets,' he said.
"'You will succeed in enticing him,' said the LORD. 'Go
and do it.'
23 "So now the LORD has put
a lying spirit in the mouths of
all these prophets of yours. The LORD has decreed disaster for you."
24 Then Zedekiah son of Kenaanah went up
and slapped Micaiah in the face. "Which way
did the spirit from[a] the LORD go when he went
from me to speak to you?" he asked.
25 Micaiah replied, "You will find out on the
day you go to hide in an inner room."
26 The king of Israel then ordered, "Take Micaiah and send him back to Amon the ruler of
the city and to Joash the king's son 27 and say,
'This is what the king says: Put this fellow in
prison and give him nothing but bread and water until I return safely.'"
28 Micaiah declared, "If you ever return
safely, the LORD has not spoken through me."
Then he added, "Mark my words, all you people!"

Ahab Killed at Ramoth Gilead

29 So the king of Israel and Jehoshaphat king
of Judah went up to Ramoth Gilead. 30 The
king of Israel said to Jehoshaphat, "I will enter
the battle in disguise, but you wear your royal
robes." So the king of Israel disguised himself
and went into battle.

[a] 24 Or *Spirit of*

Family Resemblance

Read: 1 Kings 22:41–53

MOST CHILDREN RESEMBLE their parents in some way. Sometimes the resemblance is physical: They're born with their mother's eyes or father's grin. Other times, the likeness relates to personality traits: They've inherited a hot temper from papa or a sweet disposition from mama. For Christian parents, the most important thing is not whether our kids inherit dad's curly hair or mom's way with words. The most important trait we long to pass on is our love for the Lord. We want our children to be members of the family of faith. Parents who love God want to give their children every opportunity to learn what that means.

The Bible doesn't describe Jehoshaphat's physical appearance, but it does reveal that he bore a strong family resemblance to his father Asa, who was known for opposing idolatry and worshiping God. Like father, like son. Jehoshaphat was a good and godly king who reigned over Judah for 25 years. His epitaph could be summed up in a few poignant words: "Jehoshaphat, who sought the LORD with all his heart" (2 Chronicles 22:9). By following in his godly father's footsteps, King Jehoshaphat pleased God.

It's been well said that God has no grandchildren, only children. Each and every individual has to decide whether or not to accept redemption through Jesus Christ. Children who are brought up in Christian homes have the benefit of the teaching and influence of their parents, although it's their decision to follow their parents' example or walk away. But it's a great advantage to grow up with godly role models. Just look at young Timothy, who was commended for his "sincere faith, which first lived in [his] grandmother Lois and [his] mother Eunice" (2 Timothy 1:5).

Not everyone has had the benefit of a Christian upbringing, but that in no way excludes them from the family of God. God has a way of adopting some of the most unlikely spiritual orphans. He wants you and me and others in the family to adopt them too! We can show them how to live in a holy way just as Asa showed Jehoshaphat. You may or may not have kids who have inherited your eyes and ears, but you can help others develop eyes to see God and ears to hear the gospel. Encourage those in your sphere of influence to cultivate a strong family resemblance to their heavenly Father.

1 Kings 22:42–43

Jehoshaphat was thirty-five years old when he became king, and he reigned in Jerusalem twenty-five years. His mother's name was Azubah daughter of Shilhi. In everything he walked in the ways of his father Asa and did not stray from them; he did what was right in the eyes of the LORD.

reflection

1 How did you come into God's family?

2 How have you grown to "look like" God since you joined his family?

3 Which of God's traits would you like to model to your children or your "faith children"?

RELATED READINGS

1 Kings 15:11–15;
2 Chronicles 17:3–6;
22:7–9

Monday

Go to page 441 for your next devotional reading.

31Now the king of Aram had ordered his
thirty-two chariot commanders, "Do not fight
with anyone, small or great, except the king of
Israel." 32When the chariot commanders saw
Jehoshaphat, they thought, "Surely this is the
king of Israel." So they turned to attack him,
but when Jehoshaphat cried out, 33the chariot
commanders saw that he was not the king of
Israel and stopped pursuing him.

34But someone drew his bow at random and
hit the king of Israel between the sections of his
armor. The king told his chariot driver, "Wheel
around and get me out of the fighting. I've been
wounded." 35All day long the battle raged, and
the king was propped up in his chariot facing
the Arameans. The blood from his wound ran
onto the floor of the chariot, and that evening
he died. 36As the sun was setting, a cry spread
through the army: "Every man to his town; everyone to his land!"

37So the king died and was brought to
Samaria, and they buried him there. 38They
washed the chariot at a pool in Samaria (where
the prostitutes bathed),[a] and the dogs licked
up his blood, as the word of the LORD had declared.

39As for the other events of Ahab's reign, including all he did, the palace he built and inlaid
with ivory, and the cities he fortified, are they
not written in the book of the annals of the
kings of Israel? 40Ahab rested with his fathers.
And Ahaziah his son succeeded him as king.

Jehoshaphat King of Judah

41Jehoshaphat son of Asa became king of Judah in the fourth year of Ahab king of Israel.
42Jehoshaphat was thirty-five years old when
he became king, and he reigned in Jerusalem
twenty-five years. His mother's name was Azubah daughter of Shilhi. 43In everything he
walked in the ways of his father Asa and did
not stray from them; he did what was right in
the eyes of the LORD. The high places, however,
were not removed, and the people continued
to offer sacrifices and burn incense there. 44Je-
hoshaphat was also at peace with the king of
Israel.

45As for the other events of Jehoshaphat's
reign, the things he achieved and his military
exploits, are they not written in the book of
the annals of the kings of Judah? 46He rid the
land of the rest of the male shrine prostitutes
who remained there even after the reign of his
father Asa. 47There was then no king in Edom;
a deputy ruled.

48Now Jehoshaphat built a fleet of trading
ships[b] to go to Ophir for gold, but they never
set sail—they were wrecked at Ezion Geber.
49At that time Ahaziah son of Ahab said to Jehoshaphat, "Let my men sail with your men,"
but Jehoshaphat refused.

50Then Jehoshaphat rested with his fathers
and was buried with them in the city of David
his father. And Jehoram his son succeeded
him.

Ahaziah King of Israel

51Ahaziah son of Ahab became king of
Israel in Samaria in the seventeenth year of Jehoshaphat king of Judah, and he reigned over
Israel two years. 52He did evil in the eyes of the
LORD, because he walked in the ways of his father and mother and in the ways of Jeroboam
son of Nebat, who caused Israel to sin. 53He
served and worshiped Baal and provoked the
LORD, the God of Israel, to anger, just as his father had done.

[a]38 Or *Samaria and cleaned the weapons* [b]48 Hebrew *of ships of Tarshish*

2 Kings

Second Kings continues the *stories of the kings* of Israel and Judah. Much of its storyline focuses on Elijah's successor, Elisha. Elijah's public confrontations with King Ahab are replaced with Elisha's *quieter miracles* of mercy. The ministries of several other prophets, including Isaiah, are also covered in this book. But mostly it looks at the kings—most of them forgettable.

As you read of the different kings and prophets, notice how *God used various personalities* with assorted gifts—if the leaders chose to follow him. Those who looked to God for leadership were worthy leaders to their own people, but those who tried to lead without him inevitably failed.

Author:
Unknown.

Audience:
The people of Israel.

Date:
Between 560 and 550 B.C.

Setting:
One kingdom has divided into two.

Verse to Remember:
The LORD warned Israel and Judah through all his prophets and seers: "Turn from your evil ways. Observe my commands and decrees, in accordance with the entire Law that I commanded your fathers to obey and that I delivered to you through my servants the prophets." (17:13)

The LORD's Judgment on Ahaziah

1 After Ahab's death, Moab rebelled against
Israel. 2Now Ahaziah had fallen through
the lattice of his upper room in Samaria and
injured himself. So he sent messengers, saying to them, "Go and consult Baal-Zebub, the
god of Ekron, to see if I will recover from this
injury."

3But the angel of the LORD said to Elijah the
Tishbite, "Go up and meet the messengers of
the king of Samaria and ask them, 'Is it because
there is no God in Israel that you are going
off to consult Baal-Zebub, the god of Ekron?'
4Therefore this is what the LORD says: 'You will
not leave the bed you are lying on. You will
certainly die!' " So Elijah went.

5When the messengers returned to the king,
he asked them, "Why have you come back?"
6"A man came to meet us," they replied. "And
he said to us, 'Go back to the king who sent you
and tell him, "This is what the LORD says: Is it
because there is no God in Israel that you are
sending men to consult Baal-Zebub, the god
of Ekron? Therefore you will not leave the bed
you are lying on. You will certainly die!" '"
7The king asked them, "What kind of man
was it who came to meet you and told you
this?"
8They replied, "He was a man with a garment of hair and with a leather belt around his
waist."
The king said, "That was Elijah the Tishbite."
9Then he sent to Elijah a captain with his
company of fifty men. The captain went up
to Elijah, who was sitting on the top of a hill,
and said to him, "Man of God, the king says,
'Come down!'"
10Elijah answered the captain, "If I am a
man of God, may fire come down from heaven
and consume you and your
fifty men!" Then fire fell from
heaven and consumed the captain and his men.
11At this the king sent to
Elijah another captain with his
fifty men. The captain said to
him, "Man of God, this is what
the king says, 'Come down
at once!'"
12"If I am a man of God,"
Elijah replied, "may fire come
down from heaven and con-
sume you and your fifty men!"
Then the fire of God fell from
heaven and consumed him and
his fifty men.
13So the king sent a third
captain with his fifty men. This third captain
went up and fell on his knees before Elijah.
"Man of God," he begged, "please have respect
for my life and the lives of these fifty men, your
servants! 14See, fire has fallen from heaven and
consumed the first two captains and all their
men. But now have respect for my life!"

2 Kings 1:12

God Is a Consuming Fire

"If I am a man of God," Elijah replied, "may fire come down from heaven and consume you and your fifty men!" Then the fire of God fell from heaven and consumed him and his fifty men.

15The angel of the LORD said to Elijah, "Go
down with him; do not be afraid of him." So
Elijah got up and went down with him to
the king.
16He told the king, "This is what the LORD
says: Is it because there is no God in Israel for
you to consult that you have sent messengers to
consult Baal-Zebub, the god of Ekron? Because
you have done this, you will never leave the bed
you are lying on. You will certainly die!" 17So
he died, according to the word of the LORD that
Elijah had spoken.
Because Ahaziah had no son, Joram[a]
succeeded him as king in the second year of
Jehoram son of Jehoshaphat king of Judah.
18As for all the other events of Ahaziah's reign,
and what he did, are they not written in the
book of the annals of the kings of Israel?

Elijah Taken Up to Heaven

2 When the LORD was about to take Elijah
up to heaven in a whirlwind, Elijah and
Elisha were on their way from Gilgal. 2Elijah
said to Elisha, "Stay here; the LORD has sent me
to Bethel."
But Elisha said, "As surely as
the LORD lives and as you live,
I will not leave you." So they
went down to Bethel.
3The company of the prophets at Bethel came out to Elisha
and asked, "Do you know that
the LORD is going to take your
master from you today?"
"Yes, I know," Elisha replied,
"but do not speak of it."
4Then Elijah said to him,
"Stay here, Elisha; the LORD
has sent me to Jericho."
And he replied, "As surely as
the LORD lives and as you live,
I will not leave you." So they
went to Jericho.
5The company of the prophets at Jericho
went up to Elisha and asked him, "Do you
know that the LORD is going to take your master from you today?"
"Yes, I know," he replied, "but do not speak
of it."

[a]17 Hebrew *Jehoram,* a variant of *Joram*

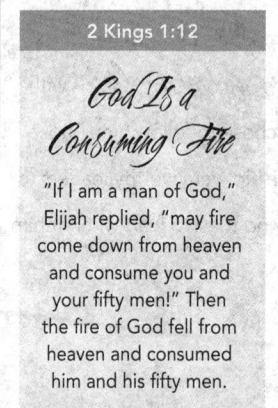

Stay With Me

Read: 2 Kings 2:1–15

WHERE HAVE ALL the mentors gone? Where are the older, wiser women who once taught younger women to bake bread, sew clothing and keep their kitchens spotless? Where are the women who once gathered in homes for coffee and encouragement? They haven't disappeared. They can be found in the church, in homes, offices, neighborhoods and schools. Their focus may have changed, but they are still there for the younger women who have much to learn from them.

Some of today's mentors are much like Elijah, who was faithfully carrying on in his role as God's prophet when he saw Elisha working in his father's fields. He saw the potential in this young man, so he threw his mantle on Elisha's shoulders, symbolically passing the leadership to the next generation. Elisha then said good-bye to his old life and moved forward, following Elijah and learning from the older man.

That's where we find the prophetic pair now: at Bethel, the house of God. Elisha had steadfastly stayed with his mentor Elijah. Even when Elijah commanded Elisha to remain in Bethel, Elisha refused, saying he would never leave the older prophet's side. Thus, Elisha expressed his love and faithfulness not only to Elijah, but also to God. Elisha vowed never to leave Elijah, and he didn't until he had gleaned everything he needed to know from this godly man, until he received the blessing of his mentor, until he watched his mentor vanish in a heavenly whirlwind.

We all need mentors like Elijah: women who have faced challenges and overcome; women who have grown through struggle and perseverance; women who have seen God perform miracles; women who have gone through hard times and experienced God's presence with them. These are the women who can pass on the news that God's Word is still active and dynamic among us. These are the ones who can place the mantle on our shoulders and confirm that we're ready to move on to greater tasks.

Who are the godly women walking along the roads in your life, willing to pass on the knowledge they've gained? Who has watched you as you've worked in your Bible study, your volunteer position or at your job? Who has seen your gifts and your potential? Try being like Elisha. Follow her and glean from her knowledge of the living God concerning how to best serve him.

2 Kings 2:2

Elijah said to Elisha, "Stay here; the LORD has sent me to Bethel." But Elisha said, "As surely as the LORD lives and as you live, I will not leave you." So they went down to Bethel.

reflection

1 Who do you see as an Elijah, faithfully serving God in your community?

2 What do you need to do to become more available to learn from a godly mentor?

3 In what ways could you become a mentor to another woman? Think of someone you know who could use a godly mentor to come alongside her in her work.

RELATED READINGS

1 Kings 19:19–21; Titus 2:1–5

Go to page 446 for your next devotional reading.

6 Then Elijah said to him, "Stay here; the
LORD has sent me to the Jordan."
And he replied, "As surely as the LORD lives
and as you live, I will not leave you." So the two
of them walked on.
7 Fifty men of the company of the prophets
went and stood at a distance, facing the place
where Elijah and Elisha had stopped at the
Jordan. 8 Elijah took his cloak, rolled it up and
struck the water with it. The water divided to
the right and to the left, and the two of them
crossed over on dry ground.
9 When they had crossed, Elijah said to Elisha, "Tell me, what can I do for you before I am
taken from you?"
"Let me inherit a double portion of your
spirit," Elisha replied.
10 "You have asked a difficult thing," Elijah
said, "yet if you see me when I am taken from
you, it will be yours—otherwise not."
11 As they were walking along and talking
together, suddenly a chariot of fire and horses
of fire appeared and separated the two of them,
and Elijah went up to heaven in a whirlwind.
12 Elisha saw this and cried out, "My father! My
father! The chariots and horsemen of Israel!"
And Elisha saw him no more. Then he took
hold of his own clothes and tore them apart.
13 He picked up the cloak that had fallen
from Elijah and went back and stood on the
bank of the Jordan. 14 Then he took the cloak
that had fallen from him and struck the water
with it. "Where now is the LORD, the God of
Elijah?" he asked. When he struck the water,
it divided to the right and to the left, and he
crossed over.
15 The company of the prophets from Jericho, who were watching, said, "The spirit of
Elijah is resting on Elisha." And they went to
meet him and bowed to the ground before
him. 16 "Look," they said, "we your servants
have fifty able men. Let them go and look for
your master. Perhaps the Spirit of the LORD
has picked him up and set him down on some
mountain or in some valley."
"No," Elisha replied, "do not send them."
17 But they persisted until he was too
ashamed to refuse. So he said, "Send them."
And they sent fifty men, who searched for
three days but did not find him. 18 When they
returned to Elisha, who was staying in Jericho,
he said to them, "Didn't I tell you not to go?"

Healing of the Water

19 The men of the city said to Elisha, "Look,
our lord, this town is well situated, as you can
see, but the water is bad and the land is unproductive."
20 "Bring me a new bowl," he said, "and put
salt in it." So they brought it to him.
21 Then he went out to the spring and threw
the salt into it, saying, "This is what the LORD
says: 'I have healed this water. Never again will
it cause death or make the land unproductive.'"
22 And the water has remained wholesome to
this day, according to the word Elisha had
spoken.

Elisha Is Jeered

23 From there Elisha went up to Bethel. As
he was walking along the road, some youths
came out of the town and jeered at him. "Go
on up, you baldhead!" they said. "Go on up,
you baldhead!" 24 He turned around, looked at
them and called down a curse on them in the
name of the LORD. Then two bears came out of
the woods and mauled forty-two of the youths.
25 And he went on to Mount Carmel and from
there returned to Samaria.

Moab Revolts

3 Joram[a] son of Ahab became king of Israel
in Samaria in the eighteenth year of Jehoshaphat king of Judah, and he reigned twelve
years. 2 He did evil in the eyes of the LORD, but
not as his father and mother had done. He
got rid of the sacred stone of Baal that his father had made. 3 Nevertheless he clung to the
sins of Jeroboam son of Nebat, which he had
caused Israel to commit; he did not turn away
from them.
4 Now Mesha king of Moab raised sheep, and
he had to supply the king of Israel with a hundred thousand lambs and with the wool of a
hundred thousand rams. 5 But after Ahab died,
the king of Moab rebelled against the king of
Israel. 6 So at that time King Joram set out from
Samaria and mobilized all Israel. 7 He also sent
this message to Jehoshaphat king of Judah:

[a] 1 Hebrew *Jehoram*, a variant of *Joram*; also in verse 6

"The king of Moab has rebelled against me. Will you go with me to fight against Moab?"

"I will go with you," he replied. "I am as you are, my people as your people, my horses as your horses."

8 "By what route shall we attack?" he asked.

"Through the Desert of Edom," he answered.

9 So the king of Israel set out with the king of Judah and the king of Edom. After a roundabout march of seven days, the army had no more water for themselves or for the animals with them.

10 "What!" exclaimed the king of Israel. "Has the LORD called us three kings together only to hand us over to Moab?"

11 But Jehoshaphat asked, "Is there no prophet of the LORD here, that we may inquire of the LORD through him?"

An officer of the king of Israel answered, "Elisha son of Shaphat is here. He used to pour water on the hands of Elijah.[a]"

12 Jehoshaphat said, "The word of the LORD is with him." So the king of Israel and Jehoshaphat and the king of Edom went down to him.

13 Elisha said to the king of Israel, "What do we have to do with each other? Go to the prophets of your father and the prophets of your mother."

"No," the king of Israel answered, "because it was the LORD who called us three kings together to hand us over to Moab."

14 Elisha said, "As surely as the LORD Almighty lives, whom I serve, if I did not have respect for the presence of Jehoshaphat king of Judah, I would not look at you or even notice you. 15 But now bring me a harpist."

While the harpist was playing, the hand of the LORD came upon Elisha 16 and he said, "This is what the LORD says: Make this valley full of ditches. 17 For this is what the LORD says: You will see neither wind nor rain, yet this valley will be filled with water, and you, your cattle and your other animals will drink. 18 This is an easy thing in the eyes of the LORD; he will also hand Moab over to you. 19 You will overthrow every fortified city and every major town. You will cut down every good tree, stop up all the springs, and ruin every good field with stones."

20 The next morning, about the time for offering the sacrifice, there it was—water flowing from the direction of Edom! And the land was filled with water.

21 Now all the Moabites had heard that the kings had come to fight against them; so every man, young and old, who could bear arms was called up and stationed on the border. 22 When they got up early in the morning, the sun was shining on the water. To the Moabites across the way, the water looked red—like blood. 23 "That's blood!" they said. "Those kings must have fought and slaughtered each other. Now to the plunder, Moab!"

24 But when the Moabites came to the camp of Israel, the Israelites rose up and fought them until they fled. And the Israelites invaded the land and slaughtered the Moabites. 25 They destroyed the towns, and each man threw a stone on every good field until it was covered. They stopped up all the springs and cut down every good tree. Only Kir Hareseth was left with its stones in place, but men armed with slings surrounded it and attacked it as well.

26 When the king of Moab saw that the battle had gone against him, he took with him seven hundred swordsmen to break through to the king of Edom, but they failed. 27 Then he took his firstborn son, who was to succeed him as king, and offered him as a sacrifice on the city wall. The fury against Israel was great; they withdrew and returned to their own land.

The Widow's Oil

4 The wife of a man from the company of the prophets cried out to Elisha, "Your servant my husband is dead, and you know that he revered the LORD. But now his creditor is coming to take my two boys as his slaves."

2 Elisha replied to her, "How can I help you? Tell me, what do you have in your house?"

"Your servant has nothing there at all," she said, "except a little oil."

3 Elisha said, "Go around and ask all your neighbors for empty jars. Don't ask for just a few. 4 Then go inside and shut the door behind you and your sons. Pour oil into all the jars, and as each is filled, put it to one side."

5 She left him and afterward shut the door

[a] 11 That is, he was Elijah's personal servant.

behind her and her sons. They brought the jars
to her and she kept pouring. 6When all the
jars were full, she said to her son, "Bring me
another one."
But he replied, "There is not a jar left." Then
the oil stopped flowing.
7She went and told the man of God, and he
said, "Go, sell the oil and pay your debts. You
and your sons can live on what is left."

The Shunammite's Son Restored to Life

8One day Elisha went to Shunem. And a
well-to-do woman was there, who urged him
to stay for a meal. So whenever he came by, he
stopped there to eat. 9She said to her husband,
"I know that this man who often comes our
way is a holy man of God. 10Let's make a small
room on the roof and put in it a bed and a table,
a chair and a lamp for him. Then he can stay
there whenever he comes to us."
11One day when Elisha came, he went up to
his room and lay down there. 12He said to his
servant Gehazi, "Call the Shunammite." So he
called her, and she stood before him. 13Elisha
said to him, "Tell her, 'You have gone to all this
trouble for us. Now what can be done for you?
Can we speak on your behalf to the king or the
commander of the army?' "
She replied, "I have a home among my
own people."
14"What can be done for her?" Elisha asked.
Gehazi said, "Well, she has no son and her
husband is old."
15Then Elisha said, "Call her." So he called
her, and she stood in the doorway. 16"About
this time next year," Elisha said, "you will hold
a son in your arms."
"No, my lord," she objected. "Don't mislead
your servant, O man of God!"
17But the woman became pregnant, and the
next year about that same time she gave birth
to a son, just as Elisha had told her.
18The child grew, and one day he went out
to his father, who was with the reapers. 19"My
head! My head!" he said to his father.
His father told a servant, "Carry him to his
mother." 20After the servant had lifted him up
and carried him to his mother, the boy sat on
her lap until noon, and then he died. 21She
went up and laid him on the bed of the man of
God, then shut the door and went out.
22She called her husband and said, "Please
send me one of the servants and a donkey so I
can go to the man of God quickly and return."
23"Why go to him today?" he asked. "It's not
the New Moon or the Sabbath."
"It's all right," she said.
24She saddled the donkey and said to her servant, "Lead on; don't slow down for me unless I
tell you." 25So she set out and came to the man
of God at Mount Carmel.
When he saw her in the distance, the man of
God said to his servant Gehazi, "Look! There's
the Shunammite! 26Run to meet her and ask
her, 'Are you all right? Is your husband all
right? Is your child all right?' "
"Everything is all right," she said.
27When she reached the man of God at the
mountain, she took hold of his feet. Gehazi
came over to push her away, but the man of
God said, "Leave her alone! She is in bitter distress, but the LORD has hidden it from me and
has not told me why."
28"Did I ask you for a son, my lord?" she said.
"Didn't I tell you, 'Don't raise my hopes'?"
29Elisha said to Gehazi, "Tuck your cloak
into your belt, take my staff in your hand and
run. If you meet anyone, do not greet him, and
if anyone greets you, do not answer. Lay my
staff on the boy's face."
30But the child's mother said, "As surely as
the LORD lives and as you live, I will not leave
you." So he got up and followed her.
31Gehazi went on ahead and laid the staff
on the boy's face, but there was no sound or
response. So Gehazi went back to meet Elisha
and told him, "The boy has not awakened."
32When Elisha reached the house, there was
the boy lying dead on his couch. 33He went in,
shut the door on the two of them and prayed
to the LORD. 34Then he got on the bed and lay
upon the boy, mouth to mouth, eyes to eyes,
hands to hands. As he stretched himself out
upon him, the boy's body grew warm. 35Elisha
turned away and walked back and forth in the
room and then got on the bed and stretched
out upon him once more. The boy sneezed
seven times and opened his eyes.
36Elisha summoned Gehazi and said, "Call
the Shunammite." And he did. When she came,
he said, "Take your son." 37She came in, fell at

his feet and bowed to the ground. Then she
took her son and went out.

Death in the Pot

38 Elisha returned to Gilgal and there was a
famine in that region. While the company of
the prophets was meeting with him, he said
to his servant, "Put on the large pot and cook
some stew for these men."
39 One of them went out into the fields to
gather herbs and found a wild vine. He gathered some of its gourds and filled the fold of
his cloak. When he returned, he cut them up
into the pot of stew, though no one knew what
they were. 40 The stew was poured out for the
men, but as they began to eat it, they cried out,
"O man of God, there is death in the pot!" And
they could not eat it.
41 Elisha said, "Get some flour." He put it into
the pot and said, "Serve it to the people to eat."
And there was nothing harmful in the pot.

Feeding of a Hundred

42 A man came from Baal
Shalishah, bringing the man
of God twenty loaves of barley
bread baked from the first ripe
grain, along with some heads
of new grain. "Give it to the
people to eat," Elisha said.
43 "How can I set this before a hundred men?" his servant asked.
But Elisha answered, "Give it
to the people to eat. For this is
what the LORD says: 'They will
eat and have some left over.'"
44 Then he set it before them,
and they ate and had some left
over, according to the word of
the LORD.

2 Kings 4:43

God Provides Abundantly

"How can I set this before a hundred men?" his servant asked. But Elisha answered, "Give it to the people to eat. For this is what the LORD says: 'They will eat and have some left over.' "

Naaman Healed of Leprosy

5 Now Naaman was commander of the
army of the king of Aram. He was a great
man in the sight of his master and highly
regarded, because through him the LORD had
given victory to Aram. He was a valiant soldier,
but he had leprosy.[a]
2 Now bands from Aram had gone out and
had taken captive a young girl from Israel, and
she served Naaman's wife. 3 She said to her mistress, "If only my master would see the prophet
who is in Samaria! He would cure him of his
leprosy."
4 Naaman went to his master and told him
what the girl from Israel had said. 5 "By all
means, go," the king of Aram replied. "I will
send a letter to the king of Israel." So Naaman
left, taking with him ten talents[b] of silver, six
thousand shekels[c] of gold and ten sets of clothing. 6 The letter that he took to the king of Israel
read: "With this letter I am sending my servant
Naaman to you so that you may cure him of
his leprosy."
7 As soon as the king of Israel read the letter,
he tore his robes and said, "Am I God? Can I
kill and bring back to life? Why does this fellow send someone to me to be cured of his
leprosy? See how he is trying to pick a quarrel
with me!"
8 When Elisha the man of
God heard that the king of
Israel had torn his robes, he
sent him this message: "Why
have you torn your robes?
Have the man come to me
and he will know that there is
a prophet in Israel." 9 So Naaman went with his horses and
chariots and stopped at the
door of Elisha's house. 10 Elisha
sent a messenger to say to him,
"Go, wash yourself seven times
in the Jordan, and your flesh
will be restored and you will
be cleansed."
11 But Naaman went away
angry and said, "I thought that
he would surely come out to
me and stand and call on the name of the LORD
his God, wave his hand over the spot and cure
me of my leprosy. 12 Are not Abana and Phar-
par, the rivers of Damascus, better than any of
the waters of Israel? Couldn't I wash in them
and be cleansed?" So he turned and went off
in a rage.
13 Naaman's servants went to him and said,

[a]1 The Hebrew word was used for various diseases affecting the skin—not necessarily leprosy; also in verses 3, 6, 7, 11 and 27.
[b]5 That is, about 750 pounds (about 340 kilograms) [c]5 That is, about 150 pounds (about 70 kilograms)

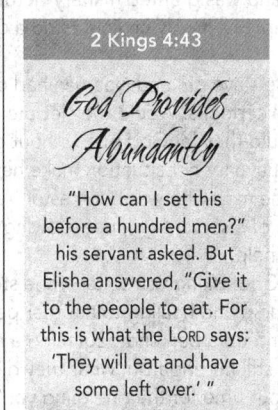

Those Exceptions of Life

Read: 2 Kings 5:1–14

2 Kings 5:1

Now Naaman was commander of the army of the king of Aram. He was a great man in the sight of his master and highly regarded, because through him the LORD had given victory to Aram. He was a valiant soldier, but he had leprosy.

reflection

1 What *except* has disrupted your life?

2 How have you handled your exception? How has this story lent some perspective on your own situation?

3 What step has God asked you to take that you are reluctant to try?

RELATED READINGS

Luke 4:24–27; John 9:1–11

IS YOUR LIFE HAPPY . . . *except* for one thing? Perhaps you enjoy a loving marriage, a beautiful home and financial ease . . . *except* you suffer from infertility. Maybe you have graduated with a master's degree, founded a business and are in top physical condition . . . *except* your parents are getting divorced. If you compiled a list of all the positives in your life, what would you include? *I have great friends; I'm an accomplished pianist; I've inherited a green thumb.* But what disrupts your sense of well-being? All of us possess at least one *except* that gets in the way of our happiness.

An unnamed slave girl experienced some poignant *excepts* in her young life. She was one of God's chosen people. She had faith in God . . . *except* she was a captive of war in a foreign land. The good news: She found herself in the household of a commander of the army.

Naaman, the commander, also experienced some significant *excepts.* He had great authority and was highly regarded by the king. Although he was a Gentile, he found favor with the God of Israel and was granted military victory. *Except* one thing plagued him: leprosy. If only he could find a cure, his life would be complete.

The slave girl and Naaman had choices to make concerning life's exceptions. Would they let the exceptions rule their lives? Or would they let God rule without exception? The slave girl could have let her situation make her bitter. Instead, she chose to help the man who was her master. And Naaman chose to take the advice of a servant girl, not allowing his pride to stand in the way of her help.

Is God asking you to take one step of obedience that may bring help and healing to another person? Perhaps it's as simple as taking up a pen and beginning a note of apology even though you're still hurting from what *they* did to *you*? Maybe you need to carve out time for the one thing you've been dreading to do. It could be you're compelled to take one act of firm discipline for the unruly child you love. That first step of obedience can bring your exception into a different light when you learn step by step what it means to trust God without exceptions.

Go to page 451 for your next devotional reading.

"My father, if the prophet had told you to do some great thing, would you not have done it? How much more, then, when he tells you, 'Wash and be cleansed'!" 14So he went down and dipped himself in the Jordan seven times, as the man of God had told him, and his flesh was restored and became clean like that of a young boy.

15Then Naaman and all his attendants went back to the man of God. He stood before him and said, "Now I know that there is no God in all the world except in Israel. Please accept now a gift from your servant."

16The prophet answered, "As surely as the LORD lives, whom I serve, I will not accept a thing." And even though Naaman urged him, he refused.

17"If you will not," said Naaman, "please let me, your servant, be given as much earth as a pair of mules can carry, for your servant will never again make burnt offerings and sacrifices to any other god but the LORD. 18But may the LORD forgive your servant for this one thing: When my master enters the temple of Rimmon to bow down and he is leaning on my arm and I bow there also—when I bow down in the temple of Rimmon, may the LORD forgive your servant for this."

19"Go in peace," Elisha said.

After Naaman had traveled some distance, 20Gehazi, the servant of Elisha the man of God, said to himself, "My master was too easy on Naaman, this Aramean, by not accepting from him what he brought. As surely as the LORD lives, I will run after him and get something from him."

21So Gehazi hurried after Naaman. When Naaman saw him running toward him, he got down from the chariot to meet him. "Is everything all right?" he asked.

22"Everything is all right," Gehazi answered. "My master sent me to say, 'Two young men from the company of the prophets have just come to me from the hill country of Ephraim. Please give them a talent[a] of silver and two sets of clothing.'"

23"By all means, take two talents," said Naaman. He urged Gehazi to accept them, and then tied up the two talents of silver in two bags, with two sets of clothing. He gave them to two of his servants, and they carried them ahead of Gehazi. 24When Gehazi came to the hill, he took the things from the servants and put them away in the house. He sent the men away and they left. 25Then he went in and stood before his master Elisha.

"Where have you been, Gehazi?" Elisha asked.

"Your servant didn't go anywhere," Gehazi answered.

26But Elisha said to him, "Was not my spirit with you when the man got down from his chariot to meet you? Is this the time to take money, or to accept clothes, olive groves, vineyards, flocks, herds, or menservants and maidservants? 27Naaman's leprosy will cling to you and to your descendants forever." Then Gehazi went from Elisha's presence and he was leprous, as white as snow.

An Axhead Floats

6 The company of the prophets said to Elisha, "Look, the place where we meet with you is too small for us. 2Let us go to the Jordan, where each of us can get a pole; and let us build a place there for us to live."

And he said, "Go."

3Then one of them said, "Won't you please come with your servants?"

"I will," Elisha replied. 4And he went with them.

They went to the Jordan and began to cut down trees. 5As one of them was cutting down a tree, the iron axhead fell into the water. "Oh, my lord," he cried out, "it was borrowed!"

6The man of God asked, "Where did it fall?" When he showed him the place, Elisha cut a stick and threw it there, and made the iron float. 7"Lift it out," he said. Then the man reached out his hand and took it.

Elisha Traps Blinded Arameans

8Now the king of Aram was at war with Israel. After conferring with his officers, he said, "I will set up my camp in such and such a place."

9The man of God sent word to the king of Israel: "Beware of passing that place, because the Arameans are going down there." 10So the

a22 That is, about 75 pounds (about 34 kilograms)

king of Israel checked on the place indicated by
the man of God. Time and again Elisha warned
the king, so that he was on his guard in such
places.
11This enraged the king of Aram. He summoned his officers and demanded of them,
“Will you not tell me which of us is on the side
of the king of Israel?”
12“None of us, my lord the king,” said one of
his officers, “but Elisha, the prophet who is in
Israel, tells the king of Israel the very words you
speak in your bedroom.”
13“Go, find out where he is,” the king ordered, “so I can send men and capture him.”
The report came back: “He is in Dothan.”
14Then he sent horses and
chariots and a strong force
there. They went by night and
surrounded the city.
15When the servant of the
man of God got up and went
out early the next morning, an
army with horses and chariots
had surrounded the city. “Oh,
my lord, what shall we do?” the
servant asked.
16“Don’t be afraid,” the
prophet answered. “Those who
are with us are more than those
who are with them.”
17And Elisha prayed, “O LORD, open his
eyes so he may see.” Then the LORD opened
the servant’s eyes, and he looked and saw
the hills full of horses and chariots of fire all
around Elisha.
18As the enemy came down toward him, Elisha prayed to the LORD, “Strike these people
with blindness.” So he struck them with blindness, as Elisha had asked.
19Elisha told them, “This is not the road and
this is not the city. Follow me, and I will lead
you to the man you are looking for.” And he led
them to Samaria.
20After they entered the city, Elisha said,
“LORD, open the eyes of these men so they can
see.” Then the LORD opened their eyes and they
looked, and there they were, inside Samaria.
21When the king of Israel saw them, he
asked Elisha, “Shall I kill them, my father? Shall
I kill them?”
22“Do not kill them,” he answered. “Would
you kill men you have captured with your own
sword or bow? Set food and water before them
so that they may eat and drink and then go
back to their master.” 23So he prepared a great
feast for them, and after they had finished eating and drinking, he sent them away, and they
returned to their master. So the bands from
Aram stopped raiding Israel’s territory.

2 Kings 6:16

God Is Greater

"Don't be afraid," the prophet answered. "Those who are with us are more than those who are with them."

Famine in Besieged Samaria

24Some time later, Ben-Hadad king of Aram
mobilized his entire army and marched up and
laid siege to Samaria. 25There
was a great famine in the city;
the siege lasted so long that a
donkey’s head sold for eighty
shekels[a] of silver, and a quarter of a cab[b] of seed pods[c] for
five shekels.[d]
26As the king of Israel
was passing by on the wall, a
woman cried to him, “Help
me, my lord the king!”
27The king replied, “If the
LORD does not help you, where
can I get help for you? From the
threshing floor? From the winepress?” 28Then
he asked her, “What’s the matter?”
She answered, “This woman said to me,
‘Give up your son so we may eat him today, and
tomorrow we’ll eat my son.’ 29So we cooked
my son and ate him. The next day I said to her,
‘Give up your son so we may eat him,’ but she
had hidden him.”
30When the king heard the woman’s words,
he tore his robes. As he went along the wall,
the people looked, and there, underneath, he
had sackcloth on his body. 31He said, “May
God deal with me, be it ever so severely, if the
head of Elisha son of Shaphat remains on his
shoulders today!”
32Now Elisha was sitting in his house, and
the elders were sitting with him. The king sent
a messenger ahead, but before he arrived, Elisha said to the elders, “Don’t you see how this

[a]25 That is, about 2 pounds (about 1 kilogram) [b]25 That is, probably about 1/2 pint (about 0.3 liter) [c]25 Or *of doves’ dung*
[d]25 That is, about 2 ounces (about 55 grams)

murderer is sending someone to cut off my
head? Look, when the messenger comes, shut
the door and hold it shut against him. Is not the
sound of his master's footsteps behind him?"
33While he was still talking to them, the messenger came down to him. And ⌊the king⌋ said,
"This disaster is from the LORD. Why should I
wait for the LORD any longer?"

7 Elisha said, "Hear the word of the LORD.
This is what the LORD says: About this
time tomorrow, a seah[a] of flour will sell for a
shekel[b] and two seahs[c] of barley for a shekel at
the gate of Samaria."
2The officer on whose arm the king was leaning said to the man of God, "Look, even if the
LORD should open the floodgates of the heavens, could this happen?"
"You will see it with your own eyes," answered Elisha, "but you will not eat any of it!"

The Siege Lifted

3Now there were four men with leprosy[d] at
the entrance of the city gate. They said to each
other, "Why stay here until we die? 4If we say,
'We'll go into the city'—the famine is there, and
we will die. And if we stay here, we will die. So
let's go over to the camp of the Arameans and
surrender. If they spare us, we live; if they kill
us, then we die."
5At dusk they got up and went to the camp
of the Arameans. When they reached the edge
of the camp, not a man was there, 6for the Lord
had caused the Arameans to hear the sound of
chariots and horses and a great army, so that
they said to one another, "Look, the king of
Israel has hired the Hittite and Egyptian kings
to attack us!" 7So they got up and fled in the
dusk and abandoned their tents and their
horses and donkeys. They left the camp as it
was and ran for their lives.
8The men who had leprosy reached the edge
of the camp and entered one of the tents. They
ate and drank, and carried away silver, gold
and clothes, and went off and hid them. They
returned and entered another tent and took
some things from it and hid them also.
9Then they said to each other, "We're not doing right. This is a day of good news and we are
keeping it to ourselves. If we wait until daylight,
punishment will overtake us. Let's go at once
and report this to the royal palace."
10So they went and called out to the city
gatekeepers and told them, "We went into the
Aramean camp and not a man was there—not
a sound of anyone—only tethered horses and
donkeys, and the tents left just as they were."
11The gatekeepers shouted the news, and it was
reported within the palace.
12The king got up in the night and said to his
officers, "I will tell you what the Arameans have
done to us. They know we are starving; so they
have left the camp to hide in the countryside,
thinking, 'They will surely come out, and then
we will take them alive and get into the city.' "
13One of his officers answered, "Have some
men take five of the horses that are left in the
city. Their plight will be like that of all the Israelites left here—yes, they will only be like all
these Israelites who are doomed. So let us send
them to find out what happened."
14So they selected two chariots with their
horses, and the king sent them after the
Aramean army. He commanded the drivers,
"Go and find out what has happened." 15They
followed them as far as the Jordan, and they
found the whole road strewn with the clothing and equipment the Arameans had thrown
away in their headlong flight. So the messengers returned and reported to the king. 16Then
the people went out and plundered the camp
of the Arameans. So a seah of flour sold for a
shekel, and two seahs of barley sold for a shekel,
as the LORD had said.
17Now the king had put the officer on whose
arm he leaned in charge of the gate, and the people trampled him in the gateway, and he died,
just as the man of God had foretold when the
king came down to his house. 18It happened as
the man of God had said to the king: "About
this time tomorrow, a seah of flour will sell for
a shekel and two seahs of barley for a shekel at
the gate of Samaria."
19The officer had said to the man of God,
"Look, even if the LORD should open the floodgates of the heavens, could this happen?" The
man of God had replied, "You will see it with

[a]1 That is, probably about 7 quarts (about 7.3 liters); also in verses 16 and 18 [b]1 That is, about 2/5 ounce (about 11 grams); also in verses 16 and 18 [c]1 That is, probably about 13 quarts (about 15 liters); also in verses 16 and 18 [d]3 The Hebrew word is used for various diseases affecting the skin—not necessarily leprosy; also in verse 8.

your own eyes, but you will not eat any of it!"
20 And that is exactly what happened to him,
for the people trampled him in the gateway,
and he died.

The Shunammite's Land Restored

8 Now Elisha had said to the woman whose
son he had restored to life, "Go away with
your family and stay for a while wherever you
can, because the LORD has decreed a famine in
the land that will last seven years." 2 The woman
proceeded to do as the man of God said. She
and her family went away and stayed in the
land of the Philistines seven years.

3 At the end of the seven years she came back
from the land of the Philistines and went to the
king to beg for her house and land. 4 The king
was talking to Gehazi, the servant of the man
of God, and had said, "Tell me about all the
great things Elisha has done." 5 Just as Gehazi
was telling the king how Elisha had restored
the dead to life, the woman whose son Elisha
had brought back to life came to beg the king
for her house and land.

Gehazi said, "This is the woman, my lord the
king, and this is her son whom Elisha restored
to life." 6 The king asked the woman about it,
and she told him.

Then he assigned an official to her case and
said to him, "Give back everything that belonged to her, including all the income from
her land from the day she left the country until now."

Hazael Murders Ben-Hadad

7 Elisha went to Damascus, and Ben-Hadad
king of Aram was ill. When the king was told,
"The man of God has come all the way up
here," 8 he said to Hazael, "Take a gift with you
and go to meet the man of God. Consult the
LORD through him; ask him, 'Will I recover
from this illness?'"

9 Hazael went to meet Elisha, taking with
him as a gift forty camel-loads of all the finest
wares of Damascus. He went in and stood before him, and said, "Your son Ben-Hadad king
of Aram has sent me to ask, 'Will I recover
from this illness?'"

10 Elisha answered, "Go and say to him,
'You will certainly recover'; but[a] the LORD has
revealed to me that he will in fact die." 11 He
stared at him with a fixed gaze until Hazael
felt ashamed. Then the man of God began
to weep.

12 "Why is my lord weeping?" asked Hazael.

"Because I know the harm you will do to
the Israelites," he answered. "You will set fire
to their fortified places, kill their young men
with the sword, dash their little children to the
ground, and rip open their pregnant women."

13 Hazael said, "How could your servant, a
mere dog, accomplish such a feat?"

"The LORD has shown me that you will become king of Aram," answered Elisha.

14 Then Hazael left Elisha and returned to
his master. When Ben-Hadad asked, "What
did Elisha say to you?" Hazael replied, "He told
me that you would certainly recover." 15 But the
next day he took a thick cloth, soaked it in water and spread it over the king's face, so that he
died. Then Hazael succeeded him as king.

Jehoram King of Judah

16 In the fifth year of Joram son of Ahab king
of Israel, when Jehoshaphat was king of Judah,
Jehoram son of Jehoshaphat began his reign as
king of Judah. 17 He was thirty-two years old
when he became king, and he reigned in Jerusalem eight years. 18 He walked in the ways of
the kings of Israel, as the house of Ahab had
done, for he married a daughter of Ahab. He
did evil in the eyes of the LORD. 19 Nevertheless,
for the sake of his servant David, the LORD was
not willing to destroy Judah. He had promised
to maintain a lamp for David and his descendants forever.

20 In the time of Jehoram, Edom rebelled
against Judah and set up its own king. 21 So Jehoram[b] went to Zair with all his chariots. The
Edomites surrounded him and his chariot commanders, but he rose up and broke through by
night; his army, however, fled back home. 22 To
this day Edom has been in rebellion against
Judah. Libnah revolted at the same time.

23 As for the other events of Jehoram's reign,
and all he did, are they not written in the book
of the annals of the kings of Judah? 24 Jehoram
rested with his fathers and was buried with

[a] 10 The Hebrew may also be read *Go and say, 'You will certainly not recover,' for.* [b] 21 Hebrew *Joram,* a variant of *Jehoram;* also in verses 23 and 24

When God Promises

Read: 2 Kings 8:16–24

THE STORY IS TOLD of a 91-year-old woman who said, "I spend about one hour each day with my Lord, reading my Bible and Christian literature. When people ask what good all my reading does if I can't remember what I've read, my answer is always the same: 'I'm in pretty good health, have a roof over my head and have plenty of food to eat. I also have two sons and one grandson who love me dearly. My cup runneth over.' I am not concerned about my memory. I just do my reading and God does the remembering."

God doesn't forget his promises; he remembers them regardless of how much time passes. King Jehoram, Judah's fifth king, reigned for eight years. Unlike his faithful father, Jehoshaphat, who worshiped the Lord, Jehoram "did evil in the eyes of the LORD" (2 Kings 8:18) and incurred God's anger. God allowed the Philistines, Arabians and Cushites to invade and plunder the land. Jehoram died a painful death and was denied burial in the tomb of the kings (see 2 Chronicles 21:16–20).

Because of Jehoram's evil actions, his reign ended painfully and abruptly. But God allowed Jehoram's grandson to survive. God remembered his promise to King David that he would preserve a godly remnant so that a Savior, his only Son, could be born through the tribe of Judah.

The people waited years for the Messiah. There were good kings and bad kings, captivity and foreign occupation. But through it all, God was mindful of his promise to send a Savior through the line of Judah. Roughly 600 years after the final book in the Old Testament was written, God kept his promise by sending Jesus in his perfect time, in his perfect way.

The sad truth is that people *do* break promises. They fail to keep their word. And this breaks our hearts. But no matter how many promises have been broken, no matter how many people have let us down, God never will. He is faithful . . . even if his promises take time to come to fruition. As the apostle Paul says, "For no matter how many promises God has made, they are 'Yes' in Christ. And so through him the 'Amen' is spoken by us to the glory of God" (2 Corinthians 1:20).

2 Kings 8:19

Nevertheless, for the sake of his servant David, the LORD was not willing to destroy Judah. He had promised to maintain a lamp for David and his descendants forever.

reflection

1 What promise have you been waiting for God to keep?

2 How have people's broken promises made it difficult for you to trust in God's promises?

3 How does it comfort you to know that God always keeps his promises? How does it challenge you to know that sometimes his promises take time to be fulfilled?

RELATED READINGS

2 Samuel 7:4–16;
Psalm 89:1–52;
2 Peter 3:8–9

Go to page 457 for your next devotional reading.

them in the City of David. And Ahaziah his
son succeeded him as king.

Ahaziah King of Judah

25 In the twelfth year of Joram son of Ahab
king of Israel, Ahaziah son of Jehoram king of
Judah began to reign. 26 Ahaziah was twenty-
two years old when he became king, and he
reigned in Jerusalem one year. His mother's
name was Athaliah, a granddaughter of Omri
king of Israel. 27 He walked in the ways of the
house of Ahab and did evil in the eyes of the
LORD, as the house of Ahab had done, for
he was related by marriage to Ahab's family.

28 Ahaziah went with Joram son of Ahab to
war against Hazael king of Aram at Ramoth
Gilead. The Arameans wounded Joram; 29 so
King Joram returned to Jezreel to recover from
the wounds the Arameans had inflicted on
him at Ramoth[a] in his battle with Hazael king
of Aram.

Then Ahaziah son of Jehoram king of Judah
went down to Jezreel to see Joram son of Ahab,
because he had been wounded.

Jehu Anointed King of Israel

9 The prophet Elisha summoned a man
from the company of the prophets and
said to him, "Tuck your cloak into your belt,
take this flask of oil with you and go to Ramoth Gilead. 2 When you get there, look for
Jehu son of Jehoshaphat, the son of Nimshi.
Go to him, get him away from his companions
and take him into an inner room. 3 Then take
the flask and pour the oil on his head and declare, 'This is what the LORD says: I anoint you
king over Israel.' Then open the door and run;
don't delay!"

4 So the young man, the prophet, went to Ramoth Gilead. 5 When he arrived, he found the
army officers sitting together. "I have a message
for you, commander," he said.

"For which of us?" asked Jehu.

"For you, commander," he replied.

6 Jehu got up and went into the house. Then
the prophet poured the oil on Jehu's head and
declared, "This is what the LORD, the God of
Israel, says: 'I anoint you king over the LORD's
people Israel. 7 You are to destroy the house of
Ahab your master, and I will avenge the blood
of my servants the prophets and the blood of
all the LORD's servants shed by Jezebel. 8 The
whole house of Ahab will perish. I will cut off
from Ahab every last male in Israel—slave or
free. 9 I will make the house of Ahab like the
house of Jeroboam son of Nebat and like the
house of Baasha son of Ahijah. 10 As for Jezebel, dogs will devour her on the plot of ground
at Jezreel, and no one will bury her.'" Then he
opened the door and ran.

11 When Jehu went out to his fellow officers,
one of them asked him, "Is everything all right?
Why did this madman come to you?"

"You know the man and the sort of things he
says," Jehu replied.

12 "That's not true!" they said. "Tell us."

Jehu said, "Here is what he told me: 'This
is what the LORD says: I anoint you king over
Israel.'"

13 They hurried and took their cloaks and
spread them under him on the bare steps. Then
they blew the trumpet and shouted, "Jehu is
king!"

Jehu Kills Joram and Ahaziah

14 So Jehu son of Jehoshaphat, the son of Nimshi, conspired against Joram. (Now Joram and
all Israel had been defending Ramoth Gilead
against Hazael king of Aram, 15 but King Joram[b] had returned to Jezreel to recover from
the wounds the Arameans had inflicted on him
in the battle with Hazael king of Aram.) Jehu
said, "If this is the way you feel, don't let anyone slip out of the city to go and tell the news
in Jezreel." 16 Then he got into his chariot and
rode to Jezreel, because Joram was resting there
and Ahaziah king of Judah had gone down to
see him.

17 When the lookout standing on the tower
in Jezreel saw Jehu's troops approaching, he
called out, "I see some troops coming."

"Get a horseman," Joram ordered. "Send
him to meet them and ask, 'Do you come in
peace?'"

18 The horseman rode off to meet Jehu and
said, "This is what the king says: 'Do you come
in peace?'"

"What do you have to do with peace?" Jehu
replied. "Fall in behind me."

[a] 29 Hebrew *Ramah,* a variant of *Ramoth*   [b] 15 Hebrew *Jehoram,* a variant of *Joram;* also in verses 17 and 21–24

The lookout reported, "The messenger has
reached them, but he isn't coming back."
19 So the king sent out a second horseman.
When he came to them he said, "This is what
the king says: 'Do you come in peace?' "
Jehu replied, "What do you have to do with
peace? Fall in behind me."
20 The lookout reported, "He has reached
them, but he isn't coming back either. The driving is like that of Jehu son of Nimshi—he drives
like a madman."
21 "Hitch up my chariot," Joram ordered.
And when it was hitched up, Joram king of
Israel and Ahaziah king of Judah rode out, each
in his own chariot, to meet Jehu. They met him
at the plot of ground that had belonged to Naboth the Jezreelite. 22 When Joram saw Jehu he
asked, "Have you come in peace, Jehu?"
"How can there be peace," Jehu replied, "as
long as all the idolatry and witchcraft of your
mother Jezebel abound?"
23 Joram turned about and fled, calling out to
Ahaziah, "Treachery, Ahaziah!"
24 Then Jehu drew his bow and shot Joram
between the shoulders. The arrow pierced his
heart and he slumped down in his chariot.
25 Jehu said to Bidkar, his chariot officer, "Pick
him up and throw him on the field that belonged to Naboth the Jezreelite. Remember
how you and I were riding together in chariots
behind Ahab his father when the LORD made
this prophecy about him: 26 'Yesterday I saw
the blood of Naboth and the blood of his sons,
declares the LORD, and I will surely make you
pay for it on this plot of ground, declares the
LORD.'[a] Now then, pick him up and throw him
on that plot, in accordance with the word of
the LORD."
27 When Ahaziah king of Judah saw what
had happened, he fled up the road to Beth
Haggan.[b] Jehu chased him, shouting, "Kill him
too!" They wounded him in his chariot on the
way up to Gur near Ibleam, but he escaped
to Megiddo and died there. 28 His servants
took him by chariot to Jerusalem and buried
him with his fathers in his tomb in the City of
David. 29 (In the eleventh year of Joram son of
Ahab, Ahaziah had become king of Judah.)

Jezebel Killed

30 Then Jehu went to Jezreel. When Jezebel
heard about it, she painted her eyes, arranged
her hair and looked out of a window. 31 As Jehu
entered the gate, she asked, "Have you come in
peace, Zimri, you murderer of your master?"[c]
32 He looked up at the window and called
out, "Who is on my side? Who?" Two or three
eunuchs looked down at him. 33 "Throw her
down!" Jehu said. So they threw her down, and
some of her blood spattered the wall and the
horses as they trampled her underfoot.
34 Jehu went in and ate and drank. "Take care
of that cursed woman," he said, "and bury her,
for she was a king's daughter." 35 But when they
went out to bury her, they found nothing except her skull, her feet and her hands. 36 They
went back and told Jehu, who said, "This is the
word of the LORD that he spoke through his servant Elijah the Tishbite: On the plot of ground
at Jezreel dogs will devour Jezebel's flesh.[d] 37 Jezebel's body will be like refuse on the ground in
the plot at Jezreel, so that no one will be able to
say, 'This is Jezebel.' "

Ahab's Family Killed

10 Now there were in Samaria seventy
sons of the house of Ahab. So Jehu
wrote letters and sent them to Samaria: to the officials of Jezreel,[e] to the elders and to the guardians of Ahab's children. He said, 2 "As soon as
this letter reaches you, since your master's sons
are with you and you have chariots and horses,
a fortified city and weapons, 3 choose the best
and most worthy of your master's sons and set
him on his father's throne. Then fight for your
master's house."
4 But they were terrified and said, "If two
kings could not resist him, how can we?"
5 So the palace administrator, the city governor, the elders and the guardians sent this message to Jehu: "We are your servants and we will
do anything you say. We will not appoint anyone as king; you do whatever you think best."
6 Then Jehu wrote them a second letter, saying, "If you are on my side and will obey me,
take the heads of your master's sons and come
to me in Jezreel by this time tomorrow."
Now the royal princes, seventy of them, were

[a] 26 See 1 Kings 21:19. [b] 27 Or *fled by way of the garden house* [c] 31 Or *"Did Zimri have peace, who murdered his master?"*
[d] 36 See 1 Kings 21:23. [e] 1 Hebrew; some Septuagint manuscripts and Vulgate *of the city*

with the leading men of the city, who were rear-
ing them. 7When the letter arrived, these men
took the princes and slaughtered all seventy of
them. They put their heads in baskets and sent
them to Jehu in Jezreel. 8When the messenger
arrived, he told Jehu, "They have brought the
heads of the princes."

Then Jehu ordered, "Put them in two piles at
the entrance of the city gate until morning."

9The next morning Jehu went out. He stood
before all the people and said, "You are innocent. It was I who conspired against my master and killed him, but who killed all these?
10Know then, that not a word the LORD has
spoken against the house of Ahab will fail. The
LORD has done what he promised through his
servant Elijah." 11So Jehu killed everyone in
Jezreel who remained of the house of Ahab, as
well as all his chief men, his close friends and
his priests, leaving him no survivor.

12Jehu then set out and went toward Samaria.
At Beth Eked of the Shepherds, 13he met some
relatives of Ahaziah king of Judah and asked,
"Who are you?"

They said, "We are relatives of Ahaziah, and
we have come down to greet the families of the
king and of the queen mother."

14"Take them alive!" he ordered. So they
took them alive and slaughtered them by the
well of Beth Eked—forty-two men. He left
no survivor.

15After he left there, he came upon Jehonadab son of Recab, who was on his way to meet
him. Jehu greeted him and said, "Are you in accord with me, as I am with you?"

"I am," Jehonadab answered.

"If so," said Jehu, "give me your hand." So he
did, and Jehu helped him up into the chariot.
16Jehu said, "Come with me and see my zeal
for the LORD." Then he had him ride along in
his chariot.

17When Jehu came to Samaria, he killed
all who were left there of Ahab's family; he
destroyed them, according to the word of the
LORD spoken to Elijah.

Ministers of Baal Killed

18Then Jehu brought all the people together
and said to them, "Ahab served Baal a little;
Jehu will serve him much. 19Now summon all
the prophets of Baal, all his ministers and all his
priests. See that no one is missing, because I am
going to hold a great sacrifice for Baal. Anyone
who fails to come will no longer live." But Jehu
was acting deceptively in order to destroy the
ministers of Baal.

20Jehu said, "Call an assembly in honor of
Baal." So they proclaimed it. 21Then he sent
word throughout Israel, and all the ministers of
Baal came; not one stayed away. They crowded
into the temple of Baal until it was full from one
end to the other. 22And Jehu said to the keeper
of the wardrobe, "Bring robes for all the ministers of Baal." So he brought out robes for them.

23Then Jehu and Jehonadab son of Recab
went into the temple of Baal. Jehu said to the
ministers of Baal, "Look around and see that
no servants of the LORD are here with you—
only ministers of Baal." 24So they went in to
make sacrifices and burnt offerings. Now Jehu
had posted eighty men outside with this warning: "If one of you lets any of the men I am placing in your hands escape, it will be your life for
his life."

25As soon as Jehu had finished making the
burnt offering, he ordered the guards and officers: "Go in and kill them; let no one escape."
So they cut them down with the sword. The
guards and officers threw the bodies out and
then entered the inner shrine of the temple of
Baal. 26They brought the sacred stone out of
the temple of Baal and burned it. 27They demolished the sacred stone of Baal and tore down
the temple of Baal, and people have used it for
a latrine to this day.

28So Jehu destroyed Baal worship in Israel.
29However, he did not turn away from the sins
of Jeroboam son of Nebat, which he had caused
Israel to commit—the worship of the golden
calves at Bethel and Dan.

30The LORD said to Jehu, "Because you have
done well in accomplishing what is right in my
eyes and have done to the house of Ahab all I
had in mind to do, your descendants will sit on
the throne of Israel to the fourth generation."
31Yet Jehu was not careful to keep the law of the
LORD, the God of Israel, with all his heart. He
did not turn away from the sins of Jeroboam,
which he had caused Israel to commit.

32In those days the LORD began to reduce
the size of Israel. Hazael overpowered the Isra-

elites throughout their territory 33 east of the
Jordan in all the land of Gilead (the region of
Gad, Reuben and Manasseh), from Aroer by
the Arnon Gorge through Gilead to Bashan.
34 As for the other events of Jehu's reign, all
he did, and all his achievements, are they not
written in the book of the an-
nals of the kings of Israel?
35 Jehu rested with his fathers
and was buried in Samaria. And
Jehoahaz his son succeeded him
as king. 36 The time that Jehu
reigned over Israel in Samaria
was twenty-eight years.

Athaliah and Joash

11 When Athaliah the
mother of Ahaziah
saw that her son was dead, she
proceeded to destroy the whole
royal family. 2 But Jehosheba,
the daughter of King Jehoram[a]
and sister of Ahaziah, took Joash son of Ahaziah and stole
him away from among the
royal princes, who were about
to be murdered. She put him and his nurse in a
bedroom to hide him from Athaliah; so he was
not killed. 3 He remained hidden with his nurse
at the temple of the LORD for six years while
Athaliah ruled the land.
4 In the seventh year Jehoiada sent for the
commanders of units of a hundred, the Carites and the guards and had them brought to
him at the temple of the LORD. He made a covenant with them and put them under oath at
the temple of the LORD. Then he showed them
the king's son. 5 He commanded them, saying,
"This is what you are to do: You who are in the
three companies that are going on duty on the
Sabbath—a third of you guarding the royal
palace, 6 a third at the Sur Gate, and a third
at the gate behind the guard, who take turns
guarding the temple— 7 and you who are in the
other two companies that normally go off Sabbath duty are all to guard the temple for the
king. 8 Station yourselves around the king, each
man with his weapon in his hand. Anyone who
approaches your ranks[b] must be put to death.
Stay close to the king wherever he goes."
9 The commanders of units of a hundred
did just as Jehoiada the priest ordered. Each
one took his men—those who were going on
duty on the Sabbath and those who were going off duty—and came to Jehoiada the priest.
10 Then he gave the commanders the spears
and shields that had belonged
to King David and that were in
the temple of the LORD. 11 The
guards, each with his weapon
in his hand, stationed themselves around the king—near
the altar and the temple, from
the south side to the north side
of the temple.
12 Jehoiada brought out the
king's son and put the crown
on him; he presented him with
a copy of the covenant and
proclaimed him king. They
anointed him, and the people clapped their hands and
shouted, "Long live the king!"
13 When Athaliah heard the
noise made by the guards and
the people, she went to the people at the temple
of the LORD. 14 She looked and there was the
king, standing by the pillar, as the custom was.
The officers and the trumpeters were beside the
king, and all the people of the land were rejoicing and blowing trumpets. Then Athaliah tore
her robes and called out, "Treason! Treason!"
15 Jehoiada the priest ordered the commanders of units of a hundred, who were in charge of
the troops: "Bring her out between the ranks[c]
and put to the sword anyone who follows her."
For the priest had said, "She must not be put
to death in the temple of the LORD." 16 So they
seized her as she reached the place where the
horses enter the palace grounds, and there she
was put to death.
17 Jehoiada then made a covenant between
the LORD and the king and people that they
would be the LORD's people. He also made a
covenant between the king and the people.
18 All the people of the land went to the temple
of Baal and tore it down. They smashed the altars and idols to pieces and killed Mattan the
priest of Baal in front of the altars.

> **2 Kings 10:30**
>
> *God Rewards Obedience*
>
> The LORD said to Jehu, "Because you have done well in accomplishing what is right in my eyes and have done to the house of Ahab all I had in mind to do, your descendants will sit on the throne of Israel to the fourth generation."

[a]2 Hebrew *Joram*, a variant of *Jehoram* [b]8 Or *approaches the precincts* [c]15 Or *out from the precincts*

Then Jehoiada the priest posted guards at
the temple of the LORD. 19He took with him
the commanders of hundreds, the Carites, the
guards and all the people of the land, and
together they brought the king down from the
temple of the LORD and went into the palace,
entering by way of the gate of the guards. The
king then took his place on the royal throne,
20and all the people of the land rejoiced. And
the city was quiet, because Athaliah had been
slain with the sword at the palace.

21Joash[a] was seven years old when he began
to reign.

Joash Repairs the Temple

12 In the seventh year of Jehu, Joash[b]
became king, and he reigned in Jerusalem forty years. His mother's name was
Zibiah; she was from Beersheba. 2Joash did
what was right in the eyes of the LORD all
the years Jehoiada the priest instructed him.
3The high places, however, were not removed;
the people continued to offer sacrifices and
burn incense there.

4Joash said to the priests, "Collect all the
money that is brought as sacred offerings to the
temple of the LORD—the money collected in
the census, the money received from personal
vows and the money brought voluntarily to the
temple. 5Let every priest receive the money from
one of the treasurers, and let it be used to repair
whatever damage is found in the temple."

6But by the twenty-third year of King Joash
the priests still had not repaired the temple.
7Therefore King Joash summoned Jehoiada
the priest and the other priests and asked them,
"Why aren't you repairing the damage done to
the temple? Take no more money from your
treasurers, but hand it over for repairing the
temple." 8The priests agreed that they would
not collect any more money from the people
and that they would not repair the temple themselves.

9Jehoiada the priest took a chest and bored a
hole in its lid. He placed it beside the altar, on the
right side as one enters the temple of the LORD.
The priests who guarded the entrance put into
the chest all the money that was brought to the
temple of the LORD. 10Whenever they saw that
there was a large amount of money in the chest,
the royal secretary and the high priest came,
counted the money that had been brought into
the temple of the LORD and put it into bags.
11When the amount had been determined,
they gave the money to the men appointed to
supervise the work on the temple. With it they
paid those who worked on the temple of the
LORD—the carpenters and builders, 12the masons and stonecutters. They purchased timber
and dressed stone for the repair of the temple
of the LORD, and met all the other expenses of
restoring the temple.

13The money brought into the temple was
not spent for making silver basins, wick trimmers, sprinkling bowls, trumpets or any other
articles of gold or silver for the temple of the
LORD; 14it was paid to the workmen, who used
it to repair the temple. 15They did not require
an accounting from those to whom they gave
the money to pay the workers, because they
acted with complete honesty. 16The money
from the guilt offerings and sin offerings was
not brought into the temple of the LORD; it belonged to the priests.

17About this time Hazael king of Aram went
up and attacked Gath and captured it. Then he
turned to attack Jerusalem. 18But Joash king
of Judah took all the sacred objects dedicated
by his fathers—Jehoshaphat, Jehoram and
Ahaziah, the kings of Judah—and the gifts he
himself had dedicated and all the gold found
in the treasuries of the temple of the LORD and
of the royal palace, and he sent them to Hazael
king of Aram, who then withdrew from Jerusalem.

19As for the other events of the reign of
Joash, and all he did, are they not written in
the book of the annals of the kings of Judah?
20His officials conspired against him and
assassinated him at Beth Millo, on the road
down to Silla. 21The officials who murdered
him were Jozabad son of Shimeath and Jehozabad son of Shomer. He died and was buried
with his fathers in the City of David. And
Amaziah his son succeeded him as king.

Jehoahaz King of Israel

13 In the twenty-third year of Joash son
of Ahaziah king of Judah, Jehoahaz
son of Jehu became king of Israel in Samaria,

[a]21 Hebrew *Jehoash,* a variant of *Joash* [b]1 Hebrew *Jehoash,* a variant of *Joash*; also in verses 2, 4, 6, 7 and 18

The Truth Will Come Out

Read: 2 Kings 12:1–21

EARLY GREEK TRAGEDIANS obsessed over deception. Reading the plays of Sophocles and Euripides, one might conclude that they lived in societies paranoid that a web of half-truths and lies prevailed. Their mythical figures spoke in riddles; those who tried to evade prophecies unwittingly played into the hands of fate. When the truth did finally come to light, it often appeared only when calamity had already struck. We may feel this way about various aspects of our lives. Paranoia may plague our opinions on politics, our neighbors, even our family. Honesty once broken takes a long time to rebuild. Thus, scrupulous honesty in our dealings with others is one of our most valuable assets.

The workers described in 2 Kings 12 realized the value of trustworthiness. They were so well known for their complete honesty that they weren't required to give an account for how they spent the vast amounts of money allotted for the temple's reconstruction.

How different that scene in 2 Kings is from the scene in Genesis 3, where God confronted Adam and Eve and demanded an accounting from them after their fateful encounter with the serpent. For the first time in this first couple's lives—which had been perfect, stress-free and marked by an ongoing, intimate relationship with their Creator—the two garden-dwellers were asked to account for their actions to God himself. Why? Because they had listened to the serpent's lies, compromised what they knew to be the truth of God's Word and allowed sin to invade paradise.

Can you relate? Maybe your lies don't seem serpent-sized, but even so-called white lies can open the door to compromise and sin. Maybe you don't tell the whole truth about the money you've spent or about why you can't take on a project or about the company supplies you took home. But even the Greek tragedians knew that lies don't stay hidden forever. When a lie is discovered, we risk losing the trust of those we most value.

Wouldn't it be better to live like the straightforward workers in this story? Their reputation for "complete honesty" went before them, gaining them the respect of their superiors and even the king.

2 Kings 12:15

They did not require an accounting from those to whom they gave the money to pay the workers, because they acted with complete honesty.

reflection

1 Have you compromised the truth and gotten caught up in "little white lies"? What was the outcome?

2 What do you want your reputation to look like? Ask God to help you become a person known for her complete honesty.

3 Can you think of any situation in which it would be right and necessary to hide the truth? (Hint: Read 2 Kings 11:1–3.)

RELATED READINGS

Genesis 3:1–24; Proverbs 16:11; Isaiah 59:12–15; Acts 5:1–11

Go to page 463 for your next devotional reading.

and he reigned seventeen years. 2He did evil
in the eyes of the LORD by following the sins
of Jeroboam son of Nebat, which he had
caused Israel to commit, and he did not turn
away from them. 3So the LORD's anger burned
against Israel, and for a long time he kept them
under the power of Hazael king of Aram and
Ben-Hadad his son.

4Then Jehoahaz sought the LORD's favor,
and the LORD listened to him, for he saw how
severely the king of Aram was oppressing Israel.
5The LORD provided a deliverer for Israel, and
they escaped from the power of Aram. So the
Israelites lived in their own homes as they had
before. 6But they did not turn away from the
sins of the house of Jeroboam, which he had
caused Israel to commit; they continued in
them. Also, the Asherah pole[a] remained standing in Samaria.

7Nothing had been left of the army of Jehoahaz except fifty horsemen, ten chariots and ten
thousand foot soldiers, for the king of Aram
had destroyed the rest and made them like the
dust at threshing time.

8As for the other events of the reign of Jehoahaz, all he did and his achievements, are
they not written in the book
of the annals of the kings of
Israel? 9Jehoahaz rested with
his fathers and was buried in
Samaria. And Jehoash[b] his son
succeeded him as king.

Jehoash King of Israel

10In the thirty-seventh year
of Joash king of Judah, Jehoash son of Jehoahaz became
king of Israel in Samaria, and
he reigned sixteen years. 11He
did evil in the eyes of the LORD
and did not turn away from
any of the sins of Jeroboam son
of Nebat, which he had caused
Israel to commit; he continued
in them.

12As for the other events of the reign of Jehoash, all he did and his achievements, including his war against Amaziah king of Judah, are
they not written in the book of the annals of
the kings of Israel? 13Jehoash rested with his
fathers, and Jeroboam succeeded him on the
throne. Jehoash was buried in Samaria with the
kings of Israel.

14Now Elisha was suffering from the illness
from which he died. Jehoash king of Israel
went down to see him and wept over him. "My
father! My father!" he cried. "The chariots and
horsemen of Israel!"

15Elisha said, "Get a bow and some arrows,"
and he did so. 16"Take the bow in your hands,"
he said to the king of Israel. When he had taken
it, Elisha put his hands on the king's hands.

17"Open the east window," he said, and he
opened it. "Shoot!" Elisha said, and he shot.
"The LORD's arrow of victory, the arrow of
victory over Aram!" Elisha declared. "You will
completely destroy the Arameans at Aphek."

18Then he said, "Take the arrows," and the
king took them. Elisha told him, "Strike the
ground." He struck it three times and stopped.
19The man of God was angry with him and
said, "You should have struck the ground five or
six times; then you would have defeated Aram
and completely destroyed it. But now you will
defeat it only three times."

20Elisha died and was buried.

Now Moabite raiders used to
enter the country every spring.
21Once while some Israelites
were burying a man, suddenly
they saw a band of raiders; so
they threw the man's body into
Elisha's tomb. When the body
touched Elisha's bones, the
man came to life and stood up
on his feet.

22Hazael king of Aram op-
pressed Israel throughout the
reign of Jehoahaz. 23But the
LORD was gracious to them and
had compassion and showed
concern for them because of
his covenant with Abraham, Isaac and Jacob.
To this day he has been unwilling to destroy
them or banish them from his presence.

2 Kings 13:23

God Is Compassionate

But the LORD was gracious to them and had compassion and showed concern for them . . . To this day he has been unwilling to destroy them or banish them from his presence.

[a]6 That is, a symbol of the goddess Asherah; here and elsewhere in 2 Kings [b]9 Hebrew *Joash,* a variant of *Jehoash*; also in verses 12–14 and 25

24 Hazael king of Aram died, and Ben-Hadad
his son succeeded him as king. 25 Then Jehoash
son of Jehoahaz recaptured from Ben-Hadad
son of Hazael the towns he had taken in battle
from his father Jehoahaz. Three times Jehoash
defeated him, and so he recovered the Israelite towns.

Amaziah King of Judah

14 In the second year of Jehoash[a] son of
Jehoahaz king of Israel, Amaziah son
of Joash king of Judah began to reign. 2 He
was twenty-five years old when he became
king, and he reigned in Jerusalem twenty-nine
years. His mother's name was Jehoaddin; she
was from Jerusalem. 3 He did what was right
in the eyes of the LORD, but not as his father
David had done. In everything he followed the
example of his father Joash. 4 The high places,
however, were not removed; the people continued to offer sacrifices and burn incense there.

5 After the kingdom was firmly in his grasp,
he executed the officials who had murdered his
father the king. 6 Yet he did not put the sons of
the assassins to death, in accordance with what
is written in the Book of the Law of Moses
where the LORD commanded: "Fathers shall
not be put to death for their children, nor children put to death for their fathers; each is to die
for his own sins."[b]

7 He was the one who defeated ten thousand
Edomites in the Valley of Salt and captured
Sela in battle, calling it Joktheel, the name it
has to this day.

8 Then Amaziah sent messengers to Jehoash son of Jehoahaz, the son of Jehu, king of
Israel, with the challenge: "Come, meet me face
to face."

9 But Jehoash king of Israel replied to
Amaziah king of Judah: "A thistle in Lebanon
sent a message to a cedar in Lebanon, 'Give
your daughter to my son in marriage.' Then a
wild beast in Lebanon came along and trampled the thistle underfoot. 10 You have indeed
defeated Edom and now you are arrogant.
Glory in your victory, but stay at home! Why
ask for trouble and cause your own downfall
and that of Judah also?"

11 Amaziah, however, would not listen, so Jehoash king of Israel attacked. He and Amaziah
king of Judah faced each other at Beth Shemesh
in Judah. 12 Judah was routed by Israel, and
every man fled to his home. 13 Jehoash king of
Israel captured Amaziah king of Judah, the son
of Joash, the son of Ahaziah, at Beth Shemesh.
Then Jehoash went to Jerusalem and broke
down the wall of Jerusalem from the Ephraim
Gate to the Corner Gate—a section about six
hundred feet long.[c] 14 He took all the gold and
silver and all the articles found in the temple
of the LORD and in the treasuries of the royal
palace. He also took hostages and returned to
Samaria.

15 As for the other events of the reign of Jehoash, what he did and his achievements, including his war against Amaziah king of Judah, are
they not written in the book of the annals of
the kings of Israel? 16 Jehoash rested with his fathers and was buried in Samaria with the kings
of Israel. And Jeroboam his son succeeded him
as king.

17 Amaziah son of Joash king of Judah lived
for fifteen years after the death of Jehoash son
of Jehoahaz king of Israel. 18 As for the other
events of Amaziah's reign, are they not written
in the book of the annals of the kings of Judah?

19 They conspired against him in Jerusalem,
and he fled to Lachish, but they sent men after
him to Lachish and killed him there. 20 He was
brought back by horse and was buried in Jerusalem with his fathers, in the City of David.

21 Then all the people of Judah took Azariah,[d]
who was sixteen years old, and made him king
in place of his father Amaziah. 22 He was the
one who rebuilt Elath and restored it to Judah
after Amaziah rested with his fathers.

Jeroboam II King of Israel

23 In the fifteenth year of Amaziah son of
Joash king of Judah, Jeroboam son of Jehoash
king of Israel became king in Samaria, and he
reigned forty-one years. 24 He did evil in the
eyes of the LORD and did not turn away from
any of the sins of Jeroboam son of Nebat, which
he had caused Israel to commit. 25 He was the
one who restored the boundaries of Israel from
Lebo[e] Hamath to the Sea of the Arabah,[f] in

[a] 1 Hebrew *Joash,* a variant of *Jehoash*; also in verses 13, 23 and 27 [b] 6 Deut. 24:16 [c] 13 Hebrew *four hundred cubits* (about 180 meters)
[d] 21 Also called *Uzziah* [e] 25 Or *from the entrance to* [f] 25 That is, the Dead Sea

accordance with the word of the LORD, the God of Israel, spoken through his servant Jonah son of Amittai, the prophet from Gath Hepher.

[26]The LORD had seen how bitterly everyone in Israel, whether slave or free, was suffering; there was no one to help them. [27]And since the LORD had not said he would blot out the name of Israel from under heaven, he saved them by the hand of Jeroboam son of Jehoash.

[28]As for the other events of Jeroboam's reign, all he did, and his military achievements, including how he recovered for Israel both Damascus and Hamath, which had belonged to Yaudi,[a] are they not written in the book of the annals of the kings of Israel? [29]Jeroboam rested with his fathers, the kings of Israel. And Zechariah his son succeeded him as king.

Azariah King of Judah

15 In the twenty-seventh year of Jeroboam king of Israel, Azariah son of Amaziah king of Judah began to reign. [2]He was sixteen years old when he became king, and he reigned in Jerusalem fifty-two years. His mother's name was Jecoliah; she was from Jerusalem. [3]He did what was right in the eyes of the LORD, just as his father Amaziah had done. [4]The high places, however, were not removed; the people continued to offer sacrifices and burn incense there.

[5]The LORD afflicted the king with leprosy[b] until the day he died, and he lived in a separate house.[c] Jotham the king's son had charge of the palace and governed the people of the land.

[6]As for the other events of Azariah's reign, and all he did, are they not written in the book of the annals of the kings of Judah? [7]Azariah rested with his fathers and was buried near them in the City of David. And Jotham his son succeeded him as king.

Zechariah King of Israel

[8]In the thirty-eighth year of Azariah king of Judah, Zechariah son of Jeroboam became king of Israel in Samaria, and he reigned six months. [9]He did evil in the eyes of the LORD, as his fathers had done. He did not turn away from the sins of Jeroboam son of Nebat, which he had caused Israel to commit.

[10]Shallum son of Jabesh conspired against Zechariah. He attacked him in front of the people,[d] assassinated him and succeeded him as king. [11]The other events of Zechariah's reign are written in the book of the annals of the kings of Israel. [12]So the word of the LORD spoken to Jehu was fulfilled: "Your descendants will sit on the throne of Israel to the fourth generation."[e]

> **2 Kings 14:27**
>
> *God Saves*
>
> And since the LORD had not said he would blot out the name of Israel from under heaven, he saved them by the hand of Jeroboam son of Jehoash.

Shallum King of Israel

[13]Shallum son of Jabesh became king in the thirty-ninth year of Uzziah king of Judah, and he reigned in Samaria one month. [14]Then Menahem son of Gadi went from Tirzah up to Samaria. He attacked Shallum son of Jabesh in Samaria, assassinated him and succeeded him as king.

[15]The other events of Shallum's reign, and the conspiracy he led, are written in the book of the annals of the kings of Israel.

[16]At that time Menahem, starting out from Tirzah, attacked Tiphsah and everyone in the city and its vicinity, because they refused to open their gates. He sacked Tiphsah and ripped open all the pregnant women.

Menahem King of Israel

[17]In the thirty-ninth year of Azariah king of Judah, Menahem son of Gadi became king of Israel, and he reigned in Samaria ten years. [18]He did evil in the eyes of the LORD. During his entire reign he did not turn away from the sins of Jeroboam son of Nebat, which he had caused Israel to commit.

[19]Then Pul[f] king of Assyria invaded the land, and Menahem gave him a thousand talents[g] of silver to gain his support and strengthen his own hold on the kingdom.

[a]28 Or *Judah* [b]5 The Hebrew word was used for various diseases affecting the skin—not necessarily leprosy. [c]5 Or *in a house where he was relieved of responsibility* [d]10 Hebrew; some Septuagint manuscripts *in Ibleam* [e]12 2 Kings 10:30 [f]19 Also called *Tiglath-Pileser* [g]19 That is, about 37 tons (about 34 metric tons)

20 Menahem exacted this money from Israel.
Every wealthy man had to contribute fifty shekels[a] of silver to be given to the king of Assyria.
So the king of Assyria withdrew and stayed in
the land no longer.
21 As for the other events of Menahem's
reign, and all he did, are they not written in the
book of the annals of the kings of Israel? 22 Menahem rested with his fathers. And Pekahiah his
son succeeded him as king.

Pekahiah King of Israel

23 In the fiftieth year of Azariah king of
Judah, Pekahiah son of Menahem became
king of Israel in Samaria, and he reigned two
years. 24 Pekahiah did evil in the eyes of the
LORD. He did not turn away from the sins of
Jeroboam son of Nebat, which he had caused
Israel to commit. 25 One of his chief officers,
Pekah son of Remaliah, conspired against
him. Taking fifty men of Gilead with him,
he assassinated Pekahiah, along with Argob
and Arieh, in the citadel of the royal palace
at Samaria. So Pekah killed Pekahiah and
succeeded him as king.
26 The other events of Pekahiah's reign, and
all he did, are written in the book of the annals
of the kings of Israel.

Pekah King of Israel

27 In the fifty-second year of Azariah king of
Judah, Pekah son of Remaliah became king of
Israel in Samaria, and he reigned twenty years.
28 He did evil in the eyes of the LORD. He did
not turn away from the sins of Jeroboam son
of Nebat, which he had caused Israel to commit.
29 In the time of Pekah king of Israel, Tiglath-Pileser king of Assyria came and took Ijon,
Abel Beth Maacah, Janoah, Kedesh and Hazor.
He took Gilead and Galilee, including all the
land of Naphtali, and deported the people to
Assyria. 30 Then Hoshea son of Elah conspired
against Pekah son of Remaliah. He attacked
and assassinated him, and then succeeded him
as king in the twentieth year of Jotham son of
Uzziah.
31 As for the other events of Pekah's reign,
and all he did, are they not written in the book
of the annals of the kings of Israel?

Jotham King of Judah

32 In the second year of Pekah son of
Remaliah king of Israel, Jotham son of Uzziah
king of Judah began to reign. 33 He was twenty-
five years old when he became king, and he
reigned in Jerusalem sixteen years. His mother's name was Jerusha daughter of Zadok. 34 He
did what was right in the eyes of the LORD,
just as his father Uzziah had done. 35 The high
places, however, were not removed; the people
continued to offer sacrifices and burn incense
there. Jotham rebuilt the Upper Gate of the
temple of the LORD.
36 As for the other events of Jotham's reign,
and what he did, are they not written in the
book of the annals of the kings of Judah? 37 (In
those days the LORD began to send Rezin king
of Aram and Pekah son of Remaliah against Judah.) 38 Jotham rested with his fathers and was
buried with them in the City of David, the city
of his father. And Ahaz his son succeeded him
as king.

Ahaz King of Judah

16 In the seventeenth year of Pekah son of
Remaliah, Ahaz son of Jotham king of
Judah began to reign. 2 Ahaz was twenty years
old when he became king, and he reigned in Jerusalem sixteen years. Unlike David his father,
he did not do what was right in the eyes of the
LORD his God. 3 He walked in the ways of the
kings of Israel and even sacrificed his son in[b]
the fire, following the detestable ways of the nations the LORD had driven out before the Israelites. 4 He offered sacrifices and burned incense
at the high places, on the hilltops and under
every spreading tree.
5 Then Rezin king of Aram and Pekah son
of Remaliah king of Israel marched up to fight
against Jerusalem and besieged Ahaz, but they
could not overpower him. 6 At that time, Rezin
king of Aram recovered Elath for Aram by driving out the men of Judah. Edomites then moved
into Elath and have lived there to this day.
7 Ahaz sent messengers to say to Tiglath-
Pileser king of Assyria, "I am your servant and
vassal. Come up and save me out of the hand of
the king of Aram and of the king of Israel, who
are attacking me." 8 And Ahaz took the silver
and gold found in the temple of the LORD and

[a] 20 That is, about 1 1/4 pounds (about 0.6 kilogram) [b] 3 Or *even made his son pass through*

in the treasuries of the royal palace and sent
it as a gift to the king of Assyria. 9The king of
Assyria complied by attacking Damascus and
capturing it. He deported its inhabitants to Kir
and put Rezin to death.
10Then King Ahaz went to Damascus to
meet Tiglath-Pileser king of Assyria. He saw an
altar in Damascus and sent to Uriah the priest
a sketch of the altar, with detailed plans for its
construction. 11So Uriah the priest built an altar in accordance with all the plans that King
Ahaz had sent from Damascus and finished it
before King Ahaz returned. 12When the king
came back from Damascus and saw the altar,
he approached it and presented offerings[a] on
it. 13He offered up his burnt offering and grain
offering, poured out his drink offering, and
sprinkled the blood of his fellowship offerings[b]
on the altar. 14The bronze altar that stood before the LORD he brought from the front of the
temple—from between the new altar and the
temple of the LORD—and put it on the north
side of the new altar.
15King Ahaz then gave these orders to Uriah
the priest: "On the large new altar, offer the
morning burnt offering and the evening grain
offering, the king's burnt offering and his grain
offering, and the burnt offering of all the people of the land, and their grain offering and
their drink offering. Sprinkle on the altar all
the blood of the burnt offerings and sacrifices.
But I will use the bronze altar for seeking guidance." 16And Uriah the priest did just as King
Ahaz had ordered.
17King Ahaz took away the side panels and
removed the basins from the movable stands.
He removed the Sea from the bronze bulls that
supported it and set it on a stone base. 18He
took away the Sabbath canopy[c] that had been
built at the temple and removed the royal entryway outside the temple of the LORD, in def-
erence to the king of Assyria.
19As for the other events of the reign of
Ahaz, and what he did, are they not written in
the book of the annals of the kings of Judah?
20Ahaz rested with his fathers and was buried
with them in the City of David. And Hezekiah
his son succeeded him as king.

Hoshea Last King of Israel

17 In the twelfth year of Ahaz king of Judah, Hoshea son of Elah became king
of Israel in Samaria, and he reigned nine years.
2He did evil in the eyes of the LORD, but not
like the kings of Israel who preceded him.
3Shalmaneser king of Assyria came up to attack Hoshea, who had been Shalmaneser's vassal and had paid him tribute. 4But the king of
Assyria discovered that Hoshea was a traitor,
for he had sent envoys to So[d] king of Egypt,
and he no longer paid tribute to the king of
Assyria, as he had done year by year. Therefore
Shalmaneser seized him and put him in prison.
5The king of Assyria invaded the entire land,
marched against Samaria and laid siege to it for
three years. 6In the ninth year of Hoshea, the
king of Assyria captured Samaria and deported
the Israelites to Assyria. He settled them in Halah, in Gozan on the Habor River and in the
towns of the Medes.

Israel Exiled Because of Sin

7All this took place because the Israelites
had sinned against the LORD their God, who
had brought them up out of Egypt from under
the power of Pharaoh king of Egypt. They worshiped other gods 8and followed the practices
of the nations the LORD had driven out before
them, as well as the practices that the kings of
Israel had introduced. 9The Israelites secretly
did things against the LORD their God that
were not right. From watchtower to fortified
city they built themselves high places in all
their towns. 10They set up sacred stones and
Asherah poles on every high hill and under every spreading tree. 11At every high place they
burned incense, as the nations whom the LORD
had driven out before them had done. They
did wicked things that provoked the LORD
to anger. 12They worshiped idols, though the
LORD had said, "You shall not do this."[e] 13The
LORD warned Israel and Judah through all his
prophets and seers: "Turn from your evil ways.
Observe my commands and decrees, in accordance with the entire Law that I commanded
your fathers to obey and that I delivered to you
through my servants the prophets."
14But they would not listen and were as

[a]12 Or *and went up* [b]13 Traditionally *peace offerings* [c]18 Or *the dais of his throne* (see Septuagint) [d]4 Or *to Sais, to the*; *So* is possibly an abbreviation for *Osorkon.* [e]12 Exodus 20:4,5

Beyond Understanding

MOTHER OF SAMSON

IT WAS BEYOND UNDERSTANDING.

She had been a faithful wife to Manoah for many years—a good wife. And although the two of them made a happy family together, they longed for the joy of raising a child. Yet for some reason, God had not entrusted her with a baby. She endured all the hurtful inquiries from insensitive neighbors and nosy relatives. When she could, she skillfully dodged questions that left her open to comments and criticisms. But sometimes the pain was inescapable. *What's wrong with me? Would I really be such a bad mother? Can God not trust me with a baby?*

So, when she heard what the man in front of her was saying, she could not take it in. *A child? A son?* One moment she was busy filling skins with water. The next, a man appeared out of nowhere, telling her the best news of her life. Not only that, but he said this child would be no ordinary child. He would be . . . *what had he said?* He would be *"set apart to God from birth"*?

It was beyond understanding.

She had a difficult time trying to explain it to Manoah that night. Even when the angel appeared to her a second time, it didn't get any easier. Thankfully, Manoah was there to talk to the man this time, but it still seemed unbelievable. When her husband asked for the angel's name, his reply struck a familiar chord within her heart.

"My name? It is beyond understanding."

Yes, it was all beyond her understanding. Why had God chosen her? Why had he allowed her to cry all those tears all those many nights? Why was he coming to her now? Why?

It was, as it was supposed to be, beyond understanding.

—Prayer—

Lord, allow me to rejoice in your perfect timing—especially when I don't understand it.

God heard Manoah, and the angel of God came again to the woman while she was out in the field.

Judges 13:9

ASSIGNED READING:

Judges 13:1–24

Weekend

Go to page 467 for your next devotional reading.

stiff-necked as their fathers, who did not trust
in the Lord their God. 15 They rejected his decrees and the covenant he had made with their
fathers and the warnings he had given them.
They followed worthless idols and themselves
became worthless. They imitated the nations
around them although the Lord had ordered
them, "Do not do as they do," and they did the
things the Lord had forbidden them to do.

16 They forsook all the commands of the
Lord their God and made for themselves two
idols cast in the shape of calves, and an Asherah pole. They bowed down to all the starry
hosts, and they worshiped Baal. 17 They sacrificed their sons and daughters in[a] the fire. They
practiced divination and sorcery and sold themselves to do evil in the eyes of the Lord, provoking him to anger.

18 So the Lord was very angry with Israel
and removed them from his presence. Only
the tribe of Judah was left, 19 and even Judah
did not keep the commands of the Lord their
God. They followed the practices Israel had
introduced. 20 Therefore the Lord rejected all
the people of Israel; he afflicted
them and gave them into the
hands of plunderers, until he
thrust them from his presence.

21 When he tore Israel away
from the house of David, they
made Jeroboam son of Nebat
their king. Jeroboam enticed
Israel away from following
the Lord and caused them to
commit a great sin. 22 The Israelites persisted in all the sins
of Jeroboam and did not turn
away from them 23 until the
Lord removed them from his
presence, as he had warned
through all his servants the
prophets. So the people of Is-
rael were taken from their homeland into exile
in Assyria, and they are still there.

> **2 Kings 17:23**
>
> *God Disciplines*
>
> The Lord removed them from his presence, as he had warned through all his servants the prophets. So the people of Israel were taken from their homeland into exile in Assyria, and they are still there.

Samaria Resettled

24 The king of Assyria brought people
from Babylon, Cuthah, Avva, Hamath and
Sepharvaim and settled them in the towns of
Samaria to replace the Israelites. They took
over Samaria and lived in its towns. 25 When
they first lived there, they did not worship the
Lord; so he sent lions among them and they
killed some of the people. 26 It was reported to
the king of Assyria: "The people you deported
and resettled in the towns of Samaria do not
know what the god of that country requires. He
has sent lions among them, which are killing
them off, because the people do not know what
he requires."

27 Then the king of Assyria gave this order:
"Have one of the priests you took captive from
Samaria go back to live there and teach the
people what the god of the land requires." 28 So
one of the priests who had been exiled from
Samaria came to live in Bethel and taught them
how to worship the Lord.

29 Nevertheless, each national group made
its own gods in the several towns where they settled, and set them up in the shrines the people
of Samaria had made at the high places. 30 The
men from Babylon made Succoth Benoth, the
men from Cuthah made Nergal, and the men
from Hamath made Ashima;
31 the Avvites made Nibhaz
and Tartak, and the Sephar-
vites burned their children in
the fire as sacrifices to Adram-
melech and Anammelech, the
gods of Sepharvaim. 32 They
worshiped the Lord, but they
also appointed all sorts of their
own people to officiate for
them as priests in the shrines
at the high places. 33 They worshiped the Lord, but they also
served their own gods in accordance with the customs of the
nations from which they had
been brought.

34 To this day they persist
in their former practices. They neither worship the Lord nor adhere to the decrees and
ordinances, the laws and commands that the
Lord gave the descendants of Jacob, whom he
named Israel. 35 When the Lord made a covenant with the Israelites, he commanded them:
"Do not worship any other gods or bow down

[a] 17 Or *They made their sons and daughters pass through*

to them, serve them or sacrifice to them. [36]But
the LORD, who brought you up out of Egypt
with mighty power and outstretched arm, is
the one you must worship. To him you shall
bow down and to him offer sacrifices. [37]You
must always be careful to keep the decrees and
ordinances, the laws and commands he wrote
for you. Do not worship other gods. [38]Do not
forget the covenant I have made with you, and
do not worship other gods. [39]Rather, worship
the LORD your God; it is he who will deliver
you from the hand of all your enemies."

[40]They would not listen, however, but
persisted in their former practices. [41]Even
while these people were worshiping the LORD,
they were serving their idols. To this day their
children and grandchildren continue to do as
their fathers did.

Hezekiah King of Judah

18 In the third year of Hoshea son of
Elah king of Israel, Hezekiah son of
Ahaz king of Judah began to reign. [2]He was
twenty-five years old when he became king,
and he reigned in Jerusalem twenty-nine
years. His mother's name was Abijah[a] daughter of Zechariah. [3]He did what was right in the
eyes of the LORD, just as his father David had
done. [4]He removed the high places, smashed
the sacred stones and cut down the Asherah
poles. He broke into pieces the bronze snake
Moses had made, for up to that time the Israelites had been burning incense to it. (It was
called[b] Nehushtan.[c])

[5]Hezekiah trusted in the LORD, the God of
Israel. There was no one like him among all the
kings of Judah, either before him or after him.
[6]He held fast to the LORD and did not cease to
follow him; he kept the commands the LORD
had given Moses. [7]And the LORD was with
him; he was successful in whatever he undertook. He rebelled against the king of Assyria
and did not serve him. [8]From watchtower to
fortified city, he defeated the Philistines, as far
as Gaza and its territory.

[9]In King Hezekiah's fourth year, which was
the seventh year of Hoshea son of Elah king
of Israel, Shalmaneser king of Assyria marched
against Samaria and laid siege to it. [10]At the
end of three years the Assyrians took it. So
Samaria was captured in Hezekiah's sixth year,
which was the ninth year of Hoshea king of
Israel. [11]The king of Assyria deported Israel to
Assyria and settled them in Halah, in Gozan
on the Habor River and in towns of the Medes.
[12]This happened because they had not obeyed
the LORD their God, but had violated his covenant—all that Moses the servant of the LORD
commanded. They neither listened to the commands nor carried them out.

[13]In the fourteenth year of King Hezekiah's
reign, Sennacherib king of Assyria attacked all
the fortified cities of Judah and captured them.
[14]So Hezekiah king of Judah sent this message to the king of Assyria at Lachish: "I have
done wrong. Withdraw from me, and I will
pay whatever you demand of me." The king of
Assyria exacted from Hezekiah king of Judah
three hundred talents[d] of silver and thirty talents[e] of gold. [15]So Hezekiah gave him all the
silver that was found in the temple of the LORD
and in the treasuries of the royal palace.

[16]At this time Hezekiah king of Judah
stripped off the gold with which he had covered the doors and doorposts of the temple of
the LORD, and gave it to the king of Assyria.

Sennacherib Threatens Jerusalem

[17]The king of Assyria sent his supreme
commander, his chief officer and his field
commander with a large army, from Lachish
to King Hezekiah at Jerusalem. They came
up to Jerusalem and stopped at the aqueduct
of the Upper Pool, on the road to the Washerman's Field. [18]They called for the king; and Eliakim son of Hilkiah the palace administrator,
Shebna the secretary, and Joah son of Asaph
the recorder went out to them.

[19]The field commander said to them, "Tell
Hezekiah:

"'This is what the great king, the king
of Assyria, says: On what are you basing
this confidence of yours? [20]You say you
have strategy and military strength—but
you speak only empty words. On whom
are you depending, that you rebel against
me? [21]Look now, you are depending on

[a]2 Hebrew *Abi,* a variant of *Abijah* [b]4 Or *He called it* [c]4 *Nehushtan* sounds like the Hebrew for *bronze* and *snake* and *unclean thing.*
[d]14 That is, about 11 tons (about 10 metric tons) [e]14 That is, about 1 ton (about 1 metric ton)

Egypt, that splintered reed of a staff, which
pierces a man's hand and wounds him if
he leans on it! Such is Pharaoh king of
Egypt to all who depend on him. 22 And if
you say to me, "We are depending on the
LORD our God"—isn't he the one whose
high places and altars Hezekiah removed,
saying to Judah and Jerusalem, "You must
worship before this altar in Jerusalem"?

23 " 'Come now, make a bargain with my
master, the king of Assyria: I will give you
two thousand horses—if you can put riders on them! 24 How can you repulse one
officer of the least of my master's officials,
even though you are depending on Egypt
for chariots and horsemen[a]? 25 Furthermore, have I come to attack and destroy
this place without word from the LORD?
The LORD himself told me to march
against this country and destroy it.' "

26 Then Eliakim son of Hilkiah, and Shebna
and Joah said to the field commander, "Please
speak to your servants in Aramaic, since we understand it. Don't speak to us in Hebrew in the
hearing of the people on the wall."

27 But the commander replied, "Was it only
to your master and you that my master sent me
to say these things, and not to the men sitting
on the wall—who, like you, will have to eat
their own filth and drink their own urine?"

28 Then the commander stood and called
out in Hebrew: "Hear the word of the great
king, the king of Assyria! 29 This is what the
king says: Do not let Hezekiah deceive you. He
cannot deliver you from my hand. 30 Do not let
Hezekiah persuade you to trust in the LORD
when he says, 'The LORD will surely deliver us;
this city will not be given into the hand of the
king of Assyria.'

31 "Do not listen to Hezekiah. This is what
the king of Assyria says: Make peace with me
and come out to me. Then every one of you will
eat from his own vine and fig tree and drink
water from his own cistern, 32 until I come and
take you to a land like your own, a land of grain
and new wine, a land of bread and vineyards, a
land of olive trees and honey. Choose life and
not death!

"Do not listen to Hezekiah, for he is misleading you when he says, 'The LORD will deliver
us.' 33 Has the god of any nation ever delivered
his land from the hand of the king of Assyria?
34 Where are the gods of Hamath and Arpad?
Where are the gods of Sepharvaim, Hena and
Ivvah? Have they rescued Samaria from my
hand? 35 Who of all the gods of these countries
has been able to save his land from me? How
then can the LORD deliver Jerusalem from my
hand?"

36 But the people remained silent and
said nothing in reply, because the king had
commanded, "Do not answer him."

37 Then Eliakim son of Hilkiah the palace administrator, Shebna the secretary and Joah son
of Asaph the recorder went to Hezekiah, with
their clothes torn, and told him what the field
commander had said.

Jerusalem's Deliverance Foretold

19 When King Hezekiah heard this, he
tore his clothes and put on sackcloth
and went into the temple of the LORD. 2 He sent
Eliakim the palace administrator, Shebna the
secretary and the leading priests, all wearing
sackcloth, to the prophet Isaiah son of Amoz.
3 They told him, "This is what Hezekiah says:
This day is a day of distress and rebuke and disgrace, as when children come to the point of
birth and there is no strength to deliver them.
4 It may be that the LORD your God will hear all
the words of the field commander, whom his
master, the king of Assyria, has sent to ridicule
the living God, and that he will rebuke him for
the words the LORD your God has heard. Therefore pray for the remnant that still survives."

5 When King Hezekiah's officials came to
Isaiah, 6 Isaiah said to them, "Tell your master,
'This is what the LORD says: Do not be afraid of
what you have heard—those words with which
the underlings of the king of Assyria have blasphemed me. 7 Listen! I am going to put such a
spirit in him that when he hears a certain report,
he will return to his own country, and there I
will have him cut down with the sword.' "

8 When the field commander heard that the
king of Assyria had left Lachish, he withdrew
and found the king fighting against Libnah.

[a]24 Or *charioteers*

Never-Fail Disaster Plan

Read: 2 Kings 18:19—19:19

ON SEVERAL OCCASIONS, Pastor Isaac Raju was beaten by Hindu neighbors who objected to the church meetings in his home. Then, when Pastor Raju's mother-in-law died, their house was surrounded by Hindu neighbors insisting that she, a Christian, be cremated according to Hindu tradition. The pastor and his wife were held against their will on the upper level of their own home as a Hindu priest chanted funeral rites on the ground floor.

A month later, in the wake of one of the most terrible tsunamis in Southeast Asia's history, the Christians reached out to their persecutors. Filled with compassion, Pastor Isaac Raju and his 25 congregants helped bury bodies and provide food and clothing for the tsunami survivors. Pastor Raju reminded his congregation, "Nothing happens without the knowledge of God. Everything is in his hands." He wanted his church to show love to their neighbors by providing physical needs like clothing, rice and cooking pots and by telling them about the love of God.

For years, Indian Christians have been marked as one of the most persecuted groups on the planet. They suffer torture, persecution and constant threats from their Hindu neighbors. Yet they didn't look away when disaster struck. They moved among the hungry, hurt and mourning, friends and enemies alike, offering fresh water and bowls of steaming rice . . . just as they knew Jesus would have done.

King Hezekiah, one of Judah's godly kings, also endured taunts and intimidation at the hands of his enemies. When a letter came from the Assyrian King Sennacherib threatening that he would conquer Judah, Hezekiah had his own disaster plan. He laid out the letter before the Lord and prayed. In his faithfulness, God listened and delivered the Israelites.

What do you do when you encounter a terrible scenario that seems to have no solution? When tragedy roars down on you like a tsunami? When something or someone truly terrifying marches your way? Do you curl up in retreat? Do you strike back in retaliation? Or do you lay the situation out before God and trust him to show you what to do?

Wouldn't it be wonderful if down the road everyone who looks at the end of your story has reason to exclaim, "Who is a God like yours!"

2 Kings 19:19

"Now, O LORD our God, deliver us from [Sennacherib's] hand, so that all kingdoms on earth may know that you alone, O LORD, are God."

reflection

1 When have you felt trapped or persecuted for your faith?

2 What are some ways you can tangibly show Christ's love to those who have hurt you?

3 What specific situation are you facing in which you require God's help and protection? Follow Hezekiah's lead and lay your problems before the Lord in prayer.

RELATED READINGS

Psalm 115:1–8;
Matthew 5:10–12;
Luke 6:27–36

Go to page 472 for your next devotional reading.

9Now Sennacherib received a report that
Tirhakah, the Cushite[a] king ⌊of Egypt⌋, was
marching out to fight against him. So he again
sent messengers to Hezekiah with this word:
10"Say to Hezekiah king of Judah: Do not let
the god you depend on deceive you when he
says, 'Jerusalem will not be handed over to the
king of Assyria.' 11Surely you have heard what
the kings of Assyria have done to all the countries, destroying them completely. And will you
be delivered? 12Did the gods of the nations that
were destroyed by my forefathers deliver them:
the gods of Gozan, Haran, Rezeph and the people of Eden who were in Tel Assar? 13Where
is the king of Hamath, the king of Arpad, the
king of the city of Sepharvaim, or of Hena or
Ivvah?"

Hezekiah's Prayer

14Hezekiah received the letter from the
messengers and read it. Then he went up to
the temple of the LORD and spread it out before the LORD. 15And Hezekiah prayed to the
LORD: "O LORD, God of Israel, enthroned between the cherubim, you alone are God over
all the kingdoms of the earth. You have made
heaven and earth. 16Give ear, O LORD, and
hear; open your eyes, O LORD, and see; listen
to the words Sennacherib has sent to insult the
living God.

17"It is true, O LORD, that the Assyrian kings
have laid waste these nations and their lands.
18They have thrown their gods into the fire
and destroyed them, for they were not gods
but only wood and stone, fashioned by men's
hands. 19Now, O LORD our God, deliver us
from his hand, so that all kingdoms on earth
may know that you alone, O LORD, are God."

Isaiah Prophesies Sennacherib's Fall

20Then Isaiah son of Amoz sent a message
to Hezekiah: "This is what the LORD, the God
of Israel, says: I have heard your prayer concerning Sennacherib king of Assyria. 21This is the
word that the LORD has spoken against him:

"'The Virgin Daughter of Zion
despises you and mocks you.
The Daughter of Jerusalem
tosses her head as you flee.
22Who is it you have insulted and
blasphemed?
Against whom have you raised your
voice
and lifted your eyes in pride?
Against the Holy One of Israel!
23By your messengers
you have heaped insults on the Lord.
And you have said,
"With my many chariots
I have ascended the heights of the
mountains,
the utmost heights of Lebanon.
I have cut down its tallest cedars,
the choicest of its pines.
I have reached its remotest parts,
the finest of its forests.
24I have dug wells in foreign lands
and drunk the water there.
With the soles of my feet
I have dried up all the streams of Egypt."

25"'Have you not heard?
Long ago I ordained it.
In days of old I planned it;
now I have brought it to pass,
that you have turned fortified cities
into piles of stone.
26Their people, drained of power,
are dismayed and put to shame.
They are like plants in the field,
like tender green shoots,
like grass sprouting on the roof,
scorched before it grows up.

27"'But I know where you stay
and when you come and go
and how you rage against me.
28Because you rage against me
and your insolence has reached my ears,
I will put my hook in your nose
and my bit in your mouth,
and I will make you return
by the way you came.'

29"This will be the sign for you, O Hezekiah:

"This year you will eat what grows by itself,
and the second year what springs from
that.

[a]9 That is, from the upper Nile region

But in the third year sow and reap,
plant vineyards and eat their fruit.
30 Once more a remnant of the house of Judah
will take root below and bear fruit above.
31 For out of Jerusalem will come a remnant,
and out of Mount Zion a band of survivors.

The zeal of the LORD Almighty will accomplish this.

32 "Therefore this is what the LORD says concerning the king of Assyria:

"He will not enter this city
or shoot an arrow here.
He will not come before it with shield
or build a siege ramp against it.
33 By the way that he came he will return;
he will not enter this city,
declares the LORD.
34 I will defend this city and save it,
for my sake and for the sake of David my servant."

35 That night the angel of
the LORD went out and put to
death a hundred and eighty-
five thousand men in the Assyrian camp. When the people
got up the next morning—there were all the
dead bodies! 36 So Sennacherib king of Assyria
broke camp and withdrew. He returned to Nineveh and stayed there.
37 One day, while he was worshiping in the
temple of his god Nisroch, his sons Adram-
melech and Sharezer cut him down with the
sword, and they escaped to the land of Ararat. And Esarhaddon his son succeeded him
as king.

Hezekiah's Illness

20 In those days Hezekiah became ill and
was at the point of death. The prophet
Isaiah son of Amoz went to him and said,
"This is what the LORD says: Put your house
in order, because you are going to die; you will
not recover."

2 Kings 19:34

God Is All Powerful

"I will defend this city and save it, for my sake and for the sake of David my servant."

2 Hezekiah turned his face to the wall and
prayed to the LORD, 3 "Remember, O LORD,
how I have walked before you faithfully and
with wholehearted devotion and have done
what is good in your eyes." And Hezekiah wept
bitterly.
4 Before Isaiah had left the middle court, the
word of the LORD came to him: 5 "Go back and
tell Hezekiah, the leader of my people, 'This is
what the LORD, the God of your father David,
says: I have heard your prayer and seen your
tears; I will heal you. On the third day from
now you will go up to the temple of the LORD.
6 I will add fifteen years to your life. And I will
deliver you and this city from the hand of the
king of Assyria. I will defend this city for my
sake and for the sake of my servant David.' "
7 Then Isaiah said, "Prepare a poultice of
figs." They did so and applied it
to the boil, and he recovered.
8 Hezekiah had asked Isaiah,
"What will be the sign that
the LORD will heal me and
that I will go up to the temple
of the LORD on the third day
from now?"
9 Isaiah answered, "This is
the LORD's sign to you that
the LORD will do what he has
promised: Shall the shadow go
forward ten steps, or shall it go
back ten steps?"
10 "It is a simple matter
for the shadow to go forward ten steps," said
Hezekiah. "Rather, have it go back ten steps."
11 Then the prophet Isaiah called upon the
LORD, and the LORD made the shadow go back
the ten steps it had gone down on the stairway
of Ahaz.

Envoys From Babylon

12 At that time Merodach-Baladan son of Baladan king of Babylon sent Hezekiah letters and
a gift, because he had heard of Hezekiah's illness. 13 Hezekiah received the messengers and
showed them all that was in his storehouses—
the silver, the gold, the spices and the fine
oil—his armory and everything found among
his treasures. There was nothing in his palace
or in all his kingdom that Hezekiah did not
show them.

14Then Isaiah the prophet went to King
Hezekiah and asked, "What did those men say,
and where did they come from?"
"From a distant land," Hezekiah replied.
"They came from Babylon."
15The prophet asked, "What did they see in
your palace?"
"They saw everything in my palace,"
Hezekiah said. "There is nothing among my
treasures that I did not show them."
16Then Isaiah said to Hezekiah, "Hear
the word of the LORD: 17The time will surely
come when everything in your palace, and all
that your fathers have stored up until this day,
will be carried off to Babylon. Nothing will be
left, says the LORD. 18And some of your descendants, your own flesh and blood, that will
be born to you, will be taken away, and they
will become eunuchs in the palace of the king
of Babylon."
19"The word of the LORD you have spoken
is good," Hezekiah replied. For he thought,
"Will there not be peace and security in my lifetime?"
20As for the other events of Hezekiah's reign,
all his achievements and how he made the pool
and the tunnel by which he brought water into
the city, are they not written in the book of
the annals of the kings of Judah? 21Hezekiah
rested with his fathers. And Manasseh his son
succeeded him as king.

Manasseh King of Judah

21 Manasseh was twelve years old when
he became king, and he reigned in Jerusalem fifty-five years. His mother's name
was Hephzibah. 2He did evil in the eyes of the
LORD, following the detestable practices of the
nations the LORD had driven out before the Israelites. 3He rebuilt the high places his father
Hezekiah had destroyed; he also erected altars
to Baal and made an Asherah pole, as Ahab
king of Israel had done. He bowed down to
all the starry hosts and worshiped them. 4He
built altars in the temple of the LORD, of which
the LORD had said, "In Jerusalem I will put my
Name." 5In both courts of the temple of the
LORD, he built altars to all the starry hosts. 6He
sacrificed his own son in[a] the fire, practiced sorcery and divination, and consulted mediums
and spiritists. He did much evil in the eyes of
the LORD, provoking him to anger.
7He took the carved Asherah pole he had
made and put it in the temple, of which the
LORD had said to David and to his son Solomon, "In this temple and in Jerusalem, which
I have chosen out of all the tribes of Israel, I will
put my Name forever. 8I will not again make
the feet of the Israelites wander from the land
I gave their forefathers, if only they will be careful to do everything I commanded them and
will keep the whole Law that my servant Moses
gave them." 9But the people did not listen. Manasseh led them astray, so that they did more
evil than the nations the LORD had destroyed
before the Israelites.
10The LORD said through his servants the
prophets: 11"Manasseh king of Judah has committed these detestable sins. He has done more
evil than the Amorites who preceded him and
has led Judah into sin with his idols. 12There-
fore this is what the LORD, the God of Israel,
says: I am going to bring such disaster on Jerusalem and Judah that the ears of everyone
who hears of it will tingle. 13I will stretch out
over Jerusalem the measuring line used against
Samaria and the plumb line used against the
house of Ahab. I will wipe out Jerusalem as
one wipes a dish, wiping it and turning it upside down. 14I will forsake the remnant of my
inheritance and hand them over to their enemies. They will be looted and plundered by all
their foes, 15because they have done evil in my
eyes and have provoked me to anger from the
day their forefathers came out of Egypt until
this day."
16Moreover, Manasseh also shed so much
innocent blood that he filled Jerusalem from
end to end—besides the sin that he had caused
Judah to commit, so that they did evil in the
eyes of the LORD.
17As for the other events of Manasseh's reign,
and all he did, including the sin he committed,
are they not written in the book of the annals of
the kings of Judah? 18Manasseh rested with his
fathers and was buried in his palace garden, the
garden of Uzza. And Amon his son succeeded
him as king.

[a]6 Or *He made his own son pass through*

Amon King of Judah

19Amon was twenty-two years old when he became king, and he reigned in Jerusalem two years. His mother's name was Meshullemeth daughter of Haruz; she was from Jotbah. 20He did evil in the eyes of the LORD, as his father Manasseh had done. 21He walked in all the ways of his father; he worshiped the idols his father had worshiped, and bowed down to them. 22He forsook the LORD, the God of his fathers, and did not walk in the way of the LORD.

23Amon's officials conspired against him and assassinated the king in his palace. 24Then the people of the land killed all who had plotted against King Amon, and they made Josiah his son king in his place.

25As for the other events of Amon's reign, and what he did, are they not written in the book of the annals of the kings of Judah? 26He was buried in his grave in the garden of Uzza. And Josiah his son succeeded him as king.

The Book of the Law Found

22 Josiah was eight years old when he became king, and he reigned in Jerusalem thirty-one years. His mother's name was Jedidah daughter of Adaiah; she was from Bozkath. 2He did what was right in the eyes of the LORD and walked in all the ways of his father David, not turning aside to the right or to the left.

3In the eighteenth year of his reign, King Josiah sent the secretary, Shaphan son of Azaliah, the son of Meshullam, to the temple of the LORD. He said: 4"Go up to Hilkiah the high priest and have him get ready the money that has been brought into the temple of the LORD, which the doorkeepers have collected from the people. 5Have them entrust it to the men appointed to supervise the work on the temple. And have these men pay the workers who repair the temple of the LORD— 6the carpenters, the builders and the masons. Also have them purchase timber and dressed stone to repair the temple. 7But they need not account for the money entrusted to them, because they are acting faithfully."

8Hilkiah the high priest said to Shaphan the secretary, "I have found the Book of the Law in the temple of the LORD." He gave it to Shaphan, who read it. 9Then Shaphan the secretary went to the king and reported to him: "Your officials have paid out the money that was in the temple of the LORD and have entrusted it to the workers and supervisors at the temple." 10Then Shaphan the secretary informed the king, "Hilkiah the priest has given me a book." And Shaphan read from it in the presence of the king.

11When the king heard the words of the Book of the Law, he tore his robes. 12He gave these orders to Hilkiah the priest, Ahikam son of Shaphan, Acbor son of Micaiah, Shaphan the secretary and Asaiah the king's attendant: 13"Go and inquire of the LORD for me and for the people and for all Judah about what is written in this book that has been found. Great is the LORD's anger that burns against us because our fathers have not obeyed the words of this book; they have not acted in accordance with all that is written there concerning us."

14Hilkiah the priest, Ahikam, Acbor, Shaphan and Asaiah went to speak to the prophetess Huldah, who was the wife of Shallum son of Tikvah, the son of Harhas, keeper of the wardrobe. She lived in Jerusalem, in the Second District.

15She said to them, "This is what the LORD, the God of Israel, says: Tell the man who sent you to me, 16'This is what the LORD says: I am going to bring disaster on this place and its people, according to everything written in the book the king of Judah has read. 17Because they have forsaken me and burned incense to other gods and provoked me to anger by all the idols their hands have made,[a] my anger will burn against this place and will not be quenched.' 18Tell the king of Judah, who sent you to inquire of the LORD, 'This is what the LORD, the God of Israel, says concerning the words you heard: 19Because your heart was responsive and you humbled yourself before the LORD when you heard what I have spoken against this place and its people, that they would become accursed and laid waste, and because you tore your robes and wept in my presence, I have heard you, declares the LORD. 20Therefore I will gather you to your fathers, and you will be buried in peace. Your eyes will not see all the disaster I am going to bring on this place.'"

So they took her answer back to the king.

17 Or *by everything they have done*

Life Condensed

2 Kings 22:1–20

2 Kings 22:2

[Josiah] did what was right in the eyes of the Lord and walked in all the ways of his father David, not turning aside to the right or to the left.

CONDENSED SOUP. CONDENSED MILK. Condensed books. We like all sorts of things that are condensed, consolidated, compressed, abridged or abbreviated. Make it short. Make it quick. Whatever saves time. Whatever gets us to the bottom line.

The condensed version of King Josiah's life is found in a single sentence. Thirty-one words in one verse sum up the essence of his entire life: "He did what was right in the eyes of the Lord and walked in all the ways of his father David, not turning aside to the right or to the left." Amazing! Concise! Josiah walked the path of righteousness without swerving.

Josiah became king at age 8 and reigned until his death at 39. His father and grandfather both reigned over Judah before him. Both "did evil in the eyes of the Lord" (2 Kings 21:20). Despite his evil legacy, Josiah turned his heart toward God. And although Judah, the nation he ruled, had turned to worship false gods, Josiah did not waver in his allegiance to the one true God. No other king before or after him stayed on course like Josiah.

If your life were condensed into a short synopsis—one brief sentence—what would be said of you? How our lives are summarized depends on the choices we make each day. We have the tendency to become distracted with the cares and responsibilities of life. Laundry piles up. Bills need to be paid. Children get sick. As we care for our families and do our work, it's easy to become sidetracked from our primary purpose: pleasing God. It is easier to give lip service to spiritual things than to stay on course, keeping in step with the Spirit (see Galatians 5:25).

How will you be remembered? Eventually, someone will write your obituary or eulogy. Your life will be abridged into a few brief sentences and paragraphs. What will be said of you? More important, how will God summarize your life?

Let it be said of you, "______________ [fill in your name] did what was right in the eyes of the Lord and walked in the way of truth, not turning aside to the right or to the left."

reflection

1 How would you describe your character when it comes to following God's ways? Write a one-sentence summary of your current life, starting with "I walk in the way of . . ."

2 What might God want to change in your life so that your life summary will be different?

3 What steps will you take today to walk in God's ways?

RELATED READINGS

2 Kings 23:8–25; Psalm 26:1–3; Isaiah 30:19–26; Galatians 5:25

Go to page 485 for your next devotional reading.

Josiah Renews the Covenant

23 Then the king called together all the
elders of Judah and Jerusalem. 2He
went up to the temple of the LORD with the men
of Judah, the people of Jerusalem, the priests
and the prophets—all the people from the least
to the greatest. He read in their hearing all the
words of the Book of the Covenant, which had
been found in the temple of the LORD. 3The
king stood by the pillar and renewed the covenant in the presence of the LORD—to follow
the LORD and keep his commands, regulations
and decrees with all his heart and all his soul,
thus confirming the words of the covenant written in this book. Then all the people pledged
themselves to the covenant.
4The king ordered Hilkiah the high priest,
the priests next in rank and the doorkeepers
to remove from the temple of the LORD all the
articles made for Baal and Asherah and all the
starry hosts. He burned them outside Jerusalem in the fields of the Kidron Valley and took
the ashes to Bethel. 5He did away with the pagan priests appointed by the kings of Judah to
burn incense on the high places of the towns of
Judah and on those around Jerusalem—those
who burned incense to Baal, to the sun and
moon, to the constellations and to all the starry
hosts. 6He took the Asherah pole from the temple of the LORD to the Kidron Valley outside
Jerusalem and burned it there. He ground it to
powder and scattered the dust over the graves
of the common people. 7He also tore down the
quarters of the male shrine prostitutes, which
were in the temple of the LORD and where
women did weaving for Asherah.
8Josiah brought all the priests from the
towns of Judah and desecrated the high places,
from Geba to Beersheba, where the priests had
burned incense. He broke down the shrines[a]
at the gates—at the entrance to the Gate of
Joshua, the city governor, which is on the left of
the city gate. 9Although the priests of the high
places did not serve at the altar of the LORD
in Jerusalem, they ate unleavened bread with
their fellow priests.
10He desecrated Topheth, which was in the
Valley of Ben Hinnom, so no one could use
it to sacrifice his son or daughter in[b] the fire
to Molech. 11He removed from the entrance
to the temple of the LORD the horses that the
kings of Judah had dedicated to the sun. They
were in the court near the room of an official
named Nathan-Melech. Josiah then burned the
chariots dedicated to the sun.
12He pulled down the altars the kings of
Judah had erected on the roof near the upper
room of Ahaz, and the altars Manasseh had
built in the two courts of the temple of the
LORD. He removed them from there, smashed
them to pieces and threw the rubble into the
Kidron Valley. 13The king also desecrated
the high places that were east of Jerusalem on
the south of the Hill of Corruption—the ones
Solomon king of Israel had built for Ashtoreth
the vile goddess of the Sidonians, for Chemosh
the vile god of Moab, and for Molech[c] the detestable god of the people of Ammon. 14Josiah
smashed the sacred stones and cut down the
Asherah poles and covered the sites with human bones.
15Even the altar at Bethel, the high place
made by Jeroboam son of Nebat, who had
caused Israel to sin—even that altar and high
place he demolished. He burned the high place
and ground it to powder, and burned the Asherah pole also. 16Then Josiah looked around,
and when he saw the tombs that were there
on the hillside, he had the bones removed
from them and burned on the altar to defile
it, in accordance with the word of the LORD
proclaimed by the man of God who foretold
these things.
17The king asked, "What is that tombstone
I see?"
The men of the city said, "It marks the tomb
of the man of God who came from Judah and
pronounced against the altar of Bethel the very
things you have done to it."
18"Leave it alone," he said. "Don't let anyone
disturb his bones." So they spared his bones
and those of the prophet who had come from
Samaria.
19Just as he had done at Bethel, Josiah removed and defiled all the shrines at the high
places that the kings of Israel had built in the
towns of Samaria that had provoked the LORD
to anger. 20Josiah slaughtered all the priests

[a]8 Or *high places* [b]10 Or *to make his son or daughter pass through* [c]13 Hebrew *Milcom*

of those high places on the altars and burned human bones on them. Then he went back to Jerusalem.

21 The king gave this order to all the people: "Celebrate the Passover to the LORD your God, as it is written in this Book of the Covenant." 22 Not since the days of the judges who led Israel, nor throughout the days of the kings of Israel and the kings of Judah, had any such Passover been observed. 23 But in the eighteenth year of King Josiah, this Passover was celebrated to the LORD in Jerusalem.

24 Furthermore, Josiah got rid of the mediums and spiritists, the household gods, the idols and all the other detestable things seen in Judah and Jerusalem. This he did to fulfill the requirements of the law written in the book that Hilkiah the priest had discovered in the temple of the LORD. 25 Neither before nor after Josiah was there a king like him who turned to the LORD as he did—with all his heart and with all his soul and with all his strength, in accordance with all the Law of Moses.

26 Nevertheless, the LORD did not turn away from the heat of his fierce anger, which burned against Judah because of all that Manasseh had done to provoke him to anger. 27 So the LORD said, "I will remove Judah also from my presence as I removed Israel, and I will reject Jerusalem, the city I chose, and this temple, about which I said, 'There shall my Name be.'[a]"

28 As for the other events of Josiah's reign, and all he did, are they not written in the book of the annals of the kings of Judah?

29 While Josiah was king, Pharaoh Neco king of Egypt went up to the Euphrates River to help the king of Assyria. King Josiah marched out to meet him in battle, but Neco faced him and killed him at Megiddo. 30 Josiah's servants brought his body in a chariot from Megiddo to Jerusalem and buried him in his own tomb. And the people of the land took Jehoahaz son of Josiah and anointed him and made him king in place of his father.

Jehoahaz King of Judah

31 Jehoahaz was twenty-three years old when he became king, and he reigned in Jerusalem three months. His mother's name was Hamutal daughter of Jeremiah; she was from Libnah. 32 He did evil in the eyes of the LORD, just as his fathers had done. 33 Pharaoh Neco put him in chains at Riblah in the land of Hamath[b] so that he might not reign in Jerusalem, and he imposed on Judah a levy of a hundred talents[c] of silver and a talent[d] of gold. 34 Pharaoh Neco made Eliakim son of Josiah king in place of his father Josiah and changed Eliakim's name to Jehoiakim. But he took Jehoahaz and carried him off to Egypt, and there he died. 35 Jehoiakim paid Pharaoh Neco the silver and gold he demanded. In order to do so, he taxed the land and exacted the silver and gold from the people of the land according to their assessments.

Jehoiakim King of Judah

36 Jehoiakim was twenty-five years old when he became king, and he reigned in Jerusalem eleven years. His mother's name was Zebidah daughter of Pedaiah; she was from Rumah. 37 And he did evil in the eyes of the LORD, just as his fathers had done.

24 During Jehoiakim's reign, Nebuchadnezzar king of Babylon invaded the land, and Jehoiakim became his vassal for three years. But then he changed his mind and rebelled against Nebuchadnezzar. 2 The LORD sent Babylonian,[e] Aramean, Moabite and Ammonite raiders against him. He sent them to destroy Judah, in accordance with the word of the LORD proclaimed by his servants the prophets. 3 Surely these things happened to Judah according to the LORD's command, in order to remove them from his presence because of the sins of Manasseh and all he had done, 4 including the shedding of innocent blood. For he had filled Jerusalem with innocent blood, and the LORD was not willing to forgive.

5 As for the other events of Jehoiakim's reign, and all he did, are they not written in the book of the annals of the kings of Judah? 6 Jehoiakim rested with his fathers. And Jehoiachin his son succeeded him as king.

7 The king of Egypt did not march out from his own country again, because the king of Babylon had taken all his territory, from the Wadi of Egypt to the Euphrates River.

[a] 27 1 Kings 8:29 [b] 33 Hebrew; Septuagint (see also 2 Chron. 36:3) *Neco at Riblah in Hamath removed him* [c] 33 That is, about 3 3/4 tons (about 3.4 metric tons) [d] 33 That is, about 75 pounds (about 34 kilograms) [e] 2 Or *Chaldean*

Jehoiachin King of Judah

8Jehoiachin was eighteen years old when he
became king, and he reigned in Jerusalem three
months. His mother's name was Nehushta
daughter of Elnathan; she was from Jerusalem.
9He did evil in the eyes of the LORD, just as his
father had done.
10At that time the officers of Nebuchadnezzar king of Babylon advanced on Jerusalem
and laid siege to it, 11and Nebuchadnezzar
himself came up to the city while his officers
were besieging it. 12Jehoiachin king of Judah,
his mother, his attendants, his nobles and his
officials all surrendered to him.
In the eighth year of the reign of the king
of Babylon, he took Jehoiachin
prisoner. 13As the LORD had
declared, Nebuchadnezzar removed all the treasures from
the temple of the LORD and
from the royal palace, and
took away all the gold articles
that Solomon king of Israel
had made for the temple of the
LORD. 14He carried into exile
all Jerusalem: all the officers
and fighting men, and all the
craftsmen and artisans—a total
of ten thousand. Only the poorest people of the land were left.
15Nebuchadnezzar took Je-
hoiachin captive to Babylon.
He also took from Jerusalem
to Babylon the king's mother,
his wives, his officials and the leading men of
the land. 16The king of Babylon also deported
to Babylon the entire force of seven thousand
fighting men, strong and fit for war, and a
thousand craftsmen and artisans. 17He made
Mattaniah, Jehoiachin's uncle, king in his place
and changed his name to Zedekiah.

Zedekiah King of Judah

18Zedekiah was twenty-one years old when
he became king, and he reigned in Jerusalem
eleven years. His mother's name was Hamutal
daughter of Jeremiah; she was from Libnah.
19He did evil in the eyes of the LORD, just as
Jehoiakim had done. 20It was because of the
LORD's anger that all this happened to Jerusalem and Judah, and in the end he thrust them
from his presence.

The Fall of Jerusalem

Now Zedekiah rebelled against the king
of Babylon.

25 So in the ninth year of Zedekiah's reign,
on the tenth day of the tenth month,
Nebuchadnezzar king of Babylon marched
against Jerusalem with his whole army. He encamped outside the city and built siege works
all around it. 2The city was kept under siege until the eleventh year of King Zedekiah. 3By the
ninth day of the ⌊fourth⌋[a] month the famine in
the city had become so severe that there was
no food for the people to eat.
4Then the city wall was broken
through, and the whole army
fled at night through the gate
between the two walls near the
king's garden, though the Babylonians[b] were surrounding
the city. They fled toward the
Arabah,[c] 5but the Babylonian[d]
army pursued the king and
overtook him in the plains of
Jericho. All his soldiers were
separated from him and scattered, 6and he was captured.
He was taken to the king of
Babylon at Riblah, where sentence was pronounced on
him. 7They killed the sons of
Zedekiah before his eyes. Then
they put out his eyes, bound him with bronze
shackles and took him to Babylon.
8On the seventh day of the fifth month, in
the nineteenth year of Nebuchadnezzar king
of Babylon, Nebuzaradan commander of the
imperial guard, an official of the king of Babylon, came to Jerusalem. 9He set fire to the
temple of the LORD, the royal palace and all the
houses of Jerusalem. Every important building he burned down. 10The whole Babylonian
army, under the commander of the imperial
guard, broke down the walls around Jerusalem.
11Nebuzaradan the commander of the guard
carried into exile the people who remained
in the city, along with the rest of the populace
and those who had gone over to the king of

2 Kings 24:13

God Is Sovereign

As the LORD had declared, Nebuchadnezzar removed all the treasures from the temple of the LORD and from the royal palace, and took away all the gold articles that Solomon king of Israel had made for the temple of the LORD.

a3 See Jer. 52:6. b4 Or *Chaldeans*; also in verses 13, 25 and 26 c4 Or *the Jordan Valley* d5 Or *Chaldean*; also in verses 10 and 24

Babylon. 12But the commander left behind
some of the poorest people of the land to work
the vineyards and fields.

13The Babylonians broke up the bronze pillars, the movable stands and the bronze Sea that
were at the temple of the LORD and they carried
the bronze to Babylon. 14They also took away
the pots, shovels, wick trimmers, dishes and
all the bronze articles used in the temple service. 15The commander of the imperial guard
took away the censers and sprinkling bowls—
all that were made of pure gold or silver.

16The bronze from the two pillars, the Sea
and the movable stands, which Solomon had
made for the temple of the LORD, was more
than could be weighed. 17Each pillar was
twenty-seven feet[a] high. The bronze capital on
top of one pillar was four and a half feet[b] high
and was decorated with a network and pomegranates of bronze all around. The other pillar,
with its network, was similar.

18The commander of the guard took as prisoners Seraiah the chief priest, Zephaniah the
priest next in rank and the three doorkeepers.
19Of those still in the city, he took the officer in
charge of the fighting men and five royal advisers. He also took the secretary who was chief officer in charge of conscripting the people of the
land and sixty of his men who were found in
the city. 20Nebuzaradan the commander took
them all and brought them to the king of Babylon at Riblah. 21There at Riblah, in the land of
Hamath, the king had them executed.

So Judah went into captivity, away from
her land.

22Nebuchadnezzar king of Babylon appointed Gedaliah son of Ahikam, the son of
Shaphan, to be over the people he had left behind in Judah. 23When all the army officers
and their men heard that the king of Babylon
had appointed Gedaliah as governor, they
came to Gedaliah at Mizpah—Ishmael son of
Nethaniah, Johanan son of Kareah, Seraiah
son of Tanhumeth the Netophathite, Jaazaniah
the son of the Maacathite, and their men.
24Gedaliah took an oath to reassure them and
their men. "Do not be afraid of the Babylonian
officials," he said. "Settle down in the land and
serve the king of Babylon, and it will go well
with you."

25In the seventh month, however, Ishmael
son of Nethaniah, the son of Elishama, who
was of royal blood, came with ten men and
assassinated Gedaliah and also the men of Judah and the Babylonians who were with him at
Mizpah. 26At this, all the people from the least
to the greatest, together with the army officers,
fled to Egypt for fear of the Babylonians.

Jehoiachin Released

27In the thirty-seventh year of the exile of
Jehoiachin king of Judah, in the year Evil-
Merodach[c] became king of Babylon, he
released Jehoiachin from prison on the twenty-
seventh day of the twelfth month. 28He spoke
kindly to him and gave him a seat of honor
higher than those of the other kings who were
with him in Babylon. 29So Jehoiachin put aside
his prison clothes and for the rest of his life ate
regularly at the king's table. 30Day by day the
king gave Jehoiachin a regular allowance as
long as he lived.

[a] 17 Hebrew *eighteen cubits* (about 8.1 meters) [b] 17 Hebrew *three cubits* (about 1.3 meters) [c] 27 Also called *Amel-Marduk*

1 Chronicles

The Chronicles were *written for a people* in the process of rebuilding—rebuilding their walls, their temple, their country, their lives. Judgment and exile were their most recent memories, and even at this point they were still subject to Persia. *They had once been God's people,* but now, with the exile over and the time for rebuilding begun, would he take them back? Would he even want them back?

"Remember," the Chronicler seems to say. Remember your past. These people in your family tree are more than just dusty old names. *They are a part of you.* Their choices are what created your history, and it is your history that shapes your present. *You would do well to learn from them.* You would do well to learn all you possibly can.

Author:
Unknown, but possibly Ezra.

Audience:
All Israel.

Date:
About 430 B.C.

Setting:
The book begins with Israel's genealogical records and then focuses on King David's reign, paralleling many of the events recorded in 2 Samuel.

Verse to Remember:
"You made your people Israel your very own forever, and you, O LORD, have become their God." (17:22)

Historical Records From Adam to Abraham

To Noah's Sons

1 Adam, Seth, Enosh, 2 Kenan, Mahalalel,
Jared, 3 Enoch, Methuselah, Lamech,
Noah.

4 The sons of Noah:[a]
Shem, Ham and Japheth.

The Japhethites

5 The sons[b] of Japheth:
Gomer, Magog, Madai, Javan, Tubal, Meshech and Tiras.
6 The sons of Gomer:
Ashkenaz, Riphath[c] and Togarmah.
7 The sons of Javan:
Elishah, Tarshish, the Kittim and the Rodanim.

[a] 4 Septuagint; Hebrew does not have this line. [b] 5 *Sons* may mean *descendants* or *successors* or *nations*; also in verses 6–10, 17 and 20.
[c] 6 Many Hebrew manuscripts and Vulgate (see also Septuagint and Gen. 10:3); most Hebrew manuscripts *Diphath*

The Hamites

8 The sons of Ham:
Cush, Mizraim,[a] Put and Canaan.
9 The sons of Cush:
Seba, Havilah, Sabta, Raamah and Sabteca.
The sons of Raamah:
Sheba and Dedan.
10 Cush was the father[b] of
Nimrod, who grew to be a mighty warrior on earth.
11 Mizraim was the father of
the Ludites, Anamites, Lehabites, Naphtuhites, 12 Pathrusites, Casluhites (from whom the Philistines came) and Caphtorites.
13 Canaan was the father of
Sidon his firstborn,[c] and of the Hittites, 14 Jebusites, Amorites, Girgashites, 15 Hivites, Arkites, Sinites, 16 Arvadites, Zemarites and Hamathites.

The Semites

17 The sons of Shem:
Elam, Asshur, Arphaxad, Lud and Aram.
The sons of Aram:[d]
Uz, Hul, Gether and Meshech.
18 Arphaxad was the father of Shelah,
and Shelah the father of Eber.
19 Two sons were born to Eber:
One was named Peleg,[e] because in his time the earth was divided; his brother was named Joktan.
20 Joktan was the father of
Almodad, Sheleph, Hazarmaveth, Jerah, 21 Hadoram, Uzal, Diklah, 22 Obal,[f] Abimael, Sheba, 23 Ophir, Havilah and Jobab. All these were sons of Joktan.

24 Shem, Arphaxad,[g] Shelah,
25 Eber, Peleg, Reu,
26 Serug, Nahor, Terah
27 and Abram (that is, Abraham).

The Family of Abraham

28 The sons of Abraham:
Isaac and Ishmael.

Descendants of Hagar

29 These were their descendants:
Nebaioth the firstborn of Ishmael, Kedar, Adbeel, Mibsam, 30 Mishma, Dumah, Massa, Hadad, Tema, 31 Jetur, Naphish and Kedemah. These were the sons of Ishmael.

Descendants of Keturah

32 The sons born to Keturah, Abraham's concubine:
Zimran, Jokshan, Medan, Midian, Ishbak and Shuah.
The sons of Jokshan:
Sheba and Dedan.
33 The sons of Midian:
Ephah, Epher, Hanoch, Abida and Eldaah.
All these were descendants of Keturah.

Descendants of Sarah

34 Abraham was the father of Isaac.
The sons of Isaac:
Esau and Israel.

Esau's Sons

35 The sons of Esau:
Eliphaz, Reuel, Jeush, Jalam and Korah.
36 The sons of Eliphaz:
Teman, Omar, Zepho,[h] Gatam and Kenaz;
by Timna: Amalek.[i]
37 The sons of Reuel:
Nahath, Zerah, Shammah and Mizzah.

The People of Seir in Edom

38 The sons of Seir:
Lotan, Shobal, Zibeon, Anah, Dishon, Ezer and Dishan.
39 The sons of Lotan:
Hori and Homam. Timna was Lotan's sister.

[a] 8 That is, Egypt; also in verse 11 [b] 10 *Father* may mean *ancestor* or *predecessor* or *founder*; also in verses 11, 13, 18 and 20. [c] 13 Or *of the Sidonians, the foremost* [d] 17 One Hebrew manuscript and some Septuagint manuscripts (see also Gen. 10:23); most Hebrew manuscripts do not have this line. [e] 19 *Peleg* means *division.* [f] 22 Some Hebrew manuscripts and Syriac (see also Gen. 10:28); most Hebrew manuscripts *Ebal* [g] 24 Hebrew; some Septuagint manuscripts *Arphaxad, Cainan* (see also note at Gen. 11:10) [h] 36 Many Hebrew manuscripts, some Septuagint manuscripts and Syriac (see also Gen. 36:11); most Hebrew manuscripts *Zephi* [i] 36 Some Septuagint manuscripts (see also Gen. 36:12); Hebrew *Gatam, Kenaz, Timna and Amalek*

40 The sons of Shobal:
Alvan,[a] Manahath, Ebal, Shepho and Onam.
The sons of Zibeon:
Aiah and Anah.
41 The son of Anah:
Dishon.
The sons of Dishon:
Hemdan,[b] Eshban, Ithran and Keran.
42 The sons of Ezer:
Bilhan, Zaavan and Akan.[c]
The sons of Dishan[d]:
Uz and Aran.

The Rulers of Edom

43 These were the kings who reigned in Edom before any Israelite king reigned[e]:
Bela son of Beor, whose city was named Dinhabah.
44 When Bela died, Jobab son of Zerah from Bozrah succeeded him as king.
45 When Jobab died, Husham from the land of the Temanites succeeded him as king.
46 When Husham died, Hadad son of Bedad, who defeated Midian in the country of Moab, succeeded him as king. His city was named Avith.
47 When Hadad died, Samlah from Masrekah succeeded him as king.
48 When Samlah died, Shaul from Rehoboth on the river[f] succeeded him as king.
49 When Shaul died, Baal-Hanan son of Acbor succeeded him as king.
50 When Baal-Hanan died, Hadad succeeded him as king. His city was named Pau,[g] and his wife's name was Mehetabel daughter of Matred, the daughter of
Me-Zahab. 51 Hadad also died.

The chiefs of Edom were:
Timna, Alvah, Jetheth, 52 Oholibamah,
Elah, Pinon, 53 Kenaz, Teman, Mibzar,
54 Magdiel and Iram. These were the chiefs of Edom.

Israel's Sons

2 These were the sons of Israel:
Reuben, Simeon, Levi, Judah, Issachar,
Zebulun, 2 Dan, Joseph, Benjamin, Naphtali, Gad and Asher.

Judah

To Hezron's Sons

3 The sons of Judah:
Er, Onan and Shelah. These three were born to him by a Canaanite woman, the daughter of Shua. Er, Judah's firstborn, was wicked in the LORD's sight; so the
LORD put him to death. 4 Tamar, Judah's daughter-in-law, bore him Perez and Zerah. Judah had five sons in all.

5 The sons of Perez:
Hezron and Hamul.
6 The sons of Zerah:
Zimri, Ethan, Heman, Calcol and Darda[h]—five in all.
7 The son of Carmi:
Achar,[i] who brought trouble on Israel by violating the ban on taking devoted things.[j]
8 The son of Ethan:
Azariah.
9 The sons born to Hezron were:
Jerahmeel, Ram and Caleb.[k]

From Ram Son of Hezron

10 Ram was the father of
Amminadab, and Amminadab the father of Nahshon, the leader of the people of Judah.
11 Nahshon was the father of Salmon,[l] Salmon the father of Boaz,
12 Boaz the father of Obed and Obed the father of Jesse.
13 Jesse was the father of
Eliab his firstborn; the second son was Abinadab, the third Shimea,
14 the fourth Nethanel, the fifth Raddai,
15 the sixth Ozem and the seventh David.
16 Their sisters were Zeruiah and

[a]40 Many Hebrew manuscripts and some Septuagint manuscripts (see also Gen. 36:23); most Hebrew manuscripts *Alian* [b]41 Many Hebrew manuscripts and some Septuagint manuscripts (see also Gen. 36:26); most Hebrew manuscripts *Hamran* [c]42 Many Hebrew and Septuagint manuscripts (see also Gen. 36:27); most Hebrew manuscripts *Zaavan, Jaakan* [d]42 Hebrew *Dishon,* a variant of *Dishan* [e]43 Or *before an Israelite king reigned over them* [f]48 Possibly the Euphrates [g]50 Many Hebrew manuscripts, some Septuagint manuscripts, Vulgate and Syriac (see also Gen. 36:39); most Hebrew manuscripts *Pai* [h]6 Many Hebrew manuscripts, some Septuagint manuscripts and Syriac (see also 1 Kings 4:31); most Hebrew manuscripts *Dara* [i]7 *Achar* means *trouble*; *Achar* is called *Achan* in Joshua. [j]7 The Hebrew term refers to the irrevocable giving over of things or persons to the LORD, often by totally destroying them. [k]9 Hebrew *Kelubai,* a variant of *Caleb* [l]11 Septuagint (see also Ruth 4:21); Hebrew *Salma*

Abigail. Zeruiah's three sons were
Abishai, Joab and Asahel. 17 Abigail was
the mother of Amasa, whose father was
Jether the Ishmaelite.

Caleb Son of Hezron

18 Caleb son of Hezron had children by his
wife Azubah (and by Jerioth). These
were her sons: Jesher, Shobab and
Ardon. 19 When Azubah died, Caleb
married Ephrath, who bore him Hur.
20 Hur was the father of Uri, and Uri the
father of Bezalel.

21 Later, Hezron lay with the daughter of Makir the father of Gilead (he had married
her when he was sixty years old), and
she bore him Segub. 22 Segub was the
father of Jair, who controlled twenty-
three towns in Gilead. 23 (But Geshur
and Aram captured Havvoth Jair,[a] as
well as Kenath with its surrounding
settlements—sixty towns.) All these
were descendants of Makir the father
of Gilead.

24 After Hezron died in Caleb Ephrathah,
Abijah the wife of Hezron bore him
Ashhur the father[b] of Tekoa.

Jerahmeel Son of Hezron

25 The sons of Jerahmeel the firstborn of
Hezron:
Ram his firstborn, Bunah, Oren, Ozem
and[c] Ahijah. 26 Jerahmeel had another
wife, whose name was Atarah; she was
the mother of Onam.

27 The sons of Ram the firstborn of Jerahmeel:
Maaz, Jamin and Eker.

28 The sons of Onam:
Shammai and Jada.
The sons of Shammai:
Nadab and Abishur.

29 Abishur's wife was named Abihail, who
bore him Ahban and Molid.

30 The sons of Nadab:
Seled and Appaim. Seled died without children.

31 The son of Appaim:
Ishi, who was the father of Sheshan.
Sheshan was the father of Ahlai.

32 The sons of Jada, Shammai's brother:
Jether and Jonathan. Jether died without children.

33 The sons of Jonathan:
Peleth and Zaza.
These were the descendants of Jerahmeel.

34 Sheshan had no sons—only daughters.
He had an Egyptian servant named
Jarha. 35 Sheshan gave his daughter in
marriage to his servant Jarha, and she
bore him Attai.

36 Attai was the father of Nathan,
Nathan the father of Zabad,
37 Zabad the father of Ephlal,
Ephlal the father of Obed,
38 Obed the father of Jehu,
Jehu the father of Azariah,
39 Azariah the father of Helez,
Helez the father of Eleasah,
40 Eleasah the father of Sismai,
Sismai the father of Shallum,
41 Shallum the father of Jekamiah,
and Jekamiah the father of Elishama.

The Clans of Caleb

42 The sons of Caleb the brother of Jerahmeel:
Mesha his firstborn, who was the father
of Ziph, and his son Mareshah,[d] who
was the father of Hebron.

43 The sons of Hebron:
Korah, Tappuah, Rekem and Shema.
44 Shema was the father of Raham, and
Raham the father of Jorkeam. Rekem
was the father of Shammai. 45 The son
of Shammai was Maon, and Maon was
the father of Beth Zur.

46 Caleb's concubine Ephah was the mother
of Haran, Moza and Gazez. Haran was
the father of Gazez.

47 The sons of Jahdai:
Regem, Jotham, Geshan, Pelet, Ephah
and Shaaph.

48 Caleb's concubine Maacah was the mother
of Sheber and Tirhanah. 49 She also
gave birth to Shaaph the father of Madmannah and to Sheva the father of Mac-
benah and Gibea. Caleb's daughter was

[a] 23 Or *captured the settlements of Jair* [b] 24 *Father* may mean *civic leader* or *military leader*; also in verses 42, 45, 49–52 and possibly elsewhere. [c] 25 Or *Oren and Ozem, by* [d] 42 The meaning of the Hebrew for this phrase is uncertain.

Acsah. [50]These were the descendants of Caleb.

The sons of Hur the firstborn of Ephrathah:
Shobal the father of Kiriath Jearim,
[51]Salma the father of Bethlehem, and
Hareph the father of Beth Gader.
[52]The descendants of Shobal the father of Kiriath Jearim were:
Haroeh, half the Manahathites, [53]and
the clans of Kiriath Jearim: the Ithrites, Puthites, Shumathites and Mishraites. From these descended the Zorathites and Eshtaolites.
[54]The descendants of Salma:
Bethlehem, the Netophathites, Atroth Beth Joab, half the Manahathites, the
Zorites, [55]and the clans of scribes[a]
who lived at Jabez: the Tirathites, Shimeathites and Sucathites. These are the Kenites who came from Hammath, the father of the house of Recab.[b]

The Sons of David

3 These were the sons of David born to him in Hebron:
The firstborn was Amnon the son of Ahinoam of Jezreel;
the second, Daniel the son of Abigail of Carmel;
[2]the third, Absalom the son of Maacah daughter of Talmai king of Geshur;
the fourth, Adonijah the son of Haggith;
[3]the fifth, Shephatiah the son of Abital;
and the sixth, Ithream, by his wife Eglah.
[4]These six were born to David in Hebron, where he reigned seven years and six months.
David reigned in Jerusalem thirty-three years,
[5]and these were the children born to him there:
Shammua,[c] Shobab, Nathan and Solomon. These four were by Bathsheba[d]
daughter of Ammiel. [6]There were also
Ibhar, Elishua,[e] Eliphelet, [7]Nogah, Nepheg, Japhia, [8]Elishama, Eliada and
Eliphelet—nine in all. [9]All these were
the sons of David, besides his sons by his concubines. And Tamar was their sister.

The Kings of Judah

[10]Solomon's son was Rehoboam,
Abijah his son,
Asa his son,
Jehoshaphat his son,
[11]Jehoram[f] his son,
Ahaziah his son,
Joash his son,
[12]Amaziah his son,
Azariah his son,
Jotham his son,
[13]Ahaz his son,
Hezekiah his son,
Manasseh his son,
[14]Amon his son,
Josiah his son.
[15]The sons of Josiah:
Johanan the firstborn,
Jehoiakim the second son,
Zedekiah the third,
Shallum the fourth.
[16]The successors of Jehoiakim:
Jehoiachin[g] his son,
and Zedekiah.

The Royal Line After the Exile

[17]The descendants of Jehoiachin the captive:
Shealtiel his son, [18]Malkiram, Pedaiah,
Shenazzar, Jekamiah, Hoshama and Nedabiah.
[19]The sons of Pedaiah:
Zerubbabel and Shimei.
The sons of Zerubbabel:
Meshullam and Hananiah.
Shelomith was their sister.
[20]There were also five others:
Hashubah, Ohel, Berekiah, Hasadiah and Jushab-Hesed.
[21]The descendants of Hananiah:
Pelatiah and Jeshaiah, and the sons of

[a]55 Or *of the Sopherites* [b]55 Or *father of Beth Recab* [c]5 Hebrew *Shimea,* a variant of *Shammua* [d]5 One Hebrew manuscript and Vulgate (see also Septuagint and 2 Samuel 11:3); most Hebrew manuscripts *Bathshua* [e]6 Two Hebrew manuscripts (see also 2 Samuel 5:15 and 1 Chron. 14:5); most Hebrew manuscripts *Elishama* [f]11 Hebrew *Joram,* a variant of *Jehoram* [g]16 Hebrew *Jeconiah,* a variant of *Jehoiachin*; also in verse 17

Rephaiah, of Arnan, of Obadiah and
of Shecaniah.
22 The descendants of Shecaniah:
Shemaiah and his sons:
Hattush, Igal, Bariah, Neariah and Shaphat—six in all.
23 The sons of Neariah:
Elioenai, Hizkiah and Azrikam—three in all.
24 The sons of Elioenai:
Hodaviah, Eliashib, Pelaiah, Akkub, Johanan, Delaiah and Anani—seven in all.

Other Clans of Judah

4 The descendants of Judah:
Perez, Hezron, Carmi, Hur and Shobal.
2 Reaiah son of Shobal was the father of Jahath, and Jahath the father of Ahumai and Lahad. These were the clans of the Zorathites.
3 These were the sons[a] of Etam:
Jezreel, Ishma and Idbash. Their sister
was named Hazzelelponi. 4 Penuel was
the father of Gedor, and Ezer the father of Hushah.
These were the descendants of Hur, the firstborn of Ephrathah and father[b] of Bethlehem.
5 Ashhur the father of Tekoa had two wives, Helah and Naarah.
6 Naarah bore him Ahuzzam, Hepher, Temeni and Haahashtari. These were the descendants of Naarah.
7 The sons of Helah:
Zereth, Zohar, Ethnan, 8 and Koz, who
was the father of Anub and Hazzobebah and of the clans of Aharhel son of Harum.

9 Jabez was more honorable than his brothers. His mother had named him Jabez,[c] saying,
"I gave birth to him in pain." 10 Jabez cried out
to the God of Israel, "Oh, that you would bless
me and enlarge my territory! Let your hand
be with me, and keep me from harm so that I
will be free from pain." And God granted his request.

1 Chronicles 4:10

God Blesses Faith

Jabez cried out to the God of Israel, "Oh, that you would bless me and enlarge my territory! Let your hand be with me, and keep me from harm so that I will be free from pain." And God granted his request.

11 Kelub, Shuhah's brother, was the father of Mehir, who was the father
of Eshton. 12 Eshton
was the father of Beth Rapha, Paseah and Tehinnah the father of Ir Nahash.[d] These were the men of Recah.
13 The sons of Kenaz:
Othniel and Seraiah.
The sons of Othniel:
Hathath and Meonothai.[e] 14 Meonothai was
the father of Ophrah.
Seraiah was the father of Joab,
the father of Ge Harashim.[f] It was called this because its people were craftsmen.
15 The sons of Caleb son of Jephunneh:
Iru, Elah and Naam.
The son of Elah:
Kenaz.
16 The sons of Jehallelel:
Ziph, Ziphah, Tiria and Asarel.
17 The sons of Ezrah:
Jether, Mered, Epher and Jalon. One of Mered's wives gave birth to Miriam, Shammai and Ishbah the father of Eshtemoa. 18 (His Judean wife gave birth
to Jered the father of Gedor, Heber the father of Soco, and Jekuthiel the father of Zanoah.) These were the children of Pharaoh's daughter Bithiah, whom Mered had married.
19 The sons of Hodiah's wife, the sister of Naham:
the father of Keilah the Garmite, and Eshtemoa the Maacathite.
20 The sons of Shimon:
Amnon, Rinnah, Ben-Hanan and Tilon.

[a] 3 Some Septuagint manuscripts (see also Vulgate); Hebrew *father* [b] 4 *Father* may mean *civic leader* or *military leader*; also in verses 12, 14, 17, 18 and possibly elsewhere. [c] 9 *Jabez* sounds like the Hebrew for *pain*. [d] 12 Or *of the city of Nahash* [e] 13 Some Septuagint manuscripts and Vulgate; Hebrew does not have *and Meonothai*. [f] 14 *Ge Harashim* means *valley of craftsmen*.

The descendants of Ishi:
Zoheth and Ben-Zoheth.
21 The sons of Shelah son of Judah:
Er the father of Lecah, Laadah the father
of Mareshah and the clans of the linen
workers at Beth Ashbea, 22 Jokim, the
men of Cozeba, and Joash and Saraph,
who ruled in Moab and Jashubi Lehem.
(These records are from ancient times.)
23 They were the potters who lived at
Netaim and Gederah; they stayed there
and worked for the king.

Simeon

24 The descendants of Simeon:
Nemuel, Jamin, Jarib, Zerah and
Shaul;
25 Shallum was Shaul's son, Mibsam his
son and Mishma his son.
26 The descendants of Mishma:
Hammuel his son, Zaccur his son and
Shimei his son.
27 Shimei had sixteen sons and six daughters,
but his brothers did not have many children;
so their entire clan did not become as numerous as the people of Judah. 28 They lived in
Beersheba, Moladah, Hazar Shual, 29 Bilhah,
Ezem, Tolad, 30 Bethuel, Hormah, Ziklag,
31 Beth Marcaboth, Hazar Susim, Beth Biri and
Shaaraim. These were their towns until the
reign of David. 32 Their surrounding villages
were Etam, Ain, Rimmon, Token and Ashan—
five towns— 33 and all the villages around these
towns as far as Baalath.[a] These were their settlements. And they kept a genealogical record.

34 Meshobab, Jamlech, Joshah son of
Amaziah, 35 Joel, Jehu son of Joshibiah,
the son of Seraiah, the son of Asiel, 36 also
Elioenai, Jaakobah, Jeshohaiah, Asaiah,
Adiel, Jesimiel, Benaiah, 37 and Ziza son
of Shiphi, the son of Allon, the son of Jedaiah, the son of Shimri, the son of Shemaiah.

38 The men listed above by name were leaders
of their clans. Their families increased greatly,
39 and they went to the outskirts of Gedor to
the east of the valley in search of pasture for
their flocks. 40 They found rich, good pasture,
and the land was spacious, peaceful and quiet.
Some Hamites had lived there formerly.

41 The men whose names were listed came
in the days of Hezekiah king of Judah. They attacked the Hamites in their dwellings and also
the Meunites who were there and completely
destroyed[b] them, as is evident to this day. Then
they settled in their place, because there was
pasture for their flocks. 42 And five hundred of
these Simeonites, led by Pelatiah, Neariah, Rephaiah and Uzziel, the sons of Ishi, invaded the
hill country of Seir. 43 They killed the remaining Amalekites who had escaped, and they
have lived there to this day.

Reuben

5 The sons of Reuben the firstborn of Israel
(he was the firstborn, but when he defiled
his father's marriage bed, his rights as firstborn
were given to the sons of Joseph son of Israel;
so he could not be listed in the genealogical
record in accordance with his birthright, 2 and
though Judah was the strongest of his brothers
and a ruler came from him, the rights of the
firstborn belonged to Joseph)— 3 the sons of
Reuben the firstborn of Israel:
Hanoch, Pallu, Hezron and Carmi.
4 The descendants of Joel:
Shemaiah his son, Gog his son,
Shimei his son, 5 Micah his son,
Reaiah his son, Baal his son,
6 and Beerah his son, whom Tiglath-Pileser[c] king of Assyria took into exile.
Beerah was a leader of the Reubenites.
7 Their relatives by clans, listed according to
their genealogical records:
Jeiel the chief, Zechariah, 8 and Bela son
of Azaz, the son of Shema, the son of
Joel. They settled in the area from Aroer
to Nebo and Baal Meon. 9 To the east
they occupied the land up to the edge
of the desert that extends to the Euphrates River, because their livestock
had increased in Gilead.
10 During Saul's reign they waged war
against the Hagrites, who were defeated at
their hands; they occupied the dwellings
of the Hagrites throughout the entire region east of Gilead.

[a] 33 Some Septuagint manuscripts (see also Joshua 19:8); Hebrew *Baal* [b] 41 The Hebrew term refers to the irrevocable giving over of things or persons to the LORD, often by totally destroying them. [c] 6 Hebrew *Tilgath-Pilneser,* a variant of *Tiglath-Pileser*; also in verse 26

Gad

11 The Gadites lived next to them in Bashan,
as far as Salecah:
12 Joel was the chief, Shapham the second,
then Janai and Shaphat, in Bashan.
13 Their relatives, by families, were:
Michael, Meshullam, Sheba, Jorai, Jacan, Zia and Eber—seven in all.
14 These were the sons of Abihail son of Huri, the son of Jaroah, the son of Gilead, the son of Michael, the son of Jeshishai, the son of Jahdo, the son of Buz.
15 Ahi son of Abdiel, the son of Guni, was head of their family.
16 The Gadites lived in Gilead, in Bashan and its outlying villages, and on all the pasturelands of Sharon as far as they extended.
17 All these were entered in the genealogical records during the reigns of Jotham king of Judah and Jeroboam king of Israel.

18 The Reubenites, the Gadites and the half-
tribe of Manasseh had 44,760 men ready for military service—able-bodied men who could handle shield and sword, who could use a bow, and who were trained for battle.
19 They waged war against the Hagrites, Jetur, Naphish and
Nodab.
20 They were helped in fighting them, and God handed the Hagrites and all their allies over to them, because they cried out to him during the battle. He answered their prayers, because they trusted in him.
21 They seized the livestock of the Hagrites—fifty thousand camels, two hundred fifty thousand sheep and two thousand donkeys. They also took one hundred thousand people captive,
22 and many others fell slain, because the battle was God's. And they occupied the land until the exile.

The Half-Tribe of Manasseh

23 The people of the half-tribe of Manasseh were numerous; they settled in the land from Bashan to Baal Hermon, that is, to Senir (Mount Hermon).
24 These were the heads of their families: Epher, Ishi, Eliel, Azriel, Jeremiah, Hodaviah and Jahdiel. They were brave warriors, famous men, and heads of their families.
25 But they were unfaithful to the God of their fathers and prostituted themselves to the gods of the peoples of the land, whom God had destroyed before
them.
26 So the God of Israel stirred up the spirit of Pul king of Assyria (that is, Tiglath-Pileser king of Assyria), who took the Reubenites, the Gadites and the half-tribe of Manasseh into exile. He took them to Halah, Habor, Hara and the river of Gozan, where they are to this day.

Levi

6 The sons of Levi:
Gershon, Kohath and Merari.
2 The sons of Kohath:
Amram, Izhar, Hebron and Uzziel.
3 The children of Amram:
Aaron, Moses and Miriam.
The sons of Aaron:
Nadab, Abihu, Eleazar and Ithamar.
4 Eleazar was the father of Phinehas,
Phinehas the father of Abishua,
5 Abishua the father of Bukki,
Bukki the father of Uzzi,
6 Uzzi the father of Zerahiah,
Zerahiah the father of Meraioth,
7 Meraioth the father of Amariah,
Amariah the father of Ahitub,
8 Ahitub the father of Zadok,
Zadok the father of Ahimaaz,
9 Ahimaaz the father of Azariah,
Azariah the father of Johanan,
10 Johanan the father of Azariah (it was he who served as priest in the temple Solomon built in Jerusalem),
11 Azariah the father of Amariah,
Amariah the father of Ahitub,
12 Ahitub the father of Zadok,
Zadok the father of Shallum,
13 Shallum the father of Hilkiah,
Hilkiah the father of Azariah,
14 Azariah the father of Seraiah,
and Seraiah the father of Jehozadak.
15 Jehozadak was deported when the LORD sent Judah and Jerusalem into exile by the hand of Nebuchadnezzar.

16 The sons of Levi:
Gershon,[a] Kohath and Merari.
17 These are the names of the sons of Gershon:

[a]16 Hebrew *Gershom*, a variant of *Gershon*; also in verses 17, 20, 43, 62 and 71

Our Secret Weapon

Read: 1 Chronicles 5:18–22

IMAGINE RANKS OF WARRIORS stretching as far as the eye can see. Their weapons glinting in the morning sunlight, spread over the villages and pastures of the land God had given them. Nearly 45,000 strapping young men—weapon-savvy, war-hungry and expertly trained—fingering their bows and sword hilts impatiently. They had trained for this battle.

In the silence you could have heard a horse snort, a fish jump in the Jordan, a scabbard ring hollow against a shield. But as the battle got underway and the screams tore at their eardrums, you could hear something else: the cries of the warriors calling out to God for help. He was the secret weapon in the battle. And they trusted him for the victory.

Let's face it; life is more a battlefield than a playground. Every day we face enemies we can't even see. We are at war "against the powers of this dark world and against the spiritual forces of evil in the heavenly realms" (Ephesians 6:12). We fight battles within ourselves—against insecurity, anxiety, depression. We fight for spiritual territory rather than for plots of land. We fight against the fallen things in this world: materialism, greed, selfishness, addiction, violence, apathy, prejudice, injustice . . . and the list goes on. Daunting enemies, indeed.

As soldiers in God's army we are called to do battle with evil by putting on the armor of God (see Ephesians 6:10–18). Every morning, picture yourself donning each piece like a modern-day Joan of Arc: the belt of God's truth, the breastplate of righteousness, the gospel of peace. Take up your shield of faith, the helmet of salvation and the sword of the Spirit. And then, like the Israelites, employ your "secret weapon": prayer. Ask God for help, "pray[ing] in the Spirit . . . with all kinds of prayers and requests" (Ephesians 6:18). One commentator said, "Satan trembles when he sees the weakest saint upon his knees." Don't hesitate to utilize your secret weapon by praying to the Lord of hosts, and trust him to hear your prayers. He's the one who will lead you to win your battle because he has already won the war.

Wednesday

1 Chronicles 5:20

They were helped in fighting them, and God handed the Hagrites and all their allies over to them, because they cried out to him during the battle. He answered their prayers, because they trusted in him.

reflection

1 Are most of your battles fought against "inward" or "outward" foes?

2 What weapons are you finding most effective against your foe?

3 How often do you utilize your "secret weapon" (prayer)?

RELATED READINGS

Psalm 24:1–10;
Philippians 4:6;
James 4:1–8;
1 Peter 3:10–16

Go to page 493 for your next devotional reading.

Libni and Shimei.
18 The sons of Kohath:
Amram, Izhar, Hebron and Uzziel.
19 The sons of Merari:
Mahli and Mushi.
These are the clans of the Levites listed according to their fathers:
20 Of Gershon:
Libni his son, Jehath his son,
Zimmah his son, 21 Joah his son,
Iddo his son, Zerah his son
and Jeatherai his son.
22 The descendants of Kohath:
Amminadab his son, Korah his son,
Assir his son, 23 Elkanah his son,
Ebiasaph his son, Assir his son,
24 Tahath his son, Uriel his son,
Uzziah his son and Shaul his son.
25 The descendants of Elkanah:
Amasai, Ahimoth,
26 Elkanah his son,[a] Zophai his son,
Nahath his son, 27 Eliab his son,
Jeroham his son, Elkanah his son
and Samuel his son.[b]
28 The sons of Samuel:
Joel[c] the firstborn
and Abijah the second son.
29 The descendants of Merari:
Mahli, Libni his son,
Shimei his son, Uzzah his son,
30 Shimea his son, Haggiah his son
and Asaiah his son.

The Temple Musicians

31 These are the men David put in charge of
the music in the house of the LORD after the ark
came to rest there. 32 They ministered with music before the tabernacle, the Tent of Meeting,
until Solomon built the temple of the LORD in
Jerusalem. They performed their duties according to the regulations laid down for them.
33 Here are the men who served, together
with their sons:
From the Kohathites:
Heman, the musician,
the son of Joel, the son of Samuel,
34 the son of Elkanah, the son of Jeroham,
the son of Eliel, the son of Toah,
35 the son of Zuph, the son of Elkanah,
the son of Mahath, the son of Amasai,
36 the son of Elkanah, the son of Joel,
the son of Azariah, the son of Zephaniah,
37 the son of Tahath, the son of Assir,
the son of Ebiasaph, the son of Korah,
38 the son of Izhar, the son of Kohath,
the son of Levi, the son of Israel;
39 and Heman's associate Asaph, who served at his right hand:
Asaph son of Berekiah, the son of Shimea,
40 the son of Michael, the son of Baaseiah,[d]
the son of Malkijah, 41 the son of Ethni,
the son of Zerah, the son of Adaiah,
42 the son of Ethan, the son of Zimmah,
the son of Shimei, 43 the son of Jahath,
the son of Gershon, the son of Levi;
44 and from their associates, the Merarites, at his left hand:
Ethan son of Kishi, the son of Abdi,
the son of Malluch, 45 the son of Hashabiah,
the son of Amaziah, the son of Hilkiah,
46 the son of Amzi, the son of Bani,
the son of Shemer, 47 the son of Mahli,
the son of Mushi, the son of Merari,
the son of Levi.

48 Their fellow Levites were assigned to all
the other duties of the tabernacle, the house of
God. 49 But Aaron and his descendants were
the ones who presented offerings on the altar
of burnt offering and on the altar of incense in
connection with all that was done in the Most
Holy Place, making atonement for Israel, in
accordance with all that Moses the servant of
God had commanded.

50 These were the descendants of Aaron:
Eleazar his son, Phinehas his son,
Abishua his son, 51 Bukki his son,
Uzzi his son, Zerahiah his son,

[a]26 Some Hebrew manuscripts, Septuagint and Syriac; most Hebrew manuscripts *Ahimoth* [26] *and Elkanah. The sons of Elkanah:*
[b]27 Some Septuagint manuscripts (see also 1 Samuel 1:19,20 and 1 Chron. 6:33,34); Hebrew does not have *and Samuel his son.*
[c]28 Some Septuagint manuscripts and Syriac (see also 1 Samuel 8:2 and 1 Chron. 6:33); Hebrew does not have *Joel.* [d]40 Most Hebrew manuscripts; some Hebrew manuscripts, one Septuagint manuscript and Syriac *Maaseiah*

52 Meraioth his son, Amariah his son,
Ahitub his son, 53 Zadok his son
and Ahimaaz his son.

54 These were the locations
of their settlements allotted as
their territory (they were assigned to the descendants of
Aaron who were from the Kohathite clan, because the first
lot was for them):
55 They were given Hebron
in Judah with its surrounding pasturelands. 56 But the
fields and villages around
the city were given to Caleb
son of Jephunneh.
57 So the descendants of
Aaron were given Hebron (a
city of refuge), and Libnah,[a]
Jattir, Eshtemoa, 58 Hilen,
Debir, 59 Ashan, Juttah[b] and
Beth Shemesh, together with
their pasturelands. 60 And
from the tribe of Benjamin they were
given Gibeon,[c] Geba, Alemeth and Anathoth, together with their pasturelands.
These towns, which were distributed
among the Kohathite clans, were thirteen
in all.
61 The rest of Kohath's descendants were allotted ten towns from the clans of half the tribe
of Manasseh.
62 The descendants of Gershon, clan by
clan, were allotted thirteen towns from the
tribes of Issachar, Asher and Naphtali, and
from the part of the tribe of Manasseh that is
in Bashan.
63 The descendants of Merari, clan by clan,
were allotted twelve towns from the tribes of
Reuben, Gad and Zebulun.
64 So the Israelites gave the Levites these
towns and their pasturelands. 65 From the
tribes of Judah, Simeon and Benjamin they allotted the previously named towns.
66 Some of the Kohathite clans were given
as their territory towns from the tribe of
Ephraim.

> 1 Chronicles 6:49
>
> **God Requires Payment for Sin**
>
> But Aaron and his descendants were the ones who presented offerings on the altar of burnt offering and on the altar of incense in connection with all that was done in the Most Holy Place, making atonement for Israel.

67 In the hill country of Ephraim they
were given Shechem (a city of refuge), and
Gezer,[d] 68 Jokmeam, Beth Horon, 69 Aijalon and Gath Rimmon,
together with their pas-
turelands.
70 And from half the
tribe of Manasseh the
Israelites gave Aner and
Bileam, together with
their pasturelands, to
the rest of the Kohath-
ite clans.

71 The Gershonites received
the following:
From the clan of the half-
tribe of Manasseh
they received Golan in
Bashan and also Ash-
taroth, together with
their pasturelands;
72 from the tribe of Issachar
they received Kedesh,
Daberath, 73 Ramoth
and Anem, together with their pasturelands;
74 from the tribe of Asher
they received Mashal, Abdon, 75 Hukok
and Rehob, together with their pasturelands;
76 and from the tribe of Naphtali
they received Kedesh in Galilee, Hammon and Kiriathaim, together with
their pasturelands.

77 The Merarites (the rest of the Levites) received the following:
From the tribe of Zebulun
they received Jokneam, Kartah,[e]
Rimmono and Tabor, together with
their pasturelands;
78 from the tribe of Reuben across the Jordan east of Jericho
they received Bezer in the desert,
Jahzah, 79 Kedemoth and Mephaath,
together with their pasturelands;
80 and from the tribe of Gad
they received Ramoth in Gilead,

[a]57 See Joshua 21:13; Hebrew *given the cities of refuge: Hebron, Libnah.* [b]59 Syriac (see also Septuagint and Joshua 21:16); Hebrew does not have *Juttah.* [c]60 See Joshua 21:17; Hebrew does not have *Gibeon.* [d]67 See Joshua 21:21; Hebrew *given the cities of refuge: Shechem, Gezer.* [e]77 See Septuagint and Joshua 21:34; Hebrew does not have *Jokneam, Kartah.*

Mahanaim, 81 Heshbon and Jazer,
together with their pasturelands.

Issachar

7 The sons of Issachar:
Tola, Puah, Jashub and Shimron—four in all.
2 The sons of Tola:
Uzzi, Rephaiah, Jeriel, Jahmai, Ibsam and Samuel—heads of their families. During the reign of David, the descendants of Tola listed as fighting men in their genealogy numbered 22,600.
3 The son of Uzzi:
Izrahiah.
The sons of Izrahiah:
Michael, Obadiah, Joel and Isshiah. All
five of them were chiefs. 4 According to
their family genealogy, they had 36,000 men ready for battle, for they had many wives and children.
5 The relatives who were fighting men belonging to all the clans of Issachar, as listed in their genealogy, were 87,000 in all.

Benjamin

6 Three sons of Benjamin:
Bela, Beker and Jediael.
7 The sons of Bela:
Ezbon, Uzzi, Uzziel, Jerimoth and Iri, heads of families—five in all. Their genealogical record listed 22,034 fighting men.
8 The sons of Beker:
Zemirah, Joash, Eliezer, Elioenai, Omri, Jeremoth, Abijah, Anathoth and
Alemeth. All these were the sons of Be-
ker. 9 Their genealogical record listed
the heads of families and 20,200 fighting men.
10 The son of Jediael:
Bilhan.
The sons of Bilhan:
Jeush, Benjamin, Ehud, Kenaanah, Ze-
than, Tarshish and Ahishahar. 11 All
these sons of Jediael were heads of families. There were 17,200 fighting men ready to go out to war.
12 The Shuppites and Huppites were the descendants of Ir, and the Hushites the descendants of Aher.

Naphtali

13 The sons of Naphtali:
Jahziel, Guni, Jezer and Shillem[a]—the descendants of Bilhah.

Manasseh

14 The descendants of Manasseh:
Asriel was his descendant through his Aramean concubine. She gave birth to
Makir the father of Gilead. 15 Makir took
a wife from among the Huppites and Shuppites. His sister's name was Maacah.
Another descendant was named Zelophehad, who had only daughters.
16 Makir's wife Maacah gave birth to a son and named him Peresh. His brother was named Sheresh, and his sons were Ulam and Rakem.
17 The son of Ulam:
Bedan.
These were the sons of Gilead son of Ma-
kir, the son of Manasseh. 18 His sister
Hammoleketh gave birth to Ishhod, Abiezer and Mahlah.
19 The sons of Shemida were:
Ahian, Shechem, Likhi and Aniam.

Ephraim

20 The descendants of Ephraim:
Shuthelah, Bered his son,
Tahath his son, Eleadah his son,
Tahath his son, 21 Zabad his son
and Shuthelah his son.
Ezer and Elead were killed by the native-born men of Gath, when they went
down to seize their livestock. 22 Their fa-
ther Ephraim mourned for them many days, and his relatives came to comfort
him. 23 Then he lay with his wife again,
and she became pregnant and gave birth to a son. He named him Beriah,[b] because there had been misfortune in his family.
24 His daughter was Sheerah, who built Lower and Upper Beth Horon as well as Uzzen Sheerah.
25 Rephah was his son, Resheph his son,[c]

[a] 13 Some Hebrew and Septuagint manuscripts (see also Gen. 46:24 and Num. 26:49); most Hebrew manuscripts *Shallum* [b] 23 *Beriah* sounds like the Hebrew for *misfortune.* [c] 25 Some Septuagint manuscripts; Hebrew does not have *his son.*

Telah his son, Tahan his son,
26 Ladan his son, Ammihud his son,
Elishama his son, 27 Nun his son
and Joshua his son.
28 Their lands and settlements included
Bethel and its surrounding villages, Naaran
to the east, Gezer and its villages to the west,
and Shechem and its villages all the way to
Ayyah and its villages. 29 Along the borders of
Manasseh were Beth Shan, Taanach, Megiddo
and Dor, together with their villages. The
descendants of Joseph son of Israel lived in
these towns.

Asher

30 The sons of Asher:
Imnah, Ishvah, Ishvi and Beriah. Their sister was Serah.
31 The sons of Beriah:
Heber and Malkiel, who was the father of Birzaith.
32 Heber was the father of Japhlet, Shomer and Hotham and of their sister Shua.
33 The sons of Japhlet:
Pasach, Bimhal and Ashvath.
These were Japhlet's sons.
34 The sons of Shomer:
Ahi, Rohgah,[a] Hubbah and Aram.
35 The sons of his brother Helem:
Zophah, Imna, Shelesh and Amal.
36 The sons of Zophah:
Suah, Harnepher, Shual, Beri, Imrah,
37 Bezer, Hod, Shamma, Shilshah, Ithran[b] and Beera.
38 The sons of Jether:
Jephunneh, Pispah and Ara.
39 The sons of Ulla:
Arah, Hanniel and Rizia.
40 All these were descendants of Asher—
heads of families, choice men, brave warriors
and outstanding leaders. The number of men
ready for battle, as listed in their genealogy,
was 26,000.

The Genealogy of Saul the Benjamite

8 Benjamin was the father of Bela his firstborn,
Ashbel the second son, Aharah the third,
2 Nohah the fourth and Rapha the fifth.
3 The sons of Bela were:
Addar, Gera, Abihud,[c] 4 Abishua, Naaman, Ahoah, 5 Gera, Shephuphan and Huram.
6 These were the descendants of Ehud, who were heads of families of those living in Geba and were deported to Manahath:
7 Naaman, Ahijah, and Gera, who deported them and who was the father of Uzza and Ahihud.
8 Sons were born to Shaharaim in Moab after he had divorced his wives Hushim and Baara.
9 By his wife Hodesh he had Jobab, Zibia, Mesha, Malcam,
10 Jeuz, Sakia and Mirmah. These were his sons, heads of families.
11 By Hushim he had Abitub and Elpaal.
12 The sons of Elpaal:
Eber, Misham, Shemed (who built Ono and Lod with its surrounding villages),
13 and Beriah and Shema, who were heads of families of those living in Aijalon and who drove out the inhabitants of Gath.
14 Ahio, Shashak, Jeremoth, 15 Zebadiah, Arad, Eder, 16 Michael, Ishpah and Joha were the sons of Beriah.
17 Zebadiah, Meshullam, Hizki, Heber, 18 Ishmerai, Izliah and Jobab were the sons of Elpaal.
19 Jakim, Zicri, Zabdi, 20 Elienai, Zillethai, Eliel, 21 Adaiah, Beraiah and Shimrath were the sons of Shimei.
22 Ishpan, Eber, Eliel, 23 Abdon, Zicri, Hanan, 24 Hananiah, Elam, Anthothijah,
25 Iphdeiah and Penuel were the sons of Shashak.
26 Shamsherai, Shehariah, Athaliah,
27 Jaareshiah, Elijah and Zicri were the sons of Jeroham.
28 All these were heads of families, chiefs as
listed in their genealogy, and they lived in Jerusalem.

29 Jeiel[d] the father[e] of Gibeon lived in Gibeon.
His wife's name was Maacah, 30 and his firstborn son was Abdon, followed by

[a] 34 Or *of his brother Shomer: Rohgah* [b] 37 Possibly a variant of *Jether* [c] 3 Or *Gera the father of Ehud* [d] 29 Some Septuagint manuscripts (see also 1 Chron. 9:35); Hebrew does not have *Jeiel.* [e] 29 *Father* may mean *civic leader* or *military leader.*

Zur, Kish, Baal, Ner,[a] Nadab, 31Gedor,
Ahio, Zeker 32and Mikloth, who was
the father of Shimeah. They too lived
near their relatives in Jerusalem.
33 Ner was the father of Kish, Kish the father
of Saul, and Saul the father of Jonathan,
Malki-Shua, Abinadab and Esh-Baal.[b]
34 The son of Jonathan:
Merib-Baal,[c] who was the father of
Micah.
35 The sons of Micah:
Pithon, Melech, Tarea and Ahaz.
36 Ahaz was the father of Jehoaddah,
Jehoaddah was the father of Alemeth,
Azmaveth and Zimri, and Zimri was
the father of Moza. 37Moza was the father of Binea; Raphah was his son, Eleasah his son and Azel his son.
38 Azel had six sons, and these were
their names:
Azrikam, Bokeru, Ishmael, Sheariah,
Obadiah and Hanan. All these were
the sons of Azel.
39 The sons of his brother Eshek:
Ulam his firstborn, Jeush the second
son and Eliphelet the third. 40The sons
of Ulam were brave warriors who could
handle the bow. They had many sons
and grandsons—150 in all.
All these were the descendants of Benjamin.

9 All Israel was listed in the genealogies recorded in the book of the kings of Israel.

The People in Jerusalem

The people of Judah were taken captive to
Babylon because of their unfaithfulness. 2Now
the first to resettle on their own property in
their own towns were some Israelites, priests,
Levites and temple servants.
3Those from Judah, from Benjamin, and
from Ephraim and Manasseh who lived in Jerusalem were:
4 Uthai son of Ammihud, the son of Omri,
the son of Imri, the son of Bani, a descendant of Perez son of Judah.
5 Of the Shilonites:
Asaiah the firstborn and his sons.
6 Of the Zerahites:
Jeuel.
The people from Judah numbered 690.
7 Of the Benjamites:
Sallu son of Meshullam, the son of
Hodaviah, the son of Hassenuah;
8 Ibneiah son of Jeroham; Elah son of
Uzzi, the son of Micri; and Meshullam
son of Shephatiah, the son of Reuel, the
son of Ibnijah.
9 The people from Benjamin, as listed
in their genealogy, numbered 956. All
these men were heads of their families.
10 Of the priests:
Jedaiah; Jehoiarib; Jakin;
11 Azariah son of Hilkiah, the son of Meshullam, the son of Zadok, the son of
Meraioth, the son of Ahitub, the official
in charge of the house of God;
12 Adaiah son of Jeroham, the son of Pashhur, the son of Malkijah; and Maasai
son of Adiel, the son of Jahzerah, the
son of Meshullam, the son of Meshille-
mith, the son of Immer.
13 The priests, who were heads of families, numbered 1,760. They were able
men, responsible for ministering in the
house of God.
14 Of the Levites:
Shemaiah son of Hasshub, the son of
Azrikam, the son of Hashabiah, a Merarite; 15Bakbakkar, Heresh, Galal and
Mattaniah son of Mica, the son of Zicri,
the son of Asaph; 16Obadiah son of
Shemaiah, the son of Galal, the son of
Jeduthun; and Berekiah son of Asa,
the son of Elkanah, who lived in the
villages of the Netophathites.
17 The gatekeepers:
Shallum, Akkub, Talmon, Ahiman
and their brothers, Shallum their chief
18being stationed at the King's Gate on
the east, up to the present time. These
were the gatekeepers belonging to the
camp of the Levites. 19Shallum son of
Kore, the son of Ebiasaph, the son of
Korah, and his fellow gatekeepers from

[a]30 Some Septuagint manuscripts (see also 1 Chron. 9:36); Hebrew does not have *Ner.* [b]33 Also known as *Ish-Bosheth* [c]34 Also known as *Mephibosheth*

his family (the Korahites) were responsible for guarding the thresholds of the Tent[a] just as their fathers had been responsible for guarding the entrance to the dwelling of the LORD. 20In earlier times Phinehas son of Eleazar was in charge of the gatekeepers, and the LORD was with him. 21Zechariah son of Meshelemiah was the gatekeeper at the entrance to the Tent of Meeting.

22Altogether, those chosen to be gatekeepers at the thresholds numbered 212. They
were registered by genealogy in their villages.
The gatekeepers had been assigned to their
positions of trust by David and Samuel the
seer. 23They and their descendants were in
charge of guarding the gates of the house of
the LORD—the house called the Tent. 24The
gatekeepers were on the four sides: east, west,
north and south. 25Their brothers in their
villages had to come from time to time and
share their duties for seven-day periods. 26But
the four principal gatekeepers, who were Levites, were entrusted with the responsibility
for the rooms and treasuries in the house of
God. 27They would spend the night stationed
around the house of God, because they had to
guard it; and they had charge of the key for
opening it each morning.

28Some of them were in charge of the articles
used in the temple service; they counted them
when they were brought in and when they
were taken out. 29Others were assigned to take
care of the furnishings and all the other articles
of the sanctuary, as well as the flour and wine,
and the oil, incense and spices. 30But some of
the priests took care of mixing the spices. 31A
Levite named Mattithiah, the firstborn son of
Shallum the Korahite, was entrusted with the
responsibility for baking the offering bread.
32Some of their Kohathite brothers were in
charge of preparing for every Sabbath the
bread set out on the table.

33Those who were musicians, heads of
Levite families, stayed in the rooms of the
temple and were exempt from other duties because they were responsible for the work day
and night.

34All these were heads of Levite families,
chiefs as listed in their genealogy, and they
lived in Jerusalem.

The Genealogy of Saul

35Jeiel the father[b] of Gibeon lived in Gibeon.
His wife's name was Maacah, 36and his
firstborn son was Abdon, followed by
Zur, Kish, Baal, Ner, Nadab, 37Gedor,
Ahio, Zechariah and Mikloth. 38Mik-
loth was the father of Shimeam. They
too lived near their relatives in Jerusalem.

39Ner was the father of Kish, Kish the father of Saul, and Saul the father of Jonathan, Malki-Shua, Abinadab and Esh-Baal.[c]

40The son of Jonathan:
Merib-Baal,[d] who was the father of Micah.

41The sons of Micah:
Pithon, Melech, Tahrea and Ahaz.[e]

42Ahaz was the father of Jadah, Jadah[f]
was the father of Alemeth, Azmaveth
and Zimri, and Zimri was the father of
Moza. 43Moza was the father of Binea;
Rephaiah was his son, Eleasah his son
and Azel his son.

44Azel had six sons, and these were their names:
Azrikam, Bokeru, Ishmael, Sheariah, Obadiah and Hanan. These were the sons of Azel.

Saul Takes His Life

10 Now the Philistines fought against
Israel; the Israelites fled before them,
and many fell slain on Mount Gilboa. 2The Philistines pressed hard after Saul and his sons,
and they killed his sons Jonathan, Abinadab
and Malki-Shua. 3The fighting grew fierce
around Saul, and when the archers overtook
him, they wounded him.

4Saul said to his armor-bearer, "Draw your
sword and run me through, or these uncircumcised fellows will come and abuse me."

But his armor-bearer was terrified and would
not do it; so Saul took his own sword and fell
on it. 5When the armor-bearer saw that Saul

a19 That is, the temple; also in verses 21 and 23 b35 *Father* may mean *civic leader* or *military leader.* c39 Also known as *Ish-Bosheth*
d40 Also known as *Mephibosheth* e41 Vulgate and Syriac (see also Septuagint and 1 Chron. 8:35); Hebrew does not have *and Ahaz.*
f42 Some Hebrew manuscripts and Septuagint (see also 1 Chron. 8:36); most Hebrew manuscripts *Jarah, Jarah*

was dead, he too fell on his sword and died. [6]So
Saul and his three sons died, and all his house
died together.
[7]When all the Israelites in the valley saw
that the army had fled and that Saul and his
sons had died, they abandoned their towns
and fled. And the Philistines came and occupied them.
[8]The next day, when the Philistines came
to strip the dead, they found Saul and his sons
fallen on Mount Gilboa. [9]They stripped him
and took his head and his armor, and sent messengers throughout the land of the Philistines
to proclaim the news among their idols and
their people. [10]They put his armor in the temple of their gods and hung up his head in the
temple of Dagon.
[11]When all the inhabitants of Jabesh Gilead
heard of everything the Philistines had done
to Saul, [12]all their valiant men went and took
the bodies of Saul and his sons and brought
them to Jabesh. Then they buried their bones
under the great tree in Jabesh, and they fasted
seven days.
[13]Saul died because he was
unfaithful to the LORD; he did
not keep the word of the LORD
and even consulted a medium
for guidance, [14]and did not inquire of the LORD. So the LORD
put him to death and turned
the kingdom over to David son
of Jesse.

> **1 Chronicles 10:13**
>
> ***God Punishes Disobedience***
>
> Saul died because he was unfaithful to the LORD; he did not keep the word of the LORD and even consulted a medium for guidance.

David Becomes King Over Israel

11 All Israel came together to David at He-
bron and said, "We are your
own flesh and blood. [2]In the
past, even while Saul was king, you were the
one who led Israel on their military campaigns.
And the LORD your God said to you, 'You will
shepherd my people Israel, and you will become their ruler.'"
[3]When all the elders of Israel had come to
King David at Hebron, he made a compact
with them at Hebron before the LORD, and they
anointed David king over Israel, as the LORD
had promised through Samuel.

David Conquers Jerusalem

[4]David and all the Israelites marched to Jerusalem (that is, Jebus). The Jebusites who lived
there [5]said to David, "You will not get in here."
Nevertheless, David captured the fortress of
Zion, the City of David.
[6]David had said, "Whoever leads the attack
on the Jebusites will become commander-in-
chief." Joab son of Zeruiah went up first, and
so he received the command.
[7]David then took up residence in the fortress, and so it was called the City of David. [8]He
built up the city around it, from the supporting
terraces[a] to the surrounding wall, while Joab restored the rest of the city. [9]And David became
more and more powerful, because the LORD Almighty was with him.

David's Mighty Men

[10]These were the chiefs of David's mighty
men—they, together with all Israel, gave his
kingship strong support to extend it over the
whole land, as the LORD had promised—
[11]this is the list of David's
mighty men:
Jashobeam,[b] a Hacmonite,
was chief of the officers[c]; he
raised his spear against three
hundred men, whom he killed
in one encounter.
[12]Next to him was Eleazar
son of Dodai the Ahohite, one
of the three mighty men. [13]He
was with David at Pas Dammim when the Philistines gathered there for battle. At a place
where there was a field full of
barley, the troops fled from the
Philistines. [14]But they took
their stand in the middle of
the field. They defended it and struck the Philistines down, and the LORD brought about a
great victory.
[15]Three of the thirty chiefs came down to David to the rock at the cave of Adullam, while a
band of Philistines was encamped in the Valley
of Rephaim. [16]At that time David was in the
stronghold, and the Philistine garrison was at
Bethlehem. [17]David longed for water and said,
"Oh, that someone would get me a drink of

[a]8 Or *the Millo* [b]11 Possibly a variant of *Jashob-Baal* [c]11 Or *Thirty*; some Septuagint manuscripts *Three* (see also 2 Samuel 23:8)

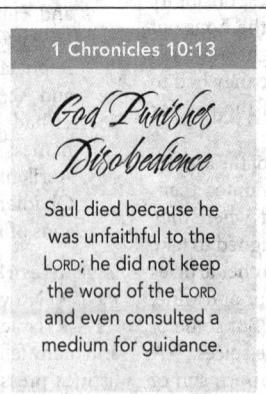

Perfect Timing

Read: 1 Chronicles 11:1–19

DO YOU EVER GET TIRED of waiting for God to keep his promises? "Lord, I know one day you're coming to bring justice, but right now there's such corruption in my city!" "God, I know Jesus is coming to judge evildoers, but some of them just broke my windshield!" "Father, you promise someday we'll all live in perfect health, but my body's failing." For those of us who long for everything to finally be all right, our heart's desire is, "Come quickly, Lord Jesus!"

The people of Israel must have felt impatience and frustration when David was anointed king by Samuel. At that time the land faced years under the rule of the unstable King Saul, from whom the Spirit of the Lord had departed because of Saul's sinful choices. The people had watched Saul disobey God by taking on the role of a priest, though he wasn't a Levite. Then he failed to kill the king of the Amalekites as he had been told. Playing politics, he fought jealously against his own warrior, David. He even had the audacity to seek advice from a medium at Endor. Surely it was time for a new king! Must they wait forever?

In time Saul died and God raised up a new king. Good-looking, strong and powerful, David was anointed king by the elders of Israel, just as Samuel had promised. Best of all, here was a king who loved God and would lead the nation back to worshiping him.

The prophets and New Testament writers have promised that the King of kings, Jesus Christ, is coming again to establish his perfect kingdom. So what is he waiting for? Haven't things gotten bad enough? Isn't there enough pain, sorrow, corruption and cruelty in the world?

When you grow weary of waiting for Christ's return, remember that God is willing to wait because he is so merciful. Peter said, "The Lord is not slow in keeping his promise, as some understand slowness. He is patient with you, not wanting anyone to perish, but everyone to come to repentance" (2 Peter 3:9). He is waiting for everyone who will to come to saving faith. When that time comes, he will keep his promise, just as he said.

1 Chronicles 11:3

When all the elders of Israel had come to King David at Hebron, he made a compact with them at Hebron before the LORD, and they anointed David king over Israel, as the LORD had promised through Samuel.

reflection

1 When in your life has God patiently waited for you to respond to him?

2 Do you know someone who still needs to know Jesus? How can you pray for that person? What can you say to him or her?

3 What does 2 Peter 3:11–14 say about being ready for the day of the Lord? How can you pray in order to be ready?

RELATED READINGS

1 Samuel 16:1–13; 28:1–25; Acts 1:7–8; 1 Thessalonians 4:15–17

"He who loves the coming of the Lord is not he who affirms it is far off, nor is it he who says it is near. It is he who, whether it be far or near, awaits it with sincere faith, steadfast hope and fervent love."

Saint Augustine

Go to page 497 for your next devotional reading.

water from the well near the gate of Bethlehem!" 18So the Three broke through the Philistine lines, drew water from the well near the
gate of Bethlehem and carried it back to David.
But he refused to drink it; instead, he poured
it out before the LORD. 19"God forbid that I
should do this!" he said. "Should I drink the
blood of these men who went at the risk of
their lives?" Because they risked their lives to
bring it back, David would not drink it.

Such were the exploits of the three
mighty men.

20Abishai the brother of Joab was chief of
the Three. He raised his spear against three
hundred men, whom he killed, and so he became as famous as the Three. 21He was doubly
honored above the Three and became their
commander, even though he was not included
among them.

22Benaiah son of Jehoiada was a valiant
fighter from Kabzeel, who performed great
exploits. He struck down two of Moab's best
men. He also went down into a pit on a snowy
day and killed a lion. 23And he struck down an
Egyptian who was seven and a half feet[a] tall.
Although the Egyptian had a spear like a weaver's rod in his hand, Benaiah went against him
with a club. He snatched the spear from the
Egyptian's hand and killed him with his own
spear. 24Such were the exploits of Benaiah son
of Jehoiada; he too was as famous as the three
mighty men. 25He was held in greater honor
than any of the Thirty, but he was not included
among the Three. And David put him in charge
of his bodyguard.

26The mighty men were:
Asahel the brother of Joab,
Elhanan son of Dodo from Bethlehem,
27Shammoth the Harorite,
Helez the Pelonite,
28Ira son of Ikkesh from Tekoa,
Abiezer from Anathoth,
29Sibbecai the Hushathite,
Ilai the Ahohite,
30Maharai the Netophathite,
Heled son of Baanah the Netophathite,
31Ithai son of Ribai from Gibeah in Benjamin,
Benaiah the Pirathonite,
32Hurai from the ravines of Gaash,
Abiel the Arbathite,
33Azmaveth the Baharumite,
Eliahba the Shaalbonite,
34the sons of Hashem the Gizonite,
Jonathan son of Shagee the Hararite,
35Ahiam son of Sacar the Hararite,
Eliphal son of Ur,
36Hepher the Mekerathite,
Ahijah the Pelonite,
37Hezro the Carmelite,
Naarai son of Ezbai,
38Joel the brother of Nathan,
Mibhar son of Hagri,
39Zelek the Ammonite,
Naharai the Berothite, the armor-
bearer of Joab son of Zeruiah,
40Ira the Ithrite,
Gareb the Ithrite,
41Uriah the Hittite,
Zabad son of Ahlai,
42Adina son of Shiza the Reubenite, who
was chief of the Reubenites, and the
thirty with him,
43Hanan son of Maacah,
Joshaphat the Mithnite,
44Uzzia the Ashterathite,
Shama and Jeiel the sons of Hotham
the Aroerite,
45Jediael son of Shimri,
his brother Joha the Tizite,
46Eliel the Mahavite,
Jeribai and Joshaviah the sons of El-
naam,
Ithmah the Moabite,
47Eliel, Obed and Jaasiel the Mezobaite.

Warriors Join David

12 These were the men who came to David at Ziklag, while he was banished
from the presence of Saul son of Kish (they
were among the warriors who helped him in
battle; 2they were armed with bows and were
able to shoot arrows or to sling stones right-
handed or left-handed; they were kinsmen of
Saul from the tribe of Benjamin):

3Ahiezer their chief and Joash the sons
of Shemaah the Gibeathite; Jeziel and Pe-

a23 Hebrew *five cubits* (about 2.3 meters)

let the sons of Azmaveth; Beracah, Jehu
the Anathothite, [4]and Ishmaiah the Gib-
eonite, a mighty man among the Thirty,
who was a leader of the Thirty; Jeremiah,
Jahaziel, Johanan, Jozabad the Gederathite,
[5]Eluzai, Jerimoth, Bealiah, Shemariah
and Shephatiah the Haruphite; [6]Elkanah,
Isshiah, Azarel, Joezer and Jashobeam the
Korahites; [7]and Joelah and Zebadiah the
sons of Jeroham from Gedor.

[8]Some Gadites defected to David at his
stronghold in the desert. They were brave warriors, ready for battle and able to handle the shield and spear. Their faces were the faces of lions, and they were as swift as gazelles in the mountains.

[9] Ezer was the chief,
Obadiah the second in command, Eliab the third,
[10] Mishmannah the fourth, Jeremiah the fifth,
[11] Attai the sixth, Eliel the seventh,
[12] Johanan the eighth, Elzabad the ninth,
[13] Jeremiah the tenth and Macbannai the eleventh.

[14]These Gadites were army commanders;
the least was a match for a hundred, and the
greatest for a thousand. [15]It was they who
crossed the Jordan in the first month when it was overflowing all its banks, and they put to flight everyone living in the valleys, to the east and to the west.

[16]Other Benjamites and some men from
Judah also came to David in his stronghold.
[17]David went out to meet them and said to
them, "If you have come to me in peace, to help me, I am ready to have you unite with me. But if you have come to betray me to my enemies when my hands are free from violence, may the God of our fathers see it and judge you."

[18]Then the Spirit came upon Amasai, chief
of the Thirty, and he said:

"We are yours, O David!
We are with you, O son of Jesse!
Success, success to you,
and success to those who help you,
for your God will help you."

So David received them and made them leaders of his raiding bands.

[19]Some of the men of Manasseh defected
to David when he went with the Philistines to fight against Saul. (He and his men did not help the Philistines because, after consultation, their rulers sent him away. They said, "It will cost us our heads if he deserts to his
master Saul.") [20]When David went to Ziklag,
these were the men of Manasseh who defected to him: Adnah, Jozabad, Jediael, Michael, Jozabad, Elihu and Zillethai, leaders of units of
a thousand in Manasseh. [21]They helped Da-
vid against raiding bands, for all of them were brave warriors, and they were commanders in
his army. [22]Day after day men came to help
David, until he had a great army, like the army of God.[a]

Others Join David at Hebron

[23]These are the numbers of the men armed
for battle who came to David at Hebron to turn Saul's kingdom over to him, as the LORD had said:

[24] men of Judah, carrying shield and spear—6,800 armed for battle;
[25] men of Simeon, warriors ready for battle—7,100;
[26] men of Levi—4,600, [27] including Jehoiada, leader of the family of Aaron, with 3,700 men, [28]and Zadok, a brave young warrior, with 22 officers from his family;
[29] men of Benjamin, Saul's kinsmen—3,000, most of whom had remained loyal to Saul's house until then;
[30] men of Ephraim, brave warriors, famous in their own clans—20,800;
[31] men of half the tribe of Manasseh, designated by name to come and make David king—18,000;
[32] men of Issachar, who understood the times and knew what Israel should do—200 chiefs, with all their relatives under their command;
[33] men of Zebulun, experienced soldiers prepared for battle with every type of weapon, to help David with undivided loyalty—50,000;
[34] men of Naphtali—1,000 officers, together

a22 Or *a great and mighty army*

with 37,000 men carrying shields and
spears;
35 men of Dan, ready for battle—28,600;
36 men of Asher, experienced soldiers prepared for battle—40,000;
37 and from east of the Jordan, men of
Reuben, Gad and the half-tribe of Manasseh, armed with every type of
weapon—120,000.

38 All these were fighting men who volunteered to serve in the ranks. They came to Hebron fully determined to make David king over
all Israel. All the rest of the Israelites were also
of one mind to make David king. 39 The men
spent three days there with David, eating and
drinking, for their families had supplied provisions for them. 40 Also, their neighbors from
as far away as Issachar, Zebulun and Naphtali
came bringing food on donkeys, camels, mules
and oxen. There were plentiful supplies of
flour, fig cakes, raisin cakes, wine, oil, cattle and
sheep, for there was joy in Israel.

Bringing Back the Ark

13 David conferred with each of his officers, the commanders of thousands
and commanders of hundreds. 2 He then said
to the whole assembly of Israel, "If it seems
good to you and if it is the will of the LORD
our God, let us send word far and wide to the
rest of our brothers throughout the territories
of Israel, and also to the priests and Levites who
are with them in their towns and pasturelands,
to come and join us. 3 Let us bring the ark of
our God back to us, for we did not inquire of[a]
it[b] during the reign of Saul." 4 The whole assembly agreed to do this, because it seemed right
to all the people.

5 So David assembled all the Israelites, from
the Shihor River in Egypt to Lebo[c] Hamath,
to bring the ark of God from Kiriath Jearim.
6 David and all the Israelites with him went to
Baalah of Judah (Kiriath Jearim) to bring up
from there the ark of God the LORD, who is enthroned between the cherubim—the ark that is
called by the Name.

7 They moved the ark of God from Abinadab's house on a new cart, with Uzzah and
Ahio guiding it. 8 David and all the Israelites
were celebrating with all their might before
God, with songs and with harps, lyres, tambourines, cymbals and trumpets.

9 When they came to the threshing floor of
Kidon, Uzzah reached out his hand to steady
the ark, because the oxen stumbled. 10 The
LORD's anger burned against Uzzah, and he
struck him down because he had put his hand
on the ark. So he died there before God.

11 Then David was angry because the LORD's
wrath had broken out against Uzzah, and to
this day that place is called Perez Uzzah.[d]

12 David was afraid of God that day and
asked, "How can I ever bring the ark of God to
me?" 13 He did not take the ark to be with him in
the City of David. Instead, he took it aside to the
house of Obed-Edom the Gittite. 14 The ark of
God remained with the family of Obed-Edom
in his house for three months, and the LORD
blessed his household and everything he had.

David's House and Family

14 Now Hiram king of Tyre sent messengers to David, along with cedar logs,
stonemasons and carpenters to build a palace
for him. 2 And David knew that the LORD had
established him as king over Israel and that his
kingdom had been highly exalted for the sake
of his people Israel.

3 In Jerusalem David took more wives and
became the father of more sons and daughters.
4 These are the names of the children born
to him there: Shammua, Shobab, Nathan,
Solomon, 5 Ibhar, Elishua, Elpelet, 6 Nogah,
Nepheg, Japhia, 7 Elishama, Beeliada[e] and
Eliphelet.

David Defeats the Philistines

8 When the Philistines heard that David had
been anointed king over all Israel, they went up
in full force to search for him, but David heard
about it and went out to meet them. 9 Now the
Philistines had come and raided the Valley of
Rephaim; 10 so David inquired of God: "Shall
I go and attack the Philistines? Will you hand
them over to me?"

The LORD answered him, "Go, I will hand
them over to you."

11 So David and his men went up to Baal Perazim, and there he defeated them. He said, "As

[a]3 Or *we neglected* [b]3 Or *him* [c]5 Or *to the entrance to* [d]11 *Perez Uzzah* means *outbreak against Uzzah.* [e]7 A variant of *Eliada*

Thinking About God

Read: 1 Chronicles 13:1–6

DRIVING TO THE GROCERY STORE after a blizzard, a woman listened on her radio to the Christian announcer say, "Our mission is to help you think more about God today than you did yesterday."

Hmmm, the woman thought, *I don't think I even thought about God yesterday.*

She remembered waking up to snow swirling outside. She'd made hot chocolate and kept the kids entertained all day until the electricity went off. Then she gathered sleeping bags and flashlights for the night. She'd watched the thermometer in the house drop and worried about staying warm through the night. She remembered feeling relieved when the electricity came back on hours later. *But, did I pray? Did I think about God?* She couldn't remember consciously giving God a thought during that busy day.

After David assumed the throne of Israel, he recognized that the people had been remiss in thinking about God. Their leader, King Saul, had been unfaithful to God and hadn't sought God's guidance for some time. So David's first royal act was to bring the ark of the covenant to Jerusalem, back to its place at the center of worship among the people of God as a physical reminder of God's presence, sovereignty and faithfulness.

Physical reminders of God can help us take time to talk to him and to listen to him. Many of the great cathedrals of Europe were built at the center of towns, the hub of people's business and worship life. Our churches today are also physical reminders of God. When we step into our church buildings, we're reminded that we meet God there.

We are also reminded of God through his people. Take a moment to express your love and thanksgiving to God for encircling you with loving friends and family.

And if we develop eyes to see, God will give us glimpses of himself through the beauty of nature: a blooming rose bush, a glorious sunset, a soft snowfall. Take time to whisper a prayer of adoration.

You can also place reminders around your home or office to trigger thoughts of God: your favorite Bible sitting by the chair; books, music and artwork placed in prominent positions. Don't let a day go by after which you wonder, *Did I think about God today?*

Go to page 499 for your next devotional reading.

1 Chronicles 13:2–3

He then said to the whole assembly of Israel, "If it seems good to you and if it is the will of the LORD our God . . . let us bring the ark of our God back to us, for we did not inquire of it during the reign of Saul."

reflection

1 Are there stretches of time when you don't think about God? How do those times affect you?

2 What brings you back to God after a time away?

3 What physical reminders do you use to prompt you to think about God? Can you think of other ways to keep God in the forefront of your mind?

RELATED READINGS

Deuteronomy 8:10–18;
1 Chronicles 10:1–14;
Acts 17:27–28

"Build yourself a cell in your heart and retire there to pray."

Catherine of Siena

waters break out, God has broken out against
my enemies by my hand." So that place was
called Baal Perazim.[a] 12 The Philistines had
abandoned their gods there, and David gave
orders to burn them in the fire.

13 Once more the Philistines raided the valley; 14 so David inquired of God again, and God
answered him, "Do not go straight up, but circle around them and attack them in front of the
balsam trees. 15 As soon as you hear the sound
of marching in the tops of the balsam trees,
move out to battle, because that will mean God
has gone out in front of you to strike the Philistine army." 16 So David did as God commanded
him, and they struck down the Philistine army,
all the way from Gibeon to Gezer.

17 So David's fame spread throughout every
land, and the LORD made all the nations
fear him.

The Ark Brought to Jerusalem

15 After David had constructed buildings
for himself in the City of David, he prepared a place for the ark of God and pitched a
tent for it. 2 Then David said, "No one but the
Levites may carry the ark of God, because the
LORD chose them to carry the ark of the LORD
and to minister before him forever."

3 David assembled all Israel in Jerusalem to
bring up the ark of the LORD to the place he
had prepared for it. 4 He called together the descendants of Aaron and the Levites:

5 From the descendants of Kohath,
Uriel the leader and 120 relatives;
6 from the descendants of Merari,
Asaiah the leader and 220 relatives;
7 from the descendants of Gershon,[b]
Joel the leader and 130 relatives;
8 from the descendants of Elizaphan,
Shemaiah the leader and 200 relatives;
9 from the descendants of Hebron,
Eliel the leader and 80 relatives;
10 from the descendants of Uzziel,
Amminadab the leader and 112 relatives.

11 Then David summoned Zadok and Abiathar the priests, and Uriel, Asaiah, Joel, Shemaiah, Eliel and Amminadab the Levites. 12 He
said to them, "You are the heads of the Levitical
families; you and your fellow Levites are to consecrate yourselves and bring up the ark of the
LORD, the God of Israel, to the place I have prepared for it. 13 It was because you, the Levites,
did not bring it up the first time that the LORD
our God broke out in anger against us. We did
not inquire of him about how to do it in the
prescribed way." 14 So the priests and Levites
consecrated themselves in order to bring up the
ark of the LORD, the God of Israel. 15 And the
Levites carried the ark of God with the poles on
their shoulders, as Moses had commanded in
accordance with the word of the LORD.

16 David told the leaders of the Levites to
appoint their brothers as singers to sing joyful
songs, accompanied by musical instruments:
lyres, harps and cymbals.

17 So the Levites appointed Heman son of
Joel; from his brothers, Asaph son of Berekiah;
and from their brothers the Merarites, Ethan
son of Kushaiah; 18 and with them their brothers next in rank: Zechariah,[c] Jaaziel, Shemiramoth, Jehiel, Unni, Eliab, Benaiah, Maaseiah,
Mattithiah, Eliphelehu, Mikneiah, Obed-Edom
and Jeiel,[d] the gatekeepers.

19 The musicians Heman, Asaph and
Ethan were to sound the bronze cymbals;
20 Zechariah, Aziel, Shemiramoth, Jehiel, Unni,
Eliab, Maaseiah and Benaiah were to play the
lyres according to *alamoth*,[e] 21 and Mattithiah,
Eliphelehu, Mikneiah, Obed-Edom, Jeiel and
Azaziah were to play the harps, directing according to *sheminith*.[e] 22 Kenaniah the head Levite was in charge of the singing; that was his
responsibility because he was skillful at it.

23 Berekiah and Elkanah were to be doorkeepers for the ark. 24 Shebaniah, Joshaphat,
Nethanel, Amasai, Zechariah, Benaiah and Eliezer the priests were to blow trumpets before
the ark of God. Obed-Edom and Jehiah were
also to be doorkeepers for the ark.

25 So David and the elders of Israel and the
commanders of units of a thousand went to
bring up the ark of the covenant of the LORD
from the house of Obed-Edom, with rejoicing.
26 Because God had helped the Levites who
were carrying the ark of the covenant of the

[a] 11 *Baal Perazim* means *the lord who breaks out.* [b] 7 Hebrew *Gershom,* a variant of *Gershon* [c] 18 Three Hebrew manuscripts and most Septuagint manuscripts (see also verse 20 and 1 Chron. 16:5); most Hebrew manuscripts *Zechariah son and* or *Zechariah, Ben and* [d] 18 Hebrew; Septuagint (see also verse 21) *Jeiel and Azaziah* [e] 20,21 Probably a musical term

Love Is Blind

DELILAH

DEAR DIARY:

If I hear one more story about how cute Samson and Delilah are together, I'm going to be sick. Ever since the two of them fell in "love" (questionable in my mind), that's all my friends talk about. They go from trying to guess when they'll marry to figuring out when they'll have a baby.

"I think it'll be a boy for sure."

"No, a girl. My mom says beautiful women always have girls first."

"What if it's twins?"

"Boy twins! Imagine two Samson hunks!"

All their squealing—as if this is the romance of the century—I just can't take it anymore.

Although he's definitely not my type, I admit he's kind of cute. Handsome, really. And all Delilah can do is toy with him like a cat playing with a mouse before she devours it. Why is it that bad girls like her always get the good guys to fall for them? She's manipulative, bossy, and when she doesn't get her way, she whines. It's so irritating.

What does Samson see in her anyway? Well, there's the obvious. But I think he even considers her little tantrums cute. Almost endearing. And that's why he continues to tease her every night, leading her on with stories about this and that. Whenever she pouts, he just calls her over and starts whispering in her ear until soon the two of them are laughing and chatting again. Sickening.

Can't he see what she's doing to him?

This week, I overheard some people in town talking about Delilah, something about money and betrayal. It figures. She always finds a way to get all the attention around here. Well maybe this little scheme will backfire. I guess we'll just have to wait and see.

—Prayer—

God, help me to learn from this story to be honest in all my relationships, to look to you only for my fulfillment and to live my life without envy or discontent.

Some time later, he fell in love with a woman in the Valley of Sorek whose name was Delilah.

Judges 16:4

ASSIGNED READING:

Judges 16:1–31

Weekend

Go to page 501 for your next devotional reading.

LORD, seven bulls and seven rams were sacrificed. 27 Now David was clothed in a robe of
fine linen, as were all the Levites who were
carrying the ark, and as were the singers, and
Kenaniah, who was in charge of the singing of
the choirs. David also wore a linen ephod. 28 So
all Israel brought up the ark of the covenant of
the LORD with shouts, with the sounding of
rams' horns and trumpets, and of cymbals, and
the playing of lyres and harps.

29 As the ark of the covenant of the LORD was
entering the City of David, Michal daughter of
Saul watched from a window. And when she
saw King David dancing and celebrating, she
despised him in her heart.

16 They brought the ark of God and set it
inside the tent that David had pitched
for it, and they presented burnt offerings and
fellowship offerings[a] before God. 2 After David
had finished sacrificing the burnt offerings and
fellowship offerings, he blessed the people in
the name of the LORD. 3 Then he gave a loaf of
bread, a cake of dates and a cake of raisins to
each Israelite man and woman.

4 He appointed some of the Levites to minister before the ark of the LORD, to make petition, to give thanks, and to praise the LORD,
the God of Israel: 5 Asaph was the chief, Zechariah second, then Jeiel, Shemiramoth, Jehiel,
Mattithiah, Eliab, Benaiah, Obed-Edom and
Jeiel. They were to play the
lyres and harps, Asaph was to
sound the cymbals, 6 and Benaiah and Jahaziel the priests
were to blow the trumpets
regularly before the ark of the
covenant of God.

David's Psalm of Thanks

7 That day David first committed to Asaph and his associates this psalm of thanks to
the LORD:

8 Give thanks to the LORD,
call on his name;
make known among the nations what he
has done.
9 Sing to him, sing praise to him;
tell of all his wonderful acts.
10 Glory in his holy name;
let the hearts of those who seek the
LORD rejoice.
11 Look to the LORD and his strength;
seek his face always.
12 Remember the wonders he has done,
his miracles, and the judgments he
pronounced,
13 O descendants of Israel his servant,
O sons of Jacob, his chosen ones.

14 He is the LORD our God;
his judgments are in all the earth.
15 He remembers[b] his covenant forever,
the word he commanded, for a thousand
generations,
16 the covenant he made with Abraham,
the oath he swore to Isaac.
17 He confirmed it to Jacob as a decree,
to Israel as an everlasting covenant:
18 "To you I will give the land of Canaan
as the portion you will inherit."

19 When they were but few in number,
few indeed, and strangers in it,
20 they[c] wandered from nation to nation,
from one kingdom to another.
21 He allowed no man to oppress them;
for their sake he rebuked kings:
22 "Do not touch my anointed ones;
do my prophets no harm."

23 Sing to the LORD, all the
earth;
proclaim his salvation
day after day.
24 Declare his glory among
the nations,
his marvelous deeds
among all
peoples.
25 For great is the LORD and
most worthy of
praise;
he is to be feared above
all gods.
26 For all the gods of the nations are idols,
but the LORD made the heavens.

1 Chronicles 16:26

God Is the True God

For all the gods of the
nations are idols,
but the LORD made
the heavens.

[a]1 Traditionally *peace offerings*; also in verse 2 [b]15 Some Septuagint manuscripts (see also Psalm 105:8); Hebrew *Remember*
[c]18–20 One Hebrew manuscript, Septuagint and Vulgate (see also Psalm 105:12); most Hebrew manuscripts *inherit, / [19] though you are but few in number, / few indeed, and strangers in it." / [20] They*

A Glorious Outpouring

Read: 1 Chronicles 16:7–36

WE OFTEN THINK of gratitude in terms of gain: Someone gives you a ride to work. A neighbor cooks a meal when you've had surgery. Your boss notices your hard work and gives you a raise. Of course you're grateful. And if you remember your mother's upbringing, you promptly write a thank-you note.

It's more astonishing to witness people overcome with an attitude of thanksgiving in dire circumstances. Think of the parents of a terminally ill child who praise God for each day of their daughter's life. You might be baffled by a family's ability to be thankful in the midst of disaster, weeping with joy that even though their house and possessions have been destroyed by flood, fire or earthquake, their family has survived.

Even deeper than gratitude for a favor or thankfulness in the midst of misery, thanksgiving can be viewed as a testament to an enduring quality in someone we admire and respect. For instance, David celebrated God's divine attributes with a heart of pure thanksgiving. With great fanfare, the ark of the covenant had finally arrived in Jerusalem and taken its place into the tent David had prepared for it. After the offerings were made and the feast was over, David's gladness spilled over into a great song of jubilant thanksgiving.

Consider the countless reasons you have to be grateful. Has something brought great joy to your life? Consider the attributes of those you love: your husband's faithfulness, your friends' trustworthiness, your parents' goodness, your child's tender heart.

Today is the perfect time to "give thanks to the LORD, for he is good." Start by expressing thanks for some of the things David included in his prayer:

- "[God's] wonderful acts . . ." (verse 9)
- "His miracles . . ." (verse 12)
- "His salvation . . ." (verse 23)
- "His glory . . ." (verse 24)
- "His marvelous deeds among all peoples . . ." (verse 24)
- "His holiness . . ." (verse 29)

Everything about God is worthy of our praise. Let us not allow anyone or anything to rob us of the gift of a thankful heart. We can sing with David, "Let the heavens rejoice, let the earth be glad; let them say among the nations, 'The LORD reigns!'" (verse 31).

1 Chronicles 16:34

Give thanks to the LORD, for he is good; his love endures forever.

reflection

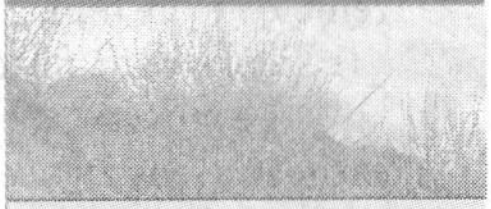

1 Do you think your friends and family would characterize you as a grateful person? Why or why not?

2 What are the characteristics of God for which you are thankful?

3 How often do you remember to thank God for his work in your life and in the world around you? Spend some time thanking God for his qualities listed in today's devotions.

RELATED READINGS

Psalms 100:1–5; 136:1–26; Colossians 3:16–17

"Thou who hast given so much to me, give me one more thing—a grateful heart!"

George Herbert

Monday

Go to page 505 for your next devotional reading.

27 Splendor and majesty are before him;
strength and joy in his dwelling place.
28 Ascribe to the LORD, O families of nations,
ascribe to the LORD glory and strength,
29 ascribe to the LORD the glory due his
name.
Bring an offering and come before him;
worship the LORD in the splendor of his[a]
holiness.
30 Tremble before him, all the earth!
The world is firmly established; it cannot
be moved.
31 Let the heavens rejoice, let the earth be
glad;
let them say among the nations, "The
LORD reigns!"
32 Let the sea resound, and all that is in it;
let the fields be jubilant, and everything
in them!
33 Then the trees of the forest will sing,
they will sing for joy before the LORD,
for he comes to judge the earth.

34 Give thanks to the LORD, for he is good;
his love endures forever.
35 Cry out, "Save us, O God our Savior;
gather us and deliver us from the
nations,
that we may give thanks to your holy
name,
that we may glory in your praise."
36 Praise be to the LORD, the God of Israel,
from everlasting to everlasting.

Then all the people said "Amen" and "Praise
the LORD."

37 David left Asaph and his associates before
the ark of the covenant of the LORD to minister there regularly, according to each day's requirements. 38 He also left Obed-Edom and his
sixty-eight associates to minister with them.
Obed-Edom son of Jeduthun, and also Hosah,
were gatekeepers.
39 David left Zadok the priest and his fellow
priests before the tabernacle of the LORD at the
high place in Gibeon 40 to present burnt offerings to the LORD on the altar of burnt offering
regularly, morning and evening, in accordance
with everything written in the Law of the LORD,
which he had given Israel. 41 With them were
Heman and Jeduthun and the rest of those chosen and designated by name to give thanks to
the LORD, "for his love endures forever." 42 Heman and Jeduthun were responsible for the
sounding of the trumpets and cymbals and for
the playing of the other instruments for sacred
song. The sons of Jeduthun were stationed at
the gate.
43 Then all the people left, each for his own
home, and David returned home to bless his
family.

God's Promise to David

17 After David was settled in his palace,
he said to Nathan the prophet, "Here I
am, living in a palace of cedar, while the ark of
the covenant of the LORD is under a tent."
2 Nathan replied to David, "Whatever you
have in mind, do it, for God is with you."
3 That night the word of God came to Nathan, saying:

4 "Go and tell my servant David, 'This is
what the LORD says: You are not the one to
build me a house to dwell in. 5 I have not
dwelt in a house from the day I brought
Israel up out of Egypt to this day. I have
moved from one tent site to another, from
one dwelling place to another. 6 Wherever
I have moved with all the Israelites, did I
ever say to any of their leaders[b] whom I
commanded to shepherd my people, "Why
have you not built me a house of cedar?"'
7 "Now then, tell my servant David,
'This is what the LORD Almighty says: I
took you from the pasture and from following the flock, to be ruler over my people Israel. 8 I have been with you wherever
you have gone, and I have cut off all your
enemies from before you. Now I will
make your name like the names of the
greatest men of the earth. 9 And I will provide a place for my people Israel and will
plant them so that they can have a home
of their own and no longer be disturbed.
Wicked people will not oppress them anymore, as they did at the beginning 10 and
have done ever since the time I appointed
leaders over my people Israel. I will also
subdue all your enemies.

[a] 29 Or *LORD with the splendor of* [b] 6 Traditionally *judges*; also in verse 10

"'I declare to you that the LORD will
build a house for you: 11When your days
are over and you go to be with your fathers, I will raise up your offspring to
succeed you, one of your own sons, and
I will establish his kingdom. 12He is the
one who will build a house for me, and I
will establish his throne forever. 13I will
be his father, and he will be my son. I
will never take my love away from him,
as I took it away from your predecessor.
14I will set him over my house and my
kingdom forever; his throne will be established forever.'"

15Nathan reported to David all the words of
this entire revelation.

David's Prayer

16Then King David went in and sat before
the LORD, and he said:

"Who am I, O LORD God, and what is
my family, that you have brought me this
far? 17And as if this were not enough in
your sight, O God, you have spoken about
the future of the house of your servant.
You have looked on me as though I were
the most exalted of men, O LORD God.

18"What more can David say to you
for honoring your servant? For you
know your servant, 19O LORD. For the
sake of your servant and according to
your will, you have done this great thing
and made known all these
great promises.

20"There is no one like
you, O LORD, and there is
no God but you, as we have
heard with our own ears.
21And who is like your people Israel—the one nation
on earth whose God went
out to redeem a people for
himself, and to make a name
for yourself, and to perform
great and awesome won-
ders by driving out nations
from before your people,
whom you redeemed from Egypt? 22You
made your people Israel your very own
forever, and you, O LORD, have become
their God.

23"And now, LORD, let the promise you
have made concerning your servant and
his house be established forever. Do as you
promised, 24so that it will be established
and that your name will be great forever.
Then men will say, 'The LORD Almighty,
the God over Israel, is Israel's God!' And
the house of your servant David will be
established before you.

25"You, my God, have revealed to your
servant that you will build a house for
him. So your servant has found courage
to pray to you. 26O LORD, you are God!
You have promised these good things
to your servant. 27Now you have been
pleased to bless the house of your servant,
that it may continue forever in your sight;
for you, O LORD, have blessed it, and it
will be blessed forever."

David's Victories

18 In the course of time, David defeated
the Philistines and subdued them, and
he took Gath and its surrounding villages from
the control of the Philistines.

2David also defeated the Moabites, and they
became subject to him and brought tribute.

3Moreover, David fought Hadadezer king
of Zobah, as far as Hamath, when he went to
establish his control along the Euphrates River.
4David captured a thousand of his chariots,
seven thousand charioteers
and twenty thousand foot soldiers. He hamstrung all but a
hundred of the chariot horses.

5When the Arameans of Da-
mascus came to help Hadadezer king of Zobah, David struck
down twenty-two thousand of
them. 6He put garrisons in the
Aramean kingdom of Damas-
cus, and the Arameans became
subject to him and brought
tribute. The LORD gave David
victory everywhere he went.

7David took the gold shields
carried by the officers of Hadadezer and
brought them to Jerusalem. 8From Tebah[a]

1 Chronicles 17:20

God Is Unsurpassed

"There is no one like you, O LORD, and there is no God but you, as we have heard with our own ears."

[a]8 Hebrew *Tibhath*, a variant of *Tebah*

and Cun, towns that belonged to Hadadezer,
David took a great quantity of bronze, which
Solomon used to make the bronze Sea, the pillars and various bronze articles.
9When Tou king of Hamath heard that David had defeated the entire army of Hadadezer
king of Zobah, 10he sent his son Hadoram to
King David to greet him and congratulate him
on his victory in battle over Hadadezer, who
had been at war with Tou. Hadoram brought all
kinds of articles of gold and silver and bronze.
11King David dedicated these articles to the
LORD, as he had done with the silver and gold
he had taken from all these nations: Edom and
Moab, the Ammonites and the Philistines,
and Amalek.
12Abishai son of Zeruiah struck down eighteen thousand Edomites in the Valley of Salt.
13He put garrisons in Edom, and all the Edomites became subject to David. The LORD gave
David victory everywhere he went.

David's Officials

14David reigned over all Israel, doing what
was just and right for all his people. 15Joab son
of Zeruiah was over the army; Jehoshaphat
son of Ahilud was recorder; 16Zadok son of
Ahitub and Ahimelech[a] son of Abiathar were
priests; Shavsha was secretary; 17Benaiah son
of Jehoiada was over the Kerethites and Pelethites; and David's sons were chief officials at
the king's side.

The Battle Against the Ammonites

19 In the course of time, Nahash king
of the Ammonites died, and his son
succeeded him as king. 2David thought, "I
will show kindness to Hanun son of Nahash,
because his father showed kindness to me." So
David sent a delegation to express his sympathy to Hanun concerning his father.
When David's men came to Hanun in the
land of the Ammonites to express sympathy
to him, 3the Ammonite nobles said to Hanun,
"Do you think David is honoring your father
by sending men to you to express sympathy?
Haven't his men come to you to explore and
spy out the country and overthrow it?" 4So Hanun seized David's men, shaved them, cut off
their garments in the middle at the buttocks,
and sent them away.
5When someone came and told David about
the men, he sent messengers to meet them, for
they were greatly humiliated. The king said,
"Stay at Jericho till your beards have grown,
and then come back."
6When the Ammonites realized that they
had become a stench in David's nostrils, Hanun and the Ammonites sent a thousand talents[b] of silver to hire chariots and charioteers
from Aram Naharaim,[c] Aram Maacah and Zobah. 7They hired thirty-two thousand chariots
and charioteers, as well as the king of Maacah
with his troops, who came and camped near
Medeba, while the Ammonites were mustered
from their towns and moved out for battle.
8On hearing this, David sent Joab out with
the entire army of fighting men. 9The Ammonites came out and drew up in battle formation
at the entrance to their city, while the kings
who had come were by themselves in the open
country.
10Joab saw that there were battle lines in
front of him and behind him; so he selected
some of the best troops in Israel and deployed
them against the Arameans. 11He put the rest
of the men under the command of Abishai his
brother, and they were deployed against the Ammonites. 12Joab said, "If the Arameans are too
strong for me, then you are to rescue me; but
if the Ammonites are too strong for you, then
I will rescue you. 13Be strong and let us fight
bravely for our people and the cities of our God.
The LORD will do what is good in his sight."
14Then Joab and the troops with him advanced to fight the Arameans, and they fled
before him. 15When the Ammonites saw that
the Arameans were fleeing, they too fled before
his brother Abishai and went inside the city. So
Joab went back to Jerusalem.
16After the Arameans saw that they had
been routed by Israel, they sent messengers
and had Arameans brought from beyond the
River,[d] with Shophach the commander of Hadadezer's army leading them.
17When David was told of this, he gathered
all Israel and crossed the Jordan; he advanced

[a]16 Some Hebrew manuscripts, Vulgate and Syriac (see also 2 Samuel 8:17); most Hebrew manuscripts *Abimelech* [b]6 That is, about 37 tons (about 34 metric tons) [c]6 That is, Northwest Mesopotamia [d]16 That is, the Euphrates

But as the angel was doing so, the LORD saw it
and was grieved because of the calamity and
said to the angel who was destroying the people, "Enough! Withdraw your hand." The angel
of the LORD was then standing at the threshing
floor of Araunah[a] the Jebusite.
16David looked up and saw the angel of the
LORD standing between heaven and earth, with
a drawn sword in his hand extended over Jerusalem. Then David and the elders, clothed in
sackcloth, fell facedown.
17David said to God, "Was it not I who ordered the fighting men to be counted? I am the
one who has sinned and done wrong. These are
but sheep. What have they done? O LORD my
God, let your hand fall upon me and my family,
but do not let this plague remain on your people."
18Then the angel of the LORD ordered Gad
to tell David to go up and build an altar to the
LORD on the threshing floor of Araunah the
Jebusite. 19So David went up in obedience to
the word that Gad had spoken in the name of
the LORD.
20While Araunah was threshing wheat, he
turned and saw the angel; his four sons who
were with him hid themselves. 21Then David approached, and when Araunah looked
and saw him, he left the threshing floor and
bowed down before David with his face to
the ground.
22David said to him, "Let me have the site of
your threshing floor so I can build an altar to
the LORD, that the plague on the people may be
stopped. Sell it to me at the full price."
23Araunah said to David, "Take it! Let my
lord the king do whatever pleases him. Look,
I will give the oxen for the burnt offerings, the
threshing sledges for the wood, and the wheat
for the grain offering. I will give all this."
24But King David replied to Araunah, "No,
I insist on paying the full price. I will not take
for the LORD what is yours, or sacrifice a burnt
offering that costs me nothing."
25So David paid Araunah six hundred shekels[b] of gold for the site. 26David built an altar
to the LORD there and sacrificed burnt offerings and fellowship offerings.[c] He called on the
LORD, and the LORD answered him with fire
from heaven on the altar of burnt offering.
27Then the LORD spoke to the angel, and
he put his sword back into its sheath. 28At
that time, when David saw that the LORD had
answered him on the threshing floor of Araunah the Jebusite, he offered sacrifices there.
29The tabernacle of the LORD, which Moses
had made in the desert, and the altar of burnt
offering were at that time on the high place at
Gibeon. 30But David could not go before it to
inquire of God, because he was afraid of the
sword of the angel of the LORD.

22 Then David said, "The house of the
LORD God is to be here, and also the
altar of burnt offering for Israel."

Preparations for the Temple

2So David gave orders to assemble the
aliens living in Israel, and from among them
he appointed stonecutters to prepare dressed
stone for building the house of God. 3He
provided a large amount of iron to make nails
for the doors of the gateways and for the fit-
tings, and more bronze than could be weighed.
4He also provided more cedar logs than could
be counted, for the Sidonians and Tyrians had
brought large numbers of them to David.
5David said, "My son Solomon is young
and inexperienced, and the house to be built
for the LORD should be of great magnificence
and fame and splendor in the sight of all the
nations. Therefore I will make preparations for
it." So David made extensive preparations before his death.
6Then he called for his son Solomon and
charged him to build a house for the LORD,
the God of Israel. 7David said to Solomon:
"My son, I had it in my heart to build a house
for the Name of the LORD my God. 8But this
word of the LORD came to me: 'You have shed
much blood and have fought many wars. You
are not to build a house for my Name, because
you have shed much blood on the earth in my
sight. 9But you will have a son who will be a
man of peace and rest, and I will give him rest
from all his enemies on every side. His name
will be Solomon,[d] and I will grant Israel peace
and quiet during his reign. 10He is the one who

[a]15 Hebrew *Ornan*, a variant of *Araunah*; also in verses 18–28 [b]25 That is, about 15 pounds (about 7 kilograms) [c]26 Traditionally *peace offerings* [d]9 *Solomon* sounds like and may be derived from the Hebrew for *peace*.

will build a house for my Name. He will be my
son, and I will be his father. And I will establish
the throne of his kingdom over
Israel forever.'
11“Now, my son, the LORD
be with you, and may you have
success and build the house of
the LORD your God, as he said
you would. 12May the LORD
give you discretion and understanding when he puts you in
command over Israel, so that
you may keep the law of the
LORD your God. 13Then you
will have success if you are careful to observe the decrees and
laws that the LORD gave Moses
for Israel. Be strong and courageous. Do not be afraid or discouraged.
14“I have taken great pains to provide for
the temple of the LORD a hundred thousand
talents[a] of gold, a million talents[b] of silver,
quantities of bronze and iron too great to be
weighed, and wood and stone. And you may
add to them. 15You have many workmen:
stonecutters, masons and carpenters, as well
as men skilled in every kind of work 16in gold
and silver, bronze and iron—craftsmen beyond
number. Now begin the work, and the LORD be
with you.”
17Then David ordered all the leaders of
Israel to help his son Solomon. 18He said to
them, “Is not the LORD your God with you?
And has he not granted you rest on every side?
For he has handed the inhabitants of the land
over to me, and the land is subject to the LORD
and to his people. 19Now devote your heart
and soul to seeking the LORD your God. Begin
to build the sanctuary of the LORD God, so that
you may bring the ark of the covenant of the
LORD and the sacred articles belonging to God
into the temple that will be built for the Name
of the LORD.”

> **1 Chronicles 22:11**
>
> *God Is With Us*
>
> “Now, my son, the LORD be with you, and may you have success and build the house of the LORD your God, as he said you would.”

The Levites

23 When David was old and full of years,
he made his son Solomon king over
Israel.
2He also gathered together all the leaders of
Israel, as well as the priests and Levites. 3The
Levites thirty years old or more were counted,
and the total number of men
was thirty-eight thousand.
4David said, “Of these, twenty-
four thousand are to supervise
the work of the temple of the
LORD and six thousand are to
be officials and judges. 5Four
thousand are to be gatekeepers
and four thousand are to praise
the LORD with the musical instruments I have provided for
that purpose.”
6David divided the Levites
into groups corresponding to
the sons of Levi: Gershon, Kohath and Merari.

Gershonites

7Belonging to the Gershonites:
Ladan and Shimei.
8 The sons of Ladan:
Jehiel the first, Zetham and Joel—three in all.
9 The sons of Shimei:
Shelomoth, Haziel and Haran—three in all.
These were the heads of the families of Ladan.
10 And the sons of Shimei:
Jahath, Ziza,[c] Jeush and Beriah.
These were the sons of Shimei—four in all.
11 Jahath was the first and Ziza the second, but Jeush and Beriah did not have many sons; so they were counted as one family with one assignment.

Kohathites

12The sons of Kohath:
Amram, Izhar, Hebron and Uzziel—four in all.
13 The sons of Amram:
Aaron and Moses.
Aaron was set apart, he and his descendants forever, to consecrate the most holy things, to offer sacrifices before the LORD, to minister before him and

[a]14 That is, about 3,750 tons (about 3,450 metric tons) [b]14 That is, about 37,500 tons (about 34,500 metric tons) [c]10 One Hebrew manuscript, Septuagint and Vulgate (see also verse 11); most Hebrew manuscripts *Zina*

to pronounce blessings in his name
forever. 14 The sons of Moses the man
of God were counted as part of the tribe
of Levi.

5 The sons of Moses:
Gershom and Eliezer.
6 The descendants of Ger-
shom:
Shubael was the first.
7 The descendants of Eliezer:
Rehabiah was the first.
Eliezer had no other sons,
but the sons of Rehabiah
were very numerous.
8 The sons of Izhar:
Shelomith was the first.
9 The sons of Hebron:
Jeriah the first, Amariah
the second, Jahaziel the
third and Jekameam the
fourth.
0 The sons of Uzziel:
Micah the first and Isshiah the second.

Merarites

1 The sons of Merari:
Mahli and Mushi.
The sons of Mahli:
Eleazar and Kish.
22 Eleazar died without having sons: he
had only daughters. Their cousins, the
sons of Kish, married them.
3 The sons of Mushi:
Mahli, Eder and Jerimoth—three in
all.

24 These were the descendants of Levi by
heir families—the heads of families as they
vere registered under their names and counted
ndividually, that is, the workers twenty years
ld or more who served in the temple of the
ORD. 25 For David had said, "Since the LORD,
he God of Israel, has granted rest to his peo-
le and has come to dwell in Jerusalem forever,
6 the Levites no longer need to carry the taber-
acle or any of the articles used in its service."
7 According to the last instructions of David,
he Levites were counted from those twenty
ears old or more.
28 The duty of the Levites was to help Aaron's
lescendants in the service of the temple of the
LORD: to be in charge of the courtyards, the side
rooms, the purification of all sacred things and
the performance of other duties at the house of
God. 29 They were in charge of the bread set out
on the table, the flour for the
grain offerings, the unleavened
wafers, the baking and the mixing, and all measurements of
quantity and size. 30 They were
also to stand every morning
to thank and praise the LORD.
They were to do the same in
the evening 31 and whenever
burnt offerings were presented
to the LORD on Sabbaths and
at New Moon festivals and at
appointed feasts. They were to
serve before the LORD regularly
in the proper number and in
the way prescribed for them.
32 And so the Levites carried out their responsibilities for the Tent of Meeting, for the
Holy Place and, under their brothers the descendants of Aaron, for the service of the temple of the LORD.

The Divisions of Priests

24 These were the divisions of the sons
of Aaron:
The sons of Aaron were Nadab, Abihu, Eleazar and Ithamar. 2 But Nadab and Abihu died
before their father did, and they had no sons;
so Eleazar and Ithamar served as the priests.
3 With the help of Zadok a descendant of Eleazar and Ahimelech a descendant of Ithamar,
David separated them into divisions for their
appointed order of ministering. 4 A larger number of leaders were found among Eleazar's
descendants than among Ithamar's, and they
were divided accordingly: sixteen heads of
families from Eleazar's descendants and eight
heads of families from Ithamar's descendants.
5 They divided them impartially by drawing
lots, for there were officials of the sanctuary
and officials of God among the descendants of
both Eleazar and Ithamar.
6 The scribe Shemaiah son of Nethanel, a Levite, recorded their names in the presence of
the king and of the officials: Zadok the priest,
Ahimelech son of Abiathar and the heads of
families of the priests and of the Levites—one

1 Chronicles 23:30

God Is Worthy of Praise

They were also to stand every morning to thank and praise the LORD. They were to do the same in the evening.

family being taken from Eleazar and then one from Ithamar.

7 The first lot fell to Jehoiarib,
the second to Jedaiah,
8 the third to Harim,
the fourth to Seorim,
9 the fifth to Malkijah,
the sixth to Mijamin,
10 the seventh to Hakkoz,
the eighth to Abijah,
11 the ninth to Jeshua,
the tenth to Shecaniah,
12 the eleventh to Eliashib,
the twelfth to Jakim,
13 the thirteenth to Huppah,
the fourteenth to Jeshebeab,
14 the fifteenth to Bilgah,
the sixteenth to Immer,
15 the seventeenth to Hezir,
the eighteenth to Happizzez,
16 the nineteenth to Pethahiah,
the twentieth to Jehezkel,
17 the twenty-first to Jakin,
the twenty-second to Gamul,
18 the twenty-third to Delaiah
and the twenty-fourth to Maaziah.

19 This was their appointed order of ministering when they entered the temple of the LORD, according to the regulations prescribed for them by their forefather Aaron, as the LORD, the God of Israel, had commanded him.

The Rest of the Levites

20 As for the rest of the descendants of Levi:
from the sons of Amram: Shubael;
from the sons of Shubael: Jehdeiah.
21 As for Rehabiah, from his sons:
Isshiah was the first.
22 From the Izharites: Shelomoth;
from the sons of Shelomoth: Jahath.
23 The sons of Hebron: Jeriah the first,[a]
Amariah the second, Jahaziel the third
and Jekameam the fourth.
24 The son of Uzziel: Micah;
from the sons of Micah: Shamir.
25 The brother of Micah: Isshiah;
from the sons of Isshiah: Zechariah.
26 The sons of Merari: Mahli and Mushi.
The son of Jaaziah: Beno.
27 The sons of Merari:
from Jaaziah: Beno, Shoham, Zaccur and Ibri.
28 From Mahli: Eleazar, who had no sons.
29 From Kish: the son of Kish:
Jerahmeel.
30 And the sons of Mushi: Mahli, Eder and Jerimoth.

These were the Levites, according to their
families. 31 They also cast lots, just as their
brothers the descendants of Aaron did, in the presence of King David and of Zadok, Ahimelech, and the heads of families of the priests and of the Levites. The families of the oldest brother were treated the same as those of the youngest.

The Singers

25 David, together with the commanders of the army, set apart some of the sons of Asaph, Heman and Jeduthun for the ministry of prophesying, accompanied by harps, lyres and cymbals. Here is the list of the men who performed this service:

2 From the sons of Asaph:
Zaccur, Joseph, Nethaniah and Asarelah. The sons of Asaph were under the supervision of Asaph, who prophesied under the king's supervision.
3 As for Jeduthun, from his sons:
Gedaliah, Zeri, Jeshaiah, Shimei,[b] Hashabiah and Mattithiah, six in all, under the supervision of their father Jeduthun, who prophesied, using the harp in thanking and praising the LORD.
4 As for Heman, from his sons:
Bukkiah, Mattaniah, Uzziel, Shubael and Jerimoth; Hananiah, Hanani, Eliathah, Giddalti and Romamti-Ezer; Joshbekashah, Mallothi, Hothir and Mahazioth.
5 All these were sons of Heman the king's
seer. They were given him through the promises of God to exalt him.[c] God gave Heman fourteen sons and three daughters.

[a]23 Two Hebrew manuscripts and some Septuagint manuscripts (see also 1 Chron. 23:19); most Hebrew manuscripts *The sons of Jeriah:*
[b]3 One Hebrew manuscript and some Septuagint manuscripts (see also verse 17); most Hebrew manuscripts do not have *Shimei.*
[c]5 Hebrew *exalt the horn*

6 All these men were under the supervision
of their fathers for the music of the temple of
the LORD, with cymbals, lyres and harps, for
the ministry at the house of God. Asaph, Jeduthun and Heman were under the supervision
of the king. 7 Along with their relatives—all
of them trained and skilled in music for the
LORD—they numbered 288. 8 Young and old
alike, teacher as well as student, cast lots for
their duties.

9 The first lot, which was for Asaph, fell
to Joseph,
his sons and relatives,[a] 12[b]
the second to Gedaliah,
he and his relatives and sons, 12
10 the third to Zaccur,
his sons and relatives, 12
11 the fourth to Izri,[c]
his sons and relatives, 12
12 the fifth to Nethaniah,
his sons and relatives, 12
13 the sixth to Bukkiah,
his sons and relatives, 12
14 the seventh to Jesarelah,[d]
his sons and relatives, 12
15 the eighth to Jeshaiah,
his sons and relatives, 12
16 the ninth to Mattaniah,
his sons and relatives, 12
17 the tenth to Shimei,
his sons and relatives, 12
18 the eleventh to Azarel,[e]
his sons and relatives, 12
19 the twelfth to Hashabiah,
his sons and relatives, 12
20 the thirteenth to Shubael,
his sons and relatives, 12
21 the fourteenth to Mattithiah,
his sons and relatives, 12
22 the fifteenth to Jerimoth,
his sons and relatives, 12
23 the sixteenth to Hananiah,
his sons and relatives, 12
24 the seventeenth to Joshbekashah,
his sons and relatives, 12
25 the eighteenth to Hanani,
his sons and relatives, 12
26 the nineteenth to Mallothi,
his sons and relatives, 12
27 the twentieth to Eliathah,
his sons and relatives, 12
28 the twenty-first to Hothir,
his sons and relatives, 12
29 the twenty-second to Giddalti,
his sons and relatives, 12
30 the twenty-third to Mahazioth,
his sons and relatives, 12
31 the twenty-fourth to Romamti-Ezer,
his sons and relatives, 12

The Gatekeepers

26 The divisions of the gatekeepers:

From the Korahites: Meshelemiah son of
Kore, one of the sons of Asaph.
2 Meshelemiah had sons:
Zechariah the firstborn,
Jediael the second,
Zebadiah the third,
Jathniel the fourth,
3 Elam the fifth,
Jehohanan the sixth
and Eliehoenai the seventh.
4 Obed-Edom also had sons:
Shemaiah the firstborn,
Jehozabad the second,
Joah the third,
Sacar the fourth,
Nethanel the fifth,
5 Ammiel the sixth,
Issachar the seventh
and Peullethai the eighth.
(For God had blessed Obed-Edom.)

6 His son Shemaiah also had sons, who
were leaders in their father's family because they were very capable men. 7 The
sons of Shemaiah: Othni, Rephael,
Obed and Elzabad; his relatives Elihu
and Semakiah were also able men. 8 All
these were descendants of Obed-Edom;
they and their sons and their relatives
were capable men with the strength to
do the work—descendants of Obed-
Edom, 62 in all.
9 Meshelemiah had sons and relatives, who
were able men—18 in all.

[a]9 See Septuagint; Hebrew does not have *his sons and relatives.* [b]9 See the total in verse 7; Hebrew does not have *twelve.*
[c]11 A variant of *Zeri* [d]14 A variant of *Asarelah* [e]18 A variant of *Uzziel*

10 Hosah the Merarite had sons: Shimri the
first (although he was not the firstborn,
his father had appointed him the first),
11 Hilkiah the second, Tabaliah the
third and Zechariah the fourth. The
sons and relatives of Hosah were 13
in all.

12 These divisions of the gatekeepers, through
their chief men, had duties for ministering in
the temple of the LORD, just as their relatives
had. 13 Lots were cast for each gate, according
to their families, young and old alike.

14 The lot for the East Gate fell to Shelemiah.[a]
Then lots were cast for his son Zechariah, a
wise counselor, and the lot for the North Gate
fell to him. 15 The lot for the South Gate fell to
Obed-Edom, and the lot for the storehouse fell
to his sons. 16 The lots for the West Gate and
the Shalleketh Gate on the upper road fell to
Shuppim and Hosah.

Guard was alongside of guard: 17 There were
six Levites a day on the east, four a day on the
north, four a day on the south and two at a
time at the storehouse. 18 As for the court to
the west, there were four at the road and two
at the court itself.

19 These were the divisions of the gatekeepers
who were descendants of Korah and Merari.

The Treasurers and Other Officials

20 Their fellow Levites were[b] in charge of the
treasuries of the house of God and the treasuries for the dedicated things.

21 The descendants of Ladan, who were Gershonites through Ladan and who were heads
of families belonging to Ladan the Gershonite,
were Jehieli, 22 the sons of Jehieli, Zetham and
his brother Joel. They were in charge of the treasuries of the temple of the LORD.

23 From the Amramites, the Izharites, the Hebronites and the Uzzielites:

24 Shubael, a descendant of Gershom son of
Moses, was the officer in charge of the
treasuries. 25 His relatives through Eliezer: Rehabiah his son, Jeshaiah his son,
Joram his son, Zicri his son and Shelomith his son. 26 Shelomith and his relatives were in charge of all the treasuries
for the things dedicated by King David,
by the heads of families who were the
commanders of thousands and commanders of hundreds, and by the other
army commanders. 27 Some of the plunder taken in battle they dedicated for
the repair of the temple of the LORD.
28 And everything dedicated by Samuel
the seer and by Saul son of Kish, Abner
son of Ner and Joab son of Zeruiah, and
all the other dedicated things were in
the care of Shelomith and his relatives.

29 From the Izharites: Kenaniah and his sons
were assigned duties away from the temple, as officials and judges over Israel.

30 From the Hebronites: Hashabiah and
his relatives—seventeen hundred able
men—were responsible in Israel west
of the Jordan for all the work of the
LORD and for the king's service. 31 As
for the Hebronites, Jeriah was their
chief according to the genealogical records of their families. In the fortieth
year of David's reign a search was made
in the records, and capable men among
the Hebronites were found at Jazer in
Gilead. 32 Jeriah had twenty-seven hundred relatives, who were able men and
heads of families, and King David put
them in charge of the Reubenites, the
Gadites and the half-tribe of Manasseh
for every matter pertaining to God and
for the affairs of the king.

Army Divisions

27 This is the list of the Israelites—heads
of families, commanders of thousands
and commanders of hundreds, and their officers, who served the king in all that concerned
the army divisions that were on duty month
by month throughout the year. Each division
consisted of 24,000 men.

2 In charge of the first division, for the first
month, was Jashobeam son of Zabdiel.
There were 24,000 men in his division. 3 He
was a descendant of Perez and chief of all
the army officers for the first month.

4 In charge of the division for the second
month was Dodai the Ahohite; Mikloth

[a] 14 A variant of *Meshelemiah* [b] 20 Septuagint; Hebrew *As for the Levites, Ahijah was*

was the leader of his division. There were
24,000 men in his division.
5 The third army commander, for the third
month, was Benaiah son of Jehoiada the
priest. He was chief and there were 24,000
men in his division. 6 This was the Benaiah
who was a mighty man among the Thirty
and was over the Thirty. His son Ammiza-
bad was in charge of his division.
7 The fourth, for the fourth month, was Asahel the brother of Joab; his son Zebadiah
was his successor. There were 24,000 men
in his division.
8 The fifth, for the fifth month, was the
commander Shamhuth the Izrahite. There
were 24,000 men in his division.
9 The sixth, for the sixth month, was Ira the
son of Ikkesh the Tekoite. There were
24,000 men in his division.
10 The seventh, for the seventh month, was Helez the Pelonite, an Ephraimite. There were
24,000 men in his division.
11 The eighth, for the eighth month, was Sibbecai the Hushathite, a Zerahite. There were
24,000 men in his division.
12 The ninth, for the ninth month, was Abiezer
the Anathothite, a Benjamite. There were
24,000 men in his division.
13 The tenth, for the tenth month, was Maharai
the Netophathite, a Zerahite. There were
24,000 men in his division.
14 The eleventh, for the eleventh month, was
Benaiah the Pirathonite, an Ephraimite.
There were 24,000 men in his division.
15 The twelfth, for the twelfth month, was Heldai the Netophathite, from the family of
Othniel. There were 24,000 men in his division.

Officers of the Tribes

16 The officers over the tribes of Israel:

over the Reubenites: Eliezer son of Zicri;
over the Simeonites: Shephatiah son of Maacah;
17 over Levi: Hashabiah son of Kemuel;
over Aaron: Zadok;
18 over Judah: Elihu, a brother of David;
over Issachar: Omri son of Michael;
19 over Zebulun: Ishmaiah son of Obadiah;
over Naphtali: Jerimoth son of Azriel;
20 over the Ephraimites: Hoshea son of Azaziah;
over half the tribe of Manasseh: Joel son of Pedaiah;
21 over the half-tribe of Manasseh in Gilead: Iddo son of Zechariah;
over Benjamin: Jaasiel son of Abner;
22 over Dan: Azarel son of Jeroham.

These were the officers over the tribes of Israel.

23 David did not take the number of the men
twenty years old or less, because the LORD had
promised to make Israel as numerous as the
stars in the sky. 24 Joab son of Zeruiah began to
count the men but did not finish. Wrath came
on Israel on account of this numbering, and
the number was not entered in the book[a] of
the annals of King David.

The King's Overseers

25 Azmaveth son of Adiel was in charge of
the royal storehouses.

Jonathan son of Uzziah was in charge of the storehouses in the outlying districts, in the towns, the villages and the watchtowers.

26 Ezri son of Kelub was in charge of the field
workers who farmed the land.

27 Shimei the Ramathite was in charge of
the vineyards.

Zabdi the Shiphmite was in charge of the produce of the vineyards for the wine vats.

28 Baal-Hanan the Gederite was in charge
of the olive and sycamore-fig trees in the western foothills.

Joash was in charge of the supplies of olive oil.

29 Shitrai the Sharonite was in charge of the
herds grazing in Sharon.

Shaphat son of Adlai was in charge of the herds in the valleys.

30 Obil the Ishmaelite was in charge of the
camels.

Jehdeiah the Meronothite was in charge of the donkeys.

31 Jaziz the Hagrite was in charge of the
flocks.

All these were the officials in charge of King David's property.

[a] 24 Septuagint; Hebrew *number*

32 Jonathan, David's uncle, was a counselor, a man of insight and a scribe. Jehiel son of Hacmoni took care of the king's sons.

33 Ahithophel was the king's counselor.

Hushai the Arkite was the king's friend. 34 Ahithophel was succeeded by Jehoiada son of Benaiah and by Abiathar.

Joab was the commander of the royal army.

David's Plans for the Temple

28 David summoned all the officials of Israel to assemble at Jerusalem: the officers over the tribes, the commanders of the divisions in the service of the king, the commanders of thousands and commanders of hundreds, and the officials in charge of all the property and livestock belonging to the king and his sons, together with the palace officials, the mighty men and all the brave warriors.

2 King David rose to his feet and said: "Listen to me, my brothers and my people. I had it in my heart to build a house as a place of rest for the ark of the covenant of the LORD, for the footstool of our God, and I made plans to build it. 3 But God said to me, 'You are not to build a house for my Name, because you are a warrior and have shed blood.'

4 "Yet the LORD, the God of Israel, chose me from my whole family to be king over Israel forever. He chose Judah as leader, and from the house of Judah he chose my family, and from my father's sons he was pleased to make me king over all Israel. 5 Of all my sons—and the LORD has given me many—he has chosen my son Solomon to sit on the throne of the kingdom of the LORD over Israel. 6 He said to me: 'Solomon your son is the one who will build my house and my courts, for I have chosen him to be my son, and I will be his father. 7 I will establish his kingdom forever if he is unswerving in carrying out my commands and laws, as is being done at this time.'

8 "So now I charge you in the sight of all Israel and of the assembly of the LORD, and in the hearing of our God: Be careful to follow all the commands of the LORD your God, that you may possess this good land and pass it on as an inheritance to your descendants forever.

9 "And you, my son Solomon, acknowledge the God of your father, and serve him with wholehearted devotion and with a willing mind, for the LORD searches every heart and understands every motive behind the thoughts. If you seek him, he will be found by you; but if you forsake him, he will reject you forever. 10 Consider now, for the LORD has chosen you to build a temple as a sanctuary. Be strong and do the work."

11 Then David gave his son Solomon the plans for the portico of the temple, its buildings, its storerooms, its upper parts, its inner rooms and the place of atonement. 12 He gave him the plans of all that the Spirit had put in his mind for the courts of the temple of the LORD and all the surrounding rooms, for the treasuries of the temple of God and for the treasuries for the dedicated things. 13 He gave him instructions for the divisions of the priests and Levites, and for all the work of serving in the temple of the LORD, as well as for all the articles to be used in its service. 14 He designated the weight of gold for all the gold articles to be used in various kinds of service, and the weight of silver for all the silver articles to be used in various kinds of service: 15 the weight of gold for the gold lampstands and their lamps, with the weight for each lampstand and its lamps; and the weight of silver for each silver lampstand and its lamps, according to the use of each lampstand; 16 the weight of gold for each table for consecrated bread; the weight of silver for the silver tables; 17 the weight of pure gold for the forks, sprinkling bowls and pitchers; the weight of gold for each gold dish; the weight of silver for each silver dish; 18 and the weight of the refined gold for the altar of incense. He also gave him the plan for the chariot, that is, the cherubim of gold

> **1 Chronicles 28:9**
>
> ### *God Can Be Found*
>
> "The LORD searches every heart and understands every motive behind the thoughts. If you seek him, he will be found by you; but if you forsake him, he will reject you forever."

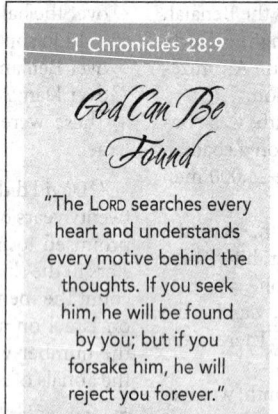

Big Plans

Read: 1 Chronicles 28:1–21

GOD HAD BIG PLANS for Solomon. He wanted him to build the temple. Solomon's dad, King David, had completed the plans and handed the task over to his son. Some parents might have said, "Be careful to follow the blueprints." Others might have said, "Be wise about the budget." But David commanded, "Be strong and courageous, and do the work." At least 30 times in Scripture God's people are told, "Be strong." Why? Because human beings are so easily discouraged. When we encounter a big task, we tend to lose courage, lose heart and sometimes even lose faith.

You might be thinking, *David had to fight giants. What kind of courage did Solomon need to build a temple?* But imagine the emotional pressure of trying to create a home for the Creator of the universe. Who wouldn't need courage to build a home beautiful enough for God? And take a moment to imagine the spiritual opposition Solomon faced. Those who don't believe in God or who don't understand the importance of God's work will always oppose it. Surely there were naysayers who objected to the cost of the materials. No doubt they grumbled about Solomon's focus on the temple at the expense of their agendas for the nation. It takes a brave leader to follow God's commands rather than collapse under the weight of criticism.

God has plans for you too. He has transformed your heart into a temple for his Holy Spirit. It takes courage to be a godly woman. There will be people who oppose God's work in your life. There will be naysayers who may try to convince you that the cost of serving God is too high or that the time and attention you pay to his Word is too great. There may be those who say you can cut corners, that you can hedge on God's intentions for the way you live. Don't believe it. The same God who helped David fight giants is the same God who enabled Solomon to build the most magnificent temple the people had ever seen. That God is *your* God, and he inhabits your heart. Therefore, "Be strong and courageous, and do the work." God was faithful to stay with Solomon and complete the work of the temple. He'll be faithful to complete the good work he began in you too.

1 Chronicles 28:20

David also said to Solomon his son, "Be strong and courageous, and do the work. Do not be afraid or discouraged, for the LORD God, my God, is with you. He will not fail you or forsake you until all the work for the service of the temple of the LORD is finished."

reflection

1. What type of construction is God doing in your "temple" right now?
2. How does the command to "be strong and courageous" encourage you?
3. Are there any naysayers in your life? Pray for the wisdom and courage to follow God's leading rather than be discouraged by their criticism.

RELATED READINGS

Joshua 1:6–9;
1 Kings 5:1–6;
Philippians 1:6

"Courage is fear that has said its prayers."

Dorothy Bernard

Wednesday

Go to page 520 for your next devotional reading.

that spread their wings and shelter the ark of
the covenant of the LORD.
19"All this," David said, "I have in writing
from the hand of the LORD upon me, and he
gave me understanding in all the details of
the plan."
20David also said to Solomon his son, "Be
strong and courageous, and do the work. Do
not be afraid or discouraged, for the LORD
God, my God, is with you. He will not fail you
or forsake you until all the work for the service
of the temple of the LORD is finished. 21The divisions of the priests and Levites are ready for
all the work on the temple of God, and every
willing man skilled in any craft will help you in
all the work. The officials and all the people will
obey your every command."

Gifts for Building the Temple

29 Then King David said to the whole
assembly: "My son Solomon, the one
whom God has chosen, is young and inexperienced. The task is great, because this palatial
structure is not for man but for the LORD God.
2With all my resources I have provided for the
temple of my God—gold for the gold work, silver for the silver, bronze for the bronze, iron
for the iron and wood for the
wood, as well as onyx for the
settings, turquoise,[a] stones of
various colors, and all kinds
of fine stone and marble—all
of these in large quantities. 3Be-
sides, in my devotion to the temple of my God I now give my
personal treasures of gold and
silver for the temple of my God,
over and above everything I
have provided for this holy
temple: 4three thousand talents[b] of gold (gold of Ophir)
and seven thousand talents[c] of
refined silver, for the overlaying
of the walls of the buildings,
5for the gold work and the silver work, and for all the work to
be done by the craftsmen. Now, who is willing
to consecrate himself today to the LORD?"

1 Chronicles 29:12

God Gives Strength and Honor

"Wealth and honor come
from you;
you are the ruler
of all things.
In your hands are
strength and power
to exalt and give
strength to all."

6Then the leaders of families, the officers of
the tribes of Israel, the commanders of thousands and commanders of hundreds, and
the officials in charge of the king's work gave
willingly. 7They gave toward the work on the
temple of God five thousand talents[d] and ten
thousand darics[e] of gold, ten thousand talents[f]
of silver, eighteen thousand talents[g] of bronze
and a hundred thousand talents[h] of iron. 8Any
who had precious stones gave them to the treasury of the temple of the LORD in the custody
of Jehiel the Gershonite. 9The people rejoiced
at the willing response of their leaders, for they
had given freely and wholeheartedly to the
LORD. David the king also rejoiced greatly.

David's Prayer

10David praised the LORD in the presence of
the whole assembly, saying,

"Praise be to you, O LORD,
God of our father Israel,
from everlasting to everlasting.
11Yours, O LORD, is the greatness and the
power
and the glory and the majesty and the
splendor,
for everything in heaven
and earth is yours.
Yours, O LORD, is the
kingdom;
you are exalted as head
over all.
12Wealth and honor come
from you;
you are the ruler of all
things.
In your hands are strength
and power
to exalt and give strength
to all.
13Now, our God, we give you
thanks,
and praise your glorious
name.

14"But who am I, and who are my people,
that we should be able to give as generously as

[a]2 The meaning of the Hebrew for this word is uncertain. [b]4 That is, about 110 tons (about 100 metric tons) [c]4 That is, about 260 tons (about 240 metric tons) [d]7 That is, about 190 tons (about 170 metric tons) [e]7 That is, about 185 pounds (about 84 kilograms) [f]7 That is, about 375 tons (about 345 metric tons) [g]7 That is, about 675 tons (about 610 metric tons) [h]7 That is, about 3,750 tons (about 3,450 metric tons)

this? Everything comes from you, and we have
given you only what comes from your hand.
15 We are aliens and strangers in your sight, as
were all our forefathers. Our days on earth are
like a shadow, without hope. 16 O LORD our
God, as for all this abundance that we have
provided for building you a temple for your
Holy Name, it comes from your hand, and all
of it belongs to you. 17 I know, my God, that you
test the heart and are pleased with integrity. All
these things have I given willingly and with
honest intent. And now I have seen with joy
how willingly your people who are here have
given to you. 18 O LORD, God of our fathers
Abraham, Isaac and Israel, keep this desire in
the hearts of your people forever, and keep
their hearts loyal to you. 19 And give my son
Solomon the wholehearted devotion to keep
your commands, requirements and decrees
and to do everything to build the palatial structure for which I have provided."

20 Then David said to the whole assembly,
"Praise the LORD your God." So they all praised
the LORD, the God of their fathers; they bowed
low and fell prostrate before the LORD and
the king.

Solomon Acknowledged as King

21 The next day they made sacrifices to the
LORD and presented burnt offerings to him: a
thousand bulls, a thousand rams and a thousand male lambs, together with their drink offerings, and other sacrifices in abundance for
all Israel. 22 They ate and drank with great joy
in the presence of the LORD that day.

Then they acknowledged Solomon son of
David as king a second time, anointing him
before the LORD to be ruler and Zadok to be
priest. 23 So Solomon sat on the throne of the
LORD as king in place of his father David. He
prospered and all Israel obeyed him. 24 All
the officers and mighty men, as well as all of
King David's sons, pledged their submission to
King Solomon.

25 The LORD highly exalted Solomon in the
sight of all Israel and bestowed on him royal
splendor such as no king over Israel ever
had before.

The Death of David

26 David son of Jesse was king over all Israel.
27 He ruled over Israel forty years—seven in
Hebron and thirty-three in Jerusalem. 28 He
died at a good old age, having enjoyed long life,
wealth and honor. His son Solomon succeeded
him as king.

29 As for the events of King David's reign,
from beginning to end, they are written in the
records of Samuel the seer, the records of Nathan the prophet and the records of Gad the
seer, 30 together with the details of his reign and
power, and the circumstances that surrounded
him and Israel and the kingdoms of all the
other lands.

2 Chronicles

Author:
Unknown,
but possibly Ezra.

Audience:
All Israel.

Date:
About 430 B.C.

Setting:
The book covers the time from Solomon's reign (970 B.C.) to the Babylonian exile (586 B.C.), paralleling many of the events of 1 and 2 Kings.

Verse to Remember:
"If my people, who are called by my name, will humble themselves and pray and seek my face and turn from their wicked ways, then will I hear from heaven and will forgive their sin and will heal their land." (7:14)

David's son Solomon is firmly established as king, and his rule starts out strong. There is one thing he desires from God more than anything else: *wisdom.* Solomon receives that gift, but by the end of his life he is often turning his back on it.

As the book goes through the roll call of various kings of Judah, good kings alternate with bad until the *Law of God is found* when Josiah becomes king—implying that at some point God's Law had actually been lost!

As illustrated by Solomon and a few other kings, it is possible to start life dedicated to God and end it distracted by false gods and wrong priorities. Even the kings of *God's own people were not immune* to the lure of self-centered desires and false gods.

Solomon Asks for Wisdom

1 Solomon son of David established himself firmly over his kingdom, for the
LORD his God was with him and made him
exceedingly great.
2Then Solomon spoke to all Israel—to the
commanders of thousands and commanders
of hundreds, to the judges and to all the leaders
in Israel, the heads of families— 3and Solomon
and the whole assembly went to the high place
at Gibeon, for God's Tent of Meeting was there,
which Moses the LORD's servant had made in
the desert. 4Now David had brought up the ark
of God from Kiriath Jearim to the place he had

prepared for it, because he had pitched a tent
for it in Jerusalem. 5But the bronze altar that
Bezalel son of Uri, the son of Hur, had made
was in Gibeon in front of the tabernacle of the
LORD; so Solomon and the assembly inquired
of him there. 6Solomon went up to the bronze
altar before the LORD in the Tent of Meeting
and offered a thousand burnt offerings on it.
7That night God appeared to Solomon and
said to him, "Ask for whatever you want me to
give you."
8Solomon answered God, "You have shown
great kindness to David my father and have
made me king in his place. 9Now, LORD God,
let your promise to my father David be confirmed, for you have made me king over a
people who are as numerous as the dust of the
earth. 10Give me wisdom and knowledge, that
I may lead this people, for who is able to govern
this great people of yours?"
11God said to Solomon,
"Since this is your heart's desire and you have not asked for
wealth, riches or honor, nor for
the death of your enemies, and
since you have not asked for a
long life but for wisdom and
knowledge to govern my people over whom I have made
you king, 12therefore wisdom
and knowledge will be given
you. And I will also give you
wealth, riches and honor, such
as no king who was before you
ever had and none after you
will have."
13Then Solomon went to Jerusalem from the high place at
Gibeon, from before the Tent
of Meeting. And he reigned over Israel.
14Solomon accumulated chariots and
horses; he had fourteen hundred chariots and
twelve thousand horses,[a] which he kept in the
chariot cities and also with him in Jerusalem.
15The king made silver and gold as common in
Jerusalem as stones, and cedar as plentiful as
sycamore-fig trees in the foothills. 16Solomon's
horses were imported from Egypt[b] and from
Kue[c]—the royal merchants purchased them
from Kue. 17They imported a chariot from
Egypt for six hundred shekels[d] of silver, and a
horse for a hundred and fifty.[e] They also
exported them to all the kings of the Hittites
and of the Arameans.

Preparations for Building the Temple

2 Solomon gave orders to build a temple for
the Name of the LORD and a royal palace
for himself. 2He conscripted seventy thousand
men as carriers and eighty thousand as stonecutters in the hills and thirty-six hundred as
foremen over them.
3Solomon sent this message to Hiram[f] king
of Tyre:

"Send me cedar logs as you did for my
father David when you sent him cedar to
build a palace to live in. 4Now I am about
to build a temple for the Name of the LORD
my God and to dedicate it to
him for burning fragrant incense before him, for setting
out the consecrated bread
regularly, and for making
burnt offerings every morning and evening and on Sabbaths and New Moons and
at the appointed feasts of the
LORD our God. This is a lasting ordinance for Israel.
5"The temple I am going
to build will be great, because
our God is greater than all
other gods. 6But who is able
to build a temple for him,
since the heavens, even the
highest heavens, cannot contain him? Who then am I to
build a temple for him, except as a place
to burn sacrifices before him?
7"Send me, therefore, a man skilled to
work in gold and silver, bronze and iron,
and in purple, crimson and blue yarn,
and experienced in the art of engraving,
to work in Judah and Jerusalem with my
skilled craftsmen, whom my father David
provided.

2 Chronicles 2:6

God Is Unfathomable

"But who is able to build a temple for him, since the heavens, even the highest heavens, cannot contain him? Who then am I to build a temple for him, except as a place to burn sacrifices before him?"

[a]14 Or *charioteers* [b]16 Or possibly *Muzur,* a region in Cilicia; also in verse 17 [c]16 Probably Cilicia [d]17 That is, about 15 pounds (about 7 kilograms) [e]17 That is, about 3 3/4 pounds (about 1.7 kilograms) [f]3 Hebrew *Huram,* a variant of *Hiram*; also in verses 11 and 12

Something Beautiful for God

Read: 2 Chronicles 2:1–6

IT'S NOT WRONG to want something for yourself—as long as you don't cling too tightly to it. When it comes to sharing, the fair split goes, "One for you, one for me."

Solomon had plenty of possessions, and he was generous and played fair. A temple for God, a palace for himself. Do you know someone who's done the same? They have the money to build a nice house for themselves, and they also fund a church project or a center for the homeless. We can be encouraged by their example and by Solomon's example: He knew that the most worthy God of the universe deserves the best workmanship, the finest materials and the choicest offerings.

What a daring project: building a house for Almighty God! Solomon understood the irony—that he, a mortal man, would do such a thing. He insisted that nothing be slipshod. He endeavored for seven years to produce the most magnificent temple possible, using gold, silver, precious stones, marble and cedar—most of it collected for years by his father, David, and the rest of it donated by the people of Israel. Even so, would it pass muster for Yahweh's majesty? Would it cause visitors and worshipers to think great and high thoughts of the God of Israel? Would it reflect God's beauty and grandeur?

God doesn't need our things. But he ordains our work and endows us with creativity and talent. He designed us to be busy about the business of doing things for him, of making all kinds of things that reflect his regenerating grace and that glorify him.

In what beautiful enterprise might God be directing you to be involved? It could be people or projects, aptitudes or art. You may have the ability to create something that reveals and reflects some of his greatness. If so, ask him to provide the resources. Find the helpers and materials needed to accomplish the goal. Go ahead and enjoy the process and the fruit of your labor, like Solomon did. But give fairly and generously to the author of your gifts and talents. Do a God-sized work for him.

2 Chronicles 2:1

Solomon gave orders to build a temple for the Name of the LORD and a royal palace for himself.

reflection

1 What problems could you foresee in constructing a building for God? What satisfactions?

2 How much of your time and possessions do you dedicate to God? Is it a fair percentage?

3 What gifts or resources has God blessed you with? How can you use something of yourself to give back to God?

RELATED READINGS

Mark 14:3–9; Acts 7:44–50

"[Work] is, or should be, the full expression of the worker's faculties, the thing in which he finds spiritual, mental and bodily satisfaction, and the medium in which he offers himself to God."

Dorothy Lee Sayers

Thursday

Go to page 524 for your next devotional reading.

8“Send me also cedar, pine and algum[a]
logs from Lebanon, for I know that your
men are skilled in cutting timber there.
My men will work with yours 9to provide me with plenty of lumber, because
the temple I build must be large and magnificent. 10I will give your servants, the
woodsmen who cut the timber, twenty
thousand cors[b] of ground wheat, twenty
thousand cors of barley, twenty thousand
baths[c] of wine and twenty thousand baths
of olive oil.”

11Hiram king of Tyre replied by letter to Solomon:

“Because the LORD loves his people, he
has made you their king.”

12And Hiram added:

“Praise be to the LORD, the God of
Israel, who made heaven and earth!
He has given King David a wise son, endowed with intelligence and discernment,
who will build a temple for the LORD and
a palace for himself.

13“I am sending you Huram-Abi, a
man of great skill, 14whose mother was
from Dan and whose father was from
Tyre. He is trained to work in gold and
silver, bronze and iron, stone and wood,
and with purple and blue and crimson
yarn and fine linen. He is experienced in
all kinds of engraving and can execute any
design given to him. He will work with
your craftsmen and with those of my lord,
David your father.

15“Now let my lord send his servants
the wheat and barley and the olive oil
and wine he promised, 16and we will cut
all the logs from Lebanon that you need
and will float them in rafts by sea down
to Joppa. You can then take them up to Jerusalem.”

17Solomon took a census of all the aliens
who were in Israel, after the census his father
David had taken; and they were found to be
153,600. 18He assigned 70,000 of them to be
carriers and 80,000 to be stonecutters in the
hills, with 3,600 foremen over them to keep
the people working.

Solomon Builds the Temple

3 Then Solomon began to build the temple of
the LORD in Jerusalem on Mount Moriah,
where the LORD had appeared to his father David. It was on the threshing floor of Araunah[d]
the Jebusite, the place provided by David. 2He
began building on the second day of the second
month in the fourth year of his reign.

3The foundation Solomon laid for building
the temple of God was sixty cubits long and
twenty cubits wide[e] (using the cubit of the old
standard). 4The portico at the front of the temple was twenty cubits[f] long across the width of
the building and twenty cubits[g] high.

He overlaid the inside with pure gold. 5He
paneled the main hall with pine and covered it
with fine gold and decorated it with palm tree
and chain designs. 6He adorned the temple with
precious stones. And the gold he used was gold
of Parvaim. 7He overlaid the ceiling beams,
doorframes, walls and doors of the temple with
gold, and he carved cherubim on the walls.

8He built the Most Holy Place, its length corresponding to the width of the temple—twenty
cubits long and twenty cubits wide. He overlaid
the inside with six hundred talents[h] of fine
gold. 9The gold nails weighed fifty shekels.[i] He
also overlaid the upper parts with gold.

10In the Most Holy Place he made a pair
of sculptured cherubim and overlaid them
with gold. 11The total wingspan of the cherubim was twenty cubits. One wing of the first
cherub was five cubits[j] long and touched the
temple wall, while its other wing, also five cubits long, touched the wing of the other cherub.
12Similarly one wing of the second cherub was
five cubits long and touched the other temple
wall, and its other wing, also five cubits long,
touched the wing of the first cherub. 13The
wings of these cherubim extended twenty
cubits. They stood on their feet, facing the
main hall.[k]

[a]8 Probably a variant of *almug*; possibly juniper [b]10 That is, probably about 125,000 bushels (about 4,400 kiloliters) [c]10 That is, probably about 115,000 gallons (about 440 kiloliters) [d]1 Hebrew *Ornan*, a variant of *Araunah* [e]3 That is, about 90 feet (about 27 meters) long and 30 feet (about 9 meters) wide [f]4 That is, about 30 feet (about 9 meters); also in verses 8, 11 and 13 [g]4 Some Septuagint and Syriac manuscripts; Hebrew *and a hundred and twenty* [h]8 That is, about 23 tons (about 21 metric tons) [i]9 That is, about 1 1/4 pounds (about 0.6 kilogram) [j]11 That is, about 7 1/2 feet (about 2.3 meters); also in verse 15 [k]13 Or *facing inward*

14 He made the curtain of blue, purple and
crimson yarn and fine linen, with cherubim
worked into it.
15 In the front of the temple he made two pillars, which ⌞together⌟ were thirty-five cubits[a]
long, each with a capital on top measuring five
cubits. 16 He made interwoven chains[b] and
put them on top of the pillars. He also made a
hundred pomegranates and attached them to
the chains. 17 He erected the pillars in the front
of the temple, one to the south and one to the
north. The one to the south he named Jakin[c]
and the one to the north Boaz.[d]

The Temple's Furnishings

4 He made a bronze altar twenty cubits long,
twenty cubits wide and ten cubits high.[e]
2 He made the Sea of cast metal, circular in shape,
measuring ten cubits from rim to rim and five
cubits[f] high. It took a line of thirty cubits[g] to measure around it. 3 Below the rim, figures of bulls
encircled it—ten to a cubit.[h] The bulls were cast
in two rows in one piece with the Sea.
4 The Sea stood on twelve bulls, three facing
north, three facing west, three facing south and
three facing east. The Sea rested on top of them,
and their hindquarters were toward the center.
5 It was a handbreadth[i] in thickness, and its rim
was like the rim of a cup, like a lily blossom. It
held three thousand baths.[j]
6 He then made ten basins for washing and
placed five on the south side and five on the
north. In them the things to be used for the
burnt offerings were rinsed, but the Sea was to
be used by the priests for washing.
7 He made ten gold lampstands according
to the specifications for them and placed them
in the temple, five on the south side and five
on the north.
8 He made ten tables and placed them in the
temple, five on the south side and five on the
north. He also made a hundred gold sprinkling
bowls.
9 He made the courtyard of the priests, and
the large court and the doors for the court, and
overlaid the doors with bronze. 10 He placed the
Sea on the south side, at the southeast corner.
11 He also made the pots and shovels and
sprinkling bowls.
So Huram finished the work he had undertaken for King Solomon in the temple of God:

12 the two pillars;
the two bowl-shaped capitals on top of the pillars;
the two sets of network decorating the two bowl-shaped capitals on top of the pillars;
13 the four hundred pomegranates for the two sets of network (two rows of pomegranates for each network, decorating the bowl-shaped capitals on top of the pillars);
14 the stands with their basins;
15 the Sea and the twelve bulls under it;
16 the pots, shovels, meat forks and all related articles.

All the objects that Huram-Abi made for
King Solomon for the temple of the LORD were
of polished bronze. 17 The king had them cast
in clay molds in the plain of the Jordan between
Succoth and Zarethan.[k] 18 All these things that
Solomon made amounted to so much that the
weight of the bronze was not determined.
19 Solomon also made all the furnishings
that were in God's temple:

the golden altar;
the tables on which was the bread of the Presence;
20 the lampstands of pure gold with their lamps, to burn in front of the inner sanctuary as prescribed;
21 the gold floral work and lamps and tongs (they were solid gold);
22 the pure gold wick trimmers, sprinkling bowls, dishes and censers; and the gold doors of the temple: the inner doors to the Most Holy Place and the doors of the main hall.

5 When all the work Solomon had done
for the temple of the LORD was finished,
he brought in the things his father David had

[a] 15 That is, about 52 feet (about 16 meters) [b] 16 Or possibly *made chains in the inner sanctuary*; the meaning of the Hebrew for this phrase is uncertain. [c] 17 *Jakin* probably means *he establishes.* [d] 17 *Boaz* probably means *in him is strength.* [e] 1 That is, about 30 feet (about 9 meters) long and wide, and about 15 feet (about 4.5 meters) high [f] 2 That is, about 7 1/2 feet (about 2.3 meters) [g] 2 That is, about 45 feet (about 13.5 meters) [h] 3 That is, about 1 1/2 feet (about 0.5 meter) [i] 5 That is, about 3 inches (about 8 centimeters) [j] 5 That is, about 17,500 gallons (about 66 kiloliters) [k] 17 Hebrew *Zeredatha,* a variant of *Zarethan*

dedicated—the silver and gold and all the furnishings—and he placed them in the treasuries
of God's temple.

The Ark Brought to the Temple

> **2 Chronicles 5:13**
>
> *God Is Good*
>
> "He is good;
> his love endures forever."

[2]Then Solomon summoned
to Jerusalem the elders of Israel,
all the heads of the tribes and
the chiefs of the Israelite families, to bring up the ark of the
LORD's covenant from Zion,
the City of David. [3]And all the
men of Israel came together to
the king at the time of the festival in the seventh month.
[4]When all the elders of Israel had arrived,
the Levites took up the ark, [5]and they brought
up the ark and the Tent of Meeting and all the
sacred furnishings in it. The priests, who were
Levites, carried them up; [6]and King Solomon
and the entire assembly of Israel that had gathered about him were before the ark, sacrificing
so many sheep and cattle that they could not be
recorded or counted.
[7]The priests then brought the ark of the
LORD's covenant to its place in the inner sanctuary of the temple, the Most Holy Place, and
put it beneath the wings of the cherubim. [8]The
cherubim spread their wings over the place of
the ark and covered the ark and its carrying
poles. [9]These poles were so long that their ends,
extending from the ark, could be seen from in
front of the inner sanctuary, but not from outside the Holy Place; and they are still there today. [10]There was nothing in the ark except the
two tablets that Moses had placed in it at Horeb, where the LORD made a covenant with the
Israelites after they came out of Egypt.
[11]The priests then withdrew from the Holy
Place. All the priests who were there had
consecrated themselves, regardless of their
divisions. [12]All the Levites who were musicians—Asaph, Heman, Jeduthun and their
sons and relatives—stood on the east side of
the altar, dressed in fine linen and playing cymbals, harps and lyres. They were accompanied
by 120 priests sounding trumpets. [13]The trumpeters and singers joined in unison, as with one
voice, to give praise and thanks to the LORD.
Accompanied by trumpets, cymbals and other
instruments, they raised their voices in praise
to the LORD and sang:

"He is good;
his love endures forever."

Then the temple of the LORD
was filled with a cloud, [14]and
the priests could not perform
their service because of the
cloud, for the glory of the LORD
filled the temple of God.

6 Then Solomon said, "The
LORD has said that he
would dwell in a dark cloud; [2]I have built a
magnificent temple for you, a place for you to
dwell forever."
[3]While the whole assembly of Israel was
standing there, the king turned around and
blessed them. [4]Then he said:

"Praise be to the LORD, the God of
Israel, who with his hands has fulfilled
what he promised with his mouth to my
father David. For he said, [5]'Since the day
I brought my people out of Egypt, I have
not chosen a city in any tribe of Israel to
have a temple built for my Name to be
there, nor have I chosen anyone to be the
leader over my people Israel. [6]But now I
have chosen Jerusalem for my Name to be
there, and I have chosen David to rule my
people Israel.'
[7]"My father David had it in his heart to
build a temple for the Name of the LORD,
the God of Israel. [8]But the LORD said to
my father David, 'Because it was in your
heart to build a temple for my Name, you
did well to have this in your heart. [9]Nev-
ertheless, you are not the one to build the
temple, but your son, who is your own
flesh and blood—he is the one who will
build the temple for my Name.'
[10]"The LORD has kept the promise he
made. I have succeeded David my father
and now I sit on the throne of Israel, just
as the LORD promised, and I have built the
temple for the Name of the LORD, the God
of Israel. [11]There I have placed the ark, in
which is the covenant of the LORD that he
made with the people of Israel."

Loose Ends

Read: 2 Chronicles 6:1–10

2 Chronicles 6:9

"Nevertheless, you are not the one to build the temple, but your son, who is your own flesh and blood—he is the one who will build the temple for my Name."

GOD TOLD DAVID that he wouldn't be the one to finish what he started. Abraham was promised descendents, but he would never bounce all of them on his knees. The prophets were promised a Messiah, but they didn't live to see him in the flesh.

We can't always finish what we start. That idea often runs counter to our sensibilities as women. Of course we have to finish. We have calendar planners. We have to-do lists. We have people depending on us. We hate loose ends. We have every intention of completing what we begin. But sometimes we're supposed to leave some loose ends dangling.

King David knew a thing or two about loose ends. He had the noble ambition of building a temple for God. He drew the blueprints according to God's specifications. He gathered the supplies. But he never set a single stone in place. He had been a warrior and had shed blood. So God had in mind a different man for the job: David's son Solomon. When Solomon became king, he picked up the loose ends his father had left and went to work. The plans were David's, but the work of constructing the temple belonged to King Solomon.

Think about it. Even King Solomon said, "There is nothing new under the sun" (Ecclesiastes 1:9). Much of the work we do for God is a continuation of what another person began. We teach a class that someone else started. We mentor a woman that someone else brought to faith. We paint walls that someone else erected. When we're gone, new voices will fill that classroom. New mentors will emerge. New hands will paint church walls. And that's as it should be.

If David had pressed ahead with constructing the temple, not only would he have been disobedient, but he also would have deprived his son of a unique opportunity to use his wisdom, gifts and talents to serve God.

Is there a task or position you are clinging to that God is asking you to release? The simple truth is that loose ends leave room for someone else to come along and continue the work in new and unique ways. And God may want you to move forward to a different phase of life. Leaving room for loose ends allows God's kingdom to extend beyond our influence and reach into eternity.

reflection

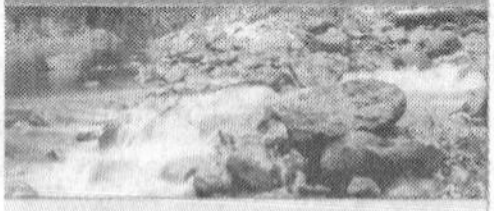

1 What loose ends have you picked up and begun working on?

2 What loose ends are you leaving for others to pick up and leave their personal touch on?

3 How does considering both those who have gone before you and those who will come after you impact the work you are doing today?

RELATED READINGS

1 Chronicles 28:2–3, 11–19;
1 Corinthians 3:10–15

Go to page 527 for your next devotional reading.

Solomon's Prayer of Dedication

12Then Solomon stood before the altar of the
LORD in front of the whole assembly of Israel
and spread out his hands. 13Now he had made
a bronze platform, five cubits[a] long, five cubits
wide and three cubits[b] high, and had placed it
in the center of the outer court. He stood on
the platform and then knelt down before the
whole assembly of Israel and spread out his
hands toward heaven. 14He said:

"O LORD, God of Israel, there is no God
like you in heaven or on earth—you who
keep your covenant of love with your servants who continue wholeheartedly in
your way. 15You have kept your promise
to your servant David my father; with
your mouth you have promised and with
your hand you have fulfilled it—as it is
today.

16"Now LORD, God of Israel, keep
for your servant David my father the
promises you made to him when you
said, 'You shall never fail to have a man
to sit before me on the throne of Israel, if
only your sons are careful in all they do
to walk before me according to my law, as
you have done.' 17And now, O LORD, God
of Israel, let your word that you promised
your servant David come true.

18"But will God really dwell on earth
with men? The heavens, even the highest
heavens, cannot contain you. How much
less this temple I have built! 19Yet give attention to your servant's prayer and his
plea for mercy, O LORD my God. Hear
the cry and the prayer that your servant
is praying in your presence. 20May your
eyes be open toward this temple day and
night, this place of which you said you
would put your Name there. May you
hear the prayer your servant prays toward this place. 21Hear the supplications
of your servant and of your people Israel
when they pray toward this place. Hear
from heaven, your dwelling place; and
when you hear, forgive.

22"When a man wrongs his neighbor
and is required to take an oath and he
comes and swears the oath before your
altar in this temple, 23then hear from
heaven and act. Judge between your servants, repaying the guilty by bringing
down on his own head what he has done.
Declare the innocent not guilty and so establish his innocence.

24"When your people Israel have been
defeated by an enemy because they have
sinned against you and when they turn
back and confess your name, praying
and making supplication before you in
this temple, 25then hear from heaven and
forgive the sin of your people Israel and
bring them back to the land you gave to
them and their fathers.

26"When the heavens are shut up and
there is no rain because your people have
sinned against you, and when they pray
toward this place and confess your name
and turn from their sin because you have
afflicted them, 27then hear from heaven
and forgive the sin of your servants, your
people Israel. Teach them the right way to
live, and send rain on the land you gave
your people for an inheritance.

28"When famine or plague comes to
the land, or blight or mildew, locusts or
grasshoppers, or when enemies besiege
them in any of their cities, whatever disaster or disease may come, 29and when
a prayer or plea is made by any of your
people Israel—each one aware of his afflictions and pains, and spreading out his
hands toward this temple— 30then hear
from heaven, your dwelling place. Forgive, and deal with each man according
to all he does, since you know his heart
(for you alone know the hearts of men),
31so that they will fear you and walk in
your ways all the time they live in the land
you gave our fathers.

32"As for the foreigner who does not belong to your people Israel but has come
from a distant land because of your great
name and your mighty hand and your
outstretched arm—when he comes and
prays toward this temple, 33then hear
from heaven, your dwelling place, and

[a]13 That is, about 7 1/2 feet (about 2.3 meters) [b]13 That is, about 4 1/2 feet (about 1.3 meters)

do whatever the foreigner asks of you, so
that all the peoples of the earth may know
your name and fear you, as do your own
people Israel, and may know that this
house I have built bears your Name.
34"When your people go to war against
their enemies, wherever you send them,
and when they pray to you toward this
city you have chosen and the temple I
have built for your Name, 35then hear
from heaven their prayer and their plea,
and uphold their cause.
36"When they sin against you—for
there is no one who does not sin—and
you become angry with them and give
them over to the enemy, who takes them
captive to a land far away or near; 37and
if they have a change of heart in the land
where they are held captive, and repent
and plead with you in the land of their
captivity and say, 'We have sinned, we
have done wrong and acted wickedly';
38and if they turn back to you with all
their heart and soul in the land of their
captivity where they were
taken, and pray toward the
land you gave their fathers,
toward the city you have chosen and toward the temple
I have built for your Name;
39then from heaven, your
dwelling place, hear their
prayer and their pleas, and
uphold their cause. And forgive your people, who have
sinned against you.
40"Now, my God, may
your eyes be open and your
ears attentive to the prayers offered in
this place.

41"Now arise, O LORD God, and come to
your resting place,
you and the ark of your might.
May your priests, O LORD God, be
clothed with salvation,
may your saints rejoice in your
goodness.
42O LORD God, do not reject your
anointed one.

2 Chronicles 6:39

God Hears Us

"Hear their prayer and their pleas, and uphold their cause. And forgive your people, who have sinned against you."

Remember the great love promised
to David your servant."

The Dedication of the Temple

7 When Solomon finished praying, fire
came down from heaven and consumed
the burnt offering and the sacrifices, and the
glory of the LORD filled the temple. 2The
priests could not enter the temple of the LORD
because the glory of the LORD filled it. 3When
all the Israelites saw the fire coming down and
the glory of the LORD above the temple, they
knelt on the pavement with their faces to the
ground, and they worshiped and gave thanks
to the LORD, saying,

"He is good;
his love endures forever."

4Then the king and all the people offered
sacrifices before the LORD. 5And King Solomon
offered a sacrifice of twenty-two thousand head
of cattle and a hundred and twenty thousand
sheep and goats. So the king and all the people dedicated the temple of God. 6The priests
took their positions, as did the
Levites with the LORD's musical instruments, which King
David had made for praising
the LORD and which were used
when he gave thanks, saying,
"His love endures forever." Opposite the Levites, the priests
blew their trumpets, and all the
Israelites were standing.
7Solomon consecrated the
middle part of the courtyard in
front of the temple of the LORD,
and there he offered burnt offerings and the fat of the fellow-
ship offerings,[a] because the bronze altar he had
made could not hold the burnt offerings, the
grain offerings and the fat portions.
8So Solomon observed the festival at that
time for seven days, and all Israel with him—a
vast assembly, people from Lebo[b] Hamath to
the Wadi of Egypt. 9On the eighth day they
held an assembly, for they had celebrated the
dedication of the altar for seven days and the
festival for seven days more. 10On the twenty-
third day of the seventh month he sent the

[a]7 Traditionally *peace offerings* [b]8 Or *from the entrance to*

Learning to Wait

NAOMI

"HOW DID IT GO, my daughter?" Naomi asked her daughter-in-law Ruth.

Ruth had just returned from spending an evening with Boaz. Like a schoolgirl describing her first experience falling in love, the words tumbled out of her.

The way her daughter-in-law smiled and mindlessly fingered a lock of her hair whenever she said Boaz' name reminded Naomi of an earlier time: a time when the very thought of her former husband, Elimelech, "Eli" as she liked to call him, sent a chill of excitement through her.

But that was before—before their hometown of Bethlehem became a poorhouse, before the famine, before the move to Moab, before immeasurable heartache and loss. When she lost her husband and then both sons, she was sure life would never be the same. And it never was. When she decided to return to Bethlehem, her friends even paid tribute to that fact.

She remembered the surprise on their faces. The words they didn't bother to whisper: "Can this be Naomi?" they wondered aloud, staring at the shadow of the woman they'd known.

Naomi had scoffed at the irony. Her mother had named her "Pleasant." What was pleasant about her life now? Instead of joy there was suffering; bitterness was her only destiny now.

However, from the ruddy soil of her sorrow, seeds of hope sprouted from one small word: *wait*.

Wait for God's timing. Bethlehem, the "house of bread," would again be filled with a luscious aroma.

Wait for God's provision. Boaz, the one-in-a-million man, would soon marry Ruth.

Wait for God's blessing. Jesus, the direct descendant of Boaz and Ruth, was coming.

So, today, when her daughter-in-law (now practically a daughter) came to her, she saw uncertainty in her eyes. She knew there were questions, unpredictable situations. Would Ruth have a chance at happiness again? Was there hope? There was no way to know for sure. But Naomi offered Ruth the best advice she could—something she'd learned the hard way.

"Wait. Wait, my daughter, until you find out what happens . . ." Just wait.

"Wait, my daughter, until you find out what happens. For the man will not rest until the matter is settled today."

Ruth 3:18

ASSIGNED READING:

Ruth 2–4

—Prayer—

Great Savior, take away the impatience in my soul so I can better see your good plans for me.

Weekend

Go to page 530 for your next devotional reading.

people to their homes, joyful and glad in heart
for the good things the LORD had done for David and Solomon and for his people Israel.

The LORD Appears to Solomon

11 When Solomon had finished the temple
of the LORD and the royal palace, and had
succeeded in carrying out all he had in mind
to do in the temple of the LORD and in his own
palace, 12 the LORD appeared to him at night
and said:

"I have heard your prayer and have chosen this place for myself as a temple for
sacrifices.
13 "When I shut up the heavens so that
there is no rain, or command locusts to
devour the land or send a plague among
my people, 14 if my people,
who are called by my name,
will humble themselves
and pray and seek my face
and turn from their wicked
ways, then will I hear from
heaven and will forgive their
sin and will heal their land.
15 Now my eyes will be open
and my ears attentive to
the prayers offered in this
place. 16 I have chosen and
consecrated this temple so
that my Name may be there
forever. My eyes and my
heart will always be there.
17 "As for you, if you walk
before me as David your
father did, and do all I command, and observe my
decrees and laws, 18 I will establish your
royal throne, as I covenanted with David
your father when I said, 'You shall never
fail to have a man to rule over Israel.'
19 "But if you[a] turn away and forsake
the decrees and commands I have given
you[a] and go off to serve other gods
and worship them, 20 then I will uproot
Israel from my land, which I have given
them, and will reject this temple I have
consecrated for my Name. I will make it
a byword and an object of ridicule among
all peoples. 21 And though this temple is
now so imposing, all who pass by will be
appalled and say, 'Why has the LORD done
such a thing to this land and to this temple?' 22 People will answer, 'Because they
have forsaken the LORD, the God of their
fathers, who brought them out of Egypt,
and have embraced other gods, worshiping and serving them—that is why he
brought all this disaster on them.'"

2 Chronicles 7:14

God Offers Forgiveness

"If my people, who are called by my name, will humble themselves and pray and seek my face and turn from their wicked ways, then will I hear from heaven and will forgive their sin and will heal their land."

Solomon's Other Activities

8 At the end of twenty years, during which
Solomon built the temple of the LORD and
his own palace, 2 Solomon rebuilt the villages
that Hiram[b] had given him, and settled Israelites in them. 3 Solomon then went to Hamath
Zobah and captured it. 4 He
also built up Tadmor in the
desert and all the store cities
he had built in Hamath. 5 He
rebuilt Upper Beth Horon and
Lower Beth Horon as fortified
cities, with walls and with gates
and bars, 6 as well as Baalath
and all his store cities, and all
the cities for his chariots and
for his horses[c]—whatever he
desired to build in Jerusalem,
in Lebanon and throughout all
the territory he ruled.
7 All the people left from the
Hittites, Amorites, Perizzites,
Hivites and Jebusites (these peoples were not Israelites), 8 that
is, their descendants remaining
in the land, whom the Israelites
had not destroyed—these Solomon conscripted
for his slave labor force, as it is to this day. 9 But
Solomon did not make slaves of the Israelites
for his work; they were his fighting men, commanders of his captains, and commanders of
his chariots and charioteers. 10 They were also
King Solomon's chief officials—two hundred
and fifty officials supervising the men.
11 Solomon brought Pharaoh's daughter up
from the City of David to the palace he had
built for her, for he said, "My wife must not live
in the palace of David king of Israel, because

[a]19 The Hebrew is plural. [b]2 Hebrew *Huram,* a variant of *Hiram;* also in verse 18 [c]6 Or *charioteers*

the places the ark of the LORD has entered
are holy."
12 On the altar of the LORD that he had built
in front of the portico, Solomon sacrificed
burnt offerings to the LORD, 13 according to the
daily requirement for offerings commanded
by Moses for Sabbaths, New Moons and the
three annual feasts—the Feast of Unleavened
Bread, the Feast of Weeks and the Feast of Tabernacles. 14 In keeping with the ordinance of
his father David, he appointed the divisions
of the priests for their duties, and the Levites
to lead the praise and to assist the priests according to each day's requirement. He also
appointed the gatekeepers by divisions for the
various gates, because this was what David the
man of God had ordered. 15 They did not devi-
ate from the king's commands to the priests or
to the Levites in any matter, including that of
the treasuries.
16 All Solomon's work was carried out, from
the day the foundation of the temple of the
LORD was laid until its completion. So the temple of the LORD was finished.
17 Then Solomon went to Ezion Geber and
Elath on the coast of Edom. 18 And Hiram sent
him ships commanded by his own officers,
men who knew the sea. These, with Solomon's
men, sailed to Ophir and brought back four
hundred and fifty talents[a] of gold, which they
delivered to King Solomon.

The Queen of Sheba Visits Solomon

9 When the queen of Sheba heard of Solomon's fame, she came to Jerusalem to
test him with hard questions. Arriving with
a very great caravan—with camels carrying
spices, large quantities of gold, and precious
stones—she came to Solomon and talked with
him about all she had on her mind. 2 Solomon
answered all her questions; nothing was too
hard for him to explain to her. 3 When the
queen of Sheba saw the wisdom of Solomon, as
well as the palace he had built, 4 the food on his
table, the seating of his officials, the attending
servants in their robes, the cupbearers in their
robes and the burnt offerings he made at[b] the
temple of the LORD, she was overwhelmed.
5 She said to the king, "The report I heard
in my own country about your achievements
and your wisdom is true. 6 But I did not believe
what they said until I came and saw with my
own eyes. Indeed, not even half the greatness
of your wisdom was told me; you have far
exceeded the report I heard. 7 How happy your
men must be! How happy your officials, who
continually stand before you and hear your
wisdom! 8 Praise be to the LORD your God,
who has delighted in you and placed you on
his throne as king to rule for the LORD your
God. Because of the love of your God for Israel
and his desire to uphold them forever, he has
made you king over them, to maintain justice
and righteousness."
9 Then she gave the king 120 talents[c] of gold,
large quantities of spices, and precious stones.
There had never been such spices as those the
queen of Sheba gave to King Solomon.
10 (The men of Hiram and the men of Solomon brought gold from Ophir; they also
brought algumwood[d] and precious stones.
11 The king used the algumwood to make steps
for the temple of the LORD and for the royal
palace, and to make harps and lyres for the musicians. Nothing like them had ever been seen
in Judah.)
12 King Solomon gave the queen of Sheba
all she desired and asked for; he gave her
more than she had brought to him. Then she
left and returned with her retinue to her own
country.

Solomon's Splendor

13 The weight of the gold that Solomon received yearly was 666 talents,[e] 14 not including
the revenues brought in by merchants and
traders. Also all the kings of Arabia and the
governors of the land brought gold and silver
to Solomon.
15 King Solomon made two hundred large
shields of hammered gold; six hundred bekas[f]
of hammered gold went into each shield. 16 He
also made three hundred small shields of hammered gold, with three hundred bekas[g] of gold
in each shield. The king put them in the Palace
of the Forest of Lebanon.

[a] 18 That is, about 17 tons (about 16 metric tons) [b] 4 Or *the ascent by which he went up to* [c] 9 That is, about 4 1/2 tons (about 4 metric tons) [d] 10 Probably a variant of *almugwood* [e] 13 That is, about 25 tons (about 23 metric tons) [f] 15 That is, about 7 1/2 pounds (about 3.5 kilograms) [g] 16 That is, about 3 3/4 pounds (about 1.7 kilograms)

The Holy Other

2 Chronicles 8:11

Solomon brought Pharaoh's daughter up from the City of David to the palace he had built for her, for he said, "My wife must not live in the palace of David king of Israel, because the places the ark of the LORD has entered are holy."

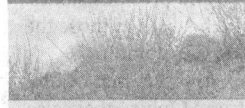

reflection

1 How do your unbelieving friends and family affect your attitude toward God?

2 What are some concrete ways you can keep holy what is holy, while still honoring and respecting the unbelievers you love?

3 Think about the burden you feel toward a spouse or loved one who wants nothing to do with the Lord. Spend time in prayer, giving your anxieties and grief about them to God.

RELATED READINGS

1 Kings 7:1–8; 11:1–13; Philippians 4:4–7; 1 Peter 3:1–6

Read: 2 Chronicles 8:1–11

DO YOU LIVE with an unbelieving husband, longing to someday witness his change of heart? Have you grown discouraged at how easily he picks apart your imperfections or the obvious faults he sees in "God's people"? Maybe it's not your husband but a parent, coworker or good friend who wants nothing to do with your faith. So you continue to suffer in silence. How can you live a life that honors God and cling to what is holy when those around you feel ambivalent, at best, or openly hostile, at worst, toward the God you love?

Solomon would have empathized with your plight. Second Chronicles 8 tells us that he married an Egyptian princess. Pharaoh's daughter was an ironic choice for the wisest man on earth. Was his memory so short that he did not recall the Israelites' miraculous escape from bondage to his wife's ancestors? And even if his wife was a believer in the true God, surely she had servants who worshiped Egyptian gods. Solomon recognized that God's holiness must take precedence over his wife's comfort, so he moved her and her household to the outskirts of Jerusalem. He separated her from God's holy place.

The princess must have known why she was being relocated. Did she resent this separation? Did she try to undermine Solomon's efforts to remain faithful to God? The Scriptural record does not say. We do learn later that in his old age, Solomon's heart was divided by the gods of his many wives. Ultimately, he could not keep his faith from being corrupted by the influence of those closest to him.

God knows the agony of loving those who, at present, want nothing to do with him. Think of all the people he created who openly reject him. Yet he still loves them and shows by example that his "kindness . . . leads [them] toward repentance" (Romans 2:4). In your own circumstances, follow God's example by being kind but firm. Be faithful to keep yourself wholly holy. By doing this you can help win your spouse, parent, child, colleague or friend to true belief. Be encouraged by Peter's words, "If any of them do not believe the word, they may be won over without words by [your] behavior" (1 Peter 3:1). You can rest in the knowledge that they are in God's loving hands . . . and so are you.

Go to page 535 for your next devotional reading.

17 Then the king made a great throne inlaid
with ivory and overlaid with pure gold. 18 The
throne had six steps, and a footstool of gold
was attached to it. On both sides of the seat
were armrests, with a lion standing beside each
of them. 19 Twelve lions stood on the six steps,
one at either end of each step. Nothing like it
had ever been made for any other kingdom.
20 All King Solomon's goblets were gold, and
all the household articles in the Palace of the
Forest of Lebanon were pure gold. Nothing was
made of silver, because silver was considered
of little value in Solomon's day. 21 The king had
a fleet of trading ships[a] manned by Hiram's[b]
men. Once every three years it returned, carrying gold, silver and ivory, and apes and baboons.

22 King Solomon was greater in riches and
wisdom than all the other kings of the earth.
23 All the kings of the earth sought audience
with Solomon to hear the wisdom God had
put in his heart. 24 Year after year, everyone
who came brought a gift—articles of silver
and gold, and robes, weapons and spices, and
horses and mules.

25 Solomon had four thousand stalls for
horses and chariots, and twelve thousand
horses,[c] which he kept in the chariot cities
and also with him in Jerusalem. 26 He ruled
over all the kings from the River[d] to the land
of the Philistines, as far as the border of Egypt.
27 The king made silver as common in Jerusalem as stones, and cedar as plentiful as sycamore-fig trees in the foothills. 28 Solomon's
horses were imported from Egypt[e] and from
all other countries.

Solomon's Death

29 As for the other events of Solomon's reign,
from beginning to end, are they not written
in the records of Nathan the prophet, in the
prophecy of Ahijah the Shilonite and in the
visions of Iddo the seer concerning Jeroboam
son of Nebat? 30 Solomon reigned in Jerusalem
over all Israel forty years. 31 Then he rested with
his fathers and was buried in the city of David
his father. And Rehoboam his son succeeded
him as king.

Israel Rebels Against Rehoboam

10 Rehoboam went to Shechem, for all the
Israelites had gone there to make him
king. 2 When Jeroboam son of Nebat heard this
(he was in Egypt, where he had fled from King
Solomon), he returned from Egypt. 3 So they
sent for Jeroboam, and he and all Israel went to
Rehoboam and said to him: 4 "Your father put
a heavy yoke on us, but now lighten the harsh
labor and the heavy yoke he put on us, and we
will serve you."

5 Rehoboam answered, "Come back to me in
three days." So the people went away.

6 Then King Rehoboam consulted the elders
who had served his father Solomon during his
lifetime. "How would you advise me to answer
these people?" he asked.

7 They replied, "If you will be kind to these
people and please them and give them a favorable answer, they will always be your servants."

8 But Rehoboam rejected the advice the elders gave him and consulted the young men
who had grown up with him and were serving
him. 9 He asked them, "What is your advice?
How should we answer these people who say to
me, 'Lighten the yoke your father put on us'?"

10 The young men who had grown up with
him replied, "Tell the people who have said to
you, 'Your father put a heavy yoke on us, but
make our yoke lighter'—tell them, 'My little
finger is thicker than my father's waist. 11 My
father laid on you a heavy yoke; I will make
it even heavier. My father scourged you with
whips; I will scourge you with scorpions.' "

12 Three days later Jeroboam and all the people returned to Rehoboam, as the king had
said, "Come back to me in three days." 13 The
king answered them harshly. Rejecting the advice of the elders, 14 he followed the advice of
the young men and said, "My father made your
yoke heavy; I will make it even heavier. My father scourged you with whips; I will scourge
you with scorpions." 15 So the king did not listen to the people, for this turn of events was
from God, to fulfill the word the LORD had spoken to Jeroboam son of Nebat through Ahijah
the Shilonite.

[a] 21 Hebrew *of ships that could go to Tarshish* [b] 21 Hebrew *Huram,* a variant of *Hiram* [c] 25 Or *charioteers* [d] 26 That is, the Euphrates
[e] 28 Or possibly *Muzur,* a region in Cilicia

16When all Israel saw that the king refused
to listen to them, they answered the king:

"What share do we have in David,
what part in Jesse's son?
To your tents, O Israel!
Look after your own house, O David!"

So all the Israelites went home. 17But as for
the Israelites who were living in the towns of
Judah, Rehoboam still ruled over them.

18King Rehoboam sent out Adoniram,[a]
who was in charge of forced labor, but the Israelites stoned him to death. King Rehoboam,
however, managed to get into his chariot and
escape to Jerusalem. 19So Israel has been in rebellion against the house of David to this day.

11 When Rehoboam arrived in Jerusalem, he mustered the house of Judah
and Benjamin—a hundred and eighty thousand fighting men—to make war against Israel
and to regain the kingdom for Rehoboam.

2But this word of the LORD came to Shemaiah the man of God: 3"Say to Rehoboam son
of Solomon king of Judah and to all the Israelites in Judah and Benjamin, 4'This is what
the LORD says: Do not go up to fight against
your brothers. Go home, every one of you, for
this is my doing.'" So they obeyed the words
of the LORD and turned back from marching
against Jeroboam.

Rehoboam Fortifies Judah

5Rehoboam lived in Jerusalem and built up
towns for defense in Judah: 6Bethlehem, Etam,
Tekoa, 7Beth Zur, Soco, Adullam, 8Gath, Mareshah, Ziph, 9Adoraim, Lachish, Azekah, 10Zo-
rah, Aijalon and Hebron. These were fortified
cities in Judah and Benjamin. 11He strengthened their defenses and put commanders in
them, with supplies of food, olive oil and wine.
12He put shields and spears in all the cities,
and made them very strong. So Judah and Benjamin were his.

13The priests and Levites from all their districts throughout Israel sided with him. 14The
Levites even abandoned their pasturelands and
property, and came to Judah and Jerusalem because Jeroboam and his sons had rejected them
as priests of the LORD. 15And he appointed his
own priests for the high places and for the
goat and calf idols he had made. 16Those from
every tribe of Israel who set their hearts on seeking the LORD, the God of Israel, followed the
Levites to Jerusalem to offer sacrifices to the
LORD, the God of their fathers. 17They strengthened the kingdom of Judah and supported
Rehoboam son of Solomon three years, walking in the ways of David and Solomon during
this time.

Rehoboam's Family

18Rehoboam married Mahalath, who was
the daughter of David's son Jerimoth and of
Abihail, the daughter of Jesse's son Eliab. 19She
bore him sons: Jeush, Shemariah and Zaham.
20Then he married Maacah daughter of Absalom, who bore him Abijah, Attai, Ziza and Shelomith. 21Rehoboam loved Maacah daughter
of Absalom more than any of his other wives
and concubines. In all, he had eighteen wives
and sixty concubines, twenty-eight sons and
sixty daughters.

22Rehoboam appointed Abijah son of Maacah to be the chief prince among his brothers,
in order to make him king. 23He acted wisely,
dispersing some of his sons throughout the districts of Judah and Benjamin, and to all the fortified cities. He gave them abundant provisions
and took many wives for them.

Shishak Attacks Jerusalem

12 After Rehoboam's position as king was
established and he had become strong,
he and all Israel[b] with him abandoned the law
of the LORD. 2Because they had been unfaithful to the LORD, Shishak king of Egypt attacked
Jerusalem in the fifth year of King Rehoboam.
3With twelve hundred chariots and sixty thousand horsemen and the innumerable troops of
Libyans, Sukkites and Cushites[c] that came with
him from Egypt, 4he captured the fortified cities of Judah and came as far as Jerusalem.

5Then the prophet Shemaiah came to
Rehoboam and to the leaders of Judah who
had assembled in Jerusalem for fear of Shishak,
and he said to them, "This is what the LORD
says, 'You have abandoned me; therefore, I now
abandon you to Shishak.'"

[a]18 Hebrew *Hadoram*, a variant of *Adoniram* [b]1 That is, Judah, as frequently in 2 Chronicles [c]3 That is, people from the upper Nile region

6The leaders of Israel and the king humbled
themselves and said, "The LORD is just."
7When the LORD saw that they humbled
themselves, this word of the LORD came to Shemaiah: "Since they have humbled themselves, I
will not destroy them but will soon give them
deliverance. My wrath will not be poured out
on Jerusalem through Shishak. 8They will,
however, become subject to him, so that they
may learn the difference between serving me
and serving the kings of other lands."
9When Shishak king of Egypt attacked Jerusalem, he carried off the treasures of the
temple of the LORD and the treasures of the
royal palace. He took everything, including
the gold shields Solomon had made. 10So King
Rehoboam made bronze shields to replace
them and assigned these to the commanders
of the guard on duty at the entrance to the
royal palace. 11Whenever the king went to the
LORD's temple, the guards went with him, bearing the shields, and afterward they returned
them to the guardroom.
12Because Rehoboam humbled himself, the
LORD's anger turned from him, and he was not
totally destroyed. Indeed, there was some good
in Judah.
13King Rehoboam established himself
firmly in Jerusalem and continued as king. He
was forty-one years old when he became king,
and he reigned seventeen years in Jerusalem,
the city the LORD had chosen out of all the
tribes of Israel in which to put his Name. His
mother's name was Naamah; she was an Ammonite. 14He did evil because he had not set
his heart on seeking the LORD.
15As for the events of Rehoboam's reign,
from beginning to end, are they not written
in the records of Shemaiah the prophet and of
Iddo the seer that deal with genealogies? There
was continual warfare between Rehoboam and
Jeroboam. 16Rehoboam rested with his fathers
and was buried in the City of David. And Abijah his son succeeded him as king.

Abijah King of Judah

13 In the eighteenth year of the reign of
Jeroboam, Abijah became king of Judah, 2and he reigned in Jerusalem three years.
His mother's name was Maacah,[a] a daughter[b]
of Uriel of Gibeah.
There was war between Abijah and Jeroboam.
3Abijah went into battle with a force of four
hundred thousand able fighting men, and
Jeroboam drew up a battle line against him
with eight hundred thousand able troops.
4Abijah stood on Mount Zemaraim, in the
hill country of Ephraim, and said, "Jeroboam
and all Israel, listen to me! 5Don't you know
that the LORD, the God of Israel, has given the
kingship of Israel to David and his descendants
forever by a covenant of salt? 6Yet Jeroboam son
of Nebat, an official of Solomon son of David,
rebelled against his master. 7Some worthless
scoundrels gathered around him and opposed
Rehoboam son of Solomon when he was
young and indecisive and not strong enough
to resist them.
8"And now you plan to resist the kingdom of
the LORD, which is in the hands of David's descendants. You are indeed a vast army and have
with you the golden calves that Jeroboam made
to be your gods. 9But didn't you drive out the
priests of the LORD, the sons of Aaron, and
the Levites, and make priests of your own as
the peoples of other lands do? Whoever comes
to consecrate himself with a young bull and
seven rams may become a priest of what are
not gods.
10"As for us, the LORD is our God, and we
have not forsaken him. The priests who serve
the LORD are sons of Aaron, and the Levites assist them. 11Every morning and evening they
present burnt offerings and fragrant incense
to the LORD. They set out the bread on the
ceremonially clean table and light the lamps on
the gold lampstand every evening. We are observing the requirements of the LORD our God.
But you have forsaken him. 12God is with us;
he is our leader. His priests with their trumpets
will sound the battle cry against you. Men of
Israel, do not fight against the LORD, the God of
your fathers, for you will not succeed."
13Now Jeroboam had sent troops around to
the rear, so that while he was in front of Judah
the ambush was behind them. 14Judah turned
and saw that they were being attacked at both
front and rear. Then they cried out to the LORD.

[a]2 Most Septuagint manuscripts and Syriac (see also 2 Chron. 11:20 and 1 Kings 15:2); Hebrew *Micaiah* [b]2 Or *granddaughter*

The priests blew their trumpets 15and the men
of Judah raised the battle cry. At the sound of
their battle cry, God routed Jeroboam and all
Israel before Abijah and Judah. 16The Israelites
fled before Judah, and God delivered them into
their hands. 17Abijah and his men inflicted
heavy losses on them, so that there were five
hundred thousand casualties among Israel's
able men. 18The men of Israel were subdued
on that occasion, and the men of Judah were
victorious because they relied on the LORD, the
God of their fathers.

19Abijah pursued Jeroboam and took from
him the towns of Bethel, Jeshanah and Ephron,
with their surrounding villages.
20Jeroboam did not regain
power during the time of Abijah. And the LORD struck him
down and he died.

21But Abijah grew in strength.
He married fourteen wives and
had twenty-two sons and sixteen daughters.

22The other events of Abijah's
reign, what he did and what he
said, are written in the annotations of the prophet Iddo.

14 And Abijah rested with
his fathers and was
buried in the City of David.
Asa his son succeeded him as
king, and in his days the country was at peace
for ten years.

> **2 Chronicles 14:11**
>
> *God Helps the Powerless*
>
> Then Asa called to the LORD his God and said, "LORD, there is no one like you to help the powerless against the mighty."

Asa King of Judah

2Asa did what was good and right in the
eyes of the LORD his God. 3He removed the foreign altars and the high places, smashed the sacred stones and cut down the Asherah poles.[a]
4He commanded Judah to seek the LORD, the
God of their fathers, and to obey his laws and
commands. 5He removed the high places and
incense altars in every town in Judah, and the
kingdom was at peace under him. 6He built up
the fortified cities of Judah, since the land was
at peace. No one was at war with him during
those years, for the LORD gave him rest.

7"Let us build up these towns," he said to Judah, "and put walls around them, with towers,
gates and bars. The land is still ours, because we
have sought the LORD our God; we sought him
and he has given us rest on every side." So they
built and prospered.

8Asa had an army of three hundred thousand men from Judah, equipped with large
shields and with spears, and two hundred and
eighty thousand from Benjamin, armed with
small shields and with bows. All these were
brave fighting men.

9Zerah the Cushite marched out against
them with a vast army[b] and three hundred
chariots, and came as far as Mareshah. 10Asa
went out to meet him, and they took up battle
positions in the Valley of Zeph-
athah near Mareshah.

11Then Asa called to the
LORD his God and said, "LORD,
there is no one like you to
help the powerless against the
mighty. Help us, O LORD our
God, for we rely on you, and
in your name we have come
against this vast army. O LORD,
you are our God; do not let
man prevail against you."

12The LORD struck down the
Cushites before Asa and Judah.
The Cushites fled, 13and Asa
and his army pursued them
as far as Gerar. Such a great
number of Cushites fell that they could not
recover; they were crushed before the LORD
and his forces. The men of Judah carried off a
large amount of plunder. 14They destroyed all
the villages around Gerar, for the terror of the
LORD had fallen upon them. They plundered
all these villages, since there was much booty
there. 15They also attacked the camps of the
herdsmen and carried off droves of sheep and
goats and camels. Then they returned to Jerusalem.

Asa's Reform

15 The Spirit of God came upon Azariah
son of Oded. 2He went out to meet
Asa and said to him, "Listen to me, Asa and
all Judah and Benjamin. The LORD is with you
when you are with him. If you seek him, he will

[a]3 That is, symbols of the goddess Asherah; here and elsewhere in 2 Chronicles [b]9 Hebrew *with an army of a thousand thousands* or *with an army of thousands upon thousands*

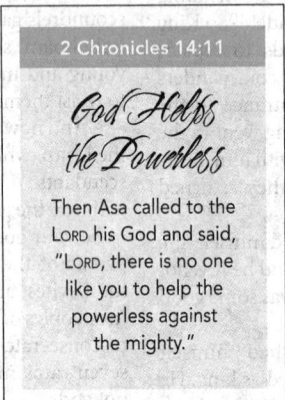

Good and Right

Read: 2 Chronicles 14:1–15

WHEN SHE WAS 11 years old, Victoria, the girl who would be queen, saw a royal family tree and supposedly remarked, "I am nearer to the throne than I thought." Then, according to her governess, she vowed, "I will be good." Queen Victoria's January 23, 1901, obituary in the New York Times said, "It was never quite so true as in her time that the British Empire was one on which the sun never set." Not only was Victoria a good queen, she was a godly queen. Engraved above the door at the Frogmore Royal Mausoleum where she lies buried beside her beloved Prince Albert are the inspiring words, "Farewell best beloved, here at last I shall rest with thee, with thee in Christ I shall rise again."

The day will come when our obituaries will be written. Others will review our lives and summarize what they saw in a few short words. We will have left our mark, and it will be too late to change it. The challenge now is to live so as to be remembered as good and godly women.

The chroniclers who wrote these books in the Bible were in large part eulogists, evaluating the lives of the kings of Israel. They recorded the good and bad history in black and white for us to read many years later. In the list of so many kings who did evil, King Asa stands out for doing what was good and right. He stepped up to a throne in a kingdom that was in spiritual disarray, and he made a deliberate choice: He and his people would seek the Lord and obey his laws.

In later days, when people reminisce about your life, what will they remember? Will they remember a woman who did what was good and right in the eyes of the Lord despite the cost? Will they remember a woman who continued to do God's work until her last days? What will your close friends remember? What about your husband, children, siblings, coworkers? As long as you draw breath, your mark on this world is still being made. It doesn't become indelible until after you're gone. There is still time to be remembered as someone who sought God and did her best to do what was "good and right."

2 Chronicles 14:2

Asa did what was good and right in the eyes of the LORD his God.

reflection

1 What kind of legacy are you leaving for those around you?

2 How can you make pleasing God the main desire of your heart? Insert your name in verse 2: "________ does what is good and right in the eyes of the LORD her God."

3 Think of one or two people you want to be at your funeral. What do you want them to remember about you?

RELATED READINGS

Ephesians 2:6–10; Colossians 3:23–25

Go to page 543 for your next devotional reading.

be found by you, but if you forsake him, he will forsake you. 3For a long time Israel was without the true God, without a priest to teach and without the law. 4But in their distress they turned to the LORD, the God of Israel, and sought him, and he was found by them. 5In those days it was not safe to travel about, for all the inhabitants of the lands were in great turmoil. 6One nation was being crushed by another and one city by another, because God was troubling them with every kind of distress. 7But as for you, be strong and do not give up, for your work will be rewarded."

> **2 Chronicles 15:7**
>
> *God Rewards*
>
> "But as for you, be strong and do not give up, for your work will be rewarded."

8When Asa heard these words and the prophecy of Azariah son of[a] Oded the prophet, he took courage. He removed the detestable idols from the whole land of Judah and Benjamin and from the towns he had captured in the hills of Ephraim. He repaired the altar of the LORD that was in front of the portico of the LORD's temple.

9Then he assembled all Judah and Benjamin and the people from Ephraim, Manasseh and Simeon who had settled among them, for large numbers had come over to him from Israel when they saw that the LORD his God was with him.

10They assembled at Jerusalem in the third month of the fifteenth year of Asa's reign. 11At that time they sacrificed to the LORD seven hundred head of cattle and seven thousand sheep and goats from the plunder they had brought back. 12They entered into a covenant to seek the LORD, the God of their fathers, with all their heart and soul. 13All who would not seek the LORD, the God of Israel, were to be put to death, whether small or great, man or woman. 14They took an oath to the LORD with loud acclamation, with shouting and with trumpets and horns. 15All Judah rejoiced about the oath because they had sworn it wholeheartedly. They sought God eagerly, and he was found by them. So the LORD gave them rest on every side.

16King Asa also deposed his grandmother Maacah from her position as queen mother, because she had made a repulsive Asherah pole. Asa cut the pole down, broke it up and burned it in the Kidron Valley. 17Although he did not remove the high places from Israel, Asa's heart was fully committed ⌞to the LORD⌟ all his life. 18He brought into the temple of God the silver and gold and the articles that he and his father had dedicated.

19There was no more war until the thirty-fifth year of Asa's reign.

Asa's Last Years

16 In the thirty-sixth year of Asa's reign Baasha king of Israel went up against Judah and fortified Ramah to prevent anyone from leaving or entering the territory of Asa king of Judah.

2Asa then took the silver and gold out of the treasuries of the LORD's temple and of his own palace and sent it to Ben-Hadad king of Aram, who was ruling in Damascus. 3"Let there be a treaty between me and you," he said, "as there was between my father and your father. See, I am sending you silver and gold. Now break your treaty with Baasha king of Israel so he will withdraw from me."

4Ben-Hadad agreed with King Asa and sent the commanders of his forces against the towns of Israel. They conquered Ijon, Dan, Abel Maim[b] and all the store cities of Naphtali. 5When Baasha heard this, he stopped building Ramah and abandoned his work. 6Then King Asa brought all the men of Judah, and they carried away from Ramah the stones and timber Baasha had been using. With them he built up Geba and Mizpah.

7At that time Hanani the seer came to Asa king of Judah and said to him: "Because you relied on the king of Aram and not on the LORD your God, the army of the king of Aram has escaped from your hand. 8Were not the Cushites[c] and Libyans a mighty army with great numbers of chariots and horsemen[d]? Yet when you relied on the LORD, he delivered them into your hand. 9For the eyes of the LORD range throughout the

[a]8 Vulgate and Syriac (see also Septuagint and verse 1); Hebrew does not have *Azariah son of.* [b]4 Also known as *Abel Beth Maacah*
[c]8 That is, people from the upper Nile region [d]8 Or *charioteers*

earth to strengthen those whose hearts are fully
committed to him. You have done a foolish
thing, and from now on you will be at war."
10 Asa was angry with the seer because of
this; he was so enraged that he
put him in prison. At the same
time Asa brutally oppressed
some of the people.
11 The events of Asa's reign,
from beginning to end, are written in the book of the kings of
Judah and Israel. 12 In the
thirty-ninth year of his reign
Asa was afflicted with a disease
in his feet. Though his disease
was severe, even in his illness
he did not seek help from the
LORD, but only from the physicians. 13 Then in the forty-first
year of his reign Asa died and
rested with his fathers. 14 They buried him in
the tomb that he had cut out for himself in the
City of David. They laid him on a bier covered
with spices and various blended perfumes, and
they made a huge fire in his honor.

> **2 Chronicles 16:9**
>
> *God Wants Committed Women*
>
> For the eyes of the LORD range throughout the earth to strengthen those whose hearts are fully committed to him.

Jehoshaphat King of Judah

17 Jehoshaphat his son succeeded him as
king and strengthened himself against
Israel. 2 He stationed troops in all the fortified
cities of Judah and put garrisons in Judah and
in the towns of Ephraim that his father Asa
had captured.
3 The LORD was with Jehoshaphat because in
his early years he walked in the ways his father
David had followed. He did not consult the
Baals 4 but sought the God of his father and followed his commands rather than the practices
of Israel. 5 The LORD established the kingdom
under his control; and all Judah brought gifts
to Jehoshaphat, so that he had great wealth and
honor. 6 His heart was devoted to the ways of
the LORD; furthermore, he removed the high
places and the Asherah poles from Judah.
7 In the third year of his reign he sent his officials Ben-Hail, Obadiah, Zechariah, Nethanel
and Micaiah to teach in the towns of Judah.
8 With them were certain Levites—Shemaiah,
Nethaniah, Zebadiah, Asahel, Shemiramoth,
Jehonathan, Adonijah, Tobijah and Tob-Ado-
nijah—and the priests Elishama and Jehoram.
9 They taught throughout Judah, taking with
them the Book of the Law of the LORD; they
went around to all the towns of Judah and
taught the people.
10 The fear of the LORD fell
on all the kingdoms of the
lands surrounding Judah, so
that they did not make war
with Jehoshaphat. 11 Some Philistines brought Jehoshaphat
gifts and silver as tribute, and
the Arabs brought him flocks:
seven thousand seven hun-
dred rams and seven thousand
seven hundred goats.
12 Jehoshaphat became more
and more powerful; he built
forts and store cities in Judah
13 and had large supplies in the
towns of Judah. He also kept experienced fighting men in Jerusalem. 14 Their
enrollment by families was as follows:

From Judah, commanders of units of 1,000:
Adnah the commander, with 300,000 fighting men;
15 next, Jehohanan the commander, with 280,000;
16 next, Amasiah son of Zicri, who volunteered himself for the service of the LORD, with 200,000.
17 From Benjamin:
Eliada, a valiant soldier, with 200,000 men armed with bows and shields;
18 next, Jehozabad, with 180,000 men armed for battle.

19 These were the men who served the king, besides those he stationed in the fortified cities
throughout Judah.

Micaiah Prophesies Against Ahab

18 Now Jehoshaphat had great wealth and
honor, and he allied himself with Ahab
by marriage. 2 Some years later he went down to
visit Ahab in Samaria. Ahab slaughtered many
sheep and cattle for him and the people with
him and urged him to attack Ramoth Gilead.
3 Ahab king of Israel asked Jehoshaphat king of
Judah, "Will you go with me against Ramoth
Gilead?"

Jehoshaphat replied, "I am as you are, and
my people as your people; we will join you
in the war." 4But Jehoshaphat also said to the
king of Israel, "First seek the counsel of the
LORD."

5So the king of Israel brought together the
prophets—four hundred men—and asked
them, "Shall we go to war against Ramoth
Gilead, or shall I refrain?"

"Go," they answered, "for God will give it
into the king's hand."

6But Jehoshaphat asked, "Is there not a
prophet of the LORD here whom we can inquire of?"

7The king of Israel answered Jehoshaphat,
"There is still one man through whom we can
inquire of the LORD, but I hate him because he
never prophesies anything good about me, but
always bad. He is Micaiah son of Imlah."

"The king should not say that," Jehoshaphat replied.

8So the king of Israel called one of his officials and said, "Bring Micaiah son of Imlah at
once."

9Dressed in their royal robes, the king of
Israel and Jehoshaphat king of Judah were sitting on their thrones at the threshing floor by
the entrance to the gate of Samaria, with all
the prophets prophesying before them. 10Now
Zedekiah son of Kenaanah had made iron
horns, and he declared, "This is what the LORD
says: 'With these you will gore the Arameans
until they are destroyed.'"

11All the other prophets were prophesying
the same thing. "Attack Ramoth Gilead and be
victorious," they said, "for the LORD will give it
into the king's hand."

12The messenger who had gone to summon
Micaiah said to him, "Look, as one man the
other prophets are predicting success for the
king. Let your word agree with theirs, and
speak favorably."

13But Micaiah said, "As surely as the LORD
lives, I can tell him only what my God says."

14When he arrived, the king asked him,
"Micaiah, shall we go to war against Ramoth
Gilead, or shall I refrain?"

"Attack and be victorious," he answered, "for
they will be given into your hand."

15The king said to him, "How many times
must I make you swear to tell me nothing but
the truth in the name of the LORD?"

16Then Micaiah answered, "I saw all Israel
scattered on the hills like sheep without a shepherd, and the LORD said, 'These people have no
master. Let each one go home in peace.'"

17The king of Israel said to Jehoshaphat,
"Didn't I tell you that he never prophesies anything good about me, but only bad?"

18Micaiah continued, "Therefore hear the
word of the LORD: I saw the LORD sitting on
his throne with all the host of heaven standing
on his right and on his left. 19And the LORD
said, 'Who will entice Ahab king of Israel into
attacking Ramoth Gilead and going to his
death there?'

"One suggested this, and another that.
20Finally, a spirit came forward, stood before
the LORD and said, 'I will entice him.'

"'By what means?' the LORD asked.

21"'I will go and be a lying spirit in the
mouths of all his prophets,' he said.

"'You will succeed in enticing him,' said the
LORD. 'Go and do it.'

22"So now the LORD has put a lying spirit
in the mouths of these prophets of yours. The
LORD has decreed disaster for you."

23Then Zedekiah son of Kenaanah went up
and slapped Micaiah in the face. "Which way
did the spirit from[a] the LORD go when he went
from me to speak to you?" he asked.

24Micaiah replied, "You will find out on the
day you go to hide in an inner room."

25The king of Israel then ordered, "Take Micaiah and send him back to Amon the ruler of
the city and to Joash the king's son, 26and say,
'This is what the king says: Put this fellow in
prison and give him nothing but bread and water until I return safely.'"

27Micaiah declared, "If you ever return
safely, the LORD has not spoken through me."
Then he added, "Mark my words, all you people!"

Ahab Killed at Ramoth Gilead

28So the king of Israel and Jehoshaphat king
of Judah went up to Ramoth Gilead. 29The
king of Israel said to Jehoshaphat, "I will enter
the battle in disguise, but you wear your royal

[a]23 Or *Spirit of*

robes." So the king of Israel disguised himself
and went into battle.
30Now the king of Aram had ordered his
chariot commanders, "Do not fight with anyone, small or great, except the king of Israel."
31When the chariot commanders saw Jehoshaphat, they thought, "This is the king of Israel."
So they turned to attack him, but Jehoshaphat
cried out, and the LORD helped him. God drew
them away from him, 32for when the chariot
commanders saw that he was not the king of
Israel, they stopped pursuing him.
33But someone drew his bow at random
and hit the king of Israel between the sections
of his armor. The king told the chariot driver,
"Wheel around and get me out of the fighting.
I've been wounded." 34All day long the battle
raged, and the king of Israel propped himself
up in his chariot facing the Arameans until evening. Then at sunset he died.

19 When Jehoshaphat king of Judah returned safely to his palace in Jerusalem, 2Jehu the seer, the son of Hanani, went
out to meet him and said to the king, "Should
you help the wicked and love[a] those who hate
the LORD? Because of this, the wrath of the
LORD is upon you. 3There is, however, some
good in you, for you have rid the land of the
Asherah poles and have set your heart on seeking God."

Jehoshaphat Appoints Judges

4Jehoshaphat lived in Jerusalem, and he went out again
among the people from Beersheba to the hill country of
Ephraim and turned them back
to the LORD, the God of their
fathers. 5He appointed judges
in the land, in each of the fortified cities of Judah. 6He told
them, "Consider carefully what
you do, because you are not
judging for man but for the
LORD, who is with you whenever you give a verdict. 7Now
let the fear of the LORD be upon
you. Judge carefully, for with the LORD our God
there is no injustice or partiality or bribery."

> 2 Chronicles 19:7
>
> *God Is Impartial*
>
> Now let the fear of the LORD be upon you. Judge carefully, for with the LORD our God there is no injustice or partiality or bribery.

8In Jerusalem also, Jehoshaphat appointed
some of the Levites, priests and heads of Israelite
families to administer the law of the LORD and
to settle disputes. And they lived in Jerusalem.
9He gave them these orders: "You must serve
faithfully and wholeheartedly in the fear of the
LORD. 10In every case that comes before you
from your fellow countrymen who live in the
cities—whether bloodshed or other concerns
of the law, commands, decrees or ordinances
—you are to warn them not to sin against the
LORD; otherwise his wrath will come on you and
your brothers. Do this, and you will not sin.
11"Amariah the chief priest will be over
you in any matter concerning the LORD, and
Zebadiah son of Ishmael, the leader of the tribe
of Judah, will be over you in any matter concerning the king, and the Levites will serve as
officials before you. Act with courage, and may
the LORD be with those who do well."

Jehoshaphat Defeats Moab and Ammon

20 After this, the Moabites and Ammonites with some of the Meunites[b] came
to make war on Jehoshaphat.
2Some men came and told Jehoshaphat, "A
vast army is coming against you from Edom,[c]
from the other side of the Sea.[d] It is already in
Hazazon Tamar" (that is, En Gedi). 3Alarmed,
Jehoshaphat resolved to inquire of the LORD,
and he proclaimed a fast for all Judah. 4The people of Judah came together to seek help from
the LORD; indeed, they came
from every town in Judah to
seek him.
5Then Jehoshaphat stood up
in the assembly of Judah and
Jerusalem at the temple of the
LORD in the front of the new
courtyard 6and said:

"O LORD, God of our fa-
thers, are you not the God
who is in heaven? You rule
over all the kingdoms of the
nations. Power and might
are in your hand, and no
one can withstand you. 7O our God, did
you not drive out the inhabitants of this

[a]2 Or *and make alliances with* [b]1 Some Septuagint manuscripts; Hebrew *Ammonites* [c]2 One Hebrew manuscript; most Hebrew manuscripts, Septuagint and Vulgate *Aram* [d]2 That is, the Dead Sea

land before your people Israel and give it
forever to the descendants of Abraham
your friend? 8They have lived in it and
have built in it a sanctuary for your Name,
saying, 9'If calamity comes upon us,
whether the sword of judgment, or plague
or famine, we will stand in your presence
before this temple that bears your Name
and will cry out to you in our distress, and
you will hear us and save us.'

10"But now here are men from Ammon, Moab and Mount Seir, whose
territory you would not allow Israel to
invade when they came from Egypt; so
they turned away from them and did not
destroy them. 11See how they are repaying us by coming to drive us out of the
possession you gave us as an inheritance.
12O our God, will you not judge them?
For we have no power to face this vast
army that is attacking us. We do not know
what to do, but our eyes are upon you."

13All the men of Judah, with their wives
and children and little ones, stood there before
the LORD.

14Then the Spirit of the LORD came upon
Jahaziel son of Zechariah, the son of Benaiah,
the son of Jeiel, the son of Mattaniah, a Levite
and descendant of Asaph, as he stood in the
assembly.

15He said: "Listen, King Jehoshaphat and all
who live in Judah and Jerusalem! This is what
the LORD says to you: 'Do not be afraid or discouraged because of this vast army. For the battle is not yours, but God's. 16Tomorrow march
down against them. They will be climbing up
by the Pass of Ziz, and you will find them at the
end of the gorge in the Desert of Jeruel. 17You
will not have to fight this battle. Take up your
positions; stand firm and see the deliverance
the LORD will give you, O Judah and Jerusalem.
Do not be afraid; do not be discouraged. Go
out to face them tomorrow, and the LORD will
be with you.'"

18Jehoshaphat bowed with his face to the
ground, and all the people of Judah and Jerusalem fell down in worship before the LORD.
19Then some Levites from the Kohathites and
Korahites stood up and praised the LORD, the
God of Israel, with a very loud voice.

20Early in the morning they left for the Desert of Tekoa. As they set out, Jehoshaphat stood
and said, "Listen to me, Judah and people of Jerusalem! Have faith in the LORD your God and
you will be upheld; have faith in his prophets
and you will be successful." 21After consulting
the people, Jehoshaphat appointed men to sing
to the LORD and to praise him for the splendor
of his[a] holiness as they went out at the head of
the army, saying:

"Give thanks to the LORD,
  for his love endures forever."

22As they began to sing and praise, the LORD
set ambushes against the men of Ammon and
Moab and Mount Seir who were invading Ju-
dah, and they were defeated. 23The men of Am-
mon and Moab rose up against the men from
Mount Seir to destroy and annihilate them.
After they finished slaughtering the men from
Seir, they helped to destroy one another.

24When the men of Judah came to the place
that overlooks the desert and looked toward
the vast army, they saw only dead bodies lying
on the ground; no one had escaped. 25So Jehoshaphat and his men went to carry off their
plunder, and they found among them a great
amount of equipment and clothing[b] and also
articles of value—more than they could take
away. There was so much plunder that it took
three days to collect it. 26On the fourth day
they assembled in the Valley of Beracah, where
they praised the LORD. This is why it is called
the Valley of Beracah[c] to this day.

27Then, led by Jehoshaphat, all the men of
Judah and Jerusalem returned joyfully to Jerusalem, for the LORD had given them cause to
rejoice over their enemies. 28They entered Jerusalem and went to the temple of the LORD with
harps and lutes and trumpets.

29The fear of God came upon all the kingdoms of the countries when they heard how
the LORD had fought against the enemies of
Israel. 30And the kingdom of Jehoshaphat was
at peace, for his God had given him rest on
every side.

[a]21 Or *him with the splendor of* [b]25 Some Hebrew manuscripts and Vulgate; most Hebrew manuscripts *corpses* [c]26 *Beracah* means *praise.*

The End of Jehoshaphat's Reign

31 So Jehoshaphat reigned over Judah. He
was thirty-five years old when
he became king of Judah,
and he reigned in Jerusalem
twenty-five years. His mother's
name was Azubah daughter
of Shilhi. 32 He walked in the
ways of his father Asa and did
not stray from them; he did
what was right in the eyes of
the LORD. 33 The high places,
however, were not removed,
and the people still had not
set their hearts on the God of
their fathers.
34 The other events of Jehoshaphat's reign, from beginning
to end, are written in the annals of Jehu son of
Hanani, which are recorded in the book of the
kings of Israel.
35 Later, Jehoshaphat king of Judah made an
alliance with Ahaziah king of Israel, who was
guilty of wickedness. 36 He agreed with him
to construct a fleet of trading ships.[a] After
these were built at Ezion Geber, 37 Eliezer son
of Dodavahu of Mareshah prophesied against
Jehoshaphat, saying, "Because you have made
an alliance with Ahaziah, the LORD will destroy
what you have made." The ships were wrecked
and were not able to set sail to trade.[b]

2 Chronicles 20:29

God Fights for His People

The fear of God came upon all the kingdoms of the countries when they heard how the LORD had fought against the enemies of Israel.

21 Then Jehoshaphat rested with his fathers and was buried with them in the
City of David. And Jehoram his son succeeded
him as king. 2 Jehoram's brothers, the sons of
Jehoshaphat, were Azariah, Jehiel, Zechariah,
Azariahu, Michael and Shephatiah. All these
were sons of Jehoshaphat king of Israel.[c] 3 Their
father had given them many gifts of silver and
gold and articles of value, as well as fortified cities in Judah, but he had given the kingdom to
Jehoram because he was his firstborn son.

Jehoram King of Judah

4 When Jehoram established himself firmly
over his father's kingdom, he put all his brothers to the sword along with some of the princes
of Israel. 5 Jehoram was thirty-two years old
when he became king, and he reigned in Jerusalem eight years. 6 He walked in the ways of
the kings of Israel, as the house of Ahab had
done, for he married a daugh-
ter of Ahab. He did evil in the
eyes of the LORD. 7 Nevertheless, because of the covenant
the LORD had made with David, the LORD was not willing
to destroy the house of David.
He had promised to maintain
a lamp for him and his descendants forever.
8 In the time of Jehoram,
Edom rebelled against Judah
and set up its own king. 9 So
Jehoram went there with his officers and all his chariots. The
Edomites surrounded him and
his chariot commanders, but he rose up and
broke through by night. 10 To this day Edom
has been in rebellion against Judah.
Libnah revolted at the same time, because Jehoram had forsaken the LORD, the God of his
fathers. 11 He had also built high places on the
hills of Judah and had caused the people of Jerusalem to prostitute themselves and had led
Judah astray.
12 Jehoram received a letter from Elijah the
prophet, which said:

"This is what the LORD, the God of your
father David, says: 'You have not walked
in the ways of your father Jehoshaphat
or of Asa king of Judah. 13 But you have
walked in the ways of the kings of Israel,
and you have led Judah and the people of
Jerusalem to prostitute themselves, just as
the house of Ahab did. You have also murdered your own brothers, members of
your father's house, men who were better
than you. 14 So now the LORD is about to
strike your people, your sons, your wives
and everything that is yours, with a heavy
blow. 15 You yourself will be very ill with a
lingering disease of the bowels, until the
disease causes your bowels to come out.'"

16 The LORD aroused against Jehoram the
hostility of the Philistines and of the Arabs
who lived near the Cushites. 17 They attacked

[a] 36 Hebrew *of ships that could go to Tarshish* [b] 37 Hebrew *sail for Tarshish* [c] 2 That is, Judah, as frequently in 2 Chronicles

Judah, invaded it and carried off all the goods
found in the king's palace, together with his
sons and wives. Not a son was left to him except Ahaziah,[a] the youngest.
18 After all this, the LORD afflicted Jehoram
with an incurable disease of the bowels. 19 In
the course of time, at the end of the second year,
his bowels came out because of the disease, and
he died in great pain. His people made no fire
in his honor, as they had for his fathers.
20 Jehoram was thirty-two years old when he
became king, and he reigned in Jerusalem eight
years. He passed away, to no one's regret, and
was buried in the City of David, but not in the
tombs of the kings.

Ahaziah King of Judah

22 The people of Jerusalem made Ahaziah, Jehoram's youngest son, king in
his place, since the raiders, who came with the
Arabs into the camp, had killed all the older
sons. So Ahaziah son of Jehoram king of Judah
began to reign.
2 Ahaziah was twenty-two[b] years old when
he became king, and he reigned in Jerusalem
one year. His mother's name was Athaliah, a
granddaughter of Omri.
3 He too walked in the ways of the house of
Ahab, for his mother encouraged him in doing
wrong. 4 He did evil in the eyes of the LORD,
as the house of Ahab had done, for after his
father's death they became his advisers, to his
undoing. 5 He also followed their counsel when
he went with Joram[c] son of Ahab king of Israel
to war against Hazael king of Aram at Ramoth
Gilead. The Arameans wounded Joram; 6 so he
returned to Jezreel to recover from the wounds
they had inflicted on him at Ramoth[d] in his
battle with Hazael king of Aram.
Then Ahaziah[e] son of Jehoram king of Judah
went down to Jezreel to see Joram son of Ahab
because he had been wounded.
7 Through Ahaziah's visit to Joram, God
brought about Ahaziah's downfall. When
Ahaziah arrived, he went out with Joram to
meet Jehu son of Nimshi, whom the LORD had
anointed to destroy the house of Ahab. 8 While
Jehu was executing judgment on the house of
Ahab, he found the princes of Judah and the
sons of Ahaziah's relatives, who had been attending Ahaziah, and he killed them. 9 He then
went in search of Ahaziah, and his men captured him while he was hiding in Samaria. He
was brought to Jehu and put to death. They buried him, for they said, "He was a son of Jehoshaphat, who sought the LORD with all his heart."
So there was no one in the house of Ahaziah
powerful enough to retain the kingdom.

Athaliah and Joash

10 When Athaliah the mother of Ahaziah
saw that her son was dead, she proceeded to
destroy the whole royal family of the house of
Judah. 11 But Jehosheba,[f] the daughter of King
Jehoram, took Joash son of Ahaziah and stole
him away from among the royal princes who
were about to be murdered and put him and
his nurse in a bedroom. Because Jehosheba,[f]
the daughter of King Jehoram and wife of the
priest Jehoiada, was Ahaziah's sister, she hid the
child from Athaliah so she could not kill him.
12 He remained hidden with them at the temple of God for six years while Athaliah ruled
the land.
23 In the seventh year Jehoiada showed
his strength. He made a covenant
with the commanders of units of a hundred:
Azariah son of Jeroham, Ishmael son of Jehohanan, Azariah son of Obed, Maaseiah son
of Adaiah, and Elishaphat son of Zicri. 2 They
went throughout Judah and gathered the Levites and the heads of Israelite families from all
the towns. When they came to Jerusalem, 3 the
whole assembly made a covenant with the king
at the temple of God.
Jehoiada said to them, "The king's son shall
reign, as the LORD promised concerning the descendants of David. 4 Now this is what you are
to do: A third of you priests and Levites who
are going on duty on the Sabbath are to keep
watch at the doors, 5 a third of you at the royal
palace and a third at the Foundation Gate, and
all the other men are to be in the courtyards of
the temple of the LORD. 6 No one is to enter the

[a] 17 Hebrew *Jehoahaz*, a variant of *Ahaziah* [b] 2 Some Septuagint manuscripts and Syriac (see also 2 Kings 8:26); Hebrew *forty-two* [c] 5 Hebrew *Jehoram*, a variant of *Joram*; also in verses 6 and 7 [d] 6 Hebrew *Ramah*, a variant of *Ramoth* [e] 6 Some Hebrew manuscripts, Septuagint, Vulgate and Syriac (see also 2 Kings 8:29); most Hebrew manuscripts *Azariah* [f] 11 Hebrew *Jehoshabeath*, a variant of *Jehosheba*

Make a Difference

Read: 2 Chronicles 22:10–12

CAN ONE WOMAN really make a difference in a community? What about in an entire nation? You might think the answer is no. But think again. When you read the story of Jehosheba in 2 Chronicles, you'll realize that the answer is a wholehearted yes.

When Jehosheba realized that Athaliah was determined to destroy the royal line of Judah, she bravely hid her nephew Joash in the temple until he was old enough to succeed to the throne. When Joash was seven years old, he ascended to the throne and later repaired the temple and tore down the altars to Baal. More important, he preserved the Messianic line. Jehosheba made a difference in the life of another person; but she also made decisions that affected the outcome of a nation, and ultimately, it made a difference for all of humanity. Because of Jehosheba's courage at this time in history, "our Lord descended from Judah" (Hebrews 7:14).

In the eleventh century, a woman of noble birth impacted a nation. Princess Margaret was exiled with her family when the Danes overran England. Educated in Hungary, she returned to England during the reign of her great-uncle, Edward the Confessor. As one of the last remaining members of the Saxon royal family, she fled north to the Royal Scots Court during the Norman Conquest. Beautiful, intelligent and devout, Margaret won the heart of the Scottish king, Malcolm Canmore, and married him in 1069. She is credited with instigating the reform of the Church of Scotland, which had reached a low point in its history. In her private life, Margaret avidly prayed and gave lavishly to the poor. Her position allowed her to free many Anglo-Saxon prisoners.

You may not see yourself as a woman of influence. You may feel shy about sharing your faith with your kids, friends, family or coworkers. But there are many ways you can make a difference. You can refuse to give in to peer pressure or refuse to give up on a prodigal. You can speak out in the voting booth or on the editorial page. When you stand up for God's standards, you might be surprised—like a small pebble thrown into a large body of water, your words, actions and prayers can ripple outward if you muster up the courage to take a stand.

2 Chronicles 22:11

But Jehosheba, the daughter of King Jehoram, took Joash son of Ahaziah and stole him away from among the royal princes who were about to be murdered and put him and his nurse in a bedroom. Because Jehosheba, the daughter of King Jehoram and wife of the priest Jehoiada, was Ahaziah's sister, she hid the child from Athaliah so she could not kill him.

reflection

1. What women in your community are having a great impact?
2. Over whom do you have the most influence?
3. As you reflect on Jehosheba and Queen Margaret, determine how you can inspire those around you for the kingdom of God.

RELATED READINGS

Exodus 1:15–17; Matthew 10:32–33; 1 Peter 2:9–10

Wednesday

Go to page 548 for your next devotional reading.

temple of the LORD except the priests and Levites on duty; they may enter because they are
consecrated, but all the other men are to guard
what the LORD has assigned to them.[a] 7The Levites are to station themselves around the king,
each man with his weapons in his hand. Anyone who enters the temple must be put to death.
Stay close to the king wherever he goes."
8The Levites and all the men of Judah did
just as Jehoiada the priest ordered. Each one
took his men—those who were going on duty
on the Sabbath and those who were going off
duty—for Jehoiada the priest had not released
any of the divisions. 9Then he gave the commanders of units of a hundred the spears and
the large and small shields that had belonged
to King David and that were in the temple of
God. 10He stationed all the men, each with his
weapon in his hand, around the king—near
the altar and the temple, from the south side to
the north side of the temple.
11Jehoiada and his sons brought out the
king's son and put the crown on him; they
presented him with a copy of the covenant and
proclaimed him king. They anointed him and
shouted, "Long live the king!"
12When Athaliah heard the noise of the people running and cheering the king, she went to
them at the temple of the LORD. 13She looked,
and there was the king, standing by his pillar at
the entrance. The officers and the trumpeters
were beside the king, and all the people of the
land were rejoicing and blowing trumpets, and
singers with musical instruments were leading
the praises. Then Athaliah tore her robes and
shouted, "Treason! Treason!"
14Jehoiada the priest sent out the commanders of units of a hundred, who were in charge
of the troops, and said to them: "Bring her out
between the ranks[b] and put to the sword anyone who follows her." For the priest had said,
"Do not put her to death at the temple of the
LORD." 15So they seized her as she reached
the entrance of the Horse Gate on the palace
grounds, and there they put her to death.
16Jehoiada then made a covenant that he and
the people and the king[c] would be the LORD's
people. 17All the people went to the temple of
Baal and tore it down. They smashed the altars
and idols and killed Mattan the priest of Baal in
front of the altars.
18Then Jehoiada placed the oversight of the
temple of the LORD in the hands of the priests,
who were Levites, to whom David had made
assignments in the temple, to present the burnt
offerings of the LORD as written in the Law of
Moses, with rejoicing and singing, as David
had ordered. 19He also stationed doorkeepers
at the gates of the LORD's temple so that no one
who was in any way unclean might enter.
20He took with him the commanders of
hundreds, the nobles, the rulers of the people
and all the people of the land and brought the
king down from the temple of the LORD. They
went into the palace through the Upper Gate
and seated the king on the royal throne, 21and
all the people of the land rejoiced. And the city
was quiet, because Athaliah had been slain
with the sword.

Joash Repairs the Temple

24 Joash was seven years old when he
became king, and he reigned in Jerusalem forty years. His mother's name was Zibiah;
she was from Beersheba. 2Joash did what was
right in the eyes of the LORD all the years of
Jehoiada the priest. 3Jehoiada chose two wives
for him, and he had sons and daughters.
4Some time later Joash decided to restore
the temple of the LORD. 5He called together
the priests and Levites and said to them, "Go
to the towns of Judah and collect the money
due annually from all Israel, to repair the temple of your God. Do it now." But the Levites did
not act at once.
6Therefore the king summoned Jehoiada the
chief priest and said to him, "Why haven't you
required the Levites to bring in from Judah and
Jerusalem the tax imposed by Moses the servant of the LORD and by the assembly of Israel
for the Tent of the Testimony?"
7Now the sons of that wicked woman Athaliah had broken into the temple of God and had
used even its sacred objects for the Baals.
8At the king's command, a chest was made
and placed outside, at the gate of the temple of
the LORD. 9A proclamation was then issued in

[a]6 Or *to observe the LORD's command ⌞not to enter⌟* [b]14 Or *out from the precincts* [c]16 Or *covenant between ⌞the LORD⌟ and the people and the king that they* (see 2 Kings 11:17)

Judah and Jerusalem that they should bring to
the LORD the tax that Moses the servant of God
had required of Israel in the desert. 10All the
officials and all the people
brought their contributions
gladly, dropping them into the
chest until it was full. 11When-
ever the chest was brought in
by the Levites to the king's officials and they saw that there
was a large amount of money,
the royal secretary and the officer of the chief priest would
come and empty the chest and
carry it back to its place. They
did this regularly and collected
a great amount of money.
12The king and Jehoiada gave it
to the men who carried out the
work required for the temple of
the LORD. They hired masons
and carpenters to restore the LORD's temple,
and also workers in iron and bronze to repair
the temple.
13The men in charge of the work were diligent, and the repairs progressed under them.
They rebuilt the temple of God according to
its original design and reinforced it. 14When
they had finished, they brought the rest of the
money to the king and Jehoiada, and with it
were made articles for the LORD's temple: articles for the service and for the burnt offerings,
and also dishes and other objects of gold and
silver. As long as Jehoiada lived, burnt offerings were presented continually in the temple
of the LORD.
15Now Jehoiada was old and full of years,
and he died at the age of a hundred and thirty.
16He was buried with the kings in the City of
David, because of the good he had done in
Israel for God and his temple.

The Wickedness of Joash

17After the death of Jehoiada, the officials of
Judah came and paid homage to the king, and
he listened to them. 18They abandoned the temple of the LORD, the God of their fathers, and
worshiped Asherah poles and idols. Because of
their guilt, God's anger came upon Judah and
Jerusalem. 19Although the LORD sent prophets
to the people to bring them back to him, and
though they testified against them, they would
not listen.

> **2 Chronicles 24:19**
>
> *God Sends People to Speak for Him*
>
> Although the LORD sent prophets to the people to bring them back to him, and though they testified against them, they would not listen.

20Then the Spirit of God
came upon Zechariah son of
Jehoiada the priest. He stood
before the people and said,
"This is what God says: 'Why
do you disobey the LORD's commands? You will not prosper.
Because you have forsaken the
LORD, he has forsaken you.' "
21But they plotted against
him, and by order of the king
they stoned him to death in the
courtyard of the LORD's temple.
22King Joash did not remember the kindness Zechariah's father Jehoiada had shown him
but killed his son, who said as
he lay dying, "May the LORD
see this and call you to account."
23At the turn of the year,[a] the army of Aram
marched against Joash; it invaded Judah and
Jerusalem and killed all the leaders of the people. They sent all the plunder to their king in
Damascus. 24Although the Aramean army
had come with only a few men, the LORD delivered into their hands a much larger army. Because Judah had forsaken the LORD, the God of
their fathers, judgment was executed on Joash.
25When the Arameans withdrew, they left Joash severely wounded. His officials conspired
against him for murdering the son of Jehoiada
the priest, and they killed him in his bed. So he
died and was buried in the City of David, but
not in the tombs of the kings.
26Those who conspired against him were Zabad,[b] son of Shimeath an Ammonite woman,
and Jehozabad, son of Shimrith[c] a Moabite
woman. 27The account of his sons, the many
prophecies about him, and the record of the
restoration of the temple of God are written in
the annotations on the book of the kings. And
Amaziah his son succeeded him as king.

Amaziah King of Judah

25 Amaziah was twenty-five years old
when he became king, and he reigned
in Jerusalem twenty-nine years. His mother's

[a]23 Probably in the spring [b]26 A variant of *Jozabad* [c]26 A variant of *Shomer*

name was Jehoaddin[a]; she was from Jerusalem. 2He did what was right in the eyes of the LORD, but not wholeheartedly. 3After the kingdom was firmly in his control, he executed the officials who had murdered his father the king. 4Yet he did not put their sons to death, but acted in accordance with what is written in the Law, in the Book of Moses, where the LORD commanded: "Fathers shall not be put to death for their children, nor children put to death for their fathers; each is to die for his own sins."[b]

5Amaziah called the people of Judah together and assigned them according to their families to commanders of thousands and commanders of hundreds for all Judah and Benjamin. He then mustered those twenty years old or more and found that there were three hundred thousand men ready for military service, able to handle the spear and shield. 6He also hired a hundred thousand fighting men from Israel for a hundred talents[c] of silver.

7But a man of God came to him and said, "O king, these troops from Israel must not march with you, for the LORD is not with Israel—not with any of the people of Ephraim. 8Even if you go and fight courageously in battle, God will overthrow you before the enemy, for God has the power to help or to overthrow."

9Amaziah asked the man of God, "But what about the hundred talents I paid for these Israelite troops?"

The man of God replied, "The LORD can give you much more than that."

10So Amaziah dismissed the troops who had come to him from Ephraim and sent them home. They were furious with Judah and left for home in a great rage.

11Amaziah then marshaled his strength and led his army to the Valley of Salt, where he killed ten thousand men of Seir. 12The army of Judah also captured ten thousand men alive, took them to the top of a cliff and threw them down so that all were dashed to pieces.

2 Chronicles 25:9

God Has Unlimited Wealth

Amaziah asked the man of God, "But what about the hundred talents I paid for these Israelite troops?" The man of God replied, "The LORD can give you much more than that."

13Meanwhile the troops that Amaziah had sent back and had not allowed to take part in the war raided Judean towns from Samaria to Beth Horon. They killed three thousand people and carried off great quantities of plunder.

14When Amaziah returned from slaughtering the Edomites, he brought back the gods of the people of Seir. He set them up as his own gods, bowed down to them and burned sacrifices to them. 15The anger of the LORD burned against Amaziah, and he sent a prophet to him, who said, "Why do you consult this people's gods, which could not save their own people from your hand?"

16While he was still speaking, the king said to him, "Have we appointed you an adviser to the king? Stop! Why be struck down?"

So the prophet stopped but said, "I know that God has determined to destroy you, because you have done this and have not listened to my counsel."

17After Amaziah king of Judah consulted his advisers, he sent this challenge to Jehoash[d] son of Jehoahaz, the son of Jehu, king of Israel: "Come, meet me face to face."

18But Jehoash king of Israel replied to Amaziah king of Judah: "A thistle in Lebanon sent a message to a cedar in Lebanon, 'Give your daughter to my son in marriage.' Then a wild beast in Lebanon came along and trampled the thistle underfoot. 19You say to yourself that you have defeated Edom, and now you are arrogant and proud. But stay at home! Why ask for trouble and cause your own downfall and that of Judah also?"

20Amaziah, however, would not listen, for God so worked that he might hand them over to ⌊Jehoash⌋, because they sought the gods of Edom. 21So Jehoash king of Israel attacked. He and Amaziah king of Judah faced each other at Beth Shemesh in Judah. 22Judah was routed by Israel, and every man fled to his home. 23Jehoash king of Israel cap-

[a]1 Hebrew *Jehoaddan*, a variant of *Jehoaddin* [b]4 Deut. 24:16 [c]6 That is, about 3 3/4 tons (about 3.4 metric tons); also in verse 9
[d]17 Hebrew *Joash*, a variant of *Jehoash*; also in verses 18, 21, 23 and 25

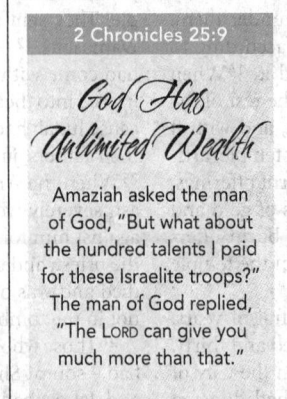

tured Amaziah king of Judah, the son of Joash,
the son of Ahaziah,[a] at Beth Shemesh. Then
Jehoash brought him to Jerusalem and broke
down the wall of Jerusalem from the Ephraim
Gate to the Corner Gate—a section about six
hundred feet[b] long. 24 He took all the gold and
silver and all the articles found in the temple of
God that had been in the care of Obed-Edom,
together with the palace treasures and the
hostages, and returned to Samaria.

25 Amaziah son of Joash king of Judah lived
for fifteen years after the death of Jehoash son
of Jehoahaz king of Israel. 26 As for the other
events of Amaziah's reign, from beginning to
end, are they not written in the book of the
kings of Judah and Israel? 27 From the time
that Amaziah turned away from following the
LORD, they conspired against him in Jerusalem
and he fled to Lachish, but they sent men after
him to Lachish and killed him there. 28 He was
brought back by horse and was buried with his
fathers in the City of Judah.

Uzziah King of Judah

26 Then all the people of Judah took
Uzziah,[c] who was sixteen years old,
and made him king in place of his father Amaziah. 2 He was the one who rebuilt Elath and
restored it to Judah after Amaziah rested with
his fathers.

3 Uzziah was sixteen years old when he became king, and he reigned in Jerusalem fifty-
two years. His mother's name was Jecoliah; she
was from Jerusalem. 4 He did what was right in
the eyes of the LORD, just as his father Amaziah
had done. 5 He sought God during the days of
Zechariah, who instructed him in the fear[d] of
God. As long as he sought the LORD, God gave
him success.

6 He went to war against the Philistines and
broke down the walls of Gath, Jabneh and Ashdod. He then rebuilt towns near Ashdod and
elsewhere among the Philistines. 7 God helped
him against the Philistines and against the
Arabs who lived in Gur Baal and against the
Meunites. 8 The Ammonites brought tribute to
Uzziah, and his fame spread as far as the border
of Egypt, because he had become very powerful.

9 Uzziah built towers in Jerusalem at the Corner Gate, at the Valley Gate and at the angle of
the wall, and he fortified them. 10 He also built
towers in the desert and dug many cisterns,
because he had much livestock in the foothills
and in the plain. He had people working his
fields and vineyards in the hills and in the fertile lands, for he loved the soil.

11 Uzziah had a well-trained army, ready
to go out by divisions according to their numbers as mustered by Jeiel the secretary and
Maaseiah the officer under the direction of
Hananiah, one of the royal officials. 12 The total number of family leaders over the fighting
men was 2,600. 13 Under their command was
an army of 307,500 men trained for war, a
powerful force to support the king against his
enemies. 14 Uzziah provided shields, spears,
helmets, coats of armor, bows and slingstones
for the entire army. 15 In Jerusalem he made
machines designed by skillful men for use on
the towers and on the corner defenses to shoot
arrows and hurl large stones. His fame spread
far and wide, for he was greatly helped until he
became powerful.

16 But after Uzziah became powerful, his
pride led to his downfall. He was unfaithful
to the LORD his God, and entered the temple
of the LORD to burn incense on the altar of incense. 17 Azariah the priest with eighty other
courageous priests of the LORD followed him
in. 18 They confronted him and said, "It is not
right for you, Uzziah, to burn incense to the
LORD. That is for the priests, the descendants
of Aaron, who have been consecrated to burn
incense. Leave the sanctuary, for you have been
unfaithful; and you will not be honored by the
LORD God."

19 Uzziah, who had a censer in his hand
ready to burn incense, became angry. While
he was raging at the priests in their presence
before the incense altar in the LORD's temple,
leprosy[e] broke out on his forehead. 20 When
Azariah the chief priest and all the other priests
looked at him, they saw that he had leprosy on
his forehead, so they hurried him out. Indeed,
he himself was eager to leave, because the LORD
had afflicted him.

[a] 23 Hebrew *Jehoahaz*, a variant of *Ahaziah* [b] 23 Hebrew *four hundred cubits* (about 180 meters) [c] 1 Also called *Azariah* [d] 5 Many Hebrew manuscripts, Septuagint and Syriac; other Hebrew manuscripts *vision* [e] 19 The Hebrew word was used for various diseases affecting the skin—not necessarily leprosy; also in verses 20, 21 and 23.

The Good and Bad of Pride

Read: 2 Chronicles 26:1–23

2 Chronicles 26:16

But after Uzziah became powerful, his pride led to his downfall.

reflection

1 What are the things you take a healthy pride in (for example, your abilities, children, etc.)? Do you have trouble acknowledging that you do some things well?

2 What things has God done in and through your life that you can boast about?

3 How does God's work in your life cause you to feel less proud and more humble?

RELATED READINGS

Psalm 10:4–18; Proverbs 16:18–20; 22:4; James 3:13–16

IT'S INTERESTING HOW one simple word can conjure up two opposing connotations. For example, when you hear the word *food*, do you respond by feeling grateful for the nutritional elements of food or are you plagued with guilt for indulging in less than healthy choices? Some foods can build up your health; other foods tear it down.

The word *pride* also has two connotations. In the context of self-respect and dignity, pride motivates us to tend to our health and general well-being and to appreciate our God-given talents and strengths. We don't often talk about this kind of pride.

The flip side of pride offers a warning—with good reason. The evil inclination of pride contains self-centeredness that leads downward. Rather than building spiritual health, the other side of pride carves out a path of destruction: arrogance, conceit and egotism.

Crowned king at the tender age of 16, Uzziah knew success as long as he sought God. But his career as king careened out of control when pride clouded his vision of himself and of God. Within this chapter, we observe how a once good king spiritually declined to a leprous and isolated man. What a prime example of the adage, "Power corrupts." King Uzziah's power and fame inflated the evil inclinations of his pride, which ultimately led to his downfall.

Have you ever witnessed the downfall of another person? Have you watched someone make a horrible choice when you knew they should stop and turn around? Maybe you watched your parents divorce, and nothing you said made a difference. Maybe right now you're watching a child that you love turn prodigal, and your heart is breaking because she's choosing not to listen to you or God.

So how do we cultivate the right kind of pride in our lives? Just as a healthy diet requires the right balance of foods, the right kind of pride requires balancing humility with a right relationship with God. When we understand that the positive and wonderful gifts he's given us come directly from him, we learn to cultivate healthy pride, not in ourselves, but in the Lord who has given us everything. As Paul wrote, "Let him who boasts boast in the Lord" (2 Corinthians 10:17).

Go to page 551 for your next devotional reading.

[21]King Uzziah had leprosy until the day he
died. He lived in a separate house[a]—leprous,
and excluded from the temple of the LORD. Jotham his son had charge of the palace and governed the people of the land.
[22]The other events of Uzziah's reign, from
beginning to end, are recorded by the prophet
Isaiah son of Amoz. [23]Uzziah rested with his
fathers and was buried near them in a field
for burial that belonged to the kings, for people said, "He had leprosy." And Jotham his son
succeeded him as king.

Jotham King of Judah

27 Jotham was twenty-five years old
when he became king, and he reigned
in Jerusalem sixteen years. His mother's name
was Jerusha daughter of Zadok. [2]He did what
was right in the eyes of the LORD, just as his
father Uzziah had done, but unlike him he did
not enter the temple of the LORD. The people,
however, continued their corrupt practices.
[3]Jotham rebuilt the Upper Gate of the temple
of the LORD and did extensive work on the
wall at the hill of Ophel. [4]He built towns in
the Judean hills and forts and towers in the
wooded areas.
[5]Jotham made war on the king of the Ammonites and conquered them. That year the
Ammonites paid him a hundred talents[b] of silver, ten thousand cors[c] of wheat and ten thousand cors of barley. The Ammonites brought
him the same amount also in the second and
third years.
[6]Jotham grew powerful because he walked
steadfastly before the LORD his God.
[7]The other events in Jotham's reign, including all his wars and the other things he did, are
written in the book of the kings of Israel and
Judah. [8]He was twenty-five years old when he
became king, and he reigned in Jerusalem sixteen years. [9]Jotham rested with his fathers and
was buried in the City of David. And Ahaz his
son succeeded him as king.

Ahaz King of Judah

28 Ahaz was twenty years old when he
became king, and he reigned in Jerusalem sixteen years. Unlike David his father,
he did not do what was right in the eyes of the
LORD. [2]He walked in the ways of the kings of
Israel and also made cast idols for worshiping
the Baals. [3]He burned sacrifices in the Valley of
Ben Hinnom and sacrificed his sons in the fire,
following the detestable ways of the nations the
LORD had driven out before the Israelites. [4]He
offered sacrifices and burned incense at the
high places, on the hilltops and under every
spreading tree.
[5]Therefore the LORD his God handed him
over to the king of Aram. The Arameans
defeated him and took many of his people as
prisoners and brought them to Damascus.
He was also given into the hands of the king
of Israel, who inflicted heavy casualties on
him. [6]In one day Pekah son of Remaliah killed
a hundred and twenty thousand soldiers in Judah—because Judah had forsaken the LORD,
the God of their fathers. [7]Zicri, an Ephraimite
warrior, killed Maaseiah the king's son, Azrikam the officer in charge of the palace, and Elkanah, second to the king. [8]The Israelites took
captive from their kinsmen two hundred thousand wives, sons and daughters. They also took
a great deal of plunder, which they carried back
to Samaria.
[9]But a prophet of the LORD named Oded
was there, and he went out to meet the army
when it returned to Samaria. He said to them,
"Because the LORD, the God of your fathers,
was angry with Judah, he gave them into your
hand. But you have slaughtered them in a rage
that reaches to heaven. [10]And now you intend
to make the men and women of Judah and Jerusalem your slaves. But aren't you also guilty of
sins against the LORD your God? [11]Now listen
to me! Send back your fellow countrymen you
have taken as prisoners, for the LORD's fierce
anger rests on you."
[12]Then some of the leaders in Ephraim—
Azariah son of Jehohanan, Berekiah son of
Meshillemoth, Jehizkiah son of Shallum, and
Amasa son of Hadlai—confronted those who
were arriving from the war. [13]"You must not
bring those prisoners here," they said, "or we
will be guilty before the LORD. Do you intend
to add to our sin and guilt? For our guilt is

[a]21 Or *in a house where he was relieved of responsibilities* [b]5 That is, about 3 3/4 tons (about 3.4 metric tons) [c]5 That is, probably about 62,000 bushels (about 2,200 kiloliters)

already great, and his fierce anger rests on
Israel."
14So the soldiers gave up the prisoners and
plunder in the presence of the officials and all
the assembly. 15The men designated by name
took the prisoners, and from the plunder they
clothed all who were naked. They provided
them with clothes and sandals, food and drink,
and healing balm. All those who were weak
they put on donkeys. So they took them back
to their fellow countrymen at Jericho, the City
of Palms, and returned to Samaria.
16At that time King Ahaz sent to the king[a]
of Assyria for help. 17The Edomites had again
come and attacked Judah and carried away
prisoners, 18while the Philistines had raided
towns in the foothills and in the Negev of Judah. They captured and occupied Beth Shemesh, Aijalon and Gederoth, as well as Soco,
Timnah and Gimzo, with their surrounding
villages. 19The LORD had humbled Judah
because of Ahaz king of Israel,[b] for he had
promoted wickedness in Judah and had been
most unfaithful to the LORD. 20Tiglath-Pileser[c]
king of Assyria came to him, but he gave him
trouble instead of help. 21Ahaz took some of
the things from the temple of the LORD and
from the royal palace and from the princes
and presented them to the king of Assyria, but
that did not help him.
22In his time of trouble King Ahaz became
even more unfaithful to the
LORD. 23He offered sacrifices
to the gods of Damascus,
who had defeated him; for he
thought, "Since the gods of
the kings of Aram have helped
them, I will sacrifice to them
so they will help me." But they
were his downfall and the
downfall of all Israel.
24Ahaz gathered together
the furnishings from the temple of God and took them
away.[d] He shut the doors of
the LORD's temple and set up
altars at every street corner in Jerusalem. 25In
every town in Judah he built high places to
burn sacrifices to other gods and provoked the
LORD, the God of his fathers, to anger.
26The other events of his reign and all his
ways, from beginning to end, are written in the
book of the kings of Judah and Israel. 27Ahaz
rested with his fathers and was buried in the
city of Jerusalem, but he was not placed in
the tombs of the kings of Israel. And Hezekiah
his son succeeded him as king.

Hezekiah Purifies the Temple

29 Hezekiah was twenty-five years old
when he became king, and he reigned
in Jerusalem twenty-nine years. His mother's
name was Abijah daughter of Zechariah. 2He
did what was right in the eyes of the LORD, just
as his father David had done.
3In the first month of the first year of his
reign, he opened the doors of the temple of the
LORD and repaired them. 4He brought in
the priests and the Levites, assembled them in
the square on the east side 5and said: "Listen to
me, Levites! Consecrate yourselves now and
consecrate the temple of the LORD, the God of
your fathers. Remove all defilement from the
sanctuary. 6Our fathers were unfaithful; they
did evil in the eyes of the LORD our God and
forsook him. They turned their faces away
from the LORD's dwelling place and turned
their backs on him. 7They also shut the doors
of the portico and put out the lamps. They did
not burn incense or present
any burnt offerings at the sanctuary to the God of Israel.
8Therefore, the anger of the
LORD has fallen on Judah and
Jerusalem; he has made them
an object of dread and horror
and scorn, as you can see with
your own eyes. 9This is why
our fathers have fallen by the
sword and why our sons and
daughters and our wives are in
captivity. 10Now I intend to
make a covenant with the
LORD, the God of Israel, so that
his fierce anger will turn away from us. 11My
sons, do not be negligent now, for the LORD has

> **2 Chronicles 29:10**
>
> *God Withholds His Wrath*
>
> "Now I intend to make a covenant with the LORD, the God of Israel, so that his fierce anger will turn away from us."

[a]16 One Hebrew manuscript, Septuagint and Vulgate (see also 2 Kings 16:7); most Hebrew manuscripts *kings* [b]19 That is, Judah, as frequently in 2 Chronicles [c]20 Hebrew *Tilgath-Pilneser,* a variant of *Tiglath-Pileser* [d]24 Or *and cut them up*

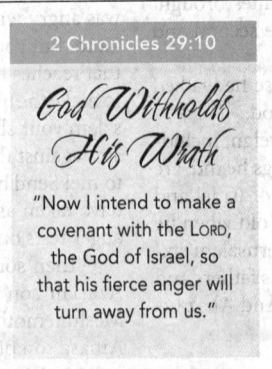

First Things First

Read: 2 Chronicles 29:1–11

WHAT WOULD YOU do if you were elected president of the world? What would be the first thing on your official to-do list? Eliminate world hunger? Disarm all nuclear weapons? Wipe out poverty?

Hezekiah was only 25 years old when he became king of Judah. His first priority was to repair the temple and reestablish worship, helping the people reconnect with God. In 2 Kings we're told that "Hezekiah trusted in the LORD, the God of Israel. There was no one like him among all the kings of Judah, either before him or after him . . . And the LORD was with him; he was successful in whatever he undertook" (2 Kings 18:5,7). Hezekiah's most notable accomplishment in his 29-year reign was drawing his people back to God.

Most likely you will not be chosen to rule a country, but you are the queen of your castle—your home. So what is the first thing on your to-do list each day? What is your number one priority? Eliminate your kids' hunger? Disarm family disputes? Tackle the budget? Or when you get up, do you put your house in order by first putting your heart in order? The best way to run a home, a business or a country is from your knees in prayer.

Take a cue from Hezekiah . . . and from David and Jesus. Each of them gave their relationship with God top priority. David wrote, "The LORD has heard my cry for mercy; the LORD accepts my prayer" (Psalm 6:9). "Jesus got up, left the house and went off to a solitary place, where he prayed" (Mark 1:35). They both put first things first by spending time with God even in the midst of other pressing needs.

Like Hezekiah, we have only a short time to make a difference to those in our small kingdoms. We cannot afford not to avail ourselves of God's wisdom and strength. Open the doors of your heart's temple and keep them open as you go about your day, submitting your thoughts and actions to God. Think of Jesus sitting beside you while you drive, in your office, at the kitchen table—and talk to him as you would a friend. And whenever possible, schedule extended prayer times into your life when you can choose "what is better" (Luke 10:42) by sitting at his feet and listening to him.

2 Chronicles 29:3
In the first month of the first year of his reign, he opened the doors of the temple of the LORD and repaired them.

reflection

1 You really are the "queen of your house." What things need your attention each day?

2 What do you see as important in your life?

3 How is God asking you to adjust your priorities to put first things first?

RELATED READINGS

2 Chronicles 7:12–16;
Psalm 5:1–3;
Luke 10:38–42;
1 Thessalonians 5:16–18

"If God is not first in our thoughts and efforts in the morning, he will be in the last place the remainder of the day."

E. M. Bounds

Go to page 564 for your next devotional reading.

chosen you to stand before him and serve him, to minister before him and to burn incense."

12 Then these Levites set to work:
from the Kohathites,
Mahath son of Amasai and Joel son of Azariah;
from the Merarites,
Kish son of Abdi and Azariah son of Jehallelel;
from the Gershonites,
Joah son of Zimmah and Eden son of Joah;
13 from the descendants of Elizaphan,
Shimri and Jeiel;
from the descendants of Asaph,
Zechariah and Mattaniah;
14 from the descendants of Heman,
Jehiel and Shimei;
from the descendants of Jeduthun,
Shemaiah and Uzziel.

15 When they had assembled their brothers
and consecrated themselves, they went in to
purify the temple of the LORD, as the king had
ordered, following the word of the LORD. 16 The
priests went into the sanctuary of the LORD to
purify it. They brought out to the courtyard of
the LORD's temple everything unclean that they
found in the temple of the LORD. The Levites
took it and carried it out to the Kidron Valley.
17 They began the consecration on the first day
of the first month, and by the eighth day of the
month they reached the portico of the LORD.
For eight more days they consecrated the temple of the LORD itself, finishing on the sixteenth day of the first month.

18 Then they went in to King Hezekiah and
reported: "We have purified the entire temple
of the LORD, the altar of burnt offering with
all its utensils, and the table for setting out the
consecrated bread, with all its articles. 19 We
have prepared and consecrated all the articles
that King Ahaz removed in his unfaithfulness
while he was king. They are now in front of the LORD's altar."

20 Early the next morning King Hezekiah
gathered the city officials together and went
up to the temple of the LORD. 21 They brought
seven bulls, seven rams, seven male lambs and
seven male goats as a sin offering for the kingdom, for the sanctuary and for Judah. The king
commanded the priests, the descendants of
Aaron, to offer these on the altar of the LORD.
22 So they slaughtered the bulls, and the priests
took the blood and sprinkled it on the altar;
next they slaughtered the rams and sprinkled
their blood on the altar; then they slaughtered
the lambs and sprinkled their blood on the altar.
23 The goats for the sin offering were brought
before the king and the assembly, and they laid
their hands on them. 24 The priests then slaughtered the goats and presented their blood on
the altar for a sin offering to atone for all Israel,
because the king had ordered the burnt offering and the sin offering for all Israel.

25 He stationed the Levites in the temple of
the LORD with cymbals, harps and lyres in the
way prescribed by David and Gad the king's seer
and Nathan the prophet; this was commanded
by the LORD through his prophets. 26 So the Levites stood ready with David's instruments, and
the priests with their trumpets.

27 Hezekiah gave the order to sacrifice the
burnt offering on the altar. As the offering began, singing to the LORD began also, accompanied by trumpets and the instruments of David
king of Israel. 28 The whole assembly bowed in
worship, while the singers sang and the trumpeters played. All this continued until the sacrifice of the burnt offering was completed.

29 When the offerings were finished, the king
and everyone present with him knelt down and
worshiped. 30 King Hezekiah and his officials
ordered the Levites to praise the LORD with the
words of David and of Asaph the seer. So they
sang praises with gladness and bowed their
heads and worshiped.

31 Then Hezekiah said, "You have now dedicated yourselves to the LORD. Come and bring
sacrifices and thank offerings to the temple of
the LORD." So the assembly brought sacrifices
and thank offerings, and all whose hearts were
willing brought burnt offerings.

32 The number of burnt offerings the assembly brought was seventy bulls, a hundred rams
and two hundred male lambs—all of them for
burnt offerings to the LORD. 33 The animals
consecrated as sacrifices amounted to six hundred bulls and three thousand sheep and goats.
34 The priests, however, were too few to skin
all the burnt offerings; so their kinsmen the Le-

vites helped them until the task was finished
and until other priests had been consecrated,
for the Levites had been more conscientious in
consecrating themselves than the priests had
been. 35 There were burnt of-
ferings in abundance, together
with the fat of the fellowship
offerings[a] and the drink offerings that accompanied the
burnt offerings.
So the service of the temple
of the LORD was reestablished.
36 Hezekiah and all the people rejoiced at what God had
brought about for his people,
because it was done so quickly.

> **2 Chronicles 30:9**
>
> *God Is Compassionate*
>
> "If you return to the LORD, then your brothers and your children will be shown compassion by their captors and will come back to this land, for the LORD your God is gracious and compassionate."

Hezekiah Celebrates the Passover

30 Hezekiah sent word to
all Israel and Judah and
also wrote letters to Ephraim
and Manasseh, inviting them
to come to the temple of the
LORD in Jerusalem and celebrate the Passover
to the LORD, the God of Israel. 2 The king and
his officials and the whole assembly in Jerusalem decided to celebrate the Passover in the
second month. 3 They had not been able to celebrate it at the regular time because not enough
priests had consecrated themselves and the people had not assembled in Jerusalem. 4 The plan
seemed right both to the king and to the whole
assembly. 5 They decided to send a proclamation throughout Israel, from Beersheba to Dan,
calling the people to come to Jerusalem and
celebrate the Passover to the LORD, the God of
Israel. It had not been celebrated in large numbers according to what was written.
6 At the king's command, couriers went
throughout Israel and Judah with letters from
the king and from his officials, which read:

"People of Israel, return to the LORD,
the God of Abraham, Isaac and Israel, that
he may return to you who are left, who
have escaped from the hand of the kings
of Assyria. 7 Do not be like your fathers
and brothers, who were unfaithful to the
LORD, the God of their fathers, so that he
made them an object of horror, as you
see. 8 Do not be stiff-necked, as your fathers were; submit to the LORD. Come to
the sanctuary, which he has consecrated
forever. Serve the LORD your
God, so that his fierce anger
will turn away from you.
9 If you return to the LORD,
then your brothers and your
children will be shown compassion by their captors and
will come back to this land,
for the LORD your God is gracious and compassionate. He
will not turn his face from
you if you return to him."

10 The couriers went from
town to town in Ephraim and
Manasseh, as far as Zebulun,
but the people scorned and
ridiculed them. 11 Nevertheless, some men of Asher, Manasseh and Zebulun humbled
themselves and went to Jerusalem. 12 Also in
Judah the hand of God was on the people to
give them unity of mind to carry out what the
king and his officials had ordered, following
the word of the LORD.
13 A very large crowd of people assembled in
Jerusalem to celebrate the Feast of Unleavened
Bread in the second month. 14 They removed
the altars in Jerusalem and cleared away the
incense altars and threw them into the Kidron Valley.
15 They slaughtered the Passover lamb on
the fourteenth day of the second month. The
priests and the Levites were ashamed and
consecrated themselves and brought burnt offerings to the temple of the LORD. 16 Then they
took up their regular positions as prescribed in
the Law of Moses the man of God. The priests
sprinkled the blood handed to them by the
Levites. 17 Since many in the crowd had not
consecrated themselves, the Levites had to kill
the Passover lambs for all those who were not
ceremonially clean and could not consecrate
⌞their lambs⌟ to the LORD. 18 Although most of
the many people who came from Ephraim, Manasseh, Issachar and Zebulun had not purified

35 Traditionally *peace offerings*

themselves, yet they ate the Passover, contrary
to what was written. But Hezekiah prayed for
them, saying, "May the LORD, who is good, pardon everyone 19who sets his heart on seeking
God—the LORD, the God of his fathers—even
if he is not clean according to the rules of the
sanctuary." 20And the LORD heard Hezekiah
and healed the people.

21The Israelites who were present in Jerusalem celebrated the Feast of Unleavened Bread
for seven days with great rejoicing, while the
Levites and priests sang to the LORD every
day, accompanied by the LORD's instruments
of praise.[a]

22Hezekiah spoke encouragingly to all the
Levites, who showed good understanding of
the service of the LORD. For the seven days
they ate their assigned portion and offered fellowship offerings[b] and praised the LORD, the
God of their fathers.

23The whole assembly then agreed to celebrate the festival seven more days; so for another
seven days they celebrated joyfully. 24Hezekiah
king of Judah provided a thousand bulls and
seven thousand sheep and goats for the assembly, and the officials provided them with
a thousand bulls and ten thousand sheep and
goats. A great number of priests consecrated
themselves. 25The entire assembly of Judah rejoiced, along with the priests and Levites and
all who had assembled from Israel, including
the aliens who had come from Israel and those
who lived in Judah. 26There was great joy in
Jerusalem, for since the days of Solomon son
of David king of Israel there had been nothing
like this in Jerusalem. 27The priests and the Levites stood to bless the people, and God heard
them, for their prayer reached heaven, his holy
dwelling place.

31 When all this had ended, the Israelites
who were there went out to the towns
of Judah, smashed the sacred stones and cut
down the Asherah poles. They destroyed the
high places and the altars throughout Judah
and Benjamin and in Ephraim and Manasseh.
After they had destroyed all of them, the Israelites returned to their own towns and to their
own property.

Contributions for Worship

2Hezekiah assigned the priests and Levites
to divisions—each of them according to their
duties as priests or Levites—to offer burnt offerings and fellowship offerings,[b] to minister,
to give thanks and to sing praises at the gates
of the LORD's dwelling. 3The king contributed
from his own possessions for the morning
and evening burnt offerings and for the burnt
offerings on the Sabbaths, New Moons and
appointed feasts as written in the Law of the
LORD. 4He ordered the people living in Jerusalem to give the portion due the priests and
Levites so they could devote themselves to the
Law of the LORD. 5As soon as the order went
out, the Israelites generously gave the firstfruits of their grain, new wine, oil and honey
and all that the fields produced. They brought
a great amount, a tithe of everything. 6The men
of Israel and Judah who lived in the towns of
Judah also brought a tithe of their herds and
flocks and a tithe of the holy things dedicated
to the LORD their God, and they piled them
in heaps. 7They began doing this in the third
month and finished in the seventh month.
8When Hezekiah and his officials came and
saw the heaps, they praised the LORD and
blessed his people Israel.

9Hezekiah asked the priests and Levites
about the heaps; 10and Azariah the chief priest,
from the family of Zadok, answered, "Since the
people began to bring their contributions to
the temple of the LORD, we have had enough
to eat and plenty to spare, because the LORD
has blessed his people, and this great amount
is left over."

11Hezekiah gave orders to prepare storerooms in the temple of the LORD, and this
was done. 12Then they faithfully brought in
the contributions, tithes and dedicated gifts.
Conaniah, a Levite, was in charge of these
things, and his brother Shimei was next in
rank. 13Jehiel, Azaziah, Nahath, Asahel, Jerimoth, Jozabad, Eliel, Ismakiah, Mahath and Benaiah were supervisors under Conaniah and
Shimei his brother, by appointment of King
Hezekiah and Azariah the official in charge of
the temple of God.

14Kore son of Imnah the Levite, keeper of

[a]21 Or *priests praised the LORD every day with resounding instruments belonging to the LORD* [b]22,2 Traditionally *peace offerings*

the East Gate, was in charge of the freewill
offerings given to God, distributing the contributions made to the LORD and also the
consecrated gifts. 15Eden, Miniamin, Jeshua,
Shemaiah, Amariah and Shecaniah assisted
him faithfully in the towns of the priests, distributing to their fellow priests according to
their divisions, old and young alike.
16In addition, they distributed to the males
three years old or more whose names were in
the genealogical records—all who would enter
the temple of the LORD to perform the daily
duties of their various tasks, according to their
responsibilities and their divi-
sions. 17And they distributed
to the priests enrolled by their
families in the genealogical
records and likewise to the Levites twenty years old or more,
according to their responsibilities and their divisions. 18They
included all the little ones, the
wives, and the sons and daughters of the whole community
listed in these genealogical records. For they were faithful in
consecrating themselves.
19As for the priests, the de-
scendants of Aaron, who lived on the farm lands
around their towns or in any other towns, men
were designated by name to distribute portions
to every male among them and to all who were
recorded in the genealogies of the Levites.
20This is what Hezekiah did throughout
Judah, doing what was good and right and
faithful before the LORD his God. 21In everything that he undertook in the service of God's
temple and in obedience to the law and the
commands, he sought his God and worked
wholeheartedly. And so he prospered.

Sennacherib Threatens Jerusalem

32 After all that Hezekiah had so faithfully
done, Sennacherib king of Assyria
came and invaded Judah. He laid siege to the
fortified cities, thinking to conquer them for
himself. 2When Hezekiah saw that Sennacherib
had come and that he intended to make war
on Jerusalem, 3he consulted with his officials
and military staff about blocking off the water from the springs outside the city, and they
helped him. 4A large force of men assembled,
and they blocked all the springs and the stream
that flowed through the land. "Why should the
kings[a] of Assyria come and find plenty of water?" they said. 5Then he worked hard repairing
all the broken sections of the wall and building
towers on it. He built another wall outside that
one and reinforced the supporting terraces[b] of
the City of David. He also made large numbers
of weapons and shields.
6He appointed military officers over the
people and assembled them before him in
the square at the city gate and
encouraged them with these
words: 7"Be strong and courageous. Do not be afraid or
discouraged because of the
king of Assyria and the vast
army with him, for there is a
greater power with us than
with him. 8With him is only
the arm of flesh, but with us is
the LORD our God to help us
and to fight our battles." And
the people gained confidence
from what Hezekiah the king
of Judah said.
9Later, when Sennacherib king of Assyria
and all his forces were laying siege to Lachish,
he sent his officers to Jerusalem with this message for Hezekiah king of Judah and for all the
people of Judah who were there:

> 10"This is what Sennacherib king of
> Assyria says: On what are you basing your
> confidence, that you remain in Jerusalem
> under siege? 11When Hezekiah says, 'The
> LORD our God will save us from the hand
> of the king of Assyria,' he is misleading
> you, to let you die of hunger and thirst.
> 12Did not Hezekiah himself remove this
> god's high places and altars, saying to Ju-
> dah and Jerusalem, 'You must worship be-
> fore one altar and burn sacrifices on it'?
> 13"Do you not know what I and my fa-
> thers have done to all the peoples of the
> other lands? Were the gods of those na-
> tions ever able to deliver their land from
> my hand? 14Who of all the gods of these

2 Chronicles 32:8

God Aids His People

"With him is only the arm of flesh, but with us is the LORD our God to help us and to fight our battles."

[a]4 Hebrew; Septuagint and Syriac *king* [b]5 Or *the Millo*

nations that my fathers destroyed has
been able to save his people from me?
How then can your god deliver you from
my hand? 15Now do not let Hezekiah deceive you and mislead you like this. Do
not believe him, for no god of any nation
or kingdom has been able to deliver his
people from my hand or the hand of my
fathers. How much less will your god
deliver you from my hand!"

16Sennacherib's officers spoke further
against the LORD God and against his servant
Hezekiah. 17The king also wrote letters insulting the LORD, the God of Israel, and saying this
against him: "Just as the gods of the peoples
of the other lands did not rescue their people
from my hand, so the god of Hezekiah will not
rescue his people from my hand." 18Then they
called out in Hebrew to the people of Jerusalem who were on the wall, to terrify them and
make them afraid in order to capture the city.
19They spoke about the God of Jerusalem as
they did about the gods of the other peoples of
the world—the work of men's hands.

20King Hezekiah and the prophet Isaiah
son of Amoz cried out in prayer to heaven
about this. 21And the LORD sent an angel,
who annihilated all the fighting men and the
leaders and officers in the camp of the Assyrian king. So he withdrew to his own land in
disgrace. And when he went into the temple of
his god, some of his sons cut him down with
the sword.

22So the LORD saved Hezekiah and the people of Jerusalem from the hand of Sennacherib
king of Assyria and from the hand of all others.
He took care of them[a] on every side. 23Many
brought offerings to Jerusalem for the LORD
and valuable gifts for Hezekiah king of Judah.
From then on he was highly regarded by all
the nations.

Hezekiah's Pride, Success and Death

24In those days Hezekiah became ill and was
at the point of death. He prayed to the LORD,
who answered him and gave him a miraculous
sign. 25But Hezekiah's heart was proud and he
did not respond to the kindness shown him;
therefore the LORD's wrath was on him and
on Judah and Jerusalem. 26Then Hezekiah
repented of the pride of his heart, as did the
people of Jerusalem; therefore the LORD's
wrath did not come upon them during the days
of Hezekiah.

27Hezekiah had very great riches and honor,
and he made treasuries for his silver and gold
and for his precious stones, spices, shields and
all kinds of valuables. 28He also made buildings
to store the harvest of grain, new wine and oil;
and he made stalls for various kinds of cattle,
and pens for the flocks. 29He built villages and
acquired great numbers of flocks and herds, for
God had given him very great riches.

30It was Hezekiah who blocked the upper
outlet of the Gihon spring and channeled the
water down to the west side of the City of David. He succeeded in everything he undertook.
31But when envoys were sent by the rulers of
Babylon to ask him about the miraculous sign
that had occurred in the land, God left him to
test him and to know everything that was in
his heart.

32The other events of Hezekiah's reign and
his acts of devotion are written in the vision
of the prophet Isaiah son of Amoz in the book
of the kings of Judah and Israel. 33Hezekiah
rested with his fathers and was buried on the
hill where the tombs of David's descendants
are. All Judah and the people of Jerusalem honored him when he died. And Manasseh his son
succeeded him as king.

Manasseh King of Judah

33 Manasseh was twelve years old when
he became king, and he reigned in Jerusalem fifty-five years. 2He did evil in the eyes
of the LORD, following the detestable practices
of the nations the LORD had driven out before
the Israelites. 3He rebuilt the high places his father Hezekiah had demolished; he also erected
altars to the Baals and made Asherah poles.
He bowed down to all the starry hosts and
worshiped them. 4He built altars in the temple
of the LORD, of which the LORD had said, "My
Name will remain in Jerusalem forever." 5In
both courts of the temple of the LORD, he built
altars to all the starry hosts. 6He sacrificed his
sons in[b] the fire in the Valley of Ben Hinnom,

[a] 22 Hebrew; Septuagint and Vulgate *He gave them rest* [b] 6 Or *He made his sons pass through*

practiced sorcery, divination and witchcraft,
and consulted mediums and spiritists. He did
much evil in the eyes of the LORD, provoking
him to anger.
7He took the carved image he had made and
put it in God's temple, of which God had said
to David and to his son Solomon, "In this temple and in Jerusalem, which I have chosen out
of all the tribes of Israel, I will put my Name
forever. 8I will not again make the feet of the
Israelites leave the land I assigned to your forefathers, if only they will be careful to do everything I commanded them concerning all the
laws, decrees and ordinances given through
Moses." 9But Manasseh led Judah and the people of Jerusalem astray, so that they did more
evil than the nations the LORD had destroyed
before the Israelites.
10The LORD spoke to Manasseh and his people, but they paid no attention. 11So the LORD
brought against them the army commanders
of the king of Assyria, who took Manasseh
prisoner, put a hook in his nose, bound him
with bronze shackles and took him to Babylon.
12In his distress he sought the favor of the LORD
his God and humbled himself greatly before
the God of his fathers. 13And when he prayed
to him, the LORD was moved by his entreaty
and listened to his plea; so he brought him back
to Jerusalem and to his kingdom. Then Manasseh knew that the LORD is God.
14Afterward he rebuilt the outer wall of the
City of David, west of the Gihon spring in the
valley, as far as the entrance of the Fish Gate
and encircling the hill of Ophel; he also made it
much higher. He stationed military commanders in all the fortified cities in Judah.
15He got rid of the foreign gods and removed the image from the temple of the LORD,
as well as all the altars he had built on the temple hill and in Jerusalem; and he threw them
out of the city. 16Then he restored the altar of
the LORD and sacrificed fellowship offerings[a]
and thank offerings on it, and told Judah to
serve the LORD, the God of Israel. 17The people, however, continued to sacrifice at the high
places, but only to the LORD their God.
18The other events of Manasseh's reign, including his prayer to his God and the words the
seers spoke to him in the name of the LORD,
the God of Israel, are written in the annals of
the kings of Israel.[b] 19His prayer and how God
was moved by his entreaty, as well as all his sins
and unfaithfulness, and the sites where he built
high places and set up Asherah poles and idols
before he humbled himself—all are written in
the records of the seers.[c] 20Manasseh rested
with his fathers and was buried in his palace.
And Amon his son succeeded him as king.

Amon King of Judah

21Amon was twenty-two years old when he
became king, and he reigned in Jerusalem two
years. 22He did evil in the eyes of the LORD,
as his father Manasseh had done. Amon worshiped and offered sacrifices to all the idols
Manasseh had made. 23But unlike his father
Manasseh, he did not humble himself before
the LORD; Amon increased his guilt.
24Amon's officials conspired against him
and assassinated him in his palace. 25Then the
people of the land killed all who had plotted
against King Amon, and they made Josiah his
son king in his place.

Josiah's Reforms

34 Josiah was eight years old when he
became king, and he reigned in Jerusalem thirty-one years. 2He did what was right in
the eyes of the LORD and walked in the ways of
his father David, not turning aside to the right
or to the left.
3In the eighth year of his reign, while he
was still young, he began to seek the God of
his father David. In his twelfth year he began
to purge Judah and Jerusalem of high places,
Asherah poles, carved idols and cast images.
4Under his direction the altars of the Baals were
torn down; he cut to pieces the incense altars
that were above them, and smashed the Asherah poles, the idols and the images. These he
broke to pieces and scattered over the graves of
those who had sacrificed to them. 5He burned
the bones of the priests on their altars, and so
he purged Judah and Jerusalem. 6In the towns
of Manasseh, Ephraim and Simeon, as far as
Naphtali, and in the ruins around them, 7he

[a]16 Traditionally *peace offerings* [b]18 That is, Judah, as frequently in 2 Chronicles [c]19 One Hebrew manuscript and Septuagint; most Hebrew manuscripts *of Hozai*

tore down the altars and the Asherah poles and
crushed the idols to powder and cut to pieces
all the incense altars throughout Israel. Then he
went back to Jerusalem.
8 In the eighteenth year of Josiah's reign, to
purify the land and the temple, he sent Shaphan son of Azaliah and Maaseiah the ruler of
the city, with Joah son of Joahaz, the recorder,
to repair the temple of the LORD his God.
9 They went to Hilkiah the high priest and
gave him the money that had been brought
into the temple of God, which the Levites who
were the doorkeepers had collected from the
people of Manasseh, Ephraim and the entire
remnant of Israel and from all the people of
Judah and Benjamin and the inhabitants of Jerusalem. 10 Then they entrusted it to the men
appointed to supervise the work on the LORD's
temple. These men paid the workers who repaired and restored the temple. 11 They also
gave money to the carpenters and builders to
purchase dressed stone, and timber for joists
and beams for the buildings that the kings of
Judah had allowed to fall into ruin.
12 The men did the work faithfully. Over
them to direct them were Jahath and Obadiah,
Levites descended from Merari, and Zechariah
and Meshullam, descended from Kohath. The
Levites—all who were skilled in playing musical instruments— 13 had charge of the laborers
and supervised all the workers
from job to job. Some of the Levites were secretaries, scribes
and doorkeepers.

The Book of the Law Found

14 While they were bring-
ing out the money that had
been taken into the temple of
the LORD, Hilkiah the priest
found the Book of the Law of
the LORD that had been given
through Moses. 15 Hilkiah
said to Shaphan the secretary,
"I have found the Book of the
Law in the temple of the LORD."
He gave it to Shaphan.
16 Then Shaphan took the book to the king
and reported to him: "Your officials are doing
everything that has been committed to them.
17 They have paid out the money that was in the
temple of the LORD and have entrusted it to
the supervisors and workers." 18 Then Shaphan
the secretary informed the king, "Hilkiah the
priest has given me a book." And Shaphan read
from it in the presence of the king.
19 When the king heard the words of the
Law, he tore his robes. 20 He gave these orders
to Hilkiah, Ahikam son of Shaphan, Abdon
son of Micah,[a] Shaphan the secretary and Asaiah the king's attendant: 21 "Go and inquire of
the LORD for me and for the remnant in Israel
and Judah about what is written in this book
that has been found. Great is the LORD's anger
that is poured out on us because our fathers
have not kept the word of the LORD; they have
not acted in accordance with all that is written
in this book."
22 Hilkiah and those the king had sent with
him[b] went to speak to the prophetess Huldah,
who was the wife of Shallum son of Tokhath,[c]
the son of Hasrah,[d] keeper of the wardrobe.
She lived in Jerusalem, in the Second District.
23 She said to them, "This is what the LORD,
the God of Israel, says: Tell the man who sent
you to me, 24 'This is what the LORD says: I
am going to bring disaster on this place and
its people—all the curses written in the book
that has been read in the pres-
ence of the king of Judah.
25 Because they have forsaken
me and burned incense to
other gods and provoked me
to anger by all that their hands
have made,[e] my anger will be
poured out on this place and
will not be quenched.' 26 Tell
the king of Judah, who sent
you to inquire of the LORD,
'This is what the LORD, the
God of Israel, says concerning
the words you heard: 27 Because your heart was responsive and you humbled yourself
before God when you heard what he spoke
against this place and its people, and because

> **2 Chronicles 34:27**
>
> *God Hears Humble People*
>
> "Because your heart was responsive and you humbled yourself before God . . . I have heard you, declares the LORD."

[a]20 Also called *Acbor son of Micaiah* [b]22 One Hebrew manuscript, Vulgate and Syriac; most Hebrew manuscripts do not have *had sent with him.* [c]22 Also called *Tikvah* [d]22 Also called *Harhas* [e]25 Or *by everything they have done*

you humbled yourself before me and tore your
robes and wept in my presence, I have heard
you, declares the LORD. 28Now I will gather
you to your fathers, and you will be buried in
peace. Your eyes will not see all the disaster I
am going to bring on this place and on those
who live here.' "

So they took her answer back to the king.

29Then the king called together all the elders of Judah and Jerusalem. 30He went up to
the temple of the LORD with the men of Judah,
the people of Jerusalem, the priests and the
Levites—all the people from the least to the
greatest. He read in their hearing all the words
of the Book of the Covenant, which had been
found in the temple of the LORD. 31The king
stood by his pillar and renewed the covenant
in the presence of the LORD—to follow the
LORD and keep his commands, regulations
and decrees with all his heart and all his soul,
and to obey the words of the covenant written
in this book.

32Then he had everyone in Jerusalem and
Benjamin pledge themselves to it; the people
of Jerusalem did this in accordance with the
covenant of God, the God of their fathers.

33Josiah removed all the detestable idols
from all the territory belonging to the Israelites, and he had all who were present in Israel
serve the LORD their God. As long as he lived,
they did not fail to follow the LORD, the God of
their fathers.

Josiah Celebrates the Passover

35 Josiah celebrated the Passover to the
LORD in Jerusalem, and the Passover
lamb was slaughtered on the fourteenth day
of the first month. 2He appointed the priests
to their duties and encouraged them in the
service of the LORD's temple. 3He said to the
Levites, who instructed all Israel and who had
been consecrated to the LORD: "Put the sacred
ark in the temple that Solomon son of David
king of Israel built. It is not to be carried about
on your shoulders. Now serve the LORD your
God and his people Israel. 4Prepare yourselves
by families in your divisions, according to the
directions written by David king of Israel and
by his son Solomon.

5"Stand in the holy place with a group of Levites for each subdivision of the families of your
fellow countrymen, the lay people. 6Slaughter
the Passover lambs, consecrate yourselves
and prepare ⌊the lambs⌋ for your fellow countrymen, doing what the LORD commanded
through Moses."

7Josiah provided for all the lay people who
were there a total of thirty thousand sheep and
goats for the Passover offerings, and also three
thousand cattle—all from the king's own possessions.

8His officials also contributed voluntarily to
the people and the priests and Levites. Hilkiah,
Zechariah and Jehiel, the administrators of
God's temple, gave the priests twenty-six hundred Passover offerings and three hundred
cattle. 9Also Conaniah along with Shemaiah
and Nethanel, his brothers, and Hashabiah,
Jeiel and Jozabad, the leaders of the Levites,
provided five thousand Passover offerings and
five hundred head of cattle for the Levites.

10The service was arranged and the priests
stood in their places with the Levites in their
divisions as the king had ordered. 11The Passover lambs were slaughtered, and the priests
sprinkled the blood handed to them, while
the Levites skinned the animals. 12They set
aside the burnt offerings to give them to the
subdivisions of the families of the people to
offer to the LORD, as is written in the Book
of Moses. They did the same with the cattle.
13They roasted the Passover animals over the
fire as prescribed, and boiled the holy offerings
in pots, caldrons and pans and served them
quickly to all the people. 14After this, they
made preparations for themselves and for the
priests, because the priests, the descendants of
Aaron, were sacrificing the burnt offerings and
the fat portions until nightfall. So the Levites
made preparations for themselves and for the
Aaronic priests.

15The musicians, the descendants of Asaph,
were in the places prescribed by David, Asaph,
Heman and Jeduthun the king's seer. The gatekeepers at each gate did not need to leave their
posts, because their fellow Levites made the
preparations for them.

16So at that time the entire service of the
LORD was carried out for the celebration of
the Passover and the offering of burnt offerings on the altar of the LORD, as King Josiah

had ordered. 17 The Israelites who were present celebrated the Passover at that time and observed the Feast of Unleavened Bread for seven days. 18 The Passover had not been observed like this in Israel since the days of the prophet Samuel; and none of the kings of Israel had ever celebrated such a Passover as did Josiah, with the priests, the Levites and all Judah and Israel who were there with the people of Jerusalem. 19 This Passover was celebrated in the eighteenth year of Josiah's reign.

The Death of Josiah

20 After all this, when Josiah had set the temple in order, Neco king of Egypt went up to fight at Carchemish on the Euphrates, and Josiah marched out to meet him in battle. 21 But Neco sent messengers to him, saying, "What quarrel is there between you and me, O king of Judah? It is not you I am attacking at this time, but the house with which I am at war. God has told me to hurry; so stop opposing God, who is with me, or he will destroy you."

22 Josiah, however, would not turn away from him, but disguised himself to engage him in battle. He would not listen to what Neco had said at God's command but went to fight him on the plain of Megiddo.

23 Archers shot King Josiah, and he told his officers, "Take me away; I am badly wounded." 24 So they took him out of his chariot, put him in the other chariot he had and brought him to Jerusalem, where he died. He was buried in the tombs of his fathers, and all Judah and Jerusalem mourned for him.

25 Jeremiah composed laments for Josiah, and to this day all the men and women singers commemorate Josiah in the laments. These became a tradition in Israel and are written in the Laments.

26 The other events of Josiah's reign and his acts of devotion, according to what is written in the Law of the LORD— 27 all the events, from beginning to end, are written in the book of the

36 kings of Israel and Judah. 1 And the people of the land took Jehoahaz son of Josiah and made him king in Jerusalem in place of his father.

Jehoahaz King of Judah

2 Jehoahaz[a] was twenty-three years old when he became king, and he reigned in Jerusalem three months. 3 The king of Egypt dethroned him in Jerusalem and imposed on Judah a levy of a hundred talents[b] of silver and a talent[c] of gold. 4 The king of Egypt made Eliakim, a brother of Jehoahaz, king over Judah and Jerusalem and changed Eliakim's name to Jehoiakim. But Neco took Eliakim's brother Jehoahaz and carried him off to Egypt.

Jehoiakim King of Judah

5 Jehoiakim was twenty-five years old when he became king, and he reigned in Jerusalem eleven years. He did evil in the eyes of the LORD his God. 6 Nebuchadnezzar king of Babylon attacked him and bound him with bronze shackles to take him to Babylon. 7 Nebuchadnezzar also took to Babylon articles from the temple of the LORD and put them in his temple[d] there.

8 The other events of Jehoiakim's reign, the detestable things he did and all that was found against him, are written in the book of the kings of Israel and Judah. And Jehoiachin his son succeeded him as king.

Jehoiachin King of Judah

9 Jehoiachin was eighteen[e] years old when he became king, and he reigned in Jerusalem three months and ten days. He did evil in the eyes of the LORD. 10 In the spring, King Nebuchadnezzar sent for him and brought him to Babylon, together with articles of value from the temple of the LORD, and he made Jehoiachin's uncle,[f] Zedekiah, king over Judah and Jerusalem.

Zedekiah King of Judah

11 Zedekiah was twenty-one years old when he became king, and he reigned in Jerusalem eleven years. 12 He did evil in the eyes of the LORD his God and did not humble himself before Jeremiah the prophet, who spoke the word of the LORD. 13 He also rebelled against King Nebuchadnezzar, who had made him take an oath in God's name. He became stiff-necked and hardened his heart and would not turn to the LORD, the God of Israel. 14 Furthermore, all the leaders of the priests and the people

[a] 2 Hebrew *Joahaz,* a variant of *Jehoahaz;* also in verse 4 [b] 3 That is, about 3 3/4 tons (about 3.4 metric tons) [c] 3 That is, about 75 pounds (about 34 kilograms) [d] 7 Or *palace* [e] 9 One Hebrew manuscript, some Septuagint manuscripts and Syriac (see also 2 Kings 24:8); most Hebrew manuscripts *eight* [f] 10 Hebrew *brother,* that is, relative (see 2 Kings 24:17)

became more and more unfaithful, following
all the detestable practices of the nations and
defiling the temple of the LORD, which he had
consecrated in Jerusalem.

The Fall of Jerusalem

15 The LORD, the God of their fathers, sent
word to them through his messengers again
and again, because he had pity on his people
and on his dwelling place. 16 But they mocked
God's messengers, despised his words and
scoffed at his prophets until the wrath of the
LORD was aroused against his people and there
was no remedy. 17 He brought up against them
the king of the Babylonians,[a] who killed their
young men with the sword in the sanctuary,
and spared neither young man nor young
woman, old man or aged. God handed all of
them over to Nebuchadnezzar. 18 He carried
to Babylon all the articles from the temple of
God, both large and small, and the treasures
of the LORD's temple and the treasures of the
king and his officials. 19 They set fire to God's
temple and broke down the wall of Jerusalem;
they burned all the palaces and destroyed everything of value there.

20 He carried into exile to Babylon the remnant, who escaped from the sword, and they
became servants to him and his sons until the
kingdom of Persia came to power. 21 The land
enjoyed its sabbath rests; all the time of its desolation it rested, until the seventy years were
completed in fulfillment of the word of the
LORD spoken by Jeremiah.

22 In the first year of Cyrus king of Persia, in
order to fulfill the word of the LORD spoken by
Jeremiah, the LORD moved the heart of Cyrus
king of Persia to make a proclamation throughout his realm and to put it in writing:

23 "This is what Cyrus king of Persia says:

"'The LORD, the God of heaven, has
given me all the kingdoms of the earth
and he has appointed me to build a temple for him at Jerusalem in Judah. Anyone
of his people among you—may the LORD
his God be with him, and let him go up.'"

[a] 17 Or *Chaldeans*

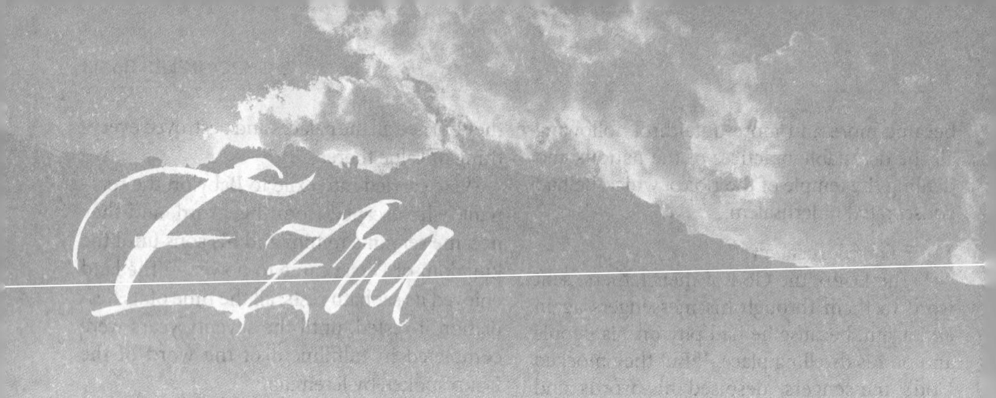

Ezra

Author:
Unknown, but possibly Ezra. (Note: There are portions written in the first person by Ezra. The author of the third person parts is debatable.)

Audience:
All Israel.

Date:
Around 440 B.C.

Setting:
The homecoming of the exiles from Babylon who will start rebuilding God's temple.

Verse to Remember:
"Though we are slaves, our God has not deserted us in our bondage. He has shown us kindness in the sight of the kings of Persia: He has granted us new life to rebuild the house of our God and repair its ruins, and he has given us a wall of protection in Judah and Jerusalem." (9:9)

A second chance is a remarkable gift. It's never deserved; it is a sheer *act of grace.* And it is precisely what God gave to his people. The same hands that brought judgment, destruction and 70 years of exile led those exiles back to the *land of promise* to start over again.

When the people reached their homeland, they made *a great beginning.* They gave freely; they offered sacrifices; they celebrated the feasts; they began rebuilding the temple—they did all the things the people of God should do. But in any work we do for God, there is opposition. For the returning exiles, it came on two fronts: *outside enemies and old tendencies.* As is often the case, the old tendencies were by far the greater threat. But greater than any enemy from within or without is a sovereign God who moves the hearts of people and who is willing to give second chances. He did both for the Israelites in Ezra's day, and *he still does both for us today.*

Cyrus Helps the Exiles to Return

1 In the first year of Cyrus king of Persia, in
order to fulfill the word of the LORD spoken by Jeremiah, the LORD moved the heart of
Cyrus king of Persia to make a proclamation
throughout his realm and to put it in writing:

2“This is what Cyrus king of Persia says:
“ ‘The LORD, the God of heaven, has
given me all the kingdoms of the earth
and he has appointed me to build a temple for him at Jerusalem in Judah. 3Any-
one of his people among you—may his
God be with him, and let him go up to
Jerusalem in Judah and build the temple
of the LORD, the God of Israel, the God
who is in Jerusalem. 4And the people of
any place where survivors may now be
living are to provide him with silver and
gold, with goods and livestock, and with
freewill offerings for the temple of God
in Jerusalem.’ ”

5Then the family heads of Judah and Benjamin, and the priests and Levites—everyone
whose heart God had moved—prepared to go
up and build the house of the LORD in Jerusalem. 6All their neighbors assisted them with
articles of silver and gold, with goods and livestock, and with valuable gifts, in addition to all
the freewill offerings. 7Moreover, King Cyrus
brought out the articles belonging to the temple of the LORD, which Nebuchadnezzar had
carried away from Jerusalem and had placed
in the temple of his god.[a] 8Cyrus king of Persia
had them brought by Mithredath the treasurer,
who counted them out to Sheshbazzar the
prince of Judah.
9This was the inventory:

	gold dishes	30
	silver dishes	1,000
	silver pans[b]	29
10	gold bowls	30
	matching silver bowls	410
	other articles	1,000

11In all, there were 5,400 articles of gold and
of silver. Sheshbazzar brought all these along
when the exiles came up from Babylon to Jerusalem.

The List of the Exiles Who Returned

2 Now these are the people of the province
who came up from the captivity of the exiles, whom Nebuchadnezzar king of Babylon
had taken captive to Babylon (they returned to
Jerusalem and Judah, each to his own town, 2in
company with Zerubbabel, Jeshua, Nehemiah,
Seraiah, Reelaiah, Mordecai, Bilshan, Mispar,
Bigvai, Rehum and Baanah):

The list of the men of the people of Israel:

3	the descendants of Parosh	2,172
4	of Shephatiah	372
5	of Arah	775
6	of Pahath-Moab (through the line of Jeshua and Joab)	2,812
7	of Elam	1,254
8	of Zattu	945
9	of Zaccai	760
10	of Bani	642
11	of Bebai	623
12	of Azgad	1,222
13	of Adonikam	666
14	of Bigvai	2,056
15	of Adin	454
16	of Ater (through Hezekiah)	98
17	of Bezai	323
18	of Jorah	112
19	of Hashum	223
20	of Gibbar	95
21	the men of Bethlehem	123
22	of Netophah	56
23	of Anathoth	128
24	of Azmaveth	42
25	of Kiriath Jearim,[c] Kephirah and Beeroth	743
26	of Ramah and Geba	621
27	of Micmash	122
28	of Bethel and Ai	223
29	of Nebo	52
30	of Magbish	156
31	of the other Elam	1,254
32	of Harim	320
33	of Lod, Hadid and Ono	725
34	of Jericho	345
35	of Senaah	3,630

36The priests:

	the descendants of Jedaiah (through the family of Jeshua)	973
37	of Immer	1,052
38	of Pashhur	1,247
39	of Harim	1,017

[a]7 Or *gods* [b]9 The meaning of the Hebrew for this word is uncertain. [c]25 See Septuagint (see also Neh. 7:29); Hebrew *Kiriath Arim.*

Life's Gamble

RUTH

"Your people will be my people and your God my God."

Ruth 1:16

ASSIGNED READING:

Ruth 1:1–22

RUTH DIDN'T BLAME ORPAH.

Not for returning to life in Moab and not for leaving Naomi.

She knew how Orpah felt. They were both young widows in the prime of their lives. In such a situation, it would be smart to stay near the familiar and enjoy the protection of family.

If that's what one wanted.

Ruth just wasn't so sure it was worth wanting.

At the same time, what was so promising or even the least bit intriguing about accompanying a withered woman to a foreign land? Ruth couldn't say for certain. Whatever it was, Orpah certainly didn't see it, couldn't see it. But Ruth saw it. Something Ruth saw in Naomi inspired her to take the greatest gamble of her young life up to that point and move to Bethlehem.

She had seen it in her father-in-law's name, "My God is King." Who was this God, and would he really rule as a righteous king? She wondered.

She had observed it in her deceased husband's godly heritage, and it touched her deep inside.

She had witnessed it in Naomi's inner strength.

Everything had been taken from her mother-in-law, and many nights Ruth had heard her crying bitter tears. Still, trouble could not completely extinguish Naomi's flicker of hope. When Naomi decided to return home to Bethlehem, instead of leaving her faith in a foreign land, she accepted her pain and determined to see what God would do. To Ruth, it spoke of perseverance, of an unconquered spirit.

Most of all, it spoke to the emptiness in Ruth's own soul. Growing up among the pagan religion of her land, she found herself unimpressed with the gods of her childhood. The brief time with Naomi's family had shown her something different. Her own "religion" had left her cold. Naomi's God, whoever he was, seemed to leave her heart strangely warmed.

If Ruth's gamble to accompany Naomi to Bethlehem didn't pay off, she might have a lifetime of loneliness to regret it. But if it did . . . well, it would change everything.

—Prayer—

"When I called you, you answered me" (Psalm 138:3).

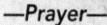

Weekend

Go to page 572 for your next devotional reading

40 The Levites:
the descendants of Jeshua and Kadmiel
(through the line of Hodaviah) 74

41 The singers:
the descendants of Asaph 128

42 The gatekeepers of the temple:
the descendants of
Shallum, Ater, Talmon,
Akkub, Hatita and Shobai 139

43 The temple servants:
the descendants of
Ziha, Hasupha, Tabbaoth,
44 Keros, Siaha, Padon,
45 Lebanah, Hagabah, Akkub,
46 Hagab, Shalmai, Hanan,
47 Giddel, Gahar, Reaiah,
48 Rezin, Nekoda, Gazzam,
49 Uzza, Paseah, Besai,
50 Asnah, Meunim, Nephusim,
51 Bakbuk, Hakupha, Harhur,
52 Bazluth, Mehida, Harsha,
53 Barkos, Sisera, Temah,
54 Neziah and Hatipha

55 The descendants of the servants of Solomon:
the descendants of
Sotai, Hassophereth, Peruda,
56 Jaala, Darkon, Giddel,
57 Shephatiah, Hattil,
Pokereth-Hazzebaim and Ami

58 The temple servants and the
descendants of the servants
of Solomon 392

59 The following came up from the
towns of Tel Melah, Tel Harsha, Kerub,
Addon and Immer, but they could not
show that their families were descended
from Israel:

60 The descendants of
Delaiah, Tobiah and Nekoda 652

61 And from among the priests:
The descendants of
Hobaiah, Hakkoz and Barzillai (a
man who had married a daughter of
Barzillai the Gileadite and was called
by that name).

62 These searched for their family records, but they could not find them and so
were excluded from the priesthood as unclean. 63 The governor ordered them not
to eat any of the most sacred food until
there was a priest ministering with the
Urim and Thummim.

64 The whole company numbered
42,360, 65 besides their 7,337 menservants
and maidservants; and they also had 200
men and women singers. 66 They had 736
horses, 245 mules, 67 435 camels and 6,720
donkeys.

68 When they arrived at the house of the
Lord in Jerusalem, some of the heads of the
families gave freewill offerings toward the rebuilding of the house of God on its site. 69 According to their ability they gave to the treasury
for this work 61,000 drachmas[a] of gold, 5,000
minas[b] of silver and 100 priestly garments.

70 The priests, the Levites, the singers, the
gatekeepers and the temple servants settled in
their own towns, along with some of the other
people, and the rest of the Israelites settled in
their towns.

Rebuilding the Altar

3 When the seventh month came and the Israelites had settled in their towns, the people assembled as one man in Jerusalem. 2 Then
Jeshua son of Jozadak and his fellow priests and
Zerubbabel son of Shealtiel and his associates
began to build the altar of the God of Israel to
sacrifice burnt offerings on it, in accordance
with what is written in the Law of Moses the
man of God. 3 Despite their fear of the peoples
around them, they built the altar on its foundation and sacrificed burnt offerings on it to the
Lord, both the morning and evening sacrifices.
4 Then in accordance with what is written, they
celebrated the Feast of Tabernacles with the required number of burnt offerings prescribed
for each day. 5 After that, they presented the regular burnt offerings, the New Moon sacrifices
and the sacrifices for all the appointed sacred

[a] 69 That is, about 1,100 pounds (about 500 kilograms) [b] 69 That is, about 3 tons (about 2.9 metric tons)

feasts of the LORD, as well as those brought as
freewill offerings to the LORD. 6On the first day
of the seventh month they began to offer burnt
offerings to the LORD, though the foundation
of the LORD's temple had not yet been laid.

Rebuilding the Temple

7Then they gave money to the masons and
carpenters, and gave food and drink and oil
to the people of Sidon and Tyre, so that they
would bring cedar logs by sea from Lebanon to
Joppa, as authorized by Cyrus king of Persia.
8In the second month of the second year
after their arrival at the house of God in Jerusalem, Zerubbabel son of Shealtiel, Jeshua son
of Jozadak and the rest of their brothers (the
priests and the Levites and all who had returned from the captivity to Jerusalem) began
the work, appointing Levites twenty years of
age and older to supervise the building of the
house of the LORD. 9Jeshua and his sons and
brothers and Kadmiel and his sons (descendants of Hodaviah[a]) and the sons of Henadad
and their sons and brothers—all Levites—
joined together in supervising those working
on the house of God.
10When the builders laid the foundation of
the temple of the LORD, the priests in their vest-
ments and with trumpets, and the Levites (the
sons of Asaph) with cymbals, took their places
to praise the LORD, as pre-
scribed by David king of Israel.
11With praise and thanksgiving they sang to the LORD:

"He is good;
his love to Israel endures
forever."

And all the people gave a great
shout of praise to the LORD,
because the foundation of the
house of the LORD was laid.
12But many of the older priests
and Levites and family heads,
who had seen the former temple, wept aloud when they
saw the foundation of this temple being laid,
while many others shouted for joy. 13No one
could distinguish the sound of the shouts of joy
from the sound of weeping, because the people
made so much noise. And the sound was heard
far away.

> **Ezra 3:11**
>
> *God's Love Endures*
>
> With praise and thanksgiving they sang to the LORD:
> "He is good;
> his love to Israel endures forever."

Opposition to the Rebuilding

4 When the enemies of Judah and Benjamin
heard that the exiles were building a temple for the LORD, the God of Israel, 2they came
to Zerubbabel and to the heads of the families
and said, "Let us help you build because, like
you, we seek your God and have been sacrificing to him since the time of Esarhaddon king
of Assyria, who brought us here."
3But Zerubbabel, Jeshua and the rest of the
heads of the families of Israel answered, "You
have no part with us in building a temple to our
God. We alone will build it for the LORD, the
God of Israel, as King Cyrus, the king of Persia,
commanded us."
4Then the peoples around them set out to
discourage the people of Judah and make them
afraid to go on building.[b] 5They hired counselors to work against them and frustrate their
plans during the entire reign of Cyrus king of
Persia and down to the reign of Darius king
of Persia.

Later Opposition Under Xerxes and Artaxerxes

6At the beginning of the reign of Xerxes,[c]
they lodged an accusation
against the people of Judah
and Jerusalem.
7And in the days of Artaxerxes king of Persia, Bishlam,
Mithredath, Tabeel and the rest
of his associates wrote a letter
to Artaxerxes. The letter was
written in Aramaic script and
in the Aramaic language.[d,e]
8Rehum the commanding
officer and Shimshai the secretary wrote a letter against Jerusalem to Artaxerxes the king
as follows:

9Rehum the commanding
officer and Shimshai the secretary, together with the rest of their associates—
the judges and officials over the men from

[a]9 Hebrew *Yehudah,* probably a variant of *Hodaviah* [b]4 Or *and troubled them as they built* [c]6 Hebrew *Ahasuerus,* a variant of Xerxes' Persian name [d]7 Or *written in Aramaic and translated* [e]7 The text of Ezra 4:8—6:18 is in Aramaic.

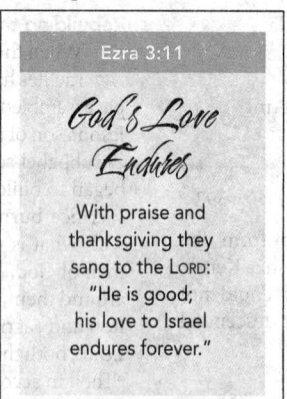

Tripolis, Persia,[a] Erech and Babylon, the
Elamites of Susa, 10 and the other people
whom the great and honorable Ashurbanipal[b] deported and settled in the
city of Samaria and elsewhere in Trans-
Euphrates.

11 (This is a copy of the letter they sent him.)

To King Artaxerxes,

From your servants, the men of Trans-
Euphrates:

12 The king should know that the Jews
who came up to us from you have gone
to Jerusalem and are rebuilding that rebellious and wicked city. They are restoring
the walls and repairing the foundations.
13 Furthermore, the king should know
that if this city is built and its walls are restored, no more taxes, tribute or duty will
be paid, and the royal revenues will suffer.
14 Now since we are under obligation to
the palace and it is not proper for us to
see the king dishonored, we are sending
this message to inform the king, 15 so that
a search may be made in the archives of
your predecessors. In these records you
will find that this city is a rebellious city,
troublesome to kings and provinces, a
place of rebellion from ancient times.
That is why this city was destroyed. 16 We
inform the king that if this city is built and
its walls are restored, you will be left with
nothing in Trans-Euphrates.

17 The king sent this reply:

To Rehum the commanding officer, Shimshai the secretary and the rest of their associates living in Samaria and elsewhere
in Trans-Euphrates:

Greetings.

18 The letter you sent us has been read
and translated in my presence. 19 I issued
an order and a search was made, and it
was found that this city has a long history
of revolt against kings and has been a place
of rebellion and sedition. 20 Jerusalem has
had powerful kings ruling over the whole
of Trans-Euphrates, and taxes, tribute and
duty were paid to them. 21 Now issue an
order to these men to stop work, so that
this city will not be rebuilt until I so order.
22 Be careful not to neglect this matter.
Why let this threat grow, to the detriment
of the royal interests?

23 As soon as the copy of the letter of King
Artaxerxes was read to Rehum and Shimshai
the secretary and their associates, they went
immediately to the Jews in Jerusalem and compelled them by force to stop.

24 Thus the work on the house of God in Jerusalem came to a standstill until the second year
of the reign of Darius king of Persia.

Tattenai's Letter to Darius

5 Now Haggai the prophet and Zechariah
the prophet, a descendant of Iddo, prophesied to the Jews in Judah and Jerusalem in the
name of the God of Israel, who was over them.
2 Then Zerubbabel son of Shealtiel and Jeshua
son of Jozadak set to work to rebuild the house
of God in Jerusalem. And the prophets of God
were with them, helping them.
3 At that time Tattenai, governor of Trans-
Euphrates, and Shethar-Bozenai and their
associates went to them and asked, "Who authorized you to rebuild this temple and restore
this structure?" 4 They also asked, "What are
the names of the men constructing this building?"[c] 5 But the eye of their God was watching
over the elders of the Jews, and they were not
stopped until a report could go to Darius and
his written reply be received.
6 This is a copy of the letter that Tattenai,
governor of Trans-Euphrates, and Shethar-
Bozenai and their associates, the officials of
Trans-Euphrates, sent to King Darius. 7 The report they sent him read as follows:

To King Darius:

Cordial greetings.

8 The king should know that we went to
the district of Judah, to the temple of the
great God. The people are building it with

[a] 9 Or *officials, magistrates and governors over the men from* [b] 10 Aramaic *Osnappar,* a variant of *Ashurbanipal* [c] 4 See Septuagint; Aramaic [4] *We told them the names of the men constructing this building.*

large stones and placing the timbers in the
walls. The work is being carried on with
diligence and is making rapid progress under their direction.
9We questioned the elders and asked
them, "Who authorized you to rebuild
this temple and restore this structure?"
10We also asked them their names, so that
we could write down the names of their
leaders for your information.
11This is the answer they gave us:

"We are the servants of the God of
heaven and earth, and we are rebuilding
the temple that was built many years ago,
one that a great king of Israel built and finished. 12But because our fathers angered
the God of heaven, he handed them over
to Nebuchadnezzar the Chaldean, king of
Babylon, who destroyed this temple and
deported the people to Babylon.
13"However, in the first year of Cyrus
king of Babylon, King Cyrus issued a decree to rebuild this house of God. 14He
even removed from the temple[a] of Babylon the gold and silver articles of the
house of God, which Nebuchadnezzar
had taken from the temple in Jerusalem
and brought to the temple[a] in Babylon.
"Then King Cyrus gave them to a
man named Sheshbazzar, whom he had
appointed governor, 15and he told him,
'Take these articles and go and deposit
them in the temple in Jerusalem. And rebuild the house of God on its site.' 16So
this Sheshbazzar came and laid the foundations of the house of God in Jerusalem.
From that day to the present it has been under construction but is not yet finished."

17Now if it pleases the king, let a search
be made in the royal archives of Babylon
to see if King Cyrus did in fact issue a decree to rebuild this house of God in Jerusalem. Then let the king send us his decision
in this matter.

The Decree of Darius

6 King Darius then issued an order, and
they searched in the archives stored in the
treasury at Babylon. 2A scroll was found in the
citadel of Ecbatana in the province of Media,
and this was written on it:

Memorandum:

3In the first year of King Cyrus, the
king issued a decree concerning the temple of God in Jerusalem:

Let the temple be rebuilt as a place to
present sacrifices, and let its foundations
be laid. It is to be ninety feet[b] high and
ninety feet wide, 4with three courses of
large stones and one of timbers. The costs
are to be paid by the royal treasury. 5Also,
the gold and silver articles of the house of
God, which Nebuchadnezzar took from
the temple in Jerusalem and brought to
Babylon, are to be returned to their places
in the temple in Jerusalem; they are to be
deposited in the house of God.

6Now then, Tattenai, governor of Trans-
Euphrates, and Shethar-Bozenai and you,
their fellow officials of that province, stay
away from there. 7Do not interfere with
the work on this temple of God. Let the
governor of the Jews and the Jewish elders
rebuild this house of God on its site.
8Moreover, I hereby decree what you
are to do for these elders of the Jews in
the construction of this house of God:
The expenses of these men are to be
fully paid out of the royal treasury, from
the revenues of Trans-Euphrates, so that
the work will not stop. 9Whatever is
needed—young bulls, rams, male lambs
for burnt offerings to the God of heaven,
and wheat, salt, wine and oil, as requested
by the priests in Jerusalem—must be
given them daily without fail, 10so that
they may offer sacrifices pleasing to the
God of heaven and pray for the well-being of the king and his sons.
11Furthermore, I decree that if anyone
changes this edict, a beam is to be pulled
from his house and he is to be lifted up
and impaled on it. And for this crime
his house is to be made a pile of rubble.
12May God, who has caused his Name to
dwell there, overthrow any king or people

[a]14 Or *palace* [b]3 Aramaic *sixty cubits* (about 27 meters)

who lifts a hand to change this decree or
to destroy this temple in Jerusalem.
I Darius have decreed it. Let it be carried out with diligence.

Completion and Dedication of the Temple

13Then, because of the decree King Darius had sent, Tattenai, governor of Trans-
Euphrates, and Shethar-Bozenai and their
associates carried it out with diligence. 14So
the elders of the Jews contin-
ued to build and prosper under the preaching of Haggai
the prophet and Zechariah, a
descendant of Iddo. They finished building the temple according to the command of the
God of Israel and the decrees of
Cyrus, Darius and Artaxerxes,
kings of Persia. 15The temple
was completed on the third
day of the month Adar, in the
sixth year of the reign of King
Darius.
16Then the people of Israel—
the priests, the Levites and the
rest of the exiles—celebrated
the dedication of the house
of God with joy. 17For the dedication of this
house of God they offered a hundred bulls, two
hundred rams, four hundred male lambs and,
as a sin offering for all Israel, twelve male goats,
one for each of the tribes of Israel. 18And they
installed the priests in their divisions and the
Levites in their groups for the service of God at
Jerusalem, according to what is written in the
Book of Moses.

> **Ezra 6:12**
>
> *God Reigns Over All*
>
> May God, who has caused his Name to dwell there, overthrow any king or people who lifts a hand to change this decree or to destroy this temple in Jerusalem.

The Passover

19On the fourteenth day of the first month,
the exiles celebrated the Passover. 20The priests
and Levites had purified themselves and were
all ceremonially clean. The Levites slaughtered
the Passover lamb for all the exiles, for their
brothers the priests and for themselves. 21So
the Israelites who had returned from the exile
ate it, together with all who had separated themselves from the unclean practices of their Gentile neighbors in order to seek the LORD, the
God of Israel. 22For seven days they celebrated
with joy the Feast of Unleavened Bread, because the LORD had filled them with joy by
changing the attitude of the king of Assyria, so
that he assisted them in the work on the house
of God, the God of Israel.

Ezra Comes to Jerusalem

7 After these things, during the reign of Artaxerxes king of Persia, Ezra son of Seraiah,
the son of Azariah, the son of Hilkiah, 2the son
of Shallum, the son of Zadok,
the son of Ahitub, 3the son of
Amariah, the son of Azariah,
the son of Meraioth, 4the son
of Zerahiah, the son of Uzzi,
the son of Bukki, 5the son of
Abishua, the son of Phinehas,
the son of Eleazar, the son of
Aaron the chief priest— 6this
Ezra came up from Babylon.
He was a teacher well versed
in the Law of Moses, which the
LORD, the God of Israel, had
given. The king had granted
him everything he asked, for
the hand of the LORD his God
was on him. 7Some of the Israelites, including priests, Le-
vites, singers, gatekeepers and temple servants,
also came up to Jerusalem in the seventh year
of King Artaxerxes.
8Ezra arrived in Jerusalem in the fifth month
of the seventh year of the king. 9He had begun
his journey from Babylon on the first day of
the first month, and he arrived in Jerusalem on
the first day of the fifth month, for the gracious
hand of his God was on him. 10For Ezra had
devoted himself to the study and observance
of the Law of the LORD, and to teaching its decrees and laws in Israel.

King Artaxerxes' Letter to Ezra

11This is a copy of the letter King Artaxerxes
had given to Ezra the priest and teacher, a man
learned in matters concerning the commands
and decrees of the LORD for Israel:

12[a]Artaxerxes, king of kings,

To Ezra the priest, a teacher of the Law of
the God of heaven:

[a]12 The text of Ezra 7:12–26 is in Aramaic.

Greetings.
13 Now I decree that any of the Israelites
in my kingdom, including priests and Levites, who wish to go to Jerusalem with
you, may go. 14 You are sent by the king
and his seven advisers to inquire about
Judah and Jerusalem with regard to the
Law of your God, which is in your hand.
15 Moreover, you are to take with you
the silver and gold that the king and his
advisers have freely given to the God of
Israel, whose dwelling is in Jerusalem,
16 together with all the silver and gold
you may obtain from the province of Babylon, as well as the freewill offerings of the
people and priests for the temple of their
God in Jerusalem. 17 With
this money be sure to buy
bulls, rams and male lambs,
together with their grain offerings and drink offerings,
and sacrifice them on the
altar of the temple of your
God in Jerusalem.
18 You and your brother
Jews may then do whatever
seems best with the rest of
the silver and gold, in accordance with the will of your
God. 19 Deliver to the God
of Jerusalem all the articles
entrusted to you for worship
in the temple of your God.
20 And anything else needed for the temple of your God that you may have occasion to supply, you may provide from the
royal treasury.
21 Now I, King Artaxerxes, order all the
treasurers of Trans-Euphrates to provide
with diligence whatever Ezra the priest, a
teacher of the Law of the God of heaven,
may ask of you— 22 up to a hundred talents[a] of silver, a hundred cors[b] of wheat,
a hundred baths[c] of wine, a hundred
baths[c] of olive oil, and salt without limit.
23 Whatever the God of heaven has prescribed, let it be done with diligence for
the temple of the God of heaven. Why
should there be wrath against the realm
of the king and of his sons? 24 You are also
to know that you have no authority to impose taxes, tribute or duty on any of the
priests, Levites, singers, gatekeepers, temple servants or other workers at this house
of God.
25 And you, Ezra, in accordance with
the wisdom of your God, which you
possess, appoint magistrates and judges
to administer justice to all the people of
Trans-Euphrates—all who know the laws
of your God. And you are to teach any
who do not know them. 26 Whoever does
not obey the law of your God and the law
of the king must surely be punished by
death, banishment, confiscation of property, or imprisonment.
27 Praise be to the LORD, the
God of our fathers, who has put
it into the king's heart to bring
honor to the house of the LORD
in Jerusalem in this way 28 and
who has extended his good favor to me before the king and
his advisers and all the king's
powerful officials. Because the
hand of the LORD my God was
on me, I took courage and gathered leading men from Israel
to go up with me.

> **Ezra 7:27**
>
> ***God Realigns Others' Plans***
>
> Praise be to the LORD, the God of our fathers, who has put it into the king's heart to bring honor to the house of the LORD in Jerusalem in this way.

List of the Family Heads Returning With Ezra

8 These are the family heads and those registered with them who came up with me
from Babylon during the reign of King Artaxerxes:

2 of the descendants of Phinehas, Gershom;
of the descendants of Ithamar, Daniel;
of the descendants of David, Hattush 3 of
the descendants of Shecaniah;

of the descendants of Parosh, Zechariah,
and with him were registered 150
men;

[a]22 That is, about 3 3/4 tons (about 3.4 metric tons) [b]22 That is, probably about 600 bushels (about 22 kiloliters) [c]22 That is, probably about 600 gallons (about 2.2 kiloliters)

4 of the descendants of Pahath-Moab, Eliehoenai son of Zerahiah, and with him 200 men;
5 of the descendants of Zattu,[a] Shecaniah son of Jahaziel, and with him 300 men;
6 of the descendants of Adin, Ebed son of Jonathan, and with him 50 men;
7 of the descendants of Elam, Jeshaiah son of Athaliah, and with him 70 men;
8 of the descendants of Shephatiah, Zebadiah son of Michael, and with him 80 men;
9 of the descendants of Joab, Obadiah son of Jehiel, and with him 218 men;
10 of the descendants of Bani,[b] Shelomith son of Josiphiah, and with him 160 men;
11 of the descendants of Bebai, Zechariah son of Bebai, and with him 28 men;
12 of the descendants of Azgad, Johanan son of Hakkatan, and with him 110 men;
13 of the descendants of Adonikam, the last ones, whose names were Eliphelet, Jeuel and Shemaiah, and with them 60 men;
14 of the descendants of Bigvai, Uthai and Zaccur, and with them 70 men.

The Return to Jerusalem

15 I assembled them at the canal that flows
toward Ahava, and we camped there three
days. When I checked among the people and
the priests, I found no Levites there. 16 So I
summoned Eliezer, Ariel, Shemaiah, Elnathan, Jarib, Elnathan, Nathan, Zechariah and
Meshullam, who were leaders, and Joiarib and
Elnathan, who were men of learning, 17 and
I sent them to Iddo, the leader in Casiphia. I
told them what to say to Iddo and his kinsmen,
the temple servants in Casiphia, so that they
might bring attendants to us for the house of
our God. 18 Because the gracious hand of our
God was on us, they brought us Sherebiah, a
capable man, from the descendants of Mahli
son of Levi, the son of Israel, and Sherebiah's
sons and brothers, 18 men; 19 and Hashabiah,
together with Jeshaiah from the descendants
of Merari, and his brothers and nephews, 20
men. 20 They also brought 220 of the temple
servants—a body that David and the officials
had established to assist the Levites. All were
registered by name.

21 There, by the Ahava Canal, I proclaimed
a fast, so that we might humble ourselves before our God and ask him for a safe journey for
us and our children, with all our possessions.
22 I was ashamed to ask the king for soldiers
and horsemen to protect us from enemies on
the road, because we had told the king, "The
gracious hand of our God is on everyone who
looks to him, but his great anger is against
all who forsake him." 23 So we fasted and petitioned our God about this, and he answered
our prayer.

24 Then I set apart twelve of the leading
priests, together with Sherebiah, Hashabiah
and ten of their brothers, 25 and I weighed out
to them the offering of silver and gold and the
articles that the king, his advisers, his officials
and all Israel present there had donated for the
house of our God. 26 I weighed out to them 650
talents[c] of silver, silver articles weighing 100 talents,[d] 100 talents[d] of gold, 27 20 bowls of gold
valued at 1,000 darics,[e] and two fine articles of
polished bronze, as precious as gold.

28 I said to them, "You as well as these articles are consecrated to the LORD. The silver
and gold are a freewill offering to the LORD, the
God of your fathers. 29 Guard them carefully
until you weigh them out in the chambers of
the house of the LORD in Jerusalem before the
leading priests and the Levites and the family
heads of Israel." 30 Then the priests and Levites
received the silver and gold and sacred articles
that had been weighed out to be taken to the
house of our God in Jerusalem.

31 On the twelfth day of the first month we
set out from the Ahava Canal to go to Jerusalem. The hand of our God was on us, and he
protected us from enemies and bandits along
the way. 32 So we arrived in Jerusalem, where
we rested three days.

33 On the fourth day, in the house of our
God, we weighed out the silver and gold and
the sacred articles into the hands of Meremoth
son of Uriah, the priest. Eleazar son of Phinehas was with him, and so were the Levites Jozabad son of Jeshua and Noadiah son of Binnui.

[a] **5** Some Septuagint manuscripts (also 1 Esdras 8:32); Hebrew does not have *Zattu.* [b] **10** Some Septuagint manuscripts (also 1 Esdras 8:36); Hebrew does not have *Bani.* [c] **26** That is, about 25 tons (about 22 metric tons) [d] **26** That is, about 3 3/4 tons (about 3.4 metric tons) [e] **27** That is, about 19 pounds (about 8.5 kilograms)

Total Dependence

Read: Ezra 8:21–34

Ezra 8:22–23

I was ashamed to ask the king for soldiers and horsemen to protect us from enemies on the road, because we had told the king, "The gracious hand of our God is on everyone who looks to him, but his great anger is against all who forsake him." So we fasted and petitioned our God about this, and he answered our prayer.

LISA REALIZED SHE needed to depend on God when she discovered she was pregnant. She was excited and happy—but the timing wasn't perfect. Her husband had two years until he finished his degree. She was supporting both of them by working two jobs. Whenever she thought about the future, she broke out in a cold sweat. How would they make the rent? Would she have to quit one of her jobs? Would her husband have to quit school? She decided that the best course was to pray for God to show them the way.

Ezra sets a great example for anyone facing an unknown future. Before he and a group of returning exiles began their 900-mile trek back to Jerusalem, they all fasted and prayed for a safe journey—literally, a "straight way." They prayed for God's favor and protection and trusted "God's gracious hand" would guide them.

God is also with you to guide you, regardless of your circumstances. Perhaps you're venturing out, depending on God for the first time. Take a step of faith and follow where he leads. He will surely guide you to the next step . . . and the next. You'll discover that faith will lead you where reason may not.

Faith and reason have been compared to two travelers. Think of Faith as a woman who can walk 20 or 30 miles at a time without flagging, while Reason is a child who can only muster the strength to go two or three miles. One day Reason said to Faith, "Oh, Faith, let me walk with you." But Faith replied, "Oh, Reason, you can never walk with me!" Nevertheless, they set out together. When they came to a deep river, Reason said, "I can never ford this," but Faith waded through it, singing. When they reached a high mountain, Reason despaired. But Faith carried Reason on her back. The writer of this old tale said, "Oh, how dependent upon Faith is Reason!"

Why has God made faith the indispensable ingredient in our journey of faith? Perhaps so that we will become totally dependent upon him. Reason tells us to stay put. Faith calls us to step out, reassuring us that "nothing is impossible with God" (Luke 1:37).

reflection

1. How have you found that your reason sometimes interferes with your faith?
2. What makes it difficult for you to depend on God?
3. How can prioritizing prayer in your life make a difference in preparing you for your faith journey?

RELATED READINGS

Proverbs 3:5–6; Isaiah 58:6–9; Hebrews 11:1–2

Go to page 577 for your next devotional reading.

34Everything was accounted for by number
and weight, and the entire weight was recorded
at that time.
35Then the exiles who had returned from
captivity sacrificed burnt offerings to the God
of Israel: twelve bulls for all Israel, ninety-six
rams, seventy-seven male lambs and, as a sin
offering, twelve male goats. All this was a burnt
offering to the LORD. 36They also delivered the
king's orders to the royal satraps and to the governors of Trans-Euphrates, who then gave assistance to the people and to the house of God.

Ezra's Prayer About Intermarriage

9 After these things had been done, the
leaders came to me and said, "The people of Israel, including the priests and the Levites, have not kept themselves separate from
the neighboring peoples with their detestable
practices, like those of the Canaanites, Hittites, Perizzites, Jebusites, Ammonites, Moabites, Egyptians and Amorites. 2They have
taken some of their daughters
as wives for themselves and
their sons, and have mingled
the holy race with the peoples
around them. And the leaders
and officials have led the way
in this unfaithfulness."
3When I heard this, I tore
my tunic and cloak, pulled
hair from my head and beard
and sat down appalled. 4Then
everyone who trembled at the
words of the God of Israel gathered around me because of this
unfaithfulness of the exiles.
And I sat there appalled until
the evening sacrifice.
5Then, at the evening sacrifice, I rose from
my self-abasement, with my tunic and cloak
torn, and fell on my knees with my hands
spread out to the LORD my God 6and prayed:

"O my God, I am too ashamed and disgraced to lift up my face to you, my God,
because our sins are higher than our heads
and our guilt has reached to the heavens.
7From the days of our forefathers until
now, our guilt has been great. Because of
our sins, we and our kings and our priests
have been subjected to the sword and
captivity, to pillage and humiliation at the
hand of foreign kings, as it is today.
8"But now, for a brief moment, the
LORD our God has been gracious in leaving us a remnant and giving us a firm
place in his sanctuary, and so our God
gives light to our eyes and a little relief in
our bondage. 9Though we are slaves, our
God has not deserted us in our bondage.
He has shown us kindness in the sight of
the kings of Persia: He has granted us new
life to rebuild the house of our God and repair its ruins, and he has given us a wall of
protection in Judah and Jerusalem.
10"But now, O our God, what can we
say after this? For we have disregarded
the commands 11you gave through your
servants the prophets when you said: 'The
land you are entering to possess is a land
polluted by the corruption of its peoples.
By their detestable practices
they have filled it with their
impurity from one end to
the other. 12Therefore, do
not give your daughters in
marriage to their sons or
take their daughters for your
sons. Do not seek a treaty of
friendship with them at any
time, that you may be strong
and eat the good things of
the land and leave it to your
children as an everlasting inheritance.'
13"What has happened to
us is a result of our evil deeds
and our great guilt, and yet,
our God, you have punished us less than
our sins have deserved and have given
us a remnant like this. 14Shall we again
break your commands and intermarry
with the peoples who commit such detestable practices? Would you not be angry
enough with us to destroy us, leaving us
no remnant or survivor? 15O LORD, God
of Israel, you are righteous! We are left
this day as a remnant. Here we are before
you in our guilt, though because of it not
one of us can stand in your presence."

Ezra 9:15

God Is Righteous

"O LORD, God of Israel, you are righteous! We are left this day as a remnant. Here we are before you in our guilt, though because of it not one of us can stand in your presence."

The People's Confession of Sin

10 While Ezra was praying and confessing, weeping and throwing himself
down before the house of God, a large crowd
of Israelites—men, women and children—gathered around him. They too wept bitterly. 2Then
Shecaniah son of Jehiel, one of the descendants
of Elam, said to Ezra, "We have been unfaithful
to our God by marrying foreign women from
the peoples around us. But in spite of this, there
is still hope for Israel. 3Now let us make a covenant before our God to send away all these
women and their children, in accordance with
the counsel of my lord and of those who fear
the commands of our God. Let it be done according to the Law. 4Rise up; this matter is in
your hands. We will support you, so take courage and do it."

5So Ezra rose up and put the leading priests
and Levites and all Israel under oath to do what
had been suggested. And they took the oath.
6Then Ezra withdrew from before the house of
God and went to the room of Jehohanan son
of Eliashib. While he was there, he ate no food
and drank no water, because he continued to
mourn over the unfaithfulness of the exiles.

7A proclamation was then issued throughout Judah and Jerusalem for all the exiles to
assemble in Jerusalem. 8Anyone who failed to
appear within three days would forfeit all his
property, in accordance with the decision of
the officials and elders, and would himself be
expelled from the assembly of the exiles.

9Within the three days, all the men of Judah
and Benjamin had gathered in Jerusalem. And
on the twentieth day of the ninth month, all
the people were sitting in the square before the
house of God, greatly distressed by the occasion
and because of the rain. 10Then Ezra the priest
stood up and said to them, "You have been
unfaithful; you have married foreign women,
adding to Israel's guilt. 11Now make confession
to the LORD, the God of your fathers, and do
his will. Separate yourselves from the peoples
around you and from your foreign wives."

12The whole assembly responded with a
loud voice: "You are right! We must do as you
say. 13But there are many people here and it is
the rainy season; so we cannot stand outside.
Besides, this matter cannot be taken care of in
a day or two, because we have sinned greatly in
this thing. 14Let our officials act for the whole
assembly. Then let everyone in our towns who
has married a foreign woman come at a set
time, along with the elders and judges of each
town, until the fierce anger of our God in this
matter is turned away from us." 15Only Jonathan son of Asahel and Jahzeiah son of Tikvah,
supported by Meshullam and Shabbethai the
Levite, opposed this.

16So the exiles did as was proposed. Ezra
the priest selected men who were family heads,
one from each family division, and all of them
designated by name. On the first day of the
tenth month they sat down to investigate the
cases, 17and by the first day of the first month
they finished dealing with all the men who had
married foreign women.

Those Guilty of Intermarriage

18 Among the descendants of the priests, the
following had married foreign women:

From the descendants of Jeshua son of
Jozadak, and his brothers: Maaseiah,
Eliezer, Jarib and Gedaliah. 19(They all
gave their hands in pledge to put away
their wives, and for their guilt they
each presented a ram from the flock as
a guilt offering.)

20 From the descendants of Immer:
Hanani and Zebadiah.

21 From the descendants of Harim:
Maaseiah, Elijah, Shemaiah, Jehiel and
Uzziah.

22 From the descendants of Pashhur:
Elioenai, Maaseiah, Ishmael, Nethanel,
Jozabad and Elasah.

23 Among the Levites:

Jozabad, Shimei, Kelaiah (that is,
Kelita), Pethahiah, Judah and Eliezer.

24 From the singers:
Eliashib.

From the gatekeepers:
Shallum, Telem and Uri.

25 And among the other Israelites:

From the descendants of Parosh:
Ramiah, Izziah, Malkijah, Mijamin, Eleazar, Malkijah and Benaiah.

26 From the descendants of Elam:
Mattaniah, Zechariah, Jehiel, Abdi, Jeremoth and Elijah.
27 From the descendants of Zattu:
Elioenai, Eliashib, Mattaniah, Jeremoth, Zabad and Aziza.
28 From the descendants of Bebai:
Jehohanan, Hananiah, Zabbai and Athlai.
29 From the descendants of Bani:
Meshullam, Malluch, Adaiah, Jashub, Sheal and Jeremoth.
30 From the descendants of Pahath-Moab:
Adna, Kelal, Benaiah, Maaseiah, Mattaniah, Bezalel, Binnui and Manasseh.
31 From the descendants of Harim:
Eliezer, Ishijah, Malkijah, Shemaiah,
Shimeon, 32 Benjamin, Malluch and
Shemariah.
33 From the descendants of Hashum:
Mattenai, Mattattah, Zabad, Eliphelet, Jeremai, Manasseh and Shimei.
34 From the descendants of Bani:
Maadai, Amram, Uel, 35 Benaiah, Bede-
iah, Keluhi, 36 Vaniah, Meremoth, Eliashib, 37 Mattaniah, Mattenai and Jaasu.
38 From the descendants of Binnui:[a]
Shimei, 39 Shelemiah, Nathan, Adaiah,
40 Macnadebai, Shashai, Sharai, 41 Azarel, Shelemiah, Shemariah, 42 Shallum,
Amariah and Joseph.
43 From the descendants of Nebo:
Jeiel, Mattithiah, Zabad, Zebina, Jaddai, Joel and Benaiah.

44 All these had married foreign women, and some of them had children by these wives.[b]

[a] 37,38 See Septuagint (also 1 Esdras 9:34); Hebrew *Jaasu* [38] *and Bani and Binnui,* [b] 44 Or *and they sent them away with their children*

Nehemiah

Author:
Unknown, but possibly Ezra or Nehemiah.

Audience:
All Israel.

Date:
Around 430 B.C.

Setting:
Battling harsh opposition, the exiles rebuild the city wall of Jerusalem.

Verse to Remember:
So the wall was completed on the twenty-fifth of Elul, in fifty-two days. When all our enemies heard about this, all the surrounding nations were afraid and lost their self-confidence, because they realized that this work had been done with the help of our God. (6:15–16)

The city of Jerusalem had been the seat of King David and Solomon. In its glory days, it was a beacon to surrounding nations of how the great *God of Israel protected his people.* But the people were disobedient, and in judgment, they were marched away to exile by their Babylonian captors. The city's glory turned to ruin and shame. After decades, many of the exiles had returned to Jerusalem, but it was still vulnerable to the violence and scorn of its enemies. The walls and gates remained in ruins. When Nehemiah, cupbearer to King Artaxerxes, heard of the city's shame, he was devastated. He knew they had to rebuild the wall to offer protection to the people and to demonstrate *God's glory once again.*

Nehemiah prayed before he spoke with the king. He prayed on the journey. He prayed when he encountered resistance. *Look for his prayers* scattered throughout the book and see what you can learn. Nehemiah also demonstrated what it means to be a godly leader, and through his leadership there was powerful unity among God's people.

Nehemiah's Prayer

1 The words of Nehemiah son of Hacaliah:

In the month of Kislev in the twentieth year,
while I was in the citadel of Susa, 2Hanani, one
of my brothers, came from Judah with some
other men, and I questioned them about the
Jewish remnant that survived the exile, and
also about Jerusalem.
3They said to me, "Those who survived the
exile and are back in the province are in great
trouble and disgrace. The wall of Jerusalem is
broken down, and its gates have been burned
with fire."

A Pattern for Prayer

Read: Nehemiah 1:1–11

IN 1960s SOUTHERN CALIFORNIA, the beaches were littered with hippies searching for the meaning of life through free love, psychedelic drugs and communal living. One day, a pastor's wife went to the beach and was distressed to see the aimless kids and began to weep. Kay Smith determined to do something, so she gathered several of her friends and, as she puts it, "saturated the air with prayer." She asked her husband, Pastor Chuck Smith, to open his church to this generation. Many people were shocked when the hippies showed up, barefoot and bedraggled, and sat on the floor rather than in the pews. But the Smiths embraced them. Their ministry was a vital part of the "Jesus Movement" that swept the country. It can be said that true revival begins with heartfelt tears but finds its voice in prayer.

Nehemiah, one of the most powerful Jews in Babylon, broke down in tears when he heard of Jerusalem's miserable condition. He mourned for God's holy city and scattered people. His compassion compelled him to pray and fast for them. His prayer reflected his heart's passion and also offers a pattern for our prayers.

First, Nehemiah acknowledged who God is: "the great and awesome God." When we focus on who God is, it helps to put our own problems into proper perspective.

Next Nehemiah acknowledged who he himself was: God's servant. When we maintain an attitude of humility toward our heavenly Father, we are reminded of our dependence on God.

Then Nehemiah confessed his own sins and the sins of the Israelites. He didn't gloss over the transgressions but stated them in honest repentance. Repentance freed him—and can free us—to make the next step in prayer.

Awed, humbled and forgiven—Nehemiah reminded God of his promises to his people. He recounted God's promises to the children of Israel and interceded for his people, asking God to hear his prayer and favor him.

What situation has brought you to tears? If it is enough to touch your heart, it's enough to bring you to your knees. Follow Nehemiah's pattern: Acknowledge who God is and who you are, confess your sins and remind God of his promises. When you do these things, you can come to God knowing that "he hears the prayer of the righteous" (Proverbs 15:29).

Nehemiah 1:4

When I heard these things, I sat down and wept. For some days I mourned and fasted and prayed before the God of heaven.

reflection

1 When was the last time you wept in prayer for someone who needed God's help?

2 What word best describes Nehemiah's heart? Ask God to give you a heart of compassion like Nehemiah's.

3 Follow Nehemiah's pattern and pray for a person or situation causing you to grieve.

RELATED READINGS

Psalm 89:5–8;
Isaiah 25:1–9;
Matthew 6:9–13

Go to page 579 for your next devotional reading.

4When I heard these things, I sat down and
wept. For some days I mourned and fasted
and prayed before the God of heaven. 5Then
I said:

"O LORD, God of heaven, the great and
awesome God, who keeps his covenant of
love with those who love him and obey
his commands, 6let your ear be attentive
and your eyes open to hear the prayer
your servant is praying before you day and night for
your servants, the people of
Israel. I confess the sins we
Israelites, including myself
and my father's house, have
committed against you. 7We
have acted very wickedly
toward you. We have not
obeyed the commands, decrees and laws you gave your
servant Moses.

8"Remember the instruction you gave your servant
Moses, saying, 'If you are
unfaithful, I will scatter you
among the nations, 9but if
you return to me and obey
my commands, then even if your exiled
people are at the farthest horizon, I will
gather them from there and bring them
to the place I have chosen as a dwelling
for my Name.'

10"They are your servants and your
people, whom you redeemed by your
great strength and your mighty hand.
11O Lord, let your ear be attentive to the
prayer of this your servant and to the
prayer of your servants who delight in revering your name. Give your servant success today by granting him favor in the
presence of this man."

I was cupbearer to the king.

Nehemiah 1:6

God Sees Our Needs

"Let your ear be attentive and your eyes open to hear the prayer your servant is praying before you day and night for your servants, the people of Israel."

Artaxerxes Sends Nehemiah to Jerusalem

2 In the month of Nisan in the twentieth
year of King Artaxerxes, when wine was
brought for him, I took the wine and gave it
to the king. I had not been sad in his presence
before; 2so the king asked me, "Why does your
face look so sad when you are not ill? This can
be nothing but sadness of heart."

I was very much afraid, 3but I said to the
king, "May the king live forever! Why should
my face not look sad when the city where my fathers are buried lies in ruins, and its gates have
been destroyed by fire?"

4The king said to me, "What is it you want?"

Then I prayed to the God of heaven, 5and I
answered the king, "If it pleases
the king and if your servant has
found favor in his sight, let him
send me to the city in Judah
where my fathers are buried so
that I can rebuild it."

6Then the king, with the
queen sitting beside him, asked
me, "How long will your journey take, and when will you
get back?" It pleased the king
to send me; so I set a time.

7I also said to him, "If it
pleases the king, may I have letters to the governors of Trans-Euphrates, so that they will
provide me safe-conduct until
I arrive in Judah? 8And may I
have a letter to Asaph, keeper of the king's forest, so he will give me timber to make beams for
the gates of the citadel by the temple and for the
city wall and for the residence I will occupy?"
And because the gracious hand of my God was
upon me, the king granted my requests. 9So I
went to the governors of Trans-Euphrates and
gave them the king's letters. The king had also
sent army officers and cavalry with me.

10When Sanballat the Horonite and Tobiah
the Ammonite official heard about this, they
were very much disturbed that someone had
come to promote the welfare of the Israelites.

Nehemiah Inspects Jerusalem's Walls

11I went to Jerusalem, and after staying there
three days 12I set out during the night with a
few men. I had not told anyone what my God
had put in my heart to do for Jerusalem. There
were no mounts with me except the one I was
riding on.

13By night I went out through the Valley
Gate toward the Jackal[a] Well and the Dung

[a]13 Or *Serpent* or *Fig*

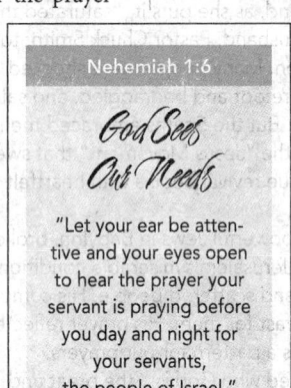

Help!

Read: Nehemiah 2:1–18

HOW WOULD YOU complete this sentence: "When I am afraid, I __________"? When things heat up do you run in the opposite direction, hide your true feelings or stick your head in the proverbial sand? Chances are you've done all three at one time or another. But here's another option: pray . . . fast!

Nehemiah faced a potentially terrifying situation. Four months before, he had discovered that the walls of Jerusalem had been destroyed and the gates burned with fire. The Jewish remnant had returned from exile, but their city was in ruins with no walls to protect them from enemy attacks and wild animals. Nehemiah longed to return to Jerusalem and help rebuild the walls, but as the king's cupbearer he was expected to be cheerful and keep his personal problems to himself. Any other response could mean death.

But Nehemiah couldn't hide his concern for God's city and people. The king noticed his servant's downcast countenance. "Why does your face look so sad?" he asked. "What do you want?"

Time must have stood still for Nehemiah. *This is what I've longed for, prayed about, dreamed of,* he may have thought. Or maybe he thought, *Oh no! This is what I feared!* But as the knot formed in Nehemiah's stomach and the lump rose in his throat, we see one of the most beautiful, spontaneous prayers in the Bible, "Then I prayed to the God of heaven."

All through the day we are faced with decisions great and small. Some require extended periods of prayer, such as Nehemiah experienced in chapter 1. Others prompt spontaneous prayers that come as easily and naturally as our very breath . . . *Help!*

What do you face today? What decisions do you have to make? You may not face a life-or-death situation like Nehemiah, but the God of heaven and earth longs to hear your simple, spontaneous prayers. *Help . . .* now!

Nehemiah 2:2,4

I was very much afraid . . . Then I prayed to the God of heaven.

reflection

1. How do you normally handle fearful situations?
2. How can you apply Nehemiah's prayer strategy to your life?
3. Have you experienced a time when God answered your specific prayer? Think of someone with whom you can share your story.

RELATED READINGS

Psalms 27:1–14; 55:16–23; 91:1–16; 1 Thessalonians 5:17

"Never be afraid to trust an unknown future to a known God."

Corrie ten Boom

Go to page 582 for your next devotional reading.

Gate, examining the walls of Jerusalem, which
had been broken down, and its gates, which
had been destroyed by fire. 14 Then I moved on
toward the Fountain Gate and the King's Pool,
but there was not enough room for my mount
to get through; 15 so I went up the valley by
night, examining the wall. Finally, I turned back
and reentered through the Valley Gate. 16 The
officials did not know where I had gone or what
I was doing, because as yet I had said nothing
to the Jews or the priests or nobles or officials
or any others who would be doing the work.

17 Then I said to them, "You see the trouble we are in: Jerusalem lies in ruins, and its
gates have been burned with fire. Come, let us
rebuild the wall of Jerusalem, and we will no
longer be in disgrace." 18 I also told them about
the gracious hand of my God upon me and
what the king had said to me.

They replied, "Let us start rebuilding." So
they began this good work.

19 But when Sanballat the Horonite, Tobiah
the Ammonite official and Geshem the Arab
heard about it, they mocked and ridiculed us.
"What is this you are doing?" they asked. "Are
you rebelling against the king?"

20 I answered them by saying, "The God of
heaven will give us success. We his servants
will start rebuilding, but as for you, you have
no share in Jerusalem or any claim or historic
right to it."

Builders of the Wall

3 Eliashib the high priest and his fellow
priests went to work and rebuilt the Sheep
Gate. They dedicated it and set its doors in
place, building as far as the Tower of the Hundred, which they dedicated, and as far as the
Tower of Hananel. 2 The men of Jericho built
the adjoining section, and Zaccur son of Imri
built next to them.

3 The Fish Gate was rebuilt by the sons of
Hassenaah. They laid its beams and put its
doors and bolts and bars in place. 4 Meremoth
son of Uriah, the son of Hakkoz, repaired the
next section. Next to him Meshullam son of
Berekiah, the son of Meshezabel, made repairs, and next to him Zadok son of Baana also
made repairs. 5 The next section was repaired
by the men of Tekoa, but their nobles would
not put their shoulders to the work under
their supervisors.[a]

6 The Jeshanah[b] Gate was repaired by Joiada
son of Paseah and Meshullam son of Besode-
iah. They laid its beams and put its doors and
bolts and bars in place. 7 Next to them, repairs
were made by men from Gibeon and Mizpah—
Melatiah of Gibeon and Jadon of Meronoth—
places under the authority of the governor of
Trans-Euphrates. 8 Uzziel son of Harhaiah, one
of the goldsmiths, repaired the next section;
and Hananiah, one of the perfume-makers,
made repairs next to that. They restored[c] Jerusalem as far as the Broad Wall. 9 Rephaiah son
of Hur, ruler of a half-district of Jerusalem,
repaired the next section. 10 Adjoining this, Jedaiah son of Harumaph made repairs opposite
his house, and Hattush son of Hashabneiah
made repairs next to him. 11 Malkijah son of
Harim and Hasshub son of Pahath-Moab repaired another section and the Tower of the
Ovens. 12 Shallum son of Hallohesh, ruler of a
half-district of Jerusalem, repaired the next section with the help of his daughters.

13 The Valley Gate was repaired by Hanun
and the residents of Zanoah. They rebuilt it and
put its doors and bolts and bars in place. They
also repaired five hundred yards[d] of the wall as
far as the Dung Gate.

14 The Dung Gate was repaired by Malkijah
son of Recab, ruler of the district of Beth Hakkerem. He rebuilt it and put its doors and bolts
and bars in place.

15 The Fountain Gate was repaired by Shal-
lun son of Col-Hozeh, ruler of the district of
Mizpah. He rebuilt it, roofing it over and putting its doors and bolts and bars in place. He
also repaired the wall of the Pool of Siloam,[e]
by the King's Garden, as far as the steps going
down from the City of David. 16 Beyond him,
Nehemiah son of Azbuk, ruler of a half-district
of Beth Zur, made repairs up to a point opposite the tombs[f] of David, as far as the artificial
pool and the House of the Heroes.

[a] 5 Or *their Lord* or *the governor* [b] 6 Or *Old* [c] 8 Or *They left out part of* [d] 13 Hebrew *a thousand cubits* (about 450 meters) [e] 15 Hebrew *Shelah,* a variant of *Shiloah,* that is, Siloam [f] 16 Hebrew; Septuagint, some Vulgate manuscripts and Syriac *tomb*

17Next to him, the repairs were made by the
Levites under Rehum son of Bani. Beside him,
Hashabiah, ruler of half the district of Keilah,
carried out repairs for his district. 18Next to
him, the repairs were made by their countrymen under Binnui[a] son of Henadad, ruler of
the other half-district of Keilah. 19Next to him,
Ezer son of Jeshua, ruler of Mizpah, repaired
another section, from a point facing the ascent
to the armory as far as the angle. 20Next to
him, Baruch son of Zabbai zealously repaired
another section, from the angle to the entrance
of the house of Eliashib the high priest. 21Next
to him, Meremoth son of Uriah, the son of
Hakkoz, repaired another section, from the entrance of Eliashib's house to the end of it.

22The repairs next to him were made by
the priests from the surrounding region. 23Be-
yond them, Benjamin and Has-
shub made repairs in front of
their house; and next to them,
Azariah son of Maaseiah, the
son of Ananiah, made repairs
beside his house. 24Next to
him, Binnui son of Henadad
repaired another section, from
Azariah's house to the angle
and the corner, 25and Palal
son of Uzai worked opposite
the angle and the tower projecting from the upper palace near
the court of the guard. Next
to him, Pedaiah son of Parosh
26and the temple servants living on the hill of Ophel made
repairs up to a point opposite the Water Gate toward the east and the projecting tower. 27Next
to them, the men of Tekoa repaired another
section, from the great projecting tower to the
wall of Ophel.

28Above the Horse Gate, the priests made
repairs, each in front of his own house. 29Next
to them, Zadok son of Immer made repairs
opposite his house. Next to him, Shemaiah
son of Shecaniah, the guard at the East Gate,
made repairs. 30Next to him, Hananiah son
of Shelemiah, and Hanun, the sixth son of Za-
laph, repaired another section. Next to them,
Meshullam son of Berekiah made repairs opposite his living quarters. 31Next to him, Malkijah, one of the goldsmiths, made repairs as far
as the house of the temple servants and the merchants, opposite the Inspection Gate, and as far
as the room above the corner; 32and between
the room above the corner and the Sheep Gate
the goldsmiths and merchants made repairs.

Opposition to the Rebuilding

4 When Sanballat heard that we were rebuilding the wall, he became angry and was
greatly incensed. He ridiculed the Jews, 2and
in the presence of his associates and the army
of Samaria, he said, "What are those feeble Jews
doing? Will they restore their wall? Will they
offer sacrifices? Will they finish in a day? Can
they bring the stones back to life from those
heaps of rubble—burned as they are?"

3Tobiah the Ammonite,
who was at his side, said,
"What they are building—if
even a fox climbed up on it, he
would break down their wall
of stones!"

4Hear us, O our God, for we
are despised. Turn their insults
back on their own heads. Give
them over as plunder in a land
of captivity. 5Do not cover up
their guilt or blot out their sins
from your sight, for they have
thrown insults in the face of[b]
the builders.

6So we rebuilt the wall till
all of it reached half its height, for the people
worked with all their heart.

7But when Sanballat, Tobiah, the Arabs,
the Ammonites and the men of Ashdod heard
that the repairs to Jerusalem's walls had gone
ahead and that the gaps were being closed, they
were very angry. 8They all plotted together to
come and fight against Jerusalem and stir up
trouble against it. 9But we prayed to our God
and posted a guard day and night to meet
this threat.

10Meanwhile, the people in Judah said,
"The strength of the laborers is giving out, and

Nehemiah 4:4

God Hears Our Prayers

Hear us, O our God, for we are despised. Turn their insults back on their own heads. Give them over as plunder in a land of captivity.

[a] 18 Two Hebrew manuscripts and Syriac (see also Septuagint and verse 24); most Hebrew manuscripts *Bavvai* [b] 5 Or *have provoked you to anger before*

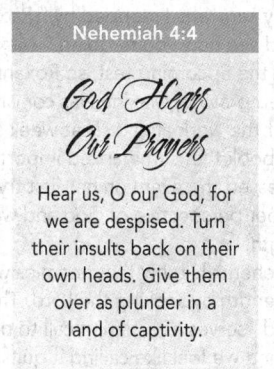

Persistence Prays

Read: Nehemiah 4:1–23

Nehemiah 4:8–10

They all plotted together to come and fight against Jerusalem and stir up trouble against it. But we prayed to our God and posted a guard day and night to meet this threat. Meanwhile, the people in Judah said, "The strength of the laborers is giving out, and there is so much rubble that we cannot rebuild the wall."

WHEN THE JEWS listened to the taunts and insults of their enemies, they felt their strength dissipating and even felt like giving up. It took the watchful eyes of Nehemiah to see the deeper spiritual realities—that God was greater than the enemy and that he would strengthen his people so that they could finish building the wall.

Maxine recalled a time when discouragement nearly won a victory in her life. She had returned to college at midlife to get her teaching certification in English. She was overwhelmed at the thought of taking the National Teacher's Examination in English, which consisted of comprehensive questions about literature titles, authors and characters—all only fuzzy memories from her young-adult college days. A friend had taken the exam twice and failed, and Maxine dreaded that possibility.

One morning Roxanne dropped by Maxine's home. "I'm not exactly sure why I stopped by," Roxanne said. "I felt a tug to come by and see how you're doing." Maxine related her apprehensions about the upcoming test, so Roxanne prayed with her. When they finished praying, Maxine was convinced that God would strengthen her for the work ahead. That week she began studying a thousand-page book that summarized important literature. Two months later she passed the exam on her first try. Through prayer, she regained a proper perspective of God and was able to find renewed strength.

Nehemiah knew that enemies were plotting, so he summoned up strength by seeking the Lord. The simple phrase "but we prayed" serves as a clarion call to prayer when the work seems too hard and we feel like calling it quits. Think about it. If Nehemiah had given up, the walls of Jerusalem would not have been rebuilt. If Maxine had given up, students might have been robbed of a godly teacher. What if Jesus had given up? We would not have a Savior to forgive our sins. Thankfully, he finished what he started.

Through prayer, you can carry on too, knowing that "he who began a good work in you will carry it on to completion until the day of Christ Jesus" (Philippians 1:6).

reflection

1 What task seems too big or too daunting for you to finish?

2 Who could you ask to come alongside you in prayer?

3 Write down some good things that might result if you do complete your task. Ask God to give you the persistence to finish what you've started.

RELATED READINGS

Isaiah 40:1–31; 2 Timothy 4:6–8; Hebrews 12:1–13

Go to page 587 for your next devotional reading.

there is so much rubble that we cannot rebuild
the wall."
[11]Also our enemies said, "Before they know
it or see us, we will be right there among them
and will kill them and put an end to the work."
[12]Then the Jews who lived near them came
and told us ten times over, "Wherever you turn,
they will attack us."
[13]Therefore I stationed some of the people
behind the lowest points of the wall at the exposed places, posting them by families, with
their swords, spears and bows. [14]After I looked
things over, I stood up and said to the nobles,
the officials and the rest of the people, "Don't
be afraid of them. Remember the Lord, who is
great and awesome, and fight for your brothers,
your sons and your daughters, your wives and
your homes."
[15]When our enemies heard that we were
aware of their plot and that God had frustrated
it, we all returned to the wall, each to his
own work.
[16]From that day on, half of my men did the
work, while the other half were equipped with
spears, shields, bows and armor. The officers
posted themselves behind all the people of Judah [17]who were building the wall. Those who
carried materials did their work with one hand
and held a weapon in the other, [18]and each of
the builders wore his sword at his side as he
worked. But the man who sounded the trumpet stayed with me.
[19]Then I said to the nobles, the officials and
the rest of the people, "The work is extensive
and spread out, and we are widely separated
from each other along the wall. [20]Wherever
you hear the sound of the trumpet, join us
there. Our God will fight for us!"
[21]So we continued the work with half the
men holding spears, from the first light of
dawn till the stars came out. [22]At that time I
also said to the people, "Have every man and
his helper stay inside Jerusalem at night, so
they can serve us as guards by night and workmen by day." [23]Neither I nor my brothers nor
my men nor the guards with me took off our
clothes; each had his weapon, even when he
went for water.[a]

Nehemiah Helps the Poor

5 Now the men and their wives raised a
great outcry against their Jewish brothers. [2]Some were saying, "We and our sons and
daughters are numerous; in order for us to eat
and stay alive, we must get grain."
[3]Others were saying, "We are mortgaging
our fields, our vineyards and our homes to get
grain during the famine."
[4]Still others were saying, "We have had to
borrow money to pay the king's tax on our
fields and vineyards. [5]Although we are of the
same flesh and blood as our countrymen and
though our sons are as good as theirs, yet we
have to subject our sons and daughters to slavery. Some of our daughters have already been
enslaved, but we are powerless, because our
fields and our vineyards belong to others."
[6]When I heard their outcry and these
charges, I was very angry. [7]I pondered them in
my mind and then accused the nobles and officials. I told them, "You are exacting usury from
your own countrymen!" So I called together a
large meeting to deal with them [8]and said: "As
far as possible, we have bought back our Jewish
brothers who were sold to the Gentiles. Now
you are selling your brothers, only for them to
be sold back to us!" They kept quiet, because
they could find nothing to say.
[9]So I continued, "What you are doing is not
right. Shouldn't you walk in the fear of our
God to avoid the reproach of our Gentile enemies? [10]I and my brothers and my men are
also lending the people money and grain. But
let the exacting of usury stop! [11]Give back to
them immediately their fields, vineyards, olive
groves and houses, and also the usury you are
charging them—the hundredth part of the
money, grain, new wine and oil."
[12]"We will give it back," they said. "And we
will not demand anything more from them.
We will do as you say."
Then I summoned the priests and made the
nobles and officials take an oath to do what
they had promised. [13]I also shook out the folds
of my robe and said, "In this way may God
shake out of his house and possessions every
man who does not keep this promise. So may
such a man be shaken out and emptied!"

[a]23 The meaning of the Hebrew for this clause is uncertain.

At this the whole assembly said, "Amen," and
praised the LORD. And the people did as they
had promised.
14 Moreover, from the twentieth year of King
Artaxerxes, when I was appointed to be their
governor in the land of Judah, until his thirty-
second year—twelve years—neither I nor my
brothers ate the food allotted to the governor.
15 But the earlier governors—those preceding
me—placed a heavy burden on the people and
took forty shekels[a] of silver from them in addition to food and wine. Their assistants also
lorded it over the people. But out of reverence
for God I did not act like that. 16 Instead, I
devoted myself to the work on this wall. All my
men were assembled there for the work; we[b]
did not acquire any land.

17 Furthermore, a hundred and fifty Jews
and officials ate at my table, as well as those
who came to us from the surrounding nations.
18 Each day one ox, six choice sheep and some
poultry were prepared for me, and every ten
days an abundant supply of wine of all kinds.
In spite of all this, I never demanded the food
allotted to the governor, because the demands
were heavy on these people.
19 Remember me with favor, O my God, for
all I have done for these people.

Further Opposition to the Rebuilding

6 When word came to Sanballat, Tobiah,
Geshem the Arab and the rest of our enemies that I had rebuilt the wall and not a gap
was left in it—though up to that time I had not
set the doors in the gates— 2 Sanballat and Geshem sent me this message: "Come, let us meet
together in one of the villages[c] on the plain
of Ono."

But they were scheming to harm me; 3 so
I sent messengers to them with this reply: "I
am carrying on a great project and cannot go
down. Why should the work stop while I leave
it and go down to you?" 4 Four times they sent
me the same message, and each time I gave
them the same answer.
5 Then, the fifth time, Sanballat sent his aide
to me with the same message, and in his hand
was an unsealed letter 6 in which was written:

"It is reported among the nations—and
Geshem[d] says it is true—that you and
the Jews are plotting to revolt, and therefore you are building the wall. Moreover,
according to these reports you are about
to become their king 7 and have even
appointed prophets to make this proclamation about you in Jerusalem: 'There is
a king in Judah!' Now this report will get
back to the king; so come, let us confer
together."

8 I sent him this reply: "Nothing like what
you are saying is happening; you are just making it up out of your head."
9 They were all trying to frighten us, thinking, "Their hands will get too weak for the
work, and it will not be completed."

⌞But I prayed,⌟ "Now strengthen my hands."
10 One day I went to the house of Shemaiah
son of Delaiah, the son of Mehetabel, who was
shut in at his home. He said, "Let us meet in
the house of God, inside the temple, and let us
close the temple doors, because men are coming to kill you—by night they are coming to
kill you."
11 But I said, "Should a man like me run
away? Or should one like me go into the temple
to save his life? I will not go!" 12 I realized that
God had not sent him, but that he had prophesied against me because Tobiah and Sanballat
had hired him. 13 He had been hired to intimidate me so that I would commit a sin by doing
this, and then they would give me a bad name
to discredit me.

14 Remember Tobiah and Sanballat, O my
God, because of what they have done; remember also the prophetess Noadiah and the rest
of the prophets who have been trying to intimidate me.

The Completion of the Wall

15 So the wall was completed on the twenty-
fifth of Elul, in fifty-two days. 16 When all our
enemies heard about this, all the surrounding nations were afraid and lost their self-
confidence, because they realized that this
work had been done with the help of our God.
17 Also, in those days the nobles of Judah

[a] 15 That is, about 1 pound (about 0.5 kilogram) [b] 16 Most Hebrew manuscripts; some Hebrew manuscripts, Septuagint, Vulgate and Syriac *I* [c] 2 Or *in Kephirim* [d] 6 Hebrew *Gashmu,* a variant of *Geshem*

were sending many letters to Tobiah, and replies from Tobiah kept coming to them. 18For
many in Judah were under oath to him, since
he was son-in-law to Shecaniah son of Arah,
and his son Jehohanan had married the daughter of Meshullam son of Berekiah. 19Moreover,
they kept reporting to me his good deeds and
then telling him what I said. And Tobiah sent
letters to intimidate me.

7 After the wall had been rebuilt and I had
set the doors in place, the gatekeepers and
the singers and the Levites were appointed. 2I
put in charge of Jerusalem my brother Hanani,
along with[a] Hananiah the commander of the
citadel, because he was a man of integrity and
feared God more than most men do. 3I said
to them, "The gates of Jerusalem are not to be
opened until the sun is hot. While the gatekeepers are still on duty, have them shut the doors
and bar them. Also appoint residents of Jerusalem as guards, some at their posts and some
near their own houses."

The List of the Exiles Who Returned

4Now the city was large and spacious, but
there were few people in it, and the houses had
not yet been rebuilt. 5So my God put it into
my heart to assemble the nobles, the officials
and the common people for registration by families. I found the genealogical record of those
who had been the first to return. This is what I
found written there:

6These are the people of the province
who came up from the captivity of the
exiles whom Nebuchadnezzar king of
Babylon had taken captive (they returned
to Jerusalem and Judah, each to his own
town, 7in company with Zerubbabel,
Jeshua, Nehemiah, Azariah, Raamiah,
Nahamani, Mordecai, Bilshan, Mispereth,
Bigvai, Nehum and Baanah):

The list of the men of Israel:

8 the descendants of Parosh	2,172
9 of Shephatiah	372
10 of Arah	652
11 of Pahath-Moab (through the line of Jeshua and Joab)	2,818
12 of Elam	1,254
13 of Zattu	845
14 of Zaccai	760
15 of Binnui	648
16 of Bebai	628
17 of Azgad	2,322
18 of Adonikam	667
19 of Bigvai	2,067
20 of Adin	655
21 of Ater (through Hezekiah)	98
22 of Hashum	328
23 of Bezai	324
24 of Hariph	112
25 of Gibeon	95
26 the men of Bethlehem and Netophah	188
27 of Anathoth	128
28 of Beth Azmaveth	42
29 of Kiriath Jearim, Kephirah and Beeroth	743
30 of Ramah and Geba	621
31 of Micmash	122
32 of Bethel and Ai	123
33 of the other Nebo	52
34 of the other Elam	1,254
35 of Harim	320
36 of Jericho	345
37 of Lod, Hadid and Ono	721
38 of Senaah	3,930

39The priests:

the descendants of Jedaiah (through the family of Jeshua)	973
40 of Immer	1,052
41 of Pashhur	1,247
42 of Harim	1,017

43The Levites:

the descendants of Jeshua (through Kadmiel through the line of Hodaviah)	74

44The singers:

the descendants of Asaph	148

45The gatekeepers:

the descendants of Shallum, Ater, Talmon, Akkub, Hatita and Shobai	138

[a] 2 Or *Hanani, that is,*

46The temple servants:

the descendants of
Ziha, Hasupha, Tabbaoth,
47 Keros, Sia, Padon,
48 Lebana, Hagaba, Shalmai,
49 Hanan, Giddel, Gahar,
50 Reaiah, Rezin, Nekoda,
51 Gazzam, Uzza, Paseah,
52 Besai, Meunim, Nephusim,
53 Bakbuk, Hakupha, Harhur,
54 Bazluth, Mehida, Harsha,
55 Barkos, Sisera, Temah,
56 Neziah and Hatipha

57The descendants of the servants of Solomon:

the descendants of
Sotai, Sophereth, Perida,
58 Jaala, Darkon, Giddel,
59 Shephatiah, Hattil,
Pokereth-Hazzebaim and Amon

60 The temple servants and the descendants of the servants of Solomon 392

61The following came up from the towns of Tel Melah, Tel Harsha, Kerub, Addon and Immer, but they could not show that their families were descended from Israel:

62 the descendants of
Delaiah, Tobiah and Nekoda 642

63 And from among the priests:

the descendants of
Hobaiah, Hakkoz and Barzillai (a man who had married a daughter of Barzillai the Gileadite and was called by that name).

64These searched for their family records, but they could not find them and so were excluded from the priesthood as unclean.
65The governor, therefore, ordered them not to eat any of the most sacred food until there should be a priest ministering with the Urim and Thummim.

66The whole company numbered 42,360,
67besides their 7,337 menservants and maidservants; and they also had 245 men and women singers.
68There were 736 horses, 245 mules,[a]
69435 camels and 6,720 donkeys.

70Some of the heads of the families contributed to the work. The governor gave to the treasury 1,000 drachmas[b] of gold, 50 bowls and 530 garments for priests.
71Some of the heads of the families gave to the treasury for the work 20,000 drachmas[c] of gold and 2,200 minas[d] of silver.
72The total given by the rest of the people was 20,000 drachmas of gold, 2,000 minas[e] of silver and 67 garments for priests.

73The priests, the Levites, the gatekeepers, the singers and the temple servants, along with certain of the people and the rest of the Israelites, settled in their own towns.

Ezra Reads the Law

8 When the seventh month came and the Israelites had settled in their towns,
1all the people assembled as one man in the square before the Water Gate. They told Ezra the scribe to bring out the Book of the Law of Moses, which the LORD had commanded for Israel.

2So on the first day of the seventh month Ezra the priest brought the Law before the assembly, which was made up of men and women and all who were able to understand.
3He read it aloud from daybreak till noon as he faced the square before the Water Gate in the presence of the men, women and others who could understand. And all the people listened attentively to the Book of the Law.

4Ezra the scribe stood on a high wooden platform built for the occasion. Beside him on his right stood Mattithiah, Shema, Anaiah, Uriah, Hilkiah and Maaseiah; and on his left were Pedaiah, Mishael, Malkijah, Hashum, Hashbaddanah, Zechariah and Meshullam.

5Ezra opened the book. All the people could see him because he was standing above them; and as he opened it, the people all stood up.

[a]68 Some Hebrew manuscripts (see also Ezra 2:66); most Hebrew manuscripts do not have this verse. [b]70 That is, about 19 pounds (about 8.5 kilograms) [c]71 That is, about 375 pounds (about 170 kilograms); also in verse 72 [d]71 That is, about 1 1/3 tons (about 1.2 metric tons) [e]72 That is, about 1 1/4 tons (about 1.1 metric tons)

Unlimited Source of Joy

Read: Nehemiah 8:1–12

WHAT A GLORIOUS DAY! The people are finally celebrating the completion of their dream—the rebuilding of the wall around Jerusalem. Yet, upon hearing the reading of God's laws, the people are cut to the heart, grieved by their sin. Nehemiah tells the people to put away their mourning, "For the joy of the LORD is your strength." How could they have joy in the face of their guilt and sorrow? How could they experience joy even when they had neglected God's ways?

Let's bring this into our own lives. Can we experience joy even in the midst of realizing how broken and needy we are? In the midst of our disappointment and struggles? Yes, we can! The joy available to us—like the joy that was available to the people of Jerusalem—is not dependent upon us or on our circumstances. It's not dependent on our temperament or hormone levels. This joy does not come from "having it all together," or from everything going well, accomplishing our goals or overcoming obstacles. No, this joy is "of the *LORD*."

Joy—true joy—originates from God and from living in close connection with God, not from our immediate situation or emotional state. Joy is always accessible to us because God has given us his Holy Spirit (see Galatians 5:22–23). Not only do we have constant access to the Spirit of joy, but this joy is also, according to Nehemiah, our very strength; and it is available now! The enemy tries to deceive us into believing we cannot experience joy—at least not just yet. We buy into the thinking that says, "When this is over, when I finish this, when I obtain that, when I've resolved this . . . *then* I can experience joy."

Yet God wants us to know his joy *now*. Not tomorrow, not when we're healed, not when sorrow has passed, not when we've become successful, not when our child or spouse changes, not when we've lost ten pounds, not when we've paid off our debt, received a promotion or bought a bigger home, but *now*—this day!

Lasting joy does not reside in God's blessings, God's favor, God's gifts or God's people, but in God *himself*. Take time this day to seek the Lord and draw upon him to find your joy—your strength.

Nehemiah 8:10

"Do not grieve, for the joy of the LORD is your strength."

reflection

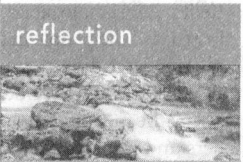

1 What's the difference between joy and feeling happy?

2 What or whom do you tend to look to first as your source of joy?

3 What are you waiting to overcome, obtain or get rid of before experiencing God's joy?

RELATED READINGS

Psalms 43:1–5; 51:1–12; 118:24;
John 15:9–17

Go to page 598 for your next devotional reading.

6Ezra praised the LORD, the great God; and all
the people lifted their hands and responded,
"Amen! Amen!" Then they bowed down and
worshiped the LORD with their faces to the
ground.
7The Levites—Jeshua, Bani, Sherebiah, Jamin, Akkub, Shabbethai, Hodiah, Maaseiah,
Kelita, Azariah, Jozabad, Hanan and Pelaiah—
instructed the people in the Law while the people were standing there. 8They read from the
Book of the Law of God, making it clear[a] and
giving the meaning so that the people could understand what was being read.
9Then Nehemiah the governor, Ezra the
priest and scribe, and the Levites who were instructing the people said to them all, "This day
is sacred to the LORD your God. Do not mourn
or weep." For all the people had been weeping
as they listened to the words of the Law.
10Nehemiah said, "Go and enjoy choice
food and sweet drinks, and send some to those
who have nothing prepared. This day is sacred
to our Lord. Do not grieve, for the joy of the
LORD is your strength."
11The Levites calmed all the
people, saying, "Be still, for this
is a sacred day. Do not grieve."
12Then all the people went
away to eat and drink, to send
portions of food and to celebrate with great joy, because
they now understood the
words that had been made
known to them.
13On the second day of the
month, the heads of all the
families, along with the priests
and the Levites, gathered
around Ezra the scribe to give
attention to the words of the
Law. 14They found written in
the Law, which the LORD had
commanded through Moses,
that the Israelites were to live in booths during the feast of the seventh month 15and that
they should proclaim this word and spread
it throughout their towns and in Jerusalem:
"Go out into the hill country and bring back
branches from olive and wild olive trees, and
from myrtles, palms and shade trees, to make
booths"—as it is written.[b]
16So the people went out and brought back
branches and built themselves booths on their
own roofs, in their courtyards, in the courts of
the house of God and in the square by the Water Gate and the one by the Gate of Ephraim.
17The whole company that had returned from
exile built booths and lived in them. From the
days of Joshua son of Nun until that day, the Israelites had not celebrated it like this. And their
joy was very great.
18Day after day, from the first day to the last,
Ezra read from the Book of the Law of God.
They celebrated the feast for seven days, and
on the eighth day, in accordance with the regulation, there was an assembly.

The Israelites Confess Their Sins

9 On the twenty-fourth day of the same
month, the Israelites gathered together,
fasting and wearing sackcloth and having dust
on their heads. 2Those of Israelite descent had
separated themselves from all
foreigners. They stood in their
places and confessed their sins
and the wickedness of their
fathers. 3They stood where
they were and read from the
Book of the Law of the LORD
their God for a quarter of
the day, and spent another
quarter in confession and in
worshiping the LORD their
God. 4Standing on the stairs
were the Levites—Jeshua,
Bani, Kadmiel, Shebaniah,
Bunni, Sherebiah, Bani and
Kenani—who called with loud
voices to the LORD their God.
5And the Levites—Jeshua,
Kadmiel, Bani, Hashabneiah,
Sherebiah, Hodiah, Shebaniah
and Pethahiah—said: "Stand up and praise
the LORD your God, who is from everlasting
to everlasting.[c]"

"Blessed be your glorious name, and
may it be exalted above all blessing and
praise. 6You alone are the LORD. You

Nehemiah 9:6

God Gives Life

"You alone are the LORD. You made the heavens, even the highest heavens, and all their starry host, the earth and all that is on it, the seas and all that is in them. You give life to everything, and the multitudes of heaven worship you."

[a]8 Or *God, translating it* [b]15 See Lev. 23:37–40. [c]5 Or *God for ever and ever*

made the heavens, even the highest heavens, and all their starry host, the earth and
all that is on it, the seas and all that is in
them. You give life to everything, and the
multitudes of heaven worship you.
7“You are the LORD God, who chose
Abram and brought him out of Ur of the
Chaldeans and named him Abraham.
8You found his heart faithful to you, and
you made a covenant with him to give to
his descendants the land of the Canaanites, Hittites, Amorites, Perizzites, Jebusites and Girgashites. You have kept your
promise because you are righteous.
9“You saw the suffering of our forefathers in Egypt; you heard their cry at the
Red Sea.[a] 10You sent miraculous signs
and wonders against Pharaoh, against all
his officials and all the people of his land,
for you knew how arrogantly the Egyptians treated them. You made a name for
yourself, which remains to this day. 11You
divided the sea before them, so that they
passed through it on dry ground, but you
hurled their pursuers into the depths, like
a stone into mighty waters. 12By day you
led them with a pillar of cloud, and by
night with a pillar of fire to give them light
on the way they were to take.
13“You came down on Mount Sinai;
you spoke to them from heaven. You gave
them regulations and laws that are just and
right, and decrees and commands that are
good. 14You made known to them your
holy Sabbath and gave them commands,
decrees and laws through your servant
Moses. 15In their hunger you gave them
bread from heaven and in their thirst you
brought them water from the rock; you
told them to go in and take possession
of the land you had sworn with uplifted
hand to give them.
16“But they, our forefathers, became
arrogant and stiff-necked, and did not
obey your commands. 17They refused
to listen and failed to remember the miracles you performed among them. They
became stiff-necked and in their rebellion
appointed a leader in order to return to
their slavery. But you are a forgiving God,
gracious and compassionate, slow to anger and abounding in love. Therefore you
did not desert them, 18even when they
cast for themselves an image of a calf and
said, ‘This is your god, who brought you
up out of Egypt,’ or when they committed
awful blasphemies.
19“Because of your great compassion
you did not abandon them in the desert.
By day the pillar of cloud did not cease to
guide them on their path, nor the pillar
of fire by night to shine on the way they
were to take. 20You gave your good Spirit
to instruct them. You did not withhold
your manna from their mouths, and you
gave them water for their thirst. 21For forty
years you sustained them in the desert; they
lacked nothing, their clothes did not wear
out nor did their feet become swollen.
22“You gave them kingdoms and nations, allotting to them even the remotest
frontiers. They took over the country of
Sihon[b] king of Heshbon and the country
of Og king of Bashan. 23You made their
sons as numerous as the stars in the sky,
and you brought them into the land that
you told their fathers to enter and possess. 24Their sons went in and took possession of the land. You subdued before
them the Canaanites, who lived in the
land; you handed the Canaanites over to
them, along with their kings and the peoples of the land, to deal with them as they
pleased. 25They captured fortified cities
and fertile land; they took possession of
houses filled with all kinds of good things,
wells already dug, vineyards, olive groves
and fruit trees in abundance. They ate to
the full and were well-nourished; they reveled in your great goodness.
26“But they were disobedient and rebelled against you; they put your law
behind their backs. They killed your
prophets, who had admonished them
in order to turn them back to you; they
committed awful blasphemies. 27So you

[a] 9 Hebrew *Yam Suph*; that is, Sea of Reeds [b] 22 One Hebrew manuscript and Septuagint; most Hebrew manuscripts *Sihon, that is, the country of the*

handed them over to their enemies, who
oppressed them. But when they were
oppressed they cried out to you. From
heaven you heard them, and in your
great compassion you gave them deliverers, who rescued them from the hand of
their enemies.
28"But as soon as they were at rest,
they again did what was evil in your
sight. Then you abandoned them to the
hand of their enemies so that they ruled
over them. And when they cried out to
you again, you heard from heaven, and
in your compassion you delivered them
time after time.
29"You warned them to return to your
law, but they became arrogant and disobeyed your commands. They sinned
against your ordinances, by which a man
will live if he obeys them. Stubbornly
they turned their backs on you, became
stiff-necked and refused to listen. 30For
many years you were patient with them.
By your Spirit you admonished them
through your prophets. Yet they paid no
attention, so you handed them over to the
neighboring peoples. 31But in your great
mercy you did not put an end to them or
abandon them, for you are a gracious and
merciful God.
32"Now therefore, O our God, the great,
mighty and awesome God, who keeps his
covenant of love, do not let all this hardship
seem trifling in your eyes—the hardship
that has come upon us, upon our kings
and leaders, upon our priests and prophets, upon our fathers and all your people,
from the days of the kings of Assyria until
today. 33In all that has happened to us, you
have been just; you have acted faithfully,
while we did wrong. 34Our kings, our leaders, our priests and our fathers did not follow your law; they did not pay attention
to your commands or the warnings you
gave them. 35Even while they were in their
kingdom, enjoying your great goodness to
them in the spacious and fertile land you
gave them, they did not serve you or turn
from their evil ways.
36"But see, we are slaves today, slaves
in the land you gave our forefathers so
they could eat its fruit and the other good
things it produces. 37Because of our sins,
its abundant harvest goes to the kings you
have placed over us. They rule over our
bodies and our cattle as they please. We
are in great distress.

The Agreement of the People

38"In view of all this, we are making a binding agreement, putting it in writing, and our
leaders, our Levites and our priests are affixing
their seals to it."

10 Those who sealed it were:

Nehemiah the governor, the son of Hacaliah.

Zedekiah, 2Seraiah, Azariah, Jeremiah,
3Pashhur, Amariah, Malkijah,
4Hattush, Shebaniah, Malluch,
5Harim, Meremoth, Obadiah,
6Daniel, Ginnethon, Baruch,
7Meshullam, Abijah, Mijamin,
8Maaziah, Bilgai and Shemaiah.
These were the priests.

9The Levites:

Jeshua son of Azaniah, Binnui of the sons
of Henadad, Kadmiel,
10and their associates: Shebaniah,
Hodiah, Kelita, Pelaiah, Hanan,
11Mica, Rehob, Hashabiah,
12Zaccur, Sherebiah, Shebaniah,
13Hodiah, Bani and Beninu.

14The leaders of the people:

Parosh, Pahath-Moab, Elam, Zattu, Bani,
15Bunni, Azgad, Bebai,
16Adonijah, Bigvai, Adin,
17Ater, Hezekiah, Azzur,
18Hodiah, Hashum, Bezai,
19Hariph, Anathoth, Nebai,
20Magpiash, Meshullam, Hezir,
21Meshezabel, Zadok, Jaddua,
22Pelatiah, Hanan, Anaiah,
23Hoshea, Hananiah, Hasshub,
24Hallohesh, Pilha, Shobek,
25Rehum, Hashabnah, Maaseiah,
26Ahiah, Hanan, Anan,
27Malluch, Harim and Baanah.

28"The rest of the people—priests, Levites, gatekeepers, singers, temple servants
and all who separated themselves from
the neighboring peoples for the sake of
the Law of God, together with their wives
and all their sons and daughters who are
able to understand— 29all these now join
their brothers the nobles, and bind themselves with a curse and an oath to follow
the Law of God given through Moses the
servant of God and to obey carefully all
the commands, regulations and decrees of
the LORD our Lord.

30"We promise not to give our daughters in marriage to the peoples around us
or take their daughters for our sons.

31"When the neighboring peoples
bring merchandise or grain to sell on the
Sabbath, we will not buy from them on
the Sabbath or on any holy day. Every seventh year we will forgo working the land
and will cancel all debts.

32"We assume the responsibility for carrying out the commands to give a third
of a shekel[a] each year for the service of
the house of our God: 33for the bread set
out on the table; for the regular grain offerings and burnt offerings; for the offerings
on the Sabbaths, New Moon festivals and
appointed feasts; for the holy offerings;
for sin offerings to make atonement for
Israel; and for all the duties of the house
of our God.

34"We—the priests, the Levites and
the people—have cast lots to determine
when each of our families is to bring to
the house of our God at set times each
year a contribution of wood to burn on
the altar of the LORD our God, as it is written in the Law.

35"We also assume responsibility for
bringing to the house of the LORD each
year the firstfruits of our crops and of
every fruit tree.

36"As it is also written in the Law, we
will bring the firstborn of our sons and of
our cattle, of our herds and of our flocks
to the house of our God, to the priests ministering there.

37"Moreover, we will bring to the storerooms of the house of our God, to the
priests, the first of our ground meal, of
our ⌞grain⌟ offerings, of the fruit of all
our trees and of our new wine and oil.
And we will bring a tithe of our crops to
the Levites, for it is the Levites who collect the tithes in all the towns where we
work. 38A priest descended from Aaron
is to accompany the Levites when they
receive the tithes, and the Levites are
to bring a tenth of the tithes up to the
house of our God, to the storerooms of
the treasury. 39The people of Israel, including the Levites, are to bring their
contributions of grain, new wine and
oil to the storerooms where the articles
for the sanctuary are kept and where the
ministering priests, the gatekeepers and
the singers stay.

"We will not neglect the house of our
God."

The New Residents of Jerusalem

11 Now the leaders of the people settled
in Jerusalem, and the rest of the people
cast lots to bring one out of every ten to live in
Jerusalem, the holy city, while the remaining
nine were to stay in their own towns. 2The people commended all the men who volunteered
to live in Jerusalem.

3These are the provincial leaders who settled
in Jerusalem (now some Israelites, priests, Levites, temple servants and descendants of Solomon's servants lived in the towns of Judah,
each on his own property in the various towns,
4while other people from both Judah and Benjamin lived in Jerusalem):

From the descendants of Judah:

Athaiah son of Uzziah, the son of
Zechariah, the son of Amariah, the son
of Shephatiah, the son of Mahalalel, a descendant of Perez; 5and Maaseiah son of
Baruch, the son of Col-Hozeh, the son of
Hazaiah, the son of Adaiah, the son of Joiarib, the son of Zechariah, a descendant
of Shelah. 6The descendants of Perez who
lived in Jerusalem totaled 468 able men.

32 That is, about 1/8 ounce (about 4 grams)

7From the descendants of Benjamin:

Sallu son of Meshullam, the son of Joed,
the son of Pedaiah, the son of Kolaiah, the
son of Maaseiah, the son of Ithiel, the son
of Jeshaiah, 8and his followers, Gabbai
and Sallai—928 men. 9Joel son of Zicri
was their chief officer, and Judah son of
Hassenuah was over the Second District
of the city.

10From the priests:

Jedaiah; the son of Joiarib; Jakin; 11Sera-
iah son of Hilkiah, the son of Meshullam,
the son of Zadok, the son of Meraioth, the
son of Ahitub, supervisor in the house of
God, 12and their associates, who carried
on work for the temple—822 men; Adaiah son of Jeroham, the son of Pelaliah, the
son of Amzi, the son of Zechariah, the son
of Pashhur, the son of Malkijah, 13and his
associates, who were heads of families—
242 men; Amashsai son of Azarel, the son
of Ahzai, the son of Meshillemoth, the
son of Immer, 14and his[a] associates, who
were able men—128. Their chief officer
was Zabdiel son of Haggedolim.

15From the Levites:

Shemaiah son of Hasshub, the son of Azrikam, the son of Hashabiah, the son of
Bunni; 16Shabbethai and Jozabad, two of
the heads of the Levites, who had charge
of the outside work of the house of God;
17Mattaniah son of Mica, the son of Zabdi,
the son of Asaph, the director who led in
thanksgiving and prayer; Bakbukiah, second among his associates; and Abda son
of Shammua, the son of Galal, the son of
Jeduthun. 18The Levites in the holy city
totaled 284.

19The gatekeepers:

Akkub, Talmon and their associates, who
kept watch at the gates—172 men.

20The rest of the Israelites, with the priests
and Levites, were in all the towns of Judah,
each on his ancestral property.

21The temple servants lived on the hill of
Ophel, and Ziha and Gishpa were in charge
of them.

22The chief officer of the Levites in Jerusalem was Uzzi son of Bani, the son of Hashabiah,
the son of Mattaniah, the son of Mica. Uzzi was
one of Asaph's descendants, who were the singers responsible for the service of the house of
God. 23The singers were under the king's orders, which regulated their daily activity.

24Pethahiah son of Meshezabel, one of the
descendants of Zerah son of Judah, was the
king's agent in all affairs relating to the people.

25As for the villages with their fields, some
of the people of Judah lived in Kiriath Arba and
its surrounding settlements, in Dibon and its
settlements, in Jekabzeel and its villages, 26in
Jeshua, in Moladah, in Beth Pelet, 27in Hazar
Shual, in Beersheba and its settlements, 28in
Ziklag, in Meconah and its settlements, 29in
En Rimmon, in Zorah, in Jarmuth, 30Zanoah,
Adullam and their villages, in Lachish and its
fields, and in Azekah and its settlements. So
they were living all the way from Beersheba to
the Valley of Hinnom.

31The descendants of the Benjamites from
Geba lived in Micmash, Aija, Bethel and its
settlements, 32in Anathoth, Nob and Ananiah,
33in Hazor, Ramah and Gittaim, 34in Hadid,
Zeboim and Neballat, 35in Lod and Ono, and
in the Valley of the Craftsmen.

36Some of the divisions of the Levites of Judah settled in Benjamin.

Priests and Levites

12 These were the priests and Levites
who returned with Zerubbabel son of
Shealtiel and with Jeshua:

Seraiah, Jeremiah, Ezra,
2 Amariah, Malluch, Hattush,
3 Shecaniah, Rehum, Meremoth,
4 Iddo, Ginnethon,[b] Abijah,
5 Mijamin,[c] Moadiah, Bilgah,
6 Shemaiah, Joiarib, Jedaiah,
7 Sallu, Amok, Hilkiah and Jedaiah.

These were the leaders of the priests and their
associates in the days of Jeshua.

8The Levites were Jeshua, Binnui, Kadmiel,
Sherebiah, Judah, and also Mattaniah, who,

[a]14 Most Septuagint manuscripts; Hebrew *their* [b]4 Many Hebrew manuscripts and Vulgate (see also Neh. 12:16); most Hebrew manuscripts *Ginnethoi* [c]5 A variant of *Miniamin*

together with his associates, was in charge of
the songs of thanksgiving. 9 Bakbukiah and
Unni, their associates, stood opposite them in
the services.

10 Jeshua was the father of Joiakim, Joiakim
the father of Eliashib, Eliashib the father of
Joiada, 11 Joiada the father of Jonathan, and Jonathan the father of Jaddua.

12 In the days of Joiakim, these were the
heads of the priestly families:

of Seraiah's family, Meraiah;
of Jeremiah's, Hananiah;
13 of Ezra's, Meshullam;
of Amariah's, Jehohanan;
14 of Malluch's, Jonathan;
of Shecaniah's,[a] Joseph;
15 of Harim's, Adna;
of Meremoth's,[b] Helkai;
16 of Iddo's, Zechariah;
of Ginnethon's, Meshullam;
17 of Abijah's, Zicri;
of Miniamin's and of Moadiah's, Piltai;
18 of Bilgah's, Shammua;
of Shemaiah's, Jehonathan;
19 of Joiarib's, Mattenai;
of Jedaiah's, Uzzi;
20 of Sallu's, Kallai;
of Amok's, Eber;
21 of Hilkiah's, Hashabiah;
of Jedaiah's, Nethanel.

22 The family heads of the Levites in the days
of Eliashib, Joiada, Johanan and Jaddua, as well
as those of the priests, were recorded in the
reign of Darius the Persian. 23 The family heads
among the descendants of Levi up to the time
of Johanan son of Eliashib were recorded in the
book of the annals. 24 And the leaders of the Levites were Hashabiah, Sherebiah, Jeshua son of
Kadmiel, and their associates, who stood opposite them to give praise and thanksgiving, one
section responding to the other, as prescribed
by David the man of God.

25 Mattaniah, Bakbukiah, Obadiah, Meshullam, Talmon and Akkub were gatekeepers who
guarded the storerooms at the gates. 26 They
served in the days of Joiakim son of Jeshua, the
son of Jozadak, and in the days of Nehemiah
the governor and of Ezra the priest and scribe.

Dedication of the Wall of Jerusalem

27 At the dedication of the wall of Jerusalem, the Levites were sought out from where
they lived and were brought to Jerusalem to
celebrate joyfully the dedication with songs
of thanksgiving and with the music of cymbals, harps and lyres. 28 The singers also were
brought together from the region around Jerusalem—from the villages of the Netophathites,
29 from Beth Gilgal, and from the area of Geba
and Azmaveth, for the singers had built villages
for themselves around Jerusalem. 30 When the
priests and Levites had purified themselves
ceremonially, they purified the people, the
gates and the wall.

31 I had the leaders of Judah go up on top[c]
of the wall. I also assigned two large choirs to
give thanks. One was to proceed on top[d] of the
wall to the right, toward the Dung Gate. 32 Hoshaiah and half the leaders of Judah followed
them, 33 along with Azariah, Ezra, Meshullam,
34 Judah, Benjamin, Shemaiah, Jeremiah, 35 as
well as some priests with trumpets, and also
Zechariah son of Jonathan, the son of Shemaiah, the son of Mattaniah, the son of Micaiah,
the son of Zaccur, the son of Asaph, 36 and his
associates—Shemaiah, Azarel, Milalai, Gilalai,
Maai, Nethanel, Judah and Hanani—with musical instruments ⌞prescribed by⌟ David the man
of God. Ezra the scribe led the procession.
37 At the Fountain Gate they continued directly
up the steps of the City of David on the ascent
to the wall and passed above the house of David to the Water Gate on the east.

38 The second choir proceeded in the opposite direction. I followed them on top[e] of the
wall, together with half the people—past the
Tower of the Ovens to the Broad Wall, 39 over
the Gate of Ephraim, the Jeshanah[f] Gate, the
Fish Gate, the Tower of Hananel and the Tower
of the Hundred, as far as the Sheep Gate. At the
Gate of the Guard they stopped.

40 The two choirs that gave thanks then
took their places in the house of God; so did
I, together with half the officials, 41 as well as
the priests—Eliakim, Maaseiah, Miniamin,
Micaiah, Elioenai, Zechariah and Hananiah
with their trumpets— 42 and also Maaseiah,

[a] 14 Very many Hebrew manuscripts, some Septuagint manuscripts and Syriac (see also Neh. 12:3); most Hebrew manuscripts *Shebaniah's*
[b] 15 Some Septuagint manuscripts (see also Neh. 12:3); Hebrew *Meraioth's* [c] 31 Or *go alongside* [d] 31 Or *proceed alongside*
[e] 38 Or *them alongside* [f] 39 Or *Old*

Shemaiah, Eleazar, Uzzi, Jehohanan, Malkijah,
Elam and Ezer. The choirs sang under the direction of Jezrahiah. 43And on that day they
offered great sacrifices, rejoicing because God
had given them great joy. The
women and children also rejoiced. The sound of rejoicing
in Jerusalem could be heard
far away.

> **Nehemiah 12:43**
>
> *God Gives Joy*
>
> And on that day they offered great sacrifices, rejoicing because God had given them great joy. The women and children also rejoiced. The sound of rejoicing in Jerusalem could be heard far away.

44At that time men were
appointed to be in charge of
the storerooms for the contributions, firstfruits and tithes.
From the fields around the
towns they were to bring into
the storerooms the portions
required by the Law for the
priests and the Levites, for Judah was pleased with the ministering priests and Levites.
45They performed the service
of their God and the service of purification,
as did also the singers and gatekeepers, according to the commands of David and his son Solomon. 46For long ago, in the days of David and
Asaph, there had been directors for the singers
and for the songs of praise and thanksgiving
to God. 47So in the days of Zerubbabel and of
Nehemiah, all Israel contributed the daily portions for the singers and gatekeepers. They also
set aside the portion for the other Levites, and
the Levites set aside the portion for the descendants of Aaron.

Nehemiah's Final Reforms

13 On that day the Book of Moses was
read aloud in the hearing of the people and there it was found written that no Ammonite or Moabite should ever be admitted
into the assembly of God, 2because they had
not met the Israelites with food and water
but had hired Balaam to call a curse down on
them. (Our God, however, turned the curse
into a blessing.) 3When the people heard this
law, they excluded from Israel all who were of
foreign descent.

4Before this, Eliashib the priest had been put
in charge of the storerooms of the house of our
God. He was closely associated with Tobiah,
5and he had provided him with a large room
formerly used to store the grain offerings and
incense and temple articles, and also the tithes
of grain, new wine and oil prescribed for the
Levites, singers and gatekeepers, as well as the
contributions for the priests.

6But while all this was going
on, I was not in Jerusalem, for
in the thirty-second year of Artaxerxes king of Babylon I had
returned to the king. Some
time later I asked his permission 7and came back to Jerusalem. Here I learned about the
evil thing Eliashib had done
in providing Tobiah a room in
the courts of the house of God.
8I was greatly displeased and
threw all Tobiah's household
goods out of the room. 9I gave
orders to purify the rooms,
and then I put back into them
the equipment of the house of
God, with the grain offerings and the incense.

10I also learned that the portions assigned
to the Levites had not been given to them, and
that all the Levites and singers responsible for
the service had gone back to their own fields.
11So I rebuked the officials and asked them,
"Why is the house of God neglected?" Then
I called them together and stationed them at
their posts.

12All Judah brought the tithes of grain,
new wine and oil into the storerooms. 13I put
Shelemiah the priest, Zadok the scribe, and a
Levite named Pedaiah in charge of the storerooms and made Hanan son of Zaccur, the
son of Mattaniah, their assistant, because these
men were considered trustworthy. They were
made responsible for distributing the supplies
to their brothers.

14Remember me for this, O my God, and do
not blot out what I have so faithfully done for
the house of my God and its services.

15In those days I saw men in Judah treading
winepresses on the Sabbath and bringing in
grain and loading it on donkeys, together with
wine, grapes, figs and all other kinds of loads.
And they were bringing all this into Jerusalem on the Sabbath. Therefore I warned them
against selling food on that day. 16Men from

Tyre who lived in Jerusalem were bringing in
fish and all kinds of merchandise and selling
them in Jerusalem on the Sabbath to the people of Judah. 17 I rebuked the nobles of Judah
and said to them, "What is this wicked thing
you are doing—desecrating the Sabbath day?
18 Didn't your forefathers do the same things,
so that our God brought all this calamity upon
us and upon this city? Now you are stirring
up more wrath against Israel by desecrating
the Sabbath."

19 When evening shadows fell on the gates
of Jerusalem before the Sabbath, I ordered the
doors to be shut and not opened until the Sabbath was over. I stationed some of my own men
at the gates so that no load could be brought in
on the Sabbath day. 20 Once or twice the merchants and sellers of all kinds of goods spent the
night outside Jerusalem. 21 But I warned them
and said, "Why do you spend the night by the
wall? If you do this again, I will lay hands on
you." From that time on they no longer came
on the Sabbath. 22 Then I commanded the Levites to purify themselves and go and guard the
gates in order to keep the Sabbath day holy.

Remember me for this also, O my God, and show mercy to me according to your great love.

23 Moreover, in those days I saw men of Judah who had married women from Ashdod,
Ammon and Moab. 24 Half of their children
spoke the language of Ashdod or the language
of one of the other peoples, and did not know
how to speak the language of Judah. 25 I rebuked them and called curses down on them.
I beat some of the men and pulled out their
hair. I made them take an oath in God's name
and said: "You are not to give your daughters
in marriage to their sons, nor are you to take
their daughters in marriage for your sons or for
yourselves. 26 Was it not because of marriages
like these that Solomon king of Israel sinned?
Among the many nations there was no king
like him. He was loved by his God, and God
made him king over all Israel, but even he was
led into sin by foreign women. 27 Must we hear
now that you too are doing all this terrible wickedness and are being unfaithful to our God by
marrying foreign women?"

28 One of the sons of Joiada son of Eliashib
the high priest was son-in-law to Sanballat the
Horonite. And I drove him away from me.

29 Remember them, O my God, because
they defiled the priestly office and the covenant
of the priesthood and of the Levites.

30 So I purified the priests and the Levites of
everything foreign, and assigned them duties,
each to his own task. 31 I also made provision
for contributions of wood at designated times,
and for the firstfruits.

Remember me with favor, O my God.

Esther

Author:
Unknown.

Audience:
All Israel.

Date:
Written in hindsight, after the events described in the book. About 460 B.C.

Setting:
Susa, the capital of the Persian Empire, during a turbulent time for the Jews.

Verse to Remember:
"And who knows but that you have come to royal position for such a time as this?" (4:14)

Silence. Utter, complete silence. We read the pages of Scripture expecting to hear God's voice, but when we turn to the book of Esther, we find only silence. Nowhere in these pages is God's name mentioned. No direct words. No prophecies. No prayers. The nation of Israel was in exile, living in subjection to a pagan king. *God was silent, but he was not absent.*

It is there, in heaven's stillness, that a young woman enters the scene. Esther is a Jew, but she finds herself upon the stage of the Persian court with all its foreign customs and intrigues. And God has a purpose for her, right where she is. As Esther's story unfolds, *watch for God's providence.* You will not see his hand, but you can see his fingerprints all over the situation.

Queen Vashti Deposed

1 This is what happened during the time of
Xerxes,[a] the Xerxes who ruled over 127
provinces stretching from India to Cush[b]: 2At
that time King Xerxes reigned from his royal
throne in the citadel of Susa, 3and in the third
year of his reign he gave a banquet for all his
nobles and officials. The military leaders of Persia and Media, the princes, and the nobles of
the provinces were present.
4For a full 180 days he displayed the vast
wealth of his kingdom and the splendor and
glory of his majesty. 5When these days were
over, the king gave a banquet, lasting seven
days, in the enclosed garden of the king's palace, for all the people from the least to the

[a]1 Hebrew *Ahasuerus*, a variant of Xerxes' Persian name; here and throughout Esther [b]1 That is, the upper Nile region

greatest, who were in the citadel of Susa. 6The
garden had hangings of white and blue linen,
fastened with cords of white linen and purple
material to silver rings on marble pillars. There
were couches of gold and silver on a mosaic
pavement of porphyry, marble, mother-of-
pearl and other costly stones. 7Wine was
served in goblets of gold, each one different
from the other, and the royal wine was abundant, in keeping with the king's liberality. 8By
the king's command each guest was allowed to
drink in his own way, for the king instructed
all the wine stewards to serve each man what
he wished.

9Queen Vashti also gave a banquet for the
women in the royal palace of King Xerxes.

10On the seventh day, when King Xerxes was
in high spirits from wine, he commanded the
seven eunuchs who served him—Mehuman,
Biztha, Harbona, Bigtha, Abagtha, Zethar and
Carcas— 11to bring before him Queen Vashti,
wearing her royal crown, in order to display
her beauty to the people and nobles, for she
was lovely to look at. 12But when the attendants delivered the king's command, Queen
Vashti refused to come. Then the king became
furious and burned with anger.

13Since it was customary for the king to
consult experts in matters of law and justice,
he spoke with the wise men who understood
the times 14and were closest to the king—
Carshena, Shethar, Admatha, Tarshish, Meres,
Marsena and Memucan, the seven nobles of
Persia and Media who had special access to the
king and were highest in the kingdom.

15"According to law, what must be done to
Queen Vashti?" he asked. "She has not obeyed
the command of King Xerxes that the eunuchs
have taken to her."

16Then Memucan replied in the presence
of the king and the nobles, "Queen Vashti has
done wrong, not only against the king but also
against all the nobles and the peoples of all the
provinces of King Xerxes. 17For the queen's
conduct will become known to all the women,
and so they will despise their husbands and
say, 'King Xerxes commanded Queen Vashti
to be brought before him, but she would not
come.' 18This very day the Persian and Median
women of the nobility who have heard about
the queen's conduct will respond to all the
king's nobles in the same way. There will be no
end of disrespect and discord.

19"Therefore, if it pleases the king, let him
issue a royal decree and let it be written in the
laws of Persia and Media, which cannot be repealed, that Vashti is never again to enter the
presence of King Xerxes. Also let the king
give her royal position to someone else who is
better than she. 20Then when the king's edict
is proclaimed throughout all his vast realm, all
the women will respect their husbands, from
the least to the greatest."

21The king and his nobles were pleased with
this advice, so the king did as Memucan proposed. 22He sent dispatches to all parts of the
kingdom, to each province in its own script and
to each people in its own language, proclaiming
in each people's tongue that every man should
be ruler over his own household.

Esther Made Queen

2 Later when the anger of King Xerxes had
subsided, he remembered Vashti and what
she had done and what he had decreed about
her. 2Then the king's personal attendants proposed, "Let a search be made for beautiful
young virgins for the king. 3Let the king appoint commissioners in every province of his
realm to bring all these beautiful girls into the
harem at the citadel of Susa. Let them be placed
under the care of Hegai, the king's eunuch, who
is in charge of the women; and let beauty treatments be given to them. 4Then let the girl who
pleases the king be queen instead of Vashti."
This advice appealed to the king, and he followed it.

5Now there was in the citadel of Susa a Jew
of the tribe of Benjamin, named Mordecai son
of Jair, the son of Shimei, the son of Kish, 6who
had been carried into exile from Jerusalem
by Nebuchadnezzar king of Babylon, among
those taken captive with Jehoiachin[a] king of Judah. 7Mordecai had a cousin named Hadassah,
whom he had brought up because she had neither father nor mother. This girl, who was also
known as Esther, was lovely in form and features, and Mordecai had taken her as his own
daughter when her father and mother died.

a6 Hebrew *Jeconiah,* a variant of *Jehoiachin*

A Rival and a Wife

PENINNAH

Because the LORD had closed her womb, her rival kept provoking her in order to irritate her. This went on year after year.

1 Samuel 1:6–7

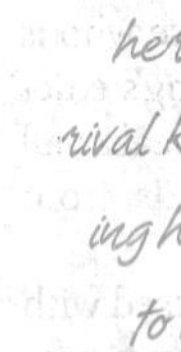

ASSIGNED READING:

1 Samuel 1:1–28

"MY FATHER MADE IT FOR THE *BAAABY*." Peninnah held a small wooden toy in her hands.

Her voice inflection rose on the last part of that sentence, stretching out the word as long as she possibly could. Peninnah was always doing that to Hannah—endlessly talking about babies, children, runny noses and nursing. Peninnah had a special knack for turning every occasion into an opportunity to make a dig at Hannah's infertility.

"Do you *like* it, Hannah?" She pushed just a little more.

Hannah didn't respond. She busied herself with that day's list of household chores. Peninnah turned away. *Score!* she thought to herself gleefully. And for a minute, she felt good.

It was hard living under the same roof 24/7. Peninnah and Hannah shared living quarters, meals, household chores and the love of a husband. Well, they sort of shared that, Peninnah thought with a pang. She recalled the way Elkanah spoke with tenderness to Hannah, how he showered her with gifts, how he always made sure she had everything she wanted—and how he *looked* at her. Peninnah saw that look. And he never looked at *her* that way. She had given Elkanah sons and daughters; he should have doted on her and loved her beyond reason for her gifts to him. Oh, he was kind to her. Nice. Pleasant. And he loved the kids. But that look. He *never* looked at *her* that way.

It was so unfair. According to the culture of that day, Peninnah was the superior wife. Any woman who remained childless was seen as a blight on society, a misfit. Hannah should have been unloved. Not Peninnah and her many sons and daughters. She knew she was better, more valuable. And she made certain Hannah never, ever, not even for one second, forgot it.

Peninnah gloated and planned her next slight. This time she'd mention something in front of Elkanah. Her children were proof that she was better than Hannah. Now, if only she could *feel* that way.

—Prayer—

Lord, sometimes in my quest to fulfill my own needs, I trample on those around me. Forgive me, and help me to treat others with love.

Weekend

Go to page 603 for your next devotional reading

8When the king's order and edict had been
proclaimed, many girls were brought to the citadel of Susa and put under the care of Hegai.
Esther also was taken to the king's palace and
entrusted to Hegai, who had charge of the
harem. 9The girl pleased him and won his favor.
Immediately he provided her with her beauty
treatments and special food. He assigned to her
seven maids selected from the king's palace and
moved her and her maids into the best place in
the harem.
10Esther had not revealed her nationality
and family background, because Mordecai had
forbidden her to do so. 11Every day he walked
back and forth near the courtyard of the harem
to find out how Esther was and what was happening to her.
12Before a girl's turn came to go in to King
Xerxes, she had to complete twelve months of
beauty treatments prescribed for the women,
six months with oil of myrrh and six with perfumes and cosmetics. 13And this is how she
would go to the king: Anything she wanted was
given her to take with her from the harem to
the king's palace. 14In the evening she would go
there and in the morning return to another part
of the harem to the care of Shaashgaz, the king's
eunuch who was in charge of the concubines.
She would not return to the king unless he was
pleased with her and summoned her by name.
15When the turn came for Esther (the girl
Mordecai had adopted, the daughter of his uncle Abihail) to go to the king, she asked for nothing other than what Hegai, the king's eunuch
who was in charge of the harem, suggested.
And Esther won the favor of everyone who
saw her. 16She was taken to King Xerxes in the
royal residence in the tenth month, the month
of Tebeth, in the seventh year of his reign.
17Now the king was attracted to Esther more
than to any of the other women, and she won
his favor and approval more than any of the
other virgins. So he set a royal crown on her
head and made her queen instead of Vashti.
18And the king gave a great banquet, Esther's
banquet, for all his nobles and officials. He proclaimed a holiday throughout the provinces
and distributed gifts with royal liberality.

Mordecai Uncovers a Conspiracy

19When the virgins were assembled a second time, Mordecai was sitting at the king's
gate. 20But Esther had kept secret her family
background and nationality just as Mordecai
had told her to do, for she continued to follow
Mordecai's instructions as she had done when
he was bringing her up.
21During the time Mordecai was sitting at
the king's gate, Bigthana[a] and Teresh, two of
the king's officers who guarded the doorway,
became angry and conspired to assassinate
King Xerxes. 22But Mordecai found out about
the plot and told Queen Esther, who in turn
reported it to the king, giving credit to Mordecai. 23And when the report was investigated
and found to be true, the two officials were
hanged on a gallows.[b] All this was recorded in
the book of the annals in the presence of the
king.

Haman's Plot to Destroy the Jews

3 After these events, King Xerxes honored
Haman son of Hammedatha, the Agagite,
elevating him and giving him a seat of honor
higher than that of all the other nobles. 2All
the royal officials at the king's gate knelt down
and paid honor to Haman, for the king had
commanded this concerning him. But Mordecai would not kneel down or pay him honor.
3Then the royal officials at the king's gate
asked Mordecai, "Why do you disobey the
king's command?" 4Day after day they spoke to
him but he refused to comply. Therefore they
told Haman about it to see whether Mordecai's
behavior would be tolerated, for he had told
them he was a Jew.
5When Haman saw that Mordecai would
not kneel down or pay him honor, he was enraged. 6Yet having learned who Mordecai's
people were, he scorned the idea of killing only
Mordecai. Instead Haman looked for a way to
destroy all Mordecai's people, the Jews, throughout the whole kingdom of Xerxes.
7In the twelfth year of King Xerxes, in the
first month, the month of Nisan, they cast the
pur (that is, the lot) in the presence of Haman
to select a day and month. And the lot fell on[c]
the twelfth month, the month of Adar.

[a] 21 Hebrew *Bigthan,* a variant of *Bigthana* [b] 23 Or *were hung* (or *impaled*) *on poles*; similarly elsewhere in Esther [c] 7 Septuagint; Hebrew does not have *And the lot fell on.*

8 Then Haman said to King Xerxes, “There is a certain people dispersed and scattered among the peoples in all the provinces of your kingdom whose customs are different from those of all other people and who do not obey the king’s laws; it is not in the king’s best interest to tolerate them. 9 If it pleases the king, let a decree be issued to destroy them, and I will put ten thousand talents[a] of silver into the royal treasury for the men who carry out this business.”

10 So the king took his signet ring from his finger and gave it to Haman son of Hammedatha, the Agagite, the enemy of the Jews. 11 “Keep the money,” the king said to Haman, “and do with the people as you please.”

12 Then on the thirteenth day of the first month the royal secretaries were summoned. They wrote out in the script of each province and in the language of each people all Haman’s orders to the king’s satraps, the governors of the various provinces and the nobles of the various peoples. These were written in the name of King Xerxes himself and sealed with his own ring. 13 Dispatches were sent by couriers to all the king’s provinces with the order to destroy, kill and annihilate all the Jews—young and old, women and little children—on a single day, the thirteenth day of the twelfth month, the month of Adar, and to plunder their goods. 14 A copy of the text of the edict was to be issued as law in every province and made known to the people of every nationality so they would be ready for that day.

15 Spurred on by the king’s command, the couriers went out, and the edict was issued in the citadel of Susa. The king and Haman sat down to drink, but the city of Susa was bewildered.

Mordecai Persuades Esther to Help

4 When Mordecai learned of all that had been done, he tore his clothes, put on sackcloth and ashes, and went out into the city, wailing loudly and bitterly. 2 But he went only as far as the king’s gate, because no one clothed in sackcloth was allowed to enter it. 3 In every province to which the edict and order of the king came, there was great mourning among the Jews, with fasting, weeping and wailing. Many lay in sackcloth and ashes.

4 When Esther’s maids and eunuchs came and told her about Mordecai, she was in great distress. She sent clothes for him to put on instead of his sackcloth, but he would not accept them. 5 Then Esther summoned Hathach, one of the king’s eunuchs assigned to attend her, and ordered him to find out what was troubling Mordecai and why.

6 So Hathach went out to Mordecai in the open square of the city in front of the king’s gate. 7 Mordecai told him everything that had happened to him, including the exact amount of money Haman had promised to pay into the royal treasury for the destruction of the Jews. 8 He also gave him a copy of the text of the edict for their annihilation, which had been published in Susa, to show to Esther and explain it to her, and he told him to urge her to go into the king’s presence to beg for mercy and plead with him for her people.

9 Hathach went back and reported to Esther what Mordecai had said. 10 Then she instructed him to say to Mordecai, 11 “All the king’s officials and the people of the royal provinces know that for any man or woman who approaches the king in the inner court without being summoned the king has but one law: that he be put to death. The only exception to this is for the king to extend the gold scepter to him and spare his life. But thirty days have passed since I was called to go to the king.”

12 When Esther’s words were reported to Mordecai, 13 he sent back this answer: “Do not think that because you are in the king’s house you alone of all the Jews will escape. 14 For if you remain silent at this time, relief and deliverance for the Jews will arise from another place, but you and your father’s family will perish. And who knows but

Esther 4:14

God Appoints for His Purpose

“And who knows but that you have come to royal position for such a time as this?”

[a]9 That is, about 375 tons (about 345 metric tons)

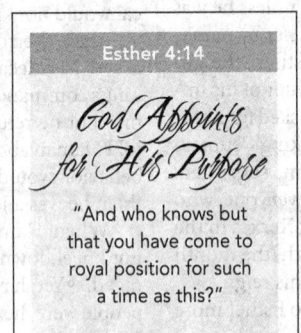

that you have come to royal position for such
a time as this?”
15Then Esther sent this reply to Mordecai:
16“Go, gather together all the Jews who are in
Susa, and fast for me. Do not eat or drink for
three days, night or day. I and my maids will
fast as you do. When this is done, I will go to
the king, even though it is against the law. And
if I perish, I perish.”
17So Mordecai went away and carried out all
of Esther’s instructions.

Esther’s Request to the King

5 On the third day Esther put on her royal
robes and stood in the inner court of the
palace, in front of the king’s hall. The king was
sitting on his royal throne in the hall, facing the
entrance. 2When he saw Queen Esther standing in the court, he was pleased with her and
held out to her the gold scepter that was in his
hand. So Esther approached and touched the
tip of the scepter.
3Then the king asked, “What is it, Queen
Esther? What is your request? Even up to half
the kingdom, it will be given you.”
4“If it pleases the king,” replied Esther, “let
the king, together with Haman, come today
to a banquet I have prepared for him.”
5“Bring Haman at once,” the king said, “so
that we may do what Esther asks.”
So the king and Haman went to the banquet
Esther had prepared. 6As they were drinking
wine, the king again asked Esther, “Now what
is your petition? It will be given you. And what
is your request? Even up to half the kingdom,
it will be granted.”
7Esther replied, “My petition and my request
is this: 8If the king regards me with favor and if
it pleases the king to grant my petition and fulfill my request, let the king and Haman come tomorrow to the banquet I will prepare for them.
Then I will answer the king’s question.”

Haman’s Rage Against Mordecai

9Haman went out that day happy and in
high spirits. But when he saw Mordecai at the
king’s gate and observed that he neither rose
nor showed fear in his presence, he was filled
with rage against Mordecai. 10Nevertheless, Haman restrained himself and went home.
Calling together his friends and Zeresh,
his wife, 11Haman boasted to them about his
vast wealth, his many sons, and all the ways
the king had honored him and how he had
elevated him above the other nobles and officials. 12“And that’s not all,” Haman added.
“I’m the only person Queen Esther invited to
accompany the king to the banquet she gave.
And she has invited me along with the king tomorrow. 13But all this gives me no satisfaction
as long as I see that Jew Mordecai sitting at the
king’s gate.”
14His wife Zeresh and all his friends said to
him, “Have a gallows built, seventy-five feet[a]
high, and ask the king in the morning to have
Mordecai hanged on it. Then go with the king
to the dinner and be happy.” This suggestion
delighted Haman, and he had the gallows
built.

Mordecai Honored

6 That night the king could not sleep; so he
ordered the book of the chronicles, the
record of his reign, to be brought in and read
to him. 2It was found recorded there that Mordecai had exposed Bigthana and Teresh, two of
the king’s officers who guarded the doorway,
who had conspired to assassinate King Xerxes.
3“What honor and recognition has Mordecai received for this?” the king asked.
“Nothing has been done for him,” his attendants answered.
4The king said, “Who is in the court?” Now
Haman had just entered the outer court of the
palace to speak to the king about hanging Mordecai on the gallows he had erected for him.
5His attendants answered, “Haman is standing in the court.”
“Bring him in,” the king ordered.
6When Haman entered, the king asked him,
“What should be done for the man the king delights to honor?”
Now Haman thought to himself, “Who is
there that the king would rather honor than
me?” 7So he answered the king, “For the man
the king delights to honor, 8have them bring
a royal robe the king has worn and a horse
the king has ridden, one with a royal crest

[a] 14 Hebrew *fifty cubits* (about 23 meters)

placed on its head. 9Then let the robe and
horse be entrusted to one of the king's most
noble princes. Let them robe the man the king
delights to honor, and lead him on the horse
through the city streets, proclaiming before
him, 'This is what is done for the man the king
delights to honor!'"
10"Go at once," the king commanded Haman. "Get the robe and the horse and do just as
you have suggested for Mordecai the Jew, who
sits at the king's gate. Do not neglect anything
you have recommended."
11So Haman got the robe and the horse. He
robed Mordecai, and led him on horseback
through the city streets, proclaiming before
him, "This is what is done for the man the king
delights to honor!"
12Afterward Mordecai returned to the king's
gate. But Haman rushed home, with his head
covered in grief, 13and told Zeresh his wife and
all his friends everything that had happened
to him.
His advisers and his wife Zeresh said to him,
"Since Mordecai, before whom your downfall
has started, is of Jewish origin, you cannot
stand against him—you will surely come to
ruin!" 14While they were still talking with him,
the king's eunuchs arrived and hurried Haman
away to the banquet Esther had prepared.

Haman Hanged

7 So the king and Haman went to dine with
Queen Esther, 2and as they were drinking
wine on that second day, the king again asked,
"Queen Esther, what is your petition? It will be
given you. What is your request? Even up to
half the kingdom, it will be granted."
3Then Queen Esther answered, "If I have
found favor with you, O king, and if it pleases
your majesty, grant me my life—this is my petition. And spare my people—this is my request.
4For I and my people have been sold for destruction and slaughter and annihilation. If we had
merely been sold as male and female slaves, I
would have kept quiet, because no such distress
would justify disturbing the king.[a]"
5King Xerxes asked Queen Esther, "Who
is he? Where is the man who has dared to do
such a thing?"
6Esther said, "The adversary and enemy is
this vile Haman."
Then Haman was terrified before the king
and queen. 7The king got up in a rage, left his
wine and went out into the palace garden. But
Haman, realizing that the king had already
decided his fate, stayed behind to beg Queen
Esther for his life.
8Just as the king returned from the palace
garden to the banquet hall, Haman was falling
on the couch where Esther was reclining.
The king exclaimed, "Will he even molest
the queen while she is with me in the house?"
As soon as the word left the king's mouth,
they covered Haman's face. 9Then Harbona,
one of the eunuchs attending the king, said,
"A gallows seventy-five feet[b] high stands by
Haman's house. He had it made for Mordecai,
who spoke up to help the king."
The king said, "Hang him on it!" 10So they
hanged Haman on the gallows he had prepared
for Mordecai. Then the king's fury subsided.

The King's Edict in Behalf of the Jews

8 That same day King Xerxes gave Queen
Esther the estate of Haman, the enemy
of the Jews. And Mordecai came into the presence of the king, for Esther had told how he
was related to her. 2The king took off his signet
ring, which he had reclaimed from Haman,
and presented it to Mordecai. And Esther
appointed him over Haman's estate.
3Esther again pleaded with the king, falling
at his feet and weeping. She begged him to put
an end to the evil plan of Haman the Agagite,
which he had devised against the Jews. 4Then
the king extended the gold scepter to Esther
and she arose and stood before him.
5"If it pleases the king," she said, "and if he
regards me with favor and thinks it the right
thing to do, and if he is pleased with me, let
an order be written overruling the dispatches
that Haman son of Hammedatha, the Agagite,
devised and wrote to destroy the Jews in all the
king's provinces. 6For how can I bear to see disaster fall on my people? How can I bear to see
the destruction of my family?"
7King Xerxes replied to Queen Esther and
to Mordecai the Jew, "Because Haman attacked

[a]4 Or *quiet, but the compensation our adversary offers cannot be compared with the loss the king would suffer* [b]9 Hebrew *fifty cubits* (about 23 meters)

Too Tired?

Read: Esther 7:1–10

ROSA LOUISE PARKS was tired. The petite African American woman sat quietly, grateful to find a seat on the bus after spending most of the day on her feet. When a white passenger demanded she give up her seat, Rosa looked up. Segregation was the law in Montgomery, Alabama, in 1955. Blacks were expected to yield their seats on public transportation to whites. To refuse meant arrest. Rosa stayed seated, and her actions helped change the landscape of the United States. Years later, Rosa wrote that it wasn't physical weariness that gave her such inner strength. She said, "Our mistreatment was just not right, and I was tired of it."

Centuries earlier, another woman was faced with a decision. Like Rosa, Esther had two strikes against her in the Persian Empire: She was female and a member of an oppressed people, the Jews. Although King Xerxes had chosen Esther to be queen, she was forbidden to approach the powerful king without an invitation. And an evil prime minister named Haman was plotting to annihilate the Jews. Esther's cousin Mordecai's plea to intervene meant risking her own life. It took courage for Queen Esther to take a stand, just as it took courage for Rosa Parks to remain seated. Both women's actions opened the door to freedom for their people.

Many of us may think we're safe from the type of persecution Rosa Parks and Esther faced. But Christians are being persecuted throughout the world in places like China, the Sudan and North Korea. Every day people die for the privilege of worshiping Jesus. It is estimated that more Christians died for their faith in the twentieth century than all the previous 19 centuries combined, and the numbers appear to be rising in the twenty-first century. Even in places where there is no outright persecution, many people think Christians are naive and out of touch with so-called reality. Some people do not really know or understand the person and mission of Jesus and will take every opportunity to slander his followers.

Wherever God has placed you, he can use you to speak his truth—words of love, justice and faith to a lost world—even if it means being misunderstood or ridiculed. Yes, it may be difficult and you may be weary; but, sister, "never tire of doing what is right" (2 Thessalonians 3:13).

Esther 7:3–4

Then Queen Esther answered, "If I have found favor with you, O king, and if it pleases your majesty, grant me my life—this is my petition. And spare my people—this is my request. For I and my people have been sold for destruction and slaughter and annihilation. If we had merely been sold as male and female slaves, I would have kept quiet, because no such distress would justify disturbing the king."

reflection

1. How did reading about Rosa Parks and Queen Esther inspire you?

2. Have you ever felt God nudging you to speak up about a situation? What happened?

3. What do you need to take a stand on in your home, neighborhood or in the political arena?

RELATED READINGS

Psalm 118:6–9;
Luke 21:5–19;
2 Timothy 3:10–17

to page 607 for your next devotional reading.

the Jews, I have given his estate to Esther, and
they have hanged him on the gallows. 8Now
write another decree in the king's name in behalf of the Jews as seems best to you, and seal
it with the king's signet ring—for no document
written in the king's name and sealed with his
ring can be revoked."

9At once the royal secretaries were summoned—on the twenty-third day of the third
month, the month of Sivan. They wrote out
all Mordecai's orders to the Jews, and to the satraps, governors and nobles of the 127 provinces
stretching from India to Cush.[a] These orders
were written in the script of each province and
the language of each people and also to the
Jews in their own script and language. 10Mor-
decai wrote in the name of King Xerxes, sealed
the dispatches with the king's signet ring, and
sent them by mounted couriers, who rode fast
horses especially bred for the king.

11The king's edict granted the Jews in every
city the right to assemble and protect themselves; to destroy, kill and annihilate any armed
force of any nationality or province that might
attack them and their women and children;
and to plunder the property of their enemies.
12The day appointed for the Jews to do this in
all the provinces of King Xerxes was the thirteenth day of the twelfth month, the month of
Adar. 13A copy of the text of the edict was to
be issued as law in every province and made
known to the people of every nationality
so that the Jews would be ready on that day to
avenge themselves on their enemies.

14The couriers, riding the royal horses,
raced out, spurred on by the king's command.
And the edict was also issued in the citadel of
Susa.

15Mordecai left the king's presence wearing
royal garments of blue and white, a large crown
of gold and a purple robe of fine linen. And the
city of Susa held a joyous celebration. 16For the
Jews it was a time of happiness and joy, gladness and honor. 17In every province and in
every city, wherever the edict of the king went,
there was joy and gladness among the Jews,
with feasting and celebrating. And many people of other nationalities became Jews because
fear of the Jews had seized them.

[a]9 That is, the upper Nile region

Triumph of the Jews

9 On the thirteenth day of the twelfth
month, the month of Adar, the edict
commanded by the king was to be carried out.
On this day the enemies of the Jews had hoped
to overpower them, but now the tables were
turned and the Jews got the upper hand over
those who hated them. 2The Jews assembled in
their cities in all the provinces of King Xerxes
to attack those seeking their destruction. No
one could stand against them, because the people of all the other nationalities were afraid of
them. 3And all the nobles of the provinces, the
satraps, the governors and the king's administrators helped the Jews, because fear of Mordecai had seized them. 4Mordecai was prominent
in the palace; his reputation spread throughout the provinces, and he became more and
more powerful.

5The Jews struck down all their enemies with
the sword, killing and destroying them, and
they did what they pleased to those who hated
them. 6In the citadel of Susa, the Jews killed and
destroyed five hundred men. 7They also killed
Parshandatha, Dalphon, Aspatha, 8Poratha,
Adalia, Aridatha, 9Parmashta, Arisai, Aridai
and Vaizatha, 10the ten sons of Haman son of
Hammedatha, the enemy of the Jews. But they
did not lay their hands on the plunder.

11The number of those slain in the citadel
of Susa was reported to the king that same day.
12The king said to Queen Esther, "The Jews
have killed and destroyed five hundred men
and the ten sons of Haman in the citadel of
Susa. What have they done in the rest of the
king's provinces? Now what is your petition? It
will be given you. What is your request? It will
also be granted."

13"If it pleases the king," Esther answered,
"give the Jews in Susa permission to carry out
this day's edict tomorrow also, and let Haman's
ten sons be hanged on gallows."

14So the king commanded that this be done.
An edict was issued in Susa, and they hanged
the ten sons of Haman. 15The Jews in Susa
came together on the fourteenth day of the
month of Adar, and they put to death in Susa
three hundred men, but they did not lay their
hands on the plunder.

16Meanwhile, the remainder of the Jews who
were in the king's provinces also assembled to
protect themselves and get relief from their
enemies. They killed seventy-five thousand of
them but did not lay their hands on the plunder. 17This happened on the thirteenth day of
the month of Adar, and on the fourteenth they
rested and made it a day of feasting and joy.

Purim Celebrated

18The Jews in Susa, however, had assembled
on the thirteenth and fourteenth, and then on
the fifteenth they rested and made it a day of
feasting and joy.
19That is why rural Jews—those living in
villages—observe the fourteenth of the month
of Adar as a day of joy and feasting, a day for
giving presents to each other.
20Mordecai recorded these events, and
he sent letters to all the Jews throughout the
provinces of King Xerxes, near and far, 21to
have them celebrate annually the fourteenth
and fifteenth days of the month of Adar 22as
the time when the Jews got re-
lief from their enemies, and as
the month when their sorrow
was turned into joy and their
mourning into a day of celebration. He wrote them to observe
the days as days of feasting and
joy and giving presents of food
to one another and gifts to
the poor.
23So the Jews agreed to
continue the celebration they
had begun, doing what Mordecai had written to them. 24For
Haman son of Hammedatha,
the Agagite, the enemy of all
the Jews, had plotted against the Jews to destroy
them and had cast the *pur* (that is, the lot) for
their ruin and destruction. 25But when the plot
came to the king's attention,[a] he issued written
orders that the evil scheme Haman had devised
against the Jews should come back onto his
own head, and that he and his sons should be
hanged on the gallows. 26(Therefore these days
were called Purim, from the word *pur*.) Because
of everything written in this letter and because
of what they had seen and what had happened
to them, 27the Jews took it upon themselves to
establish the custom that they and their descendants and all who join them should without fail
observe these two days every year, in the way
prescribed and at the time appointed. 28These
days should be remembered and observed in
every generation by every family, and in every
province and in every city. And these days of
Purim should never cease to be celebrated by
the Jews, nor should the memory of them die
out among their descendants.
29So Queen Esther, daughter of Abihail,
along with Mordecai the Jew, wrote with full
authority to confirm this second letter concerning Purim. 30And Mordecai sent letters
to all the Jews in the 127 provinces of the kingdom of Xerxes—words of goodwill and assurance— 31to establish these days of Purim at
their designated times, as Mordecai the Jew
and Queen Esther had decreed
for them, and as they had established for themselves and
their descendants in regard to
their times of fasting and lamentation. 32Esther's decree confirmed these regulations about
Purim, and it was written down
in the records.

Esther 9:22

God Relieves Sorrow

The Jews got relief from their enemies, and . . . their sorrow was turned into joy and their mourning into a day of celebration.

The Greatness of Mordecai

10 King Xerxes imposed
tribute throughout the
empire, to its distant shores.
2And all his acts of power and
might, together with a full account of the greatness of Mor-
decai to which the king had raised him, are
they not written in the book of the annals of
the kings of Media and Persia? 3Mordecai the
Jew was second in rank to King Xerxes, preeminent among the Jews, and held in high esteem
by his many fellow Jews, because he worked for
the good of his people and spoke up for the welfare of all the Jews.

[a] 25 Or *when Esther came before the king*

Job

Author:
Unknown.

Audience:
God's people.

Date:
Unknown B.C.

Setting:
Job lived in Uz, east of Canaan. His story is one of personal tragedy.

Verse to Remember:
"Naked I came from my mother's womb, and naked I will depart. The LORD gave and the LORD has taken away; may the name of the LORD be praised." (1:21)

One of the best-known stories in Scripture, the book of Job *demonstrates God's providence in a believer's suffering.* Satan challenged God that Job was righteous only because of his wealth. Job's friends insisted that his suffering proved he was guilty of hidden sin and that God was displeased with him. Then God himself showed up with a long list of questions, demonstrating how *his creation reveals* his majesty and mystery—a mystery hidden from Job until he saw God himself and submitted before him. At the end of the story, Job's wealth was restored and his family grew. But more than that, *Job had seen God* and *knew God's goodness* even in suffering.

Prologue

1 In the land of Uz there lived a man whose
name was Job. This man was blameless
and upright; he feared God and shunned evil.
2 He had seven sons and three daughters, 3 and
he owned seven thousand sheep, three thousand camels, five hundred yoke of oxen and
five hundred donkeys, and had a large number
of servants. He was the greatest man among all
the people of the East.
4 His sons used to take turns holding feasts in
their homes, and they would invite their three
sisters to eat and drink with them. 5 When a
period of feasting had run its course, Job would
send and have them purified. Early in the morning he would sacrifice a burnt offering for each
of them, thinking, "Perhaps my children have
sinned and cursed God in their hearts." This
was Job's regular custom.

Job's First Test

6 One day the angels[a] came to present themselves before the LORD, and Satan[b] also came
with them. 7 The LORD said to Satan, "Where
have you come from?"
Satan answered the LORD, "From roaming

[a]6 Hebrew *the sons of God* [b]6 *Satan* means *accuser.*

To Know God Is to Trust God

Read: Job 1:1–22

IMAGINE THAT YOUR NEIGHBOR calls you at work, telling you the terrible news that your house and vehicles have been destroyed by fire, and while that person is still speaking, you learn that you've been fired from your job. While those words are still coming out of your employer's mouth, your husband calls: your kids and all their families have been killed while they were vacationing together.

These are the unimaginable circumstances Job encountered. Devastating messages assaulted him again and again—each one coming while the messenger "was still speaking." Who can even begin to comprehend his sheer horror at learning that all ten of his children were dead?

What did Job do? What was his initial response upon hearing of the loss of all he owned and of all he held dear? First, he grieved. He physically responded in the Eastern mode of grief by tearing his robe and shaving his head to display his deep sorrow. Yet no outward sign of grief could capture the inward torture Job felt.

Job's next step demonstrates faithfulness toward God. He fell to the ground and worshiped. That's right—he didn't berate God or ask "Why me?" or "Why them?" Instead, he acknowledged that everything comes from God, and he praised the name of the Lord. Try envisioning that scene. It will take your breath away. Picture this man, deep in the throes of grief, praising God. In light of the horrific blows dealt to him, how did he do that?

Only one answer suffices: Job knew God—*really* knew him with an uncommon intimacy. His close communion with God had taught him that God was the only one who could give him any kind of real comfort. Job's knowledge yielded a deep trust in an infallible Lord—a trust that enabled Job's heart to keep beating even in the face of overwhelming heartbreak. It enabled him to respond to horrible pain with worship and praise.

Yes, times of seeking for answers and grappling for understanding followed that day of destruction, but Job's initial response reflected a heart that knew and trusted God. What an amazing and beautiful image!

Job 1:20–21

Then he fell to the ground in worship and said: "Naked I came from my mother's womb, and naked I will depart. The LORD gave and the LORD has taken away; may the name of the LORD be praised."

reflection

1. How have you responded to bad news in the past? With praise? Anger? Despair? Confusion?

2. Job knew God well enough to turn to him in grief. How deep does your knowledge of God go? How close is your heart attuned to his?

3. How might going through tough times or experiencing pain and grief help someone know God?

RELATED READINGS

Deuteronomy 32:36–39; Psalms 42:1–11; 86:1–17

Go to page 609 for your next devotional reading.

through the earth and going back and forth in it."

8Then the LORD said to Satan, "Have you considered my servant Job? There is no one on earth like him; he is blameless and upright, a man who fears God and shuns evil."

9"Does Job fear God for nothing?" Satan replied. 10"Have you not put a hedge around him and his household and everything he has? You have blessed the work of his hands, so that his flocks and herds are spread throughout the land. 11But stretch out your hand and strike everything he has, and he will surely curse you to your face."

12The LORD said to Satan, "Very well, then, everything he has is in your hands, but on the man himself do not lay a finger."

Then Satan went out from the presence of the LORD.

13One day when Job's sons and daughters were feasting and drinking wine at the oldest brother's house, 14a messenger came to Job and said, "The oxen were plowing and the donkeys were grazing nearby, 15and the Sabeans attacked and carried them off. They put the servants to the sword, and I am the only one who has escaped to tell you!"

16While he was still speaking, another messenger came and said, "The fire of God fell from the sky and burned up the sheep and the servants, and I am the only one who has escaped to tell you!"

17While he was still speaking, another messenger came and said, "The Chaldeans formed three raiding parties and swept down on your camels and carried them off. They put the servants to the sword, and I am the only one who has escaped to tell you!"

18While he was still speaking, yet another messenger came and said, "Your sons and daughters were feasting and drinking wine at the oldest brother's house, 19when suddenly a mighty wind swept in from the desert and struck the four corners of the house. It collapsed on them and they are dead, and I am the only one who has escaped to tell you!"

20At this, Job got up and tore his robe and shaved his head. Then he fell to the ground in worship 21and said:

"Naked I came from my
    mother's womb,
  and naked I will depart.[a]
The LORD gave and the
    LORD has taken
    away;
  may the name of the
    LORD be praised."

22In all this, Job did not sin by charging God with wrongdoing.

Job 1:21

God Gives and Takes Away

"Naked I came from my
mother's womb,
and naked I will depart.
The LORD gave and the
LORD has taken away;
may the name of the
LORD be praised."

Job's Second Test

2 On another day the angels[b] came to present themselves before the LORD, and Satan also came with them to present himself before him. 2And the LORD said to Satan, "Where have you come from?"

Satan answered the LORD, "From roaming through the earth and going back and forth in it."

3Then the LORD said to Satan, "Have you considered my servant Job? There is no one on earth like him; he is blameless and upright, a man who fears God and shuns evil. And he still maintains his integrity, though you incited me against him to ruin him without any reason."

4"Skin for skin!" Satan replied. "A man will give all he has for his own life. 5But stretch out your hand and strike his flesh and bones, and he will surely curse you to your face."

6The LORD said to Satan, "Very well, then, he is in your hands; but you must spare his life."

7So Satan went out from the presence of the LORD and afflicted Job with painful sores from the soles of his feet to the top of his head. 8Then Job took a piece of broken pottery and scraped himself with it as he sat among the ashes.

9His wife said to him, "Are you still holding on to your integrity? Curse God and die!"

[a]21 Or *will return there* [b]1 Hebrew *the sons of God*

Silence Is Golden

Read: Job 2:9–13

THERE'S NO "HOW-TO" MANUAL describing what to say or do for someone who has suffered a great loss. A mother loses her child to disease, a wife loses her husband to divorce, a family loses their home to fire. What do you say?

Job was suffering. All of his children, servants, flocks and herds were gone. His health and well-being were decimated. Job's wife bitterly responded, "Curse God and die!" As much as she, too, must have been suffering, Job's wife talked too much and too soon.

When Job's three friends, Eliphaz, Bildad and Zophar, came to see him, the Bible tells us that Job had been disfigured by grief. Job's friends wept aloud, tore their robes and threw dust into the air—the ancient mourning rituals for death or tragic loss. For seven days and nights they did not utter a word. They simply sat beside him in silence.

Later on, Job's friends tried to explain away his misfortunes and wrongly blamed Job. But at the beginning, they got it right by recognizing that nothing they could say could assuage his grief. Here, they offered him not words but the comfort of their presence.

When we encounter friends who have suffered great loss, it is easy to drop off a casserole, send a sympathy card or say, "Call me if you need anything." We often rely on pat answers: "God knows best; all things work together for good." Sometimes we speak too much or too soon. Maybe we're fearful in the presence of others' pain, so we babble about meaningless things. Sometimes we're fearful of the roiling emotions lurking below the surface, so we don't even make contact.

Perhaps Job's friends stumbled onto one key to mourning with those who mourn: Have the wisdom to know when to talk and when to stay silent. Solomon said, "There is a time for everything . . . a time to weep and time to laugh . . . a time to be silent and a time to speak" (Ecclesiastes 3:1,4,7). You can pray for the wisdom to realize when your presence will speak louder than words. Your presence says, "I'm here for you. I love you. I am walking through this valley with you."

The next time you find yourself eye-to-eye with someone in grief, don't worry about what you will say. God will give you words to speak and the wisdom to know when to keep silent.

Job 2:13

Then they sat on the ground with him for seven days and seven nights. No one said a word to him, because they saw how great his suffering was.

reflection

1 Has there ever been a time when you were grieving or struggling and someone's advice or comments were like pouring salt on a wound? How did it affect you?

2 What was the most helpful thing that anyone has ever done for you during a time of loss or great struggle?

3 How can you show support to someone you know who is struggling?

RELATED READINGS

Proverbs 20:15; 25:20; Romans 12:15; 2 Corinthians 1:3–11

Go to page 615 for your next devotional reading.

10He replied, "You are talking like a foolish[a] woman. Shall we accept good from God, and not trouble?"

In all this, Job did not sin in what he said.

Job's Three Friends

11When Job's three friends, Eliphaz the Temanite, Bildad the Shuhite and Zophar the Naamathite, heard about all the troubles that had come upon him, they set out from their homes and met together by agreement to go and sympathize with him and comfort him.
12When they saw him from a distance, they could hardly recognize him; they began to weep aloud, and they tore their robes and sprinkled dust on their heads. 13Then they sat on the ground with him for seven days and seven nights. No one said a word to him, because they saw how great his suffering was.

Job Speaks

3 After this, Job opened his mouth and cursed the day of his birth. 2He said:

3 "May the day of my birth perish,
and the night it was said, 'A boy is born!'
4 That day—may it turn to darkness;
may God above not care about it;
may no light shine upon it.
5 May darkness and deep shadow[b] claim it once more;
may a cloud settle over it;
may blackness overwhelm its light.
6 That night—may thick darkness seize it;
may it not be included among the days of the year
nor be entered in any of the months.
7 May that night be barren;
may no shout of joy be heard in it.
8 May those who curse days[c] curse that day,
those who are ready to rouse Leviathan.
9 May its morning stars become dark;
may it wait for daylight in vain
and not see the first rays of dawn,
10 for it did not shut the doors of the womb on me
to hide trouble from my eyes.

11 "Why did I not perish at birth,
and die as I came from the womb?
12 Why were there knees to receive me
and breasts that I might be nursed?
13 For now I would be lying down in peace;
I would be asleep and at rest
14 with kings and counselors of the earth,
who built for themselves places now lying in ruins,
15 with rulers who had gold,
who filled their houses with silver.
16 Or why was I not hidden in the ground like a stillborn child,
like an infant who never saw the light of day?
17 There the wicked cease from turmoil,
and there the weary are at rest.
18 Captives also enjoy their ease;
they no longer hear the slave driver's shout.
19 The small and the great are there,
and the slave is freed from his master.

20 "Why is light given to those in misery,
and life to the bitter of soul,
21 to those who long for death that does not come,
who search for it more than for hidden treasure,
22 who are filled with gladness
and rejoice when they reach the grave?
23 Why is life given to a man
whose way is hidden,
whom God has hedged in?
24 For sighing comes to me instead of food;
my groans pour out like water.
25 What I feared has come upon me;
what I dreaded has happened to me.
26 I have no peace, no quietness;
I have no rest, but only turmoil."

Eliphaz

4 Then Eliphaz the Temanite replied:

2 "If someone ventures a word with you, will you be impatient?
But who can keep from speaking?
3 Think how you have instructed many,
how you have strengthened feeble hands.
4 Your words have supported those who stumbled;
you have strengthened faltering knees.

[a] 10 The Hebrew word rendered *foolish* denotes moral deficiency. [b] 5 Or *and the shadow of death* [c] 8 Or *the sea*

5 But now trouble comes to you, and you are
discouraged;
it strikes you, and you are dismayed.
6 Should not your piety be your confidence
and your blameless ways your hope?

7 "Consider now: Who, being innocent, has
ever perished?
Where were the upright ever destroyed?
8 As I have observed, those who plow evil
and those who sow trouble reap it.
9 At the breath of God they are destroyed;
at the blast of his anger they perish.
10 The lions may roar and growl,
yet the teeth of the great lions are
broken.
11 The lion perishes for lack of prey,
and the cubs of the lioness are scattered.

12 "A word was secretly brought to me,
my ears caught a whisper of it.
13 Amid disquieting dreams in the night,
when deep sleep falls on men,
14 fear and trembling seized me
and made all my bones shake.
15 A spirit glided past my face,
and the hair on my body stood on end.
16 It stopped,
but I could not tell what it was.
A form stood before my
eyes,
and I heard a hushed
voice:
17 'Can a mortal be more
righteous than
God?
Can a man be more pure
than his Maker?
18 If God places no trust in his
servants,
if he charges his angels
with error,
19 how much more those who live in houses
of clay,
whose foundations are in the dust,
who are crushed more readily than a
moth!
20 Between dawn and dusk they are broken to
pieces;
unnoticed, they perish forever.
21 Are not the cords of their tent pulled up,
so that they die without wisdom?'[a]

5 "Call if you will, but who will answer
you?
To which of the holy ones will you turn?
2 Resentment kills a fool,
and envy slays the simple.
3 I myself have seen a fool taking root,
but suddenly his house was cursed.
4 His children are far from safety,
crushed in court without a defender.
5 The hungry consume his harvest,
taking it even from among thorns,
and the thirsty pant after his wealth.
6 For hardship does not spring from the
soil,
nor does trouble sprout from the
ground.
7 Yet man is born to trouble
as surely as sparks fly upward.

8 "But if it were I, I would appeal to God;
I would lay my cause before him.
9 He performs wonders that cannot be
fathomed,
miracles that cannot be counted.
10 He bestows rain on the earth;
he sends water upon the countryside.
11 The lowly he sets on high,
and those who mourn
are lifted to safety.
12 He thwarts the plans of the
crafty,
so that their hands
achieve no success.
13 He catches the wise in their
craftiness,
and the schemes of the
wily are swept away.
14 Darkness comes upon
them in the
daytime;
at noon they grope as in the night.
15 He saves the needy from the sword in their
mouth;
he saves them from the clutches of the
powerful.
16 So the poor have hope,
and injustice shuts its mouth.

> **Job 4:17**
>
> *God Is Pure*
>
> "Can a mortal be more righteous than God? Can a man be more pure than his Maker?"

[a]21 Some interpreters end the quotation after verse 17.

17 "Blessed is the man whom God corrects;
so do not despise the discipline of the Almighty.[a]
18 For he wounds, but he also binds up;
he injures, but his hands also heal.
19 From six calamities he will rescue you;
in seven no harm will befall you.
20 In famine he will ransom you from death,
and in battle from the stroke of the sword.
21 You will be protected from the lash of the tongue,
and need not fear when destruction comes.
22 You will laugh at destruction and famine,
and need not fear the beasts of the earth.
23 For you will have a covenant with the stones of the field,
and the wild animals will be at peace with you.
24 You will know that your tent is secure;
you will take stock of your property and find nothing missing.
25 You will know that your children will be many,
and your descendants like the grass of the earth.
26 You will come to the grave in full vigor,
like sheaves gathered in season.

27 "We have examined this, and it is true.
So hear it and apply it to yourself."

Job 5:17

God Disciplines Us

"Blessed is the man whom God corrects; so do not despise the discipline of the Almighty."

Job
6 Then Job replied:

2 "If only my anguish could be weighed
and all my misery be placed on the scales!
3 It would surely outweigh the sand of the seas—
no wonder my words have been impetuous.
4 The arrows of the Almighty are in me,
my spirit drinks in their poison;
God's terrors are marshaled against me.
5 Does a wild donkey bray when it has grass,
or an ox bellow when it has fodder?
6 Is tasteless food eaten without salt,
or is there flavor in the white of an egg[b]?
7 I refuse to touch it;
such food makes me ill.
8 "Oh, that I might have my request,
that God would grant what I hope for,
9 that God would be willing to crush me,
to let loose his hand and cut me off!
10 Then I would still have this consolation—
my joy in unrelenting pain—
that I had not denied the words of the Holy One.

11 "What strength do I have, that I should still hope?
What prospects, that I should be patient?
12 Do I have the strength of stone?
Is my flesh bronze?
13 Do I have any power to help myself,
now that success has been driven from me?

14 "A despairing man should have the devotion of his friends,
even though he forsakes the fear of the Almighty.
15 But my brothers are as undependable as intermittent streams,
as the streams that overflow
16 when darkened by thawing ice
and swollen with melting snow,
17 but that cease to flow in the dry season,
and in the heat vanish from their channels.
18 Caravans turn aside from their routes;
they go up into the wasteland and perish.
19 The caravans of Tema look for water,

[a]17 Hebrew *Shaddai*; here and throughout Job [b]6 The meaning of the Hebrew for this phrase is uncertain.

the traveling merchants of Sheba look
in hope.
20 They are distressed, because they had been
confident;
they arrive there, only to be
disappointed.
21 Now you too have proved to be of no help;
you see something dreadful and are
afraid.
22 Have I ever said, 'Give something on my
behalf,
pay a ransom for me from your wealth,
23 deliver me from the hand of the enemy,
ransom me from the clutches of the
ruthless'?
24 "Teach me, and I will be quiet;
show me where I have been wrong.
25 How painful are honest words!
But what do your arguments prove?
26 Do you mean to correct what I say,
and treat the words of a despairing man
as wind?
27 You would even cast lots for the fatherless
and barter away your friend.
28 "But now be so kind as to look at me.
Would I lie to your face?
29 Relent, do not be unjust;
reconsider, for my integrity is at stake.[a]
30 Is there any wickedness on my lips?
Can my mouth not discern malice?

7 "Does not man have hard service on
earth?
Are not his days like
those of a hired
man?
2 Like a slave longing for the
evening shadows,
or a hired man waiting
eagerly for his
wages,
3 so I have been allotted
months of futility,
and nights of misery
have been assigned
to me.
4 When I lie down I think,
'How long before I get up?'
The night drags on, and I toss till dawn.
5 My body is clothed with worms and scabs,
my skin is broken and festering.
6 "My days are swifter than a weaver's
shuttle,
and they come to an end without hope.
7 Remember, O God, that my life is but a
breath;
my eyes will never see happiness again.
8 The eye that now sees me will see me no
longer;
you will look for me, but I will be no
more.
9 As a cloud vanishes and is gone,
so he who goes down to the grave[b] does
not return.
10 He will never come to his house again;
his place will know him no more.
11 "Therefore I will not keep silent;
I will speak out in the anguish of my
spirit,
I will complain in the bitterness of my
soul.
12 Am I the sea, or the monster of the deep,
that you put me under guard?
13 When I think my bed will comfort me
and my couch will ease my complaint,
14 even then you frighten me with dreams
and terrify me with visions,
15 so that I prefer strangling and death,
rather than this body of mine.
16 I despise my life; I would not live forever.
Let me alone; my days
have no meaning.
17 "What is man that you
make so much of
him,
that you give him so
much attention,
18 that you examine him
every morning
and test him every
moment?
19 Will you never look away
from me,
or let me alone even for
an instant?

> **Job 7:1**
>
> *God Appoints Difficult Times*
>
> "Does not man have hard service on earth? Are not his days like those of a hired man?"

[a]29 Or *my righteousness still stands* [b]9 Hebrew *Sheol*

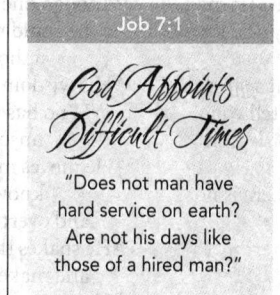

20 If I have sinned, what have I done to you,
O watcher of men?
Why have you made me your target?
Have I become a burden to you?[a]
21 Why do you not pardon my offenses
and forgive my sins?
For I will soon lie down in the dust;
you will search for me, but I will be no
more."

Bildad

8 Then Bildad the Shuhite replied:

2 "How long will you say such things?
Your words are a
blustering wind.
3 Does God pervert justice?
Does the Almighty
pervert what is
right?
4 When your children sinned
against him,
he gave them over to the
penalty of their sin.
5 But if you will look to God
and plead with the
Almighty,
6 if you are pure and upright,
even now he will rouse
himself on your behalf
and restore you to your rightful place.
7 Your beginnings will seem humble,
so prosperous will your future be.

8 "Ask the former generations
and find out what their fathers learned,
9 for we were born only yesterday and know
nothing,
and our days on earth are but a shadow.
10 Will they not instruct you and tell you?
Will they not bring forth words from
their understanding?
11 Can papyrus grow tall where there is no
marsh?
Can reeds thrive without water?
12 While still growing and uncut,
they wither more quickly than grass.
13 Such is the destiny of all who forget God;
so perishes the hope of the godless.
14 What he trusts in is fragile[b];
what he relies on is a spider's web.
15 He leans on his web, but it gives way;
he clings to it, but it does not hold.
16 He is like a well-watered plant in the
sunshine,
spreading its shoots over the garden;
17 it entwines its roots around a pile of rocks
and looks for a place among the stones.
18 But when it is torn from its spot,
that place disowns it and says, 'I never
saw you.'
19 Surely its life withers away,
and[c] from the soil other plants grow.

> **Job 8:3**
>
> *God's Judgment Is Right*
>
> "Does God pervert justice? Does the Almighty pervert what is right?"

20 "Surely God does not reject
a blameless man
or strengthen the hands
of evildoers.
21 He will yet fill your mouth
with laughter
and your lips with shouts
of joy.
22 Your enemies will be
clothed in shame,
and the tents of the
wicked will be no
more."

Job

9 Then Job replied:

2 "Indeed, I know that this is true.
But how can a mortal be righteous
before God?
3 Though one wished to dispute with him,
he could not answer him one time out of
a thousand.
4 His wisdom is profound, his power is vast.
Who has resisted him and come out
unscathed?
5 He moves mountains without their
knowing it
and overturns them in his anger.
6 He shakes the earth from its place
and makes its pillars tremble.
7 He speaks to the sun and it does not shine;
he seals off the light of the stars.
8 He alone stretches out the heavens

[a] 20 A few manuscripts of the Masoretic Text, an ancient Hebrew scribal tradition and Septuagint; most manuscripts of the Masoretic Text *I have become a burden to myself.* [b] 14 The meaning of the Hebrew for this word is uncertain. [c] 19 Or *Surely all the joy it has / is that*

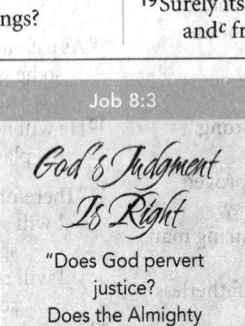

Beyond the Questions

Read: Job 9:1–35

ZELIE GUERIN MARTIN could have chosen to believe that God was not fair. She was born in 1831 in Alencon, France, and described her childhood as "dismal," recounting how she received little love or affection from her parents. After she married her husband, Louis, she began what started as a happy life as a wife and mother. But tragedy soon struck when four of her nine children died within three years of one another. She lamented, "I haven't a penny's worth of courage." She could have questioned God's love and goodness in the midst of such raw pain. Instead, she looked beyond her present suffering toward a hopeful eternity. The book of Job says, "Man born of woman is of few days and full of trouble" (Job 14:1). Zelie echoed Job's outlook when her life was derailed by death: "My children were not lost forever; life is short and full of miseries, and we shall find our little ones again up above."

The death of Job's children and the loss of all he possessed were inexplicable from a human perspective. It just didn't seem fair. Job longed to argue with God and plead his case, but he realized that God "is not a man like me that I might answer him" (Job 9:32). He longed for someone to "arbitrate" between them.

As mere mortals, it's simply not possible to look beyond heaven's veil to see why God allows things to happen as they do. The simple truth is that God is God, and we are not. And let's face it: Sometimes the things that happen don't seem fair. But thankfully, God *has* sent an arbitrator in the form of his Son, Jesus Christ, to mediate between humans and our holy God. The Bible tells us that Jesus "is able to save completely those who come to God through him, because he always lives to intercede for them" (Hebrews 7:25).

Though we may suffer temporarily on this earth—and no one is denying the intense grief we experience as human beings—through faith in Christ, we can rest assured of an eternity where "there will be no more death or mourning or crying or pain" (Revelation 21:4).

Thursday

Job 9:32–33

"He is not a man like me that I might answer him, that we might confront each other in court. If only there were someone to arbitrate between us, to lay his hand upon us both."

reflection

1 Describe a time when you wanted to question God. What did you want to dispute or ask?

2 Do you feel closer to God or farther away from him when you question the unfairness of life?

3 Have you asked Jesus to be your arbitrator so that you can enter eternity? If you have not, will you do so now, so you can rest assured of an eternal life in Christ?

RELATED READINGS

Isaiah 55:8–11;
Romans 8:31–39;
James 5:7–11

Go to page 620 for your next devotional reading.

and treads on the waves of the sea.
9 He is the Maker of the Bear and Orion,
the Pleiades and the constellations of the south.
10 He performs wonders that cannot be fathomed,
miracles that cannot be counted.
11 When he passes me, I cannot see him;
when he goes by, I cannot perceive him.
12 If he snatches away, who can stop him?
Who can say to him, 'What are you doing?'
13 God does not restrain his anger;
even the cohorts of Rahab cowered at his feet.

14 "How then can I dispute with him?
How can I find words to argue with him?
15 Though I were innocent, I could not answer him;
I could only plead with my Judge for mercy.
16 Even if I summoned him and he responded,
I do not believe he would give me a hearing.
17 He would crush me with a storm
and multiply my wounds for no reason.
18 He would not let me regain my breath
but would overwhelm me with misery.
19 If it is a matter of strength, he is mighty!
And if it is a matter of justice, who will summon him[a]?
20 Even if I were innocent, my mouth would condemn me;
if I were blameless, it would pronounce me guilty.

21 "Although I am blameless,
I have no concern for myself;
I despise my own life.
22 It is all the same; that is why I say,
'He destroys both the blameless and the wicked.'
23 When a scourge brings sudden death,
he mocks the despair of the innocent.
24 When a land falls into the hands of the wicked,
he blindfolds its judges.
If it is not he, then who is it?

25 "My days are swifter than a runner;
they fly away without a glimpse of joy.
26 They skim past like boats of papyrus,
like eagles swooping down on their prey.
27 If I say, 'I will forget my complaint,
I will change my expression, and smile,'
28 I still dread all my sufferings,
for I know you will not hold me innocent.
29 Since I am already found guilty,
why should I struggle in vain?
30 Even if I washed myself with soap[b]
and my hands with washing soda,
31 you would plunge me into a slime pit
so that even my clothes would detest me.

32 "He is not a man like me that I might answer him,
that we might confront each other in court.
33 If only there were someone to arbitrate between us,
to lay his hand upon us both,
34 someone to remove God's rod from me,
so that his terror would frighten me no more.
35 Then I would speak up without fear of him,
but as it now stands with me, I cannot.

Job 9:32

God Is Superior to Humans

"He is not a man like me that I might answer him, that we might confront each other in court."

10 "I loathe my very life;
therefore I will give free rein to my complaint
and speak out in the bitterness of my soul.
2 I will say to God: Do not condemn me,
but tell me what charges you have against me.
3 Does it please you to oppress me,
to spurn the work of your hands,

[a] 19 See Septuagint; Hebrew *me.* [b] 30 Or *snow*

while you smile on the schemes of the
wicked?
4 Do you have eyes of flesh?
Do you see as a mortal sees?
5 Are your days like those of a mortal
or your years like those of a man,
6 that you must search out my faults
and probe after my sin—
7 though you know that I am not guilty
and that no one can rescue me from
your hand?

8 "Your hands shaped me and made me.
Will you now turn and destroy me?
9 Remember that you molded me like clay.
Will you now turn me to dust again?
10 Did you not pour me out like milk
and curdle me like cheese,
11 clothe me with skin and flesh
and knit me together with bones and
sinews?
12 You gave me life and showed me kindness,
and in your providence watched over
my spirit.

13 "But this is what you concealed in your
heart,
and I know that this was in your mind:
14 If I sinned, you would be watching me
and would not let
my offense go
unpunished.
15 If I am guilty—woe to me!
Even if I am innocent, I
cannot lift my head,
for I am full of shame
and drowned in[a] my
affliction.
16 If I hold my head high, you
stalk me like a lion
and again display your
awesome power
against me.
17 You bring new witnesses against me
and increase your anger toward me;
your forces come against me wave upon
wave.

18 "Why then did you bring me out of the
womb?
I wish I had died before any eye saw me.
19 If only I had never come into being,
or had been carried straight from the
womb to the grave!
20 Are not my few days almost over?
Turn away from me so I can have a
moment's joy
21 before I go to the place of no return,
to the land of gloom and deep shadow,[b]
22 to the land of deepest night,
of deep shadow and disorder,
where even the light is like darkness."

Zophar

11 Then Zophar the Naamathite replied:

2 "Are all these words to go unanswered?
Is this talker to be vindicated?
3 Will your idle talk reduce men to silence?
Will no one rebuke you when you
mock?
4 You say to God, 'My beliefs are flawless
and I am pure in your sight.'
5 Oh, how I wish that God would speak,
that he would open his lips against you
6 and disclose to you the secrets of wisdom,
for true wisdom has two sides.
Know this: God has even
forgotten some of
your sin.

7 "Can you fathom the
mysteries of God?
Can you probe the limits
of the Almighty?
8 They are higher than the
heavens—what can
you do?
They are deeper than
the depths of the
grave[c]—what can
you know?
9 Their measure is longer
than the earth
and wider than the sea.

10 "If he comes along and confines you in
prison
and convenes a court, who can oppose
him?

Job 11:7

God Is Mysterious

"Can you fathom the
mysteries of God?
Can you probe the limits
of the Almighty?"

[a]15 Or *and aware of* [b]21 Or *and the shadow of death*; also in verse 22 [c]8 Hebrew *than Sheol*

11 Surely he recognizes deceitful men;
and when he sees evil, does he not take note?
12 But a witless man can no more become wise
than a wild donkey's colt can be born a man.[a]

13 "Yet if you devote your heart to him
and stretch out your hands to him,
14 if you put away the sin that is in your hand
and allow no evil to dwell in your tent,
15 then you will lift up your face without shame;
you will stand firm and without fear.
16 You will surely forget your trouble,
recalling it only as waters gone by.
17 Life will be brighter than noonday,
and darkness will become like morning.
18 You will be secure, because there is hope;
you will look about you and take your rest in safety.
19 You will lie down, with no one to make you afraid,
and many will court your favor.
20 But the eyes of the wicked will fail,
and escape will elude them;
their hope will become a dying gasp."

Job 12

12 Then Job replied:

2 "Doubtless you are the people,
and wisdom will die with you!
3 But I have a mind as well as you;
I am not inferior to you.
Who does not know all these things?

4 "I have become a laughingstock to my friends,
though I called upon God and he answered—
a mere laughingstock, though righteous and blameless!
5 Men at ease have contempt for misfortune
as the fate of those whose feet are slipping.
6 The tents of marauders are undisturbed,
and those who provoke God are secure—
those who carry their god in their hands.[b]

7 "But ask the animals, and they will teach you,
or the birds of the air, and they will tell you;
8 or speak to the earth, and it will teach you,
or let the fish of the sea inform you.
9 Which of all these does not know
that the hand of the LORD has done this?
10 In his hand is the life of every creature
and the breath of all mankind.
11 Does not the ear test words
as the tongue tastes food?
12 Is not wisdom found among the aged?
Does not long life bring understanding?

13 "To God belong wisdom and power;
counsel and understanding are his.
14 What he tears down cannot be rebuilt;
the man he imprisons cannot be released.
15 If he holds back the waters, there is drought;
if he lets them loose, they devastate the land.
16 To him belong strength and victory;
both deceived and deceiver are his.
17 He leads counselors away stripped
and makes fools of judges.
18 He takes off the shackles put on by kings
and ties a loincloth[c] around their waist.
19 He leads priests away stripped
and overthrows men long established.
20 He silences the lips of trusted advisers
and takes away the discernment of elders.
21 He pours contempt on nobles
and disarms the mighty.
22 He reveals the deep things of darkness
and brings deep shadows into the light.
23 He makes nations great, and destroys them;
he enlarges nations, and disperses them.
24 He deprives the leaders of the earth of their reason;
he sends them wandering through a trackless waste.
25 They grope in darkness with no light;
he makes them stagger like drunkards.

[a] 12 Or *wild donkey can be born tame* [b] 6 Or *secure / in what God's hand brings them* [c] 18 Or *shackles of kings / and ties a belt*

13 “My eyes have seen all this,
my ears have heard and understood it.
2 What you know, I also know;
I am not inferior to you.
3 But I desire to speak to the Almighty
and to argue my case with God.
4 You, however, smear me with lies;
you are worthless physicians, all of you!
5 If only you would be altogether silent!
For you, that would be wisdom.
6 Hear now my argument;
listen to the plea of my lips.
7 Will you speak wickedly on God’s behalf?
Will you speak deceitfully for him?
8 Will you show him partiality?
Will you argue the case for God?
9 Would it turn out well if he examined you?
Could you deceive him as you might deceive men?
10 He would surely rebuke you
if you secretly showed partiality.
11 Would not his splendor terrify you?
Would not the dread of him fall on you?
12 Your maxims are proverbs of ashes;
your defenses are defenses of clay.

13 “Keep silent and let me speak;
then let come to me what may.
14 Why do I put myself in jeopardy
and take my life in my hands?
15 Though he slay me, yet will I hope in him;
I will surely[a] defend my ways to his face.
16 Indeed, this will turn out for my deliverance,
for no godless man would dare come before him!
17 Listen carefully to my words;
let your ears take in what I say.
18 Now that I have prepared my case,
I know I will be vindicated.
19 Can anyone bring charges against me?
If so, I will be silent and die.

20 “Only grant me these two things, O God,
and then I will not hide from you:
21 Withdraw your hand far from me,
and stop frightening me with your terrors.
22 Then summon me and I will answer,
or let me speak, and you reply.
23 How many wrongs and sins have I committed?
Show me my offense and my sin.
24 Why do you hide your face
and consider me your enemy?
25 Will you torment a windblown leaf?
Will you chase after dry chaff?
26 For you write down bitter things against me
and make me inherit the sins of my youth.
27 You fasten my feet in shackles;
you keep close watch on all my paths
by putting marks on the soles of my feet.

28 “So man wastes away like something rotten,
like a garment eaten by moths.

14 “Man born of woman
is of few days and full of trouble.
2 He springs up like a flower and withers away;
like a fleeting shadow, he does not endure.
3 Do you fix your eye on such a one?
Will you bring him[b] before you for judgment?
4 Who can bring what is pure from the impure?
No one!
5 Man’s days are determined;
you have decreed the number of his months
and have set limits he cannot exceed.
6 So look away from him and let him alone,
till he has put in his time like a hired man.

> **Job 13:15**
>
> ***God Is Trustworthy***
>
> “Though he slay me, yet will I hope in him;
> I will surely defend my ways to his face.”

[a] 15 Or *He will surely slay me; I have no hope — / yet I will* [b] 3 Septuagint, Vulgate and Syriac; Hebrew *me*

The Patience of Job

Read: Job 13:1–28

Job 13:15

"Though he slay me, yet will I hope in him."

reflection

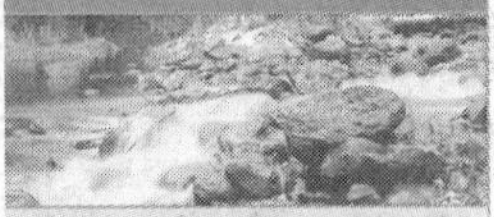

1 Have you ever wondered if suffering is the result of sinfulness?

2 Has this devotional caused you to rethink your position? Why or why not?

3 Make Job's proclamation personal to your situation: "Though he ____________, yet will I hope in him." (For example: "Though he allows breast cancer, yet will I hope in him.")

RELATED READINGS

Job 1:1–22;
Romans 5:1–5;
2 Corinthians 12:7–10

CARING FOR A PARENT with Alzheimer's disease takes what Carolyn Sherman calls "the patience of Job." Carolyn and Sandy Sherman have cared for both their mothers for ten years. For two of those years the two older women lived at home with the Shermans. Carolyn says she prayed many times for the patience and strength to see this through. "You do get irritated. You do lose it sometimes," said Carolyn. "I never realized that it would take so much time and so much patience." Carolyn went on to say that she had prayed many times for the ability to see it through.

Even well-intentioned people, like Job's foolish counselors, believe that all suffering or sickness is the direct result of sin. Throughout the book of Job we've seen Job's friends try to convince him that he had done something to displease God, that somehow Job was responsible for the horrible things that had happened to him. But this could not be further from the truth. Everyone suffers—the righteous and the unrighteous—including Job, who "was blameless and upright; he feared God and shunned evil" (Job 1:1). For some reason God chose to use Job as an example of patience in the midst of great suffering.

When something tragic happens, we often scramble to figure out why. Did I sin? Did they sin? If we didn't sin, then who sinned? Like Job's friends, we just want to affix blame so we can make some kind of sense out of the seemingly senseless. But not all suffering is the direct result of sin. Paul's thorn in the flesh was not given to him because he was such a sinner, but because God wanted him to understand something important about suffering. God said, "My grace is sufficient for you, for my power is made perfect in weakness" (2 Corinthians 12:9).

The simple truth is that God is not constrained to tell us *why* bad things happen to us. But he will let us know *how* to walk through them . . . with patience and hope. Yes, Job had some questions he wanted God to answer. But despite his questions Job could still faithfully proclaim, "Though he slay me, yet will I hope in him." Can the same be said of you?

Go to page 630 for your next devotional reading.

7 "At least there is hope for a tree:
If it is cut down, it will sprout again,
and its new shoots will not fail.
8 Its roots may grow old in the ground
and its stump die in the soil,
9 yet at the scent of water it will bud
and put forth shoots like a plant.
10 But man dies and is laid low;
he breathes his last and is no more.
11 As water disappears from the sea
or a riverbed becomes parched and dry,
12 so man lies down and does not rise;
till the heavens are no more, men will not awake
or be roused from their sleep.

13 "If only you would hide me in the grave[a]
and conceal me till your anger has passed!
If only you would set me a time
and then remember me!
14 If a man dies, will he live again?
All the days of my hard service
I will wait for my renewal[b] to come.
15 You will call and I will answer you;
you will long for the creature your hands have made.
16 Surely then you will count my steps
but not keep track of my sin.
17 My offenses will be sealed up in a bag;
you will cover over my sin.

18 "But as a mountain erodes and crumbles
and as a rock is moved from its place,
19 as water wears away stones
and torrents wash away the soil,
so you destroy man's hope.
20 You overpower him once for all, and he is gone;
you change his countenance and send him away.
21 If his sons are honored, he does not know it;
if they are brought low, he does not see it.
22 He feels but the pain of his own body
and mourns only for himself."

Eliphaz

15 Then Eliphaz the Temanite replied:

2 "Would a wise man answer with empty notions
or fill his belly with the hot east wind?
3 Would he argue with useless words,
with speeches that have no value?
4 But you even undermine piety
and hinder devotion to God.
5 Your sin prompts your mouth;
you adopt the tongue of the crafty.
6 Your own mouth condemns you, not mine;
your own lips testify against you.

7 "Are you the first man ever born?
Were you brought forth before the hills?
8 Do you listen in on God's council?
Do you limit wisdom to yourself?
9 What do you know that we do not know?
What insights do you have that we do not have?
10 The gray-haired and the aged are on our side,
men even older than your father.
11 Are God's consolations not enough for you,
words spoken gently to you?
12 Why has your heart carried you away,
and why do your eyes flash,
13 so that you vent your rage against God
and pour out such words from your mouth?

14 "What is man, that he could be pure,
or one born of woman, that he could be righteous?
15 If God places no trust in his holy ones,
if even the heavens are not pure in his eyes,
16 how much less man, who is vile and corrupt,
who drinks up evil like water!

17 "Listen to me and I will explain to you;
let me tell you what I have seen,
18 what wise men have declared,
hiding nothing received from their fathers
19 (to whom alone the land was given
when no alien passed among them):
20 All his days the wicked man suffers torment,
the ruthless through all the years stored up for him.
21 Terrifying sounds fill his ears;

[a] 13 Hebrew *Sheol* [b] 14 Or *release*

when all seems well, marauders attack
him.
22 He despairs of escaping the darkness;
he is marked for the sword.
23 He wanders about—food for vultures[a];
he knows the day of darkness is at
hand.
24 Distress and anguish fill him with terror;
they overwhelm him, like a king poised
to attack,
25 because he shakes his fist at God
and vaunts himself against the
Almighty,
26 defiantly charging against him
with a thick, strong shield.
27 "Though his face is covered with fat
and his waist bulges with flesh,
28 he will inhabit ruined towns
and houses where no one lives,
houses crumbling to rubble.
29 He will no longer be rich and his wealth
will not endure,
nor will his possessions spread over the
land.
30 He will not escape the darkness;
a flame will wither his shoots,
and the breath of God's mouth will
carry him away.
31 Let him not deceive himself by trusting
what is worthless,
for he will get nothing in return.
32 Before his time he will be paid in full,
and his branches will not flourish.
33 He will be like a vine stripped of its unripe
grapes,
like an olive tree shedding its blossoms.
34 For the company of the godless will be
barren,
and fire will consume the tents of those
who love bribes.
35 They conceive trouble and give birth to
evil;
their womb fashions deceit."

Job 16

Then Job replied:
2 "I have heard many things like these;
miserable comforters are you all!
3 Will your long-winded speeches never
end?
What ails you that you keep on arguing?
4 I also could speak like you,
if you were in my place;
I could make fine speeches against you
and shake my head at you.
5 But my mouth would encourage you;
comfort from my lips would bring you
relief.

6 "Yet if I speak, my pain is not relieved;
and if I refrain, it does not go away.
7 Surely, O God, you have worn me out;
you have devastated my entire
household.
8 You have bound me—and it has become a
witness;
my gauntness rises up and testifies
against me.
9 God assails me and tears me in his anger
and gnashes his teeth at me;
my opponent fastens on me his piercing
eyes.
10 Men open their mouths to jeer at me;
they strike my cheek in scorn
and unite together against me.
11 God has turned me over to evil men
and thrown me into the clutches of the
wicked.
12 All was well with me, but he shattered me;
he seized me by the neck and crushed
me.
He has made me his target;
13 his archers surround me.
Without pity, he pierces my kidneys
and spills my gall on the ground.
14 Again and again he bursts upon me;
he rushes at me like a warrior.

15 "I have sewed sackcloth over my skin
and buried my brow in the dust.
16 My face is red with weeping,
deep shadows ring my eyes;
17 yet my hands have been free of violence
and my prayer is pure.

18 "O earth, do not cover my blood;
may my cry never be laid to rest!
19 Even now my witness is in heaven;

[a] 23 Or *about, looking for food*

my advocate is on high.
20 My intercessor is my friend[a]
as my eyes pour out tears
to God;
21 on behalf of a man he
pleads with God
as a man pleads for his
friend.

22 "Only a few years will pass
before I go on the
journey of no
return.

17 1 My spirit is broken,
my days are cut short,
the grave awaits me.
2 Surely mockers surround
me;
my eyes must dwell on their hostility.

3 "Give me, O God, the pledge you demand.
Who else will put up security for me?
4 You have closed their minds to
understanding;
therefore you will not let them triumph.
5 If a man denounces his friends for reward,
the eyes of his children will fail.

6 "God has made me a byword to everyone,
a man in whose face people spit.
7 My eyes have grown dim with grief;
my whole frame is but a shadow.
8 Upright men are appalled at this;
the innocent are aroused against the
ungodly.
9 Nevertheless, the righteous will hold to
their ways,
and those with clean hands will grow
stronger.

10 "But come on, all of you, try again!
I will not find a wise man among you.
11 My days have passed, my plans are
shattered,
and so are the desires of my heart.
12 These men turn night into day;
in the face of darkness they say, 'Light
is near.'
13 If the only home I hope for is the grave,[b]
if I spread out my bed in darkness,
14 if I say to corruption, 'You are my father,'
and to the worm, 'My mother' or 'My
sister,'
15 where then is my hope?
Who can see any hope
for me?
16 Will it go down to the gates
of death[b]?
Will we descend together
into the dust?"

Job 16:19

God Is Our Advocate

"Even now my witness
is in heaven;
my advocate is on high."

Bildad

18 Then Bildad the Shu-
hite replied:

2 "When will you end these
speeches?
Be sensible, and then we
can talk.
3 Why are we regarded as cattle
and considered stupid in your sight?
4 You who tear yourself to pieces in your
anger,
is the earth to be abandoned for your
sake?
Or must the rocks be moved from their
place?

5 "The lamp of the wicked is snuffed out;
the flame of his fire stops burning.
6 The light in his tent becomes dark;
the lamp beside him goes out.
7 The vigor of his step is weakened;
his own schemes throw him down.
8 His feet thrust him into a net
and he wanders into its mesh.
9 A trap seizes him by the heel;
a snare holds him fast.
10 A noose is hidden for him on the ground;
a trap lies in his path.
11 Terrors startle him on every side
and dog his every step.
12 Calamity is hungry for him;
disaster is ready for him when he falls.
13 It eats away parts of his skin;
death's firstborn devours his limbs.
14 He is torn from the security of his tent
and marched off to the king of terrors.
15 Fire resides[c] in his tent;
burning sulfur is scattered over his
dwelling.
16 His roots dry up below

[a] **20** Or *My friends treat me with scorn* [b] **13,16** Hebrew *Sheol* [c] **15** Or *Nothing he had remains*

and his branches wither above.
17 The memory of him perishes from the
earth;
he has no name in the land.
18 He is driven from light into darkness
and is banished from the world.
19 He has no offspring or descendants among
his people,
no survivor where once he lived.
20 Men of the west are appalled at his fate;
men of the east are seized with horror.
21 Surely such is the dwelling of an evil
man;
such is the place of one who knows not
God."

Job
19
Then Job replied:
2 "How long will you torment me
and crush me with words?
3 Ten times now you have reproached me;
shamelessly you attack me.
4 If it is true that I have gone astray,
my error remains my concern alone.
5 If indeed you would exalt yourselves above
me
and use my humiliation against me,
6 then know that God has wronged me
and drawn his net around me.

7 "Though I cry, 'I've been
wronged!' I get no
response;
though I call for help,
there is no justice.
8 He has blocked my way so I
cannot pass;
he has shrouded my
paths in darkness.
9 He has stripped me of my
honor
and removed the crown
from my head.
10 He tears me down on every side till I am
gone;
he uproots my hope like a tree.
11 His anger burns against me;
he counts me among his enemies.
12 His troops advance in force;
they build a siege ramp against me
and encamp around my tent.

13 "He has alienated my brothers from me;
my acquaintances are completely
estranged from me.
14 My kinsmen have gone away;
my friends have forgotten me.
15 My guests and my maidservants count me
a stranger;
they look upon me as an alien.
16 I summon my servant, but he does not
answer,
though I beg him with my own mouth.
17 My breath is offensive to my wife;
I am loathsome to my own brothers.
18 Even the little boys scorn me;
when I appear, they ridicule me.
19 All my intimate friends detest me;
those I love have turned against me.
20 I am nothing but skin and bones;
I have escaped with only the skin of my
teeth.[a]

21 "Have pity on me, my friends, have pity,
for the hand of God has struck me.
22 Why do you pursue me as God does?
Will you never get enough of my flesh?

23 "Oh, that my words were recorded,
that they were written on
a scroll,
24 that they were inscribed
with an iron tool
on[b] lead,
or engraved in rock
forever!
25 I know that my Redeemer[c]
lives,
and that in the end he
will stand upon the
earth.[d]
26 And after my skin has been
destroyed,
yet[e] in[f] my flesh I will see God;
27 I myself will see him
with my own eyes—I, and not another.
How my heart yearns within me!

Job 19:25

God Lives

"I know that my
Redeemer lives,
and that in the end he will
stand upon the earth."

[a]20 Or *only my gums* [b]24 Or *and* [c]25 Or *defender* [d]25 Or *upon my grave* [e]26 Or *And after I awake, / though this ⌞body⌟ has been destroyed, / then* [f]26 Or */ apart from*

28 "If you say, 'How we will hound him,
since the root of the trouble lies in
him,[a]'
29 you should fear the sword yourselves;
for wrath will bring punishment by the
sword,
and then you will know that there is
judgment.[b]"

Zophar

20 Then Zophar the Naamathite replied:

2 "My troubled thoughts prompt me to
answer
because I am greatly disturbed.
3 I hear a rebuke that dishonors me,
and my understanding inspires me to
reply.

4 "Surely you know how it has been from of
old,
ever since man[c] was placed on the
earth,
5 that the mirth of the wicked is brief,
the joy of the godless lasts but a
moment.
6 Though his pride reaches to the heavens
and his head touches the clouds,
7 he will perish forever, like his own dung;
those who have seen him will say,
'Where is he?'
8 Like a dream he flies away, no more to be
found,
banished like a vision of the night.
9 The eye that saw him will not see him
again;
his place will look on him no more.
10 His children must make amends to the
poor;
his own hands must give back his
wealth.
11 The youthful vigor that fills his bones
will lie with him in the dust.

12 "Though evil is sweet in his mouth
and he hides it under his tongue,
13 though he cannot bear to let it go
and keeps it in his mouth,
14 yet his food will turn sour in his
stomach;
it will become the venom of serpents
within him.
15 He will spit out the riches he swallowed;
God will make his stomach vomit them
up.
16 He will suck the poison of serpents;
the fangs of an adder will kill him.
17 He will not enjoy the streams,
the rivers flowing with honey and
cream.
18 What he toiled for he must give back
uneaten;
he will not enjoy the profit from his
trading.
19 For he has oppressed the poor and left
them destitute;
he has seized houses he did not build.

20 "Surely he will have no respite from his
craving;
he cannot save himself by his
treasure.
21 Nothing is left for him to devour;
his prosperity will not endure.
22 In the midst of his plenty, distress will
overtake him;
the full force of misery will come upon
him.
23 When he has filled his belly,
God will vent his burning anger against
him
and rain down his blows upon him.
24 Though he flees from an iron weapon,
a bronze-tipped arrow pierces him.
25 He pulls it out of his back,
the gleaming point out of his liver.
Terrors will come over him;
26 total darkness lies in wait for his
treasures.
A fire unfanned will consume him
and devour what is left in his tent.
27 The heavens will expose his guilt;
the earth will rise up against him.
28 A flood will carry off his house,
rushing waters[d] on the day of God's
wrath.
29 Such is the fate God allots the wicked,
the heritage appointed for them by
God."

[a] 28 Many Hebrew manuscripts, Septuagint and Vulgate; most Hebrew manuscripts *me* [b] 29 Or / *that you may come to know the Almighty* [c] 4 Or *Adam* [d] 28 Or *The possessions in his house will be carried off, / washed away*

Job
21 Then Job replied:

2 "Listen carefully to my words;
let this be the consolation you give me.
3 Bear with me while I speak,
and after I have spoken, mock on.

4 "Is my complaint directed to man?
Why should I not be impatient?
5 Look at me and be astonished;
clap your hand over your mouth.
6 When I think about this, I am terrified;
trembling seizes my body.
7 Why do the wicked live on,
growing old and increasing in power?
8 They see their children established around them,
their offspring before their eyes.
9 Their homes are safe and free from fear;
the rod of God is not upon them.
10 Their bulls never fail to breed;
their cows calve and do not miscarry.
11 They send forth their children as a flock;
their little ones dance about.
12 They sing to the music of tambourine and harp;
they make merry to the sound of the flute.
13 They spend their years in prosperity
and go down to the grave[a] in peace.[b]
14 Yet they say to God, 'Leave us alone!
We have no desire to know your ways.
15 Who is the Almighty, that we should serve him?
What would we gain by praying to him?'
16 But their prosperity is not in their own hands,
so I stand aloof from the counsel of the wicked.

17 "Yet how often is the lamp of the wicked snuffed out?
How often does calamity come upon them,
the fate God allots in his anger?
18 How often are they like straw before the wind,
like chaff swept away by a gale?
19 ⌊It is said,⌋ 'God stores up a man's punishment for his sons.'
Let him repay the man himself, so that he will know it!
20 Let his own eyes see his destruction;
let him drink of the wrath of the Almighty.[c]
21 For what does he care about the family he leaves behind
when his allotted months come to an end?

22 "Can anyone teach knowledge to God,
since he judges even the highest?
23 One man dies in full vigor,
completely secure and at ease,
24 his body[d] well nourished,
his bones rich with marrow.
25 Another man dies in bitterness of soul,
never having enjoyed anything good.
26 Side by side they lie in the dust,
and worms cover them both.

27 "I know full well what you are thinking,
the schemes by which you would wrong me.
28 You say, 'Where now is the great man's house,
the tents where wicked men lived?'
29 Have you never questioned those who travel?
Have you paid no regard to their accounts—
30 that the evil man is spared from the day of calamity,
that he is delivered from[e] the day of wrath?
31 Who denounces his conduct to his face?
Who repays him for what he has done?
32 He is carried to the grave,
and watch is kept over his tomb.
33 The soil in the valley is sweet to him;
all men follow after him,
and a countless throng goes[f] before him.

34 "So how can you console me with your nonsense?
Nothing is left of your answers but falsehood!"

[a]13 Hebrew *Sheol* [b]13 Or *in an instant* [c]17–20 Verses 17 and 18 may be taken as exclamations and 19 and 20 as declarations. [d]24 The meaning of the Hebrew for this word is uncertain. [e]30 Or *man is reserved for the day of calamity, / that he is brought forth to* [f]33 Or / *as a countless throng went*

Eliphaz

22 Then Eliphaz the Temanite replied:

2 "Can a man be of benefit to God?
Can even a wise man benefit him?
3 What pleasure would it give the Almighty
if you were righteous?
What would he gain if your ways were
blameless?

4 "Is it for your piety that he rebukes you
and brings charges against you?
5 Is not your wickedness great?
Are not your sins endless?
6 You demanded security from your
brothers for no reason;
you stripped men of their clothing,
leaving them naked.
7 You gave no water to the weary
and you withheld food from the hungry,
8 though you were a powerful man, owning
land—
an honored man, living on it.
9 And you sent widows away empty-handed
and broke the strength of the fatherless.
10 That is why snares are all around you,
why sudden peril terrifies you,
11 why it is so dark you cannot see,
and why a flood of water covers you.

12 "Is not God in the heights of heaven?
And see how lofty are the highest stars!
13 Yet you say, 'What does God know?
Does he judge through such darkness?
14 Thick clouds veil him, so he does not see us
as he goes about in the vaulted heavens.'
15 Will you keep to the old path
that evil men have trod?
16 They were carried off before their time,
their foundations washed away by a
flood.
17 They said to God, 'Leave us alone!
What can the Almighty do to us?'
18 Yet it was he who filled their houses with
good things,
so I stand aloof from the counsel of the
wicked.

19 "The righteous see their ruin and rejoice;
the innocent mock them, saying,
20 'Surely our foes are destroyed,
and fire devours their wealth.'

21 "Submit to God and be at peace with him;
in this way prosperity will come to you.
22 Accept instruction from his mouth
and lay up his words in your heart.
23 If you return to the Almighty, you will be
restored:
If you remove wickedness far from your
tent
24 and assign your nuggets to the dust,
your gold of Ophir to the rocks in the
ravines,
25 then the Almighty will be your gold,
the choicest silver for you.
26 Surely then you will find delight in the
Almighty
and will lift up your face to God.
27 You will pray to him, and he will hear you,
and you will fulfill your vows.
28 What you decide on will be done,
and light will shine on your ways.
29 When men are brought low and you say,
'Lift them up!'
then he will save the downcast.
30 He will deliver even one who is not
innocent,
who will be delivered through the
cleanness of your hands."

Job

23 Then Job replied:

2 "Even today my complaint is bitter;
his hand[a] is heavy in spite of[b] my
groaning.
3 If only I knew where to find him;
if only I could go to his dwelling!
4 I would state my case before him
and fill my mouth with arguments.
5 I would find out what he would answer me,
and consider what he would say.
6 Would he oppose me with great power?
No, he would not press charges against
me.
7 There an upright man could present his
case before him,
and I would be delivered forever from
my judge.

[a]2 Septuagint and Syriac; Hebrew / *the hand on me* [b]2 Or *heavy on me in*

8 "But if I go to the east, he is not there;
if I go to the west, I do not find him.
9 When he is at work in the north, I do not see him;
when he turns to the south, I catch no glimpse of him.
10 But he knows the way that I take;
when he has tested me, I will come forth as gold.
11 My feet have closely followed his steps;
I have kept to his way without turning aside.
12 I have not departed from the commands of his lips;
I have treasured the words of his mouth more than my daily bread.

13 "But he stands alone, and who can oppose him?
He does whatever he pleases.
14 He carries out his decree against me,
and many such plans he still has in store.
15 That is why I am terrified before him;
when I think of all this, I fear him.
16 God has made my heart faint;
the Almighty has terrified me.
17 Yet I am not silenced by the darkness,
by the thick darkness that covers my face.

24 "Why does the Almighty not set times for judgment?
Why must those who know him look in vain for such days?
2 Men move boundary stones;
they pasture flocks they have stolen.
3 They drive away the orphan's donkey
and take the widow's ox in pledge.
4 They thrust the needy from the path
and force all the poor of the land into hiding.
5 Like wild donkeys in the desert,
the poor go about their labor of foraging food;
the wasteland provides food for their children.
6 They gather fodder in the fields
and glean in the vineyards of the wicked.
7 Lacking clothes, they spend the night naked;
they have nothing to cover themselves in the cold.
8 They are drenched by mountain rains
and hug the rocks for lack of shelter.
9 The fatherless child is snatched from the breast;
the infant of the poor is seized for a debt.
10 Lacking clothes, they go about naked;
they carry the sheaves, but still go hungry.
11 They crush olives among the terraces[a];
they tread the winepresses, yet suffer thirst.
12 The groans of the dying rise from the city,
and the souls of the wounded cry out for help.
But God charges no one with wrongdoing.

13 "There are those who rebel against the light,
who do not know its ways
or stay in its paths.
14 When daylight is gone, the murderer rises up
and kills the poor and needy;
in the night he steals forth like a thief.
15 The eye of the adulterer watches for dusk;
he thinks, 'No eye will see me,'
and he keeps his face concealed.
16 In the dark, men break into houses,
but by day they shut themselves in;
they want nothing to do with the light.
17 For all of them, deep darkness is their morning[b];
they make friends with the terrors of darkness.[c]

Job 23:13

God Is Unchangeable

"But he stands alone, and who can oppose him? He does whatever he pleases."

[a]11 Or *olives between the millstones*; the meaning of the Hebrew for this word is uncertain. [b]17 Or *them, their morning is like the shadow of death* [c]17 Or *of the shadow of death*

18 "Yet they are foam on the surface of the water;
their portion of the land is cursed,
so that no one goes to the vineyards.
19 As heat and drought snatch away the melted snow,
so the grave[a] snatches away those who have sinned.
20 The womb forgets them,
the worm feasts on them;
evil men are no longer remembered
but are broken like a tree.
21 They prey on the barren and childless woman,
and to the widow show no kindness.
22 But God drags away the mighty by his power;
though they become established, they have no assurance of life.
23 He may let them rest in a feeling of security,
but his eyes are on their ways.
24 For a little while they are exalted, and then they are gone;
they are brought low and gathered up like all others;
they are cut off like heads of grain.

25 "If this is not so, who can prove me false
and reduce my words to nothing?"

Bildad

25 Then Bildad the Shuhite replied:

2 "Dominion and awe belong to God;
he establishes order in the heights of heaven.
3 Can his forces be numbered?
Upon whom does his light not rise?
4 How then can a man be righteous before God?
How can one born of woman be pure?
5 If even the moon is not bright
and the stars are not pure in his eyes,
6 how much less man, who is but a maggot—
a son of man, who is only a worm!"

Job

26 Then Job replied:

2 "How you have helped the powerless!
How you have saved the arm that is feeble!
3 What advice you have offered to one without wisdom!
And what great insight you have displayed!
4 Who has helped you utter these words?
And whose spirit spoke from your mouth?

5 "The dead are in deep anguish,
those beneath the waters and all that live in them.
6 Death[a] is naked before God;
Destruction[b] lies uncovered.
7 He spreads out the northern ⌊skies⌋ over empty space;
he suspends the earth over nothing.
8 He wraps up the waters in his clouds,
yet the clouds do not burst under their weight.
9 He covers the face of the full moon,
spreading his clouds over it.
10 He marks out the horizon on the face of the waters
for a boundary between light and darkness.
11 The pillars of the heavens quake,
aghast at his rebuke.
12 By his power he churned up the sea;
by his wisdom he cut Rahab to pieces.
13 By his breath the skies became fair;
his hand pierced the gliding serpent.
14 And these are but the outer fringe of his works;
how faint the whisper we hear of him!

Job 26:7

God Sustains the World

"He spreads out the northern skies over empty space;
he suspends the earth over nothing."

[a] 19,6 Hebrew *Sheol* [b] 6 Hebrew *Abaddon*

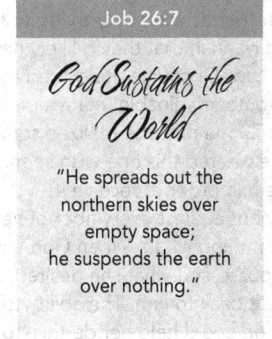

Release

HANNAH

O Lord Almighty, if you will only look upon your servant's misery and remember me, and not forget your servant but give her a son, then I will give him to the Lord for all the days of his life, and no razor will ever be used on his head.

1 Samuel 1:11

ASSIGNED READING:

1 Samuel 1–2

SHE DIDN'T NEED THREE WISHES.

She only needed one. What she most wanted in life could be summed up in a single wish. For so many years, she'd thought about it to the point where realizing that dream became an all-consuming pursuit. Waking and sleeping, it was her primary focus. It preoccupied her mind like background noise—a constant loop reminding her over and over again that what she wanted most she couldn't have.

"Have you tried some herbs from the midwife? I hear they can really help."

"Did you offer a sacrifice? God will answer you."

"Have you talked with your husband about it?"

"Have you . . ."

Her friends were only trying to help, but they just served to remind Hannah that they'd likely never wanted something as badly as she had. *Of course* she'd tried everything. She'd been down every route imaginable, many times; and still nothing.

Until, one day, she realized something.

She wanted this one wish so much that she was willing to release it in order to receive it.

It went against every fiber of her being, but she knew it was the right thing to do. When God answered her prayer, and she finally possessed what she desired, she knew that she would have to give it back to him. The ability to do that came from him too. Only God could help her do this, to understand that she was to hold her precious gift loosely, open-palmed, so that in God's time, when he received it back from her, he would not have to pry away her fingers.

For the first time in a long time, she felt release and a sense of peace when she quietly prayed, "I will give him to the Lord for all the days of his life."

—Prayer—

Gracious God, thank you for the wisdom and grace to make tough decisions in your name.

Weekend

Go to page 635 for your next devotional reading

Who then can understand the thunder
of his power?"

27 And Job continued his discourse:

2 "As surely as God lives, who has denied me
justice,
the Almighty, who has made me taste
bitterness of soul,
3 as long as I have life within me,
the breath of God in my nostrils,
4 my lips will not speak wickedness,
and my tongue will utter no deceit.
5 I will never admit you are in the right;
till I die, I will not deny my integrity.
6 I will maintain my righteousness and
never let go of it;
my conscience will not reproach me as
long as I live.

7 "May my enemies be like the wicked,
my adversaries like the unjust!
8 For what hope has the godless when he is
cut off,
when God takes away his life?
9 Does God listen to his cry
when distress comes upon him?
10 Will he find delight in the Almighty?
Will he call upon God at all times?

11 "I will teach you about the power of God;
the ways of the Almighty I will not
conceal.
12 You have all seen this yourselves.
Why then this meaningless talk?

13 "Here is the fate God allots to the wicked,
the heritage a ruthless man receives
from the Almighty:
14 However many his children, their fate is
the sword;
his offspring will never have enough to
eat.
15 The plague will bury those who survive
him,
and their widows will not weep for
them.
16 Though he heaps up silver like dust
and clothes like piles of clay,
17 what he lays up the righteous will wear,
and the innocent will divide his silver.
18 The house he builds is like a moth's
cocoon,
like a hut made by a watchman.
19 He lies down wealthy, but will do so no
more;
when he opens his eyes, all is gone.
20 Terrors overtake him like a flood;
a tempest snatches him away in the
night.
21 The east wind carries him off, and he is
gone;
it sweeps him out of his place.
22 It hurls itself against him without mercy
as he flees headlong from its power.
23 It claps its hands in derision
and hisses him out of his place.

28 "There is a mine for silver
and a place where gold is refined.
2 Iron is taken from the earth,
and copper is smelted from ore.
3 Man puts an end to the darkness;
he searches the farthest recesses
for ore in the blackest darkness.
4 Far from where people dwell he cuts a
shaft,
in places forgotten by the foot of man;
far from men he dangles and sways.
5 The earth, from which food comes,
is transformed below as by fire;
6 sapphires[a] come from its rocks,
and its dust contains nuggets of gold.
7 No bird of prey knows that hidden path,
no falcon's eye has seen it.
8 Proud beasts do not set foot on it,
and no lion prowls there.
9 Man's hand assaults the flinty rock
and lays bare the roots of the mountains.
10 He tunnels through the rock;
his eyes see all its treasures.
11 He searches[b] the sources of the rivers
and brings hidden things to light.

12 "But where can wisdom be found?
Where does understanding dwell?
13 Man does not comprehend its worth;
it cannot be found in the land of the
living.
14 The deep says, 'It is not in me';
the sea says, 'It is not with me.'

[a]6 Or *lapis lazuli*; also in verse 16 [b]11 Septuagint, Aquila and Vulgate; Hebrew *He dams up*

15 It cannot be bought with the finest gold,
nor can its price be weighed in silver.
16 It cannot be bought with the gold of Ophir,
with precious onyx or sapphires.
17 Neither gold nor crystal can compare with it,
nor can it be had for jewels of gold.
18 Coral and jasper are not worthy of mention;
the price of wisdom is beyond rubies.
19 The topaz of Cush cannot compare with it;
it cannot be bought with pure gold.

20 "Where then does wisdom come from?
Where does understanding dwell?
21 It is hidden from the eyes of every living thing,
concealed even from the birds of the air.
22 Destruction[a] and Death say,
'Only a rumor of it has reached our ears.'
23 God understands the way to it
and he alone knows where it dwells,
24 for he views the ends of the earth
and sees everything under the heavens.
25 When he established the force of the wind
and measured out the waters,
26 when he made a decree for the rain
and a path for the thunderstorm,
27 then he looked at wisdom and appraised it;
he confirmed it and tested it.
28 And he said to man,
'The fear of the Lord—that is wisdom,
and to shun evil is understanding.'"

Job 28:28

God Is to Be Revered

"And he said to man,
'The fear of the Lord—
that is wisdom,
and to shun evil is
understanding.'"

29

Job continued his discourse:

2 "How I long for the months gone by,
for the days when God watched over me,
3 when his lamp shone upon my head
and by his light I walked through darkness!
4 Oh, for the days when I was in my prime,
when God's intimate friendship blessed my house,
5 when the Almighty was still with me
and my children were around me,
6 when my path was drenched with cream
and the rock poured out for me streams of olive oil.

7 "When I went to the gate of the city
and took my seat in the public square,
8 the young men saw me and stepped aside
and the old men rose to their feet;
9 the chief men refrained from speaking
and covered their mouths with their hands;
10 the voices of the nobles were hushed,
and their tongues stuck to the roof of their mouths.
11 Whoever heard me spoke well of me,
and those who saw me commended me,
12 because I rescued the poor who cried for help,
and the fatherless who had none to assist him.
13 The man who was dying blessed me;
I made the widow's heart sing.
14 I put on righteousness as my clothing;
justice was my robe and my turban.
15 I was eyes to the blind
and feet to the lame.
16 I was a father to the needy;
I took up the case of the stranger.
17 I broke the fangs of the wicked
and snatched the victims from their teeth.

18 "I thought, 'I will die in my own house,
my days as numerous as the grains of sand.
19 My roots will reach to the water,
and the dew will lie all night on my branches.
20 My glory will remain fresh in me,
the bow ever new in my hand.'

[a] 22 Hebrew *Abaddon*

21 "Men listened to me expectantly,
waiting in silence for my counsel.
22 After I had spoken, they spoke no more;
my words fell gently on their ears.
23 They waited for me as for showers
and drank in my words as the spring rain.
24 When I smiled at them, they scarcely believed it;
the light of my face was precious to them.[a]
25 I chose the way for them and sat as their chief;
I dwelt as a king among his troops;
I was like one who comforts mourners.

30 "But now they mock me,
men younger than I,
whose fathers I would have disdained
to put with my sheep dogs.
2 Of what use was the strength of their hands to me,
since their vigor had gone from them?
3 Haggard from want and hunger,
they roamed[b] the parched land
in desolate wastelands at night.
4 In the brush they gathered salt herbs,
and their food[c] was the root of the broom tree.
5 They were banished from their fellow men,
shouted at as if they were thieves.
6 They were forced to live in the dry stream beds,
among the rocks and in holes in the ground.
7 They brayed among the bushes
and huddled in the undergrowth.
8 A base and nameless brood,
they were driven out of the land.

9 "And now their sons mock me in song;
I have become a byword among them.
10 They detest me and keep their distance;
they do not hesitate to spit in my face.
11 Now that God has unstrung my bow and afflicted me,
they throw off restraint in my presence.
12 On my right the tribe[d] attacks;
they lay snares for my feet,
they build their siege ramps against me.
13 They break up my road;
they succeed in destroying me—
without anyone's helping them.[e]
14 They advance as through a gaping breach;
amid the ruins they come rolling in.
15 Terrors overwhelm me;
my dignity is driven away as by the wind,
my safety vanishes like a cloud.

16 "And now my life ebbs away;
days of suffering grip me.
17 Night pierces my bones;
my gnawing pains never rest.
18 In his great power ⌊God⌋ becomes like clothing to me[f];
he binds me like the neck of my garment.
19 He throws me into the mud,
and I am reduced to dust and ashes.

20 "I cry out to you, O God, but you do not answer;
I stand up, but you merely look at me.
21 You turn on me ruthlessly;
with the might of your hand you attack me.
22 You snatch me up and drive me before the wind;
you toss me about in the storm.
23 I know you will bring me down to death,
to the place appointed for all the living.

24 "Surely no one lays a hand on a broken man
when he cries for help in his distress.
25 Have I not wept for those in trouble?
Has not my soul grieved for the poor?
26 Yet when I hoped for good, evil came;
when I looked for light, then came darkness.
27 The churning inside me never stops;
days of suffering confront me.
28 I go about blackened, but not by the sun;
I stand up in the assembly and cry for help.
29 I have become a brother of jackals,
a companion of owls.
30 My skin grows black and peels;

[a]24 The meaning of the Hebrew for this clause is uncertain. [b]3 Or *gnawed* [c]4 Or *fuel* [d]12 The meaning of the Hebrew for this word is uncertain. [e]13 Or *me. / 'No one can help him,' ⌊they say⌋.* [f]18 Hebrew; Septuagint *⌊God⌋ grasps my clothing*

my body burns with fever.
31 My harp is tuned to mourning,
and my flute to the sound of wailing.

31 "I made a covenant with my eyes
not to look lustfully at a girl.
2 For what is man's lot from God above,
his heritage from the Almighty on high?
3 Is it not ruin for the wicked,
disaster for those who do
wrong?
4 Does he not see my ways
and count my every step?

5 "If I have walked in
falsehood
or my foot has hurried
after deceit—
6 let God weigh me in honest
scales
and he will know that I
am blameless—
7 if my steps have turned from the path,
if my heart has been led by my eyes,
or if my hands have been defiled,
8 then may others eat what I have sown,
and may my crops be uprooted.

9 "If my heart has been enticed by a woman,
or if I have lurked at my neighbor's door,
10 then may my wife grind another man's
grain,
and may other men sleep with her.
11 For that would have been shameful,
a sin to be judged.
12 It is a fire that burns to Destruction[a];
it would have uprooted my harvest.

13 "If I have denied justice to my menservants
and maidservants
when they had a grievance against me,
14 what will I do when God confronts me?
What will I answer when called to
account?
15 Did not he who made me in the womb
make them?
Did not the same one form us both
within our mothers?

16 "If I have denied the desires of the poor
or let the eyes of the widow grow weary,
17 if I have kept my bread to myself,
not sharing it with the fatherless—
18 but from my youth I reared him as would a
father,
and from my birth I guided the widow—
19 if I have seen anyone perishing for lack of
clothing,
or a needy man without a garment,
20 and his heart did not bless
me
for warming him with
the fleece from my
sheep,
21 if I have raised my hand
against the
fatherless,
knowing that I had
influence in court,
22 then let my arm fall from
the shoulder,
let it be broken off at the joint.
23 For I dreaded destruction from God,
and for fear of his splendor I could not
do such things.

24 "If I have put my trust in gold
or said to pure gold, 'You are my
security,'
25 if I have rejoiced over my great wealth,
the fortune my hands had gained,
26 if I have regarded the sun in its radiance
or the moon moving in splendor,
27 so that my heart was secretly enticed
and my hand offered them a kiss of
homage,
28 then these also would be sins to be
judged,
for I would have been unfaithful to God
on high.

29 "If I have rejoiced at my enemy's
misfortune
or gloated over the trouble that came to
him—
30 I have not allowed my mouth to sin
by invoking a curse against his life—
31 if the men of my household have never
said,
'Who has not had his fill of Job's
meat?'—

Job 31:4

God Sees All

"Does he not see my ways
and count my
every step?"

[a]12 Hebrew *Abaddon*

Hanging on to Hope

Read: Job 31:1–40

"SOMETIMES FAITH IS just hanging on in the dark." These words, spoken by a wise woman, were offered as solace to a suffering friend. Sometimes things just don't make sense. Sometimes we simply can't see beyond the pain. Sometimes we can't even manage to utter a prayer.

In those dark nights—when life seems to suffocate us with sorrow—faith compels us to hang on. We've seen that Job, who suffered great losses, felt that way. Job 31 records the final words of Job's defense before God after his three friends filled the air with their empty explanations of why Job had suffered so greatly.

Think about it. We know the conversation God had with Satan at the beginning of this account, yet we are still appalled by the tragic events of Job's life. Job had no idea Satan was tempting him because God was allowing his faith to be tested. No wonder Job reeled from his losses and grasped for answers. We can feel the pain and desperation in his voice when he cried, "Oh, that I had someone to hear me!" But throughout his trial, throughout his test, Job knew the Almighty was listening.

Have you ever felt that way? Perhaps your heart's cry surfaced in a winter season of your life—cold, dark and endless. Did your winter only worsen when you received heartless indictments from your "friends" rather than warm words of understanding and consolation? You may be in that barren season even now, with no one to offer you comfort or relief. Allow Job's words to comfort you as a fellow traveler on your journey: "Let the Almighty answer me."

Job recounted his actions based on his heart for God, although he never knew what had happened in heaven to instigate his suffering. While we may learn God's reasons later (sometimes only in eternity), for now all that is required is for us to "hang on in the dark" until God's light illumines the way again.

Job 31:35

"Oh, that I had someone to hear me! I sign now my defense—let the Almighty answer me; let my accuser put his indictment in writing."

reflection

1 What have been the darkest days of your life?

2 In what ways did God shine hope through your darkness?

3 Do you know someone who is echoing Job's plea to be heard? Try offering the warmth of comfort and a listening ear.

RELATED READINGS

Isaiah 55:6–13; Lamentations 3:18–26; Micah 7:1–9

Go to page 640 for your next devotional reading.

32 but no stranger had to spend the night in
the street,
for my door was always open to the
traveler—
33 if I have concealed my sin as men do,[a]
by hiding my guilt in my heart
34 because I so feared the crowd
and so dreaded the contempt of the
clans
that I kept silent and would not go
outside

35 ("Oh, that I had someone to hear me!
I sign now my defense—let the
Almighty answer me;
let my accuser put his indictment in
writing.
36 Surely I would wear it on my shoulder,
I would put it on like a crown.
37 I would give him an account of my every
step;
like a prince I would approach him.)—
38 "if my land cries out against me
and all its furrows are wet with tears,
39 if I have devoured its yield without
payment
or broken the spirit of its tenants,
40 then let briers come up instead of wheat
and weeds instead of barley."

The words of Job are ended.

Elihu

32 So these three men stopped answering Job, because he was righteous in
his own eyes. 2 But Elihu son of Barakel the
Buzite, of the family of Ram, became very angry with Job for justifying himself rather than
God. 3 He was also angry with the three friends,
because they had found no way to refute Job,
and yet had condemned him.[b] 4 Now Elihu
had waited before speaking to Job because they
were older than he. 5 But when he saw that the
three men had nothing more to say, his anger
was aroused.
6 So Elihu son of Barakel the Buzite said:

"I am young in years,
and you are old;
that is why I was fearful,
not daring to tell you what I know.
7 I thought, 'Age should speak;
advanced years should teach wisdom.'
8 But it is the spirit[c] in a man,
the breath of the Almighty, that gives
him understanding.
9 It is not only the old[d] who are wise,
not only the aged who understand what
is right.

10 "Therefore I say: Listen to me;
I too will tell you what I know.
11 I waited while you spoke,
I listened to your reasoning;
while you were searching for words,
12 I gave you my full attention.
But not one of you has proved Job wrong;
none of you has answered his
arguments.
13 Do not say, 'We have found wisdom;
let God refute him, not man.'
14 But Job has not marshaled his words
against me,
and I will not answer him with your
arguments.

15 "They are dismayed and have no more to
say;
words have failed them.
16 Must I wait, now that they are silent,
now that they stand there with no reply?
17 I too will have my say;
I too will tell what I know.
18 For I am full of words,
and the spirit within me compels me;
19 inside I am like bottled-up wine,
like new wineskins ready to burst.
20 I must speak and find relief;
I must open my lips and reply.
21 I will show partiality to no one,
nor will I flatter any man;
22 for if I were skilled in flattery,
my Maker would soon take me away.

33 "But now, Job, listen to my words;
pay attention to everything I say.
2 I am about to open my mouth;
my words are on the tip of my tongue.
3 My words come from an upright heart;
my lips sincerely speak what I know.

[a]33 Or *as Adam did* [b]3 Masoretic Text; an ancient Hebrew scribal tradition *Job, and so had condemned God* [c]8 Or *Spirit*; also in verse 18 [d]9 Or *many*; or *great*

4 The Spirit of God has made me;
the breath of the Almighty gives me life.
5 Answer me then, if you can;
prepare yourself and confront me.
6 I am just like you before God;
I too have been taken
from clay.
7 No fear of me should alarm
you,
nor should my hand be
heavy upon you.

8 "But you have said in my
hearing—
I heard the very words—
9 'I am pure and without sin;
I am clean and free from
guilt.
10 Yet God has found fault with me;
he considers me his enemy.
11 He fastens my feet in shackles;
he keeps close watch on all my paths.'

Job 33:4

God Created Us

"The Spirit of God
has made me;
the breath of the
Almighty gives me life."

12 "But I tell you, in this you are not right,
for God is greater than man.
13 Why do you complain to him
that he answers none of man's words[a]?
14 For God does speak—now one way, now
another—
though man may not perceive it.
15 In a dream, in a vision of the night,
when deep sleep falls on men
as they slumber in their beds,
16 he may speak in their ears
and terrify them with warnings,
17 to turn man from wrongdoing
and keep him from pride,
18 to preserve his soul from the pit,[b]
his life from perishing by the sword.[c]
19 Or a man may be chastened on a bed of
pain
with constant distress in his bones,
20 so that his very being finds food repulsive
and his soul loathes the choicest meal.
21 His flesh wastes away to nothing,
and his bones, once hidden, now stick
out.
22 His soul draws near to the pit,[d]
and his life to the messengers of death.[e]
23 "Yet if there is an angel on his side
as a mediator, one out of a thousand,
to tell a man what is right for him,
24 to be gracious to him and say,
'Spare him from going
down to the pit[f];
I have found a ransom
for him'—
25 then his flesh is renewed
like a child's;
it is restored as in the
days of his youth.
26 He prays to God and finds
favor with him,
he sees God's face and
shouts for joy;
he is restored by God to
his righteous state.
27 Then he comes to men and says,
'I sinned, and perverted what was right,
but I did not get what I deserved.
28 He redeemed my soul from going down to
the pit,[g]
and I will live to enjoy the light.'

29 "God does all these things to a man—
twice, even three times—
30 to turn back his soul from the pit,[h]
that the light of life may shine on him.

31 "Pay attention, Job, and listen to me;
be silent, and I will speak.
32 If you have anything to say, answer me;
speak up, for I want you to be cleared.
33 But if not, then listen to me;
be silent, and I will teach you wisdom."

34

Then Elihu said:

2 "Hear my words, you wise men;
listen to me, you men of learning.
3 For the ear tests words
as the tongue tastes food.
4 Let us discern for ourselves what is right;
let us learn together what is good.

5 "Job says, 'I am innocent,
but God denies me justice.
6 Although I am right,
I am considered a liar;

[a]13 Or *that he does not answer for any of his actions* [b]18 Or *preserve him from the grave* [c]18 Or *from crossing the River* [d]22 Or *He draws near to the grave* [e]22 Or *to the dead* [f]24 Or *grave* [g]28 Or *redeemed me from going down to the grave* [h]30 Or *turn him back from the grave*

although I am guiltless,
his arrow inflicts an incurable wound.'
7 What man is like Job,
who drinks scorn like water?
8 He keeps company with evildoers;
he associates with wicked men.
9 For he says, 'It profits a man nothing
when he tries to please God.'

10 "So listen to me, you men of
understanding.
Far be it from God to do evil,
from the Almighty to do wrong.
11 He repays a man for what he has done;
he brings upon him what his conduct
deserves.
12 It is unthinkable that God would do
wrong,
that the Almighty would pervert justice.
13 Who appointed him over the earth?
Who put him in charge of the whole
world?
14 If it were his intention
and he withdrew his spirit[a] and breath,
15 all mankind would perish together
and man would return to the dust.

16 "If you have understanding, hear this;
listen to what I say.
17 Can he who hates justice govern?
Will you condemn the just and mighty
One?
18 Is he not the One who says to kings, 'You
are worthless,'
and to nobles, 'You are wicked,'
19 who shows no partiality to princes
and does not favor the rich over the
poor,
for they are all the work of his hands?
20 They die in an instant, in the middle of the
night;
the people are shaken and they pass
away;
the mighty are removed without human
hand.

21 "His eyes are on the ways of men;
he sees their every step.
22 There is no dark place, no deep shadow,
where evildoers can hide.
23 God has no need to examine men further,
that they should come before him for
judgment.
24 Without inquiry he shatters the mighty
and sets up others in their place.
25 Because he takes note of their deeds,
he overthrows them in the night and
they are crushed.
26 He punishes them for their wickedness
where everyone can see them,
27 because they turned from following him
and had no regard for any of his ways.
28 They caused the cry of the poor to come
before him,
so that he heard the cry of the needy.
29 But if he remains silent, who can condemn
him?
If he hides his face, who can see him?
Yet he is over man and nation alike,
30 to keep a godless man from ruling,
from laying snares for the people.

31 "Suppose a man says to God,
'I am guilty but will offend no more.
32 Teach me what I cannot see;
if I have done wrong, I will not do so
again.'
33 Should God then reward you on your
terms,
when you refuse to repent?
You must decide, not I;
so tell me what you know.

34 "Men of understanding declare,
wise men who hear me say to me,
35 'Job speaks without knowledge;
his words lack insight.'
36 Oh, that Job might be tested to the utmost
for answering like a wicked man!
37 To his sin he adds rebellion;
scornfully he claps his hands among us
and multiplies his words against God."

35 Then Elihu said:

2 "Do you think this is just?
You say, 'I will be cleared by God.[b]'
3 Yet you ask him, 'What profit is it to me,[c]
and what do I gain by not sinning?'

4 "I would like to reply to you

[a]14 Or *Spirit* [b]2 Or *My righteousness is more than God's* [c]3 Or *you*

and to your friends with you.
5 Look up at the heavens and see;
gaze at the clouds so high above you.
6 If you sin, how does that affect him?
If your sins are many, what does that do to him?
7 If you are righteous, what do you give to him,
or what does he receive from your hand?
8 Your wickedness affects only a man like yourself,
and your righteousness only the sons of men.

Job 35:7

God Is Self-Sufficient

"If you are righteous,
what do you give to him,
or what does he receive
from your hand?"

9 "Men cry out under a load of oppression;
they plead for relief from the arm of the powerful.
10 But no one says, 'Where is God my Maker,
who gives songs in the night,
11 who teaches more to us than to[a] the beasts of the earth
and makes us wiser than[b] the birds of the air?'
12 He does not answer when men cry out
because of the arrogance of the wicked.
13 Indeed, God does not listen to their empty plea;
the Almighty pays no attention to it.
14 How much less, then, will he listen
when you say that you do not see him,
that your case is before him
and you must wait for him,
15 and further, that his anger never punishes
and he does not take the least notice of wickedness.[c]
16 So Job opens his mouth with empty talk;
without knowledge he multiplies words."

36 Elihu continued:

2 "Bear with me a little longer and I will show you
that there is more to be said in God's behalf.
3 I get my knowledge from afar;
I will ascribe justice to my Maker.
4 Be assured that my words are not false;
one perfect in knowledge is with you.

5 "God is mighty, but does not despise men;
he is mighty, and firm in his purpose.
6 He does not keep the wicked alive
but gives the afflicted their rights.
7 He does not take his eyes off the righteous;
he enthrones them with kings
and exalts them forever.
8 But if men are bound in chains,
held fast by cords of affliction,
9 he tells them what they have done—
that they have sinned arrogantly.
10 He makes them listen to correction
and commands them to repent of their evil.
11 If they obey and serve him,
they will spend the rest of their days in prosperity
and their years in contentment.
12 But if they do not listen,
they will perish by the sword[d]
and die without knowledge.

13 "The godless in heart harbor resentment;
even when he fetters them, they do not cry for help.
14 They die in their youth,
among male prostitutes of the shrines.
15 But those who suffer he delivers in their suffering;
he speaks to them in their affliction.

16 "He is wooing you from the jaws of distress
to a spacious place free from restriction,
to the comfort of your table laden with choice food.
17 But now you are laden with the judgment due the wicked;

[a]11 Or *teaches us by* [b]11 Or *us wise by* [c]15 Symmachus, Theodotion and Vulgate; the meaning of the Hebrew for this word is uncertain.
[d]12 Or *will cross the River*

Who?

Read: Job 36:21–33

Job 36:27–28

"He draws up the drops of water, which distill as rain to the streams; the clouds pour down their moisture and abundant showers fall on mankind."

METEOROLOGISTS HAVE STUDIED weather patterns to discover the what, when, where and how of rain, thunder, lightning, hail, drought and monsoons. They have pondered why deserts receive less than an inch of rain per year, while India's monsoons pour down over 400 inches annually. Why does lightning strike? What causes hail? How can we predict hurricanes?

While great strides have been made in observing, predicting and understanding the weather, no one has been able to change it. Why? Because while human beings have studied the what, when, where and how, they often have forgotten to ask the most important question of all: *Who?*

Job's friend, Elihu, didn't subscribe to the weather channel or own a farmer's almanac. He understood, however, that God controls it all: "He draws up the drops of water, which distill as rain to the streams; the clouds pour down their moisture and abundant showers fall on mankind." He could have said, "I don't understand the process of condensation and precipitation, but I do understand that God is in control."

The first words in the Bible are, "In the beginning God." While we might not understand all the intricate details and secrets of life, we can hold on to this: *God set the universe in motion and sustains it.* Paul wrote, "He is before all things, and in him [Jesus Christ] all things hold together" (Colossians 1:17). "Sovereign LORD, you have made the heavens and the earth by your great power and outstretched arm. Nothing is too hard for you" (Jeremiah 32:17).

Are you going through a difficult situation in your life right now? Are there circumstances that you cannot understand? Instead of trying to fix it or control it, rather than trying to figure out the what, when, where and why of your struggle, focus instead on *Who*:

God is *Elohim*—the Creator, who made you for a purpose.

God is *El Elyon*—God Most High, whose ways are higher than your ways.

God is *El Roi*—the God who sees and knows where you are and how you feel.

God is *El Shaddai*—the Lord God Almighty, the one who can change you or walk with you through your circumstances as surely as he can send rain from heaven.

reflection

1 What circumstances can only God change? Do you trust him to do that?

2 Do you have trouble believing that nothing is too difficult for God? Why or why not?

3 Take some time to reflect on God's names mentioned in today's devotional. Which of his names are the most meaningful to you in your present circumstances?

RELATED READINGS

Psalms 24:1–2; 104:1–35; Isaiah 40:28–31; Hebrews 11:1–3

Go to page 643 for your next devotional reading.

judgment and justice have taken hold
of you.
18 Be careful that no one entices you by
riches;
do not let a large bribe turn you aside.
19 Would your wealth
or even all your mighty efforts
sustain you so you would not be in
distress?
20 Do not long for the night,
to drag people away from their homes.[a]
21 Beware of turning to evil,
which you seem to prefer to affliction.

22 "God is exalted in his power.
Who is a teacher like him?
23 Who has prescribed his ways for him,
or said to him, 'You have done wrong'?
24 Remember to extol his work,
which men have praised
in song.
25 All mankind has seen it;
men gaze on it from afar.
26 How great is God—beyond
our understanding!
The number of his years
is past finding out.

27 "He draws up the drops of
water,
which distill as rain to
the streams[b];
28 the clouds pour down their
moisture
and abundant showers
fall on mankind.
29 Who can understand how he spreads out
the clouds,
how he thunders from his pavilion?
30 See how he scatters his lightning about
him,
bathing the depths of the sea.
31 This is the way he governs[c] the nations
and provides food in abundance.
32 He fills his hands with lightning
and commands it to strike its mark.
33 His thunder announces the coming storm;
even the cattle make known its
approach.[d]

Job 36:26

God Is Past Comprehension

"How great is God—beyond our understanding! The number of his years is past finding out."

37 "At this my heart pounds
and leaps from its place.
2 Listen! Listen to the roar of his voice,
to the rumbling that comes from his
mouth.
3 He unleashes his lightning beneath the
whole heaven
and sends it to the ends of the earth.
4 After that comes the sound of his roar;
he thunders with his majestic voice.
When his voice resounds,
he holds nothing back.
5 God's voice thunders in marvelous ways;
he does great things beyond our
understanding.
6 He says to the snow, 'Fall on the earth,'
and to the rain shower, 'Be a mighty
downpour.'
7 So that all men he has made
may know his work,
he stops every man from
his labor.[e]
8 The animals take cover;
they remain in their
dens.
9 The tempest comes out
from its chamber,
the cold from the driving
winds.
10 The breath of God
produces ice,
and the broad waters
become frozen.
11 He loads the clouds with
moisture;
he scatters his lightning through them.
12 At his direction they swirl around
over the face of the whole earth
to do whatever he commands them.
13 He brings the clouds to punish men,
or to water his earth[f] and show his love.

14 "Listen to this, Job;
stop and consider God's wonders.
15 Do you know how God controls the clouds
and makes his lightning flash?
16 Do you know how the clouds hang poised,
those wonders of him who is perfect in
knowledge?

[a] 20 The meaning of the Hebrew for verses 18–20 is uncertain. [b] 27 Or *distill from the mist as rain* [c] 31 Or *nourishes*
[d] 33 Or *announces his coming— / the One zealous against evil* [e] 7 Or */ he fills all men with fear by his power* [f] 13 Or *to favor them*

17 You who swelter in your clothes
when the land lies hushed under the south wind,
18 can you join him in spreading out the skies,
hard as a mirror of cast bronze?

19 "Tell us what we should say to him;
we cannot draw up our case because of our darkness.
20 Should he be told that I want to speak?
Would any man ask to be swallowed up?
21 Now no one can look at the sun,
bright as it is in the skies
after the wind has swept them clean.
22 Out of the north he comes in golden splendor;
God comes in awesome majesty.
23 The Almighty is beyond our reach and exalted in power;
in his justice and great righteousness, he does not oppress.
24 Therefore, men revere him,
for does he not have regard for all the wise in heart?[a]"

Job 37:23

God Is Righteous

The Almighty is beyond our reach and exalted in power;
in his justice and great righteousness, he does not oppress.

The Lord Speaks

38 Then the Lord answered Job out of the storm. He said:

2 "Who is this that darkens my counsel
with words without knowledge?
3 Brace yourself like a man;
I will question you,
and you shall answer me.

4 "Where were you when I laid the earth's foundation?
Tell me, if you understand.
5 Who marked off its dimensions? Surely you know!
Who stretched a measuring line across it?
6 On what were its footings set,
or who laid its cornerstone—
7 while the morning stars sang together
and all the angels[b] shouted for joy?

8 "Who shut up the sea behind doors
when it burst forth from the womb,
9 when I made the clouds its garment
and wrapped it in thick darkness,
10 when I fixed limits for it
and set its doors and bars in place,
11 when I said, 'This far you may come and no farther;
here is where your proud waves halt'?

12 "Have you ever given orders to the morning,
or shown the dawn its place,
13 that it might take the earth by the edges
and shake the wicked out of it?
14 The earth takes shape like clay under a seal;
its features stand out like those of a garment.
15 The wicked are denied their light,
and their upraised arm is broken.

16 "Have you journeyed to the springs of the sea
or walked in the recesses of the deep?
17 Have the gates of death been shown to you?
Have you seen the gates of the shadow of death[c]?
18 Have you comprehended the vast expanses of the earth?
Tell me, if you know all this.

19 "What is the way to the abode of light?
And where does darkness reside?
20 Can you take them to their places?
Do you know the paths to their dwellings?
21 Surely you know, for you were already born!
You have lived so many years!

22 "Have you entered the storehouses of the snow
or seen the storehouses of the hail,
23 which I reserve for times of trouble,
for days of war and battle?
24 What is the way to the place where the lightning is dispersed,

a 24 Or *for he does not have regard for any who think they are wise.* b 7 Hebrew *the sons of God* c 17 Or *gates of deep shadows*

God Speaks

Read: Job 38:1–41

FOR 37 CHAPTERS Job and his friends have grappled with the question of suffering. Why do people suffer? Is it because God isn't there? Because God doesn't care? Because the one suffering has done something to displease God? Job and his friends have gone around and around and still come up empty. Finally God "answered Job out of the storm" (Job 38:1).

God didn't deign to tell Job the reason for Job's suffering, but he did remind Job that he is the mighty God who marked the dimensions of the earth, fixed the limits of the sea and blanketed the sky with clouds. This is the God whom Job and his friends dared to question. The audacity of trying to bring God down to their level! But when God spoke, he showed them how much bigger and more magnificent were his ways than their ways.

In the midst of God's glory, Job gained a proper perspective on his suffering. The same is true for us. When we hear God speak and remember his glory, we know our suffering is not in vain. Henry Gariepy wrote, "Many who have trod the path of suffering and sensed the Presence on the road will share the sentiment of the unknown poet":

I walked a mile with Pleasure,
  She chatted all the way,
But left me none the wiser
  For all she had to say.

I walked a mile with Sorrow,
  And ne'r a word said she,
But, oh, the thing I learned from her
  When Sorrow walked with me!

Have you been grappling with pain and suffering? Are you trying to figure out why God has allowed sorrow and trouble to come into your life? The best solution isn't to talk endlessly with your friends and try to figure out the reasons for your suffering. Wait for God, the one who gave "orders to the morning" (Job 38:12), to speak with you in the midst of the storm.

Wednesday

Job 38:1

Then the LORD answered Job out of the storm.

reflection

1 When you suffer, whom do you tend to talk to?

2 Has any human philosopher, speaker or writer been able to comfort you when you've suffered?

3 Does it comfort you to know that while God is powerful enough to create the vast universe, he is interested enough to speak to you personally?

RELATED READINGS

Nahum 1:3–5;
2 Peter 1:16–21

"Absolutely everything that can happen to us—good, bad or indifferent—God knows and cares about."

Thelma Wells

Go to page 646 for your next devotional reading.

or the place where the east winds are
scattered over the earth?
25 Who cuts a channel for the torrents of rain,
and a path for the thunderstorm,
26 to water a land where no man lives,
a desert with no one in it,
27 to satisfy a desolate wasteland
and make it sprout with grass?
28 Does the rain have a father?
Who fathers the drops of dew?
29 From whose womb comes the ice?
Who gives birth to the frost from the
heavens
30 when the waters become hard as stone,
when the surface of the deep is frozen?

31 "Can you bind the beautiful[a] Pleiades?
Can you loose the cords of Orion?
32 Can you bring forth the constellations in
their seasons[b]
or lead out the Bear[c] with its cubs?
33 Do you know the laws of the heavens?
Can you set up ⌞God's[d]⌟ dominion over
the earth?

34 "Can you raise your voice to the clouds
and cover yourself with a flood of water?
35 Do you send the lightning bolts on their
way?
Do they report to you, 'Here we are'?
36 Who endowed the heart[e] with wisdom
or gave understanding to the mind[e]?
37 Who has the wisdom to count the clouds?
Who can tip over the water jars of the
heavens
38 when the dust becomes hard
and the clods of earth stick together?

39 "Do you hunt the prey for the lioness
and satisfy the hunger of the lions
40 when they crouch in their dens
or lie in wait in a thicket?
41 Who provides food for the raven
when its young cry out to God
and wander about for lack of food?

39 "Do you know when the mountain
goats give birth?
Do you watch when the doe bears her
fawn?
2 Do you count the months till they bear?
Do you know the time they give birth?
3 They crouch down and bring forth their
young;
their labor pains are ended.
4 Their young thrive and grow strong in the
wilds;
they leave and do not return.

5 "Who let the wild donkey go free?
Who untied his ropes?
6 I gave him the wasteland as his home,
the salt flats as his habitat.
7 He laughs at the commotion in the town;
he does not hear a driver's shout.
8 He ranges the hills for his pasture
and searches for any green thing.

9 "Will the wild ox consent to serve you?
Will he stay by your manger at night?
10 Can you hold him to the furrow with a
harness?
Will he till the valleys behind you?
11 Will you rely on him for his great
strength?
Will you leave your heavy work to him?
12 Can you trust him to bring in your grain
and gather it to your threshing floor?

13 "The wings of the ostrich flap joyfully,
but they cannot compare with the
pinions and feathers of the stork.
14 She lays her eggs on the ground
and lets them warm in the sand,
15 unmindful that a foot may crush them,
that some wild animal may trample
them.
16 She treats her young harshly, as if they
were not hers;
she cares not that her labor was in vain,
17 for God did not endow her with wisdom
or give her a share of good sense.
18 Yet when she spreads her feathers to run,
she laughs at horse and rider.

19 "Do you give the horse his strength
or clothe his neck with a flowing mane?
20 Do you make him leap like a locust,
striking terror with his proud snorting?
21 He paws fiercely, rejoicing in his strength,

[a]31 Or *the twinkling*; or *the chains of the* [b]32 Or *the morning star in its season* [c]32 Or *out Leo* [d]33 Or *his*; or *their*
[e]36 The meaning of the Hebrew for this word is uncertain.

and charges into the fray.
22 He laughs at fear, afraid of nothing;
he does not shy away from the sword.
23 The quiver rattles against his side,
along with the flashing spear and lance.
24 In frenzied excitement he eats up the
ground;
he cannot stand still when the trumpet
sounds.
25 At the blast of the trumpet he snorts, 'Aha!'
He catches the scent of battle from afar,
the shout of commanders and the battle
cry.

26 "Does the hawk take flight by your wisdom
and spread his wings toward the south?
27 Does the eagle soar at your command
and build his nest on high?
28 He dwells on a cliff and stays there at night;
a rocky crag is his stronghold.
29 From there he seeks out his food;
his eyes detect it from afar.
30 His young ones feast on blood,
and where the slain are, there is he."

40 The LORD said to Job:

2 "Will the one who contends with the
Almighty correct him?
Let him who accuses God answer him!"

3 Then Job answered the LORD:

4 "I am unworthy—how can I reply to you?
I put my hand over my mouth.
5 I spoke once, but I have no answer—
twice, but I will say no more."

6 Then the LORD spoke to Job out of the storm:

7 "Brace yourself like a man;
I will question you,
and you shall answer me.

8 "Would you discredit my justice?
Would you condemn me to justify
yourself?
9 Do you have an arm like God's,
and can your voice thunder like his?
10 Then adorn yourself with glory and
splendor,
and clothe yourself in honor and
majesty.
11 Unleash the fury of your wrath,
look at every proud man and bring him
low,
12 look at every proud man and humble him,
crush the wicked where they stand.
13 Bury them all in the dust together;
shroud their faces in the grave.
14 Then I myself will admit to you
that your own right hand can save you.

15 "Look at the behemoth,[a]
which I made along with you
and which feeds on grass like an ox.
16 What strength he has in his loins,
what power in the muscles of his belly!
17 His tail[b] sways like a cedar;
the sinews of his thighs are close-knit.
18 His bones are tubes of bronze,
his limbs like rods of iron.
19 He ranks first among the works of God,
yet his Maker can approach him with
his sword.
20 The hills bring him their produce,
and all the wild animals play nearby.
21 Under the lotus plants he lies,
hidden among the reeds in the marsh.
22 The lotuses conceal him in their shadow;
the poplars by the stream surround him.
23 When the river rages, he is not alarmed;
he is secure, though the Jordan should
surge against his mouth.
24 Can anyone capture him by the eyes,[c]
or trap him and pierce his nose?

41 "Can you pull in the leviathan[d] with
a fishhook
or tie down his tongue with a rope?
2 Can you put a cord through his nose
or pierce his jaw with a hook?
3 Will he keep begging you for mercy?
Will he speak to you with gentle words?
4 Will he make an agreement with you
for you to take him as your slave for life?
5 Can you make a pet of him like a bird
or put him on a leash for your girls?
6 Will traders barter for him?
Will they divide him up among the
merchants?

[a] 15 Possibly the hippopotamus or the elephant [b] 17 Possibly trunk [c] 24 Or *by a water hole* [d] 1 Possibly the crocodile

Say No More

Read: Job 40:1–14

Job 40:3–5

Then Job answered the LORD: "I am unworthy—how can I reply to you? I put my hand over my mouth. I spoke once, but I have no answer—twice, but I will say no more."

WHO HASN'T WANTED to shake her fist at God and scream, "Why?"

The question catches in your throat when you visit your friend who is barely recognizable, ravaged by chemotherapy. It comes to mind when a friend's baby dies or a spouse has an affair. *Why? Why did my baby die? Why did my husband leave me? Why did we lose all our savings in a bad investment?* These questions wrack our thoughts and challenge our faith. How can a loving God allow so much pain?

When we consider the mystery of suffering, the story of Job inevitably comes to mind. At this point in the story, Job has suffered horribly, and he has boldly questioned God, protesting that he didn't deserve to lose his family, his health and his possessions. Well-intentioned friends have come alongside him, offering unhelpful explanations and pat answers. Job has cried out to God, and God has answered him with amazing words and unfathomable questions. The Lord challenged him with questions that reveal Job's limitations. No, Job does not have power like God's. He cannot adorn himself with glory and splendor. He cannot judge the wicked. Only God is sovereign. Job is merely human. Job began to understand and bowed in silence to the Creator of the universe, saying, "I am unworthy . . . I will say no more" (Job 40:4–5).

But notice something else. God loved Job enough to be with him in his suffering—and that made all the difference. Job didn't need to keep asking the questions because he had discovered that God himself was the answer. He didn't need the specifics; he finally rested in the truth that God is God . . . and that was enough.

Sometimes, when we reach the end of ourselves, when we reach the end of the tears and the rage and the questions, when we are quiet, we hear him say, "I am God. I am here."

reflection

1 Think of a time when you have wondered, *Why, God?* What was the situation?

2 In what ways do you need to be quiet, to repent and to humbly bow before God as Job did?

3 What have you learned about God through your difficult experiences?

RELATED READINGS

Psalm 46:8–10; Zephaniah 3:17; Romans 8:18–39; 1 Peter 4:12–19

Go to page 650 for your next devotional reading.

7 Can you fill his hide with harpoons
or his head with fishing spears?
8 If you lay a hand on him,
you will remember the struggle and
never do it again!
9 Any hope of subduing him is false;
the mere sight of him is overpowering.
10 No one is fierce enough to rouse him.
Who then is able to stand against me?
11 Who has a claim against me that I must
pay?
Everything under heaven belongs to me.
12 "I will not fail to speak of his limbs,
his strength and his graceful form.
13 Who can strip off his outer coat?
Who would approach him with a bridle?
14 Who dares open the doors of his mouth,
ringed about with his fearsome teeth?
15 His back has[a] rows of shields
tightly sealed together;
16 each is so close to the next
that no air can pass between.
17 They are joined fast to one another;
they cling together and cannot be
parted.
18 His snorting throws out flashes of light;
his eyes are like the rays of dawn.
19 Firebrands stream from his
mouth;
sparks of fire shoot out.
20 Smoke pours from his
nostrils
as from a boiling pot
over a fire of reeds.
21 His breath sets coals ablaze,
and flames dart from his
mouth.
22 Strength resides in his
neck;
dismay goes before him.
23 The folds of his flesh are
tightly joined;
they are firm and immovable.
24 His chest is hard as rock,
hard as a lower millstone.
25 When he rises up, the mighty are terrified;
they retreat before his thrashing.
26 The sword that reaches him has no effect,
nor does the spear or the dart or the
javelin.
27 Iron he treats like straw
and bronze like rotten wood.
28 Arrows do not make him flee;
slingstones are like chaff to him.
29 A club seems to him but a piece of straw;
he laughs at the rattling of the lance.
30 His undersides are jagged potsherds,
leaving a trail in the mud like a
threshing sledge.
31 He makes the depths churn like a boiling
caldron
and stirs up the sea like a pot of
ointment.
32 Behind him he leaves a glistening wake;
one would think the deep had white
hair.
33 Nothing on earth is his equal—
a creature without fear.
34 He looks down on all that are haughty;
he is king over all that are proud."

Job

42

Then Job replied to the LORD:

2 "I know that you can do all things;
no plan of yours can be thwarted.
3 ⌊You asked,⌋ 'Who is this
that obscures my
counsel without
knowledge?'
Surely I spoke of things I
did not understand,
things too wonderful for
me to know.

4 ⌊"You said,⌋ 'Listen now,
and I will speak;
I will question you,
and you shall answer me.'
5 My ears had heard of you
but now my eyes have
seen you.
6 Therefore I despise myself
and repent in dust and ashes."

Epilogue

7 After the LORD had said these things to
Job, he said to Eliphaz the Temanite, "I am

Job 42:2

God Can Do All Things

"I know that you can
do all things;
no plan of yours can
be thwarted."

[a] 15 Or *His pride is his*

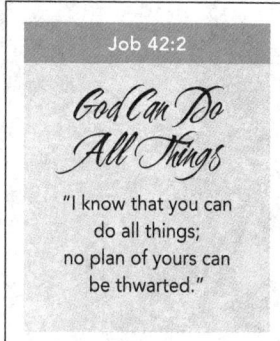

angry with you and your two friends, because
you have not spoken of me what is right, as
my servant Job has. 8So now take seven bulls
and seven rams and go to my servant Job and
sacrifice a burnt offering for yourselves. My
servant Job will pray for you, and I will accept
his prayer and not deal with you according to
your folly. You have not spoken of me what is
right, as my servant Job has." 9So Eliphaz the
Temanite, Bildad the Shuhite and Zophar the
Naamathite did what the LORD told them; and
the LORD accepted Job's prayer.

10After Job had prayed for his friends, the
LORD made him prosperous again and gave
him twice as much as he had before. 11All his
brothers and sisters and everyone who had
known him before came and ate with him in
his house. They comforted and consoled him
over all the trouble the LORD had brought upon
him, and each one gave him a piece of silver[a]
and a gold ring.

12The LORD blessed the latter part of Job's
life more than the first. He had fourteen thousand sheep, six thousand camels, a thousand
yoke of oxen and a thousand donkeys. 13And
he also had seven sons and three daughters.
14The first daughter he named Jemimah, the
second Keziah and the third Keren-Happuch.
15Nowhere in all the land were there found
women as beautiful as Job's daughters, and
their father granted them an inheritance along
with their brothers.

16After this, Job lived a hundred and forty
years; he saw his children and their children to
the fourth generation. 17And so he died, old
and full of years.

[a]11 Hebrew *him a kesitah*; a kesitah was a unit of money of unknown weight and value.

Psalms

Every congregation needs a songbook, for it is our songs that unite us in one voice and one purpose: *worshiping God.* The musical meters for the psalms collected here have been lost to time, but the words remain, striking chords of their own with their vivid language, beautiful artistry and startling honesty.

We find in the psalms *a mirror to our human existence.* There are psalms that overflow with praise and adoration and others that are heavy with grief and sorrow. There are psalms expressing frustration that God is not helping or even listening, and there are psalms of wide-eyed wonder about who we are in relation to this omniscient, omnipotent God.

The psalms are songs and poems, but they are also prayers. In reading them we learn to pray from the heart, to lay ourselves open before *a God who already knows the depths* of what lurks within us, who gives us freedom to bring those depths to the light, and who loves us still.

Author:
David, Asaph, the sons of Korah, Solomon, Heman, Ethan and Moses.

Audience:
All Israel.

Date:
Written between the time of Moses (about 1440 B.C.) and the time following the Babylonian captivity (after 538 B.C.).

Setting:
Picture a passionate worship service in God's temple with God's people.

Verse to Remember:
Your word is a lamp to my feet and a light for my path. (119:105)

BOOK I

Psalms 1–41

Psalm 1

1 Blessed is the man
who does not walk in the counsel of the wicked
or stand in the way of sinners
or sit in the seat of mockers.
2 But his delight is in the law of the LORD,
and on his law he meditates day and night.
3 He is like a tree planted by streams of water,
which yields its fruit in season
and whose leaf does not wither.
Whatever he does prospers.

Like a Tree

Read: Psalm 1:1–6

Psalm 1:2–3

But his delight is in the law of the LORD, and on his law he meditates day and night. He is like a tree planted by streams of water, which yields its fruit in season and whose leaf does not wither. Whatever he does prospers.

WHAT GIVES YOU DELIGHT? You know, that sense of unparalleled joy, that amazing degree of enjoyment and pleasure, even to the point of rapture. That's how the dictionary defines delight. But how do *you* define delight? Is it playing with your baby, reading a good book, walking on the beach at sunset or working on scrapbook pages? Maybe you delight in running through rain-washed streets in the early morning or hiking in the mountains on a sunny autumn day. Maybe your delight is getting lost in playing games or listening to music.

The psalmist defines delight as immersing oneself in the law of the Lord. He sings of the person who finds joy in listening to God's voice in Scripture, who discovers with pleasure "the riches of the wisdom and knowledge of God" (Romans 11:33). For this person, meditating on the Scriptures is not a duty that fulfills a certain obligation, but it is willingly devoting spare time, staying up late into the night immersed in the Bible.

And what is the result of this constant delight in God's Word? One becomes like a tree planted by a river. You've seen them—tall, vital trees, well-watered because they are rooted deep in the stream. This tree is resplendent with foliage in rich shades of green. It's a tree that can withstand biting frost, harsh winds and blazing sun.

A person who delights in God's Word will prosper and have integrity, will speak truthfully and exhibit stability and strength. This is the person who will reflect the face of God like a river reflects the sun in dappled waves. This one is truly blessed.

The book of Psalms is a wonderful place to introduce yourself to the idea of *delighting* in God's Word. The poetic music of the psalms is rich in metaphors and images that let your imagination soar with the grandeur, majesty, wisdom and unsurpassing love of God. You will see him as a rock, a fortress, a strong tower, a nurturing mother and so much more. He rides on the wind and shows himself in the starry heavens. Delight yourself in singing along with the psalmist and plant your roots deep in the nourishing living water of God's Word.

reflection

1 What three adjectives would describe your interest in the Scriptures? Is "delightful" on your list?

2 Does the idea of delighting in God's Word attract you to the Bible? What other things motivate you to spend time in God's Word?

3 How is your spiritual life growing like a prosperous fruit tree? Find a picture of a beautiful tree to use as a bookmark to remind you of Psalm 1.

RELATED READINGS

Psalms 112:1–10; 119:9–16; Jeremiah 17:7–8; John 7:38; Revelation 7:17

Go to page 654 for your next devotional reading.

4 Not so the wicked!
They are like chaff
that the wind blows away.
5 Therefore the wicked will not stand in the judgment,
nor sinners in the assembly of the righteous.
6 For the LORD watches over the way of the righteous,
but the way of the wicked will perish.

Psalm 2

1 Why do the nations conspire[a]
and the peoples plot in vain?
2 The kings of the earth take their stand
and the rulers gather together
against the LORD
and against his Anointed One.[b]
3 "Let us break their chains," they say,
"and throw off their fetters."

4 The One enthroned in heaven laughs;
the Lord scoffs at them.
5 Then he rebukes them in his anger
and terrifies them in his wrath, saying,
6 "I have installed my King[c]
on Zion, my holy hill."

7 I will proclaim the decree of the LORD:

He said to me, "You are my Son[d];
today I have become your Father.[e]
8 Ask of me,
and I will make the nations your inheritance,
the ends of the earth your possession.
9 You will rule them with an iron scepter[f];
you will dash them to pieces like pottery."

10 Therefore, you kings, be wise;
be warned, you rulers of the earth.
11 Serve the LORD with fear
and rejoice with trembling.
12 Kiss the Son, lest he be angry
and you be destroyed in your way,
for his wrath can flare up in a moment.
Blessed are all who take refuge in him.

> **Psalm 1:6**
>
> *God Watches Over Us*
>
> For the LORD watches over the way of the righteous, but the way of the wicked will perish.

Psalm 3

A psalm of David. When he fled from his son Absalom.

1 O LORD, how many are my foes!
How many rise up against me!
2 Many are saying of me,
"God will not deliver him." *Selah*[g]

3 But you are a shield around me, O LORD;
you bestow glory on me and lift[h] up my head.
4 To the LORD I cry aloud,
and he answers me from his holy hill. *Selah*

5 I lie down and sleep;
I wake again, because the LORD sustains me.
6 I will not fear the tens of thousands
drawn up against me on every side.

7 Arise, O LORD!
Deliver me, O my God!
Strike all my enemies on the jaw;
break the teeth of the wicked.
8 From the LORD comes deliverance.
May your blessing be on your people. *Selah*

Psalm 4

For the director of music. With stringed instruments. A psalm of David.

1 Answer me when I call to you,
O my righteous God.
Give me relief from my distress;
be merciful to me and hear my prayer.

2 How long, O men, will you turn my glory into shame[i]?

[a]1 Hebrew; Septuagint *rage* [b]2 Or *anointed one* [c]6 Or *king* [d]7 Or *son*; also in verse 12 [e]7 Or *have begotten you* [f]9 Or *will break them with a rod of iron* [g]2 A word of uncertain meaning, occurring frequently in the Psalms; possibly a musical term [h]3 Or *LORD, / my Glorious One, who lifts* [i]2 Or *you dishonor my Glorious One*

How long will you love delusions and
seek false gods[a]? *Selah*
3 Know that the LORD has set apart the
godly for himself;
the LORD will hear when I call to him.

4 In your anger do not sin;
when you are on your beds,
search your hearts and be silent. *Selah*
5 Offer right sacrifices
and trust in the LORD.

6 Many are asking, "Who can
show us any good?"
Let the light of your
face shine upon us,
O LORD.
7 You have filled my heart
with greater joy
than when their grain
and new wine
abound.
8 I will lie down and sleep in
peace,
for you alone, O LORD,
make me dwell in safety.

Psalm 5

For the director of music. For flutes.
A psalm of David.

1 Give ear to my words, O LORD,
consider my sighing.
2 Listen to my cry for help,
my King and my God,
for to you I pray.
3 In the morning, O LORD, you hear my
voice;
in the morning I lay my requests before
you
and wait in expectation.

4 You are not a God who takes pleasure in
evil;
with you the wicked cannot dwell.
5 The arrogant cannot stand in your presence;
you hate all who do wrong.
6 You destroy those who tell lies;
bloodthirsty and deceitful men
the LORD abhors.

7 But I, by your great mercy,
will come into your house;
in reverence will I bow down
toward your holy temple.
8 Lead me, O LORD, in your righteousness
because of my enemies—
make straight your way before me.

9 Not a word from their mouth can be
trusted;
their heart is filled with destruction.
Their throat is an open grave;
with their tongue they
speak deceit.
10 Declare them guilty,
O God!
Let their intrigues be
their downfall.
Banish them for their
many sins,
for they have rebelled
against you.

11 But let all who take refuge
in you be glad;
let them ever sing for joy.
Spread your protection
over them,
that those who love your name may
rejoice in you.
12 For surely, O LORD, you bless the
righteous;
you surround them with your favor as
with a shield.

Psalm 6

For the director of music. With stringed
instruments. According to *sheminith*.[b]
A psalm of David.

1 O LORD, do not rebuke me in your
anger
or discipline me in your wrath.
2 Be merciful to me, LORD, for I am faint;
O LORD, heal me, for my bones are in
agony.
3 My soul is in anguish.
How long, O LORD, how long?

4 Turn, O LORD, and deliver me;
save me because of your unfailing
love.
5 No one remembers you when he is dead.
Who praises you from the grave[c]?

Psalm 5:11

God Offers Refuge

But let all who take
refuge in you be glad;
let them ever sing for joy.
Spread your protection
over them,
that those who love your
name may rejoice in you.

[a]2 Or *seek lies* [b]Title: Probably a musical term [c]5 Hebrew *Sheol*

6 I am worn out from groaning;
all night long I flood my bed with weeping
and drench my couch with tears.
7 My eyes grow weak with sorrow;
they fail because of all my foes.

8 Away from me, all you who do evil,
for the LORD has heard my weeping.
9 The LORD has heard my cry for mercy;
the LORD accepts my prayer.
10 All my enemies will be ashamed and dismayed;
they will turn back in sudden disgrace.

Psalm 7

A *shiggaion*[a] of David, which he sang to the LORD concerning Cush, a Benjamite.

1 O LORD my God, I take refuge in you;
save and deliver me from all who pursue me,
2 or they will tear me like a lion
and rip me to pieces with no one to rescue me.

3 O LORD my God, if I have done this
and there is guilt on my hands—
4 if I have done evil to him who is at peace with me
or without cause have robbed my foe—
5 then let my enemy pursue and overtake me;
let him trample my life to the ground
and make me sleep in the dust. *Selah*

6 Arise, O LORD, in your anger;
rise up against the rage of my enemies.
Awake, my God; decree justice.
7 Let the assembled peoples gather around you.
Rule over them from on high;
8 let the LORD judge the peoples.
Judge me, O LORD, according to my righteousness,
according to my integrity, O Most High.
9 O righteous God,
who searches minds and hearts,
bring to an end the violence of the wicked
and make the righteous secure.

10 My shield[b] is God Most High,
who saves the upright in heart.
11 God is a righteous judge,
a God who expresses his wrath every day.
12 If he does not relent,
he[c] will sharpen his sword;
he will bend and string his bow.
13 He has prepared his deadly weapons;
he makes ready his flaming arrows.

14 He who is pregnant with evil
and conceives trouble gives birth to disillusionment.
15 He who digs a hole and scoops it out
falls into the pit he has made.
16 The trouble he causes recoils on himself;
his violence comes down on his own head.

17 I will give thanks to the LORD because of his righteousness
and will sing praise to the name of the LORD Most High.

Psalm 7:17

God Is Righteous

I will give thanks to the LORD because of his righteousness and will sing praise to the name of the LORD Most High.

Psalm 8

For the director of music. According to *gittith*.[d] A psalm of David.

1 O LORD, our Lord,
how majestic is your name in all the earth!

You have set your glory
above the heavens.
2 From the lips of children and infants
you have ordained praise[e]
because of your enemies,
to silence the foe and the avenger.

3 When I consider your heavens,
the work of your fingers,

[a]Title: Probably a literary or musical term [b]10 Or *sovereign* [c]12 Or *If a man does not repent, / God* [d]Title: Probably a musical term
[e]2 Or *strength*

Love Gone Wrong

MICHAL

And Michal daughter of Saul had no children to the day of her death.

2 Samuel 6:23

ASSIGNED READING:
1 Samuel 18:1—19:17; 25:44; 2 Samuel 3:6–21; 6:1–23

MICHAL HATED TO REHASH an old event, but she always found herself powerless against the tug of her memories.

She remembered it had started out so well. Boy meets girl. Girl falls for boy. Soon, rumors were circulating throughout the kingdom that something was afoot between a princess and a warrior. Michal remembered how the women, busy with their daily chores in the market or at the wells, could not keep from chattering.

"I heard the princess has a crush on David."

"That's so yesterday. I heard they're in love. And Saul wants them to be married as soon as possible."

"Not only that, I heard the groom is giving the bride's father a really strange wedding gift . . ."

(Whispers) "A hundred what?"

She recalled how the excitement brewing back in those days had made the kingdom seem electric. Of course, there were those who tried to tell her that it would not be easy to love a headstrong soldier: the long nights away from home, the constant danger, the family allegiances and betrayals. But in the innocent throes of love, she didn't want to imagine how difficult her relationship with David might turn out to be.

She found herself falling more in love with David with each passing day, but her father Saul only grew increasingly jealous. David held full sway over her allegiance, and her father couldn't stand it. So, he did what only the king could do: He sent her away and even forced her to marry someone else.

Even though she made her way back to David in time, it was never the same. Their love, if it had ever truly existed, had completely unraveled. To Michal, it felt as if resuming her place as David's wife was now only a business arrangement, an attempt to fulfill an obligation. No longer in love, they stayed together for the kingdom's sake.

Whenever she allowed the memories to surface, they always ended the same way. She was left with only a cruel snapshot of love gone wrong—a miserable, spiteful woman and a man ready to move on.

—Prayer—

God, things don't always work out the way I want them to. Give me wisdom and grace to accept life's disappointments.

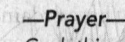

Weekend

Go to page 658 for your next devotional reading.

the moon and the stars,
which you have set in place,
4 what is man that you are mindful of him,
the son of man that you care for him?
5 You made him a little lower than the heavenly beings[a]
and crowned him with glory and honor.

6 You made him ruler over the works of your hands;
you put everything under his feet:
7 all flocks and herds,
and the beasts of the field,
8 the birds of the air,
and the fish of the sea,
all that swim the paths of the seas.

9 O LORD, our Lord,
how majestic is your name in all the earth!

Psalm 9[b]

For the director of music. To ⌊the tune of⌋ "The Death of the Son." A psalm of David.

1 I will praise you, O LORD, with all my heart;
I will tell of all your wonders.
2 I will be glad and rejoice in you;
I will sing praise to your name, O Most High.

3 My enemies turn back;
they stumble and perish before you.
4 For you have upheld my right and my cause;
you have sat on your throne, judging righteously.
5 You have rebuked the nations and destroyed the wicked;
you have blotted out their name for ever and ever.
6 Endless ruin has overtaken the enemy,
you have uprooted their cities;
even the memory of them has perished.

7 The LORD reigns forever;
he has established his throne for judgment.
8 He will judge the world in righteousness;
he will govern the peoples with justice.
9 The LORD is a refuge for the oppressed,
a stronghold in times of trouble.
10 Those who know your name will trust in you,
for you, LORD, have never forsaken those who seek you.

11 Sing praises to the LORD, enthroned in Zion;
proclaim among the nations what he has done.
12 For he who avenges blood remembers;
he does not ignore the cry of the afflicted.

13 O LORD, see how my enemies persecute me!
Have mercy and lift me up from the gates of death,
14 that I may declare your praises
in the gates of the Daughter of Zion
and there rejoice in your salvation.
15 The nations have fallen into the pit they have dug;
their feet are caught in the net they have hidden.
16 The LORD is known by his justice;
the wicked are ensnared by the work of their hands. *Higgaion.*[c] *Selah*
17 The wicked return to the grave,[d]
all the nations that forget God.
18 But the needy will not always be forgotten,
nor the hope of the afflicted ever perish.

19 Arise, O LORD, let not man triumph;
let the nations be judged in your presence.
20 Strike them with terror, O LORD;
let the nations know they are but men. *Selah*

Psalm 10[b]

1 Why, O LORD, do you stand far off?
Why do you hide yourself in times of trouble?

2 In his arrogance the wicked man hunts down the weak,
who are caught in the schemes he devises.
3 He boasts of the cravings of his heart;
he blesses the greedy and reviles the LORD.

[a]5 Or *than God* [b]Psalms 9 and 10 may have been originally a single acrostic poem, the stanzas of which begin with the successive letters of the Hebrew alphabet. In the Septuagint they constitute one psalm. [c]16 Or *Meditation*; possibly a musical notation [d]17 Hebrew *Sheol*

4 In his pride the wicked does not seek him;
in all his thoughts there is no room for
God.
5 His ways are always prosperous;
he is haughty and your laws are far from
him;
he sneers at all his enemies.
6 He says to himself, "Nothing will shake
me;
I'll always be happy and never have
trouble."
7 His mouth is full of curses
and lies and threats;
trouble and evil are
under his tongue.
8 He lies in wait near the
villages;
from ambush he murders
the innocent,
watching in secret for his
victims.
9 He lies in wait like a lion in
cover;
he lies in wait to catch
the helpless;
he catches the helpless
and drags them off in his net.
10 His victims are crushed, they collapse;
they fall under his strength.
11 He says to himself, "God has forgotten;
he covers his face and never sees."

12 Arise, LORD! Lift up your hand, O God.
Do not forget the helpless.
13 Why does the wicked man revile God?
Why does he say to himself,
"He won't call me to account"?
14 But you, O God, do see trouble and grief;
you consider it to take it in hand.
The victim commits himself to you;
you are the helper of the fatherless.
15 Break the arm of the wicked and evil
man;
call him to account for his wickedness
that would not be found out.

16 The LORD is King for ever and ever;
the nations will perish from his land.
17 You hear, O LORD, the desire of the
afflicted;
you encourage them, and you listen to
their cry,
18 defending the fatherless and the
oppressed,
in order that man, who is of the earth,
may terrify no more.

Psalm 10:17

God Encourages the Afflicted

You hear, O LORD, the
desire of the afflicted;
you encourage them,
and you listen
to their cry.

Psalm 11

For the director of music. Of David.

1 In the LORD I take refuge.
How then can you say to me:
"Flee like a bird to your
mountain.
2 For look, the wicked bend
their bows;
they set their arrows
against the strings
to shoot from the
shadows
at the upright in heart.
3 When the foundations are
being destroyed,
what can the righteous
do[a]?"

4 The LORD is in his holy
temple;
the LORD is on his heavenly throne.
He observes the sons of men;
his eyes examine them.
5 The LORD examines the righteous,
but the wicked[b] and those who love
violence
his soul hates.
6 On the wicked he will rain
fiery coals and burning sulfur;
a scorching wind will be their lot.

7 For the LORD is righteous,
he loves justice;
upright men will see his face.

Psalm 12

For the director of music. According to *sheminith.*[c]
A psalm of David.

1 Help, LORD, for the godly are no more;
the faithful have vanished from among
men.
2 Everyone lies to his neighbor;
their flattering lips speak with
deception.

a3 Or *what is the Righteous One doing* b5 Or *The LORD, the Righteous One, examines the wicked, /* cTitle: Probably a musical term

3 May the LORD cut off all flattering lips
and every boastful tongue
4 that says, "We will triumph with our tongues;
we own our lips[a]—who is our master?"

5 "Because of the oppression of the weak
and the groaning of the needy,
I will now arise," says the LORD.
"I will protect them from those who malign them."
6 And the words of the LORD are flawless,
like silver refined in a furnace of clay,
purified seven times.

7 O LORD, you will keep us safe
and protect us from such people forever.
8 The wicked freely strut about
when what is vile is honored among men.

Psalm 12:6

God Is Truthful

And the words of the LORD are flawless,
like silver refined in
a furnace of clay,
purified seven times.

Psalm 13

For the director of music. A psalm of David.

1 How long, O LORD? Will you forget me forever?
How long will you hide your face from me?
2 How long must I wrestle with my thoughts
and every day have sorrow in my heart?
How long will my enemy triumph over me?

3 Look on me and answer, O LORD my God.
Give light to my eyes, or I will sleep in death;
4 my enemy will say, "I have overcome him,"
and my foes will rejoice when I fall.

5 But I trust in your unfailing love;
my heart rejoices in your salvation.
6 I will sing to the LORD,
for he has been good to me.

Psalm 14

For the director of music. Of David.

1 The fool[b] says in his heart,
"There is no God."
They are corrupt, their deeds are vile;
there is no one who does good.

2 The LORD looks down from heaven
on the sons of men
to see if there are any who understand,
any who seek God.
3 All have turned aside,
they have together become corrupt;
there is no one who does good,
not even one.

4 Will evildoers never learn—
those who devour my people as men eat bread
and who do not call on the LORD?
5 There they are, overwhelmed with dread,
for God is present in the company of the righteous.
6 You evildoers frustrate the plans of the poor,
but the LORD is their refuge.

7 Oh, that salvation for Israel would come out of Zion!
When the LORD restores the fortunes of his people,
let Jacob rejoice and Israel be glad!

Psalm 15

A psalm of David.

1 LORD, who may dwell in your sanctuary?
Who may live on your holy hill?

2 He whose walk is blameless
and who does what is righteous,
who speaks the truth from his heart
3 and has no slander on his tongue,
who does his neighbor no wrong
and casts no slur on his fellowman,
4 who despises a vile man
but honors those who fear the LORD,
who keeps his oath
even when it hurts,
5 who lends his money without usury
and does not accept a bribe against the innocent.

[a]4 Or / *our lips are our plowshares* [b]1 The Hebrew words rendered *fool* in Psalms denote one who is morally deficient.

Never Alone

Read: Psalm 13:1–6

Psalm 13:5
But I trust in your unfailing love; my heart rejoices in your salvation.

reflection

1 Have you experienced a time when you couldn't feel God's presence? When?

2 How did you respond? What did you do?

3 Based on your understanding of Psalm 13, what will you do next time you find yourself feeling this way?

RELATED READINGS
Deuteronomy 31:1–6; Isaiah 54:1–17; Lamentations 3:31–33

AT AGE 46, PETER MARSHALL, chaplain of the United States Senate, died of a heart attack. Soon after he died, his wife, Catherine Marshall, stood beside his body. Later she wrote how the presence of God comforted her:

"As I opened the door," she wrote, "there was the instantaneous awareness that I was not alone. Yet the man I loved was not in the still form on the bed. I knew that Peter was near and alive. And beside him was another presence of transcendent glory, the Lord he had served through long years." God stood beside Catherine to comfort her in her deepest grief.

In this psalm, the writer found himself feeling so alone, so seemingly abandoned by God, that he was plunged into a deep depression and despair that took him to the edge of death. He was wrestling with his thoughts. His sorrow was overwhelming.

Perhaps you can relate to such feelings. Perhaps you know what it's like when your thoughts are whirling around in aching confusion. You may know what it's like to plead with God for light, for peace, for an alternative to the spiritual death you think is imminent.

Then comes the "*but*." The psalmist, even as he was suffering terribly, stopped himself with that little word. David chose to trust in God's goodness even when his heart was failing and grieving. Because he knew God, he chose to trust in God's unfailing love and rejoice even in the midst of sorrow.

Did you get that? He said, "But . . . I will" (verses 5–6). The psalmist made a choice. He made a conscious decision to trust in God's love even when the dark clouds of terror and depression hid God's face.

David knew this as a fact. And you can know it too: You are never alone. God is always nearby . . . even when you can't see his face or feel his presence. When you feel alone, call out to him. No matter how you feel, the fact remains: He is here. He is everywhere. And he hears your cries.

Monday

Go to page 662 for your next devotional reading.

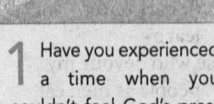

He who does these things
will never be shaken.

Psalm 16

A *miktam*[a] of David.

1 Keep me safe, O God,
for in you I take refuge.

2 I said to the LORD, "You are my Lord;
apart from you I have no good thing."
3 As for the saints who are in the land,
they are the glorious ones in whom is all my delight.[b]
4 The sorrows of those will increase
who run after other gods.
I will not pour out their libations of blood
or take up their names on my lips.

5 LORD, you have assigned me my portion and my cup;
you have made my lot secure.
6 The boundary lines have fallen for me in pleasant places;
surely I have a delightful inheritance.

7 I will praise the LORD, who counsels me;
even at night my heart instructs me.
8 I have set the LORD always before me.
Because he is at my right hand,
I will not be shaken.

9 Therefore my heart is glad and my tongue rejoices;
my body also will rest secure,
10 because you will not abandon me to the grave,[c]
nor will you let your Holy One[d] see decay.
11 You have made[e] known to me the path of life;
you will fill me with joy in your presence,
with eternal pleasures at your right hand.

Psalm 16:5

God Offers Security

LORD, you have assigned me my portion and my cup; you have made my lot secure.

Psalm 17

A prayer of David.

1 Hear, O LORD, my righteous plea;
listen to my cry.
Give ear to my prayer—
it does not rise from deceitful lips.
2 May my vindication come from you;
may your eyes see what is right.

3 Though you probe my heart and examine me at night,
though you test me, you will find nothing;
I have resolved that my mouth will not sin.
4 As for the deeds of men—
by the word of your lips
I have kept myself
from the ways of the violent.
5 My steps have held to your paths;
my feet have not slipped.

6 I call on you, O God, for you will answer me;
give ear to me and hear my prayer.
7 Show the wonder of your great love,
you who save by your right hand
those who take refuge in you from their foes.
8 Keep me as the apple of your eye;
hide me in the shadow of your wings
9 from the wicked who assail me,
from my mortal enemies who surround me.

10 They close up their callous hearts,
and their mouths speak with arrogance.
11 They have tracked me down, they now surround me,
with eyes alert, to throw me to the ground.
12 They are like a lion hungry for prey,
like a great lion crouching in cover.

[a] Title: Probably a literary or musical term [b] 3 Or *As for the pagan priests who are in the land / and the nobles in whom all delight, I said:* [c] 10 Hebrew *Sheol* [d] 10 Or *your faithful one* [e] 11 Or *You will make*

13 Rise up, O LORD, confront them, bring
them down;
rescue me from the wicked by your
sword.
14 O LORD, by your hand save
me from such men,
from men of this world
whose reward is in
this life.
You still the hunger of
those you cherish;
their sons have plenty,
and they store up wealth
for their children.
15 And I—in righteousness I
will see your face;
when I awake, I will be
satisfied with seeing
your likeness.

Psalm 17:15

God Provides Satisfaction

And I—in righteousness
I will see your face;
when I awake, I will be
satisfied with seeing
your likeness.

Psalm 18

For the director of music. Of David the servant of the LORD. He sang to the LORD the words of this song when the LORD delivered him from the hand of all his enemies and from the hand of Saul. He said:

1 I love you, O LORD, my strength.

2 The LORD is my rock, my fortress and my
deliverer;
my God is my rock, in whom I take
refuge.
He is my shield and the horn[a] of my
salvation, my stronghold.
3 I call to the LORD, who is worthy of praise,
and I am saved from my enemies.

4 The cords of death entangled me;
the torrents of destruction overwhelmed
me.
5 The cords of the grave[b] coiled around me;
the snares of death confronted me.
6 In my distress I called to the LORD;
I cried to my God for help.
From his temple he heard my voice;
my cry came before him, into his ears.

7 The earth trembled and quaked,
and the foundations of the mountains
shook;
they trembled because he was angry.
8 Smoke rose from his nostrils;
consuming fire came from his mouth,
burning coals blazed out of it.
9 He parted the heavens and
came down;
dark clouds were under
his feet.
10 He mounted the cherubim
and flew;
he soared on the wings
of the wind.
11 He made darkness his
covering, his
canopy around
him—
the dark rain clouds of
the sky.
12 Out of the brightness of
his presence clouds
advanced,
with hailstones and bolts of lightning.
13 The LORD thundered from heaven;
the voice of the Most High resounded.[c]
14 He shot his arrows and scattered ⌊the
enemies⌋,
great bolts of lightning and routed
them.
15 The valleys of the sea were exposed
and the foundations of the earth laid
bare
at your rebuke, O LORD,
at the blast of breath from your nostrils.

16 He reached down from on high and took
hold of me;
he drew me out of deep waters.
17 He rescued me from my powerful enemy,
from my foes, who were too strong for
me.
18 They confronted me in the day of my
disaster,
but the LORD was my support.
19 He brought me out into a spacious place;
he rescued me because he delighted in
me.

20 The LORD has dealt with me according to
my righteousness;

[a]2 *Horn* here symbolizes strength. [b]5 Hebrew *Sheol* [c]13 Some Hebrew manuscripts and Septuagint (see also 2 Samuel 22:14); most Hebrew manuscripts *resounded, / amid hailstones and bolts of lightning*

according to the cleanness of my hands
he has rewarded me.
21 For I have kept the ways of the LORD;
I have not done evil by turning from my God.
22 All his laws are before me;
I have not turned away from his decrees.
23 I have been blameless before him
and have kept myself from sin.
24 The LORD has rewarded me according to my righteousness,
according to the cleanness of my hands in his sight.

25 To the faithful you show yourself faithful,
to the blameless you show yourself blameless,
26 to the pure you show yourself pure,
but to the crooked you show yourself shrewd.
27 You save the humble
but bring low those whose eyes are haughty.
28 You, O LORD, keep my lamp burning;
my God turns my darkness into light.
29 With your help I can advance against a troop[a];
with my God I can scale a wall.

30 As for God, his way is perfect;
the word of the LORD is flawless.
He is a shield
for all who take refuge in him.
31 For who is God besides the LORD?
And who is the Rock except our God?
32 It is God who arms me with strength
and makes my way perfect.
33 He makes my feet like the feet of a deer;
he enables me to stand on the heights.
34 He trains my hands for battle;
my arms can bend a bow of bronze.
35 You give me your shield of victory,
and your right hand sustains me;
you stoop down to make me great.
36 You broaden the path beneath me,
so that my ankles do not turn.

37 I pursued my enemies and overtook them;
I did not turn back till they were destroyed.
38 I crushed them so that they could not rise;
they fell beneath my feet.
39 You armed me with strength for battle;
you made my adversaries bow at my feet.
40 You made my enemies turn their backs in flight,
and I destroyed my foes.
41 They cried for help, but there was no one to save them—
to the LORD, but he did not answer.
42 I beat them as fine as dust borne on the wind;
I poured them out like mud in the streets.

43 You have delivered me from the attacks of the people;
you have made me the head of nations;
people I did not know are subject to me.
44 As soon as they hear me, they obey me;
foreigners cringe before me.
45 They all lose heart;
they come trembling from their strongholds.

46 The LORD lives! Praise be to my Rock!
Exalted be God my Savior!
47 He is the God who avenges me,
who subdues nations under me,
48 who saves me from my enemies.
You exalted me above my foes;
from violent men you rescued me.
49 Therefore I will praise you among the nations, O LORD;
I will sing praises to your name.
50 He gives his king great victories;
he shows unfailing kindness to his anointed,
to David and his descendants forever.

Psalm 19

For the director of music. A psalm of David.

1 The heavens declare the glory of God;
the skies proclaim the work of his hands.
2 Day after day they pour forth speech;
night after night they display knowledge.
3 There is no speech or language
where their voice is not heard.[b]

[a]29 Or *can run through a barricade* [b]3 Or *They have no speech, there are no words; / no sound is heard from them*

An Articulate Creation

Psalm 19:1

The heavens declare the glory of God; the skies proclaim the work of his hands.

reflection

1 Which aspects of nature resonate with you? Perhaps you enjoy a beautiful sunset or bird watching; whatever the particular expression, think about how you can incorporate worship or prayer into the time you spend appreciating the natural world.

2 How can you reconcile the importance of worshiping the Creator with the responsibility of stewardship of God's creation?

3 Think about the last time nature made a strong impression on you—good or bad. How can you subject your emotional responses to the cosmos to the psalmist's idea that the creation proclaims God's invisible qualities?

RELATED READINGS

Job 38:1–41;
Isaiah 65:17–25;
Romans 8:18–27

Read: Psalm 19:1–14

WE LIVE IN TUMULTUOUS TIMES of natural disaster. The news carries stories of devastating earthquakes, floods and tropical storms that careen along coastlines and cause massive losses of property and life in the cities, towns and individual households they invade. Amidst screaming natural forces it may be easy to forget that even the winds and rains submit to God's voice. Although the natural world does not glorify itself, the booming truths pounding in the surf and soaring through the skies fall on many a deaf ear. But nature's voice "goes out into all the earth" proclaiming the articulate truth that God is in his heaven and watching over his creation.

In an urban setting, where smog blankets the sky and artificial light dulls the stars, seeing God's imprint may be difficult. Natural disasters may strike us more as an example of nature's random savagery than the handiwork of our all-powerful God. Certainly the creation groans under the curse of sin, just as we do. We cannot pretend to understand the reasons for earthquakes, floods or fires, but we do know the One who controls the universe, and we can cling to him amidst the rising waters.

The next time you witness a flower growing between the sidewalk cracks, a raging thunderstorm or a magnificent sunset, remember that creation acts as a signpost, pointing to Someone greater than "Mother Nature." It reveals the God who wants all people of all nations to recognize his majesty, to worship the One whose infinite creativity and power produced the spectacular displays found in the natural world.

The natural world is a testimony to God's magnificent creatorship and also should be the object of our diligent stewardship. However, we must flee the two extremes—either fearing nature's power or worshiping creation and not the Creator. Even today, the creation is God's universal proclamation of his nature, underpinning his special revelation through Christ and the Scriptures. As women who love and appreciate the beauty of the world, may we always remember to listen closely to the deeper truths of God's goodness and grandeur that whisper from the rushing stream or shout from the thunderclap.

Go to page 667 for your next devotional reading.

4 Their voice[a] goes out into all the earth,
their words to the ends of the world.

In the heavens he has pitched a tent for the sun,
5 which is like a bridegroom coming forth from his pavilion,
like a champion rejoicing to run his course.
6 It rises at one end of the heavens
and makes its circuit to the other;
nothing is hidden from its heat.

7 The law of the LORD is perfect,
reviving the soul.
The statutes of the LORD are trustworthy,
making wise the simple.
8 The precepts of the LORD are right,
giving joy to the heart.
The commands of the LORD are radiant,
giving light to the eyes.
9 The fear of the LORD is pure,
enduring forever.
The ordinances of the LORD are sure
and altogether righteous.
10 They are more precious than gold,
than much pure gold;
they are sweeter than honey,
than honey from the comb.
11 By them is your servant warned;
in keeping them there is great reward.

12 Who can discern his errors?
Forgive my hidden faults.
13 Keep your servant also from willful sins;
may they not rule over me.
Then will I be blameless,
innocent of great transgression.

14 May the words of my mouth and the meditation of my heart
be pleasing in your sight,
O LORD, my Rock and my Redeemer.

Psalm 20

For the director of music. A psalm of David.

1 May the LORD answer you when you are in distress;
may the name of the God of Jacob protect you.
2 May he send you help from the sanctuary
and grant you support from Zion.
3 May he remember all your sacrifices
and accept your burnt offerings. *Selah*
4 May he give you the desire of your heart
and make all your plans succeed.
5 We will shout for joy when you are victorious
and will lift up our banners in the name of our God.

May the LORD grant all your requests.

6 Now I know that the LORD saves his anointed;
he answers him from his holy heaven
with the saving power of his right hand.
7 Some trust in chariots and some in horses,
but we trust in the name of the LORD our God.
8 They are brought to their knees and fall,
but we rise up and stand firm.

9 O LORD, save the king!
Answer[b] us when we call!

Psalm 21

For the director of music. A psalm of David.

1 O LORD, the king rejoices in your strength.
How great is his joy in the victories you give!
2 You have granted him the desire of his heart
and have not withheld the request of his lips. *Selah*
3 You welcomed him with rich blessings
and placed a crown of pure gold on his head.
4 He asked you for life, and you gave it to him—
length of days, for ever and ever.
5 Through the victories you gave, his glory is great;
you have bestowed on him splendor and majesty.
6 Surely you have granted him eternal blessings
and made him glad with the joy of your presence.
7 For the king trusts in the LORD;

[a]4 Septuagint, Jerome and Syriac; Hebrew *line* [b]9 Or *save! / O King, answer*

through the unfailing love of the Most
High
he will not be shaken.
8 Your hand will lay hold on all your enemies;
your right hand will seize your foes.
9 At the time of your appearing
you will make them like a fiery furnace.
In his wrath the LORD will swallow them
up,
and his fire will consume them.
10 You will destroy their descendants from
the earth,
their posterity from mankind.
11 Though they plot evil against you
and devise wicked schemes, they cannot
succeed;
12 for you will make them turn their backs
when you aim at them with drawn bow.

13 Be exalted, O LORD, in your strength;
we will sing and praise your might.

Psalm 22

For the director of music. To ⌊the tune of⌋ "The Doe of the Morning." A psalm of David.

1 My God, my God, why have you forsaken
me?
Why are you so far from saving me,
so far from the words of my groaning?
2 O my God, I cry out by day, but you do not
answer,
by night, and am not
silent.
3 Yet you are enthroned as
the Holy One;
you are the praise of
Israel.[a]
4 In you our fathers put their
trust;
they trusted and you
delivered them.
5 They cried to you and were
saved;
in you they trusted and were not
disappointed.

6 But I am a worm and not a man,
scorned by men and despised by the
people.
7 All who see me mock me;
they hurl insults, shaking their heads:
8 "He trusts in the LORD;
let the LORD rescue him.
Let him deliver him,
since he delights in him."

9 Yet you brought me out of the womb;
you made me trust in you
even at my mother's breast.
10 From birth I was cast upon you;
from my mother's womb you have been
my God.
11 Do not be far from me,
for trouble is near
and there is no one to help.

12 Many bulls surround me;
strong bulls of Bashan encircle me.
13 Roaring lions tearing their prey
open their mouths wide against me.
14 I am poured out like water,
and all my bones are out of joint.
My heart has turned to wax;
it has melted away within me.
15 My strength is dried up like a potsherd,
and my tongue sticks to the roof of my
mouth;
you lay me[b] in the dust of death.
16 Dogs have surrounded me;
a band of evil men has encircled me,
they have pierced[c] my
hands and my
feet.
17 I can count all my bones;
people stare and gloat
over me.
18 They divide my garments
among them
and cast lots for my
clothing.

19 But you, O LORD, be not far
off;
O my Strength, come
quickly to help me.
20 Deliver my life from the sword,
my precious life from the power of the
dogs.
21 Rescue me from the mouth of the lions;

Psalm 22:3

God Is Holy

Yet you are enthroned as the Holy One; you are the praise of Israel.

[a]3 Or *Yet you are holy, / enthroned on the praises of Israel* [b]15 Or */ I am laid* [c]16 Some Hebrew manuscripts, Septuagint and Syriac; most Hebrew manuscripts */ like the lion,*

save[a] me from the horns of the wild
oxen.

22 I will declare your name to my brothers;
in the congregation I will praise you.
23 You who fear the LORD, praise him!
All you descendants of Jacob, honor him!
Revere him, all you descendants of
Israel!
24 For he has not despised or disdained
the suffering of the afflicted one;
he has not hidden his face from him
but has listened to his cry for help.

25 From you comes the theme of my praise in
the great assembly;
before those who fear you[b] will I fulfill
my vows.
26 The poor will eat and be satisfied;
they who seek the LORD will praise
him—
may your hearts live forever!
27 All the ends of the earth
will remember and turn to the LORD,
and all the families of the nations
will bow down before him,
28 for dominion belongs to the LORD
and he rules over the
nations.

29 All the rich of the earth will
feast and worship;
all who go down to the
dust will kneel
before him—
those who cannot keep
themselves alive.
30 Posterity will serve him;
future generations will
be told about the
Lord.
31 They will proclaim his
righteousness
to a people yet unborn—
for he has done it.

Psalm 23

A psalm of David.

1 The LORD is my shepherd, I shall not be in
want.
2 He makes me lie down in green
pastures,
he leads me beside quiet waters,
3 he restores my soul.
He guides me in paths of righteousness
for his name's sake.
4 Even though I walk
through the valley of the shadow of
death,[c]
I will fear no evil,
for you are with me;
your rod and your staff,
they comfort me.

5 You prepare a table before me
in the presence of my enemies.
You anoint my head with oil;
my cup overflows.
6 Surely goodness and love will follow me
all the days of my life,
and I will dwell in the house of the LORD
forever.

Psalm 24

Of David. A psalm.

1 The earth is the LORD's, and everything
in it,
the world, and all who
live in it;
2 for he founded it upon the
seas
and established it upon
the waters.

3 Who may ascend the hill of
the LORD?
Who may stand in his
holy place?
4 He who has clean hands
and a pure heart,
who does not lift up his
soul to an idol
or swear by what is false.[d]
5 He will receive blessing from the LORD
and vindication from God his Savior.
6 Such is the generation of those who seek
him,
who seek your face, O God of
Jacob.[e] *Selah*

Psalm 24:1

God Owns Everything

The earth is the LORD's,
and everything in it,
the world, and all
who live in it.

[a]21 Or / *you have heard* [b]25 Hebrew *him* [c]4 Or *through the darkest valley* [d]4 Or *swear falsely* [e]6 Two Hebrew manuscripts and Syriac (see also Septuagint); most Hebrew manuscripts *face, Jacob*

7 Lift up your heads, O you gates;
be lifted up, you ancient doors,
that the King of glory may come in.
8 Who is this King of glory?
The LORD strong and mighty,
the LORD mighty in battle.
9 Lift up your heads, O you gates;
lift them up, you ancient doors,
that the King of glory may come in.
10 Who is he, this King of glory?
The LORD Almighty—
he is the King of glory. *Selah*

Psalm 25[a]

Of David.

1 To you, O LORD, I lift up my soul;
2 in you I trust, O my God.
Do not let me be put to shame,
nor let my enemies triumph over me.
3 No one whose hope is in you
will ever be put to shame,
but they will be put to shame
who are treacherous without excuse.

4 Show me your ways, O LORD,
teach me your paths;
5 guide me in your truth and teach me,
for you are God my Savior,
and my hope is in you all day long.
6 Remember, O LORD, your great mercy and love,
for they are from of old.
7 Remember not the sins of my youth
and my rebellious ways;
according to your love remember me,
for you are good, O LORD.

8 Good and upright is the LORD;
therefore he instructs sinners in his ways.
9 He guides the humble in what is right
and teaches them his way.
10 All the ways of the LORD are loving and faithful
for those who keep the demands of his covenant.
11 For the sake of your name, O LORD,
forgive my iniquity, though it is great.
12 Who, then, is the man that fears the LORD?
He will instruct him in the way chosen for him.
13 He will spend his days in prosperity,
and his descendants will inherit the land.
14 The LORD confides in those who fear him;
he makes his covenant known to them.
15 My eyes are ever on the LORD,
for only he will release my feet from the snare.

16 Turn to me and be gracious to me,
for I am lonely and afflicted.
17 The troubles of my heart have multiplied;
free me from my anguish.
18 Look upon my affliction and my distress
and take away all my sins.
19 See how my enemies have increased
and how fiercely they hate me!
20 Guard my life and rescue me;
let me not be put to shame,
for I take refuge in you.
21 May integrity and uprightness protect me,
because my hope is in you.

22 Redeem Israel, O God,
from all their troubles!

Psalm 26

Of David.

1 Vindicate me, O LORD,
for I have led a blameless life;
I have trusted in the LORD
without wavering.
2 Test me, O LORD, and try me,
examine my heart and my mind;
3 for your love is ever before me,
and I walk continually in your truth.
4 I do not sit with deceitful men,
nor do I consort with hypocrites;
5 I abhor the assembly of evildoers
and refuse to sit with the wicked.
6 I wash my hands in innocence,
and go about your altar, O LORD,
7 proclaiming aloud your praise
and telling of all your wonderful deeds.
8 I love the house where you live, O LORD,
the place where your glory dwells.

9 Do not take away my soul along with sinners,
my life with bloodthirsty men,
10 in whose hands are wicked schemes,

[a] This psalm is an acrostic poem, the verses of which begin with the successive letters of the Hebrew alphabet.

Coming Clean

Read: Psalm 24:1–10

THE VIENNA MATERNITY HOSPITAL was the largest maternity hospital in the world in the middle of the nineteenth century. It was considered a safer place to deliver a child than a home. Yet the mortality rates for mothers giving birth were alarming. Studies done from 1839 to 1847 revealed that women attended by medical students were dying at nearly triple the rate of those attended by midwives. The cause? Unwashed hands. Doctors would routinely conduct post-mortems and then proceed directly to the maternity wards to deliver babies. Finally, a Hungarian doctor named Ignaz Phillip Semmelweis introduced the doctors to hand washing with a chlorine solution between procedures. Only then did the mortality rates of mothers of newborns drop dramatically.

Today we understand to a far greater degree the role of bacteria in producing and spreading disease. Medical personnel and restaurant workers alike are required to wash their hands regularly. And how often do we hear mothers urge their children, "Wash your hands before you come to the table!"

Just as external cleanliness promotes physical health, having "clean hands" before God promotes spiritual health. Scrubbing up spiritually involves repentance—confessing our sins, coming clean—before God so that we can experience spiritual well-being. The psalmist pleaded, "Create in me a pure heart, O God, and renew a steadfast spirit within me" (Psalm 51:10).

In her book *With My Whole Heart*, author Karen Mains writes, "Spiritual awakening always begins with cleansing. It begins in the heart of the individual who suddenly says to herself, 'I'm dirty.' And that is painful, particularly if we've been pretending all along to be clean."

If you long for greater intimacy with God, ask him to examine your heart to see if there are any areas in which you need to come clean before him. Confession, in its most elemental form, simply means agreeing with God that you've departed from his ways and fallen short of his standards. Admit to him—and to yourself—that you are in need of a spiritual bath. Be prepared, like a little child, to squirm a little when he reminds you to wash behind your ears. But, oh, the joy of coming clean!

Wednesday

Go to page 669 for your next devotional reading.

Psalm 24:3–4

Who may ascend the hill of the LORD? Who may stand in his holy place? He who has clean hands and a pure heart.

reflection

1 When was the last time you "washed your hands" by spending time in confession to God?

2 Ask God to bring things to mind that you need to confess to him today.

3 Spend some time asking God to forgive you of those things that displease him. Thank him that "if we confess our sins, he is faithful and just and will forgive us our sins and purify us from all unrighteousness" (1 John 1:9).

RELATED READINGS

2 Samuel 12:1–13; Psalm 51:1–19; Matthew 5:8

whose right hands are full of bribes.
11 But I lead a blameless life;
redeem me and be merciful to me.

12 My feet stand on level ground;
in the great assembly I will praise the LORD.

Psalm 27

Of David.

1 The LORD is my light and my salvation—
whom shall I fear?
The LORD is the stronghold of my life—
of whom shall I be afraid?
2 When evil men advance against me
to devour my flesh,[a]
when my enemies and my foes attack me,
they will stumble and fall.
3 Though an army besiege me,
my heart will not fear;
though war break out against me,
even then will I be confident.

4 One thing I ask of the LORD,
this is what I seek:
that I may dwell in the house of the LORD
all the days of my life,
to gaze upon the beauty of the LORD
and to seek him in his temple.
5 For in the day of trouble
he will keep me safe in his dwelling;
he will hide me in the shelter of his tabernacle
and set me high upon a rock.
6 Then my head will be exalted
above the enemies who surround me;
at his tabernacle will I sacrifice with shouts of joy;
I will sing and make music to the LORD.

7 Hear my voice when I call, O LORD;
be merciful to me and answer me.
8 My heart says of you, "Seek his[b] face!"
Your face, LORD, I will seek.
9 Do not hide your face from me,
do not turn your servant away in anger;
you have been my helper.
Do not reject me or forsake me,
O God my Savior.
10 Though my father and mother forsake me,
the LORD will receive me.
11 Teach me your way, O LORD;
lead me in a straight path
because of my oppressors.
12 Do not turn me over to the desire of my foes,
for false witnesses rise up against me,
breathing out violence.

13 I am still confident of this:
I will see the goodness of the LORD
in the land of the living.
14 Wait for the LORD;
be strong and take heart
and wait for the LORD.

Psalm 27:1

God Is My Salvation

The LORD is my light and my salvation—
whom shall I fear?
The LORD is the stronghold of my life—
of whom shall I be afraid?

Psalm 28

Of David.

1 To you I call, O LORD my Rock;
do not turn a deaf ear to me.
For if you remain silent,
I will be like those who have gone down to the pit.
2 Hear my cry for mercy
as I call to you for help,
as I lift up my hands
toward your Most Holy Place.

3 Do not drag me away with the wicked,
with those who do evil,
who speak cordially with their neighbors
but harbor malice in their hearts.
4 Repay them for their deeds
and for their evil work;
repay them for what their hands have done
and bring back upon them what they deserve.
5 Since they show no regard for the works of the LORD
and what his hands have done,

[a]2 Or *to slander me* [b]8 Or *To you, O my heart, he has said, "Seek my*

Fearless

Read: Psalm 27:1–14

WHOM DO YOU FEAR? Let's face it: It's a scary world out there. All kinds of people may do us harm—from the stranger lurking on the corner to the terrorist lurking behind a computer somewhere, from a drunken driver to a corrupt investment firm.

Sometimes we fear people who may harm us in more personal ways—the boss who has it out for us or the woman who dislikes us. We may find ourselves working harder when the boss is around or walking on eggshells around the neighborhood gossip. We may violate our own consciences so we don't offend those who make sure their opinions are heard. We are afraid of those peers who like to put pressure on us.

David, who wrote this psalm, had many enemies chasing him at one time or another. He was no stranger to danger. But he also knew that God was powerful and knowledgeable enough to thwart the plans others might have to harm him. He knew that God could intervene on his behalf. He knew that God had plans for him. He knew that God had his best interests at heart. So in this ringing statement of trust, he put his fate in the hands of God who would be his "stronghold" (Psalm 27:1).

We can learn from David one key to facing our fears. David escaped the pressure of fear and warfare by retreating into God's holy presence in the tabernacle. He proclaimed, "I will sing and make music to the LORD" (verse 6). Praise and worship can help to take our minds off of our fears by placing our thoughts on our powerful God.

David also reminds us to "wait for the LORD; be strong and take heart and wait for the LORD" (verse 14). Though God's answer may not come when or how we expect it, we can trust that he is more faithful than even a parent. Even if our boss fires us, our best friend gossips behind our back or our retirement fund is drained, God will surround us with his love. In spite of anything that can happen, God will be there for us. Ultimately, we who trust in him find safety for our souls. Since that is the case, whom on earth should we fear?

Thursday

Go to page 676 for your next devotional reading.

Psalm 27:1

The LORD is my light
and my salvation—
whom shall I fear?
The LORD is the strong-
hold of my life—of
whom shall I be afraid?

reflection

1 Whom do you fear and why?

2 How has God shielded you when you have been in a frightening situation?

3 How do you reconcile this psalm and its implications with the realization that some faithful people do come to physical harm?

RELATED READINGS

Joshua 1:5–9;
Luke 12:4–7;
Romans 8:35–39;
1 John 4:14–18

"Where are the men and women who love God supremely and fear nothing and no one but God?"

Nancy Leigh DeMoss

he will tear them down
and never build them up again.

6 Praise be to the LORD,
for he has heard my cry for mercy.
7 The LORD is my strength and my shield;
my heart trusts in him, and I am helped.
My heart leaps for joy
and I will give thanks to him in song.

8 The LORD is the strength of his people,
a fortress of salvation for his anointed one.
9 Save your people and bless your inheritance;
be their shepherd and carry them forever.

Psalm 29

A psalm of David.

1 Ascribe to the LORD, O mighty ones,
ascribe to the LORD glory and strength.
2 Ascribe to the LORD the glory due his name;
worship the LORD in the splendor of his[a] holiness.

3 The voice of the LORD is over the waters;
the God of glory thunders,
the LORD thunders over the mighty waters.
4 The voice of the LORD is powerful;
the voice of the LORD is majestic.
5 The voice of the LORD breaks the cedars;
the LORD breaks in pieces the cedars of Lebanon.
6 He makes Lebanon skip like a calf,
Sirion[b] like a young wild ox.
7 The voice of the LORD strikes
with flashes of lightning.
8 The voice of the LORD shakes the desert;
the LORD shakes the Desert of Kadesh.
9 The voice of the LORD twists the oaks[c]
and strips the forests bare.
And in his temple all cry, "Glory!"

10 The LORD sits[d] enthroned over the flood;
the LORD is enthroned as King forever.
11 The LORD gives strength to his people;
the LORD blesses his people with peace.

Psalm 30

A psalm. A song. For the dedication of the temple.[e] Of David.

1 I will exalt you, O LORD,
for you lifted me out of the depths
and did not let my enemies gloat over me.
2 O LORD my God, I called to you for help
and you healed me.
3 O LORD, you brought me up from the grave[f];
you spared me from going down into the pit.

4 Sing to the LORD, you saints of his;
praise his holy name.
5 For his anger lasts only a moment,
but his favor lasts a lifetime;
weeping may remain for a night,
but rejoicing comes in the morning.

6 When I felt secure, I said,
"I will never be shaken."
7 O LORD, when you favored me,
you made my mountain[g] stand firm;
but when you hid your face,
I was dismayed.

8 To you, O LORD, I called;
to the Lord I cried for mercy:
9 "What gain is there in my destruction,[h]
in my going down into the pit?
Will the dust praise you?
Will it proclaim your faithfulness?
10 Hear, O LORD, and be merciful to me;
O LORD, be my help."
11 You turned my wailing into dancing;
you removed my sackcloth and clothed me with joy,
12 that my heart may sing to you and not be silent.
O LORD my God, I will give you thanks forever.

Psalm 31

For the director of music. A psalm of David.

1 In you, O LORD, I have taken refuge;
let me never be put to shame;
deliver me in your righteousness.
2 Turn your ear to me,

[a]2 Or *LORD with the splendor of* [b]6 That is, Mount Hermon [c]9 Or *LORD makes the deer give birth* [d]10 Or *sat* [e]Title: Or *palace*
[f]3 Hebrew *Sheol* [g]7 Or *hill country* [h]9 Or *there if I am silenced*

come quickly to my rescue;
be my rock of refuge,
a strong fortress to save me.
3 Since you are my rock and my fortress,
for the sake of your name lead and guide me.
4 Free me from the trap that is set for me,
for you are my refuge.
5 Into your hands I commit my spirit;
redeem me, O LORD, the God of truth.

6 I hate those who cling to worthless idols;
I trust in the LORD.
7 I will be glad and rejoice in your love,
for you saw my affliction
and knew the anguish of my soul.
8 You have not handed me over to the enemy
but have set my feet in a spacious place.

9 Be merciful to me, O LORD, for I am in distress;
my eyes grow weak with sorrow,
my soul and my body with grief.
10 My life is consumed by anguish
and my years by groaning;
my strength fails because of my affliction,[a]
and my bones grow weak.
11 Because of all my enemies,
I am the utter contempt of my neighbors;
I am a dread to my friends—
those who see me on the street flee from me.
12 I am forgotten by them as though I were dead;
I have become like broken pottery.
13 For I hear the slander of many;
there is terror on every side;
they conspire against me
and plot to take my life.

14 But I trust in you, O LORD;
I say, "You are my God."
15 My times are in your hands;
deliver me from my enemies
and from those who pursue me.
16 Let your face shine on your servant;
save me in your unfailing love.
17 Let me not be put to shame, O LORD,
for I have cried out to you;
but let the wicked be put to shame
and lie silent in the grave.[b]
18 Let their lying lips be silenced,
for with pride and contempt
they speak arrogantly against the righteous.

19 How great is your goodness,
which you have stored up for those who fear you,
which you bestow in the sight of men
on those who take refuge in you.
20 In the shelter of your presence you hide them
from the intrigues of men;
in your dwelling you keep them safe
from accusing tongues.

21 Praise be to the LORD,
for he showed his wonderful love to me
when I was in a besieged city.
22 In my alarm I said,
"I am cut off from your sight!"
Yet you heard my cry for mercy
when I called to you for help.

23 Love the LORD, all his saints!
The LORD preserves the faithful,
but the proud he pays back in full.
24 Be strong and take heart,
all you who hope in the LORD.

Psalm 31:7

God Sees Our Pain

I will be glad and rejoice in your love, for you saw my affliction and knew the anguish of my soul.

Psalm 32

Of David. A *maskil*.[c]

1 Blessed is he
whose transgressions are forgiven,

[a]10 Or *guilt* [b]17 Hebrew *Sheol* [c]Title: Probably a literary or musical term

whose sins are covered.
2 Blessed is the man
whose sin the LORD does not count against him
and in whose spirit is no deceit.

3 When I kept silent,
my bones wasted away
through my groaning all day long.
4 For day and night
your hand was heavy upon me;
my strength was sapped
as in the heat of summer. *Selah*
5 Then I acknowledged my sin to you
and did not cover up my iniquity.
I said, "I will confess
my transgressions to the LORD"—
and you forgave
the guilt of my sin. *Selah*

6 Therefore let everyone who is godly pray to you
while you may be found;
surely when the mighty waters rise,
they will not reach him.
7 You are my hiding place;
you will protect me from trouble
and surround me with songs of deliverance. *Selah*

8 I will instruct you and teach you in the way you should go;
I will counsel you and watch over you.
9 Do not be like the horse or the mule,
which have no understanding
but must be controlled by bit and bridle
or they will not come to you.
10 Many are the woes of the wicked,
but the LORD's unfailing love
surrounds the man who trusts in him.

11 Rejoice in the LORD and be glad, you righteous;
sing, all you who are upright in heart!

Psalm 33

1 Sing joyfully to the LORD, you righteous;
it is fitting for the upright to praise him.
2 Praise the LORD with the harp;
make music to him on the ten-stringed lyre.
3 Sing to him a new song;
play skillfully, and shout for joy.

4 For the word of the LORD is right and true;
he is faithful in all he does.
5 The LORD loves righteousness and justice;
the earth is full of his unfailing love.

6 By the word of the LORD were the heavens made,
their starry host by the breath of his mouth.
7 He gathers the waters of the sea into jars[a];
he puts the deep into storehouses.
8 Let all the earth fear the LORD;
let all the people of the world revere him.
9 For he spoke, and it came to be;
he commanded, and it stood firm.
10 The LORD foils the plans of the nations;
he thwarts the purposes of the peoples.
11 But the plans of the LORD stand firm forever,
the purposes of his heart through all generations.

12 Blessed is the nation whose God is the LORD,
the people he chose for his inheritance.
13 From heaven the LORD looks down
and sees all mankind;
14 from his dwelling place he watches
all who live on earth—
15 he who forms the hearts of all,
who considers everything they do.
16 No king is saved by the size of his army;
no warrior escapes by his great strength.
17 A horse is a vain hope for deliverance;
despite all its great strength it cannot save.
18 But the eyes of the LORD are on those who fear him,
on those whose hope is in his unfailing love,

Psalm 32:8

God Counsels Us

I will instruct you and teach you in the way you should go; I will counsel you and watch over you.

[a] 7 Or *sea as into a heap*

19 to deliver them from death
and keep them alive in famine.

20 We wait in hope for the LORD;
he is our help and our shield.
21 In him our hearts rejoice,
for we trust in his holy name.
22 May your unfailing love rest upon us,
O LORD,
even as we put our hope in you.

Psalm 34[a]

Of David. When he pretended to be insane before Abimelech, who drove him away, and he left.

1 I will extol the LORD at all times;
his praise will always be on my lips.
2 My soul will boast in the LORD;
let the afflicted hear and rejoice.
3 Glorify the LORD with me;
let us exalt his name together.

4 I sought the LORD, and he answered me;
he delivered me from all my fears.
5 Those who look to him are radiant;
their faces are never covered with shame.
6 This poor man called, and the LORD heard
him;
he saved him out of all his troubles.
7 The angel of the LORD encamps around
those who fear him,
and he delivers them.

8 Taste and see that the LORD is good;
blessed is the man who takes refuge in
him.
9 Fear the LORD, you his saints,
for those who fear him lack nothing.
10 The lions may grow weak and hungry,
but those who seek the LORD lack no
good thing.

11 Come, my children, listen to me;
I will teach you the fear of the LORD.
12 Whoever of you loves life
and desires to see many good days,
13 keep your tongue from evil
and your lips from speaking lies.
14 Turn from evil and do good;
seek peace and pursue it.

15 The eyes of the LORD are on the righteous
and his ears are attentive to their cry;
16 the face of the LORD is against those who
do evil,
to cut off the memory of them from the
earth.

17 The righteous cry out, and the LORD hears
them;
he delivers them from all their troubles.
18 The LORD is close to the brokenhearted
and saves those who are crushed in
spirit.

19 A righteous man may have many troubles,
but the LORD delivers him from them
all;
20 he protects all his bones,
not one of them will be broken.

21 Evil will slay the wicked;
the foes of the righteous will be
condemned.
22 The LORD redeems his servants;
no one will be condemned who takes
refuge in him.

Psalm 35

Of David.

1 Contend, O LORD, with those who contend
with me;
fight against those who fight against me.
2 Take up shield and buckler;
arise and come to my aid.
3 Brandish spear and javelin[b]
against those who pursue me.
Say to my soul,
"I am your salvation."

4 May those who seek my life
be disgraced and put to shame;
may those who plot my ruin
be turned back in dismay.
5 May they be like chaff before the wind,
with the angel of the LORD driving them
away;
6 may their path be dark and slippery,
with the angel of the LORD pursuing
them.
7 Since they hid their net for me without
cause
and without cause dug a pit for me,
8 may ruin overtake them by surprise—

[a] This psalm is an acrostic poem, the verses of which begin with the successive letters of the Hebrew alphabet. [b] 3 Or *and block the way*

may the net they hid entangle them,
may they fall into the pit, to their ruin.
9 Then my soul will rejoice in the LORD
and delight in his salvation.
10 My whole being will exclaim,
"Who is like you, O LORD?
You rescue the poor from those too strong for them,
the poor and needy from those who rob them."

11 Ruthless witnesses come forward;
they question me on things I know nothing about.
12 They repay me evil for good
and leave my soul forlorn.
13 Yet when they were ill, I put on sackcloth
and humbled myself with fasting.
When my prayers returned to me unanswered,
14 I went about mourning
as though for my friend or brother.
I bowed my head in grief
as though weeping for my mother.
15 But when I stumbled, they gathered in glee;
attackers gathered against me when I was unaware.
They slandered me without ceasing.
16 Like the ungodly they maliciously mocked[a];
they gnashed their teeth at me.
17 O Lord, how long will you look on?
Rescue my life from their ravages,
my precious life from these lions.
18 I will give you thanks in the great assembly;
among throngs of people I will praise you.

19 Let not those gloat over me
who are my enemies without cause;
let not those who hate me without reason
maliciously wink the eye.
20 They do not speak peaceably,
but devise false accusations
against those who live quietly in the land.
21 They gape at me and say, "Aha! Aha!
With our own eyes we have seen it."
22 O LORD, you have seen this; be not silent.
Do not be far from me, O Lord.
23 Awake, and rise to my defense!
Contend for me, my God and Lord.
24 Vindicate me in your righteousness,
O LORD my God;
do not let them gloat over me.
25 Do not let them think, "Aha, just what we wanted!"
or say, "We have swallowed him up."

26 May all who gloat over my distress
be put to shame and confusion;
may all who exalt themselves over me
be clothed with shame and disgrace.
27 May those who delight in my vindication
shout for joy and gladness;
may they always say, "The LORD be exalted,
who delights in the well-being of his servant."
28 My tongue will speak of your righteousness
and of your praises all day long.

Psalm 36

For the director of music. Of David the servant of the LORD.

1 An oracle is within my heart
concerning the sinfulness of the wicked:[b]
There is no fear of God
before his eyes.
2 For in his own eyes he flatters himself
too much to detect or hate his sin.
3 The words of his mouth are wicked and deceitful;
he has ceased to be wise and to do good.
4 Even on his bed he plots evil;
he commits himself to a sinful course
and does not reject what is wrong.

5 Your love, O LORD, reaches to the heavens,
your faithfulness to the skies.
6 Your righteousness is like the mighty mountains,
your justice like the great deep.
O LORD, you preserve both man and beast.
7 How priceless is your unfailing love!
Both high and low among men

[a]16 Septuagint; Hebrew may mean *ungodly circle of mockers.* [b]1 Or *heart: / Sin proceeds from the wicked.*

find[a] refuge in the shadow of your wings.
8 They feast on the abundance of your house;
you give them drink
from your river of
delights.
9 For with you is the fountain
of life;
in your light we see light.

10 Continue your love to those
who know you,
your righteousness to the
upright in heart.
11 May the foot of the proud
not come against
me,
nor the hand of the
wicked drive me away.
12 See how the evildoers lie fallen—
thrown down, not able to rise!

Psalm 36:5

God Offers Loyalty

Your love, O LORD,
reaches to the heavens,
your faithfulness
to the skies.

Psalm 37[b]

Of David.

1 Do not fret because of evil men
or be envious of those who do wrong;
2 for like the grass they will soon wither,
like green plants they will soon die away.

3 Trust in the LORD and do good;
dwell in the land and enjoy safe pasture.
4 Delight yourself in the LORD
and he will give you the desires of your
heart.

5 Commit your way to the LORD;
trust in him and he will do this:
6 He will make your righteousness shine like
the dawn,
the justice of your cause like the
noonday sun.

7 Be still before the LORD and wait patiently
for him;
do not fret when men succeed in their
ways,
when they carry out their wicked
schemes.

8 Refrain from anger and turn from wrath;
do not fret—it leads only to evil.
9 For evil men will be cut off,
but those who hope in the LORD will
inherit the land.

10 A little while, and the
wicked will be no
more;
though you look for
them, they will not
be found.
11 But the meek will inherit
the land
and enjoy great peace.

12 The wicked plot against the
righteous
and gnash their teeth at
them;
13 but the Lord laughs at the wicked,
for he knows their day is coming.

14 The wicked draw the sword
and bend the bow
to bring down the poor and needy,
to slay those whose ways are upright.
15 But their swords will pierce their own
hearts,
and their bows will be broken.

16 Better the little that the righteous have
than the wealth of many wicked;
17 for the power of the wicked will be
broken,
but the LORD upholds the righteous.

18 The days of the blameless are known to the
LORD,
and their inheritance will endure
forever.
19 In times of disaster they will not wither;
in days of famine they will enjoy
plenty.

20 But the wicked will perish:
The LORD's enemies will be like the
beauty of the fields,
they will vanish—vanish like smoke.

21 The wicked borrow and do not repay,
but the righteous give generously;
22 those the LORD blesses will inherit the
land,
but those he curses will be cut off.

[a]7 Or *love, O God! / Men find*; or *love! / Both heavenly beings and men / find* [b]This psalm is an acrostic poem, the stanzas of which begin with the successive letters of the Hebrew alphabet.

It's Not Fair!

Read: Psalm 37:1–11

Psalm 37:1–2
Do not fret because of evil men or be envious of those who do wrong;
for like the grass they will soon wither,
like green plants they will soon die away.

BEING THE VICTIM OF INJUSTICE can test the very roots of our faith. Lori discovered this when her husband, Sam, was accused of animal abuse the winter several of his cattle died in a blizzard. Although autopsies revealed the animals had been well fed, a key defense witness wasn't allowed to testify and important evidence was not submitted. Still, Lori and Sam trusted the jury to sift through the case and find him innocent. Instead, he was convicted and sentenced to five years probation and a large fine. They could have allowed bitterness and anger to cloud their lives, but instead they chose to hang on to the promises of God that David describes in Psalm 37.

Almost everyone at one time or another has experienced a situation where they find themselves saying, "That's not fair!" The psalmist faced such a situation when he saw his enemies prosper while he suffered. David, however, turned his focus to God; he found hope in knowing that God would set things right. What was the path David took to finding peace in the midst of injustice?

♦ "Trust in the LORD." Every event in our lives—good and bad—is filtered through God's sovereign hands. We can trust God to use for our good anything that others intend as evil.

♦ "Do good." Whatever happens, despite the injustices that we suffer, we are to choose the higher path that demonstrates God's Spirit within us.

♦ "Dwell in the land." Though we may feel like running away from conflict or trying to hide from challenges, doing so robs us of experiencing how God can provide a place of rest and safety: "I will lie down and sleep in peace, for you alone, O LORD, make me dwell in safety" (Psalm 4:8).

♦ "Delight yourself in the LORD." Rather than getting depressed about our tough situation, turning our thoughts to God's presence and singing his praise songs will lift our spirits.

♦ "Commit your way to the LORD." We can decide to follow God, regardless of what others do or say.

♦ "Be still before the LORD." We can afford a lifetime of patience, for we know that God will make things right. He is a just God who will one day rule and reign with complete fairness and impartiality.

reflection

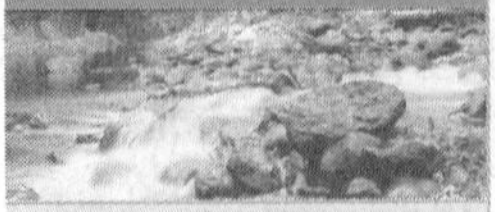

1 When have you suffered from injustice?

2 How did you react to the situation?

3 What do you need to do to learn to trust God more?

RELATED READINGS
Genesis 50:15–21;
Psalm 1:1–6;
Romans 8:18–28

Go to page 679 for your next devotional reading.

23 If the LORD delights in a man's way,
he makes his steps firm;
24 though he stumble, he will not fall,
for the LORD upholds him with his hand.

25 I was young and now I am old,
yet I have never seen the righteous forsaken
or their children begging bread.
26 They are always generous and lend freely;
their children will be blessed.

27 Turn from evil and do good;
then you will dwell in the land forever.
28 For the LORD loves the just
and will not forsake his faithful ones.

They will be protected forever,
but the offspring of the wicked will be cut off;
29 the righteous will inherit the land
and dwell in it forever.

30 The mouth of the righteous man utters wisdom,
and his tongue speaks what is just.
31 The law of his God is in his heart;
his feet do not slip.

32 The wicked lie in wait for the righteous,
seeking their very lives;
33 but the LORD will not leave them in their power
or let them be condemned when brought to trial.

34 Wait for the LORD
and keep his way.
He will exalt you to inherit the land;
when the wicked are cut off, you will see it.

35 I have seen a wicked and ruthless man
flourishing like a green tree in its native soil,
36 but he soon passed away and was no more;
though I looked for him, he could not be found.

37 Consider the blameless, observe the upright;
there is a future[a] for the man of peace.
38 But all sinners will be destroyed;
the future[b] of the wicked will be cut off.

39 The salvation of the righteous comes from the LORD;
he is their stronghold in time of trouble.
40 The LORD helps them and delivers them;
he delivers them from the wicked and saves them,
because they take refuge in him.

Psalm 38

A psalm of David. A petition.

1 O LORD, do not rebuke me in your anger
or discipline me in your wrath.
2 For your arrows have pierced me,
and your hand has come down upon me.
3 Because of your wrath there is no health in my body;
my bones have no soundness because of my sin.
4 My guilt has overwhelmed me
like a burden too heavy to bear.

5 My wounds fester and are loathsome
because of my sinful folly.
6 I am bowed down and brought very low;
all day long I go about mourning.
7 My back is filled with searing pain;
there is no health in my body.
8 I am feeble and utterly crushed;
I groan in anguish of heart.

9 All my longings lie open before you, O Lord;
my sighing is not hidden from you.
10 My heart pounds, my strength fails me;
even the light has gone from my eyes.
11 My friends and companions avoid me
because of my wounds;
my neighbors stay far away.

> **Psalm 38:9**
>
> *God Knows Our Desires*
>
> All my longings lie open before you, O LORD;
> my sighing is not hidden from you.

[a] 37 Or *there will be posterity* [b] 38 Or *posterity*

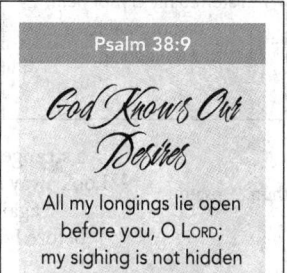

12 Those who seek my life set their traps,
those who would harm me talk of my ruin;
all day long they plot deception.
13 I am like a deaf man, who cannot hear,
like a mute, who cannot open his mouth;
14 I have become like a man who does not hear,
whose mouth can offer no reply.
15 I wait for you, O LORD;
you will answer, O Lord my God.
16 For I said, "Do not let them gloat
or exalt themselves over me when my foot slips."
17 For I am about to fall,
and my pain is ever with me.
18 I confess my iniquity;
I am troubled by my sin.
19 Many are those who are my vigorous enemies;
those who hate me without reason are numerous.
20 Those who repay my good with evil
slander me when I pursue what is good.
21 O LORD, do not forsake me;
be not far from me, O my God.
22 Come quickly to help me,
O Lord my Savior.

Psalm 39:12

God Knows Our Needs

Hear my prayer, O LORD,
listen to my cry for help;
be not deaf to
my weeping.

Psalm 39

For the director of music. For Jeduthun. A psalm of David.

1 I said, "I will watch my ways
and keep my tongue from sin;
I will put a muzzle on my mouth
as long as the wicked are in my presence."
2 But when I was silent and still,
not even saying anything good,
my anguish increased.
3 My heart grew hot within me,
and as I meditated, the fire burned;
then I spoke with my tongue:
4 "Show me, O LORD, my life's end
and the number of my days;
let me know how fleeting is my life.
5 You have made my days a mere handbreadth;
the span of my years is as nothing before you.
Each man's life is but a breath. *Selah*
6 Man is a mere phantom as he goes to and fro:
He bustles about, but only in vain;
he heaps up wealth, not knowing who will get it.

7 "But now, Lord, what do I look for?
My hope is in you.
8 Save me from all my transgressions;
do not make me the scorn of fools.
9 I was silent; I would not open my mouth,
for you are the one who has done this.
10 Remove your scourge from me;
I am overcome by the blow of your hand.
11 You rebuke and discipline men for their sin;
you consume their wealth like a moth—
each man is but a breath. *Selah*

12 "Hear my prayer, O LORD,
listen to my cry for help;
be not deaf to my weeping.
For I dwell with you as an alien,
a stranger, as all my fathers were.
13 Look away from me, that I may rejoice again
before I depart and am no more."

Psalm 40

For the director of music. Of David. A psalm.

1 I waited patiently for the LORD;
he turned to me and heard my cry.
2 He lifted me out of the slimy pit,
out of the mud and mire;
he set my feet on a rock
and gave me a firm place to stand.
3 He put a new song in my mouth,
a hymn of praise to our God.

A Second Chance at Love

ABIGAIL

"HOW DID A SMART WOMAN like you end up with a man like Nabal?"

It wasn't the first time Abigail had heard a question like that. Even when people didn't have the nerve to ask it outright, Abigail knew what they were thinking. And she agreed. A brash, outspoken nitwit, Nabal was not exactly a perfect match for her.

Where he was quick to anger, she thought of herself as more of a slow boil. Whereas he reacted, she preferred to patiently contemplate her next move. No one ever had to guess what Nabal was thinking. His mouth ran ahead of his thoughts on a regular basis. Not Abigail. She liked choosing her words carefully—which is why it was so frustrating that his indiscretions always landed both of them in trouble.

"I don't know how you remain so patient," said her friends, looking at her with pity.

"Couldn't you just kill him when he acts like that?" inquired others sarcastically.

Even when Nabal insulted David, and she could have allowed him to suffer for his actions, she wouldn't let herself do it. She couldn't, even though she knew many women would have been happy to sit back and watch their husbands reap the consequences of their actions. But there were too many other issues at stake, too many other people whose lives depended on her husband. She gathered up her supplies and rushed to her donkey.

It wasn't the first time she'd had to clean up after him—something an outspoken neighbor rudely emphasized as Abigail rushed to meet David with a peace offering to cover Nabal's latest offense. "And it won't be the *last* time either . . ." she added as Abigail made her way down the pathway.

But it was.

—Prayer—

Help me to be faithful, Lord, wherever you've called me to be.

May my lord pay no attention to that wicked man Nabal. He is just like his name—his name is Fool, and folly goes with him.

1 Samuel 25:25

ASSIGNED READING:

1 Samuel 25:1–44

Weekend

Go to page 682 for your next devotional reading.

Many will see and fear
and put their trust in the LORD.

4 Blessed is the man
who makes the LORD his trust,
who does not look to the proud,
to those who turn aside to false gods.[a]
5 Many, O LORD my God,
are the wonders you have done.
The things you planned for us
no one can recount to you;
were I to speak and tell of them,
they would be too many to declare.

6 Sacrifice and offering you did not desire,
but my ears you have pierced[b,c];
burnt offerings and sin offerings
you did not require.
7 Then I said, "Here I am, I have come—
it is written about me in the scroll.[d]
8 I desire to do your will, O my God;
your law is within my heart."

9 I proclaim righteousness in the great
assembly;
I do not seal my lips,
as you know, O LORD.
10 I do not hide your righteousness in my
heart;
I speak of your faithfulness and
salvation.
I do not conceal your love and your truth
from the great assembly.

11 Do not withhold your mercy from me,
O LORD;
may your love and your truth always
protect me.
12 For troubles without number surround me;
my sins have overtaken me, and I
cannot see.
They are more than the hairs of my head,
and my heart fails within me.

13 Be pleased, O LORD, to save me;
O LORD, come quickly to help me.
14 May all who seek to take my life
be put to shame and confusion;
may all who desire my ruin
be turned back in disgrace.
15 May those who say to me, "Aha! Aha!"
be appalled at their own shame.
16 But may all who seek you
rejoice and be glad in you;
may those who love your salvation always
say,
"The LORD be exalted!"

17 Yet I am poor and needy;
may the Lord think of me.
You are my help and my deliverer;
O my God, do not delay.

Psalm 41

For the director of music. A psalm of David.

1 Blessed is he who has regard for the weak;
the LORD delivers him in times of
trouble.
2 The LORD will protect him and preserve
his life;
he will bless him in the land
and not surrender him to the desire of
his foes.
3 The LORD will sustain him on his sickbed
and restore him from his bed of illness.

4 I said, "O LORD, have mercy on me;
heal me, for I have sinned against you."
5 My enemies say of me in malice,
"When will he die and his name
perish?"
6 Whenever one comes to see me,
he speaks falsely, while his heart gathers
slander;
then he goes out and spreads it abroad.

7 All my enemies whisper together against
me;
they imagine the worst for me, saying,
8 "A vile disease has beset him;
he will never get up from the place
where he lies."
9 Even my close friend, whom I trusted,
he who shared my bread,
has lifted up his heel against me.

10 But you, O LORD, have mercy on me;
raise me up, that I may repay them.
11 I know that you are pleased with me,
for my enemy does not triumph over me.
12 In my integrity you uphold me
and set me in your presence forever.

[a]4 Or *to falsehood* [b]6 Hebrew; Septuagint *but a body you have prepared for me* (see also Symmachus and Theodotion) [c]6 Or *opened*
[d]7 Or *come / with the scroll written for me*

13 Praise be to the LORD, the God of Israel,
from everlasting to everlasting.
Amen and Amen.

BOOK II
Psalms 42–72

Psalm 42[a]
For the director of music.
A *maskil*[b] of the Sons of Korah.

1 As the deer pants for streams of water,
so my soul pants for you, O God.
2 My soul thirsts for God, for the living God.
When can I go and meet
with God?
3 My tears have been my food
day and night,
while men say to me all day
long,
"Where is your God?"
4 These things I remember
as I pour out my soul:
how I used to go with the
multitude,
leading the procession to
the house of God,
with shouts of joy and
thanksgiving
among the festive
throng.

5 Why are you downcast, O my soul?
Why so disturbed within me?
Put your hope in God,
for I will yet praise him,
my Savior and 6 my God.

My[c] soul is downcast within me;
therefore I will remember you
from the land of the Jordan,
the heights of Hermon—from Mount
Mizar.
7 Deep calls to deep
in the roar of your waterfalls;
all your waves and breakers
have swept over me.

8 By day the LORD directs his love,
at night his song is with me—
a prayer to the God of my life.

9 I say to God my Rock,
"Why have you forgotten me?
Why must I go about mourning,
oppressed by the enemy?"
10 My bones suffer mortal agony
as my foes taunt me,
saying to me all day long,
"Where is your God?"

11 Why are you downcast, O my soul?
Why so disturbed within me?
Put your hope in God,
for I will yet praise him,
my Savior and my God.

Psalm 43[a]
1 Vindicate me, O God,
and plead my cause
against an ungodly
nation;
rescue me from deceitful
and wicked men.
2 You are God my
stronghold.
Why have you rejected
me?
Why must I go about
mourning,
oppressed by the enemy?
3 Send forth your light and
your truth,
let them guide me;
let them bring me to your holy mountain,
to the place where you dwell.
4 Then will I go to the altar of God,
to God, my joy and my delight.
I will praise you with the harp,
O God, my God.

5 Why are you downcast, O my soul?
Why so disturbed within me?
Put your hope in God,
for I will yet praise him,
my Savior and my God.

Psalm 44
For the director of music. Of the Sons of Korah.
A *maskil.*[b]

1 We have heard with our ears, O God;
our fathers have told us

Psalm 43:3

God Brings Us to Him

Send forth your light
and your truth,
let them guide me;
let them bring me to
your holy mountain,
to the place where
you dwell.

[a]In many Hebrew manuscripts Psalms 42 and 43 constitute one psalm. [b]Title: Probably a literary or musical term
5,6 A few Hebrew manuscripts, Septuagint and Syriac; most Hebrew manuscripts *praise him for his saving help. / [6] O my God, my*

From Despair to Hope

Read: Psalm 42:1–11

Psalm 42:5

Why are you downcast, O my soul? Why so disturbed within me? Put your hope in God, for I will yet praise him, my Savior and my God.

THROUGHOUT THE DAY, many thoughts flow through our minds—from what we will cook for dinner to wondering if our friend's struggling marriage will survive. In the midst of our thinking, an undercurrent of despair can creep in while we watch the nightly news, hear of a cancer diagnosis, sort out a misunderstanding or deal with whatever we're facing that day.

Exiled north to Jordan and overflowing with a longing to return to Jerusalem, the psalmist voiced his deep sadness. Rather than denying or minimizing his pain, he clearly identified his sorrow and proclaimed his thirst for God.

Then what? The psalmist spoke to his soul! Was he mad? Did he have a personality disorder? No! He practiced the secret to overcoming hopelessness—the hopelessness that can trickle into our hearts and minds until we find ourselves in the rushing current, tumbling toward a waterfall of despair. Three times in Psalms 42 and 43, the psalmist admonishes his soul to "hope in God, for I will yet praise him!"

The psalmist encouraged his soul to praise God—in other words, to acknowledge, affirm and adore God's character, even when he was feeling downcast in spirit or disturbed in heart. Our souls need similar encouragement. When we choose to dwell upon God's character, we always have something to praise him about: his loving-kindness, goodness, power, faithfulness and mercy. If we want to bolster our souls with hope, we can start by filling our mouths with praise. When we choose to dwell on God's light and truth, our souls can overflow with the comfort of being guided by God (see Psalm 43:3). When we choose to live close to God's heart, we overflow with delight and joy (see verse 4).

If you are submerged in pain, sorrow, despair or confusion, maybe you need to give your soul a good talking to. What will you say?

reflection

1 What thoughts are threatening to overflow and leave you feeling hopeless?

2 What words does your soul need to hear right now?

3 What are some specific reasons why you can hope in God? Spend some time meditating on God's loving-kindness, goodness, power, faithfulness and mercy. Practice sitting quietly in his presence.

RELATED READINGS

Psalm 27:13–14; 43:1–5; 84:1–12; Hebrews 6:13–20

Go to page 688 for your next devotional reading.

what you did in their days,
in days long ago.
2 With your hand you drove out the nations
and planted our fathers;
you crushed the peoples
and made our fathers flourish.
3 It was not by their sword that they won the land,
nor did their arm bring them victory;
it was your right hand, your arm,
and the light of your face, for you loved them.

4 You are my King and my God,
who decrees[a] victories for Jacob.
5 Through you we push back our enemies;
through your name we trample our foes.
6 I do not trust in my bow,
my sword does not bring me victory;
7 but you give us victory over our enemies,
you put our adversaries to shame.
8 In God we make our boast all day long,
and we will praise your name
forever. *Selah*

9 But now you have rejected and humbled us;
you no longer go out with our armies.
10 You made us retreat before the enemy,
and our adversaries have plundered us.
11 You gave us up to be devoured like sheep
and have scattered us among the nations.
12 You sold your people for a pittance,
gaining nothing from their sale.

13 You have made us a reproach to our neighbors,
the scorn and derision of those around us.
14 You have made us a byword among the nations;
the peoples shake their heads at us.
15 My disgrace is before me all day long,
and my face is covered with shame
16 at the taunts of those who reproach and revile me,
because of the enemy, who is bent on revenge.

17 All this happened to us,
though we had not forgotten you
or been false to your covenant.
18 Our hearts had not turned back;
our feet had not strayed from your path.
19 But you crushed us and made us a haunt for jackals
and covered us over with deep darkness.

20 If we had forgotten the name of our God
or spread out our hands to a foreign god,
21 would not God have discovered it,
since he knows the secrets of the heart?
22 Yet for your sake we face death all day long;
we are considered as sheep to be slaughtered.

23 Awake, O Lord! Why do you sleep?
Rouse yourself! Do not reject us forever.
24 Why do you hide your face
and forget our misery and oppression?

25 We are brought down to the dust;
our bodies cling to the ground.
26 Rise up and help us;
redeem us because of your unfailing love.

Psalm 45

For the director of music. To ⌊the tune of⌋ "Lilies." Of the Sons of Korah. A *maskil*.[b] A wedding song.

1 My heart is stirred by a noble theme
as I recite my verses for the king;
my tongue is the pen of a skillful writer.

2 You are the most excellent of men
and your lips have been anointed with grace,
since God has blessed you forever.
3 Gird your sword upon your side, O mighty one;
clothe yourself with splendor and majesty.
4 In your majesty ride forth victoriously
in behalf of truth, humility and righteousness;
let your right hand display awesome deeds.
5 Let your sharp arrows pierce the hearts of the king's enemies;
let the nations fall beneath your feet.

[a] 4 Septuagint, Aquila and Syriac; Hebrew *King, O God; / command* [b] Title: Probably a literary or musical term

6 Your throne, O God, will last for ever and ever;
a scepter of justice will be the scepter of your kingdom.
7 You love righteousness and hate wickedness;
therefore God, your God, has set you above your companions
by anointing you with the oil of joy.
8 All your robes are fragrant with myrrh and aloes and cassia;
from palaces adorned with ivory
the music of the strings makes you glad.
9 Daughters of kings are among your honored women;
at your right hand is the royal bride in gold of Ophir.
10 Listen, O daughter, consider and give ear:
Forget your people and your father's house.
11 The king is enthralled by your beauty;
honor him, for he is your lord.
12 The Daughter of Tyre will come with a gift,[a]
men of wealth will seek your favor.

13 All glorious is the princess within ⌊her chamber⌋;
her gown is interwoven with gold.
14 In embroidered garments she is led to the king;
her virgin companions follow her
and are brought to you.
15 They are led in with joy and gladness;
they enter the palace of the king.

16 Your sons will take the place of your fathers;
you will make them princes throughout the land.
17 I will perpetuate your memory through all generations;
therefore the nations will praise you for ever and ever.

Psalm 46

For the director of music. Of the Sons of Korah. According to *alamoth*.[b] A song.

1 God is our refuge and strength,
an ever-present help in trouble.
2 Therefore we will not fear, though the earth give way
and the mountains fall into the heart of the sea,
3 though its waters roar and foam
and the mountains quake with their surging. *Selah*

Psalm 46:1

God Is Our Strength

God is our refuge and strength, an ever-present help in trouble.

4 There is a river whose streams make glad the city of God,
the holy place where the Most High dwells.
5 God is within her, she will not fall;
God will help her at break of day.
6 Nations are in uproar, kingdoms fall;
he lifts his voice, the earth melts.

7 The LORD Almighty is with us;
the God of Jacob is our fortress. *Selah*

8 Come and see the works of the LORD,
the desolations he has brought on the earth.
9 He makes wars cease to the ends of the earth;
he breaks the bow and shatters the spear,
he burns the shields[c] with fire.
10 "Be still, and know that I am God;
I will be exalted among the nations,
I will be exalted in the earth."

11 The LORD Almighty is with us;
the God of Jacob is our fortress. *Selah*

Psalm 47

For the director of music. Of the Sons of Korah. A psalm.

1 Clap your hands, all you nations;
shout to God with cries of joy.
2 How awesome is the LORD Most High,

[a] 12 Or *A Tyrian robe is among the gifts* [b] Title: Probably a musical term [c] 9 Or *chariots*

the great King over all the earth!
3 He subdued nations under us,
peoples under our feet.
4 He chose our inheritance for us,
the pride of Jacob, whom he loved. *Selah*
5 God has ascended amid shouts of joy,
the LORD amid the sounding of trumpets.
6 Sing praises to God, sing praises;
sing praises to our King, sing praises.

7 For God is the King of all the earth;
sing to him a psalm[a] of praise.
8 God reigns over the nations;
God is seated on his holy throne.
9 The nobles of the nations assemble
as the people of the God of Abraham,
for the kings[b] of the earth belong to God;
he is greatly exalted.

Psalm 48

A song. A psalm of the Sons of Korah.

1 Great is the LORD, and most worthy of praise,
in the city of our God, his holy mountain.
2 It is beautiful in its loftiness,
the joy of the whole earth.
Like the utmost heights of Zaphon[c] is Mount Zion,
the[d] city of the Great King.
3 God is in her citadels;
he has shown himself to be her fortress.

4 When the kings joined forces,
when they advanced together,
5 they saw ⌊her⌋ and were astounded;
they fled in terror.
6 Trembling seized them there,
pain like that of a woman in labor.
7 You destroyed them like ships of Tarshish
shattered by an east wind.

8 As we have heard,
so have we seen
in the city of the LORD Almighty,
in the city of our God:
God makes her secure forever. *Selah*
9 Within your temple, O God,
we meditate on your unfailing love.
10 Like your name, O God,
your praise reaches to the ends of the earth;
your right hand is filled with righteousness.
11 Mount Zion rejoices,
the villages of Judah are glad
because of your judgments.

12 Walk about Zion, go around her,
count her towers,
13 consider well her ramparts,
view her citadels,
that you may tell of them to the next generation.
14 For this God is our God for ever and ever;
he will be our guide even to the end.

Psalm 48:14

God Provides Guidance

For this God is our God
for ever and ever;
he will be our guide
even to the end.

Psalm 49

For the director of music. Of the Sons of Korah. A psalm.

1 Hear this, all you peoples;
listen, all who live in this world,
2 both low and high,
rich and poor alike:
3 My mouth will speak words of wisdom;
the utterance from my heart will give understanding.
4 I will turn my ear to a proverb;
with the harp I will expound my riddle:

5 Why should I fear when evil days come,
when wicked deceivers surround me—
6 those who trust in their wealth
and boast of their great riches?
7 No man can redeem the life of another
or give to God a ransom for him—
8 the ransom for a life is costly,

[a]7 Or *a maskil* (probably a literary or musical term) [b]9 Or *shields* [c]2 *Zaphon* can refer to a sacred mountain or the direction north.
[d]2 Or *earth, / Mount Zion, on the northern side / of the*

no payment is ever enough—
9 that he should live on forever
and not see decay.

10 For all can see that wise men die;
the foolish and the senseless alike perish
and leave their wealth to others.
11 Their tombs will remain their houses[a]
forever,
their dwellings for endless generations,
though they had[b] named lands after
themselves.

12 But man, despite his riches, does not
endure;
he is[c] like the beasts that perish.

13 This is the fate of those who trust in
themselves,
and of their followers, who approve their
sayings. *Selah*
14 Like sheep they are destined for the grave,[d]
and death will feed on them.
The upright will rule over them in the
morning;
their forms will decay in the grave,[d]
far from their princely mansions.
15 But God will redeem my life[e] from the
grave;
he will surely take me to himself. *Selah*

16 Do not be overawed when a man grows
rich,
when the splendor of his house increases;
17 for he will take nothing with him when he
dies,
his splendor will not descend with him.
18 Though while he lived he counted himself
blessed—
and men praise you when you prosper—
19 he will join the generation of his fathers,
who will never see the light ⌞of life⌟.

20 A man who has riches without
understanding
is like the beasts that perish.

Psalm 50

A psalm of Asaph.

1 The Mighty One, God, the LORD,
speaks and summons the earth
from the rising of the sun to the place
where it sets.
2 From Zion, perfect in beauty,
God shines forth.
3 Our God comes and will not be silent;
a fire devours before him,
and around him a tempest rages.
4 He summons the heavens above,
and the earth, that he may judge his
people:
5 "Gather to me my consecrated ones,
who made a covenant with me by
sacrifice."
6 And the heavens proclaim his
righteousness,
for God himself is judge. *Selah*

7 "Hear, O my people, and I will speak,
O Israel, and I will testify against you:
I am God, your God.
8 I do not rebuke you for your sacrifices
or your burnt offerings, which are ever
before me.
9 I have no need of a bull from your stall
or of goats from your pens,
10 for every animal of the forest is mine,
and the cattle on a thousand hills.
11 I know every bird in the mountains,
and the creatures of the field are mine.
12 If I were hungry I would not tell you,
for the world is mine, and all that is in it.
13 Do I eat the flesh of bulls
or drink the blood of goats?
14 Sacrifice thank offerings to God,
fulfill your vows to the Most High,
15 and call upon me in the day of trouble;
I will deliver you, and you will honor
me."

16 But to the wicked, God says:
"What right have you to recite my laws
or take my covenant on your lips?
17 You hate my instruction
and cast my words behind you.
18 When you see a thief, you join with him;
you throw in your lot with adulterers.
19 You use your mouth for evil
and harness your tongue to deceit.
20 You speak continually against your brother

[a] 11 Septuagint and Syriac; Hebrew *In their thoughts their houses will remain* [b] 11 Or / *for they have* [c] 12 Hebrew; Septuagint and Syriac read verse 12 the same as verse 20. [d] 14 Hebrew *Sheol*; also in verse 15 [e] 15 Or *soul*

and slander your own mother's son.
21 These things you have done and I kept silent;
you thought I was altogether[a] like you.
But I will rebuke you
and accuse you to your face.

22 "Consider this, you who forget God,
or I will tear you to pieces, with none to rescue:
23 He who sacrifices thank offerings honors me,
and he prepares the way
so that I may show him[b] the salvation of God."

Psalm 51

For the director of music. A psalm of David. When the prophet Nathan came to him after David had committed adultery with Bathsheba.

1 Have mercy on me, O God,
according to your unfailing love;
according to your great compassion
blot out my transgressions.
2 Wash away all my iniquity
and cleanse me from my sin.

3 For I know my transgressions,
and my sin is always before me.
4 Against you, you only, have I sinned
and done what is evil in your sight,
so that you are proved right when you speak
and justified when you judge.
5 Surely I was sinful at birth,
sinful from the time my mother conceived me.
6 Surely you desire truth in the inner parts[c];
you teach[d] me wisdom in the inmost place.

7 Cleanse me with hyssop, and I will be clean;
wash me, and I will be whiter than snow.
8 Let me hear joy and gladness;
let the bones you have crushed rejoice.
9 Hide your face from my sins
and blot out all my iniquity.

10 Create in me a pure heart, O God,
and renew a steadfast spirit within me.
11 Do not cast me from your presence
or take your Holy Spirit from me.
12 Restore to me the joy of your salvation
and grant me a willing spirit, to sustain me.

13 Then I will teach transgressors your ways,
and sinners will turn back to you.
14 Save me from bloodguilt, O God,
the God who saves me,
and my tongue will sing of your righteousness.
15 O Lord, open my lips,
and my mouth will declare your praise.
16 You do not delight in sacrifice, or I would bring it;
you do not take pleasure in burnt offerings.
17 The sacrifices of God are[e] a broken spirit;
a broken and contrite heart,
O God, you will not despise.

18 In your good pleasure make Zion prosper;
build up the walls of Jerusalem.
19 Then there will be righteous sacrifices,
whole burnt offerings to delight you;
then bulls will be offered on your altar.

Psalm 52

For the director of music. A *maskil*[f] of David. When Doeg the Edomite had gone to Saul and told him: "David has gone to the house of Ahimelech."

1 Why do you boast of evil, you mighty man?
Why do you boast all day long,
you who are a disgrace in the eyes of God?
2 Your tongue plots destruction;
it is like a sharpened razor,
you who practice deceit.
3 You love evil rather than good,
falsehood rather than speaking the truth. *Selah*
4 You love every harmful word,
O you deceitful tongue!

5 Surely God will bring you down to everlasting ruin:
He will snatch you up and tear you from your tent;

[a]21 Or *thought the 'I AM' was* [b]23 Or *and to him who considers his way / I will show* [c]6 The meaning of the Hebrew for this phrase is uncertain. [d]6 Or *you desired . . . ; / you taught* [e]17 Or *My sacrifice, O God, is* [f]Title: Probably a literary or musical term

O God, Have Mercy

Read: Psalm 51:1–19

Psalm 51:1

Have mercy on me, O God, according to your unfailing love; according to your great compassion blot out my transgressions.

reflection

1 What excuses have you recently made to God, others and yourself for your sin?

2 How have you renamed your sin to make it sound better?

3 How does it comfort you that God doesn't forgive excuses but that he does forgive sin?

RELATED READINGS

2 Samuel 11:1—12:25; Psalm 103:8–18; Romans 3:21–24

"If we cover our sin, God will expose it. If we expose our sin, God will cover it."

Unknown

WE EXCUSE OURSELVES so easily. I was tired. He started it. That's the way I was raised. Everyone else does it. The woman you put here with me—she gave me some fruit from the tree, and I ate it. It's his fault. It's her fault. Maybe it's even God's fault. But surely it's not my fault!

O God, have mercy.

Until we stop making excuses, we aren't ready to be forgiven. Whether we think we're above the law (as David apparently thought when he chose to send for the married Bathsheba) or that our action is okay if others started it (as Adam thought in the garden) or that it isn't really worth God's notice (as Ananias and Sapphira may have thought when they lied about their offering to the church), our excuses cover us as poorly as Adam and Eve's fig leaves in the Garden of Eden.

Sometimes we change the name to cover our sin: It's not gossip; it's sharing. It's not coveting; it's admiring. It's not lying; it's explaining. David even planned to have his lover's husband killed in war to make the object of his lust a widow, thinking that would redefine adultery. But God didn't buy it.

O God, have mercy.

God doesn't forgive excuses. But God *does* forgive sin. He's waiting for us to call it what he calls it: sin. When we acknowledge our sin and repent, God removes sin as far as the east is from the west. Picture a globe in your mind. No matter how far you go, you'll never discover west by traveling east. That's how far God is willing to cleanse, forgive and make us new.

When the prophet Nathan confronted King David about his sin, David's repentance was deep and real. In Psalm 51 he put his feelings into words. He cried out for God's mercy, asking God to cleanse him of his sin, to teach him wisdom and to heal his conscience and his emotions. David's song of confession and restoration can give us courage to confess our wrongs, no matter how great our wrongdoings seem to us and no matter how far away from God we feel.

Repentance frees us. Honesty renews us. God's mercy cleanses us.

Go to page 692 for your next devotional reading.

he will uproot you from the land of the
living. *Selah*
6 The righteous will see and fear;
they will laugh at him, saying,
7 "Here now is the man
who did not make God his stronghold
but trusted in his great wealth
and grew strong by destroying others!"

8 But I am like an olive tree
flourishing in the house of God;
I trust in God's unfailing love
for ever and ever.
9 I will praise you forever for what you have
done;
in your name I will hope, for your name
is good.
I will praise you in the presence of your
saints.

Psalm 53

For the director of music. According to *mahalath*.[a]
A *maskil*[b] of David.

1 The fool says in his heart,
"There is no God."
They are corrupt, and their
ways are vile;
there is no one who does
good.

2 God looks down from
heaven
on the sons of men
to see if there are any who
understand,
any who seek God.
3 Everyone has turned away,
they have together
become corrupt;
there is no one who does
good,
not even one.

4 Will the evildoers never learn—
those who devour my people as men eat
bread
and who do not call on God?
5 There they were, overwhelmed with dread,
where there was nothing to dread.
God scattered the bones of those who
attacked you;
you put them to shame, for God
despised them.

6 Oh, that salvation for Israel would come
out of Zion!
When God restores the fortunes of his
people,
let Jacob rejoice and Israel be glad!

Psalm 54

For the director of music. With stringed instruments. A *maskil*[b] of David. When the Ziphites had gone to Saul and said, "Is not David hiding among us?"

1 Save me, O God, by your name;
vindicate me by your might.
2 Hear my prayer, O God;
listen to the words of my mouth.

3 Strangers are attacking me;
ruthless men seek my life—
men without regard for God. *Selah*

4 Surely God is my help;
the Lord is the one who sustains me.

5 Let evil recoil on those who
slander me;
in your faithfulness
destroy them.

6 I will sacrifice a freewill
offering to you;
I will praise your name,
O LORD,
for it is good.
7 For he has delivered
me from all my
troubles,
and my eyes have looked
in triumph on my
foes.

> **Psalm 53:1**
>
> *God Can Be Known*
>
> The fool says in his heart,
> "There is no God."
> They are corrupt, and
> their ways are vile;
> there is no one who
> does good.

Psalm 55

For the director of music. With stringed instruments. A *maskil*[b] of David.

1 Listen to my prayer, O God,
do not ignore my plea;
2 hear me and answer me.
My thoughts trouble me and I am
distraught
3 at the voice of the enemy,
at the stares of the wicked;

[a]Title: Probably a musical term [b]Title: Probably a literary or musical term

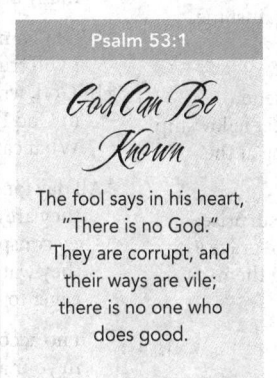

for they bring down suffering upon me
and revile me in their anger.

4 My heart is in anguish within me;
the terrors of death assail me.
5 Fear and trembling have beset me;
horror has overwhelmed me.
6 I said, "Oh, that I had the wings of a dove!
I would fly away and be at rest—
7 I would flee far away
and stay in the desert; *Selah*
8 I would hurry to my place of shelter,
far from the tempest and storm."

9 Confuse the wicked, O Lord, confound their speech,
for I see violence and strife in the city.
10 Day and night they prowl about on its walls;
malice and abuse are within it.
11 Destructive forces are at work in the city;
threats and lies never leave its streets.

12 If an enemy were insulting me,
I could endure it;
if a foe were raising himself against me,
I could hide from him.
13 But it is you, a man like myself,
my companion, my close friend,
14 with whom I once enjoyed sweet fellowship
as we walked with the throng at the house of God.

15 Let death take my enemies by surprise;
let them go down alive to the grave,[a]
for evil finds lodging among them.

16 But I call to God,
and the LORD saves me.
17 Evening, morning and noon
I cry out in distress,
and he hears my voice.
18 He ransoms me unharmed
from the battle waged against me,
even though many oppose me.
19 God, who is enthroned forever,
will hear them and afflict them— *Selah*
men who never change their ways
and have no fear of God.

20 My companion attacks his friends;
he violates his covenant.
21 His speech is smooth as butter,
yet war is in his heart;
his words are more soothing than oil,
yet they are drawn swords.

22 Cast your cares on the LORD
and he will sustain you;
he will never let the righteous fall.
23 But you, O God, will bring down the wicked
into the pit of corruption;
bloodthirsty and deceitful men
will not live out half their days.

But as for me, I trust in you.

Psalm 56

For the director of music. To ⌊the tune of⌋ "A Dove on Distant Oaks." Of David. A *miktam.*[b] When the Philistines had seized him in Gath.

1 Be merciful to me, O God, for men hotly pursue me;
all day long they press their attack.
2 My slanderers pursue me all day long;
many are attacking me in their pride.

3 When I am afraid,
I will trust in you.
4 In God, whose word I praise,
in God I trust; I will not be afraid.
What can mortal man do to me?

5 All day long they twist my words;
they are always plotting to harm me.
6 They conspire, they lurk,
they watch my steps,
eager to take my life.
7 On no account let them escape;
in your anger, O God, bring down the nations.
8 Record my lament;
list my tears on your scroll[c]—
are they not in your record?

9 Then my enemies will turn back
when I call for help.
By this I will know that God is for me.
10 In God, whose word I praise,
in the LORD, whose word I praise—
11 in God I trust; I will not be afraid.
What can man do to me?

[a]15 Hebrew *Sheol* [b]Title: Probably a literary or musical term [c]8 Or / *put my tears in your wineskin*

12 I am under vows to you, O God;
I will present my thank offerings to you.
13 For you have delivered me[a] from death
and my feet from stumbling,
that I may walk before God
in the light of life.[b]

Psalm 57

For the director of music. ⌊To the tune of⌋ "Do Not Destroy." Of David. A *miktam*.[c] When he had fled from Saul into the cave.

1 Have mercy on me, O God, have mercy on me,
for in you my soul takes refuge.
I will take refuge in the shadow of your wings
until the disaster has passed.

2 I cry out to God Most High,
to God, who fulfills ⌊his purpose⌋ for me.
3 He sends from heaven and saves me,
rebuking those who hotly pursue me;
Selah
God sends his love and his faithfulness.

4 I am in the midst of lions;
I lie among ravenous beasts—
men whose teeth are spears and arrows,
whose tongues are sharp swords.
5 Be exalted, O God, above the heavens;
let your glory be over all the earth.

6 They spread a net for my feet—
I was bowed down in distress.
They dug a pit in my path—
but they have fallen into it themselves.
Selah

7 My heart is steadfast, O God,
my heart is steadfast;
I will sing and make music.
8 Awake, my soul!
Awake, harp and lyre!
I will awaken the dawn.
9 I will praise you, O Lord, among the nations;
I will sing of you among the peoples.
10 For great is your love, reaching to the heavens;
your faithfulness reaches to the skies.

11 Be exalted, O God, above the heavens;
let your glory be over all the earth.

Psalm 57:3

God Shelters Us

He sends from heaven
and saves me,
rebuking those who
hotly pursue me;
God sends his love and
his faithfulness.

Psalm 58

For the director of music. ⌊To the tune of⌋ "Do Not Destroy." Of David. A *miktam*.[c]

1 Do you rulers indeed speak justly?
Do you judge uprightly among men?
2 No, in your heart you devise injustice,
and your hands mete out violence on the earth.
3 Even from birth the wicked go astray;
from the womb they are wayward and speak lies.
4 Their venom is like the venom of a snake,
like that of a cobra that has stopped its ears,
5 that will not heed the tune of the charmer,
however skillful the enchanter may be.

6 Break the teeth in their mouths, O God;
tear out, O LORD, the fangs of the lions!
7 Let them vanish like water that flows away;
when they draw the bow, let their arrows be blunted.
8 Like a slug melting away as it moves along,
like a stillborn child, may they not see the sun.

9 Before your pots can feel ⌊the heat of⌋ the thorns—
whether they be green or dry—the wicked will be swept away.[d]
10 The righteous will be glad when they are avenged,

[a]13 Or *my soul* [b]13 Or *the land of the living* [c]Title: Probably a literary or musical term [d]9 The meaning of the Hebrew for this verse is uncertain.

Light in a Dark Cave

Psalm 57:2–3

I cry out to God Most High, to God, who fulfills his purpose for me. He sends from heaven and saves me, rebuking those who hotly pursue me; God sends his love and his faithfulness.

reflection

1 Have you ever found yourself in a dark cave? Describe it.

2 What can you learn from David regarding worshiping God even in the midst of hard times? Spend some time working through the four steps from worry to worship found in Psalm 57. Write them down, personalizing them if you can.

3 Read Psalm 57 aloud as a praise song to God.

RELATED READINGS

1 Samuel 24:1–22; Luke 1:69–75; Acts 16:22–34; 1 Peter 3:13–16

Read: Psalm 57:1–11

DAVID FOUND HIMSELF in a lonely, dark cave at En Gedi. He was hiding from King Saul, in fear for his life and pursued by thousands of his own countrymen.

How did David climb out from his soul's dark hiding place? We find some clues in Psalm 57, penned while David lived in the cave. This page from David's songbook reflects the roller coaster of emotions he experienced. You might recognize some of his feelings: fear turned to faith, panic rolled toward hope, terror shifted to trust, dependence circled to dread. Up and down, around and around, back and forth . . . but David always returned to God—worshiping him even in a dark cave.

In his grotto hiding place, David cried out to God for help, "Have mercy on me, O God" (verse 1). What a great place to start when we're in a dark place. Then, he wrote what he knew to be true about his God, saying, "God sends his love and his faithfulness" (verse 3). Recounting God's character traits helps to take our focus off ourselves and place our focus rightly on him. Next, David verbalized his fears, saying, "I am in the midst of lions" (verse 4). Naming our fears can make our enemies seem smaller in the context of the Creator of the universe. Finally, he relinquished his circumstances to God's glory, saying, "Be exalted, O God, above the heavens" (verse 5). Like Jesus during his dark night in the garden of Gethsemane, David sought God's will above his own. This progression toward trusting God lit David's way from a place of worry to one of worship; he chose to hide in the shadow of God's wings, whether he lived in a cave or in a palace. When Saul came to En Gedi and entered the cave, David had the courage to do the right thing: He spared the life of the king God had anointed, and he sought reconciliation with Saul, even though it might mean death for him.

If you're in the dark, follow David's steps and walk toward the light: (1) Cry out for mercy. (2) Remember God's love and faithfulness. (3) Verbalize your fears. (4) Pray that God's will be accomplished in your life for his glory. Then choose to worship God wherever you may be.

Go to page 701 for your next devotional reading.

when they bathe their feet in the blood
of the wicked.
11 Then men will say,
"Surely the righteous still are rewarded;
surely there is a God who
judges the earth."

Psalm 59

For the director of music. ⌊To the tune of⌋ "Do Not Destroy." Of David. A *miktam*.[a] When Saul had sent men to watch David's house in order to kill him.

1 Deliver me from my
enemies, O God;
protect me from those
who rise up against
me.
2 Deliver me from evildoers
and save me from
bloodthirsty men.

3 See how they lie in wait for me!
Fierce men conspire against me
for no offense or sin of mine, O LORD.
4 I have done no wrong, yet they are ready to
attack me.
Arise to help me; look on my plight!
5 O LORD God Almighty, the God of Israel,
rouse yourself to punish all the nations;
show no mercy to wicked traitors. *Selah*

6 They return at evening,
snarling like dogs,
and prowl about the city.
7 See what they spew from their mouths—
they spew out swords from their lips,
and they say, "Who can hear us?"
8 But you, O LORD, laugh at them;
you scoff at all those nations.

9 O my Strength, I watch for you;
you, O God, are my fortress, 10 my
loving God.

God will go before me
and will let me gloat over those who
slander me.
11 But do not kill them, O Lord our shield,[b]
or my people will forget.
In your might make them wander about,
and bring them down.
12 For the sins of their mouths,
for the words of their lips,
let them be caught in their pride.
For the curses and lies they
utter,
13 consume them in wrath,
consume them till they
are no more.
Then it will be known
to the ends of the
earth
that God rules over
Jacob. *Selah*

14 They return at evening,
snarling like dogs,
and prowl about the city.
15 They wander about for food
and howl if not satisfied.
16 But I will sing of your strength,
in the morning I will sing of your love;
for you are my fortress,
my refuge in times of trouble.

17 O my Strength, I sing praise to you;
you, O God, are my fortress, my loving
God.

> **Psalm 58:11**
>
> *God Rewards the Righteous*
>
> Then men will say,
> "Surely the righteous still
> are rewarded;
> surely there is a God who
> judges the earth."

Psalm 60

For the director of music. To ⌊the tune of⌋ "The Lily of the Covenant." A *miktam*[a] of David. For teaching. When he fought Aram Naharaim[c] and Aram Zobah,[d] and when Joab returned and struck down twelve thousand Edomites in the Valley of Salt.

1 You have rejected us, O God, and burst
forth upon us;
you have been angry—now restore us!
2 You have shaken the land and torn it open;
mend its fractures, for it is quaking.
3 You have shown your people desperate
times;
you have given us wine that makes us
stagger.

4 But for those who fear you, you have raised
a banner
to be unfurled against the bow. *Selah*

5 Save us and help us with your right hand,

[a]Title: Probably a literary or musical term [b]11 Or *sovereign* [c]Title: That is, Arameans of Northwest Mesopotamia [d]Title: That is, Arameans of central Syria

that those you love may be delivered.
6 God has spoken from his sanctuary:
"In triumph I will parcel out Shechem
and measure off the Valley of Succoth.
7 Gilead is mine, and Manasseh is mine;
Ephraim is my helmet,
Judah my scepter.
8 Moab is my washbasin,
upon Edom I toss my sandal;
over Philistia I shout in triumph."

9 Who will bring me to the fortified city?
Who will lead me to Edom?
10 Is it not you, O God, you who have
rejected us
and no longer go out with our armies?
11 Give us aid against the enemy,
for the help of man is worthless.
12 With God we will gain the victory,
and he will trample down our enemies.

Psalm 61

For the director of music. With stringed instruments. Of David.

1 Hear my cry, O God;
listen to my prayer.

2 From the ends of the earth
I call to you,
I call as my heart grows
faint;
lead me to the rock that
is higher than I.
3 For you have been my
refuge,
a strong tower against
the foe.

4 I long to dwell in your tent
forever
and take refuge in the
shelter of your wings. *Selah*
5 For you have heard my vows, O God;
you have given me the heritage of those
who fear your name.

6 Increase the days of the king's life,
his years for many generations.
7 May he be enthroned in God's presence
forever;
appoint your love and faithfulness to
protect him.

8 Then will I ever sing praise to your name
and fulfill my vows day after day.

Psalm 61:3

God Is a Strong Tower

For you have been
my refuge,
a strong tower against
the foe.

Psalm 62

For the director of music. For Jeduthun.
A psalm of David.

1 My soul finds rest in God alone;
my salvation comes from him.
2 He alone is my rock and my salvation;
he is my fortress, I will never be
shaken.

3 How long will you assault a man?
Would all of you throw him down—
this leaning wall, this tottering fence?
4 They fully intend to topple him
from his lofty place;
they take delight in lies.
With their mouths they bless,
but in their hearts they curse. *Selah*

5 Find rest, O my soul, in God alone;
my hope comes from him.
6 He alone is my rock and my salvation;
he is my fortress, I will not be shaken.
7 My salvation and my honor
depend on God[a];
he is my mighty rock, my
refuge.
8 Trust in him at all times,
O people;
pour out your hearts to
him,
for God is our refuge.
Selah
9 Lowborn men are but a
breath,
the highborn are but
a lie;
if weighed on a balance,
they are nothing;
together they are only a breath.
10 Do not trust in extortion
or take pride in stolen goods;
though your riches increase,
do not set your heart on them.

11 One thing God has spoken,
two things have I heard:
that you, O God, are strong,
12 and that you, O Lord, are loving.

[a]7 Or / *God Most High is my salvation and my honor*

Surely you will reward each person
according to what he has done.

Psalm 63

A psalm of David. When he was in the Desert of Judah.

1 O God, you are my God,
earnestly I seek you;
my soul thirsts for you,
my body longs for you,
in a dry and weary land
where there is no water.

2 I have seen you in the sanctuary
and beheld your power and your glory.
3 Because your love is better than life,
my lips will glorify you.
4 I will praise you as long as I live,
and in your name I will lift up my hands.
5 My soul will be satisfied as with the richest of foods;
with singing lips my mouth will praise you.

6 On my bed I remember you;
I think of you through the watches of the night.
7 Because you are my help,
I sing in the shadow of your wings.
8 My soul clings to you;
your right hand upholds me.

9 They who seek my life will be destroyed;
they will go down to the depths of the earth.
10 They will be given over to the sword
and become food for jackals.
11 But the king will rejoice in God;
all who swear by God's name will praise him,
while the mouths of liars will be silenced.

Psalm 64

For the director of music. A psalm of David.

1 Hear me, O God, as I voice my complaint;
protect my life from the threat of the enemy.
2 Hide me from the conspiracy of the wicked,
from that noisy crowd of evildoers.

3 They sharpen their tongues like swords
and aim their words like deadly arrows.
4 They shoot from ambush at the innocent man;
they shoot at him suddenly, without fear.

5 They encourage each other in evil plans,
they talk about hiding their snares;
they say, "Who will see them[a]?"
6 They plot injustice and say,
"We have devised a perfect plan!"
Surely the mind and heart of man are cunning.

7 But God will shoot them with arrows;
suddenly they will be struck down.
8 He will turn their own tongues against them
and bring them to ruin;
all who see them will shake their heads in scorn.

9 All mankind will fear;
they will proclaim the works of God
and ponder what he has done.
10 Let the righteous rejoice in the LORD
and take refuge in him;
let all the upright in heart praise him!

Psalm 65

For the director of music. A psalm of David. A song.

1 Praise awaits[b] you, O God, in Zion;
to you our vows will be fulfilled.
2 O you who hear prayer,
to you all men will come.
3 When we were overwhelmed by sins,
you forgave[c] our transgressions.
4 Blessed are those you choose
and bring near to live in your courts!
We are filled with the good things of your house,
of your holy temple.

5 You answer us with awesome deeds of righteousness,
O God our Savior,
the hope of all the ends of the earth
and of the farthest seas,
6 who formed the mountains by your power,
having armed yourself with strength,

a5 Or *us* b1 Or *befits*; the meaning of the Hebrew for this word is uncertain. c3 Or *made atonement for*

7 who stilled the roaring of the seas,
the roaring of their waves,
and the turmoil of the nations.
8 Those living far away fear your wonders;
where morning dawns and evening fades
you call forth songs of joy.

9 You care for the land and water it;
you enrich it abundantly.
The streams of God are filled with water
to provide the people with grain,
for so you have ordained it.[a]
10 You drench its furrows
and level its ridges;
you soften it with showers
and bless its crops.
11 You crown the year with your bounty,
and your carts overflow with abundance.
12 The grasslands of the desert overflow;
the hills are clothed with gladness.
13 The meadows are covered with flocks
and the valleys are mantled with grain;
they shout for joy and sing.

Psalm 66

For the director of music. A song. A psalm.

1 Shout with joy to God, all the earth!
2 Sing the glory of his name;
make his praise glorious!
3 Say to God, "How awesome are your deeds!
So great is your power
that your enemies cringe before you.
4 All the earth bows down to you;
they sing praise to you,
they sing praise to your name." *Selah*

5 Come and see what God has done,
how awesome his works in man's behalf!
6 He turned the sea into dry land,
they passed through the waters on foot—
come, let us rejoice in him.
7 He rules forever by his power,
his eyes watch the nations—
let not the rebellious rise up against him. *Selah*

8 Praise our God, O peoples,
let the sound of his praise be heard;
9 he has preserved our lives
and kept our feet from slipping.
10 For you, O God, tested us;
you refined us like silver.
11 You brought us into prison
and laid burdens on our backs.
12 You let men ride over our heads;
we went through fire and water,
but you brought us to a place of abundance.

13 I will come to your temple with burnt offerings
and fulfill my vows to you—
14 vows my lips promised and my mouth spoke
when I was in trouble.
15 I will sacrifice fat animals to you
and an offering of rams;
I will offer bulls and goats. *Selah*

16 Come and listen, all you who fear God;
let me tell you what he has done for me.
17 I cried out to him with my mouth;
his praise was on my tongue.
18 If I had cherished sin in my heart,
the Lord would not have listened;
19 but God has surely listened
and heard my voice in prayer.
20 Praise be to God,
who has not rejected my prayer
or withheld his love from me!

Psalm 67

For the director of music. With stringed instruments. A psalm. A song.

1 May God be gracious to us and bless us
and make his face shine upon us, *Selah*
2 that your ways may be known on earth,
your salvation among all nations.

3 May the peoples praise you, O God;
may all the peoples praise you.
4 May the nations be glad and sing for joy,
for you rule the peoples justly
and guide the nations of the earth. *Selah*
5 May the peoples praise you, O God;
may all the peoples praise you.

[a]9 Or *for that is how you prepare the land*

6 Then the land will yield its harvest,
and God, our God, will bless us.
7 God will bless us,
and all the ends of the earth will fear him.

Psalm 68

For the director of music. Of David. A psalm. A song.

1 May God arise, may his enemies be scattered;
may his foes flee before him.
2 As smoke is blown away by the wind,
may you blow them away;
as wax melts before the fire,
may the wicked perish before God.
3 But may the righteous be glad
and rejoice before God;
may they be happy and joyful.

4 Sing to God, sing praise to his name,
extol him who rides on the clouds[a]—
his name is the LORD—
and rejoice before him.
5 A father to the fatherless, a defender of widows,
is God in his holy dwelling.
6 God sets the lonely in families,[b]
he leads forth the prisoners with singing;
but the rebellious live in a sun-scorched land.

7 When you went out before your people, O God,
when you marched through the wasteland, *Selah*
8 the earth shook,
the heavens poured down rain,
before God, the One of Sinai,
before God, the God of Israel.
9 You gave abundant showers, O God;
you refreshed your weary inheritance.
10 Your people settled in it,
and from your bounty, O God, you provided for the poor.

11 The Lord announced the word,
and great was the company of those who proclaimed it:
12 "Kings and armies flee in haste;
in the camps men divide the plunder.
13 Even while you sleep among the campfires,[c]
the wings of ⌞my⌟ dove are sheathed with silver,
its feathers with shining gold."
14 When the Almighty[d] scattered the kings in the land,
it was like snow fallen on Zalmon.

15 The mountains of Bashan are majestic mountains;
rugged are the mountains of Bashan.
16 Why gaze in envy, O rugged mountains,
at the mountain where God chooses to reign,
where the LORD himself will dwell forever?
17 The chariots of God are tens of thousands
and thousands of thousands;
the Lord ⌞has come⌟ from Sinai into his sanctuary.
18 When you ascended on high,
you led captives in your train;
you received gifts from men,
even from[e] the rebellious—
that you,[f] O LORD God, might dwell there.

19 Praise be to the Lord, to God our Savior,
who daily bears our burdens. *Selah*
20 Our God is a God who saves;
from the Sovereign LORD comes escape from death.

21 Surely God will crush the heads of his enemies,
the hairy crowns of those who go on in their sins.

Psalm 68:4

God Is Majestic

Sing to God, sing praise
to his name,
extol him who rides
on the clouds—
his name is the LORD—
and rejoice before him.

[a]4 Or */ prepare the way for him who rides through the deserts* [b]6 Or *the desolate in a homeland* [c]13 Or *saddlebags* [d]14 Hebrew *Shaddai* [e]18 Or *gifts for men, / even* [f]18 Or *they*

22 The Lord says, "I will bring them from
Bashan;
I will bring them from the depths of the
sea,
23 that you may plunge your feet in the blood
of your foes,
while the tongues of your dogs have
their share."

24 Your procession has come into view,
O God,
the procession of my God and King into
the sanctuary.
25 In front are the singers, after them the
musicians;
with them are the maidens playing
tambourines.
26 Praise God in the great congregation;
praise the LORD in the assembly of
Israel.
27 There is the little tribe of Benjamin,
leading them,
there the great throng of Judah's
princes,
and there the princes of Zebulun and of
Naphtali.

28 Summon your power, O God[a];
show us your strength, O God, as you
have done before.
29 Because of your temple at Jerusalem
kings will bring you gifts.
30 Rebuke the beast among the reeds,
the herd of bulls among the calves of the
nations.
Humbled, may it bring bars of silver.
Scatter the nations who delight in
war.
31 Envoys will come from Egypt;
Cush[b] will submit herself to God.

32 Sing to God, O kingdoms of the earth,
sing praise to the Lord, *Selah*
33 to him who rides the ancient skies above,
who thunders with mighty voice.
34 Proclaim the power of God,
whose majesty is over Israel,
whose power is in the skies.
35 You are awesome, O God, in your
sanctuary;
the God of Israel gives power and
strength to his people.

Praise be to God!

Psalm 69

For the director of music. To ⌊the tune of⌋ "Lilies."
Of David.

1 Save me, O God,
for the waters have come up to my neck.
2 I sink in the miry depths,
where there is no foothold.
I have come into the deep waters;
the floods engulf me.
3 I am worn out calling for help;
my throat is parched.
My eyes fail,
looking for my God.
4 Those who hate me without reason
outnumber the hairs of my head;
many are my enemies without cause,
those who seek to destroy me.
I am forced to restore
what I did not steal.

5 You know my folly, O God;
my guilt is not hidden from you.

6 May those who hope in you
not be disgraced because of me,
O Lord, the LORD Almighty;
may those who seek you
not be put to shame because of me,
O God of Israel.
7 For I endure scorn for your sake,
and shame covers my face.
8 I am a stranger to my brothers,
an alien to my own mother's sons;
9 for zeal for your house consumes me,
and the insults of those who insult you
fall on me.
10 When I weep and fast,
I must endure scorn;
11 when I put on sackcloth,
people make sport of me.
12 Those who sit at the gate mock me,
and I am the song of the drunkards.

13 But I pray to you, O LORD,
in the time of your favor;
in your great love, O God,

[a]28 Many Hebrew manuscripts, Septuagint and Syriac; most Hebrew manuscripts *Your God has summoned power for you* [b]31 That is, the upper Nile region

answer me with your sure salvation.
14 Rescue me from the mire,
do not let me sink;
deliver me from those who hate me,
from the deep waters.
15 Do not let the floodwaters engulf me
or the depths swallow me up
or the pit close its mouth over me.
16 Answer me, O LORD, out of the goodness
of your love;
in your great mercy turn to me.
17 Do not hide your face from your servant;
answer me quickly, for I am in trouble.
18 Come near and rescue me;
redeem me because of my foes.

19 You know how I am scorned, disgraced
and shamed;
all my enemies are before you.
20 Scorn has broken my heart
and has left me helpless;
I looked for sympathy, but there was
none,
for comforters, but I found none.
21 They put gall in my food
and gave me vinegar for my thirst.

22 May the table set before them become a
snare;
may it become retribution and[a] a trap.
23 May their eyes be darkened so they cannot
see,
and their backs be bent
forever.
24 Pour out your wrath on
them;
let your fierce anger
overtake them.
25 May their place be deserted;
let there be no one to
dwell in their tents.
26 For they persecute those
you wound
and talk about the pain
of those you hurt.
27 Charge them with crime
upon crime;
do not let them share in your salvation.
28 May they be blotted out of the book of life
and not be listed with the righteous.

29 I am in pain and distress;
may your salvation, O God, protect me.

30 I will praise God's name in song
and glorify him with thanksgiving.
31 This will please the LORD more than an ox,
more than a bull with its horns and hoofs.
32 The poor will see and be glad—
you who seek God, may your hearts live!
33 The LORD hears the needy
and does not despise his captive people.

34 Let heaven and earth praise him,
the seas and all that move in them,
35 for God will save Zion
and rebuild the cities of Judah.
Then people will settle there and possess it;
36 the children of his servants will inherit
it,
and those who love his name will dwell
there.

Psalm 70

For the director of music. Of David. A petition.

1 Hasten, O God, to save me;
O LORD, come quickly to help me.
2 May those who seek my life
be put to shame and confusion;
may all who desire my ruin
be turned back in disgrace.
3 May those who say to me, "Aha! Aha!"
turn back because of
their shame.
4 But may all who seek you
rejoice and be glad in
you;
may those who love your
salvation always say,
"Let God be exalted!"

5 Yet I am poor and needy;
come quickly to me,
O God.
You are my help and my
deliverer;
O LORD, do not delay.

Psalm 71

1 In you, O LORD, I have taken refuge;
let me never be put to shame.
2 Rescue me and deliver me in your
righteousness;

Psalm 70:5

God Rescues Us

Yet I am poor and needy;
come quickly to me,
O God.
You are my help and
my deliverer;
O LORD, do not delay.

[a]22 Or *snare / and their fellowship become*

turn your ear to me and save me.
3 Be my rock of refuge,
to which I can always go;
give the command to save me,
for you are my rock and my fortress.
4 Deliver me, O my God,
from the hand of the wicked,
from the grasp of evil and cruel men.
5 For you have been my hope,
O Sovereign LORD,
my confidence since my youth.
6 From birth I have relied on you;
you brought me forth from my mother's womb.
I will ever praise you.
7 I have become like a portent to many,
but you are my strong refuge.
8 My mouth is filled with your praise,
declaring your splendor all day long.

9 Do not cast me away when I am old;
do not forsake me when my strength is gone.
10 For my enemies speak against me;
those who wait to kill me conspire together.
11 They say, "God has forsaken him;
pursue him and seize him,
for no one will rescue him."
12 Be not far from me, O God;
come quickly, O my God, to help me.
13 May my accusers perish in shame;
may those who want to harm me
be covered with scorn and disgrace.

14 But as for me, I will always have hope;
I will praise you more and more.
15 My mouth will tell of your righteousness,
of your salvation all day long,
though I know not its measure.
16 I will come and proclaim your mighty acts,
O Sovereign LORD;
I will proclaim your righteousness,
yours alone.

Psalm 71:5

God Inspires Confidence

For you have been my hope, O Sovereign LORD, my confidence since my youth.

17 Since my youth, O God, you have taught me,
and to this day I declare your marvelous deeds.
18 Even when I am old and gray,
do not forsake me, O God,
till I declare your power to the next generation,
your might to all who are to come.

19 Your righteousness reaches to the skies, O God,
you who have done great things.
Who, O God, is like you?
20 Though you have made me see troubles, many and bitter,
you will restore my life again;
from the depths of the earth
you will again bring me up.
21 You will increase my honor
and comfort me once again.

22 I will praise you with the harp
for your faithfulness, O my God;
I will sing praise to you with the lyre,
O Holy One of Israel.
23 My lips will shout for joy
when I sing praise to you—
I, whom you have redeemed.
24 My tongue will tell of your righteous acts
all day long,
for those who wanted to harm me
have been put to shame and confusion.

Psalm 72

Of Solomon.

1 Endow the king with your justice, O God,
the royal son with your righteousness.
2 He will[a] judge your people in righteousness,
your afflicted ones with justice.
3 The mountains will bring prosperity to the people,
the hills the fruit of righteousness.
4 He will defend the afflicted among the people

[a]2 Or *May he*; similarly in verses 3–11 and 17

Unshakable Confidence

Read: Psalm 71:1–24

WHAT DO YOU RELY ON to give you confidence? Your skills, your degrees, your accomplishments? What about when you sense a call to do a task for which you feel unqualified? Have you ever found yourself wondering, "Who am I to _____ [lead this group, start this ministry, supervise these employees, organize this fundraiser, teach these children . . .]?" Have you ever thought, "You picked the wrong woman for this job, Lord"?

If we rely on ourselves, we will *not* be qualified for that which God calls us. In fact, throughout Scripture we see that God often chose people who felt unqualified for the tasks God laid before them: Abraham, Sarah, Moses, David, Esther and Mary all felt unequal to the task. But if God can use a roaming Bedouin to birth a nation, a stuttering speaker to confront Egypt's pharaoh, a shepherd boy to lead a nation, an exiled Jewish girl to rescue her people and a timid teenager to bear the Son of God, then God can use us! The critical question isn't, "Can I do this?" The better question is, "Can God do this through me?" The answer is a resounding "Yes!"

When the psalmist asked God to be a refuge and rescuer in Psalm 71, he boldly proclaimed his dependence upon the Sovereign Lord. The psalmist knew that every breath he had taken had occurred because God had given it. Throughout his lifetime he had been dependent on God.

When we feel weak-kneed and lack confidence, we are most open to relying on God. The Bible gives us affirmation after affirmation of God's strength in the face of our limited ability: "I can do everything through him who gives me strength" (Philippians 4:13). "Nothing is impossible with God" (Luke 1:37). "Nothing is too hard for [the Lord]" (Jeremiah 32:17). "In all these things we are more than conquerors through him who loved us" (Romans 8:37). "My grace is sufficient for you, for my power is made perfect in weakness" (2 Corinthians 12:9). Nothing silences the voice of timidity as powerfully as the voice of Scripture.

So if you find yourself in a new situation today, make sure you don't rely on your own limited talents or skills, but that you place your unshakable confidence in the limitless God.

Psalm 71:5–6

For you have been my hope, O Sovereign Lord, my confidence since my youth. From birth I have relied on you.

reflection

1 On what or on whom do you tend to rely when feeling out of your comfort zone?

2 Is there an area in your life in which God might be calling you to move out in faith? What fears do you have about that situation?

3 How does the psalmist's reliance on God in Psalm 71 encourage you and renew your confidence in God's ability to help you?

RELATED READINGS

Exodus 3:1–15;
Joshua 1:1–9;
Luke 1:26–38;
2 Corinthians 3:4–6;
2 Timothy 1:7–12

Thursday

Go to page 712 for your next devotional reading.

and save the children of the needy;
he will crush the oppressor.

5 He will endure[a] as long as the sun,
as long as the moon, through all generations.
6 He will be like rain falling on a mown field,
like showers watering the earth.
7 In his days the righteous will flourish;
prosperity will abound till the moon is no more.

8 He will rule from sea to sea
and from the River[b] to the ends of the earth.[c]
9 The desert tribes will bow before him
and his enemies will lick the dust.
10 The kings of Tarshish and of distant shores
will bring tribute to him;
the kings of Sheba and Seba
will present him gifts.
11 All kings will bow down to him
and all nations will serve him.

12 For he will deliver the needy who cry out,
the afflicted who have no one to help.
13 He will take pity on the weak and the needy
and save the needy from death.
14 He will rescue them from oppression and violence,
for precious is their blood in his sight.

15 Long may he live!
May gold from Sheba be given him.
May people ever pray for him
and bless him all day long.
16 Let grain abound throughout the land;
on the tops of the hills may it sway.
Let its fruit flourish like Lebanon;
let it thrive like the grass of the field.
17 May his name endure forever;
may it continue as long as the sun.

All nations will be blessed through him,
and they will call him blessed.

18 Praise be to the LORD God, the God of Israel,
who alone does marvelous deeds.
19 Praise be to his glorious name forever;
may the whole earth be filled with his glory.
Amen and Amen.

20 This concludes the prayers of David son of Jesse.

BOOK III
Psalms 73–89

Psalm 73

A psalm of Asaph.

1 Surely God is good to Israel,
to those who are pure in heart.

2 But as for me, my feet had almost slipped;
I had nearly lost my foothold.
3 For I envied the arrogant
when I saw the prosperity of the wicked.

4 They have no struggles;
their bodies are healthy and strong.[d]
5 They are free from the burdens common to man;
they are not plagued by human ills.
6 Therefore pride is their necklace;
they clothe themselves with violence.
7 From their callous hearts comes iniquity[e];
the evil conceits of their minds know no limits.
8 They scoff, and speak with malice;
in their arrogance they threaten oppression.
9 Their mouths lay claim to heaven,
and their tongues take possession of the earth.
10 Therefore their people turn to them
and drink up waters in abundance.[f]
11 They say, "How can God know?
Does the Most High have knowledge?"

12 This is what the wicked are like—
always carefree, they increase in wealth.

13 Surely in vain have I kept my heart pure;
in vain have I washed my hands in innocence.
14 All day long I have been plagued;
I have been punished every morning.

[a] 5 Septuagint; Hebrew *You will be feared* [b] 8 That is, the Euphrates [c] 8 Or *the end of the land* [d] 4 With a different word division of the Hebrew; Masoretic Text *struggles at their death; / their bodies are healthy* [e] 7 Syriac (see also Septuagint); Hebrew *Their eyes bulge with fat* [f] 10 The meaning of the Hebrew for this verse is uncertain.

15 If I had said, "I will speak thus,"
I would have betrayed your children.
16 When I tried to understand all this,
it was oppressive to me
17 till I entered the sanctuary of God;
then I understood their final destiny.

18 Surely you place them on slippery ground;
you cast them down to ruin.
19 How suddenly are they destroyed,
completely swept away by terrors!
20 As a dream when one awakes,
so when you arise, O Lord,
you will despise them as fantasies.

21 When my heart was grieved
and my spirit embittered,
22 I was senseless and ignorant;
I was a brute beast before you.

23 Yet I am always with you;
you hold me by my right hand.
24 You guide me with your counsel,
and afterward you will take me into glory.
25 Whom have I in heaven but you?
And earth has nothing I desire besides you.
26 My flesh and my heart may fail,
but God is the strength of my heart
and my portion forever.

27 Those who are far from you will perish;
you destroy all who are unfaithful to you.
28 But as for me, it is good to be near God.
I have made the Sovereign LORD my refuge;
I will tell of all your deeds.

Psalm 74

A *maskil*[a] of Asaph.

1 Why have you rejected us forever, O God?
Why does your anger smolder against the sheep of your pasture?
2 Remember the people you purchased of old,
the tribe of your inheritance, whom you redeemed—
Mount Zion, where you dwelt.
3 Turn your steps toward these everlasting ruins,
all this destruction the enemy has brought on the sanctuary.

4 Your foes roared in the place where you met with us;
they set up their standards as signs.
5 They behaved like men wielding axes
to cut through a thicket of trees.
6 They smashed all the carved paneling
with their axes and hatchets.
7 They burned your sanctuary to the ground;
they defiled the dwelling place of your Name.
8 They said in their hearts, "We will crush them completely!"
They burned every place where God was worshiped in the land.
9 We are given no miraculous signs;
no prophets are left,
and none of us knows how long this will be.

10 How long will the enemy mock you, O God?
Will the foe revile your name forever?
11 Why do you hold back your hand, your right hand?
Take it from the folds of your garment and destroy them!

12 But you, O God, are my king from of old;
you bring salvation upon the earth.
13 It was you who split open the sea by your power;
you broke the heads of the monster in the waters.
14 It was you who crushed the heads of Leviathan
and gave him as food to the creatures of the desert.
15 It was you who opened up springs and streams;
you dried up the ever flowing rivers.
16 The day is yours, and yours also the night;
you established the sun and moon.

[a]Title: Probably a literary or musical term

17 It was you who set all the boundaries of the
earth;
you made both summer and winter.
18 Remember how the enemy has mocked
you, O LORD,
how foolish people have reviled your
name.
19 Do not hand over the life of your dove to
wild beasts;
do not forget the lives of your afflicted
people forever.
20 Have regard for your covenant,
because haunts of violence fill the dark
places of the land.
21 Do not let the oppressed retreat in
disgrace;
may the poor and needy praise your
name.
22 Rise up, O God, and defend your cause;
remember how fools mock you all day
long.
23 Do not ignore the clamor of your
adversaries,
the uproar of your enemies, which rises
continually.

Psalm 75

For the director of music. ⌞To the tune of⌟ "Do Not Destroy." A psalm of Asaph. A song.

1 We give thanks to you,
O God,
we give thanks, for your
Name is near;
men tell of your
wonderful deeds.
2 You say, "I choose the
appointed time;
it is I who judge
uprightly.
3 When the earth and all its
people quake,
it is I who hold its pillars
firm. *Selah*
4 To the arrogant I say, 'Boast
no more,'
and to the wicked, 'Do not lift up your
horns.
5 Do not lift your horns against heaven;
do not speak with outstretched neck.'"
6 No one from the east or the west
or from the desert can exalt a man.
7 But it is God who judges:
He brings one down, he exalts another.
8 In the hand of the LORD is a cup
full of foaming wine mixed with
spices;
he pours it out, and all the wicked of the
earth
drink it down to its very dregs.
9 As for me, I will declare this forever;
I will sing praise to the God of Jacob.
10 I will cut off the horns of all the wicked,
but the horns of the righteous will be
lifted up.

> **Psalm 75:1**
>
> *God Has Earned Our Gratitude*
>
> We give thanks to you,
> O God,
> we give thanks, for
> your Name is near;
> men tell of your
> wonderful deeds.

Psalm 76

For the director of music. With stringed instruments. A psalm of Asaph. A song.

1 In Judah God is known;
his name is great in Israel.
2 His tent is in Salem,
his dwelling place in Zion.
3 There he broke the flashing arrows,
the shields and the swords, the weapons
of war. *Selah*
4 You are resplendent with light,
more majestic than mountains rich with
game.
5 Valiant men lie plundered,
they sleep their last
sleep;
not one of the warriors
can lift his hands.
6 At your rebuke, O God of
Jacob,
both horse and chariot
lie still.
7 You alone are to be feared.
Who can stand before
you when you are
angry?
8 From heaven you
pronounced
judgment,
and the land feared and
was quiet—
9 when you, O God, rose up to judge,
to save all the afflicted of the land.
Selah

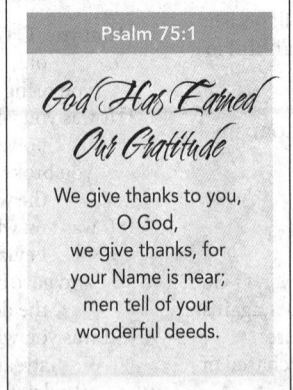

10 Surely your wrath against men brings you
praise,
and the survivors of your wrath are
restrained.[a]

11 Make vows to the LORD your God and
fulfill them;
let all the neighboring lands
bring gifts to the One to be feared.
12 He breaks the spirit of rulers;
he is feared by the kings of the earth.

Psalm 77

For the director of music. For Jeduthun. Of Asaph.
A psalm.

1 I cried out to God for help;
I cried out to God to hear me.
2 When I was in distress, I sought the Lord;
at night I stretched out untiring hands
and my soul refused to be comforted.

3 I remembered you, O God, and I groaned;
I mused, and my spirit grew faint.
Selah
4 You kept my eyes from closing;
I was too troubled to speak.
5 I thought about the former days,
the years of long ago;
6 I remembered my songs in the night.
My heart mused and my spirit inquired:

7 "Will the Lord reject
forever?
Will he never show his
favor again?
8 Has his unfailing love
vanished forever?
Has his promise failed
for all time?
9 Has God forgotten to be
merciful?
Has he in anger withheld
his compassion?"
Selah

10 Then I thought, "To this I
will appeal:
the years of the right
hand of the Most
High."
11 I will remember the deeds of the LORD;
yes, I will remember your miracles of
long ago.
12 I will meditate on all your works
and consider all your mighty deeds.

13 Your ways, O God, are holy.
What god is so great as our God?
14 You are the God who performs miracles;
you display your power among the
peoples.
15 With your mighty arm you redeemed your
people,
the descendants of Jacob and Joseph.
Selah

16 The waters saw you, O God,
the waters saw you and writhed;
the very depths were convulsed.
17 The clouds poured down water,
the skies resounded with thunder;
your arrows flashed back and forth.
18 Your thunder was heard in the whirlwind,
your lightning lit up the world;
the earth trembled and quaked.
19 Your path led through the sea,
your way through the mighty waters,
though your footprints were not seen.

20 You led your people like a flock
by the hand of Moses and Aaron.

Psalm 78:4

God Is Praiseworthy

We will not hide them
from their children;
we will tell the
next generation
the praiseworthy deeds
of the LORD,
his power, and the
wonders he has done.

Psalm 78

A *maskil*[b] of Asaph.

1 O my people, hear my
teaching;
listen to the words of my
mouth.
2 I will open my mouth in
parables,
I will utter hidden
things, things from
of old—
3 what we have heard and
known,
what our fathers have
told us.
4 We will not hide them
from their children;
we will tell the next
generation

[a]10 Or *Surely the wrath of men brings you praise, / and with the remainder of wrath you arm yourself* [b]Title: Probably a literary or musical term

the praiseworthy deeds of the LORD,
his power, and the wonders he has done.
5 He decreed statutes for Jacob
and established the law in Israel,
which he commanded our forefathers
to teach their children,
6 so the next generation would know them,
even the children yet to be born,
and they in turn would tell their
children.
7 Then they would put their trust in God
and would not forget his deeds
but would keep his commands.
8 They would not be like their forefathers—
a stubborn and rebellious generation,
whose hearts were not loyal to God,
whose spirits were not faithful to him.

9 The men of Ephraim, though armed with
bows,
turned back on the day of battle;
10 they did not keep God's covenant
and refused to live by his law.
11 They forgot what he had done,
the wonders he had shown them.
12 He did miracles in the sight of their fathers
in the land of Egypt, in the region of
Zoan.
13 He divided the sea and led them through;
he made the water stand firm like a wall.
14 He guided them with the cloud by day
and with light from the fire all night.
15 He split the rocks in the desert
and gave them water as abundant as the
seas;
16 he brought streams out of a rocky crag
and made water flow down like rivers.

17 But they continued to sin against him,
rebelling in the desert against the Most
High.
18 They willfully put God to the test
by demanding the food they craved.
19 They spoke against God, saying,
"Can God spread a table in the desert?
20 When he struck the rock, water gushed out,
and streams flowed abundantly.
But can he also give us food?
Can he supply meat for his people?"
21 When the LORD heard them, he was very
angry;
his fire broke out against Jacob,
and his wrath rose against Israel,
22 for they did not believe in God
or trust in his deliverance.
23 Yet he gave a command to the skies above
and opened the doors of the heavens;
24 he rained down manna for the people to
eat,
he gave them the grain of heaven.
25 Men ate the bread of angels;
he sent them all the food they could eat.
26 He let loose the east wind from the heavens
and led forth the south wind by his
power.
27 He rained meat down on them like dust,
flying birds like sand on the seashore.
28 He made them come down inside their
camp,
all around their tents.
29 They ate till they had more than enough,
for he had given them what they craved.
30 But before they turned from the food they
craved,
even while it was still in their mouths,
31 God's anger rose against them;
he put to death the sturdiest among
them,
cutting down the young men of Israel.

32 In spite of all this, they kept on sinning;
in spite of his wonders, they did not
believe.
33 So he ended their days in futility
and their years in terror.
34 Whenever God slew them, they would seek
him;
they eagerly turned to him again.
35 They remembered that God was their
Rock,
that God Most High was their
Redeemer.
36 But then they would flatter him with their
mouths,
lying to him with their tongues;
37 their hearts were not loyal to him,
they were not faithful to his covenant.
38 Yet he was merciful;
he forgave their iniquities
and did not destroy them.
Time after time he restrained his anger
and did not stir up his full wrath.

39 He remembered that they were but flesh,
a passing breeze that does not return.
40 How often they rebelled against him in the desert
and grieved him in the wasteland!
41 Again and again they put God to the test;
they vexed the Holy One of Israel.
42 They did not remember his power—
the day he redeemed them from the oppressor,
43 the day he displayed his miraculous signs in Egypt,
his wonders in the region of Zoan.
44 He turned their rivers to blood;
they could not drink from their streams.
45 He sent swarms of flies that devoured them,
and frogs that devastated them.
46 He gave their crops to the grasshopper,
their produce to the locust.
47 He destroyed their vines with hail
and their sycamore-figs with sleet.
48 He gave over their cattle to the hail,
their livestock to bolts of lightning.
49 He unleashed against them his hot anger,
his wrath, indignation and hostility—
a band of destroying angels.
50 He prepared a path for his anger;
he did not spare them from death
but gave them over to the plague.
51 He struck down all the firstborn of Egypt,
the firstfruits of manhood in the tents of Ham.
52 But he brought his people out like a flock;
he led them like sheep through the desert.
53 He guided them safely, so they were unafraid;
but the sea engulfed their enemies.
54 Thus he brought them to the border of his holy land,
to the hill country his right hand had taken.
55 He drove out nations before them
and allotted their lands to them as an inheritance;
he settled the tribes of Israel in their homes.

56 But they put God to the test
and rebelled against the Most High;
they did not keep his statutes.
57 Like their fathers they were disloyal and faithless,
as unreliable as a faulty bow.
58 They angered him with their high places;
they aroused his jealousy with their idols.
59 When God heard them, he was very angry;
he rejected Israel completely.
60 He abandoned the tabernacle of Shiloh,
the tent he had set up among men.
61 He sent ⌊the ark of⌋ his might into captivity,
his splendor into the hands of the enemy.
62 He gave his people over to the sword;
he was very angry with his inheritance.
63 Fire consumed their young men,
and their maidens had no wedding songs;
64 their priests were put to the sword,
and their widows could not weep.
65 Then the Lord awoke as from sleep,
as a man wakes from the stupor of wine.
66 He beat back his enemies;
he put them to everlasting shame.
67 Then he rejected the tents of Joseph,
he did not choose the tribe of Ephraim;
68 but he chose the tribe of Judah,
Mount Zion, which he loved.
69 He built his sanctuary like the heights,
like the earth that he established forever.
70 He chose David his servant
and took him from the sheep pens;
71 from tending the sheep he brought him
to be the shepherd of his people Jacob,
of Israel his inheritance.
72 And David shepherded them with integrity of heart;
with skillful hands he led them.

Psalm 79

A psalm of Asaph.

1 O God, the nations have invaded your inheritance;
they have defiled your holy temple,
they have reduced Jerusalem to rubble.
2 They have given the dead bodies of your servants
as food to the birds of the air,

the flesh of your saints to the beasts of
the earth.
3 They have poured out blood like water
all around Jerusalem,
and there is no one to bury the dead.
4 We are objects of reproach to our
neighbors,
of scorn and derision to those around
us.

5 How long, O LORD? Will you be angry
forever?
How long will your jealousy burn like
fire?
6 Pour out your wrath on the nations
that do not acknowledge you,
on the kingdoms
that do not call on your name;
7 for they have devoured Jacob
and destroyed his homeland.
8 Do not hold against us the sins of the
fathers;
may your mercy come quickly to meet
us,
for we are in desperate need.

9 Help us, O God our Savior,
for the glory of your name;
deliver us and forgive our sins
for your name's sake.
10 Why should the nations say,
"Where is their God?"
Before our eyes, make known among the
nations
that you avenge the outpoured blood of
your servants.
11 May the groans of the prisoners come
before you;
by the strength of your arm
preserve those condemned to die.

12 Pay back into the laps of our neighbors
seven times
the reproach they have hurled at you,
O Lord.
13 Then we your people, the sheep of your
pasture,
will praise you forever;
from generation to generation
we will recount your praise.

Psalm 80

For the director of music. To ⌊the tune of⌋ "The Lilies of the Covenant." Of Asaph. A psalm.

1 Hear us, O Shepherd of Israel,
you who lead Joseph like a flock;
you who sit enthroned between the
cherubim, shine forth
2 before Ephraim, Benjamin and
Manasseh.
Awaken your might;
come and save us.

3 Restore us, O God;
make your face shine upon us,
that we may be saved.

4 O LORD God Almighty,
how long will your anger smolder
against the prayers of your people?
5 You have fed them with the bread of tears;
you have made them drink tears by the
bowlful.
6 You have made us a source of contention to
our neighbors,
and our enemies mock us.

7 Restore us, O God Almighty;
make your face shine upon us,
that we may be saved.

8 You brought a vine out of Egypt;
you drove out the nations and planted it.
9 You cleared the ground for it,
and it took root and filled the land.
10 The mountains were covered with its
shade,
the mighty cedars with its branches.
11 It sent out its boughs to the Sea,[a]
its shoots as far as the River.[b]

12 Why have you broken down its walls
so that all who pass by pick its grapes?
13 Boars from the forest ravage it
and the creatures of the field feed on it.
14 Return to us, O God Almighty!
Look down from heaven and see!
Watch over this vine,
15 the root your right hand has planted,
the son[c] you have raised up for yourself.

16 Your vine is cut down, it is burned with
fire;

[a] 11 Probably the Mediterranean [b] 11 That is, the Euphrates [c] 15 Or *branch*

at your rebuke your people perish.
17 Let your hand rest on the man at your right hand,
the son of man you have raised up for yourself.
18 Then we will not turn away from you;
revive us, and we will call on your name.

19 Restore us, O LORD God Almighty;
make your face shine upon us,
that we may be saved.

Psalm 81

For the director of music. According to *gittith.*[a] Of Asaph.

1 Sing for joy to God our strength;
shout aloud to the God of Jacob!
2 Begin the music, strike the tambourine,
play the melodious harp and lyre.

3 Sound the ram's horn at the New Moon,
and when the moon is full, on the day of our Feast;
4 this is a decree for Israel,
an ordinance of the God of Jacob.
5 He established it as a statute for Joseph
when he went out against Egypt,
where we heard a language we did not understand.[b]

6 He says, "I removed the burden from their shoulders;
their hands were set free from the basket.
7 In your distress you called and I rescued you,
I answered you out of a thundercloud;
I tested you at the waters of Meribah. *Selah*

8 "Hear, O my people, and I will warn you—
if you would but listen to me, O Israel!
9 You shall have no foreign god among you;
you shall not bow down to an alien god.
10 I am the LORD your God,
who brought you up out of Egypt.
Open wide your mouth and I will fill it.

11 "But my people would not listen to me;
Israel would not submit to me.
12 So I gave them over to their stubborn hearts
to follow their own devices.

13 "If my people would but listen to me,
if Israel would follow my ways,
14 how quickly would I subdue their enemies
and turn my hand against their foes!
15 Those who hate the LORD would cringe before him,
and their punishment would last forever.
16 But you would be fed with the finest of wheat;
with honey from the rock I would satisfy you."

Psalm 81:1

God Is Strong

Sing for joy to God our strength; shout aloud to the God of Jacob!

Psalm 82

A psalm of Asaph.

1 God presides in the great assembly;
he gives judgment among the "gods":

2 "How long will you[c] defend the unjust
and show partiality to the wicked? *Selah*
3 Defend the cause of the weak and fatherless;
maintain the rights of the poor and oppressed.
4 Rescue the weak and needy;
deliver them from the hand of the wicked.

5 "They know nothing, they understand nothing.
They walk about in darkness;
all the foundations of the earth are shaken.

6 "I said, 'You are "gods";
you are all sons of the Most High.'
7 But you will die like mere men;
you will fall like every other ruler."

8 Rise up, O God, judge the earth,
for all the nations are your inheritance.

[a]Title: Probably a musical term [b]5 Or / *and we heard a voice we had not known* [c]2 The Hebrew is plural.

Psalm 83

A song. A psalm of Asaph.

1 O God, do not keep silent;
be not quiet, O God, be not still.
2 See how your enemies are astir,
how your foes rear their heads.
3 With cunning they conspire against your
people;
they plot against those you cherish.
4 "Come," they say, "let us destroy them as a
nation,
that the name of Israel be remembered
no more."

5 With one mind they plot together;
they form an alliance against you—
6 the tents of Edom and the Ishmaelites,
of Moab and the Hagrites,
7 Gebal,[a] Ammon and Amalek,
Philistia, with the people of Tyre.
8 Even Assyria has joined them
to lend strength to the descendants of
Lot. *Selah*

9 Do to them as you did to Midian,
as you did to Sisera and Jabin at the river
Kishon,
10 who perished at Endor
and became like refuse on the ground.
11 Make their nobles like Oreb and Zeeb,
all their princes like Zebah and
Zalmunna,
12 who said, "Let us take possession
of the pasturelands of God."

13 Make them like tumbleweed, O my God,
like chaff before the wind.
14 As fire consumes the forest
or a flame sets the mountains ablaze,
15 so pursue them with your tempest
and terrify them with your storm.
16 Cover their faces with shame
so that men will seek your name,
O LORD.

17 May they ever be ashamed and dismayed;
may they perish in disgrace.
18 Let them know that you, whose name is
the LORD—
that you alone are the Most High over
all the earth.

Psalm 84

For the director of music. According to *gittith.*[b]
Of the Sons of Korah. A psalm.

1 How lovely is your dwelling place,
O LORD Almighty!
2 My soul yearns, even faints,
for the courts of the LORD;
my heart and my flesh cry out
for the living God.

3 Even the sparrow has found a home,
and the swallow a nest for herself,
where she may have her young—
a place near your altar,
O LORD Almighty, my King and my
God.
4 Blessed are those who dwell in your house;
they are ever praising you. *Selah*

5 Blessed are those whose strength is in you,
who have set their hearts on pilgrimage.
6 As they pass through the Valley of Baca,
they make it a place of springs;
the autumn rains also cover it with
pools.[c]
7 They go from strength to strength,
till each appears before God in Zion.

8 Hear my prayer, O LORD God Almighty;
listen to me, O God of Jacob. *Selah*
9 Look upon our shield,[d] O God;
look with favor on your anointed one.

10 Better is one day in your courts
than a thousand elsewhere;
I would rather be a doorkeeper in the
house of my God
than dwell in the tents of the wicked.
11 For the LORD God is a sun and shield;
the LORD bestows favor and honor;
no good thing does he withhold
from those whose walk is blameless.

12 O LORD Almighty,
blessed is the man who trusts in you.

Psalm 85

For the director of music. Of the Sons of Korah.
A psalm.

1 You showed favor to your land, O LORD;
you restored the fortunes of Jacob.
2 You forgave the iniquity of your people

[a]7 That is, Byblos [b]Title: Probably a musical term [c]6 Or *blessings* [d]9 Or *sovereign*

and covered all their sins. *Selah*
3 You set aside all your wrath
and turned from your fierce anger.

4 Restore us again, O God our Savior,
and put away your displeasure toward us.
5 Will you be angry with us forever?
Will you prolong your anger through all generations?
6 Will you not revive us again,
that your people may rejoice in you?
7 Show us your unfailing love, O LORD,
and grant us your salvation.

8 I will listen to what God the LORD will say;
he promises peace to his people, his saints—
but let them not return to folly.
9 Surely his salvation is near those who fear him,
that his glory may dwell in our land.

10 Love and faithfulness meet together;
righteousness and peace kiss each other.
11 Faithfulness springs forth from the earth,
and righteousness looks down from heaven.
12 The LORD will indeed give what is good,
and our land will yield its harvest.
13 Righteousness goes before him
and prepares the way for his steps.

Psalm 85:8

God Promises Peace

I will listen to what God the LORD will say;
he promises peace to his people, his saints—
but let them not return to folly.

Psalm 86

A prayer of David.

1 Hear, O LORD, and answer me,
for I am poor and needy.
2 Guard my life, for I am devoted to you.
You are my God; save your servant
who trusts in you.
3 Have mercy on me, O Lord,
for I call to you all day long.
4 Bring joy to your servant,
for to you, O Lord,
I lift up my soul.

5 You are forgiving and good, O Lord,
abounding in love to all who call to you.
6 Hear my prayer, O LORD;
listen to my cry for mercy.
7 In the day of my trouble I will call to you,
for you will answer me.

8 Among the gods there is none like you, O Lord;
no deeds can compare with yours.
9 All the nations you have made
will come and worship before you, O Lord;
they will bring glory to your name.
10 For you are great and do marvelous deeds;
you alone are God.

11 Teach me your way, O LORD,
and I will walk in your truth;
give me an undivided heart,
that I may fear your name.
12 I will praise you, O Lord my God, with all my heart;
I will glorify your name forever.
13 For great is your love toward me;
you have delivered me from the depths of the grave.[a]

14 The arrogant are attacking me, O God;
a band of ruthless men seeks my life—
men without regard for you.
15 But you, O Lord, are a compassionate and gracious God,
slow to anger, abounding in love and faithfulness.
16 Turn to me and have mercy on me;
grant your strength to your servant
and save the son of your maidservant.[b]
17 Give me a sign of your goodness,
that my enemies may see it and be put to shame,
for you, O LORD, have helped me and comforted me.

[a]13 Hebrew *Sheol* [b]16 Or *save your faithful son*

Will the Real God Please Stand Up?

Psalm 86:15

But you, O Lord, are a compassionate and gracious God, slow to anger, abounding in love and faithfulness.

Read: Psalm 86:1–17

WHEN YOU APPROACH GOD in prayer, what are the "givens" you believe about him? That he hears you, forgives you and loves you with a steadfast love? That's how the psalmist describes God. But do you sometimes secretly picture him as an unmerciful judge, wondering if he really will forgive *this* sin—the one you find yourself repeatedly battling? Or does God seem like an absentee parent who is unresponsive to your needs rather than a loving Father who understands your pain? When you've blown it again, do you sense that God has a scowl of disappointment on his face rather than open, welcoming arms?

Sometimes without realizing it, we project upon God images of our own making—a demanding taskmaster for whom we never can do enough, an exacting parent we can never quite please, a short-tempered boss we easily anger. Yet, this is not the God of the Bible, the God of David, and this is not the real God.

Listen to David's description of the God he knew so intimately: "You are . . . abounding in love to all who call to you" (verse 5). God is not an unmerciful, cruel master but a "forgiving and good" heavenly Father. He is not skimpy with his love, and he does not play favorites. He is not a God who gives love conditionally. No, this God—our God—is overflowing with love. Even when he was poor, weak, needy and in trouble, David proclaimed, "Great is your love toward me" (verse 13).

Who is this God we serve? This is no impotent God: "You are great and do marvelous deeds" (verse 10). This is no uncaring, unaware, neglectful God who tells us, "Get over it." Rather, he is a "compassionate and gracious God" (verse 15) who comforts us in our tears. He is not a temperamental, grumpy, quick-to-anger God, but one who is "slow to anger" (verse 15). He is not an unpredictable, fickle, unreliable God, but one "abounding in . . . faithfulness" (verse 15). There is no God like him!

When you find yourself hesitant to come before God or to wholly trust him, consider what image of God you're holding onto. Is it the real God of Scripture or an impostor? Worship the real God, in spirit and in truth.

reflection

1 What false images of God do you have that keep you from coming boldly before his throne?

2 How has a parent shaped your image of God, positively or negatively? How have other relationships in your life shaped your image of God?

3 Choose one character trait of God's that is listed in this psalm and meditate on it today. What new insights do you gain?

RELATED READINGS

Psalms 103:1–22; 145:1–21; Lamentations 3:22–23; John 4:24

Go to page 716 for your next devotional reading.

Psalm 87

Of the Sons of Korah. A psalm. A song.

1 He has set his foundation on the holy mountain;
2 the LORD loves the gates of Zion
more than all the dwellings of Jacob.
3 Glorious things are said of you,
O city of God: *Selah*
4 "I will record Rahab[a] and Babylon
among those who acknowledge me—
Philistia too, and Tyre, along with Cush[b]—
and will say, 'This[c] one was born in Zion.' "
5 Indeed, of Zion it will be said,
"This one and that one were born in her,
and the Most High himself will establish her."
6 The LORD will write in the register of the peoples:
"This one was born in Zion." *Selah*
7 As they make music they will sing,
"All my fountains are in you."

Psalm 88

A song. A psalm of the Sons of Korah. For the director of music. According to *mahalath leannoth.*[d] A *maskil*[e] of Heman the Ezrahite.

1 O LORD, the God who saves me,
day and night I cry out before you.
2 May my prayer come before you;
turn your ear to my cry.

3 For my soul is full of trouble
and my life draws near the grave.[f]
4 I am counted among those who go down to the pit;
I am like a man without strength.
5 I am set apart with the dead,
like the slain who lie in the grave,
whom you remember no more,
who are cut off from your care.
6 You have put me in the lowest pit,
in the darkest depths.
7 Your wrath lies heavily upon me;
you have overwhelmed me with all your waves. *Selah*
8 You have taken from me my closest friends
and have made me repulsive to them.
I am confined and cannot escape;
9 my eyes are dim with grief.

I call to you, O LORD, every day;
I spread out my hands to you.
10 Do you show your wonders to the dead?
Do those who are dead rise up and praise you? *Selah*
11 Is your love declared in the grave,
your faithfulness in Destruction[g]?
12 Are your wonders known in the place of darkness,
or your righteous deeds in the land of oblivion?

13 But I cry to you for help, O LORD;
in the morning my prayer comes before you.
14 Why, O LORD, do you reject me
and hide your face from me?

15 From my youth I have been afflicted and close to death;
I have suffered your terrors and am in despair.
16 Your wrath has swept over me;
your terrors have destroyed me.
17 All day long they surround me like a flood;
they have completely engulfed me.
18 You have taken my companions and loved ones from me;
the darkness is my closest friend.

Psalm 89:1

God Is Faithful

I will sing of the LORD's great love forever; with my mouth I will make your faithfulness known through all generations.

Psalm 89

A *maskil*[e] of Ethan the Ezrahite.

1 I will sing of the LORD's great love forever;
with my mouth I will make your faithfulness known through all generations.

[a]4 A poetic name for Egypt [b]4 That is, the upper Nile region [c]4 Or *"O Rahab and Babylon, / Philistia, Tyre and Cush, / I will record concerning those who acknowledge me: / 'This* [d]Title: Possibly a tune, "The Suffering of Affliction" [e]Title: Probably a literary or musical term [f]3 Hebrew *Sheol* [g]11 Hebrew *Abaddon*

2 I will declare that your love stands firm
forever,
that you established your faithfulness in
heaven itself.
3 You said, "I have made a covenant with my
chosen one,
I have sworn to David my servant,
4 'I will establish your line forever
and make your throne firm through all
generations.'" *Selah*

5 The heavens praise your wonders, O LORD,
your faithfulness too, in the assembly of
the holy ones.
6 For who in the skies above can compare
with the LORD?
Who is like the LORD among the
heavenly beings?
7 In the council of the holy ones God is
greatly feared;
he is more awesome than all who
surround him.
8 O LORD God Almighty, who is like you?
You are mighty, O LORD, and your
faithfulness surrounds you.
9 You rule over the surging sea;
when its waves mount up, you still them.
10 You crushed Rahab like one of the slain;
with your strong arm you scattered your
enemies.
11 The heavens are yours, and yours also the
earth;
you founded the world and all that is
in it.
12 You created the north and the south;
Tabor and Hermon sing for joy at your
name.
13 Your arm is endued with power;
your hand is strong, your right hand
exalted.

14 Righteousness and justice are the
foundation of your throne;
love and faithfulness go before you.
15 Blessed are those who have learned to
acclaim you,
who walk in the light of your presence,
O LORD.
16 They rejoice in your name all day long;
they exult in your righteousness.
17 For you are their glory and strength,
and by your favor you exalt our horn.[a]
18 Indeed, our shield[b] belongs to the LORD,
our king to the Holy One of Israel.

19 Once you spoke in a vision,
to your faithful people you said:
"I have bestowed strength on a warrior;
I have exalted a young man from among
the people.
20 I have found David my servant;
with my sacred oil I have anointed him.
21 My hand will sustain him;
surely my arm will strengthen him.
22 No enemy will subject him to tribute;
no wicked man will oppress him.
23 I will crush his foes before him
and strike down his adversaries.
24 My faithful love will be with him,
and through my name his horn[c] will be
exalted.
25 I will set his hand over the sea,
his right hand over the rivers.
26 He will call out to me, 'You are my
Father,
my God, the Rock my Savior.'
27 I will also appoint him my firstborn,
the most exalted of the kings of the
earth.
28 I will maintain my love to him forever,
and my covenant with him will never
fail.
29 I will establish his line forever,
his throne as long as the heavens
endure.

30 "If his sons forsake my law
and do not follow my statutes,
31 if they violate my decrees
and fail to keep my commands,
32 I will punish their sin with the rod,
their iniquity with flogging;
33 but I will not take my love from him,
nor will I ever betray my faithfulness.
34 I will not violate my covenant
or alter what my lips have uttered.
35 Once for all, I have sworn by my holiness—
and I will not lie to David—
36 that his line will continue forever

[a]17 *Horn* here symbolizes strong one. [b]18 Or *sovereign* [c]24 *Horn* here symbolizes strength.

and his throne endure before me like
the sun;
37 it will be established forever like the moon,
the faithful witness in the sky." *Selah*

38 But you have rejected, you have spurned,
you have been very angry with your
anointed one.
39 You have renounced the covenant with
your servant
and have defiled his crown in the dust.
40 You have broken through all his walls
and reduced his strongholds to ruins.
41 All who pass by have plundered him;
he has become the scorn of his
neighbors.
42 You have exalted the right hand of his foes;
you have made all his enemies rejoice.
43 You have turned back the edge of his
sword
and have not supported him in battle.
44 You have put an end to his splendor
and cast his throne to the ground.
45 You have cut short the days of his youth;
you have covered him with a mantle of
shame. *Selah*

46 How long, O LORD? Will you hide yourself
forever?
How long will your wrath burn like fire?
47 Remember how fleeting is my life.
For what futility you have created all
men!
48 What man can live and not see death,
or save himself from the power of the
grave[a]? *Selah*
49 O Lord, where is your former great love,
which in your faithfulness you swore to
David?
50 Remember, Lord, how your servant has[b]
been mocked,
how I bear in my heart the taunts of all
the nations,
51 the taunts with which your enemies have
mocked, O LORD,
with which they have mocked every step
of your anointed one.

52 Praise be to the LORD forever!
Amen and Amen.

BOOK IV
Psalms 90–106

Psalm 90
A prayer of Moses the man of God.

1 Lord, you have been our dwelling place
throughout all generations.
2 Before the mountains were born
or you brought forth the earth and the
world,
from everlasting to everlasting you are
God.

3 You turn men back to dust,
saying, "Return to dust, O sons of men."
4 For a thousand years in your sight
are like a day that has just gone by,
or like a watch in the night.
5 You sweep men away in the sleep of
death;
they are like the new grass of the
morning—
6 though in the morning it springs up new,
by evening it is dry and withered.

7 We are consumed by your anger
and terrified by your indignation.
8 You have set our iniquities before you,
our secret sins in the light of your
presence.
9 All our days pass away under your wrath;
we finish our years with a moan.
10 The length of our days is seventy years—
or eighty, if we have the strength;
yet their span[c] is but trouble and sorrow,
for they quickly pass, and we fly away.

11 Who knows the power of your anger?
For your wrath is as great as the fear that
is due you.
12 Teach us to number our days aright,
that we may gain a heart of wisdom.

13 Relent, O LORD! How long will it be?
Have compassion on your servants.
14 Satisfy us in the morning with your
unfailing love,
that we may sing for joy and be glad all
our days.
15 Make us glad for as many days as you have
afflicted us,

[a] 48 Hebrew *Sheol* [b] 50 Or *your servants have* [c] 10 Or *yet the best of them*

Unthinkable

BATHSHEBA

David pleaded with God for the child. He fasted and went into his house and spent the nights lying on the ground.

2 Samuel 12:16

"THE SON BORN to you will die."

As David recounted what the prophet had told him, Bathsheba shuddered. Her breath froze in her lungs so that she could neither inhale nor exhale. Like a wounded animal, an involuntary moan escaped her lips. She felt her face flush as she reached out to steady herself on David's arm.

David, too, was visibly shaken. His bloodshot eyes stared into hers.

"No. It couldn't be . . ." Her first thoughts denied the truth. Their baby boy, barely a week old, had been the picture of health just that morning. But now, with David's words ringing in her ears, she gathered the hem of her dress and ran down the palace hallway to his room. His elderly nanny met her at the doorway, frantic with concern.

"Your Highness . . . the baby . . ." her words swam together in confusion. "Something is wrong."

Bathsheba rushed to where he lay, scooping the limp figure into her arms. His breathing was shallow and ragged. Her perfectly healthy boy, their son, was now dying.

She sank to her knees in a crumpled heap and pushed back her hair with her palms. *This couldn't be happening.* First her husband, Uriah, and now the unthinkable. How much more could she take?

She realized what the prophet said regarding sin, but who could think about blame at a time like this? The overwhelming pain of losing a child eclipsed everything else. And watching David suffer heightened her agony. For the next few days, she watched helplessly as grief threatened to drown her husband. He wouldn't eat. He wouldn't sleep.

If they had lost their child suddenly in an accident, perhaps it wouldn't hurt so badly. But she was sure that this relentless swell of heartache upon heartache each passing day was much worse.

Finally, at the end of the week, the tide receded. And what remained, mingled with the pain and heartache, was the strangest sensation of peace and relief.

—Prayer—

Gracious Lord, forgive my sin, heal my heart and give me peace.

ASSIGNED READING:

2 Samuel 11:1—12:25; 1 Kings 1–2; Psalm 51:1–19

Weekend

Go to page 718 for your next devotional reading.

for as many years as we have seen
trouble.
16 May your deeds be shown to your servants,
your splendor to their children.

17 May the favor[a] of the Lord our God rest
upon us;
establish the work of our hands for us—
yes, establish the work of our hands.

Psalm 91

1 He who dwells in the shelter of the Most
High
will rest in the shadow of the Almighty.[b]
2 I will say[c] of the LORD, "He is my refuge
and my fortress,
my God, in whom I trust."

3 Surely he will save you from the fowler's
snare
and from the deadly pestilence.
4 He will cover you with his feathers,
and under his wings you will find
refuge;
his faithfulness will be your shield and
rampart.
5 You will not fear the terror of night,
nor the arrow that flies
by day,
6 nor the pestilence that
stalks in the
darkness,
nor the plague that
destroys at midday.
7 A thousand may fall at your
side,
ten thousand at your
right hand,
but it will not come near
you.
8 You will only observe with
your eyes
and see the punishment of the wicked.

9 If you make the Most High your
dwelling—
even the LORD, who is my refuge—
10 then no harm will befall you,
no disaster will come near your tent.
11 For he will command his angels
concerning you
to guard you in all your ways;
12 they will lift you up in their hands,
so that you will not strike your foot
against a stone.
13 You will tread upon the lion and the cobra;
you will trample the great lion and the
serpent.

14 "Because he loves me," says the LORD, "I
will rescue him;
I will protect him, for he acknowledges
my name.
15 He will call upon me, and I will answer
him;
I will be with him in trouble,
I will deliver him and honor him.
16 With long life will I satisfy him
and show him my salvation."

Psalm 91:4

God Shields Us

He will cover you with
his feathers,
and under his wings
you will find refuge;
his faithfulness will be
your shield and rampart.

Psalm 92

A psalm. A song. For the Sabbath day.

1 It is good to praise the LORD
and make music to your name, O Most
High,
2 to proclaim your love in the morning
and your faithfulness at night,
3 to the music of the ten-
stringed lyre
and the melody of the
harp.

4 For you make me glad
by your deeds,
O LORD;
I sing for joy at the works
of your hands.
5 How great are your works,
O LORD,
how profound your
thoughts!
6 The senseless man does not
know,
fools do not understand,
7 that though the wicked spring up like grass
and all evildoers flourish,
they will be forever destroyed.

8 But you, O LORD, are exalted forever.

9 For surely your enemies, O LORD,
surely your enemies will perish;

[a]17 Or *beauty* [b]1 Hebrew *Shaddai* [c]2 Or *He says*

All Creation Praises Him

Psalm 92:1–2

It is good to praise the LORD and make music to your name, O Most High, to proclaim your love in the morning and your faithfulness at night.

reflection

1 What beautiful creations has God put in your neighborhood or hometown for which you can praise him?

2 How has God surprised you with his love and creativity?

3 What are five things you can praise God for today?

RELATED READINGS

Psalms 19:1–14; 96:1–13; 148:1–14; Luke 19:28–40

"What an inexpressible joy for me, to look up through the apple blossoms and the fluttering leaves, and to see God's love there."

Elizabeth Charles

Read: Psalm 92:1–15

INSTEAD OF GREETING the morning with a grunt and a cup of coffee, birds wake up singing. Every morning around daybreak neighborhoods fill with birdsong. Referred to by bird-watchers as "the dawn chorus," the daily songfest marks a bird's territory and communicates to our ears a sound of reckless, warbling joy. True, birdsong is glorious, but only human beings sing words of praise. And our God who filled his universe with all sorts of wonderful extras *wants* our praise. He wants *our* praise. Why? Because God is worthy. Jesus said that if his followers "keep quiet, the stones will cry out" (Luke 19:40).

God, who gave the crow his harsh caw and dark plumage, also granted the cardinal his lovely song and a coat that can be seen half a block away. The God who created broccoli also surprises us with the taste of watermelon in the season we need it most. The Creator sprinkled the world with butterflies and fireflies and gave us noisy, refreshing creeks and waterfalls. He hid treasures of gold and copper, diamonds and rubies inside his mountains. And he gave us voices and even rounded up psalmists to write some of the words we can sing.

In Psalm 92 the psalmist recites several reasons why "it is good to praise the LORD":

- For who God is—exalted, the Most High, upright, a Rock, loving and faithful
- For what he does—great works and profound thoughts, judges the wicked, defeats enemies

This God deserves the praises of all his creatures: people, birds—and even the stones of the field. Whether our instrument is a flute, a guitar or our own off-key singing voices, God wants our praise. Declaring his love and faithfulness morning, noon and night is good. The ability to praise our Maker in song and words is a gift that only humans have. Use that gift and lift up a chorus of praise today.

Go to page 723 for your next devotional reading.

all evildoers will be scattered.
10 You have exalted my horn[a] like that of a
wild ox;
fine oils have been poured upon me.
11 My eyes have seen the defeat of my
adversaries;
my ears have heard the rout of my
wicked foes.
12 The righteous will flourish like a palm tree,
they will grow like a cedar of Lebanon;
13 planted in the house of the LORD,
they will flourish in the courts of our
God.
14 They will still bear fruit in old age,
they will stay fresh and green,
15 proclaiming, "The LORD is upright;
he is my Rock, and there is no
wickedness in him."

Psalm 93

1 The LORD reigns, he is robed in majesty;
the LORD is robed in majesty
and is armed with strength.
The world is firmly established;
it cannot be moved.
2 Your throne was established long ago;
you are from all eternity.

3 The seas have lifted up,
O LORD,
the seas have lifted up
their voice;
the seas have lifted up
their pounding
waves.
4 Mightier than the thunder
of the great waters,
mightier than the
breakers of the
sea—
the LORD on high is
mighty.

5 Your statutes stand firm;
holiness adorns your house
for endless days, O LORD.

Psalm 94

1 O LORD, the God who avenges,
O God who avenges, shine forth.
2 Rise up, O Judge of the earth;
pay back to the proud what they deserve.
3 How long will the wicked, O LORD,
how long will the wicked be jubilant?
4 They pour out arrogant words;
all the evildoers are full of boasting.
5 They crush your people, O LORD;
they oppress your inheritance.
6 They slay the widow and the alien;
they murder the fatherless.
7 They say, "The LORD does not see;
the God of Jacob pays no heed."

8 Take heed, you senseless ones among the
people;
you fools, when will you become wise?
9 Does he who implanted the ear not hear?
Does he who formed the eye not see?
10 Does he who disciplines nations not
punish?
Does he who teaches man lack
knowledge?
11 The LORD knows the thoughts of man;
he knows that they are futile.

12 Blessed is the man you discipline, O LORD,
the man you teach from your law;
13 you grant him relief from days of trouble,
till a pit is dug for the
wicked.
14 For the LORD will not reject
his people;
he will never forsake his
inheritance.
15 Judgment will again
be founded on
righteousness,
and all the upright in
heart will follow it.

16 Who will rise up for me
against the wicked?
Who will take a stand
for me against
evildoers?
17 Unless the LORD had given me help,
I would soon have dwelt in the silence
of death.
18 When I said, "My foot is slipping,"
your love, O LORD, supported me.

Psalm 94:14

God Keeps His People

For the LORD will not
reject his people;
he will never forsake
his inheritance.

[a] 10 *Horn* here symbolizes strength.

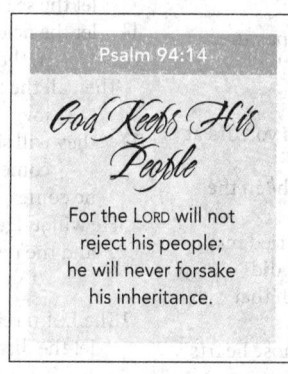

19 When anxiety was great within me,
your consolation brought joy to my soul.
20 Can a corrupt throne be allied with you—
one that brings on misery by its decrees?
21 They band together against the righteous
and condemn the innocent to death.
22 But the LORD has become my fortress,
and my God the rock in whom I take refuge.
23 He will repay them for their sins
and destroy them for their wickedness;
the LORD our God will destroy them.

Psalm 95

1 Come, let us sing for joy to the LORD;
let us shout aloud to the Rock of our salvation.
2 Let us come before him with thanksgiving
and extol him with music and song.

3 For the LORD is the great God,
the great King above all gods.
4 In his hand are the depths of the earth,
and the mountain peaks belong to him.
5 The sea is his, for he made it,
and his hands formed the dry land.

6 Come, let us bow down in worship,
let us kneel before the LORD our Maker;
7 for he is our God
and we are the people of his pasture,
the flock under his care.

Today, if you hear his voice,
8 do not harden your hearts as you did at Meribah,[a]
as you did that day at Massah[b] in the desert,
9 where your fathers tested and tried me,
though they had seen what I did.
10 For forty years I was angry with that generation;
I said, "They are a people whose hearts go astray,
and they have not known my ways."
11 So I declared on oath in my anger,
"They shall never enter my rest."

Psalm 96

1 Sing to the LORD a new song;
sing to the LORD, all the earth.
2 Sing to the LORD, praise his name;
proclaim his salvation day after day.
3 Declare his glory among the nations,
his marvelous deeds among all peoples.

4 For great is the LORD and most worthy of praise;
he is to be feared above all gods.
5 For all the gods of the nations are idols,
but the LORD made the heavens.
6 Splendor and majesty are before him;
strength and glory are in his sanctuary.

7 Ascribe to the LORD, O families of nations,
ascribe to the LORD glory and strength.
8 Ascribe to the LORD the glory due his name;
bring an offering and come into his courts.
9 Worship the LORD in the splendor of his[c] holiness;
tremble before him, all the earth.

10 Say among the nations, "The LORD reigns."
The world is firmly established, it cannot be moved;
he will judge the peoples with equity.
11 Let the heavens rejoice, let the earth be glad;
let the sea resound, and all that is in it;
12 let the fields be jubilant, and everything in them.
Then all the trees of the forest will sing for joy;
13 they will sing before the LORD, for he comes,
he comes to judge the earth.
He will judge the world in righteousness
and the peoples in his truth.

Psalm 97

1 The LORD reigns, let the earth be glad;
let the distant shores rejoice.

2 Clouds and thick darkness surround him;
righteousness and justice are the foundation of his throne.
3 Fire goes before him
and consumes his foes on every side.
4 His lightning lights up the world;
the earth sees and trembles.

[a] 8 *Meribah* means *quarreling.* [b] 8 *Massah* means *testing.* [c] 9 Or LORD *with the splendor of*

5 The mountains melt like wax before the LORD,
before the Lord of all the earth.
6 The heavens proclaim his righteousness,
and all the peoples see his glory.

7 All who worship images are put to shame,
those who boast in idols—
worship him, all you gods!

8 Zion hears and rejoices
and the villages of Judah are glad
because of your judgments, O LORD.
9 For you, O LORD, are the Most High over all the earth;
you are exalted far above all gods.

10 Let those who love the LORD hate evil,
for he guards the lives of his faithful ones
and delivers them from the hand of the wicked.
11 Light is shed upon the righteous
and joy on the upright in heart.
12 Rejoice in the LORD, you who are righteous,
and praise his holy name.

Psalm 98

A psalm.

1 Sing to the LORD a new song,
for he has done marvelous things;
his right hand and his holy arm
have worked salvation for him.
2 The LORD has made his salvation known
and revealed his righteousness to the nations.
3 He has remembered his love
and his faithfulness to the house of Israel;
all the ends of the earth have seen
the salvation of our God.

4 Shout for joy to the LORD, all the earth,
burst into jubilant song with music;
5 make music to the LORD with the harp,
with the harp and the sound of singing,
6 with trumpets and the blast of the ram's horn—
shout for joy before the LORD, the King.

7 Let the sea resound, and everything in it,
the world, and all who live in it.
8 Let the rivers clap their hands,
let the mountains sing together for joy;
9 let them sing before the LORD,
for he comes to judge the earth.
He will judge the world in righteousness
and the peoples with equity.

Psalm 99

1 The LORD reigns,
let the nations tremble;
he sits enthroned between the cherubim,
let the earth shake.
2 Great is the LORD in Zion;
he is exalted over all the nations.
3 Let them praise your great and awesome name—
he is holy.
4 The King is mighty, he loves justice—
you have established equity;
in Jacob you have done
what is just and right.
5 Exalt the LORD our God
and worship at his footstool;
he is holy.

6 Moses and Aaron were among his priests,
Samuel was among those who called on his name;
they called on the LORD
and he answered them.
7 He spoke to them from the pillar of cloud;
they kept his statutes and the decrees he gave them.

8 O LORD our God,
you answered them;
you were to Israel[a] a forgiving God,
though you punished their misdeeds.[b]
9 Exalt the LORD our God

Psalm 99:1

God Rules All Nations

The LORD reigns,
let the nations tremble;
he sits enthroned
between the cherubim,
let the earth shake.

[a]8 Hebrew *them* [b]8 Or / *an avenger of the wrongs done to them*

and worship at his holy mountain,
for the LORD our God is holy.

Psalm 100

A psalm. For giving thanks.

1 Shout for joy to the LORD, all the earth.
2 Worship the LORD with gladness;
come before him with joyful songs.
3 Know that the LORD is God.
It is he who made us, and we are his[a];
we are his people, the sheep of his pasture.

4 Enter his gates with thanksgiving
and his courts with praise;
give thanks to him and praise his name.
5 For the LORD is good and his love endures forever;
his faithfulness continues through all generations.

Psalm 101

Of David. A psalm.

1 I will sing of your love and justice;
to you, O LORD, I will sing praise.
2 I will be careful to lead a blameless life—
when will you come to me?

I will walk in my house
with blameless heart.
3 I will set before my eyes
no vile thing.

The deeds of faithless men I hate;
they will not cling to me.
4 Men of perverse heart shall be far from me;
I will have nothing to do with evil.

5 Whoever slanders his neighbor in secret,
him will I put to silence;
whoever has haughty eyes and a proud heart,
him will I not endure.

6 My eyes will be on the faithful in the land,
that they may dwell with me;
he whose walk is blameless
will minister to me.

7 No one who practices deceit
will dwell in my house;
no one who speaks falsely
will stand in my presence.

8 Every morning I will put to silence
all the wicked in the land;
I will cut off every evildoer
from the city of the LORD.

Psalm 102

A prayer of an afflicted man. When he is faint and pours out his lament before the LORD.

1 Hear my prayer, O LORD;
let my cry for help come to you.
2 Do not hide your face from me
when I am in distress.
Turn your ear to me;
when I call, answer me quickly.

3 For my days vanish like smoke;
my bones burn like glowing embers.
4 My heart is blighted and withered like grass;
I forget to eat my food.
5 Because of my loud groaning
I am reduced to skin and bones.
6 I am like a desert owl,
like an owl among the ruins.
7 I lie awake; I have become
like a bird alone on a roof.
8 All day long my enemies taunt me;
those who rail against me use my name as a curse.
9 For I eat ashes as my food
and mingle my drink with tears
10 because of your great wrath,
for you have taken me up and thrown me aside.
11 My days are like the evening shadow;
I wither away like grass.

12 But you, O LORD, sit enthroned forever;
your renown endures through all generations.
13 You will arise and have compassion on Zion,
for it is time to show favor to her;
the appointed time has come.
14 For her stones are dear to your servants;
her very dust moves them to pity.
15 The nations will fear the name of the LORD,
all the kings of the earth will revere your glory.
16 For the LORD will rebuild Zion

[a] 3 Or *and not we ourselves*

The Wow in Worship

Read: Psalm 100:1–5

SOMETIMES WE LACK THE *WOW* in our worship. Psalm 100 offers us a spiritual pick-me-up. It reveals that the more you know about God's nature, the more you'll express your love for him. Information leads to adoration. When the psalmist reflected on the Lord as God, Creator and Shepherd, it resulted in worship, gladness and joyful songs. It's true; to know him is to love him.

Knowing that "the LORD is God" (verse 3) identifies him as the only true God. He exists before all, after all and above all. He possesses power unlimited, knowledge unfathomable and a presence unavoidable. He is indescribable, indispensable and indisputable. God is big!

A little girl listened as her father read family devotions. She seemed awed by her parents' talk of God's limitless power. "Daddy," she asked, "how big is God?" Her father answered, "Honey, he is always a lot bigger than what you need." Believing that God is bigger than your situation produces passion in your praise.

Knowing that "it is he who made us" (verse 3) reveals him as Creator, the One who fashioned us into his very image (see Genesis 1:27). He displays his creativity through forming humans who are diverse yet distinct. But why did God create us? The psalmist says we were created to become his people—those of his highest priority. Your value lies not in *who* you are but in *whose* you are. Belonging to God adds awe to your adoration.

Knowing that "we are . . . the sheep of his pasture" (verse 3) can help us understand the tender care God shows his people. Shepherds are responsible for every aspect of their flock's well-being and take these responsibilities very seriously. They make sure their sheep have protection, guidance, pasture, sustenance and rest. Your Good Shepherd is like that. He leads his sheep to "green pastures" (Psalm 23:2), "calls his own sheep by name" (John 10:3) and "lays down his life for the sheep" (John 10:11). Showing gratitude to your Shepherd can engender gladness in your heart.

Understanding that the Lord is bigger than any of your needs, that he is *your* Creator—you belong to him—can't help but put the wow back into your worship!

Psalm 100:2–3

Worship the LORD with gladness; come before him with joyful songs. Know that the LORD is God. It is he who made us, and we are his; we are his people, the sheep of his pasture.

reflection

1 On a scale of one to ten, how would you rank the intensity of your worship?

2 List some of the attributes of God. In what ways has he revealed himself to you?

3 How does knowing the nature of God affect how you praise him? Now take some time to enter his gates with a joyful song that celebrates his character.

RELATED READINGS

Psalm 23:1–6;
Isaiah 42:5–6;
Romans 9:25–26;
Colossians 1:16–17

Go to page 726 for your next devotional reading.

and appear in his glory.
17 He will respond to the prayer of the
destitute;
he will not despise their plea.

18 Let this be written for a future generation,
that a people not yet created may praise
the LORD:
19 "The LORD looked down from his
sanctuary on high,
from heaven he viewed the earth,
20 to hear the groans of the prisoners
and release those condemned to death."
21 So the name of the LORD will be declared
in Zion
and his praise in Jerusalem
22 when the peoples and the kingdoms
assemble to worship the LORD.

23 In the course of my life[a] he
broke my strength;
he cut short my days.
24 So I said:
"Do not take me away,
O my God, in the
midst of my days;
your years go on through
all generations.
25 In the beginning you laid
the foundations of
the earth,
and the heavens are the
work of your hands.
26 They will perish, but you
remain;
they will all wear out like a garment.
Like clothing you will change them
and they will be discarded.
27 But you remain the same,
and your years will never end.
28 The children of your servants will live in
your presence;
their descendants will be established
before you."

Psalm 102:25

God Made Everything

In the beginning you laid
the foundations
of the earth,
and the heavens are the
work of your hands.

Psalm 103

Of David.

1 Praise the LORD, O my soul;
all my inmost being, praise his holy
name.
2 Praise the LORD, O my soul,
and forget not all his benefits—
3 who forgives all your sins
and heals all your diseases,
4 who redeems your life from the pit
and crowns you with love and
compassion,
5 who satisfies your desires with good
things
so that your youth is renewed like the
eagle's.

6 The LORD works righteousness
and justice for all the oppressed.

7 He made known his ways to Moses,
his deeds to the people of Israel:
8 The LORD is compassionate and gracious,
slow to anger, abounding in love.
9 He will not always accuse,
nor will he harbor his
anger forever;
10 he does not treat us as our
sins deserve
or repay us according to
our iniquities.
11 For as high as the heavens
are above the earth,
so great is his love for
those who fear him;
12 as far as the east is from the
west,
so far has he removed
our transgressions
from us.
13 As a father has compassion on his
children,
so the LORD has compassion on those
who fear him;
14 for he knows how we are formed,
he remembers that we are dust.
15 As for man, his days are like grass,
he flourishes like a flower of the field;
16 the wind blows over it and it is gone,
and its place remembers it no more.
17 But from everlasting to everlasting
the LORD's love is with those who fear
him,
and his righteousness with their
children's children—

[a]23 Or *By his power*

18 with those who keep his covenant
and remember to obey his precepts.

19 The LORD has established his throne in heaven,
and his kingdom rules over all.

20 Praise the LORD, you his angels,
you mighty ones who do his bidding,
who obey his word.
21 Praise the LORD, all his heavenly hosts,
you his servants who do his will.
22 Praise the LORD, all his works
everywhere in his dominion.

Praise the LORD, O my soul.

Psalm 104

1 Praise the LORD, O my soul.

O LORD my God, you are very great;
you are clothed with splendor and majesty.
2 He wraps himself in light as with a garment;
he stretches out the heavens like a tent
3 and lays the beams of his upper chambers on their waters.
He makes the clouds his chariot
and rides on the wings of the wind.
4 He makes winds his messengers,[a]
flames of fire his servants.

5 He set the earth on its foundations;
it can never be moved.
6 You covered it with the deep as with a garment;
the waters stood above the mountains.
7 But at your rebuke the waters fled,
at the sound of your thunder they took to flight;
8 they flowed over the mountains,
they went down into the valleys,
to the place you assigned for them.
9 You set a boundary they cannot cross;
never again will they cover the earth.

10 He makes springs pour water into the ravines;
it flows between the mountains.
11 They give water to all the beasts of the field;
the wild donkeys quench their thirst.
12 The birds of the air nest by the waters;
they sing among the branches.
13 He waters the mountains from his upper chambers;
the earth is satisfied by the fruit of his work.
14 He makes grass grow for the cattle,
and plants for man to cultivate—
bringing forth food from the earth:
15 wine that gladdens the heart of man,
oil to make his face shine,
and bread that sustains his heart.
16 The trees of the LORD are well watered,
the cedars of Lebanon that he planted.
17 There the birds make their nests;
the stork has its home in the pine trees.
18 The high mountains belong to the wild goats;
the crags are a refuge for the coneys.[b]

19 The moon marks off the seasons,
and the sun knows when to go down.
20 You bring darkness, it becomes night,
and all the beasts of the forest prowl.
21 The lions roar for their prey
and seek their food from God.
22 The sun rises, and they steal away;
they return and lie down in their dens.
23 Then man goes out to his work,
to his labor until evening.

24 How many are your works, O LORD!
In wisdom you made them all;
the earth is full of your creatures.
25 There is the sea, vast and spacious,
teeming with creatures beyond number—
living things both large and small.
26 There the ships go to and fro,
and the leviathan, which you formed to frolic there.

27 These all look to you
to give them their food at the proper time.
28 When you give it to them,
they gather it up;
when you open your hand,
they are satisfied with good things.
29 When you hide your face,
they are terrified;
when you take away their breath,

a4 Or *angels* b18 That is, the hyrax or rock badger

Grow Up, Not Old

Read: Psalm 103:1–22

"I USED TO BE CUTE, BUT NOW I feel invisible," said the 50-something lady as she laughed nervously, but her eyes glistened with tears. A 30-something woman expressed the same feelings, saying, "When I was in my 20s, I turned a few heads, but now, hey, I'm a mom of four. What do I expect?" Both women are attractive . . . some might even say they're beautiful. But they each struggle with their self-image because our culture is not kind to aging women. Physical beauty and glamorized sexuality are prized above character and inner loveliness. God's view—the Biblical view—of growing older makes the world's view of beauty seem silly and nonsensical. But it takes mental discipline to focus on God's standards of worth and beauty when so many media outlets suggest that anyone over 30 is past their prime.

God doesn't pretend that growing older is easy. He acknowledges that our days are as fleeting as the grass growing in the field. We all realize that our outward beauty will fade away like a flower that blooms for a season and then disappears. Thankfully, our heavenly Father values the inner beauty that will never perish, an eternal beauty that comes from a heart radiating with God's love.

Yes, aging is hard. For most of us, getting older means losing our youthful beauty and experiencing the breakdown of our bodies. But God tells us that there is a loveliness that comes with maturity. When we know Jesus as our Savior, we are more aware that each day brings us closer to that place where there will be no more tears, no more sorrow, no more death. Growing older for the child of God does not mean feeling useless and ugly. It means growing up and maturing into a person who looks like God—exhibiting his qualities of compassion, abounding love and mercy. The truth is, you're getting older every day. Embrace aging as your pathway to being ever growing, ever green with an eternal purpose.

Psalm 103:15–16

As for man, his days are like grass, he flourishes like a flower of the field; the wind blows over it and it is gone, and its place remembers it no more.

reflection

1 How has your culture's view of aging affected your self-image?

2 How does knowing that God views you as lovely make you feel?

3 As you've grown older, how has your wisdom increased?

RELATED READINGS

Psalm 71:17–21; Proverbs 16:31; Isaiah 46:3–4

"By focusing our heart's desire on Christ and letting the Holy Spirit transform us from the inside out, we are indeed becoming beautiful where it really counts."

Debra Evans

Go to page 734 for your next devotional reading.

they die and return to the dust.
30 When you send your Spirit,
they are created,
and you renew the face of the earth.

31 May the glory of the LORD endure forever;
may the LORD rejoice in his works—
32 he who looks at the earth, and it trembles,
who touches the mountains, and they smoke.

33 I will sing to the LORD all my life;
I will sing praise to my God as long as I live.
34 May my meditation be pleasing to him,
as I rejoice in the LORD.
35 But may sinners vanish from the earth
and the wicked be no more.

Praise the LORD, O my soul.

Praise the LORD.[a]

Psalm 105

1 Give thanks to the LORD, call on his name;
make known among the nations what he has done.
2 Sing to him, sing praise to him;
tell of all his wonderful acts.
3 Glory in his holy name;
let the hearts of those who seek the LORD rejoice.
4 Look to the LORD and his strength;
seek his face always.

5 Remember the wonders he has done,
his miracles, and the judgments he pronounced,
6 O descendants of Abraham his servant,
O sons of Jacob, his chosen ones.
7 He is the LORD our God;
his judgments are in all the earth.

8 He remembers his covenant forever,
the word he commanded, for a thousand generations,
9 the covenant he made with Abraham,
the oath he swore to Isaac.
10 He confirmed it to Jacob as a decree,
to Israel as an everlasting covenant:
11 "To you I will give the land of Canaan
as the portion you will inherit."

12 When they were but few in number,
few indeed, and strangers in it,
13 they wandered from nation to nation,
from one kingdom to another.
14 He allowed no one to oppress them;
for their sake he rebuked kings:
15 "Do not touch my anointed ones;
do my prophets no harm."

16 He called down famine on the land
and destroyed all their supplies of food;
17 and he sent a man before them—
Joseph, sold as a slave.
18 They bruised his feet with shackles,
his neck was put in irons,
19 till what he foretold came to pass,
till the word of the LORD proved him true.
20 The king sent and released him,
the ruler of peoples set him free.
21 He made him master of his household,
ruler over all he possessed,
22 to instruct his princes as he pleased
and teach his elders wisdom.

> Psalm 105:8
>
> *God Remembers His Promises*
>
> He remembers his covenant forever, the word he commanded, for a thousand generations.

23 Then Israel entered Egypt;
Jacob lived as an alien in the land of Ham.
24 The LORD made his people very fruitful;
he made them too numerous for their foes,
25 whose hearts he turned to hate his people,
to conspire against his servants.
26 He sent Moses his servant,
and Aaron, whom he had chosen.
27 They performed his miraculous signs among them,
his wonders in the land of Ham.

[a] 35 Hebrew *Hallelu Yah*; in the Septuagint this line stands at the beginning of Psalm 105.

28 He sent darkness and made the land
dark—
for had they not rebelled against his
words?
29 He turned their waters into blood,
causing their fish to die.
30 Their land teemed with frogs,
which went up into the bedrooms of
their rulers.
31 He spoke, and there came swarms of
flies,
and gnats throughout their country.
32 He turned their rain into hail,
with lightning throughout their land;
33 he struck down their vines and fig trees
and shattered the trees of their country.
34 He spoke, and the locusts came,
grasshoppers without number;
35 they ate up every green thing in their land,
ate up the produce of their soil.
36 Then he struck down all the firstborn in
their land,
the firstfruits of all their manhood.

37 He brought out Israel, laden with silver
and gold,
and from among their tribes no one
faltered.
38 Egypt was glad when they left,
because dread of Israel had fallen on
them.
39 He spread out a cloud as a covering,
and a fire to give light at night.
40 They asked, and he brought them quail
and satisfied them with the bread of
heaven.
41 He opened the rock, and water gushed out;
like a river it flowed in the desert.

42 For he remembered his holy promise
given to his servant Abraham.
43 He brought out his people with rejoicing,
his chosen ones with shouts of joy;
44 he gave them the lands of the nations,
and they fell heir to what others had
toiled for—
45 that they might keep his precepts
and observe his laws.

Praise the LORD.[a]

Psalm 106

1 Praise the LORD.[b]

Give thanks to the LORD, for he is good;
his love endures forever.
2 Who can proclaim the mighty acts of the
LORD
or fully declare his praise?
3 Blessed are they who maintain justice,
who constantly do what is right.
4 Remember me, O LORD, when you show
favor to your people,
come to my aid when you save them,
5 that I may enjoy the prosperity of your
chosen ones,
that I may share in the joy of your nation
and join your inheritance in giving
praise.

6 We have sinned, even as our fathers did;
we have done wrong and acted wickedly.
7 When our fathers were in Egypt,
they gave no thought to your miracles;
they did not remember your many
kindnesses,
and they rebelled by the sea, the Red
Sea.[c]
8 Yet he saved them for his name's sake,
to make his mighty power known.
9 He rebuked the Red Sea, and it dried up;
he led them through the depths as
through a desert.
10 He saved them from the hand of the foe;
from the hand of the enemy he
redeemed them.
11 The waters covered their adversaries;
not one of them survived.
12 Then they believed his promises
and sang his praise.

13 But they soon forgot what he had done
and did not wait for his counsel.
14 In the desert they gave in to their craving;
in the wasteland they put God to the
test.
15 So he gave them what they asked for,
but sent a wasting disease upon them.

16 In the camp they grew envious of Moses
and of Aaron, who was consecrated to
the LORD.

[a]45 Hebrew *Hallelu Yah* [b]1 Hebrew *Hallelu Yah*; also in verse 48 [c]7 Hebrew *Yam Suph*; that is, Sea of Reeds; also in verses 9 and 22

17 The earth opened up and swallowed
Dathan;
it buried the company of Abiram.
18 Fire blazed among their followers;
a flame consumed the wicked.

19 At Horeb they made a calf
and worshiped an idol cast from metal.
20 They exchanged their Glory
for an image of a bull, which eats grass.
21 They forgot the God who saved them,
who had done great things in Egypt,
22 miracles in the land of Ham
and awesome deeds by the Red Sea.
23 So he said he would destroy them—
had not Moses, his chosen one,
stood in the breach before him
to keep his wrath from destroying them.

24 Then they despised the pleasant land;
they did not believe his promise.
25 They grumbled in their tents
and did not obey the LORD.
26 So he swore to them with uplifted hand
that he would make them fall in the
desert,
27 make their descendants fall among the
nations
and scatter them throughout the lands.

28 They yoked themselves to the Baal of Peor
and ate sacrifices offered to lifeless gods;
29 they provoked the LORD to anger by their
wicked deeds,
and a plague broke out among them.
30 But Phinehas stood up and intervened,
and the plague was checked.
31 This was credited to him as righteousness
for endless generations to come.

32 By the waters of Meribah they angered the
LORD,
and trouble came to Moses because of
them;
33 for they rebelled against the Spirit of God,
and rash words came from Moses' lips.[a]

34 They did not destroy the peoples
as the LORD had commanded them,
35 but they mingled with the nations
and adopted their customs.
36 They worshiped their idols,
which became a snare to them.
37 They sacrificed their sons
and their daughters to demons.
38 They shed innocent blood,
the blood of their sons and daughters,
whom they sacrificed to the idols of
Canaan,
and the land was desecrated by their
blood.
39 They defiled themselves by what they did;
by their deeds they prostituted
themselves.

40 Therefore the LORD was angry with his
people
and abhorred his inheritance.
41 He handed them over to the nations,
and their foes ruled over them.
42 Their enemies oppressed them
and subjected them to their power.
43 Many times he delivered them,
but they were bent on rebellion
and they wasted away in their sin.

44 But he took note of their distress
when he heard their cry;
45 for their sake he remembered his covenant
and out of his great love he relented.
46 He caused them to be pitied
by all who held them captive.

47 Save us, O LORD our God,
and gather us from the nations,
that we may give thanks to your holy name
and glory in your praise.

48 Praise be to the LORD, the God of Israel,
from everlasting to everlasting.
Let all the people say, "Amen!"

Praise the LORD.

BOOK V
Psalms 107–150

Psalm 107

1 Give thanks to the LORD, for he is good;
his love endures forever.
2 Let the redeemed of the LORD say this—
those he redeemed from the hand of the
foe,

33 Or *against his spirit, / and rash words came from his lips*

3 those he gathered from the lands,
from east and west, from north and south.[a]

4 Some wandered in desert wastelands,
finding no way to a city where they could settle.
5 They were hungry and thirsty,
and their lives ebbed away.
6 Then they cried out to the LORD in their trouble,
and he delivered them from their distress.
7 He led them by a straight way
to a city where they could settle.
8 Let them give thanks to the LORD for his unfailing love
and his wonderful deeds for men,
9 for he satisfies the thirsty
and fills the hungry with good things.

10 Some sat in darkness and the deepest gloom,
prisoners suffering in iron chains,
11 for they had rebelled against the words of God
and despised the counsel of the Most High.
12 So he subjected them to bitter labor;
they stumbled, and there was no one to help.
13 Then they cried to the LORD in their trouble,
and he saved them from their distress.
14 He brought them out of darkness and the deepest gloom
and broke away their chains.
15 Let them give thanks to the LORD for his unfailing love
and his wonderful deeds for men,
16 for he breaks down gates of bronze
and cuts through bars of iron.

17 Some became fools through their rebellious ways
and suffered affliction because of their iniquities.
18 They loathed all food
and drew near the gates of death.
19 Then they cried to the LORD in their trouble,
and he saved them from their distress.
20 He sent forth his word and healed them;
he rescued them from the grave.
21 Let them give thanks to the LORD for his unfailing love
and his wonderful deeds for men.
22 Let them sacrifice thank offerings
and tell of his works with songs of joy.

23 Others went out on the sea in ships;
they were merchants on the mighty waters.
24 They saw the works of the LORD,
his wonderful deeds in the deep.
25 For he spoke and stirred up a tempest
that lifted high the waves.
26 They mounted up to the heavens and went down to the depths;
in their peril their courage melted away.
27 They reeled and staggered like drunken men;
they were at their wits' end.
28 Then they cried out to the LORD in their trouble,
and he brought them out of their distress.
29 He stilled the storm to a whisper;
the waves of the sea were hushed.
30 They were glad when it grew calm,
and he guided them to their desired haven.
31 Let them give thanks to the LORD for his unfailing love
and his wonderful deeds for men.
32 Let them exalt him in the assembly of the people
and praise him in the council of the elders.

Psalm 107:8

God Gives Unfailing Love

Let them give thanks
to the LORD for his
unfailing love
and his wonderful
deeds for men.

[a]3 Hebrew *north and the sea*

33 He turned rivers into a desert,
flowing springs into thirsty ground,
34 and fruitful land into a salt waste,
because of the wickedness of those who lived there.
35 He turned the desert into pools of water
and the parched ground into flowing springs;
36 there he brought the hungry to live,
and they founded a city where they could settle.
37 They sowed fields and planted vineyards
that yielded a fruitful harvest;
38 he blessed them, and their numbers greatly increased,
and he did not let their herds diminish.

39 Then their numbers decreased, and they were humbled
by oppression, calamity and sorrow;
40 he who pours contempt on nobles
made them wander in a trackless waste.
41 But he lifted the needy out of their affliction
and increased their families like flocks.
42 The upright see and rejoice,
but all the wicked shut their mouths.

43 Whoever is wise, let him heed these things
and consider the great love of the LORD.

Psalm 108

A song. A psalm of David.

1 My heart is steadfast, O God;
I will sing and make music with all my soul.
2 Awake, harp and lyre!
I will awaken the dawn.
3 I will praise you, O LORD, among the nations;
I will sing of you among the peoples.
4 For great is your love, higher than the heavens;
your faithfulness reaches to the skies.
5 Be exalted, O God, above the heavens,
and let your glory be over all the earth.
6 Save us and help us with your right hand,
that those you love may be delivered.
7 God has spoken from his sanctuary:
"In triumph I will parcel out Shechem
and measure off the Valley of Succoth.
8 Gilead is mine, Manasseh is mine;
Ephraim is my helmet,
Judah my scepter.
9 Moab is my washbasin,
upon Edom I toss my sandal;
over Philistia I shout in triumph."

10 Who will bring me to the fortified city?
Who will lead me to Edom?
11 Is it not you, O God, you who have rejected us
and no longer go out with our armies?
12 Give us aid against the enemy,
for the help of man is worthless.
13 With God we will gain the victory,
and he will trample down our enemies.

Psalm 109

For the director of music. Of David. A psalm.

1 O God, whom I praise,
do not remain silent,
2 for wicked and deceitful men
have opened their mouths against me;
they have spoken against me with lying tongues.
3 With words of hatred they surround me;
they attack me without cause.
4 In return for my friendship they accuse me,
but I am a man of prayer.
5 They repay me evil for good,
and hatred for my friendship.

6 Appoint[a] an evil man[b] to oppose him;
let an accuser[c] stand at his right hand.
7 When he is tried, let him be found guilty,
and may his prayers condemn him.
8 May his days be few;
may another take his place of leadership.
9 May his children be fatherless
and his wife a widow.
10 May his children be wandering beggars;
may they be driven[d] from their ruined homes.
11 May a creditor seize all he has;
may strangers plunder the fruits of his labor.
12 May no one extend kindness to him

[a]6 Or ⌊They say:⌋ "Appoint (with quotation marks at the end of verse 19) [b]6 Or *the Evil One* [c]6 Or *let Satan* [d]10 Septuagint; Hebrew *sought*

or take pity on his fatherless children.
13 May his descendants be cut off,
their names blotted out from the next generation.
14 May the iniquity of his fathers be remembered before the LORD;
may the sin of his mother never be blotted out.
15 May their sins always remain before the LORD,
that he may cut off the memory of them from the earth.

16 For he never thought of doing a kindness,
but hounded to death the poor
and the needy and the brokenhearted.
17 He loved to pronounce a curse—
may it[a] come on him;
he found no pleasure in blessing—
may it be[b] far from him.
18 He wore cursing as his garment;
it entered into his body like water,
into his bones like oil.
19 May it be like a cloak wrapped about him,
like a belt tied forever around him.
20 May this be the LORD's payment to my accusers,
to those who speak evil of me.

21 But you, O Sovereign LORD,
deal well with me for your name's sake;
out of the goodness of your love, deliver me.
22 For I am poor and needy,
and my heart is wounded within me.
23 I fade away like an evening shadow;
I am shaken off like a locust.
24 My knees give way from fasting;
my body is thin and gaunt.
25 I am an object of scorn to my accusers;
when they see me, they shake their heads.

26 Help me, O LORD my God;
save me in accordance with your love.
27 Let them know that it is your hand,
that you, O LORD, have done it.
28 They may curse, but you will bless;
when they attack they will be put to shame,
but your servant will rejoice.
29 My accusers will be clothed with disgrace
and wrapped in shame as in a cloak.

30 With my mouth I will greatly extol the LORD;
in the great throng I will praise him.
31 For he stands at the right hand of the needy one,
to save his life from those who condemn him.

Psalm 110

Of David. A psalm.

1 The LORD says to my Lord:
"Sit at my right hand
until I make your enemies
a footstool for your feet."

2 The LORD will extend your mighty scepter from Zion;
you will rule in the midst of your enemies.

3 Your troops will be willing
on your day of battle.
Arrayed in holy majesty,
from the womb of the dawn
you will receive the dew of your youth.[c]

4 The LORD has sworn
and will not change his mind:
"You are a priest forever,
in the order of Melchizedek."

5 The Lord is at your right hand;
he will crush kings on the day of his wrath.
6 He will judge the nations, heaping up the dead
and crushing the rulers of the whole earth.
7 He will drink from a brook beside the way[d];
therefore he will lift up his head.

Psalm 111[e]

1 Praise the LORD.[f]

I will extol the LORD with all my heart
in the council of the upright and in the assembly.

[a]17 Or *curse, / and it has* [b]17 Or *blessing, / and it is* [c]3 Or / *your young men will come to you like the dew* [d]7 Or / *The One who grants succession will set him in authority* [e]This psalm is an acrostic poem, the lines of which begin with the successive letters of the Hebrew alphabet. [f]1 Hebrew *Hallelu Yah*

2 Great are the works of the LORD;
they are pondered by all who delight in them.
3 Glorious and majestic are his deeds,
and his righteousness endures forever.
4 He has caused his wonders to be remembered;
the LORD is gracious and compassionate.
5 He provides food for those who fear him;
he remembers his covenant forever.
6 He has shown his people the power of his works,
giving them the lands of other nations.
7 The works of his hands are faithful and just;
all his precepts are trustworthy.
8 They are steadfast for ever and ever,
done in faithfulness and uprightness.
9 He provided redemption for his people;
he ordained his covenant forever—
holy and awesome is his name.

10 The fear of the LORD is the beginning of wisdom;
all who follow his precepts have good understanding.
To him belongs eternal praise.

Psalm 111:10

God Gives Wisdom

The fear of the LORD is the beginning of wisdom;
all who follow his precepts have good understanding.
To him belongs eternal praise.

Psalm 112[a]

1 Praise the LORD.[b]

Blessed is the man who fears the LORD,
who finds great delight in his commands.

2 His children will be mighty in the land;
the generation of the upright will be blessed.
3 Wealth and riches are in his house,
and his righteousness endures forever.
4 Even in darkness light dawns for the upright,
for the gracious and compassionate and righteous man.[c]
5 Good will come to him who is generous and lends freely,
who conducts his affairs with justice.
6 Surely he will never be shaken;
a righteous man will be remembered forever.
7 He will have no fear of bad news;
his heart is steadfast, trusting in the LORD.
8 His heart is secure, he will have no fear;
in the end he will look in triumph on his foes.
9 He has scattered abroad his gifts to the poor,
his righteousness endures forever;
his horn[d] will be lifted high in honor.

10 The wicked man will see and be vexed,
he will gnash his teeth and waste away;
the longings of the wicked will come to nothing.

Psalm 113

1 Praise the LORD.[e]

Praise, O servants of the LORD,
praise the name of the LORD.
2 Let the name of the LORD be praised,
both now and forevermore.
3 From the rising of the sun to the place where it sets,
the name of the LORD is to be praised.

4 The LORD is exalted over all the nations,
his glory above the heavens.
5 Who is like the LORD our God,
the One who sits enthroned on high,
6 who stoops down to look
on the heavens and the earth?

[a]This psalm is an acrostic poem, the lines of which begin with the successive letters of the Hebrew alphabet. [b]1 Hebrew *Hallelu Yah*
[c]4 Or / *for* ⌊*the LORD*⌋ *is gracious and compassionate and righteous* [d]9 *Horn* here symbolizes dignity. [e]1 Hebrew *Hallelu Yah*; also in verse 9

A Checklist of Delight

Psalm 112:1

Praise the LORD. Blessed is the man who fears the LORD, who finds great delight in his commands.

reflection

1 What keeps you from acknowledging God's gifts to you?

2 What could you do to live a more mindful and thankful life?

3 Why does God tell you to praise him? What will you praise him for today?

RELATED READINGS

1 Chronicles 29:20; Psalms 65:1–13; 103:1–22; 104:1–35

"Celebrating each new day helps us develop the ability to be grateful for all new moments and for the God who is in each one."

Karen Burton Mains

Read: Psalm 112:1–10

LIFE. CHECK. *OXYGEN*. CHECK. *Food*. Check. *Ability to read*. Check.

How long has it been since you listed the good things God has given you? He created a beautiful world full of all you need: air, water, thousands of varieties of food and much more. In giving you your family, your ability to smell and your sense of humor, God has given you precious gifts. From telling Old Testament tales of his long-suffering to letting you see behind the scenes of his Son's trip to Earth, his Word is an extra-special love gift.

The psalms give many examples of praise and list many good reasons for thanksgiving. *Give thanks in all circumstances?* Check. Even in the midst of trials, praise is appropriate because God is keeping track of your enemies while you sleep. *Give praise for dark times?* Check. Even in darkness his light dawns. *Thank him for family?* Check. God will meet your needs and watch over your children. *Delight in God's commands?* Check. Even God's commands are counted among his gracious blessings, for they bring us life.

Scripture never promises believers a trial-free life. But God's Word does promise a life of purpose, direction and blessing under his watchful care. It does promise that the one who trusts God is secure.

Have you thanked God for gravity lately? For clouds that shade you from the summer sun, provide the rain and glow at sunrise? For your ears, your nose, your eyes? For giving humankind the ability to create penicillin, the electric light, the telephone, the means of preserving food? For loving you enough to claim you as his child? For watching over you even when you are busy or distracted and you forget him? For protecting you and giving you purpose and hope? Make your own checklist. He is worthy of your praise.

Go to page 738 for your next devotional reading.

7 He raises the poor from the dust
and lifts the needy from the ash heap;
8 he seats them with princes,
with the princes of their people.
9 He settles the barren woman in her home
as a happy mother of children.

Praise the LORD.

Psalm 114

1 When Israel came out of Egypt,
the house of Jacob from a people of foreign tongue,
2 Judah became God's sanctuary,
Israel his dominion.

3 The sea looked and fled,
the Jordan turned back;
4 the mountains skipped like rams,
the hills like lambs.

5 Why was it, O sea, that you fled,
O Jordan, that you turned back,
6 you mountains, that you skipped like rams,
you hills, like lambs?

7 Tremble, O earth, at the presence of the Lord,
at the presence of the God of Jacob,
8 who turned the rock into a pool,
the hard rock into springs of water.

Psalm 115

1 Not to us, O LORD, not to us
but to your name be the glory,
because of your love and faithfulness.

2 Why do the nations say,
"Where is their God?"
3 Our God is in heaven;
he does whatever pleases him.
4 But their idols are silver and gold,
made by the hands of men.
5 They have mouths, but cannot speak,
eyes, but they cannot see;
6 they have ears, but cannot hear,
noses, but they cannot smell;
7 they have hands, but cannot feel,
feet, but they cannot walk;
nor can they utter a sound with their throats.

8 Those who make them will be like them,
and so will all who trust in them.

9 O house of Israel, trust in the LORD—
he is their help and shield.
10 O house of Aaron, trust in the LORD—
he is their help and shield.
11 You who fear him, trust in the LORD—
he is their help and shield.

12 The LORD remembers us and will bless us:
He will bless the house of Israel,
he will bless the house of Aaron,
13 he will bless those who fear the LORD—
small and great alike.

14 May the LORD make you increase,
both you and your children.
15 May you be blessed by the LORD,
the Maker of heaven and earth.

16 The highest heavens belong to the LORD,
but the earth he has given to man.
17 It is not the dead who praise the LORD,
those who go down to silence;
18 it is we who extol the LORD,
both now and forevermore.

Praise the LORD.[a]

Psalm 116

1 I love the LORD, for he heard my voice;
he heard my cry for mercy.
2 Because he turned his ear to me,
I will call on him as long as I live.

3 The cords of death entangled me,
the anguish of the grave[b] came upon me;
I was overcome by trouble and sorrow.
4 Then I called on the name of the LORD:
"O LORD, save me!"

5 The LORD is gracious and righteous;
our God is full of compassion.
6 The LORD protects the simplehearted;
when I was in great need, he saved me.

7 Be at rest once more, O my soul,
for the LORD has been good to you.

8 For you, O LORD, have delivered my soul from death,
my eyes from tears,

[a]18 Hebrew *Hallelu Yah* [b]3 Hebrew *Sheol*

my feet from stumbling,
9 that I may walk before the LORD
in the land of the living.
10 I believed; therefore[a] I said,
"I am greatly afflicted."
11 And in my dismay I said,
"All men are liars."

12 How can I repay the LORD
for all his goodness to me?
13 I will lift up the cup of salvation
and call on the name of
the LORD.
14 I will fulfill my vows to the
LORD
in the presence of all his
people.

15 Precious in the sight of the
LORD
is the death of his saints.
16 O LORD, truly I am your
servant;
I am your servant,
the son of your
maidservant[b];
you have freed me from my chains.

17 I will sacrifice a thank offering to you
and call on the name of the LORD.
18 I will fulfill my vows to the LORD
in the presence of all his people,
19 in the courts of the house of the LORD—
in your midst, O Jerusalem.

Praise the LORD.[c]

Psalm 117

1 Praise the LORD, all you nations;
extol him, all you peoples.
2 For great is his love toward us,
and the faithfulness of the LORD
endures forever.

Praise the LORD.[c]

Psalm 118

1 Give thanks to the LORD, for he is good;
his love endures forever.

2 Let Israel say:
"His love endures forever."
3 Let the house of Aaron say:
"His love endures forever."
4 Let those who fear the LORD say:
"His love endures forever."

5 In my anguish I cried to the LORD,
and he answered by setting me free.
6 The LORD is with me; I will not be afraid.
What can man do to me?
7 The LORD is with me; he is my helper.
I will look in triumph on my enemies.

8 It is better to take refuge in the LORD
than to trust in man.
9 It is better to take refuge in
the LORD
than to trust in princes.
10 All the nations surrounded
me,
but in the name of the
LORD I cut them off.
11 They surrounded me on
every side,
but in the name of the
LORD I cut them off.
12 They swarmed around me
like bees,
but they died out as quickly as burning
thorns;
in the name of the LORD I cut them off.

13 I was pushed back and about to fall,
but the LORD helped me.
14 The LORD is my strength and my song;
he has become my salvation.

15 Shouts of joy and victory
resound in the tents of the righteous:
"The LORD's right hand has done mighty
things!
16 The LORD's right hand is lifted high;
the LORD's right hand has done mighty
things!"

17 I will not die but live,
and will proclaim what the LORD has
done.
18 The LORD has chastened me severely,
but he has not given me over to death.

19 Open for me the gates of righteousness;
I will enter and give thanks to the LORD.

Psalm 116:15

God Welcomes Us to Heaven

Precious in the sight
of the LORD
is the death of his saints.

[a]10 Or *believed even when* [b]16 Or *servant, your faithful son* [c]19,2 Hebrew *Hallelu Yah*

20 This is the gate of the LORD
through which the righteous may enter.
21 I will give you thanks, for you answered me;
you have become my salvation.

22 The stone the builders rejected
has become the capstone;
23 the LORD has done this,
and it is marvelous in our eyes.
24 This is the day the LORD has made;
let us rejoice and be glad in it.

25 O LORD, save us;
O LORD, grant us success.
26 Blessed is he who comes in the name of the LORD.
From the house of the LORD we bless you.[a]
27 The LORD is God,
and he has made his light shine upon us.
With boughs in hand, join in the festal procession
up[b] to the horns of the altar.

28 You are my God, and I will give you thanks;
you are my God, and I will exalt you.

29 Give thanks to the LORD, for he is good;
his love endures forever.

Psalm 119[c]

א Aleph

1 Blessed are they whose ways are blameless,
who walk according to the law of the LORD.
2 Blessed are they who keep his statutes
and seek him with all their heart.
3 They do nothing wrong;
they walk in his ways.
4 You have laid down precepts
that are to be fully obeyed.
5 Oh, that my ways were steadfast
in obeying your decrees!
6 Then I would not be put to shame
when I consider all your commands.
7 I will praise you with an upright heart
as I learn your righteous laws.
8 I will obey your decrees;
do not utterly forsake me.

ב Beth

9 How can a young man keep his way pure?
By living according to your word.
10 I seek you with all my heart;
do not let me stray from your commands.
11 I have hidden your word in my heart
that I might not sin against you.
12 Praise be to you, O LORD;
teach me your decrees.
13 With my lips I recount
all the laws that come from your mouth.
14 I rejoice in following your statutes
as one rejoices in great riches.
15 I meditate on your precepts
and consider your ways.
16 I delight in your decrees;
I will not neglect your word.

ג Gimel

17 Do good to your servant, and I will live;
I will obey your word.
18 Open my eyes that I may see
wonderful things in your law.
19 I am a stranger on earth;
do not hide your commands from me.
20 My soul is consumed with longing
for your laws at all times.
21 You rebuke the arrogant, who are cursed
and who stray from your commands.
22 Remove from me scorn and contempt,
for I keep your statutes.
23 Though rulers sit together and slander me,
your servant will meditate on your decrees.
24 Your statutes are my delight;
they are my counselors.

ד Daleth

25 I am laid low in the dust;
preserve my life according to your word.
26 I recounted my ways and you answered me;
teach me your decrees.

[a] 26 The Hebrew is plural. [b] 27 Or *Bind the festal sacrifice with ropes / and take it* [c] This psalm is an acrostic poem; the verses of each stanza begin with the same letter of the Hebrew alphabet.

It's Later Than You Think

Read: Psalm 118:1–29

Psalm 118:24

This is the day the LORD has made; let us rejoice and be glad in it.

reflection

1 How can you relate to Luci's thoughts on how we strive to save time, but in the process, we're missing out on somethings?

2 How will you follow her suggestion to take the time to do something beautifully?

3 Memorize Psalm 118:24, "This is the day the LORD has made; let us rejoice and be glad in it." Whenever you find yourself in a hurry, bring this Scripture to mind, and rejoice in the Lord!

RELATED READINGS

Romans 5:1–5;
Philippians 4:4–7

WHEN I WAS A CHILD, our family had a chiming clock that had been handed down through the generations and was a well-loved treasure. On the hour, of course, it would chime out the time, and by it we kept on schedule with meals and departures and awakening and bedtime. Many nights, from our respective bedrooms, each of us would call out the number of chimes until the last one stopped.

One night, after we had all gone to bed about midnight, the clock began to gong and we started our audible ritual: "Nine . . . ten . . . eleven . . . twelve." Just as we closed our mouths after shouting out TWELVE! the clock struck thirteen. We could hardly believe our ears. Where did that come from? I wondered, as we all laughed heartily from our beds. Then, almost in perfect unison, we called out: "It's later than you think!"

For most of us, that's the problem: Our greatest fear is running out of time. So we hurry through life trying desperately to get everything done: working overtime, eating fast food in the car, racing down the freeway. We've gone from The One Minute Manager to The One Minute Mother to One Minute Wisdom. Life itself encourages us to hurry. I can do my laundry twice as fast as my grandmother did; I can travel coast to coast faster than my father ever could; I can handle correspondence that took my mother hours with a few keystrokes and mouse clicks. And yet, I seem to have less time than they did. What has happened?

In our quest to save time, we're losing something. I thought the other day about how my grandparents valued time. They always had time for my parents and my brothers and me; they had time for music in their home (each of them was a competent musician); they emphasized beautifully served meals, family reunions and long conversations. It seemed they had time for everything in life that was important, because they took time to live . . .

Today, this very day, why don't you think of something that takes a bit of extra time to do and do it. Do it for yourself. Do it for a family member. Do it for a neighbor or friend. Do it for the Lord . . . Don't wait for another time. Rejoice in this day and be glad! Tonight, your clock could strike thirteen.

—Luci Swindoll

Go to page 745 for your next devotional reading.

27 Let me understand the teaching of your
precepts;
then I will meditate on your wonders.
28 My soul is weary with sorrow;
strengthen me according to your word.
29 Keep me from deceitful ways;
be gracious to me through your law.
30 I have chosen the way of truth;
I have set my heart on your laws.
31 I hold fast to your statutes, O LORD;
do not let me be put to shame.
32 I run in the path of your commands,
for you have set my heart free.

ה He

33 Teach me, O LORD, to follow your decrees;
then I will keep them to the end.
34 Give me understanding, and I will keep
your law
and obey it with all my heart.
35 Direct me in the path of your commands,
for there I find delight.
36 Turn my heart toward your statutes
and not toward selfish gain.
37 Turn my eyes away from worthless things;
preserve my life according to your
word.[a]
38 Fulfill your promise to your servant,
so that you may be feared.
39 Take away the disgrace I dread,
for your laws are good.
40 How I long for your precepts!
Preserve my life in your righteousness.

ו Waw

41 May your unfailing love come to me,
O LORD,
your salvation according to your promise;
42 then I will answer the one who taunts me,
for I trust in your word.
43 Do not snatch the word of truth from my
mouth,
for I have put my hope in your laws.
44 I will always obey your law,
for ever and ever.
45 I will walk about in freedom,
for I have sought out your precepts.
46 I will speak of your statutes before kings
and will not be put to shame,
47 for I delight in your commands
because I love them.
48 I lift up my hands to[b] your commands,
which I love,
and I meditate on your decrees.

ז Zayin

49 Remember your word to your servant,
for you have given me hope.
50 My comfort in my suffering is this:
Your promise preserves my life.
51 The arrogant mock me without restraint,
but I do not turn from your law.
52 I remember your ancient laws, O LORD,
and I find comfort in them.
53 Indignation grips me because of the
wicked,
who have forsaken your law.
54 Your decrees are the theme of my song
wherever I lodge.
55 In the night I remember your name,
O LORD,
and I will keep your law.
56 This has been my practice:
I obey your precepts.

ח Heth

57 You are my portion, O LORD;
I have promised to obey your words.
58 I have sought your face with all my heart;
be gracious to me according to your
promise.
59 I have considered my ways
and have turned my steps to your
statutes.
60 I will hasten and not delay
to obey your commands.
61 Though the wicked bind me with ropes,
I will not forget your law.
62 At midnight I rise to give you thanks
for your righteous laws.
63 I am a friend to all who fear you,
to all who follow your precepts.
64 The earth is filled with your love, O LORD;
teach me your decrees.

ט Teth

65 Do good to your servant
according to your word, O LORD.

[a]37 Two manuscripts of the Masoretic Text and Dead Sea Scrolls; most manuscripts of the Masoretic Text *life in your way* [b]48 Or *for*

66 Teach me knowledge and good judgment,
for I believe in your commands.
67 Before I was afflicted I went astray,
but now I obey your word.
68 You are good, and what you do is good;
teach me your decrees.
69 Though the arrogant have smeared me
with lies,
I keep your precepts with all my heart.
70 Their hearts are callous and unfeeling,
but I delight in your law.
71 It was good for me to be afflicted
so that I might learn your decrees.
72 The law from your mouth is more precious
to me
than thousands of pieces of silver and
gold.

י Yodh

73 Your hands made me and formed me;
give me understanding to learn your
commands.
74 May those who fear you rejoice when they
see me,
for I have put my hope in your word.
75 I know, O LORD, that your laws are
righteous,
and in faithfulness you have afflicted
me.
76 May your unfailing love be my comfort,
according to your promise to your
servant.
77 Let your compassion come to me that I
may live,
for your law is my delight.
78 May the arrogant be put to shame for
wronging me without cause;
but I will meditate on your precepts.
79 May those who fear you turn to me,
those who understand your statutes.
80 May my heart be blameless toward your
decrees,
that I may not be put to shame.

כ Kaph

81 My soul faints with longing for your
salvation,
but I have put my hope in your word.
82 My eyes fail, looking for your promise;
I say, "When will you comfort me?"
83 Though I am like a wineskin in the
smoke,
I do not forget your decrees.
84 How long must your servant wait?
When will you punish my persecutors?
85 The arrogant dig pitfalls for me,
contrary to your law.
86 All your commands are trustworthy;
help me, for men persecute me without
cause.
87 They almost wiped me from the earth,
but I have not forsaken your precepts.
88 Preserve my life according to your love,
and I will obey the statutes of your
mouth.

ל Lamedh

89 Your word, O LORD, is eternal;
it stands firm in the heavens.
90 Your faithfulness continues through all
generations;
you established the earth, and it
endures.
91 Your laws endure to this day,
for all things serve you.
92 If your law had not been my delight,
I would have perished in my affliction.
93 I will never forget your precepts,
for by them you have preserved my life.
94 Save me, for I am yours;
I have sought out your precepts.
95 The wicked are waiting to destroy me,
but I will ponder your statutes.
96 To all perfection I see a limit;
but your commands are boundless.

מ Mem

97 Oh, how I love your law!
I meditate on it all day long.
98 Your commands make me wiser than
my enemies,
for they are ever with me.
99 I have more insight than all my teachers,
for I meditate on your statutes.
100 I have more understanding than
the elders,
for I obey your precepts.
101 I have kept my feet from every evil path
so that I might obey your word.
102 I have not departed from your laws,

for you yourself have taught me.
103 How sweet are your words to my taste,
sweeter than honey to my mouth!
104 I gain understanding from your precepts;
therefore I hate every wrong path.

נ Nun

105 Your word is a lamp to my feet
and a light for my path.
106 I have taken an oath and
confirmed it,
that I will follow your
righteous laws.
107 I have suffered much;
preserve my life,
O LORD, according
to your word.
108 Accept, O LORD, the
willing praise of
my mouth,
and teach me your laws.
109 Though I constantly take
my life in my hands,
I will not forget your law.
110 The wicked have set a snare for me,
but I have not strayed from your
precepts.
111 Your statutes are my heritage forever;
they are the joy of my heart.
112 My heart is set on keeping your decrees
to the very end.

ס Samekh

113 I hate double-minded men,
but I love your law.
114 You are my refuge and my shield;
I have put my hope in your word.
115 Away from me, you evildoers,
that I may keep the commands of my
God!
116 Sustain me according to your promise,
and I will live;
do not let my hopes be dashed.
117 Uphold me, and I will be delivered;
I will always have regard for your
decrees.
118 You reject all who stray from your decrees,
for their deceitfulness is in vain.
119 All the wicked of the earth you discard
like dross;
therefore I love your statutes.
120 My flesh trembles in fear of you;
I stand in awe of your laws.

ע Ayin

121 I have done what is righteous and just;
do not leave me to my oppressors.
122 Ensure your servant's well-being;
let not the arrogant
oppress me.

Psalm 119:105

God Gives Instruction

Your word is a lamp
to my feet
and a light for my path.

123 My eyes fail, looking for
your salvation,
looking for your
righteous promise.
124 Deal with your servant
according to
your love
and teach me your
decrees.
125 I am your servant; give
me discernment
that I may understand
your statutes.
126 It is time for you to act, O LORD;
your law is being broken.
127 Because I love your commands
more than gold, more than pure gold,
128 and because I consider all your
precepts right,
I hate every wrong path.

פ Pe

129 Your statutes are wonderful;
therefore I obey them.
130 The unfolding of your words gives light;
it gives understanding to the simple.
131 I open my mouth and pant,
longing for your commands.
132 Turn to me and have mercy on me,
as you always do to those who love
your name.
133 Direct my footsteps according to
your word;
let no sin rule over me.
134 Redeem me from the oppression of men,
that I may obey your precepts.
135 Make your face shine upon your servant
and teach me your decrees.
136 Streams of tears flow from my eyes,
for your law is not obeyed.

צ Tsadhe

137 Righteous are you, O LORD,
and your laws are right.
138 The statutes you have laid down
are righteous;
they are fully trustworthy.
139 My zeal wears me out,
for my enemies ignore your words.
140 Your promises have been
thoroughly tested,
and your servant loves them.
141 Though I am lowly and despised,
I do not forget your precepts.
142 Your righteousness is everlasting
and your law is true.
143 Trouble and distress have come upon me,
but your commands are my delight.
144 Your statutes are forever right;
give me understanding that I may live.

ק Qoph

145 I call with all my heart; answer me,
O LORD,
and I will obey your decrees.
146 I call out to you; save me
and I will keep your statutes.
147 I rise before dawn and cry for help;
I have put my hope in your word.
148 My eyes stay open through the watches of
the night,
that I may meditate on your promises.
149 Hear my voice in accordance with
your love;
preserve my life, O LORD, according to
your laws.
150 Those who devise wicked schemes
are near,
but they are far from your law.
151 Yet you are near, O LORD,
and all your commands are true.
152 Long ago I learned from your statutes
that you established them to last forever.

ר Resh

153 Look upon my suffering and deliver me,
for I have not forgotten your law.
154 Defend my cause and redeem me;
preserve my life according to your
promise.
155 Salvation is far from the wicked,
for they do not seek out your decrees.
156 Your compassion is great, O LORD;
preserve my life according to your laws.
157 Many are the foes who persecute me,
but I have not turned from your statutes.
158 I look on the faithless with loathing,
for they do not obey your word.
159 See how I love your precepts;
preserve my life, O LORD, according to
your love.
160 All your words are true;
all your righteous laws are eternal.

ש Sin and Shin

161 Rulers persecute me without cause,
but my heart trembles at your word.
162 I rejoice in your promise
like one who finds great spoil.
163 I hate and abhor falsehood
but I love your law.
164 Seven times a day I praise you
for your righteous laws.
165 Great peace have they who love your law,
and nothing can make them stumble.
166 I wait for your salvation, O LORD,
and I follow your commands.
167 I obey your statutes,
for I love them greatly.
168 I obey your precepts and your statutes,
for all my ways are known to you.

ת Taw

169 May my cry come before you, O LORD;
give me understanding according to
your word.
170 May my supplication come before you;
deliver me according to your promise.
171 May my lips overflow with praise,
for you teach me your decrees.
172 May my tongue sing of your word,
for all your commands are righteous.
173 May your hand be ready to help me,
for I have chosen your precepts.
174 I long for your salvation, O LORD,
and your law is my delight.
175 Let me live that I may praise you,
and may your laws sustain me.
176 I have strayed like a lost sheep.
Seek your servant,
for I have not forgotten your commands.

Psalm 120

A song of ascents.

1 I call on the LORD in my distress,
and he answers me.
2 Save me, O LORD, from lying lips
and from deceitful tongues.

3 What will he do to you,
and what more besides, O deceitful
tongue?
4 He will punish you with a warrior's sharp
arrows,
with burning coals of the broom tree.

5 Woe to me that I dwell in Meshech,
that I live among the tents of Kedar!
6 Too long have I lived
among those who hate peace.
7 I am a man of peace;
but when I speak, they are for war.

Psalm 121

A song of ascents.

1 I lift up my eyes to the hills—
where does my help come from?
2 My help comes from the LORD,
the Maker of heaven and
earth.

3 He will not let your foot
slip—
he who watches over you
will not slumber;
4 indeed, he who watches
over Israel
will neither slumber nor
sleep.

5 The LORD watches over
you—
the LORD is your shade at
your right hand;
6 the sun will not harm you by day,
nor the moon by night.

7 The LORD will keep you from all harm—
he will watch over your life;
8 the LORD will watch over your coming and
going
both now and forevermore.

> **Psalm 121:2**
>
> *God Is Our Help*
>
> My help comes from the LORD, the Maker of heaven and earth.

Psalm 122

A song of ascents. Of David.

1 I rejoiced with those who said to me,
"Let us go to the house of the LORD."
2 Our feet are standing
in your gates, O Jerusalem.

3 Jerusalem is built like a city
that is closely compacted together.
4 That is where the tribes go up,
the tribes of the LORD,
to praise the name of the LORD
according to the statute given to Israel.
5 There the thrones for judgment stand,
the thrones of the house of David.

6 Pray for the peace of Jerusalem:
"May those who love you be secure.
7 May there be peace within your walls
and security within your citadels."
8 For the sake of my brothers and friends,
I will say, "Peace be within you."
9 For the sake of the house of the LORD our
God,
I will seek your prosperity.

Psalm 123

A song of ascents.

1 I lift up my eyes to you,
to you whose throne is in
heaven.
2 As the eyes of slaves look
to the hand of their
master,
as the eyes of a maid look
to the hand of her
mistress,
so our eyes look to the
LORD our God,
till he shows us his
mercy.

3 Have mercy on us, O LORD,
have mercy on us,
for we have endured much contempt.
4 We have endured much ridicule from the
proud,
much contempt from the arrogant.

Psalm 124

A song of ascents. Of David.

1 If the LORD had not been on our side—
let Israel say—
2 if the LORD had not been on our side
when men attacked us,
3 when their anger flared against us,

they would have swallowed us alive;
4 the flood would have engulfed us,
the torrent would have swept over us,
5 the raging waters
would have swept us away.

6 Praise be to the LORD,
who has not let us be torn by their teeth.
7 We have escaped like a bird
out of the fowler's snare;
the snare has been broken,
and we have escaped.
8 Our help is in the name of the LORD,
the Maker of heaven and earth.

Psalm 125

A song of ascents.

1 Those who trust in the LORD are like
Mount Zion,
which cannot be shaken
but endures forever.
2 As the mountains surround
Jerusalem,
so the LORD surrounds
his people
both now and
forevermore.

3 The scepter of the wicked
will not remain
over the land allotted to
the righteous,
for then the righteous might use
their hands to do evil.

4 Do good, O LORD, to those who are good,
to those who are upright in heart.
5 But those who turn to crooked ways
the LORD will banish with the
evildoers.

Peace be upon Israel.

Psalm 126

A song of ascents.

1 When the LORD brought back the captives
to[a] Zion,
we were like men who dreamed.[b]
2 Our mouths were filled with laughter,
our tongues with songs of joy.
Then it was said among the nations,
"The LORD has done great things for
them."
3 The LORD has done great things for us,
and we are filled with joy.

4 Restore our fortunes,[c] O LORD,
like streams in the Negev.
5 Those who sow in tears
will reap with songs of joy.
6 He who goes out weeping,
carrying seed to sow,
will return with songs of joy,
carrying sheaves with him.

Psalm 127

A song of ascents. Of Solomon.

1 Unless the LORD builds the house,
its builders labor in vain.
Unless the LORD watches
over the city,
the watchmen stand
guard in vain.
2 In vain you rise early
and stay up late,
toiling for food to eat—
for he grants sleep to[d]
those he loves.

3 Sons are a heritage from
the LORD,
children a reward from
him.
4 Like arrows in the hands of a warrior
are sons born in one's youth.
5 Blessed is the man
whose quiver is full of them.
They will not be put to shame
when they contend with their enemies
in the gate.

> **Psalm 127:1**
>
> *God Offers Firm Foundations*
>
> Unless the LORD builds the house,
> its builders labor in vain.

Psalm 128

A song of ascents.

1 Blessed are all who fear the LORD,
who walk in his ways.
2 You will eat the fruit of your labor;
blessings and prosperity will be yours.
3 Your wife will be like a fruitful vine
within your house;
your sons will be like olive shoots
around your table.

[a]1 Or *LORD restored the fortunes of* [b]1 Or *men restored to health* [c]4 Or *Bring back our captives* [d]2 Or *eat— / for while they sleep he provides for*

What Might Have Been

TAMAR

THINGS WERE NOT as they should have been.

For one thing, Tamar now lived with her brother, isolated from her other virgin sisters. She could no longer call the house they had shared her "home." She was different from all of them, tainted. Her change of address seemed to mirror her change in life. She could never go back. Her home was not, nor would it ever be, as it should have been.

Secondly, the richly ornamented robe she used to wear so proudly was now merely a shredded scrap, a visible symbol that her personality and purity were forever altered. Her view of herself, as well as the way others looked at her, was altered and would never be as it once had been.

On top of all that, she would never marry. *What man would have her?* she wondered. Who could see beauty in a crushed rose? One day, she was a young woman with her whole life ahead of her. The next day, all of that changed. Her options were no longer as they once had been.

She would never have children. She was, after all, "damaged goods," "used." Imaginary adjectives swirled around her in a dark cloud, publicly labeling her disgrace. Her future would never be as it should have been.

Her father overlooked it. Her brother downplayed it. Those who should have been her avengers were, instead, passive. It shouldn't have been that way.

The stronger took advantage of the weaker.

Evil overcame good.

She was innocent but somehow made to feel guilty.

Nothing, *nothing,* is as it should be in a fallen world. Not for Tamar; and, really, not for any woman before or since.

What happened to Tamar wasn't something that should have happened. And she had to find a way to go on.

"What about me? Where could I get rid of my disgrace?"

2 Samuel 13:13

ASSIGNED READING:

2 Samuel 13:1–39

—Prayer—

Loving Savior, I pray for healing of the painful experiences in my life, and in the lives of those around me.

Weekend

Go to page 749 for your next devotional reading.

4 Thus is the man blessed
who fears the LORD.

5 May the LORD bless you from Zion
all the days of your life;
may you see the prosperity of Jerusalem,
6 and may you live to see your children's
children.

Peace be upon Israel.

Psalm 129

A song of ascents.

1 They have greatly oppressed me from my
youth—
let Israel say—
2 they have greatly oppressed me from my
youth,
but they have not gained the victory
over me.
3 Plowmen have plowed my back
and made their furrows long.
4 But the LORD is righteous;
he has cut me free from the cords of the
wicked.

5 May all who hate Zion
be turned back in shame.
6 May they be like grass on the roof,
which withers before it can grow;
7 with it the reaper cannot fill his hands,
nor the one who gathers fill his arms.
8 May those who pass by not say,
"The blessing of the LORD be upon
you;
we bless you in the name of the LORD."

Psalm 130

A song of ascents.

1 Out of the depths I cry to you, O LORD;
2 O Lord, hear my voice.
Let your ears be attentive
to my cry for mercy.

3 If you, O LORD, kept a record of sins,
O Lord, who could stand?
4 But with you there is forgiveness;
therefore you are feared.

5 I wait for the LORD, my soul waits,
and in his word I put my hope.
6 My soul waits for the Lord
more than watchmen wait for the
morning,
more than watchmen wait for the
morning.

7 O Israel, put your hope in the LORD,
for with the LORD is unfailing love
and with him is full redemption.
8 He himself will redeem Israel
from all their sins.

Psalm 131

A song of ascents. Of David.

1 My heart is not proud, O LORD,
my eyes are not haughty;
I do not concern myself with great matters
or things too wonderful for me.
2 But I have stilled and quieted my soul;
like a weaned child with its mother,
like a weaned child is my soul within me.

3 O Israel, put your hope in the LORD
both now and forevermore.

Psalm 132

A song of ascents.

1 O LORD, remember David
and all the hardships he endured.

2 He swore an oath to the LORD
and made a vow to the Mighty One of
Jacob:
3 "I will not enter my house
or go to my bed—
4 I will allow no sleep to my eyes,
no slumber to my eyelids,
5 till I find a place for the LORD,
a dwelling for the Mighty One of Jacob."

6 We heard it in Ephrathah,
we came upon it in the fields of Jaar[a]:[b]
7 "Let us go to his dwelling place;
let us worship at his footstool—
8 arise, O LORD, and come to your resting
place,
you and the ark of your might.
9 May your priests be clothed with
righteousness;
may your saints sing for joy."

10 For the sake of David your servant,
do not reject your anointed one.

[a] 6 That is, Kiriath Jearim [b] 6 Or *heard of it in Ephrathah, / we found it in the fields of Jaar.* (And no quotes around verses 7–9)

11 The LORD swore an oath to David,
a sure oath that he will not revoke:
"One of your own descendants
I will place on your throne—
12 if your sons keep my covenant
and the statutes I teach them,
then their sons will sit
on your throne for ever and ever."

13 For the LORD has chosen Zion,
he has desired it for his dwelling:
14 "This is my resting place for ever and
ever;
here I will sit enthroned, for I have
desired it—
15 I will bless her with abundant provisions;
her poor will I satisfy with food.
16 I will clothe her priests with salvation,
and her saints will ever
sing for joy.

17 "Here I will make a horn[a]
grow for David
and set up a lamp for my
anointed one.
18 I will clothe his enemies
with shame,
but the crown on
his head will be
resplendent."

Psalm 133

A song of ascents. Of David.

1 How good and pleasant it is
when brothers live
together in unity!
2 It is like precious oil poured on the head,
running down on the beard,
running down on Aaron's beard,
down upon the collar of his robes.
3 It is as if the dew of Hermon
were falling on Mount Zion.
For there the LORD bestows his blessing,
even life forevermore.

Psalm 134

A song of ascents.

1 Praise the LORD, all you servants of the
LORD
who minister by night in the house of
the LORD.
2 Lift up your hands in the sanctuary
and praise the LORD.

3 May the LORD, the Maker of heaven and
earth,
bless you from Zion.

Psalm 135

1 Praise the LORD.[b]

Praise the name of the LORD;
praise him, you servants of the LORD,
2 you who minister in the house of the
LORD,
in the courts of the house of our God.
3 Praise the LORD, for the LORD is good;
sing praise to his name, for that is
pleasant.
4 For the LORD has chosen
Jacob to be his
own,
Israel to be his treasured
possession.
5 I know that the LORD is
great,
that our Lord is greater
than all gods.
6 The LORD does whatever
pleases him,
in the heavens and on
the earth,
in the seas and all their
depths.
7 He makes clouds rise from
the ends of the
earth;
he sends lightning with the rain
and brings out the wind from his
storehouses.
8 He struck down the firstborn of Egypt,
the firstborn of men and animals.
9 He sent his signs and wonders into your
midst, O Egypt,
against Pharaoh and all his servants.
10 He struck down many nations
and killed mighty kings—
11 Sihon king of the Amorites,
Og king of Bashan
and all the kings of Canaan—

Psalm 135:6

God Answers to Himself

The LORD does whatever
pleases him,
in the heavens and
on the earth,
in the seas and all
their depths.

a17 *Horn* here symbolizes strong one, that is, king. b1 Hebrew *Hallelu Yah*; also in verses 3 and 21

12 and he gave their land as an inheritance,
an inheritance to his people Israel.

13 Your name, O LORD, endures forever,
your renown, O LORD, through all
generations.
14 For the LORD will vindicate his people
and have compassion on his servants.

15 The idols of the nations are silver and gold,
made by the hands of men.
16 They have mouths, but cannot speak,
eyes, but they cannot see;
17 they have ears, but cannot hear,
nor is there breath in their mouths.
18 Those who make them will be like them,
and so will all who trust in them.

19 O house of Israel, praise the LORD;
O house of Aaron, praise the LORD;
20 O house of Levi, praise the LORD;
you who fear him, praise the LORD.
21 Praise be to the LORD from Zion,
to him who dwells in Jerusalem.

Praise the LORD.

Psalm 136

1 Give thanks to the LORD, for he is good.
His love endures forever.
2 Give thanks to the God of gods.
His love endures forever.
3 Give thanks to the Lord of lords:
His love endures forever.

4 to him who alone does great wonders,
His love endures forever.
5 who by his understanding made the
heavens,
His love endures forever.
6 who spread out the earth upon the waters,
His love endures forever.
7 who made the great lights—
His love endures forever.
8 the sun to govern the day,
His love endures forever.
9 the moon and stars to govern the night;
His love endures forever.

10 to him who struck down the firstborn of
Egypt
His love endures forever.
11 and brought Israel out from among them
His love endures forever.
12 with a mighty hand and outstretched arm;
His love endures forever.

13 to him who divided the Red Sea[a] asunder
His love endures forever.
14 and brought Israel through the midst of it,
His love endures forever.
15 but swept Pharaoh and his army into the
Red Sea;
His love endures forever.

16 to him who led his people through the
desert,
His love endures forever.
17 who struck down great kings,
His love endures forever.
18 and killed mighty kings—
His love endures forever.
19 Sihon king of the Amorites
His love endures forever.
20 and Og king of Bashan—
His love endures forever.
21 and gave their land as an inheritance,
His love endures forever.
22 an inheritance to his servant Israel;
His love endures forever.

23 to the One who remembered us in our low
estate
His love endures forever.
24 and freed us from our enemies,
His love endures forever.
25 and who gives food to every creature.
His love endures forever.

26 Give thanks to the God of heaven.
His love endures forever.

Psalm 137

1 By the rivers of Babylon we sat and wept
when we remembered Zion.
2 There on the poplars
we hung our harps,
3 for there our captors asked us for songs,
our tormentors demanded songs of joy;
they said, "Sing us one of the songs of
Zion!"

4 How can we sing the songs of the LORD
while in a foreign land?

[a] 13 Hebrew *Yam Suph*; that is, Sea of Reeds; also in verse 15

Enduring, Endearing Love

Read: Psalm 136:1–26

"DIAMONDS ARE FOREVER"—at least that's what the jewelry industry hopes enamored couples everywhere will believe. One advertiser boasted, "Since diamonds last forever, a diamond engagement ring tells your sweetheart that your love for her will be unwavering on into eternity." Unfortunately, a diamond often outlasts the marriage it was meant to symbolize. Human love is not flawless.

So, where can you find flawless and eternal love? Psalm 136 asserts repeatedly that God's love "endures forever." This antiphonal song served as an anthem or pledge of mutual love between God and his people. Old Testament priests sang the first phrase in these verses while the congregation answered with the refrain: "His love endures forever." It was much like an exchange of wedding vows between God and his bride, the nation of Israel (see Isaiah 62:5).

God desires the closeness of such a relationship with each of us for eternity. And his love lasts beyond a lifetime. Not only does God offer us *enduring* love, he also extends to us *endearing* love, a strong affection that lifts one higher or increases the value of the one beloved. *Enduring* speaks of the *quantity* of God's love while *endearing* portrays the *quality*. The psalmist says that God is "the One who remembered us in our low estate" (verse 23). We are nothing. But God loved us before we were lovely. We are his diamonds in the rough.

In the rough, a diamond looks like a common pebble. The stone must undergo a finishing process to bring out its full radiance. It is then held against a large grinding wheel to cut and polish the stone. Many meticulous hours are spent perfecting it.

Like the nation of Israel, God has lifted you out of the rubble of a worthless life. He is polishing and chiseling you into a jewel of great beauty. You are his diamond. You are like a bride being prepared for the bridegroom. *And his love endures forever.*

Monday

Psalm 136:1,23

Give thanks . . . to the One who remembered us in our low estate . . . *His love endures forever.*

reflection

1 In what ways has the human love you've experienced been flawed and temporary?

2 In what ways have you experienced God's enduring love personally?

3 How does it make you feel to know that God values you as a priceless diamond? How does it make you feel to know that he is chiseling and polishing you into a jewel of great beauty?

RELATED READINGS

Isaiah 62:1–5;
Zechariah 9:14–17;
Revelation 19:5–10

Go to page 755 for your next devotional reading.

5 If I forget you, O Jerusalem,
may my right hand forget ⌊its skill⌋.
6 May my tongue cling to the roof of my mouth
if I do not remember you,
if I do not consider Jerusalem
my highest joy.

7 Remember, O LORD, what the Edomites did
on the day Jerusalem fell.
"Tear it down," they cried,
"tear it down to its foundations!"
8 O Daughter of Babylon, doomed to destruction,
happy is he who repays you
for what you have done to us—
9 he who seizes your infants
and dashes them against the rocks.

> **Psalm 138:8**
>
> *God Has a Purpose*
>
> The LORD will fulfill his purpose for me; your love, O LORD, endures forever— do not abandon the works of your hands.

Psalm 138

Of David.

1 I will praise you, O LORD, with all my heart;
before the "gods" I will sing your praise.
2 I will bow down toward your holy temple
and will praise your name
for your love and your faithfulness,
for you have exalted above all things
your name and your word.
3 When I called, you answered me;
you made me bold and stouthearted.

4 May all the kings of the earth praise you, O LORD,
when they hear the words of your mouth.
5 May they sing of the ways of the LORD,
for the glory of the LORD is great.

6 Though the LORD is on high, he looks upon the lowly,
but the proud he knows from afar.
7 Though I walk in the midst of trouble,
you preserve my life;
you stretch out your hand against the anger of my foes,
with your right hand you save me.
8 The LORD will fulfill ⌊his purpose⌋ for me;
your love, O LORD, endures forever—
do not abandon the works of your hands.

Psalm 139

For the director of music. Of David. A psalm.

1 O LORD, you have searched me
and you know me.
2 You know when I sit and when I rise;
you perceive my thoughts from afar.
3 You discern my going out and my lying down;
you are familiar with all my ways.
4 Before a word is on my tongue
you know it completely, O LORD.

5 You hem me in—behind and before;
you have laid your hand upon me.
6 Such knowledge is too wonderful for me,
too lofty for me to attain.

7 Where can I go from your Spirit?
Where can I flee from your presence?
8 If I go up to the heavens, you are there;
if I make my bed in the depths,[a] you are there.
9 If I rise on the wings of the dawn,
if I settle on the far side of the sea,
10 even there your hand will guide me,
your right hand will hold me fast.

11 If I say, "Surely the darkness will hide me
and the light become night around me,"
12 even the darkness will not be dark to you;
the night will shine like the day,
for darkness is as light to you.

13 For you created my inmost being;
you knit me together in my mother's womb.

[a] 8 Hebrew *Sheol*

14 I praise you because I am fearfully and
wonderfully made;
your works are wonderful,
I know that full well.
15 My frame was not hidden from you
when I was made in the secret place.
When I was woven together in the depths
of the earth,
16 your eyes saw my unformed body.
All the days ordained for me
were written in your book
before one of them came to be.

17 How precious to[a] me are your thoughts,
O God!
How vast is the sum of them!
18 Were I to count them,
they would outnumber the grains of sand.
When I awake,
I am still with you.

19 If only you would slay the wicked, O God!
Away from me, you bloodthirsty men!
20 They speak of you with evil intent;
your adversaries misuse your name.
21 Do I not hate those who hate you, O LORD,
and abhor those who rise up against
you?
22 I have nothing but hatred for them;
I count them my enemies.
23 Search me, O God, and know my heart;
test me and know my anxious thoughts.
24 See if there is any offensive way in me,
and lead me in the way everlasting.

Psalm 140

For the director of music. A psalm of David.

1 Rescue me, O LORD, from evil men;
protect me from men of violence,
2 who devise evil plans in their hearts
and stir up war every day.
3 They make their tongues as sharp as a
serpent's;
the poison of vipers is on their lips.
Selah

4 Keep me, O LORD, from the hands of the
wicked;
protect me from men of violence
who plan to trip my feet.
5 Proud men have hidden a snare for me;
they have spread out the cords of their
net
and have set traps for me along my path.
Selah

6 O LORD, I say to you, "You are my God."
Hear, O LORD, my cry for mercy.
7 O Sovereign LORD, my strong deliverer,
who shields my head in the day of
battle—
8 do not grant the wicked their desires,
O LORD;
do not let their plans succeed,
or they will become proud. *Selah*

9 Let the heads of those who surround me
be covered with the trouble their lips
have caused.
10 Let burning coals fall upon them;
may they be thrown into the fire,
into miry pits, never to rise.
11 Let slanderers not be established in the
land;
may disaster hunt down men of violence.

12 I know that the LORD secures justice for
the poor
and upholds the cause of the needy.
13 Surely the righteous will praise your name
and the upright will live before you.

Psalm 141

A psalm of David.

1 O LORD, I call to you; come quickly to me.
Hear my voice when I call to you.
2 May my prayer be set before you like
incense;
may the lifting up of my hands be like
the evening sacrifice.

3 Set a guard over my mouth, O LORD;
keep watch over the door of my lips.
4 Let not my heart be drawn to what is evil,
to take part in wicked deeds
with men who are evildoers;
let me not eat of their delicacies.

5 Let a righteous man[b] strike me—it is a
kindness;
let him rebuke me—it is oil on my head.
My head will not refuse it.

[a]17 Or *concerning* [b]5 Or *Let the Righteous One*

Yet my prayer is ever against the deeds of
evildoers;
6 their rulers will be thrown down from
the cliffs,
and the wicked will learn that my words
were well spoken.
7 ⌊They will say,⌋ "As one plows and breaks
up the earth,
so our bones have been scattered at the
mouth of the grave.[a]"

8 But my eyes are fixed on you, O Sovereign
LORD;
in you I take refuge—do not give me
over to death.
9 Keep me from the snares they have laid for
me,
from the traps set by evildoers.
10 Let the wicked fall into their own nets,
while I pass by in safety.

Psalm 142

A *maskil*[b] of David. When he was in the cave. A prayer.

1 I cry aloud to the LORD;
I lift up my voice to the LORD for
mercy.
2 I pour out my complaint before him;
before him I tell my trouble.

3 When my spirit grows faint within me,
it is you who know my way.
In the path where I walk
men have hidden a snare for me.
4 Look to my right and see;
no one is concerned for me.
I have no refuge;
no one cares for my life.

5 I cry to you, O LORD;
I say, "You are my refuge,
my portion in the land of the living."
6 Listen to my cry,
for I am in desperate need;
rescue me from those who pursue me,
for they are too strong for me.
7 Set me free from my prison,
that I may praise your name.

Then the righteous will gather about me
because of your goodness to me.

Psalm 143

A psalm of David.

1 O LORD, hear my prayer,
listen to my cry for mercy;
in your faithfulness and righteousness
come to my relief.
2 Do not bring your servant into judgment,
for no one living is righteous before
you.

3 The enemy pursues me,
he crushes me to the ground;
he makes me dwell in darkness
like those long dead.
4 So my spirit grows faint within me;
my heart within me is dismayed.

5 I remember the days of long ago;
I meditate on all your works
and consider what your hands have
done.
6 I spread out my hands to you;
my soul thirsts for you like a parched
land. *Selah*

7 Answer me quickly, O LORD;
my spirit fails.
Do not hide your face from me
or I will be like those who go down to
the pit.
8 Let the morning bring me word of your
unfailing love,
for I have put my trust in you.
Show me the way I should go,
for to you I lift up my soul.
9 Rescue me from my enemies, O LORD,
for I hide myself in you.
10 Teach me to do your will,
for you are my God;
may your good Spirit
lead me on level ground.

11 For your name's sake, O LORD, preserve
my life;
in your righteousness, bring me out of
trouble.
12 In your unfailing love, silence my
enemies;
destroy all my foes,
for I am your servant.

[a]7 Hebrew *Sheol* [b]Title: Probably a literary or musical term

Psalm 144

Of David.

1 Praise be to the LORD my Rock,
who trains my hands for war,
my fingers for battle.
2 He is my loving God and my fortress,
my stronghold and my deliverer,
my shield, in whom I take refuge,
who subdues peoples[a] under me.

3 O LORD, what is man that you care for him,
the son of man that you think of him?
4 Man is like a breath;
his days are like a fleeting shadow.

5 Part your heavens, O LORD, and come down;
touch the mountains, so that they smoke.
6 Send forth lightning and scatter ⌊the enemies⌋;
shoot your arrows and rout them.
7 Reach down your hand from on high;
deliver me and rescue me
from the mighty waters,
from the hands of foreigners
8 whose mouths are full of lies,
whose right hands are deceitful.

9 I will sing a new song to you, O God;
on the ten-stringed lyre I will make music to you,
10 to the One who gives victory to kings,
who delivers his servant David from the deadly sword.

11 Deliver me and rescue me
from the hands of foreigners
whose mouths are full of lies,
whose right hands are deceitful.

12 Then our sons in their youth
will be like well-nurtured plants,
and our daughters will be like pillars
carved to adorn a palace.
13 Our barns will be filled
with every kind of provision.
Our sheep will increase by thousands,
by tens of thousands in our fields;
14 our oxen will draw heavy loads.[b]
There will be no breaching of walls,
no going into captivity,
no cry of distress in our streets.

15 Blessed are the people of whom this is true;
blessed are the people whose God is the LORD.

Psalm 145[c]

A psalm of praise. Of David.

1 I will exalt you, my God the King;
I will praise your name for ever and ever.
2 Every day I will praise you
and extol your name for ever and ever.

3 Great is the LORD and most worthy of praise;
his greatness no one can fathom.
4 One generation will commend your works to another;
they will tell of your mighty acts.
5 They will speak of the glorious splendor of your majesty,
and I will meditate on your wonderful works.[d]
6 They will tell of the power of your awesome works,
and I will proclaim your great deeds.
7 They will celebrate your abundant goodness
and joyfully sing of your righteousness.

8 The LORD is gracious and compassionate,
slow to anger and rich in love.
9 The LORD is good to all;
he has compassion on all he has made.

Psalm 145:8

God Is Enduring

The LORD is gracious and compassionate,
slow to anger and rich in love.

[a]2 Many manuscripts of the Masoretic Text, Dead Sea Scrolls, Aquila, Jerome and Syriac; most manuscripts of the Masoretic Text *subdues my people* [b]14 Or *our chieftains will be firmly established* [c]This psalm is an acrostic poem, the verses of which (including verse 13b) begin with the successive letters of the Hebrew alphabet. [d]5 Dead Sea Scrolls and Syriac (see also Septuagint); Masoretic Text *On the glorious splendor of your majesty / and on your wonderful works I will meditate*

10 All you have made will praise you,
O LORD;
your saints will extol you.
11 They will tell of the glory of your
kingdom
and speak of your might,
12 so that all men may know of your mighty
acts
and the glorious splendor of your
kingdom.
13 Your kingdom is an everlasting kingdom,
and your dominion endures through all
generations.

The LORD is faithful to all his promises
and loving toward all he has made.[a]
14 The LORD upholds all those who fall
and lifts up all who are bowed down.
15 The eyes of all look to you,
and you give them their food at the
proper time.
16 You open your hand
and satisfy the desires of every living
thing.

17 The LORD is righteous in all his ways
and loving toward all he has made.
18 The LORD is near to all who call on him,
to all who call on him in truth.
19 He fulfills the desires of those who fear
him;
he hears their cry and saves them.
20 The LORD watches over all who love
him,
but all the wicked he will
destroy.

21 My mouth will speak in
praise of the LORD.
Let every creature praise
his holy name
for ever and ever.

Psalm 146

1 Praise the LORD.[b]

Praise the LORD, O my
soul.
2 I will praise the LORD all my life;
I will sing praise to my God as long as
I live.
3 Do not put your trust in princes,
in mortal men, who cannot save.
4 When their spirit departs, they return to
the ground;
on that very day their plans come to
nothing.
5 Blessed is he whose help is the God of
Jacob,
whose hope is in the LORD his God,
6 the Maker of heaven and earth,
the sea, and everything in them—
the LORD, who remains faithful forever.
7 He upholds the cause of the oppressed
and gives food to the hungry.
The LORD sets prisoners free,
8 the LORD gives sight to the blind,
the LORD lifts up those who are bowed
down,
the LORD loves the righteous.
9 The LORD watches over the alien
and sustains the fatherless and the
widow,
but he frustrates the ways of the
wicked.

10 The LORD reigns forever,
your God, O Zion, for all generations.

Praise the LORD.

Psalm 147

1 Praise the LORD.[c]

How good it is to sing praises to our God,
how pleasant and fitting
to praise him!

2 The LORD builds up
Jerusalem;
he gathers the exiles of
Israel.
3 He heals the brokenhearted
and binds up their
wounds.

4 He determines the number
of the stars
and calls them each by
name.
5 Great is our Lord and mighty in power;
his understanding has no limit.

> **Psalm 147:5**
>
> *God Is Limitless*
>
> Great is our Lord and mighty in power; his understanding has no limit.

[a]13 One manuscript of the Masoretic Text, Dead Sea Scrolls and Syriac (see also Septuagint); most manuscripts of the Masoretic Text do not have the last two lines of verse 13. [b]1 Hebrew *Hallelu Yah*; also in verse 10 [c]1 Hebrew *Hallelu Yah*; also in verse 20

God in Your Brag Book

Read: Psalm 145:1–21

WHOM DO YOU BRAG ABOUT? Do your friends hear about your brilliant daughter, your generous sister, your adorable puppy? Have you in turn seen every photo of a friend's grandchild, heard about every new word, every tooth and every step?

How often do you brag about God? People in your life need to hear from you about him—your children, nieces and nephews, godchildren, neighborhood kids, everyone. They will someday have their own stories of how their prayers were answered. They will learn about God's faithfulness as they go through hard times. God will bless them with delightful surprises. They will experience God's mercy and tenderness for themselves. But until they have their own stories, they need to hear *yours*. Your stories will "prime the pump" as it were and alert them to watch for God as they "live and move and have [their] being" in him (Acts 17:28).

Scripture tells us that God is gracious and compassionate, patient and merciful. King David knew this from his own experience. God protected him from many who would have killed him, including his own king and father-in-law, King Saul, and later his son Absalom, who wanted to be king himself. David knew God as the only King who is always righteous. David also knew God as the One who forgives, who washes away devastating sins instead of killing the sinner. David knew God in a surprisingly intimate way. The shepherd knew God as his Shepherd. The king called God his own King.

It's easy to complain about inefficient checkout clerks, dangerous drivers and ungrateful relatives. It's natural to tell our stories of financial hardship and illness and slights from our friends. It's great to have funny stories to tell about what has happened to us. But it's so much sweeter and deeper to bless others with stories about the good things, the true things, the beautiful and enduring things that we've experienced with God. It's so rewarding to look for opportunities to praise God and to remember how he has been good to us. It's so wonderfully fun to brag about God.

Psalm 145:4
One generation will commend your works to another; they will tell of your mighty acts.

reflection

1 Why do you think David spent so much time praising God?

2 What special reasons do you have to praise God?

3 How can you brag about God to someone today?

RELATED READINGS
Deuteronomy 6:1–9;
Psalm 105:1–5;
Philippians 4:4–9

Go to page 759 for your next devotional reading.

6 The LORD sustains the humble
but casts the wicked to the ground.

7 Sing to the LORD with thanksgiving;
make music to our God on the harp.
8 He covers the sky with clouds;
he supplies the earth with rain
and makes grass grow on the hills.
9 He provides food for the cattle
and for the young ravens when they call.

10 His pleasure is not in the strength of the horse,
nor his delight in the legs of a man;
11 the LORD delights in those who fear him,
who put their hope in his unfailing love.

12 Extol the LORD, O Jerusalem;
praise your God, O Zion,
13 for he strengthens the bars of your gates
and blesses your people within you.
14 He grants peace to your borders
and satisfies you with the finest of wheat.

15 He sends his command to the earth;
his word runs swiftly.
16 He spreads the snow like wool
and scatters the frost like ashes.
17 He hurls down his hail like pebbles.
Who can withstand his icy blast?
18 He sends his word and melts them;
he stirs up his breezes, and the waters flow.

19 He has revealed his word to Jacob,
his laws and decrees to Israel.
20 He has done this for no other nation;
they do not know his laws.

Praise the LORD.

Psalm 148

1 Praise the LORD.[a]

Praise the LORD from the heavens,
praise him in the heights above.
2 Praise him, all his angels,
praise him, all his heavenly hosts.
3 Praise him, sun and moon,
praise him, all you shining stars.
4 Praise him, you highest heavens
and you waters above the skies.
5 Let them praise the name of the LORD,
for he commanded and they were created.
6 He set them in place for ever and ever;
he gave a decree that will never pass away.

7 Praise the LORD from the earth,
you great sea creatures and all ocean depths,
8 lightning and hail, snow and clouds,
stormy winds that do his bidding,
9 you mountains and all hills,
fruit trees and all cedars,
10 wild animals and all cattle,
small creatures and flying birds,
11 kings of the earth and all nations,
you princes and all rulers on earth,
12 young men and maidens,
old men and children.

13 Let them praise the name of the LORD,
for his name alone is exalted;
his splendor is above the earth and the heavens.
14 He has raised up for his people a horn,[b]
the praise of all his saints,
of Israel, the people close to his heart.

Praise the LORD.

Psalm 149

1 Praise the LORD.[c]

Sing to the LORD a new song,
his praise in the assembly of the saints.

2 Let Israel rejoice in their Maker;
let the people of Zion be glad in their King.
3 Let them praise his name with dancing
and make music to him with tambourine and harp.
4 For the LORD takes delight in his people;
he crowns the humble with salvation.
5 Let the saints rejoice in this honor
and sing for joy on their beds.

6 May the praise of God be in their mouths
and a double-edged sword in their hands,
7 to inflict vengeance on the nations
and punishment on the peoples,

[a]1 Hebrew *Hallelu Yah*; also in verse 14 [b]14 *Horn* here symbolizes strong one, that is, king. [c]1 Hebrew *Hallelu Yah*; also in verse 9

8 to bind their kings with fetters,
their nobles with shackles of iron,
9 to carry out the sentence written against them.
This is the glory of all his saints.

Praise the LORD.

Psalm 150

1 Praise the LORD.[a]

Praise God in his sanctuary;
praise him in his mighty heavens.
2 Praise him for his acts of power;
praise him for his surpassing greatness.
3 Praise him with the sounding of the trumpet,
praise him with the harp and lyre,
4 praise him with tambourine and dancing,
praise him with the strings and flute,
5 praise him with the clash of cymbals,
praise him with resounding cymbals.

6 Let everything that has breath praise the LORD.

Praise the LORD.

a1 Hebrew *Hallelu Yah*; also in verse 6

Proverbs

Author:
Primarily King Solomon.

Audience:
All Israel.

Date:
Solomon wrote most of the proverbs during his reign (970 to 930 B.C.), but the book wasn't fully compiled until around 700 B.C.

Setting:
Written during Solomon's wiser days. Solomon had great wisdom, but he gave in to temptation later on in his life.

Verse to Remember:
The fear of the LORD is the beginning of knowledge, but fools despise wisdom and discipline. (1:7)

Wisdom is at the heart of Proverbs. Most of the book was written by King Solomon, whom *God blessed with the gift* of great wisdom. Delving into subjects as varied as money, relationships, folly, adultery, child-rearing, contentment and choosing good companions, the book is a treasure trove of advice.

Godly wisdom is one of life's most important and valuable pursuits, *worth much more* than material wealth. Many people choose to read this book monthly, one chapter each day, to be sure to keep the lessons learned at the front of their minds.

Prologue: Purpose and Theme

1 The proverbs of Solomon son of David, king of Israel:

2 for attaining wisdom and discipline;
for understanding words of insight;
3 for acquiring a disciplined and prudent life,
doing what is right and just and fair;
4 for giving prudence to the simple,
knowledge and discretion to the young—
5 let the wise listen and add to their learning,
and let the discerning get guidance—
6 for understanding proverbs and parables,
the sayings and riddles of the wise.

7 The fear of the LORD is the beginning of knowledge,

Perpetual Puberty

Read: Proverbs 1:1–33

JUNIOR HIGH. The place where we transitioned to adolescence with pimply faces and few social skills. A time when it was uncool to listen to authority. When sarcasm and spite peppered our speech. We thought we knew it all. Now—after 20, 30 or 40 years—many of us look back with regret on some of the choices we made then. We still wince when we remember the wounds we received from cutting words; we still wince when we remember the wounds we inflicted on others. What was missing during that season of life? Could it have been wisdom?

Actually, wisdom was there all the time, but we probably ignored it. When we allow wisdom to go unheeded, we're like a teenager stuck in perpetual puberty. In Proverbs 1, Solomon describes the unwise as those who "delight in mockery" (verse 22), reject help (verse 24) and ignore advice (verse 25). It sounds like Solomon knew more than a few spiritual adolescents, doesn't it?

He goes on to say that those who reject God's knowledge will "eat the fruit of their ways and be filled with the fruit of their schemes" (verse 31). In other words, we will reap what we sow, or in popular jargon, "we'll get what we deserve." Wisdom's warning is appropriate for all of us, regardless of our age.

Where are you on your spiritual journey? Are you stuck in perpetual spiritual puberty? Here are a few signs: You constantly worry about what others think of you. You overreact to stressful situations. You're too proud or stubborn to listen to those older and wiser. You stay with one group and ridicule others. If you've found yourself in perpetual puberty, then seek wisdom.

God's wisdom isn't reserved for a few scholars; it's available to everyone. Wisdom is found in the book that holds eternal truth—God's Word. According to Solomon, wisdom comes from listening to God (one of the most frequent commands in the Old Testament) and obeying him. Wisdom comes from letting the Holy Spirit live within you. Wisdom grows when, "like newborn babies, [you] crave pure spiritual milk, so that by it you may grow up in your salvation, now that you have tasted that the Lord is good" (1 Peter 2:2–3). If you're stuck in spiritual adolescence, listen, learn and grow spiritually mature.

Wednesday

Proverbs 1:24–25

You rejected me when I called and no one gave heed when I stretched out my hand . . . You ignored all my advice and would not accept my rebuke.

reflection

1 When you think back to your junior high years, what feelings do you experience?

2 Describe a time when you disregarded wisdom. What was the result?

3 How will you go about growing more and seeking wisdom?

RELATED READINGS

Psalm 81:8–16; Jeremiah 13:15–17; Galatians 6:6–10

Go to page 765 for your next devotional reading.

but fools[a] despise wisdom and
discipline.

Exhortations to Embrace Wisdom

Warning Against Enticement

8 Listen, my son, to your father's instruction
and do not forsake your mother's
teaching.
9 They will be a garland to grace your head
and a chain to adorn your neck.

10 My son, if sinners entice you,
do not give in to them.
11 If they say, "Come along with us;
let's lie in wait for someone's blood,
let's waylay some harmless soul;
12 let's swallow them alive, like the grave,[b]
and whole, like those who go down to
the pit;
13 we will get all sorts of valuable things
and fill our houses with plunder;
14 throw in your lot with us,
and we will share a common purse"—
15 my son, do not go along with them,
do not set foot on their paths;
16 for their feet rush into sin,
they are swift to shed blood.
17 How useless to spread a net
in full view of all the birds!
18 These men lie in wait for their own blood;
they waylay only themselves!
19 Such is the end of all who go after
ill-gotten gain;
it takes away the lives of those who get it.

Warning Against Rejecting Wisdom

20 Wisdom calls aloud in the street,
she raises her voice in the public
squares;
21 at the head of the noisy streets[c] she cries
out,
in the gateways of the city she makes her
speech:

22 "How long will you simple ones[d] love your
simple ways?
How long will mockers delight in
mockery
and fools hate knowledge?
23 If you had responded to my rebuke,
I would have poured out my heart to you
and made my thoughts known to you.
24 But since you rejected me when I called
and no one gave heed when I stretched
out my hand,
25 since you ignored all my advice
and would not accept my rebuke,
26 I in turn will laugh at your disaster;
I will mock when calamity overtakes
you—
27 when calamity overtakes you like a storm,
when disaster sweeps over you like a
whirlwind,
when distress and trouble overwhelm
you.

28 "Then they will call to me but I will not
answer;
they will look for me but will not find
me.
29 Since they hated knowledge
and did not choose to fear the LORD,
30 since they would not accept my advice
and spurned my rebuke,
31 they will eat the fruit of their ways
and be filled with the fruit of their
schemes.
32 For the waywardness of the simple will kill
them,
and the complacency of fools will
destroy them;
33 but whoever listens to me will live in safety
and be at ease, without fear of harm."

Moral Benefits of Wisdom

2 My son, if you accept my words
and store up my commands within you,
2 turning your ear to wisdom
and applying your heart to
understanding,
3 and if you call out for insight
and cry aloud for understanding,
4 and if you look for it as for silver
and search for it as for hidden treasure,
5 then you will understand the fear of the
LORD
and find the knowledge of God.
6 For the LORD gives wisdom,

[a]7 The Hebrew words rendered *fool* in Proverbs, and often elsewhere in the Old Testament, denote one who is morally deficient.
[b]12 Hebrew *Sheol* [c]21 Hebrew; Septuagint / *on the tops of the walls* [d]22 The Hebrew word rendered *simple* in Proverbs generally denotes one without moral direction and inclined to evil.

and from his mouth come knowledge
and understanding.
7 He holds victory in store for the upright,
he is a shield to those whose walk is
blameless,
8 for he guards the course of the just
and protects the way of his faithful ones.

9 Then you will understand what is right and
just
and fair—every good
path.
10 For wisdom will enter your
heart,
and knowledge will be
pleasant to your
soul.
11 Discretion will protect you,
and understanding will
guard you.

12 Wisdom will save you from
the ways of wicked
men,
from men whose words are perverse,
13 who leave the straight paths
to walk in dark ways,
14 who delight in doing wrong
and rejoice in the perverseness of evil,
15 whose paths are crooked
and who are devious in their ways.

16 It will save you also from the adulteress,
from the wayward wife with her
seductive words,
17 who has left the partner of her youth
and ignored the covenant she made
before God.[a]
18 For her house leads down to death
and her paths to the spirits of the dead.
19 None who go to her return
or attain the paths of life.

20 Thus you will walk in the ways of good
men
and keep to the paths of the righteous.
21 For the upright will live in the land,
and the blameless will remain in it;
22 but the wicked will be cut off from the
land,
and the unfaithful will be torn from it.

Proverbs 3:6

God Gives Guidance

In all your ways
acknowledge him,
and he will make your
paths straight.

Further Benefits of Wisdom

3 My son, do not forget my teaching,
but keep my commands in your heart,
2 for they will prolong your life many years
and bring you prosperity.

3 Let love and faithfulness never leave you;
bind them around your neck,
write them on the tablet of your heart.
4 Then you will win favor
and a good name
in the sight of God and
man.

5 Trust in the LORD with all
your heart
and lean not on your
own understanding;
6 in all your ways
acknowledge him,
and he will make your
paths straight.[b]

7 Do not be wise in your own
eyes;
fear the LORD and shun evil.
8 This will bring health to your body
and nourishment to your bones.

9 Honor the LORD with your wealth,
with the firstfruits of all your crops;
10 then your barns will be filled to
overflowing,
and your vats will brim over with new
wine.

11 My son, do not despise the LORD's
discipline
and do not resent his rebuke,
12 because the LORD disciplines those he
loves,
as a father[c] the son he delights in.

13 Blessed is the man who finds wisdom,
the man who gains understanding,
14 for she is more profitable than silver
and yields better returns than gold.
15 She is more precious than rubies;
nothing you desire can compare with
her.
16 Long life is in her right hand;
in her left hand are riches and honor.

[a] 17 Or *covenant of her God* [b] 6 Or *will direct your paths* [c] 12 Hebrew; Septuagint / *and he punishes*

17 Her ways are pleasant ways,
and all her paths are peace.
18 She is a tree of life to those who embrace her;
those who lay hold of her will be blessed.

19 By wisdom the LORD laid the earth's foundations,
by understanding he set the heavens in place;
20 by his knowledge the deeps were divided,
and the clouds let drop the dew.

21 My son, preserve sound judgment and discernment,
do not let them out of your sight;
22 they will be life for you,
an ornament to grace your neck.
23 Then you will go on your way in safety,
and your foot will not stumble;
24 when you lie down, you will not be afraid;
when you lie down, your sleep will be sweet.
25 Have no fear of sudden disaster
or of the ruin that overtakes the wicked,
26 for the LORD will be your confidence
and will keep your foot from being snared.

27 Do not withhold good from those who deserve it,
when it is in your power to act.
28 Do not say to your neighbor,
"Come back later; I'll give it tomorrow"—
when you now have it with you.

29 Do not plot harm against your neighbor,
who lives trustfully near you.
30 Do not accuse a man for no reason—
when he has done you no harm.

31 Do not envy a violent man
or choose any of his ways,
32 for the LORD detests a perverse man
but takes the upright into his confidence.

33 The LORD's curse is on the house of the wicked,
but he blesses the home of the righteous.
34 He mocks proud mockers
but gives grace to the humble.
35 The wise inherit honor,
but fools he holds up to shame.

Wisdom Is Supreme

4 Listen, my sons, to a father's instruction;
pay attention and gain understanding.
2 I give you sound learning,
so do not forsake my teaching.
3 When I was a boy in my father's house,
still tender, and an only child of my mother,
4 he taught me and said,
"Lay hold of my words with all your heart;
keep my commands and you will live.
5 Get wisdom, get understanding;
do not forget my words or swerve from them.
6 Do not forsake wisdom, and she will protect you;
love her, and she will watch over you.
7 Wisdom is supreme; therefore get wisdom.
Though it cost all you have,[a] get understanding.
8 Esteem her, and she will exalt you;
embrace her, and she will honor you.
9 She will set a garland of grace on your head
and present you with a crown of splendor."

10 Listen, my son, accept what I say,
and the years of your life will be many.
11 I guide you in the way of wisdom
and lead you along straight paths.
12 When you walk, your steps will not be hampered;
when you run, you will not stumble.
13 Hold on to instruction, do not let it go;
guard it well, for it is your life.
14 Do not set foot on the path of the wicked
or walk in the way of evil men.
15 Avoid it, do not travel on it;
turn from it and go on your way.
16 For they cannot sleep till they do evil;
they are robbed of slumber till they make someone fall.
17 They eat the bread of wickedness
and drink the wine of violence.

[a]7 Or *Whatever else you get*

18 The path of the righteous is like the first
gleam of dawn,
shining ever brighter till the full light
of day.
19 But the way of the wicked is like deep
darkness;
they do not know what makes them
stumble.

20 My son, pay attention to what I say;
listen closely to my words.
21 Do not let them out of your sight,
keep them within your heart;
22 for they are life to those who find them
and health to a man's whole body.
23 Above all else, guard your heart,
for it is the wellspring of life.
24 Put away perversity from your mouth;
keep corrupt talk far from your lips.
25 Let your eyes look straight ahead,
fix your gaze directly before you.
26 Make level[a] paths for your feet
and take only ways that are firm.
27 Do not swerve to the right or the left;
keep your foot from evil.

Warning Against Adultery

5 My son, pay attention to my wisdom,
listen well to my words of insight,
2 that you may maintain discretion
and your lips may preserve knowledge.
3 For the lips of an adulteress
drip honey,
and her speech is
smoother than oil;
4 but in the end she is bitter
as gall,
sharp as a double-edged
sword.
5 Her feet go down to death;
her steps lead straight to
the grave.[b]
6 She gives no thought to the
way of life;
her paths are crooked,
but she knows it
not.

7 Now then, my sons, listen to me;
do not turn aside from what I say.
8 Keep to a path far from her,
do not go near the door of her house,
9 lest you give your best strength to
others
and your years to one who is cruel,
10 lest strangers feast on your wealth
and your toil enrich another man's
house.
11 At the end of your life you will groan,
when your flesh and body are
spent.
12 You will say, "How I hated discipline!
How my heart spurned correction!
13 I would not obey my teachers
or listen to my instructors.
14 I have come to the brink of utter ruin
in the midst of the whole assembly."

15 Drink water from your own cistern,
running water from your own well.
16 Should your springs overflow in the
streets,
your streams of water in the public
squares?
17 Let them be yours alone,
never to be shared with strangers.
18 May your fountain be blessed,
and may you rejoice in the wife of your
youth.
19 A loving doe, a graceful deer—
may her breasts satisfy
you always,
may you ever be
captivated by her
love.
20 Why be captivated, my son,
by an adulteress?
Why embrace the bosom
of another man's
wife?

21 For a man's ways are in full
view of the LORD,
and he examines all his
paths.
22 The evil deeds of a wicked
man ensnare him;
the cords of his sin hold him fast.
23 He will die for lack of discipline,
led astray by his own great folly.

> **Proverbs 5:21**
>
> *God Examines Hearts*
>
> For a man's ways are in full view of the LORD, and he examines all his paths.

[a] 26 Or *Consider the* [b] 5 Hebrew *Sheol*

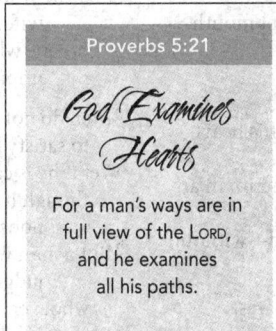

Warnings Against Folly

6 My son, if you have put up security for
your neighbor,
if you have struck hands in pledge for
another,
2 if you have been trapped by what you said,
ensnared by the words of your mouth,
3 then do this, my son, to free yourself,
since you have fallen into your
neighbor's hands:
Go and humble yourself;
press your plea with your neighbor!
4 Allow no sleep to your eyes,
no slumber to your eyelids.
5 Free yourself, like a gazelle from the hand
of the hunter,
like a bird from the snare of the fowler.

6 Go to the ant, you sluggard;
consider its ways and be wise!
7 It has no commander,
no overseer or ruler,
8 yet it stores its provisions in summer
and gathers its food at harvest.

9 How long will you lie there, you sluggard?
When will you get up from your sleep?
10 A little sleep, a little slumber,
a little folding of the hands to rest—
11 and poverty will come on you like a bandit
and scarcity like an armed man.[a]

12 A scoundrel and villain,
who goes about with a corrupt mouth,
13 who winks with his eye,
signals with his feet
and motions with his fingers,
14 who plots evil with deceit in his heart—
he always stirs up dissension.
15 Therefore disaster will overtake him in an
instant;
he will suddenly be destroyed—without
remedy.

16 There are six things the LORD hates,
seven that are detestable to him:
17 haughty eyes,
a lying tongue,
hands that shed innocent blood,
18 a heart that devises wicked schemes,
feet that are quick to rush into evil,
19 a false witness who pours out lies
and a man who stirs up dissension
among brothers.

Warning Against Adultery

20 My son, keep your father's commands
and do not forsake your mother's
teaching.
21 Bind them upon your heart forever;
fasten them around your neck.
22 When you walk, they will guide you;
when you sleep, they will watch over
you;
when you awake, they will speak to you.
23 For these commands are a lamp,
this teaching is a light,
and the corrections of discipline
are the way to life,
24 keeping you from the immoral woman,
from the smooth tongue of the wayward
wife.
25 Do not lust in your heart after her beauty
or let her captivate you with her eyes,
26 for the prostitute reduces you to a loaf of
bread,
and the adulteress preys upon your very
life.
27 Can a man scoop fire into his lap
without his clothes being burned?
28 Can a man walk on hot coals
without his feet being scorched?
29 So is he who sleeps with another man's
wife;
no one who touches her will go
unpunished.

30 Men do not despise a thief if he steals
to satisfy his hunger when he is starving.
31 Yet if he is caught, he must pay sevenfold,
though it costs him all the wealth of his
house.
32 But a man who commits adultery lacks
judgment;
whoever does so destroys himself.
33 Blows and disgrace are his lot,
and his shame will never be wiped away;
34 for jealousy arouses a husband's fury,
and he will show no mercy when he
takes revenge.
35 He will not accept any compensation;

[a] 11 Or *like a vagrant / and scarcity like a beggar*

Things God Hates

Read: Proverbs 6:16–19

HATE IS A SEVERE WORD. It expresses an intense hostility or extreme dislike. Many children use the word without thought, and most parents admonish them, "We don't use the word *hate*." But inevitably the harsh word slips out: "I hate vegetables!" "I hate my little brother!" Many adults aren't much better, and the word slips out all too easily: "I hate it when the pastor's wife gets all the glory." "I hate that man's singing." "I hate skinny models." "I hate to cook dinner."

What do you hate? What things do you avoid at all costs? For some the thought of a certain activity causes intense agitation. Perhaps your first auto accident occurred during a blizzard. To this day, you hate getting behind the steering wheel when the fluffy flakes appear. Everybody hates something. And strange as it may seem, the Bible says that even the all-loving God hates some things.

It may seem strange to us to read the words "hate" and "God" in the same sentence. If God is love, then what does he hate? Solomon lists the top seven things God hates: (1) a prideful sneer, (2) fraud, (3) bloodshed, (4) conspiracy, (5) evil intent, (6) perjury and (7) inciting division among God's people. Bible commentator Matthew Henry wrote, "God hates sin; he hates every sin; he can never be reconciled to it; he hates nothing but sin," but apparently these sins are especially repugnant to him.

This list possesses a common thread; it includes sins particularly harmful to others. Since human beings are God's special creation, he is exceptionally sensitive to sins that cause grief for others. The list also crescendos: the first six sins place emphasis on the seventh. It's bad for you to sin, but it is "detestable" to start a chain reaction—causing others to sin too.

What are the top seven things you hate? The psalmist said, "Let those who love the LORD hate evil" (Psalm 97:10). To love God is to hate what he hates. Instead of despising veggies or hating to drive on icy roads, go a little deeper. Really think about what's on God's "hate" list. Then banish those things from your house and your heart.

Thursday

Go to page 769 for your next devotional reading.

Proverbs 6:16

There are six things the LORD hates, seven that are detestable to him.

reflection

1 What on God's list of things to hate surprises you?

2 Ask God to show you if you have ever practiced anything on this list. If so, what? (Be honest.)

3 How will you banish the things on God's list from your life?

RELATED READINGS

Psalm 101:1–8;
Proverbs 8:13;
Romans 1:18–20

he will refuse the bribe, however great
it is.

Warning Against the Adulteress

7 My son, keep my words
and store up my commands within you.
2 Keep my commands and you will live;
guard my teachings as the apple of your
eye.
3 Bind them on your fingers;
write them on the tablet of your heart.
4 Say to wisdom, "You are my sister,"
and call understanding your kinsman;
5 they will keep you from the adulteress,
from the wayward wife with her
seductive words.

6 At the window of my house
I looked out through the lattice.
7 I saw among the simple,
I noticed among the young men,
a youth who lacked judgment.
8 He was going down the street near her
corner,
walking along in the direction of her
house
9 at twilight, as the day was fading,
as the dark of night set in.

10 Then out came a woman to meet him,
dressed like a prostitute and with crafty
intent.
11 (She is loud and defiant,
her feet never stay at home;
12 now in the street, now in the squares,
at every corner she lurks.)
13 She took hold of him and kissed him
and with a brazen face she said:

14 "I have fellowship offerings[a] at home;
today I fulfilled my vows.
15 So I came out to meet you;
I looked for you and have found you!
16 I have covered my bed
with colored linens from Egypt.
17 I have perfumed my bed
with myrrh, aloes and cinnamon.
18 Come, let's drink deep of love till morning;
let's enjoy ourselves with love!
19 My husband is not at home;
he has gone on a long journey.
20 He took his purse filled with money
and will not be home till full moon."

21 With persuasive words she led him astray;
she seduced him with her smooth talk.
22 All at once he followed her
like an ox going to the slaughter,
like a deer[b] stepping into a noose[c]
23 till an arrow pierces his liver,
like a bird darting into a snare,
little knowing it will cost him his life.

24 Now then, my sons, listen to me;
pay attention to what I say.
25 Do not let your heart turn to her ways
or stray into her paths.
26 Many are the victims she has brought
down;
her slain are a mighty throng.
27 Her house is a highway to the grave,[d]
leading down to the chambers of death.

Wisdom's Call

8 Does not wisdom call out?
Does not understanding raise her voice?
2 On the heights along the way,
where the paths meet, she takes her
stand;
3 beside the gates leading into the city,
at the entrances, she cries aloud:
4 "To you, O men, I call out;
I raise my voice to all mankind.
5 You who are simple, gain prudence;
you who are foolish, gain
understanding.
6 Listen, for I have worthy things to say;
I open my lips to speak what is right.
7 My mouth speaks what is true,
for my lips detest wickedness.
8 All the words of my mouth are just;
none of them is crooked or perverse.
9 To the discerning all of them are right;
they are faultless to those who have
knowledge.
10 Choose my instruction instead of silver,
knowledge rather than choice gold,
11 for wisdom is more precious than rubies,
and nothing you desire can compare
with her.

[a]14 Traditionally *peace offerings* [b]22 Syriac (see also Septuagint); Hebrew *fool* [c]22 The meaning of the Hebrew for this line is uncertain. [d]27 Hebrew *Sheol*

12 "I, wisdom, dwell together with prudence;
I possess knowledge and discretion.
13 To fear the LORD is to hate evil;
I hate pride and arrogance,
evil behavior and perverse speech.
14 Counsel and sound judgment are mine;
I have understanding and power.
15 By me kings reign
and rulers make laws that are just;
16 by me princes govern,
and all nobles who rule on earth.[a]
17 I love those who love me,
and those who seek me find me.
18 With me are riches and honor,
enduring wealth and prosperity.
19 My fruit is better than fine gold;
what I yield surpasses choice silver.
20 I walk in the way of righteousness,
along the paths of justice,
21 bestowing wealth on those who love me
and making their treasuries full.

22 "The LORD brought me forth as the first of his works,[b,c]
before his deeds of old;
23 I was appointed[d] from eternity,
from the beginning, before the world began.
24 When there were no oceans, I was given birth,
when there were no springs abounding with water;
25 before the mountains were settled in place,
before the hills, I was given birth,
26 before he made the earth or its fields
or any of the dust of the world.
27 I was there when he set the heavens in place,
when he marked out the horizon on the face of the deep,
28 when he established the clouds above
and fixed securely the fountains of the deep,
29 when he gave the sea its boundary
so the waters would not overstep his command,
and when he marked out the foundations of the earth.
30 Then I was the craftsman at his side.
I was filled with delight day after day,
rejoicing always in his presence,
31 rejoicing in his whole world
and delighting in mankind.

32 "Now then, my sons, listen to me;
blessed are those who keep my ways.
33 Listen to my instruction and be wise;
do not ignore it.
34 Blessed is the man who listens to me,
watching daily at my doors,
waiting at my doorway.
35 For whoever finds me finds life
and receives favor from the LORD.
36 But whoever fails to find me harms himself;
all who hate me love death."

Invitations of Wisdom and of Folly

9 Wisdom has built her house;
she has hewn out its seven pillars.
2 She has prepared her meat and mixed her wine;
she has also set her table.
3 She has sent out her maids, and she calls
from the highest point of the city.
4 "Let all who are simple come in here!"
she says to those who lack judgment.
5 "Come, eat my food
and drink the wine I have mixed.
6 Leave your simple ways and you will live;
walk in the way of understanding.

7 "Whoever corrects a mocker invites insult;
whoever rebukes a wicked man incurs abuse.
8 Do not rebuke a mocker or he will hate you;
rebuke a wise man and he will love you.
9 Instruct a wise man and he will be wiser still;
teach a righteous man and he will add to his learning.

10 "The fear of the LORD is the beginning of wisdom,
and knowledge of the Holy One is understanding.
11 For through me your days will be many,
and years will be added to your life.

[a]16 Many Hebrew manuscripts and Septuagint; most Hebrew manuscripts *and nobles—all righteous rulers* [b]22 Or *way*; or *dominion* [c]22 Or *The LORD possessed me at the beginning of his work*; or *The LORD brought me forth at the beginning of his work* [d]23 Or *fashioned*

12 If you are wise, your wisdom will reward
you;
if you are a mocker, you alone will
suffer."

13 The woman Folly is loud;
she is undisciplined and without
knowledge.
14 She sits at the door of her house,
on a seat at the highest point of the city,
15 calling out to those who pass by,
who go straight on their way.
16 "Let all who are simple come in here!"
she says to those who lack judgment.
17 "Stolen water is sweet;
food eaten in secret is delicious!"
18 But little do they know that the dead are
there,
that her guests are in the depths of the
grave.[a]

Proverbs of Solomon

10 The proverbs of Solomon:

A wise son brings joy to his father,
but a foolish son grief to his mother.

2 Ill-gotten treasures are of no value,
but righteousness delivers from death.

3 The LORD does not let the righteous go
hungry
but he thwarts the craving of the
wicked.

4 Lazy hands make a man poor,
but diligent hands bring wealth.

5 He who gathers crops in summer is a wise
son,
but he who sleeps during harvest is a
disgraceful son.

6 Blessings crown the head of the righteous,
but violence overwhelms the mouth of
the wicked.[b]

7 The memory of the righteous will be a
blessing,
but the name of the wicked will rot.

8 The wise in heart accept commands,
but a chattering fool comes to ruin.

9 The man of integrity walks securely,
but he who takes crooked paths will be
found out.

10 He who winks maliciously causes grief,
and a chattering fool comes to ruin.

11 The mouth of the righteous is a fountain of
life,
but violence overwhelms the mouth of
the wicked.

12 Hatred stirs up dissension,
but love covers over all wrongs.

13 Wisdom is found on the lips of the
discerning,
but a rod is for the back of him who
lacks judgment.

14 Wise men store up knowledge,
but the mouth of a fool invites ruin.

15 The wealth of the rich is their fortified city,
but poverty is the ruin of the poor.

16 The wages of the righteous bring them
life,
but the income of the wicked brings
them punishment.

17 He who heeds discipline shows the way to
life,
but whoever ignores correction leads
others astray.

18 He who conceals his hatred has lying lips,
and whoever spreads slander is a fool.

19 When words are many, sin is not absent,
but he who holds his tongue is wise.

20 The tongue of the righteous is choice
silver,
but the heart of the wicked is of little
value.

21 The lips of the righteous nourish many,
but fools die for lack of judgment.

22 The blessing of the LORD brings wealth,
and he adds no trouble to it.

23 A fool finds pleasure in evil conduct,
but a man of understanding delights in
wisdom.

[a] 18 Hebrew *Sheol* [b] 6 Or *but the mouth of the wicked conceals violence*; also in verse 11

Nourishing Words

Read: Proverbs 10:16–22

DURING WORLD WAR II the Office of War developed a media campaign called "Loose lips sink ships!" to help the citizenry maintain a code of silence. With Japanese and German submarines patrolling the coastlines of the United States, those leading the Office of War realized that silence meant security. One of their most memorable posters depicted a fiery ship sinking into the ocean.

Such urgent statements may have invited skepticism, but, to the soldier on the ground, stray comments presented very present dangers. A careless word could cost lives. King Solomon would not have laughed at such dire warnings. The sagacious king understood the power words have to destroy. In Proverbs 10 he reminds us we have the power to raise or sink the spirits of the people around us with our words.

Take a moment to think about your recent conversations. Have you felt nourished by someone's encouraging words? How did those words lift you up? How did you respond? Or perhaps you remember when someone's language wounded your spirit. Maybe you were torpedoed by a thoughtless comment from a neighbor or struck down by a destructive argument with a family member or friend. We have all experienced the withering force of cruel words. But consider the effects of good and kind speech. Just as foolish talk can bring death, truth spoken with love can lift the discouraged soul, restore dignity to the oppressed and heal the brokenhearted. God places great importance on our words. The apostle Paul did too. He said, "Let your conversation be always full of grace, seasoned with salt, so that you may know how to answer everyone" (Colossians 4:6).

Your words have the power of life or death. You can wound another's spirit or protect another's dignity by the words you speak. Choose your words wisely. Kindly nourish and uplift those around you.

Proverbs 10:21

The lips of the righteous nourish many, but fools die for lack of judgment.

reflection

1 Describe a time when your words wounded someone's spirit or nourished someone's spirit.

2 What has been the tone of the words coming out of your mouth today? How do they reflect what's in your heart?

3 How has God's Word proven to have power in your life?

RELATED READINGS

Ecclesiastes 5:2–3; 10:12–14; James 3:1–12

Go to page 775 for your next devotional reading.

24 What the wicked dreads will overtake him;
what the righteous desire will be
granted.

25 When the storm has swept by, the wicked
are gone,
but the righteous stand firm forever.

26 As vinegar to the teeth and smoke to the
eyes,
so is a sluggard to those who send him.

27 The fear of the LORD adds length to life,
but the years of the wicked are cut short.

28 The prospect of the righteous is joy,
but the hopes of the wicked come to
nothing.

29 The way of the LORD is a refuge for the
righteous,
but it is the ruin of those who do evil.

30 The righteous will never be uprooted,
but the wicked will not remain in the
land.

31 The mouth of the righteous brings forth
wisdom,
but a perverse tongue will be cut out.

32 The lips of the righteous know what is
fitting,
but the mouth of the wicked only what
is perverse.

11 The LORD abhors dishonest scales,
but accurate weights are his delight.

2 When pride comes, then comes disgrace,
but with humility comes
wisdom.

3 The integrity of the upright
guides them,
but the unfaithful are
destroyed by their
duplicity.

4 Wealth is worthless in the
day of wrath,
but righteousness
delivers from death.

5 The righteousness of the
blameless makes a
straight way for them,
but the wicked are brought down by
their own wickedness.

6 The righteousness of the upright delivers
them,
but the unfaithful are trapped by evil
desires.

7 When a wicked man dies, his hope
perishes;
all he expected from his power comes to
nothing.

8 The righteous man is rescued from
trouble,
and it comes on the wicked instead.

9 With his mouth the godless destroys his
neighbor,
but through knowledge the righteous
escape.

10 When the righteous prosper, the city
rejoices;
when the wicked perish, there are shouts
of joy.

11 Through the blessing of the upright a city
is exalted,
but by the mouth of the wicked it is
destroyed.

12 A man who lacks judgment derides his
neighbor,
but a man of understanding holds his
tongue.

13 A gossip betrays a confidence,
but a trustworthy man keeps a secret.

14 For lack of guidance a
nation falls,
but many advisers make
victory sure.

15 He who puts up security for
another will surely
suffer,
but whoever refuses
to strike hands in
pledge is safe.

16 A kindhearted woman
gains respect,
but ruthless men gain
only wealth.

Proverbs 11:1

God Loves Honesty

The LORD abhors
dishonest scales,
but accurate weights
are his delight.

17 A kind man benefits himself,
but a cruel man brings trouble on himself.

18 The wicked man earns deceptive wages,
but he who sows righteousness reaps a sure reward.

19 The truly righteous man attains life,
but he who pursues evil goes to his death.

20 The LORD detests men of perverse heart
but he delights in those whose ways are blameless.

21 Be sure of this: The wicked will not go unpunished,
but those who are righteous will go free.

22 Like a gold ring in a pig's snout
is a beautiful woman who shows no discretion.

23 The desire of the righteous ends only in good,
but the hope of the wicked only in wrath.

24 One man gives freely, yet gains even more;
another withholds unduly, but comes to poverty.

25 A generous man will prosper;
he who refreshes others will himself be refreshed.

26 People curse the man who hoards grain,
but blessing crowns him who is willing to sell.

27 He who seeks good finds goodwill,
but evil comes to him who searches for it.

28 Whoever trusts in his riches will fall,
but the righteous will thrive like a green leaf.

29 He who brings trouble on his family will inherit only wind,
and the fool will be servant to the wise.

30 The fruit of the righteous is a tree of life,
and he who wins souls is wise.

31 If the righteous receive their due on earth,
how much more the ungodly and the sinner!

> **Proverbs 12:2**
>
> ***God Hates Deceit***
>
> A good man obtains favor from the LORD,
> but the LORD condemns a crafty man.

12 Whoever loves discipline loves knowledge,
but he who hates correction is stupid.

2 A good man obtains favor from the LORD,
but the LORD condemns a crafty man.

3 A man cannot be established through wickedness,
but the righteous cannot be uprooted.

4 A wife of noble character is her husband's crown,
but a disgraceful wife is like decay in his bones.

5 The plans of the righteous are just,
but the advice of the wicked is deceitful.

6 The words of the wicked lie in wait for blood,
but the speech of the upright rescues them.

7 Wicked men are overthrown and are no more,
but the house of the righteous stands firm.

8 A man is praised according to his wisdom,
but men with warped minds are despised.

9 Better to be a nobody and yet have a servant
than pretend to be somebody and have no food.

10 A righteous man cares for the needs of his animal,

but the kindest acts of the wicked are
cruel.

11 He who works his land will have abundant
food,
but he who chases fantasies lacks
judgment.

12 The wicked desire the plunder of evil men,
but the root of the righteous flourishes.

13 An evil man is trapped by his sinful talk,
but a righteous man escapes trouble.

14 From the fruit of his lips a man is filled
with good things
as surely as the work of his hands
rewards him.

15 The way of a fool seems right to him,
but a wise man listens to advice.

16 A fool shows his annoyance at once,
but a prudent man overlooks an insult.

17 A truthful witness gives honest testimony,
but a false witness tells lies.

18 Reckless words pierce like a sword,
but the tongue of the wise brings healing.

19 Truthful lips endure forever,
but a lying tongue lasts only a moment.

20 There is deceit in the hearts of those who
plot evil,
but joy for those who promote peace.

21 No harm befalls the righteous,
but the wicked have their fill of trouble.

22 The LORD detests lying lips,
but he delights in men who are truthful.

23 A prudent man keeps his knowledge to
himself,
but the heart of fools blurts out folly.

24 Diligent hands will rule,
but laziness ends in slave labor.

25 An anxious heart weighs a man down,
but a kind word cheers him up.

26 A righteous man is cautious in friendship,[a]
but the way of the wicked leads them
astray.

27 The lazy man does not roast[b] his game,
but the diligent man prizes his
possessions.

28 In the way of righteousness there is life;
along that path is immortality.

13 A wise son heeds his father's
instruction,
but a mocker does not listen to rebuke.

2 From the fruit of his lips a man enjoys
good things,
but the unfaithful have a craving for
violence.

3 He who guards his lips guards his life,
but he who speaks rashly will come to
ruin.

4 The sluggard craves and gets nothing,
but the desires of the diligent are fully
satisfied.

5 The righteous hate what is false,
but the wicked bring shame and
disgrace.

6 Righteousness guards the man of
integrity,
but wickedness overthrows the sinner.

7 One man pretends to be rich, yet has
nothing;
another pretends to be poor, yet has
great wealth.

8 A man's riches may ransom his life,
but a poor man hears no threat.

9 The light of the righteous shines brightly,
but the lamp of the wicked is snuffed
out.

10 Pride only breeds quarrels,
but wisdom is found in those who take
advice.

11 Dishonest money dwindles away,
but he who gathers money little by little
makes it grow.

12 Hope deferred makes the heart sick,
but a longing fulfilled is a tree of life.

13 He who scorns instruction will pay for it,

[a]26 Or *man is a guide to his neighbor* [b]27 The meaning of the Hebrew for this word is uncertain.

but he who respects a command is
rewarded.

14 The teaching of the wise is a fountain of
life,
turning a man from the snares of death.

15 Good understanding wins favor,
but the way of the unfaithful is hard.[a]

16 Every prudent man acts out of knowledge,
but a fool exposes his folly.

17 A wicked messenger falls into trouble,
but a trustworthy envoy brings
healing.

18 He who ignores discipline comes to
poverty and shame,
but whoever heeds correction is
honored.

19 A longing fulfilled is sweet to the soul,
but fools detest turning from evil.

20 He who walks with the wise grows wise,
but a companion of fools suffers harm.

21 Misfortune pursues the sinner,
but prosperity is the reward of the
righteous.

22 A good man leaves an inheritance for his
children's children,
but a sinner's wealth is stored up for the
righteous.

23 A poor man's field may produce abundant
food,
but injustice sweeps it away.

24 He who spares the rod hates his son,
but he who loves him is careful to
discipline him.

25 The righteous eat to their hearts' content,
but the stomach of the wicked goes
hungry.

14 The wise woman builds her house,
but with her own hands the foolish
one tears hers down.

2 He whose walk is upright fears the LORD,
but he whose ways are devious despises
him.

3 A fool's talk brings a rod to his back,
but the lips of the wise protect them.

4 Where there are no oxen, the manger is
empty,
but from the strength of an ox comes an
abundant harvest.

5 A truthful witness does not deceive,
but a false witness pours out lies.

6 The mocker seeks wisdom and finds none,
but knowledge comes easily to the
discerning.

7 Stay away from a foolish man,
for you will not find knowledge on his
lips.

8 The wisdom of the prudent is to give
thought to their ways,
but the folly of fools is deception.

9 Fools mock at making amends for sin,
but goodwill is found among the
upright.

10 Each heart knows its own bitterness,
and no one else can share its joy.

11 The house of the wicked will be destroyed,
but the tent of the upright will flourish.

12 There is a way that seems right to a man,
but in the end it leads to death.

13 Even in laughter the heart may ache,
and joy may end in grief.

14 The faithless will be fully repaid for their
ways,
and the good man rewarded for his.

15 A simple man believes anything,
but a prudent man gives thought to his
steps.

16 A wise man fears the LORD and shuns evil,
but a fool is hotheaded and reckless.

17 A quick-tempered man does foolish things,
and a crafty man is hated.

18 The simple inherit folly,
but the prudent are crowned with
knowledge.

[a]15 Or *unfaithful does not endure*

19 Evil men will bow down in the presence of
the good,
and the wicked at the gates of the
righteous.

20 The poor are shunned even by their
neighbors,
but the rich have many friends.

21 He who despises his neighbor sins,
but blessed is he who is kind to the
needy.

22 Do not those who plot evil go astray?
But those who plan what is good find[a]
love and faithfulness.

23 All hard work brings a profit,
but mere talk leads only to poverty.

24 The wealth of the wise is their crown,
but the folly of fools yields folly.

25 A truthful witness saves
lives,
but a false witness is
deceitful.

26 He who fears the LORD has
a secure fortress,
and for his children it
will be a refuge.

27 The fear of the LORD is a
fountain of life,
turning a man from the
snares of death.

28 A large population is a
king's glory,
but without subjects a prince is ruined.

29 A patient man has great understanding,
but a quick-tempered man displays folly.

30 A heart at peace gives life to the body,
but envy rots the bones.

31 He who oppresses the poor shows
contempt for their Maker,
but whoever is kind to the needy honors
God.

32 When calamity comes, the wicked are
brought down,
but even in death the righteous have a
refuge.

33 Wisdom reposes in the heart of the
discerning
and even among fools she lets herself be
known.[b]

34 Righteousness exalts a nation,
but sin is a disgrace to any people.

35 A king delights in a wise servant,
but a shameful servant incurs his wrath.

15 A gentle answer turns away wrath,
but a harsh word stirs up anger.

2 The tongue of the wise commends
knowledge,
but the mouth of the fool gushes folly.

3 The eyes of the LORD are everywhere,
keeping watch on the wicked and the
good.

Proverbs 14:26

God Gives Security

He who fears the LORD
has a secure fortress,
and for his children it
will be a refuge.

4 The tongue that brings
healing is a tree of
life,
but a deceitful tongue
crushes the spirit.

5 A fool spurns his father's
discipline,
but whoever heeds
correction shows
prudence.

6 The house of the righteous
contains great
treasure,
but the income of the wicked brings
them trouble.

7 The lips of the wise spread knowledge;
not so the hearts of fools.

8 The LORD detests the sacrifice of the wicked,
but the prayer of the upright pleases him.

9 The LORD detests the way of the wicked
but he loves those who pursue
righteousness.

10 Stern discipline awaits him who leaves the
path;
he who hates correction will die.

[a]22 Or *show* [b]33 Hebrew; Septuagint and Syriac / *but in the heart of fools she is not known*

Life's Questions

QUEEN OF SHEBA

SHE HAD QUESTIONS. And she didn't think twice about traveling 1500 miles, one way, to get answers.

Over the years, her wise, elderly subjects often told her that the longer she lived, the more mysterious life would seem. "Life brings all kinds of questions our way," they would say. "Live long enough and you'll find this to be truer by the day."

All she knew was that she'd already lived long enough and seen enough of the world to have questions—lots of them. *Why does poverty exist? Why do the innocent suffer? What is the meaning of life? Is this all there is?*

She came to Jerusalem with much on her mind, determined to leave with a sense of satisfaction. And Solomon did not disappoint. To her delight, not only did Solomon answer all of her questions, he also explained them in a way that made sense to her.

She enjoyed the challenge of bringing her strictly pagan viewpoint into conversation with the God-fearing Solomon. She loved that he didn't blindly agree with her every thought—a welcome relief from the palace back home, where no one dared oppose her. Posing her pagan perspective against his faith lent itself to lively discussion in their late-night talks, afternoon debates and intellectual jousts.

"Naturally," she would later tell her people back home, "there were some questions Solomon didn't have to answer." *Was the God of Israel as great as he claimed? Does he really bless those who serve him? Is there no end to his resources and might?* The evidence, she concluded, spoke for itself. She merely had to look around for the answer. Forty thousand horses, expansive borders and a palace dripping with gold and silver spoke more than words ever could.

"Not the half has been told," she would often recall of her time with Solomon. "Not the half."

—Prayer—

Great God, I have many questions. Grant me the wisdom to see your truth all around me.

She came to Solomon and talked with him about all that she had on her mind.

1 Kings 10:2

ASSIGNED READING:

1 Kings 10:1–29;
2 Chronicles 9:1–28

Weekend

Go to page 781 for your next devotional reading.

11 Death and Destruction[a] lie open before
the LORD—
how much more the hearts of men!

12 A mocker resents correction;
he will not consult the wise.

13 A happy heart makes the face cheerful,
but heartache crushes the spirit.

14 The discerning heart seeks knowledge,
but the mouth of a fool feeds on folly.

15 All the days of the oppressed are
wretched,
but the cheerful heart has a continual
feast.

16 Better a little with the fear of the LORD
than great wealth with turmoil.

17 Better a meal of vegetables where there is
love
than a fattened calf with hatred.

18 A hot-tempered man stirs up dissension,
but a patient man calms a quarrel.

19 The way of the sluggard is blocked with
thorns,
but the path of the upright is a highway.

20 A wise son brings joy to his father,
but a foolish man despises his mother.

21 Folly delights a man who lacks judgment,
but a man of understanding keeps a
straight course.

22 Plans fail for lack of
counsel,
but with many advisers
they succeed.

23 A man finds joy in giving
an apt reply—
and how good is a timely
word!

24 The path of life leads
upward for the wise
to keep him from going
down to the grave.[b]

25 The LORD tears down the proud man's
house
but he keeps the widow's boundaries
intact.

26 The LORD detests the thoughts of the
wicked,
but those of the pure are pleasing to him.

27 A greedy man brings trouble to his family,
but he who hates bribes will live.

28 The heart of the righteous weighs its
answers,
but the mouth of the wicked gushes evil.

29 The LORD is far from the wicked
but he hears the prayer of the righteous.

30 A cheerful look brings joy to the heart,
and good news gives health to the bones.

31 He who listens to a life-giving rebuke
will be at home among the wise.

32 He who ignores discipline despises
himself,
but whoever heeds correction gains
understanding.

33 The fear of the LORD teaches a man
wisdom,[c]
and humility comes before honor.

16 To man belong the plans of the heart,
but from the LORD comes the reply
of the tongue.

2 All a man's ways seem
innocent to him,
but motives are weighed
by the LORD.

3 Commit to the LORD
whatever you do,
and your plans will
succeed.

4 The LORD works out
everything for his
own ends—
even the wicked for a day
of disaster.

5 The LORD detests all the proud of heart.
Be sure of this: They will not go
unpunished.

Proverbs 16:1

God Gives Us Words

To man belong the
plans of the heart,
but from the LORD comes
the reply of the tongue.

[a]11 Hebrew *Sheol and Abaddon* [b]24 Hebrew *Sheol* [c]33 Or *Wisdom teaches the fear of the LORD*

6 Through love and faithfulness sin is atoned for;
through the fear of the LORD a man avoids evil.

7 When a man's ways are pleasing to the LORD,
he makes even his enemies live at peace with him.

8 Better a little with righteousness
than much gain with injustice.

9 In his heart a man plans his course,
but the LORD determines his steps.

10 The lips of a king speak as an oracle,
and his mouth should not betray justice.

11 Honest scales and balances are from the LORD;
all the weights in the bag are of his making.

12 Kings detest wrongdoing,
for a throne is established through righteousness.

13 Kings take pleasure in honest lips;
they value a man who speaks the truth.

14 A king's wrath is a messenger of death,
but a wise man will appease it.

15 When a king's face brightens, it means life;
his favor is like a rain cloud in spring.

16 How much better to get wisdom than gold,
to choose understanding rather than silver!

17 The highway of the upright avoids evil;
he who guards his way guards his life.

18 Pride goes before destruction,
a haughty spirit before a fall.

19 Better to be lowly in spirit and among the oppressed
than to share plunder with the proud.

20 Whoever gives heed to instruction prospers,
and blessed is he who trusts in the LORD.

21 The wise in heart are called discerning,
and pleasant words promote instruction.[a]

22 Understanding is a fountain of life to those who have it,
but folly brings punishment to fools.

23 A wise man's heart guides his mouth,
and his lips promote instruction.[b]

24 Pleasant words are a honeycomb,
sweet to the soul and healing to the bones.

25 There is a way that seems right to a man,
but in the end it leads to death.

26 The laborer's appetite works for him;
his hunger drives him on.

27 A scoundrel plots evil,
and his speech is like a scorching fire.

28 A perverse man stirs up dissension,
and a gossip separates close friends.

29 A violent man entices his neighbor
and leads him down a path that is not good.

30 He who winks with his eye is plotting perversity;
he who purses his lips is bent on evil.

31 Gray hair is a crown of splendor;
it is attained by a righteous life.

32 Better a patient man than a warrior,
a man who controls his temper than one who takes a city.

33 The lot is cast into the lap,
but its every decision is from the LORD.

17 Better a dry crust with peace and quiet
than a house full of feasting,[c] with strife.

2 A wise servant will rule over a disgraceful son,
and will share the inheritance as one of the brothers.

3 The crucible for silver and the furnace for gold,
but the LORD tests the heart.

4 A wicked man listens to evil lips;
a liar pays attention to a malicious tongue.

a21 Or *words make a man persuasive* b23 Or *mouth / and makes his lips persuasive* c1 Hebrew *sacrifices*

5 He who mocks the poor shows contempt
for their Maker;
whoever gloats over disaster will not go
unpunished.

6 Children's children are a crown to the
aged,
and parents are the pride of their
children.

7 Arrogant[a] lips are unsuited to a fool—
how much worse lying lips to a ruler!

8 A bribe is a charm to the one who gives it;
wherever he turns, he succeeds.

9 He who covers over an offense promotes
love,
but whoever repeats the matter separates
close friends.

10 A rebuke impresses a man of discernment
more than a hundred lashes a fool.

11 An evil man is bent only on rebellion;
a merciless official will be sent against
him.

12 Better to meet a bear robbed of her cubs
than a fool in his folly.

13 If a man pays back evil for good,
evil will never leave his house.

14 Starting a quarrel is like breaching a dam;
so drop the matter before a dispute
breaks out.

15 Acquitting the guilty and condemning the
innocent—
the LORD detests them both.

16 Of what use is money in the hand of a fool,
since he has no desire to get wisdom?

17 A friend loves at all times,
and a brother is born for adversity.

18 A man lacking in judgment strikes hands
in pledge
and puts up security for his neighbor.

19 He who loves a quarrel loves sin;
he who builds a high gate invites
destruction.

20 A man of perverse heart does not prosper;
he whose tongue is deceitful falls into
trouble.

21 To have a fool for a son brings grief;
there is no joy for the father of a fool.

22 A cheerful heart is good medicine,
but a crushed spirit dries up the bones.

23 A wicked man accepts a bribe in secret
to pervert the course of justice.

24 A discerning man keeps wisdom in view,
but a fool's eyes wander to the ends of
the earth.

25 A foolish son brings grief to his father
and bitterness to the one who bore him.

26 It is not good to punish an innocent man,
or to flog officials for their integrity.

27 A man of knowledge uses words with
restraint,
and a man of understanding is even-
tempered.

28 Even a fool is thought wise if he keeps
silent,
and discerning if he holds his tongue.

18 An unfriendly man pursues selfish
ends;
he defies all sound judgment.

2 A fool finds no pleasure in understanding
but delights in airing his own opinions.

3 When wickedness comes, so does
contempt,
and with shame comes disgrace.

4 The words of a man's mouth are deep
waters,
but the fountain of wisdom is a bubbling
brook.

5 It is not good to be partial to the wicked
or to deprive the innocent of justice.

6 A fool's lips bring him strife,
and his mouth invites a beating.

7 A fool's mouth is his undoing,
and his lips are a snare to his soul.

[a]7 Or *Eloquent*

8 The words of a gossip are like choice morsels;
they go down to a man's inmost parts.

9 One who is slack in his work
is brother to one who destroys.

10 The name of the LORD is a
strong tower;
the righteous run to it
and are safe.

11 The wealth of the rich is
their fortified city;
they imagine it an
unscalable wall.

12 Before his downfall a man's
heart is proud,
but humility comes
before honor.

13 He who answers before
listening—
that is his folly and his shame.

14 A man's spirit sustains him in sickness,
but a crushed spirit who can bear?

15 The heart of the discerning acquires
knowledge;
the ears of the wise seek it out.

16 A gift opens the way for the giver
and ushers him into the presence of the
great.

17 The first to present his case seems right,
till another comes forward and
questions him.

18 Casting the lot settles disputes
and keeps strong opponents apart.

19 An offended brother is more unyielding
than a fortified city,
and disputes are like the barred gates of
a citadel.

20 From the fruit of his mouth a man's
stomach is filled;
with the harvest from his lips he is
satisfied.

21 The tongue has the power of life and death,
and those who love it will eat its fruit.

22 He who finds a wife finds what is good
and receives favor from the LORD.

23 A poor man pleads for mercy,
but a rich man answers harshly.

24 A man of many
companions may
come to ruin,
but there is a friend who
sticks closer than a
brother.

Proverbs 18:24

God Is a Lasting Friend

A man of many
companions may
come to ruin,
but there is a friend
who sticks closer
than a brother.

19 Better a poor man
whose walk is
blameless
than a fool whose lips are
perverse.

2 It is not good to have zeal
without knowledge,
nor to be hasty and miss
the way.

3 A man's own folly ruins his life,
yet his heart rages against the LORD.

4 Wealth brings many friends,
but a poor man's friend deserts him.

5 A false witness will not go unpunished,
and he who pours out lies will not go
free.

6 Many curry favor with a ruler,
and everyone is the friend of a man who
gives gifts.

7 A poor man is shunned by all his
relatives—
how much more do his friends avoid
him!
Though he pursues them with pleading,
they are nowhere to be found.[a]

8 He who gets wisdom loves his own soul;
he who cherishes understanding
prospers.

9 A false witness will not go unpunished,
and he who pours out lies will perish.

10 It is not fitting for a fool to live in luxury—
how much worse for a slave to rule over
princes!

[a] 7 The meaning of the Hebrew for this sentence is uncertain.

11 A man's wisdom gives him patience;
it is to his glory to overlook an offense.

12 A king's rage is like the roar of a lion,
but his favor is like dew on the grass.

13 A foolish son is his father's ruin,
and a quarrelsome wife is like a constant dripping.

14 Houses and wealth are inherited from parents,
but a prudent wife is from the LORD.

15 Laziness brings on deep sleep,
and the shiftless man goes hungry.

16 He who obeys instructions guards his life,
but he who is contemptuous of his ways will die.

17 He who is kind to the poor lends to the LORD,
and he will reward him for what he has done.

18 Discipline your son, for in that there is hope;
do not be a willing party to his death.

19 A hot-tempered man must pay the penalty;
if you rescue him, you will have to do it again.

20 Listen to advice and accept instruction,
and in the end you will be wise.

21 Many are the plans in a man's heart,
but it is the LORD's purpose that prevails.

22 What a man desires is unfailing love[a];
better to be poor than a liar.

23 The fear of the LORD leads to life:
Then one rests content, untouched by trouble.

24 The sluggard buries his hand in the dish;
he will not even bring it back to his mouth!

Proverbs 19:21

God Prevails in His Plans

Many are the plans in
a man's heart,
but it is the LORD's
purpose that prevails.

25 Flog a mocker, and the simple will learn prudence;
rebuke a discerning man, and he will gain knowledge.

26 He who robs his father and drives out his mother
is a son who brings shame and disgrace.

27 Stop listening to instruction, my son,
and you will stray from the words of knowledge.

28 A corrupt witness mocks at justice,
and the mouth of the wicked gulps down evil.

29 Penalties are prepared for mockers,
and beatings for the backs of fools.

20 Wine is a mocker and beer a brawler;
whoever is led astray by them is not wise.

2 A king's wrath is like the roar of a lion;
he who angers him forfeits his life.

3 It is to a man's honor to avoid strife,
but every fool is quick to quarrel.

4 A sluggard does not plow in season;
so at harvest time he looks but finds nothing.

5 The purposes of a man's heart are deep waters,
but a man of understanding draws them out.

6 Many a man claims to have unfailing love,
but a faithful man who can find?

7 The righteous man leads a blameless life;
blessed are his children after him.

8 When a king sits on his throne to judge,
he winnows out all evil with his eyes.

[a]22 Or *A man's greed is his shame*

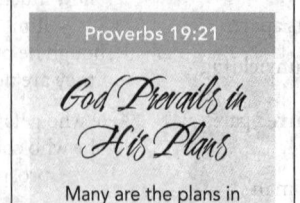

Paybacks

Read: Proverbs 20:1–22

REVENGE ISN'T SWEET; instead, it makes us sour. Studies have shown an association between negative emotions such as anger and revenge with a variety of destructive physical symptoms, including headaches, backaches, allergic disorders, ulcers, nausea, high blood pressure and heart attacks. Sadly, while vengeful people plot another's demise, they themselves often develop a painful health problem. Paybacks have a way of paying us back.

Revenge is an outward manifestation of an underlying problem: anger. Anger left unchecked will deepen into bitter roots of resentment or jealousy. And when these unbiblical attitudes are full-grown, the desire for revenge springs up. Revenge opposes the Golden Rule: "Do to others what you would have them do to you" (Matthew 7:12). Instead of taking things into our own hands, this proverb encourages us to let go and let God deal with our enemies. Because God is just, those who are wicked will eventually get their "just desserts."

Louis XII of France is said to have treated his enemies in an unexpected manner after ascending to the throne. Before coming to power, he had been cast into prison and kept in chains. Later when he did become king, he was urged to seek revenge on those who had opposed him, but he refused. Instead, he prepared a scroll on which he listed all who had perpetrated crimes against him. Behind every man's name he placed a cross in red ink. When the guilty heard about this, they feared for their lives and fled. Then the king explained, "The cross which I drew beside each name was not a sign of punishment, but a pledge of forgiveness extended for the sake of the crucified Savior, who upon His cross forgave His enemies and prayed for them."

Getting revenge may get us even with our enemies, but forgiveness places us above them. In fact, we are never more like God than when we turn the other cheek. In the Lord's Prayer, the only petition that is conditional is forgiveness: "Forgive us our debts, as we also have forgiven our debtors" (Matthew 6:12). Why can we forego revenge and offer forgiveness? Because we have been forgiven by God. To issue payback is human, but to pardon is divine.

Go to page 784 for your next devotional reading.

Proverbs 20:22

Do not say, "I'll pay you back for this wrong!" Wait for the LORD, and he will deliver you.

reflection

1 Have you been contemplating a payback? Are you experiencing any painful physical, emotional or spiritual consequences?

2 What are some of the things God has forgiven you for?

3 How does reviewing how you've been forgiven help you let go of revenge and let God handle the paybacks?

RELATED READINGS

Matthew 6:12–15;
Luke 6:27–36;
Romans 12:14–21

"Forgiveness is the key that unlocks the door of resentment and the handcuffs of hate. It is a power that breaks the chains of bitterness and the shackles of selfishness."

Corrie ten Boom

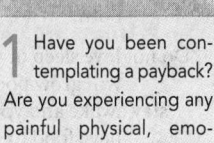

9 Who can say, "I have kept my heart pure;
I am clean and without sin"?

10 Differing weights and differing
measures—
the LORD detests them both.

11 Even a child is known by
his actions,
by whether his conduct is
pure and right.

12 Ears that hear and eyes that
see—
the LORD has made them
both.

13 Do not love sleep or you
will grow poor;
stay awake and you will
have food to spare.

14 "It's no good, it's no good!" says the buyer;
then off he goes and boasts about his
purchase.

15 Gold there is, and rubies in abundance,
but lips that speak knowledge are a rare
jewel.

16 Take the garment of one who puts up
security for a stranger;
hold it in pledge if he does it for a
wayward woman.

17 Food gained by fraud tastes sweet to a
man,
but he ends up with a mouth full of
gravel.

18 Make plans by seeking advice;
if you wage war, obtain guidance.

19 A gossip betrays a confidence;
so avoid a man who talks too much.

20 If a man curses his father or mother,
his lamp will be snuffed out in pitch
darkness.

21 An inheritance quickly gained at the
beginning
will not be blessed at the end.

22 Do not say, "I'll pay you back for this
wrong!"
Wait for the LORD, and he will deliver
you.

23 The LORD detests differing weights,
and dishonest scales do not please him.

24 A man's steps are directed
by the LORD.
How then can anyone
understand his own
way?

25 It is a trap for a man to
dedicate something
rashly
and only later to consider
his vows.

26 A wise king winnows out
the wicked;
he drives the threshing
wheel over them.

27 The lamp of the LORD searches the spirit of
a man[a];
it searches out his inmost being.

28 Love and faithfulness keep a king safe;
through love his throne is made
secure.

29 The glory of young men is their
strength,
gray hair the splendor of the old.

30 Blows and wounds cleanse away evil,
and beatings purge the inmost
being.

21 The king's heart is in the hand of the
LORD;
he directs it like a watercourse wherever
he pleases.

2 All a man's ways seem right to him,
but the LORD weighs the heart.

3 To do what is right and just
is more acceptable to the LORD than
sacrifice.

4 Haughty eyes and a proud heart,
the lamp of the wicked, are sin!

5 The plans of the diligent lead to profit
as surely as haste leads to poverty.

Proverbs 20:24

God Directs Steps

A man's steps are
directed by the LORD.
How then can anyone
understand his own way?

[a]27 Or *The spirit of man is the LORD's lamp*

6 A fortune made by a lying tongue
is a fleeting vapor and a deadly snare.[a]

7 The violence of the wicked will drag them away,
for they refuse to do what is right.

8 The way of the guilty is devious,
but the conduct of the innocent is upright.

9 Better to live on a corner of the roof
than share a house with a quarrelsome wife.

10 The wicked man craves evil;
his neighbor gets no mercy from him.

11 When a mocker is punished, the simple gain wisdom;
when a wise man is instructed, he gets knowledge.

12 The Righteous One[b] takes note of the house of the wicked
and brings the wicked to ruin.

13 If a man shuts his ears to the cry of the poor,
he too will cry out and not be answered.

14 A gift given in secret soothes anger,
and a bribe concealed in the cloak pacifies great wrath.

15 When justice is done, it brings joy to the righteous
but terror to evildoers.

16 A man who strays from the path of understanding
comes to rest in the company of the dead.

17 He who loves pleasure will become poor;
whoever loves wine and oil will never be rich.

18 The wicked become a ransom for the righteous,
and the unfaithful for the upright.

19 Better to live in a desert
than with a quarrelsome and ill-tempered wife.

20 In the house of the wise are stores of choice food and oil,
but a foolish man devours all he has.

21 He who pursues righteousness and love
finds life, prosperity[c] and honor.

22 A wise man attacks the city of the mighty
and pulls down the stronghold in which they trust.

23 He who guards his mouth and his tongue
keeps himself from calamity.

24 The proud and arrogant man—"Mocker" is his name;
he behaves with overweening pride.

25 The sluggard's craving will be the death of him,
because his hands refuse to work.

26 All day long he craves for more,
but the righteous give without sparing.

27 The sacrifice of the wicked is detestable—
how much more so when brought with evil intent!

28 A false witness will perish,
and whoever listens to him will be destroyed forever.[d]

29 A wicked man puts up a bold front,
but an upright man gives thought to his ways.

30 There is no wisdom, no insight, no plan
that can succeed against the LORD.

31 The horse is made ready for the day of battle,
but victory rests with the LORD.

22 A good name is more desirable than great riches;
to be esteemed is better than silver or gold.

2 Rich and poor have this in common:
The LORD is the Maker of them all.

3 A prudent man sees danger and takes refuge,
but the simple keep going and suffer for it.

[a]6 Some Hebrew manuscripts, Septuagint and Vulgate; most Hebrew manuscripts *vapor for those who seek death* [b]12 Or *The righteous man* [c]21 Or *righteousness* [d]28 Or / *but the words of an obedient man will live on*

Investments of the Heart

Proverbs 22:4

Humility and the fear of the LORD bring wealth and honor and life.

reflection

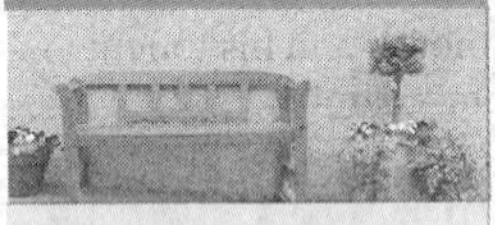

1 How do you define wealth? How does God?

2 What, in your own life, does it look like to "fear God"?

3 How do you invest the riches you've been given by God (your money, time, talents, etc.)?

RELATED READINGS

Psalm 37:1–6; Proverbs 3:1–10; Mark 12:43–44; 1 Timothy 6:17–19

Read: Proverbs 22:1–11

IF DR. SEUSS HAD ENDED UP on Wall Street instead of Mulberry Street, perhaps his book titles may have sounded something like this: Great Day for the Dow! Horton Hears a Hedge and a High Index; Green Backs and Pork. The growth of investment companies and of commercialism demonstrates the continuing deification of the almighty dollar.

We all know that money can't buy love, happiness or redemption. So why does the book of Proverbs imply that wealth, honor and life will come to those who are humble and fear the Lord? There are Christians who are not wealthy by any stretch of the imagination, just as there are wealthy Christians who don't seem humble. Just what is the principle behind this proverb?

First, God's definition of "wealth" isn't the same as the world's definition. King Solomon's riches were legendary; his yearly income amounted to 25 tons of gold, not counting outside revenues from merchants and traders (see 1 Kings 10:14–15). In terms of finance, King Solomon was clearly qualified to write about wealth and prosperity. But the king soon discovered that God's inheritance isn't about quarterly dividends, accelerated land accumulation or a vast collection of chariots and horses. Rather, it is about the heart. In God's eyes, spiritual riches are acquired by being rich toward him—by exhibiting a humble reverence for his awesome holiness. Spiritual wealth is laced with integrity, bejeweled by honor and polished for eternity. Spiritual riches will pay dividends in prudence, humility, honor, discipline, generosity, purity and graciousness.

This proverb is not a guide for earning wealth but a general principle for living wisely. Although this is not a guarantee that God will make us rich, spiritual riches can help reap financial stability (see Proverbs 21:20). Prudence will teach us to save for a rainy day rather than spend heedlessly. Disciplined giving can benefit us financially as well as spiritually. God delights in giving to the giver. Jesus said, "Give, and it will be given to you. A good measure, pressed down, shaken together and running over, will be poured into your lap" (Luke 6:38). But more important than financial wealth is the richness of living a godly life. We may not live on Wall Street, but we can make investments every day that will yield the benefits of humility, the fear of the Lord, honor and eternal life.

Go to page 788 for your next devotional reading.

4 Humility and the fear of the LORD
bring wealth and honor and life.

5 In the paths of the wicked lie thorns and snares,
but he who guards his soul stays far from them.

6 Train[a] a child in the way he should go,
and when he is old he will not turn from it.

7 The rich rule over the poor,
and the borrower is servant to the lender.

8 He who sows wickedness reaps trouble,
and the rod of his fury will be destroyed.

9 A generous man will himself be blessed,
for he shares his food with the poor.

10 Drive out the mocker, and out goes strife;
quarrels and insults are ended.

11 He who loves a pure heart and whose speech is gracious
will have the king for his friend.

12 The eyes of the LORD keep watch over knowledge,
but he frustrates the words of the unfaithful.

13 The sluggard says, "There is a lion outside!"
or, "I will be murdered in the streets!"

14 The mouth of an adulteress is a deep pit;
he who is under the LORD's wrath will fall into it.

15 Folly is bound up in the heart of a child,
but the rod of discipline will drive it far from him.

16 He who oppresses the poor to increase his wealth
and he who gives gifts to the rich—both come to poverty.

Sayings of the Wise

17 Pay attention and listen to the sayings of the wise;
apply your heart to what I teach,
18 for it is pleasing when you keep them in your heart
and have all of them ready on your lips.
19 So that your trust may be in the LORD,
I teach you today, even you.
20 Have I not written thirty[b] sayings for you,
sayings of counsel and knowledge,
21 teaching you true and reliable words,
so that you can give sound answers
to him who sent you?

22 Do not exploit the poor because they are poor
and do not crush the needy in court,
23 for the LORD will take up their case
and will plunder those who plunder them.

24 Do not make friends with a hot-tempered man,
do not associate with one easily angered,
25 or you may learn his ways
and get yourself ensnared.

26 Do not be a man who strikes hands in pledge
or puts up security for debts;
27 if you lack the means to pay,
your very bed will be snatched from under you.

28 Do not move an ancient boundary stone
set up by your forefathers.

29 Do you see a man skilled in his work?
He will serve before kings;
he will not serve before obscure men.

23 When you sit to dine with a ruler,
note well what[c] is before you,
2 and put a knife to your throat
if you are given to gluttony.
3 Do not crave his delicacies,
for that food is deceptive.

4 Do not wear yourself out to get rich;
have the wisdom to show restraint.
5 Cast but a glance at riches, and they are gone,
for they will surely sprout wings
and fly off to the sky like an eagle.

6 Do not eat the food of a stingy man,
do not crave his delicacies;
7 for he is the kind of man

a6 Or *Start* b20 Or *not formerly written*; or *not written excellent* c1 Or *who*

who is always thinking about the cost.[a]
"Eat and drink," he says to you,
but his heart is not with you.
8 You will vomit up the little you have eaten
and will have wasted your compliments.

9 Do not speak to a fool,
for he will scorn the wisdom of your words.

10 Do not move an ancient boundary stone
or encroach on the fields of the fatherless,
11 for their Defender is strong;
he will take up their case against you.

12 Apply your heart to instruction
and your ears to words of knowledge.

13 Do not withhold discipline from a child;
if you punish him with the rod, he will not die.
14 Punish him with the rod
and save his soul from death.[b]

15 My son, if your heart is wise,
then my heart will be glad;
16 my inmost being will rejoice
when your lips speak what is right.

17 Do not let your heart envy sinners,
but always be zealous for the fear of the LORD.
18 There is surely a future hope for you,
and your hope will not be cut off.

19 Listen, my son, and be wise,
and keep your heart on the right path.
20 Do not join those who drink too much wine
or gorge themselves on meat,
21 for drunkards and gluttons become poor,
and drowsiness clothes them in rags.

22 Listen to your father, who gave you life,
and do not despise your mother when she is old.
23 Buy the truth and do not sell it;
get wisdom, discipline and understanding.
24 The father of a righteous man has great joy;
he who has a wise son delights in him.
25 May your father and mother be glad;
may she who gave you birth rejoice!

26 My son, give me your heart
and let your eyes keep to my ways,
27 for a prostitute is a deep pit
and a wayward wife is a narrow well.
28 Like a bandit she lies in wait,
and multiplies the unfaithful among men.

29 Who has woe? Who has sorrow?
Who has strife? Who has complaints?
Who has needless bruises? Who has bloodshot eyes?
30 Those who linger over wine,
who go to sample bowls of mixed wine.
31 Do not gaze at wine when it is red,
when it sparkles in the cup,
when it goes down smoothly!
32 In the end it bites like a snake
and poisons like a viper.
33 Your eyes will see strange sights
and your mind imagine confusing things.
34 You will be like one sleeping on the high seas,
lying on top of the rigging.
35 "They hit me," you will say, "but I'm not hurt!
They beat me, but I don't feel it!
When will I wake up
so I can find another drink?"

24 Do not envy wicked men,
do not desire their company;
2 for their hearts plot violence,
and their lips talk about making trouble.

3 By wisdom a house is built,
and through understanding it is established;
4 through knowledge its rooms are filled
with rare and beautiful treasures.

5 A wise man has great power,
and a man of knowledge increases strength;
6 for waging war you need guidance,
and for victory many advisers.

[a]7 Or *for as he thinks within himself, / so he is*; or *for as he puts on a feast, / so he is* [b]14 Hebrew *Sheol*

7 Wisdom is too high for a fool;
in the assembly at the gate he has
nothing to say.

8 He who plots evil
will be known as a schemer.
9 The schemes of folly are sin,
and men detest a mocker.

10 If you falter in times of trouble,
how small is your strength!

11 Rescue those being led away to death;
hold back those staggering toward
slaughter.
12 If you say, "But we knew nothing about this,"
does not he who weighs the heart
perceive it?
Does not he who guards your life know it?
Will he not repay each person according
to what he has done?

13 Eat honey, my son, for it is good;
honey from the comb is sweet to your
taste.
14 Know also that wisdom is sweet to your
soul;
if you find it, there is a future hope for
you,
and your hope will not be cut off.

15 Do not lie in wait like an outlaw against a
righteous man's house,
do not raid his dwelling place;
16 for though a righteous man falls seven
times, he rises again,
but the wicked are brought down by
calamity.

17 Do not gloat when your enemy falls;
when he stumbles, do not let your heart
rejoice,
18 or the LORD will see and disapprove
and turn his wrath away from him.

19 Do not fret because of evil men
or be envious of the wicked,
20 for the evil man has no future hope,
and the lamp of the wicked will be
snuffed out.

21 Fear the LORD and the king, my son,
and do not join with the rebellious,
22 for those two will send sudden destruction
upon them,
and who knows what calamities they
can bring?

Further Sayings of the Wise

23 These also are sayings of the wise:

To show partiality in judging is not good:
24 Whoever says to the guilty, "You are
innocent"—
peoples will curse him and nations
denounce him.
25 But it will go well with those who convict
the guilty,
and rich blessing will come upon them.

26 An honest answer
is like a kiss on the lips.

27 Finish your outdoor work
and get your fields ready;
after that, build your house.

28 Do not testify against your neighbor
without cause,
or use your lips to deceive.
29 Do not say, "I'll do to him as he has done to
me;
I'll pay that man back for what he did."

30 I went past the field of the sluggard,
past the vineyard of the man who lacks
judgment;
31 thorns had come up everywhere,
the ground was covered with weeds,
and the stone wall was in ruins.
32 I applied my heart to what I observed
and learned a lesson from what I saw:
33 A little sleep, a little slumber,
a little folding of the hands to rest—
34 and poverty will come on you like a bandit
and scarcity like an armed man.[a]

More Proverbs of Solomon

25 These are more proverbs of Solomon, copied by the men of Hezekiah king of Judah:

2 It is the glory of God to conceal a matter;
to search out a matter is the glory of
kings.

[a]34 Or *like a vagrant / and scarcity like a beggar*

Apples of Gold

Read: Proverbs 25:1–15

Proverbs 25:11
A word aptly spoken
is like apples of gold
in settings of silver.

IN THE 1950s, Mary grew up knowing she was different from other kids . . . and she hated it. Because she had a cleft palate, she had learned to steel herself against the jokes and stares of children who teased her about her misshapen lip, crooked nose and garbled speech. Mary was convinced that no one outside her family could ever love her . . . until she entered Mrs. Leonard's class. Mrs. Leonard had a warm smile, a round face and beautiful brown hair. All of the children liked Mrs. Leonard, but Mary grew to love her.

In those days, teachers administered a hearing test in the classroom. Unfortunately, Mary not only had a speech impediment due to her cleft palate, she was also partially deaf in one ear. Determined not to let the children have something else to tease her about, she thought of a way to cheat on the hearing test: She could pass the "whisper test" by covering her bad ear and turning her good ear toward her teacher. On the day of the dreaded hearing test, surely God put seven words in Mrs. Leonard's mouth that changed Mary's life forever. When it was time for Mary's "whisper test," she clearly heard the words: "I wish you were my little girl."

Solomon called these kinds of words "apples of gold in settings of silver." They are words that can erase years of pain and sorrow. They are words filled with love and acceptance. They are words that are priceless to those who hear them.

If someone listened in on your conversations, would their lives be changed for better or worse? Would they hear you speaking about the character flaws of others as if they were physical defects or would they hear that you consider others as beautiful in God's eyes? Ask yourself if your words build up or tear down. Do your words push others away from you or draw others near? Most important, do they draw others to God?

It's never too late to dispense apples of gold in settings of silver. Seek someone who is downcast and whisper a word of encouragement. You never know who needs to hear the words, "I wish you were my friend."

reflection

1 How have you been affected negatively by hurtful words? In what ways are you guilty of hurting others with your words?

2 Can you think of a time when you have been on the receiving end of positive and encouraging words? How did they affect you?

3 Ask God to show you someone to whisper words of encouragement to today.

RELATED READINGS

Proverbs 12:25; Colossians 3:12–14; 1 Timothy 4:12; 1 Peter 3:9–12

"If I can enjoy a joke at the expense of another; if I can in any way slight another in conversation, or even in thought, then I know nothing of Calvary's love."

Amy Carmichael

Wednesday

Go to page 795 for your next devotional reading.

3 As the heavens are high and the earth is deep,
so the hearts of kings are unsearchable.

4 Remove the dross from the silver,
and out comes material for[a] the silversmith;
5 remove the wicked from the king's presence,
and his throne will be established through righteousness.

6 Do not exalt yourself in the king's presence,
and do not claim a place among great men;
7 it is better for him to say to you, "Come up here,"
than for him to humiliate you before a nobleman.

What you have seen with your eyes
8 do not bring[b] hastily to court,
for what will you do in the end
if your neighbor puts you to shame?

9 If you argue your case with a neighbor,
do not betray another man's confidence,
10 or he who hears it may shame you
and you will never lose your bad reputation.

11 A word aptly spoken
is like apples of gold in settings of silver.

12 Like an earring of gold or an ornament of fine gold
is a wise man's rebuke to a listening ear.

13 Like the coolness of snow at harvest time
is a trustworthy messenger to those who send him;
he refreshes the spirit of his masters.

14 Like clouds and wind without rain
is a man who boasts of gifts he does not give.

15 Through patience a ruler can be persuaded,
and a gentle tongue can break a bone.

16 If you find honey, eat just enough—
too much of it, and you will vomit.

17 Seldom set foot in your neighbor's house—
too much of you, and he will hate you.

18 Like a club or a sword or a sharp arrow
is the man who gives false testimony against his neighbor.

19 Like a bad tooth or a lame foot
is reliance on the unfaithful in times of trouble.

20 Like one who takes away a garment on a cold day,
or like vinegar poured on soda,
is one who sings songs to a heavy heart.

21 If your enemy is hungry, give him food to eat;
if he is thirsty, give him water to drink.
22 In doing this, you will heap burning coals on his head,
and the LORD will reward you.

23 As a north wind brings rain,
so a sly tongue brings angry looks.

24 Better to live on a corner of the roof
than share a house with a quarrelsome wife.

25 Like cold water to a weary soul
is good news from a distant land.

26 Like a muddied spring or a polluted well
is a righteous man who gives way to the wicked.

27 It is not good to eat too much honey,
nor is it honorable to seek one's own honor.

28 Like a city whose walls are broken down
is a man who lacks self-control.

26 Like snow in summer or rain in harvest,
honor is not fitting for a fool.

2 Like a fluttering sparrow or a darting swallow,
an undeserved curse does not come to rest.

[a]4 Or *comes a vessel from* [b]7,8 Or *nobleman / on whom you had set your eyes. /* [8]*Do not go*

3 A whip for the horse, a halter for the donkey,
and a rod for the backs of fools!

4 Do not answer a fool according to his folly,
or you will be like him yourself.

5 Answer a fool according to his folly,
or he will be wise in his own eyes.

6 Like cutting off one's feet or drinking violence
is the sending of a message by the hand of a fool.

7 Like a lame man's legs that hang limp
is a proverb in the mouth of a fool.

8 Like tying a stone in a sling
is the giving of honor to a fool.

9 Like a thornbush in a drunkard's hand
is a proverb in the mouth of a fool.

10 Like an archer who wounds at random
is he who hires a fool or any passer-by.

11 As a dog returns to its vomit,
so a fool repeats his folly.

12 Do you see a man wise in his own eyes?
There is more hope for a fool than for him.

13 The sluggard says, "There is a lion in the road,
a fierce lion roaming the streets!"

14 As a door turns on its hinges,
so a sluggard turns on his bed.

15 The sluggard buries his hand in the dish;
he is too lazy to bring it back to his mouth.

16 The sluggard is wiser in his own eyes
than seven men who answer discreetly.

17 Like one who seizes a dog by the ears
is a passer-by who meddles in a quarrel not his own.

18 Like a madman shooting
firebrands or deadly arrows
19 is a man who deceives his neighbor
and says, "I was only joking!"

20 Without wood a fire goes out;
without gossip a quarrel dies down.

21 As charcoal to embers and as wood to fire,
so is a quarrelsome man for kindling strife.

22 The words of a gossip are like choice morsels;
they go down to a man's inmost parts.

23 Like a coating of glaze[a] over earthenware
are fervent lips with an evil heart.

24 A malicious man disguises himself with his lips,
but in his heart he harbors deceit.

25 Though his speech is charming, do not believe him,
for seven abominations fill his heart.

26 His malice may be concealed by deception,
but his wickedness will be exposed in the assembly.

27 If a man digs a pit, he will fall into it;
if a man rolls a stone, it will roll back on him.

28 A lying tongue hates those it hurts,
and a flattering mouth works ruin.

27 Do not boast about tomorrow,
for you do not know what a day may bring forth.

2 Let another praise you,
and not your own mouth;
someone else, and not your own lips.

3 Stone is heavy and sand a burden,
but provocation by a fool is heavier than both.

Proverbs 27:2

God Commends Humility

Let another praise you,
and not your own mouth;
someone else, and
not your own lips.

[a]23 With a different word division of the Hebrew; Masoretic Text *of silver dross*

4 Anger is cruel and fury overwhelming,
but who can stand before jealousy?

5 Better is open rebuke
than hidden love.

6 Wounds from a friend can be trusted,
but an enemy multiplies kisses.

7 He who is full loathes honey,
but to the hungry even what is bitter
tastes sweet.

8 Like a bird that strays from its nest
is a man who strays from his home.

9 Perfume and incense bring joy to the heart,
and the pleasantness of one's friend
springs from his earnest counsel.

10 Do not forsake your friend and the friend
of your father,
and do not go to your brother's house
when disaster strikes you—
better a neighbor nearby than a brother
far away.

11 Be wise, my son, and bring joy to my heart;
then I can answer anyone who treats me
with contempt.

12 The prudent see danger and take refuge,
but the simple keep going and suffer
for it.

13 Take the garment of one who puts up
security for a stranger;
hold it in pledge if he does it for a
wayward woman.

14 If a man loudly blesses his neighbor early
in the morning,
it will be taken as a curse.

15 A quarrelsome wife is like
a constant dripping on a rainy day;
16 restraining her is like restraining the wind
or grasping oil with the hand.

17 As iron sharpens iron,
so one man sharpens another.

18 He who tends a fig tree will eat its fruit,
and he who looks after his master will be
honored.

19 As water reflects a face,
so a man's heart reflects the man.

20 Death and Destruction[a] are never satisfied,
and neither are the eyes of man.

21 The crucible for silver and the furnace for
gold,
but man is tested by the praise he
receives.

22 Though you grind a fool in a mortar,
grinding him like grain with a pestle,
you will not remove his folly from him.

23 Be sure you know the condition of your
flocks,
give careful attention to your herds;
24 for riches do not endure forever,
and a crown is not secure for all
generations.
25 When the hay is removed and new growth
appears
and the grass from the hills is gathered
in,
26 the lambs will provide you with clothing,
and the goats with the price of a field.
27 You will have plenty of goats' milk
to feed you and your family
and to nourish your servant girls.

28 The wicked man flees though no one
pursues,
but the righteous are as bold as a lion.

2 When a country is rebellious, it has many
rulers,
but a man of understanding and
knowledge maintains order.

3 A ruler[b] who oppresses the poor
is like a driving rain that leaves no crops.

4 Those who forsake the law praise the
wicked,
but those who keep the law resist them.

5 Evil men do not understand justice,
but those who seek the LORD
understand it fully.

6 Better a poor man whose walk is blameless
than a rich man whose ways are
perverse.

[a] 20 Hebrew *Sheol and Abaddon* [b] 3 Or *A poor man*

7 He who keeps the law is a discerning son,
but a companion of gluttons disgraces his father.

8 He who increases his wealth by exorbitant interest
amasses it for another, who will be kind to the poor.

9 If anyone turns a deaf ear to the law,
even his prayers are detestable.

10 He who leads the upright along an evil path
will fall into his own trap,
but the blameless will receive a good inheritance.

11 A rich man may be wise in his own eyes,
but a poor man who has discernment sees through him.

12 When the righteous triumph, there is great elation;
but when the wicked rise to power, men go into hiding.

13 He who conceals his sins does not prosper,
but whoever confesses and renounces them finds mercy.

14 Blessed is the man who always fears the LORD,
but he who hardens his heart falls into trouble.

15 Like a roaring lion or a charging bear
is a wicked man ruling over a helpless people.

16 A tyrannical ruler lacks judgment,
but he who hates ill-gotten gain will enjoy a long life.

17 A man tormented by the guilt of murder
will be a fugitive till death;
let no one support him.

18 He whose walk is blameless is kept safe,
but he whose ways are perverse will suddenly fall.

19 He who works his land will have abundant food,
but the one who chases fantasies will have his fill of poverty.

20 A faithful man will be richly blessed,
but one eager to get rich will not go unpunished.

21 To show partiality is not good—
yet a man will do wrong for a piece of bread.

22 A stingy man is eager to get rich
and is unaware that poverty awaits him.

23 He who rebukes a man will in the end gain more favor
than he who has a flattering tongue.

24 He who robs his father or mother
and says, "It's not wrong"—
he is partner to him who destroys.

25 A greedy man stirs up dissension,
but he who trusts in the LORD will prosper.

26 He who trusts in himself is a fool,
but he who walks in wisdom is kept safe.

27 He who gives to the poor will lack nothing,
but he who closes his eyes to them receives many curses.

28 When the wicked rise to power, people go into hiding;
but when the wicked perish, the righteous thrive.

29 A man who remains stiff-necked after many rebukes
will suddenly be destroyed—without remedy.

2 When the righteous thrive, the people rejoice;
when the wicked rule, the people groan.

3 A man who loves wisdom brings joy to his father,
but a companion of prostitutes squanders his wealth.

4 By justice a king gives a country stability,
but one who is greedy for bribes tears it down.

5 Whoever flatters his neighbor
is spreading a net for his feet.

6 An evil man is snared by his own sin,
but a righteous one can sing and be glad.

7 The righteous care about justice for the poor,
but the wicked have no such concern.

8 Mockers stir up a city,
but wise men turn away anger.

9 If a wise man goes to court with a fool,
the fool rages and scoffs, and there is no peace.

10 Bloodthirsty men hate a man of integrity
and seek to kill the upright.

11 A fool gives full vent to his anger,
but a wise man keeps himself under control.

12 If a ruler listens to lies,
all his officials become wicked.

13 The poor man and the oppressor have this in common:
The LORD gives sight to the eyes of both.

14 If a king judges the poor with fairness,
his throne will always be secure.

15 The rod of correction imparts wisdom,
but a child left to himself disgraces his mother.

16 When the wicked thrive, so does sin,
but the righteous will see their downfall.

17 Discipline your son, and he will give you peace;
he will bring delight to your soul.

18 Where there is no revelation, the people cast off restraint;
but blessed is he who keeps the law.

19 A servant cannot be corrected by mere words;
though he understands, he will not respond.

20 Do you see a man who speaks in haste?
There is more hope for a fool than for him.

21 If a man pampers his servant from youth,
he will bring grief[a] in the end.

22 An angry man stirs up dissension,
and a hot-tempered one commits many sins.

23 A man's pride brings him low,
but a man of lowly spirit gains honor.

24 The accomplice of a thief is his own enemy;
he is put under oath and dare not testify.

25 Fear of man will prove to be a snare,
but whoever trusts in the LORD is kept safe.

26 Many seek an audience with a ruler,
but it is from the LORD that man gets justice.

27 The righteous detest the dishonest;
the wicked detest the upright.

Proverbs 29:18

God Blesses His Followers

Where there is no revelation, the people cast off restraint; but blessed is he who keeps the law.

Sayings of Agur

30 The sayings of Agur son of Jakeh—an oracle[b]:

This man declared to Ithiel,
to Ithiel and to Ucal:[c]

2 "I am the most ignorant of men;
I do not have a man's understanding.
3 I have not learned wisdom,
nor have I knowledge of the Holy One.
4 Who has gone up to heaven and come down?
Who has gathered up the wind in the hollow of his hands?
Who has wrapped up the waters in his cloak?
Who has established all the ends of the earth?

[a]21 The meaning of the Hebrew for this word is uncertain. [b]1 Or *Jakeh of Massa* [c]1 Masoretic Text; with a different word division of the Hebrew *declared, "I am weary, O God; / I am weary, O God, and faint.*

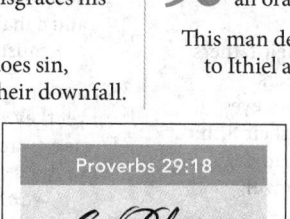

What is his name, and the name of his
son?
Tell me if you know!

5 "Every word of God is
flawless;
he is a shield to those
who take refuge in
him.
6 Do not add to his words,
or he will rebuke you and
prove you a liar.

7 "Two things I ask of you,
O LORD;
do not refuse me before
I die:
8 Keep falsehood and lies far
from me;
give me neither poverty nor riches,
but give me only my daily bread.
9 Otherwise, I may have too much and
disown you
and say, 'Who is the LORD?'
Or I may become poor and steal,
and so dishonor the name of my God.

10 "Do not slander a servant to his master,
or he will curse you, and you will pay
for it.

11 "There are those who curse their fathers
and do not bless their mothers;
12 those who are pure in their own eyes
and yet are not cleansed of their filth;
13 those whose eyes are ever so haughty,
whose glances are so disdainful;
14 those whose teeth are swords
and whose jaws are set with knives
to devour the poor from the earth,
the needy from among mankind.

15 "The leech has two daughters.
'Give! Give!' they cry.

"There are three things that are never
satisfied,
four that never say, 'Enough!':
16 the grave,[a] the barren womb,
land, which is never satisfied with water,
and fire, which never says, 'Enough!'

Proverbs 30:5

God Is Flawless

Every word of God
is flawless;
he is a shield to those
who take refuge in him.

17 "The eye that mocks a father,
that scorns obedience to a mother,
will be pecked out by the ravens of the
valley,
will be eaten by the
vultures.

18 "There are three things that
are too amazing for
me,
four that I do not
understand:
19 the way of an eagle in the
sky,
the way of a snake on a
rock,
the way of a ship on the
high seas,
and the way of a man
with a maiden.

20 "This is the way of an adulteress:
She eats and wipes her mouth
and says, 'I've done nothing wrong.'

21 "Under three things the earth trembles,
under four it cannot bear up:
22 a servant who becomes king,
a fool who is full of food,
23 an unloved woman who is married,
and a maidservant who displaces her
mistress.

24 "Four things on earth are small,
yet they are extremely wise:
25 Ants are creatures of little strength,
yet they store up their food in the
summer;
26 coneys[b] are creatures of little power,
yet they make their home in the
crags;
27 locusts have no king,
yet they advance together in ranks;
28 a lizard can be caught with the hand,
yet it is found in kings' palaces.

29 "There are three things that are stately in
their stride,
four that move with stately bearing:
30 a lion, mighty among beasts,
who retreats before nothing;

[a]16 Hebrew *Sheol* [b]26 That is, the hyrax or rock badger

You Gotta Laugh

Read: Proverbs 31:10–31

OH, THE UNIQUE CHALLENGES awaiting the woman approaching middle age! Imagine waking up one morning to find your face sort of lying in a pool beside you. Your once tight abs have been replaced with something rather squishy that has to be gathered up (starting somewhere around the knees) and tucked into industrial–strength, control-top pantyhose. Imagine suddenly realizing that your thighs almost create sparks when you walk. Your biceps are so deflated that in a strong breeze you worry that they might actually make a flapping sound. Maybe you don't have to imagine it. Maybe you're living it.

God might have knit these bodies together out of a more "permanent press" kind of fabric. He could have built in a kind of stretch that wouldn't lose its elasticity around middle age. But he didn't. And through our aging and all the challenges we live through, he teaches us what's really important.

The Proverbs 31 "virtuous woman" got in on that teaching. She could "laugh at the days to come" (verse 25). Her future held flabby abs and combustible thighs too. But she could laugh. Why?

The passage describes a woman who seems just about perfect. Many Bible teachers call her the "virtuous woman," and she makes Martha Stewart look like a novice. She keeps her husband happy; she works eagerly; she gets up early and stays up late. She gives to others generously, makes her own clothes, is an eloquent teacher, and her kids love her. A woman like this "who can find," indeed! She is a formidable pattern, an intimidating example.

But look past the outward layer. Look deeper. You'll see a woman of wisdom who fully understood what was really important. She understood what it meant to work hard and to serve God with her whole heart. She understood that everything of consequence was wrapped up in him. Serving others came as a natural extension of serving him.

There's only one metamorphosis that matters—and it will keep every woman eternally beautiful. It's a metamorphosis of the heart. The Scripture says, "Therefore, if anyone is in Christ, he is a new creation; the old has gone, the new has come!" (2 Corinthians 5:17). Having a heart of unselfish service that has been transformed by Christ—that's what's important. And that is what gives us the ability to laugh at the future . . . even if it involves flabby thighs.

Thursday

Go to page 799 for your next devotional reading.

Proverbs 31:25,30

She is clothed with strength and dignity; she can laugh at the days to come . . . Charm is deceptive, and beauty is fleeting; but a woman who fears the LORD is to be praised.

reflection

1 When your attention to appearance gets out of whack and your focus is more on looks than on eternal things, how might "fearing the Lord" turn your focus back to where it needs to be?

2 What are some of the ways the woman in Proverbs 31:10–31 served others?

3 How many different types of people did her daily life and ministry touch? How might you underestimate the many lives you touch each day?

RELATED READINGS

Psalm 139:1–24;
Romans 12:1–12;
Galatians 6:9–10;
1 Peter 3:1–6

31 a strutting rooster, a he-goat,
and a king with his army around him.[a]

32 "If you have played the fool and exalted yourself,
or if you have planned evil,
clap your hand over your mouth!
33 For as churning the milk produces butter,
and as twisting the nose produces blood,
so stirring up anger produces strife."

Sayings of King Lemuel

31 The sayings of King Lemuel—an oracle[b] his mother taught him:

2 "O my son, O son of my womb,
O son of my vows,[c]
3 do not spend your strength on women,
your vigor on those who ruin kings.

4 "It is not for kings, O Lemuel—
not for kings to drink wine,
not for rulers to crave beer,
5 lest they drink and forget what the law decrees,
and deprive all the oppressed of their rights.
6 Give beer to those who are perishing,
wine to those who are in anguish;
7 let them drink and forget their poverty
and remember their misery no more.

8 "Speak up for those who cannot speak for themselves,
for the rights of all who are destitute.
9 Speak up and judge fairly;
defend the rights of the poor and needy."

Epilogue: The Wife of Noble Character

10[d] A wife of noble character who can find?
She is worth far more than rubies.
11 Her husband has full confidence in her
and lacks nothing of value.
12 She brings him good, not harm,
all the days of her life.
13 She selects wool and flax
and works with eager hands.
14 She is like the merchant ships,
bringing her food from afar.
15 She gets up while it is still dark;
she provides food for her family
and portions for her servant girls.
16 She considers a field and buys it;
out of her earnings she plants a vineyard.
17 She sets about her work vigorously;
her arms are strong for her tasks.
18 She sees that her trading is profitable,
and her lamp does not go out at night.
19 In her hand she holds the distaff
and grasps the spindle with her fingers.
20 She opens her arms to the poor
and extends her hands to the needy.
21 When it snows, she has no fear for her household;
for all of them are clothed in scarlet.
22 She makes coverings for her bed;
she is clothed in fine linen and purple.
23 Her husband is respected at the city gate,
where he takes his seat among the elders of the land.
24 She makes linen garments and sells them,
and supplies the merchants with sashes.
25 She is clothed with strength and dignity;
she can laugh at the days to come.
26 She speaks with wisdom,
and faithful instruction is on her tongue.
27 She watches over the affairs of her household
and does not eat the bread of idleness.
28 Her children arise and call her blessed;
her husband also, and he praises her:
29 "Many women do noble things,
but you surpass them all."
30 Charm is deceptive, and beauty is fleeting;
but a woman who fears the LORD is to be praised.
31 Give her the reward she has earned,
and let her works bring her praise at the city gate.

[a]31 Or *king secure against revolt* [b]1 Or *of Lemuel king of Massa, which* [c]2 Or */ the answer to my prayers* [d]10 Verses 10–31 are an acrostic, each verse beginning with a successive letter of the Hebrew alphabet.

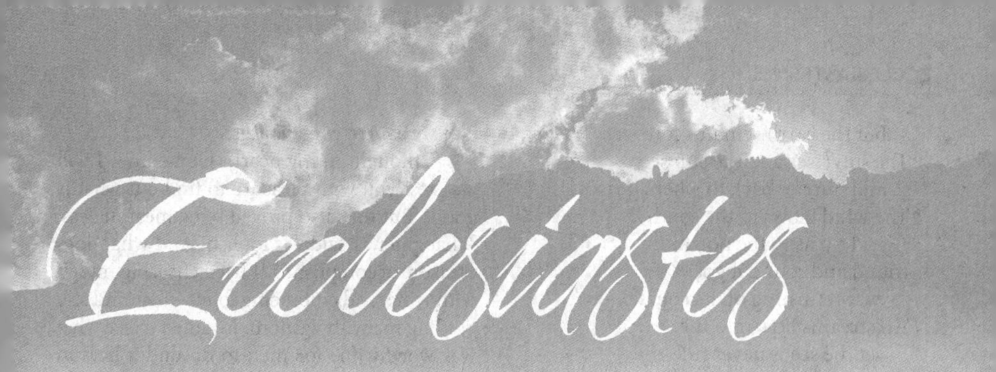

Ecclesiastes

The book of Ecclesiastes takes the reader along on the *adventurous quest for meaning in life.* It's a search we are all on to some degree or another as we live our lives each day. We want to spend our time and energy on what is meaningful and on what will last. But finding those things—*that's the challenge.*

As we follow the Teacher's trail, we find that he's already looked for meaning in most places we would try. Wisdom—a good place to start—he's already plumbed. Pleasures and work and money and getting ahead—he's been there. Even madness and folly—he's tried those too. He's lived long and seen much, and he's found little that has meaning. But the meaning *is* there. *There is treasure at the end of the quest,* and along the way are insights, truths and intriguing ways of looking at life from someone who has examined it from every angle.

Author:
The Teacher, who was probably King Solomon.

Audience:
All Israel.

Date:
Most likely near the end of Solomon's life, 930 B.C.

Setting:
In the twilight of his life, the wise Teacher reflects on human existence.

Verse to Remember:
Now all has been heard; here is the conclusion of the matter: Fear God and keep his commandments, for this is the whole duty of man. (12:13)

Everything Is Meaningless

1 The words of the Teacher,[a] son of David,
king in Jerusalem:

2 "Meaningless! Meaningless!"
says the Teacher.
"Utterly meaningless!
Everything is meaningless."

3 What does man gain from all his labor
at which he toils under the sun?
4 Generations come and generations go,

[a]1 Or *leader of the assembly;* also in verses 2 and 12

but the earth remains forever.
5 The sun rises and the sun sets,
and hurries back to where it rises.
6 The wind blows to the south
and turns to the north;
round and round it goes,
ever returning on its course.
7 All streams flow into the sea,
yet the sea is never full.
To the place the streams come from,
there they return again.
8 All things are wearisome,
more than one can say.
The eye never has enough of seeing,
nor the ear its fill of hearing.
9 What has been will be again,
what has been done will be done again;
there is nothing new under the sun.
10 Is there anything of which one can say,
"Look! This is something new"?
It was here already, long ago;
it was here before our time.
11 There is no remembrance of men of old,
and even those who are yet to come
will not be remembered
by those who follow.

Wisdom Is Meaningless

12 I, the Teacher, was king over Israel in Jerusalem. 13 I devoted myself to study and to explore by wisdom all that is done under heaven.
What a heavy burden God has laid on men! 14 I
have seen all the things that are done under the
sun; all of them are meaningless, a chasing after
the wind.

15 What is twisted cannot be straightened;
what is lacking cannot be counted.

16 I thought to myself, "Look, I have grown
and increased in wisdom more than anyone
who has ruled over Jerusalem before me; I have
experienced much of wisdom and knowledge."
17 Then I applied myself to the understanding
of wisdom, and also of madness and folly,
but I learned that this, too, is a chasing after
the wind.

18 For with much wisdom comes much
sorrow;
the more knowledge, the more grief.

Pleasures Are Meaningless

2 I thought in my heart, "Come now, I will
test you with pleasure to find out what is
good." But that also proved to be meaningless.
2 "Laughter," I said, "is foolish. And what does
pleasure accomplish?" 3 I tried cheering myself
with wine, and embracing folly—my mind still
guiding me with wisdom. I wanted to see what
was worthwhile for men to do under heaven
during the few days of their lives.

4 I undertook great projects: I built houses
for myself and planted vineyards. 5 I made gardens and parks and planted all kinds of fruit
trees in them. 6 I made reservoirs to water
groves of flourishing trees. 7 I bought male and
female slaves and had other slaves who were
born in my house. I also owned more herds
and flocks than anyone in Jerusalem before me.
8 I amassed silver and gold for myself, and the
treasure of kings and provinces. I acquired men
and women singers, and a harem[a] as well—the
delights of the heart of man. 9 I became greater
by far than anyone in Jerusalem before me. In
all this my wisdom stayed with me.

10 I denied myself nothing my eyes desired;
I refused my heart no pleasure.
My heart took delight in all my work,
and this was the reward for all my labor.
11 Yet when I surveyed all that my hands had
done
and what I had toiled to achieve,
everything was meaningless, a chasing
after the wind;
nothing was gained under the sun.

Wisdom and Folly Are Meaningless

12 Then I turned my thoughts to consider
wisdom,
and also madness and folly.
What more can the king's successor do
than what has already been done?
13 I saw that wisdom is better than folly,
just as light is better than darkness.
14 The wise man has eyes in his head,
while the fool walks in the darkness;
but I came to realize
that the same fate overtakes them both.

15 Then I thought in my heart,

[a] 8 The meaning of the Hebrew for this phrase is uncertain.

Wind Catchers

Read: Ecclesiastes 2:1–11

HAVE YOU EVER TRIED to catch the wind? Perhaps you once launched a kite on a passing breeze or trimmed your sails to harness the swirling air currents to propel your sailboat forward. But did you honestly catch the wind—or did it catch you? Wind is elusive. It is intangible. Chimes or catchers hanging on your back porch may detect its presence or point out its direction, but they'll never contain it.

Solomon discovered that finding pleasure is as elusive as catching the wind. He pursued everything imaginable to achieve lasting bliss. But the smartest man alive still had a restless mind. The richest man in the world couldn't buy happiness. The most powerful person in the kingdom was unable to satisfy his own heart. And although he had 700 wives and 300 concubines, he never found true love. His conclusion? These pursuits were meaningless, completely unsatisfying.

Securing happiness on our own is like trying to catch the wind. We can try to chase it, but it will always remain just out of reach. The Bible teaches us that instead of searching for happiness, we should allow God's joy and peace to reign in our hearts. Instead of striving for the things we think will satisfy, we can learn to find true contentment by looking to God, whatever our circumstance.

The Bible often uses the word *blessed*, which means "oh, how happy." To God, blessed people are happy people and happy people are blessed. Solomon's father, King David, said blessed are those whose sins are forgiven (see Psalm 32:1), who trust in the Lord (see Psalm 40:4) and who draw near to God (see Psalm 65:4). The true source of pleasure is God. Don't waste your time trying to catch the wind; instead, find true happiness by laying hold of the Wind Maker.

Go to page 801 for your next devotional reading.

Ecclesiastes 2:11

Yet when I surveyed all that my hands had done and what I had toiled to achieve, everything was meaningless, a chasing after the wind; nothing was gained under the sun.

reflection

1 In what ways have you chased after something but found it meaningless?

2 What are some things "in your own backyard" that bring you joy?

3 When have you experienced a time of real contentment?

RELATED READINGS

Psalms 68:3; 84:1–12;
John 3:5–8;
1 Timothy 6:6–10

"Many persons have a wrong idea of what constitutes true happiness. It is not attained through self-gratification but through fidelity to a worthy purpose."

Helen Adams Keller

"The fate of the fool will overtake me
also.
What then do I gain by being wise?"
I said in my heart,
"This too is meaningless."
16 For the wise man, like the fool, will not be
long remembered;
in days to come both will be forgotten.
Like the fool, the wise man too must die!

Toil Is Meaningless

17 So I hated life, because the work that is
done under the sun was grievous to me. All of
it is meaningless, a chasing after the wind. 18 I
hated all the things I had toiled for under the
sun, because I must leave them to the one who
comes after me. 19 And who knows whether he
will be a wise man or a fool? Yet he will have
control over all the work into which I have
poured my effort and skill under the sun. This
too is meaningless. 20 So my heart began to despair over all my toilsome labor under the sun.
21 For a man may do his work with wisdom,
knowledge and skill, and then he must leave all
he owns to someone who has not worked for it.
This too is meaningless and a great misfortune.
22 What does a man get for all the toil and anxious striving with which he labors under the
sun? 23 All his days his work is pain and grief;
even at night his mind does not rest. This too
is meaningless.

24 A man can do nothing better than to eat and drink and
find satisfaction in his work.
This too, I see, is from the hand
of God, 25 for without him, who
can eat or find enjoyment? 26 To
the man who pleases him, God
gives wisdom, knowledge and
happiness, but to the sinner
he gives the task of gathering
and storing up wealth to hand
it over to the one who pleases
God. This too is meaningless, a
chasing after the wind.

Ecclesiastes 2:24

God Provides Satisfaction

A man can do nothing better than to eat and drink and find satisfaction in his work. This too, I see, is from the hand of God.

A Time for Everything

3 There is a time for everything,
and a season for every activity under
heaven:

2 a time to be born and a time to die,
a time to plant and a time to uproot,
3 a time to kill and a time to heal,
a time to tear down and a time to build,
4 a time to weep and a time to laugh,
a time to mourn and a time to dance,
5 a time to scatter stones and a time to
gather them,
a time to embrace and a time to refrain,
6 a time to search and a time to give up,
a time to keep and a time to throw away,
7 a time to tear and a time to mend,
a time to be silent and a time to speak,
8 a time to love and a time to hate,
a time for war and a time for peace.

9 What does the worker gain from his toil?
10 I have seen the burden God has laid on men.
11 He has made everything beautiful in its time.
He has also set eternity in the hearts of men;
yet they cannot fathom what God has done
from beginning to end. 12 I know that there is
nothing better for men than to be happy and
do good while they live. 13 That everyone may
eat and drink, and find satisfaction in all his
toil—this is the gift of God. 14 I know that everything God does will endure forever; nothing
can be added to it and nothing taken from it.
God does it so that men will revere him.

15 Whatever is has already
been,
and what will be has
been before;
and God will call the
past to account.[a]

16 And I saw something else
under the sun:
In the place of judgment—
wickedness was
there,
in the place of justice—
wickedness was
there.

17 I thought in my heart,

"God will bring to judgment
both the righteous and the wicked,
for there will be a time for every activity,
a time for every deed."

[a]15 Or *God calls back the past*

Power of Persuasion

JEZEBEL

"WHO'S GOING TO STOP ME?"

She didn't really expect anyone to respond. She already knew the answer. Sure, her husband was technically king. But all she had to do was make one comment, quip a phrase or even raise one of her pointed eyebrows, and she had his ear. Everyone in the palace, from the lowest servant to the highest official, knew who wore the royal pants in the family. She wasn't the most powerful woman in the land for nothing.

Keeping her husband in line was easy. In fact, with her persuasive talents, she wielded control over an entire kingdom to serve her religious ideals. She motivated some 850 pagan priests to do her bidding and ever-increase her influence. She came to be known as a woman who always got her way—and a woman dedicated to expanding the worship of Baal. Throughout her reign in the northern kingdom of Israel, she ensured that Baal worship flourished. She even convinced her husband to build a temple to Baal in Samaria, the capital.

However, her reign did not go unchallenged. "Those cursed God-fearing Israelites drive me mad," she would often say. Despite her many supporters, the opposition (no matter how small compared to her supporters) irritated her to no end. If someone questioned her, she had them arrested. If someone spoke against her, she silenced them. Permanently. Still, despite the numbers she persecuted, it seemed like more opponents cropped up every day. She heard rumors that there were those who had never worshiped Baal—and did not intend to.

Toward the end, she might have sensed her days were numbered and so became even more ravenously devoted to her cause, driven by a devilish force she may not have fully understood. And ironically, although she devoted herself to making an indelible impression on others for the sake of her cause, within moments of her death, not an earthly remnant of her remained.

—Prayer—

Jesus, give me strength to stand against evil. Give me wisdom to keep my heart pure.

There was never a man like Ahab, who sold himself to do evil in the eyes of the LORD, urged on by Jezebel his wife.

1 Kings 21:25

ASSIGNED READING:

1 Kings 16:29–33; 18:1—19:18; 21:1–29; 2 Kings 9:1–37

Weekend

Go to page 805 for your next devotional reading.

18 I also thought, "As for men, God tests
them so that they may see that they are like the
animals. 19 Man's fate is like that of the animals;
the same fate awaits them both: As one dies, so
dies the other. All have the same breath[a]; man
has no advantage over the animal. Everything
is meaningless. 20 All go to the same place; all
come from dust, and to dust all return. 21 Who
knows if the spirit of man rises upward and
if the spirit of the animal[b] goes down into
the earth?"

22 So I saw that there is nothing better for a
man than to enjoy his work, because that is his
lot. For who can bring him to see what will happen after him?

Oppression, Toil, Friendlessness

4 Again I looked and saw all the oppression that was taking place under the sun:

I saw the tears of the oppressed—
  and they have no comforter;
power was on the side of their
    oppressors—
  and they have no comforter.
2 And I declared that the dead,
  who had already died,
are happier than the living,
  who are still alive.
3 But better than both
  is he who has not yet been,
who has not seen the evil
  that is done under the sun.

4 And I saw that all labor and all achievement spring from man's envy of his neighbor. This too is meaningless, a chasing after the wind.

5 The fool folds his hands
  and ruins himself.
6 Better one handful with tranquillity
  than two handfuls with toil
  and chasing after the wind.

7 Again I saw something meaningless under the sun:

8 There was a man all alone;
  he had neither son nor brother.
There was no end to his toil,
  yet his eyes were not content with his
    wealth.
"For whom am I toiling," he asked,
  "and why am I depriving myself of
    enjoyment?"
This too is meaningless—
  a miserable business!

9 Two are better than one,
  because they have a good return for
    their work:
10 If one falls down,
  his friend can help him up.
But pity the man who falls
  and has no one to help him up!
11 Also, if two lie down together, they will
    keep warm.
  But how can one keep warm alone?
12 Though one may be overpowered,
  two can defend themselves.
A cord of three strands is not quickly
    broken.

Advancement Is Meaningless

13 Better a poor but wise youth than an old
but foolish king who no longer knows how to
take warning. 14 The youth may have come
from prison to the kingship, or he may have
been born in poverty within his kingdom. 15 I
saw that all who lived and walked under the
sun followed the youth, the king's successor.
16 There was no end to all the people who were
before them. But those who came later were not
pleased with the successor. This too is meaningless, a chasing after the wind.

Stand in Awe of God

5 Guard your steps when you go to the house of God. Go near to listen rather than to offer the sacrifice of fools, who do not know that they do wrong.

2 Do not be quick with your mouth,
  do not be hasty in your heart
  to utter anything before God.
God is in heaven
  and you are on earth,
  so let your words be few.
3 As a dream comes when there are many
    cares,
  so the speech of a fool when there are
    many words.

[a]19 Or *spirit* [b]21 Or *Who knows the spirit of man, which rises upward, or the spirit of the animal, which*

4When you make a vow to God, do not delay in fulfilling it. He has no pleasure in fools;
fulfill your vow. 5It is better not to vow than
to make a vow and not fulfill it. 6Do not let
your mouth lead you into sin. And do not protest to the ⌊temple⌋ messenger, "My vow was a
mistake." Why should God be angry at what
you say and destroy the work of your hands?
7Much dreaming and many words are meaningless. Therefore stand in awe of God.

Riches Are Meaningless

8If you see the poor oppressed in a district,
and justice and rights denied, do not be surprised at such things; for one official is eyed
by a higher one, and over them both are others higher still. 9The increase from the land
is taken by all; the king himself profits from
the fields.

10 Whoever loves money never has money
        enough;
    whoever loves wealth is never satisfied
        with his income.
  This too is meaningless.

11 As goods increase,
    so do those who consume them.
  And what benefit are they to the owner
    except to feast his eyes on them?

12 The sleep of a laborer is sweet,
    whether he eats little or much,
  but the abundance of a rich man
    permits him no sleep.

13I have seen a grievous evil under the sun:

  wealth hoarded to the harm of its owner,
14   or wealth lost through some misfortune,
  so that when he has a son
    there is nothing left for him.
15 Naked a man comes from his mother's
        womb,
    and as he comes, so he departs.
  He takes nothing from his labor
    that he can carry in his hand.

16This too is a grievous evil:

  As a man comes, so he departs,
    and what does he gain,
    since he toils for the wind?
17 All his days he eats in darkness,
    with great frustration, affliction and
        anger.

18Then I realized that it is good and proper
for a man to eat and drink, and to find satisfaction in his toilsome labor under the sun during
the few days of life God has given him—for
this is his lot. 19Moreover, when God gives any
man wealth and possessions, and enables him
to enjoy them, to accept his lot and be happy in
his work—this is a gift of God. 20He seldom reflects on the days of his life, because God keeps
him occupied with gladness of heart.

6 I have seen another evil under the sun,
and it weighs heavily on men: 2God gives
a man wealth, possessions and honor, so that
he lacks nothing his heart desires, but God
does not enable him to enjoy them, and a
stranger enjoys them instead. This is meaningless, a grievous evil.
3A man may have a hundred children and
live many years; yet no matter how long he
lives, if he cannot enjoy his prosperity and does
not receive proper burial, I say that a stillborn
child is better off than he. 4It comes without
meaning, it departs in darkness, and in darkness its name is shrouded. 5Though it never
saw the sun or knew anything, it has more
rest than does that man— 6even if he lives a
thousand years twice over but fails to enjoy his
prosperity. Do not all go to the same place?

7 All man's efforts are for his mouth,
    yet his appetite is never satisfied.
8 What advantage has a wise man
    over a fool?
  What does a poor man gain
    by knowing how to conduct himself
        before others?
9 Better what the eye sees
    than the roving of the appetite.
  This too is meaningless,
    a chasing after the wind.

10 Whatever exists has already been named,
    and what man is has been known;
  no man can contend
    with one who is stronger than he.
11 The more the words,
    the less the meaning,
    and how does that profit anyone?

12 For who knows what is good for a man in
life, during the few and meaningless days he
passes through like a shadow? Who can tell
him what will happen under the sun after he
is gone?

Wisdom

7 A good name is better
than fine perfume,
and the day of death
better than the day
of birth.
2 It is better to go to a house
of mourning
than to go to a house of
feasting,
for death is the destiny of
every man;
the living should take
this to heart.
3 Sorrow is better than laughter,
because a sad face is good for the heart.
4 The heart of the wise is in the house of
mourning,
but the heart of fools is in the house of
pleasure.
5 It is better to heed a wise man's rebuke
than to listen to the song of fools.
6 Like the crackling of thorns under the pot,
so is the laughter of fools.
This too is meaningless.
7 Extortion turns a wise man into a fool,
and a bribe corrupts the heart.
8 The end of a matter is better than its
beginning,
and patience is better than pride.
9 Do not be quickly provoked in your spirit,
for anger resides in the lap of fools.

10 Do not say, "Why were the old days better
than these?"
For it is not wise to ask such questions.

11 Wisdom, like an inheritance, is a good
thing
and benefits those who see the sun.
12 Wisdom is a shelter
as money is a shelter,
but the advantage of knowledge is this:
that wisdom preserves the life of its
possessor.

13 Consider what God has done:

Who can straighten
what he has made
crooked?
14 When times are good, be
happy;
but when times are bad,
consider:
God has made the one
as well as the other.
Therefore, a man cannot
discover
anything about his
future.
15 In this meaningless life of
mine I have seen
both of these:

a righteous man perishing in his
righteousness,
and a wicked man living long in his
wickedness.
16 Do not be overrighteous,
neither be overwise—
why destroy yourself?
17 Do not be overwicked,
and do not be a fool—
why die before your time?
18 It is good to grasp the one
and not let go of the other.
The man who fears God will avoid all
⌊extremes⌋.[a]

19 Wisdom makes one wise man more
powerful
than ten rulers in a city.

20 There is not a righteous man on earth
who does what is right and never sins.

21 Do not pay attention to every word people
say,
or you may hear your servant cursing
you—
22 for you know in your heart
that many times you yourself have
cursed others.

Ecclesiastes 7:13

God Is Omnipotent

Consider what God
has done:
Who can straighten
what he has made
crooked?

[a]18 Or *will follow them both*

Remember the Good Ol' Days?

Read: Ecclesiastes 7:2–14

IT'S EASY TO THINK THE PAST was better than today. Most of us have selective memories. We only remember what we want to remember. We reminisce about our fun-loving college days but forget how we stayed up all night to study, subsisting on Ramen noodles and completely stressing out because no one had asked us to the upcoming party. We remember being single—enjoying the freedom to have ice cream for dinner—but forget how lonely we felt eating by ourselves. We recall our children as darling babies but don't remember how frustrated we were when the "terrible twos" hit.

You could make the case that it's good to forget the bad. However, when we look at the past through rose-colored glasses, we run the risk of being ungrateful for what we have right now. Rather than seeing today's gifts, we yearn for yesterday's fun and games, conveniently glossing over the past's difficulties.

Our days, months and years are made up of both good times and bad. The tapestry of life's events makes up the very essence of who we are. Think about today and the difficulties you are encountering: The laundry is piling up. The roof needs fixing. Your kids aren't listening to you. Now consider some of the memories you're making today: Your baby took his first steps. Your daughter graduated from kindergarten, high school or college. You got that big promotion. You finally started your own business.

Thank God for all your wonderful memories. Take the difficult things to God in prayer. Ask him what he wants you to learn from your present situation. God doesn't waste any of our experiences. He can use the good ol' days, as well as the not-so-great days, to benefit us, if we let him. The key is to remember things as they really were, to be content with things as they really are and to trust God to take care of the future.

Ecclesiastes 7:10,14

Do not say, "Why were the old days better than these?" For it is not wise to ask such questions . . . When times are good, be happy; but when times are bad, consider: God has made the one as well as the other. Therefore, a man cannot discover anything about his future.

reflection

1. Name some difficulties you've faced in the past. What good came out of them?

2. What difficulties are you facing right now? How might God use them for your good or the good of someone else?

3. Name some of the women you know who have used their difficulties to help others. How have they glorified God?

RELATED READINGS

Exodus 16:1–8;
Isaiah 40:28–31;
43:18–19

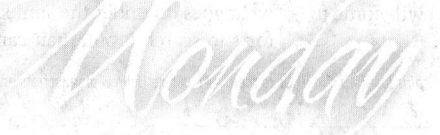

Go to page 813 for your next devotional reading.

23 All this I tested by wisdom and I said,

"I am determined to be wise"—
but this was beyond me.
24 Whatever wisdom may be,
it is far off and most profound—
who can discover it?
25 So I turned my mind to understand,
to investigate and to search out wisdom
and the scheme of things
and to understand the stupidity of
wickedness
and the madness of folly.

26 I find more bitter than death
the woman who is a snare,
whose heart is a trap
and whose hands are chains.
The man who pleases God will escape her,
but the sinner she will ensnare.

27 "Look," says the Teacher,[a] "this is what I
have discovered:

"Adding one thing to another to discover
the scheme of things—
28 while I was still searching
but not finding—
I found one ⌊upright⌋ man among a
thousand,
but not one ⌊upright⌋ woman among
them all.
29 This only have I found:
God made mankind upright,
but men have gone in search of many
schemes."

8 Who is like the wise man?
Who knows the explanation of things?
Wisdom brightens a man's face
and changes its hard appearance.

Obey the King

2 Obey the king's command, I say, because
you took an oath before God. 3 Do not be in a
hurry to leave the king's presence. Do not stand
up for a bad cause, for he will do whatever he
pleases. 4 Since a king's word is supreme, who
can say to him, "What are you doing?"

5 Whoever obeys his command will come to
no harm,
and the wise heart will know the proper
time and procedure.
6 For there is a proper time and procedure
for every matter,
though a man's misery weighs heavily
upon him.

7 Since no man knows the future,
who can tell him what is to come?
8 No man has power over the wind to
contain it[b];
so no one has power over the day of his
death.
As no one is discharged in time of war,
so wickedness will not release those who
practice it.

9 All this I saw, as I applied my mind to everything done under the sun. There is a time when
a man lords it over others to his own[c] hurt.
10 Then too, I saw the wicked buried—those
who used to come and go from the holy place
and receive praise[d] in the city where they did
this. This too is meaningless.
11 When the sentence for a crime is not
quickly carried out, the hearts of the people are
filled with schemes to do wrong. 12 Although
a wicked man commits a hundred crimes and
still lives a long time, I know that it will go better with God-fearing men, who are reverent before God. 13 Yet because the wicked do not fear
God, it will not go well with them, and their
days will not lengthen like a shadow.
14 There is something else meaningless that
occurs on earth: righteous men who get what
the wicked deserve, and wicked men who get
what the righteous deserve. This too, I say, is
meaningless. 15 So I commend the enjoyment
of life, because nothing is better for a man under the sun than to eat and drink and be glad.
Then joy will accompany him in his work all
the days of the life God has given him under
the sun.

16 When I applied my mind to know wisdom
and to observe man's labor on earth—his eyes
not seeing sleep day or night— 17 then I saw all
that God has done. No one can comprehend
what goes on under the sun. Despite all his efforts to search it out, man cannot discover its

[a]27 Or *leader of the assembly* [b]8 Or *over his spirit to retain it* [c]9 Or *to their* [d]10 Some Hebrew manuscripts and Septuagint (Aquila); most Hebrew manuscripts *and are forgotten*

meaning. Even if a wise man claims he knows, he cannot really comprehend it.

A Common Destiny for All

9 So I reflected on all this and concluded
that the righteous and the wise and what
they do are in God's hands, but no man knows
whether love or hate awaits him. 2All share
a common destiny—the righteous and the
wicked, the good and the bad,[a] the clean and
the unclean, those who offer sacrifices and
those who do not.

As it is with the good man,
so with the sinner;
as it is with those who take oaths,
so with those who are afraid to take them.

3This is the evil in everything that happens
under the sun: The same destiny overtakes all.
The hearts of men, moreover, are full of evil
and there is madness in their hearts while they
live, and afterward they join the dead. 4Anyone
who is among the living has hope[b]—even a live
dog is better off than a dead lion!

5 For the living know that they will die,
but the dead know nothing;
they have no further reward,
and even the memory of them is forgotten.
6 Their love, their hate
and their jealousy have long since vanished;
never again will they have a part
in anything that happens under the sun.

7Go, eat your food with gladness, and drink
your wine with a joyful heart, for it is now that
God favors what you do. 8Always be clothed
in white, and always anoint your head with
oil. 9Enjoy life with your wife, whom you love,
all the days of this meaningless life that God
has given you under the sun—all your meaningless days. For this is your lot in life and in
your toilsome labor under the sun. 10Whatever
your hand finds to do, do it with all your might,
for in the grave,[c] where you are going, there is
neither working nor planning nor knowledge
nor wisdom.

11I have seen something else under the sun:

The race is not to the swift
or the battle to the strong,
nor does food come to the wise
or wealth to the brilliant
or favor to the learned;
but time and chance happen to them all.

12Moreover, no man knows when his hour
will come:

As fish are caught in a cruel net,
or birds are taken in a snare,
so men are trapped by evil times
that fall unexpectedly upon them.

Wisdom Better Than Folly

13I also saw under the sun this example of
wisdom that greatly impressed me: 14There
was once a small city with only a few people in it. And a powerful king came against
it, surrounded it and built huge siegeworks
against it. 15Now there lived in that city a man
poor but wise, and he saved the city by his wisdom. But nobody remembered that poor man.
16So I said, "Wisdom is better than strength."
But the poor man's wisdom is despised, and his
words are no longer heeded.

17 The quiet words of the wise are more to be heeded
than the shouts of a ruler of fools.
18 Wisdom is better than weapons of war,
but one sinner destroys much good.

10 As dead flies give perfume a bad smell,
so a little folly outweighs wisdom and honor.
2 The heart of the wise inclines to the right,
but the heart of the fool to the left.
3 Even as he walks along the road,
the fool lacks sense
and shows everyone how stupid he is.
4 If a ruler's anger rises against you,
do not leave your post;
calmness can lay great errors to rest.

5 There is an evil I have seen under the sun,
the sort of error that arises from a ruler:
6 Fools are put in many high positions,

[a]2 Septuagint (Aquila), Vulgate and Syriac; Hebrew does not have *and the bad.* [b]4 Or *What then is to be chosen? With all who live, there is hope* [c]10 Hebrew *Sheol*

while the rich occupy the low ones.
7 I have seen slaves on horseback,
while princes go on foot like slaves.

8 Whoever digs a pit may fall into it;
whoever breaks through a wall may be bitten by a snake.
9 Whoever quarries stones may be injured by them;
whoever splits logs may be endangered by them.

10 If the ax is dull
and its edge unsharpened,
more strength is needed
but skill will bring success.

11 If a snake bites before it is charmed,
there is no profit for the charmer.

12 Words from a wise man's mouth are gracious,
but a fool is consumed by his own lips.
13 At the beginning his words are folly;
at the end they are wicked madness—
14 and the fool multiplies words.

No one knows what is coming—
who can tell him what will happen after him?

15 A fool's work wearies him;
he does not know the way to town.

16 Woe to you, O land whose king was a servant[a]
and whose princes feast in the morning.
17 Blessed are you, O land whose king is of noble birth
and whose princes eat at a proper time—
for strength and not for drunkenness.

18 If a man is lazy, the rafters sag;
if his hands are idle, the house leaks.

19 A feast is made for laughter,
and wine makes life merry,
but money is the answer for everything.

20 Do not revile the king even in your thoughts,
or curse the rich in your bedroom,
because a bird of the air may carry your words,
and a bird on the wing may report what you say.

Bread Upon the Waters

11 Cast your bread upon the waters,
for after many days you will find it again.
2 Give portions to seven, yes to eight,
for you do not know what disaster may come upon the land.

3 If clouds are full of water,
they pour rain upon the earth.
Whether a tree falls to the south or to the north,
in the place where it falls, there will it lie.
4 Whoever watches the wind will not plant;
whoever looks at the clouds will not reap.

5 As you do not know the path of the wind,
or how the body is formed[b] in a mother's womb,
so you cannot understand the work of God,
the Maker of all things.

6 Sow your seed in the morning,
and at evening let not your hands be idle,
for you do not know which will succeed,
whether this or that,
or whether both will do equally well.

Remember Your Creator While Young

7 Light is sweet,
and it pleases the eyes to see the sun.
8 However many years a man may live,
let him enjoy them all.
But let him remember the days of darkness,
for they will be many.
Everything to come is meaningless.

9 Be happy, young man, while you are young,
and let your heart give you joy in the days of your youth.
Follow the ways of your heart
and whatever your eyes see,
but know that for all these things
God will bring you to judgment.

[a]16 Or *king is a child* [b]5 Or *know how life* (or *the spirit*) / *enters the body being formed*

10 So then, banish anxiety from your heart
and cast off the troubles of your body,
for youth and vigor are meaningless.

12 Remember your Creator
in the days of your youth,
before the days of trouble come
and the years approach when you will say,
"I find no pleasure in them"—
2 before the sun and the light
and the moon and the stars grow dark,
and the clouds return after the rain;
3 when the keepers of the house tremble,
and the strong men stoop,
when the grinders cease because they are few,
and those looking through the windows grow dim;
4 when the doors to the street are closed
and the sound of grinding fades;
when men rise up at the sound of birds,
but all their songs grow faint;
5 when men are afraid of heights
and of dangers in the streets;
when the almond tree blossoms
and the grasshopper drags himself along
and desire no longer is stirred.
Then man goes to his eternal home
and mourners go about the streets.

6 Remember him—before the silver cord is severed,
or the golden bowl is broken;
before the pitcher is shattered at the spring,
or the wheel broken at the well,
7 and the dust returns to the ground it came from,
and the spirit returns to God who gave it.

8 "Meaningless! Meaningless!" says the Teacher.[a]
"Everything is meaningless!"

The Conclusion of the Matter

9 Not only was the Teacher wise, but also
he imparted knowledge to the people. He pondered and searched out and set in order many
proverbs. 10 The Teacher searched to find just
the right words, and what he wrote was upright
and true.
11 The words of the wise are like goads, their
collected sayings like firmly embedded nails—
given by one Shepherd. 12 Be warned, my son,
of anything in addition to them.
Of making many books there is no end, and much study wearies the body.

13 Now all has been heard;
here is the conclusion of the matter:
Fear God and keep his commandments,
for this is the whole ⌊duty⌋ of man.
14 For God will bring every deed into judgment,
including every hidden thing,
whether it is good or evil.

> **Ecclesiastes 12:14**
>
> *God Exposes Secrets*
>
> For God will bring every deed into judgment, including every hidden thing, whether it is good or evil.

[a] 8 Or *the leader of the assembly*; also in verses 9 and 10

Song of Songs

Author:
Probably King Solomon.

Audience:
All Israel.

Date:
Most likely early in Solomon's reign, around 965 B.C.

Setting:
Storybook romance and steamy dialogue between two God-fearing, passionate lovers.

Verse to Remember:
Many waters cannot quench love; rivers cannot wash it away. If one were to give all the wealth of his house for love, it would be utterly scorned. (8:7)

What's *that* book doing in the Bible? Song of Songs is anything but the typical book of Scripture. A love song that ranges from the softly romantic to the wildly erotic, *Song of Songs celebrates the gift* of marital love. Readers are cautioned not to "arouse or awaken love" too early. But for this husband and wife, much joy is to be found in their private, tender love. They kiss and caress and whisper to each other. They belong to each other, rejoice in each other and brag on each other. Many of the metaphors for the lovers' beauty are agricultural and may sound unusual to our ears, but the love and desire translate into any culture.

Not only did God create marriage, but the inclusion of this book in Scripture says that he rejoices in married love and wants his people to rejoice in it too.

1 Solomon's Song of Songs.

Beloved[a]

2 Let him kiss me with the kisses of his
mouth—
for your love is more delightful than
wine.
3 Pleasing is the fragrance of your perfumes;
your name is like perfume poured out.
No wonder the maidens love you!
4 Take me away with you—let us hurry!
Let the king bring me into his
chambers.

Friends

We rejoice and delight in you[b];
we will praise your love more than wine.

[a] Primarily on the basis of the gender of the Hebrew pronouns used, male and female speakers are indicated in the margins by the captions *Lover* and *Beloved* respectively. The words of others are marked *Friends*. In some instances the divisions and their captions are debatable.
[b] 4 The Hebrew is masculine singular.

Beloved

How right they are to adore you!

5 Dark am I, yet lovely,
O daughters of Jerusalem,
dark like the tents of Kedar,
like the tent curtains of Solomon.[a]
6 Do not stare at me because I am dark,
because I am darkened by the sun.
My mother's sons were angry with me
and made me take care of the vineyards;
my own vineyard I have neglected.
7 Tell me, you whom I love, where you graze
your flock
and where you rest your sheep at midday.
Why should I be like a veiled woman
beside the flocks of your friends?

Friends

8 If you do not know, most beautiful of
women,
follow the tracks of the sheep
and graze your young goats
by the tents of the shepherds.

Lover

9 I liken you, my darling, to a mare
harnessed to one of the chariots of
Pharaoh.
10 Your cheeks are beautiful with earrings,
your neck with strings of jewels.
11 We will make you earrings of gold,
studded with silver.

Beloved

12 While the king was at his table,
my perfume spread its fragrance.
13 My lover is to me a sachet of myrrh
resting between my breasts.
14 My lover is to me a cluster of henna
blossoms
from the vineyards of En Gedi.

Lover

15 How beautiful you are, my darling!
Oh, how beautiful!
Your eyes are doves.

Beloved

16 How handsome you are, my lover!
Oh, how charming!
And our bed is verdant.

Lover

17 The beams of our house are cedars;
our rafters are firs.

Beloved[b]

2 I am a rose[c] of Sharon,
a lily of the valleys.

Lover

2 Like a lily among thorns
is my darling among the maidens.

Beloved

3 Like an apple tree among the trees of the
forest
is my lover among the young men.
I delight to sit in his shade,
and his fruit is sweet to my taste.
4 He has taken me to the banquet hall,
and his banner over me is love.
5 Strengthen me with raisins,
refresh me with apples,
for I am faint with love.
6 His left arm is under my head,
and his right arm embraces me.
7 Daughters of Jerusalem, I charge you
by the gazelles and by the does of the
field:
Do not arouse or awaken love
until it so desires.

8 Listen! My lover!
Look! Here he comes,
leaping across the mountains,
bounding over the hills.
9 My lover is like a gazelle or a young stag.
Look! There he stands behind our wall,
gazing through the windows,
peering through the lattice.
10 My lover spoke and said to me,
"Arise, my darling,
my beautiful one, and come with me.
11 See! The winter is past;
the rains are over and gone.
12 Flowers appear on the earth;
the season of singing has come,
the cooing of doves
is heard in our land.
13 The fig tree forms its early fruit;
the blossoming vines spread their
fragrance.

[a]5 Or *Salma* [b]Or *Lover* [c]1 Possibly a member of the crocus family

Arise, come, my darling;
my beautiful one, come with me."

Lover

14 My dove in the clefts of the rock,
in the hiding places on the mountainside,
show me your face,
let me hear your voice;
for your voice is sweet,
and your face is lovely.
15 Catch for us the foxes,
the little foxes
that ruin the vineyards,
our vineyards that are in bloom.

Beloved

16 My lover is mine and I am his;
he browses among the lilies.
17 Until the day breaks
and the shadows flee,
turn, my lover,
and be like a gazelle
or like a young stag
on the rugged hills.[a]

3 All night long on my bed
I looked for the one my heart loves;
I looked for him but did not find him.
2 I will get up now and go about the city,
through its streets and squares;
I will search for the one my heart loves.
So I looked for him but did not find him.
3 The watchmen found me
as they made their rounds in the city.
"Have you seen the one my heart loves?"
4 Scarcely had I passed them
when I found the one my heart loves.
I held him and would not let him go
till I had brought him to my mother's house,
to the room of the one who conceived me.
5 Daughters of Jerusalem, I charge you
by the gazelles and by the does of the field:
Do not arouse or awaken love
until it so desires.

Song of Songs 2:16

God Has Affection for Us

My lover is mine and I am his.

6 Who is this coming up from the desert
like a column of smoke,
perfumed with myrrh and incense
made from all the spices of the merchant?
7 Look! It is Solomon's carriage,
escorted by sixty warriors,
the noblest of Israel,
8 all of them wearing the sword,
all experienced in battle,
each with his sword at his side,
prepared for the terrors of the night.
9 King Solomon made for himself the carriage;
he made it of wood from Lebanon.
10 Its posts he made of silver,
its base of gold.
Its seat was upholstered with purple,
its interior lovingly inlaid
by[b] the daughters of Jerusalem.
11 Come out, you daughters of Zion,
and look at King Solomon wearing the crown,
the crown with which his mother crowned him
on the day of his wedding,
the day his heart rejoiced.

Lover

4 How beautiful you are, my darling!
Oh, how beautiful!
Your eyes behind your veil are doves.
Your hair is like a flock of goats
descending from Mount Gilead.
2 Your teeth are like a flock of sheep just shorn,
coming up from the washing.
Each has its twin;
not one of them is alone.
3 Your lips are like a scarlet ribbon;
your mouth is lovely.
Your temples behind your veil
are like the halves of a pomegranate.
4 Your neck is like the tower of David,
built with elegance[c];

[a] 17 Or *the hills of Bether* [b] 10 Or *its inlaid interior a gift of love / from* [c] 4 The meaning of the Hebrew for this word is uncertain.

Picture Perfect Bride

Read: Song of Songs 4:1–16

OURS WAS A WEDDING unlike any other, I'm sure . . .

When the organ music began, I wheeled toward the door, stopping for a moment in front of a full-length mirror. I looked a little like a float in the Rose Parade.

The glass doors of the sanctuary opened, and I positioned myself at the top of the aisle, breathing deeply to steady my nerves. Daddy looked resplendent in his gray morning suit and a Windsor cravat. I'd never seen him so formally attired, nor he me. He smiled in a way that told me, *You're not my little pal anymore, not my cowgirl. And I'm glad.*

I leaned toward his ear, and above the organ music I explained in a loud whisper that I would wheel slowly so he could keep up with me. He handed Judy one of his crutches and held onto the armrest of my chair for support.

"You're marrying a good one, honey-girl," he told me . . .

Just before the wedding march began, I looked down at my gown. *Aaugh!* I groaned—I had wheeled over the hem and left a huge, greasy tire mark. It didn't help that my dress hung clumped and uneven. And even though my chair was spiffed up, the wheels and gears were still visible through the wire mesh. My bouquet of daisies was off center on my lap, because my hands couldn't hold them. I was not a picture perfect bride.

As my last bridesmaid finished her walk, the organ pipes crescendoed, and I inched my chair closer to the last pew, wanting to catch a glimpse of Ken. Suddenly, I spotted him down front, standing at attention and looking tall and elegant in his tuxedo. I looked down, my face hot and my heart pounding. It was a flush of nerves I'd never felt before. When I looked up again, I saw him craning to look up the aisle, to find me. Our eyes met, and—it was amazing—from that point, everything changed.

How I looked no longer mattered. I forgot all about my wheelchair. Grease stains? Flowers? No longer did I feel ugly or unworthy. The love in Ken's eyes washed it all away. I was the pure and perfect bride—his bride. That's what he saw, and that's what changed me.

—Joni Eareckson Tada

Song of Songs 4:9

You have stolen my heart, my sister, my bride; you have stolen my heart with one glance of your eyes, with one jewel of your necklace.

reflection

1 Think about a wedding you witnessed. How did everything else fade away once the bride and groom saw one another face-to-face?

2 Does it surprise you that God takes such delight in marriages? Why or why not?

3 What especially moved you about Joni's story? How have you felt ugly or unworthy in your life? How has the love of another person (a friend, relative, child or spouse) changed that? How has God's love changed your life?

RELATED READINGS

Genesis 2:18–25;
1 Corinthians 13:1–13;
Ephesians 5:21–33

Go to page 817 for your next devotional reading.

on it hang a thousand shields,
all of them shields of warriors.
5 Your two breasts are like two fawns,
like twin fawns of a gazelle
that browse among the lilies.
6 Until the day breaks
and the shadows flee,
I will go to the mountain of myrrh
and to the hill of incense.
7 All beautiful you are, my darling;
there is no flaw in you.

8 Come with me from Lebanon, my bride,
come with me from Lebanon.
Descend from the crest of Amana,
from the top of Senir, the summit of Hermon,
from the lions' dens
and the mountain haunts of the leopards.
9 You have stolen my heart, my sister, my bride;
you have stolen my heart
with one glance of your eyes,
with one jewel of your necklace.
10 How delightful is your love, my sister, my bride!
How much more pleasing is your love than wine,
and the fragrance of your perfume than any spice!
11 Your lips drop sweetness as the honeycomb, my bride;
milk and honey are under your tongue.
The fragrance of your garments is like that of Lebanon.
12 You are a garden locked up, my sister, my bride;
you are a spring enclosed, a sealed fountain.
13 Your plants are an orchard of pomegranates
with choice fruits,
with henna and nard,
14 nard and saffron,
calamus and cinnamon,
with every kind of incense tree,
with myrrh and aloes
and all the finest spices.
15 You are[a] a garden fountain,
a well of flowing water
streaming down from Lebanon.

Beloved

16 Awake, north wind,
and come, south wind!
Blow on my garden,
that its fragrance may spread abroad.
Let my lover come into his garden
and taste its choice fruits.

Lover

5 I have come into my garden, my sister, my bride;
I have gathered my myrrh with my spice.
I have eaten my honeycomb and my honey;
I have drunk my wine and my milk.

Friends

Eat, O friends, and drink;
drink your fill, O lovers.

Beloved

2 I slept but my heart was awake.
Listen! My lover is knocking:
"Open to me, my sister, my darling,
my dove, my flawless one.
My head is drenched with dew,
my hair with the dampness of the night."
3 I have taken off my robe—
must I put it on again?
I have washed my feet—
must I soil them again?
4 My lover thrust his hand through the latch-opening;
my heart began to pound for him.
5 I arose to open for my lover,
and my hands dripped with myrrh,
my fingers with flowing myrrh,
on the handles of the lock.
6 I opened for my lover,
but my lover had left; he was gone.
My heart sank at his departure.[b]
I looked for him but did not find him.
I called him but he did not answer.
7 The watchmen found me
as they made their rounds in the city.
They beat me, they bruised me;

[a]15 Or *I am* (spoken by the *Beloved*) [b]6 Or *heart had gone out to him when he spoke*

they took away my cloak,
those watchmen of the walls!
8 O daughters of Jerusalem, I charge you—
if you find my lover,
what will you tell him?
Tell him I am faint with love.

Friends

9 How is your beloved better than others,
most beautiful of women?
How is your beloved better than others,
that you charge us so?

Beloved

10 My lover is radiant and ruddy,
outstanding among ten thousand.
11 His head is purest gold;
his hair is wavy
and black as a raven.
12 His eyes are like doves
by the water streams,
washed in milk,
mounted like jewels.
13 His cheeks are like beds of spice
yielding perfume.
His lips are like lilies
dripping with myrrh.
14 His arms are rods of gold
set with chrysolite.
His body is like polished ivory
decorated with sapphires.[a]
15 His legs are pillars of marble
set on bases of pure gold.
His appearance is like Lebanon,
choice as its cedars.
16 His mouth is sweetness itself;
he is altogether lovely.
This is my lover, this my friend,
O daughters of Jerusalem.

Friends

6 Where has your lover gone,
most beautiful of women?
Which way did your lover turn,
that we may look for him with you?

Beloved

2 My lover has gone down to his garden,
to the beds of spices,
to browse in the gardens
and to gather lilies.
3 I am my lover's and my lover is mine;
he browses among the lilies.

Lover

4 You are beautiful, my darling, as Tirzah,
lovely as Jerusalem,
majestic as troops with banners.
5 Turn your eyes from me;
they overwhelm me.
Your hair is like a flock of goats
descending from Gilead.
6 Your teeth are like a flock of sheep
coming up from the washing.
Each has its twin,
not one of them is alone.
7 Your temples behind your veil
are like the halves of a pomegranate.
8 Sixty queens there may be,
and eighty concubines,
and virgins beyond number;
9 but my dove, my perfect one, is unique,
the only daughter of her mother,
the favorite of the one who bore her.
The maidens saw her and called her blessed;
the queens and concubines praised her.

Friends

10 Who is this that appears like the dawn,
fair as the moon, bright as the sun,
majestic as the stars in procession?

Lover

11 I went down to the grove of nut trees
to look at the new growth in the valley,
to see if the vines had budded
or the pomegranates were in bloom.
12 Before I realized it,
my desire set me among the royal
chariots of my people.[b]

Friends

13 Come back, come back, O Shulammite;
come back, come back, that we may gaze
on you!

Lover

Why would you gaze on the Shulammite
as on the dance of Mahanaim?

7 How beautiful your sandaled feet,
O prince's daughter!
Your graceful legs are like jewels,

[a] 14 Or *lapis lazuli* [b] 12 Or *among the chariots of Amminadab*; or *among the chariots of the people of the prince*

the work of a craftsman's hands.
2 Your navel is a rounded goblet
that never lacks blended wine.
Your waist is a mound of wheat
encircled by lilies.
3 Your breasts are like two fawns,
twins of a gazelle.
4 Your neck is like an ivory tower.
Your eyes are the pools of Heshbon
by the gate of Bath Rabbim.
Your nose is like the tower of Lebanon
looking toward Damascus.
5 Your head crowns you like Mount Carmel.
Your hair is like royal tapestry;
the king is held captive by its tresses.
6 How beautiful you are and how pleasing,
O love, with your delights!
7 Your stature is like that of the palm,
and your breasts like clusters of fruit.
8 I said, "I will climb the palm tree;
I will take hold of its fruit."
May your breasts be like the clusters of the vine,
the fragrance of your breath like apples,
9 and your mouth like the best wine.

Beloved

May the wine go straight to my lover,
flowing gently over lips and teeth.[a]
10 I belong to my lover,
and his desire is for me.
11 Come, my lover, let us go to the countryside,
let us spend the night in the villages.[b]
12 Let us go early to the vineyards
to see if the vines have budded,
if their blossoms have opened,
and if the pomegranates are in bloom—
there I will give you my love.
13 The mandrakes send out their fragrance,
and at our door is every delicacy,
both new and old,
that I have stored up for you, my lover.

Song of Songs 8:6

God Gives Unyielding Love

For love is as strong
as death,
its jealousy unyielding
as the grave.
It burns like
blazing fire,
like a mighty flame.

8 If only you were to me like a brother,
who was nursed at my mother's breasts!
Then, if I found you outside,
I would kiss you,
and no one would despise me.
2 I would lead you
and bring you to my mother's house—
she who has taught me.
I would give you spiced wine to drink,
the nectar of my pomegranates.
3 His left arm is under my head
and his right arm embraces me.
4 Daughters of Jerusalem, I charge you:
Do not arouse or awaken love
until it so desires.

Friends

5 Who is this coming up from the desert
leaning on her lover?

Beloved

Under the apple tree I roused you;
there your mother conceived you,
there she who was in labor gave you birth.
6 Place me like a seal over your heart,
like a seal on your arm;
for love is as strong as death,
its jealousy[c] unyielding as the grave.[d]
It burns like blazing fire,
like a mighty flame.[e]
7 Many waters cannot quench love;
rivers cannot wash it away.
If one were to give
all the wealth of his house for love,
it[f] would be utterly scorned.

Friends

8 We have a young sister,
and her breasts are not yet grown.
What shall we do for our sister
for the day she is spoken for?
9 If she is a wall,

[a]9 Septuagint, Aquila, Vulgate and Syriac; Hebrew *lips of sleepers* [b]11 Or *henna bushes* [c]6 Or *ardor* [d]6 Hebrew *Sheol* [e]6 Or / *like the very flame of the Lord* [f]7 Or *he*

The Strongest Love

Read: Song of Songs 8:1–7

FROM *ROMEO AND JULIET* to the movie *Titanic,* books, films and stories tell us that there is a love that is great enough to die for. Many women would say their greatest earthly desire is for true intimacy with a man—not a vague commitment or wishy-washy affection. Some might say they want a love worth dying for. Maybe you feel the same way. In fact, if you are honest, on many days you long more for the affirmation and passion of a husband or boyfriend than you ache for the love of God.

God is love—even your desire for love points to him as the source of all love. The love between a man and a woman is a beautiful reflection of God's love, but you only desire that kind of love because God has placed that desire in you.

The Song of Songs presents a picture of love between a man and a woman that reflects the love of God. God doesn't love you at a distance or remember you as an afterthought. Look at the words used to express his love: *seal, strong, unyielding, blazing* and *unquenchable.* He loves everything about you, the way you walk, talk, laugh and brush your hair. He loves you in more ways than you can ever know because he knows you through and through. He knows your thoughts, when you sit, when you rise and when you lie down (see Psalm 139).

God wants you to believe that he loves you! He doesn't put conditions on his love. He only asks that you respond to his love: "Place me like a seal over your heart." Imagine God saying to you, "*I love you so much that I want to be with you intimately, at all times.*" God loves you with the strongest love imaginable—a love that is as strong as death. In fact, he proved his love through Christ's sacrifice on the cross. This ultimate gift showed us that his love for us was, in fact, a love worth dying for.

Wednesday

Song of Songs 8:6

Place me like a seal over your heart, like a seal on your arm; for love is as strong as death, its jealousy unyielding as the grave. It burns like blazing fire, like a mighty flame.

reflection

1 What keeps you from believing and fully accepting God's love?

2 How would your thoughts and actions be different this week if you fully believed that God loved you?

3 Read Psalm 139. Memorize as much of it as you can. How does it change your view of yourself to realize how intimately God knows you and loves you?

RELATED READINGS

Psalm 136:1–26;
Ephesians 3:14–19;
1 John 4:7–12

"There is no need to plead that the love of God shall fill our heart as though he were unwilling to fill us. He is willing as light is willing to flood a room that is opened to its brightness."

Amy Carmichael

Go to page 826 for your next devotional reading.

we will build towers of silver on her.
If she is a door,
we will enclose her with panels of cedar.

Beloved

10 I am a wall,
and my breasts are like towers.
Thus I have become in his eyes
like one bringing contentment.
11 Solomon had a vineyard in Baal Hamon;
he let out his vineyard to tenants.
Each was to bring for its fruit
a thousand shekels[a] of silver.
12 But my own vineyard is mine to give;
the thousand shekels are for you,
O Solomon,
and two hundred[b] are for those who
tend its fruit.

Lover

13 You who dwell in the gardens
with friends in attendance,
let me hear your voice!

Beloved

14 Come away, my lover,
and be like a gazelle
or like a young stag
on the spice-laden mountains.

[a]11 That is, about 25 pounds (about 11.5 kilograms); also in verse 12 [b]12 That is, about 5 pounds (about 2.3 kilograms)

Isaiah

When God chose Israel to be his own people, he told them plainly that *they were to worship him alone.* But the people failed to obey. They worshiped false gods, and though God repeatedly warned them to return to him, they stubbornly clung to their idols and pagan alliances.

Isaiah paints in bold strokes the sins of a people who had *denied their allegiance to God.* In equally bold strokes is the response that God's holiness demands. But the picture is not painted in black and white. It is in full color, complete with shadings and depths that reach far into the future. Yes, *God would judge* his people. But he would do more than that. He would redeem them. In the darkest place of judgment, *the light of a Redeemer still shines through.*

The book of Isaiah has been described as a condensed version of the Bible, for it captures the essence of both the Old and New Testaments. Through Isaiah's poetic words we see that God is both loving and just, a shepherd and a warrior. And above all, he is a holy God who loves his people and *will go to any lengths to redeem them.*

Author:
Isaiah.

Audience:
Judah, Israel, surrounding pagan nations.

Date:
Between 701 and 681 B.C.

Setting:
Judgment is on the horizon for Judah as the Assyrians threaten to overtake them.

Verse to Remember:
"Though the mountains be shaken and the hills be removed, yet my unfailing love for you will not be shaken nor my covenant of peace be removed," says the LORD, who has compassion on you. (54:10)

1 The vision concerning Judah and Jerusalem that Isaiah son of Amoz saw during the reigns of Uzziah, Jotham, Ahaz and Hezekiah, kings of Judah.

A Rebellious Nation

2 Hear, O heavens! Listen, O earth!
For the LORD has spoken:
"I reared children and brought them up,

but they have rebelled against me.
3 The ox knows his master,
the donkey his owner's manger,
but Israel does not know,
my people do not understand."

4 Ah, sinful nation,
a people loaded with guilt,
a brood of evildoers,
children given to corruption!
They have forsaken the LORD;
they have spurned the Holy One of Israel
and turned their backs on him.

5 Why should you be beaten anymore?
Why do you persist in rebellion?
Your whole head is injured,
your whole heart afflicted.
6 From the sole of your foot to the top of your head
there is no soundness—
only wounds and welts
and open sores,
not cleansed or bandaged
or soothed with oil.

7 Your country is desolate,
your cities burned with fire;
your fields are being stripped by foreigners
right before you,
laid waste as when overthrown by strangers.
8 The Daughter of Zion is left
like a shelter in a vineyard,
like a hut in a field of melons,
like a city under siege.
9 Unless the LORD Almighty
had left us some survivors,
we would have become like Sodom,
we would have been like Gomorrah.

10 Hear the word of the LORD,
you rulers of Sodom;
listen to the law of our God,
you people of Gomorrah!
11 "The multitude of your sacrifices—
what are they to me?" says the LORD.
"I have more than enough of burnt offerings,
of rams and the fat of fattened animals;
I have no pleasure
in the blood of bulls and lambs and goats.
12 When you come to appear before me,
who has asked this of you,
this trampling of my courts?
13 Stop bringing meaningless offerings!
Your incense is detestable to me.
New Moons, Sabbaths and convocations—
I cannot bear your evil assemblies.
14 Your New Moon festivals and your appointed feasts
my soul hates.
They have become a burden to me;
I am weary of bearing them.
15 When you spread out your hands in prayer,
I will hide my eyes from you;
even if you offer many prayers,
I will not listen.
Your hands are full of blood;
16 wash and make yourselves clean.
Take your evil deeds
out of my sight!
Stop doing wrong,
17 learn to do right!
Seek justice,
encourage the oppressed.[a]
Defend the cause of the fatherless,
plead the case of the widow.

18 "Come now, let us reason together,"
says the LORD.
"Though your sins are like scarlet,
they shall be as white as snow;
though they are red as crimson,
they shall be like wool.
19 If you are willing and obedient,
you will eat the best from the land;
20 but if you resist and rebel,
you will be devoured by the sword."
For the mouth of the LORD has spoken.

21 See how the faithful city
has become a harlot!
She once was full of justice;
righteousness used to dwell in her—
but now murderers!
22 Your silver has become dross,
your choice wine is diluted with water.
23 Your rulers are rebels,

[a] 17 Or / *rebuke the oppressor*

companions of thieves;
they all love bribes
and chase after gifts.
They do not defend the cause of the fatherless;
the widow's case does not come before them.
24 Therefore the Lord, the LORD Almighty,
the Mighty One of Israel, declares:
"Ah, I will get relief from my foes
and avenge myself on my enemies.
25 I will turn my hand against you;
I will thoroughly purge away your dross
and remove all your impurities.
26 I will restore your judges as in days of old,
your counselors as at the beginning.
Afterward you will be called
the City of Righteousness,
the Faithful City."

27 Zion will be redeemed with justice,
her penitent ones with righteousness.
28 But rebels and sinners will both be broken,
and those who forsake the LORD will perish.
29 "You will be ashamed because of the sacred oaks
in which you have delighted;
you will be disgraced because of the gardens
that you have chosen.
30 You will be like an oak with fading leaves,
like a garden without water.
31 The mighty man will become tinder
and his work a spark;
both will burn together,
with no one to quench the fire."

The Mountain of the LORD

2 This is what Isaiah son of Amoz saw concerning Judah and Jerusalem:

2 In the last days
the mountain of the LORD's temple will be established
as chief among the mountains;
it will be raised above the hills,
and all nations will stream to it.
3 Many peoples will come and say,

"Come, let us go up to the mountain of the LORD,
to the house of the God of Jacob.
He will teach us his ways,
so that we may walk in his paths."
The law will go out from Zion,
the word of the LORD from Jerusalem.
4 He will judge between the nations
and will settle disputes for many peoples.
They will beat their swords into plowshares
and their spears into pruning hooks.
Nation will not take up sword against nation,
nor will they train for war anymore.

5 Come, O house of Jacob,
let us walk in the light of the LORD.

The Day of the LORD

6 You have abandoned your people,
the house of Jacob.
They are full of superstitions from the East;
they practice divination like the Philistines
and clasp hands with pagans.
7 Their land is full of silver and gold;
there is no end to their treasures.
Their land is full of horses;
there is no end to their chariots.
8 Their land is full of idols;
they bow down to the work of their hands,
to what their fingers have made.
9 So man will be brought low
and mankind humbled—
do not forgive them.[a]

10 Go into the rocks,
hide in the ground
from dread of the LORD

> **Isaiah 2:10**
>
> *God Is Majestic*
>
> Go into the rocks,
> hide in the ground
> from dread of the LORD
> and the splendor
> of his majesty!

a 9 Or *not raise them up*

and the splendor of his majesty!
11 The eyes of the arrogant man will be
humbled
and the pride of men brought low;
the LORD alone will be exalted in that day.

12 The LORD Almighty has a day in store
for all the proud and lofty,
for all that is exalted
(and they will be humbled),
13 for all the cedars of Lebanon, tall and lofty,
and all the oaks of Bashan,
14 for all the towering mountains
and all the high hills,
15 for every lofty tower
and every fortified wall,
16 for every trading ship[a]
and every stately vessel.
17 The arrogance of man will be brought low
and the pride of men humbled;
the LORD alone will be exalted in that day,
18 and the idols will totally disappear.

19 Men will flee to caves in the rocks
and to holes in the ground
from dread of the LORD
and the splendor of his majesty,
when he rises to shake the earth.
20 In that day men will throw away
to the rodents and bats
their idols of silver and idols of gold,
which they made to worship.
21 They will flee to caverns in the rocks
and to the overhanging crags
from dread of the LORD
and the splendor of his majesty,
when he rises to shake the earth.

22 Stop trusting in man,
who has but a breath in his nostrils.
Of what account is he?

Judgment on Jerusalem and Judah

3 See now, the Lord,
the LORD Almighty,
is about to take from Jerusalem and Judah
both supply and support:
all supplies of food and all supplies of
water,
2 the hero and warrior,
the judge and prophet,
the soothsayer and elder,
3 the captain of fifty and man of rank,
the counselor, skilled craftsman and
clever enchanter.

4 I will make boys their officials;
mere children will govern them.
5 People will oppress each other—
man against man, neighbor against
neighbor.
The young will rise up against the old,
the base against the honorable.

6 A man will seize one of his brothers
at his father's home, and say,
"You have a cloak, you be our leader;
take charge of this heap of ruins!"
7 But in that day he will cry out,
"I have no remedy.
I have no food or clothing in my house;
do not make me the leader of the
people."

8 Jerusalem staggers,
Judah is falling;
their words and deeds are against the LORD,
defying his glorious presence.
9 The look on their faces testifies against
them;
they parade their sin like Sodom;
they do not hide it.
Woe to them!
They have brought disaster upon
themselves.

10 Tell the righteous it will be well with them,
for they will enjoy the fruit of their
deeds.
11 Woe to the wicked! Disaster is upon them!
They will be paid back for what their hands
have done.

12 Youths oppress my people,
women rule over them.
O my people, your guides lead you astray;
they turn you from the path.

13 The LORD takes his place in court;
he rises to judge the people.
14 The LORD enters into judgment
against the elders and leaders of his
people:

[a]16 Hebrew *every ship of Tarshish*

"It is you who have ruined my vineyard;
the plunder from the poor is in your houses.
15 What do you mean by crushing my people
and grinding the faces of the poor?"
declares the Lord, the LORD Almighty.

16 The LORD says,
"The women of Zion are haughty,
walking along with outstretched necks,
flirting with their eyes,
tripping along with mincing steps,
with ornaments jingling on their ankles.
17 Therefore the Lord will bring sores on the heads of the women of Zion;
the LORD will make their scalps bald."

18 In that day the Lord will snatch away their
finery: the bangles and headbands and crescent
necklaces, 19 the earrings and bracelets and
veils, 20 the headdresses and ankle chains and
sashes, the perfume bottles and charms, 21 the
signet rings and nose rings, 22 the fine robes and
the capes and cloaks, the purses 23 and mirrors,
and the linen garments and tiaras and shawls.

24 Instead of fragrance there will be a stench;
instead of a sash, a rope;
instead of well-dressed hair, baldness;
instead of fine clothing, sackcloth;
instead of beauty, branding.
25 Your men will fall by the sword,
your warriors in battle.
26 The gates of Zion will lament and mourn;
destitute, she will sit on the ground.

4 1 In that day seven women
will take hold of one man
and say, "We will eat our own food
and provide our own clothes;
only let us be called by your name.
Take away our disgrace!"

The Branch of the LORD

2 In that day the Branch of the LORD will be
beautiful and glorious, and the fruit of the land
will be the pride and glory of the survivors in
Israel. 3 Those who are left in Zion, who remain
in Jerusalem, will be called holy, all who are
recorded among the living in Jerusalem. 4 The
Lord will wash away the filth of the women of
Zion; he will cleanse the bloodstains from Jerusalem by a spirit[a] of judgment and a spirit[a]
of fire. 5 Then the LORD will create over all of
Mount Zion and over those who assemble
there a cloud of smoke by day and a glow of
flaming fire by night; over all the glory will be a
canopy. 6 It will be a shelter and shade from the
heat of the day, and a refuge and hiding place
from the storm and rain.

The Song of the Vineyard

5 I will sing for the one I love
a song about his vineyard:
My loved one had a vineyard
on a fertile hillside.
2 He dug it up and cleared it of stones
and planted it with the choicest vines.
He built a watchtower in it
and cut out a winepress as well.
Then he looked for a crop of good grapes,
but it yielded only bad fruit.

3 "Now you dwellers in Jerusalem and men of Judah,
judge between me and my vineyard.
4 What more could have been done for my vineyard
than I have done for it?
When I looked for good grapes,
why did it yield only bad?
5 Now I will tell you
what I am going to do to my vineyard:
I will take away its hedge,
and it will be destroyed;
I will break down its wall,
and it will be trampled.
6 I will make it a wasteland,
neither pruned nor cultivated,
and briers and thorns will grow there.
I will command the clouds
not to rain on it."

7 The vineyard of the LORD Almighty
is the house of Israel,
and the men of Judah
are the garden of his delight.
And he looked for justice, but saw bloodshed;
for righteousness, but heard cries of distress.

[a] 4 Or *the Spirit*

Woes and Judgments

8 Woe to you who add house to house
and join field to field
till no space is left
and you live alone in the land.

9 The LORD Almighty has declared in my hearing:

"Surely the great houses will become desolate,
the fine mansions left without occupants.
10 A ten-acre[a] vineyard will produce only a bath[b] of wine,
a homer[c] of seed only an ephah[d] of grain."

11 Woe to those who rise early in the morning
to run after their drinks,
who stay up late at night
till they are inflamed with wine.
12 They have harps and lyres at their banquets,
tambourines and flutes and wine,
but they have no regard for the deeds of the LORD,
no respect for the work of his hands.
13 Therefore my people will go into exile
for lack of understanding;
their men of rank will die of hunger
and their masses will be parched with thirst.
14 Therefore the grave[e] enlarges its appetite
and opens its mouth without limit;
into it will descend their nobles and masses
with all their brawlers and revelers.
15 So man will be brought low
and mankind humbled,
the eyes of the arrogant humbled.
16 But the LORD Almighty will be exalted by his justice,
and the holy God will show himself holy
by his righteousness.
17 Then sheep will graze as in their own pasture;
lambs will feed[f] among the ruins of the rich.

18 Woe to those who draw sin along with cords of deceit,
and wickedness as with cart ropes,
19 to those who say, "Let God hurry,
let him hasten his work
so we may see it.
Let it approach,
let the plan of the Holy One of Israel come,
so we may know it."

20 Woe to those who call evil good
and good evil,
who put darkness for light
and light for darkness,
who put bitter for sweet
and sweet for bitter.

21 Woe to those who are wise in their own eyes
and clever in their own sight.

22 Woe to those who are heroes at drinking wine
and champions at mixing drinks,
23 who acquit the guilty for a bribe,
but deny justice to the innocent.
24 Therefore, as tongues of fire lick up straw
and as dry grass sinks down in the flames,
so their roots will decay
and their flowers blow away like dust;
for they have rejected the law of the LORD Almighty
and spurned the word of the Holy One of Israel.
25 Therefore the LORD's anger burns against his people;

Isaiah 5:16

God Is Just

But the LORD Almighty
will be exalted by
his justice,
and the holy God will
show himself holy by
his righteousness.

[a]10 Hebrew *ten-yoke,* that is, the land plowed by 10 yoke of oxen in one day [b]10 That is, probably about 6 gallons (about 22 liters) [c]10 That is, probably about 6 bushels (about 220 liters) [d]10 That is, probably about 3/5 bushel (about 22 liters) [e]14 Hebrew *Sheol*
[f]17 Septuagint; Hebrew / *strangers will eat*

his hand is raised and he strikes them
down.
The mountains shake,
and the dead bodies are like refuse in
the streets.
Yet for all this, his anger is not turned
away,
his hand is still upraised.

26 He lifts up a banner for the distant
nations,
he whistles for those at the ends of the
earth.
Here they come,
swiftly and speedily!
27 Not one of them grows tired or stumbles,
not one slumbers or sleeps;
not a belt is loosened at the waist,
not a sandal thong is broken.
28 Their arrows are sharp,
all their bows are strung;
their horses' hoofs seem like flint,
their chariot wheels like a whirlwind.
29 Their roar is like that of the lion,
they roar like young lions;
they growl as they seize their prey
and carry it off with no one to rescue.
30 In that day they will roar over it
like the roaring of the sea.
And if one looks at the land,
he will see darkness and distress;
even the light will be darkened by the
clouds.

Isaiah's Commission

6 In the year that King Uzziah died, I saw
the Lord seated on a throne, high and
exalted, and the train of his robe filled the
temple.
2 Above him were seraphs, each with
six wings: With two wings they covered their
faces, with two they covered their feet, and
with two they were flying.
3 And they were call-
ing to one another:

"Holy, holy, holy is the LORD Almighty;
the whole earth is full of his glory."

4 At the sound of their voices the doorposts
and thresholds shook and the temple was filled
with smoke.

5 "Woe to me!" I cried. "I am ruined! For I
am a man of unclean lips, and I live among a
people of unclean lips, and my eyes have seen
the King, the LORD Almighty."

6 Then one of the seraphs flew to me with a
live coal in his hand, which he had taken with
tongs from the altar.
7 With it he touched my
mouth and said, "See, this has touched your
lips; your guilt is taken away and your sin
atoned for."

8 Then I heard the voice of the Lord saying,
"Whom shall I send? And who will go for us?"
And I said, "Here am I. Send me!"
9 He said, "Go and tell this people:

"'Be ever hearing, but never
understanding;
be ever seeing, but never perceiving.'
10 Make the heart of this people calloused;
make their ears dull
and close their eyes.[a]
Otherwise they might see with their eyes,
hear with their ears,
understand with their hearts,
and turn and be healed."

11 Then I said, "For how long, O Lord?"
And he answered:

"Until the cities lie ruined
and without inhabitant,
until the houses are left deserted
and the fields ruined and ravaged,
12 until the LORD has sent everyone far away
and the land is utterly forsaken.
13 And though a tenth remains in the land,
it will again be laid waste.
But as the terebinth and oak
leave stumps when they are cut down,
so the holy seed will be the stump in the
land."

The Sign of Immanuel

7 When Ahaz son of Jotham, the son of
Uzziah, was king of Judah, King Rezin of
Aram and Pekah son of Remaliah king of Israel
marched up to fight against Jerusalem, but they
could not overpower it.

2 Now the house of David was told, "Aram
has allied itself with[b] Ephraim"; so the hearts of

[a] 9,10 Hebrew; Septuagint *'You will be ever hearing, but never understanding; / you will be ever seeing, but never perceiving.' /* [10] *This people's heart has become calloused; / they hardly hear with their ears, / and they have closed their eyes* [b] 2 Or *has set up camp in*

Isaiah 6:8

Then I heard the voice of the Lord saying, "Whom shall I send? And who will go for us?" And I said, "Here am I. Send me!"

reflection

1 In what ways has worship sustained and encouraged you in the past?

2 What difficult task is God calling you to now? Will you say, like Isaiah, "Here am I, send me"?

3 Take some time to sit quietly and think about God. Let yourself think of his holiness, his majesty, his power, his love. Be still and know that he is God.

RELATED READINGS

1 Kings 17:1–6; Isaiah 50:4–10; Hebrews 13:20–21

Read: Isaiah 6:1–8

WHO LIKES TO TAKE ON TROUBLE? Worse yet, to do so singlehandedly? The task Isaiah faced was a difficult and undesirable one. The Israelites were in a mess—again. They were suffering because of their sinful ways. The problem was so immense and overwhelming that no one seemed able or even available to help.

God himself asked the question, "Whom shall I send? And who will go for us?" Isaiah answered, "Here am I. Send me!"

Wait a minute. What made Isaiah run *to* the problem rather than following the instinct to avoid conflict and personal danger? Isaiah wasn't a damage-control expert or a crisis-management counselor. He was a lone prophet. So how was he equipped to intervene?

What prompted Isaiah to step forward and offer himself to God was an experience in worship that altered him forever. Isaiah saw God seated on his throne in heaven. His senses were overwhelmed with the magnificence of God's presence. He heard the antiphonal singing of the seraphs, whose voices shook the doorposts and thresholds. Smoke filled the sanctuary. Isaiah was humbled and awestruck.

Everything pointed the prophet beyond the current task to the eternal glory of God. The weight of coming face-to-face with God was so intense that it nearly crushed Isaiah. Yet at the same time it revived and rejuvenated him. Seeing God in all his glory and splendor and worshiping him equipped Isaiah to serve God.

Has God called you to a task for which you feel completely inadequate? Perhaps you're parenting a child with a disability, disciplining a rebellious son, caring for an elderly parent, battling to preserve a broken marriage. The key to taking on the extraordinary challenge is to worship God, to spend time in his presence meditating on just how awesome he is. When we praise God's holiness and majesty, when we focus on his strength and wisdom, then we are assured of the courage and vigor he makes available to us—the power to go one more mile, to endure one more day, to love one more hour, to forgive one more time. Like Isaiah, we can face these hard assignments with confidence that if God has called us, he will equip us.

Go to page 829 for your next devotional reading.

Ahaz and his people were shaken, as the trees
of the forest are shaken by the wind.
3Then the LORD said to Isaiah, "Go out, you
and your son Shear-Jashub,[a] to meet Ahaz at
the end of the aqueduct of the Upper Pool, on
the road to the Washerman's Field. 4Say to him,
'Be careful, keep calm and don't be afraid. Do
not lose heart because of these two smoldering
stubs of firewood—because of the fierce anger
of Rezin and Aram and of the son of Remaliah.
5Aram, Ephraim and Remaliah's son have plotted your ruin, saying, 6"Let us invade Judah; let
us tear it apart and divide it among ourselves,
and make the son of Tabeel king over it." 7Yet
this is what the Sovereign LORD says:

"'It will not take place,
it will not happen,
8for the head of Aram is Damascus,
and the head of Damascus is only Rezin.
Within sixty-five years
Ephraim will be too shattered to be a
people.
9The head of Ephraim is Samaria,
and the head of Samaria is only
Remaliah's son.
If you do not stand firm in your faith,
you will not stand at all.'"

10Again the LORD spoke to Ahaz, 11"Ask the
LORD your God for a sign, whether in the deepest depths or in the highest heights."
12But Ahaz said, "I will not ask; I will not put
the LORD to the test."
13Then Isaiah said, "Hear now, you house of
David! Is it not enough to try the patience of
men? Will you try the patience of my God also?
14Therefore the Lord himself will give you[b] a
sign: The virgin will be with child and will give
birth to a son, and[c] will call him Immanuel.[d]
15He will eat curds and honey when he knows
enough to reject the wrong and choose the
right. 16But before the boy knows enough to
reject the wrong and choose the right, the land
of the two kings you dread will be laid waste.
17The LORD will bring on you and on your
people and on the house of your father a time
unlike any since Ephraim broke away from Judah—he will bring the king of Assyria."
18In that day the LORD will whistle for flies
from the distant streams of Egypt and for bees
from the land of Assyria. 19They will all come
and settle in the steep ravines and in the crevices
in the rocks, on all the thornbushes and at all
the water holes. 20In that day the Lord will use
a razor hired from beyond the River[e]—the king
of Assyria—to shave your head and the hair of
your legs, and to take off your beards also. 21In
that day, a man will keep alive a young cow and
two goats. 22And because of the abundance of
the milk they give, he will have curds to eat.
All who remain in the land will eat curds and
honey. 23In that day, in every place where there
were a thousand vines worth a thousand silver
shekels,[f] there will be only briers and thorns.
24Men will go there with bow and arrow, for
the land will be covered with briers and thorns.
25As for all the hills once cultivated by the hoe,
you will no longer go there for fear of the briers
and thorns; they will become places where cattle are turned loose and where sheep run.

Assyria, the LORD's Instrument

8 The LORD said to me, "Take a large scroll
and write on it with an ordinary pen: Maher-Shalal-Hash-Baz.[g] 2And I will call in Uriah
the priest and Zechariah son of Jeberekiah as
reliable witnesses for me."
3Then I went to the prophetess, and she conceived and gave birth to a son. And the LORD
said to me, "Name him Maher-Shalal-Hash-
Baz. 4Before the boy knows how to say 'My father' or 'My mother,' the wealth of Damascus
and the plunder of Samaria will be carried off
by the king of Assyria."
5The LORD spoke to me again:

6"Because this people has rejected
the gently flowing waters of Shiloah
and rejoices over Rezin
and the son of Remaliah,
7therefore the Lord is about to bring against
them
the mighty floodwaters of the River[e]—
the king of Assyria with all his pomp.
It will overflow all its channels,
run over all its banks
8and sweep on into Judah, swirling over it,

[a]3 *Shear-Jashub* means *a remnant will return.* [b]14 The Hebrew is plural. [c]14 Masoretic Text; Dead Sea Scrolls *and he* or *and they* [d]14 *Immanuel* means *God with us.* [e]20,7 That is, the Euphrates [f]23 That is, about 25 pounds (about 11.5 kilograms) [g]1 *Maher-Shalal-Hash-Baz* means *quick to the plunder, swift to the spoil*; also in verse 3.

passing through it and reaching up to
the neck.
Its outspread wings will cover the breadth
of your land,
O Immanuel[a]!"
9 Raise the war cry,[b] you nations, and be
shattered!
Listen, all you distant lands.
Prepare for battle, and be shattered!
Prepare for battle, and be shattered!
10 Devise your strategy, but it will be
thwarted;
propose your plan, but it will not stand,
for God is with us.[c]

Fear God

11 The LORD spoke to me with his strong
hand upon me, warning me not to follow the
way of this people. He said:

12 "Do not call conspiracy
everything that these people call
conspiracy[d];
do not fear what they fear,
and do not dread it.
13 The LORD Almighty is
the one you are to
regard as holy,
he is the one you are to
fear,
he is the one you are to
dread,
14 and he will be a sanctuary;
but for both houses of
Israel he will be
a stone that causes men to
stumble
and a rock that makes
them fall.
And for the people of
Jerusalem he will be
a trap and a snare.
15 Many of them will stumble;
they will fall and be broken,
they will be snared and captured."

16 Bind up the testimony
and seal up the law among my disciples.
17 I will wait for the LORD,
who is hiding his face from the house of
Jacob.
I will put my trust in him.

18 Here am I, and the children the LORD
has given me. We are signs and symbols in
Israel from the LORD Almighty, who dwells on
Mount Zion.

19 When men tell you to consult mediums
and spiritists, who whisper and mutter, should
not a people inquire of their God? Why consult the dead on behalf of the living? 20 To the
law and to the testimony! If they do not speak
according to this word, they have no light of
dawn. 21 Distressed and hungry, they will roam
through the land; when they are famished, they
will become enraged and, looking upward, will
curse their king and their God. 22 Then they
will look toward the earth and see only distress
and darkness and fearful gloom, and they will
be thrust into utter darkness.

To Us a Child Is Born

9 Nevertheless, there will be no more gloom
for those who were in distress. In the past
he humbled the land of Zebulun and the land
of Naphtali, but in the future
he will honor Galilee of the
Gentiles, by the way of the sea,
along the Jordan—

2 The people walking in
darkness
have seen a great light;
on those living in the land
of the shadow of
death[e]
a light has dawned.
3 You have enlarged the
nation
and increased their joy;
they rejoice before you
as people rejoice at the harvest,
as men rejoice
when dividing the plunder.
4 For as in the day of Midian's defeat,
you have shattered
the yoke that burdens them,
the bar across their shoulders,
the rod of their oppressor.

> Isaiah 8:13
>
> *God Is Holy*
>
> "The LORD Almighty is the one you are to regard as holy, he is the one you are to fear, he is the one you are to dread."

[a]8 *Immanuel* means *God with us.* [b]9 Or *Do your worst* [c]10 Hebrew *Immanuel* [d]12 Or *Do not call for a treaty / every time these people call for a treaty* [e]2 Or *land of darkness*

A King by Any Other Name

Read: Isaiah 9:2–7

ACCORDING TO THE SOCIAL SECURITY ADMINISTRATION, Minnie, Ida and Bertha were just a few of the top ten girls' names in the 1880s. Today those names have given way to names such as Kaitlyn, Sarah, Emily and Natalie.

Names are important. Expectant parents spend hours choosing the perfect name for their baby, speaking the names aloud and looking up the meanings. They imagine what their child's name will communicate and how others will respond when they hear the name. Names can shape the child's life in many ways.

God gave his Son Jesus many names when Isaiah recorded this prophecy. The Messiah was to come as a dawning light for the people of God who were living in the darkness of their sins. He was to be a Wonderful Counselor, Mighty God, Everlasting Father and Prince of Peace.

We sometimes don't really think about these names because they are so familiar to us. Speak them slowly aloud. Concentrate on absorbing the meaning of each one.

When Isaiah spoke each of these names to the people of Judah and Israel, he proclaimed the reality of the coming Messiah and of all he would mean to the nation—a nation that was crying out for direction, deliverance and light. The Messiah's names indicate all that he would be to them: One who would listen and guide, One who would rescue them, One who was timeless, One who would care for them like a parent, One who would bring justice and peace to their land.

Which of these names of Jesus holds the most meaning for you today? Do you most need a Wonderful Counselor? Are you most aware of the Mighty God? Perhaps you seek the direction of an Everlasting Father or crave the presence of the Prince of Peace. Whatever name you choose, write it on your daily calendar or put it on a sticky note on your fridge. Throughout the day, think about that name. Ask God to show you how he fulfills all the promise his name holds out to you.

Isaiah 9:6

For to us a child is born,
to us a son is given,
and the government
will be on his shoulders.
And he will be called
Wonderful Counselor,
Mighty God, Everlasting
Father, Prince of Peace.

reflection

1 Which of God's attributes are reflected in the names for Christ given in this passage? Pray and ask God to reveal all that they can mean to you personally.

2 What name do you commonly use to refer to Jesus? How might referring to his various names affect the way you approach times of prayer and solitude with him?

3 How can these names of Jesus be useful in telling others about him?

RELATED READINGS

Exodus 3:13–15;
Luke 1:31–33;
John 8:58

Go to page 833 for your next devotional reading.

5 Every warrior's boot used in battle
and every garment rolled in blood
will be destined for burning,
will be fuel for the fire.
6 For to us a child is born,
to us a son is given,
and the government will
be on his shoulders.
And he will be called
Wonderful Counselor,[a]
Mighty God,
Everlasting Father,
Prince of Peace.
7 Of the increase of his
government and
peace
there will be no end.
He will reign on David's
throne
and over his kingdom,
establishing and upholding
it
with justice and
righteousness
from that time on and forever.
The zeal of the LORD Almighty
will accomplish this.

The LORD's Anger Against Israel

8 The Lord has sent a message against Jacob;
it will fall on Israel.
9 All the people will know it—
Ephraim and the inhabitants of
Samaria—
who say with pride
and arrogance of heart,
10 "The bricks have fallen down,
but we will rebuild with dressed stone;
the fig trees have been felled,
but we will replace them with cedars."
11 But the LORD has strengthened Rezin's foes
against them
and has spurred their enemies on.
12 Arameans from the east and Philistines
from the west
have devoured Israel with open mouth.

Yet for all this, his anger is not turned
away,
his hand is still upraised.

Isaiah 9:6

God Gives Us Hope

For to us a child is born,
to us a son is given,
and the government will
be on his shoulders.
And he will be called
Wonderful Counselor,
Mighty God,
Everlasting Father,
Prince of Peace.

13 But the people have not returned to him
who struck them,
nor have they sought the LORD
Almighty.
14 So the LORD will cut off
from Israel both
head and tail,
both palm branch and
reed in a single day;
15 the elders and prominent
men are the head,
the prophets who teach
lies are the tail.
16 Those who guide this
people mislead
them,
and those who are
guided are led
astray.
17 Therefore the Lord will
take no pleasure in
the young men,
nor will he pity the
fatherless and
widows,
for everyone is ungodly and wicked,
every mouth speaks vileness.

Yet for all this, his anger is not turned
away,
his hand is still upraised.

18 Surely wickedness burns like a fire;
it consumes briers and thorns,
it sets the forest thickets ablaze,
so that it rolls upward in a column of
smoke.
19 By the wrath of the LORD Almighty
the land will be scorched
and the people will be fuel for the fire;
no one will spare his brother.
20 On the right they will devour,
but still be hungry;
on the left they will eat,
but not be satisfied.
Each will feed on the flesh of his own
offspring[b]:
21 Manasseh will feed on Ephraim, and
Ephraim on Manasseh;
together they will turn against Judah.

[a]6 Or *Wonderful, Counselor* [b]20 Or *arm*

Yet for all this, his anger is not turned
away,
his hand is still upraised.

10 Woe to those who make unjust laws,
to those who issue oppressive
decrees,
2 to deprive the poor of their rights
and withhold justice from the oppressed
of my people,
making widows their prey
and robbing the fatherless.
3 What will you do on the day of reckoning,
when disaster comes from afar?
To whom will you run for help?
Where will you leave your riches?
4 Nothing will remain but to cringe among
the captives
or fall among the slain.
Yet for all this, his anger is not turned
away,
his hand is still upraised.

God's Judgment on Assyria

5 "Woe to the Assyrian, the rod of my anger,
in whose hand is the club of my wrath!
6 I send him against a godless nation,
I dispatch him against a people who
anger me,
to seize loot and snatch plunder,
and to trample them down like mud in
the streets.
7 But this is not what he intends,
this is not what he has in mind;
his purpose is to destroy,
to put an end to many nations.
8 'Are not my commanders all kings?' he
says.
9 'Has not Calno fared like Carchemish?
Is not Hamath like Arpad,
and Samaria like Damascus?
10 As my hand seized the kingdoms of the
idols,
kingdoms whose images excelled those
of Jerusalem and Samaria—
11 shall I not deal with Jerusalem and her
images
as I dealt with Samaria and her idols?'"

12 When the Lord has finished all his work
against Mount Zion and Jerusalem, he will say,
"I will punish the king of Assyria for the willful
pride of his heart and the haughty look in his
eyes. 13 For he says:

"'By the strength of my hand I have done
this,
and by my wisdom, because I have
understanding.
I removed the boundaries of nations,
I plundered their treasures;
like a mighty one I subdued[a] their kings.
14 As one reaches into a nest,
so my hand reached for the wealth of the
nations;
as men gather abandoned eggs,
so I gathered all the countries;
not one flapped a wing,
or opened its mouth to chirp.'"

15 Does the ax raise itself above him who
swings it,
or the saw boast against him who uses
it?
As if a rod were to wield him who lifts it
up,
or a club brandish him who is not wood!
16 Therefore, the Lord, the LORD Almighty,
will send a wasting disease upon his
sturdy warriors;
under his pomp a fire will be kindled
like a blazing flame.
17 The Light of Israel will become a fire,
their Holy One a flame;
in a single day it will burn and consume
his thorns and his briers.
18 The splendor of his forests and fertile fields
it will completely destroy,
as when a sick man wastes away.
19 And the remaining trees of his forests will
be so few
that a child could write them down.

The Remnant of Israel

20 In that day the remnant of Israel,
the survivors of the house of Jacob,
will no longer rely on him
who struck them down
but will truly rely on the LORD,

[a] 13 Or *I subdued the mighty,*

the Holy One of Israel.
21 A remnant will return,[a] a remnant of Jacob
will return to the Mighty God.
22 Though your people, O Israel, be like the sand by the sea,
only a remnant will return.
Destruction has been decreed,
overwhelming and righteous.
23 The Lord, the LORD Almighty, will carry out
the destruction decreed upon the whole land.

24 Therefore, this is what the Lord, the LORD Almighty, says:

"O my people who live in Zion,
do not be afraid of the Assyrians,
who beat you with a rod
and lift up a club against you, as Egypt did.
25 Very soon my anger against you will end
and my wrath will be directed to their destruction."

26 The LORD Almighty will lash them with a whip,
as when he struck down Midian at the rock of Oreb;
and he will raise his staff over the waters,
as he did in Egypt.
27 In that day their burden will be lifted from your shoulders,
their yoke from your neck;
the yoke will be broken because you have grown so fat.[b]

Isaiah 11:4

God Is Righteous

But with righteousness he will judge the needy, with justice he will give decisions for the poor of the earth.

28 They enter Aiath;
they pass through Migron;
they store supplies at Micmash.
29 They go over the pass, and say,
"We will camp overnight at Geba."
Ramah trembles;
Gibeah of Saul flees.
30 Cry out, O Daughter of Gallim!
Listen, O Laishah!
Poor Anathoth!
31 Madmenah is in flight;
the people of Gebim take cover.
32 This day they will halt at Nob;
they will shake their fist
at the mount of the Daughter of Zion,
at the hill of Jerusalem.

33 See, the Lord, the LORD Almighty,
will lop off the boughs with great power.
The lofty trees will be felled,
the tall ones will be brought low.
34 He will cut down the forest thickets with an ax;
Lebanon will fall before the Mighty One.

The Branch From Jesse

11 A shoot will come up from the stump of Jesse;
from his roots a Branch will bear fruit.
2 The Spirit of the LORD will rest on him—
the Spirit of wisdom and of understanding,
the Spirit of counsel and of power,
the Spirit of knowledge and of the fear of the LORD—
3 and he will delight in the fear of the LORD.

He will not judge by what he sees with his eyes,
or decide by what he hears with his ears;
4 but with righteousness he will judge the needy,
with justice he will give decisions for the poor of the earth.
He will strike the earth with the rod of his mouth;
with the breath of his lips he will slay the wicked.
5 Righteousness will be his belt
and faithfulness the sash around his waist.
6 The wolf will live with the lamb,
the leopard will lie down with the goat,

[a] 21 Hebrew *shear-jashub*; also in verse 22 [b] 27 Hebrew; Septuagint *broken / from your shoulders*

Perfect Timing

NAAMAN'S WIFE'S SERVANT GIRL

IT WAS A SIMPLE CASE of being in the wrong place at the wrong time. Or was it?

After all, she hadn't signed up to be his household servant. The fact was that she had been kidnapped to serve in Aram (also known as Syria). If anyone had a right to be angry, it was her. She remembered the day the Aramean rabble-rousers crossed her path as if it were yesterday.

She had simply been minding her own business in her homeland of Israel (just southwest of Aram). Sure, she'd heard the stories about the Arameans taking children away from their families. After all, the two countries had several generations of animosity between them. Under King David's rule, Aram had actually paid tribute to Israel. But now Aram had become a powerful threat, and their surprise raids occurred more frequently. All the village mothers warned their children not to linger too long at the well or play outside after dark. *But nothing would happen to her, would it?*

But something did happen to her. She ended up in the enemy's lair—destined to grow up as a servant in a strange land. Wrong place, wrong time. Right?

Right, except the evidence spoke otherwise.

"If it weren't for me," she reasoned, "my master, Naaman, would never have seen Elisha for a cure." And if he hadn't seen Elisha and experienced miraculous healing, he would never have been witness to the power of God. He would never have become the unmistakable, living proof for Israel's God among the very people who'd kidnapped her.

So, was she in the wrong place at the wrong time? "Yes and no," she would later conclude when telling the story to the neighborhood children. It was the worst thing that had ever happened to her, but it was also a great thing that changed the lives of many people.

Certainly, she would have rather stayed near her home in Israel. But God gave her a chance to speak just the right thing, at just the right time, in just the place where God could use her.

—Prayer—

I open myself to your leading, Father. I will be ready when I hear your call, ready to answer in a way that is pleasing to you.

She said to her mistress, "If only my master would see the prophet who is in Samaria! He would cure him of his leprosy."

2 Kings 5:3

ASSIGNED READING:

2 Kings 5:1–27

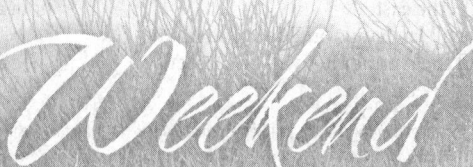

Weekend

Go to page 840 for your next devotional reading.

the calf and the lion and the yearling[a]
together;
and a little child will lead them.
7 The cow will feed with the bear,
their young will lie down together,
and the lion will eat straw like the ox.
8 The infant will play near the hole of the
cobra,
and the young child put his hand into
the viper's nest.
9 They will neither harm nor destroy
on all my holy mountain,
for the earth will be full of the knowledge
of the LORD
as the waters cover the sea.

10 In that day the Root of Jesse will stand
as a banner for the peoples;
the nations will rally to him,
and his place of rest will be
glorious. 11 In that day the
Lord will reach out his hand
a second time to reclaim the
remnant that is left of his people from Assyria, from Lower
Egypt, from Upper Egypt,[b]
from Cush,[c] from Elam, from
Babylonia,[d] from Hamath and
from the islands of the sea.

Isaiah 12:2

God Is Our Salvation

"Surely God is my salvation;
I will trust and not be afraid.
The LORD, the LORD, is my strength and my song;
he has become my salvation."

12 He will raise a banner for
the nations
and gather the exiles of
Israel;
he will assemble the
scattered people of
Judah
from the four quarters of the earth.
13 Ephraim's jealousy will vanish,
and Judah's enemies[e] will be cut off;
Ephraim will not be jealous of Judah,
nor Judah hostile toward Ephraim.
14 They will swoop down on the slopes of
Philistia to the west;
together they will plunder the people to
the east.
They will lay hands on Edom and Moab,
and the Ammonites will be subject to
them.
15 The LORD will dry up
the gulf of the Egyptian sea;
with a scorching wind he will sweep his
hand
over the Euphrates River.[f]
He will break it up into seven streams
so that men can cross over in sandals.
16 There will be a highway for the remnant of
his people
that is left from Assyria,
as there was for Israel
when they came up from Egypt.

Songs of Praise

12 In that day you will say:

"I will praise you, O LORD.
Although you were angry with me,
your anger has turned
away
and you have comforted
me.
2 Surely God is my salvation;
I will trust and not be
afraid.
The LORD, the LORD, is my
strength and my
song;
he has become my
salvation."
3 With joy you will draw
water
from the wells of
salvation.

4 In that day you will say:

"Give thanks to the LORD, call on his
name;
make known among the nations what he
has done,
and proclaim that his name is
exalted.
5 Sing to the LORD, for he has done glorious
things;
let this be known to all the world.
6 Shout aloud and sing for joy, people of
Zion,
for great is the Holy One of Israel among
you."

[a] 6 Hebrew; Septuagint *lion will feed* [b] 11 Hebrew *from Pathros* [c] 11 That is, the upper Nile region [d] 11 Hebrew *Shinar* [e] 13 Or *hostility*
[f] 15 Hebrew *the River*

A Prophecy Against Babylon

13 An oracle concerning Babylon that Isaiah son of Amoz saw:

2 Raise a banner on a bare hilltop,
shout to them;
beckon to them
to enter the gates of the nobles.
3 I have commanded my holy ones;
I have summoned my warriors to carry out my wrath—
those who rejoice in my triumph.

4 Listen, a noise on the mountains,
like that of a great multitude!
Listen, an uproar among the kingdoms,
like nations massing together!
The LORD Almighty is mustering
an army for war.
5 They come from faraway lands,
from the ends of the heavens—
the LORD and the weapons of his wrath—
to destroy the whole country.

6 Wail, for the day of the LORD is near;
it will come like destruction from the Almighty.[a]
7 Because of this, all hands will go limp,
every man's heart will melt.
8 Terror will seize them,
pain and anguish will grip them;
they will writhe like a woman in labor.
They will look aghast at each other,
their faces aflame.

9 See, the day of the LORD is coming
—a cruel day, with wrath and fierce anger—
to make the land desolate
and destroy the sinners within it.
10 The stars of heaven and their constellations
will not show their light.
The rising sun will be darkened
and the moon will not give its light.
11 I will punish the world for its evil,
the wicked for their sins.
I will put an end to the arrogance of the haughty
and will humble the pride of the ruthless.
12 I will make man scarcer than pure gold,
more rare than the gold of Ophir.
13 Therefore I will make the heavens tremble;
and the earth will shake from its place
at the wrath of the LORD Almighty,
in the day of his burning anger.

14 Like a hunted gazelle,
like sheep without a shepherd,
each will return to his own people,
each will flee to his native land.
15 Whoever is captured will be thrust through;
all who are caught will fall by the sword.
16 Their infants will be dashed to pieces
before their eyes;
their houses will be looted and their wives ravished.

17 See, I will stir up against them the Medes,
who do not care for silver
and have no delight in gold.
18 Their bows will strike down the young men;
they will have no mercy on infants
nor will they look with compassion on children.
19 Babylon, the jewel of kingdoms,
the glory of the Babylonians'[b] pride,
will be overthrown by God
like Sodom and Gomorrah.
20 She will never be inhabited
or lived in through all generations;
no Arab will pitch his tent there,
no shepherd will rest his flocks there.

> **Isaiah 13:9**
>
> *God Will Exercise His Wrath*
>
> See, the day of the LORD is coming
> —a cruel day, with wrath and fierce anger—
> to make the land desolate
> and destroy the sinners within it.

[a] 6 Hebrew *Shaddai* [b] 19 Or *Chaldeans'*

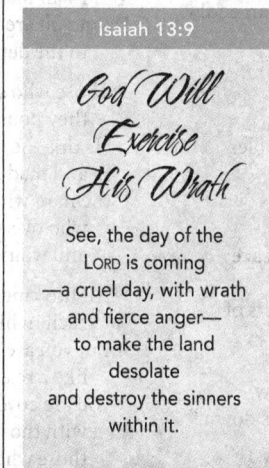

21 But desert creatures will lie there,
jackals will fill her houses;
there the owls will dwell,
and there the wild goats will leap about.
22 Hyenas will howl in her strongholds,
jackals in her luxurious palaces.
Her time is at hand,
and her days will not be prolonged.

14 The LORD will have compassion on Jacob;
once again he will choose Israel
and will settle them in their own land.
Aliens will join them
and unite with the house of Jacob.
2 Nations will take them
and bring them to their own place.
And the house of Israel will possess the nations
as menservants and maidservants in the LORD's land.
They will make captives of their captors
and rule over their oppressors.

3 On the day the LORD gives you relief from
suffering and turmoil and cruel bondage, 4 you
will take up this taunt against the king of Babylon:

How the oppressor has come to an end!
How his fury[a] has ended!
5 The LORD has broken the rod of the wicked,
the scepter of the rulers,
6 which in anger struck down peoples
with unceasing blows,
and in fury subdued nations
with relentless aggression.
7 All the lands are at rest and at peace;
they break into singing.
8 Even the pine trees and the cedars of Lebanon
exult over you and say,
"Now that you have been laid low,
no woodsman comes to cut us down."

9 The grave[b] below is all astir
to meet you at your coming;
it rouses the spirits of the departed to greet you—
all those who were leaders in the world;
it makes them rise from their thrones—
all those who were kings over the nations.
10 They will all respond,
they will say to you,
"You also have become weak, as we are;
you have become like us."
11 All your pomp has been brought down to the grave,
along with the noise of your harps;
maggots are spread out beneath you
and worms cover you.

12 How you have fallen from heaven,
O morning star, son of the dawn!
You have been cast down to the earth,
you who once laid low the nations!
13 You said in your heart,
"I will ascend to heaven;
I will raise my throne
above the stars of God;
I will sit enthroned on the mount of assembly,
on the utmost heights of the sacred mountain.[c]
14 I will ascend above the tops of the clouds;
I will make myself like the Most High."
15 But you are brought down to the grave,
to the depths of the pit.

16 Those who see you stare at you,
they ponder your fate:
"Is this the man who shook the earth
and made kingdoms tremble,
17 the man who made the world a desert,
who overthrew its cities
and would not let his captives go home?"

18 All the kings of the nations lie in state,
each in his own tomb.
19 But you are cast out of your tomb
like a rejected branch;
you are covered with the slain,
with those pierced by the sword,
those who descend to the stones of the pit.
Like a corpse trampled underfoot,
20 you will not join them in burial,

[a]4 Dead Sea Scrolls, Septuagint and Syriac; the meaning of the word in the Masoretic Text is uncertain. [b]9 Hebrew *Sheol*; also in verses 11 and 15 [c]13 Or *the north*; Hebrew *Zaphon*

for you have destroyed your land
and killed your people.

The offspring of the wicked
will never be mentioned again.
21 Prepare a place to slaughter his sons
for the sins of their forefathers;
they are not to rise to inherit the land
and cover the earth with their cities.

22 "I will rise up against them,"
declares the LORD Almighty.
"I will cut off from Babylon her name and survivors,
her offspring and descendants,"
declares the LORD.
23 "I will turn her into a place for owls
and into swampland;
I will sweep her with the broom of destruction,"
declares the LORD Almighty.

A Prophecy Against Assyria

24 The LORD Almighty has sworn,

"Surely, as I have planned, so it will be,
and as I have purposed, so it will stand.
25 I will crush the Assyrian in my land;
on my mountains I will trample him down.
His yoke will be taken from my people,
and his burden removed from their shoulders."

26 This is the plan determined for the whole world;
this is the hand stretched out over all nations.
27 For the LORD Almighty has purposed, and who can thwart him?
His hand is stretched out, and who can turn it back?

A Prophecy Against the Philistines

28 This oracle came in the year King Ahaz died:

29 Do not rejoice, all you Philistines,
that the rod that struck you is broken;
from the root of that snake will spring up a viper,
its fruit will be a darting, venomous serpent.
30 The poorest of the poor will find pasture,
and the needy will lie down in safety.
But your root I will destroy by famine;
it will slay your survivors.

31 Wail, O gate! Howl, O city!
Melt away, all you Philistines!
A cloud of smoke comes from the north,
and there is not a straggler in its ranks.
32 What answer shall be given
to the envoys of that nation?
"The LORD has established Zion,
and in her his afflicted people will find refuge."

A Prophecy Against Moab

15 An oracle concerning Moab:

Ar in Moab is ruined,
destroyed in a night!
Kir in Moab is ruined,
destroyed in a night!
2 Dibon goes up to its temple,
to its high places to weep;
Moab wails over Nebo and Medeba.
Every head is shaved
and every beard cut off.
3 In the streets they wear sackcloth;
on the roofs and in the public squares
they all wail,
prostrate with weeping.
4 Heshbon and Elealeh cry out,
their voices are heard all the way to Jahaz.
Therefore the armed men of Moab cry out,
and their hearts are faint.

5 My heart cries out over Moab;
her fugitives flee as far as Zoar,
as far as Eglath Shelishiyah.
They go up the way to Luhith,
weeping as they go;
on the road to Horonaim
they lament their destruction.
6 The waters of Nimrim are dried up
and the grass is withered;
the vegetation is gone
and nothing green is left.
7 So the wealth they have acquired and stored up
they carry away over the Ravine of the Poplars.

8 Their outcry echoes along the border of
Moab;
their wailing reaches as far as Eglaim,
their lamentation as far as Beer Elim.
9 Dimon's[a] waters are full of blood,
but I will bring still more upon
Dimon[a]—
a lion upon the fugitives of Moab
and upon those who remain in the land.

16 Send lambs as tribute
to the ruler of the land,
from Sela, across the desert,
to the mount of the Daughter of Zion.
2 Like fluttering birds
pushed from the nest,
so are the women of Moab
at the fords of the Arnon.

3 "Give us counsel,
render a decision.
Make your shadow like night—
at high noon.
Hide the fugitives,
do not betray the refugees.
4 Let the Moabite fugitives stay with you;
be their shelter from the destroyer."

The oppressor will come to an end,
and destruction will cease;
the aggressor will vanish from the land.
5 In love a throne will be established;
in faithfulness a man will sit on it—
one from the house[b] of David—
one who in judging seeks justice
and speeds the cause of righteousness.

6 We have heard of Moab's pride—
her overweening pride and conceit,
her pride and her insolence—
but her boasts are empty.
7 Therefore the Moabites wail,
they wail together for Moab.
Lament and grieve
for the men[c] of Kir Hareseth.
8 The fields of Heshbon wither,
the vines of Sibmah also.
The rulers of the nations
have trampled down the choicest vines,
which once reached Jazer
and spread toward the desert.
Their shoots spread out
and went as far as the sea.
9 So I weep, as Jazer weeps,
for the vines of Sibmah.
O Heshbon, O Elealeh,
I drench you with tears!
The shouts of joy over your ripened fruit
and over your harvests have been stilled.
10 Joy and gladness are taken away from the
orchards;
no one sings or shouts in the vineyards;
no one treads out wine at the presses,
for I have put an end to the shouting.
11 My heart laments for Moab like a harp,
my inmost being for Kir Hareseth.
12 When Moab appears at her high place,
she only wears herself out;
when she goes to her shrine to pray,
it is to no avail.

13 This is the word the LORD has already spoken concerning Moab. 14 But now the LORD
says: "Within three years, as a servant bound
by contract would count them, Moab's splendor and all her many people will be despised,
and her survivors will be very few and feeble."

An Oracle Against Damascus

17 An oracle concerning Damascus:

"See, Damascus will no longer be a city
but will become a heap of ruins.
2 The cities of Aroer will be deserted
and left to flocks, which will lie down,
with no one to make them afraid.
3 The fortified city will disappear from
Ephraim,
and royal power from Damascus;
the remnant of Aram will be
like the glory of the Israelites,"
declares the LORD Almighty.

4 "In that day the glory of Jacob will fade;
the fat of his body will waste away.
5 It will be as when a reaper gathers the
standing grain
and harvests the grain with his arm—
as when a man gleans heads of grain
in the Valley of Rephaim.

[a]9 Masoretic Text; Dead Sea Scrolls, some Septuagint manuscripts and Vulgate *Dibon* [b]5 Hebrew *tent* [c]7 Or "*raisin cakes*," a wordplay

6 Yet some gleanings will remain,
as when an olive tree is beaten,
leaving two or three olives on the topmost branches,
four or five on the fruitful boughs,"
declares the LORD, the God of Israel.

7 In that day men will look to their Maker
and turn their eyes to the Holy One of Israel.
8 They will not look to the altars,
the work of their hands,
and they will have no regard for the Asherah poles[a]
and the incense altars their fingers have made.

Isaiah 17:7

God Is Our Maker

In that day men will look
to their Maker
and turn their eyes to the
Holy One of Israel.

9 In that day their strong cities, which they left because of
the Israelites, will be like places
abandoned to thickets and undergrowth. And all will be desolation.

10 You have forgotten God your Savior;
you have not remembered the Rock,
your fortress.
Therefore, though you set out the finest plants
and plant imported vines,
11 though on the day you set them out, you make them grow,
and on the morning when you plant them, you bring them to bud,
yet the harvest will be as nothing
in the day of disease and incurable pain.

12 Oh, the raging of many nations—
they rage like the raging sea!
Oh, the uproar of the peoples—
they roar like the roaring of great waters!
13 Although the peoples roar like the roar of surging waters,
when he rebukes them they flee far away,
driven before the wind like chaff on the hills,
like tumbleweed before a gale.
14 In the evening, sudden terror!
Before the morning, they are gone!
This is the portion of those who loot us,
the lot of those who plunder us.

A Prophecy Against Cush

18 Woe to the land of whirring wings[b]
along the rivers of Cush,[c]
2 which sends envoys by sea
in papyrus boats over the water.

Go, swift messengers,
to a people tall and smooth-skinned,
to a people feared far and wide,
an aggressive nation of strange speech,
whose land is divided by rivers.

3 All you people of the world,
you who live on the earth,
when a banner is raised on the mountains,
you will see it,
and when a trumpet sounds,
you will hear it.
4 This is what the LORD says to me:
"I will remain quiet and will look on
from my dwelling place,
like shimmering heat in the sunshine,
like a cloud of dew in the heat of harvest."
5 For, before the harvest, when the blossom is gone
and the flower becomes a ripening grape,
he will cut off the shoots with pruning knives,
and cut down and take away the spreading branches.
6 They will all be left to the mountain birds of prey
and to the wild animals;
the birds will feed on them all summer,
the wild animals all winter.

7 At that time gifts will be brought to the
LORD Almighty

[a] 8 That is, symbols of the goddess Asherah [b] 1 Or *of locusts* [c] 1 That is, the upper Nile region

Remember

Read: Isaiah 17:7–14

Isaiah 17:10–11

You have forgotten God your Savior; you have not remembered the Rock, your fortress. Therefore, though you set out the finest plants and plant imported vines, though on the day you set them out, you make them grow, and on the morning when you plant them, you bring them to bud, yet the harvest will be as nothing in the day of disease and incurable pain.

IT IS AMAZING THAT we can inhabit creation on this marvelous planet—in the midst of the changing seasons, with natural wonders surrounding us—and not always be aware of our Creator. Yet it happens. The momentum of life picks up, the to-do lists lengthen, the needs around us scream for attention, and before we know it, we have forgotten what is most important.

It's not a new problem. Throughout the Old Testament, God used prophets like Isaiah to confront his people about this very thing. God reminded the people to be mindful of him, to remember their history, to keep their priorities in line—but they had trouble listening. Therefore, their efforts came up empty. They spent time doing what they thought was important, but they harvested only unexpected suffering. Anything they planted and nurtured without consulting the Gardener would come to ruin and disease. Isaiah prophesied that when they forgot that God was their source of life, they would harvest only dead vines and shriveled fruit.

Centuries later, Jesus brought this same metaphor home to his disciples: "I am the true vine, and my Father is the gardener . . . I am the vine; you are the branches. If a man remains in me and I in him, he will bear much fruit; apart from me you can do nothing" (John 15:1,5).

No matter what we do, whether it's planting a vineyard, starting a business, raising children or running a ministry, if we do not consult God, if we are not connected to the Vine, we will not yield a harvest.

It's essential to remember that God is the One who causes us to bear fruit. When life is off kilter, what reminders can you plant in your life to bring you into his presence? Ancient Jews practiced several reminders of God's presence. Their daily rituals and yearly feasts symbolized and celebrated their history with God.

It's important to practice daily and weekly habits that remind us of God's presence. Simple things can help us grow in our faith life: meditating on God's goodness while in the car-pool line, posting a Scripture verse in the kitchen, listening to worship music while getting ready in the morning or taking a prayer walk each day. Be creative in the ways you find to stay connected to the Vine.

reflection

1. Think about a moment when you were especially aware of God's presence in your life. What did that feel like?
2. What do you have in your home that can be your morning and evening reminder of God's presence and power?
3. What difference does it make in your day when you are mindful of God's presence?

RELATED READINGS

Deuteronomy 4:5–9; Psalm 42:1–2; Proverbs 3:1–6

Monday

Go to page 847 for your next devotional reading.

from a people tall and smooth-skinned,
from a people feared far and wide,
an aggressive nation of strange speech,
whose land is divided by rivers—
the gifts will be brought to Mount Zion, the place of the Name of the LORD Almighty.

A Prophecy About Egypt

19 An oracle concerning Egypt:

See, the LORD rides on a swift cloud
and is coming to Egypt.
The idols of Egypt tremble before him,
and the hearts of the Egyptians melt
within them.

2 "I will stir up Egyptian against Egyptian—
brother will fight against brother,
neighbor against neighbor,
city against city,
kingdom against kingdom.
3 The Egyptians will lose heart,
and I will bring their plans to nothing;
they will consult the idols and the spirits of
the dead,
the mediums and the spiritists.
4 I will hand the Egyptians over
to the power of a cruel master,
and a fierce king will rule over them,"
declares the Lord, the LORD Almighty.

5 The waters of the river will dry up,
and the riverbed will be parched and
dry.
6 The canals will stink;
the streams of Egypt will dwindle and
dry up.
The reeds and rushes will wither,
7 also the plants along the Nile,
at the mouth of the river.
Every sown field along the Nile
will become parched, will blow away
and be no more.
8 The fishermen will groan and lament,
all who cast hooks into the Nile;
those who throw nets on the water
will pine away.
9 Those who work with combed flax will
despair,
the weavers of fine linen will lose hope.
10 The workers in cloth will be dejected,
and all the wage earners will be sick at
heart.

11 The officials of Zoan are nothing but fools;
the wise counselors of Pharaoh give
senseless advice.
How can you say to Pharaoh,
"I am one of the wise men,
a disciple of the ancient kings"?
12 Where are your wise men now?
Let them show you and make known
what the LORD Almighty
has planned against Egypt.
13 The officials of Zoan have become fools,
the leaders of Memphis[a] are deceived;
the cornerstones of her peoples
have led Egypt astray.
14 The LORD has poured into them
a spirit of dizziness;
they make Egypt stagger in all that she does,
as a drunkard staggers around in his
vomit.
15 There is nothing Egypt can do—
head or tail, palm branch or reed.

16 In that day the Egyptians will be like
women. They will shudder with fear at the
uplifted hand that the LORD Almighty raises
against them. 17 And the land of Judah will
bring terror to the Egyptians; everyone to
whom Judah is mentioned will be terrified, because of what the LORD Almighty is planning
against them.
18 In that day five cities in Egypt will speak
the language of Canaan and swear allegiance to
the LORD Almighty. One of them will be called
the City of Destruction.[b]
19 In that day there will be an altar to the
LORD in the heart of Egypt, and a monument
to the LORD at its border. 20 It will be a sign and
witness to the LORD Almighty in the land of
Egypt. When they cry out to the LORD because
of their oppressors, he will send them a savior
and defender, and he will rescue them. 21 So the
LORD will make himself known to the Egyptians, and in that day they will acknowledge the
LORD. They will worship with sacrifices and

[a] 13 Hebrew *Noph* [b] 18 Most manuscripts of the Masoretic Text; some manuscripts of the Masoretic Text, Dead Sea Scrolls and Vulgate *City of the Sun* (that is, Heliopolis)

grain offerings; they will make vows to the
LORD and keep them. 22The LORD will strike
Egypt with a plague; he will strike them and
heal them. They will turn to the LORD, and he
will respond to their pleas and heal them.
23In that day there will be a highway from
Egypt to Assyria. The Assyrians will go to
Egypt and the Egyptians to Assyria. The Egyptians and Assyrians will worship together. 24In
that day Israel will be the third, along with
Egypt and Assyria, a blessing on the earth.
25The LORD Almighty will bless them, saying,
"Blessed be Egypt my people, Assyria my handiwork, and Israel my inheritance."

A Prophecy Against Egypt and Cush

20 In the year that the supreme commander, sent by Sargon king of Assyria,
came to Ashdod and attacked and captured
it— 2at that time the LORD spoke through
Isaiah son of Amoz. He said to him, "Take off
the sackcloth from your body and the sandals
from your feet." And he did so, going around
stripped and barefoot.
3Then the LORD said, "Just as my servant
Isaiah has gone stripped and barefoot for three
years, as a sign and portent against Egypt and
Cush,[a] 4so the king of Assyria will lead away
stripped and barefoot the Egyptian captives
and Cushite exiles, young and old, with buttocks bared—to Egypt's shame. 5Those who
trusted in Cush and boasted in Egypt will be
afraid and put to shame. 6In that day the people who live on this coast will say, 'See what has
happened to those we relied on, those we fled
to for help and deliverance from the king of
Assyria! How then can we escape?'"

A Prophecy Against Babylon

21 An oracle concerning the Desert by
the Sea:

Like whirlwinds sweeping through the
southland,
an invader comes from the desert,
from a land of terror.

2 A dire vision has been shown to me:
The traitor betrays, the looter takes loot.
Elam, attack! Media, lay siege!
I will bring to an end all the groaning
she caused.

3 At this my body is racked with pain,
pangs seize me, like those of a woman
in labor;
I am staggered by what I hear,
I am bewildered by what I see.
4 My heart falters,
fear makes me tremble;
the twilight I longed for
has become a horror to me.

5 They set the tables,
they spread the rugs,
they eat, they drink!
Get up, you officers,
oil the shields!

6This is what the Lord says to me:

"Go, post a lookout
and have him report what he sees.
7 When he sees chariots
with teams of horses,
riders on donkeys
or riders on camels,
let him be alert,
fully alert."

8And the lookout[b] shouted,

"Day after day, my lord, I stand on the
watchtower;
every night I stay at my post.
9 Look, here comes a man in a chariot
with a team of horses.
And he gives back the answer:
'Babylon has fallen, has fallen!
All the images of its gods
lie shattered on the ground!'"

10 O my people, crushed on the threshing
floor,
I tell you what I have heard
from the LORD Almighty,
from the God of Israel.

A Prophecy Against Edom

11 An oracle concerning Dumah[c]:

Someone calls to me from Seir,
"Watchman, what is left of the night?

[a] 3 That is, the upper Nile region; also in verse 5 [b] 8 Dead Sea Scrolls and Syriac; Masoretic Text *A lion* [c] 11 *Dumah* means *silence* or *stillness*, a wordplay on *Edom*.

Watchman, what is left of the night?"
12 The watchman replies,
"Morning is coming, but also the night.
If you would ask, then ask;
and come back yet again."

A Prophecy Against Arabia

13 An oracle concerning Arabia:

You caravans of Dedanites,
who camp in the thickets of Arabia,
14 bring water for the thirsty;
you who live in Tema,
bring food for the fugitives.
15 They flee from the sword,
from the drawn sword,
from the bent bow
and from the heat of battle.

16 This is what the Lord says to me: "Within
one year, as a servant bound by contract would
count it, all the pomp of Kedar will come to an
end. 17 The survivors of the bowmen, the warriors of Kedar, will be few." The LORD, the God
of Israel, has spoken.

A Prophecy About Jerusalem

22 An oracle concerning the Valley of Vision:

What troubles you now,
that you have all gone up on the roofs,
2 O town full of commotion,
O city of tumult and revelry?
Your slain were not killed by the sword,
nor did they die in battle.
3 All your leaders have fled together;
they have been captured without using the bow.
All you who were caught were taken prisoner together,
having fled while the enemy was still far away.
4 Therefore I said, "Turn away from me;
let me weep bitterly.
Do not try to console me
over the destruction of my people."

5 The Lord, the LORD Almighty, has a day
of tumult and trampling and terror
in the Valley of Vision,
a day of battering down walls
and of crying out to the mountains.
6 Elam takes up the quiver,
with her charioteers and horses;
Kir uncovers the shield.
7 Your choicest valleys are full of chariots,
and horsemen are posted at the city gates;
8 the defenses of Judah are stripped away.

And you looked in that day
to the weapons in the Palace of the Forest;
9 you saw that the City of David
had many breaches in its defenses;
you stored up water
in the Lower Pool.
10 You counted the buildings in Jerusalem
and tore down houses to strengthen the wall.
11 You built a reservoir between the two walls
for the water of the Old Pool,
but you did not look to the One who made it,
or have regard for the One who planned it long ago.

12 The Lord, the LORD Almighty,
called you on that day
to weep and to wail,
to tear out your hair and put on sackcloth.
13 But see, there is joy and revelry,
slaughtering of cattle and killing of sheep,
eating of meat and drinking of wine!
"Let us eat and drink," you say,
"for tomorrow we die!"

14 The LORD Almighty has revealed this in
my hearing: "Till your dying day this sin will
not be atoned for," says the Lord, the LORD Almighty.

15 This is what the Lord, the LORD Almighty,
says:

"Go, say to this steward,
to Shebna, who is in charge of the palace:
16 What are you doing here and who gave you permission
to cut out a grave for yourself here,
hewing your grave on the height
and chiseling your resting place in the rock?

17 "Beware, the LORD is about to take firm hold of you
and hurl you away, O you mighty man.
18 He will roll you up tightly like a ball
and throw you into a large country.
There you will die
and there your splendid chariots will remain—
you disgrace to your master's house!
19 I will depose you from your office,
and you will be ousted from your position.

20 "In that day I will summon my servant, Eliakim son of Hilkiah. 21 I will clothe him with
your robe and fasten your sash around him and
hand your authority over to him. He will be a
father to those who live in Jerusalem and to the
house of Judah. 22 I will place on his shoulder
the key to the house of David; what he opens
no one can shut, and what he shuts no one can
open. 23 I will drive him like a peg into a firm
place; he will be a seat[a] of honor for the house
of his father. 24 All the glory of his family will
hang on him: its offspring and offshoots—all
its lesser vessels, from the bowls to all the jars.

25 "In that day," declares the LORD Almighty,
"the peg driven into the firm place will give
way; it will be sheared off and will fall, and the
load hanging on it will be cut
down." The LORD has spoken.

A Prophecy About Tyre

23 An oracle concerning Tyre:

Wail, O ships of Tarshish!
For Tyre is destroyed
and left without house or harbor.
From the land of Cyprus[b]
word has come to them.

2 Be silent, you people of the island
and you merchants of Sidon,
whom the seafarers have enriched.
3 On the great waters
came the grain of the Shihor;
the harvest of the Nile[c] was the revenue of Tyre,
and she became the marketplace of the nations.

4 Be ashamed, O Sidon, and you, O fortress of the sea,
for the sea has spoken:
"I have neither been in labor nor given birth;
I have neither reared sons nor brought up daughters."
5 When word comes to Egypt,
they will be in anguish at the report from Tyre.

6 Cross over to Tarshish;
wail, you people of the island.
7 Is this your city of revelry,
the old, old city,
whose feet have taken her
to settle in far-off lands?
8 Who planned this against Tyre,
the bestower of crowns,
whose merchants are princes,
whose traders are renowned in the earth?
9 The LORD Almighty planned it,
to bring low the pride of all glory
and to humble all who are renowned on the earth.

10 Till[d] your land as along the Nile,
O Daughter of Tarshish,
for you no longer have a harbor.
11 The LORD has stretched out his hand over the sea
and made its kingdoms tremble.
He has given an order concerning Phoenicia[e]

> **Isaiah 23:11**
>
> *God Surpasses All*
>
> The LORD has stretched out his hand over the sea and made its kingdoms tremble.
> He has given an order concerning Phoenicia that her fortresses be destroyed.

[a] 23 Or *throne* [b] 1 Hebrew *Kittim* [c] 2,3 Masoretic Text; one Dead Sea Scroll *Sidon, / who cross over the sea; / your envoys* [3] *are on the great waters. / The grain of the Shihor, / the harvest of the Nile,* [d] 10 Dead Sea Scrolls and some Septuagint manuscripts; Masoretic Text *Go through* [e] 11 Hebrew *Canaan*

that her fortresses be destroyed.
12 He said, "No more of your reveling,
O Virgin Daughter of Sidon, now crushed!

"Up, cross over to Cyprus[a];
even there you will find no rest."
13 Look at the land of the Babylonians,[b]
this people that is now of no account!
The Assyrians have made it
a place for desert creatures;
they raised up their siege towers,
they stripped its fortresses bare
and turned it into a ruin.

14 Wail, you ships of Tarshish;
your fortress is destroyed!

15 At that time Tyre will be forgotten for
seventy years, the span of a king's life. But at
the end of these seventy years, it will happen to
Tyre as in the song of the prostitute:

16 "Take up a harp, walk through the city,
O prostitute forgotten;
play the harp well, sing many a song,
so that you will be remembered."

17 At the end of seventy years, the LORD will
deal with Tyre. She will return to her hire as
a prostitute and will ply her trade with all the
kingdoms on the face of the earth. 18 Yet her
profit and her earnings will be set apart for the
LORD; they will not be stored up or hoarded.
Her profits will go to those who live before the
LORD, for abundant food and fine clothes.

The LORD's Devastation of the Earth

24 See, the LORD is going to lay waste
the earth
and devastate it;
he will ruin its face
and scatter its inhabitants—
2 it will be the same
for priest as for people,
for master as for servant,
for mistress as for maid,
for seller as for buyer,
for borrower as for lender,
for debtor as for creditor.
3 The earth will be completely laid waste
and totally plundered.
The LORD has spoken this word.

4 The earth dries up and withers,
the world languishes and withers,
the exalted of the earth languish.
5 The earth is defiled by its people;
they have disobeyed the laws,
violated the statutes
and broken the everlasting covenant.
6 Therefore a curse consumes the earth;
its people must bear their guilt.
Therefore earth's inhabitants are burned
up,
and very few are left.
7 The new wine dries up and the vine
withers;
all the merrymakers groan.
8 The gaiety of the tambourines is stilled,
the noise of the revelers has stopped,
the joyful harp is silent.
9 No longer do they drink wine with a song;
the beer is bitter to its drinkers.
10 The ruined city lies desolate;
the entrance to every house is barred.
11 In the streets they cry out for wine;
all joy turns to gloom,
all gaiety is banished from the earth.
12 The city is left in ruins,
its gate is battered to pieces.
13 So will it be on the earth
and among the nations,
as when an olive tree is beaten,
or as when gleanings are left after the
grape harvest.

14 They raise their voices, they shout for joy;
from the west they acclaim the LORD's
majesty.
15 Therefore in the east give glory to the
LORD;
exalt the name of the LORD, the God of
Israel,
in the islands of the sea.
16 From the ends of the earth we hear
singing:
"Glory to the Righteous One."

But I said, "I waste away, I waste away!
Woe to me!
The treacherous betray!
With treachery the treacherous betray!"
17 Terror and pit and snare await you,

[a]12 Hebrew *Kittim* [b]13 Or *Chaldeans*

O people of the earth.
18 Whoever flees at the sound of terror
will fall into a pit;
whoever climbs out of the pit
will be caught in a snare.

The floodgates of the heavens are opened,
the foundations of the earth shake.
19 The earth is broken up,
the earth is split asunder,
the earth is thoroughly shaken.
20 The earth reels like a drunkard,
it sways like a hut in the wind;
so heavy upon it is the guilt of its rebellion
that it falls—never to rise again.

21 In that day the LORD will punish
the powers in the heavens above
and the kings on the earth below.
22 They will be herded together
like prisoners bound in a dungeon;
they will be shut up in prison
and be punished[a] after many days.
23 The moon will be abashed, the sun
ashamed;
for the LORD Almighty will reign
on Mount Zion and in Jerusalem,
and before its elders, gloriously.

Praise to the LORD

25 O LORD, you are my God;
I will exalt you and
praise your name,
for in perfect faithfulness
you have done marvelous
things,
things planned long ago.
2 You have made the city a
heap of rubble,
the fortified town a ruin,
the foreigners' stronghold a
city no more;
it will never be rebuilt.
3 Therefore strong peoples
will honor you;
cities of ruthless nations
will revere you.
4 You have been a refuge for
the poor,
a refuge for the needy in his distress,
a shelter from the storm
and a shade from the heat.
For the breath of the ruthless
is like a storm driving against a wall
5 and like the heat of the desert.
You silence the uproar of foreigners;
as heat is reduced by the shadow of a
cloud,
so the song of the ruthless is stilled.

6 On this mountain the LORD Almighty will
prepare
a feast of rich food for all peoples,
a banquet of aged wine—
the best of meats and the finest of wines.
7 On this mountain he will destroy
the shroud that enfolds all peoples,
the sheet that covers all nations;
8 he will swallow up death forever.
The Sovereign LORD will wipe away the
tears
from all faces;
he will remove the disgrace of his people
from all the earth.
The LORD has spoken.

9 In that day they will say,

"Surely this is our God;
we trusted in him, and he saved us.
This is the LORD, we trusted in him;
let us rejoice and be glad
in his salvation."
10 The hand of the LORD
will rest on this
mountain;
but Moab will be
trampled under
him
as straw is trampled
down in the
manure.
11 They will spread out their
hands in it,
as a swimmer spreads
out his hands to
swim.
God will bring down their
pride
despite the cleverness[b] of their hands.

Isaiah 25:1

God Is Constantly Faithful

O LORD, you are my God;
I will exalt you and praise
your name,
for in perfect faithfulness
you have done marvelous
things,
things planned long ago.

[a] 22 Or *released* [b] 11 The meaning of the Hebrew for this word is uncertain.

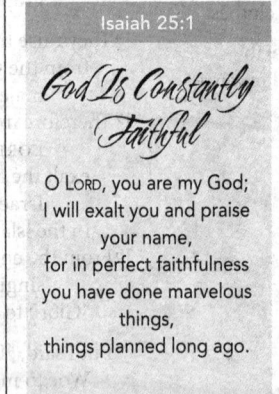

Thank You!

Read: Isaiah 25:1–9

DESPITE ALL THE PROMISES and reminders, sometimes the stain of my sin seems so repugnant and the gift of His grace seems so extravagant that I can hardly believe He bestows it on us ruined sinners so freely. But He does. His Word tells us, "If we confess our sins, he is faithful and just and will forgive us our sins and purify us from all unrighteousness."

Still, I sometimes find myself asking, *Lord, did we hear You right? Did You say* all *unrighteousness? Do You mean* all *my sin, past, present, and future? Even if it's sin I consider little and insignificant, like gossip; or medium-sized, like losing my temper; or great big, like murder and adultery and stealing? Did You really mean* all *my sin is forgiven?*

Then I hear Him whispering to my heart—listen, and you may hear him too: "Anne, the blood of Jesus . . . purifies you from all sin . . . In him you have redemption through his blood, the forgiveness of sins, in accordance with the riches of God's grace . . . Because it is impossible for the blood of bulls and goats to take away your sins . . . Christ came into the world . . . You have been made holy through the sacrifice of the body of Jesus Christ once for all . . . The Holy Spirit also testifies to you about this . . . Your sins and lawless acts I will remember no more."

Hearing these words in my heart, I cry out in gratitude, *Thank You! Thank You! Thank You, dear Jesus, for cleansing me and washing me by Your blood! Based on Your Word, I know I am clean and forgiven. Amen.*

Whew! I feel better. Like I've had a shower after a strenuous work-out! Now . . . *now*, I'm finally ready to *really* talk to Him. And I sense that He is waiting, listening, gently inviting: *Therefore, Anne, since you have confidence to enter the Most Holy Place by the blood of Jesus, by a new and living way opened for you through the curtain, that is, his body, and since you have a great priest over the house of God, draw near to God with a sincere heart in full assurance of faith, having your heart sprinkled to cleanse you from a guilty conscience* [see Hebrews 10:19–22].

—*Anne Graham Lotz*

Isaiah 25:9

In that day they will say, "Surely this is our God; we trusted in him, and he saved us. This is the LORD, we trusted in him; let us rejoice and be glad in his salvation."

reflection

1 Do you, like Anne Graham Lotz, have a difficult time believing that God can forgive you of *all* unrighteousness?

2 Take a few moments to meditate on today's devotional passage. Listen for the voice of assurance in your heart that you have, indeed, been forgiven if you've accepted Christ's sacrifice.

3 Now take the time to "rejoice and be glad in his salvation" (Isaiah 25:9).

RELATED READINGS

Psalms 32:1–2; 103:11–12; Micah 7:19; Mark 2:1–12

Go to page 849 for your next devotional reading.

12 He will bring down your high fortified
walls
and lay them low;
he will bring them down to the ground,
to the very dust.

A Song of Praise

26

In that day this song will be sung in the land of Judah:

We have a strong city;
God makes salvation
its walls and ramparts.
2 Open the gates
that the righteous nation
may enter,
the nation that keeps
faith.
3 You will keep in perfect
peace
him whose mind is
steadfast,
because he trusts in you.

> Isaiah 26:3
>
> *God Brings Peace*
>
> You will keep in
> perfect peace
> him whose mind
> is steadfast,
> because he trusts in you.

4 Trust in the LORD forever,
for the LORD, the LORD,
is the Rock eternal.
5 He humbles those who
dwell on high,
he lays the lofty city low;
he levels it to the ground
and casts it down to the dust.
6 Feet trample it down—
the feet of the oppressed,
the footsteps of the poor.

7 The path of the righteous is level;
O upright One, you make the way of the
righteous smooth.
8 Yes, LORD, walking in the way of your
laws,[a]
we wait for you;
your name and renown
are the desire of our hearts.
9 My soul yearns for you in the night;
in the morning my spirit longs for you.
When your judgments come upon the
earth,
the people of the world learn
righteousness.
10 Though grace is shown to the wicked,
they do not learn righteousness;
even in a land of uprightness they go on
doing evil
and regard not the majesty of the LORD.
11 O LORD, your hand is lifted high,
but they do not see it.
Let them see your zeal for your people and
be put to shame;
let the fire reserved for your enemies
consume them.

12 LORD, you establish peace for us;
all that we have accomplished you have
done for us.
13 O LORD, our God, other
lords besides you
have ruled over us,
but your name alone do
we honor.
14 They are now dead, they
live no more;
those departed spirits do
not rise.
You punished them and
brought them to
ruin;
you wiped out all
memory of them.
15 You have enlarged the
nation, O LORD;
you have enlarged the nation.
You have gained glory for yourself;
you have extended all the borders of the
land.

16 LORD, they came to you in their distress;
when you disciplined them,
they could barely whisper a prayer.[b]
17 As a woman with child and about to give
birth
writhes and cries out in her pain,
so were we in your presence, O LORD.
18 We were with child, we writhed in pain,
but we gave birth to wind.
We have not brought salvation to the earth;
we have not given birth to people of the
world.

19 But your dead will live;
their bodies will rise.
You who dwell in the dust,
wake up and shout for joy.

[a] 8 Or *judgments* [b] 16 The meaning of the Hebrew for this clause is uncertain.

Traveling Heavenward

Read: Isaiah 26:1–21

MARKIE, WHO WAS FIVE YEARS OLD, seemed unusually fixated on heaven because so many people he loved were already there. "Why would anyone rather stay on earth when heaven is such a great place?" he often asked.

"Grammy, I want to go to heaven today!" said Markie.

Grandma laughed and agreed, "Me, too, Markie!"

"Let's go!" he yelled.

She sighed before responding, "Mark, only Jesus can decide when it's time for us to go to heaven."

He paused before asking, "Well, why won't he let us go today?"

"We can't leave earth until our work is done."

The boy processed that thought. Then he noticed the piles of Christmas packages and wrapping paper supplies and exclaimed, "Okay, Grammy, let's get these packages wrapped so we can get our work done, and then Jesus will let us go to heaven."

"Well, he might have other tasks for us to do, too, before our work is over."

Satisfied with that answer, they tackled the packages and talked about what other "jobs" God might have for them that day.

Markie is not the first person to feel the tension of longing for heaven while still living here on earth. The prophet Isaiah spoke for generations of believers who have God's promise that this life is not all there is. There is life after death, and one day we'll wake up in heaven. Our time here is only a tiny dash in the line that stretches toward eternity.

We have the rest of our lives to look forward to, and yet we must focus on the rest of today first. We're headed for home, but we're still on the journey.

Isaiah 26:19

But your dead will live; their bodies will rise. You who dwell in the dust, wake up and shout for joy. Your dew is like the dew of the morning; the earth will give birth to her dead.

reflection

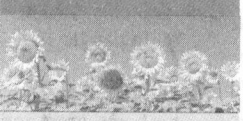

1 What work does God have for you today?

2 How would seeing each day in the context of heaven deepen your desire for intimacy with Jesus?

3 What would happen if, before getting out of bed tomorrow morning, you asked yourself, "How will I travel heavenward today?"

RELATED READINGS

Psalm 84:1–7; 1 Thessalonians 4:13–18; Hebrews 11:1–40

Wednesday

Go to page 852 for your next devotional reading.

Your dew is like the dew of the morning;
the earth will give birth to her dead.

20 Go, my people, enter your rooms
and shut the doors behind you;
hide yourselves for a little while
until his wrath has passed by.
21 See, the LORD is coming out of his dwelling
to punish the people of the earth for their sins.
The earth will disclose the blood shed upon her;
she will conceal her slain no longer.

Deliverance of Israel

27 In that day,

the LORD will punish with his sword,
his fierce, great and powerful sword,
Leviathan the gliding serpent,
Leviathan the coiling serpent;
he will slay the monster of the sea.

2 In that day—

"Sing about a fruitful vineyard:
3 I, the LORD, watch over it;
I water it continually.
I guard it day and night
so that no one may harm it.
4 I am not angry.
If only there were briers and thorns confronting me!
I would march against them in battle;
I would set them all on fire.
5 Or else let them come to me for refuge;
let them make peace with me,
yes, let them make peace with me."

6 In days to come Jacob will take root,
Israel will bud and blossom
and fill all the world with fruit.

7 Has ⌊the LORD⌋ struck her
as he struck down those who struck her?
Has she been killed
as those were killed who killed her?
8 By warfare[a] and exile you contend with her—
with his fierce blast he drives her out,
as on a day the east wind blows.
9 By this, then, will Jacob's guilt be atoned for,
and this will be the full fruitage of the removal of his sin:
When he makes all the altar stones
to be like chalk stones crushed to pieces,
no Asherah poles[b] or incense altars
will be left standing.
10 The fortified city stands desolate,
an abandoned settlement, forsaken like the desert;
there the calves graze,
there they lie down;
they strip its branches bare.
11 When its twigs are dry, they are broken off
and women come and make fires with them.
For this is a people without understanding;
so their Maker has no compassion on them,
and their Creator shows them no favor.

12 In that day the LORD will thresh from
the flowing Euphrates[c] to the Wadi of Egypt,
and you, O Israelites, will be gathered up one
by one. 13 And in that day a great trumpet will
sound. Those who were perishing in Assyria
and those who were exiled in Egypt will come
and worship the LORD on the holy mountain
in Jerusalem.

Woe to Ephraim

28 Woe to that wreath, the pride of Ephraim's drunkards,
to the fading flower, his glorious beauty,
set on the head of a fertile valley—
to that city, the pride of those laid low by wine!
2 See, the Lord has one who is powerful and strong.
Like a hailstorm and a destructive wind,
like a driving rain and a flooding downpour,
he will throw it forcefully to the ground.
3 That wreath, the pride of Ephraim's drunkards,
will be trampled underfoot.
4 That fading flower, his glorious beauty,
set on the head of a fertile valley,
will be like a fig ripe before harvest—

[a] 8 See Septuagint; the meaning of the Hebrew for this word is uncertain. [b] 9 That is, symbols of the goddess Asherah [c] 12 Hebrew *River*

as soon as someone sees it and takes it in
his hand,
he swallows it.

5 In that day the LORD Almighty
will be a glorious crown,
a beautiful wreath
for the remnant of his people.
6 He will be a spirit of justice
to him who sits in judgment,
a source of strength
to those who turn back the battle at the
gate.
7 And these also stagger from wine
and reel from beer:
Priests and prophets stagger from beer
and are befuddled with wine;
they reel from beer,
they stagger when seeing visions,
they stumble when rendering decisions.
8 All the tables are covered with vomit
and there is not a spot without filth.
9 "Who is it he is trying to teach?
To whom is he explaining his message?
To children weaned from their milk,
to those just taken from the breast?
10 For it is:
Do and do, do and do,
rule on rule, rule on rule[a];
a little here, a little there."
11 Very well then, with foreign lips and
strange tongues
God will speak to this people,
12 to whom he said,
"This is the resting place, let the weary
rest";
and, "This is the place of repose"—
but they would not listen.
13 So then, the word of the LORD to them will
become:
Do and do, do and do,
rule on rule, rule on rule;
a little here, a little there—
so that they will go and fall backward,
be injured and snared and captured.

14 Therefore hear the word of the LORD, you
scoffers
who rule this people in Jerusalem.
15 You boast, "We have entered into a
covenant with death,
with the grave[b] we have made an
agreement.
When an overwhelming scourge sweeps by,
it cannot touch us,
for we have made a lie our refuge
and falsehood[c] our hiding place."

16 So this is what the Sovereign LORD says:

"See, I lay a stone in Zion,
a tested stone,
a precious cornerstone for a sure
foundation;
the one who trusts will never be
dismayed.
17 I will make justice the measuring line
and righteousness the plumb line;
hail will sweep away your refuge, the lie,
and water will overflow your hiding
place.
18 Your covenant with death will be annulled;
your agreement with the grave will not
stand.
When the overwhelming scourge sweeps
by,
you will be beaten down by it.
19 As often as it comes it will carry you away;
morning after morning, by day and by
night,
it will sweep through."

The understanding of this message
will bring sheer terror.
20 The bed is too short to stretch out on,
the blanket too narrow to wrap around
you.
21 The LORD will rise up as he did at Mount
Perazim,
he will rouse himself as in the Valley of
Gibeon—
to do his work, his strange work,
and perform his task, his alien task.
22 Now stop your mocking,
or your chains will become heavier;
the Lord, the LORD Almighty, has told me
of the destruction decreed against the
whole land.

[a]10 Hebrew / *sav lasav sav lasav* / *kav lakav kav lakav* (possibly meaningless sounds; perhaps a mimicking of the prophet's words); also in verse 13 [b]15 Hebrew *Sheol*; also in verse 18 [c]15 Or *false gods*

Crowned With Hope

Read: Isaiah 28:1–6

IN THE MIDDLE OF A GRAY TENEMENT BUILDING, there is a cheerful wreath brightening a doorway. Among the broken bottles and litter in a run-down neighborhood, there is a carefully tended garden of flowers. These surprises stand out like beacons, saying, "In this house, hope flourishes. In this house, we believe, even in the midst of deferred dreams and dismal surroundings." Think about a woman you know whose home life you certainly don't envy, yet she holds her head up with dignity and grace. She always imparts a word of encouragement and joy. God encircles her life like a golden crown. She stands out like a beacon of God's presence.

Ephraim, the northern kingdom of Israel, was facing a dismal future as it slid into idolatry. Its wreath of glory was fading fast. Amid Isaiah's prophecy of doom, however, there was a gleam of hope. God had a remnant of faithful people, and God promised to encircle their lives like a glorious crown of strength and hope.

We all can sympathize with the feeling of being trapped in dismal or destructive situations. Perhaps you work with people who see nothing wrong with dishonesty, and you're waging what feels like a losing battle for the truth. Maybe your husband does nothing but discourage or criticize, and you feel yourself fading daily beneath the weight of his words. To those hoping in the darkness, God promises to adorn us with his glory, to encircle our bowed and tired heads with a magnificent wreath: his presence.

God has a special place in his heart for the downtrodden. In reality, we're all beaten back by the world at some point in our day or week. When you feel discouraged or oppressed, picture God's presence, like a lovely wreath, resting on you and strengthening you. Then stand out like a beacon that shines in a world badly in need of hope.

Isaiah 28:5

In that day the LORD Almighty will be a glorious crown, a beautiful wreath for the remnant of his people.

reflection

1 Who do you know who is an example of hope amid dark circumstances? How do you feel when you're around that person?

2 When your surroundings seem dismal, how does God's presence give you renewed hope?

3 God's presence in your life can shine as a beacon to others. Think of a relationship or circumstance in your life that needs an infusion of light today. Pray for God's presence in that situation.

RELATED READINGS

Leviticus 25:35–43; Isaiah 61:1—62:5; Jonah 3:1–10; Romans 8:18–39

Go to page 858 for your next devotional reading.

23 Listen and hear my voice;
pay attention and hear what I say.
24 When a farmer plows for planting, does he plow continually?
Does he keep on breaking up and harrowing the soil?
25 When he has leveled the surface,
does he not sow caraway and scatter cummin?
Does he not plant wheat in its place,[a]
barley in its plot,[a]
and spelt in its field?
26 His God instructs him
and teaches him the right way.

27 Caraway is not threshed with a sledge,
nor is a cartwheel rolled over cummin;
caraway is beaten out with a rod,
and cummin with a stick.
28 Grain must be ground to make bread;
so one does not go on threshing it forever.
Though he drives the wheels of his threshing cart over it,
his horses do not grind it.
29 All this also comes from the LORD Almighty,
wonderful in counsel and magnificent in wisdom.

Woe to David's City

29 Woe to you, Ariel, Ariel,
the city where David settled!
Add year to year
and let your cycle of festivals go on.
2 Yet I will besiege Ariel;
she will mourn and lament,
she will be to me like an altar hearth.[b]
3 I will encamp against you all around;
I will encircle you with towers
and set up my siege works against you.
4 Brought low, you will speak from the ground;
your speech will mumble out of the dust.
Your voice will come ghostlike from the earth;
out of the dust your speech will whisper.
5 But your many enemies will become like fine dust,
the ruthless hordes like blown chaff.
Suddenly, in an instant,
6 the LORD Almighty will come
with thunder and earthquake and great noise,
with windstorm and tempest and flames of a devouring fire.
7 Then the hordes of all the nations that fight against Ariel,
that attack her and her fortress and besiege her,
will be as it is with a dream,
with a vision in the night—
8 as when a hungry man dreams that he is eating,
but he awakens, and his hunger remains;
as when a thirsty man dreams that he is drinking,
but he awakens faint, with his thirst unquenched.
So will it be with the hordes of all the nations
that fight against Mount Zion.

9 Be stunned and amazed,
blind yourselves and be sightless;
be drunk, but not from wine,
stagger, but not from beer.
10 The LORD has brought over you a deep sleep:
He has sealed your eyes (the prophets);
he has covered your heads (the seers).

11 For you this whole vision is nothing but
words sealed in a scroll. And if you give the
scroll to someone who can read, and say to him,
"Read this, please," he will answer, "I can't; it is
sealed." 12 Or if you give the scroll to someone
who cannot read, and say, "Read this, please,"
he will answer, "I don't know how to read."

13 The Lord says:

"These people come near to me with their mouth
and honor me with their lips,
but their hearts are far from me.
Their worship of me
is made up only of rules taught by men.[c]

[a]25 The meaning of the Hebrew for this word is uncertain. [b]2 The Hebrew for *altar hearth* sounds like the Hebrew for *Ariel.* [c]13 Hebrew; Septuagint *They worship me in vain; / their teachings are but rules taught by men*

14 Therefore once more I will astound these
people
with wonder upon wonder;
the wisdom of the wise will perish,
the intelligence of the intelligent will
vanish."
15 Woe to those who go to
great depths
to hide their plans from
the LORD,
who do their work in
darkness and think,
"Who sees us? Who will
know?"
16 You turn things upside
down,
as if the potter were
thought to be like
the clay!
Shall what is formed say to
him who formed it,
"He did not make me"?
Can the pot say of the
potter,
"He knows nothing"?
17 In a very short time, will not Lebanon be
turned into a fertile field
and the fertile field seem like a forest?
18 In that day the deaf will hear the words of
the scroll,
and out of gloom and darkness
the eyes of the blind will see.
19 Once more the humble will rejoice in the
LORD;
the needy will rejoice in the Holy One
of Israel.
20 The ruthless will vanish,
the mockers will disappear,
and all who have an eye for evil will be
cut down—
21 those who with a word make a man out to
be guilty,
who ensnare the defender in court
and with false testimony deprive the
innocent of justice.

22 Therefore this is what the LORD, who redeemed Abraham, says to the house of Jacob:

"No longer will Jacob be ashamed;
no longer will their faces grow pale.
23 When they see among them their children,
the work of my hands,
they will keep my name holy;
they will acknowledge the holiness of
the Holy One of Jacob,
and will stand in awe of
the God of Israel.
24 Those who are wayward
in spirit will gain
understanding;
those who complain will
accept instruction."

Isaiah 29:15

God Knows All Plans

Woe to those who go to
great depths
to hide their plans
from the LORD,
who do their work in
darkness and think,
"Who sees us? Who
will know?"

Woe to the Obstinate Nation

30 "Woe to the obstinate
children,"
declares the LORD,
"to those who carry out
plans that are not
mine,
forming an alliance, but
not by my Spirit,
heaping sin upon sin;
2 who go down to Egypt
without consulting me;
who look for help to Pharaoh's protection,
to Egypt's shade for refuge.
3 But Pharaoh's protection will be to your
shame,
Egypt's shade will bring you disgrace.
4 Though they have officials in Zoan
and their envoys have arrived in
Hanes,
5 everyone will be put to shame
because of a people useless to them,
who bring neither help nor advantage,
but only shame and disgrace."

6 An oracle concerning the animals of the Negev:

Through a land of hardship and distress,
of lions and lionesses,
of adders and darting snakes,
the envoys carry their riches on donkeys'
backs,
their treasures on the humps of camels,
to that unprofitable nation,
7 to Egypt, whose help is utterly useless.
Therefore I call her
Rahab the Do-Nothing.

8 Go now, write it on a tablet for them,
inscribe it on a scroll,
that for the days to come
it may be an everlasting witness.
9 These are rebellious people, deceitful children,
children unwilling to listen to the Lord's instruction.
10 They say to the seers,
"See no more visions!"
and to the prophets,
"Give us no more visions of what is right!
Tell us pleasant things,
prophesy illusions.
11 Leave this way,
get off this path,
and stop confronting us
with the Holy One of Israel!"

12 Therefore, this is what the Holy One of Israel says:

"Because you have rejected this message,
relied on oppression
and depended on deceit,
13 this sin will become for you
like a high wall, cracked and bulging,
that collapses suddenly, in an instant.
14 It will break in pieces like pottery,
shattered so mercilessly
that among its pieces not
a fragment will be found
for taking coals from a hearth
or scooping water out of a cistern."

15 This is what the Sovereign Lord, the Holy One of Israel, says:

"In repentance and rest is your salvation,
in quietness and trust is your strength,
but you would have none of it.
16 You said, 'No, we will flee on horses.'
Therefore you will flee!
You said, 'We will ride off on swift horses.'
Therefore your pursuers will be swift!
17 A thousand will flee
at the threat of one;
at the threat of five
you will all flee away,
till you are left
like a flagstaff on a mountaintop,
like a banner on a hill."

18 Yet the Lord longs to be gracious to you;
he rises to show you compassion.
For the Lord is a God of justice.
Blessed are all who wait for him!

19 O people of Zion, who live in Jerusalem,
you will weep no more. How gracious he will
be when you cry for help! As soon as he hears,
he will answer you. 20 Although the Lord gives
you the bread of adversity and the water of
affliction, your teachers will be hidden no
more; with your own eyes you will see them.
21 Whether you turn to the right or to the left,
your ears will hear a voice behind you, saying,
"This is the way; walk in it." 22 Then you will
defile your idols overlaid with silver and your
images covered with gold; you will throw them
away like a menstrual cloth and say to them,
"Away with you!"

23 He will also send you rain for the seed you
sow in the ground, and the food that comes
from the land will be rich and
plentiful. In that day your cattle will graze in broad meadows. 24 The oxen and donkeys
that work the soil will eat fodder and mash, spread out with
fork and shovel. 25 In the day
of great slaughter, when the
towers fall, streams of water
will flow on every high mountain and every lofty hill. 26 The
moon will shine like the sun,
and the sunlight will be seven
times brighter, like the light of
seven full days, when the Lord
binds up the bruises of his people and heals the wounds he
inflicted.

27 See, the Name of the Lord comes from afar,

Isaiah 30:27

God Is a Consuming Fire

See, the Name of the Lord comes from afar, with burning anger and dense clouds of smoke; his lips are full of wrath, and his tongue is a consuming fire.

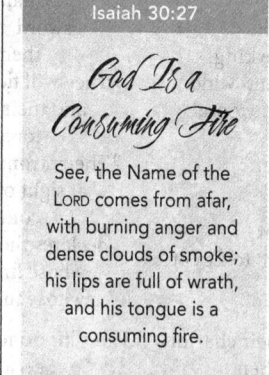

with burning anger and dense clouds of smoke;
his lips are full of wrath,
and his tongue is a consuming fire.
28 His breath is like a rushing torrent,
rising up to the neck.
He shakes the nations in the sieve of destruction;
he places in the jaws of the peoples
a bit that leads them astray.
29 And you will sing
as on the night you celebrate a holy festival;
your hearts will rejoice
as when people go up with flutes
to the mountain of the LORD,
to the Rock of Israel.
30 The LORD will cause men to hear his majestic voice
and will make them see his arm coming down
with raging anger and consuming fire,
with cloudburst, thunderstorm and hail.
31 The voice of the LORD will shatter Assyria;
with his scepter he will strike them down.
32 Every stroke the LORD lays on them
with his punishing rod
will be to the music of tambourines and harps,
as he fights them in battle with the blows of his arm.
33 Topheth has long been prepared;
it has been made ready for the king.
Its fire pit has been made deep and wide,
with an abundance of fire and wood;
the breath of the LORD,
like a stream of burning sulfur,
sets it ablaze.

Woe to Those Who Rely on Egypt

31 Woe to those who go down to Egypt for help,
who rely on horses,
who trust in the multitude of their chariots
and in the great strength of their horsemen,
but do not look to the Holy One of Israel,
or seek help from the LORD.
2 Yet he too is wise and can bring disaster;
he does not take back his words.
He will rise up against the house of the wicked,
against those who help evildoers.
3 But the Egyptians are men and not God;
their horses are flesh and not spirit.
When the LORD stretches out his hand,
he who helps will stumble,
he who is helped will fall;
both will perish together.

4 This is what the LORD says to me:

"As a lion growls,
a great lion over his prey—
and though a whole band of shepherds
is called together against him,
he is not frightened by their shouts
or disturbed by their clamor—
so the LORD Almighty will come down
to do battle on Mount Zion and on its heights.
5 Like birds hovering overhead,
the LORD Almighty will shield Jerusalem;
he will shield it and deliver it,
he will 'pass over' it and will rescue it."

6 Return to him you have so greatly revolted
against, O Israelites. 7 For in that day every one
of you will reject the idols of silver and gold
your sinful hands have made.

8 "Assyria will fall by a sword that is not of man;
a sword, not of mortals, will devour them.
They will flee before the sword
and their young men will be put to forced labor.
9 Their stronghold will fall because of terror;
at sight of the battle standard their commanders will panic,"
declares the LORD,
whose fire is in Zion,
whose furnace is in Jerusalem.

The Kingdom of Righteousness

32 See, a king will reign in righteousness
and rulers will rule with justice.
2 Each man will be like a shelter from the wind
and a refuge from the storm,

like streams of water in the desert
and the shadow of a great rock in a thirsty land.

3 Then the eyes of those who see will no longer be closed,
and the ears of those who hear will listen.
4 The mind of the rash will know and understand,
and the stammering tongue will be fluent and clear.
5 No longer will the fool be called noble
nor the scoundrel be highly respected.
6 For the fool speaks folly,
his mind is busy with evil:
He practices ungodliness
and spreads error concerning the LORD;
the hungry he leaves empty
and from the thirsty he withholds water.
7 The scoundrel's methods are wicked,
he makes up evil schemes
to destroy the poor with lies,
even when the plea of the needy is just.
8 But the noble man makes noble plans,
and by noble deeds he stands.

The Women of Jerusalem

9 You women who are so complacent,
rise up and listen to me;
you daughters who feel secure,
hear what I have to say!
10 In little more than a year
you who feel secure will tremble;
the grape harvest will fail,
and the harvest of fruit will not come.
11 Tremble, you complacent women;
shudder, you daughters who feel secure!
Strip off your clothes,
put sackcloth around your waists.
12 Beat your breasts for the pleasant fields,
for the fruitful vines
13 and for the land of my people,
a land overgrown with thorns and briers—
yes, mourn for all houses of merriment
and for this city of revelry.
14 The fortress will be abandoned,
the noisy city deserted;
citadel and watchtower will become a wasteland forever,
the delight of donkeys, a pasture for flocks,
15 till the Spirit is poured upon us from on high,
and the desert becomes a fertile field,
and the fertile field seems like a forest.
16 Justice will dwell in the desert
and righteousness live in the fertile field.
17 The fruit of righteousness will be peace;
the effect of righteousness will be quietness and confidence forever.
18 My people will live in peaceful dwelling places,
in secure homes,
in undisturbed places of rest.
19 Though hail flattens the forest
and the city is leveled completely,
20 how blessed you will be,
sowing your seed by every stream,
and letting your cattle and donkeys range free.

Distress and Help

33 Woe to you, O destroyer,
you who have not been destroyed!
Woe to you, O traitor,
you who have not been betrayed!
When you stop destroying,
you will be destroyed;
when you stop betraying,
you will be betrayed.

2 O LORD, be gracious to us;
we long for you.
Be our strength every morning,
our salvation in time of distress.
3 At the thunder of your voice, the peoples flee;

Isaiah 33:2

God Gives Daily Strength

O LORD, be gracious to us;
we long for you.
Be our strength every morning,
our salvation in time of distress.

Security

Read: Isaiah 32:9–20

Isaiah 32:9

You women who are so complacent, rise up and listen to me; you daughters who feel secure, hear what I have to say!

SURELY ISAIAH IS ADDRESSING rich women with time to lounge around in opulent comfort, isn't he? Yes, but the complacent women Isaiah describes are nevertheless some of God's chosen and beloved people. Instead of staying true to their covenant with God, they grew accustomed to their easy, luxurious lives and content with empty, religious rituals. Instead of finding their security in God, the strength and resources of their circumstances had sidetracked their loyalty. As a result, Isaiah used them as an example of how the people of Jerusalem had let their values become skewed, and now he had to warn them of an impending disaster.

"In little more than a year you who feel secure will tremble" (verse 10). Why? Because the Assyrians, the most brutal army on the planet, would soon invade their land. Their fields would be trampled, their children viciously slaughtered and the rest of the people taken into captivity. Every ounce of smugness would be shattered; every strain of security, obliterated.

Who has the luxury to be complacent? We've got careers, kids and cleaning to manage. But Isaiah could just as easily be addressing many of us today. External things and relationships so easily distract us from finding our security in God. We all have different methods of trying to find our security outside of God. Some of us try to find security in our looks, while others are affirmation junkies—always looking for one more accolade. Some look for security in a savings account or stock portfolio, having their kids in the "best" schools or living in a safe neighborhood. They have a job, insurance, a healthy body and a healthy checking account. They vacation twice a year and drive a new car. What more could they need?

While some of us may allow these things to lull us into a false sense of security, any one of them could be gone in a moment. Beauty fades, stocks tumble, houses deteriorate and people disappoint us. Hurricanes hit, terrorists strike and cancer can be only a few multiplying cells away. The fact is there is no real security while we live on this earth. It's a frightening fact, but true. God does not want us to live in fear because he promises to be with his people. But only he can provide "secure homes," "peaceful dwelling places," "fertile fields," "quietness and confidence" and "undisturbed places of rest" (verses 15–18).

reflection

1 What source of false security might be the cause of complacency in your life?

2 What distracts you from placing all your trust in God?

3 Write a prayer today that expresses your desire to trust in God as your "soul" security.

RELATED READINGS

Isaiah 31:1–3; 65:17–25; Jeremiah 9:23–24; Haggai 1:3–11; Revelation 21:1–5

"The center of God's will is our only safety."

Betsie ten Boom

Go to page 861 for your next devotional reading.

when you rise up, the nations scatter.
4 Your plunder, O nations, is harvested as
by young locusts;
like a swarm of locusts men pounce
on it.

5 The LORD is exalted, for he dwells on high;
he will fill Zion with justice and
righteousness.
6 He will be the sure foundation for your
times,
a rich store of salvation and wisdom and
knowledge;
the fear of the LORD is the key to this
treasure.[a]
7 Look, their brave men cry aloud in the
streets;
the envoys of peace weep bitterly.
8 The highways are deserted,
no travelers are on the roads.
The treaty is broken,
its witnesses[b] are despised,
no one is respected.
9 The land mourns[c] and wastes away,
Lebanon is ashamed and withers;
Sharon is like the Arabah,
and Bashan and Carmel drop their
leaves.

10 "Now will I arise," says the LORD.
"Now will I be exalted;
now will I be lifted up.
11 You conceive chaff,
you give birth to straw;
your breath is a fire that consumes you.
12 The peoples will be burned as if to lime;
like cut thornbushes they will be set
ablaze."
13 You who are far away, hear what I have
done;
you who are near, acknowledge my
power!
14 The sinners in Zion are terrified;
trembling grips the godless:
"Who of us can dwell with the consuming
fire?
Who of us can dwell with everlasting
burning?"
15 He who walks righteously
and speaks what is right,
who rejects gain from extortion
and keeps his hand from accepting
bribes,
who stops his ears against plots of murder
and shuts his eyes against contemplating
evil—
16 this is the man who will dwell on the
heights,
whose refuge will be the mountain
fortress.
His bread will be supplied,
and water will not fail him.

17 Your eyes will see the king in his beauty
and view a land that stretches afar.
18 In your thoughts you will ponder the
former terror:
"Where is that chief officer?
Where is the one who took the revenue?
Where is the officer in charge of the
towers?"
19 You will see those arrogant people no
more,
those people of an obscure speech,
with their strange, incomprehensible
tongue.

20 Look upon Zion, the city of our festivals;
your eyes will see Jerusalem,
a peaceful abode, a tent that will not be
moved;
its stakes will never be pulled up,
nor any of its ropes broken.
21 There the LORD will be our Mighty One.
It will be like a place of broad rivers and
streams.
No galley with oars will ride them,
no mighty ship will sail them.
22 For the LORD is our judge,
the LORD is our lawgiver,
the LORD is our king;
it is he who will save us.

23 Your rigging hangs loose:
The mast is not held secure,
the sail is not spread.
Then an abundance of spoils will be
divided
and even the lame will carry off plunder.

[a]6 Or *is a treasure from him* [b]8 Dead Sea Scrolls; Masoretic Text / *the cities* [c]9 Or *dries up*

24 No one living in Zion will say, "I am ill";
and the sins of those who dwell there
will be forgiven.

Judgment Against the Nations

34 Come near, you nations, and listen;
pay attention, you peoples!
Let the earth hear, and all that is in it,
the world, and all that comes out of it!
2 The LORD is angry with all nations;
his wrath is upon all their armies.
He will totally destroy[a] them,
he will give them over to slaughter.
3 Their slain will be thrown out,
their dead bodies will send up a stench;
the mountains will be soaked with their
blood.
4 All the stars of the heavens will be
dissolved
and the sky rolled up like a scroll;
all the starry host will fall
like withered leaves from the vine,
like shriveled figs from the fig tree.

5 My sword has drunk its fill in the
heavens;
see, it descends in judgment on Edom,
the people I have totally destroyed.
6 The sword of the LORD is bathed in blood,
it is covered with fat—
the blood of lambs and goats,
fat from the kidneys of rams.
For the LORD has a sacrifice in Bozrah
and a great slaughter in Edom.
7 And the wild oxen will fall with them,
the bull calves and the great bulls.
Their land will be drenched with blood,
and the dust will be soaked with fat.

8 For the LORD has a day of vengeance,
a year of retribution, to uphold Zion's
cause.
9 Edom's streams will be turned into pitch,
her dust into burning sulfur;
her land will become blazing pitch!
10 It will not be quenched night and day;
its smoke will rise forever.
From generation to generation it will lie
desolate;
no one will ever pass through it again.
11 The desert owl[b] and screech owl[b] will
possess it;
the great owl[b] and the raven will nest
there.
God will stretch out over Edom
the measuring line of chaos
and the plumb line of desolation.
12 Her nobles will have nothing there to be
called a kingdom,
all her princes will vanish away.
13 Thorns will overrun her citadels,
nettles and brambles her strongholds.
She will become a haunt for jackals,
a home for owls.
14 Desert creatures will meet with hyenas,
and wild goats will bleat to each other;
there the night creatures will also repose
and find for themselves places of rest.
15 The owl will nest there and lay eggs,
she will hatch them, and care for her
young under the shadow of her
wings;
there also the falcons will gather,
each with its mate.

16 Look in the scroll of the LORD and read:

None of these will be missing,
not one will lack her mate.
For it is his mouth that has given the order,
and his Spirit will gather them together.
17 He allots their portions;
his hand distributes them by measure.
They will possess it forever
and dwell there from generation to
generation.

Joy of the Redeemed

35 The desert and the parched land will
be glad;
the wilderness will rejoice and blossom.
Like the crocus, 2 it will burst into bloom;
it will rejoice greatly and shout for joy.
The glory of Lebanon will be given to it,
the splendor of Carmel and Sharon;
they will see the glory of the LORD,
the splendor of our God.

3 Strengthen the feeble hands,
steady the knees that give way;

[a] 2 The Hebrew term refers to the irrevocable giving over of things or persons to the LORD, often by totally destroying them; also in verse 5.
[b] 11 The precise identification of these birds is uncertain.

Family Ties

ATHALIAH

LIKE ANY BRIDE, she made sure her wedding day was all she had dreamed of. But unlike other brides, she intended for her marriage to go down in history—for all the wrong reasons.

On the groom's side of the family: Jehoram, the firstborn son of King Jehoshaphat, king of Judah—a bold leader with a wicked weakness for nepotism. And on the bride's? King Ahab, renowned for his Baal worship and evil choices. Athaliah and her betrothed had been anticipating this day for a long time, the day they would be joined in a partnership that would advance their mutual agendas: reigning with a singleminded focus and making sure there was no one left alive to make a counterclaim to the throne.

But if Athaliah was going to make history, she would have to surpass someone she had known and watched throughout her formative years: Queen Jezebel, King Ahab's infamous wife. Jezebel was considered as one of the most ruthless rulers in the history of Israel. And growing up in the palace, Athaliah had seen Jezebel persecute the opposition without mercy.

With her eye on her goal, it didn't take long for her treachery to trump that of her murderous family. Instead of grieving her son's tragic death, she seized the moment. She nonchalantly killed all of his children—her own grandchildren—in order to solidify her position as queen. Therefore, nothing stood in the way as she seized power. Athaliah finally put all that she'd learned into practice. And then some. In her mind, she was unstoppable.

Just like Jezebel had once thought too.

—Prayer—

"A good name is more desirable than great riches; to be esteemed is better than silver or gold" (Proverbs 22:1).

All the people of the land rejoiced. And the city was quiet, because Athaliah had been slain with the sword.

2 Chronicles 23:21

ASSIGNED READING:

2 Kings 8:25—11:20;
2 Chronicles 22:10–12; 24:1–8

Weekend

Go to page 863 for your next devotional reading.

4 say to those with fearful hearts,
"Be strong, do not fear;
your God will come,
he will come with vengeance;
with divine retribution
he will come to save you."

5 Then will the eyes of the blind be opened
and the ears of the deaf unstopped.
6 Then will the lame leap like a deer,
and the mute tongue shout for joy.
Water will gush forth in the wilderness
and streams in the desert.
7 The burning sand will become a pool,
the thirsty ground bubbling springs.
In the haunts where jackals once lay,
grass and reeds and papyrus will grow.

8 And a highway will be there;
it will be called the Way of Holiness.
The unclean will not journey on it;
it will be for those who walk in that
Way;
wicked fools will not go about on it.[a]
9 No lion will be there,
nor will any ferocious
beast get up on it;
they will not be found
there.
But only the redeemed will
walk there,
10 and the ransomed of the
Lord will return.
They will enter Zion with
singing;
everlasting joy will
crown their heads.
Gladness and joy will
overtake them,
and sorrow and sighing
will flee away.

Isaiah 35:10

God Extends Everlasting Joy

And the ransomed of the Lord will return. They will enter Zion with singing; everlasting joy will crown their heads.

Sennacherib Threatens Jerusalem

36 In the fourteenth year of King Hezekiah's reign, Sennacherib king of
Assyria attacked all the fortified cities of Judah and captured them. 2Then the king of
Assyria sent his field commander with a large
army from Lachish to King Hezekiah at Jerusalem. When the commander stopped at the
aqueduct of the Upper Pool, on the road
to the Washerman's Field, 3Eliakim son of
Hilkiah the palace administrator, Shebna the
secretary, and Joah son of Asaph the recorder
went out to him.

4The field commander said to them, "Tell
Hezekiah,

"'This is what the great king, the king
of Assyria, says: On what are you basing
this confidence of yours? 5You say you
have strategy and military strength—but
you speak only empty words. On whom
are you depending, that you rebel against
me? 6Look now, you are depending on
Egypt, that splintered reed of a staff,
which pierces a man's hand and wounds
him if he leans on it! Such is Pharaoh
king of Egypt to all who depend on
him. 7And if you say to me, "We are depending on the Lord our God"—isn't
he the one whose high places and
altars Hezekiah removed, saying to Judah
and Jerusalem, "You must worship before
this altar"?

8"'Come now, make a
bargain with my master, the
king of Assyria: I will give
you two thousand horses—if
you can put riders on them!
9How then can you repulse
one officer of the least of
my master's officials, even
though you are depending
on Egypt for chariots and
horsemen? 10Furthermore,
have I come to attack and destroy this land without the
Lord? The Lord himself
told me to march against this
country and destroy it.'"

11Then Eliakim, Shebna and Joah said to
the field commander, "Please speak to your
servants in Aramaic, since we understand it.
Don't speak to us in Hebrew in the hearing of
the people on the wall."

12But the commander replied, "Was it only
to your master and you that my master sent me
to say these things, and not to the men sitting

[a] 8 Or / *the simple will not stray from it*

Are We There Yet?

Read: Isaiah 35:1–10

ANYONE WHO HAS EVER TAKEN a road trip with small children can anticipate the question. Kids seldom understand the concept of time and distance. It might be many miles yet to Grandma's house, but restless children pepper their parents with questions before they've even reached the turnpike. "Are we there yet?"

Scripture often describes our lives in terms of a spiritual journey. "Therefore, strengthen your feeble arms and weak knees. Make level paths for your feet," wrote the author of Hebrews (Hebrews 12:12–13). The prophet Jeremiah gave this travel advisory: "Set up road signs; put up guideposts. Take note of the highway, the road that you take" (Jeremiah 31:21).

Some stretches of our spiritual roadway are straight and smooth; others are marred by a habitual sin, a time of distance from God or another difficulty that makes our path "rocky." Isaiah wrote of a different kind of highway: a highway of holiness. In Biblical times, certain roads between temples could only be used by those who were ceremonially clean; therefore, "the Way of Holiness" refers to an actual, literal road.

Spiritually speaking, we are on a path that is leading somewhere. How do we know if we are on the highway of holiness in our own journeys? The book of Romans contains signposts often referred to as the "Roman Road," and the direction they point concludes with this promise: "If you confess with your mouth, 'Jesus is Lord,' and believe in your heart that God raised him from the dead, you will be saved" (Romans 10:9). When it comes to our final destination, none of us is "there yet," but we have God's Word to lead us in the right direction. Author and speaker Patsy Clairmont wrote, "I don't know where the long and winding road is leading you, but I do know this: if you remember passing Calvary, you are on the right road."

Isaiah 35:8

And a highway will be there; it will be called the Way of Holiness. The unclean will not journey on it; it will be for those who walk in that Way; wicked fools will not go about on it.

reflection

1. What does the concept of a "highway of holiness" mean to you personally?
2. How do you reconcile the disparity between God's holiness and your own imperfections?
3. Take a look at Romans 3–10 and identify the various signposts of faith on "the Roman Road."

RELATED READINGS

Isaiah 40:3–5;
Romans 3:23; 5:8; 6:23; 10:9–13

"We have ample evidence that the Lord is able to guide."

Elisabeth Elliot

Go to page 868 for your next devotional reading.

on the wall—who, like you, will have to eat
their own filth and drink their own urine?"
13 Then the commander stood and called out
in Hebrew, "Hear the words of the great king,
the king of Assyria! 14 This is what the king says:
Do not let Hezekiah deceive you. He cannot
deliver you! 15 Do not let Hezekiah persuade
you to trust in the LORD when he says, 'The
LORD will surely deliver us; this city will not be
given into the hand of the king of Assyria.'
16 "Do not listen to Hezekiah. This is what
the king of Assyria says: Make peace with me
and come out to me. Then every one of you will
eat from his own vine and fig tree and drink
water from his own cistern, 17 until I come and
take you to a land like your own—a land of
grain and new wine, a land of bread and vineyards.
18 "Do not let Hezekiah mislead you when
he says, 'The LORD will deliver us.' Has the
god of any nation ever delivered his land from
the hand of the king of Assyria? 19 Where
are the gods of Hamath and Arpad? Where are
the gods of Sepharvaim? Have they rescued
Samaria from my hand? 20 Who of all the gods
of these countries has been able to save his land
from me? How then can the LORD deliver Jerusalem from my hand?"
21 But the people remained silent and said
nothing in reply, because the king had commanded, "Do not answer him."
22 Then Eliakim son of Hilkiah the palace administrator, Shebna the secretary, and Joah son
of Asaph the recorder went to Hezekiah, with
their clothes torn, and told him what the field
commander had said.

Jerusalem's Deliverance Foretold

37 When King Hezekiah heard this, he
tore his clothes and put on sackcloth
and went into the temple of the LORD. 2 He sent
Eliakim the palace administrator, Shebna the
secretary, and the leading priests, all wearing
sackcloth, to the prophet Isaiah son of Amoz.
3 They told him, "This is what Hezekiah says:
This day is a day of distress and rebuke and disgrace, as when children come to the point of
birth and there is no strength to deliver them.
4 It may be that the LORD your God will hear
the words of the field commander, whom his
master, the king of Assyria, has sent to ridicule
the living God, and that he will rebuke him for
the words the LORD your God has heard. Therefore pray for the remnant that still survives."
5 When King Hezekiah's officials came to
Isaiah, 6 Isaiah said to them, "Tell your master,
'This is what the LORD says: Do not be afraid of
what you have heard—those words with which
the underlings of the king of Assyria have blasphemed me. 7 Listen! I am going to put a spirit
in him so that when he hears a certain report,
he will return to his own country, and there I
will have him cut down with the sword.'"
8 When the field commander heard that the
king of Assyria had left Lachish, he withdrew
and found the king fighting against Libnah.
9 Now Sennacherib received a report that
Tirhakah, the Cushite[a] king ⌞of Egypt⌟, was
marching out to fight against him. When he
heard it, he sent messengers to Hezekiah with
this word: 10 "Say to Hezekiah king of Judah:
Do not let the god you depend on deceive you
when he says, 'Jerusalem will not be handed
over to the king of Assyria.' 11 Surely you have
heard what the kings of Assyria have done to
all the countries, destroying them completely.
And will you be delivered? 12 Did the gods of
the nations that were destroyed by my forefathers deliver them—the gods of Gozan, Haran,
Rezeph and the people of Eden who were in Tel
Assar? 13 Where is the king of Hamath, the king
of Arpad, the king of the city of Sepharvaim, or
of Hena or Ivvah?"

Hezekiah's Prayer

14 Hezekiah received the letter from the messengers and read it. Then he went up to the temple of the LORD and spread it out before the
LORD. 15 And Hezekiah prayed to the LORD:
16 "O LORD Almighty, God of Israel, enthroned
between the cherubim, you alone are God over
all the kingdoms of the earth. You have made
heaven and earth. 17 Give ear, O LORD, and
hear; open your eyes, O LORD, and see; listen
to all the words Sennacherib has sent to insult
the living God.
18 "It is true, O LORD, that the Assyrian kings
have laid waste all these peoples and their
lands. 19 They have thrown their gods into the
fire and destroyed them, for they were not gods

[a] 9 That is, from the upper Nile region

but only wood and stone, fashioned by human
hands. 20Now, O LORD our God, deliver us
from his hand, so that all kingdoms on earth
may know that you alone, O LORD, are God.[a]"

Sennacherib's Fall

21Then Isaiah son of Amoz sent a message
to Hezekiah: "This is what the LORD, the God
of Israel, says: Because you have prayed to me
concerning Sennacherib king of Assyria, 22this
is the word the LORD has spoken against him:

"The Virgin Daughter of Zion
despises and mocks you.
The Daughter of Jerusalem
tosses her head as you flee.
23Who is it you have insulted and blasphemed?
Against whom have you raised your voice
and lifted your eyes in pride?
Against the Holy One of Israel!
24By your messengers
you have heaped insults on the Lord.
And you have said,
'With my many chariots
I have ascended the heights of the mountains,
the utmost heights of Lebanon.
I have cut down its tallest cedars,
the choicest of its pines.
I have reached its remotest heights,
the finest of its forests.
25I have dug wells in foreign lands[b]
and drunk the water there.
With the soles of my feet
I have dried up all the streams of Egypt.'

26"Have you not heard?
Long ago I ordained it.
In days of old I planned it;
now I have brought it to pass,
that you have turned fortified cities
into piles of stone.
27Their people, drained of power,
are dismayed and put to shame.
They are like plants in the field,
like tender green shoots,
like grass sprouting on the roof,
scorched[c] before it grows up.

28"But I know where you stay
and when you come and go
and how you rage against me.
29Because you rage against me
and because your insolence has reached my ears,
I will put my hook in your nose
and my bit in your mouth,
and I will make you return
by the way you came.

30"This will be the sign for you, O Hezekiah:

"This year you will eat what grows by itself,
and the second year what springs from that.
But in the third year sow and reap,
plant vineyards and eat their fruit.
31Once more a remnant of the house of Judah
will take root below and bear fruit above.
32For out of Jerusalem will come a remnant,
and out of Mount Zion a band of survivors.
The zeal of the LORD Almighty
will accomplish this.

33"Therefore this is what the LORD says concerning the king of Assyria:

"He will not enter this city
or shoot an arrow here.
He will not come before it with shield
or build a siege ramp against it.
34By the way that he came he will return;
he will not enter this city,"
declares the LORD.
35"I will defend this city and save it,
for my sake and for the sake of David
my servant!"

36Then the angel of the LORD went out and
put to death a hundred and eighty-five thousand men in the Assyrian camp. When the people got up the next morning—there were all the
dead bodies! 37So Sennacherib king of Assyria

[a] 20 Dead Sea Scrolls (see also 2 Kings 19:19); Masoretic Text *alone are the LORD* [b] 25 Dead Sea Scrolls (see also 2 Kings 19:24); Masoretic Text does not have *in foreign lands.* [c] 27 Some manuscripts of the Masoretic Text, Dead Sea Scrolls and some Septuagint manuscripts (see also 2 Kings 19:26); most manuscripts of the Masoretic Text *roof / and terraced fields*

broke camp and withdrew. He returned to Nineveh and stayed there.
38One day, while he was worshiping in the
temple of his god Nisroch, his sons Adram-
melech and Sharezer cut him down with the
sword, and they escaped to the land of Ararat. And Esarhaddon his son succeeded him
as king.

Hezekiah's Illness

38 In those days Hezekiah became ill and
was at the point of death. The prophet
Isaiah son of Amoz went to him and said,
"This is what the LORD says: Put your house
in order, because you are going to die; you will
not recover."
2Hezekiah turned his face to the wall and
prayed to the LORD, 3"Remember, O LORD,
how I have walked before you faithfully and
with wholehearted devotion and have done
what is good in your eyes." And Hezekiah wept
bitterly.
4Then the word of the LORD came to Isaiah: 5"Go and tell Hezekiah, 'This is what the
LORD, the God of your father David, says: I
have heard your prayer and seen your tears; I
will add fifteen years to your life. 6And I will
deliver you and this city from the hand of the
king of Assyria. I will defend this city.
7" 'This is the LORD's sign to you that the
LORD will do what he has promised: 8I will
make the shadow cast by the sun go back the
ten steps it has gone down on
the stairway of Ahaz.'" So the
sunlight went back the ten
steps it had gone down.

9A writing of Hezekiah king
of Judah after his illness and recovery:

10I said, "In the prime of my
life
must I go through the
gates of death[a]
and be robbed of the rest
of my years?"
11I said, "I will not again see
the LORD,
the LORD, in the land of the living;
no longer will I look on mankind,
or be with those who now dwell in this
world.[b]
12Like a shepherd's tent my house
has been pulled down and taken from
me.
Like a weaver I have rolled up my life,
and he has cut me off from the loom;
day and night you made an end of me.
13I waited patiently till dawn,
but like a lion he broke all my bones;
day and night you made an end of me.
14I cried like a swift or thrush,
I moaned like a mourning dove.
My eyes grew weak as I looked to the
heavens.
I am troubled; O Lord, come to my
aid!"

15But what can I say?
He has spoken to me, and he himself has
done this.
I will walk humbly all my years
because of this anguish of my soul.
16Lord, by such things men live;
and my spirit finds life in them too.
You restored me to health
and let me live.
17Surely it was for my benefit
that I suffered such anguish.
In your love you kept me
from the pit of destruction;
you have put all my sins
behind your back.
18For the grave[a] cannot
praise you,
death cannot sing your
praise;
those who go down to the
pit
cannot hope for your
faithfulness.
19The living, the living—they
praise you,
as I am doing today;
fathers tell their children
about your faithfulness.

20The LORD will save me,
and we will sing with stringed
instruments

> **Isaiah 38:19**
>
> *God Is Dependable*
>
> The living, the living—
> they praise you,
> as I am doing today;
> fathers tell their children
> about your faithfulness.

[a]10,18 Hebrew *Sheol* [b]11 A few Hebrew manuscripts; most Hebrew manuscripts *in the place of cessation*

all the days of our lives
in the temple of the LORD.

21 Isaiah had said, "Prepare a poultice of figs
and apply it to the boil, and he will recover."
22 Hezekiah had asked, "What will be the sign
that I will go up to the temple of the LORD?"

Envoys From Babylon

39 At that time Merodach-Baladan son of Baladan king of Babylon sent Hezekiah letters and a gift, because he had heard of his illness and recovery. 2 Hezekiah received the envoys gladly and showed them what was in his storehouses—the silver, the gold, the spices, the fine oil, his entire armory and everything found among his treasures. There was nothing in his palace or in all his kingdom that Hezekiah did not show them.

3 Then Isaiah the prophet went to King Hezekiah and asked, "What did those men say, and where did they come from?"

"From a distant land," Hezekiah replied. "They came to me from Babylon."

4 The prophet asked, "What did they see in your palace?"

"They saw everything in my palace," Hezekiah said. "There is nothing among my treasures that I did not show them."

5 Then Isaiah said to Hezekiah, "Hear the
word of the LORD Almighty: 6 The time will surely come when everything in your palace, and all that your fathers have stored up until this day, will be carried off to Babylon. Nothing will be left, says the LORD.
7 And some of your descendants, your own flesh and blood who will be born to you, will be taken away, and they will become eunuchs in the palace of the king of Babylon."

8 "The word of the LORD you have spoken is good," Hezekiah replied. For he thought, "There will be peace and security in my lifetime."

Comfort for God's People

40 Comfort, comfort my people,
says your God.
2 Speak tenderly to Jerusalem,
and proclaim to her
that her hard service has been completed,
that her sin has been paid for,
that she has received from the LORD's hand
double for all her sins.

3 A voice of one calling:
"In the desert prepare
the way for the LORD[a];
make straight in the wilderness
a highway for our God.[b]
4 Every valley shall be raised up,
every mountain and hill made low;
the rough ground shall become level,
the rugged places a plain.
5 And the glory of the LORD will be revealed,
and all mankind together will see it.
For the mouth of the LORD
has spoken."

6 A voice says, "Cry out."
And I said, "What shall I cry?"
"All men are like grass,
and all their glory is like the flowers of the field.
7 The grass withers and the flowers fall,
because the breath of the LORD blows on them.
Surely the people are grass.
8 The grass withers and the flowers fall,
but the word of our God stands forever."

9 You who bring good tidings to Zion,
go up on a high mountain.
You who bring good tidings to Jerusalem,[c]
lift up your voice with a shout,
lift it up, do not be afraid;
say to the towns of Judah,
"Here is your God!"
10 See, the Sovereign LORD comes with power,
and his arm rules for him.
See, his reward is with him,
and his recompense accompanies him.
11 He tends his flock like a shepherd:
He gathers the lambs in his arms
and carries them close to his heart;
he gently leads those that have young.

12 Who has measured the waters in the hollow of his hand,
or with the breadth of his hand marked off the heavens?

a3 Or *A voice of one calling in the desert: / "Prepare the way for the LORD* b3 Hebrew; Septuagint *make straight the paths of our God*
c9 Or *O Zion, bringer of good tidings, / go up on a high mountain. / O Jerusalem, bringer of good tidings*

The God of All Comfort

Read: Isaiah 40:1–20

Isaiah 40:1–2

Comfort, comfort my people, says your God. Speak tenderly to Jerusalem, and proclaim to her that her hard service has been completed, that her sin has been paid for, that she has received from the LORD's hand double for all her sins.

HUMANS CRAVE COMFORT. From infancy, we cry for our mother's arms. When we are hurt, we long for tenderness; even hardened criminals weep for compassion in the isolation of a prison cell.

Though Israel didn't yet realize it, Isaiah was envisioning a day when its people would long for comfort like they longed for their next breath. Isaiah repeatedly warned them that sorrow and degradation awaited them because of their sin, and the outlook didn't look good. They would be exiled to Babylon because of their rebellion, and compassion would seem far from reach.

Even in the midst of their pain, though, God promised his people lavish solace: "Comfort, comfort my people," he said. Remarkable, isn't he? It's one thing to comfort someone who has been wronged, to nurse their wounds and soothe their pain. But what if that person has *done* wrong and is suffering for it? Justice says that they deserve what they get. But God spoke these gracious and merciful words through Isaiah: God will comfort those who have wronged *him*.

Isaiah's prophecy not only looked forward to a time when God would restore Israel, but it also looked ahead to the time when John the Baptist would announce the coming of Jesus, whom God would send as the ultimate comfort. Jesus would offer himself as a final sacrifice—the Lamb of God—and he would take on himself the pain of sin on behalf of those who believe in him.

Through Isaiah, a glorious love song radiates hope to a people caught up in the current of sin. Though justice says we deserve to suffer, God's compassionate grace says, "Comfort, comfort my people." The God of all comfort longs to take us in his arms and comfort us.

reflection

1 Read through this chapter again. What phrases give you great comfort?

2 What painful sins do you need forgiveness and comfort for? Meditate on the mystery of comfort from a God *you* have wronged.

3 Where can you reflect the gift of God's righteousness today?

RELATED READINGS

Lamentations 3:19–26; Hosea 2:14–23; John 1:19–28; 2 Corinthians 1:3–4

Go to page 885 for your next devotional reading.

Who has held the dust of the earth in a basket,
or weighed the mountains on the scales
and the hills in a balance?
13 Who has understood the mind[a] of the LORD,
or instructed him as his counselor?
14 Whom did the LORD consult to enlighten him,
and who taught him the right way?
Who was it that taught him knowledge
or showed him the path of understanding?

15 Surely the nations are like a drop in a bucket;
they are regarded as dust on the scales;
he weighs the islands as though they were fine dust.
16 Lebanon is not sufficient for altar fires,
nor its animals enough for burnt offerings.
17 Before him all the nations are as nothing;
they are regarded by him as worthless
and less than nothing.

18 To whom, then, will you compare God?
What image will you compare him to?
19 As for an idol, a craftsman casts it,
and a goldsmith overlays it with gold
and fashions silver chains for it.
20 A man too poor to present such an offering
selects wood that will not rot.
He looks for a skilled craftsman
to set up an idol that will not topple.

21 Do you not know?
Have you not heard?
Has it not been told you from the beginning?
Have you not understood since the earth was founded?
22 He sits enthroned above the circle of the earth,
and its people are like grasshoppers.
He stretches out the heavens like a canopy,
and spreads them out like a tent to live in.
23 He brings princes to naught
and reduces the rulers of this world to nothing.
24 No sooner are they planted,
no sooner are they sown,
no sooner do they take root in the ground,
than he blows on them and they wither,
and a whirlwind sweeps them away like chaff.

25 "To whom will you compare me?
Or who is my equal?" says the Holy One.
26 Lift your eyes and look to the heavens:
Who created all these?
He who brings out the starry host one by one,
and calls them each by name.
Because of his great power and mighty strength,
not one of them is missing.

27 Why do you say, O Jacob,
and complain, O Israel,
"My way is hidden from the LORD;
my cause is disregarded by my God"?
28 Do you not know?
Have you not heard?
The LORD is the everlasting God,
the Creator of the ends of the earth.
He will not grow tired or weary,
and his understanding no one can fathom.
29 He gives strength to the weary
and increases the power of the weak.
30 Even youths grow tired and weary,
and young men stumble and fall;
31 but those who hope in the LORD
will renew their strength.
They will soar on wings like eagles;
they will run and not grow weary,
they will walk and not be faint.

The Helper of Israel

41 "Be silent before me, you islands!
Let the nations renew their strength!
Let them come forward and speak;
let us meet together at the place of judgment.

2 "Who has stirred up one from the east,
calling him in righteousness to his service[b]?
He hands nations over to him

[a]13 Or *Spirit*; or *spirit* [b]2 Or / *whom victory meets at every step*

and subdues kings before him.
He turns them to dust with his sword,
to windblown chaff with his bow.
3 He pursues them and moves on unscathed,
by a path his feet have not traveled
before.
4 Who has done this and carried it through,
calling forth the generations from the
beginning?
I, the LORD—with the first of them
and with the last—I am he."

5 The islands have seen it and fear;
the ends of the earth tremble.
They approach and come forward;
6 each helps the other
and says to his brother, "Be strong!"
7 The craftsman encourages the goldsmith,
and he who smooths with the hammer
spurs on him who strikes the anvil.
He says of the welding, "It is good."
He nails down the idol so it will not
topple.

8 "But you, O Israel, my servant,
Jacob, whom I have chosen,
you descendants of Abraham my
friend,
9 I took you from the ends of the earth,
from its farthest corners I called you.
I said, 'You are my servant';
I have chosen you and
have not rejected
you.
10 So do not fear, for I am with
you;
do not be dismayed, for I
am your God.
I will strengthen you and
help you;
I will uphold you with
my righteous right
hand.

11 "All who rage against you
will surely be ashamed
and disgraced;
those who oppose you
will be as nothing and
perish.
12 Though you search for your enemies,
you will not find them.
Those who wage war against you
will be as nothing at all.
13 For I am the LORD, your God,
who takes hold of your right hand
and says to you, Do not fear;
I will help you.
14 Do not be afraid, O worm Jacob,
O little Israel,
for I myself will help you," declares the
LORD,
your Redeemer, the Holy One of Israel.
15 "See, I will make you into a threshing
sledge,
new and sharp, with many teeth.
You will thresh the mountains and crush
them,
and reduce the hills to chaff.
16 You will winnow them, the wind will pick
them up,
and a gale will blow them away.
But you will rejoice in the LORD
and glory in the Holy One of Israel.

17 "The poor and needy search for water,
but there is none;
their tongues are parched with thirst.
But I the LORD will answer them;
I, the God of Israel, will not forsake
them.
18 I will make rivers flow on barren heights,
and springs within the
valleys.
I will turn the desert into
pools of water,
and the parched ground
into springs.
19 I will put in the desert
the cedar and the acacia,
the myrtle and the
olive.
I will set pines in the
wasteland,
the fir and the cypress
together,
20 so that people may see and
know,
may consider and
understand,
that the hand of the LORD
has done this,
that the Holy One of Israel has created it.

Isaiah 41:10

God Strengthens Us

"So do not fear, for
I am with you;
do not be dismayed, for
I am your God.
I will strengthen you
and help you;
I will uphold you with my
righteous right hand."

21 "Present your case," says the LORD.
"Set forth your arguments," says Jacob's King.
22 "Bring in ⌞your idols⌟ to tell us
what is going to happen.
Tell us what the former things were,
so that we may consider them
and know their final outcome.
Or declare to us the things to come,
23 tell us what the future holds,
so we may know that you are gods.
Do something, whether good or bad,
so that we will be dismayed and filled with fear.
24 But you are less than nothing
and your works are utterly worthless;
he who chooses you is detestable.

25 "I have stirred up one from the north, and he comes—
one from the rising sun who calls on my name.
He treads on rulers as if they were mortar,
as if he were a potter treading the clay.
26 Who told of this from the beginning, so we could know,
or beforehand, so we could say, 'He was right'?
No one told of this,
no one foretold it,
no one heard any words from you.
27 I was the first to tell Zion, 'Look, here they are!'
I gave to Jerusalem a messenger of good tidings.
28 I look but there is no one—
no one among them to give counsel,
no one to give answer when I ask them.
29 See, they are all false!
Their deeds amount to nothing;
their images are but wind and confusion.

The Servant of the LORD

42 "Here is my servant, whom I uphold,
my chosen one in whom I delight;
I will put my Spirit on him
and he will bring justice to the nations.
2 He will not shout or cry out,
or raise his voice in the streets.
3 A bruised reed he will not break,
and a smoldering wick he will not snuff out.
In faithfulness he will bring forth justice;
4 he will not falter or be discouraged
till he establishes justice on earth.
In his law the islands will put their hope."

5 This is what God the LORD says—
he who created the heavens and stretched them out,
who spread out the earth and all that comes out of it,
who gives breath to its people,
and life to those who walk on it:
6 "I, the LORD, have called you in righteousness;
I will take hold of your hand.
I will keep you and will make you
to be a covenant for the people
and a light for the Gentiles,
7 to open eyes that are blind,
to free captives from prison
and to release from the dungeon those who sit in darkness.

8 "I am the LORD; that is my name!
I will not give my glory to another
or my praise to idols.
9 See, the former things have taken place,
and new things I declare;
before they spring into being
I announce them to you."

Song of Praise to the LORD

10 Sing to the LORD a new song,
his praise from the ends of the earth,
you who go down to the sea, and all that is in it,
you islands, and all who live in them.
11 Let the desert and its towns raise their voices;
let the settlements where Kedar lives rejoice.
Let the people of Sela sing for joy;
let them shout from the mountaintops.
12 Let them give glory to the LORD
and proclaim his praise in the islands.
13 The LORD will march out like a mighty man,
like a warrior he will stir up his zeal;

with a shout he will raise the battle cry
and will triumph over his enemies.

14 "For a long time I have kept silent,
I have been quiet and held myself back.
But now, like a woman in childbirth,
I cry out, I gasp and pant.
15 I will lay waste the mountains and hills
and dry up all their vegetation;
I will turn rivers into islands
and dry up the pools.
16 I will lead the blind by ways they have not known,
along unfamiliar paths I will guide them;
I will turn the darkness into light before them
and make the rough places smooth.
These are the things I will do;
I will not forsake them.
17 But those who trust in idols,
who say to images, 'You are our gods,'
will be turned back in utter shame.

Israel Blind and Deaf

18 "Hear, you deaf;
look, you blind, and see!
19 Who is blind but my servant,
and deaf like the messenger I send?
Who is blind like the one committed to me,
blind like the servant of the LORD?
20 You have seen many things,
but have paid no attention;
your ears are open, but you hear nothing."
21 It pleased the LORD
for the sake of his righteousness
to make his law great and glorious.
22 But this is a people plundered and looted,
all of them trapped in pits
or hidden away in prisons.
They have become plunder,
with no one to rescue them;
they have been made loot,
with no one to say, "Send them back."
23 Which of you will listen to this
or pay close attention in time to come?
24 Who handed Jacob over to become loot,
and Israel to the plunderers?
Was it not the LORD,
against whom we have sinned?
For they would not follow his ways;
they did not obey his law.
25 So he poured out on them his burning anger,
the violence of war.
It enveloped them in flames, yet they did not understand;
it consumed them, but they did not take it to heart.

Israel's Only Savior

43 But now, this is what the LORD says—
he who created you, O Jacob,
he who formed you, O Israel:
"Fear not, for I have redeemed you;
I have summoned you by name; you are mine.
2 When you pass through the waters,
I will be with you;
and when you pass through the rivers,
they will not sweep over you.
When you walk through the fire,
you will not be burned;
the flames will not set you ablaze.
3 For I am the LORD, your God,
the Holy One of Israel, your Savior;
I give Egypt for your ransom,
Cush[a] and Seba in your stead.
4 Since you are precious and honored in my sight,
and because I love you,
I will give men in exchange for you,
and people in exchange for your life.

Isaiah 43:1

God Created Us

But now, this is what
the LORD says—
he who created you,
O Jacob,
he who formed you,
O Israel:
"Fear not, for I have
redeemed you;
I have summoned you by
name; you are mine."

[a]3 That is, the upper Nile region

5 Do not be afraid, for I am with you;
I will bring your children from the east
and gather you from the west.
6 I will say to the north, 'Give them up!'
and to the south, 'Do not hold them back.'
Bring my sons from afar
and my daughters from the ends of the earth—
7 everyone who is called by my name,
whom I created for my glory,
whom I formed and made."

8 Lead out those who have eyes but are blind,
who have ears but are deaf.
9 All the nations gather together
and the peoples assemble.
Which of them foretold this
and proclaimed to us the former things?
Let them bring in their witnesses to prove they were right,
so that others may hear and say, "It is true."
10 "You are my witnesses," declares the LORD,
"and my servant whom I have chosen,
so that you may know and believe me
and understand that I am he.
Before me no god was formed,
nor will there be one after me.
11 I, even I, am the LORD,
and apart from me there is no savior.
12 I have revealed and saved and proclaimed—
I, and not some foreign god among you.
You are my witnesses," declares the LORD,
"that I am God.
13 Yes, and from ancient days I am he.
No one can deliver out of my hand.
When I act, who can reverse it?"

God's Mercy and Israel's Unfaithfulness

14 This is what the LORD says—
your Redeemer, the Holy One of Israel:
"For your sake I will send to Babylon
and bring down as fugitives all the Babylonians,[a]
in the ships in which they took pride.
15 I am the LORD, your Holy One,
Israel's Creator, your King."

16 This is what the LORD says—
he who made a way through the sea,
a path through the mighty waters,
17 who drew out the chariots and horses,
the army and reinforcements together,
and they lay there, never to rise again,
extinguished, snuffed out like a wick:
18 "Forget the former things;
do not dwell on the past.
19 See, I am doing a new thing!
Now it springs up; do you not perceive it?
I am making a way in the desert
and streams in the wasteland.
20 The wild animals honor me,
the jackals and the owls,
because I provide water in the desert
and streams in the wasteland,
to give drink to my people, my chosen,
21 the people I formed for myself
that they may proclaim my praise.

22 "Yet you have not called upon me, O Jacob,
you have not wearied yourselves for me, O Israel.
23 You have not brought me sheep for burnt offerings,
nor honored me with your sacrifices.
I have not burdened you with grain offerings
nor wearied you with demands for incense.
24 You have not bought any fragrant calamus for me,
or lavished on me the fat of your sacrifices.
But you have burdened me with your sins
and wearied me with your offenses.

25 "I, even I, am he who blots out
your transgressions, for my own sake,
and remembers your sins no more.
26 Review the past for me,
let us argue the matter together;
state the case for your innocence.
27 Your first father sinned;
your spokesmen rebelled against me.
28 So I will disgrace the dignitaries of your temple,

14 Or *Chaldeans*

and I will consign Jacob to destruction[a]
and Israel to scorn.

Israel the Chosen

44 "But now listen, O Jacob, my servant,
Israel, whom I have chosen.
2 This is what the LORD says—
he who made you, who formed you in the womb,
and who will help you:
Do not be afraid, O Jacob, my servant,
Jeshurun, whom I have chosen.
3 For I will pour water on the thirsty land,
and streams on the dry ground;
I will pour out my Spirit on your offspring,
and my blessing on your descendants.
4 They will spring up like grass in a meadow,
like poplar trees by flowing streams.
5 One will say, 'I belong to the LORD';
another will call himself by the name of Jacob;
still another will write on his hand, 'The LORD's,'
and will take the name Israel.

The LORD, Not Idols

6 "This is what the LORD says—
Israel's King and Redeemer, the LORD Almighty:
I am the first and I am the last;
apart from me there is no God.
7 Who then is like me? Let him proclaim it.
Let him declare and lay out before me
what has happened since I established my ancient people,
and what is yet to come—
yes, let him foretell what will come.
8 Do not tremble, do not be afraid.
Did I not proclaim this and foretell it long ago?
You are my witnesses. Is there any God besides me?
No, there is no other Rock; I know not one."
9 All who make idols are nothing,
and the things they treasure are worthless.
Those who would speak up for them are blind;
they are ignorant, to their own shame.
10 Who shapes a god and casts an idol,
which can profit him nothing?
11 He and his kind will be put to shame;
craftsmen are nothing but men.
Let them all come together and take their stand;
they will be brought down to terror and infamy.

12 The blacksmith takes a tool
and works with it in the coals;
he shapes an idol with hammers,
he forges it with the might of his arm.
He gets hungry and loses his strength;
he drinks no water and grows faint.
13 The carpenter measures with a line
and makes an outline with a marker;
he roughs it out with chisels
and marks it with compasses.
He shapes it in the form of man,
of man in all his glory,
that it may dwell in a shrine.
14 He cut down cedars,
or perhaps took a cypress or oak.
He let it grow among the trees of the forest,
or planted a pine, and the rain made it grow.
15 It is man's fuel for burning;
some of it he takes and warms himself,
he kindles a fire and bakes bread.
But he also fashions a god and worships it;
he makes an idol and bows down to it.
16 Half of the wood he burns in the fire;
over it he prepares his meal,
he roasts his meat and eats his fill.
He also warms himself and says,
"Ah! I am warm; I see the fire."
17 From the rest he makes a god, his idol;
he bows down to it and worships.
He prays to it and says,
"Save me; you are my god."
18 They know nothing, they understand nothing;
their eyes are plastered over so they cannot see,
and their minds closed so they cannot understand.
19 No one stops to think,

[a] 28 The Hebrew term refers to the irrevocable giving over of things or persons to the LORD, often by totally destroying them.

no one has the knowledge or
understanding to say,
"Half of it I used for fuel;
I even baked bread over its coals,
I roasted meat and I ate.
Shall I make a detestable thing from what
is left?
Shall I bow down to a block of wood?"
20 He feeds on ashes, a deluded heart
misleads him;
he cannot save himself, or say,
"Is not this thing in my right hand a
lie?"

21 "Remember these things, O Jacob,
for you are my servant, O Israel.
I have made you, you are my servant;
O Israel, I will not forget you.
22 I have swept away your offenses like a
cloud,
your sins like the morning mist.
Return to me,
for I have redeemed you."

23 Sing for joy, O heavens, for the LORD has
done this;
shout aloud, O earth beneath.
Burst into song, you mountains,
you forests and all your trees,
for the LORD has redeemed Jacob,
he displays his glory in Israel.

Jerusalem to Be Inhabited

24 "This is what the LORD says—
your Redeemer, who formed you in the
womb:

I am the LORD,
who has made all things,
who alone stretched out the heavens,
who spread out the earth by myself,
25 who foils the signs of false prophets
and makes fools of diviners,
who overthrows the learning of the wise
and turns it into nonsense,
26 who carries out the words of his servants
and fulfills the predictions of his
messengers,

who says of Jerusalem, 'It shall be
inhabited,'
of the towns of Judah, 'They shall be
built,'
and of their ruins, 'I will restore them,'
27 who says to the watery deep, 'Be dry,
and I will dry up your streams,'
28 who says of Cyrus, 'He is my shepherd
and will accomplish all that I please;
he will say of Jerusalem, "Let it be
rebuilt,"
and of the temple, "Let its foundations
be laid."'

45 "This is what the LORD says to his
anointed,
to Cyrus, whose right hand I take
hold of
to subdue nations before him
and to strip kings of their armor,
to open doors before him
so that gates will not be shut:
2 I will go before you
and will level the mountains[a];
I will break down gates of bronze
and cut through bars of iron.
3 I will give you the treasures of darkness,
riches stored in secret places,
so that you may know that I am the LORD,
the God of Israel, who summons you by
name.
4 For the sake of Jacob my servant,
of Israel my chosen,
I summon you by name
and bestow on you a title of honor,
though you do not acknowledge me.
5 I am the LORD, and there is no other;
apart from me there is no God.
I will strengthen you,
though you have not acknowledged me,
6 so that from the rising of the sun
to the place of its setting
men may know there is none besides me.
I am the LORD, and there is no other.
7 I form the light and create darkness,
I bring prosperity and create disaster;
I, the LORD, do all these things.
8 "You heavens above, rain down
righteousness;
let the clouds shower it down.

[a] 2 Dead Sea Scrolls and Septuagint; the meaning of the word in the Masoretic Text is uncertain.

Let the earth open wide,
let salvation spring up,
let righteousness grow with it;
I, the LORD, have created it.

9 "Woe to him who quarrels with his Maker,
to him who is but a potsherd among the
potsherds on the ground.
Does the clay say to the potter,
'What are you making?'
Does your work say,
'He has no hands'?
10 Woe to him who says to his father,
'What have you begotten?'
or to his mother,
'What have you brought to birth?'

11 "This is what the LORD says—
the Holy One of Israel, and its Maker:
Concerning things to come,
do you question me about my children,
or give me orders about the work of my
hands?
12 It is I who made the earth
and created mankind upon it.
My own hands stretched out the heavens;
I marshaled their starry hosts.
13 I will raise up Cyrus[a] in my
righteousness:
I will make all his ways straight.
He will rebuild my city
and set my exiles free,
but not for a price or reward,
says the LORD Almighty."

14 This is what the LORD says:

"The products of Egypt and
the merchandise of
Cush,[b]
and those tall Sabeans—
they will come over to you
and will be yours;
they will trudge behind
you,
coming over to you in
chains.
They will bow down before
you
and plead with you,
saying,
'Surely God is with you, and there is no
other;
there is no other god.'"
15 Truly you are a God who hides himself,
O God and Savior of Israel.
16 All the makers of idols will be put to shame
and disgraced;
they will go off into disgrace together.
17 But Israel will be saved by the LORD
with an everlasting salvation;
you will never be put to shame or disgraced,
to ages everlasting.

18 For this is what the LORD says—
he who created the heavens,
he is God;
he who fashioned and made the earth,
he founded it;
he did not create it to be empty,
but formed it to be inhabited—
he says:
"I am the LORD,
and there is no other.
19 I have not spoken in secret,
from somewhere in a land of darkness;
I have not said to Jacob's descendants,
'Seek me in vain.'
I, the LORD, speak the truth;
I declare what is right.

20 "Gather together and come;
assemble, you fugitives from the nations.
Ignorant are those who carry about idols
of wood,
who pray to gods that cannot save.
21 Declare what is to be,
present it—
let them take counsel
together.
Who foretold this long ago,
who declared it from the
distant past?
Was it not I, the LORD?
And there is no God
apart from me,
a righteous God and a
Savior;
there is none but me.
22 "Turn to me and be saved,

Isaiah 45:22

God Offers Salvation

"Turn to me and be saved,
all you ends of the earth;
for I am God, and
there is no other."

[a]13 Hebrew *him* [b]14 That is, the upper Nile region

all you ends of the earth;
for I am God, and there is no other.
23 By myself I have sworn,
my mouth has uttered in all integrity
a word that will not be revoked:
Before me every knee will bow;
by me every tongue will swear.
24 They will say of me, 'In the LORD alone
are righteousness and strength.'"
All who have raged against him
will come to him and be put to shame.
25 But in the LORD all the descendants of Israel
will be found righteous and will exult.

Gods of Babylon

46 Bel bows down, Nebo stoops low;
their idols are borne by beasts of burden.[a]
The images that are carried about are burdensome,
a burden for the weary.
2 They stoop and bow down together;
unable to rescue the burden,
they themselves go off into captivity.

3 "Listen to me, O house of Jacob,
all you who remain of the house of Israel,
you whom I have upheld since you were conceived,
and have carried since your birth.
4 Even to your old age and gray hairs
I am he, I am he who will sustain you.
I have made you and I will carry you;
I will sustain you and I will rescue you.

5 "To whom will you compare me or count me equal?
To whom will you liken me that we may be compared?
6 Some pour out gold from their bags
and weigh out silver on the scales;
they hire a goldsmith to make it into a god,
and they bow down and worship it.
7 They lift it to their shoulders and carry it;
they set it up in its place, and there it stands.
From that spot it cannot move.
Though one cries out to it, it does not answer;
it cannot save him from his troubles.

8 "Remember this, fix it in mind,
take it to heart, you rebels.
9 Remember the former things, those of long ago;
I am God, and there is no other;
I am God, and there is none like me.
10 I make known the end from the beginning,
from ancient times, what is still to come.
I say: My purpose will stand,
and I will do all that I please.
11 From the east I summon a bird of prey;
from a far-off land, a man to fulfill my purpose.
What I have said, that will I bring about;
what I have planned, that will I do.
12 Listen to me, you stubborn-hearted,
you who are far from righteousness.
13 I am bringing my righteousness near,
it is not far away;
and my salvation will not be delayed.
I will grant salvation to Zion,
my splendor to Israel.

The Fall of Babylon

47 "Go down, sit in the dust,
Virgin Daughter of Babylon;
sit on the ground without a throne,
Daughter of the Babylonians.[b]
No more will you be called
tender or delicate.
2 Take millstones and grind flour;
take off your veil.
Lift up your skirts, bare your legs,
and wade through the streams.
3 Your nakedness will be exposed
and your shame uncovered.
I will take vengeance;
I will spare no one."

4 Our Redeemer—the LORD Almighty is his name—
is the Holy One of Israel.

5 "Sit in silence, go into darkness,
Daughter of the Babylonians;
no more will you be called
queen of kingdoms.
6 I was angry with my people
and desecrated my inheritance;
I gave them into your hand,

a1 Or *are but beasts and cattle* b1 Or *Chaldeans*; also in verse 5

and you showed them no mercy.
Even on the aged
you laid a very heavy yoke.
7 You said, 'I will continue forever—
the eternal queen!'
But you did not consider these things
or reflect on what might happen.

8 "Now then, listen, you wanton creature,
lounging in your security
and saying to yourself,
'I am, and there is none besides me.
I will never be a widow
or suffer the loss of children.'
9 Both of these will overtake you
in a moment, on a single day:
loss of children and widowhood.
They will come upon you in full measure,
in spite of your many sorceries
and all your potent spells.
10 You have trusted in your wickedness
and have said, 'No one sees me.'
Your wisdom and knowledge mislead you
when you say to yourself,
'I am, and there is none besides me.'
11 Disaster will come upon you,
and you will not know how to conjure
it away.
A calamity will fall upon you
that you cannot ward off with a ransom;
a catastrophe you cannot foresee
will suddenly come upon you.

12 "Keep on, then, with your magic spells
and with your many sorceries,
which you have labored at since
childhood.
Perhaps you will succeed,
perhaps you will cause terror.
13 All the counsel you have received has only
worn you out!
Let your astrologers come forward,
those stargazers who make predictions
month by month,
let them save you from what is coming
upon you.
14 Surely they are like stubble;
the fire will burn them up.
They cannot even save themselves
from the power of the flame.
Here are no coals to warm anyone;
here is no fire to sit by.
15 That is all they can do for you—
these you have labored with
and trafficked with since childhood.
Each of them goes on in his error;
there is not one that can save you.

Stubborn Israel

48 "Listen to this, O house of Jacob,
you who are called by the name of
Israel
and come from the line of Judah,
you who take oaths in the name of the
Lord
and invoke the God of Israel—
but not in truth or righteousness—
2 you who call yourselves citizens of the holy
city
and rely on the God of Israel—
the Lord Almighty is his name:
3 I foretold the former things long ago,
my mouth announced them and I made
them known;
then suddenly I acted, and they came
to pass.
4 For I knew how stubborn you were;
the sinews of your neck were iron,
your forehead was bronze.
5 Therefore I told you these things long ago;
before they happened I announced them
to you
so that you could not say,
'My idols did them;
my wooden image and metal god
ordained them.'
6 You have heard these things; look at them
all.
Will you not admit them?

"From now on I will tell you of new things,
of hidden things unknown to you.
7 They are created now, and not long ago;
you have not heard of them before
today.
So you cannot say,
'Yes, I knew of them.'
8 You have neither heard nor understood;
from of old your ear has not been open.
Well do I know how treacherous you are;
you were called a rebel from birth.
9 For my own name's sake I delay my wrath;

for the sake of my praise I hold it back
from you,
so as not to cut you off.
10 See, I have refined you, though not as
silver;
I have tested you in the
furnace of affliction.
11 For my own sake, for my
own sake, I do this.
How can I let myself be
defamed?
I will not yield my glory
to another.

Israel Freed

12 "Listen to me, O Jacob,
Israel, whom I have
called:
I am he;
I am the first and I am
the last.
13 My own hand laid the foundations of the
earth,
and my right hand spread out the
heavens;
when I summon them,
they all stand up together.

14 "Come together, all of you, and listen:
Which of ⌊the idols⌋ has foretold these
things?
The LORD's chosen ally
will carry out his purpose against
Babylon;
his arm will be against the
Babylonians.[a]
15 I, even I, have spoken;
yes, I have called him.
I will bring him,
and he will succeed in his mission.

16 "Come near me and listen to this:

"From the first announcement I have not
spoken in secret;
at the time it happens, I am there."

And now the Sovereign LORD has sent me,
with his Spirit.

17 This is what the LORD says—
your Redeemer, the Holy One of Israel:
"I am the LORD your God,
who teaches you what is best for you,
who directs you in the way you should
go.
18 If only you had paid
attention to my
commands,
your peace would have
been like a river,
your righteousness like
the waves of the
sea.
19 Your descendants would
have been like the
sand,
your children like its
numberless grains;
their name would never be
cut off
nor destroyed from
before me."

Isaiah 48:17

God Is Our Redeemer

This is what the
LORD says—
your Redeemer, the
Holy One of Israel:
"I am the LORD
your God."

20 Leave Babylon,
flee from the Babylonians!
Announce this with shouts of joy
and proclaim it.
Send it out to the ends of the earth;
say, "The LORD has redeemed his
servant Jacob."
21 They did not thirst when he led them
through the deserts;
he made water flow for them from the
rock;
he split the rock
and water gushed out.

22 "There is no peace," says the LORD, "for the
wicked."

The Servant of the LORD

49 Listen to me, you islands;
hear this, you distant nations:
Before I was born the LORD called me;
from my birth he has made mention of
my name.
2 He made my mouth like a sharpened
sword,
in the shadow of his hand he hid me;
he made me into a polished arrow
and concealed me in his quiver.
3 He said to me, "You are my servant,

[a] 14 Or *Chaldeans*; also in verse 20

Israel, in whom I will display my
splendor."
4 But I said, "I have labored to no purpose;
I have spent my strength in vain and for
nothing.
Yet what is due me is in the LORD's hand,
and my reward is with my God."

5 And now the LORD says—
he who formed me in the womb to be
his servant
to bring Jacob back to him
and gather Israel to himself,
for I am honored in the eyes of the LORD
and my God has been my strength—
6 he says:
"It is too small a thing for you to be my
servant
to restore the tribes of Jacob
and bring back those of Israel I have
kept.
I will also make you a light for the
Gentiles,
that you may bring my salvation to the
ends of the earth."

7 This is what the LORD
says—
the Redeemer and Holy
One of Israel—
to him who was despised
and abhorred by the
nation,
to the servant of rulers:
"Kings will see you and
rise up,
princes will see and bow
down,
because of the LORD, who is
faithful,
the Holy One of Israel,
who has chosen
you."

Restoration of Israel

8 This is what the LORD says:

"In the time of my favor I will answer you,
and in the day of salvation I will help
you;
I will keep you and will make you
to be a covenant for the people,
to restore the land
and to reassign its desolate inheritances,
9 to say to the captives, 'Come out,'
and to those in darkness, 'Be free!'

"They will feed beside the roads
and find pasture on every barren hill.
10 They will neither hunger nor thirst,
nor will the desert heat or the sun beat
upon them.
He who has compassion on them will
guide them
and lead them beside springs of water.
11 I will turn all my mountains into roads,
and my highways will be raised up.
12 See, they will come from afar—
some from the north, some from the
west,
some from the region of Aswan.[a]"

13 Shout for joy, O heavens;
rejoice, O earth;
burst into song, O mountains!
For the LORD comforts his people
and will have
compassion on his
afflicted ones.

14 But Zion said, "The LORD
has forsaken me,
the Lord has forgotten
me."

15 "Can a mother forget the
baby at her breast
and have no compassion
on the child she has
borne?
Though she may forget,
I will not forget you!
16 See, I have engraved you
on the palms of my
hands;
your walls are ever before me.
17 Your sons hasten back,
and those who laid you waste depart
from you.
18 Lift up your eyes and look around;
all your sons gather and come to you.
As surely as I live," declares the LORD,

Isaiah 49:15

God Doesn't Forget Us

"Can a mother forget the
baby at her breast
and have no compassion
on the child she
has borne?
Though she may forget,
I will not forget you!"

[a] 12 Dead Sea Scrolls; Masoretic Text *Sinim*

"you will wear them all as ornaments;
you will put them on, like a bride.

19 "Though you were ruined and made desolate
and your land laid waste,
now you will be too small for your people,
and those who devoured you will be far away.
20 The children born during your bereavement
will yet say in your hearing,
'This place is too small for us;
give us more space to live in.'
21 Then you will say in your heart,
'Who bore me these?
I was bereaved and barren;
I was exiled and rejected.
Who brought these up?
I was left all alone,
but these—where have they come from?'"

22 This is what the Sovereign LORD says:

"See, I will beckon to the Gentiles,
I will lift up my banner to the peoples;
they will bring your sons in their arms
and carry your daughters on their shoulders.
23 Kings will be your foster fathers,
and their queens your nursing mothers.
They will bow down before you with their faces to the ground;
they will lick the dust at your feet.
Then you will know that I am the LORD;
those who hope in me will not be disappointed."
24 Can plunder be taken from warriors,
or captives rescued from the fierce[a]?

25 But this is what the LORD says:

"Yes, captives will be taken from warriors,
and plunder retrieved from the fierce;
I will contend with those who contend with you,
and your children I will save.
26 I will make your oppressors eat their own flesh;
they will be drunk on their own blood,
as with wine.
Then all mankind will know
that I, the LORD, am your Savior,
your Redeemer, the Mighty One of Jacob."

Israel's Sin and the Servant's Obedience

50 This is what the LORD says:

"Where is your mother's certificate of divorce
with which I sent her away?
Or to which of my creditors
did I sell you?
Because of your sins you were sold;
because of your transgressions your mother was sent away.
2 When I came, why was there no one?
When I called, why was there no one to answer?
Was my arm too short to ransom you?
Do I lack the strength to rescue you?
By a mere rebuke I dry up the sea,
I turn rivers into a desert;
their fish rot for lack of water
and die of thirst.
3 I clothe the sky with darkness
and make sackcloth its covering."
4 The Sovereign LORD has given me an instructed tongue,
to know the word that sustains the weary.
He wakens me morning by morning,
wakens my ear to listen like one being taught.
5 The Sovereign LORD has opened my ears,
and I have not been rebellious;
I have not drawn back.
6 I offered my back to those who beat me,
my cheeks to those who pulled out my beard;
I did not hide my face
from mocking and spitting.
7 Because the Sovereign LORD helps me,
I will not be disgraced.
Therefore have I set my face like flint,
and I know I will not be put to shame.
8 He who vindicates me is near.

24 Dead Sea Scrolls, Vulgate and Syriac (see also Septuagint and verse 25); Masoretic Text *righteous*

Who then will bring charges against me?
Let us face each other!
Who is my accuser?
Let him confront me!
9 It is the Sovereign LORD who helps me.
Who is he that will condemn me?
They will all wear out like a garment;
the moths will eat them up.

10 Who among you fears the LORD
and obeys the word of his servant?
Let him who walks in the dark,
who has no light,
trust in the name of the LORD
and rely on his God.
11 But now, all you who light fires
and provide yourselves with flaming torches,
go, walk in the light of your fires
and of the torches you have set ablaze.
This is what you shall receive from my hand:
You will lie down in torment.

Everlasting Salvation for Zion

51 "Listen to me, you who pursue righteousness
and who seek the LORD:
Look to the rock from which you were cut
and to the quarry from which you were hewn;
2 look to Abraham, your father,
and to Sarah, who gave you birth.
When I called him he was but one,
and I blessed him and made him many.
3 The LORD will surely comfort Zion
and will look with compassion on all her ruins;
he will make her deserts like Eden,
her wastelands like the garden of the LORD.
Joy and gladness will be found in her,
thanksgiving and the sound of singing.

4 "Listen to me, my people;
hear me, my nation:
The law will go out from me;
my justice will become a light to the nations.
5 My righteousness draws near speedily,
my salvation is on the way,
and my arm will bring justice to the nations.
The islands will look to me
and wait in hope for my arm.
6 Lift up your eyes to the heavens,
look at the earth beneath;
the heavens will vanish like smoke,
the earth will wear out like a garment
and its inhabitants die like flies.
But my salvation will last forever,
my righteousness will never fail.

7 "Hear me, you who know what is right,
you people who have my law in your hearts:
Do not fear the reproach of men
or be terrified by their insults.
8 For the moth will eat them up like a garment;
the worm will devour them like wool.
But my righteousness will last forever,
my salvation through all generations."

9 Awake, awake! Clothe yourself with strength,
O arm of the LORD;
awake, as in days gone by,
as in generations of old.
Was it not you who cut Rahab to pieces,
who pierced that monster through?
10 Was it not you who dried up the sea,
the waters of the great deep,
who made a road in the depths of the sea
so that the redeemed might cross over?
11 The ransomed of the LORD will return.
They will enter Zion with singing;
everlasting joy will crown their heads.
Gladness and joy will overtake them,
and sorrow and sighing will flee away.

12 "I, even I, am he who comforts you.
Who are you that you fear mortal men,
the sons of men, who are but grass,
13 that you forget the LORD your Maker,
who stretched out the heavens
and laid the foundations of the earth,
that you live in constant terror every day
because of the wrath of the oppressor,
who is bent on destruction?
For where is the wrath of the oppressor?
14 The cowering prisoners will soon be set free;

they will not die in their dungeon,
nor will they lack bread.
15 For I am the LORD your God,
who churns up the sea so that its waves roar—
the LORD Almighty is his name.
16 I have put my words in your mouth
and covered you with the shadow of my hand—
I who set the heavens in place,
who laid the foundations of the earth,
and who say to Zion, 'You are my people.'"

The Cup of the LORD's Wrath

17 Awake, awake!
Rise up, O Jerusalem,
you who have drunk from the hand of the LORD
the cup of his wrath,
you who have drained to its dregs
the goblet that makes men stagger.
18 Of all the sons she bore
there was none to guide her;
of all the sons she reared
there was none to take her by the hand.
19 These double calamities have come upon you—
who can comfort you?—
ruin and destruction,
famine and sword—
who can[a] console you?
20 Your sons have fainted;
they lie at the head of every street,
like antelope caught in a net.
They are filled with the wrath of the LORD
and the rebuke of your God.
21 Therefore hear this, you afflicted one,
made drunk, but not with wine.
22 This is what your Sovereign LORD says,
your God, who defends his people:
"See, I have taken out of your hand
the cup that made you stagger;
from that cup, the goblet of my wrath,
you will never drink again.
23 I will put it into the hands of your tormentors,
who said to you,
'Fall prostrate that we may walk over you.'
And you made your back like the ground,
like a street to be walked over."

52 Awake, awake, O Zion,
clothe yourself with strength.
Put on your garments of splendor,
O Jerusalem, the holy city.
The uncircumcised and defiled
will not enter you again.
2 Shake off your dust;
rise up, sit enthroned, O Jerusalem.
Free yourself from the chains on your neck,
O captive Daughter of Zion.

3 For this is what the LORD says:

"You were sold for nothing,
and without money you will be redeemed."

4 For this is what the Sovereign LORD says:

"At first my people went down to Egypt to live;
lately, Assyria has oppressed them.

5 "And now what do I have here?" declares the LORD.

"For my people have been taken away for nothing,
and those who rule them mock,[b]"
declares the LORD.
"And all day long
my name is constantly blasphemed.

Isaiah 51:12

God Comforts His People

"I, even I, am he who comforts you. Who are you that you fear mortal men, the sons of men, who are but grass?"

[a] 19 Dead Sea Scrolls, Septuagint, Vulgate and Syriac; Masoretic Text / *how can I* [b] 5 Dead Sea Scrolls and Vulgate; Masoretic Text *wail*

6 Therefore my people will know my name;
therefore in that day they will know
that it is I who foretold it.
Yes, it is I."

7 How beautiful on the mountains
are the feet of those who bring good news,
who proclaim peace,
who bring good tidings,
who proclaim salvation,
who say to Zion,
"Your God reigns!"
8 Listen! Your watchmen lift up their voices;
together they shout for joy.
When the LORD returns to Zion,
they will see it with their own eyes.
9 Burst into songs of joy together,
you ruins of Jerusalem,
for the LORD has comforted his people,
he has redeemed Jerusalem.
10 The LORD will lay bare his holy arm
in the sight of all the nations,
and all the ends of the earth will see
the salvation of our God.

11 Depart, depart, go out from there!
Touch no unclean thing!
Come out from it and be pure,
you who carry the vessels of the LORD.
12 But you will not leave in haste
or go in flight;
for the LORD will go before you,
the God of Israel will be your rear guard.

The Suffering and Glory of the Servant

13 See, my servant will act wisely[a];
he will be raised and lifted up and highly exalted.
14 Just as there were many who were appalled at him[b]—
his appearance was so disfigured beyond that of any man
and his form marred beyond human likeness—
15 so will he sprinkle many nations,[c]
and kings will shut their mouths because of him.
For what they were not told, they will see,
and what they have not heard, they will understand.

53 Who has believed our message
and to whom has the arm of the LORD been revealed?
2 He grew up before him like a tender shoot,
and like a root out of dry ground.
He had no beauty or majesty to attract us to him,
nothing in his appearance that we should desire him.
3 He was despised and rejected by men,
a man of sorrows, and familiar with suffering.
Like one from whom men hide their faces
he was despised, and we esteemed him not.

4 Surely he took up our infirmities
and carried our sorrows,
yet we considered him stricken by God,
smitten by him, and afflicted.
5 But he was pierced for our transgressions,
he was crushed for our iniquities;
the punishment that brought us peace was upon him,
and by his wounds we are healed.
6 We all, like sheep, have gone astray,
each of us has turned to his own way;
and the LORD has laid on him
the iniquity of us all.

7 He was oppressed and afflicted,
yet he did not open his mouth;
he was led like a lamb to the slaughter,
and as a sheep before her shearers is silent,
so he did not open his mouth.
8 By oppression[d] and judgment he was taken away.

Isaiah 52:7

God Reigns Over the World

How beautiful on the mountains
are the feet of those who bring good news . . .
"Your God reigns!"

[a]13 Or *will prosper* [b]14 Hebrew *you* [c]15 Hebrew; Septuagint *so will many nations marvel at him* [d]8 Or *From arrest*

Rejoice in Suffering?

Read: Isaiah 53:1–12

DID YOU WONDER IF you read that Scripture verse right? God *willed* for Jesus to suffer. Those are difficult words to understand. We don't want to believe it. After all, if God intended for Jesus to suffer, he might want us to suffer too. And we're not sure we're up for that calling.

"Isn't God loving?" we reason. "If so, why would he want us to suffer? It doesn't make sense. Shouldn't God want his children to live in a world with no difficulties, disease or death?"

Ah, but God *did* create the world perfect and without suffering in a garden long ago. We all have an Eden-like yearning because God created us to live there. But we sinned, and suffering was the penalty for sin. Therefore, in this life, we will experience suffering and death. In fact, as the Isaiah passage reveals, God actually *intended* for Jesus to suffer during his earthly life so that we could be saved.

In Romans, Paul tells us to expect suffering on earth—and even to rejoice in it. Why rejoice? Because God uses it to produce perseverance, character and hope. God doesn't waste any suffering we experience. He uses it for our good if we let him.

However, God isn't callous to our suffering. He cares deeply. Jesus showed us that when he came to earth. He healed those who were suffering. He wept because people were suffering. And now he has conquered suffering. He is seated at the right hand of God. We will suffer on earth, but the story doesn't end there. Go back to Isaiah 53:11: "After the suffering of his soul, he will see the light of life." That was true for Jesus, and it's true for all those who believe Jesus is Lord. Your suffering is not the end of the story. If you're a believer, you will one day live in a perfect place: "Then I saw a new heaven and a new earth . . . There will be no more death or mourning or crying or pain, for the old order of things has passed away" (Revelation 21:1,4).

Isaiah 53:10–11

Yet it was the LORD's will to crush him and cause him to suffer, and though the LORD makes his life a guilt offering, he will see his offspring and prolong his days, and the will of the LORD will prosper in his hand. After the suffering of his soul, he will see the light of life and be satisfied; by his knowledge my righteous servant will justify many, and he will bear their iniquities.

reflection

1. Where do you see suffering today?
2. Can you give examples of how God has comforted you during a time of suffering or has brought you through a trial?
3. Think of someone you can encourage who is suffering. Which of God's promises can you share?

RELATED READINGS

Exodus 3:7–9;
Romans 5:3–8; 8:17–25;
James 1:2–4

Go to page 894 for your next devotional reading.

And who can speak of his descendants?
For he was cut off from the land of the living;
for the transgression of my people he was stricken.[a]
9 He was assigned a grave with the wicked,
and with the rich in his death,
though he had done no violence,
nor was any deceit in his mouth.
10 Yet it was the LORD's will to crush him and cause him to suffer,
and though the LORD makes[b] his life a guilt offering,
he will see his offspring and prolong his days,
and the will of the LORD will prosper in his hand.
11 After the suffering of his soul,
he will see the light ⌞of life⌟[c] and be satisfied[d];
by his knowledge[e] my righteous servant will justify many,
and he will bear their iniquities.
12 Therefore I will give him a portion among the great,[f]
and he will divide the spoils with the strong,[g]
because he poured out his life unto death,
and was numbered with the transgressors.
For he bore the sin of many,
and made intercession for the transgressors.

The Future Glory of Zion

54 "Sing, O barren woman,
you who never bore a child;
burst into song, shout for joy,
you who were never in labor;
because more are the children of the desolate woman
than of her who has a husband,"
says the LORD.
2 "Enlarge the place of your tent,
stretch your tent curtains wide,
do not hold back;
lengthen your cords,
strengthen your stakes.
3 For you will spread out to the right and to the left;
your descendants will dispossess nations
and settle in their desolate cities.

4 "Do not be afraid; you will not suffer shame.
Do not fear disgrace; you will not be humiliated.
You will forget the shame of your youth
and remember no more the reproach of your widowhood.
5 For your Maker is your husband—
the LORD Almighty is his name—
the Holy One of Israel is your Redeemer;
he is called the God of all the earth.
6 The LORD will call you back
as if you were a wife deserted and distressed in spirit—
a wife who married young,
only to be rejected," says your God.
7 "For a brief moment I abandoned you,
but with deep compassion I will bring you back.
8 In a surge of anger
I hid my face from you for a moment,
but with everlasting kindness
I will have compassion on you,"
says the LORD your Redeemer.

9 "To me this is like the days of Noah,
when I swore that the waters of Noah would never again cover the earth.
So now I have sworn not to be angry with you,
never to rebuke you again.
10 Though the mountains be shaken
and the hills be removed,
yet my unfailing love for you will not be shaken
nor my covenant of peace be removed,"
says the LORD, who has compassion on you.

11 "O afflicted city, lashed by storms and not comforted,

[a]8 Or *away. / Yet who of his generation considered / that he was cut off from the land of the living / for the transgression of my people, / to whom the blow was due?* [b]10 Hebrew *though you make* [c]11 Dead Sea Scrolls (see also Septuagint); Masoretic Text does not have *the light ⌞of life⌟*. [d]11 Or (with Masoretic Text) [11] *He will see the result of the suffering of his soul / and be satisfied* [e]11 Or *by knowledge of him* [f]12 Or *many* [g]12 Or *numerous*

I will build you with stones of
turquoise,[a]
your foundations with sapphires.[b]
12 I will make your battlements of rubies,
your gates of sparkling jewels,
and all your walls of precious stones.
13 All your sons will be taught by the LORD,
and great will be your children's peace.
14 In righteousness you will be established:
Tyranny will be far from you;
you will have nothing to fear.
Terror will be far removed;
it will not come near you.
15 If anyone does attack you, it will not be my
doing;
whoever attacks you will surrender to
you.

16 "See, it is I who created the blacksmith
who fans the coals into flame
and forges a weapon fit for its work.
And it is I who have created the destroyer
to work havoc;
17 no weapon forged against you will
prevail,
and you will refute every tongue that
accuses you.
This is the heritage of the servants of the
LORD,
and this is their
vindication from
me,"
declares the LORD.

Invitation to the Thirsty

55 "Come, all you who
are thirsty,
come to the waters;
and you who have no
money,
come, buy and eat!
Come, buy wine and milk
without money and
without cost.
2 Why spend money on what
is not bread,
and your labor on what
does not satisfy?
Listen, listen to me, and eat
what is good,

> **Isaiah 55:2**
>
> ### God Provides Satisfaction
>
> "Why spend money on
> what is not bread,
> and your labor on what
> does not satisfy?
> Listen, listen to me, and
> eat what is good,
> and your soul will delight
> in the richest of fare."

and your soul will delight in the richest
of fare.
3 Give ear and come to me;
hear me, that your soul may live.
I will make an everlasting covenant with
you,
my faithful love promised to David.
4 See, I have made him a witness to the
peoples,
a leader and commander of the peoples.
5 Surely you will summon nations you know
not,
and nations that do not know you will
hasten to you,
because of the LORD your God,
the Holy One of Israel,
for he has endowed you with splendor."

6 Seek the LORD while he may be found;
call on him while he is near.
7 Let the wicked forsake his way
and the evil man his thoughts.
Let him turn to the LORD, and he will have
mercy on him,
and to our God, for he will freely
pardon.

8 "For my thoughts are not your thoughts,
neither are your ways my ways,"
declares the LORD.
9 "As the heavens are higher
than the earth,
so are my ways higher
than your ways
and my thoughts than
your thoughts.
10 As the rain and the snow
come down from heaven,
and do not return to it
without watering the
earth
and making it bud and
flourish,
so that it yields seed for
the sower and bread
for the eater,
11 so is my word that goes out
from my mouth:
It will not return to me
empty,

[a] 11 The meaning of the Hebrew for this word is uncertain. [b] 11 Or *lapis lazuli*

but will accomplish what I desire
and achieve the purpose for which I sent it.
12 You will go out in joy
and be led forth in peace;
the mountains and hills
will burst into song before you,
and all the trees of the field
will clap their hands.
13 Instead of the thornbush will grow the pine tree,
and instead of briers the myrtle will grow.
This will be for the LORD's renown,
for an everlasting sign,
which will not be destroyed."

Salvation for Others

56 This is what the LORD says:

"Maintain justice
and do what is right,
for my salvation is close at hand
and my righteousness will soon be revealed.
2 Blessed is the man who does this,
the man who holds it fast,
who keeps the Sabbath without desecrating it,
and keeps his hand from doing any evil."

3 Let no foreigner who has bound himself to the LORD say,
"The LORD will surely exclude me from his people."
And let not any eunuch complain,
"I am only a dry tree."
4 For this is what the LORD says:

"To the eunuchs who keep my Sabbaths,
who choose what pleases me
and hold fast to my covenant—
5 to them I will give within my temple and its walls
a memorial and a name
better than sons and daughters;
I will give them an everlasting name
that will not be cut off.
6 And foreigners who bind themselves to the LORD
to serve him,
to love the name of the LORD,
and to worship him,
all who keep the Sabbath without desecrating it
and who hold fast to my covenant—
7 these I will bring to my holy mountain
and give them joy in my house of prayer.
Their burnt offerings and sacrifices
will be accepted on my altar;
for my house will be called
a house of prayer for all nations."
8 The Sovereign LORD declares—
he who gathers the exiles of Israel:
"I will gather still others to them
besides those already gathered."

God's Accusation Against the Wicked

9 Come, all you beasts of the field,
come and devour, all you beasts of the forest!
10 Israel's watchmen are blind,
they all lack knowledge;
they are all mute dogs,
they cannot bark;
they lie around and dream,
they love to sleep.
11 They are dogs with mighty appetites;
they never have enough.
They are shepherds who lack understanding;
they all turn to their own way,
each seeks his own gain.
12 "Come," each one cries, "let me get wine!
Let us drink our fill of beer!
And tomorrow will be like today,
or even far better."

57 The righteous perish,
and no one ponders it in his heart;
devout men are taken away,
and no one understands
that the righteous are taken away
to be spared from evil.
2 Those who walk uprightly
enter into peace;
they find rest as they lie in death.

3 "But you—come here, you sons of a sorceress,

you offspring of adulterers and
prostitutes!
4 Whom are you mocking?
At whom do you sneer
and stick out your tongue?
Are you not a brood of rebels,
the offspring of liars?
5 You burn with lust among the oaks
and under every spreading tree;
you sacrifice your children in the ravines
and under the overhanging crags.
6 ⌊The idols⌋ among the smooth stones of the
ravines are your portion;
they, they are your lot.
Yes, to them you have poured out drink
offerings
and offered grain offerings.
In the light of these things, should I
relent?
7 You have made your bed on a high and
lofty hill;
there you went up to offer your
sacrifices.
8 Behind your doors and your doorposts
you have put your pagan symbols.
Forsaking me, you uncovered your bed,
you climbed into it and opened it wide;
you made a pact with those whose beds
you love,
and you looked on their nakedness.
9 You went to Molech[a] with olive oil
and increased your perfumes.
You sent your ambassadors[b] far away;
you descended to the grave[c] itself!
10 You were wearied by all your ways,
but you would not say, 'It is hopeless.'
You found renewal of your strength,
and so you did not faint.

11 "Whom have you so dreaded and feared
that you have been false to me,
and have neither remembered me
nor pondered this in your hearts?
Is it not because I have long been silent
that you do not fear me?
12 I will expose your righteousness and your
works,
and they will not benefit you.
13 When you cry out for help,
let your collection ⌊of idols⌋ save you!
The wind will carry all of them off,
a mere breath will blow them away.
But the man who makes me his refuge
will inherit the land
and possess my holy mountain."

Comfort for the Contrite

14 And it will be said:

"Build up, build up, prepare the road!
Remove the obstacles out of the way of
my people."
15 For this is what the high and lofty One
says—
he who lives forever, whose name is
holy:
"I live in a high and holy place,
but also with him who is contrite and
lowly in spirit,
to revive the spirit of the lowly
and to revive the heart of the contrite.
16 I will not accuse forever,
nor will I always be angry,
for then the spirit of man would grow faint
before me—
the breath of man that I have created.
17 I was enraged by his sinful greed;
I punished him, and hid my face in
anger,
yet he kept on in his willful ways.
18 I have seen his ways, but I will heal him;
I will guide him and restore comfort to
him,
19 creating praise on the lips of the
mourners in Israel.
Peace, peace, to those far and near,"
says the LORD. "And I will heal them."
20 But the wicked are like the tossing sea,
which cannot rest,
whose waves cast up mire and mud.
21 "There is no peace," says my God, "for the
wicked."

True Fasting

58 "Shout it aloud, do not hold back.
Raise your voice like a trumpet.
Declare to my people their rebellion
and to the house of Jacob their sins.
2 For day after day they seek me out;

[a]9 Or *to the king* [b]9 Or *idols* [c]9 Hebrew *Sheol*

they seem eager to know my ways,
as if they were a nation that does what is right
and has not forsaken the commands of its God.
They ask me for just decisions
and seem eager for God to come near them.
3 'Why have we fasted,' they say,
'and you have not seen it?
Why have we humbled ourselves,
and you have not noticed?'

"Yet on the day of your fasting, you do as you please
and exploit all your workers.
4 Your fasting ends in quarreling and strife,
and in striking each other with wicked fists.
You cannot fast as you do today
and expect your voice to be heard on high.
5 Is this the kind of fast I have chosen,
only a day for a man to humble himself?
Is it only for bowing one's head like a reed
and for lying on sackcloth and ashes?
Is that what you call a fast,
a day acceptable to the LORD?

6 "Is not this the kind of fasting I have chosen:
to loose the chains of injustice
and untie the cords of the yoke,
to set the oppressed free
and break every yoke?
7 Is it not to share your food with the hungry
and to provide the poor wanderer with shelter—
when you see the naked, to clothe him,
and not to turn away from your own flesh and blood?
8 Then your light will break forth like the dawn,
and your healing will quickly appear;
then your righteousness[a] will go before you,
and the glory of the LORD will be your rear guard.
9 Then you will call, and the LORD will answer;
you will cry for help, and he will say: Here am I.

"If you do away with the yoke of oppression,
with the pointing finger and malicious talk,
10 and if you spend yourselves in behalf of the hungry
and satisfy the needs of the oppressed,
then your light will rise in the darkness,
and your night will become like the noonday.
11 The LORD will guide you always;
he will satisfy your needs in a sun-scorched land
and will strengthen your frame.
You will be like a well-watered garden,
like a spring whose waters never fail.
12 Your people will rebuild the ancient ruins
and will raise up the age-old foundations;
you will be called Repairer of Broken Walls,
Restorer of Streets with Dwellings.

13 "If you keep your feet from breaking the Sabbath
and from doing as you please on my holy day,
if you call the Sabbath a delight
and the LORD's holy day honorable,
and if you honor it by not going your own way
and not doing as you please or speaking idle words,

Isaiah 58:11

God Carries Us Through

"The LORD will guide you always;
he will satisfy your needs
in a sun-scorched land
and will strengthen
your frame."

[a]8 Or *your righteous One*

14 then you will find your joy in the LORD,
and I will cause you to ride on the heights of the land
and to feast on the inheritance of your father Jacob."
The mouth of the LORD has spoken.

Sin, Confession and Redemption

59 Surely the arm of the LORD is not too short to save,
nor his ear too dull to hear.
2 But your iniquities have separated you from your God;
your sins have hidden his face from you, so that he will not hear.
3 For your hands are stained with blood,
your fingers with guilt.
Your lips have spoken lies,
and your tongue mutters wicked things.
4 No one calls for justice;
no one pleads his case with integrity.
They rely on empty arguments and speak lies;
they conceive trouble and give birth to evil.
5 They hatch the eggs of vipers
and spin a spider's web.
Whoever eats their eggs will die,
and when one is broken, an adder is hatched.
6 Their cobwebs are useless for clothing;
they cannot cover themselves with what they make.
Their deeds are evil deeds,
and acts of violence are in their hands.
7 Their feet rush into sin;
they are swift to shed innocent blood.
Their thoughts are evil thoughts;
ruin and destruction mark their ways.
8 The way of peace they do not know;
there is no justice in their paths.
They have turned them into crooked roads;
no one who walks in them will know peace.
9 So justice is far from us,
and righteousness does not reach us.
We look for light, but all is darkness;
for brightness, but we walk in deep shadows.
10 Like the blind we grope along the wall,
feeling our way like men without eyes.
At midday we stumble as if it were twilight;
among the strong, we are like the dead.
11 We all growl like bears;
we moan mournfully like doves.
We look for justice, but find none;
for deliverance, but it is far away.

12 For our offenses are many in your sight,
and our sins testify against us.
Our offenses are ever with us,
and we acknowledge our iniquities:
13 rebellion and treachery against the LORD,
turning our backs on our God,
fomenting oppression and revolt,
uttering lies our hearts have conceived.
14 So justice is driven back,
and righteousness stands at a distance;
truth has stumbled in the streets,
honesty cannot enter.
15 Truth is nowhere to be found,
and whoever shuns evil becomes a prey.

The LORD looked and was displeased
that there was no justice.
16 He saw that there was no one,
he was appalled that there was no one to intervene;
so his own arm worked salvation for him,
and his own righteousness sustained him.
17 He put on righteousness as his breastplate,
and the helmet of salvation on his head;
he put on the garments of vengeance
and wrapped himself in zeal as in a cloak.
18 According to what they have done,
so will he repay
wrath to his enemies
and retribution to his foes;
he will repay the islands their due.
19 From the west, men will fear the name of the LORD,
and from the rising of the sun, they will revere his glory.
For he will come like a pent-up flood
that the breath of the LORD drives along.[a]

[a] 19 Or *When the enemy comes in like a flood, / the Spirit of the LORD will put him to flight*

20 "The Redeemer will come to Zion,
to those in Jacob who repent of their sins,"
declares the LORD.

21 "As for me, this is my covenant with them,"
says the LORD. "My Spirit, who is on you, and
my words that I have put in your mouth will not
depart from your mouth, or from the mouths
of your children, or from the mouths of their
descendants from this time on and forever,"
says the LORD.

The Glory of Zion

60 "Arise, shine, for your light has come,
and the glory of the LORD rises upon you.
2 See, darkness covers the earth
and thick darkness is over the peoples,
but the LORD rises upon you
and his glory appears over you.
3 Nations will come to your light,
and kings to the brightness of your dawn.

4 "Lift up your eyes and look about you:
All assemble and come to you;
your sons come from afar,
and your daughters are carried on the arm.
5 Then you will look and be radiant,
your heart will throb and swell with joy;
the wealth on the seas will be brought to you,
to you the riches of the nations will come.
6 Herds of camels will cover your land,
young camels of Midian and Ephah.
And all from Sheba will come,
bearing gold and incense
and proclaiming the praise of the LORD.
7 All Kedar's flocks will be gathered to you,
the rams of Nebaioth will serve you;
they will be accepted as offerings on my altar,
and I will adorn my glorious temple.

8 "Who are these that fly along like clouds,
like doves to their nests?
9 Surely the islands look to me;
in the lead are the ships of Tarshish,[a]
bringing your sons from afar,
with their silver and gold,
to the honor of the LORD your God,
the Holy One of Israel,
for he has endowed you with splendor.

10 "Foreigners will rebuild your walls,
and their kings will serve you.
Though in anger I struck you,
in favor I will show you compassion.
11 Your gates will always stand open,
they will never be shut, day or night,
so that men may bring you the wealth of the nations—
their kings led in triumphal procession.
12 For the nation or kingdom that will not serve you will perish;
it will be utterly ruined.

13 "The glory of Lebanon will come to you,
the pine, the fir and the cypress together,
to adorn the place of my sanctuary;
and I will glorify the place of my feet.
14 The sons of your oppressors will come bowing before you;
all who despise you will bow down at your feet
and will call you the City of the LORD,
Zion of the Holy One of Israel.

15 "Although you have been forsaken and hated,
with no one traveling through,
I will make you the everlasting pride
and the joy of all generations.
16 You will drink the milk of nations
and be nursed at royal breasts.
Then you will know that I, the LORD, am your Savior,
your Redeemer, the Mighty One of Jacob.
17 Instead of bronze I will bring you gold,
and silver in place of iron.
Instead of wood I will bring you bronze,
and iron in place of stones.
I will make peace your governor
and righteousness your ruler.
18 No longer will violence be heard in your land,

[a]9 Or *the trading ships*

nor ruin or destruction within your
borders,
but you will call your walls Salvation
and your gates Praise.
19 The sun will no more be your light by day,
nor will the brightness of the moon
shine on you,
for the LORD will be your everlasting light,
and your God will be your glory.
20 Your sun will never set again,
and your moon will wane no more;
the LORD will be your everlasting light,
and your days of sorrow will end.
21 Then will all your people be righteous
and they will possess the land forever.
They are the shoot I have planted,
the work of my hands,
for the display of my splendor.
22 The least of you will become a thousand,
the smallest a mighty nation.
I am the LORD;
in its time I will do this swiftly."

The Year of the LORD's Favor

61 The Spirit of the Sovereign LORD is
on me,
because the LORD has anointed me
to preach good news to the poor.
He has sent me to bind up the
brokenhearted,
to proclaim freedom for the captives
and release from
darkness for the
prisoners,[a]
2 to proclaim the year of the
LORD's favor
and the day of vengeance
of our God,
to comfort all who mourn,
3 and provide for those
who grieve in
Zion—
to bestow on them a crown
of beauty
instead of ashes,
the oil of gladness
instead of mourning,
and a garment of praise
instead of a spirit of despair.
They will be called oaks of righteousness,
a planting of the LORD
for the display of his splendor.

4 They will rebuild the ancient ruins
and restore the places long devastated;
they will renew the ruined cities
that have been devastated for
generations.
5 Aliens will shepherd your flocks;
foreigners will work your fields and
vineyards.
6 And you will be called priests of the LORD,
you will be named ministers of our God.
You will feed on the wealth of nations,
and in their riches you will boast.

7 Instead of their shame
my people will receive a double portion,
and instead of disgrace
they will rejoice in their inheritance;
and so they will inherit a double portion in
their land,
and everlasting joy will be theirs.

8 "For I, the LORD, love justice;
I hate robbery and iniquity.
In my faithfulness I will reward them
and make an everlasting covenant with
them.
9 Their descendants will be known among
the nations
and their offspring among the peoples.
All who see them will
acknowledge
that they are a people the
LORD has blessed."

10 I delight greatly in the
LORD;
my soul rejoices in my
God.
For he has clothed me
with garments of
salvation
and arrayed me in a robe
of righteousness,
as a bridegroom adorns his
head like a priest,
and as a bride adorns herself with her
jewels.
11 For as the soil makes the sprout come up

Isaiah 61:10

God Saves

I delight greatly in
the LORD . . .
For he has clothed
me with garments of
salvation
and arrayed me in a robe
of righteousness.

[a]1 Hebrew; Septuagint *the blind*

Splendor

Read: Isaiah 61:1–6

Isaiah 61:3

[He will] provide for those who grieve in Zion—to bestow on them a crown of beauty instead of ashes, the oil of gladness instead of mourning, and a garment of praise instead of a spirit of despair. They will be called oaks of righteousness, a planting of the LORD for the display of his splendor.

MARY WAS BORN INTO A DIRTY and crowded working-class district in Scotland in 1848. Her father sometimes threw her out on the streets when he arrived home drunk, and by age 14 she was working ten-hour shifts at the textile mill to support her family.

But God exchanged Mary Slessor's misery for something better when she began working at a city mission in Dundee. While there, she was inspired to sail to West Africa as a missionary to Calabar. Mary was no richer in Africa than she had been in Scotland—in fact, she now made her home in a mud hut. Throughout her 39 years in Africa, she never married. She was not even always in good health: Malaria and boils plagued her.

Yet, despite the pain she suffered, God displayed his splendor through Mary and her work. She found joy in rescuing children from ritual murder. She discovered pleasure and purpose serving as a peacemaker with the Okoyong people. And she adopted a family. "If anyone may testify as to the reality of his presence and power, it is surely this unworthy servant," she wrote to a friend. "He and his Word are a living bright reality for sure . . . I mean to glorify him and to magnify his grace."

The Israelites also had their share of misery. The Assyrians swept them from their homeland, destroying all they loved and everything familiar. However, their story, like Mary's, didn't end in misery. In fact, Isaiah predicted joy was ahead. God planned to exchange their mourning and despair for gladness and praise. Why? So that once rescued, God's people would be living demonstrations of his splendor.

We each suffer our own miseries, and we think things will never change. Perhaps you've experienced burdensome memories, a scarring divorce or a difficult diagnosis. However, can you sense any hope? Can you see God on the march, gradually transforming the pain into something you can endure? You never know; up ahead you just might see the possibility of joy. Like the Jews in exile, and like Mary Slessor in Scotland, you can trust that, despite the present pain, God has plans for your future. He is able to use whatever you go through today to display his splendor through you tomorrow.

reflection

1 How does this passage bring hope to your times of misery?

2 How does God's ability to transform your grief into joy demonstrate his power?

3 How might God be planning to display his splendor through your current difficult circumstance?

RELATED READINGS

Psalm 92:12–13; Isaiah 44:23; Jeremiah 31:13; 1 Peter 4:12–13

Go to page 905 for your next devotional reading.

and a garden causes seeds to grow,
so the Sovereign LORD will make
righteousness and praise
spring up before all nations.

Zion's New Name

62 For Zion's sake I will not keep silent,
for Jerusalem's sake I will not remain
quiet,
till her righteousness shines out like the
dawn,
her salvation like a blazing torch.
2 The nations will see your righteousness,
and all kings your glory;
you will be called by a new name
that the mouth of the LORD will
bestow.
3 You will be a crown of splendor in the
LORD's hand,
a royal diadem in the hand of your
God.
4 No longer will they call you Deserted,
or name your land Desolate.
But you will be called Hephzibah,[a]
and your land Beulah[b];
for the LORD will take delight in you,
and your land will be married.
5 As a young man marries a maiden,
so will your sons[c] marry you;
as a bridegroom rejoices over his bride,
so will your God rejoice over you.

6 I have posted watchmen on your walls,
O Jerusalem;
they will never be silent day or night.
You who call on the LORD,
give yourselves no rest,
7 and give him no rest till he establishes
Jerusalem
and makes her the praise of the earth.

8 The LORD has sworn by his right hand
and by his mighty arm:
"Never again will I give your grain
as food for your enemies,
and never again will foreigners drink the
new wine
for which you have toiled;
9 but those who harvest it will eat it
and praise the LORD,
and those who gather the grapes will
drink it
in the courts of my sanctuary."

10 Pass through, pass through the gates!
Prepare the way for the people.
Build up, build up the highway!
Remove the stones.
Raise a banner for the nations.

11 The LORD has made proclamation
to the ends of the earth:
"Say to the Daughter of Zion,
'See, your Savior comes!
See, his reward is with him,
and his recompense accompanies him.'"
12 They will be called the Holy People,
the Redeemed of the LORD;
and you will be called Sought After,
the City No Longer Deserted.

God's Day of Vengeance and Redemption

63 Who is this coming from Edom,
from Bozrah, with his garments
stained crimson?
Who is this, robed in splendor,
striding forward in the greatness of his
strength?

"It is I, speaking in righteousness,
mighty to save."

2 Why are your garments red,
like those of one treading the winepress?

3 "I have trodden the winepress alone;
from the nations no one was with me.
I trampled them in my anger
and trod them down in my wrath;
their blood spattered my garments,
and I stained all my clothing.
4 For the day of vengeance was in my heart,
and the year of my redemption has
come.
5 I looked, but there was no one to help,
I was appalled that no one gave support;
so my own arm worked salvation for me,
and my own wrath sustained me.
6 I trampled the nations in my anger;
in my wrath I made them drunk
and poured their blood on the ground."

[a] 4 *Hephzibah* means *my delight is in her.* [b] 4 *Beulah* means *married.* [c] 5 Or *Builder*

Praise and Prayer

7 I will tell of the kindnesses of the LORD,
the deeds for which he is to be praised,
according to all the LORD has done for us—
yes, the many good things he has done
for the house of Israel,
according to his compassion and many kindnesses.
8 He said, "Surely they are my people,
sons who will not be false to me";
and so he became their Savior.
9 In all their distress he too was distressed,
and the angel of his presence saved them.
In his love and mercy he redeemed them;
he lifted them up and carried them
all the days of old.
10 Yet they rebelled
and grieved his Holy Spirit.
So he turned and became their enemy
and he himself fought against them.

11 Then his people recalled[a] the days of old,
the days of Moses and his people—
where is he who brought them through the sea,
with the shepherd of his flock?
Where is he who set
his Holy Spirit among them,
12 who sent his glorious arm of power
to be at Moses' right hand,
who divided the waters before them,
to gain for himself everlasting renown,
13 who led them through the depths?
Like a horse in open country,
they did not stumble;
14 like cattle that go down to the plain,
they were given rest by the Spirit of the LORD.
This is how you guided your people
to make for yourself a glorious name.

15 Look down from heaven and see
from your lofty throne, holy and glorious.
Where are your zeal and your might?
Your tenderness and compassion are withheld from us.
16 But you are our Father,
though Abraham does not know us
or Israel acknowledge us;
you, O LORD, are our Father,
our Redeemer from of old is your name.
17 Why, O LORD, do you make us wander from your ways
and harden our hearts so we do not revere you?
Return for the sake of your servants,
the tribes that are your inheritance.
18 For a little while your people possessed your holy place,
but now our enemies have trampled down your sanctuary.
19 We are yours from of old;
but you have not ruled over them,
they have not been called by your name.[b]

64 Oh, that you would rend the heavens
and come down,
that the mountains would tremble before you!
2 As when fire sets twigs ablaze
and causes water to boil,
come down to make your name known to your enemies
and cause the nations to quake before you!
3 For when you did awesome things that we did not expect,
you came down, and the mountains trembled before you.
4 Since ancient times no one has heard,
no ear has perceived,
no eye has seen any God besides you,

Isaiah 64:1

God Is Powerful

Oh, that you would rend the heavens and come down, that the mountains would tremble before you!

[a]11 Or *But may he recall* [b]19 Or *We are like those you have never ruled, / like those never called by your name*

who acts on behalf of those who wait
for him.
5 You come to the help of those who gladly
do right,
who remember your ways.
But when we continued to sin against
them,
you were angry.
How then can we be saved?
6 All of us have become like one who is
unclean,
and all our righteous acts are like filthy
rags;
we all shrivel up like a leaf,
and like the wind our sins sweep us
away.
7 No one calls on your name
or strives to lay hold of you;
for you have hidden your face from us
and made us waste away because of our
sins.

8 Yet, O LORD, you are our Father.
We are the clay, you are the potter;
we are all the work of your hand.
9 Do not be angry beyond measure, O LORD;
do not remember our sins forever.
Oh, look upon us, we pray,
for we are all your people.
10 Your sacred cities have become a desert;
even Zion is a desert, Jerusalem a
desolation.
11 Our holy and glorious temple, where our
fathers praised you,
has been burned with fire,
and all that we treasured lies in ruins.
12 After all this, O LORD, will you hold
yourself back?
Will you keep silent and punish us
beyond measure?

Judgment and Salvation

65 "I revealed myself to those who did
not ask for me;
I was found by those who did not seek
me.
To a nation that did not call on my name,
I said, 'Here am I, here am I.'
2 All day long I have held out my hands
to an obstinate people,
who walk in ways not good,
pursuing their own imaginations—
3 a people who continually provoke me
to my very face,
offering sacrifices in gardens
and burning incense on altars of brick;
4 who sit among the graves
and spend their nights keeping secret
vigil;
who eat the flesh of pigs,
and whose pots hold broth of unclean
meat;
5 who say, 'Keep away; don't come near me,
for I am too sacred for you!'
Such people are smoke in my nostrils,
a fire that keeps burning all day.

6 "See, it stands written before me:
I will not keep silent but will pay back
in full;
I will pay it back into their laps—
7 both your sins and the sins of your
fathers,"
says the LORD.
"Because they burned sacrifices on the
mountains
and defied me on the hills,
I will measure into their laps
the full payment for their former deeds."

8 This is what the LORD says:

"As when juice is still found in a cluster of
grapes
and men say, 'Don't destroy it,
there is yet some good in it,'
so will I do in behalf of my servants;
I will not destroy them all.
9 I will bring forth descendants from Jacob,
and from Judah those who will possess
my mountains;
my chosen people will inherit them,
and there will my servants live.
10 Sharon will become a pasture for flocks,
and the Valley of Achor a resting place
for herds,
for my people who seek me.

11 "But as for you who forsake the LORD
and forget my holy mountain,
who spread a table for Fortune
and fill bowls of mixed wine for Destiny,
12 I will destine you for the sword,

and you will all bend down for the
slaughter;
for I called but you did not answer,
I spoke but you did not listen.
You did evil in my sight
and chose what displeases me."

13 Therefore this is what the Sovereign LORD says:

"My servants will eat,
but you will go hungry;
my servants will drink,
but you will go thirsty;
my servants will rejoice,
but you will be put to shame.
14 My servants will sing
out of the joy of their hearts,
but you will cry out
from anguish of heart
and wail in brokenness
of spirit.
15 You will leave your name
to my chosen ones as a
curse;
the Sovereign LORD will
put you to death,
but to his servants he will
give another name.
16 Whoever invokes a blessing
in the land
will do so by the God of
truth;
he who takes an oath in the
land
will swear by the God of truth.
For the past troubles will be forgotten
and hidden from my eyes.

New Heavens and a New Earth

17 "Behold, I will create
new heavens and a new earth.
The former things will not be remembered,
nor will they come to mind.
18 But be glad and rejoice forever
in what I will create,
for I will create Jerusalem to be a delight
and its people a joy.
19 I will rejoice over Jerusalem
and take delight in my people;
the sound of weeping and of crying
will be heard in it no more.
20 "Never again will there be in it
an infant who lives but a few days,
or an old man who does not live out his
years;
he who dies at a hundred
will be thought a mere youth;
he who fails to reach[a] a hundred
will be considered accursed.
21 They will build houses and dwell in them;
they will plant vineyards and eat their
fruit.
22 No longer will they build houses and
others live in them,
or plant and others eat.
For as the days of a tree,
so will be the days of my people;
my chosen ones will long
enjoy
the works of their hands.
23 They will not toil in vain
or bear children doomed
to misfortune;
for they will be a people
blessed by the
LORD,
they and their
descendants with
them.
24 Before they call I will
answer;
while they are still
speaking I will hear.
25 The wolf and the lamb will feed together,
and the lion will eat straw like the ox,
but dust will be the serpent's food.
They will neither harm nor destroy
on all my holy mountain,"
says the LORD.

Isaiah 65:24

God Has Quick Answers

"Before they call
I will answer;
while they are still
speaking I will hear."

Judgment and Hope

66

This is what the LORD says:

"Heaven is my throne,
and the earth is my footstool.
Where is the house you will build for me?
Where will my resting place be?
2 Has not my hand made all these things,

[a] 20 Or *I the sinner who reaches*

and so they came into being?"
declares the LORD.

"This is the one I esteem:
he who is humble and contrite in spirit,
and trembles at my word.
3 But whoever sacrifices a bull
is like one who kills a man,
and whoever offers a lamb,
like one who breaks a dog's neck;
whoever makes a grain offering
is like one who presents pig's blood,
and whoever burns memorial incense,
like one who worships an idol.
They have chosen their own ways,
and their souls delight in their
abominations;
4 so I also will choose harsh treatment for
them
and will bring upon them what they
dread.
For when I called, no one answered,
when I spoke, no one listened.
They did evil in my sight
and chose what displeases me."

5 Hear the word of the LORD,
you who tremble at his word:
"Your brothers who hate you,
and exclude you because of my name,
have said,
'Let the LORD be glorified,
that we may see your joy!'
Yet they will be put to shame.
6 Hear that uproar from the city,
hear that noise from the temple!
It is the sound of the LORD
repaying his enemies all they deserve.

7 "Before she goes into labor,
she gives birth;
before the pains come upon her,
she delivers a son.
8 Who has ever heard of such a thing?
Who has ever seen such things?
Can a country be born in a day
or a nation be brought forth in a
moment?
Yet no sooner is Zion in labor
than she gives birth to her children.
9 Do I bring to the moment of birth
and not give delivery?" says the LORD.
"Do I close up the womb
when I bring to delivery?" says your
God.
10 "Rejoice with Jerusalem and be glad for
her,
all you who love her;
rejoice greatly with her,
all you who mourn over her.
11 For you will nurse and be satisfied
at her comforting breasts;
you will drink deeply
and delight in her overflowing
abundance."

12 For this is what the LORD says:

"I will extend peace to her like a river,
and the wealth of nations like a flooding
stream;
you will nurse and be carried on her arm
and dandled on her knees.
13 As a mother comforts her child,
so will I comfort you;
and you will be comforted over
Jerusalem."

14 When you see this, your heart will rejoice
and you will flourish like grass;
the hand of the LORD will be made known
to his servants,
but his fury will be shown to his foes.
15 See, the LORD is coming with fire,
and his chariots are like a whirlwind;
he will bring down his anger with fury,
and his rebuke with flames of fire.
16 For with fire and with his sword
the LORD will execute judgment upon
all men,
and many will be those slain by the
LORD.

17 "Those who consecrate and purify themselves to go into the gardens, following the one in the midst of[a] those who eat the flesh of pigs and rats and other abominable things—they will meet their end together," declares the LORD.

18 "And I, because of their actions and their imaginations, am about to come[b] and gather

[a]17 Or *gardens behind one of your temples, and* [b]18 The meaning of the Hebrew for this clause is uncertain.

all nations and tongues, and they will come and
see my glory.
19"I will set a sign among them, and I will
send some of those who survive to the nations—to Tarshish, to the Libyans[a] and Lydi-
ans (famous as archers), to Tubal and Greece,
and to the distant islands that have not heard of
my fame or seen my glory. They will proclaim
my glory among the nations. 20And they will
bring all your brothers, from all the nations, to
my holy mountain in Jerusalem as an offering
to the LORD—on horses, in chariots and wagons, and on mules and camels," says the LORD.
"They will bring them, as the Israelites bring
their grain offerings, to the temple of the LORD
in ceremonially clean vessels. 21And I will
select some of them also to be priests and Levites," says the LORD.

22"As the new heavens and the new earth
that I make will endure before me," declares
the LORD, "so will your name and descendants
endure. 23From one New Moon to another
and from one Sabbath to another, all mankind
will come and bow down before me," says the
LORD. 24"And they will go out and look upon
the dead bodies of those who rebelled against
me; their worm will not die, nor will their fire
be quenched, and they will be loathsome to
all mankind."

[a]19 Some Septuagint manuscripts *Put* (Libyans); Hebrew *Pul*

Jeremiah

The people of Jerusalem used to love God with the love of a new bride for her husband; now even the priests, lawmakers, leaders and prophets have begun to worship Baal and other false gods. God has warned the people for 23 years, and *now his patience* is coming to an end. Judah is about to go into exile for 70 years. They had broken God's covenant, and now they would suffer the consequences.

Even in the prediction of doom, *there is hope.* The time of exile will not last forever; God's people will be restored. God's prophet, Jeremiah, is to buy a field to emphasize that point. But notice how Jeremiah and his message were received. Yet Jeremiah is obedient to God, and *God is faithful to his promises.*

Author:
Jeremiah.

Audience:
Jerusalem—Judah's capital city.

Date:
Jeremiah wrote from 626 B.C. through sometime after the fall of Jerusalem in 586 B.C.

Setting:
Jeremiah's message is Judah's last hope before God allows Babylon to sweep the country away.

Verse to Remember:
"My people have committed two sins: They have forsaken me, the spring of living water, and have dug their own cisterns, broken cisterns that cannot hold water." (2:13)

1 The words of Jeremiah son of Hilkiah, one
of the priests at Anathoth in the territory
of Benjamin. 2The word of the LORD came to
him in the thirteenth year of the reign of Josiah
son of Amon king of Judah, 3and through the
reign of Jehoiakim son of Josiah king of Judah,
down to the fifth month of the eleventh year of
Zedekiah son of Josiah king of Judah, when the
people of Jerusalem went into exile.

The Call of Jeremiah

4The word of the LORD came to me, saying,
5"Before I formed you in the womb I knew[a]
you,

[a]5 Or *chose*

before you were born I set you apart;
I appointed you as a prophet to the
nations."

6"Ah, Sovereign LORD," I said, "I do not
know how to speak; I am only a child."
7But the LORD said to me, "Do not say, 'I am
only a child.' You must go to everyone I send
you to and say whatever I command you. 8Do
not be afraid of them, for I am with you and
will rescue you," declares the LORD.
9Then the LORD reached out his hand and
touched my mouth and said to me, "Now, I
have put my words in your mouth. 10See, today
I appoint you over nations and kingdoms to uproot and tear down, to destroy and overthrow,
to build and to plant."
11The word of the LORD came to me: "What
do you see, Jeremiah?"

"I see the branch of an almond tree," I replied.
12The LORD said to me, "You have seen
correctly, for I am watching[a] to see that my
word is fulfilled."
13The word of the LORD came to me again:
"What do you see?"

"I see a boiling pot, tilting away from the
north," I answered.
14The LORD said to me, "From the north disaster will be poured out on all who live in the
land. 15I am about to summon all the peoples
of the northern kingdoms," declares the LORD.

"Their kings will come and set up their
thrones
in the entrance of the gates of
Jerusalem;
they will come against all her surrounding
walls
and against all the towns of Judah.
16I will pronounce my judgments on my
people
because of their wickedness in forsaking
me,
in burning incense to other gods
and in worshiping what their hands
have made.

17"Get yourself ready! Stand up and say to
them whatever I command you. Do not be
terrified by them, or I will terrify you before
them. 18Today I have made you a fortified city,
an iron pillar and a bronze wall to stand against
the whole land—against the kings of Judah, its
officials, its priests and the people of the land.
19They will fight against you but will not overcome you, for I am with you and will rescue
you," declares the LORD.

Israel Forsakes God

2 The word of the LORD came to me: 2"Go
and proclaim in the hearing of Jerusalem:

"'I remember the devotion of your youth,
how as a bride you loved me
and followed me through the desert,
through a land not sown.
3Israel was holy to the LORD,
the firstfruits of his harvest;
all who devoured her were held guilty,
and disaster overtook them,'"
declares the LORD.

4Hear the word of the LORD, O house of
Jacob,
all you clans of the house of Israel.

5This is what the LORD says:

"What fault did your fathers find in me,
that they strayed so far from me?
They followed worthless idols
and became worthless themselves.
6They did not ask, 'Where is the LORD,
who brought us up out of Egypt
and led us through the barren
wilderness,
through a land of deserts and rifts,
a land of drought and darkness,[b]
a land where no one travels and no one
lives?'
7I brought you into a fertile land
to eat its fruit and rich produce.
But you came and defiled my land
and made my inheritance detestable.
8The priests did not ask,
'Where is the LORD?'
Those who deal with the law did not know
me;
the leaders rebelled against me.
The prophets prophesied by Baal,
following worthless idols.

[a] 12 The Hebrew for *watching* sounds like the Hebrew for *almond tree.* [b] 6 Or *and the shadow of death*

9 "Therefore I bring charges against you
again,"
declares the LORD.
"And I will bring charges against your
children's children.
10 Cross over to the coasts of Kittim[a] and
look,
send to Kedar[b] and observe closely;
see if there has ever been anything like
this:
11 Has a nation ever changed its gods?
(Yet they are not gods at all.)
But my people have exchanged their[c] Glory
for worthless idols.
12 Be appalled at this, O heavens,
and shudder with great horror,"
declares the LORD.
13 "My people have committed two sins:
They have forsaken me,
the spring of living water,
and have dug their own
cisterns,
broken cisterns that
cannot hold water.
14 Is Israel a servant, a slave by
birth?
Why then has he become
plunder?
15 Lions have roared;
they have growled at him.
They have laid waste his
land;
his towns are burned and
deserted.
16 Also, the men of Memphis[d]
and Tahpanhes
have shaved the crown of your head.[e]
17 Have you not brought this on yourselves
by forsaking the LORD your God
when he led you in the way?
18 Now why go to Egypt
to drink water from the Shihor[f]?
And why go to Assyria
to drink water from the River[g]?
19 Your wickedness will punish you;
your backsliding will rebuke you.
Consider then and realize
how evil and bitter it is for you
when you forsake the LORD your God
and have no awe of me,"
declares the Lord, the LORD Almighty.
20 "Long ago you broke off your yoke
and tore off your bonds;
you said, 'I will not serve you!'
Indeed, on every high hill
and under every spreading tree
you lay down as a prostitute.
21 I had planted you like a choice vine
of sound and reliable stock.
How then did you turn against me
into a corrupt, wild vine?
22 Although you wash yourself with soda
and use an abundance of soap,
the stain of your guilt is still before me,"
declares the Sovereign LORD.
23 "How can you say, 'I am not defiled;
I have not run after the
Baals'?
See how you behaved in the
valley;
consider what you have
done.
You are a swift she-camel
running here and there,
24 a wild donkey accustomed
to the desert,
sniffing the wind in her
craving—
in her heat who can
restrain her?
Any males that pursue
her need not tire
themselves;
at mating time they will find her.
25 Do not run until your feet are bare
and your throat is dry.
But you said, 'It's no use!
I love foreign gods,
and I must go after them.'
26 "As a thief is disgraced when he is caught,
so the house of Israel is disgraced—
they, their kings and their officials,
their priests and their prophets.
27 They say to wood, 'You are my father,'
and to stone, 'You gave me birth.'

Jeremiah 2:13

God Is a Spring of Life

"My people have
committed two sins:
They have forsaken me,
the spring of living water,
and have dug their
own cisterns."

[a]10 That is, Cyprus and western coastlands [b]10 The home of Bedouin tribes in the Syro-Arabian desert [c]11 Masoretic Text; an ancient Hebrew scribal tradition *my* [d]16 Hebrew *Noph* [e]16 Or *have cracked your skull* [f]18 That is, a branch of the Nile [g]18 That is, the Euphrates

They have turned their backs to me
and not their faces;
yet when they are in trouble, they say,
'Come and save us!'
28 Where then are the gods you made for yourselves?
Let them come if they can save you
when you are in trouble!
For you have as many gods
as you have towns, O Judah.

29 "Why do you bring charges against me?
You have all rebelled against me,"
declares the LORD.
30 "In vain I punished your people;
they did not respond to correction.
Your sword has devoured your prophets
like a ravening lion.

31 "You of this generation, consider the word of the LORD:

"Have I been a desert to Israel
or a land of great darkness?
Why do my people say, 'We are free to roam;
we will come to you no more'?
32 Does a maiden forget her jewelry,
a bride her wedding ornaments?
Yet my people have forgotten me,
days without number.
33 How skilled you are at pursuing love!
Even the worst of women can learn from your ways.
34 On your clothes men find
the lifeblood of the innocent poor,
though you did not catch them breaking in.
Yet in spite of all this
35 you say, 'I am innocent;
he is not angry with me.'
But I will pass judgment on you
because you say, 'I have not sinned.'
36 Why do you go about so much,
changing your ways?
You will be disappointed by Egypt
as you were by Assyria.
37 You will also leave that place
with your hands on your head,
for the LORD has rejected those you trust;
you will not be helped by them.

3 "If a man divorces his wife
and she leaves him and marries another man,
should he return to her again?
Would not the land be completely defiled?
But you have lived as a prostitute with many lovers—
would you now return to me?"
declares the LORD.

2 "Look up to the barren heights and see.
Is there any place where you have not been ravished?
By the roadside you sat waiting for lovers,
sat like a nomad[a] in the desert.
You have defiled the land
with your prostitution and wickedness.
3 Therefore the showers have been withheld,
and no spring rains have fallen.
Yet you have the brazen look of a prostitute;
you refuse to blush with shame.
4 Have you not just called to me:
'My Father, my friend from my youth,
5 will you always be angry?
Will your wrath continue forever?'
This is how you talk,
but you do all the evil you can."

Unfaithful Israel

6 During the reign of King Josiah, the LORD
said to me, "Have you seen what faithless Israel
has done? She has gone up on every high hill
and under every spreading tree and has committed adultery there. 7 I thought that after she
had done all this she would return to me but
she did not, and her unfaithful sister Judah saw
it. 8 I gave faithless Israel her certificate of divorce and sent her away because of all her adulteries. Yet I saw that her unfaithful sister Judah
had no fear; she also went out and committed
adultery. 9 Because Israel's immorality mattered
so little to her, she defiled the land and committed adultery with stone and wood. 10 In spite
of all this, her unfaithful sister Judah did not
return to me with all her heart, but only in pretense," declares the LORD.

11 The LORD said to me, "Faithless Israel is
more righteous than unfaithful Judah. 12 Go,
proclaim this message toward the north:

[a]2 Or *an Arab*

Inside Out

Read: Jeremiah 2:32–33

LIKE MANY WOMEN each morning, perhaps you wake up, pour yourself a cup of caffeine, take a shower and then get ready to meet the world. You pick out an outfit (preferably one that makes you look five to ten pounds lighter), do your hair and put on makeup. Finally, you add jewelry, a belt and maybe a purse. Voilà! You're ready to meet the day.

The care involved in our routines begs the question: How much time do we spend getting ready *spiritually* each morning? Do we take any time at all to ask God to guide us during our day? Do we read the Scriptures, meditate or pray so that we can be more patient, kind and loving with our spouse and children? Or do we worry more about getting out the door than about the condition of our hearts?

Caring for our outward appearance is not wrong . . . as long as we don't neglect focusing on our inner thoughts and attitudes too. The prophet Jeremiah noted that women are unlikely to forget their accessories, but God's people are prone to forget him. If we're honest, we'll admit that we are much like the Israelites. In the midst of our busy lives, God often gets pushed to the bottom of our to-do lists. But spiritual growth happens from the inside out.

Try this: Tomorrow as you shower, praise God for the cleansing that Jesus' forgiveness provides. As you're getting dressed, thank God for clothing you with Christ's righteousness. When you put on your moisturizer, ask God to soften your heart to his leading throughout the day. As you apply your makeup, thank him for being the foundation of your life. When you put in your contacts, ask God to give you eyes to see his workings in the world. And as you put on your earrings, thank him for beautifying your life with the fruits of the Spirit.

Who knows? After talking to God throughout the morning, you might not even need caffeine!

Jeremiah 2:32

"Does a maiden forget her jewelry, a bride her wedding ornaments? Yet my people have forgotten me, days without number."

reflection

1 What "enemies of the soul" (busyness, etc.) cause you to sometimes forget to take time with God?

2 How much time do you spend daily in prayer and Bible study, preparing your heart for the day?

3 What are some ways you can become more balanced in your life?

RELATED READINGS

Psalm 5:1–3; Proverbs 31:30; Romans 12:1–2; Ephesians 4:21–24; 1 Peter 3:3–6

"Help me, God, to slow down, to be silent, so I can hear You and do Your will and not mine."

Marian Wright Edelman

Go to page 915 for your next devotional reading.

"'Return, faithless Israel,' declares the LORD,
'I will frown on you no longer,
for I am merciful,' declares the LORD,
'I will not be angry forever.
13 Only acknowledge your guilt—
you have rebelled against the LORD your God,
you have scattered your favors to foreign gods
under every spreading tree,
and have not obeyed me,'"
declares the LORD.

14 "Return, faithless people," declares the
LORD, "for I am your husband. I will choose
you—one from a town and two from a clan—
and bring you to Zion. 15 Then
I will give you shepherds after
my own heart, who will lead
you with knowledge and understanding. 16 In those days, when
your numbers have increased
greatly in the land," declares
the LORD, "men will no longer
say, 'The ark of the covenant of
the LORD.' It will never enter
their minds or be remembered;
it will not be missed, nor will
another one be made. 17 At that
time they will call Jerusalem
The Throne of the LORD, and
all nations will gather in Jerusalem to honor the name of the LORD. No longer
will they follow the stubbornness of their evil
hearts. 18 In those days the house of Judah will
join the house of Israel, and together they will
come from a northern land to the land I gave
your forefathers as an inheritance.

Jeremiah 3:15

God Commissions Caretakers

"Then I will give you shepherds after my own heart, who will lead you with knowledge and understanding."

19 "I myself said,

"'How gladly would I treat you like sons
and give you a desirable land,
the most beautiful inheritance of any nation.'
I thought you would call me 'Father'
and not turn away from following me.
20 But like a woman unfaithful to her husband,
so you have been unfaithful to me,
O house of Israel,"
declares the LORD.

21 A cry is heard on the barren heights,
the weeping and pleading of the people of Israel,
because they have perverted their ways
and have forgotten the LORD their God.

22 "Return, faithless people;
I will cure you of backsliding."

"Yes, we will come to you,
for you are the LORD our God.
23 Surely the ⌊idolatrous⌋ commotion on the hills
and mountains is a deception;
surely in the LORD our God
is the salvation of Israel.
24 From our youth shameful gods have consumed
the fruits of our fathers' labor—
their flocks and herds,
their sons and daughters.
25 Let us lie down in our shame,
and let our disgrace cover us.
We have sinned against the LORD our God,
both we and our fathers;
from our youth till this day
we have not obeyed the LORD our God."

4 "If you will return, O Israel,
return to me,"
declares the LORD.
"If you put your detestable idols out of my sight
and no longer go astray,
2 and if in a truthful, just and righteous way
you swear, 'As surely as the LORD lives,'
then the nations will be blessed by him
and in him they will glory."

3 This is what the LORD says to the men of Judah and to Jerusalem:

"Break up your unplowed ground
and do not sow among thorns.
4 Circumcise yourselves to the LORD,
circumcise your hearts,

you men of Judah and people of
Jerusalem,
or my wrath will break out and burn like
fire
because of the evil you have done—
burn with no one to quench it.

Disaster From the North

5 "Announce in Judah and proclaim in
Jerusalem and say:
'Sound the trumpet throughout the
land!'
Cry aloud and say:
'Gather together!
Let us flee to the fortified cities!'
6 Raise the signal to go to Zion!
Flee for safety without delay!
For I am bringing disaster from the north,
even terrible destruction."

7 A lion has come out of his lair;
a destroyer of nations has set out.
He has left his place
to lay waste your land.
Your towns will lie in ruins
without inhabitant.
8 So put on sackcloth,
lament and wail,
for the fierce anger of the LORD
has not turned away from us.

9 "In that day," declares the LORD,
"the king and the officials will lose
heart,
the priests will be horrified,
and the prophets will be appalled."

10 Then I said, "Ah, Sovereign LORD, how
completely you have deceived this people and
Jerusalem by saying, 'You will have peace,'
when the sword is at our throats."
11 At that time this people and Jerusalem
will be told, "A scorching wind from the barren heights in the desert blows toward my people, but not to winnow or cleanse; 12 a wind
too strong for that comes from me.[a] Now I pronounce my judgments against them."

13 Look! He advances like the clouds,
his chariots come like a whirlwind,
his horses are swifter than eagles.
Woe to us! We are ruined!
14 O Jerusalem, wash the evil from your heart
and be saved.
How long will you harbor wicked
thoughts?
15 A voice is announcing from Dan,
proclaiming disaster from the hills of
Ephraim.
16 "Tell this to the nations,
proclaim it to Jerusalem:
'A besieging army is coming from a distant
land,
raising a war cry against the cities of
Judah.
17 They surround her like men guarding a
field,
because she has rebelled against me,'"
declares the LORD.
18 "Your own conduct and actions
have brought this upon you.
This is your punishment.
How bitter it is!
How it pierces to the heart!"

19 Oh, my anguish, my anguish!
I writhe in pain.
Oh, the agony of my heart!
My heart pounds within me,
I cannot keep silent.
For I have heard the sound of the trumpet;
I have heard the battle cry.
20 Disaster follows disaster;
the whole land lies in ruins.
In an instant my tents are destroyed,
my shelter in a moment.
21 How long must I see the battle standard
and hear the sound of the trumpet?

22 "My people are fools;
they do not know me.
They are senseless children;
they have no understanding.
They are skilled in doing evil;
they know not how to do good."

23 I looked at the earth,
and it was formless and empty;
and at the heavens,
and their light was gone.
24 I looked at the mountains,
and they were quaking;
all the hills were swaying.

[a] 12 Or *comes at my command*

25 I looked, and there were no people;
every bird in the sky had flown away.
26 I looked, and the fruitful land was a desert;
all its towns lay in ruins
before the LORD, before his fierce anger.

27 This is what the LORD says:

"The whole land will be ruined,
though I will not destroy it completely.
28 Therefore the earth will mourn
and the heavens above grow dark,
because I have spoken and will not relent,
I have decided and will not turn back."

29 At the sound of horsemen and archers
every town takes to flight.
Some go into the thickets;
some climb up among the rocks.
All the towns are deserted;
no one lives in them.

30 What are you doing, O devastated one?
Why dress yourself in scarlet
and put on jewels of gold?
Why shade your eyes with paint?
You adorn yourself in vain.
Your lovers despise you;
they seek your life.

31 I hear a cry as of a woman in labor,
a groan as of one bearing her first child—
the cry of the Daughter of Zion gasping for breath,
stretching out her hands and saying,
"Alas! I am fainting;
my life is given over to murderers."

Not One Is Upright

5 "Go up and down the streets of Jerusalem,
look around and consider,
search through her squares.
If you can find but one person
who deals honestly and seeks the truth,
I will forgive this city.
2 Although they say, 'As surely as the LORD lives,'
still they are swearing falsely."
3 O LORD, do not your eyes look for truth?
You struck them, but they felt no pain;
you crushed them, but they refused correction.
They made their faces harder than stone
and refused to repent.
4 I thought, "These are only the poor;
they are foolish,
for they do not know the way of the LORD,
the requirements of their God.
5 So I will go to the leaders
and speak to them;
surely they know the way of the LORD,
the requirements of their God."
But with one accord they too had broken off the yoke
and torn off the bonds.
6 Therefore a lion from the forest will attack them,
a wolf from the desert will ravage them,
a leopard will lie in wait near their towns
to tear to pieces any who venture out,
for their rebellion is great
and their backslidings many.

7 "Why should I forgive you?
Your children have forsaken me
and sworn by gods that are not gods.
I supplied all their needs,
yet they committed adultery
and thronged to the houses of prostitutes.
8 They are well-fed, lusty stallions,
each neighing for another man's wife.
9 Should I not punish them for this?"
declares the LORD.
"Should I not avenge myself
on such a nation as this?

10 "Go through her vineyards and ravage them,
but do not destroy them completely.
Strip off her branches,
for these people do not belong to the LORD.
11 The house of Israel and the house of Judah
have been utterly unfaithful to me,"
declares the LORD.

12 They have lied about the LORD;
they said, "He will do nothing!
No harm will come to us;
we will never see sword or famine.
13 The prophets are but wind
and the word is not in them;
so let what they say be done to them."

14Therefore this is what the LORD God Almighty says:

"Because the people have spoken these words,
I will make my words in your mouth a fire
and these people the wood it consumes.
15O house of Israel," declares the LORD,
"I am bringing a distant nation against you—
an ancient and enduring nation,
a people whose language you do not know,
whose speech you do not understand.
16Their quivers are like an open grave;
all of them are mighty warriors.
17They will devour your harvests and food,
devour your sons and daughters;
they will devour your flocks and herds,
devour your vines and fig trees.
With the sword they will destroy
the fortified cities in which you trust.

18"Yet even in those days,"
declares the LORD, "I will not
destroy you completely. 19And
when the people ask, 'Why has
the LORD our God done all
this to us?' you will tell them,
'As you have forsaken me and
served foreign gods in your
own land, so now you will
serve foreigners in a land not
your own.'

Jeremiah 5:18

God Shows Mercy

"Yet even in those days,"
declares the LORD,
"I will not destroy you
completely."

20"Announce this to the house of Jacob
and proclaim it in Judah:
21Hear this, you foolish and senseless people,
who have eyes but do not see,
who have ears but do not hear:
22Should you not fear me?" declares the LORD.
"Should you not tremble in my presence?
I made the sand a boundary for the sea,
an everlasting barrier it cannot cross.
The waves may roll, but they cannot prevail;
they may roar, but they cannot cross it.
23But these people have stubborn and rebellious hearts;
they have turned aside and gone away.
24They do not say to themselves,
'Let us fear the LORD our God,
who gives autumn and spring rains in season,
who assures us of the regular weeks of harvest.'
25Your wrongdoings have kept these away;
your sins have deprived you of good.

26"Among my people are wicked men
who lie in wait like men who snare birds
and like those who set traps to catch men.
27Like cages full of birds,
their houses are full of deceit;
they have become rich and powerful
28 and have grown fat and sleek.
Their evil deeds have no limit;
they do not plead the case of the fatherless to win it,
they do not defend the rights of the poor.
29Should I not punish them for this?"
declares the LORD.
"Should I not avenge myself
on such a nation as this?

30"A horrible and shocking thing
has happened in the land:
31The prophets prophesy lies,
the priests rule by their own authority,
and my people love it this way.
But what will you do in the end?

Jerusalem Under Siege

6 "Flee for safety, people of Benjamin!
Flee from Jerusalem!
Sound the trumpet in Tekoa!
Raise the signal over Beth Hakkerem!
For disaster looms out of the north,
even terrible destruction.
2I will destroy the Daughter of Zion,
so beautiful and delicate.
3Shepherds with their flocks will come against her;

they will pitch their tents around her,
each tending his own portion."

4 "Prepare for battle against her!
Arise, let us attack at noon!
But, alas, the daylight is fading,
and the shadows of evening grow long.
5 So arise, let us attack at night
and destroy her fortresses!"

6 This is what the LORD Almighty says:

"Cut down the trees
and build siege ramps against Jerusalem.
This city must be punished;
it is filled with oppression.
7 As a well pours out its water,
so she pours out her wickedness.
Violence and destruction resound in her;
her sickness and wounds are ever before me.
8 Take warning, O Jerusalem,
or I will turn away from you
and make your land desolate
so no one can live in it."

9 This is what the LORD Almighty says:

"Let them glean the remnant of Israel
as thoroughly as a vine;
pass your hand over the branches again,
like one gathering grapes."

10 To whom can I speak and give warning?
Who will listen to me?
Their ears are closed[a]
so they cannot hear.
The word of the LORD is offensive to them;
they find no pleasure in it.
11 But I am full of the wrath of the LORD,
and I cannot hold it in.

"Pour it out on the children in the street
and on the young men gathered together;
both husband and wife will be caught in it,
and the old, those weighed down with years.
12 Their houses will be turned over to others,
together with their fields and their wives,
when I stretch out my hand
against those who live in the land,"
declares the LORD.
13 "From the least to the greatest,
all are greedy for gain;
prophets and priests alike,
all practice deceit.
14 They dress the wound of my people
as though it were not serious.
'Peace, peace,' they say,
when there is no peace.
15 Are they ashamed of their loathsome conduct?
No, they have no shame at all;
they do not even know how to blush.
So they will fall among the fallen;
they will be brought down when I punish them,"
says the LORD.

16 This is what the LORD says:

"Stand at the crossroads and look;
ask for the ancient paths,
ask where the good way is, and walk in it,
and you will find rest for your souls.
But you said, 'We will not walk in it.'
17 I appointed watchmen over you and said,
'Listen to the sound of the trumpet!'
But you said, 'We will not listen.'
18 Therefore hear, O nations;
observe, O witnesses,
what will happen to them.
19 Hear, O earth:
I am bringing disaster on this people,
the fruit of their schemes,
because they have not listened to my words
and have rejected my law.
20 What do I care about incense from Sheba
or sweet calamus from a distant land?
Your burnt offerings are not acceptable;
your sacrifices do not please me."

21 Therefore this is what the LORD says:

"I will put obstacles before this people.
Fathers and sons alike will stumble over them;
neighbors and friends will perish."

22 This is what the LORD says:

[a] 10 Hebrew *uncircumcised*

"Look, an army is coming
from the land of the north;
a great nation is being stirred up
from the ends of the earth.
23 They are armed with bow and spear;
they are cruel and show no mercy.
They sound like the roaring sea
as they ride on their horses;
they come like men in battle formation
to attack you, O Daughter of Zion."

24 We have heard reports about them,
and our hands hang limp.
Anguish has gripped us,
pain like that of a woman in labor.
25 Do not go out to the fields
or walk on the roads,
for the enemy has a sword,
and there is terror on every side.
26 O my people, put on sackcloth
and roll in ashes;
mourn with bitter wailing
as for an only son,
for suddenly the destroyer
will come upon us.

27 "I have made you a tester of metals
and my people the ore,
that you may observe
and test their ways.
28 They are all hardened rebels,
going about to slander.
They are bronze and iron;
they all act corruptly.
29 The bellows blow fiercely
to burn away the lead with fire,
but the refining goes on in vain;
the wicked are not purged out.
30 They are called rejected silver,
because the LORD has rejected them."

False Religion Worthless

7 This is the word that came to Jeremiah
from the LORD: 2 "Stand at the gate of the
LORD's house and there proclaim this message:
"'Hear the word of the LORD, all you people of Judah who come through these gates
to worship the LORD. 3 This is what the LORD
Almighty, the God of Israel, says: Reform your
ways and your actions, and I will let you live
in this place. 4 Do not trust in deceptive words
and say, "This is the temple of the LORD, the
temple of the LORD, the temple of the LORD!"
5 If you really change your ways and your actions and deal with each other justly, 6 if you
do not oppress the alien, the fatherless or the
widow and do not shed innocent blood in this
place, and if you do not follow other gods to
your own harm, 7 then I will let you live in this
place, in the land I gave your forefathers for
ever and ever. 8 But look, you are trusting in deceptive words that are worthless.
9 "'Will you steal and murder, commit adultery and perjury,[a] burn incense to Baal and
follow other gods you have not known, 10 and
then come and stand before me in this house,
which bears my Name, and say, "We are safe"—
safe to do all these detestable things? 11 Has this
house, which bears my Name, become a den
of robbers to you? But I have been watching!
declares the LORD.
12 "'Go now to the place in Shiloh where I
first made a dwelling for my Name, and see
what I did to it because of the wickedness of
my people Israel. 13 While you were doing all
these things, declares the LORD, I spoke to you
again and again, but you did not listen; I called
you, but you did not answer. 14 Therefore, what
I did to Shiloh I will now do to the house that
bears my Name, the temple you trust in, the
place I gave to you and your fathers. 15 I will
thrust you from my presence, just as I did all
your brothers, the people of Ephraim.'
16 "So do not pray for this people nor offer
any plea or petition for them; do not plead with
me, for I will not listen to you. 17 Do you not
see what they are doing in the towns of Judah
and in the streets of Jerusalem? 18 The children
gather wood, the fathers light the fire, and the
women knead the dough and make cakes of
bread for the Queen of Heaven. They pour out
drink offerings to other gods to provoke me to
anger. 19 But am I the one they are provoking?
declares the LORD. Are they not rather harming themselves, to their own shame?
20 "'Therefore this is what the Sovereign
LORD says: My anger and my wrath will be
poured out on this place, on man and beast,
on the trees of the field and on the fruit of the
ground, and it will burn and not be quenched.

[a] 9 Or *and swear by false gods*

21"'This is what the LORD Almighty, the
God of Israel, says: Go ahead, add your burnt
offerings to your other sacrifices and eat the
meat yourselves! 22For when I brought your
forefathers out of Egypt and spoke to them, I
did not just give them commands about burnt
offerings and sacrifices, 23but I gave them this
command: Obey me, and I will be your God
and you will be my people. Walk in all the ways
I command you, that it may go well with you.
24But they did not listen or pay attention; instead, they followed the stubborn inclinations
of their evil hearts. They went backward and
not forward. 25From the time your forefathers
left Egypt until now, day after day, again and
again I sent you my servants the prophets.
26But they did not listen to me or pay attention.
They were stiff-necked and did more evil than
their forefathers.'

27"When you tell them all this, they will not
listen to you; when you call to them, they will
not answer. 28Therefore say to them, 'This is
the nation that has not obeyed the LORD its
God or responded to correction. Truth has
perished; it has vanished from their lips. 29Cut
off your hair and throw it away; take up a lament on the barren heights, for the LORD has
rejected and abandoned this generation that is
under his wrath.

The Valley of Slaughter

30"'The people of Judah have done evil in
my eyes, declares the LORD. They have set up
their detestable idols in the house that bears
my Name and have defiled it. 31They have built
the high places of Topheth in the Valley of Ben
Hinnom to burn their sons and daughters in
the fire—something I did not command, nor
did it enter my mind. 32So beware, the days are
coming, declares the LORD, when people will
no longer call it Topheth or the Valley of Ben
Hinnom, but the Valley of Slaughter, for they
will bury the dead in Topheth until there is no
more room. 33Then the carcasses of this people
will become food for the birds of the air and the
beasts of the earth, and there will be no one to
frighten them away. 34I will bring an end to the
sounds of joy and gladness and to the voices of
bride and bridegroom in the towns of Judah
and the streets of Jerusalem, for the land will
become desolate.

8 "'At that time, declares the LORD, the
bones of the kings and officials of Judah,
the bones of the priests and prophets, and the
bones of the people of Jerusalem will be removed from their graves. 2They will be exposed
to the sun and the moon and all the stars of the
heavens, which they have loved and served and
which they have followed and consulted and
worshiped. They will not be gathered up or buried, but will be like refuse lying on the ground.
3Wherever I banish them, all the survivors of
this evil nation will prefer death to life, declares
the LORD Almighty.'

Sin and Punishment

4"Say to them, 'This is what the LORD says:

"'When men fall down, do they not
get up?
When a man turns away, does he not
return?
5 Why then have these people turned away?
Why does Jerusalem always turn away?
They cling to deceit;
they refuse to return.
6 I have listened attentively,
but they do not say what is right.
No one repents of his wickedness,
saying, "What have I done?"
Each pursues his own course
like a horse charging into battle.
7 Even the stork in the sky
knows her appointed seasons,
and the dove, the swift and the thrush
observe the time of their migration.
But my people do not know
the requirements of the LORD.

8"'How can you say, "We are wise,
for we have the law of the LORD,"
when actually the lying pen of the scribes
has handled it falsely?
9 The wise will be put to shame;
they will be dismayed and trapped.
Since they have rejected the word of the
LORD,
what kind of wisdom do they have?
10 Therefore I will give their wives to other
men
and their fields to new owners.
From the least to the greatest,
all are greedy for gain;

prophets and priests alike,
all practice deceit.
11 They dress the wound of my people
as though it were not serious.
"Peace, peace," they say,
when there is no peace.
12 Are they ashamed of their
loathsome conduct?
No, they have no shame
at all;
they do not even know
how to blush.
So they will fall among the
fallen;
they will be brought
down when they are
punished,
says the LORD.

Jeremiah 8:18

God Is Our Comforter

O my Comforter
in sorrow,
my heart is faint
within me.

13 "'I will take away their
harvest,
declares the LORD.
There will be no grapes on the vine.
There will be no figs on the tree,
and their leaves will wither.
What I have given them
will be taken from them.[a]'"

14 "Why are we sitting here?
Gather together!
Let us flee to the fortified cities
and perish there!
For the LORD our God has doomed us to
perish
and given us poisoned water to
drink,
because we have sinned against him.
15 We hoped for peace
but no good has come,
for a time of healing
but there was only terror.
16 The snorting of the enemy's horses
is heard from Dan;
at the neighing of their stallions
the whole land trembles.
They have come to devour
the land and everything in it,
the city and all who live there."

17 "See, I will send venomous snakes among
you,
vipers that cannot be charmed,
and they will bite you,"
declares the LORD.

18 O my Comforter[a] in sorrow,
my heart is faint within
me.
19 Listen to the cry of my
people
from a land far away:
"Is the LORD not in Zion?
Is her King no longer
there?"
"Why have they provoked
me to anger with
their images,
with their worthless
foreign idols?"

20 "The harvest is past,
the summer has ended,
and we are not saved."

21 Since my people are crushed, I am
crushed;
I mourn, and horror grips me.
22 Is there no balm in Gilead?
Is there no physician there?
Why then is there no healing
for the wound of my people?

9 1 Oh, that my head were a spring of water
and my eyes a fountain of tears!
I would weep day and night
for the slain of my people.
2 Oh, that I had in the desert
a lodging place for travelers,
so that I might leave my people
and go away from them;
for they are all adulterers,
a crowd of unfaithful people.

3 "They make ready their tongue
like a bow, to shoot lies;
it is not by truth
that they triumph[b] in the land.
They go from one sin to another;
they do not acknowledge me,"
declares the LORD.
4 "Beware of your friends;
do not trust your brothers.
For every brother is a deceiver,[c]

[a] 13,18 The meaning of the Hebrew for this sentence is uncertain. [b] 3 Or *lies; / they are not valiant for truth* [c] 4 Or *a deceiving Jacob*

and every friend a slanderer.
5 Friend deceives friend,
and no one speaks the truth.
They have taught their tongues to lie;
they weary themselves with sinning.
6 You[a] live in the midst of deception;
in their deceit they refuse to
acknowledge me,"
declares the LORD.

7 Therefore this is what the LORD Almighty says:

"See, I will refine and test them,
for what else can I do
because of the sin of my people?
8 Their tongue is a deadly arrow;
it speaks with deceit.
With his mouth each speaks cordially to
his neighbor,
but in his heart he sets a trap for him.
9 Should I not punish them for this?"
declares the LORD.
"Should I not avenge myself
on such a nation as this?"

10 I will weep and wail for the mountains
and take up a lament concerning the
desert pastures.
They are desolate and untraveled,
and the lowing of cattle is not heard.
The birds of the air have fled
and the animals are gone.

11 "I will make Jerusalem a heap of ruins,
a haunt of jackals;
and I will lay waste the towns of Judah
so no one can live there."

12 What man is wise enough to understand
this? Who has been instructed by the LORD
and can explain it? Why has the land been ruined and laid waste like a desert that no one
can cross?
13 The LORD said, "It is because they have
forsaken my law, which I set before them; they
have not obeyed me or followed my law. 14 Instead, they have followed the stubbornness of
their hearts; they have followed the Baals, as
their fathers taught them." 15 Therefore, this
is what the LORD Almighty, the God of Israel,
says: "See, I will make this people eat bitter food
and drink poisoned water. 16 I will scatter them
among nations that neither they nor their fathers have known, and I will pursue them with
the sword until I have destroyed them."

17 This is what the LORD Almighty says:

"Consider now! Call for the wailing
women to come;
send for the most skillful of them.
18 Let them come quickly
and wail over us
till our eyes overflow with tears
and water streams from our eyelids.
19 The sound of wailing is heard from Zion:
'How ruined we are!
How great is our shame!
We must leave our land
because our houses are in ruins.'"

20 Now, O women, hear the word of the
LORD;
open your ears to the words of his
mouth.
Teach your daughters how to wail;
teach one another a lament.
21 Death has climbed in through our
windows
and has entered our fortresses;
it has cut off the children from the streets
and the young men from the public
squares.

22 Say, "This is what the LORD declares:

"'The dead bodies of men will lie
like refuse on the open field,
like cut grain behind the reaper,
with no one to gather them.'"

23 This is what the LORD says:

"Let not the wise man boast of his wisdom
or the strong man boast of his strength
or the rich man boast of his riches,
24 but let him who boasts boast about this:
that he understands and knows me,
that I am the LORD, who exercises
kindness,
justice and righteousness on earth,
for in these I delight,"
declares the LORD.

[a]6 That is, Jeremiah (the Hebrew is singular)

Staying Spiritually Sage

HULDAH

READY IN A PINCH. That was Huldah, a prophetess in Judah. The thing about being one of God's messengers was that people usually didn't turn to her until it was a time of crisis. When the people needed to hear a word from God, then they turned to the resident prophetess for answers.

It didn't rattle her, this last-minute urgency. It came with the territory.

"I guess I'm used to it by now," she mused, as she patiently listened to the king's officials recount how they made the exciting discovery. Although she could name several male prophets in her people's history, only two other women knew her particular job stress. She shared her esteemed title of "prophetess" with Miriam (see Exodus 15:20) and Deborah (see Judges 4:4). With a reputation for integrity, truthfulness and spiritual discernment, she was the natural choice to handle such sensitive information related to the newly rediscovered Book of the Law.

Unlike her friends who worked in the fields or the market, she didn't keep office hours. "I never know when someone will need me," she often said.

She never knew when she would need to share a word of wisdom or petition the Lord on the people's behalf, so she had to stay prepared. She couldn't slack off, spiritually speaking. She drew strength by reminding herself that she couldn't afford to miss an opportunity to be available and useful to God. And on this day, she was able to deliver the timely and sensitive message that God wanted Judah to hear.

"You never know when someone will show up on your doorstep seeking spiritual wisdom," Huldah would often say. "Sometimes, it's your friend or neighbor. Sometimes it's the king. No matter who shows up, God has a word for them. And it's good to be prepared."

—Prayer—

Gracious God, keep me prepared so that I may be of service to others in need. Give me the wisdom and discernment to find the right words to help where I can.

Hilkiah the priest, Ahikam, Acbor, Shaphan and Asaiah went to speak to the prophetess Huldah.

2 Kings 22:14

ASSIGNED READING:

2 Kings 22:14–20

Weekend

Go to page 919 for your next devotional reading.

25 "The days are coming," declares the LORD,
"when I will punish all who are circumcised
only in the flesh— 26 Egypt, Judah, Edom, Ammon, Moab and all who live in the desert in
distant places.[a] For all these nations are really
uncircumcised, and even the whole house of
Israel is uncircumcised in heart."

God and Idols

10 Hear what the LORD says to you,
O house of Israel. 2 This is what the
LORD says:

"Do not learn the ways of the nations
or be terrified by signs in the sky,
though the nations are terrified by them.
3 For the customs of the peoples are
worthless;
they cut a tree out of the forest,
and a craftsman shapes it with his chisel.
4 They adorn it with silver and gold;
they fasten it with hammer and nails
so it will not totter.
5 Like a scarecrow in a melon patch,
their idols cannot speak;
they must be carried
because they cannot walk.
Do not fear them;
they can do no harm
nor can they do any
good."

6 No one is like you, O LORD;
you are great,
and your name is mighty
in power.
7 Who should not revere you,
O King of the nations?
This is your due.
Among all the wise men of
the nations
and in all their
kingdoms,
there is no one like you.
8 They are all senseless and foolish;
they are taught by worthless wooden
idols.
9 Hammered silver is brought from Tarshish
and gold from Uphaz.
What the craftsman and goldsmith have
made
is then dressed in blue and purple—
all made by skilled workers.
10 But the LORD is the true God;
he is the living God, the eternal King.
When he is angry, the earth trembles;
the nations cannot endure his wrath.

11 "Tell them this: 'These gods, who did not
make the heavens and the earth, will perish
from the earth and from under the heavens.'"[b]

12 But God made the earth by his power;
he founded the world by his wisdom
and stretched out the heavens by his
understanding.
13 When he thunders, the waters in the
heavens roar;
he makes clouds rise from the ends of
the earth.
He sends lightning with the rain
and brings out the wind from his
storehouses.

14 Everyone is senseless and without
knowledge;
every goldsmith is shamed by his idols.
His images are a fraud;
they have no breath in them.
15 They are worthless, the
objects of
mockery;
when their judgment
comes, they will
perish.
16 He who is the Portion of
Jacob is not like
these,
for he is the Maker of all
things,
including Israel, the tribe
of his inheritance—
the LORD Almighty is his
name.

Jeremiah 10:7

God Is King of the Nations

"Who should not
revere you,
O King of the nations?"

Coming Destruction

17 Gather up your belongings to leave the
land,
you who live under siege.
18 For this is what the LORD says:
"At this time I will hurl out
those who live in this land;

[a] 26 Or *desert and who clip the hair by their foreheads* [b] 11 The text of this verse is in Aramaic.

I will bring distress on them
so that they may be captured."

19 Woe to me because of my injury!
My wound is incurable!
Yet I said to myself,
"This is my sickness, and I must endure it."
20 My tent is destroyed;
all its ropes are snapped.
My sons are gone from me and are no more;
no one is left now to pitch my tent
or to set up my shelter.
21 The shepherds are senseless
and do not inquire of the LORD;
so they do not prosper
and all their flock is scattered.
22 Listen! The report is coming—
a great commotion from the land of the north!
It will make the towns of Judah desolate,
a haunt of jackals.

Jeremiah's Prayer

23 I know, O LORD, that a man's life is not his own;
it is not for man to direct his steps.
24 Correct me, LORD, but only with justice—
not in your anger,
lest you reduce me to nothing.
25 Pour out your wrath on the nations
that do not acknowledge you,
on the peoples who do not call on your name.
For they have devoured Jacob;
they have devoured him completely
and destroyed his homeland.

The Covenant Is Broken

11 This is the word that came to Jeremiah
from the LORD: 2 "Listen to the terms
of this covenant and tell them to the people of
Judah and to those who live in Jerusalem. 3 Tell
them that this is what the LORD, the God of
Israel, says: 'Cursed is the man who does not
obey the terms of this covenant— 4 the terms I
commanded your forefathers when I brought
them out of Egypt, out of the iron-smelting
furnace.' I said, 'Obey me and do everything I
command you, and you will be my people, and
I will be your God. 5 Then I will fulfill the oath
I swore to your forefathers, to give them a land
flowing with milk and honey'—the land you
possess today."

I answered, "Amen, LORD."

6 The LORD said to me, "Proclaim all these
words in the towns of Judah and in the streets
of Jerusalem: 'Listen to the terms of this covenant and follow them. 7 From the time I
brought your forefathers up from Egypt until
today, I warned them again and again, saying,
"Obey me." 8 But they did not listen or pay attention; instead, they followed the stubbornness
of their evil hearts. So I brought on them all the
curses of the covenant I had commanded them
to follow but that they did not keep.'"

9 Then the LORD said to me, "There is a
conspiracy among the people of Judah and
those who live in Jerusalem. 10 They have returned to the sins of their forefathers, who refused to listen to my words. They have followed
other gods to serve them. Both the house of
Israel and the house of Judah have broken the
covenant I made with their forefathers. 11 Therefore this is what the LORD says: 'I will bring on
them a disaster they cannot escape. Although
they cry out to me, I will not listen to them.
12 The towns of Judah and the people of Jerusalem will go and cry out to the gods to whom
they burn incense, but they will not help them
at all when disaster strikes. 13 You have as many
gods as you have towns, O Judah; and the altars
you have set up to burn incense to that shameful god Baal are as many as the streets of Jerusalem.'

14 "Do not pray for this people nor offer any
plea or petition for them, because I will not listen when they call to me in the time of their
distress.

15 "What is my beloved doing in my temple
as she works out her evil schemes with many?
Can consecrated meat avert ⌞your punishment⌟?
When you engage in your wickedness,
then you rejoice.[a]"

16 The LORD called you a thriving olive tree
with fruit beautiful in form.

[a]15 Or *Could consecrated meat avert your punishment? / Then you would rejoice*

But with the roar of a mighty storm
he will set it on fire,
and its branches will be broken.

17 The LORD Almighty, who planted you, has
decreed disaster for you, because the house of
Israel and the house of Judah have done evil
and provoked me to anger by burning incense
to Baal.

Plot Against Jeremiah

18 Because the LORD revealed their plot to
me, I knew it, for at that time he showed me
what they were doing. 19 I had been like a gentle lamb led to the slaughter; I did not realize
that they had plotted against me, saying,

"Let us destroy the tree and its fruit;
let us cut him off from the land of the
living,
that his name be remembered no more."
20 But, O LORD Almighty, you who judge
righteously
and test the heart and mind,
let me see your vengeance upon them,
for to you I have committed my cause.

21 "Therefore this is what the LORD says about
the men of Anathoth who are seeking your life
and saying, 'Do not prophesy in the name of the
LORD or you will die by our hands'— 22 therefore this is what the LORD Almighty says: 'I
will punish them. Their young men will die by
the sword, their sons and daughters by famine.
23 Not even a remnant will be left to them, because I will bring disaster on the men of Anathoth in the year of their punishment.' "

Jeremiah's Complaint

12 You are always righteous, O LORD,
when I bring a case before you.
Yet I would speak with you about your
justice:
Why does the way of the wicked
prosper?
Why do all the faithless live at ease?
2 You have planted them, and they have
taken root;
they grow and bear fruit.
You are always on their lips
but far from their hearts.
3 Yet you know me, O LORD;
you see me and test my thoughts about
you.
Drag them off like sheep to be butchered!
Set them apart for the day of slaughter!
4 How long will the land lie parched[a]
and the grass in every field be withered?
Because those who live in it are wicked,
the animals and birds have perished.
Moreover, the people are saying,
"He will not see what happens to us."

God's Answer

5 "If you have raced with men on foot
and they have worn you out,
how can you compete with horses?
If you stumble in safe country,[b]
how will you manage in the thickets by[c]
the Jordan?
6 Your brothers, your own family—
even they have betrayed you;
they have raised a loud cry against you.
Do not trust them,
though they speak well of you.

7 "I will forsake my house,
abandon my inheritance;
I will give the one I love
into the hands of her enemies.
8 My inheritance has become to me
like a lion in the forest.
She roars at me;
therefore I hate her.
9 Has not my inheritance become to me
like a speckled bird of prey
that other birds of prey surround and
attack?
Go and gather all the wild beasts;
bring them to devour.
10 Many shepherds will ruin my vineyard
and trample down my field;
they will turn my pleasant field
into a desolate wasteland.
11 It will be made a wasteland,
parched and desolate before me;
the whole land will be laid waste
because there is no one who cares.
12 Over all the barren heights in the desert
destroyers will swarm,
for the sword of the LORD will devour
from one end of the land to the other;

[a] 4 Or *land mourn* [b] 5 Or *If you put your trust in a land of safety* [c] 5 Or *the flooding of*

Why Do the Wicked Prosper?

Read: Jeremiah 12:1–17

WE'VE ALL ASKED QUESTIONS similar to Jeremiah's at least once:

Why does she get the promotion even though she makes unethical decisions?

Why did her children turn out better than mine even though she seemed to neglect them?

Why do they have what they need and more when they don't know what it *means* to tithe?

It's hard to understand why God appears to sanction those who openly disregard him. In Jeremiah's case, it was people in his own hometown he was trying to help who had turned against him. They even plotted to kill him!

Sometimes we may feel that God has given a greater measure of his protection and provision to people who don't live upright lives. It's hard to reconcile God's nature when we see injustice all around us. We wonder why he doesn't intervene immediately to punish those who make sinful choices.

If you sometimes question God's actions, you're in good company. Throughout history, God's people have wrestled with the same issues. We look at martyrs, missionaries and others serving God who experience horrible suffering and pain. Why do evildoers often seem to have the easiest lives, while people of faith struggle? Shouldn't it be the other way around? This side of heaven, we may never be able to answer such questions.

Even so, we know our God knows the hearts and motives of all people. He sees when innocents are harmed and the upright are dealt injustice. And he does care. It may look like he isn't intervening now, but a time is coming when each person must account for his or her life. As Jesus said, "Will not God bring about justice for his chosen ones, who cry out to him day and night? Will he keep putting them off? I tell you, he will see that they get justice, and quickly. However, when the Son of Man comes, will he find faith on the earth?" (Luke 18:7–8).

While we may not understand God's ways, we know that he is all-wise, all-knowing and just. He watches over us and will make everything right in its time. The key is for each of us to remain faithful to him until then.

Jeremiah 12:1–2

You are always righteous, O LORD, when I bring a case before you. Yet I would speak with you about your justice: Why does the way of the wicked prosper? Why do all the faithless live at ease? You have planted them, and they have taken root; they grow and bear fruit. You are always on their lips but far from their hearts.

reflection

1 What situation has caused you to wonder why the wicked prosper?

2 When you're tempted to question God's actions, what steps can you take to remember his wisdom?

3 What assurance do you have that God will render his justice one day?

RELATED READINGS

Job 21:7–21;
Psalms 73:1–28;
145:17–20;
Proverbs 11:21–23

Go to page 924 for your next devotional reading.

no one will be safe.
13 They will sow wheat but reap thorns;
they will wear themselves out but gain nothing.
So bear the shame of your harvest
because of the LORD's fierce anger."

14 This is what the LORD says: "As for all my
wicked neighbors who seize the inheritance I
gave my people Israel, I will uproot them from
their lands and I will uproot the house of Judah
from among them. 15 But after I uproot them, I
will again have compassion and will bring each
of them back to his own inheritance and his
own country. 16 And if they learn well the ways
of my people and swear by my name, saying,
'As surely as the LORD lives'—even as they once
taught my people to swear by Baal—then they
will be established among my people. 17 But if
any nation does not listen, I will completely uproot and destroy it," declares the LORD.

A Linen Belt

13 This is what the LORD said to me: "Go
and buy a linen belt and put it around
your waist, but do not let it touch water." 2 So I
bought a belt, as the LORD directed, and put it
around my waist.

3 Then the word of the LORD
came to me a second time:
4 "Take the belt you bought and
are wearing around your waist,
and go now to Perath[a] and
hide it there in a crevice in the
rocks." 5 So I went and hid it at
Perath, as the LORD told me.

6 Many days later the LORD
said to me, "Go now to Perath
and get the belt I told you to
hide there." 7 So I went to Perath and dug up the belt and
took it from the place where I
had hidden it, but now it was
ruined and completely useless.

8 Then the word of the LORD came to me:
9 "This is what the LORD says: 'In the same way
I will ruin the pride of Judah and the great
pride of Jerusalem. 10 These wicked people,
who refuse to listen to my words, who follow
the stubbornness of their hearts and go after
other gods to serve and worship them, will be
like this belt—completely useless! 11 For as a
belt is bound around a man's waist, so I bound
the whole house of Israel and the whole house
of Judah to me,' declares the LORD, 'to be my
people for my renown and praise and honor.
But they have not listened.'

Wineskins

12 "Say to them: 'This is what the LORD, the
God of Israel, says: Every wineskin should be
filled with wine.' And if they say to you, 'Don't
we know that every wineskin should be filled
with wine?' 13 then tell them, 'This is what
the LORD says: I am going to fill with drunkenness all who live in this land, including the
kings who sit on David's throne, the priests, the
prophets and all those living in Jerusalem. 14 I
will smash them one against the other, fathers
and sons alike, declares the LORD. I will allow
no pity or mercy or compassion to keep me
from destroying them.'"

Threat of Captivity

15 Hear and pay attention,
do not be arrogant,
for the LORD has spoken.
16 Give glory to the LORD your God
before he brings the darkness,
before your feet stumble
on the darkening hills.
You hope for light,
but he will turn it to thick darkness
and change it to deep gloom.
17 But if you do not listen,
I will weep in secret
because of your pride;
my eyes will weep bitterly,
overflowing with tears,
because the LORD's flock
will be taken captive.

18 Say to the king and to the queen mother,
"Come down from your thrones,
for your glorious crowns
will fall from your heads."
19 The cities in the Negev will be shut up,

> **Jeremiah 13:16**
>
> *God Is Worthy of Praise*
>
> Give glory to the LORD
> your God
> before he brings
> the darkness,
> before your feet stumble
> on the darkening hills.

[a]4 Or possibly *the Euphrates*; also in verses 5–7

and there will be no one to open them.
All Judah will be carried into exile,
carried completely away.

20 Lift up your eyes and see
those who are coming from the north.
Where is the flock that was entrusted to you,
the sheep of which you boasted?
21 What will you say when ⌊the LORD⌋ sets over you
those you cultivated as your special allies?
Will not pain grip you
like that of a woman in labor?
22 And if you ask yourself,
"Why has this happened to me?"—
it is because of your many sins
that your skirts have been torn off
and your body mistreated.
23 Can the Ethiopian[a] change his skin
or the leopard its spots?
Neither can you do good
who are accustomed to doing evil.

24 "I will scatter you like chaff
driven by the desert wind.
25 This is your lot,
the portion I have decreed for you,"
declares the LORD,
"because you have forgotten me
and trusted in false gods.
26 I will pull up your skirts over your face
that your shame may be seen—
27 your adulteries and lustful neighings,
your shameless prostitution!
I have seen your detestable acts
on the hills and in the fields.
Woe to you, O Jerusalem!
How long will you be unclean?"

Drought, Famine, Sword

14 This is the word of the LORD to Jeremiah concerning the drought:

2 "Judah mourns,
her cities languish;
they wail for the land,
and a cry goes up from Jerusalem.
3 The nobles send their servants for water;
they go to the cisterns
but find no water.
They return with their jars unfilled;
dismayed and despairing,
they cover their heads.
4 The ground is cracked
because there is no rain in the land;
the farmers are dismayed
and cover their heads.
5 Even the doe in the field
deserts her newborn fawn
because there is no grass.
6 Wild donkeys stand on the barren heights
and pant like jackals;
their eyesight fails
for lack of pasture."

Jeremiah 14:7

God Honors His Name

"Although our sins testify against us, O LORD, do something for the sake of your name. For our backsliding is great; we have sinned against you."

7 Although our sins testify against us,
O LORD, do something for the sake of your name.
For our backsliding is great;
we have sinned against you.
8 O Hope of Israel,
its Savior in times of distress,
why are you like a stranger in the land,
like a traveler who stays only a night?
9 Why are you like a man taken by surprise,
like a warrior powerless to save?
You are among us, O LORD,
and we bear your name;
do not forsake us!

10 This is what the LORD says about this people:

"They greatly love to wander;
they do not restrain their feet.
So the LORD does not accept them;

[a] 23 Hebrew *Cushite* (probably a person from the upper Nile region)

he will now remember their wickedness
and punish them for their sins."

11 Then the LORD said to me, "Do not pray
for the well-being of this people. 12 Although
they fast, I will not listen to their cry; though
they offer burnt offerings and grain offerings,
I will not accept them. Instead, I will destroy
them with the sword, famine and plague."

13 But I said, "Ah, Sovereign LORD, the prophets keep telling them, 'You will not see the
sword or suffer famine. Indeed, I will give you
lasting peace in this place.' "

14 Then the LORD said to me, "The prophets are prophesying lies in my name. I have
not sent them or appointed them or spoken
to them. They are prophesying to you false
visions, divinations, idolatries[a] and the delusions of their own minds. 15 Therefore, this is
what the LORD says about the prophets who
are prophesying in my name: I did not send
them, yet they are saying, 'No sword or famine
will touch this land.' Those same prophets will
perish by sword and famine. 16 And the people
they are prophesying to will be thrown out into
the streets of Jerusalem because of the famine
and sword. There will be no one to bury them
or their wives, their sons or their daughters.
I will pour out on them the calamity they deserve.

17 "Speak this word to them:

" 'Let my eyes overflow with tears
night and day without ceasing;
for my virgin daughter—my people—
has suffered a grievous wound,
a crushing blow.
18 If I go into the country,
I see those slain by the sword;
if I go into the city,
I see the ravages of famine.
Both prophet and priest
have gone to a land they know not.' "
19 Have you rejected Judah completely?
Do you despise Zion?
Why have you afflicted us
so that we cannot be healed?
We hoped for peace
but no good has come,
for a time of healing
but there is only terror.
20 O LORD, we acknowledge our wickedness
and the guilt of our fathers;
we have indeed sinned against you.
21 For the sake of your name do not despise
us;
do not dishonor your glorious throne.
Remember your covenant with us
and do not break it.
22 Do any of the worthless idols of the nations
bring rain?
Do the skies themselves send down
showers?
No, it is you, O LORD our God.
Therefore our hope is in you,
for you are the one who does all this.

15 Then the LORD said to me: "Even if
Moses and Samuel were to stand be-
fore me, my heart would not go out to this people. Send them away from my presence! Let
them go! 2 And if they ask you, 'Where shall we
go?' tell them, 'This is what the LORD says:

" 'Those destined for death, to death;
those for the sword, to the sword;
those for starvation, to starvation;
those for captivity, to captivity.'

3 "I will send four kinds of destroyers against
them," declares the LORD, "the sword to kill and
the dogs to drag away and the birds of the air
and the beasts of the earth to devour and destroy. 4 I will make them abhorrent to all the
kingdoms of the earth because of what Manasseh son of Hezekiah king of Judah did in Jerusalem.

5 "Who will have pity on you, O Jerusalem?
Who will mourn for you?
Who will stop to ask how you are?
6 You have rejected me," declares the LORD.
"You keep on backsliding.
So I will lay hands on you and destroy you;
I can no longer show compassion.
7 I will winnow them with a winnowing fork
at the city gates of the land.
I will bring bereavement and destruction
on my people,
for they have not changed their ways.

[a] 14 Or *visions, worthless divinations*

8 I will make their widows more numerous
than the sand of the sea.
At midday I will bring a destroyer
against the mothers of their young men;
suddenly I will bring down on them
anguish and terror.
9 The mother of seven will grow faint
and breathe her last.
Her sun will set while it is still day;
she will be disgraced and humiliated.
I will put the survivors to the sword
before their enemies,"
declares the LORD.

10 Alas, my mother, that you gave me birth,
a man with whom the whole land strives
and contends!
I have neither lent nor borrowed,
yet everyone curses me.

11 The LORD said,

"Surely I will deliver you for a good
purpose;
surely I will make your enemies plead
with you
in times of disaster and times of distress.

12 "Can a man break iron—
iron from the north—or bronze?
13 Your wealth and your treasures
I will give as plunder, without charge,
because of all your sins
throughout your country.
14 I will enslave you to your enemies
in[a] a land you do not know,
for my anger will kindle a fire
that will burn against you."

15 You understand, O LORD;
remember me and care for me.
Avenge me on my persecutors.
You are long-suffering—do not take me
away;
think of how I suffer reproach for your
sake.
16 When your words came, I ate them;
they were my joy and my heart's delight,
for I bear your name,
O LORD God Almighty.
17 I never sat in the company of revelers,
never made merry with them;
I sat alone because your hand was on me
and you had filled me with indignation.
18 Why is my pain unending
and my wound grievous and incurable?
Will you be to me like a deceptive brook,
like a spring that fails?

19 Therefore this is what the LORD says:

"If you repent, I will restore you
that you may serve me;
if you utter worthy, not worthless, words,
you will be my spokesman.
Let this people turn to you,
but you must not turn to them.
20 I will make you a wall to this people,
a fortified wall of bronze;
they will fight against you
but will not overcome you,
for I am with you
to rescue and save you,"
declares the LORD.
21 "I will save you from the hands of the
wicked
and redeem you from the grasp of the
cruel."

Day of Disaster

16 Then the word of the LORD came to
me: 2 "You must not marry and have
sons or daughters in this place." 3 For this is
what the LORD says about the sons and daughters born in this land and about the women
who are their mothers and the men who are
their fathers: 4 "They will die of deadly diseases.
They will not be mourned or buried but will be
like refuse lying on the ground. They will perish by sword and famine, and their dead bodies
will become food for the birds of the air and the
beasts of the earth."

5 For this is what the LORD says: "Do not enter a house where there is a funeral meal; do
not go to mourn or show sympathy, because
I have withdrawn my blessing, my love and
my pity from this people," declares the LORD.
6 "Both high and low will die in this land. They
will not be buried or mourned, and no one
will cut himself or shave his head for them.
7 No one will offer food to comfort those who

[a] 14 Some Hebrew manuscripts, Septuagint and Syriac (see also Jer. 17:4); most Hebrew manuscripts *I will cause your enemies to bring you into*

Intimate Doubt

Read: Jeremiah 15:1–21

Jeremiah 15:18

Why is my pain unending and my wound grievous and incurable? Will you be to me like a deceptive brook, like a spring that fails?

HELP WANTED:

Who: An ordained spokesperson who is passionate, committed, can endure criticism and perhaps even personal injury and imprisonment. Must be willing to look ridiculous and bear the scorn of peers. Personal characteristics: introverted, unmarried, childless and prone to melancholy. Can be a person who cries easily.

What: Tell the people of Judah that their revival is superficial and unpleasing to the Lord and that God will therefore judge them.

When: Starts immediately—never mind the economic, political and social collapse of Judah.

Pay: None

Any takers? Didn't think so.

No wonder no prophet ever chose his job. Being a prophet was, no doubt, the most discouraging job on the planet. However, that doesn't mean that God is a cosmic taskmaster who doles out difficult assignments to teach people like Jeremiah to trust him more.

Instead, God gave Jeremiah the freedom to express his doubts. Jeremiah did so on several occasions, and the audacity in Jeremiah's words reveals his intimacy with God. They're the kind of words one might hear in a lover's quarrel: "Don't you care? Aren't you going to notice me? I feel so alone." We don't speak that way to a stranger or even an acquaintance; words like this we only speak to someone we love. In this case, doubt is not an indication of failure. It's an indication of intimacy.

In turn, the Lord responded to Jeremiah with firm grace: "If you repent, I will restore you that you may [continue to] serve me" (verse 19). In other words, there is a time to express doubt; but there is also a point at which we must return to our senses before we forget who God is and what he's called us to do. Talk to God about your doubts and your questions, but don't go so far that you begin to lose focus of who you are and who God is.

Are you in the middle of a seemingly impossible assignment? Are you wondering if God really knows how much you can take? God knows your limits; he realizes that he calls flawed people to enormous tasks. Yet his promise is forever the same: "I am with you always, to the very end of the age" (Matthew 28:20).

reflection

1 Describe the most discouraging job or task that you've ever undertaken. What made it difficult? What were your complaints?

2 What feels impossible and discouraging to you right now? How is it affecting you?

3 Write out your "intimate doubts" and express your needs to God. When you are finished, reclaim his promise to be with you as you follow him.

RELATED READINGS

Jeremiah 1:4–8; 12:1–3; 20:7–12; Jude 22

Go to page 927 for your next devotional reading.

mourn for the dead—not even for a father or a
mother—nor will anyone give them a drink to
console them.

8“And do not enter a house where there is
feasting and sit down to eat and drink. 9For
this is what the LORD Almighty, the God of
Israel, says: Before your eyes and in your days I
will bring an end to the sounds of joy and gladness and to the voices of bride and bridegroom
in this place.

10“When you tell these people all this and they ask you,
‘Why has the LORD decreed
such a great disaster against
us? What wrong have we
done? What sin have we committed against the LORD our
God?’ 11then say to them, ‘It
is because your fathers forsook
me,’ declares the LORD, ‘and followed other gods and served
and worshiped them. They forsook me and did not keep my
law. 12But you have behaved
more wickedly than your fathers. See how each
of you is following the stubbornness of his evil
heart instead of obeying me. 13So I will throw
you out of this land into a land neither you nor
your fathers have known, and there you will
serve other gods day and night, for I will show
you no favor.’

14“However, the days are coming,” declares
the LORD, “when men will no longer say, ‘As
surely as the LORD lives, who brought the Israelites up out of Egypt,’ 15but they will say,
‘As surely as the LORD lives, who brought the
Israelites up out of the land of the north and
out of all the countries where he had banished
them.’ For I will restore them to the land I gave
their forefathers.

16“But now I will send for many fishermen,”
declares the LORD, “and they will catch them.
After that I will send for many hunters, and
they will hunt them down on every mountain
and hill and from the crevices of the rocks.
17My eyes are on all their ways; they are not hidden from me, nor is their sin concealed from
my eyes. 18I will repay them double for their
wickedness and their sin, because they have
defiled my land with the lifeless forms of their
vile images and have filled my inheritance with
their detestable idols.”

19O LORD, my strength and my fortress,
my refuge in time of distress,
to you the nations will come
from the ends of the earth and say,
“Our fathers possessed nothing but false gods,
worthless idols that did them no good.
20Do men make their own gods?
Yes, but they are not gods!”

21“Therefore I will teach them—
this time I will teach them
my power and might.
Then they will know
that my name is the LORD.

Jeremiah 16:21

God Teaches Us

“Therefore I will
teach them—
this time I will teach them
my power and might.
Then they will know
that my name is the LORD.”

17 “Judah’s sin is engraved with an iron tool,
inscribed with a flint point,
on the tablets of their hearts
and on the horns of their altars.
2Even their children remember
their altars and Asherah poles[a]
beside the spreading trees
and on the high hills.
3My mountain in the land
and your[b] wealth and all your treasures
I will give away as plunder,
together with your high places,
because of sin throughout your country.
4Through your own fault you will lose
the inheritance I gave you.
I will enslave you to your enemies
in a land you do not know,
for you have kindled my anger,
and it will burn forever.”

5This is what the LORD says:

“Cursed is the one who trusts in man,
who depends on flesh for his strength

[a]2 That is, symbols of the goddess Asherah [b]2,3 Or *hills / 3and the mountains of the land. / Your*

and whose heart turns away from the
LORD.
6 He will be like a bush in the wastelands;
he will not see prosperity when it comes.
He will dwell in the parched places of the
desert,
in a salt land where no one lives.

7 "But blessed is the man who trusts in the
LORD,
whose confidence is in him.
8 He will be like a tree planted by the water
that sends out its roots by the stream.
It does not fear when heat comes;
its leaves are always green.
It has no worries in a year of drought
and never fails to bear fruit."

9 The heart is deceitful above all things
and beyond cure.
Who can understand it?

10 "I the LORD search the heart
and examine the mind,
to reward a man according to his conduct,
according to what his deeds deserve."
11 Like a partridge that hatches eggs it did not
lay
is the man who gains riches by unjust
means.
When his life is half gone, they will desert
him,
and in the end he will prove to be a fool.

12 A glorious throne, exalted from the
beginning,
is the place of our sanctuary.
13 O LORD, the hope of Israel,
all who forsake you will be put to shame.
Those who turn away from you will be
written in the dust
because they have forsaken the LORD,
the spring of living water.

14 Heal me, O LORD, and I will be healed;
save me and I will be saved,
for you are the one I praise.
15 They keep saying to me,
"Where is the word of the LORD?
Let it now be fulfilled!"
16 I have not run away from being your
shepherd;
you know I have not desired the day of
despair.
What passes my lips is open before you.
17 Do not be a terror to me;
you are my refuge in the day of disaster.
18 Let my persecutors be put to shame,
but keep me from shame;
let them be terrified,
but keep me from terror.
Bring on them the day of disaster;
destroy them with double destruction.

Keeping the Sabbath Holy

19 This is what the LORD said to me: "Go
and stand at the gate of the people, through
which the kings of Judah go in and out; stand
also at all the other gates of Jerusalem.
20 Say
to them, 'Hear the word of the LORD, O kings
of Judah and all people of Judah and everyone
living in Jerusalem who come through these
gates.
21 This is what the LORD says: Be careful not to carry a load on the Sabbath day or
bring it through the gates of Jerusalem.
22 Do
not bring a load out of your houses or do any
work on the Sabbath, but keep the Sabbath day
holy, as I commanded your forefathers.
23 Yet
they did not listen or pay attention; they were
stiff-necked and would not listen or respond to
discipline.
24 But if you are careful to obey me,
declares the LORD, and bring no load through
the gates of this city on the Sabbath, but keep
the Sabbath day holy by not doing any work on
it,
25 then kings who sit on David's throne will
come through the gates of this city with their
officials. They and their officials will come riding in chariots and on horses, accompanied by
the men of Judah and those living in Jerusalem,
and this city will be inhabited forever.
26 People
will come from the towns of Judah and the
villages around Jerusalem, from the territory
of Benjamin and the western foothills, from
the hill country and the Negev, bringing burnt
offerings and sacrifices, grain offerings, incense
and thank offerings to the house of the LORD.
27 But if you do not obey me to keep the Sabbath day holy by not carrying any load as you
come through the gates of Jerusalem on the
Sabbath day, then I will kindle an unquenchable fire in the gates of Jerusalem that will consume her fortresses.'"

Saving a Terminal Heart

Read: Jeremiah 17:5–14

WHEN YOU HEAR THE WORDS "heart failure," a pang of panic, regret or sorrow may surge through you. Many women have lost parents, friends or a husband to a weakly pumping heart. Maybe you suffer from heart disease. But even if your physical heart is healthy, your spiritual heart is a terminal case. The prophet Jeremiah described it this way: "The heart is . . . beyond cure."

Maybe you believe your own spiritual heart works just fine, thank you. Your own efforts will cure you—or so you think. "Go with your heart," the world says. What do you believe? Do you agree with Jeremiah's assessment or are you feeling that the world is right on this point?

To determine the state of your heart you need the help of a professional. Better than any doctor's diagnosis, God probes the inner workings of our hearts. Just as a woman with a feeble heart can only guess at the true condition of her ventricles without an expert exam, so each of us must rely on God's perfect knowledge of our soul. When you have to choose between your own assessment of your heart and God's, do you believe your prognosis or do you listen to the One with the power to heal?

Most of us would use any means possible to halt progressive heart failure, but we still face the temptation to doubt the doctor's orders. Maybe we're told to eat right and exercise, but it seems too hard to keep on living a healthy lifestyle. In the same way, we might disbelieve that God's searching eyes can see the areas of our hearts we try to hide. Or we tell ourselves that what is wrong won't likely kill us—at least today. So we ignore it. Not doing what we need to do to heal our physical heart will allow the damage to progress. Disregard of our spiritual health is just as devastating.

The bad news: You have a broken heart. The good news: God can cure the incurable.

Jeremiah 17:9–10

The heart is deceitful above all things and beyond cure. Who can understand it? "I the LORD search the heart and examine the mind, to reward a man according to his conduct, according to what his deeds deserve."

reflection

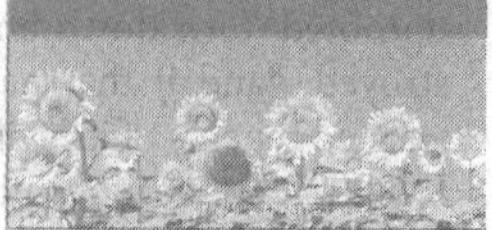

1. In what areas of your life do you suffer from spiritual heart disease?

2. What keeps you from following the Great Physician's orders?

3. In what ways can you entrust your *whole* heart to God's care?

RELATED READINGS

Isaiah 58:6–14;
Matthew 15:18;
Acts 15:8–9;
Hebrews 4:12–13

Go to page 929 for your next devotional reading.

At the Potter's House

18 This is the word that came to Jeremiah
from the LORD: 2“Go down to the potter's house, and there I will give you my message.” 3So I went down to the potter's house,
and I saw him working at the wheel. 4But the
pot he was shaping from the clay was marred in
his hands; so the potter formed it into another
pot, shaping it as seemed best to him.

5Then the word of the LORD came to me: 6“O
house of Israel, can I not do with you as this potter does?” declares the LORD. “Like clay in the
hand of the potter, so are you
in my hand, O house of Israel.
7If at any time I announce that
a nation or kingdom is to be
uprooted, torn down and destroyed, 8and if that nation I
warned repents of its evil, then
I will relent and not inflict on
it the disaster I had planned.
9And if at another time I announce that a nation or kingdom is to be built up and
planted, 10and if it does evil in
my sight and does not obey me,
then I will reconsider the good
I had intended to do for it.

11“Now therefore say to the people of Judah
and those living in Jerusalem, ‘This is what the
LORD says: Look! I am preparing a disaster for
you and devising a plan against you. So turn
from your evil ways, each one of you, and reform your ways and your actions.’ 12But they
will reply, ‘It's no use. We will continue with our
own plans; each of us will follow the stubbornness of his evil heart.’ ”

Jeremiah 18:6

God Shapes Us

“O house of Israel, can
I not do with you as this
potter does?” declares
the LORD. “Like clay in the
hand of the potter, so
are you in my hand,
O house of Israel.”

13Therefore this is what the LORD says:

“Inquire among the nations:
  Who has ever heard anything like this?
A most horrible thing has been done
  by Virgin Israel.
14Does the snow of Lebanon
  ever vanish from its rocky slopes?
Do its cool waters from distant sources
  ever cease to flow?[a]
15Yet my people have forgotten me;
  they burn incense to worthless idols,
which made them stumble in their ways
  and in the ancient paths.
They made them walk in bypaths
  and on roads not built up.
16Their land will be laid waste,
  an object of lasting scorn;
all who pass by will be appalled
  and will shake their heads.
17Like a wind from the east,
  I will scatter them before their enemies;
I will show them my back and not my face
  in the day of their disaster.”

18They said, “Come, let's
make plans against Jeremiah;
for the teaching of the law by
the priest will not be lost, nor
will counsel from the wise, nor
the word from the prophets. So
come, let's attack him with our
tongues and pay no attention
to anything he says.”

19Listen to me, O LORD;
  hear what my accusers
    are saying!
20Should good be repaid with
    evil?
  Yet they have dug a pit
    for me.
Remember that I stood before you
  and spoke in their behalf
  to turn your wrath away from them.
21So give their children over to famine;
  hand them over to the power of the
    sword.
Let their wives be made childless and
    widows;
  let their men be put to death,
  their young men slain by the sword in
    battle.
22Let a cry be heard from their houses
  when you suddenly bring invaders
    against them,
for they have dug a pit to capture me
  and have hidden snares for my feet.
23But you know, O LORD,
  all their plots to kill me.
Do not forgive their crimes
  or blot out their sins from your sight.

[a]14 The meaning of the Hebrew for this sentence is uncertain.

Pain at the Potter's Wheel

Read: Jeremiah 18:1–10

HAVE YOU SEEN A POTTER at the wheel lately? As modern-day thinkers, we might wonder why God sent Jeremiah down to the potter's house. We may not know much about pottery, except that it's beautiful and expensive. But in Jeremiah's day, pottery was essential for everyday living. Seeing a potter at work was probably as common then as seeing an office worker at a keyboard today.

So when God sent Jeremiah to the potter's wheel, he drew on an image that was very familiar to the Israelites in order to highlight the difference between the Creator and the created being, the sovereign versus the subject. The potter is highly skilled, imaginative and purposefully intent upon the outcome of his creation. In contrast, the clay is crude and unformed, misshapen and useless without the intervention of the master potter. By observing a potter at work, it becomes clear who is doing the shaping and who is being shaped.

How odd it would be for the clay to call out to the potter, "Hey, ease up there. Not so rough!" It's ridiculous to envision. And yet, Jeremiah's lesson of the potter still resonates with us. It is often painful to be the clay. At times we are pressed, pushed, molded and remolded. Our Potter may crush us from time to time when he encounters residual clumps that need smoothing over.

However, our master Potter knows his business far better than we do. We are a marred and messy mixture of clay and water. In the hands of our skilled Potter, the outcome is a beautiful and unique work of art.

This week try to remember the picture of a potter and his clay. Consider the difference between the Creator and the creation. It may help to remember that our wise and loving God knows the beautiful vessel he alone is capable of fashioning.

Thursday

Jeremiah 18:4

But the pot he was shaping from the clay was marred in his hands; so the potter formed it into another pot, shaping it as seemed best to him.

reflection

1. How do you feel about the analogy of being made and shaped by the Potter?
2. Describe a time when you were in need of reshaping by God. In what ways has God proven himself a trustworthy Potter?
3. What do you think God is trying to create in your life right now?

RELATED READINGS

Isaiah 45:9–12; 64:8; Romans 9:20–21

Go to page 933 for your next devotional reading.

Let them be overthrown before you;
deal with them in the time of your
anger.

19 This is what the LORD says: "Go and
buy a clay jar from a potter. Take along
some of the elders of the people and of the
priests 2 and go out to the Valley of Ben Hinnom, near the entrance of the Potsherd Gate.
There proclaim the words I tell you, 3 and say,
'Hear the word of the LORD, O kings of Judah
and people of Jerusalem. This is what the LORD
Almighty, the God of Israel, says: Listen! I am
going to bring a disaster on this place that will
make the ears of everyone who hears of it tingle. 4 For they have forsaken me and made
this a place of foreign gods; they have burned
sacrifices in it to gods that neither they nor
their fathers nor the kings of Judah ever knew,
and they have filled this place with the blood of
the innocent. 5 They have built the high places
of Baal to burn their sons in the fire as offerings to Baal—something I did not command
or mention, nor did it enter my mind. 6 So beware, the days are coming, declares the LORD,
when people will no longer call this place Topheth or the Valley of Ben Hinnom, but the
Valley of Slaughter.

7 "'In this place I will ruin[a] the plans of Judah and Jerusalem. I will make them fall by
the sword before their enemies, at the hands of
those who seek their lives, and I will give their
carcasses as food to the birds of the air and the
beasts of the earth. 8 I will devastate this city
and make it an object of scorn; all who pass by
will be appalled and will scoff because of all its
wounds. 9 I will make them eat the flesh of their
sons and daughters, and they will eat one another's flesh during the stress of the siege imposed
on them by the enemies who seek their lives.'

10 "Then break the jar while those who go
with you are watching, 11 and say to them, 'This
is what the LORD Almighty says: I will smash
this nation and this city just as this potter's jar
is smashed and cannot be repaired. They will
bury the dead in Topheth until there is no more
room. 12 This is what I will do to this place and
to those who live here, declares the LORD. I will
make this city like Topheth. 13 The houses in Jerusalem and those of the kings of Judah will be
defiled like this place, Topheth—all the houses
where they burned incense on the roofs to all
the starry hosts and poured out drink offerings
to other gods.'"

14 Jeremiah then returned from Topheth,
where the LORD had sent him to prophesy,
and stood in the court of the LORD's temple
and said to all the people, 15 "This is what the
LORD Almighty, the God of Israel, says: 'Listen! I am going to bring on this city and the
villages around it every disaster I pronounced
against them, because they were stiff-necked
and would not listen to my words.'"

Jeremiah and Pashhur

20 When the priest Pashhur son of Immer, the chief officer in the temple of
the LORD, heard Jeremiah prophesying these
things, 2 he had Jeremiah the prophet beaten
and put in the stocks at the Upper Gate of
Benjamin at the LORD's temple. 3 The next day,
when Pashhur released him from the stocks,
Jeremiah said to him, "The LORD's name for
you is not Pashhur, but Magor-Missabib.[b] 4 For
this is what the LORD says: 'I will make you a terror to yourself and to all your friends; with your
own eyes you will see them fall by the sword
of their enemies. I will hand all Judah over to
the king of Babylon, who will carry them away
to Babylon or put them to the sword. 5 I will
hand over to their enemies all the wealth of this
city—all its products, all its valuables and all the
treasures of the kings of Judah. They will take
it away as plunder and carry it off to Babylon.
6 And you, Pashhur, and all who live in your
house will go into exile to Babylon. There you
will die and be buried, you and all your friends
to whom you have prophesied lies.'"

Jeremiah's Complaint

7 O LORD, you deceived[c] me, and I was
deceived[c];
you overpowered me and prevailed.
I am ridiculed all day long;
everyone mocks me.
8 Whenever I speak, I cry out
proclaiming violence and destruction.
So the word of the LORD has brought me

[a] 7 The Hebrew for *ruin* sounds like the Hebrew for *jar* (see verses 1 and 10). [b] 3 *Magor-Missabib* means *terror on every side.*
[c] 7 Or *persuaded*

insult and reproach all day long.
9 But if I say, "I will not mention him
or speak any more in his name,"
his word is in my heart like a fire,
a fire shut up in my bones.
I am weary of holding it in;
indeed, I cannot.
10 I hear many whispering,
"Terror on every side!
Report him! Let's report him!"
All my friends
are waiting for me to slip, saying,
"Perhaps he will be deceived;
then we will prevail over him
and take our revenge on him."

11 But the LORD is with me like a mighty warrior;
so my persecutors will stumble and not prevail.
They will fail and be thoroughly disgraced;
their dishonor will never be forgotten.
12 O LORD Almighty, you who examine the righteous
and probe the heart and mind,
let me see your vengeance upon them,
for to you I have committed my cause.

13 Sing to the LORD!
Give praise to the LORD!
He rescues the life of the needy
from the hands of the wicked.

14 Cursed be the day I was born!
May the day my mother bore me not be blessed!
15 Cursed be the man who brought my father the news,
who made him very glad, saying,
"A child is born to you—a son!"
16 May that man be like the towns
the LORD overthrew without pity.
May he hear wailing in the morning,
a battle cry at noon.
17 For he did not kill me in the womb,
with my mother as my grave,
her womb enlarged forever.
18 Why did I ever come out of the womb
to see trouble and sorrow
and to end my days in shame?

> **Jeremiah 20:13**
>
> *God Rescues*
>
> Sing to the LORD!
> Give praise to the LORD!
> He rescues the life
> of the needy
> from the hands
> of the wicked.

God Rejects Zedekiah's Request

21 The word came to Jeremiah from the
LORD when King Zedekiah sent to
him Pashhur son of Malkijah and the priest
Zephaniah son of Maaseiah. They said: 2 "Inquire now of the LORD for us because Nebuchadnezzar[a] king of Babylon is attacking us.
Perhaps the LORD will perform wonders for
us as in times past so that he will withdraw
from us."
3 But Jeremiah answered them, "Tell Zedekiah, 4 'This is what the LORD, the God of Israel,
says: I am about to turn against you the weapons
of war that are in your hands, which you are
using to fight the king of Babylon and the Babylonians[b] who are outside the wall besieging
you. And I will gather them inside this city.
5 I myself will fight against you with an outstretched hand and a mighty
arm in anger and fury and great
wrath. 6 I will strike down those
who live in this city—both
men and animals—and they
will die of a terrible plague.
7 After that, declares the LORD,
I will hand over Zedekiah king
of Judah, his officials and the
people in this city who survive
the plague, sword and famine,
to Nebuchadnezzar king of
Babylon and to their enemies
who seek their lives. He will
put them to the sword; he will
show them no mercy or pity or compassion.'
8 "Furthermore, tell the people, 'This is what
the LORD says: See, I am setting before you the
way of life and the way of death. 9 Whoever
stays in this city will die by the sword, famine
or plague. But whoever goes out and surrenders to the Babylonians who are besieging you
will live; he will escape with his life. 10 I have
determined to do this city harm and not good,

[a] 2 Hebrew *Nebuchadrezzar,* of which *Nebuchadnezzar* is a variant; here and often in Jeremiah and Ezekiel [b] 4 Or *Chaldeans;* also in verse 9

declares the LORD. It will be given into the
hands of the king of Babylon, and he will destroy it with fire.'

11 "Moreover, say to the royal house of Judah, 'Hear the word of the LORD; 12 O house of
David, this is what the LORD says:

"'Administer justice every morning;
 rescue from the hand of his oppressor
 the one who has been robbed,
or my wrath will break out and burn like
 fire
 because of the evil you have done—
 burn with no one to quench it.
13 I am against you, ⌞Jerusalem,⌟
 you who live above this valley
 on the rocky plateau,
 declares the LORD—
you who say, "Who can come against us?
 Who can enter our refuge?"
14 I will punish you as your deeds deserve,
 declares the LORD.
I will kindle a fire in your forests
 that will consume everything around
 you.'"

Judgment Against Evil Kings

22 This is what the LORD says: "Go down
to the palace of the king of Judah and
proclaim this message there: 2 'Hear the word
of the LORD, O king of Judah, you who sit on
David's throne—you, your officials and your
people who come through these gates. 3 This is
what the LORD says: Do what is just and right.
Rescue from the hand of his oppressor the one
who has been robbed. Do no wrong or violence
to the alien, the fatherless or the widow, and do
not shed innocent blood in this place. 4 For if
you are careful to carry out these commands,
then kings who sit on David's throne will come
through the gates of this palace, riding in chariots and on horses, accompanied by their officials and their people. 5 But if you do not obey
these commands, declares the LORD, I swear by
myself that this palace will become a ruin.'"

6 For this is what the LORD says about the palace of the king of Judah:

"Though you are like Gilead to me,
 like the summit of Lebanon,
I will surely make you like a desert,
 like towns not inhabited.
7 I will send destroyers against you,
 each man with his weapons,
and they will cut up your fine cedar beams
 and throw them into the fire.

8 "People from many nations will pass by
this city and will ask one another, 'Why has
the LORD done such a thing to this great city?'
9 And the answer will be: 'Because they have
forsaken the covenant of the LORD their God
and have worshiped and served other gods.'"

10 Do not weep for the dead ⌞king⌟ or mourn
 his loss;
 rather, weep bitterly for him who is
 exiled,
because he will never return
 nor see his native land again.

11 For this is what the LORD says about Shallum[a] son of Josiah, who succeeded his father
as king of Judah but has gone from this place:
"He will never return. 12 He will die in the place
where they have led him captive; he will not see
this land again."

13 "Woe to him who builds his palace by
 unrighteousness,
 his upper rooms by injustice,
making his countrymen work for nothing,
 not paying them for their labor.
14 He says, 'I will build myself a great palace
 with spacious upper rooms.'
So he makes large windows in it,
 panels it with cedar
 and decorates it in red.

15 "Does it make you a king
 to have more and more cedar?
Did not your father have food and drink?
 He did what was right and just,
 so all went well with him.
16 He defended the cause of the poor and
 needy,
 and so all went well.
Is that not what it means to know me?"
 declares the LORD.
17 "But your eyes and your heart
 are set only on dishonest gain,
on shedding innocent blood
 and on oppression and extortion."

[a] 11 Also called *Jehoahaz*

What God Values

Read: Jeremiah 22:1–5

IN THE MIDDLE OF A TUMULTUOUS TIME in American history, an activist arose who did what was right for the oppressed. Coretta Scott, a vivacious young woman studying voice and violin at the New England Conservatory, met a charismatic young doctoral student in Boston who shared her passions. She swept Martin Luther King Jr. off his feet. They married and became partners in a tireless fight for social justice and the civil rights of all Americans.

For 38 years following her husband's tragic death, Mrs. King traveled the world, speaking out against all manner of injustice and oppression, received by heads of state and even preaching in St. Paul's Cathedral in Rome. With her passing in 2006, Coretta Scott King left a rich living legacy of welcoming the alien, caring for the widow and orphan, and fighting for the freedom of all people regardless of race, creed or culture. She cared about what God cared about.

The kingdom of Judah was corrupt and rebellious, and in response, God was sending judgment. Jeremiah had an urgent message from God that would save the kingdom. Was it to build up their armies? Was it to build a new city wall? Was it to go to war? No. Jeremiah said, "Do what is right. Rescue the oppressed. If you do, then the kingdom will last; if you don't, then the kingdom will end in ruins." But the people didn't listen. They didn't care about what God valued. And it cost them everything.

Fast-forward several centuries to scenes of our world, and things haven't changed all that much. The world today doesn't care much about what God cares about. It's easy to talk about justice, but it's another thing to do what is just and right. It's easy to remain comfortable and complacent, but it's hard to move out of our comfort zone. But loving God means loving what he values. And God cares about those who suffer injustice and oppression.

Jeremiah 22:3

"This is what the LORD says: Do what is just and right. Rescue from the hand of his oppressor the one who has been robbed. Do no wrong or violence to the alien, the fatherless or the widow, and do not shed innocent blood in this place."

reflection

1 As we become women after God's own heart and learn to value what he values, our awareness of the needs around us increases. What injustices do you witness around you, and what can you do to help the situation?

2 How does the gospel provide an answer to the suffering endured by so many in this world?

3 What steps can you take to serve someone who is oppressed politically, socially, economically or spiritually?

RELATED READINGS

Isaiah 58:6–14; James 2:14–26

Go to page 935 for your next devotional reading.

18 Therefore this is what the LORD says about
Jehoiakim son of Josiah king of Judah:

"They will not mourn for him:
'Alas, my brother! Alas, my sister!'
They will not mourn for him:
'Alas, my master! Alas, his splendor!'
19 He will have the burial of a donkey—
dragged away and thrown
outside the gates of Jerusalem."

20 "Go up to Lebanon and cry out,
let your voice be heard in Bashan,
cry out from Abarim,
for all your allies are crushed.
21 I warned you when you felt secure,
but you said, 'I will not listen!'
This has been your way from your youth;
you have not obeyed me.
22 The wind will drive all your shepherds
away,
and your allies will go into exile.
Then you will be ashamed and disgraced
because of all your wickedness.
23 You who live in 'Lebanon,[a]'
who are nestled in cedar buildings,
how you will groan when pangs come
upon you,
pain like that of a woman in labor!

24 "As surely as I live," declares the LORD,
"even if you, Jehoiachin[b] son of Jehoiakim
king of Judah, were a signet ring on my right
hand, I would still pull you off. 25 I will hand
you over to those who seek your life, those you
fear—to Nebuchadnezzar king of Babylon and
to the Babylonians.[c] 26 I will hurl you and the
mother who gave you birth into another country, where neither of you was born, and there
you both will die. 27 You will never come back
to the land you long to return to."

28 Is this man Jehoiachin a despised, broken
pot,
an object no one wants?
Why will he and his children be hurled
out,
cast into a land they do not know?
29 O land, land, land,
hear the word of the LORD!
30 This is what the LORD says:
"Record this man as if childless,
a man who will not prosper in his
lifetime,
for none of his offspring will prosper,
none will sit on the throne of David
or rule anymore in Judah."

The Righteous Branch

23 "Woe to the shepherds who are destroying and scattering the sheep of my pasture!" declares the LORD. 2 Therefore this is
what the LORD, the God of Israel, says to the
shepherds who tend my people: "Because you
have scattered my flock and driven them away
and have not bestowed care on them, I will bestow punishment on you for the evil you have
done," declares the LORD. 3 "I myself will gather
the remnant of my flock out of all the countries
where I have driven them and will bring them
back to their pasture, where they will be fruitful and increase in number. 4 I will place shepherds over them who will tend them, and they
will no longer be afraid or terrified, nor will any
be missing," declares the LORD.

5 "The days are coming," declares the LORD,
"when I will raise up to David[d] a
righteous Branch,
a King who will reign wisely
and do what is just and right in the land.
6 In his days Judah will be saved
and Israel will live in safety.
This is the name by which he will be called:
The LORD Our Righteousness.

7 "So then, the days are coming," declares the
LORD, "when people will no longer say, 'As
surely as the LORD lives, who brought the Israelites up out of Egypt,' 8 but they will say, 'As
surely as the LORD lives, who brought the descendants of Israel up out of the land of the
north and out of all the countries where he
had banished them.' Then they will live in their
own land."

Lying Prophets

9 Concerning the prophets:

My heart is broken within me;
all my bones tremble.

[a] 23 That is, the palace in Jerusalem (see 1 Kings 7:2) [b] 24 Hebrew *Coniah,* a variant of *Jehoiachin*; also in verse 28 [c] 25 Or *Chaldeans*
[d] 5 Or *up from David's line*

More Than a Pretty Face

ESTHER

SHE BREATHED A SIGH of relief. He hadn't forgotten.

In the midst of scheduling important meetings, summoning officials and juggling all of his other kingly duties, King Xerxes had not allowed his wife's request to go unnoticed. In fact, she'd seen how his eyes darted her way throughout the banquet that night as he spoke to his guest, Haman, and quietly directed the royal stewards throughout the meal.

Esther was aware of the allure of her beauty. She knew garnering the king's eye was rarely an issue. She was, after all, ravishing—among a thousand women in the land, she was indisputably the most beautiful. Ever since she was a little girl, she'd realized there was something special about her. Women in the marketplace would point to her and smile softly, admiring the length of her rich hair or her sculpted features. Whenever strangers lathered compliments on her, her family beamed with joy, and Esther blushed on more than one occasion.

However, what she had to do tonight would require more than her looks. When Mordecai sought her out for the sake of their people, he wasn't necessarily addressing Esther, the beauty. He was summoning something he'd seen deep inside her that others, so taken with her outward appearance, had hardly noticed. It would take more than a pretty face to convince the king to reverse his order against her people, the Jews. It would exact from Esther the whole of who she was—her mind, her heart and her strength.

As King Xerxes raised the sweet-tasting wine to his lips, he spoke to her. "Queen Esther, what is your petition? It will be given you. What is your request?"

At that moment, Esther did not think about the style of her hair. She did not wonder if her face looked radiant or her lips plump. She did not inwardly debate whether her thighs were too big or her hips too wide. She looked deep within herself, called up her courage, engaged her mind and made her request.

—Prayer—

Thank you, God, for equipping women like Esther to be examples of strength and courage for women throughout the years.

Then Queen Esther answered, "If I have found favor with you, O king, and if it pleases your majesty, grant me my life—this is my petition."

Esther 7:3

ASSIGNED READING:

Esther

Weekend

Go to page 941 for your next devotional reading.

I am like a drunken man,
like a man overcome by wine,
because of the LORD
and his holy words.
10 The land is full of adulterers;
because of the curse[a] the land lies parched[b]
and the pastures in the desert are withered.
The ⌊prophets⌋ follow an evil course
and use their power unjustly.

11 "Both prophet and priest are godless;
even in my temple I find their wickedness,"
declares the LORD.
12 "Therefore their path will become slippery;
they will be banished to darkness
and there they will fall.
I will bring disaster on them
in the year they are punished,"
declares the LORD.

13 "Among the prophets of Samaria
I saw this repulsive thing:
They prophesied by Baal
and led my people Israel astray.
14 And among the prophets of Jerusalem
I have seen something horrible:
They commit adultery and live a lie.
They strengthen the hands of evildoers,
so that no one turns from his wickedness.
They are all like Sodom to me;
the people of Jerusalem are like Gomorrah."

15 Therefore, this is what the LORD Almighty says concerning the prophets:

"I will make them eat bitter food
and drink poisoned water,
because from the prophets of Jerusalem
ungodliness has spread throughout the land."

16 This is what the LORD Almighty says:

"Do not listen to what the prophets are prophesying to you;
they fill you with false hopes.
They speak visions from their own minds,
not from the mouth of the LORD.
17 They keep saying to those who despise me,
'The LORD says: You will have peace.'
And to all who follow the stubbornness of their hearts
they say, 'No harm will come to you.'
18 But which of them has stood in the council of the LORD
to see or to hear his word?
Who has listened and heard his word?
19 See, the storm of the LORD
will burst out in wrath,
a whirlwind swirling down
on the heads of the wicked.
20 The anger of the LORD will not turn back
until he fully accomplishes
the purposes of his heart.
In days to come
you will understand it clearly.
21 I did not send these prophets,
yet they have run with their message;
I did not speak to them,
yet they have prophesied.
22 But if they had stood in my council,
they would have proclaimed my words to my people
and would have turned them from their evil ways
and from their evil deeds.

23 "Am I only a God nearby,"
declares the LORD,
"and not a God far away?
24 Can anyone hide in secret places
so that I cannot see him?"
declares the LORD.
"Do not I fill heaven and earth?"
declares the LORD.

25 "I have heard what the prophets say who
prophesy lies in my name. They say, 'I had a

Jeremiah 23:24

God Sees Everything

"Can anyone hide in secret places so that I cannot see him?" declares the LORD.

[a] 10 Or *because of these things* [b] 10 Or *land mourns*

dream! I had a dream!' 26 How long will this
continue in the hearts of these lying prophets, who prophesy the delusions of their own
minds? 27 They think the dreams they tell one
another will make my people forget my name,
just as their fathers forgot my name through
Baal worship. 28 Let the prophet who has a
dream tell his dream, but let the one who has
my word speak it faithfully. For what has straw
to do with grain?" declares the LORD. 29 "Is not
my word like fire," declares the LORD, "and like
a hammer that breaks a rock in pieces?

30 "Therefore," declares the LORD, "I am
against the prophets who steal from one
another words supposedly from me. 31 Yes,"
declares the LORD, "I am against the prophets
who wag their own tongues and yet declare,
'The LORD declares.' 32 Indeed, I am against
those who prophesy false dreams," declares
the LORD. "They tell them and lead my people
astray with their reckless lies, yet I did not send
or appoint them. They do not benefit these people in the least," declares the LORD.

False Oracles and False Prophets

33 "When these people, or a prophet or
a priest, ask you, 'What is the oracle[a] of the
LORD?' say to them, 'What oracle?[b] I will forsake you, declares the LORD.' 34 If a prophet or
a priest or anyone else claims, 'This is the oracle of the LORD,' I will punish that man and his
household. 35 This is what each of you keeps
on saying to his friend or relative: 'What is the
LORD's answer?' or 'What has the LORD spoken?' 36 But you must not mention 'the oracle
of the LORD' again, because every man's own
word becomes his oracle and so you distort the
words of the living God, the LORD Almighty,
our God. 37 This is what you keep saying to a
prophet: 'What is the LORD's answer to you?'
or 'What has the LORD spoken?' 38 Although
you claim, 'This is the oracle of the LORD,' this
is what the LORD says: You used the words,
'This is the oracle of the LORD,' even though I
told you that you must not claim, 'This is the
oracle of the LORD.' 39 Therefore, I will surely
forget you and cast you out of my presence
along with the city I gave to you and your
fathers. 40 I will bring upon you everlasting
disgrace—everlasting shame that will not be
forgotten."

Two Baskets of Figs

24 After Jehoiachin[c] son of Jehoiakim
king of Judah and the officials, the
craftsmen and the artisans of Judah were carried into exile from Jerusalem to Babylon by
Nebuchadnezzar king of Babylon, the LORD
showed me two baskets of figs placed in front
of the temple of the LORD. 2 One basket had
very good figs, like those that ripen early; the
other basket had very poor figs, so bad they
could not be eaten.

3 Then the LORD asked me, "What do you
see, Jeremiah?"

"Figs," I answered. "The good ones are very
good, but the poor ones are so bad they cannot
be eaten."

4 Then the word of the LORD came to me:
5 "This is what the LORD, the God of Israel, says:
'Like these good figs, I regard as good the exiles
from Judah, whom I sent away from this place
to the land of the Babylonians.[d] 6 My eyes will
watch over them for their good, and I will bring
them back to this land. I will build them up and
not tear them down; I will plant them and not
uproot them. 7 I will give them a heart to know
me, that I am the LORD. They will be my people, and I will be their God, for they will return
to me with all their heart.

8 "'But like the poor figs, which are so bad
they cannot be eaten,' says the LORD, 'so will I
deal with Zedekiah king of Judah, his officials
and the survivors from Jerusalem, whether
they remain in this land or live in Egypt. 9 I
will make them abhorrent and an offense to
all the kingdoms of the earth, a reproach and
a byword, an object of ridicule and cursing,
wherever I banish them. 10 I will send the
sword, famine and plague against them until
they are destroyed from the land I gave to them
and their fathers.'"

Seventy Years of Captivity

25 The word came to Jeremiah concerning all the people of Judah in
the fourth year of Jehoiakim son of Josiah
king of Judah, which was the first year of

33 Or *burden* (see Septuagint and Vulgate) [b]33 Hebrew; Septuagint and Vulgate *'You are the burden.* (The Hebrew for *oracle* and *burden*
s the same.) [c]1 Hebrew *Jeconiah,* a variant of *Jehoiachin* [d]5 Or *Chaldeans*

Nebuchadnezzar king of Babylon. 2So Jeremiah the prophet said to all the people of
Judah and to all those living in Jerusalem:
3For twenty-three years—from the thirteenth
year of Josiah son of Amon king of Judah until this very day—the word of the LORD has
come to me and I have spoken to you again
and again, but you have not listened.

4And though the LORD has sent all his servants the prophets to you again and again, you
have not listened or paid any attention. 5They
said, "Turn now, each of you, from your evil
ways and your evil practices, and you can stay
in the land the LORD gave to you and your fathers for ever and ever. 6Do not follow other
gods to serve and worship them; do not provoke me to anger with what your hands have
made. Then I will not harm you."

7"But you did not listen to me," declares the
LORD, "and you have provoked me with what
your hands have made, and you have brought
harm to yourselves."

8Therefore the LORD Almighty says this:
"Because you have not listened to my words,
9I will summon all the peoples of the north
and my servant Nebuchadnezzar king of Babylon," declares the LORD, "and I will bring them
against this land and its inhabitants and against
all the surrounding nations. I will completely
destroy[a] them and make them an object of horror and scorn, and an everlasting ruin. 10I will
banish from them the sounds of joy and gladness, the voices of bride and bridegroom, the
sound of millstones and the light of the lamp.
11This whole country will become a desolate
wasteland, and these nations will serve the king
of Babylon seventy years.

12"But when the seventy years are fulfilled, I
will punish the king of Babylon and his nation,
the land of the Babylonians,[b] for their guilt,"
declares the LORD, "and will make it desolate
forever. 13I will bring upon that land all the
things I have spoken against it, all that are written in this book and prophesied by Jeremiah
against all the nations. 14They themselves will
be enslaved by many nations and great kings; I
will repay them according to their deeds and
the work of their hands."

The Cup of God's Wrath

15This is what the LORD, the God of Israel,
said to me: "Take from my hand this cup filled
with the wine of my wrath and make all the
nations to whom I send you drink it. 16When
they drink it, they will stagger and go mad because of the sword I will send among them."

17So I took the cup from the LORD's hand
and made all the nations to whom he sent me
drink it: 18Jerusalem and the towns of Judah,
its kings and officials, to make them a ruin and
an object of horror and scorn and cursing, as
they are today; 19Pharaoh king of Egypt, his attendants, his officials and all his people, 20and
all the foreign people there; all the kings of Uz;
all the kings of the Philistines (those of Ashkelon, Gaza, Ekron, and the people left at Ashdod); 21Edom, Moab and Ammon; 22all the
kings of Tyre and Sidon; the kings of the coastlands across the sea; 23Dedan, Tema, Buz and
all who are in distant places[c]; 24all the kings of
Arabia and all the kings of the foreign people
who live in the desert; 25all the kings of Zimri,
Elam and Media; 26and all the kings of the
north, near and far, one after the other—all the
kingdoms on the face of the earth. And after
all of them, the king of Sheshach[d] will drink
it too.

27"Then tell them, 'This is what the LORD
Almighty, the God of Israel, says: Drink, get
drunk and vomit, and fall to rise no more
because of the sword I will send among you.'
28But if they refuse to take the cup from your
hand and drink, tell them, 'This is what the
LORD Almighty says: You must drink it! 29See,
I am beginning to bring disaster on the city
that bears my Name, and will you indeed go
unpunished? You will not go unpunished, for I
am calling down a sword upon all who live on
the earth, declares the LORD Almighty.'

30"Now prophesy all these words against
them and say to them:

"'The LORD will roar from on high;
he will thunder from his holy dwelling
and roar mightily against his land.
He will shout like those who tread the
grapes,
shout against all who live on the earth.

[a]9 The Hebrew term refers to the irrevocable giving over of things or persons to the LORD, often by totally destroying them.
[b]12 Or *Chaldeans* [c]23 Or *who clip the hair by their foreheads* [d]26 *Sheshach* is a cryptogram for Babylon.

31 The tumult will resound to the ends of the
earth,
for the LORD will bring charges against
the nations;
he will bring judgment on
all mankind
and put the wicked to the
sword,'"
declares the LORD.

32 This is what the LORD Almighty says:

"Look! Disaster is
spreading
from nation to nation;
a mighty storm is rising
from the ends of the
earth."

33 At that time those slain by
the LORD will be everywhere—
from one end of the earth to
the other. They will not be mourned or gathered up or buried, but will be like refuse lying
on the ground.

34 Weep and wail, you shepherds;
roll in the dust, you leaders of the flock.
For your time to be slaughtered has come;
you will fall and be shattered like fine
pottery.
35 The shepherds will have nowhere to flee,
the leaders of the flock no place to
escape.
36 Hear the cry of the shepherds,
the wailing of the leaders of the flock,
for the LORD is destroying their pasture.
37 The peaceful meadows will be laid waste
because of the fierce anger of the LORD.
38 Like a lion he will leave his lair,
and their land will become desolate
because of the sword[a] of the oppressor
and because of the LORD's fierce anger.

Jeremiah Threatened With Death

26 Early in the reign of Jehoiakim son of
Josiah king of Judah, this word came
from the LORD: 2 "This is what the LORD says:
Stand in the courtyard of the LORD's house and
speak to all the people of the towns of Judah
who come to worship in the house of the LORD.
Tell them everything I command you; do not
omit a word. 3 Perhaps they will listen and each
will turn from his evil way. Then I will relent
and not bring on them the di-
saster I was planning because
of the evil they have done. 4 Say
to them, 'This is what the LORD
says: If you do not listen to me
and follow my law, which I
have set before you, 5 and if
you do not listen to the words
of my servants the prophets,
whom I have sent to you again
and again (though you have
not listened), 6 then I will make
this house like Shiloh and this
city an object of cursing among
all the nations of the earth.'"

7 The priests, the proph-
ets and all the people heard
Jeremiah speak these words in
the house of the LORD. 8 But as soon as Jeremiah
finished telling all the people everything the
LORD had commanded him to say, the priests,
the prophets and all the people seized him and
said, "You must die! 9 Why do you prophesy in
the LORD's name that this house will be like Shiloh and this city will be desolate and deserted?"
And all the people crowded around Jeremiah
in the house of the LORD.

10 When the officials of Judah heard about
these things, they went up from the royal palace to the house of the LORD and took their
places at the entrance of the New Gate of the
LORD's house. 11 Then the priests and the prophets said to the officials and all the people, "This
man should be sentenced to death because he
has prophesied against this city. You have heard
it with your own ears!"

12 Then Jeremiah said to all the officials and
all the people: "The LORD sent me to prophesy
against this house and this city all the things
you have heard. 13 Now reform your ways and
your actions and obey the LORD your God.
Then the LORD will relent and not bring the disaster he has pronounced against you. 14 As for
me, I am in your hands; do with me whatever
you think is good and right. 15 Be assured,
however, that if you put me to death, you will

> **Jeremiah 26:3**
>
> ***God Withholds His Wrath***
>
> "Perhaps they will listen and each will turn from his evil way. Then I will relent and not bring on them the disaster I was planning because of the evil they have done."

[a] 38 Some Hebrew manuscripts and Septuagint (see also Jer. 46:16 and 50:16); most Hebrew manuscripts *anger*

bring the guilt of innocent blood on yourselves
and on this city and on those who live in it, for
in truth the LORD has sent me to you to speak
all these words in your hearing."
16 Then the officials and all the people said to
the priests and the prophets, "This man should
not be sentenced to death! He has spoken to us
in the name of the LORD our God."
17 Some of the elders of the
land stepped forward and said
to the entire assembly of people,
18 "Micah of Moresheth prophesied in the days of Hezekiah
king of Judah. He told all the
people of Judah, 'This is what
the LORD Almighty says:

"'Zion will be plowed like
a field,
Jerusalem will become a
heap of rubble,
the temple hill a mound
overgrown with
thickets.'[a]

19 "Did Hezekiah king of Judah
or anyone else in Judah put him to death? Did
not Hezekiah fear the LORD and seek his favor?
And did not the LORD relent, so that he did
not bring the disaster he pronounced against
them? We are about to bring a terrible disaster
on ourselves!"
20 (Now Uriah son of Shemaiah from Kiriath Jearim was another man who prophesied
in the name of the LORD; he prophesied the
same things against this city and this land as
Jeremiah did. 21 When King Jehoiakim and all
his officers and officials heard his words, the
king sought to put him to death. But Uriah
heard of it and fled in fear to Egypt. 22 King Jehoiakim, however, sent Elnathan son of Acbor
to Egypt, along with some other men. 23 They
brought Uriah out of Egypt and took him to
King Jehoiakim, who had him struck down
with a sword and his body thrown into the
burial place of the common people.)
24 Furthermore, Ahikam son of Shaphan
supported Jeremiah, and so he was not handed
over to the people to be put to death.

Jeremiah 27:5

God Gives at His Discretion

"With my great power and outstretched arm I made the earth and its people and the animals that are on it, and I give it to anyone I please."

Judah to Serve Nebuchadnezzar

27 Early in the reign of Zedekiah[b] son of
Josiah king of Judah, this word came to
Jeremiah from the LORD: 2 This is what the LORD
said to me: "Make a yoke out of straps and crossbars and put it on your neck. 3 Then send word
to the kings of Edom, Moab, Ammon, Tyre and
Sidon through the envoys who have come to
Jerusalem to Zedekiah king of
Judah. 4 Give them a message
for their masters and say, 'This
is what the LORD Almighty, the
God of Israel, says: "Tell this to
your masters: 5 With my great
power and outstretched arm
I made the earth and its people and the animals that are
on it, and I give it to anyone
I please. 6 Now I will hand all
your countries over to my servant Nebuchadnezzar king of
Babylon; I will make even the
wild animals subject to him.
7 All nations will serve him and
his son and his grandson until
the time for his land comes; then many nations
and great kings will subjugate him.
8 "'"If, however, any nation or kingdom will
not serve Nebuchadnezzar king of Babylon or
bow its neck under his yoke, I will punish that
nation with the sword, famine and plague, declares the LORD, until I destroy it by his hand.
9 So do not listen to your prophets, your diviners, your interpreters of dreams, your mediums
or your sorcerers who tell you, 'You will not
serve the king of Babylon.' 10 They prophesy
lies to you that will only serve to remove you
far from your lands; I will banish you and
you will perish. 11 But if any nation will bow
its neck under the yoke of the king of Babylon
and serve him, I will let that nation remain in
its own land to till it and to live there, declares
the LORD."'"
12 I gave the same message to Zedekiah king
of Judah. I said, "Bow your neck under the yoke
of the king of Babylon; serve him and his people, and you will live. 13 Why will you and your
people die by the sword, famine and plague

[a] 18 Micah 3:12 [b] 1 A few Hebrew manuscripts and Syriac (see also Jer. 27:3, 12 and 28:1); most Hebrew manuscripts *Jehoiakim* (Most Septuagint manuscripts do not have this verse.)

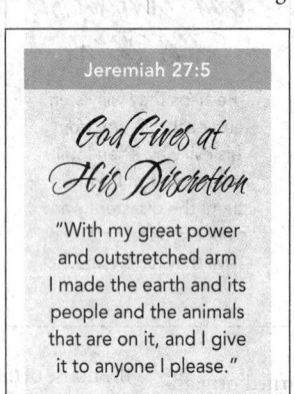

Primary Source

Read: Jeremiah 27:1–22

IN THE INFORMATION AGE, there is no shortage of perspectives. Newscasts, blogs, radio, movies, television and opinion polls constantly assail us with how we should feel and think about all kinds of issues. However, when believers need perspective, where do we turn? Whose voice echoes in our ears?

We like to say that we turn to God and to the Scriptures. But if we're truthful, we're a lot like the children of Israel. Instead of getting information from the primary source, they sought out false prophets. If they had listened to Jeremiah, they would have known God was saying just the opposite of what they were hearing.

Today, it's unlikely that a believer would seek out mediums or psychics for advice on life—although they are readily available. However, a number of other sources influence our thoughts and decisions, and not all of them are godly. From social trends to cultural mores, other people greatly affect how we see life. And Satan is aware of just how much "airtime" is available to influence us throughout our day.

Case in point: What are you worried about today? Headlines like terrorism, war, financial collapse? If those threats don't concern you, perhaps daytime television has convinced you that your children might be on meth or that your husband might be having an affair. And we wonder why we sometimes live with a vague sense of dread much of the time! Maybe instead of turning to God for perspective, we've been turning elsewhere.

It's normal to be concerned about our lives and our loved ones . . . but if we're not careful, anxiety can all too quickly imprison us. When you feel the cords of anxiety and worry tightening around you, think about the Lord's promises, his sovereignty and his goodness. Why not start by reading less of the newspaper and more of God's Word? Try turning off the television and tuning into praise music. You don't need to completely hide from the world, but try spending as much time hearing from God as you do hearing from other sources. The more you dwell on God's faithfulness, the less likely you'll view life from the wrong perspective. Go to the primary source for wisdom and insight.

Jeremiah 27:9

"So do not listen to your prophets, your diviners, your interpreters of dreams, your mediums or your sorcerers who tell you, 'You will not serve the king of Babylon.' "

reflection

1 What "voices" are you listening to each day?

2 In what ways do you struggle with worry and fear? Be specific.

3 Think of three ways you can dwell on God's promises—instead of what you fear—today.

RELATED READINGS

2 Kings 24:8–17; Psalms 27:1–3; 94:19; Philippians 4:4–9

"How do we find the peace and simplicity we crave in our lives? I think the answer lies in patience and prayer."

Ellyn Sanna

Monday

Go to page 944 for your next devotional reading.

with which the LORD has threatened any nation
that will not serve the king of Babylon? [14]Do
not listen to the words of the prophets who say
to you, 'You will not serve the king of Babylon,'
for they are prophesying lies to you. [15]'I have
not sent them,' declares the LORD. 'They are
prophesying lies in my name. Therefore, I will
banish you and you will perish, both you and
the prophets who prophesy to you.' "

[16]Then I said to the priests and all these people, "This is what the LORD says: Do not listen
to the prophets who say, 'Very soon now the
articles from the LORD's house will be brought
back from Babylon.' They are prophesying lies
to you. [17]Do not listen to them. Serve the king
of Babylon, and you will live. Why should this
city become a ruin? [18]If they are prophets and
have the word of the LORD, let them plead
with the LORD Almighty that the furnishings
remaining in the house of the LORD and in the
palace of the king of Judah and in Jerusalem
not be taken to Babylon. [19]For this is what the
LORD Almighty says about the pillars, the Sea,
the movable stands and the other furnishings
that are left in this city, [20]which Nebuchadnezzar king of Babylon did not take away when
he carried Jehoiachin[a] son of Jehoiakim king
of Judah into exile from Jerusalem to Babylon,
along with all the nobles of Judah and Jerusalem— [21]yes, this is what the LORD Almighty,
the God of Israel, says about the things that are
left in the house of the LORD and in the palace
of the king of Judah and in Jerusalem: [22]'They
will be taken to Babylon and there they will remain until the day I come for them,' declares
the LORD. 'Then I will bring them back and restore them to this place.' "

The False Prophet Hananiah

28 In the fifth month of that same year,
the fourth year, early in the reign of
Zedekiah king of Judah, the prophet Hananiah
son of Azzur, who was from Gibeon, said to
me in the house of the LORD in the presence of
the priests and all the people: [2]"This is what the
LORD Almighty, the God of Israel, says: 'I will
break the yoke of the king of Babylon. [3]Within
two years I will bring back to this place all the
articles of the LORD's house that Nebuchadnezzar king of Babylon removed from here and
took to Babylon. [4]I will also bring back to this
place Jehoiachin[a] son of Jehoiakim king of Judah and all the other exiles from Judah who
went to Babylon,' declares the LORD, 'for I will
break the yoke of the king of Babylon.' "

[5]Then the prophet Jeremiah replied to the
prophet Hananiah before the priests and all
the people who were standing in the house of
the LORD. [6]He said, "Amen! May the LORD do
so! May the LORD fulfill the words you have
prophesied by bringing the articles of the
LORD's house and all the exiles back to this
place from Babylon. [7]Nevertheless, listen to
what I have to say in your hearing and in the
hearing of all the people: [8]From early times
the prophets who preceded you and me have
prophesied war, disaster and plague against
many countries and great kingdoms. [9]But the
prophet who prophesies peace will be recognized as one truly sent by the LORD only if his
prediction comes true."

[10]Then the prophet Hananiah took the yoke
off the neck of the prophet Jeremiah and broke
it, [11]and he said before all the people, "This is
what the LORD says: 'In the same way will I
break the yoke of Nebuchadnezzar king of Babylon off the neck of all the nations within two
years.' " At this, the prophet Jeremiah went on
his way.

[12]Shortly after the prophet Hananiah had
broken the yoke off the neck of the prophet Jeremiah, the word of the LORD came to Jeremiah:
[13]"Go and tell Hananiah, 'This is what the LORD
says: You have broken a wooden yoke, but in its
place you will get a yoke of iron. [14]This is what
the LORD Almighty, the God of Israel, says: I
will put an iron yoke on the necks of all these
nations to make them serve Nebuchadnezzar
king of Babylon, and they will serve him. I will
even give him control over the wild animals.' "

[15]Then the prophet Jeremiah said to
Hananiah the prophet, "Listen, Hananiah! The
LORD has not sent you, yet you have persuaded
this nation to trust in lies. [16]Therefore, this is
what the LORD says: 'I am about to remove you
from the face of the earth. This very year you
are going to die, because you have preached rebellion against the LORD.' "

[a]20,4 Hebrew *Jeconiah,* a variant of *Jehoiachin*

17 In the seventh month of that same year,
Hananiah the prophet died.

A Letter to the Exiles

29 This is the text of the letter that the
prophet Jeremiah sent from Jerusalem
to the surviving elders among the exiles and to
the priests, the prophets and all the other people Nebuchadnezzar had carried into exile from
Jerusalem to Babylon. 2 (This was after King Jehoiachin[a] and the queen mother, the court officials and the leaders of Judah and Jerusalem,
the craftsmen and the artisans had gone into
exile from Jerusalem.) 3 He entrusted the letter
to Elasah son of Shaphan and to Gemariah son
of Hilkiah, whom Zedekiah king of Judah sent
to King Nebuchadnezzar in Babylon. It said:

4 This is what the LORD Almighty, the
God of Israel, says to all those I carried
into exile from Jerusalem to Babylon:
5 "Build houses and settle down; plant gardens and eat what they produce. 6 Marry
and have sons and daughters; find wives
for your sons and give your daughters in
marriage, so that they too may have sons
and daughters. Increase in number there;
do not decrease. 7 Also, seek the peace and
prosperity of the city to which I have carried you into exile. Pray to the LORD for
it, because if it prospers, you
too will prosper." 8 Yes, this
is what the LORD Almighty,
the God of Israel, says: "Do
not let the prophets and diviners among you deceive
you. Do not listen to the
dreams you encourage them
to have. 9 They are prophesying lies to you in my name. I
have not sent them," declares
the LORD.

10 This is what the LORD
says: "When seventy years
are completed for Babylon,
I will come to you and fulfill my gracious promise
to bring you back to this place. 11 For I
know the plans I have for you," declares
the LORD, "plans to prosper you and not
to harm you, plans to give you hope and a
future. 12 Then you will call upon me and
come and pray to me, and I will listen to
you. 13 You will seek me and find me when
you seek me with all your heart. 14 I will
be found by you," declares the LORD, "and
will bring you back from captivity.[b] I will
gather you from all the nations and places
where I have banished you," declares the
LORD, "and will bring you back to the
place from which I carried you into exile."

15 You may say, "The LORD has raised
up prophets for us in Babylon," 16 but this
is what the LORD says about the king who
sits on David's throne and all the people
who remain in this city, your countrymen
who did not go with you into exile—
17 yes, this is what the LORD Almighty
says: "I will send the sword, famine and
plague against them and I will make them
like poor figs that are so bad they cannot
be eaten. 18 I will pursue them with the
sword, famine and plague and will make
them abhorrent to all the kingdoms of the
earth and an object of cursing and horror,
of scorn and reproach, among all the nations where I drive them. 19 For they have
not listened to my words," declares the
LORD, "words that I sent to
them again and again by my
servants the prophets. And
you exiles have not listened
either," declares the LORD.

20 Therefore, hear the
word of the LORD, all you exiles whom I have sent away
from Jerusalem to Babylon.
21 This is what the LORD Almighty, the God of Israel,
says about Ahab son of Kolaiah and Zedekiah son of
Maaseiah, who are prophesying lies to you in my name:
"I will hand them over to
Nebuchadnezzar king of Bab-
ylon, and he will put them to death before
your very eyes. 22 Because of them, all the
exiles from Judah who are in Babylon

> **Jeremiah 29:11**
>
> *God Has Good Planned*
>
> "For I know the plans I have for you," declares the LORD, "plans to prosper you and not to harm you, plans to give you hope and a future."

[a] 2 Hebrew *Jeconiah,* a variant of *Jehoiachin* [b] 14 Or *will restore your fortunes*

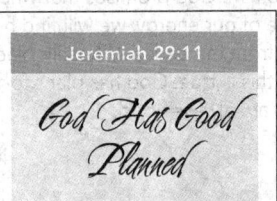

God Owns Time

Read: Jeremiah 29:4–14

IT'S SO HARD TO LOOK beyond our circumstances. For the Jews in the time of Jeremiah, it seemed impossible. The Babylonians had whisked them from their homes and settled them in enemy territory. Into this depressing scene, God sent Jeremiah, the anguished prophet of judgment. But his message this time was one of hope. In essence, he said, "Though your circumstances look bleak, your confinement will be limited. So settle in and make a home away from home for yourselves. As incredible as it sounds, look for and enjoy the moments of joy, even in this place. It won't be long before the worst will be over."

Today endless darkness may seem to surround you, just as the Israelites experienced. Maybe it is hard to remember the last time you felt free or comfortable. You've watched your business struggle, your friend fight disease or a child disown you. And you may have lived in this place for such a long time that you consider it a second home.

Whether or not the darkness is of your own making, and whether or not you can see its end, remember this: God owns time. Though he rarely shares his reasons with us, he knows why he allows the pain to continue. And he also knows the date—the day, the hour and the precise minute—when the agony will end. Not only that, but he also knows what he has in store for us when it's over.

Through Jeremiah, God invited the exiles to look to him, to call to him. God promises that when we search for him with every ounce of our energy, we will find him. In his time, he will bring us back from the dark and hostile places. As difficult as it is to imagine now, this is true: God has plans for us. And because he's God, his plans are always good.

Jeremiah 29:11–14

"I know the plans I have for you," declares the LORD, "plans to prosper you and not to harm you, plans to give you hope and a future. Then you will call upon me and come and pray to me, and I will listen to you. You will seek me and find me when you seek me with all your heart. I will be found by you," declares the LORD, "and will bring you back from captivity."

reflection

1 When was a time you felt surrounded by darkness?

2 How can knowing that God owns time give you perspective on a difficult situation?

3 If you're in a tough place right now, spend some time crying out to God. Ask him for renewed hope, for the strength to lean on him and for the wisdom to know what to ask for.

RELATED READINGS

2 Chronicles 7:12–16;
Psalm 40:1–17;
Isaiah 55:1–13

Go to page 949 for your next devotional reading.

will use this curse: 'The LORD treat you
like Zedekiah and Ahab, whom the king
of Babylon burned in the fire.' [23]For they
have done outrageous things in Israel;
they have committed adultery with their
neighbors' wives and in my name have
spoken lies, which I did not tell them to
do. I know it and am a witness to it," declares the LORD.

Message to Shemaiah

[24]Tell Shemaiah the Nehelamite, [25]"This is
what the LORD Almighty, the God of Israel,
says: You sent letters in your own name to all
the people in Jerusalem, to Zephaniah son
of Maaseiah the priest, and to all the other
priests. You said to Zephaniah, [26]'The LORD
has appointed you priest in place of Jehoiada
to be in charge of the house of the LORD;
you should put any madman who acts like a
prophet into the stocks and neck-irons. [27]So
why have you not reprimanded Jeremiah from
Anathoth, who poses as a prophet among you?
[28]He has sent this message to us in Babylon:
It will be a long time. Therefore build houses
and settle down; plant gardens and eat what
they produce.'"

[29]Zephaniah the priest, however, read the
letter to Jeremiah the prophet. [30]Then the word
of the LORD came to Jeremiah: [31]"Send this
message to all the exiles: 'This
is what the LORD says about
Shemaiah the Nehelamite: Because Shemaiah has prophesied to you, even though I did
not send him, and has led you
to believe a lie, [32]this is what
the LORD says: I will surely punish Shemaiah the Nehelamite
and his descendants. He will
have no one left among this
people, nor will he see the good
things I will do for my people,
declares the LORD, because he has preached rebellion against me.'"

Restoration of Israel

30 This is the word that came to Jeremiah
from the LORD: [2]"This is what the
LORD, the God of Israel, says: 'Write in a book
all the words I have spoken to you. [3]The days
are coming,' declares the LORD, 'when I will
bring my people Israel and Judah back from
captivity[a] and restore them to the land I gave
their forefathers to possess,' says the LORD."

[4]These are the words the LORD spoke concerning Israel and Judah: [5]"This is what the
LORD says:

"'Cries of fear are heard—
terror, not peace.
[6]Ask and see:
Can a man bear children?
Then why do I see every strong man
with his hands on his stomach like a woman in labor,
every face turned deathly pale?
[7]How awful that day will be!
None will be like it.
It will be a time of trouble for Jacob,
but he will be saved out of it.

[8]"'In that day,' declares the LORD Almighty,
'I will break the yoke off their necks
and will tear off their bonds;
no longer will foreigners enslave them.
[9]Instead, they will serve the LORD their God
and David their king,
whom I will raise up for them.

[10]"'So do not fear, O Jacob my servant;
do not be dismayed, O Israel,'
declares the LORD.
'I will surely save you out of a distant place,
your descendants from the land of their exile.
Jacob will again have peace and security,
and no one will make him afraid.
[11]I am with you and will save you,'
declares the LORD.
'Though I completely destroy all the nations
among which I scatter you,
I will not completely destroy you.

Jeremiah 30:11

God Saves His People

"I am with you and will save you," declares the LORD.

[a]3 Or *will restore the fortunes of my people Israel and Judah*

I will discipline you but only with justice;
I will not let you go entirely
unpunished.'

12 "This is what the LORD says:

"'Your wound is incurable,
your injury beyond healing.
13 There is no one to plead your cause,
no remedy for your sore,
no healing for you.
14 All your allies have forgotten you;
they care nothing for you.
I have struck you as an enemy would
and punished you as would the cruel,
because your guilt is so great
and your sins so many.
15 Why do you cry out over your wound,
your pain that has no cure?
Because of your great guilt and many sins
I have done these things to you.

16 "'But all who devour you will be devoured;
all your enemies will go into exile.
Those who plunder you will be plundered;
all who make spoil of you I will despoil.
17 But I will restore you to health
and heal your wounds,'
declares the LORD,
'because you are called an outcast,
Zion for whom no one cares.'

18 "This is what the LORD says:

"'I will restore the fortunes of Jacob's tents
and have compassion on his dwellings;
the city will be rebuilt on her ruins,
and the palace will stand in its proper
place.
19 From them will come songs of
thanksgiving
and the sound of rejoicing.
I will add to their numbers,
and they will not be decreased;
I will bring them honor,
and they will not be disdained.
20 Their children will be as in days of old,
and their community will be established
before me;
I will punish all who oppress them.
21 Their leader will be one of their own;
their ruler will arise from among them.
I will bring him near and he will come
close to me,
for who is he who will devote himself
to be close to me?'
declares the LORD.
22 "'So you will be my people,
and I will be your God.'"

23 See, the storm of the LORD
will burst out in wrath,
a driving wind swirling down
on the heads of the wicked.
24 The fierce anger of the LORD will not turn
back
until he fully accomplishes
the purposes of his heart.
In days to come
you will understand this.

31 "At that time," declares the LORD, "I
will be the God of all the clans of Israel,
and they will be my people."

2 This is what the LORD says:

"The people who survive the sword
will find favor in the desert;
I will come to give rest to Israel."

3 The LORD appeared to us in the past,[a] saying:

"I have loved you with an everlasting love;
I have drawn you with loving-kindness.
4 I will build you up again
and you will be rebuilt, O Virgin Israel.
Again you will take up your tambourines
and go out to dance with the joyful.
5 Again you will plant vineyards
on the hills of Samaria;
the farmers will plant them
and enjoy their fruit.
6 There will be a day when watchmen cry
out
on the hills of Ephraim,
'Come, let us go up to Zion,
to the LORD our God.'"

7 This is what the LORD says:

"Sing with joy for Jacob;
shout for the foremost of the nations.
Make your praises heard, and say,
'O LORD, save your people,

[a] 3 Or *LORD has appeared to us from afar*

the remnant of Israel.'
8 See, I will bring them from the land of the north
and gather them from the ends of the earth.
Among them will be the blind and the lame,
expectant mothers and women in labor;
a great throng will return.
9 They will come with weeping;
they will pray as I bring them back.
I will lead them beside streams of water
on a level path where they will not stumble,
because I am Israel's father,
and Ephraim is my firstborn son.

10 "Hear the word of the LORD, O nations;
proclaim it in distant coastlands:
'He who scattered Israel will gather them
and will watch over his flock like a shepherd.'
11 For the LORD will ransom Jacob
and redeem them from the hand of those stronger than they.
12 They will come and shout for joy on the heights of Zion;
they will rejoice in the bounty of the LORD—
the grain, the new wine and the oil,
the young of the flocks and herds.
They will be like a well-watered garden,
and they will sorrow no more.
13 Then maidens will dance and be glad,
young men and old as well.
I will turn their mourning into gladness;
I will give them comfort and joy instead of sorrow.
14 I will satisfy the priests with abundance,
and my people will be filled with my bounty,"
declares the LORD.

15 This is what the LORD says:

"A voice is heard in Ramah,
mourning and great weeping,
Rachel weeping for her children
and refusing to be comforted,
because her children are no more."

16 This is what the LORD says:

"Restrain your voice from weeping
and your eyes from tears,
for your work will be rewarded,"
declares the LORD.
"They will return from the land of the enemy.
17 So there is hope for your future,"
declares the LORD.
"Your children will return to their own land.

18 "I have surely heard Ephraim's moaning:
'You disciplined me like an unruly calf,
and I have been disciplined.
Restore me, and I will return,
because you are the LORD my God.
19 After I strayed,
I repented;
after I came to understand,
I beat my breast.
I was ashamed and humiliated
because I bore the disgrace of my youth.'
20 Is not Ephraim my dear son,
the child in whom I delight?
Though I often speak against him,
I still remember him.
Therefore my heart yearns for him;
I have great compassion for him,"
declares the LORD.

21 "Set up road signs;
put up guideposts.
Take note of the highway,
the road that you take.
Return, O Virgin Israel,
return to your towns.
22 How long will you wander,
O unfaithful daughter?
The LORD will create a new thing on earth—
a woman will surround[a] a man."

23 This is what the LORD Almighty, the God
of Israel, says: "When I bring them back from
captivity,[b] the people in the land of Judah and
in its towns will once again use these words:
'The LORD bless you, O righteous dwelling,
O sacred mountain.' 24 People will live together
in Judah and all its towns—farmers and those

[a] 22 Or *will go about* ⌞*seeking*⌟; or *will protect* [b] 23 Or *I restore their fortunes*

who move about with their flocks. 25I will refresh the weary and satisfy the faint."
26At this I awoke and looked around. My
sleep had been pleasant to me.
27"The days are coming," declares the LORD,
"when I will plant the house of Israel and the
house of Judah with the offspring of men and
of animals. 28Just as I watched over them to uproot and tear down, and to overthrow, destroy
and bring disaster, so I will watch over them
to build and to plant," declares the LORD. 29"In
those days people will no longer say,

'The fathers have eaten sour grapes,
and the children's teeth are set on edge.'

30Instead, everyone will die for his own sin;
whoever eats sour grapes—his own teeth will
be set on edge.

31"The time is coming," declares the LORD,
"when I will make a new covenant
with the house of Israel
and with the house of Judah.
32It will not be like the covenant
I made with their forefathers
when I took them by the hand
to lead them out of Egypt,
because they broke my covenant,
though I was a husband to[a] them,[b]"
declares the LORD.
33"This is the covenant I will make with the
house of Israel
after that time," declares the LORD.
"I will put my law in their minds
and write it on their hearts.
I will be their God,
and they will be my people.
34No longer will a man teach his neighbor,
or a man his brother, saying, 'Know the
LORD,'
because they will all know me,
from the least of them to the greatest,"
declares the LORD.
"For I will forgive their wickedness
and will remember their sins no more."

35This is what the LORD says,

he who appoints the sun
to shine by day,
who decrees the moon and stars
to shine by night,
who stirs up the sea
so that its waves roar—
the LORD Almighty is his name:
36"Only if these decrees vanish from my
sight,"
declares the LORD,
"will the descendants of Israel ever cease
to be a nation before me."

37This is what the LORD says:

"Only if the heavens above can be
measured
and the foundations of the earth below
be searched out
will I reject all the descendants of Israel
because of all they have done,"
declares the LORD.

38"The days are coming," declares the LORD,
"when this city will be rebuilt for me from the
Tower of Hananel to the Corner Gate. 39The
measuring line will stretch from there straight
to the hill of Gareb and then turn to Goah.
40The whole valley where dead bodies and
ashes are thrown, and all the terraces out to the
Kidron Valley on the east as far as the corner
of the Horse Gate, will be holy to the LORD.
The city will never again be uprooted or demolished."

Jeremiah Buys a Field

32 This is the word that came to Jeremiah
from the LORD in the tenth year of
Zedekiah king of Judah, which was the eighteenth year of Nebuchadnezzar. 2The army of
the king of Babylon was then besieging Jerusalem, and Jeremiah the prophet was confined in
the courtyard of the guard in the royal palace
of Judah.
3Now Zedekiah king of Judah had imprisoned him there, saying, "Why do you prophesy
as you do? You say, 'This is what the LORD says:
I am about to hand this city over to the king of
Babylon, and he will capture it. 4Zedekiah king
of Judah will not escape out of the hands of the
Babylonians[c] but will certainly be handed over
to the king of Babylon, and will speak with him

[a]32 Hebrew; Septuagint and Syriac / *and I turned away from* [b]32 Or *was their master* [c]4 Or *Chaldeans*; also in verses 5, 24, 25, 28, 29 and 43

Written on Our Hearts

Read: Jeremiah 31:31–37

OUR DAYS ARE FILLED with juggling and struggling. We struggle to get the kids to school on time, to get to the office on time and then to get back home on time. We contend with our schedules to get the house clean, the project done, the meals made and the mortgage paid. We juggle returning e-mails and phone calls to our friends. We may even have the same approach in our relationship with God. In the midst of the tumult and pressure, it's hard to fit it all in.

The reality is, we don't always "want" God enough to fit him into our schedule. We will never get closer to God if we rely on our effort and willpower alone. Jeremiah reminds us of a life-changing truth: God *wants* to be near us. You may know that on some level already. But when it comes to reading the Bible when you are exhausted at the end of the day, do you feel *desired*? When it comes to prayer, do you believe God is tired of your mumblings or that he is still eager to hear your voice? Is it hard to imagine that you could commit a thousand sins today and still be confident that God wants to be with you as much as he would if you had lived perfectly?

God wants to be with you. God wants you to know him. He wants you to live a life full of freedom and abundance (see John 10:10; Hebrews 2:14–15). He wants to give you good things. He wants this so much that he took the initiative to write his laws in your heart and mind so you would never be without them.

In the midst of your working, pushing and hurrying, the God of the universe isn't waiting for an opening in your schedule. He has already come to you. What does it look like to respond to his desire for intimacy? It might mean simply acknowledging his presence, recognizing the truth already written on your heart. It might mean enjoying the freedom that comes when you quit striving and working and rest in the power of his presence and forgiveness.

No matter how you respond, know that he is there waiting for you.

Jeremiah 31:33–34

"This is the covenant I will make with the house of Israel after that time," declares the LORD. "I will put my law in their minds and write it on their hearts. I will be their God, and they will be my people. No longer will a man teach his neighbor, or a man his brother, saying, 'Know the LORD,' because they will all know me, from the least of them to the greatest," declares the LORD. "For I will forgive their wickedness and will remember their sins no more."

reflection

1 Why is it important to remember that God took the initiative in his relationship with you?

2 In what ways does the pace of your days affect your relationship with God?

3 Do you like the idea of God wanting you? How do you respond to the measures God takes to seek you and find you?

RELATED READINGS

Psalm 62:1–8;
Isaiah 65:1–3,17–25;
Hosea 11:1–8

Go to page 955 for your next devotional reading.

face to face and see him with his own eyes. 5 He
will take Zedekiah to Babylon, where he will remain until I deal with him, declares the LORD.
If you fight against the Babylonians, you will
not succeed.' "

6 Jeremiah said, "The word of the LORD came
to me: 7 Hanamel son of Shallum your uncle is
going to come to you and say, 'Buy my field at
Anathoth, because as nearest relative it is your
right and duty to buy it.'

8 "Then, just as the LORD had said, my cousin
Hanamel came to me in the courtyard of the
guard and said, 'Buy my field at Anathoth in
the territory of Benjamin. Since it is your right
to redeem it and possess it, buy it for yourself.'

"I knew that this was the word of the LORD;
9 so I bought the field at Anathoth from my
cousin Hanamel and weighed out for him
seventeen shekels[a] of silver. 10 I signed and
sealed the deed, had it witnessed, and weighed
out the silver on the scales. 11 I took the deed
of purchase—the sealed copy containing the
terms and conditions, as well as the unsealed
copy— 12 and I gave this deed to Baruch son of
Neriah, the son of Mahseiah, in the presence of
my cousin Hanamel and of the witnesses who
had signed the deed and of all the Jews sitting
in the courtyard of the guard.

13 "In their presence I gave
Baruch these instructions:
14 'This is what the LORD Almighty, the God of Israel, says:
Take these documents, both
the sealed and unsealed copies
of the deed of purchase, and
put them in a clay jar so they
will last a long time. 15 For this
is what the LORD Almighty, the
God of Israel, says: Houses,
fields and vineyards will again
be bought in this land.'

16 "After I had given the deed
of purchase to Baruch son of
Neriah, I prayed to the LORD:

> 17 "Ah, Sovereign LORD, you have made
> the heavens and the earth by your great
> power and outstretched arm. Nothing
> is too hard for you. 18 You show love to
> thousands but bring the punishment for
> the fathers' sins into the laps of their chil-
> dren after them. O great and powerful
> God, whose name is the LORD Almighty,
> 19 great are your purposes and mighty
> are your deeds. Your eyes are open to all
> the ways of men; you reward everyone ac-
> cording to his conduct and as his deeds de-
> serve. 20 You performed miraculous signs
> and wonders in Egypt and have continued
> them to this day, both in Israel and among
> all mankind, and have gained the renown
> that is still yours. 21 You brought your
> people Israel out of Egypt with signs and
> wonders, by a mighty hand and an out-
> stretched arm and with great terror. 22 You
> gave them this land you had sworn to give
> their forefathers, a land flowing with milk
> and honey. 23 They came in and took pos-
> session of it, but they did not obey you or
> follow your law; they did not do what you
> commanded them to do. So you brought
> all this disaster upon them.
>
> 24 "See how the siege ramps are built
> up to take the city. Because of the sword,
> famine and plague, the city will be handed
> over to the Babylonians who are attacking
> it. What you said has happened, as you
> now see. 25 And though the city will be
> handed over to the Babylonians, you, O Sovereign LORD,
> say to me, 'Buy the field with
> silver and have the transac-
> tion witnessed.' "

26 Then the word of the
LORD came to Jeremiah: 27 "I
am the LORD, the God of all
mankind. Is anything too hard
for me? 28 Therefore, this is
what the LORD says: I am about
to hand this city over to the
Babylonians and to Nebuchadnezzar king of Babylon, who
will capture it. 29 The Babylonians who are attacking this city
will come in and set it on fire; they will burn it
down, along with the houses where the people
provoked me to anger by burning incense on
the roofs to Baal and by pouring out drink offerings to other gods.

Jeremiah 32:17

God Is Sovereign

"Ah, Sovereign LORD,
you have made the
heavens and the earth
by your great power
and outstretched arm.
Nothing is too
hard for you."

[a] 9 That is, about 7 ounces (about 200 grams)

30 “The people of Israel and Judah have done nothing but evil in my sight from their youth; indeed, the people of Israel have done nothing but provoke me with what their hands have made, declares the LORD. 31 From the day it was built until now, this city has so aroused my anger and wrath that I must remove it from my sight. 32 The people of Israel and Judah have provoked me by all the evil they have done—they, their kings and officials, their priests and prophets, the men of Judah and the people of Jerusalem. 33 They turned their backs to me and not their faces; though I taught them again and again, they would not listen or respond to discipline. 34 They set up their abominable idols in the house that bears my Name and defiled it. 35 They built high places for Baal in the Valley of Ben Hinnom to sacrifice their sons and daughters[a] to Molech, though I never commanded, nor did it enter my mind, that they should do such a detestable thing and so make Judah sin.

36 “You are saying about this city, ‘By the sword, famine and plague it will be handed over to the king of Babylon’; but this is what the LORD, the God of Israel, says: 37 I will surely gather them from all the lands where I banish them in my furious anger and great wrath; I will bring them back to this place and let them live in safety. 38 They will be my people, and I will be their God. 39 I will give them singleness of heart and action, so that they will always fear me for their own good and the good of their children after them. 40 I will make an everlasting covenant with them: I will never stop doing good to them, and I will inspire them to fear me, so that they will never turn away from me. 41 I will rejoice in doing them good and will assuredly plant them in this land with all my heart and soul.

42 “This is what the LORD says: As I have brought all this great calamity on this people, so I will give them all the prosperity I have promised them. 43 Once more fields will be bought in this land of which you say, ‘It is a desolate waste, without men or animals, for it has been handed over to the Babylonians.’ 44 Fields will be bought for silver, and deeds will be signed, sealed and witnessed in the territory of Benjamin, in the villages around Jerusalem, in the towns of Judah and in the towns of the hill country, of the western foothills and of the Negev, because I will restore their fortunes,[b] declares the LORD.”

> **Jeremiah 33:3**
>
> *God Answers Prayers*
>
> “Call to me and I will answer you and tell you great and unreachable things you do not know.”

Promise of Restoration

33 While Jeremiah was still confined in the courtyard of the guard, the word of the LORD came to him a second time: 2 “This is what the LORD says, he who made the earth, the LORD who formed it and established it—the LORD is his name: 3 ‘Call to me and I will answer you and tell you great and unsearchable things you do not know.’ 4 For this is what the LORD, the God of Israel, says about the houses in this city and the royal palaces of Judah that have been torn down to be used against the siege ramps and the sword 5 in the fight with the Babylonians[c]: ‘They will be filled with the dead bodies of the men I will slay in my anger and wrath. I will hide my face from this city because of all its wickedness.

6 “ ‘Nevertheless, I will bring health and healing to it; I will heal my people and will let them enjoy abundant peace and security. 7 I will bring Judah and Israel back from captivity[d] and will rebuild them as they were before. 8 I will cleanse them from all the sin they have committed against me and will forgive all their sins of rebellion against me. 9 Then this city will bring me renown, joy, praise and honor before all nations on earth that hear of all the good things I do for it; and they will be in awe and will tremble at the abundant prosperity and peace I provide for it.’

10 “This is what the LORD says: ‘You say about this place, “It is a desolate waste, without men or animals.” Yet in the towns of Judah and the streets of Jerusalem that are deserted, inhabited

[a] 35 Or *to make their sons and daughters pass through* ⌞*the fire*⌟ [b] 44 Or *will bring them back from captivity* [c] 5 Or *Chaldeans*
[d] 7 Or *will restore the fortunes of Judah and Israel*

by neither men nor animals, there will be heard
once more 11the sounds of joy and gladness,
the voices of bride and bridegroom, and the
voices of those who bring thank offerings to
the house of the LORD, saying,

"Give thanks to the LORD Almighty,
for the LORD is good;
his love endures forever."

For I will restore the fortunes of the land as
they were before,' says the LORD.

12"This is what the LORD Almighty says:
'In this place, desolate and without men or
animals—in all its towns there will again be
pastures for shepherds to rest their flocks. 13In
the towns of the hill country, of the western
foothills and of the Negev, in the territory of
Benjamin, in the villages around Jerusalem and
in the towns of Judah, flocks will again pass under the hand of the one who counts them,' says
the LORD.

14" 'The days are coming,' declares the LORD,
'when I will fulfill the gracious promise I made
to the house of Israel and to the house of Judah.

15" 'In those days and at that time
I will make a righteous Branch sprout
from David's line;
he will do what is just and right in the
land.
16In those days Judah will be saved
and Jerusalem will live in safety.
This is the name by which it[a] will be called:
The LORD Our Righteousness.'

17For this is what the LORD says: 'David will
never fail to have a man to sit on the throne
of the house of Israel, 18nor will the priests,
who are Levites, ever fail to have a man to
stand before me continually to offer burnt offerings, to burn grain offerings and to present
sacrifices.' "

19The word of the LORD came to Jeremiah:
20"This is what the LORD says: 'If you can
break my covenant with the day and my covenant with the night, so that day and night no
longer come at their appointed time, 21then
my covenant with David my servant—and my
covenant with the Levites who are priests ministering before me—can be broken and David
will no longer have a descendant to reign on his
throne. 22I will make the descendants of David
my servant and the Levites who minister before me as countless as the stars of the sky and
as measureless as the sand on the seashore.' "

23The word of the LORD came to Jeremiah:
24"Have you not noticed that these people are
saying, 'The LORD has rejected the two kingdoms[b] he chose'? So they despise my people
and no longer regard them as a nation. 25This
is what the LORD says: 'If I have not established
my covenant with day and night and the fixed
laws of heaven and earth, 26then I will reject
the descendants of Jacob and David my servant
and will not choose one of his sons to rule over
the descendants of Abraham, Isaac and Jacob.
For I will restore their fortunes[c] and have compassion on them.' "

Warning to Zedekiah

34 While Nebuchadnezzar king of Babylon and all his army and all the kingdoms and peoples in the empire he ruled were
fighting against Jerusalem and all its surrounding towns, this word came to Jeremiah from
the LORD: 2"This is what the LORD, the God
of Israel, says: Go to Zedekiah king of Judah
and tell him, 'This is what the LORD says: I am
about to hand this city over to the king of Babylon, and he will burn it down. 3You will not escape from his grasp but will surely be captured
and handed over to him. You will see the king
of Babylon with your own eyes, and he will
speak with you face to face. And you will go
to Babylon.

4" 'Yet hear the promise of the LORD, O
Zedekiah king of Judah. This is what the LORD
says concerning you: You will not die by the
sword; 5you will die peacefully. As people
made a funeral fire in honor of your fathers,
the former kings who preceded you, so they
will make a fire in your honor and lament,
"Alas, O master!" I myself make this promise,
declares the LORD.' "

6Then Jeremiah the prophet told all this to
Zedekiah king of Judah, in Jerusalem, 7while
the army of the king of Babylon was fighting
against Jerusalem and the other cities of Judah

[a]16 Or *he* [b]24 Or *families* [c]26 Or *will bring them back from captivity*

that were still holding out—Lachish and Azekah. These were the only fortified cities left
in Judah.

Freedom for Slaves

8The word came to Jeremiah from the LORD
after King Zedekiah had made a covenant with
all the people in Jerusalem to proclaim freedom for the slaves. 9Everyone was to free his
Hebrew slaves, both male and female; no one
was to hold a fellow Jew in bondage. 10So all
the officials and people who entered into this
covenant agreed that they would free their
male and female slaves and no longer hold
them in bondage. They agreed, and set them
free. 11But afterward they changed their minds
and took back the slaves they had freed and enslaved them again.

12Then the word of the LORD came to
Jeremiah: 13"This is what the LORD, the God of
Israel, says: I made a covenant with your forefathers when I brought them out of Egypt, out of
the land of slavery. I said, 14'Every seventh year
each of you must free any fellow Hebrew who
has sold himself to you. After he has served
you six years, you must let him go free.'[a] Your
fathers, however, did not listen to me or pay
attention to me. 15Recently you repented and
did what is right in my sight: Each of you proclaimed freedom to his countrymen. You even
made a covenant before me in the house that
bears my Name. 16But now you have turned
around and profaned my name; each of you
has taken back the male and female slaves you
had set free to go where they wished. You have
forced them to become your slaves again.

17"Therefore, this is what the LORD says: You
have not obeyed me; you have not proclaimed
freedom for your fellow countrymen. So I
now proclaim 'freedom' for you, declares the
LORD—'freedom' to fall by the sword, plague
and famine. I will make you abhorrent to all
the kingdoms of the earth. 18The men who
have violated my covenant and have not fulfilled the terms of the covenant they made
before me, I will treat like the calf they cut in
two and then walked between its pieces. 19The
leaders of Judah and Jerusalem, the court officials, the priests and all the people of the land
who walked between the pieces of the calf, 20I
will hand over to their enemies who seek their
lives. Their dead bodies will become food for
the birds of the air and the beasts of the earth.

21"I will hand Zedekiah king of Judah and
his officials over to their enemies who seek their
lives, to the army of the king of Babylon, which
has withdrawn from you. 22I am going to give
the order, declares the LORD, and I will bring
them back to this city. They will fight against it,
take it and burn it down. And I will lay waste
the towns of Judah so no one can live there."

The Recabites

35 This is the word that came to Jeremiah
from the LORD during the reign of Jehoiakim son of Josiah king of Judah: 2"Go to
the Recabite family and invite them to come to
one of the side rooms of the house of the LORD
and give them wine to drink."

3So I went to get Jaazaniah son of Jeremiah,
the son of Habazziniah, and his brothers and all
his sons—the whole family of the Recabites. 4I
brought them into the house of the LORD, into
the room of the sons of Hanan son of Igdaliah
the man of God. It was next to the room of the
officials, which was over that of Maaseiah son
of Shallum the doorkeeper. 5Then I set bowls
full of wine and some cups before the men of
the Recabite family and said to them, "Drink
some wine."

6But they replied, "We do not drink wine,
because our forefather Jonadab son of Recab
gave us this command: 'Neither you nor your
descendants must ever drink wine. 7Also you
must never build houses, sow seed or plant vineyards; you must never have any of these things,
but must always live in tents. Then you will live
a long time in the land where you are nomads.'
8We have obeyed everything our forefather Jonadab son of Recab commanded us. Neither we
nor our wives nor our sons and daughters have
ever drunk wine 9or built houses to live in or
had vineyards, fields or crops. 10We have lived
in tents and have fully obeyed everything our
forefather Jonadab commanded us. 11But when
Nebuchadnezzar king of Babylon invaded this
land, we said, 'Come, we must go to Jerusalem
to escape the Babylonian[b] and Aramean armies.' So we have remained in Jerusalem."

12Then the word of the LORD came to

[a]14 Deut. 15:12 [b]11 Or *Chaldean*

Jeremiah, saying: 13"This is what the LORD
Almighty, the God of Israel, says: Go and tell
the men of Judah and the people of Jerusalem, 'Will you not learn a lesson and obey my
words?' declares the LORD. 14'Jonadab son of
Recab ordered his sons not to drink wine and
this command has been kept. To this day they
do not drink wine, because they obey their forefather's command. But I have spoken to you
again and again, yet you have not obeyed me.
15Again and again I sent all my servants the
prophets to you. They said, "Each of you must
turn from your wicked ways and reform your
actions; do not follow other gods to serve them.
Then you will live in the land I have given to
you and your fathers." But you have not paid
attention or listened to me. 16The descendants
of Jonadab son of Recab have carried out the
command their forefather gave them, but these
people have not obeyed me.'

17"Therefore, this is what the LORD God Almighty, the God of Israel, says: 'Listen! I am going to bring on Judah and on everyone living in
Jerusalem every disaster I pronounced against
them. I spoke to them, but they did not listen; I
called to them, but they did not answer.' "

18Then Jeremiah said to the family of the
Recabites, "This is what the LORD Almighty,
the God of Israel, says: 'You have obeyed the
command of your forefather Jonadab and have
followed all his instructions and have done everything he ordered.' 19Therefore, this is what
the LORD Almighty, the God of Israel, says: 'Jonadab son of Recab will never fail to have a man
to serve me.' "

Jehoiakim Burns Jeremiah's Scroll

36 In the fourth year of Jehoiakim son of
Josiah king of Judah, this word came
to Jeremiah from the LORD: 2"Take a scroll and
write on it all the words I have spoken to you
concerning Israel, Judah and all the other nations from the time I began speaking to you
in the reign of Josiah till now. 3Perhaps when
the people of Judah hear about every disaster I
plan to inflict on them, each of them will turn
from his wicked way; then I will forgive their
wickedness and their sin."

4So Jeremiah called Baruch son of Neriah,
and while Jeremiah dictated all the words the
LORD had spoken to him, Baruch wrote them
on the scroll. 5Then Jeremiah told Baruch, "I
am restricted; I cannot go to the LORD's temple. 6So you go to the house of the LORD on a
day of fasting and read to the people from the
scroll the words of the LORD that you wrote as
I dictated. Read them to all the people of Judah
who come in from their towns. 7Perhaps they
will bring their petition before the LORD, and
each will turn from his wicked ways, for the anger and wrath pronounced against this people
by the LORD are great."

8Baruch son of Neriah did everything
Jeremiah the prophet told him to do; at the
LORD's temple he read the words of the LORD
from the scroll. 9In the ninth month of the fifth
year of Jehoiakim son of Josiah king of Judah, a
time of fasting before the LORD was proclaimed
for all the people in Jerusalem and those who
had come from the towns of Judah. 10From
the room of Gemariah son of Shaphan the secretary, which was in the upper courtyard at the
entrance of the New Gate of the temple, Baruch
read to all the people at the LORD's temple the
words of Jeremiah from the scroll.

11When Micaiah son of Gemariah, the son
of Shaphan, heard all the words of the LORD
from the scroll, 12he went down to the secretary's room in the royal palace, where all the
officials were sitting: Elishama the secretary,
Delaiah son of Shemaiah, Elnathan son of Acbor, Gemariah son of Shaphan, Zedekiah son
of Hananiah, and all the other officials. 13After
Micaiah told them everything he had heard
Baruch read to the people from the scroll, 14all
the officials sent Jehudi son of Nethaniah, the
son of Shelemiah, the son of Cushi, to say to
Baruch, "Bring the scroll from which you have
read to the people and come." So Baruch son
of Neriah went to them with the scroll in his
hand. 15They said to him, "Sit down, please,
and read it to us."

So Baruch read it to them. 16When they
heard all these words, they looked at each other
in fear and said to Baruch, "We must report all
these words to the king." 17Then they asked
Baruch, "Tell us, how did you come to write all
this? Did Jeremiah dictate it?"

18"Yes," Baruch replied, "he dictated all
these words to me, and I wrote them in ink on
the scroll."

Personal Delivery

Read: Jeremiah 36:1–32

"PUT IT IN WRITING."

Those four words get results. Have a complaint? Put it in writing. Have a deal? Put it in writing. Need to clarify something? Put it in writing. And so when God wanted to get someone's attention, that's exactly what he did: He put it in writing.

Through the prophet Jeremiah and his faithful scribe, Baruch, God dictated a personal message to King Jehoiakim and his people: "Dear Jehoiakim: Here is the word of the Lord . . ." While we don't know exactly what part of Jeremiah's prophecy was written down for the king, we know this much: The king didn't like it. In fact, not only did the king refuse to comply, but he treated God's words with contempt by burning the scroll piece by piece—an unthinkable, unspeakable atrocity. No one in his right mind would treat the words of God in such a way, right?

And yet, have you ever disrespected God's Word? Think about it. You may not torch its pages, but have you ever just ignored it? You may not outwardly rebel, but have you refused to let the words of the Bible touch your life? God has put his love story in writing for us to enjoy. Yet we so often ignore it, downplay it or even entirely forget about it in the course of our daily lives.

"Dear ______: Here are my words for you . . ."

Put your name in the blank. Think of God's story as a first-class letter addressed to you. Think of his words as intimate and deeply personal—something he wants you to know, something straight from his heart. When God had something important to say, he could have used a number of means to communicate it. But he chose to put it in writing.

Every day this week, carve out a few quiet minutes, find a cozy corner and open his "letter." Find out what he wants to say to you personally.

Jeremiah 36:2–3

"Take a scroll and write on it all the words I have spoken to you concerning Israel, Judah and all the other nations from the time I began speaking to you in the reign of Josiah till now. Perhaps when the people of Judah hear about every disaster I plan to inflict on them, each of them will turn from his wicked way; then I will forgive their wickedness and their sin."

reflection

1 Why do you think King Jehoiakim reacted with so much hostility to God's words?

2 What is your favorite part of God's "letter" to you, the Bible? Why?

3 How does it make you feel to know God wrote this letter with you in mind?

RELATED READINGS

2 Kings 23:36—24:6;
John 16:12–16;
2 Thessalonians 1:5–10;
2 Peter 1:19–21

Go to page 960 for your next devotional reading.

19 Then the officials said to Baruch, "You and
Jeremiah, go and hide. Don't let anyone know
where you are."
20 After they put the scroll in the room of
Elishama the secretary, they went to the king in
the courtyard and reported everything to him.
21 The king sent Jehudi to get the scroll, and
Jehudi brought it from the room of Elishama
the secretary and read it to the king and all the
officials standing beside him. 22 It was the ninth
month and the king was sitting in the winter
apartment, with a fire burning in the firepot
in front of him. 23 Whenever Jehudi had read
three or four columns of the scroll, the king
cut them off with a scribe's knife and threw
them into the firepot, until the entire scroll
was burned in the fire. 24 The king and all his
attendants who heard all these words showed
no fear, nor did they tear their clothes. 25 Even
though Elnathan, Delaiah and Gemariah urged
the king not to burn the scroll, he would not listen to them. 26 Instead, the king commanded
Jerahmeel, a son of the king, Seraiah son of
Azriel and Shelemiah son of Abdeel to arrest
Baruch the scribe and Jeremiah the prophet.
But the LORD had hidden them.
27 After the king burned the scroll containing the words that Baruch had written at Jeremiah's dictation, the word of the LORD came
to Jeremiah: 28 "Take another scroll and write
on it all the words that were on the first scroll,
which Jehoiakim king of Judah burned up.
29 Also tell Jehoiakim king of Judah, 'This is
what the LORD says: You burned that scroll and
said, "Why did you write on it that the king of
Babylon would certainly come and destroy this
land and cut off both men and animals from
it?" 30 Therefore, this is what the LORD says
about Jehoiakim king of Judah: He will have no
one to sit on the throne of David; his body will
be thrown out and exposed to the heat by day
and the frost by night. 31 I will punish him and
his children and his attendants for their wickedness; I will bring on them and those living in Jerusalem and the people of Judah every disaster
I pronounced against them, because they have
not listened.'"
32 So Jeremiah took another scroll and gave
it to the scribe Baruch son of Neriah, and as
Jeremiah dictated, Baruch wrote on it all the
words of the scroll that Jehoiakim king of Judah had burned in the fire. And many similar
words were added to them.

Jeremiah in Prison

37 Zedekiah son of Josiah was made king
of Judah by Nebuchadnezzar king of
Babylon; he reigned in place of Jehoiachin[a] son
of Jehoiakim. 2 Neither he nor his attendants
nor the people of the land paid any attention
to the words the LORD had spoken through
Jeremiah the prophet.
3 King Zedekiah, however, sent Jehucal son
of Shelemiah with the priest Zephaniah son
of Maaseiah to Jeremiah the prophet with this
message: "Please pray to the LORD our God for
us."
4 Now Jeremiah was free to come and go
among the people, for he had not yet been put
in prison. 5 Pharaoh's army had marched out of
Egypt, and when the Babylonians[b] who were
besieging Jerusalem heard the report about
them, they withdrew from Jerusalem.
6 Then the word of the LORD came to
Jeremiah the prophet: 7 "This is what the LORD,
the God of Israel, says: Tell the king of Judah,
who sent you to inquire of me, 'Pharaoh's army,
which has marched out to support you, will go
back to its own land, to Egypt. 8 Then the Babylonians will return and attack this city; they
will capture it and burn it down.'
9 "This is what the LORD says: Do not deceive yourselves, thinking, 'The Babylonians
will surely leave us.' They will not! 10 Even if
you were to defeat the entire Babylonian[c] army
that is attacking you and only wounded men
were left in their tents, they would come out
and burn this city down."
11 After the Babylonian army had withdrawn
from Jerusalem because of Pharaoh's army,
12 Jeremiah started to leave the city to go to
the territory of Benjamin to get his share of
the property among the people there. 13 But
when he reached the Benjamin Gate, the captain of the guard, whose name was Irijah son
of Shelemiah, the son of Hananiah, arrested
him and said, "You are deserting to the Babylonians!"

[a] 1 Hebrew *Coniah,* a variant of *Jehoiachin* [b] 5 Or *Chaldeans*; also in verses 8, 9, 13 and 14 [c] 10 Or *Chaldean*; also in verse 11

14“That’s not true!” Jeremiah said. “I am not deserting to the Babylonians.” But Irijah would not listen to him; instead, he arrested Jeremiah and brought him to the officials. 15They were angry with Jeremiah and had him beaten and imprisoned in the house of Jonathan the secretary, which they had made into a prison.

16Jeremiah was put into a vaulted cell in a dungeon, where he remained a long time. 17Then King Zedekiah sent for him and had him brought to the palace, where he asked him privately, “Is there any word from the LORD?”

“Yes,” Jeremiah replied, “you will be handed over to the king of Babylon.”

18Then Jeremiah said to King Zedekiah, “What crime have I committed against you or your officials or this people, that you have put me in prison? 19Where are your prophets who prophesied to you, ‘The king of Babylon will not attack you or this land’? 20But now, my lord the king, please listen. Let me bring my petition before you: Do not send me back to the house of Jonathan the secretary, or I will die there.”

21King Zedekiah then gave orders for Jeremiah to be placed in the courtyard of the guard and given bread from the street of the bakers each day until all the bread in the city was gone. So Jeremiah remained in the courtyard of the guard.

Jeremiah Thrown Into a Cistern

38 Shephatiah son of Mattan, Gedaliah son of Pashhur, Jehucal[a] son of Shelemiah, and Pashhur son of Malkijah heard what Jeremiah was telling all the people when he said, 2“This is what the LORD says: ‘Whoever stays in this city will die by the sword, famine or plague, but whoever goes over to the Babylonians[b] will live. He will escape with his life; he will live.’ 3And this is what the LORD says: ‘This city will certainly be handed over to the army of the king of Babylon, who will capture it.’ ”

4Then the officials said to the king, “This man should be put to death. He is discouraging the soldiers who are left in this city, as well as all the people, by the things he is saying to them. This man is not seeking the good of these people but their ruin.”

5“He is in your hands,” King Zedekiah answered. “The king can do nothing to oppose you.”

6So they took Jeremiah and put him into the cistern of Malkijah, the king’s son, which was in the courtyard of the guard. They lowered Jeremiah by ropes into the cistern; it had no water in it, only mud, and Jeremiah sank down into the mud.

7But Ebed-Melech, a Cushite,[c] an official[d] in the royal palace, heard that they had put Jeremiah into the cistern. While the king was sitting in the Benjamin Gate, 8Ebed-Melech went out of the palace and said to him, 9“My lord the king, these men have acted wickedly in all they have done to Jeremiah the prophet. They have thrown him into a cistern, where he will starve to death when there is no longer any bread in the city.”

10Then the king commanded Ebed-Melech the Cushite, “Take thirty men from here with you and lift Jeremiah the prophet out of the cistern before he dies.”

11So Ebed-Melech took the men with him and went to a room under the treasury in the palace. He took some old rags and worn-out clothes from there and let them down with ropes to Jeremiah in the cistern. 12Ebed-Melech the Cushite said to Jeremiah, “Put these old rags and worn-out clothes under your arms to pad the ropes.” Jeremiah did so, 13and they pulled him up with the ropes and lifted him out of the cistern. And Jeremiah remained in the courtyard of the guard.

Zedekiah Questions Jeremiah Again

14Then King Zedekiah sent for Jeremiah the prophet and had him brought to the third entrance to the temple of the LORD. “I am going to ask you something,” the king said to Jeremiah. “Do not hide anything from me.”

15Jeremiah said to Zedekiah, “If I give you an answer, will you not kill me? Even if I did give you counsel, you would not listen to me.”

16But King Zedekiah swore this oath secretly to Jeremiah: “As surely as the LORD lives, who has given us breath, I will neither kill you nor hand you over to those who are seeking your life.”

17Then Jeremiah said to Zedekiah, “This

[a]1 Hebrew *Jucal,* a variant of *Jehucal* [b]2 Or *Chaldeans*; also in verses 18, 19 and 23 [c]7 Probably from the upper Nile region [d]7 Or *a eunuch*

is what the LORD God Almighty, the God of
Israel, says: 'If you surrender to the officers of
the king of Babylon, your life will be spared
and this city will not be burned down; you and
your family will live. 18But if you will not surrender to the officers of the king of Babylon,
this city will be handed over to the Babylonians
and they will burn it down; you yourself will
not escape from their hands.' "
19King Zedekiah said to Jeremiah, "I am
afraid of the Jews who have gone over to the
Babylonians, for the Babylonians may hand me
over to them and they will mistreat me."
20"They will not hand you over," Jeremiah replied. "Obey the LORD by doing what I tell you.
Then it will go well with you, and your life will
be spared. 21But if you refuse to surrender, this
is what the LORD has revealed to me: 22All the
women left in the palace of the king of Judah
will be brought out to the officials of the king of
Babylon. Those women will say to you:

" 'They misled you and overcame you—
those trusted friends of yours.
Your feet are sunk in the mud;
your friends have deserted you.'

23"All your wives and children will be
brought out to the Babylonians. You yourself
will not escape from their hands but will be captured by the king of Babylon; and this city will[a]
be burned down."
24Then Zedekiah said to Jeremiah, "Do not
let anyone know about this conversation, or
you may die. 25If the officials hear that I talked
with you, and they come to you and say, 'Tell
us what you said to the king and what the king
said to you; do not hide it from us or we will kill
you,' 26then tell them, 'I was pleading with the
king not to send me back to Jonathan's house
to die there.' "
27All the officials did come to Jeremiah and
question him, and he told them everything the
king had ordered him to say. So they said no
more to him, for no one had heard his conversation with the king.
28And Jeremiah remained in the courtyard
of the guard until the day Jerusalem was captured.

The Fall of Jerusalem

39 This is how Jerusalem was taken: 1In
the ninth year of Zedekiah king of
Judah, in the tenth month, Nebuchadnezzar
king of Babylon marched against Jerusalem
with his whole army and laid siege to it. 2And
on the ninth day of the fourth month of Zedekiah's eleventh year, the city wall was broken
through. 3Then all the officials of the king of
Babylon came and took seats in the Middle
Gate: Nergal-Sharezer of Samgar, Nebo-Sar-
sekim[b] a chief officer, Nergal-Sharezer a high
official and all the other officials of the king of
Babylon. 4When Zedekiah king of Judah and
all the soldiers saw them, they fled; they left
the city at night by way of the king's garden,
through the gate between the two walls, and
headed toward the Arabah.[c]
5But the Babylonian[d] army pursued them
and overtook Zedekiah in the plains of Jericho.
They captured him and took him to Nebuchadnezzar king of Babylon at Riblah in the land
of Hamath, where he pronounced sentence
on him. 6There at Riblah the king of Babylon
slaughtered the sons of Zedekiah before his eyes
and also killed all the nobles of Judah. 7Then he
put out Zedekiah's eyes and bound him with
bronze shackles to take him to Babylon.
8The Babylonians[e] set fire to the royal palace and the houses of the people and broke
down the walls of Jerusalem. 9Nebuzaradan
commander of the imperial guard carried into
exile to Babylon the people who remained in
the city, along with those who had gone over to
him, and the rest of the people. 10But Nebuzaradan the commander of the guard left behind
in the land of Judah some of the poor people,
who owned nothing; and at that time he gave
them vineyards and fields.
11Now Nebuchadnezzar king of Babylon had
given these orders about Jeremiah through Nebuzaradan commander of the imperial guard:
12"Take him and look after him; don't harm
him but do for him whatever he asks." 13So
Nebuzaradan the commander of the guard,
Nebushazban a chief officer, Nergal-Sharezer
a high official and all the other officers of the
king of Babylon 14sent and had Jeremiah taken

[a]23 Or *and you will cause this city to* [b]3 Or *Nergal-Sharezer, Samgar-Nebo, Sarsekim* [c]4 Or *the Jordan Valley* [d]5 Or *Chaldean*
[e]8 Or *Chaldeans*

out of the courtyard of the guard. They turned
him over to Gedaliah son of Ahikam, the son
of Shaphan, to take him back to his home. So
he remained among his own people.
[15]While Jeremiah had been confined in the
courtyard of the guard, the word of the LORD
came to him: [16]“Go and tell Ebed-Melech the
Cushite, ‘This is what the LORD
Almighty, the God of Israel,
says: I am about to fulfill my
words against this city through
disaster, not prosperity. At that
time they will be fulfilled before
your eyes. [17]But I will rescue
you on that day, declares the
LORD; you will not be handed
over to those you fear. [18]I will
save you; you will not fall by
the sword but will escape with
your life, because you trust in
me, declares the LORD.’ ”

> Jeremiah 39:18
>
> *God Saves Those Who Trust*
>
> “I will save you; you will not fall by the sword but will escape with your life, because you trust in me, declares the LORD.”

Jeremiah Freed

40 The word came to Jeremiah from the
LORD after Nebuzaradan commander
of the imperial guard had released him at Ramah. He had found Jeremiah bound in chains
among all the captives from Jerusalem and
Judah who were being carried into exile to
Babylon. [2]When the commander of the guard
found Jeremiah, he said to him, “The LORD
your God decreed this disaster for this place.
[3]And now the LORD has brought it about; he
has done just as he said he would. All this happened because you people sinned against the
LORD and did not obey him. [4]But today I am
freeing you from the chains on your wrists.
Come with me to Babylon, if you like, and I
will look after you; but if you do not want to,
then don't come. Look, the whole country lies
before you; go wherever you please.” [5]However,
before Jeremiah turned to go,[a] Nebuzaradan
added, “Go back to Gedaliah son of Ahikam,
the son of Shaphan, whom the king of Babylon
has appointed over the towns of Judah, and live
with him among the people, or go anywhere
else you please.”
Then the commander gave him provisions
and a present and let him go. [6]So Jeremiah
went to Gedaliah son of Ahikam at Mizpah
and stayed with him among the people who
were left behind in the land.

Gedaliah Assassinated

[7]When all the army officers and their men
who were still in the open country heard that
the king of Babylon had appointed Gedaliah
son of Ahikam as governor
over the land and had put him
in charge of the men, women
and children who were the
poorest in the land and who
had not been carried into exile to Babylon, [8]they came to
Gedaliah at Mizpah—Ishmael
son of Nethaniah, Johanan and
Jonathan the sons of Kareah,
Seraiah son of Tanhumeth, the
sons of Ephai the Netophathite,
and Jaazaniah[b] the son of the
Maacathite, and their men.
[9]Gedaliah son of Ahikam, the
son of Shaphan, took an oath
to reassure them and their men. “Do not be
afraid to serve the Babylonians,[c]” he said. “Settle down in the land and serve the king of Babylon, and it will go well with you. [10]I myself
will stay at Mizpah to represent you before the
Babylonians who come to us, but you are to harvest the wine, summer fruit and oil, and put
them in your storage jars, and live in the towns
you have taken over.”
[11]When all the Jews in Moab, Ammon,
Edom and all the other countries heard that the
king of Babylon had left a remnant in Judah and
had appointed Gedaliah son of Ahikam, the
son of Shaphan, as governor over them, [12]they
all came back to the land of Judah, to Gedaliah
at Mizpah, from all the countries where they
had been scattered. And they harvested an
abundance of wine and summer fruit.
[13]Johanan son of Kareah and all the army
officers still in the open country came to
Gedaliah at Mizpah [14]and said to him, “Don't
you know that Baalis king of the Ammonites
has sent Ishmael son of Nethaniah to take your
life?” But Gedaliah son of Ahikam did not believe them.
[15]Then Johanan son of Kareah said privately
to Gedaliah in Mizpah, “Let me go and kill

[a]5 Or *Jeremiah answered* [b]8 Hebrew *Jezaniah,* a variant of *Jaazaniah* [c]9 Or *Chaldeans*; also in verse 10

Queen of Denial

Read: Jeremiah 40:1–6

HAVE YOU EVER IGNORED specific warnings and then faced the consequences? You should have seen it coming—in fact, you did. But you just drifted along on your raft of denial, like a complacent Queen Cleopatra drifting on her barge down the Nile. Before you knew it, it was too late.

Jeremiah's hometown was in ruins—Jerusalem had fallen, just as God said it would. The most important religious symbols of the Jews had been desecrated. Everything Jeremiah's nation stood for was devastated. And according to the commander of the guard who released Jeremiah from his chains, even Israel's enemies knew that Jerusalem's destruction was because of the people's disobedience.

For generations, God had warned the Israelites that if they let themselves slide spiritually, they would suffer as a nation. He called them back to himself as king after king led the people further away from their spiritual roots. He sent prophets like Jeremiah with messages that were both harsh and hopeful. Through these prophets, God practically begged his people to repent.

They had seen it coming, but it was too late now.

There is hope after this kind of judgment, but the road back is long and hard. The citizens of Jerusalem did return—70 years later. Those who had been carried away as children were old by the time they began to rebuild their country.

What warnings about tomorrow are you not heeding today? What river of denial are you white-water rafting on? Are you thinking God will overlook your trifling with his commands? God *will* discipline us because he loves us. He would no more let us get away with our destructive behavior than good parents would overlook rebellion.

Don't let complacency keep you from action. More than likely, something in your life—a thought pattern, an attitude or an action—needs adjustment today so that you can stay on the path God has for you. You've been thinking about addressing it, wondering if it was God's voice you were hearing. Don't stay in denial. Respond today to avoid repercussions tomorrow.

Jeremiah 40:2–3

When the commander of the guard found Jeremiah, he said to him, "The LORD your God decreed this disaster for this place. And now the LORD has brought it about; he has done just as he said he would. All this happened because you people sinned against the LORD and did not obey him."

reflection

1. When have you specifically ignored warning signs and faced a consequence as a result?
2. In what ways has God spoken to you when you strayed off the path he set out for you?
3. What area related to obedience do you struggle with the most?

RELATED READINGS

Deuteronomy 30:1–10; Psalm 94:12; Isaiah 55:6–7; Hebrews 12:5–6

Go to page 964 for your next devotional reading.

Ishmael son of Nethaniah, and no one will
know it. Why should he take your life and
cause all the Jews who are gathered around
you to be scattered and the remnant of Judah
to perish?"

16 But Gedaliah son of Ahikam said to Johanan son of Kareah, "Don't do such a thing! What
you are saying about Ishmael is not true."

41 In the seventh month Ishmael son of
Nethaniah, the son of Elishama, who
was of royal blood and had been one of the
king's officers, came with ten men to Gedaliah
son of Ahikam at Mizpah. While they were eating together there, 2 Ishmael son of Nethaniah
and the ten men who were with him got up
and struck down Gedaliah son of Ahikam, the
son of Shaphan, with the sword, killing the one
whom the king of Babylon had appointed as
governor over the land. 3 Ishmael also killed
all the Jews who were with Gedaliah at Mizpah, as well as the Babylonian[a] soldiers who
were there.

4 The day after Gedaliah's assassination, before anyone knew about it, 5 eighty men who
had shaved off their beards, torn their clothes
and cut themselves came from Shechem, Shiloh and Samaria, bringing grain offerings and
incense with them to the house of the LORD.
6 Ishmael son of Nethaniah went out from Mizpah to meet them, weeping as he went. When
he met them, he said, "Come to Gedaliah son
of Ahikam." 7 When they went into the city,
Ishmael son of Nethaniah and the men who
were with him slaughtered them and threw
them into a cistern. 8 But ten of them said to
Ishmael, "Don't kill us! We have wheat and
barley, oil and honey, hidden in a field." So
he let them alone and did not kill them with
the others. 9 Now the cistern where he threw
all the bodies of the men he had killed along
with Gedaliah was the one King Asa had made
as part of his defense against Baasha king of
Israel. Ishmael son of Nethaniah filled it with
the dead.

10 Ishmael made captives of all the rest of the
people who were in Mizpah—the king's daughters along with all the others who were left
there, over whom Nebuzaradan commander
of the imperial guard had appointed Gedaliah
son of Ahikam. Ishmael son of Nethaniah
took them captive and set out to cross over to
the Ammonites.

11 When Johanan son of Kareah and all the
army officers who were with him heard about
all the crimes Ishmael son of Nethaniah had
committed, 12 they took all their men and went
to fight Ishmael son of Nethaniah. They caught
up with him near the great pool in Gibeon.
13 When all the people Ishmael had with him
saw Johanan son of Kareah and the army officers who were with him, they were glad. 14 All
the people Ishmael had taken captive at Mizpah turned and went over to Johanan son of
Kareah. 15 But Ishmael son of Nethaniah and
eight of his men escaped from Johanan and
fled to the Ammonites.

Flight to Egypt

16 Then Johanan son of Kareah and all the
army officers who were with him led away all
the survivors from Mizpah whom he had recovered from Ishmael son of Nethaniah after he
had assassinated Gedaliah son of Ahikam: the
soldiers, women, children and court officials
he had brought from Gibeon. 17 And they went
on, stopping at Geruth Kimham near Bethlehem on their way to Egypt 18 to escape the Babylonians.[b] They were afraid of them because
Ishmael son of Nethaniah had killed Gedaliah
son of Ahikam, whom the king of Babylon had
appointed as governor over the land.

42 Then all the army officers, including
Johanan son of Kareah and Jezaniah[c]
son of Hoshaiah, and all the people from the
least to the greatest approached 2 Jeremiah the
prophet and said to him, "Please hear our petition and pray to the LORD your God for this
entire remnant. For as you now see, though we
were once many, now only a few are left. 3 Pray
that the LORD your God will tell us where we
should go and what we should do."

4 "I have heard you," replied Jeremiah the
prophet. "I will certainly pray to the LORD your
God as you have requested; I will tell you everything the LORD says and will keep nothing
back from you."

5 Then they said to Jeremiah, "May the LORD
be a true and faithful witness against us if we

[a] 3 Or *Chaldean* [b] 18 Or *Chaldeans* [c] 1 Hebrew; Septuagint (see also 43:2) *Azariah*

do not act in accordance with everything the
LORD your God sends you to tell us. [6]Whether
it is favorable or unfavorable, we will obey
the LORD our God, to whom
we are sending you, so that it
will go well with us, for we will
obey the LORD our God."
[7]Ten days later the word of
the LORD came to Jeremiah.
[8]So he called together Johanan
son of Kareah and all the army
officers who were with him and
all the people from the least to
the greatest. [9]He said to them,
"This is what the LORD, the God
of Israel, to whom you sent me
to present your petition, says:
[10]'If you stay in this land, I will
build you up and not tear you
down; I will plant you and not
uproot you, for I am grieved
over the disaster I have inflicted on you. [11]Do
not be afraid of the king of Babylon, whom you
now fear. Do not be afraid of him, declares the
LORD, for I am with you and will save you and
deliver you from his hands. [12]I will show you
compassion so that he will have compassion on
you and restore you to your land.'
[13]"However, if you say, 'We will not stay in
this land,' and so disobey the LORD your God,
[14]and if you say, 'No, we will go and live in
Egypt, where we will not see war or hear the
trumpet or be hungry for bread,' [15]then hear
the word of the LORD, O remnant of Judah.
This is what the LORD Almighty, the God of
Israel, says: 'If you are determined to go to
Egypt and you do go to settle there, [16]then the
sword you fear will overtake you there, and the
famine you dread will follow you into Egypt,
and there you will die. [17]Indeed, all who are
determined to go to Egypt to settle there will
die by the sword, famine and plague; not one
of them will survive or escape the disaster I
will bring on them.' [18]This is what the LORD
Almighty, the God of Israel, says: 'As my anger
and wrath have been poured out on those who
lived in Jerusalem, so will my wrath be poured
out on you when you go to Egypt. You will be
an object of cursing and horror, of condemnation and reproach; you will never see this
place again.'
[19]"O remnant of Judah, the LORD has told
you, 'Do not go to Egypt.' Be
sure of this: I warn you today
[20]that you made a fatal mistake[a] when you sent me to the
LORD your God and said, 'Pray
to the LORD our God for us;
tell us everything he says and
we will do it.' [21]I have told you
today, but you still have not
obeyed the LORD your God in
all he sent me to tell you. [22]So
now, be sure of this: You will
die by the sword, famine and
plague in the place where you
want to go to settle."

Jeremiah 42:6

God Seeks Obedience

"Whether it is favorable or unfavorable, we will obey the LORD our God, to whom we are sending you, so that it will go well with us, for we will obey the LORD our God."

43
When Jeremiah fin-
ished telling the peo-
ple all the words of the LORD
their God—everything the LORD had sent him
to tell them— [2]Azariah son of Hoshaiah and Johanan son of Kareah and all the arrogant men
said to Jeremiah, "You are lying! The LORD our
God has not sent you to say, 'You must not go
to Egypt to settle there.' [3]But Baruch son of
Neriah is inciting you against us to hand us
over to the Babylonians,[b] so they may kill us or
carry us into exile to Babylon."
[4]So Johanan son of Kareah and all the army
officers and all the people disobeyed the LORD's
command to stay in the land of Judah. [5]In-
stead, Johanan son of Kareah and all the army
officers led away all the remnant of Judah who
had come back to live in the land of Judah from
all the nations where they had been scattered.
[6]They also led away all the men, women and
children and the king's daughters whom Nebuzaradan commander of the imperial guard
had left with Gedaliah son of Ahikam, the son
of Shaphan, and Jeremiah the prophet and
Baruch son of Neriah. [7]So they entered Egypt
in disobedience to the LORD and went as far
as Tahpanhes.
[8]In Tahpanhes the word of the LORD came
to Jeremiah: [9]"While the Jews are watching,
take some large stones with you and bury them
in clay in the brick pavement at the entrance

[a]20 Or *you erred in your hearts* [b]3 Or *Chaldeans*

to Pharaoh's palace in Tahpanhes. 10Then say
to them, 'This is what the LORD Almighty, the
God of Israel, says: I will send for my servant
Nebuchadnezzar king of Babylon, and I will
set his throne over these stones I have buried
here; he will spread his royal canopy above
them. 11He will come and attack Egypt, bringing death to those destined for death, captivity
to those destined for captivity, and the sword
to those destined for the sword. 12He[a] will set
fire to the temples of the gods of Egypt; he will
burn their temples and take their gods captive.
As a shepherd wraps his garment around him,
so will he wrap Egypt around himself and depart from there unscathed. 13There in the temple of the sun[b] in Egypt he will demolish the
sacred pillars and will burn down the temples
of the gods of Egypt.'"

Disaster Because of Idolatry

44 This word came to Jeremiah concerning
all the Jews living in Lower Egypt—in
Migdol, Tahpanhes and Memphis[c]—and in Upper Egypt[d]: 2"This is what the LORD Almighty,
the God of Israel, says: You saw the great disaster I brought on Jerusalem and on all the towns
of Judah. Today they lie deserted and in ruins
3because of the evil they have done. They provoked me to anger by burning incense and by
worshiping other gods that neither they nor you
nor your fathers ever knew. 4Again and again
I sent my servants the prophets, who said, 'Do
not do this detestable thing that I hate!' 5But
they did not listen or pay attention; they did
not turn from their wickedness or stop burning
incense to other gods. 6Therefore, my fierce anger was poured out; it raged against the towns
of Judah and the streets of Jerusalem and made
them the desolate ruins they are today.

7"Now this is what the LORD God Almighty,
the God of Israel, says: Why bring such great disaster on yourselves by cutting off from Judah
the men and women, the children and infants,
and so leave yourselves without a remnant?
8Why provoke me to anger with what your
hands have made, burning incense to other
gods in Egypt, where you have come to live?
You will destroy yourselves and make yourselves an object of cursing and reproach among
all the nations on earth. 9Have you forgotten
the wickedness committed by your fathers and
by the kings and queens of Judah and the wickedness committed by you and your wives in the
land of Judah and the streets of Jerusalem? 10To
this day they have not humbled themselves or
shown reverence, nor have they followed my
law and the decrees I set before you and your fathers.

11"Therefore, this is what the LORD Almighty, the God of Israel, says: I am determined to bring disaster on you and to destroy
all Judah. 12I will take away the remnant of Judah who were determined to go to Egypt to settle there. They will all perish in Egypt; they will
fall by the sword or die from famine. From the
least to the greatest, they will die by sword or
famine. They will become an object of cursing
and horror, of condemnation and reproach. 13I
will punish those who live in Egypt with the
sword, famine and plague, as I punished Jerusalem. 14None of the remnant of Judah who have
gone to live in Egypt will escape or survive to
return to the land of Judah, to which they long
to return and live; none will return except a few
fugitives."

15Then all the men who knew that their
wives were burning incense to other gods,
along with all the women who were present—a
large assembly—and all the people living in
Lower and Upper Egypt,[e] said to Jeremiah,
16"We will not listen to the message you have
spoken to us in the name of the LORD! 17We
will certainly do everything we said we would:
We will burn incense to the Queen of Heaven
and will pour out drink offerings to her just as
we and our fathers, our kings and our officials
did in the towns of Judah and in the streets of
Jerusalem. At that time we had plenty of food
and were well off and suffered no harm. 18But
ever since we stopped burning incense to the
Queen of Heaven and pouring out drink offerings to her, we have had nothing and have been
perishing by sword and famine."

19The women added, "When we burned incense to the Queen of Heaven and poured out
drink offerings to her, did not our husbands
know that we were making cakes like her image and pouring out drink offerings to her?"

20Then Jeremiah said to all the people, both

[a]12 Or *I* [b]13 Or *in Heliopolis* [c]1 Hebrew *Noph* [d]1 Hebrew *in Pathros* [e]15 Hebrew *in Egypt and Pathros*

Quit!

JOB'S WIFE

His wife said to him, "Are you still holding on to your integrity? Curse God and die!"

Job 2:9

SHE WAS AT HER WIT'S END.

Emotionally depleted from her grievous losses, Job's wife had nothing left to give to her husband. She'd wept so much in such a short time that she was sure she'd cried her last tear. Life seemed hopeless and, worse yet, she felt like God did not seem to care. Everything she'd cherished was now nothing but a memory.

And even the memories were starting to blur. One day, she had the frightening experience of suddenly not being able to picture her loved ones' faces in her mind—her sons and daughters, their spouses. What did they look like? Could she remember clearly? Under the stress of her situation, she suffered untold emotional and psychological distress, digressing into symptoms of physical pain. She wasn't eating. She wasn't sleeping.

So, perhaps it's not that surprising that the day she saw her husband covered in boils and scraping himself with a shard of pottery, she just lost it. Job's wife fell to pieces emotionally and spiritually.

Her tirade may have been a long time in coming—it's unclear from the details in the story. Maybe she had resented Job's piety and devotion to God for a while. On the other hand, maybe she had actually been on the same level spiritually as her husband before her tragic loss and was simply responding under stress in exactly the way some of us might in a similar situation. Only in her instance, her breakdown was recorded for posterity.

We know Job was a righteous man—but, the truth is, we don't know if his wife ever got back on track with God. We can't say with certainty if she ever returned to faith in him (if she'd ever had faith at all). What we do know about her story is that life hurts sometimes. And if we all really spoke our mind during the times when it hurts us the most, we might sound more like her than we care to admit.

—Prayer—
Heavenly Father, life is so difficult sometimes. Help me to remember to turn to you when I need support and encouragement.

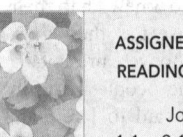

ASSIGNED READING:
Job 1:1—2:10

Weekend

Go to page 982 for your next devotional reading

men and women, who were answering him,
21"Did not the LORD remember and think
about the incense burned in the towns of Judah
and the streets of Jerusalem by you and your
fathers, your kings and your officials and the
people of the land? 22When the LORD could
no longer endure your wicked actions and the
detestable things you did, your land became an
object of cursing and a desolate waste without
inhabitants, as it is today. 23Because you have
burned incense and have sinned against the
LORD and have not obeyed him or followed his
law or his decrees or his stipulations, this disaster has come upon you, as you now see."

24Then Jeremiah said to all the people, including the women, "Hear the word of the
LORD, all you people of Judah in Egypt. 25This
is what the LORD Almighty, the God of Israel,
says: You and your wives have shown by your
actions what you promised when you said, 'We
will certainly carry out the vows we made to
burn incense and pour out drink offerings to
the Queen of Heaven.'

"Go ahead then, do what you promised!
Keep your vows! 26But hear the word of the
LORD, all Jews living in Egypt: 'I swear by my
great name,' says the LORD, 'that no one from
Judah living anywhere in Egypt will ever again
invoke my name or swear, "As surely as the Sovereign LORD lives." 27For I am watching over
them for harm, not for good; the Jews in Egypt
will perish by sword and famine until they are
all destroyed. 28Those who escape the sword
and return to the land of Judah from Egypt will
be very few. Then the whole remnant of Judah
who came to live in Egypt will know whose
word will stand—mine or theirs.

29" 'This will be the sign to you that I will punish you in this place,' declares the LORD, 'so that
you will know that my threats of harm against
you will surely stand.' 30This is what the LORD
says: 'I am going to hand Pharaoh Hophra king
of Egypt over to his enemies who seek his life,
just as I handed Zedekiah king of Judah over to
Nebuchadnezzar king of Babylon, the enemy
who was seeking his life.' "

A Message to Baruch

45 This is what Jeremiah the prophet told
Baruch son of Neriah in the fourth
year of Jehoiakim son of Josiah king of Judah,
after Baruch had written on a scroll the words
Jeremiah was then dictating: 2"This is what the
LORD, the God of Israel, says to you, Baruch:
3You said, 'Woe to me! The LORD has added sorrow to my pain; I am worn out with groaning
and find no rest.' "

4⌞The LORD said,⌟ "Say this to him: 'This is
what the LORD says: I will overthrow what I
have built and uproot what I have planted,
throughout the land. 5Should you then seek
great things for yourself? Seek them not. For
I will bring disaster on all people, declares the
LORD, but wherever you go I will let you escape
with your life.' "

A Message About Egypt

46 This is the word of the LORD that came
to Jeremiah the prophet concerning
the nations:

2Concerning Egypt:

This is the message against the army of Pharaoh Neco king of Egypt, which was defeated at
Carchemish on the Euphrates River by Nebuchadnezzar king of Babylon in the fourth year
of Jehoiakim son of Josiah king of Judah:

3"Prepare your shields, both large and
small,
and march out for battle!
4Harness the horses,
mount the steeds!
Take your positions
with helmets on!
Polish your spears,
put on your armor!
5What do I see?
They are terrified,
they are retreating,
their warriors are defeated.
They flee in haste
without looking back,
and there is terror on every side,"
declares the LORD.

6"The swift cannot flee
nor the strong escape.
In the north by the River Euphrates
they stumble and fall.

7"Who is this that rises like the Nile,
like rivers of surging waters?

8 Egypt rises like the Nile,
like rivers of surging waters.
She says, 'I will rise and cover the earth;
I will destroy cities and their people.'
9 Charge, O horses!
Drive furiously, O charioteers!
March on, O warriors—
men of Cush[a] and Put who carry shields,
men of Lydia who draw the bow.
10 But that day belongs to the Lord, the LORD Almighty—
a day of vengeance, for vengeance on his foes.
The sword will devour till it is satisfied,
till it has quenched its thirst with blood.
For the Lord, the LORD Almighty, will offer sacrifice
in the land of the north by the River Euphrates.

11 "Go up to Gilead and get balm,
O Virgin Daughter of Egypt.
But you multiply remedies in vain;
there is no healing for you.
12 The nations will hear of your shame;
your cries will fill the earth.
One warrior will stumble over another;
both will fall down together."

13 This is the message the LORD spoke to Jeremiah the prophet about the coming of Nebuchadnezzar king of Babylon to attack Egypt:

14 "Announce this in Egypt, and proclaim it in Migdol;
proclaim it also in Memphis[b] and Tahpanhes:
'Take your positions and get ready,
for the sword devours those around you.'
15 Why will your warriors be laid low?
They cannot stand, for the LORD will push them down.
16 They will stumble repeatedly;
they will fall over each other.
They will say, 'Get up, let us go back
to our own people and our native lands,
away from the sword of the oppressor.'
17 There they will exclaim,
'Pharaoh king of Egypt is only a loud noise;
he has missed his opportunity.'

18 "As surely as I live," declares the King,
whose name is the LORD Almighty,
"one will come who is like Tabor among the mountains,
like Carmel by the sea.
19 Pack your belongings for exile,
you who live in Egypt,
for Memphis will be laid waste
and lie in ruins without inhabitant.

20 "Egypt is a beautiful heifer,
but a gadfly is coming
against her from the north.
21 The mercenaries in her ranks
are like fattened calves.
They too will turn and flee together,
they will not stand their ground,
for the day of disaster is coming upon them,
the time for them to be punished.
22 Egypt will hiss like a fleeing serpent
as the enemy advances in force;
they will come against her with axes,
like men who cut down trees.
23 They will chop down her forest,"
declares the LORD,
"dense though it be.
They are more numerous than locusts,
they cannot be counted.
24 The Daughter of Egypt will be put to shame,
handed over to the people of the north."

25 The LORD Almighty, the God of Israel, says: "I am about to bring punishment on Amon god of Thebes,[c] on Pharaoh, on Egypt and her gods and her kings, and on those who rely on Pharaoh.
26 I will hand them over to those who seek their lives, to Nebuchadnezzar king of Babylon and his officers. Later, however, Egypt will be inhabited as in times past," declares the LORD.

27 "Do not fear, O Jacob my servant;
do not be dismayed, O Israel.
I will surely save you out of a distant place,
your descendants from the land of their exile.

[a] 9 That is, the upper Nile region [b] 14 Hebrew *Noph*; also in verse 19 [c] 25 Hebrew *No*

Jacob will again have peace and security,
and no one will make him afraid.
28 Do not fear, O Jacob my servant,
for I am with you,"
declares the LORD.
"Though I completely
destroy all the
nations
among which I scatter
you,
I will not completely
destroy you.
I will discipline you but
only with justice;
I will not let you
go entirely
unpunished."

Jeremiah 46:28

God Protects His Own

"Do not fear, O Jacob
my servant,
for I am with you,"
declares the LORD.

A Message About the Philistines

47 This is the word of the LORD that came
to Jeremiah the prophet concerning
the Philistines before Pharaoh attacked Gaza:

2 This is what the LORD says:

"See how the waters are rising in the north;
they will become an overflowing torrent.
They will overflow the land and everything
in it,
the towns and those who live in them.
The people will cry out;
all who dwell in the land will wail
3 at the sound of the hoofs of galloping
steeds,
at the noise of enemy chariots
and the rumble of their wheels.
Fathers will not turn to help their children;
their hands will hang limp.
4 For the day has come
to destroy all the Philistines
and to cut off all survivors
who could help Tyre and Sidon.
The LORD is about to destroy the
Philistines,
the remnant from the coasts of
Caphtor.[a]
5 Gaza will shave her head in mourning;
Ashkelon will be silenced.
O remnant on the plain,
how long will you cut yourselves?

6 "'Ah, sword of the LORD,' ⌊you cry,⌋
'how long till you rest?
Return to your scabbard;
cease and be still.'
7 But how can it rest
when the LORD has
commanded it,
when he has ordered it
to attack Ashkelon and
the coast?"

A Message About Moab

48 Concerning Moab:

This is what the LORD Almighty, the God of Israel, says:

"Woe to Nebo, for it will be
ruined.
Kiriathaim will be disgraced and
captured;
the stronghold[b] will be disgraced and
shattered.
2 Moab will be praised no more;
in Heshbon[c] men will plot her downfall:
'Come, let us put an end to that nation.'
You too, O Madmen,[d] will be silenced;
the sword will pursue you.
3 Listen to the cries from Horonaim,
cries of great havoc and destruction.
4 Moab will be broken;
her little ones will cry out.[e]
5 They go up the way to Luhith,
weeping bitterly as they go;
on the road down to Horonaim
anguished cries over the destruction are
heard.
6 Flee! Run for your lives;
become like a bush[f] in the desert.
7 Since you trust in your deeds and riches,
you too will be taken captive,
and Chemosh will go into exile,
together with his priests and officials.
8 The destroyer will come against every
town,
and not a town will escape.
The valley will be ruined
and the plateau destroyed,
because the LORD has spoken.

[a]4 That is, Crete [b]1 Or / *Misgab* [c]2 The Hebrew for *Heshbon* sounds like the Hebrew for *plot.* [d]2 The name of the Moabite town Madmen sounds like the Hebrew for *be silenced.* [e]4 Hebrew; Septuagint / *proclaim it to Zoar* [f]6 Or *like Aroer*

9 Put salt on Moab,
for she will be laid waste[a];
her towns will become desolate,
with no one to live in them.

10 "A curse on him who is lax in doing the LORD's work!
A curse on him who keeps his sword from bloodshed!

11 "Moab has been at rest from youth,
like wine left on its dregs,
not poured from one jar to another—
she has not gone into exile.
So she tastes as she did,
and her aroma is unchanged.
12 But days are coming,"
declares the LORD,
"when I will send men who pour from jars,
and they will pour her out;
they will empty her jars
and smash her jugs.
13 Then Moab will be ashamed of Chemosh,
as the house of Israel was ashamed
when they trusted in Bethel.

14 "How can you say, 'We are warriors,
men valiant in battle'?
15 Moab will be destroyed and her towns invaded;
her finest young men will go down in the slaughter,"
declares the King, whose name is the LORD Almighty.
16 "The fall of Moab is at hand;
her calamity will come quickly.
17 Mourn for her, all who live around her,
all who know her fame;
say, 'How broken is the mighty scepter,
how broken the glorious staff!'

18 "Come down from your glory
and sit on the parched ground,
O inhabitants of the Daughter of Dibon,
for he who destroys Moab
will come up against you
and ruin your fortified cities.
19 Stand by the road and watch,
you who live in Aroer.
Ask the man fleeing and the woman escaping,
ask them, 'What has happened?'
20 Moab is disgraced, for she is shattered.
Wail and cry out!
Announce by the Arnon
that Moab is destroyed.
21 Judgment has come to the plateau—
to Holon, Jahzah and Mephaath,
22 to Dibon, Nebo and Beth Diblathaim,
23 to Kiriathaim, Beth Gamul and Beth Meon,
24 to Kerioth and Bozrah—
to all the towns of Moab, far and near.
25 Moab's horn[b] is cut off;
her arm is broken,"
declares the LORD.

26 "Make her drunk,
for she has defied the LORD.
Let Moab wallow in her vomit;
let her be an object of ridicule.
27 Was not Israel the object of your ridicule?
Was she caught among thieves,
that you shake your head in scorn
whenever you speak of her?
28 Abandon your towns and dwell among the rocks,
you who live in Moab.
Be like a dove that makes its nest
at the mouth of a cave.

29 "We have heard of Moab's pride—
her overweening pride and conceit,
her pride and arrogance
and the haughtiness of her heart.
30 I know her insolence but it is futile,"
declares the LORD,
"and her boasts accomplish nothing.
31 Therefore I wail over Moab,
for all Moab I cry out,
I moan for the men of Kir Hareseth.
32 I weep for you, as Jazer weeps,
O vines of Sibmah.
Your branches spread as far as the sea;
they reached as far as the sea of Jazer.
The destroyer has fallen
on your ripened fruit and grapes.
33 Joy and gladness are gone
from the orchards and fields of Moab.
I have stopped the flow of wine from the presses;

[a]9 Or *Give wings to Moab, / for she will fly away* [b]25 *Horn* here symbolizes strength.

no one treads them with shouts of joy.
Although there are shouts,
they are not shouts of joy.

34 "The sound of their cry rises
from Heshbon to Elealeh and Jahaz,
from Zoar as far as Horonaim and Eglath Shelishiyah,
for even the waters of Nimrim are dried up.
35 In Moab I will put an end
to those who make offerings on the high places
and burn incense to their gods,"
declares the LORD.
36 "So my heart laments for Moab like a flute;
it laments like a flute for the men of Kir Hareseth.
The wealth they acquired is gone.
37 Every head is shaved
and every beard cut off;
every hand is slashed
and every waist is covered with sackcloth.
38 On all the roofs in Moab
and in the public squares
there is nothing but mourning,
for I have broken Moab
like a jar that no one wants,"
declares the LORD.
39 "How shattered she is! How they wail!
How Moab turns her back in shame!
Moab has become an object of ridicule,
an object of horror to all those around her."

40 This is what the LORD says:

"Look! An eagle is swooping down,
spreading its wings over Moab.
41 Kerioth[a] will be captured
and the strongholds taken.
In that day the hearts of Moab's warriors
will be like the heart of a woman in labor.
42 Moab will be destroyed as a nation
because she defied the LORD.
43 Terror and pit and snare await you,
O people of Moab,"
declares the LORD.
44 "Whoever flees from the terror
will fall into a pit,
whoever climbs out of the pit
will be caught in a snare;
for I will bring upon Moab
the year of her punishment,"
declares the LORD.
45 "In the shadow of Heshbon
the fugitives stand helpless,
for a fire has gone out from Heshbon,
a blaze from the midst of Sihon;
it burns the foreheads of Moab,
the skulls of the noisy boasters.
46 Woe to you, O Moab!
The people of Chemosh are destroyed;
your sons are taken into exile
and your daughters into captivity.

47 "Yet I will restore the fortunes of Moab
in days to come,"
declares the LORD.

Here ends the judgment on Moab.

A Message About Ammon

49 Concerning the Ammonites:

This is what the LORD says:

"Has Israel no sons?
Has she no heirs?
Why then has Molech[b] taken possession of Gad?
Why do his people live in its towns?
2 But the days are coming,"
declares the LORD,
"when I will sound the battle cry
against Rabbah of the Ammonites;
it will become a mound of ruins,
and its surrounding villages will be set on fire.
Then Israel will drive out
those who drove her out,"
says the LORD.
3 "Wail, O Heshbon, for Ai is destroyed!
Cry out, O inhabitants of Rabbah!
Put on sackcloth and mourn;
rush here and there inside the walls,
for Molech will go into exile,
together with his priests and officials.

[a]41 Or *The cities* [b]1 Or *their king*; Hebrew *malcam*; also in verse 3

4 Why do you boast of your valleys,
boast of your valleys so fruitful?
O unfaithful daughter,
you trust in your riches and say,
'Who will attack me?'
5 I will bring terror on you
from all those around you,"
declares the Lord, the LORD Almighty.
"Every one of you will be driven away,
and no one will gather the fugitives.

6 "Yet afterward, I will restore the fortunes
of the Ammonites,"
declares the LORD.

A Message About Edom

7 Concerning Edom:

This is what the LORD Almighty says:

"Is there no longer wisdom in Teman?
Has counsel perished from the prudent?
Has their wisdom decayed?
8 Turn and flee, hide in deep caves,
you who live in Dedan,
for I will bring disaster on Esau
at the time I punish him.
9 If grape pickers came to you,
would they not leave a few grapes?
If thieves came during the night,
would they not steal only as much as
they wanted?
10 But I will strip Esau bare;
I will uncover his hiding places,
so that he cannot conceal himself.
His children, relatives and neighbors will
perish,
and he will be no more.
11 Leave your orphans; I will protect their
lives.
Your widows too can trust in me."

12 This is what the LORD says: "If those who
do not deserve to drink the cup must drink it,
why should you go unpunished? You will not
go unpunished, but must drink it. 13 I swear by
myself," declares the LORD, "that Bozrah will
become a ruin and an object of horror, of reproach and of cursing; and all its towns will be
in ruins forever."

14 I have heard a message from the LORD:
An envoy was sent to the nations to say,
"Assemble yourselves to attack it!
Rise up for battle!"

15 "Now I will make you small among the
nations,
despised among men.
16 The terror you inspire
and the pride of your heart have
deceived you,
you who live in the clefts of the rocks,
who occupy the heights of the hill.
Though you build your nest as high as the
eagle's,
from there I will bring you down,"
declares the LORD.
17 "Edom will become an object of horror;
all who pass by will be appalled and will
scoff
because of all its wounds.
18 As Sodom and Gomorrah were
overthrown,
along with their neighboring towns,"
says the LORD,
"so no one will live there;
no man will dwell in it.

19 "Like a lion coming up from Jordan's
thickets
to a rich pastureland,
I will chase Edom from its land in an
instant.
Who is the chosen one I will appoint for
this?
Who is like me and who can challenge me?
And what shepherd can stand against
me?"
20 Therefore, hear what the LORD has planned
against Edom,
what he has purposed against those who
live in Teman:
The young of the flock will be dragged
away;
he will completely destroy their pasture
because of them.
21 At the sound of their fall the earth will
tremble;
their cry will resound to the Red Sea.[a]
22 Look! An eagle will soar and swoop down,
spreading its wings over Bozrah.

[a]21 Hebrew *Yam Suph*; that is, Sea of Reeds

In that day the hearts of Edom's warriors
will be like the heart of a woman in labor.

A Message About Damascus

23 Concerning Damascus:

"Hamath and Arpad are dismayed,
for they have heard bad news.
They are disheartened,
troubled like[a] the restless sea.
24 Damascus has become feeble,
she has turned to flee
and panic has gripped her;
anguish and pain have seized her,
pain like that of a woman in labor.
25 Why has the city of renown not been abandoned,
the town in which I delight?
26 Surely, her young men will fall in the streets;
all her soldiers will be silenced in that day,"
declares the LORD Almighty.
27 "I will set fire to the walls of Damascus;
it will consume the fortresses of Ben-Hadad."

A Message About Kedar and Hazor

28 Concerning Kedar and the kingdoms of
Hazor, which Nebuchadnezzar king of Babylon
attacked:

This is what the LORD says:

"Arise, and attack Kedar
and destroy the people of the East.
29 Their tents and their flocks will be taken;
their shelters will be carried off
with all their goods and camels.
Men will shout to them,
'Terror on every side!'
30 "Flee quickly away!
Stay in deep caves, you who live in Hazor,"
declares the LORD.
"Nebuchadnezzar king of Babylon has plotted against you;
he has devised a plan against you.
31 "Arise and attack a nation at ease,
which lives in confidence,"
declares the LORD,
"a nation that has neither gates nor bars;
its people live alone.
32 Their camels will become plunder,
and their large herds will be booty.
I will scatter to the winds those who are in distant places[b]
and will bring disaster on them from every side,"
declares the LORD.
33 "Hazor will become a haunt of jackals,
a desolate place forever.
No one will live there;
no man will dwell in it."

A Message About Elam

34 This is the word of the LORD that came to
Jeremiah the prophet concerning Elam, early
in the reign of Zedekiah king of Judah:

35 This is what the LORD Almighty says:

"See, I will break the bow of Elam,
the mainstay of their might.
36 I will bring against Elam the four winds
from the four quarters of the heavens;
I will scatter them to the four winds,
and there will not be a nation
where Elam's exiles do not go.
37 I will shatter Elam before their foes,
before those who seek their lives;
I will bring disaster upon them,
even my fierce anger,"
declares the LORD.
"I will pursue them with the sword
until I have made an end of them.
38 I will set my throne in Elam
and destroy her king and officials,"
declares the LORD.
39 "Yet I will restore the fortunes of Elam
in days to come,"
declares the LORD.

A Message About Babylon

50 This is the word the LORD spoke
through Jeremiah the prophet concerning Babylon and the land of the Babylonians[c]:

2 "Announce and proclaim among the nations,
lift up a banner and proclaim it;
keep nothing back, but say,

[a] 23 Hebrew *on* or *by* [b] 32 Or *who clip the hair by their foreheads* [c] 1 Or *Chaldeans*; also in verses 8, 25, 35 and 45

'Babylon will be captured;
Bel will be put to shame,
Marduk filled with terror.
Her images will be put to shame
and her idols filled with terror.'
3 A nation from the north will attack her
and lay waste her land.
No one will live in it;
both men and animals will flee away.

4 "In those days, at that time,"
declares the LORD,
"the people of Israel and the people of Judah together
will go in tears to seek the LORD their God.
5 They will ask the way to Zion
and turn their faces toward it.
They will come and bind themselves to the LORD
in an everlasting covenant
that will not be forgotten.

6 "My people have been lost sheep;
their shepherds have led them astray
and caused them to roam on the mountains.
They wandered over mountain and hill
and forgot their own resting place.
7 Whoever found them devoured them;
their enemies said, 'We are not guilty,
for they sinned against the LORD, their true pasture,
the LORD, the hope of their fathers.'

8 "Flee out of Babylon;
leave the land of the Babylonians,
and be like the goats that lead the flock.
9 For I will stir up and bring against Babylon
an alliance of great nations from the land of the north.
They will take up their positions against her,
and from the north she will be captured.
Their arrows will be like skilled warriors
who do not return empty-handed.
10 So Babylonia[a] will be plundered;
all who plunder her will have their fill,"
declares the LORD.

11 "Because you rejoice and are glad,
you who pillage my inheritance,
because you frolic like a heifer threshing grain
and neigh like stallions,
12 your mother will be greatly ashamed;
she who gave you birth will be disgraced.
She will be the least of the nations—
a wilderness, a dry land, a desert.
13 Because of the LORD's anger she will not be inhabited
but will be completely desolate.
All who pass Babylon will be horrified and scoff
because of all her wounds.

14 "Take up your positions around Babylon,
all you who draw the bow.
Shoot at her! Spare no arrows,
for she has sinned against the LORD.
15 Shout against her on every side!
She surrenders, her towers fall,
her walls are torn down.
Since this is the vengeance of the LORD,
take vengeance on her;
do to her as she has done to others.
16 Cut off from Babylon the sower,
and the reaper with his sickle at harvest.
Because of the sword of the oppressor
let everyone return to his own people,
let everyone flee to his own land.

17 "Israel is a scattered flock
that lions have chased away.
The first to devour him
was the king of Assyria;
the last to crush his bones
was Nebuchadnezzar king of Babylon."

18 Therefore this is what the LORD Almighty, the God of Israel, says:

"I will punish the king of Babylon and his land
as I punished the king of Assyria.
19 But I will bring Israel back to his own pasture
and he will graze on Carmel and Bashan;
his appetite will be satisfied
on the hills of Ephraim and Gilead.
20 In those days, at that time,"

[a] 10 Or *Chaldea*

declares the LORD,
"search will be made for Israel's guilt,
but there will be none,
and for the sins of Judah,
but none will be found,
for I will forgive the
remnant I spare.

21 "Attack the land of
Merathaim
and those who live in
Pekod.
Pursue, kill and completely
destroy[a] them,"
declares the LORD.
"Do everything I have
commanded you.
22 The noise of battle is in the
land,
the noise of great
destruction!
23 How broken and shattered
is the hammer of the
whole earth!
How desolate is Babylon
among the nations!
24 I set a trap for you, O Babylon,
and you were caught before you knew it;
you were found and captured
because you opposed the LORD.
25 The LORD has opened his arsenal
and brought out the weapons of his wrath,
for the Sovereign LORD Almighty has work
to do
in the land of the Babylonians.
26 Come against her from afar.
Break open her granaries;
pile her up like heaps of grain.
Completely destroy her
and leave her no remnant.
27 Kill all her young bulls;
let them go down to the slaughter!
Woe to them! For their day has come,
the time for them to be punished.
28 Listen to the fugitives and refugees from
Babylon
declaring in Zion
how the LORD our God has taken
vengeance,
vengeance for his temple.

Jeremiah 50:20

God Forgives His People

"In those days, at
that time,"
declares the LORD,
"search will be made
for Israel's guilt,
but there will be none,
and for the sins of Judah,
but none will be found,
for I will forgive the
remnant I spare."

29 "Summon archers against Babylon,
all those who draw the bow.
Encamp all around her;
let no one escape.
Repay her for her deeds;
do to her as she has done.
For she has defied the
LORD,
the Holy One of Israel.
30 Therefore, her young men
will fall in the
streets;
all her soldiers will be
silenced in that
day,"
declares the LORD.
31 "See, I am against you,
O arrogant one,"
declares the Lord, the
LORD Almighty,
"for your day has come,
the time for you to be
punished.
32 The arrogant one will stumble and fall
and no one will help her up;
I will kindle a fire in her towns
that will consume all who are around
her."

33 This is what the LORD Almighty says:

"The people of Israel are oppressed,
and the people of Judah as well.
All their captors hold them fast,
refusing to let them go.
34 Yet their Redeemer is strong;
the LORD Almighty is his name.
He will vigorously defend their cause
so that he may bring rest to their land,
but unrest to those who live in Babylon.

35 "A sword against the Babylonians!"
declares the LORD—
"against those who live in Babylon
and against her officials and wise men!
36 A sword against her false prophets!
They will become fools.
A sword against her warriors!
They will be filled with terror.
37 A sword against her horses and chariots
and all the foreigners in her ranks!

21 The Hebrew term refers to the irrevocable giving over of things or persons to the LORD, often by totally destroying them; also in verse 26.

They will become women.
A sword against her treasures!
They will be plundered.
38 A drought on[a] her waters!
They will dry up.
For it is a land of idols,
idols that will go mad with terror.

39 "So desert creatures and hyenas will live there,
and there the owl will dwell.
It will never again be inhabited
or lived in from generation to generation.
40 As God overthrew Sodom and Gomorrah
along with their neighboring towns,"
declares the LORD,
"so no one will live there;
no man will dwell in it.

41 "Look! An army is coming from the north;
a great nation and many kings
are being stirred up from the ends of the earth.
42 They are armed with bows and spears;
they are cruel and without mercy.
They sound like the roaring sea
as they ride on their horses;
they come like men in battle formation
to attack you, O Daughter of Babylon.
43 The king of Babylon has heard reports about them,
and his hands hang limp.
Anguish has gripped him,
pain like that of a woman in labor.
44 Like a lion coming up from Jordan's thickets
to a rich pastureland,
I will chase Babylon from its land in an instant.
Who is the chosen one I will appoint for this?
Who is like me and who can challenge me?
And what shepherd can stand against me?"
45 Therefore, hear what the LORD has planned against Babylon,
what he has purposed against the land of the Babylonians:
The young of the flock will be dragged away;
he will completely destroy their pasture because of them.
46 At the sound of Babylon's capture the earth will tremble;
its cry will resound among the nations.

51 This is what the LORD says:

"See, I will stir up the spirit of a destroyer
against Babylon and the people of Leb Kamai.[b]
2 I will send foreigners to Babylon
to winnow her and to devastate her land;
they will oppose her on every side
in the day of her disaster.
3 Let not the archer string his bow,
nor let him put on his armor.
Do not spare her young men;
completely destroy[c] her army.
4 They will fall down slain in Babylon,[d]
fatally wounded in her streets.
5 For Israel and Judah have not been forsaken
by their God, the LORD Almighty,
though their land[e] is full of guilt
before the Holy One of Israel.

6 "Flee from Babylon!
Run for your lives!
Do not be destroyed because of her sins.
It is time for the LORD's vengeance;
he will pay her what she deserves.
7 Babylon was a gold cup in the LORD's hand;
she made the whole earth drunk.
The nations drank her wine;
therefore they have now gone mad.
8 Babylon will suddenly fall and be broken.
Wail over her!
Get balm for her pain;
perhaps she can be healed.

9 " 'We would have healed Babylon,
but she cannot be healed;
let us leave her and each go to his own land,
for her judgment reaches to the skies,
it rises as high as the clouds.'

[a] 38 Or *A sword against* [b] 1 *Leb Kamai* is a cryptogram for Chaldea, that is, Babylonia. [c] 3 The Hebrew term refers to the irrevocable giving over of things or persons to the LORD, often by totally destroying them. [d] 4 Or *Chaldea* [e] 5 Or / *and the land of the Babylonians*

10 " 'The LORD has vindicated us;
come, let us tell in Zion
what the LORD our God has done.'

11 "Sharpen the arrows,
take up the shields!
The LORD has stirred up the kings of the Medes,
because his purpose is to destroy Babylon.
The LORD will take vengeance,
vengeance for his temple.
12 Lift up a banner against the walls of Babylon!
Reinforce the guard,
station the watchmen,
prepare an ambush!
The LORD will carry out his purpose,
his decree against the people of Babylon.
13 You who live by many waters
and are rich in treasures,
your end has come,
the time for you to be cut off.
14 The LORD Almighty has sworn by himself:
I will surely fill you with men, as with a swarm of locusts,
and they will shout in triumph over you.

15 "He made the earth by his power;
he founded the world by his wisdom
and stretched out the heavens by his understanding.
16 When he thunders, the waters in the heavens roar;
he makes clouds rise from the ends of the earth.
He sends lightning with the rain
and brings out the wind from his storehouses.

17 "Every man is senseless and without knowledge;
every goldsmith is shamed by his idols.
His images are a fraud;
they have no breath in them.
18 They are worthless, the objects of mockery;
when their judgment comes, they will perish.
19 He who is the Portion of Jacob is not like these,
for he is the Maker of all things,
including the tribe of his inheritance—
the LORD Almighty is his name.

Jeremiah 51:15

God Created the World

"He made the earth
by his power;
he founded the world
by his wisdom
and stretched out
the heavens by his
understanding."

20 "You are my war club,
my weapon for battle—
with you I shatter nations,
with you I destroy kingdoms,
21 with you I shatter horse and rider,
with you I shatter chariot and driver,
22 with you I shatter man and woman,
with you I shatter old man and youth,
with you I shatter young man and maiden,
23 with you I shatter shepherd and flock,
with you I shatter farmer and oxen,
with you I shatter governors and officials.

24 "Before your eyes I will repay Babylon and all who live in Babylonia[a] for all the wrong they have done in Zion," declares the LORD.

25 "I am against you, O destroying mountain,
you who destroy the whole earth,"
declares the LORD.
"I will stretch out my hand against you,
roll you off the cliffs,
and make you a burned-out mountain.
26 No rock will be taken from you for a cornerstone,
nor any stone for a foundation,
for you will be desolate forever,"
declares the LORD.

27 "Lift up a banner in the land!
Blow the trumpet among the nations!

[a]24 Or *Chaldea*; also in verse 35

Prepare the nations for battle against her;
summon against her these kingdoms:
Ararat, Minni and Ashkenaz.
Appoint a commander against her;
send up horses like a swarm of locusts.
28 Prepare the nations for battle against her—
the kings of the Medes,
their governors and all their officials,
and all the countries they rule.
29 The land trembles and writhes,
for the LORD's purposes against Babylon stand—
to lay waste the land of Babylon
so that no one will live there.
30 Babylon's warriors have stopped fighting;
they remain in their strongholds.
Their strength is exhausted;
they have become like women.
Her dwellings are set on fire;
the bars of her gates are broken.
31 One courier follows another
and messenger follows messenger
to announce to the king of Babylon
that his entire city is captured,
32 the river crossings seized,
the marshes set on fire,
and the soldiers terrified."

33 This is what the LORD Almighty, the God of Israel, says:

"The Daughter of Babylon is like a threshing floor
at the time it is trampled;
the time to harvest her will soon come."

34 "Nebuchadnezzar king of Babylon has devoured us,
he has thrown us into confusion,
he has made us an empty jar.
Like a serpent he has swallowed us
and filled his stomach with our delicacies,
and then has spewed us out.
35 May the violence done to our flesh[a] be upon Babylon,"
say the inhabitants of Zion.
"May our blood be on those who live in Babylonia,"
says Jerusalem.

36 Therefore, this is what the LORD says:

"See, I will defend your cause
and avenge you;
I will dry up her sea
and make her springs dry.
37 Babylon will be a heap of ruins,
a haunt of jackals,
an object of horror and scorn,
a place where no one lives.
38 Her people all roar like young lions,
they growl like lion cubs.
39 But while they are aroused,
I will set out a feast for them
and make them drunk,
so that they shout with laughter—
then sleep forever and not awake,"
declares the LORD.

40 "I will bring them down
like lambs to the slaughter,
like rams and goats.

41 "How Sheshach[b] will be captured,
the boast of the whole earth seized!
What a horror Babylon will be
among the nations!
42 The sea will rise over Babylon;
its roaring waves will cover her.
43 Her towns will be desolate,
a dry and desert land,
a land where no one lives,
through which no man travels.
44 I will punish Bel in Babylon
and make him spew out what he has swallowed.
The nations will no longer stream to him.
And the wall of Babylon will fall.

45 "Come out of her, my people!
Run for your lives!
Run from the fierce anger of the LORD.
46 Do not lose heart or be afraid
when rumors are heard in the land;
one rumor comes this year, another the next,
rumors of violence in the land
and of ruler against ruler.
47 For the time will surely come
when I will punish the idols of Babylon;
her whole land will be disgraced

[a]35 Or *done to us and to our children* [b]41 *Sheshach* is a cryptogram for Babylon.

and her slain will all lie fallen within her.
48 Then heaven and earth and all that is in
them
will shout for joy over Babylon,
for out of the north
destroyers will attack her,"
declares the LORD.

49 "Babylon must fall because of Israel's slain,
just as the slain in all the earth
have fallen because of Babylon.
50 You who have escaped the sword,
leave and do not linger!
Remember the LORD in a distant land,
and think on Jerusalem."

51 "We are disgraced,
for we have been insulted
and shame covers our faces,
because foreigners have entered
the holy places of the LORD's house."

52 "But days are coming," declares the LORD,
"when I will punish her idols,
and throughout her land
the wounded will groan.
53 Even if Babylon reaches the sky
and fortifies her lofty stronghold,
I will send destroyers against her,"
declares the LORD.

54 "The sound of a cry comes from Babylon,
the sound of great destruction
from the land of the Babylonians.[a]
55 The LORD will destroy Babylon;
he will silence her noisy din.
Waves ⌊of enemies⌋ will rage like great
waters;
the roar of their voices will resound.
56 A destroyer will come against Babylon;
her warriors will be captured,
and their bows will be broken.
For the LORD is a God of retribution;
he will repay in full.
57 I will make her officials and wise men
drunk,
her governors, officers and warriors as
well;
they will sleep forever and not awake,"
declares the King, whose name is the
LORD Almighty.

58 This is what the LORD Almighty says:

"Babylon's thick wall will be leveled
and her high gates set on fire;
the peoples exhaust themselves for
nothing,
the nations' labor is only fuel for the
flames."

59 This is the message Jeremiah gave to the
staff officer Seraiah son of Neriah, the son of
Mahseiah, when he went to Babylon with
Zedekiah king of Judah in the fourth year of
his reign. 60 Jeremiah had written on a scroll
about all the disasters that would come upon
Babylon—all that had been recorded concerning Babylon. 61 He said to Seraiah, "When
you get to Babylon, see that you read all these
words aloud. 62 Then say, 'O LORD, you have
said you will destroy this place, so that neither
man nor animal will live in it; it will be desolate
forever.' 63 When you finish reading this scroll,
tie a stone to it and throw it into the Euphrates. 64 Then say, 'So will Babylon sink to rise no
more because of the disaster I will bring upon
her. And her people will fall.'"

The words of Jeremiah end here.

The Fall of Jerusalem

52 Zedekiah was twenty-one years old
when he became king, and he reigned
in Jerusalem eleven years. His mother's name
was Hamutal daughter of Jeremiah; she was
from Libnah. 2 He did evil in the eyes of the
LORD, just as Jehoiakim had done. 3 It was
because of the LORD's anger that all this happened to Jerusalem and Judah, and in the end
he thrust them from his presence.

Now Zedekiah rebelled against the king
of Babylon.

4 So in the ninth year of Zedekiah's reign, on
the tenth day of the tenth month, Nebuchadnezzar king of Babylon marched against Jerusalem with his whole army. They camped outside
the city and built siege works all around it. 5 The
city was kept under siege until the eleventh year
of King Zedekiah.

6 By the ninth day of the fourth month
the famine in the city had become so severe
that there was no food for the people to eat.

[a] 54 Or *Chaldeans*

7Then the city wall was broken through, and
the whole army fled. They left the city at night
through the gate between the two walls near
the king's garden, though the Babylonians[a]
were surrounding the city. They fled toward the
Arabah,[b] 8but the Babylonian[c] army pursued
King Zedekiah and overtook him in the plains
of Jericho. All his soldiers were separated from
him and scattered, 9and he was captured.

He was taken to the king of Babylon at Riblah
in the land of Hamath, where he pronounced
sentence on him. 10There at Riblah the king
of Babylon slaughtered the sons of Zedekiah
before his eyes; he also killed all the officials
of Judah. 11Then he put out Zedekiah's eyes,
bound him with bronze shackles and took him
to Babylon, where he put him in prison till the
day of his death.

12On the tenth day of the fifth month, in the
nineteenth year of Nebuchadnezzar king of
Babylon, Nebuzaradan commander of the imperial guard, who served the king of Babylon,
came to Jerusalem. 13He set fire to the temple of
the LORD, the royal palace and all the houses of
Jerusalem. Every important building he burned
down. 14The whole Babylonian army under the
commander of the imperial guard broke down
all the walls around Jerusalem. 15Nebuzaradan
the commander of the guard carried into exile
some of the poorest people and those who remained in the city, along with the rest of the
craftsmen[d] and those who had gone over to
the king of Babylon. 16But Nebuzaradan left
behind the rest of the poorest people of the land
to work the vineyards and fields.

17The Babylonians broke up the bronze pillars, the movable stands and the bronze Sea
that were at the temple of the LORD and they carried all the bronze to Babylon. 18They also took
away the pots, shovels, wick trimmers, sprinkling bowls, dishes and all the bronze articles
used in the temple service. 19The commander
of the imperial guard took away the basins, censers, sprinkling bowls, pots, lampstands, dishes
and bowls used for drink offerings—all that
were made of pure gold or silver.

20The bronze from the two pillars, the Sea
and the twelve bronze bulls under it, and the
movable stands, which King Solomon had
made for the temple of the LORD, was more
than could be weighed. 21Each of the pillars
was eighteen cubits high and twelve cubits in
circumference[e]; each was four fingers thick,
and hollow. 22The bronze capital on top of
the one pillar was five cubits[f] high and was
decorated with a network and pomegranates
of bronze all around. The other pillar, with
its pomegranates, was similar. 23There were
ninety-six pomegranates on the sides; the total
number of pomegranates above the surrounding network was a hundred.

24The commander of the guard took as prisoners Seraiah the chief priest, Zephaniah the
priest next in rank and the three doorkeepers.
25Of those still in the city, he took the officer
in charge of the fighting men, and seven royal
advisers. He also took the secretary who was
chief officer in charge of conscripting the
people of the land and sixty of his men who
were found in the city. 26Nebuzaradan the
commander took them all and brought them
to the king of Babylon at Riblah. 27There at
Riblah, in the land of Hamath, the king had
them executed.

So Judah went into captivity, away from her
land. 28This is the number of the people Nebuchadnezzar carried into exile:

in the seventh year, 3,023 Jews;
29 in Nebuchadnezzar's eighteenth year,
832 people from Jerusalem;
30 in his twenty-third year,
745 Jews taken into exile by Nebuzaradan the commander of the imperial
guard.
There were 4,600 people in all.

Jehoiachin Released

31In the thirty-seventh year of the exile of
Jehoiachin king of Judah, in the year Evil-Me-
rodach[g] became king of Babylon, he released
Jehoiachin king of Judah and freed him from
prison on the twenty-fifth day of the twelfth
month. 32He spoke kindly to him and gave
him a seat of honor higher than those of the

[a]7 Or *Chaldeans*; also in verse 17 [b]7 Or *the Jordan Valley* [c]8 Or *Chaldean*; also in verse 14 [d]15 Or *populace* [e]21 That is, about 27 feet (about 8.1 meters) high and 18 feet (about 5.4 meters) in circumference [f]22 That is, about 7 1/2 feet (about 2.3 meters) [g]31 Also called *Amel-Marduk*

other kings who were with him in Babylon.
33So Jehoiachin put aside his prison clothes
and for the rest of his life ate regularly at the
king's table. 34Day by day the king of Babylon
gave Jehoiachin a regular allowance as long as
he lived, till the day of his death.

Lamentations

Author:
Anonymous (possibly Jeremiah).

Audience:
All who mourned Jerusalem's destruction.

Date:
Shortly after the fall of Jerusalem in 586 B.C.

Setting:
The Babylonians had destroyed God's holy city of Jerusalem. Those who weren't killed or tortured were taken as prisoners.

Verse to Remember:
How deserted lies the city, once so full of people! How like a widow is she, who once was great among the nations! She who was queen among the provinces has now become a slave. (1:1)

Jerusalem has been destroyed. The beautiful city with its glorious temple representing God's presence has been nearly leveled, with most of its people killed or taken prisoner. The few people left in the city are destitute, hopeless and frightened.

The book of Lamentations is a series of poems—five stanzas of 22 or 66 verses each. Each poem is a lament, and in chapter 5, the climax of the book, *all joy is gone,* and the author pleads for God to return to his people. Other places in Scripture make clear that *God shared the sorrow* of his prophets and his people as they lamented the destruction of Jerusalem and the hard times its people were facing.

1 [a] How deserted lies the city,
once so full of people!
How like a widow is she,
who once was great among the nations!
She who was queen among the provinces
has now become a slave.

2 Bitterly she weeps at night,
tears are upon her cheeks.
Among all her lovers
there is none to comfort her.
All her friends have betrayed her;
they have become her enemies.

[a] This chapter is an acrostic poem, the verses of which begin with the successive letters of the Hebrew alphabet.

3 After affliction and harsh labor,
Judah has gone into exile.
She dwells among the nations;
she finds no resting place.
All who pursue her have overtaken her
in the midst of her distress.

4 The roads to Zion mourn,
for no one comes to her appointed feasts.
All her gateways are desolate,
her priests groan,
her maidens grieve,
and she is in bitter anguish.

5 Her foes have become her masters;
her enemies are at ease.
The LORD has brought her grief
because of her many sins.
Her children have gone into exile,
captive before the foe.

6 All the splendor has departed
from the Daughter of Zion.
Her princes are like deer
that find no pasture;
in weakness they have fled
before the pursuer.

7 In the days of her affliction and wandering
Jerusalem remembers all the treasures
that were hers in days of old.
When her people fell into enemy hands,
there was no one to help her.
Her enemies looked at her
and laughed at her destruction.

8 Jerusalem has sinned greatly
and so has become unclean.
All who honored her despise her,
for they have seen her nakedness;
she herself groans
and turns away.

9 Her filthiness clung to her skirts;
she did not consider her future.
Her fall was astounding;
there was none to comfort her.
"Look, O LORD, on my affliction,
for the enemy has triumphed."

10 The enemy laid hands
on all her treasures;
she saw pagan nations
enter her sanctuary—
those you had forbidden
to enter your assembly.

11 All her people groan
as they search for bread;
they barter their treasures for food
to keep themselves alive.
"Look, O LORD, and consider,
for I am despised."

12 "Is it nothing to you, all you who pass by?
Look around and see.
Is any suffering like my suffering
that was inflicted on me,
that the LORD brought on me
in the day of his fierce anger?

13 "From on high he sent fire,
sent it down into my bones.
He spread a net for my feet
and turned me back.
He made me desolate,
faint all the day long.

14 "My sins have been bound into a yoke[a];
by his hands they were woven together.
They have come upon my neck
and the Lord has sapped my strength.
He has handed me over
to those I cannot withstand.

15 "The Lord has rejected
all the warriors in my midst;
he has summoned an army against me
to[b] crush my young men.
In his winepress the Lord has trampled
the Virgin Daughter of Judah.

16 "This is why I weep
and my eyes overflow with tears.
No one is near to comfort me,
no one to restore my spirit.
My children are destitute
because the enemy has prevailed."

17 Zion stretches out her hands,
but there is no one to comfort her.
The LORD has decreed for Jacob
that his neighbors become his foes;
Jerusalem has become
an unclean thing among them.

[a] 14 Most Hebrew manuscripts; Septuagint *He kept watch over my sins* [b] 15 Or *has set a time for me / when he will*

Brought to Grief

Read: Lamentations 1:1–11

Lamentations 1:5

The LORD has brought her grief because of her many sins.

CAROL DIDN'T WANT to believe her daughter's news.

Rachel had always been a good kid who went to church every Sunday. She had vowed to remain sexually pure until marriage. She didn't even have a boyfriend. So Carol was surprised when Rachel called from a friend's house at 3:00 A.M. in tears. In between her sobs, it sounded as if Rachel said she was pregnant.

Carol felt a rush of feelings all at once—disbelief, fear, anger, helplessness. All she could do for the moment was cry with her daughter. And just as Rachel had to face the consequences of her sin, so did her mother. Grief overwhelmed them both.

In Lamentations, Jeremiah felt overwhelmed too. He wept over the consequences of Judah's sin. The Babylonian army destroyed the beautiful temple, killed most of the people of Jerusalem and captured the rest. Jeremiah groaned over the people's suffering and their broken relationship with God. He longed for them to repent, so God would restore them.

Likewise, Carol, with lots of tears, prayed for her daughter's restoration to God. The road seemed long at the time, but she kept praying. When finally Rachel's selfish tears turned into repentance, God welcomed her warmly. He lavished forgiveness upon her and began to bless her obedience.

Carol walked her own journey with God during those tough nine months, and she came out of it with a new ministry. She now volunteers each week with the local Crisis Pregnancy Center where she gives practical and spiritual help to young women just like Rachel.

While sin brings regret and consequences we cannot change, God is still good. He forgives us, restores us and renews us in ways we never thought possible.

reflection

1. When was the last time you wept over sin—in your life or in the lives of others?
2. Why does grief accompany sin?
3. Is there a friend or family member who needs your prayers? How can you pray for them? How can you help them in their grief?

RELATED READINGS

Psalm 30:4–5; Jeremiah 13:16–17; 29:11–14; Joel 2:25–26; Micah 7:18–20; 1 John 1:8–9

Go to page 986 for your next devotional reading.

18 "The LORD is righteous,
yet I rebelled against his command.
Listen, all you peoples;
look upon my suffering.
My young men and maidens
have gone into exile.

19 "I called to my allies
but they betrayed me.
My priests and my elders
perished in the city
while they searched for food
to keep themselves alive.

20 "See, O LORD, how
distressed I am!
I am in torment within,
and in my heart I am
disturbed,
for I have been most
rebellious.
Outside, the sword
bereaves;
inside, there is only
death.

21 "People have heard my
groaning,
but there is no one to comfort me.
All my enemies have heard of my distress;
they rejoice at what you have done.
May you bring the day you have announced
so they may become like me.

22 "Let all their wickedness come before you;
deal with them
as you have dealt with me
because of all my sins.
My groans are many
and my heart is faint."

Lamentations 1:20

God Sees Affliction

"See, O LORD, how
distressed I am!
I am in torment within,
and in my heart
I am disturbed."

2

[a] How the Lord has covered the
Daughter of Zion
with the cloud of his anger[b]!
He has hurled down the splendor of Israel
from heaven to earth;
he has not remembered his footstool
in the day of his anger.

2 Without pity the Lord has swallowed up
all the dwellings of Jacob;
in his wrath he has torn down
the strongholds of the Daughter of
Judah.
He has brought her kingdom and its
princes
down to the ground in dishonor.

3 In fierce anger he has cut off
every horn[c] of Israel.
He has withdrawn his right hand
at the approach of the enemy.
He has burned in Jacob
like a flaming fire
that consumes
everything around
it.

4 Like an enemy he has
strung his bow;
his right hand is ready.
Like a foe he has slain
all who were pleasing to
the eye;
he has poured out his
wrath like fire
on the tent of the
Daughter of Zion.

5 The Lord is like an enemy;
he has swallowed up Israel.
He has swallowed up all her palaces
and destroyed her strongholds.
He has multiplied mourning and
lamentation
for the Daughter of Judah.

6 He has laid waste his dwelling like a
garden;
he has destroyed his place of meeting.
The LORD has made Zion forget
her appointed feasts and her Sabbaths;
in his fierce anger he has spurned
both king and priest.

7 The Lord has rejected his altar
and abandoned his sanctuary.
He has handed over to the enemy
the walls of her palaces;
they have raised a shout in the house of the
LORD
as on the day of an appointed feast.

[a] This chapter is an acrostic poem, the verses of which begin with the successive letters of the Hebrew alphabet. [b] 1 Or *How the Lord in his anger / has treated the Daughter of Zion with contempt* [c] 3 Or / *all the strength*; or *every king*; *horn* here symbolizes strength.

8 The LORD determined to tear down
the wall around the Daughter of Zion.
He stretched out a measuring line
and did not withhold his hand from destroying.
He made ramparts and walls lament;
together they wasted away.

9 Her gates have sunk into the ground;
their bars he has broken and destroyed.
Her king and her princes are exiled among the nations,
the law is no more,
and her prophets no longer find
visions from the LORD.

10 The elders of the Daughter of Zion
sit on the ground in silence;
they have sprinkled dust on their heads
and put on sackcloth.
The young women of Jerusalem
have bowed their heads to the ground.

11 My eyes fail from weeping,
I am in torment within,
my heart is poured out on the ground
because my people are destroyed,
because children and infants faint
in the streets of the city.

12 They say to their mothers,
"Where is bread and wine?"
as they faint like wounded men
in the streets of the city,
as their lives ebb away
in their mothers' arms.

13 What can I say for you?
With what can I compare you,
O Daughter of Jerusalem?
To what can I liken you,
that I may comfort you,
O Virgin Daughter of Zion?
Your wound is as deep as the sea.
Who can heal you?

14 The visions of your prophets
were false and worthless;
they did not expose your sin
to ward off your captivity.
The oracles they gave you
were false and misleading.

15 All who pass your way
clap their hands at you;
they scoff and shake their heads
at the Daughter of Jerusalem:
"Is this the city that was called
the perfection of beauty,
the joy of the whole earth?"

16 All your enemies open their mouths
wide against you;
they scoff and gnash their teeth
and say, "We have swallowed her up.
This is the day we have waited for;
we have lived to see it."

17 The LORD has done what he planned;
he has fulfilled his word,
which he decreed long ago.
He has overthrown you without pity,
he has let the enemy gloat over you,
he has exalted the horn[a] of your foes.

18 The hearts of the people
cry out to the Lord.
O wall of the Daughter of Zion,
let your tears flow like a river
day and night;
give yourself no relief,
your eyes no rest.

19 Arise, cry out in the night,
as the watches of the night begin;
pour out your heart like water
in the presence of the Lord.
Lift up your hands to him
for the lives of your children,
who faint from hunger
at the head of every street.

Lamentations 2:17

God Does As He Planned

The LORD has done what he planned;
he has fulfilled his word,
which he decreed long ago.

[a]17 *Horn* here symbolizes strength.

20 “Look, O LORD, and consider:
Whom have you ever treated like this?
Should women eat their offspring,
the children they have cared for?
Should priest and prophet be killed
in the sanctuary of the Lord?

21 “Young and old lie together
in the dust of the streets;
my young men and maidens
have fallen by the sword.
You have slain them in the day of your anger;
you have slaughtered them without pity.

22 “As you summon to a feast day,
so you summoned against me terrors on every side.
In the day of the LORD’s anger
no one escaped or survived;
those I cared for and reared,
my enemy has destroyed.”

3

3[a] I am the man who has seen affliction
by the rod of his wrath.
2 He has driven me away and made me walk
in darkness rather than light;
3 indeed, he has turned his hand against me
again and again, all day long.
4 He has made my skin and my flesh grow old
and has broken my bones.
5 He has besieged me and surrounded me
with bitterness and hardship.
6 He has made me dwell in darkness
like those long dead.

Lamentations 3:22

God Has Unfailing Compassion

Because of the LORD’s great love we are not consumed, for his compassions never fail.

7 He has walled me in so I cannot escape;
he has weighed me down with chains.
8 Even when I call out or cry for help,
he shuts out my prayer.
9 He has barred my way with blocks of stone;
he has made my paths crooked.

10 Like a bear lying in wait,
like a lion in hiding,
11 he dragged me from the path and mangled me
and left me without help.
12 He drew his bow
and made me the target for his arrows.

13 He pierced my heart
with arrows from his quiver.
14 I became the laughingstock of all my people;
they mock me in song all day long.
15 He has filled me with bitter herbs
and sated me with gall.

16 He has broken my teeth with gravel;
he has trampled me in the dust.
17 I have been deprived of peace;
I have forgotten what prosperity is.
18 So I say, “My splendor is gone
and all that I had hoped from the LORD.”

19 I remember my affliction and my wandering,
the bitterness and the gall.
20 I well remember them,
and my soul is downcast within me.
21 Yet this I call to mind
and therefore I have hope:

22 Because of the LORD’s great love we are not consumed,
for his compassions never fail.
23 They are new every morning;
great is your faithfulness.
24 I say to myself, “The LORD is my portion;
therefore I will wait for him.”

25 The LORD is good to those whose hope is in him,
to the one who seeks him;
26 it is good to wait quietly
for the salvation of the LORD.
27 It is good for a man to bear the yoke
while he is young.

[a] This chapter is an acrostic poem; the verses of each stanza begin with the successive letters of the Hebrew alphabet, and the verses within each stanza begin with the same letter.

A Fresh Start

Read: Lamentations 3:21–51

STARTING OVER. It's the second chance we didn't think we'd have. It's a wave of relief that washes over our past mistakes. It is a gift from God we don't deserve.

In the book of Lamentations, the prophet Jeremiah looks back at the destruction of Jerusalem. God promised that his people would face punishment for their sinful choices, and he was true to his word. Their city had been ravaged, and they were now living in exile. The temple was completely destroyed.

In the midst of Jeremiah's lament, however, he remembers the mercy of God. Were it not for God's mercy, every one of God's people would have perished. The judgment on them was painful, but God would not leave them ruined. Eventually, after they acknowledged their disobedience and confessed their sin, God would forgive and restore them. He would allow them to start over once more. And he does the same for us.

Maybe you have experienced the discipline of God in your own life. You have suffered painful consequences for sinful choices you have made. Perhaps you feel that God has left you there. If so, remember that although God is just, he is also full of mercy. His compassions never fail. He promises to forgive us when we come to him and confess what we have done or not done. No matter how you have offended God, you can have hope because of his great mercy. You can always have a fresh start with him because his compassions are "new every morning."

Take some time to thank God for the specific ways he has acted mercifully toward you. Thank him for forgiving your sin. Express gratitude to him for actively restoring you. You may even want to sing or pray the words to the hymn, "Great Is Thy Faithfulness":

> "Pardon for sin and a peace that endureth
> Thine own dear presence to cheer and to guide;
> Strength for today and bright hope for tomorrow,
> Blessings all mine, with ten thousand beside!"

Lamentations 3:21–23

Yet this I call to mind and therefore I have hope: Because of the LORD's great love we are not consumed, for his compassions never fail. They are new every morning; great is your faithfulness.

reflection

1 Recall a time in your life when you experienced God's discipline for disobedient choices. How did you feel?

2 When you disobey God, do you quickly respond with repentance and confession? Why or why not?

3 In what way have you experienced the ever-new compassion of God?

RELATED READINGS

Jeremiah 3:12–13; Zechariah 10:6; Luke 15:3–24

Go to page 992 for your next devotional reading.

28 Let him sit alone in silence,
for the LORD has laid it on him.
29 Let him bury his face in the dust—
there may yet be hope.
30 Let him offer his cheek to one who would strike him,
and let him be filled with disgrace.

31 For men are not cast off
by the Lord forever.
32 Though he brings grief, he will show compassion,
so great is his unfailing love.
33 For he does not willingly bring affliction
or grief to the children of men.

34 To crush underfoot
all prisoners in the land,
35 to deny a man his rights
before the Most High,
36 to deprive a man of justice—
would not the Lord see such things?

37 Who can speak and have it happen
if the Lord has not decreed it?
38 Is it not from the mouth of the Most High
that both calamities and good things come?
39 Why should any living man complain
when punished for his sins?

40 Let us examine our ways and test them,
and let us return to the LORD.
41 Let us lift up our hearts and our hands
to God in heaven, and say:
42 "We have sinned and rebelled
and you have not forgiven.

43 "You have covered yourself with anger and pursued us;
you have slain without pity.
44 You have covered yourself with a cloud
so that no prayer can get through.
45 You have made us scum and refuse
among the nations.

46 "All our enemies have opened their mouths
wide against us.
47 We have suffered terror and pitfalls,
ruin and destruction."
48 Streams of tears flow from my eyes
because my people are destroyed.

49 My eyes will flow unceasingly,
without relief,
50 until the LORD looks down
from heaven and sees.
51 What I see brings grief to my soul
because of all the women of my city.

52 Those who were my enemies without cause
hunted me like a bird.
53 They tried to end my life in a pit
and threw stones at me;
54 the waters closed over my head,
and I thought I was about to be cut off.

55 I called on your name, O LORD,
from the depths of the pit.
56 You heard my plea: "Do not close your ears
to my cry for relief."
57 You came near when I called you,
and you said, "Do not fear."

58 O Lord, you took up my case;
you redeemed my life.
59 You have seen, O LORD, the wrong done to me.
Uphold my cause!
60 You have seen the depth of their vengeance,
all their plots against me.

61 O LORD, you have heard their insults,
all their plots against me—
62 what my enemies whisper and mutter
against me all day long.
63 Look at them! Sitting or standing,
they mock me in their songs.

64 Pay them back what they deserve, O LORD,
for what their hands have done.
65 Put a veil over their hearts,
and may your curse be on them!
66 Pursue them in anger and destroy them
from under the heavens of the LORD.

4 [a] How the gold has lost its luster,
the fine gold become dull!
The sacred gems are scattered
at the head of every street.

2 How the precious sons of Zion,
once worth their weight in gold,

[a]This chapter is an acrostic poem, the verses of which begin with the successive letters of the Hebrew alphabet.

are now considered as pots of clay,
the work of a potter's hands!

3 Even jackals offer their breasts
to nurse their young,
but my people have become heartless
like ostriches in the desert.

4 Because of thirst the infant's tongue
sticks to the roof of its mouth;
the children beg for bread,
but no one gives it to them.

5 Those who once ate delicacies
are destitute in the streets.
Those nurtured in purple
now lie on ash heaps.

6 The punishment of my people
is greater than that of Sodom,
which was overthrown in a moment
without a hand turned to help her.

7 Their princes were brighter than snow
and whiter than milk,
their bodies more ruddy than rubies,
their appearance like sapphires.[a]

8 But now they are blacker than soot;
they are not recognized in the streets.
Their skin has shriveled on their bones;
it has become as dry as a stick.

9 Those killed by the sword are better off
than those who die of famine;
racked with hunger, they waste away
for lack of food from the field.

10 With their own hands compassionate
women
have cooked their own children,
who became their food
when my people were destroyed.

11 The LORD has given full vent to his wrath;
he has poured out his fierce anger.
He kindled a fire in Zion
that consumed her foundations.

12 The kings of the earth did not believe,
nor did any of the world's people,
that enemies and foes could enter
the gates of Jerusalem.

13 But it happened because of the sins of her
prophets
and the iniquities of her priests,
who shed within her
the blood of the righteous.

14 Now they grope through the streets
like men who are blind.
They are so defiled with blood
that no one dares to touch their
garments.

15 "Go away! You are unclean!" men cry to
them.
"Away! Away! Don't touch us!"
When they flee and wander about,
people among the nations say,
"They can stay here no longer."

16 The LORD himself has scattered them;
he no longer watches over them.
The priests are shown no honor,
the elders no favor.

17 Moreover, our eyes failed,
looking in vain for help;
from our towers we watched
for a nation that could not save us.

18 Men stalked us at every step,
so we could not walk in our streets.
Our end was near, our days were
numbered,
for our end had come.

19 Our pursuers were swifter
than eagles in the sky;
they chased us over the mountains
and lay in wait for us in the desert.

20 The LORD's anointed, our very life breath,
was caught in their traps.
We thought that under his shadow
we would live among the nations.

21 Rejoice and be glad, O Daughter of Edom,
you who live in the land of Uz.
But to you also the cup will be passed;
you will be drunk and stripped naked.

22 O Daughter of Zion, your punishment will
end;
he will not prolong your exile.

[a]7 Or *lapis lazuli*

But, O Daughter of Edom, he will punish
your sin
and expose your wickedness.

5 Remember, O LORD, what has happened
to us;
look, and see our disgrace.
2 Our inheritance has been turned over to
aliens,
our homes to foreigners.
3 We have become orphans and fatherless,
our mothers like widows.
4 We must buy the water we drink;
our wood can be had only at a price.
5 Those who pursue us are at our heels;
we are weary and find no rest.
6 We submitted to Egypt and
Assyria
to get enough bread.
7 Our fathers sinned and are
no more,
and we bear their
punishment.
8 Slaves rule over us,
and there is none to free
us from their hands.
9 We get our bread at the risk
of our lives
because of the sword in
the desert.
10 Our skin is hot as an oven,
feverish from hunger.
11 Women have been ravished in Zion,
and virgins in the towns of Judah.
12 Princes have been hung up by their hands;
elders are shown no respect.
13 Young men toil at the millstones;
boys stagger under loads of wood.
14 The elders are gone from the city gate;
the young men have stopped their
music.
15 Joy is gone from our hearts;
our dancing has turned to mourning.
16 The crown has fallen from our head.
Woe to us, for we have sinned!
17 Because of this our hearts are faint,
because of these things our eyes grow
dim
18 for Mount Zion, which lies desolate,
with jackals prowling
over it.
19 You, O LORD, reign
forever;
your throne endures
from generation to
generation.
20 Why do you always forget
us?
Why do you forsake us
so long?
21 Restore us to yourself,
O LORD, that we
may return;
renew our days as of old
22 unless you have utterly rejected us
and are angry with us beyond measure.

> **Lamentations 5:21**
>
> *God Can Restore Us*
>
> Restore us to yourself,
> O LORD, that we
> may return;
> renew our days as of old.

Ezekiel

Author: Ezekiel.

Audience: Ezekiel's fellow Jewish exiles in Babylon.

Date: Between 593 and 571 B.C.

Setting: The priest Ezekiel prophesied to his fellow Jews, who were taken as prisoners to Babylon in 597 B.C.

Verse to Remember: "I will give you a new heart and put a new spirit in you; I will remove from you your heart of stone and give you a heart of flesh." (36:26)

Throughout Israel's recorded history in the Old Testament, *God outlined the way to blessing.* But he also outlined the consequences that would result from disobedience. Enter Ezekiel. Ezekiel was a prophet who warned God's people of their impending judgment, often using creative and stark analogies. At the same time, he spoke of hope for the future restoration of Israel. He described a time when the people's hard hearts would be softened and God's Spirit would dwell within them.

From the first chapter of Ezekiel until the last, we see *portraits of the sovereignty of God.* He is in control over nature, people and history. At least 65 times in this one book, God says, "Then they will know that I am the LORD." He did not orchestrate the fall of Jerusalem, the destruction of the temple or the judgment of the nations without an end result in mind. His glory and honor are always at stake. What a joy as we turn the final pages of this book of judgment to see that *a plan for deliverance is always in God's mind*—a plan of ultimate revival, redemption and restoration.

The Living Creatures and the Glory of the LORD

1 In the[a] thirtieth year, in the fourth month
on the fifth day, while I was among the
exiles by the Kebar River, the heavens were
opened and I saw visions of God.
2On the fifth of the month—it was the fifth
year of the exile of King Jehoiachin— 3the word
of the LORD came to Ezekiel the priest, the son
of Buzi,[b] by the Kebar River in the land of the
Babylonians.[c] There the hand of the LORD was
upon him.

[a]1 Or ⌊my⌋ [b]3 Or *Ezekiel son of Buzi the priest* [c]3 Or *Chaldeans*

4 I looked, and I saw a windstorm coming
out of the north—an immense cloud with flashing lightning and surrounded by brilliant light.
The center of the fire looked like glowing metal,
5 and in the fire was what looked like four living
creatures. In appearance their form was that of
a man, 6 but each of them had four faces and
four wings. 7 Their legs were straight; their feet
were like those of a calf and gleamed like burnished bronze. 8 Under their wings on their
four sides they had the hands of a man. All four
of them had faces and wings, 9 and their wings
touched one another. Each one went straight
ahead; they did not turn as they moved.
10 Their faces looked like this: Each of the
four had the face of a man, and on the right
side each had the face of a lion, and on the
left the face of an ox; each also had the face of
an eagle. 11 Such were their faces. Their wings
were spread out upward; each had two wings,
one touching the wing of another creature on
either side, and two wings covering its body.
12 Each one went straight ahead. Wherever the
spirit would go, they would go, without turning
as they went. 13 The appearance of the living
creatures was like burning coals of fire or like
torches. Fire moved back and forth among the
creatures; it was bright, and lightning flashed
out of it. 14 The creatures sped back and forth
like flashes of lightning.
15 As I looked at the living creatures, I saw
a wheel on the ground beside each creature
with its four faces. 16 This was the appearance
and structure of the wheels: They sparkled like
chrysolite, and all four looked alike. Each appeared to be made like a wheel intersecting a
wheel. 17 As they moved, they would go in any
one of the four directions the creatures faced;
the wheels did not turn about[a] as the creatures
went. 18 Their rims were high and awesome,
and all four rims were full of eyes all around.
19 When the living creatures moved, the
wheels beside them moved; and when the living creatures rose from the ground, the wheels
also rose. 20 Wherever the spirit would go, they
would go, and the wheels would rise along
with them, because the spirit of the living creatures was in the wheels. 21 When the creatures
moved, they also moved; when the creatures
stood still, they also stood still; and when the
creatures rose from the ground, the wheels rose
along with them, because the spirit of the living
creatures was in the wheels.
22 Spread out above the heads of the living
creatures was what looked like an expanse,
sparkling like ice, and awesome. 23 Under the
expanse their wings were stretched out one
toward the other, and each had two wings covering its body. 24 When the creatures moved, I
heard the sound of their wings, like the roar of
rushing waters, like the voice of the Almighty,[b]
like the tumult of an army. When they stood
still, they lowered their wings.
25 Then there came a voice from above the
expanse over their heads as they stood with
lowered wings. 26 Above the expanse over
their heads was what looked like a throne of
sapphire,[c] and high above on the throne was
a figure like that of a man. 27 I saw that from
what appeared to be his waist up he looked like
glowing metal, as if full of fire, and that from
there down he looked like fire; and brilliant
light surrounded him. 28 Like the appearance
of a rainbow in the clouds on a rainy day, so
was the radiance around him.
This was the appearance of the likeness of
the glory of the LORD. When I saw it, I fell facedown, and I heard the voice of one speaking.

Ezekiel's Call

2 He said to me, "Son of man, stand up on
your feet and I will speak to you." 2 As he
spoke, the Spirit came into me and raised me to
my feet, and I heard him speaking to me.
3 He said: "Son of man, I am sending you to
the Israelites, to a rebellious nation that has rebelled against me; they and their fathers have
been in revolt against me to this very day. 4 The
people to whom I am sending you are obstinate and stubborn. Say to them, 'This is what
the Sovereign LORD says.' 5 And whether they
listen or fail to listen—for they are a rebellious
house—they will know that a prophet has been
among them. 6 And you, son of man, do not be
afraid of them or their words. Do not be afraid,
though briers and thorns are all around you
and you live among scorpions. Do not be afraid
of what they say or terrified by them, though

[a]17 Or *aside* [b]24 Hebrew *Shaddai* [c]26 Or *lapis lazuli*

Wild Inspiration

Read: Ezekiel 1:1–28

Ezekiel 1:28

Like the appearance of a rainbow in the clouds on a rainy day, so was the radiance around him. This was the appearance of the likeness of the glory of the LORD. When I saw it, I fell facedown, and I heard the voice of one speaking.

DO YOU EVER READ Bible passages and just scratch your head in confusion? For most non-scholarly Bible readers, the book of Ezekiel is chock-full of kaleidoscopic visions that seem more like *Star Wars* than Scripture. After reading Ezekiel 1, can you imagine what fun Hollywood would have in creating their rendition of this scene? Even animatronics wizards might struggle to come up with a four-winged human being with four faces (that of a man, lion, ox and eagle)—on wheels, no less. God is, indeed, more creative than any human being's imagination.

Why would God give this wild vision to Ezekiel?

The answer might have to do with inspiration. It seems that what enabled the prophet Ezekiel and his contemporaries to press on in their difficult ministries was a powerful, majestic vision of God. Ezekiel's particular vision left an indelible impression: God was the absolute Sovereign over all of creation and history. The prophet would remember this one-of-a-kind experience and return to it all of his life.

Ezekiel could describe the cherubim in this vision with great detail. However, when he saw "the appearance of the likeness of the glory of the LORD," he groped for words and ultimately could not respond. He could only fall facedown—awestruck by God's holiness and glory.

Ezekiel, like most Biblical prophets, endured his share of shame and often appeared foolish to his contemporaries. He did not have a dream job . . . so he needed a vision. His visions of God sustained, encouraged, strengthened and directed him in an otherwise difficult and thankless task.

What is your vision of God? What keeps you staying with the job God has called you to do? Is your motivation based on who God has revealed himself to be? Whatever your task today, dare to ask the wild, holy, Sovereign God of Ezekiel to reveal his majesty to encourage and strengthen you.

reflection

1. Do you ever feel uninspired and unrewarded in your ministry, task or job?
2. Where do you usually look for motivation?
3. How has God revealed himself to you in a way that has strengthened and encouraged you?

RELATED READINGS

Isaiah 6:1–13; Ezekiel 3:22–23; 8:1–4; 10:3–5; Acts 9:1–9; 2 Corinthians 12:2–6

"God is compelled to conceal himself in a measure from the natural world, for the divine illumination would blind the eyes of mortal man were it to shine upon him in full strength."

L. S. Thornton

Go to page 996 for your next devotional reading.

they are a rebellious house. 7You must speak
my words to them, whether they listen or fail
to listen, for they are rebellious. 8But you, son
of man, listen to what I say to you. Do not rebel like that rebellious house; open your mouth
and eat what I give you."
9Then I looked, and I saw a hand stretched
out to me. In it was a scroll, 10which he un-
rolled before me. On both sides of it were written words of lament and mourning and woe.

3 And he said to me, "Son of man, eat what
is before you, eat this scroll; then go and
speak to the house of Israel." 2So I opened my
mouth, and he gave me the scroll to eat.
3Then he said to me, "Son of man, eat
this scroll I am giving you and fill your stomach with it." So I ate it, and it
tasted as sweet as honey in
my mouth.
4He then said to me: "Son
of man, go now to the house of
Israel and speak my words to
them. 5You are not being sent
to a people of obscure speech
and difficult language, but
to the house of Israel— 6not
to many peoples of obscure
speech and difficult language,
whose words you cannot understand. Surely if I had sent
you to them, they would have
listened to you. 7But the house
of Israel is not willing to listen
to you because they are not
willing to listen to me, for the
whole house of Israel is hard-
ened and obstinate. 8But I will make you as unyielding and hardened as they are. 9I will make
your forehead like the hardest stone, harder
than flint. Do not be afraid of them or terrified
by them, though they are a rebellious house."
10And he said to me, "Son of man, listen
carefully and take to heart all the words I speak
to you. 11Go now to your countrymen in exile
and speak to them. Say to them, 'This is what
the Sovereign LORD says,' whether they listen
or fail to listen."
12Then the Spirit lifted me up, and I heard
behind me a loud rumbling sound—May the
glory of the LORD be praised in his dwelling
place!— 13the sound of the wings of the living
creatures brushing against each other and the
sound of the wheels beside them, a loud rumbling sound. 14The Spirit then lifted me up and
took me away, and I went in bitterness and in
the anger of my spirit, with the strong hand of
the LORD upon me. 15I came to the exiles who
lived at Tel Abib near the Kebar River. And
there, where they were living, I sat among them
for seven days—overwhelmed.

Ezekiel 3:18

God Holds Us Accountable

"When I say to a wicked man, 'You will surely die,' and you do not warn him or speak out to dissuade him from his evil ways in order to save his life, that wicked man will die for his sin, and I will hold you accountable."

Warning to Israel

16At the end of seven days the word of the
LORD came to me: 17"Son of man, I have made
you a watchman for the house of Israel; so hear
the word I speak and give them
warning from me. 18When
I say to a wicked man, 'You
will surely die,' and you do not
warn him or speak out to dissuade him from his evil ways
in order to save his life, that
wicked man will die for[a] his
sin, and I will hold you accountable for his blood. 19But if you
do warn the wicked man and
he does not turn from his wickedness or from his evil ways, he
will die for his sin; but you will
have saved yourself.
20"Again, when a righteous
man turns from his righteousness and does evil, and I put a
stumbling block before him, he
will die. Since you did not warn
him, he will die for his sin. The righteous things
he did will not be remembered, and I will hold
you accountable for his blood. 21But if you do
warn the righteous man not to sin and he does
not sin, he will surely live because he took warning, and you will have saved yourself."
22The hand of the LORD was upon me there,
and he said to me, "Get up and go out to the
plain, and there I will speak to you." 23So I got
up and went out to the plain. And the glory
of the LORD was standing there, like the glory
I had seen by the Kebar River, and I fell facedown.

[a]18 Or *in*; also in verses 19 and 20

24Then the Spirit came into me and raised
me to my feet. He spoke to me and said: "Go,
shut yourself inside your house. 25And you,
son of man, they will tie with ropes; you will
be bound so that you cannot go out among the
people. 26I will make your tongue stick to the
roof of your mouth so that you will be silent
and unable to rebuke them, though they are a
rebellious house. 27But when I speak to you,
I will open your mouth and you shall say to
them, 'This is what the Sovereign LORD says.'
Whoever will listen let him listen, and whoever
will refuse let him refuse; for they are a rebellious house.

Siege of Jerusalem Symbolized

4 "Now, son of man, take a clay tablet, put
it in front of you and draw the city of Jerusalem on it. 2Then lay siege to it: Erect siege
works against it, build a ramp up to it, set up
camps against it and put battering rams around
it. 3Then take an iron pan, place it as an iron
wall between you and the city and turn your
face toward it. It will be under siege, and you
shall besiege it. This will be a sign to the house
of Israel.

4"Then lie on your left side and put the sin
of the house of Israel upon yourself.[a] You are
to bear their sin for the number of days you
lie on your side. 5I have assigned you the same
number of days as the years of their sin. So for
390 days you will bear the sin of the house of
Israel.

6"After you have finished this, lie down
again, this time on your right side, and bear
the sin of the house of Judah. I have assigned
you 40 days, a day for each year. 7Turn your
face toward the siege of Jerusalem and with
bared arm prophesy against her. 8I will tie you
up with ropes so that you cannot turn from
one side to the other until you have finished
the days of your siege.

9"Take wheat and barley, beans and lentils,
millet and spelt; put them in a storage jar and
use them to make bread for yourself. You are to
eat it during the 390 days you lie on your side.
10Weigh out twenty shekels[b] of food to eat each
day and eat it at set times. 11Also measure out a
sixth of a hin[c] of water and drink it at set times.
12Eat the food as you would a barley cake; bake
it in the sight of the people, using human excrement for fuel." 13The LORD said, "In this way
the people of Israel will eat defiled food among
the nations where I will drive them."

14Then I said, "Not so, Sovereign LORD! I
have never defiled myself. From my youth until now I have never eaten anything found dead
or torn by wild animals. No unclean meat has
ever entered my mouth."

15"Very well," he said, "I will let you bake
your bread over cow manure instead of human excrement."

16He then said to me: "Son of man, I will cut
off the supply of food in Jerusalem. The people
will eat rationed food in anxiety and drink rationed water in despair, 17for food and water
will be scarce. They will be appalled at the sight
of each other and will waste away because of[d]
their sin.

5 "Now, son of man, take a sharp sword
and use it as a barber's razor to shave your
head and your beard. Then take a set of scales
and divide up the hair. 2When the days of your
siege come to an end, burn a third of the hair
with fire inside the city. Take a third and strike
it with the sword all around the city. And scatter a third to the wind. For I will pursue them
with drawn sword. 3But take a few strands of
hair and tuck them away in the folds of your
garment. 4Again, take a few of these and throw
them into the fire and burn them up. A fire will
spread from there to the whole house of Israel.

5"This is what the Sovereign LORD says: This
is Jerusalem, which I have set in the center of
the nations, with countries all around her. 6Yet
in her wickedness she has rebelled against my
laws and decrees more than the nations and
countries around her. She has rejected my laws
and has not followed my decrees.

7"Therefore this is what the Sovereign LORD
says: You have been more unruly than the nations around you and have not followed my
decrees or kept my laws. You have not even[e]
conformed to the standards of the nations
around you.

8"Therefore this is what the Sovereign LORD
says: I myself am against you, Jerusalem, and

[a]4 Or *your side* [b]10 That is, about 8 ounces (about 0.2 kilogram) [c]11 That is, about 2/3 quart (about 0.6 liter) [d]17 Or *away in*
[e]7 Most Hebrew manuscripts; some Hebrew manuscripts and Syriac *You have*

I will inflict punishment on you in the sight
of the nations. 9Because of all your detestable
idols, I will do to you what I have never done
before and will never do again.
10Therefore in your midst fathers will eat their children,
and children will eat their fathers. I will inflict punishment
on you and will scatter all your
survivors to the winds. 11There-
fore as surely as I live, declares
the Sovereign LORD, because
you have defiled my sanctuary
with all your vile images and detestable practices, I myself will
withdraw my favor; I will not
look on you with pity or spare
you. 12A third of your people
will die of the plague or perish
by famine inside you; a third
will fall by the sword outside
your walls; and a third I will
scatter to the winds and pursue
with drawn sword.

> **Ezekiel 5:11**
>
> *God Can Withdraw Favor*
>
> "Therefore as surely as I live, declares the Sovereign LORD, because you have defiled my sanctuary with all your vile images and detestable practices, I myself will withdraw my favor; I will not look on you with pity or spare you."

13"Then my anger will cease and my wrath
against them will subside, and I will be avenged.
And when I have spent my wrath upon them,
they will know that I the LORD have spoken in
my zeal.
14"I will make you a ruin and a reproach
among the nations around you, in the sight of
all who pass by. 15You will be a reproach and a
taunt, a warning and an object of horror to the
nations around you when I inflict punishment
on you in anger and in wrath and with sting-
ing rebuke. I the LORD have spoken. 16When
I shoot at you with my deadly and destructive
arrows of famine, I will shoot to destroy you.
I will bring more and more famine upon you
and cut off your supply of food. 17I will send
famine and wild beasts against you, and they
will leave you childless. Plague and bloodshed
will sweep through you, and I will bring the
sword against you. I the LORD have spoken."

A Prophecy Against the Mountains of Israel

6 The word of the LORD came to me: 2"Son
of man, set your face against the mountains of Israel; prophesy against them 3and
say: 'O mountains of Israel, hear the word of
the Sovereign LORD. This is what the Sovereign LORD says to the mountains and hills, to
the ravines and valleys: I am about to bring a
sword against you, and I will destroy your high
places. 4Your altars will be demolished and your incense
altars will be smashed; and I
will slay your people in front of
your idols. 5I will lay the dead
bodies of the Israelites in front
of their idols, and I will scatter
your bones around your altars.
6Wherever you live, the towns
will be laid waste and the high
places demolished, so that your
altars will be laid waste and
devastated, your idols smashed
and ruined, your incense altars
broken down, and what you
have made wiped out. 7Your
people will fall slain among
you, and you will know that I
am the LORD.
8"'But I will spare some, for
some of you will escape the
sword when you are scattered among the lands
and nations. 9Then in the nations where they
have been carried captive, those who escape
will remember me—how I have been grieved
by their adulterous hearts, which have turned
away from me, and by their eyes, which have
lusted after their idols. They will loathe themselves for the evil they have done and for all
their detestable practices. 10And they will
know that I am the LORD; I did not threaten in
vain to bring this calamity on them.
11"'This is what the Sovereign LORD says:
Strike your hands together and stamp your feet
and cry out "Alas!" because of all the wicked and
detestable practices of the house of Israel, for
they will fall by the sword, famine and plague.
12He that is far away will die of the plague, and
he that is near will fall by the sword, and he
that survives and is spared will die of famine.
So will I spend my wrath upon them. 13And
they will know that I am the LORD, when their
people lie slain among their idols around their
altars, on every high hill and on all the mountaintops, under every spreading tree and every
leafy oak—places where they offered fragrant
incense to all their idols. 14And I will stretch

Renewal by Fire

Read: Ezekiel 6:1–14

Ezekiel 6:6

"Wherever you live, the towns will be laid waste and the high places demolished, so that your altars will be laid waste and devastated, your idols smashed and ruined, your incense altars broken down, and what you have made wiped out."

reflection

1 How about you? Do you have deadwood accumulating in your soul that needs God's renewing discipline?

2 Why is God's discipline a sign of his love?

3 How will you praise God for his "controlled burning" in your life?

RELATED READINGS

Exodus 32:1–35; Judges 3:7–14; Jeremiah 44:1–30; Hebrews 12:4–11

NEARLY EIGHT MILLION ACRES of forest area burned across America in 2004. In the past, the common thought was that no fire was a good fire. But conservation experts tell us that forest fires actually contribute to the health and well-being of the forest.

Amid densely packed old-growth trees, leaves, branches and other debris constantly accumulate on the woodland floor. If not consumed in small, natural fires, this deadwood over time will continue to build and become susceptible to even larger, more intense fires that are more difficult to control.

In addition, trees such as the jack pine actually *require* a blaze to crack their seeds and begin the process of rebirth. Amidst the devastation wrought by wildfire, these hard seeds burst forth with new life as the forest slowly rebuilds. New growth provides a better habitat for many animals so that biodiversity improves. New initiatives for "controlled burning" have emerged to help forests return to their natural cycles of renewal through fire.

The prophet Ezekiel railed against people weighed down by some serious "deadwood"—disobedience and idolatry—that had accumulated over years. Ezekiel informed the people that God was enraged by their rebellion. God's anger, however, was not simply a punishment, but a necessary means by which their love and devotion to him would be renewed. How is that? God's judgment rejuvenated the hearts of his people from the damaging effects of apathy, just as forest fires cleanse the forest of stagnation and decay.

Discipline gets our attention. Consequences alert us that something is wrong. If God simply left us alone, negative attitudes would slowly accumulate in our hearts. Unchecked, we would become prime candidates for uncontrolled disaster.

Have you ever experienced a time when your sin resulted in painful consequences? Can you see how those consequences might have served to renew your relationship with God? Were there signs of renewal in your attitude toward him because you learned from your mistakes? Ezekiel understood the principle of renewal; he longed to see God's rebuke result in repentance for his people. Though God may choose to burn out the deadwood in your life, he does so for a good reason. Don't fight it. Learn from it.

Go to page 1000 for your next devotional reading.

out my hand against them and make the land
a desolate waste from the desert to Diblah[a]—
wherever they live. Then they will know that I
am the LORD.' "

The End Has Come

7 The word of the LORD came to me: 2"Son
of man, this is what the Sovereign LORD
says to the land of Israel: The end! The end has
come upon the four corners of the land. 3The
end is now upon you and I will unleash my anger against you. I will judge you according to
your conduct and repay you for all your detestable practices. 4I will not look on you with pity
or spare you; I will surely repay you for your
conduct and the detestable practices among
you. Then you will know that I am the LORD.

5"This is what the Sovereign LORD says:
Disaster! An unheard-of[b] disaster is coming.
6The end has come! The end has come! It has
roused itself against you. It has come! 7Doom
has come upon you—you who dwell in the
land. The time has come, the day is near; there
is panic, not joy, upon the mountains. 8I am
about to pour out my wrath on you and spend
my anger against you; I will judge you according to your conduct and repay you for all your
detestable practices. 9I will not look on you
with pity or spare you; I will repay you in accordance with your conduct and the detestable
practices among you. Then you will know that
it is I the LORD who strikes the blow.

10"The day is here! It has come! Doom has
burst forth, the rod has budded, arrogance has
blossomed! 11Violence has grown into[c] a rod to
punish wickedness; none of the people will be
left, none of that crowd—no wealth, nothing of
value. 12The time has come, the day has arrived.
Let not the buyer rejoice nor the seller grieve,
for wrath is upon the whole crowd. 13The seller
will not recover the land he has sold as long
as both of them live, for the vision concerning
the whole crowd will not be reversed. Because
of their sins, not one of them will preserve his
life. 14Though they blow the trumpet and get
everything ready, no one will go into battle, for
my wrath is upon the whole crowd.

15"Outside is the sword, inside are plague
and famine; those in the country will die by the
sword, and those in the city will be devoured by
famine and plague. 16All who survive and escape will be in the mountains, moaning like
doves of the valleys, each because of his sins.
17Every hand will go limp, and every knee will
become as weak as water. 18They will put on
sackcloth and be clothed with terror. Their
faces will be covered with shame and their
heads will be shaved. 19They will throw
their silver into the streets, and their gold will
be an unclean thing. Their silver and gold will
not be able to save them in the day of the LORD's
wrath. They will not satisfy their hunger or fill
their stomachs with it, for it has made them
stumble into sin. 20They were proud of their
beautiful jewelry and used it to make their detestable idols and vile images. Therefore I will
turn these into an unclean thing for them. 21I
will hand it all over as plunder to foreigners
and as loot to the wicked of the earth, and they
will defile it. 22I will turn my face away from
them, and they will desecrate my treasured
place; robbers will enter it and desecrate it.

23"Prepare chains, because the land is full of
bloodshed and the city is full of violence. 24I
will bring the most wicked of the nations to
take possession of their houses; I will put an
end to the pride of the mighty, and their sanctuaries will be desecrated. 25When terror comes,
they will seek peace, but there will be none.
26Calamity upon calamity will come, and rumor upon rumor. They will try to get a vision
from the prophet; the teaching of the law by
the priest will be lost, as will the counsel of the
elders. 27The king will mourn, the prince will
be clothed with despair, and the hands of the
people of the land will tremble. I will deal with
them according to their conduct, and by their
own standards I will judge them. Then they
will know that I am the LORD."

Idolatry in the Temple

8 In the sixth year, in the sixth month on the
fifth day, while I was sitting in my house
and the elders of Judah were sitting before me,
the hand of the Sovereign LORD came upon me
there. 2I looked, and I saw a figure like that of
a man.[d] From what appeared to be his waist
down he was like fire, and from there up his

[a]14 Most Hebrew manuscripts; a few Hebrew manuscripts *Riblah* [b]5 Most Hebrew manuscripts; some Hebrew manuscripts and Syriac *Disaster after* [c]11 Or *The violent one has become* [d]2 Or *saw a fiery figure*

appearance was as bright as glowing metal. 3He
stretched out what looked like a hand and took
me by the hair of my head. The Spirit lifted me
up between earth and heaven and in visions of
God he took me to Jerusalem, to the entrance
to the north gate of the inner court, where the
idol that provokes to jealousy stood. 4And there
before me was the glory of the God of Israel, as
in the vision I had seen in the plain.

5Then he said to me, "Son of man, look
toward the north." So I looked, and in the entrance north of the gate of the altar I saw this
idol of jealousy.

6And he said to me, "Son of man, do you
see what they are doing—the utterly detestable
things the house of Israel is doing here, things
that will drive me far from my sanctuary? But
you will see things that are even more detestable."

7Then he brought me to the entrance to the
court. I looked, and I saw a hole in the wall.
8He said to me, "Son of man, now dig into the
wall." So I dug into the wall and saw a doorway there.

9And he said to me, "Go in and see the
wicked and detestable things they are doing
here." 10So I went in and looked, and I saw
portrayed all over the walls all kinds of crawling things and detestable animals and all the
idols of the house of Israel. 11In front of them
stood seventy elders of the house of Israel, and
Jaazaniah son of Shaphan was standing among
them. Each had a censer in his hand, and a fragrant cloud of incense was rising.

12He said to me, "Son of man, have you seen
what the elders of the house of Israel are doing
in the darkness, each at the shrine of his own
idol? They say, 'The LORD does not see us; the
LORD has forsaken the land.'" 13Again, he said,
"You will see them doing things that are even
more detestable."

14Then he brought me to the entrance to the
north gate of the house of the LORD, and I saw
women sitting there, mourning for Tammuz.
15He said to me, "Do you see this, son of man?
You will see things that are even more detestable than this."

16He then brought me into the inner court
of the house of the LORD, and there at the entrance to the temple, between the portico and
the altar, were about twenty-five men. With
their backs toward the temple of the LORD and
their faces toward the east, they were bowing
down to the sun in the east.

17He said to me, "Have you seen this, son of
man? Is it a trivial matter for the house of Judah
to do the detestable things they are doing here?
Must they also fill the land with violence and
continually provoke me to anger? Look at them
putting the branch to their nose! 18Therefore I
will deal with them in anger; I will not look on
them with pity or spare them. Although they
shout in my ears, I will not listen to them."

Idolaters Killed

9 Then I heard him call out in a loud voice,
"Bring the guards of the city here, each
with a weapon in his hand." 2And I saw six men
coming from the direction of the upper gate,
which faces north, each with a deadly weapon
in his hand. With them was a man clothed in
linen who had a writing kit at his side. They
came in and stood beside the bronze altar.

3Now the glory of the God of Israel went up
from above the cherubim, where it had been,
and moved to the threshold of the temple.
Then the LORD called to the man clothed in
linen who had the writing kit at his side 4and
said to him, "Go throughout the city of Jerusalem and put a mark on the foreheads of those
who grieve and lament over all the detestable
things that are done in it."

5As I listened, he said to the others, "Follow
him through the city and kill, without showing
pity or compassion. 6Slaughter old men, young
men and maidens, women and children, but
do not touch anyone who has the mark. Begin
at my sanctuary." So they began with the elders
who were in front of the temple.

7Then he said to them, "Defile the temple
and fill the courts with the slain. Go!" So they
went out and began killing throughout the city.
8While they were killing and I was left alone,
I fell facedown, crying out, "Ah, Sovereign
LORD! Are you going to destroy the entire remnant of Israel in this outpouring of your wrath
on Jerusalem?"

9He answered me, "The sin of the house of
Israel and Judah is exceedingly great; the land is
full of bloodshed and the city is full of injustice.
They say, 'The LORD has forsaken the land; the

LORD does not see.' 10So I will not look on them with pity or spare them, but I will bring down on their own heads what they have done."

11Then the man in linen with the writing kit at his side brought back word, saying, "I have done as you commanded."

The Glory Departs From the Temple

10 I looked, and I saw the likeness of a throne of sapphire[a] above the expanse that was over the heads of the cherubim. 2The LORD said to the man clothed in linen, "Go in among the wheels beneath the cherubim. Fill your hands with burning coals from among the cherubim and scatter them over the city." And as I watched, he went in.

3Now the cherubim were standing on the south side of the temple when the man went in, and a cloud filled the inner court. 4Then the glory of the LORD rose from above the cherubim and moved to the threshold of the temple. The cloud filled the temple, and the court was full of the radiance of the glory of the LORD. 5The sound of the wings of the cherubim could be heard as far away as the outer court, like the voice of God Almighty[b] when he speaks.

> Ezekiel 10:4
>
> *God Is Radiant*
>
> Then the glory of the LORD rose from above the cherubim and moved to the threshold of the temple. The cloud filled the temple, and the court was full of the radiance of the glory of the LORD.

6When the LORD commanded the man in linen, "Take fire from among the wheels, from among the cherubim," the man went in and stood beside a wheel. 7Then one of the cherubim reached out his hand to the fire that was among them. He took up some of it and put it into the hands of the man in linen, who took it and went out. 8(Under the wings of the cherubim could be seen what looked like the hands of a man.)

9I looked, and I saw beside the cherubim four wheels, one beside each of the cherubim; the wheels sparkled like chrysolite. 10As for their appearance, the four of them looked alike; each was like a wheel intersecting a wheel. 11As they moved, they would go in any one of the four directions the cherubim faced; the wheels did not turn about[c] as the cherubim went. The cherubim went in whatever direction the head faced, without turning as they went. 12Their entire bodies, including their backs, their hands and their wings, were completely full of eyes, as were their four wheels. 13I heard the wheels being called "the whirling wheels." 14Each of the cherubim had four faces: One face was that of a cherub, the second the face of a man, the third the face of a lion, and the fourth the face of an eagle.

15Then the cherubim rose upward. These were the living creatures I had seen by the Kebar River. 16When the cherubim moved, the wheels beside them moved; and when the cherubim spread their wings to rise from the ground, the wheels did not leave their side. 17When the cherubim stood still, they also stood still; and when the cherubim rose, they rose with them, because the spirit of the living creatures was in them.

18Then the glory of the LORD departed from over the threshold of the temple and stopped above the cherubim. 19While I watched, the cherubim spread their wings and rose from the ground, and as they went, the wheels went with them. They stopped at the entrance to the east gate of the LORD's house, and the glory of the God of Israel was above them.

20These were the living creatures I had seen beneath the God of Israel by the Kebar River, and I realized that they were cherubim. 21Each had four faces and four wings, and under their wings was what looked like the hands of a man. 22Their faces had the same appearance as those I had seen by the Kebar River. Each one went straight ahead.

Judgment on Israel's Leaders

11 Then the Spirit lifted me up and brought me to the gate of the house of the LORD that faces east. There at the entrance to the gate were twenty-five men, and I saw among them Jaazaniah son of Azzur and

[a]1 Or *lapis lazuli* [b]5 Hebrew *El-Shaddai* [c]11 Or *aside*

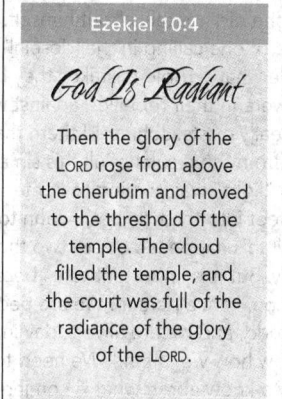

Light the Way

Read: Ezekiel 10:1–22

Ezekiel 10:4

Then the glory of the LORD rose from above the cherubim and moved to the threshold of the temple. The cloud filled the temple, and the court was full of the radiance of the glory of the LORD.

GOD SPEAKS TO US of "light" and "dark" to help us to understand that we can make such terrible mistakes about what the world is, what the universe is, who we are ourselves, whether there is any life after we die, whether there is a place called heaven. We can make such terrible mistakes about whether God made the world or whether it came by chance. We can make such terrible mistakes about whom to believe, and just believe lies instead of the truth. God tells us that believing lies and making such mistakes about life is like sitting in dark darkness. Then He says that because people are in such dark darkness, one of three Persons, God the Son, came to be born as a baby, to grow up to teach and live so that people would have light to see and understand what mistakes they had made.

John did not talk about himself. He even called himself a "voice of one calling in the [desert]" (Luke 3:4)! Constantly he told people what terrible mistakes they had made, and what sinners they were in their rebellion against what is true, and against God who really exists. John told them that a Savior was coming to save them from the results of all this sin and rebellion. John told people that a "light" was coming to lighten their darkness, and to guide their feet into the true path. John told people the truth.

All this happened about two thousand years ago. Now it is history. But it is important to us because it is true history. You are a person. I am a person. We are people who have been born into the world, and we are alive today in this time of history. We need to know how we "fit in." We need to know about the past, and we need to know about what is coming in the future, but we need to know what we are meant to do right now. One thing we are meant to do is to give light to others sitting in darkness.

—*Edith Schaeffer*

reflection

1 How does it comfort you to know that God's glory radiates in heaven?

2 What are some of the lies that comprise the "dark darkness" described in today's devotional? How do these lies affect *your* life?

3 How will you glorify God by helping those who are sitting in darkness to see the light?

RELATED READINGS

Psalm 138:1–8; Habakkuk 3:3–4; John 1:6–9

Go to page 1002 for your next devotional reading.

Pelatiah son of Benaiah, leaders of the people.
2The LORD said to me, "Son of man, these
are the men who are plotting evil and giving
wicked advice in this city. 3They say, 'Will it not
soon be time to build houses?[a] This city is a
cooking pot, and we are the meat.' 4Therefore
prophesy against them; prophesy, son of man."
5Then the Spirit of the LORD came upon me,
and he told me to say: "This is what the LORD
says: That is what you are saying, O house of
Israel, but I know what is going through your
mind. 6You have killed many people in this
city and filled its streets with
the dead.
7"Therefore this is what the
Sovereign LORD says: The bodies you have thrown there are
the meat and this city is the
pot, but I will drive you out
of it. 8You fear the sword, and
the sword is what I will bring
against you, declares the Sovereign LORD. 9I will drive you
out of the city and hand you
over to foreigners and inflict
punishment on you. 10You will
fall by the sword, and I will execute judgment on you at the
borders of Israel. Then you will
know that I am the LORD. 11This city will not
be a pot for you, nor will you be the meat in it;
I will execute judgment on you at the borders
of Israel. 12And you will know that I am the
LORD, for you have not followed my decrees or
kept my laws but have conformed to the standards of the nations around you."
13Now as I was prophesying, Pelatiah son of
Benaiah died. Then I fell facedown and cried
out in a loud voice, "Ah, Sovereign LORD!
Will you completely destroy the remnant of
Israel?"
14The word of the LORD came to me: 15"Son
of man, your brothers—your brothers who are
your blood relatives[b] and the whole house of
Israel—are those of whom the people of Jerusalem have said, 'They are[c] far away from the
LORD; this land was given to us as our possession.'

> **Ezekiel 11:19**
>
> *God Renews Hearts*
>
> "I will give them an undivided heart and put a new spirit in them; I will remove from them their heart of stone and give them a heart of flesh."

Promised Return of Israel

16"Therefore say: 'This is what the Sovereign LORD says: Although I sent them far away
among the nations and scattered them among
the countries, yet for a little while I have been a
sanctuary for them in the countries where they
have gone.'
17"Therefore say: 'This is what the Sovereign
LORD says: I will gather you from the nations
and bring you back from the countries where
you have been scattered, and I will give you
back the land of Israel again.'
18"They will return to it and
remove all its vile images and
detestable idols. 19I will give
them an undivided heart and
put a new spirit in them; I will
remove from them their heart
of stone and give them a heart
of flesh. 20Then they will follow my decrees and be careful to keep my laws. They will
be my people, and I will be
their God. 21But as for those
whose hearts are devoted to
their vile images and detestable idols, I will bring down
on their own heads what they
have done, declares the Sovereign LORD."
22Then the cherubim, with the wheels beside them, spread their wings, and the glory of
the God of Israel was above them. 23The glory
of the LORD went up from within the city and
stopped above the mountain east of it. 24The
Spirit lifted me up and brought me to the exiles
in Babylonia[d] in the vision given by the Spirit
of God.
Then the vision I had seen went up from me,
25and I told the exiles everything the LORD had
shown me.

The Exile Symbolized

12 The word of the LORD came to me:
2"Son of man, you are living among a
rebellious people. They have eyes to see but do
not see and ears to hear but do not hear, for
they are a rebellious people.

[a]3 Or *This is not the time to build houses.* [b]15 Or *are in exile with you* (see Septuagint and Syriac) [c]15 Or *those to whom the people of Jerusalem have said, 'Stay* [d]24 Or *Chaldea*

Unfailing Love

GOMER

"Sow for yourselves righteousness, reap the fruit of unfailing love."

Hosea 10:12

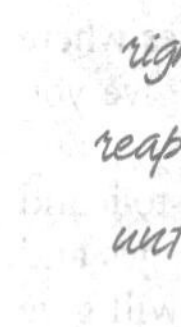

ASSIGNED READING:

Hosea 1–3

"HOW DOES HE DO IT?"

"He's a fool for her, I tell you."

"Senseless. You tell him she's a tramp . . . a vixen . . . and it's as if he doesn't hear you at all."

"Somebody told me he's not even the father of those children."

The chatter in the marketplace among the women rose to a crescendo as they daily observed the strange and wonderful relationship between Gomer and her husband. She was strange, and he was wonderful—too wonderful for her.

"Why does he put up with her?" they all wanted to know. How could a prophet—a prophet of God—put up with the wandering eye and straying heart of an out-and-out adulteress and still claim unfailing love for her? It was a mystery to the townspeople.

And to Gomer.

It seemed no matter how deeply she wounded her husband, he would not give up on her. She habitually ran from the security of his love to find solace in the arms of strangers. She preferred the emotionless physicality of those she met on the street to his unfailing, undying love. Instead of loving the one who called her by name, she preferred the anonymity of someone with no name, no home and no family.

Gomer herself must have wondered sometimes about the contradictions. Did she ever stop to ask why Hosea so relentlessly and tenderly loved her? Or why she rejected his love? Did she ever doubt her own emotional stability since she proved incapable of commitment? Some say the definition of insanity is repeating the same action over and over again but expecting a different response. In Gomer's case, she was "crazy" to think that her loveless pursuits could satisfy the core needs for fulfillment and security that every woman has. However, it didn't keep her from running away from the very thing she desperately wanted to find—unfailing love.

—Prayer—

"Give thanks to the LORD, for he is good; his love endures forever" (1 Chronicles 16:34).

Weekend

Go to page 1004 for your next devotional reading.

3“Therefore, son of man, pack your belongings for exile and in the daytime, as they watch,
set out and go from where you are to another
place. Perhaps they will understand, though
they are a rebellious house. 4During the daytime, while they watch, bring out your belongings packed for exile. Then in the evening,
while they are watching, go out like those who
go into exile. 5While they watch, dig through
the wall and take your belongings out through
it. 6Put them on your shoulder as they are
watching and carry them out at dusk. Cover
your face so that you cannot see the land, for I
have made you a sign to the house of Israel.”

7So I did as I was commanded. During the
day I brought out my things packed for exile.
Then in the evening I dug through the wall
with my hands. I took my belongings out at
dusk, carrying them on my shoulders while
they watched.

8In the morning the word of the LORD came
to me: 9“Son of man, did not that rebellious
house of Israel ask you, ‘What are you doing?’

10“Say to them, ‘This is what the Sovereign
LORD says: This oracle concerns the prince in Jerusalem and the whole house of Israel who are
there.’ 11Say to them, ‘I am a sign to you.’

“As I have done, so it will be done to them.
They will go into exile as captives.

12“The prince among them will put his
things on his shoulder at dusk and leave, and
a hole will be dug in the wall for him to go
through. He will cover his face so that he cannot see the land. 13I will spread my net for him,
and he will be caught in my snare; I will bring
him to Babylonia, the land of the Chaldeans,
but he will not see it, and there he will die. 14I
will scatter to the winds all those around him—
his staff and all his troops—and I will pursue
them with drawn sword.

15“They will know that I am the LORD, when
I disperse them among the nations and scatter
them through the countries. 16But I will spare
a few of them from the sword, famine and
plague, so that in the nations where they go they
may acknowledge all their detestable practices.
Then they will know that I am the LORD.”

17The word of the LORD came to me: 18“Son
of man, tremble as you eat your food, and shudder in fear as you drink your water. 19Say to the
people of the land: ‘This is what the Sovereign
LORD says about those living in Jerusalem and
in the land of Israel: They will eat their food
in anxiety and drink their water in despair, for
their land will be stripped of everything in it
because of the violence of all who live there.
20The inhabited towns will be laid waste and
the land will be desolate. Then you will know
that I am the LORD.’ ”

21The word of the LORD came to me: 22“Son
of man, what is this proverb you have in the
land of Israel: ‘The days go by and every vision
comes to nothing’? 23Say to them, ‘This is what
the Sovereign LORD says: I am going to put an
end to this proverb, and they will no longer
quote it in Israel.’ Say to them, ‘The days are
near when every vision will be fulfilled. 24For
there will be no more false visions or flattering
divinations among the people of Israel. 25But
I the LORD will speak what I will, and it shall
be fulfilled without delay. For in your days, you
rebellious house, I will fulfill whatever I say, declares the Sovereign LORD.’ ”

26The word of the LORD came to me: 27“Son
of man, the house of Israel is saying, ‘The vision he sees is for many years from now, and
he prophesies about the distant future.’

28“Therefore say to them, ‘This is what the
Sovereign LORD says: None of my words will
be delayed any longer; whatever I say will be
fulfilled, declares the Sovereign LORD.’ ”

False Prophets Condemned

13 The word of the LORD came to me:
2“Son of man, prophesy against the
prophets of Israel who are now prophesying.
Say to those who prophesy out of their own
imagination: ‘Hear the word of the LORD!
3This is what the Sovereign LORD says: Woe
to the foolish[a] prophets who follow their own
spirit and have seen nothing! 4Your prophets,
O Israel, are like jackals among ruins. 5You
have not gone up to the breaks in the wall to
repair it for the house of Israel so that it will
stand firm in the battle on the day of the LORD.
6Their visions are false and their divinations a
lie. They say, “The LORD declares,” when the
LORD has not sent them; yet they expect their
words to be fulfilled. 7Have you not seen false

[a] 3 Or *wicked*

Shelter in a Strange Land

Read: Ezekiel 11:16–25

Ezekiel 11:16

"Therefore say: 'This is what the Sovereign LORD says: Although I sent them far away among the nations and scattered them among the countries, yet for a little while I have been a sanctuary for them in the countries where they have gone.'"

THE PAST TWO CENTURIES have produced an unprecedented shrinking of time and distance. Journeys that once required days or weeks have now been reduced to hours with trains, automobiles and air travel—methods of transportation that would have seemed fantastical a hundred years ago. Yet the availability of these means of travel has also introduced a new level of fragmentation. Perhaps you've moved far from your parents; perhaps your job requires you to travel to a different city every day; perhaps your children or grandchildren live a long plane ride from you. As a result, you sometimes feel isolated from your friends and family. Though you long for closeness with others, you often find only loneliness.

The Israelites had slavery to add to their dislocation anxiety. God scattered them among foreign nations, fulfilling his promise to send them into captivity if they forgot to keep him first and foremost in their lives. In strange lands, far from temple life and the comfort of communal worship, God promised to be their sanctuary in the midst of their isolation. The abiding presence of the Lord would go with the scattered people into foreign lands.

We, too, long to be hidden in the presence of God. Following Christ can be a lonely journey in a hostile world. Many of us sit in silent agony at meetings as colleagues ridicule some aspect of our faith. Many of us can relate to feelings of abiding isolation not too different from the Israelites' alien existence as they groaned before God. They longed to return to their country from the foreign lands where everything seemed antagonistic to the faith they had earlier taken for granted.

God wants us to learn an important lesson from these seasons of loneliness: Our true citizenship is in heaven. When you feel like an outsider, remember that you are a citizen of heaven, and God promises to be your sanctuary in these foreign lands.

reflection

1 How do you react to feelings of loneliness or isolation in your life?

2 Remembering that God provides you with sanctuary isn't always easy. During difficult times when you may not feel his presence, how can you practically remind yourself of this truth?

3 Spend some time praying for things that seem "far off"—family, friends, even a place you dearly miss. Ask the Lord to satisfy these longings in you. Ask him to ultimately satisfy you with himself.

RELATED READINGS

Isaiah 4:5–6; Jeremiah 1:17–19; Luke 18:28–30

Go to page 1009 for your next devotional reading.

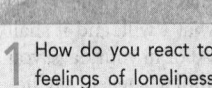

visions and uttered lying divinations when
you say, "The LORD declares," though I have
not spoken?
8"'Therefore this is what the Sovereign
LORD says: Because of your false words and
lying visions, I am against you, declares the
Sovereign LORD. 9My hand will be against the
prophets who see false visions and utter lying
divinations. They will not belong to the council
of my people or be listed in the records of the
house of Israel, nor will they enter the land of
Israel. Then you will know that I am the Sovereign LORD.
10"'Because they lead my people astray, saying, "Peace," when there is no peace, and because, when a flimsy wall is built, they cover
it with whitewash, 11therefore tell those who
cover it with whitewash that it is going to fall.
Rain will come in torrents, and I will send hailstones hurtling down, and violent winds will
burst forth. 12When the wall collapses, will people not ask you, "Where is the whitewash you
covered it with?"
13"'Therefore this is what the Sovereign
LORD says: In my wrath I will unleash a violent
wind, and in my anger hailstones and torrents
of rain will fall with destructive fury. 14I will
tear down the wall you have covered with whitewash and will level it to the ground so that its
foundation will be laid bare. When it[a] falls,
you will be destroyed in it; and you will know
that I am the LORD. 15So I will spend my wrath
against the wall and against those who covered
it with whitewash. I will say to you, "The wall
is gone and so are those who whitewashed it,
16those prophets of Israel who prophesied to
Jerusalem and saw visions of peace for her
when there was no peace, declares the Sovereign LORD."'
17"Now, son of man, set your face against
the daughters of your people who prophesy
out of their own imagination. Prophesy against
them 18and say, 'This is what the Sovereign
LORD says: Woe to the women who sew magic
charms on all their wrists and make veils of various lengths for their heads in order to ensnare
people. Will you ensnare the lives of my people
but preserve your own? 19You have profaned
me among my people for a few handfuls of
barley and scraps of bread. By lying to my people, who listen to lies, you have killed those
who should not have died and have spared
those who should not live.
20"'Therefore this is what the Sovereign
LORD says: I am against your magic charms
with which you ensnare people like birds and I
will tear them from your arms; I will set free the
people that you ensnare like birds. 21I will tear
off your veils and save my people from your
hands, and they will no longer fall prey to your
power. Then you will know that I am the LORD.
22Because you disheartened the righteous with
your lies, when I had brought them no grief,
and because you encouraged the wicked not to
turn from their evil ways and so save their lives,
23therefore you will no longer see false visions
or practice divination. I will save my people
from your hands. And then you will know that
I am the LORD.'"

Idolaters Condemned

14 Some of the elders of Israel came to me
and sat down in front of me. 2Then the
word of the LORD came to me: 3"Son of man,
these men have set up idols in their hearts and
put wicked stumbling blocks before their faces.
Should I let them inquire of me at all? 4There-
fore speak to them and tell them, 'This is what
the Sovereign LORD says: When any Israelite
sets up idols in his heart and puts a wicked
stumbling block before his face and then goes
to a prophet, I the LORD will answer him myself
in keeping with his great idolatry. 5I will do this
to recapture the hearts of the people of Israel,
who have all deserted me for their idols.'
6"Therefore say to the house of Israel, 'This
is what the Sovereign LORD says: Repent! Turn
from your idols and renounce all your detestable practices!
7"'When any Israelite or any alien living in
Israel separates himself from me and sets up
idols in his heart and puts a wicked stumbling
block before his face and then goes to a prophet
to inquire of me, I the LORD will answer him
myself. 8I will set my face against that man and
make him an example and a byword. I will cut
him off from my people. Then you will know
that I am the LORD.
9"'And if the prophet is enticed to utter

[a]14 Or *the city*

a prophecy, I the LORD have enticed that
prophet, and I will stretch out my hand against
him and destroy him from among my people
Israel. 10They will bear their guilt—the prophet
will be as guilty as the one who consults him.
11Then the people of Israel will no longer
stray from me, nor will they defile themselves
anymore with all their sins. They will be my
people, and I will be their God, declares the
Sovereign LORD.' "

Judgment Inescapable

12The word of the LORD came to me: 13"Son
of man, if a country sins against me by being
unfaithful and I stretch out my hand against
it to cut off its food supply and send famine
upon it and kill its men and their animals,
14even if these three men—Noah, Daniel[a]
and Job—were in it, they could save only themselves by their righteousness, declares the Sovereign LORD.

15"Or if I send wild beasts through that country and they leave it childless and it becomes
desolate so that no one can pass through it because of the beasts, 16as surely as I live, declares
the Sovereign LORD, even if these three men
were in it, they could not save their own sons
or daughters. They alone would be saved, but
the land would be desolate.

17"Or if I bring a sword against that country
and say, 'Let the sword pass throughout the
land,' and I kill its men and their animals, 18as
surely as I live, declares the Sovereign LORD,
even if these three men were in it, they could
not save their own sons or daughters. They
alone would be saved.

19"Or if I send a plague into that land and
pour out my wrath upon it through bloodshed,
killing its men and their animals, 20as surely
as I live, declares the Sovereign LORD, even if
Noah, Daniel and Job were in it, they could
save neither son nor daughter. They would save
only themselves by their righteousness.

21"For this is what the Sovereign LORD says:
How much worse will it be when I send against
Jerusalem my four dreadful judgments—sword
and famine and wild beasts and plague—to kill
its men and their animals! 22Yet there will be
some survivors—sons and daughters who will
be brought out of it. They will come to you, and
when you see their conduct and their actions,
you will be consoled regarding the disaster I
have brought upon Jerusalem—every disaster
I have brought upon it. 23You will be consoled
when you see their conduct and their actions,
for you will know that I have done nothing in it
without cause, declares the Sovereign LORD."

Jerusalem, A Useless Vine

15 The word of the LORD came to me:
2"Son of man, how is the wood of a
vine better than that of a branch on any of the
trees in the forest? 3Is wood ever taken from
it to make anything useful? Do they make
pegs from it to hang things on? 4And after it
is thrown on the fire as fuel and the fire burns
both ends and chars the middle, is it then useful for anything? 5If it was not useful for anything when it was whole, how much less can it
be made into something useful when the fire
has burned it and it is charred?

6"Therefore this is what the Sovereign LORD
says: As I have given the wood of the vine
among the trees of the forest as fuel for the fire,
so will I treat the people living in Jerusalem. 7I
will set my face against them. Although they
have come out of the fire, the fire will yet consume them. And when I set my face against
them, you will know that I am the LORD. 8I will
make the land desolate because they have been
unfaithful, declares the Sovereign LORD."

An Allegory of Unfaithful Jerusalem

16 The word of the LORD came to me:
2"Son of man, confront Jerusalem with
her detestable practices 3and say, 'This is what
the Sovereign LORD says to Jerusalem: Your
ancestry and birth were in the land of the Canaanites; your father was an Amorite and your
mother a Hittite. 4On the day you were born
your cord was not cut, nor were you washed with
water to make you clean, nor were you rubbed
with salt or wrapped in cloths. 5No one looked
on you with pity or had compassion enough to
do any of these things for you. Rather, you were
thrown out into the open field, for on the day
you were born you were despised.

6" 'Then I passed by and saw you kicking
about in your blood, and as you lay there in

[a] 14 Or *Danel*; the Hebrew spelling may suggest a person other than the prophet Daniel; also in verse 20.

your blood I said to you, "Live!"[a] 7I made you
grow like a plant of the field. You grew up and
developed and became the most beautiful of
jewels.[b] Your breasts were formed and your
hair grew, you who were naked and bare.
8"'Later I passed by, and when I looked at
you and saw that you were old enough for love,
I spread the corner of my garment over you
and covered your nakedness. I gave you my
solemn oath and entered into a covenant with
you, declares the Sovereign LORD, and you became mine.
9"'I bathed[c] you with water and washed the
blood from you and put ointments on you. 10I
clothed you with an embroidered dress and put
leather sandals on you. I dressed you in fine
linen and covered you with costly garments.
11I adorned you with jewelry: I put bracelets
on your arms and a necklace around your
neck, 12and I put a ring on your nose, earrings
on your ears and a beautiful crown on your
head. 13So you were adorned with gold and silver; your clothes were of fine linen and costly
fabric and embroidered cloth. Your food was
fine flour, honey and olive oil. You became very
beautiful and rose to be a queen. 14And your
fame spread among the nations on account of
your beauty, because the splendor I had given
you made your beauty perfect, declares the Sovereign LORD.
15"'But you trusted in your beauty and used
your fame to become a prostitute. You lavished
your favors on anyone who passed by and your
beauty became his.[d] 16You took some of your
garments to make gaudy high places, where
you carried on your prostitution. Such things
should not happen, nor should they ever occur.
17You also took the fine jewelry I gave you, the
jewelry made of my gold and silver, and you
made for yourself male idols and engaged in
prostitution with them. 18And you took your
embroidered clothes to put on them, and you
offered my oil and incense before them. 19Also
the food I provided for you—the fine flour, olive oil and honey I gave you to eat—you offered
as fragrant incense before them. That is what
happened, declares the Sovereign LORD.
20"'And you took your sons and daughters
whom you bore to me and sacrificed them as
food to the idols. Was your prostitution not
enough? 21You slaughtered my children and
sacrificed them[e] to the idols. 22In all your detestable practices and your prostitution you
did not remember the days of your youth,
when you were naked and bare, kicking about
in your blood.
23"'Woe! Woe to you, declares the Sovereign
LORD. In addition to all your other wickedness,
24you built a mound for yourself and made a
lofty shrine in every public square. 25At the
head of every street you built your lofty shrines
and degraded your beauty, offering your body
with increasing promiscuity to anyone who
passed by. 26You engaged in prostitution with
the Egyptians, your lustful neighbors, and provoked me to anger with your increasing promiscuity. 27So I stretched out my hand against
you and reduced your territory; I gave you over
to the greed of your enemies, the daughters of
the Philistines, who were shocked by your lewd
conduct. 28You engaged in prostitution with
the Assyrians too, because you were insatiable;
and even after that, you still were not satisfied.
29Then you increased your promiscuity to include Babylonia,[f] a land of merchants, but even
with this you were not satisfied.
30"'How weak-willed you are, declares the
Sovereign LORD, when you do all these things,
acting like a brazen prostitute! 31When you
built your mounds at the head of every street
and made your lofty shrines in every public
square, you were unlike a prostitute, because
you scorned payment.
32"'You adulterous wife! You prefer strangers to your own husband! 33Every prostitute receives a fee, but you give gifts to all your lovers,
bribing them to come to you from everywhere
for your illicit favors. 34So in your prostitution
you are the opposite of others; no one runs after you for your favors. You are the very opposite, for you give payment and none is given to
you.
35"'Therefore, you prostitute, hear the word
of the LORD! 36This is what the Sovereign LORD
says: Because you poured out your wealth[g] and
exposed your nakedness in your promiscuity

[a]6 A few Hebrew manuscripts, Septuagint and Syriac; most Hebrew manuscripts *"Live!" And as you lay there in your blood I said to you, "Live!"* [b]7 Or *became mature* [c]9 Or *I had bathed* [d]15 Most Hebrew manuscripts; one Hebrew manuscript (see some Septuagint manuscripts) *by. Such a thing should not happen* [e]21 Or *and made them pass through ⌊the fire⌋* [f]29 Or *Chaldea* [g]36 Or *lust*

with your lovers, and because of all your detestable idols, and because you gave them your children's blood, 37therefore I am going to gather
all your lovers, with whom you found pleasure,
those you loved as well as those you hated. I
will gather them against you from all around
and will strip you in front of them, and they
will see all your nakedness. 38I will sentence
you to the punishment of women who commit adultery and who shed blood; I will bring
upon you the blood vengeance of my wrath
and jealous anger. 39Then I will hand you over
to your lovers, and they will tear down your
mounds and destroy your lofty shrines. They
will strip you of your clothes and take your fine
jewelry and leave you naked and bare. 40They
will bring a mob against you, who will stone
you and hack you to pieces with their swords.
41They will burn down your houses and inflict punishment on you in the sight of many
women. I will put a stop to your prostitution,
and you will no longer pay your lovers. 42Then
my wrath against you will subside and my jealous anger will turn away from you; I will be
calm and no longer angry.

43" 'Because you did not remember the days
of your youth but enraged me with all these
things, I will surely bring down on your head
what you have done, declares the Sovereign
LORD. Did you not add lewdness to all your
other detestable practices?

44" 'Everyone who quotes proverbs will
quote this proverb about you: "Like mother,
like daughter." 45You are a true daughter of
your mother, who despised her husband and
her children; and you are a true sister of your
sisters, who despised their husbands and their
children. Your mother was a Hittite and your
father an Amorite. 46Your older sister was
Samaria, who lived to the north of you with
her daughters; and your younger sister, who
lived to the south of you with her daughters,
was Sodom. 47You not only walked in their
ways and copied their detestable practices,
but in all your ways you soon became more depraved than they. 48As surely as I live, declares
the Sovereign LORD, your sister Sodom and her
daughters never did what you and your daughters have done.

49" 'Now this was the sin of your sister
Sodom: She and her daughters were arrogant,
overfed and unconcerned; they did not help
the poor and needy. 50They were haughty and
did detestable things before me. Therefore I did
away with them as you have seen. 51Samaria
did not commit half the sins you did. You have
done more detestable things than they, and
have made your sisters seem righteous by all
these things you have done. 52Bear your disgrace, for you have furnished some justification for your sisters. Because your sins were
more vile than theirs, they appear more righteous than you. So then, be ashamed and bear
your disgrace, for you have made your sisters
appear righteous.

53" 'However, I will restore the fortunes of
Sodom and her daughters and of Samaria and
her daughters, and your fortunes along with
them, 54so that you may bear your disgrace and
be ashamed of all you have done in giving them
comfort. 55And your sisters, Sodom with her
daughters and Samaria with her daughters, will
return to what they were before; and you and
your daughters will return to what you were
before. 56You would not even mention your
sister Sodom in the day of your pride, 57before
your wickedness was uncovered. Even so, you
are now scorned by the daughters of Edom[a]
and all her neighbors and the daughters of the
Philistines—all those around you who despise
you. 58You will bear the consequences of your
lewdness and your detestable practices, declares the LORD.

59" 'This is what the Sovereign LORD says: I
will deal with you as you deserve, because you
have despised my oath by breaking the covenant. 60Yet I will remember the covenant I
made with you in the days of your youth, and I
will establish an everlasting covenant with you.
61Then you will remember your ways and be
ashamed when you receive your sisters, both
those who are older than you and those who
are younger. I will give them to you as daughters, but not on the basis of my covenant with
you. 62So I will establish my covenant with
you, and you will know that I am the LORD.
63Then, when I make atonement for you for
all you have done, you will remember and be

[a] 57 Many Hebrew manuscripts and Syriac; most Hebrew manuscripts, Septuagint and Vulgate *Aram*

Turn Around

Read: Ezekiel 16:1–63

CHOICES CAN DETERMINE the course of a life. They can establish the legacy of a family. And they can affect the destiny of a nation. Wise choices will bring blessing; foolish ones will bring destruction and pain. Some choices can cost us nearly everything.

This passage tells an allegory of how the people of Jerusalem betrayed God. The language paints a picture of a loving God who had compassion on people who had nothing of their own, who were alone and helpless. God's tender care is beautiful to see. But we are shocked as the story continues. The people betray God—they abandon their Savior and pursue other gods. God's love is spurned by the people's willful and selfish choices.

Maybe you've made some poor choices too. Have you chosen to walk your own road, going against what you know to be right? Has the allure of illicit love, personal ambition, intriguing philosophies or accumulating things or anything else caused you to overlook what is really important? Have you realized yet that God is not going to change the rules or make an exception for you? God will deal with you. There is no getting around that. He loves you too much to leave you to follow your own ways or the ways of the world.

The next choice you make could be the one that changes your life. Instead of going your own way, return to the Lover of your soul. Rather than making choices on a whim, think carefully and wisely. Be honest with God about the mistakes you've made. Let go of your self-centered ways—completely—and turn full-faced toward God. Be intentional. Deliberate. And choose to "offer your bodies as living sacrifices, holy and pleasing to God—this is your spiritual act of worship. Do not conform any longer to the pattern of this world, but be transformed by the renewing of your mind. Then you will be able to test and approve what God's will is—his good, pleasing and perfect will" (Romans 12:1–2).

Ezekiel 16:60–61
"Yet I will remember the covenant I made with you in the days of your youth, and I will establish an everlasting covenant with you. Then you will remember your ways and be ashamed."

reflection

1 How have the choices you have made, good and bad, affected the course of your life?

2 Is there an area of your life in which you need to turn from disobedience? If so, will you do so today?

3 What tangible steps will you take to turn toward God?

RELATED READINGS

Ezekiel 36:24–27;
Hebrews 12:14–29;
1 Peter 3:8–12

"Turn to God from idols. For the sword of His wrath that had been aimed at you has been sheathed into the heart of His Son... Because He has died for you, you were forgiven."

Paris Reidhead

Go to page 1012 for your next devotional reading.

ashamed and never again open your mouth
because of your humiliation, declares the Sovereign LORD.’”

Two Eagles and a Vine

17 The word of the LORD came to me:
2“Son of man, set forth an allegory
and tell the house of Israel a parable. 3Say to
them, ‘This is what the Sovereign LORD says:
A great eagle with powerful wings, long feathers and full plumage of varied colors came to
Lebanon. Taking hold of the top of a cedar, 4he
broke off its topmost shoot and carried it away
to a land of merchants, where he planted it in
a city of traders.
5“ ‘He took some of the seed of your land
and put it in fertile soil. He planted it like a willow by abundant water, 6and it sprouted and became a low, spreading vine. Its branches turned
toward him, but its roots remained under it. So
it became a vine and produced branches and
put out leafy boughs.
7“ ‘But there was another great eagle with
powerful wings and full plumage. The vine
now sent out its roots toward him from the
plot where it was planted and stretched out its
branches to him for water. 8It had been planted
in good soil by abundant water so that it would
produce branches, bear fruit and become a
splendid vine.’
9“Say to them, ‘This is what the Sovereign LORD says: Will it thrive? Will it not be
uprooted and stripped of its fruit so that it withers? All its new growth will wither. It will not
take a strong arm or many people to pull it up
by the roots. 10Even if it is transplanted, will
it thrive? Will it not wither completely when
the east wind strikes it—wither away in the plot
where it grew?’”
11Then the word of the LORD came to me:
12“Say to this rebellious house, ‘Do you not
know what these things mean?’ Say to them:
‘The king of Babylon went to Jerusalem and carried off her king and her nobles, bringing them
back with him to Babylon. 13Then he took a
member of the royal family and made a treaty
with him, putting him under oath. He also carried away the leading men of the land, 14so that
the kingdom would be brought low, unable to
rise again, surviving only by keeping his treaty.
15But the king rebelled against him by sending
his envoys to Egypt to get horses and a large
army. Will he succeed? Will he who does such
things escape? Will he break the treaty and
yet escape?
16“ ‘As surely as I live, declares the Sovereign
LORD, he shall die in Babylon, in the land of the
king who put him on the throne, whose oath
he despised and whose treaty he broke. 17Phar-
aoh with his mighty army and great horde will
be of no help to him in war, when ramps are
built and siege works erected to destroy many
lives. 18He despised the oath by breaking the
covenant. Because he had given his hand in
pledge and yet did all these things, he shall
not escape.
19“ ‘Therefore this is what the Sovereign
LORD says: As surely as I live, I will bring down
on his head my oath that he despised and my
covenant that he broke. 20I will spread my net
for him, and he will be caught in my snare. I
will bring him to Babylon and execute judgment upon him there because he was unfaithful to me. 21All his fleeing troops will fall by
the sword, and the survivors will be scattered
to the winds. Then you will know that I the
LORD have spoken.
22“ ‘This is what the Sovereign LORD says: I
myself will take a shoot from the very top of
a cedar and plant it; I will break off a tender
sprig from its topmost shoots and plant it on a
high and lofty mountain. 23On the mountain
heights of Israel I will plant it; it will produce
branches and bear fruit and become a splendid
cedar. Birds of every kind will nest in it; they
will find shelter in the shade of its branches.
24All the trees of the field will know that I the
LORD bring down the tall tree and make the
low tree grow tall. I dry up the green tree and
make the dry tree flourish.
“ ‘I the LORD have spoken, and I will do it.’”

The Soul Who Sins Will Die

18 The word of the LORD came to me:
2“What do you people mean by quot-
ing this proverb about the land of Israel:

“ ‘The fathers eat sour grapes,
and the children’s teeth are set on edge’?

3“As surely as I live, declares the Sovereign
LORD, you will no longer quote this proverb in
Israel. 4For every living soul belongs to me, the

father as well as the son—both alike belong to
me. The soul who sins is the one who will die.

5 “Suppose there is a
righteous man
who does what is just
and right.
6 He does not eat at the
mountain shrines
or look to the idols of the
house of Israel.
He does not defile his
neighbor’s wife
or lie with a woman
during her period.
7 He does not oppress
anyone,
but returns what he took
in pledge for a loan.
He does not commit robbery
but gives his food to the hungry
and provides clothing for the naked.
8 He does not lend at usury
or take excessive interest.[a]
He withholds his hand from doing wrong
and judges fairly between man and man.
9 He follows my decrees
and faithfully keeps my laws.
That man is righteous;
he will surely live,
declares the Sovereign LORD.

10 “Suppose he has a violent son, who sheds
blood or does any of these other things[b]
11 (though the father has done none of them):

“He eats at the mountain shrines.
He defiles his neighbor’s wife.
12 He oppresses the poor and needy.
He commits robbery.
He does not return what he took in pledge.
He looks to the idols.
He does detestable things.
13 He lends at usury and takes excessive
interest.

Will such a man live? He will not! Because he
has done all these detestable things, he will
surely be put to death and his blood will be on
his own head.
14 “But suppose this son has a son who sees
all the sins his father commits, and though he
sees them, he does not do such things:

15 “He does not eat at the
mountain shrines
or look to the idols of the
house of Israel.
He does not defile his
neighbor’s wife.
16 He does not oppress
anyone
or require a pledge for a
loan.
He does not commit
robbery
but gives his food to the
hungry
and provides clothing for
the naked.
17 He withholds his hand from sin[c]
and takes no usury or excessive interest.
He keeps my laws and follows my decrees.

He will not die for his father’s sin; he will surely
live. 18 But his father will die for his own sin, because he practiced extortion, robbed his brother
and did what was wrong among his people.
19 “Yet you ask, ‘Why does the son not share
the guilt of his father?’ Since the son has done
what is just and right and has been careful to
keep all my decrees, he will surely live. 20 The
soul who sins is the one who will die. The son
will not share the guilt of the father, nor will the
father share the guilt of the son. The righteousness of the righteous man will be credited to
him, and the wickedness of the wicked will be
charged against him.
21 “But if a wicked man turns away from all
the sins he has committed and keeps all my
decrees and does what is just and right, he
will surely live; he will not die. 22 None of the
offenses he has committed will be remembered
against him. Because of the righteous things he
has done, he will live. 23 Do I take any pleasure
in the death of the wicked? declares the Sovereign LORD. Rather, am I not pleased when they
turn from their ways and live?
24 “But if a righteous man turns from his righteousness and commits sin and does the same
detestable things the wicked man does, will he

Ezekiel 18:4

God Is Over All

“For every living soul belongs to me, the father as well as the son—both alike belong to me. The soul who sins is the one who will die.”

[a] 8 Or *take interest*; similarly in verses 13 and 17 [b] 10 Or *things to a brother* [c] 17 Septuagint (see also verse 8); Hebrew *from the poor*

Family Folly

Ezekiel 18:18–19

"But his father will die for his own sin, because he practiced extortion, robbed his brother and did what was wrong among his people. Yet you ask, 'Why does the son not share the guilt of his father?' Since the son has done what is just and right and has been careful to keep all my decrees, he will surely live."

Read: Ezekiel 18:1–18

SINGER AND AUTHOR STORMIE OMARTIAN has written candidly of the horrors she survived as a child. Stormie's abusive mother was mentally ill. As a result, Stormie was neglected and tragically abused. For much of her early childhood, Stormie remained locked in a closet by her unstable mother, and Stormie's father did nothing to intervene. As an adult, Stormie found hope and healing through her relationship with Jesus Christ. She chose to walk a different path than her parents and in faith guide her children down a godly path.

Perhaps you can relate to Stormie's story. Maybe you grew up in a dysfunctional, abusive or unbelieving home and are tempted to believe that you are destined to repeat the same unhealthy behaviors you witnessed there. Just as heart disease or breast cancer can run in a family, sometimes behavior modeled by certain influential family members can spread throughout the entire family. However, Scripture makes it clear that we are not doomed to repeat the mistakes of others. We can be liberated from the bondage of sin through the freedom found in the perfect role model, Jesus Christ. Jesus said, "So if the Son sets you free, you will be free indeed" (John 8:36). The key is to walk in freedom and faith, obedience and blessing.

While God does not *punish* us for the sins of our family members or caregivers, their sins may cause us to be more likely to make poor choices, exhibit unhealthy patterns or otherwise suffer from their actions. We must remember that we are not responsible for their wrongs. Although affected, we are not condemned because we grew up in an abusive or unbelieving home. Nor are we saved by the faith of godly parents. Each one of us is accountable before God for our own actions.

If someone's sins against you have resulted in fear, unforgiveness or despair, take courage from the fact that God's grace is greater than any wrong. Step into the freedom he has for you today.

reflection

1 What unhealthy behavioral patterns can you identify in past generations of your family?

2 How do these negative actions impact your life today?

3 How can you begin to establish a new spiritual legacy for yourself and your family?

RELATED READINGS

Leviticus 20:9–12; Isaiah 58:12; Matthew 16:27

Go to page 1018 for your next devotional reading.

live? None of the righteous things he has done
will be remembered. Because of the unfaithfulness he is guilty of and because of the sins he
has committed, he will die.
25"Yet you say, 'The way of the Lord is not
just.' Hear, O house of Israel: Is my way unjust?
Is it not your ways that are unjust? 26If a righteous man turns from his righteousness and
commits sin, he will die for it; because of the sin
he has committed he will die. 27But if a wicked
man turns away from the wickedness he has
committed and does what is just and right, he
will save his life. 28Because he considers all
the offenses he has committed and turns away
from them, he will surely live; he will not die.
29Yet the house of Israel says, 'The way of the
Lord is not just.' Are my ways unjust, O house
of Israel? Is it not your ways that are unjust?
30"Therefore, O house of Israel, I will judge
you, each one according to his ways, declares
the Sovereign LORD. Repent! Turn away from
all your offenses; then sin will not be your
downfall. 31Rid yourselves of all the offenses
you have committed, and get a new heart and a
new spirit. Why will you die, O house of Israel?
32For I take no pleasure in the death of anyone,
declares the Sovereign LORD. Repent and live!

A Lament for Israel's Princes

19 "Take up a lament concerning the
princes of Israel 2and say:

"'What a lioness was your mother
among the lions!
She lay down among the young lions
and reared her cubs.
3She brought up one of her cubs,
and he became a strong lion.
He learned to tear the prey
and he devoured men.
4The nations heard about him,
and he was trapped in their pit.
They led him with hooks
to the land of Egypt.
5"'When she saw her hope unfulfilled,
her expectation gone,
she took another of her cubs
and made him a strong lion.
6He prowled among the lions,
for he was now a strong lion.
He learned to tear the prey
and he devoured men.
7He broke down[a] their strongholds
and devastated their towns.
The land and all who were in it
were terrified by his roaring.
8Then the nations came against him,
those from regions round about.
They spread their net for him,
and he was trapped in their pit.
9With hooks they pulled him into a cage
and brought him to the king of Babylon.
They put him in prison,
so his roar was heard no longer
on the mountains of Israel.

10"'Your mother was like a vine in your
vineyard[b]
planted by the water;
it was fruitful and full of branches
because of abundant water.
11Its branches were strong,
fit for a ruler's scepter.
It towered high
above the thick foliage,
conspicuous for its height
and for its many branches.
12But it was uprooted in fury
and thrown to the ground.
The east wind made it shrivel,
it was stripped of its fruit;
its strong branches withered
and fire consumed them.
13Now it is planted in the desert,
in a dry and thirsty land.
14Fire spread from one of its main[c] branches
and consumed its fruit.
No strong branch is left on it
fit for a ruler's scepter.'

This is a lament and is to be used as a lament."

Rebellious Israel

20 In the seventh year, in the fifth month
on the tenth day, some of the elders of
Israel came to inquire of the LORD, and they sat
down in front of me.
2Then the word of the LORD came to me:
3"Son of man, speak to the elders of Israel

[a]7 Targum (see Septuagint); Hebrew *He knew* [b]10 Two Hebrew manuscripts; most Hebrew manuscripts *your blood* [c]14 Or *from under its*

and say to them, 'This is what the Sovereign LORD says: Have you come to inquire of me? As surely as I live, I will not let you inquire of me, declares the Sovereign LORD.'

4"Will you judge them? Will you judge them, son of man? Then confront them with the detestable practices of their fathers 5and say to them: 'This is what the Sovereign LORD says: On the day I chose Israel, I swore with uplifted hand to the descendants of the house of Jacob and revealed myself to them in Egypt. With uplifted hand I said to them, "I am the LORD your God." 6On that day I swore to them that I would bring them out of Egypt into a land I had searched out for them, a land flowing with milk and honey, the most beautiful of all lands. 7And I said to them, "Each of you, get rid of the vile images you have set your eyes on, and do not defile yourselves with the idols of Egypt. I am the LORD your God."

8" 'But they rebelled against me and would not listen to me; they did not get rid of the vile images they had set their eyes on, nor did they forsake the idols of Egypt. So I said I would pour out my wrath on them and spend my anger against them in Egypt. 9But for the sake of my name I did what would keep it from being profaned in the eyes of the nations they lived among and in whose sight I had revealed myself to the Israelites by bringing them out of Egypt. 10Therefore I led them out of Egypt and brought them into the desert. 11I gave them my decrees and made known to them my laws, for the man who obeys them will live by them. 12Also I gave them my Sabbaths as a sign between us, so they would know that I the LORD made them holy.

13" 'Yet the people of Israel rebelled against me in the desert. They did not follow my decrees but rejected my laws—although the man who obeys them will live by them—and they utterly desecrated my Sabbaths. So I said I would pour out my wrath on them and destroy them in the desert. 14But for the sake of my name I did what would keep it from being profaned in the eyes of the nations in whose sight I had brought them out. 15Also with uplifted hand I swore to them in the desert that I would not bring them into the land I had given them—a land flowing with milk and honey, most beautiful of all lands— 16because they rejected my laws and did not follow my decrees and desecrated my Sabbaths. For their hearts were devoted to their idols. 17Yet I looked on them with pity and did not destroy them or put an end to them in the desert. 18I said to their children in the desert, "Do not follow the statutes of your fathers or keep their laws or defile yourselves with their idols. 19I am the LORD your God; follow my decrees and be careful to keep my laws. 20Keep my Sabbaths holy, that they may be a sign between us. Then you will know that I am the LORD your God."

21" 'But the children rebelled against me: They did not follow my decrees, they were not careful to keep my laws—although the man who obeys them will live by them—and they desecrated my Sabbaths. So I said I would pour out my wrath on them and spend my anger against them in the desert. 22But I withheld my hand, and for the sake of my name I did what would keep it from being profaned in the eyes of the nations in whose sight I had brought them out. 23Also with uplifted hand I swore to them in the desert that I would disperse them among the nations and scatter them through the countries, 24because they had not obeyed my laws but had rejected my decrees and desecrated my Sabbaths, and their eyes ⌊lusted⌋ after their fathers' idols. 25I also gave them over to statutes that were not good and laws they could not live by; 26I let them become defiled through their gifts—the sacrifice of every firstborn[a]—that I might fill them with horror so they would know that I am the LORD.'

27"Therefore, son of man, speak to the people of Israel and say to them, 'This is what the Sovereign LORD says: In this also your fathers

Ezekiel 20:19

God Expects Obedience

"I am the LORD your God; follow my decrees and be careful to keep my laws."

[a]26 Or *—making every firstborn pass through ⌊the fire⌋*

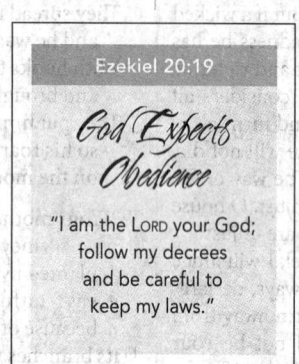

blasphemed me by forsaking me: 28When I
brought them into the land I had sworn to give
them and they saw any high hill or any leafy
tree, there they offered their sacrifices, made
offerings that provoked me to anger, presented
their fragrant incense and poured out their
drink offerings. 29Then I said to them: What is
this high place you go to?' " (It is called Bamah[a]
to this day.)

Judgment and Restoration

30"Therefore say to the house of Israel: 'This
is what the Sovereign LORD says: Will you defile yourselves the way your fathers did and
lust after their vile images? 31When you offer
your gifts—the sacrifice of your sons in[b] the
fire—you continue to defile yourselves with all
your idols to this day. Am I to let you inquire
of me, O house of Israel? As surely as I live, declares the Sovereign LORD, I will not let you inquire of me.
32" 'You say, "We want to be like the nations,
like the peoples of the world, who serve wood
and stone." But what you have in mind will
never happen. 33As surely as I live, declares
the Sovereign LORD, I will rule over you with a
mighty hand and an outstretched arm and with
outpoured wrath. 34I will bring you from the nations and gather you from the countries where
you have been scattered—with a mighty hand
and an outstretched arm and with outpoured
wrath. 35I will bring you into the desert of the
nations and there, face to face, I will execute
judgment upon you. 36As I judged your fathers
in the desert of the land of Egypt, so I will judge
you, declares the Sovereign LORD. 37I will take
note of you as you pass under my rod, and I
will bring you into the bond of the covenant.
38I will purge you of those who revolt and rebel against me. Although I will bring them out
of the land where they are living, yet they will
not enter the land of Israel. Then you will know
that I am the LORD.
39" 'As for you, O house of Israel, this is what
the Sovereign LORD says: Go and serve your
idols, every one of you! But afterward you will
surely listen to me and no longer profane my
holy name with your gifts and idols. 40For
on my holy mountain, the high mountain of
Israel, declares the Sovereign LORD, there in
the land the entire house of Israel will serve
me, and there I will accept them. There I will
require your offerings and your choice gifts,[c]
along with all your holy sacrifices. 41I will accept you as fragrant incense when I bring you
out from the nations and gather you from the
countries where you have been scattered, and
I will show myself holy among you in the sight
of the nations. 42Then you will know that I
am the LORD, when I bring you into the land
of Israel, the land I had sworn with uplifted
hand to give to your fathers. 43There you will
remember your conduct and all the actions by
which you have defiled yourselves, and you
will loathe yourselves for all the evil you have
done. 44You will know that I am the LORD,
when I deal with you for my name's sake and
not according to your evil ways and your corrupt practices, O house of Israel, declares the
Sovereign LORD.' "

Prophecy Against the South

45The word of the LORD came to me: 46"Son
of man, set your face toward the south; preach
against the south and prophesy against the forest of the southland. 47Say to the southern forest: 'Hear the word of the LORD. This is what
the Sovereign LORD says: I am about to set
fire to you, and it will consume all your trees,
both green and dry. The blazing flame will not
be quenched, and every face from south to
north will be scorched by it. 48Everyone will
see that I the LORD have kindled it; it will not
be quenched.' "
49Then I said, "Ah, Sovereign LORD! They are
saying of me, 'Isn't he just telling parables?' "

Babylon, God's Sword of Judgment

21 The word of the LORD came to me:
2"Son of man, set your face against
Jerusalem and preach against the sanctuary.
Prophesy against the land of Israel 3and say to
her: 'This is what the LORD says: I am against
you. I will draw my sword from its scabbard
and cut off from you both the righteous and
the wicked. 4Because I am going to cut off the
righteous and the wicked, my sword will be
unsheathed against everyone from south to
north. 5Then all people will know that I the

[a]29 *Bamah* means *high place.* [b]31 Or *—making your sons pass through* [c]40 Or *and the gifts of your firstfruits*

LORD have drawn my sword from its scabbard;
it will not return again.’
6 “Therefore groan, son of man! Groan before them with broken heart and bitter grief.
7 And when they ask you, ‘Why are you groaning?’ you shall say, ‘Because of the news that
is coming. Every heart will melt and every
hand go limp; every spirit will become faint
and every knee become as weak as water.’ It is
coming! It will surely take place, declares the
Sovereign LORD.”
8 The word of the LORD came to me: 9 “Son
of man, prophesy and say, ‘This is what the
Lord says:

“ ‘A sword, a sword,
sharpened and polished—
10 sharpened for the slaughter,
polished to flash like lightning!

“ ‘Shall we rejoice in the scepter of my son
⌊Judah⌋? The sword despises every such stick.

11 “ ‘The sword is appointed to be polished,
to be grasped with the hand;
it is sharpened and polished,
made ready for the hand of the slayer.
12 Cry out and wail, son of man,
for it is against my people;
it is against all the princes of Israel.
They are thrown to the sword
along with my people.
Therefore beat your breast.

13 “ ‘Testing will surely come. And what
if the scepter ⌊of Judah⌋, which the sword
despises, does not continue? declares the Sovereign LORD.’

14 “So then, son of man, prophesy
and strike your hands together.
Let the sword strike twice,
even three times.
It is a sword for slaughter—
a sword for great slaughter,
closing in on them from every side.
15 So that hearts may melt
and the fallen be many,
I have stationed the sword for slaughter[a]
at all their gates.
Oh! It is made to flash like lightning,
it is grasped for slaughter.
16 O sword, slash to the right,
then to the left,
wherever your blade is turned.
17 I too will strike my hands together,
and my wrath will subside.
I the LORD have spoken.”

18 The word of the LORD came to me: 19 “Son
of man, mark out two roads for the sword of
the king of Babylon to take, both starting from
the same country. Make a signpost where the
road branches off to the city. 20 Mark out one
road for the sword to come against Rabbah of
the Ammonites and another against Judah and
fortified Jerusalem. 21 For the king of Babylon
will stop at the fork in the road, at the junction
of the two roads, to seek an omen: He will cast
lots with arrows, he will consult his idols, he
will examine the liver. 22 Into his right hand
will come the lot for Jerusalem, where he is to
set up battering rams, to give the command to
slaughter, to sound the battle cry, to set battering rams against the gates, to build a ramp and
to erect siege works. 23 It will seem like a false
omen to those who have sworn allegiance to
him, but he will remind them of their guilt and
take them captive.
24 “Therefore this is what the Sovereign
LORD says: ‘Because you people have brought
to mind your guilt by your open rebellion, revealing your sins in all that you do—because
you have done this, you will be taken captive.
25 “ ‘O profane and wicked prince of Israel,
whose day has come, whose time of punishment has reached its climax, 26 this is what
the Sovereign LORD says: Take off the turban,
remove the crown. It will not be as it was: The
lowly will be exalted and the exalted will be
brought low. 27 A ruin! A ruin! I will make it
a ruin! It will not be restored until he comes
to whom it rightfully belongs; to him I will
give it.’
28 “And you, son of man, prophesy and say,
‘This is what the Sovereign LORD says about the
Ammonites and their insults:

“ ‘A sword, a sword,
drawn for the slaughter,
polished to consume

[a] 15 Septuagint; the meaning of the Hebrew for this word is uncertain.

and to flash like lightning!
29 Despite false visions concerning you
and lying divinations about you,
it will be laid on the necks
of the wicked who are to be slain,
whose day has come,
whose time of punishment has reached
its climax.
30 Return the sword to its scabbard.
In the place where you were created,
in the land of your ancestry,
I will judge you.
31 I will pour out my wrath upon you
and breathe out my fiery
anger against you;
I will hand you over to
brutal men,
men skilled in
destruction.
32 You will be fuel for the fire,
your blood will be shed
in your land,
you will be remembered no
more;
for I the LORD have
spoken.' "

> **Ezekiel 22:14**
>
> *God Follows Through*
>
> "Will your courage endure or your hands be strong in the day I deal with you? I the LORD have spoken, and I will do it."

Jerusalem's Sins

22 The word of the LORD came to me:
2 "Son of man, will you judge her? Will
you judge this city of bloodshed? Then confront her with all her detestable practices 3 and
say: 'This is what the Sovereign LORD says:
O city that brings on herself doom by shedding blood in her midst and defiles herself by
making idols, 4 you have become guilty because
of the blood you have shed and have become
defiled by the idols you have made. You have
brought your days to a close, and the end of
your years has come. Therefore I will make you
an object of scorn to the nations and a laughingstock to all the countries. 5 Those who are near
and those who are far away will mock you, O
infamous city, full of turmoil.
6 " 'See how each of the princes of Israel who
are in you uses his power to shed blood. 7 In you
they have treated father and mother with contempt; in you they have oppressed the alien and
mistreated the fatherless and the widow. 8 You
have despised my holy things and desecrated
my Sabbaths. 9 In you are slanderous men bent
on shedding blood; in you are those who eat at
the mountain shrines and commit lewd acts.
10 In you are those who dishonor their fathers'
bed; in you are those who violate women during their period, when they are ceremonially
unclean. 11 In you one man commits a detestable offense with his neighbor's wife, another
shamefully defiles his daughter-in-law, and
another violates his sister, his own father's
daughter. 12 In you men accept bribes to shed
blood; you take usury and excessive interest[a]
and make unjust gain from
your neighbors by extortion.
And you have forgotten me, declares the Sovereign LORD.
13 " 'I will surely strike my
hands together at the unjust
gain you have made and at the
blood you have shed in your
midst. 14 Will your courage endure or your hands be strong
in the day I deal with you? I
the LORD have spoken, and I
will do it. 15 I will disperse you
among the nations and scatter
you through the countries; and
I will put an end to your uncleanness. 16 When
you have been defiled[b] in the eyes of the nations, you will know that I am the LORD.' "
17 Then the word of the LORD came to me:
18 "Son of man, the house of Israel has become
dross to me; all of them are the copper, tin,
iron and lead left inside a furnace. They are but
the dross of silver. 19 Therefore this is what the
Sovereign LORD says: 'Because you have all become dross, I will gather you into Jerusalem.
20 As men gather silver, copper, iron, lead and
tin into a furnace to melt it with a fiery blast,
so will I gather you in my anger and my wrath
and put you inside the city and melt you. 21 I
will gather you and I will blow on you with my
fiery wrath, and you will be melted inside her.
22 As silver is melted in a furnace, so you will be
melted inside her, and you will know that I the
LORD have poured out my wrath upon you.' "
23 Again the word of the LORD came to me:
24 "Son of man, say to the land, 'You are a land

[a] 12 Or *usury and interest* [b] 16 Or *When I have allotted you your inheritance*

Hard Truth

Read: Ezekiel 22:17–22

HOW DO YOU EXPLAIN the presence of pain?

In his book *Celebrating the Wrath of God*, Jim McGuiggan writes of a young Christian couple who longed to have a baby. After years of prayer, they finally had a child, but the little one had severe spina bifida and did not live long. How could God allow such loss? McGuiggan writes that as long as we continue to think of God as a warm and fuzzy deity, we will be unable to understand the presence of pain in the world and the power of God to redeem our pain.

It may seem easier to focus on the "nice" passages of Scripture that speak clearly of God's love; however, to ignore the passages about God's anger, vengeance and jealousy is to miss who God is. In Ezekiel 22, the prophet speaks hard truth to the nation of Israel. It may have been easier for Israel to hear of God's affection for them, but that would have been counter to God's nature. God hates anything and everything that destroys the people and the world he created. He is angry with those who participate in that destruction. He is jealous of anything that breaks his covenant of love with his people. God loves what he created, and he will pour out his righteous wrath as a reflection of that love. Read that again, slowly.

Sin alters the created order so significantly that it leads to the sickness, disease, sadness, stress and fatigue that we experience. God hates all the sin and sorrow that causes suffering and has sent the Messiah to redeem the world from it. The good news is that suffering can point us to God's power to console and redeem.

Just as the Israelites in Ezekiel's time suffered, we, too, will suffer . . . it's a Biblical promise: "It has been granted to you on behalf of Christ not only to believe on him, but also to suffer for him" (Philippians 1:29). Sometimes suffering is the direct result of our sin. Sometimes suffering is simply a consequence of the fact that we are fragile human beings. Sometimes we suffer as the result of other people's sins. But while we live on this earth, we will endure pain and suffering. Won't you allow God to use your pain to draw you closer to him?

Ezekiel 22:22

"As silver is melted in a furnace, so you will be melted inside her, and you will know that I the LORD have poured out my wrath upon you."

reflection

1 How do you think suffering can strengthen your relationship with God?

2 Have you experienced pain that drew you closer to God?

3 What would it be like for you to embrace the difficult things of your life today—physical pain, a strained relationship or a major disappointment—as part of God's redemptive work in you?

RELATED READINGS

Psalm 103:1–22; Zechariah 7:8–14; Revelation 20:1–4

"Suffering is the very best gift God has to give us. He gives it only to his chosen friends."

Therese of Liseux

Thursday

Go to page 1022 for your next devotional reading.

that has had no rain or showers[a] in the day of
wrath.' 25There is a conspiracy of her princes[b]
within her like a roaring lion tearing its prey;
they devour people, take treasures and precious things and make many widows within
her. 26Her priests do violence to my law and
profane my holy things; they do not distinguish
between the holy and the common; they teach
that there is no difference between the unclean
and the clean; and they shut their eyes to the
keeping of my Sabbaths, so that I am profaned
among them. 27Her officials within her are like
wolves tearing their prey; they shed blood and
kill people to make unjust gain. 28Her prophets whitewash these deeds for them by false
visions and lying divinations. They say, 'This
is what the Sovereign LORD says'—when the
LORD has not spoken. 29The people of the land
practice extortion and commit robbery; they
oppress the poor and needy and mistreat the
alien, denying them justice.

30"I looked for a man among them who
would build up the wall and stand before me
in the gap on behalf of the land so I would not
have to destroy it, but I found none. 31So I
will pour out my wrath on them and consume
them with my fiery anger, bringing down on
their own heads all they have done, declares the
Sovereign LORD."

Two Adulterous Sisters

23 The word of the LORD came to me:
2"Son of man, there were two women,
daughters of the same mother. 3They became
prostitutes in Egypt, engaging in prostitution
from their youth. In that land their breasts
were fondled and their virgin bosoms caressed.
4The older was named Oholah, and her sister
was Oholibah. They were mine and gave birth
to sons and daughters. Oholah is Samaria, and
Oholibah is Jerusalem.

5"Oholah engaged in prostitution while she
was still mine; and she lusted after her lovers,
the Assyrians—warriors 6clothed in blue, governors and commanders, all of them handsome young men, and mounted horsemen.
7She gave herself as a prostitute to all the elite
of the Assyrians and defiled herself with all the
idols of everyone she lusted after. 8She did not
give up the prostitution she began in Egypt,
when during her youth men slept with her, caressed her virgin bosom and poured out their
lust upon her.

9"Therefore I handed her over to her lovers,
the Assyrians, for whom she lusted. 10They
stripped her naked, took away her sons and
daughters and killed her with the sword. She
became a byword among women, and punishment was inflicted on her.

11"Her sister Oholibah saw this, yet in her
lust and prostitution she was more depraved
than her sister. 12She too lusted after the Assyrians—governors and commanders, warriors in
full dress, mounted horsemen, all handsome
young men. 13I saw that she too defiled herself;
both of them went the same way.

14"But she carried her prostitution still further. She saw men portrayed on a wall, figures
of Chaldeans[c] portrayed in red, 15with belts
around their waists and flowing turbans on
their heads; all of them looked like Babylonian
chariot officers, natives of Chaldea.[d] 16As soon
as she saw them, she lusted after them and sent
messengers to them in Chaldea. 17Then the
Babylonians came to her, to the bed of love, and
in their lust they defiled her. After she had been
defiled by them, she turned away from them in
disgust. 18When she carried on her prostitution openly and exposed her nakedness, I
turned away from her in disgust, just as I had
turned away from her sister. 19Yet she became
more and more promiscuous as she recalled
the days of her youth, when she was a prostitute in Egypt. 20There she lusted after her
lovers, whose genitals were like those of donkeys and whose emission was like that of
horses. 21So you longed for the lewdness of
your youth, when in Egypt your bosom was
caressed and your young breasts fondled.[e]

22"Therefore, Oholibah, this is what the
Sovereign LORD says: I will stir up your lovers against you, those you turned away from
in disgust, and I will bring them against you
from every side— 23the Babylonians and all
the Chaldeans, the men of Pekod and Shoa
and Koa, and all the Assyrians with them,
handsome young men, all of them governors

[a]24 Septuagint; Hebrew *has not been cleansed or rained on* [b]25 Septuagint; Hebrew *prophets* [c]14 Or *Babylonians* [d]15 Or *Babylonia*; also in verse 16 [e]21 Syriac (see also verse 3); Hebrew *caressed because of your young breasts*

and commanders, chariot officers and men of
high rank, all mounted on horses. 24They will
come against you with weapons,[a] chariots and
wagons and with a throng of people; they will
take up positions against you on every side
with large and small shields and with helmets. I
will turn you over to them for punishment, and
they will punish you according to their standards. 25I will direct my jealous anger against
you, and they will deal with you in fury. They
will cut off your noses and your ears, and those
of you who are left will fall by the sword. They
will take away your sons and daughters, and
those of you who are left will be consumed by
fire. 26They will also strip you of your clothes
and take your fine jewelry. 27So I will put a stop
to the lewdness and prostitution you began in
Egypt. You will not look on these things with
longing or remember Egypt anymore.

28"For this is what the Sovereign LORD says:
I am about to hand you over to those you hate,
to those you turned away from in disgust.
29They will deal with you in hatred and take
away everything you have worked for. They
will leave you naked and bare, and the shame
of your prostitution will be exposed. Your lewdness and promiscuity 30have brought this upon
you, because you lusted after the nations and
defiled yourself with their idols. 31You have
gone the way of your sister; so I will put her
cup into your hand.

32"This is what the Sovereign LORD says:

"You will drink your sister's cup,
  a cup large and deep;
it will bring scorn and derision,
  for it holds so much.
33You will be filled with drunkenness and
    sorrow,
  the cup of ruin and desolation,
  the cup of your sister Samaria.
34You will drink it and drain it dry;
  you will dash it to pieces
  and tear your breasts.

I have spoken, declares the Sovereign LORD.

35"Therefore this is what the Sovereign
LORD says: Since you have forgotten me and
thrust me behind your back, you must bear
the consequences of your lewdness and prostitution."

36The LORD said to me: "Son of man, will
you judge Oholah and Oholibah? Then confront them with their detestable practices, 37for
they have committed adultery and blood is on
their hands. They committed adultery with
their idols; they even sacrificed their children,
whom they bore to me,[b] as food for them.
38They have also done this to me: At that same
time they defiled my sanctuary and desecrated
my Sabbaths. 39On the very day they sacrificed
their children to their idols, they entered my
sanctuary and desecrated it. That is what they
did in my house.

40"They even sent messengers for men who
came from far away, and when they arrived
you bathed yourself for them, painted your
eyes and put on your jewelry. 41You sat on an
elegant couch, with a table spread before it on
which you had placed the incense and oil that
belonged to me.

42"The noise of a carefree crowd was around
her; Sabeans[c] were brought from the desert
along with men from the rabble, and they put
bracelets on the arms of the woman and her
sister and beautiful crowns on their heads.
43Then I said about the one worn out by adultery, 'Now let them use her as a prostitute, for
that is all she is.' 44And they slept with her. As
men sleep with a prostitute, so they slept with
those lewd women, Oholah and Oholibah.
45But righteous men will sentence them to the
punishment of women who commit adultery
and shed blood, because they are adulterous
and blood is on their hands.

46"This is what the Sovereign LORD says:
Bring a mob against them and give them over
to terror and plunder. 47The mob will stone
them and cut them down with their swords;
they will kill their sons and daughters and burn
down their houses.

48"So I will put an end to lewdness in the
land, that all women may take warning and
not imitate you. 49You will suffer the penalty
for your lewdness and bear the consequences
of your sins of idolatry. Then you will know
that I am the Sovereign LORD."

[a]24 The meaning of the Hebrew for this word is uncertain. [b]37 Or *even made the children they bore to me pass through ⌊the fire⌋*
[c]42 Or *drunkards*

The Cooking Pot

24 In the ninth year, in the tenth month
on the tenth day, the word of the LORD
came to me: 2"Son of man, record this date, this
very date, because the king of Babylon has laid
siege to Jerusalem this very day. 3Tell this rebellious house a parable and say to them: 'This is
what the Sovereign LORD says:

"'Put on the cooking pot; put it on
and pour water into it.
4 Put into it the pieces of meat,
all the choice pieces—the leg and the
shoulder.
Fill it with the best of these bones;
5 take the pick of the flock.
Pile wood beneath it for the bones;
bring it to a boil
and cook the bones in it.

6"'For this is what the Sovereign LORD says:

"'Woe to the city of bloodshed,
to the pot now encrusted,
whose deposit will not go away!
Empty it piece by piece
without casting lots for them.

7"'For the blood she shed is in her midst:
She poured it on the bare rock;
she did not pour it on the ground,
where the dust would cover it.
8 To stir up wrath and take revenge
I put her blood on the bare rock,
so that it would not be covered.

9"'Therefore this is what the Sovereign LORD
says:

"'Woe to the city of bloodshed!
I, too, will pile the wood high.
10 So heap on the wood
and kindle the fire.
Cook the meat well,
mixing in the spices;
and let the bones be charred.
11 Then set the empty pot on the coals
till it becomes hot and its copper
glows
so its impurities may be melted
and its deposit burned away.
12 It has frustrated all efforts;
its heavy deposit has not been removed,
not even by fire.

13"'Now your impurity is lewdness. Because
I tried to cleanse you but you would not be
cleansed from your impurity, you will not be
clean again until my wrath against you has
subsided.

14"'I the LORD have spoken. The time has
come for me to act. I will not hold back; I will
not have pity, nor will I relent. You will be
judged according to your conduct and your actions, declares the Sovereign LORD.'"

Ezekiel's Wife Dies

15The word of the LORD came to me: 16"Son
of man, with one blow I am about to take away
from you the delight of your eyes. Yet do not
lament or weep or shed any tears. 17Groan
quietly; do not mourn for the dead. Keep your
turban fastened and your sandals on your feet;
do not cover the lower part of your face or eat
the customary food ⌞of mourners⌟."

18So I spoke to the people in the morning,
and in the evening my wife died. The next
morning I did as I had been commanded.

19Then the people asked me, "Won't you tell
us what these things have to do with us?"

20So I said to them, "The word of the LORD
came to me: 21Say to the house of Israel, 'This
is what the Sovereign LORD says: I am about
to desecrate my sanctuary—the stronghold
in which you take pride, the delight of your
eyes, the object of your affection. The sons
and daughters you left behind will fall by the
sword. 22And you will do as I have done. You
will not cover the lower part of your face or eat
the customary food ⌞of mourners⌟. 23You will
keep your turbans on your heads and your sandals on your feet. You will not mourn or weep
but will waste away because of[a] your sins and
groan among yourselves. 24Ezekiel will be a
sign to you; you will do just as he has done.
When this happens, you will know that I am
the Sovereign LORD.'

25"And you, son of man, on the day I take
away their stronghold, their joy and glory, the
delight of their eyes, their heart's desire, and
their sons and daughters as well— 26on that
day a fugitive will come to tell you the news.

[a]23 Or *away in*

Signposts

Ezekiel 24:18

So I spoke to the people in the morning, and in the evening my wife died. The next morning I did as I had been commanded.

reflection

1 How do you think that Ezekiel was able to do what God asked?

2 What do you think the people learned from Ezekiel's actions?

3 What can others learn about God from watching how you handle life's challenges?

RELATED READINGS

Ezekiel 12:9–11; Matthew 5:16; Luke 11:30; 1 Timothy 4:15–16; 1 Peter 2:12

Read: Ezekiel 24:15–27

IMAGES OF JOHN F. KENNEDY'S assassination on November 22, 1963, are seared on many people's memories. We remember the Dallas motorcade, with the Camelot couple smiling and waving. We remember Jackie in her pink suit and pillbox hat. Then the shock of the shots from the Texas School Book Depository. Who can forget the dignified stance of Jacqueline Kennedy or the heart-wrenching icon of John Jr. standing at attention, saluting his father's flag-draped casket as it passed by on the horse-drawn caisson? Though the family's loss was very public, their grief was dignified and private.

When God told Ezekiel that his wife, whom he deeply loved, was going to die, it had the same sense of tragedy. And Ezekiel, too, was required to deal with his sorrow before a watching world.

God used Ezekiel's tragedy as a symbol that the Israelite people could learn from. His wife's death foreshadowed a time when the sanctuary would be desecrated and the people's children would be killed. God insisted that Ezekiel not grieve his loss publicly, only privately. When the people asked why Ezekiel was not grieving, he was able to explain God's prophecy: The people would not be able to publicly mourn their losses. Instead, they would privately grieve over their own sin that caused such destruction. Ezekiel's loss was altogether real, deep and painful. Yet God used that experience.

God used Ezekiel as a signpost to direct others to him and to help them know he was the Lord (verse 27). Ezekiel said, "I did as I had been commanded," and he turned his tragedy into a life that pointed to God. Our lives also have the potential to reveal who God is. While an entire nation might not be watching, those closest to us are key viewers when it comes to watching the drama of our lives unfold. How we handle a number of plots—loss, success, friendship, marriage, finances—gives others an opportunity to see the difference that being a disciple of Jesus makes.

Go to page 1034 for your next devotional reading.

27 At that time your mouth will be opened; you
will speak with him and will no longer be silent. So you will be a sign to them, and they will
know that I am the LORD."

A Prophecy Against Ammon

25 The word of the LORD came to me:
2 "Son of man, set your face against the
Ammonites and prophesy against them. 3 Say
to them, 'Hear the word of the Sovereign LORD.
This is what the Sovereign LORD says: Because
you said "Aha!" over my sanctuary when it was
desecrated and over the land of Israel when it
was laid waste and over the people of Judah
when they went into exile, 4 therefore I am going to give you to the people of the East as a possession. They will set up their camps and pitch
their tents among you; they will eat your fruit
and drink your milk. 5 I will turn Rabbah into
a pasture for camels and Ammon into a resting
place for sheep. Then you will know that I am
the LORD. 6 For this is what the Sovereign LORD
says: Because you have clapped your hands and
stamped your feet, rejoicing with all the malice
of your heart against the land of Israel, 7 therefore I will stretch out my hand against you and
give you as plunder to the nations. I will cut
you off from the nations and exterminate you
from the countries. I will destroy you, and you
will know that I am the LORD.'"

A Prophecy Against Moab

8 "This is what the Sovereign LORD says: 'Because Moab and Seir said, "Look, the house of
Judah has become like all the other nations,"
9 therefore I will expose the flank of Moab, beginning at its frontier towns—Beth Jeshimoth,
Baal Meon and Kiriathaim—the glory of that
land. 10 I will give Moab along with the Ammonites to the people of the East as a possession, so
that the Ammonites will not be remembered
among the nations; 11 and I will inflict punishment on Moab. Then they will know that I am
the LORD.'"

A Prophecy Against Edom

12 "This is what the Sovereign LORD says:
'Because Edom took revenge on the house
of Judah and became very guilty by doing so,
13 therefore this is what the Sovereign LORD
says: I will stretch out my hand against Edom
and kill its men and their animals. I will lay it
waste, and from Teman to Dedan they will fall
by the sword. 14 I will take vengeance on Edom
by the hand of my people Israel, and they will
deal with Edom in accordance with my anger
and my wrath; they will know my vengeance,
declares the Sovereign LORD.'"

A Prophecy Against Philistia

15 "This is what the Sovereign LORD says: 'Because the Philistines acted in vengeance and
took revenge with malice in their hearts, and
with ancient hostility sought to destroy Judah,
16 therefore this is what the Sovereign LORD
says: I am about to stretch out my hand against
the Philistines, and I will cut off the Kerethites
and destroy those remaining along the coast.
17 I will carry out great vengeance on them and
punish them in my wrath. Then they will know
that I am the LORD, when I take vengeance
on them.'"

A Prophecy Against Tyre

26 In the eleventh year, on the first day of
the month, the word of the LORD came
to me: 2 "Son of man, because Tyre has said of
Jerusalem, 'Aha! The gate to the nations is broken, and its doors have swung open to me; now
that she lies in ruins I will prosper,' 3 therefore
this is what the Sovereign LORD says: I am
against you, O Tyre, and I will bring many
nations against you, like the sea casting up its
waves. 4 They will destroy the walls of Tyre and
pull down her towers; I will scrape away her
rubble and make her a bare rock. 5 Out in the
sea she will become a place to spread fishnets,
for I have spoken, declares the Sovereign LORD.
She will become plunder for the nations, 6 and
her settlements on the mainland will be ravaged by the sword. Then they will know that
I am the LORD.

7 "For this is what the Sovereign LORD says:
From the north I am going to bring against
Tyre Nebuchadnezzar[a] king of Babylon, king of
kings, with horses and chariots, with horsemen
and a great army. 8 He will ravage your settlements on the mainland with the sword; he will
set up siege works against you, build a ramp up
to your walls and raise his shields against you.

a7 Hebrew *Nebuchadrezzar,* of which *Nebuchadnezzar* is a variant; here and often in Ezekiel and Jeremiah

9He will direct the blows of his battering rams
against your walls and demolish your towers
with his weapons. 10His horses will be so many
that they will cover you with dust. Your walls
will tremble at the noise of the war horses, wagons and chariots when he enters your gates as
men enter a city whose walls have been broken
through. 11The hoofs of his horses will trample
all your streets; he will kill your people with the
sword, and your strong pillars will fall to the
ground. 12They will plunder your wealth and
loot your merchandise; they will break down
your walls and demolish your fine houses and
throw your stones, timber and rubble into the
sea. 13I will put an end to your noisy songs, and
the music of your harps will be heard no more.
14I will make you a bare rock, and you will become a place to spread fishnets. You will never
be rebuilt, for I the LORD have spoken, declares
the Sovereign LORD.

15"This is what the Sovereign LORD says to
Tyre: Will not the coastlands tremble at the
sound of your fall, when the wounded groan
and the slaughter takes place in you? 16Then
all the princes of the coast will step down from
their thrones and lay aside their robes and take
off their embroidered garments. Clothed with
terror, they will sit on the ground, trembling
every moment, appalled at you. 17Then they
will take up a lament concerning you and say
to you:

"'How you are destroyed, O city of
renown,
peopled by men of the sea!
You were a power on the seas,
you and your citizens;
you put your terror
on all who lived there.
18Now the coastlands tremble
on the day of your fall;
the islands in the sea
are terrified at your collapse.'

19"This is what the Sovereign LORD says:
When I make you a desolate city, like cities no
longer inhabited, and when I bring the ocean
depths over you and its vast waters cover you,
20then I will bring you down with those who
go down to the pit, to the people of long ago.
I will make you dwell in the earth below, as in
ancient ruins, with those who go down to the
pit, and you will not return or take your place[a]
in the land of the living. 21I will bring you to a
horrible end and you will be no more. You will
be sought, but you will never again be found,
declares the Sovereign LORD."

A Lament for Tyre

27 The word of the LORD came to me:
2"Son of man, take up a lament concerning Tyre. 3Say to Tyre, situated at the gateway to the sea, merchant of peoples on many
coasts, 'This is what the Sovereign LORD says:

"'You say, O Tyre,
"I am perfect in beauty."
4Your domain was on the high seas;
your builders brought your beauty to
perfection.
5They made all your timbers
of pine trees from Senir[b];
they took a cedar from Lebanon
to make a mast for you.
6Of oaks from Bashan
they made your oars;
of cypress wood[c] from the coasts of
Cyprus[d]
they made your deck, inlaid with ivory.
7Fine embroidered linen from Egypt was
your sail
and served as your banner;
your awnings were of blue and purple
from the coasts of Elishah.
8Men of Sidon and Arvad were your
oarsmen;
your skilled men, O Tyre, were aboard
as your seamen.
9Veteran craftsmen of Gebal[e] were on board
as shipwrights to caulk your seams.
All the ships of the sea and their sailors
came alongside to trade for your wares.

10"'Men of Persia, Lydia and Put
served as soldiers in your army.
They hung their shields and helmets on
your walls,
bringing you splendor.
11Men of Arvad and Helech

[a]20 Septuagint; Hebrew *return, and I will give glory* [b]5 That is, Hermon [c]6 Targum; the Masoretic Text has a different division of the consonants. [d]6 Hebrew *Kittim* [e]9 That is, Byblos

manned your walls on every side;
men of Gammad
were in your towers.
They hung their shields around your walls;
they brought your beauty to perfection.

12 " 'Tarshish did business with you because
of your great wealth of goods; they exchanged
silver, iron, tin and lead for your merchandise.
13 " 'Greece, Tubal and Meshech traded with
you; they exchanged slaves and articles of
bronze for your wares.
14 " 'Men of Beth Togarmah exchanged work
horses, war horses and mules for your merchandise.
15 " 'The men of Rhodes[a] traded with you,
and many coastlands were your customers;
they paid you with ivory tusks and ebony.
16 " 'Aram[b] did business with you because
of your many products; they exchanged turquoise, purple fabric, embroidered work, fine
linen, coral and rubies for your merchandise.
17 " 'Judah and Israel traded with you; they
exchanged wheat from Minnith and confec-
tions,[c] honey, oil and balm for your wares.
18 " 'Damascus, because of your many products and great wealth of goods, did business
with you in wine from Helbon and wool from
Zahar.
19 " 'Danites and Greeks from Uzal bought
your merchandise; they exchanged wrought
iron, cassia and calamus for your wares.
20 " 'Dedan traded in saddle blankets with
you.
21 " 'Arabia and all the princes of Kedar were
your customers; they did business with you in
lambs, rams and goats.
22 " 'The merchants of Sheba and Raamah
traded with you; for your merchandise they
exchanged the finest of all kinds of spices and
precious stones, and gold.
23 " 'Haran, Canneh and Eden and merchants
of Sheba, Asshur and Kilmad traded with you.
24 In your marketplace they traded with you
beautiful garments, blue fabric, embroidered
work and multicolored rugs with cords twisted
and tightly knotted.

25 " 'The ships of Tarshish serve
as carriers for your wares.
You are filled with heavy cargo
in the heart of the sea.
26 Your oarsmen take you
out to the high seas.
But the east wind will break you to pieces
in the heart of the sea.
27 Your wealth, merchandise and wares,
your mariners, seamen and shipwrights,
your merchants and all your soldiers,
and everyone else on board
will sink into the heart of the sea
on the day of your shipwreck.
28 The shorelands will quake
when your seamen cry out.
29 All who handle the oars
will abandon their ships;
the mariners and all the seamen
will stand on the shore.
30 They will raise their voice
and cry bitterly over you;
they will sprinkle dust on their heads
and roll in ashes.
31 They will shave their heads because of you
and will put on sackcloth.
They will weep over you with anguish of
soul
and with bitter mourning.
32 As they wail and mourn over you,
they will take up a lament concerning
you:
"Who was ever silenced like Tyre,
surrounded by the sea?"
33 When your merchandise went out on the
seas,
you satisfied many nations;
with your great wealth and your wares
you enriched the kings of the earth.
34 Now you are shattered by the sea
in the depths of the waters;
your wares and all your company
have gone down with you.
35 All who live in the coastlands
are appalled at you;
their kings shudder with horror
and their faces are distorted with fear.
36 The merchants among the nations hiss at
you;
you have come to a horrible end
and will be no more.' "

[a]15 Septuagint; Hebrew *Dedan* [b]16 Most Hebrew manuscripts; some Hebrew manuscripts and Syriac *Edom* [c]17 The meaning of the Hebrew for this word is uncertain.

A Prophecy Against the King of Tyre

28 The word of the LORD came to me:
2 "Son of man, say to the ruler of Tyre,
'This is what the Sovereign LORD says:

" 'In the pride of your heart
you say, "I am a god;
I sit on the throne of a god
in the heart of the seas."
But you are a man and not a god,
though you think you are as wise as a god.
3 Are you wiser than Daniel[a]?
Is no secret hidden from you?
4 By your wisdom and understanding
you have gained wealth for yourself
and amassed gold and silver
in your treasuries.
5 By your great skill in trading
you have increased your wealth,
and because of your wealth
your heart has grown proud.

6 " 'Therefore this is what the Sovereign
LORD says:

" 'Because you think you are wise,
as wise as a god,
7 I am going to bring foreigners against you,
the most ruthless of nations;
they will draw their swords
against your beauty and wisdom
and pierce your shining splendor.
8 They will bring you down to the pit,
and you will die a violent death
in the heart of the seas.
9 Will you then say, "I am a god,"
in the presence of those who kill you?
You will be but a man, not a god,
in the hands of those who slay you.
10 You will die the death of the uncircumcised
at the hands of foreigners.
I have spoken, declares the Sovereign LORD.' "

11 The word of the LORD came to me: 12 "Son
of man, take up a lament concerning the king
of Tyre and say to him: 'This is what the Sovereign LORD says:

" 'You were the model of perfection,
full of wisdom and perfect in beauty.
13 You were in Eden,
the garden of God;
every precious stone adorned you:
ruby, topaz and emerald,
chrysolite, onyx and jasper,
sapphire,[b] turquoise and beryl.[c]
Your settings and mountings[d] were made of gold;
on the day you were created they were prepared.
14 You were anointed as a guardian cherub,
for so I ordained you.
You were on the holy mount of God;
you walked among the fiery stones.
15 You were blameless in your ways
from the day you were created
till wickedness was found in you.
16 Through your widespread trade
you were filled with violence,
and you sinned.
So I drove you in disgrace from the mount of God,
and I expelled you, O guardian cherub,
from among the fiery stones.
17 Your heart became proud
on account of your beauty,
and you corrupted your wisdom
because of your splendor.
So I threw you to the earth;
I made a spectacle of you before kings.
18 By your many sins and dishonest trade
you have desecrated your sanctuaries.
So I made a fire come out from you,
and it consumed you,

> **Ezekiel 28:17**
>
> *God Judges Pride*
>
> "Your heart became proud on account of your beauty, and you corrupted your wisdom because of your splendor."

[a] 3 Or *Danel*; the Hebrew spelling may suggest a person other than the prophet Daniel. [b] 13 Or *lapis lazuli* [c] 13 The precise identification of some of these precious stones is uncertain. [d] 13 The meaning of the Hebrew for this phrase is uncertain.

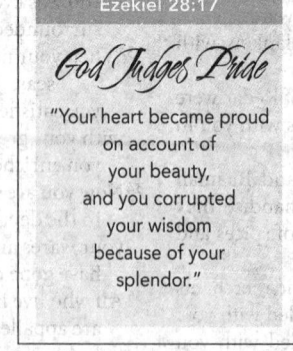

and I reduced you to ashes on the ground
in the sight of all who were watching.
19 All the nations who knew you
are appalled at you;
you have come to a horrible end
and will be no more.' "

A Prophecy Against Sidon

20 The word of the LORD came to me: 21 "Son
of man, set your face against Sidon; prophesy
against her 22 and say: 'This is what the Sovereign LORD says:

" 'I am against you, O Sidon,
and I will gain glory within you.
They will know that I am the LORD,
when I inflict punishment on her
and show myself holy within her.
23 I will send a plague upon her
and make blood flow in her streets.
The slain will fall within her,
with the sword against her on every side.
Then they will know that I am the LORD.

24 " 'No longer will the people of Israel have
malicious neighbors who are painful briers and
sharp thorns. Then they will know that I am
the Sovereign LORD.
25 " 'This is what the Sovereign LORD says:
When I gather the people of Israel from the
nations where they have been scattered, I will
show myself holy among them in the sight of
the nations. Then they will live in their own
land, which I gave to my servant Jacob. 26 They
will live there in safety and will build houses
and plant vineyards; they will live in safety
when I inflict punishment on all their neighbors who maligned them. Then they will know
that I am the LORD their God.' "

A Prophecy Against Egypt

29 In the tenth year, in the tenth month on
the twelfth day, the word of the LORD
came to me: 2 "Son of man, set your face against
Pharaoh king of Egypt and prophesy against
him and against all Egypt. 3 Speak to him and
say: 'This is what the Sovereign LORD says:

" 'I am against you, Pharaoh king of Egypt,
you great monster lying among your
streams.
You say, "The Nile is mine;
I made it for myself."
4 But I will put hooks in your jaws
and make the fish of your streams stick
to your scales.
I will pull you out from among your
streams,
with all the fish sticking to your scales.
5 I will leave you in the desert,
you and all the fish of your streams.
You will fall on the open field
and not be gathered or picked up.
I will give you as food
to the beasts of the earth and the birds
of the air.

6 Then all who live in Egypt will know that I
am the LORD.

" 'You have been a staff of reed for the house
of Israel. 7 When they grasped you with their
hands, you splintered and you tore open their
shoulders; when they leaned on you, you broke
and their backs were wrenched.[a]
8 " 'Therefore this is what the Sovereign
LORD says: I will bring a sword against you and
kill your men and their animals. 9 Egypt will
become a desolate wasteland. Then they will
know that I am the LORD.
" 'Because you said, "The Nile is mine; I made
it," 10 therefore I am against you and against
your streams, and I will make the land of Egypt
a ruin and a desolate waste from Migdol to Aswan, as far as the border of Cush.[b] 11 No foot of
man or animal will pass through it; no one will
live there for forty years. 12 I will make the land
of Egypt desolate among devastated lands, and
her cities will lie desolate forty years among ruined cities. And I will disperse the Egyptians
among the nations and scatter them through
the countries.
13 " 'Yet this is what the Sovereign LORD says:
At the end of forty years I will gather the Egyptians from the nations where they were scattered. 14 I will bring them back from captivity
and return them to Upper Egypt,[c] the land of
their ancestry. There they will be a lowly kingdom. 15 It will be the lowliest of kingdoms and
will never again exalt itself above the other

[a] 7 Syriac (see also Septuagint and Vulgate); Hebrew *and you caused their backs to stand* [b] 10 That is, the upper Nile region
[c] 14 Hebrew *to Pathros*

nations. I will make it so weak that it will never
again rule over the nations. 16 Egypt will no longer be a source of confidence for the people of
Israel but will be a reminder of their sin in turning to her for help. Then they will know that I
am the Sovereign LORD.' "

17 In the twenty-seventh year, in the first
month on the first day, the word of the LORD
came to me: 18 "Son of man, Nebuchadnezzar
king of Babylon drove his army in a hard campaign against Tyre; every head was rubbed bare
and every shoulder made raw. Yet he and his
army got no reward from the campaign he led
against Tyre. 19 Therefore this is what the Sovereign LORD says: I am going to give Egypt to
Nebuchadnezzar king of Babylon, and he will
carry off its wealth. He will loot and plunder
the land as pay for his army. 20 I have given
him Egypt as a reward for his efforts because
he and his army did it for me, declares the Sovereign LORD.

21 "On that day I will make a horn[a] grow for
the house of Israel, and I will open your mouth
among them. Then they will know that I am
the LORD."

A Lament for Egypt

30 The word of the LORD came to me:
2 "Son of man, prophesy and say: 'This
is what the Sovereign LORD says:

" 'Wail and say,
"Alas for that day!"
3 For the day is near,
the day of the LORD is near—
a day of clouds,
a time of doom for the nations.
4 A sword will come against Egypt,
and anguish will come upon Cush.[b]
When the slain fall in Egypt,
her wealth will be carried away
and her foundations torn down.

5 Cush and Put, Lydia and all Arabia, Libya[c]
and the people of the covenant land will fall by
the sword along with Egypt.

6 " 'This is what the LORD says:

" 'The allies of Egypt will fall
and her proud strength will fail.
From Migdol to Aswan
they will fall by the sword within her,
declares the Sovereign LORD.
7 " 'They will be desolate
among desolate lands,
and their cities will lie
among ruined cities.
8 Then they will know that I am the LORD,
when I set fire to Egypt
and all her helpers are crushed.

9 " 'On that day messengers will go out
from me in ships to frighten Cush out of her
complacency. Anguish will take hold of them
on the day of Egypt's doom, for it is sure to
come.

10 " 'This is what the Sovereign LORD says:

" 'I will put an end to the hordes of Egypt
by the hand of Nebuchadnezzar king of
Babylon.
11 He and his army—the most ruthless of
nations—
will be brought in to destroy the land.
They will draw their swords against Egypt
and fill the land with the slain.
12 I will dry up the streams of the Nile
and sell the land to evil men;
by the hand of foreigners
I will lay waste the land and everything
in it.
I the LORD have spoken.

13 " 'This is what the Sovereign LORD says:

" 'I will destroy the idols
and put an end to the images in
Memphis.[d]
No longer will there be a prince in Egypt,
and I will spread fear throughout the
land.
14 I will lay waste Upper Egypt,[e]
set fire to Zoan
and inflict punishment on Thebes.[f]
15 I will pour out my wrath on Pelusium,[g]
the stronghold of Egypt,
and cut off the hordes of Thebes.
16 I will set fire to Egypt;
Pelusium will writhe in agony.

[a] 21 *Horn* here symbolizes strength. [b] 4 That is, the upper Nile region; also in verses 5 and 9 [c] 5 Hebrew *Cub* [d] 13 Hebrew *Noph*; also in verse 16 [e] 14 Hebrew *waste Pathros* [f] 14 Hebrew *No*; also in verses 15 and 16 [g] 15 Hebrew *Sin*; also in verse 16

Thebes will be taken by storm;
Memphis will be in constant distress.
17 The young men of Heliopolis[a] and Bubastis[b]
will fall by the sword,
and the cities themselves will go into captivity.
18 Dark will be the day at Tahpanhes
when I break the yoke of Egypt;
there her proud strength will come to an end.
She will be covered with clouds,
and her villages will go into captivity.
19 So I will inflict punishment on Egypt,
and they will know that I am the LORD.' "

20 In the eleventh year, in the first month on
the seventh day, the word of the LORD came
to me: 21 "Son of man, I have broken the arm
of Pharaoh king of Egypt. It has not been
bound up for healing or put in a splint so as
to become strong enough to hold a sword.
22 Therefore this is what the Sovereign LORD
says: I am against Pharaoh king of Egypt. I will
break both his arms, the good arm as well as
the broken one, and make the sword fall from
his hand. 23 I will disperse the Egyptians among
the nations and scatter them through the countries. 24 I will strengthen the arms of the king
of Babylon and put my sword in his hand, but
I will break the arms of Pharaoh, and he will
groan before him like a mortally wounded
man. 25 I will strengthen the arms of the king
of Babylon, but the arms of Pharaoh will fall
limp. Then they will know that I am the LORD,
when I put my sword into the hand of the king
of Babylon and he brandishes it against Egypt.
26 I will disperse the Egyptians among the nations and scatter them through the countries.
Then they will know that I am the LORD."

A Cedar in Lebanon

31 In the eleventh year, in the third month
on the first day, the word of the LORD
came to me: 2 "Son of man, say to Pharaoh king
of Egypt and to his hordes:

" 'Who can be compared with you in majesty?
3 Consider Assyria, once a cedar in Lebanon,
with beautiful branches overshadowing the forest;
it towered on high,
its top above the thick foliage.
4 The waters nourished it,
deep springs made it grow tall;
their streams flowed
all around its base
and sent their channels
to all the trees of the field.
5 So it towered higher
than all the trees of the field;
its boughs increased
and its branches grew long,
spreading because of abundant waters.
6 All the birds of the air
nested in its boughs,
all the beasts of the field
gave birth under its branches;
all the great nations
lived in its shade.
7 It was majestic in beauty,
with its spreading boughs,
for its roots went down
to abundant waters.
8 The cedars in the garden of God
could not rival it,
nor could the pine trees
equal its boughs,
nor could the plane trees
compare with its branches—
no tree in the garden of God
could match its beauty.
9 I made it beautiful
with abundant branches,
the envy of all the trees of Eden
in the garden of God.

10 " 'Therefore this is what the Sovereign
LORD says: Because it towered on high, lifting
its top above the thick foliage, and because it
was proud of its height, 11 I handed it over to
the ruler of the nations, for him to deal with according to its wickedness. I cast it aside, 12 and
the most ruthless of foreign nations cut it down
and left it. Its boughs fell on the mountains and
in all the valleys; its branches lay broken in all
the ravines of the land. All the nations of the
earth came out from under its shade and left
it. 13 All the birds of the air settled on the fallen

[a] 17 Hebrew *Awen* (or *On*) [b] 17 Hebrew *Pi Beseth*

tree, and all the beasts of the field were among
its branches. 14 Therefore no other trees by the
waters are ever to tower proudly on high, lifting their tops above the thick foliage. No other
trees so well-watered are ever to reach such a
height; they are all destined for death, for the
earth below, among mortal men, with those
who go down to the pit.
15 " 'This is what the Sovereign LORD says:
On the day it was brought down to the grave[a]
I covered the deep springs with mourning for
it; I held back its streams, and its abundant waters were restrained. Because of it I clothed Lebanon with gloom, and all the trees of the field
withered away. 16 I made the nations tremble at
the sound of its fall when I brought it down to
the grave with those who go down to the pit.
Then all the trees of Eden, the choicest and best
of Lebanon, all the trees that were well-watered,
were consoled in the earth below. 17 Those who
lived in its shade, its allies among the nations,
had also gone down to the grave with it, joining
those killed by the sword.
18 " 'Which of the trees of Eden can be
compared with you in splendor and majesty?
Yet you, too, will be brought down with the
trees of Eden to the earth below; you will lie
among the uncircumcised, with those killed by
the sword.

" 'This is Pharaoh and all his hordes, declares the Sovereign LORD.' "

A Lament for Pharaoh

32 In the twelfth year, in the twelfth
month on the first day, the word of the
LORD came to me: 2 "Son of man, take up a lament concerning Pharaoh king of Egypt and
say to him:

" 'You are like a lion among the nations;
you are like a monster in the seas
thrashing about in your streams,
churning the water with your feet
and muddying the streams.

3 " 'This is what the Sovereign LORD says:

" 'With a great throng of people
I will cast my net over you,
and they will haul you up in my net.
4 I will throw you on the land
and hurl you on the open field.
I will let all the birds of the air settle on you
and all the beasts of the earth gorge
themselves on you.
5 I will spread your flesh on the mountains
and fill the valleys with your remains.
6 I will drench the land with your flowing
blood
all the way to the mountains,
and the ravines will be filled with your
flesh.
7 When I snuff you out, I will cover the
heavens
and darken their stars;
I will cover the sun with a cloud,
and the moon will not give its light.
8 All the shining lights in the heavens
I will darken over you;
I will bring darkness over your land,
declares the Sovereign LORD.
9 I will trouble the hearts of many peoples
when I bring about your destruction
among the nations,
among[b] lands you have not known.
10 I will cause many peoples to be appalled at
you,
and their kings will shudder with horror
because of you
when I brandish my sword before them.
On the day of your downfall
each of them will tremble
every moment for his life.

11 " 'For this is what the Sovereign LORD
says:

" 'The sword of the king of Babylon
will come against you.
12 I will cause your hordes to fall
by the swords of mighty men—
the most ruthless of all nations.
They will shatter the pride of Egypt,
and all her hordes will be overthrown.
13 I will destroy all her cattle
from beside abundant waters
no longer to be stirred by the foot of man
or muddied by the hoofs of cattle.
14 Then I will let her waters settle
and make her streams flow like oil,
declares the Sovereign LORD.

[a] 15 Hebrew *Sheol*; also in verses 16 and 17 [b] 9 Hebrew; Septuagint *bring you into captivity among the nations, / to*

15 When I make Egypt desolate
and strip the land of everything in it,
when I strike down all who live there,
then they will know that I am the LORD.'

16 "This is the lament they will chant for her.
The daughters of the nations will chant it; for
Egypt and all her hordes they will chant it, de-
clares the Sovereign LORD."

17 In the twelfth year, on the fifteenth day of
the month, the word of the LORD came to me:
18 "Son of man, wail for the hordes of Egypt
and consign to the earth below both her and
the daughters of mighty nations, with those
who go down to the pit. 19 Say to them, 'Are
you more favored than others? Go down and
be laid among the uncircumcised.' 20 They
will fall among those killed by the sword. The
sword is drawn; let her be dragged off with
all her hordes. 21 From within the grave[a] the
mighty leaders will say of Egypt and her allies,
'They have come down and they lie with the uncircumcised, with those killed by the sword.'
22 "Assyria is there with her whole army; she
is surrounded by the graves of all her slain, all
who have fallen by the sword. 23 Their graves
are in the depths of the pit and her army lies
around her grave. All who had spread terror
in the land of the living are slain, fallen by
the sword.
24 "Elam is there, with all her hordes around
her grave. All of them are slain, fallen by the
sword. All who had spread terror in the land
of the living went down uncircumcised to the
earth below. They bear their shame with those
who go down to the pit. 25 A bed is made for
her among the slain, with all her hordes around
her grave. All of them are uncircumcised, killed
by the sword. Because their terror had spread
in the land of the living, they bear their shame
with those who go down to the pit; they are laid
among the slain.
26 "Meshech and Tubal are there, with all
their hordes around their graves. All of them
are uncircumcised, killed by the sword because
they spread their terror in the land of the living. 27 Do they not lie with the other uncircumcised warriors who have fallen, who went
down to the grave with their weapons of war,
whose swords were placed under their heads?
The punishment for their sins rested on their
bones, though the terror of these warriors had
stalked through the land of the living.
28 "You too, O Pharaoh, will be broken and
will lie among the uncircumcised, with those
killed by the sword.
29 "Edom is there, her kings and all her
princes; despite their power, they are laid with
those killed by the sword. They lie with the
uncircumcised, with those who go down to
the pit.
30 "All the princes of the north and all the
Sidonians are there; they went down with the
slain in disgrace despite the terror caused by
their power. They lie uncircumcised with those
killed by the sword and bear their shame with
those who go down to the pit.
31 "Pharaoh—he and all his army—will see
them and he will be consoled for all his hordes
that were killed by the sword, declares the Sovereign LORD. 32 Although I had him spread terror in the land of the living, Pharaoh and all his
hordes will be laid among the uncircumcised,
with those killed by the sword, declares the Sovereign LORD."

Ezekiel a Watchman

33 The word of the LORD came to me:
2 "Son of man, speak to your countrymen and say to them: 'When I bring the
sword against a land, and the people of the
land choose one of their men and make him
their watchman, 3 and he sees the sword coming against the land and blows the trumpet
to warn the people, 4 then if anyone hears the
trumpet but does not take warning and the
sword comes and takes his life, his blood will
be on his own head. 5 Since he heard the sound
of the trumpet but did not take warning, his
blood will be on his own head. If he had taken
warning, he would have saved himself. 6 But if
the watchman sees the sword coming and does
not blow the trumpet to warn the people and
the sword comes and takes the life of one of
them, that man will be taken away because of
his sin, but I will hold the watchman accountable for his blood.'
7 "Son of man, I have made you a watchman

[a] 21 Hebrew *Sheol*; also in verse 27

for the house of Israel; so hear the word I speak and give them warning from me. 8When I say to the wicked, 'O wicked man, you will surely die,' and you do not speak out to dissuade him from his ways, that wicked man will die for[a] his sin, and I will hold you accountable for his blood. 9But if you do warn the wicked man to turn from his ways and he does not do so, he will die for his sin, but you will have saved yourself.

10"Son of man, say to the house of Israel, 'This is what you are saying: "Our offenses and sins weigh us down, and we are wasting away because of[b] them. How then can we live?"' 11Say to them, 'As surely as I live, declares the Sovereign LORD, I take no pleasure in the death of the wicked, but rather that they turn from their ways and live. Turn! Turn from your evil ways! Why will you die, O house of Israel?'

12"Therefore, son of man, say to your countrymen, 'The righteousness of the righteous man will not save him when he disobeys, and the wickedness of the wicked man will not cause him to fall when he turns from it. The righteous man, if he sins, will not be allowed to live because of his former righteousness.' 13If I tell the righteous man that he will surely live, but then he trusts in his righteousness and does evil, none of the righteous things he has done will be remembered; he will die for the evil he has done. 14And if I say to the wicked man, 'You will surely die,' but he then turns away from his sin and does what is just and right— 15if he gives back what he took in pledge for a loan, returns what he has stolen, follows the decrees that give life, and does no evil, he will surely live; he will not die. 16None of the sins he has committed will be remembered against him. He has done what is just and right; he will surely live.

17"Yet your countrymen say, 'The way of the Lord is not just.' But it is their way that is not just. 18If a righteous man turns from his righteousness and does evil, he will die for it. 19And if a wicked man turns away from his wickedness and does what is just and right, he will live by doing so. 20Yet, O house of Israel, you say, 'The way of the Lord is not just.' But I will judge each of you according to his own ways."

Ezekiel 33:11

God Calls for Repentance

"As surely as I live, declares the Sovereign LORD, I take no pleasure in the death of the wicked, but rather that they turn from their ways and live. Turn! Turn from your evil ways! Why will you die, O house of Israel?"

Jerusalem's Fall Explained

21In the twelfth year of our exile, in the tenth month on the fifth day, a man who had escaped from Jerusalem came to me and said, "The city has fallen!" 22Now the evening before the man arrived, the hand of the LORD was upon me, and he opened my mouth before the man came to me in the morning. So my mouth was opened and I was no longer silent.

23Then the word of the LORD came to me: 24"Son of man, the people living in those ruins in the land of Israel are saying, 'Abraham was only one man, yet he possessed the land. But we are many; surely the land has been given to us as our possession.' 25Therefore say to them, 'This is what the Sovereign LORD says: Since you eat meat with the blood still in it and look to your idols and shed blood, should you then possess the land? 26You rely on your sword, you do detestable things, and each of you defiles his neighbor's wife. Should you then possess the land?'

27"Say this to them: 'This is what the Sovereign LORD says: As surely as I live, those who are left in the ruins will fall by the sword, those out in the country I will give to the wild animals to be devoured, and those in strongholds and caves will die of a plague. 28I will make the land a desolate waste, and her proud strength will come to an end, and the mountains of Israel will become desolate so that no one will cross them. 29Then they will know that I am the LORD, when I have made the land a deso-

[a]8 Or *in*; also in verse 9 [b]10 Or *away in*

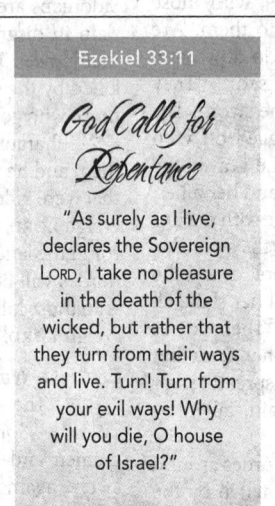

late waste because of all the detestable things
they have done.’

30“As for you, son of man, your countrymen
are talking together about you by the walls and
at the doors of the houses, saying to each other,
‘Come and hear the message that has come
from the LORD.’ 31My people come to you, as
they usually do, and sit before you to listen to
your words, but they do not put them into practice. With their mouths they express devotion,
but their hearts are greedy for unjust gain. 32In-
deed, to them you are nothing more than one
who sings love songs with a beautiful voice and
plays an instrument well, for they hear your
words but do not put them into practice.

33“When all this comes true—and it surely
will—then they will know that a prophet has
been among them.”

Shepherds and Sheep

34 The word of the LORD came to me:
2“Son of man, prophesy against the
shepherds of Israel; prophesy and say to them:
‘This is what the Sovereign LORD says: Woe to
the shepherds of Israel who only take care of
themselves! Should not shepherds take care of
the flock? 3You eat the curds, clothe yourselves
with the wool and slaughter the choice animals,
but you do not take care of the flock. 4You have
not strengthened the weak or healed the sick
or bound up the injured. You have not brought
back the strays or searched for the lost. You
have ruled them harshly and brutally. 5So they
were scattered because there was no shepherd,
and when they were scattered they became
food for all the wild animals. 6My sheep wandered over all the mountains and on every high
hill. They were scattered over the whole earth,
and no one searched or looked for them.

7“ ‘Therefore, you shepherds, hear the word
of the LORD: 8As surely as I live, declares the
Sovereign LORD, because my flock lacks a shepherd and so has been plundered and has become food for all the wild animals, and because
my shepherds did not search for my flock but
cared for themselves rather than for my flock,
9therefore, O shepherds, hear the word of the
LORD: 10This is what the Sovereign LORD says:
I am against the shepherds and will hold them
accountable for my flock. I will remove them
from tending the flock so that the shepherds
can no longer feed themselves. I will rescue my
flock from their mouths, and it will no longer
be food for them.

11“ ‘For this is what the Sovereign LORD says:
I myself will search for my sheep and look after
them. 12As a shepherd looks after his scattered
flock when he is with them, so will I look after
my sheep. I will rescue them from all the places
where they were scattered on a day of clouds
and darkness. 13I will bring them out from the
nations and gather them from the countries,
and I will bring them into their own land. I will
pasture them on the mountains of Israel, in the
ravines and in all the settlements in the land.
14I will tend them in a good pasture, and the
mountain heights of Israel will be their grazing
land. There they will lie down in good grazing
land, and there they will feed in a rich pasture
on the mountains of Israel. 15I myself will tend
my sheep and have them lie down, declares the
Sovereign LORD. 16I will search for the lost and
bring back the strays. I will bind up the injured
and strengthen the weak, but the sleek and the
strong I will destroy. I will shepherd the flock
with justice.

17“ ‘As for you, my flock, this is what the Sovereign LORD says: I will judge between one
sheep and another, and between rams and
goats. 18Is it not enough for you to feed on the
good pasture? Must you also trample the rest of
your pasture with your feet? Is it not enough
for you to drink clear water? Must you also
muddy the rest with your feet? 19Must my flock
feed on what you have trampled and drink
what you have muddied with your feet?

20“ ‘Therefore this is what the Sovereign
LORD says to them: See, I myself will judge
between the fat sheep and the lean sheep.
21Because you shove with flank and shoulder,
butting all the weak sheep with your horns until you have driven them away, 22I will save my
flock, and they will no longer be plundered. I
will judge between one sheep and another. 23I
will place over them one shepherd, my servant
David, and he will tend them; he will tend
them and be their shepherd. 24I the LORD will
be their God, and my servant David will be
prince among them. I the LORD have spoken.

25“ ‘I will make a covenant of peace with
them and rid the land of wild beasts so that

Treasured

MARY

"DID YOU HEAR ANYTHING I JUST SAID?"

Startled by the piercing tone of the market manager's voice, Mary blinked rapidly as if awakening from a deep dream. She quickly responded, "Yes . . . so sorry. That challah loaf there—that's fine. And these too," she added, clutching three heads of garlic in her hand. Mary quickly paid the manager his due and headed home before her young son awoke from his nap.

So much had happened in her life, she'd hardly taken time to think through all of it. At any given moment, her mind would suddenly float away to memories. Yet she could never grasp their full meaning.

As the afternoon sun cast the shadow of her small frame on the dirt path, various scenes surfaced: that first day in the temple; the look of rapture on the face of the prophetess Anna as she blessed Mary's child. And what did Simeon mean—something about a sword piercing her own soul someday?

Mary turned a corner and saw the familiar roofline of her home in the distance. Almost home. She smiled to herself, recalling the warm feeling of security that had washed over her when they had first seen the outline of the sleepy town of Nazareth. They had been so frightened, but Joseph felt God leading them there through his dreams. And now, though not his birthplace, their son would come to know it as "home." Jesus of Nazareth.

"You are to give him the name Jesus. He will be great and will be called the Son of the Most High" (Luke 1:31–32).

Like a thousand times before, her mind pondered the angel's words and the Magi's posture before her child—all as if for the first time. Mary stored each moment and memory surrounding her precious baby boy inside of her heart. Tucked away treasures, they were her comfort and her assurance. Most of all, they were hers and hers alone to ponder. No one else could share her chosen place—the earthly mother of the Son of God.

—Prayer—

You have chosen me to live in this place and time, Lord. May I live out my days for your glory.

But Mary treasured up all these things and pondered them in her heart.

Luke 2:19

ASSIGNED READING:
Luke 2:19, 21–40

Weekend

Go to page 1038 for your next devotional reading.

they may live in the desert and sleep in the forests in safety. 26I will bless them and the places
surrounding my hill.[a] I will send down showers in season; there will be showers of blessing.
27The trees of the field will yield their fruit and
the ground will yield its crops; the people will
be secure in their land. They will know that I
am the LORD, when I break the bars of their
yoke and rescue them from the hands of those
who enslaved them. 28They will no longer be
plundered by the nations, nor will wild animals
devour them. They will live in safety, and no
one will make them afraid. 29I will provide for
them a land renowned for its crops, and they
will no longer be victims of famine in the land
or bear the scorn of the nations. 30Then they
will know that I, the LORD their God, am with
them and that they, the house of Israel, are my
people, declares the Sovereign LORD. 31You my
sheep, the sheep of my pasture, are people, and
I am your God, declares the Sovereign LORD.' "

A Prophecy Against Edom

35 The word of the LORD came to me:
2"Son of man, set your face against
Mount Seir; prophesy against it 3and say: 'This
is what the Sovereign LORD says: I am against
you, Mount Seir, and I will stretch out my hand
against you and make you a desolate waste. 4I
will turn your towns into ruins and you will
be desolate. Then you will know that I am
the LORD.

5" 'Because you harbored an ancient hostility
and delivered the Israelites over to the sword at
the time of their calamity, the time their punishment reached its climax, 6therefore as surely as
I live, declares the Sovereign LORD, I will give
you over to bloodshed and it will pursue you.
Since you did not hate bloodshed, bloodshed
will pursue you. 7I will make Mount Seir a desolate waste and cut off from it all who come and
go. 8I will fill your mountains with the slain;
those killed by the sword will fall on your hills
and in your valleys and in all your ravines. 9I
will make you desolate forever; your towns will
not be inhabited. Then you will know that I am
the LORD.

10" 'Because you have said, "These two nations and countries will be ours and we will
take possession of them," even though I the
LORD was there, 11therefore as surely as I live,
declares the Sovereign LORD, I will treat you
in accordance with the anger and jealousy you
showed in your hatred of them and I will make
myself known among them when I judge you.
12Then you will know that I the LORD have
heard all the contemptible things you have said
against the mountains of Israel. You said, "They
have been laid waste and have been given over
to us to devour." 13You boasted against me and
spoke against me without restraint, and I heard
it. 14This is what the Sovereign LORD says:
While the whole earth rejoices, I will make
you desolate. 15Because you rejoiced when the
inheritance of the house of Israel became desolate, that is how I will treat you. You will be desolate, O Mount Seir, you and all of Edom. Then
they will know that I am the LORD.' "

A Prophecy to the Mountains of Israel

36 "Son of man, prophesy to the mountains of Israel and say, 'O mountains
of Israel, hear the word of the LORD. 2This is
what the Sovereign LORD says: The enemy said
of you, "Aha! The ancient heights have become
our possession." ' 3Therefore prophesy and say,
'This is what the Sovereign LORD says: Because
they ravaged and hounded you from every side
so that you became the possession of the rest of
the nations and the object of people's malicious
talk and slander, 4therefore, O mountains of
Israel, hear the word of the Sovereign LORD:
This is what the Sovereign LORD says to the
mountains and hills, to the ravines and valleys,
to the desolate ruins and the deserted towns
that have been plundered and ridiculed by the
rest of the nations around you— 5this is what
the Sovereign LORD says: In my burning zeal
I have spoken against the rest of the nations,
and against all Edom, for with glee and with
malice in their hearts they made my land their
own possession so that they might plunder
its pastureland.' 6Therefore prophesy concerning the land of Israel and say to the mountains
and hills, to the ravines and valleys: 'This is
what the Sovereign LORD says: I speak in my
jealous wrath because you have suffered the
scorn of the nations. 7Therefore this is what

[a] **26** Or *I will make them and the places surrounding my hill a blessing*

the Sovereign LORD says: I swear with uplifted
hand that the nations around you will also suffer scorn.

8 "'But you, O mountains of Israel, will produce branches and fruit for my people Israel,
for they will soon come home. 9 I am concerned
for you and will look on you with favor; you will
be plowed and sown, 10 and I will multiply the
number of people upon you, even the whole
house of Israel. The towns will be inhabited and
the ruins rebuilt. 11 I will increase the number
of men and animals upon you, and they will be
fruitful and become numerous. I will settle people on you as in the past and will make you prosper more than before. Then you will know that
I am the LORD. 12 I will cause people, my people Israel, to walk upon you. They will possess
you, and you will be their inheritance; you will
never again deprive them of their children.

13 "'This is what the Sovereign LORD says:
Because people say to you, "You devour men
and deprive your nation of its children," 14 therefore you will no longer devour men or make
your nation childless, declares the Sovereign
LORD. 15 No longer will I make you hear the
taunts of the nations, and no longer will you
suffer the scorn of the peoples or cause your nation to fall, declares the Sovereign LORD.'"

16 Again the word of the LORD came to me:
17 "Son of man, when the people of Israel were
living in their own land, they defiled it by their
conduct and their actions. Their conduct was
like a woman's monthly uncleanness in my
sight. 18 So I poured out my wrath on them
because they had shed blood in the land and
because they had defiled it with their idols. 19 I
dispersed them among the nations, and they
were scattered through the countries; I judged
them according to their conduct and their actions. 20 And wherever they went among the
nations they profaned my holy name, for it
was said of them, 'These are the LORD's people, and yet they had to leave his land.' 21 I had
concern for my holy name, which the house of
Israel profaned among the nations where they
had gone.

22 "Therefore say to the house of Israel, 'This
is what the Sovereign LORD says: It is not for
your sake, O house of Israel, that I am going
to do these things, but for the sake of my holy
name, which you have profaned among the nations where you have gone. 23 I will show the
holiness of my great name, which has been profaned among the nations, the name you have
profaned among them. Then the nations will
know that I am the LORD, declares the Sovereign LORD, when I show myself holy through
you before their eyes.

24 "'For I will take you out of the nations;
I will gather you from all the countries and
bring you back into your own land. 25 I will
sprinkle clean water on you, and you will be
clean; I will cleanse you from all your impurities and from all your idols. 26 I will give
you a new heart and put a new spirit in you;
I will remove from you your heart of stone
and give you a heart of flesh. 27 And I will put
my Spirit in you and move you to follow my
decrees and be careful to keep my laws. 28 You
will live in the land I gave your forefathers;
you will be my people, and I will be your God.
29 I will save you from all your uncleanness.
I will call for the grain and make it plentiful
and will not bring famine upon you. 30 I will increase the fruit of the trees and the crops of the
field, so that you will no longer suffer disgrace
among the nations because of famine. 31 Then
you will remember your evil ways and wicked
deeds, and you will loathe yourselves for your
sins and detestable practices. 32 I want you to
know that I am not doing this for your sake,
declares the Sovereign LORD. Be ashamed and
disgraced for your conduct, O house of Israel!

33 "'This is what the Sovereign LORD says:
On the day I cleanse you from all your sins, I
will resettle your towns, and the ruins will be
rebuilt. 34 The desolate land will be cultivated
instead of lying desolate in the sight of all who
pass through it. 35 They will say, "This land that
was laid waste has become like the garden of
Eden; the cities that were lying in ruins, desolate and destroyed, are now fortified and
inhabited." 36 Then the nations around you that
remain will know that I the LORD have rebuilt
what was destroyed and have replanted what
was desolate. I the LORD have spoken, and I
will do it.'

37 "This is what the Sovereign LORD says:
Once again I will yield to the plea of the house
of Israel and do this for them: I will make their

people as numerous as sheep, 38as numerous
as the flocks for offerings at Jerusalem during
her appointed feasts. So will the ruined cities
be filled with flocks of people. Then they will
know that I am the LORD."

The Valley of Dry Bones

37 The hand of the LORD
was upon me, and he
brought me out by the Spirit
of the LORD and set me in the
middle of a valley; it was full
of bones. 2He led me back and
forth among them, and I saw a
great many bones on the floor
of the valley, bones that were
very dry. 3He asked me, "Son
of man, can these bones live?"

I said, "O Sovereign LORD,
you alone know."

4Then he said to me, "Prophesy to these bones and say to
them, 'Dry bones, hear the
word of the LORD! 5This is what the Sovereign
LORD says to these bones: I will make breath[a]
enter you, and you will come to life. 6I will attach tendons to you and make flesh come upon
you and cover you with skin; I will put breath
in you, and you will come to life. Then you will
know that I am the LORD.' "

7So I prophesied as I was commanded. And
as I was prophesying, there was a noise, a rattling sound, and the bones came together, bone
to bone. 8I looked, and tendons and flesh appeared on them and skin covered them, but
there was no breath in them.

9Then he said to me, "Prophesy to the breath;
prophesy, son of man, and say to it, 'This is
what the Sovereign LORD says: Come from the
four winds, O breath, and breathe into these
slain, that they may live.' " 10So I prophesied as
he commanded me, and breath entered them;
they came to life and stood up on their feet—a
vast army.

11Then he said to me: "Son of man, these
bones are the whole house of Israel. They say,
'Our bones are dried up and our hope is gone;
we are cut off.' 12Therefore prophesy and say to
them: 'This is what the Sovereign LORD says:
O my people, I am going to open your graves
and bring you up from them; I will bring you
back to the land of Israel. 13Then you, my people, will know that I am the LORD, when I open
your graves and bring you up
from them. 14I will put my
Spirit in you and you will live,
and I will settle you in your
own land. Then you will know
that I the LORD have spoken,
and I have done it, declares the
LORD.' "

> **Ezekiel 36:36**
>
> *God Rebuilds Lives*
>
> "Then the nations around you that remain will know that I the LORD have rebuilt what was destroyed and have replanted what was desolate. I the LORD have spoken, and I will do it."

One Nation Under One King

15The word of the LORD
came to me: 16"Son of man,
take a stick of wood and write
on it, 'Belonging to Judah and
the Israelites associated with
him.' Then take another stick
of wood, and write on it, 'Ephraim's stick, belonging to Joseph
and all the house of Israel
associated with him.' 17Join them together
into one stick so that they will become one in
your hand.

18"When your countrymen ask you, 'Won't
you tell us what you mean by this?' 19say to
them, 'This is what the Sovereign LORD says: I
am going to take the stick of Joseph—which is
in Ephraim's hand—and of the Israelite tribes
associated with him, and join it to Judah's stick,
making them a single stick of wood, and they
will become one in my hand.' 20Hold before
their eyes the sticks you have written on 21and
say to them, 'This is what the Sovereign LORD
says: I will take the Israelites out of the nations
where they have gone. I will gather them from
all around and bring them back into their own
land. 22I will make them one nation in the
land, on the mountains of Israel. There will be
one king over all of them and they will never
again be two nations or be divided into two
kingdoms. 23They will no longer defile themselves with their idols and vile images or with
any of their offenses, for I will save them from
all their sinful backsliding,[b] and I will cleanse
them. They will be my people, and I will be
their God.

[a]5 The Hebrew for this word can also mean *wind* or *spirit* (see verses 6–14). [b]23 Many Hebrew manuscripts (see also Septuagint); most Hebrew manuscripts *all their dwelling places where they sinned*

Life From Death

Read: Ezekiel 37:1–14

IN ONE OF THE MOST STRIKING parts of Ezekiel's prophecy, God gave him a vision right out of a fright night for middle schoolers—a valley of death full of skeletons so decayed they were just piles of bones.

Nevertheless, God's message wasn't about death; it was about life. It was about God's power to bring life from death. It doesn't matter if the body is in the ground—or if what's left of it is on the ground. It doesn't matter if the skeleton has come apart and is mixed in with other old bones. God has the power to bring life out of a valley of death.

We may be physically alive, but sometimes we feel as if we're wandering in that valley. We feel as spiritually, emotionally or even relationally as dead as an old pile of bones. Inside we may feel as useless as old skeletons. If we're stuck in our old patterns, we may feel that it's too late to change. If we've been waiting to serve God in a specific way, we may fear that we've waited too long. We are oh-so-certain that our chance to be all God wants us to be has passed us by. But Ezekiel's vision reminds us that nothing and no one is too far gone for God to regenerate. God is able to resurrect dead dreams, missed opportunities, dying marriages and terminal friendships. He is God, and he can do anything.

Instead of believing that your mistakes and regrets pose too much of an obstacle to him, do you believe God can energize you with new life and purpose? Can you look beyond the vulture-picked-over-dry-bones of your missteps, rebellions and outright mess-ups? Will you see that the hope of your life is wrapped up not in your own power to overcome your inertia and bad habits but in God's desire to renew you, to call you to something more?

Ezekiel 37:3–4

He asked me, "Son of man, can these bones live?" I said, "O Sovereign LORD, you alone know." Then he said to me, "Prophesy to these bones and say to them, 'Dry bones, hear the word of the LORD!' "

reflection

1. How far are you in the process of regeneration? Where is God continuing to work on you?
2. What keeps you from believing that God can restore the parts of your life that feel dead or broken?
3. What is the "something more" God may be calling you to?

RELATED READINGS

Genesis 2:7; John 8:3–11; Romans 6:3–4; 2 Corinthians 3:18

Monday

Go to page 1046 for your next devotional reading.

24“‘My servant David will be king over
them, and they will all have one shepherd. They
will follow my laws and be careful to keep my
decrees. 25They will live in the land I gave to
my servant Jacob, the land where your fathers
lived. They and their children and their children’s children will live there forever, and David my servant will be their prince forever. 26I
will make a covenant of peace with them; it will
be an everlasting covenant. I will establish them
and increase their numbers, and I will put my
sanctuary among them forever. 27My dwelling
place will be with them; I will be their God, and
they will be my people. 28Then the nations will
know that I the LORD make Israel holy, when
my sanctuary is among them forever.’ ”

A Prophecy Against Gog

38 The word of the LORD came to me:
2“Son of man, set your face against
Gog, of the land of Magog, the chief prince
of[a] Meshech and Tubal; prophesy against him
3and say: ‘This is what the Sovereign LORD says:
I am against you, O Gog, chief prince of[b] Meshech and Tubal. 4I will turn you around, put
hooks in your jaws and bring you out with your
whole army—your horses, your horsemen fully
armed, and a great horde with large and small
shields, all of them brandishing their swords.
5Persia, Cush[c] and Put will be with them, all
with shields and helmets, 6also Gomer with
all its troops, and Beth Togarmah from the far
north with all its troops—the many nations
with you.

7“‘Get ready; be prepared, you and all the
hordes gathered about you, and take command
of them. 8After many days you will be called
to arms. In future years you will invade a land
that has recovered from war, whose people
were gathered from many nations to the mountains of Israel, which had long been desolate.
They had been brought out from the nations,
and now all of them live in safety. 9You and all
your troops and the many nations with you will
go up, advancing like a storm; you will be like a
cloud covering the land.

10“‘This is what the Sovereign LORD says:
On that day thoughts will come into your mind
and you will devise an evil scheme. 11You will
say, “I will invade a land of unwalled villages;
I will attack a peaceful and unsuspecting people—all of them living without walls and without gates and bars. 12I will plunder and loot
and turn my hand against the resettled ruins
and the people gathered from the nations, rich
in livestock and goods, living at the center of
the land.” 13Sheba and Dedan and the merchants of Tarshish and all her villages[d] will say
to you, “Have you come to plunder? Have you
gathered your hordes to loot, to carry off silver
and gold, to take away livestock and goods and
to seize much plunder?” ’

14“Therefore, son of man, prophesy and say
to Gog: ‘This is what the Sovereign LORD says:
In that day, when my people Israel are living in
safety, will you not take notice of it? 15You will
come from your place in the far north, you and
many nations with you, all of them riding on
horses, a great horde, a mighty army. 16You will
advance against my people Israel like a cloud
that covers the land. In days to come, O Gog,
I will bring you against my land, so that the nations may know me when I show myself holy
through you before their eyes.

17“‘This is what the Sovereign LORD says:
Are you not the one I spoke of in former days
by my servants the prophets of Israel? At that
time they prophesied for years that I would
bring you against them. 18This is what will happen in that day: When Gog attacks the land of
Israel, my hot anger will be aroused, declares
the Sovereign LORD. 19In my zeal and fiery
wrath I declare that at that time there shall be
a great earthquake in the land of Israel. 20The
fish of the sea, the birds of the air, the beasts of
the field, every creature that moves along the
ground, and all the people on the face of the
earth will tremble at my presence. The mountains will be overturned, the cliffs will crumble and every wall will fall to the ground. 21I
will summon a sword against Gog on all my
mountains, declares the Sovereign LORD. Every
man’s sword will be against his brother. 22I will
execute judgment upon him with plague and
bloodshed; I will pour down torrents of rain,
hailstones and burning sulfur on him and on
his troops and on the many nations with him.
23And so I will show my greatness and my

[a]2 Or *the prince of Rosh,* [b]3 Or *Gog, prince of Rosh,* [c]5 That is, the upper Nile region [d]13 Or *her strong lions*

holiness, and I will make myself known in the
sight of many nations. Then they will know
that I am the LORD.'

39 "Son of man, prophesy
against Gog and say:
'This is what the Sovereign
LORD says: I am against you,
O Gog, chief prince of[a] Meshech and Tubal. 2I will turn
you around and drag you
along. I will bring you from the
far north and send you against
the mountains of Israel. 3Then
I will strike your bow from
your left hand and make your
arrows drop from your right
hand. 4On the mountains of
Israel you will fall, you and all
your troops and the nations
with you. I will give you as food
to all kinds of carrion birds and to the wild animals. 5You will fall in the open field, for I have
spoken, declares the Sovereign LORD. 6I will
send fire on Magog and on those who live in
safety in the coastlands, and they will know
that I am the LORD.
7" 'I will make known my holy name among
my people Israel. I will no longer let my holy
name be profaned, and the nations will know
that I the LORD am the Holy One in Israel. 8It
is coming! It will surely take place, declares
the Sovereign LORD. This is the day I have spoken of.
9" 'Then those who live in the towns of Israel
will go out and use the weapons for fuel and
burn them up—the small and large shields, the
bows and arrows, the war clubs and spears. For
seven years they will use them for fuel. 10They
will not need to gather wood from the fields
or cut it from the forests, because they will use
the weapons for fuel. And they will plunder
those who plundered them and loot those who
looted them, declares the Sovereign LORD.
11" 'On that day I will give Gog a burial place
in Israel, in the valley of those who travel east
toward[b] the Sea.[c] It will block the way of travelers, because Gog and all his hordes will be
buried there. So it will be called the Valley of
Hamon Gog.[d]

Ezekiel 38:23

God Reveals His Greatness

"And so I will show my greatness and my holiness, and I will make myself known in the sight of many nations. Then they will know that I am the LORD."

12" 'For seven months the house of Israel will
be burying them in order to cleanse the land.
13All the people of the land
will bury them, and the day I
am glorified will be a memorable day for them, declares the
Sovereign LORD.
14" 'Men will be regularly
employed to cleanse the land.
Some will go throughout the
land and, in addition to them,
others will bury those that remain on the ground. At the end
of the seven months they will
begin their search. 15As they
go through the land and one
of them sees a human bone, he
will set up a marker beside it
until the gravediggers have buried it in the Valley of Hamon
Gog. 16(Also a town called Hamonah[e] will be
there.) And so they will cleanse the land.'
17"Son of man, this is what the Sovereign
LORD says: Call out to every kind of bird and all
the wild animals: 'Assemble and come together
from all around to the sacrifice I am preparing
for you, the great sacrifice on the mountains of
Israel. There you will eat flesh and drink blood.
18You will eat the flesh of mighty men and
drink the blood of the princes of the earth as if
they were rams and lambs, goats and bulls—all
of them fattened animals from Bashan. 19At the
sacrifice I am preparing for you, you will eat fat
till you are glutted and drink blood till you are
drunk. 20At my table you will eat your fill of
horses and riders, mighty men and soldiers of
every kind,' declares the Sovereign LORD.
21"I will display my glory among the nations,
and all the nations will see the punishment I inflict and the hand I lay upon them. 22From that
day forward the house of Israel will know that
I am the LORD their God. 23And the nations
will know that the people of Israel went into
exile for their sin, because they were unfaithful
to me. So I hid my face from them and handed
them over to their enemies, and they all fell by
the sword. 24I dealt with them according to
their uncleanness and their offenses, and I hid
my face from them.

[a]1 Or *Gog, prince of Rosh,* [b]11 Or *of* [c]11 That is, the Dead Sea [d]11 *Hamon Gog* means *hordes of Gog.* [e]16 *Hamonah* means *horde.*

25“Therefore this is what the Sovereign
LORD says: I will now bring Jacob back from
captivity[a] and will have compassion on all
the people of Israel, and I will be zealous for
my holy name. 26They will forget their shame
and all the unfaithfulness they showed toward
me when they lived in safety
in their land with no one to
make them afraid. 27When I
have brought them back from
the nations and have gathered
them from the countries of
their enemies, I will show myself holy through them in the
sight of many nations. 28Then
they will know that I am the
LORD their God, for though
I sent them into exile among
the nations, I will gather them
to their own land, not leaving
any behind. 29I will no longer
hide my face from them, for I
will pour out my Spirit on the
house of Israel, declares the
Sovereign LORD.”

> **Ezekiel 39:25**
>
> *God Protects His Reputation*
>
> “Therefore this is what the Sovereign LORD says: I will now bring Jacob back from captivity and will have compassion on all the people of Israel, and I will be zealous for my holy name.”

The New Temple Area

40 In the twenty-fifth year of our exile, at
the beginning of the year, on the tenth
of the month, in the fourteenth year after the
fall of the city—on that very day the hand of
the LORD was upon me and he took me there.
2In visions of God he took me to the land of
Israel and set me on a very high mountain,
on whose south side were some buildings that
looked like a city. 3He took me there, and I saw
a man whose appearance was like bronze; he
was standing in the gateway with a linen cord
and a measuring rod in his hand. 4The man
said to me, “Son of man, look with your eyes
and hear with your ears and pay attention to
everything I am going to show you, for that
is why you have been brought here. Tell the
house of Israel everything you see.”

The East Gate to the Outer Court

5I saw a wall completely surrounding the
temple area. The length of the measuring rod
in the man’s hand was six long cubits, each of
which was a cubit[b] and a handbreadth.[c] He
measured the wall; it was one measuring rod
thick and one rod high.
6Then he went to the gate facing east. He
climbed its steps and measured the threshold of the gate; it was one rod
deep.[d] 7The alcoves for the
guards were one rod long and
one rod wide, and the projecting walls between the alcoves
were five cubits thick. And the
threshold of the gate next to
the portico facing the temple
was one rod deep.
8Then he measured the portico of the gateway; 9it[e] was
eight cubits deep and its jambs
were two cubits thick. The
portico of the gateway faced
the temple.
10Inside the east gate were
three alcoves on each side;
the three had the same measurements, and the faces of
the projecting walls on each side had the
same measurements. 11Then he measured the
width of the entrance to the gateway; it was
ten cubits and its length was thirteen cubits.
12In front of each alcove was a wall one cubit
high, and the alcoves were six cubits square.
13Then he measured the gateway from the top
of the rear wall of one alcove to the top of the
opposite one; the distance was twenty-five cubits from one parapet opening to the opposite
one. 14He measured along the faces of the projecting walls all around the inside of the gateway—sixty cubits. The measurement was up
to the portico[f] facing the courtyard.[g] 15The
distance from the entrance of the gateway to
the far end of its portico was fifty cubits. 16The
alcoves and the projecting walls inside the
gateway were surmounted by narrow parapet
openings all around, as was the portico; the
openings all around faced inward. The faces
of the projecting walls were decorated with
palm trees.

[a] 25 Or *now restore the fortunes of Jacob* [b] 5 The common cubit was about 1 1/2 feet (about 0.5 meter). [c] 5 That is, about 3 inches (about 8 centimeters) [d] 6 Septuagint; Hebrew *deep, the first threshold, one rod deep* [e] 8,9 Many Hebrew manuscripts, Septuagint, Vulgate and Syriac; most Hebrew manuscripts *gateway facing the temple; it was one rod deep. 9Then he measured the portico of the gateway; it* [f] 14 Septuagint; Hebrew *projecting wall* [g] 14 The meaning of the Hebrew for this verse is uncertain.

The Outer Court

17 Then he brought me into the outer court. There I saw some rooms and a pavement that had been constructed all around the court; there were thirty rooms along the pavement. 18 It abutted the sides of the gateways and was as wide as they were long; this was the lower pavement. 19 Then he measured the distance from the inside of the lower gateway to the outside of the inner court; it was a hundred cubits on the east side as well as on the north.

The North Gate

20 Then he measured the length and width of the gate facing north, leading into the outer court. 21 Its alcoves—three on each side—its projecting walls and its portico had the same measurements as those of the first gateway. It was fifty cubits long and twenty-five cubits wide. 22 Its openings, its portico and its palm tree decorations had the same measurements as those of the gate facing east. Seven steps led up to it, with its portico opposite them. 23 There was a gate to the inner court facing the north gate, just as there was on the east. He measured from one gate to the opposite one; it was a hundred cubits.

The South Gate

24 Then he led me to the south side and I saw a gate facing south. He measured its jambs and its portico, and they had the same measurements as the others. 25 The gateway and its portico had narrow openings all around, like the openings of the others. It was fifty cubits long and twenty-five cubits wide. 26 Seven steps led up to it, with its portico opposite them; it had palm tree decorations on the faces of the projecting walls on each side. 27 The inner court also had a gate facing south, and he measured from this gate to the outer gate on the south side; it was a hundred cubits.

Gates to the Inner Court

28 Then he brought me into the inner court through the south gate, and he measured the south gate; it had the same measurements as the others. 29 Its alcoves, its projecting walls and its portico had the same measurements as the others. The gateway and its portico had openings all around. It was fifty cubits long and twenty-five cubits wide. 30 (The porticoes of the gateways around the inner court were twenty-five cubits wide and five cubits deep.) 31 Its portico faced the outer court; palm trees decorated its jambs, and eight steps led up to it.

32 Then he brought me to the inner court on the east side, and he measured the gateway; it had the same measurements as the others. 33 Its alcoves, its projecting walls and its portico had the same measurements as the others. The gateway and its portico had openings all around. It was fifty cubits long and twenty-five cubits wide. 34 Its portico faced the outer court; palm trees decorated the jambs on either side, and eight steps led up to it.

35 Then he brought me to the north gate and measured it. It had the same measurements as the others, 36 as did its alcoves, its projecting walls and its portico, and it had openings all around. It was fifty cubits long and twenty-five cubits wide. 37 Its portico[a] faced the outer court; palm trees decorated the jambs on either side, and eight steps led up to it.

The Rooms for Preparing Sacrifices

38 A room with a doorway was by the portico in each of the inner gateways, where the burnt offerings were washed. 39 In the portico of the gateway were two tables on each side, on which the burnt offerings, sin offerings and guilt offerings were slaughtered. 40 By the outside wall of the portico of the gateway, near the steps at the entrance to the north gateway were two tables, and on the other side of the steps were two tables. 41 So there were four tables on one side of the gateway and four on the other—eight tables in all—on which the sacrifices were slaughtered. 42 There were also four tables of dressed stone for the burnt offerings, each a cubit and a half long, a cubit and a half wide and a cubit high. On them were placed the utensils for slaughtering the burnt offerings and the other sacrifices. 43 And double-pronged hooks, each a handbreadth long, were attached to the wall all around. The tables were for the flesh of the offerings.

Rooms for the Priests

44 Outside the inner gate, within the inner court, were two rooms, one[b] at the side of the

[a] 37 Septuagint (see also verses 31 and 34); Hebrew *jambs* [b] 44 Septuagint; Hebrew *were rooms for singers, which were*

north gate and facing south, and another at the
side of the south[a] gate and facing north. 45He
said to me, "The room facing south is for the
priests who have charge of the temple, 46and
the room facing north is for the priests who
have charge of the altar. These are the sons of
Zadok, who are the only Levites who may draw
near to the LORD to minister before him."
47Then he measured the court: It was
square—a hundred cubits long and a hundred cubits wide. And the altar was in front of
the temple.

The Temple

48He brought me to the portico of the temple and measured the jambs of the portico;
they were five cubits wide on either side. The
width of the entrance was fourteen cubits and
its projecting walls were[b] three cubits wide on
either side. 49The portico was twenty cubits
wide, and twelve[c] cubits from front to back.
It was reached by a flight of stairs,[d] and there
were pillars on each side of the jambs.

41 Then the man brought me to the outer
sanctuary and measured the jambs;
the width of the jambs was six cubits[e] on each
side.[f] 2The entrance was ten cubits wide, and
the projecting walls on each side of it were five
cubits wide. He also measured the outer sanctuary; it was forty cubits long and twenty cubits wide.
3Then he went into the inner sanctuary and
measured the jambs of the entrance; each was
two cubits wide. The entrance was six cubits
wide, and the projecting walls on each side of
it were seven cubits wide. 4And he measured
the length of the inner sanctuary; it was twenty
cubits, and its width was twenty cubits across
the end of the outer sanctuary. He said to me,
"This is the Most Holy Place."
5Then he measured the wall of the temple;
it was six cubits thick, and each side room
around the temple was four cubits wide. 6The
side rooms were on three levels, one above
another, thirty on each level. There were ledges
all around the wall of the temple to serve as supports for the side rooms, so that the supports
were not inserted into the wall of the temple.
7The side rooms all around the temple were
wider at each successive level. The structure
surrounding the temple was built in ascending
stages, so that the rooms widened as one went
upward. A stairway went up from the lowest
floor to the top floor through the middle floor.
8I saw that the temple had a raised base all
around it, forming the foundation of the side
rooms. It was the length of the rod, six long cubits. 9The outer wall of the side rooms was five
cubits thick. The open area between the side
rooms of the temple 10and the ⌊priests'⌋ rooms
was twenty cubits wide all around the temple.
11There were entrances to the side rooms from
the open area, one on the north and another on
the south; and the base adjoining the open area
was five cubits wide all around.
12The building facing the temple courtyard
on the west side was seventy cubits wide. The
wall of the building was five cubits thick all
around, and its length was ninety cubits.
13Then he measured the temple; it was a hundred cubits long, and the temple courtyard and
the building with its walls were also a hundred
cubits long. 14The width of the temple courtyard on the east, including the front of the temple, was a hundred cubits.
15Then he measured the length of the building facing the courtyard at the rear of the temple, including its galleries on each side; it was a
hundred cubits.
The outer sanctuary, the inner sanctuary
and the portico facing the court, 16as well as
the thresholds and the narrow windows and
galleries around the three of them—everything beyond and including the threshold was
covered with wood. The floor, the wall up to
the windows, and the windows were covered.
17In the space above the outside of the entrance to the inner sanctuary and on the walls
at regular intervals all around the inner and
outer sanctuary 18were carved cherubim and
palm trees. Palm trees alternated with cherubim. Each cherub had two faces: 19the face of
a man toward the palm tree on one side and
the face of a lion toward the palm tree on the
other. They were carved all around the whole
temple. 20From the floor to the area above the

[a] 44 Septuagint; Hebrew *east* [b] 48 Septuagint; Hebrew *entrance was* [c] 49 Septuagint; Hebrew *eleven* [d] 49 Hebrew; Septuagint *Ten steps led up to it* [e] 1 The common cubit was about 1 1/2 feet (about 0.5 meter). [f] 1 One Hebrew manuscript and Septuagint; most Hebrew manuscripts *side, the width of the tent*

entrance, cherubim and palm trees were carved
on the wall of the outer sanctuary.
21The outer sanctuary had a rectangular
doorframe, and the one at the front of the Most
Holy Place was similar. 22There was a wooden
altar three cubits high and two cubits square[a];
its corners, its base[b] and its sides were of wood.
The man said to me, "This is the table that is
before the LORD." 23Both the outer sanctuary
and the Most Holy Place had double doors.
24Each door had two leaves—two hinged
leaves for each door. 25And on the doors of
the outer sanctuary were carved cherubim and
palm trees like those carved on the walls, and
there was a wooden overhang on the front of
the portico. 26On the sidewalls of the portico
were narrow windows with palm trees carved
on each side. The side rooms of the temple also
had overhangs.

Rooms for the Priests

42 Then the man led me northward into
the outer court and brought me to the
rooms opposite the temple courtyard and opposite the outer wall on the north side. 2The
building whose door faced north was a hundred cubits[c] long and fifty cubits wide. 3Both in
the section twenty cubits from the inner court
and in the section opposite the pavement of the
outer court, gallery faced gallery at the three
levels. 4In front of the rooms was an inner passageway ten cubits wide and a hundred cubits[d]
long. Their doors were on the north. 5Now the
upper rooms were narrower, for the galleries
took more space from them than from the
rooms on the lower and middle floors of the
building. 6The rooms on the third floor had no
pillars, as the courts had; so they were smaller
in floor space than those on the lower and middle floors. 7There was an outer wall parallel to
the rooms and the outer court; it extended in
front of the rooms for fifty cubits. 8While the
row of rooms on the side next to the outer court
was fifty cubits long, the row on the side nearest the sanctuary was a hundred cubits long.
9The lower rooms had an entrance on the east
side as one enters them from the outer court.
10On the south side[e] along the length of the
wall of the outer court, adjoining the temple
courtyard and opposite the outer wall, were
rooms 11with a passageway in front of them.
These were like the rooms on the north; they
had the same length and width, with similar
exits and dimensions. Similar to the doorways
on the north 12were the doorways of the rooms
on the south. There was a doorway at the beginning of the passageway that was parallel to
the corresponding wall extending eastward, by
which one enters the rooms.
13Then he said to me, "The north and south
rooms facing the temple courtyard are the
priests' rooms, where the priests who approach
the LORD will eat the most holy offerings. There
they will put the most holy offerings—the grain
offerings, the sin offerings and the guilt offerings—for the place is holy. 14Once the priests
enter the holy precincts, they are not to go into
the outer court until they leave behind the garments in which they minister, for these are holy.
They are to put on other clothes before they go
near the places that are for the people."
15When he had finished measuring what
was inside the temple area, he led me out by
the east gate and measured the area all around:
16He measured the east side with the measuring rod; it was five hundred cubits.[f] 17He
measured the north side; it was five hundred
cubits[g] by the measuring rod. 18He measured
the south side; it was five hundred cubits by the
measuring rod. 19Then he turned to the west
side and measured; it was five hundred cubits
by the measuring rod. 20So he measured the
area on all four sides. It had a wall around it,
five hundred cubits long and five hundred cubits wide, to separate the holy from the common.

The Glory Returns to the Temple

43 Then the man brought me to the gate
facing east, 2and I saw the glory of the
God of Israel coming from the east. His voice
was like the roar of rushing waters, and the land
was radiant with his glory. 3The vision I saw
was like the vision I had seen when he[h] came to
destroy the city and like the visions I had seen
by the Kebar River, and I fell facedown. 4The

[a]22 Septuagint; Hebrew *long* [b]22 Septuagint; Hebrew *length* [c]2 The common cubit was about 1 1/2 feet (about 0.5 meter).
[d]4 Septuagint and Syriac; Hebrew *and one cubit* [e]10 Septuagint; Hebrew *Eastward* [f]16 See Septuagint of verse 17; Hebrew *rods*; also in verses 18 and 19. [g]17 Septuagint; Hebrew *rods* [h]3 Some Hebrew manuscripts and Vulgate; most Hebrew manuscripts *I*

glory of the LORD entered the temple through
the gate facing east. 5Then the Spirit lifted me
up and brought me into the inner court, and
the glory of the LORD filled the temple.

6While the man was stand-
ing beside me, I heard someone
speaking to me from inside the
temple. 7He said: "Son of man,
this is the place of my throne
and the place for the soles of
my feet. This is where I will live
among the Israelites forever.
The house of Israel will never
again defile my holy name—
neither they nor their kings—
by their prostitution[a] and the
lifeless idols[b] of their kings at
their high places. 8When they
placed their threshold next to
my threshold and their doorposts beside my doorposts,
with only a wall between me
and them, they defiled my holy name by their
detestable practices. So I destroyed them in my
anger. 9Now let them put away from me their
prostitution and the lifeless idols of their kings,
and I will live among them forever.

10"Son of man, describe the temple to the
people of Israel, that they may be ashamed of
their sins. Let them consider the plan, 11and if
they are ashamed of all they have done, make
known to them the design of the temple—its
arrangement, its exits and entrances—its whole
design and all its regulations[c] and laws. Write
these down before them so that they may be
faithful to its design and follow all its regulations.

12"This is the law of the temple: All the surrounding area on top of the mountain will be
most holy. Such is the law of the temple.

The Altar

13"These are the measurements of the altar
in long cubits, that cubit being a cubit[d] and a
handbreadth[e]: Its gutter is a cubit deep and a
cubit wide, with a rim of one span[f] around the
edge. And this is the height of the altar: 14From
the gutter on the ground up to the lower ledge
it is two cubits high and a cubit wide, and from
the smaller ledge up to the larger ledge it is four
cubits high and a cubit wide. 15The altar hearth
is four cubits high, and four horns project upward from the hearth. 16The
altar hearth is square, twelve
cubits long and twelve cubits
wide. 17The upper ledge also
is square, fourteen cubits long
and fourteen cubits wide, with
a rim of half a cubit and a gutter of a cubit all around. The
steps of the altar face east."

18Then he said to me, "Son
of man, this is what the Sovereign LORD says: These will be
the regulations for sacrificing
burnt offerings and sprinkling
blood upon the altar when it is
built: 19You are to give a young
bull as a sin offering to the
priests, who are Levites, of the
family of Zadok, who come near to minister
before me, declares the Sovereign LORD. 20You
are to take some of its blood and put it on the
four horns of the altar and on the four corners
of the upper ledge and all around the rim, and
so purify the altar and make atonement for it.
21You are to take the bull for the sin offering
and burn it in the designated part of the temple
area outside the sanctuary.

22"On the second day you are to offer a male
goat without defect for a sin offering, and the
altar is to be purified as it was purified with the
bull. 23When you have finished purifying it,
you are to offer a young bull and a ram from
the flock, both without defect. 24You are to offer them before the LORD, and the priests are
to sprinkle salt on them and sacrifice them as a
burnt offering to the LORD.

25"For seven days you are to provide a male
goat daily for a sin offering; you are also to provide a young bull and a ram from the flock,
both without defect. 26For seven days they are
to make atonement for the altar and cleanse it;
thus they will dedicate it. 27At the end of these
days, from the eighth day on, the priests are to
present your burnt offerings and fellowship

Ezekiel 43:2

God Displays His Glory

And I saw the glory of the God of Israel coming from the east. His voice was like the roar of rushing waters, and the land was radiant with his glory.

[a]7 Or *their spiritual adultery*; also in verse 9 [b]7 Or *the corpses*; also in verse 9 [c]11 Some Hebrew manuscripts and Septuagint; most Hebrew manuscripts *regulations and its whole design* [d]13 The common cubit was about 1 1/2 feet (about 0.5 meter). [e]13 That is, about 3 inches (about 8 centimeters) [f]13 That is, about 9 inches (about 22 centimeters)

God in You

Read: Ezekiel 43:1–12

Ezekiel 43:5

Then the Spirit lifted me up and brought me into the inner court, and the glory of the LORD filled the temple.

PICTURE A CONSUMING FIRE, a cumulus cloud, a rainbow on an overcast day. In the Old Testament, God gives us many compelling images of his glory. At that time, his glory dwelled in temples made by human hands. And one day, as Ezekiel's grandiose vision details, his glory will fill the temple once again.

The unifying theme of God's glory, in both the Old and New Testaments, is holiness: the purity of a consuming fire (Exodus 24:17), the stark contrast of a white cloud against the sky (Exodus 40:35), and the hope that a colorful rainbow inspires on a rainy day (Ezekiel 1:28). God's glory is another way to speak of his holiness.

While we wait for God's glory to fill the temple one day, the God of the universe makes his home in human hearts. When Jesus returned to heaven, he left the Holy Spirit to fill the hearts of his people. God resides within those who have invited him. Our bodies are temples of the Lord, says the apostle Paul in 1 Corinthians 6:19, so we must honor them by pursuing and practicing holiness.

We see a pattern through the Old and New Testaments of sin destroying the temple. The same thing happens today with our temples (bodies). Sin drives out holiness and destroys our fellowship with God.

Ezekiel's vision should challenge us to make a choice. We can fill our temple with sin or with God's glory . . . but there is not room for both. Either sin will fill our temple and destroy us body and soul, or God's holiness, the righteousness that comes from him, will find a home in our hearts.

Ezekiel's vision ultimately speaks of a time when the temple will no longer be defiled by sin. Instead, God's glory, his beauty, splendor and majesty will fill the temple.

reflection

1 What sinful habit, if you allow it to continue, could destroy your temple?

2 How could you better care for your temple?

3 What does God's glory look like in your life? (For some help, see Galatians 5:22–23.)

RELATED READINGS

1 Kings 6:1–38; 8:57–61; 9:6–9; John 2:18–22; 1 Corinthians 6:19–20

Tuesday

Go to page 1050 for your next devotional reading.

offerings[a] on the altar. Then I will accept you,
declares the Sovereign LORD."

The Prince, the Levites, the Priests

44 Then the man brought me back to the
outer gate of the sanctuary, the one
facing east, and it was shut. 2The LORD said to
me, "This gate is to remain shut. It must not be
opened; no one may enter through it. It is to remain shut because the LORD, the God of Israel,
has entered through it. 3The prince himself is
the only one who may sit inside the gateway to
eat in the presence of the LORD. He is to enter
by way of the portico of the gateway and go out
the same way."

4Then the man brought me by way of the
north gate to the front of the temple. I looked
and saw the glory of the LORD filling the temple
of the LORD, and I fell facedown.

5The LORD said to me, "Son of man, look
carefully, listen closely and give attention to
everything I tell you concerning all the regulations regarding the temple of the LORD.
Give attention to the entrance of the temple
and all the exits of the sanctuary. 6Say to the
rebellious house of Israel, 'This is what the Sovereign LORD says: Enough of your detestable
practices, O house of Israel! 7In addition to all
your other detestable practices, you brought foreigners uncircumcised in heart and flesh into
my sanctuary, desecrating my temple while
you offered me food, fat and blood, and you
broke my covenant. 8Instead of carrying out
your duty in regard to my holy things, you put
others in charge of my sanctuary. 9This is what
the Sovereign LORD says: No foreigner uncircumcised in heart and flesh is to enter my sanctuary, not even the foreigners who live among
the Israelites.

10" 'The Levites who went far from me when
Israel went astray and who wandered from me
after their idols must bear the consequences of
their sin. 11They may serve in my sanctuary,
having charge of the gates of the temple and
serving in it; they may slaughter the burnt offerings and sacrifices for the people and stand
before the people and serve them. 12But because they served them in the presence of their
idols and made the house of Israel fall into sin,
therefore I have sworn with uplifted hand that
they must bear the consequences of their sin,
declares the Sovereign LORD. 13They are not to
come near to serve me as priests or come near
any of my holy things or my most holy offerings; they must bear the shame of their detestable practices. 14Yet I will put them in charge
of the duties of the temple and all the work that
is to be done in it.

15" 'But the priests, who are Levites and descendants of Zadok and who faithfully carried
out the duties of my sanctuary when the Israelites went astray from me, are to come near to
minister before me; they are to stand before me
to offer sacrifices of fat and blood, declares the
Sovereign LORD. 16They alone are to enter my
sanctuary; they alone are to come near my table to minister before me and perform my service.

17" 'When they enter the gates of the inner
court, they are to wear linen clothes; they must
not wear any woolen garment while ministering at the gates of the inner court or inside the
temple. 18They are to wear linen turbans on
their heads and linen undergarments around
their waists. They must not wear anything
that makes them perspire. 19When they go
out into the outer court where the people are,
they are to take off the clothes they have been
ministering in and are to leave them in the sacred rooms, and put on other clothes, so that
they do not consecrate the people by means of
their garments.

20" 'They must not shave their heads or let
their hair grow long, but they are to keep the
hair of their heads trimmed. 21No priest is to
drink wine when he enters the inner court.
22They must not marry widows or divorced
women; they may marry only virgins of Israelite descent or widows of priests. 23They are
to teach my people the difference between
the holy and the common and show them
how to distinguish between the unclean and
the clean.

24" 'In any dispute, the priests are to serve
as judges and decide it according to my
ordinances. They are to keep my laws and my
decrees for all my appointed feasts, and they
are to keep my Sabbaths holy.

[a] 27 Traditionally *peace offerings*

25“ ‘A priest must not defile himself by going
near a dead person; however, if the dead person was his father or mother, son or daughter,
brother or unmarried sister, then he may defile
himself. 26After he is cleansed, he must wait
seven days. 27On the day he goes into the inner
court of the sanctuary to minister in the sanctuary, he is to offer a sin offering for himself,
declares the Sovereign LORD.

28“ ‘I am to be the only inheritance the priests have. You are
to give them no possession in
Israel; I will be their possession.
29They will eat the grain offerings, the sin offerings and the
guilt offerings; and everything
in Israel devoted[a] to the LORD
will belong to them. 30The best
of all the firstfruits and of all
your special gifts will belong
to the priests. You are to give
them the first portion of your
ground meal so that a blessing
may rest on your household.
31The priests must not eat anything, bird or animal, found
dead or torn by wild animals.

Division of the Land

45 “ ‘When you allot the land as an inheritance, you are to present to the LORD a
portion of the land as a sacred district, 25,000
cubits long and 20,000[b] cubits wide; the entire
area will be holy. 2Of this, a section 500 cubits
square is to be for the sanctuary, with 50 cubits
around it for open land. 3In the sacred district,
measure off a section 25,000 cubits[c] long and
10,000 cubits[d] wide. In it will be the sanctuary,
the Most Holy Place. 4It will be the sacred portion of the land for the priests, who minister
in the sanctuary and who draw near to minister before the LORD. It will be a place for their
houses as well as a holy place for the sanctuary.
5An area 25,000 cubits long and 10,000 cubits
wide will belong to the Levites, who serve in
the temple, as their possession for towns to
live in.[e]

Ezekiel 45:9

God Hates Oppression

"This is what the Sovereign LORD says: You have gone far enough, O princes of Israel! Give up your violence and oppression and do what is just and right. Stop dispossessing my people, declares the Sovereign LORD."

6“ ‘You are to give the city as its property an
area 5,000 cubits wide and 25,000 cubits long,
adjoining the sacred portion; it will belong to
the whole house of Israel.

7“ ‘The prince will have the land bordering
each side of the area formed by the sacred district and the property of the city. It will extend
westward from the west side and eastward
from the east side, running
lengthwise from the western to
the eastern border parallel to
one of the tribal portions. 8This
land will be his possession in
Israel. And my princes will no
longer oppress my people but
will allow the house of Israel to
possess the land according to
their tribes.

9“ ‘This is what the Sovereign LORD says: You have gone
far enough, O princes of Israel!
Give up your violence and oppression and do what is just
and right. Stop dispossessing
my people, declares the Sovereign LORD. 10You are to use
accurate scales, an accurate
ephah[f] and an accurate bath.[g]
11The ephah and the bath are
to be the same size, the bath containing a tenth
of a homer[h] and the ephah a tenth of a homer;
the homer is to be the standard measure for
both. 12The shekel[i] is to consist of twenty gerahs. Twenty shekels plus twenty-five shekels
plus fifteen shekels equal one mina.[j]

Offerings and Holy Days

13“ ‘This is the special gift you are to offer:
a sixth of an ephah from each homer of wheat
and a sixth of an ephah from each homer of
barley. 14The prescribed portion of oil, measured by the bath, is a tenth of a bath from each
cor (which consists of ten baths or one homer,
for ten baths are equivalent to a homer). 15Also
one sheep is to be taken from every flock of
two hundred from the well-watered pastures
of Israel. These will be used for the grain offer-

[a]29 The Hebrew term refers to the irrevocable giving over of things or persons to the LORD. [b]1 Septuagint (see also verses 3 and 5 and 48:9); Hebrew *10,000* [c]3 That is, about 7 miles (about 12 kilometers) [d]3 That is, about 3 miles (about 5 kilometers) [e]5 Septuagint; Hebrew *temple; they will have as their possession 20 rooms* [f]10 An ephah was a dry measure. [g]10 A bath was a liquid measure. [h]11 A homer was a dry measure. [i]12 A shekel weighed about 2/5 ounce (about 11.5 grams). [j]12 That is, 60 shekels; the common mina was 50 shekels.

ings, burnt offerings and fellowship offerings[a]
to make atonement for the people, declares the
Sovereign LORD. 16All the people of the land
will participate in this special gift for the use
of the prince in Israel. 17It will be the duty of
the prince to provide the burnt offerings, grain
offerings and drink offerings at the festivals,
the New Moons and the Sabbaths—at all the
appointed feasts of the house of Israel. He will
provide the sin offerings, grain offerings, burnt
offerings and fellowship offerings to make
atonement for the house of Israel.

18" 'This is what the Sovereign LORD says: In
the first month on the first day you are to take
a young bull without defect and purify the sanctuary. 19The priest is to take some of the blood
of the sin offering and put it on the doorposts
of the temple, on the four corners of the upper
ledge of the altar and on the gateposts of the
inner court. 20You are to do the same on the
seventh day of the month for anyone who sins
unintentionally or through ignorance; so you
are to make atonement for the temple.

21" 'In the first month on the fourteenth day
you are to observe the Passover, a feast lasting
seven days, during which you shall eat bread
made without yeast. 22On that day the prince
is to provide a bull as a sin offering for himself
and for all the people of the land. 23Every day
during the seven days of the Feast he is to provide seven bulls and seven rams without defect
as a burnt offering to the LORD, and a male
goat for a sin offering. 24He is to provide as a
grain offering an ephah for each bull and an
ephah for each ram, along with a hin[b] of oil for
each ephah.

25" 'During the seven days of the Feast,
which begins in the seventh month on the fifteenth day, he is to make the same provision
for sin offerings, burnt offerings, grain offerings and oil.

46 " 'This is what the Sovereign LORD says:
The gate of the inner court facing east
is to be shut on the six working days, but on the
Sabbath day and on the day of the New Moon
it is to be opened. 2The prince is to enter from
the outside through the portico of the gateway
and stand by the gatepost. The priests are to
sacrifice his burnt offering and his fellowship
offerings.[c] He is to worship at the threshold of
the gateway and then go out, but the gate will
not be shut until evening. 3On the Sabbaths
and New Moons the people of the land are to
worship in the presence of the LORD at the entrance to that gateway. 4The burnt offering the
prince brings to the LORD on the Sabbath day
is to be six male lambs and a ram, all without
defect. 5The grain offering given with the ram
is to be an ephah,[d] and the grain offering with
the lambs is to be as much as he pleases, along
with a hin[b] of oil for each ephah. 6On the day
of the New Moon he is to offer a young bull,
six lambs and a ram, all without defect. 7He is
to provide as a grain offering one ephah with
the bull, one ephah with the ram, and with the
lambs as much as he wants to give, along with
a hin of oil with each ephah. 8When the prince
enters, he is to go in through the portico of the
gateway, and he is to come out the same way.

9" 'When the people of the land come before
the LORD at the appointed feasts, whoever enters by the north gate to worship is to go out
the south gate; and whoever enters by the south
gate is to go out the north gate. No one is to return through the gate by which he entered, but
each is to go out the opposite gate. 10The prince
is to be among them, going in when they go in
and going out when they go out.

11" 'At the festivals and the appointed feasts,
the grain offering is to be an ephah with a bull,
an ephah with a ram, and with the lambs as
much as one pleases, along with a hin of oil
for each ephah. 12When the prince provides a
freewill offering to the LORD—whether a burnt
offering or fellowship offerings—the gate facing east is to be opened for him. He shall offer
his burnt offering or his fellowship offerings
as he does on the Sabbath day. Then he shall
go out, and after he has gone out, the gate will
be shut.

13" 'Every day you are to provide a year-old
lamb without defect for a burnt offering to the
LORD; morning by morning you shall provide
it. 14You are also to provide with it morning
by morning a grain offering, consisting of a
sixth of an ephah with a third of a hin of oil to

[a]15 Traditionally *peace offerings*; also in verse 17 [b]24,5 That is, probably about 4 quarts (about 4 liters) [c]2 Traditionally *peace offerings*; also in verse 12 [d]5 That is, probably about 3/5 bushel (about 22 liters)

Once and for All

Read: Ezekiel 45:18–25

Ezekiel 45:22–23

"On that day the prince is to provide a bull as a sin offering for himself and for all the people of the land. Every day during the seven days of the Feast he is to provide seven bulls and seven rams without defect as a burnt offering to the LORD, and a male goat for a sin offering."

IMAGINE YOUR CALENDAR reading something like this:

9:00 A.M.	Dentist
10:00 A.M.	Cleaners, bank
12:30 P.M.	Lunch meeting
2:30 P.M.	Pick up kids/goat
4:00 P.M.	Stop by altar for sacrifice
Note to self:	Make sacrifice third Tuesday of every month.

Are you nagged by guilty feelings over your sins? Do you replay mistakes in your head over and over? For the Israelites, sin must have been almost continually on their minds. Just when they finished one sacrifice, it was time for another. The Old Testament sacrificial system was extremely complex, with many dates and details to remember. Sacrifices were made again and again—for the same individuals. Because they could not permanently remove the sin of the people, the blood of countless animals spilled down the altar year after year.

Only one sacrifice has ever been sufficient to atone for people's sin once for all time. Through Jesus Christ's death on the cross we can receive forgiveness from sin—permanently. There is no additional sacrifice needed.

Maybe you have personally received Christ's gift of forgiveness, but you wrestle with guilt over past sins. If that is the case, you probably don't need a calendar like the Israelites' had to remind you of your sin; you may even have plenty of people in your life that won't let you forget it. Your thoughts constantly accuse you, and you feel that Christ's sacrifice wasn't enough to pay for your failures and mistakes.

These thoughts and feelings are not from God. Satan would like nothing more than to make us feel that we are not forgiven. Satan reminds us of our sins, holding them over our heads. But when we believe his lies, we deny the truth of what Christ accomplished.

The next time you feel guilt start to surface, recall the permanent and perfect sacrifice of Christ. He paid for your sin. All of it.

reflection

1 How does the sacrifice of Jesus reveal his love for you?

2 Whenever you struggle with feelings of guilt over confessed sin, what can you do to remind yourself that you are forgiven?

3 What action can you take today that will show that you believe that your sin is paid for?

RELATED READINGS

Psalm 103:11–12; Hebrews 9:11–14; 10:1–14

Wednesday

Go to page 1057 for your next devotional reading.

moisten the flour. The presenting of this grain offering to the LORD is a lasting ordinance. 15So the lamb and the grain offering and the oil shall be provided morning by morning for a regular burnt offering.

16" 'This is what the Sovereign LORD says: If the prince makes a gift from his inheritance to one of his sons, it will also belong to his descendants; it is to be their property by inheritance. 17If, however, he makes a gift from his inheritance to one of his servants, the servant may keep it until the year of freedom; then it will revert to the prince. His inheritance belongs to his sons only; it is theirs. 18The prince must not take any of the inheritance of the people, driving them off their property. He is to give his sons their inheritance out of his own property, so that none of my people will be separated from his property.' "

19Then the man brought me through the entrance at the side of the gate to the sacred rooms facing north, which belonged to the priests, and showed me a place at the western end. 20He said to me, "This is the place where the priests will cook the guilt offering and the sin offering and bake the grain offering, to avoid bringing them into the outer court and consecrating the people."

21He then brought me to the outer court and led me around to its four corners, and I saw in each corner another court. 22In the four corners of the outer court were enclosed[a] courts, forty cubits long and thirty cubits wide; each of the courts in the four corners was the same size. 23Around the inside of each of the four courts was a ledge of stone, with places for fire built all around under the ledge. 24He said to me, "These are the kitchens where those who minister at the temple will cook the sacrifices of the people."

The River From the Temple

47 The man brought me back to the entrance of the temple, and I saw water coming out from under the threshold of the temple toward the east (for the temple faced east). The water was coming down from under the south side of the temple, south of the altar. 2He then brought me out through the north gate and led me around the outside to the outer gate facing east, and the water was flowing from the south side.

3As the man went eastward with a measuring line in his hand, he measured off a thousand cubits[b] and then led me through water that was ankle-deep. 4He measured off another thousand cubits and led me through water that was knee-deep. He measured off another thousand and led me through water that was up to the waist. 5He measured off another thousand, but now it was a river that I could not cross, because the water had risen and was deep enough to swim in—a river that no one could cross. 6He asked me, "Son of man, do you see this?"

Then he led me back to the bank of the river. 7When I arrived there, I saw a great number of trees on each side of the river. 8He said to me, "This water flows toward the eastern region and goes down into the Arabah,[c] where it enters the Sea.[d] When it empties into the Sea,[d] the water there becomes fresh. 9Swarms of living creatures will live wherever the river flows. There will be large numbers of fish, because this water flows there and makes the salt water fresh; so where the river flows everything will live. 10Fishermen will stand along the shore; from En Gedi to En Eglaim there will be places for spreading nets. The fish will be of many kinds—like the fish of the Great Sea.[e] 11But the swamps and marshes will not become fresh; they will be left for salt. 12Fruit trees of all kinds will grow on both banks of the river. Their leaves will not wither, nor will their fruit fail. Every month they will bear, because the water from the sanctuary flows to them. Their fruit will serve for food and their leaves for healing."

The Boundaries of the Land

13This is what the Sovereign LORD says: "These are the boundaries by which you are to divide the land for an inheritance among the twelve tribes of Israel, with two portions for Joseph. 14You are to divide it equally among them. Because I swore with uplifted hand to give it to your forefathers, this land will become your inheritance.

[a]22 The meaning of the Hebrew for this word is uncertain. [b]3 That is, about 1,500 feet (about 450 meters) [c]8 Or *the Jordan Valley*
[d]8 That is, the Dead Sea [e]10 That is, the Mediterranean; also in verses 15, 19 and 20

15 “This is to be the boundary of the land:
“On the north side it will run from the Great
Sea by the Hethlon road past Lebo[a] Hamath to Zedad, 16 Berothah[b] and Sibraim
(which lies on the border between Damascus and Hamath), as far as Hazer Hatticon,
which is on the border of Hauran. 17 The
boundary will extend from the sea to Hazar Enan,[c] along the northern border of Damascus, with the border of Hamath to the
north. This will be the north boundary.
18 “On the east side the boundary will run between Hauran and Damascus, along the
Jordan between Gilead and the land of
Israel, to the eastern sea and as far as Tamar.[d] This will be the east boundary.
19 “On the south side it will run from Tamar as
far as the waters of Meribah Kadesh, then
along the Wadi ⌊of Egypt⌋ to the Great Sea.
This will be the south boundary.
20 “On the west side, the Great Sea will be the
boundary to a point opposite Lebo[e] Hamath. This will be the west boundary.

21 “You are to distribute this land among
yourselves according to the tribes of Israel.
22 You are to allot it as an inheritance for yourselves and for the aliens who have settled
among you and who have children. You are to
consider them as native-born Israelites; along
with you they are to be allotted an inheritance
among the tribes of Israel. 23 In whatever tribe
the alien settles, there you are to give him his
inheritance,” declares the Sovereign LORD.

The Division of the Land

48 “These are the tribes, listed by name:
At the northern frontier, Dan will have
one portion; it will follow the Hethlon road
to Lebo[f] Hamath; Hazar Enan and the northern border of Damascus next to Hamath will
be part of its border from the east side to the
west side.
2 “Asher will have one portion; it will border
the territory of Dan from east to west.
3 “Naphtali will have one portion; it will border the territory of Asher from east to west.
4 “Manasseh will have one portion; it will border the territory of Naphtali from east to west.
5 “Ephraim will have one portion; it will
border the territory of Manasseh from east
to west.
6 “Reuben will have one portion; it will border the territory of Ephraim from east to west.
7 “Judah will have one portion; it will border
the territory of Reuben from east to west.
8 “Bordering the territory of Judah from east
to west will be the portion you are to present
as a special gift. It will be 25,000 cubits[g] wide,
and its length from east to west will equal one
of the tribal portions; the sanctuary will be in
the center of it.
9 “The special portion you are to offer to the
LORD will be 25,000 cubits long and 10,000 cubits[h] wide. 10 This will be the sacred portion for
the priests. It will be 25,000 cubits long on the
north side, 10,000 cubits wide on the west side,
10,000 cubits wide on the east side and 25,000
cubits long on the south side. In the center of
it will be the sanctuary of the LORD. 11 This will
be for the consecrated priests, the Zadokites,
who were faithful in serving me and did not
go astray as the Levites did when the Israelites
went astray. 12 It will be a special gift to them
from the sacred portion of the land, a most
holy portion, bordering the territory of the Levites.
13 “Alongside the territory of the priests, the
Levites will have an allotment 25,000 cubits
long and 10,000 cubits wide. Its total length will
be 25,000 cubits and its width 10,000 cubits.
14 They must not sell or exchange any of it. This
is the best of the land and must not pass into
other hands, because it is holy to the LORD.
15 “The remaining area, 5,000 cubits wide
and 25,000 cubits long, will be for the common
use of the city, for houses and for pastureland.
The city will be in the center of it 16 and will
have these measurements: the north side 4,500
cubits, the south side 4,500 cubits, the east side
4,500 cubits, and the west side 4,500 cubits.
17 The pastureland for the city will be 250 cubits on the north, 250 cubits on the south, 250
cubits on the east, and 250 cubits on the west.
18 What remains of the area, bordering on the
sacred portion and running the length of it, will

[a] 15 Or *past the entrance to* [b] 15,16 See Septuagint and Ezekiel 48:1; Hebrew *road to go into Zedad, 16 Hamath, Berothah* [c] 17 Hebrew *Enon,* a variant of *Enan* [d] 18 Septuagint and Syriac; Hebrew *Israel. You will measure to the eastern sea* [e] 20 Or *opposite the entrance to* [f] 1 Or *to the entrance to* [g] 8 That is, about 7 miles (about 12 kilometers) [h] 9 That is, about 3 miles (about 5 kilometers)

be 10,000 cubits on the east side and 10,000 cubits on the west side. Its produce will supply
food for the workers of the city. 19 The workers
from the city who farm it will come from all the
tribes of Israel. 20 The entire portion will be a
square, 25,000 cubits on each side. As a special
gift you will set aside the sacred portion, along
with the property of the city.
21 "What remains on both sides of the area
formed by the sacred portion and the city
property will belong to the prince. It will extend eastward from the 25,000 cubits of the
sacred portion to the eastern border, and westward from the 25,000 cubits to the western border. Both these areas running the length of the
tribal portions will belong to the prince, and
the sacred portion with the temple sanctuary
will be in the center of them. 22 So the property
of the Levites and the property of the city will
lie in the center of the area that belongs to the
prince. The area belonging to the prince will
lie between the border of Judah and the border
of Benjamin.
23 "As for the rest of the tribes: Benjamin will
have one portion; it will extend from the east
side to the west side.
24 "Simeon will have one portion; it will
border the territory of Benjamin from east
to west.
25 "Issachar will have one portion; it will border the territory of Simeon from east to west.
26 "Zebulun will have one portion; it will border the territory of Issachar from east to west.
27 "Gad will have one portion; it will border
the territory of Zebulun from east to west.
28 "The southern boundary of Gad will run
south from Tamar to the waters of Meribah
Kadesh, then along the Wadi ⌞of Egypt⌟ to the
Great Sea.[a]
29 "This is the land you are to allot as an inheritance to the tribes of Israel, and these will be
their portions," declares the Sovereign LORD.

The Gates of the City

30 "These will be the exits of the city: Beginning on the north side, which is 4,500 cubits
long, 31 the gates of the city will be named after
the tribes of Israel. The three gates on the north
side will be the gate of Reuben, the gate of Judah and the gate of Levi.
32 "On the east side, which is 4,500 cubits
long, will be three gates: the gate of Joseph, the
gate of Benjamin and the gate of Dan.
33 "On the south side, which measures 4,500
cubits, will be three gates: the gate of Simeon,
the gate of Issachar and the gate of Zebulun.
34 "On the west side, which is 4,500 cubits
long, will be three gates: the gate of Gad, the
gate of Asher and the gate of Naphtali.
35 "The distance all around will be 18,000 cubits.

"And the name of the city from that time on
will be:

THE LORD IS THERE."

[a] 28 That is, the Mediterranean

Daniel

Author:
Daniel.

Audience:
Exiles in Babylon and all of God's people.

Date:
About 530 B.C.

Setting:
The Jews are taken into captivity by the Babylonians.

Verses to Remember:
"If we are thrown into the blazing furnace, the God we serve is able to save us from it, and he will rescue us from your hand, O king. But even if he does not, we want you to know, O king, that we will not serve your gods or worship the image of gold you have set up." (3:17–18)

Time and eternity intertwine in this book written during the days of exile. There are backward glances at *past sins that need to be confessed.* There are present tests and challenges to be faced. And there are prophetic visions that reach far into the future. At a time when the people of Israel wondered if God's covenant with them had been destroyed along with the temple, we find God is not only present, *but he is actively working* on behalf of his people, both for Daniel's generation and for the generations to come.

A window opens in this book, and we catch a *glimpse of the workings of heaven,* of angels delayed while they battle resistance, of visions that strike terror and of explanations that are only partially understood. *But we also see life on this earth,* specifically life in exile, away from the land of promise, away from home. And we see that this life is fraught with *challenges that lead us to make the choice* between saving our own skin or entrusting ourselves to God's protection.

Daniel's Training in Babylon

1 In the third year of the reign of Jehoiakim
king of Judah, Nebuchadnezzar king of
Babylon came to Jerusalem and besieged it.
2And the Lord delivered Jehoiakim king of Judah into his hand, along with some of the articles from the temple of God. These he carried
off to the temple of his god in Babylonia[a] and
put in the treasure house of his god.
3Then the king ordered Ashpenaz, chief of
his court officials, to bring in some of the Israelites from the royal family and the nobility—

[a]2 Hebrew *Shinar*

4 young men without any physical defect,
handsome, showing aptitude for every kind of
learning, well informed, quick to understand,
and qualified to serve in the king's palace. He
was to teach them the language and literature
of the Babylonians.[a] 5 The king assigned them
a daily amount of food and wine from the
king's table. They were to be trained for three
years, and after that they were to enter the
king's service.

6 Among these were some from Judah: Daniel, Hananiah, Mishael and Azariah. 7 The chief
official gave them new names: to Daniel, the
name Belteshazzar; to Hananiah, Shadrach; to
Mishael, Meshach; and to Azariah, Abednego.

8 But Daniel resolved not to defile himself
with the royal food and wine, and he asked the
chief official for permission not to defile himself this way. 9 Now God had caused the official
to show favor and sympathy to Daniel, 10 but
the official told Daniel, "I am afraid of my lord
the king, who has assigned your[b] food and
drink. Why should he see you looking worse
than the other young men your age? The king
would then have my head because of you."

11 Daniel then said to the guard whom
the chief official had appointed over Daniel,
Hananiah, Mishael and Azariah, 12 "Please test
your servants for ten days: Give us nothing but
vegetables to eat and water to drink. 13 Then
compare our appearance with that of the young
men who eat the royal food, and treat your servants in accordance with what you see." 14 So he
agreed to this and tested them for ten days.

15 At the end of the ten days they looked
healthier and better nourished than any of
the young men who ate the royal food. 16 So
the guard took away their choice food and the
wine they were to drink and gave them vegetables instead.

17 To these four young men God gave
knowledge and understanding of all kinds of
literature and learning. And Daniel could understand visions and dreams of all kinds.

18 At the end of the time set by the king to
bring them in, the chief official presented
them to Nebuchadnezzar. 19 The king talked
with them, and he found none equal to Daniel, Hananiah, Mishael and Azariah; so they
entered the king's service. 20 In every matter
of wisdom and understanding about which
the king questioned them, he found them ten
times better than all the magicians and enchanters in his whole kingdom.

21 And Daniel remained there until the first
year of King Cyrus.

Nebuchadnezzar's Dream

2 In the second year of his reign, Nebuchadnezzar had dreams; his mind was troubled
and he could not sleep. 2 So the king summoned
the magicians, enchanters, sorcerers and astrologers[c] to tell him what he had dreamed. When
they came in and stood before the king, 3 he
said to them, "I have had a dream that troubles
me and I want to know what it means.[d]"

4 Then the astrologers answered the king in
Aramaic,[e] "O king, live forever! Tell your servants the dream, and we will interpret it."

5 The king replied to the astrologers, "This
is what I have firmly decided: If you do not
tell me what my dream was and interpret it, I
will have you cut into pieces and your houses
turned into piles of rubble. 6 But if you tell me
the dream and explain it, you will receive from
me gifts and rewards and great honor. So tell
me the dream and interpret it for me."

7 Once more they replied, "Let the king
tell his servants the dream, and we will interpret it."

8 Then the king answered, "I am certain
that you are trying to gain time, because you
realize that this is what I have firmly decided:
9 If you do not tell me the dream, there is just
one penalty for you. You have conspired to
tell me misleading and wicked things, hoping
the situation will change. So then, tell me the
dream, and I will know that you can interpret
it for me."

10 The astrologers answered the king, "There
is not a man on earth who can do what the
king asks! No king, however great and mighty,
has ever asked such a thing of any magician
or enchanter or astrologer. 11 What the king
asks is too difficult. No one can reveal it to
the king except the gods, and they do not live
among men."

[a] 4 Or *Chaldeans* [b] 10 The Hebrew for *your* and *you* in this verse is plural. [c] 2 Or *Chaldeans*; also in verses 4, 5 and 10 [d] 3 Or *was*
[e] 4 The text from here through chapter 7 is in Aramaic.

12This made the king so angry and furious that he ordered the execution of all the wise men of Babylon. 13So the decree was issued to put the wise men to death, and men were sent to look for Daniel and his friends to put them to death.

14When Arioch, the commander of the king's guard, had gone out to put to death the wise men of Babylon, Daniel spoke to him with wisdom and tact. 15He asked the king's officer, "Why did the king issue such a harsh decree?" Arioch then explained the matter to Daniel. 16At this, Daniel went in to the king and asked for time, so that he might interpret the dream for him.

17Then Daniel returned to his house and explained the matter to his friends Hananiah, Mishael and Azariah. 18He urged them to plead for mercy from the God of heaven concerning this mystery, so that he and his friends might not be executed with the rest of the wise men of Babylon. 19During the night the mystery was revealed to Daniel in a vision. Then Daniel praised the God of heaven 20and said:

"Praise be to the name of God for ever and ever;
wisdom and power are his.
21He changes times and seasons;
he sets up kings and deposes them.
He gives wisdom to the wise
and knowledge to the discerning.
22He reveals deep and hidden things;
he knows what lies in darkness,
and light dwells with him.
23I thank and praise you, O God of my fathers:
You have given me wisdom and power,
you have made known to me what we asked of you,
you have made known to us the dream of the king."

Daniel 2:28

God Reveals Mysteries

"There is a God in heaven who reveals mysteries. He has shown King Nebuchadnezzar what will happen in days to come. Your dream and the visions that passed through your mind as you lay on your bed are these."

Daniel Interprets the Dream

24Then Daniel went to Arioch, whom the king had appointed to execute the wise men of Babylon, and said to him, "Do not execute the wise men of Babylon. Take me to the king, and I will interpret his dream for him."

25Arioch took Daniel to the king at once and said, "I have found a man among the exiles from Judah who can tell the king what his dream means."

26The king asked Daniel (also called Belteshazzar), "Are you able to tell me what I saw in my dream and interpret it?"

27Daniel replied, "No wise man, enchanter, magician or diviner can explain to the king the mystery he has asked about, 28but there is a God in heaven who reveals mysteries. He has shown King Nebuchadnezzar what will happen in days to come. Your dream and the visions that passed through your mind as you lay on your bed are these:

29"As you were lying there, O king, your mind turned to things to come, and the revealer of mysteries showed you what is going to happen. 30As for me, this mystery has been revealed to me, not because I have greater wisdom than other living men, but so that you, O king, may know the interpretation and that you may understand what went through your mind.

31"You looked, O king, and there before you stood a large statue—an enormous, dazzling statue, awesome in appearance. 32The head of the statue was made of pure gold, its chest and arms of silver, its belly and thighs of bronze, 33its legs of iron, its feet partly of iron and partly of baked clay. 34While you were watching, a rock was cut out, but not by human hands. It struck the statue on its feet of iron and clay and smashed them. 35Then the iron, the clay, the bronze, the silver and the gold were broken to pieces at the same time and became like chaff on a threshing floor in the summer. The wind

Dream Weaver

Read: Daniel 2:24–47

AS YOU APPROACH THE KING'S THRONE, a swarm of whispers fills the room.

"Who does she think she is?" "She'll never be able to do it."

Striding steadily forward, and struggling with your own self-doubts, you wonder, "Will all these gawking eyes witness an execution or a miracle today?"

While these thoughts took place in your imagination, a similar situation occurred in Daniel's reality. He stood face-to-face with an unpredictable despot, King Nebuchadnezzar, who had murdered many of Daniel's family and friends during their exile to Babylon. Now Daniel's own life was in danger (along with all the other scholars and key advisers of the nation) unless someone—anyone—could interpret the king's strange dream. Daniel's life depended upon being able to do what no one had been able to do—not even the king's "wise men."

Talk about stress. Daniel faced a seemingly impossible and dangerous circumstance requiring the utmost wisdom and bravery. Not only had he been exiled to Babylon (modern-day Baghdad), but now he faced an even more pressing drama.

How did Daniel handle this super-dramatic, high-stress situation? He coped with it by cultivating a close relationship with God and depending on God for wisdom and power (verses 20–23). When the drama heated up, when asked if he could interpret Nebuchadnezzar's dream, Daniel did not talk himself up. He humbly responded, "No [one] can explain to the king the mystery he has asked about, but there is a God in heaven who reveals mysteries" (verses 27–28). Daniel invited God into his drama.

In the course of our lives, we're sometimes called to deal with stressful or uncomfortable situations. You may work as the only female in your church's leadership; you may care for your aging in-laws, who have never thought you were good enough for their son. No matter what the situation, the best way to handle it with grace and wisdom is to invite God to direct the circumstance. Let him weave your way through with his wisdom. Lean on his strength. Rely on his insights. You may not feel like you can handle the stress, but with God's help, you can.

Go to page 1060 for your next devotional reading.

Daniel 2:24

"Take me to the king, and I will interpret his dream for him."

reflection

1 What difficult circumstances are you facing right now?

2 How does your heart feel in the midst of your own drama? Small? Broken? Weak?

3 Share your feelings with a trusted friend and together invite the God of wisdom and power into the situation.

RELATED READINGS

Genesis 41:15–16; Esther 3:12–15; 5:1–3; Daniel 2:1–23

swept them away without leaving a trace. But
the rock that struck the statue became a huge
mountain and filled the whole earth.

36“This was the dream, and now we will
interpret it to the king. 37You, O king, are the
king of kings. The God of heaven has given you
dominion and power and might and glory;
38in your hands he has placed mankind and
the beasts of the field and the birds of the air.
Wherever they live, he has made you ruler over
them all. You are that head of gold.

39“After you, another kingdom will rise,
inferior to yours. Next, a third kingdom, one
of bronze, will rule over the whole earth.
40Finally, there will be a fourth kingdom,
strong as iron—for iron breaks and smashes everything—and as iron breaks things to pieces,
so it will crush and break all the others. 41Just
as you saw that the feet and toes were partly
of baked clay and partly of iron, so this will
be a divided kingdom; yet it will have some of
the strength of iron in it, even as you saw iron
mixed with clay. 42As the toes were partly iron
and partly clay, so this kingdom will be partly
strong and partly brittle. 43And just as you saw
the iron mixed with baked clay, so the people
will be a mixture and will not remain united,
any more than iron mixes with clay.

44“In the time of those kings, the God of
heaven will set up a kingdom that will never be
destroyed, nor will it be left to another people.
It will crush all those kingdoms and bring them
to an end, but it will itself endure forever. 45This
is the meaning of the vision of the rock cut out
of a mountain, but not by human hands—a
rock that broke the iron, the bronze, the clay,
the silver and the gold to pieces.

“The great God has shown the king what
will take place in the future. The dream is true
and the interpretation is trustworthy.”

46Then King Nebuchadnezzar fell prostrate
before Daniel and paid him honor and ordered
that an offering and incense be presented to
him. 47The king said to Daniel, “Surely your
God is the God of gods and the Lord of kings
and a revealer of mysteries, for you were able to
reveal this mystery.”

48Then the king placed Daniel in a high
position and lavished many gifts on him. He
made him ruler over the entire province of
Babylon and placed him in charge of all its
wise men. 49Moreover, at Daniel’s request
the king appointed Shadrach, Meshach and
Abednego administrators over the province of
Babylon, while Daniel himself remained at the
royal court.

The Image of Gold and the Fiery Furnace

3 King Nebuchadnezzar made an image of
gold, ninety feet high and nine feet[a] wide,
and set it up on the plain of Dura in the province of Babylon. 2He then summoned the satraps, prefects, governors, advisers, treasurers,
judges, magistrates and all the other provincial
officials to come to the dedication of the image
he had set up. 3So the satraps, prefects, governors, advisers, treasurers, judges, magistrates
and all the other provincial officials assembled
for the dedication of the image that King Nebuchadnezzar had set up, and they stood before it.

4Then the herald loudly proclaimed, “This is
what you are commanded to do, O peoples, nations and men of every language: 5As soon as
you hear the sound of the horn, flute, zither, lyre,
harp, pipes and all kinds of music, you must fall
down and worship the image of gold that King
Nebuchadnezzar has set up. 6Whoever does
not fall down and worship will immediately be
thrown into a blazing furnace.”

7Therefore, as soon as they heard the sound
of the horn, flute, zither, lyre, harp and all kinds
of music, all the peoples, nations and men of
every language fell down and worshiped the
image of gold that King Nebuchadnezzar had
set up.

8At this time some astrologers[b] came forward and denounced the Jews. 9They said to
King Nebuchadnezzar, “O king, live forever!
10You have issued a decree, O king, that everyone who hears the sound of the horn, flute,
zither, lyre, harp, pipes and all kinds of music
must fall down and worship the image of gold,
11and that whoever does not fall down and
worship will be thrown into a blazing furnace.
12But there are some Jews whom you have set
over the affairs of the province of Babylon—
Shadrach, Meshach and Abednego—who pay

[a]1 Aramaic *sixty cubits high and six cubits wide* (about 27 meters high and 2.7 meters wide) [b]8 Or *Chaldeans*

no attention to you, O king. They neither serve
your gods nor worship the image of gold you
have set up."
13 Furious with rage, Nebuchadnezzar summoned Shadrach, Meshach and Abednego.
So these men were brought before the king,
14 and Nebuchadnezzar said to them, "Is it
true, Shadrach, Meshach and Abednego, that
you do not serve my gods or worship the image
of gold I have set up? 15 Now when you hear
the sound of the horn, flute, zither, lyre, harp,
pipes and all kinds of music, if you are ready to
fall down and worship the image I made, very
good. But if you do not worship it, you will be
thrown immediately into a blazing furnace.
Then what god will be able to rescue you from
my hand?"
16 Shadrach, Meshach and Abednego replied to the king, "O Nebuchadnezzar, we do
not need to defend ourselves before you in this
matter. 17 If we are thrown into the blazing furnace, the God we serve is able to save us from it,
and he will rescue us from your hand, O king.
18 But even if he does not, we want you to know,
O king, that we will not serve your gods or worship the image of gold you have set up."
19 Then Nebuchadnezzar was furious with
Shadrach, Meshach and Abednego, and his attitude toward them changed. He ordered the
furnace heated seven times hotter than usual
20 and commanded some of the strongest soldiers in his army to tie up Shadrach, Meshach
and Abednego and throw them into the blazing furnace. 21 So these men, wearing their
robes, trousers, turbans and other clothes, were
bound and thrown into the blazing furnace.
22 The king's command was so urgent and the
furnace so hot that the flames of the fire killed
the soldiers who took up Shadrach, Meshach
and Abednego, 23 and these three men, firmly
tied, fell into the blazing furnace.
24 Then King Nebuchadnezzar leaped to
his feet in amazement and asked his advisers,
"Weren't there three men that we tied up and
threw into the fire?"
They replied, "Certainly, O king."
25 He said, "Look! I see four men walking
around in the fire, unbound and unharmed,
and the fourth looks like a son of the gods."
26 Nebuchadnezzar then approached the
opening of the blazing furnace and shouted,
"Shadrach, Meshach and Abednego, servants
of the Most High God, come out! Come
here!"
So Shadrach, Meshach and Abednego came
out of the fire, 27 and the satraps, prefects, governors and royal advisers crowded around them.
They saw that the fire had not harmed their
bodies, nor was a hair of their heads singed;
their robes were not scorched, and there was
no smell of fire on them.
28 Then Nebuchadnezzar said, "Praise be to
the God of Shadrach, Meshach and Abednego,
who has sent his angel and rescued his servants! They trusted in him and defied the
king's command and were willing to give up
their lives rather than serve or worship any
god except their own God. 29 Therefore I decree that the people of any nation or language
who say anything against the God of Shadrach, Meshach and Abednego be cut into
pieces and their houses be turned into piles of
rubble, for no other god can save in this way."
30 Then the king promoted Shadrach, Meshach and Abednego in the province of Babylon.

Nebuchadnezzar's Dream of a Tree

4 King Nebuchadnezzar,

To the peoples, nations and men of every language, who live in all the world:

May you prosper greatly!

2 It is my pleasure to tell you about the
miraculous signs and wonders that the
Most High God has performed for me.

3 How great are his signs,
how mighty his wonders!
His kingdom is an eternal kingdom;
his dominion endures from
generation to generation.

4 I, Nebuchadnezzar, was at home in my
palace, contented and prosperous. 5 I had
a dream that made me afraid. As I was lying in my bed, the images and visions that
passed through my mind terrified me.
6 So I commanded that all the wise men of
Babylon be brought before me to interpret
the dream for me. 7 When the magicians,

Able to Save

Read: Daniel 3:1–30

Daniel 3:17–18

"If we are thrown into the blazing furnace, the God we serve is able to save us from it, and he will rescue us from your hand, O king. But even if he does not, we want you to know, O king, that we will not serve your gods or worship the image of gold you have set up."

SHADRACH, MESHACH AND ABEDNEGO survived a close encounter with martyrdom. Because they defied the ruling authority, they were scheduled to be thrown into a furnace. But trusting God to honor their faithfulness, they vowed fidelity—even if it cost them their lives. While *we* know the end of the story (they lived), *they* had no certainty that they would survive the raging blaze of Nebuchadnezzar's furnace when they stood up for God. And though they were certain of God's power and willingness to protect them, they didn't demand that he save them.

Now consider this story that occurred centuries later: A judge summoned Perpetua, age 26, and commanded her to deny God or face certain death. Perpetua, with a newborn infant, faced a dilemma. North African Christians under Roman rule in A.D. 200 ran the risk of being put to death for openly acknowledging their faith. As her father looked on, urging her to save herself for her child cradled in his arms, still she would not do as she was commanded and sacrifice to idols.

Perpetua held fast in her conviction and faith in the living God. When the wild bull that was released to attack her and another believer failed to kill them, the Romans sent in the gladiators. A terrified young man approached her and made several ineffectual stabs. In a final act of mercy, she steered his sword into the lethal blow and died.

Many Christians face persecution today. At some point many more may have to make the choice to denounce God or risk everything they hold dear, including their lives. And many face such choices now, though with less threatening consequences: We may be ostracized from our families or passed over for promotions. We may be treated unjustly or misunderstood.

Have you ever thought about what you would do if you were faced with dire persecution? Are you willing to risk everything because you are convinced that loving God is worth whatever sacrifices you face? When faced with the choice to remain faithful or cave in to fear, think of the three young men in Babylon and Perpetua in North Africa who counted their own lives as nothing compared to the grace they had been given.

reflection

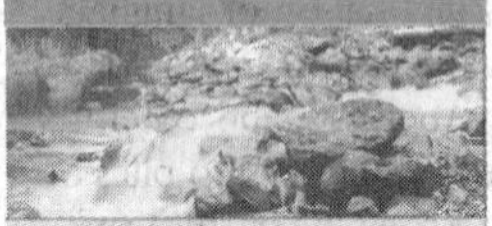

1. What kind of persecution do you face for being a Christian? How do you deal with it?
2. What would it be like to face dire persecution like so many people around the world today?
3. What lessons have you learned from Perpetua and Daniel's three friends?

RELATED READINGS

Psalm 124:1–8; Isaiah 43:1–13; Matthew 5:11,44; Luke 21:12–19

Go to page 1063 for your next devotional reading.

enchanters, astrologers[a] and diviners
came, I told them the dream, but they
could not interpret it for me. 8Finally,
Daniel came into my presence and I told
him the dream. (He is called Belteshazzar,
after the name of my god, and the spirit of
the holy gods is in him.)
9I said, "Belteshazzar, chief of the magicians, I know that the spirit of the holy
gods is in you, and no mystery is too difficult for you. Here is my dream; interpret it
for me. 10These are the visions I saw while
lying in my bed: I looked, and there before
me stood a tree in the middle of the land.
Its height was enormous. 11The tree grew
large and strong and its top touched the
sky; it was visible to the ends of the earth.
12Its leaves were beautiful, its fruit abundant, and on it was food for all. Under it
the beasts of the field found shelter, and
the birds of the air lived in its branches;
from it every creature was fed.
13"In the visions I saw while lying in
my bed, I looked, and there before me
was a messenger,[b] a holy one, coming
down from heaven. 14He called in a loud
voice: 'Cut down the tree and trim off its
branches; strip off its leaves and scatter its
fruit. Let the animals flee from under it
and the birds from its branches. 15But let
the stump and its roots, bound with iron
and bronze, remain in the ground, in the
grass of the field.
" 'Let him be drenched with the dew of
heaven, and let him live with the animals
among the plants of the earth. 16Let his
mind be changed from that of a man and
let him be given the mind of an animal,
till seven times[c] pass by for him.
17" 'The decision is announced by messengers, the holy ones declare the verdict,
so that the living may know that the
Most High is sovereign over the kingdoms of men and gives them to anyone
he wishes and sets over them the lowliest
of men.'
18"This is the dream that I, King Nebuchadnezzar, had. Now, Belteshazzar, tell
me what it means, for none of the wise
men in my kingdom can interpret it for
me. But you can, because the spirit of the
holy gods is in you."

Daniel Interprets the Dream

19Then Daniel (also called Belteshazzar) was greatly perplexed for a time, and
his thoughts terrified him. So the king
said, "Belteshazzar, do not let the dream
or its meaning alarm you."
Belteshazzar answered, "My lord, if only
the dream applied to your enemies and its
meaning to your adversaries! 20The tree
you saw, which grew large and strong,
with its top touching the sky, visible to
the whole earth, 21with beautiful leaves
and abundant fruit, providing food for
all, giving shelter to the beasts of the field,
and having nesting places in its branches
for the birds of the air— 22you, O king,
are that tree! You have become great and
strong; your greatness has grown until it
reaches the sky, and your dominion extends to distant parts of the earth.
23"You, O king, saw a messenger, a
holy one, coming down from heaven and
saying, 'Cut down the tree and destroy
it, but leave the stump, bound with iron
and bronze, in the grass of the field, while
its roots remain in the ground. Let him
be drenched with the dew of heaven; let
him live like the wild animals, until seven
times pass by for him.'
24"This is the interpretation, O king,
and this is the decree the Most High has issued against my lord the king: 25You will
be driven away from people and will live
with the wild animals; you will eat grass
like cattle and be drenched with the dew
of heaven. Seven times will pass by for
you until you acknowledge that the Most
High is sovereign over the kingdoms of
men and gives them to anyone he wishes.
26The command to leave the stump of the
tree with its roots means that your kingdom will be restored to you when you
acknowledge that Heaven rules. 27There-
fore, O king, be pleased to accept my advice: Renounce your sins by doing what is
right, and your wickedness by being kind

[a]7 Or *Chaldeans* [b]13 Or *watchman*; also in verses 17 and 23 [c]16 Or *years*; also in verses 23, 25 and 32

to the oppressed. It may be that then your prosperity will continue."

The Dream Is Fulfilled

28 All this happened to King Nebuchadnezzar. 29 Twelve months later, as the king was walking on the roof of the royal palace of Babylon, 30 he said, "Is not this the great Babylon I have built as the royal residence, by my mighty power and for the glory of my majesty?"

31 The words were still on his lips when a voice came from heaven, "This is what is decreed for you, King Nebuchadnezzar: Your royal authority has been taken from you. 32 You will be driven away from people and will live with the wild animals; you will eat grass like cattle. Seven times will pass by for you until you acknowledge that the Most High is sovereign over the kingdoms of men and gives them to anyone he wishes."

33 Immediately what had been said about Nebuchadnezzar was fulfilled. He was driven away from people and ate grass like cattle. His body was drenched with the dew of heaven until his hair grew like the feathers of an eagle and his nails like the claws of a bird.

34 At the end of that time, I, Nebuchadnezzar, raised my eyes toward heaven, and my sanity was restored. Then I praised the Most High; I honored and glorified him who lives forever.

His dominion is an eternal dominion;
  his kingdom endures from generation to generation.
35 All the peoples of the earth
  are regarded as nothing.
He does as he pleases
  with the powers of heaven
  and the peoples of the earth.
No one can hold back his hand
  or say to him: "What have you done?"

36 At the same time that my sanity was restored, my honor and splendor were returned to me for the glory of my kingdom. My advisers and nobles sought me out, and I was restored to my throne and became even greater than before. 37 Now I, Nebuchadnezzar, praise and exalt and glorify the King of heaven, because everything he does is right and all his ways are just. And those who walk in pride he is able to humble.

> **Daniel 4:37**
>
> ***God Is King of Heaven***
>
> Now I, Nebuchadnezzar, praise and exalt and glorify the King of heaven, because everything he does is right and all his ways are just. And those who walk in pride he is able to humble.

The Writing on the Wall

5 King Belshazzar gave a great banquet for a thousand of his nobles and drank wine with them. 2 While Belshazzar was drinking his wine, he gave orders to bring in the gold and silver goblets that Nebuchadnezzar his father[a] had taken from the temple in Jerusalem, so that the king and his nobles, his wives and his concubines might drink from them. 3 So they brought in the gold goblets that had been taken from the temple of God in Jerusalem, and the king and his nobles, his wives and his concubines drank from them. 4 As they drank the wine, they praised the gods of gold and silver, of bronze, iron, wood and stone.

5 Suddenly the fingers of a human hand appeared and wrote on the plaster of the wall, near the lampstand in the royal palace. The king watched the hand as it wrote. 6 His face turned pale and he was so frightened that his knees knocked together and his legs gave way.

7 The king called out for the enchanters, astrologers[b] and diviners to be brought and said to these wise men of Babylon, "Whoever reads this writing and tells me what it means will be clothed in purple and have a gold chain placed around his neck, and he will be made the third highest ruler in the kingdom."

8 Then all the king's wise men came in, but

[a] 2 Or *ancestor*; or *predecessor*; also in verses 11, 13 and 18 [b] 7 Or *Chaldeans*; also in verse 11

Dear John

ELIZABETH

DEAREST JOHN:

I'm writing to you, my son, so you will always know how much your mother loved you. Before you were even a twinkle in your daddy's eye, we prayed for your arrival and safekeeping. True, we'd practically given up on having a child of our own. But how glad we are to finally say that you belong to us!

I remember when your father came home and "told" me the news that we were going to have a son. Of course, he couldn't speak a word of the wonderful message God's angel had delivered to him that day. But we managed to get it out of him anyway! My first thought was, *The Lord has done this for me*. Already, God determined that you would bring me so much happiness.

The next few months flew by. Son, I have to tell you that I was pretty nervous about being pregnant for the first time. Every woman I'd ever known had these horror stories about morning sickness. Of course, I would never tell them this, but I was strangely pleased to go through this rite of passage. Instead of dreading the nausea and queasiness, it reminded me that my body was undergoing wonderful changes to prepare a home for you to live in for the next few months. Every kick, every gurgle, reminded me that I was no longer alone. You were there with me, my son, throughout my day. And I would soon see you face-to-face!

Of course, your Aunt Mary and I were pregnant at about the same time. We couldn't have been happier! Apparently, you felt the same way about her baby boy. You won't remember this, but you leaped in my womb when the two of you first "met"! Mary and I couldn't believe it, and together we praised God for his two gracious gifts. That day, we agreed that we were the most blessed women on earth because we believed that God would do what he said he would do. My John, never forget that you are a miracle.

Love,
Mother

—Prayer—
Giving Father, thank you for the gift of love.

[Zechariah's] wife Elizabeth was also a descendant of Aaron. Both of them were upright in the sight of God, observing all the Lord's commandments and regulations blamelessly.

Luke 1:5–6

ASSIGNED READING:
Luke 1:5–80

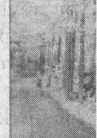

Weekend

Go to page 1067 for your next devotional reading.

they could not read the writing or tell the king
what it meant. 9So King Belshazzar became
even more terrified and his face grew more
pale. His nobles were baffled.
10The queen,[a] hearing the voices of the
king and his nobles, came into the banquet
hall. "O king, live forever!" she said. "Don't
be alarmed! Don't look so pale! 11There is a
man in your kingdom who has the spirit of the
holy gods in him. In the time of your father
he was found to have insight and intelligence
and wisdom like that of the gods. King Nebuchadnezzar your father—your father the king, I
say—appointed him chief of the magicians, enchanters, astrologers and diviners. 12This man
Daniel, whom the king called Belteshazzar, was
found to have a keen mind and knowledge and
understanding, and also the ability to interpret
dreams, explain riddles and solve difficult problems. Call for Daniel, and he will tell you what
the writing means."
13So Daniel was brought before the king,
and the king said to him, "Are you Daniel, one
of the exiles my father the king brought from
Judah? 14I have heard that the spirit of the gods
is in you and that you have insight, intelligence
and outstanding wisdom. 15The wise men and
enchanters were brought before me to read
this writing and tell me what it means, but they
could not explain it. 16Now I have heard that
you are able to give interpretations and to solve
difficult problems. If you can read this writing
and tell me what it means, you will be clothed
in purple and have a gold chain placed around
your neck, and you will be made the third highest ruler in the kingdom."
17Then Daniel answered the king, "You
may keep your gifts for yourself and give your
rewards to someone else. Nevertheless, I will
read the writing for the king and tell him what
it means.
18"O king, the Most High God gave your
father Nebuchadnezzar sovereignty and greatness and glory and splendor. 19Because of the
high position he gave him, all the peoples and
nations and men of every language dreaded
and feared him. Those the king wanted to put
to death, he put to death; those he wanted to
spare, he spared; those he wanted to promote,
he promoted; and those he wanted to humble,
he humbled. 20But when his heart became arrogant and hardened with pride, he was deposed
from his royal throne and stripped of his glory.
21He was driven away from people and given
the mind of an animal; he lived with the wild
donkeys and ate grass like cattle; and his body
was drenched with the dew of heaven, until he
acknowledged that the Most High God is sovereign over the kingdoms of men and sets over
them anyone he wishes.
22"But you his son,[b] O Belshazzar, have not
humbled yourself, though you knew all this.
23Instead, you have set yourself up against the
Lord of heaven. You had the goblets from his
temple brought to you, and you and your nobles, your wives and your concubines drank
wine from them. You praised the gods of silver and gold, of bronze, iron, wood and stone,
which cannot see or hear or understand. But
you did not honor the God who holds in his
hand your life and all your ways. 24Therefore
he sent the hand that wrote the inscription.
25"This is the inscription that was written:

MENE, MENE, TEKEL, PARSIN[c]

26"This is what these words mean:

Mene[d]: God has numbered the days
of your reign and brought it to
an end.
27 *Tekel*[e]: You have been weighed on
the scales and found wanting.
28 *Peres*[f]: Your kingdom is divided and
given to the Medes and Persians."

29Then at Belshazzar's command, Daniel
was clothed in purple, a gold chain was placed
around his neck, and he was proclaimed the
third highest ruler in the kingdom.
30That very night Belshazzar, king of the Babylonians,[g] was slain, 31and Darius the Mede
took over the kingdom, at the age of sixty-two.

Daniel in the Den of Lions

6 It pleased Darius to appoint 120 satraps
to rule throughout the kingdom, 2with
three administrators over them, one of whom

[a]10 Or *queen mother* [b]22 Or *descendant*; or *successor* [c]25 Aramaic *UPARSIN* (that is, *AND PARSIN*) [d]26 *Mene* can mean *numbered* or *mina* (a unit of money). [e]27 *Tekel* can mean *weighed* or *shekel*. [f]28 *Peres* (the singular of *Parsin*) can mean *divided* or *Persia* or *a half mina* or *a half shekel*. [g]30 Or *Chaldeans*

was Daniel. The satraps were made accountable to them so that the king might not suffer
loss. 3Now Daniel so distinguished himself
among the administrators and the satraps by
his exceptional qualities that the king planned
to set him over the whole kingdom. 4At this,
the administrators and the satraps tried to find
grounds for charges against
Daniel in his conduct of government affairs, but they were
unable to do so. They could
find no corruption in him, because he was trustworthy and
neither corrupt nor negligent.
5Finally these men said, "We
will never find any basis for
charges against this man Daniel unless it has something to
do with the law of his God."

6So the administrators and
the satraps went as a group
to the king and said: "O King
Darius, live forever! 7The royal
administrators, prefects, satraps, advisers and governors
have all agreed that the king should issue an
edict and enforce the decree that anyone who
prays to any god or man during the next thirty
days, except to you, O king, shall be thrown
into the lions' den. 8Now, O king, issue the
decree and put it in writing so that it cannot
be altered—in accordance with the laws of the
Medes and Persians, which cannot be repealed."
9So King Darius put the decree in writing.

10Now when Daniel learned that the decree
had been published, he went home to his upstairs room where the windows opened toward
Jerusalem. Three times a day he got down on
his knees and prayed, giving thanks to his God,
just as he had done before. 11Then these men
went as a group and found Daniel praying and
asking God for help. 12So they went to the king
and spoke to him about his royal decree: "Did
you not publish a decree that during the next
thirty days anyone who prays to any god or
man except to you, O king, would be thrown
into the lions' den?"

The king answered, "The decree stands—in
accordance with the laws of the Medes and Persians, which cannot be repealed."

Daniel 6:16

God Rescues His People

So the king gave the order, and they brought Daniel and threw him into the lions' den. The king said to Daniel, "May your God, whom you serve continually, rescue you!"

13Then they said to the king, "Daniel, who is
one of the exiles from Judah, pays no attention
to you, O king, or to the decree you put in writing. He still prays three times a day." 14When
the king heard this, he was greatly distressed;
he was determined to rescue Daniel and made
every effort until sundown to save him.

15Then the men went as a
group to the king and said to
him, "Remember, O king, that
according to the law of the
Medes and Persians no decree
or edict that the king issues can
be changed."

16So the king gave the order,
and they brought Daniel and
threw him into the lions' den.
The king said to Daniel, "May
your God, whom you serve
continually, rescue you!"

17A stone was brought and
placed over the mouth of the
den, and the king sealed it
with his own signet ring and
with the rings of his nobles, so
that Daniel's situation might not be changed.
18Then the king returned to his palace and
spent the night without eating and without any
entertainment being brought to him. And he
could not sleep.

19At the first light of dawn, the king got up
and hurried to the lions' den. 20When he came
near the den, he called to Daniel in an anguished
voice, "Daniel, servant of the living God, has
your God, whom you serve continually, been
able to rescue you from the lions?"

21Daniel answered, "O king, live forever!
22My God sent his angel, and he shut the
mouths of the lions. They have not hurt me,
because I was found innocent in his sight.
Nor have I ever done any wrong before you,
O king."

23The king was overjoyed and gave orders
to lift Daniel out of the den. And when Daniel
was lifted from the den, no wound was found
on him, because he had trusted in his God.

24At the king's command, the men who had
falsely accused Daniel were brought in and
thrown into the lions' den, along with their
wives and children. And before they reached

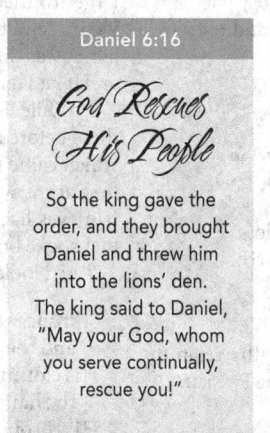

the floor of the den, the lions overpowered
them and crushed all their bones.
25 Then King Darius wrote to all the peoples,
nations and men of every language throughout
the land:

"May you prosper greatly!

26 "I issue a decree that in every part of
my kingdom people must fear and reverence the God of Daniel.

"For he is the living God
and he endures forever;
his kingdom will not be destroyed,
his dominion will never end.
27 He rescues and he saves;
he performs signs and wonders
in the heavens and on the earth.
He has rescued Daniel
from the power of the lions."

28 So Daniel prospered during the reign of
Darius and the reign of Cyrus[a] the Persian.

Daniel's Dream of Four Beasts

7 In the first year of Belshazzar king of Babylon, Daniel had a dream, and visions
passed through his mind as he was lying on
his bed. He wrote down the substance of
his dream.
2 Daniel said: "In my vision at night I looked,
and there before me were the four winds of
heaven churning up the great sea. 3 Four great
beasts, each different from the
others, came up out of the sea.
4 "The first was like a lion,
and it had the wings of an eagle. I watched until its wings
were torn off and it was lifted
from the ground so that it
stood on two feet like a man,
and the heart of a man was
given to it.
5 "And there before me was
a second beast, which looked
like a bear. It was raised up on
one of its sides, and it had three
ribs in its mouth between its
teeth. It was told, 'Get up and
eat your fill of flesh!'
6 "After that, I looked, and there before me
was another beast, one that looked like a leopard. And on its back it had four wings like those
of a bird. This beast had four heads, and it was
given authority to rule.
7 "After that, in my vision at night I looked,
and there before me was a fourth beast—terrifying and frightening and very powerful. It had
large iron teeth; it crushed and devoured its
victims and trampled underfoot whatever was
left. It was different from all the former beasts,
and it had ten horns.
8 "While I was thinking about the horns,
there before me was another horn, a little one,
which came up among them; and three of the
first horns were uprooted before it. This horn
had eyes like the eyes of a man and a mouth
that spoke boastfully.
9 "As I looked,

"thrones were set in place,
and the Ancient of Days took his seat.
His clothing was as white as snow;
the hair of his head was white like wool.
His throne was flaming with fire,
and its wheels were all ablaze.
10 A river of fire was flowing,
coming out from before him.
Thousands upon thousands attended him;
ten thousand times ten thousand stood
before him.
The court was seated,
and the books were opened.

11 "Then I continued to
watch because of the boastful
words the horn was speak-
ing. I kept looking until the
beast was slain and its body
destroyed and thrown into the
blazing fire. 12 (The other beasts
had been stripped of their
authority, but were allowed to
live for a period of time.)
13 "In my vision at night I
looked, and there before me
was one like a son of man, coming with the clouds of heaven.
He approached the Ancient of
Days and was led into his presence. 14 He was
given authority, glory and sovereign power; all

Daniel 7:14

God Is the God of All Nations

"He was given authority, glory and sovereign power; all peoples, nations and men of every language worshiped him."

[a] 28 Or *Darius, that is, the reign of Cyrus*

Princes of Pride

Read: Daniel 6:1–28

DON'T YOU HATE IT when someone "steals your thunder" or takes your job and performs it better than you did? Then perhaps you understand the 120 sneering satraps from Daniel 6, because that's exactly what Daniel did, much to their dismay.

The "satraps" (also translated "captains" or "princes") were politicians and possibly royalty. They were men of power, prestige and persuasion, and they were also prideful—and that's a deadly combination.

Through God's power, Daniel obtained the favor of the king and thereby received a much-coveted position of authority. The satraps' unchecked pride eventually festered into a full-blown contagion. In presenting their strategy to eliminate Daniel, they preyed upon the king's own sense of pride. And because Daniel failed to give in to their demands, he incurred the penalty of the king's decree.

Pride. Pride. Pride. It's everywhere in this story.

Except in the heart of Daniel, the second most powerful leader in the land. His answer is laden with humility; the credit to his survival goes to God alone. What a difference from those prideful princes. Daniel refused to be sucked into the princes' vortex of pride. Because that's what pride does; it draws others in, destroying everyone in its path.

Those who are slaves to pride do anything to maintain the illusion that they are more capable, more worthy and more significant than others. Pride prompts people to do any number of horrible acts to those they think are lesser beings than themselves. Pride is the original sin—it was Satan's sin in heaven and the sin he promotes among human beings (see Isaiah 14:13).

And pride before God is absurd as well as deadly. "The LORD sustains the humble but casts the wicked to the ground," says Psalm 147:6; and that's exactly what happened in this story. While Daniel lived on in the good graces of the king, the prideful satraps were thrown into the same hole they had dug for Daniel.

The cure for pride is cultivating humility. Humility is being honest about who we really are before God. Humility is recognizing who God is: the King of kings and Lord of lords. Being empty before God is the only way he can fill us with himself.

Daniel 6:22

"My God sent his angel, and he shut the mouths of the lions. They have not hurt me, because I was found innocent in his sight. Nor have I ever done any wrong before you, O king."

reflection

1 Why do you think God hates pride?

2 When was the last time you asked God to show you your pride?

3 How can you be more like Daniel and less like the prideful satraps?

RELATED READINGS

Proverbs 3:34; 11:2; 16:18; Matthew 11:29; Ephesians 4:2; James 4:10

"Humility is strong—not bold; quiet—not speechless; sure—not arrogant."

Estelle Smith

Go to page 1077 for your next devotional reading.

peoples, nations and men of every language
worshiped him. His dominion is an everlasting
dominion that will not pass away, and his kingdom is one that will never be destroyed.

The Interpretation of the Dream

15"I, Daniel, was troubled in spirit, and the
visions that passed through my mind disturbed
me. 16I approached one of those standing there
and asked him the true meaning of all this.

"So he told me and gave me the interpretation of these things: 17'The four great beasts
are four kingdoms that will rise from the earth.
18But the saints of the Most High will receive
the kingdom and will possess it forever—yes,
for ever and ever.'

19"Then I wanted to know the true meaning
of the fourth beast, which was different from
all the others and most terrifying, with its iron
teeth and bronze claws—the beast that crushed
and devoured its victims and trampled underfoot whatever was left. 20I also wanted to know
about the ten horns on its head and about the
other horn that came up, before which three
of them fell—the horn that looked more imposing than the others and that had eyes and
a mouth that spoke boastfully. 21As I watched,
this horn was waging war against the saints and
defeating them, 22until the Ancient of Days
came and pronounced judgment in favor of
the saints of the Most High, and the time came
when they possessed the kingdom.

23"He gave me this explanation: 'The fourth
beast is a fourth kingdom that will appear on
earth. It will be different from all the other
kingdoms and will devour the whole earth,
trampling it down and crushing it. 24The ten
horns are ten kings who will come from this
kingdom. After them another king will arise,
different from the earlier ones; he will subdue
three kings. 25He will speak against the Most
High and oppress his saints and try to change
the set times and the laws. The saints will be
handed over to him for a time, times and half
a time.[a]

26" 'But the court will sit, and his power
will be taken away and completely destroyed
forever. 27Then the sovereignty, power and
greatness of the kingdoms under the whole
heaven will be handed over to the saints, the
people of the Most High. His kingdom will be
an everlasting kingdom, and all rulers will worship and obey him.'

28"This is the end of the matter. I, Daniel,
was deeply troubled by my thoughts, and my
face turned pale, but I kept the matter to myself."

Daniel's Vision of a Ram and a Goat

8 In the third year of King Belshazzar's
reign, I, Daniel, had a vision, after the one
that had already appeared to me. 2In my vision
I saw myself in the citadel of Susa in the province of Elam; in the vision I was beside the Ulai
Canal. 3I looked up, and there before me was
a ram with two horns, standing beside the canal, and the horns were long. One of the horns
was longer than the other but grew up later.
4I watched the ram as he charged toward the
west and the north and the south. No animal
could stand against him, and none could rescue from his power. He did as he pleased and
became great.

5As I was thinking about this, suddenly a
goat with a prominent horn between his eyes
came from the west, crossing the whole earth
without touching the ground. 6He came toward
the two-horned ram I had seen standing beside
the canal and charged at him in great rage. 7I
saw him attack the ram furiously, striking the
ram and shattering his two horns. The ram
was powerless to stand against him; the goat
knocked him to the ground and trampled on
him, and none could rescue the ram from his
power. 8The goat became very great, but at the
height of his power his large horn was broken
off, and in its place four prominent horns grew
up toward the four winds of heaven.

9Out of one of them came another horn,
which started small but grew in power to the
south and to the east and toward the Beautiful
Land. 10It grew until it reached the host of the
heavens, and it threw some of the starry host
down to the earth and trampled on them. 11It
set itself up to be as great as the Prince of the
host; it took away the daily sacrifice from him,
and the place of his sanctuary was brought low.
12Because of rebellion, the host ⌞of the saints⌟[b]

[a]25 Or *for a year, two years and half a year* [b]12 Or *rebellion, the armies*

and the daily sacrifice were given over to it. It
prospered in everything it did, and truth was
thrown to the ground.
13Then I heard a holy one speaking, and
another holy one said to him, "How long will
it take for the vision to be fulfilled—the vision
concerning the daily sacrifice, the rebellion
that causes desolation, and the surrender of
the sanctuary and of the host that will be trampled underfoot?"
14He said to me, "It will take 2,300 evenings
and mornings; then the sanctuary will be
reconsecrated."

The Interpretation of the Vision

15While I, Daniel, was watching the vision
and trying to understand it, there before me
stood one who looked like a man. 16And I
heard a man's voice from the Ulai calling, "Gabriel, tell this man the meaning of the vision."
17As he came near the place where I was
standing, I was terrified and fell prostrate. "Son
of man," he said to me, "understand that the
vision concerns the time of the end."
18While he was speaking to me, I was in a
deep sleep, with my face to the ground. Then
he touched me and raised me to my feet.
19He said: "I am going to tell you what will
happen later in the time of wrath, because the
vision concerns the appointed time of the end.[a]
20The two-horned ram that you saw represents
the kings of Media and Persia. 21The shaggy
goat is the king of Greece, and the large horn
between his eyes is the first king. 22The four
horns that replaced the one that was broken off
represent four kingdoms that will emerge from
his nation but will not have the same power.
23"In the latter part of their reign, when rebels have become completely wicked, a stern-
faced king, a master of intrigue, will arise.
24He will become very strong, but not by his
own power. He will cause astounding devastation and will succeed in whatever he does. He
will destroy the mighty men and the holy people. 25He will cause deceit to prosper, and he
will consider himself superior. When they feel
secure, he will destroy many and take his stand
against the Prince of princes. Yet he will be destroyed, but not by human power.
26"The vision of the evenings and mornings
that has been given you is true, but seal up the
vision, for it concerns the distant future."
27I, Daniel, was exhausted and lay ill for
several days. Then I got up and went about the
king's business. I was appalled by the vision; it
was beyond understanding.

Daniel's Prayer

9 In the first year of Darius son of Xerxes[b]
(a Mede by descent), who was made ruler
over the Babylonian[c] kingdom— 2in the first
year of his reign, I, Daniel, understood from the
Scriptures, according to the word of the LORD
given to Jeremiah the prophet, that the desolation of Jerusalem would last seventy years. 3So
I turned to the Lord God and pleaded with him
in prayer and petition, in fasting, and in sackcloth and ashes.
4I prayed to the LORD my God and confessed:

"O Lord, the great and awesome God,
who keeps his covenant of love with all
who love him and obey his commands,
5we have sinned and done wrong. We
have been wicked and have rebelled; we
have turned away from your commands
and laws. 6We have not listened to your
servants the prophets, who spoke in your
name to our kings, our princes and our fathers, and to all the people of the land.
7"Lord, you are righteous, but this day
we are covered with shame—the men of
Judah and people of Jerusalem and all
Israel, both near and far, in all the countries where you have scattered us because
of our unfaithfulness to you. 8O LORD, we
and our kings, our princes and our fathers
are covered with shame because we have
sinned against you. 9The Lord our God is
merciful and forgiving, even though we
have rebelled against him; 10we have not
obeyed the LORD our God or kept the laws
he gave us through his servants the prophets. 11All Israel has transgressed your law
and turned away, refusing to obey you.
"Therefore the curses and sworn judgments written in the Law of Moses, the servant of God, have been poured out on us,

[a]19 Or *because the end will be at the appointed time* [b]1 Hebrew *Ahasuerus* [c]1 Or *Chaldean*

because we have sinned against you. 12You
have fulfilled the words spoken against us
and against our rulers by bringing upon
us great disaster. Under the whole heaven
nothing has ever been done like what has
been done to Jerusalem. 13Just as it is written in the Law of Moses, all this disaster
has come upon us, yet we have not sought
the favor of the LORD our God by turning from our sins and giving attention to
your truth. 14The LORD did not hesitate to
bring the disaster upon us, for the LORD
our God is righteous in everything he
does; yet we have not obeyed him.

15"Now, O Lord our God, who brought
your people out of Egypt with a mighty
hand and who made for yourself a name
that endures to this day, we have sinned,
we have done wrong. 16O Lord, in keeping with all your righteous acts, turn
away your anger and your wrath from
Jerusalem, your city, your holy hill. Our
sins and the iniquities of our fathers have
made Jerusalem and your people an object of scorn to all those around us.

17"Now, our God, hear the prayers and
petitions of your servant. For your sake,
O Lord, look with favor on your desolate
sanctuary. 18Give ear, O God, and hear;
open your eyes and see the desolation of
the city that bears your Name. We do not
make requests of you because we are righteous, but because of your great mercy.
19O Lord, listen! O Lord, forgive! O Lord,
hear and act! For your sake, O my God,
do not delay, because your city and your
people bear your Name."

The Seventy "Sevens"

20While I was speaking and praying, confessing my sin and the sin of my people Israel
and making my request to the LORD my God
for his holy hill— 21while I was still in prayer,
Gabriel, the man I had seen in the earlier vision, came to me in swift flight about the time
of the evening sacrifice. 22He instructed me
and said to me, "Daniel, I have now come to
give you insight and understanding. 23As soon
as you began to pray, an answer was given,
which I have come to tell you, for you are highly
esteemed. Therefore, consider the message and
understand the vision:

24"Seventy 'sevens'[a] are decreed for your
people and your holy city to finish[b] transgression, to put an end to sin, to atone for wickedness, to bring in everlasting righteousness, to
seal up vision and prophecy and to anoint the
most holy.[c]

25"Know and understand this: From the
issuing of the decree[d] to restore and rebuild
Jerusalem until the Anointed One,[e] the ruler,
comes, there will be seven 'sevens,' and sixty-
two 'sevens.' It will be rebuilt with streets and
a trench, but in times of trouble. 26After the
sixty-two 'sevens,' the Anointed One will be cut
off and will have nothing.[f] The people of the
ruler who will come will destroy the city and
the sanctuary. The end will come like a flood:
War will continue until the end, and desolations have been decreed. 27He will confirm a
covenant with many for one 'seven.'[g] In the middle of the 'seven'[g] he will put an end to sacrifice
and offering. And on a wing ⌊of the temple⌋ he
will set up an abomination that causes desolation, until the end that is decreed is poured out
on him.[h]"[i]

Daniel's Vision of a Man

10 In the third year of Cyrus king of Persia, a revelation was given to Daniel
(who was called Belteshazzar). Its message
was true and it concerned a great war.[j] The
understanding of the message came to him in
a vision.

2At that time I, Daniel, mourned for three
weeks. 3I ate no choice food; no meat or wine
touched my lips; and I used no lotions at all
until the three weeks were over.

4On the twenty-fourth day of the first
month, as I was standing on the bank of the
great river, the Tigris, 5I looked up and there
before me was a man dressed in linen, with a
belt of the finest gold around his waist. 6His
body was like chrysolite, his face like lightning,

[a]24 Or *'weeks'*; also in verses 25 and 26 [b]24 Or *restrain* [c]24 Or *Most Holy Place*; or *most holy One* [d]25 Or *word* [e]25 Or *an anointed one*; also in verse 26 [f]26 Or *off and will have no one*; or *off, but not for himself* [g]27 Or *'week'* [h]27 Or *it* [i]27 Or *And one who causes desolation will come upon the pinnacle of the abominable ⌊temple⌋, until the end that is decreed is poured out on the desolated ⌊city⌋* [j]1 Or *true and burdensome*

his eyes like flaming torches, his arms and legs
like the gleam of burnished bronze, and his
voice like the sound of a multitude.
7 I, Daniel, was the only one who saw the vision; the men with me did not see it, but such
terror overwhelmed them that they fled and
hid themselves. 8 So I was left alone, gazing at
this great vision; I had no strength left, my face
turned deathly pale and I was helpless. 9 Then I
heard him speaking, and as I listened to him, I
fell into a deep sleep, my face to the ground.
10 A hand touched me and set me trembling
on my hands and knees. 11 He said, "Daniel, you
who are highly esteemed, consider carefully the
words I am about to speak to you, and stand
up, for I have now been sent to you." And when
he said this to me, I stood up trembling.
12 Then he continued, "Do not be afraid, Daniel. Since the first day that you set your mind
to gain understanding and to humble yourself
before your God, your words were heard, and
I have come in response to them. 13 But the
prince of the Persian kingdom resisted me
twenty-one days. Then Michael, one of the
chief princes, came to help me, because I was
detained there with the king of Persia. 14 Now I
have come to explain to you what will happen
to your people in the future, for the vision concerns a time yet to come."
15 While he was saying this to me, I bowed
with my face toward the ground and was
speechless. 16 Then one who looked like a man[a]
touched my lips, and I opened my mouth and
began to speak. I said to the one standing before me, "I am overcome with anguish because
of the vision, my lord, and I am helpless. 17 How
can I, your servant, talk with you, my lord? My
strength is gone and I can hardly breathe."
18 Again the one who looked like a man
touched me and gave me strength. 19 "Do not
be afraid, O man highly esteemed," he said.
"Peace! Be strong now; be strong."

When he spoke to me, I was strengthened
and said, "Speak, my lord, since you have given
me strength."
20 So he said, "Do you know why I have
come to you? Soon I will return to fight against
the prince of Persia, and when I go, the prince
of Greece will come; 21 but first I will tell you
what is written in the Book of Truth. (No one
supports me against them except Michael,
11 your prince. 1 And in the first year of
Darius the Mede, I took my stand to
support and protect him.)

The Kings of the South and the North

2 "Now then, I tell you the truth: Three more
kings will appear in Persia, and then a fourth,
who will be far richer than all the others. When
he has gained power by his wealth, he will stir
up everyone against the kingdom of Greece.
3 Then a mighty king will appear, who will rule
with great power and do as he pleases. 4 After
he has appeared, his empire will be broken
up and parceled out toward the four winds of
heaven. It will not go to his descendants, nor
will it have the power he exercised, because his
empire will be uprooted and given to others.
5 "The king of the South will become strong,
but one of his commanders will become even
stronger than he and will rule his own kingdom
with great power. 6 After some years, they will
become allies. The daughter of the king of the
South will go to the king of the North to make
an alliance, but she will not retain her power,
and he and his power[b] will not last. In those
days she will be handed over, together with her
royal escort and her father[c] and the one who
supported her.
7 "One from her family line will arise to take
her place. He will attack the forces of the king
of the North and enter his fortress; he will fight
against them and be victorious. 8 He will also
seize their gods, their metal images and their
valuable articles of silver and gold and carry
them off to Egypt. For some years he will leave
the king of the North alone. 9 Then the king of
the North will invade the realm of the king of
the South but will retreat to his own country.
10 His sons will prepare for war and assemble a
great army, which will sweep on like an irresist-
ible flood and carry the battle as far as his fortress.
11 "Then the king of the South will march
out in a rage and fight against the king of the
North, who will raise a large army, but it will
be defeated. 12 When the army is carried off,

[a] 16 Most manuscripts of the Masoretic Text; one manuscript of the Masoretic Text, Dead Sea Scrolls and Septuagint *Then something that looked like a man's hand* [b] 6 Or *offspring* [c] 6 Or *child* (see Vulgate and Syriac)

the king of the South will be filled with pride
and will slaughter many thousands, yet he will
not remain triumphant. 13For the king of the
North will muster another army, larger than
the first; and after several years, he will advance
with a huge army fully equipped.
14"In those times many will rise against the
king of the South. The violent men among your
own people will rebel in fulfillment of the vision, but without success. 15Then the king of
the North will come and build up siege ramps
and will capture a fortified city. The forces of
the South will be powerless to resist; even their
best troops will not have the strength to stand.
16The invader will do as he pleases; no one will
be able to stand against him. He will establish
himself in the Beautiful Land and will have
the power to destroy it. 17He will determine
to come with the might of his entire kingdom
and will make an alliance with the king of the
South. And he will give him a daughter in marriage in order to overthrow the kingdom, but
his plans[a] will not succeed or help him. 18Then
he will turn his attention to the coastlands and
will take many of them, but a commander
will put an end to his insolence and will turn
his insolence back upon him. 19After this, he
will turn back toward the fortresses of his own
country but will stumble and fall, to be seen
no more.
20"His successor will send out a tax collector
to maintain the royal splendor. In a few years,
however, he will be destroyed, yet not in anger
or in battle.
21"He will be succeeded by a contemptible
person who has not been given the honor of
royalty. He will invade the kingdom when its
people feel secure, and he will seize it through
intrigue. 22Then an overwhelming army will
be swept away before him; both it and a prince
of the covenant will be destroyed. 23After
coming to an agreement with him, he will act
deceitfully, and with only a few people he will
rise to power. 24When the richest provinces
feel secure, he will invade them and will
achieve what neither his fathers nor his forefathers did. He will distribute plunder, loot and
wealth among his followers. He will plot the
overthrow of fortresses—but only for a time.
25"With a large army he will stir up his
strength and courage against the king of the
South. The king of the South will wage war
with a large and very powerful army, but he
will not be able to stand because of the plots
devised against him. 26Those who eat from the
king's provisions will try to destroy him; his
army will be swept away, and many will fall in
battle. 27The two kings, with their hearts bent
on evil, will sit at the same table and lie to each
other, but to no avail, because an end will still
come at the appointed time. 28The king of the
North will return to his own country with great
wealth, but his heart will be set against the holy
covenant. He will take action against it and
then return to his own country.
29"At the appointed time he will invade the
South again, but this time the outcome will be
different from what it was before. 30Ships of
the western coastlands[b] will oppose him, and
he will lose heart. Then he will turn back and
vent his fury against the holy covenant. He will
return and show favor to those who forsake the
holy covenant.
31"His armed forces will rise up to desecrate
the temple fortress and will abolish the daily
sacrifice. Then they will set up the abomination
that causes desolation. 32With flattery he will
corrupt those who have violated the covenant,
but the people who know their God will firmly
resist him.
33"Those who are wise will instruct many,
though for a time they will fall by the sword or
be burned or captured or plundered. 34When
they fall, they will receive a little help, and
many who are not sincere will join them.
35Some of the wise will stumble, so that they
may be refined, purified and made spotless until the time of the end, for it will still come at
the appointed time.

The King Who Exalts Himself

36"The king will do as he pleases. He will exalt and magnify himself above every god and
will say unheard-of things against the God of
gods. He will be successful until the time of
wrath is completed, for what has been determined must take place. 37He will show no regard for the gods of his fathers or for the one
desired by women, nor will he regard any god,

[a]17 Or *but she* [b]30 Hebrew *of Kittim*

but will exalt himself above them all. 38Instead
of them, he will honor a god of fortresses; a god
unknown to his fathers he will honor with gold
and silver, with precious stones and costly gifts.
39He will attack the mightiest fortresses with
the help of a foreign god and will greatly honor
those who acknowledge him. He will make
them rulers over many people and will distribute the land at a price.[a]
40"At the time of the end the king of the
South will engage him in battle, and the king of
the North will storm out against him with chariots and cavalry and a great fleet of ships. He
will invade many countries and sweep through
them like a flood. 41He will also invade the
Beautiful Land. Many countries will fall, but
Edom, Moab and the leaders of Ammon will
be delivered from his hand. 42He will extend
his power over many countries; Egypt will not
escape. 43He will gain control of the treasures
of gold and silver and all the riches of Egypt,
with the Libyans and Nubians in submission.
44But reports from the east and the north will
alarm him, and he will set out in a great rage to
destroy and annihilate many.
45He will pitch his royal tents
between the seas at[b] the beautiful holy mountain. Yet he will
come to his end, and no one
will help him.

The End Times

12 "At that time Michael,
the great prince who
protects your people, will arise.
There will be a time of distress
such as has not happened from
the beginning of nations until
then. But at that time your people—everyone whose name is
found written in the book—
will be delivered. 2Multitudes
who sleep in the dust of the
earth will awake: some to everlasting life, others to shame and everlasting contempt. 3Those
who are wise[c] will shine like the brightness of
the heavens, and those who lead many to righteousness, like the stars for ever and ever. 4But
you, Daniel, close up and seal the words of the
scroll until the time of the end. Many will go
here and there to increase knowledge."

5Then I, Daniel, looked, and there before
me stood two others, one on this bank of the
river and one on the opposite bank. 6One of
them said to the man clothed in linen, who
was above the waters of the river, "How long
will it be before these astonishing things are fulfilled?"
7The man clothed in linen, who was above
the waters of the river, lifted his right hand and
his left hand toward heaven, and I heard him
swear by him who lives forever, saying, "It will
be for a time, times and half a time.[d] When the
power of the holy people has been finally broken, all these things will be completed."
8I heard, but I did not understand. So I
asked, "My lord, what will the outcome of all
this be?"
9He replied, "Go your way,
Daniel, because the words are
closed up and sealed until the
time of the end. 10Many will
be purified, made spotless and
refined, but the wicked will
continue to be wicked. None
of the wicked will understand,
but those who are wise will understand.
11"From the time that the
daily sacrifice is abolished and
the abomination that causes
desolation is set up, there will
be 1,290 days. 12Blessed is the
one who waits for and reaches
the end of the 1,335 days.
13"As for you, go your way
till the end. You will rest, and
then at the end of the days you will rise to receive your allotted inheritance."

Daniel 12:2

God Will Resurrect the Dead

"Multitudes who sleep in the dust of the earth will awake: some to everlasting life, others to shame and everlasting contempt."

[a]39 Or *land for a reward* [b]45 Or *the sea and* [c]3 Or *who impart wisdom* [d]7 Or *a year, two years and half a year*

Hosea

Author:
Hosea.

Audience:
The northern kingdom of Israel and all of God's people.

Date:
About 715 B.C.

Setting:
Hosea lived during the time of the end of the northern kingdom, which fell in 722 B.C.

Verse to Remember:
The LORD said to [Hosea], "Go, take to yourself an adulterous wife and children of unfaithfulness, because the land is guilty of the vilest adultery in departing from the LORD." (1:2)

God's prophets did more than give sermons warning of God's judgments. Sometimes their lives were the people's lessons. *God asked Hosea to do a difficult thing:* He was to marry a woman who would abuse his love. As the people of Israel prostituted themselves with false gods, so Hosea's wife, Gomer, would leave him for other men.

Each of Gomer's three children received a name that told of God's dissatisfaction with Israel's spiritual adultery. And as Hosea bought his wife and brought her back home, so the nation was charged *to return to God and be faithful to him.* God's yearning love had been disdained, yet it still endured.

1 The word of the LORD that came to Hosea son of Beeri during the reigns of Uzziah, Jotham, Ahaz and Hezekiah, kings of Judah, and during the reign of Jeroboam son of Jehoash[a] king of Israel:

Hosea's Wife and Children

2 When the LORD began to speak through Hosea, the LORD said to him, "Go, take to yourself an adulterous wife and children of unfaithfulness, because the land is guilty of the vilest

[a]1 Hebrew *Joash,* a variant of *Jehoash*

adultery in departing from the LORD." 3So he
married Gomer daughter of Diblaim, and she
conceived and bore him a son.
4Then the LORD said to Hosea, "Call him
Jezreel, because I will soon punish the house of
Jehu for the massacre at Jezreel, and I will put
an end to the kingdom of Israel. 5In that day
I will break Israel's bow in the
Valley of Jezreel."
6Gomer conceived again
and gave birth to a daughter.
Then the LORD said to Hosea,
"Call her Lo-Ruhamah,[a] for I
will no longer show love to the
house of Israel, that I should
at all forgive them. 7Yet I will
show love to the house of Judah; and I will save them—not
by bow, sword or battle, or by
horses and horsemen, but by
the LORD their God."
8After she had weaned Lo-Ruhamah, Gomer had another
son. 9Then the LORD said,
"Call him Lo-Ammi,[b] for you
are not my people, and I am not your God.
10"Yet the Israelites will be like the sand on
the seashore, which cannot be measured or
counted. In the place where it was said to them,
'You are not my people,' they will be called 'sons
of the living God.' 11The people of Judah and
the people of Israel will be reunited, and they
will appoint one leader and will come up out of
the land, for great will be the day of Jezreel.

Hosea 1:7

God Demonstrates Love

"Yet I will show love to the house of Judah; and I will save them—not by bow, sword or battle, or by horses and horsemen, but by the LORD their God."

2 "Say of your brothers, 'My people,' and of
your sisters, 'My loved one.'

Israel Punished and Restored

2"Rebuke your mother, rebuke her,
for she is not my wife,
and I am not her husband.
Let her remove the adulterous look from her face
and the unfaithfulness from between her breasts.
3Otherwise I will strip her naked
and make her as bare as on the day she was born;
I will make her like a desert,
turn her into a parched land,
and slay her with thirst.
4I will not show my love to her children,
because they are the children of adultery.
5Their mother has been unfaithful
and has conceived them in disgrace.
She said, 'I will go after my lovers,
who give me my food and my water,
my wool and my linen,
my oil and my drink.'
6Therefore I will block her path with thornbushes;
I will wall her in so that she cannot find her way.
7She will chase after her lovers but not catch them;
she will look for them but not find them.
Then she will say,
'I will go back to my husband as at first,
for then I was better off than now.'
8She has not acknowledged that I was the one
who gave her the grain, the new wine and oil,
who lavished on her the silver and gold—
which they used for Baal.
9"Therefore I will take away my grain when it ripens,
and my new wine when it is ready.
I will take back my wool and my linen,
intended to cover her nakedness.
10So now I will expose her lewdness
before the eyes of her lovers;
no one will take her out of my hands.
11I will stop all her celebrations:
her yearly festivals, her New Moons,
her Sabbath days—all her appointed feasts.
12I will ruin her vines and her fig trees,
which she said were her pay from her lovers;
I will make them a thicket,

[a]6 *Lo-Ruhamah* means *not loved.* [b]9 *Lo-Ammi* means *not my people.*

and wild animals will devour them.
13 I will punish her for the days
she burned incense to the Baals;
she decked herself with rings and jewelry,
and went after her lovers,
but me she forgot,"
declares the LORD.

14 "Therefore I am now going to allure her;
I will lead her into the desert
and speak tenderly to her.
15 There I will give her back her vineyards,
and will make the Valley of Achor[a] a door of hope.
There she will sing[b] as in the days of her youth,
as in the day she came up out of Egypt.

16 "In that day," declares the LORD,
"you will call me 'my husband';
you will no longer call me 'my master.[c]'
17 I will remove the names of the Baals from her lips;
no longer will their names be invoked.
18 In that day I will make a covenant for them
with the beasts of the field and the birds of the air
and the creatures that move along the ground.
Bow and sword and battle
I will abolish from the land,
so that all may lie down in safety.
19 I will betroth you to me forever;
I will betroth you in[d] righteousness and justice,
in[e] love and compassion.
20 I will betroth you in faithfulness,
and you will acknowledge the LORD.

21 "In that day I will respond,"
declares the LORD—
"I will respond to the skies,
and they will respond to the earth;
22 and the earth will respond to the grain,
the new wine and oil,
and they will respond to Jezreel.[f]
23 I will plant her for myself in the land;
I will show my love to the one I called
'Not my loved one.[g]'
I will say to those called 'Not my people,[h]'
'You are my people';
and they will say, 'You are my God.'"

Hosea's Reconciliation With His Wife

3 The LORD said to me, "Go, show your love
to your wife again, though she is loved by
another and is an adulteress. Love her as the
LORD loves the Israelites, though they turn to
other gods and love the sacred raisin cakes."
2 So I bought her for fifteen shekels[i] of silver and about a homer and a lethek[j] of barley.
3 Then I told her, "You are to live with[k] me many
days; you must not be a prostitute or be intimate with any man, and I will live with[k] you."
4 For the Israelites will live many days without king or prince, without sacrifice or sacred
stones, without ephod or idol. 5 Afterward the
Israelites will return and seek the LORD their
God and David their king. They will come
trembling to the LORD and to his blessings in
the last days.

The Charge Against Israel

4 Hear the word of the LORD, you Israelites,
because the LORD has a charge to bring
against you who live in the land:
"There is no faithfulness,
no love,
no acknowledgment of God in the land.
2 There is only cursing,[l] lying
and murder,
stealing and adultery;
they break all bounds,
and bloodshed follows bloodshed.
3 Because of this the land mourns,[m]
and all who live in it waste away;

> **Hosea 2:20**
>
> *God Is Faithful*
>
> "I will betroth you in faithfulness, and you will acknowledge the LORD."

[a] 15 *Achor* means *trouble.* [b] 15 Or *respond* [c] 16 Hebrew *baal* [d] 19 Or *with*; also in verse 20 [e] 19 Or *with* [f] 22 *Jezreel* means *God plants.* [g] 23 Hebrew *Lo-Ruhamah* [h] 23 Hebrew *Lo-Ammi* [i] 2 That is, about 6 ounces (about 170 grams) [j] 2 That is, probably about 10 bushels (about 330 liters) [k] 3 Or *wait for* [l] 2 That is, to pronounce a curse upon [m] 3 Or *dries up*

Real Joy

Read: Hosea 3:1–5

SEVERAL YEARS AGO I SPOKE at a women's retreat where their theme was "Experiencing the Joy!" I remember telling them that "real joy is knowing the depth of your sin and the extent of your idolatry." Until you believe with your whole being that, given the right set of circumstances, you are capable of committing any sin, and until you know that apart from Christ there is nothing that's naturally good in you, then you will never know real joy.

Real joy is knowing how bad I am and then comparing it to how much I have been forgiven. Jesus said it himself: Those who have been forgiven much, love much. Their gratitude spills over, and they find themselves crazy in love with God, falling at his feet, worshiping with abandon. They find themselves loving others extravagantly and forgiving others from the heart. For not only do those who have been forgiven much love much, but they forgive much too. As the Bible instructs, we are to "be kind and compassionate to one another, forgiving each other, just as in Christ God forgave you" (Ephesians 4:32).

Although some sins are more heinous than others—murder is more detrimental to society than entertaining lustful thoughts or stealing a packet of Sweet 'N Low—all sin is grievous to God. All sin separates us from him. All sin is serious . . .

Whenever my heart starts to grow cold, when I take comfort in being "not so bad" and seek satisfaction in feeling superior to others, all I need is to look at the cross of Christ. Then, once I see clearly that it was me who put Jesus there, I remember his words to another sinful woman: "Your sins are forgiven . . . Your faith has saved you; go in peace" (Luke 7:48,50).

—Nancy Kennedy

Hosea 3:1

The LORD said to me, "Go, show your love to your wife again, though she is loved by another and is an adulteress. Love her as the LORD loves the Israelites, though they turn to other gods and love the sacred raisin cakes."

reflection

1 Put yourself in Hosea's place. How do you think he felt when he was asked to take back an adulteress wife?

2 Now put yourself in Hosea's wife's place. How grateful do you think she was for Hosea's love? How does it make you feel to know that God is *always* willing to take you back—regardless of how "bad" you are?

3 Spend some time reflecting on the thought that real joy is knowing how much you've been forgiven. Thank your heavenly Husband for forgiving you and loving you enough to send his Son to provide perfect peace and joy.

RELATED READINGS

Psalm 103:8–12;
Isaiah 38:16–19;
Acts 3:19

Go to page 1080 for your next devotional reading.

the beasts of the field and the birds of the air
and the fish of the sea are dying.

4 "But let no man bring a charge,
let no man accuse another,
for your people are like those
who bring charges against a priest.
5 You stumble day and night,
and the prophets stumble with you.
So I will destroy your mother—
6 my people are destroyed from lack of knowledge.

"Because you have rejected knowledge,
I also reject you as my priests;
because you have ignored the law of your God,
I also will ignore your children.
7 The more the priests increased,
the more they sinned against me;
they exchanged[a] their[b] Glory for something disgraceful.
8 They feed on the sins of my people
and relish their wickedness.
9 And it will be: Like people, like priests.
I will punish both of them for their ways
and repay them for their deeds.

10 "They will eat but not have enough;
they will engage in prostitution but not increase,
because they have deserted the LORD
to give themselves 11 to prostitution,
to old wine and new,
which take away the understanding 12 of my people.
They consult a wooden idol
and are answered by a stick of wood.
A spirit of prostitution leads them astray;
they are unfaithful to their God.
13 They sacrifice on the mountaintops
and burn offerings on the hills,
under oak, poplar and terebinth,
where the shade is pleasant.
Therefore your daughters turn to prostitution
and your daughters-in-law to adultery.

14 "I will not punish your daughters
when they turn to prostitution,
nor your daughters-in-law
when they commit adultery,
because the men themselves consort with harlots
and sacrifice with shrine prostitutes—
a people without understanding will come to ruin!

15 "Though you commit adultery, O Israel,
let not Judah become guilty.

"Do not go to Gilgal;
do not go up to Beth Aven.[c]
And do not swear, 'As surely as the LORD lives!'
16 The Israelites are stubborn,
like a stubborn heifer.
How then can the LORD pasture them
like lambs in a meadow?
17 Ephraim is joined to idols;
leave him alone!
18 Even when their drinks are gone,
they continue their prostitution;
their rulers dearly love shameful ways.
19 A whirlwind will sweep them away,
and their sacrifices will bring them shame.

Judgment Against Israel

5 "Hear this, you priests!
Pay attention, you Israelites!
Listen, O royal house!
This judgment is against you:
You have been a snare at Mizpah,
a net spread out on Tabor.
2 The rebels are deep in slaughter.
I will discipline all of them.
3 I know all about Ephraim;
Israel is not hidden from me.
Ephraim, you have now turned to prostitution;
Israel is corrupt.

4 "Their deeds do not permit them
to return to their God.
A spirit of prostitution is in their heart;
they do not acknowledge the LORD.
5 Israel's arrogance testifies against them;

[a]7 Syriac and an ancient Hebrew scribal tradition; Masoretic Text *I will exchange* [b]7 Masoretic Text; an ancient Hebrew scribal tradition *my* [c]15 *Beth Aven* means *house of wickedness* (a name for Bethel, which means *house of God*).

the Israelites, even Ephraim, stumble in
their sin;
Judah also stumbles with them.
6 When they go with their flocks and herds
to seek the LORD,
they will not find him;
he has withdrawn himself from them.
7 They are unfaithful to the LORD;
they give birth to illegitimate children.
Now their New Moon festivals
will devour them and their fields.

8 "Sound the trumpet in Gibeah,
the horn in Ramah.
Raise the battle cry in Beth Aven[a];
lead on, O Benjamin.
9 Ephraim will be laid waste
on the day of reckoning.
Among the tribes of Israel
I proclaim what is certain.
10 Judah's leaders are like those
who move boundary stones.
I will pour out my wrath on them
like a flood of water.
11 Ephraim is oppressed,
trampled in judgment,
intent on pursuing
idols.[b]
12 I am like a moth to
Ephraim,
like rot to the people of
Judah.
13 "When Ephraim saw his
sickness,
and Judah his sores,
then Ephraim turned to
Assyria,
and sent to the great king
for help.
But he is not able to cure
you,
not able to heal your sores.
14 For I will be like a lion to Ephraim,
like a great lion to Judah.
I will tear them to pieces and go away;
I will carry them off, with no one to
rescue them.
15 Then I will go back to my place
until they admit their guilt.
And they will seek my face;
in their misery they will earnestly seek
me."

Israel Unrepentant

6 "Come, let us return to the LORD.
He has torn us to pieces
but he will heal us;
he has injured us
but he will bind up our wounds.
2 After two days he will revive us;
on the third day he will restore us,
that we may live in his presence.
3 Let us acknowledge the LORD;
let us press on to acknowledge him.
As surely as the sun rises,
he will appear;
he will come to us like the winter rains,
like the spring rains that water the
earth."

4 "What can I do with you, Ephraim?
What can I do with you, Judah?
Your love is like the morning mist,
like the early dew that disappears.
5 Therefore I cut you in
pieces with my
prophets,
I killed you with the
words of my mouth;
my judgments flashed
like lightning upon
you.
6 For I desire mercy, not
sacrifice,
and acknowledgment
of God rather than
burnt offerings.
7 Like Adam,[c] they have
broken the
covenant—
they were unfaithful to me there.
8 Gilead is a city of wicked men,
stained with footprints of blood.
9 As marauders lie in ambush for a man,
so do bands of priests;
they murder on the road to Shechem,
committing shameful crimes.

Hosea 6:6

God Desires Obedience

"For I desire mercy,
not sacrifice,
and acknowledgment
of God rather than
burnt offerings."

[a]8 *Beth Aven* means *house of wickedness* (a name for Bethel, which means *house of God*). [b]11 The meaning of the Hebrew for this word is uncertain. [c]7 Or *As at Adam*; or *Like men*

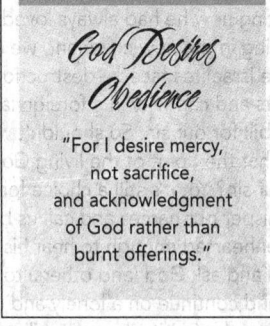

Come Clean

Read: Hosea 6:1–3

Hosea 6:1

"Come, let us return to the LORD. He has torn us to pieces but he will heal us; he has injured us but he will bind up our wounds."

SHERRY'S HUSBAND, RON, was out of town, and she ended up going out to dinner with a male coworker. But since the evening wasn't romantic, she decided not to tell Ron. After all, Sherry reasoned, he'd most likely be angry—and nothing had happened. But as she talked to Ron on the phone that night, a voice inside her whispered, *Come clean.*

Amelia's two boys were extremely rowdy at the restaurant. Since she was looking forward to having a long conversation with a friend who had come along, she was angrier than usual—and she yelled at the kids on the way home. As the boys slunk into the house, shoulders sagging, Amelia's conscience urged her to apologize. She ignored it, but she couldn't sleep that night.

A friend shares something confidential with you, and you tell some of your friends from church about it as a "prayer request." Immediately, you feel ashamed. Later, you want to confess your wrongdoing, but something inside you hesitates.

Human beings, every one, tend to be like the children of Israel. Time and time again God sent prophets to warn them of the consequences of their sins. Godly people like Hosea wept as they told the people that God longed for them to soften their hearts and come back to him like a wife would return to her husband. Sometimes they listened to the warnings, but usually they continued down the destructive vortex, making light of God's mercy and forgetting how he had always loved them.

Living in the new covenant, we don't fear the kind of destruction the Israelites faced—destruction at the hands of foreign oppressors and captivity in a foreign land. Jesus has already paid the whole bill for our sin. So shouldn't we be extra sensitive when we know that the Spirit of the living God is nudging us to come clean with our sin? Yet it's still a choice for each one of us. The Spirit can whisper our names and call us back, but we have to listen and be openhearted enough to hear his still, small voice. We can turn around and ask God (and others) to forgive us or risk grieving the Spirit and continue on a lonely and ultimately destructive path.

When the Spirit whispers, will you listen?

reflection

1. How often do you recognize the Holy Spirit's voice when he nudges you to confess your sins?

2. Is anything holding you back from coming clean before God and others? Is it pride, shame, fear or something else?

3. Do you believe that God is ready to forgive you? Now, will you let him?

RELATED READINGS

Psalms 32:5–6; 130:3–8; Romans 8:26–27; Galatians 6:8; Ephesians 4:30

Go to page 1085 for your next devotional reading.

10 I have seen a horrible thing
in the house of Israel.
There Ephraim is given to prostitution
and Israel is defiled.

11 "Also for you, Judah,
a harvest is appointed.

"Whenever I would restore the fortunes of
my people,

7 1 whenever I would heal Israel,
the sins of Ephraim are exposed
and the crimes of Samaria revealed.
They practice deceit,
thieves break into houses,
bandits rob in the streets;
2 but they do not realize
that I remember all their evil deeds.
Their sins engulf them;
they are always before me.

3 "They delight the king with their
wickedness,
the princes with their lies.
4 They are all adulterers,
burning like an oven
whose fire the baker need not stir
from the kneading of the dough till it
rises.
5 On the day of the festival of our king
the princes become inflamed with
wine,
and he joins hands with the mockers.
6 Their hearts are like an oven;
they approach him with intrigue.
Their passion smolders all night;
in the morning it blazes like a flaming
fire.
7 All of them are hot as an oven;
they devour their rulers.
All their kings fall,
and none of them calls on me.

8 "Ephraim mixes with the nations;
Ephraim is a flat cake not turned over.
9 Foreigners sap his strength,
but he does not realize it.
His hair is sprinkled with gray,
but he does not notice.
10 Israel's arrogance testifies against him,
but despite all this
he does not return to the LORD his God
or search for him.

11 "Ephraim is like a dove,
easily deceived and senseless—
now calling to Egypt,
now turning to Assyria.
12 When they go, I will throw my net over
them;
I will pull them down like birds of the
air.
When I hear them flocking together,
I will catch them.
13 Woe to them,
because they have strayed from me!
Destruction to them,
because they have rebelled against me!
I long to redeem them
but they speak lies against me.
14 They do not cry out to me from their
hearts
but wail upon their beds.
They gather together[a] for grain and new
wine
but turn away from me.
15 I trained them and strengthened them,
but they plot evil against me.
16 They do not turn to the Most High;
they are like a faulty bow.
Their leaders will fall by the sword
because of their insolent words.
For this they will be ridiculed
in the land of Egypt.

Israel to Reap the Whirlwind

8 "Put the trumpet to your lips!
An eagle is over the house of the LORD
because the people have broken my
covenant
and rebelled against my law.
2 Israel cries out to me,
'O our God, we acknowledge you!'
3 But Israel has rejected what is good;
an enemy will pursue him.
4 They set up kings without my consent;
they choose princes without my
approval.
With their silver and gold
they make idols for themselves
to their own destruction.

[a] 14 Most Hebrew manuscripts; some Hebrew manuscripts and Septuagint *They slash themselves*

5 Throw out your calf-idol, O Samaria!
My anger burns against them.
How long will they be incapable of purity?
6 They are from Israel!
This calf—a craftsman has made it;
it is not God.
It will be broken in pieces,
that calf of Samaria.

7 "They sow the wind
and reap the whirlwind.
The stalk has no head;
it will produce no flour.
Were it to yield grain,
foreigners would swallow it up.
8 Israel is swallowed up;
now she is among the nations
like a worthless thing.
9 For they have gone up to Assyria
like a wild donkey wandering alone.
Ephraim has sold herself to lovers.
10 Although they have sold themselves
among the nations,
I will now gather them together.
They will begin to waste away
under the oppression of the mighty
king.

11 "Though Ephraim built many altars for sin
offerings,
these have become altars for sinning.
12 I wrote for them the many things of my
law,
but they regarded them as something
alien.
13 They offer sacrifices given to me
and they eat the meat,
but the LORD is not pleased with them.
Now he will remember their wickedness
and punish their sins:
They will return to Egypt.
14 Israel has forgotten his Maker
and built palaces;
Judah has fortified many towns.
But I will send fire upon their cities
that will consume their fortresses."

Punishment for Israel

9 Do not rejoice, O Israel;
do not be jubilant like the other nations.
For you have been unfaithful to your God;
you love the wages of a prostitute
at every threshing floor.
2 Threshing floors and winepresses will not
feed the people;
the new wine will fail them.
3 They will not remain in the LORD's land;
Ephraim will return to Egypt
and eat unclean[a] food in Assyria.
4 They will not pour out wine offerings to
the LORD,
nor will their sacrifices please him.
Such sacrifices will be to them like the
bread of mourners;
all who eat them will be unclean.
This food will be for themselves;
it will not come into the temple of the
LORD.

5 What will you do on the day of your
appointed feasts,
on the festival days of the LORD?
6 Even if they escape from destruction,
Egypt will gather them,
and Memphis will bury them.
Their treasures of silver will be taken over
by briers,
and thorns will overrun their tents.
7 The days of punishment are coming,
the days of reckoning are at hand.
Let Israel know this.
Because your sins are so many
and your hostility so great,
the prophet is considered a fool,
the inspired man a maniac.
8 The prophet, along with my God,
is the watchman over Ephraim,[b]
yet snares await him on all his paths,
and hostility in the house of his God.
9 They have sunk deep into corruption,
as in the days of Gibeah.
God will remember their wickedness
and punish them for their sins.

10 "When I found Israel,
it was like finding grapes in the
desert;
when I saw your fathers,
it was like seeing the early fruit on the
fig tree.
But when they came to Baal Peor,

[a] 3 That is, ceremonially unclean [b] 8 Or *The prophet is the watchman over Ephraim, / the people of my God*

they consecrated themselves to that
shameful idol
and became as vile as the thing they
loved.
11 Ephraim's glory will fly away like a bird—
no birth, no pregnancy, no conception.
12 Even if they rear children,
I will bereave them of every one.
Woe to them
when I turn away from them!
13 I have seen Ephraim, like Tyre,
planted in a pleasant place.
But Ephraim will bring out
their children to the slayer."

14 Give them, O LORD—
what will you give them?
Give them wombs that miscarry
and breasts that are dry.

15 "Because of all their wickedness in Gilgal,
I hated them there.
Because of their sinful deeds,
I will drive them out of my house.
I will no longer love them;
all their leaders are rebellious.
16 Ephraim is blighted,
their root is withered,
they yield no fruit.
Even if they bear children,
I will slay their cherished offspring."

17 My God will reject them
because they have not obeyed him;
they will be wanderers among the
nations.

10 Israel was a spreading vine;
he brought forth fruit for himself.
As his fruit increased,
he built more altars;
as his land prospered,
he adorned his sacred stones.
2 Their heart is deceitful,
and now they must bear their guilt.
The LORD will demolish their altars
and destroy their sacred stones.

3 Then they will say, "We have no king
because we did not revere the LORD.
But even if we had a king,
what could he do for us?"
4 They make many promises,
take false oaths
and make agreements;
therefore lawsuits spring up
like poisonous weeds in a plowed field.
5 The people who live in Samaria fear
for the calf-idol of Beth Aven.[a]
Its people will mourn over it,
and so will its idolatrous priests,
those who had rejoiced over its splendor,
because it is taken from them into exile.
6 It will be carried to Assyria
as tribute for the great king.
Ephraim will be disgraced;
Israel will be ashamed of its wooden
idols.[b]
7 Samaria and its king will float away
like a twig on the surface of the waters.
8 The high places of wickedness[c] will be
destroyed—
it is the sin of Israel.
Thorns and thistles will grow up
and cover their altars.
Then they will say to the mountains,
"Cover us!"
and to the hills, "Fall on us!"

9 "Since the days of Gibeah, you have
sinned, O Israel,
and there you have remained.[d]
Did not war overtake
the evildoers in Gibeah?
10 When I please, I will punish them;
nations will be gathered against them
to put them in bonds for their double
sin.
11 Ephraim is a trained heifer
that loves to thresh;
so I will put a yoke
on her fair neck.
I will drive Ephraim,
Judah must plow,
and Jacob must break up the ground.
12 Sow for yourselves righteousness,
reap the fruit of unfailing love,
and break up your unplowed ground;
for it is time to seek the LORD,
until he comes

[a] 5 *Beth Aven* means *house of wickedness* (a name for Bethel, which means *house of God*). [b] 6 Or *its counsel* [c] 8 Hebrew *aven*, a reference to Beth Aven (a derogatory name for Bethel) [d] 9 Or *there a stand was taken*

and showers righteousness on you.
13 But you have planted wickedness,
you have reaped evil,
you have eaten the fruit of deception.
Because you have depended on your own strength
and on your many warriors,
14 the roar of battle will rise against your people,
so that all your fortresses will be devastated—
as Shalman devastated Beth Arbel on the day of battle,
when mothers were dashed to the ground with their children.
15 Thus will it happen to you, O Bethel,
because your wickedness is great.
When that day dawns,
the king of Israel will be completely destroyed.

God's Love for Israel

11 "When Israel was a child, I loved him,
and out of Egypt I called my son.
2 But the more I[a] called Israel,
the further they went from me.[b]
They sacrificed to the Baals
and they burned incense to images.
3 It was I who taught Ephraim to walk,
taking them by the arms;
but they did not realize
it was I who healed them.
4 I led them with cords of human kindness,
with ties of love;
I lifted the yoke from their neck
and bent down to feed them.

5 "Will they not return to Egypt
and will not Assyria rule over them
because they refuse to repent?
6 Swords will flash in their cities,
will destroy the bars of their gates
and put an end to their plans.
7 My people are determined to turn from me.
Even if they call to the Most High,
he will by no means exalt them.

8 "How can I give you up, Ephraim?
How can I hand you over, Israel?
How can I treat you like Admah?
How can I make you like Zeboiim?
My heart is changed within me;
all my compassion is aroused.
9 I will not carry out my fierce anger,
nor will I turn and devastate Ephraim.
For I am God, and not man—
the Holy One among you.
I will not come in wrath.[c]
10 They will follow the LORD;
he will roar like a lion.
When he roars,
his children will come trembling from the west.
11 They will come trembling
like birds from Egypt,
like doves from Assyria.
I will settle them in their homes,"
declares the LORD.

Israel's Sin

12 Ephraim has surrounded me with lies,
the house of Israel with deceit.
And Judah is unruly against God,
even against the faithful Holy One.

12 1 Ephraim feeds on the wind;
he pursues the east wind all day
and multiplies lies and violence.
He makes a treaty with Assyria
and sends olive oil to Egypt.
2 The LORD has a charge to bring against Judah;
he will punish Jacob[d] according to his ways
and repay him according to his deeds.
3 In the womb he grasped his brother's heel;
as a man he struggled with God.
4 He struggled with the angel and overcame him;
he wept and begged for his favor.
He found him at Bethel
and talked with him there—
5 the LORD God Almighty,
the LORD is his name of renown!
6 But you must return to your God;
maintain love and justice,
and wait for your God always.

[a] 2 Some Septuagint manuscripts; Hebrew *they* [b] 2 Septuagint; Hebrew *them* [c] 9 Or *come against any city* [d] 2 *Jacob* means *he grasps the heel* (figuratively, *he deceives*).

Stop Running Away

Read: Hosea 11:1–11

HE DIDN'T JUST WALK AWAY from God. He ran. After leaving home, the young North African pursued his study of philosophy—and his appetites—in Carthage, Rome and then Milan. Over time, he grew dissatisfied. Finally, in anguish in his Milan garden, he cried out to God. He then heard a child's voice singing what he understood to be a message from God: "Take up and read." He picked up a nearby copy of the apostle Paul's epistles. What he read changed his life.

Augustine would become the bishop of Hippo. His defense of the Christian faith would serve as a foundation for the church for the following one thousand years. "Go on, O Lord, and act," this sinner-turned-priest wrote. "Stir us up and call us back; inflame us and draw us to thee; stir us up and grow sweet to us; let us now love thee, let us run to thee."

Hosea likewise describes a God who leads his people and loves them like the perfect Father he is, a father who has every reason to be angry with his children when they run in the opposite direction, discounting the gifts he has given them, honoring everything and anything but him, and refusing to listen or to come home to him. Even so, God's "compassion is aroused," writes the prophet Hosea. Though the people deserve it, he "will not come in wrath." Instead, he comes to them in love.

Hosea reminds his people that it is time to stop running away and start running back into God's open arms. God will not give up. No, he cannot. His love constrains him. God's restraint allowed Augustine and the children of Israel the opportunity to stop being headstrong and run in the right direction—toward him.

No matter how many miles from home you feel, no matter how long it's been since you whispered a prayer or listened for God's voice, the journey back to where you belong is one step away. "Come trembling" to him like a dove, and he will settle you in his home (see verse 11).

Thursday

Hosea 11:7–9

"My people are determined to turn from me. Even if they call to the Most High, he will by no means exalt them. How can I give you up, Ephraim? How can I hand you over, Israel? How can I treat you like Admah? How can I make you like Zeboiim? My heart is changed within me; all my compassion is aroused. I will not carry out my fierce anger, nor will I turn and devastate Ephraim. For I am God, and not man—the Holy One among you. I will not come in wrath."

reflection

1 When are you tempted to run from God?

2 What would happen if God's love did not restrain him from expressing his full anger toward his people?

3 How can you express your gratitude for God's restraint? Spend some time journaling or praying your response.

RELATED READINGS

2 Kings 13:22–23;
Joel 2:13–14;
Matthew 18:12–14;
Luke 15:11–24

Go to page 1092 for your next devotional reading.

7 The merchant uses dishonest scales;
he loves to defraud.
8 Ephraim boasts,
"I am very rich; I have become wealthy.
With all my wealth they
will not find in me
any iniquity or sin."
9 "I am the LORD your God,
⌊who brought you⌋ out
of[a] Egypt;
I will make you live in tents
again,
as in the days of your
appointed feasts.
10 I spoke to the prophets,
gave them many visions
and told parables
through them."
11 Is Gilead wicked?
Its people are worthless!
Do they sacrifice bulls in
Gilgal?
Their altars will be like piles of stones
on a plowed field.
12 Jacob fled to the country of Aram[b];
Israel served to get a wife,
and to pay for her he tended sheep.
13 The LORD used a prophet to bring Israel up
from Egypt,
by a prophet he cared for him.
14 But Ephraim has bitterly provoked him to
anger;
his Lord will leave upon him the guilt of
his bloodshed
and will repay him for his contempt.

The LORD's Anger Against Israel

13 When Ephraim spoke, men
trembled;
he was exalted in Israel.
But he became guilty of Baal worship
and died.
2 Now they sin more and more;
they make idols for themselves from
their silver,
cleverly fashioned images,
all of them the work of craftsmen.
It is said of these people,
"They offer human sacrifice
and kiss[c] the calf-idols."
3 Therefore they will be like the morning
mist,
like the early dew that
disappears,
like chaff swirling from a
threshing floor,
like smoke escaping
through a window.
4 "But I am the LORD your
God,
⌊who brought you⌋ out
of[a] Egypt.
You shall acknowledge no
God but me,
no Savior except me.
5 I cared for you in the
desert,
in the land of burning
heat.
6 When I fed them, they were satisfied;
when they were satisfied, they became
proud;
then they forgot me.
7 So I will come upon them like a lion,
like a leopard I will lurk by the path.
8 Like a bear robbed of her cubs,
I will attack them and rip them open.
Like a lion I will devour them;
a wild animal will tear them apart.
9 "You are destroyed, O Israel,
because you are against me, against your
helper.
10 Where is your king, that he may save
you?
Where are your rulers in all your
towns,
of whom you said,
'Give me a king and princes'?
11 So in my anger I gave you a king,
and in my wrath I took him away.
12 The guilt of Ephraim is stored up,
his sins are kept on record.
13 Pains as of a woman in childbirth come to
him,
but he is a child without wisdom;
when the time arrives,

Hosea 13:4

God Is the Only God

"But I am the LORD
your God,
who brought you
out of Egypt.
You shall acknowledge
no God but me,
no Savior except me."

[a] 9,4 Or *God / ever since you were in* [b] 12 That is, Northwest Mesopotamia [c] 2 Or *"Men who sacrifice / kiss*

he does not come to the opening of the
womb.

14 "I will ransom them from the power of the
grave[a];
I will redeem them from death.
Where, O death, are your plagues?
Where, O grave,[a] is your destruction?

"I will have no compassion,
15 even though he thrives among his
brothers.
An east wind from the LORD will come,
blowing in from the desert;
his spring will fail
and his well dry up.
His storehouse will be plundered
of all its treasures.
16 The people of Samaria must bear their
guilt,
because they have rebelled against their
God.
They will fall by the sword;
their little ones will be dashed to the
ground,
their pregnant women
ripped open."

Repentance to Bring Blessing

14 Return, O Israel, to
the LORD your God.
Your sins have been your
downfall!
2 Take words with you
and return to the LORD.
Say to him:
"Forgive all our sins
and receive us graciously,
that we may offer the
fruit of our lips.[b]
3 Assyria cannot save us;
we will not mount war-horses.
We will never again say 'Our gods'
to what our own hands have made,
for in you the fatherless find
compassion."

4 "I will heal their waywardness
and love them freely,
for my anger has turned away from
them.
5 I will be like the dew to Israel;
he will blossom like a lily.
Like a cedar of Lebanon
he will send down his roots;
6 his young shoots will grow.
His splendor will be like an olive tree,
his fragrance like a cedar of Lebanon.
7 Men will dwell again in his shade.
He will flourish like the grain.
He will blossom like a vine,
and his fame will be like the wine from
Lebanon.
8 O Ephraim, what more have I[c] to do with
idols?
I will answer him and
care for him.
I am like a green pine tree;
your fruitfulness comes
from me."
9 Who is wise? He will
realize these things.
Who is discerning? He
will understand
them.
The ways of the LORD are
right;
the righteous walk in
them,
but the rebellious stumble in them.

Hosea 14:9

God Does Right

The ways of the LORD
are right;
the righteous walk
in them,
but the rebellious
stumble in them.

[a]14 Hebrew *Sheol* [b]2 Or *offer our lips as sacrifices of bulls* [c]8 Or *What more has Ephraim*

Joel

Author:
Joel.

Audience:
The southern kingdom (Judah) and all of God's people.

Date:
About 835 B.C.

Setting:
The people of Judah trusted in their great wealth, not in God.

Verse to Remember:
Rend your heart and not your garments. Return to the LORD your God, for he is gracious and compassionate, slow to anger and abounding in love, and he relents from sending calamity. (2:13)

The land of Judah lay in ruins. Locusts of many varieties had eaten every green thing. Every blade of grass, every ear of grain, every leaf off the trees. The cattle grew gaunt and bawled out their hunger. The sheep wandered in confusion. The people were also beginning to go hungry, and *their hearts were far from God.* And now maybe, just maybe, God could finally get their attention. After the devastation of the locusts, God stepped in through the prophet Joel's words: *"The day of the Lord is coming.* A day of great darkness and gloom and judgment." But God didn't stop there. "Repent, and *I will show pity.* Come to me with a right heart, rather than with sacrifices that you don't really want to give, and I will be gracious. And someday your children will know me too."

This brief book is packed with *the awesome reality of God's power* over all events—past, present and future. And it's also packed with the hope of God's great compassion and love for his people.

1 The word of the LORD that came to Joel son of Pethuel.

An Invasion of Locusts

2 Hear this, you elders;
listen, all who live in the land.
Has anything like this ever happened in your days
or in the days of your forefathers?
3 Tell it to your children,
and let your children tell it to their children,
and their children to the next generation.
4 What the locust swarm has left
the great locusts have eaten;
what the great locusts have left
the young locusts have eaten;

what the young locusts have left
other locusts[a] have eaten.

5 Wake up, you drunkards, and weep!
Wail, all you drinkers of wine;
wail because of the new wine,
for it has been snatched from your lips.
6 A nation has invaded my land,
powerful and without number;
it has the teeth of a lion,
the fangs of a lioness.
7 It has laid waste my vines
and ruined my fig trees.
It has stripped off their bark
and thrown it away,
leaving their branches white.

8 Mourn like a virgin[b] in sackcloth
grieving for the husband[c] of her youth.
9 Grain offerings and drink offerings
are cut off from the house of the LORD.
The priests are in mourning,
those who minister before the LORD.
10 The fields are ruined,
the ground is dried up[d];
the grain is destroyed,
the new wine is dried up,
the oil fails.
11 Despair, you farmers,
wail, you vine growers;
grieve for the wheat and the barley,
because the harvest of the field is
destroyed.
12 The vine is dried up
and the fig tree is withered;
the pomegranate, the palm and the apple
tree—
all the trees of the field—are dried up.
Surely the joy of mankind
is withered away.

A Call to Repentance

13 Put on sackcloth, O priests, and mourn;
wail, you who minister before the altar.
Come, spend the night in sackcloth,
you who minister before my God;
for the grain offerings and drink offerings
are withheld from the house of your
God.
14 Declare a holy fast;
call a sacred assembly.
Summon the elders
and all who live in the land
to the house of the LORD your God,
and cry out to the LORD.

15 Alas for that day!
For the day of the LORD is near;
it will come like destruction from the
Almighty.[e]

16 Has not the food been cut off
before our very eyes—
joy and gladness
from the house of our God?
17 The seeds are shriveled
beneath the clods.[f]
The storehouses are in ruins,
the granaries have been broken down,
for the grain has dried up.
18 How the cattle moan!
The herds mill about
because they have no pasture;
even the flocks of sheep are suffering.

19 To you, O LORD, I call,
for fire has devoured the open pastures
and flames have burned up all the trees
of the field.
20 Even the wild animals pant for you;
the streams of water have dried up
and fire has devoured the open pastures.

An Army of Locusts

2 Blow the trumpet in Zion;
sound the alarm on my holy hill.
Let all who live in the land tremble,
for the day of the LORD is coming.
It is close at hand—
2 a day of darkness and gloom,
a day of clouds and blackness.
Like dawn spreading across the mountains
a large and mighty army comes,
such as never was of old
nor ever will be in ages to come.

3 Before them fire devours,
behind them a flame blazes.
Before them the land is like the garden of
Eden,
behind them, a desert waste—

[a]4 The precise meaning of the four Hebrew words used here for locusts is uncertain. [b]8 Or *young woman* [c]8 Or *betrothed*
[d]10 Or *ground mourns* [e]15 Hebrew *Shaddai* [f]17 The meaning of the Hebrew for this word is uncertain.

nothing escapes them.
4 They have the appearance of horses;
they gallop along like cavalry.
5 With a noise like that of chariots
they leap over the mountaintops,
like a crackling fire consuming stubble,
like a mighty army drawn up for battle.

6 At the sight of them, nations are in anguish;
every face turns pale.
7 They charge like warriors;
they scale walls like soldiers.
They all march in line,
not swerving from their course.
8 They do not jostle each other;
each marches straight ahead.
They plunge through defenses
without breaking ranks.
9 They rush upon the city;
they run along the wall.
They climb into the houses;
like thieves they enter through the windows.

10 Before them the earth shakes,
the sky trembles,
the sun and moon are darkened,
and the stars no longer shine.
11 The LORD thunders
at the head of his army;
his forces are beyond number,
and mighty are those who obey his command.
The day of the LORD is great;
it is dreadful.
Who can endure it?

Rend Your Heart

12 "Even now," declares the LORD,
"return to me with all your heart,
with fasting and weeping and mourning."

> Joel 2:13
>
> **God Is Slow to Anger**
>
> Return to the LORD your God,
> for he is gracious and compassionate,
> slow to anger and abounding in love,
> and he relents from sending calamity.

13 Rend your heart
and not your garments.
Return to the LORD your God,
for he is gracious and compassionate,
slow to anger and abounding in love,
and he relents from sending calamity.
14 Who knows? He may turn and have pity
and leave behind a blessing—
grain offerings and drink offerings
for the LORD your God.

15 Blow the trumpet in Zion,
declare a holy fast,
call a sacred assembly.
16 Gather the people,
consecrate the assembly;
bring together the elders,
gather the children,
those nursing at the breast.
Let the bridegroom leave his room
and the bride her chamber.
17 Let the priests, who minister before the LORD,
weep between the temple porch and the altar.
Let them say, "Spare your people, O LORD.
Do not make your inheritance an object of scorn,
a byword among the nations.
Why should they say among the peoples,
'Where is their God?' "

The LORD's Answer

18 Then the LORD will be jealous for his land
and take pity on his people.

19 The LORD will reply[a] to them:

"I am sending you grain, new wine and oil,
enough to satisfy you fully;
never again will I make you
an object of scorn to the nations.

20 "I will drive the northern army far from you,

[a] 18,19 Or *LORD was jealous . . . / and took pity . . . / 19 The LORD replied*

pushing it into a parched and barren land,
with its front columns going into the eastern sea[a]
and those in the rear into the western sea.[b]
And its stench will go up;
its smell will rise."

Surely he has done great things.[c]
21 Be not afraid, O land;
be glad and rejoice.
Surely the LORD has done great things.
22 Be not afraid, O wild animals,
for the open pastures are becoming green.
The trees are bearing their fruit;
the fig tree and the vine yield their riches.
23 Be glad, O people of Zion,
rejoice in the LORD your God,
for he has given you
the autumn rains in righteousness.[d]
He sends you abundant showers,
both autumn and spring rains, as before.
24 The threshing floors will be filled with grain;
the vats will overflow with new wine and oil.
25 "I will repay you for the years the locusts have eaten—
the great locust and the young locust,
the other locusts and the locust swarm[e]—
my great army that I sent among you.
26 You will have plenty to eat, until you are full,
and you will praise the name of the LORD your God,
who has worked wonders for you;
never again will my people be shamed.
27 Then you will know that I am in Israel,
that I am the LORD your God,
and that there is no other;
never again will my people be shamed.

The Day of the LORD

28 "And afterward,
I will pour out my Spirit on all people.
Your sons and daughters will prophesy,
your old men will dream dreams,
your young men will see visions.
29 Even on my servants, both men and women,
I will pour out my Spirit in those days.
30 I will show wonders in the heavens
and on the earth,
blood and fire and billows of smoke.
31 The sun will be turned to darkness
and the moon to blood
before the coming of the great and dreadful day of the LORD.
32 And everyone who calls
on the name of the LORD will be saved;
for on Mount Zion and in Jerusalem
there will be deliverance,
as the LORD has said,
among the survivors
whom the LORD calls.

The Nations Judged

3 "In those days and at that time,
when I restore the fortunes of Judah and Jerusalem,
2 I will gather all nations
and bring them down to the Valley of Jehoshaphat.[f]
There I will enter into judgment against them
concerning my inheritance, my people Israel,
for they scattered my people among the nations
and divided up my land.
3 They cast lots for my people
and traded boys for prostitutes;
they sold girls for wine
that they might drink.

4 "Now what have you against me, O Tyre
and Sidon and all you regions of Philistia? Are
you repaying me for something I have done?
If you are paying me back, I will swiftly and
speedily return on your own heads what you
have done. 5 For you took my silver and my
gold and carried off my finest treasures to your
temples. 6 You sold the people of Judah and

[a] 20 That is, the Dead Sea [b] 20 That is, the Mediterranean [c] 20 Or *rise. / Surely it has done great things."* [d] 23 Or / *the teacher for righteousness:* [e] 25 The precise meaning of the four Hebrew words used here for locusts is uncertain. [f] 2 *Jehoshaphat* means *the LORD judges*; also in verse 12.

But for a Moment

Read: Joel 2:1–32

Joel 2:25,27

"I will repay you for the years the locusts have eaten—the great locust and the young locust, the other locusts and the locust swarm—my great army that I sent among you . . . Then you will know that I am in Israel, that I am the LORD your God, and that there is no other; never again will my people be shamed."

AFTER THE WICKED KING LOUIS XIV OF FRANCE revoked the Edict of Nantes and condemned tens of thousands of the noblest men and women of France to torture and to death, many brave women were imprisoned in a huge tower called the Tour de Constance. The dungeon was a terrible place; its walls were 15 feet thick, and it was lighted only by narrow embrasures. The sister of a martyred minister lived for 36 years in that prison, and never gave way.

When at last the Huguenot women were released in 1768, someone found a word scored in the middle of the hard stone floor. The inscription is hardly readable, and to see it on a fine summer day, one has to kneel down and have a candle lighted; otherwise it is too dark. That one word is *Resist.* It is thought that some woman carved it, perhaps with a needle (the tracing is so faint), toiling at that word to help and strengthen herself and others, so that after she was gone they might be encouraged in their resolve to endure till the end. Surely the powers of endurance that God can give to the human soul are beyond our understanding. These women had not even the comfort of their Bibles. They had nothing, *nothing*—but God. Can the God who so gloriously nourished them with heavenly strength not feed us also, in our lesser needs, as we wait day by day upon Him?

When we think of suffering, such as myriads have endured in all ages, in all lands, and of the suffering, too, that many are enduring today, our own little troubles and difficulties seem too small to think about at all, and we can only find relief in praying for those who suffer. And yet, though this is so, sometimes our trifles can try us a good deal, and those words, "And even this shall pass," may perhaps bring comfort to some among us. At longest it is "but for a moment," and then . . . ?

—*Amy Carmichael*

reflection

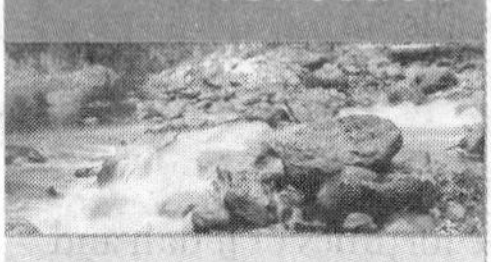

1 What area of your life seems lost or hopeless? Ask God for the strength to resist giving way to discouragement.

2 How does God's promise to "repay you for the years the locusts have eaten" give you hope?

3 How does the thought that what you are enduring is "but for a moment" in light of eternity bring you comfort?

RELATED READINGS

Psalm 103:1–22; 2 Corinthians 4:16–17; Revelation 2:20–29

Go to page 1097 for your next devotional reading.

Jerusalem to the Greeks, that you might send
them far from their homeland.
7 "See, I am going to rouse
them out of the places to
which you sold them, and I
will return on your own heads
what you have done. 8 I will sell
your sons and daughters to the
people of Judah, and they will
sell them to the Sabeans, a nation far away." The LORD has
spoken.

> Joel 3:16
>
> *God Is a Powerful Refuge*
>
> But the LORD will be a refuge for his people, a stronghold for the people of Israel.

9 Proclaim this among the
nations:
Prepare for war!
Rouse the warriors!
Let all the fighting men draw near and
attack.
10 Beat your plowshares into swords
and your pruning hooks into spears.
Let the weakling say,
"I am strong!"
11 Come quickly, all you nations from every
side,
and assemble there.

Bring down your warriors, O LORD!

12 "Let the nations be roused;
let them advance into the Valley of
Jehoshaphat,
for there I will sit
to judge all the nations on every side.
13 Swing the sickle,
for the harvest is ripe.
Come, trample the grapes,
for the winepress is full
and the vats overflow—
so great is their wickedness!"

14 Multitudes, multitudes
in the valley of decision!
For the day of the LORD is near
in the valley of decision.
15 The sun and moon will be darkened,
and the stars no longer
shine.
16 The LORD will roar from
Zion
and thunder from
Jerusalem;
the earth and the sky
will tremble.
But the LORD will be
a refuge for his
people,
a stronghold for the
people of Israel.

Blessings for God's People

17 "Then you will know that I, the LORD your
God,
dwell in Zion, my holy hill.
Jerusalem will be holy;
never again will foreigners invade her.

18 "In that day the mountains will drip new
wine,
and the hills will flow with milk;
all the ravines of Judah will run with
water.
A fountain will flow out of the LORD's
house
and will water the valley of acacias.[a]
19 But Egypt will be desolate,
Edom a desert waste,
because of violence done to the people of
Judah,
in whose land they shed innocent blood.
20 Judah will be inhabited forever
and Jerusalem through all generations.
21 Their bloodguilt, which I have not
pardoned,
I will pardon."

The LORD dwells in Zion!

[a] 18 Or *Valley of Shittim*

Amos

Author:
Amos.

Audience:
The northern kingdom (Israel) and all of God's people.

Date:
About 760–750 B.C.

Setting:
Wealthy people were oppressing the poor in Israel.

Verse to Remember:
Seek good, not evil, that you may live. Then the LORD God Almighty will be with you, just as you say he is. (5:14)

Being God's chosen people is a privileged position to hold. But it comes with certain risks, namely complacency. Israel was enjoying a season of prosperity when Amos came preaching his message of doom. The people had fancy clothes, fine houses (sometimes two of them), plenty to eat and drink—no one wanted to listen to tales of destruction. They felt quite secure in what they presumed was God's blessing.

Their prosperity, however, was a facade. They had bought it at the price of injustice. They oppressed the poor and cheated in the courts. Worst of all, they kept up their religious appearances, making the prescribed offerings and celebrating the designated feasts, thinking that doing so would keep God placated. *They thought if they performed the right rituals,* they could live however they wanted. But they were dead wrong.

Amos preaches a point-blank message: God cannot be manipulated. And God's message then is the same message for us today. *God isn't looking for the right rituals;* he is looking for right living. And right living begins with justice and fairness for those who are most vulnerable.

1 The words of Amos, one of the shepherds of Tekoa—what he saw concerning Israel two years before the earthquake, when Uzziah was king of Judah and Jeroboam son of Jehoash[a] was king of Israel.

2 He said:

"The LORD roars from Zion
and thunders from Jerusalem;
the pastures of the shepherds dry up,[b]
and the top of Carmel withers."

Judgment on Israel's Neighbors

3 This is what the LORD says:

"For three sins of Damascus,
even for four, I will not turn back ⌊my wrath⌋.
Because she threshed Gilead
with sledges having iron teeth,
4 I will send fire upon the house of Hazael
that will consume the fortresses of Ben-Hadad.
5 I will break down the gate of Damascus;
I will destroy the king who is in[c] the Valley of Aven[d]
and the one who holds the scepter in Beth Eden.
The people of Aram will go into exile to Kir,"
says the LORD.

6 This is what the LORD says:

"For three sins of Gaza,
even for four, I will not turn back ⌊my wrath⌋.
Because she took captive whole communities
and sold them to Edom,
7 I will send fire upon the walls of Gaza
that will consume her fortresses.
8 I will destroy the king[e] of Ashdod
and the one who holds the scepter in Ashkelon.
I will turn my hand against Ekron,
till the last of the Philistines is dead,"
says the Sovereign LORD.

9 This is what the LORD says:

"For three sins of Tyre,
even for four, I will not turn back ⌊my wrath⌋.
Because she sold whole communities of captives to Edom,
disregarding a treaty of brotherhood,
10 I will send fire upon the walls of Tyre
that will consume her fortresses."

11 This is what the LORD says:

"For three sins of Edom,
even for four, I will not turn back ⌊my wrath⌋.
Because he pursued his brother with a sword,
stifling all compassion,[f]
because his anger raged continually
and his fury flamed unchecked,
12 I will send fire upon Teman
that will consume the fortresses of Bozrah."

13 This is what the LORD says:

"For three sins of Ammon,
even for four, I will not turn back ⌊my wrath⌋.
Because he ripped open the pregnant women of Gilead
in order to extend his borders,
14 I will set fire to the walls of Rabbah
that will consume her fortresses
amid war cries on the day of battle,
amid violent winds on a stormy day.
15 Her king[g] will go into exile,
he and his officials together,"
says the LORD.

2 This is what the LORD says:

"For three sins of Moab,
even for four, I will not turn back ⌊my wrath⌋.
Because he burned, as if to lime,
the bones of Edom's king,
2 I will send fire upon Moab
that will consume the fortresses of Kerioth.[h]
Moab will go down in great tumult

[a] 1 Hebrew *Joash,* a variant of *Jehoash* [b] 2 Or *shepherds mourn* [c] 5 Or *the inhabitants of* [d] 5 *Aven* means *wickedness.* [e] 8 Or *inhabitants* [f] 11 Or *sword / and destroyed his allies* [g] 15 Or / *Molech;* Hebrew *malcam* [h] 2 Or *of her cities*

amid war cries and the blast of the
trumpet.
3 I will destroy her ruler
and kill all her officials with him,"
says the LORD.

4 This is what the LORD says:

"For three sins of Judah,
even for four, I will not turn back ⌊my
wrath⌋.
Because they have rejected the law of the
LORD
and have not kept his decrees,
because they have been led astray by false
gods,[a]
the gods[b] their ancestors followed,
5 I will send fire upon Judah
that will consume the fortresses of
Jerusalem."

Judgment on Israel

6 This is what the LORD says:

"For three sins of Israel,
even for four, I will not turn back ⌊my
wrath⌋.
They sell the righteous for silver,
and the needy for a pair of sandals.
7 They trample on the heads of the poor
as upon the dust of the ground
and deny justice to the oppressed.
Father and son use the same girl
and so profane my holy name.
8 They lie down beside every altar
on garments taken in pledge.
In the house of their god
they drink wine taken as fines.

9 "I destroyed the Amorite before them,
though he was tall as the cedars
and strong as the oaks.
I destroyed his fruit above
and his roots below.

10 "I brought you up out of Egypt,
and I led you forty years in the desert
to give you the land of the Amorites.
11 I also raised up prophets from among your
sons
and Nazirites from among your young
men.
Is this not true, people of Israel?"
declares the LORD.
12 "But you made the Nazirites drink wine
and commanded the prophets not to
prophesy.

13 "Now then, I will crush you
as a cart crushes when loaded with
grain.
14 The swift will not escape,
the strong will not muster their
strength,
and the warrior will not save his life.
15 The archer will not stand his ground,
the fleet-footed soldier will not get
away,
and the horseman will not save his life.
16 Even the bravest warriors
will flee naked on that day,"
declares the LORD.

Witnesses Summoned Against Israel

3 Hear this word the LORD has spoken
against you, O people of Israel—against
the whole family I brought up out of Egypt:

2 "You only have I chosen
of all the families of the earth;
therefore I will punish you
for all your sins."

3 Do two walk together
unless they have agreed to do so?
4 Does a lion roar in the thicket
when he has no prey?
Does he growl in his den
when he has caught nothing?
5 Does a bird fall into a trap on the ground
where no snare has been set?
Does a trap spring up from the earth
when there is nothing to catch?
6 When a trumpet sounds in a city,
do not the people tremble?
When disaster comes to a city,
has not the LORD caused it?

7 Surely the Sovereign LORD does nothing
without revealing his plan
to his servants the prophets.

8 The lion has roared—
who will not fear?

[a]4 Or *by lies* [b]4 Or *lies*

Perfect Timing

ANNA

SHE'D WAITED A LIFETIME for this one moment. When she saw the baby, nestled in Simeon's arms, she gasped.

This is no ordinary child, she thought to herself.

She carefully watched from a distance as the three of them stood in the temple with the baby—mother, father and Simeon. Simeon's strong voice rang out as he blessed the child and his parents.

"My eyes have seen your salvation," Simeon exclaimed.

Anna felt the corners of her wrinkled lips curve as she drew a ragged breath and whispered, "As have mine."

Although she had worshiped at the temple day and night continually, she still marveled at the timing. An elderly widow, she had lived just long enough to see the Messiah with her own eyes. She realized she would likely never see him as an adult man or even as a young boy. But she saw in this tiny newborn a promise that extended beyond the realm of time and into eternity.

When Simeon returned the baby to his mother, Anna raised a slender, shaky finger. She bid Mary to come closer. The child's face, plump and peaceful as he slept soundly on his mother's breast, made her smile. Mary watched Anna respond to him with a precious combination of grandmotherly affection and austere reverence. Looking into the face of the child-King, she probably didn't know at that moment whether to kiss his face or kneel at his feet.

Feeling as though she were in a dream, she took Jesus' delicate hand in her own and patted it softly, tracing his tiny nails and fingertips as she began a prayer of thanks. She exclaimed. She whispered. She gave thanks to God for this astonishing gift. When she finished, she smiled a knowing smile at his young mother who was, by now, beaming.

"Yes, this was a day worth waiting for," she concluded. The Messiah had made his journey from heaven to earth, and she had been among the first witnesses.

—Prayer—

God, thank you for the precious gift of your Son, Jesus.

Coming up to them at that very moment, she gave thanks to God and spoke about the child to all who were looking forward to the redemption of Jerusalem.

Luke 2:38

ASSIGNED READING:

Luke 2:36–38

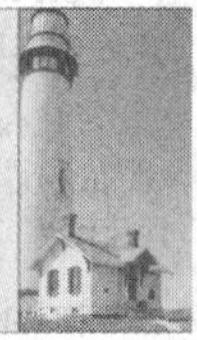

Weekend

Go to page 1103 for your next devotional reading.

The Sovereign LORD has spoken—
who can but prophesy?

9 Proclaim to the fortresses of Ashdod
and to the fortresses of Egypt:
"Assemble yourselves on the mountains of Samaria;
see the great unrest within her
and the oppression among her people."

10 "They do not know how to do right,"
declares the LORD,
"who hoard plunder and loot in their fortresses."

11 Therefore this is what the Sovereign
LORD says:

"An enemy will overrun the land;
he will pull down your strongholds
and plunder your fortresses."

12 This is what the LORD says:

"As a shepherd saves from the lion's mouth
only two leg bones or a piece of an ear,
so will the Israelites be saved,
those who sit in Samaria
on the edge of their beds
and in Damascus on their couches.[a]"

13 "Hear this and testify against the house
of Jacob," declares the Lord, the LORD God Almighty.

14 "On the day I punish Israel for her sins,
I will destroy the altars of Bethel;
the horns of the altar will be cut off
and fall to the ground.
15 I will tear down the winter house
along with the summer house;
the houses adorned with ivory will be destroyed
and the mansions will be demolished,"
declares the LORD.

Israel Has Not Returned to God

4 Hear this word, you cows of Bashan on Mount Samaria,
you women who oppress the poor and crush the needy
and say to your husbands, "Bring us some drinks!"
2 The Sovereign LORD has sworn by his holiness:
"The time will surely come
when you will be taken away with hooks,
the last of you with fishhooks.
3 You will each go straight out
through breaks in the wall,
and you will be cast out toward Harmon,[b]"
declares the LORD.

4 "Go to Bethel and sin;
go to Gilgal and sin yet more.
Bring your sacrifices every morning,
your tithes every three years.[c]
5 Burn leavened bread as a thank offering
and brag about your freewill offerings—
boast about them, you Israelites,
for this is what you love to do,"
declares the Sovereign LORD.

6 "I gave you empty stomachs[d] in every city
and lack of bread in every town,
yet you have not returned to me,"
declares the LORD.

7 "I also withheld rain from you
when the harvest was still three months away.
I sent rain on one town,
but withheld it from another.
One field had rain;
another had none and dried up.
8 People staggered from town to town for water
but did not get enough to drink,
yet you have not returned to me,"
declares the LORD.

9 "Many times I struck your gardens and vineyards,
I struck them with blight and mildew.
Locusts devoured your fig and olive trees,
yet you have not returned to me,"
declares the LORD.

10 "I sent plagues among you
as I did to Egypt.
I killed your young men with the sword,
along with your captured horses.

[a] 12 The meaning of the Hebrew for this line is uncertain. [b] 3 Masoretic Text; with a different word division of the Hebrew (see Septuagint) *out, O mountain of oppression* [c] 4 Or *tithes on the third day* [d] 6 Hebrew *you cleanness of teeth*

I filled your nostrils with the stench of
your camps,
yet you have not returned to me,"
declares the LORD.

11 "I overthrew some of you
as I[a] overthrew Sodom and Gomorrah.
You were like a burning stick snatched
from the fire,
yet you have not returned to me,"
declares the LORD.

12 "Therefore this is what I will do to you,
Israel,
and because I will do this to you,
prepare to meet your
God, O Israel."

13 He who forms the
mountains,
creates the wind,
and reveals his thoughts
to man,
he who turns dawn to
darkness,
and treads the high
places of the earth—
the LORD God Almighty
is his name.

> **Amos 4:13**
>
> *God Is Almighty*
>
> He who forms the
> mountains,
> creates the wind . . .
> the LORD God Almighty
> is his name.

A Lament and Call to Repentance

5 Hear this word, O house of Israel, this lament I take up concerning you:

2 "Fallen is Virgin Israel,
never to rise again,
deserted in her own land,
with no one to lift her up."

3 This is what the Sovereign LORD says:

"The city that marches out a thousand
strong for Israel
will have only a hundred left;
the town that marches out a hundred
strong
will have only ten left."

4 This is what the LORD says to the house of
Israel:

"Seek me and live;
5 do not seek Bethel,
do not go to Gilgal,
do not journey to Beersheba.
For Gilgal will surely go into exile,
and Bethel will be reduced to nothing.[b]"
6 Seek the LORD and live,
or he will sweep through the house of
Joseph like a fire;
it will devour,
and Bethel will have no one to quench it.

7 You who turn justice into bitterness
and cast righteousness to the ground
8 (he who made the Pleiades and Orion,
who turns blackness into dawn
and darkens day into night,
who calls for the waters of
the sea
and pours them out
over the face of the
land—
the LORD is his name—
9 he flashes destruction on
the stronghold
and brings the fortified
city to ruin),
10 you hate the one who
reproves in court
and despise him who
tells the truth.

11 You trample on the poor
and force him to give you grain.
Therefore, though you have built stone
mansions,
you will not live in them;
though you have planted lush vineyards,
you will not drink their wine.
12 For I know how many are your offenses
and how great your sins.

You oppress the righteous and take bribes
and you deprive the poor of justice in
the courts.
13 Therefore the prudent man keeps quiet in
such times,
for the times are evil.

14 Seek good, not evil,
that you may live.
Then the LORD God Almighty will be with
you,

[a]11 Hebrew *God* [b]5 Or *grief*; or *wickedness*; Hebrew *aven*, a reference to Beth Aven (a derogatory name for Bethel)

just as you say he is.
15 Hate evil, love good;
maintain justice in the courts.
Perhaps the LORD God Almighty will have mercy
on the remnant of Joseph.

16 Therefore this is what the Lord, the LORD God Almighty, says:

"There will be wailing in all the streets
and cries of anguish in every public square.
The farmers will be summoned to weep
and the mourners to wail.
17 There will be wailing in all the vineyards,
for I will pass through your midst,"
says the LORD.

The Day of the LORD

18 Woe to you who long
for the day of the LORD!
Why do you long for the day of the LORD?
That day will be darkness, not light.
19 It will be as though a man fled from a lion
only to meet a bear,
as though he entered his house
and rested his hand on the wall
only to have a snake bite him.
20 Will not the day of the LORD be darkness, not light—
pitch-dark, without a ray of brightness?

21 "I hate, I despise your religious feasts;
I cannot stand your assemblies.
22 Even though you bring me burnt offerings
and grain offerings,
I will not accept them.
Though you bring choice fellowship offerings,[a]
I will have no regard for them.
23 Away with the noise of your songs!
I will not listen to the music of your harps.
24 But let justice roll on like a river,
righteousness like a never-failing stream!

> **Amos 5:24**
>
> *God Desires Justice*
>
> "But let justice roll on like a river, righteousness like a never-failing stream!"

25 "Did you bring me sacrifices and offerings
forty years in the desert, O house of Israel?
26 You have lifted up the shrine of your king,
the pedestal of your idols,
the star of your god[b]—
which you made for yourselves.
27 Therefore I will send you into exile beyond Damascus,"
says the LORD, whose name is God Almighty.

Woe to the Complacent

6 Woe to you who are complacent in Zion,
and to you who feel secure on Mount Samaria,
you notable men of the foremost nation,
to whom the people of Israel come!
2 Go to Calneh and look at it;
go from there to great Hamath,
and then go down to Gath in Philistia.
Are they better off than your two kingdoms?
Is their land larger than yours?
3 You put off the evil day
and bring near a reign of terror.
4 You lie on beds inlaid with ivory
and lounge on your couches.
You dine on choice lambs
and fattened calves.
5 You strum away on your harps like David
and improvise on musical instruments.
6 You drink wine by the bowlful
and use the finest lotions,
but you do not grieve over the ruin of Joseph.
7 Therefore you will be among the first to go into exile;
your feasting and lounging will end.

[a] 22 Traditionally *peace offerings* [b] 26 Or *lifted up Sakkuth your king / and Kaiwan your idols, / your star-gods*; Septuagint *lifted up the shrine of Molech / and the star of your god Rephan, / their idols*

The LORD Abhors the Pride of Israel

8 The Sovereign LORD has sworn by himself—the LORD God Almighty declares:

"I abhor the pride of Jacob
  and detest his fortresses;
I will deliver up the city
  and everything in it."

9 If ten men are left in one house, they too
will die. 10 And if a relative who is to burn the
bodies comes to carry them out of the house
and asks anyone still hiding there, "Is anyone
with you?" and he says, "No," then he will say,
"Hush! We must not mention the name of
the LORD."

11 For the LORD has given the command,
  and he will smash the great house into
    pieces
  and the small house into bits.

12 Do horses run on the rocky crags?
  Does one plow there with oxen?
But you have turned justice into poison
  and the fruit of righteousness into
    bitterness—
13 you who rejoice in the conquest of Lo
    Debar[a]
  and say, "Did we not take Karnaim[b] by
    our own strength?"

14 For the LORD God Almighty declares,
  "I will stir up a nation against you,
    O house of Israel,
that will oppress you all the way
  from Lebo[c] Hamath to the valley of the
    Arabah."

Locusts, Fire and a Plumb Line

7 This is what the Sovereign LORD showed
me: He was preparing swarms of locusts
after the king's share had been harvested and
just as the second crop was coming up. 2 When
they had stripped the land clean, I cried out,
"Sovereign LORD, forgive! How can Jacob survive? He is so small!"

3 So the LORD relented.

"This will not happen," the LORD said.

4 This is what the Sovereign LORD showed
me: The Sovereign LORD was calling for judgment by fire; it dried up the great deep and devoured the land. 5 Then I cried out, "Sovereign
LORD, I beg you, stop! How can Jacob survive?
He is so small!"

6 So the LORD relented.

"This will not happen either," the Sovereign
LORD said.

7 This is what he showed me: The Lord was
standing by a wall that had been built true to
plumb, with a plumb line in his hand. 8 And the
LORD asked me, "What do you see, Amos?"

"A plumb line," I replied.

Then the Lord said, "Look, I am setting a
plumb line among my people Israel; I will spare
them no longer.

9 "The high places of Isaac will be destroyed
  and the sanctuaries of Israel will be
    ruined;
  with my sword I will rise against the
    house of Jeroboam."

Amos and Amaziah

10 Then Amaziah the priest of Bethel sent
a message to Jeroboam king of Israel: "Amos
is raising a conspiracy against you in the very
heart of Israel. The land cannot bear all his
words. 11 For this is what Amos is saying:

"'Jeroboam will die by the sword,
  and Israel will surely go into exile,
  away from their native land.'"

12 Then Amaziah said to Amos, "Get out, you
seer! Go back to the land of Judah. Earn your
bread there and do your prophesying there.
13 Don't prophesy anymore at Bethel, because
this is the king's sanctuary and the temple of
the kingdom."

14 Amos answered Amaziah, "I was neither
a prophet nor a prophet's son, but I was a shepherd, and I also took care of sycamore-fig trees.
15 But the LORD took me from tending the flock
and said to me, 'Go, prophesy to my people
Israel.' 16 Now then, hear the word of the LORD.
You say,

"'Do not prophesy against Israel,
  and stop preaching against the house of
    Isaac.'

17 "Therefore this is what the LORD says:

[a] 13 *Lo Debar* means *nothing.* [b] 13 *Karnaim* means *horns*; *horn* here symbolizes strength. [c] 14 Or *from the entrance to*

"'Your wife will become a prostitute in the city,
and your sons and daughters will fall by the sword.
Your land will be measured and divided up,
and you yourself will die in a pagan[a] country.
And Israel will certainly go into exile,
away from their native land.'"

A Basket of Ripe Fruit

8 This is what the Sovereign LORD showed
me: a basket of ripe fruit. 2"What do you
see, Amos?" he asked.

"A basket of ripe fruit," I answered.

Then the LORD said to me, "The time is ripe
for my people Israel; I will spare them no longer.

3"In that day," declares the Sovereign LORD,
"the songs in the temple will turn to wailing.[b]
Many, many bodies—flung everywhere! Silence!"

4 Hear this, you who trample the needy
and do away with the poor of the land,
5 saying,

"When will the New Moon be over
that we may sell grain,
and the Sabbath be ended
that we may market wheat?"—
skimping the measure,
boosting the price
and cheating with dishonest scales,
6 buying the poor with silver
and the needy for a pair of sandals,
selling even the sweepings with the wheat.

7 The LORD has sworn by the Pride of Jacob:
"I will never forget anything they have done.

8 "Will not the land tremble for this,
and all who live in it mourn?
The whole land will rise like the Nile;
it will be stirred up and then sink
like the river of Egypt.

9 "In that day," declares the Sovereign LORD,

"I will make the sun go down at noon
and darken the earth in broad daylight.
10 I will turn your religious feasts into mourning
and all your singing into weeping.
I will make all of you wear sackcloth
and shave your heads.
I will make that time like mourning for an only son
and the end of it like a bitter day.

11 "The days are coming," declares the Sovereign LORD,
"when I will send a famine through the land—
not a famine of food or a thirst for water,
but a famine of hearing the words of the LORD.
12 Men will stagger from sea to sea
and wander from north to east,
searching for the word of the LORD,
but they will not find it.

13 "In that day

"the lovely young women and strong young men
will faint because of thirst.
14 They who swear by the shame[c] of Samaria,
or say, 'As surely as your god lives, O Dan,'
or, 'As surely as the god[d] of Beersheba lives'—
they will fall,
never to rise again."

Israel to Be Destroyed

9 I saw the Lord standing by the altar, and
he said:

"Strike the tops of the pillars
so that the thresholds shake.
Bring them down on the heads of all the people;
those who are left I will kill with the sword.
Not one will get away,
none will escape.
2 Though they dig down to the depths of the grave,[e]
from there my hand will take them.
Though they climb up to the heavens,
from there I will bring them down.

[a] 17 Hebrew *an unclean* [b] 3 Or *"the temple singers will wail* [c] 14 Or *by Ashima*; or *by the idol* [d] 14 Or *power* [e] 2 Hebrew *to Sheol*

What About the Poor?

Read: Amos 8:1–14

ASK YOUR NEIGHBOR OR COWORKER to list the "top ten" sins, and you will probably hear a version of the Ten Commandments. Murder, stealing, lying and adultery would probably head the list.

But when God revealed to Amos that he was about to bring judgment upon his people, he cited Israel's treatment of the poor as cause for punishment. In startling imagery, God said Israel had "trampled" the needy and cheated the poor. The poor, the victims of Israel's greed and exploitation, had no recourse but to appeal to God. And God listened.

In the New Testament, Jesus repeatedly takes up the often-overlooked cause of the poor. When Jesus preached in the synagogue in Luke 4:16–21, the prophecy he chose to read to reveal who he was came from Isaiah 61:1–2: "The Spirit of the Lord is on me, because he has anointed me to preach good news to the poor." When Jesus described final judgment in Matthew 25:31–46, he evaluated how well people cared for the hungry, the thirsty, the stranger, the needy and the imprisoned. Jesus so identifies with the poor in this passage that he says that the good deeds done to the "least of these" were counted as being done to him!

How does the way you live reveal your concern for the poor? Are the poor an afterthought? A nuisance? A perplexing problem you've quit trying to solve? For many of us, Amos's message challenges us to serve the poverty stricken in ways besides simply giving money. Volunteering in a food pantry or rescue mission may be the first step to helping poor people with their immediate needs. Working directly with people who are poor helps us to put names and faces on poverty. When we do that, we can no longer objectify and ignore the needy. But are there ways to take our compassion one step further? How can we speak up to make sure the poor aren't exploited? How can we work to make sure our institutions don't make the problem worse? How can we vote for policies and practices that are equitable?

It is God's desire that we be willing to share what we have with those in need and help the poor whenever we can. When we do, our hearts beat in time with his.

Amos 8:4–5

Hear this, you who trample the needy and do away with the poor of the land, saying, "When will the New Moon be over that we may sell grain, and the Sabbath be ended that we may market wheat?"—skimping the measure, boosting the price and cheating with dishonest scales.

reflection

1. What are your assumptions about why someone might be poor?
2. Have you ever been without what you needed to live? What did you do?
3. Why do you think God identifies himself with the poor? What does that tell you about his character?

RELATED READINGS

Isaiah 61:1–3; Matthew 25:31–46; Luke 4:16–21

Monday

Go to page 1109 for your next devotional reading.

3 Though they hide themselves on the top of
Carmel,
there I will hunt them down and seize
them.
Though they hide from me at the bottom
of the sea,
there I will command the serpent to bite
them.
4 Though they are driven into exile by their
enemies,
there I will command the sword to slay
them.
I will fix my eyes upon them
for evil and not for good."

5 The Lord, the LORD Almighty,
he who touches the earth and it melts,
and all who live in it mourn—
the whole land rises like the Nile,
then sinks like the river of Egypt—
6 he who builds his lofty palace[a] in the
heavens
and sets its foundation[b] on the earth,
who calls for the waters of the sea
and pours them out over the face of the
land—
the LORD is his name.

7 "Are not you Israelites
the same to me as the Cushites[c]?"
declares the LORD.
"Did I not bring Israel up from Egypt,
the Philistines from Caphtor[d]
and the Arameans from Kir?

8 "Surely the eyes of the Sovereign LORD
are on the sinful kingdom.
I will destroy it
from the face of the earth—
yet I will not totally destroy
the house of Jacob,"
declares the LORD.

9 "For I will give the command,
and I will shake the house of Israel
among all the nations
as grain is shaken in a sieve,
and not a pebble will reach the ground.
10 All the sinners among my people
will die by the sword,
all those who say,
'Disaster will not overtake or meet us.'

Israel's Restoration

11 "In that day I will restore
David's fallen tent.
I will repair its broken places,
restore its ruins,
and build it as it used to be,
12 so that they may possess the remnant of
Edom
and all the nations that bear my name,[e]"
declares the LORD, who will
do these things.

13 "The days are coming," declares the
LORD,
"when the reaper will be overtaken by the
plowman
and the planter by the one treading
grapes.
New wine will drip from the mountains
and flow from all the hills.
14 I will bring back my exiled[f] people Israel;
they will rebuild the ruined cities and
live in them.
They will plant vineyards and drink their
wine;
they will make gardens and eat their
fruit.
15 I will plant Israel in their own land,
never again to be uprooted
from the land I have given them,"
says the LORD your God.

[a]6 The meaning of the Hebrew for this phrase is uncertain. [b]6 The meaning of the Hebrew for this word is uncertain. [c]7 That is, people from the upper Nile region [d]7 That is, Crete [e]12 Hebrew; Septuagint *so that the remnant of men / and all the nations that bear my name may seek ⌊the Lord⌋* [f]14 Or *will restore the fortunes of my*

Obadiah

The people of Edom, descendants of Jacob's brother Esau, *forgot brotherly kindness.* God told them they were proud, but he would soon humble them. Since they lived on a mountain, they looked down on everyone else. Not only were they pleased when the people of Israel suffered at the hands of their enemies, but they also helped themselves to the plunder as the city was destroyed. But God would punish the Edomites and show his love to the Israelites by doing so.

Those who mess with God's people challenge God himself. *Our protection is a job he takes personally* because he takes affronts against his people seriously. He may not act when or how we want him to, but we can rest assured that he will act. Like the people of Israel, *we are under his protection and his lasting covenant of love.*

Author:
Obadiah.

Audience:
The Edomites, Judah and all of God's people.

Date:
Probably during the Babylonian attacks on Jerusalem (605–586 B.C.).

Setting:
The Edomites, who were descendants of Esau and related to the Israelites, were harassing the people of Israel.

Verse to Remember:
"Because of the violence against your brother Jacob, you will be covered with shame; you will be destroyed forever." (10)

1 The vision of Obadiah.

This is what the Sovereign LORD says about Edom—

We have heard a message from the LORD:
An envoy was sent to the nations to say,
"Rise, and let us go against her for battle"—

2 "See, I will make you small among the nations;
you will be utterly despised.
3 The pride of your heart has deceived you,

you who live in the clefts of the rocks[a]
and make your home on the heights,
you who say to yourself,
'Who can bring me down to the ground?'
4 Though you soar like the eagle
and make your nest among the stars,
from there I will bring you down,"
declares the LORD.
5 "If thieves came to you,
if robbers in the night—
Oh, what a disaster awaits you—
would they not steal only as much as they wanted?
If grape pickers came to you,
would they not leave a few grapes?
6 But how Esau will be ransacked,
his hidden treasures pillaged!
7 All your allies will force you to the border;
your friends will deceive and overpower you;
those who eat your bread will set a trap for you,[b]
but you will not detect it.

8 "In that day," declares the LORD,
"will I not destroy the wise men of Edom,
men of understanding in the mountains of Esau?
9 Your warriors, O Teman, will be terrified,
and everyone in Esau's mountains
will be cut down in the slaughter.
10 Because of the violence against your brother Jacob,
you will be covered with shame;
you will be destroyed forever.
11 On the day you stood aloof
while strangers carried off his wealth
and foreigners entered his gates
and cast lots for Jerusalem,
you were like one of them.
12 You should not look down on your brother
in the day of his misfortune,
nor rejoice over the people of Judah
in the day of their destruction,
nor boast so much
in the day of their trouble.
13 You should not march through the gates of my people
in the day of their disaster,
nor look down on them in their calamity
in the day of their disaster,
nor seize their wealth
in the day of their disaster.
14 You should not wait at the crossroads
to cut down their fugitives,
nor hand over their survivors
in the day of their trouble.

15 "The day of the LORD is near
for all nations.
As you have done, it will be done to you;
your deeds will return upon your own head.
16 Just as you drank on my holy hill,
so all the nations will drink continually;
they will drink and drink
and be as if they had never been.
17 But on Mount Zion will be deliverance;
it will be holy,
and the house of Jacob
will possess its inheritance.
18 The house of Jacob will be a fire
and the house of Joseph a flame;
the house of Esau will be stubble,
and they will set it on fire and consume it.
There will be no survivors
from the house of Esau."
The LORD has spoken.

19 People from the Negev will occupy
the mountains of Esau,
and people from the foothills will possess
the land of the Philistines.
They will occupy the fields of Ephraim and Samaria,
and Benjamin will possess Gilead.
20 This company of Israelite exiles who are in Canaan
will possess ⌊the land⌋ as far as Zarephath;
the exiles from Jerusalem who are in Sepharad
will possess the towns of the Negev.
21 Deliverers will go up on[c] Mount Zion
to govern the mountains of Esau.
And the kingdom will be the LORD's.

[a]3 Or *of Sela* [b]7 The meaning of the Hebrew for this clause is uncertain. [c]21 Or *from*

Jonah

God's choice of workers rarely falls along the lines of human logic. God wanted to have his words preached in the capital city of Assyria. He wanted the people of Nineveh, who were pagans and also Israel's enemy, to humble themselves and repent. And so he picked a prejudiced, stubborn, complaining man to be his mouthpiece. Jonah didn't want the job from the start. *But God wanted Jonah,* and he pursued him when he could have washed his hands of him and chosen someone else.

Jonah's story illustrates *God's boundless love.* We see God reaching across the boundaries of Israel into enemy territory. We see him reaching into the depths of the sea to save a rebellious man. And we see him patiently working with Jonah, and working with him again, to help him understand something of that boundless love. Jonah may not be the most admirable prophet God used, but he is exceedingly human. *And it is humans, including women like you, that God uses to do his work.*

Author:
Jonah.

Audience:
Israel and all of God's people.

Date:
Probably about 785–750 B.C.

Setting:
God sends a reluctant Jonah to Nineveh, the capital city of the dreaded nation of Assyria, to preach repentance.

Verse to Remember:
"O LORD, is this not what I said when I was still at home? That is why I was so quick to flee to Tarshish. I knew that you are a gracious and compassionate God, slow to anger and abounding in love, a God who relents from sending calamity." (4:2)

Jonah Flees From the LORD

1 The word of the LORD came to Jonah son
of Amittai: 2"Go to the great city of Nineveh and preach against it, because its wickedness has come up before me."
3But Jonah ran away from the LORD and
headed for Tarshish. He went down to Joppa,
where he found a ship bound for that port. After paying the fare, he went aboard and sailed
for Tarshish to flee from the LORD.

4 Then the LORD sent a great wind on the sea,
and such a violent storm arose that the ship
threatened to break up. 5 All the sailors were
afraid and each cried out to his own god. And
they threw the cargo into the sea to lighten
the ship.
But Jonah had gone below deck, where he
lay down and fell into a deep sleep. 6 The captain went to him and said, "How can you sleep?
Get up and call on your god! Maybe he will
take notice of us, and we will not perish."
7 Then the sailors said to each other, "Come,
let us cast lots to find out who is responsible
for this calamity." They cast lots and the lot fell
on Jonah.
8 So they asked him, "Tell us, who is responsible for making all this trouble for us? What
do you do? Where do you come from? What is
your country? From what people are you?"
9 He answered, "I am a Hebrew and I worship the LORD, the God of heaven, who made
the sea and the land."
10 This terrified them and they asked, "What
have you done?" (They knew he was running
away from the LORD, because he had already
told them so.)
11 The sea was getting rougher and rougher.
So they asked him, "What should we do to you
to make the sea calm down for us?"
12 "Pick me up and throw me
into the sea," he replied, "and it
will become calm. I know that
it is my fault that this great
storm has come upon you."
13 Instead, the men did their
best to row back to land. But
they could not, for the sea
grew even wilder than before.
14 Then they cried to the LORD,
"O LORD, please do not let us
die for taking this man's life.
Do not hold us accountable for
killing an innocent man, for
you, O LORD, have done as you
pleased." 15 Then they took Jonah and threw him overboard,
and the raging sea grew calm. 16 At this the
men greatly feared the LORD, and they offered
a sacrifice to the LORD and made vows to him.

> **Jonah 2:7**
>
> *God Hears Prayer*
>
> "When my life was ebbing away, I remembered you, LORD, and my prayer rose to you, to your holy temple."

17 But the LORD provided a great fish to swallow Jonah, and Jonah was inside the fish three
days and three nights.

Jonah's Prayer

2 From inside the fish Jonah prayed to the
LORD his God. 2 He said:

"In my distress I called to the LORD,
and he answered me.
From the depths of the grave[a] I called for help,
and you listened to my cry.
3 You hurled me into the deep,
into the very heart of the seas,
and the currents swirled about me;
all your waves and breakers
swept over me.
4 I said, 'I have been banished
from your sight;
yet I will look again
toward your holy temple.'
5 The engulfing waters threatened me,[b]
the deep surrounded me;
seaweed was wrapped around my head.
6 To the roots of the mountains I sank down;
the earth beneath barred me in forever.
But you brought my life up from the pit,
O LORD my God.
7 "When my life was ebbing away,
I remembered you, LORD,
and my prayer rose to you,
to your holy temple.
8 "Those who cling to worthless idols
forfeit the grace that could be theirs.
9 But I, with a song of thanksgiving,
will sacrifice to you.
What I have vowed I will make good.
Salvation comes from the LORD."

[a] 2 Hebrew *Sheol* [b] 5 Or *waters were at my throat*

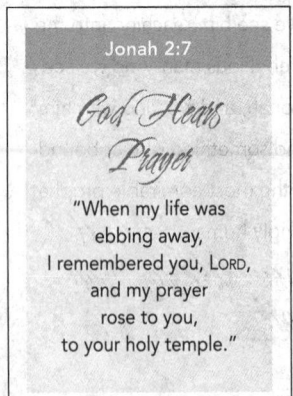

Wishing Them Well

Read: Jonah 3:1–10

HAVE YOU EVER HAD A FRIEND or acquaintance who made a wrong choice for every right choice you made, yet in the end your friend seemed to face none of the consequences you faced? It's hard to take, watching someone come out smelling like roses when you know the stinky stuff they've been rooted in.

If you can relate, then you can empathize with Jonah when God told him to go to Nineveh. Now, that was not just *any* field of service for the ancient prophet. It was Israel's greatest national enemy. The Ninevites were citizens of Assyria, a brutal nation to the east, and Israel's greatest threat.

It's no wonder that when the people of Nineveh did clean up their act (for a while anyway), Jonah was distressed. How could God sanction the redemption of a country like that? It didn't seem fair. And in truth, at least from Jonah's perspective, it probably wasn't.

It's tough to just do what's asked of you and leave the fairness issue to God, isn't it? It's hard to see people receive good things when they've caused you (or someone you love) pain. Like when your ex-son-in-law remarries or when the disloyal secretary down the hall gets a promotion you deserved. It's even harder to facilitate their good fortune, like Jonah did. Jesus said to love our enemies, but when it comes right down to it, we'd rather not.

How do we get past our feelings and wish our enemies well? We grace them with the same kind of mercy with which God graced us without expectation of getting anything back in return (see Luke 6:35–36). We focus on God and on the good things he has given us and done for us. The key to countering the envy of another's fortune is to be grateful for our own. And when we do that, we let go of the part of God's job that we'd like to do—the finger-pointing. It's just too hard to do our own work and God's too. And he does it so much better! Since we don't have his insight into the hearts and minds of those people we'd like to judge and condemn, it's better for us to push aside our limited understanding of justice and just trust him instead.

Jonah 3:1–2

Then the word of the LORD came to Jonah a second time: "Go to the great city of Nineveh and proclaim to it the message I give you."

reflection

1 Think about the feelings you have toward people who live under a completely different set of values than you do. How do your feelings for them compare to the love God has for them?

2 When it comes to people you dislike, why is it difficult to "wish them well"?

3 What keeps you from being able to leave that person solely accountable to God? Fear? Anger? Jealousy?

RELATED READINGS

Psalm 3:1–8; Matthew 5:43–47; 20:1–16

Tuesday

Go to page 1115 for your next devotional reading.

10 And the LORD commanded the fish, and it vomited Jonah onto dry land.

Jonah Goes to Nineveh

3 Then the word of the LORD came to Jonah a second time: 2 "Go to the great city of Nineveh and proclaim to it the message I give you."

3 Jonah obeyed the word of the LORD and went to Nineveh. Now Nineveh was a very important city—a visit required three days. 4 On the first day, Jonah started into the city. He proclaimed: "Forty more days and Nineveh will be overturned." 5 The Ninevites believed God. They declared a fast, and all of them, from the greatest to the least, put on sackcloth.

6 When the news reached the king of Nineveh, he rose from his throne, took off his royal robes, covered himself with sackcloth and sat down in the dust. 7 Then he issued a proclamation in Nineveh:

> "By the decree of the king and his nobles:
>
> Do not let any man or beast, herd or flock, taste anything; do not let them eat or drink. 8 But let man and beast be covered with sackcloth. Let everyone call urgently on God. Let them give up their evil ways and their violence. 9 Who knows? God may yet relent and with compassion turn from his fierce anger so that we will not perish."

10 When God saw what they did and how they turned from their evil ways, he had compassion and did not bring upon them the destruction he had threatened.

> Jonah 4:2
>
> *God Is Gracious*
>
> "I knew that you are a gracious and compassionate God, slow to anger and abounding in love, a God who relents from sending calamity."

Jonah's Anger at the LORD's Compassion

4 But Jonah was greatly displeased and became angry. 2 He prayed to the LORD, "O LORD, is this not what I said when I was still at home? That is why I was so quick to flee to Tarshish. I knew that you are a gracious and compassionate God, slow to anger and abounding in love, a God who relents from sending calamity. 3 Now, O LORD, take away my life, for it is better for me to die than to live."

4 But the LORD replied, "Have you any right to be angry?"

5 Jonah went out and sat down at a place east of the city. There he made himself a shelter, sat in its shade and waited to see what would happen to the city. 6 Then the LORD God provided a vine and made it grow up over Jonah to give shade for his head to ease his discomfort, and Jonah was very happy about the vine. 7 But at dawn the next day God provided a worm, which chewed the vine so that it withered. 8 When the sun rose, God provided a scorching east wind, and the sun blazed on Jonah's head so that he grew faint. He wanted to die, and said, "It would be better for me to die than to live."

9 But God said to Jonah, "Do you have a right to be angry about the vine?"

"I do," he said. "I am angry enough to die."

10 But the LORD said, "You have been concerned about this vine, though you did not tend it or make it grow. It sprang up overnight and died overnight. 11 But Nineveh has more than a hundred and twenty thousand people who cannot tell their right hand from their left, and many cattle as well. Should I not be concerned about that great city?"

Micah

God is a God of mercy. But make no mistake about it; *he will not let the wicked go unpunished.* The book of Micah places us on a pendulum that swings from blessing to judgment. The prophet Micah is brokenhearted over the rebellion of God's chosen people, and he urges them *to turn their hearts back to God.* Micah prophesies the downfall of the rich and powerful. He draws attention to the plight of the poor. His warnings to the Israelites are not popular. The people don't want to hear that their actions will have disastrous consequences. Micah sees that the people's earthly riches will leave them spiritually and emotionally bankrupt, and he encourages them to return to *the only One who can bring true fulfillment and joy.* Like a loving but stern parent, Micah holds their faces in his hands and says, in effect, "Listen to me" (Micah 1:2; 3:1; 6:1), as he promises the people that God will forgive them if they turn back to him.

Author:
Micah.

Audience:
The southern kingdom (Judah) and northern kingdom (Israel).

Date:
Likely between 742 and 687 B.C., during the time of Isaiah and Hosea.

Setting:
Political mayhem has the kingdoms reeling from one bad king to another. Micah steps in to prophesy judgment.

Verse to Remember:
He has showed you,
O man, what is good. And what does the LORD require of you? To act justly and to love mercy and to walk humbly with your God.
(6:8)

1 The word of the LORD that came to Micah of Moresheth during the reigns of Jotham, Ahaz and Hezekiah, kings of Judah—the vision he saw concerning Samaria and Jerusalem.

2 Hear, O peoples, all of you,
listen, O earth and all who are in it,
that the Sovereign LORD may witness against you,
the Lord from his holy temple.

Judgment Against Samaria and Jerusalem

3 Look! The LORD is coming from his dwelling place;

he comes down and treads the high
places of the earth.
4 The mountains melt beneath him
and the valleys split apart,
like wax before the fire,
like water rushing down a slope.
5 All this is because of Jacob's transgression,
because of the sins of the house of Israel.
What is Jacob's transgression?
Is it not Samaria?
What is Judah's high place?
Is it not Jerusalem?

6 "Therefore I will make Samaria a heap of
rubble,
a place for planting vineyards.
I will pour her stones into the valley
and lay bare her foundations.
7 All her idols will be broken to pieces;
all her temple gifts will be burned with
fire;
I will destroy all her images.
Since she gathered her gifts from the wages
of prostitutes,
as the wages of prostitutes they will
again be used."

Weeping and Mourning

8 Because of this I will weep and wail;
I will go about barefoot and naked.
I will howl like a jackal
and moan like an owl.
9 For her wound is incurable;
it has come to Judah.
It[a] has reached the very gate of my people,
even to Jerusalem itself.
10 Tell it not in Gath[b];
weep not at all.[c]
In Beth Ophrah[d]
roll in the dust.
11 Pass on in nakedness and shame,
you who live in Shaphir.[e]
Those who live in Zaanan[f]
will not come out.
Beth Ezel is in mourning;
its protection is taken from you.
12 Those who live in Maroth[g] writhe in pain,
waiting for relief,
because disaster has come from the LORD,
even to the gate of Jerusalem.
13 You who live in Lachish,[h]
harness the team to the chariot.
You were the beginning of sin
to the Daughter of Zion,
for the transgressions of Israel
were found in you.
14 Therefore you will give parting gifts
to Moresheth Gath.
The town of Aczib[i] will prove deceptive
to the kings of Israel.
15 I will bring a conqueror against you
who live in Mareshah.[j]
He who is the glory of Israel
will come to Adullam.
16 Shave your heads in mourning
for the children in whom you delight;
make yourselves as bald as the vulture,
for they will go from you into exile.

Man's Plans and God's

2 Woe to those who plan iniquity,
to those who plot evil on their beds!
At morning's light they carry it out
because it is in their power to do it.
2 They covet fields and seize them,
and houses, and take them.
They defraud a man of his home,
a fellowman of his inheritance.
3 Therefore, the LORD says:

"I am planning disaster against this
people,
from which you cannot save yourselves.
You will no longer walk proudly,
for it will be a time of calamity.
4 In that day men will ridicule you;
they will taunt you with this mournful
song:
'We are utterly ruined;
my people's possession is divided up.
He takes it from me!
He assigns our fields to traitors.'"

5 Therefore you will have no one in the
assembly of the LORD
to divide the land by lot.

[a]9 Or *He* [b]10 *Gath* sounds like the Hebrew for *tell.* [c]10 Hebrew; Septuagint may suggest *not in Acco.* The Hebrew for *in Acco* sounds like the Hebrew for *weep.* [d]10 *Beth Ophrah* means *house of dust.* [e]11 *Shaphir* means *pleasant.* [f]11 *Zaanan* sounds like the Hebrew for *come out.* [g]12 *Maroth* sounds like the Hebrew for *bitter.* [h]13 *Lachish* sounds like the Hebrew for *team.* [i]14 *Aczib* means *deception.* [j]15 *Mareshah* sounds like the Hebrew for *conqueror.*

False Prophets

6 "Do not prophesy," their prophets say.
"Do not prophesy about these things;
disgrace will not overtake us."
7 Should it be said, O house of Jacob:
"Is the Spirit of the LORD angry?
Does he do such things?"

"Do not my words do good
to him whose ways are upright?
8 Lately my people have risen up
like an enemy.
You strip off the rich robe
from those who pass by
without a care,
like men returning from
battle.
9 You drive the women of my
people
from their pleasant
homes.
You take away my blessing
from their children
forever.
10 Get up, go away!
For this is not your
resting place,
because it is defiled,
it is ruined, beyond all
remedy.
11 If a liar and deceiver comes and says,
'I will prophesy for you plenty of wine
and beer,'
he would be just the prophet for this
people!

Deliverance Promised

12 "I will surely gather all of you, O Jacob;
I will surely bring together the remnant
of Israel.
I will bring them together like sheep in a
pen,
like a flock in its pasture;
the place will throng with people.
13 One who breaks open the way will go up
before them;
they will break through the gate and go
out.
Their king will pass through before
them,
the LORD at their head."

Leaders and Prophets Rebuked

3 Then I said,

"Listen, you leaders of Jacob,
you rulers of the house of Israel.
Should you not know justice,
2 you who hate good and love evil;
who tear the skin from my people
and the flesh from their bones;
3 who eat my people's flesh,
strip off their skin
and break their bones in
pieces;
who chop them up like
meat for the pan,
like flesh for the pot?"

4 Then they will cry out to
the LORD,
but he will not answer
them.
At that time he will hide
his face from them
because of the evil they
have done.

5 This is what the LORD says:

"As for the prophets
who lead my people
astray,
if one feeds them,
they proclaim 'peace';
if he does not,
they prepare to wage war against him.
6 Therefore night will come over you,
without visions,
and darkness, without divination.
The sun will set for the prophets,
and the day will go dark for them.
7 The seers will be ashamed
and the diviners disgraced.
They will all cover their faces
because there is no answer from God."

8 But as for me, I am filled with power,
with the Spirit of the LORD,
and with justice and might,
to declare to Jacob his transgression,
to Israel his sin.
9 Hear this, you leaders of the house of
Jacob,

> **Micah 3:4**
>
> *God Cannot Look on Evil*
>
> Then they will cry out to the LORD, but he will not answer them. At that time he will hide his face from them because of the evil they have done.

you rulers of the house of Israel,
who despise justice
and distort all that is right;
10 who build Zion with bloodshed,
and Jerusalem with wickedness.
11 Her leaders judge for a bribe,
her priests teach for a price,
and her prophets tell fortunes for money.
Yet they lean upon the LORD and say,
"Is not the LORD among us?
No disaster will come upon us."
12 Therefore because of you,
Zion will be plowed like a field,
Jerusalem will become a heap of rubble,
the temple hill a mound overgrown with thickets.

The Mountain of the LORD

4 In the last days

the mountain of the LORD's temple will be established
as chief among the mountains;
it will be raised above the hills,
and peoples will stream to it.

2 Many nations will come and say,

"Come, let us go up to the mountain of the LORD,
to the house of the God of Jacob.
He will teach us his ways,
so that we may walk in his paths."
The law will go out from Zion,
the word of the LORD from Jerusalem.
3 He will judge between many peoples
and will settle disputes for strong nations far and wide.
They will beat their swords into plowshares
and their spears into pruning hooks.
Nation will not take up sword against nation,
nor will they train for war anymore.
4 Every man will sit under his own vine
and under his own fig tree,
and no one will make them afraid,
for the LORD Almighty has spoken.
5 All the nations may walk
in the name of their gods;
we will walk in the name of the LORD
our God for ever and ever.

The LORD's Plan

6 "In that day," declares the LORD,

"I will gather the lame;
I will assemble the exiles
and those I have brought to grief.
7 I will make the lame a remnant,
those driven away a strong nation.
The LORD will rule over them in Mount Zion
from that day and forever.
8 As for you, O watchtower of the flock,
O stronghold[a] of the Daughter of Zion,
the former dominion will be restored to you;
kingship will come to the Daughter of Jerusalem."
9 Why do you now cry aloud—
have you no king?
Has your counselor perished,
that pain seizes you like that of a woman in labor?
10 Writhe in agony, O Daughter of Zion,
like a woman in labor,
for now you must leave the city
to camp in the open field.
You will go to Babylon;
there you will be rescued.
There the LORD will redeem you
out of the hand of your enemies.

11 But now many nations
are gathered against you.
They say, "Let her be defiled,
let our eyes gloat over Zion!"
12 But they do not know
the thoughts of the LORD;
they do not understand his plan,
he who gathers them like sheaves to the threshing floor.

13 "Rise and thresh, O Daughter of Zion,
for I will give you horns of iron;
I will give you hoofs of bronze
and you will break to pieces many nations."

[a] 8 Or *hill*

God's Better Way

Read: Micah 4:1–13

THINGS WEREN'T GOING LUCI'S WAY at work. She worked longer and harder than ever without recognition and with no promotion in sight.

Even though she didn't like change, she started looking for another job. The one most intriguing to her seemed like a long shot—way out of her league. However, just as she was getting ready to accept another offer, the long shot came in. She was the company's top pick.

It was a perfect match. Luci couldn't have dreamed of a better job. Looking back, she realized she would never have sought the job if things at her old company hadn't become difficult. She wouldn't have *chosen* to have things turn sour so she would want to leave. At the time, the thought of moving to a new job seemed impossible. And scary.

But God wanted her to experience more. He wanted the best for her. And she would never have found his best if she hadn't experienced trouble at work. God allowed the problems and ultimately used them for her good, even though at the time it had been a mystery to her. She did not "know the thoughts of the LORD" (verse 12). Many times, neither do we.

Micah spoke of a future time when Jerusalem would experience peace . . . a time when war would end. At the time, it seemed like a crazy message. Things were more than uncomfortable; they were downright horrible. The armies of Babylon had destroyed the temple, killed people and tortured many more. Yet Micah said peace was coming. It didn't seem possible.

Sometimes, the things God promises for our future don't seem at all likely in light of what we're experiencing today. From our limited perspective, we don't see the big picture, only a tiny thumbnail print. Like Luci, we may be experiencing something difficult or uncomfortable that will result in something better. It's important to remember that sometimes our troubles are only a momentary detour leading us to God's best for us.

Micah 4:12

But they do not know the thoughts of the LORD; they do not understand his plan, he who gathers them like sheaves to the threshing floor.

reflection

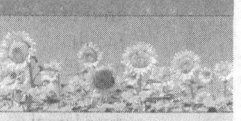

1 How has God used a difficult situation in your past for your good?

2 Is there a situation in your life right now that you can look at from a fresh perspective?

3 How can you share your experiences with someone else who needs encouragement today?

RELATED READINGS

Psalms 92:4–5; 94:11; Isaiah 55:8–9; 1 Corinthians 3:18–20

Wednesday

Go to page 1118 for your next devotional reading.

You will devote their ill-gotten gains to the
LORD,
their wealth to the Lord of all the earth.

A Promised Ruler From Bethlehem

5 Marshal your troops, O city of troops,[a]
for a siege is laid against us.
They will strike Israel's ruler
on the cheek with a rod.

2 "But you, Bethlehem
Ephrathah,
though you are small
among the clans[b] of
Judah,
out of you will come for me
one who will be ruler
over Israel,
whose origins[c] are from
of old,
from ancient times.[d]"

3 Therefore Israel will be
abandoned
until the time when she
who is in labor gives
birth
and the rest of his brothers
return
to join the Israelites.
4 He will stand and shepherd his flock
in the strength of the LORD,
in the majesty of the name of the LORD
his God.
And they will live securely, for then his
greatness
will reach to the ends of the earth.
5 And he will be their peace.

Deliverance and Destruction

When the Assyrian invades our land
and marches through our fortresses,
we will raise against him seven shepherds,
even eight leaders of men.
6 They will rule[e] the land of Assyria with the
sword,
the land of Nimrod with drawn sword.[f]
He will deliver us from the Assyrian
when he invades our land
and marches into our borders.

Micah 5:2

God Knows the Future

"But you, Bethlehem
Ephrathah,
though you are small
among the clans
of Judah,
out of you will
come for me
one who will be ruler
over Israel."

7 The remnant of Jacob will be
in the midst of many peoples
like dew from the LORD,
like showers on the grass,
which do not wait for man
or linger for mankind.
8 The remnant of Jacob will be among the
nations,
in the midst of many peoples,
like a lion among the
beasts of the forest,
like a young lion among
flocks of sheep,
which mauls and mangles
as it goes,
and no one can rescue.
9 Your hand will be lifted
up in triumph over
your enemies,
and all your foes will be
destroyed.

10 "In that day," declares the
LORD,

"I will destroy your horses
from among you
and demolish your
chariots.
11 I will destroy the cities of
your land
and tear down all your strongholds.
12 I will destroy your witchcraft
and you will no longer cast spells.
13 I will destroy your carved images
and your sacred stones from among you;
you will no longer bow down
to the work of your hands.
14 I will uproot from among you your
Asherah poles[g]
and demolish your cities.
15 I will take vengeance in anger and wrath
upon the nations that have not obeyed
me."

The LORD's Case Against Israel

6 Listen to what the LORD says:

"Stand up, plead your case before the
mountains;

[a]1 Or *Strengthen your walls, O walled city* [b]2 Or *rulers* [c]2 Hebrew *goings out* [d]2 Or *from days of eternity* [e]6 Or *crush* [f]6 Or *Nimrod in its gates* [g]14 That is, symbols of the goddess Asherah

let the hills hear what you have to say.
2 Hear, O mountains, the LORD's accusation;
listen, you everlasting foundations of the earth.
For the LORD has a case against his people;
he is lodging a charge against Israel.

3 "My people, what have I done to you?
How have I burdened you? Answer me.
4 I brought you up out of Egypt
and redeemed you from the land of slavery.
I sent Moses to lead you,
also Aaron and Miriam.
5 My people, remember
what Balak king of Moab counseled
and what Balaam son of Beor answered.
Remember ⌞your journey⌟ from Shittim to Gilgal,
that you may know the righteous acts of the LORD."

6 With what shall I come before the LORD
and bow down before the exalted God?
Shall I come before him with burnt offerings,
with calves a year old?
7 Will the LORD be pleased
with thousands of rams,
with ten thousand rivers of oil?
Shall I offer my firstborn for my transgression,
the fruit of my body for the sin of my soul?
8 He has showed you, O man,
what is good.
And what does the LORD
require of you?
To act justly and to love mercy
and to walk humbly with your God.

Micah 6:8

God Requires Humility

He has showed you,
O man, what is good.
And what does the LORD
require of you?
To act justly and to
love mercy
and to walk humbly
with your God.

Israel's Guilt and Punishment

9 Listen! The LORD is calling to the city—
and to fear your name is wisdom—
"Heed the rod and the One who appointed it.[a]
10 Am I still to forget, O wicked house,
your ill-gotten treasures
and the short ephah,[b] which is accursed?
11 Shall I acquit a man with dishonest scales,
with a bag of false weights?
12 Her rich men are violent;
her people are liars
and their tongues speak deceitfully.
13 Therefore, I have begun to destroy you,
to ruin you because of your sins.
14 You will eat but not be satisfied;
your stomach will still be empty.[c]
You will store up but save nothing,
because what you save I will give to the sword.
15 You will plant but not harvest;
you will press olives but not use the oil on yourselves,
you will crush grapes but not drink the wine.
16 You have observed the statutes of Omri
and all the practices of Ahab's house,
and you have followed their traditions.
Therefore I will give you over to ruin
and your people to derision;
you will bear the scorn of the nations.[d]"

Israel's Misery

7 What misery is mine!
I am like one who gathers summer fruit
at the gleaning of the vineyard;
there is no cluster of grapes to eat,
none of the early figs that I crave.
2 The godly have been swept from the land;
not one upright man remains.
All men lie in wait to shed blood;
each hunts his brother with a net.
3 Both hands are skilled in doing evil;

[a]9 The meaning of the Hebrew for this line is uncertain. [b]10 An ephah was a dry measure. [c]14 The meaning of the Hebrew for this word is uncertain. [d]16 Septuagint; Hebrew *scorn due my people*

Walk Humbly

Read: Micah 6:1–9

Micah 6:8

He has showed you, O man, what is good. And what does the LORD require of you? To act justly and to love mercy and to walk humbly with your God.

reflection

1 What are some ways you have tried to sacrifice to God without having an obedient heart?

2 In what concrete way can you extend justice and mercy today?

3 What changes do you need to make so that you fulfill the call to walk humbly with God?

RELATED READINGS

Deuteronomy 11:1; 1 Samuel 15:22–23; Romans 12:1–3

"The pearl of justice is found in the heart of mercy."

Catherine of Siena

PICTURE A COURTROOM. The judge enters the room, his long robe flowing. From your angle, you can't see his face. But when he sits down at the bench, his identity is finally revealed. God is the judge. And his people are on trial.

The charges are as follows: They have turned away from God. They have forgotten his merciful help and deliverance from the past. They have taken his blessings for granted.

What can they do to find favor with God? Is there a sacrifice they can make? What penance is required? The people have tried to pacify him with offerings, large and costly. But Micah reminds us that God sees the heart. He knows these are not genuine, humble expressions of repentance. He sees that the sacrifices are an attempt to replace approaching God honestly.

Look over the list of requirements in today's passage. Do you deal with people and situations in a fair and honest way? Do you extend mercy even when it hurts to do so? Thankfully, what God requires is not a catalog of regulations and sacrifices. Instead, he simply issues a call to live in relationship with him. Day by day.

Attempting to appease God with offerings doesn't work. Like the Israelites, we are so often tempted to go through the motions and "pay God off." Giving tithes, attending church regularly and teaching are all good things, but they cannot take the place of identifying so closely with God that we almost automatically do that which is closest to his heart: *Act justly, love mercy and walk humbly with God.* That's what obedience really is. And obedience, which can sound like a dutiful word, or a grudging business exchange, should be a joyful word. It becomes so when we stop calculating the cost of doing what God commands and instead respond with abandon to the One who loves us.

God sees the motives hidden behind our every word and action. He tells us to come humbly, as children. Stop hedging. Stop making excuses. Just listen and follow. Let him show you who he really is. Above all, love him. Simply love him most of all.

Go to page 1122 for your next devotional reading.

the ruler demands gifts,
the judge accepts bribes,
the powerful dictate what they desire—
they all conspire together.
4 The best of them is like a brier,
the most upright worse than a thorn hedge.
The day of your watchmen has come,
the day God visits you.
Now is the time of their confusion.
5 Do not trust a neighbor;
put no confidence in a friend.
Even with her who lies in your embrace
be careful of your words.
6 For a son dishonors his father,
a daughter rises up against her mother,
a daughter-in-law against her mother-in-law—
a man's enemies are the members of his own household.

7 But as for me, I watch in hope for the LORD,
I wait for God my Savior;
my God will hear me.

Israel Will Rise

8 Do not gloat over me, my enemy!
Though I have fallen, I will rise.
Though I sit in darkness,
the LORD will be my light.
9 Because I have sinned against him,
I will bear the LORD's wrath,
until he pleads my case
and establishes my right.
He will bring me out into the light;
I will see his righteousness.
10 Then my enemy will see it
and will be covered with shame,
she who said to me,
"Where is the LORD your God?"
My eyes will see her downfall;
even now she will be trampled underfoot
like mire in the streets.

11 The day for building your walls will come,
the day for extending your boundaries.
12 In that day people will come to you
from Assyria and the cities of Egypt,
even from Egypt to the Euphrates
and from sea to sea
and from mountain to mountain.
13 The earth will become desolate because of its inhabitants,
as the result of their deeds.

Prayer and Praise

14 Shepherd your people with your staff,
the flock of your inheritance,
which lives by itself in a forest,
in fertile pasturelands.[a]
Let them feed in Bashan and Gilead
as in days long ago.

15 "As in the days when you came out of Egypt,
I will show them my wonders."

16 Nations will see and be ashamed,
deprived of all their power.
They will lay their hands on their mouths
and their ears will become deaf.
17 They will lick dust like a snake,
like creatures that crawl on the ground.
They will come trembling out of their dens;
they will turn in fear to the LORD our God
and will be afraid of you.
18 Who is a God like you,
who pardons sin and forgives the transgression
of the remnant of his inheritance?
You do not stay angry forever
but delight to show mercy.
19 You will again have compassion on us;
you will tread our sins underfoot
and hurl all our iniquities into the depths of the sea.
20 You will be true to Jacob,
and show mercy to Abraham,
as you pledged on oath to our fathers
in days long ago.

Micah 7:18

God Pardons Sins

Who is a God like you,
who pardons sin
and forgives the
transgression?

[a]14 Or *in the middle of Carmel*

Nahum

Author:
Nahum.

Audience:
The residents of Nineveh and Judah.

Date:
Likely written shortly before the fall of Nineveh in 612 B.C.

Setting:
Assyria had just conquered the Egyptian city of Thebes in 663 B.C., and Judah seemed to be next. However, Assyria would fall in 612 B.C.

Verse to Remember:
The LORD has given a command concerning you, Nineveh: "You will have no descendants to bear your name. I will destroy the carved images and cast idols that are in the temple of your gods. I will prepare your grave, for you are vile." (1:14)

The people of Nineveh had had their chance.

A little over one hundred years earlier, the people of Nineveh had been warned by the reluctant prophet Jonah about impending judgment. The people repented and turned from their evil ways. Now, however, those who had heeded God's call to repentance had failed to pass on their fear of the Lord to their descendants. And so the wicked capital city of Assyria had returned to its vile, violent ways.

God speaks hotly of the residents of Nineveh—they are his enemies, his foes. They want to destroy God's people, Judah, *but God will destroy them.* Nineveh was a "city of blood, full of lies, full of plunder, never without victims" (Nahum 3:1). Now the violence was coming to them instead, and they would be utterly ruined. *God would break their pride.* Their destruction would cause the neighboring nations to rejoice. God will not let evil go unpunished. He will deal with it in his time.

1 An oracle concerning Nineveh. The book of the vision of Nahum the Elkoshite.

The LORD's Anger Against Nineveh

2 The LORD is a jealous and avenging God;
the LORD takes vengeance and is filled with wrath.
The LORD takes vengeance on his foes
and maintains his wrath against his enemies.
3 The LORD is slow to anger and great in power;
the LORD will not leave the guilty unpunished.
His way is in the whirlwind and the storm,
and clouds are the dust of his feet.
4 He rebukes the sea and dries it up;
he makes all the rivers run dry.
Bashan and Carmel wither
and the blossoms of Lebanon fade.
5 The mountains quake before him
and the hills melt away.
The earth trembles at his presence,
the world and all who live in it.
6 Who can withstand his indignation?
Who can endure his fierce anger?
His wrath is poured out like fire;
the rocks are shattered before him.

7 The LORD is good,
a refuge in times of trouble.
He cares for those who trust in him,
8 but with an overwhelming flood
he will make an end of ⌊Nineveh⌋;
he will pursue his foes into darkness.

9 Whatever they plot against the LORD
he[a] will bring to an end;
trouble will not come a second time.
10 They will be entangled among thorns
and drunk from their wine;
they will be consumed like dry stubble.[b]
11 From you, ⌊O Nineveh,⌋ has one come forth
who plots evil against the LORD
and counsels wickedness.

12 This is what the LORD says:

"Although they have allies and are numerous,
they will be cut off and pass away.
Although I have afflicted you, ⌊O Judah,⌋
I will afflict you no more.
13 Now I will break their yoke from your neck
and tear your shackles away."

14 The LORD has given a command concerning you, ⌊Nineveh⌋:
"You will have no descendants to bear your name.
I will destroy the carved images and cast idols
that are in the temple of your gods.
I will prepare your grave,
for you are vile."

15 Look, there on the mountains,
the feet of one who brings good news,
who proclaims peace!
Celebrate your festivals, O Judah,
and fulfill your vows.
No more will the wicked invade you;
they will be completely destroyed.

Nahum 1:7

God Is a Refuge

The LORD is good,
a refuge in times
of trouble.
He cares for those who
trust in him.

Nineveh to Fall

2 An attacker advances against you, ⌊Nineveh⌋.
Guard the fortress,
watch the road,
brace yourselves,
marshal all your strength!

2 The LORD will restore the splendor of Jacob
like the splendor of Israel,
though destroyers have laid them waste
and have ruined their vines.

3 The shields of his soldiers are red;
the warriors are clad in scarlet.

[a]9 Or *What do you foes plot against the LORD? / He* [b]10 The meaning of the Hebrew for this verse is uncertain.

Bullies

Read: Nahum 1:1–15

Nahum 1:3

The LORD is slow to anger and great in power; the LORD will not leave the guilty unpunished. His way is in the whirlwind and the storm, and clouds are the dust of his feet.

EVERY SCHOOLYARD HAS THEM. They're the nemesis of every 43-pound weakling and pig-tailed girl with lunch money. They are the menaces of the playground. It seems they never get caught—and there are very few who can or will stand up to them.

At this time in history, the biggest bullies on Israel's block were the Assyrians. The Ninevites, who lived in the capital city of Assyria, were vicious and arrogant. Hearing their name made the Israelites cringe and whimper. One hundred years earlier, Jonah had tried to run away from them, and for good reason. Their war crimes were legendary.

And dear Nahum, whose name means, "comfort," brings Israel some good news: The big bully is finally going to get his due. And who will avenge them? God himself. Jonah had demonstrated God's compassion toward the bullies and had given them a chance to change. Now, a century after their short-lived revival, Nahum lets them have it.

Nahum draws a terrifying cosmic portrait of the God who can make short work of any bully, no matter how big and pushy. God is slow to anger; he is not impulsive. But when he has waited with infinite patience for the guilty to change, watch out! The most powerful forces of nature—the whirlwind, the storm, the earthquake and the flood—are but a shadow of God's awesome power; they are his tools, as a hammer is the tool of a worker. The real force is the strength behind the hammer. And this worker, Israel's God, has declared of the bullies, "They will be cut off and pass away" (verse 12).

But Nahum's portrait is a study in contrasts and mystery: God is also "good, a refuge in times of trouble. He cares for those who trust in him" (verse 7). God is both stern *and* kind, just *and* loving.

The world is full of bullies. Maybe they've never looked at Nahum's portrait of God. The sight should strike as much terror in their hearts as looking up into the eye of a whirlwind. But as for you, keep Nahum's portrait in mind the next time you face a bully. God sees injustice and, in his time, will avenge the helpless and the innocent. If Jonah's story reminds us that their day may not be today, then Nahum assures us that their day will certainly come.

reflection

1 Do you have experience with being "bullied"? Describe what it feels like.

2 Describe what it is like to finally have someone stick up for you.

3 Who are the "big bullies" in your present circumstances? Ask God to deal with them and be your "refuge in times of trouble."

RELATED READINGS

Psalms 62:11–12; 77:14–20; Jonah 1:1–3; Nahum 3:1–3,10

Go to page 1127 for your next devotional reading.

The metal on the chariots flashes
on the day they are made ready;
the spears of pine are brandished.[a]
4 The chariots storm through the streets,
rushing back and forth through the squares.
They look like flaming torches;
they dart about like lightning.

5 He summons his picked troops,
yet they stumble on their way.
They dash to the city wall;
the protective shield is put in place.
6 The river gates are thrown open
and the palace collapses.
7 It is decreed[b] that ⌊the city⌋
be exiled and carried away.
Its slave girls moan like doves
and beat upon their breasts.
8 Nineveh is like a pool,
and its water is draining away.
"Stop! Stop!" they cry,
but no one turns back.
9 Plunder the silver!
Plunder the gold!
The supply is endless,
the wealth from all its treasures!
10 She is pillaged, plundered, stripped!
Hearts melt, knees give way,
bodies tremble, every face grows pale.

11 Where now is the lions' den,
the place where they fed their young,
where the lion and lioness went,
and the cubs, with nothing to fear?
12 The lion killed enough for his cubs
and strangled the prey for his mate,
filling his lairs with the kill
and his dens with the prey.

13 "I am against you,"
declares the LORD Almighty.
"I will burn up your chariots in smoke,
and the sword will devour your young lions.
I will leave you no prey on the earth.
The voices of your messengers
will no longer be heard."

Woe to Nineveh

3 Woe to the city of blood,
full of lies,
full of plunder,
never without victims!
2 The crack of whips,
the clatter of wheels,
galloping horses
and jolting chariots!
3 Charging cavalry,
flashing swords
and glittering spears!
Many casualties,
piles of dead,
bodies without number,
people stumbling over the corpses—
4 all because of the wanton lust of a harlot,
alluring, the mistress of sorceries,
who enslaved nations by her prostitution
and peoples by her witchcraft.

5 "I am against you," declares the LORD Almighty.
"I will lift your skirts over your face.
I will show the nations your nakedness
and the kingdoms your shame.
6 I will pelt you with filth,
I will treat you with contempt
and make you a spectacle.
7 All who see you will flee from you and say,
'Nineveh is in ruins—who will mourn for her?'
Where can I find anyone to comfort you?"

8 Are you better than Thebes,[c]
situated on the Nile,
with water around her?
The river was her defense,
the waters her wall.
9 Cush[d] and Egypt were her boundless strength;
Put and Libya were among her allies.
10 Yet she was taken captive
and went into exile.
Her infants were dashed to pieces
at the head of every street.
Lots were cast for her nobles,
and all her great men were put in chains.

[a]3 Hebrew; Septuagint and Syriac / *the horsemen rush to and fro* [b]7 The meaning of the Hebrew for this word is uncertain. [c]8 Hebrew *No Amon* [d]9 That is, the upper Nile region

11 You too will become drunk;
you will go into hiding
and seek refuge from the enemy.

12 All your fortresses are like fig trees
with their first ripe fruit;
when they are shaken,
the figs fall into the mouth of the eater.
13 Look at your troops—
they are all women!
The gates of your land
are wide open to your enemies;
fire has consumed their bars.

14 Draw water for the siege,
strengthen your defenses!
Work the clay,
tread the mortar,
repair the brickwork!
15 There the fire will devour you;
the sword will cut you down
and, like grasshoppers, consume you.
Multiply like grasshoppers,
multiply like locusts!

16 You have increased the number of your
merchants
till they are more than the stars of the
sky,
but like locusts they strip the land
and then fly away.
17 Your guards are like locusts,
your officials like swarms of locusts
that settle in the walls on a cold day—
but when the sun appears they fly away,
and no one knows where.

18 O king of Assyria, your shepherds[a]
slumber;
your nobles lie down to rest.
Your people are scattered on the mountains
with no one to gather them.
19 Nothing can heal your wound;
your injury is fatal.
Everyone who hears the news about you
claps his hands at your fall,
for who has not felt
your endless cruelty?

[a] 18 Or *rulers*

Habakkuk

While most prophets delivered a message from God to his people, *the book of Habakkuk is a conversation* between God and the prophet himself. During his lifetime, Habakkuk not only experienced the prosperity and promise of spiritual renewal in Judah, but he also witnessed its decline. The conversation recorded in his book was not delivered directly to Israel but instead was about Israel and its impending destruction by the violent Babylonians.

Habakkuk addresses two main questions to God: How can you let such evil run rampant in the land? How can you use such godless people as the Babylonians to exact judgment? God did not answer all of Habakkuk's questions, but he did assure Habakkuk that *he was in control and would triumph in the end.* In conclusion, Habakkuk made a decision. In so many words, he said, *"God, you are awesome.* I will praise you no matter what. You are my strength."

Author:
Habakkuk.

Audience:
The southern kingdom of Judah and all of God's people.

Date:
About 605 B.C.

Setting:
Babylon was about to destroy Judah.

Verse to Remember:
LORD, I have heard of your fame; I stand in awe of your deeds, O LORD. Renew them in our day, in our time make them known; in wrath remember mercy. (3:2)

1 The oracle that Habakkuk the prophet received.

Habakkuk's Complaint

2 How long, O LORD, must I call for help,
but you do not listen?
Or cry out to you, "Violence!"
but you do not save?
3 Why do you make me look at injustice?
Why do you tolerate wrong?
Destruction and violence are before me;
there is strife, and conflict abounds.
4 Therefore the law is paralyzed,
and justice never prevails.
The wicked hem in the righteous,
so that justice is perverted.

The LORD's Answer

5 "Look at the nations and watch—
and be utterly amazed.
For I am going to do something in your days
that you would not believe,
even if you were told.
6 I am raising up the Babylonians,[a]
that ruthless and impetuous people,
who sweep across the whole earth
to seize dwelling places not their own.
7 They are a feared and dreaded people;
they are a law to themselves
and promote their own honor.
8 Their horses are swifter than leopards,
fiercer than wolves at dusk.
Their cavalry gallops headlong;
their horsemen come from afar.
They fly like a vulture swooping to devour;
9 they all come bent on violence.
Their hordes[b] advance like a desert wind
and gather prisoners like sand.
10 They deride kings
and scoff at rulers.
They laugh at all fortified cities;
they build earthen ramps and capture them.
11 Then they sweep past like the wind and go on—
guilty men, whose own strength is their god."

Habakkuk's Second Complaint

12 O LORD, are you not from everlasting?
My God, my Holy One, we will not die.
O LORD, you have appointed them to execute judgment;
O Rock, you have ordained them to punish.
13 Your eyes are too pure to look on evil;
you cannot tolerate wrong.
Why then do you tolerate the treacherous?
Why are you silent while the wicked
swallow up those more righteous than themselves?
14 You have made men like fish in the sea,
like sea creatures that have no ruler.
15 The wicked foe pulls all of them up with hooks,
he catches them in his net,
he gathers them up in his dragnet;
and so he rejoices and is glad.
16 Therefore he sacrifices to his net
and burns incense to his dragnet,
for by his net he lives in luxury
and enjoys the choicest food.
17 Is he to keep on emptying his net,
destroying nations without mercy?

2 I will stand at my watch
and station myself on the ramparts;
I will look to see what he will say to me,
and what answer I am to give to this complaint.[c]

The LORD's Answer

2 Then the LORD replied:

"Write down the revelation
and make it plain on tablets
so that a herald[d] may run with it.
3 For the revelation awaits an appointed time;
it speaks of the end
and will not prove false.
Though it linger, wait for it;
it[e] will certainly come and will not delay.

4 "See, he is puffed up;
his desires are not upright—
but the righteous will live by his faith[f]—
5 indeed, wine betrays him;
he is arrogant and never at rest.

Habakkuk 1:5

God Will Amaze

"Look at the nations
and watch—
and be utterly amazed.
For I am going to do
something in your days
that you would
not believe,
even if you were told."

a6 Or *Chaldeans* b9 The meaning of the Hebrew for this word is uncertain. c1 Or *and what to answer when I am rebuked* d2 Or *so that whoever reads it* e3 Or *Though he linger, wait for him; / he* f4 Or *faithfulness*

Deep Waters

SAMARITAN WOMAN

SHE WAS NOT USED TO THIS KIND of male attention. Usually, men were interested in her for what they could get from her: good times and a few laughs—and sex. And then they were gone.

This man was different, she realized.

It was the first time in her life that she ever felt appreciated—not for what she could do but for who she was. This Jewish stranger told her things about her past she'd never told any other person, not even her closest friend. His familiarity startled, but did not frighten, her. It drew her in like the warmth from a fire on a bitterly cold day. He—dare she say it—loved her. He did.

And she knew it from the moment she saw him sitting there by the well.

But he was a Jew and she was a Samaritan. Jews and Samaritans did not associate with each other. When this man asked her for something to drink, he was violating the laws of his people, going against the customs of the time. A Jew would become ceremonially unclean after touching a Samaritan's jar of water. She marveled at his boldness. They weren't supposed to be talking. They weren't supposed to have anything to do with each other. But yet there he sat, talking to her like she was a person. Like she mattered. Like she was someone worth loving. She was amazed at his love.

What she didn't know was that as he drew from the deep and mysterious waters of her own soul, he had also unearthed a reciprocal love for him. She discovered that, in the few moments they shared, he had produced a pool of pure love within her. A love that she'd always longed to give to someone but thought no one would want. Her lovers certainly hadn't wanted it. But here, on a random day in Sychar, she'd finally found someone who did. Rather, that someone had found her.

—Prayer—

Wonderful Savior, thank you for your great love for me. Let your love inspire me to show love to others.

"Sir," the woman said, "you have nothing to draw with and the well is deep. Where can you get this living water?"

John 4:11

ASSIGNED READING:

John 4:1–42

Weekend

Go to page 1133 for your next devotional reading.

Because he is as greedy as the grave[a]
and like death is never satisfied,
he gathers to himself all the nations
and takes captive all the peoples.

6 "Will not all of them taunt him with ridicule and scorn, saying,

" 'Woe to him who piles up stolen goods
and makes himself wealthy by extortion!
How long must this go on?'
7 Will not your debtors[b] suddenly arise?
Will they not wake up and make you tremble?
Then you will become their victim.
8 Because you have plundered many nations,
the peoples who are left will plunder you.
For you have shed man's blood;
you have destroyed lands and cities and everyone in them.

9 "Woe to him who builds his realm by unjust gain
to set his nest on high,
to escape the clutches of ruin!
10 You have plotted the ruin of many peoples,
shaming your own house
and forfeiting your life.
11 The stones of the wall will cry out,
and the beams of the woodwork will echo it.

12 "Woe to him who builds a city with bloodshed
and establishes a town by crime!
13 Has not the LORD Almighty determined
that the people's labor is only fuel for the fire,
that the nations exhaust themselves for nothing?
14 For the earth will be filled with the knowledge of the glory of the LORD,
as the waters cover the sea.

Habakkuk 2:20

God Deserves Respect

"But the LORD is in his holy temple;
let all the earth be silent before him."

15 "Woe to him who gives drink to his neighbors,
pouring it from the wineskin till they are drunk,
so that he can gaze on their naked bodies.
16 You will be filled with shame instead of glory.
Now it is your turn! Drink and be exposed[c]!
The cup from the LORD's right hand is coming around to you,
and disgrace will cover your glory.
17 The violence you have done to Lebanon will overwhelm you,
and your destruction of animals will terrify you.
For you have shed man's blood;
you have destroyed lands and cities and everyone in them.

18 "Of what value is an idol, since a man has carved it?
Or an image that teaches lies?
For he who makes it trusts in his own creation;
he makes idols that cannot speak.
19 Woe to him who says to wood, 'Come to life!'
Or to lifeless stone, 'Wake up!'
Can it give guidance?
It is covered with gold and silver;
there is no breath in it.
20 But the LORD is in his holy temple;
let all the earth be silent before him."

Habakkuk's Prayer

3 A prayer of Habakkuk the prophet. On *shigionoth*.[d]

2 LORD, I have heard of your fame;
I stand in awe of your deeds,
O LORD.
Renew them in our day,

[a] 5 Hebrew *Sheol* [b] 7 Or *creditors* [c] 16 Masoretic Text; Dead Sea Scrolls, Aquila, Vulgate and Syriac (see also Septuagint) *and stagger* [d] 1 Probably a literary or musical term

in our time make them known;
in wrath remember mercy.

3 God came from Teman,
the Holy One from Mount Paran.
Selah[a]
His glory covered the heavens
and his praise filled the earth.
4 His splendor was like the sunrise;
rays flashed from his hand,
where his power was hidden.
5 Plague went before him;
pestilence followed his steps.
6 He stood, and shook the earth;
he looked, and made the nations
tremble.
The ancient mountains crumbled
and the age-old hills collapsed.
His ways are eternal.
7 I saw the tents of Cushan in distress,
the dwellings of Midian in anguish.

8 Were you angry with the rivers, O LORD?
Was your wrath against the streams?
Did you rage against the sea
when you rode with your horses
and your victorious chariots?
9 You uncovered your bow,
you called for many arrows. *Selah*
You split the earth with rivers;
10 the mountains saw you and writhed.
Torrents of water swept by;
the deep roared
and lifted its waves on high.

11 Sun and moon stood still in the heavens
at the glint of your flying arrows,
at the lightning of your flashing spear.
12 In wrath you strode through the earth
and in anger you threshed the nations.
13 You came out to deliver your people,
to save your anointed one.
You crushed the leader of the land of
wickedness,
you stripped him from head to foot.
Selah
14 With his own spear you pierced his head
when his warriors stormed out to scatter
us,
gloating as though about to devour
the wretched who were in hiding.
15 You trampled the sea with your horses,
churning the great waters.

16 I heard and my heart pounded,
my lips quivered at the sound;
decay crept into my bones,
and my legs trembled.
Yet I will wait patiently for the day of
calamity
to come on the nation invading us.
17 Though the fig tree does not bud
and there are no grapes on the vines,
though the olive crop fails
and the fields produce no food,
though there are no sheep in the pen
and no cattle in the stalls,
18 yet I will rejoice in the LORD,
I will be joyful in God my Savior.

19 The Sovereign LORD is my strength;
he makes my feet like the feet of a deer,
he enables me to go on the heights.

For the director of music. On my stringed
instruments.

[a] 3 A word of uncertain meaning; possibly a musical term; also in verses 9 and 13

Zephaniah

Author:
Zephaniah.

Audience:
Judah and all nations.

Date:
Likely during the early years of the reign of King Josiah (640–609 B.C.).

Setting:
Zephaniah's prophecy encouraged King Josiah to bring spiritual reform to Judah.

Verse to Remember:
"The LORD your God is with you, he is mighty to save. He will take great delight in you, he will quiet you with his love, he will rejoice over you with singing."
(3:17)

When sin goes unchecked for any length of time, it's easy to grow complacent, to think that God will never do anything about it, that nothing will ever change. *Our tolerance for sin increases over time,* and what once seemed abhorrent becomes acceptable, or at least not worth bothering with.

Zephaniah preached his message during a time when sin and idolatry had become the comfortable norm in Judah. His message was both broad and dire: *Destruction is coming.* God will punish the nations, and Judah and Jerusalem will not be exempt. God will deal with sin. And it will be devastating.

But, Zephaniah said, the devastation will not last forever. One day the shame and disgrace will be lifted. And a quiet season of healing and restoration will begin.

It's easy to skip to the end of the book and read the words of comfort. It's much harder to trudge through the words of judgment. But the order is there for a reason. *First sin must be dealt with.* Then, and only then, is restoration possible.

1 The word of the LORD that came to Zephaniah son of Cushi, the son of Gedaliah, the son of Amariah, the son of Hezekiah, during the reign of Josiah son of Amon king of Judah:

Warning of Coming Destruction

2 "I will sweep away everything
from the face of the earth,"
declares the LORD.
3 "I will sweep away both men and animals;

I will sweep away the birds of the air
and the fish of the sea.
The wicked will have only heaps of rubble[a]
when I cut off man from the face of the earth,"
declares the LORD.

Against Judah

4 "I will stretch out my hand against Judah
and against all who live in Jerusalem.
I will cut off from this place every remnant of Baal,
the names of the pagan and the idolatrous priests—
5 those who bow down on the roofs
to worship the starry host,
those who bow down and swear by the LORD
and who also swear by Molech,[b]
6 those who turn back from following the LORD
and neither seek the LORD nor inquire of him.
7 Be silent before the Sovereign LORD,
for the day of the LORD is near.
The LORD has prepared a sacrifice;
he has consecrated those he has invited.
8 On the day of the LORD's sacrifice
I will punish the princes
and the king's sons
and all those clad
in foreign clothes.
9 On that day I will punish
all who avoid stepping on the threshold,[c]
who fill the temple of their gods
with violence and deceit.
10 "On that day," declares the LORD,
"a cry will go up from the Fish Gate,
wailing from the New Quarter,
and a loud crash from the hills.
11 Wail, you who live in the market district[d];
all your merchants will be wiped out,
all who trade with[e] silver will be ruined.
12 At that time I will search Jerusalem with lamps
and punish those who are complacent,
who are like wine left on its dregs,
who think, 'The LORD will do nothing,
either good or bad.'
13 Their wealth will be plundered,
their houses demolished.
They will build houses
but not live in them;
they will plant vineyards
but not drink the wine.

The Great Day of the LORD

14 "The great day of the LORD is near—
near and coming quickly.
Listen! The cry on the day of the LORD will be bitter,
the shouting of the warrior there.
15 That day will be a day of wrath,
a day of distress and anguish,
a day of trouble and ruin,
a day of darkness and gloom,
a day of clouds and blackness,
16 a day of trumpet and battle cry
against the fortified cities
and against the corner towers.
17 I will bring distress on the people
and they will walk like blind men,
because they have sinned against the LORD.
Their blood will be poured out like dust
and their entrails like filth.
18 Neither their silver nor their gold
will be able to save them
on the day of the LORD's wrath.
In the fire of his jealousy
the whole world will be consumed,
for he will make a sudden end
of all who live in the earth."

2 Gather together, gather together,
O shameful nation,
2 before the appointed time arrives
and that day sweeps on like chaff,
before the fierce anger of the LORD comes upon you,
before the day of the LORD's wrath
comes upon you.
3 Seek the LORD, all you humble of the land,
you who do what he commands.
Seek righteousness, seek humility;
perhaps you will be sheltered
on the day of the LORD's anger.

[a]3 The meaning of the Hebrew for this line is uncertain. [b]5 Hebrew *Malcam*, that is, Milcom [c]9 See 1 Samuel 5:5. [d]11 Or *the Mortar* [e]11 Or *in*

Against Philistia

4 Gaza will be abandoned
and Ashkelon left in ruins.
At midday Ashdod will be emptied
and Ekron uprooted.
5 Woe to you who live by the sea,
O Kerethite people;
the word of the LORD is against you,
O Canaan, land of the Philistines.

"I will destroy you,
and none will be left."

6 The land by the sea, where the Kerethites[a] dwell,
will be a place for shepherds and sheep pens.
7 It will belong to the remnant of the house of Judah;
there they will find pasture.
In the evening they will lie down
in the houses of Ashkelon.
The LORD their God will care for them;
he will restore their fortunes.[b]

Against Moab and Ammon

8 "I have heard the insults of Moab
and the taunts of the Ammonites,
who insulted my people
and made threats against their land.
9 Therefore, as surely as I live,"
declares the LORD Almighty, the God of Israel,
"surely Moab will become like Sodom,
the Ammonites like Gomorrah—
a place of weeds and salt pits,
a wasteland forever.
The remnant of my people will plunder them;
the survivors of my nation will inherit their land."
10 This is what they will get in return for their pride,
for insulting and mocking the people of the LORD Almighty.
11 The LORD will be awesome to them
when he destroys all the gods of the land.
The nations on every shore will worship him,
every one in its own land.

Against Cush

12 "You too, O Cushites,[c]
will be slain by my sword."

Against Assyria

13 He will stretch out his hand against the north
and destroy Assyria,
leaving Nineveh utterly desolate
and dry as the desert.
14 Flocks and herds will lie down there,
creatures of every kind.
The desert owl and the screech owl
will roost on her columns.
Their calls will echo through the windows,
rubble will be in the doorways,
the beams of cedar will be exposed.
15 This is the carefree city
that lived in safety.
She said to herself,
"I am, and there is none besides me."
What a ruin she has become,
a lair for wild beasts!
All who pass by her scoff
and shake their fists.

The Future of Jerusalem

3 Woe to the city of oppressors,
rebellious and defiled!
2 She obeys no one,
she accepts no correction.
She does not trust in the LORD,
she does not draw near to her God.
3 Her officials are roaring lions,
her rulers are evening wolves,
who leave nothing for the morning.
4 Her prophets are arrogant;
they are treacherous men.
Her priests profane the sanctuary
and do violence to the law.
5 The LORD within her is righteous;
he does no wrong.
Morning by morning he dispenses his justice,
and every new day he does not fail,
yet the unrighteous know no shame.
6 "I have cut off nations;
their strongholds are demolished.
I have left their streets deserted,

[a] 6 The meaning of the Hebrew for this word is uncertain. [b] 7 Or *will bring back their captives* [c] 12 That is, people from the upper Nile region

Going Home

Read: Zephaniah 3:14–20

THE TWENTIETH CENTURY was the bloodiest century in history. Amid millions of lives lost to warfare and violent conflict, international homelessness reached its zenith. Ethnic and religious groups on the fringes of society, hated and destroyed by neighbors, did not merely live without four walls and a roof—they literally had no home. *Home* embodies a state of well-being to which many will never return.

Some of the displaced peoples even bear the marks of their nomadic past in their names. With a name that can be translated "wanderer," the *Csángó* trace their ancestry back to the nomadic Asians of the Carpathian Mountains. Straddling the modern Romanian-Moldavian border, the Csángó people have never known what it feels like to be "home."

Many of us can relate to the wandering of the Csángó people. While we may have the physical comforts of a house, we still experience an indefinable, heartsick longing for home. Even women who appear to lead the ideal life—a seemingly perfect family, a good job, honor and respect within the community—can suffer silently from feelings of alienation. It's possible to feel displaced instead of secure in the arms of those we love. At the end of the day, lying in bed, one can be safely home and still feel profoundly *lost*.

In truth, we are all outsiders and wanderers according to God. Imagine what it would mean for a Csángó woman, always the alien, to hear God's promise through Zephaniah: "*I will bring you home.*" Now imagine the hopeful imagery of the joyous homecoming awaiting all of us. We may never experience what it's like to find our home in an earthly sense. But then again, maybe that's just as God intended. That homesick feeling reminds us that we're not yet really home.

Whenever your heart swells with longings for security and rest, remember God's promise to one day bring you safely home to his house, where he has prepared a room for you (see John 14:1–4).

Monday

Zephaniah 3:19–20

"At that time I will deal with all who oppressed you; I will rescue the lame and gather those who have been scattered. I will give them praise and honor in every land where they were put to shame. At that time I will gather you; at that time I will bring you home. I will give you honor and praise among all the peoples of the earth when I restore your fortunes before your very eyes," says the LORD.

reflection

1 Zephaniah describes *home* in terms of gathering the scattered. In what areas of your life do you feel scattered instead of grounded?

2 Why do you think women are vulnerable to feeling emotionally homeless?

3 How does the future promise of home affect your life today?

RELATED READINGS

Psalm 61:1–5;
Micah 4:6–8;
Hebrews 11:8–9;
Revelation 7:9–17

Go to page 1140 for your next devotional reading.

with no one passing through.
Their cities are destroyed;
no one will be left—no one at all.
7 I said to the city,
'Surely you will fear me
and accept correction!'
Then her dwelling would not be cut off,
nor all my punishments come upon her.
But they were still eager
to act corruptly in all they did.
8 Therefore wait for me," declares the LORD,
"for the day I will stand up to testify.[a]
I have decided to assemble the nations,
to gather the kingdoms
and to pour out my wrath
on them—
all my fierce anger.
The whole world will be
consumed
by the fire of my jealous
anger.

9 "Then will I purify the lips
of the peoples,
that all of them may call
on the name of the
LORD
and serve him shoulder
to shoulder.
10 From beyond the rivers of
Cush[b]
my worshipers, my
scattered people,
will bring me offerings.
11 On that day you will not be put to shame
for all the wrongs you have done to me,
because I will remove from this city
those who rejoice in their pride.
Never again will you be haughty
on my holy hill.
12 But I will leave within you
the meek and humble,
who trust in the name of the LORD.
13 The remnant of Israel will do no wrong;
they will speak no lies,
nor will deceit be found in their mouths.
They will eat and lie down
and no one will make them afraid."
14 Sing, O Daughter of Zion;
shout aloud, O Israel!
Be glad and rejoice with all your heart,
O Daughter of Jerusalem!
15 The LORD has taken away your
punishment,
he has turned back your enemy.
The LORD, the King of Israel, is with you;
never again will you fear any harm.
16 On that day they will say to Jerusalem,
"Do not fear, O Zion;
do not let your hands
hang limp.
17 The LORD your God is with
you,
he is mighty to save.
He will take great delight
in you,
he will quiet you with his
love,
he will rejoice over you
with singing."
18 "The sorrows for the
appointed feasts
I will remove from you;
they are a burden and a
reproach to you.[c]
19 At that time I will deal
with all who oppressed
you;
I will rescue the lame
and gather those who have been
scattered.
I will give them praise and honor
in every land where they were put to
shame.
20 At that time I will gather you;
at that time I will bring you home.
I will give you honor and praise
among all the peoples of the earth
when I restore your fortunes[d]
before your very eyes,"
says the LORD.

Zephaniah 3:17

God Rejoices Over Us

"The LORD your
God is with you,
he is mighty to save.
He will take great
delight in you,
he will quiet you
with his love,
he will rejoice over
you with singing."

[a]8 Septuagint and Syriac; Hebrew *will rise up to plunder* [b]10 That is, the upper Nile region [c]18 Or *"I will gather you who mourn for the appointed feasts; / your reproach is a burden to you* [d]20 Or *I bring back your captives*

Haggai

Haggai, the second shortest book in the Old Testament, has one central theme: *What are you waiting for? Build God's house!* Throughout the Old Testament, having a place to worship God was of paramount importance. The Israelites built the tabernacle in the wilderness. Then Solomon built the magnificent temple in Jerusalem, which was destroyed by King Nebuchadnezzar when he conquered the land. In the book of Haggai, the exiled Israelites have returned to Jerusalem. *They start out with good intentions* to rebuild the temple, but their enthusiasm wanes as they face opposition and become distracted with building their own homes. Haggai speaks out, telling the Israelites to put aside their own personal agendas and finish the task set before them. *Make worshiping God a top priority,* he reminds them.

Author:
Haggai.

Audience:
The exiles who returned to Jerusalem.

Date:
520 B.C.

Setting:
The Persian king Cyrus allowed the Jews to return to Jerusalem to rebuild the temple. However, misplaced priorities and local opposition brought work to a halt.

Verse to Remember:
"You expected much, but see, it turned out to be little. What you brought home, I blew away. Why?" declares the LORD Almighty. "Because of my house, which remains a ruin, while each of you is busy with his own house." (1:9)

A Call to Build the House of the LORD

1 In the second year of King Darius, on the
first day of the sixth month, the word of
the LORD came through the prophet Haggai
to Zerubbabel son of Shealtiel, governor of
Judah, and to Joshua[a] son of Jehozadak, the
high priest:
2 This is what the LORD Almighty says:
"These people say, 'The time has not yet come
for the LORD's house to be built.'"

[a]1 A variant of *Jeshua*; here and elsewhere in Haggai

3Then the word of the LORD came through
the prophet Haggai: 4"Is it a time for you yourselves to be living in your paneled houses, while
this house remains a ruin?"
5Now this is what the LORD Almighty says:
"Give careful thought to your ways. 6You have
planted much, but have harvested little. You
eat, but never have enough. You drink, but
never have your fill. You put on clothes, but are
not warm. You earn wages, only to put them in
a purse with holes in it."
7This is what the LORD Almighty says: "Give
careful thought to your ways. 8Go up into the
mountains and bring down timber and build
the house, so that I may take pleasure in it and
be honored," says the LORD. 9"You expected
much, but see, it turned out to be little. What
you brought home, I blew away. Why?" declares the LORD Almighty. "Because of my
house, which remains a ruin, while each of
you is busy with his own house. 10Therefore,
because of you the heavens have withheld their
dew and the earth its crops. 11I called for a
drought on the fields and the mountains, on
the grain, the new wine, the oil and whatever
the ground produces, on men and cattle, and
on the labor of your hands."

12Then Zerubbabel son of
Shealtiel, Joshua son of Jehozadak, the high priest, and the
whole remnant of the people
obeyed the voice of the LORD
their God and the message of
the prophet Haggai, because
the LORD their God had sent
him. And the people feared
the LORD.
13Then Haggai, the LORD's
messenger, gave this message
of the LORD to the people: "I
am with you," declares the
LORD. 14So the LORD stirred up the spirit of Zerubbabel son of Shealtiel, governor of Judah,
and the spirit of Joshua son of Jehozadak, the
high priest, and the spirit of the whole remnant
of the people. They came and began to work
on the house of the LORD Almighty, their God,
15on the twenty-fourth day of the sixth month
in the second year of King Darius.

> **Haggai 1:13**
>
> *God Is With Us*
>
> Then Haggai, the LORD's messenger, gave this message of the LORD to the people: "I am with you," declares the LORD.

The Promised Glory of the New House

2 On the twenty-first day of the seventh
month, the word of the LORD came
through the prophet Haggai: 2"Speak to Zerubbabel son of Shealtiel, governor of Judah, to
Joshua son of Jehozadak, the high priest, and
to the remnant of the people. Ask them, 3'Who
of you is left who saw this house in its former
glory? How does it look to you now? Does it not
seem to you like nothing? 4But now be strong,
O Zerubbabel,' declares the LORD. 'Be strong,
O Joshua son of Jehozadak, the high priest. Be
strong, all you people of the land,' declares the
LORD, 'and work. For I am with you,' declares
the LORD Almighty. 5'This is what I covenanted
with you when you came out of Egypt. And my
Spirit remains among you. Do not fear.'
6"This is what the LORD Almighty says: 'In
a little while I will once more shake the heavens and the earth, the sea and the dry land. 7I
will shake all nations, and the desired of all nations will come, and I will fill this house with
glory,' says the LORD Almighty. 8'The silver is
mine and the gold is mine,' declares the LORD
Almighty. 9'The glory of this present house will
be greater than the glory of the former house,'
says the LORD Almighty. 'And
in this place I will grant peace,'
declares the LORD Almighty."

Blessings for a Defiled People

10On the twenty-fourth day
of the ninth month, in the second year of Darius, the word of
the LORD came to the prophet
Haggai: 11"This is what the
LORD Almighty says: 'Ask the
priests what the law says: 12If
a person carries consecrated
meat in the fold of his garment,
and that fold touches some
bread or stew, some wine, oil or other food,
does it become consecrated?'"
The priests answered, "No."
13Then Haggai said, "If a person defiled by
contact with a dead body touches one of these
things, does it become defiled?"
"Yes," the priests replied, "it becomes defiled."

14 Then Haggai said, " 'So it is with this people and this nation in my sight,' declares the
LORD. 'Whatever they do and whatever they
offer there is defiled.

15 " 'Now give careful thought to this from
this day on[a]—consider how things were before
one stone was laid on another in the LORD's temple. 16 When anyone came to a heap of twenty
measures, there were only ten. When anyone
went to a wine vat to draw fifty measures, there
were only twenty. 17 I struck all the work of
your hands with blight, mildew and hail, yet
you did not turn to me,' declares the LORD.
18 'From this day on, from this twenty-fourth
day of the ninth month, give careful thought to
the day when the foundation of the LORD's temple was laid. Give careful thought: 19 Is there yet
any seed left in the barn? Until now, the vine
and the fig tree, the pomegranate and the olive
tree have not borne fruit.

" 'From this day on I will bless you.' "

Zerubbabel the LORD's Signet Ring

20 The word of the LORD came to Haggai a
second time on the twenty-fourth day of the
month: 21 "Tell Zerubbabel governor of Judah
that I will shake the heavens and the earth.
22 I will overturn royal thrones and shatter
the power of the foreign kingdoms. I will overthrow chariots and their drivers; horses and
their riders will fall, each by the sword of his
brother.

23 " 'On that day,' declares the LORD Almighty,
'I will take you, my servant Zerubbabel son of
Shealtiel,' declares the LORD, 'and I will make
you like my signet ring, for I have chosen you,'
declares the LORD Almighty."

[a] 15 Or *to the days past*

Zechariah

Author:
Zechariah.

Audience:
The exiles who returned to Jerusalem.

Date:
Between about 520 and 480 B.C.

Setting:
Zechariah, like Haggai, encouraged the exiles who had returned to Jerusalem from Babylon to complete the rebuilding of the temple.

Verse to Remember:
Therefore tell the people: This is what the LORD Almighty says: "Return to me," declares the LORD Almighty, "and I will return to you," says the LORD Almighty. (1:3)

God's anger against his people will not last forever. At the end of the 70 years of Judah's captivity, *God sent messages of mercy to his people.* It was time to return and rebuild. The temple would be built again, and God would once again dwell among his people and make them prosper. In addition, God himself would judge their enemies. A series of *visions in Zechariah tell of cleansing and renewal*—of restored hope. The vision of the priest with filthy garments, reclothed by God in glistening, pure clothes, is a fitting image of the restoration of the people. And Zechariah's prophecies about the Messiah offered hope and inspiration to the people.

A Call to Return to the LORD

1 In the eighth month of the second year
of Darius, the word of the LORD came to
the prophet Zechariah son of Berekiah, the son
of Iddo:
2"The LORD was very angry with your forefathers. 3Therefore tell the people: This is what
the LORD Almighty says: 'Return to me,' declares the LORD Almighty, 'and I will return to
you,' says the LORD Almighty. 4Do not be like
your forefathers, to whom the earlier prophets
proclaimed: This is what the LORD Almighty
says: 'Turn from your evil ways and your evil
practices.' But they would not listen or pay attention to me, declares the LORD. 5Where are
your forefathers now? And the prophets, do

they live forever? 6But did not my words and
my decrees, which I commanded my servants
the prophets, overtake your forefathers?
"Then they repented and said, 'The LORD Almighty has done to us what our
ways and practices deserve, just
as he determined to do.'"

The Man Among the Myrtle Trees

7On the twenty-fourth day
of the eleventh month, the
month of Shebat, in the second year of Darius, the word of
the LORD came to the prophet
Zechariah son of Berekiah, the
son of Iddo.
8During the night I had a
vision—and there before me
was a man riding a red horse!
He was standing among the
myrtle trees in a ravine. Behind him were red, brown and
white horses.
9I asked, "What are these, my lord?"
The angel who was talking with me answered, "I will show you what they are."
10Then the man standing among the myrtle
trees explained, "They are the ones the LORD
has sent to go throughout the earth."
11And they reported to the angel of the
LORD, who was standing among the myrtle
trees, "We have gone throughout the earth and
found the whole world at rest and in peace."
12Then the angel of the LORD said, "LORD
Almighty, how long will you withhold mercy
from Jerusalem and from the towns of Judah,
which you have been angry with these seventy
years?" 13So the LORD spoke kind and comforting words to the angel who talked with me.
14Then the angel who was speaking to me
said, "Proclaim this word: This is what the
LORD Almighty says: 'I am very jealous for Jerusalem and Zion, 15but I am very angry with
the nations that feel secure. I was only a little
angry, but they added to the calamity.'
16"Therefore, this is what the LORD says: 'I
will return to Jerusalem with mercy, and there
my house will be rebuilt. And the measuring
line will be stretched out over Jerusalem,' declares the LORD Almighty.
17"Proclaim further: This is what the LORD
Almighty says: 'My towns will again overflow
with prosperity, and the LORD will again comfort Zion and choose Jerusalem.'"

> **Zechariah 1:3**
>
> *God Calls Wayward People*
>
> "Therefore tell the people: This is what the LORD Almighty says: 'Return to me,' declares the LORD Almighty, 'and I will return to you,' says the LORD Almighty."

Four Horns and Four Craftsmen

18Then I looked up—and
there before me were four
horns! 19I asked the angel who
was speaking to me, "What are
these?"
He answered me, "These are
the horns that scattered Judah,
Israel and Jerusalem."
20Then the LORD showed
me four craftsmen. 21I asked,
"What are these coming to
do?"
He answered, "These are
the horns that scattered Judah
so that no one could raise his
head, but the craftsmen have
come to terrify them and throw
down these horns of the nations who lifted up
their horns against the land of Judah to scatter
its people."

A Man With a Measuring Line

2 Then I looked up—and there before me
was a man with a measuring line in his
hand! 2I asked, "Where are you going?"
He answered me, "To measure Jerusalem, to
find out how wide and how long it is."
3Then the angel who was speaking to me
left, and another angel came to meet him 4and
said to him: "Run, tell that young man, 'Jerusalem will be a city without walls because of the
great number of men and livestock in it. 5And
I myself will be a wall of fire around it,' declares
the LORD, 'and I will be its glory within.'
6"Come! Come! Flee from the land of the
north," declares the LORD, "for I have scattered
you to the four winds of heaven," declares
the LORD.
7"Come, O Zion! Escape, you who live in
the Daughter of Babylon!" 8For this is what
the LORD Almighty says: "After he has honored me and has sent me against the nations
that have plundered you—for whoever touches
you touches the apple of his eye— 9I will surely

Blessed Are the Desperate

Read: Zechariah 1:1–21

I'M A COLORFUL SINNER, and I've fallen woefully short of God's glory. I'm desperate for divine help. We all are.

C.S. Lewis paints a vivid description of how we humans seem to desecrate every good thing God does for us. In his book *Letters to Malcolm*, Lewis writes, "We poison the wine as He decants it into us; murder a melody He would play with us as the instrument. We caricature the self-portrait He would paint. Hence all sin, whatever else it is, is a sacrilege . . ."

Maybe you expect rejection from a perfect God because of your less-than-perfect past. Or maybe you're spiritually crippled by a sin that seems unforgivable. But the good news of the gospel is that our heavenly Father loves us with an everlasting love . . .

We need to acknowledge the fact that we're crippled—that there is nothing righteous in us, that we are desperate for His mercy. And when the Spirit prompts us to recognize our need for salvation, God provides a Savior through the sacrifice of His only son, Jesus, who rescues us from barren places and gives us a seat next to Him at the Lord's banquet table.

Because of God's mercy, our stained hearts have been bleached by the blood of the Lamb. The God who spoke the universe into existence, who breathed life into Adam, who stretched out the heavens and the necks of giraffes, has looked down, taken our hand in His, and said, "Yep, she's Mine." Even though we're crippled, we have been royally adopted by the King of Kings and Lord of Lords. We are listed as His next of Kin. Our names are written on His hands and in His book of life. His love for us is based on His character, not our performance. And it is greater than we could ever hope for or imagine.

> He himself bore our sins in his body on the tree, so that we might die to sins and live for righteousness; by his wounds you have been healed. (1 Peter 2:24)

Blessed are the desperate.

—Lisa Harper

Tuesday

Zechariah 1:4–6

"Do not be like your forefathers, to whom the earlier prophets proclaimed: This is what the LORD Almighty says: 'Turn from your evil ways and your evil practices.' But they would not listen or pay attention to me, declares the LORD . . . But did not my words and my decrees, which I commanded my servants the prophets, overtake your forefathers?"

reflection

1 Describe a time when you felt desperate for God's mercy. How did God rescue you from the barren place?

2 When did you know that you belonged to God? How does knowing that your name is written on his hand and in his book of life comfort you?

3 In today's passage, the Lord spoke of those who would not listen to him. Do you know people like that? Spend time praying that they will begin to hear God's voice and turn or return to his Son.

RELATED READINGS

Isaiah 55:6–13;
Malachi 3:6–7;
1 Peter 2:22–24

Go to page 1142 for your next devotional reading.

raise my hand against them so that their slaves
will plunder them.[a] Then you will know that
the LORD Almighty has sent me.
10“Shout and be glad, O Daughter of Zion.
For I am coming, and I will live among you,”
declares the LORD. 11“Many nations will be
joined with the LORD in that day and will become my people. I will live among you and you
will know that the LORD Almighty has sent me
to you. 12The LORD will inherit Judah as his
portion in the holy land and will again choose
Jerusalem. 13Be still before the LORD, all mankind, because he has roused himself from his
holy dwelling.”

Clean Garments for the High Priest

3 Then he showed me Joshua[b] the high
priest standing before the angel of the
LORD, and Satan[c] standing at his right side
to accuse him. 2The LORD said to Satan, “The
LORD rebuke you, Satan! The LORD, who has
chosen Jerusalem, rebuke you!
Is not this man a burning stick
snatched from the fire?”
3Now Joshua was dressed
in filthy clothes as he stood
before the angel. 4The angel
said to those who were standing before him, “Take off his
filthy clothes.”
Then he said to Joshua, “See,
I have taken away your sin,
and I will put rich garments on
you.”
5Then I said, “Put a clean
turban on his head.” So they
put a clean turban on his head
and clothed him, while the angel of the LORD
stood by.
6The angel of the LORD gave this charge
to Joshua: 7“This is what the LORD Almighty
says: ‘If you will walk in my ways and keep my
requirements, then you will govern my house
and have charge of my courts, and I will give
you a place among these standing here.
8“ ‘Listen, O high priest Joshua and your associates seated before you, who are men symbolic
of things to come: I am going to bring my servant, the Branch. 9See, the stone I have set in
front of Joshua! There are seven eyes[d] on that
one stone, and I will engrave an inscription on
it,’ says the LORD Almighty, ‘and I will remove
the sin of this land in a single day.
10“ ‘In that day each of you will invite his
neighbor to sit under his vine and fig tree,’ declares the LORD Almighty.”

The Gold Lampstand and the Two Olive Trees

4 Then the angel who talked with me returned and wakened me, as a man is wakened from his sleep. 2He asked me, “What do
you see?”
I answered, “I see a solid gold lampstand
with a bowl at the top and seven lights on it,
with seven channels to the lights. 3Also there
are two olive trees by it, one on the right of the
bowl and the other on its left.”
4I asked the angel who talked with me,
“What are these, my lord?”
5He answered, “Do you not
know what these are?”
“No, my lord,” I replied.
6So he said to me, “This is
the word of the LORD to Zerubbabel: ‘Not by might nor by
power, but by my Spirit,’ says
the LORD Almighty.
7“What[e] are you, O mighty
mountain? Before Zerubbabel
you will become level ground.
Then he will bring out the capstone to shouts of ‘God bless it!
God bless it!’ ”
8Then the word of the LORD
came to me: 9“The hands of Zerubbabel have laid the foundation of this temple; his hands will also complete it. Then you
will know that the LORD Almighty has sent me
to you.
10“Who despises the day of small things?
Men will rejoice when they see the plumb line
in the hand of Zerubbabel.
“(These seven are the eyes of the LORD,
which range throughout the earth.)”
11Then I asked the angel, “What are these
two olive trees on the right and the left of the
lampstand?”

Zechariah 4:6

God Is Spirit

So he said to me, “This is the word of the LORD to Zerubbabel: ‘Not by might nor by power, but by my Spirit,’ says the LORD Almighty.”

[a] 8,9 Or *says after … eye:* 9 *“I … plunder them.”* [b] 1 A variant of *Jeshua*; here and elsewhere in Zechariah [c] 1 *Satan* means *accuser.*
[d] 9 Or *facets* [e] 7 Or *Who*

The Garments of Forgiveness

Read: Zechariah 3:1–10

Zechariah 3:3–4

Now Joshua was dressed in filthy clothes as he stood before the angel. The angel said to those who were standing before him, "Take off his filthy clothes." Then he said to Joshua, "See, I have taken away your sin, and I will put rich garments on you."

THERE'S NOTHING LIKE RETAIL THERAPY. Although not for everyone, a day spent perusing the latest fashions can do wonders for a litany of woes—at least temporarily. However much we like shopping for the new, in many ways we enjoy the old: the comfort of a ratty sweatshirt, the security of tradition, the familiarity of a well-traveled path.

Our sinful nature looks a lot like the comfort of a worn, old sweatshirt; it's familiar, well-fitted, and after a while we don't notice the rips and smudges. God, however, knows our desperate need for new clothes—not the materialistic, worldly kind; rather, the heavenly, eternal kind hemmed in heaven.

Our past mistakes and wrongs are like Joshua's dirty garments; they're stinky, stained and in need of a makeover. Zechariah's vision shows that instead of merely washing Joshua's clothing, God gives him an entire new outfit. That's retail therapy at its best.

Zechariah 3 reveals God's desire to remove Joshua's garments of sin and shame and to replace them—permanently. The new robes are perfectly pure, symbolizing cleansing and forgiveness. How strange it would be if Joshua refused the gift, only to cling to his filthy clothes. In this sense, rejecting God's forgiveness makes as much sense as a woman turning down a free shopping spree. And yet it happens every day. Rather than accepting God's gift of forgiveness, many individuals choose the familiarity of guilt and the comfort of self-condemnation.

God offers forgiveness to us free of charge. It's free because Jesus already paid the bill on the cross; Jesus' resurrection gives incalculable value to the robes of forgiveness. If he had not defeated death, the new clothes he offers would only be temporary. Because he lives, they will never fade or wear out.

Don't settle for grungy, old rags. Hand your "wardrobe" over, so God can give you a whole new look.

reflection

1. What often holds women back from fully accepting God's forgiveness?
2. Why do we grow comfortable in the grungy clothes of sinful habits and patterns?
3. How would you look wearing God's beautiful garments of forgiveness?

RELATED READINGS

Psalms 51:2–7; 130:3–4; Isaiah 1:18; Jeremiah 33:6–8; Revelation 7:9–14

Wednesday

Go to page 1145 for your next devotional reading.

12 Again I asked him, "What are these two
olive branches beside the two gold pipes that
pour out golden oil?"
13 He replied, "Do you not know what these
are?"
"No, my lord," I said.
14 So he said, "These are the two who are
anointed to[a] serve the Lord of all the earth."

The Flying Scroll

5 I looked again—and there before me was
a flying scroll!
2 He asked me, "What do you see?"
I answered, "I see a flying scroll, thirty feet
long and fifteen feet wide.[b]"
3 And he said to me, "This is the curse that
is going out over the whole land; for according to what it says on one side, every thief will
be banished, and according to what it says on
the other, everyone who swears falsely will be
banished. 4 The LORD Almighty declares, 'I will
send it out, and it will enter the house of the
thief and the house of him who swears falsely
by my name. It will remain in his house and destroy it, both its timbers and its stones.' "

The Woman in a Basket

5 Then the angel who was speaking to me
came forward and said to me, "Look up and
see what this is that is appearing."
6 I asked, "What is it?"
He replied, "It is a measuring basket.[c]" And
he added, "This is the iniquity[d] of the people
throughout the land."
7 Then the cover of lead was raised, and there
in the basket sat a woman! 8 He said, "This is
wickedness," and he pushed her back into the
basket and pushed the lead cover down over
its mouth.
9 Then I looked up—and there before me
were two women, with the wind in their wings!
They had wings like those of a stork, and they
lifted up the basket between heaven and earth.
10 "Where are they taking the basket?" I
asked the angel who was speaking to me.
11 He replied, "To the country of Babylonia[e]
to build a house for it. When it is ready, the basket will be set there in its place."

Four Chariots

6 I looked up again—and there before me
were four chariots coming out from between two mountains—mountains of bronze!
2 The first chariot had red horses, the second
black, 3 the third white, and the fourth dappled—all of them powerful. 4 I asked the angel who was speaking to me, "What are these,
my lord?"
5 The angel answered me, "These are the four
spirits[f] of heaven, going out from standing in
the presence of the Lord of the whole world.
6 The one with the black horses is going toward
the north country, the one with the white
horses toward the west,[g] and the one with the
dappled horses toward the south."
7 When the powerful horses went out, they
were straining to go throughout the earth. And
he said, "Go throughout the earth!" So they
went throughout the earth.
8 Then he called to me, "Look, those going toward the north country have given my Spirit[h]
rest in the land of the north."

A Crown for Joshua

9 The word of the LORD came to me: 10 "Take
⌞silver and gold⌟ from the exiles Heldai, Tobijah and Jedaiah, who have arrived from Babylon. Go the same day to the house of Josiah
son of Zephaniah. 11 Take the silver and gold
and make a crown, and set it on the head of
the high priest, Joshua son of Jehozadak. 12 Tell
him this is what the LORD Almighty says:
'Here is the man whose name is the Branch,
and he will branch out from his place and
build the temple of the LORD. 13 It is he who
will build the temple of the LORD, and he will
be clothed with majesty and will sit and rule
on his throne. And he will be a priest on his
throne. And there will be harmony between
the two.' 14 The crown will be given to Heldai,[i]
Tobijah, Jedaiah and Hen[j] son of Zephaniah
as a memorial in the temple of the LORD.
15 Those who are far away will come and help
to build the temple of the LORD, and you will
know that the LORD Almighty has sent me to
you. This will happen if you diligently obey the
LORD your God."

[a] 14 Or *two who bring oil and* [b] 2 Hebrew *twenty cubits long and ten cubits wide* (about 9 meters long and 4.5 meters wide) [c] 6 Hebrew *an ephah*; also in verses 7–11 [d] 6 Or *appearance* [e] 11 Hebrew *Shinar* [f] 5 Or *winds* [g] 6 Or *horses after them* [h] 8 Or *spirit* [i] 14 Syriac; Hebrew *Helem* [j] 14 Or *and the gracious one, the*

Justice and Mercy, Not Fasting

7 In the fourth year of King Darius, the
word of the LORD came to Zechariah on
the fourth day of the ninth month, the month
of Kislev. 2The people of Bethel had sent Sharezer and Regem-Melech, together with their
men, to entreat the LORD 3by asking the priests
of the house of the LORD Almighty and the
prophets, "Should I mourn and fast in the fifth
month, as I have done for so many years?"
4Then the word of the LORD Almighty came
to me: 5"Ask all the people of the land and the
priests, 'When you fasted and mourned in the
fifth and seventh months for the past seventy
years, was it really for me that you fasted? 6And
when you were eating and drinking, were you
not just feasting for yourselves? 7Are these
not the words the LORD proclaimed through
the earlier prophets when Jerusalem and its
surrounding towns were at rest and prosperous, and the Negev and the western foothills
were settled?' "
8And the word of the LORD came again to
Zechariah: 9"This is what the LORD Almighty
says: 'Administer true justice; show mercy and
compassion to one another. 10Do not oppress
the widow or the fatherless, the alien or the
poor. In your hearts do not think evil of each
other.'
11"But they refused to pay attention; stubbornly they turned their backs and stopped up
their ears. 12They made their hearts as hard
as flint and would not listen to the law or to
the words that the LORD Almighty had sent by
his Spirit through the earlier prophets. So the
LORD Almighty was very angry.
13" 'When I called, they did not listen; so
when they called, I would not listen,' says the
LORD Almighty. 14'I scattered them with a
whirlwind among all the nations, where they
were strangers. The land was left so desolate behind them that no one could come or go. This
is how they made the pleasant land desolate.' "

The LORD Promises to Bless Jerusalem

8 Again the word of the LORD Almighty
came to me. 2This is what the LORD Almighty says: "I am very jealous for Zion; I am
burning with jealousy for her."
3This is what the LORD says: "I will return to
Zion and dwell in Jerusalem. Then Jerusalem
will be called the City of Truth, and the mountain of the LORD Almighty will be called the
Holy Mountain."
4This is what the LORD Almighty says: "Once
again men and women of ripe old age will sit in
the streets of Jerusalem, each with cane in hand
because of his age. 5The city streets will be filled
with boys and girls playing there."
6This is what the LORD Almighty says: "It
may seem marvelous to the remnant of this
people at that time, but will it seem marvelous
to me?" declares the LORD Almighty.
7This is what the LORD Almighty says: "I will
save my people from the countries of the east
and the west. 8I will bring them back to live in
Jerusalem; they will be my people, and I will be
faithful and righteous to them as their God."
9This is what the LORD Almighty says: "You
who now hear these words spoken by the
prophets who were there when the foundation
was laid for the house of the LORD Almighty,
let your hands be strong so that the temple
may be built. 10Before that time there were
no wages for man or beast. No one could go
about his business safely because of his enemy,
for I had turned every man against his neighbor. 11But now I will not deal with the remnant
of this people as I did in the past," declares the
LORD Almighty.
12"The seed will grow well, the vine will yield
its fruit, the ground will produce its crops, and
the heavens will drop their dew. I will give all
these things as an inheritance to the remnant
of this people. 13As you have been an object of
cursing among the nations, O Judah and Israel,
so will I save you, and you will be a blessing. Do
not be afraid, but let your hands be strong."
14This is what the LORD Almighty says: "Just
as I had determined to bring disaster upon you
and showed no pity when your fathers angered
me," says the LORD Almighty, 15"so now I have
determined to do good again to Jerusalem and
Judah. Do not be afraid. 16These are the things
you are to do: Speak the truth to each other,
and render true and sound judgment in your
courts; 17do not plot evil against your neighbor, and do not love to swear falsely. I hate all
this," declares the LORD.
18Again the word of the LORD Almighty
came to me. 19This is what the LORD Almighty

Failure to Communicate

Read: Zechariah 7:8–14

PERHAPS ONE OF THE MOST memorable movie lines of all times comes from the classic film *Cool Hand Luke* starring Paul Newman. A captain, played by Strother Martin, said these famous words, "What we've got here is failure to communicate. Some men you just can't reach, so you get what we had here last week which is the way he wants it. Well, he gets it." It's true, sometimes we get what we want.

The Israelites had a massive breakdown in communication with God. They did not listen when he called them. So when they finally called upon him, he would not listen to them. They got what they wanted.

The Lord had told his people to be truthful and just, merciful and compassionate, to care for each other and for strangers, and to think well of each other. They failed to listen to their God. Thus, Zechariah 7:13 is perhaps one of the saddest verses in Scripture. The Israelites did not avail themselves of the relationship God wanted with them. They thought they would avoid the consequences of miscommunication. Instead, God was unreachable for a time. They ended up in a land of desolation.

Desolation. A sorry sort of word. A sorry sort of life. We each know what that looks like. Not an inviting image. We don't really want to end up desolate and unheard, as the Israelites did, but how do we avoid it? How do we listen to God?

The Word of God is the framework from which we listen. When we know it and absorb it, it is dynamic and living. Scripture intersects with our thoughts, feelings and spirit. We create an open space for that to happen by dedicating time and attention to study and prayer. Out of love and respect for God, we concentrate on listening to him—as if he were the only other being in the universe. Listening means that we are receptive; like soft ground that soaks up the rain, so the Word can yield rich fruit in our lives. Listening to God, and heeding what God says, is the way to keep the "pleasant land" fruitful and to prevent it from becoming desolate (see verse 14). It's the only way to remain attuned to God and his voice.

Zechariah 7:13

"'When I called, they did not listen; so when they called, I would not listen,' says the LORD Almighty."

reflection

1 Can you think of a time you listened to God and were blessed? How about a time when you didn't and suffered for it?

2 How can you remind yourself to listen to God?

3 What are some concrete ways you can love your Father by listening to him?

RELATED READINGS

Leviticus 26:14–28;
Psalm 81:8–16;
Matthew 13:13–23

Go to page 1153 for your next devotional reading.

says: "The fasts of the fourth, fifth, seventh and
tenth months will become joyful and glad occasions and happy festivals for Judah. Therefore
love truth and peace."
20 This is what the LORD Almighty says:
"Many peoples and the inhabitants of many
cities will yet come, 21 and the inhabitants of
one city will go to another and say, 'Let us go
at once to entreat the LORD and seek the LORD
Almighty. I myself am going.' 22 And many
peoples and powerful nations will come to Jerusalem to seek the LORD Almighty and to entreat him."
23 This is what the LORD Almighty says: "In
those days ten men from all languages and nations will take firm hold of one Jew by the hem
of his robe and say, 'Let us go with you, because
we have heard that God is with you.'"

Judgment on Israel's Enemies

An Oracle

9 The word of the LORD is against the land
of Hadrach
and will rest upon Damascus—
for the eyes of men and all the tribes of
Israel
are on the LORD—[a]
2 and upon Hamath too, which borders on
it,
and upon Tyre and Sidon, though they
are very skillful.
3 Tyre has built herself a stronghold;
she has heaped up silver like dust,
and gold like the dirt of the streets.
4 But the Lord will take away her possessions
and destroy her power on the sea,
and she will be consumed by fire.
5 Ashkelon will see it and fear;
Gaza will writhe in agony,
and Ekron too, for her hope will wither.
Gaza will lose her king
and Ashkelon will be deserted.
6 Foreigners will occupy Ashdod,
and I will cut off the pride of the
Philistines.
7 I will take the blood from their mouths,
the forbidden food from between their
teeth.
Those who are left will belong to our God
and become leaders in Judah,
and Ekron will be like the Jebusites.
8 But I will defend my house
against marauding forces.
Never again will an oppressor overrun my
people,
for now I am keeping watch.

The Coming of Zion's King

9 Rejoice greatly, O Daughter of Zion!
Shout, Daughter of Jerusalem!
See, your king[b] comes to you,
righteous and having salvation,
gentle and riding on a donkey,
on a colt, the foal of a donkey.
10 I will take away the chariots from Ephraim
and the war-horses from Jerusalem,
and the battle bow will be broken.
He will proclaim peace to the nations.
His rule will extend from sea to sea
and from the River[c] to the ends of the
earth.[d]
11 As for you, because of the blood of my
covenant with you,
I will free your prisoners from the
waterless pit.
12 Return to your fortress, O prisoners of
hope;
even now I announce that I will restore
twice as much to you.
13 I will bend Judah as I bend my bow
and fill it with Ephraim.
I will rouse your sons, O Zion,
against your sons, O Greece,
and make you like a warrior's sword.

The LORD Will Appear

14 Then the LORD will appear over them;
his arrow will flash like lightning.
The Sovereign LORD will sound the
trumpet;
he will march in the storms of the south,
15 and the LORD Almighty will shield
them.
They will destroy
and overcome with slingstones.
They will drink and roar as with wine;
they will be full like a bowl

[a]1 Or *Damascus. / For the eye of the LORD is on all mankind, / as well as on the tribes of Israel,* [b]9 Or *King* [c]10 That is, the Euphrates
[d]10 Or *the end of the land*

used for sprinkling[a] the corners of the altar.
16 The LORD their God will save them on that day
as the flock of his people.
They will sparkle in his land
like jewels in a crown.
17 How attractive and beautiful they will be!
Grain will make the young men thrive,
and new wine the young women.

The LORD Will Care for Judah

10 Ask the LORD for rain in the springtime;
it is the LORD who makes the storm clouds.
He gives showers of rain to men,
and plants of the field to everyone.
2 The idols speak deceit,
diviners see visions that lie;
they tell dreams that are false,
they give comfort in vain.
Therefore the people wander like sheep
oppressed for lack of a shepherd.

3 "My anger burns against the shepherds,
and I will punish the leaders;
for the LORD Almighty will care
for his flock, the house of Judah,
and make them like a proud horse in battle.
4 From Judah will come the cornerstone,
from him the tent peg,
from him the battle bow,
from him every ruler.
5 Together they[b] will be like mighty men
trampling the muddy streets in battle.
Because the LORD is with them,
they will fight and overthrow the horsemen.

6 "I will strengthen the house of Judah
and save the house of Joseph.
I will restore them
because I have compassion on them.
They will be as though
I had not rejected them,
for I am the LORD their God
and I will answer them.
7 The Ephraimites will become like mighty men,
and their hearts will be glad as with wine.
Their children will see it and be joyful;
their hearts will rejoice in the LORD.
8 I will signal for them
and gather them in.
Surely I will redeem them;
they will be as numerous as before.
9 Though I scatter them among the peoples,
yet in distant lands they will remember me.
They and their children will survive,
and they will return.
10 I will bring them back from Egypt
and gather them from Assyria.
I will bring them to Gilead and Lebanon,
and there will not be room enough for them.
11 They will pass through the sea of trouble;
the surging sea will be subdued
and all the depths of the Nile will dry up.
Assyria's pride will be brought down
and Egypt's scepter will pass away.
12 I will strengthen them in the LORD
and in his name they will walk,"
declares the LORD.

> **Zechariah 10:12**
>
> *God Strengthens Us*
>
> "I will strengthen them
> in the LORD
> and in his name they
> will walk,"
> declares the LORD.

11 Open your doors, O Lebanon,
so that fire may devour your cedars!
2 Wail, O pine tree, for the cedar has fallen;
the stately trees are ruined!
Wail, oaks of Bashan;
the dense forest has been cut down!
3 Listen to the wail of the shepherds;

[a] 15 Or *bowl, / like* [b] 4,5 Or *ruler, all of them together. / [5] They*

their rich pastures are destroyed!
Listen to the roar of the lions;
the lush thicket of the Jordan is ruined!

Two Shepherds

4 This is what the LORD my God says: "Pasture the flock marked for slaughter. 5 Their buy-
ers slaughter them and go unpunished. Those
who sell them say, 'Praise the LORD, I am rich!'
Their own shepherds do not spare them. 6 For
I will no longer have pity on the people of the
land," declares the LORD. "I will hand everyone
over to his neighbor and his king. They will oppress the land, and I will not rescue them from
their hands."

7 So I pastured the flock marked for slaughter, particularly the oppressed of the flock.
Then I took two staffs and called one Favor and
the other Union, and I pastured the flock. 8 In
one month I got rid of the three shepherds.

The flock detested me, and I grew weary of
them 9 and said, "I will not be your shepherd.
Let the dying die, and the perishing perish. Let
those who are left eat one another's flesh."

10 Then I took my staff called Favor and broke
it, revoking the covenant I had made with all
the nations. 11 It was revoked on that day, and
so the afflicted of the flock who were watching
me knew it was the word of the LORD.

12 I told them, "If you think it best, give me
my pay; but if not, keep it." So they paid me
thirty pieces of silver.

13 And the LORD said to me, "Throw it to the
potter"—the handsome price at which they
priced me! So I took the thirty pieces of silver
and threw them into the house of the LORD to
the potter.

14 Then I broke my second staff called Union,
breaking the brotherhood between Judah and
Israel.

15 Then the LORD said to me, "Take again the
equipment of a foolish shepherd. 16 For I am
going to raise up a shepherd over the land who
will not care for the lost, or seek the young, or
heal the injured, or feed the healthy, but will
eat the meat of the choice sheep, tearing off
their hoofs.

17 "Woe to the worthless shepherd,
who deserts the flock!
May the sword strike his arm and his right
eye!
May his arm be completely withered,
his right eye totally blinded!"

Jerusalem's Enemies to Be Destroyed

An Oracle

12 This is the word of the LORD concerning Israel. The LORD, who stretches out
the heavens, who lays the foundation of the
earth, and who forms the spirit of man within
him, declares: 2 "I am going to make Jerusalem a
cup that sends all the surrounding peoples reeling. Judah will be besieged as well as Jerusalem.
3 On that day, when all the nations of the earth
are gathered against her, I will make Jerusalem
an immovable rock for all the nations. All who
try to move it will injure themselves. 4 On that
day I will strike every horse with panic and its
rider with madness," declares the LORD. "I will
keep a watchful eye over the house of Judah,
but I will blind all the horses of the nations.
5 Then the leaders of Judah will say in their
hearts, 'The people of Jerusalem are strong, because the LORD Almighty is their God.'

6 "On that day I will make the leaders of Judah like a firepot in a woodpile, like a flaming
torch among sheaves. They will consume right
and left all the surrounding peoples, but Jerusalem will remain intact in her place.

7 "The LORD will save the dwellings of Judah
first, so that the honor of the house of David
and of Jerusalem's inhabitants may not be
greater than that of Judah. 8 On that day the
LORD will shield those who live in Jerusalem,
so that the feeblest among them will be like David, and the house of David will be like God,
like the Angel of the LORD going before them.
9 On that day I will set out to destroy all the nations that attack Jerusalem.

Mourning for the One They Pierced

10 "And I will pour out on the house of David and the inhabitants of Jerusalem a spirit[a] of
grace and supplication. They will look on[b] me,
the one they have pierced, and they will mourn
for him as one mourns for an only child, and
grieve bitterly for him as one grieves for a firstborn son. 11 On that day the weeping in Jerusalem will be great, like the weeping of Hadad

[a] 10 Or *the Spirit* [b] 10 Or *to*

Rimmon in the plain of Megiddo. 12 The land
will mourn, each clan by itself, with their wives
by themselves: the clan of the house of David
and their wives, the clan of the house of Nathan and their wives, 13 the clan of the house
of Levi and their wives, the clan of Shimei and
their wives, 14 and all the rest of the clans and
their wives.

Cleansing From Sin

13 "On that day a fountain will be opened
to the house of David and the inhabitants of Jerusalem, to cleanse them from sin
and impurity.
2 "On that day, I will banish the names of the
idols from the land, and they will be remembered no more," declares the LORD Almighty.
"I will remove both the prophets and the spirit
of impurity from the land. 3 And if anyone still
prophesies, his father and mother, to whom
he was born, will say to him, 'You must die, because you have told lies in the LORD's name.'
When he prophesies, his own parents will
stab him.
4 "On that day every prophet will be
ashamed of his prophetic vision. He will not
put on a prophet's garment of hair in order to
deceive. 5 He will say, 'I am not a prophet. I am
a farmer; the land has been my livelihood since
my youth.[a]' 6 If someone asks him, 'What are
these wounds on your body[b]?'
he will answer, 'The wounds
I was given at the house of
my friends.'

The Shepherd Struck, the Sheep Scattered

7 "Awake, O sword, against
my shepherd,
against the man who is
close to me!"
declares the LORD
Almighty.
"Strike the shepherd,
and the sheep will be
scattered,
and I will turn my hand against the little
ones.
8 In the whole land," declares the LORD,
"two-thirds will be struck down and
perish;
yet one-third will be left in it.
9 This third I will bring into the fire;
I will refine them like silver
and test them like gold.
They will call on my name
and I will answer them;
I will say, 'They are my people,'
and they will say, 'The LORD is our
God.'"

The LORD Comes and Reigns

14 A day of the LORD is coming when your
plunder will be divided among you.
2 I will gather all the nations to Jerusalem to
fight against it; the city will be captured, the
houses ransacked, and the women raped. Half
of the city will go into exile, but the rest of the
people will not be taken from the city.
3 Then the LORD will go out and fight against
those nations, as he fights in the day of battle.
4 On that day his feet will stand on the Mount
of Olives, east of Jerusalem, and the Mount of
Olives will be split in two from east to west,
forming a great valley, with half of the mountain moving north and half moving south.
5 You will flee by my mountain valley, for it will
extend to Azel. You will flee as you fled from
the earthquake[c] in the days of Uzziah king of
Judah. Then the LORD my God
will come, and all the holy ones
with him.
6 On that day there will be
no light, no cold or frost. 7 It
will be a unique day, without
daytime or nighttime—a day
known to the LORD. When evening comes, there will be light.
8 On that day living water
will flow out from Jerusalem,
half to the eastern sea[d] and half
to the western sea,[e] in summer
and in winter.
9 The LORD will be king over the whole earth.
On that day there will be one LORD, and his
name the only name.
10 The whole land, from Geba to Rimmon,
south of Jerusalem, will become like the Arabah.

> **Zechariah 14:9**
>
> ***God Is One***
>
> The LORD will be king over the whole earth. On that day there will be one LORD, and his name the only name.

[a]5 Or *farmer; a man sold me in my youth* [b]6 Or *wounds between your hands* [c]5 Or [5]*My mountain valley will be blocked and will extend to Azel. It will be blocked as it was blocked because of the earthquake* [d]8 That is, the Dead Sea [e]8 That is, the Mediterranean

But Jerusalem will be raised up and remain in
its place, from the Benjamin Gate to the site of
the First Gate, to the Corner Gate, and from
the Tower of Hananel to the royal winepresses.
11 It will be inhabited; never again will it be destroyed. Jerusalem will be secure.

12 This is the plague with which the LORD
will strike all the nations that fought against
Jerusalem: Their flesh will rot while they are
still standing on their feet, their eyes will rot in
their sockets, and their tongues will rot in their
mouths. 13 On that day men will be stricken by
the LORD with great panic. Each man will seize
the hand of another, and they will attack each
other. 14 Judah too will fight at Jerusalem. The
wealth of all the surrounding nations will be
collected—great quantities of gold and silver
and clothing. 15 A similar plague will strike the
horses and mules, the camels and donkeys, and
all the animals in those camps.

16 Then the survivors from all the nations
that have attacked Jerusalem will go up year
after year to worship the King, the LORD Almighty, and to celebrate the Feast of Tabernacles. 17 If any of the peoples of the earth do not
go up to Jerusalem to worship the King, the
LORD Almighty, they will have no rain. 18 If the
Egyptian people do not go up and take part,
they will have no rain. The LORD[a] will bring
on them the plague he inflicts on the nations
that do not go up to celebrate the Feast of Tabernacles. 19 This will be the punishment of Egypt
and the punishment of all the nations that do
not go up to celebrate the Feast of Tabernacles.

20 On that day HOLY TO THE LORD will be
inscribed on the bells of the horses, and the
cooking pots in the LORD's house will be like
the sacred bowls in front of the altar. 21 Every
pot in Jerusalem and Judah will be holy to the
LORD Almighty, and all who come to sacrifice
will take some of the pots and cook in them.
And on that day there will no longer be a Canaanite[b] in the house of the LORD Almighty.

[a] 18 Or *part, then the LORD* [b] 21 Or *merchant*

Malachi

Again and again God had shown his love for his people. Yet their love for him was sorely lacking. After returning to their homeland, the people embraced God's laws for a time, but they eventually became complacent. *Their worship involved merely following tradition*—and barely even that. The animals they sacrificed were ones they couldn't sell—crippled and blind animals. God's people, even the priests, were shortchanging him. They were even stealing from him in their refusal to give the tithe he had commanded. Then they had the gall to say, "It's futile to serve God," as though they resented what little they gave him. *"Come worship me when you mean it"* seems to be God's disgusted response.

Author:
Malachi.

Audience:
Jews in Jerusalem and all of God's people.

Date:
About 430 B.C.

Setting:
Although the temple in Jerusalem and the city walls had been rebuilt, the Jews languished in their worship.

Verse to Remember:
"My name will be great among the nations, from the rising to the setting of the sun. In every place incense and pure offerings will be brought to my name, because my name will be great among the nations," says the LORD Almighty. (1:11)

1 An oracle: The word of the LORD to Israel
through Malachi.[a]

Jacob Loved, Esau Hated

2 "I have loved you," says the LORD.
"But you ask, 'How have you loved us?'
"Was not Esau Jacob's brother?" the LORD
says. "Yet I have loved Jacob, 3 but Esau I have
hated, and I have turned his mountains into a
wasteland and left his inheritance to the desert jackals."
4 Edom may say, "Though we have been
crushed, we will rebuild the ruins."
But this is what the LORD Almighty says:

[a]1 *Malachi* means *my messenger.*

"They may build, but I will demolish. They will
be called the Wicked Land, a people always under the wrath of the LORD. 5You will see it with
your own eyes and say, 'Great is the LORD—
even beyond the borders of Israel!'

Blemished Sacrifices

6"A son honors his father, and a servant his
master. If I am a father, where is the honor due
me? If I am a master, where is the respect due
me?" says the LORD Almighty. "It is you, O
priests, who show contempt for my name.

"But you ask, 'How have we shown contempt
for your name?'

7"You place defiled food on my altar.

"But you ask, 'How have we defiled you?'

"By saying that the LORD's table is contemptible. 8When you bring blind animals for sacrifice, is that not wrong? When you sacrifice
crippled or diseased animals, is that not wrong?
Try offering them to your governor! Would he
be pleased with you? Would he accept you?"
says the LORD Almighty.

9"Now implore God to be
gracious to us. With such offerings from your hands, will
he accept you?"—says the
LORD Almighty.

10"Oh, that one of you would
shut the temple doors, so that
you would not light useless
fires on my altar! I am not
pleased with you," says the
LORD Almighty, "and I will accept no offering from your
hands. 11My name will be great
among the nations, from the
rising to the setting of the sun.
In every place incense and pure
offerings will be brought to my
name, because my name will
be great among the nations,"
says the LORD Almighty.

12"But you profane it by saying of the Lord's
table, 'It is defiled,' and of its food, 'It is contemptible.' 13And you say, 'What a burden!'
and you sniff at it contemptuously," says the
LORD Almighty.

"When you bring injured, crippled or diseased animals and offer them as sacrifices,
should I accept them from your hands?" says
the LORD. 14"Cursed is the cheat who has an
acceptable male in his flock and vows to give
it, but then sacrifices a blemished animal to the
Lord. For I am a great king," says the LORD Almighty, "and my name is to be feared among
the nations.

> **Malachi 1:11**
>
> ***God Surpasses All***
>
> "My name will be great among the nations, from the rising to the setting of the sun. In every place incense and pure offerings will be brought to my name, because my name will be great among the nations," says the LORD Almighty.

Admonition for the Priests

2 "And now this admonition is for you,
O priests. 2If you do not listen, and if you
do not set your heart to honor my name," says
the LORD Almighty, "I will send a curse upon
you, and I will curse your blessings. Yes, I have
already cursed them, because you have not set
your heart to honor me.

3"Because of you I will rebuke[a] your descendants[b]; I will spread on your faces the offal
from your festival sacrifices, and you will be
carried off with it. 4And you will know that I
have sent you this admonition so that my covenant with Levi may continue,"
says the LORD Almighty. 5"My
covenant was with him, a covenant of life and peace, and I
gave them to him; this called
for reverence and he revered
me and stood in awe of my
name. 6True instruction was
in his mouth and nothing
false was found on his lips. He
walked with me in peace and
uprightness, and turned many
from sin.

7"For the lips of a priest
ought to preserve knowledge,
and from his mouth men
should seek instruction—because he is the messenger of
the LORD Almighty. 8But you
have turned from the way and
by your teaching have caused
many to stumble; you have violated the covenant with Levi," says the LORD Almighty.
9"So I have caused you to be despised and
humiliated before all the people, because you
have not followed my ways but have shown
partiality in matters of the law."

[a]3 Or *cut off* (see Septuagint) [b]3 Or *will blight your grain*

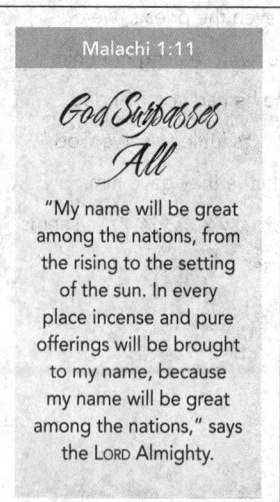

Mine?

Read: Malachi 3:1–18

HAVE YOU EVER TRIED to take a toy from a toddler? If so, then you know it's hardly worth the effort. Even though the child probably doesn't know where the toy came from, the words *my* and *mine* repeatedly resound. It's hers and no one else's.

Mine. It's one of the first words we learn as children. No one has to teach us to be possessive. Hoarding comes naturally. Maybe we fear that we won't have what we need or that someone will take what we think rightfully belongs to us. Learning to share is so often the challenge.

God instituted the concept of tithing during Moses' time. Not only was it the way God provided for the Levites, but it was also a spiritual discipline to teach his people to rely on him. By giving God the first tenth of their produce, they acknowledged that all they had was from his hand. In this passage, God lamented that the people were robbing him by withholding their tithe. He asked them to "test" his generosity. And wow! God can pass *that* test, opening the floodgates of heaven and pouring out so much blessing that there will not be enough room for it.

With a return like that, who wouldn't want to give to God? But God doesn't ask us to give out of his own need or for what we receive in return. He asks us to give as a reflection of how generous he has been to us. He has, indeed, poured out mercy, forgiveness, provision and everything else we need. Jesus said, "Give, and it will be given to you. A good measure, pressed down, shaken together and running over, will be poured into your lap. For with the measure you use, it will be measured to you" (Luke 6:38). The Old Testament tithe was a requirement, but the New Testament offering is a test of the heart. Giving is not a duty but a joyous outpouring of gratitude. And giving is God's way of making us, his people, a conduit of his love to others.

We cannot receive God's gifts with closed fists. No, receiving requires open hands. What God pours into our hands, we pour out. And in God's kingdom, there is always more to spare.

Malachi 3:10

"Bring the whole tithe into the storehouse, that there may be food in my house. Test me in this," says the LORD Almighty, "and see if I will not throw open the floodgates of heaven and pour out so much blessing that you will not have room enough for it."

reflection

1. Are your hands open or are you tightfisted, like a child with a toy?
2. Have you practiced the grace of generous giving? If so, what happened? How did giving affect you?
3. Why would giving to God in order to receive from God not be a good motive? What's wrong with this way of thinking?

RELATED READINGS

Proverbs 3:9–10;
Luke 21:1–4;
2 Corinthians 9:6–8

"Giving is a joy if we do it in the right spirit. It all depends on whether we think of it as 'What can I spare?' or as 'What can I share?'"

Esther York Burkholder

Go to page 1155 for your next devotional reading.

Judah Unfaithful

10Have we not all one Father[a]? Did not one
God create us? Why do we profane the covenant of our fathers by breaking faith with one
another?
11Judah has broken faith. A detestable thing
has been committed in Israel and in Jerusalem:
Judah has desecrated the sanctuary the LORD
loves, by marrying the daughter of a foreign
god. 12As for the man who does this, whoever
he may be, may the LORD cut him off from the
tents of Jacob[b]—even though he brings offerings to the LORD Almighty.
13Another thing you do: You flood the
LORD's altar with tears. You weep and wail
because he no longer pays attention to your
offerings or accepts them with pleasure from
your hands. 14You ask, "Why?" It is because the
LORD is acting as the witness between you and
the wife of your youth, because you have broken faith with her, though she is your partner,
the wife of your marriage covenant.
15Has not ⌊the LORD⌋ made them one? In
flesh and spirit they are his. And why one?
Because he was seeking godly offspring.[c] So
guard yourself in your spirit, and do not break
faith with the wife of your youth.
16"I hate divorce," says the LORD God of
Israel, "and I hate a man's covering himself[d]
with violence as well as with his garment," says
the LORD Almighty.

So guard yourself in your spirit, and do not
break faith.

The Day of Judgment

17You have wearied the LORD with your
words.

"How have we wearied him?" you ask.

By saying, "All who do evil are good in the
eyes of the LORD, and he is pleased with them"
or "Where is the God of justice?"

3 "See, I will send my messenger, who will
prepare the way before me. Then suddenly
the Lord you are seeking will come to his temple; the messenger of the covenant, whom you
desire, will come," says the LORD Almighty.
2But who can endure the day of his coming? Who can stand when he appears? For he
will be like a refiner's fire or a launderer's soap.
3He will sit as a refiner and purifier of silver;
he will purify the Levites and refine them like
gold and silver. Then the LORD will have men
who will bring offerings in righteousness, 4and
the offerings of Judah and Jerusalem will be acceptable to the LORD, as in days gone by, as in
former years.
5"So I will come near to you for judgment. I
will be quick to testify against sorcerers, adulterers and perjurers, against those who defraud laborers of their wages, who oppress the widows
and the fatherless, and deprive aliens of justice,
but do not fear me," says the LORD Almighty.

Robbing God

6"I the LORD do not change. So you, O descendants of Jacob, are not destroyed. 7Ever
since the time of your forefathers you have
turned away from my decrees and have not
kept them. Return to me, and I will return to
you," says the LORD Almighty.

"But you ask, 'How are we to return?'

8"Will a man rob God? Yet you rob me.

"But you ask, 'How do we rob you?'

"In tithes and offerings. 9You are under a
curse—the whole nation of you—because you
are robbing me. 10Bring the whole tithe into
the storehouse, that there may be food in my
house. Test me in this," says the LORD Almighty,
"and see if I will not throw open the floodgates
of heaven and pour out so much blessing that
you will not have room enough for it. 11I will
prevent pests from devouring your crops, and
the vines in your fields will not cast their fruit,"
says the LORD Almighty. 12"Then all the nations will call you blessed, for yours will be a
delightful land," says the LORD Almighty.
13"You have said harsh things against me,"
says the LORD.

"Yet you ask, 'What have we said against
you?'

14"You have said, 'It is futile to serve God.
What did we gain by carrying out his requirements and going about like mourners before
the LORD Almighty? 15But now we call the arrogant blessed. Certainly the evildoers prosper,
and even those who challenge God escape.'"

[a]10 Or *father* [b]12 Or *12May the LORD cut off from the tents of Jacob anyone who gives testimony in behalf of the man who does this*
[c]15 Or *15But the one ⌊who is our father⌋ did not do this, not as long as life remained in him. And what was he seeking? An offspring from God* [d]16 Or *his wife*

Just a Touch

SUFFERING WOMAN

"IF I ONLY TOUCH HIS CLOAK, I will be healed." Her thoughts were single-focused; her intention was simple.

"If *I* only touch his cloak . . ."

No one could do it for her. She had to be the one who touched him. She had to draw on her fortitude to make her way through the crowd surrounding Jesus. She alone could summon the inner strength to step out in faith toward the Healer. Others had experienced healing, but no one could transfer the power to her. She had to encounter Jesus personally. She had suffered for 12 years alone. And she could not depend on anyone else to bring her to this moment. She had to do it herself.

"If I only *touch* his cloak . . ." How great was her faith in the Master! She surmised she only had to graze his power in order to be changed. She willingly believed that he would not require her to go to great lengths to receive what she needed. She did not intend to jump through hoops, recite a mantra or go through the motions to receive mercy. Her approach was simple and heartfelt. If reaching out to him in faith did not work, she had no other option.

"If I only touch *his* cloak . . ." She knew the source of the power. Those whom she'd sought assistance from before—doctors, priests, family and friends—had only let her down. None could give her relief. But when she saw Jesus and witnessed his miracles firsthand, she knew he was the One who would not disappoint. The disciples and the host of followers surrounding him may have intimidated her, but they did not distract her. She did not pull one of them aside and issue her request. She was laser-focused on the Father's Son.

"If I only touch his cloak, I will be *healed*." She did. And she was.

—Prayer—

God, give me faith like this woman . . . and heal me.

Just then a woman who had been subject to bleeding for twelve years came up behind him and touched the edge of his cloak.

Matthew 9:20

ASSIGNED READING:

Matthew 9:20–22; Mark 5:25–34; Luke 8:43–48

Weekend

Go to page 1161 for your next devotional reading.

16 Then those who feared the LORD talked
with each other, and the LORD listened and
heard. A scroll of remembrance
was written in his presence concerning those who feared the
LORD and honored his name.
17 "They will be mine," says
the LORD Almighty, "in the day
when I make up my treasured
possession.[a] I will spare them,
just as in compassion a man
spares his son who serves him.
18 And you will again see the
distinction between the righteous and the wicked, between
those who serve God and those
who do not.

> **Malachi 4:6**
>
> *God Can Turn Hearts*
>
> "He will turn the hearts of the fathers to their children, and the hearts of the children to their fathers; or else I will come and strike the land with a curse."

The Day of the LORD

4 "Surely the day is coming; it will burn
like a furnace. All the arrogant and every
evildoer will be stubble, and that day that is
coming will set them on fire," says the LORD
Almighty. "Not a root or a branch will be left
to them. 2 But for you who revere my name,
the sun of righteousness will
rise with healing in its wings.
And you will go out and leap
like calves released from the
stall. 3 Then you will trample
down the wicked; they will
be ashes under the soles of
your feet on the day when I do
these things," says the LORD Almighty.
4 "Remember the law of my
servant Moses, the decrees and
laws I gave him at Horeb for
all Israel.
5 "See, I will send you the
prophet Elijah before that great
and dreadful day of the LORD
comes. 6 He will turn the hearts of the fathers to
their children, and the hearts of the children to
their fathers; or else I will come and strike the
land with a curse."

[a]17 Or *Almighty, "my treasured possession, in the day when I act*

The New Testament

Matthew

A silent interval of 400 years passed between the Old and New Testaments. Scripture says nothing of those years, but history tells us that they included times of peace and then *persecution for the people of God,* culminating with the oppression of the Roman Empire. It is to this Roman-ruled nation of Jews that Matthew primarily addresses his Gospel. A Jew himself, he was also a tax collector—a Roman puppet. Tax collectors were notorious cheaters, squeezing whatever they could out of their fellow citizens so they could skim a healthy profit off the top for themselves. But whatever Matthew once was, when he encountered Jesus, *he became a devoted disciple.*

This Gospel gives us an up-close-and-personal view of Jesus as teacher and healer, as well as a wide panoramic view showing how *Jesus fulfilled the ancient prophecies* that pointed to the promised King and Messiah. Jesus didn't just burst onto the scene. His life and his death were planned from the foundation of the world. Matthew shows us that *the whole of Scripture is one continuous story.*

Author:
Matthew, also called Levi.

Audience:
Followers of Jesus. Matthew wrote with a Jewish audience in mind.

Date:
Probably between A.D. 60 and 70.

Setting:
Matthew most likely wrote from Israel, though some believe he wrote from Syrian Antioch.

Verse to Remember:
This was to fulfill what was spoken through the prophet Isaiah: "He took up our infirmities and carried our diseases." (8:17)

The Genealogy of Jesus

1 A record of the genealogy of Jesus Christ the son of David, the son of Abraham:
2 Abraham was the father of Isaac,
Isaac the father of Jacob,
Jacob the father of Judah and his brothers,
3 Judah the father of Perez and Zerah, whose mother was Tamar,
Perez the father of Hezron,

Hezron the father of Ram,
4 Ram the father of Amminadab,
Amminadab the father of Nahshon,
Nahshon the father of Salmon,
5 Salmon the father of Boaz, whose mother was Rahab,
Boaz the father of Obed, whose mother was Ruth,
Obed the father of Jesse,
6 and Jesse the father of King David.

David was the father of Solomon, whose mother had been Uriah's wife,
7 Solomon the father of Rehoboam,
Rehoboam the father of Abijah,
Abijah the father of Asa,
8 Asa the father of Jehoshaphat,
Jehoshaphat the father of Jehoram,
Jehoram the father of Uzziah,
9 Uzziah the father of Jotham,
Jotham the father of Ahaz,
Ahaz the father of Hezekiah,
10 Hezekiah the father of Manasseh,
Manasseh the father of Amon,
Amon the father of Josiah,
11 and Josiah the father of Jeconiah[a] and his brothers at the time of the exile to Babylon.

12 After the exile to Babylon:
Jeconiah was the father of Shealtiel,
Shealtiel the father of Zerubbabel,
13 Zerubbabel the father of Abiud,
Abiud the father of Eliakim,
Eliakim the father of Azor,
14 Azor the father of Zadok,
Zadok the father of Akim,
Akim the father of Eliud,
15 Eliud the father of Eleazar,
Eleazar the father of Matthan,
Matthan the father of Jacob,
16 and Jacob the father of Joseph, the husband of Mary, of whom was born Jesus, who is called Christ.

17 Thus there were fourteen generations in
all from Abraham to David, fourteen from David to the exile to Babylon, and fourteen from the exile to the Christ.[b]

Matthew 1:21

God Reaches Out to Save

"She will give birth to a son, and you are to give him the name Jesus, because he will save his people from their sins."

The Birth of Jesus Christ

18 This is how the birth of Jesus Christ came
about: His mother Mary was pledged to be married to Joseph, but before they came together, she was found to be with child through the
Holy Spirit. 19 Because Joseph her husband
was a righteous man and did not want to expose her to public disgrace, he had in mind to divorce her quietly.
20 But after he had considered this, an angel
of the Lord appeared to him in a dream and said, "Joseph son of David, do not be afraid to take Mary home as your wife, because what is conceived in her
is from the Holy Spirit. 21 She
will give birth to a son, and you are to give him the name Jesus,[c] because he will save his people from their sins."
22 All this took place to fulfill
what the Lord had said through
the prophet: 23 "The virgin will
be with child and will give birth to a son, and they will call him Immanuel"[d]—which means, "God with us."
24 When Joseph woke up, he did what the an-
gel of the Lord had commanded him and took
Mary home as his wife. 25 But he had no union
with her until she gave birth to a son. And he gave him the name Jesus.

The Visit of the Magi

2 After Jesus was born in Bethlehem in Judea, during the time of King Herod, Magi[e]
from the east came to Jerusalem 2 and asked,
"Where is the one who has been born king of the Jews? We saw his star in the east[f] and have come to worship him."

[a] 11 That is, Jehoiachin; also in verse 12 [b] 17 Or *Messiah.* "The Christ" (Greek) and "the Messiah" (Hebrew) both mean "the Anointed One." [c] 21 *Jesus* is the Greek form of *Joshua,* which means *the LORD saves.* [d] 23 Isaiah 7:14 [e] 1 Traditionally *Wise Men* [f] 2 Or *star when it rose*

Impossible Dream

Read: Matthew 1:18–25

FOR CENTURIES GOD'S PEOPLE had been waiting for the promised Messiah, each family hoping he would be born to them. Then in an "impossible" dream, Joseph received a revelation from heaven telling him that Mary, his betrothed, was going to bear God's son. An angel of the Lord instructed Joseph not to shame her, but to marry her and raise the Son of God as his own child. In this dream, God revealed that the coming baby was the promised one, the Messiah.

But was the dream really a nightmare for Joseph? Joseph must have wrestled with all that this news implied. For the rest of his life he might live with the whispers—whispers that he hadn't been able to wait until the marriage bed, or, worse, that he was raising another man's child. For a righteous man like Joseph, the prospect of living with this shame might have been just as impossible to understand as a pregnant virgin.

Joseph probably considered the weight of responsibility—and its impact on his fiancée, Mary. How could *he* teach God's Son anything? Would the Son of God want to play? Would he lead the Son of God in prayer? How would their own children feel? But Joseph put his doubts and questions aside and decided to accept the charge God had given him, regardless of the personal implications. And God blessed him, entrusting him with Jesus, who surely must have been a profound joy to have as his child.

You may have dreamed an impossible dream only to have it turn into a nightmare. Perhaps it was the dream of a perfect child who has turned into a challenging teenager. Maybe you dreamed of a new start but are now struggling to make a blended family work. Perhaps the whispers of others are shouting louder than their praise. You have a world of responsibilities sitting on your shoulders, and you're just not sure you can handle it all.

Do what Joseph did when facing the impossible. Bring Jesus into your home and invite him into your heart. He doesn't know the word *impossible* because with him all things are possible.

Matthew 1:24–25

When Joseph woke up, he did what the angel of the Lord had commanded him and took Mary home as his wife. But he had no union with her until she gave birth to a son. And he gave him the name Jesus.

reflection

1 What "impossible" news do you face?

2 What comfort do you find in the angel's words, "Do not be afraid"?

3 If you haven't asked Jesus to reside in your heart, say a prayer now, asking him to take up residence. Ask him to make the impossible possible by filling you with his Spirit and by giving you new life.

RELATED READINGS

Mark 10:26–29;
Luke 1:37;
Romans 8:28

Monday

Go to page 1168 for your next devotional reading.

3When King Herod heard this he was disturbed, and all Jerusalem with him. 4When he
had called together all the people's chief priests
and teachers of the law, he asked them where
the Christ[a] was to be born. 5"In Bethlehem
in Judea," they replied, "for this is what the
prophet has written:

6"'But you, Bethlehem, in the land of Judah,
are by no means least among the rulers
of Judah;
for out of you will come a ruler
who will be the shepherd of my people
Israel.'[b]"

7Then Herod called the Magi secretly and
found out from them the exact time the star
had appeared. 8He sent them to Bethlehem
and said, "Go and make a careful search for the
child. As soon as you find him, report to me, so
that I too may go and worship him."
9After they had heard the king, they went on
their way, and the star they had seen in the east[c]
went ahead of them until it stopped over the
place where the child was. 10When they saw
the star, they were overjoyed. 11On coming to
the house, they saw the child with his mother
Mary, and they bowed down and worshiped
him. Then they opened their treasures and
presented him with gifts of gold and of incense
and of myrrh. 12And having been warned in a
dream not to go back to Herod, they returned
to their country by another route.

The Escape to Egypt

13When they had gone, an angel of the Lord
appeared to Joseph in a dream. "Get up," he
said, "take the child and his mother and escape
to Egypt. Stay there until I tell you, for Herod is
going to search for the child to kill him."
14So he got up, took the child and his mother
during the night and left for Egypt, 15where he
stayed until the death of Herod. And so was
fulfilled what the Lord had said through the
prophet: "Out of Egypt I called my son."[d]
16When Herod realized that he had been out-
witted by the Magi, he was furious, and he gave
orders to kill all the boys in Bethlehem and its
vicinity who were two years old and under, in
accordance with the time he had learned from
the Magi. 17Then what was said through the
prophet Jeremiah was fulfilled:

18"A voice is heard in Ramah,
weeping and great mourning,
Rachel weeping for her children
and refusing to be comforted,
because they are no more."[e]

The Return to Nazareth

19After Herod died, an angel of the Lord
appeared in a dream to Joseph in Egypt 20and
said, "Get up, take the child and his mother and
go to the land of Israel, for those who were trying to take the child's life are dead."
21So he got up, took the child and his mother
and went to the land of Israel. 22But when he
heard that Archelaus was reigning in Judea in
place of his father Herod, he was afraid to go
there. Having been warned in a dream, he withdrew to the district of Galilee, 23and he went
and lived in a town called Nazareth. So was fulfilled what was said through the prophets: "He
will be called a Nazarene."

John the Baptist Prepares the Way

3 In those days John the Baptist came,
preaching in the Desert of Judea 2and
saying, "Repent, for the kingdom of heaven is
near." 3This is he who was spoken of through
the prophet Isaiah:

"A voice of one calling in the desert,
'Prepare the way for the Lord,
make straight paths for him.'"[f]

4John's clothes were made of camel's hair,
and he had a leather belt around his waist. His
food was locusts and wild honey. 5People went
out to him from Jerusalem and all Judea and
the whole region of the Jordan. 6Confessing
their sins, they were baptized by him in the Jordan River.
7But when he saw many of the Pharisees and
Sadducees coming to where he was baptizing,
he said to them: "You brood of vipers! Who
warned you to flee from the coming wrath?
8Produce fruit in keeping with repentance.
9And do not think you can say to yourselves,
'We have Abraham as our father.' I tell you that
out of these stones God can raise up children

[a]4 Or *Messiah* [b]6 Micah 5:2 [c]9 Or *seen when it rose* [d]15 Hosea 11:1 [e]18 Jer. 31:15 [f]3 Isaiah 40:3

for Abraham. 10The ax is already at the root of
the trees, and every tree that does not produce
good fruit will be cut down and thrown into
the fire.
11"I baptize you with[a] water for repentance.
But after me will come one who is more powerful than I, whose sandals I am not fit to carry.
He will baptize you with the Holy Spirit and
with fire. 12His winnowing fork is in his hand,
and he will clear his threshing floor, gathering
his wheat into the barn and burning up the
chaff with unquenchable fire."

The Baptism of Jesus

13Then Jesus came from Galilee to the Jordan to be baptized by John. 14But John tried
to deter him, saying, "I need to be baptized by
you, and do you come to me?"
15Jesus replied, "Let it be so now; it is proper
for us to do this to fulfill all righteousness."
Then John consented.
16As soon as Jesus was baptized, he went up
out of the water. At that moment heaven was
opened, and he saw the Spirit of God descending like a dove and lighting on him. 17And a
voice from heaven said, "This is my Son, whom
I love; with him I am well pleased."

The Temptation of Jesus

4 Then Jesus was led by the Spirit into the
desert to be tempted by the devil. 2After
fasting forty days and forty nights, he was hungry. 3The tempter came to him and said, "If
you are the Son of God, tell these stones to become bread."
4Jesus answered, "It is written: 'Man does
not live on bread alone, but on every word that
comes from the mouth of God.'[b]"
5Then the devil took him to the holy city
and had him stand on the highest point of the
temple. 6"If you are the Son of God," he said,
"throw yourself down. For it is written:

"'He will command his angels concerning
you,
and they will lift you up in their hands,
so that you will not strike your foot against
a stone.'[c]"

7Jesus answered him, "It is also written: 'Do
not put the Lord your God to the test.'[d]"
8Again, the devil took him to a very high
mountain and showed him all the kingdoms of
the world and their splendor. 9"All this I will
give you," he said, "if you will bow down and
worship me."
10Jesus said to him, "Away from me, Satan!
For it is written: 'Worship the Lord your God,
and serve him only.'[e]"
11Then the devil left him, and angels came
and attended him.

Jesus Begins to Preach

12When Jesus heard that John had been put
in prison, he returned to Galilee. 13Leaving Nazareth, he went and lived in Capernaum, which
was by the lake in the area of Zebulun and
Naphtali— 14to fulfill what was said through
the prophet Isaiah:

15"Land of Zebulun and land of Naphtali,
the way to the sea, along the Jordan,
Galilee of the Gentiles—
16the people living in darkness
have seen a great light;
on those living in the land of the shadow
of death
a light has dawned."[f]

17From that time on Jesus began to preach,
"Repent, for the kingdom of heaven is near."

The Calling of the First Disciples

18As Jesus was walking beside the Sea of
Galilee, he saw two brothers, Simon called Peter and his brother Andrew. They were casting
a net into the lake, for they were fishermen.
19"Come, follow me," Jesus said, "and I will
make you fishers of men." 20At once they left
their nets and followed him.
21Going on from there, he saw two other
brothers, James son of Zebedee and his brother
John. They were in a boat with their father Zebedee, preparing their nets. Jesus called them,
22and immediately they left the boat and their
father and followed him.

Jesus Heals the Sick

23Jesus went throughout Galilee, teaching
in their synagogues, preaching the good news
of the kingdom, and healing every disease and
sickness among the people. 24News about him

[a]11 Or *in* [b]4 Deut. 8:3 [c]6 Psalm 91:11,12 [d]7 Deut. 6:16 [e]10 Deut. 6:13 [f]16 Isaiah 9:1,2

spread all over Syria, and people brought to him
all who were ill with various diseases, those suffering severe pain, the demon-possessed, those
having seizures, and the paralyzed, and he
healed them. 25 Large crowds from Galilee, the
Decapolis,[a] Jerusalem, Judea and the region
across the Jordan followed him.

The Beatitudes

5 Now when he saw the crowds, he went
up on a mountainside and sat down. His
disciples came to him, 2 and he began to teach
them, saying:

3 "Blessed are the poor in spirit,
for theirs is the kingdom of heaven.
4 Blessed are those who mourn,
for they will be comforted.
5 Blessed are the meek,
for they will inherit the earth.
6 Blessed are those who hunger and thirst
for righteousness,
for they will be filled.
7 Blessed are the merciful,
for they will be shown mercy.
8 Blessed are the pure in heart,
for they will see God.
9 Blessed are the peacemakers,
for they will be called sons of God.
10 Blessed are those who are persecuted
because of righteousness,
for theirs is the kingdom of heaven.

11 "Blessed are you when people insult you,
persecute you and falsely say all kinds of evil
against you because of me. 12 Rejoice and be
glad, because great is your reward in heaven,
for in the same way they persecuted the prophets who were before you.

Salt and Light

13 "You are the salt of the earth. But if the
salt loses its saltiness, how can it be made salty
again? It is no longer good for anything, except
to be thrown out and trampled by men.
14 "You are the light of the world. A city on
a hill cannot be hidden. 15 Neither do people
light a lamp and put it under a bowl. Instead
they put it on its stand, and it gives light to everyone in the house. 16 In the same way, let your
light shine before men, that they may see your
good deeds and praise your Father in heaven.

The Fulfillment of the Law

17 "Do not think that I have come to abolish
the Law or the Prophets; I have not come to
abolish them but to fulfill them. 18 I tell you
the truth, until heaven and earth disappear,
not the smallest letter, not the least stroke of
a pen, will by any means disappear from the
Law until everything is accomplished. 19 Anyone who breaks one of the least of these commandments and teaches others to do the same
will be called least in the kingdom of heaven,
but whoever practices and teaches these commands will be called great in the kingdom of
heaven. 20 For I tell you that unless your righteousness surpasses that of the Pharisees and
the teachers of the law, you will certainly not
enter the kingdom of heaven.

Murder

21 "You have heard that it was said to the people long ago, 'Do not murder,[b] and anyone who
murders will be subject to judgment.' 22 But I tell
you that anyone who is angry with his brother[c]
will be subject to judgment. Again, anyone
who says to his brother, 'Raca,[d]' is answerable
to the Sanhedrin. But anyone who says, 'You
fool!' will be in danger of the fire of hell.
23 "Therefore, if you are offering your gift at
the altar and there remember that your brother
has something against you, 24 leave your gift
there in front of the altar. First go and be reconciled to your brother; then come and offer
your gift.
25 "Settle matters quickly with your adversary who is taking you to court. Do it while you
are still with him on the way, or he may hand
you over to the judge, and the judge may hand
you over to the officer, and you may be thrown
into prison. 26 I tell you the truth, you will not
get out until you have paid the last penny.[e]

Adultery

27 "You have heard that it was said, 'Do not
commit adultery.'[f] 28 But I tell you that anyone
who looks at a woman lustfully has already
committed adultery with her in his heart. 29 If
your right eye causes you to sin, gouge it out

[a] 25 That is, the Ten Cities [b] 21 Exodus 20:13 [c] 22 Some manuscripts *brother without cause* [d] 22 An Aramaic term of contempt
[e] 26 Greek *kodrantes* [f] 27 Exodus 20:14

and throw it away. It is better for you to lose one part of your body than for your whole body to be thrown into hell. 30And if your right hand causes you to sin, cut it off and throw it away. It is better for you to lose one part of your body than for your whole body to go into hell.

Divorce

31"It has been said, 'Anyone who divorces his wife must give her a certificate of divorce.'[a] 32But I tell you that anyone who divorces his wife, except for marital unfaithfulness, causes her to become an adulteress, and anyone who marries the divorced woman commits adultery.

Oaths

33"Again, you have heard that it was said to the people long ago, 'Do not break your oath, but keep the oaths you have made to the Lord.' 34But I tell you, Do not swear at all: either by heaven, for it is God's throne; 35or by the earth, for it is his footstool; or by Jerusalem, for it is the city of the Great King. 36And do not swear by your head, for you cannot make even one hair white or black. 37Simply let your 'Yes' be 'Yes,' and your 'No,' 'No'; anything beyond this comes from the evil one.

An Eye for an Eye

38"You have heard that it was said, 'Eye for eye, and tooth for tooth.'[b] 39But I tell you, Do not resist an evil person. If someone strikes you on the right cheek, turn to him the other also. 40And if someone wants to sue you and take your tunic, let him have your cloak as well. 41If someone forces you to go one mile, go with him two miles. 42Give to the one who asks you, and do not turn away from the one who wants to borrow from you.

Love for Enemies

43"You have heard that it was said, 'Love your neighbor[c] and hate your enemy.' 44But I tell you: Love your enemies[d] and pray for those who persecute you, 45that you may be sons of your Father in heaven. He causes his sun to rise on the evil and the good, and sends rain on the righteous and the unrighteous. 46If you love those who love you, what reward will you get? Are not even the tax collectors doing that? 47And if you greet only your brothers, what are you doing more than others? Do not even pagans do that? 48Be perfect, therefore, as your heavenly Father is perfect.

Giving to the Needy

6 "Be careful not to do your 'acts of righteousness' before men, to be seen by them. If you do, you will have no reward from your Father in heaven.

2"So when you give to the needy, do not announce it with trumpets, as the hypocrites do in the synagogues and on the streets, to be honored by men. I tell you the truth, they have received their reward in full. 3But when you give to the needy, do not let your left hand know what your right hand is doing, 4so that your giving may be in secret. Then your Father, who sees what is done in secret, will reward you.

> **Matthew 6:1**
>
> *God Rewards Sincere Service*
>
> "Be careful not to do your 'acts of righteousness' before men, to be seen by them. If you do, you will have no reward from your Father in heaven."

Prayer

5"And when you pray, do not be like the hypocrites, for they love to pray standing in the synagogues and on the street corners to be seen by men. I tell you the truth, they have received their reward in full. 6But when you pray, go into your room, close the door and pray to your Father, who is unseen. Then your Father, who sees what is done in secret, will reward you. 7And when you pray, do not keep on babbling like pagans, for they think they will be heard because of their many words. 8Do not be like them, for your Father knows what you need before you ask him.

9"This, then, is how you should pray:

"'Our Father in heaven,
hallowed be your name,
10your kingdom come,

[a]31 Deut. 24:1 [b]38 Exodus 21:24; Lev. 24:20; Deut. 19:21 [c]43 Lev. 19:18 [d]44 Some late manuscripts *enemies, bless those who curse you, do good to those who hate you*

your will be done
on earth as it is in heaven.
11 Give us today our daily bread.
12 Forgive us our debts,
as we also have forgiven our debtors.
13 And lead us not into temptation,
but deliver us from the evil one.[a]'

14 For if you forgive men when they sin against
you, your heavenly Father will also forgive you.
15 But if you do not forgive men their sins, your
Father will not forgive your sins.

Fasting

16 "When you fast, do not look somber as the
hypocrites do, for they disfigure their faces to
show men they are fasting. I tell you the truth,
they have received their reward in full. 17 But
when you fast, put oil on your head and wash
your face, 18 so that it will not be obvious to
men that you are fasting, but only to your Father, who is unseen; and your Father, who sees
what is done in secret, will reward you.

Treasures in Heaven

19 "Do not store up for yourselves treasures
on earth, where moth and rust destroy, and
where thieves break in and steal. 20 But store up
for yourselves treasures in heaven, where moth
and rust do not destroy, and where thieves do
not break in and steal. 21 For where your treasure is, there your heart will be also.

22 "The eye is the lamp of the body. If your
eyes are good, your whole body will be full of
light. 23 But if your eyes are bad, your whole
body will be full of darkness. If then the light
within you is darkness, how great is that darkness!

24 "No one can serve two masters. Either he
will hate the one and love the other, or he will
be devoted to the one and despise the other.
You cannot serve both God and Money.

Do Not Worry

25 "Therefore I tell you, do not worry about
your life, what you will eat or drink; or about
your body, what you will wear. Is not life more
important than food, and the body more important than clothes? 26 Look at the birds of
the air; they do not sow or reap or store away
in barns, and yet your heavenly Father feeds
them. Are you not much more valuable than
they? 27 Who of you by worrying can add a single hour to his life[b]?

28 "And why do you worry about clothes?
See how the lilies of the field grow. They do not
labor or spin. 29 Yet I tell you that not even Solomon in all his splendor was dressed like one
of these. 30 If that is how God clothes the grass
of the field, which is here today and tomorrow
is thrown into the fire, will he not much more
clothe you, O you of little faith? 31 So do not
worry, saying, 'What shall we eat?' or 'What
shall we drink?' or 'What shall we wear?' 32 For
the pagans run after all these things, and your
heavenly Father knows that you need them.
33 But seek first his kingdom and his righteousness, and all these things will be given to you
as well. 34 Therefore do not worry about tomorrow, for tomorrow will worry about itself. Each
day has enough trouble of its own.

Judging Others

7 "Do not judge, or you too will be judged.
2 For in the same way you judge others,
you will be judged, and with the measure you
use, it will be measured to you.

3 "Why do you look at the speck of sawdust
in your brother's eye and pay no attention to
the plank in your own eye? 4 How can you say
to your brother, 'Let me take the speck out of
your eye,' when all the time there is a plank
in your own eye? 5 You hypocrite, first take
the plank out of your own eye, and then you
will see clearly to remove the speck from your
brother's eye.

6 "Do not give dogs what is sacred; do not
throw your pearls to pigs. If you do, they may
trample them under their feet, and then turn
and tear you to pieces.

Ask, Seek, Knock

7 "Ask and it will be given to you; seek and you
will find; knock and the door will be opened to
you. 8 For everyone who asks receives; he who
seeks finds; and to him who knocks, the door
will be opened.

9 "Which of you, if his son asks for bread, will
give him a stone? 10 Or if he asks for a fish, will

[a] 13 Or *from evil*; some late manuscripts *one, / for yours is the kingdom and the power and the glory forever. Amen.* [b] 27 Or *single cubit to his height*

give him a snake? 11If you, then, though you are evil, know how to give good gifts to your children, how much more will your Father in heaven give good gifts to those who ask him! 12So in everything, do to others what you would have them do to you, for this sums up the Law and the Prophets.

The Narrow and Wide Gates

13"Enter through the narrow gate. For wide is the gate and broad is the road that leads to destruction, and many enter through it. 14But small is the gate and narrow the road that leads to life, and only a few find it.

A Tree and Its Fruit

15"Watch out for false prophets. They come to you in sheep's clothing, but inwardly they are ferocious wolves. 16By their fruit you will recognize them. Do people pick grapes from thornbushes, or figs from thistles? 17Likewise every good tree bears good fruit, but a bad tree bears bad fruit. 18A good tree cannot bear bad fruit, and a bad tree cannot bear good fruit. 19Every tree that does not bear good fruit is cut down and thrown into the fire. 20Thus, by their fruit you will recognize them.

21"Not everyone who says to me, 'Lord, Lord,' will enter the kingdom of heaven, but only he who does the will of my Father who is in heaven. 22Many will say to me on that day, 'Lord, Lord, did we not prophesy in your name, and in your name drive out demons and perform many miracles?' 23Then I will tell them plainly, 'I never knew you. Away from me, you evildoers!'

The Wise and Foolish Builders

24"Therefore everyone who hears these words of mine and puts them into practice is like a wise man who built his house on the rock. 25The rain came down, the streams rose, and the winds blew and beat against that house; yet it did not fall, because it had its foundation on the rock. 26But everyone who hears these words of mine and does not put them into practice is like a foolish man who built his house on sand. 27The rain came down, the streams rose, and the winds blew and beat against that house, and it fell with a great crash."

28When Jesus had finished saying these things, the crowds were amazed at his teaching, 29because he taught as one who had authority, and not as their teachers of the law.

The Man With Leprosy

8 When he came down from the mountainside, large crowds followed him. 2A man with leprosy[a] came and knelt before him and said, "Lord, if you are willing, you can make me clean."

3Jesus reached out his hand and touched the man. "I am willing," he said. "Be clean!" Immediately he was cured[b] of his leprosy. 4Then Jesus said to him, "See that you don't tell anyone. But go, show yourself to the priest and offer the gift Moses commanded, as a testimony to them."

The Faith of the Centurion

5When Jesus had entered Capernaum, a centurion came to him, asking for help. 6"Lord," he said, "my servant lies at home paralyzed and in terrible suffering."

7Jesus said to him, "I will go and heal him."

8The centurion replied, "Lord, I do not deserve to have you come under my roof. But just say the word, and my servant will be healed. 9For I myself am a man under authority, with soldiers under me. I tell this one, 'Go,' and he goes; and that one, 'Come,' and he comes. I say to my servant, 'Do this,' and he does it."

10When Jesus heard this, he was astonished and said to those following him, "I tell you the truth, I have not found anyone in Israel with such great faith. 11I say to you that many will come from the east and the west, and will take their places at the feast with Abraham, Isaac and Jacob in the kingdom of heaven. 12But the subjects of the kingdom will be thrown outside, into the darkness, where there will be weeping and gnashing of teeth."

13Then Jesus said to the centurion, "Go! It will be done just as you believed it would." And his servant was healed at that very hour.

Jesus Heals Many

14When Jesus came into Peter's house, he saw Peter's mother-in-law lying in bed with a fever. 15He touched her hand and the fever

[a]2 The Greek word was used for various diseases affecting the skin—not necessarily leprosy. [b]3 Greek *made clean*

The Giver

Read: Matthew 7:7–29

Matthew 7:11
"If you, then, though you are evil, know how to give good gifts to your children, how much more will your Father in heaven give good gifts to those who ask him!"

ACCORDING TO RECENT STATISTICS, parents spend an average of $1,500 a year on clothes for their kids and $450 a year on furnishings for their kids' rooms. Children as young as elementary school age have cell phones, portable digital audio players, high-definition televisions and multiple video game platforms. Every year, parents in the United States spend tens of billions of dollars on Christmas gifts for their kids.

These statistics reflect more than rampant consumerism. They reflect the desire of parents to give gifts to their kids. Parents have always wanted their children to have good things.

Jesus used this universal truth to teach us of the power of prayer. It is a natural instinct to care for our child, to respond when our child asks for help or food or even a present. How much more will our heavenly Father give good gifts to his children!

Unlike earthly parents, God the Father gives *perfect* gifts because they are spiritual gifts uniquely suited to each of us. There's no such thing as a Christian who's been spoiled rotten with spiritual gifts. God gives us gifts that fit us perfectly, gifts that fill and complete us. How are we to respond to such generosity? By using those gifts to the utmost. Isn't that what every parent wants their child to do? We offer our children good things, so they'll know they are loved. But we want them to use their gifts often and take care of them.

And God wants us to *delight* in his good gifts. What parent wants a child to put a present back under the Christmas tree and walk away disappointed? We want to see joy on our child's face as she receives gifts from us. We want her to enjoy what we have given her. We know she loves her doll if she picks it up and hugs it. We're sure he loves his bike if he climbs on and rides it. Our heavenly Father longs for us to enjoy the gifts he gives, to wrap our arms around them and use them for his good pleasure. God's gifts are there for the taking . . . with pleasure.

reflection

1 What is one good gift that God has offered you today? How have you embraced it?

2 In what ways do your memories of your earthly parents affect how you read this passage?

3 What spiritual gifts have you been given? Spend some time in prayer, asking your heavenly Father for gifts to build his body, the church.

RELATED READINGS

Romans 12:3–8; 1 Corinthians 12:4–31; Ephesians 3:14–21; James 1:17–18

"To remain a child before God is to recognize our nothingness, to expect everything from God as a little child expects everything from its father."

Therese of Liseux

Go to page 1171 for your next devotional reading.

left her, and she got up and began to wait on
him.
16When evening came, many who were demon-possessed were brought to him, and he
drove out the spirits with a word and healed all
the sick. 17This was to fulfill what was spoken
through the prophet Isaiah:

"He took up our infirmities
and carried our diseases."[a]

The Cost of Following Jesus

18When Jesus saw the crowd around him,
he gave orders to cross to the other side of the
lake. 19Then a teacher of the law came to him
and said, "Teacher, I will follow you wherever
you go."
20Jesus replied, "Foxes have holes and birds
of the air have nests, but the Son of Man has no
place to lay his head."
21Another disciple said to him, "Lord, first
let me go and bury my father."
22But Jesus told him, "Follow me, and let the
dead bury their own dead."

Jesus Calms the Storm

23Then he got into the boat
and his disciples followed him.
24Without warning, a furious
storm came up on the lake, so
that the waves swept over the
boat. But Jesus was sleeping.
25The disciples went and woke
him, saying, "Lord, save us!
We're going to drown!"
26He replied, "You of little
faith, why are you so afraid?"
Then he got up and rebuked
the winds and the waves, and
it was completely calm.
27The men were amazed
and asked, "What kind of man
is this? Even the winds and the waves obey
him!"

The Healing of Two Demon-possessed Men

28When he arrived at the other side in the region of the Gadarenes,[b] two demon-possessed
men coming from the tombs met him. They
were so violent that no one could pass that way.
29"What do you want with us, Son of God?"
they shouted. "Have you come here to torture
us before the appointed time?"
30Some distance from them a large herd of
pigs was feeding. 31The demons begged Jesus,
"If you drive us out, send us into the herd
of pigs."
32He said to them, "Go!" So they came out
and went into the pigs, and the whole herd
rushed down the steep bank into the lake and
died in the water. 33Those tending the pigs ran
off, went into the town and reported all this, including what had happened to the demon-possessed men. 34Then the whole town went out
to meet Jesus. And when they saw him, they
pleaded with him to leave their region.

Jesus Heals a Paralytic

9 Jesus stepped into a boat, crossed over and
came to his own town. 2Some men brought
to him a paralytic, lying on a mat. When Jesus
saw their faith, he said to the paralytic, "Take
heart, son; your sins are forgiven."
3At this, some of the teachers of the law said
to themselves, "This fellow is
blaspheming!"
4Knowing their thoughts,
Jesus said, "Why do you entertain evil thoughts in your
hearts? 5Which is easier: to
say, 'Your sins are forgiven,' or
to say, 'Get up and walk'? 6But
so that you may know that
the Son of Man has authority
on earth to forgive sins..."
Then he said to the paralytic,
"Get up, take your mat and
go home." 7And the man got
up and went home. 8When
the crowd saw this, they were
filled with awe; and they
praised God, who had given
such authority to men.

The Calling of Matthew

9As Jesus went on from there, he saw a man
named Matthew sitting at the tax collector's
booth. "Follow me," he told him, and Matthew
got up and followed him.
10While Jesus was having dinner at Matthew's house, many tax collectors and "sinners"

> **Matthew 9:6**
>
> *God Forgives Sins*
>
> "But so that you may know that the Son of Man has authority on earth to forgive sins . . ." Then he said to the paralytic, "Get up, take your mat and go home."

[a]17 Isaiah 53:4 [b]28 Some manuscripts *Gergesenes*; others *Gerasenes*

came and ate with him and his disciples.
11 When the Pharisees saw this, they asked his
disciples, "Why does your teacher eat with tax
collectors and 'sinners'?"

12 On hearing this, Jesus said, "It is not the
healthy who need a doctor, but the sick. 13 But
go and learn what this means: 'I desire mercy,
not sacrifice.'[a] For I have not come to call the
righteous, but sinners."

Jesus Questioned About Fasting

14 Then John's disciples came and asked him,
"How is it that we and the Pharisees fast, but
your disciples do not fast?"

15 Jesus answered, "How can the guests of
the bridegroom mourn while he is with them?
The time will come when the bridegroom will
be taken from them; then they will fast.

16 "No one sews a patch of unshrunk cloth
on an old garment, for the patch will pull away
from the garment, making the tear worse. 17 Neither do men pour new wine into old wineskins.
If they do, the skins will burst, the wine will run
out and the wineskins will be ruined. No, they
pour new wine into new wineskins, and both
are preserved."

A Dead Girl and a Sick Woman

18 While he was saying this, a ruler came and
knelt before him and said, "My daughter has
just died. But come and put your hand on her,
and she will live." 19 Jesus got up and went with
him, and so did his disciples.

20 Just then a woman who had been subject
to bleeding for twelve years came up behind
him and touched the edge of his cloak. 21 She
said to herself, "If I only touch his cloak, I will
be healed."

22 Jesus turned and saw her. "Take heart,
daughter," he said, "your faith has healed you."
And the woman was healed from that moment.

23 When Jesus entered the ruler's house and
saw the flute players and the noisy crowd, 24 he
said, "Go away. The girl is not dead but asleep."
But they laughed at him. 25 After the crowd had
been put outside, he went in and took the girl
by the hand, and she got up. 26 News of this
spread through all that region.

Jesus Heals the Blind and Mute

27 As Jesus went on from there, two blind
men followed him, calling out, "Have mercy
on us, Son of David!"

28 When he had gone indoors, the blind men
came to him, and he asked them, "Do you believe that I am able to do this?"

"Yes, Lord," they replied.

29 Then he touched their eyes and said, "According to your faith will it be done to you";
30 and their sight was restored. Jesus warned
them sternly, "See that no one knows about
this." 31 But they went out and spread the news
about him all over that region.

32 While they were going out, a man who
was demon-possessed and could not talk was
brought to Jesus. 33 And when the demon was
driven out, the man who had been mute spoke.
The crowd was amazed and said, "Nothing like
this has ever been seen in Israel."

34 But the Pharisees said, "It is by the prince
of demons that he drives out demons."

The Workers Are Few

35 Jesus went through all the towns and
villages, teaching in their synagogues, preaching the good news of the kingdom and healing
every disease and sickness. 36 When he saw the
crowds, he had compassion on them, because
they were harassed and helpless, like sheep without a shepherd. 37 Then he said to his disciples,
"The harvest is plentiful but the workers are
few. 38 Ask the Lord of the harvest, therefore,
to send out workers into his harvest field."

Jesus Sends Out the Twelve

10 He called his twelve disciples to him
and gave them authority to drive out
evil[b] spirits and to heal every disease and sickness.

2 These are the names of the twelve apostles: first, Simon (who is called Peter) and his
brother Andrew; James son of Zebedee, and
his brother John; 3 Philip and Bartholomew;
Thomas and Matthew the tax collector; James
son of Alphaeus, and Thaddaeus; 4 Simon the
Zealot and Judas Iscariot, who betrayed him.

5 These twelve Jesus sent out with the following instructions: "Do not go among the Gentiles or enter any town of the Samaritans. 6 Go

[a] 13 Hosea 6:6 [b] 1 Greek *unclean*

Press Toward Jesus

Read: Matthew 9:20–22

JOANNA LOOKED AT HERSELF in the mirror and sighed—a sigh of total, utter exhaustion. She felt much older than her 34 years. It felt as though she had been struggling with insomnia, muscle pain and fatigue forever. One doctor diagnosed her with Epstein Barr. Another with depression. Another simply said she didn't have a diagnosis. One seemed to hint that she was making up her symptoms.

Joanna knew God was in control, but it was hard to trust on days like this when all she wanted to do was crawl under the covers and sob. "God, where are you?" she cried. "How much longer do I have to go through this?" Joanna was desperate, so she leaned on Jesus. No, he didn't miraculously heal her. But he graciously helped her each and every day as she leaned on him for strength.

The woman who touched Jesus' cloak must have felt the same sort of desperation. The Bible says she had been bleeding for 12 years. Not only was she suffering physically, she was also probably suffering emotionally. In Jewish society, such a woman would have been labeled "unclean." Because of this status, she would have been considered an outcast. The loneliness and isolation must have felt overwhelming. No wonder she pressed through the multitude of people who were following the Messiah. She must have believed that touching him was her only hope.

Imagine her breathless expectation as she reached toward Jesus . . . and her overwhelming relief when she realized that he had, indeed, relieved her suffering. What joy must have flooded her the very instant she touched the hem of his cloak!

Are you feeling desperate like these two women? Do you cry for relief from a lingering illness? If so, take comfort in the fact that Jesus is near and that he is the Great Physician. Sometimes, he heals in an instant, as he did in this story. At other times, he heals over a period of years or he waits to heal, allowing us to press into him so that he can "strengthen [us] with power through his Spirit in [our] inner being" (Ephesians 3:16). At still other times, he does not heal. Then, like Paul, we learn that "[God's] power is made perfect in weakness" (2 Corinthians 12:9).

The ways in which God ministers to people are as varied as the people he touches—but he is *always* faithful to bring peace and joy, even in midst of our suffering. Today, press close to him. You'll experience his power.

Matthew 9:20–21

Just then a woman who had been subject to bleeding for twelve years came up behind him and touched the edge of his cloak. She said to herself, "If I only touch his cloak, I will be healed."

reflection

1 Describe an area of your life in which you feel truly desperate.

2 How have you felt isolated from others because of your circumstances?

3 Press into Jesus in prayer. Ask him to restore you to fellowship with him and fellowship with believers. Ask him to heal you physically, emotionally and spiritually. If he chooses not to heal you this day, ask him to strengthen you with his power instead.

RELATED READINGS

Luke 4:16–19;
2 Corinthians 12:7–9;
Hebrews 10:19–25

Go to page 1176 for your next devotional reading.

rather to the lost sheep of Israel. 7As you go, preach this message: 'The kingdom of heaven is near.' 8Heal the sick, raise the dead, cleanse those who have leprosy,[a] drive out demons. Freely you have received, freely give. 9Do not take along any gold or silver or copper in your belts; 10take no bag for the journey, or extra tunic, or sandals or a staff; for the worker is worth his keep.

11"Whatever town or village you enter, search for some worthy person there and stay at his house until you leave. 12As you enter the home, give it your greeting. 13If the home is deserving, let your peace rest on it; if it is not, let your peace return to you. 14If anyone will not welcome you or listen to your words, shake the dust off your feet when you leave that home or town. 15I tell you the truth, it will be more bearable for Sodom and Gomorrah on the day of judgment than for that town. 16I am sending you out like sheep among wolves. Therefore be as shrewd as snakes and as innocent as doves.

17"Be on your guard against men; they will hand you over to the local councils and flog you in their synagogues. 18On my account you will be brought before governors and kings as witnesses to them and to the Gentiles. 19But when they arrest you, do not worry about what to say or how to say it. At that time you will be given what to say, 20for it will not be you speaking, but the Spirit of your Father speaking through you.

21"Brother will betray brother to death, and a father his child; children will rebel against their parents and have them put to death. 22All men will hate you because of me, but he who stands firm to the end will be saved. 23When you are persecuted in one place, flee to another. I tell you the truth, you will not finish going through the cities of Israel before the Son of Man comes.

24"A student is not above his teacher, nor a servant above his master. 25It is enough for the student to be like his teacher, and the servant like his master. If the head of the house has been called Beelzebub,[b] how much more the members of his household!

26"So do not be afraid of them. There is nothing concealed that will not be disclosed, or hidden that will not be made known. 27What I tell you in the dark, speak in the daylight; what is whispered in your ear, proclaim from the roofs. 28Do not be afraid of those who kill the body but cannot kill the soul. Rather, be afraid of the One who can destroy both soul and body in hell. 29Are not two sparrows sold for a penny[c]? Yet not one of them will fall to the ground apart from the will of your Father. 30And even the very hairs of your head are all numbered. 31So don't be afraid; you are worth more than many sparrows.

32"Whoever acknowledges me before men, I will also acknowledge him before my Father in heaven. 33But whoever disowns me before men, I will disown him before my Father in heaven.

34"Do not suppose that I have come to bring peace to the earth. I did not come to bring peace, but a sword. 35For I have come to turn

"'a man against his father,
a daughter against her mother,
a daughter-in-law against her mother-in-law—
36 a man's enemies will be the members of his own household.'[d]

37"Anyone who loves his father or mother more than me is not worthy of me; anyone who loves his son or daughter more than me is not worthy of me; 38and anyone who does not take his cross and follow me is not worthy of me. 39Whoever finds his life will lose it, and whoever loses his life for my sake will find it.

40"He who receives you receives me, and he who receives me receives the one who sent me.

Matthew 10:29

God Watches Over All

"Are not two sparrows sold for a penny? Yet not one of them will fall to the ground apart from the will of your Father."

[a]8 The Greek word was used for various diseases affecting the skin—not necessarily leprosy. [b]25 Greek *Beezeboul* or *Beelzeboul*
[c]29 Greek *an assarion* [d]36 Micah 7:6

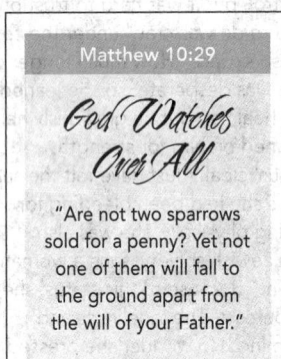

41 Anyone who receives a prophet because he is
a prophet will receive a prophet's reward, and
anyone who receives a righteous man because
he is a righteous man will receive a righteous
man's reward. 42 And if anyone gives even a cup
of cold water to one of these little ones because
he is my disciple, I tell you the truth, he will
certainly not lose his reward."

Jesus and John the Baptist

11 After Jesus had finished instructing his
twelve disciples, he went on from there
to teach and preach in the towns of Galilee.[a]
2 When John heard in prison what Christ
was doing, he sent his disciples 3 to ask him,
"Are you the one who was to come, or should
we expect someone else?"
4 Jesus replied, "Go back and report to John
what you hear and see: 5 The blind receive
sight, the lame walk, those who have leprosy[b]
are cured, the deaf hear, the dead are raised,
and the good news is preached to the poor.
6 Blessed is the man who does not fall away on
account of me."
7 As John's disciples were leaving, Jesus began to speak to the crowd about John: "What
did you go out into the desert to see? A reed
swayed by the wind? 8 If not, what did you
go out to see? A man dressed in fine clothes?
No, those who wear fine clothes are in kings'
palaces. 9 Then what did you go out to see?
A prophet? Yes, I tell you, and more than a
prophet. 10 This is the one about whom it is
written:

"'I will send my messenger ahead of you,
who will prepare your way before you.'[c]

11 I tell you the truth: Among those born of
women there has not risen anyone greater
than John the Baptist; yet he who is least in
the kingdom of heaven is greater than he.
12 From the days of John the Baptist until now,
the kingdom of heaven has been forcefully
advancing, and forceful men lay hold of it.
13 For all the Prophets and the Law prophesied
until John. 14 And if you are willing to accept
it, he is the Elijah who was to come. 15 He who
has ears, let him hear.
16 "To what can I compare this generation?
They are like children sitting in the marketplaces and calling out to others:

17 "'We played the flute for you,
and you did not dance;
we sang a dirge,
and you did not mourn.'

18 For John came neither eating nor drinking,
and they say, 'He has a demon.' 19 The Son of
Man came eating and drinking, and they say,
'Here is a glutton and a drunkard, a friend of
tax collectors and "sinners."' But wisdom is
proved right by her actions."

Woe on Unrepentant Cities

20 Then Jesus began to denounce the cities
in which most of his miracles had been performed, because they did not repent. 21 "Woe
to you, Korazin! Woe to you, Bethsaida! If the
miracles that were performed in you had been
performed in Tyre and Sidon, they would have
repented long ago in sackcloth and ashes. 22 But
I tell you, it will be more bearable for Tyre and
Sidon on the day of judgment than for you.
23 And you, Capernaum, will you be lifted
up to the skies? No, you will go down to the
depths.[d] If the miracles that were performed in
you had been performed in Sodom, it would
have remained to this day. 24 But I tell you that
it will be more bearable for Sodom on the day
of judgment than for you."

Rest for the Weary

25 At that time Jesus said, "I praise you, Father, Lord of heaven and earth, because you
have hidden these things from the wise and
learned, and revealed them to little children.
26 Yes, Father, for this was your good pleasure.
27 "All things have been committed to me by
my Father. No one knows the Son except the
Father, and no one knows the Father except
the Son and those to whom the Son chooses
to reveal him.
28 "Come to me, all you who are weary and
burdened, and I will give you rest. 29 Take my
yoke upon you and learn from me, for I am
gentle and humble in heart, and you will find
rest for your souls. 30 For my yoke is easy and
my burden is light."

[a] 1 Greek *in their towns* [b] 5 The Greek word was used for various diseases affecting the skin—not necessarily leprosy. [c] 10 Mal. 3:1
[d] 23 Greek *Hades*

Lord of the Sabbath

12 At that time Jesus went through the
grainfields on the Sabbath. His disciples
were hungry and began to pick
some heads of grain and eat
them. 2When the Pharisees saw
this, they said to him, "Look!
Your disciples are doing what
is unlawful on the Sabbath."
3He answered, "Haven't you
read what David did when he
and his companions were hungry? 4He entered the house
of God, and he and his companions ate the consecrated
bread—which was not lawful
for them to do, but only for the priests. 5Or
haven't you read in the Law that on the Sabbath
the priests in the temple desecrate the day and
yet are innocent? 6I tell you that one[a] greater
than the temple is here. 7If you had known what
these words mean, 'I desire mercy, not sacrifice,'[b]
you would not have condemned the innocent.
8For the Son of Man is Lord of the Sabbath."
9Going on from that place, he went into
their synagogue, 10and a man with a shriveled
hand was there. Looking for a reason to accuse
Jesus, they asked him, "Is it lawful to heal on
the Sabbath?"
11He said to them, "If any of you has a sheep
and it falls into a pit on the Sabbath, will you
not take hold of it and lift it out? 12How much
more valuable is a man than a sheep! Therefore
it is lawful to do good on the Sabbath."
13Then he said to the man, "Stretch out
your hand." So he stretched it out and it was
completely restored, just as sound as the other.
14But the Pharisees went out and plotted how
they might kill Jesus.

> Matthew 11:28
>
> *God Gives Rest to the Weary*
>
> "Come to me, all you who are weary and burdened, and I will give you rest."

God's Chosen Servant

15Aware of this, Jesus withdrew from that
place. Many followed him, and he healed all
their sick, 16warning them not to tell who
he was. 17This was to fulfill what was spoken
through the prophet Isaiah:

18"Here is my servant whom I have chosen,
the one I love, in whom I delight;
I will put my Spirit on him,
and he will proclaim justice to the
nations.
19He will not quarrel or cry out;
no one will hear his voice
in the streets.
20A bruised reed he will not
break,
and a smoldering wick
he will not snuff
out,
till he leads justice to
victory.
21 In his name the nations
will put their
hope."[c]

Jesus and Beelzebub

22Then they brought him a demon-possessed man who was blind and mute, and Jesus
healed him, so that he could both talk and see.
23All the people were astonished and said,
"Could this be the Son of David?"
24But when the Pharisees heard this, they
said, "It is only by Beelzebub,[d] the prince of demons, that this fellow drives out demons."
25Jesus knew their thoughts and said to
them, "Every kingdom divided against itself
will be ruined, and every city or household
divided against itself will not stand. 26If Satan
drives out Satan, he is divided against himself.
How then can his kingdom stand? 27And if I
drive out demons by Beelzebub, by whom do
your people drive them out? So then, they will
be your judges. 28But if I drive out demons by
the Spirit of God, then the kingdom of God has
come upon you.
29"Or again, how can anyone enter a strong
man's house and carry off his possessions unless he first ties up the strong man? Then he
can rob his house.
30"He who is not with me is against me,
and he who does not gather with me scatters.
31And so I tell you, every sin and blasphemy
will be forgiven men, but the blasphemy against
the Spirit will not be forgiven. 32Anyone who
speaks a word against the Son of Man will be
forgiven, but anyone who speaks against the
Holy Spirit will not be forgiven, either in this
age or in the age to come.

[a]6 Or *something*; also in verses 41 and 42 [b]7 Hosea 6:6 [c]21 Isaiah 42:1–4 [d]24 Greek *Beezeboul* or *Beelzeboul*; also in verse 27

33“Make a tree good and its fruit will be
good, or make a tree bad and its fruit will be
bad, for a tree is recognized by its fruit. 34You
brood of vipers, how can you who are evil say
anything good? For out of the overflow of
the heart the mouth speaks. 35The good man
brings good things out of the good stored up
in him, and the evil man brings evil things out
of the evil stored up in him. 36But I tell you
that men will have to give account on the day of
judgment for every careless word they have spoken. 37For by your words you will be acquitted,
and by your words you will be condemned.”

The Sign of Jonah

38Then some of the Pharisees and teachers
of the law said to him, “Teacher, we want to see
a miraculous sign from you.”

39He answered, “A wicked and adulterous
generation asks for a miraculous sign! But none
will be given it except the sign of the prophet
Jonah. 40For as Jonah was three days and three
nights in the belly of a huge fish, so the Son
of Man will be three days and three nights in
the heart of the earth. 41The men of Nineveh
will stand up at the judgment with this generation and condemn it; for they repented at the
preaching of Jonah, and now one[a] greater than
Jonah is here. 42The Queen of the South will
rise at the judgment with this generation and
condemn it; for she came from the ends of the
earth to listen to Solomon’s wisdom, and now
one greater than Solomon is here.

43“When an evil[b] spirit comes out of a man,
it goes through arid places seeking rest and
does not find it. 44Then it says, ‘I will return
to the house I left.’ When it arrives, it finds the
house unoccupied, swept clean and put in order. 45Then it goes and takes with it seven other
spirits more wicked than itself, and they go in
and live there. And the final condition of that
man is worse than the first. That is how it will
be with this wicked generation.”

Jesus’ Mother and Brothers

46While Jesus was still talking to the crowd,
his mother and brothers stood outside, wanting to speak to him. 47Someone told him,
“Your mother and brothers are standing outside, wanting to speak to you.”[c]

48He replied to him, “Who is my mother,
and who are my brothers?” 49Pointing to his
disciples, he said, “Here are my mother and
my brothers. 50For whoever does the will of
my Father in heaven is my brother and sister
and mother.”

The Parable of the Sower

13 That same day Jesus went out of the
house and sat by the lake. 2Such large
crowds gathered around him that he got into a
boat and sat in it, while all the people stood on
the shore. 3Then he told them many things in
parables, saying: “A farmer went out to sow his
seed. 4As he was scattering the seed, some fell
along the path, and the birds came and ate it
up. 5Some fell on rocky places, where it did not
have much soil. It sprang up quickly, because
the soil was shallow. 6But when the sun came
up, the plants were scorched, and they withered because they had no root. 7Other seed
fell among thorns, which grew up and choked
the plants. 8Still other seed fell on good soil,
where it produced a crop—a hundred, sixty or
thirty times what was sown. 9He who has ears,
let him hear.”

10The disciples came to him and asked, “Why
do you speak to the people in parables?”

11He replied, “The knowledge of the secrets
of the kingdom of heaven has been given to
you, but not to them. 12Whoever has will be
given more, and he will have an abundance.
Whoever does not have, even what he has will
be taken from him. 13This is why I speak to
them in parables:

> “Though seeing, they do not see;
> though hearing, they do not hear or
> understand.

14In them is fulfilled the prophecy of Isaiah:

> “ ‘You will be ever hearing but never
> understanding;
> you will be ever seeing but never
> perceiving.
> 15For this people’s heart has become
> calloused;
> they hardly hear with their ears,
> and they have closed their eyes.
> Otherwise they might see with their eyes,

[a]41 Or *something;* also in verse 42 [b]43 Greek *unclean* [c]47 Some manuscripts do not have verse 47.

Buried Treasure

Matthew 13:13

"This is why I speak to them in parables."

reflection

1 What Bible study tools or methods do you use on a daily basis?

2 Which of the following would you use to describe your time with God's Word: skimming the surface or digging for treasure?

3 What new treasure has God revealed to you lately? What could you do with that new insight?

RELATED READINGS

Psalm 78:1–4; Proverbs 1:5–7; 2:3–5; Mark 4:10–12; Romans 11:33

Read: Matthew 13:1–58

ARE YOU DIGGING for buried treasure? If not, you should know that it's waiting there for you.

But wait. Don't reach for a shovel just yet. For this kind of digging, you need other kinds of tools: your Bible, a concordance and maybe a reliable commentary or two. And bring along your mind, heart, time and a bit of patience. You may ask, "What kind of treasure can I find with these tools?" The answer is profound. You'll find a wealth of God's wisdom that can only be found when you search for it as if you were digging for gold or silver buried beneath the earth's surface.

You may have noticed that if you read Scripture simply to check it off your to-do list, you don't gain much insight. But when you pray, when you compare one Scripture with another, when you meditate on verses, then you gain insight—then you find the golden nuggets of wisdom and truth that have been there all the time, buried beneath the surface.

In Matthew 11 and 12, Jesus had pronounced judgment on the unrepentant and especially the religious leaders who were uniting against him. But in Matthew 13, Jesus changed his approach in speaking to the crowds. He started teaching in parables—earthly stories with heavenly meanings. Only those who wanted to dig deep enough could understand what he was really saying. Others might pass Christ's teachings off as simple stories. But these "simple stories" were eternal stories—helping generations understand spiritual principles through physical metaphors. Rural folk could grasp the kingdom of heaven by looking at a farmer working in the fields. People in business could comprehend the kingdom of heaven through stories of faithful or evil servants. All could look forward to Christ's return via the story of a wedding and bridegroom. Simple stories—profound truth.

Jesus gladly answered his disciples' questions about his parables and gave them the interpretations. His hidden truths are an open secret for those who are really looking. When you ask the Holy Spirit to give you ears to hear and eyes to see, God will open his treasure house and give you fresh insight into his parables. Ask him for understanding, and he'll help you unearth buried treasure.

Thursday

Go to page 1181 for your next devotional reading.

hear with their ears,
understand with their hearts
and turn, and I would heal them.'[a]

16 But blessed are your eyes because they see,
and your ears because they hear. 17 For I tell you
the truth, many prophets and righteous men
longed to see what you see but did not see it,
and to hear what you hear but did not hear it.
18 "Listen then to what the parable of the
sower means: 19 When anyone hears the message about the kingdom and does not understand it, the evil one comes and snatches
away what was sown in his heart. This is the
seed sown along the path. 20 The one who received the seed that fell on rocky places is the
man who hears the word and at once receives
it with joy. 21 But since he has no root, he lasts
only a short time. When trouble or persecution
comes because of the word, he quickly falls
away. 22 The one who received the seed that
fell among the thorns is the man who hears the
word, but the worries of this life and the deceitfulness of wealth choke it, making it unfruitful.
23 But the one who received the seed that fell on
good soil is the man who hears the word and
understands it. He produces a crop, yielding a
hundred, sixty or thirty times what was sown."

The Parable of the Weeds

24 Jesus told them another parable: "The kingdom of heaven is like a man who sowed good
seed in his field. 25 But while everyone was
sleeping, his enemy came and sowed weeds
among the wheat, and went away. 26 When the
wheat sprouted and formed heads, then the
weeds also appeared.
27 "The owner's servants came to him and
said, 'Sir, didn't you sow good seed in your
field? Where then did the weeds come from?'
28 " 'An enemy did this,' he replied.
"The servants asked him, 'Do you want us to
go and pull them up?'
29 " 'No,' he answered, 'because while you are
pulling the weeds, you may root up the wheat
with them. 30 Let both grow together until the
harvest. At that time I will tell the harvesters:
First collect the weeds and tie them in bundles
to be burned; then gather the wheat and bring
it into my barn.' "

The Parables of the Mustard Seed and the Yeast

31 He told them another parable: "The kingdom of heaven is like a mustard seed, which
a man took and planted in his field. 32 Though
it is the smallest of all your seeds, yet when it
grows, it is the largest of garden plants and becomes a tree, so that the birds of the air come
and perch in its branches."
33 He told them still another parable: "The
kingdom of heaven is like yeast that a woman
took and mixed into a large amount[b] of flour
until it worked all through the dough."
34 Jesus spoke all these things to the crowd in
parables; he did not say anything to them without using a parable. 35 So was fulfilled what was
spoken through the prophet:

"I will open my mouth in parables,
I will utter things hidden since the
creation of the world."[c]

The Parable of the Weeds Explained

36 Then he left the crowd and went into the
house. His disciples came to him and said, "Explain to us the parable of the weeds in the field."
37 He answered, "The one who sowed the
good seed is the Son of Man. 38 The field is the
world, and the good seed stands for the sons of
the kingdom. The weeds are the sons of the evil
one, 39 and the enemy who sows them is the
devil. The harvest is the end of the age, and the
harvesters are angels.
40 "As the weeds are pulled up and burned
in the fire, so it will be at the end of the age.
41 The Son of Man will send out his angels, and
they will weed out of his kingdom everything
that causes sin and all who do evil. 42 They will
throw them into the fiery furnace, where there
will be weeping and gnashing of teeth. 43 Then
the righteous will shine like the sun in the
kingdom of their Father. He who has ears, let
him hear.

The Parables of the Hidden Treasure and the Pearl

44 "The kingdom of heaven is like treasure
hidden in a field. When a man found it, he hid
it again, and then in his joy went and sold all he
had and bought that field.

[a] 15 Isaiah 6:9,10 [b] 33 Greek *three satas* (probably about 1/2 bushel or 22 liters) [c] 35 Psalm 78:2

45“Again, the kingdom of heaven is like a
merchant looking for fine pearls. 46When he
found one of great value, he went away and
sold everything he had and bought it.

The Parable of the Net

47“Once again, the kingdom of heaven is like
a net that was let down into the lake and caught
all kinds of fish. 48When it was full, the fishermen pulled it up on the shore. Then they sat
down and collected the good fish in baskets,
but threw the bad away. 49This is how it will be
at the end of the age. The angels will come and
separate the wicked from the righteous 50and
throw them into the fiery furnace, where there
will be weeping and gnashing of teeth.
51“Have you understood all these things?”
Jesus asked.
“Yes,” they replied.
52He said to them, “Therefore every teacher
of the law who has been instructed about the
kingdom of heaven is like the owner of a house
who brings out of his storeroom new treasures
as well as old.”

A Prophet Without Honor

53When Jesus had finished these parables,
he moved on from there. 54Coming to his
hometown, he began teaching the people in
their synagogue, and they were
amazed. “Where did this man
get this wisdom and these miraculous powers?” they asked.
55“Isn’t this the carpenter’s son?
Isn’t his mother’s name Mary,
and aren’t his brothers James,
Joseph, Simon and Judas?
56Aren’t all his sisters with us?
Where then did this man get all
these things?” 57And they took
offense at him.
But Jesus said to them,
“Only in his hometown and
in his own house is a prophet
without honor.”
58And he did not do many miracles there because of their lack of faith.

John the Baptist Beheaded

14 At that time Herod the tetrarch heard
the reports about Jesus, 2and he said to
his attendants, “This is John the Baptist; he has
risen from the dead! That is why miraculous
powers are at work in him.”
3Now Herod had arrested John and bound
him and put him in prison because of Herodias,
his brother Philip’s wife, 4for John had been saying to him: “It is not lawful for you to have her.”
5Herod wanted to kill John, but he was afraid
of the people, because they considered him a
prophet.
6On Herod’s birthday the daughter of
Herodias danced for them and pleased Herod
so much 7that he promised with an oath to
give her whatever she asked. 8Prompted by her
mother, she said, “Give me here on a platter
the head of John the Baptist.” 9The king was distressed, but because of his oaths and his dinner
guests, he ordered that her request be granted
10and had John beheaded in the prison. 11His
head was brought in on a platter and given to
the girl, who carried it to her mother. 12John’s
disciples came and took his body and buried it.
Then they went and told Jesus.

Jesus Feeds the Five Thousand

13When Jesus heard what had happened, he
withdrew by boat privately to a solitary place.
Hearing of this, the crowds followed him on
foot from the towns. 14When Jesus landed and
saw a large crowd, he had compassion on them
and healed their sick.
15As evening approached,
the disciples came to him and
said, “This is a remote place,
and it’s already getting late.
Send the crowds away, so they
can go to the villages and buy
themselves some food.”
16Jesus replied, “They do
not need to go away. You give
them something to eat.”
17“We have here only five
loaves of bread and two fish,”
they answered.
18“Bring them here to me,”
he said. 19And he directed the people to sit
down on the grass. Taking the five loaves and
the two fish and looking up to heaven, he gave
thanks and broke the loaves. Then he gave them
to the disciples, and the disciples gave them to
the people. 20They all ate and were satisfied,
and the disciples picked up twelve basketfuls

> Matthew 14:14
>
> *God Has Compassion*
>
> When Jesus landed and saw a large crowd, he had compassion on them and healed their sick.

of broken pieces that were left over. 21The number of those who ate was about five thousand
men, besides women and children.

Jesus Walks on the Water

22Immediately Jesus made the disciples
get into the boat and go on ahead of him to
the other side, while he dismissed the crowd.
23After he had dismissed them, he went up on
a mountainside by himself to pray. When evening came, he was there alone, 24but the boat
was already a considerable distance[a] from
land, buffeted by the waves because the wind
was against it.
25During the fourth watch of the night Jesus
went out to them, walking on the lake. 26When
the disciples saw him walking on the lake, they
were terrified. "It's a ghost," they said, and cried
out in fear.
27But Jesus immediately said to them: "Take
courage! It is I. Don't be afraid."
28"Lord, if it's you," Peter replied, "tell me to
come to you on the water."
29"Come," he said.
Then Peter got down out of the boat, walked
on the water and came toward Jesus. 30But
when he saw the wind, he was afraid and, beginning to sink, cried out, "Lord, save me!"
31Immediately Jesus reached out his hand
and caught him. "You of little faith," he said,
"why did you doubt?"
32And when they climbed into the boat, the
wind died down. 33Then those who were in the
boat worshiped him, saying, "Truly you are the
Son of God."
34When they had crossed over, they landed
at Gennesaret. 35And when the men of that
place recognized Jesus, they sent word to all the
surrounding country. People brought all their
sick to him 36and begged him to let the sick
just touch the edge of his cloak, and all who
touched him were healed.

Clean and Unclean

15 Then some Pharisees and teachers of
the law came to Jesus from Jerusalem
and asked, 2"Why do your disciples break the
tradition of the elders? They don't wash their
hands before they eat!"
3Jesus replied, "And why do you break the
command of God for the sake of your tradition? 4For God said, 'Honor your father and
mother'[b] and 'Anyone who curses his father
or mother must be put to death.'[c] 5But you
say that if a man says to his father or mother,
'Whatever help you might otherwise have received from me is a gift devoted to God,' 6he
is not to 'honor his father[d]' with it. Thus you
nullify the word of God for the sake of your tradition. 7You hypocrites! Isaiah was right when
he prophesied about you:

8" 'These people honor me with their lips,
but their hearts are far from me.
9They worship me in vain;
their teachings are but rules taught by
men.'[e]"

10Jesus called the crowd to him and said,
"Listen and understand. 11What goes into a
man's mouth does not make him 'unclean,' but
what comes out of his mouth, that is what
makes him 'unclean.' "
12Then the disciples came to him and asked,
"Do you know that the Pharisees were offended
when they heard this?"
13He replied, "Every plant that my heavenly
Father has not planted will be pulled up by the
roots. 14Leave them; they are blind guides.[f] If
a blind man leads a blind man, both will fall
into a pit."
15Peter said, "Explain the parable to us."
16"Are you still so dull?" Jesus asked them.
17"Don't you see that whatever enters the
mouth goes into the stomach and then out
of the body? 18But the things that come out
of the mouth come from the heart, and these
make a man 'unclean.' 19For out of the heart
come evil thoughts, murder, adultery, sexual
immorality, theft, false testimony, slander.
20These are what make a man 'unclean'; but
eating with unwashed hands does not make
him 'unclean.' "

The Faith of the Canaanite Woman

21Leaving that place, Jesus withdrew to
the region of Tyre and Sidon. 22A Canaanite
woman from that vicinity came to him, crying
out, "Lord, Son of David, have mercy on me!

[a]24 Greek *many stadia* [b]4 Exodus 20:12; Deut. 5:16 [c]4 Exodus 21:17; Lev. 20:9 [d]6 Some manuscripts *father or his mother*
[e]9 Isaiah 29:13 [f]14 Some manuscripts *guides of the blind*

My daughter is suffering terribly from demon-
possession."
23 Jesus did not answer a word. So his disciples came to him and urged him, "Send her
away, for she keeps crying out after us."
24 He answered, "I was sent only to the lost
sheep of Israel."
25 The woman came and knelt before him.
"Lord, help me!" she said.
26 He replied, "It is not right to take the children's bread and toss it to their dogs."
27 "Yes, Lord," she said, "but even the dogs
eat the crumbs that fall from their masters'
table."
28 Then Jesus answered, "Woman, you have
great faith! Your request is granted." And her
daughter was healed from that very hour.

Jesus Feeds the Four Thousand

29 Jesus left there and went along the Sea of
Galilee. Then he went up on a mountainside
and sat down. 30 Great crowds came to him,
bringing the lame, the blind, the crippled, the
mute and many others, and laid them at his
feet; and he healed them. 31 The people were
amazed when they saw the mute speaking,
the crippled made well, the lame walking and
the blind seeing. And they praised the God of
Israel.
32 Jesus called his disciples to him and said,
"I have compassion for these people; they have
already been with me three days and have nothing to eat. I do not want to send them away
hungry, or they may collapse on the way."
33 His disciples answered, "Where could we
get enough bread in this remote place to feed
such a crowd?"
34 "How many loaves do you have?" Jesus
asked.
"Seven," they replied, "and a few small fish."
35 He told the crowd to sit down on the
ground. 36 Then he took the seven loaves and
the fish, and when he had given thanks, he
broke them and gave them to the disciples, and
they in turn to the people. 37 They all ate and
were satisfied. Afterward the disciples picked
up seven basketfuls of broken pieces that were
left over. 38 The number of those who ate was
four thousand, besides women and children.
39 After Jesus had sent the crowd away, he got
into the boat and went to the vicinity of Mag-
adan.

The Demand for a Sign

16 The Pharisees and Sadducees came to
Jesus and tested him by asking him to
show them a sign from heaven.
2 He replied,[a] "When evening comes, you
say, 'It will be fair weather, for the sky is red,'
3 and in the morning, 'Today it will be stormy,
for the sky is red and overcast.' You know how
to interpret the appearance of the sky, but you
cannot interpret the signs of the times. 4 A
wicked and adulterous generation looks for a
miraculous sign, but none will be given it except the sign of Jonah." Jesus then left them and
went away.

The Yeast of the Pharisees and Sadducees

5 When they went across the lake, the disciples forgot to take bread. 6 "Be careful," Jesus
said to them. "Be on your guard against the
yeast of the Pharisees and Sadducees."
7 They discussed this among themselves
and said, "It is because we didn't bring any
bread."
8 Aware of their discussion, Jesus asked, "You
of little faith, why are you talking among yourselves about having no bread? 9 Do you still
not understand? Don't you remember the five
loaves for the five thousand, and how many basketfuls you gathered? 10 Or the seven loaves for
the four thousand, and how many basketfuls
you gathered? 11 How is it you don't understand
that I was not talking to you about bread? But
be on your guard against the yeast of the Pharisees and Sadducees." 12 Then they understood
that he was not telling them to guard against
the yeast used in bread, but against the teaching of the Pharisees and Sadducees.

Peter's Confession of Christ

13 When Jesus came to the region of Caesarea Philippi, he asked his disciples, "Who do
people say the Son of Man is?"
14 They replied, "Some say John the Baptist;
others say Elijah; and still others, Jeremiah or
one of the prophets."

[a] 2 Some early manuscripts do not have the rest of verse 2 and all of verse 3.

Jesus: Our Everything

Read: Matthew 16:13–26

"JESUS IS EVERYTHING." Mother Teresa's words were demonstrated by her selfless, Christlike actions—she was a friend to the poor, unabashedly loving society's rejects and giving hope to the hopeless in her adopted country of India. How broken her heart must have been every time she lifted an untouchable out of the gutter to die in her arms or she fed and bathed a hungry, dirty orphan.

Through her actions, this humble woman proved that Jesus was more than a good man, a brilliant teacher or even a prophet sent from God. She knew in her heart that Jesus is the Messiah, the Son of the living God, and that knowledge empowered her with enough love for a lifetime of service.

In Matthew 16, Jesus asked his disciples who they thought he was. Peter aced the pop quiz, calling him "the Son of the living God." We all know Peter wasn't perfect. He was the one who had the tendency to speak first and think later. He was the one who denied Christ three times at Jesus' trial. Yet at this key moment, he comprehended that Jesus was the Messiah God had promised for centuries. After Pentecost, Peter's boldness allowed him to proclaim Christ's identity whenever and wherever he could, regardless of the persecution and suffering it invited. Eventually, he was crucified for spreading the news that Jesus was God's Son. The ancient writer Origen records that Peter was crucified head down because he felt unworthy to die in the same manner as Jesus. To the apostle who had once denied him, Jesus was everything; in fact, Jesus was the only thing.

The One who lived among us was God's hands and feet. He gave us the very words of his Father. He taught us how to love. He taught us how to give. And he taught us to die as a grain of wheat dies, so that the seeds of life are multiplied (see John 12:24).

Mother Teresa and Simon Peter understood that with Jesus, there was no such thing as loving moderately. They showed others that Jesus was Lord of their lives by loving as he loved and serving as he served—continually, wholeheartedly and sacrificially.

Matthew 16:15–16

"But what about you?" he asked. "Who do you say I am?" Simon Peter answered, "You are the Christ, the Son of the living God."

reflection

1 Fill in the blank with the words of your choice: Jesus is __________________________________.

2 How does your answer to the above question affect how you live?

3 On a scale of one to ten, how well are you loving others continually, wholeheartedly and sacrificially?

RELATED READINGS

John 11:25–27; 13:34–35;
1 John 3:1–3,16–24

Go to page 1184 for your next devotional reading.

15“But what about you?” he asked. “Who do you say I am?”

16Simon Peter answered, “You are the Christ,[a] the Son of the living God.”

17Jesus replied, “Blessed are you, Simon son of Jonah, for this was not revealed to you by man, but by my Father in heaven. 18And I tell you that you are Peter,[b] and on this rock I will build my church, and the gates of Hades[c] will not overcome it.[d] 19I will give you the keys of the kingdom of heaven; whatever you bind on earth will be[e] bound in heaven, and whatever you loose on earth will be[e] loosed in heaven.” 20Then he warned his disciples not to tell anyone that he was the Christ.

Jesus Predicts His Death

21From that time on Jesus began to explain to his disciples that he must go to Jerusalem and suffer many things at the hands of the elders, chief priests and teachers of the law, and that he must be killed and on the third day be raised to life.

22Peter took him aside and began to rebuke him. “Never, Lord!” he said. “This shall never happen to you!”

23Jesus turned and said to Peter, “Get behind me, Satan! You are a stumbling block to me; you do not have in mind the things of God, but the things of men.”

24Then Jesus said to his disciples, “If anyone would come after me, he must deny himself and take up his cross and follow me. 25For whoever wants to save his life[f] will lose it, but whoever loses his life for me will find it. 26What good will it be for a man if he gains the whole world, yet forfeits his soul? Or what can a man give in exchange for his soul? 27For the Son of Man is going to come in his Father’s glory with his angels, and then he will reward each person according to what he has done. 28I tell you the truth, some who are standing here will not taste death before they see the Son of Man coming in his kingdom.”

> **Matthew 16:25**
>
> *God Is Life*
>
> “For whoever wants to save his life will lose it, but whoever loses his life for me will find it.”

The Transfiguration

17 After six days Jesus took with him Peter, James and John the brother of James, and led them up a high mountain by themselves. 2There he was transfigured before them. His face shone like the sun, and his clothes became as white as the light. 3Just then there appeared before them Moses and Elijah, talking with Jesus.

4Peter said to Jesus, “Lord, it is good for us to be here. If you wish, I will put up three shelters—one for you, one for Moses and one for Elijah.”

5While he was still speaking, a bright cloud enveloped them, and a voice from the cloud said, “This is my Son, whom I love; with him I am well pleased. Listen to him!”

6When the disciples heard this, they fell facedown to the ground, terrified. 7But Jesus came and touched them. “Get up,” he said. “Don’t be afraid.” 8When they looked up, they saw no one except Jesus.

9As they were coming down the mountain, Jesus instructed them, “Don’t tell anyone what you have seen, until the Son of Man has been raised from the dead.”

10The disciples asked him, “Why then do the teachers of the law say that Elijah must come first?”

11Jesus replied, “To be sure, Elijah comes and will restore all things. 12But I tell you, Elijah has already come, and they did not recognize him, but have done to him everything they wished. In the same way the Son of Man is going to suffer at their hands.” 13Then the disciples understood that he was talking to them about John the Baptist.

The Healing of a Boy With a Demon

14When they came to the crowd, a man approached Jesus and knelt before him. 15“Lord, have mercy on my son,” he said. “He has seizures and is suffering greatly. He often falls into the fire or into the water. 16I brought him to your disciples, but they could not heal him.”

[a]16 Or *Messiah*; also in verse 20 [b]18 *Peter* means *rock.* [c]18 Or *hell* [d]18 Or *not prove stronger than it* [e]19 Or *have been*
[f]25 The Greek word means either *life* or *soul*; also in verse 26.

17“O unbelieving and perverse generation,”
Jesus replied, “how long shall I stay with you?
How long shall I put up with you? Bring the
boy here to me.” 18Jesus rebuked the demon,
and it came out of the boy, and he was healed
from that moment.
19Then the disciples came to Jesus in private
and asked, “Why couldn’t we drive it out?”
20He replied, “Because you have so little
faith. I tell you the truth, if you have faith as
small as a mustard seed, you can say to this
mountain, ‘Move from here to there’ and it
will move. Nothing will be impossible for
you.[a]”
22When they came together in Galilee, he
said to them, “The Son of Man is going to
be betrayed into the hands of men. 23They
will kill him, and on the third day he will be
raised to life.” And the disciples were filled
with grief.

The Temple Tax

24After Jesus and his disciples arrived in
Capernaum, the collectors of the two-drachma
tax came to Peter and asked, “Doesn’t your
teacher pay the temple tax[b]?”
25“Yes, he does,” he replied.
When Peter came into the house, Jesus was
the first to speak. “What do you think, Simon?”
he asked. “From whom do the kings of the
earth collect duty and taxes—from their own
sons or from others?”
26“From others,” Peter answered.
“Then the sons are exempt,” Jesus said to
him. 27“But so that we may not offend them,
go to the lake and throw out your line. Take the
first fish you catch; open its mouth and you will
find a four-drachma coin. Take it and give it to
them for my tax and yours.”

The Greatest in the Kingdom of Heaven

18 At that time the disciples came to Jesus
and asked, “Who is the greatest in the
kingdom of heaven?”
2He called a little child and had him stand
among them. 3And he said: “I tell you the
truth, unless you change and become like little
children, you will never enter the kingdom of
heaven. 4Therefore, whoever humbles himself
like this child is the greatest in the kingdom of
heaven.
5“And whoever welcomes a little child like
this in my name welcomes me. 6But if anyone
causes one of these little ones who believe in
me to sin, it would be better for him to have a
large millstone hung around his neck and to be
drowned in the depths of the sea.
7“Woe to the world because of the things
that cause people to sin! Such things must
come, but woe to the man through whom they
come! 8If your hand or your foot causes you to
sin, cut it off and throw it away. It is better for
you to enter life maimed or crippled than to
have two hands or two feet and be thrown into
eternal fire. 9And if your eye causes you to sin,
gouge it out and throw it away. It is better for
you to enter life with one eye than to have two
eyes and be thrown into the fire of hell.

The Parable of the Lost Sheep

10“See that you do not look down on one of
these little ones. For I tell you that their angels
in heaven always see the face of my Father in
heaven.[c]
12“What do you think? If a man owns a hundred sheep, and one of them wanders away,
will he not leave the ninety-nine on the hills
and go to look for the one that wandered off?
13And if he finds it, I tell you the truth, he is
happier about that one sheep than about the
ninety-nine that did not wander off. 14In the
same way your Father in heaven is not willing
that any of these little ones should be lost.

A Brother Who Sins Against You

15“If your brother sins against you,[d] go and
show him his fault, just between the two of you.
If he listens to you, you have won your brother
over. 16But if he will not listen, take one or
two others along, so that ‘every matter may be
established by the testimony of two or three
witnesses.’[e] 17If he refuses to listen to them, tell
it to the church; and if he refuses to listen even
to the church, treat him as you would a pagan
or a tax collector.
18“I tell you the truth, whatever you bind on
earth will be[f] bound in heaven, and whatever
you loose on earth will be[f] loosed in heaven.

[a]20 Some manuscripts *you.* [21] *But this kind does not go out except by prayer and fasting.* [b]24 Greek *the two drachmas* [c]10 Some manuscripts *heaven.* [11] *The Son of Man came to save what was lost.* [d]15 Some manuscripts do not have *against you.* [e]16 Deut. 19:15 [f]18 Or *have been*

Scorned

HERODIAS

So Herodias nursed a grudge against John and wanted to kill him.

Mark 6:19

"WHAT SHALL I ASK FOR?" asked her daughter, dressed in her beautiful dancing costume, as she stood impatiently before her mother.

Herodias paused a moment before answering. A thousand options came to mind. It wasn't every day that one had the chance to receive anything within a king's grasp. As queen, her own powers had limits. But this, this was an exceptional opportunity. And it required careful consideration.

Anything I ask for, I can receive . . . up to half of the kingdom . . . Herodias mused silently, mindlessly tapping her lips with her slender finger. *What should it be?*

Jewelry? Clothes? A statue in her honor?

Horses? Land? A new palace?

Amid a myriad of alternatives, suddenly she snapped to attention. She knew without a doubt what she wanted. It was something better than material objects, fame, riches or glory. It was something only the king could provide: revenge.

With it, she reasoned, maybe she could finally get a good night's sleep instead of laying awake at night thinking how one man named John had absolutely ruined her life.

With it, she hoped she could finally take the sting out of John's slanderous accusations. His judgmental attitude toward her constantly rang in her ears and gave her no peace.

With it, maybe this self-righteous know-it-all would stop haunting her thoughts and whipping her into such a frenzy that she could hardly think straight.

Yes, revenge was what she wanted.

And when it was served to her on a fine piece of dishware, she gloated. But only for a moment. As it turned out, her sleep from that night onward likely wasn't as restful as she'd hoped. The sting to her conscience wasn't any less painful; if she were truthful, it was actually much worse. And, though we can't be sure, one can guess that sometimes (if not every night) she still saw John in her dreams.

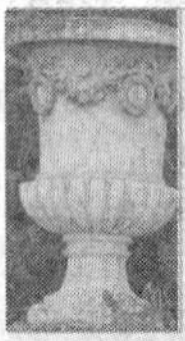

ASSIGNED READING:
Matthew 14:1–12; Mark 6:14–29

—Prayer—

Lord God, teach me to handle my anger and hurt in a godly manner. Help me not to desire revenge, but help me to overcome evil with good.

Weekend

Go to page 1186 for your next devotional reading.

19“Again, I tell you that if two of you on earth agree about anything you ask for, it will be done for you by my Father in heaven. 20For where two or three come together in my name, there am I with them.”

The Parable of the Unmerciful Servant

21Then Peter came to Jesus and asked, “Lord, how many times shall I forgive my brother when he sins against me? Up to seven times?”

22Jesus answered, “I tell you, not seven times, but seventy-seven times.[a]

23“Therefore, the kingdom of heaven is like a king who wanted to settle accounts with his servants. 24As he began the settlement, a man who owed him ten thousand talents[b] was brought to him. 25Since he was not able to pay, the master ordered that he and his wife and his children and all that he had be sold to repay the debt.

26“The servant fell on his knees before him. ‘Be patient with me,’ he begged, ‘and I will pay back everything.’ 27The servant’s master took pity on him, canceled the debt and let him go.

28“But when that servant went out, he found one of his fellow servants who owed him a hundred denarii.[c] He grabbed him and began to choke him. ‘Pay back what you owe me!’ he demanded.

29“His fellow servant fell to his knees and begged him, ‘Be patient with me, and I will pay you back.’

30“But he refused. Instead, he went off and had the man thrown into prison until he could pay the debt. 31When the other servants saw what had happened, they were greatly distressed and went and told their master everything that had happened.

32“Then the master called the servant in. ‘You wicked servant,’ he said, ‘I canceled all that debt of yours because you begged me to. 33Shouldn’t you have had mercy on your fellow servant just as I had on you?’ 34In anger his master turned him over to the jailers to be tortured, until he should pay back all he owed.

35“This is how my heavenly Father will treat each of you unless you forgive your brother from your heart.”

Divorce

19 When Jesus had finished saying these things, he left Galilee and went into the region of Judea to the other side of the Jordan. 2Large crowds followed him, and he healed them there.

3Some Pharisees came to him to test him. They asked, “Is it lawful for a man to divorce his wife for any and every reason?”

4“Haven’t you read,” he replied, “that at the beginning the Creator ‘made them male and female,’[d] 5and said, ‘For this reason a man will leave his father and mother and be united to his wife, and the two will become one flesh’[e]? 6So they are no longer two, but one. Therefore what God has joined together, let man not separate.”

7“Why then,” they asked, “did Moses command that a man give his wife a certificate of divorce and send her away?”

8Jesus replied, “Moses permitted you to divorce your wives because your hearts were hard. But it was not this way from the beginning. 9I tell you that anyone who divorces his wife, except for marital unfaithfulness, and marries another woman commits adultery.”

10The disciples said to him, “If this is the situation between a husband and wife, it is better not to marry.”

11Jesus replied, “Not everyone can accept this word, but only those to whom it has been given. 12For some are eunuchs because they were born that way; others were made that way by men; and others have renounced marriage[f] because of the kingdom of heaven. The one who can accept this should accept it.”

The Little Children and Jesus

13Then little children were brought to Jesus for him to place his hands on them and pray for them. But the disciples rebuked those who brought them.

14Jesus said, “Let the little children come to me, and do not hinder them, for the kingdom of heaven belongs to such as these.” 15When he had placed his hands on them, he went on from there.

[a]22 Or *seventy times seven* [b]24 That is, millions of dollars [c]28 That is, a few dollars [d]4 Gen. 1:27 [e]5 Gen. 2:24 [f]12 Or *have made themselves eunuchs*

Superglue

Read: Matthew 19:1–12

SUPERGLUE WORKS. Once two items are glued together, separation becomes a painful, sticky mess. Paper tears and fabric frays if you divide the two pieces that have melded into one. Once separated, the original items are never the same—each inevitably retains fragments of the other. Think of two pieces of paper glued together—after they've been torn apart, each piece is ragged and weak. That's why superglue comes with a label advising the consumer to use extreme caution when handling it.

We might think of marriage as something like God's superglue because it weaves two lives intricately into one. After this blessed blending, attempts at separation cause irreparable damage. Hearts break, commitments crumble and families split. God's intertwining of husband and wife extends to children, friends and families related to the union. God's Word also provides a strong warning: "What God has joined together, let man not separate."

When Ruth Bell was a teenage girl, she left her childhood home in China to attend school in Korea. Her idea of the future? She fully intended to be an old maid missionary in Tibet. However, she did give the thought of a husband some serious consideration. So she wrote the following list of particulars:

"If I marry: He must be so tall that when he is on his knees, as one has said, he reaches all the way to heaven. His shoulders must be broad enough to bear the burden of a family. His lips must be strong enough to smile, firm enough to say no, and tender enough to kiss. Love must be so deep that it takes its stand in Christ and so wide that it takes the whole lost world in. He must be active enough to save souls. He must be big enough to be gentle and great enough to be thoughtful. His arms must be strong enough to carry a little child."

Ruth eventually found a man who fit her qualifications; she married evangelist Billy Graham. Ruth and Billy Graham realize that their marriage has endured the test of time not because they are perfect people, but because God is at the center of their relationship.

It takes supernatural empowerment and a determined effort on the part of both husband and wife to keep the bond of marriage strong. Only through God's strength can couples remain "superglued" together. As Solomon wisely said, "A cord of three strands is not quickly broken" (Ecclesiastes 4:12).

Monday

Go to page 1195 for your next devotional reading.

Matthew 19:4–6

"Haven't you read . . . 'For this reason a man will leave his father and mother and be united to his wife, and the two will become one flesh'? So they are no longer two, but one. Therefore what God has joined together, let man not separate."

reflection

1 Have you ever tried to separate something that was superglued together? What was the result?

2 Think of someone—perhaps even yourself—who has experienced divorce. What were the residual effects? If you've been divorced, ask God to heal the hurts of your separation.

3 If you're married, list some practical ways you and your husband can stick together when the world tries to pull you apart.

RELATED READINGS

Genesis 2:19–25;
1 Corinthians 7:10–16;
Ephesians 5:21–33

"A good marriage is the union of two forgivers."

Ruth Graham

The Rich Young Man

16Now a man came up to Jesus and asked,
"Teacher, what good thing must I do to get eternal life?"
17"Why do you ask me about what is good?"
Jesus replied. "There is only One who is good.
If you want to enter life, obey the commandments."
18"Which ones?" the man inquired.
Jesus replied, "'Do not murder, do not commit adultery, do not steal, do not give false
testimony, 19honor your father and mother,'[a]
and 'love your neighbor as yourself.'[b]"
20"All these I have kept," the young man said.
"What do I still lack?"
21Jesus answered, "If you want to be perfect,
go, sell your possessions and give to the poor,
and you will have treasure in heaven. Then
come, follow me."
22When the young man heard this, he went
away sad, because he had great wealth.
23Then Jesus said to his disciples, "I tell you
the truth, it is hard for a rich man to enter the
kingdom of heaven. 24Again I tell you, it is
easier for a camel to go through the eye of a
needle than for a rich man to enter the kingdom of God."
25When the disciples heard
this, they were greatly astonished and asked, "Who then
can be saved?"
26Jesus looked at them and
said, "With man this is impossible, but with God all things are
possible."
27Peter answered him, "We
have left everything to follow
you! What then will there be
for us?"
28Jesus said to them, "I tell
you the truth, at the renewal
of all things, when the Son
of Man sits on his glorious
throne, you who have followed me will also
sit on twelve thrones, judging the twelve tribes
of Israel. 29And everyone who has left houses
or brothers or sisters or father or mother[c] or
children or fields for my sake will receive a hundred times as much and will inherit eternal life.
30But many who are first will be last, and many
who are last will be first.

> **Matthew 19:26**
>
> *God Does the Impossible*
>
> Jesus looked at them and said, "With man this is impossible, but with God all things are possible."

The Parable of the Workers in the Vineyard

20 "For the kingdom of heaven is like a
landowner who went out early in the
morning to hire men to work in his vineyard.
2He agreed to pay them a denarius for the day
and sent them into his vineyard.
3"About the third hour he went out and saw
others standing in the marketplace doing nothing. 4He told them, 'You also go and work in
my vineyard, and I will pay you whatever is
right.' 5So they went.
"He went out again about the sixth hour and
the ninth hour and did the same thing. 6About
the eleventh hour he went out and found still
others standing around. He asked them, 'Why
have you been standing here all day long doing nothing?'
7"'Because no one has hired us,' they answered.
"He said to them, 'You also go and work in
my vineyard.'
8"When evening came, the owner of the
vineyard said to his foreman, 'Call the workers
and pay them their wages, beginning with the
last ones hired and going on to
the first.'
9"The workers who were
hired about the eleventh
hour came and each received
a denarius. 10So when those
came who were hired first,
they expected to receive
more. But each one of them
also received a denarius.
11When they received it, they
began to grumble against the
landowner. 12'These men who
were hired last worked only
one hour,' they said, 'and you
have made them equal to us
who have borne the burden of the work and
the heat of the day.'
13"But he answered one of them, 'Friend, I
am not being unfair to you. Didn't you agree to
work for a denarius? 14Take your pay and go.
I want to give the man who was hired last the

[a] 19 Exodus 20:12–16; Deut. 5:16–20 [b] 19 Lev. 19:18 [c] 29 Some manuscripts *mother or wife*

same as I gave you. 15 Don't I have the right to do what I want with my own money? Or are you envious because I am generous?'

16 "So the last will be first, and the first will be last."

Jesus Again Predicts His Death

17 Now as Jesus was going up to Jerusalem, he took the twelve disciples aside and said to them, 18 "We are going up to Jerusalem, and the Son of Man will be betrayed to the chief priests and the teachers of the law. They will condemn him to death 19 and will turn him over to the Gentiles to be mocked and flogged and crucified. On the third day he will be raised to life!"

A Mother's Request

20 Then the mother of Zebedee's sons came to Jesus with her sons and, kneeling down, asked a favor of him.

21 "What is it you want?" he asked.

She said, "Grant that one of these two sons of mine may sit at your right and the other at your left in your kingdom."

22 "You don't know what you are asking," Jesus said to them. "Can you drink the cup I am going to drink?"

"We can," they answered.

23 Jesus said to them, "You will indeed drink from my cup, but to sit at my right or left is not for me to grant. These places belong to those for whom they have been prepared by my Father."

24 When the ten heard about this, they were indignant with the two brothers. 25 Jesus called them together and said, "You know that the rulers of the Gentiles lord it over them, and their high officials exercise authority over them. 26 Not so with you. Instead, whoever wants to become great among you must be your servant, 27 and whoever wants to be first must be your slave— 28 just as the Son of Man did not come to be served, but to serve, and to give his life as a ransom for many."

Two Blind Men Receive Sight

29 As Jesus and his disciples were leaving Jericho, a large crowd followed him. 30 Two blind men were sitting by the roadside, and when they heard that Jesus was going by, they shouted, "Lord, Son of David, have mercy on us!"

31 The crowd rebuked them and told them to be quiet, but they shouted all the louder, "Lord, Son of David, have mercy on us!"

32 Jesus stopped and called them. "What do you want me to do for you?" he asked.

33 "Lord," they answered, "we want our sight."

34 Jesus had compassion on them and touched their eyes. Immediately they received their sight and followed him.

The Triumphal Entry

21 As they approached Jerusalem and came to Bethphage on the Mount of Olives, Jesus sent two disciples, 2 saying to them, "Go to the village ahead of you, and at once you will find a donkey tied there, with her colt by her. Untie them and bring them to me. 3 If anyone says anything to you, tell him that the Lord needs them, and he will send them right away."

4 This took place to fulfill what was spoken through the prophet:

5 "Say to the Daughter of Zion,
'See, your king comes to you,
gentle and riding on a donkey,
on a colt, the foal of a donkey.'"[a]

6 The disciples went and did as Jesus had instructed them. 7 They brought the donkey and the colt, placed their cloaks on them, and Jesus sat on them. 8 A very large crowd spread their cloaks on the road, while others cut branches from the trees and spread them on the road. 9 The crowds that went ahead of him and those that followed shouted,

"Hosanna[b] to the Son of David!"

"Blessed is he who comes in the name of the Lord!"[c]

"Hosanna[b] in the highest!"

10 When Jesus entered Jerusalem, the whole city was stirred and asked, "Who is this?"

11 The crowds answered, "This is Jesus, the prophet from Nazareth in Galilee."

[a] 5 Zech. 9:9 [b] 9 A Hebrew expression meaning "Save!" which became an exclamation of praise; also in verse 15 [c] 9 Psalm 118:26

Jesus at the Temple

12 Jesus entered the temple area and drove out all who were buying and selling there. He overturned the tables of the money changers and the benches of those selling doves. 13 "It is written," he said to them, " 'My house will be called a house of prayer,'[a] but you are making it a 'den of robbers.'[b]"

14 The blind and the lame came to him at the temple, and he healed them. 15 But when the chief priests and the teachers of the law saw the wonderful things he did and the children shouting in the temple area, "Hosanna to the Son of David," they were indignant.

16 "Do you hear what these children are saying?" they asked him.

"Yes," replied Jesus, "have you never read,

" 'From the lips of children and infants
you have ordained praise'[c]?"

17 And he left them and went out of the city to Bethany, where he spent the night.

The Fig Tree Withers

18 Early in the morning, as he was on his way back to the city, he was hungry. 19 Seeing a fig tree by the road, he went up to it but found nothing on it except leaves. Then he said to it, "May you never bear fruit again!" Immediately the tree withered.

20 When the disciples saw this, they were amazed. "How did the fig tree wither so quickly?" they asked.

21 Jesus replied, "I tell you the truth, if you have faith and do not doubt, not only can you do what was done to the fig tree, but also you can say to this mountain, 'Go, throw yourself into the sea,' and it will be done. 22 If you believe, you will receive whatever you ask for in prayer."

The Authority of Jesus Questioned

23 Jesus entered the temple courts, and, while he was teaching, the chief priests and the elders of the people came to him. "By what authority are you doing these things?" they asked. "And who gave you this authority?"

24 Jesus replied, "I will also ask you one question. If you answer me, I will tell you by what authority I am doing these things. 25 John's baptism—where did it come from? Was it from heaven, or from men?"

They discussed it among themselves and said, "If we say, 'From heaven,' he will ask, 'Then why didn't you believe him?' 26 But if we say, 'From men'—we are afraid of the people, for they all hold that John was a prophet."

27 So they answered Jesus, "We don't know."

Then he said, "Neither will I tell you by what authority I am doing these things.

The Parable of the Two Sons

28 "What do you think? There was a man who had two sons. He went to the first and said, 'Son, go and work today in the vineyard.'

29 " 'I will not,' he answered, but later he changed his mind and went.

30 "Then the father went to the other son and said the same thing. He answered, 'I will, sir,' but he did not go.

31 "Which of the two did what his father wanted?"

"The first," they answered.

Jesus said to them, "I tell you the truth, the tax collectors and the prostitutes are entering the kingdom of God ahead of you. 32 For John came to you to show you the way of righteousness, and you did not believe him, but the tax collectors and the prostitutes did. And even after you saw this, you did not repent and believe him.

The Parable of the Tenants

33 "Listen to another parable: There was a landowner who planted a vineyard. He put a wall around it, dug a winepress in it and built a watchtower. Then he rented the vineyard to some farmers and went away on a journey. 34 When the harvest time approached, he sent his servants to the tenants to collect his fruit.

35 "The tenants seized his servants; they beat one, killed another, and stoned a third. 36 Then he sent other servants to them, more than the first time, and the tenants treated them the same way. 37 Last of all, he sent his son to them. 'They will respect my son,' he said.

38 "But when the tenants saw the son, they said to each other, 'This is the heir. Come, let's kill him and take his inheritance.' 39 So they took him and threw him out of the vineyard and killed him.

[a] 13 Isaiah 56:7 [b] 13 Jer. 7:11 [c] 16 Psalm 8:2

40"Therefore, when the owner of the vineyard comes, what will he do to those tenants?"
41"He will bring those wretches to a
wretched end," they replied, "and he will rent
the vineyard to other tenants, who will give
him his share of the crop at harvest time."
42Jesus said to them, "Have you never read
in the Scriptures:

"'The stone the builders rejected
has become the capstone[a];
the Lord has done this,
and it is marvelous in our eyes'[b]?

43"Therefore I tell you that the kingdom of
God will be taken away from you and given to
a people who will produce its fruit. 44He who
falls on this stone will be broken to pieces, but
he on whom it falls will be crushed."[c]
45When the chief priests and the Pharisees
heard Jesus' parables, they knew he was talking
about them. 46They looked for a way to arrest
him, but they were afraid of the crowd because
the people held that he was a prophet.

The Parable of the Wedding Banquet

22 Jesus spoke to them again in parables,
saying: 2"The kingdom of heaven is
like a king who prepared a wedding banquet
for his son. 3He sent his servants to those who
had been invited to the banquet to tell them to
come, but they refused to come.
4"Then he sent some more servants and said,
'Tell those who have been invited that I have
prepared my dinner: My oxen and fattened
cattle have been butchered, and everything is
ready. Come to the wedding banquet.'
5"But they paid no attention and went off—
one to his field, another to his business. 6The
rest seized his servants, mistreated them and
killed them. 7The king was enraged. He sent
his army and destroyed those murderers and
burned their city.
8"Then he said to his servants, 'The wedding
banquet is ready, but those I invited did not deserve to come. 9Go to the street corners and invite to the banquet anyone you find.' 10So the
servants went out into the streets and gathered
all the people they could find, both good and bad,
and the wedding hall was filled with guests.
11"But when the king came in to see the
guests, he noticed a man there who was not
wearing wedding clothes. 12'Friend,' he asked,
'how did you get in here without wedding
clothes?' The man was speechless.
13"Then the king told the attendants, 'Tie
him hand and foot, and throw him outside,
into the darkness, where there will be weeping
and gnashing of teeth.'
14"For many are invited, but few are chosen."

Paying Taxes to Caesar

15Then the Pharisees went out and laid plans
to trap him in his words. 16They sent their
disciples to him along with the Herodians.
"Teacher," they said, "we know you are a man
of integrity and that you teach the way of God
in accordance with the truth. You aren't swayed
by men, because you pay no attention to who
they are. 17Tell us then, what is your opinion?
Is it right to pay taxes to Caesar or not?"
18But Jesus, knowing their evil intent, said,
"You hypocrites, why are you trying to trap
me? 19Show me the coin used for paying the
tax." They brought him a denarius, 20and
he asked them, "Whose portrait is this? And
whose inscription?"
21"Caesar's," they replied.
Then he said to them, "Give to Caesar what
is Caesar's, and to God what is God's."
22When they heard this, they were amazed.
So they left him and went away.

Marriage at the Resurrection

23That same day the Sadducees, who say
there is no resurrection, came to him with a
question. 24"Teacher," they said, "Moses told us
that if a man dies without having children, his
brother must marry the widow and have children for him. 25Now there were seven brothers among us. The first one married and died,
and since he had no children, he left his wife
to his brother. 26The same thing happened to
the second and third brother, right on down to
the seventh. 27Finally, the woman died. 28Now
then, at the resurrection, whose wife will she
be of the seven, since all of them were married
to her?"
29Jesus replied, "You are in error because

[a]42 Or *cornerstone* [b]42 Psalm 118:22,23 [c]44 Some manuscripts do not have verse 44.

you do not know the Scriptures or the power of God. 30 At the resurrection people will neither marry nor be given in marriage; they will be like the angels in heaven. 31 But about the resurrection of the dead—have you not read what God said to you, 32 'I am the God of Abraham, the God of Isaac, and the God of Jacob'[a]? He is not the God of the dead but of the living."

33 When the crowds heard this, they were astonished at his teaching.

The Greatest Commandment

34 Hearing that Jesus had silenced the Sadducees, the Pharisees got together. 35 One of them, an expert in the law, tested him with this question: 36 "Teacher, which is the greatest commandment in the Law?"

37 Jesus replied: " 'Love the Lord your God with all your heart and with all your soul and with all your mind.'[b] 38 This is the first and greatest commandment. 39 And the second is like it: 'Love your neighbor as yourself.'[c] 40 All the Law and the Prophets hang on these two commandments."

Whose Son Is the Christ?

41 While the Pharisees were gathered together, Jesus asked them, 42 "What do you think about the Christ[d]? Whose son is he?"

"The son of David," they replied.

43 He said to them, "How is it then that David, speaking by the Spirit, calls him 'Lord'? For he says,

44 " 'The Lord said to my Lord:
"Sit at my right hand
until I put your enemies
under your feet." '[e]

45 If then David calls him 'Lord,' how can he be his son?" 46 No one could say a word in reply, and from that day on no one dared to ask him any more questions.

Seven Woes

23 Then Jesus said to the crowds and to his disciples: 2 "The teachers of the law and the Pharisees sit in Moses' seat. 3 So you must obey them and do everything they tell you. But do not do what they do, for they do not practice what they preach. 4 They tie up heavy loads and put them on men's shoulders, but they themselves are not willing to lift a finger to move them.

5 "Everything they do is done for men to see: They make their phylacteries[f] wide and the tassels on their garments long; 6 they love the place of honor at banquets and the most important seats in the synagogues; 7 they love to be greeted in the marketplaces and to have men call them 'Rabbi.'

8 "But you are not to be called 'Rabbi,' for you have only one Master and you are all brothers. 9 And do not call anyone on earth 'father,' for you have one Father, and he is in heaven. 10 Nor are you to be called 'teacher,' for you have one Teacher, the Christ.[d] 11 The greatest among you will be your servant. 12 For whoever exalts himself will be humbled, and whoever humbles himself will be exalted.

13 "Woe to you, teachers of the law and Pharisees, you hypocrites! You shut the kingdom of heaven in men's faces. You yourselves do not enter, nor will you let those enter who are trying to.[g]

15 "Woe to you, teachers of the law and Pharisees, you hypocrites! You travel over land and sea to win a single convert, and when he becomes one, you make him twice as much a son of hell as you are.

16 "Woe to you, blind guides! You say, 'If anyone swears by the temple, it means nothing; but if anyone swears by the gold of the temple, he is bound by his oath.' 17 You blind fools! Which is greater: the gold, or the temple that makes the gold sacred? 18 You also say, 'If anyone swears by the altar, it means nothing; but if anyone swears by the gift on it, he is bound by his oath.' 19 You blind men! Which is greater: the gift, or the altar that makes the gift sacred? 20 Therefore, he who swears by the altar swears by it and by everything on it. 21 And he who swears by the temple swears by it and by the one who dwells in it. 22 And he who swears by heaven swears by God's throne and by the one who sits on it.

23 "Woe to you, teachers of the law and

[a] 32 Exodus 3:6 [b] 37 Deut. 6:5 [c] 39 Lev. 19:18 [d] 42,10 Or *Messiah* [e] 44 Psalm 110:1 [f] 5 That is, boxes containing Scripture verses, worn on forehead and arm [g] 13 Some manuscripts *to.* [14] *Woe to you, teachers of the law and Pharisees, you hypocrites! You devour widows' houses and for a show make lengthy prayers. Therefore you will be punished more severely.*

Pharisees, you hypocrites! You give a tenth of
your spices—mint, dill and cummin. But you
have neglected the more important matters of
the law—justice, mercy and faithfulness. You
should have practiced the latter, without neglecting the former. 24You blind guides! You
strain out a gnat but swallow a camel.

25"Woe to you, teachers of the law and Pharisees, you hypocrites! You clean the outside
of the cup and dish, but inside they are full of
greed and self-indulgence. 26Blind Pharisee!
First clean the inside of the cup and dish, and
then the outside also will be clean.

27"Woe to you, teachers of the law and Pharisees, you hypocrites! You are like whitewashed
tombs, which look beautiful on the outside but
on the inside are full of dead men's bones and
everything unclean. 28In the same way, on the
outside you appear to people as righteous but
on the inside you are full of hypocrisy and wickedness.

29"Woe to you, teachers of the law and Pharisees, you hypocrites! You build tombs for the
prophets and decorate the graves of the righteous. 30And you say, 'If we had lived in the
days of our forefathers, we would not have
taken part with them in shedding the blood
of the prophets.' 31So you testify against yourselves that you are the descendants of those
who murdered the prophets. 32Fill up, then,
the measure of the sin of your forefathers!

33"You snakes! You brood of vipers! How
will you escape being condemned to hell?
34Therefore I am sending you prophets and
wise men and teachers. Some of them you will
kill and crucify; others you will flog in your synagogues and pursue from town to town. 35And
so upon you will come all the righteous blood
that has been shed on earth, from the blood of
righteous Abel to the blood of Zechariah son
of Berekiah, whom you murdered between the
temple and the altar. 36I tell you the truth, all
this will come upon this generation.

37"O Jerusalem, Jerusalem, you who kill the
prophets and stone those sent to you, how often
I have longed to gather your children together,
as a hen gathers her chicks under her wings,
but you were not willing. 38Look, your house is
left to you desolate. 39For I tell you, you will not
see me again until you say, 'Blessed is he who
comes in the name of the Lord.'[a]"

Signs of the End of the Age

24 Jesus left the temple and was walking
away when his disciples came up to
him to call his attention to its buildings. 2"Do
you see all these things?" he asked. "I tell you
the truth, not one stone here will be left on
another; every one will be thrown down."

3As Jesus was sitting on the Mount of Olives,
the disciples came to him privately. "Tell us,"
they said, "when will this happen, and what
will be the sign of your coming and of the end
of the age?"

4Jesus answered: "Watch out that no one deceives you. 5For many will come in my name,
claiming, 'I am the Christ,[b]' and will deceive
many. 6You will hear of wars and rumors of
wars, but see to it that you are not alarmed.
Such things must happen, but the end is still
to come. 7Nation will rise against nation, and
kingdom against kingdom. There will be famines and earthquakes in various places. 8All
these are the beginning of birth pains.

9"Then you will be handed over to be
persecuted and put to death, and you will be
hated by all nations because of me. 10At that
time many will turn away from the faith and
will betray and hate each other, 11and many
false prophets will appear and deceive many
people. 12Because of the increase of wickedness, the love of most will grow cold, 13but he
who stands firm to the end will be saved. 14And
this gospel of the kingdom will be preached in
the whole world as a testimony to all nations,
and then the end will come.

15"So when you see standing in the holy
place 'the abomination that causes desolation,'[c]
spoken of through the prophet Daniel—let the
reader understand— 16then let those who are
in Judea flee to the mountains. 17Let no one on
the roof of his house go down to take anything
out of the house. 18Let no one in the field go
back to get his cloak. 19How dreadful it will be
in those days for pregnant women and nursing
mothers! 20Pray that your flight will not take
place in winter or on the Sabbath. 21For then
there will be great distress, unequaled from the

[a]39 Psalm 118:26 [b]5 Or *Messiah*; also in verse 23 [c]15 Daniel 9:27; 11:31; 12:11

beginning of the world until now—and never to
be equaled again. 22 If those days had not been
cut short, no one would survive, but for the
sake of the elect those days will be shortened.
23 At that time if anyone says to you, 'Look, here
is the Christ!' or, 'There he is!' do not believe it.
24 For false Christs and false prophets will appear and perform great signs and miracles to
deceive even the elect—if that were possible.
25 See, I have told you ahead of time.

26 "So if anyone tells you, 'There he is, out in
the desert,' do not go out; or, 'Here he is, in the
inner rooms,' do not believe it. 27 For as lightning that comes from the east is visible even
in the west, so will be the coming of the Son of
Man. 28 Wherever there is a carcass, there the
vultures will gather.

29 "Immediately after the distress of those
days

"'the sun will be darkened,
  and the moon will not give its light;
the stars will fall from the sky,
  and the heavenly bodies will be
    shaken.'[a]

30 "At that time the sign of the Son of Man
will appear in the sky, and all the nations of the
earth will mourn. They will see the Son of Man
coming on the clouds of the sky, with power
and great glory. 31 And he will send his angels
with a loud trumpet call, and
they will gather his elect from
the four winds, from one end
of the heavens to the other.

32 "Now learn this lesson
from the fig tree: As soon as its
twigs get tender and its leaves
come out, you know that summer is near. 33 Even so, when
you see all these things, you
know that it[b] is near, right at
the door. 34 I tell you the truth,
this generation[c] will certainly not pass away
until all these things have happened. 35 Heaven
and earth will pass away, but my words will
never pass away.

> Matthew 24:35
>
> *God Is Eternal*
>
> "Heaven and earth will pass away, but my words will never pass away."

The Day and Hour Unknown

36 "No one knows about that day or hour, not
even the angels in heaven, nor the Son,[d] but
only the Father. 37 As it was in the days of Noah,
so it will be at the coming of the Son of Man.
38 For in the days before the flood, people were
eating and drinking, marrying and giving in
marriage, up to the day Noah entered the ark;
39 and they knew nothing about what would
happen until the flood came and took them all
away. That is how it will be at the coming of the
Son of Man. 40 Two men will be in the field; one
will be taken and the other left. 41 Two women
will be grinding with a hand mill; one will be
taken and the other left.

42 "Therefore keep watch, because you do
not know on what day your Lord will come.
43 But understand this: If the owner of the
house had known at what time of night the
thief was coming, he would have kept watch
and would not have let his house be broken
into. 44 So you also must be ready, because the
Son of Man will come at an hour when you do
not expect him.

45 "Who then is the faithful and wise servant,
whom the master has put in charge of the servants in his household to give them their food
at the proper time? 46 It will be good for that servant whose master finds him doing so when he
returns. 47 I tell you the truth, he will put him
in charge of all his possessions. 48 But suppose
that servant is wicked and says to himself, 'My
master is staying away a long time,' 49 and he
then begins to beat his fellow
servants and to eat and drink
with drunkards. 50 The master
of that servant will come on a
day when he does not expect
him and at an hour he is not
aware of. 51 He will cut him to
pieces and assign him a place
with the hypocrites, where
there will be weeping and
gnashing of teeth.

The Parable of the Ten Virgins

25 "At that time the kingdom of heaven
will be like ten virgins who took their
lamps and went out to meet the bridegroom.
2 Five of them were foolish and five were wise.
3 The foolish ones took their lamps but did not
take any oil with them. 4 The wise, however,
took oil in jars along with their lamps. 5 The

[a] 29 Isaiah 13:10; 34:4 [b] 33 Or *he* [c] 34 Or *race* [d] 36 Some manuscripts do not have *nor the Son.*

bridegroom was a long time in coming, and
they all became drowsy and fell asleep.
6“At midnight the cry rang out: ‘Here’s the
bridegroom! Come out to meet him!’
7“Then all the virgins woke up and trimmed
their lamps. 8The foolish ones said to the wise,
‘Give us some of your oil; our lamps are going out.’
9“ ‘No,’ they replied, ‘there may not be enough
for both us and you. Instead, go to those who
sell oil and buy some for yourselves.’
10“But while they were on their way to buy
the oil, the bridegroom arrived. The virgins
who were ready went in with him to the wedding banquet. And the door was shut.
11“Later the others also came. ‘Sir! Sir!’ they
said. ‘Open the door for us!’
12“But he replied, ‘I tell you the truth, I don’t
know you.’
13“Therefore keep watch, because you do
not know the day or the hour.

The Parable of the Talents

14“Again, it will be like a man going on a
journey, who called his servants and entrusted
his property to them. 15To one he gave five talents[a] of money, to another two talents, and to
another one talent, each according to his ability.
Then he went on his journey. 16The man who
had received the five talents went at once and
put his money to work and gained five more.
17So also, the one with the two talents gained
two more. 18But the man who had received the
one talent went off, dug a hole in the ground
and hid his master’s money.
19“After a long time the master of those
servants returned and settled accounts with
them. 20The man who had received the five
talents brought the other five. ‘Master,’ he said,
‘you entrusted me with five talents. See, I have
gained five more.’
21“His master replied, ‘Well done, good and
faithful servant! You have been faithful with
a few things; I will put you in charge of many
things. Come and share your master’s happiness!’
22“The man with the two talents also came.
‘Master,’ he said, ‘you entrusted me with two
talents; see, I have gained two more.’
23“His master replied, ‘Well done, good and
faithful servant! You have been faithful with
a few things; I will put you in charge of many
things. Come and share your master’s happiness!’
24“Then the man who had received the one
talent came. ‘Master,’ he said, ‘I knew that you
are a hard man, harvesting where you have not
sown and gathering where you have not scattered seed. 25So I was afraid and went out and
hid your talent in the ground. See, here is what
belongs to you.’
26“His master replied, ‘You wicked, lazy servant! So you knew that I harvest where I have
not sown and gather where I have not scattered seed? 27Well then, you should have put
my money on deposit with the bankers, so that
when I returned I would have received it back
with interest.
28“ ‘Take the talent from him and give it to
the one who has the ten talents. 29For everyone
who has will be given more, and he will have an
abundance. Whoever does not have, even what
he has will be taken from him. 30And throw
that worthless servant outside, into the darkness, where there will be weeping and gnashing of teeth.’

The Sheep and the Goats

31“When the Son of Man comes in his glory,
and all the angels with him, he will sit on his
throne in heavenly glory. 32All the nations will
be gathered before him, and he will separate
the people one from another as a shepherd separates the sheep from the goats. 33He will put
the sheep on his right and the goats on his left.
34“Then the King will say to those on his
right, ‘Come, you who are blessed by my Father;
take your inheritance, the kingdom prepared
for you since the creation of the world. 35For
I was hungry and you gave me something to
eat, I was thirsty and you gave me something to
drink, I was a stranger and you invited me in,
36I needed clothes and you clothed me, I was
sick and you looked after me, I was in prison
and you came to visit me.’
37“Then the righteous will answer him,
‘Lord, when did we see you hungry and feed
you, or thirsty and give you something to

[a]15 A talent was worth more than a thousand dollars.

Always a Bridesmaid

Read: Matthew 25:1–13

DO YOU REMEMBER playing bride? Digging through the dress-up clothes to find the shiny white dress, high-heeled shoes and beautiful white veil? If you were playing with a group of friends, didn't you argue over who would "have to" be the bridesmaids and who would "get to" be the bride?

As we grew older, our imaginary play turned into the real event: picking the right dress, choosing the flowers and asking our sisters, friends and family members to serve as bridesmaids. But those women who remained unmarried were doomed to hear the tired old phrase "Always a bridesmaid, never a bride." But what's wrong with being a bridesmaid?

In the parable of the ten virgins, Jesus encouraged all believers to be like eager bridesmaids, ready and waiting for the coming of the bridegroom. In Jesus' wedding scenario, the wise bridesmaids, called "virgins," didn't carry bouquets of flowers; they carried oil-filled lamps. So why should we want to be like the bridesmaids? The secret is found in the symbolism behind the story.

The ancient Israelites considered marriage to be the greatest of life's events. When the time came for the wedding, the groom and his friends would dress in their finest clothes and parade to the home of the bride, usually by night, to bring the bride and her attendants to the groom's home. This was why it was so important for the bridesmaids to keep oil in their lamps . . . so they could light the way to the groom's home. Now you know where we probably got the idea for candlelight weddings!

But the oil in the lamps holds far more significance than its practical ability to illuminate the path or its romantic quality of providing ambience for the wedding. In Scripture, oil symbolizes the presence of the Holy Spirit (see 1 Samuel 16:13). Through this story, Jesus was symbolically reminding people that when he returns, he will be coming for those who are wise enough to be filled with the Holy Spirit. Are you ready? Are you like a wise bridesmaid with oil in your lamp?

Matthew 25:1–4

"At that time the kingdom of heaven will be like ten virgins who took their lamps and went out to meet the bridegroom. Five of them were foolish and five were wise. The foolish ones took their lamps but did not take any oil with them. The wise, however, took oil in jars along with their lamps."

reflection

1 How does this parable help you anticipate more fully Jesus Christ's return?

2 How do you know that the "lamp" of your heart is filled with the oil of the Holy Spirit?

3 Ask God to help you keep your lamp continually filled so you will be always ready and eagerly awaiting his coming.

RELATED READINGS

Acts 2:38–39;
Ephesians 5:15–18;
2 Timothy 1:13–14

Go to page 1197 for your next devotional reading.

drink? 38When did we see you a stranger and
invite you in, or needing clothes and clothe
you? 39When did we see you sick or in prison
and go to visit you?'
40"The King will reply, 'I tell you the truth,
whatever you did for one of the least of these
brothers of mine, you did for me.'
41"Then he will say to those on his left, 'Depart from me, you who are cursed, into the eternal fire prepared for the devil and his angels.
42For I was hungry and you gave me nothing
to eat, I was thirsty and you gave me nothing to
drink, 43I was a stranger and you did not invite
me in, I needed clothes and you did not clothe
me, I was sick and in prison and you did not
look after me.'
44"They also will answer, 'Lord, when did
we see you hungry or thirsty or a stranger or
needing clothes or sick or in prison, and did
not help you?'
45"He will reply, 'I tell you the truth, whatever
you did not do for one of the least of these, you
did not do for me.'
46"Then they will go away to eternal punishment, but the righteous to eternal life."

The Plot Against Jesus

26 When Jesus had finished saying all
these things, he said to his disciples,
2"As you know, the Passover is two days
away—and the Son of Man will be handed over
to be crucified."
3Then the chief priests and the elders of the
people assembled in the palace of the high
priest, whose name was Caiaphas, 4and they
plotted to arrest Jesus in some sly way and kill
him. 5"But not during the Feast," they said, "or
there may be a riot among the people."

Jesus Anointed at Bethany

6While Jesus was in Bethany in the home of
a man known as Simon the Leper, 7a woman
came to him with an alabaster jar of very expensive perfume, which she poured on his head as
he was reclining at the table.
8When the disciples saw this, they were indignant. "Why this waste?" they asked. 9"This
perfume could have been sold at a high price
and the money given to the poor."
10Aware of this, Jesus said to them, "Why
are you bothering this woman? She has done
a beautiful thing to me. 11The poor you will
always have with you, but you will not always
have me. 12When she poured this perfume on
my body, she did it to prepare me for burial.
13I tell you the truth, wherever this gospel is
preached throughout the world, what she has
done will also be told, in memory of her."

Judas Agrees to Betray Jesus

14Then one of the Twelve—the one called
Judas Iscariot—went to the chief priests 15and
asked, "What are you willing to give me if I
hand him over to you?" So they counted out for
him thirty silver coins. 16From then on Judas
watched for an opportunity to hand him over.

The Lord's Supper

17On the first day of the Feast of Unleavened
Bread, the disciples came to Jesus and asked,
"Where do you want us to make preparations
for you to eat the Passover?"
18He replied, "Go into the city to a certain man and tell him, 'The Teacher says: My
appointed time is near. I am going to celebrate
the Passover with my disciples at your house.'"
19So the disciples did as Jesus had directed
them and prepared the Passover.
20When evening came, Jesus was reclining
at the table with the Twelve. 21And while they
were eating, he said, "I tell you the truth, one of
you will betray me."
22They were very sad and began to say to
him one after the other, "Surely not I, Lord?"
23Jesus replied, "The one who has dipped
his hand into the bowl with me will betray me.
24The Son of Man will go just as it is written
about him. But woe to that man who betrays
the Son of Man! It would be better for him if
he had not been born."
25Then Judas, the one who would betray
him, said, "Surely not I, Rabbi?"
Jesus answered, "Yes, it is you."[a]
26While they were eating, Jesus took bread,
gave thanks and broke it, and gave it to his disciples, saying, "Take and eat; this is my body."
27Then he took the cup, gave thanks and offered it to them, saying, "Drink from it, all of
you. 28This is my blood of the[b] covenant, which
is poured out for many for the forgiveness of

[a]25 Or *"You yourself have said it"* [b]28 Some manuscripts *the new*

Extravagant Love

Read: Matthew 26:6–13

"EXTRAVAGANT." "OVER THE TOP." "Totally in character for *her*," the disciples around the table might have thought. This woman did not follow convention. She didn't care that the men in the room were watching or what they thought. She just acted, and as a result, she is remembered to this day.

This scene continues to be an example of extravagant love. We know from John's Gospel that the woman mentioned here is Mary of Bethany, the sister of Lazarus and Martha. This event took place during the final week of Jesus' life, after he had raised Mary's brother from the dead and wept with her and her sister. Mary's life and faith must have undergone significant transformation in those following days and weeks. Although we can't know for sure what Mary was thinking, her act echoed the preparation of a body for burial. Mary's act wittingly or unwittingly foreshadowed Jesus' coming death on the cross.

Put yourself in Mary's shoes. Perhaps she had followed Christ and heard his predictions about the signs of the end times. Maybe she had heard him tell the parable of the ten virgins. She must have sensed something was different about Jesus that night. Although she may not have understood the full meaning of Jesus' words, Mary poured out her expensive perfume from an alabaster jar, anointing Jesus with her love. Most likely, she gave her Lord the most valuable thing she possessed. Though others criticized her, Jesus praised her for her extravagant expression of love for him, for preparing him for his burial in a symbolic way.

Abraham loved his son Isaac, yet he willingly offered him to God; and God gave him back as a blessing. Hannah offered Samuel to the Lord's service and has gone down in history as a woman most blessed. Mary had an alabaster jar of perfume. She broke it open and poured it out as a love offering. Jesus praised her actions and promised she would always be remembered.

What is your most precious possession? Are you willing to pour out your time? Your money? Your gifts? Your talents? When you give your best to Jesus, he will accept your offering of extravagant love with joy.

Wednesday

Matthew 26:10–12

Jesus said to them, "Why are you bothering this woman? She has done a beautiful thing to me. The poor you will always have with you, but you will not always have me. When she poured this perfume on my body, she did it to prepare me for burial."

reflection

1 What are you willing to offer Jesus today?

2 What are you holding back?

3 Do you ever worry about what others will think of your actions? Ask God for courage and willingness to act for Jesus no matter what others may think.

RELATED READINGS

Genesis 22:1–19;
1 Samuel 1:21—2:11;
Mark 14:3–9;
Luke 6:38

"We can do no great things—only small things with great love."

Mother Teresa

Go to page 1205 for your next devotional reading.

sins. 29I tell you, I will not drink of this fruit of
the vine from now on until that day when I
drink it anew with you in my Father's kingdom."

30When they had sung a hymn, they went
out to the Mount of Olives.

Jesus Predicts Peter's Denial

31Then Jesus told them, "This very night
you will all fall away on account of me, for it
is written:

> "'I will strike the shepherd,
> and the sheep of the flock will be
> scattered.'[a]

32But after I have risen, I will go ahead of you
into Galilee."

33Peter replied, "Even if all fall away on account of you, I never will."

34"I tell you the truth," Jesus answered, "this
very night, before the rooster crows, you will
disown me three times."

35But Peter declared, "Even if I have to die
with you, I will never disown you." And all the
other disciples said the same.

Gethsemane

36Then Jesus went with his disciples to a
place called Gethsemane, and he said to them,
"Sit here while I go over there and pray." 37He
took Peter and the two sons of Zebedee along
with him, and he began to be sorrowful and
troubled. 38Then he said to them, "My soul
is overwhelmed with sorrow to the point of
death. Stay here and keep watch with me."

39Going a little farther, he fell with his face
to the ground and prayed, "My Father, if it is
possible, may this cup be taken from me. Yet
not as I will, but as you will."

40Then he returned to his disciples and
found them sleeping. "Could you men not
keep watch with me for one hour?" he asked
Peter. 41"Watch and pray so that you will not
fall into temptation. The spirit is willing, but
the body is weak."

42He went away a second time and prayed,
"My Father, if it is not possible for this cup to
be taken away unless I drink it, may your will
be done."

43When he came back, he again found them
sleeping, because their eyes were heavy. 44So he
left them and went away once more and prayed
the third time, saying the same thing.

45Then he returned to the disciples and said
to them, "Are you still sleeping and resting?
Look, the hour is near, and the Son of Man is
betrayed into the hands of sinners. 46Rise, let
us go! Here comes my betrayer!"

Jesus Arrested

47While he was still speaking, Judas, one
of the Twelve, arrived. With him was a large
crowd armed with swords and clubs, sent from
the chief priests and the elders of the people.
48Now the betrayer had arranged a signal with
them: "The one I kiss is the man; arrest him."
49Going at once to Jesus, Judas said, "Greetings, Rabbi!" and kissed him.

50Jesus replied, "Friend, do what you came
for."[b]

Then the men stepped forward, seized Jesus
and arrested him. 51With that, one of Jesus'
companions reached for his sword, drew it out
and struck the servant of the high priest, cutting off his ear.

52"Put your sword back in its place," Jesus
said to him, "for all who draw the sword will
die by the sword. 53Do you think I cannot call
on my Father, and he will at once put at my
disposal more than twelve legions of angels?
54But how then would the Scriptures be fulfilled that say it must happen in this way?"

55At that time Jesus said to the crowd, "Am I
leading a rebellion, that you have come out
with swords and clubs to capture me? Every
day I sat in the temple courts teaching, and
you did not arrest me. 56But this has all taken
place that the writings of the prophets might
be fulfilled." Then all the disciples deserted him
and fled.

Before the Sanhedrin

57Those who had arrested Jesus took him to
Caiaphas, the high priest, where the teachers
of the law and the elders had assembled. 58But
Peter followed him at a distance, right up to the
courtyard of the high priest. He entered and sat
down with the guards to see the outcome.

59The chief priests and the whole Sanhedrin
were looking for false evidence against Jesus so

[a]31 Zech. 13:7 [b]50 Or *"Friend, why have you come?"*

that they could put him to death. 60But they
did not find any, though many false witnesses
came forward.
Finally two came forward 61and declared,
"This fellow said, 'I am able to destroy the temple of God and rebuild it in three days.'"
62Then the high priest stood up and said
to Jesus, "Are you not going to answer? What
is this testimony that these men are bringing
against you?" 63But Jesus remained silent.
The high priest said to him, "I charge you
under oath by the living God: Tell us if you are
the Christ,[a] the Son of God."
64"Yes, it is as you say," Jesus
replied. "But I say to all of
you: In the future you will see
the Son of Man sitting at the
right hand of the Mighty One
and coming on the clouds of
heaven."
65Then the high priest tore
his clothes and said, "He has
spoken blasphemy! Why do
we need any more witnesses?
Look, now you have heard
the blasphemy. 66What do
you think?"
"He is worthy of death,"
they answered.
67Then they spit in his face
and struck him with their fists.
Others slapped him 68and said,
"Prophesy to us, Christ. Who hit you?"

> **Matthew 26:64**
>
> *God Is the Mighty One*
>
> "Yes, it is as you say," Jesus replied. "But I say to all of you: In the future you will see the Son of Man sitting at the right hand of the Mighty One and coming on the clouds of heaven."

Peter Disowns Jesus

69Now Peter was sitting out in the courtyard,
and a servant girl came to him. "You also were
with Jesus of Galilee," she said.
70But he denied it before them all. "I don't
know what you're talking about," he said.
71Then he went out to the gateway, where
another girl saw him and said to the people
there, "This fellow was with Jesus of Nazareth."
72He denied it again, with an oath: "I don't
know the man!"
73After a little while, those standing there
went up to Peter and said, "Surely you are one
of them, for your accent gives you away."
74Then he began to call down curses on
himself and he swore to them, "I don't know
the man!"
Immediately a rooster crowed. 75Then Peter remembered the word Jesus had spoken:
"Before the rooster crows, you will disown me
three times." And he went outside and wept
bitterly.

Judas Hangs Himself

27 Early in the morning, all the chief
priests and the elders of the people
came to the decision to put Jesus to death.
2They bound him, led him
away and handed him over to
Pilate, the governor.
3When Judas, who had be-
trayed him, saw that Jesus was
condemned, he was seized
with remorse and returned the
thirty silver coins to the chief
priests and the elders. 4"I have
sinned," he said, "for I have betrayed innocent blood."
"What is that to us?" they
replied. "That's your responsibility."
5So Judas threw the money
into the temple and left. Then
he went away and hanged himself.
6The chief priests picked up
the coins and said, "It is against the law to put
this into the treasury, since it is blood money."
7So they decided to use the money to buy
the potter's field as a burial place for foreigners. 8That is why it has been called the Field
of Blood to this day. 9Then what was spoken
by Jeremiah the prophet was fulfilled: "They
took the thirty silver coins, the price set on
him by the people of Israel, 10and they used
them to buy the potter's field, as the Lord
commanded me."[b]

Jesus Before Pilate

11Meanwhile Jesus stood before the governor, and the governor asked him, "Are you the
king of the Jews?"
"Yes, it is as you say," Jesus replied.
12When he was accused by the chief priests

[a]63 Or *Messiah*; also in verse 68 [b]10 See Zech. 11:12,13; Jer. 19:1–13; 32:6–9.

and the elders, he gave no answer. 13Then Pilate asked him, "Don't you hear the testimony
they are bringing against you?" 14But Jesus
made no reply, not even to a single charge—to
the great amazement of the governor.
15Now it was the governor's custom at the
Feast to release a prisoner chosen by the crowd.
16At that time they had a notorious prisoner,
called Barabbas. 17So when the crowd had
gathered, Pilate asked them, "Which one do
you want me to release to you: Barabbas, or
Jesus who is called Christ?" 18For he knew it
was out of envy that they had handed Jesus
over to him.
19While Pilate was sitting on the judge's seat,
his wife sent him this message: "Don't have anything to do with that innocent man, for I have
suffered a great deal today in a dream because
of him."
20But the chief priests and the elders
persuaded the crowd to ask for Barabbas and
to have Jesus executed.
21"Which of the two do you want me to release to you?" asked the governor.
"Barabbas," they answered.
22"What shall I do, then, with Jesus who is
called Christ?" Pilate asked.
They all answered, "Crucify him!"
23"Why? What crime has he committed?"
asked Pilate.
But they shouted all the louder, "Crucify
him!"
24When Pilate saw that he was getting nowhere, but that instead an uproar was starting,
he took water and washed his hands in front of
the crowd. "I am innocent of this man's blood,"
he said. "It is your responsibility!"
25All the people answered, "Let his blood be
on us and on our children!"
26Then he released Barabbas to them. But
he had Jesus flogged, and handed him over to
be crucified.

The Soldiers Mock Jesus

27Then the governor's soldiers took Jesus
into the Praetorium and gathered the whole
company of soldiers around him. 28They
stripped him and put a scarlet robe on him,
29and then twisted together a crown of thorns
and set it on his head. They put a staff in his right
hand and knelt in front of him and mocked
him. "Hail, king of the Jews!" they said. 30They
spit on him, and took the staff and struck him
on the head again and again. 31After they had
mocked him, they took off the robe and put his
own clothes on him. Then they led him away to
crucify him.

The Crucifixion

32As they were going out, they met a man
from Cyrene, named Simon, and they forced
him to carry the cross. 33They came to a place
called Golgotha (which means The Place of
the Skull). 34There they offered Jesus wine to
drink, mixed with gall; but after tasting it, he
refused to drink it. 35When they had crucified
him, they divided up his clothes by casting
lots.[a] 36And sitting down, they kept watch over
him there. 37Above his head they placed the
written charge against him: THIS IS JESUS, THE
KING OF THE JEWS. 38Two robbers were crucified with him, one on his right and one on his
left. 39Those who passed by hurled insults at
him, shaking their heads 40and saying, "You
who are going to destroy the temple and build
it in three days, save yourself! Come down
from the cross, if you are the Son of God!"
41In the same way the chief priests, the
teachers of the law and the elders mocked him.
42"He saved others," they said, "but he can't
save himself! He's the King of Israel! Let him
come down now from the cross, and we will
believe in him. 43He trusts in God. Let God rescue him now if he wants him, for he said, 'I am
the Son of God.' " 44In the same way the robbers who were crucified with him also heaped
insults on him.

The Death of Jesus

45From the sixth hour until the ninth hour
darkness came over all the land. 46About the
ninth hour Jesus cried out in a loud voice, *"Eloi,
Eloi,*[b] *lama sabachthani?"*—which means, "My
God, my God, why have you forsaken me?"[c]
47When some of those standing there heard
this, they said, "He's calling Elijah."
48Immediately one of them ran and got a
sponge. He filled it with wine vinegar, put it on

[a]35 A few late manuscripts *lots that the word spoken by the prophet might be fulfilled: "They divided my garments among themselves and cast lots for my clothing"* (Psalm 22:18) [b]46 Some manuscripts *Eli, Eli* [c]46 Psalm 22:1

a stick, and offered it to Jesus to drink. 49 The
rest said, "Now leave him alone. Let's see if Elijah comes to save him."
50 And when Jesus had cried out again in a
loud voice, he gave up his spirit.
51 At that moment the curtain of the temple was torn in two from top to bottom. The
earth shook and the rocks split. 52 The tombs
broke open and the bodies of many holy people
who had died were raised to life. 53 They came
out of the tombs, and after Jesus' resurrection
they went into the holy city and appeared to
many people.
54 When the centurion and those with him
who were guarding Jesus saw the earthquake
and all that had happened, they were terrified, and exclaimed, "Surely he was the Son[a]
of God!"
55 Many women were there, watching from
a distance. They had followed Jesus from Galilee to care for his needs. 56 Among them were
Mary Magdalene, Mary the mother of James
and Joses, and the mother of Zebedee's sons.

The Burial of Jesus

57 As evening approached, there came a rich
man from Arimathea, named Joseph, who had
himself become a disciple of Jesus. 58 Going to
Pilate, he asked for Jesus' body, and Pilate ordered that it be given to him. 59 Joseph took the
body, wrapped it in a clean linen cloth, 60 and
placed it in his own new tomb that he had cut
out of the rock. He rolled a big stone in front
of the entrance to the tomb and went away.
61 Mary Magdalene and the other Mary were
sitting there opposite the tomb.

The Guard at the Tomb

62 The next day, the one after Preparation
Day, the chief priests and the Pharisees went
to Pilate. 63 "Sir," they said, "we remember that
while he was still alive that deceiver said, 'After
three days I will rise again.' 64 So give the order
for the tomb to be made secure until the third
day. Otherwise, his disciples may come and
steal the body and tell the people that he has
been raised from the dead. This last deception
will be worse than the first."
65 "Take a guard," Pilate answered. "Go, make
the tomb as secure as you know how." 66 So they
went and made the tomb secure by putting a
seal on the stone and posting the guard.

The Resurrection

28 After the Sabbath, at dawn on the first
day of the week, Mary Magdalene and
the other Mary went to look at the tomb.
2 There was a violent earthquake, for an angel
of the Lord came down from heaven and, going
to the tomb, rolled back the stone and sat on
it. 3 His appearance was like lightning, and his
clothes were white as snow. 4 The guards were
so afraid of him that they shook and became
like dead men.
5 The angel said to the women, "Do not be
afraid, for I know that you are looking for Jesus,
who was crucified. 6 He is not here; he has risen,
just as he said. Come and see the place where
he lay. 7 Then go quickly and tell his disciples:
'He has risen from the dead and is going ahead
of you into Galilee. There you will see him.'
Now I have told you."
8 So the women hurried away from the tomb,
afraid yet filled with joy, and ran to tell his disciples. 9 Suddenly Jesus met them. "Greetings,"
he said. They came to him, clasped his feet and
worshiped him. 10 Then Jesus said to them, "Do
not be afraid. Go and tell my brothers to go to
Galilee; there they will see me."

The Guards' Report

11 While the women were on their way, some
of the guards went into the city and reported to
the chief priests everything that had happened.
12 When the chief priests had met with the elders and devised a plan, they gave the soldiers
a large sum of money, 13 telling them, "You are
to say, 'His disciples came during the night
and stole him away while we were asleep.' 14 If
this report gets to the governor, we will satisfy
him and keep you out of trouble." 15 So the
soldiers took the money and did as they were
instructed. And this story has been widely
circulated among the Jews to this very day.

The Great Commission

16 Then the eleven disciples went to Galilee,
to the mountain where Jesus had told them to
go. 17 When they saw him, they worshiped him;
but some doubted. 18 Then Jesus came to them
and said, "All authority in heaven and on earth

[a] 54 Or *a son*

has been given to me. 19 Therefore go and make
disciples of all nations, baptizing them in[a] the
name of the Father and of the Son and of the
Holy Spirit, 20 and teaching them to obey everything I have commanded you. And surely I am
with you always, to the very end of the age."

[a] 19 Or *into*; see Acts 8:16; 19:5; Romans 6:3; 1 Cor. 1:13; 10:2 and Gal. 3:27.

Mark

The story of Jesus' life, death and resurrection is told in the first four books of the New Testament. Of these four eyewitness accounts, the Gospel of Mark is *the most fast-paced narrative*. Historians are not exactly sure of Mark's identity, but most agree that he was a friend of Peter's, obtaining the information about the life of Jesus from him. Mark's excitement in telling his story is underscored by his repeated use of the words "immediately" and "at once."

The word *gospel* means "good news," and Mark emphasizes the "good news" of Jesus' ministry of salvation. *Mark is very clear about the deity of Christ* but also goes to great lengths to show his humanity. While he does not neglect recounting the teachings of Jesus, it is the actions of Jesus that stir his heart. The purpose of this Gospel is to tell Jesus' life story so that all will come to the conclusion that, *"Yes, Jesus is the Son of God."*

Author:
John Mark.

Audience:
Followers of Jesus. Mark wrote with a Roman audience in mind.

Date:
Probably between A.D. 55 and 65.

Setting:
Mark most likely wrote from Rome. Early church sources tell us the apostle Peter relayed information to Mark for his Gospel.

Verse to Remember:
Then a cloud appeared and enveloped them, and a voice came from the cloud: "This is my Son, whom I love. Listen to him!" (9:7)

John the Baptist Prepares the Way

1 The beginning of the gospel about Jesus
Christ, the Son of God.[a]

2 It is written in Isaiah the prophet:

"I will send my messenger ahead of you,
who will prepare your way"[b]—
3 "a voice of one calling in the desert,
'Prepare the way for the Lord,
make straight paths for him.'"[c]

4 And so John came, baptizing in the desert region and preaching a baptism of repentance for
the forgiveness of sins. 5 The whole Judean countryside and all the people of Jerusalem went out

[a]1 Some manuscripts do not have *the Son of God.* [b]2 Mal. 3:1 [c]3 Isaiah 40:3

to him. Confessing their sins, they were baptized
by him in the Jordan River. 6John wore clothing
made of camel's hair, with a leather belt around
his waist, and he ate locusts and wild honey.
7And this was his message: "After me will come
one more powerful than I, the thongs of whose
sandals I am not worthy to stoop down and untie. 8I baptize you with[a] water, but he will baptize you with the Holy Spirit."

The Baptism and Temptation of Jesus

9At that time Jesus came from Nazareth in
Galilee and was baptized by John in the Jordan.
10As Jesus was coming up out of the water, he
saw heaven being torn open and the Spirit descending on him like a dove. 11And a voice
came from heaven: "You are my Son, whom I
love; with you I am well pleased."

12At once the Spirit sent him out into the
desert, 13and he was in the desert forty days,
being tempted by Satan. He was with the wild
animals, and angels attended him.

The Calling of the First Disciples

14After John was put in prison, Jesus went
into Galilee, proclaiming the good news of
God. 15"The time has come," he said. "The
kingdom of God is near. Repent and believe
the good news!"

16As Jesus walked beside the Sea of Galilee,
he saw Simon and his brother Andrew casting
a net into the lake, for they were fishermen.
17"Come, follow me," Jesus said, "and I will
make you fishers of men." 18At once they left
their nets and followed him.

19When he had gone a little farther, he saw
James son of Zebedee and his brother John in
a boat, preparing their nets. 20Without delay
he called them, and they left their father Zebedee in the boat with the hired men and followed him.

Jesus Drives Out an Evil Spirit

21They went to Capernaum, and when the
Sabbath came, Jesus went into the synagogue
and began to teach. 22The people were amazed
at his teaching, because he taught them as
one who had authority, not as the teachers of
the law. 23Just then a man in their synagogue
who was possessed by an evil[b] spirit cried out,
24"What do you want with us, Jesus of Nazareth? Have you come to destroy us? I know
who you are—the Holy One of God!"

25"Be quiet!" said Jesus sternly. "Come out of
him!" 26The evil spirit shook the man violently
and came out of him with a shriek.

27The people were all so amazed that they
asked each other, "What is this? A new teaching—and with authority! He even gives orders
to evil spirits and they obey him." 28News
about him spread quickly over the whole region of Galilee.

Jesus Heals Many

29As soon as they left the synagogue, they
went with James and John to the home of Simon and Andrew. 30Simon's mother-in-law
was in bed with a fever, and they told Jesus
about her. 31So he went to her, took her hand
and helped her up. The fever left her and she
began to wait on them.

32That evening after sunset the people
brought to Jesus all the sick and demon-
possessed. 33The whole town gathered at the
door, 34and Jesus healed many who had various diseases. He also drove out many demons,
but he would not let the demons speak because
they knew who he was.

Jesus Prays in a Solitary Place

35Very early in the morning, while it was still
dark, Jesus got up, left the house and went off to
a solitary place, where he prayed. 36Simon and
his companions went to look for him, 37and
when they found him, they exclaimed: "Everyone is looking for you!"

38Jesus replied, "Let us go somewhere else—
to the nearby villages—so I can preach there
also. That is why I have come." 39So he traveled
throughout Galilee, preaching in their synagogues and driving out demons.

A Man With Leprosy

40A man with leprosy[c] came to him and
begged him on his knees, "If you are willing,
you can make me clean."

41Filled with compassion, Jesus reached out
his hand and touched the man. "I am willing,"
he said. "Be clean!" 42Immediately the leprosy
left him and he was cured.

[a] 8 Or *in* [b] 23 Greek *unclean*; also in verses 26 and 27 [c] 40 The Greek word was used for various diseases affecting the skin—not necessarily leprosy.

Expect the Extraordinary

Read: Mark 1:14–20

IT WAS A DAY LIKE ANY OTHER. It's likely the four men kissed their families good-bye and went down to the shore—just as they did every day. They probably told jokes, talked about their hopes and dreams, and bragged about how many fish they'd catch. This was the life they knew, the life they thought they were destined to live. Being fishermen was more than what they did; it was who they were.

Then something extraordinary happened. Jesus came on the scene.

When the divine intersects with the ordinary, everything changes. An ordinary man who catches fish becomes a disciple who fishes for people. A mother whose daily life consists of changing diapers and folding laundry becomes a shepherdess of young lives. A smart businesswoman becomes a spiritual leader. A teacher becomes a mentor. A friend becomes an intercessor. A student becomes a missionary. A tongue-tied wallflower blossoms into a gifted speaker. When Jesus enters the scene, we can expect the extraordinary.

The four Galileans could never have guessed the turn their lives would take that day. They were ordinary men living ordinary lives. But they recognized the extraordinary when they saw it, left everything they knew and chose to follow him.

There were other people at the lake that day who saw Jesus, other people who heard him speak. The father of James and John was there. So were some hired men. They heard and they saw, but they stayed with their nets and fished for fish.

When Jesus calls us to follow him, he is looking for people who are willing to let go of the ordinary and look for the extraordinary. Sometimes that means we're called to leave everything—our nets and our families—and go where he tells us. Other times, following him means we keep doing what we've been doing, only with a shift in our perspective: We still change diapers, but we focus on raising godly children. We still do laundry, but as we do, we remember that we serve the God of holiness. We still do business, but we remember that it's all kingdom business. We still go fishing, but now we fish for people as well as fish.

Mark 1:17

"Come, follow me," Jesus said, "and I will make you fishers of men."

reflection

1 When you heard Jesus' call for the first time, what changed for you?

2 Do you identify more with the men who left everything to follow Jesus or with those who stayed with their nets?

3 Jesus called fishermen to become "fishers of men." What is he calling you to do today?

RELATED READINGS

1 Corinthians 1:26–31; 1 Peter 2:9–10

Go to page 1208 for your next devotional reading.

43 Jesus sent him away at once with a strong
warning: 44 "See that you don't tell this to anyone. But go, show yourself to the priest and
offer the sacrifices that Moses commanded
for your cleansing, as a testimony to them."
45 Instead he went out and began to talk freely,
spreading the news. As a result, Jesus could no
longer enter a town openly but stayed outside
in lonely places. Yet the people still came to
him from everywhere.

Jesus Heals a Paralytic

2 A few days later, when Jesus again entered
Capernaum, the people heard that he had
come home. 2 So many gathered that there was
no room left, not even outside the door, and he
preached the word to them. 3 Some men came,
bringing to him a paralytic, carried by four of
them. 4 Since they could not get him to Jesus
because of the crowd, they made an opening in
the roof above Jesus and, after digging through
it, lowered the mat the paralyzed man was lying on. 5 When Jesus saw their faith, he said to
the paralytic, "Son, your sins are forgiven."

6 Now some teachers of the law were sitting
there, thinking to themselves, 7 "Why does this
fellow talk like that? He's blaspheming! Who
can forgive sins but God alone?"

8 Immediately Jesus knew in his spirit that
this was what they were thinking in their
hearts, and he said to them, "Why are you
thinking these things? 9 Which is easier: to say
to the paralytic, 'Your sins are forgiven,' or to
say, 'Get up, take your mat and walk'? 10 But
that you may know that the Son of Man has
authority on earth to forgive sins..." He said
to the paralytic, 11 "I tell you, get up, take your
mat and go home." 12 He got up, took his mat
and walked out in full view of them all. This
amazed everyone and they praised God, saying, "We have never seen anything like this!"

The Calling of Levi

13 Once again Jesus went out beside the lake.
A large crowd came to him, and he began to
teach them. 14 As he walked along, he saw Levi
son of Alphaeus sitting at the tax collector's
booth. "Follow me," Jesus told him, and Levi
got up and followed him.

15 While Jesus was having dinner at Levi's
house, many tax collectors and "sinners" were
eating with him and his disciples, for there were
many who followed him. 16 When the teachers
of the law who were Pharisees saw him eating with the "sinners" and tax collectors, they
asked his disciples: "Why does he eat with tax
collectors and 'sinners'?"

17 On hearing this, Jesus said to them, "It is
not the healthy who need a doctor, but the sick.
I have not come to call the righteous, but sinners."

Jesus Questioned About Fasting

18 Now John's disciples and the Pharisees
were fasting. Some people came and asked
Jesus, "How is it that John's disciples and the
disciples of the Pharisees are fasting, but yours
are not?"

19 Jesus answered, "How can the guests of the
bridegroom fast while he is with them? They
cannot, so long as they have him with them.
20 But the time will come when the bridegroom
will be taken from them, and on that day they
will fast.

21 "No one sews a patch of unshrunk cloth
on an old garment. If he does, the new piece
will pull away from the old, making the tear
worse. 22 And no one pours new wine into old
wineskins. If he does, the wine will burst the
skins, and both the wine and the wineskins
will be ruined. No, he pours new wine into
new wineskins."

Lord of the Sabbath

23 One Sabbath Jesus was going through the
grainfields, and as his disciples walked along,
they began to pick some heads of grain. 24 The
Pharisees said to him, "Look, why are they doing what is unlawful on the Sabbath?"

25 He answered, "Have you never read what
David did when he and his companions were
hungry and in need? 26 In the days of Abiathar
the high priest, he entered the house of God
and ate the consecrated bread, which is lawful
only for priests to eat. And he also gave some
to his companions."

27 Then he said to them, "The Sabbath was
made for man, not man for the Sabbath. 28 So
the Son of Man is Lord even of the Sabbath."

3 Another time he went into the synagogue,
and a man with a shriveled hand was there.
2 Some of them were looking for a reason to ac-

cuse Jesus, so they watched him closely to see if
he would heal him on the Sabbath. 3Jesus said
to the man with the shriveled hand, "Stand up
in front of everyone."
4Then Jesus asked them, "Which is lawful on
the Sabbath: to do good or to do evil, to save
life or to kill?" But they remained silent.
5He looked around at them in anger and,
deeply distressed at their stubborn hearts,
said to the man, "Stretch out your hand." He
stretched it out, and his hand was completely
restored. 6Then the Pharisees went out and began to plot with the Herodians how they might
kill Jesus.

Crowds Follow Jesus

7Jesus withdrew with his disciples to the
lake, and a large crowd from Galilee followed.
8When they heard all he was doing, many
people came to him from Judea, Jerusalem, Id-
umea, and the regions across the Jordan and
around Tyre and Sidon. 9Because of the crowd
he told his disciples to have a small boat ready
for him, to keep the people from crowding him.
10For he had healed many, so that those with
diseases were pushing forward to touch him.
11Whenever the evil[a] spirits saw him, they fell
down before him and cried out, "You are the
Son of God." 12But he gave them strict orders
not to tell who he was.

The Appointing of the Twelve Apostles

13Jesus went up on a mountainside and called to him those
he wanted, and they came to
him. 14He appointed twelve—
designating them apostles[b]—
that they might be with him
and that he might send them
out to preach 15and to have
authority to drive out demons.
16These are the twelve he
appointed: Simon (to whom he gave the name
Peter); 17James son of Zebedee and his brother
John (to them he gave the name Boanerges,
which means Sons of Thunder); 18Andrew,
Philip, Bartholomew, Matthew, Thomas, James
son of Alphaeus, Thaddaeus, Simon the Zealot
19and Judas Iscariot, who betrayed him.

> **Mark 3:35**
>
> *God Is Our Family*
>
> "Whoever does God's will is my brother and sister and mother."

Jesus and Beelzebub

20Then Jesus entered a house, and again a
crowd gathered, so that he and his disciples
were not even able to eat. 21When his family
heard about this, they went to take charge of
him, for they said, "He is out of his mind."
22And the teachers of the law who came
down from Jerusalem said, "He is possessed by
Beelzebub[c]! By the prince of demons he is driving out demons."
23So Jesus called them and spoke to them
in parables: "How can Satan drive out Satan?
24If a kingdom is divided against itself, that
kingdom cannot stand. 25If a house is divided
against itself, that house cannot stand. 26And
if Satan opposes himself and is divided, he cannot stand; his end has come. 27In fact, no one
can enter a strong man's house and carry off
his possessions unless he first ties up the strong
man. Then he can rob his house. 28I tell you the
truth, all the sins and blasphemies of men will
be forgiven them. 29But whoever blasphemes
against the Holy Spirit will never be forgiven;
he is guilty of an eternal sin."
30He said this because they were saying, "He
has an evil spirit."

Jesus' Mother and Brothers

31Then Jesus' mother and brothers arrived.
Standing outside, they sent
someone in to call him. 32A
crowd was sitting around
him, and they told him, "Your
mother and brothers are outside looking for you."
33"Who are my mother and
my brothers?" he asked.
34Then he looked at those
seated in a circle around him
and said, "Here are my mother
and my brothers! 35Whoever
does God's will is my brother
and sister and mother."

The Parable of the Sower

4 Again Jesus began to teach by the lake.
The crowd that gathered around him was
so large that he got into a boat and sat in it out
on the lake, while all the people were along
the shore at the water's edge. 2He taught them

[a]11 Greek *unclean*; also in verse 30 [b]14 Some manuscripts do not have *designating them apostles.* [c]22 Greek *Beezeboul* or *Beelzeboul*

Something Wonderful

Read: Mark 3:1–19

Mark 3:13

Jesus went up on a mountainside and called to him those he wanted, and they came to him.

reflection

1 What is God asking you to do that you are afraid to undertake?

2 What excuses have you been giving for not accepting the task?

3 What are the spiritual and physical resources you need to accept God's call? Ask God to give them to you.

RELATED READINGS

Exodus 3:1–12;
Romans 1:1–7;
1 Corinthians 1:26–31

"WHO, ME, LORD?"

"Yes, you. I'm calling you."

"But what you're asking of me is too difficult. I don't have the skills or the training. I can't possibly succeed at this!"

Does this conversation sound familiar? Many of us know the experience of being asked to take on a task that seems much too demanding for us. We're afraid of failure. We make excuses. But by doing so, we may miss the joy of being part of something wonderful.

In *The Purpose Driven Life*, author Rick Warren responds to those who make excuses concerning why they cannot serve the Lord: "Abraham was old, Jacob was insecure, Leah was unattractive, Joseph was abused, Moses stuttered, Gideon was poor, Samson was codependent, Rahab was immoral, David had an affair and all kinds of family problems, Elijah was suicidal, Jeremiah was depressed, Jonah was reluctant, Naomi was a widow, John the Baptist was eccentric to say the least, Peter was impulsive and hot-tempered, Martha worried a lot, the Samaritan woman had several failed marriages, Zacchaeus was unpopular, Thomas had doubts, Paul had poor health, and Timothy was timid."

The 12 men Jesus asked to be his apostles could have offered lots of reasons why they were not fit to serve. They were common men with no special standing in the eyes of the world. Yet when Jesus called, they came: fishermen, tax collectors and even revolutionaries. History shows that their faith and obedience to Jesus Christ changed the world profoundly.

When Jesus calls us to follow him, he's not looking for the smartest or the strongest or the most brave. He doesn't check our resume or call our list of references. Scripture is full of stories of women and men who were used powerfully by God despite their lack of experience or expertise. How about you? Is God asking you to accept an assignment that seems far beyond your comfort zone? Are you afraid that you might fail? Are you afraid that you might succeed?

Take heart from this account of those whom Jesus chose to be his closest companions—those who would carry on his work. They changed the world not because of what they had in themselves, but because of the One who empowered them. And they were part of something wonderful.

Go to page 1211 for your next devotional reading.

many things by parables, and in his teaching
said: 3“Listen! A farmer went out to sow his
seed. 4As he was scattering the seed, some fell
along the path, and the birds came and ate it
up. 5Some fell on rocky places, where it did not
have much soil. It sprang up quickly, because
the soil was shallow. 6But when the sun came
up, the plants were scorched, and they withered because they had no root. 7Other seed fell
among thorns, which grew up and choked the
plants, so that they did not bear grain. 8Still
other seed fell on good soil. It came up, grew
and produced a crop, multiplying thirty, sixty,
or even a hundred times.”

9Then Jesus said, “He who has ears to hear,
let him hear.”

10When he was alone, the Twelve and the
others around him asked him about the parables. 11He told them, “The secret of the kingdom of God has been given to you. But to those
on the outside everything is said in parables
12so that,

“ ‘they may be ever seeing but never
perceiving,
and ever hearing but never
understanding;
otherwise they might turn and be
forgiven!’[a]”

13Then Jesus said to them, “Don’t you understand this parable? How then will you
understand any parable? 14The farmer sows
the word. 15Some people are like seed along
the path, where the word is sown. As soon
as they hear it, Satan comes and takes away
the word that was sown in them. 16Others,
like seed sown on rocky places, hear the word
and at once receive it with joy. 17But since
they have no root, they last only a short time.
When trouble or persecution comes because
of the word, they quickly fall away. 18Still
others, like seed sown among thorns, hear
the word; 19but the worries of this life, the deceitfulness of wealth and the desires for other
things come in and choke the word, making it
unfruitful. 20Others, like seed sown on good
soil, hear the word, accept it, and produce a
crop—thirty, sixty or even a hundred times
what was sown.”

[a]12 Isaiah 6:9,10

A Lamp on a Stand

21He said to them, “Do you bring in a lamp
to put it under a bowl or a bed? Instead, don’t
you put it on its stand? 22For whatever is hidden is meant to be disclosed, and whatever
is concealed is meant to be brought out into
the open. 23If anyone has ears to hear, let
him hear.”

24“Consider carefully what you hear,” he
continued. “With the measure you use, it will be
measured to you—and even more. 25Whoever
has will be given more; whoever does not have,
even what he has will be taken from him.”

The Parable of the Growing Seed

26He also said, “This is what the kingdom of
God is like. A man scatters seed on the ground.
27Night and day, whether he sleeps or gets up,
the seed sprouts and grows, though he does
not know how. 28All by itself the soil produces
grain—first the stalk, then the head, then the
full kernel in the head. 29As soon as the grain
is ripe, he puts the sickle to it, because the harvest has come.”

The Parable of the Mustard Seed

30Again he said, “What shall we say the kingdom of God is like, or what parable shall we use
to describe it? 31It is like a mustard seed, which is
the smallest seed you plant in the ground. 32Yet
when planted, it grows and becomes the largest
of all garden plants, with such big branches that
the birds of the air can perch in its shade.”

33With many similar parables Jesus spoke
the word to them, as much as they could understand. 34He did not say anything to them
without using a parable. But when he was
alone with his own disciples, he explained everything.

Jesus Calms the Storm

35That day when evening came, he said to
his disciples, “Let us go over to the other side.”
36Leaving the crowd behind, they took him
along, just as he was, in the boat. There were
also other boats with him. 37A furious squall
came up, and the waves broke over the boat,
so that it was nearly swamped. 38Jesus was in
the stern, sleeping on a cushion. The disciples
woke him and said to him, “Teacher, don’t you
care if we drown?”

39He got up, rebuked the wind and said to the waves, "Quiet! Be still!" Then the wind died down and it was completely calm.

40He said to his disciples, "Why are you so afraid? Do you still have no faith?"

41They were terrified and asked each other, "Who is this? Even the wind and the waves obey him!"

The Healing of a Demon-possessed Man

5 They went across the lake to the region of the Gerasenes.[a] 2When Jesus got out of the boat, a man with an evil[b] spirit came from the tombs to meet him. 3This man lived in the tombs, and no one could bind him any more, not even with a chain. 4For he had often been chained hand and foot, but he tore the chains apart and broke the irons on his feet. No one was strong enough to subdue him. 5Night and day among the tombs and in the hills he would cry out and cut himself with stones.

6When he saw Jesus from a distance, he ran and fell on his knees in front of him. 7He shouted at the top of his voice, "What do you want with me, Jesus, Son of the Most High God? Swear to God that you won't torture me!" 8For Jesus had said to him, "Come out of this man, you evil spirit!"

9Then Jesus asked him, "What is your name?"

"My name is Legion," he replied, "for we are many." 10And he begged Jesus again and again not to send them out of the area.

11A large herd of pigs was feeding on the nearby hillside. 12The demons begged Jesus, "Send us among the pigs; allow us to go into them." 13He gave them permission, and the evil spirits came out and went into the pigs. The herd, about two thousand in number, rushed down the steep bank into the lake and were drowned.

14Those tending the pigs ran off and reported this in the town and countryside, and the people went out to see what had happened. 15When they came to Jesus, they saw the man who had been possessed by the legion of demons, sitting there, dressed and in his right mind; and they were afraid. 16Those who had seen it told the people what had happened to the demon-possessed man—and told about the pigs as well. 17Then the people began to plead with Jesus to leave their region.

18As Jesus was getting into the boat, the man who had been demon-possessed begged to go with him. 19Jesus did not let him, but said, "Go home to your family and tell them how much the Lord has done for you, and how he has had mercy on you." 20So the man went away and began to tell in the Decapolis[c] how much Jesus had done for him. And all the people were amazed.

A Dead Girl and a Sick Woman

21When Jesus had again crossed over by boat to the other side of the lake, a large crowd gathered around him while he was by the lake. 22Then one of the synagogue rulers, named Jairus, came there. Seeing Jesus, he fell at his feet 23and pleaded earnestly with him, "My little daughter is dying. Please come and put your hands on her so that she will be healed and live." 24So Jesus went with him.

A large crowd followed and pressed around him. 25And a woman was there who had been subject to bleeding for twelve years. 26She had suffered a great deal under the care of many doctors and had spent all she had, yet instead of getting better she grew worse. 27When she heard about Jesus, she came up behind him in the crowd and touched his cloak, 28because she thought, "If I just touch his clothes, I will be healed." 29Immediately her bleeding stopped and she felt in her body that she was freed from her suffering.

30At once Jesus realized that power had gone out from him. He turned around in the crowd and asked, "Who touched my clothes?"

31"You see the people crowding against you," his disciples answered, "and yet you can ask, 'Who touched me?' "

32But Jesus kept looking around to see who had done it. 33Then the woman, knowing what had happened to her, came and fell at his feet and, trembling with fear, told him the whole truth. 34He said to her, "Daughter, your faith has healed you. Go in peace and be freed from your suffering."

35While Jesus was still speaking, some men

[a]1 Some manuscripts *Gadarenes*; other manuscripts *Gergesenes* [b]2 Greek *unclean*; also in verses 8 and 13 [c]20 That is, the Ten Cities

A Mother's Request

CANAANITE WOMAN

"HOW DID HE HEAL ME, Mother? Were you there when it happened?"

"My daughter, you ask me to tell you a story you've heard many times."

"I know, Mother." The young girl paused as if she were in deep thought. "But I still don't understand how Jesus could heal me when he wasn't even there in my room."

"You speak of a great mystery as if I can tell you the answer. I don't know how he did it. I just know he did. Now, come. We have much to do today."

Her daughter was not quite ready just yet. She slowly lifted her eyes to meet her mother's. "You must have loved me very much to go to him."

"Yes, very much, my daughter." Her mother smiled and tousled the young girl's hair.

This Canaanite mother knew she would never be able to express just how much she loved her child. How much she'd risked to save her. How far she'd pushed. How great her faith.

She could hardly bear to think back to the time when her daughter had been so sick that she'd almost lost her. Her pale skin, now ruddy with health, had then made her look more like an old spirit than a young girl. Her worst fear had come true before her eyes: her daughter was dying.

Is it any wonder that this mother would not take no for an answer from Jesus? Her faith compelled her to push past any limits. Love propelled her to pursue him with all her heart. Despite the fact that Jews regarded Canaanites as longtime enemies and even subhuman, she dared to make her request. She was willing to risk being seen as a fool, a "dog" no less, if it meant her daughter would live.

The girl took up her basket. "I'm ready, Mother."

Her mother smiled. It was worth every risk. Every single one.

—Prayer—

God in heaven, when might I take a risk in the name of faith? I pray I will be ready when God opens the door.

Then Jesus answered, "Woman, you have great faith! Your request is granted." And her daughter was healed from that very hour.

Matthew 15:28

ASSIGNED READING:

Matthew 15:21–28; Mark 7:24–30

Weekend

Go to page 1215 for your next devotional reading.

came from the house of Jairus, the synagogue ruler. "Your daughter is dead," they said. "Why bother the teacher any more?"

36 Ignoring what they said, Jesus told the synagogue ruler, "Don't be afraid; just believe."

37 He did not let anyone follow him except Peter, James and John the brother of James. 38 When they came to the home of the synagogue ruler, Jesus saw a commotion, with people crying and wailing loudly. 39 He went in and said to them, "Why all this commotion and wailing? The child is not dead but asleep." 40 But they laughed at him.

After he put them all out, he took the child's father and mother and the disciples who were with him, and went in where the child was. 41 He took her by the hand and said to her, *"Talitha koum!"* (which means, "Little girl, I say to you, get up!"). 42 Immediately the girl stood up and walked around (she was twelve years old). At this they were completely astonished. 43 He gave strict orders not to let anyone know about this, and told them to give her something to eat.

A Prophet Without Honor

6 Jesus left there and went to his hometown, accompanied by his disciples. 2 When the Sabbath came, he began to teach in the synagogue, and many who heard him were amazed.

"Where did this man get these things?" they asked. "What's this wisdom that has been given him, that he even does miracles! 3 Isn't this the carpenter? Isn't this Mary's son and the brother of James, Joseph,[a] Judas and Simon? Aren't his sisters here with us?" And they took offense at him.

4 Jesus said to them, "Only in his hometown, among his relatives and in his own house is a prophet without honor." 5 He could not do any miracles there, except lay his hands on a few sick people and heal them. 6 And he was amazed at their lack of faith.

Jesus Sends Out the Twelve

Then Jesus went around teaching from village to village. 7 Calling the Twelve to him, he sent them out two by two and gave them authority over evil[b] spirits.

8 These were his instructions: "Take nothing for the journey except a staff—no bread, no bag, no money in your belts. 9 Wear sandals but not an extra tunic. 10 Whenever you enter a house, stay there until you leave that town. 11 And if any place will not welcome you or listen to you, shake the dust off your feet when you leave, as a testimony against them."

12 They went out and preached that people should repent. 13 They drove out many demons and anointed many sick people with oil and healed them.

John the Baptist Beheaded

14 King Herod heard about this, for Jesus' name had become well known. Some were saying,[c] "John the Baptist has been raised from the dead, and that is why miraculous powers are at work in him."

15 Others said, "He is Elijah."

And still others claimed, "He is a prophet, like one of the prophets of long ago."

16 But when Herod heard this, he said, "John, the man I beheaded, has been raised from the dead!"

17 For Herod himself had given orders to have John arrested, and he had him bound and put in prison. He did this because of Herodias, his brother Philip's wife, whom he had married. 18 For John had been saying to Herod, "It is not lawful for you to have your brother's wife." 19 So Herodias nursed a grudge against John and wanted to kill him. But she was not able to, 20 because Herod feared John and protected him, knowing him to be a righteous and holy man. When Herod heard John, he was greatly puzzled[d]; yet he liked to listen to him.

21 Finally the opportune time came. On his birthday Herod gave a banquet for his high officials and military commanders and the leading men of Galilee. 22 When the daughter of Herodias came in and danced, she pleased Herod and his dinner guests.

The king said to the girl, "Ask me for anything you want, and I'll give it to you." 23 And he promised her with an oath, "Whatever you ask I will give you, up to half my kingdom."

24 She went out and said to her mother, "What shall I ask for?"

[a] 3 Greek *Joses,* a variant of *Joseph* [b] 7 Greek *unclean* [c] 14 Some early manuscripts *He was saying* [d] 20 Some early manuscripts *he did many things*

"The head of John the Baptist," she answered.

25 At once the girl hurried in to the king with the request: "I want you to give me right now the head of John the Baptist on a platter."

26 The king was greatly distressed, but because of his oaths and his dinner guests, he did not want to refuse her. 27 So he immediately sent an executioner with orders to bring John's head. The man went, beheaded John in the prison, 28 and brought back his head on a platter. He presented it to the girl, and she gave it to her mother. 29 On hearing of this, John's disciples came and took his body and laid it in a tomb.

Jesus Feeds the Five Thousand

30 The apostles gathered around Jesus and reported to him all they had done and taught. 31 Then, because so many people were coming and going that they did not even have a chance to eat, he said to them, "Come with me by yourselves to a quiet place and get some rest."

32 So they went away by themselves in a boat to a solitary place. 33 But many who saw them leaving recognized them and ran on foot from all the towns and got there ahead of them. 34 When Jesus landed and saw a large crowd, he had compassion on them, because they were like sheep without a shepherd. So he began teaching them many things.

35 By this time it was late in the day, so his disciples came to him. "This is a remote place," they said, "and it's already very late. 36 Send the people away so they can go to the surrounding countryside and villages and buy themselves something to eat."

37 But he answered, "You give them something to eat."

They said to him, "That would take eight months of a man's wages[a]! Are we to go and spend that much on bread and give it to them to eat?"

38 "How many loaves do you have?" he asked. "Go and see."

When they found out, they said, "Five—and two fish."

39 Then Jesus directed them to have all the people sit down in groups on the green grass. 40 So they sat down in groups of hundreds and fifties. 41 Taking the five loaves and the two fish and looking up to heaven, he gave thanks and broke the loaves. Then he gave them to his disciples to set before the people. He also divided the two fish among them all. 42 They all ate and were satisfied, 43 and the disciples picked up twelve basketfuls of broken pieces of bread and fish. 44 The number of the men who had eaten was five thousand.

Jesus Walks on the Water

45 Immediately Jesus made his disciples get into the boat and go on ahead of him to Bethsaida, while he dismissed the crowd. 46 After leaving them, he went up on a mountainside to pray.

47 When evening came, the boat was in the middle of the lake, and he was alone on land. 48 He saw the disciples straining at the oars, because the wind was against them. About the fourth watch of the night he went out to them, walking on the lake. He was about to pass by them, 49 but when they saw him walking on the lake, they thought he was a ghost. They cried out, 50 because they all saw him and were terrified.

Immediately he spoke to them and said, "Take courage! It is I. Don't be afraid." 51 Then he climbed into the boat with them, and the wind died down. They were completely amazed, 52 for they had not understood about the loaves; their hearts were hardened.

53 When they had crossed over, they landed at Gennesaret and anchored there. 54 As soon as they got out of the boat, people recognized Jesus. 55 They ran throughout that whole region and carried the sick on mats to wherever they

Mark 6:31

God Values Rest

Then, because so many people were coming and going that they did not even have a chance to eat, he said to them, "Come with me by yourselves to a quiet place and get some rest."

[a]37 Greek *take two hundred denarii*

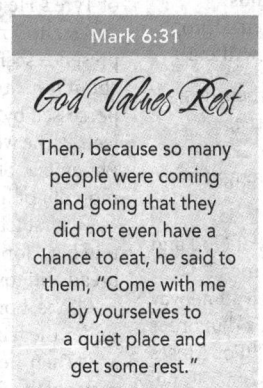

heard he was. 56 And wherever he went—into
villages, towns or countryside—they placed
the sick in the marketplaces. They begged him
to let them touch even the edge of his cloak,
and all who touched him were healed.

Clean and Unclean

7 The Pharisees and some of the teachers
of the law who had come from Jerusalem
gathered around Jesus and 2 saw some of his
disciples eating food with hands that were "unclean," that is, unwashed. 3 (The Pharisees and
all the Jews do not eat unless they give their
hands a ceremonial washing, holding to the tradition of the elders. 4 When they come from the
marketplace they do not eat unless they wash.
And they observe many other traditions, such
as the washing of cups, pitchers and kettles.[a])
5 So the Pharisees and teachers of the law
asked Jesus, "Why don't your disciples live according to the tradition of the elders instead of
eating their food with 'unclean' hands?"
6 He replied, "Isaiah was right when he prophesied about you hypocrites; as it is written:

> " 'These people honor me with their lips,
> but their hearts are far from me.
> 7 They worship me in vain;
> their teachings are but rules taught by
> men.'[b]

8 You have let go of the commands of God and
are holding on to the traditions of men."
9 And he said to them: "You have a fine way
of setting aside the commands of God in order
to observe[c] your own traditions! 10 For Moses
said, 'Honor your father and your mother,'[d] and,
'Anyone who curses his father or mother must
be put to death.'[e] 11 But you say that if a man
says to his father or mother: 'Whatever help
you might otherwise have received from me is
Corban' (that is, a gift devoted to God), 12 then
you no longer let him do anything for his father
or mother. 13 Thus you nullify the word of God
by your tradition that you have handed down.
And you do many things like that."
14 Again Jesus called the crowd to him
and said, "Listen to me, everyone, and understand this. 15 Nothing outside a man can make
him 'unclean' by going into him. Rather, it is
what comes out of a man that makes him 'unclean.'[f]"
17 After he had left the crowd and entered
the house, his disciples asked him about this
parable. 18 "Are you so dull?" he asked. "Don't
you see that nothing that enters a man from
the outside can make him 'unclean'? 19 For it
doesn't go into his heart but into his stomach,
and then out of his body." (In saying this, Jesus
declared all foods "clean.")
20 He went on: "What comes out of a man is
what makes him 'unclean.' 21 For from within,
out of men's hearts, come evil thoughts, sexual
immorality, theft, murder, adultery, 22 greed,
malice, deceit, lewdness, envy, slander, arrogance and folly. 23 All these evils come from
inside and make a man 'unclean.' "

The Faith of a Syrophoenician Woman

24 Jesus left that place and went to the vicinity
of Tyre.[g] He entered a house and did not want
anyone to know it; yet he could not keep his
presence secret. 25 In fact, as soon as she heard
about him, a woman whose little daughter was
possessed by an evil[h] spirit came and fell at his
feet. 26 The woman was a Greek, born in Syrian
Phoenicia. She begged Jesus to drive the demon out of her daughter.
27 "First let the children eat all they want," he
told her, "for it is not right to take the children's
bread and toss it to their dogs."
28 "Yes, Lord," she replied, "but even the dogs
under the table eat the children's crumbs."
29 Then he told her, "For such a reply, you
may go; the demon has left your daughter."
30 She went home and found her child lying
on the bed, and the demon gone.

The Healing of a Deaf and Mute Man

31 Then Jesus left the vicinity of Tyre and
went through Sidon, down to the Sea of Galilee
and into the region of the Decapolis.[i] 32 There
some people brought to him a man who was
deaf and could hardly talk, and they begged
him to place his hand on the man.
33 After he took him aside, away from the
crowd, Jesus put his fingers into the man's ears.

[a] 4 Some early manuscripts *pitchers, kettles and dining couches* [b] 6,7 Isaiah 29:13 [c] 9 Some manuscripts *set up* [d] 10 Exodus 20:12; Deut. 5:16 [e] 10 Exodus 21:17; Lev. 20:9 [f] 15 Some early manuscripts *'unclean.' 16 If anyone has ears to hear, let him hear.*
[g] 24 Many early manuscripts *Tyre and Sidon* [h] 25 Greek *unclean* [i] 31 That is, the Ten Cities

A Strong-Willed Woman

Read: Mark 7:24–36

SO WHAT DOES IT TAKE to have the distinction of being a genuinely strong-willed woman? After all, every woman has opportunities to use some degree of strong will at various times in her life . . . But for those of us who fit the description of the strong-willed woman, it can be said that we use our strong wills almost as often as we breathe. It is so deeply ingrained in us we often struggle to understand why everyone doesn't share the depth and strength of our convictions.

I met Emily after one of my learning styles seminars for public school teachers. She had not grown up in a Christian home, but she had attended a conservative church off and on during her youth. She thanked me, not only for the seminar but for weaving my faith into the presentation. Then she hesitantly asked me, "Do you believe it's even possible for a strong-willed woman to be a Christian?" I was startled by the question, and she went on to confess that she had very deliberately stayed away from church the past few years because she knew she had a stubborn and independent nature. Half of her was afraid God wouldn't even want her, and the other half was afraid he would demand she give up her strong will if she did decide to give her heart to Christ. Emily is certainly not alone. There are many strong-willed women whose hearts and souls long to know Christ but whose self-sufficient natures won't even consider the possibility of surrendering their hard-won independence. These are women who can and will change the world one way or another—and it's never been more important to find a way to recognize and validate their worth in the kingdom of God.

Many of us may have secretly wondered if there was something wrong with us, if perhaps we just weren't trying hard enough to be good, conforming Christian women. So let's come together and identify ourselves to each other and the world. Let's discover and celebrate the fact that God has placed in the heart of many of his human creations an undercurrent so strong and so solid it carries us from birth to death.

—*Cynthia Ulrich Tobias*

Mark 7:26–28

The woman was a Greek, born in Syrian Phoenicia. She begged Jesus to drive the demon out of her daughter. "First let the children eat all they want," he told her, "for it is not right to take the children's bread and toss it to their dogs." "Yes, Lord," she replied, "but even the dogs under the table eat the children's crumbs."

reflection

1 How did the woman in today's Scripture passage prove to be strong-willed? How did Jesus reward her for her determination?

2 Do you consider yourself a strong-willed woman? In what ways?

3 Ask God to make you strong enough to allow your will to become his will. Make your prayer the prayer of Jesus: "Not my will, but yours be done" (Luke 22:42).

RELATED READINGS

Matthew 15:21–28; Ephesians 6:5–8

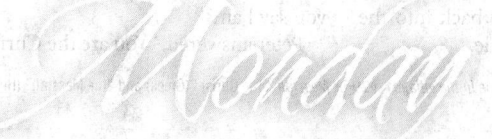

Go to page 1220 for your next devotional reading.

Then he spit and touched the man's tongue.
34 He looked up to heaven and with a deep
sigh said to him, *"Ephphatha!"* (which means,
"Be opened!"). 35 At this, the man's ears were
opened, his tongue was loosened and he began
to speak plainly.
36 Jesus commanded them not to tell anyone.
But the more he did so, the more they kept talking about it. 37 People were overwhelmed with
amazement. "He has done everything well,"
they said. "He even makes the deaf hear and
the mute speak."

Jesus Feeds the Four Thousand

8 During those days another large crowd
gathered. Since they had nothing to eat,
Jesus called his disciples to him and said, 2 "I
have compassion for these people; they have
already been with me three days and have nothing to eat. 3 If I send them home hungry, they
will collapse on the way, because some of them
have come a long distance."
4 His disciples answered, "But where in this
remote place can anyone get enough bread to
feed them?"
5 "How many loaves do you have?" Jesus
asked.
"Seven," they replied.
6 He told the crowd to sit down on the
ground. When he had taken the seven loaves
and given thanks, he broke them and gave
them to his disciples to set before the people,
and they did so. 7 They had a few small fish
as well; he gave thanks for them also and told
the disciples to distribute them. 8 The people
ate and were satisfied. Afterward the disciples
picked up seven basketfuls of broken pieces
that were left over. 9 About four thousand men
were present. And having sent them away, 10 he
got into the boat with his disciples and went to
the region of Dalmanutha.
11 The Pharisees came and began to question
Jesus. To test him, they asked him for a sign
from heaven. 12 He sighed deeply and said,
"Why does this generation ask for a miraculous
sign? I tell you the truth, no sign will be given
to it." 13 Then he left them, got back into the
boat and crossed to the other side.

The Yeast of the Pharisees and Herod

14 The disciples had forgotten to bring
bread, except for one loaf they had with them
in the boat. 15 "Be careful," Jesus warned them.
"Watch out for the yeast of the Pharisees and
that of Herod."
16 They discussed this with one another and
said, "It is because we have no bread."
17 Aware of their discussion, Jesus asked
them: "Why are you talking about having no
bread? Do you still not see or understand? Are
your hearts hardened? 18 Do you have eyes but
fail to see, and ears but fail to hear? And don't
you remember? 19 When I broke the five loaves
for the five thousand, how many basketfuls of
pieces did you pick up?"
"Twelve," they replied.
20 "And when I broke the seven loaves for the
four thousand, how many basketfuls of pieces
did you pick up?"
They answered, "Seven."
21 He said to them, "Do you still not understand?"

The Healing of a Blind Man at Bethsaida

22 They came to Bethsaida, and some people
brought a blind man and begged Jesus to touch
him. 23 He took the blind man by the hand and
led him outside the village. When he had spit
on the man's eyes and put his hands on him,
Jesus asked, "Do you see anything?"
24 He looked up and said, "I see people; they
look like trees walking around."
25 Once more Jesus put his hands on the
man's eyes. Then his eyes were opened, his
sight was restored, and he saw everything
clearly. 26 Jesus sent him home, saying, "Don't
go into the village.[a]"

Peter's Confession of Christ

27 Jesus and his disciples went on to the
villages around Caesarea Philippi. On the way
he asked them, "Who do people say I am?"
28 They replied, "Some say John the Baptist; others say Elijah; and still others, one of
the prophets."
29 "But what about you?" he asked. "Who do
you say I am?"
Peter answered, "You are the Christ.[b]"

[a] 26 Some manuscripts *Don't go and tell anyone in the village* [b] 29 Or *Messiah.* "The Christ" (Greek) and "the Messiah" (Hebrew) both mean "the Anointed One."

30Jesus warned them not to tell anyone
about him.

Jesus Predicts His Death

31He then began to teach them that the
Son of Man must suffer many things and be
rejected by the elders, chief priests and teachers of the law, and that he must be killed and
after three days rise again. 32He spoke plainly
about this, and Peter took him aside and began
to rebuke him.

33But when Jesus turned and looked at his
disciples, he rebuked Peter. "Get behind me,
Satan!" he said. "You do not have in mind the
things of God, but the things of men."

34Then he called the crowd to him along
with his disciples and said: "If anyone would
come after me, he must deny himself and take
up his cross and follow me. 35For whoever
wants to save his life[a] will lose it, but whoever
loses his life for me and for the gospel will
save it. 36What good is it for a man to gain the
whole world, yet forfeit his soul? 37Or what
can a man give in exchange for his soul? 38If
anyone is ashamed of me and my words in this
adulterous and sinful generation, the Son of
Man will be ashamed of him when he comes
in his Father's glory with the holy angels."

9 And he said to them, "I tell you the truth,
some who are standing here will not taste
death before they see the kingdom of God
come with power."

The Transfiguration

2After six days Jesus took Peter, James and
John with him and led them up a high mountain, where they were all alone. There he was
transfigured before them. 3His clothes became
dazzling white, whiter than anyone in the
world could bleach them. 4And there appeared
before them Elijah and Moses, who were talking with Jesus.

5Peter said to Jesus, "Rabbi, it is good for us
to be here. Let us put up three shelters—one for
you, one for Moses and one for Elijah." 6(He
did not know what to say, they were so frightened.)

7Then a cloud appeared and enveloped
them, and a voice came from the cloud: "This
is my Son, whom I love. Listen to him!"

8Suddenly, when they looked around, they
no longer saw anyone with them except Jesus.

9As they were coming down the mountain, Jesus gave them orders not to tell anyone
what they had seen until the Son of Man had
risen from the dead. 10They kept the matter to
themselves, discussing what "rising from the
dead" meant.

11And they asked him, "Why do the teachers of the law say that Elijah must come first?"

12Jesus replied, "To be sure, Elijah does come
first, and restores all things. Why then is it written that the Son of Man must suffer much and
be rejected? 13But I tell you, Elijah has come,
and they have done to him everything they
wished, just as it is written about him."

The Healing of a Boy With an Evil Spirit

14When they came to the other disciples,
they saw a large crowd around them and the
teachers of the law arguing with them. 15As
soon as all the people saw Jesus, they were overwhelmed with wonder and ran to greet him.

16"What are you arguing with them about?"
he asked.

17A man in the crowd answered, "Teacher, I
brought you my son, who is possessed by a spirit
that has robbed him of speech. 18Whenever it
seizes him, it throws him to the ground. He
foams at the mouth, gnashes his teeth and becomes rigid. I asked your disciples to drive out
the spirit, but they could not."

19"O unbelieving generation," Jesus replied,
"how long shall I stay with you? How long shall
I put up with you? Bring the boy to me."

20So they brought him. When the spirit
saw Jesus, it immediately threw the boy into
a convulsion. He fell to the ground and rolled
around, foaming at the mouth.

21Jesus asked the boy's father, "How long has
he been like this?"

"From childhood," he answered. 22"It has often thrown him into fire or water to kill him.
But if you can do anything, take pity on us and
help us."

23" 'If you can'?" said Jesus. "Everything is
possible for him who believes."

24Immediately the boy's father exclaimed, "I
do believe; help me overcome my unbelief!"

[a]35 The Greek word means either *life* or *soul*; also in verse 36.

25 When Jesus saw that a crowd was running
to the scene, he rebuked the evil[a] spirit. "You
deaf and mute spirit," he said, "I command you,
come out of him and never enter him again."

26 The spirit shrieked, convulsed him
violently and came out. The boy looked so
much like a corpse that many said, "He's dead."
27 But Jesus took him by the hand and lifted
him to his feet, and he stood up.

28 After Jesus had gone indoors, his disciples
asked him privately, "Why couldn't we drive it
out?"

29 He replied, "This kind can come out only
by prayer.[b]"

30 They left that place and passed through
Galilee. Jesus did not want anyone to know
where they were, 31 because he was teaching
his disciples. He said to them, "The Son of
Man is going to be betrayed into the hands of
men. They will kill him, and after three days
he will rise." 32 But they did not understand
what he meant and were afraid to ask him
about it.

Who Is the Greatest?

33 They came to Capernaum. When he was
in the house, he asked them, "What were you
arguing about on the road?" 34 But they kept
quiet because on the way they had argued
about who was the greatest.

35 Sitting down, Jesus called the Twelve and
said, "If anyone wants to be first, he must be the
very last, and the servant of all."

36 He took a little child and had him stand
among them. Taking him in his arms, he said
to them, 37 "Whoever welcomes one of these
little children in my name welcomes me; and
whoever welcomes me does not welcome me
but the one who sent me."

Whoever Is Not Against Us Is for Us

38 "Teacher," said John, "we saw a man driving out demons in your name and we told him
to stop, because he was not one of us."

39 "Do not stop him," Jesus said. "No one
who does a miracle in my name can in the next
moment say anything bad about me, 40 for
whoever is not against us is for us. 41 I tell you
the truth, anyone who gives you a cup of water
in my name because you belong to Christ will
certainly not lose his reward.

Causing to Sin

42 "And if anyone causes one of these little
ones who believe in me to sin, it would be better for him to be thrown into the sea with a
large millstone tied around his neck. 43 If your
hand causes you to sin, cut it off. It is better
for you to enter life maimed than with two
hands to go into hell, where the fire never goes
out.[c] 45 And if your foot causes you to sin, cut
it off. It is better for you to enter life crippled
than to have two feet and be thrown into hell.[d]
47 And if your eye causes you to sin, pluck it
out. It is better for you to enter the kingdom of
God with one eye than to have two eyes and be
thrown into hell, 48 where

"'their worm does not die,
and the fire is not quenched.'[e]

49 Everyone will be salted with fire.

50 "Salt is good, but if it loses its saltiness,
how can you make it salty again? Have salt in
yourselves, and be at peace with each other."

Divorce

10 Jesus then left that place and went into
the region of Judea and across the Jordan. Again crowds of people came to him, and
as was his custom, he taught them.

2 Some Pharisees came and tested him
by asking, "Is it lawful for a man to divorce
his wife?"

3 "What did Moses command you?" he replied.

4 They said, "Moses permitted a man to write
a certificate of divorce and send her away."

5 "It was because your hearts were hard that
Moses wrote you this law," Jesus replied. 6 "But
at the beginning of creation God 'made them
male and female.'[f] 7 'For this reason a man will
leave his father and mother and be united to
his wife,[g] 8 and the two will become one flesh.'[h]
So they are no longer two, but one. 9 Therefore
what God has joined together, let man not separate."

10 When they were in the house again, the disciples asked Jesus about this. 11 He answered,

[a] 25 Greek *unclean* [b] 29 Some manuscripts *prayer and fasting* [c] 43 Some manuscripts *out,* 44 *where / "'their worm does not die, / and the fire is not quenched.'* [d] 45 Some manuscripts *hell,* 46 *where / "'their worm does not die, / and the fire is not quenched.'*
[e] 48 Isaiah 66:24 [f] 6 Gen. 1:27 [g] 7 Some early manuscripts do not have *and be united to his wife.* [h] 8 Gen. 2:24

"Anyone who divorces his wife and marries another woman commits adultery against her. 12 And if she divorces her husband and marries another man, she commits adultery."

The Little Children and Jesus

13 People were bringing little children to Jesus to have him touch them, but the disciples rebuked them. 14 When Jesus saw this, he was indignant. He said to them, "Let the little children come to me, and do not hinder them, for the kingdom of God belongs to such as these. 15 I tell you the truth, anyone who will not receive the kingdom of God like a little child will never enter it." 16 And he took the children in his arms, put his hands on them and blessed them.

The Rich Young Man

17 As Jesus started on his way, a man ran up to him and fell on his knees before him. "Good teacher," he asked, "what must I do to inherit eternal life?"

18 "Why do you call me good?" Jesus answered. "No one is good—except God alone. 19 You know the commandments: 'Do not murder, do not commit adultery, do not steal, do not give false testimony, do not defraud, honor your father and mother.'[a]"

20 "Teacher," he declared, "all these I have kept since I was a boy."

21 Jesus looked at him and loved him. "One thing you lack," he said. "Go, sell everything you have and give to the poor, and you will have treasure in heaven. Then come, follow me."

22 At this the man's face fell. He went away sad, because he had great wealth.

23 Jesus looked around and said to his disciples, "How hard it is for the rich to enter the kingdom of God!"

24 The disciples were amazed at his words. But Jesus said again, "Children, how hard it is[b] to enter the kingdom of God! 25 It is easier for a camel to go through the eye of a needle than for a rich man to enter the kingdom of God."

26 The disciples were even more amazed, and said to each other, "Who then can be saved?"

27 Jesus looked at them and said, "With man this is impossible, but not with God; all things are possible with God."

28 Peter said to him, "We have left everything to follow you!"

29 "I tell you the truth," Jesus replied, "no one who has left home or brothers or sisters or mother or father or children or fields for me and the gospel 30 will fail to receive a hundred times as much in this present age (homes, brothers, sisters, mothers, children and fields—and with them, persecutions) and in the age to come, eternal life. 31 But many who are first will be last, and the last first."

Jesus Again Predicts His Death

32 They were on their way up to Jerusalem, with Jesus leading the way, and the disciples were astonished, while those who followed were afraid. Again he took the Twelve aside and told them what was going to happen to him. 33 "We are going up to Jerusalem," he said, "and the Son of Man will be betrayed to the chief priests and teachers of the law. They will condemn him to death and will hand him over to the Gentiles, 34 who will mock him and spit on him, flog him and kill him. Three days later he will rise."

The Request of James and John

35 Then James and John, the sons of Zebedee, came to him. "Teacher," they said, "we want you to do for us whatever we ask."

36 "What do you want me to do for you?" he asked.

37 They replied, "Let one of us sit at your right and the other at your left in your glory."

38 "You don't know what you are asking," Jesus said. "Can you drink the cup I drink or be baptized with the baptism I am baptized with?"

39 "We can," they answered.

Jesus said to them, "You will drink the cup I drink and be baptized with the baptism I am baptized with, 40 but to sit at my right or left is not for me to grant. These places belong to those for whom they have been prepared."

41 When the ten heard about this, they became indignant with James and John. 42 Jesus called them together and said, "You know that those who are regarded as rulers of the Gentiles lord it over them, and their high officials exercise authority over them. 43 Not so with you.

[a] 19 Exodus 20:12–16; Deut. 5:16–20 [b] 24 Some manuscripts *is for those who trust in riches*

Like a Lamb

Mark 10:15–16

"I tell you the truth, anyone who will not receive the kingdom of God like a little child will never enter it." And he took the children in his arms, put his hands on them and blessed them.

reflection

1 What circumstance are you in right now in which you need to trust God as a child trusts her daddy?

2 Name some ways in which you know that your God—your *Abba*—protects you.

3 How can you become more like a child in the kingdom of God? Ask God to help you take the first step.

RELATED READINGS

Matthew 18:1–6; 21:14–16; Romans 8:28–31; 1 John 3:1–3

Read: Mark 10:13–16

AUTHOR AND SHEPHERD PHILLIP KELLER writes about coming home to his humble cottage one stormy night with a couple of shivering baby lambs. He wrapped them inside his big, wool jacket and snuggled them against his chest. Sleet, snow and chilling rain lashed against his body, but within his embrace, the lambs were safe and warm.

Children, like lambs, trust us to meet their needs and provide for their safety. With a natural tendency to believe, they don't weigh issues with cynicism like adults do. Jesus made it clear that the kingdom of God belongs to people with a childlike faith—those who don't receive the kingdom like a child "will never enter it." This concept is hard for skeptical adults to accept. Many of us have grown oversophisticated, and our hearts have grown hard. Somewhere along the way we got tougher and more callous, turning to self-sufficiency and believing we could handle our lives by using our own resources. We've forgotten what it's like to believe as we might have when were little girls, looking up to God with childlike wonder and adoration.

Throughout Scripture, God continually encourages us to rely on him like a child relies on a parent. Some of us may have lost the ability to trust because our parents never provided adequately for our needs, while others of us may have lost our ability to trust through circumstances—a failed job, the death of a loved one, a lost desire. But God has revealed time and again that he can help us relearn that childlike faith if we let him. It's a matter of cultivating a relationship with him and letting him show himself faithful as he works good out of our circumstances.

Isaiah 40:11 paints a warm and inviting picture of perfect trust in Jesus: "He tends his flock like a shepherd: He gathers the lambs in his arms and carries them close to his heart."

Close your eyes and picture yourself resting your head on Jesus' chest. Can you hear his heart beating with love for you?

Go to page 1224 for your next devotional reading.

Instead, whoever wants to become great among
you must be your servant, 44 and whoever
wants to be first must be slave of all. 45 For even
the Son of Man did not come to be served, but
to serve, and to give his life as a
ransom for many."

> **Mark 10:45**
>
> *God Loves Service*
>
> "For even the Son of Man did not come to be served, but to serve, and to give his life as a ransom for many."

Blind Bartimaeus Receives His Sight

46 Then they came to Jericho. As Jesus and his disciples,
together with a large crowd,
were leaving the city, a blind
man, Bartimaeus (that is, the
Son of Timaeus), was sitting by
the roadside begging. 47 When
he heard that it was Jesus of
Nazareth, he began to shout,
"Jesus, Son of David, have
mercy on me!"

48 Many rebuked him and told him to be
quiet, but he shouted all the more, "Son of David, have mercy on me!"

49 Jesus stopped and said, "Call him."

So they called to the blind man, "Cheer up!
On your feet! He's calling you." 50 Throwing his
cloak aside, he jumped to his feet and came
to Jesus.

51 "What do you want me to do for you?"
Jesus asked him.

The blind man said, "Rabbi, I want to see."

52 "Go," said Jesus, "your faith has healed
you." Immediately he received his sight and followed Jesus along the road.

The Triumphal Entry

11 As they approached Jerusalem and
came to Bethphage and Bethany at the
Mount of Olives, Jesus sent two of his disciples,
2 saying to them, "Go to the village ahead of
you, and just as you enter it, you will find a colt
tied there, which no one has ever ridden. Untie
it and bring it here. 3 If anyone asks you, 'Why
are you doing this?' tell him, 'The Lord needs it
and will send it back here shortly.'"

4 They went and found a colt outside in the
street, tied at a doorway. As they untied it,
5 some people standing there asked, "What are
you doing, untying that colt?" 6 They answered
as Jesus had told them to, and the people let
them go. 7 When they brought the colt to Jesus
and threw their cloaks over it, he sat on it.
8 Many people spread their cloaks on the road,
while others spread branches
they had cut in the fields.
9 Those who went ahead and
those who followed shouted,

"Hosanna![a]"

"Blessed is he who comes
in the name of the
Lord!"[b]

10 "Blessed is the coming
kingdom of our
father David!"

"Hosanna in the highest!"

11 Jesus entered Jerusalem
and went to the temple. He looked around at everything, but since it was already late, he went
out to Bethany with the Twelve.

Jesus Clears the Temple

12 The next day as they were leaving Bethany,
Jesus was hungry. 13 Seeing in the distance a fig
tree in leaf, he went to find out if it had any
fruit. When he reached it, he found nothing
but leaves, because it was not the season for
figs. 14 Then he said to the tree, "May no one
ever eat fruit from you again." And his disciples
heard him say it.

15 On reaching Jerusalem, Jesus entered
the temple area and began driving out those
who were buying and selling there. He overturned the tables of the money changers and
the benches of those selling doves, 16 and
would not allow anyone to carry merchandise
through the temple courts. 17 And as he taught
them, he said, "Is it not written:

"'My house will be called
a house of prayer for all nations'[c]?

But you have made it 'a den of robbers.'[d]"

18 The chief priests and the teachers of the
law heard this and began looking for a way to
kill him, for they feared him, because the whole
crowd was amazed at his teaching.

[a] 9 A Hebrew expression meaning "Save!" which became an exclamation of praise; also in verse 10 [b] 9 Psalm 118:25,26 [c] 17 Isaiah 56:7
[d] 17 Jer. 7:11

19When evening came, they[a] went out of
the city.

The Withered Fig Tree

20In the morning, as they went along, they
saw the fig tree withered from the roots. 21Pe-
ter remembered and said to Jesus, "Rabbi, look!
The fig tree you cursed has withered!"
22"Have[b] faith in God," Jesus answered. 23"I
tell you the truth, if anyone says to this mountain, 'Go, throw yourself into the sea,' and does
not doubt in his heart but believes that what
he says will happen, it will be done for him.
24Therefore I tell you, whatever you ask for in
prayer, believe that you have received it, and it
will be yours. 25And when you stand praying,
if you hold anything against anyone, forgive
him, so that your Father in heaven may forgive
you your sins.[c]"

The Authority of Jesus Questioned

27They arrived again in Jerusalem, and
while Jesus was walking in the temple courts,
the chief priests, the teachers of the law and the
elders came to him. 28"By what authority are
you doing these things?" they asked. "And who
gave you authority to do this?"
29Jesus replied, "I will ask you one question.
Answer me, and I will tell you by what authority I am doing these things. 30John's baptism—
was it from heaven, or from men? Tell me!"
31They discussed it among themselves and
said, "If we say, 'From heaven,' he will ask,
'Then why didn't you believe him?' 32But if we
say, 'From men'..." (They feared the people, for
everyone held that John really was a prophet.)
33So they answered Jesus, "We don't know."
Jesus said, "Neither will I tell you by what
authority I am doing these things."

The Parable of the Tenants

12 He then began to speak to them in parables: "A man planted a vineyard. He
put a wall around it, dug a pit for the winepress
and built a watchtower. Then he rented the vineyard to some farmers and went away on a journey. 2At harvest time he sent a servant to the
tenants to collect from them some of the fruit
of the vineyard. 3But they seized him, beat him
and sent him away empty-handed. 4Then he
sent another servant to them; they struck this
man on the head and treated him shamefully.
5He sent still another, and that one they killed.
He sent many others; some of them they beat,
others they killed.
6"He had one left to send, a son, whom he
loved. He sent him last of all, saying, 'They will
respect my son.'
7"But the tenants said to one another, 'This
is the heir. Come, let's kill him, and the inheritance will be ours.' 8So they took him and killed
him, and threw him out of the vineyard.
9"What then will the owner of the vineyard
do? He will come and kill those tenants and
give the vineyard to others. 10Haven't you read
this scripture:

"'The stone the builders rejected
has become the capstone[d];
11the Lord has done this,
and it is marvelous in our eyes'[e]?"

12Then they looked for a way to arrest him
because they knew he had spoken the parable against them. But they were afraid of the
crowd; so they left him and went away.

Paying Taxes to Caesar

13Later they sent some of the Pharisees and
Herodians to Jesus to catch him in his words.
14They came to him and said, "Teacher, we
know you are a man of integrity. You aren't
swayed by men, because you pay no attention
to who they are; but you teach the way of God
in accordance with the truth. Is it right to pay
taxes to Caesar or not? 15Should we pay or
shouldn't we?"
But Jesus knew their hypocrisy. "Why are
you trying to trap me?" he asked. "Bring me a
denarius and let me look at it." 16They brought
the coin, and he asked them, "Whose portrait
is this? And whose inscription?"
"Caesar's," they replied.
17Then Jesus said to them, "Give to Caesar
what is Caesar's and to God what is God's."
And they were amazed at him.

Marriage at the Resurrection

18Then the Sadducees, who say there is no
resurrection, came to him with a question.

[a]19 Some early manuscripts *he* [b]22 Some early manuscripts *If you have* [c]25 Some manuscripts *sins.* 26*But if you do not forgive, neither will your Father who is in heaven forgive your sins.* [d]10 Or *cornerstone* [e]11 Psalm 118:22,23

19“Teacher,” they said, “Moses wrote for us
that if a man’s brother dies and leaves a wife but
no children, the man must marry the widow
and have children for his brother. 20Now there
were seven brothers. The first one married and
died without leaving any children. 21The second one married the widow, but he also died,
leaving no child. It was the same with the third.
22In fact, none of the seven left any children.
Last of all, the woman died too. 23At the resurrection[a] whose wife will she be, since the seven
were married to her?”

24Jesus replied, “Are you not in error because you do not know the Scriptures or the
power of God? 25When the dead rise, they will
neither marry nor be given in marriage; they
will be like the angels in heaven. 26Now about
the dead rising—have you not read in the book
of Moses, in the account of the bush, how God
said to him, ‘I am the God of Abraham, the
God of Isaac, and the God of Jacob’[b]? 27He is
not the God of the dead, but of the living. You
are badly mistaken!”

The Greatest Commandment

28One of the teachers of the law came and
heard them debating. Noticing that Jesus had
given them a good answer, he asked him, “Of
all the commandments, which is the most important?”

29“The most important one,” answered Jesus,
“is this: ‘Hear, O Israel, the Lord our God, the
Lord is one.[c] 30Love the Lord your God with
all your heart and with all your soul and with
all your mind and with all your strength.’[d]
31The second is this: ‘Love your neighbor as
yourself.’[e] There is no commandment greater
than these.”

32“Well said, teacher,” the man replied. “You
are right in saying that God is one and there is
no other but him. 33To love him with all your
heart, with all your understanding and with
all your strength, and to love your neighbor as
yourself is more important than all burnt offerings and sacrifices.”

34When Jesus saw that he had answered
wisely, he said to him, “You are not far from
the kingdom of God.” And from then on no
one dared ask him any more questions.

Whose Son Is the Christ?

35While Jesus was teaching in the temple
courts, he asked, “How is it that the teachers
of the law say that the Christ[f] is the son of David? 36David himself, speaking by the Holy
Spirit, declared:

“ ‘The Lord said to my Lord:
“Sit at my right hand
until I put your enemies
under your feet.” ’[g]

37David himself calls him ‘Lord.’ How then can
he be his son?”

The large crowd listened to him with delight.

38As he taught, Jesus said, “Watch out
for the teachers of the law. They like to walk
around in flowing robes and be greeted in the
marketplaces, 39and have the most important
seats in the synagogues and the places of honor
at banquets. 40They devour widows’ houses
and for a show make lengthy prayers. Such
men will be punished most severely.”

The Widow’s Offering

41Jesus sat down opposite the place where
the offerings were put and watched the crowd
putting their money into the temple treasury.
Many rich people threw in large amounts.
42But a poor widow came and put in two very
small copper coins,[h] worth only a fraction of
a penny.[i]

43Calling his disciples to him, Jesus said,
“I tell you the truth, this poor widow has put
more into the treasury than all the others.
44They all gave out of their wealth; but she, out
of her poverty, put in everything—all she had
to live on.”

Signs of the End of the Age

13 As he was leaving the temple, one
of his disciples said to him, “Look,
Teacher! What massive stones! What magnificent buildings!”

2“Do you see all these great buildings?” replied Jesus. “Not one stone here will be left on
another; every one will be thrown down.”

3As Jesus was sitting on the Mount of Olives
opposite the temple, Peter, James, John and

[a]23 Some manuscripts *resurrection, when men rise from the dead,* [b]26 Exodus 3:6 [c]29 Or *the Lord our God is one Lord*
[d]30 Deut. 6:4,5 [e]31 Lev. 19:18 [f]35 Or *Messiah* [g]36 Psalm 110:1 [h]42 Greek *two lepta* [i]42 Greek *kodrantes*

Trusting in the Rock

Read: Mark 12:28–44

Mark 12:41–42

Many rich people threw in large amounts. But a poor widow came and put in two very small copper coins, worth only a fraction of a penny.

reflection

1 What has suddenly disappeared from your life? How has it affected your ability to trust in God?

2 Who do you most identify with in this Scripture passage—the crowd who gave a portion of their income or the widow who gave sacrificially?

3 What is God asking you to put into his hands today?

RELATED READINGS

Deuteronomy 32:3–4; Psalms 62:1–12; 95:1–11; 1 Timothy 6:17–19

IN MAY 2003 A HEAVY FOG covered the White Mountains of New Hampshire. When the dense haze lifted, residents were shocked to see that The Old Man of the Mountain had disappeared. The 40-foot-tall natural outcropping of granite ledges had looked like the profile of an old man. This natural wonder inspired Nathaniel Hawthorne's famous story, "The Great Stone Face," over 200 years ago. Its image graced New Hampshire license plates, quarters and tourist souvenirs. As the official state emblem, The Old Man of the Mountain had endured for centuries. But then the 700-ton face fell. New Hampshire's governor said: "This rugged yet beautiful monument fit the character of the pioneers who founded this state, the immigrants who built it, and the spirit of those who live here today. It was the ultimate symbol of those who would 'Live Free or Die.' "

Sometimes, like New Hampshire's state symbol, those things we trust disappear. They fade away in the night with one sudden phone call or car ride or decision. Perhaps we knew, deep down, that the person could not be counted on, the job could not last, the relationship would not weather the storm, but we decided to believe it was timeless anyway. When we carry many responsibilities—children, a marriage, a job, parents, a home—we often come to trust ourselves as well. *Who else will keep things going?* we wonder. So we hold on tightly to keep everything together, to stay in control.

God's desire is the opposite of our human inclination: He wants us to release our tight-fisted control. He wants us to give him the control of everything in our lives. The widow who gave two small copper coins showed her trust in God to provide for her, even if her every material possession was gone. The crowd who went before her gave a lot, but in proportion to what they owned, they gave but little. They were holding back. This faithful woman "put in everything—all she had to live on" (verse 44).

God wants you to place everything in his hands, not because he wants you to be empty, but because he wants to fill you to overflowing. Of all the things we look to for stability and permanence, he is the only true Rock who will never fall or fade away.

Go to page 1227 for your next devotional reading.

Andrew asked him privately, 4“Tell us, when
will these things happen? And what will be the
sign that they are all about to be fulfilled?”

5Jesus said to them: “Watch out that no
one deceives you. 6Many will come in my
name, claiming, ‘I am he,’ and will deceive
many. 7When you hear of wars and rumors
of wars, do not be alarmed. Such things must
happen, but the end is still to come. 8Nation
will rise against nation, and kingdom against
kingdom. There will be earthquakes in various
places, and famines. These are the beginning
of birth pains.

9“You must be on your guard. You will be
handed over to the local councils and flogged
in the synagogues. On account of me you will
stand before governors and
kings as witnesses to them.
10And the gospel must first
be preached to all nations.
11Whenever you are arrested
and brought to trial, do not
worry beforehand about what
to say. Just say whatever is
given you at the time, for it is
not you speaking, but the Holy
Spirit.

12“Brother will betray brother to death, and a father his
child. Children will rebel against
their parents and have them
put to death. 13All men will hate
you because of me, but he who stands firm to
the end will be saved.

14“When you see ‘the abomination that
causes desolation’[a] standing where it[b] does not
belong—let the reader understand—then let
those who are in Judea flee to the mountains.
15Let no one on the roof of his house go down
or enter the house to take anything out. 16Let
no one in the field go back to get his cloak.
17How dreadful it will be in those days for
pregnant women and nursing mothers! 18Pray
that this will not take place in winter, 19because
those will be days of distress unequaled from
the beginning, when God created the world,
until now—and never to be equaled again. 20If
the Lord had not cut short those days, no one
would survive. But for the sake of the elect,
whom he has chosen, he has shortened them.
21At that time if anyone says to you, ‘Look, here
is the Christ[c]!’ or, ‘Look, there he is!’ do not believe it. 22For false Christs and false prophets
will appear and perform signs and miracles to
deceive the elect—if that were possible. 23So
be on your guard; I have told you everything
ahead of time.

24“But in those days, following that distress,

“ ‘the sun will be darkened,
and the moon will not give its light;
25the stars will fall from the sky,
and the heavenly bodies will be
shaken.’[d]

26“At that time men will
see the Son of Man coming
in clouds with great power
and glory. 27And he will send
his angels and gather his elect
from the four winds, from the
ends of the earth to the ends of
the heavens.

28“Now learn this lesson
from the fig tree: As soon as its
twigs get tender and its leaves
come out, you know that summer is near. 29Even so, when
you see these things happening, you know that it is near,
right at the door. 30I tell you
the truth, this generation[e] will certainly not
pass away until all these things have happened.
31Heaven and earth will pass away, but my
words will never pass away.

Mark 13:26

God Will Return With Power

“At that time men will see the Son of Man coming in clouds with great power and glory.”

The Day and Hour Unknown

32“No one knows about that day or hour,
not even the angels in heaven, nor the Son, but
only the Father. 33Be on guard! Be alert[f]! You
do not know when that time will come. 34It’s
like a man going away: He leaves his house
and puts his servants in charge, each with his
assigned task, and tells the one at the door to
keep watch.

35“Therefore keep watch because you do not
know when the owner of the house will come
back—whether in the evening, or at midnight,

[a] 14 Daniel 9:27; 11:31; 12:11 [b] 14 Or *he*; also in verse 29 [c] 21 Or *Messiah* [d] 25 Isaiah 13:10; 34:4 [e] 30 Or *race* [f] 33 Some manuscripts *alert and pray*

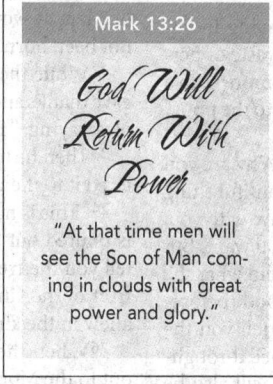

or when the rooster crows, or at dawn. 36 If
he comes suddenly, do not let him find you
sleeping. 37 What I say to you, I say to everyone: 'Watch!'"

Jesus Anointed at Bethany

14 Now the Passover and the Feast of Unleavened Bread were only two days
away, and the chief priests and the teachers of
the law were looking for some sly way to arrest
Jesus and kill him. 2 "But not during the Feast,"
they said, "or the people may riot."

3 While he was in Bethany, reclining at the
table in the home of a man known as Simon
the Leper, a woman came with an alabaster jar
of very expensive perfume, made of pure nard.
She broke the jar and poured the perfume on
his head.

4 Some of those present were saying indig-
nantly to one another, "Why this waste of perfume? 5 It could have been sold for more than a
year's wages[a] and the money given to the poor."
And they rebuked her harshly.

6 "Leave her alone," said Jesus. "Why are you
bothering her? She has done a beautiful thing
to me. 7 The poor you will always have with you,
and you can help them any time you want. But
you will not always have me. 8 She did what she
could. She poured perfume on my body beforehand to prepare for my burial. 9 I tell you the
truth, wherever the gospel is preached throughout the world, what she has done will also be
told, in memory of her."

10 Then Judas Iscariot, one of the Twelve,
went to the chief priests to betray Jesus to
them. 11 They were delighted to hear this and
promised to give him money. So he watched
for an opportunity to hand him over.

The Lord's Supper

12 On the first day of the Feast of Unleavened Bread, when it was customary to sacrifice
the Passover lamb, Jesus' disciples asked him,
"Where do you want us to go and make preparations for you to eat the Passover?"

13 So he sent two of his disciples, telling
them, "Go into the city, and a man carrying a
jar of water will meet you. Follow him. 14 Say to
the owner of the house he enters, 'The Teacher
asks: Where is my guest room, where I may
eat the Passover with my disciples?' 15 He will
show you a large upper room, furnished and
ready. Make preparations for us there."

16 The disciples left, went into the city and
found things just as Jesus had told them. So
they prepared the Passover.

17 When evening came, Jesus arrived with
the Twelve. 18 While they were reclining at the
table eating, he said, "I tell you the truth, one
of you will betray me—one who is eating with
me."

19 They were saddened, and one by one they
said to him, "Surely not I?"

20 "It is one of the Twelve," he replied, "one
who dips bread into the bowl with me. 21 The
Son of Man will go just as it is written about
him. But woe to that man who betrays the Son
of Man! It would be better for him if he had
not been born."

22 While they were eating, Jesus took bread,
gave thanks and broke it, and gave it to his disciples, saying, "Take it; this is my body."

23 Then he took the cup, gave thanks and offered it to them, and they all drank from it.

24 "This is my blood of the[b] covenant, which
is poured out for many," he said to them. 25 "I
tell you the truth, I will not drink again of the
fruit of the vine until that day when I drink it
anew in the kingdom of God."

26 When they had sung a hymn, they went
out to the Mount of Olives.

Jesus Predicts Peter's Denial

27 "You will all fall away," Jesus told them,
"for it is written:

"'I will strike the shepherd,
and the sheep will be scattered.'[c]

28 But after I have risen, I will go ahead of you
into Galilee."

29 Peter declared, "Even if all fall away, I will
not."

30 "I tell you the truth," Jesus answered, "today—yes, tonight—before the rooster crows
twice[d] you yourself will disown me three
times."

31 But Peter insisted emphatically, "Even if I
have to die with you, I will never disown you."
And all the others said the same.

[a] 5 Greek *than three hundred denarii* [b] 24 Some manuscripts *the new* [c] 27 Zech. 13:7 [d] 30 Some early manuscripts do not have *twice.*

Worship and Witness

Read: Mark 14:1–72

OUR LORD JESUS CHRIST is the preeminent one and the head of the church. We worship him because he deserves all of our allegiance and our love. We sing, "He is Lord"; but is he truly *Lord*? Remember, Jesus is Lord *of* all, or not Lord *at* all. It is a contradiction in terms to say that Jesus is Lord of part of my life. He must be Lord of *all!*

We agree that first things must be first in our lives, but how many of us, if we carefully examined our hearts, would find that often the truly important things in life are last, and the least important things are right up there in first place?

More and more we need to realize that we have been saved for two great purposes in life—the first is to *worship,* and the second is to *witness.* If you and I are not a worshiping people, then the witness of our lives will be weak and fruitless. There are two aspects of worship that are vital. The first is the personal quiet place of communion with God. This is where we spend time in praise, adoration and thankfulness for all that God is and for all that our preeminent Lord Jesus has done for us. The second crucial aspect is our public worship, where we join with fellow believers in church and together worship God. Never treat public worship lightly.

Out of worship flows our witness. If Christ is preeminent in our hearts then "out of the overflow of the heart the mouth speaks" (Matthew 12:34). When Christ is Lord of all, the Holy Spirit fills our lives, and we can't help but overflow in witness (see John 7:38–39).

Dear heavenly Father, you have exalted your Son, Jesus, to be both Lord and Christ. Can I do anything less? I pray that he may have preeminence in every area of my life for his name's sake. Amen.

—Barbara Hughes

Mark 14:6–9

"She has done a beautiful thing to me. The poor you will always have with you, and you can help them any time you want. But you will not always have me. She did what she could. She poured perfume on my body beforehand to prepare for my burial. I tell you the truth, wherever the gospel is preached throughout the world, what she has done will also be told, in memory of her."

reflection

1 How did the woman in today's Scripture passage show that Jesus was Lord in her life?

2 How did this prove to be a lasting witness to him?

3 In what ways can you pour out your love to Jesus today in personal worship? To whom will you then witness about your love for the Lord?

RELATED READINGS

Psalm 45;
Matthew 28:16–20;
Acts 1:6–8

Go to page 1231 for your next devotional reading.

Gethsemane

32 They went to a place called Gethsemane,
and Jesus said to his disciples, "Sit here while
I pray." 33 He took Peter, James and John along
with him, and he began to be deeply distressed
and troubled. 34 "My soul is overwhelmed with
sorrow to the point of death," he said to them.
"Stay here and keep watch."

35 Going a little farther, he fell to the ground
and prayed that if possible the hour might pass
from him. 36 "*Abba*,[a] Father," he said, "everything is possible for you. Take this cup from
me. Yet not what I will, but what you will."

37 Then he returned to his disciples and
found them sleeping. "Simon," he said to Peter,
"are you asleep? Could you not keep watch for
one hour? 38 Watch and pray so that you will
not fall into temptation. The spirit is willing,
but the body is weak."

39 Once more he went away and prayed the
same thing. 40 When he came back, he again
found them sleeping, because their eyes were
heavy. They did not know what to say to him.
41 Returning the third time, he said to them,
"Are you still sleeping and resting? Enough!
The hour has come. Look, the Son of Man is
betrayed into the hands of sinners. 42 Rise! Let
us go! Here comes my betrayer!"

Jesus Arrested

43 Just as he was speaking, Judas, one of
the Twelve, appeared. With him was a crowd
armed with swords and clubs, sent from the
chief priests, the teachers of the law, and the elders.

44 Now the betrayer had arranged a signal
with them: "The one I kiss is the man; arrest
him and lead him away under guard." 45 Going
at once to Jesus, Judas said, "Rabbi!" and kissed
him. 46 The men seized Jesus and arrested him.
47 Then one of those standing near drew his
sword and struck the servant of the high priest,
cutting off his ear.

48 "Am I leading a rebellion," said Jesus, "that
you have come out with swords and clubs to
capture me? 49 Every day I was with you, teaching in the temple courts, and you did not arrest me. But the Scriptures must be fulfilled."
50 Then everyone deserted him and fled.

51 A young man, wearing nothing but a
linen garment, was following Jesus. When they
seized him, 52 he fled naked, leaving his garment behind.

Before the Sanhedrin

53 They took Jesus to the high priest, and
all the chief priests, elders and teachers of
the law came together. 54 Peter followed him
at a distance, right into the courtyard of the
high priest. There he sat with the guards and
warmed himself at the fire.

55 The chief priests and the whole Sanhedrin
were looking for evidence against Jesus so that
they could put him to death, but they did not
find any. 56 Many testified falsely against him,
but their statements did not agree.

57 Then some stood up and gave this false
testimony against him: 58 "We heard him say,
'I will destroy this man-made temple and in
three days will build another, not made by
man.'" 59 Yet even then their testimony did
not agree.

60 Then the high priest stood up before them
and asked Jesus, "Are you not going to answer?
What is this testimony that these men are
bringing against you?" 61 But Jesus remained
silent and gave no answer.

Again the high priest asked him, "Are you
the Christ,[b] the Son of the Blessed One?"

62 "I am," said Jesus. "And you will see the Son
of Man sitting at the right hand of the Mighty
One and coming on the clouds of heaven."

63 The high priest tore his clothes. "Why
do we need any more witnesses?" he asked.
64 "You have heard the blasphemy. What do
you think?"

They all condemned him as worthy of
death. 65 Then some began to spit at him; they
blindfolded him, struck him with their fists,
and said, "Prophesy!" And the guards took him
and beat him.

Peter Disowns Jesus

66 While Peter was below in the courtyard,
one of the servant girls of the high priest came
by. 67 When she saw Peter warming himself,
she looked closely at him.

"You also were with that Nazarene, Jesus,"
she said.

68 But he denied it. "I don't know or under-

[a] 36 Aramaic for *Father* [b] 61 Or *Messiah*

stand what you're talking about," he said, and went out into the entryway.[a]

69 When the servant girl saw him there, she said again to those standing around, "This fellow is one of them." 70 Again he denied it.

After a little while, those standing near said to Peter, "Surely you are one of them, for you are a Galilean."

71 He began to call down curses on himself, and he swore to them, "I don't know this man you're talking about."

72 Immediately the rooster crowed the second time.[b] Then Peter remembered the word Jesus had spoken to him: "Before the rooster crows twice[c] you will disown me three times." And he broke down and wept.

Jesus Before Pilate

15 Very early in the morning, the chief priests, with the elders, the teachers of the law and the whole Sanhedrin, reached a decision. They bound Jesus, led him away and handed him over to Pilate.

2 "Are you the king of the Jews?" asked Pilate.

"Yes, it is as you say," Jesus replied.

3 The chief priests accused him of many things. 4 So again Pilate asked him, "Aren't you going to answer? See how many things they are accusing you of."

5 But Jesus still made no reply, and Pilate was amazed.

6 Now it was the custom at the Feast to release a prisoner whom the people requested. 7 A man called Barabbas was in prison with the insurrectionists who had committed murder in the uprising. 8 The crowd came up and asked Pilate to do for them what he usually did.

9 "Do you want me to release to you the king of the Jews?" asked Pilate, 10 knowing it was out of envy that the chief priests had handed Jesus over to him. 11 But the chief priests stirred up the crowd to have Pilate release Barabbas instead.

12 "What shall I do, then, with the one you call the king of the Jews?" Pilate asked them.

13 "Crucify him!" they shouted.

14 "Why? What crime has he committed?" asked Pilate.

But they shouted all the louder, "Crucify him!"

15 Wanting to satisfy the crowd, Pilate released Barabbas to them. He had Jesus flogged, and handed him over to be crucified.

The Soldiers Mock Jesus

16 The soldiers led Jesus away into the palace (that is, the Praetorium) and called together the whole company of soldiers. 17 They put a purple robe on him, then twisted together a crown of thorns and set it on him. 18 And they began to call out to him, "Hail, king of the Jews!" 19 Again and again they struck him on the head with a staff and spit on him. Falling on their knees, they paid homage to him. 20 And when they had mocked him, they took off the purple robe and put his own clothes on him. Then they led him out to crucify him.

The Crucifixion

21 A certain man from Cyrene, Simon, the father of Alexander and Rufus, was passing by on his way in from the country, and they forced him to carry the cross. 22 They brought Jesus to the place called Golgotha (which means The Place of the Skull). 23 Then they offered him wine mixed with myrrh, but he did not take it. 24 And they crucified him. Dividing up his clothes, they cast lots to see what each would get.

25 It was the third hour when they crucified him. 26 The written notice of the charge against him read: THE KING OF THE JEWS. 27 They crucified two robbers with him, one on his right and one on his left.[d] 29 Those who passed by hurled insults at him, shaking their heads and saying, "So! You who are going to destroy the temple and build it in three days, 30 come down from the cross and save yourself!"

31 In the same way the chief priests and the teachers of the law mocked him among themselves. "He saved others," they said, "but he can't save himself! 32 Let this Christ,[e] this King of Israel, come down now from the cross, that we may see and believe." Those crucified with him also heaped insults on him.

[a] 68 Some early manuscripts *entryway and the rooster crowed* [b] 72 Some early manuscripts do not have *the second time.* [c] 72 Some early manuscripts do not have *twice.* [d] 27 Some manuscripts *left,* [28] *and the scripture was fulfilled which says, "He was counted with the lawless ones"* (Isaiah 53:12) [e] 32 Or *Messiah*

The Death of Jesus

33 At the sixth hour darkness came over the
whole land until the ninth hour. 34 And at the
ninth hour Jesus cried out in a loud voice, *"Eloi,
Eloi, lama sabachthani?"*—which means, "My
God, my God, why have you forsaken me?"[a]
35 When some of those standing near heard
this, they said, "Listen, he's calling Elijah."
36 One man ran, filled a sponge with wine
vinegar, put it on a stick, and offered it to Jesus
to drink. "Now leave him alone. Let's see if Elijah comes to take him down," he said.
37 With a loud cry, Jesus breathed his last.
38 The curtain of the temple was torn in two
from top to bottom. 39 And when the centurion,
who stood there in front of Jesus, heard his cry
and[b] saw how he died, he said, "Surely this man
was the Son[c] of God!"
40 Some women were watching from a distance. Among them were Mary Magdalene,
Mary the mother of James the younger and of
Joses, and Salome. 41 In Galilee these women
had followed him and cared for his needs.
Many other women who had come up with
him to Jerusalem were also there.

The Burial of Jesus

42 It was Preparation Day (that is, the day before the Sabbath). So as evening approached,
43 Joseph of Arimathea, a prominent member
of the Council, who was himself waiting for
the kingdom of God, went boldly to Pilate and
asked for Jesus' body. 44 Pilate was surprised to
hear that he was already dead. Summoning the
centurion, he asked him if Jesus had already
died. 45 When he learned from the centurion
that it was so, he gave the body to Joseph. 46 So
Joseph bought some linen cloth, took down
the body, wrapped it in the linen, and placed
it in a tomb cut out of rock. Then he rolled a
stone against the entrance of the tomb. 47 Mary
Magdalene and Mary the mother of Joses saw
where he was laid.

The Resurrection

16 When the Sabbath was over, Mary Magdalene, Mary the mother of James, and
Salome bought spices so that they might go
to anoint Jesus' body. 2 Very early on the first
day of the week, just after sunrise, they were
on their way to the tomb 3 and they asked each
other, "Who will roll the stone away from the
entrance of the tomb?"
4 But when they looked up, they saw that the
stone, which was very large, had been rolled
away. 5 As they entered the tomb, they saw a
young man dressed in a white robe sitting on
the right side, and they were alarmed.
6 "Don't be alarmed," he said. "You are looking for Jesus the Nazarene, who was crucified.
He has risen! He is not here. See the place where
they laid him. 7 But go, tell his disciples and
Peter, 'He is going ahead of you into Galilee.
There you will see him, just as he told you.' "
8 Trembling and bewildered, the women
went out and fled from the tomb. They said
nothing to anyone, because they were afraid.

[The earliest manuscripts and some other ancient
witnesses do not have Mark 16:9–20.]

9 When Jesus rose early on the first day of the
week, he appeared first to Mary Magdalene, out
of whom he had driven seven demons. 10 She
went and told those who had been with him
and who were mourning and weeping. 11 When
they heard that Jesus was alive and that she had
seen him, they did not believe it.
12 Afterward Jesus appeared in a different
form to two of them while they were walking
in the country. 13 These returned and reported
it to the rest; but they did not believe them either.
14 Later Jesus appeared to the Eleven as they
were eating; he rebuked them for their lack of
faith and their stubborn refusal to believe those
who had seen him after he had risen.
15 He said to them, "Go into all the world
and preach the good news to all creation.
16 Whoever believes and is baptized will be
saved, but whoever does not believe will be condemned. 17 And these signs will accompany
those who believe: In my name they will drive
out demons; they will speak in new tongues;
18 they will pick up snakes with their hands;
and when they drink deadly poison, it will not

[a] 34 Psalm 22:1 [b] 39 Some manuscripts do not have *heard his cry and* [c] 39 Or *a son*

Don't Be Afraid

Read: Mark 16:1–13

JESUS WAS DEAD. Crucified. And in his empty tomb sat an angel telling the grieving women who came to minister to their fallen master's body, "Don't be alarmed."

Of course, Jesus had told his followers what to expect. He would die . . . which he did. He would be buried . . . which he was. And in three days he would rise again. Now he wasn't in the tomb. And there was an angel who understated the situation by saying, "Don't be alarmed." Of course they were alarmed, afraid and distressed: The soldiers had crucified Jesus; he had lain in the tomb three days; the huge stone they had worried about had been rolled away; there was an angel standing there . . . talking to them!

It's easy to look at ancient Bible characters and second-guess their responses: "Why didn't they get it?" We like to think *we* would have gotten it. *We* would have understood Jesus words' about his death and resurrection. *We'd* have comprehended that he must first suffer as our Savior before he could return as King of kings. The knowledge that the sign of Jonah meant Jesus would lie three days in the tomb would have been a breeze for us to comprehend, or so we like to think.

But really, if we had been there, encountering an angel in a dark, empty tomb, we would have probably run away in terror or stood there quaking in our sandals. We might have been like the women who "said nothing to anyone, because they were afraid" (verse 8). What were they afraid of? Perhaps they were afraid of the Roman soldiers; they may have been afraid people would think they were crazy; they may have been afraid they wouldn't relay the angel's message correctly.

Do you hold back from telling people that Jesus is risen? Maybe you're afraid you'll be mocked or laughed at. Or maybe you're afraid people will think you've gone off the religious deep end. Or maybe you're afraid you won't know the right words to say. Listen to the angel's words again: "Don't be alarmed . . . He has risen!"

Friday

Mark 16:6

"Don't be alarmed," [the angel] said. "You are looking for Jesus the Nazarene, who was crucified. He has risen! He is not here. See the place where they laid him."

reflection

1 Put yourself in the women's shoes. What emotions other than fear might they have been feeling?

2 Are you afraid to tell others Jesus is risen?

3 Who needs to hear this Good News? Pray for the faith to overcome your fear.

RELATED READINGS

Romans 8:35–39;
1 Corinthians 15:54–58;
1 Peter 1:3–9;
1 John 4:16–18

Go to page 1235 for your next devotional reading.

hurt them at all; they will place their hands on sick people, and they will get well."
19 After the Lord Jesus had spoken to them, he was taken up into heaven and he sat at the right hand of God.
20 Then the disciples went out and preached everywhere, and the Lord worked with them and confirmed his word by the signs that accompanied it.

Luke

Luke, the physician, *meticulously researched the details* for his book, talking with people who had known Jesus well. The Gospels of Matthew and Luke record Jesus' birth, but Luke is the only one that reports Mary's song, *the Magnificat,* and the announcement to the shepherds. He shows Jesus' divinity, but emphasizes his humanity as well, calling him the *"Son of Man."* Luke spends much time telling us about common people's encounters with Christ through which we see Jesus' heart for people. Luke's Gospel concludes with the ascension, at which time Jesus was taken up to heaven. *The story then continues* in Luke's second volume, the book of Acts.

Author:
Luke, a doctor and a Gentile (Greek) Christian.

Audience:
Followers of Jesus. Luke appealed to the Gentiles.

Date:
Probably about A.D. 60.

Setting:
Luke wrote to the Gentiles from Rome or perhaps Caesarea, Achaia or Ephesus.

Verse to Remember:
"For the Son of Man came to seek and to save what was lost." (19:10)

Introduction

1 Many have undertaken to draw up an
account of the things that have been fulfilled[a] among us, 2just as they were handed
down to us by those who from the first were
eyewitnesses and servants of the word. 3There-
fore, since I myself have carefully investigated
everything from the beginning, it seemed good
also to me to write an orderly account for you,
most excellent Theophilus, 4so that you may
know the certainty of the things you have
been taught.

The Birth of John the Baptist Foretold

5In the time of Herod king of Judea there
was a priest named Zechariah, who belonged
to the priestly division of Abijah; his wife
Elizabeth was also a descendant of Aaron.

[a] 1 Or *been surely believed*

6 Both of them were upright in the sight of God,
observing all the Lord's commandments and
regulations blamelessly. 7 But they had no children, because Elizabeth was barren; and they
were both well along in years.
8 Once when Zechariah's division was on
duty and he was serving as priest before God,
9 he was chosen by lot, according to the custom
of the priesthood, to go into the temple of the
Lord and burn incense. 10 And when the time
for the burning of incense came, all the assembled worshipers were praying outside.
11 Then an angel of the Lord appeared to
him, standing at the right side of the altar of incense. 12 When Zechariah saw him, he was startled and was gripped with fear. 13 But the angel
said to him: "Do not be afraid, Zechariah; your
prayer has been heard. Your wife Elizabeth will
bear you a son, and you are to give him the
name John. 14 He will be a joy and delight to
you, and many will rejoice because of his birth,
15 for he will be great in the sight of the Lord. He
is never to take wine or other fermented drink,
and he will be filled with the Holy Spirit even
from birth.[a] 16 Many of the people of Israel will
he bring back to the Lord their God. 17 And
he will go on before the Lord, in the spirit and
power of Elijah, to turn the hearts of the fathers
to their children and the disobedient to the wisdom of the righteous—to make ready a people
prepared for the Lord."
18 Zechariah asked the angel, "How can I be
sure of this? I am an old man and my wife is
well along in years."
19 The angel answered, "I am
Gabriel. I stand in the presence
of God, and I have been sent to
speak to you and to tell you this
good news. 20 And now you will
be silent and not able to speak
until the day this happens, because you did not believe my
words, which will come true at
their proper time."
21 Meanwhile, the people
were waiting for Zechariah and
wondering why he stayed so long in the temple. 22 When he came out, he could not speak
to them. They realized he had seen a vision in
the temple, for he kept making signs to them
but remained unable to speak.
23 When his time of service was completed,
he returned home. 24 After this his wife Elizabeth became pregnant and for five months remained in seclusion. 25 "The Lord has done this
for me," she said. "In these days he has shown
his favor and taken away my disgrace among
the people."

Luke 1:37

God Can Do Anything

"For nothing is impossible with God."

The Birth of Jesus Foretold

26 In the sixth month, God sent the angel
Gabriel to Nazareth, a town in Galilee, 27 to a
virgin pledged to be married to a man named
Joseph, a descendant of David. The virgin's
name was Mary. 28 The angel went to her and
said, "Greetings, you who are highly favored!
The Lord is with you."
29 Mary was greatly troubled at his words and
wondered what kind of greeting this might be.
30 But the angel said to her, "Do not be afraid,
Mary, you have found favor with God. 31 You
will be with child and give birth to a son, and
you are to give him the name Jesus. 32 He will
be great and will be called the Son of the Most
High. The Lord God will give him the throne
of his father David, 33 and he will reign over
the house of Jacob forever; his kingdom will
never end."
34 "How will this be," Mary asked the angel,
"since I am a virgin?"
35 The angel answered, "The Holy Spirit will
come upon you, and the power of the Most
High will overshadow you. So
the holy one to be born will be
called[b] the Son of God. 36 Even
Elizabeth your relative is going
to have a child in her old age,
and she who was said to be
barren is in her sixth month.
37 For nothing is impossible
with God."
38 "I am the Lord's servant,"
Mary answered. "May it be to
me as you have said." Then the
angel left her.

Mary Visits Elizabeth

39 At that time Mary got ready and hurried
to a town in the hill country of Judea, 40 where

[a] 15 Or *from his mother's womb* [b] 35 Or *So the child to be born will be called holy,*

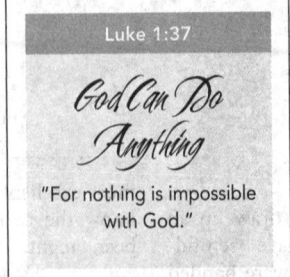

Waiting Game

MARTHA

THE DAYS SEEMED TO STRETCH on forever, and the nights were almost unbearable. The minutes turned into hours; one day turned into two—two of the longest days of her life. Certainly, the message that Lazarus was sick had reached Jesus by now. So, why wasn't he here already? Martha paced outside her home, deliberating the questions. She was confused by his delay. Didn't he care about her brother? Or *her* for that matter?

She decided to give him some more time. He was on his way, she felt sure. He had to be. Even when Lazarus's last breaths rattled in his chest, she kept casting her eyes toward the doorway. She expected Jesus to come through the door at any moment. And when he did, he would restore health and harmony in her family.

But he never came.

After Lazarus died, Mary (always the more emotional one) sobbed hysterically. The other mourners wrapped their arms around her in an effort to console her. Her body heaved with her loud sobs. Meanwhile, Martha responded as only Martha could. She made a mental list of what needed to be done to prepare her brother's body. She began at the top of her list and worked her way down. Mechanically, she sat and tore strips of material in which to wrap him. She fought against the tears welling in her eyes and bit her bottom lip until she thought it would bleed.

Later, she watched as the strong men shouldered her brother's body and carried it to his grave. She instinctively put her arm around her sister, and they both shuddered at the finality of the stone settling into place across the entrance. Martha silently crossed the last item off her list. It was over. Finished. There was nothing more to be done.

Just then, she saw a small crowd of people coming down the road toward her home. From a distance, she recognized a familiar figure striding toward her. In an instant, she knew who he was.

—Prayer—
Jesus, grant me patience in prayer and complete trust in your Word.

"Lord," Martha said to Jesus, "if you had been here, my brother would not have died. But I know that even now God will give you whatever you ask."

John 11:21–22

ASSIGNED READING:
Luke 10:38–42; John 11:17–44

Weekend

Go to page 1238 for your next devotional reading.

she entered Zechariah's home and greeted Elizabeth. 41 When Elizabeth heard Mary's greeting,
the baby leaped in her womb, and Elizabeth
was filled with the Holy Spirit. 42 In a loud
voice she exclaimed: "Blessed are you among
women, and blessed is the child you will bear!
43 But why am I so favored, that the mother of
my Lord should come to me? 44 As soon as the
sound of your greeting reached my ears, the
baby in my womb leaped for joy. 45 Blessed is
she who has believed that what the Lord has
said to her will be accomplished!"

Mary's Song

46 And Mary said:

"My soul glorifies the Lord
47 and my spirit rejoices in God my Savior,
48 for he has been mindful
of the humble state of his servant.
From now on all generations will call me
blessed,
49 for the Mighty One has done great
things for me—
holy is his name.
50 His mercy extends to those who fear him,
from generation to generation.
51 He has performed mighty deeds with his
arm;
he has scattered those who are proud in
their inmost thoughts.
52 He has brought down rulers from their
thrones
but has lifted up the humble.
53 He has filled the hungry with good things
but has sent the rich away empty.
54 He has helped his servant Israel,
remembering to be merciful
55 to Abraham and his descendants forever,
even as he said to our fathers."

56 Mary stayed with Elizabeth for about three
months and then returned home.

The Birth of John the Baptist

57 When it was time for Elizabeth to have her
baby, she gave birth to a son. 58 Her neighbors
and relatives heard that the Lord had shown
her great mercy, and they shared her joy.
59 On the eighth day they came to circumcise
the child, and they were going to name him after his father Zechariah, 60 but his mother spoke
up and said, "No! He is to be called John."
61 They said to her, "There is no one among
your relatives who has that name."
62 Then they made signs to his father, to find
out what he would like to name the child. 63 He
asked for a writing tablet, and to everyone's
astonishment he wrote, "His name is John."
64 Immediately his mouth was opened and
his tongue was loosed, and he began to speak,
praising God. 65 The neighbors were all filled
with awe, and throughout the hill country of Judea people were talking about all these things.
66 Everyone who heard this wondered about it,
asking, "What then is this child going to be?"
For the Lord's hand was with him.

Zechariah's Song

67 His father Zechariah was filled with the
Holy Spirit and prophesied:

68 "Praise be to the Lord, the God of Israel,
because he has come and has redeemed
his people.
69 He has raised up a horn[a] of salvation for us
in the house of his servant David
70 (as he said through his holy prophets of
long ago),
71 salvation from our enemies
and from the hand of all who hate us—
72 to show mercy to our fathers
and to remember his holy covenant,
73 the oath he swore to our father Abraham:
74 to rescue us from the hand of our enemies,
and to enable us to serve him without
fear
75 in holiness and righteousness before
him all our days.

76 And you, my child, will be called a prophet
of the Most High;
for you will go on before the Lord to
prepare the way for him,
77 to give his people the knowledge of
salvation
through the forgiveness of their sins,
78 because of the tender mercy of our God,
by which the rising sun will come to us
from heaven
79 to shine on those living in darkness

[a] 69 *Horn* here symbolizes strength.

and in the shadow of death,
to guide our feet into the path of peace."

80 And the child grew and became strong
in spirit; and he lived in the desert until he appeared publicly to Israel.

The Birth of Jesus

2 In those days Caesar Augustus issued a decree that a census should be taken of the
entire Roman world. 2 (This was the first census
that took place while Quirinius was governor
of Syria.) 3 And everyone went to his own town
to register.

4 So Joseph also went up from the town of
Nazareth in Galilee to Judea, to Bethlehem
the town of David, because he belonged to the
house and line of David. 5 He went there to
register with Mary, who was pledged to be married to him and was expecting a child. 6 While
they were there, the time came for the baby to
be born, 7 and she gave birth to her firstborn,
a son. She wrapped him in cloths and placed
him in a manger, because there was no room
for them in the inn.

The Shepherds and the Angels

8 And there were shepherds living out in the
fields nearby, keeping watch over their flocks at
night. 9 An angel of the Lord appeared to them,
and the glory of the Lord shone around them,
and they were terrified. 10 But the angel said
to them, "Do not be afraid. I bring you good
news of great joy that will be for all the people.
11 Today in the town of David a Savior has been
born to you; he is Christ[a] the Lord. 12 This will
be a sign to you: You will find a baby wrapped
in cloths and lying in a manger."

13 Suddenly a great company of the heavenly
host appeared with the angel, praising God
and saying,

14 "Glory to God in the highest,
and on earth peace to men on whom his
favor rests."

15 When the angels had left them and gone
into heaven, the shepherds said to one another,
"Let's go to Bethlehem and see this thing
that has happened, which the Lord has told
us about."

16 So they hurried off and found Mary and
Joseph, and the baby, who was lying in the manger. 17 When they had seen him, they spread
the word concerning what had been told them
about this child, 18 and all who heard it were
amazed at what the shepherds said to them.
19 But Mary treasured up all these things and
pondered them in her heart. 20 The shepherds
returned, glorifying and praising God for all
the things they had heard and seen, which were
just as they had been told.

Jesus Presented in the Temple

21 On the eighth day, when it was time to circumcise him, he was named Jesus, the name
the angel had given him before he had been
conceived.

22 When the time of their purification according to the Law of Moses had been completed,
Joseph and Mary took him to Jerusalem to present him to the Lord 23 (as it is written in the
Law of the Lord, "Every firstborn male is to
be consecrated to the Lord"[b]), 24 and to offer
a sacrifice in keeping with what is said in the
Law of the Lord: "a pair of doves or two young
pigeons."[c]

25 Now there was a man in Jerusalem called
Simeon, who was righteous and devout. He
was waiting for the consolation of Israel, and
the Holy Spirit was upon him. 26 It had been revealed to him by the Holy Spirit that he would
not die before he had seen the Lord's Christ.
27 Moved by the Spirit, he went into the temple
courts. When the parents brought in the child
Jesus to do for him what the custom of the Law
required, 28 Simeon took him in his arms and
praised God, saying:

29 "Sovereign Lord, as you have promised,
you now dismiss[d] your servant in peace.
30 For my eyes have seen your salvation,
31 which you have prepared in the sight of
all people,
32 a light for revelation to the Gentiles
and for glory to your people Israel."

33 The child's father and mother marveled
at what was said about him. 34 Then Simeon
blessed them and said to Mary, his mother:
"This child is destined to cause the falling and

[a] 11 Or *Messiah.* "The Christ" (Greek) and "the Messiah" (Hebrew) both mean "the Anointed One"; also in verse 26. [b] 23 Exodus 13:2,12
[c] 24 Lev. 12:8 [d] 29 Or *promised, / now dismiss*

Luke 2:36–38

There was also a prophetess, Anna, the daughter of Phanuel, of the tribe of Asher. She was very old; she had lived with her husband seven years after her marriage, and then was a widow until she was eighty-four. She never left the temple but worshiped night and day, fasting and praying. Coming up to them at that very moment, she gave thanks to God and spoke about the child to all who were looking forward to the redemption of Jerusalem.

reflection

1 What encourages you about the story of Anna in the temple?

2 Physical limitations sometimes come with age, but what do you see as the positive aspects of advancing years?

3 How might your opportunities to serve God be broader now than they were when you were younger?

RELATED READINGS

Genesis 24:34–36; Exodus 15:19–21; 1 Samuel 2:1–10; Acts 2:14–21

No Age Barrier

Read: Luke 2:25–39

BY ANYONE'S DEFINITION, Anna was old. Married for only 7 years, a widow until age 84, Anna had witnessed the passing of decade after decade. Her world was not a large one, as she was consigned to living in the temple and devoted herself to fasting and prayer; she mostly worshiped and waited. The years of waiting were finally over when she spotted *him*: the precious infant lying in the young mother's arms. Angels had announced this child's birth. Now an aged woman became another in the line of those who sang the chorus of annunciation: The Messiah had come! What a beautiful message from a beautiful woman who had waited years to proclaim her prophetic message.

Nineteenth-century author and abolitionist Harriet Beecher Stowe once wrote, "So much had been said and sung of beautiful young girls, why don't somebody wake up to the beauty of old women?"

We live in a youth-oriented culture. American women spend millions of dollars each year on products designed to keep us young—or at least to help us appear that way. Older women can easily feel marginalized—as if their days of usefulness are past. Yet Scripture reminds us that God reserves some of his most significant assignments to women who have attained the maturity to handle them—like Anna the prophetess.

As the years pass, do you sometimes wonder whether the best ones are now behind you? Do your options seem limited and your value diminished? When you set your heart to serve God, you can continue to do so whatever your health, age or personal circumstances.

Angels and an elderly woman announced the birth of the Savior of the world. Approximately 33 years later, angels and a select group of women proclaimed the astounding news of his resurrection from the dead. Age and gender present no barrier when God entrusts us with a divine message or mission.

Go to page 1241 for your next devotional reading.

rising of many in Israel, and to be a sign that
will be spoken against, 35so that the thoughts
of many hearts will be revealed. And a sword
will pierce your own soul too."
36There was also a prophetess, Anna, the
daughter of Phanuel, of the tribe of Asher. She
was very old; she had lived with her husband
seven years after her marriage, 37and then was
a widow until she was eighty-four.[a] She never
left the temple but worshiped night and day,
fasting and praying. 38Coming up to them at
that very moment, she gave thanks to God and
spoke about the child to all who were looking
forward to the redemption of Jerusalem.
39When Joseph and Mary had done everything required by the Law of the Lord, they
returned to Galilee to their own town of Nazareth. 40And the child grew and became strong;
he was filled with wisdom, and the grace of
God was upon him.

The Boy Jesus at the Temple

41Every year his parents went to Jerusalem
for the Feast of the Passover. 42When he was
twelve years old, they went up to the Feast, according to the custom. 43After the Feast was
over, while his parents were returning home,
the boy Jesus stayed behind in Jerusalem, but
they were unaware of it. 44Thinking he was
in their company, they traveled on for a day.
Then they began looking for him among their
relatives and friends. 45When they did not
find him, they went back to Jerusalem to look
for him. 46After three days they found him in
the temple courts, sitting among the teachers,
listening to them and asking them questions.
47Everyone who heard him was amazed at
his understanding and his answers. 48When
his parents saw him, they were astonished.
His mother said to him, "Son, why have you
treated us like this? Your father and I have been
anxiously searching for you."
49"Why were you searching for me?" he
asked. "Didn't you know I had to be in my Father's house?" 50But they did not understand
what he was saying to them.
51Then he went down to Nazareth with them
and was obedient to them. But his mother treasured all these things in her heart. 52And Jesus
grew in wisdom and stature, and in favor with
God and men.

John the Baptist Prepares the Way

3 In the fifteenth year of the reign of Tiberius
Caesar—when Pontius Pilate was governor of Judea, Herod tetrarch of Galilee, his
brother Philip tetrarch of Iturea and Traconitis,
and Lysanias tetrarch of Abilene— 2during the
high priesthood of Annas and Caiaphas, the
word of God came to John son of Zechariah in
the desert. 3He went into all the country around
the Jordan, preaching a baptism of repentance
for the forgiveness of sins. 4As is written in the
book of the words of Isaiah the prophet:

"A voice of one calling in the desert,
'Prepare the way for the Lord,
make straight paths for him.
5 Every valley shall be filled in,
every mountain and hill made low.
The crooked roads shall become straight,
the rough ways smooth.
6 And all mankind will see God's
salvation.'"[b]

7John said to the crowds coming out to be
baptized by him, "You brood of vipers! Who
warned you to flee from the coming wrath?
8Produce fruit in keeping with repentance.
And do not begin to say to yourselves, 'We have
Abraham as our father.' For I tell you that out of
these stones God can raise up children for Abraham. 9The ax is already at the root of the trees,
and every tree that does not produce good fruit
will be cut down and thrown into the fire."
10"What should we do then?" the crowd
asked.
11John answered, "The man with two tunics
should share with him who has none, and the
one who has food should do the same."
12Tax collectors also came to be baptized.
"Teacher," they asked, "what should we do?"
13"Don't collect any more than you are required to," he told them.
14Then some soldiers asked him, "And what
should we do?"
He replied, "Don't extort money and
don't accuse people falsely—be content with
your pay."

[a]37 Or *widow for eighty-four years* [b]6 Isaiah 40:3–5

15The people were waiting expectantly and
were all wondering in their hearts if John might
possibly be the Christ.[a] 16John answered them
all, "I baptize you with[b] water. But one more
powerful than I will come, the thongs of whose
sandals I am not worthy to untie. He will baptize you with the Holy Spirit and with fire.
17His winnowing fork is in his hand to clear
his threshing floor and to gather the wheat into
his barn, but he will burn up the chaff with
unquenchable fire." 18And with many other
words John exhorted the people and preached
the good news to them.
19But when John rebuked Herod the tetrarch
because of Herodias, his brother's wife, and all
the other evil things he had done, 20Herod
added this to them all: He locked John up in
prison.

The Baptism and Genealogy of Jesus

21When all the people were being baptized,
Jesus was baptized too. And as he was praying, heaven was opened 22and the Holy Spirit
descended on him in bodily form like a dove.
And a voice came from heaven: "You are my
Son, whom I love; with you I am well pleased."
23Now Jesus himself was about thirty years
old when he began his ministry. He was the
son, so it was thought, of Joseph,

the son of Heli, 24the son of Matthat,
the son of Levi, the son of Melki,
the son of Jannai, the son of Joseph,
25 the son of Mattathias, the son of Amos,
the son of Nahum, the son of Esli,
the son of Naggai, 26the son of Maath,
the son of Mattathias, the son of Semein,
the son of Josech, the son of Joda,
27 the son of Joanan, the son of Rhesa,
the son of Zerubbabel, the son of Shealtiel,
the son of Neri, 28the son of Melki,
the son of Addi, the son of Cosam,
the son of Elmadam, the son of Er,
29 the son of Joshua, the son of Eliezer,
the son of Jorim, the son of Matthat,
the son of Levi, 30the son of Simeon,
the son of Judah, the son of Joseph,
the son of Jonam, the son of Eliakim,
31 the son of Melea, the son of Menna,
the son of Mattatha, the son of Nathan,
the son of David, 32the son of Jesse,
the son of Obed, the son of Boaz,
the son of Salmon,[c] the son of Nahshon,
33 the son of Amminadab, the son of Ram,[d]
the son of Hezron, the son of Perez,
the son of Judah, 34the son of Jacob,
the son of Isaac, the son of Abraham,
the son of Terah, the son of Nahor,
35 the son of Serug, the son of Reu,
the son of Peleg, the son of Eber,
the son of Shelah, 36the son of Cainan,
the son of Arphaxad, the son of Shem,
the son of Noah, the son of Lamech,
37 the son of Methuselah, the son of Enoch,
the son of Jared, the son of Mahalalel,
the son of Kenan, 38the son of Enosh,
the son of Seth, the son of Adam,
the son of God.

The Temptation of Jesus

4 Jesus, full of the Holy Spirit, returned from
the Jordan and was led by the Spirit in the
desert, 2where for forty days he was tempted
by the devil. He ate nothing during those days,
and at the end of them he was hungry.
3The devil said to him, "If you are the Son of
God, tell this stone to become bread."
4Jesus answered, "It is written: 'Man does
not live on bread alone.'[e]"
5The devil led him up to a high place and
showed him in an instant all the kingdoms of
the world. 6And he said to him, "I will give
you all their authority and splendor, for it has
been given to me, and I can give it to anyone
I want to. 7So if you worship me, it will all be
yours."
8Jesus answered, "It is written: 'Worship the
Lord your God and serve him only.'[f]"
9The devil led him to Jerusalem and had
him stand on the highest point of the temple.
"If you are the Son of God," he said, "throw
yourself down from here. 10For it is written:

"'He will command his angels concerning
you
to guard you carefully;
11 they will lift you up in their hands,

[a]15 Or *Messiah* [b]16 Or *in* [c]32 Some early manuscripts *Sala* [d]33 Some manuscripts *Amminadab, the son of Admin, the son of Arni*; other manuscripts vary widely. [e]4 Deut. 8:3 [f]8 Deut. 6:13

From Suffering to Serving

Read: Luke 4:1–44

LUKE, THE PHYSICIAN, tells us that Simon's mother-in-law was sick with a high fever. This was no ordinary cold. She was really, really sick and suffering. You know what it's like to have a fever. First you have the chills, so you pile the blankets high. Then you get too hot, so you throw the blankets off. Then you're hit with a blazing headache. Soon your whole body begins to ache. Finally, you're so worn out, you lay there lethargically, unable to move a muscle. It's miserable.

In this case, the disciples didn't run to the local apothecary; "they asked Jesus to help her" (verse 38). The Great Physician bent over the tired woman's body and told the fever to leave—and it left! Amazingly, she didn't need rest to recover from her ordeal. She wasn't just partially healed, she was so completely healed that "she got up at once and began to wait on them" (verse 39).

Now this was a no-nonsense kind of woman. She probably could have stayed on her sickbed for a few days, let other people wait on her, gotten a little more sympathy and emotional mileage out of that fever, and no one would have known (except Jesus). But some women have a gift for serving others, no matter what. They serve until they can't stand up anymore. And as soon as they're a bit better, they're up and at it again. They are always busy and always concerned for those around them. You know the type; they are often the silent strength behind those men and women who have the showier, more "glamorous" jobs.

You might *be* one of those women. You think, *I don't have time to rest, and I really don't have time to be sick.* But let's face it: sometimes our human bodies wear out. We get sick . . . or just sick and tired. That's when we can ask for help from the One who is the source of healing and strength. Jesus is still in the miracle business. Ask him to heal you body, mind and spirit. And keep in mind that there's nothing wrong with finding the healthy balance between meeting your own needs so you can continue to meet the needs of others.

Luke 4:38–39

Now Simon's mother-in-law was suffering from a high fever, and they asked Jesus to help her. So he bent over her and rebuked the fever, and it left her. She got up at once and began to wait on them.

reflection

1 Assess your life. Are you both serving others and caring for your own needs? How are you balancing the competing needs of those around you?

2 Are you chronically ill? How can you serve where you are?

3 Do you know someone who is sick and suffering? How can you pray for her? How can you help her in practical ways?

RELATED READINGS

Psalm 30:2; Matthew 9:20–22; James 5:14–16

"The definition of a servant: One who is doing the will of another with the resources of another for the benefit of another."

Cosette Conaway

Go to page 1246 for your next devotional reading.

so that you will not strike your foot
against a stone.'[a]"

12 Jesus answered, "It says: 'Do not put the Lord your God to the test.'[b]"

13 When the devil had finished all this tempting, he left him until an opportune time.

Jesus Rejected at Nazareth

14 Jesus returned to Galilee in the power of the Spirit, and news about him spread through the whole countryside. 15 He taught in their synagogues, and everyone praised him.

16 He went to Nazareth, where he had been brought up, and on the Sabbath day he went into the synagogue, as was his custom. And he stood up to read. 17 The scroll of the prophet Isaiah was handed to him. Unrolling it, he found the place where it is written:

18 "The Spirit of the Lord is on me,
because he has anointed me
to preach good news to the poor.
He has sent me to proclaim freedom for the prisoners
and recovery of sight for the blind,
to release the oppressed,
19 to proclaim the year of the Lord's favor."[c]

> **Luke 4:18**
>
> *God Cares for the Oppressed*
>
> "The Spirit of the Lord is on me . . .
> to preach good news to the poor.
> He has sent me to proclaim freedom for the prisoners
> and recovery of sight for the blind,
> to release the oppressed."

20 Then he rolled up the scroll, gave it back to the attendant and sat down. The eyes of everyone in the synagogue were fastened on him, 21 and he began by saying to them, "Today this scripture is fulfilled in your hearing."

22 All spoke well of him and were amazed at the gracious words that came from his lips. "Isn't this Joseph's son?" they asked.

23 Jesus said to them, "Surely you will quote this proverb to me: 'Physician, heal yourself! Do here in your hometown what we have heard that you did in Capernaum.'"

24 "I tell you the truth," he continued, "no prophet is accepted in his hometown. 25 I assure you that there were many widows in Israel in Elijah's time, when the sky was shut for three and a half years and there was a severe famine throughout the land. 26 Yet Elijah was not sent to any of them, but to a widow in Zarephath in the region of Sidon. 27 And there were many in Israel with leprosy[d] in the time of Elisha the prophet, yet not one of them was cleansed—only Naaman the Syrian."

28 All the people in the synagogue were furious when they heard this. 29 They got up, drove him out of the town, and took him to the brow of the hill on which the town was built, in order to throw him down the cliff. 30 But he walked right through the crowd and went on his way.

Jesus Drives Out an Evil Spirit

31 Then he went down to Capernaum, a town in Galilee, and on the Sabbath began to teach the people. 32 They were amazed at his teaching, because his message had authority.

33 In the synagogue there was a man possessed by a demon, an evil[e] spirit. He cried out at the top of his voice, 34 "Ha! What do you want with us, Jesus of Nazareth? Have you come to destroy us? I know who you are—the Holy One of God!"

35 "Be quiet!" Jesus said sternly. "Come out of him!" Then the demon threw the man down before them all and came out without injuring him.

36 All the people were amazed and said to each other, "What is this teaching? With authority and power he gives orders to evil spirits and they come out!" 37 And the news about him spread throughout the surrounding area.

Jesus Heals Many

38 Jesus left the synagogue and went to the home of Simon. Now Simon's mother-in-law was suffering from a high fever, and they asked

[a] 11 Psalm 91:11,12 [b] 12 Deut. 6:16 [c] 19 Isaiah 61:1,2 [d] 27 The Greek word was used for various diseases affecting the skin—not necessarily leprosy. [e] 33 Greek *unclean*; also in verse 36

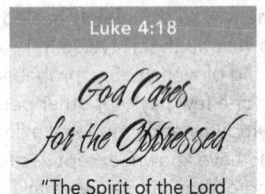

Jesus to help her. 39 So he bent over her and rebuked the fever, and it left her. She got up at
once and began to wait on them.
40 When the sun was setting, the people
brought to Jesus all who had various kinds of
sickness, and laying his hands on each one, he
healed them. 41 Moreover, demons came out
of many people, shouting, "You are the Son of
God!" But he rebuked them and would not allow them to speak, because they knew he was
the Christ.[a]
42 At daybreak Jesus went out to a solitary
place. The people were looking for him and
when they came to where he was, they tried
to keep him from leaving them. 43 But he said,
"I must preach the good news of the kingdom
of God to the other towns also, because that is
why I was sent." 44 And he kept on preaching in
the synagogues of Judea.[b]

The Calling of the First Disciples

5 One day as Jesus was standing by the Lake
of Gennesaret,[c] with the people crowding
around him and listening to the word of God,
2 he saw at the water's edge two boats, left there
by the fishermen, who were washing their nets.
3 He got into one of the boats, the one belonging to Simon, and asked him to put out a little
from shore. Then he sat down and taught the
people from the boat.
4 When he had finished speaking, he said to
Simon, "Put out into deep water, and let down[d]
the nets for a catch."
5 Simon answered, "Master, we've worked
hard all night and haven't caught anything. But
because you say so, I will let down the nets."
6 When they had done so, they caught such
a large number of fish that their nets began to
break. 7 So they signaled their partners in the
other boat to come and help them, and they
came and filled both boats so full that they began to sink.
8 When Simon Peter saw this, he fell at Jesus'
knees and said, "Go away from me, Lord; I am
a sinful man!" 9 For he and all his companions
were astonished at the catch of fish they had
taken, 10 and so were James and John, the sons
of Zebedee, Simon's partners.
Then Jesus said to Simon, "Don't be afraid;
from now on you will catch men." 11 So they
pulled their boats up on shore, left everything
and followed him.

The Man With Leprosy

12 While Jesus was in one of the towns, a man
came along who was covered with leprosy.[e]
When he saw Jesus, he fell with his face to the
ground and begged him, "Lord, if you are willing, you can make me clean."
13 Jesus reached out his hand and touched
the man. "I am willing," he said. "Be clean!"
And immediately the leprosy left him.
14 Then Jesus ordered him, "Don't tell anyone, but go, show yourself to the priest and
offer the sacrifices that Moses commanded for
your cleansing, as a testimony to them."
15 Yet the news about him spread all the more,
so that crowds of people came to hear him and
to be healed of their sicknesses. 16 But Jesus often withdrew to lonely places and prayed.

Jesus Heals a Paralytic

17 One day as he was teaching, Pharisees
and teachers of the law, who had come from
every village of Galilee and from Judea and Jerusalem, were sitting there. And the power of
the Lord was present for him to heal the sick.
18 Some men came carrying a paralytic on a
mat and tried to take him into the house to lay
him before Jesus. 19 When they could not find a
way to do this because of the crowd, they went
up on the roof and lowered him on his mat
through the tiles into the middle of the crowd,
right in front of Jesus.
20 When Jesus saw their faith, he said,
"Friend, your sins are forgiven."
21 The Pharisees and the teachers of the law
began thinking to themselves, "Who is this fellow who speaks blasphemy? Who can forgive
sins but God alone?"
22 Jesus knew what they were thinking and
asked, "Why are you thinking these things in
your hearts? 23 Which is easier: to say, 'Your sins
are forgiven,' or to say, 'Get up and walk'? 24 But
that you may know that the Son of Man has
authority on earth to forgive sins..." He said to
the paralyzed man, "I tell you, get up, take your
mat and go home." 25 Immediately he stood up

[a]41 Or *Messiah* [b]44 Or *the land of the Jews*; some manuscripts *Galilee* [c]1 That is, Sea of Galilee [d]4 The Greek verb is plural.
[e]12 The Greek word was used for various diseases affecting the skin—not necessarily leprosy.

in front of them, took what he had been lying on and went home praising God. 26 Everyone was amazed and gave praise to God. They were filled with awe and said, "We have seen remarkable things today."

The Calling of Levi

27 After this, Jesus went out and saw a tax collector by the name of Levi sitting at his tax booth. "Follow me," Jesus said to him, 28 and Levi got up, left everything and followed him.

29 Then Levi held a great banquet for Jesus at his house, and a large crowd of tax collectors and others were eating with them. 30 But the Pharisees and the teachers of the law who belonged to their sect complained to his disciples, "Why do you eat and drink with tax collectors and 'sinners'?"

31 Jesus answered them, "It is not the healthy who need a doctor, but the sick. 32 I have not come to call the righteous, but sinners to repentance."

Jesus Questioned About Fasting

33 They said to him, "John's disciples often fast and pray, and so do the disciples of the Pharisees, but yours go on eating and drinking."

34 Jesus answered, "Can you make the guests of the bridegroom fast while he is with them? 35 But the time will come when the bridegroom will be taken from them; in those days they will fast."

36 He told them this parable: "No one tears a patch from a new garment and sews it on an old one. If he does, he will have torn the new garment, and the patch from the new will not match the old. 37 And no one pours new wine into old wineskins. If he does, the new wine will burst the skins, the wine will run out and the wineskins will be ruined. 38 No, new wine must be poured into new wineskins. 39 And no one after drinking old wine wants the new, for he says, 'The old is better.' "

Lord of the Sabbath

6 One Sabbath Jesus was going through the grainfields, and his disciples began to pick some heads of grain, rub them in their hands and eat the kernels. 2 Some of the Pharisees asked, "Why are you doing what is unlawful on the Sabbath?"

3 Jesus answered them, "Have you never read what David did when he and his companions were hungry? 4 He entered the house of God, and taking the consecrated bread, he ate what is lawful only for priests to eat. And he also gave some to his companions." 5 Then Jesus said to them, "The Son of Man is Lord of the Sabbath."

6 On another Sabbath he went into the synagogue and was teaching, and a man was there whose right hand was shriveled. 7 The Pharisees and the teachers of the law were looking for a reason to accuse Jesus, so they watched him closely to see if he would heal on the Sabbath. 8 But Jesus knew what they were thinking and said to the man with the shriveled hand, "Get up and stand in front of everyone." So he got up and stood there.

9 Then Jesus said to them, "I ask you, which is lawful on the Sabbath: to do good or to do evil, to save life or to destroy it?"

10 He looked around at them all, and then said to the man, "Stretch out your hand." He did so, and his hand was completely restored. 11 But they were furious and began to discuss with one another what they might do to Jesus.

The Twelve Apostles

12 One of those days Jesus went out to a mountainside to pray, and spent the night praying to God. 13 When morning came, he called his disciples to him and chose twelve of them, whom he also designated apostles: 14 Simon (whom he named Peter), his brother Andrew, James, John, Philip, Bartholomew, 15 Matthew, Thomas, James son of Alphaeus, Simon who was called the Zealot, 16 Judas son of James, and Judas Iscariot, who became a traitor.

Blessings and Woes

17 He went down with them and stood on a level place. A large crowd of his disciples was there and a great number of people from all over Judea, from Jerusalem, and from the coast of Tyre and Sidon, 18 who had come to hear him and to be healed of their diseases. Those troubled by evil[a] spirits were cured, 19 and the people all tried to touch him, because power was coming from him and healing them all.

20 Looking at his disciples, he said:

[a] 18 Greek *unclean*

"Blessed are you who are poor,
for yours is the kingdom of God.
21 Blessed are you who hunger now,
for you will be satisfied.
Blessed are you who weep now,
for you will laugh.
22 Blessed are you when men hate you,
when they exclude you and insult you
and reject your name as evil,
because of the Son of Man.

23 "Rejoice in that day and
leap for joy, because great is
your reward in heaven. For
that is how their fathers treated
the prophets.

24 "But woe to you who are rich,
for you have already received your comfort.
25 Woe to you who are well fed now,
for you will go hungry.
Woe to you who laugh now,
for you will mourn and weep.
26 Woe to you when all men speak well of you,
for that is how their fathers treated the false prophets.

Love for Enemies

27 "But I tell you who hear me: Love your enemies, do good to those who hate you, 28 bless
those who curse you, pray for those who mistreat you. 29 If someone strikes you on one
cheek, turn to him the other also. If someone
takes your cloak, do not stop him from taking
your tunic. 30 Give to everyone who asks you,
and if anyone takes what belongs to you, do not
demand it back. 31 Do to others as you would
have them do to you.
32 "If you love those who love you, what
credit is that to you? Even 'sinners' love those
who love them. 33 And if you do good to those
who are good to you, what credit is that to you?
Even 'sinners' do that. 34 And if you lend to
those from whom you expect repayment, what
credit is that to you? Even 'sinners' lend to 'sinners,' expecting to be repaid in full. 35 But love
your enemies, do good to them, and lend to
them without expecting to get
anything back. Then your reward will be great, and you will
be sons of the Most High, because he is kind to the ungrateful and wicked. 36 Be merciful,
just as your Father is merciful.

Luke 6:35

God Shows Kindness

"But love your enemies, do good to them, and lend to them without expecting to get anything back. Then your reward will be great, and you will be sons of the Most High, because he is kind to the ungrateful and wicked."

Judging Others

37 "Do not judge, and you
will not be judged. Do not condemn, and you will not be condemned. Forgive, and you will
be forgiven. 38 Give, and it will
be given to you. A good measure, pressed down, shaken
together and running over,
will be poured into your lap.
For with the measure you use,
it will be measured to you."
39 He also told them this par-
able: "Can a blind man lead a blind man? Will
they not both fall into a pit? 40 A student is not
above his teacher, but everyone who is fully
trained will be like his teacher.
41 "Why do you look at the speck of sawdust
in your brother's eye and pay no attention to
the plank in your own eye? 42 How can you say
to your brother, 'Brother, let me take the speck
out of your eye,' when you yourself fail to see
the plank in your own eye? You hypocrite, first
take the plank out of your eye, and then you
will see clearly to remove the speck from your
brother's eye.

A Tree and Its Fruit

43 "No good tree bears bad fruit, nor does
a bad tree bear good fruit. 44 Each tree is recognized by its own fruit. People do not pick
figs from thornbushes, or grapes from briers.
45 The good man brings good things out of the
good stored up in his heart, and the evil man
brings evil things out of the evil stored up in
his heart. For out of the overflow of his heart
his mouth speaks.

The Wise and Foolish Builders

46 "Why do you call me, 'Lord, Lord,' and do
not do what I say? 47 I will show you what he

Rock Solid

Read: Luke 6:27–49

Luke 6:47–48

I will show you what he is like who comes to me and hears my words and puts them into practice. He is like a man building a house, who dug down deep and laid the foundation on rock. When a flood came, the torrent struck that house but could not shake it, because it was well built.

THE FUTURISTIC SPACE NEEDLE SPIKES from the Seattle skyline. Stretching approximately 605 feet into the sky, its spire pierces the clouds that often veil the earthquake-prone city. Although its height can seem frightening, especially when the Needle sways, it is actually safer than many tall buildings. The architects who designed the stunning structure kept one principle firmly in mind: the larger and higher the building, the stronger the base needs to be.

The Space Needle's foundation is 30 feet deep, weighs 5,850 tons and contains 250 tons of reinforcing steel. The foundation is as heavy as the Needle, enabling the airy structure to withstand a wind velocity of 200 miles per hour. In 2001 it withstood an earthquake of 6.8 on the Richter scale. It is estimated that it can endure even greater shocks because the architects doubled the 1962 building code requirements.

Jesus, the master builder of strong, resilient women, likens our spiritual foundation to a building with a strong, immovable base. In his analogy, he tells of a wise builder who "laid the foundation on rock" (verse 48). We know that sooner or later, floods *will* come in one form or another: illness, financial problems, a relationship breakdown, societal calamities, terrorism or natural disasters. If we don't take Jesus' words to heart and put them into practice, we are on shaky ground. But if we build our spiritual lives on what he says, we can withstand anything that shakes us.

And what strong words had Jesus given his followers? Love your enemies and be good to them (see verses 27–36). Exchange kindness for anger, silence for gossip, a sweet spirit for bitterness. Don't judge others but accept them as God has accepted you. Forgive, because you have been forgiven (see verse 37). Be generous, and generosity will come back to you when you most need it (see verse 38). Be more concerned with your own purity than about the purity of others (see verses 41–42). Care about the goodness of your heart because your words will reveal, no matter how good an actress you are, what's really inside (see verses 44–45). The rock solid foundation isn't an abstract notion. The "rocks," ironically, are a soft heart and a gentle spirit. And those can only come from the Rock of Ages, Jesus Christ.

reflection

1. What storm is threatening to sway you?
2. How deep is your foundation in Jesus? How much deeper would you like it to go?
3. What will you do to develop a deeper and stronger foundation?

RELATED READINGS

1 Corinthians 3:10–16; 1 Peter 2:4–12; Jude 20–21

Wednesday

Go to page 1250 for your next devotional reading.

is like who comes to me and hears my words
and puts them into practice. 48 He is like a man
building a house, who dug down deep and laid
the foundation on rock. When a flood came,
the torrent struck that house but could not
shake it, because it was well built. 49 But the one
who hears my words and does not put them
into practice is like a man who built a house on
the ground without a foundation. The moment
the torrent struck that house, it collapsed and
its destruction was complete."

The Faith of the Centurion

7 When Jesus had finished saying all this
in the hearing of the people, he entered
Capernaum. 2 There a centurion's servant,
whom his master valued highly, was sick and
about to die. 3 The centurion heard of Jesus and
sent some elders of the Jews to him, asking him
to come and heal his servant. 4 When they came
to Jesus, they pleaded earnestly with him, "This
man deserves to have you do this, 5 because he
loves our nation and has built our synagogue."
6 So Jesus went with them.

He was not far from the house when the
centurion sent friends to say to him: "Lord,
don't trouble yourself, for I do not deserve to
have you come under my roof. 7 That is why I
did not even consider myself worthy to come
to you. But say the word, and my servant will
be healed. 8 For I myself am a man under
authority, with soldiers under me. I tell this
one, 'Go,' and he goes; and that one, 'Come,'
and he comes. I say to my servant, 'Do this,'
and he does it."

9 When Jesus heard this, he was amazed at
him, and turning to the crowd following him,
he said, "I tell you, I have not found such great
faith even in Israel." 10 Then the men who had
been sent returned to the house and found the
servant well.

Jesus Raises a Widow's Son

11 Soon afterward, Jesus went to a town called
Nain, and his disciples and a large crowd went
along with him. 12 As he approached the town
gate, a dead person was being carried out—the
only son of his mother, and she was a widow.
And a large crowd from the town was with her.
13 When the Lord saw her, his heart went out to
her and he said, "Don't cry."

14 Then he went up and touched the coffin, and those carrying it stood still. He said,
"Young man, I say to you, get up!" 15 The dead
man sat up and began to talk, and Jesus gave
him back to his mother.

16 They were all filled with awe and praised
God. "A great prophet has appeared among us,"
they said. "God has come to help his people."
17 This news about Jesus spread throughout
Judea[a] and the surrounding country.

Jesus and John the Baptist

18 John's disciples told him about all these
things. Calling two of them, 19 he sent them to
the Lord to ask, "Are you the one who was to
come, or should we expect someone else?"

20 When the men came to Jesus, they said,
"John the Baptist sent us to you to ask, 'Are you
the one who was to come, or should we expect
someone else?'"

21 At that very time Jesus cured many who
had diseases, sicknesses and evil spirits, and
gave sight to many who were blind. 22 So he replied to the messengers, "Go back and report to
John what you have seen and heard: The blind
receive sight, the lame walk, those who have
leprosy[b] are cured, the deaf hear, the dead are
raised, and the good news is preached to the
poor. 23 Blessed is the man who does not fall
away on account of me."

24 After John's messengers left, Jesus began to
speak to the crowd about John: "What did you
go out into the desert to see? A reed swayed
by the wind? 25 If not, what did you go out to
see? A man dressed in fine clothes? No, those
who wear expensive clothes and indulge in
luxury are in palaces. 26 But what did you go
out to see? A prophet? Yes, I tell you, and more
than a prophet. 27 This is the one about whom
it is written:

> "'I will send my messenger ahead of you,
> who will prepare your way before you.'[c]

28 I tell you, among those born of women there
is no one greater than John; yet the one who is
least in the kingdom of God is greater than he."

29 (All the people, even the tax collectors,

[a] 17 Or *the land of the Jews* [b] 22 The Greek word was used for various diseases affecting the skin—not necessarily leprosy.
[c] 27 Mal. 3:1

when they heard Jesus' words, acknowledged
that God's way was right, because they had
been baptized by John. 30But the Pharisees
and experts in the law rejected God's purpose
for themselves, because they had not been baptized by John.)

31"To what, then, can I compare the people
of this generation? What are they like? 32They
are like children sitting in the marketplace and
calling out to each other:

"'We played the flute for you,
and you did not dance;
we sang a dirge,
and you did not cry.'

33For John the Baptist came neither eating
bread nor drinking wine, and you say, 'He has
a demon.' 34The Son of Man came eating and
drinking, and you say, 'Here is a glutton and
a drunkard, a friend of tax collectors and "sinners."' 35But wisdom is proved right by all her
children."

Jesus Anointed by a Sinful Woman

36Now one of the Pharisees invited Jesus to
have dinner with him, so he went to the Pharisee's house and reclined at the table. 37When a
woman who had lived a sinful life in that town
learned that Jesus was eating at the Pharisee's
house, she brought an alabaster jar of perfume,
38and as she stood behind him at his feet weeping, she began to wet his feet with her tears.
Then she wiped them with her hair, kissed
them and poured perfume on them.

39When the Pharisee who had invited him
saw this, he said to himself, "If this man were a
prophet, he would know who is touching him
and what kind of woman she is—that she is a
sinner."

40Jesus answered him, "Simon, I have something to tell you."

"Tell me, teacher," he said.

41"Two men owed money to a certain moneylender. One owed him five hundred denarii,[a]
and the other fifty. 42Neither of them had the
money to pay him back, so he canceled the
debts of both. Now which of them will love
him more?"

43Simon replied, "I suppose the one who
had the bigger debt canceled."

"You have judged correctly," Jesus said.

44Then he turned toward the woman and
said to Simon, "Do you see this woman? I came
into your house. You did not give me any water for my feet, but she wet my feet with her
tears and wiped them with her hair. 45You did
not give me a kiss, but this woman, from the
time I entered, has not stopped kissing my feet.
46You did not put oil on my head, but she has
poured perfume on my feet. 47Therefore, I tell
you, her many sins have been forgiven—for she
loved much. But he who has been forgiven little
loves little."

48Then Jesus said to her, "Your sins are forgiven."

49The other guests began to say among themselves, "Who is this who even forgives sins?"

50Jesus said to the woman, "Your faith has
saved you; go in peace."

The Parable of the Sower

8 After this, Jesus traveled about from one
town and village to another, proclaiming
the good news of the kingdom of God. The
Twelve were with him, 2and also some women
who had been cured of evil spirits and diseases:
Mary (called Magdalene) from whom seven demons had come out; 3Joanna the wife of Cuza,
the manager of Herod's household; Susanna;
and many others. These women were helping
to support them out of their own means.

4While a large crowd was gathering and people were coming to Jesus from town after town,
he told this parable: 5"A farmer went out to sow
his seed. As he was scattering the seed, some
fell along the path; it was trampled on, and the
birds of the air ate it up. 6Some fell on rock, and
when it came up, the plants withered because
they had no moisture. 7Other seed fell among
thorns, which grew up with it and choked the
plants. 8Still other seed fell on good soil. It
came up and yielded a crop, a hundred times
more than was sown."

When he said this, he called out, "He who
has ears to hear, let him hear."

9His disciples asked him what this parable
meant. 10He said, "The knowledge of the secrets of the kingdom of God has been given to
you, but to others I speak in parables, so that,

[a]41 A denarius was a coin worth about a day's wages.

“ ‘though seeing, they may not see;
though hearing, they may not
understand.’[a]

11“This is the meaning of the parable: The
seed is the word of God. 12Those along the
path are the ones who hear, and then the devil
comes and takes away the word from their
hearts, so that they may not believe and be
saved. 13Those on the rock are the ones who
receive the word with joy when they hear it,
but they have no root. They believe for a while,
but in the time of testing they fall away. 14The
seed that fell among thorns stands for those
who hear, but as they go on their way they are
choked by life’s worries, riches and pleasures,
and they do not mature. 15But the seed on
good soil stands for those with a noble and
good heart, who hear the word, retain it, and
by persevering produce a crop.

A Lamp on a Stand

16“No one lights a lamp and hides it in a jar
or puts it under a bed. Instead, he puts it on a
stand, so that those who come in can see the
light. 17For there is nothing hidden that will
not be disclosed, and nothing concealed that
will not be known or brought out into the open.
18Therefore consider carefully how you listen.
Whoever has will be given more; whoever does
not have, even what he thinks he has will be
taken from him.”

Jesus’ Mother and Brothers

19Now Jesus’ mother and brothers came to
see him, but they were not able to get near him
because of the crowd. 20Someone told him,
“Your mother and brothers are standing outside, wanting to see you.”

21He replied, “My mother and brothers are
those who hear God’s word and put it into practice.”

Jesus Calms the Storm

22One day Jesus said to his disciples, “Let’s
go over to the other side of the lake.” So they
got into a boat and set out. 23As they sailed,
he fell asleep. A squall came down on the lake,
so that the boat was being swamped, and they
were in great danger.

24The disciples went and woke him, saying,
“Master, Master, we’re going to drown!”

He got up and rebuked the wind and the
raging waters; the storm subsided, and all was
calm. 25“Where is your faith?” he asked his disciples.

In fear and amazement they asked one
another, “Who is this? He commands even the
winds and the water, and they obey him.”

The Healing of a Demon-possessed Man

26They sailed to the region of the Gerasenes,[b] which is across the lake from Galilee.
27When Jesus stepped ashore, he was met by
a demon-possessed man from the town. For
a long time this man had not worn clothes or
lived in a house, but had lived in the tombs.
28When he saw Jesus, he cried out and fell at
his feet, shouting at the top of his voice, “What
do you want with me, Jesus, Son of the Most
High God? I beg you, don’t torture me!” 29For
Jesus had commanded the evil[c] spirit to come
out of the man. Many times it had seized him,
and though he was chained hand and foot and
kept under guard, he had broken his chains
and had been driven by the demon into solitary places.

30Jesus asked him, “What is your name?”

“Legion,” he replied, because many demons
had gone into him. 31And they begged him
repeatedly not to order them to go into the
Abyss.

32A large herd of pigs was feeding there
on the hillside. The demons begged Jesus to
let them go into them, and he gave them permission. 33When the demons came out of the
man, they went into the pigs, and the herd
rushed down the steep bank into the lake and
was drowned.

34When those tending the pigs saw what
had happened, they ran off and reported this
in the town and countryside, 35and the people
went out to see what had happened. When they
came to Jesus, they found the man from whom
the demons had gone out, sitting at Jesus’ feet,
dressed and in his right mind; and they were
afraid. 36Those who had seen it told the people how the demon-possessed man had been
cured. 37Then all the people of the region of the

[a] **10** Isaiah 6:9 [b] **26** Some manuscripts *Gadarenes*; other manuscripts *Gergesenes*; also in verse 37 [c] **29** Greek *unclean*

Travels With the Messiah

Read: Luke 8:22–39

Luke 8:25

"Where is your faith?" [Jesus] asked his disciples. In fear and amazement they asked one another, "Who is this? He commands even the winds and the water, and they obey him."

AS THE DISCIPLES TRAVELED with Jesus, there were a few surprises along the way. First Jesus had turned water into wine at a wedding. That was an "inside" secret because the guests never knew what had happened. But the disciples knew that Jesus' mother had urged him to do it. Then he started healing people. Those healings were startling, clearly miraculous. This man who'd called them to be his disciples didn't just heal people hidden away for years in back bedrooms, unknown even to their neighbors. He healed beggars known to the whole town, relatives of prominent officials, men and women with obvious, disfiguring handicaps.

Still, the disciples needed to see a miracle that hit them closer to home; they had to get to the point of really *personal* need before they could understand the Master's true identity. It took a storm at sea, and the disciples' own terror and helplessness, before they really sat up and took notice that Jesus was not just a good man but—could it be?—God *become* man. When their friend and master stilled the angry sea with a single word, they were amazed . . . and afraid. Suddenly, it wasn't the waves that were so intimidating, but the man in the boat with them who commanded the waves.

As they continued their travels with Jesus, they would need to know that he was more than a man . . . that he was the Christ. They would need this awareness as they stepped ashore after their traumatic boat trip. They would need to remember again and again that the teacher who was so precious to them could command the wind and waves. Because when they reached the shore, there were no banners saying "Welcome, Jesus and Friends." No, their welcoming committee was a screaming, naked man who lived among the tombs. The demons within this poor man knew who Jesus was and feared him. Perhaps now, after experiencing his power to save them and calm the elements, the disciples feared the demons less because they had grown to trust Jesus more personally than ever before.

reflection

1 As you've traveled with Jesus, what has most intrigued you about him?

2 Which of Jesus' miracles would you most like to have observed and why?

3 What life experiences have helped you to trust Jesus more and fear the world around you less?

RELATED READINGS

Matthew 16:13–17; John 2:1–11

Go to page 1255 for your next devotional reading.

Gerasenes asked Jesus to leave them, because
they were overcome with fear. So he got into
the boat and left.
38The man from whom the demons had
gone out begged to go with him, but Jesus sent
him away, saying, 39"Return home and tell how
much God has done for you." So the man went
away and told all over town how much Jesus
had done for him.

A Dead Girl and a Sick Woman

40Now when Jesus returned, a crowd welcomed him, for they were all expecting him.
41Then a man named Jairus, a ruler of the synagogue, came and fell at Jesus' feet, pleading with
him to come to his house 42because his only
daughter, a girl of about twelve, was dying.
As Jesus was on his way, the crowds almost
crushed him. 43And a woman was there who
had been subject to bleeding for twelve years,[a]
but no one could heal her. 44She came up behind him and touched the edge of his cloak,
and immediately her bleeding stopped.
45"Who touched me?" Jesus asked.
When they all denied it, Peter said, "Master, the people are crowding and pressing
against you."
46But Jesus said, "Someone touched me; I
know that power has gone out from me."
47Then the woman, seeing that she could
not go unnoticed, came trembling and fell at
his feet. In the presence of all the people, she
told why she had touched him and how she
had been instantly healed. 48Then he said to
her, "Daughter, your faith has healed you. Go
in peace."
49While Jesus was still speaking, someone
came from the house of Jairus, the synagogue
ruler. "Your daughter is dead," he said. "Don't
bother the teacher any more."
50Hearing this, Jesus said to Jairus, "Don't be
afraid; just believe, and she will be healed."
51When he arrived at the house of Jairus,
he did not let anyone go in with him except Peter, John and James, and the child's father and
mother. 52Meanwhile, all the people were wailing and mourning for her. "Stop wailing," Jesus
said. "She is not dead but asleep."
53They laughed at him, knowing that she
was dead. 54But he took her by the hand and
said, "My child, get up!" 55Her spirit returned,
and at once she stood up. Then Jesus told them
to give her something to eat. 56Her parents
were astonished, but he ordered them not to
tell anyone what had happened.

Jesus Sends Out the Twelve

9 When Jesus had called the Twelve together,
he gave them power and authority to drive
out all demons and to cure diseases, 2and he
sent them out to preach the kingdom of God
and to heal the sick. 3He told them: "Take nothing for the journey—no staff, no bag, no bread,
no money, no extra tunic. 4Whatever house
you enter, stay there until you leave that town.
5If people do not welcome you, shake the dust
off your feet when you leave their town, as a
testimony against them." 6So they set out and
went from village to village, preaching the gospel and healing people everywhere.
7Now Herod the tetrarch heard about all
that was going on. And he was perplexed, because some were saying that John had been
raised from the dead, 8others that Elijah had appeared, and still others that one of the prophets
of long ago had come back to life. 9But Herod
said, "I beheaded John. Who, then, is this I hear
such things about?" And he tried to see him.

Jesus Feeds the Five Thousand

10When the apostles returned, they reported
to Jesus what they had done. Then he took
them with him and they withdrew by themselves to a town called Bethsaida, 11but the
crowds learned about it and followed him.
He welcomed them and spoke to them about
the kingdom of God, and healed those who
needed healing.
12Late in the afternoon the Twelve came to
him and said, "Send the crowd away so they
can go to the surrounding villages and countryside and find food and lodging, because we are
in a remote place here."
13He replied, "You give them something to
eat."
They answered, "We have only five loaves of
bread and two fish—unless we go and buy food
for all this crowd." 14(About five thousand men
were there.)

[a]43 Many manuscripts *years, and she had spent all she had on doctors*

But he said to his disciples, "Have them sit
down in groups of about fifty each." 15The disciples did so, and everybody sat down. 16Tak-
ing the five loaves and the two fish and looking
up to heaven, he gave thanks and broke them.
Then he gave them to the disciples to set before
the people. 17They all ate and were satisfied,
and the disciples picked up twelve basketfuls
of broken pieces that were left over.

Peter's Confession of Christ

18Once when Jesus was praying in private
and his disciples were with him, he asked them,
"Who do the crowds say I am?"

19They replied, "Some say John the Baptist;
others say Elijah; and still others, that one of the
prophets of long ago has come back to life."

20"But what about you?" he asked. "Who do
you say I am?"

Peter answered, "The Christ[a] of God."

21Jesus strictly warned them not to tell this
to anyone. 22And he said, "The Son of Man
must suffer many things and be rejected by the
elders, chief priests and teachers of the law, and
he must be killed and on the third day be raised
to life."

23Then he said to them all: "If anyone would
come after me, he must deny himself and take
up his cross daily and follow me. 24For whoever
wants to save his life will lose it, but whoever
loses his life for me will save it. 25What good
is it for a man to gain the whole world, and
yet lose or forfeit his very self? 26If anyone is
ashamed of me and my words, the Son of Man
will be ashamed of him when he comes in his
glory and in the glory of the Father and of the
holy angels. 27I tell you the truth, some who are
standing here will not taste death before they
see the kingdom of God."

The Transfiguration

28About eight days after Jesus said this,
he took Peter, John and James with him and
went up onto a mountain to pray. 29As he was
praying, the appearance of his face changed,
and his clothes became as bright as a flash of
lightning. 30Two men, Moses and Elijah, 31ap-
peared in glorious splendor, talking with Jesus.
They spoke about his departure, which he was
about to bring to fulfillment at Jerusalem. 32Pe-
ter and his companions were very sleepy, but
when they became fully awake, they saw his
glory and the two men standing with him. 33As
the men were leaving Jesus, Peter said to him,
"Master, it is good for us to be here. Let us put
up three shelters—one for you, one for Moses
and one for Elijah." (He did not know what he
was saying.)

34While he was speaking, a cloud appeared
and enveloped them, and they were afraid as
they entered the cloud. 35A voice came from
the cloud, saying, "This is my Son, whom I
have chosen; listen to him." 36When the voice
had spoken, they found that Jesus was alone.
The disciples kept this to themselves, and told
no one at that time what they had seen.

The Healing of a Boy With an Evil Spirit

37The next day, when they came down from
the mountain, a large crowd met him. 38A man
in the crowd called out, "Teacher, I beg you to
look at my son, for he is my only child. 39A
spirit seizes him and he suddenly screams; it
throws him into convulsions so that he foams
at the mouth. It scarcely ever leaves him and
is destroying him. 40I begged your disciples to
drive it out, but they could not."

41"O unbelieving and perverse generation,"
Jesus replied, "how long shall I stay with you
and put up with you? Bring your son here."

42Even while the boy was coming, the demon threw him to the ground in a convulsion.
But Jesus rebuked the evil[b] spirit, healed the
boy and gave him back to his father. 43And
they were all amazed at the greatness of God.

While everyone was marveling at all that
Jesus did, he said to his disciples, 44"Listen
carefully to what I am about to tell you: The
Son of Man is going to be betrayed into the
hands of men." 45But they did not understand
what this meant. It was hidden from them, so
that they did not grasp it, and they were afraid
to ask him about it.

Who Will Be the Greatest?

46An argument started among the disciples
as to which of them would be the greatest. 47Je-
sus, knowing their thoughts, took a little child
and had him stand beside him. 48Then he said
to them, "Whoever welcomes this little child

[a]20 Or *Messiah* [b]42 Greek *unclean*

in my name welcomes me; and whoever welcomes me welcomes the one who sent me. For
he who is least among you all—he is the greatest.”
49 “Master,” said John, “we saw a man driving
out demons in your name and we tried to stop
him, because he is not one of us.”
50 “Do not stop him,” Jesus said, “for whoever
is not against you is for you.”

Samaritan Opposition

51 As the time approached for him to be
taken up to heaven, Jesus resolutely set out for
Jerusalem. 52 And he sent messengers on ahead,
who went into a Samaritan village to get things
ready for him; 53 but the people there did not
welcome him, because he was heading for Jerusalem. 54 When the disciples James and John
saw this, they asked, “Lord, do you want us to
call fire down from heaven to destroy them[a]?”
55 But Jesus turned and rebuked them, 56 and[b]
they went to another village.

The Cost of Following Jesus

57 As they were walking along the road, a
man said to him, “I will follow you wherever
you go.”
58 Jesus replied, “Foxes have holes and birds
of the air have nests, but the Son of Man has no
place to lay his head.”
59 He said to another man, “Follow me.”
But the man replied, “Lord, first let me go
and bury my father.”
60 Jesus said to him, “Let the dead bury their
own dead, but you go and proclaim the kingdom of God.”
61 Still another said, “I will follow you, Lord;
but first let me go back and say good-by to my
family.”
62 Jesus replied, “No one who puts his hand
to the plow and looks back is fit for service in
the kingdom of God.”

Jesus Sends Out the Seventy-two

10 After this the Lord appointed seventy-
two[c] others and sent them two by two
ahead of him to every town and place where he
was about to go. 2 He told them, “The harvest is
plentiful, but the workers are few. Ask the Lord
of the harvest, therefore, to send out workers
into his harvest field. 3 Go! I am sending you
out like lambs among wolves. 4 Do not take a
purse or bag or sandals; and do not greet anyone on the road.
5 “When you enter a house, first say, ‘Peace
to this house.’ 6 If a man of peace is there, your
peace will rest on him; if not, it will return to
you. 7 Stay in that house, eating and drinking
whatever they give you, for the worker deserves his wages. Do not move around from
house to house.
8 “When you enter a town and are welcomed,
eat what is set before you. 9 Heal the sick who
are there and tell them, ‘The kingdom of God
is near you.’ 10 But when you enter a town and
are not welcomed, go into its streets and say,
11 ‘Even the dust of your town that sticks to our
feet we wipe off against you. Yet be sure of this:
The kingdom of God is near.’ 12 I tell you, it will
be more bearable on that day for Sodom than
for that town.
13 “Woe to you, Korazin! Woe to you, Bethsaida! For if the miracles that were performed
in you had been performed in Tyre and Sidon,
they would have repented long ago, sitting in
sackcloth and ashes. 14 But it will be more bearable for Tyre and Sidon at the judgment than
for you. 15 And you, Capernaum, will you be
lifted up to the skies? No, you will go down to
the depths.[d]
16 “He who listens to you listens to me; he
who rejects you rejects me; but he who rejects
me rejects him who sent me.”
17 The seventy-two returned with joy and
said, “Lord, even the demons submit to us in
your name.”
18 He replied, “I saw Satan fall like lightning
from heaven. 19 I have given you authority to
trample on snakes and scorpions and to overcome all the power of the enemy; nothing will
harm you. 20 However, do not rejoice that the
spirits submit to you, but rejoice that your
names are written in heaven.”
21 At that time Jesus, full of joy through the
Holy Spirit, said, “I praise you, Father, Lord of
heaven and earth, because you have hidden
these things from the wise and learned, and

[a] 54 Some manuscripts *them, even as Elijah did* [b] 55,56 Some manuscripts *them. And he said, “You do not know what kind of spirit you are of, for the Son of Man did not come to destroy men’s lives, but to save them.” 56 And* [c] 1 Some manuscripts *seventy*; also in verse 17
[d] 15 Greek *Hades*

revealed them to little children. Yes, Father, for
this was your good pleasure.
[22]“All things have been committed to me
by my Father. No one knows who the Son is
except the Father, and no one knows who the
Father is except the Son and those to whom the
Son chooses to reveal him.”
[23]Then he turned to his disciples and said
privately, “Blessed are the eyes that see what
you see. [24]For I tell you that many prophets
and kings wanted to see what you see but did
not see it, and to hear what you hear but did
not hear it.”

The Parable of the Good Samaritan

[25]On one occasion an expert in the law
stood up to test Jesus. “Teacher,” he asked,
“what must I do to inherit eternal life?”
[26]“What is written in the Law?” he replied.
“How do you read it?”
[27]He answered: “ ‘Love the Lord your God
with all your heart and with all your soul and
with all your strength and with all your mind’[a];
and, ‘Love your neighbor as yourself.’[b]”
[28]“You have answered correctly,” Jesus replied. “Do this and you will live.”
[29]But he wanted to justify himself, so he
asked Jesus, “And who is my neighbor?”
[30]In reply Jesus said: “A man was going
down from Jerusalem to Jericho, when he fell
into the hands of robbers. They stripped him
of his clothes, beat him and went away, leaving
him half dead. [31]A priest happened to be going down the same road, and when he saw the
man, he passed by on the other side. [32]So too, a
Levite, when he came to the place and saw him,
passed by on the other side. [33]But a Samaritan,
as he traveled, came where the man was; and
when he saw him, he took pity on him. [34]He
went to him and bandaged his wounds, pouring on oil and wine. Then he put the man on
his own donkey, took him to an inn and took
care of him. [35]The next day he took out two
silver coins[c] and gave them to the innkeeper.
‘Look after him,’ he said, ‘and when I return, I
will reimburse you for any extra expense you
may have.’
[36]“Which of these three do you think was
a neighbor to the man who fell into the hands
of robbers?”
[37]The expert in the law replied, “The one
who had mercy on him.”
Jesus told him, “Go and do likewise.”

At the Home of Martha and Mary

[38]As Jesus and his disciples were on their
way, he came to a village where a woman
named Martha opened her home to him. [39]She
had a sister called Mary, who sat at the Lord’s
feet listening to what he said. [40]But Martha was
distracted by all the preparations that had to be
made. She came to him and asked, “Lord, don’t
you care that my sister has left me to do the
work by myself? Tell her to help me!”
[41]“Martha, Martha,” the Lord answered,
“you are worried and upset about many things,
[42]but only one thing is needed.[d] Mary has chosen what is better, and it will not be taken away
from her.”

Jesus’ Teaching on Prayer

11 One day Jesus was praying in a certain
place. When he finished, one of his disciples said to him, “Lord, teach us to pray, just
as John taught his disciples.”
[2]He said to them, “When you pray, say:

“ ‘Father,[e]
hallowed be your name,
your kingdom come.[f]
[3]Give us each day our daily bread.
[4]Forgive us our sins,
for we also forgive everyone who sins
against us.[g]
And lead us not into temptation.[h]’ ”

[5]Then he said to them, “Suppose one of
you has a friend, and he goes to him at midnight and says, ‘Friend, lend me three loaves of
bread, [6]because a friend of mine on a journey
has come to me, and I have nothing to set before him.’
[7]“Then the one inside answers, ‘Don’t
bother me. The door is already locked, and my
children are with me in bed. I can’t get up and
give you anything.’ [8]I tell you, though he will
not get up and give him the bread because he

[a]27 Deut. 6:5 [b]27 Lev. 19:18 [c]35 Greek *two denarii* [d]42 Some manuscripts *but few things are needed—or only one* [e]2 Some manuscripts *Our Father in heaven* [f]2 Some manuscripts *come. May your will be done on earth as it is in heaven.* [g]4 Greek *everyone who is indebted to us* [h]4 Some manuscripts *temptation but deliver us from the evil one*

Too Busy

Read: Luke 10:38–42

WE FACE THE SAME CHOICE that confronted Martha. We can dismiss the implications of Jesus' words for us, especially when our time is limited and we are juggling so many other demands. Or we can face our need and begin working to know God better. Whatever we decide, we must not forget who puts this challenge before us and the depth of his concern. The real choice is not whether we will become thinkers or doers. We are called to be both. But we will be better at both if we heed Christ's call to dig deeply into the heart of God. This never means stepping out of life to devote ourselves to something abstract and useless; rather it means to plunge into the very essence of life. We were made for this, and it is only as we grow in our understanding of God that we will satisfy the deepest longings of our hearts and find the meaning we ache for.

But even more, we need to know him. Mary and Martha learned the hard way, and we do too. If my own struggles have taught me anything, it is that my greatest need is to know God better, and I am not alone. To be blunt, life is simply too demanding and overwhelming at times to think I can manage without knowing the one who rules the winds and waves that batter my little vessel. We ask too much of ourselves to try to trust a stranger. Neglecting our need to know him better is, as Dr. Packer so wisely warns, "to sentence ourselves to stumble and blunder through life, blindfolded, as it were, with no sense of direction and no understanding of what surrounds you." We hurt ourselves if we shrug our shoulders and walk away.

It is time we started. There is much to do and more to learn.

Not even a lifetime will be enough to know God completely. But our smallest efforts will be richly rewarded, for "the time it takes to dig deep into the heart of God is often repaid by striking a vein of gold or an oil gusher. The effort is repaid with joy and power beyond all expectation."

—*Carolyn Custis James*

Luke 10:41–42

"Martha, Martha," the Lord answered, "you are worried and upset about many things, but only one thing is needed. Mary has chosen what is better, and it will not be taken away from her."

reflection

1 Do you consider yourself to be more like Mary or Martha?

2 How did this devotional help you to realize that you can be both a thinker and a doer?

3 What can you set aside right now in order to still your mind and hands long enough to listen for God's voice? Deliberately sit still for a few minutes and ask him to reveal himself to you in a new way.

RELATED READINGS

Psalm 46:10–11; Matthew 6:25–34; 11:28–30; Philippians 4:6–7

Go to page 1259 for your next devotional reading.

is his friend, yet because of the man's boldness[a]
he will get up and give him as
much as he needs.
9“So I say to you: Ask and it
will be given to you; seek and
you will find; knock and the
door will be opened to you.
10For everyone who asks receives; he who seeks finds; and
to him who knocks, the door
will be opened.
11“Which of you fathers, if
your son asks for[b] a fish, will
give him a snake instead? 12Or
if he asks for an egg, will give
him a scorpion? 13If you then,
though you are evil, know how
to give good gifts to your children, how much more will
your Father in heaven give the Holy Spirit to
those who ask him!”

> Luke 11:13
>
> *God Gives His Spirit*
>
> “If you then, though you are evil, know how to give good gifts to your children, how much more will your Father in heaven give the Holy Spirit to those who ask him!”

Jesus and Beelzebub

14Jesus was driving out a demon that was
mute. When the demon left, the man who had
been mute spoke, and the crowd was amazed.
15But some of them said, “By Beelzebub,[c] the
prince of demons, he is driving out demons.”
16Others tested him by asking for a sign from
heaven.
17Jesus knew their thoughts and said to
them: “Any kingdom divided against itself will
be ruined, and a house divided against itself
will fall. 18If Satan is divided against himself,
how can his kingdom stand? I say this because
you claim that I drive out demons by Beelzebub. 19Now if I drive out demons by Beelzebub, by whom do your followers drive them
out? So then, they will be your judges. 20But if
I drive out demons by the finger of God, then
the kingdom of God has come to you.
21“When a strong man, fully armed, guards
his own house, his possessions are safe. 22But
when someone stronger attacks and overpow-
ers him, he takes away the armor in which the
man trusted and divides up the spoils.
23“He who is not with me is against me, and
he who does not gather with me, scatters.
24“When an evil[d] spirit comes out of a man,
it goes through arid places seeking rest and
does not find it. Then it says,
‘I will return to the house I
left.’ 25When it arrives, it finds
the house swept clean and put
in order. 26Then it goes and
takes seven other spirits more
wicked than itself, and they go
in and live there. And the final
condition of that man is worse
than the first.”
27As Jesus was saying these
things, a woman in the crowd
called out, “Blessed is the mother who gave you birth and
nursed you.”
28He replied, “Blessed rather
are those who hear the word of
God and obey it.”

The Sign of Jonah

29As the crowds increased, Jesus said, “This
is a wicked generation. It asks for a miraculous
sign, but none will be given it except the sign
of Jonah. 30For as Jonah was a sign to the Ninevites, so also will the Son of Man be to this
generation. 31The Queen of the South will rise
at the judgment with the men of this generation and condemn them; for she came from
the ends of the earth to listen to Solomon's wisdom, and now one[e] greater than Solomon is
here. 32The men of Nineveh will stand up at the
judgment with this generation and condemn
it; for they repented at the preaching of Jonah,
and now one greater than Jonah is here.

The Lamp of the Body

33“No one lights a lamp and puts it in a place
where it will be hidden, or under a bowl. Instead he puts it on its stand, so that those who
come in may see the light. 34Your eye is the
lamp of your body. When your eyes are good,
your whole body also is full of light. But when
they are bad, your body also is full of darkness.
35See to it, then, that the light within you is not
darkness. 36Therefore, if your whole body is
full of light, and no part of it dark, it will be
completely lighted, as when the light of a lamp
shines on you.”

[a]8 Or *persistence* [b]11 Some manuscripts *for bread, will give him a stone; or if he asks for* [c]15 Greek *Beezeboul* or *Beelzeboul*; also in verses 18 and 19 [d]24 Greek *unclean* [e]31 Or *something*; also in verse 32

Six Woes

37When Jesus had finished speaking, a Pharisee invited him to eat with him; so he went
in and reclined at the table. 38But the Pharisee,
noticing that Jesus did not first wash before the
meal, was surprised.
39Then the Lord said to him, "Now then,
you Pharisees clean the outside of the cup and
dish, but inside you are full of greed and wickedness. 40You foolish people! Did not the one
who made the outside make the inside also?
41But give what is inside ⌊the dish⌋[a] to the poor,
and everything will be clean for you.
42"Woe to you Pharisees, because you give
God a tenth of your mint, rue and all other
kinds of garden herbs, but you neglect justice
and the love of God. You should have practiced
the latter without leaving the former undone.
43"Woe to you Pharisees, because you love
the most important seats in the synagogues
and greetings in the marketplaces.
44"Woe to you, because you are like unmarked graves, which men walk over without
knowing it."
45One of the experts in the law answered
him, "Teacher, when you say these things, you
insult us also."
46Jesus replied, "And you
experts in the law, woe to you,
because you load people down
with burdens they can hardly
carry, and you yourselves
will not lift one finger to help
them.
47"Woe to you, because you
build tombs for the prophets,
and it was your forefathers
who killed them. 48So you
testify that you approve of
what your forefathers did; they
killed the prophets, and you
build their tombs. 49Because of
this, God in his wisdom said, 'I
will send them prophets and apostles, some of
whom they will kill and others they will persecute.' 50Therefore this generation will be held
responsible for the blood of all the prophets
that has been shed since the beginning of the
world, 51from the blood of Abel to the blood
of Zechariah, who was killed between the altar
and the sanctuary. Yes, I tell you, this generation will be held responsible for it all.
52"Woe to you experts in the law, because
you have taken away the key to knowledge. You
yourselves have not entered, and you have hindered those who were entering."
53When Jesus left there, the Pharisees and
the teachers of the law began to oppose him
fiercely and to besiege him with questions,
54waiting to catch him in something he might
say.

Warnings and Encouragements

12 Meanwhile, when a crowd of many
thousands had gathered, so that they
were trampling on one another, Jesus began to
speak first to his disciples, saying: "Be on your
guard against the yeast of the Pharisees, which
is hypocrisy. 2There is nothing concealed that
will not be disclosed, or hidden that will not be
made known. 3What you have said in the dark
will be heard in the daylight, and what you
have whispered in the ear in the inner rooms
will be proclaimed from the roofs.
4"I tell you, my friends, do not be afraid of
those who kill the body and af-
ter that can do no more. 5But
I will show you whom you
should fear: Fear him who, after the killing of the body, has
power to throw you into hell.
Yes, I tell you, fear him. 6Are
not five sparrows sold for two
pennies[b]? Yet not one of them
is forgotten by God. 7Indeed,
the very hairs of your head are
all numbered. Don't be afraid;
you are worth more than many
sparrows.
8"I tell you, whoever ac-
knowledges me before men,
the Son of Man will also acknowledge him before the angels of God. 9But
he who disowns me before men will be disowned before the angels of God. 10And everyone who speaks a word against the Son of Man
will be forgiven, but anyone who blasphemes
against the Holy Spirit will not be forgiven.

Luke 12:7

God Treasures Us

"Indeed, the very hairs of your head are all numbered. Don't be afraid; you are worth more than many sparrows."

[a]41 Or *what you have* [b]6 Greek *two assaria*

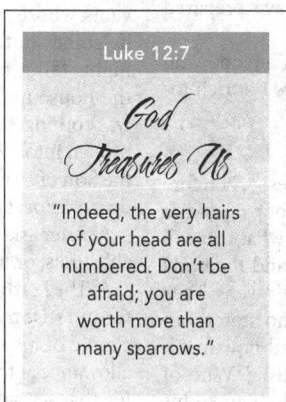

11“When you are brought before synagogues, rulers and authorities, do not worry about how you will defend yourselves or what you will say, 12for the Holy Spirit will teach you at that time what you should say.”

The Parable of the Rich Fool

13Someone in the crowd said to him, “Teacher, tell my brother to divide the inheritance with me.”

14Jesus replied, “Man, who appointed me a judge or an arbiter between you?” 15Then he said to them, “Watch out! Be on your guard against all kinds of greed; a man’s life does not consist in the abundance of his possessions.”

16And he told them this parable: “The ground of a certain rich man produced a good crop. 17He thought to himself, ‘What shall I do? I have no place to store my crops.’

18“Then he said, ‘This is what I’ll do. I will tear down my barns and build bigger ones, and there I will store all my grain and my goods. 19And I’ll say to myself, “You have plenty of good things laid up for many years. Take life easy; eat, drink and be merry.” ’

20“But God said to him, ‘You fool! This very night your life will be demanded from you. Then who will get what you have prepared for yourself?’

21“This is how it will be with anyone who stores up things for himself but is not rich toward God.”

Do Not Worry

22Then Jesus said to his disciples: “Therefore I tell you, do not worry about your life, what you will eat; or about your body, what you will wear. 23Life is more than food, and the body more than clothes. 24Consider the ravens: They do not sow or reap, they have no storeroom or barn; yet God feeds them. And how much more valuable you are than birds! 25Who of you by worrying can add a single hour to his life[a]? 26Since you cannot do this very little thing, why do you worry about the rest?

27“Consider how the lilies grow. They do not labor or spin. Yet I tell you, not even Solomon in all his splendor was dressed like one of these. 28If that is how God clothes the grass of the field, which is here today, and tomorrow is thrown into the fire, how much more will he clothe you, O you of little faith! 29And do not set your heart on what you will eat or drink; do not worry about it. 30For the pagan world runs after all such things, and your Father knows that you need them. 31But seek his kingdom, and these things will be given to you as well.

32“Do not be afraid, little flock, for your Father has been pleased to give you the kingdom. 33Sell your possessions and give to the poor. Provide purses for yourselves that will not wear out, a treasure in heaven that will not be exhausted, where no thief comes near and no moth destroys. 34For where your treasure is, there your heart will be also.

Watchfulness

35“Be dressed ready for service and keep your lamps burning, 36like men waiting for their master to return from a wedding banquet, so that when he comes and knocks they can immediately open the door for him. 37It will be good for those servants whose master finds them watching when he comes. I tell you the truth, he will dress himself to serve, will have them recline at the table and will come and wait on them. 38It will be good for those servants whose master finds them ready, even if he comes in the second or third watch of the night. 39But understand this: If the owner of the house had known at what hour the thief was coming, he would not have let his house be broken into. 40You also must be ready, because the Son of Man will come at an hour when you do not expect him.”

41Peter asked, “Lord, are you telling this parable to us, or to everyone?”

42The Lord answered, “Who then is the faithful and wise manager, whom the master puts in charge of his servants to give them their food allowance at the proper time? 43It will be good for that servant whom the master finds doing so when he returns. 44I tell you the truth, he will put him in charge of all his possessions. 45But suppose the servant says to himself, ‘My master is taking a long time in coming,’ and he then begins to beat the menservants and maidservants and to eat and drink and get drunk. 46The master of that servant will come on a day

[a]25 Or *single cubit to his height*

Scandalous Reckoning

MARY OF BETHANY

DAYS BEFORE CHRIST'S CRUCIFIXION, only one person seemed to understand the gravity of the situation: Jesus was going to die. Although he had said many times that he must come to Jerusalem to die, the disciples could not seem to grasp it. Mary of Bethany, at least in part, somehow understood.

That's why she chose to do something that shocked and confounded the men who followed Jesus. They didn't get it. But that didn't matter to Mary. She knew what she had to do.

The disciples were in denial. Their focus remained steadfastly in the present. They couldn't see that what she was doing was admirable. Instead, they worried about the cost of the perfume (it was worth a large sum of money); the customs of the day (it was traditional practice to give to the poor on the evening of the Passover); and their own opinions (without waiting for direction from Jesus, to whom the action was directed, they started to rebuke her).

Mary remained squarely transfixed on the horizon of events, though even she did not anticipate all that would transpire.

She could not have fully comprehended the significance; it was still the mystery of God. But the events taking place were not entirely lost on her, as they apparently were on the others. Intuitively, she sensed that what lay before her Lord was unimaginable pain, suffering and death. And she came to terms with it. Her ceremonial preparation for his burial confirmed her understanding.

As she carefully poured the nard on his head, the perfume traced the familiar features of his face: a brow she'd seen furrowed with concern; cheeks she'd seen wet with tears at the death of her brother; lips that had spoken truth to her. Her extravagance confounded the witnesses, but her comprehension of Christ's destiny touched the very heart of God.

—Prayer—

Dear God, I give everything I have to you, for you have made me rich with your love.

"I tell you the truth, wherever this gospel is preached throughout the world, what she has done will also be told, in memory of her."

Matthew 26:13

ASSIGNED READING:

Matthew 26:6–13; Luke 10:38–42; John 11:17—12:11

Weekend

Go to page 1261 for your next devotional reading.

when he does not expect him and at an hour he is not aware of. He will cut him to pieces and assign him a place with the unbelievers.

47“That servant who knows his master’s will and does not get ready or does not do what his master wants will be beaten with many blows. 48But the one who does not know and does things deserving punishment will be beaten with few blows. From everyone who has been given much, much will be demanded; and from the one who has been entrusted with much, much more will be asked.

Not Peace but Division

49“I have come to bring fire on the earth, and how I wish it were already kindled! 50But I have a baptism to undergo, and how distressed I am until it is completed! 51Do you think I came to bring peace on earth? No, I tell you, but division. 52From now on there will be five in one family divided against each other, three against two and two against three. 53They will be divided, father against son and son against father, mother against daughter and daughter against mother, mother-in-law against daughter-in-law and daughter-in-law against mother-in-law.”

Interpreting the Times

54He said to the crowd: “When you see a cloud rising in the west, immediately you say, ‘It’s going to rain,’ and it does. 55And when the south wind blows, you say, ‘It’s going to be hot,’ and it is. 56Hypocrites! You know how to interpret the appearance of the earth and the sky. How is it that you don’t know how to interpret this present time?

57“Why don’t you judge for yourselves what is right? 58As you are going with your adversary to the magistrate, try hard to be reconciled to him on the way, or he may drag you off to the judge, and the judge turn you over to the officer, and the officer throw you into prison. 59I tell you, you will not get out until you have paid the last penny.[a]”

Repent or Perish

13 Now there were some present at that time who told Jesus about the Galileans whose blood Pilate had mixed with their sacrifices. 2Jesus answered, “Do you think that these Galileans were worse sinners than all the other Galileans because they suffered this way? 3I tell you, no! But unless you repent, you too will all perish. 4Or those eighteen who died when the tower in Siloam fell on them—do you think they were more guilty than all the others living in Jerusalem? 5I tell you, no! But unless you repent, you too will all perish.”

6Then he told this parable: “A man had a fig tree, planted in his vineyard, and he went to look for fruit on it, but did not find any. 7So he said to the man who took care of the vineyard, ‘For three years now I’ve been coming to look for fruit on this fig tree and haven’t found any. Cut it down! Why should it use up the soil?’

8“ ‘Sir,’ the man replied, ‘leave it alone for one more year, and I’ll dig around it and fertilize it. 9If it bears fruit next year, fine! If not, then cut it down.’ ”

A Crippled Woman Healed on the Sabbath

10On a Sabbath Jesus was teaching in one of the synagogues, 11and a woman was there who had been crippled by a spirit for eighteen years. She was bent over and could not straighten up at all. 12When Jesus saw her, he called her forward and said to her, “Woman, you are set free from your infirmity.” 13Then he put his hands on her, and immediately she straightened up and praised God.

14Indignant because Jesus had healed on the Sabbath, the synagogue ruler said to the people, “There are six days for work. So come and be healed on those days, not on the Sabbath.”

15The Lord answered him, “You hypocrites! Doesn’t each of you on the Sabbath untie his ox or donkey from the stall and lead it out to give it water? 16Then should not this woman, a daughter of Abraham, whom Satan has kept bound for eighteen long years, be set free on the Sabbath day from what bound her?”

17When he said this, all his opponents were humiliated, but the people were delighted with all the wonderful things he was doing.

The Parables of the Mustard Seed and the Yeast

18Then Jesus asked, “What is the kingdom of God like? What shall I compare it to? 19It is like a mustard seed, which a man took and planted

[a]59 Greek *lepton*

When Jesus Sees

Read: Luke 13:10–21

FROM AN EARLY AGE, we're taught to look away from those who are different. "Don't stare," we're told. "It's rude!" Often people with disabilities make us uncomfortable, so we learn to pretend we don't notice that someone has a deformity or scars or walks with a limp or moves around in a chair. Unfortunately, we sometimes take it one step further and pretend we don't see the person at all.

The woman in the synagogue had spent 18 years being overlooked. She was bent over like a question mark, staring at the ground and her own two feet. She couldn't see the faces behind the words, but she knew the tones, the jokes and the whispers. She could hear people hurrying past and skirting around her. And while plenty of people looked at her, many probably looked the other way. Only one truly saw her.

When Jesus saw her, he didn't turn away. He didn't pretend not to see her. Instead, he spoke to her and touched her. She was set free from her infirmity. Her 18 years of living with a crooked body dropped away, and she stood straight and tall, seeing Jesus face-to-face.

In that compassionate interaction, Jesus had an encounter with someone the world tends to overlook. He showed us that, first of all, we need to see others—to look at them and acknowledge their presence as God's creation, precious in his sight. When we look into their eyes, we'll see a human being and not a deformity, disability or limitation.

Second, we need to speak to that person as we would anyone. Conversing normally shows that we're not intimidated by the person's disability. Even if we're just talking about the weather, we are expressing our interest in the other person's words and opinions.

Third, we need to be willing to touch them if it's appropriate. Human touch is a mysterious, powerful tool that communicates worth and significance through something as simple as a handshake, a touch on the shoulder or a hug.

Everyone needs to know that they are valued. When we begin to see others as Jesus does—as human beings with value and significance—we might become the window through which they can see Jesus for themselves.

Luke 13:12

When Jesus saw her, he called her forward and said to her, "Woman, you are set free from your infirmity."

reflection

1 How do you tend to respond to people with disabilities?

2 What does Jesus' example with the woman teach you about relating to others with or without physical disabilities?

3 Whom do you need to see as Jesus sees them?

RELATED READINGS

1 Samuel 16:6–7;
2 Samuel 9:1–13;
2 Corinthians 4:16–18

"I would rather be in this chair knowing him, than on my feet without him."

Joni Eareckson Tada

Monday

Go to page 1264 for your next devotional reading.

in his garden. It grew and became a tree, and the birds of the air perched in its branches."

20Again he asked, "What shall I compare the kingdom of God to? 21It is like yeast that a woman took and mixed into a large amount[a] of flour until it worked all through the dough."

The Narrow Door

22Then Jesus went through the towns and villages, teaching as he made his way to Jerusalem. 23Someone asked him, "Lord, are only a few people going to be saved?"

He said to them, 24"Make every effort to enter through the narrow door, because many, I tell you, will try to enter and will not be able to. 25Once the owner of the house gets up and closes the door, you will stand outside knocking and pleading, 'Sir, open the door for us.'

"But he will answer, 'I don't know you or where you come from.'

26"Then you will say, 'We ate and drank with you, and you taught in our streets.'

27"But he will reply, 'I don't know you or where you come from. Away from me, all you evildoers!'

28"There will be weeping there, and gnashing of teeth, when you see Abraham, Isaac and Jacob and all the prophets in the kingdom of God, but you yourselves thrown out. 29People will come from east and west and north and south, and will take their places at the feast in the kingdom of God. 30Indeed there are those who are last who will be first, and first who will be last."

Jesus' Sorrow for Jerusalem

31At that time some Pharisees came to Jesus and said to him, "Leave this place and go somewhere else. Herod wants to kill you."

32He replied, "Go tell that fox, 'I will drive out demons and heal people today and tomorrow, and on the third day I will reach my goal.' 33In any case, I must keep going today and tomorrow and the next day—for surely no prophet can die outside Jerusalem!

34"O Jerusalem, Jerusalem, you who kill the prophets and stone those sent to you, how often I have longed to gather your children together, as a hen gathers her chicks under her wings, but you were not willing! 35Look, your house is left to you desolate. I tell you, you will not see me again until you say, 'Blessed is he who comes in the name of the Lord.'[b]"

Luke 13:34

God Weeps for His People

"O Jerusalem, Jerusalem, you who kill the prophets and stone those sent to you, how often I have longed to gather your children together, as a hen gathers her chicks under her wings, but you were not willing!"

Jesus at a Pharisee's House

14 One Sabbath, when Jesus went to eat in the house of a prominent Pharisee, he was being carefully watched. 2There in front of him was a man suffering from dropsy. 3Jesus asked the Pharisees and experts in the law, "Is it lawful to heal on the Sabbath or not?" 4But they remained silent. So taking hold of the man, he healed him and sent him away.

5Then he asked them, "If one of you has a son[c] or an ox that falls into a well on the Sabbath day, will you not immediately pull him out?" 6And they had nothing to say.

7When he noticed how the guests picked the places of honor at the table, he told them this parable: 8"When someone invites you to a wedding feast, do not take the place of honor, for a person more distinguished than you may have been invited. 9If so, the host who invited both of you will come and say to you, 'Give this man your seat.' Then, humiliated, you will have to take the least important place. 10But when you are invited, take the lowest place, so that when your host comes, he will say to you, 'Friend, move up to a better place.' Then you will be honored in the presence of all your fellow guests. 11For everyone who exalts himself will be humbled, and he who humbles himself will be exalted."

12Then Jesus said to his host, "When you give a luncheon or dinner, do not invite your friends, your brothers or relatives, or your rich

[a]21 Greek *three satas* (probably about 1/2 bushel or 22 liters) [b]35 Psalm 118:26 [c]5 Some manuscripts *donkey*

neighbors; if you do, they may invite you back and so you will be repaid. 13But when you give a banquet, invite the poor, the crippled, the lame, the blind, 14and you will be blessed. Although they cannot repay you, you will be repaid at the resurrection of the righteous."

The Parable of the Great Banquet

15When one of those at the table with him heard this, he said to Jesus, "Blessed is the man who will eat at the feast in the kingdom of God."

16Jesus replied: "A certain man was preparing a great banquet and invited many guests. 17At the time of the banquet he sent his servant to tell those who had been invited, 'Come, for everything is now ready.'

18"But they all alike began to make excuses. The first said, 'I have just bought a field, and I must go and see it. Please excuse me.'

19"Another said, 'I have just bought five yoke of oxen, and I'm on my way to try them out. Please excuse me.'

20"Still another said, 'I just got married, so I can't come.'

21"The servant came back and reported this to his master. Then the owner of the house became angry and ordered his servant, 'Go out quickly into the streets and alleys of the town and bring in the poor, the crippled, the blind and the lame.'

22" 'Sir,' the servant said, 'what you ordered has been done, but there is still room.'

23"Then the master told his servant, 'Go out to the roads and country lanes and make them come in, so that my house will be full. 24I tell you, not one of those men who were invited will get a taste of my banquet.' "

The Cost of Being a Disciple

25Large crowds were traveling with Jesus, and turning to them he said: 26"If anyone comes to me and does not hate his father and mother, his wife and children, his brothers and sisters—yes, even his own life—he cannot be my disciple. 27And anyone who does not carry his cross and follow me cannot be my disciple.

28"Suppose one of you wants to build a tower. Will he not first sit down and estimate the cost to see if he has enough money to complete it? 29For if he lays the foundation and is not able to finish it, everyone who sees it will ridicule him, 30saying, 'This fellow began to build and was not able to finish.'

31"Or suppose a king is about to go to war against another king. Will he not first sit down and consider whether he is able with ten thousand men to oppose the one coming against him with twenty thousand? 32If he is not able, he will send a delegation while the other is still a long way off and will ask for terms of peace. 33In the same way, any of you who does not give up everything he has cannot be my disciple.

34"Salt is good, but if it loses its saltiness, how can it be made salty again? 35It is fit neither for the soil nor for the manure pile; it is thrown out.

"He who has ears to hear, let him hear."

The Parable of the Lost Sheep

15 Now the tax collectors and "sinners" were all gathering around to hear him. 2But the Pharisees and the teachers of the law muttered, "This man welcomes sinners and eats with them."

3Then Jesus told them this parable: 4"Suppose one of you has a hundred sheep and loses one of them. Does he not leave the ninety-nine in the open country and go after the lost sheep until he finds it? 5And when he finds it, he joyfully puts it on his shoulders 6and goes home. Then he calls his friends and neighbors together and says, 'Rejoice with me; I have found my lost sheep.' 7I tell you that in the same way there will be more rejoicing in heaven over one sinner who repents than over ninety-nine righteous persons who do not need to repent.

The Parable of the Lost Coin

8"Or suppose a woman has ten silver coins[a] and loses one. Does she not light a lamp, sweep the house and search carefully until she finds it? 9And when she finds it, she calls her friends and neighbors together and says, 'Rejoice with me; I have found my lost coin.' 10In the same way, I tell you, there is rejoicing in the presence of the angels of God over one sinner who repents."

[a]8 Greek *ten drachmas*, each worth about a day's wages

Lost and Found

Luke 15:10

"There is rejoicing in the presence of the angels of God over one sinner who repents."

reflection

1 What are some things that cause you to rejoice?

2 Jesus searched diligently for lost individuals. Who would you go out of your way to find?

3 When was the last time you felt spiritually lost? Do you feel lost right now? If you have lost your way, spend some time asking God to show you the way back home to him.

RELATED READINGS

Psalms 23:1–4; 139:1–24; Luke 19:1–10; John 10:14–16

Read: Luke 15:1–32

HERE'S AN INTERESTING BIT of trivia: According to the Department of Statistics, the average American spends one full year of their life looking for lost things. One year! Have you ever misplaced your car keys just when you urgently needed to get somewhere on time? or looked for those eyeglasses that were sitting on top of your head? or searched high and low for the book you wanted to take on vacation? You probably felt as if you searched an entire year just for one lost item.

Jesus spent *three* years searching . . . his entire ministry. But he did not search for material things, such as keys, glasses and books. No, Jesus looked for lost people. He searched among the sinners and found such unpopular people as Matthew, the tax collector, and Mary Magdalene, the woman tormented by seven demons. He searched in the region of Galilee and found the likes of Peter and John and many women followers. He searched among the rebellious and found Zacchaeus. He went into Samaria, an area shunned by orthodox Jews, and met the woman who lived in sin getting water at a well.

Jesus still searches for the lost. Where did he find you? At a nightclub? Living life as a rebel? Riding the subway in a big city? Buried under a pile of books at a university? Or perhaps he found you sitting in a church pew, convinced you had everything together, that you could set things right with God on your own terms . . . sort of like Nicodemus, the learned Pharisee and member of the Sanhedrin. Yet even to him, Jesus said, "You must be born again" (John 3:7).

Wherever you were, the Savior came looking for you because you are valuable to him. You are worth every moment of the search. For when you answered his call, he and the angels in heaven rejoiced. And now you are his beloved child, one of his "chosen people, a royal priesthood, a holy nation, a people belonging to God, that you may declare the praises of him who called you out of darkness into his wonderful light" (1 Peter 2:9).

There is so much, so very much for you to rejoice in.

Go to page 1268 for your next devotional reading.

The Parable of the Lost Son

11 Jesus continued: "There was a man who
had two sons. 12 The younger one said to his father, 'Father, give me my share of the estate.' So
he divided his property between them.

13 "Not long after that, the younger son got
together all he had, set off for a distant country
and there squandered his wealth in wild living.
14 After he had spent everything, there was a
severe famine in that whole country, and he began to be in need. 15 So he went and hired himself out to a citizen of that country, who sent
him to his fields to feed pigs. 16 He longed to
fill his stomach with the pods that the pigs were
eating, but no one gave him anything.

17 "When he came to his senses, he said,
'How many of my father's hired men have food
to spare, and here I am starving to death! 18 I
will set out and go back to my father and say
to him: Father, I have sinned against heaven
and against you. 19 I am no longer worthy to be
called your son; make me like one of your hired
men.' 20 So he got up and went
to his father.

"But while he was still a long
way off, his father saw him and
was filled with compassion for
him; he ran to his son, threw
his arms around him and
kissed him.

21 "The son said to him,
'Father, I have sinned against
heaven and against you. I am
no longer worthy to be called
your son.[a]'

22 "But the father said to his
servants, 'Quick! Bring the best
robe and put it on him. Put a
ring on his finger and sandals
on his feet. 23 Bring the fattened
calf and kill it. Let's have a feast
and celebrate. 24 For this son of mine was dead
and is alive again; he was lost and is found.' So
they began to celebrate.

25 "Meanwhile, the older son was in the field.
When he came near the house, he heard music
and dancing. 26 So he called one of the servants
and asked him what was going on. 27 'Your
brother has come,' he replied, 'and your father
has killed the fattened calf because he has him
back safe and sound.'

28 "The older brother became angry and
refused to go in. So his father went out and
pleaded with him. 29 But he answered his father, 'Look! All these years I've been slaving for
you and never disobeyed your orders. Yet you
never gave me even a young goat so I could celebrate with my friends. 30 But when this son of
yours who has squandered your property with
prostitutes comes home, you kill the fattened
calf for him!'

31 " 'My son,' the father said, 'you are always
with me, and everything I have is yours. 32 But
we had to celebrate and be glad, because this
brother of yours was dead and is alive again; he
was lost and is found.' "

> **Luke 15:20**
>
> *God Welcomes the Prodigal*
>
> "So he got up and went to his father. But while he was still a long way off, his father saw him and was filled with compassion for him; he ran to his son, threw his arms around him and kissed him."

The Parable of the Shrewd Manager

16 Jesus told his disciples: "There was a
rich man whose manager was accused
of wasting his possessions. 2 So
he called him in and asked
him, 'What is this I hear about
you? Give an account of your
management, because you cannot be manager any longer.'

3 "The manager said to himself, 'What shall I do now? My
master is taking away my job.
I'm not strong enough to dig,
and I'm ashamed to beg— 4 I
know what I'll do so that, when
I lose my job here, people will
welcome me into their houses.'

5 "So he called in each one of
his master's debtors. He asked
the first, 'How much do you
owe my master?'

6 " 'Eight hundred gallons[b]
of olive oil,' he replied.

"The manager told him, 'Take your bill, sit
down quickly, and make it four hundred.'

7 "Then he asked the second, 'And how much
do you owe?'

" 'A thousand bushels[c] of wheat,' he replied.

"He told him, 'Take your bill and make it
eight hundred.'

[a] 21 Some early manuscripts *son. Make me like one of your hired men.*
[b] 6 Greek *one hundred batous* (probably about 3 kiloliters)
[c] 7 Greek *one hundred korous* (probably about 35 kiloliters)

8“The master commended the dishonest
manager because he had acted shrewdly. For
the people of this world are more shrewd in
dealing with their own kind than are the people of the light. 9I tell you, use worldly wealth
to gain friends for yourselves, so that when it is
gone, you will be welcomed into eternal dwellings.
10“Whoever can be trusted with very little
can also be trusted with much, and whoever is
dishonest with very little will also be dishonest
with much. 11So if you have not been trustworthy in handling worldly wealth, who will trust
you with true riches? 12And if you have not
been trustworthy with someone else’s property,
who will give you property of your own?
13“No servant can serve two masters. Either
he will hate the one and love the other, or he
will be devoted to the one and despise the other.
You cannot serve both God and Money.”
14The Pharisees, who loved money, heard all
this and were sneering at Jesus. 15He said to
them, “You are the ones who justify yourselves
in the eyes of men, but God knows your hearts.
What is highly valued among men is detestable
in God’s sight.

Additional Teachings

16“The Law and the Prophets were proclaimed until John. Since that time, the good
news of the kingdom of God is being preached,
and everyone is forcing his way into it. 17It is
easier for heaven and earth to disappear than
for the least stroke of a pen to drop out of the
Law.
18“Anyone who divorces his wife and marries another woman commits adultery, and
the man who marries a divorced woman commits adultery.

The Rich Man and Lazarus

19“There was a rich man who was dressed
in purple and fine linen and lived in luxury every day. 20At his gate was laid a beggar named
Lazarus, covered with sores 21and longing to
eat what fell from the rich man’s table. Even the
dogs came and licked his sores.
22“The time came when the beggar died and
the angels carried him to Abraham’s side. The
rich man also died and was buried. 23In hell,[a]
where he was in torment, he looked up and saw
Abraham far away, with Lazarus by his side.
24So he called to him, ‘Father Abraham, have
pity on me and send Lazarus to dip the tip of
his finger in water and cool my tongue, because
I am in agony in this fire.’
25“But Abraham replied, ‘Son, remember
that in your lifetime you received your good
things, while Lazarus received bad things, but
now he is comforted here and you are in agony.
26And besides all this, between us and you a
great chasm has been fixed, so that those who
want to go from here to you cannot, nor can
anyone cross over from there to us.’
27“He answered, ‘Then I beg you, father,
send Lazarus to my father’s house, 28for I have
five brothers. Let him warn them, so that they
will not also come to this place of torment.’
29“Abraham replied, ‘They have Moses and
the Prophets; let them listen to them.’
30“ ‘No, father Abraham,’ he said, ‘but if
someone from the dead goes to them, they will
repent.’
31“He said to him, ‘If they do not listen to
Moses and the Prophets, they will not be convinced even if someone rises from the dead.’ ”

Sin, Faith, Duty

17 Jesus said to his disciples: “Things that
cause people to sin are bound to come,
but woe to that person through whom they
come. 2It would be better for him to be thrown
into the sea with a millstone tied around his
neck than for him to cause one of these little
ones to sin. 3So watch yourselves.
“If your brother sins, rebuke him, and if he repents, forgive him. 4If he sins against you seven
times in a day, and seven times comes back to
you and says, ‘I repent,’ forgive him.”
5The apostles said to the Lord, “Increase
our faith!”
6He replied, “If you have faith as small as
a mustard seed, you can say to this mulberry
tree, ‘Be uprooted and planted in the sea,’ and
it will obey you.
7“Suppose one of you had a servant plowing or looking after the sheep. Would he say to
the servant when he comes in from the field,
‘Come along now and sit down to eat’? 8Would
he not rather say, ‘Prepare my supper, get your-

[a]23 Greek *Hades*

self ready and wait on me while I eat and drink;
after that you may eat and drink'? 9Would he
thank the servant because he did what he was
told to do? 10So you also, when you have done
everything you were told to do, should say,
'We are unworthy servants; we have only done
our duty.'"

Ten Healed of Leprosy

11Now on his way to Jerusalem, Jesus traveled along the border between Samaria and
Galilee. 12As he was going into a village, ten
men who had leprosy[a] met him. They stood
at a distance 13and called out in a loud voice,
"Jesus, Master, have pity on us!"

14When he saw them, he said, "Go, show
yourselves to the priests." And as they went,
they were cleansed.

15One of them, when he saw he was healed,
came back, praising God in a loud voice. 16He
threw himself at Jesus' feet and thanked him—
and he was a Samaritan.

17Jesus asked, "Were not all ten cleansed?
Where are the other nine? 18Was no one found
to return and give praise to God except this
foreigner?" 19Then he said to him, "Rise and
go; your faith has made you well."

The Coming of the Kingdom of God

20Once, having been asked by the Pharisees
when the kingdom of God would come, Jesus
replied, "The kingdom of God does not come
with your careful observation, 21nor will people say, 'Here it is,' or 'There it is,' because the
kingdom of God is within[b] you."

22Then he said to his disciples, "The time is
coming when you will long to see one of the
days of the Son of Man, but you will not see
it. 23Men will tell you, 'There he is!' or 'Here
he is!' Do not go running off after them. 24For
the Son of Man in his day[c] will be like the lightning, which flashes and lights up the sky from
one end to the other. 25But first he must suffer many things and be rejected by this generation.

26"Just as it was in the days of Noah, so also
will it be in the days of the Son of Man. 27Peo-
ple were eating, drinking, marrying and being
given in marriage up to the day Noah entered
the ark. Then the flood came and destroyed
them all.

28"It was the same in the days of Lot. People were eating and drinking, buying and selling, planting and building. 29But the day Lot
left Sodom, fire and sulfur rained down from
heaven and destroyed them all.

30"It will be just like this on the day the Son
of Man is revealed. 31On that day no one who
is on the roof of his house, with his goods inside, should go down to get them. Likewise, no
one in the field should go back for anything.
32Remember Lot's wife! 33Whoever tries to
keep his life will lose it, and whoever loses his
life will preserve it. 34I tell you, on that night
two people will be in one bed; one will be taken
and the other left. 35Two women will be grinding grain together; one will be taken and the
other left.[d]"

37"Where, Lord?" they asked.

He replied, "Where there is a dead body,
there the vultures will gather."

The Parable of the Persistent Widow

18 Then Jesus told his disciples a parable
to show them that they should always
pray and not give up. 2He said: "In a certain
town there was a judge who neither feared God
nor cared about men. 3And there was a widow
in that town who kept coming to him with the
plea, 'Grant me justice against my adversary.'

4"For some time he refused. But finally he
said to himself, 'Even though I don't fear God
or care about men, 5yet because this widow
keeps bothering me, I will see that she gets justice, so that she won't eventually wear me out
with her coming!'"

6And the Lord said, "Listen to what the unjust judge says. 7And will not God bring about
justice for his chosen ones, who cry out to him
day and night? Will he keep putting them off?
8I tell you, he will see that they get justice, and
quickly. However, when the Son of Man comes,
will he find faith on the earth?"

The Parable of the Pharisee and the Tax Collector

9To some who were confident of their own
righteousness and looked down on everybody

[a]12 The Greek word was used for various diseases affecting the skin—not necessarily leprosy. [b]21 Or *among* [c]24 Some manuscripts do not have *in his day.* [d]35 Some manuscripts *left.* 36*Two men will be in the field; one will be taken and the other left.*

Knocking on God's Door

Read: Luke 18:1–17

Luke 18:7

"And will not God bring about justice for his chosen ones, who cry out to him day and night? Will he keep putting them off?"

reflection

1 Would you describe your prayer life as strong, weak or improving?

2 When God doesn't answer your prayer in the way you wanted, how do you handle it?

3 What specific steps will you take to grow in your prayer life?

RELATED READINGS

1 Samuel 1:1–20; Isaiah 62:6–7; Matthew 5:5; 7:7–11

"I'VE BEEN LAID OFF AGAIN," said Jim.

"But that's the third time in five years," said Nan. "What will we do? Do you have severance pay?" Jim shook his head no.

Nan collapsed onto a kitchen chair, tears slipping down her cheeks. "I can't go through this again."

They were both middle-aged, and jobs were hard to find. They had children who needed clothing, parents who needed help. Together, they decided to place their future in God's hands and plead their case before him day and night. Every morning, they read God's Word together and prayed. At dinnertime they prayed too, asking God to provide a job.

Several weeks later, a woman they'd met at a job center told them about an opening. Armed with the knowledge that God is faithful and that he answers prayer according to his purpose, Jim applied for the job. Jim and Nan had knocked long and hard on heaven's door for job openings, and it took a long time for their prayers to be answered. This time, within a week, Jim was hired.

Unlike the widow in Jesus' parable who went before an unjust judge, Jim and Nan called upon a loving Father. The widow had no friend to speak for her, but Jim and Nan had Jesus—the One who lives to intercede. The widow only had access to the judge at certain times, while this couple had access to their heavenly Father morning, noon and night. In one area they were similar: like the widow, Jim and Nan were persistent; they did not give up.

And God answered.

You may be praying and waiting for something: a baby, a job, a husband, a ministry. Keep praying. Day and night. He will answer in the way that he sees fit. The answer may not look like what you were imagining, but it will be for your good.

Go to page 1271 for your next devotional reading.

else, Jesus told this parable: 10“Two men went
up to the temple to pray, one a Pharisee and
the other a tax collector. 11The Pharisee stood
up and prayed about[a] himself: ‘God, I thank
you that I am not like other men—robbers,
evildoers, adulterers—or even like this tax collector. 12I fast twice a week and give a tenth of
all I get.’
13“But the tax collector stood at a distance.
He would not even look up to heaven, but beat
his breast and said, ‘God, have mercy on me,
a sinner.’
14“I tell you that this man, rather than the
other, went home justified before God. For everyone who exalts himself will be humbled,
and he who humbles himself will be exalted.”

The Little Children and Jesus

15People were also bringing babies to Jesus
to have him touch them. When the disciples
saw this, they rebuked them. 16But Jesus called
the children to him and said, “Let the little children come to me, and do not hinder them, for
the kingdom of God belongs to such as these.
17I tell you the truth, anyone who will not receive the kingdom of God like a little child will
never enter it.”

The Rich Ruler

18A certain ruler asked him, “Good teacher,
what must I do to inherit eternal life?”
19“Why do you call me good?” Jesus answered. “No one is good—except God alone.
20You know the commandments: ‘Do not commit adultery, do not murder, do not steal, do
not give false testimony, honor your father and
mother.’[b]”
21“All these I have kept since I was a boy,”
he said.
22When Jesus heard this, he said to him,
“You still lack one thing. Sell everything you
have and give to the poor, and you will have
treasure in heaven. Then come, follow me.”
23When he heard this, he became very sad,
because he was a man of great wealth. 24Jesus
looked at him and said, “How hard it is for the
rich to enter the kingdom of God! 25Indeed, it
is easier for a camel to go through the eye of
a needle than for a rich man to enter the kingdom of God.”
26Those who heard this asked, “Who then
can be saved?”
27Jesus replied, “What is impossible with
men is possible with God.”
28Peter said to him, “We have left all we had
to follow you!”
29“I tell you the truth,” Jesus said to them,
“no one who has left home or wife or brothers
or parents or children for the sake of the kingdom of God 30will fail to receive many times
as much in this age and, in the age to come,
eternal life.”

Jesus Again Predicts His Death

31Jesus took the Twelve aside and told them,
“We are going up to Jerusalem, and everything
that is written by the prophets about the Son
of Man will be fulfilled. 32He will be handed
over to the Gentiles. They will mock him, insult
him, spit on him, flog him and kill him. 33On
the third day he will rise again.”
34The disciples did not understand any of
this. Its meaning was hidden from them, and
they did not know what he was talking about.

A Blind Beggar Receives His Sight

35As Jesus approached Jericho, a blind man
was sitting by the roadside begging. 36When
he heard the crowd going by, he asked what
was happening. 37They told him, “Jesus of Nazareth is passing by.”
38He called out, “Jesus, Son of David, have
mercy on me!”
39Those who led the way rebuked him and
told him to be quiet, but he shouted all the
more, “Son of David, have mercy on me!”
40Jesus stopped and ordered the man to be
brought to him. When he came near, Jesus
asked him, 41“What do you want me to do for
you?”
“Lord, I want to see,” he replied.
42Jesus said to him, “Receive your sight;
your faith has healed you.” 43Immediately he
received his sight and followed Jesus, praising
God. When all the people saw it, they also
praised God.

Zacchaeus the Tax Collector

19 Jesus entered Jericho and was passing
through. 2A man was there by the
name of Zacchaeus; he was a chief tax collector

[a] 11 Or *to* [b] 20 Exodus 20:12–16; Deut. 5:16–20

and was wealthy. 3He wanted to see who Jesus
was, but being a short man he could not, because of the crowd. 4So he ran ahead and
climbed a sycamore-fig tree to see him, since
Jesus was coming that way.

5When Jesus reached the spot, he looked
up and said to him, "Zacchaeus, come down
immediately. I must stay at your house today."
6So he came down at once and welcomed him
gladly.

7All the people saw this and began to mutter,
"He has gone to be the guest of a 'sinner.'"

8But Zacchaeus stood up
and said to the Lord, "Look,
Lord! Here and now I give half
of my possessions to the poor,
and if I have cheated anybody
out of anything, I will pay back
four times the amount."

9Jesus said to him, "Today
salvation has come to this
house, because this man, too,
is a son of Abraham. 10For the
Son of Man came to seek and
to save what was lost."

> **Luke 19:10**
>
> *God Saves the Lost*
>
> "For the Son of Man came to seek and to save what was lost."

The Parable of the Ten Minas

11While they were listening to this, he went
on to tell them a parable, because he was near
Jerusalem and the people thought that the kingdom of God was going to appear at once. 12He
said: "A man of noble birth went to a distant
country to have himself appointed king and
then to return. 13So he called ten of his servants
and gave them ten minas.[a] 'Put this money to
work,' he said, 'until I come back.'

14"But his subjects hated him and sent a delegation after him to say, 'We don't want this man
to be our king.'

15"He was made king, however, and returned home. Then he sent for the servants to
whom he had given the money, in order to find
out what they had gained with it.

16"The first one came and said, 'Sir, your
mina has earned ten more.'

17"'Well done, my good servant!' his master
replied. 'Because you have been trustworthy in
a very small matter, take charge of ten cities.'

18"The second came and said, 'Sir, your
mina has earned five more.'

19"His master answered, 'You take charge of
five cities.'

20"Then another servant came and said, 'Sir,
here is your mina; I have kept it laid away in a
piece of cloth. 21I was afraid of you, because
you are a hard man. You take out what you did
not put in and reap what you did not sow.'

22"His master replied, 'I will judge you by
your own words, you wicked servant! You
knew, did you, that I am a hard man, taking out
what I did not put in, and reaping what I did
not sow? 23Why then didn't you put my money
on deposit, so that when I came
back, I could have collected it
with interest?'

24"Then he said to those
standing by, 'Take his mina
away from him and give it to
the one who has ten minas.'

25"'Sir,' they said, 'he already
has ten!'

26"He replied, 'I tell you that
to everyone who has, more
will be given, but as for the one
who has nothing, even what he
has will be taken away. 27But
those enemies of mine who did not want me to
be king over them—bring them here and kill
them in front of me.'"

The Triumphal Entry

28After Jesus had said this, he went on ahead,
going up to Jerusalem. 29As he approached
Bethphage and Bethany at the hill called the
Mount of Olives, he sent two of his disciples,
saying to them, 30"Go to the village ahead of
you, and as you enter it, you will find a colt
tied there, which no one has ever ridden. Untie it and bring it here. 31If anyone asks you,
'Why are you untying it?' tell him, 'The Lord
needs it.'"

32Those who were sent ahead went and
found it just as he had told them. 33As they
were untying the colt, its owners asked them,
"Why are you untying the colt?"

34They replied, "The Lord needs it."

35They brought it to Jesus, threw their
cloaks on the colt and put Jesus on it. 36As he
went along, people spread their cloaks on the
road.

[a] 13 A mina was about three months' wages.

A Desirable Donkey?

Read: Luke 19:28–44

THINK OF THE ANIMAL that you most identify with. Perhaps you thought of a species that you physically resemble. Long neck? A giraffe. Sleek? A panther. Bookish? An owl. More than likely you picked an animal that shares a characteristic common to you: silly like a monkey, clever as a fox or resourceful like a squirrel. Answering this question reveals a lot about a person. Possums enjoy sleep. Birds crave freedom. And hyenas laugh from the belly. Which animal do you most closely resemble?

You probably didn't pick the donkey with its enormous ears, obstinate will and annoying bray. Notoriously stubborn and simpleminded, the donkey or donkey colt is mentioned frequently in the Bible. It served as the common beast of burden for the poor. Unlike the noble horse, which was coveted by the rich and royal, the donkey was an animal for blue-collar workers. Donkeys are low-maintenance animals with great endurance. They have the ability to live and work under hot, difficult conditions. Sometimes they were used for riding but mostly they pulled loads and carts, worked mills and threshers or carried heavy burdens.

Jesus chose to ride a donkey's colt when making his triumphal entry into Jerusalem. Although the King of kings deserved a fine steed, he humbly rode a big-eared burro. It was prophesied, "See, your king comes to you, gentle and riding on a donkey, on a colt, the foal of a donkey" (Matthew 21:5).

Doesn't that give you reassurance? If the Lord "needs" a stubborn, lowly donkey, perhaps he could use a whimsical woman. Maybe your plodding steadiness is just what he can use. Maybe your stubbornness looks more like persistence and perseverance to God. Perhaps your down-to-earth personality fits right into his plans. Paul said, "[God] chose the lowly things of this world and the despised things—and the things that are not—to nullify the things that are, so that no one may boast before him" (1 Corinthians 1:28–29).

Whether you resemble a parrot, a peacock or a porcupine, God needs *you*.

Luke 19:30–31

"Go to the village ahead of you, and as you enter it, you will find a [donkey's] colt tied there, which no one has ever ridden. Untie it and bring it here. If anyone asks you, 'Why are you untying it?' tell him, 'The Lord needs it.'"

reflection

1 What animal do you most identify with?

2 Why do you think Jesus chose a donkey to ride on into Jerusalem?

3 How might God use *your* personality traits for his glory?

RELATED READINGS

Proverbs 29:23;
Zechariah 9:9;
1 Corinthians 12:1–26

Go to page 1276 for your next devotional reading.

37 When he came near the place where the
road goes down the Mount of Olives, the whole
crowd of disciples began joyfully to praise God
in loud voices for all the miracles they had
seen:

38 "Blessed is the king who comes in the
name of the Lord!"[a]

"Peace in heaven and glory in the highest!"

39 Some of the Pharisees in the crowd said to
Jesus, "Teacher, rebuke your disciples!"
40 "I tell you," he replied, "if they keep quiet,
the stones will cry out."
41 As he approached Jerusalem and saw the
city, he wept over it 42 and said, "If you, even
you, had only known on this day what would
bring you peace—but now it is hidden from
your eyes. 43 The days will come upon you
when your enemies will build an embankment
against you and encircle you and hem you in on
every side. 44 They will dash you to the ground,
you and the children within your walls. They
will not leave one stone on another, because
you did not recognize the time of God's coming to you."

Jesus at the Temple

45 Then he entered the temple area and began driving out those who were selling. 46 "It is
written," he said to them, " 'My house will be a
house of prayer'[b]; but you have made it 'a den
of robbers.'[c]"
47 Every day he was teaching at the temple.
But the chief priests, the teachers of the law and
the leaders among the people were trying to kill
him. 48 Yet they could not find any way to do it,
because all the people hung on his words.

The Authority of Jesus Questioned

20 One day as he was teaching the people
in the temple courts and preaching
the gospel, the chief priests and the teachers of
the law, together with the elders, came up to
him. 2 "Tell us by what authority you are doing
these things," they said. "Who gave you this
authority?"
3 He replied, "I will also ask you a question.
Tell me, 4 John's baptism—was it from heaven,
or from men?"
5 They discussed it among themselves and
said, "If we say, 'From heaven,' he will ask, 'Why
didn't you believe him?' 6 But if we say, 'From
men,' all the people will stone us, because they
are persuaded that John was a prophet."
7 So they answered, "We don't know where
it was from."
8 Jesus said, "Neither will I tell you by what
authority I am doing these things."

The Parable of the Tenants

9 He went on to tell the people this parable:
"A man planted a vineyard, rented it to some
farmers and went away for a long time. 10 At
harvest time he sent a servant to the tenants
so they would give him some of the fruit of the
vineyard. But the tenants beat him and sent
him away empty-handed. 11 He sent another
servant, but that one also they beat and treated
shamefully and sent away empty-handed. 12 He
sent still a third, and they wounded him and
threw him out.
13 "Then the owner of the vineyard said,
'What shall I do? I will send my son, whom I
love; perhaps they will respect him.'
14 "But when the tenants saw him, they
talked the matter over. 'This is the heir,' they
said. 'Let's kill him, and the inheritance will be
ours.' 15 So they threw him out of the vineyard
and killed him.
"What then will the owner of the vineyard
do to them? 16 He will come and kill those tenants and give the vineyard to others."
When the people heard this, they said, "May
this never be!"
17 Jesus looked directly at them and asked,
"Then what is the meaning of that which is written:

" 'The stone the builders rejected
has become the capstone'[d,e]?

18 Everyone who falls on that stone will be broken to pieces, but he on whom it falls will be
crushed."
19 The teachers of the law and the chief priests
looked for a way to arrest him immediately, because they knew he had spoken this parable
against them. But they were afraid of the people.

[a] 38 Psalm 118:26 [b] 46 Isaiah 56:7 [c] 46 Jer. 7:11 [d] 17 Or *cornerstone* [e] 17 Psalm 118:22

Paying Taxes to Caesar

20Keeping a close watch on him, they sent
spies, who pretended to be honest. They hoped
to catch Jesus in something he said so that
they might hand him over to the power and
authority of the governor. 21So the spies questioned him: "Teacher, we know that you speak
and teach what is right, and that you do not
show partiality but teach the way of God in accordance with the truth. 22Is it right for us to
pay taxes to Caesar or not?"
23He saw through their duplicity and said to
them, 24"Show me a denarius. Whose portrait
and inscription are on it?"
25"Caesar's," they replied.

He said to them, "Then give to Caesar what
is Caesar's, and to God what is God's."
26They were unable to trap him in what he
had said there in public. And astonished by his
answer, they became silent.

The Resurrection and Marriage

27Some of the Sadducees, who say there is
no resurrection, came to Jesus with a question.
28"Teacher," they said, "Moses wrote for us that
if a man's brother dies and leaves a wife but no
children, the man must marry the widow and
have children for his brother. 29Now there were
seven brothers. The first one married a woman
and died childless. 30The second 31and then
the third married her, and in the same way the
seven died, leaving no children. 32Finally, the
woman died too. 33Now then, at the resurrection whose wife will she be, since the seven
were married to her?"
34Jesus replied, "The people of this age
marry and are given in marriage. 35But those
who are considered worthy of taking part in
that age and in the resurrection from the dead
will neither marry nor be given in marriage,
36and they can no longer die; for they are like
the angels. They are God's children, since they
are children of the resurrection. 37But in the
account of the bush, even Moses showed that
the dead rise, for he calls the Lord 'the God of
Abraham, and the God of Isaac, and the God
of Jacob.'[a] 38He is not the God of the dead, but
of the living, for to him all are alive."
39Some of the teachers of the law responded,
"Well said, teacher!" 40And no one dared to ask
him any more questions.

Whose Son Is the Christ?

41Then Jesus said to them, "How is it that
they say the Christ[b] is the Son of David? 42Da-
vid himself declares in the Book of Psalms:

"'The Lord said to my Lord:
  "Sit at my right hand
43until I make your enemies
  a footstool for your feet."'[c]

44David calls him 'Lord.' How then can he be
his son?"
45While all the people were listening, Jesus
said to his disciples, 46"Beware of the teachers
of the law. They like to walk around in flowing
robes and love to be greeted in the marketplaces
and have the most important seats in the synagogues and the places of honor at banquets.
47They devour widows' houses and for a show
make lengthy prayers. Such men will be punished most severely."

The Widow's Offering

21 As he looked up, Jesus saw the rich
putting their gifts into the temple treasury. 2He also saw a poor widow put in two
very small copper coins.[d] 3"I tell you the truth,"
he said, "this poor widow has put in more than
all the others. 4All these people gave their gifts
out of their wealth; but she out of her poverty
put in all she had to live on."

Signs of the End of the Age

5Some of his disciples were remarking
about how the temple was adorned with beautiful stones and with gifts dedicated to God.
But Jesus said, 6"As for what you see here, the
time will come when not one stone will be left
on another; every one of them will be thrown
down."
7"Teacher," they asked, "when will these
things happen? And what will be the sign that
they are about to take place?"
8He replied: "Watch out that you are not
deceived. For many will come in my name,
claiming, 'I am he,' and, 'The time is near.' Do
not follow them. 9When you hear of wars and
revolutions, do not be frightened. These things

[a]37 Exodus 3:6 [b]41 Or *Messiah* [c]43 Psalm 110:1 [d]2 Greek *two lepta*

must happen first, but the end will not come right away."

10Then he said to them: "Nation will rise against nation, and kingdom against kingdom. 11There will be great earthquakes, famines and pestilences in various places, and fearful events and great signs from heaven.

12"But before all this, they will lay hands on you and persecute you. They will deliver you to synagogues and prisons, and you will be brought before kings and governors, and all on account of my name. 13This will result in your being witnesses to them. 14But make up your mind not to worry beforehand how you will defend yourselves. 15For I will give you words and wisdom that none of your adversaries will be able to resist or contradict. 16You will be betrayed even by parents, brothers, relatives and friends, and they will put some of you to death. 17All men will hate you because of me. 18But not a hair of your head will perish. 19By standing firm you will gain life.

20"When you see Jerusalem being surrounded by armies, you will know that its desolation is near. 21Then let those who are in Judea flee to the mountains, let those in the city get out, and let those in the country not enter the city. 22For this is the time of punishment in fulfillment of all that has been written. 23How dreadful it will be in those days for pregnant women and nursing mothers! There will be great distress in the land and wrath against this people. 24They will fall by the sword and will be taken as prisoners to all the nations. Jerusalem will be trampled on by the Gentiles until the times of the Gentiles are fulfilled.

25"There will be signs in the sun, moon and stars. On the earth, nations will be in anguish and perplexity at the roaring and tossing of the sea. 26Men will faint from terror, apprehensive of what is coming on the world, for the heavenly bodies will be shaken. 27At that time they will see the Son of Man coming in a cloud with power and great glory. 28When these things begin to take place, stand up and lift up your heads, because your redemption is drawing near."

29He told them this parable: "Look at the fig tree and all the trees. 30When they sprout leaves, you can see for yourselves and know that summer is near. 31Even so, when you see these things happening, you know that the kingdom of God is near.

32"I tell you the truth, this generation[a] will certainly not pass away until all these things have happened. 33Heaven and earth will pass away, but my words will never pass away.

34"Be careful, or your hearts will be weighed down with dissipation, drunkenness and the anxieties of life, and that day will close on you unexpectedly like a trap. 35For it will come upon all those who live on the face of the whole earth. 36Be always on the watch, and pray that you may be able to escape all that is about to happen, and that you may be able to stand before the Son of Man."

37Each day Jesus was teaching at the temple, and each evening he went out to spend the night on the hill called the Mount of Olives, 38and all the people came early in the morning to hear him at the temple.

Judas Agrees to Betray Jesus

22 Now the Feast of Unleavened Bread, called the Passover, was approaching, 2and the chief priests and the teachers of the law were looking for some way to get rid of Jesus, for they were afraid of the people. 3Then Satan entered Judas, called Iscariot, one of the Twelve. 4And Judas went to the chief priests and the officers of the temple guard and discussed with them how he might betray Jesus. 5They were delighted and agreed to give him money. 6He consented, and watched for an opportunity to hand Jesus over to them when no crowd was present.

The Last Supper

7Then came the day of Unleavened Bread on which the Passover lamb had to be sacrificed. 8Jesus sent Peter and John, saying, "Go and make preparations for us to eat the Passover."

9"Where do you want us to prepare for it?" they asked.

10He replied, "As you enter the city, a man carrying a jar of water will meet you. Follow him to the house that he enters, 11and say to the owner of the house, 'The Teacher asks: Where is the guest room, where I may eat the

[a]32 Or *race*

Passover with my disciples?' 12He will show
you a large upper room, all furnished. Make
preparations there."
13They left and found things just as Jesus
had told them. So they prepared the Passover.
14When the hour came, Jesus and his apostles reclined at the table. 15And he said to them,
"I have eagerly desired to eat this Passover with
you before I suffer. 16For I tell you, I will not eat
it again until it finds fulfillment in the kingdom
of God."
17After taking the cup, he gave thanks and
said, "Take this and divide it among you. 18For
I tell you I will not drink again of the fruit of
the vine until the kingdom of God comes."
19And he took bread, gave thanks and broke
it, and gave it to them, saying,
"This is my body given for
you; do this in remembrance
of me."
20In the same way, after the
supper he took the cup, saying,
"This cup is the new covenant
in my blood, which is poured
out for you. 21But the hand of
him who is going to betray me
is with mine on the table. 22The
Son of Man will go as it has
been decreed, but woe to that
man who betrays him." 23They
began to question among themselves which of them it might
be who would do this.
24Also a dispute arose among them as to
which of them was considered to be greatest.
25Jesus said to them, "The kings of the Gentiles lord it over them; and those who exercise
authority over them call themselves Benefac-
tors. 26But you are not to be like that. Instead,
the greatest among you should be like the youngest, and the one who rules like the one who
serves. 27For who is greater, the one who is at
the table or the one who serves? Is it not the
one who is at the table? But I am among you
as one who serves. 28You are those who have
stood by me in my trials. 29And I confer on you
a kingdom, just as my Father conferred one on
me, 30so that you may eat and drink at my table
in my kingdom and sit on thrones, judging the
twelve tribes of Israel.
31"Simon, Simon, Satan has asked to sift
you[a] as wheat. 32But I have prayed for you, Simon, that your faith may not fail. And when
you have turned back, strengthen your brothers."
33But he replied, "Lord, I am ready to go
with you to prison and to death."
34Jesus answered, "I tell you, Peter, before
the rooster crows today, you will deny three
times that you know me."
35Then Jesus asked them, "When I sent you
without purse, bag or sandals, did you lack anything?"
"Nothing," they answered.
36He said to them, "But now if you have a
purse, take it, and also a bag;
and if you don't have a sword,
sell your cloak and buy one.
37It is written: 'And he was numbered with the transgressors'[b];
and I tell you that this must be
fulfilled in me. Yes, what is written about me is reaching its fulfillment."
38The disciples said, "See,
Lord, here are two swords."
"That is enough," he replied.

Luke 22:20

God Covenants With Us

In the same way, after the supper he took the cup, saying, "This cup is the new covenant in my blood, which is poured out for you."

Jesus Prays on the Mount of Olives

39Jesus went out as usual
to the Mount of Olives, and
his disciples followed him. 40On reaching the
place, he said to them, "Pray that you will not
fall into temptation." 41He withdrew about a
stone's throw beyond them, knelt down and
prayed, 42"Father, if you are willing, take this
cup from me; yet not my will, but yours be
done." 43An angel from heaven appeared to
him and strengthened him. 44And being in anguish, he prayed more earnestly, and his sweat
was like drops of blood falling to the ground.[c]
45When he rose from prayer and went
back to the disciples, he found them asleep,
exhausted from sorrow. 46"Why are you sleeping?" he asked them. "Get up and pray so that
you will not fall into temptation."

[a]31 The Greek is plural. [b]37 Isaiah 53:12 [c]44 Some early manuscripts do not have verses 43 and 44.

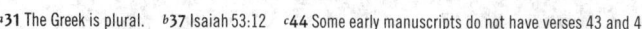

Not My Will

Read: Luke 22:39–46

Luke 22:41–42

[Jesus] withdrew about a stone's throw beyond them, knelt down and prayed, "Father, if you are willing, take this cup from me; yet not my will, but yours be done."

WHEN I WAS YOUNG I had the idea (I am sure I must have heard sermons on this) that I would somehow have to annihilate my own will before I could properly pray to God for his. "You must have absolutely no will of your own in the matter," someone had said. This sounded all right to me, and I spent a lot of time and energy trying to follow this advice. Finally I saw that no such thing was required. The struggle Jesus had in the Garden of Gethsemane showed me this. A conflict was taking place—not to annihilate his own will but to accept the will of the Father, which was *other* than his. It did not end with Jesus saying, "My will is now thine" but with, "Not my will but thine be done." The act of praying, far from divesting us of human desires, enables us to lay them before God as very real and pressing and say to him, "Not mine, Lord. Yours." (If we had gotten rid of them, there would be nothing to lay down.)

There is something terribly down-to earth about this. They are my own requests I am supposed to "make known" to God. They are things I feel strongly about. They may be sinful. If they are, making them known to God might make plain to me their true nature. But I start by making them known. I pray for what I want, as a child asks its father for whatever it wants. This is faith's legitimate activity.

Sometimes a father's answer to his child is no. If God, like a father, denies us what we want now, it is in order to give us some far better thing later on. The will of God, we can rest assured, is invariably a better thing, but our having asked for what we wanted now provides the occasion for us to say, "Nevertheless, not my will but thine be done."

—Elisabeth Elliot

reflection

1 Describe the area of your life where you are struggling to accept the will of the Father.

2 How has this devotional helped you in understanding the difference between annihilating your will and submitting your will to God?

3 Can you now pray, "Nevertheless, not my will but thine be done"? Proclaim in faith that God's will is invariably the best thing for your life and the lives of those you love.

RELATED READINGS

Psalm 143; Matthew 6:9–13; John 10:15–18; Romans 12:1–2

Go to page 1279 for your next devotional reading.

Jesus Arrested

47While he was still speaking a crowd came
up, and the man who was called Judas, one of
the Twelve, was leading them. He approached
Jesus to kiss him, 48but Jesus asked him, "Judas,
are you betraying the Son of Man with a kiss?"
49When Jesus' followers saw what was going
to happen, they said, "Lord, should we strike
with our swords?" 50And one of them struck
the servant of the high priest, cutting off his
right ear.
51But Jesus answered, "No more of this!"
And he touched the man's ear and healed him.
52Then Jesus said to the chief priests, the officers of the temple guard, and the elders, who
had come for him, "Am I leading a rebellion,
that you have come with swords and clubs?
53Every day I was with you in the temple
courts, and you did not lay a hand on me. But
this is your hour—when darkness reigns."

Peter Disowns Jesus

54Then seizing him, they led him away and
took him into the house of the high priest. Peter followed at a distance. 55But when they had
kindled a fire in the middle of the courtyard
and had sat down together, Peter sat down with
them. 56A servant girl saw him seated there in
the firelight. She looked closely at him and said,
"This man was with him."
57But he denied it. "Woman, I don't know
him," he said.
58A little later someone else saw him and
said, "You also are one of them."
"Man, I am not!" Peter replied.
59About an hour later another asserted,
"Certainly this fellow was with him, for he is
a Galilean."
60Peter replied, "Man, I don't know what
you're talking about!" Just as he was speaking,
the rooster crowed. 61The Lord turned and
looked straight at Peter. Then Peter remembered the word the Lord had spoken to him:
"Before the rooster crows today, you will disown me three times." 62And he went outside
and wept bitterly.

The Guards Mock Jesus

63The men who were guarding Jesus began
mocking and beating him. 64They blindfolded
him and demanded, "Prophesy! Who hit you?"
65And they said many other insulting things
to him.

Jesus Before Pilate and Herod

66At daybreak the council of the elders of
the people, both the chief priests and teachers
of the law, met together, and Jesus was led before them. 67"If you are the Christ,[a]" they said,
"tell us."
Jesus answered, "If I tell you, you will not believe me, 68and if I asked you, you would not
answer. 69But from now on, the Son of Man
will be seated at the right hand of the mighty
God."
70They all asked, "Are you then the Son of
God?"
He replied, "You are right in saying I am."
71Then they said, "Why do we need any
more testimony? We have heard it from his
own lips."

23 Then the whole assembly rose and led
him off to Pilate. 2And they began to
accuse him, saying, "We have found this man
subverting our nation. He opposes payment
of taxes to Caesar and claims to be Christ,[b]
a king."
3So Pilate asked Jesus, "Are you the king of
the Jews?"
"Yes, it is as you say," Jesus replied.
4Then Pilate announced to the chief priests
and the crowd, "I find no basis for a charge
against this man."
5But they insisted, "He stirs up the people all
over Judea[c] by his teaching. He started in Galilee and has come all the way here."
6On hearing this, Pilate asked if the man was
a Galilean. 7When he learned that Jesus was under Herod's jurisdiction, he sent him to Herod,
who was also in Jerusalem at that time.
8When Herod saw Jesus, he was greatly
pleased, because for a long time he had been
wanting to see him. From what he had heard
about him, he hoped to see him perform some
miracle. 9He plied him with many questions,
but Jesus gave him no answer. 10The chief
priests and the teachers of the law were standing there, vehemently accusing him. 11Then
Herod and his soldiers ridiculed and mocked

[a]67 Or *Messiah* [b]2 Or *Messiah*; also in verses 35 and 39 [c]5 Or *over the land of the Jews*

him. Dressing him in an elegant robe, they sent
him back to Pilate. 12That day Herod and Pilate
became friends—before this they had been enemies.
13Pilate called together the chief priests, the
rulers and the people, 14and said to them, "You
brought me this man as one who was inciting
the people to rebellion. I have examined him in
your presence and have found no basis for your
charges against him. 15Neither has Herod, for
he sent him back to us; as you can see, he has
done nothing to deserve death. 16Therefore, I
will punish him and then release him.[a]"
18With one voice they cried out, "Away with
this man! Release Barabbas to us!" 19(Barabbas
had been thrown into prison for an insurrection in the city, and for murder.)
20Wanting to release Jesus, Pilate appealed to
them again. 21But they kept shouting, "Crucify
him! Crucify him!"
22For the third time he spoke to them:
"Why? What crime has this man committed?
I have found in him no grounds for the death
penalty. Therefore I will have him punished
and then release him."
23But with loud shouts they insistently
demanded that he be crucified, and their
shouts prevailed. 24So Pilate decided to grant
their demand. 25He released the man who had
been thrown into prison for insurrection and
murder, the one they asked for, and surrendered Jesus to their will.

The Crucifixion

26As they led him away, they
seized Simon from Cyrene,
who was on his way in from
the country, and put the cross
on him and made him carry it
behind Jesus. 27A large number
of people followed him, including women who mourned and
wailed for him. 28Jesus turned
and said to them, "Daughters
of Jerusalem, do not weep for
me; weep for yourselves and
for your children. 29For the
time will come when you will
say, 'Blessed are the barren women, the wombs
that never bore and the breasts that never
nursed!' 30Then

> "'they will say to the mountains, "Fall on us!"
> and to the hills, "Cover us!"'[b]

31For if men do these things when the tree is
green, what will happen when it is dry?"
32Two other men, both criminals, were also
led out with him to be executed. 33When they
came to the place called the Skull, there they
crucified him, along with the criminals—one
on his right, the other on his left. 34Jesus said,
"Father, forgive them, for they do not know
what they are doing."[c] And they divided up his
clothes by casting lots.
35The people stood watching, and the rulers
even sneered at him. They said, "He saved others; let him save himself if he is the Christ of
God, the Chosen One."
36The soldiers also came up and mocked
him. They offered him wine vinegar 37and said,
"If you are the king of the Jews, save yourself."
38There was a written notice above him,
which read: THIS IS THE KING OF THE JEWS.
39One of the criminals who hung there
hurled insults at him: "Aren't you the Christ?
Save yourself and us!"
40But the other criminal rebuked him.
"Don't you fear God," he said, "since you are
under the same sentence? 41We are punished
justly, for we are getting what our deeds deserve. But this man has done
nothing wrong."
42Then he said, "Jesus, remember me when you come
into your kingdom.[d]"
43Jesus answered him, "I tell
you the truth, today you will be
with me in paradise."

> **Luke 23:43**
>
> *God Grants Salvation*
>
> Jesus answered him, "I tell you the truth, today you will be with me in paradise."

Jesus' Death

44It was now about the sixth
hour, and darkness came over
the whole land until the ninth
hour, 45for the sun stopped
shining. And the curtain of the
temple was torn in two. 46Jesus
called out with a loud voice, "Father, into your

[a]16 Some manuscripts *him."* [17] *Now he was obliged to release one man to them at the Feast.* [b]30 Hosea 10:8 [c]34 Some early manuscripts do not have this sentence. [d]42 Some manuscripts *come with your kingly power*

Nightmare

PILATE'S WIFE

SHE AWOKE WITH A START. Beads of sweat ran down the middle of her back. Her face was flushed, her breathing ragged and quick.

It took a few moments to reorient herself to her bedroom. Where was she? How long had she been sleeping?

She'd had the most terrifying nightmare. Even now, fully awake, the events seemed so real—she could recall every detail.

"Jesus . . ." she whispered to herself as she mindlessly smoothed the bed linens with her palms. Her dream had been about the man they called Jesus. He was a prisoner—brought before her husband, Pilate. But why? What crime had he committed?

Something about him in her dream led her to believe he was innocent. Completely innocent. She didn't know exactly how to explain it. She wasn't a Jew, and she couldn't begin to understand why these religious leaders had worked themselves into a frenzy over this man, but she knew without a doubt that they were dead wrong.

If only they could be more like the Romans . . . civilized, orderly, she thought to herself. Nevertheless, she was convinced. Her husband could be responsible for convicting an innocent man—to death!

Her stomach began to knot just thinking about it. Waves of nausea swept over her as she struggled out of bed. She knew what she had to do. She'd heard the commotion of the gathering crowd.

"It must be nearly time," she mumbled. She recalled her husband's annual duty to release one of the prisoners for Passover. "I have to hurry before it's too late . . ."

She called out for one of her aides. "Quick! Get a message to my husband immediately. He must not go ahead with the execution of that man. I don't care what you tell him, just tell him not to go through with it. He's innocent!"

The messenger left her chambers, and she collapsed back on the bed. Her mind raced with adrenaline, and her stomach ached as she wondered if the message would get to him in time.

—Prayer—

Lord God, help me to have a pure heart and to do what I know is right.

While Pilate was sitting on the judge's seat, his wife sent him this message: "Don't have anything to do with that innocent man, for I have suffered a great deal today in a dream because of him."

Matthew 27:19

ASSIGNED READING:

Matthew 27:11–26

Weekend

Go to page 1284 for your next devotional reading.

hands I commit my spirit." When he had said
this, he breathed his last.
47The centurion, seeing what had happened,
praised God and said, "Surely this was a righteous man." 48When all the people who had
gathered to witness this sight saw what took
place, they beat their breasts and went away.
49But all those who knew him, including the
women who had followed him from Galilee,
stood at a distance, watching these things.

Jesus' Burial

50Now there was a man named Joseph, a
member of the Council, a good and upright
man, 51who had not consented to their decision
and action. He came from the Judean town of
Arimathea and he was waiting for the kingdom
of God. 52Going to Pilate, he asked for Jesus'
body. 53Then he took it down, wrapped it in
linen cloth and placed it in a tomb cut in the
rock, one in which no one had yet been laid.
54It was Preparation Day, and the Sabbath was
about to begin.
55The women who had come with Jesus
from Galilee followed Joseph and saw the tomb
and how his body was laid in it. 56Then they
went home and prepared spices and perfumes.
But they rested on the Sabbath in obedience to
the commandment.

The Resurrection

24 On the first day of the week, very early
in the morning, the women took the
spices they had prepared and went to the tomb.
2They found the stone rolled away from the
tomb, 3but when they entered, they did not
find the body of the Lord Jesus. 4While they
were wondering about this, suddenly two men
in clothes that gleamed like lightning stood beside them. 5In their fright the women bowed
down with their faces to the ground, but the
men said to them, "Why do you look for the
living among the dead? 6He is not here; he has
risen! Remember how he told you, while he was
still with you in Galilee: 7'The Son of Man must
be delivered into the hands of sinful men, be
crucified and on the third day be raised again.'"
8Then they remembered his words.
9When they came back from the tomb, they
told all these things to the Eleven and to all
the others. 10It was Mary Magdalene, Joanna,
Mary the mother of James, and the others
with them who told this to the apostles. 11But
they did not believe the women, because their
words seemed to them like nonsense. 12Peter,
however, got up and ran to the tomb. Bending
over, he saw the strips of linen lying by themselves, and he went away, wondering to himself
what had happened.

On the Road to Emmaus

13Now that same day two of them were going to a village called Emmaus, about seven
miles[a] from Jerusalem. 14They were talking
with each other about everything that had happened. 15As they talked and discussed these
things with each other, Jesus himself came up
and walked along with them; 16but they were
kept from recognizing him.
17He asked them, "What are you discussing
together as you walk along?"
They stood still, their faces downcast. 18One
of them, named Cleopas, asked him, "Are
you only a visitor to Jerusalem and do not
know the things that have happened there in
these days?"
19"What things?" he asked.
"About Jesus of Nazareth," they replied. "He
was a prophet, powerful in word and deed before God and all the people. 20The chief priests
and our rulers handed him over to be sentenced
to death, and they crucified him; 21but we had
hoped that he was the one who was going to
redeem Israel. And what is more, it is the third
day since all this took place. 22In addition,
some of our women amazed us. They went to
the tomb early this morning 23but didn't find
his body. They came and told us that they had
seen a vision of angels, who said he was alive.
24Then some of our companions went to the
tomb and found it just as the women had said,
but him they did not see."
25He said to them, "How foolish you are,
and how slow of heart to believe all that the
prophets have spoken! 26Did not the Christ[b]
have to suffer these things and then enter his
glory?" 27And beginning with Moses and all
the Prophets, he explained to them what was
said in all the Scriptures concerning himself.

[a]13 Greek *sixty stadia* (about 11 kilometers) [b]26 Or *Messiah*; also in verse 46

28As they approached the village to which
they were going, Jesus acted as if he were going
farther. 29But they urged him strongly, "Stay
with us, for it is nearly evening; the day is almost over." So he went in to stay with them.
30When he was at the table with them, he
took bread, gave thanks, broke it and began to
give it to them. 31Then their eyes were opened
and they recognized him, and he disappeared
from their sight. 32They asked each other,
"Were not our hearts burning within us while
he talked with us on the road and opened the
Scriptures to us?"
33They got up and returned at once to Jerusalem. There they found the Eleven and those
with them, assembled together 34and saying,
"It is true! The Lord has risen and has appeared
to Simon." 35Then the two told what had happened on the way, and how Jesus was recognized by them when he broke the bread.

Jesus Appears to the Disciples

36While they were still talking about this,
Jesus himself stood among them and said to
them, "Peace be with you."
37They were startled and frightened, thinking they saw a ghost. 38He said to them, "Why
are you troubled, and why do doubts rise in
your minds? 39Look at my hands and my feet.
It is I myself! Touch me and see; a ghost does
not have flesh and bones, as you see I have."
40When he had said this, he showed them
his hands and feet. 41And while they still did
not believe it because of joy and amazement,
he asked them, "Do you have anything here to
eat?" 42They gave him a piece of broiled fish,
43and he took it and ate it in their presence.
44He said to them, "This is what I told you
while I was still with you: Everything must be
fulfilled that is written about me in the Law of
Moses, the Prophets and the Psalms."
45Then he opened their minds so they could
understand the Scriptures. 46He told them,
"This is what is written: The Christ will suffer and rise from the dead on the third day,
47and repentance and forgiveness of sins will
be preached in his name to all nations, beginning at Jerusalem. 48You are witnesses of these
things. 49I am going to send you what my Father has promised; but stay in the city until you
have been clothed with power from on high."

The Ascension

50When he had led them out to the vicinity
of Bethany, he lifted up his hands and blessed
them. 51While he was blessing them, he left
them and was taken up into heaven. 52Then
they worshiped him and returned to Jerusalem
with great joy. 53And they stayed continually at
the temple, praising God.

John

Author:
The apostle John.

Audience:
Followers of Jesus. John wrote to convince unbelievers and the doubting.

Date:
About A.D. 85–90, before John's exile to the island of Patmos.

Setting:
John's eyewitness account is presumably the last Gospel written.

Verse to Remember:
Jesus answered, "I am the way and the truth and the life. No one comes to the Father except through me." (14:6)

John's Gospel stands apart from the other three, shedding new light on what has by now become a familiar story. There are fewer parables, fewer instances of Jesus' public speaking and fewer miracles, but there are more conversations, more personal encounters and more interactions among the disciples. It is John who records *Jesus' seven "I am" statements* that give us tangible descriptions of who this Son of God is.

Nearly half of John's Gospel is devoted to the final week of Jesus' life. John is the only disciple who followed Jesus all the way to the cross, and as we look through his eyes, we feel his shock and deep grief, but we also experience something else—something that so overwhelmed John he incorporated it into how he described himself even years later when he wrote his Gospel. *We experience love.*

John always referred to himself as "the disciple whom Jesus loved," as though the concept still left him slack-jawed with awe. As we follow John's footsteps, listening to Jesus, witnessing his death and rejoicing at his resurrection, we experience that awe for ourselves. For we realize that we, too, are *the disciples whom Jesus loves.*

The Word Became Flesh

1 In the beginning was the Word, and the
Word was with God, and the Word was
God. 2He was with God in the beginning.
3Through him all things were made; without
him nothing was made that has been made. 4In
him was life, and that life was the light of men.
5The light shines in the darkness, but the darkness has not understood[a] it.
6There came a man who was sent from God;

[a]5 Or *darkness, and the darkness has not overcome*

his name was John. 7He came as a witness to
testify concerning that light, so that through
him all men might believe. 8He himself was
not the light; he came only as a witness to the
light. 9The true light that gives light to every
man was coming into the world.[a]

10He was in the world, and though the world
was made through him, the world did not recognize him. 11He came to that which was his
own, but his own did not receive him. 12Yet to
all who received him, to those who believed
in his name, he gave the right to become children of God— 13children born not of natural
descent,[b] nor of human decision or a husband's
will, but born of God.

14The Word became flesh and made his
dwelling among us. We have seen his glory, the
glory of the One and Only,[c]
who came from the Father, full
of grace and truth.

15John testifies concerning
him. He cries out, saying, "This
was he of whom I said, 'He who
comes after me has surpassed
me because he was before me.'"
16From the fullness of his grace
we have all received one blessing after another. 17For the
law was given through Moses;
grace and truth came through
Jesus Christ. 18No one has ever
seen God, but God the One and
Only,[c,d] who is at the Father's
side, has made him known.

John 1:14

God Reveals Himself

The Word became flesh and made his dwelling among us. We have seen his glory, the glory of the One and Only, who came from the Father, full of grace and truth.

John the Baptist Denies Being the Christ

19Now this was John's testimony when the
Jews of Jerusalem sent priests and Levites to ask
him who he was. 20He did not fail to confess,
but confessed freely, "I am not the Christ.[e]"

21They asked him, "Then who are you? Are
you Elijah?"

He said, "I am not."

"Are you the Prophet?"

He answered, "No."

22Finally they said, "Who are you? Give us
an answer to take back to those who sent us.
What do you say about yourself?"

23John replied in the words of Isaiah the
prophet, "I am the voice of one calling in the
desert, 'Make straight the way for the Lord.'"[f]

24Now some Pharisees who had been sent
25questioned him, "Why then do you baptize
if you are not the Christ, nor Elijah, nor the
Prophet?"

26"I baptize with[g] water," John replied, "but
among you stands one you do not know. 27He
is the one who comes after me, the thongs of
whose sandals I am not worthy to untie."

28This all happened at Bethany on the other
side of the Jordan, where John was baptizing.

Jesus the Lamb of God

29The next day John saw Jesus coming toward him and said, "Look, the Lamb of God,
who takes away the sin of
the world! 30This is the one I
meant when I said, 'A man who
comes after me has surpassed
me because he was before me.'
31I myself did not know him,
but the reason I came baptizing
with water was that he might
be revealed to Israel."

32Then John gave this
testimony: "I saw the Spirit
come down from heaven as a
dove and remain on him. 33I
would not have known him,
except that the one who sent
me to baptize with water told
me, 'The man on whom you
see the Spirit come down and
remain is he who will baptize with the Holy
Spirit.' 34I have seen and I testify that this is the
Son of God."

Jesus' First Disciples

35The next day John was there again with
two of his disciples. 36When he saw Jesus passing by, he said, "Look, the Lamb of God!"

37When the two disciples heard him say this,
they followed Jesus. 38Turning around, Jesus
saw them following and asked, "What do you
want?"

They said, "Rabbi" (which means Teacher),
"where are you staying?"

[a]9 Or *This was the true light that gives light to every man who comes into the world* [b]13 Greek *of bloods* [c]14,18 Or *the Only Begotten* [d]18 Some manuscripts *but the only* (or *only begotten*) *Son* [e]20 Or *Messiah.* "The Christ" (Greek) and "the Messiah" (Hebrew) both mean "the Anointed One"; also in verse 25. [f]23 Isaiah 40:3 [g]26 Or *in*; also in verses 31 and 33

Light Keepers

Read: John 1:1–18

John 1:7–9

[John] came as a witness to testify concerning that light, so that through him all men might believe. He himself was not the light; he came only as a witness to the light. The true light that gives light to every man was coming into the world.

reflection

1 What are your favorite types of light (lamps, candles, firelight, sunshine)? List them.

2 What positive feeling do you derive from each light source you listed?

3 How can you emit a Christlike light in your home or workplace?

RELATED READINGS

Matthew 5:14–16; John 3:16–21; 8:12

GURNET POINT LIGHT in Plymouth, Massachusetts, is distinct from any other lighthouse in the United States: It is associated with Hannah Thomas, the first female lighthouse keeper in America. When Hannah's husband went off to fight in the War for Independence, Hannah remained behind to keep the great lamp burning to guide ships out at sea.

In spiritual terms, women have been keepers of the light for centuries: Agnes of Rome was martyred for refusing to sacrifice to pagan gods. Glady Aylward was a missionary to China who shared the gospel in villages and prisons and among lepers. Rose Lathrop, daughter of Nathaniel Hawthorne, established homes in the late 1800s for young women suffering from cancer. Like John the Baptist, these women directed and guided others toward the true light that came into the world: Jesus.

Have you ever watched the sun reflecting off prisms hanging from a crystal chandelier? The prisms themselves are not the light; they merely reflect the light produced by the chandelier. Yet they are capable of throwing hundreds of sparkling rainbows throughout a room. In his book *Desiring God,* John Piper wrote, "We were made to be prisms refracting the light of God's glory into all of life. Why God should want to give us a share in shining with his glory—*shekinah*—is a great mystery. Call it grace or mercy or love—it is an unspeakable wonder!"

To reflect the light of God's presence in a dark and damaged world, we have to stay close to the source: the Son. The more we let his light shine into our eyes and reflect into the eyes of others, the more we become like him. "And we, who with unveiled faces all reflect the Lord's glory, are being transformed into his likeness with ever-increasing glory, which comes from the Lord, who is the Spirit" (2 Corinthians 3:18).

Let's be keepers of God's light—ensuring that the light of his love burns brightly. We can also reflect that light into the lives of others. It only takes a small beacon of light to dispel the darkness.

Go to page 1286 for your next devotional reading.

39"Come," he replied, "and you will see."
So they went and saw where he was staying,
and spent that day with him. It was about the
tenth hour.
40Andrew, Simon Peter's brother, was one
of the two who heard what John had said and
who had followed Jesus. 41The first thing Andrew did was to find his brother Simon and tell
him, "We have found the Messiah" (that is, the
Christ). 42And he brought him to Jesus.
Jesus looked at him and said, "You are Simon
son of John. You will be called Cephas" (which,
when translated, is Peter[a]).

Jesus Calls Philip and Nathanael

43The next day Jesus decided to leave for
Galilee. Finding Philip, he said to him, "Follow
me."
44Philip, like Andrew and Peter, was from the
town of Bethsaida. 45Philip found Nathanael
and told him, "We have found the one Moses
wrote about in the Law, and about whom the
prophets also wrote—Jesus of Nazareth, the
son of Joseph."
46"Nazareth! Can anything good come from
there?" Nathanael asked.
"Come and see," said Philip.
47When Jesus saw Nathanael approaching,
he said of him, "Here is a true Israelite, in
whom there is nothing false."
48"How do you know me?" Nathanael asked.
Jesus answered, "I saw you while you were still
under the fig tree before Philip called you."
49Then Nathanael declared, "Rabbi, you are
the Son of God; you are the King of Israel."
50Jesus said, "You believe[b] because I told
you I saw you under the fig tree. You shall see
greater things than that." 51He then added, "I
tell you[c] the truth, you[c] shall see heaven open,
and the angels of God ascending and descending on the Son of Man."

Jesus Changes Water to Wine

2 On the third day a wedding took place at
Cana in Galilee. Jesus' mother was there,
2and Jesus and his disciples had also been
invited to the wedding. 3When the wine was
gone, Jesus' mother said to him, "They have no
more wine."
4"Dear woman, why do you involve me?"
Jesus replied. "My time has not yet come."
5His mother said to the servants, "Do
whatever he tells you."
6Nearby stood six stone water jars, the kind
used by the Jews for ceremonial washing, each
holding from twenty to thirty gallons.[d]
7Jesus said to the servants, "Fill the jars with
water"; so they filled them to the brim.
8Then he told them, "Now draw some out
and take it to the master of the banquet."
They did so, 9and the master of the banquet
tasted the water that had been turned into
wine. He did not realize where it had come
from, though the servants who had drawn the
water knew. Then he called the bridegroom
aside 10and said, "Everyone brings out the
choice wine first and then the cheaper wine after the guests have had too much to drink; but
you have saved the best till now."
11This, the first of his miraculous signs,
Jesus performed at Cana in Galilee. He thus
revealed his glory, and his disciples put their
faith in him.

Jesus Clears the Temple

12After this he went down to Capernaum
with his mother and brothers and his disciples.
There they stayed for a few days.
13When it was almost time for the Jewish
Passover, Jesus went up to Jerusalem. 14In
the temple courts he found men selling cattle,
sheep and doves, and others sitting at tables ex-
changing money. 15So he made a whip out of
cords, and drove all from the temple area, both
sheep and cattle; he scattered the coins of the
money changers and overturned their tables.
16To those who sold doves he said, "Get these
out of here! How dare you turn my Father's
house into a market!"
17His disciples remembered that it is written: "Zeal for your house will consume me."[e]
18Then the Jews demanded of him, "What
miraculous sign can you show us to prove your
authority to do all this?"
19Jesus answered them, "Destroy this temple, and I will raise it again in three days."
20The Jews replied, "It has taken forty-six
years to build this temple, and you are going to

[a]42 Both *Cephas* (Aramaic) and *Peter* (Greek) mean *rock.* [b]50 Or *Do you believe . . . ?* [c]51 The Greek is plural. [d]6 Greek *two to three metretes* (probably about 75 to 115 liters) [e]17 Psalm 69:9

The Wedding Guest

Read: John 2:1–11

John 2:9

The master of the banquet tasted the water that had been turned into wine. He did not realize where it had come from, though the servants who had drawn the water knew.

YEARS AGO WHEN JOHNNY CARSON was the host of *The Tonight Show,* he interviewed an eight-year-old boy. The young man was asked to appear because he had rescued two friends from a coal mine outside his hometown in West Virginia. As Johnny questioned the boy, it became apparent to him and the audience that the young man was a Christian. So Johnny asked him if he attended Sunday school. When the boy said he did, Johnny asked, "What are you learning in Sunday school?" "Last week our lesson was about when Jesus went to a wedding and turned water into wine." The audience roared, but Johnny tried to keep a straight face. Then he said, "And what did you learn from that story?" The boy squirmed in his chair. It was apparent he hadn't thought about this. But then he lifted up his face and said, "If you're going to have a wedding, make sure you invite Jesus!"

Jesus' first miracle occurred at a wedding he'd been invited to. It clearly announced his nature, showing that he came to bring joy to his people. God delights in his children. Our joy pleases him. When we celebrate, he celebrates with us.

The hosts of the wedding celebration would have been embarrassed if the wine had run dry. Knowing this, Jesus' mother turned to the One who can turn sorrow into gladness. Jesus quietly worked behind the scenes to turn the water into wine. When the banquet master tasted the wine, he was surprised that it was better than what had been served at first.

When we invite Jesus into every aspect of our lives, he can exchange our past pain for present comfort and turn our deep sorrow into divine delight. He can take old wounds and turn them into fresh wisdom. He can turn stale, old thoughts into new ideas and creative ways to solve our problems. He can take a cold silence and turn it once again into a warm conversation. If we just ask, he can take those things that we are ashamed of and cast them into a sea of forgetfulness, allowing us to experience true and deep joy. He does not save the best for *last,* he saves the best for *now.*

Those who drew the water knew the secret: Jesus has the power to change things. Just imagine what he can change if you only issue the invitation. He's the guest who can never stay too long.

reflection

1 How has Jesus changed difficult circumstances for you in the past?

2 What would you exchange right now if you could—gladness for mourning, praise for despair, beauty for ashes? Invite Jesus to work a divine exchange for you as only he can.

3 Who will you share the knowledge of the joy of the Lord with today?

RELATED READINGS

Isaiah 61:1–3; 65:17–25; Revelation 21:5

Go to page 1288 for your next devotional reading.

raise it in three days?" 21But the temple he had spoken of was his body. 22After he was raised from the dead, his disciples recalled what he had said. Then they believed the Scripture and the words that Jesus had spoken.

23Now while he was in Jerusalem at the Passover Feast, many people saw the miraculous signs he was doing and believed in his name.[a] 24But Jesus would not entrust himself to them, for he knew all men. 25He did not need man's testimony about man, for he knew what was in a man.

Jesus Teaches Nicodemus

3 Now there was a man of the Pharisees named Nicodemus, a member of the Jewish ruling council. 2He came to Jesus at night and said, "Rabbi, we know you are a teacher who has come from God. For no one could perform the miraculous signs you are doing if God were not with him."

3In reply Jesus declared, "I tell you the truth, no one can see the kingdom of God unless he is born again.[b]"

4"How can a man be born when he is old?" Nicodemus asked. "Surely he cannot enter a second time into his mother's womb to be born!"

5Jesus answered, "I tell you the truth, no one can enter the kingdom of God unless he is born of water and the Spirit. 6Flesh gives birth to flesh, but the Spirit[c] gives birth to spirit. 7You should not be surprised at my saying, 'You[d] must be born again.' 8The wind blows wherever it pleases. You hear its sound, but you cannot tell where it comes from or where it is going. So it is with everyone born of the Spirit."

9"How can this be?" Nicodemus asked.

10"You are Israel's teacher," said Jesus, "and do you not understand these things? 11I tell you the truth, we speak of what we know, and we testify to what we have seen, but still you people do not accept our testimony. 12I have spoken to you of earthly things and you do not believe; how then will you believe if I speak of heavenly things? 13No one has ever gone into heaven except the one who came from heaven—the Son of Man.[e] 14Just as Moses lifted up the snake in the desert, so the Son of Man must be lifted up, 15that everyone who believes in him may have eternal life.[f]

16"For God so loved the world that he gave his one and only Son,[g] that whoever believes in him shall not perish but have eternal life. 17For God did not send his Son into the world to condemn the world, but to save the world through him. 18Whoever believes in him is not condemned, but whoever does not believe stands condemned already because he has not believed in the name of God's one and only Son.[h] 19This is the verdict: Light has come into the world, but men loved darkness instead of light because their deeds were evil. 20Everyone who does evil hates the light, and will not come into the light for fear that his deeds will be exposed. 21But whoever lives by the truth comes into the light, so that it may be seen plainly that what he has done has been done through God."[i]

John the Baptist's Testimony About Jesus

22After this, Jesus and his disciples went out into the Judean countryside, where he spent some time with them, and baptized. 23Now John also was baptizing at Aenon near Salim, because there was plenty of water, and people were constantly coming to be baptized. 24(This was before John was put in prison.) 25An argument developed between some of John's disciples and a certain Jew[j] over the matter of ceremonial washing. 26They came to John and said to him, "Rabbi, that man who was with you on the other side of the Jordan—the one you testified about—well, he is baptizing, and everyone is going to him."

John 3:15–16

God Offers Eternal Life

"Everyone who believes in him may have eternal life. For God so loved the world that he gave his one and only Son, that whoever believes in him shall not perish but have eternal life."

[a]23 Or *and believed in him* [b]3 Or *born from above*; also in verse 7 [c]6 Or *but spirit* [d]7 The Greek is plural. [e]13 Some manuscripts *Man, who is in heaven* [f]15 Or *believes may have eternal life in him* [g]16 Or *his only begotten Son* [h]18 Or *God's only begotten Son* [i]21 Some interpreters end the quotation after verse 15. [j]25 Some manuscripts *and certain Jews*

No Condemnation

Read John 3:1–21

WE OFTEN GO THROUGH THE DAY feeling as if someone is looking over our shoulder ready to judge our actions. *My husband probably wonders why dinner isn't made yet . . . My boss is thinking I'm taking too long with that project . . . . Amber's teacher doesn't understand why we were late this morning . . . This isn't how Mom would have done it . . .* And perhaps the voice we hear the most is our own: *Why aren't you good enough?*

Even if others praise us, the pressure we put on ourselves can drown out the latest acclaim. We put pressure on ourselves to do more—and do it better and quicker. *How could God be pleased with us,* we wonder, *when we feel so weak?*

Listen to the words in this chapter of John's Gospel. God wants a relationship with us—not to condemn us, but to free us. He offers redemption through Jesus—not because we have *done* something to deserve it, but because he loves us.

Though we may read those words again and again, they can be hard to believe. But try to wrap your brain around this truth: God does not condemn you. None of the pressure you feel throughout the day is from God. In truth, you may be trying to please others or achieve your own goals more than you are trying to please God. You may feel guilty because you keep changing the standard.

Richard Foster writes, "The less we are manipulated by the expectations of others, the more we are open to the expectations of God." Yes, we are weak. Yes, we often fail to meet our own expectations. But what does God expect of us today? To believe in his Son who set us free from sin. To believe that he is stronger than our doubts, fears, pride and ambition. To believe that he does not condemn us for who we were before we met his Son. To discover who we are in the light of his love, freedom and grace.

John 3:17

"For God did not send his Son into the world to condemn the world, but to save the world through him."

reflection

1 How have you experienced self-condemnation?

2 Reread the words and personalize them by filling in your name: "*God did not send his Son into the world to condemn ________________, but to save ________________ through him.*"

3 How often do you feel judged by others throughout your day? Remember whose opinion really counts. Ask God to show you who you are in the light of his love.

RELATED READINGS

John 5:24;
Romans 8:1–4;
1 John 3:19–24

Go to page 1291 for your next devotional reading.

27To this John replied, "A man can receive
only what is given him from heaven. 28You
yourselves can testify that I said, 'I am not the
Christ[a] but am sent ahead of him.' 29The bride
belongs to the bridegroom. The friend who
attends the bridegroom waits and listens for
him, and is full of joy when he hears the bridegroom's voice. That joy is mine, and it is now
complete. 30He must become greater; I must
become less.

31"The one who comes from above is above
all; the one who is from the earth belongs to the
earth, and speaks as one from the earth. The
one who comes from heaven is above all. 32He
testifies to what he has seen and heard, but no
one accepts his testimony. 33The man who has
accepted it has certified that God is truthful.
34For the one whom God has sent speaks the
words of God, for God[b] gives the Spirit without limit. 35The Father loves the Son and has
placed everything in his hands. 36Whoever believes in the Son has eternal life, but whoever
rejects the Son will not see life, for God's wrath
remains on him."[c]

Jesus Talks With a Samaritan Woman

4 The Pharisees heard that Jesus was gaining
and baptizing more disciples than John,
2although in fact it was not Jesus who baptized,
but his disciples. 3When the Lord learned of
this, he left Judea and went back once more to
Galilee.

4Now he had to go through Samaria. 5So he
came to a town in Samaria called Sychar, near
the plot of ground Jacob had given to his son
Joseph. 6Jacob's well was there, and Jesus, tired
as he was from the journey, sat down by the
well. It was about the sixth hour.

7When a Samaritan woman came to draw
water, Jesus said to her, "Will you give me a
drink?" 8(His disciples had gone into the town
to buy food.)

9The Samaritan woman said to him, "You
are a Jew and I am a Samaritan woman. How
can you ask me for a drink?" (For Jews do not
associate with Samaritans.[d])

10Jesus answered her, "If you knew the gift
of God and who it is that asks you for a drink,
you would have asked him and he would have
given you living water."

11"Sir," the woman said, "you have nothing
to draw with and the well is deep. Where can
you get this living water? 12Are you greater
than our father Jacob, who gave us the well and
drank from it himself, as did also his sons and
his flocks and herds?"

13Jesus answered, "Everyone who drinks
this water will be thirsty again, 14but whoever
drinks the water I give him will never thirst. Indeed, the water I give him will become in him a
spring of water welling up to eternal life."

15The woman said to him, "Sir, give me this
water so that I won't get thirsty and have to
keep coming here to draw water."

16He told her, "Go, call your husband and
come back."

17"I have no husband," she replied.

Jesus said to her, "You are right when you say
you have no husband. 18The fact is, you have
had five husbands, and the man you now have
is not your husband. What you have just said
is quite true."

19"Sir," the woman said, "I can see that you
are a prophet. 20Our fathers worshiped on this
mountain, but you Jews claim that the place
where we must worship is in Jerusalem."

21Jesus declared, "Believe me, woman, a time
is coming when you will worship the Father neither on this mountain nor in Jerusalem. 22You
Samaritans worship what you do not know;
we worship what we do know, for salvation is
from the Jews. 23Yet a time is coming and has
now come when the true worshipers will worship the Father in spirit and truth, for they are
the kind of worshipers the Father seeks. 24God
is spirit, and his worshipers must worship in
spirit and in truth."

25The woman said, "I know that Messiah"
(called Christ) "is coming. When he comes, he
will explain everything to us."

26Then Jesus declared, "I who speak to you
am he."

The Disciples Rejoin Jesus

27Just then his disciples returned and were
surprised to find him talking with a woman.
But no one asked, "What do you want?" or
"Why are you talking with her?"

28Then, leaving her water jar, the woman
went back to the town and said to the people,

[a]28 Or *Messiah* [b]34 Greek *he* [c]36 Some interpreters end the quotation after verse 30. [d]9 Or *do not use dishes Samaritans have used*

29 “Come, see a man who told me everything
I ever did. Could this be the Christ[a]?” 30 They
came out of the town and made their way toward him.
31 Meanwhile his disciples urged him,
“Rabbi, eat something.”
32 But he said to them, “I have food to eat
that you know nothing about.”
33 Then his disciples said to each other,
“Could someone have brought him food?”
34 “My food,” said Jesus, “is to do the will of
him who sent me and to finish his work. 35 Do
you not say, ‘Four months more and then the
harvest’? I tell you, open your eyes and look
at the fields! They are ripe for harvest. 36 Even
now the reaper draws his wages, even now he
harvests the crop for eternal life, so that the
sower and the reaper may be glad together.
37 Thus the saying ‘One sows and another
reaps’ is true. 38 I sent you to reap what you
have not worked for. Others have done the
hard work, and you have reaped the benefits
of their labor.”

Many Samaritans Believe

39 Many of the Samaritans from that town
believed in him because of the woman’s testimony, “He told me everything
I ever did.” 40 So when the Samaritans came to him, they
urged him to stay with them,
and he stayed two days. 41 And
because of his words many
more became believers.
42 They said to the woman,
“We no longer believe just because of what you said; now we
have heard for ourselves, and
we know that this man really is
the Savior of the world.”

Jesus Heals the Official’s Son

43 After the two days he
left for Galilee. 44 (Now Jesus
himself had pointed out that
a prophet has no honor in his own country.)
45 When he arrived in Galilee, the Galileans welcomed him. They had seen all that he had done
in Jerusalem at the Passover Feast, for they also
had been there.
46 Once more he visited Cana in Galilee,
where he had turned the water into wine. And
there was a certain royal official whose son lay
sick at Capernaum. 47 When this man heard
that Jesus had arrived in Galilee from Judea, he
went to him and begged him to come and heal
his son, who was close to death.
48 “Unless you people see miraculous signs
and wonders,” Jesus told him, “you will never
believe.”
49 The royal official said, “Sir, come down before my child dies.”
50 Jesus replied, “You may go. Your son will
live.”
The man took Jesus at his word and departed.
51 While he was still on the way, his servants
met him with the news that his boy was living.
52 When he inquired as to the time when his
son got better, they said to him, “The fever left
him yesterday at the seventh hour.”
53 Then the father realized that this was the
exact time at which Jesus had said to him,
“Your son will live.” So he and all his household believed.
54 This was the second miraculous sign that Jesus performed, having come from
Judea to Galilee.

John 4:42

God Employs Women

They said to the woman, “We no longer believe just because of what you said; now we have heard for ourselves, and we know that this man really is the Savior of the world.”

The Healing at the Pool

5 Some time later, Jesus
went up to Jerusalem for
a feast of the Jews. 2 Now there
is in Jerusalem near the Sheep
Gate a pool, which in Aramaic
is called Bethesda[b] and which
is surrounded by five covered
colonnades. 3 Here a great number of disabled people used to
lie—the blind, the lame, the
paralyzed.[c] 5 One who was
there had been an invalid for
thirty-eight years. 6 When Jesus
saw him lying there and learned that he had
been in this condition for a long time, he asked
him, “Do you want to get well?”

[a] 29 Or *Messiah* [b] 2 Some manuscripts *Bethzatha*; other manuscripts *Bethsaida* [c] 3 Some less important manuscripts *paralyzed—and they waited for the moving of the waters. 4 From time to time an angel of the Lord would come down and stir up the waters. The first one into the pool after each such disturbance would be cured of whatever disease he had.*

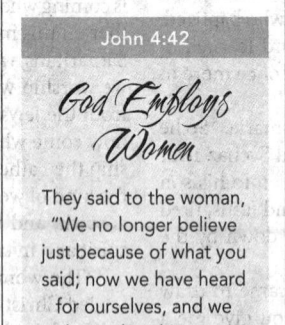

The Wellspring

Read: John 4:3–30

MOVING WATER HAS A FASCINATION of its own. Creeks gurgle, waterfalls plummet, springs bubble, ocean tides crash. The bubbles, foam and noise draw us. The water sustains us. We need water for our physical life, but it also somehow soothes our spirit.

Desert animals travel many miles to find a water hole. City birds cluster in birdbaths or rain puddles. Grocery shoppers pay several dollars for plastic bottles of water. For thousands of years springs and wells provided the only access to clean water. City planners designed their locations around reliable water sources. Hauling water from long distances was hard, thirst-inducing work.

When Jesus compared life with him to a never-ending, thirst-quenching spring, the image resonated with a hardworking Samaritan woman. Water got her attention, for she was thirsty. Though she had come to the well to draw water, Jesus knew she needed more than physical water; she needed him. She had tried to find satisfaction drinking from the wells of the world, but no man had truly quenched her thirst. Then she met Jesus, who knew everything she ever did. This man became a wellspring of life-giving truth that overflowed to her community.

What are you really thirsty for? Do you long to know the meaning of your life? Are you longing for the kind of love that fills you up rather than drains you? Are you forever trying to find acceptance and respect? Or are those longings so deep and buried that you can't even say what you want or need? Perhaps you can't even get beyond just feeling . . . empty.

Only Jesus can identify those deep longings and fill your thirsty soul. Seek out the One who offers you living water. Come to him. He won't be surprised at how empty you are. He knows everything you ever did. He's the wellspring who will fill you to overflowing with his goodness and love.

John 4:14

"Whoever drinks the water I give him will never thirst. Indeed, the water I give him will become in him a spring of water welling up to eternal life."

reflection

1 Would you describe your relationship with Jesus as a life-giving stream or a parched desert?

2 When and where do you feel closest to Jesus?

3 How has Jesus satisfied your spiritual thirst?

RELATED READINGS

Psalm 42:1–11;
John 7:37–39;
Revelation 7:16–17

Go to page 1300 for your next devotional reading.

7“Sir,” the invalid replied, “I have no one to help me into the pool when the water is stirred. While I am trying to get in, someone else goes down ahead of me.”

8Then Jesus said to him, “Get up! Pick up your mat and walk.” 9At once the man was cured; he picked up his mat and walked.

The day on which this took place was a Sabbath, 10and so the Jews said to the man who had been healed, “It is the Sabbath; the law forbids you to carry your mat.”

11But he replied, “The man who made me well said to me, ‘Pick up your mat and walk.’ ”

12So they asked him, “Who is this fellow who told you to pick it up and walk?”

> **John 5:26**
>
> *God Is Life*
>
> “For as the Father has life in himself, so he has granted the Son to have life in himself.”

13The man who was healed had no idea who it was, for Jesus had slipped away into the crowd that was there.

14Later Jesus found him at the temple and said to him, “See, you are well again. Stop sinning or something worse may happen to you.” 15The man went away and told the Jews that it was Jesus who had made him well.

Life Through the Son

16So, because Jesus was doing these things on the Sabbath, the Jews persecuted him. 17Jesus said to them, “My Father is always at his work to this very day, and I, too, am working.” 18For this reason the Jews tried all the harder to kill him; not only was he breaking the Sabbath, but he was even calling God his own Father, making himself equal with God.

19Jesus gave them this answer: “I tell you the truth, the Son can do nothing by himself; he can do only what he sees his Father doing, because whatever the Father does the Son also does. 20For the Father loves the Son and shows him all he does. Yes, to your amazement he will show him even greater things than these. 21For just as the Father raises the dead and gives them life, even so the Son gives life to whom he is pleased to give it. 22Moreover, the Father judges no one, but has entrusted all judgment to the Son, 23that all may honor the Son just as they honor the Father. He who does not honor the Son does not honor the Father, who sent him.

24“I tell you the truth, whoever hears my word and believes him who sent me has eternal life and will not be condemned; he has crossed over from death to life. 25I tell you the truth, a time is coming and has now come when the dead will hear the voice of the Son of God and those who hear will live. 26For as the Father has life in himself, so he has granted the Son to have life in himself. 27And he has given him authority to judge because he is the Son of Man.

28“Do not be amazed at this, for a time is coming when all who are in their graves will hear his voice 29and come out—those who have done good will rise to live, and those who have done evil will rise to be condemned. 30By myself I can do nothing; I judge only as I hear, and my judgment is just, for I seek not to please myself but him who sent me.

Testimonies About Jesus

31“If I testify about myself, my testimony is not valid. 32There is another who testifies in my favor, and I know that his testimony about me is valid.

33“You have sent to John and he has testified to the truth. 34Not that I accept human testimony; but I mention it that you may be saved. 35John was a lamp that burned and gave light, and you chose for a time to enjoy his light.

36“I have testimony weightier than that of John. For the very work that the Father has given me to finish, and which I am doing, testifies that the Father has sent me. 37And the Father who sent me has himself testified concerning me. You have never heard his voice nor seen his form, 38nor does his word dwell in you, for you do not believe the one he sent. 39You diligently study[a] the Scriptures because you think that by them you possess eternal life. These are the Scriptures that testify about me, 40yet you refuse to come to me to have life.

[a] 39 Or *Study diligently* (the imperative)

41“I do not accept praise from men, 42but
I know you. I know that you do not have the
love of God in your hearts. 43I have come in
my Father’s name, and you do not accept me;
but if someone else comes in his own name,
you will accept him. 44How can you believe if
you accept praise from one another, yet make
no effort to obtain the praise that comes from
the only God[a]?

45“But do not think I will accuse you before
the Father. Your accuser is Moses, on whom
your hopes are set. 46If you believed Moses,
you would believe me, for he wrote about me.
47But since you do not believe what he wrote,
how are you going to believe what I say?”

Jesus Feeds the Five Thousand

6 Some time after this, Jesus crossed to the
far shore of the Sea of Galilee (that is, the
Sea of Tiberias), 2and a great crowd of people
followed him because they saw the miraculous
signs he had performed on the sick. 3Then
Jesus went up on a mountainside and sat down
with his disciples. 4The Jewish Passover Feast
was near.

5When Jesus looked up and saw a great
crowd coming toward him, he said to Philip,
“Where shall we buy bread for these people to
eat?” 6He asked this only to test him, for he already had in mind what he was going to do.

7Philip answered him, “Eight months’
wages[b] would not buy enough bread for each
one to have a bite!”

8Another of his disciples, Andrew, Simon Peter’s brother, spoke up, 9“Here is a boy with five
small barley loaves and two small fish, but how
far will they go among so many?”

10Jesus said, “Have the people sit down.”
There was plenty of grass in that place, and the
men sat down, about five thousand of them.
11Jesus then took the loaves, gave thanks, and
distributed to those who were seated as much
as they wanted. He did the same with the fish.

12When they had all had enough to eat, he
said to his disciples, “Gather the pieces that
are left over. Let nothing be wasted.” 13So they
gathered them and filled twelve baskets with
the pieces of the five barley loaves left over by
those who had eaten.

14After the people saw the miraculous sign
that Jesus did, they began to say, “Surely this
is the Prophet who is to come into the world.”
15Jesus, knowing that they intended to come
and make him king by force, withdrew again
to a mountain by himself.

Jesus Walks on the Water

16When evening came, his disciples went
down to the lake, 17where they got into a boat
and set off across the lake for Capernaum. By
now it was dark, and Jesus had not yet joined
them. 18A strong wind was blowing and the waters grew rough. 19When they had rowed three
or three and a half miles,[c] they saw Jesus approaching the boat, walking on the water; and
they were terrified. 20But he said to them, “It
is I; don’t be afraid.” 21Then they were willing
to take him into the boat, and immediately the
boat reached the shore where they were heading.

22The next day the crowd that had stayed
on the opposite shore of the lake realized that
only one boat had been there, and that Jesus
had not entered it with his disciples, but that
they had gone away alone. 23Then some boats
from Tiberias landed near the place where the
people had eaten the bread after the Lord had
given thanks. 24Once the crowd realized that
neither Jesus nor his disciples were there, they
got into the boats and went to Capernaum in
search of Jesus.

Jesus the Bread of Life

25When they found him on the other side
of the lake, they asked him, “Rabbi, when did
you get here?”

26Jesus answered, “I tell you the truth, you
are looking for me, not because you saw miraculous signs but because you ate the loaves and
had your fill. 27Do not work for food that spoils,
but for food that endures to eternal life, which
the Son of Man will give you. On him God the
Father has placed his seal of approval.”

28Then they asked him, “What must we do
to do the works God requires?”

29Jesus answered, “The work of God is this:
to believe in the one he has sent.”

30So they asked him, “What miraculous sign

[a]44 Some early manuscripts *the Only One* [b]7 Greek *two hundred denarii* [c]19 Greek *rowed twenty-five or thirty stadia* (about 5 or 6 kilometers)

then will you give that we may see it and believe you? What will you do? 31 Our forefathers
ate the manna in the desert; as it is written: 'He
gave them bread from heaven to eat.'[a]"
32 Jesus said to them, "I tell you the truth,
it is not Moses who has given you the bread
from heaven, but it is my Father who gives you
the true bread from heaven. 33 For the bread of
God is he who comes down from heaven and
gives life to the world."
34 "Sir," they said, "from now on give us this
bread."
35 Then Jesus declared, "I am the bread of
life. He who comes to me will never go hungry,
and he who believes in me will
never be thirsty. 36 But as I told
you, you have seen me and still
you do not believe. 37 All that
the Father gives me will come
to me, and whoever comes
to me I will never drive away.
38 For I have come down from
heaven not to do my will but to
do the will of him who sent me.
39 And this is the will of him
who sent me, that I shall lose
none of all that he has given
me, but raise them up at the
last day. 40 For my Father's will
is that everyone who looks to the Son and believes in him shall have eternal life, and I will
raise him up at the last day."
41 At this the Jews began to grumble about
him because he said, "I am the bread that came
down from heaven." 42 They said, "Is this not
Jesus, the son of Joseph, whose father and
mother we know? How can he now say, 'I came
down from heaven'?"
43 "Stop grumbling among yourselves," Jesus
answered. 44 "No one can come to me unless
the Father who sent me draws him, and I will
raise him up at the last day. 45 It is written in
the Prophets: 'They will all be taught by God.'[b]
Everyone who listens to the Father and learns
from him comes to me. 46 No one has seen the
Father except the one who is from God; only
he has seen the Father. 47 I tell you the truth,
he who believes has everlasting life. 48 I am the
bread of life. 49 Your forefathers ate the manna

John 6:37

God Doesn't Push Us Away

"All that the Father gives me will come to me, and whoever comes to me I will never drive away."

in the desert, yet they died. 50 But here is the
bread that comes down from heaven, which
a man may eat and not die. 51 I am the living
bread that came down from heaven. If anyone eats of this bread, he will live forever. This
bread is my flesh, which I will give for the life
of the world."
52 Then the Jews began to argue sharply
among themselves, "How can this man give us
his flesh to eat?"
53 Jesus said to them, "I tell you the truth,
unless you eat the flesh of the Son of Man
and drink his blood, you have no life in you.
54 Whoever eats my flesh and drinks my blood
has eternal life, and I will raise
him up at the last day. 55 For
my flesh is real food and my
blood is real drink. 56 Whoever
eats my flesh and drinks my
blood remains in me, and I
in him. 57 Just as the living Father sent me and I live because
of the Father, so the one who
feeds on me will live because
of me. 58 This is the bread that
came down from heaven. Your
forefathers ate manna and
died, but he who feeds on this
bread will live forever." 59 He
said this while teaching in the synagogue in
Capernaum.

Many Disciples Desert Jesus

60 On hearing it, many of his disciples said,
"This is a hard teaching. Who can accept it?"
61 Aware that his disciples were grumbling
about this, Jesus said to them, "Does this offend
you? 62 What if you see the Son of Man ascend
to where he was before! 63 The Spirit gives life;
the flesh counts for nothing. The words I have
spoken to you are spirit[c] and they are life. 64 Yet
there are some of you who do not believe." For
Jesus had known from the beginning which of
them did not believe and who would betray
him. 65 He went on to say, "This is why I told
you that no one can come to me unless the Father has enabled him."
66 From this time many of his disciples
turned back and no longer followed him.

[a] 31 Exodus 16:4; Neh. 9:15; Psalm 78:24,25 [b] 45 Isaiah 54:13 [c] 63 Or *Spirit*

67"You do not want to leave too, do you?"
Jesus asked the Twelve.
68Simon Peter answered him, "Lord, to
whom shall we go? You have the words of eternal life. 69We believe and know that you are the
Holy One of God."
70Then Jesus replied, "Have I not chosen
you, the Twelve? Yet one of you is a devil!"
71(He meant Judas, the son of Simon Iscariot,
who, though one of the Twelve, was later to betray him.)

Jesus Goes to the Feast of Tabernacles

7 After this, Jesus went around in Galilee,
purposely staying away from Judea because the Jews there were waiting to take his
life. 2But when the Jewish Feast of Tabernacles
was near, 3Jesus' brothers said to him, "You
ought to leave here and go to Judea, so that
your disciples may see the miracles you do.
4No one who wants to become a public figure
acts in secret. Since you are doing these things,
show yourself to the world." 5For even his own
brothers did not believe in him.
6Therefore Jesus told them, "The right time
for me has not yet come; for you any time is
right. 7The world cannot hate you, but it hates
me because I testify that what it does is evil.
8You go to the Feast. I am not yet[a] going up
to this Feast, because for me the right time has
not yet come." 9Having said this, he stayed in
Galilee.
10However, after his brothers had left for the
Feast, he went also, not publicly, but in secret.
11Now at the Feast the Jews were watching for
him and asking, "Where is that man?"
12Among the crowds there was widespread
whispering about him. Some said, "He is a
good man."
Others replied, "No, he deceives the people." 13But no one would say anything publicly
about him for fear of the Jews.

Jesus Teaches at the Feast

14Not until halfway through the Feast did
Jesus go up to the temple courts and begin
to teach. 15The Jews were amazed and asked,
"How did this man get such learning without
having studied?"
16Jesus answered, "My teaching is not my
own. It comes from him who sent me. 17If
anyone chooses to do God's will, he will find
out whether my teaching comes from God or
whether I speak on my own. 18He who speaks
on his own does so to gain honor for himself,
but he who works for the honor of the one who
sent him is a man of truth; there is nothing false
about him. 19Has not Moses given you the law?
Yet not one of you keeps the law. Why are you
trying to kill me?"
20"You are demon-possessed," the crowd answered. "Who is trying to kill you?"
21Jesus said to them, "I did one miracle, and
you are all astonished. 22Yet, because Moses
gave you circumcision (though actually it did
not come from Moses, but from the patriarchs),
you circumcise a child on the Sabbath. 23Now
if a child can be circumcised on the Sabbath so
that the law of Moses may not be broken, why
are you angry with me for healing the whole
man on the Sabbath? 24Stop judging by mere
appearances, and make a right judgment."

Is Jesus the Christ?

25At that point some of the people of Jerusalem began to ask, "Isn't this the man they are
trying to kill? 26Here he is, speaking publicly,
and they are not saying a word to him. Have
the authorities really concluded that he is the
Christ[b]? 27But we know where this man is
from; when the Christ comes, no one will
know where he is from."
28Then Jesus, still teaching in the temple
courts, cried out, "Yes, you know me, and you
know where I am from. I am not here on my
own, but he who sent me is true. You do not
know him, 29but I know him because I am
from him and he sent me."
30At this they tried to seize him, but no
one laid a hand on him, because his time had
not yet come. 31Still, many in the crowd put
their faith in him. They said, "When the Christ
comes, will he do more miraculous signs than
this man?"
32The Pharisees heard the crowd whispering
such things about him. Then the chief priests
and the Pharisees sent temple guards to arrest
him.
33Jesus said, "I am with you for only a short

[a]8 Some early manuscripts do not have *yet.* [b]26 Or *Messiah;* also in verses 27, 31, 41 and 42

time, and then I go to the one who sent me.
34 You will look for me, but you will not find
me; and where I am, you cannot come."
35 The Jews said to one another, "Where does
this man intend to go that we cannot find him?
Will he go where our people
live scattered among the Greeks,
and teach the Greeks? 36 What
did he mean when he said, 'You
will look for me, but you will
not find me,' and 'Where I am,
you cannot come'?"
37 On the last and greatest
day of the Feast, Jesus stood
and said in a loud voice, "If anyone is thirsty, let him come to
me and drink. 38 Whoever believes in me, as[a] the Scripture
has said, streams of living water will flow from within him."
39 By this he meant the Spirit,
whom those who believed in
him were later to receive. Up to that time the
Spirit had not been given, since Jesus had not
yet been glorified.
40 On hearing his words, some of the people
said, "Surely this man is the Prophet."
41 Others said, "He is the Christ."
Still others asked, "How can the Christ come
from Galilee? 42 Does not the Scripture say that
the Christ will come from David's family[b] and
from Bethlehem, the town where David lived?"
43 Thus the people were divided because of
Jesus. 44 Some wanted to seize him, but no one
laid a hand on him.

> **John 7:37**
>
> **God Offers Fulfillment**
>
> On the last and greatest day of the Feast, Jesus stood and said in a loud voice, "If anyone is thirsty, let him come to me and drink."

Unbelief of the Jewish Leaders

45 Finally the temple guards went back to the
chief priests and Pharisees, who asked them,
"Why didn't you bring him in?"
46 "No one ever spoke the way this man
does," the guards declared.
47 "You mean he has deceived you also?" the
Pharisees retorted. 48 "Has any of the rulers or
of the Pharisees believed in him? 49 No! But
this mob that knows nothing of the law—there
is a curse on them."
50 Nicodemus, who had gone to Jesus earlier
and who was one of their own number, asked,
51 "Does our law condemn anyone without first
hearing him to find out what he is doing?"
52 They replied, "Are you from Galilee, too?
Look into it, and you will find that a prophet[c]
does not come out of Galilee."

[The earliest manuscripts and many other ancient witnesses do not have John 7:53—8:11.]

53 Then each went to his own
home.
8 But Jesus went to the
Mount of Olives. 2 At
dawn he appeared again in
the temple courts, where all
the people gathered around
him, and he sat down to teach
them. 3 The teachers of the law
and the Pharisees brought in
a woman caught in adultery. They made her
stand before the group 4 and said to Jesus,
"Teacher, this woman was caught in the act of
adultery. 5 In the Law Moses commanded us
to stone such women. Now what do you say?"
6 They were using this question as a trap, in order to have a basis for accusing him.
But Jesus bent down and started to write on
the ground with his finger. 7 When they kept on
questioning him, he straightened up and said
to them, "If any one of you is without sin, let
him be the first to throw a stone at her." 8 Again
he stooped down and wrote on the ground.
9 At this, those who heard began to go away
one at a time, the older ones first, until only
Jesus was left, with the woman still standing
there. 10 Jesus straightened up and asked her,
"Woman, where are they? Has no one condemned you?"
11 "No one, sir," she said.
"Then neither do I condemn you," Jesus declared. "Go now and leave your life of sin."

The Validity of Jesus' Testimony

12 When Jesus spoke again to the people, he
said, "I am the light of the world. Whoever fol-

[a] 37,38 Or *If anyone is thirsty, let him come to me. / And let him drink,* [38] *who believes in me. / As* [b] 42 Greek *seed* [c] 52 Two early manuscripts *the Prophet*

lows me will never walk in darkness, but will
have the light of life."
13 The Pharisees challenged him, "Here
you are, appearing as your own witness; your
testimony is not valid."
14 Jesus answered, "Even if I testify on my
own behalf, my testimony is valid, for I know
where I came from and where I am going. But
you have no idea where I come from or where
I am going. 15 You judge by human standards;
I pass judgment on no one. 16 But if I do judge,
my decisions are right, because I am not alone.
I stand with the Father, who sent me. 17 In
your own Law it is written that the testimony
of two men is valid. 18 I am one who testifies
for myself; my other witness is the Father, who
sent me."
19 Then they asked him, "Where is your father?"
"You do not know me or my Father," Jesus
replied. "If you knew me, you would know my
Father also." 20 He spoke these words while
teaching in the temple area near the place
where the offerings were put. Yet no one seized
him, because his time had not yet come.
21 Once more Jesus said to them, "I am going
away, and you will look for me, and you will die
in your sin. Where I go, you cannot come."
22 This made the Jews ask, "Will he kill himself? Is that why he says, 'Where I go, you cannot come'?"
23 But he continued, "You are from below;
I am from above. You are of this world; I am
not of this world. 24 I told you that you would
die in your sins; if you do not believe that I am
⌊the one I claim to be⌋,[a] you will indeed die in
your sins."
25 "Who are you?" they asked.
"Just what I have been claiming all along,"
Jesus replied. 26 "I have much to say in judgment of you. But he who sent me is reliable, and
what I have heard from him I tell the world."
27 They did not understand that he was telling them about his Father. 28 So Jesus said,
"When you have lifted up the Son of Man, then
you will know that I am ⌊the one I claim to be⌋
and that I do nothing on my own but speak just
what the Father has taught me. 29 The one who
sent me is with me; he has not left me alone,
for I always do what pleases him." 30 Even as he
spoke, many put their faith in him.

The Children of Abraham

31 To the Jews who had believed him, Jesus
said, "If you hold to my teaching, you are really
my disciples. 32 Then you will know the truth,
and the truth will set you free."
33 They answered him, "We are Abraham's
descendants[b] and have never been slaves
of anyone. How can you say that we shall be
set free?"
34 Jesus replied, "I tell you the truth, everyone who sins is a slave to sin. 35 Now a slave
has no permanent place in the family, but a
son belongs to it forever. 36 So if the Son sets
you free, you will be free indeed. 37 I know you
are Abraham's descendants. Yet you are ready
to kill me, because you have no room for my
word. 38 I am telling you what I have seen in the
Father's presence, and you do what you have
heard from your father.[c]"
39 "Abraham is our father," they answered.
"If you were Abraham's children," said Jesus,
"then you would[d] do the things Abraham did.
40 As it is, you are determined to kill me, a man
who has told you the truth that I heard from
God. Abraham did not do such things. 41 You
are doing the things your own father does."
"We are not illegitimate children," they
protested. "The only Father we have is God
himself."

The Children of the Devil

42 Jesus said to them, "If God were your Father, you would love me, for I came from God
and now am here. I have not come on my own;
but he sent me. 43 Why is my language not clear
to you? Because you are unable to hear what I
say. 44 You belong to your father, the devil, and
you want to carry out your father's desire. He
was a murderer from the beginning, not holding to the truth, for there is no truth in him.
When he lies, he speaks his native language, for
he is a liar and the father of lies. 45 Yet because
I tell the truth, you do not believe me! 46 Can
any of you prove me guilty of sin? If I am telling the truth, why don't you believe me? 47 He

[a] 24 Or *I am he*; also in verse 28 [b] 33 Greek *seed*; also in verse 37 [c] 38 Or *presence. Therefore do what you have heard from the Father.*
[d] 39 Some early manuscripts *"If you are Abraham's children," said Jesus, "then*

who belongs to God hears what God says. The
reason you do not hear is that you do not belong to God."

The Claims of Jesus About Himself

48The Jews answered him, "Aren't we right
in saying that you are a Samaritan and demon-
possessed?"

49"I am not possessed by a demon," said
Jesus, "but I honor my Father and you dishonor
me. 50I am not seeking glory for myself; but
there is one who seeks it, and he is the judge.
51I tell you the truth, if anyone keeps my word,
he will never see death."

52At this the Jews exclaimed, "Now we know
that you are demon-possessed! Abraham died
and so did the prophets, yet you say that if anyone keeps your word, he will never taste death.
53Are you greater than our father Abraham?
He died, and so did the prophets. Who do you
think you are?"

54Jesus replied, "If I glorify myself, my glory
means nothing. My Father, whom you claim
as your God, is the one who glorifies me.
55Though you do not know him, I know him.
If I said I did not, I would be a liar like you, but
I do know him and keep his word. 56Your father Abraham rejoiced at the thought of seeing
my day; he saw it and was glad."

57"You are not yet fifty years
old," the Jews said to him, "and
you have seen Abraham!"

58"I tell you the truth," Jesus
answered, "before Abraham
was born, I am!" 59At this,
they picked up stones to stone
him, but Jesus hid himself,
slipping away from the temple
grounds.

John 8:58

God Is Eternal

"I tell you the truth,"
Jesus answered, "before
Abraham was born,
I am!"

Jesus Heals a Man Born Blind

9 As he went along, he saw a man blind from
birth. 2His disciples asked him, "Rabbi,
who sinned, this man or his parents, that he
was born blind?"

3"Neither this man nor his parents sinned,"
said Jesus, "but this happened so that the work
of God might be displayed in his life. 4As long
as it is day, we must do the work of him who
sent me. Night is coming, when no one can
work. 5While I am in the world, I am the light
of the world."

6Having said this, he spit on the ground,
made some mud with the saliva, and put it
on the man's eyes. 7"Go," he told him, "wash
in the Pool of Siloam" (this word means Sent).
So the man went and washed, and came home
seeing.

8His neighbors and those who had formerly
seen him begging asked, "Isn't this the same
man who used to sit and beg?" 9Some claimed
that he was.

Others said, "No, he only looks like him."

But he himself insisted, "I am the man."

10"How then were your eyes opened?" they
demanded.

11He replied, "The man they call Jesus made
some mud and put it on my eyes. He told me to
go to Siloam and wash. So I went and washed,
and then I could see."

12"Where is this man?" they asked him.

"I don't know," he said.

The Pharisees Investigate the Healing

13They brought to the Pharisees the man
who had been blind. 14Now the day on which
Jesus had made the mud and opened the man's
eyes was a Sabbath. 15Therefore the Pharisees
also asked him how he had received his sight.
"He put mud on my eyes," the
man replied, "and I washed,
and now I see."

16Some of the Pharisees said,
"This man is not from God, for
he does not keep the Sabbath."

But others asked, "How can
a sinner do such miraculous
signs?" So they were divided.

17Finally they turned again
to the blind man, "What have
you to say about him? It was
your eyes he opened."

The man replied, "He is a prophet."

18The Jews still did not believe that he had
been blind and had received his sight until they
sent for the man's parents. 19"Is this your son?"
they asked. "Is this the one you say was born
blind? How is it that now he can see?"

20"We know he is our son," the parents answered, "and we know he was born blind. 21But
how he can see now, or who opened his eyes,

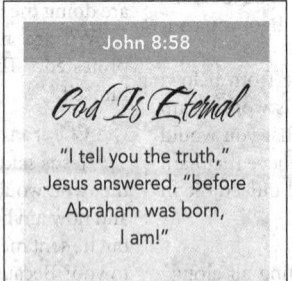

we don't know. Ask him. He is of age; he will
speak for himself." 22His parents said this because they were afraid of the Jews, for already
the Jews had decided that anyone who acknowledged that Jesus was the Christ[a] would be put
out of the synagogue. 23That was why his parents said, "He is of age; ask him."
24A second time they summoned the man
who had been blind. "Give glory to God,[b]"
they said. "We know this man is a sinner."
25He replied, "Whether he is a sinner or not,
I don't know. One thing I do know. I was blind
but now I see!"
26Then they asked him, "What did he do to
you? How did he open your eyes?"
27He answered, "I have told you already
and you did not listen. Why do you want to
hear it again? Do you want to become his disciples, too?"
28Then they hurled insults at him and said,
"You are this fellow's disciple! We are disciples
of Moses! 29We know that God spoke to Moses, but as for this fellow, we don't even know
where he comes from."
30The man answered, "Now that is remarkable! You don't know where he comes from, yet
he opened my eyes. 31We know that God does
not listen to sinners. He listens to the godly
man who does his will. 32No-
body has ever heard of opening
the eyes of a man born blind.
33If this man were not from
God, he could do nothing."
34To this they replied, "You
were steeped in sin at birth;
how dare you lecture us!" And
they threw him out.

Spiritual Blindness

35Jesus heard that they had
thrown him out, and when he
found him, he said, "Do you believe in the Son of Man?"
36"Who is he, sir?" the man asked. "Tell me
so that I may believe in him."
37Jesus said, "You have now seen him; in
fact, he is the one speaking with you."
38Then the man said, "Lord, I believe," and
he worshiped him.
39Jesus said, "For judgment I have come into
this world, so that the blind will see and those
who see will become blind."
40Some Pharisees who were with him
heard him say this and asked, "What? Are we
blind too?"
41Jesus said, "If you were blind, you would
not be guilty of sin; but now that you claim you
can see, your guilt remains.

The Shepherd and His Flock

10 "I tell you the truth, the man who does
not enter the sheep pen by the gate,
but climbs in by some other way, is a thief and
a robber. 2The man who enters by the gate is
the shepherd of his sheep. 3The watchman
opens the gate for him, and the sheep listen
to his voice. He calls his own sheep by name
and leads them out. 4When he has brought out
all his own, he goes on ahead of them, and his
sheep follow him because they know his voice.
5But they will never follow a stranger; in fact,
they will run away from him because they do
not recognize a stranger's voice." 6Jesus used
this figure of speech, but they did not understand what he was telling them.
7Therefore Jesus said again, "I tell you the
truth, I am the gate for the sheep. 8All who
ever came before me were thieves and robbers,
but the sheep did not listen to
them. 9I am the gate; whoever
enters through me will be
saved.[c] He will come in and
go out, and find pasture. 10The
thief comes only to steal and
kill and destroy; I have come
that they may have life, and
have it to the full.
11"I am the good shepherd.
The good shepherd lays down
his life for the sheep. 12The
hired hand is not the shepherd
who owns the sheep. So when
he sees the wolf coming, he
abandons the sheep and runs away. Then the
wolf attacks the flock and scatters it. 13The man
runs away because he is a hired hand and cares
nothing for the sheep.
14"I am the good shepherd; I know my
sheep and my sheep know me— 15just as the
Father knows me and I know the Father—and

John 10:11

God Is the Good Shepherd

"I am the good shepherd.
The good shepherd
lays down his life
for the sheep."

[a]22 Or *Messiah* [b]24 A solemn charge to tell the truth (see Joshua 7:19) [c]9 Or *kept safe*

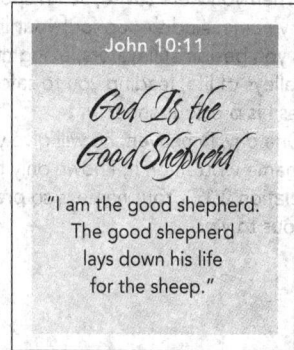

He Knows Your Name

John 10:3

"The watchman opens the gate for him, and the sheep listen to his voice. He calls his own sheep by name and leads them out."

Read: John 10:1–18

"THE SWEETEST SOUND in the world is the sound of a person's own name," wrote Dale Carnegie in his all-time bestseller *How to Win Friends and Influence People.* There's nothing more embarrassing than being at a social event and seeing someone you know and not remembering their name. There's nothing more humiliating than greeting someone you thought you knew well with a hug and a personal hello only to have them look back with the deer-in-the-headlights look. You just know they're thinking, *Now what is her name?*

Our name reflects who we are. It gives us a sense of belonging, a sense of identity. If someone knows our name, it means they know *us.* It's hard not to take it personally when someone forgets our name. Unfortunately, parents do it. They call us by our sibling's name or jumble our names into one long name: "JimmySueBob, get over here." Bosses do it. They point and say, "You, I need that report." Teachers do it. They mistakenly call us by our classmate's name. But if our closest friend, boyfriend or husband forgot our name—forget about it! It would be an almost unforgivable offense.

Thankfully, Jesus knows your name. In this passage of John we learn that Jesus calls us each "by name." The Creator of the universe, the One who determined the number of stars in the sky and called each of them by name, knows *your* name. Not only does he *know* your name, but he *calls* you by name.

When you were saved, Jesus spoke to you personally. He called you by name. And throughout your life, he calls your name as he leads you beside still waters, along the mountaintops and through the valleys of life, leading you to safe pastures as a shepherd guides his precious sheep.

One day, in heaven, he will give you "a white stone with a new name written on it, known only to him who receives it" (Revelation 2:17). Your name is so precious to Jesus. Is his name precious to you?

reflection

1 Spend some time thinking about Jesus' names. Which is your favorite and why?

2 How does it make you feel that Jesus knows and calls you by name?

3 What does it mean to you to know that he has a new, special name waiting for you?

RELATED READINGS

Psalm 23; Isaiah 9:6; Ezekiel 34:25–31; Revelation 2:17

"The name we give to something shapes our attitude toward it."

Katherine Paterson

Go to page 1303 for your next devotional reading.

I lay down my life for the sheep. 16 I have other sheep that are not of this sheep pen. I must bring them also. They too will listen to my voice, and there shall be one flock and one shepherd. 17 The reason my Father loves me is that I lay down my life—only to take it up again. 18 No one takes it from me, but I lay it down of my own accord. I have authority to lay it down and authority to take it up again. This command I received from my Father."

19 At these words the Jews were again divided. 20 Many of them said, "He is demon-possessed and raving mad. Why listen to him?"

21 But others said, "These are not the sayings of a man possessed by a demon. Can a demon open the eyes of the blind?"

The Unbelief of the Jews

22 Then came the Feast of Dedication[a] at Jerusalem. It was winter, 23 and Jesus was in the temple area walking in Solomon's Colonnade. 24 The Jews gathered around him, saying, "How long will you keep us in suspense? If you are the Christ,[b] tell us plainly."

25 Jesus answered, "I did tell you, but you do not believe. The miracles I do in my Father's name speak for me, 26 but you do not believe because you are not my sheep. 27 My sheep listen to my voice; I know them, and they follow me. 28 I give them eternal life, and they shall never perish; no one can snatch them out of my hand. 29 My Father, who has given them to me, is greater than all[c]; no one can snatch them out of my Father's hand. 30 I and the Father are one."

31 Again the Jews picked up stones to stone him, 32 but Jesus said to them, "I have shown you many great miracles from the Father. For which of these do you stone me?"

33 "We are not stoning you for any of these," replied the Jews, "but for blasphemy, because you, a mere man, claim to be God."

34 Jesus answered them, "Is it not written in your Law, 'I have said you are gods'[d]? 35 If he called them 'gods,' to whom the word of God came—and the Scripture cannot be broken—36 what about the one whom the Father set apart as his very own and sent into the world? Why then do you accuse me of blasphemy because I said, 'I am God's Son'? 37 Do not believe me unless I do what my Father does. 38 But if I do it, even though you do not believe me, believe the miracles, that you may know and understand that the Father is in me, and I in the Father." 39 Again they tried to seize him, but he escaped their grasp.

40 Then Jesus went back across the Jordan to the place where John had been baptizing in the early days. Here he stayed 41 and many people came to him. They said, "Though John never performed a miraculous sign, all that John said about this man was true." 42 And in that place many believed in Jesus.

The Death of Lazarus

11 Now a man named Lazarus was sick. He was from Bethany, the village of Mary and her sister Martha. 2 This Mary, whose brother Lazarus now lay sick, was the same one who poured perfume on the Lord and wiped his feet with her hair. 3 So the sisters sent word to Jesus, "Lord, the one you love is sick."

4 When he heard this, Jesus said, "This sickness will not end in death. No, it is for God's glory so that God's Son may be glorified through it." 5 Jesus loved Martha and her sister and Lazarus. 6 Yet when he heard that Lazarus was sick, he stayed where he was two more days.

7 Then he said to his disciples, "Let us go back to Judea."

8 "But Rabbi," they said, "a short while ago the Jews tried to stone you, and yet you are going back there?"

9 Jesus answered, "Are there not twelve hours of daylight? A man who walks by day will not stumble, for he sees by this world's light. 10 It is when he walks by night that he stumbles, for he has no light."

11 After he had said this, he went on to tell them, "Our friend Lazarus has fallen asleep; but I am going there to wake him up."

12 His disciples replied, "Lord, if he sleeps, he will get better." 13 Jesus had been speaking of his death, but his disciples thought he meant natural sleep.

14 So then he told them plainly, "Lazarus is dead, 15 and for your sake I am glad I was not

[a]22 That is, Hanukkah [b]24 Or *Messiah* [c]29 Many early manuscripts *What my Father has given me is greater than all* [d]34 Psalm 82:6

there, so that you may believe. But let us go to
him."
16 Then Thomas (called Didymus) said to
the rest of the disciples, "Let us also go, that we
may die with him."

Jesus Comforts the Sisters

17 On his arrival, Jesus found that Lazarus
had already been in the tomb for four days.
18 Bethany was less than two miles[a] from Jerusalem, 19 and many Jews had come to Martha
and Mary to comfort them in the loss of their
brother. 20 When Martha heard that Jesus was
coming, she went out to meet him, but Mary
stayed at home.
21 "Lord," Martha said to Jesus, "if you had
been here, my brother would not have died.
22 But I know that even now God will give you
whatever you ask."
23 Jesus said to her, "Your brother will rise
again."
24 Martha answered, "I know he will rise
again in the resurrection at the last day."
25 Jesus said to her, "I am the resurrection
and the life. He who believes in me will live,
even though he dies; 26 and whoever lives and
believes in me will never die. Do you believe
this?"
27 "Yes, Lord," she told him, "I believe that
you are the Christ,[b] the Son of God, who was
to come into the world."
28 And after she had said this, she went back
and called her sister Mary aside. "The Teacher
is here," she said, "and is asking for you."
29 When Mary heard this, she got up quickly
and went to him. 30 Now Jesus had not yet entered the village, but was still at the place where
Martha had met him. 31 When the Jews who
had been with Mary in the house, comforting
her, noticed how quickly she got up and went
out, they followed her, supposing she was going to the tomb to mourn there.
32 When Mary reached the place where Jesus
was and saw him, she fell at his feet and said,
"Lord, if you had been here, my brother would
not have died."
33 When Jesus saw her weeping, and the Jews
who had come along with her also weeping,
he was deeply moved in spirit and troubled.
34 "Where have you laid him?" he asked.
"Come and see, Lord," they replied.
35 Jesus wept.
36 Then the Jews said, "See how he loved
him!"
37 But some of them said, "Could not he who
opened the eyes of the blind man have kept this
man from dying?"

Jesus Raises Lazarus From the Dead

38 Jesus, once more deeply moved, came to
the tomb. It was a cave with a stone laid across
the entrance. 39 "Take away the stone," he said.
"But, Lord," said Martha, the sister of the
dead man, "by this time there is a bad odor, for
he has been there four days."
40 Then Jesus said, "Did I not tell you that
if you believed, you would see the glory of
God?"
41 So they took away the stone. Then Jesus
looked up and said, "Father, I thank you that
you have heard me. 42 I knew that you always
hear me, but I said this for the benefit of the
people standing here, that they may believe
that you sent me."
43 When he had said this, Jesus called in a
loud voice, "Lazarus, come out!" 44 The dead
man came out, his hands and feet wrapped with
strips of linen, and a cloth around his face.
Jesus said to them, "Take off the grave clothes
and let him go."

The Plot to Kill Jesus

45 Therefore many of the Jews who had come
to visit Mary, and had seen what Jesus did, put
their faith in him. 46 But some of them went
to the Pharisees and told them what Jesus had
done. 47 Then the chief priests and the Pharisees called a meeting of the Sanhedrin.
"What are we accomplishing?" they asked.
"Here is this man performing many miraculous signs. 48 If we let him go on like this, everyone will believe in him, and then the Romans
will come and take away both our place[c] and
our nation."
49 Then one of them, named Caiaphas, who
was high priest that year, spoke up, "You know
nothing at all! 50 You do not realize that it is better for you that one man die for the people than
that the whole nation perish."
51 He did not say this on his own, but as high

[a] 18 Greek *fifteen stadia* (about 3 kilometers) [b] 27 Or *Messiah* [c] 48 Or *temple*

First and Last

MARY MAGDALENE

SEVEN. THAT'S THE NUMBER of demons who daily assaulted Mary of Magdala without remorse.

Unimaginable. That's what the tormented nights were like as Mary battled frightening forces she didn't understand—evil forces that brought fitful sleep and days filled with anguish. We'll likely never know the depth of relief she experienced at the healing hands of Jesus. Mary, changed by the power of love, was forever indebted to him. Following him was not an option; it was a necessity.

Three. That's the number of agonizingly long days Mary endured after Jesus' death; they must have seemed an eternity. She had stood at a distance from the cross, huddled together with her fellow sisters. None of them could believe the cruel scene unfolding before their eyes. The hands that had released indomitable power in her life, and in the lives of so many others, now hung limp on the wooden beams, pierced and bloody.

Last. That's what Mary was on Friday evening. She was one of the last to see Jesus alive. One of the last to leave his ravaged body and return home for Passover preparations. For all she knew, evil had just extinguished the light of the world forever. Lost without him, she stumbled home in the encroaching darkness that obscured her path and clung to her soul.

Among the first. That's what Mary was on resurrection morning. She was among the first at the tomb. Among the first to peer into the empty blackness of the cool enclosure. Among the first to see the glory of an angel, cleverly cloaked in the clothes of a gardener. She was first to ask the obvious and assume the worst. Ironically, the person God chose to see Jesus first was the last person most people would have expected to receive the honor (a demon-possessed woman?). Nevertheless, Mary Magdalene holds the envious position in history of being among the first—the first to see Jesus alive and the first to carry back to a waiting world the glorious gospel of Good News.

—Prayer—

Jesus, friend and Savior, thank you for the miracles you've worked in my life.

Mary Magdalene went to the disciples with the news: "I have seen the Lord!"

John 20:18

ASSIGNED READING:

Matthew 27–28; Mark 15–16; Luke 24:1–12; John 19–20

Weekend

Go to page 1307 for your next devotional reading.

priest that year he prophesied that Jesus would
die for the Jewish nation, 52 and not only for
that nation but also for the scattered children
of God, to bring them together and make them
one. 53 So from that day on they plotted to take
his life.
54 Therefore Jesus no longer moved about
publicly among the Jews. Instead he withdrew
to a region near the desert, to a village called
Ephraim, where he stayed with his disciples.
55 When it was almost time for the Jewish
Passover, many went up from the country to Jerusalem for their ceremonial cleansing before
the Passover. 56 They kept looking for Jesus,
and as they stood in the temple area they asked
one another, "What do you think? Isn't he coming to the Feast at all?" 57 But the chief priests
and Pharisees had given orders that if anyone
found out where Jesus was, he should report it
so that they might arrest him.

Jesus Anointed at Bethany

12 Six days before the Passover, Jesus arrived at Bethany, where Lazarus lived,
whom Jesus had raised from the dead. 2 Here
a dinner was given in Jesus' honor. Martha
served, while Lazarus was among those reclining at the table with him. 3 Then Mary took
about a pint[a] of pure nard, an expensive perfume; she poured it on Jesus' feet and wiped
his feet with her hair. And the house was filled
with the fragrance of the perfume.
4 But one of his disciples, Judas Iscariot, who
was later to betray him, objected, 5 "Why wasn't
this perfume sold and the money given to the
poor? It was worth a year's wages.[b]" 6 He did
not say this because he cared about the poor
but because he was a thief; as keeper of the
money bag, he used to help himself to what
was put into it.
7 "Leave her alone," Jesus replied. "⌊It was
intended⌋ that she should save this perfume
for the day of my burial. 8 You will always have
the poor among you, but you will not always
have me."
9 Meanwhile a large crowd of Jews found
out that Jesus was there and came, not only because of him but also to see Lazarus, whom he
had raised from the dead. 10 So the chief priests
made plans to kill Lazarus as well, 11 for on account of him many of the Jews were going over
to Jesus and putting their faith in him.

The Triumphal Entry

12 The next day the great crowd that had
come for the Feast heard that Jesus was on his
way to Jerusalem. 13 They took palm branches
and went out to meet him, shouting,

"Hosanna![c]"

"Blessed is he who comes in the name of
the Lord!"[d]

"Blessed is the King of Israel!"

14 Jesus found a young donkey and sat upon it,
as it is written,

15 "Do not be afraid, O Daughter of Zion;
see, your king is coming,
seated on a donkey's colt."[e]

16 At first his disciples did not understand
all this. Only after Jesus was glorified did they
realize that these things had been written
about him and that they had done these things
to him.
17 Now the crowd that was with him when
he called Lazarus from the tomb and raised
him from the dead continued to spread the
word. 18 Many people, because they had heard
that he had given this miraculous sign, went
out to meet him. 19 So the Pharisees said to one
another, "See, this is getting us nowhere. Look
how the whole world has gone after him!"

Jesus Predicts His Death

20 Now there were some Greeks among those
who went up to worship at the Feast. 21 They
came to Philip, who was from Bethsaida in Galilee, with a request. "Sir," they said, "we would
like to see Jesus." 22 Philip went to tell Andrew;
Andrew and Philip in turn told Jesus.
23 Jesus replied, "The hour has come for the
Son of Man to be glorified. 24 I tell you the truth,
unless a kernel of wheat falls to the ground and
dies, it remains only a single seed. But if it dies,
it produces many seeds. 25 The man who loves
his life will lose it, while the man who hates
his life in this world will keep it for eternal life.

[a] 3 Greek *a litra* (probably about 0.5 liter) [b] 5 Greek *three hundred denarii* [c] 13 A Hebrew expression meaning "Save!" which became an exclamation of praise [d] 13 Psalm 118:25,26 [e] 15 Zech. 9:9

26Whoever serves me must follow me; and
where I am, my servant also will be. My Father
will honor the one who serves me.
27"Now my heart is troubled, and what shall
I say? 'Father, save me from this hour'? No, it
was for this very reason I came to this hour.
28Father, glorify your name!"
Then a voice came from heaven, "I have glorified it, and will glorify it again." 29The crowd
that was there and heard it said it had thundered; others said an angel had spoken to him.
30Jesus said, "This voice was for your benefit,
not mine. 31Now is the time for
judgment on this world; now
the prince of this world will be
driven out. 32But I, when I am
lifted up from the earth, will
draw all men to myself." 33He
said this to show the kind of
death he was going to die.
34The crowd spoke up, "We
have heard from the Law that
the Christ[a] will remain forever,
so how can you say, 'The Son of
Man must be lifted up'? Who is
this 'Son of Man'?"

> **John 12:46**
>
> *God Is Light*
>
> "I have come into the world as a light, so that no one who believes in me should stay in darkness."

35Then Jesus told them, "You are going to
have the light just a little while longer. Walk
while you have the light, before darkness overtakes you. The man who walks in the dark
does not know where he is going. 36Put your
trust in the light while you have it, so that
you may become sons of light." When he had
finished speaking, Jesus left and hid himself
from them.

The Jews Continue in Their Unbelief

37Even after Jesus had done all these miraculous signs in their presence, they still would not
believe in him. 38This was to fulfill the word of
Isaiah the prophet:

"Lord, who has believed our message
and to whom has the arm of the Lord
been revealed?"[b]

39For this reason they could not believe, because, as Isaiah says elsewhere:

40"He has blinded their eyes
and deadened their hearts,
so they can neither see with their eyes,
nor understand with their hearts,
nor turn—and I would heal them."[c]

41Isaiah said this because he saw Jesus' glory
and spoke about him.
42Yet at the same time many even among
the leaders believed in him. But because of the
Pharisees they would not confess their faith for
fear they would be put out of the synagogue;
43for they loved praise from men more than
praise from God.
44Then Jesus cried out,
"When a man believes in me,
he does not believe in me only,
but in the one who sent me.
45When he looks at me, he sees
the one who sent me. 46I have
come into the world as a light,
so that no one who believes in
me should stay in darkness.
47"As for the person who
hears my words but does not
keep them, I do not judge him.
For I did not come to judge the
world, but to save it. 48There is
a judge for the one who rejects me and does
not accept my words; that very word which I
spoke will condemn him at the last day. 49For I
did not speak of my own accord, but the Father
who sent me commanded me what to say and
how to say it. 50I know that his command leads
to eternal life. So whatever I say is just what the
Father has told me to say."

Jesus Washes His Disciples' Feet

13 It was just before the Passover Feast.
Jesus knew that the time had come
for him to leave this world and go to the Father. Having loved his own who were in the
world, he now showed them the full extent of
his love.[d]
2The evening meal was being served, and the
devil had already prompted Judas Iscariot, son
of Simon, to betray Jesus. 3Jesus knew that the
Father had put all things under his power, and
that he had come from God and was returning
to God; 4so he got up from the meal, took off
his outer clothing, and wrapped a towel around
his waist. 5After that, he poured water into a

[a]34 Or *Messiah* [b]38 Isaiah 53:1 [c]40 Isaiah 6:10 [d]1 Or *he loved them to the last*

basin and began to wash his disciples' feet,
drying them with the towel that was wrapped
around him.
6He came to Simon Peter, who said to him,
"Lord, are you going to wash my feet?"
7Jesus replied, "You do not realize now what
I am doing, but later you will understand."
8"No," said Peter, "you shall never wash my
feet."
Jesus answered, "Unless I wash you, you
have no part with me."
9"Then, Lord," Simon Peter replied, "not just
my feet but my hands and my head as well!"
10Jesus answered, "A person who has had
a bath needs only to wash his feet; his whole
body is clean. And you are clean, though not
every one of you." 11For he knew who was going to betray him, and that was why he said not
every one was clean.
12When he had finished washing their feet,
he put on his clothes and returned to his place.
"Do you understand what I have done for
you?" he asked them. 13"You call me 'Teacher'
and 'Lord,' and rightly so, for that is what I am.
14Now that I, your Lord and Teacher, have
washed your feet, you also should wash one another's feet. 15I have set you an example that
you should do as I have done for you. 16I tell
you the truth, no servant is greater than his
master, nor is a messenger greater than the
one who sent him. 17Now that you know these
things, you will be blessed if you do them.

Jesus Predicts His Betrayal

18"I am not referring to all of you; I know
those I have chosen. But this is to fulfill the
scripture: 'He who shares my bread has lifted
up his heel against me.'[a]
19"I am telling you now before it happens, so
that when it does happen you will believe that
I am He. 20I tell you the truth, whoever accepts
anyone I send accepts me; and whoever accepts
me accepts the one who sent me."
21After he had said this, Jesus was troubled
in spirit and testified, "I tell you the truth, one
of you is going to betray me."
22His disciples stared at one another, at a
loss to know which of them he meant. 23One
of them, the disciple whom Jesus loved, was reclining next to him. 24Simon Peter motioned
to this disciple and said, "Ask him which one
he means."
25Leaning back against Jesus, he asked him,
"Lord, who is it?"
26Jesus answered, "It is the one to whom I
will give this piece of bread when I have dipped
it in the dish." Then, dipping the piece of bread,
he gave it to Judas Iscariot, son of Simon. 27As
soon as Judas took the bread, Satan entered
into him.
"What you are about to do, do quickly," Jesus
told him, 28but no one at the meal understood
why Jesus said this to him. 29Since Judas had
charge of the money, some thought Jesus was
telling him to buy what was needed for the
Feast, or to give something to the poor. 30As
soon as Judas had taken the bread, he went out.
And it was night.

Jesus Predicts Peter's Denial

31When he was gone, Jesus said, "Now is
the Son of Man glorified and God is glorified
in him. 32If God is glorified in him,[b] God will
glorify the Son in himself, and will glorify him
at once.
33"My children, I will be with you only a little longer. You will look for me, and just as I
told the Jews, so I tell you now: Where I am
going, you cannot come.
34"A new command I give you: Love one
another. As I have loved you, so you must love
one another. 35By this all men will know that
you are my disciples, if you love one another."
36Simon Peter asked him, "Lord, where are
you going?"
Jesus replied, "Where I am going, you cannot follow now, but you will follow later."
37Peter asked, "Lord, why can't I follow you
now? I will lay down my life for you."
38Then Jesus answered, "Will you really
lay down your life for me? I tell you the truth,
before the rooster crows, you will disown me
three times!

Jesus Comforts His Disciples

14 "Do not let your hearts be troubled.
Trust in God[c]; trust also in me. 2In my
Father's house are many rooms; if it were not
so, I would have told you. I am going there to

[a]18 Psalm 41:9 [b]32 Many early manuscripts do not have *If God is glorified in him.* [c]1 Or *You trust in God*

Servant Leaders

Read: John 13:1–17

NBC'S *DATELINE* NEWSMAGAZINE did a segment on a "revolutionary" idea for the business world: servant-leadership. Stone Phillips wondered, "Can humility and faith be good for business? Was Jesus the ultimate CEO? It's an image nearly 2,000 years old and a message that true leaders are servants first. It's an idea that's finding new disciples in corporate America."

Stone Phillips interviewed Larry Spears, who owns a worldwide nonprofit organization headquartered in Indianapolis. Larry suggested a leadership model based on sacrifice and service by those at the top toward those below them in the chain of command. He said, "Servant-leadership sort of challenges people to be brave and courageous, and to bring ideas like friendship and perhaps even love to the work place."

Jesus was the ultimate servant-leader. He knew he would be putting his mission in the hands of the disciples in the coming hours as he headed to the cross. It would soon be their turn to spread the Good News of the gospel message. So he demonstrated servant-leadership in a profoundly beautiful way. On the night before his trial and crucifixion, Jesus took the lead by humbly, lovingly kneeling at the feet of his followers and washing the dirt from their feet.

Perhaps he was thinking of how their feet would carry them to parts of the world they probably hadn't even yet heard about as they spread the Good News about the Messiah. Perhaps he reminisced about the places they had walked together. Perhaps he prayed that their feet would stand strong when they faced the persecution to come. This was surely a precious, intimate moment with his friends.

We women have grown accustomed to serving our friends and family. We serve dinner and wash dishes. We wash dirty faces. We wash loads and loads of laundry. As we carry out our roles as servants, may we humbly lead those we love to the servant-leader Jesus, the One who was willing to humble himself and wash us "whiter than snow" (Psalm 51:7).

John 13:15–16

"I have set you an example that you should do as I have done for you. I tell you the truth, no servant is greater than his master, nor is a messenger greater than the one who sent him."

reflection

1 Where are some of the places your feet have carried you for the Lord?

2 What leadership roles has God allowed you to undertake for him?

3 Knowing that Jesus was willing to washing his disciples' feet, how will you humbly serve those whom you lead?

RELATED READINGS

Matthew 23:8–12;
Mark 9:33–35;
Philippians 2:1–8

Go to page 1309 for your next devotional reading.

prepare a place for you. 3And if I go and prepare a place for you, I will come back and take you to be with me that you also may be where I am. 4You know the way to the place where I am going."

Jesus the Way to the Father

5Thomas said to him, "Lord, we don't know where you are going, so how can we know the way?"

6Jesus answered, "I am the way and the truth and the life. No one comes to the Father except through me. 7If you really knew me, you would know[a] my Father as well. From now on, you do know him and have seen him."

8Philip said, "Lord, show us the Father and that will be enough for us."

9Jesus answered: "Don't you know me, Philip, even after I have been among you such a long time? Anyone who has seen me has seen the Father. How can you say, 'Show us the Father'? 10Don't you believe that I am in the Father, and that the Father is in me? The words I say to you are not just my own. Rather, it is the Father, living in me, who is doing his work. 11Believe me when I say that I am in the Father and the Father is in me; or at least believe on the evidence of the miracles themselves. 12I tell you the truth, anyone who has faith in me will do what I have been doing. He will do even greater things than these, because I am going to the Father. 13And I will do whatever you ask in my name, so that the Son may bring glory to the Father. 14You may ask me for anything in my name, and I will do it.

Jesus Promises the Holy Spirit

15"If you love me, you will obey what I command. 16And I will ask the Father, and he will give you another Counselor to be with you forever— 17the Spirit of truth. The world cannot accept him, because it neither sees him nor knows him. But you know him, for he lives with you and will be[b] in you. 18I will not leave you as orphans; I will come to you. 19Before long, the world will not see me anymore, but you will see me. Because I live, you also will live. 20On that day you will realize that I am in my Father, and you are in me, and I am in you. 21Whoever has my commands and obeys them, he is the one who loves me. He who loves me will be loved by my Father, and I too will love him and show myself to him."

22Then Judas (not Judas Iscariot) said, "But, Lord, why do you intend to show yourself to us and not to the world?"

23Jesus replied, "If anyone loves me, he will obey my teaching. My Father will love him, and we will come to him and make our home with him. 24He who does not love me will not obey my teaching. These words you hear are not my own; they belong to the Father who sent me.

25"All this I have spoken while still with you. 26But the Counselor, the Holy Spirit, whom the Father will send in my name, will teach you all things and will remind you of everything I have said to you. 27Peace I leave with you; my peace I give you. I do not give to you as the world gives. Do not let your hearts be troubled and do not be afraid.

28"You heard me say, 'I am going away and I am coming back to you.' If you loved me, you would be glad that I am going to the Father, for the Father is greater than I. 29I have told you now before it happens, so that when it does happen you will believe. 30I will not speak with you much longer, for the prince of this world is coming. He has no hold on me, 31but the world must learn that I love the Father and that I do exactly what my Father has commanded me.

"Come now; let us leave.

The Vine and the Branches

15 "I am the true vine, and my Father is the gardener. 2He cuts off every branch in me that bears no fruit, while every branch that does bear fruit he prunes[c] so that it will be even more fruitful. 3You are already clean because of the word I have spoken to you. 4Remain in me, and I will remain in you. No branch can bear fruit by itself; it must remain in the vine. Neither can you bear fruit unless you remain in me.

5"I am the vine; you are the branches. If a man remains in me and I in him, he will bear much fruit; apart from me you can do nothing. 6If anyone does not remain in me, he is like a branch that is thrown away and withers; such

[a]7 Some early manuscripts *If you really have known me, you will know* [b]17 Some early manuscripts *and is* [c]2 The Greek for *prunes* also means *cleans.*

Faithfully Available

Read: John 14:1–31

WHAT ASSIGNMENT HAS GOD GIVEN YOU? Would you ask Him? I know He has one in mind for you because He told us clearly, through the words of the apostle Paul, that "we are God's workmanship, created in Christ Jesus to do good works, which God prepared in advance for us to do."

Don't dodge your assignment because it seems to lack any chance for success. Don't miss your assignment because it seems such an insignificant, small thing. The church in Europe was birthed when Paul spoke to a handful of women on a river bank. The size and scope of the assignment are up to Him, and the effectiveness and lasting impact of your service are also His responsibility. You and I are simply to be faithfully available . . . and obedient.

The assignments God has given me have taken me way beyond my comfort zone. While some of them have begun small and stayed small, others have begun small and grown larger, while still others were begun large and blossomed into major tasks.

There have been times when I have argued, resisted, procrastinated, and questioned, but in the end I always give in, because He is my Lord . . . I have "seen" Him . . . and I love Him. I don't serve Him because I have to. I serve Him because I want to do something for Him. And in the process of being obedient, I have come to know Him. He has "made known to me the path of life. He has filled me with joy in His presence, with eternal pleasures at His right hand."

With eagerness and enthusiasm, I put my feet in motion. I want to serve Him all the days of my life. I want to stay awake to His glorious vision forever. I am now on a passionate pursuit for more of Jesus. I embrace the Cross that shatters the stranglehold of self and enlarges my capacity to receive more. I long . . .

- to gaze on His visible face,
- to hear His audible voice,
- to feel His unmistakable touch,
- to become an eyewitness of His glory.

In the meantime, I refuse to sleep one more minute. I'm awake . . . with eyes opened, heart rended, and knees bent while I whisper, "Yes . . . Yes, Lord! . . . Yes, Sir!" then raise my hand as I move my feet. "I'm available for service. Send me. I'll go. I want to stay awake forever . . ."

—*Anne Graham Lotz*

John 14:25–26

"All this I have spoken while still with you. But the Counselor, the Holy Spirit, whom the Father will send in my name, will teach you all things and will remind you of everything I have said to you."

reflection

1 What assignment has God given to you?

2 What is the first step of obedience you need to take in order to begin fulfilling that special assignment?

3 Whisper, "Yes . . . Yes, Lord!" and ask the Holy Spirit to teach you how to complete the assignment in a way that perfectly glorifies God and brings you to a greater knowledge of him.

RELATED READINGS

1 Chronicles 9:22–27; Psalm 16; Ephesians 2:4–10; Hebrews 5:5–10

Go to page 1312 for your next devotional reading.

branches are picked up, thrown into the fire and burned. 7If you remain in me and my words remain in you, ask whatever you wish, and it will be given you. 8This is to my Father's glory, that you bear much fruit, showing yourselves to be my disciples.

9"As the Father has loved me, so have I loved you. Now remain in my love. 10If you obey my commands, you will remain in my love, just as I have obeyed my Father's commands and remain in his love. 11I have told you this so that my joy may be in you and that your joy may be complete. 12My command is this: Love each other as I have loved you. 13Greater love has no one than this, that he lay down his life for his friends. 14You are my friends if you do what I command. 15I no longer call you servants, because a servant does not know his master's business. Instead, I have called you friends, for everything that I learned from my Father I have made known to you. 16You did not choose me, but I chose you and appointed you to go and bear fruit—fruit that will last. Then the Father will give you whatever you ask in my name. 17This is my command: Love each other.

> John 15:7
>
> *God Gives Good Gifts*
>
> "If you remain in me and my words remain in you, ask whatever you wish, and it will be given you."

The World Hates the Disciples

18"If the world hates you, keep in mind that it hated me first. 19If you belonged to the world, it would love you as its own. As it is, you do not belong to the world, but I have chosen you out of the world. That is why the world hates you. 20Remember the words I spoke to you: 'No servant is greater than his master.'[a] If they persecuted me, they will persecute you also. If they obeyed my teaching, they will obey yours also. 21They will treat you this way because of my name, for they do not know the One who sent me. 22If I had not come and spoken to them, they would not be guilty of sin. Now, however, they have no excuse for their sin. 23He who hates me hates my Father as well. 24If I had not done among them what no one else did, they would not be guilty of sin. But now they have seen these miracles, and yet they have hated both me and my Father. 25But this is to fulfill what is written in their Law: 'They hated me without reason.'[b]

26"When the Counselor comes, whom I will send to you from the Father, the Spirit of truth who goes out from the Father, he will testify about me. 27And you also must testify, for you have been with me from the beginning.

16 "All this I have told you so that you will not go astray. 2They will put you out of the synagogue; in fact, a time is coming when anyone who kills you will think he is offering a service to God. 3They will do such things because they have not known the Father or me. 4I have told you this, so that when the time comes you will remember that I warned you. I did not tell you this at first because I was with you.

The Work of the Holy Spirit

5"Now I am going to him who sent me, yet none of you asks me, 'Where are you going?' 6Because I have said these things, you are filled with grief. 7But I tell you the truth: It is for your good that I am going away. Unless I go away, the Counselor will not come to you; but if I go, I will send him to you. 8When he comes, he will convict the world of guilt[c] in regard to sin and righteousness and judgment: 9in regard to sin, because men do not believe in me; 10in regard to righteousness, because I am going to the Father, where you can see me no longer; 11and in regard to judgment, because the prince of this world now stands condemned.

12"I have much more to say to you, more than you can now bear. 13But when he, the Spirit of truth, comes, he will guide you into all truth. He will not speak on his own; he will speak only what he hears, and he will tell you what is yet to come. 14He will bring glory to me by taking from what is mine and making it known to you. 15All that belongs to the Father is mine. That is why I said the Spirit will take from what is mine and make it known to you.

16"In a little while you will see me no more, and then after a little while you will see me."

[a]20 John 13:16 [b]25 Psalms 35:19; 69:4 [c]8 Or *will expose the guilt of the world*

The Disciples' Grief Will Turn to Joy

17Some of his disciples said to one another,
"What does he mean by saying, 'In a little while
you will see me no more, and then after a little
while you will see me,' and 'Because I am going
to the Father'?" 18They kept
asking, "What does he mean
by 'a little while'? We don't understand what he is saying."
19Jesus saw that they wanted
to ask him about this, so he said
to them, "Are you asking one
another what I meant when I
said, 'In a little while you will
see me no more, and then after
a little while you will see me'?
20I tell you the truth, you will
weep and mourn while the
world rejoices. You will grieve,
but your grief will turn to joy.
21A woman giving birth to a
child has pain because her time
has come; but when her baby is
born she forgets the anguish because of her joy
that a child is born into the world. 22So with
you: Now is your time of grief, but I will see you
again and you will rejoice, and no one will take
away your joy. 23In that day you will no longer
ask me anything. I tell you the truth, my Father
will give you whatever you ask in my name.
24Until now you have not asked for anything
in my name. Ask and you will receive, and your
joy will be complete.
25"Though I have been speaking figuratively,
a time is coming when I will no longer use this
kind of language but will tell you plainly about
my Father. 26In that day you will ask in my
name. I am not saying that I will ask the Father
on your behalf. 27No, the Father himself loves
you because you have loved me and have believed that I came from God. 28I came from the
Father and entered the world; now I am leaving
the world and going back to the Father."
29Then Jesus' disciples said, "Now you are
speaking clearly and without figures of speech.
30Now we can see that you know all things and
that you do not even need to have anyone ask
you questions. This makes us believe that you
came from God."

John 16:33

God Has Overcome the World

"I have told you these things, so that in me you may have peace. In this world you will have trouble. But take heart! I have overcome the world."

31"You believe at last!"[a] Jesus answered.
32"But a time is coming, and has come, when
you will be scattered, each to his own home.
You will leave me all alone. Yet I am not alone,
for my Father is with me.
33"I have told you these
things, so that in me you may
have peace. In this world
you will have trouble. But
take heart! I have overcome
the world."

Jesus Prays for Himself

17 After Jesus said this, he
looked toward heaven
and prayed:

"Father, the time has
come. Glorify your Son,
that your Son may glorify
you. 2For you granted him
authority over all people
that he might give eternal
life to all those you have
given him. 3Now this is eternal life: that
they may know you, the only true God,
and Jesus Christ, whom you have sent. 4I
have brought you glory on earth by completing the work you gave me to do. 5And
now, Father, glorify me in your presence
with the glory I had with you before the
world began.

Jesus Prays for His Disciples

6"I have revealed you[b] to those whom
you gave me out of the world. They were
yours; you gave them to me and they have
obeyed your word. 7Now they know that
everything you have given me comes from
you. 8For I gave them the words you gave
me and they accepted them. They knew
with certainty that I came from you, and
they believed that you sent me. 9I pray
for them. I am not praying for the world,
but for those you have given me, for they
are yours. 10All I have is yours, and all
you have is mine. And glory has come to
me through them. 11I will remain in the
world no longer, but they are still in the
world, and I am coming to you. Holy Father, protect them by the power of your

[a]31 Or *"Do you now believe?"* [b]6 Greek *your name*; also in verse 26

Full of Joy

Read: John 17:1–26

John 17:13

"I am coming to you now, but I say these things while I am still in the world, so that they may have the full measure of my joy within them."

reflection

1 On a scale of one to ten, how would you rate your joy factor?

2 After reading Nadine's comments, do you relate to her when she talks about allowing imaginary troubles to interrupt joy?

3 What might you do today to experience more joy?

RELATED READINGS

Acts 14:15–17;
Romans 14:17–18;
Hebrews 1:8–9;
1 Peter 1:8–9

"I'D MAKE MORE MISTAKES next time," said 85-year-old Nadine Stair when asked what she would do if she had her life to live over again. "I'd relax. I would limber up. I would be sillier than I have been this trip. I would take fewer things seriously. I would take more chances. I would climb more mountains and swim more rivers. I would eat more ice cream and less beans. I would perhaps have more actual troubles, but I'd have fewer imaginary ones. You see, I'm one of those people who live sensibly and sanely hour after hour, day after day. Oh, I've had my moments, and if I had to do it over again, I'd have more of them. In fact, I'd try to have nothing else—just moments, one after another, instead of living so many years ahead of each day. I've been one of those persons who never goes anywhere without a thermometer, a hot water bottle and a raincoat. If I had to do it over again, I would travel lighter than I have. If I had my life to live over, I would start barefoot earlier in the spring and stay that way later in the fall. I would go to more dances. I would ride more merry-go-rounds. I would pick more daisies."

In his final prayer, Jesus prayed that his disciples would experience the full measure of his joy—now. He prayed for us to have his joy in the middle of rush-hour traffic, screaming kids and a darkening world. He doesn't want us to wait for heaven to be full of joy.

Jesus' joy has a divine purpose: to reveal him. He desires to fill us with overflowing joy, to proclaim his victory to the world over life's worst conditions—even in the face of hurricanes, plagues, terrorism and nuclear disaster.

But as Nadine tells us, joy flows from a foundation of *truth*. So many times we focus on imaginary troubles. But Jesus reminds us that joy comes from knowing the Father through the Son. As you reflect on your life, whether you're 18, 38, 48 or 88, choose to live in fullness of joy by taking the time to pick more daisies . . . and by living each moment fully aware of God's love for you.

Wednesday

Go to page 1316 for your next devotional reading.

name—the name you gave me—so that they may be one as we are one. [12]While I was with them, I protected them and kept them safe by that name you gave me. None has been lost except the one doomed to destruction so that Scripture would be fulfilled.

[13]"I am coming to you now, but I say these things while I am still in the world, so that they may have the full measure of my joy within them. [14]I have given them your word and the world has hated them, for they are not of the world any more than I am of the world. [15]My prayer is not that you take them out of the world but that you protect them from the evil one. [16]They are not of the world, even as I am not of it. [17]Sanctify[a] them by the truth; your word is truth. [18]As you sent me into the world, I have sent them into the world. [19]For them I sanctify myself, that they too may be truly sanctified.

Jesus Prays for All Believers

[20]"My prayer is not for them alone. I pray also for those who will believe in me through their message, [21]that all of them may be one, Father, just as you are in me and I am in you. May they also be in us so that the world may believe that you have sent me. [22]I have given them the glory that you gave me, that they may be one as we are one: [23]I in them and you in me. May they be brought to complete unity to let the world know that you sent me and have loved them even as you have loved me.

[24]"Father, I want those you have given me to be with me where I am, and to see my glory, the glory you have given me because you loved me before the creation of the world.

[25]"Righteous Father, though the world does not know you, I know you, and they know that you have sent me. [26]I have made you known to them, and will continue to make you known in order that the love you have for me may be in them and that I myself may be in them."

Jesus Arrested

18 When he had finished praying, Jesus left with his disciples and crossed the Kidron Valley. On the other side there was an olive grove, and he and his disciples went into it.

[2]Now Judas, who betrayed him, knew the place, because Jesus had often met there with his disciples. [3]So Judas came to the grove, guiding a detachment of soldiers and some officials from the chief priests and Pharisees. They were carrying torches, lanterns and weapons.

[4]Jesus, knowing all that was going to happen to him, went out and asked them, "Who is it you want?"

[5]"Jesus of Nazareth," they replied.

"I am he," Jesus said. (And Judas the traitor was standing there with them.) [6]When Jesus said, "I am he," they drew back and fell to the ground.

[7]Again he asked them, "Who is it you want?"

And they said, "Jesus of Nazareth."

[8]"I told you that I am he," Jesus answered. "If you are looking for me, then let these men go." [9]This happened so that the words he had spoken would be fulfilled: "I have not lost one of those you gave me."[b]

[10]Then Simon Peter, who had a sword, drew it and struck the high priest's servant, cutting off his right ear. (The servant's name was Malchus.)

[11]Jesus commanded Peter, "Put your sword away! Shall I not drink the cup the Father has given me?"

Jesus Taken to Annas

[12]Then the detachment of soldiers with its commander and the Jewish officials arrested Jesus. They bound him [13]and brought him first to Annas, who was the father-in-law of Caiaphas, the high priest that year. [14]Caiaphas was the one who had advised the Jews that it would be good if one man died for the people.

Peter's First Denial

[15]Simon Peter and another disciple were following Jesus. Because this disciple was known to the high priest, he went with Jesus into the high priest's courtyard, [16]but Peter had to wait

[a]17 Greek *hagiazo (set apart for sacred use* or *make holy)*; also in verse 19 [b]9 John 6:39

outside at the door. The other disciple, who was
known to the high priest, came back, spoke to
the girl on duty there and brought Peter in.
17"You are not one of his disciples, are you?"
the girl at the door asked Peter.
He replied, "I am not."
18It was cold, and the servants and officials
stood around a fire they had made to keep
warm. Peter also was standing with them,
warming himself.

The High Priest Questions Jesus

19Meanwhile, the high priest questioned
Jesus about his disciples and his teaching.
20"I have spoken openly to the world," Jesus
replied. "I always taught in synagogues or at
the temple, where all the Jews come together.
I said nothing in secret. 21Why question me?
Ask those who heard me. Surely they know
what I said."
22When Jesus said this, one of the officials
nearby struck him in the face. "Is this the way
you answer the high priest?" he demanded.
23"If I said something wrong," Jesus replied,
"testify as to what is wrong. But if I spoke the
truth, why did you strike me?" 24Then Annas
sent him, still bound, to Caiaphas the high
priest.[a]

Peter's Second and Third Denials

25As Simon Peter stood warming himself,
he was asked, "You are not one of his disciples,
are you?"
He denied it, saying, "I am not."
26One of the high priest's servants, a relative
of the man whose ear Peter had cut off, challenged him, "Didn't I see you with him in the
olive grove?" 27Again Peter denied it, and at
that moment a rooster began to crow.

Jesus Before Pilate

28Then the Jews led Jesus from Caiaphas to
the palace of the Roman governor. By now it
was early morning, and to avoid ceremonial
uncleanness the Jews did not enter the palace;
they wanted to be able to eat the Passover. 29So
Pilate came out to them and asked, "What
charges are you bringing against this man?"
30"If he were not a criminal," they replied,
"we would not have handed him over to you."
31Pilate said, "Take him yourselves and
judge him by your own law."
"But we have no right to execute anyone,"
the Jews objected. 32This happened so that the
words Jesus had spoken indicating the kind of
death he was going to die would be fulfilled.
33Pilate then went back inside the palace,
summoned Jesus and asked him, "Are you the
king of the Jews?"
34"Is that your own idea," Jesus asked, "or
did others talk to you about me?"
35"Am I a Jew?" Pilate replied. "It was your
people and your chief priests who handed you
over to me. What is it you have done?"
36Jesus said, "My kingdom is not of this
world. If it were, my servants would fight to
prevent my arrest by the Jews. But now my kingdom is from another place."
37"You are a king, then!" said Pilate.
Jesus answered, "You are right in saying I
am a king. In fact, for this reason I was born,
and for this I came into the world, to testify to
the truth. Everyone on the side of truth listens
to me."
38"What is truth?" Pilate asked. With this he
went out again to the Jews and said, "I find no
basis for a charge against him. 39But it is your
custom for me to release to you one prisoner
at the time of the Passover. Do you want me to
release 'the king of the Jews'?"
40They shouted back, "No, not him! Give us
Barabbas!" Now Barabbas had taken part in a
rebellion.

Jesus Sentenced to Be Crucified

19 Then Pilate took Jesus and had him
flogged. 2The soldiers twisted together
a crown of thorns and put it on his head. They
clothed him in a purple robe 3and went up to
him again and again, saying, "Hail, king of the
Jews!" And they struck him in the face.
4Once more Pilate came out and said to the
Jews, "Look, I am bringing him out to you to
let you know that I find no basis for a charge
against him." 5When Jesus came out wearing
the crown of thorns and the purple robe, Pilate
said to them, "Here is the man!"
6As soon as the chief priests and their officials
saw him, they shouted, "Crucify! Crucify!"

[a]24 Or *(Now Annas had sent him, still bound, to Caiaphas the high priest.)*

But Pilate answered, "You take him and
crucify him. As for me, I find no basis for a
charge against him."
7 The Jews insisted, "We have a law, and according to that law he must die, because he
claimed to be the Son of God."
8 When Pilate heard this, he was even more
afraid, 9 and he went back inside the palace.
"Where do you come from?" he asked Jesus,
but Jesus gave him no answer.

> **John 19:11**
>
> *God Appoints Those in Authority*
>
> Jesus answered, "You would have no power over me if it were not given to you from above. Therefore the one who handed me over to you is guilty of a greater sin."

10 "Do you refuse to speak to
me?" Pilate said. "Don't you realize I have power either to free
you or to crucify you?"
11 Jesus answered, "You
would have no power over me
if it were not given to you from
above. Therefore the one who
handed me over to you is guilty
of a greater sin."
12 From then on, Pilate tried
to set Jesus free, but the Jews
kept shouting, "If you let this
man go, you are no friend of
Caesar. Anyone who claims to
be a king opposes Caesar."
13 When Pilate heard this,
he brought Jesus out and sat
down on the judge's seat at a
place known as the Stone Pavement (which in
Aramaic is Gabbatha). 14 It was the day of Preparation of Passover Week, about the sixth hour.
"Here is your king," Pilate said to the Jews.
15 But they shouted, "Take him away! Take
him away! Crucify him!"
"Shall I crucify your king?" Pilate asked.
"We have no king but Caesar," the chief
priests answered.
16 Finally Pilate handed him over to them to
be crucified.

The Crucifixion

So the soldiers took charge of Jesus. 17 Carrying his own cross, he went out to the place
of the Skull (which in Aramaic is called Golgotha). 18 Here they crucified him, and with
him two others—one on each side and Jesus
in the middle.
19 Pilate had a notice prepared and fastened
to the cross. It read: JESUS OF NAZARETH, THE
KING OF THE JEWS. 20 Many of the Jews read
this sign, for the place where Jesus was crucified was near the city, and the sign was written in Aramaic, Latin and Greek. 21 The chief
priests of the Jews protested to Pilate, "Do not
write 'The King of the Jews,' but that this man
claimed to be king of the Jews."
22 Pilate answered, "What I have written, I
have written."
23 When the soldiers crucified Jesus, they took his clothes,
dividing them into four shares,
one for each of them, with the
undergarment remaining. This
garment was seamless, woven
in one piece from top to bottom.
24 "Let's not tear it," they said
to one another. "Let's decide by
lot who will get it."
This happened that the scripture might be fulfilled which
said,

"They divided my
garments among
them
and cast lots for my
clothing."[a]

So this is what the soldiers did.
25 Near the cross of Jesus stood his mother,
his mother's sister, Mary the wife of Clopas,
and Mary Magdalene. 26 When Jesus saw his
mother there, and the disciple whom he loved
standing nearby, he said to his mother, "Dear
woman, here is your son," 27 and to the disciple,
"Here is your mother." From that time on, this
disciple took her into his home.

The Death of Jesus

28 Later, knowing that all was now completed,
and so that the Scripture would be fulfilled,
Jesus said, "I am thirsty." 29 A jar of wine vinegar
was there, so they soaked a sponge in it, put
the sponge on a stalk of the hyssop plant, and
lifted it to Jesus' lips. 30 When he had received
the drink, Jesus said, "It is finished." With that,
he bowed his head and gave up his spirit.
31 Now it was the day of Preparation, and the
next day was to be a special Sabbath. Because

[a] 24 Psalm 22:18

It Is Finished

John 19:30

Jesus said, "It is finished." With that, he bowed his head and gave up his spirit.

reflection

1 Have you accepted Jesus' death as full payment for your sins? How does it feel to be completely forgiven and free from eternal death?

2 Who are the people in your life who have not accepted Jesus' death as payment for their sins? Pray for those you know who haven't asked for his forgiveness.

3 What are different ways you can thank Jesus for the wonderful love gift that only he could give? Pray and thank him right now.

RELATED READINGS

Genesis 3:14–16; Isaiah 53:1–12; Hebrews 9:11–22

Read: John 19:25–42

ALL OF HUMAN HISTORY has been moving toward one climactic moment: the death of Jesus Christ. From the first hint in Genesis 3:15 that the serpent would strike the heel of the man to Simeon's prophecy to Mary that a sword would pierce her soul (see Luke 2:34–35), history has held its breath—waiting for the promise to be fulfilled. Those prophecies were finally, painfully fulfilled as the Lifegiver gave up his spirit on the cross.

All of the Old Testament sacrifices pointed to this moment. At this juncture, the great High Priest became the sacrificial Lamb. The symbolism and mysterious predictions became reality in the life and death of this man who was God. This God-man who turned himself over to death so that his murderers could be forgiven. This man-God whose death would remove the sins of his own mother, who watched with sorrow as the prophecies became reality on that hideous cross. This God-man whose willing sacrifice sufficiently, completely covered the sins of men and women past, present and future.

Angels, prophets and Jesus Christ himself predicted his death at the hands of sinners. But his death was also *for* those sinners. God's justice demands death for sin. God's mercy provided the willing, perfect sacrifice for sin. The cross is God's love gift. On that cross love made a man die so that his enemies could live. There, the only perfect human died so that we sinners can be forgiven. On that day, everything that separates people from God was torn in the brutal tearing of Christ's body.

He did it for you. This sacrifice was the only way your sins could be paid for without your own eternal death. Christ's death paid the price of your sin. When Jesus said, "It is finished," he meant there was nothing else to do, nothing left to pay. He paid it all—totally, completely, permanently.

It is finished.

Thursday

Go to page 1318 for your next devotional reading.

the Jews did not want the bodies left on the
crosses during the Sabbath, they asked Pilate
to have the legs broken and the bodies taken
down. 32The soldiers therefore came and broke
the legs of the first man who had been crucified with Jesus, and then those of the other.
33But when they came to Jesus and found
that he was already dead, they did not break
his legs. 34Instead, one of the soldiers pierced
Jesus' side with a spear, bringing a sudden flow
of blood and water. 35The man who saw it has
given testimony, and his testimony is true. He
knows that he tells the truth, and he testifies so
that you also may believe. 36These things happened so that the scripture would be fulfilled:
"Not one of his bones will be broken,"[a] 37and,
as another scripture says, "They will look on
the one they have pierced."[b]

The Burial of Jesus

38Later, Joseph of Arimathea asked Pilate for
the body of Jesus. Now Joseph was a disciple of
Jesus, but secretly because he feared the Jews.
With Pilate's permission, he came and took the
body away. 39He was accompanied by Nicodemus, the man who earlier had visited Jesus at
night. Nicodemus brought a mixture of myrrh
and aloes, about seventy-five pounds.[c] 40Tak-
ing Jesus' body, the two of them wrapped it,
with the spices, in strips of linen. This was in accordance with Jewish burial customs. 41At the
place where Jesus was crucified, there was a garden, and in the garden a new tomb, in which
no one had ever been laid. 42Because it was the
Jewish day of Preparation and since the tomb
was nearby, they laid Jesus there.

The Empty Tomb

20 Early on the first day of the week, while
it was still dark, Mary Magdalene went
to the tomb and saw that the stone had been
removed from the entrance. 2So she came running to Simon Peter and the other disciple, the
one Jesus loved, and said, "They have taken the
Lord out of the tomb, and we don't know where
they have put him!"

3So Peter and the other disciple started for
the tomb. 4Both were running, but the other
disciple outran Peter and reached the tomb
first. 5He bent over and looked in at the strips
of linen lying there but did not go in. 6Then
Simon Peter, who was behind him, arrived and
went into the tomb. He saw the strips of linen
lying there, 7as well as the burial cloth that had
been around Jesus' head. The cloth was folded
up by itself, separate from the linen. 8Finally
the other disciple, who had reached the tomb
first, also went inside. He saw and believed.
9(They still did not understand from Scripture
that Jesus had to rise from the dead.)

Jesus Appears to Mary Magdalene

10Then the disciples went back to their
homes, 11but Mary stood outside the tomb
crying. As she wept, she bent over to look into
the tomb 12and saw two angels in white, seated
where Jesus' body had been, one at the head
and the other at the foot.

13They asked her, "Woman, why are you crying?"

"They have taken my Lord away," she said,
"and I don't know where they have put him."
14At this, she turned around and saw Jesus
standing there, but she did not realize that it
was Jesus.

15"Woman," he said, "why are you crying?
Who is it you are looking for?"

Thinking he was the gardener, she said, "Sir,
if you have carried him away, tell me where you
have put him, and I will get him."

16Jesus said to her, "Mary."

She turned toward him and cried out in
Aramaic, "Rabboni!" (which means Teacher).

17Jesus said, "Do not hold on to me, for I
have not yet returned to the Father. Go instead
to my brothers and tell them, 'I am returning
to my Father and your Father, to my God and
your God.'"

18Mary Magdalene went to the disciples
with the news: "I have seen the Lord!" And she
told them that he had said these things to her.

Jesus Appears to His Disciples

19On the evening of that first day of the
week, when the disciples were together, with
the doors locked for fear of the Jews, Jesus
came and stood among them and said, "Peace
be with you!" 20After he said this, he showed
them his hands and side. The disciples were
overjoyed when they saw the Lord.

[a] 36 Exodus 12:46; Num. 9:12; Psalm 34:20 [b] 37 Zech. 12:10 [c] 39 Greek *a hundred litrai* (about 34 kilograms)

The Real Jesus

Read: John 20:11–31

John 20:31

But these are written that you may believe that Jesus is the Christ, the Son of God, and that by believing you may have life in his name.

IMAGINE JESUS SAVORING boiled fish for breakfast. See his face light up as he delights in a child's antics. Observe him as he keeps the party going, turning water at a wedding into choice wine.

This is the human Jesus—a man who cried, laughed, slept, conversed and shared affection freely. Few knew Jesus' personal habits like his 12 disciples. And John, who Jesus called "beloved," may have known him best of all.

As an insider, John offers an up-close view of seven of Jesus' miracles and shares the compelling details of Jesus' death and resurrection. After all of these real-life stories, John is quick to admit that Jesus did many more miracles: "But these are written that you may believe that Jesus is the Christ, the Son of God, and that by believing you may have life in his name" (verse 31).

"Trust me," John seems to say. "I knew him. I loved him. I watched him do miracles, die and come back to life again. Jesus is God's Son. He proved it!" Though we cannot walk beside the human Jesus today, millions have seen him through John's eyes.

Centuries later, a Jesus-follower named Sundar Singh said this about knowing Jesus Christ: "There are many Christians who do not feel his glorious presence as something real . . . only when someone surrenders his heart to Jesus can he find him." Singh knew in his mind who Jesus Christ was—but when he surrendered his heart, he found peace even while he was in prison.

How do you know Jesus? Knowing details about his life and ministry isn't enough. When you receive his forgiveness, you can go beyond knowing him to loving him. When you spend time with him in prayer, you can go beyond loving him to sensing his presence. Reflect today on how you can experience his presence in all of your daily moments. The real Jesus longs to hold a place in your heart.

reflection

1. Do you think you *know* Jesus or just know *about* Jesus?
2. How much time each day do you spend with him?
3. How has time in his Word and in prayer helped you to know and love him more?

RELATED READINGS

John 3:16–21; 6:41–58; 1 John 5:1–5

"I must make a conscious, deliberate, daily choice to sit at His feet, to listen to His Word, to receive His love, to let Him change me and to pour out my heart's devotion to Him."

Nancy Leigh DeMoss

Go to page 1320 for your next devotional reading.

21 Again Jesus said, "Peace be with you! As
the Father has sent me, I am sending you."
22 And with that he breathed on them and said,
"Receive the Holy Spirit. 23 If you forgive anyone his sins, they are forgiven; if you do not
forgive them, they are not forgiven."

Jesus Appears to Thomas

24 Now Thomas (called Didymus), one of the
Twelve, was not with the disciples when Jesus
came. 25 So the other disciples told him, "We
have seen the Lord!"

But he said to them, "Unless I see the nail
marks in his hands and put my finger where
the nails were, and put my hand into his side, I
will not believe it."

26 A week later his disciples were in the house
again, and Thomas was with them. Though the
doors were locked, Jesus came and stood among
them and said, "Peace be with you!" 27 Then he
said to Thomas, "Put your finger here; see my
hands. Reach out your hand and put it into my
side. Stop doubting and believe."

28 Thomas said to him, "My Lord and my
God!"

29 Then Jesus told him, "Because you have
seen me, you have believed; blessed are those
who have not seen and yet have believed."

30 Jesus did many other miraculous signs
in the presence of his disciples, which are not
recorded in this book. 31 But these are written
that you may[a] believe that Jesus is the Christ,
the Son of God, and that by believing you may
have life in his name.

Jesus and the Miraculous Catch of Fish

21 Afterward Jesus appeared again to his
disciples, by the Sea of Tiberias.[b] It happened this way: 2 Simon Peter, Thomas (called
Didymus), Nathanael from Cana in Galilee,
the sons of Zebedee, and two other disciples
were together. 3 "I'm going out to fish," Simon
Peter told them, and they said, "We'll go with
you." So they went out and got into the boat,
but that night they caught nothing.

4 Early in the morning, Jesus stood on the
shore, but the disciples did not realize that it
was Jesus.

5 He called out to them, "Friends, haven't you
any fish?"

"No," they answered.

6 He said, "Throw your net on the right side
of the boat and you will find some." When they
did, they were unable to haul the net in because
of the large number of fish.

7 Then the disciple whom Jesus loved said to
Peter, "It is the Lord!" As soon as Simon Peter
heard him say, "It is the Lord," he wrapped his
outer garment around him (for he had taken it
off) and jumped into the water. 8 The other disciples followed in the boat, towing the net full
of fish, for they were not far from shore, about a
hundred yards.[c] 9 When they landed, they saw
a fire of burning coals there with fish on it, and
some bread.

10 Jesus said to them, "Bring some of the fish
you have just caught."

11 Simon Peter climbed aboard and dragged
the net ashore. It was full of large fish, 153, but
even with so many the net was not torn. 12 Jesus said to them, "Come and have breakfast."
None of the disciples dared ask him, "Who are
you?" They knew it was the Lord. 13 Jesus came,
took the bread and gave it to them, and did the
same with the fish. 14 This was now the third
time Jesus appeared to his disciples after he was
raised from the dead.

Jesus Reinstates Peter

15 When they had finished eating, Jesus said
to Simon Peter, "Simon son of John, do you
truly love me more than these?"

"Yes, Lord," he said, "you know that I love
you."

Jesus said, "Feed my lambs."

16 Again Jesus said, "Simon son of John, do
you truly love me?"

He answered, "Yes, Lord, you know that I
love you."

Jesus said, "Take care of my sheep."

17 The third time he said to him, "Simon son
of John, do you love me?"

Peter was hurt because Jesus asked him the
third time, "Do you love me?" He said, "Lord,
you know all things; you know that I love
you."

Jesus said, "Feed my sheep. 18 I tell you the
truth, when you were younger you dressed
yourself and went where you wanted; but when
you are old you will stretch out your hands,

[a] 31 Some manuscripts *may continue to* [b] 1 That is, Sea of Galilee [c] 8 Greek *about two hundred cubits* (about 90 meters)

Making History

SALOME

Some women were watching from a distance. Among them were Mary Magdalene, Mary the mother of James the younger and of Joses, and Salome.

Mark 15:40

ASSIGNED READING:

Mark 15:40; 16:1–8

SALOME HAD A STRANGE FEELING. Something told her that the climactic meeting in Jerusalem for Passover had a greater significance this year. Surely, as one of Jesus' closest followers and supporters, she was aware of the mounting controversy surrounding him at this time. People were more and more divided because of her Master. Most no longer perceived him as merely a popular miracle worker and generous benefactor. No. His recent messages about sacrifice and commitment were too intense and demanding for that description anymore.

She'd seen the reaction of the crowds. She'd observed how the religious leaders scowled and huddled in groups. Her intuition told her something was afoot.

Was she so surprised, then, when the assembly of Jews turned on him at the end of the week? After hearing of his predawn arrest in the garden of Gethsemane, she'd lingered nearby as they took him to the religious leaders and eventually to Pilate. She'd heard the commotion of jealous leaders shouting mercilessly for his execution.

Now, with the other women at the foot of the cross, this spiritual sisterhood formed the foundation for future Christian women's groups across the world. They could not have known history would record their names: Salome (probably the mother of James and John, Zebedee's sons), Mary Magdalene, Mary the wife of Clopas, Jesus' mother Mary and Mary the mother of James and Joses. Together, their synergy supported and encouraged Jesus on a regular basis. In pairs, triads and even as a group, they—and other women, such as Joanna, Mary of Bethany, Martha and Susanna—appear in Scripture alongside him on many occasions.

The last snapshot of Salome in Scripture is of her walking to the tomb on Sunday, spices in hand, to prepare Jesus' body. Perhaps on the way there, the strange feeling returned that she'd not been able to shake since arriving in Jerusalem. Only this time, by the time she reached the empty tomb, it brought an unexpected smile to her lips.

—Prayer—

Dear God, thank you for the women in my life who support me and love me.

Weekend

Go to page 1323 for your next devotional reading.

and someone else will dress you and lead you where you do not want to go." 19Jesus said this to indicate the kind of death by which Peter would glorify God. Then he said to him, "Follow me!"

20Peter turned and saw that the disciple whom Jesus loved was following them. (This was the one who had leaned back against Jesus at the supper and had said, "Lord, who is going to betray you?") 21When Peter saw him, he asked, "Lord, what about him?"

22Jesus answered, "If I want him to remain alive until I return, what is that to you? You must follow me." 23Because of this, the rumor spread among the brothers that this disciple would not die. But Jesus did not say that he would not die; he only said, "If I want him to remain alive until I return, what is that to you?"

24This is the disciple who testifies to these things and who wrote them down. We know that his testimony is true.

25Jesus did many other things as well. If every one of them were written down, I suppose that even the whole world would not have room for the books that would be written.

Acts

Author:
Luke, a physician, and a Gentile (Greek) Christian.

Audience:
Specifically, Theophilus, whose name means "dear friend who loves God." He is the same high official for whom the book of Luke was written (see Luke 1:1).

Date:
Probably about A.D. 63.

Setting:
The gospel is spreading to all parts of the Roman Empire.

Verse to Remember:
"But you will receive power when the Holy Spirit comes on you; and you will be my witnesses in Jerusalem, and in all Judea and Samaria, and to the ends of the earth." (1:8)

The book of Acts, the second book written by Luke, *is full of firsts*: Peter's first sermon, the first mass evangelism meeting, the birth of the first church, the first martyr, the first Christian missionaries and the first Gentile additions to the new church. The new Christian church, composed of followers of Jesus, is a vibrant young church, *filled with the Holy Spirit* and quickly making a mark on the world. The arrival of the promised Holy Spirit makes the book of Acts exciting and unpredictable. Watch for *miracles and imprisonments and unexpected conversions*. See the Christians' hesitation as the persecuting Saul becomes the missionary Paul.

And watch persecution begin as the gospel spreads to Gentiles and around the known world.

Jesus Taken Up Into Heaven

1 In my former book, Theophilus, I wrote
about all that Jesus began to do and to
teach 2until the day he was taken up to heaven,
after giving instructions through the Holy
Spirit to the apostles he had chosen. 3After his
suffering, he showed himself to these men and
gave many convincing proofs that he was alive.
He appeared to them over a period of forty days
and spoke about the kingdom of God. 4On one
occasion, while he was eating with them, he
gave them this command: "Do not leave Jerusalem, but wait for the gift my Father promised,
which you have heard me speak about. 5For

A Mother's Prayers

Read: Acts 1:1–14

MONICA NEVER STOPPED PRAYING for her son. She had raised Augustine in the Christian faith in their small town in Algeria, but when he was a teenager the family moved to Carthage in North Africa. Possessed of a brilliant intellect and an even stronger will, Augustine rejected his mother's faith and instead chose a life in pursuit of immorality. In his autobiographical book *Confessions*, Augustine spoke of his years of debauchery: "Years passed, in which I wallowed in the mire of that deep pit, and the darkness of falsehood . . . All which time that chaste, godly and sober widow . . . ceased not at all hours of her devotions to bewail my case unto You. And her prayers entered into Your presence . . ."

Three hundred years before the birth of Augustine, we can only imagine how another mother labored in prayer for her children. In addition to Jesus, her firstborn, Mary of Nazareth had several other children. And yet their family was spiritually divided. John's Gospel clearly tells us that "even his own brothers did not believe in him" (John 7:5). The skepticism of her younger sons toward their elder half brother must have pierced Mary's heart.

The black Friday when her oldest son hung on a Roman cross had to be the worst day of Mary's life. And the Sunday when he rose again was the very best. Among those to whom Christ appeared after his resurrection was his brother James. We don't need to know the words that passed between them. It's enough to know that when the disciples and the women gathered to pray in the upper room following Jesus' ascension into heaven, Mary was among them. And her other sons were with her! *Praying.* The One they had rejected in life was the One in whom they now placed their faith for eternity.

Monica's prodigal son Augustine became one of the most famously devout fourth-century Christians: the Bishop of Hippo. *The Confessions of St. Augustine* is a classic of the Christian faith. Mary's son James became leader of the church in Jerusalem and wrote the New Testament book that bears his name.

Do you have children, grandchildren or children whom you love—related to you or not—who have turned away from God? Years may pass without any apparent external change. But heaven hears your loving intercession on their behalf. Take heart! God hears your prayers for your children.

Monday

Acts 1:14

They all joined together constantly in prayer, along with the women and Mary the mother of Jesus, and with his brothers.

reflection

1 Speculate on why it wasn't until the resurrection that Jesus' brothers believed he was who he said he was.

2 If you have a prodigal or know a prodigal, how does this devotional offer you hope?

3 Spend some time praying for those who have walked away from the faith of their mothers. Ask God to hear your prayers and bring the straying children home.

RELATED READINGS

Matthew 18:12–14;
Luke 15:11–32;
2 Timothy 1:5–7

Go to page 1328 for your next devotional reading.

John baptized with[a] water, but in a few days
you will be baptized with the Holy Spirit."
6 So when they met together, they asked him,
"Lord, are you at this time going to restore the
kingdom to Israel?"
7 He said to them: "It is not for you to know
the times or dates the Father has set by his own
authority. 8 But you will receive power when
the Holy Spirit comes on you; and you will be
my witnesses in Jerusalem, and in all Judea and
Samaria, and to the ends of the earth."
9 After he said this, he was taken up before
their very eyes, and a cloud hid him from their
sight.
10 They were looking intently up into the
sky as he was going, when suddenly two men
dressed in white stood beside them. 11 "Men
of Galilee," they said, "why do you stand here
looking into the sky? This same Jesus, who has
been taken from you into heaven, will come
back in the same way you have seen him go
into heaven."

Matthias Chosen to Replace Judas

12 Then they returned to Jerusalem from the
hill called the Mount of Olives, a Sabbath day's
walk[b] from the city. 13 When they arrived, they
went upstairs to the room where they were staying. Those present were Peter, John, James and
Andrew; Philip and Thomas, Bartholomew and
Matthew; James son of Alphaeus and Simon
the Zealot, and Judas son of James. 14 They all
joined together constantly in prayer, along with
the women and Mary the mother of Jesus, and
with his brothers.
15 In those days Peter stood up among the
believers[c] (a group numbering about a hundred and twenty) 16 and said, "Brothers, the
Scripture had to be fulfilled which the Holy
Spirit spoke long ago through the mouth of David concerning Judas, who served as guide for
those who arrested Jesus— 17 he was one of our
number and shared in this ministry."
18 (With the reward he got for his wickedness, Judas bought a field; there he fell headlong, his body burst open and all his intestines
spilled out. 19 Everyone in Jerusalem heard
about this, so they called that field in their language Akeldama, that is, Field of Blood.)
20 "For," said Peter, "it is written in the book
of Psalms,

> "'May his place be deserted;
> let there be no one to dwell in it,'[d]

and,

> "'May another take his place of
> leadership.'[e]

21 Therefore it is necessary to choose one of the
men who have been with us the whole time
the Lord Jesus went in and out among us, 22 beginning from John's baptism to the time when
Jesus was taken up from us. For one of these
must become a witness with us of his resurrection."
23 So they proposed two men: Joseph called
Barsabbas (also known as Justus) and Matthias.
24 Then they prayed, "Lord, you know everyone's heart. Show us which of these two you
have chosen 25 to take over this apostolic ministry, which Judas left to go where he belongs."
26 Then they cast lots, and the lot fell to Matthias;
so he was added to the eleven apostles.

The Holy Spirit Comes at Pentecost

2 When the day of Pentecost came, they
were all together in one place. 2 Suddenly
a sound like the blowing of a violent wind came
from heaven and filled the whole house where
they were sitting. 3 They saw what seemed to be
tongues of fire that separated and came to rest
on each of them. 4 All of them were filled with
the Holy Spirit and began to speak in other
tongues[f] as the Spirit enabled them.
5 Now there were staying in Jerusalem God-
fearing Jews from every nation under heaven.
6 When they heard this sound, a crowd came
together in bewilderment, because each one
heard them speaking in his own language.
7 Utterly amazed, they asked: "Are not all these
men who are speaking Galileans? 8 Then how
is it that each of us hears them in his own native language? 9 Parthians, Medes and Elamites; residents of Mesopotamia, Judea and
Cappadocia, Pontus and Asia, 10 Phrygia and
Pamphylia, Egypt and the parts of Libya near
Cyrene; visitors from Rome 11 (both Jews and
converts to Judaism); Cretans and Arabs—we

[a] 5 Or *in* [b] 12 That is, about 3/4 mile (about 1,100 meters) [c] 15 Greek *brothers* [d] 20 Psalm 69:25 [e] 20 Psalm 109:8 [f] 4 Or *languages*; also in verse 11

hear them declaring the wonders of God in our
own tongues!" 12 Amazed and perplexed, they
asked one another, "What does this mean?"
13 Some, however, made fun of them and
said, "They have had too much wine.[a]"

Peter Addresses the Crowd

14 Then Peter stood up with the Eleven,
raised his voice and addressed the crowd: "Fellow Jews and all of you who live in Jerusalem,
let me explain this to you; listen carefully to
what I say. 15 These men are not drunk, as you
suppose. It's only nine in the morning! 16 No,
this is what was spoken by the prophet Joel:

17 " 'In the last days, God says,
I will pour out my Spirit on all people.
Your sons and daughters will prophesy,
your young men will see
visions,
your old men will dream
dreams.
18 Even on my servants, both
men and women,
I will pour out my Spirit
in those days,
and they will prophesy.
19 I will show wonders in the
heaven above
and signs on the earth
below,
blood and fire and
billows of smoke.
20 The sun will be turned to
darkness
and the moon to blood
before the coming of the great and
glorious day of the Lord.
21 And everyone who calls
on the name of the Lord will be saved.'[b]

22 "Men of Israel, listen to this: Jesus of Nazareth was a man accredited by God to you by
miracles, wonders and signs, which God did
among you through him, as you yourselves
know. 23 This man was handed over to you by
God's set purpose and foreknowledge; and you,
with the help of wicked men,[c] put him to death
by nailing him to the cross. 24 But God raised
him from the dead, freeing him from the agony
of death, because it was impossible for death to
keep its hold on him. 25 David said about him:

" 'I saw the Lord always before me.
Because he is at my right hand,
I will not be shaken.
26 Therefore my heart is glad and my tongue
rejoices;
my body also will live in hope,
27 because you will not abandon me to the
grave,
nor will you let your Holy One see decay.
28 You have made known to me the paths of
life;
you will fill me with joy in your
presence.'[d]

29 "Brothers, I can tell you confidently that
the patriarch David died and
was buried, and his tomb is
here to this day. 30 But he was
a prophet and knew that God
had promised him on oath
that he would place one of his
descendants on his throne.
31 Seeing what was ahead, he
spoke of the resurrection of
the Christ,[e] that he was not
abandoned to the grave, nor
did his body see decay. 32 God
has raised this Jesus to life, and
we are all witnesses of the fact.
33 Exalted to the right hand of
God, he has received from the
Father the promised Holy Spirit
and has poured out what you now see and hear.
34 For David did not ascend to heaven, and yet
he said,

" 'The Lord said to my Lord:
"Sit at my right hand
35 until I make your enemies
a footstool for your feet." '[f]

36 "Therefore let all Israel be assured of this:
God has made this Jesus, whom you crucified,
both Lord and Christ."
37 When the people heard this, they were
cut to the heart and said to Peter and the other
apostles, "Brothers, what shall we do?"

Acts 2:33

God Pours Out His Spirit

"Exalted to the right hand of God, he has received from the Father the promised Holy Spirit and has poured out what you now see and hear."

[a] 13 Or *sweet wine* [b] 21 Joel 2:28–32 [c] 23 Or *of those not having the law* (that is, Gentiles) [d] 28 Psalm 16:8–11 [e] 31 Or *Messiah.* "The Christ" (Greek) and "the Messiah" (Hebrew) both mean "the Anointed One"; also in verse 36. [f] 35 Psalm 110:1

38Peter replied, "Repent and be baptized,
every one of you, in the name of Jesus Christ
for the forgiveness of your sins. And you will
receive the gift of the Holy Spirit. 39The promise is for you and your children and for all who
are far off—for all whom the Lord our God
will call."

40With many other words he warned them;
and he pleaded with them, "Save yourselves
from this corrupt generation." 41Those who
accepted his message were baptized, and about
three thousand were added to their number
that day.

The Fellowship of the Believers

42They devoted themselves to the apostles'
teaching and to the fellowship, to the breaking
of bread and to prayer. 43Everyone was filled
with awe, and many wonders and miraculous
signs were done by the apostles. 44All the believers were together and had everything in
common. 45Selling their possessions and
goods, they gave to anyone as he had need.
46Every day they continued to meet together
in the temple courts. They broke bread in their
homes and ate together with glad and sincere
hearts, 47praising God and enjoying the favor
of all the people. And the Lord added to their
number daily those who were being saved.

Peter Heals the Crippled Beggar

3 One day Peter and John were going up
to the temple at the time of prayer—at
three in the afternoon. 2Now a man crippled
from birth was being carried to the temple
gate called Beautiful, where he was put every
day to beg from those going into the temple
courts. 3When he saw Peter and John about to
enter, he asked them for money. 4Peter looked
straight at him, as did John. Then Peter said,
"Look at us!" 5So the man gave them his attention, expecting to get something from them.

6Then Peter said, "Silver or gold I do not
have, but what I have I give you. In the name of
Jesus Christ of Nazareth, walk." 7Taking him by
the right hand, he helped him up, and instantly
the man's feet and ankles became strong. 8He
jumped to his feet and began to walk. Then he
went with them into the temple courts, walking and jumping, and praising God. 9When all
the people saw him walking and praising God,
10they recognized him as the same man who
used to sit begging at the temple gate called
Beautiful, and they were filled with wonder
and amazement at what had happened to him.

Peter Speaks to the Onlookers

11While the beggar held on to Peter and
John, all the people were astonished and came
running to them in the place called Solomon's
Colonnade. 12When Peter saw this, he said to
them: "Men of Israel, why does this surprise
you? Why do you stare at us as if by our own
power or godliness we had made this man
walk? 13The God of Abraham, Isaac and Jacob,
the God of our fathers, has glorified his servant
Jesus. You handed him over to be killed, and
you disowned him before Pilate, though he had
decided to let him go. 14You disowned the Holy
and Righteous One and asked that a murderer
be released to you. 15You killed the author of
life, but God raised him from the dead. We
are witnesses of this. 16By faith in the name of
Jesus, this man whom you see and know was
made strong. It is Jesus' name and the faith that
comes through him that has given this complete healing to him, as you can all see.

17"Now, brothers, I know that you acted
in ignorance, as did your leaders. 18But this
is how God fulfilled what he had foretold
through all the prophets, saying that his
Christ[a] would suffer. 19Repent, then, and turn
to God, so that your sins may be wiped out,
that times of refreshing may come from the
Lord, 20and that he may send the Christ, who
has been appointed for you—even Jesus. 21He
must remain in heaven until the time comes
for God to restore everything, as he promised
long ago through his holy prophets. 22For Moses said, 'The Lord your God will raise up for
you a prophet like me from among your own
people; you must listen to everything he tells
you. 23Anyone who does not listen to him will
be completely cut off from among his people.'[b]

24"Indeed, all the prophets from Samuel on,
as many as have spoken, have foretold these
days. 25And you are heirs of the prophets and
of the covenant God made with your fathers.
He said to Abraham, 'Through your offspring

[a]18 Or *Messiah*; also in verse 20 [b]23 Deut. 18:15,18,19

all peoples on earth will be blessed.'[a] 26When
God raised up his servant, he sent him first to
you to bless you by turning each of you from
your wicked ways."

Peter and John Before the Sanhedrin

4 The priests and the captain of the temple
guard and the Sadducees came up to Peter and John while they were speaking to the
people. 2They were greatly disturbed because
the apostles were teaching the people and proclaiming in Jesus the resurrection of the dead.
3They seized Peter and John, and because it
was evening, they put them in jail until the
next day. 4But many who heard the message
believed, and the number of men grew to about
five thousand.

5The next day the rulers, elders and teachers
of the law met in Jerusalem. 6Annas the high
priest was there, and so were Caiaphas, John,
Alexander and the other men of the high priest's
family. 7They had Peter and John brought before them and began to question them: "By
what power or what name did you do this?"

8Then Peter, filled with the Holy Spirit,
said to them: "Rulers and elders of the people! 9If we are being called to account today
for an act of kindness shown to a cripple and
are asked how he was healed, 10then know
this, you and all the people of Israel: It is by
the name of Jesus Christ of
Nazareth, whom you crucified
but whom God raised from
the dead, that this man stands
before you healed. 11He is

"'the stone you builders
rejected,
which has become the
capstone.'[b,c]

12Salvation is found in no one
else, for there is no other name
under heaven given to men by
which we must be saved."

13When they saw the cour-
age of Peter and John and realized that they were unschooled,
ordinary men, they were astonished and they took note that
these men had been with Jesus. 14But since
they could see the man who had been healed
standing there with them, there was nothing
they could say. 15So they ordered them to withdraw from the Sanhedrin and then conferred
together. 16"What are we going to do with these
men?" they asked. "Everybody living in Jerusalem knows they have done an outstanding miracle, and we cannot deny it. 17But to stop this
thing from spreading any further among the
people, we must warn these men to speak no
longer to anyone in this name."

18Then they called them in again and commanded them not to speak or teach at all in the
name of Jesus. 19But Peter and John replied,
"Judge for yourselves whether it is right in
God's sight to obey you rather than God. 20For
we cannot help speaking about what we have
seen and heard."

21After further threats they let them go.
They could not decide how to punish them,
because all the people were praising God for
what had happened. 22For the man who was
miraculously healed was over forty years old.

The Believers' Prayer

23On their release, Peter and John went
back to their own people and reported all that
the chief priests and elders had said to them.
24When they heard this, they raised their
voices together in prayer to God. "Sovereign
Lord," they said, "you made the
heaven and the earth and the
sea, and everything in them.
25You spoke by the Holy Spirit
through the mouth of your servant, our father David:

"'Why do the nations rage
and the peoples plot in
vain?
26The kings of the earth take
their stand
and the rulers gather
together
against the Lord
and against his Anointed
One.'[d,e]

27Indeed Herod and Pontius
Pilate met together with the
Gentiles and the people[f] of Israel in this city to

> **Acts 4:13**
>
> *God Gives Boldness*
>
> When they saw the courage of Peter and John and realized that they were unschooled, ordinary men, they were astonished and they took note that these men had been with Jesus.

[a]25 Gen. 22:18; 26:4 [b]11 Or *cornerstone* [c]11 Psalm 118:22 [d]26 That is, Christ or Messiah [e]26 Psalm 2:1,2 [f]27 The Greek is plural.

Transformed by Jesus

Read: Acts 4:1–37

Acts 4:13

When they saw the courage of Peter and John and realized that they were unschooled, ordinary men, they were astonished and they took note that these men had been with Jesus.

WHEN WOMEN KINDLY ASK me to sign their copies of my books, I sometimes write, "To Susan the Beautiful!"

"Oh, no!" Susan (or Kathy or Linda) will protest, turning red. "I'm not beautiful."

"Sure you are," I insist, as I add my signature. "It says so right in the Bible." As further proof, I jot down "Psalm 149:4" and encourage them to look it up. You see, it's God's gift of salvation that makes us truly beautiful, inside and out. Nothing transforms a woman's appearance more than being covered from head to toe in the grace of God's Son.

I know this beautifying process is legitimate because I've seen it happen again and again. When women come to know the Lord in a real and personal way, their frown lines begin to soften. A sparkle appears in their eyes, and a radiance falls over their countenance.

We have proven scientifically that such physical changes occur when we fall in love: glowing skin, sparkling eyes, increased heart rate. And for some of us, similar improvements take place when we're expecting a child. Conventional wisdom says that "all brides are beautiful" and "pregnant women glow." It's chemical, hormonal, and very real.

Why not at the spiritual level too? When you allow the Lord to fill your heart with his boundless love, it shows on the outside. This beauty has nothing to do with cosmetics or plastic surgery. On the contrary, it's an inside job: A heart full of love produces a face full of joy.

When I stepped into a church for the first time as an adult, I was amazed to see pew after pew of attractive women. Is this a requirement of membership? I wondered. Maybe they're all Mary Kay consultants . . .

Soon I learned the happy truth: Such beauty is a gift from God. Unlike lipstick and blush, which seldom last longer than a few hours, spiritual beauty is timeless. It literally pours out of your pores and alters your appearance in a most appealing way. People will think you've had a face-lift, when in fact you've had a faith-lift.

—Liz Curtis Higgs

reflection

1 Why were people so astounded by Peter and John's courage?

2 Based on your knowledge of the Bible, what had happened to transform them so radically?

3 How have you experienced a "faith-lift" since walking with Christ? How does it reflect outwardly?

RELATED READINGS

Psalm 149:1–9; Isaiah 61:1–3; 1 Corinthians 1:26–31

Go to page 1335 for your next devotional reading.

conspire against your holy servant Jesus, whom you anointed. 28They did what your power and will had decided beforehand should happen. 29Now, Lord, consider their threats and enable your servants to speak your word with great boldness. 30Stretch out your hand to heal and perform miraculous signs and wonders through the name of your holy servant Jesus."

31After they prayed, the place where they were meeting was shaken. And they were all filled with the Holy Spirit and spoke the word of God boldly.

The Believers Share Their Possessions

32All the believers were one in heart and mind. No one claimed that any of his possessions was his own, but they shared everything they had. 33With great power the apostles continued to testify to the resurrection of the Lord Jesus, and much grace was upon them all. 34There were no needy persons among them. For from time to time those who owned lands or houses sold them, brought the money from the sales 35and put it at the apostles' feet, and it was distributed to anyone as he had need.

36Joseph, a Levite from Cyprus, whom the apostles called Barnabas (which means Son of Encouragement), 37sold a field he owned and brought the money and put it at the apostles' feet.

Ananias and Sapphira

5 Now a man named Ananias, together with his wife Sapphira, also sold a piece of property. 2With his wife's full knowledge he kept back part of the money for himself, but brought the rest and put it at the apostles' feet.

3Then Peter said, "Ananias, how is it that Satan has so filled your heart that you have lied to the Holy Spirit and have kept for yourself some of the money you received for the land? 4Didn't it belong to you before it was sold? And after it was sold, wasn't the money at your disposal? What made you think of doing such a thing? You have not lied to men but to God."

5When Ananias heard this, he fell down and died. And great fear seized all who heard what had happened. 6Then the young men came forward, wrapped up his body, and carried him out and buried him.

7About three hours later his wife came in, not knowing what had happened. 8Peter asked her, "Tell me, is this the price you and Ananias got for the land?"

"Yes," she said, "that is the price."

9Peter said to her, "How could you agree to test the Spirit of the Lord? Look! The feet of the men who buried your husband are at the door, and they will carry you out also."

10At that moment she fell down at his feet and died. Then the young men came in and, finding her dead, carried her out and buried her beside her husband. 11Great fear seized the whole church and all who heard about these events.

The Apostles Heal Many

12The apostles performed many miraculous signs and wonders among the people. And all the believers used to meet together in Solomon's Colonnade. 13No one else dared join them, even though they were highly regarded by the people. 14Nevertheless, more and more men and women believed in the Lord and were added to their number. 15As a result, people brought the sick into the streets and laid them on beds and mats so that at least Peter's shadow might fall on some of them as he passed by. 16Crowds gathered also from the towns around Jerusalem, bringing their sick and those tormented by evil[a] spirits, and all of them were healed.

The Apostles Persecuted

17Then the high priest and all his associates, who were members of the party of the Sadducees, were filled with jealousy. 18They arrested the apostles and put them in the public jail. 19But during the night an angel of the Lord opened the doors of the jail and brought them out. 20"Go, stand in the temple courts," he said, "and tell the people the full message of this new life."

21At daybreak they entered the temple courts, as they had been told, and began to teach the people.

When the high priest and his associates arrived, they called together the Sanhedrin—the full assembly of the elders of Israel—and sent to the jail for the apostles. 22But on arriving at

[a]16 Greek *unclean*

the jail, the officers did not find them there. So they went back and reported, 23“We found the jail securely locked, with the guards standing at the doors; but when we opened them, we found no one inside.” 24On hearing this report, the captain of the temple guard and the chief priests were puzzled, wondering what would come of this.

25Then someone came and said, “Look! The men you put in jail are standing in the temple courts teaching the people.” 26At that, the captain went with his officers and brought the apostles. They did not use force, because they feared that the people would stone them.

27Having brought the apostles, they made them appear before the Sanhedrin to be questioned by the high priest. 28“We gave you strict orders not to teach in this name,” he said. “Yet you have filled Jerusalem with your teaching and are determined to make us guilty of this man's blood.”

29Peter and the other apostles replied: “We must obey God rather than men! 30The God of our fathers raised Jesus from the dead—whom you had killed by hanging him on a tree. 31God exalted him to his own right hand as Prince and Savior that he might give repentance and forgiveness of sins to Israel. 32We are witnesses of these things, and so is the Holy Spirit, whom God has given to those who obey him.”

33When they heard this, they were furious and wanted to put them to death. 34But a Pharisee named Gamaliel, a teacher of the law, who was honored by all the people, stood up in the Sanhedrin and ordered that the men be put outside for a little while. 35Then he addressed them: “Men of Israel, consider carefully what you intend to do to these men. 36Some time ago Theudas appeared, claiming to be somebody, and about four hundred men rallied to him. He was killed, all his followers were dispersed, and it all came to nothing. 37After him, Judas the Galilean appeared in the days of the census and led a band of people in revolt. He too was killed, and all his followers were scattered. 38Therefore, in the present case I advise you: Leave these men alone! Let them go! For if their purpose or activity is of human origin, it will fail. 39But if it is from God, you will not be able to stop these men; you will only find yourselves fighting against God.”

40His speech persuaded them. They called the apostles in and had them flogged. Then they ordered them not to speak in the name of Jesus, and let them go.

41The apostles left the Sanhedrin, rejoicing because they had been counted worthy of suffering disgrace for the Name. 42Day after day, in the temple courts and from house to house, they never stopped teaching and proclaiming the good news that Jesus is the Christ.[a]

The Choosing of the Seven

6 In those days when the number of disciples was increasing, the Grecian Jews among them complained against the Hebraic Jews because their widows were being overlooked in the daily distribution of food. 2So the Twelve gathered all the disciples together and said, “It would not be right for us to neglect the ministry of the word of God in order to wait on tables. 3Brothers, choose seven men from among you who are known to be full of the Spirit and wisdom. We will turn this responsibility over to them 4and will give our attention to prayer and the ministry of the word.”

5This proposal pleased the whole group. They chose Stephen, a man full of faith and of the Holy Spirit; also Philip, Procorus, Nicanor, Timon, Parmenas, and Nicolas from Antioch, a convert to Judaism. 6They presented these men to the apostles, who prayed and laid their hands on them.

7So the word of God spread. The number of disciples in Jerusalem increased rapidly, and a large number of priests became obedient to the faith.

Stephen Seized

8Now Stephen, a man full of God's grace and power, did great wonders and miraculous signs among the people. 9Opposition arose, however, from members of the Synagogue of the Freedmen (as it was called)—Jews of Cyrene and Alexandria as well as the provinces of Cilicia and Asia. These men began to argue with Stephen, 10but they could not stand up against his wisdom or the Spirit by whom he spoke.

11Then they secretly persuaded some men

[a]42 Or *Messiah*

to say, "We have heard Stephen speak words of
blasphemy against Moses and against God."
12 So they stirred up the people and the elders and the teachers of the law. They seized Stephen and brought him before the Sanhedrin.
13 They produced false witnesses, who testified,
"This fellow never stops speaking against this
holy place and against the law. 14 For we have
heard him say that this Jesus of Nazareth will
destroy this place and change the customs Moses handed down to us."
15 All who were sitting in the Sanhedrin
looked intently at Stephen, and they saw that
his face was like the face of an angel.

Stephen's Speech to the Sanhedrin

7 Then the high priest asked him, "Are these
charges true?"
2 To this he replied: "Brothers and fathers, listen to me! The God of glory appeared to our
father Abraham while he was still in Mesopotamia, before he lived in Haran. 3 'Leave your
country and your people,' God said, 'and go to
the land I will show you.'[a]
4 "So he left the land of the Chaldeans and
settled in Haran. After the death of his father,
God sent him to this land where you are now
living. 5 He gave him no inheritance here, not
even a foot of ground. But God promised him
that he and his descendants after him would
possess the land, even though at that time
Abraham had no child. 6 God spoke to him in
this way: 'Your descendants will be strangers
in a country not their own, and they will be
enslaved and mistreated four hundred years.
7 But I will punish the nation they serve as
slaves,' God said, 'and afterward they will come
out of that country and worship me in this
place.'[b] 8 Then he gave Abraham the covenant
of circumcision. And Abraham became the father of Isaac and circumcised him eight days
after his birth. Later Isaac became the father
of Jacob, and Jacob became the father of the
twelve patriarchs.
9 "Because the patriarchs were jealous of Joseph, they sold him as a slave into Egypt. But
God was with him 10 and rescued him from
all his troubles. He gave Joseph wisdom and
enabled him to gain the goodwill of Pharaoh
king of Egypt; so he made him ruler over Egypt
and all his palace.
11 "Then a famine struck all Egypt and Canaan, bringing great suffering, and our fathers
could not find food. 12 When Jacob heard that
there was grain in Egypt, he sent our fathers
on their first visit. 13 On their second visit, Joseph told his brothers who he was, and Pharaoh learned about Joseph's family. 14 After this,
Joseph sent for his father Jacob and his whole
family, seventy-five in all. 15 Then Jacob went
down to Egypt, where he and our fathers died.
16 Their bodies were brought back to Shechem
and placed in the tomb that Abraham had
bought from the sons of Hamor at Shechem
for a certain sum of money.
17 "As the time drew near for God to fulfill his
promise to Abraham, the number of our people in Egypt greatly increased. 18 Then another
king, who knew nothing about Joseph, became
ruler of Egypt. 19 He dealt treacherously with
our people and oppressed our forefathers by
forcing them to throw out their newborn babies so that they would die.
20 "At that time Moses was born, and he was
no ordinary child.[c] For three months he was
cared for in his father's house. 21 When he was
placed outside, Pharaoh's daughter took him
and brought him up as her own son. 22 Moses
was educated in all the wisdom of the Egyptians and was powerful in speech and action.
23 "When Moses was forty years old, he
decided to visit his fellow Israelites. 24 He saw
one of them being mistreated by an Egyptian,
so he went to his defense and avenged him by
killing the Egyptian. 25 Moses thought that his
own people would realize that God was using
him to rescue them, but they did not. 26 The
next day Moses came upon two Israelites who
were fighting. He tried to reconcile them by saying, 'Men, you are brothers; why do you want
to hurt each other?'
27 "But the man who was mistreating the
other pushed Moses aside and said, 'Who
made you ruler and judge over us? 28 Do you
want to kill me as you killed the Egyptian yesterday?'[d] 29 When Moses heard this, he fled to
Midian, where he settled as a foreigner and had
two sons.

[a] 3 Gen. 12:1 [b] 7 Gen. 15:13,14 [c] 20 Or *was fair in the sight of God* [d] 28 Exodus 2:14

30“After forty years had passed, an angel
appeared to Moses in the flames of a burning
bush in the desert near Mount Sinai. 31When
he saw this, he was amazed at the sight. As he
went over to look more closely, he heard the
Lord’s voice: 32‘I am the God of your fathers,
the God of Abraham, Isaac and Jacob.’[a] Moses
trembled with fear and did not dare to look.

33“Then the Lord said to him, ‘Take off your
sandals; the place where you are standing is
holy ground. 34I have indeed seen the oppression of my people in Egypt. I have heard their
groaning and have come down to set them free.
Now come, I will send you back to Egypt.’[b]

35“This is the same Moses whom they had
rejected with the words, ‘Who made you ruler
and judge?’ He was sent to be
their ruler and deliverer by
God himself, through the angel who appeared to him in
the bush. 36He led them out of
Egypt and did wonders and miraculous signs in Egypt, at the
Red Sea[c] and for forty years in
the desert.

37“This is that Moses who
told the Israelites, ‘God will
send you a prophet like me
from your own people.’[d] 38He
was in the assembly in the desert, with the angel who spoke
to him on Mount Sinai, and
with our fathers; and he received living words
to pass on to us.

39“But our fathers refused to obey him. Instead, they rejected him and in their hearts
turned back to Egypt. 40They told Aaron,
‘Make us gods who will go before us. As for
this fellow Moses who led us out of Egypt—we
don’t know what has happened to him!’[e] 41That
was the time they made an idol in the form of
a calf. They brought sacrifices to it and held a
celebration in honor of what their hands had
made. 42But God turned away and gave them
over to the worship of the heavenly bodies.
This agrees with what is written in the book of
the prophets:

“ ‘Did you bring me sacrifices and offerings
forty years in the desert, O house of
Israel?
43You have lifted up the shrine of Molech
and the star of your god Rephan,
the idols you made to worship.
Therefore I will send you into exile’[f]
beyond Babylon.

44“Our forefathers had the tabernacle of the
Testimony with them in the desert. It had been
made as God directed Moses, according to the
pattern he had seen. 45Having received the
tabernacle, our fathers under Joshua brought
it with them when they took the land from
the nations God drove out before them. It remained in the land until the time of David,
46who enjoyed God’s favor and asked that he
might provide a dwelling place
for the God of Jacob.[g] 47But
it was Solomon who built the
house for him.

48“However, the Most High
does not live in houses made
by men. As the prophet says:

49“ ‘Heaven is my throne,
and the earth is my
footstool.
What kind of house will
you build for me?
says the Lord.
Or where will my resting
place be?
50Has not my hand made all these things?’[h]

51“You stiff-necked people, with uncircumcised hearts and ears! You are just like your fathers: You always resist the Holy Spirit! 52Was
there ever a prophet your fathers did not persecute? They even killed those who predicted the
coming of the Righteous One. And now you
have betrayed and murdered him— 53you who
have received the law that was put into effect
through angels but have not obeyed it.”

The Stoning of Stephen

54When they heard this, they were furious
and gnashed their teeth at him. 55But Stephen,
full of the Holy Spirit, looked up to heaven and
saw the glory of God, and Jesus standing at the

> **Acts 7:49**
>
> *God Is Infinite*
>
> “Heaven is my throne,
> and the earth is
> my footstool.
> What kind of house will
> you build for me?
> says the Lord.”

[a]32 Exodus 3:6 [b]34 Exodus 3:5,7,8,10 [c]36 That is, Sea of Reeds [d]37 Deut. 18:15 [e]40 Exodus 32:1 [f]43 Amos 5:25–27
[g]46 Some early manuscripts *the house of Jacob* [h]50 Isaiah 66:1,2

right hand of God. 56“Look,” he said, “I see heaven open and the Son of Man standing at the right hand of God.”

57At this they covered their ears and, yelling at the top of their voices, they all rushed at him, 58dragged him out of the city and began to stone him. Meanwhile, the witnesses laid their clothes at the feet of a young man named Saul.

59While they were stoning him, Stephen prayed, “Lord Jesus, receive my spirit.” 60Then he fell on his knees and cried out, “Lord, do not hold this sin against them.” When he had said this, he fell asleep.

8 And Saul was there, giving approval to his death.

The Church Persecuted and Scattered

On that day a great persecution broke out against the church at Jerusalem, and all except the apostles were scattered throughout Judea and Samaria. 2Godly men buried Stephen and mourned deeply for him. 3But Saul began to destroy the church. Going from house to house, he dragged off men and women and put them in prison.

Philip in Samaria

4Those who had been scattered preached the word wherever they went. 5Philip went down to a city in Samaria and proclaimed the Christ[a] there. 6When the crowds heard Philip and saw the miraculous signs he did, they all paid close attention to what he said. 7With shrieks, evil[b] spirits came out of many, and many paralytics and cripples were healed. 8So there was great joy in that city.

Simon the Sorcerer

9Now for some time a man named Simon had practiced sorcery in the city and amazed all the people of Samaria. He boasted that he was someone great, 10and all the people, both high and low, gave him their attention and exclaimed, “This man is the divine power known as the Great Power.” 11They followed him because he had amazed them for a long time with his magic. 12But when they believed Philip as he preached the good news of the kingdom of God and the name of Jesus Christ, they were baptized, both men and women. 13Simon himself believed and was baptized. And he followed Philip everywhere, astonished by the great signs and miracles he saw.

14When the apostles in Jerusalem heard that Samaria had accepted the word of God, they sent Peter and John to them. 15When they arrived, they prayed for them that they might receive the Holy Spirit, 16because the Holy Spirit had not yet come upon any of them; they had simply been baptized into[c] the name of the Lord Jesus. 17Then Peter and John placed their hands on them, and they received the Holy Spirit.

18When Simon saw that the Spirit was given at the laying on of the apostles’ hands, he offered them money 19and said, “Give me also this ability so that everyone on whom I lay my hands may receive the Holy Spirit.”

20Peter answered: “May your money perish with you, because you thought you could buy the gift of God with money! 21You have no part or share in this ministry, because your heart is not right before God. 22Repent of this wickedness and pray to the Lord. Perhaps he will forgive you for having such a thought in your heart. 23For I see that you are full of bitterness and captive to sin.”

24Then Simon answered, “Pray to the Lord for me so that nothing you have said may happen to me.”

25When they had testified and proclaimed the word of the Lord, Peter and John returned to Jerusalem, preaching the gospel in many Samaritan villages.

Philip and the Ethiopian

26Now an angel of the Lord said to Philip, “Go south to the road—the desert road—that goes down from Jerusalem to Gaza.” 27So he started out, and on his way he met an Ethiopian[d] eunuch, an important official in charge of all the treasury of Candace, queen of the Ethiopians. This man had gone to Jerusalem to worship, 28and on his way home was sitting in his chariot reading the book of Isaiah the prophet. 29The Spirit told Philip, “Go to that chariot and stay near it.”

30Then Philip ran up to the chariot and heard the man reading Isaiah the prophet. “Do you understand what you are reading?” Philip asked.

[a]5 Or *Messiah* [b]7 Greek *unclean* [c]16 Or *in* [d]27 That is, from the upper Nile region

31"How can I," he said, "unless someone explains it to me?" So he invited Philip to come
up and sit with him.
32The eunuch was reading this passage
of Scripture:

"He was led like a sheep to the slaughter,
and as a lamb before the shearer is silent,
so he did not open his mouth.
33In his humiliation he was deprived of
justice.
Who can speak of his descendants?
For his life was taken from the earth."[a]

34The eunuch asked Philip, "Tell me, please,
who is the prophet talking about, himself or
someone else?" 35Then Philip began with that
very passage of Scripture and told him the
good news about Jesus.
36As they traveled along the road, they came
to some water and the eunuch said, "Look, here
is water. Why shouldn't I be baptized?"[b] 38And
he gave orders to stop the chariot. Then both
Philip and the eunuch went down into the
water and Philip baptized him. 39When they
came up out of the water, the Spirit of the Lord
suddenly took Philip away, and the eunuch did
not see him again, but went on his way rejoicing. 40Philip, however, appeared at Azotus and
traveled about, preaching the gospel in all the
towns until he reached Caesarea.

Saul's Conversion

9 Meanwhile, Saul was still breathing out
murderous threats against the Lord's disciples. He went to the high priest 2and asked him
for letters to the synagogues in Damascus, so
that if he found any there who belonged to the
Way, whether men or women, he might take
them as prisoners to Jerusalem. 3As he neared
Damascus on his journey, suddenly a light
from heaven flashed around him. 4He fell to
the ground and heard a voice say to him, "Saul,
Saul, why do you persecute me?"
5"Who are you, Lord?" Saul asked.
"I am Jesus, whom you are persecuting," he
replied. 6"Now get up and go into the city, and
you will be told what you must do."
7The men traveling with Saul stood there
speechless; they heard the sound but did not
see anyone. 8Saul got up from the ground, but
when he opened his eyes he could see nothing.
So they led him by the hand into Damascus.
9For three days he was blind, and did not eat
or drink anything.
10In Damascus there was a disciple named
Ananias. The Lord called to him in a vision,
"Ananias!"
"Yes, Lord," he answered.
11The Lord told him, "Go to the house of Judas on Straight Street and ask for a man from
Tarsus named Saul, for he is praying. 12In
a vision he has seen a man named Ananias
come and place his hands on him to restore
his sight."
13"Lord," Ananias answered, "I have heard
many reports about this man and all the harm
he has done to your saints in Jerusalem. 14And
he has come here with authority from the chief
priests to arrest all who call on your name."
15But the Lord said to Ananias, "Go! This
man is my chosen instrument to carry my
name before the Gentiles and their kings and
before the people of Israel. 16I will show him
how much he must suffer for my name."
17Then Ananias went to the house and entered it. Placing his hands on Saul, he said,
"Brother Saul, the Lord—Jesus, who appeared
to you on the road as you were coming here—
has sent me so that you may see again and be
filled with the Holy Spirit." 18Immediately,
something like scales fell from Saul's eyes, and
he could see again. He got up and was baptized,
19and after taking some food, he regained
his strength.

Saul in Damascus and Jerusalem

Saul spent several days with the disciples in
Damascus. 20At once he began to preach in
the synagogues that Jesus is the Son of God.
21All those who heard him were astonished
and asked, "Isn't he the man who raised havoc
in Jerusalem among those who call on this
name? And hasn't he come here to take them
as prisoners to the chief priests?" 22Yet Saul
grew more and more powerful and baffled the
Jews living in Damascus by proving that Jesus
is the Christ.[c]
23After many days had gone by, the Jews

[a]33 Isaiah 53:7,8 [b]36 Some late manuscripts *baptized?" 37Philip said, "If you believe with all your heart, you may." The eunuch answered, "I believe that Jesus Christ is the Son of God."* [c]22 Or *Messiah*

"Get Up!"

Read: Acts 9:1–43

"GET UP!"

Did your parents use those words to rouse you out of sleep when you were a teenager? Are *you* now using those very words to wake those unwilling to rise from their warm, comfy beds in the morning? When you read through Acts 9, you'll notice that the phrase, "Get up," occurs in contrasting settings. A closer look moves these words from the commonplace to the compelling. Let's explore why this simple command warrants our attention.

On the road to Damascus, Saul was flattened to the ground by a blazing light and a surprising voice. After the Lord identified himself as Jesus, his first command to Saul was, "Now get up."

In the latter part of the chapter there are two accounts where Peter issued the command, "Get up." In the first, Peter instructed Aeneas, the paralytic in Lydda, to "get up and take care of your mat," after declaring, "Jesus Christ heals you" (verse 34).

Nearby in Joppa, a much-beloved saint named Tabitha, or Dorcas, had died. Peter went to the upstairs room where she lay. After he knelt and prayed, he turned toward the dead woman and said, "Tabitha, get up" (verse 40).

The Greek phrase "get up" has several meanings. It can be used in the sense of waking someone up from sleep. It can also mean to rise from a prone position as one who is ill. The deeper meaning is profound. It is the same root word used for resurrection—meaning to arise from the dead.

Saul, Aeneas and Dorcas were trapped in different realms of death—sin, paralysis and physical death—that required resurrection power. They heard the words, "Get up," and responded with immediate obedience.

Do you feel spiritually asleep—maybe even dead? As a wise person once counseled, "Just move your feet, and God will guide you where to go." But first, you have to "Get up!"

Acts 9:5–6

"Who are you, Lord?" Saul asked. "I am Jesus, whom you are persecuting," he replied. "Now get up and go into the city, and you will be told what you must do."

reflection

1 Spiritually, do you most relate to Saul, the opponent of Christ; Aeneas, the paralytic; or Dorcas, the woman who had died? Depending upon your answer, ask God to either knock you off your horse, heal you or resurrect you.

2 In what way is "getting up" a response of faith? What is keeping you from "getting up" to do what God has asked you to do?

3 Who in your life needs to know about Jesus' healing power? Whom can you be a "Peter" to? Pray for opportunities to talk with that person about Jesus.

RELATED READINGS

1 Kings 19:5;
Matthew 9:5;
Luke 8:49–56;
Acts 22:6–16;
Romans 1:1–4

Wednesday

Go to page 1338 for your next devotional reading.

conspired to kill him, 24but Saul learned of
their plan. Day and night they kept close watch
on the city gates in order to kill him. 25But his
followers took him by night and lowered him
in a basket through an opening in the wall.

26When he came to Jerusalem, he tried to
join the disciples, but they were all afraid of
him, not believing that he really was a disciple.
27But Barnabas took him and brought him to
the apostles. He told them how Saul on his journey had seen the Lord and that the Lord had
spoken to him, and how in Damascus he had
preached fearlessly in the name of Jesus. 28So
Saul stayed with them and moved about freely
in Jerusalem, speaking boldly in the name
of the Lord. 29He talked and debated with
the Grecian Jews, but they tried to kill him.
30When the brothers learned of this, they took
him down to Caesarea and sent him off to Tarsus.

31Then the church throughout Judea, Galilee and Samaria enjoyed a time of peace. It
was strengthened; and encouraged by the Holy
Spirit, it grew in numbers, living in the fear of
the Lord.

Aeneas and Dorcas

32As Peter traveled about the country, he
went to visit the saints in Lydda. 33There he
found a man named Aeneas, a paralytic who
had been bedridden for eight years. 34"Aeneas,"
Peter said to him, "Jesus Christ heals you. Get
up and take care of your mat." Immediately
Aeneas got up. 35All those who lived in Lydda
and Sharon saw him and turned to the Lord.

36In Joppa there was a disciple named Tabitha (which, when translated, is Dorcas[a]), who
was always doing good and helping the poor.
37About that time she became sick and died,
and her body was washed and placed in an upstairs room. 38Lydda was near Joppa; so when
the disciples heard that Peter was in Lydda,
they sent two men to him and urged him,
"Please come at once!"

39Peter went with them, and when he arrived he was taken upstairs to the room. All the
widows stood around him, crying and showing
him the robes and other clothing that Dorcas
had made while she was still with them.

40Peter sent them all out of the room; then
he got down on his knees and prayed. Turning
toward the dead woman, he said, "Tabitha, get
up." She opened her eyes, and seeing Peter she
sat up. 41He took her by the hand and helped
her to her feet. Then he called the believers
and the widows and presented her to them
alive. 42This became known all over Joppa,
and many people believed in the Lord. 43Peter
stayed in Joppa for some time with a tanner
named Simon.

Cornelius Calls for Peter

10 At Caesarea there was a man named
Cornelius, a centurion in what was
known as the Italian Regiment. 2He and all
his family were devout and God-fearing; he
gave generously to those in need and prayed
to God regularly. 3One day at about three in
the afternoon he had a vision. He distinctly saw
an angel of God, who came to him and said,
"Cornelius!"

4Cornelius stared at him in fear. "What is it,
Lord?" he asked.

The angel answered, "Your prayers and gifts
to the poor have come up as a memorial offering before God. 5Now send men to Joppa to
bring back a man named Simon who is called
Peter. 6He is staying with Simon the tanner,
whose house is by the sea."

7When the angel who spoke to him had
gone, Cornelius called two of his servants and
a devout soldier who was one of his attendants.
8He told them everything that had happened
and sent them to Joppa.

Peter's Vision

9About noon the following day as they were
on their journey and approaching the city, Peter went up on the roof to pray. 10He became
hungry and wanted something to eat, and
while the meal was being prepared, he fell into
a trance. 11He saw heaven opened and something like a large sheet being let down to earth
by its four corners. 12It contained all kinds of
four-footed animals, as well as reptiles of the
earth and birds of the air. 13Then a voice told
him, "Get up, Peter. Kill and eat."

14"Surely not, Lord!" Peter replied. "I have
never eaten anything impure or unclean."

15The voice spoke to him a second time,

[a]36 Both *Tabitha* (Aramaic) and *Dorcas* (Greek) mean *gazelle*.

"Do not call anything impure that God has
made clean."
16This happened three times, and
immediately the sheet was taken back to
heaven.
17While Peter was wondering about the
meaning of the vision, the men sent by Cornelius found out where Simon's house was and
stopped at the gate. 18They called out, asking
if Simon who was known as Peter was staying there.
19While Peter was still thinking about the vision, the Spirit said to him, "Simon, three[a] men
are looking for you. 20So get up
and go downstairs. Do not hesitate to go with them, for I have
sent them."
21Peter went down and said
to the men, "I'm the one you're
looking for. Why have you
come?"
22The men replied, "We
have come from Cornelius the
centurion. He is a righteous
and God-fearing man, who is
respected by all the Jewish people. A holy angel told him to
have you come to his house so that he could
hear what you have to say." 23Then Peter invited
the men into the house to be his guests.

Acts 10:35

God Accepts People

"[God] accepts men from every nation who fear him and do what is right."

Peter at Cornelius's House

The next day Peter started out with them,
and some of the brothers from Joppa went
along. 24The following day he arrived in Caesarea. Cornelius was expecting them and had
called together his relatives and close friends.
25As Peter entered the house, Cornelius met
him and fell at his feet in reverence. 26But Peter made him get up. "Stand up," he said, "I am
only a man myself."
27Talking with him, Peter went inside and
found a large gathering of people. 28He said to
them: "You are well aware that it is against our
law for a Jew to associate with a Gentile or visit
him. But God has shown me that I should not
call any man impure or unclean. 29So when I
was sent for, I came without raising any objec-
tion. May I ask why you sent for me?"
30Cornelius answered: "Four days ago I was
in my house praying at this hour, at three in the
afternoon. Suddenly a man in shining clothes
stood before me 31and said, 'Cornelius, God
has heard your prayer and remembered your
gifts to the poor. 32Send to Joppa for Simon
who is called Peter. He is a guest in the home
of Simon the tanner, who lives by the sea.' 33So
I sent for you immediately, and it was good of
you to come. Now we are all here in the presence of God to listen to everything the Lord
has commanded you to tell us."
34Then Peter began to speak: "I now realize
how true it is that God does
not show favoritism 35but accepts men from every nation
who fear him and do what is
right. 36You know the message God sent to the people of
Israel, telling the good news
of peace through Jesus Christ,
who is Lord of all. 37You know
what has happened throughout Judea, beginning in Galilee after the baptism that
John preached— 38how God
anointed Jesus of Nazareth
with the Holy Spirit and power, and how he
went around doing good and healing all who
were under the power of the devil, because
God was with him.
39"We are witnesses of everything he did in
the country of the Jews and in Jerusalem. They
killed him by hanging him on a tree, 40but God
raised him from the dead on the third day and
caused him to be seen. 41He was not seen by
all the people, but by witnesses whom God
had already chosen—by us who ate and drank
with him after he rose from the dead. 42He
commanded us to preach to the people and to
testify that he is the one whom God appointed
as judge of the living and the dead. 43All the
prophets testify about him that everyone who
believes in him receives forgiveness of sins
through his name."
44While Peter was still speaking these words,
the Holy Spirit came on all who heard the message. 45The circumcised believers who had
come with Peter were astonished that the gift

[a]19 One early manuscript *two*; other manuscripts do not have the number.

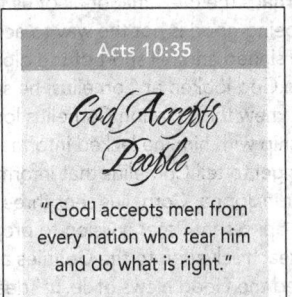

Is Good, Good Enough?

Read: Acts 10:1–48

Acts 10:22

The men replied, "We have come from Cornelius the centurion. He is a righteous and God-fearing man, who is respected by all the Jewish people. A holy angel told him to have you come to his house so that he could hear what you have to say."

HOW MANY *GOOD* PEOPLE do you know? People who give to the poor, volunteer at the homeless shelter, travel on mission trips, tutor children in the projects, sort items at the relief agency or visit the elderly?

Cornelius the centurion was such a man. He was one of the *good* people. He had diligently worked his way through the ranks to take command of over 100 Roman soldiers. He was a God-fearing, devout man who gave to those in need. He was also a man of prayer. But though he was good, it was not enough.

That's the dilemma for all of us. No matter how good we try to be, being good is not the way to acceptance by a holy God, "for all have sinned and fall short of the glory of God" (Romans 3:23). But when God looked at Cornelius, he saw a willing and open heart. God knew that, though Cornelius longed to have an intimate relationship with him, he lacked information about Jesus. So God sent an angel to tell Cornelius that information could be attained from Peter in Joppa. Cornelius sent three men to find Peter. Then the Holy Spirit sent Peter a vision to prepare him for the mission ahead: to preach salvation to the Gentiles as well as the Jews. When Peter shared the Good News of Jesus' death and resurrection, Cornelius and his entire family received the gift of eternal life and the Holy Spirit.

Have you, like Cornelius, been working really hard to be good? That's good. But do you, like Cornelius, have a religion of good works without a real relationship with Jesus? Then God has the same message for you that he delivered to Cornelius and his family: "Everyone who believes in [Jesus] receives forgiveness of sins through his name" (verse 43). The only path to a relationship with the Father is to believe that Jesus is "the way and the truth and the life. No one comes to the Father except through [him]" (John 14:6).

reflection

1 How do you find yourself working to please God?

2 What steps did God take to bring the gospel to you? Who were his messengers?

3 What would your life look like if you truly believed Jesus was the only way to the Father?

RELATED READINGS

Matthew 7:21–23; Romans 1:16–18

"There is no better measure of a person than what he does when he is absolutely free to choose."

Wilma Askinas

Thursday

Go to page 1341 for your next devotional reading.

of the Holy Spirit had been poured out even on
the Gentiles. 46For they heard them speaking
in tongues[a] and praising God.
Then Peter said, 47"Can anyone keep these
people from being baptized with water? They
have received the Holy Spirit just as we have."
48So he ordered that they be baptized in the
name of Jesus Christ. Then they asked Peter to
stay with them for a few days.

Peter Explains His Actions

11 The apostles and the brothers throughout Judea heard that the Gentiles also
had received the word of God. 2So when Peter
went up to Jerusalem, the circumcised believers criticized
him 3and said, "You went into
the house of uncircumcised
men and ate with them."
4Peter began and explained
everything to them precisely
as it had happened: 5"I was in
the city of Joppa praying, and
in a trance I saw a vision. I saw
something like a large sheet being let down from heaven by its
four corners, and it came down
to where I was. 6I looked into it
and saw four-footed animals of
the earth, wild beasts, reptiles,
and birds of the air. 7Then I heard a voice telling me, 'Get up, Peter. Kill and eat.'
8"I replied, 'Surely not, Lord! Nothing impure or unclean has ever entered my mouth.'
9"The voice spoke from heaven a second
time, 'Do not call anything impure that God
has made clean.' 10This happened three times,
and then it was all pulled up to heaven again.
11"Right then three men who had been sent
to me from Caesarea stopped at the house
where I was staying. 12The Spirit told me to
have no hesitation about going with them.
These six brothers also went with me, and we
entered the man's house. 13He told us how he
had seen an angel appear in his house and say,
'Send to Joppa for Simon who is called Peter.
14He will bring you a message through which
you and all your household will be saved.'
15"As I began to speak, the Holy Spirit came
on them as he had come on us at the beginning. 16Then I remembered what the Lord had
said: 'John baptized with[b] water, but you will be
baptized with the Holy Spirit.' 17So if God gave
them the same gift as he gave us, who believed
in the Lord Jesus Christ, who was I to think
that I could oppose God?"
18When they heard this, they had no further
objections and praised God, saying, "So then,
God has granted even the Gentiles repentance
unto life."

The Church in Antioch

19Now those who had been scattered by
the persecution in connection with Stephen
traveled as far as Phoenicia, Cyprus and Antioch, telling the
message only to Jews. 20Some
of them, however, men from
Cyprus and Cyrene, went to
Antioch and began to speak
to Greeks also, telling them
the good news about the Lord
Jesus. 21The Lord's hand was
with them, and a great number
of people believed and turned
to the Lord.
22News of this reached the
ears of the church at Jerusalem, and they sent Barnabas
to Antioch. 23When he arrived
and saw the evidence of the grace of God, he
was glad and encouraged them all to remain
true to the Lord with all their hearts. 24He was
a good man, full of the Holy Spirit and faith,
and a great number of people were brought to
the Lord.
25Then Barnabas went to Tarsus to look for
Saul, 26and when he found him, he brought
him to Antioch. So for a whole year Barnabas
and Saul met with the church and taught great
numbers of people. The disciples were called
Christians first at Antioch.
27During this time some prophets came
down from Jerusalem to Antioch. 28One of
them, named Agabus, stood up and through
the Spirit predicted that a severe famine would
spread over the entire Roman world. (This happened during the reign of Claudius.) 29The disciples, each according to his ability, decided to
provide help for the brothers living in Judea.

Acts 11:21

God Guides People

The Lord's hand was with them, and a great number of people believed and turned to the Lord.

[a]46 Or *other languages* [b]16 Or *in*

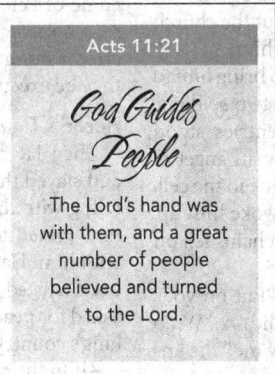

30 This they did, sending their gift to the elders
by Barnabas and Saul.

Peter's Miraculous Escape From Prison

12 It was about this time that King Herod
arrested some who belonged to the
church, intending to persecute them. 2 He had
James, the brother of John, put to death with
the sword. 3 When he saw that this pleased the
Jews, he proceeded to seize Peter also. This happened during the Feast of Unleavened Bread.
4 After arresting him, he put him in prison,
handing him over to be guarded by four squads
of four soldiers each. Herod intended to bring
him out for public trial after the Passover.

5 So Peter was kept in prison, but the church
was earnestly praying to God for him.

6 The night before Herod was to bring him to
trial, Peter was sleeping between two soldiers,
bound with two chains, and sentries stood
guard at the entrance. 7 Suddenly an angel of
the Lord appeared and a light shone in the cell.
He struck Peter on the side and woke him up.
"Quick, get up!" he said, and the chains fell off
Peter's wrists.

8 Then the angel said to him, "Put on your
clothes and sandals." And Peter did so. "Wrap
your cloak around you and follow me," the angel told him. 9 Peter followed him out of the
prison, but he had no idea that what the angel
was doing was really happening; he thought he
was seeing a vision. 10 They passed the first and
second guards and came to the iron gate leading to the city. It opened for them by itself, and
they went through it. When they had walked
the length of one street, suddenly the angel
left him.

11 Then Peter came to himself and said,
"Now I know without a doubt that the Lord
sent his angel and rescued me from Herod's
clutches and from everything the Jewish people were anticipating."

12 When this had dawned on him, he went to
the house of Mary the mother of John, also
called Mark, where many people had gathered
and were praying. 13 Peter knocked at the outer
entrance, and a servant girl named Rhoda
came to answer the door. 14 When she recognized Peter's voice, she was so overjoyed she
ran back without opening it and exclaimed,
"Peter is at the door!"

15 "You're out of your mind," they told her.
When she kept insisting that it was so, they
said, "It must be his angel."

16 But Peter kept on knocking, and when
they opened the door and saw him, they were
astonished. 17 Peter motioned with his hand for
them to be quiet and described how the Lord
had brought him out of prison. "Tell James and
the brothers about this," he said, and then he
left for another place.

18 In the morning, there was no small commotion among the soldiers as to what had become of Peter. 19 After Herod had a thorough
search made for him and did not find him, he
cross-examined the guards and ordered that
they be executed.

Herod's Death

Then Herod went from Judea to Caesarea
and stayed there a while. 20 He had been quarreling with the people of Tyre and Sidon; they
now joined together and sought an audience
with him. Having secured the support of Blas-
tus, a trusted personal servant of the king, they
asked for peace, because they depended on the
king's country for their food supply.

21 On the appointed day Herod, wearing his
royal robes, sat on his throne and delivered a
public address to the people. 22 They shouted,
"This is the voice of a god, not of a man."
23 Immediately, because Herod did not give
praise to God, an angel of the Lord struck him
down, and he was eaten by worms and died.

24 But the word of God continued to increase
and spread.

25 When Barnabas and Saul had finished
their mission, they returned from[a] Jerusalem,
taking with them John, also called Mark.

Barnabas and Saul Sent Off

13 In the church at Antioch there were
prophets and teachers: Barnabas, Simeon called Niger, Lucius of Cyrene, Manaen
(who had been brought up with Herod the tetrarch) and Saul. 2 While they were worshiping
the Lord and fasting, the Holy Spirit said, "Set
apart for me Barnabas and Saul for the work to
which I have called them." 3 So after they had

[a] 25 Some manuscripts *to*

Praying Through

Read: Acts 12:1–17

DURING WORLD WAR II, Bible College of Wales founder Rees Howells regularly led his students in prayer. On September 9, 1943, the day the allies invaded Salerno, Italy, he called an extra prayer meeting at 9:45 P.M. and began with this message: "The Lord has burdened me between the meetings with the invasion of Salerno. I believe our men are in great difficulties, and the Lord has told me that unless we can pray through, they are in danger of losing their hold." The students fell to their knees and began praying. Then, at 11:00 P.M., they spontaneously began to sing, praising God for his intervention.

The next day the newspaper reported that the Nazis' artillery had been so heavy that establishing a beachhead required nothing short of a miracle. But a miracle had occurred. For no explainable reason, the enemy's artillery had ceased—at precisely 11:00 P.M.

Something mysterious takes place when we pray. God doesn't *need* our prayers, yet he uses them. In the inexplicable workings of heaven and earth, our prayers make a difference.

In this passage in the book of Acts, the believers who had gathered at Mary's house had just witnessed the death of James. They knew that Peter was next in line for Herod's sword, and they knew that they were powerless to do anything about it. But when they prayed to God for Peter, something miraculous happened. An angel stepped into the jail cell, Peter's chains fell off and the locked doors opened. On what might have been Peter's last night alive, God intervened in ways neither Peter nor the praying Christians could fathom.

We can never know how God will answer the prayers of his people. We only know that he tells us to pray about anything and everything. We may feel powerless in ourselves, but when we lift our prayers to God, when we "pray through" our difficulties, the door is opened for God to step in and do the miraculous.

Acts 12:5

So Peter was kept in prison, but the church was earnestly praying to God for him.

reflection

1 When has God answered your prayers in a way that exceeded your expectations?

2 Do you pray about everything or only about "big" things? Why or why not?

3 What difficulty might God be asking you to "pray through"?

RELATED READINGS

Matthew 7:7–11;
John 14:13–14;
1 Thessalonians 5:17;
James 5:13–16

"The more you pray, the more you will find to pray about."

Stormie Omartian

Go to page 1347 for your next devotional reading.

fasted and prayed, they placed their hands on
them and sent them off.

On Cyprus

4 The two of them, sent on their way by the
Holy Spirit, went down to Seleucia and sailed
from there to Cyprus. 5 When they arrived at
Salamis, they proclaimed the word of God in
the Jewish synagogues. John was with them as
their helper.

6 They traveled through the whole island
until they came to Paphos. There they met a
Jewish sorcerer and false prophet named Bar-
Jesus, 7 who was an attendant of the proconsul,
Sergius Paulus. The proconsul, an intelligent
man, sent for Barnabas and Saul because he
wanted to hear the word of God. 8 But Elymas
the sorcerer (for that is what his name means)
opposed them and tried to turn the proconsul
from the faith. 9 Then Saul, who was also called
Paul, filled with the Holy Spirit, looked straight
at Elymas and said, 10 "You are a child of the
devil and an enemy of everything that is right!
You are full of all kinds of deceit and trickery.
Will you never stop perverting the right ways
of the Lord? 11 Now the hand of the Lord is
against you. You are going to be blind, and
for a time you will be unable to see the light
of the sun."

Immediately mist and darkness came over
him, and he groped about, seeking someone to
lead him by the hand. 12 When the proconsul
saw what had happened, he believed, for he
was amazed at the teaching about the Lord.

In Pisidian Antioch

13 From Paphos, Paul and his companions
sailed to Perga in Pamphylia, where John left
them to return to Jerusalem. 14 From Perga they
went on to Pisidian Antioch. On the Sabbath
they entered the synagogue and sat down. 15 After the reading from the Law and the Prophets,
the synagogue rulers sent word to them, saying, "Brothers, if you have a message of encouragement for the people, please speak."

16 Standing up, Paul motioned with his hand
and said: "Men of Israel and you Gentiles who
worship God, listen to me! 17 The God of the
people of Israel chose our fathers; he made the
people prosper during their stay in Egypt, with
mighty power he led them out of that country,
18 he endured their conduct[a] for about forty
years in the desert, 19 he overthrew seven nations in Canaan and gave their land to his people as their inheritance. 20 All this took about
450 years.

"After this, God gave them judges until the
time of Samuel the prophet. 21 Then the people
asked for a king, and he gave them Saul son of
Kish, of the tribe of Benjamin, who ruled forty
years. 22 After removing Saul, he made David
their king. He testified concerning him: 'I have
found David son of Jesse a man after my own
heart; he will do everything I want him to do.'

23 "From this man's descendants God has
brought to Israel the Savior Jesus, as he promised. 24 Before the coming of Jesus, John
preached repentance and baptism to all the
people of Israel. 25 As John was completing his
work, he said: 'Who do you think I am? I am
not that one. No, but he is coming after me,
whose sandals I am not worthy to untie.'

26 "Brothers, children of Abraham, and you
God-fearing Gentiles, it is to us that this message of salvation has been sent. 27 The people
of Jerusalem and their rulers did not recognize
Jesus, yet in condemning him they fulfilled the
words of the prophets that are read every Sabbath. 28 Though they found no proper ground
for a death sentence, they asked Pilate to have
him executed. 29 When they had carried out
all that was written about him, they took him
down from the tree and laid him in a tomb.
30 But God raised him from the dead, 31 and for
many days he was seen by those who had traveled with him from Galilee to Jerusalem. They
are now his witnesses to our people.

32 "We tell you the good news: What God
promised our fathers 33 he has fulfilled for us,
their children, by raising up Jesus. As it is written in the second Psalm:

"'You are my Son;
today I have become your Father.[b,c]

34 The fact that God raised him from the dead,
never to decay, is stated in these words:

"'I will give you the holy and sure blessings
promised to David.'[d]

[a]18 Some manuscripts *and cared for them* [b]33 Or *have begotten you* [c]33 Psalm 2:7 [d]34 Isaiah 55:3

35 So it is stated elsewhere:

"'You will not let your Holy One see
decay.'[a]

36 "For when David had served God's purpose in his own generation, he fell asleep; he
was buried with his fathers and his body decayed. 37 But the one whom God raised from
the dead did not see decay.

38 "Therefore, my brothers, I want you to
know that through Jesus the forgiveness of sins
is proclaimed to you. 39 Through him everyone
who believes is justified from everything you
could not be justified from by the law of Moses.
40 Take care that what the prophets have said
does not happen to you:

41 "'Look, you scoffers,
wonder and perish,
for I am going to do something in your
days
that you would never believe,
even if someone told you.'[b]"

42 As Paul and Barnabas were leaving the
synagogue, the people invited them to speak
further about these things on the next Sabbath. 43 When the congregation was dismissed,
many of the Jews and devout converts to Judaism followed Paul and Barnabas, who talked
with them and urged them to continue in the
grace of God.

44 On the next Sabbath almost the whole city
gathered to hear the word of the Lord. 45 When
the Jews saw the crowds, they were filled with
jealousy and talked abusively against what Paul
was saying.

46 Then Paul and Barnabas answered them
boldly: "We had to speak the word of God to
you first. Since you reject it and do not consider
yourselves worthy of eternal life, we now turn
to the Gentiles. 47 For this is what the Lord has
commanded us:

"'I have made you[c] a light for the Gentiles,
that you[c] may bring salvation to the
ends of the earth.'[d]"

48 When the Gentiles heard this, they were
glad and honored the word of the Lord; and all
who were appointed for eternal life believed.

49 The word of the Lord spread through
the whole region. 50 But the Jews incited the
God-fearing women of high standing and the
leading men of the city. They stirred up persecution against Paul and Barnabas, and expelled
them from their region. 51 So they shook the
dust from their feet in protest against them
and went to Iconium. 52 And the disciples were
filled with joy and with the Holy Spirit.

In Iconium

14 At Iconium Paul and Barnabas went as
usual into the Jewish synagogue. There
they spoke so effectively that a great number
of Jews and Gentiles believed. 2 But the Jews
who refused to believe stirred up the Gentiles
and poisoned their minds against the brothers.
3 So Paul and Barnabas spent considerable time
there, speaking boldly for the Lord, who confirmed the message of his grace by enabling
them to do miraculous signs and wonders.
4 The people of the city were divided; some
sided with the Jews, others with the apostles.
5 There was a plot afoot among the Gentiles
and Jews, together with their leaders, to mistreat them and stone them. 6 But they found
out about it and fled to the Lycaonian cities
of Lystra and Derbe and to the surrounding
country, 7 where they continued to preach the
good news.

In Lystra and Derbe

8 In Lystra there sat a man crippled in his
feet, who was lame from birth and had never
walked. 9 He listened to Paul as he was speaking. Paul looked directly at him, saw that he
had faith to be healed 10 and called out, "Stand
up on your feet!" At that, the man jumped up
and began to walk.

11 When the crowd saw what Paul had done,
they shouted in the Lycaonian language, "The
gods have come down to us in human form!"
12 Barnabas they called Zeus, and Paul they
called Hermes because he was the chief speaker.
13 The priest of Zeus, whose temple was just outside the city, brought bulls and wreaths to the
city gates because he and the crowd wanted to
offer sacrifices to them.

14 But when the apostles Barnabas and Paul
heard of this, they tore their clothes and rushed

[a] 35 Psalm 16:10 [b] 41 Hab. 1:5 [c] 47 The Greek is singular. [d] 47 Isaiah 49:6

out into the crowd, shouting: 15“Men, why are you doing this? We too are only men, human like you. We are bringing you good news, telling you to turn from these worthless things to the living God, who made heaven and earth and sea and everything in them. 16In the past, he let all nations go their own way. 17Yet he has not left himself without testimony: He has shown kindness by giving you rain from heaven and crops in their seasons; he provides you with plenty of food and fills your hearts with joy.” 18Even with these words, they had difficulty keeping the crowd from sacrificing to them.

19Then some Jews came from Antioch and Iconium and won the crowd over. They stoned Paul and dragged him outside the city, thinking he was dead. 20But after the disciples had gathered around him, he got up and went back into the city. The next day he and Barnabas left for Derbe.

The Return to Antioch in Syria

21They preached the good news in that city and won a large number of disciples. Then they returned to Lystra, Iconium and Antioch, 22strengthening the disciples and encouraging them to remain true to the faith. “We must go through many hardships to enter the kingdom of God,” they said. 23Paul and Barnabas appointed elders[a] for them in each church and, with prayer and fasting, committed them to the Lord, in whom they had put their trust. 24After going through Pisidia, they came into Pamphylia, 25and when they had preached the word in Perga, they went down to Attalia.

26From Attalia they sailed back to Antioch, where they had been committed to the grace of God for the work they had now completed. 27On arriving there, they gathered the church together and reported all that God had done through them and how he had opened the door of faith to the Gentiles. 28And they stayed there a long time with the disciples.

> **Acts 15:11**
>
> *God Saves Through Grace*
>
> “No! We believe it is through the grace of our Lord Jesus that we are saved, just as they are.”

The Council at Jerusalem

15 Some men came down from Judea to Antioch and were teaching the brothers: “Unless you are circumcised, according to the custom taught by Moses, you cannot be saved.” 2This brought Paul and Barnabas into sharp dispute and debate with them. So Paul and Barnabas were appointed, along with some other believers, to go up to Jerusalem to see the apostles and elders about this question. 3The church sent them on their way, and as they traveled through Phoenicia and Samaria, they told how the Gentiles had been converted. This news made all the brothers very glad. 4When they came to Jerusalem, they were welcomed by the church and the apostles and elders, to whom they reported everything God had done through them.

5Then some of the believers who belonged to the party of the Pharisees stood up and said, “The Gentiles must be circumcised and required to obey the law of Moses.”

6The apostles and elders met to consider this question. 7After much discussion, Peter got up and addressed them: “Brothers, you know that some time ago God made a choice among you that the Gentiles might hear from my lips the message of the gospel and believe. 8God, who knows the heart, showed that he accepted them by giving the Holy Spirit to them, just as he did to us. 9He made no distinction between us and them, for he purified their hearts by faith. 10Now then, why do you try to test God by putting on the necks of the disciples a yoke that neither we nor our fathers have been able to bear? 11No! We believe it is through the grace of our Lord Jesus that we are saved, just as they are.”

12The whole assembly became silent as they listened to Barnabas and Paul telling about the miraculous signs and wonders God had done among the Gentiles through them. 13When they finished, James spoke up: “Brothers, listen to me. 14Simon[b] has described to us how God

[a]23 Or *Barnabas ordained elders*; or *Barnabas had elders elected* [b]14 Greek *Simeon*, a variant of *Simon*; that is, Peter

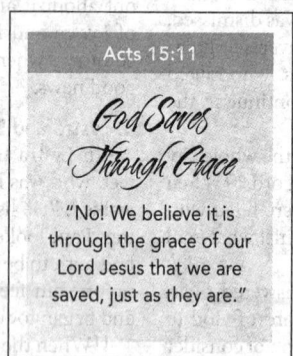

at first showed his concern by taking from the
Gentiles a people for himself. 15The words of
the prophets are in agreement with this, as it
is written:

16"'After this I will return
and rebuild David's fallen tent.
Its ruins I will rebuild,
and I will restore it,
17that the remnant of men may seek the Lord,
and all the Gentiles who bear my name,
says the Lord, who does these things'[a]
18 that have been known for ages.[b]

19"It is my judgment, therefore, that we
should not make it difficult for the Gentiles
who are turning to God. 20Instead we should
write to them, telling them to abstain from
food polluted by idols, from sexual immorality,
from the meat of strangled animals and from
blood. 21For Moses has been preached in every
city from the earliest times and is read in the
synagogues on every Sabbath."

The Council's Letter to Gentile Believers

22Then the apostles and elders, with the
whole church, decided to choose some of their
own men and send them to Antioch with Paul
and Barnabas. They chose Judas (called Barsabbas) and Silas, two men who were leaders
among the brothers. 23With them they sent the
following letter:

The apostles and elders, your brothers,

To the Gentile believers in Antioch, Syria
and Cilicia:

Greetings.

24We have heard that some went out
from us without our authorization and
disturbed you, troubling your minds by
what they said. 25So we all agreed to choose
some men and send them to you with our
dear friends Barnabas and Paul— 26men
who have risked their lives for the name
of our Lord Jesus Christ. 27Therefore we
are sending Judas and Silas to confirm by
word of mouth what we are writing. 28It
seemed good to the Holy Spirit and to us
not to burden you with anything beyond
the following requirements: 29You are to
abstain from food sacrificed to idols, from
blood, from the meat of strangled animals
and from sexual immorality. You will do
well to avoid these things.

Farewell.

30The men were sent off and went down
to Antioch, where they gathered the church
together and delivered the letter. 31The people read it and were glad for its encouraging
message. 32Judas and Silas, who themselves
were prophets, said much to encourage and
strengthen the brothers. 33After spending
some time there, they were sent off by the
brothers with the blessing of peace to return
to those who had sent them.[c] 35But Paul and
Barnabas remained in Antioch, where they and
many others taught and preached the word of
the Lord.

Disagreement Between Paul and Barnabas

36Some time later Paul said to Barnabas,
"Let us go back and visit the brothers in all
the towns where we preached the word of
the Lord and see how they are doing." 37Bar-
nabas wanted to take John, also called Mark,
with them, 38but Paul did not think it wise to
take him, because he had deserted them in
Pamphylia and had not continued with them
in the work. 39They had such a sharp disagree-
ment that they parted company. Barnabas took
Mark and sailed for Cyprus, 40but Paul chose
Silas and left, commended by the brothers to
the grace of the Lord. 41He went through Syria
and Cilicia, strengthening the churches.

Timothy Joins Paul and Silas

16 He came to Derbe and then to Lystra,
where a disciple named Timothy lived,
whose mother was a Jewess and a believer, but
whose father was a Greek. 2The brothers at
Lystra and Iconium spoke well of him. 3Paul
wanted to take him along on the journey, so
he circumcised him because of the Jews who
lived in that area, for they all knew that his father was a Greek. 4As they traveled from town
to town, they delivered the decisions reached

[a]17 Amos 9:11,12 [b]17,18 Some manuscripts *things'— / 18known to the Lord for ages is his work* [c]33 Some manuscripts *them, 34but Silas decided to remain there*

by the apostles and elders in Jerusalem for the
people to obey. 5So the churches were strengthened in the faith and grew daily in numbers.

Paul's Vision of the Man of Macedonia

6Paul and his companions traveled throughout the region of Phrygia and Galatia, having
been kept by the Holy Spirit from preaching
the word in the province of Asia. 7When they
came to the border of Mysia, they tried to enter Bithynia, but the Spirit of Jesus would not
allow them to. 8So they passed by Mysia and
went down to Troas. 9During the night Paul
had a vision of a man of Macedonia standing
and begging him, "Come over to Macedonia
and help us." 10After Paul had seen the vision,
we got ready at once to leave for Macedonia,
concluding that God had called us to preach
the gospel to them.

Lydia's Conversion in Philippi

11From Troas we put out to sea and sailed
straight for Samothrace, and the next day on to
Neapolis. 12From there we traveled to Philippi,
a Roman colony and the leading city of that
district of Macedonia. And we stayed there
several days.

13On the Sabbath we went outside the city
gate to the river, where we expected to find
a place of prayer. We sat down and began to
speak to the women who had gathered there.
14One of those listening was a
woman named Lydia, a dealer
in purple cloth from the city of
Thyatira, who was a worshiper
of God. The Lord opened her
heart to respond to Paul's message. 15When she and the members of her household were
baptized, she invited us to her
home. "If you consider me a
believer in the Lord," she said,
"come and stay at my house."
And she persuaded us.

> **Acts 16:31**
>
> *God Saves Through Faith*
>
> They replied, "Believe in the Lord Jesus, and you will be saved—you and your household."

Paul and Silas in Prison

16Once when we were going to the place of
prayer, we were met by a slave girl who had a
spirit by which she predicted the future. She
earned a great deal of money for her owners
by fortune-telling. 17This girl followed Paul
and the rest of us, shouting, "These men are
servants of the Most High God, who are telling
you the way to be saved." 18She kept this up
for many days. Finally Paul became so troubled
that he turned around and said to the spirit,
"In the name of Jesus Christ I command you
to come out of her!" At that moment the spirit
left her.

19When the owners of the slave girl realized
that their hope of making money was gone,
they seized Paul and Silas and dragged them
into the marketplace to face the authorities.
20They brought them before the magistrates
and said, "These men are Jews, and are throwing our city into an uproar 21by advocating
customs unlawful for us Romans to accept
or practice."

22The crowd joined in the attack against Paul
and Silas, and the magistrates ordered them to
be stripped and beaten. 23After they had been
severely flogged, they were thrown into prison,
and the jailer was commanded to guard them
carefully. 24Upon receiving such orders, he put
them in the inner cell and fastened their feet
in the stocks.

25About midnight Paul and Silas were praying and singing hymns to God, and the other
prisoners were listening to them. 26Suddenly
there was such a violent earthquake that the
foundations of the prison were shaken. At once
all the prison doors flew open, and everybody's
chains came loose. 27The jailer
woke up, and when he saw the
prison doors open, he drew his
sword and was about to kill
himself because he thought the
prisoners had escaped. 28But
Paul shouted, "Don't harm
yourself! We are all here!"

29The jailer called for lights,
rushed in and fell trembling
before Paul and Silas. 30He
then brought them out and
asked, "Sirs, what must I do to
be saved?"

31They replied, "Believe in the Lord Jesus,
and you will be saved—you and your household." 32Then they spoke the word of the Lord
to him and to all the others in his house. 33At
that hour of the night the jailer took them and
washed their wounds; then immediately he

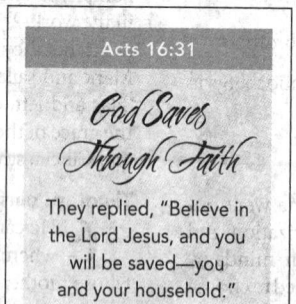

Little White Lie

SAPPHIRA

WHAT WAS THE PRICE we agreed to say we paid again?

Sapphira silently calculated the cost of the land once more for good measure.

Nine . . . plus . . .

Take away half . . . add . . . or was it add half and take away . . . ?

She muttered to herself as she made her way through the city streets. *I'm never going to get this right.* Her husband, Ananias, had been over this with her a hundred times, but still she tended to forget things whenever she was nervous. One little mistake, and their charade would be over.

"I'll go first and lay the money at the apostles' feet," he'd told her. "I'll tell them that the amount was the full price we got for the property. Then, if anyone asks you about it, you just back me up. Got it?"

She got it alright. How else were they going to make ends meet if they didn't keep a little kickback for themselves?

She'd been astonished lately at her friends and even perfect strangers. What had gotten into them? Everyone was out of their minds with generosity—selling houses and land as routinely as if they were eggs and butter.

Inside, she may have secretly wished she could be like the other churchgoers she admired.

But I'm just too practical, she reasoned. *Maybe when Ananias and I get ahead, then we'll be able to give like they do.*

In the meantime, she had to say that she was fairly impressed with the amount they *had* agreed to give to the church. She reassured herself on her way to meet Ananias. That gift would certainly outweigh any little white lie she or her husband would tell.

And maybe, with a little luck, Ananias would have already taken care of it and no one would ask her anything. Then she wouldn't have to tell a lie; she'd only have to live one.

—Prayer—

Heavenly Father, I am sorry for the lies that I participate in. Forgive me and help me to live a life of honesty.

Peter asked her, "Tell me, is this the price you and Ananias got for the land?" "Yes," she said, "that is the price."

Acts 5:8

ASSIGNED READING:

Acts 5:1–11

Weekend

Go to page 1349 for your next devotional reading.

and all his family were baptized. 34 The jailer brought them into his house and set a meal before them; he was filled with joy because he had come to believe in God—he and his whole family.

35 When it was daylight, the magistrates sent their officers to the jailer with the order: "Release those men." 36 The jailer told Paul, "The magistrates have ordered that you and Silas be released. Now you can leave. Go in peace."

37 But Paul said to the officers: "They beat us publicly without a trial, even though we are Roman citizens, and threw us into prison. And now do they want to get rid of us quietly? No! Let them come themselves and escort us out."

38 The officers reported this to the magistrates, and when they heard that Paul and Silas were Roman citizens, they were alarmed. 39 They came to appease them and escorted them from the prison, requesting them to leave the city. 40 After Paul and Silas came out of the prison, they went to Lydia's house, where they met with the brothers and encouraged them. Then they left.

In Thessalonica

17 When they had passed through Amphipolis and Apollonia, they came to Thessalonica, where there was a Jewish synagogue. 2 As his custom was, Paul went into the synagogue, and on three Sabbath days he reasoned with them from the Scriptures, 3 explaining and proving that the Christ[a] had to suffer and rise from the dead. "This Jesus I am proclaiming to you is the Christ,[a]" he said. 4 Some of the Jews were persuaded and joined Paul and Silas, as did a large number of God-fearing Greeks and not a few prominent women.

5 But the Jews were jealous; so they rounded up some bad characters from the marketplace, formed a mob and started a riot in the city. They rushed to Jason's house in search of Paul and Silas in order to bring them out to the crowd.[b] 6 But when they did not find them, they dragged Jason and some other brothers before the city officials, shouting: "These men who have caused trouble all over the world have now come here, 7 and Jason has welcomed them into his house. They are all defying Caesar's decrees, saying that there is another king, one called Jesus." 8 When they heard this, the crowd and the city officials were thrown into turmoil. 9 Then they made Jason and the others post bond and let them go.

In Berea

10 As soon as it was night, the brothers sent Paul and Silas away to Berea. On arriving there, they went to the Jewish synagogue. 11 Now the Bereans were of more noble character than the Thessalonians, for they received the message with great eagerness and examined the Scriptures every day to see if what Paul said was true. 12 Many of the Jews believed, as did also a number of prominent Greek women and many Greek men.

13 When the Jews in Thessalonica learned that Paul was preaching the word of God at Berea, they went there too, agitating the crowds and stirring them up. 14 The brothers immediately sent Paul to the coast, but Silas and Timothy stayed at Berea. 15 The men who escorted Paul brought him to Athens and then left with instructions for Silas and Timothy to join him as soon as possible.

In Athens

16 While Paul was waiting for them in Athens, he was greatly distressed to see that the city was full of idols. 17 So he reasoned in the synagogue with the Jews and the God-fearing Greeks, as well as in the marketplace day by day with those who happened to be there. 18 A group of Epicurean and Stoic philosophers began to dispute with him. Some of them asked, "What is this babbler trying to say?" Others remarked, "He seems to be advocating foreign gods." They said this because Paul was preaching the good news about Jesus and the resurrection. 19 Then they took him and brought him to a meeting of the Areopagus, where they said to him, "May we know what this new teaching is that you are presenting? 20 You are bringing some strange ideas to our ears, and we want to know what they mean." 21 (All the Athenians and the foreigners who lived there spent their time doing nothing but talking about and listening to the latest ideas.)

22 Paul then stood up in the meeting of the

[a] 3 Or *Messiah* [b] 5 Or *the assembly of the people*

Reaching

Read: Acts 17:16–34

WHEN PEOPLE DREAM about what they can achieve, they are often told to "reach for the stars." Well, we all know one can reach, at least metaphorically, but never touch. The nearest star, our sun, is 93 million miles away, and if anyone even got much closer to it than we are now, they'd be incinerated. The temperature even on Venus, our next closest planetary neighbor, is 720 degrees Kelvin. The surface of the sun is a whopping 5800 degrees Kelvin. Does that tell you anything about the power of the Creator of the sun?

Happily, there's no danger of incineration when we reach for God. What Paul preached to the people of Athens is still true. Paul told them in chapter 17 that God revealed himself to us as the One who made everything and the One who dictates the rise and fall of nations. He revealed himself as the One in control of all things. Why does God go to such lengths to reveal himself? So that perhaps we might seek him. It's as if God is holding his breath, willing each and every person to reach out to him.

God promises that when we search for him, we'll find him and be satisfied. Living in God's realm is like being returned to our natural element. Our every breath is in his hands: "For in him we live and move and have our being" (verse 28). Otherwise we are spiritually like fish out of water; we can do nothing to help ourselves; we cannot move, and our spirits cannot stay alive.

Imagine the God of the universe wanting you to reach out to him—waiting in eager anticipation. Do you know what's really remarkable? As you begin reaching toward God, you'll find you don't need to reach at all. He is not far. There's no stretch. Our loving God is as close as your next breath—your next prayer. Jesus says, "Here I am! I stand at the door and knock. If anyone hears my voice and opens the door, I will come in and eat with him, and he with me" (Revelation 3:20).

Acts 17:27–28

"God did this so that men would seek him and perhaps reach out for him and find him, though he is not far from each one of us. 'For in him we live and move and have our being.' As some of your own poets have said, 'We are his offspring.' "

reflection

1 How is God revealing himself to you these days?

2 Can you remember what life was like before you first reached out to God? In what ways are you able to move and breathe and live in God?

3 Do you need to reach out to God now? If so, spend some time in his presence right now.

RELATED READINGS

1 Chronicles 16:10–11; Isaiah 55:6–7; Hebrews 11:6

Go to page 1352 for your next devotional reading.

Areopagus and said: "Men of Athens! I see that
in every way you are very religious. 23For as
I walked around and looked carefully at your
objects of worship, I even found an altar with
this inscription: TO AN UNKNOWN GOD. Now
what you worship as something unknown I am
going to proclaim to you.

24"The God who made the world and everything in it is the Lord of heaven and earth and
does not live in temples built by hands. 25And
he is not served by human hands, as if he needed
anything, because he himself gives all men life
and breath and everything else. 26From one
man he made every nation of
men, that they should inhabit
the whole earth; and he determined the times set for them
and the exact places where
they should live. 27God did
this so that men would seek
him and perhaps reach out
for him and find him, though
he is not far from each one of
us. 28'For in him we live and
move and have our being.' As
some of your own poets have
said, 'We are his offspring.'

29"Therefore since we are
God's offspring, we should not think that the
divine being is like gold or silver or stone—an
image made by man's design and skill. 30In the
past God overlooked such ignorance, but now
he commands all people everywhere to repent.
31For he has set a day when he will judge the
world with justice by the man he has appointed.
He has given proof of this to all men by raising
him from the dead."

32When they heard about the resurrection
of the dead, some of them sneered, but others
said, "We want to hear you again on this subject." 33At that, Paul left the Council. 34A few
men became followers of Paul and believed.
Among them was Dionysius, a member of the
Areopagus, also a woman named Damaris, and
a number of others.

Acts 17:27

God Is Near

"God did this so that men would seek him and perhaps reach out for him and find him, though he is not far from each one of us."

In Corinth

18 After this, Paul left Athens and went to
Corinth. 2There he met a Jew named
Aquila, a native of Pontus, who had recently
come from Italy with his wife Priscilla, because
Claudius had ordered all the Jews to leave
Rome. Paul went to see them, 3and because
he was a tentmaker as they were, he stayed
and worked with them. 4Every Sabbath he
reasoned in the synagogue, trying to persuade
Jews and Greeks.

5When Silas and Timothy came from Macedonia, Paul devoted himself exclusively to
preaching, testifying to the Jews that Jesus was
the Christ.[a] 6But when the Jews opposed Paul
and became abusive, he shook out his clothes
in protest and said to them, "Your blood be on
your own heads! I am clear of
my responsibility. From now on
I will go to the Gentiles."

7Then Paul left the synagogue
and went next door to the house
of Titius Justus, a worshiper of
God. 8Crispus, the synagogue
ruler, and his entire household
believed in the Lord; and many
of the Corinthians who heard
him believed and were baptized.

9One night the Lord spoke
to Paul in a vision: "Do not be
afraid; keep on speaking, do not
be silent. 10For I am with you, and no one is
going to attack and harm you, because I have
many people in this city." 11So Paul stayed
for a year and a half, teaching them the word
of God.

12While Gallio was proconsul of Achaia, the
Jews made a united attack on Paul and brought
him into court. 13"This man," they charged, "is
persuading the people to worship God in ways
contrary to the law."

14Just as Paul was about to speak, Gallio
said to the Jews, "If you Jews were making a
complaint about some misdemeanor or serious
crime, it would be reasonable for me to listen
to you. 15But since it involves questions about
words and names and your own law—settle
the matter yourselves. I will not be a judge of
such things." 16So he had them ejected from
the court. 17Then they all turned on Sosthenes
the synagogue ruler and beat him in front of the
court. But Gallio showed no concern whatever.

[a]5 Or *Messiah;* also in verse 28

Priscilla, Aquila and Apollos

18 Paul stayed on in Corinth for some time.
Then he left the brothers and sailed for Syria,
accompanied by Priscilla and Aquila. Before
he sailed, he had his hair cut off at Cenchrea
because of a vow he had taken. 19 They arrived
at Ephesus, where Paul left Priscilla and Aquila.
He himself went into the synagogue and reasoned with the Jews. 20 When they asked him
to spend more time with them, he declined.
21 But as he left, he promised, "I will come back
if it is God's will." Then he set sail from Ephesus. 22 When he landed at Caesarea, he went up
and greeted the church and then went down
to Antioch.

23 After spending some time in Antioch,
Paul set out from there and traveled from place
to place throughout the region of Galatia and
Phrygia, strengthening all the disciples.

24 Meanwhile a Jew named Apollos, a native of Alexandria, came to Ephesus. He was
a learned man, with a thorough knowledge of
the Scriptures. 25 He had been instructed in the
way of the Lord, and he spoke with great fervor[a]
and taught about Jesus accurately, though he
knew only the baptism of John. 26 He began to
speak boldly in the synagogue. When Priscilla
and Aquila heard him, they invited him to their
home and explained to him the way of God
more adequately.

27 When Apollos wanted to go to Achaia, the
brothers encouraged him and wrote to the disciples there to welcome him. On arriving, he was
a great help to those who by grace had believed.
28 For he vigorously refuted the Jews in public
debate, proving from the Scriptures that Jesus
was the Christ.

Paul in Ephesus

19 While Apollos was at Corinth, Paul
took the road through the interior and
arrived at Ephesus. There he found some disciples 2 and asked them, "Did you receive the
Holy Spirit when[b] you believed?"

They answered, "No, we have not even heard
that there is a Holy Spirit."

3 So Paul asked, "Then what baptism did
you receive?"

"John's baptism," they replied.

4 Paul said, "John's baptism was a baptism
of repentance. He told the people to believe in
the one coming after him, that is, in Jesus." 5 On
hearing this, they were baptized into[c] the name
of the Lord Jesus. 6 When Paul placed his hands
on them, the Holy Spirit came on them, and
they spoke in tongues[d] and prophesied. 7 There
were about twelve men in all.

8 Paul entered the synagogue and spoke
boldly there for three months, arguing per-
suasively about the kingdom of God. 9 But
some of them became obstinate; they refused
to believe and publicly maligned the Way. So
Paul left them. He took the disciples with him
and had discussions daily in the lecture hall of
Tyrannus. 10 This went on for two years, so that
all the Jews and Greeks who lived in the province of Asia heard the word of the Lord.

11 God did extraordinary miracles through
Paul, 12 so that even handkerchiefs and aprons
that had touched him were taken to the sick,
and their illnesses were cured and the evil spirits left them.

13 Some Jews who went around driving out
evil spirits tried to invoke the name of the Lord
Jesus over those who were demon-possessed.
They would say, "In the name of Jesus, whom
Paul preaches, I command you to come out."
14 Seven sons of Sceva, a Jewish chief priest,
were doing this. 15 ⌞One day⌟ the evil spirit answered them, "Jesus I know, and I know about
Paul, but who are you?" 16 Then the man who
had the evil spirit jumped on them and overpowered them all. He gave them such a beating
that they ran out of the house naked and bleeding.

17 When this became known to the Jews and
Greeks living in Ephesus, they were all seized
with fear, and the name of the Lord Jesus was
held in high honor. 18 Many of those who believed now came and openly confessed their
evil deeds. 19 A number who had practiced sorcery brought their scrolls together and burned
them publicly. When they calculated the value
of the scrolls, the total came to fifty thousand
drachmas.[e] 20 In this way the word of the Lord
spread widely and grew in power.

21 After all this had happened, Paul decided

[a] 25 Or *with fervor in the Spirit* [b] 2 Or *after* [c] 5 Or *in* [d] 6 Or *other languages* [e] 19 A drachma was a silver coin worth about a day's wages.

Name-Droppers

Read: Acts 19:1–20

Acts 19:15–16

The evil spirit answered them, "Jesus I know, and I know about Paul, but who are you?" Then the man who had the evil spirit jumped on them and overpowered them all.

NAME-DROPPERS ARE KNOWN for annoying those who overhear their outrageous claims. Casually sprinkling their conversations with the names of famous people, they aim to impress their listeners. Some imply a familiarity with illustrious people, as if they are on a first-name basis.

In Acts 19, we meet the seven sons of Sceva, who employed name-dropping in their profession as exorcists. They incorporated the name of Jesus into their effort to drive out demons. But it backfired. The would-be exorcists were pummeled as the demon-possessed man overpowered them. The question is, if the disciples were able to cast out demons in Jesus' name, why couldn't the sons of Sceva? It was largely because they profaned God's name by taking it in vain. They knew the name of the Lord, but not the Lord of the name.

The demoniac's reply, "Who are you?" revealed that these men didn't have a personal relationship with Jesus nor did they believe Paul's teachings. Jesus had promised, "Signs will accompany those who believe: In my name they will drive out demons" (Mark 16:17). Tragically, these imposters thought they could use Jesus' name to work some magic.

The sons of Sceva presumptuously took Christ's name in vain. But there are other ways to take God's name in vain. Other forms of dropping God's name in a negative way:

- ♦ Repeating the Lord's name as a part of rote or routine (Matthew 6:7)
- ♦ Professing to be a Christian without obeying God's commands (Matthew 7:21–23)
- ♦ Praising God with the lips but not from the heart (Matthew 15:7–9)

There is power in God's name, but we can learn from this story to be careful not to drop God's name unless we have a personal relationship with him. The sons of Sceva were punished, beaten by the very demon they were trying to cast out. When we honor the Lord's name, we are honoring our Lord.

reflection

1 Have you ever been a name-dropper in some way? When?

2 Have you ever seen people call on God even though they didn't believe in him? What were the circumstances? What were the results?

3 In what ways can you bring honor to Jesus' name?

RELATED READINGS

Matthew 12:22–32; Mark 16:15–18; Luke 10:18–20

Go to page 1361 for your next devotional reading.

Tuesday

to go to Jerusalem, passing through Macedonia
and Achaia. "After I have been there," he said, "I
must visit Rome also." 22He sent two of his helpers, Timothy and Erastus, to Macedonia, while
he stayed in the province of Asia a little longer.

The Riot in Ephesus

23About that time there arose a great disturbance about the Way. 24A silversmith named
Demetrius, who made silver shrines of Artemis, brought in no little business for the craftsmen. 25He called them together, along with
the workmen in related trades, and said: "Men,
you know we receive a good income from this
business. 26And you see and hear how this fellow Paul has convinced and led astray large
numbers of people here in Ephesus and in
practically the whole province of Asia. He says
that man-made gods are no gods at all. 27There
is danger not only that our trade will lose its
good name, but also that the temple of the
great goddess Artemis will be discredited, and
the goddess herself, who is worshiped throughout the province of Asia and the world, will be
robbed of her divine majesty."

28When they heard this, they were furious
and began shouting: "Great is Artemis of the
Ephesians!" 29Soon the whole city was in an uproar. The people seized Gaius and Aristarchus,
Paul's traveling companions from Macedonia,
and rushed as one man into the theater. 30Paul
wanted to appear before the crowd, but the disciples would not let him. 31Even some of the
officials of the province, friends of Paul, sent
him a message begging him not to venture into
the theater.

32The assembly was in confusion: Some were
shouting one thing, some another. Most of the
people did not even know why they were there.
33The Jews pushed Alexander to the front, and
some of the crowd shouted instructions to
him. He motioned for silence in order to make
a defense before the people. 34But when they
realized he was a Jew, they all shouted in unison for about two hours: "Great is Artemis of
the Ephesians!"

35The city clerk quieted the crowd and said:
"Men of Ephesus, doesn't all the world know
that the city of Ephesus is the guardian of the
temple of the great Artemis and of her image,
which fell from heaven? 36Therefore, since
these facts are undeniable, you ought to be
quiet and not do anything rash. 37You have
brought these men here, though they have
neither robbed temples nor blasphemed our
goddess. 38If, then, Demetrius and his fellow
craftsmen have a grievance against anybody,
the courts are open and there are proconsuls.
They can press charges. 39If there is anything
further you want to bring up, it must be settled
in a legal assembly. 40As it is, we are in danger
of being charged with rioting because of today's events. In that case we would not be able
to account for this commotion, since there is
no reason for it." 41After he had said this, he
dismissed the assembly.

Through Macedonia and Greece

20 When the uproar had ended, Paul sent
for the disciples and, after encouraging them, said good-by and set out for Macedonia. 2He traveled through that area, speaking
many words of encouragement to the people,
and finally arrived in Greece, 3where he stayed
three months. Because the Jews made a plot
against him just as he was about to sail for
Syria, he decided to go back through Macedonia. 4He was accompanied by Sopater son of
Pyrrhus from Berea, Aristarchus and Secundus
from Thessalonica, Gaius from Derbe, Timothy also, and Tychicus and Trophimus from the
province of Asia. 5These men went on ahead
and waited for us at Troas. 6But we sailed from
Philippi after the Feast of Unleavened Bread,
and five days later joined the others at Troas,
where we stayed seven days.

Eutychus Raised From the Dead at Troas

7On the first day of the week we came
together to break bread. Paul spoke to the people and, because he intended to leave the next
day, kept on talking until midnight. 8There
were many lamps in the upstairs room where
we were meeting. 9Seated in a window was a
young man named Eutychus, who was sinking into a deep sleep as Paul talked on and
on. When he was sound asleep, he fell to the
ground from the third story and was picked
up dead. 10Paul went down, threw himself on
the young man and put his arms around him.
"Don't be alarmed," he said. "He's alive!" 11Then
he went upstairs again and broke bread and ate.

After talking until daylight, he left. 12 The people took the young man home alive and were
greatly comforted.

Paul's Farewell to the Ephesian Elders

13 We went on ahead to the ship and sailed
for Assos, where we were going to take Paul
aboard. He had made this arrangement because he was going there on foot. 14 When he
met us at Assos, we took him aboard and went
on to Mitylene. 15 The next day we set sail from
there and arrived off Kios. The day after that
we crossed over to Samos, and on the following
day arrived at Miletus. 16 Paul had decided to
sail past Ephesus to avoid spending time in the
province of Asia, for he was in a hurry to reach
Jerusalem, if possible, by the day of Pentecost.

17 From Miletus, Paul sent to Ephesus for the
elders of the church. 18 When they arrived, he
said to them: "You know how I lived the whole
time I was with you, from the
first day I came into the province of Asia. 19 I served the Lord
with great humility and with
tears, although I was severely
tested by the plots of the Jews.
20 You know that I have not
hesitated to preach anything
that would be helpful to you
but have taught you publicly
and from house to house. 21 I
have declared to both Jews and
Greeks that they must turn to
God in repentance and have
faith in our Lord Jesus.

22 "And now, compelled by the Spirit, I am
going to Jerusalem, not knowing what will happen to me there. 23 I only know that in every
city the Holy Spirit warns me that prison and
hardships are facing me. 24 However, I consider
my life worth nothing to me, if only I may finish the race and complete the task the Lord
Jesus has given me—the task of testifying to
the gospel of God's grace.

25 "Now I know that none of you among
whom I have gone about preaching the kingdom will ever see me again. 26 Therefore, I declare to you today that I am innocent of the
blood of all men. 27 For I have not hesitated to
proclaim to you the whole will of God. 28 Keep
watch over yourselves and all the flock of
which the Holy Spirit has made you overseers.[a]
Be shepherds of the church of God,[b] which he
bought with his own blood. 29 I know that after I leave, savage wolves will come in among
you and will not spare the flock. 30 Even from
your own number men will arise and distort
the truth in order to draw away disciples after
them. 31 So be on your guard! Remember that
for three years I never stopped warning each of
you night and day with tears.

32 "Now I commit you to God and to the
word of his grace, which can build you up and
give you an inheritance among all those who
are sanctified. 33 I have not coveted anyone's silver or gold or clothing. 34 You yourselves know
that these hands of mine have supplied my own
needs and the needs of my companions. 35 In
everything I did, I showed you that by this kind
of hard work we must help the
weak, remembering the words
the Lord Jesus himself said: 'It
is more blessed to give than
to receive.'"

36 When he had said this, he
knelt down with all of them
and prayed. 37 They all wept as
they embraced him and kissed
him. 38 What grieved them
most was his statement that
they would never see his face
again. Then they accompanied
him to the ship.

Acts 20:21

God Saves

"I have declared to both
Jews and Greeks that
they must turn to God
in repentance and have
faith in our Lord Jesus."

On to Jerusalem

21 After we had torn ourselves away from
them, we put out to sea and sailed
straight to Cos. The next day we went to Rhodes
and from there to Patara. 2 We found a ship
crossing over to Phoenicia, went on board and
set sail. 3 After sighting Cyprus and passing to
the south of it, we sailed on to Syria. We landed
at Tyre, where our ship was to unload its cargo.
4 Finding the disciples there, we stayed with
them seven days. Through the Spirit they urged
Paul not to go on to Jerusalem. 5 But when our
time was up, we left and continued on our way.
All the disciples and their wives and children
accompanied us out of the city, and there on
the beach we knelt to pray. 6 After saying good-

[a]28 Traditionally *bishops* [b]28 Many manuscripts *of the Lord*

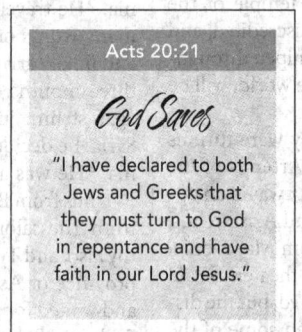

by to each other, we went aboard the ship, and
they returned home.
7 We continued our voyage from Tyre and
landed at Ptolemais, where we greeted the
brothers and stayed with them for a day. 8 Leaving the next day, we reached Caesarea and
stayed at the house of Philip the evangelist, one
of the Seven. 9 He had four unmarried daughters who prophesied.
10 After we had been there a number of days,
a prophet named Agabus came down from Judea. 11 Coming over to us, he took Paul's belt,
tied his own hands and feet with it and said,
"The Holy Spirit says, 'In this way the Jews of
Jerusalem will bind the owner of this belt and
will hand him over to the Gentiles.'"
12 When we heard this, we and the people
there pleaded with Paul not to go up to Jerusalem. 13 Then Paul answered, "Why are you
weeping and breaking my heart? I am ready
not only to be bound, but also to die in Jerusalem for the name of the Lord Jesus." 14 When he
would not be dissuaded, we gave up and said,
"The Lord's will be done."
15 After this, we got ready and went up to Jerusalem. 16 Some of the disciples from Caesarea
accompanied us and brought us to the home of
Mnason, where we were to stay. He was a man
from Cyprus and one of the early disciples.

Paul's Arrival at Jerusalem

17 When we arrived at Jerusalem, the brothers received us warmly. 18 The next day Paul
and the rest of us went to see James, and all the
elders were present. 19 Paul greeted them and
reported in detail what God had done among
the Gentiles through his ministry.
20 When they heard this, they praised God.
Then they said to Paul: "You see, brother, how
many thousands of Jews have believed, and all
of them are zealous for the law. 21 They have
been informed that you teach all the Jews who
live among the Gentiles to turn away from Moses, telling them not to circumcise their children or live according to our customs. 22 What
shall we do? They will certainly hear that you
have come, 23 so do what we tell you. There are
four men with us who have made a vow. 24 Take
these men, join in their purification rites and
pay their expenses, so that they can have their
heads shaved. Then everybody will know there
is no truth in these reports about you, but that
you yourself are living in obedience to the law.
25 As for the Gentile believers, we have written
to them our decision that they should abstain
from food sacrificed to idols, from blood,
from the meat of strangled animals and from
sexual immorality."
26 The next day Paul took the men and purified himself along with them. Then he went to
the temple to give notice of the date when the
days of purification would end and the offering
would be made for each of them.

Paul Arrested

27 When the seven days were nearly over,
some Jews from the province of Asia saw Paul
at the temple. They stirred up the whole crowd
and seized him, 28 shouting, "Men of Israel,
help us! This is the man who teaches all men
everywhere against our people and our law and
this place. And besides, he has brought Greeks
into the temple area and defiled this holy place."
29 (They had previously seen Trophimus the
Ephesian in the city with Paul and assumed that
Paul had brought him into the temple area.)
30 The whole city was aroused, and the people
came running from all directions. Seizing Paul,
they dragged him from the temple, and immediately the gates were shut. 31 While they were
trying to kill him, news reached the commander
of the Roman troops that the whole city of Jerusalem was in an uproar. 32 He at once took some
officers and soldiers and ran down to the crowd.
When the rioters saw the commander and his
soldiers, they stopped beating Paul.
33 The commander came up and arrested him
and ordered him to be bound with two chains.
Then he asked who he was and what he had
done. 34 Some in the crowd shouted one thing
and some another, and since the commander
could not get at the truth because of the uproar,
he ordered that Paul be taken into the barracks.
35 When Paul reached the steps, the violence of
the mob was so great he had to be carried by
the soldiers. 36 The crowd that followed kept
shouting, "Away with him!"

Paul Speaks to the Crowd

37 As the soldiers were about to take Paul
into the barracks, he asked the commander,
"May I say something to you?"

"Do you speak Greek?" he replied. 38"Aren't
you the Egyptian who started a revolt and led
four thousand terrorists out into the desert
some time ago?"

39Paul answered, "I am a Jew, from Tarsus in
Cilicia, a citizen of no ordinary city. Please let
me speak to the people."

40Having received the commander's permission, Paul stood on the steps and motioned to
the crowd. When they were all silent, he said to
22 them in Aramaic[a]: 1"Brothers and fathers, listen now to my defense."

2When they heard him speak to them in
Aramaic, they became very quiet.

Then Paul said: 3"I am a Jew, born in Tarsus of Cilicia, but brought up in this city. Under Gamaliel I was thoroughly trained in the
law of our fathers and was just as zealous for
God as any of you are today. 4I persecuted the
followers of this Way to their death, arresting
both men and women and throwing them into
prison, 5as also the high priest and all the Council can testify. I even obtained letters from them
to their brothers in Damascus, and went there
to bring these people as prisoners to Jerusalem
to be punished.

6"About noon as I came near Damascus,
suddenly a bright light from heaven flashed
around me. 7I fell to the ground and heard a
voice say to me, 'Saul! Saul! Why do you persecute me?'

8" 'Who are you, Lord?' I asked.

" 'I am Jesus of Nazareth, whom you are persecuting,' he replied. 9My companions saw the
light, but they did not understand the voice of
him who was speaking to me.

10" 'What shall I do, Lord?' I asked.

" 'Get up,' the Lord said, 'and go into Damascus. There you will be told all that you have
been assigned to do.' 11My companions led me
by the hand into Damascus, because the brilliance of the light had blinded me.

12"A man named Ananias came to see me.
He was a devout observer of the law and highly
respected by all the Jews living there. 13He
stood beside me and said, 'Brother Saul, receive
your sight!' And at that very moment I was able
to see him.

14"Then he said: 'The God of our fathers has
chosen you to know his will and to see the Righteous One and to hear words from his mouth.
15You will be his witness to all men of what you
have seen and heard. 16And now what are you
waiting for? Get up, be baptized and wash your
sins away, calling on his name.'

17"When I returned to Jerusalem and was
praying at the temple, I fell into a trance 18and
saw the Lord speaking. 'Quick!' he said to me.
'Leave Jerusalem immediately, because they
will not accept your testimony about me.'

19" 'Lord,' I replied, 'these men know that
I went from one synagogue to another to
imprison and beat those who believe in you.
20And when the blood of your martyr[b] Stephen
was shed, I stood there giving my approval and
guarding the clothes of those who were killing him.'

21"Then the Lord said to me, 'Go; I will send
you far away to the Gentiles.' "

Paul the Roman Citizen

22The crowd listened to Paul until he said
this. Then they raised their voices and shouted,
"Rid the earth of him! He's not fit to live!"

23As they were shouting and throwing off
their cloaks and flinging dust into the air, 24the
commander ordered Paul to be taken into the
barracks. He directed that he be flogged and
questioned in order to find out why the people were shouting at him like this. 25As they
stretched him out to flog him, Paul said to the
centurion standing there, "Is it legal for you
to flog a Roman citizen who hasn't even been
found guilty?"

26When the centurion heard this, he went
to the commander and reported it. "What are
you going to do?" he asked. "This man is a Roman citizen."

27The commander went to Paul and asked,
"Tell me, are you a Roman citizen?"

"Yes, I am," he answered.

28Then the commander said, "I had to pay a
big price for my citizenship."

"But I was born a citizen," Paul replied.

29Those who were about to question him
withdrew immediately. The commander himself was alarmed when he realized that he had
put Paul, a Roman citizen, in chains.

[a]40 Or possibly *Hebrew*; also in 22:2 [b]20 Or *witness*

Before the Sanhedrin

30The next day, since the commander
wanted to find out exactly why Paul was being
accused by the Jews, he released him and ordered the chief priests and all the Sanhedrin to
assemble. Then he brought Paul and had him
stand before them.

23 Paul looked straight at the Sanhedrin
and said, "My brothers, I have fulfilled
my duty to God in all good conscience to this
day." 2At this the high priest Ananias ordered
those standing near Paul to strike him on the
mouth. 3Then Paul said to him, "God will strike
you, you whitewashed wall! You sit there to
judge me according to the law, yet you yourself
violate the law by commanding that I be struck!"

4Those who were standing near Paul said,
"You dare to insult God's high priest?"

5Paul replied, "Brothers, I did not realize that
he was the high priest; for it is written: 'Do not
speak evil about the ruler of your people.'[a]"

6Then Paul, knowing that some of them
were Sadducees and the others Pharisees,
called out in the Sanhedrin, "My brothers, I am
a Pharisee, the son of a Pharisee. I stand on trial
because of my hope in the resurrection of the
dead." 7When he said this, a dispute broke out
between the Pharisees and the Sadducees, and
the assembly was divided. 8(The Sadducees say
that there is no resurrection, and that there are
neither angels nor spirits, but the Pharisees acknowledge them all.)

9There was a great uproar, and some of the
teachers of the law who were Pharisees stood
up and argued vigorously. "We find nothing
wrong with this man," they said. "What if a
spirit or an angel has spoken to him?" 10The
dispute became so violent that the commander
was afraid Paul would be torn to pieces by
them. He ordered the troops to go down and
take him away from them by force and bring
him into the barracks.

11The following night the Lord stood near
Paul and said, "Take courage! As you have testified about me in Jerusalem, so you must also
testify in Rome."

The Plot to Kill Paul

12The next morning the Jews formed a
conspiracy and bound themselves with an
oath not to eat or drink until they had killed
Paul. 13More than forty men were involved in
this plot. 14They went to the chief priests and
elders and said, "We have taken a solemn oath
not to eat anything until we have killed Paul.
15Now then, you and the Sanhedrin petition
the commander to bring him before you on the
pretext of wanting more accurate information
about his case. We are ready to kill him before
he gets here."

16But when the son of Paul's sister heard of
this plot, he went into the barracks and told
Paul.

17Then Paul called one of the centurions and
said, "Take this young man to the commander;
he has something to tell him." 18So he took him
to the commander.

The centurion said, "Paul, the prisoner, sent
for me and asked me to bring this young man
to you because he has something to tell you."

19The commander took the young man by
the hand, drew him aside and asked, "What is
it you want to tell me?"

20He said: "The Jews have agreed to ask you
to bring Paul before the Sanhedrin tomorrow
on the pretext of wanting more accurate information about him. 21Don't give in to them, because more than forty of them are waiting in
ambush for him. They have taken an oath not
to eat or drink until they have killed him. They
are ready now, waiting for your consent to their
request."

22The commander dismissed the young man
and cautioned him, "Don't tell anyone that you
have reported this to me."

Paul Transferred to Caesarea

23Then he called two of his centurions and
ordered them, "Get ready a detachment of two
hundred soldiers, seventy horsemen and two
hundred spearmen[b] to go to Caesarea at nine
tonight. 24Provide mounts for Paul so that he
may be taken safely to Governor Felix."

25He wrote a letter as follows:

26Claudius Lysias,

To His Excellency, Governor Felix:

Greetings.

[a]5 Exodus 22:28 [b]23 The meaning of the Greek for this word is uncertain.

27This man was seized by the Jews and they were about to kill him, but I came with my troops and rescued him, for I had learned that he is a Roman citizen. 28I wanted to know why they were accusing him, so I brought him to their Sanhedrin. 29I found that the accusation had to do with questions about their law, but there was no charge against him that deserved death or imprisonment. 30When I was informed of a plot to be carried out against the man, I sent him to you at once. I also ordered his accusers to present to you their case against him.

31So the soldiers, carrying out their orders, took Paul with them during the night and brought him as far as Antipatris. 32The next day they let the cavalry go on with him, while they returned to the barracks. 33When the cavalry arrived in Caesarea, they delivered the letter to the governor and handed Paul over to him. 34The governor read the letter and asked what province he was from. Learning that he was from Cilicia, 35he said, "I will hear your case when your accusers get here." Then he ordered that Paul be kept under guard in Herod's palace.

The Trial Before Felix

24 Five days later the high priest Ananias went down to Caesarea with some of the elders and a lawyer named Tertullus, and they brought their charges against Paul before the governor. 2When Paul was called in, Tertullus presented his case before Felix: "We have enjoyed a long period of peace under you, and your foresight has brought about reforms in this nation. 3Everywhere and in every way, most excellent Felix, we acknowledge this with profound gratitude. 4But in order not to weary you further, I would request that you be kind enough to hear us briefly.

5"We have found this man to be a troublemaker, stirring up riots among the Jews all over the world. He is a ringleader of the Nazarene sect 6and even tried to desecrate the temple; so we seized him. 8By[a] examining him yourself you will be able to learn the truth about all these charges we are bringing against him."

9The Jews joined in the accusation, asserting that these things were true.

10When the governor motioned for him to speak, Paul replied: "I know that for a number of years you have been a judge over this nation; so I gladly make my defense. 11You can easily verify that no more than twelve days ago I went up to Jerusalem to worship. 12My accusers did not find me arguing with anyone at the temple, or stirring up a crowd in the synagogues or anywhere else in the city. 13And they cannot prove to you the charges they are now making against me. 14However, I admit that I worship the God of our fathers as a follower of the Way, which they call a sect. I believe everything that agrees with the Law and that is written in the Prophets, 15and I have the same hope in God as these men, that there will be a resurrection of both the righteous and the wicked. 16So I strive always to keep my conscience clear before God and man.

17"After an absence of several years, I came to Jerusalem to bring my people gifts for the poor and to present offerings. 18I was ceremonially clean when they found me in the temple courts doing this. There was no crowd with me, nor was I involved in any disturbance. 19But there are some Jews from the province of Asia, who ought to be here before you and bring charges if they have anything against me. 20Or these who are here should state what crime they found in me when I stood before the Sanhedrin— 21unless it was this one thing I shouted as I stood in their presence: 'It is concerning the resurrection of the dead that I am on trial before you today.'"

22Then Felix, who was well acquainted with

Acts 24:15

God Will Resurrect

"I have the same hope in God as these men, that there will be a resurrection of both the righteous and the wicked."

[a] 6–8 Some manuscripts *him and wanted to judge him according to our law. 7But the commander, Lysias, came and with the use of much force snatched him from our hands 8and ordered his accusers to come before you. By*

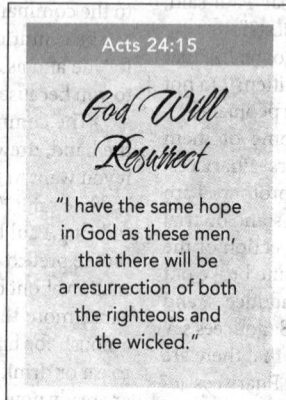

the Way, adjourned the proceedings. "When Lysias the commander comes," he said, "I will decide your case." 23He ordered the centurion to keep Paul under guard but to give him some freedom and permit his friends to take care of his needs.

24Several days later Felix came with his wife Drusilla, who was a Jewess. He sent for Paul and listened to him as he spoke about faith in Christ Jesus. 25As Paul discoursed on righteousness, self-control and the judgment to come, Felix was afraid and said, "That's enough for now! You may leave. When I find it convenient, I will send for you." 26At the same time he was hoping that Paul would offer him a bribe, so he sent for him frequently and talked with him.

27When two years had passed, Felix was succeeded by Porcius Festus, but because Felix wanted to grant a favor to the Jews, he left Paul in prison.

The Trial Before Festus

25 Three days after arriving in the province, Festus went up from Caesarea to Jerusalem, 2where the chief priests and Jewish leaders appeared before him and presented the charges against Paul. 3They urgently requested Festus, as a favor to them, to have Paul transferred to Jerusalem, for they were preparing an ambush to kill him along the way. 4Festus answered, "Paul is being held at Caesarea, and I myself am going there soon. 5Let some of your leaders come with me and press charges against the man there, if he has done anything wrong."

6After spending eight or ten days with them, he went down to Caesarea, and the next day he convened the court and ordered that Paul be brought before him. 7When Paul appeared, the Jews who had come down from Jerusalem stood around him, bringing many serious charges against him, which they could not prove.

8Then Paul made his defense: "I have done nothing wrong against the law of the Jews or against the temple or against Caesar."

9Festus, wishing to do the Jews a favor, said to Paul, "Are you willing to go up to Jerusalem and stand trial before me there on these charges?"

10Paul answered: "I am now standing before Caesar's court, where I ought to be tried. I have not done any wrong to the Jews, as you yourself know very well. 11If, however, I am guilty of doing anything deserving death, I do not refuse to die. But if the charges brought against me by these Jews are not true, no one has the right to hand me over to them. I appeal to Caesar!"

12After Festus had conferred with his council, he declared: "You have appealed to Caesar. To Caesar you will go!"

Festus Consults King Agrippa

13A few days later King Agrippa and Bernice arrived at Caesarea to pay their respects to Festus. 14Since they were spending many days there, Festus discussed Paul's case with the king. He said: "There is a man here whom Felix left as a prisoner. 15When I went to Jerusalem, the chief priests and elders of the Jews brought charges against him and asked that he be condemned.

16"I told them that it is not the Roman custom to hand over any man before he has faced his accusers and has had an opportunity to defend himself against their charges. 17When they came here with me, I did not delay the case, but convened the court the next day and ordered the man to be brought in. 18When his accusers got up to speak, they did not charge him with any of the crimes I had expected. 19Instead, they had some points of dispute with him about their own religion and about a dead man named Jesus who Paul claimed was alive. 20I was at a loss how to investigate such matters; so I asked if he would be willing to go to Jerusalem and stand trial there on these charges. 21When Paul made his appeal to be held over for the Emperor's decision, I ordered him held until I could send him to Caesar."

22Then Agrippa said to Festus, "I would like to hear this man myself."

He replied, "Tomorrow you will hear him."

Paul Before Agrippa

23The next day Agrippa and Bernice came with great pomp and entered the audience room with the high ranking officers and the leading men of the city. At the command of Festus, Paul was brought in. 24Festus said: "King Agrippa, and all who are present with us, you see this man! The whole Jewish community

has petitioned me about him in Jerusalem and
here in Caesarea, shouting that he ought not to
live any longer. 25I found he had done nothing
deserving of death, but because he made his appeal to the Emperor I decided to send him to
Rome. 26But I have nothing definite to write
to His Majesty about him. Therefore I have
brought him before all of you, and especially
before you, King Agrippa, so that as a result
of this investigation I may have something to
write. 27For I think it is unreasonable to send
on a prisoner without specifying the charges
against him."

26 Then Agrippa said to Paul, "You have
permission to speak for yourself."

So Paul motioned with his hand and began
his defense: 2"King Agrippa, I consider myself
fortunate to stand before you today as I make
my defense against all the accusations of the
Jews, 3and especially so because you are well
acquainted with all the Jewish customs and
controversies. Therefore, I beg you to listen to
me patiently.

4"The Jews all know the way I have lived
ever since I was a child, from the beginning of
my life in my own country, and also in Jerusalem. 5They have known me for a long time and
can testify, if they are willing, that according
to the strictest sect of our religion, I lived as a
Pharisee. 6And now it is because of my hope
in what God has promised our fathers that
I am on trial today. 7This is the promise our
twelve tribes are hoping to see fulfilled as they
earnestly serve God day and night. O king, it is
because of this hope that the Jews are accusing
me. 8Why should any of you consider it incredible that God raises the dead?

9"I too was convinced that I ought to do all
that was possible to oppose the name of Jesus
of Nazareth. 10And that is just what I did in Jerusalem. On the authority of the chief priests I
put many of the saints in prison, and when they
were put to death, I cast my vote against them.
11Many a time I went from one synagogue to
another to have them punished, and I tried
to force them to blaspheme. In my obsession
against them, I even went to foreign cities to
persecute them.

12"On one of these journeys I was going to
Damascus with the authority and commission
of the chief priests. 13About noon, O king, as
I was on the road, I saw a light from heaven,
brighter than the sun, blazing around me and
my companions. 14We all fell to the ground,
and I heard a voice saying to me in Aramaic,[a]
'Saul, Saul, why do you persecute me? It is hard
for you to kick against the goads.'

15"Then I asked, 'Who are you, Lord?'

"'I am Jesus, whom you are persecuting,' the
Lord replied. 16'Now get up and stand on your
feet. I have appeared to you to appoint you as
a servant and as a witness of what you have
seen of me and what I will show you. 17I will
rescue you from your own people and from
the Gentiles. I am sending you to them 18to
open their eyes and turn them from darkness
to light, and from the power of Satan to God,
so that they may receive forgiveness of sins and
a place among those who are sanctified by faith
in me.'

19"So then, King Agrippa, I was not disobedient to the vision from heaven. 20First to those
in Damascus, then to those in Jerusalem and in
all Judea, and to the Gentiles also, I preached
that they should repent and turn to God and
prove their repentance by their deeds. 21That
is why the Jews seized me in the temple courts
and tried to kill me. 22But I have had God's
help to this very day, and so I stand here and
testify to small and great alike. I am saying
nothing beyond what the prophets and Moses
said would happen— 23that the Christ[b] would
suffer and, as the first to rise from the dead,
would proclaim light to his own people and to
the Gentiles."

24At this point Festus interrupted Paul's
defense. "You are out of your mind, Paul!" he
shouted. "Your great learning is driving you insane."

25"I am not insane, most excellent Festus,"
Paul replied. "What I am saying is true and
reasonable. 26The king is familiar with these
things, and I can speak freely to him. I am convinced that none of this has escaped his notice,
because it was not done in a corner. 27King
Agrippa, do you believe the prophets? I know
you do."

28Then Agrippa said to Paul, "Do you think

[a]14 Or *Hebrew* [b]23 Or *Messiah*

The King and I

Read: Acts 26:1–32

THE KING AND I tells the story of an English widow named Anna who accepted the king of Siam's invitation to become his children's governess. Before she could meet the king, she had to learn court etiquette. One of the rules of the court was that her head always had to be lower than his. Upon meeting the king, he tested her by lowering his head closer and closer to the floor. Being used to a mere curtsy, which would have been adequate for meeting English royalty, Anna had difficulty managing her voluminous skirts and bobbing hoops as she went from curtsy to stooping to a prone position.

Paul's audience before King Agrippa defied protocol. He wore chains rather than formal attire, and he stretched out his hands rather than bowing his head. Paul didn't choose to talk about the weather or share a witty anecdote as if he were meeting royalty. If he had titled his audience before the king, it could have been called *The King of Kings and I*. Paul gave his testimony because he understood that telling a personal story could persuade both people and monarchs to follow Christ. His conversion story included three elements common to the stories of all who claim Christ as King:

(1) Encountering Christ in the present: Paul, breathing murderous threats, had bullied the disciples throughout Judea. But one day the light of Jesus' presence, "brighter than the sun" (verse 13), stopped him dead in his tracks. From then on, Paul called Jesus Lord instead of liar.

(2) Repenting of past sin: Paul confessed that he'd done many things in opposition to the name of Jesus (see verse 9), specifically, persecuting the church. Jesus took this personally, saying, "I am Jesus, whom you are persecuting" (verse 15). On that day, Paul's evil crusade ended when he turned from his sin and turned to Christ.

(3) Witnessing to others in the future: Paul was obedient to "the vision from heaven" (verse 19), declaring the gospel in Jerusalem, Judea and then to the Gentiles, "that they should repent" (verse 20). Because of Paul's obedience, the world heard Christ's message and was never to be the same.

Acts 26:14–15

"We all fell to the ground, and I heard a voice saying to me in Aramaic, 'Saul, Saul, why do you persecute me? It is hard for you to kick against the goads.' Then I asked, 'Who are you, Lord?' 'I am Jesus, whom you are persecuting,' the Lord replied."

reflection

1 Do you feel awkward or emboldened when telling others your *King of Kings and I* story?

2 How does your personal testimony include the same three elements as Paul's: encountering Christ, repenting of sin and witnessing to others?

3 What is your favorite way to address the King of kings, and what kinds of things do you discuss with him on a daily basis?

RELATED READINGS

Matthew 10:16–20;
Mark 13:9–11;
Acts 9:1–17

"The risen life is the best testimony to a risen Christ."
Unknown

Wednesday

Go to page 1364 for your next devotional reading.

that in such a short time you can persuade me to be a Christian?"

29 Paul replied, "Short time or long—I pray God that not only you but all who are listening to me today may become what I am, except for these chains."

30 The king rose, and with him the governor and Bernice and those sitting with them. 31 They left the room, and while talking with one another, they said, "This man is not doing anything that deserves death or imprisonment."

32 Agrippa said to Festus, "This man could have been set free if he had not appealed to Caesar."

Paul Sails for Rome

27 When it was decided that we would sail for Italy, Paul and some other prisoners were handed over to a centurion named Julius, who belonged to the Imperial Regiment. 2 We boarded a ship from Adramyttium about to sail for ports along the coast of the province of Asia, and we put out to sea. Aristarchus, a Macedonian from Thessalonica, was with us.

3 The next day we landed at Sidon; and Julius, in kindness to Paul, allowed him to go to his friends so they might provide for his needs. 4 From there we put out to sea again and passed to the lee of Cyprus because the winds were against us. 5 When we had sailed across the open sea off the coast of Cilicia and Pamphylia, we landed at Myra in Lycia. 6 There the centurion found an Alexandrian ship sailing for Italy and put us on board. 7 We made slow headway for many days and had difficulty arriving off Cnidus. When the wind did not allow us to hold our course, we sailed to the lee of Crete, opposite Salmone. 8 We moved along the coast with difficulty and came to a place called Fair Havens, near the town of Lasea.

9 Much time had been lost, and sailing had already become dangerous because by now it was after the Fast.[a] So Paul warned them, 10 "Men, I can see that our voyage is going to be disastrous and bring great loss to ship and cargo, and to our own lives also." 11 But the centurion, instead of listening to what Paul said, followed the advice of the pilot and of the owner of the ship. 12 Since the harbor was unsuitable to winter in, the majority decided that we should sail on, hoping to reach Phoenix and winter there. This was a harbor in Crete, facing both southwest and northwest.

The Storm

13 When a gentle south wind began to blow, they thought they had obtained what they wanted; so they weighed anchor and sailed along the shore of Crete. 14 Before very long, a wind of hurricane force, called the "northeaster," swept down from the island. 15 The ship was caught by the storm and could not head into the wind; so we gave way to it and were driven along. 16 As we passed to the lee of a small island called Cauda, we were hardly able to make the lifeboat secure. 17 When the men had hoisted it aboard, they passed ropes under the ship itself to hold it together. Fearing that they would run aground on the sandbars of Syrtis, they lowered the sea anchor and let the ship be driven along. 18 We took such a violent battering from the storm that the next day they began to throw the cargo overboard. 19 On the third day, they threw the ship's tackle overboard with their own hands. 20 When neither sun nor stars appeared for many days and the storm continued raging, we finally gave up all hope of being saved.

21 After the men had gone a long time without food, Paul stood up before them and said: "Men, you should have taken my advice not to sail from Crete; then you would have spared yourselves this damage and loss. 22 But now I urge you to keep up your courage, because not one of you will be lost; only the ship will be destroyed. 23 Last night an angel of the God whose I am and whom I serve stood beside me 24 and said, 'Do not be afraid, Paul. You must stand trial before Caesar; and God has graciously given you the lives of all who sail with you.' 25 So keep up your courage, men, for I have faith in God that it will happen just as he told me. 26 Nevertheless, we must run aground on some island."

The Shipwreck

27 On the fourteenth night we were still being driven across the Adriatic[b] Sea, when

[a] 9 That is, the Day of Atonement (Yom Kippur) [b] 27 In ancient times the name referred to an area extending well south of Italy.

about midnight the sailors sensed they were
approaching land. 28 They took soundings
and found that the water was a hundred and
twenty feet[a] deep. A short time later they
took soundings again and found it was ninety
feet[b] deep. 29 Fearing that we would be dashed
against the rocks, they dropped four anchors
from the stern and prayed for daylight. 30 In
an attempt to escape from the ship, the sailors
let the lifeboat down into the sea, pretending
they were going to lower some anchors from
the bow. 31 Then Paul said to the centurion and
the soldiers, "Unless these men stay with the
ship, you cannot be saved." 32 So the soldiers
cut the ropes that held the lifeboat and let it
fall away.

33 Just before dawn Paul urged them all to
eat. "For the last fourteen days," he said, "you
have been in constant suspense and have gone
without food—you haven't eaten anything.
34 Now I urge you to take some food. You
need it to survive. Not one of you will lose a
single hair from his head." 35 After he said this,
he took some bread and gave thanks to God
in front of them all. Then he broke it and began to eat. 36 They were all encouraged and ate
some food themselves. 37 Altogether there were
276 of us on board. 38 When they had eaten as
much as they wanted, they lightened the ship
by throwing the grain into the sea.

39 When daylight came, they did not recognize the land, but they saw a bay with a
sandy beach, where they decided to run the
ship aground if they could. 40 Cutting loose
the anchors, they left them in the sea and at
the same time untied the ropes that held the
rudders. Then they hoisted the foresail to the
wind and made for the beach. 41 But the ship
struck a sandbar and ran aground. The bow
stuck fast and would not move, and the stern
was broken to pieces by the pounding of the
surf.

42 The soldiers planned to kill the prisoners
to prevent any of them from swimming away
and escaping. 43 But the centurion wanted to
spare Paul's life and kept them from carrying
out their plan. He ordered those who could
swim to jump overboard first and get to land.
44 The rest were to get there on planks or on
pieces of the ship. In this way everyone reached
land in safety.

Ashore on Malta

28 Once safely on shore, we found out
that the island was called Malta. 2 The
islanders showed us unusual kindness. They
built a fire and welcomed us all because it
was raining and cold. 3 Paul gathered a pile
of brushwood and, as he put it on the fire, a
viper, driven out by the heat, fastened itself on
his hand. 4 When the islanders saw the snake
hanging from his hand, they said to each other,
"This man must be a murderer; for though he
escaped from the sea, Justice has not allowed
him to live." 5 But Paul shook the snake off into
the fire and suffered no ill effects. 6 The people
expected him to swell up or suddenly fall dead,
but after waiting a long time and seeing nothing unusual happen to him, they changed their
minds and said he was a god.

7 There was an estate nearby that belonged
to Publius, the chief official of the island. He
welcomed us to his home and for three days
entertained us hospitably. 8 His father was sick
in bed, suffering from fever and dysentery. Paul
went in to see him and, after prayer, placed his
hands on him and healed him. 9 When this had
happened, the rest of the sick on the island came
and were cured. 10 They honored us in many
ways and when we were ready to sail, they furnished us with the supplies we needed.

Arrival at Rome

11 After three months we put out to sea in
a ship that had wintered in the island. It was
an Alexandrian ship with the figurehead of the
twin gods Castor and Pollux. 12 We put in at
Syracuse and stayed there three days. 13 From
there we set sail and arrived at Rhegium. The
next day the south wind came up, and on the
following day we reached Puteoli. 14 There we
found some brothers who invited us to spend
a week with them. And so we came to Rome.
15 The brothers there had heard that we were
coming, and they traveled as far as the Forum
of Appius and the Three Taverns to meet us. At
the sight of these men Paul thanked God and
was encouraged. 16 When we got to Rome, Paul

[a] 28 Greek *twenty orguias* (about 37 meters) [b] 28 Greek *fifteen orguias* (about 27 meters)

The Power of Pain

Read: Acts 28:17–31

SUFFERING AND PAIN can lead to powerful ministry. Amy Carmichael established a home to rescue children from temple prostitution in India. When she fell ill and was confined to her bed, she wrote inspirational books and poems that continue to encourage generations of readers. Here's a beautiful example:

Our Father knows what's best for us, so why should we
complain?
We always want the sunshine, but he knows there must be
rain.
We love the sound of laughter and the merriment of cheer,
But our hearts would lose their tenderness if we never shed
a tear.
For growing trees are strengthened when they withstand
the storm,
And the sharp cut of the chisel gives the diamond grace
and form.
God never hurts us needlessly, and he never wastes our pain,
For every loss he sends to us is followed by rich gain.
And when we count the blessings that God so freely sent,
We'll find no cause for murmuring, and no time to lament.
For our Father loves his children, and to him all things are
plain,
So he never sends us pleasure when the soul's deep need
is pain.
So whenever we are troubled, and when everything goes
wrong,
We know God's working in our hearts, to make our spirit
strong.

When he was in chains, Paul preached to the Roman Jews and many of them believed in Jesus. He also wrote many letters, including the joy-filled letter to the Philippians, from a jail cell.

We all have experienced suffering. What is your unique story? No matter how universal the trauma, your situation and your response are personal to you. Others can learn from what you have gone through. Ask God for opportunities to share what you've learned about God's grace through your experience with suffering. Then stand back and be amazed at how God can use you to touch other people's lives.

Acts 28:30–31

For two whole years Paul stayed there in his own rented house and welcomed all who came to see him. Boldly and without hindrance he preached the kingdom of God and taught about the Lord Jesus Christ.

reflection

1 How has suffering drawn you closer to God?

2 Has someone else's suffering impacted your life in a positive way?

3 How willing are you to allow God to use your pain for his glory? Pray now for willingness.

RELATED READINGS

Exodus 18:7–11; 2 Corinthians 4:7–18; 12:7–10

Go to page 1368 for your next devotional reading.

was allowed to live by himself, with a soldier to
guard him.

Paul Preaches at Rome Under Guard

17 Three days later he called together the leaders of the Jews. When they had assembled, Paul
said to them: "My brothers, although I have
done nothing against our people or against the
customs of our ancestors, I was arrested in Jerusalem and handed over to the Romans. 18 They
examined me and wanted to release me, because I was not guilty of any crime deserving
death. 19 But when the Jews objected, I was compelled to appeal to Caesar—not that I had any
charge to bring against my own people. 20 For
this reason I have asked to see you and talk
with you. It is because of the hope of Israel that
I am bound with this chain."

21 They replied, "We have
not received any letters from Judea concerning you, and none
of the brothers who have come
from there has reported or said
anything bad about you. 22 But
we want to hear what your
views are, for we know that
people everywhere are talking
against this sect."

23 They arranged to meet
Paul on a certain day, and came
in even larger numbers to the
place where he was staying.
From morning till evening he
explained and declared to them the kingdom
of God and tried to convince them about Jesus
from the Law of Moses and from the Prophets.
24 Some were convinced by what he said, but
others would not believe. 25 They disagreed
among themselves and began to leave after
Paul had made this final statement: "The Holy
Spirit spoke the truth to your forefathers when
he said through Isaiah the prophet:

26 " 'Go to this people and say,
"You will be ever hearing but never
understanding;
you will be ever seeing but never
perceiving."
27 For this people's heart has become
calloused;
they hardly hear with their ears,
and they have closed their eyes.
Otherwise they might see
with their eyes,
hear with their ears,
understand with their
hearts
and turn, and I would heal
them.'[a]

28 "Therefore I want you to
know that God's salvation has
been sent to the Gentiles, and
they will listen!"[b]

30 For two whole years Paul
stayed there in his own rented
house and welcomed all who
came to see him. 31 Boldly and
without hindrance he preached
the kingdom of God and taught about the Lord
Jesus Christ.

> **Acts 28:28**
>
> *God Extends Salvation*
>
> "Therefore I want you to know that God's salvation has been sent to the Gentiles, and they will listen!"

[a]27 Isaiah 6:9,10 [b]28 Some manuscripts *listen!" 29 After he said this, the Jews left, arguing vigorously among themselves.*

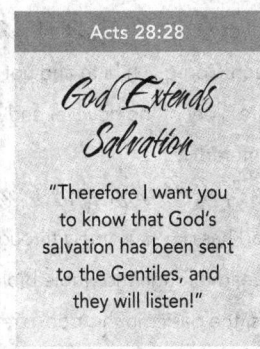

Romans

Author:
The apostle Paul.

Audience:
Followers of Jesus; originally written to Christians in Rome.

Date:
About A.D. 57.

Setting:
Paul wrote from Corinth regarding his pending visit to Rome via Jerusalem.

Verse to Remember:
"I am not ashamed of the gospel, because it is the power of God for the salvation of everyone who believes: first for the Jew, then for the Gentile." (1:16)

The Christians in Rome had not yet met Paul, and he was excited about meeting them soon. But before he went to see them, he sent them this letter, perhaps his most straightforward theological essay in print. Starting with the sinfulness of humans and the wrath of God against sin, he moves on to tell of *God's grace in salvation,* which comes to us through God-given faith and not our works. He then tells of the future glory of the believer and gives some principles for God-centered living.

This is the book to read and study to understand what God has given us freely through Christ. Whether you've not yet read through the whole Bible or you've studied it for years, the basics in this book are worth dwelling on.

God's gift of salvation is extraordinary. And so is the new life we have begun.

1 Paul, a servant of Christ Jesus, called to
be an apostle and set apart for the gospel
of God— 2 the gospel he promised beforehand
through his prophets in the Holy Scriptures 3 regarding his Son, who as to his human nature
was a descendant of David, 4 and who through
the Spirit[a] of holiness was declared with power
to be the Son of God[b] by his resurrection from
the dead: Jesus Christ our Lord. 5 Through him
and for his name's sake, we received grace and
apostleship to call people from among all the
Gentiles to the obedience that comes from

[a] 4 Or *who as to his spirit* [b] 4 Or *was appointed to be the Son of God with power*

faith. 6And you also are among those who are
called to belong to Jesus Christ.

7To all in Rome who are loved by God and
called to be saints:

Grace and peace to you from God our Father and from the Lord Jesus Christ.

Paul's Longing to Visit Rome

8First, I thank my God through Jesus
Christ for all of you, because your faith is being reported all over the world. 9God, whom
I serve with my whole heart in preaching the
gospel of his Son, is my witness how constantly
I remember you 10in my prayers at all times;
and I pray that now at last by God's will the way
may be opened for me to come to you.

11I long to see you so that I may impart to you
some spiritual gift to make you strong— 12that
is, that you and I may be mutually encouraged
by each other's faith. 13I do not want you to be
unaware, brothers, that I planned many times
to come to you (but have been prevented from
doing so until now) in order that I might have
a harvest among you, just as I have had among
the other Gentiles.

14I am obligated both to Greeks and non-
Greeks, both to the wise and the foolish. 15That
is why I am so eager to preach the gospel also to
you who are at Rome.

16I am not ashamed of the gospel, because
it is the power of God for the salvation of everyone who believes: first for the Jew, then for
the Gentile. 17For in the gospel a righteousness
from God is revealed, a righteousness that is by
faith from first to last,[a] just as it is written: "The
righteous will live by faith."[b]

God's Wrath Against Mankind

18The wrath of God is being revealed from
heaven against all the godlessness and wickedness of men who suppress the truth by their
wickedness, 19since what may be known about
God is plain to them, because God has made it
plain to them. 20For since the creation of the
world God's invisible qualities—his eternal
power and divine nature—have been clearly
seen, being understood from what has been
made, so that men are without excuse.

21For although they knew God, they neither glorified him as God nor gave thanks to
him, but their thinking became futile and their
foolish hearts were darkened. 22Although they
claimed to be wise, they became fools 23and
exchanged the glory of the immortal God for
images made to look like mortal man and birds
and animals and reptiles.

24Therefore God gave them over in the sinful desires of their hearts to sexual impurity
for the degrading of their bodies with one
another. 25They exchanged the truth of God
for a lie, and worshiped and served created
things rather than the Creator—who is forever
praised. Amen.

26Because of this, God gave them over to
shameful lusts. Even their women exchanged
natural relations for unnatural ones. 27In the
same way the men also abandoned natural relations with women and were inflamed with lust
for one another. Men committed indecent acts
with other men, and received in themselves the
due penalty for their perversion.

28Furthermore, since they did not think it
worthwhile to retain the knowledge of God,
he gave them over to a depraved mind, to do
what ought not to be done. 29They have become filled with every kind of wickedness, evil,
greed and depravity. They are full of envy, murder, strife, deceit and malice. They are gossips,
30slanderers, God-haters, insolent, arrogant
and boastful; they invent ways of doing evil;
they disobey their parents; 31they are senseless, faithless, heartless, ruthless. 32Although
they know God's righteous decree that those
who do such things deserve death, they not
only continue to do these very things but also
approve of those who practice them.

God's Righteous Judgment

2 You, therefore, have no excuse, you who
pass judgment on someone else, for at
whatever point you judge the other, you are
condemning yourself, because you who pass
judgment do the same things. 2Now we know
that God's judgment against those who do such
things is based on truth. 3So when you, a mere
man, pass judgment on them and yet do the
same things, do you think you will escape God's
judgment? 4Or do you show contempt for the
riches of his kindness, tolerance and patience,

[a]17 Or *is from faith to faith* [b]17 Hab. 2:4

Not Ashamed

Romans 1:16

I am not ashamed of the gospel, because it is the power of God for the salvation of everyone who believes: first for the Jew, then for the Gentile.

Read: Romans 1:8–17

WHAT CAUSED YOUR CHEEKS to blush red in elementary school? Being picked last for recess games? Not knowing the answer when called on? Now think about your adolescent days. Were you embarrassed if a cute boy looked your way—or if he didn't? If someone pointed out that your clothes weren't like those of the other girls? Did you cower in humiliation if you were forced to give a speech or forgot your lines in the school play?

Today we might be ashamed if our children get in trouble or if we fail to keep our temper. We may feel ashamed if we neglect prayer or realize we haven't done much for anyone but ourselves for a long while. Not to worry, God has freed us to walk in this world unashamed. In Christ there is forgiveness and a new start. Later in the book of Romans Paul proclaimed, "There is now no condemnation for those who are in Christ Jesus" (Romans 8:1). In fact, there is only one real reason to be ashamed: if we're ashamed of the gospel message. Paul made sure his readers knew that he was not ashamed of the gospel of Christ. Indeed, he was eager to tell everyone about it—Greeks and non-Greeks, intellectuals and the uneducated, the wise and the foolish.

Maybe you're embarrassed to let people know you are a Christian. You think it might not be accepted in more "sophisticated" circles. You worry that you'll be labeled a "Jesus Freak," a "religious fanatic" or someone who needs a "crutch."

Maybe you don't share your faith because you think your credentials aren't good enough. You're afraid that you don't have the right education or that you haven't memorized enough Scripture or that you haven't been a believer long enough. But think of the many people who were saved in the Bible who immediately went and told others about their encounter with Christ. The key is that they told *their* story—and you know *your* story backward and forward.

If you're not ashamed of Jesus, the best way to overcome fear or speaking out is to "just do it." Keep it simple, keep it honest, but talk to your neighbors, tell your friends and family, and share the story about how Jesus redeemed you. The more you speak, the more your confidence will grow . . . and the more God will be glorified.

reflection

1 Would you describe yourself as easily embarrassed, extremely bold or somewhere in-between?

2 Are you ever in situations in which you don't want to seem "too Christian"? Who are you afraid of? What are you afraid of?

3 When were you ever embarrassed to share your faith? Describe how you felt. Ask God to help you be bold and unafraid to tell others about the gospel.

RELATED READINGS

Matthew 10:32–33; Mark 8:34–38; 2 Timothy 1:8–12

"The Christian message is for those who have done their best and failed!"

Unknown

Go to page 1370 for your next devotional reading.

not realizing that God's kindness leads you toward repentance?

5 But because of your stubbornness and your unrepentant heart, you are storing up wrath against yourself for the day of God's wrath, when his righteous judgment will be revealed. 6 God "will give to each person according to what he has done."[a] 7 To those who by persistence in doing good seek glory, honor and immortality, he will give eternal life. 8 But for those who are self-seeking and who reject the truth and follow evil, there will be wrath and anger. 9 There will be trouble and distress for every human being who does evil: first for the Jew, then for the Gentile; 10 but glory, honor and peace for everyone who does good: first for the Jew, then for the Gentile. 11 For God does not show favoritism.

12 All who sin apart from the law will also perish apart from the law, and all who sin under the law will be judged by the law. 13 For it is not those who hear the law who are righteous in God's sight, but it is those who obey the law who will be declared righteous. 14 (Indeed, when Gentiles, who do not have the law, do by nature things required by the law, they are a law for themselves, even though they do not have the law, 15 since they show that the requirements of the law are written on their hearts, their consciences also bearing witness, and their thoughts now accusing, now even defending them.) 16 This will take place on the day when God will judge men's secrets through Jesus Christ, as my gospel declares.

The Jews and the Law

17 Now you, if you call yourself a Jew; if you rely on the law and brag about your relationship to God; 18 if you know his will and approve of what is superior because you are instructed by the law; 19 if you are convinced that you are a guide for the blind, a light for those who are in the dark, 20 an instructor of the foolish, a teacher of infants, because you have in the law the embodiment of knowledge and truth— 21 you, then, who teach others, do you not teach yourself? You who preach against stealing, do you steal? 22 You who say that people should not commit adultery, do you commit adultery? You who abhor idols, do you rob temples? 23 You who brag about the law, do you dishonor God by breaking the law? 24 As it is written: "God's name is blasphemed among the Gentiles because of you."[b]

25 Circumcision has value if you observe the law, but if you break the law, you have become as though you had not been circumcised. 26 If those who are not circumcised keep the law's requirements, will they not be regarded as though they were circumcised? 27 The one who is not circumcised physically and yet obeys the law will condemn you who, even though you have the[c] written code and circumcision, are a lawbreaker.

28 A man is not a Jew if he is only one outwardly, nor is circumcision merely outward and physical. 29 No, a man is a Jew if he is one inwardly; and circumcision is circumcision of the heart, by the Spirit, not by the written code. Such a man's praise is not from men, but from God.

God's Faithfulness

3 What advantage, then, is there in being a Jew, or what value is there in circumcision? 2 Much in every way! First of all, they have been entrusted with the very words of God.

3 What if some did not have faith? Will their lack of faith nullify God's faithfulness? 4 Not at all! Let God be true, and every man a liar. As it is written:

> "So that you may be proved right when you speak
> and prevail when you judge."[d]

5 But if our unrighteousness brings out God's righteousness more clearly, what shall we say? That God is unjust in bringing his wrath on us? (I am using a human argument.) 6 Certainly not! If that were so, how could God judge the world? 7 Someone might argue, "If my falsehood enhances God's truthfulness and so increases his glory, why am I still condemned as a sinner?" 8 Why not say—as we are being slanderously reported as saying and as some claim that we say—"Let us do evil that good may result"? Their condemnation is deserved.

[a] 6 Psalm 62:12; Prov. 24:12 [b] 24 Isaiah 52:5; Ezek. 36:22 [c] 27 Or *who, by means of a* [d] 4 Psalm 51:4

Indisputable

DORCAS (TABITHA)

Peter sent them all out of the room; then he got down on his knees and prayed. Turning toward the dead woman, he said, "Tabitha, get up."

Acts 9:40

ASSIGNED READING:

Acts 9:32–42

"SHE WAS DEAD, I tell you." Several heads in the crowd of widows nodded.

"All of you were there and saw this with your own eyes?" asked the incredulous stranger. She was new in town and wasn't entirely convinced that these ladies weren't pulling her leg.

"Yes. I was there."

"Me too." The other voices in the crowd continued peppering their assurances.

One old woman stepped forward, clutching her robes so she would not step on the hem. "I've seen plenty of dead people in my day," she said with immitigable authority. "And I am certain she was *dead*."

Dorcas (the previously deceased and, thus, central figure in the story), was a staple of society and a well-known person in the community. Her generosity toward the poor was legendary, and her kindness seemed to know no bounds. She sewed robes and other clothing for widows in Joppa, staying up late into the evening until her fingers nearly blistered. Her death was a considerable loss to the community. No one could replace her. Not easily, anyway.

This is why it was such a miracle when Peter prayed for her and God brought her back to life. Not only was a dead woman now alive, but the dead woman was a treasure like Dorcas. Having her back in the world was a double delight.

But back to the doubting newcomer…

It was a fanciful story, of course. It's not every day that one hears about someone coming back from the dead. So, the doubters were not necessarily unexpected. Besides, the disciples definitely attracted their share of controversy. One never knew what was true nowadays. Rumors took flight in the town as often as the birds.

Only something irrefutable could prove their story beyond a doubt. And, as it turned out, while they were still talking, the irrefutable walked up and introduced herself to the newcomer.

"Hello and welcome," she said kindly. "My name is Dorcas. And you are?"

—Prayer—

I pray that I can be a witness to those who doubt in your power, Lord. I want to glorify your name.

Weekend

Go to page 1376 for your next devotional reading.

No One Is Righteous

9What shall we conclude then? Are we any
better[a]? Not at all! We have already made the
charge that Jews and Gentiles alike are all under sin. 10As it is written:

"There is no one righteous, not even one;
11 there is no one who understands,
no one who seeks God.
12 All have turned away,
they have together become worthless;
there is no one who does good,
not even one."[b]
13 "Their throats are open graves;
their tongues practice deceit."[c]
"The poison of vipers is on their lips."[d]
14 "Their mouths are full of cursing and
bitterness."[e]
15 "Their feet are swift to shed blood;
16 ruin and misery mark their ways,
17 and the way of peace they do not know."[f]
18 "There is no fear of God before their
eyes."[g]

19Now we know that whatever the law says,
it says to those who are under the law, so that
every mouth may be silenced and the whole
world held accountable to God. 20Therefore
no one will be declared righteous in his sight
by observing the law; rather, through the law
we become conscious of sin.

Righteousness Through Faith

21But now a righteousness
from God, apart from law, has
been made known, to which
the Law and the Prophets
testify. 22This righteousness
from God comes through faith
in Jesus Christ to all who believe. There is no difference,
23for all have sinned and fall
short of the glory of God, 24and
are justified freely by his grace
through the redemption that
came by Christ Jesus. 25God
presented him as a sacrifice of
atonement,[h] through faith in
his blood. He did this to demonstrate his justice, because in his forbearance he had left the
sins committed beforehand unpunished— 26he
did it to demonstrate his justice at the present
time, so as to be just and the one who justifies
those who have faith in Jesus.

27Where, then, is boasting? It is excluded.
On what principle? On that of observing the
law? No, but on that of faith. 28For we maintain
that a man is justified by faith apart from observing the law. 29Is God the God of Jews only?
Is he not the God of Gentiles too? Yes, of Gentiles too, 30since there is only one God, who
will justify the circumcised by faith and the uncircumcised through that same faith. 31Do we,
then, nullify the law by this faith? Not at all!
Rather, we uphold the law.

> **Romans 3:22**
>
> *God Gives Righteousness*
>
> This righteousness from God comes through faith in Jesus Christ to all who believe.

Abraham Justified by Faith

4 What then shall we say that Abraham,
our forefather, discovered in this matter?
2If, in fact, Abraham was justified by works,
he had something to boast about—but not before God. 3What does the Scripture say? "Abraham believed God, and it was credited to him
as righteousness."[i]

4Now when a man works, his wages are not
credited to him as a gift, but as an obligation.
5However, to the man who does not work but
trusts God who justifies the wicked, his faith
is credited as righteousness. 6David says the
same thing when he speaks of the blessedness
of the man to whom God credits righteousness
apart from works:

7 "Blessed are they
whose transgressions are
forgiven,
whose sins are covered.
8 Blessed is the man
whose sin the Lord will
never count against
him."[j]

9Is this blessedness only for
the circumcised, or also for
the uncircumcised? We have
been saying that Abraham's
faith was credited to him as
righteousness. 10Under what
circumstances was it credited? Was it after he
was circumcised, or before? It was not after, but

[a]9 Or *worse* [b]12 Psalms 14:1–3; 53:1–3; Eccles. 7:20 [c]13 Psalm 5:9 [d]13 Psalm 140:3 [e]14 Psalm 10:7 [f]17 Isaiah 59:7,8
[g]18 Psalm 36:1 [h]25 Or *as the one who would turn aside his wrath, taking away sin* [i]3 Gen. 15:6; also in verse 22 [j]8 Psalm 32:1,2

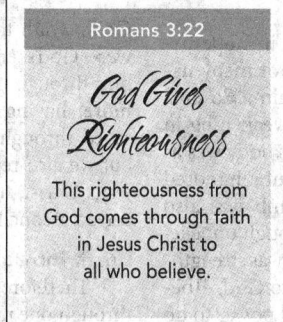

before! 11 And he received the sign of circumcision, a seal of the righteousness that he had by
faith while he was still uncircumcised. So then,
he is the father of all who believe but have not
been circumcised, in order that righteousness
might be credited to them. 12 And he is also the
father of the circumcised who not only are circumcised but who also walk in the footsteps of
the faith that our father Abraham had before he
was circumcised.

13 It was not through law that Abraham
and his offspring received the promise that he
would be heir of the world, but through the righteousness that comes by faith. 14 For if those
who live by law are heirs, faith has no value and
the promise is worthless, 15 be-
cause law brings wrath. And
where there is no law there is
no transgression.

16 Therefore, the promise
comes by faith, so that it may
be by grace and may be guaranteed to all Abraham's offspring—not only to those who
are of the law but also to those
who are of the faith of Abraham. He is the father of us all.
17 As it is written: "I have made
you a father of many nations."[a]
He is our father in the sight of
God, in whom he believed—
the God who gives life to the
dead and calls things that are
not as though they were.

18 Against all hope, Abraham in hope believed and so became the father of many nations, just as it had been said to him, "So shall
your offspring be."[b] 19 Without weakening in
his faith, he faced the fact that his body was as
good as dead—since he was about a hundred
years old—and that Sarah's womb was also
dead. 20 Yet he did not waver through unbelief
regarding the promise of God, but was strengthened in his faith and gave glory to God, 21 being fully persuaded that God had power to do
what he had promised. 22 This is why "it was
credited to him as righteousness." 23 The words
"it was credited to him" were written not for
him alone, 24 but also for us, to whom God will
credit righteousness—for us who believe in
him who raised Jesus our Lord from the dead.
25 He was delivered over to death for our sins
and was raised to life for our justification.

Peace and Joy

5 Therefore, since we have been justified
through faith, we[c] have peace with God
through our Lord Jesus Christ, 2 through
whom we have gained access by faith into this
grace in which we now stand. And we[c] rejoice
in the hope of the glory of God. 3 Not only so,
but we[c] also rejoice in our sufferings, because
we know that suffering produces perseverance;
4 perseverance, character; and character, hope.
5 And hope does not disappoint
us, because God has poured
out his love into our hearts by
the Holy Spirit, whom he has
given us.

6 You see, at just the right
time, when we were still powerless, Christ died for the
ungodly. 7 Very rarely will anyone die for a righteous man,
though for a good man someone might possibly dare to die.
8 But God demonstrates his
own love for us in this: While
we were still sinners, Christ
died for us.

9 Since we have now been justified by his blood, how much
more shall we be saved from
God's wrath through him! 10 For if, when we
were God's enemies, we were reconciled to
him through the death of his Son, how much
more, having been reconciled, shall we be
saved through his life! 11 Not only is this so,
but we also rejoice in God through our Lord
Jesus Christ, through whom we have now received reconciliation.

Death Through Adam, Life Through Christ

12 Therefore, just as sin entered the world
through one man, and death through sin, and
in this way death came to all men, because all
sinned— 13 for before the law was given, sin
was in the world. But sin is not taken into account when there is no law. 14 Nevertheless,

> **Romans 5:8**
>
> *God Reveals His Love in Christ*
>
> But God demonstrates his own love for us in this: While we were still sinners, Christ died for us.

[a] 17 Gen. 17:5 [b] 18 Gen. 15:5 [c] 1,2,3 Or *let us*

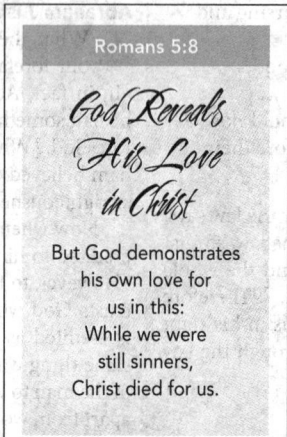

death reigned from the time of Adam to the time of Moses, even over those who did not sin by breaking a command, as did Adam, who was a pattern of the one to come.

15But the gift is not like the trespass. For if the many died by the trespass of the one man, how much more did God's grace and the gift that came by the grace of the one man, Jesus Christ, overflow to the many! 16Again, the gift of God is not like the result of the one man's sin: The judgment followed one sin and brought condemnation, but the gift followed many trespasses and brought justification. 17For if, by the trespass of the one man, death reigned through that one man, how much more will those who receive God's abundant provision of grace and of the gift of righteousness reign in life through the one man, Jesus Christ.

18Consequently, just as the result of one trespass was condemnation for all men, so also the result of one act of righteousness was justification that brings life for all men. 19For just as through the disobedience of the one man the many were made sinners, so also through the obedience of the one man the many will be made righteous.

20The law was added so that the trespass might increase. But where sin increased, grace increased all the more, 21so that, just as sin reigned in death, so also grace might reign through righteousness to bring eternal life through Jesus Christ our Lord.

Dead to Sin, Alive in Christ

6 What shall we say, then? Shall we go on sinning so that grace may increase? 2By no means! We died to sin; how can we live in it any longer? 3Or don't you know that all of us who were baptized into Christ Jesus were baptized into his death? 4We were therefore buried with him through baptism into death in order that, just as Christ was raised from the dead through the glory of the Father, we too may live a new life.

5If we have been united with him like this in his death, we will certainly also be united with him in his resurrection. 6For we know that our old self was crucified with him so that the body of sin might be done away with,[a] that we should no longer be slaves to sin— 7because anyone who has died has been freed from sin.

> **Romans 6:11**
>
> *God Gives Our Spirits Life*
>
> In the same way, count yourselves dead to sin but alive to God in Christ Jesus.

8Now if we died with Christ, we believe that we will also live with him. 9For we know that since Christ was raised from the dead, he cannot die again; death no longer has mastery over him. 10The death he died, he died to sin once for all; but the life he lives, he lives to God.

11In the same way, count yourselves dead to sin but alive to God in Christ Jesus. 12Therefore do not let sin reign in your mortal body so that you obey its evil desires. 13Do not offer the parts of your body to sin, as instruments of wickedness, but rather offer yourselves to God, as those who have been brought from death to life; and offer the parts of your body to him as instruments of righteousness. 14For sin shall not be your master, because you are not under law, but under grace.

Slaves to Righteousness

15What then? Shall we sin because we are not under law but under grace? By no means! 16Don't you know that when you offer yourselves to someone to obey him as slaves, you are slaves to the one whom you obey—whether you are slaves to sin, which leads to death, or to obedience, which leads to righteousness? 17But thanks be to God that, though you used to be slaves to sin, you wholeheartedly obeyed the form of teaching to which you were entrusted. 18You have been set free from sin and have become slaves to righteousness.

19I put this in human terms because you are weak in your natural selves. Just as you used to offer the parts of your body in slavery to impurity and to ever-increasing wickedness, so now offer them in slavery to righteousness leading to holiness. 20When you were slaves to sin, you were free from the control of righteousness.

[a]6 Or *be rendered powerless*

21What benefit did you reap at that time from
the things you are now ashamed of? Those
things result in death! 22But now that you have
been set free from sin and have become slaves
to God, the benefit you reap leads to holiness,
and the result is eternal life. 23For the wages of
sin is death, but the gift of God is eternal life in[a]
Christ Jesus our Lord.

An Illustration From Marriage

7 Do you not know, brothers—for I am
speaking to men who know the law—that
the law has authority over a man only as long
as he lives? 2For example, by law a married
woman is bound to her husband as long as
he is alive, but if her husband dies, she is released from the law of marriage. 3So then, if
she marries another man while her husband is
still alive, she is called an adulteress. But if her
husband dies, she is released from that law and
is not an adulteress, even though she marries
another man.

4So, my brothers, you also died to the law
through the body of Christ, that you might belong to another, to him who was raised from
the dead, in order that we might bear fruit to
God. 5For when we were controlled by the sinful nature,[b] the sinful passions aroused by the
law were at work in our bodies, so that we bore
fruit for death. 6But now, by dying to what once
bound us, we have been released from the law
so that we serve in the new way of the Spirit,
and not in the old way of the written code.

Struggling With Sin

7What shall we say, then? Is the law sin? Certainly not! Indeed I would not have known
what sin was except through the law. For I
would not have known what coveting really was
if the law had not said, "Do not covet."[c] 8But
sin, seizing the opportunity afforded by the
commandment, produced in me every kind of
covetous desire. For apart from law, sin is dead.
9Once I was alive apart from law; but when the
commandment came, sin sprang to life and I
died. 10I found that the very commandment
that was intended to bring life actually brought
death. 11For sin, seizing the opportunity
afforded by the commandment, deceived me,
and through the commandment put me to
death. 12So then, the law is holy, and the commandment is holy, righteous and good.

13Did that which is good, then, become
death to me? By no means! But in order that
sin might be recognized as sin, it produced
death in me through what was good, so that
through the commandment sin might become
utterly sinful.

14We know that the law is spiritual; but I am
unspiritual, sold as a slave to sin. 15I do not understand what I do. For what I want to do I do
not do, but what I hate I do. 16And if I do what
I do not want to do, I agree that the law is good.
17As it is, it is no longer I myself who do it,
but it is sin living in me. 18I know that nothing
good lives in me, that is, in my sinful nature.[d]
For I have the desire to do what is good, but I
cannot carry it out. 19For what I do is not the
good I want to do; no, the evil I do not want to
do—this I keep on doing. 20Now if I do what
I do not want to do, it is no longer I who do it,
but it is sin living in me that does it.

21So I find this law at work: When I want to
do good, evil is right there with me. 22For in
my inner being I delight in God's law; 23but I
see another law at work in the members of my
body, waging war against the law of my mind
and making me a prisoner of the law of sin at
work within my members. 24What a wretched
man I am! Who will rescue me from this body
of death? 25Thanks be to God—through Jesus
Christ our Lord!

So then, I myself in my mind am a slave to
God's law, but in the sinful nature a slave to the
law of sin.

Life Through the Spirit

8 Therefore, there is now no condemnation for those who are in Christ Jesus,[e]
2because through Christ Jesus the law of the
Spirit of life set me free from the law of sin and
death. 3For what the law was powerless to do
in that it was weakened by the sinful nature,[f]
God did by sending his own Son in the likeness
of sinful man to be a sin offering.[g] And so he
condemned sin in sinful man,[h] 4in order that
the righteous requirements of the law might be

[a]23 Or *through* [b]5 Or *the flesh*; also in verse 25 [c]7 Exodus 20:17; Deut. 5:21 [d]18 Or *my flesh* [e]1 Some later manuscripts *Jesus, who do not live according to the sinful nature but according to the Spirit,* [f]3 Or *the flesh*; also in verses 4, 5, 8, 9, 12 and 13 [g]3 Or *man, for sin* [h]3 Or *in the flesh*

fully met in us, who do not live according to
the sinful nature but according to the Spirit.
5 Those who live according to the sinful nature have their minds set on what that nature
desires; but those who live in accordance with
the Spirit have their minds set on what the
Spirit desires. 6 The mind of sinful man[a] is
death, but the mind controlled by the Spirit is
life and peace; 7 the sinful mind[b] is hostile to
God. It does not submit to God's law, nor can
it do so. 8 Those controlled by the sinful nature
cannot please God.
9 You, however, are controlled not by the sinful nature but by the Spirit, if the Spirit of God
lives in you. And if anyone does not have the
Spirit of Christ, he does not belong to Christ.
10 But if Christ is in you, your body is dead because of sin, yet your spirit is alive because of
righteousness. 11 And if the Spirit of him who
raised Jesus from the dead is living in you, he
who raised Christ from the dead will also give
life to your mortal bodies through his Spirit,
who lives in you.
12 Therefore, brothers, we have an obligation—but it is not to the sinful nature, to live
according to it. 13 For if you live
according to the sinful nature,
you will die; but if by the Spirit
you put to death the misdeeds
of the body, you will live, 14 because those who are led by the
Spirit of God are sons of God.
15 For you did not receive a
spirit that makes you a slave
again to fear, but you received
the Spirit of sonship.[c] And by
him we cry, *"Abba,*[d] Father."
16 The Spirit himself testifies
with our spirit that we are
God's children. 17 Now if we
are children, then we are heirs—heirs of God
and co-heirs with Christ, if indeed we share in
his sufferings in order that we may also share
in his glory.

Future Glory

18 I consider that our present sufferings are
not worth comparing with the glory that will
be revealed in us. 19 The creation waits in eager
expectation for the sons of God to be revealed.
20 For the creation was subjected to frustration,
not by its own choice, but by the will of the one
who subjected it, in hope 21 that[e] the creation itself will be liberated from its bondage to decay
and brought into the glorious freedom of the
children of God.
22 We know that the whole creation has been
groaning as in the pains of childbirth right up
to the present time. 23 Not only so, but we ourselves, who have the firstfruits of the Spirit,
groan inwardly as we wait eagerly for our adoption as sons, the redemption of our bodies.
24 For in this hope we were saved. But hope that
is seen is no hope at all. Who hopes for what he
already has? 25 But if we hope for what we do
not yet have, we wait for it patiently.
26 In the same way, the Spirit helps us in our
weakness. We do not know what we ought to
pray for, but the Spirit himself intercedes for us
with groans that words cannot express. 27 And
he who searches our hearts knows the mind of
the Spirit, because the Spirit intercedes for the
saints in accordance with God's will.

More Than Conquerors

28 And we know that in all
things God works for the good
of those who love him,[f] who[g]
have been called according to
his purpose. 29 For those God
foreknew he also predestined
to be conformed to the likeness
of his Son, that he might be the
firstborn among many brothers. 30 And those he predestined, he also called; those he
called, he also justified; those
he justified, he also glorified.
31 What, then, shall we say in response to
this? If God is for us, who can be against us?
32 He who did not spare his own Son, but gave
him up for us all—how will he not also, along
with him, graciously give us all things? 33 Who
will bring any charge against those whom God
has chosen? It is God who justifies. 34 Who is
he that condemns? Christ Jesus, who died—

> **Romans 8:28**
>
> *God Works Good*
>
> And we know that in all things God works for the good of those who love him, who have been called according to his purpose.

[a]6 Or *mind set on the flesh* [b]7 Or *the mind set on the flesh* [c]15 Or *adoption* [d]15 Aramaic for *Father* [e]20,21 Or *subjected it in hope. 21For* [f]28 Some manuscripts *And we know that all things work together for good to those who love God* [g]28 Or *works together with those who love him to bring about what is good—with those who*

When Words Fail

Romans 8:26

In the same way, the Spirit helps us in our weakness. We do not know what we ought to pray for, but the Spirit himself intercedes for us with groans that words cannot express.

reflection

1 Describe your prayer life. Do you struggle with it or does it flow naturally? Is it structured or hit-and-miss?

2 Have you ever been at a loss for words during a time of prayer? How did the Holy Spirit intercede on your behalf? (For example: in song, in tears or in inexpressible ways.)

3 Examine your heart. What things in your life have you been unable to express to God? Now, let the Holy Spirit lift these struggles from you and carry them before the Father.

RELATED READINGS

Psalm 94:1–23; Habakkuk 3:1–19; Philippians 1:3–11

Read: Romans 8:26–27

BEADS OF PERSPIRATION form on your brow, your heart flutters, your mind swims. An endless loop replays in your head: the scathing, screaming argument with your mother; the prognosis from the doctor; a schedule so full you can't calm your thoughts enough to fall asleep at night.

You've probably been there at some point in your life: You rush before God like an eager child bursting into a room full of toys only to find that you have no idea how to begin to pray. You don't know if you should be asking for guidance, protection or forgiveness—or all of the above. And what about how to order your list? And should you say special words? How does this prayer thing work?

Maybe you've finally got a minute to yourself, so you grab your Bible, look up to the ceiling and think, *Now what?* That list you've been building in your mind goes blank. The phone rings. The kids cry. The TV blares from another room. The dog barks. Anything . . . everything interrupts the moment. *Help!* How do you pray when words fail?

Enter the Holy Spirit. He perceives our heart's agony and comforts us in our weakness. He knows our spiritual battle often burns hottest when we fight within ourselves. We wrestle with how to prioritize our prayers. We struggle with imposing our human agendas on a holy God. We cross our arms, grit our teeth and mentally stomp our feet when things don't turn out as we desperately prayed they would. Life's frustrations can mute us spiritually: "We do not know what we ought to pray for" (verse 26). But God does not stop hearing us when we're dumbstruck before him. Both in silence and when our words flow in a jumbled torrent, the Holy Spirit intercedes on our behalf to the Father. He *does* know what to pray for.

The next time your spirit groans with a weight heavier than you can bear, trust that even when you might not be able to find words to pray, God clearly hears your cries through the intervention of the Holy Spirit. He knows your heart, your thoughts and your greatest needs better than you do yourself. Though your words may fail, your intercessor will never fail you.

Monday

Go to page 1381 for your next devotional reading.

more than that, who was raised to life—is at
the right hand of God and is also interceding
for us. 35 Who shall separate us from the love
of Christ? Shall trouble or hardship or persecution or famine or nakedness or danger or
sword? 36 As it is written:

"For your sake we face death all day long;
we are considered as sheep to be
slaughtered."[a]

37 No, in all these things we are more than conquerors through him who loved us. 38 For I am
convinced that neither death nor life, neither
angels nor demons,[b] neither the present nor
the future, nor any powers, 39 neither height
nor depth, nor anything else in all creation, will
be able to separate us from the love of God that
is in Christ Jesus our Lord.

God's Sovereign Choice

9 I speak the truth in Christ—I am not lying, my conscience confirms it in the Holy
Spirit— 2 I have great sorrow and unceasing anguish in my heart. 3 For I could wish that I myself were cursed and cut off from Christ for the
sake of my brothers, those of my own race, 4 the
people of Israel. Theirs is the adoption as sons;
theirs the divine glory, the covenants, the receiving of the law, the temple worship and the
promises. 5 Theirs are the patriarchs, and from
them is traced the human ancestry of Christ,
who is God over all, forever praised![c] Amen.
6 It is not as though God's word had failed.
For not all who are descended from Israel are
Israel. 7 Nor because they are his descendants
are they all Abraham's children. On the contrary, "It is through Isaac that your offspring
will be reckoned."[d] 8 In other words, it is not the
natural children who are God's children, but it
is the children of the promise who are regarded
as Abraham's offspring. 9 For this was how the
promise was stated: "At the appointed time I
will return, and Sarah will have a son."[e]
10 Not only that, but Rebekah's children
had one and the same father, our father Isaac.
11 Yet, before the twins were born or had done
anything good or bad—in order that God's purpose in election might stand: 12 not by works
but by him who calls—she was told, "The older
will serve the younger."[f] 13 Just as it is written:
"Jacob I loved, but Esau I hated."[g]
14 What then shall we say? Is God unjust?
Not at all! 15 For he says to Moses,

"I will have mercy on whom I have mercy,
and I will have compassion on whom I
have compassion."[h]

16 It does not, therefore, depend on man's desire
or effort, but on God's mercy. 17 For the Scripture says to Pharaoh: "I raised you up for this
very purpose, that I might display my power in
you and that my name might be proclaimed in
all the earth."[i] 18 Therefore God has mercy on
whom he wants to have mercy, and he hardens
whom he wants to harden.
19 One of you will say to me: "Then why
does God still blame us? For who resists his
will?" 20 But who are you, O man, to talk back
to God? "Shall what is formed say to him who
formed it, 'Why did you make me like this?'"[j]
21 Does not the potter have the right to make
out of the same lump of clay some pottery for
noble purposes and some for common use?
22 What if God, choosing to show his wrath
and make his power known, bore with great
patience the objects of his wrath—prepared
for destruction? 23 What if he did this to make
the riches of his glory known to the objects of
his mercy, whom he prepared in advance for
glory— 24 even us, whom he also called, not
only from the Jews but also from the Gentiles?
25 As he says in Hosea:

"I will call them 'my people' who are not
my people;
and I will call her 'my loved one' who is
not my loved one,"[k]

26 and,

"It will happen that in the very place where
it was said to them,
'You are not my people,'
they will be called 'sons of the living
God.'"[l]

27 Isaiah cries out concerning Israel:

[a]36 Psalm 44:22 [b]38 Or *nor heavenly rulers* [c]5 Or *Christ, who is over all. God be forever praised!* Or *Christ. God who is over all be forever praised!* [d]7 Gen. 21:12 [e]9 Gen. 18:10,14 [f]12 Gen. 25:23 [g]13 Mal. 1:2,3 [h]15 Exodus 33:19 [i]17 Exodus 9:16 [j]20 Isaiah 29:16; 45:9 [k]25 Hosea 2:23 [l]26 Hosea 1:10

“Though the number of the Israelites be
like the sand by the sea,
only the remnant will be saved.
28 For the Lord will carry out
his sentence on earth
with speed and
finality.”[a]
29 It is just as Isaiah said
previously:

“Unless the Lord Almighty
had left us descendants,
we would have become like
Sodom,
we would have been like
Gomorrah.”[b]

Romans 10:9

God Saves

That if you confess with your mouth, "Jesus is Lord," and believe in your heart that God raised him from the dead, you will be saved.

Israel’s Unbelief

30 What then shall we say? That the Gentiles,
who did not pursue righteousness, have obtained it, a righteousness that is by faith; 31 but
Israel, who pursued a law of righteousness, has
not attained it. 32 Why not? Because they pursued it not by faith but as if it were by works.
They stumbled over the “stumbling stone.”
33 As it is written:

“See, I lay in Zion a stone that causes men
to stumble
and a rock that makes them fall,
and the one who trusts in him will never
be put to shame.”[c]

10 Brothers, my heart’s desire and prayer
to God for the Israelites is that they
may be saved. 2 For I can testify about them
that they are zealous for God, but their zeal is
not based on knowledge. 3 Since they did not
know the righteousness that comes from God
and sought to establish their own, they did not
submit to God’s righteousness. 4 Christ is the
end of the law so that there may be righteousness for everyone who believes.
5 Moses describes in this way the righteousness that is by the law: “The man who does
these things will live by them.”[d] 6 But the righteousness that is by faith says: “Do not say in
your heart, ‘Who will ascend into heaven?’[e]”
(that is, to bring Christ down) 7 “or ‘Who will descend into the deep?’[f]” (that is, to bring Christ
up from the dead). 8 But what does it say? “The
word is near you; it is in your mouth and in
your heart,”[g] that is, the word of faith we are
proclaiming: 9 That if you con-
fess with your mouth, “Jesus is
Lord,” and believe in your heart
that God raised him from the
dead, you will be saved. 10 For
it is with your heart that you
believe and are justified, and
it is with your mouth that you
confess and are saved. 11 As
the Scripture says, “Anyone
who trusts in him will never
be put to shame.”[h] 12 For there
is no difference between Jew
and Gentile—the same Lord is
Lord of all and richly blesses all
who call on him, 13 for, “Everyone who calls on
the name of the Lord will be saved.”[i]
14 How, then, can they call on the one they
have not believed in? And how can they believe in the one of whom they have not heard?
And how can they hear without someone
preaching to them? 15 And how can they
preach unless they are sent? As it is written,
“How beautiful are the feet of those who bring
good news!”[j]
16 But not all the Israelites accepted the good
news. For Isaiah says, “Lord, who has believed
our message?”[k] 17 Consequently, faith comes
from hearing the message, and the message is
heard through the word of Christ. 18 But I ask:
Did they not hear? Of course they did:

“Their voice has gone out into all the earth,
their words to the ends of the world.”[l]

19 Again I ask: Did Israel not understand? First,
Moses says,

“I will make you envious by those who are
not a nation;
I will make you angry by a nation that
has no understanding.”[m]

20 And Isaiah boldly says,

“I was found by those who did not seek me;
I revealed myself to those who did not
ask for me.”[n]

[a] 28 Isaiah 10:22,23 [b] 29 Isaiah 1:9 [c] 33 Isaiah 8:14; 28:16 [d] 5 Lev. 18:5 [e] 6 Deut. 30:12 [f] 7 Deut. 30:13 [g] 8 Deut. 30:14
[h] 11 Isaiah 28:16 [i] 13 Joel 2:32 [j] 15 Isaiah 52:7 [k] 16 Isaiah 53:1 [l] 18 Psalm 19:4 [m] 19 Deut. 32:21 [n] 20 Isaiah 65:1

21 But concerning Israel he says,

"All day long I have held out my hands
to a disobedient and obstinate people."[a]

The Remnant of Israel

11 I ask then: Did God reject his people?
By no means! I am an Israelite myself,
a descendant of Abraham, from the tribe of
Benjamin. 2 God did not reject his people,
whom he foreknew. Don't you know what the
Scripture says in the passage about Elijah—how
he appealed to God against Israel: 3 "Lord, they
have killed your prophets and torn down your
altars; I am the only one left, and they are trying to kill me"[b]? 4 And what was God's answer
to him? "I have reserved for myself seven thousand who have not bowed the knee to Baal."[c]
5 So too, at the present time there is a remnant
chosen by grace. 6 And if by grace, then it is no
longer by works; if it were, grace would no longer be grace.[d]
7 What then? What Israel sought so earnestly
it did not obtain, but the elect did. The others
were hardened, 8 as it is written:

"God gave them a spirit of stupor,
eyes so that they could not see
and ears so that they could not hear,
to this very day."[e]

9 And David says:

"May their table become a snare and a trap,
a stumbling block and a retribution for
them.
10 May their eyes be darkened so they cannot
see,
and their backs be bent forever."[f]

Ingrafted Branches

11 Again I ask: Did they stumble so as to fall
beyond recovery? Not at all! Rather, because of
their transgression, salvation has come to the
Gentiles to make Israel envious. 12 But if their
transgression means riches for the world, and
their loss means riches for the Gentiles, how
much greater riches will their fullness bring!
13 I am talking to you Gentiles. Inasmuch as
I am the apostle to the Gentiles, I make much
of my ministry 14 in the hope that I may somehow arouse my own people to envy and save
some of them. 15 For if their rejection is the reconciliation of the world, what will their acceptance be but life from the dead? 16 If the part of
the dough offered as firstfruits is holy, then the
whole batch is holy; if the root is holy, so are
the branches.
17 If some of the branches have been broken
off, and you, though a wild olive shoot, have
been grafted in among the others and now
share in the nourishing sap from the olive root,
18 do not boast over those branches. If you do,
consider this: You do not support the root, but
the root supports you. 19 You will say then,
"Branches were broken off so that I could be
grafted in." 20 Granted. But they were broken
off because of unbelief, and you stand by faith.
Do not be arrogant, but be afraid. 21 For if God
did not spare the natural branches, he will not
spare you either.
22 Consider therefore the kindness and sternness of God: sternness to those who fell, but
kindness to you, provided that you continue in
his kindness. Otherwise, you also will be cut
off. 23 And if they do not persist in unbelief,
they will be grafted in, for God is able to graft
them in again. 24 After all, if you were cut out
of an olive tree that is wild by nature, and contrary to nature were grafted into a cultivated
olive tree, how much more readily will these,
the natural branches, be grafted into their own
olive tree!

All Israel Will Be Saved

25 I do not want you to be ignorant of this
mystery, brothers, so that you may not be
conceited: Israel has experienced a hardening
in part until the full number of the Gentiles has
come in. 26 And so all Israel will be saved, as it
is written:

"The deliverer will come from Zion;
he will turn godlessness away from
Jacob.
27 And this is[g] my covenant with them
when I take away their sins."[h]

28 As far as the gospel is concerned, they are
enemies on your account; but as far as election

[a]21 Isaiah 65:2 [b]3 1 Kings 19:10,14 [c]4 1 Kings 19:18 [d]6 Some manuscripts *be grace. But if by works, then it is no longer grace; if it were, work would no longer be work.* [e]8 Deut. 29:4; Isaiah 29:10 [f]10 Psalm 69:22,23 [g]27 Or *will be* [h]27 Isaiah 59:20,21; 27:9; Jer. 31:33,34

is concerned, they are loved on account of the patriarchs, 29for God's gifts and his call are irrevocable. 30Just as you who were at one time disobedient to God have now received mercy as a result of their disobedience, 31so they too have now become disobedient in order that they too may now[a] receive mercy as a result of God's mercy to you. 32For God has bound all men over to disobedience so that he may have mercy on them all.

Doxology

33Oh, the depth of the riches
of the wisdom and[b]
knowledge of God!
How unsearchable his
judgments,
and his paths beyond
tracing out!
34"Who has known the mind
of the Lord?
Or who has been his
counselor?"[c]
35"Who has ever given to
God,
that God should repay
him?"[d]
36For from him and through
him and to him are
all things.
To him be the glory
forever! Amen.

Living Sacrifices

12 Therefore, I urge you, brothers, in view of God's mercy, to offer your bodies as living sacrifices, holy and pleasing to God—this is your spiritual[e] act of worship. 2Do not conform any longer to the pattern of this world, but be transformed by the renewing of your mind. Then you will be able to test and approve what God's will is—his good, pleasing and perfect will.

3For by the grace given me I say to every one of you: Do not think of yourself more highly than you ought, but rather think of yourself with sober judgment, in accordance with the measure of faith God has given you. 4Just as each of us has one body with many members, and these members do not all have the same function, 5so in Christ we who are many form one body, and each member belongs to all the others. 6We have different gifts, according to the grace given us. If a man's gift is prophesying, let him use it in proportion to his[f] faith. 7If it is serving, let him serve; if it is teaching, let him teach; 8if it is encouraging, let him encourage; if it is contributing to the needs of others, let him give generously; if it is leadership, let him govern diligently; if it is showing mercy, let him do it cheerfully.

> **Romans 11:33**
>
> *God Cannot Be Fully Understood*
>
> Oh, the depth of the riches of the wisdom and knowledge of God! How unsearchable his judgments, and his paths beyond tracing out!

Love

9Love must be sincere. Hate what is evil; cling to what is good. 10Be devoted to one another in brotherly love. Honor one another above yourselves. 11Never be lacking in zeal, but keep your spiritual fervor, serving the Lord. 12Be joyful in hope, patient in affliction, faithful in prayer. 13Share with God's people who are in need. Practice hospitality.

14Bless those who persecute you; bless and do not curse. 15Rejoice with those who rejoice; mourn with those who mourn. 16Live in harmony with one another. Do not be proud, but be willing to associate with people of low position.[g] Do not be conceited.

17Do not repay anyone evil for evil. Be careful to do what is right in the eyes of everybody. 18If it is possible, as far as it depends on you, live at peace with everyone. 19Do not take revenge, my friends, but leave room for God's wrath, for it is written: "It is mine to avenge; I will repay,"[h] says the Lord. 20On the contrary:

"If your enemy is hungry, feed him;
if he is thirsty, give him something to
drink.
In doing this, you will heap burning coals
on his head."[i]

21Do not be overcome by evil, but overcome evil with good.

[a]31 Some manuscripts do not have *now.* [b]33 Or *riches and the wisdom and the* [c]34 Isaiah 40:13 [d]35 Job 41:11 [e]1 Or *reasonable* [f]6 Or *in agreement with the* [g]16 Or *willing to do menial work* [h]19 Deut. 32:35 [i]20 Prov. 25:21,22

Scoot Down Low

Read Romans 12:1–21

"HUMBLE" COMES FROM THE WORD *HUMUS*, meaning "earth" or "brought down low." Yes, the Creator of the universe who flung the stars into space is also a very down-to-earth God. Why was Jesus "brought down low"—why did he come down to earth in our form?

I was pondering that thought one day as I was busy in the kitchen, my "hive of five" grandkids buzzing around the living room. I put dinner on the table and gave the "y'all come" signal. My grown children and their children began to make their way toward the feast and the smells of my home-cooked turnip greens, buttered carrots, okra gumbo, mashed potatoes, brisket, baked chicken and corn bread (with ice cream waiting in the freezer to top it all off a little later)!

But two of my darlin's were too busy playing to answer the call. "Alyssa! Alaya!" I called again. Still they paid no attention. So I did the only thing I could do. I went over to where they were engrossed in their baby dolls and scooted down on my achy knees to look them in the eyes.

Now I had their full attention. "Girls," I said with loving firmness, "did you not hear me calling you?"

They shook their heads no, their dark braids flying, their brown eyes wide with surprise.

"Well, sweet things, now that I have your attention, help your old Grammy up and let's go eat." Together the girls tugged on my arms and off we went toward the banquet.

As I walked with them, I thought about having to go to all that trouble, to physically scoot down low to get the attention of my granddaughters. It was then I realized that this is exactly what Jesus did for me.

God had a wonderful feast prepared for us in heaven and he called his people to come and eat and enjoy! But most often, caught up in their own little dramas, they ignored his call. So, in the form of his Son, Jesus "scooted down low" and became one of us. Why? To get our attention, to meet us eye to eye—to take us by the hand and lead us to the feast.

—*Carol Kent, Thelma Wells*

Romans 12:16

Live in harmony with one another. Do not be proud, but be willing to associate with people of low position. Do not be conceited.

reflection

1 How have you gotten caught up in "little dramas" that make it hard to live in harmony with others?

2 How does it help to remember that the Creator of the universe "scooted down low" to become one of us?

3 Do you need to "scoot down low" to make things right with someone? When and how will you do that so you can restore harmony to the relationship?

RELATED READINGS

Colossians 3:12–14; James 4:7–10

"What makes humility so desirable is the marvelous thing it does to us; it creates in us a capacity for the closest possible intimacy with God."

Monica Baldwin

Go to page 1384 for your next devotional reading.

Submission to the Authorities

13 Everyone must submit himself to the
governing authorities, for there is no
authority except that which God has established. The authorities that exist have been
established by God. 2Consequently, he who
rebels against the authority is rebelling against
what God has instituted, and those who do so
will bring judgment on themselves. 3For rulers
hold no terror for those who do right, but for
those who do wrong. Do you want to be free
from fear of the one in authority? Then do what
is right and he will commend you. 4For he is
God's servant to do you good. But if you do
wrong, be afraid, for he does not bear the sword
for nothing. He is God's servant, an agent of
wrath to bring punishment on the wrongdoer.
5Therefore, it is necessary to submit to the authorities, not only because of possible punishment but also because of conscience.

6This is also why you pay taxes, for the authorities are God's servants,
who give their full time to governing. 7Give everyone what
you owe him: If you owe taxes,
pay taxes; if revenue, then revenue; if respect, then respect; if
honor, then honor.

Love, for the Day Is Near

8Let no debt remain out-
standing, except the continuing debt to love one another,
for he who loves his fellowman
has fulfilled the law. 9The commandments, "Do not commit
adultery," "Do not murder," "Do
not steal," "Do not covet,"[a] and whatever other
commandment there may be, are summed up
in this one rule: "Love your neighbor as yourself."[b] 10Love does no harm to its neighbor.
Therefore love is the fulfillment of the law.

11And do this, understanding the present
time. The hour has come for you to wake up
from your slumber, because our salvation is
nearer now than when we first believed. 12The
night is nearly over; the day is almost here. So
let us put aside the deeds of darkness and put
on the armor of light. 13Let us behave decently,
as in the daytime, not in orgies and drunkenness, not in sexual immorality and debauchery,
not in dissension and jealousy. 14Rather, clothe
yourselves with the Lord Jesus Christ, and do
not think about how to gratify the desires of
the sinful nature.[c]

The Weak and the Strong

14 Accept him whose faith is weak, without passing judgment on disputable
matters. 2One man's faith allows him to eat
everything, but another man, whose faith is
weak, eats only vegetables. 3The man who eats
everything must not look down on him who
does not, and the man who does not eat everything must not condemn the man who does,
for God has accepted him. 4Who are you to
judge someone else's servant? To his own master he stands or falls. And he will stand, for the
Lord is able to make him stand.

5One man considers one day more sacred
than another; another man considers every
day alike. Each one should be fully convinced
in his own mind. 6He who re-
gards one day as special, does
so to the Lord. He who eats
meat, eats to the Lord, for he
gives thanks to God; and he
who abstains, does so to the
Lord and gives thanks to God.
7For none of us lives to himself
alone and none of us dies to
himself alone. 8If we live, we
live to the Lord; and if we die,
we die to the Lord. So, whether
we live or die, we belong to
the Lord.

9For this very reason, Christ
died and returned to life so that he might be
the Lord of both the dead and the living. 10You,
then, why do you judge your brother? Or why
do you look down on your brother? For we
will all stand before God's judgment seat. 11It
is written:

> "'As surely as I live,' says the Lord,
> 'every knee will bow before me;
> every tongue will confess to God.'"[d]

12So then, each of us will give an account of
himself to God.

13Therefore let us stop passing judgment

> **Romans 14:9**
>
> *God Is Lord of All*
>
> For this very reason, Christ died and returned to life so that he might be the Lord of both the dead and the living.

[a]9 Exodus 20:13–15,17; Deut. 5:17–19,21 [b]9 Lev. 19:18 [c]14 Or *the flesh* [d]11 Isaiah 45:23

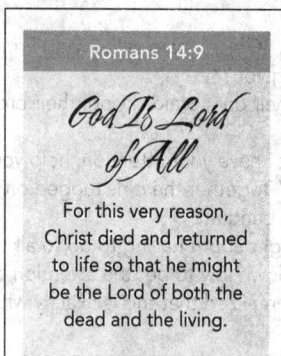

on one another. Instead, make up your mind
not to put any stumbling block or obstacle
in your brother's way. 14 As one who is in the
Lord Jesus, I am fully convinced that no food[a]
is unclean in itself. But if anyone regards something as unclean, then for him it is unclean.
15 If your brother is distressed because of what
you eat, you are no longer acting in love. Do
not by your eating destroy your brother for
whom Christ died. 16 Do not allow what you
consider good to be spoken of as evil. 17 For the
kingdom of God is not a matter of eating and
drinking, but of righteousness, peace and joy
in the Holy Spirit, 18 because anyone who
serves Christ in this way is pleasing to God and
approved by men.

19 Let us therefore make every effort to do
what leads to peace and to mutual edification.
20 Do not destroy the work of God for the sake
of food. All food is clean, but it is wrong for
a man to eat anything that causes someone
else to stumble. 21 It is better not to eat meat
or drink wine or to do anything else that will
cause your brother to fall.

22 So whatever you believe about these things
keep between yourself and God. Blessed is the
man who does not condemn himself by what
he approves. 23 But the man who has doubts is
condemned if he eats, because his eating is not
from faith; and everything that does not come
from faith is sin.

15 We who are strong ought to bear with
the failings of the weak and not to
please ourselves. 2 Each of us should please his
neighbor for his good, to build him up. 3 For
even Christ did not please himself but, as it is
written: "The insults of those who insult you
have fallen on me."[b] 4 For everything that was
written in the past was written to teach us, so
that through endurance and the encouragement of the Scriptures we might have hope.

5 May the God who gives endurance and encouragement give you a spirit of unity among
yourselves as you follow Christ Jesus, 6 so that
with one heart and mouth you may glorify the
God and Father of our Lord Jesus Christ.

7 Accept one another, then, just as Christ
accepted you, in order to bring praise to God.
8 For I tell you that Christ has become a servant of the Jews[c] on behalf of God's truth, to
confirm the promises made to the patriarchs
9 so that the Gentiles may glorify God for his
mercy, as it is written:

"Therefore I will praise you among the
Gentiles;
I will sing hymns to your name."[d]

10 Again, it says,

"Rejoice, O Gentiles, with his people."[e]

11 And again,

"Praise the Lord, all you Gentiles,
and sing praises to him, all you
peoples."[f]

12 And again, Isaiah says,

"The Root of Jesse will spring up,
one who will arise to rule over the
nations;
the Gentiles will hope in him."[g]

13 May the God of hope fill you with all joy
and peace as you trust in him, so that you may
overflow with hope by the power of the Holy
Spirit.

Paul the Minister to the Gentiles

14 I myself am convinced, my brothers, that
you yourselves are full of goodness, complete
in knowledge and competent to instruct one
another. 15 I have written you quite boldly on
some points, as if to remind you of them again,
because of the grace God gave me 16 to be a
minister of Christ Jesus to the Gentiles with
the priestly duty of proclaiming the gospel of
God, so that the Gentiles might become an offering acceptable to God, sanctified by the Holy
Spirit.

17 Therefore I glory in Christ Jesus in my service to God. 18 I will not venture to speak of
anything except what Christ has accomplished
through me in leading the Gentiles to obey God
by what I have said and done— 19 by the power
of signs and miracles, through the power of the
Spirit. So from Jerusalem all the way around
to Illyricum, I have fully proclaimed the gospel
of Christ. 20 It has always been my ambition to

[a] 14 Or *that nothing* [b] 3 Psalm 69:9 [c] 8 Greek *circumcision* [d] 9 2 Samuel 22:50; Psalm 18:49 [e] 10 Deut. 32:43 [f] 11 Psalm 117:1
[g] 12 Isaiah 11:10

Overflowing Hope

Read: Romans 15:1–13

Romans 15:13

May the God of hope fill you with all joy and peace as you trust in him, so that you may overflow with hope by the power of the Holy Spirit.

reflection

1 Would you describe your glass of hope as empty, half full or overflowing?

2 What situation is God asking you to endure right now? How have you found hope in the midst of it?

3 If you could only have one page of the Bible to sustain you for the rest of your life, what page would it be?

RELATED READINGS

Lamentations 3:21–26; Romans 5:3–5

READING THE NEWSPAPER HEADLINES on any given day can cause our hope to evaporate. Yet in Romans 15:13 Paul prays that the "God of hope" will fill us with joy and peace so that we might "overflow with hope." In the midst of a world filled with despair, only God can fill us with hope. In verse 4, Paul revealed two keys to hope: "Through endurance and the encouragement of the Scriptures we might have hope."

Key 1: Endurance. The Greek word for *endurance* means "to bear up under pressure" or "to be courageous." It takes endurance and courage to keep going when circumstances tempt us to give up. But like athletes who know they will receive a prize, believers can continue the race of faith fully confident that God will keep his promises.

Key 2: Encouragement of the Scriptures. The Greek word for *encouragement* means "comfort" or "solace." Reading God's Word fills us with hope because it comforts our souls. We read of God's ability to perform wonders and miracles in impossible situations and his power to turn intended evil to our good. We read of God's ability to redeem, protect and heal us, his children. We can rest, knowing that God loves us deeply and has our very best interests in his big Abba Father's heart.

Years ago, a caravan crossed the north of India. A missionary traveled with the group. As the caravan journeyed, a poor, old man was overcome by the heat and labor of the trip. The heartless caravan leader left him to perish alone on the road. The missionary saw him and went to comfort the dying man. She knelt beside him and whispered in his ear, "Brother, what is your hope?" With great effort, the man replied, "The blood of Jesus, his son Christ . . . purifies . . . from all sin" (see 1 John 1:7).

As the missionary held the dying man in her arms, she saw a piece of paper grasped tightly in his hands. It was a single page of the Bible containing the passage from which these words are found. The elderly man had walked a long journey, clearly enduring until the very end with only a few words of Scripture to fill his heart to overflowing with hope.

What is your hope?

Go to page 1389 for your next devotional reading.

preach the gospel where Christ was not known,
so that I would not be building on someone
else's foundation. 21 Rather, as it is written:

"Those who were not told about him will
see,
and those who have not heard will
understand."[a]

22 This is why I have often been hindered from
coming to you.

Paul's Plan to Visit Rome

23 But now that there is no more place for me
to work in these regions, and since I have been
longing for many years to see you, 24 I plan to
do so when I go to Spain. I hope to visit you
while passing through and to have you assist
me on my journey there, after I have enjoyed
your company for a while. 25 Now, however, I
am on my way to Jerusalem in the service of
the saints there. 26 For Macedonia and Achaia
were pleased to make a contribution for the
poor among the saints in Jerusalem. 27 They
were pleased to do it, and indeed they owe it
to them. For if the Gentiles have shared in the
Jews' spiritual blessings, they owe it to the Jews
to share with them their material blessings.
28 So after I have completed this task and have
made sure that they have received this fruit, I
will go to Spain and visit you on the way. 29 I
know that when I come to you, I will come in
the full measure of the blessing of Christ.

30 I urge you, brothers, by our Lord Jesus
Christ and by the love of the Spirit, to join
me in my struggle by praying to God for me.
31 Pray that I may be rescued from the unbelievers in Judea and that my service in Jerusalem
may be acceptable to the saints there, 32 so that
by God's will I may come to you with joy and
together with you be refreshed. 33 The God of
peace be with you all. Amen.

Personal Greetings

16 I commend to you our sister Phoebe, a
servant[b] of the church in Cenchrea. 2 I
ask you to receive her in the Lord in a way worthy of the saints and to give her any help she
may need from you, for she has been a great
help to many people, including me.

3 Greet Priscilla[c] and Aquila, my fellow workers in Christ Jesus. 4 They risked their lives
for me. Not only I but all the churches of
the Gentiles are grateful to them.
5 Greet also the church that meets at their
house.
Greet my dear friend Epenetus, who was
the first convert to Christ in the province
of Asia.
6 Greet Mary, who worked very hard for you.
7 Greet Andronicus and Junias, my relatives
who have been in prison with me. They are
outstanding among the apostles, and they
were in Christ before I was.
8 Greet Ampliatus, whom I love in the Lord.
9 Greet Urbanus, our fellow worker in Christ,
and my dear friend Stachys.
10 Greet Apelles, tested and approved in
Christ.
Greet those who belong to the household of
Aristobulus.
11 Greet Herodion, my relative.
Greet those in the household of Narcissus
who are in the Lord.
12 Greet Tryphena and Tryphosa, those women
who work hard in the Lord.
Greet my dear friend Persis, another woman
who has worked very hard in the Lord.
13 Greet Rufus, chosen in the Lord, and his
mother, who has been a mother to me,
too.
14 Greet Asyncritus, Phlegon, Hermes, Patro-
bas, Hermas and the brothers with them.
15 Greet Philologus, Julia, Nereus and his sister, and Olympas and all the saints with
them.
16 Greet one another with a holy kiss.
All the churches of Christ send greetings.

17 I urge you, brothers, to watch out for those
who cause divisions and put obstacles in your
way that are contrary to the teaching you have
learned. Keep away from them. 18 For such people are not serving our Lord Christ, but their
own appetites. By smooth talk and flattery they
deceive the minds of naive people. 19 Everyone
has heard about your obedience, so I am full of
joy over you; but I want you to be wise about
what is good, and innocent about what is evil.

[a] 21 Isaiah 52:15 [b] 1 Or *deaconess* [c] 3 Greek *Prisca*, a variant of *Priscilla*

20The God of peace will soon crush Satan
under your feet.
The grace of our Lord Jesus be with you.
21Timothy, my fellow worker, sends his
greetings to you, as do Lucius, Jason and Sosip-
ater, my relatives.
22I, Tertius, who wrote down this letter,
greet you in the Lord.
23Gaius, whose hospitality I and the whole
church here enjoy, sends you his greetings.
Erastus, who is the city's director of public works, and our brother Quartus send you
their greetings.[a]
25Now to him who is able to establish you by
my gospel and the proclamation of Jesus Christ,
according to the revelation of the mystery hidden for long ages past, 26but now revealed and
made known through the prophetic writings
by the command of the eternal God, so that all
nations might believe and obey him— 27to the
only wise God be glory forever through Jesus
Christ! Amen.

[a]23 Some manuscripts *their greetings.* 24*May the grace of our Lord Jesus Christ be with all of you. Amen.*

1 Corinthians

Corinth was a wealthy and prosperous center of commerce and trade when Paul wrote this letter. Morally, however, it was bankrupt. The term *Corinthian* came to be synonymous with immorality. And there, in the center of this immoral society, was a young Christian church struggling to survive.

Paul's words to the Corinthians are exceptionally modern in their *relevance to churches of today*. The problems that surfaced in the congregation in Corinth are the same problems that have plagued churches throughout the ages. There were divisions, questions about marriage and divorce, concerns about how to relate to a pagan world, lawsuits and immorality—difficult issues that no one wanted to deal with.

Paul addresses these issues head-on, giving specific advice about how to live as God's people in a fallen world. Nothing ever really changes where human nature is concerned, but Paul reminds us that we are not subjects to the whims of that nature. He points us to the resurrection when we will all be changed, clothed with immortality and bearing the likeness of Christ. He reminds us that *our lives are to be lived not for this world* but in preparation for that imperishable world that is to come.

Author:
The apostle Paul.

Audience:
Followers of Jesus; originally written to the church in Corinth.

Date:
About A.D. 55.

Setting:
Paul wrote from Ephesus to the church in Corinth, a pagan cosmopolitan city in Greece. He started this church during his second missionary journey.

Verse to Remember:
No temptation has seized you except what is common to man. And God is faithful; he will not let you be tempted beyond what you can bear. But when you are tempted, he will also provide a way out so that you can stand up under it. (10:13)

1 Paul, called to be an apostle of Christ Jesus by the will of God, and our brother Sosthenes,

2 To the church of God in Corinth, to those sanctified in Christ Jesus and called to be holy, together with all those everywhere who call on the name of our Lord Jesus Christ—their Lord and ours:

3 Grace and peace to you from God our Father and the Lord Jesus Christ.

Thanksgiving

4 I always thank God for you because of his grace given you in Christ Jesus. 5 For in him you have been enriched in every way—in all your speaking and in all your knowledge— 6 because our testimony about Christ was confirmed in you. 7 Therefore you do not lack any spiritual gift as you eagerly wait for our Lord Jesus Christ to be revealed. 8 He will keep you strong to the end, so that you will be blameless on the day of our Lord Jesus Christ. 9 God, who has called you into fellowship with his Son Jesus Christ our Lord, is faithful.

> **1 Corinthians 1:8**
>
> *God Keeps Us Strong*
>
> He will keep you strong to the end, so that you will be blameless on the day of our Lord Jesus Christ.

Divisions in the Church

10 I appeal to you, brothers, in the name of our Lord Jesus Christ, that all of you agree with one another so that there may be no divisions among you and that you may be perfectly united in mind and thought. 11 My brothers, some from Chloe's household have informed me that there are quarrels among you. 12 What I mean is this: One of you says, "I follow Paul"; another, "I follow Apollos"; another, "I follow Cephas[a]"; still another, "I follow Christ."

13 Is Christ divided? Was Paul crucified for you? Were you baptized into[b] the name of Paul? 14 I am thankful that I did not baptize any of you except Crispus and Gaius, 15 so no one can say that you were baptized into my name. 16 (Yes, I also baptized the household of Stephanas; beyond that, I don't remember if I baptized anyone else.) 17 For Christ did not send me to baptize, but to preach the gospel—not with words of human wisdom, lest the cross of Christ be emptied of its power.

Christ the Wisdom and Power of God

18 For the message of the cross is foolishness to those who are perishing, but to us who are being saved it is the power of God. 19 For it is written:

> "I will destroy the wisdom of the wise;
> the intelligence of the intelligent I will
> frustrate."[c]

20 Where is the wise man? Where is the scholar? Where is the philosopher of this age? Has not God made foolish the wisdom of the world? 21 For since in the wisdom of God the world through its wisdom did not know him, God was pleased through the foolishness of what was preached to save those who believe. 22 Jews demand miraculous signs and Greeks look for wisdom, 23 but we preach Christ crucified: a stumbling block to Jews and foolishness to Gentiles, 24 but to those whom God has called, both Jews and Greeks, Christ the power of God and the wisdom of God. 25 For the foolishness of God is wiser than man's wisdom, and the weakness of God is stronger than man's strength.

26 Brothers, think of what you were when you were called. Not many of you were wise by human standards; not many were influential; not many were of noble birth. 27 But God chose the foolish things of the world to shame the wise; God chose the weak things of the world to shame the strong. 28 He chose the lowly things of this world and the despised things—and the things that are not—to nullify the things that are, 29 so that no one may boast before him. 30 It is because of him that you are in Christ Jesus, who has become for us wisdom from God—that is, our righteousness, holiness and redemption. 31 Therefore, as it is written: "Let him who boasts boast in the Lord."[d]

[a] 12 That is, Peter [b] 13 Or *in*; also in verse 15 [c] 19 Isaiah 29:14 [d] 31 Jer. 9:24

The Foolish Things

Read: 1 Corinthians 1:18–31

THE LAWS OF NATURE as shown in cartoons are not to be trusted. Take the law of gravity, for instance. Aren't you amazed that a cartoon character can run off the edge of a cliff and keep running in place for several seconds before gravity finally kicks in? When gravity finally does regain its pull, why is it that the cartoon character's feet go first, stretching him to about ten times his original height, then the body goes, then the eyeballs follow a couple of seconds later?

And how is it those 200-foot falls are never fatal? Explosions don't kill either. No matter how many kilotons, the cartoon character never dies. He just turns black and smoky. After a second or two, even that goes away. Remarkable.

Nope, you can't trust the laws of nature in cartoon life.

Scripture teaches that we can't trust in our own cleverness any more than we can trust in our own righteousness. The fallen nature tells us that life is hard and then we die. If we have many resources, we might become hedonists and say "Eat, drink and be merry, for tomorrow we die." But just as the seemingly simple Roadrunner outwits the clever Wile E. Coyote every time, God's wisdom confounds the world's wisdom. The seemingly foolish things of God are really wise, while the seemingly wise things of the world really are foolish.

God used simple people to proclaim his simple message: Jesus Christ is our miraculous tunnel of escape from the curse of death issued when Adam and Eve fell. Any other route will leave us empty and forlorn. This may seem foolishly simpleminded to some, but it is the simple truth of the gospel; easy enough for a child to understand, yet profound enough for an intellectual to dwell on for eternity.

1 Corinthians 1:27

But God chose the foolish things of the world to shame the wise; God chose the weak things of the world to shame the strong.

reflection

1 When have you been considered foolish for believing the simple truth of the gospel?

2 How has God used your weakness to show himself strong?

3 This week, ask God to use you in spite of your weaknesses in the area he sees fit.

RELATED READINGS

Psalm 37:3–6;
1 Corinthians 3:18–23;
2 Corinthians 11:16–33

"Our Father stands with open arms and asks us to trust in His faithfulness . . . Truly, He is steady, and He firmly grasps us as we reach out to Him."

Cynthia Heald

Go to page 1394 for your next devotional reading.

2 When I came to you, brothers, I did not come with eloquence or superior wisdom as I proclaimed to you the testimony about God.[a] 2For I resolved to know nothing while I was with you except Jesus Christ and him crucified. 3I came to you in weakness and fear, and with much trembling. 4My message and my preaching were not with wise and persuasive words, but with a demonstration of the Spirit's power, 5so that your faith might not rest on men's wisdom, but on God's power.

Wisdom From the Spirit

6We do, however, speak a message of wisdom among the mature, but not the wisdom of this age or of the rulers of this age, who are coming to nothing. 7No, we speak of God's secret wisdom, a wisdom that has been hidden and that God destined for our glory before time began. 8None of the rulers of this age understood it, for if they had, they would not have crucified the Lord of glory. 9However, as it is written:

"No eye has seen,
no ear has heard,
no mind has conceived
what God has prepared
for those who love
him"[b]—

> 1 Corinthians 2:9
>
> *God Plans a Wondrous Future*
>
> "No eye has seen,
> no ear has heard,
> no mind has conceived
> what God has prepared
> for those who love him."

10but God has revealed it to us by his Spirit.

The Spirit searches all things, even the deep things of God. 11For who among men knows the thoughts of a man except the man's spirit within him? In the same way no one knows the thoughts of God except the Spirit of God. 12We have not received the spirit of the world but the Spirit who is from God, that we may understand what God has freely given us. 13This is what we speak, not in words taught us by human wisdom but in words taught by the Spirit, expressing spiritual truths in spiritual words.[c] 14The man without the Spirit does not accept the things that come from the Spirit of God, for they are foolishness to him, and he cannot understand them, because they are spiritually discerned. 15The spiritual man makes judgments about all things, but he himself is not subject to any man's judgment:

16"For who has known the mind of the Lord
that he may instruct him?"[d]

But we have the mind of Christ.

On Divisions in the Church

3 Brothers, I could not address you as spiritual but as worldly—mere infants in Christ. 2I gave you milk, not solid food, for you were not yet ready for it. Indeed, you are still not ready. 3You are still worldly. For since there is jealousy and quarreling among you, are you not worldly? Are you not acting like mere men? 4For when one says, "I follow Paul," and another, "I follow Apollos," are you not mere men?

5What, after all, is Apollos? And what is Paul? Only servants, through whom you came to believe—as the Lord has assigned to each his task. 6I planted the seed, Apollos watered it, but God made it grow. 7So neither he who plants nor he who waters is anything, but only God, who makes things grow. 8The man who plants and the man who waters have one purpose, and each will be rewarded according to his own labor. 9For we are God's fellow workers; you are God's field, God's building.

10By the grace God has given me, I laid a foundation as an expert builder, and someone else is building on it. But each one should be careful how he builds. 11For no one can lay any foundation other than the one already laid, which is Jesus Christ. 12If any man builds on this foundation using gold, silver, costly stones, wood, hay or straw, 13his work will be shown for what it is, because the Day will bring it to light. It will be revealed with fire, and the fire will test the quality of each man's work. 14If what he has built survives, he will receive his reward. 15If it is burned up, he will suffer loss; he

[a]1 Some manuscripts *as I proclaimed to you God's mystery* [b]9 Isaiah 64:4 [c]13 Or *Spirit, interpreting spiritual truths to spiritual men*
[d]16 Isaiah 40:13

himself will be saved, but only as one escaping
through the flames.
16Don't you know that you yourselves are
God's temple and that God's Spirit lives in you?
17If anyone destroys God's temple, God will destroy him; for God's temple is sacred, and you
are that temple.
18Do not deceive yourselves. If any one of
you thinks he is wise by the standards of this
age, he should become a "fool" so that he may
become wise. 19For the wisdom of this world is
foolishness in God's sight. As it is written: "He
catches the wise in their craftiness"[a]; 20and
again, "The Lord knows that the thoughts of
the wise are futile."[b] 21So then, no more boasting about men! All things are yours, 22whether
Paul or Apollos or Cephas[c] or the world or life
or death or the present or the future—all are
yours, 23and you are of Christ, and Christ is
of God.

Apostles of Christ

4 So then, men ought to regard us as servants of Christ and as those entrusted
with the secret things of God. 2Now it is required that those who have been given a trust
must prove faithful. 3I care very little if I am
judged by you or by any human court; indeed,
I do not even judge myself. 4My conscience is
clear, but that does not make me innocent. It
is the Lord who judges me. 5Therefore judge
nothing before the appointed time; wait till the
Lord comes. He will bring to light what is hidden in darkness and will expose the motives of
men's hearts. At that time each will receive his
praise from God.
6Now, brothers, I have applied these things
to myself and Apollos for your benefit, so that
you may learn from us the meaning of the saying, "Do not go beyond what is written." Then
you will not take pride in one man over against
another. 7For who makes you different from
anyone else? What do you have that you did
not receive? And if you did receive it, why do
you boast as though you did not?
8Already you have all you want! Already you
have become rich! You have become kings—
and that without us! How I wish that you really
had become kings so that we might be kings
with you! 9For it seems to me that God has put
us apostles on display at the end of the procession, like men condemned to die in the arena.
We have been made a spectacle to the whole
universe, to angels as well as to men. 10We are
fools for Christ, but you are so wise in Christ!
We are weak, but you are strong! You are honored, we are dishonored! 11To this very hour
we go hungry and thirsty, we are in rags, we are
brutally treated, we are homeless. 12We work
hard with our own hands. When we are cursed,
we bless; when we are persecuted, we endure
it; 13when we are slandered, we answer kindly.
Up to this moment we have become the scum
of the earth, the refuse of the world.
14I am not writing this to shame you, but to
warn you, as my dear children. 15Even though
you have ten thousand guardians in Christ,
you do not have many fathers, for in Christ
Jesus I became your father through the gospel.
16Therefore I urge you to imitate me. 17For
this reason I am sending to you Timothy, my
son whom I love, who is faithful in the Lord.
He will remind you of my way of life in Christ
Jesus, which agrees with what I teach everywhere in every church.
18Some of you have become arrogant, as if
I were not coming to you. 19But I will come to
you very soon, if the Lord is willing, and then
I will find out not only how these arrogant
people are talking, but what power they have.
20For the kingdom of God is not a matter of
talk but of power. 21What do you prefer? Shall
I come to you with a whip, or in love and with
a gentle spirit?

Expel the Immoral Brother!

5 It is actually reported that there is sexual
immorality among you, and of a kind that
does not occur even among pagans: A man has
his father's wife. 2And you are proud! Shouldn't
you rather have been filled with grief and have
put out of your fellowship the man who did
this? 3Even though I am not physically present, I am with you in spirit. And I have already
passed judgment on the one who did this, just
as if I were present. 4When you are assembled
in the name of our Lord Jesus and I am with
you in spirit, and the power of our Lord Jesus

[a]19 Job 5:13 [b]20 Psalm 94:11 [c]22 That is, Peter

is present, [5]hand this man over to Satan, so
that the sinful nature[a] may be destroyed and
his spirit saved on the day of the Lord.
[6]Your boasting is not good. Don't you know
that a little yeast works through the whole
batch of dough? [7]Get rid of the old yeast that
you may be a new batch without yeast—as you
really are. For Christ, our Passover lamb, has
been sacrificed. [8]Therefore let us keep the Festival, not with the old yeast, the yeast of malice
and wickedness, but with bread without yeast,
the bread of sincerity and truth.
[9]I have written you in my letter not to associate with sexually immoral people— [10]not at
all meaning the people of this world who are
immoral, or the greedy and swindlers, or idolaters. In that case you would have to leave this
world. [11]But now I am writing you that you
must not associate with anyone who calls himself a brother but is sexually immoral or greedy,
an idolater or a slanderer, a drunkard or a swindler. With such a man do not even eat.
[12]What business is it of mine to judge those
outside the church? Are you not to judge those
inside? [13]God will judge those outside. "Expel
the wicked man from among you."[b]

Lawsuits Among Believers

6 If any of you has a dispute with another,
dare he take it before the ungodly for judgment instead of before the saints? [2]Do you
not know that the saints will
judge the world? And if you
are to judge the world, are you
not competent to judge trivial
cases? [3]Do you not know that
we will judge angels? How
much more the things of this
life! [4]Therefore, if you have
disputes about such matters,
appoint as judges even men of
little account in the church![c] [5]I
say this to shame you. Is it possible that there is nobody among
you wise enough to judge a
dispute between believers? [6]But instead, one
brother goes to law against another—and this
in front of unbelievers!
[7]The very fact that you have lawsuits among
you means you have been completely defeated
already. Why not rather be wronged? Why
not rather be cheated? [8]Instead, you yourselves cheat and do wrong, and you do this to
your brothers.
[9]Do you not know that the wicked will not
inherit the kingdom of God? Do not be deceived: Neither the sexually immoral nor idolaters nor adulterers nor male prostitutes nor
homosexual offenders [10]nor thieves nor the
greedy nor drunkards nor slanderers nor swindlers will inherit the kingdom of God. [11]And
that is what some of you were. But you were
washed, you were sanctified, you were justified
in the name of the Lord Jesus Christ and by the
Spirit of our God.

Sexual Immorality

[12]"Everything is permissible for me"—but
not everything is beneficial. "Everything is
permissible for me"—but I will not be mastered by anything. [13]"Food for the stomach
and the stomach for food"—but God will destroy them both. The body is not meant for
sexual immorality, but for the Lord, and the
Lord for the body. [14]By his power God raised
the Lord from the dead, and he will raise us
also. [15]Do you not know that your bodies are
members of Christ himself? Shall I then take
the members of Christ and unite them with
a prostitute? Never! [16]Do you not know that
he who unites himself with
a prostitute is one with her
in body? For it is said, "The
two will become one flesh."[d]
[17]But he who unites himself
with the Lord is one with him
in spirit.
[18]Flee from sexual immorality. All other sins a man
commits are outside his body,
but he who sins sexually sins
against his own body. [19]Do
you not know that your body
is a temple of the Holy Spirit,
who is in you, whom you have received from
God? You are not your own; [20]you were
bought at a price. Therefore honor God with
your body.

1 Corinthians 6:20

God Bought Us at a Price

You were bought at a price. Therefore honor God with your body.

[a]5 Or *that his body;* or *that the flesh* [b]13 Deut. 17:7; 19:19; 21:21; 22:21,24; 24:7 [c]4 Or *matters, do you appoint as judges men of little account in the church?* [d]16 Gen. 2:24

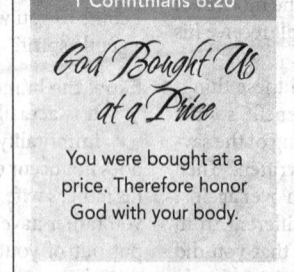

Marriage

7 Now for the matters you wrote about: It is
good for a man not to marry.[a] 2 But since
there is so much immorality, each man should
have his own wife, and each woman her own
husband. 3 The husband should fulfill his marital duty to his wife, and likewise the wife to
her husband. 4 The wife's body does not belong
to her alone but also to her husband. In the
same way, the husband's body does not belong
to him alone but also to his wife. 5 Do not deprive each other except by mutual consent and
for a time, so that you may devote yourselves
to prayer. Then come together again so that Satan will not tempt you because of your lack of
self-control. 6 I say this as a concession, not as
a command. 7 I wish that all men were as I am.
But each man has his own gift from God; one
has this gift, another has that.

8 Now to the unmarried and the widows I
say: It is good for them to stay unmarried, as
I am. 9 But if they cannot control themselves,
they should marry, for it is better to marry than
to burn with passion.

10 To the married I give this command (not
I, but the Lord): A wife must not separate from
her husband. 11 But if she does, she must remain unmarried or else be reconciled to her
husband. And a husband must not divorce his
wife.

12 To the rest I say this (I, not the Lord): If
any brother has a wife who is not a believer
and she is willing to live with him, he must
not divorce her. 13 And if a woman has a husband who is not a believer and he is willing to
live with her, she must not divorce him. 14 For
the unbelieving husband has been sanctified
through his wife, and the unbelieving wife has
been sanctified through her believing husband.
Otherwise your children would be unclean, but
as it is, they are holy.

15 But if the unbeliever leaves, let him do so.
A believing man or woman is not bound in
such circumstances; God has called us to live in
peace. 16 How do you know, wife, whether you
will save your husband? Or, how do you know,
husband, whether you will save your wife?

17 Nevertheless, each one should retain the
place in life that the Lord assigned to him and
to which God has called him. This is the rule
I lay down in all the churches. 18 Was a man
already circumcised when he was called? He
should not become uncircumcised. Was a man
uncircumcised when he was called? He should
not be circumcised. 19 Circumcision is nothing
and uncircumcision is nothing. Keeping God's
commands is what counts. 20 Each one should
remain in the situation which he was in when
God called him. 21 Were you a slave when you
were called? Don't let it trouble you—although
if you can gain your freedom, do so. 22 For he
who was a slave when he was called by the Lord
is the Lord's freedman; similarly, he who was a
free man when he was called is Christ's slave.
23 You were bought at a price; do not become
slaves of men. 24 Brothers, each man, as responsible to God, should remain in the situation
God called him to.

25 Now about virgins: I have no command
from the Lord, but I give a judgment as one
who by the Lord's mercy is trustworthy. 26 Because of the present crisis, I think that it is good
for you to remain as you are. 27 Are you married? Do not seek a divorce. Are you unmarried? Do not look for a wife. 28 But if you do
marry, you have not sinned; and if a virgin marries, she has not sinned. But those who marry
will face many troubles in this life, and I want
to spare you this.

29 What I mean, brothers, is that the time
is short. From now on those who have wives
should live as if they had none; 30 those who
mourn, as if they did not; those who are happy,
as if they were not; those who buy something,
as if it were not theirs to keep; 31 those who use
the things of the world, as if not engrossed in
them. For this world in its present form is passing away.

32 I would like you to be free from concern.
An unmarried man is concerned about the
Lord's affairs—how he can please the Lord.
33 But a married man is concerned about the
affairs of this world—how he can please his
wife— 34 and his interests are divided. An unmarried woman or virgin is concerned about
the Lord's affairs: Her aim is to be devoted to
the Lord in both body and spirit. But a married woman is concerned about the affairs of

[a] 1 Or "*It is good for a man not to have sexual relations with a woman.*"

No Distractions

1 Corinthians 7:1–2

Now for the matters you wrote about: It is good for a man not to marry. But since there is so much immorality, each man should have his own wife, and each woman her own husband.

Read: 1 Corinthians 7:1–17

WHAT ARE YOU DOING right now that is keeping you from enjoying what God has for you? Satan will turn this plot around in a number of ways. For example, he often tries to get us so bothered by the one thing we have been commanded by God not to do, that we spend far too much time thinking about it. Ultimately it distracts us from obeying God in other areas.

We become so preoccupied with certain restrictions that God has placed on our lives that we forget, just as Eve did, that those restrictions are for our own good. Without them we would be in big trouble. Sometimes single women and men are so consumed with "trying not to have sex," or at least trying not to go too far, that they are not enjoying the gift of being single. They see physical intimacy as something that they have to spend inordinate amounts of time and attention trying to avoid. Although they should indeed avoid having sex outside of marriage, singles often get so upset about the fact that they cannot have sex that they miss out on what God does want them to be doing in their relationship—learning about one another.

What joy there is in simply enjoying what God has for us right now. But in order to do that, we must not be consumed with what He has asked us *not* to do. The rate of adultery in our country has skyrocketed in recent years, and this can, at least in part, be attributed to a simple thing: Satan has dangled the carrot of singleness before the eyes of those who are married, and they have been carried away by curiosity and craving.

If you are single, he tries to cause you to become powerless in your singleness. If you are married, he seeks to make you powerless in your marriage. If you are working in the ministry, he wants you to yearn for more money. If you have children, he wants you to long to be free to do whatever *you* want, at the risk of abandoning your family. Whatever it is that God has *not* called you to do right now in your life, Satan will do his best to entice you with that very thing. Beware!

—Priscilla Evans Shirer

reflection

1. Are you surprised that God talks about sex in such a candid way? Why?
2. Do you find yourself focusing on God's restrictions rather than on what God encourages you to enjoy? How does this impact your view of God?
3. What has God called you to do right now? Ask God to give you joy in that thing and to keep Satan from tempting you away from the pleasures God's calling brings.

RELATED READINGS

Genesis 2:18–25;
1 Corinthians 6:12–20; 7:25–40;
1 Peter 3:1–7

Go to page 1397 for your next devotional reading.

this world—how she can please her husband. 35 I am saying this for your own good, not to restrict you, but that you may live in a right way in undivided devotion to the Lord.

36 If anyone thinks he is acting improperly toward the virgin he is engaged to, and if she is getting along in years and he feels he ought to marry, he should do as he wants. He is not sinning. They should get married. 37 But the man who has settled the matter in his own mind, who is under no compulsion but has control over his own will, and who has made up his mind not to marry the virgin—this man also does the right thing. 38 So then, he who marries the virgin does right, but he who does not marry her does even better.[a]

39 A woman is bound to her husband as long as he lives. But if her husband dies, she is free to marry anyone she wishes, but he must belong to the Lord. 40 In my judgment, she is happier if she stays as she is—and I think that I too have the Spirit of God.

Food Sacrificed to Idols

8 Now about food sacrificed to idols: We know that we all possess knowledge.[b] Knowledge puffs up, but love builds up. 2 The man who thinks he knows something does not yet know as he ought to know. 3 But the man who loves God is known by God.

4 So then, about eating food sacrificed to idols: We know that an idol is nothing at all in the world and that there is no God but one. 5 For even if there are so-called gods, whether in heaven or on earth (as indeed there are many "gods" and many "lords"), 6 yet for us there is but one God, the Father, from whom all things came and for whom we live; and there is but one Lord, Jesus Christ, through whom all things came and through whom we live.

7 But not everyone knows this. Some people are still so accustomed to idols that when they eat such food they think of it as having been sacrificed to an idol, and since their conscience is weak, it is defiled. 8 But food does not bring us near to God; we are no worse if we do not eat, and no better if we do.

9 Be careful, however, that the exercise of your freedom does not become a stumbling block to the weak. 10 For if anyone with a weak conscience sees you who have this knowledge eating in an idol's temple, won't he be emboldened to eat what has been sacrificed to idols? 11 So this weak brother, for whom Christ died, is destroyed by your knowledge. 12 When you sin against your brothers in this way and wound their weak conscience, you sin against Christ. 13 Therefore, if what I eat causes my brother to fall into sin, I will never eat meat again, so that I will not cause him to fall.

The Rights of an Apostle

9 Am I not free? Am I not an apostle? Have I not seen Jesus our Lord? Are you not the result of my work in the Lord? 2 Even though I may not be an apostle to others, surely I am to you! For you are the seal of my apostleship in the Lord.

3 This is my defense to those who sit in judgment on me. 4 Don't we have the right to food and drink? 5 Don't we have the right to take a believing wife along with us, as do the other apostles and the Lord's brothers and Cephas[c]? 6 Or is it only I and Barnabas who must work for a living?

7 Who serves as a soldier at his own expense? Who plants a vineyard and does not eat of its grapes? Who tends a flock and does not drink of the milk? 8 Do I say this merely from a human point of view? Doesn't the Law say the same thing? 9 For it is written in the Law of Moses: "Do not muzzle an ox while it is treading out the grain."[d] Is it about oxen that God is concerned? 10 Surely he says this for us, doesn't he? Yes, this was written for us, because when the plowman plows and the thresher threshes, they ought to do so in the hope of sharing in the harvest. 11 If we have sown spiritual seed among you, is it too much if we reap a material harvest from you? 12 If others have this right of support from you, shouldn't we have it all the more?

But we did not use this right. On the contrary, we put up with anything rather than hinder the gospel of Christ. 13 Don't you know that

[a] 36–38 Or *36 If anyone thinks he is not treating his daughter properly, and if she is getting along in years, and he feels she ought to marry, he should do as he wants. He is not sinning. He should let her get married. 37 But the man who has settled the matter in his own mind, who is under no compulsion but has control over his own will, and who has made up his mind to keep the virgin unmarried—this man also does the right thing. 38 So then, he who gives his virgin in marriage does right, but he who does not give her in marriage does even better.*
[b] 1 Or *"We all possess knowledge," as you say* [c] 5 That is, Peter [d] 9 Deut. 25:4

those who work in the temple get their food from the temple, and those who serve at the altar share in what is offered on the altar? 14In the same way, the Lord has commanded that those who preach the gospel should receive their living from the gospel.

15But I have not used any of these rights. And I am not writing this in the hope that you will do such things for me. I would rather die than have anyone deprive me of this boast. 16Yet when I preach the gospel, I cannot boast, for I am compelled to preach. Woe to me if I do not preach the gospel! 17If I preach voluntarily, I have a reward; if not voluntarily, I am simply discharging the trust committed to me. 18What then is my reward? Just this: that in preaching the gospel I may offer it free of charge, and so not make use of my rights in preaching it.

19Though I am free and belong to no man, I make myself a slave to everyone, to win as many as possible. 20To the Jews I became like a Jew, to win the Jews. To those under the law I became like one under the law (though I myself am not under the law), so as to win those under the law. 21To those not having the law I became like one not having the law (though I am not free from God's law but am under Christ's law), so as to win those not having the law. 22To the weak I became weak, to win the weak. I have become all things to all men so that by all possible means I might save some. 23I do all this for the sake of the gospel, that I may share in its blessings.

24Do you not know that in a race all the runners run, but only one gets the prize? Run in such a way as to get the prize. 25Everyone who competes in the games goes into strict training. They do it to get a crown that will not last; but we do it to get a crown that will last forever. 26Therefore I do not run like a man running aimlessly; I do not fight like a man beating the air. 27No, I beat my body and make it my slave so that after I have preached to others, I myself will not be disqualified for the prize.

Warnings From Israel's History

10 For I do not want you to be ignorant of the fact, brothers, that our forefathers were all under the cloud and that they all passed through the sea. 2They were all baptized into Moses in the cloud and in the sea. 3They all ate the same spiritual food 4and drank the same spiritual drink; for they drank from the spiritual rock that accompanied them, and that rock was Christ. 5Nevertheless, God was not pleased with most of them; their bodies were scattered over the desert.

6Now these things occurred as examples[a] to keep us from setting our hearts on evil things as they did. 7Do not be idolaters, as some of them were; as it is written: "The people sat down to eat and drink and got up to indulge in pagan revelry."[b] 8We should not commit sexual immorality, as some of them did—and in one day twenty-three thousand of them died. 9We should not test the Lord, as some of them did—and were killed by snakes. 10And do not grumble, as some of them did—and were killed by the destroying angel.

11These things happened to them as examples and were written down as warnings for us, on whom the fulfillment of the ages has come. 12So, if you think you are standing firm, be careful that you don't fall! 13No temptation has seized you except what is common to man. And God is faithful; he will not let you be tempted beyond what you can bear. But when you are tempted, he will also provide a way out so that you can stand up under it.

> **1 Corinthians 10:13**
>
> *God Is Faithful*
>
> And God is faithful;
> he will not let you be
> tempted beyond what
> you can bear. But when
> you are tempted,
> he will also provide a way
> out so that you can
> stand up under it.

Idol Feasts and the Lord's Supper

14Therefore, my dear friends, flee from idolatry. 15I speak to sensible people; judge for yourselves what I say. 16Is not the cup of thanksgiving for which we give thanks a participation in the blood of Christ? And is not the bread that we break a participation in the body of Christ? 17Because there is one loaf, we,

[a]6 Or *types*; also in verse 11 [b]7 Exodus 32:6

Unbelievable

RHODA

"YOU'RE OUT OF YOUR MIND."

That's the first thing the other believers said when she ran into the room, stammering that Peter was standing at the front door.

"Excuse me . . . but it's . . . it's *him*."

"Who are you talking about, Rhoda?" they countered.

"Pet–P–P–Peter! He's there. I mean, he's here."

So much for being the bearer of good news. Instead of elation, they met her announcement with frustration. A servant girl did not always get a lot of respect. Sure, it was a lowly job. But why did they think she would lie about something like this?

Rhoda hardly knew what to do with their cavalier response. She even reached down and pinched herself to make sure she wasn't dreaming.

No, it was real. How could she get them to believe her?

Of course, she could hardly believe it herself. One minute several houseguests had gathered together at her mistress's house to pray for Peter's release from prison. The next minute, she'd heard Peter's authoritative voice just outside.

"Rhoda! Open the door!"

Could she dare to believe the power of God unfolding before her eyes? Would she? Should she? She knew James was already dead by Herod's decree. And Peter was scheduled to be next in line for public trial after the Passover. But she was certain it was Peter's voice she'd heard—alive and well. And that could only mean one thing: God himself had rescued Peter and sent him to their home, her home.

In an instant, she had flung open the door of her heart to believe in the miracle. But in her enthusiasm, she had left Peter standing outside.

"Rhoda! Open the door!"

—Prayer—

God, your blessings and miracles surround me every day. Open my eyes to the wonder of your presence.

When she recognized Peter's voice, she was so overjoyed she ran back without opening it and exclaimed, "Peter is at the door!"

Acts 12:14

ASSIGNED READING:

Acts 12:1–17

Weekend

Go to page 1401 for your next devotional reading.

who are many, are one body, for we all partake
of the one loaf.
18Consider the people of Israel: Do not those
who eat the sacrifices participate in the altar?
19Do I mean then that a sacrifice offered to an
idol is anything, or that an idol is anything?
20No, but the sacrifices of pagans are offered to
demons, not to God, and I do not want you to
be participants with demons. 21You cannot
drink the cup of the Lord and the cup of demons too; you cannot have a part in both the
Lord's table and the table of demons. 22Are we
trying to arouse the Lord's jealousy? Are we
stronger than he?

The Believer's Freedom

23"Everything is permissible"—but not everything is beneficial. "Everything is permissible"—but not everything is constructive.
24Nobody should seek his own good, but the
good of others.
25Eat anything sold in the meat market without raising questions of conscience, 26for, "The
earth is the Lord's, and everything in it."[a]
27If some unbeliever invites you to a meal
and you want to go, eat whatever is put before
you without raising questions of conscience.
28But if anyone says to you, "This has been offered in sacrifice," then do not eat it, both for
the sake of the man who told you and for conscience' sake[b]— 29the other man's conscience, I
mean, not yours. For why should my freedom be
judged by another's conscience? 30If I take part
in the meal with thankfulness, why am I denounced because of something I thank God for?
31So whether you eat or drink or whatever
you do, do it all for the glory of God. 32Do not
cause anyone to stumble, whether Jews, Greeks
or the church of God— 33even as I try to please
everybody in every way. For I am not seeking
my own good but the good of many, so that
11 they may be saved. 1Follow my example, as I follow the example of Christ.

Propriety in Worship

2I praise you for remembering me in everything and for holding to the teachings,[c] just as
I passed them on to you.
3Now I want you to realize that the head
of every man is Christ, and the head of the
woman is man, and the head of Christ is God.
4Every man who prays or prophesies with his
head covered dishonors his head. 5And every
woman who prays or prophesies with her head
uncovered dishonors her head—it is just as
though her head were shaved. 6If a woman
does not cover her head, she should have her
hair cut off; and if it is a disgrace for a woman
to have her hair cut or shaved off, she should
cover her head. 7A man ought not to cover his
head,[d] since he is the image and glory of God;
but the woman is the glory of man. 8For man
did not come from woman, but woman from
man; 9neither was man created for woman,
but woman for man. 10For this reason, and because of the angels, the woman ought to have a
sign of authority on her head.
11In the Lord, however, woman is not independent of man, nor is man independent of
woman. 12For as woman came from man, so
also man is born of woman. But everything
comes from God. 13Judge for yourselves: Is it
proper for a woman to pray to God with her
head uncovered? 14Does not the very nature of
things teach you that if a man has long hair, it
is a disgrace to him, 15but that if a woman has
long hair, it is her glory? For long hair is given
to her as a covering. 16If anyone wants to be
contentious about this, we have no other practice—nor do the churches of God.

The Lord's Supper

17In the following directives I have no praise
for you, for your meetings do more harm than
good. 18In the first place, I hear that when
you come together as a church, there are divisions among you, and to some extent I believe
it. 19No doubt there have to be differences
among you to show which of you have God's
approval. 20When you come together, it is not
the Lord's Supper you eat, 21for as you eat, each
of you goes ahead without waiting for anybody
else. One remains hungry, another gets drunk.
22Don't you have homes to eat and drink in? Or
do you despise the church of God and humili-

[a]26 Psalm 24:1 [b]28 Some manuscripts *conscience' sake, for "the earth is the Lord's and everything in it"* [c]2 Or *traditions* [d]4–7 Or *4Every man who prays or prophesies with long hair dishonors his head. 5And every woman who prays or prophesies with no covering ⌊of hair⌋ on her head dishonors her head—she is just like one of the "shorn women." 6If a woman has no covering, let her be for now with short hair, but since it is a disgrace for a woman to have her hair shorn or shaved, she should grow it again. 7A man ought not to have long hair*

ate those who have nothing? What shall I say to you? Shall I praise you for this? Certainly not!

23For I received from the Lord what I also passed on to you: The Lord Jesus, on the night he was betrayed, took bread, 24and when he had given thanks, he broke it and said, "This is my body, which is for you; do this in remembrance of me." 25In the same way, after supper he took the cup, saying, "This cup is the new covenant in my blood; do this, whenever you drink it, in remembrance of me." 26For whenever you eat this bread and drink this cup, you proclaim the Lord's death until he comes.

27Therefore, whoever eats the bread or drinks the cup of the Lord in an unworthy manner will be guilty of sinning against the body and blood of the Lord. 28A man ought to examine himself before he eats of the bread and drinks of the cup. 29For anyone who eats and drinks without recognizing the body of the Lord eats and drinks judgment on himself. 30That is why many among you are weak and sick, and a number of you have fallen asleep. 31But if we judged ourselves, we would not come under judgment. 32When we are judged by the Lord, we are being disciplined so that we will not be condemned with the world.

33So then, my brothers, when you come together to eat, wait for each other. 34If anyone is hungry, he should eat at home, so that when you meet together it may not result in judgment.

And when I come I will give further directions.

Spiritual Gifts

12 Now about spiritual gifts, brothers, I do not want you to be ignorant. 2You know that when you were pagans, somehow or other you were influenced and led astray to mute idols. 3Therefore I tell you that no one who is speaking by the Spirit of God says, "Jesus be cursed," and no one can say, "Jesus is Lord," except by the Holy Spirit.

4There are different kinds of gifts, but the same Spirit. 5There are different kinds of service, but the same Lord. 6There are different kinds of working, but the same God works all of them in all men.

7Now to each one the manifestation of the Spirit is given for the common good. 8To one there is given through the Spirit the message of wisdom, to another the message of knowledge by means of the same Spirit, 9to another faith by the same Spirit, to another gifts of healing by that one Spirit, 10to another miraculous powers, to another prophecy, to another distinguishing between spirits, to another speaking in different kinds of tongues,[a] and to still another the interpretation of tongues.[a] 11All these are the work of one and the same Spirit, and he gives them to each one, just as he determines.

One Body, Many Parts

12The body is a unit, though it is made up of many parts; and though all its parts are many, they form one body. So it is with Christ. 13For we were all baptized by[b] one Spirit into one body—whether Jews or Greeks, slave or free—and we were all given the one Spirit to drink.

14Now the body is not made up of one part but of many. 15If the foot should say, "Because I am not a hand, I do not belong to the body," it would not for that reason cease to be part of the body. 16And if the ear should say, "Because I am not an eye, I do not belong to the body," it would not for that reason cease to be part of the body. 17If the whole body were an eye, where would the sense of hearing be? If the whole body were an ear, where would the sense of smell be? 18But in fact God has arranged the parts in the body, every one of them, just as he wanted them to be. 19If they were all one part, where would the body be? 20As it is, there are many parts, but one body.

21The eye cannot say to the hand, "I don't need you!" And the head cannot say to the feet, "I don't need you!" 22On the contrary, those parts of the body that seem to be weaker are indispensable, 23and the parts that we think are less honorable we treat with special honor. And the parts that are unpresentable are treated with special modesty, 24while our presentable parts need no special treatment. But God has combined the members of the body and has given greater honor to the parts that lacked it, 25so that there should be no division in the body, but that its parts should have equal concern for each other. 26If one part suffers, every part

[a]10 Or *languages*; also in verse 28 [b]13 Or *with*; or *in*

suffers with it; if one part is honored, every part
rejoices with it.
27 Now you are the body of Christ, and each
one of you is a part of it. 28 And in the church
God has appointed first of all apostles, second
prophets, third teachers, then workers of miracles, also those having gifts of healing, those
able to help others, those with gifts of administration, and those speaking in different kinds
of tongues. 29 Are all apostles? Are all prophets?
Are all teachers? Do all work miracles? 30 Do all
have gifts of healing? Do all speak in tongues[a]?
Do all interpret? 31 But eagerly desire[b] the
greater gifts.

Love

And now I will show you the most excellent way.

13 If I speak in the tongues[c] of men and of
angels, but have not love, I am only a resounding gong or a clanging cymbal. 2 If I have
the gift of prophecy and can fathom all mysteries and all knowledge, and if I have a faith that
can move mountains, but have not love, I am
nothing. 3 If I give all I possess to the poor and
surrender my body to the flames,[d] but have not
love, I gain nothing.
4 Love is patient, love is kind. It does not
envy, it does not boast, it is not proud. 5 It is
not rude, it is not self-seeking, it is not easily angered, it keeps no record of wrongs. 6 Love does
not delight in evil but rejoices with the truth.
7 It always protects, always trusts, always hopes,
always perseveres.
8 Love never fails. But where there are prophecies, they will cease; where there are tongues,
they will be stilled; where there is knowledge,
it will pass away. 9 For we know in part and
we prophesy in part, 10 but when perfection
comes, the imperfect disappears. 11 When I was
a child, I talked like a child, I thought like a
child, I reasoned like a child. When I became a
man, I put childish ways behind me. 12 Now we
see but a poor reflection as in a mirror; then we
shall see face to face. Now I know in part; then I
shall know fully, even as I am fully known.
13 And now these three remain: faith, hope
and love. But the greatest of these is love.

Gifts of Prophecy and Tongues

14 Follow the way of love and eagerly desire spiritual gifts, especially the gift of
prophecy. 2 For anyone who speaks in a tongue[e]
does not speak to men but to God. Indeed, no
one understands him; he utters mysteries with
his spirit.[f] 3 But everyone who prophesies speaks
to men for their strengthening, encouragement
and comfort. 4 He who speaks in a tongue edifies himself, but he who prophesies edifies
the church. 5 I would like every one of you to
speak in tongues,[g] but I would rather have you
prophesy. He who prophesies is greater than
one who speaks in tongues,[g] unless he interprets, so that the church may be edified.
6 Now, brothers, if I come to you and speak
in tongues, what good will I be to you, unless
I bring you some revelation or knowledge or
prophecy or word of instruction? 7 Even in the
case of lifeless things that make sounds, such
as the flute or harp, how will anyone know
what tune is being played unless there is a distinction in the notes? 8 Again, if the trumpet
does not sound a clear call, who will get ready
for battle? 9 So it is with you. Unless you speak
intelligible words with your tongue, how will
anyone know what you are saying? You will
just be speaking into the air. 10 Undoubtedly
there are all sorts of languages in the world, yet
none of them is without meaning. 11 If then I
do not grasp the meaning of what someone is
saying, I am a foreigner to the speaker, and he
is a foreigner to me. 12 So it is with you. Since
you are eager to have spiritual gifts, try to excel
in gifts that build up the church.
13 For this reason anyone who speaks in a
tongue should pray that he may interpret what
he says. 14 For if I pray in a tongue, my spirit
prays, but my mind is unfruitful. 15 So what
shall I do? I will pray with my spirit, but I will
also pray with my mind; I will sing with my
spirit, but I will also sing with my mind. 16 If
you are praising God with your spirit, how can
one who finds himself among those who do
not understand[h] say "Amen" to your thanksgiving, since he does not know what you are saying? 17 You may be giving thanks well enough,
but the other man is not edified.

[a] 30 Or *other languages* [b] 31 Or *But you are eagerly desiring* [c] 1 Or *languages* [d] 3 Some early manuscripts *body that I may boast*
[e] 2 Or *another language*; also in verses 4, 13, 14, 19, 26 and 27 [f] 2 Or *by the Spirit* [g] 5 Or *other languages*; also in verses 6, 18, 22, 23 and 39 [h] 16 Or *among the inquirers*

One-Hit Wonderful

Read: 1 Corinthians 13:1–13

IN THE MUSIC INDUSTRY, a one-hit wonder is a musician famous for one smash hit. Their tunes are faddish and their popularity short-lived. Future generations adopt them because they define an era. Dancers know the moves to *Disco Duck*, *The Monster Mash* and *The Macarena*. The Surfaris' song *Wipe Out* captured California's beach scene in the 60s. People from the 70s can't forget Carl Douglas's *Kung Fu Fighting*. Those hits may have been great songs, but the musicians weren't able to keep the momentum going. And thus they aren't counted among the great acts of their eras.

In 1 Corinthians 13:1–3, Paul listed some attributes that fall into the great, but not greatest, category of one-hit wonders known to human beings: faith and hope. But nothing can compete with the greatest attribute of all: love. In God's book, love is one-hit wonderful. If you're going to be known for anything, let it be love. Your lifelong goal should be to embody the diverse characteristics of love found in 1 Corinthians 13.

Unfortunately, the English language is limited to only one word to describe the many types of love. As a result, our understanding of genuine love is inadequate; we tend to confuse one kind with another. The Greek language, however, has several words for *love*, such as *eros*, meaning romantic love, and *philia*, or friendship. And there are others. But Paul used the Greek word *agape* to describe love that is divine; this type of love originates with God. It is eternal; it never fails. Verses 4–7 describe the many facets of this preeminent type of love: patience, kindness, perseverance and hope.

Here's a challenge for you: Live today seeking the greatest of all attributes. Try to express the heart of Biblical love in all that you say and do. Let today be your love song, your one-hit wonderful to everyone you encounter.

1 Corinthians 13:13

And now these three remain: faith, hope and love. But the greatest of these is love.

reflection

1 How has God shown his love for you in a very tangible, personal way? How can you show him you love him in return?

2 Review verses 4–7. Which aspect of love is the most difficult for you to express?

3 How will you show love to those you encounter today?

RELATED READINGS

Matthew 5:43–48;
John 15:9–17;
1 John 4:7–21

"Love is . . . the gift of oneself."

Jean Anouilh

Go to page 1404 for your next devotional reading.

18I thank God that I speak in tongues more than all of you. 19But in the church I would rather speak five intelligible words to instruct others than ten thousand words in a tongue.

20Brothers, stop thinking like children. In regard to evil be infants, but in your thinking be adults. 21In the Law it is written:

"Through men of strange
tongues
and through the lips of
foreigners
I will speak to this people,
but even then they will
not listen to me,"[a]

says the Lord.

22Tongues, then, are a sign, not for believers but for unbelievers; prophecy, however, is for believers, not for unbelievers. 23So if the whole church comes together and everyone speaks in tongues, and some who do not understand[b] or some unbelievers come in, will they not say that you are out of your mind? 24But if an unbeliever or someone who does not understand[c] comes in while everybody is prophesying, he will be convinced by all that he is a sinner and will be judged by all, 25and the secrets of his heart will be laid bare. So he will fall down and worship God, exclaiming, "God is really among you!"

Orderly Worship

26What then shall we say, brothers? When you come together, everyone has a hymn, or a word of instruction, a revelation, a tongue or an interpretation. All of these must be done for the strengthening of the church. 27If anyone speaks in a tongue, two—or at the most three—should speak, one at a time, and someone must interpret. 28If there is no interpreter, the speaker should keep quiet in the church and speak to himself and God.

29Two or three prophets should speak, and the others should weigh carefully what is said. 30And if a revelation comes to someone who is sitting down, the first speaker should stop. 31For you can all prophesy in turn so that everyone may be instructed and encouraged. 32The spirits of prophets are subject to the control of prophets. 33For God is not a God of disorder but of peace.

> 1 Corinthians 14:33
>
> *God Is Peaceful*
>
> For God is not a God of disorder but of peace.

As in all the congregations of the saints, 34women should remain silent in the churches. They are not allowed to speak, but must be in submission, as the Law says. 35If they want to inquire about something, they should ask their own husbands at home; for it is disgraceful for a woman to speak in the church.

36Did the word of God originate with you? Or are you the only people it has reached? 37If anybody thinks he is a prophet or spiritually gifted, let him acknowledge that what I am writing to you is the Lord's command. 38If he ignores this, he himself will be ignored.[d]

39Therefore, my brothers, be eager to prophesy, and do not forbid speaking in tongues. 40But everything should be done in a fitting and orderly way.

The Resurrection of Christ

15 Now, brothers, I want to remind you of the gospel I preached to you, which you received and on which you have taken your stand. 2By this gospel you are saved, if you hold firmly to the word I preached to you. Otherwise, you have believed in vain.

3For what I received I passed on to you as of first importance[e]: that Christ died for our sins according to the Scriptures, 4that he was buried, that he was raised on the third day according to the Scriptures, 5and that he appeared to Peter,[f] and then to the Twelve. 6After that, he appeared to more than five hundred of the brothers at the same time, most of whom are still living, though some have fallen asleep. 7Then he appeared to James, then to all the apostles, 8and last of all he appeared to me also, as to one abnormally born.

9For I am the least of the apostles and do not even deserve to be called an apostle, because I persecuted the church of God. 10But by the grace of God I am what I am, and his grace to

[a]21 Isaiah 28:11,12 [b]23 Or *some inquirers* [c]24 Or *or some inquirer* [d]38 Some manuscripts *If he is ignorant of this, let him be ignorant* [e]3 Or *you at the first* [f]5 Greek *Cephas*

me was not without effect. No, I worked harder
than all of them—yet not I, but the grace of
God that was with me. 11Whether, then, it was
I or they, this is what we preach, and this is
what you believed.

The Resurrection of the Dead

12But if it is preached that Christ has been
raised from the dead, how can some of you say
that there is no resurrection of the dead? 13If
there is no resurrection of the dead, then not
even Christ has been raised. 14And if Christ
has not been raised, our preaching is useless
and so is your faith. 15More than that, we are
then found to be false witnesses about God,
for we have testified about God that he raised
Christ from the dead. But he did not raise him
if in fact the dead are not raised. 16For if the
dead are not raised, then Christ has not been
raised either. 17And if Christ has not been
raised, your faith is futile; you are still in your
sins. 18Then those also who have fallen asleep
in Christ are lost. 19If only for this life we have
hope in Christ, we are to be pitied more than
all men.

20But Christ has indeed been raised from
the dead, the firstfruits of those who have
fallen asleep. 21For since death came through
a man, the resurrection of the dead comes also
through a man. 22For as in Adam all die, so in
Christ all will be made alive. 23But each in his
own turn: Christ, the firstfruits; then, when he
comes, those who belong to him. 24Then the
end will come, when he hands over the kingdom to God the Father after he has destroyed
all dominion, authority and power. 25For he
must reign until he has put all his enemies under his feet. 26The last enemy to be destroyed is
death. 27For he "has put everything under his
feet."[a] Now when it says that "everything" has
been put under him, it is clear that this does
not include God himself, who put everything
under Christ. 28When he has done this, then
the Son himself will be made subject to him
who put everything under him, so that God
may be all in all.

29Now if there is no resurrection, what will
those do who are baptized for the dead? If the
dead are not raised at all, why are people baptized for them? 30And as for us, why do we
endanger ourselves every hour? 31I die every
day—I mean that, brothers—just as surely as
I glory over you in Christ Jesus our Lord. 32If
I fought wild beasts in Ephesus for merely human reasons, what have I gained? If the dead
are not raised,

"Let us eat and drink,
for tomorrow we die."[b]

33Do not be misled: "Bad company corrupts
good character." 34Come back to your senses
as you ought, and stop sinning; for there are
some who are ignorant of God—I say this to
your shame.

The Resurrection Body

35But someone may ask, "How are the
dead raised? With what kind of body will they
come?" 36How foolish! What you sow does
not come to life unless it dies. 37When you
sow, you do not plant the body that will be,
but just a seed, perhaps of wheat or of something else. 38But God gives it a body as he has
determined, and to each kind of seed he gives
its own body. 39All flesh is not the same: Men
have one kind of flesh, animals have another,
birds another and fish another. 40There are also
heavenly bodies and there are earthly bodies;
but the splendor of the heavenly bodies is one
kind, and the splendor of the earthly bodies is
another. 41The sun has one kind of splendor,
the moon another and the stars another; and
star differs from star in splendor.

42So will it be with the resurrection of the
dead. The body that is sown is perishable, it is
raised imperishable; 43it is sown in dishonor,
it is raised in glory; it is sown in weakness, it is
raised in power; 44it is sown a natural body, it
is raised a spiritual body.

If there is a natural body, there is also a
spiritual body. 45So it is written: "The first
man Adam became a living being"[c]; the last
Adam, a life-giving spirit. 46The spiritual did
not come first, but the natural, and after that
the spiritual. 47The first man was of the dust of
the earth, the second man from heaven. 48As

[a]27 Psalm 8:6 [b]32 Isaiah 22:13 [c]45 Gen. 2:7

Why the Resurrection Matters

1 Corinthians 15:54

When the perishable has been clothed with the imperishable, and the mortal with immortality, then the saying that is written will come true: "Death has been swallowed up in victory."

reflection

1 Have you ever experienced a loss like that of Sandra or C. S. Lewis? If so, what emotions and questions did you experience?

2 How does it help you to know that in heaven there is no sorrow?

3 If you don't currently live as if the resurrection is true, how could you begin to make it a daily source of encouragement and strength?

RELATED READINGS

Romans 6:4–11;
1 Thessalonians 4:13–18;
1 Peter 1:3–7;
Revelation 21:1–4

"Death is the golden key that opens the palace of eternity."

John Milton

Read: 1 Corinthians 15:1–58

SANDRA'S HUSBAND OF TEN YEARS died of a sudden heart attack last year, leaving her to raise three daughters alone. On certain days, she keeps busy enough to keep the tears at bay. But on others, she wonders if she'll ever recover from the loss. She misses her husband's arms around her, his head on the pillow beside her and his guidance in making big decisions. *God, why did he have to leave us so soon?* she asks. *Why didn't you heal him so he could live to watch his girls grow up?*

C. S. Lewis asked similar questions after he lost his wife, Joy, to cancer. In *A Grief Observed*, he wrote, "How often—will it be for always?—how often will the vast emptiness astonish me like a complete novelty and make me say, 'I never realized my loss till this moment'? The same leg is cut off time after time. The first plunge of the knife into the flesh is felt again and again."

It's normal—and healthy—to grieve when those we love are taken from us. But in 1 Corinthians 15, Paul explains why the resurrection of Jesus matters so much to those who believe: This earthly chapter is not the end of the eternal story; the pain of death will one day be only a memory.

When we leave our physical bodies behind at death, we'll be ushered into God's presence, where we'll feel his healing embrace. We'll be enveloped by his all-consuming love. And suddenly, in the light of God's face, and in the face of his passion for us, all our questions, our grief—and our sorrows—will fade away. And one day, at the resurrection, our perishable bodies will be "clothed with the imperishable." We'll be transformed so that we can live forever with Christ in holy joy.

If you are grieving, hold on to the promise of the resurrection. It will make all the difference in this world—and in the next.

Go to page 1410 for your next devotional reading.

was the earthly man, so are those who are of
the earth; and as is the man from heaven, so
also are those who are of heaven. 49 And just
as we have borne the likeness of the earthly
man, so shall we[a] bear the likeness of the man
from heaven.
50 I declare to you, brothers, that flesh and
blood cannot inherit the kingdom of God, nor
does the perishable inherit the imperishable.
51 Listen, I tell you a mystery: We will not all
sleep, but we will all be changed— 52 in a flash,
in the twinkling of an eye, at the last trumpet.
For the trumpet will sound, the dead will be
raised imperishable, and we will be changed.
53 For the perishable must clothe itself with the
imperishable, and the mortal with immortality.
54 When the perishable has been clothed
with the imperishable, and the mortal with
immortality, then the saying that is written will
come true: "Death has been swallowed up in
victory."[b]

55 "Where, O death, is your
victory?
Where, O death, is your
sting?"[c]

56 The sting of death is sin, and
the power of sin is the law.
57 But thanks be to God! He
gives us the victory through
our Lord Jesus Christ.
58 Therefore, my dear brothers, stand firm. Let nothing
move you. Always give yourselves fully to the work of the
Lord, because you know that
your labor in the Lord is not in vain.

> **1 Corinthians 15:57**
>
> *God Gives Victory*
>
> But thanks be to God!
> He gives us the victory
> through our
> Lord Jesus Christ.

The Collection for God's People

16 Now about the collection for God's
people: Do what I told the Galatian
churches to do. 2 On the first day of every
week, each one of you should set aside a sum
of money in keeping with his income, saving
it up, so that when I come no collections will
have to be made. 3 Then, when I arrive, I will
give letters of introduction to the men you approve and send them with your gift to Jerusalem. 4 If it seems advisable for me to go also,
they will accompany me.

Personal Requests

5 After I go through Macedonia, I will come
to you—for I will be going through Macedonia.
6 Perhaps I will stay with you awhile, or even
spend the winter, so that you can help me on
my journey, wherever I go. 7 I do not want to
see you now and make only a passing visit; I
hope to spend some time with you, if the Lord
permits. 8 But I will stay on at Ephesus until
Pentecost, 9 because a great door for effective
work has opened to me, and there are many
who oppose me.
10 If Timothy comes, see to it that he has
nothing to fear while he is with you, for he is
carrying on the work of the Lord, just as I am.
11 No one, then, should refuse to accept him.
Send him on his way in peace so that he may
return to me. I am expecting him along with
the brothers.
12 Now about our brother
Apollos: I strongly urged him
to go to you with the brothers.
He was quite unwilling to go
now, but he will go when he
has the opportunity.
13 Be on your guard; stand
firm in the faith; be men of
courage; be strong. 14 Do everything in love.
15 You know that the household of Stephanas were the first
converts in Achaia, and they
have devoted themselves to
the service of the saints. I urge
you, brothers, 16 to submit to such as these and
to everyone who joins in the work, and labors
at it. 17 I was glad when Stephanas, Fortunatus
and Achaicus arrived, because they have supplied what was lacking from you. 18 For they
refreshed my spirit and yours also. Such men
deserve recognition.

Final Greetings

19 The churches in the province of Asia send
you greetings. Aquila and Priscilla[d] greet you
warmly in the Lord, and so does the church

[a] 49 Some early manuscripts *so let us* [b] 54 Isaiah 25:8 [c] 55 Hosea 13:14 [d] 19 Greek *Prisca*, a variant of *Priscilla*

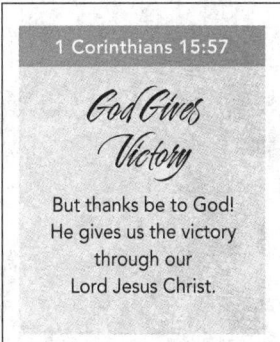

that meets at their house. 20All the brothers
here send you greetings. Greet one another
with a holy kiss.
21I, Paul, write this greeting in my own
hand.
22If anyone does not love the Lord—a curse
be on him. Come, O Lord[a]!
23The grace of the Lord Jesus be with you.
24My love to all of you in Christ Jesus.
Amen.[b]

[a]22 In Aramaic the expression *Come, O Lord* is *Marana tha.* [b]24 Some manuscripts do not have *Amen.*

2 Corinthians

Author:
The apostle Paul.

Audience:
Followers of Jesus; originally written to the church in Corinth.

Date:
About A.D. 55.

Setting:
False teachers in the church at Corinth were denying Paul's authority over them as an apostle.

Verse to Remember:
You yourselves are our letter, written on our hearts, known and read by everybody. You show that you are a letter from Christ, the result of our ministry, written not with ink but with the Spirit of the living God, not on tablets of stone but on tablets of human hearts. (3:2–3)

What would you write to your children or someone you loved if you knew they were facing difficult circumstances of their own making? This is the situation Paul was in. He had traveled to Corinth in the past and had already written a severe letter of correction to the church there. *Now he needed to confront them again.* He was distressed for their comfort and salvation (see 2 Corinthians 1:6). Like a father, Paul encouraged his spiritual children to *stand firm in the faith,* represent Christ well, give generously, beware of false prophets and take every thought captive to the obedience of Christ.

Paul told his brothers and sisters in Christ that they themselves were a "letter . . . known and read by everybody." We've often heard the saying, "Read my lips." Paul is saying that *others will "read our lives."* By our actions, words and deeds, we are living, walking, breathing letters from Christ for all to read.

1 Paul, an apostle of Christ Jesus by the will of God, and Timothy our brother,

To the church of God in Corinth, together with all the saints throughout Achaia:

2 Grace and peace to you from God our Father and the Lord Jesus Christ.

The God of All Comfort

3 Praise be to the God and Father of our Lord Jesus Christ, the Father of compassion and the God of all comfort, 4 who comforts us in all our troubles, so that we can comfort those in any trouble with the comfort we ourselves have received from God. 5 For just as the sufferings of

Christ flow over into our lives, so also through
Christ our comfort overflows. 6If we are distressed, it is for your comfort and salvation; if
we are comforted, it is for your comfort, which
produces in you patient endurance of the same
sufferings we suffer. 7And our hope for you is
firm, because we know that just as you share
in our sufferings, so also you share in our comfort.

8We do not want you to be uninformed,
brothers, about the hardships we suffered in
the province of Asia. We were under great
pressure, far beyond our ability to endure, so
that we despaired even of life. 9Indeed, in our
hearts we felt the sentence of death. But this
happened that we might not rely on ourselves
but on God, who raises the dead. 10He has delivered us from such a deadly peril, and he will
deliver us. On him we have set our hope that
he will continue to deliver us, 11as you help us
by your prayers. Then many will give thanks on
our[a] behalf for the gracious favor granted us in
answer to the prayers of many.

Paul's Change of Plans

12Now this is our boast: Our conscience testifies that we have conducted ourselves in the
world, and especially in our relations with you,
in the holiness and sincerity that are from God.
We have done so not according to worldly wisdom but according to God's grace. 13For we do
not write you anything you cannot read or understand. And I hope that, 14as you have understood us in part, you will come to understand
fully that you can boast of us just as we will
boast of you in the day of the Lord Jesus.

15Because I was confident of this, I planned
to visit you first so that you might benefit twice.
16I planned to visit you on my way to Macedonia and to come back to you from Macedonia,
and then to have you send me on my way to Judea. 17When I planned this, did I do it lightly?
Or do I make my plans in a worldly manner
so that in the same breath I say, "Yes, yes" and
"No, no"?

18But as surely as God is faithful, our message to you is not "Yes" and "No." 19For the Son
of God, Jesus Christ, who was preached among
you by me and Silas[b] and Timothy, was not
"Yes" and "No," but in him it has always been
"Yes." 20For no matter how many promises
God has made, they are "Yes" in Christ. And so
through him the "Amen" is spoken by us to the
glory of God. 21Now it is God who makes both
us and you stand firm in Christ. He anointed
us, 22set his seal of ownership on us, and put
his Spirit in our hearts as a deposit, guaranteeing what is to come.

23I call God as my witness that it was in order to spare you that I did not return to Corinth. 24Not that we lord it over your faith, but
we work with you for your joy, because it is by
2 faith you stand firm. 1So I made up my
mind that I would not make another painful visit to you. 2For if I grieve you, who is left
to make me glad but you whom I have grieved?
3I wrote as I did so that when I came I should
not be distressed by those who ought to make
me rejoice. I had confidence in all of you, that
you would all share my joy. 4For I wrote you
out of great distress and anguish of heart and
with many tears, not to grieve you but to let
you know the depth of my love for you.

Forgiveness for the Sinner

5If anyone has caused grief, he has not so
much grieved me as he has grieved all of you,
to some extent—not to put it too severely. 6The
punishment inflicted on him by the majority
is sufficient for him. 7Now instead, you ought
to forgive and comfort him, so that he will not
be overwhelmed by excessive sorrow. 8I urge
you, therefore, to reaffirm your love for him.
9The reason I wrote you was to see if you would
stand the test and be obedient in everything.
10If you forgive anyone, I also forgive him.
And what I have forgiven—if there was anything to forgive—I have forgiven in the sight
of Christ for your sake, 11in order that Satan
might not outwit us. For we are not unaware
of his schemes.

Ministers of the New Covenant

12Now when I went to Troas to preach the
gospel of Christ and found that the Lord had
opened a door for me, 13I still had no peace of
mind, because I did not find my brother Titus
there. So I said good-by to them and went on
to Macedonia.

14But thanks be to God, who always leads us

[a]11 Many manuscripts *your* [b]19 Greek *Silvanus*, a variant of *Silas*

in triumphal procession in Christ and through us spreads everywhere the fragrance of the knowledge of him. 15For we are to God the aroma of Christ among those who are being saved and those who are perishing. 16To the one we are the smell of death; to the other, the fragrance of life. And who is equal to such a task? 17Unlike so many, we do not peddle the word of God for profit. On the contrary, in Christ we speak before God with sincerity, like men sent from God.

3 Are we beginning to commend ourselves again? Or do we need, like some people, letters of recommendation to you or from you? 2You yourselves are our letter, written on our hearts, known and read by everybody. 3You show that you are a letter from Christ, the result of our ministry, written not with ink but with the Spirit of the living God, not on tablets of stone but on tablets of human hearts.

4Such confidence as this is ours through Christ before God. 5Not that we are competent in ourselves to claim anything for ourselves, but our competence comes from God. 6He has made us competent as ministers of a new covenant—not of the letter but of the Spirit; for the letter kills, but the Spirit gives life.

The Glory of the New Covenant

7Now if the ministry that brought death, which was engraved in letters on stone, came with glory, so that the Israelites could not look steadily at the face of Moses because of its glory, fading though it was, 8will not the ministry of the Spirit be even more glorious? 9If the ministry that condemns men is glorious, how much more glorious is the ministry that brings righteousness! 10For what was glorious has no glory now in comparison with the surpassing glory. 11And if what was fading away came with glory, how much greater is the glory of that which lasts!

12Therefore, since we have such a hope, we are very bold. 13We are not like Moses, who would put a veil over his face to keep the Israelites from gazing at it while the radiance was fading away. 14But their minds were made dull, for to this day the same veil remains when the old covenant is read. It has not been removed, because only in Christ is it taken away. 15Even to this day when Moses is read, a veil covers their hearts. 16But whenever anyone turns to the Lord, the veil is taken away. 17Now the Lord is the Spirit, and where the Spirit of the Lord is, there is freedom. 18And we, who with unveiled faces all reflect[a] the Lord's glory, are being transformed into his likeness with ever-increasing glory, which comes from the Lord, who is the Spirit.

Treasures in Jars of Clay

4 Therefore, since through God's mercy we have this ministry, we do not lose heart. 2Rather, we have renounced secret and shameful ways; we do not use deception, nor do we distort the word of God. On the contrary, by setting forth the truth plainly we commend ourselves to every man's conscience in the sight of God. 3And even if our gospel is veiled, it is veiled to those who are perishing. 4The god of this age has blinded the minds of unbelievers, so that they cannot see the light of the gospel of the glory of Christ, who is the image of God. 5For we do not preach ourselves, but Jesus Christ as Lord, and ourselves as your servants for Jesus' sake. 6For God, who said, "Let light shine out of darkness,"[b] made his light shine in our hearts to give us the light of the knowledge of the glory of God in the face of Christ.

7But we have this treasure in jars of clay to show that this all-surpassing power is from God and not from us. 8We are hard pressed on every side, but not crushed; perplexed, but not in despair; 9persecuted, but not abandoned; struck down, but not destroyed. 10We always carry around in our body the death of Jesus, so that the life of Jesus may also be revealed in our body. 11For we who are alive are always being given over to death for Jesus' sake, so that his life may be revealed in our mortal body. 12So then, death is at work in us, but life is at work in you.

13It is written: "I believed; therefore I have spoken."[c] With that same spirit of faith we also believe and therefore speak, 14because we know that the one who raised the Lord Jesus from the dead will also raise us with Jesus and present us with you in his presence. 15All this is

[a]18 Or *contemplate* [b]6 Gen. 1:3 [c]13 Psalm 116:10

Humble Competence

Read: 2 Corinthians 3:4–18

2 Corinthians 3:4–5

Such confidence as this is ours through Christ before God. Not that we are competent in ourselves to claim anything for ourselves, but our competence comes from God.

YOU PROBABLY KNOW SOMEONE who overestimates her competence. She might be a member of your Bible study who has a subtle way of telling others how to run their lives. Maybe it's a coworker who takes control of everything around her.

On the other end of the scale are those (often women) who revel in false humility. They tell themselves and everyone else how incapable of anything they are.

In contrast, there are those who understand that their abilities are God-given. They realize that their talents are gifts, recognize their limitations and welcome others' input. They don't think of themselves as superior but consider others' needs before their own. Being around these people frees others to be the best they can be.

True competence begins with humility, recognizing our natural abilities but acknowledging that they can only carry us so far. With that knowledge, we begin to realize that our incompetence is merely a starting point. We don't have to be perfect; we have the freedom to be the uniquely gifted, talented and competent women God created.

Elisa Morgan, president of MOPS (Mothers of Preschoolers) International, wrote:

> "I'm probably the least likely person to head a mothering organization. I grew up in a broken home. My parents were divorced when I was 5. My older sister, younger brother, and I were raised by my alcoholic mother.
>
> "While my mother meant well—truly she did—most of my memories are of me mothering her rather than her mothering me. Alcohol altered her love, turning it into something that wasn't love . . .
>
> "Ten years ago, when I was asked to consider leading MOPS International, a vital ministry that nurtures mothers, I went straight to my knees—and then to the therapist's office. How could God use me—who had never been mothered—to nurture other mothers?
>
> "The answer came as I gazed into the eyes of other moms around me and saw their needs mirroring my own. God seemed to take my deficits and make them my offering."

reflection

1 How have you found your natural abilities insufficient?

2 How does knowing that you can rely on God's competence give you confidence?

3 What might you try to do for God's kingdom if you knew you could not fail?

RELATED READINGS

Exodus 4:10–12; 2 Corinthians 12:7–10; James 1:16–18

Wednesday

Go to page 1412 for your next devotional reading.

for your benefit, so that the grace that is reaching more and more people may cause thanksgiving to overflow to the glory of God.

16 Therefore we do not lose heart. Though outwardly we are wasting away, yet inwardly we are being renewed day by day. 17 For our light and momentary troubles are achieving for us an eternal glory that far outweighs them all. 18 So we fix our eyes not on what is seen, but on what is unseen. For what is seen is temporary, but what is unseen is eternal.

> **2 Corinthians 4:17**
>
> *God Will Reward*
>
> For our light and momentary troubles are achieving for us an eternal glory that far outweighs them all.

Our Heavenly Dwelling

5 Now we know that if the earthly tent we live in is destroyed, we have a building from God, an eternal house in heaven, not built by human hands. 2 Meanwhile we groan, longing to be clothed with our heavenly dwelling, 3 because when we are clothed, we will not be found naked. 4 For while we are in this tent, we groan and are burdened, because we do not wish to be unclothed but to be clothed with our heavenly dwelling, so that what is mortal may be swallowed up by life. 5 Now it is God who has made us for this very purpose and has given us the Spirit as a deposit, guaranteeing what is to come.

6 Therefore we are always confident and know that as long as we are at home in the body we are away from the Lord. 7 We live by faith, not by sight. 8 We are confident, I say, and would prefer to be away from the body and at home with the Lord. 9 So we make it our goal to please him, whether we are at home in the body or away from it. 10 For we must all appear before the judgment seat of Christ, that each one may receive what is due him for the things done while in the body, whether good or bad.

The Ministry of Reconciliation

11 Since, then, we know what it is to fear the Lord, we try to persuade men. What we are is plain to God, and I hope it is also plain to your conscience. 12 We are not trying to commend ourselves to you again, but are giving you an opportunity to take pride in us, so that you can answer those who take pride in what is seen rather than in what is in the heart. 13 If we are out of our mind, it is for the sake of God; if we are in our right mind, it is for you. 14 For Christ's love compels us, because we are convinced that one died for all, and therefore all died. 15 And he died for all, that those who live should no longer live for themselves but for him who died for them and was raised again.

16 So from now on we regard no one from a worldly point of view. Though we once regarded Christ in this way, we do so no longer. 17 Therefore, if anyone is in Christ, he is a new creation; the old has gone, the new has come! 18 All this is from God, who reconciled us to himself through Christ and gave us the ministry of reconciliation: 19 that God was reconciling the world to himself in Christ, not counting men's sins against them. And he has committed to us the message of reconciliation. 20 We are therefore Christ's ambassadors, as though God were making his appeal through us. We implore you on Christ's behalf: Be reconciled to God. 21 God made him who had no sin to be sin[a] for us, so that in him we might become the righteousness of God.

6 As God's fellow workers we urge you not to receive God's grace in vain. 2 For he says,

> "In the time of my favor I heard you,
> and in the day of salvation I helped you."[b]

I tell you, now is the time of God's favor, now is the day of salvation.

Paul's Hardships

3 We put no stumbling block in anyone's path, so that our ministry will not be discredited. 4 Rather, as servants of God we commend ourselves in every way: in great endurance; in troubles, hardships and distresses; 5 in beatings, imprisonments and riots; in hard work, sleepless nights and hunger; 6 in purity, understanding, patience and kindness; in the Holy Spirit and in sincere love; 7 in truthful

[a]21 Or *be a sin offering* [b]2 Isaiah 49:8

The "Me Disease"

2 Corinthians 5:15

And he died for all, that those who live should no longer live for themselves but for him who died for them and was raised again.

reflection

1 What causes you to become overly focused on your own life rather than looking out for the needs of others?

2 How will becoming less self-involved help you better live for Jesus Christ?

3 On whom can you shower God's love today?

RELATED READINGS

John 13:34–38; Galatians 6:2–3; Philippians 2:3–11; 1 John 3:16–18

Read: 2 Corinthians 5:1–21

LIKE A DEADLY VIRUS, the disease of self-centeredness permeates our culture. From the driver who blatantly cuts us off in traffic to the friend who talks only about her kids, her job, her *everything*, we're saturated with symptoms of the "Me Disease." The symptoms are rude behavior, selfish conversations and sheer indifference.

The deterioration in our society can be traced to decades of feeding the needs of the "me generation" that lives by the maxim, "I can do whatever I want as long as it doesn't hurt anyone." Unfortunately, the "me" attitudes aren't confined to secular society. Even many Christians quickly claim their "rights" when they're offended.

The antidote to this malady is found in today's Scripture passage: "Those who live should no longer live for themselves." But it doesn't stop there. We are instructed to live "for him who died . . . and was raised again." No higher price could have been paid to provide us with a life worth living.

So how do we follow this command in our busy and self-involved lives? How do we live for others—and, therefore, for Jesus Christ—rather than living for ourselves? We cannot physically anoint his feet with oil as the woman in Luke 7:46 did. And it isn't as if our Lord needs anything; he owns "the cattle on a thousand hills" (Psalm 50:10). The divine prescription for the "Me Disease" is this: Jesus said, "Whatever you did for one of the least of these brothers of mine, you did for me" (Matthew 25:40).

You live for Jesus when you take soup and muffins to a shut-in. You live for Jesus when you watch your neighbor's toddlers so she can run errands. You live for Jesus when you dare to look into the eyes of the down-and-out with respect and dignity. You live for Jesus when you speak up for the poor and stand up for justice. Today may our prayer be "to cease living for me and live only for Thee."

Go to page 1418 for your next devotional reading.

speech and in the power of God; with weapons
of righteousness in the right hand and in the
left; 8through glory and dishonor, bad report
and good report; genuine, yet regarded as impostors; 9known, yet regarded as unknown;
dying, and yet we live on; beaten, and yet not
killed; 10sorrowful, yet always rejoicing; poor,
yet making many rich; having nothing, and yet
possessing everything.
11We have spoken freely to you, Corinthians, and opened wide our hearts to you. 12We
are not withholding our affection from you, but
you are withholding yours from us. 13As a fair
exchange—I speak as to my children—open
wide your hearts also.

Do Not Be Yoked With Unbelievers

14Do not be yoked together with unbelievers. For what do righteousness and wickedness
have in common? Or what fellowship can
light have with darkness? 15What harmony is
there between Christ and Belial[a]? What does a
believer have in common with an unbeliever?
16What agreement is there between the temple
of God and idols? For we are the temple of the
living God. As God has said: "I will live with
them and walk among them, and I will be their
God, and they will be my people."[b]

17"Therefore come out from them
and be separate,
says the Lord.
Touch no unclean thing,
and I will receive you."[c]
18"I will be a Father to you,
and you will be my sons
and daughters,
says the Lord
Almighty."[d]

7 Since we have these promises, dear friends, let us
purify ourselves from everything that contaminates body
and spirit, perfecting holiness
out of reverence for God.

Paul's Joy

2Make room for us in your hearts. We have
wronged no one, we have corrupted no one,
we have exploited no one. 3I do not say this
to condemn you; I have said before that you
have such a place in our hearts that we would
live or die with you. 4I have great confidence
in you; I take great pride in you. I am greatly
encouraged; in all our troubles my joy knows
no bounds.
5For when we came into Macedonia, this
body of ours had no rest, but we were harassed
at every turn—conflicts on the outside, fears
within. 6But God, who comforts the downcast,
comforted us by the coming of Titus, 7and not
only by his coming but also by the comfort you
had given him. He told us about your longing
for me, your deep sorrow, your ardent concern
for me, so that my joy was greater than ever.
8Even if I caused you sorrow by my letter, I
do not regret it. Though I did regret it—I see
that my letter hurt you, but only for a little
while— 9yet now I am happy, not because you
were made sorry, but because your sorrow led
you to repentance. For you became sorrowful
as God intended and so were not harmed in
any way by us. 10Godly sorrow brings repentance that leads to salvation and leaves no regret, but worldly sorrow brings death. 11See
what this godly sorrow has produced in you:
what earnestness, what eagerness to clear yourselves, what indignation, what alarm, what
longing, what concern, what readiness to see
justice done. At every point
you have proved yourselves
to be innocent in this matter.
12So even though I wrote to
you, it was not on account of
the one who did the wrong or
of the injured party, but rather
that before God you could see
for yourselves how devoted
to us you are. 13By all this we
are encouraged.
In addition to our own
encouragement, we were especially delighted to see how
happy Titus was, because his
spirit has been refreshed by all
of you. 14I had boasted to him
about you, and you have not embarrassed me.
But just as everything we said to you was true,
so our boasting about you to Titus has proved

> **2 Corinthians 7:1**
>
> *God Desires Our Purity*
>
> Since we have these promises, dear friends, let us purify ourselves from everything that contaminates body and spirit, perfecting holiness out of reverence for God.

[a]15 Greek *Beliar*, a variant of *Belial* [b]16 Lev. 26:12; Jer. 32:38; Ezek. 37:27 [c]17 Isaiah 52:11; Ezek. 20:34,41 [d]18 2 Samuel 7:14; 7:8

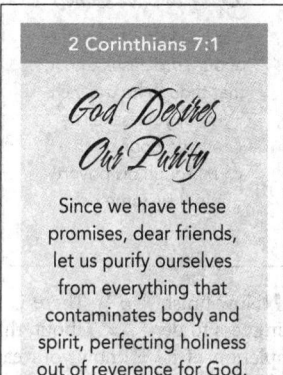

to be true as well. 15 And his affection for you is all the greater when he remembers that you were all obedient, receiving him with fear and trembling. 16 I am glad I can have complete confidence in you.

Generosity Encouraged

8 And now, brothers, we want you to know about the grace that God has given the Macedonian churches. 2 Out of the most severe trial, their overflowing joy and their extreme poverty welled up in rich generosity. 3 For I testify that they gave as much as they were able, and even beyond their ability. Entirely on their own, 4 they urgently pleaded with us for the privilege of sharing in this service to the saints. 5 And they did not do as we expected, but they gave themselves first to the Lord and then to us in keeping with God's will. 6 So we urged Titus, since he had earlier made a beginning, to bring also to completion this act of grace on your part. 7 But just as you excel in everything—in faith, in speech, in knowledge, in complete earnestness and in your love for us[a]—see that you also excel in this grace of giving.

8 I am not commanding you, but I want to test the sincerity of your love by comparing it with the earnestness of others. 9 For you know the grace of our Lord Jesus Christ, that though he was rich, yet for your sakes he became poor, so that you through his poverty might become rich.

10 And here is my advice about what is best for you in this matter: Last year you were the first not only to give but also to have the desire to do so. 11 Now finish the work, so that your eager willingness to do it may be matched by your completion of it, according to your means. 12 For if the willingness is there, the gift is acceptable according to what one has, not according to what he does not have.

13 Our desire is not that others might be relieved while you are hard pressed, but that there might be equality. 14 At the present time your plenty will supply what they need, so that in turn their plenty will supply what you need. Then there will be equality, 15 as it is written: "He who gathered much did not have too much, and he who gathered little did not have too little."[b]

> **2 Corinthians 8:9**
>
> *God Offers Spiritual Riches*
>
> For you know the grace of our Lord Jesus Christ, that though he was rich, yet for your sakes he became poor, so that you through his poverty might become rich.

Titus Sent to Corinth

16 I thank God, who put into the heart of Titus the same concern I have for you. 17 For Titus not only welcomed our appeal, but he is coming to you with much enthusiasm and on his own initiative. 18 And we are sending along with him the brother who is praised by all the churches for his service to the gospel. 19 What is more, he was chosen by the churches to accompany us as we carry the offering, which we administer in order to honor the Lord himself and to show our eagerness to help. 20 We want to avoid any criticism of the way we administer this liberal gift. 21 For we are taking pains to do what is right, not only in the eyes of the Lord but also in the eyes of men.

22 In addition, we are sending with them our brother who has often proved to us in many ways that he is zealous, and now even more so because of his great confidence in you. 23 As for Titus, he is my partner and fellow worker among you; as for our brothers, they are representatives of the churches and an honor to Christ. 24 Therefore show these men the proof of your love and the reason for our pride in you, so that the churches can see it.

9 There is no need for me to write to you about this service to the saints. 2 For I know your eagerness to help, and I have been boasting about it to the Macedonians, telling them that since last year you in Achaia were ready to give; and your enthusiasm has stirred most of them to action. 3 But I am sending the brothers in order that our boasting about you in this matter should not prove hollow, but

[a] 7 Some manuscripts *in our love for you* [b] 15 Exodus 16:18

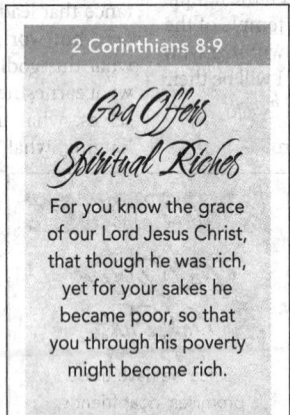

that you may be ready, as I said you would be. 4For if any Macedonians come with me and find you unprepared, we—not to say anything about you—would be ashamed of having been so confident. 5So I thought it necessary to urge the brothers to visit you in advance and finish the arrangements for the generous gift you had promised. Then it will be ready as a generous gift, not as one grudgingly given.

Sowing Generously

6Remember this: Whoever sows sparingly will also reap sparingly, and whoever sows generously will also reap generously. 7Each man should give what he has decided in his heart to give, not reluctantly or under compulsion, for God loves a cheerful giver. 8And God is able to make all grace abound to you, so that in all things at all times, having all that you need, you will abound in every good work. 9As it is written:

"He has scattered abroad his gifts to the
poor;
his righteousness endures forever."[a]

10Now he who supplies seed to the sower and bread for food will also supply and increase your store of seed and will enlarge the harvest of your righteousness. 11You will be made rich in every way so that you can be generous on every occasion, and through us your generosity will result in thanksgiving to God.

12This service that you perform is not only supplying the needs of God's people but is also overflowing in many expressions of thanks to God. 13Because of the service by which you have proved yourselves, men will praise God for the obedience that accompanies your confession of the gospel of Christ, and for your generosity in sharing with them and with everyone else. 14And in their prayers for you their hearts will go out to you, because of the surpassing grace God has given you. 15Thanks be to God for his indescribable gift!

Paul's Defense of His Ministry

10 By the meekness and gentleness of Christ, I appeal to you—I, Paul, who am "timid" when face to face with you, but "bold" when away! 2I beg you that when I come I may not have to be as bold as I expect to be toward some people who think that we live by the standards of this world. 3For though we live in the world, we do not wage war as the world does. 4The weapons we fight with are not the weapons of the world. On the contrary, they have divine power to demolish strongholds. 5We demolish arguments and every pretension that sets itself up against the knowledge of God, and we take captive every thought to make it obedient to Christ. 6And we will be ready to punish every act of disobedience, once your obedience is complete.

7You are looking only on the surface of things.[b] If anyone is confident that he belongs to Christ, he should consider again that we belong to Christ just as much as he. 8For even if I boast somewhat freely about the authority the Lord gave us for building you up rather than pulling you down, I will not be ashamed of it. 9I do not want to seem to be trying to frighten you with my letters. 10For some say, "His letters are weighty and forceful, but in person he is unimpressive and his speaking amounts to nothing." 11Such people should realize that what we are in our letters when we are absent, we will be in our actions when we are present.

12We do not dare to classify or compare ourselves with some who commend themselves. When they measure themselves by themselves and compare themselves with themselves, they are not wise. 13We, however, will not boast beyond proper limits, but will confine our boasting to the field God has assigned to us, a field that reaches even to you. 14We are not going too far in our boasting, as would be the case if we had not come to you, for we did get as far as you with the gospel of Christ. 15Neither do we go beyond our limits by boasting of work done by others.[c] Our hope is that, as your faith continues to grow, our area of activity among you will greatly expand, 16so that we can preach the gospel in the regions beyond you. For we do not want to boast about work already done in another man's territory. 17But, "Let him who boasts boast in the Lord."[d] 18For it is not the one who

[a]9 Psalm 112:9 [b]7 Or *Look at the obvious facts* [c]13–15 Or [13]*We, however, will not boast about things that cannot be measured, but we will boast according to the standard of measurement that the God of measure has assigned us—a measurement that relates even to you.* [14]*…*[15]*Neither do we boast about things that cannot be measured in regard to the work done by others.* [d]17 Jer. 9:24

commends himself who is approved, but the
one whom the Lord commends.

Paul and the False Apostles

11 I hope you will put up with a little of
my foolishness; but you are already
doing that. 2I am jealous for you with a godly
jealousy. I promised you to one husband, to
Christ, so that I might present you as a pure virgin to him. 3But I am afraid that just as Eve was
deceived by the serpent's cunning, your minds
may somehow be led astray from your sincere
and pure devotion to Christ. 4For if someone
comes to you and preaches a Jesus other than
the Jesus we preached, or if you receive a different spirit from the one you received, or a different gospel from the one you accepted, you put
up with it easily enough. 5But I do not think
I am in the least inferior to those "super-apostles." 6I may not be a trained speaker, but I do
have knowledge. We have made this perfectly
clear to you in every way.

7Was it a sin for me to lower myself in order to elevate you by preaching the gospel of
God to you free of charge? 8I robbed other
churches by receiving support from them so as
to serve you. 9And when I was with you and
needed something, I was not a burden to anyone, for the brothers who came from Macedonia supplied what I needed. I have kept myself
from being a burden to you in any way, and
will continue to do so. 10As surely as the truth
of Christ is in me, nobody in the regions of
Achaia will stop this boasting of mine. 11Why?
Because I do not love you? God knows I do!
12And I will keep on doing what I am doing in
order to cut the ground from under those who
want an opportunity to be considered equal
with us in the things they boast about.

13For such men are false apostles, deceitful
workmen, masquerading as apostles of Christ.
14And no wonder, for Satan himself masquer-
ades as an angel of light. 15It is not surprising,
then, if his servants masquerade as servants of
righteousness. Their end will be what their actions deserve.

Paul Boasts About His Sufferings

16I repeat: Let no one take me for a fool. But
if you do, then receive me just as you would
a fool, so that I may do a little boasting. 17In
this self-confident boasting I am not talking as
the Lord would, but as a fool. 18Since many are
boasting in the way the world does, I too will
boast. 19You gladly put up with fools since you
are so wise! 20In fact, you even put up with anyone who enslaves you or exploits you or takes
advantage of you or pushes himself forward or
slaps you in the face. 21To my shame I admit
that we were too weak for that!

What anyone else dares to boast about—I am
speaking as a fool—I also dare to boast about.
22Are they Hebrews? So am I. Are they Israelites? So am I. Are they Abraham's descendants?
So am I. 23Are they servants of Christ? (I am
out of my mind to talk like this.) I am more.
I have worked much harder, been in prison
more frequently, been flogged more severely,
and been exposed to death again and again.
24Five times I received from the Jews the forty
lashes minus one. 25Three times I was beaten
with rods, once I was stoned, three times I
was shipwrecked, I spent a night and a day in
the open sea, 26I have been constantly on the
move. I have been in danger from rivers, in danger from bandits, in danger from my own countrymen, in danger from Gentiles; in danger in
the city, in danger in the country, in danger at
sea; and in danger from false brothers. 27I have
labored and toiled and have often gone without
sleep; I have known hunger and thirst and have
often gone without food; I have been cold and
naked. 28Besides everything else, I face daily
the pressure of my concern for all the churches.
29Who is weak, and I do not feel weak? Who is
led into sin, and I do not inwardly burn?

30If I must boast, I will boast of the things
that show my weakness. 31The God and Father
of the Lord Jesus, who is to be praised forever,
knows that I am not lying. 32In Damascus the
governor under King Aretas had the city of the
Damascenes guarded in order to arrest me.
33But I was lowered in a basket from a window
in the wall and slipped through his hands.

Paul's Vision and His Thorn

12 I must go on boasting. Although there
is nothing to be gained, I will go on
to visions and revelations from the Lord. 2I
know a man in Christ who fourteen years ago
was caught up to the third heaven. Whether it
was in the body or out of the body I do not

know—God knows. 3And I know that this
man—whether in the body or apart from the
body I do not know, but God knows— 4was
caught up to paradise. He heard inexpressible
things, things that man is not permitted to
tell. 5I will boast about a man like that, but I
will not boast about myself,
except about my weaknesses.
6Even if I should choose to
boast, I would not be a fool, because I would be speaking the
truth. But I refrain, so no one
will think more of me than is
warranted by what I do or say.
7To keep me from becom-
ing conceited because of these
surpassingly great revelations,
there was given me a thorn in
my flesh, a messenger of Satan,
to torment me. 8Three times I
pleaded with the Lord to take
it away from me. 9But he said
to me, "My grace is sufficient
for you, for my power is made
perfect in weakness." Therefore
I will boast all the more gladly
about my weaknesses, so that Christ's power
may rest on me. 10That is why, for Christ's sake,
I delight in weaknesses, in insults, in hardships,
in persecutions, in difficulties. For when I am
weak, then I am strong.

2 Corinthians 12:9

God's Grace Is Sufficient

But he said to me, "My grace is sufficient for you, for my power is made perfect in weakness." Therefore I will boast all the more gladly about my weaknesses, so that Christ's power may rest on me.

Paul's Concern for the Corinthians

11I have made a fool of myself, but you drove
me to it. I ought to have been commended by
you, for I am not in the least inferior to the
"super-apostles," even though I am nothing.
12The things that mark an apostle—signs, wonders and miracles—were done among you with
great perseverance. 13How were you inferior to
the other churches, except that I was never a
burden to you? Forgive me this wrong!
14Now I am ready to visit you for the third
time, and I will not be a burden to you, because
what I want is not your possessions but you.
After all, children should not have to save up
for their parents, but parents for their children.
15So I will very gladly spend for you everything
I have and expend myself as well. If I love you
more, will you love me less? 16Be that as it may,
I have not been a burden to you. Yet, crafty fellow that I am, I caught you by trickery! 17Did
I exploit you through any of the men I sent
you? 18I urged Titus to go to you and I sent our
brother with him. Titus did not exploit you, did
he? Did we not act in the same spirit and follow
the same course?
19Have you been thinking
all along that we have been defending ourselves to you? We
have been speaking in the sight
of God as those in Christ; and
everything we do, dear friends,
is for your strengthening. 20For
I am afraid that when I come I
may not find you as I want you
to be, and you may not find me
as you want me to be. I fear that
there may be quarreling, jealousy, outbursts of anger, factions, slander, gossip, arrogance
and disorder. 21I am afraid that
when I come again my God
will humble me before you, and
I will be grieved over many
who have sinned earlier and
have not repented of the impurity, sexual sin
and debauchery in which they have indulged.

Final Warnings

13 This will be my third visit to you. "Every matter must be established by the
testimony of two or three witnesses."[a] 2I already
gave you a warning when I was with you the second time. I now repeat it while absent: On my
return I will not spare those who sinned earlier
or any of the others, 3since you are demanding
proof that Christ is speaking through me. He is
not weak in dealing with you, but is powerful
among you. 4For to be sure, he was crucified
in weakness, yet he lives by God's power. Likewise, we are weak in him, yet by God's power
we will live with him to serve you.
5Examine yourselves to see whether you
are in the faith; test yourselves. Do you not
realize that Christ Jesus is in you—unless, of
course, you fail the test? 6And I trust that you
will discover that we have not failed the test.
7Now we pray to God that you will not do anything wrong. Not that people will see that we

[a] 1 Deut. 19:15

Diamonds on Black Velvet

2 Corinthians 12:9

But he said to me, "My grace is sufficient for you, for my power is made perfect in weakness."

reflection

1 What would you say is your particular "thorn in the flesh"?

2 How might you have grown prideful had it not been for this "thorn"?

3 How has God proven himself strong on your behalf?

RELATED READINGS

Proverbs 18:12;
James 1:6–10;
1 Peter 1:6–7

Read: 2 Corinthians 12:7–10

"WHY WON'T GOD HEAL ME? Doesn't he love me?" Perhaps you've asked similar questions. Maybe you've been frustrated because God didn't answer a prayer the way you had hoped. Could it be that he is using those very difficulties to keep you dependent on him? Like placing sparkling diamonds on black velvet, our human weakness provides a contrasting backdrop against which God's power can be displayed.

Paul was faced with such a dilemma. He came from the best family line, studied at the best schools and encountered Jesus on the road to Damascus. He experienced revelations from God. It would have been easy for him to be proud. But Paul suffered a thorn in the flesh. Three times Paul asked God to remove his thorn. Three times God said no. Did that mean God didn't love Paul? Absolutely not! It simply meant that God decided to empower Paul despite his thorn, to keep Paul dependent on God's strength. God proved to Paul that God's power was made perfect in Paul's weakness.

Paul didn't tell his readers the nature of his thorn. If he had, we might be able to dismiss his words as not applying to us. Because he did not, we can identify with him—and wonder what our own thorns are. Is it a chronic illness, a debilitating disease we've suffered with or a painful injury we've sustained? Is it a chemical depression or bipolar illness? Is it cancer or chronic fatigue?

All of these "thorns" are hard to live with, especially if we've asked repeatedly for healing. They can make us feel weak and spiritually deficient. They can make us feel isolated, undeserving and ineffective. They can cause us to become self-absorbed and self-pitying. But there is another way to look at them: We can offer our illness or disability sacrificially to God and allow it to keep us on our knees, asking God for strength. We can allow God's love and power to push us through difficult and painful times, to use our "thorns" to make us more tenderhearted toward others. We can see them as the black velvet against which God's grace glitters.

Memorize God's words to Paul, and every time you are tempted to feel that your "thorn" disqualifies you from God's work, remember them: "My grace is sufficient for you, for my power is made perfect in weakness."

Go to page 1423 for your next devotional reading.

have stood the test but that you will do what is
right even though we may seem to have failed.
8 For we cannot do anything against the truth,
but only for the truth. 9 We are glad whenever
we are weak but you are strong; and our prayer
is for your perfection. 10 This is why I write
these things when I am absent, that when I
come I may not have to be harsh in my use of
authority—the authority the Lord gave me for
building you up, not for tearing you down.

Final Greetings

11 Finally, brothers, good-by. Aim for perfection, listen to my appeal, be of one mind, live in peace. And the God of love and peace will be with you.

12 Greet one another with a holy kiss. 13 All
the saints send their greetings.

14 May the grace of the Lord Jesus Christ, and the love of God, and the fellowship of the Holy Spirit be with you all.

Galatians

Author:
The apostle Paul.

Audience:
Followers of Jesus; originally written to the churches in Galatia.

Date:
About A.D. 50.

Setting:
Judaizers were falsely telling Gentiles that they had to obey the Jewish laws in order to be saved by Christ.

Verse to Remember:
I am astonished that you are so quickly deserting the one who called you by the grace of Christ and are turning to a different gospel—which is really no gospel at all. (1:6–7)

"Are you crazy?" It's hard to know how to answer such a question! Or what about, "How could you do something so stupid?" *Paul's question to his readers* is just as blunt: "Who has bewitched you?" (Galatians 3:1). One can picture him pulling on his hair in frustration or, if he were writing in English, using extra exclamation points. His readers knew the gospel. Yet they had willingly accepted a false gospel of human effort. So Paul looked in some detail at what the law can and cannot do. It can't save. It can't bring righteousness, before or after salvation. It can't provide any *power* at all, just a list of dos and don'ts. *Only the Holy Spirit provides the power* to keep the law.

No matter how hard we try, we cannot please God by our human effort, by following laws to earn "credit" with God. We could work 25 hours out of 24, and we'd still fall short. Our own efforts distract us from Christ and his glorious gospel. *Through him, we are saved by grace.* Without him, the law is only a list of legal obligations that remind us how far we fall short.

1 Paul, an apostle—sent not from men nor
by man, but by Jesus Christ and God the
Father, who raised him from the dead— 2and
all the brothers with me,

To the churches in Galatia:

3Grace and peace to you from God our
Father and the Lord Jesus Christ, 4who gave
himself for our sins to rescue us from the present evil age, according to the will of our God
and Father, 5to whom be glory for ever and
ever. Amen.

No Other Gospel

6I am astonished that you are so quickly deserting the one who called you by the grace of

Christ and are turning to a different gospel—
7 which is really no gospel at all. Evidently some
people are throwing you into confusion and are
trying to pervert the gospel of Christ. 8 But even
if we or an angel from heaven should preach a
gospel other than the one we preached to you,
let him be eternally condemned! 9 As we have
already said, so now I say again: If anybody is
preaching to you a gospel other than what you
accepted, let him be eternally condemned!
10 Am I now trying to win the approval of
men, or of God? Or am I trying to please men?
If I were still trying to please men, I would not
be a servant of Christ.

Paul Called by God

11 I want you to know, brothers, that the gospel I preached is not something that man made
up. 12 I did not receive it from any man, nor
was I taught it; rather, I received it by revelation
from Jesus Christ.
13 For you have heard of my previous way of
life in Judaism, how intensely I persecuted the
church of God and tried to destroy it. 14 I was
advancing in Judaism beyond many Jews of
my own age and was extremely zealous for the
traditions of my fathers. 15 But when God, who
set me apart from birth[a] and called me by his
grace, was pleased 16 to reveal his Son in me so
that I might preach him among the Gentiles, I
did not consult any man, 17 nor did I go up to Jerusalem to see those who were apostles before
I was, but I went immediately into Arabia and
later returned to Damascus.
18 Then after three years, I went up to Jerusalem to get acquainted with Peter[b] and stayed
with him fifteen days. 19 I saw none of the other
apostles—only James, the Lord's brother. 20 I assure you before God that what I am writing you
is no lie. 21 Later I went to Syria and Cilicia. 22 I
was personally unknown to the churches of Judea that are in Christ. 23 They only heard the
report: "The man who formerly persecuted us
is now preaching the faith he once tried to destroy." 24 And they praised God because of me.

Paul Accepted by the Apostles

2 Fourteen years later I went up again to Jerusalem, this time with Barnabas. I took
Titus along also. 2 I went in response to a revelation and set before them the gospel that I
preach among the Gentiles. But I did this
privately to those who seemed to be leaders,
for fear that I was running or had run my race
in vain. 3 Yet not even Titus, who was with me,
was compelled to be circumcised, even though
he was a Greek. 4 ⌞This matter arose⌟ because
some false brothers had infiltrated our ranks to
spy on the freedom we have in Christ Jesus and
to make us slaves. 5 We did not give in to them
for a moment, so that the truth of the gospel
might remain with you.
6 As for those who seemed to be important—
whatever they were makes no difference to me;
God does not judge by external appearance—
those men added nothing to my message. 7 On
the contrary, they saw that I had been entrusted
with the task of preaching the gospel to the
Gentiles,[c] just as Peter had been to the Jews.[d]
8 For God, who was at work in the ministry of
Peter as an apostle to the Jews, was also at work
in my ministry as an apostle to the Gentiles.
9 James, Peter[e] and John, those reputed to be pillars, gave me and Barnabas the right hand of fellowship when they recognized the grace given
to me. They agreed that we should go to the
Gentiles, and they to the Jews. 10 All they asked
was that we should continue to remember the
poor, the very thing I was eager to do.

Paul Opposes Peter

11 When Peter came to Antioch, I opposed
him to his face, because he was clearly in the
wrong. 12 Before certain men came from James,
he used to eat with the Gentiles. But when
they arrived, he began to draw back and separate himself from the Gentiles because he was
afraid of those who belonged to the circumcision group. 13 The other Jews joined him in his
hypocrisy, so that by their hypocrisy even Barnabas was led astray.
14 When I saw that they were not acting in
line with the truth of the gospel, I said to Peter in front of them all, "You are a Jew, yet you
live like a Gentile and not like a Jew. How is it,
then, that you force Gentiles to follow Jewish
customs?
15 "We who are Jews by birth and not 'Gentile
sinners' 16 know that a man is not justified by

[a] 15 Or *from my mother's womb* [b] 18 Greek *Cephas* [c] 7 Greek *uncircumcised* [d] 7 Greek *circumcised*; also in verses 8 and 9
[e] 9 Greek *Cephas*; also in verses 11 and 14

observing the law, but by faith in Jesus Christ.
So we, too, have put our faith in Christ Jesus
that we may be justified by faith in Christ and
not by observing the law, because by observing
the law no one will be justified.
17“If, while we seek to be justified in Christ,
it becomes evident that we our-
selves are sinners, does that
mean that Christ promotes
sin? Absolutely not! 18If I rebuild what I destroyed, I prove
that I am a lawbreaker. 19For
through the law I died to the
law so that I might live for God.
20I have been crucified with
Christ and I no longer live, but
Christ lives in me. The life I live
in the body, I live by faith in the
Son of God, who loved me and
gave himself for me. 21I do not
set aside the grace of God, for if
righteousness could be gained
through the law, Christ died
for nothing!”[a]

> Galatians 2:20
>
> *God Lives in the Christian*
>
> “I have been crucified with Christ and I no longer live, but Christ lives in me. The life I live in the body, I live by faith in the Son of God, who loved me and gave himself for me.”

Faith or Observance of the Law

3 You foolish Galatians! Who has bewitched
you? Before your very eyes Jesus Christ
was clearly portrayed as crucified. 2I would
like to learn just one thing from you: Did you
receive the Spirit by observing the law, or by
believing what you heard? 3Are you so foolish?
After beginning with the Spirit, are you now
trying to attain your goal by human effort?
4Have you suffered so much for nothing—if it
really was for nothing? 5Does God give you his
Spirit and work miracles among you because
you observe the law, or because you believe
what you heard?
6Consider Abraham: “He believed God,
and it was credited to him as righteousness.”[b]
7Understand, then, that those who believe are
children of Abraham. 8The Scripture foresaw
that God would justify the Gentiles by faith,
and announced the gospel in advance to Abraham: “All nations will be blessed through you.”[c]
9So those who have faith are blessed along with
Abraham, the man of faith.
10All who rely on observing the law are under a curse, for it is written: “Cursed is everyone who does not continue to do everything
written in the Book of the Law.”[d] 11Clearly no
one is justified before God by the law, because,
“The righteous will live by faith.”[e] 12The law is
not based on faith; on the contrary, “The man
who does these things will live
by them.”[f] 13Christ redeemed
us from the curse of the law by
becoming a curse for us, for it
is written: “Cursed is everyone
who is hung on a tree.”[g] 14He
redeemed us in order that the
blessing given to Abraham
might come to the Gentiles
through Christ Jesus, so that
by faith we might receive the
promise of the Spirit.

The Law and the Promise

15Brothers, let me take an
example from everyday life.
Just as no one can set aside or
add to a human covenant that
has been duly established, so it
is in this case. 16The promises were spoken to
Abraham and to his seed. The Scripture does
not say “and to seeds,” meaning many people,
but “and to your seed,”[h] meaning one person,
who is Christ. 17What I mean is this: The law,
introduced 430 years later, does not set aside
the covenant previously established by God
and thus do away with the promise. 18For if the
inheritance depends on the law, then it no longer depends on a promise; but God in his grace
gave it to Abraham through a promise.
19What, then, was the purpose of the law? It
was added because of transgressions until the
Seed to whom the promise referred had come.
The law was put into effect through angels by a
mediator. 20A mediator, however, does not represent just one party; but God is one.
21Is the law, therefore, opposed to the
promises of God? Absolutely not! For if a law
had been given that could impart life, then
righteousness would certainly have come by
the law. 22But the Scripture declares that the
whole world is a prisoner of sin, so that what
was promised, being given through faith in

[a]21 Some interpreters end the quotation after verse 14. [b]6 Gen. 15:6 [c]8 Gen. 12:3; 18:18; 22:18 [d]10 Deut. 27:26 [e]11 Hab. 2:4
[f]12 Lev. 18:5 [g]13 Deut. 21:23 [h]16 Gen. 12:7; 13:15; 24:7

Convert

LYDIA

"SO, YOU'RE PRETTY IMPORTANT in this church, huh?" The newcomer seemed intrigued.

Lydia, never one to seek prestigious titles, responded, "No, I was just following God's guidance when I accepted Paul's message by faith." Something she could not explain had happened when she'd heard Paul's words. "All I know is that I was changed. And I want to help others make the same discovery."

Lydia realized she may have seemed to her new friend as an unlikely candidate for conversion. She was a woman, and women rarely had the opportunity to sit at the feet of a highly trained and renowned teacher like Paul. But those closest to Lydia knew she seldom followed cultural norms or listened to what society said she should be or do.

"Seems like you've been cutting your own path for years," the newcomer remarked, as she heard more of Lydia's story.

"No, I wasn't a Jew," Lydia continued, as she shared her testimony with her guest. But she'd already found her way to the God of Israel, which is why some elements of Paul's message were already familiar to her. Before her guest could even ask it aloud, Lydia knew what she was thinking.

"Okay, then how did a Gentile, God-fearing woman from Asia Minor end up in Philippi?" There weren't even enough resident Jews to form a respectable synagogue there! It was hard to say. But it was out of the norm, and Lydia liked it that way.

"So, you see a day when many more of us will worship the true God?" her friend asked incredulously.

That was okay. Not everyone had to share Lydia's enthusiasm. She had reached the zenith of her profession in the clothing industry. Her company's P&L (profit and loss) statement read like a dream, and she enjoyed a position of influence among her peers and in the city. "So, why not dream big about the future of the church?" she countered. Now that she knew the full story of God's plan to redeem the world, she planned to be part of it.

—Prayer—

Dear God, thank you for bringing me into your faith family and adopting me as your child. You are a glorious Father indeed!

One of those listening was a woman named Lydia . . . The Lord opened her heart to respond to Paul's message.

Acts 16:14

ASSIGNED READING:

Acts 16:11–40

Weekend

Go to page 1426 for your next devotional reading.

Jesus Christ, might be given to those who believe.
23Before this faith came, we were held prisoners by the law, locked up until faith should
be revealed. 24So the law was put in charge to
lead us to Christ[a] that we might be justified by
faith. 25Now that faith has come, we are no longer under the supervision of the law.

Sons of God

26You are all sons of God through faith in
Christ Jesus, 27for all of you who were baptized into Christ have clothed yourselves with
Christ. 28There is neither Jew nor Greek, slave
nor free, male nor female, for you are all one
in Christ Jesus. 29If you belong to Christ, then
you are Abraham's seed, and heirs according to
the promise.
4 What I am saying is that as long as the heir
is a child, he is no different from a slave,
although he owns the whole estate. 2He is subject to guardians and trustees until the time set
by his father. 3So also, when we were children,
we were in slavery under the basic principles of
the world. 4But when the time had fully come,
God sent his Son, born of a woman, born under law, 5to redeem those under law, that we
might receive the full rights of sons. 6Because
you are sons, God sent the Spirit of his Son into
our hearts, the Spirit who calls out, "*Abba*,[b] Father." 7So you are no longer a slave, but a son;
and since you are a son, God has made you also
an heir.

Paul's Concern for the Galatians

8Formerly, when you did not know God,
you were slaves to those who by nature are
not gods. 9But now that you know God—or
rather are known by God—how is it that you
are turning back to those weak and miserable
principles? Do you wish to be enslaved by them
all over again? 10You are observing special days
and months and seasons and years! 11I fear for
you, that somehow I have wasted my efforts
on you.
12I plead with you, brothers, become like
me, for I became like you. You have done me
no wrong. 13As you know, it was because of
an illness that I first preached the gospel to
you. 14Even though my illness was a trial to
you, you did not treat me with contempt or
scorn. Instead, you welcomed me as if I were
an angel of God, as if I were Christ Jesus himself. 15What has happened to all your joy? I
can testify that, if you could have done so, you
would have torn out your eyes and given them
to me. 16Have I now become your enemy by
telling you the truth?
17Those people are zealous to win you over,
but for no good. What they want is to alienate
you ⌊from us⌋, so that you may be zealous for
them. 18It is fine to be zealous, provided the
purpose is good, and to be so always and not
just when I am with you. 19My dear children,
for whom I am again in the pains of childbirth
until Christ is formed in you, 20how I wish I
could be with you now and change my tone,
because I am perplexed about you!

Hagar and Sarah

21Tell me, you who want to be under the law,
are you not aware of what the law says? 22For
it is written that Abraham had two sons, one
by the slave woman and the other by the free
woman. 23His son by the slave woman was
born in the ordinary way; but his son by the
free woman was born as the result of a promise.
24These things may be taken figuratively,
for the women represent two covenants. One
covenant is from Mount Sinai and bears children who are to be slaves: This is Hagar. 25Now
Hagar stands for Mount Sinai in Arabia and
corresponds to the present city of Jerusalem, because she is in slavery with her children. 26But
the Jerusalem that is above is free, and she is
our mother. 27For it is written:

"Be glad, O barren woman,
who bears no children;
break forth and cry aloud,
you who have no labor pains;
because more are the children of the
desolate woman
than of her who has a husband."[c]

28Now you, brothers, like Isaac, are children
of promise. 29At that time the son born in the
ordinary way persecuted the son born by the
power of the Spirit. It is the same now. 30But

[a] 24 Or *charge until Christ came* [b] 6 Aramaic for *Father* [c] 27 Isaiah 54:1

what does the Scripture say? "Get rid of the
slave woman and her son, for the slave woman's son will never share in the inheritance with
the free woman's son."[a] 31 Therefore, brothers,
we are not children of the slave woman, but of
the free woman.

Freedom in Christ

5 It is for freedom that Christ has set us free.
Stand firm, then, and do not let yourselves
be burdened again by a yoke of slavery.

2 Mark my words! I, Paul, tell you that if you
let yourselves be circumcised, Christ will be of
no value to you at all. 3 Again I declare to every
man who lets himself be circumcised that he
is obligated to obey the whole
law. 4 You who are trying to
be justified by law have been
alienated from Christ; you
have fallen away from grace.
5 But by faith we eagerly await
through the Spirit the righteousness for which we hope.
6 For in Christ Jesus neither circumcision nor uncircumcision
has any value. The only thing
that counts is faith expressing
itself through love.

7 You were running a good
race. Who cut in on you and
kept you from obeying the
truth? 8 That kind of persuasion
does not come from the one
who calls you. 9 "A little yeast works through
the whole batch of dough." 10 I am confident in
the Lord that you will take no other view. The
one who is throwing you into confusion will
pay the penalty, whoever he may be. 11 Brothers, if I am still preaching circumcision, why
am I still being persecuted? In that case the offense of the cross has been abolished. 12 As for
those agitators, I wish they would go the whole
way and emasculate themselves!

13 You, my brothers, were called to be free.
But do not use your freedom to indulge the sinful nature[b]; rather, serve one another in love.
14 The entire law is summed up in a single command: "Love your neighbor as yourself."[c] 15 If
you keep on biting and devouring each other,
watch out or you will be destroyed by each
other.

Life by the Spirit

16 So I say, live by the Spirit, and you will
not gratify the desires of the sinful nature.
17 For the sinful nature desires what is contrary
to the Spirit, and the Spirit what is contrary
to the sinful nature. They are in conflict with
each other, so that you do not do what you
want. 18 But if you are led by the Spirit, you are
not under law.

19 The acts of the sinful nature are obvious:
sexual immorality, impurity and debauchery;
20 idolatry and witchcraft; hatred, discord,
jealousy, fits of rage, selfish
ambition, dissensions, factions
21 and envy; drunkenness, orgies, and the like. I warn you,
as I did before, that those who
live like this will not inherit the
kingdom of God.

22 But the fruit of the Spirit is
love, joy, peace, patience, kindness, goodness, faithfulness,
23 gentleness and self-control.
Against such things there is
no law. 24 Those who belong
to Christ Jesus have crucified
the sinful nature with its passions and desires. 25 Since we
live by the Spirit, let us keep
in step with the Spirit. 26 Let us
not become conceited, provoking and envying
each other.

Doing Good to All

6 Brothers, if someone is caught in a sin,
you who are spiritual should restore him
gently. But watch yourself, or you also may be
tempted. 2 Carry each other's burdens, and in
this way you will fulfill the law of Christ. 3 If anyone thinks he is something when he is nothing,
he deceives himself. 4 Each one should test his
own actions. Then he can take pride in himself,
without comparing himself to somebody else,
5 for each one should carry his own load.

6 Anyone who receives instruction in the
word must share all good things with his instructor.

> **Galatians 5:22–23**
>
> *God Changes Lives*
>
> But the fruit of the Spirit is love, joy, peace, patience, kindness, goodness, faithfulness, gentleness and self-control. Against such things there is no law.

[a] 30 Gen. 21:10 [b] 13 Or *the flesh*; also in verses 16, 17, 19 and 24 [c] 14 Lev. 19:18

Keeping in Step

Read: Galatians 5:13–25

Galatians 5:18,25

But if you are led by the Spirit, you are not under law . . . Since we live by the Spirit, let us keep in step with the Spirit.

"LET US KEEP IN STEP with the Spirit." It's as if Paul is describing those who are led by the Spirit as dancers who are in step with the perfect partner. In contrast, when moved by the flesh—impulses and thoughts that tell us to do as *we* desire—it's as if we are experiencing the clumsiness of a partner who keeps stepping on our toes and leading us in the wrong direction.

Like a dancer constantly tuned to the beat of the music, we must continually tune in to the voice of the Spirit and follow his lead. But, oh, how difficult it can be. The Spirit moves us to places where we might not feel quite comfortable, to step back when we want to step forward, to step forward when we want to step back. The rhythm might be too slow or too fast. Following the Spirit means resisting the urge to dance through life *our* way. It means relinquishing control.

How difficult it can be to be led by the Spirit and to hold our tongue. How difficult it is not to dance to the tune of popularity and to repeat that juicy piece of gossip we heard over coffee with friends. How humbling it is when the Spirit leads us to go low and say, "I'm sorry." How difficult it is to make the move to release resentment when we feel we've been wronged or unappreciated. When the enemy cuts in, he whispers in our ear, "What's a missed step here and there? No big deal. You can make up for it later," fueling the battle between flesh and Spirit.

Throughout the day we should ask ourselves, "Who am I being led by? My self, with its emotions, worries, pride, fears and selfishness? Am I being led by the enemy with his discordant tunes? Or am I being led by the Holy Spirit?"

Each time we move in step with the Spirit, we are saying yes to God. We're no longer bound to follow the whims of our flesh or the whisperings of the evil one. We can choose to move in sync with the Spirit.

reflection

1. What steps is the Spirit prompting you to take today?
2. How have you resisted the Spirit's leading lately?
3. How strong is your desire to "keep in step with the Spirit"? Confess your resistance to his leading, and ask him to help you stay in step with him.

RELATED READINGS

Romans 6:6–14; 8:5–8; 1 Corinthians 3:16

Monday

Go to page 1433 for your next devotional reading.

[7]Do not be deceived: God cannot be
mocked. A man reaps what he sows. [8]The one
who sows to please his sinful nature, from that
nature[a] will reap destruction; the one who
sows to please the Spirit, from the Spirit will
reap eternal life. [9]Let us not become weary in
doing good, for at the proper time we will reap
a harvest if we do not give up. [10]Therefore,
as we have opportunity, let us do good to all
people, especially to those who belong to the
family of believers.

Not Circumcision but a New Creation

[11]See what large letters I use as I write to you
with my own hand!

[12]Those who want to make a good impression outwardly are trying to compel you to
be circumcised. The only reason they do this
is to avoid being persecuted for the cross of
Christ. [13]Not even those who are circumcised
obey the law, yet they want you to be circumcised that they may boast about your flesh.
[14]May I never boast except in the cross of our
Lord Jesus Christ, through which[b] the world
has been crucified to me, and I to the world.
[15]Neither circumcision nor uncircumcision
means anything; what counts is a new creation.
[16]Peace and mercy to all who follow this rule,
even to the Israel of God.

[17]Finally, let no one cause me trouble, for I
bear on my body the marks of Jesus.

[18]The grace of our Lord Jesus Christ be with
your spirit, brothers. Amen.

[a]8 Or *his flesh, from the flesh* [b]14 Or *whom*

Ephesians

Author:
The apostle Paul.

Audience:
Followers of Jesus; originally written to the church in Ephesus.

Date:
About A.D. 60.

Setting:
Paul penned this letter from a Roman prison to encourage all the Christians in Ephesus and other areas.

Verse to Remember:
As a prisoner for the Lord, then, I urge you to live a life worthy of the calling you have received. (4:1)

It is a high privilege to be saved by grace.

While we can never earn our salvation, it does come with responsibilities. We have a calling to live up to. What we do or don't do is a reflection on Jesus, either good or bad.

Paul wrote this letter to a young church set in the heart of a pagan society. Ephesus was a thriving commercial center, but in order for the church to thrive, its members needed to know how to live, how to *stand apart as different* and yet still be able *to influence* their society.

Paul covers a broad spectrum of conduct and relationships, for every part of our life is a part of our calling. He tells us to be imitators of God, a task that would be impossible except for one thing: *We are not alone.* We have the Spirit in our inner being, and we have the protection of the full armor of God. It's up to us, however, to use what we've been given. Paul's letter instructs us how to do that.

1 Paul, an apostle of Christ Jesus by the will
of God,

To the saints in Ephesus,[a] the faithful[b] in
Christ Jesus:

2Grace and peace to you from God our Father and the Lord Jesus Christ.

Spiritual Blessings in Christ

3Praise be to the God and Father of our
Lord Jesus Christ, who has blessed us in the
heavenly realms with every spiritual blessing
in Christ. 4For he chose us in him before the
creation of the world to be holy and blameless
in his sight. In love 5he[c] predestined us to be

[a]1 Some early manuscripts do not have *in Ephesus.* [b]1 Or *believers who are* [c]4,5 Or *sight in love.* 5He

adopted as his sons through Jesus Christ, in accordance with his pleasure and will— [6]to the
praise of his glorious grace, which he has freely
given us in the One he loves. [7]In him we have
redemption through his blood, the forgiveness
of sins, in accordance with the riches of God's
grace [8]that he lavished on us with all wisdom
and understanding. [9]And he[a] made known
to us the mystery of his will according to his
good pleasure, which he purposed in Christ,
[10]to be put into effect when the times will have
reached their fulfillment—to bring all things in
heaven and on earth together under one head,
even Christ.

[11]In him we were also chosen,[b] having been
predestined according to the plan of him who
works out everything in conformity with the
purpose of his will, [12]in order that we, who
were the first to hope in Christ, might be for
the praise of his glory. [13]And you also were
included in Christ when you heard the word
of truth, the gospel of your salvation. Having
believed, you were marked in him with a seal,
the promised Holy Spirit, [14]who is a deposit
guaranteeing our inheritance until the redemption of those who are God's possession—to the
praise of his glory.

Thanksgiving and Prayer

[15]For this reason, ever since I heard about
your faith in the Lord Jesus and your love for all
the saints, [16]I have not stopped giving thanks
for you, remembering you in my prayers. [17]I
keep asking that the God of our Lord Jesus
Christ, the glorious Father, may give you the
Spirit[c] of wisdom and revelation, so that you
may know him better. [18]I pray also that the
eyes of your heart may be enlightened in order
that you may know the hope to which he has
called you, the riches of his glorious inheritance
in the saints, [19]and his incomparably great
power for us who believe. That power is like
the working of his mighty strength, [20]which
he exerted in Christ when he raised him from
the dead and seated him at his right hand in
the heavenly realms, [21]far above all rule and
authority, power and dominion, and every title that can be given, not only in the present
age but also in the one to come. [22]And God
placed all things under his feet and appointed
him to be head over everything for the church,
[23]which is his body, the fullness of him who
fills everything in every way.

Made Alive in Christ

2 As for you, you were dead in your transgressions and sins, [2]in which you used
to live when you followed the ways of this
world and of the ruler of the kingdom of the
air, the spirit who is now at work in those who
are disobedient. [3]All of us also lived among
them at one time, gratifying the cravings of
our sinful nature[d] and following its desires and
thoughts. Like the rest, we were by nature objects of wrath. [4]But because of his great love
for us, God, who is rich in mercy, [5]made us
alive with Christ even when we were dead in
transgressions—it is by grace you have been
saved. [6]And God raised us up with Christ and
seated us with him in the heavenly realms in
Christ Jesus, [7]in order that in the coming ages
he might show the incomparable riches of his
grace, expressed in his kindness to us in Christ
Jesus. [8]For it is by grace you have been saved,
through faith—and this not from yourselves,
it is the gift of God— [9]not by works, so that
no one can boast. [10]For we are God's workmanship, created in Christ Jesus to do good works,
which God prepared in advance for us to do.

One in Christ

[11]Therefore, remember that formerly you
who are Gentiles by birth and called "uncircumcised" by those who call themselves "the
circumcision" (that done in the body by the
hands of men)— [12]remember that at that time
you were separate from Christ, excluded from
citizenship in Israel and foreigners to the covenants of the promise, without hope and without God in the world. [13]But now in Christ Jesus
you who once were far away have been brought
near through the blood of Christ.

[14]For he himself is our peace, who has made
the two one and has destroyed the barrier, the
dividing wall of hostility, [15]by abolishing in
his flesh the law with its commandments and
regulations. His purpose was to create in himself one new man out of the two, thus making
peace, [16]and in this one body to reconcile both

[a]8,9 Or *us. With all wisdom and understanding, [9]he* [b]11 Or *were made heirs* [c]17 Or *a spirit* [d]3 Or *our flesh*

of them to God through the cross, by which he put to death their hostility. 17He came and preached peace to you who were far away and peace to those who were near. 18For through him we both have access to the Father by one Spirit.

19Consequently, you are no longer foreigners and aliens, but fellow citizens with God's people and members of God's household, 20built on the foundation of the apostles and prophets, with Christ Jesus himself as the chief cornerstone. 21In him the whole building is joined together and rises to become a holy temple in the Lord. 22And in him you too are being built together to become a dwelling in which God lives by his Spirit.

Paul the Preacher to the Gentiles

3 For this reason I, Paul, the prisoner of Christ Jesus for the sake of you Gentiles—

2Surely you have heard about the administration of God's grace that was given to me for you, 3that is, the mystery made known to me by revelation, as I have already written briefly. 4In reading this, then, you will be able to understand my insight into the mystery of Christ, 5which was not made known to men in other generations as it has now been revealed by the Spirit to God's holy apostles and prophets. 6This mystery is that through the gospel the Gentiles are heirs together with Israel, members together of one body, and sharers together in the promise in Christ Jesus.

7I became a servant of this gospel by the gift of God's grace given me through the working of his power. 8Although I am less than the least of all God's people, this grace was given me: to preach to the Gentiles the unsearchable riches of Christ, 9and to make plain to everyone the administration of this mystery, which for ages past was kept hidden in God, who created all things. 10His intent was that now, through the church, the manifold wisdom of God should be made known to the rulers and authorities in the heavenly realms, 11according to his eternal purpose which he accomplished in Christ Jesus our Lord. 12In him and through faith in him we may approach God with freedom and confidence. 13I ask you, therefore, not to be discouraged because of my sufferings for you, which are your glory.

A Prayer for the Ephesians

14For this reason I kneel before the Father, 15from whom his whole family[a] in heaven and on earth derives its name. 16I pray that out of his glorious riches he may strengthen you with power through his Spirit in your inner being, 17so that Christ may dwell in your hearts through faith. And I pray that you, being rooted and established in love, 18may have power, together with all the saints, to grasp how wide and long and high and deep is the love of Christ, 19and to know this love that surpasses knowledge—that you may be filled to the measure of all the fullness of God.

20Now to him who is able to do immeasurably more than all we ask or imagine, according to his power that is at work within us, 21to him be glory in the church and in Christ Jesus throughout all generations, for ever and ever! Amen.

Unity in the Body of Christ

4 As a prisoner for the Lord, then, I urge you to live a life worthy of the calling you have received. 2Be completely humble and gentle; be patient, bearing with one another in love. 3Make every effort to keep the unity of the Spirit through the bond of peace. 4There is one body and one Spirit—just as you were called to one hope when you were called— 5one Lord, one faith, one baptism; 6one God and Father of all, who is over all and through all and in all.

7But to each one of us grace has been given as Christ apportioned it. 8This is why it[b] says:

"When he ascended on high,
he led captives in his train
and gave gifts to men."[c]

9(What does "he ascended" mean except that he also descended to the lower, earthly regions[d]? 10He who descended is the very one who ascended higher than all the heavens, in order to fill the whole universe.) 11It was he who gave some to be apostles, some to be prophets, some to be evangelists, and some to be pastors and teachers, 12to prepare God's people for

[a]15 Or *whom all fatherhood* [b]8 Or *God* [c]8 Psalm 68:18 [d]9 Or *the depths of the earth*

works of service, so that the body of Christ may
be built up 13until we all reach unity in the faith
and in the knowledge of the Son of God and become mature, attaining to the
whole measure of the fullness
of Christ.
14Then we will no longer be
infants, tossed back and forth
by the waves, and blown here
and there by every wind of
teaching and by the cunning
and craftiness of men in their
deceitful scheming. 15Instead,
speaking the truth in love, we
will in all things grow up into
him who is the Head, that is,
Christ. 16From him the whole
body, joined and held together by every supporting ligament, grows and builds itself up in
love, as each part does its work.

> Ephesians 4:32
>
> *God Forgives*
>
> Be kind and compassionate to one another, forgiving each other, just as in Christ God forgave you.

Living as Children of Light

17So I tell you this, and insist on it in the
Lord, that you must no longer live as the Gentiles do, in the futility of their thinking. 18They
are darkened in their understanding and
separated from the life of God because of the
ignorance that is in them due to the hardening of their hearts. 19Having lost all sensitivity,
they have given themselves over to sensuality
so as to indulge in every kind of impurity, with
a continual lust for more.

20You, however, did not come to know
Christ that way. 21Surely you heard of him
and were taught in him in accordance with the
truth that is in Jesus. 22You were taught, with regard to your former way of life, to put off your
old self, which is being corrupted by its deceitful desires; 23to be made new in the attitude
of your minds; 24and to put on the new self,
created to be like God in true righteousness
and holiness.

25Therefore each of you must put off falsehood and speak truthfully to his neighbor, for
we are all members of one body. 26"In your anger do not sin"[a]: Do not let the sun go down
while you are still angry, 27and do not give the
devil a foothold. 28He who has been stealing
must steal no longer, but must work, doing
something useful with his own hands, that
he may have something to share with those
in need.

29Do not let any unwholesome talk come
out of your mouths, but only
what is helpful for building others up according to their needs,
that it may benefit those who
listen. 30And do not grieve the
Holy Spirit of God, with whom
you were sealed for the day of
redemption. 31Get rid of all bitterness, rage and anger, brawl-
ing and slander, along with every form of malice. 32Be kind
and compassionate to one another, forgiving each other, just
as in Christ God forgave you.

5 Be imitators of God, therefore, as dearly
loved children 2and live a life of love, just
as Christ loved us and gave himself up for us as
a fragrant offering and sacrifice to God.

3But among you there must not be even
a hint of sexual immorality, or of any kind
of impurity, or of greed, because these are
improper for God's holy people. 4Nor should
there be obscenity, foolish talk or coarse joking, which are out of place, but rather thanksgiving. 5For of this you can be sure: No
immoral, impure or greedy person—such a
man is an idolater—has any inheritance in the
kingdom of Christ and of God.[b] 6Let no one
deceive you with empty words, for because of
such things God's wrath comes on those who
are disobedient. 7Therefore do not be partners
with them.

8For you were once darkness, but now you
are light in the Lord. Live as children of light
9(for the fruit of the light consists in all goodness, righteousness and truth) 10and find out
what pleases the Lord. 11Have nothing to do
with the fruitless deeds of darkness, but rather
expose them. 12For it is shameful even to mention what the disobedient do in secret. 13But everything exposed by the light becomes visible,
14for it is light that makes everything visible.
This is why it is said:

"Wake up, O sleeper,
  rise from the dead,
and Christ will shine on you."

[a]26 Psalm 4:4 [b]5 Or *kingdom of the Christ and God*

15Be very careful, then, how you live—not
as unwise but as wise, 16making the most of
every opportunity, because the days are evil.
17Therefore do not be foolish, but understand what the Lord's will is. 18Do not get
drunk on wine, which leads to debauchery.
Instead, be filled with the Spirit. 19Speak to
one another with psalms, hymns and spiritual
songs. Sing and make music in your heart to
the Lord, 20always giving thanks to God the
Father for everything, in the name of our Lord
Jesus Christ.

21Submit to one another out of reverence
for Christ.

Wives and Husbands

22Wives, submit to your husbands as to the
Lord. 23For the husband is the head of the wife
as Christ is the head of the church, his body,
of which he is the Savior. 24Now as the church
submits to Christ, so also wives should submit
to their husbands in everything.

25Husbands, love your wives, just as Christ
loved the church and gave himself up for her
26to make her holy, cleansing[a] her by the
washing with water through the word, 27and
to present her to himself as a radiant church,
without stain or wrinkle or any other blemish,
but holy and blameless. 28In this same way,
husbands ought to love their wives as their
own bodies. He who loves his wife loves himself. 29After all, no one ever hated his own
body, but he feeds and cares for it, just as
Christ does the church— 30for we are members of his body. 31"For this reason a man will
leave his father and mother and be united to
his wife, and the two will become one flesh."[b]
32This is a profound mystery—but I am talking about Christ and the church. 33However,
each one of you also must love his wife as he
loves himself, and the wife must respect her
husband.

Children and Parents

6 Children, obey your parents in the Lord,
for this is right. 2"Honor your father and
mother"—which is the first commandment
with a promise— 3"that it may go well with
you and that you may enjoy long life on the
earth."[c]

4Fathers, do not exasperate your children;
instead, bring them up in the training and instruction of the Lord.

Slaves and Masters

5Slaves, obey your earthly masters with respect and fear, and with sincerity of heart, just
as you would obey Christ. 6Obey them not
only to win their favor when their eye is on
you, but like slaves of Christ, doing the will of
God from your heart. 7Serve wholeheartedly,
as if you were serving the Lord, not men, 8be-
cause you know that the Lord will reward everyone for whatever good he does, whether he
is slave or free.

9And masters, treat your slaves in the same
way. Do not threaten them, since you know
that he who is both their Master and yours
is in heaven, and there is no favoritism with
him.

The Armor of God

10Finally, be strong in the Lord and in his
mighty power. 11Put on the full armor of God
so that you can take your stand against the devil's schemes. 12For our struggle is not against
flesh and blood, but against the rulers, against
the authorities, against the powers of this dark
world and against the spiritual forces of evil in
the heavenly realms. 13Therefore put on the
full armor of God, so that when the day of evil
comes, you may be able to stand your ground,
and after you have done everything, to stand.
14Stand firm then, with the belt of truth buck-
led around your waist, with the breastplate of
righteousness in place, 15and with your feet
fitted with the readiness that comes from the
gospel of peace. 16In addition to all this, take
up the shield of faith, with which you can extinguish all the flaming arrows of the evil
one. 17Take the helmet of salvation and the
sword of the Spirit, which is the word of God.
18And pray in the Spirit on all occasions with
all kinds of prayers and requests. With this in
mind, be alert and always keep on praying for
all the saints.

19Pray also for me, that whenever I open
my mouth, words may be given me so that I
will fearlessly make known the mystery of the
gospel, 20for which I am an ambassador in

[a]26 Or *having cleansed* [b]31 Gen. 2:24 [c]3 Deut. 5:16

Meeting the Enemy

Read: Ephesians 6:1–24

THE IDEA OF THE DEVIL more often solicits smirks than fear or caution in the world today. In his classic work *The Screwtape Letters*, C. S. Lewis writes from the point of view of a senior demon, Screwtape, giving advice to his protégé, Wormwood, on how to influence his target. Screwtape tells Wormwood, "The fact that 'devils' are predominately *comic* figures in the modern imagination will help you. If any faint suspicion of your existence begins to arise in his mind, suggest to him a picture of something in red tights, and persuade him that since he cannot believe in that (it is an old textbook method of confusing them) he therefore cannot believe in you."

The Bible is clear that the devil *is* real and his schemes can be traced back to Eden. Beyond our limited vision lies a spiritual realm where the war for souls is waged. Jesus Christ has already won the ultimate victory, but battles still rage as Satan tries to make Christians and Christianity ineffective and impotent. Those battles play out in various arenas. Paul described them as "rulers," "authorities," "powers of this dark world" and "spiritual forces of evil in the heavenly realms." Spiritual warfare in unseen realms is as real as the battles waged here on earth.

There are also battles that occur within our thoughts, our relationships, our attitudes and our everyday choices. If the devil can wear us down so that we snap at our children or belittle our husband or pass on a tidbit of gossip, he has weakened our witness.

For every battle we face, God provides us with a full set of spiritual armor. God's armor is based on truth and righteousness, faith and peace. He asks us to be armed with his attributes, not our own. Above all, we have prayer, which reaches into the spiritual realm and places the battle into the hands of the One who has already won the war.

The presence of evil need not make us suspicious or fearful. We don't need to look for a demon behind every door. But we should be alert and prayerful so that we are aware of the devil's schemes when they come and so we can fight the battle in the spiritual realm.

Tuesday

Ephesians 6:12

For our struggle is not against flesh and blood, but against the rulers, against the authorities, against the powers of this dark world and against the spiritual forces of evil in the heavenly realms.

reflection

1 How do you picture the devil and the battle in the spiritual realm?

2 What schemes of the devil have you seen in your own life?

3 What piece of God's armor do you most need right now?

RELATED READINGS

Hebrews 2:14–18;
1 Peter 5:8–9;
1 John 4:1–4

Go to page 1439 for your next devotional reading.

chains. Pray that I may declare it fearlessly, as I should.

Final Greetings

21 Tychicus, the dear brother and faithful servant in the Lord, will tell you everything, so that you also may know how I am and what I am doing.
22 I am sending him to you for this very purpose, that you may know how we are, and that he may encourage you.

23 Peace to the brothers, and love with faith from God the Father and the Lord Jesus Christ.
24 Grace to all who love our Lord Jesus Christ with an undying love.

Philippians

Although he is in prison, this letter from Paul brims with the *theme of Christian joy.* Paul is joyful as he thinks of the Christians in Philippi. He rejoices that even his imprisonment advances the gospel. He is happy that his readers have willingly suffered for Christ as well, and *he finds great gain in Christ.* Paul is particularly pleased to hear of the Philippians' unity in Christ. They are like-minded, working together for the sake of the gospel and for one another, and Paul rejoices in that fact.

This book gives wonderful advice on putting perspective on life's bumps and bruises. The Christian life brings suffering, pain and even persecution. Yet the believer never suffers alone. *The presence of Christ Jesus brings joy* even in the midst of suffering. Read Philippians to see some of the many ways God shows himself faithful in hard times.

Author:
The apostle Paul.

Audience:
The church in Philippi and all followers of Jesus.

Date:
About A.D. 61.

Setting:
Under house arrest in Rome, Paul writes a letter to the believers in Philippi, the location of the first European church.

Verse to Remember:
Being confident of this, that he who began a good work in you will carry it on to completion until the day of Christ Jesus. (1:6)

1 Paul and Timothy, servants of Christ
Jesus,

To all the saints in Christ Jesus at Philippi,
together with the overseers[a] and deacons:

2 Grace and peace to you from God our Father and the Lord Jesus Christ.

Thanksgiving and Prayer

3 I thank my God every time I remember
you. 4 In all my prayers for all of you, I always
pray with joy 5 because of your partnership in
the gospel from the first day until now, 6 being
confident of this, that he who began a good
work in you will carry it on to completion until
the day of Christ Jesus.

7 It is right for me to feel this way about all of
you, since I have you in my heart; for whether I
am in chains or defending and confirming the
gospel, all of you share in God's grace with me.
8 God can testify how I long for all of you with
the affection of Christ Jesus.

[a]1 Traditionally *bishops*

9 And this is my prayer: that your love may
abound more and more in knowledge and
depth of insight, 10 so that you may be able
to discern what is best and may be pure and
blameless until the day of Christ, 11 filled with
the fruit of righteousness that comes through
Jesus Christ—to the glory and praise of God.

Paul's Chains Advance the Gospel

12 Now I want you to know, brothers, that
what has happened to me has really served to
advance the gospel. 13 As a result, it has become
clear throughout the whole palace guard[a] and
to everyone else that I am in chains for Christ.
14 Because of my chains, most of the brothers
in the Lord have been encouraged to speak
the word of God more courageously and fearlessly.

15 It is true that some preach Christ out of
envy and rivalry, but others out of goodwill.
16 The latter do so in love, knowing that I am
put here for the defense of the gospel. 17 The
former preach Christ out of selfish ambition,
not sincerely, supposing that they can stir up
trouble for me while I am in chains.[b] 18 But
what does it matter? The important thing is
that in every way, whether from false motives
or true, Christ is preached. And because of this
I rejoice.

Yes, and I will continue to rejoice, 19 for I
know that through your prayers and the help
given by the Spirit of Jesus Christ, what has
happened to me will turn out for my deliverance.[c] 20 I eagerly expect and hope that I will
in no way be ashamed, but will have sufficient
courage so that now as always Christ will be
exalted in my body, whether by life or by death.
21 For to me, to live is Christ and to die is gain.
22 If I am to go on living in the body, this will
mean fruitful labor for me. Yet what shall I
choose? I do not know! 23 I am torn between
the two: I desire to depart and be with Christ,
which is better by far; 24 but it is more necessary for you that I remain in the body. 25 Convinced of this, I know that I will remain, and I
will continue with all of you for your progress
and joy in the faith, 26 so that through my being with you again your joy in Christ Jesus will
overflow on account of me.

27 Whatever happens, conduct yourselves in
a manner worthy of the gospel of Christ. Then,
whether I come and see you or only hear about
you in my absence, I will know that you stand
firm in one spirit, contending as one man for
the faith of the gospel 28 without being frightened in any way by those who oppose you. This
is a sign to them that they will be destroyed,
but that you will be saved—and that by God.
29 For it has been granted to you on behalf of
Christ not only to believe on him, but also to
suffer for him, 30 since you are going through
the same struggle you saw I had, and now hear
that I still have.

Imitating Christ's Humility

2 If you have any encouragement from being united with Christ, if any comfort
from his love, if any fellowship with the Spirit,
if any tenderness and compassion, 2 then make
my joy complete by being like-minded, having
the same love, being one in spirit and purpose.
3 Do nothing out of selfish ambition or vain conceit, but in humility consider others better than
yourselves. 4 Each of you should look not only
to your own interests, but also to the interests
of others.

5 Your attitude should be the same as that of
Christ Jesus:

6 Who, being in very nature[d] God,
did not consider equality with God
something to be grasped,
7 but made himself nothing,
taking the very nature[e] of a servant,
being made in human likeness.
8 And being found in appearance as a
man,
he humbled himself
and became obedient to death—
even death on a cross!
9 Therefore God exalted him to the highest
place
and gave him the name that is above
every name,
10 that at the name of Jesus every knee should
bow,
in heaven and on earth and under the
earth,

[a]13 Or *whole palace* [b]16,17 Some late manuscripts have verses 16 and 17 in reverse order. [c]19 Or *salvation* [d]6 Or *in the form of*
[e]7 Or *the form*

11 and every tongue confess that Jesus Christ
is Lord,
to the glory of God the Father.

Shining as Stars

12 Therefore, my dear friends,
as you have always obeyed—
not only in my presence, but
now much more in my ab-
sence—continue to work out
your salvation with fear and
trembling, 13 for it is God who
works in you to will and to act
according to his good purpose.
14 Do everything without
complaining or arguing, 15 so
that you may become blameless and pure, children of God
without fault in a crooked and depraved generation, in which you shine like stars in the universe 16 as you hold out[a] the word of life—in
order that I may boast on the day of Christ that
I did not run or labor for nothing. 17 But even
if I am being poured out like a drink offering
on the sacrifice and service coming from your
faith, I am glad and rejoice with all of you. 18 So
you too should be glad and rejoice with me.

> **Philippians 2:11**
>
> *God Is Lord of All*
>
> Every tongue confess
> that Jesus Christ is Lord,
> to the glory of
> God the Father.

Timothy and Epaphroditus

19 I hope in the Lord Jesus to send Timothy
to you soon, that I also may be cheered when
I receive news about you. 20 I have no one else
like him, who takes a genuine interest in your
welfare. 21 For everyone looks out for his own
interests, not those of Jesus Christ. 22 But you
know that Timothy has proved himself, because
as a son with his father he has served with me
in the work of the gospel. 23 I hope, therefore,
to send him as soon as I see how things go with
me. 24 And I am confident in the Lord that I myself will come soon.
25 But I think it is necessary to send back to
you Epaphroditus, my brother, fellow worker
and fellow soldier, who is also your messenger,
whom you sent to take care of my needs. 26 For
he longs for all of you and is distressed because
you heard he was ill. 27 Indeed he was ill, and
almost died. But God had mercy on him, and
not on him only but also on me, to spare me
sorrow upon sorrow. 28 Therefore I am all the
more eager to send him, so that when you see
him again you may be glad and I may have
less anxiety. 29 Welcome him
in the Lord with great joy, and
honor men like him, 30 because
he almost died for the work of
Christ, risking his life to make
up for the help you could not
give me.

No Confidence in the Flesh

3 Finally, my brothers, rejoice in the Lord! It is no
trouble for me to write the
same things to you again, and
it is a safeguard for you.
2 Watch out for those dogs,
those men who do evil, those
mutilators of the flesh. 3 For it is we who are the
circumcision, we who worship by the Spirit of
God, who glory in Christ Jesus, and who put
no confidence in the flesh— 4 though I myself
have reasons for such confidence.
If anyone else thinks he has reasons to put
confidence in the flesh, I have more: 5 circumcised on the eighth day, of the people of Israel,
of the tribe of Benjamin, a Hebrew of Hebrews;
in regard to the law, a Pharisee; 6 as for zeal, persecuting the church; as for legalistic righteousness, faultless.
7 But whatever was to my profit I now
consider loss for the sake of Christ. 8 What is
more, I consider everything a loss compared
to the surpassing greatness of knowing Christ
Jesus my Lord, for whose sake I have lost all
things. I consider them rubbish, that I may gain
Christ 9 and be found in him, not having a righteousness of my own that comes from the law,
but that which is through faith in Christ—the
righteousness that comes from God and is by
faith. 10 I want to know Christ and the power
of his resurrection and the fellowship of sharing in his sufferings, becoming like him in his
death, 11 and so, somehow, to attain to the resurrection from the dead.

Pressing on Toward the Goal

12 Not that I have already obtained all this, or
have already been made perfect, but I press on

[a] 16 Or *hold on to*

to take hold of that for which Christ Jesus took hold of me. 13 Brothers, I do not consider myself yet to have taken hold of it. But one thing I do: Forgetting what is behind and straining toward what is ahead, 14 I press on toward the goal to win the prize for which God has called me heavenward in Christ Jesus.

15 All of us who are mature should take such a view of things. And if on some point you think differently, that too God will make clear to you. 16 Only let us live up to what we have already attained.

17 Join with others in following my example, brothers, and take note of those who live according to the pattern we gave you. 18 For, as I have often told you before and now say again even with tears, many live as enemies of the cross of Christ. 19 Their destiny is destruction, their god is their stomach, and their glory is in their shame. Their mind is on earthly things. 20 But our citizenship is in heaven. And we eagerly await a Savior from there, the Lord Jesus Christ, 21 who, by the power that enables him to bring everything under his control, will transform our lowly bodies so that they will be like his glorious body.

4 Therefore, my brothers, you whom I love and long for, my joy and crown, that is how you should stand firm in the Lord, dear friends!

Exhortations

2 I plead with Euodia and I plead with Syntyche to agree with each other in the Lord. 3 Yes, and I ask you, loyal yokefellow,[a] help these women who have contended at my side in the cause of the gospel, along with Clement and the rest of my fellow workers, whose names are in the book of life.

4 Rejoice in the Lord always. I will say it again: Rejoice! 5 Let your gentleness be evident to all. The Lord is near. 6 Do not be anxious about anything, but in everything, by prayer and petition, with thanksgiving, present your requests to God. 7 And the peace of God, which transcends all understanding, will guard your hearts and your minds in Christ Jesus.

8 Finally, brothers, whatever is true, whatever is noble, whatever is right, whatever is pure, whatever is lovely, whatever is admirable—if anything is excellent or praiseworthy—think about such things. 9 Whatever you have learned or received or heard from me, or seen in me—put it into practice. And the God of peace will be with you.

Thanks for Their Gifts

10 I rejoice greatly in the Lord that at last you have renewed your concern for me. Indeed, you have been concerned, but you had no opportunity to show it. 11 I am not saying this because I am in need, for I have learned to be content whatever the circumstances. 12 I know what it is to be in need, and I know what it is to have plenty. I have learned the secret of being content in any and every situation, whether well fed or hungry, whether living in plenty or in want. 13 I can do everything through him who gives me strength.

14 Yet it was good of you to share in my troubles. 15 Moreover, as you Philippians know, in the early days of your acquaintance with the gospel, when I set out from Macedonia, not one church shared with me in the matter of giving and receiving, except you only; 16 for even when I was in Thessalonica, you sent me aid again and again when I was in need. 17 Not that I am looking for a gift, but I am looking for what may be credited to your account. 18 I have received full payment and even more; I am amply supplied, now that I have received from Epaphroditus the gifts you sent. They are a fragrant offering, an acceptable sacrifice, pleasing to God. 19 And my God will meet all your needs according to his glorious riches in Christ Jesus.

20 To our God and Father be glory for ever and ever. Amen.

Final Greetings

21 Greet all the saints in Christ Jesus. The brothers who are with me send greetings. 22 All the saints send you greetings, especially those who belong to Caesar's household.

23 The grace of the Lord Jesus Christ be with your spirit. Amen.[b]

[a] 3 Or *loyal Syzygus* [b] 23 Some manuscripts do not have *Amen.*

A Gentle Spirit

Read: Philippians 4:1–13

IF YOU WALKED DOWN the street and asked five people what they thought the word *gentleness* meant, how many would say that a gentle person is docile, easily intimidated or passive? Or that gentleness would be a good quality for a pet or a horse? In our culture, assertiveness and forthrightness are more highly valued personality traits for human beings than gentleness.

But the Scriptures value gentleness. Here Paul explains what it means to be virtuous, especially in view of the disputes that had arisen among the Philippians. How were they to build unity? First, they were to rejoice. If they concentrated on rejoicing in the risen Christ, they would focus on their common joy rather than on the differences that could divide them. Next, they were to "let [their] gentleness be evident to all." Gentleness carries the idea of being reasonable. It does not mean that truth is compromised; rather, it means that the truth is defended with thoughtful consideration for the other's point of view. In other words, the people involved come to a meeting of the minds. There is a winsome quality in gentleness that diffuses anger and hostility.

A supervisor named Ann was gentle. She never raised her voice and never threatened. She had a steely calm about her. She smiled while explaining to vendors or employees exactly what was expected of them. She clearly stated the consequences if they didn't fulfill their obligations. But her subordinates never seemed defensive or discouraged; rather, they worked hard to live up to the expectations she laid out.

Paul reminded the Philippians that the key to peace was grateful prayer. He admonished them to give their every anxiety over to God as they gave thanks (verses 6–7). More than that, Paul encouraged his readers—including us—to focus on things that are beautiful, pure and positive (verses 8–9). Meditating on such things develops our ability to notice and appreciate small beauties and increases a sense of thanksgiving to God. A spirit of contentment and gratitude brings peace.

A woman who speaks words of encouragement and has an attitude of contentment is inviting; she draws people to her, even if she faces times of crisis and pain. When your gentleness is evident to all, others will know that the Lord is near and they, too, will rejoice.

Wednesday

Philippians 4:4–5

Rejoice in the Lord always. I will say it again: Rejoice! Let your gentleness be evident to all. The Lord is near.

reflection

1 What three words do you think others would use to describe you?

2 What reputation would you most like to have?

3 What is currently challenging your ability to rejoice? How can you praise God anyway?

RELATED READINGS

Exodus 16:1–8; 17:1–7; Acts 16:16–40

"In the world's eyes, especially in the business world, gentleness is often thought of as wimpy, but God says, 'The unfading beauty of a gentle and quiet spirit . . . is of great worth in God's sight.'"

Judith Couchman

Go to page 1442 for your next devotional reading.

Colossians

Author:
The apostle Paul.

Audience:
The church in Colosse (modern-day Turkey) and all followers of Jesus.

Date:
About A.D. 60.

Setting:
Paul writes from house arrest in Rome to dispel false teachings in Colosse.

Verse to Remember:
And whatever you do, whether in word or deed, do it all in the name of the Lord Jesus, giving thanks to God the Father through him. (3:17)

Jesus Christ is all you need; don't be distracted by lesser things. Christ is supreme, the Creator, the reconciler. Paul had heard of the Colossians' faith and love, but he wanted to be sure that they did not lose sight of Christ and focus on mere rules and religious traditions. If they focused on Christ, *Jesus could lead them on to maturity.*

The young church at Colosse had become a target of heretical attack. Some religious teachers insisted they had additional knowledge that was necessary for salvation. Paul's letter refutes the false teachers by *asserting the supremacy of Christ.*

1 Paul, an apostle of Christ Jesus by the will
of God, and Timothy our brother,

2 To the holy and faithful[a] brothers in Christ
at Colosse:

Grace and peace to you from God our Father.[b]

Thanksgiving and Prayer

3 We always thank God, the Father of our
Lord Jesus Christ, when we pray for you, 4 because we have heard of your faith in Christ Jesus
and of the love you have for all the saints— 5 the
faith and love that spring from the hope that
is stored up for you in heaven and that you
have already heard about in the word of truth,
the gospel 6 that has come to you. All over the
world this gospel is bearing fruit and growing,
just as it has been doing among you since the
day you heard it and understood God's grace in
all its truth. 7 You learned it from Epaphras, our
dear fellow servant, who is a faithful minister

[a] 2 Or *believing* [b] 2 Some manuscripts *Father and the Lord Jesus Christ*

of Christ on our[a] behalf, 8and who also told us of your love in the Spirit.

9For this reason, since the day we heard about you, we have not stopped praying for you and asking God to fill you with the knowledge of his will through all spiritual wisdom and understanding. 10And we pray this in order that you may live a life worthy of the Lord and may please him in every way: bearing fruit in every good work, growing in the knowledge of God, 11being strengthened with all power according to his glorious might so that you may have great endurance and patience, and joyfully 12giving thanks to the Father, who has qualified you[b] to share in the inheritance of the saints in the kingdom of light. 13For he has rescued us from the dominion of darkness and brought us into the kingdom of the Son he loves, 14in whom we have redemption,[c] the forgiveness of sins.

The Supremacy of Christ

15He is the image of the invisible God, the firstborn over all creation. 16For by him all things were created: things in heaven and on earth, visible and invisible, whether thrones or powers or rulers or authorities; all things were created by him and for him. 17He is before all things, and in him all things hold together. 18And he is the head of the body, the church; he is the beginning and the firstborn from among the dead, so that in everything he might have the supremacy. 19For God was pleased to have all his fullness dwell in him, 20and through him to reconcile to himself all things, whether things on earth or things in heaven, by making peace through his blood, shed on the cross.

> **Colossians 1:17**
>
> *God Superintends All*
>
> He is before all things, and in him all things hold together.

21Once you were alienated from God and were enemies in your minds because of[d] your evil behavior. 22But now he has reconciled you by Christ's physical body through death to present you holy in his sight, without blemish and free from accusation— 23if you continue in your faith, established and firm, not moved from the hope held out in the gospel. This is the gospel that you heard and that has been proclaimed to every creature under heaven, and of which I, Paul, have become a servant.

Paul's Labor for the Church

24Now I rejoice in what was suffered for you, and I fill up in my flesh what is still lacking in regard to Christ's afflictions, for the sake of his body, which is the church. 25I have become its servant by the commission God gave me to present to you the word of God in its fullness— 26the mystery that has been kept hidden for ages and generations, but is now disclosed to the saints. 27To them God has chosen to make known among the Gentiles the glorious riches of this mystery, which is Christ in you, the hope of glory.

28We proclaim him, admonishing and teaching everyone with all wisdom, so that we may present everyone perfect in Christ. 29To this end I labor, struggling with all his energy, which so powerfully works in me.

2 I want you to know how much I am struggling for you and for those at Laodicea, and for all who have not met me personally. 2My purpose is that they may be encouraged in heart and united in love, so that they may have the full riches of complete understanding, in order that they may know the mystery of God, namely, Christ, 3in whom are hidden all the treasures of wisdom and knowledge. 4I tell you this so that no one may deceive you by fine-sounding arguments. 5For though I am absent from you in body, I am present with you in spirit and delight to see how orderly you are and how firm your faith in Christ is.

Freedom From Human Regulations Through Life With Christ

6So then, just as you received Christ Jesus as Lord, continue to live in him, 7rooted and built up in him, strengthened in the faith as you were taught, and overflowing with thankfulness.

8See to it that no one takes you captive through hollow and deceptive philosophy,

[a]7 Some manuscripts *your* [b]12 Some manuscripts *us* [c]14 A few late manuscripts *redemption through his blood* [d]21 Or *minds, as shown by*

Bridge Builders

Read: Colossians 1:9–23

Colossians 1:22–23

But now he has reconciled you by Christ's physical body through death to present you holy in his sight, without blemish and free from accusation—if you continue in your faith, established and firm, not moved from the hope held out in the gospel.

PRIMITIVE BRIDGES WERE MADE from logs or vines extending across streams. According to historians, the first bridge was an arch bridge built in Babylon about 2200 B.C. The ancient Chinese, Egyptians, Greeks and Romans also built arch bridges out of bricks and stone. By modern times bridge builders began to use reinforced concrete and steel so the bridges would be sturdy.

A bridge must be strong enough to support its own weight as well as the people and vehicles that cross it. It must also be able to resist natural forces, such as earthquakes, strong winds and climate changes. Without bridges, people would be greatly inconvenienced, needing boats to cross waterways or being forced to travel long distances to traverse obstacles like canyons or ravines. At the worst, without bridges, people would be more isolated from one another.

The greatest bridge builder known to the world was and is Jesus Christ. When Christ stretched out his arms over the cross, he bridged the chasm that separates sinful people from a holy God. Through his blood our sins were forgiven and God's justice appeased.

But just like an expansion bridge, contrary forces can threaten our access to God: unforgiveness, unconfessed sin and unclaimed promises can corrode the foundation of our faith. Perhaps you've received a phone call: "Your son's been in an accident"; or a diagnosis: "It's breast cancer"; or a letter: "It's over."

Life has a way of crashing in on us. That's why Paul exhorts us to "continue in [our] faith, established and firm." Many times we are tempted to turn back before we reach the other side. But Christ's body and blood are strong enough to ensure our continued access to God. No opposing force "will be able to separate us from the love of God that is in Christ Jesus our Lord" (Romans 8:39).

reflection

1 What past sins have caused you to feel separated from God?

2 What are the outward circumstances or inward attitudes that may threaten your present access to God?

3 What are some steps you can take to help you continue steadfastly in the faith?

RELATED READINGS

Romans 5:8–11; 8:35–39; 2 Corinthians 5:17–21

Thursday

Go to page 1447 for your next devotional reading.

which depends on human tradition and the
basic principles of this world rather than on
Christ.
9For in Christ all the fullness of the Deity
lives in bodily form, 10and you have been given
fullness in Christ, who is the head over every
power and authority. 11In him you were also
circumcised, in the putting off of the sinful
nature,[a] not with a circumcision done by the
hands of men but with the circumcision done
by Christ, 12having been buried with him in
baptism and raised with him
through your faith in the
power of God, who raised him
from the dead.
13When you were dead in
your sins and in the uncircumcision of your sinful nature,[b]
God made you[c] alive with
Christ. He forgave us all our
sins, 14having canceled the
written code, with its regulations, that was against us and
that stood opposed to us; he
took it away, nailing it to the cross. 15And having disarmed the powers and authorities, he
made a public spectacle of them, triumphing
over them by the cross.[d]
16Therefore do not let anyone judge you
by what you eat or drink, or with regard to a
religious festival, a New Moon celebration or
a Sabbath day. 17These are a shadow of the
things that were to come; the reality, however,
is found in Christ. 18Do not let anyone who
delights in false humility and the worship of angels disqualify you for the prize. Such a person
goes into great detail about what he has seen,
and his unspiritual mind puffs him up with
idle notions. 19He has lost connection with the
Head, from whom the whole body, supported
and held together by its ligaments and sinews,
grows as God causes it to grow.
20Since you died with Christ to the basic
principles of this world, why, as though you still
belonged to it, do you submit to its rules: 21"Do
not handle! Do not taste! Do not touch!"?
22These are all destined to perish with use, because they are based on human commands and
teachings. 23Such regulations indeed have an
appearance of wisdom, with their self-imposed
worship, their false humility and their harsh
treatment of the body, but they lack any value
in restraining sensual indulgence.

Rules for Holy Living

3 Since, then, you have been raised with
Christ, set your hearts on things above,
where Christ is seated at the right hand of
God. 2Set your minds on things above, not on
earthly things. 3For you died,
and your life is now hidden
with Christ in God. 4When
Christ, who is your[e] life, appears, then you also will appear
with him in glory.
5Put to death, therefore,
whatever belongs to your
earthly nature: sexual immorality, impurity, lust, evil desires
and greed, which is idolatry.
6Because of these, the wrath of
God is coming.[f] 7You used to
walk in these ways, in the life you once lived.
8But now you must rid yourselves of all such
things as these: anger, rage, malice, slander, and
filthy language from your lips. 9Do not lie to
each other, since you have taken off your old
self with its practices 10and have put on the
new self, which is being renewed in knowledge
in the image of its Creator. 11Here there is no
Greek or Jew, circumcised or uncircumcised,
barbarian, Scythian, slave or free, but Christ is
all, and is in all.
12Therefore, as God's chosen people, holy
and dearly loved, clothe yourselves with compassion, kindness, humility, gentleness and
patience. 13Bear with each other and forgive
whatever grievances you may have against
one another. Forgive as the Lord forgave you.
14And over all these virtues put on love, which
binds them all together in perfect unity.
15Let the peace of Christ rule in your hearts,
since as members of one body you were called
to peace. And be thankful. 16Let the word of
Christ dwell in you richly as you teach and admonish one another with all wisdom, and as

Colossians 3:4

God Is Life

When Christ, who is your life, appears, then you also will appear with him in glory.

[a]11 Or *the flesh* [b]13 Or *your flesh* [c]13 Some manuscripts *us* [d]15 Or *them in him* [e]4 Some manuscripts *our* [f]6 Some early manuscripts *coming on those who are disobedient*

you sing psalms, hymns and spiritual songs with gratitude in your hearts to God. 17And whatever you do, whether in word or deed, do it all in the name of the Lord Jesus, giving thanks to God the Father through him.

Rules for Christian Households

18Wives, submit to your husbands, as is fitting in the Lord.

19Husbands, love your wives and do not be harsh with them.

20Children, obey your parents in everything, for this pleases the Lord.

21Fathers, do not embitter your children, or they will become discouraged.

22Slaves, obey your earthly masters in everything; and do it, not only when their eye is on you and to win their favor, but with sincerity of heart and reverence for the Lord. 23Whatever you do, work at it with all your heart, as working for the Lord, not for men, 24since you know that you will receive an inheritance from the Lord as a reward. It is the Lord Christ you are serving. 25Anyone who does wrong will be repaid for his wrong, and there is no favoritism.

4 Masters, provide your slaves with what is right and fair, because you know that you also have a Master in heaven.

Further Instructions

2Devote yourselves to prayer, being watchful and thankful. 3And pray for us, too, that God may open a door for our message, so that we may proclaim the mystery of Christ, for which I am in chains. 4Pray that I may proclaim it clearly, as I should. 5Be wise in the way you act toward outsiders; make the most of every opportunity. 6Let your conversation be always full of grace, seasoned with salt, so that you may know how to answer everyone.

Final Greetings

7Tychicus will tell you all the news about me. He is a dear brother, a faithful minister and fellow servant in the Lord. 8I am sending him to you for the express purpose that you may know about our[a] circumstances and that he may encourage your hearts. 9He is coming with Onesimus, our faithful and dear brother, who is one of you. They will tell you everything that is happening here.

10My fellow prisoner Aristarchus sends you his greetings, as does Mark, the cousin of Barnabas. (You have received instructions about him; if he comes to you, welcome him.) 11Jesus, who is called Justus, also sends greetings. These are the only Jews among my fellow workers for the kingdom of God, and they have proved a comfort to me. 12Epaphras, who is one of you and a servant of Christ Jesus, sends greetings. He is always wrestling in prayer for you, that you may stand firm in all the will of God, mature and fully assured. 13I vouch for him that he is working hard for you and for those at Laodicea and Hierapolis. 14Our dear friend Luke, the doctor, and Demas send greetings. 15Give my greetings to the brothers at Laodicea, and to Nympha and the church in her house.

16After this letter has been read to you, see that it is also read in the church of the Laodiceans and that you in turn read the letter from Laodicea.

17Tell Archippus: "See to it that you complete the work you have received in the Lord."

18I, Paul, write this greeting in my own hand. Remember my chains. Grace be with you.

a8 Some manuscripts *that he may know about your*

1 Thessalonians

Is there any earthly relationship more tender than that of a mother and her baby or a father and the child on his knee? In this letter to the Thessalonians, Paul compares himself and *his love for the church* to both (see 1 Thessalonians 2:7,11). This was one of Paul's first letters to the churches, and it contains what Paul felt was of *paramount importance for new believers.* The letter came as a response to Timothy's visit and addresses some specific difficulties the church was facing: fierce opposition, efforts to undermine Paul's reputation and sincerity, uncertainty about Jesus' return, and confusion about how to live a life of holiness.

Every parent would love to be able to assure their children of a promising future, but predicting such is only conjecture. Paul, however, could assure his spiritual children of *Christ's return and ultimate eternal life* in God's presence as fact. How comforting to understand that no matter what difficulties we face in this life, *we know how the story is going to end.* "The one who calls you is faithful and he will do it" (1 Thessalonians 5:24).

Author:
The apostle Paul.

Audience:
The church in Thessalonica (modern-day northern Greece) and all followers of Jesus.

Date:
About A.D. 51.

Setting:
Paul wrote from Corinth to encourage the persecuted Christians in Thessalonica.

Verse to Remember:
For the Lord himself will come down from heaven, with a loud command, with the voice of the archangel and with the trumpet call of God, and the dead in Christ will rise first. (4:16)

1

1 Paul, Silas[a] and Timothy,

To the church of the Thessalonians in God
the Father and the Lord Jesus Christ:

Grace and peace to you.[b]

Thanksgiving for the Thessalonians' Faith

2We always thank God for all of you, mentioning you in our prayers. 3We continually
remember before our God and Father your
work produced by faith, your labor prompted
by love, and your endurance inspired by hope
in our Lord Jesus Christ.
4For we know, brothers loved by God, that
he has chosen you, 5because our gospel came
to you not simply with words, but also with
power, with the Holy Spirit and with deep conviction. You know how we lived among you for
your sake. 6You became imitators of us and of
the Lord; in spite of severe suffering, you welcomed the message with the joy given by the
Holy Spirit. 7And so you became a model to all
the believers in Macedonia and Achaia. 8The
Lord's message rang out from you not only in
Macedonia and Achaia—your faith in God has
become known everywhere. Therefore we do
not need to say anything about it, 9for they
themselves report what kind of reception you
gave us. They tell how you turned to God from
idols to serve the living and true God, 10and to
wait for his Son from heaven, whom he raised
from the dead—Jesus, who rescues us from the
coming wrath.

Paul's Ministry in Thessalonica

2

2 You know, brothers, that our visit to you
was not a failure. 2We had previously suffered and been insulted in Philippi, as you know,
but with the help of our God we dared to tell you
his gospel in spite of strong opposition. 3For the
appeal we make does not spring from error or
impure motives, nor are we trying to trick you.
4On the contrary, we speak as men approved
by God to be entrusted with the gospel. We are
not trying to please men but God, who tests our
hearts. 5You know we never used flattery, nor
did we put on a mask to cover up greed—God
is our witness. 6We were not looking for praise
from men, not from you or anyone else.
As apostles of Christ we could have been
a burden to you, 7but we were gentle among
you, like a mother caring for her little children.
8We loved you so much that we were delighted
to share with you not only the gospel of God
but our lives as well, because you had become
so dear to us. 9Surely you remember, brothers,
our toil and hardship; we worked night and day
in order not to be a burden to anyone while we
preached the gospel of God to you.
10You are witnesses, and so is God, of how
holy, righteous and blameless we were among
you who believed. 11For you know that we
dealt with each of you as a father deals with his
own children, 12encouraging, comforting and
urging you to live lives worthy of God, who
calls you into his kingdom and glory.
13And we also thank God continually because, when you received the word of God,
which you heard from us, you accepted it not
as the word of men, but as it actually is, the
word of God, which is at work in you who believe. 14For you, brothers, became imitators of
God's churches in Judea, which are in Christ
Jesus: You suffered from your own countrymen
the same things those churches suffered from
the Jews, 15who killed the Lord Jesus and the
prophets and also drove us out. They displease
God and are hostile to all men 16in their effort
to keep us from speaking to the Gentiles so that
they may be saved. In this way they always heap
up their sins to the limit. The wrath of God has
come upon them at last.[c]

Paul's Longing to See the Thessalonians

17But, brothers, when we were torn away
from you for a short time (in person, not in
thought), out of our intense longing we made
every effort to see you. 18For we wanted to
come to you—certainly I, Paul, did, again and
again—but Satan stopped us. 19For what is our
hope, our joy, or the crown in which we will
glory in the presence of our Lord Jesus when
he comes? Is it not you? 20Indeed, you are our
glory and joy.

3

3 So when we could stand it no longer, we
thought it best to be left by ourselves in
Athens. 2We sent Timothy, who is our brother
and God's fellow worker[d] in spreading the

[a]1 Greek *Silvanus*, a variant of *Silas* [b]1 Some early manuscripts *you from God our Father and the Lord Jesus Christ* [c]16 Or *them fully*
[d]2 Some manuscripts *brother and fellow worker*; other manuscripts *brother and God's servant*

Best of Parents

Read: 1 Thessalonians 1:1–10

ONE OF THE MOST ILLUMINATING names of God is the one especially revealed by our Lord Jesus Christ, the name of Father. I say especially revealed by Christ, because, while God had been called throughout the ages by many other names, expressing other aspects of His character, Christ alone has revealed Him to us under the all inclusive name of Father—a name that holds within itself all other names of wisdom and power, and above all [a name] of love and goodness, a name that embodies for us a perfect supply for all our needs. Christ, who was the only begotten Son in the bosom of the Father, was the only one who could reveal this name, for He alone knew the Father . . .

But before I go any farther I must make it plain that it is a Father, such as our highest instincts tell us a good father ought to be, of whom I am speaking. Sometimes earthly fathers are unkind, or tyrannical, or selfish, or even cruel, or they are merely indifferent and neglectful; but none of these can by any stretch of charity be called good fathers. But God, who is good, must be a good father or not a father at all . . . All of us have known good fathers in this world, or at least can imagine them. I knew one, and he filled my childhood with sunshine by his most lovely fatherhood. I can remember vividly with what confidence and triumph I walked through my days, absolutely secure in the knowledge that I had a father. And I am very sure that I have learned to know a little more about the perfect fatherhood of God, because of my experience with this lovely earthly father . . .

But God is not only a father, He is a mother as well, and we have all of us known mothers whose love and tenderness have been without bound or limit. And it is very certain that the God who created them both, and who is Himself father and mother in one, could never have created earthly fathers and mothers who were more tender and more loving than He is Himself. Therefore if we want to know what sort of a Father He is, we must heap together all the best of all the fathers and mothers we have ever known or can imagine, and we must tell ourselves that this is only a faint image of God, our Father in Heaven.

—*Hannah Whitall Smith*

Go to page 1452 for your next devotional reading.

1 Thessalonians 1:3

We continually remember before our God and Father your work produced by faith, your labor prompted by love, and your endurance inspired by hope in our Lord Jesus Christ.

reflection

1. How do you typically address God? Do you call him Father, Lord or friend?
2. What things do you need from your heavenly Father?
3. Since Jesus revealed God as Father, pray to him as your *Abba* Father. Ask him to love you with the perfect father's love. If your earthly father has disappointed you, come to your heavenly Father with the expectation that he will never leave you nor forsake you.

RELATED READINGS

Exodus 15:1–5;
Matthew 6:9–13;
Galatians 4:1–6

"Trying to build the brotherhood of man without the fatherhood of God is like trying to make a wheel without a hub."

Irene Dunne

gospel of Christ, to strengthen and encourage
you in your faith, 3so that no one would be
unsettled by these trials. You know quite well
that we were destined for them. 4In fact, when
we were with you, we kept telling you that we
would be persecuted. And it turned out that
way, as you well know. 5For this reason, when
I could stand it no longer, I sent to find out
about your faith. I was afraid that in some way
the tempter might have tempted you and our
efforts might have been useless.

Timothy's Encouraging Report

6But Timothy has just now come to us from
you and has brought good news about your
faith and love. He has told us that you always
have pleasant memories of us and that you
long to see us, just as we also long to see you.
7Therefore, brothers, in all our distress and
persecution we were encouraged about you
because of your faith. 8For now we really live,
since you are standing firm in the Lord. 9How
can we thank God enough for you in return for
all the joy we have in the presence of our God
because of you? 10Night and day we pray most
earnestly that we may see you again and supply
what is lacking in your faith.
11Now may our God and Father himself
and our Lord Jesus clear the way for us to
come to you. 12May the Lord
make your love increase and
overflow for each other and for
everyone else, just as ours does
for you. 13May he strengthen
your hearts so that you will be
blameless and holy in the presence of our God and Father
when our Lord Jesus comes
with all his holy ones.

Living to Please God

4 Finally, brothers, we instructed you how to live in
order to please God, as in fact
you are living. Now we ask you
and urge you in the Lord Jesus
to do this more and more. 2For
you know what instructions we gave you by the
authority of the Lord Jesus.
3It is God's will that you should be sanctified: that you should avoid sexual immorality;
4that each of you should learn to control his
own body[a] in a way that is holy and honorable, 5not in passionate lust like the heathen,
who do not know God; 6and that in this matter no one should wrong his brother or take
advantage of him. The Lord will punish men
for all such sins, as we have already told you
and warned you. 7For God did not call us to
be impure, but to live a holy life. 8Therefore,
he who rejects this instruction does not reject man but God, who gives you his Holy
Spirit.
9Now about brotherly love we do not need
to write to you, for you yourselves have been
taught by God to love each other. 10And in fact,
you do love all the brothers throughout Macedonia. Yet we urge you, brothers, to do so more
and more.
11Make it your ambition to lead a quiet life,
to mind your own business and to work with
your hands, just as we told you, 12so that your
daily life may win the respect of outsiders
and so that you will not be dependent on anybody.

The Coming of the Lord

13Brothers, we do not want you to be ignorant about those who fall
asleep, or to grieve like the rest
of men, who have no hope.
14We believe that Jesus died
and rose again and so we believe that God will bring with
Jesus those who have fallen
asleep in him. 15According to
the Lord's own word, we tell
you that we who are still alive,
who are left till the coming
of the Lord, will certainly not
precede those who have fallen
asleep. 16For the Lord himself
will come down from heaven,
with a loud command, with
the voice of the archangel and
with the trumpet call of God,
and the dead in Christ will rise first. 17After
that, we who are still alive and are left will be

> **1 Thessalonians 4:16**
>
> ***God Will Call Us Home***
>
> For the Lord himself will come down from heaven, with a loud command, with the voice of the archangel and with the trumpet call of God, and the dead in Christ will rise first.

[a]4 Or *learn to live with his own wife*; or *learn to acquire a wife*

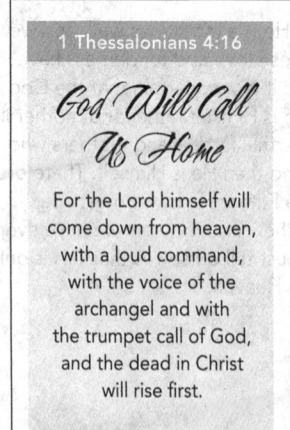

caught up together with them in the clouds to
meet the Lord in the air. And so we will be with
the Lord forever. [18]Therefore encourage each
other with these words.

5 Now, brothers, about times and dates we
do not need to write to you, [2]for you know
very well that the day of the Lord will come like
a thief in the night. [3]While people are saying,
"Peace and safety," destruction will come on
them suddenly, as labor pains on a pregnant
woman, and they will not escape.

[4]But you, brothers, are not in darkness so
that this day should surprise you like a thief.
[5]You are all sons of the light and sons of the
day. We do not belong to the night or to the
darkness. [6]So then, let us not be like others,
who are asleep, but let us be alert and self-controlled. [7]For those who sleep, sleep at night,
and those who get drunk, get drunk at night.
[8]But since we belong to the day, let us be self-
controlled, putting on faith and love as a breastplate, and the hope of salvation
as a helmet. [9]For God did not
appoint us to suffer wrath but
to receive salvation through
our Lord Jesus Christ. [10]He
died for us so that, whether we
are awake or asleep, we may
live together with him. [11]There-
fore encourage one another
and build each other up, just as
in fact you are doing.

> **1 Thessalonians 5:24**
>
> *God Is Faithful*
>
> The one who calls you is faithful and he will do it.

Final Instructions

[12]Now we ask you, brothers, to respect those
who work hard among you, who are over you in
the Lord and who admonish you. [13]Hold them
in the highest regard in love because of their
work. Live in peace with each other. [14]And we
urge you, brothers, warn those who are idle,
encourage the timid, help the weak, be patient
with everyone. [15]Make sure that nobody pays
back wrong for wrong, but always try to be
kind to each other and to everyone else.

[16]Be joyful always; [17]pray continually;
[18]give thanks in all circumstances, for this is
God's will for you in Christ Jesus.

[19]Do not put out the Spirit's fire; [20]do not
treat prophecies with contempt. [21]Test everything. Hold on to the good. [22]Avoid every kind
of evil.

[23]May God himself, the God of peace,
sanctify you through and through. May your
whole spirit, soul and body be kept blameless
at the coming of our Lord Jesus
Christ. [24]The one who calls you
is faithful and he will do it.

[25]Brothers, pray for us.
[26]Greet all the brothers with a
holy kiss. [27]I charge you before
the Lord to have this letter read
to all the brothers.

[28]The grace of our Lord
Jesus Christ be with you.

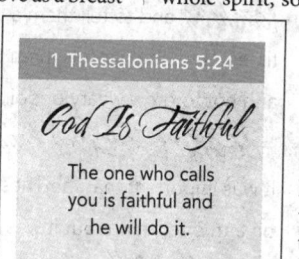

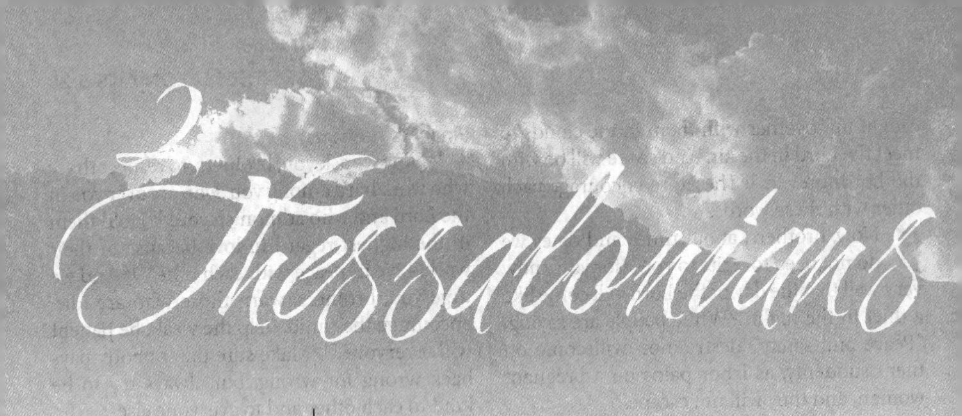

2 Thessalonians

Author:
The apostle Paul.

Audience:
The church in Thessalonica (modern-day northern Greece) and all followers of Jesus.

Date:
About A.D. 51 or 52, six months after the writing of 1 Thessalonians.

Setting:
The Christians in Thessalonica thought that Christ would return immediately. They became confused and disappointed when he didn't return on their timetable.

Verse to Remember:
"May the Lord direct your hearts into God's love and Christ's perseverance." (3:5)

The Thessalonians were enduring trials and growing in their faith. But a new trial had entered the scene and frightened some of them—the false teaching that the day of the Lord had already come. Paul writes to reassure them and to caution them to *beware of false teaching* and to tell them a little bit about the end times. He also counsels them to work hard, not to be idle and not to grow weary of doing good.

Correct teaching leads to correct living.

It was important that the Thessalonians base their actions on a true teaching. But it was also important that they *knew the truth* that God expected them to work to earn the food they ate. Notice how carefully and gently Paul corrects the believers who had been taught incorrectly but who wanted to know the truth.

1

Paul, Silas[a] and Timothy,

To the church of the Thessalonians in God our Father and the Lord Jesus Christ:

2 Grace and peace to you from God the Father and the Lord Jesus Christ.

Thanksgiving and Prayer

3 We ought always to thank God for you, brothers, and rightly so, because your faith is growing more and more, and the love every one of you has for each other is increasing. 4 Therefore, among God's churches we boast about your perseverance and faith in all the persecutions and trials you are enduring.

5 All this is evidence that God's judgment is right, and as a result you will be counted worthy of the kingdom of God, for which you are suffering. 6 God is just: He will pay back trouble to those who trouble you 7 and give relief to you who are troubled, and to us as well. This will happen when the Lord Jesus is revealed from heaven in blazing fire with his powerful angels. 8 He will punish those who do not know God and do not obey the gospel of our Lord Jesus. 9 They will be punished with everlasting destruction and shut out from the presence of the Lord and from the majesty of his power 10 on the day he comes to be glorified in his holy people and to be marveled at among all those who have believed. This includes you, because you believed our testimony to you.

> **2 Thessalonians 1:6**
>
> *God Is Just*
>
> God is just: He will pay back trouble to those who trouble you.

11 With this in mind, we constantly pray for you, that our God may count you worthy of his calling, and that by his power he may fulfill every good purpose of yours and every act prompted by your faith. 12 We pray this so that the name of our Lord Jesus may be glorified in you, and you in him, according to the grace of our God and the Lord Jesus Christ.[b]

The Man of Lawlessness

2

Concerning the coming of our Lord Jesus Christ and our being gathered to him, we ask you, brothers, 2 not to become easily unsettled or alarmed by some prophecy, report or letter supposed to have come from us, saying that the day of the Lord has already come. 3 Don't let anyone deceive you in any way, for ⌊that day will not come⌋ until the rebellion occurs and the man of lawlessness[c] is revealed, the man doomed to destruction. 4 He will oppose and will exalt himself over everything that is called God or is worshiped, so that he sets himself up in God's temple, proclaiming himself to be God.

5 Don't you remember that when I was with you I used to tell you these things? 6 And now you know what is holding him back, so that he may be revealed at the proper time. 7 For the secret power of lawlessness is already at work; but the one who now holds it back will continue to do so till he is taken out of the way. 8 And then the lawless one will be revealed, whom the Lord Jesus will overthrow with the breath of his mouth and destroy by the splendor of his coming. 9 The coming of the lawless one will be in accordance with the work of Satan displayed in all kinds of counterfeit miracles, signs and wonders, 10 and in every sort of evil that deceives those who are perishing. They perish because they refused to love the truth and so be saved. 11 For this reason God sends them a powerful delusion so that they will believe the lie 12 and so that all will be condemned who have not believed the truth but have delighted in wickedness.

Stand Firm

13 But we ought always to thank God for you, brothers loved by the Lord, because from the beginning God chose you[d] to be saved through the sanctifying work of the Spirit and through belief in the truth. 14 He called you to this through our gospel, that you might share in the glory of our Lord Jesus Christ. 15 So then, brothers, stand firm and hold to the teachings[e] we passed on to you, whether by word of mouth or by letter.

16 May our Lord Jesus Christ himself and

[a] 1 Greek *Silvanus*, a variant of *Silas* [b] 12 Or *God and Lord, Jesus Christ* [c] 3 Some manuscripts *sin* [d] 13 Some manuscripts *because God chose you as his firstfruits* [e] 15 Or *traditions*

Controversy

PRISCILLA

There [Paul] met a Jew named Aquila . . . who had recently come from Italy with his wife Priscilla, because Claudius had ordered all the Jews to leave Rome.

Acts 18:2

ASSIGNED READING:

Acts 18:1–28; Romans 16:3–5

"YOU'VE GOT TO BE KIDDING." Priscilla's neighbor was always getting the story wrong. She was sure that's what was happening now. No, her neighbor said emphatically, Emperor Claudius had served the entire neighborhood eviction notices. It was true.

Every Jew—each man, woman and child—received the royal edict to pack up and leave the Roman capital at once. Apparently, the emperor was weary of the Jews' arguments over the new Christian religion (inferred from the historical reference to "Chrestus"), so he summarily sent them packing.

Priscilla never forgot those first few panicked hours after the audacious ruling. Oh, the rush to get her and her husband Aquila's belongings together! As they joined their fellow deportees for a one-way ticket out of Rome, she cast one last glance at her home. "I wonder if I'll ever return home," she wondered, with tears threatening to spill.

Out of all the cities they could have chosen, the couple settled in the Greek city of Corinth, home to one of the largest gatherings of pagan worship on earth at that time.

"Lord, I know you can sometimes create controversy," she would later pray. "But I seem to be a magnet for it!"

Priscilla and her husband found themselves in a spiritual struggle between the overindulgent lifestyle of their neighbors and their Christian faith. On the way to the market or synagogue, she was assaulted by images and trinkets—ranging from the mundane to the obscene—all dedicated to the goddess of love, Aphrodite.

"Is it always going to be a tug-of-war? Why is it so hard to be a Christian?" Prayers filled her thoughts as she contemplated how her faith had affected the course of her everyday life.

When she and her husband moved to Ephesus to assist Paul in his missionary work, it didn't become any easier. Growing opposition, eventually erupting into full-scale rioting, tested her mettle. Priscilla could bear witness that being a Christian in the early church was not for the faint of heart. The social and political pressure likely claimed a number of spiritual casualties. However, with the encouragement of her husband, her friend Paul and a host of other new believers, her faith held fast and her legacy continues to this day.

—Prayer—

Lord, give me strength to do your will wherever my path leads.

Weekend

Go to page 1456 for your next devotional reading.

God our Father, who loved us and by his grace
gave us eternal encouragement and good hope,
17 encourage your hearts and strengthen you in
every good deed and word.

Request for Prayer

3 Finally, brothers, pray for us that the message of the Lord may spread rapidly and
be honored, just as it was with you. 2 And pray
that we may be delivered from
wicked and evil men, for not
everyone has faith. 3 But the
Lord is faithful, and he will
strengthen and protect you
from the evil one. 4 We have confidence in the Lord that you are
doing and will continue to do
the things we command. 5 May
the Lord direct your hearts into
God's love and Christ's perseverance.

> **2 Thessalonians 3:5**
>
> *God Directs Us*
>
> May the Lord direct your hearts into God's love and Christ's perseverance.

Warning Against Idleness

6 In the name of the Lord Jesus Christ, we
command you, brothers, to keep away from every brother who is idle and does not live according to the teaching[a] you received from us. 7 For
you yourselves know how you ought to follow
our example. We were not idle when we were
with you, 8 nor did we eat anyone's food without
paying for it. On the contrary, we worked night
and day, laboring and toiling so that we would
not be a burden to any of you. 9 We did this, not
because we do not have the right to such help,
but in order to make ourselves a model for you
to follow. 10 For even when we were with you,
we gave you this rule: "If a man will not work,
he shall not eat."

11 We hear that some among you are idle.
They are not busy; they are busybodies. 12 Such
people we command and urge in the Lord
Jesus Christ to settle down and
earn the bread they eat. 13 And
as for you, brothers, never tire
of doing what is right.

14 If anyone does not obey
our instruction in this letter,
take special note of him. Do
not associate with him, in order that he may feel ashamed.
15 Yet do not regard him as
an enemy, but warn him as a
brother.

Final Greetings

16 Now may the Lord of peace himself give
you peace at all times and in every way. The
Lord be with all of you.

17 I, Paul, write this greeting in my own
hand, which is the distinguishing mark in all
my letters. This is how I write.

18 The grace of our Lord Jesus Christ be with
you all.

[a]6 Or *tradition*

1 Timothy

Author:
The apostle Paul.

Audience:
Timothy, Paul's young protégé, young church leaders and all believers everywhere.

Date:
About A.D. 64, probably between Paul's first and second imprisonments in Rome.

Setting:
Timothy, the young pastor of the church of Ephesus, receives instructions from Paul on church management.

Verse to Remember:
Timothy, my son, I give you this instruction in keeping with the prophecies once made about you, so that by following them you may fight the good fight, holding on to faith and a good conscience. (1:18–19)

A friend in the faith is one of the greatest blessings God gives us. We need the companionship and encouragement of others, and we also need the loving honesty of someone *who wants us to grow* in our walk with Christ. That kind of friendship is what we see between Paul and Timothy in this first of the Pastoral Letters. In fact, Paul thought of Timothy as a son. Timothy had been Paul's loyal companion since joining him on his second missionary journey, staying with him even during Paul's imprisonment.

But *friends don't always get to remain together.* When Paul needed someone to pastor the church in Ephesus, he chose Timothy for the job. It meant they would no longer travel together as they once had, but it also gave Timothy an opportunity to grow in his faith and ministry. Paul's letter provides Timothy with the building blocks he needed to further the work in Ephesus. *He covers everything* from choosing leaders to caring for the needy. And he does it from one friend to another, seeking the best for Timothy and for the congregation he serves.

1

Paul, an apostle of Christ Jesus by the command of God our Savior and of Christ Jesus our hope,

2To Timothy my true son in the faith:

Grace, mercy and peace from God the Father and Christ Jesus our Lord.

Warning Against False Teachers of the Law

3As I urged you when I went into Macedonia, stay there in Ephesus so that you may command certain men not to teach false doctrines any longer 4nor to devote themselves to myths and endless genealogies. These promote controversies rather than God's work—which is by faith. 5The goal of this command is love, which comes from a pure heart and a good conscience and a sincere faith. 6Some have wandered away from these and turned to meaningless talk. 7They want to be teachers of the law, but they do not know what they are talking about or what they so confidently affirm.

8We know that the law is good if one uses it properly. 9We also know that law[a] is made not for the righteous but for lawbreakers and rebels, the ungodly and sinful, the unholy and irreligious; for those who kill their fathers or mothers, for murderers, 10for adulterers and perverts, for slave traders and liars and perjurers—and for whatever else is contrary to the sound doctrine 11that conforms to the glorious gospel of the blessed God, which he entrusted to me.

The Lord's Grace to Paul

12I thank Christ Jesus our Lord, who has given me strength, that he considered me faithful, appointing me to his service. 13Even though I was once a blasphemer and a persecutor and a violent man, I was shown mercy because I acted in ignorance and unbelief. 14The grace of our Lord was poured out on me abundantly, along with the faith and love that are in Christ Jesus.

15Here is a trustworthy saying that deserves full acceptance: Christ Jesus came into the world to save sinners—of whom I am the worst. 16But for that very reason I was shown mercy so that in me, the worst of sinners, Christ Jesus might display his unlimited patience as an example for those who would believe on him and receive eternal life. 17Now to the King eternal, immortal, invisible, the only God, be honor and glory for ever and ever. Amen.

18Timothy, my son, I give you this instruction in keeping with the prophecies once made about you, so that by following them you may fight the good fight, 19holding on to faith and a good conscience. Some have rejected these and so have shipwrecked their faith. 20Among them are Hymenaeus and Alexander, whom I have handed over to Satan to be taught not to blaspheme.

> 1 Timothy 1:17
>
> *God Is Immortal*
>
> Now to the King eternal,
> immortal, invisible,
> the only God, be honor
> and glory for ever
> and ever. Amen.

Instructions on Worship

2

I urge, then, first of all, that requests, prayers, intercession and thanksgiving be made for everyone— 2for kings and all those in authority, that we may live peaceful and quiet lives in all godliness and holiness. 3This is good, and pleases God our Savior, 4who wants all men to be saved and to come to a knowledge of the truth. 5For there is one God and one mediator between God and men, the man Christ Jesus, 6who gave himself as a ransom for all men—the testimony given in its proper time. 7And for this purpose I was appointed a herald and an apostle—I am telling the truth, I am not lying—and a teacher of the true faith to the Gentiles.

8I want men everywhere to lift up holy hands in prayer, without anger or disputing.

9I also want women to dress modestly, with decency and propriety, not with braided hair or gold or pearls or expensive clothes, 10but with good deeds, appropriate for women who profess to worship God.

11A woman should learn in quietness and full submission. 12I do not permit a woman to teach or to have authority over a man; she must

[a]9 Or *that the law*

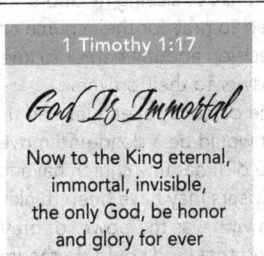

Prayer for All

Read: 1 Timothy 2:1–15

WHEN THE YOUNG PASTOR went to visit his new church, five women of all ages, shapes and sizes greeted him.

"We've been praying you would come," a spry 90-year-old woman said with a smile. "I've been a member here since I was a girl." They showed him into the small, country church that had been at risk of closing its doors. She and her four friends had decided to pray for their church and for those who would make the decision about whether to keep its doors open. The pastor was the answer to their prayers.

The pastor's colleagues had urged him not to accept the position. It would be a dead-end move for his career, they said. What chance did that tiny church have for survival in such a remote area? His advisers may have been thinking logically, but what they didn't reckon with was the power of prayer. These five faithful women believed that God could do the impossible—and he did. No one could have predicted the large numbers of people who decided to move from the city to the suburbs. Years later, the small, country church has continued to grow into a thriving ministry under the leadership of the man who felt compelled to accept the small pastorate.

Paul's letter to Timothy encourages us to pray for everyone. How easy it is to become complacent and believe that the prayers of one person don't really matter. But wouldn't it be better to spend our time praying, rather than giving up in frustration, second-guessing or criticizing others?

Just imagine what would happen if each of us took on the serious business of praying for those around us. Not just *saying* we'll pray, but *really* praying—asking for God's wisdom, guidance and protection, and giving thanks for people's willingness to serve. Five women prayed that God would make a difference in their church, and he did. Think of what God might do when *you* commit to pray for the people you know.

1 Timothy 2:1–4

I urge, then, first of all, that requests, prayers, intercession and thanksgiving be made for everyone—for kings and all those in authority, that we may live peaceful and quiet lives in all godliness and holiness. This is good, and pleases God our Savior, who wants all men to be saved and to come to a knowledge of the truth.

reflection

1. Describe a time when you knew that your prayers made a difference.
2. What priority does prayer have in your life?
3. How often do you take the time to pray for those around you? Do you know someone who needs prayer right now? Then pray right now.

RELATED READINGS

Psalm 67:1–7; Matthew 6:5–13; 7:7–12; James 5:13–16

Monday

Go to page 1462 for your next devotional reading.

be silent. 13For Adam was formed first, then Eve. 14And Adam was not the one deceived; it was the woman who was deceived and became a sinner. 15But women[a] will be saved[b] through childbearing—if they continue in faith, love and holiness with propriety.

> 1 Timothy 3:16
>
> *God Became Human*
>
> Beyond all question,
> the mystery of
> godliness is great:
> He appeared in a body.

Overseers and Deacons

3 Here is a trustworthy saying: If anyone sets his heart on being an overseer,[c] he desires a noble task. 2Now the overseer must be above reproach, the husband of but one wife, temperate, self-controlled, respectable, hospitable, able to teach, 3not given to drunkenness, not violent but gentle, not quarrelsome, not a lover of money. 4He must manage his own family well and see that his children obey him with proper respect. 5(If anyone does not know how to manage his own family, how can he take care of God's church?) 6He must not be a recent convert, or he may become conceited and fall under the same judgment as the devil. 7He must also have a good reputation with outsiders, so that he will not fall into disgrace and into the devil's trap.

8Deacons, likewise, are to be men worthy of respect, sincere, not indulging in much wine, and not pursuing dishonest gain. 9They must keep hold of the deep truths of the faith with a clear conscience. 10They must first be tested; and then if there is nothing against them, let them serve as deacons.

11In the same way, their wives[d] are to be women worthy of respect, not malicious talkers but temperate and trustworthy in everything.

12A deacon must be the husband of but one wife and must manage his children and his household well. 13Those who have served well gain an excellent standing and great assurance in their faith in Christ Jesus.

14Although I hope to come to you soon, I am writing you these instructions so that, 15if I am delayed, you will know how people ought to conduct themselves in God's household, which is the church of the living God, the pillar and foundation of the truth. 16Beyond all question, the mystery of godliness is great:

He[e] appeared in a body,[f]
was vindicated by the Spirit,
was seen by angels,
was preached among the nations,
was believed on in the world,
was taken up in glory.

Instructions to Timothy

4 The Spirit clearly says that in later times some will abandon the faith and follow deceiving spirits and things taught by demons. 2Such teachings come through hypocritical liars, whose consciences have been seared as with a hot iron. 3They forbid people to marry and order them to abstain from certain foods, which God created to be received with thanksgiving by those who believe and who know the truth. 4For everything God created is good, and nothing is to be rejected if it is received with thanksgiving, 5because it is consecrated by the word of God and prayer.

6If you point these things out to the brothers, you will be a good minister of Christ Jesus, brought up in the truths of the faith and of the good teaching that you have followed. 7Have nothing to do with godless myths and old wives' tales; rather, train yourself to be godly. 8For physical training is of some value, but godliness has value for all things, holding promise for both the present life and the life to come.

9This is a trustworthy saying that deserves full acceptance 10(and for this we labor and strive), that we have put our hope in the living God, who is the Savior of all men, and especially of those who believe.

11Command and teach these things. 12Don't let anyone look down on you because you are young, but set an example for the believers in speech, in life, in love, in faith and in purity. 13Until I come, devote yourself to the public reading of Scripture, to preaching and to teaching. 14Do not neglect your gift, which was

[a] 15 Greek *she* [b] 15 Or *restored* [c] 1 Traditionally *bishop*; also in verse 2 [d] 11 Or *way, deaconesses* [e] 16 Some manuscripts *God*
[f] 16 Or *in the flesh*

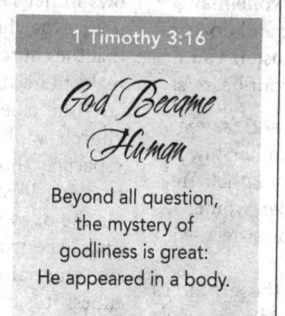

given you through a prophetic message when the body of elders laid their hands on you.

15 Be diligent in these matters; give yourself wholly to them, so that everyone may see your progress. 16 Watch your life and doctrine closely. Persevere in them, because if you do, you will save both yourself and your hearers.

Advice About Widows, Elders and Slaves

5 Do not rebuke an older man harshly, but exhort him as if he were your father. Treat younger men as brothers, 2 older women as mothers, and younger women as sisters, with absolute purity.

3 Give proper recognition to those widows who are really in need. 4 But if a widow has children or grandchildren, these should learn first of all to put their religion into practice by caring for their own family and so repaying their parents and grandparents, for this is pleasing to God. 5 The widow who is really in need and left all alone puts her hope in God and continues night and day to pray and to ask God for help. 6 But the widow who lives for pleasure is dead even while she lives. 7 Give the people these instructions, too, so that no one may be open to blame. 8 If anyone does not provide for his relatives, and especially for his immediate family, he has denied the faith and is worse than an unbeliever.

9 No widow may be put on the list of widows unless she is over sixty, has been faithful to her husband,[a] 10 and is well known for her good deeds, such as bringing up children, showing hospitality, washing the feet of the saints, helping those in trouble and devoting herself to all kinds of good deeds.

11 As for younger widows, do not put them on such a list. For when their sensual desires overcome their dedication to Christ, they want to marry. 12 Thus they bring judgment on themselves, because they have broken their first pledge. 13 Besides, they get into the habit of being idle and going about from house to house. And not only do they become idlers, but also gossips and busybodies, saying things they ought not to. 14 So I counsel younger widows to marry, to have children, to manage their homes and to give the enemy no opportunity for slander. 15 Some have in fact already turned away to follow Satan.

16 If any woman who is a believer has widows in her family, she should help them and not let the church be burdened with them, so that the church can help those widows who are really in need.

17 The elders who direct the affairs of the church well are worthy of double honor, especially those whose work is preaching and teaching. 18 For the Scripture says, "Do not muzzle the ox while it is treading out the grain,"[b] and "The worker deserves his wages."[c] 19 Do not entertain an accusation against an elder unless it is brought by two or three witnesses. 20 Those who sin are to be rebuked publicly, so that the others may take warning.

21 I charge you, in the sight of God and Christ Jesus and the elect angels, to keep these instructions without partiality, and to do nothing out of favoritism.

22 Do not be hasty in the laying on of hands, and do not share in the sins of others. Keep yourself pure.

23 Stop drinking only water, and use a little wine because of your stomach and your frequent illnesses.

24 The sins of some men are obvious, reaching the place of judgment ahead of them; the sins of others trail behind them. 25 In the same way, good deeds are obvious, and even those that are not cannot be hidden.

6 All who are under the yoke of slavery should consider their masters worthy of full respect, so that God's name and our teaching may not be slandered. 2 Those who have believing masters are not to show less respect for them because they are brothers. Instead, they are to serve them even better, because those who benefit from their service are believers, and dear to them. These are the things you are to teach and urge on them.

Love of Money

3 If anyone teaches false doctrines and does not agree to the sound instruction of our Lord Jesus Christ and to godly teaching, 4 he is conceited and understands nothing. He has an unhealthy interest in controversies and

[a] 9 Or *has had but one husband* [b] 18 Deut. 25:4 [c] 18 Luke 10:7

quarrels about words that result in envy, strife,
malicious talk, evil suspicions [5]and constant
friction between men of corrupt mind, who
have been robbed of the truth and who think
that godliness is a means to financial gain.
[6]But godliness with contentment is great
gain. [7]For we brought nothing into the world,
and we can take nothing out of it. [8]But if we
have food and clothing, we will be content
with that. [9]People who want to get rich fall
into temptation and a trap and into many foolish and harmful desires that plunge men into
ruin and destruction. [10]For the love of money
is a root of all kinds of evil. Some people, eager
for money, have wandered from the faith and
pierced themselves with many griefs.

Paul's Charge to Timothy

[11]But you, man of God, flee from all this,
and pursue righteousness, godliness, faith,
love, endurance and gentleness. [12]Fight the
good fight of the faith. Take hold of the eternal
life to which you were called when you made
your good confession in the presence of many
witnesses. [13]In the sight of God, who gives life
to everything, and of Christ Jesus, who while
testifying before Pontius Pilate made the good
confession, I charge you [14]to keep this command without spot or blame until the appearing of our Lord Jesus Christ, [15]which God will
bring about in his own time—God, the blessed
and only Ruler, the King of kings and Lord of
lords, [16]who alone is immortal and who lives
in unapproachable light, whom no one has
seen or can see. To him be honor and might
forever. Amen.

[17]Command those who are rich in this present world not to be arrogant nor to put their
hope in wealth, which is so uncertain, but to
put their hope in God, who richly provides us
with everything for our enjoyment. [18]Com-
mand them to do good, to be rich in good
deeds, and to be generous and willing to share.
[19]In this way they will lay up treasure for themselves as a firm foundation for the coming age,
so that they may take hold of the life that is
truly life.
[20]Timothy, guard what has been entrusted
to your care. Turn away from godless chatter
and the opposing ideas of what is falsely called
knowledge, [21]which some have professed and
in so doing have wandered from the faith.
Grace be with you.

2 Timothy

Author:
The apostle Paul.

Audience:
Timothy and Christians everywhere.

Date:
About A.D. 66 or 67.

Setting:
Paul penned this, his last letter, from a Roman dungeon shortly before he was executed for his faith.

Verse to Remember:
Do your best to present yourself to God as one approved, a workman who does not need to be ashamed and who correctly handles the word of truth. (2:15)

Paul's letter to his young disciple, Timothy, is personal and tender. Paul is in prison in Rome and expects to die soon, and he has words of counsel for the young pastor. Addressing him as "my dear son," Paul exhorts Timothy to be faithful and *not to be ashamed of Christ.* He urges Timothy to stay true to his calling and to continue to teach others. More than anything else, *he is to preach the Word.* Paul gives his farewell and passes the baton, but he also urges Timothy to come to see him. His personal requests to this spiritual son come at the end of the letter.

After Paul's conversion, he lived a fruitful, busy—even hectic—life. Yet *he still found time* to invest personally in individuals.

---

1 Paul, an apostle of Christ Jesus by the will
of God, according to the promise of life
that is in Christ Jesus,

2To Timothy, my dear son:

Grace, mercy and peace from God the Father and Christ Jesus our Lord.

Encouragement to Be Faithful

3I thank God, whom I serve, as my forefathers did, with a clear conscience, as night and
day I constantly remember you in my prayers.
4Recalling your tears, I long to see you, so that
I may be filled with joy. 5I have been reminded
of your sincere faith, which first lived in your
grandmother Lois and in your mother Eunice
and, I am persuaded, now lives in you also.
6For this reason I remind you to fan into flame
the gift of God, which is in you through the laying on of my hands. 7For God did not give us
a spirit of timidity, but a spirit of power, of love
and of self-discipline.

8So do not be ashamed to testify about our
Lord, or ashamed of me his prisoner. But join
with me in suffering for the gospel, by the
power of God, 9who has saved us and called
us to a holy life—not because of anything we
have done but because of his own purpose
and grace. This grace was given us in Christ
Jesus before the beginning of time, 10but it
has now been revealed through the appearing
of our Savior, Christ Jesus, who has destroyed
death and has brought life and
immortality to light through
the gospel. 11And of this gospel I was appointed a herald
and an apostle and a teacher.
12That is why I am suffering as
I am. Yet I am not ashamed, because I know whom I have believed, and am convinced that
he is able to guard what I have
entrusted to him for that day.
13What you heard from me,
keep as the pattern of sound
teaching, with faith and love in
Christ Jesus. 14Guard the good
deposit that was entrusted to
you—guard it with the help of
the Holy Spirit who lives in us.
15You know that everyone in the province
of Asia has deserted me, including Phygelus
and Hermogenes.
16May the Lord show mercy to the household of Onesiphorus, because he often refreshed me and was not ashamed of my chains.
17On the contrary, when he was in Rome, he
searched hard for me until he found me. 18May
the Lord grant that he will find mercy from the
Lord on that day! You know very well in how
many ways he helped me in Ephesus.

2 You then, my son, be strong in the grace
that is in Christ Jesus. 2And the things
you have heard me say in the presence of many
witnesses entrust to reliable men who will also
be qualified to teach others. 3Endure hardship
with us like a good soldier of Christ Jesus. 4No
one serving as a soldier gets involved in civil-
ian affairs—he wants to please his commanding officer. 5Similarly, if anyone competes as an
athlete, he does not receive the victor's crown
unless he competes according to the rules.
6The hardworking farmer should be the first to
receive a share of the crops. 7Reflect on what
I am saying, for the Lord will give you insight
into all this.
8Remember Jesus Christ, raised from the
dead, descended from David. This is my gospel,
9for which I am suffering even to the point of
being chained like a criminal. But God's word
is not chained. 10Therefore I endure everything
for the sake of the elect, that
they too may obtain the salvation that is in Christ Jesus, with
eternal glory.
11Here is a trustworthy saying:

If we died with him,
we will also live with him;
12if we endure,
we will also reign with him.
If we disown him,
he will also disown us;
13if we are faithless,
he will remain faithful,
for he cannot disown himself.

2 Timothy 2:11–12

God Will Bring Us to Heaven

If we died with him,
we will also live with him;
if we endure,
we will also reign
with him.

A Workman Approved by God

14Keep reminding them of these things.
Warn them before God against quarreling
about words; it is of no value, and only ruins
those who listen. 15Do your best to present
yourself to God as one approved, a workman
who does not need to be ashamed and who
correctly handles the word of truth. 16Avoid
godless chatter, because those who indulge in
it will become more and more ungodly. 17Their
teaching will spread like gangrene. Among
them are Hymenaeus and Philetus, 18who have
wandered away from the truth. They say that
the resurrection has already taken place, and
they destroy the faith of some. 19Nevertheless,
God's solid foundation stands firm, sealed with
this inscription: "The Lord knows those who
are his,"[a] and, "Everyone who confesses the
name of the Lord must turn away from wickedness."

[a]19 Num. 16:5 (see Septuagint)

From Cowardice to Compassion

2 Timothy 1:7

For God did not give us a spirit of timidity, but a spirit of power, of love and of self-discipline.

reflection

1 In what situations have you suffered from the "Cowardly Lion" syndrome?

2 How does it make you feel to know that God has given you a spirit of love, power and self-discipline?

3 How would your perspective change if you knew you had only a month—or a day—left to tell those you love about Jesus?

RELATED READINGS

Psalm 40:5–10; Acts 4:13–31; Colossians 4:2–6

Read: 2 Timothy 1:7–14

THREE TO ONE—that's God's ratio for success, according to 2 Timothy 1:7. A trio of God-given attributes—power, love and self-discipline—offsets one characteristic that doesn't come from him: timidity. The Greek word translated here as "timidity" also means "fear" or "cowardice." Can you relate? Who hasn't shrunk back, like the Cowardly Lion in *The Wizard of Oz*, when faced with opposition or an opportunity to speak about God to others?

But here's a refreshing perspective when confronting our own cowardice: Rather than looking at people with fear, we can see them as Jesus did. He was willing to go out and seek each one like a shepherd looks for a lost sheep. He saw each person's potential to become a child of God. We should see each person, not as a foe, but as a potential brother or sister. Do you see the difference such a change in perspective could make? It can move us from cowardice to compassion.

Who do you know that needs to hear about Jesus? A family member, a coworker, a next-door neighbor? Have they heard you speak on every subject except eternity? Regardless of what is holding you back, God has already replaced your timidity with power, love and self-discipline.

Power: We can be confident in sharing God's message because he offers us the very same power that raised Jesus from the dead. Paul reminded the Corinthians that he came "in truthful speech and in the power of God" (2 Corinthians 6:7). That same power is alive and real and available to you.

Love: God, who is love, can fill us so that we can invite others into his welcoming embrace. Love that "never fails" (see 1 Corinthians 13:8) gives us the desire to share the very best news with others.

Self-discipline: Self-discipline means that we have a sound mind, good judgment and discretion. These concepts dovetail to make us women who have the wisdom to tell others about Jesus. We will meet people where they are, discern what their needs are, sense where the "door" to their heart is, and walk through it with the gospel message.

Go to page 1467 for your next devotional reading.

[20]In a large house there are articles not only
of gold and silver, but also of wood and clay;
some are for noble purposes and some for igno-
ble. [21]If a man cleanses himself from the latter,
he will be an instrument for noble purposes,
made holy, useful to the Master and prepared
to do any good work.
[22]Flee the evil desires of youth, and pursue
righteousness, faith, love and
peace, along with those who
call on the Lord out of a pure
heart. [23]Don't have anything
to do with foolish and stupid
arguments, because you know
they produce quarrels. [24]And
the Lord's servant must not
quarrel; instead, he must be
kind to everyone, able to teach,
not resentful. [25]Those who
oppose him he must gently
instruct, in the hope that God
will grant them repentance
leading them to a knowledge
of the truth, [26]and that they
will come to their senses and escape from the
trap of the devil, who has taken them captive
to do his will.

Godlessness in the Last Days

3 But mark this: There will be terrible times
in the last days. [2]People will be lovers of
themselves, lovers of money, boastful, proud,
abusive, disobedient to their parents, ungrateful, unholy, [3]without love, unforgiving, slanderous, without self-control, brutal, not lovers of
the good, [4]treacherous, rash, conceited, lovers
of pleasure rather than lovers of God— [5]hav-
ing a form of godliness but denying its power.
Have nothing to do with them.
[6]They are the kind who worm their way
into homes and gain control over weak-willed
women, who are loaded down with sins and
are swayed by all kinds of evil desires, [7]always
learning but never able to acknowledge the
truth. [8]Just as Jannes and Jambres opposed
Moses, so also these men oppose the truth—
men of depraved minds, who, as far as the faith
is concerned, are rejected. [9]But they will not
get very far because, as in the case of those
men, their folly will be clear to everyone.

Paul's Charge to Timothy

[10]You, however, know all about my teaching, my way of life, my purpose, faith, patience,
love, endurance, [11]persecutions, sufferings—
what kinds of things happened to me in Antioch, Iconium and Lystra, the persecutions I
endured. Yet the Lord rescued me from all of
them. [12]In fact, everyone who wants to live a
godly life in Christ Jesus will be
persecuted, [13]while evil men
and impostors will go from
bad to worse, deceiving and
being deceived. [14]But as for
you, continue in what you have
learned and have become convinced of, because you know
those from whom you learned
it, [15]and how from infancy
you have known the holy Scriptures, which are able to make
you wise for salvation through
faith in Christ Jesus. [16]All
Scripture is God-breathed and
is useful for teaching, rebuk-
ing, correcting and training in righteousness,
[17]so that the man of God may be thoroughly
equipped for every good work.

4 In the presence of God and of Christ Jesus,
who will judge the living and the dead,
and in view of his appearing and his kingdom,
I give you this charge: [2]Preach the Word; be
prepared in season and out of season; correct,
rebuke and encourage—with great patience
and careful instruction. [3]For the time will
come when men will not put up with sound
doctrine. Instead, to suit their own desires,
they will gather around them a great number
of teachers to say what their itching ears want
to hear. [4]They will turn their ears away from
the truth and turn aside to myths. [5]But you,
keep your head in all situations, endure hardship, do the work of an evangelist, discharge all
the duties of your ministry.
[6]For I am already being poured out like a
drink offering, and the time has come for my
departure. [7]I have fought the good fight, I have
finished the race, I have kept the faith. [8]Now
there is in store for me the crown of righteousness, which the Lord, the righteous Judge, will
award to me on that day—and not only to me,

2 Timothy 3:16

God Inspired Scripture

All Scripture is God-breathed and is useful for teaching, rebuking, correcting and training in righteousness.

but also to all who have longed for his appearing.

Personal Remarks

9Do your best to come to me quickly, 10for
Demas, because he loved this world, has
deserted me and has gone to Thessalonica.
Crescens has gone to Galatia, and Titus to Dal-
matia. 11Only Luke is with me. Get Mark and
bring him with you, because he is helpful to me
in my ministry. 12I sent Tychicus to Ephesus.
13When you come, bring the cloak that I left
with Carpus at Troas, and my scrolls, especially
the parchments.
14Alexander the metalworker did me a
great deal of harm. The Lord will repay him
for what he has done. 15You too should be on
your guard against him, because he strongly opposed our message.
16At my first defense, no one came to my
support, but everyone deserted me. May it not
be held against them. 17But the Lord stood at
my side and gave me strength, so that through
me the message might be fully proclaimed and
all the Gentiles might hear it. And I was delivered from the lion's mouth. 18The Lord will rescue me from every evil attack and will bring
me safely to his heavenly kingdom. To him be
glory for ever and ever. Amen.

Final Greetings

19Greet Priscilla[a] and Aquila and the household of Onesiphorus. 20Erastus stayed in Corinth, and I left Trophimus sick in Miletus. 21Do
your best to get here before winter. Eubulus
greets you, and so do Pudens, Linus, Claudia
and all the brothers.
22The Lord be with your spirit. Grace be
with you.

[a]19 Greek *Prisca,* a variant of *Priscilla*

Titus

Unfinished business can be extremely messy, and it tends to only grow worse with time if not attended to. The fledgling Christian community on the island of Crete had plenty of unfinished business after Paul's visit. A Cretan poet described his fellow citizens as "always liars, evil brutes, lazy gluttons" (Titus 1:12). But all people, brutes or otherwise, *need God's love,* and so when it was time for Paul to travel on, he left the unfinished business of sharing the gospel and building the church in the capable hands of his missionary companion Titus.

Paul's letter was written both to encourage Titus and to give him guidance in instructing these new believers. This book *contains sound advice* for anyone involved in the work of encouraging others, whether within our own families or within a larger circle of ministry. Paul reminds Titus and us, that we, too, were once like the Cretans, ignorantly wallowing in our sin. It is *only through Christ's mercy* that we have the hope of eternal life. It's a perspective that reminds us that Paul's words apply to us as much they do to those we are discipling.

Author:
The apostle Paul.

Audience:
Titus, a Greek Christian, and followers of Jesus everywhere.

Date:
Probably about A.D. 64.

Setting:
Paul left Titus in charge of the churches on the Mediterranean island of Crete.

Verse to Remember:
Remind the people to be subject to rulers and authorities, to be obedient, to be ready to do whatever is good. (3:1)

1 Paul, a servant of God and an apostle of
Jesus Christ for the faith of God's elect
nd the knowledge of the truth that leads to
odliness— 2a faith and knowledge resting on
e hope of eternal life, which God, who does
ot lie, promised before the beginning of time,
3and at his appointed season he brought his
word to light through the preaching entrusted
to me by the command of God our Savior,

4To Titus, my true son in our common
faith:

Grace and peace from God the Father and
Christ Jesus our Savior.

Titus's Task on Crete

5 The reason I left you in Crete was that
you might straighten out what was left unfinished and appoint[a] elders in every town, as I
directed you. 6 An elder must be blameless, the
husband of but one wife, a man whose children
believe and are not open to the charge of being
wild and disobedient. 7 Since an overseer[b] is
entrusted with God's work, he must be blameless—not overbearing, not quick-tempered,
not given to drunkenness, not violent, not
pursuing dishonest gain. 8 Rather he must be
hospitable, one who loves what is good, who
is self-controlled, upright, holy and disciplined.
9 He must hold firmly to the trustworthy message as it has been taught, so that he can encourage others by sound doctrine and refute those
who oppose it.

10 For there are many rebellious people, mere
talkers and deceivers, especially those of the circumcision group. 11 They must
be silenced, because they are
ruining whole households by
teaching things they ought not
to teach—and that for the sake
of dishonest gain. 12 Even one
of their own prophets has said,
"Cretans are always liars, evil
brutes, lazy gluttons." 13 This
testimony is true. Therefore,
rebuke them sharply, so that
they will be sound in the faith
14 and will pay no attention to
Jewish myths or to the commands of those who reject the
truth. 15 To the pure, all things are pure, but to
those who are corrupted and do not believe,
nothing is pure. In fact, both their minds and
consciences are corrupted. 16 They claim to
know God, but by their actions they deny him.
They are detestable, disobedient and unfit for
doing anything good.

What Must Be Taught to Various Groups

2 You must teach what is in accord with
sound doctrine. 2 Teach the older men to
be temperate, worthy of respect, self-controlled,
and sound in faith, in love and in endurance.
3 Likewise, teach the older women to be reverent in the way they live, not to be slanderers
or addicted to much wine, but to teach what is
good. 4 Then they can train the younger women
to love their husbands and children, 5 to be self-
controlled and pure, to be busy at home, to be
kind, and to be subject to their husbands, so
that no one will malign the word of God.

6 Similarly, encourage the young men to be
self-controlled. 7 In everything set them an example by doing what is good. In your teaching
show integrity, seriousness 8 and soundness
of speech that cannot be condemned, so that
those who oppose you may be ashamed because they have nothing bad to say about us.

9 Teach slaves to be subject to their masters
in everything, to try to please them, not to talk
back to them, 10 and not to steal from them, but
to show that they can be fully trusted, so that
in every way they will make the teaching about
God our Savior attractive.

11 For the grace of God that
brings salvation has appeared
to all men. 12 It teaches us to
say "No" to ungodliness and
worldly passions, and to live
self-controlled, upright and
godly lives in this present age,
13 while we wait for the blessed
hope—the glorious appearing
of our great God and Savior,
Jesus Christ, 14 who gave himself for us to redeem us from
all wickedness and to purify
for himself a people that are
his very own, eager to do what
is good.

> **Titus 2:13**
>
> *God Will Come Again*
>
> While we wait for the blessed hope—the glorious appearing of our great God and Savior, Jesus Christ.

15 These, then, are the things you should
teach. Encourage and rebuke with all authority.
Do not let anyone despise you.

Doing What Is Good

3 Remind the people to be subject to rulers
and authorities, to be obedient, to be ready
to do whatever is good, 2 to slander no one, to
be peaceable and considerate, and to show true
humility toward all men.

3 At one time we too were foolish, disobedient, deceived and enslaved by all kinds of

[a]5 Or *ordain* [b]7 Traditionally *bishop*

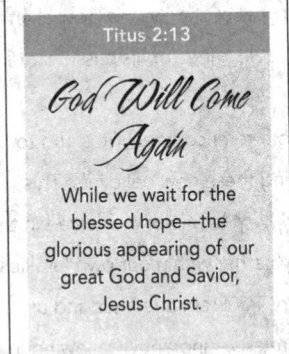

Lights in the Fog

Read: Titus 2:1–15

HAVE YOU EVER BEEN DRIVING down a road at night when the fog rolled in so thick you couldn't see five feet in front of you? It can be pretty scary. However, if you have a car's taillights ahead of you to guide you, suddenly it is not so frightening.

That is the message of Titus 2. Older women can serve as guiding lights for those coming after them. For many women, juggling all our roles—student, employee, boss, wife, mother—can be overwhelming, like walking through life in a fog. But God never intended for us to figure things out on our own—to simply muddle through. Just as he gave Ruth to Naomi and Mary to Elizabeth, God gives us each other to help, encourage and provide one another with companionship, to share ideas and wisdom and humor. When you live in community with others, you can see how other women raise and nurture their children. You can note how persistent someone is in cultivating and preserving her marriage and how it is serving her well. You can watch as women make their way in the marketplace with dignity and integrity.

It may be that the "older" woman isn't chronologically older at all. Perhaps God has gifted a younger woman with particular knowledge and wisdom that you might be in need of. We should be open to different generations reaching out to each other and bridging the years with love and laughter. We have more in common than we have differences.

In our day it's easy to become isolated and withdrawn. We don't often get together as women did in times gone by for quilting bees and church socials and over-the-fence visits. You may long for a woman to mentor you and advise you regarding how to handle your many roles and responsibilities. If so, ask God to send you someone who is wise and supportive. And keep your eyes open for such a woman so you can befriend her. She may need you as much as you need her. Perhaps God is nudging you to become a mentor to a younger woman. Pray that God will lead you to her and that you will have the courage to be a light in the fog.

Wednesday

Titus 2:3–5

Teach the older women to be reverent in the way they live, not to be slanderers or addicted to much wine, but to teach what is good. Then they can train the younger women to love their husbands and children, to be self-controlled and pure, to be busy at home, to be kind, and to be subject to their husbands, so that no one will malign the word of God.

reflection

1 What are the characteristics of your ideal mentor? Do you know someone who fits that description?

2 What are some ways that you can reach out to an older, wiser woman and invite her to be a part of your life?

3 What life experiences do you have to offer another woman? Ask God to show you someone open to being mentored.

RELATED READINGS

Proverbs 31:10–31;
Ephesians 5:21;
1 Peter 3:1–6

Go to page 1475 for your next devotional reading.

passions and pleasures. We lived in malice
and envy, being hated and hating one another.
4 But when the kindness and love of God our
Savior appeared, 5 he saved us, not because of
righteous things we had done, but because
of his mercy. He saved us
through the washing of rebirth
and renewal by the Holy Spirit,
6 whom he poured out on
us generously through Jesus
Christ our Savior, 7 so that,
having been justified by his
grace, we might become heirs
having the hope of eternal life.
8 This is a trustworthy saying.
And I want you to stress these
things, so that those who have
trusted in God may be careful
to devote themselves to doing
what is good. These things are
excellent and profitable for everyone.
9 But avoid foolish controversies and genealogies and arguments and
quarrels about the law, because these are unprofitable and useless. 10 Warn a divisive person once, and then warn him a second time.
After that, have nothing to do with him. 11 You
may be sure that such a man is warped and sinful; he is self-condemned.

Final Remarks

12 As soon as I send Artemas
or Tychicus to you, do your best
to come to me at Nicopolis, because I have decided to winter
there. 13 Do everything you
can to help Zenas the lawyer
and Apollos on their way and
see that they have everything
they need. 14 Our people must
learn to devote themselves to
doing what is good, in order
that they may provide for daily
necessities and not live unproductive lives.
15 Everyone with me sends
you greetings. Greet those who
love us in the faith.
Grace be with you all.

Titus 3:5

God Saves Us Through Mercy

He saved us, not because of righteous things we had done, but because of his mercy. He saved us through the washing of rebirth and renewal by the Holy Spirit.

Philemon

This little letter packs a big wallop. Paul's personal note to Philemon is *a fine example of how to deal gently* with a potentially tricky subject. One of Paul's new converts, Onesimus, was a slave who had run away from his master, Philemon, perhaps even stealing from him. Now Onesimus is a Christian, and Paul sends him back with this letter, urging that Philemon welcome his runaway slave as a Christian brother. To be sure that nothing would be held against the new convert, Paul promises that *he himself will pay any debt* that Onesimus may owe.

Between the lines of this letter is an appeal for trust and forgiveness, in Christ's name. When Paul instructs Philemon to charge a debt to him, Philemon knows he can trust Paul to pay it. And Paul is careful to tell Philemon that *Onesimus is a changed man,* deserving of forgiveness and acceptance.

Author:
The apostle Paul.

Audience:
Philemon, who was likely a member of the Colossian church, and all followers of Jesus.

Date:
About A.D. 60.

Setting:
Paul wrote to his friend Philemon, asking him to forgive a runaway slave, Onesimus.

Verse to Remember:
I appeal to you for my son Onesimus, who became my son while I was in chains. (10)

1 Paul, a prisoner of Christ Jesus, and Timothy our brother,

To Philemon our dear friend and fellow
worker, 2 to Apphia our sister, to Archippus our
fellow soldier and to the church that meets in
your home:

3 Grace to you and peace from God our Father and the Lord Jesus Christ.

Thanksgiving and Prayer

4 I always thank my God as I remember you
in my prayers, 5 because I hear about your faith
in the Lord Jesus and your love for all the saints.

6 I pray that you may be active in sharing your faith, so that you will have a full understanding of every good thing we have in Christ. 7 Your love has given me great joy and encouragement, because you, brother, have refreshed the hearts of the saints.

Paul's Plea for Onesimus

8 Therefore, although in Christ I could be bold and order you to do what you ought to do, 9 yet I appeal to you on the basis of love. I then, as Paul—an old man and now also a prisoner of Christ Jesus— 10 I appeal to you for my son Onesimus,[a] who became my son while I was in chains. 11 Formerly he was useless to you, but now he has become useful both to you and to me.

12 I am sending him—who is my very heart—back to you. 13 I would have liked to keep him with me so that he could take your place in helping me while I am in chains for the gospel. 14 But I did not want to do anything without your consent, so that any favor you do will be spontaneous and not forced. 15 Perhaps the reason he was separated from you for a little while was that you might have him back for good— 16 no longer as a slave, but better than a slave, as a dear brother. He is very dear to me but even dearer to you, both as a man and as a brother in the Lord.

17 So if you consider me a partner, welcome him as you would welcome me. 18 If he has done you any wrong or owes you anything, charge it to me. 19 I, Paul, am writing this with my own hand. I will pay it back—not to mention that you owe me your very self. 20 I do wish, brother, that I may have some benefit from you in the Lord; refresh my heart in Christ. 21 Confident of your obedience, I write to you, knowing that you will do even more than I ask.

22 And one thing more: Prepare a guest room for me, because I hope to be restored to you in answer to your prayers.

23 Epaphras, my fellow prisoner in Christ Jesus, sends you greetings. 24 And so do Mark, Aristarchus, Demas and Luke, my fellow workers.

25 The grace of the Lord Jesus Christ be with your spirit.

Philemon 15–16

God Can Unify All People

You might have him back for good—no longer as a slave, but better than a slave, as a dear brother. He is very dear to me but even dearer to you, both as a man and as a brother in the Lord.

[a] 10 *Onesimus* means *useful.*

Hebrews

Most of the letters in the New Testament address the basics of the faith and Christian living. The book of *Hebrews addresses deeper theological issues.* It explains many Old Testament symbols of worship—the high priest, the sacrifices, the covenant—in the light of the new covenant brought by Jesus. Jesus is greater than the angels, greater than Moses, greater than any high priest, greater than the old covenant. *Jesus is the perfect and final blood sacrifice* for our sins.

Because of who Christ is and what he did on the cross, we can have full assurance and confidence to enter the presence of God. In the Old Testament Jewish tradition, only the high priest could enter behind the curtain into the holy presence of God once a year. The writer of Hebrews *flings wide the torn veil* that separated sinful humanity from God. He invites all of us to accept Christ as Savior and enter into a relationship with God with confidence and joy.

Author:
Unknown.

Audience:
Hebrew Christians and all followers of Jesus.

Date:
Sometime before the destruction of the temple in Jerusalem in A.D. 70.

Setting:
Jewish Christians were being persecuted, probably by both Jews and Romans, and were growing weary.

Verse to Remember:
Let us hold unswervingly to the hope we profess, for he who promised is faithful. (10:23)

The Son Superior to Angels

1 In the past God spoke to our forefathers
through the prophets at many times and
in various ways, 2but in these last days he has
spoken to us by his Son, whom he appointed
heir of all things, and through whom he made
the universe. 3The Son is the radiance of God's
glory and the exact representation of his being,
sustaining all things by his powerful word. After he had provided purification for sins, he
sat down at the right hand of the Majesty in
heaven. 4So he became as much superior to the
angels as the name he has inherited is superior
to theirs.

5 For to which of the angels did God ever
say,

"You are my Son;
today I have become your Father[a]"[b]?

Or again,

"I will be his Father,
and he will be my Son"[c]?

6 And again, when God brings his firstborn
into the world, he says,

"Let all God's angels worship him."[d]

7 In speaking of the angels he says,

"He makes his angels winds,
his servants flames of fire."[e]

8 But about the Son he says,

"Your throne, O God, will last for ever and ever,
and righteousness will be the scepter of your kingdom.
9 You have loved righteousness and hated wickedness;
therefore God, your God, has set you above your companions
by anointing you with the oil of joy."[f]

10 He also says,

"In the beginning, O Lord, you laid the foundations of the earth,
and the heavens are the work of your hands.
11 They will perish, but you remain;
they will all wear out like a garment.
12 You will roll them up like a robe;
like a garment they will be changed.
But you remain the same,
and your years will never end."[g]

13 To which of the angels did God ever say,

"Sit at my right hand
until I make your enemies
a footstool for your feet"[h]?

14 Are not all angels ministering spirits sent to
serve those who will inherit salvation?

Warning to Pay Attention

2 We must pay more careful attention, therefore, to what we have heard, so that we do
not drift away. 2 For if the message spoken by
angels was binding, and every violation and disobedience received its just punishment, 3 how
shall we escape if we ignore such a great salvation? This salvation, which was first announced
by the Lord, was confirmed to us by those who
heard him. 4 God also testified to it by signs,
wonders and various miracles, and gifts of the
Holy Spirit distributed according to his will.

Jesus Made Like His Brothers

5 It is not to angels that he has subjected the
world to come, about which we are speaking.
6 But there is a place where someone has testified:

"What is man that you are mindful of him,
the son of man that you care for him?
7 You made him a little[i] lower than the angels;
you crowned him with glory and honor
8 and put everything under his feet."[j]

In putting everything under him, God left
nothing that is not subject to him. Yet at present
we do not see everything subject to him. 9 But
we see Jesus, who was made a little lower than
the angels, now crowned with glory and honor
because he suffered death, so that by the grace
of God he might taste death for everyone.
10 In bringing many sons to glory, it was fitting that God, for whom and through whom everything exists, should make the author of their
salvation perfect through suffering. 11 Both the
one who makes men holy and those who are
made holy are of the same family. So Jesus is
not ashamed to call them brothers. 12 He says,

"I will declare your name to my brothers;
in the presence of the congregation I will sing your praises."[k]

13 And again,

"I will put my trust in him."[l]

And again he says,

[a] 5 Or *have begotten you* [b] 5 Psalm 2:7 [c] 5 2 Samuel 7:14; 1 Chron. 17:13 [d] 6 Deut. 32:43 (see Dead Sea Scrolls and Septuagint) [e] 7 Psalm 104:4 [f] 9 Psalm 45:6,7 [g] 12 Psalm 102:25–27 [h] 13 Psalm 110:1 [i] 7 Or *him for a little while*; also in verse 9 [j] 8 Psalm 8:4–6 [k] 12 Psalm 22:22 [l] 13 Isaiah 8:17

"Here am I, and the children God has
given me."[a]

14Since the children have flesh and blood,
he too shared in their humanity so that by his
death he might destroy him who holds the
power of death—that is, the devil— 15and free
those who all their lives were held in slavery by
their fear of death. 16For surely it is not angels
he helps, but Abraham's descendants. 17For
this reason he had to be made like his brothers
in every way, in order that he might become a
merciful and faithful high priest in service to
God, and that he might make atonement for[b]
the sins of the people. 18Because he himself suffered when he was tempted, he is able to help
those who are being tempted.

Jesus Greater Than Moses

3 Therefore, holy brothers, who share in
the heavenly calling, fix your thoughts
on Jesus, the apostle and high priest whom
we confess. 2He was faithful to the one who
appointed him, just as Moses was faithful in all
God's house. 3Jesus has been found worthy of
greater honor than Moses, just as the builder of
a house has greater honor than the house itself.
4For every house is built by someone, but God
is the builder of everything. 5Moses was faithful as a servant in all God's house, testifying to
what would be said in the future. 6But Christ is
faithful as a son over God's house. And we are
his house, if we hold on to our courage and the
hope of which we boast.

Warning Against Unbelief

7So, as the Holy Spirit says:

"Today, if you hear his voice,
8 do not harden your hearts
as you did in the rebellion,
during the time of testing in the
desert,
9where your fathers tested and tried me
and for forty years saw what I did.
10That is why I was angry with that
generation,
and I said, 'Their hearts are always going
astray,
and they have not known my ways.'
11So I declared on oath in my anger,
'They shall never enter my rest.'"[c]

12See to it, brothers, that none of you has a
sinful, unbelieving heart that turns away from
the living God. 13But encourage one another
daily, as long as it is called Today, so that none
of you may be hardened by sin's deceitfulness.
14We have come to share in Christ if we hold
firmly till the end the confidence we had at
first. 15As has just been said:

"Today, if you hear his voice,
do not harden your hearts
as you did in the rebellion."[d]

16Who were they who heard and rebelled?
Were they not all those Moses led out of Egypt?
17And with whom was he angry for forty
years? Was it not with those who sinned, whose
bodies fell in the desert? 18And to whom did
God swear that they would never enter his
rest if not to those who disobeyed[e]? 19So we
see that they were not able to enter, because of
their unbelief.

A Sabbath-Rest for the People of God

4 Therefore, since the promise of entering
his rest still stands, let us be careful that
none of you be found to have fallen short of it.
2For we also have had the gospel preached to
us, just as they did; but the message they heard
was of no value to them, because those who
heard did not combine it with faith.[f] 3Now we
who have believed enter that rest, just as God
has said,

"So I declared on oath in my anger,
'They shall never enter my rest.'"[g]

And yet his work has been finished since the
creation of the world. 4For somewhere he has
spoken about the seventh day in these words:
"And on the seventh day God rested from all
his work."[h] 5And again in the passage above he
says, "They shall never enter my rest."
6It still remains that some will enter that
rest, and those who formerly had the gospel
preached to them did not go in, because of
their disobedience. 7Therefore God again set a
certain day, calling it Today, when a long time

[a]13 Isaiah 8:18 [b]17 Or *and that he might turn aside God's wrath, taking away* [c]11 Psalm 95:7–11 [d]15 Psalm 95:7,8
[e]18 Or *disbelieved* [f]2 Many manuscripts *because they did not share in the faith of those who obeyed* [g]3 Psalm 95:11; also in verse 5
[h]4 Gen. 2:2

later he spoke through David, as was said before:

> "Today, if you hear his voice,
> do not harden your hearts."[a]

8For if Joshua had given them rest, God would
not have spoken later about another day. 9There
remains, then, a Sabbath-rest for the people of
God; 10for anyone who enters God's rest also
rests from his own work, just as God did from
his. 11Let us, therefore, make every effort to enter that rest, so that no one will fall by following
their example of disobedience.

12For the word of God is living and active.
Sharper than any double-edged sword, it penetrates even to dividing soul and spirit, joints
and marrow; it judges the thoughts and attitudes of the heart. 13Nothing in all creation is
hidden from God's sight. Everything is uncovered and laid bare before the eyes of him to
whom we must give account.

Jesus the Great High Priest

14Therefore, since we have a
great high priest who has gone
through the heavens,[b] Jesus the
Son of God, let us hold firmly
to the faith we profess. 15For we
do not have a high priest who
is unable to sympathize with
our weaknesses, but we have
one who has been tempted in
every way, just as we are—yet
was without sin. 16Let us then
approach the throne of grace
with confidence, so that we
may receive mercy and find
grace to help us in our time of need.

> **Hebrews 4:16**
>
> *God Invites Us*
>
> Let us then approach the throne of grace with confidence, so that we may receive mercy and find grace to help us in our time of need.

5 Every high priest is selected from among
men and is appointed to represent them
in matters related to God, to offer gifts and
sacrifices for sins. 2He is able to deal gently
with those who are ignorant and are going
astray, since he himself is subject to weakness.
3This is why he has to offer sacrifices for his
own sins, as well as for the sins of the people.

4No one takes this honor upon himself;
he must be called by God, just as Aaron was.
5So Christ also did not take upon himself the
glory of becoming a high priest. But God said
to him,

> "You are my Son;
> today I have become your Father.[c]"[d]

6And he says in another place,

> "You are a priest forever,
> in the order of Melchizedek."[e]

7During the days of Jesus' life on earth, he
offered up prayers and petitions with loud cries
and tears to the one who could save him from
death, and he was heard because of his reverent submission. 8Although he was a son, he
learned obedience from what he suffered 9and,
once made perfect, he became the source of
eternal salvation for all who obey him 10and
was designated by God to be high priest in the
order of Melchizedek.

Warning Against Falling Away

11We have much to say about this, but it is
hard to explain because you are
slow to learn. 12In fact, though
by this time you ought to be
teachers, you need someone
to teach you the elementary
truths of God's word all over
again. You need milk, not solid
food! 13Anyone who lives on
milk, being still an infant, is
not acquainted with the teaching about righteousness. 14But
solid food is for the mature,
who by constant use have
trained themselves to distinguish good from evil.

6 Therefore let us leave the elementary teachings about Christ and go on to maturity,
not laying again the foundation of repentance
from acts that lead to death,[f] and of faith in
God, 2instruction about baptisms, the laying
on of hands, the resurrection of the dead, and
eternal judgment. 3And God permitting, we
will do so.

4It is impossible for those who have once
been enlightened, who have tasted the heavenly
gift, who have shared in the Holy Spirit, 5who
have tasted the goodness of the word of God

[a] 7 Psalm 95:7,8 [b] 14 Or *gone into heaven* [c] 5 Or *have begotten you* [d] 5 Psalm 2:7 [e] 6 Psalm 110:4 [f] 1 Or *from useless rituals*

The Throne of Grace

Read: Hebrews 4:1–16

DO YOU FIND IT DIFFICULT to approach God when you encounter a tempting situation? How quickly do you come to him when your attitude needs adjustment or when you are about to engage in a habit you know is unhealthy? What about those times you face difficult circumstances—a marital rift, a bad diagnosis, physical or emotional struggles? To whom do you turn? Do you turn to God or to human comforters?

Often our greatest comforters are those who have struggled with what we're facing. Why? Because they've been there. They've felt the pain, cried the buckets of tears, felt the anxiety and stayed up nights. They can sympathize in ways even our best friends cannot. But even their help is sometimes not enough. We need help from the throne of grace, the source of all comfort.

Throughout Jewish history, the high priest held the supreme position in the priestly hierarchy. The people looked to him to make the sin offering on the Day of Atonement. Only he could enter the most sacred place in the temple: the Most Holy Place, where the mercy seat rested. Jesus, as our high priest, offered the ultimate sacrifice of his own body so that no other sin offering will ever be required. When he hung on the cross, the curtain preventing access to the Most Holy Place ripped in two (see Matthew 27:51). Now everyone has access to the mercy seat. Our great high priest has opened the way for everyone to confidently enter the throne room of God.

No wonder Jesus extends amazing sympathy. He opened the way to forgiveness of sin and access to the Father. And beyond sympathy, Jesus offers empathy because he has suffered in ways no mere human has. Yes, Jesus encountered fear, exhaustion, weakness, abandonment and grief. He was misunderstood, mistreated, insulted, questioned, doubted, betrayed and so much more. He was "tempted in every way, just as we are—yet was without sin" (Hebrews 4:15). Moreover, he suffered all the horror and terrors of punishment for our sin.

Jesus knows. He feels what you feel; he sees deep into your soul. You can approach his throne with confidence, sit at his feet and weep with him. He's waiting for you.

Thursday

Hebrews 4:15–16

For we do not have a high priest who is unable to sympathize with our weaknesses, but we have one who has been tempted in every way, just as we are—yet was without sin. Let us then approach the throne of grace with confidence, so that we may receive mercy and find grace to help us in our time of need.

reflection

1 When you encounter trials or temptations, to whom do you turn?

2 Do you feel confident that you will find an empathetic ear with Jesus?

3 Describe a time when you know, without a doubt, that Jesus answered your prayer for help in a time of need?

RELATED READINGS

Lamentations 3:22–23; Matthew 27:50–54; John 1:14–16; Hebrews 2:10–18

Go to page 1478 for your next devotional reading.

and the powers of the coming age, 6if they
fall away, to be brought back to repentance,
because[a] to their loss they are crucifying the
Son of God all over again and subjecting him
to public disgrace.
7Land that drinks in the rain often falling on
it and that produces a crop useful to those for
whom it is farmed receives the blessing of God.
8But land that produces thorns and thistles is
worthless and is in danger of being cursed. In
the end it will be burned.
9Even though we speak like this, dear
friends, we are confident of better things in
your case—things that accompany salvation.
10God is not unjust; he will not forget your
work and the love you have shown him as you
have helped his people and continue to help
them. 11We want each of you to show this same
diligence to the very end, in order to make your
hope sure. 12We do not want you to become
lazy, but to imitate those who through faith and
patience inherit what has been promised.

The Certainty of God's Promise

13When God made his promise to Abraham,
since there was no one greater for him to swear
by, he swore by himself, 14saying, "I will surely
bless you and give you many descendants."[b]
15And so after waiting patiently, Abraham received what was promised.
16Men swear by someone greater than themselves, and the oath confirms what is said and
puts an end to all argument. 17Because God
wanted to make the unchanging nature of his
purpose very clear to the heirs of what was
promised, he confirmed it with an oath. 18God
did this so that, by two unchangeable things in
which it is impossible for God to lie, we who
have fled to take hold of the hope offered to
us may be greatly encouraged. 19We have this
hope as an anchor for the soul, firm and secure. It enters the inner sanctuary behind the
curtain, 20where Jesus, who went before us, has
entered on our behalf. He has become a high
priest forever, in the order of Melchizedek.

Melchizedek the Priest

7 This Melchizedek was king of Salem and
priest of God Most High. He met Abraham returning from the defeat of the kings
and blessed him, 2and Abraham gave him a
tenth of everything. First, his name means
"king of righteousness"; then also, "king of Salem" means "king of peace." 3Without father or
mother, without genealogy, without beginning
of days or end of life, like the Son of God he
remains a priest forever.
4Just think how great he was: Even the patriarch Abraham gave him a tenth of the plunder! 5Now the law requires the descendants
of Levi who become priests to collect a tenth
from the people—that is, their brothers—even
though their brothers are descended from
Abraham. 6This man, however, did not trace
his descent from Levi, yet he collected a tenth
from Abraham and blessed him who had
the promises. 7And without doubt the lesser
person is blessed by the greater. 8In the one
case, the tenth is collected by men who die;
but in the other case, by him who is declared
to be living. 9One might even say that Levi,
who collects the tenth, paid the tenth through
Abraham, 10because when Melchizedek met
Abraham, Levi was still in the body of his ancestor.

Jesus Like Melchizedek

11If perfection could have been attained
through the Levitical priesthood (for on the
basis of it the law was given to the people),
why was there still need for another priest to
come—one in the order of Melchizedek, not
in the order of Aaron? 12For when there is a
change of the priesthood, there must also be a
change of the law. 13He of whom these things
are said belonged to a different tribe, and no
one from that tribe has ever served at the altar.
14For it is clear that our Lord descended from
Judah, and in regard to that tribe Moses said
nothing about priests. 15And what we have
said is even more clear if another priest like
Melchizedek appears, 16one who has become
a priest not on the basis of a regulation as to
his ancestry but on the basis of the power of an
indestructible life. 17For it is declared:

"You are a priest forever,
in the order of Melchizedek."[c]

18The former regulation is set aside because
it was weak and useless 19(for the law made

[a]6 Or *repentance while* [b]14 Gen. 22:17 [c]17 Psalm 110:4

nothing perfect), and a better hope is introduced, by which we draw near to God.
20 And it was not without an oath! Others became priests without any oath, 21 but he became
a priest with an oath when God said to him:

"The Lord has sworn
and will not change his mind:
'You are a priest forever.'"[a]

22 Because of this oath, Jesus has become the
guarantee of a better covenant.
23 Now there have been
many of those priests, since
death prevented them from
continuing in office; 24 but because Jesus lives forever, he
has a permanent priesthood.
25 Therefore he is able to save
completely[b] those who come
to God through him, because
he always lives to intercede for
them.
26 Such a high priest meets
our need—one who is holy,
blameless, pure, set apart from
sinners, exalted above the heavens. 27 Unlike the other high
priests, he does not need to offer sacrifices day
after day, first for his own sins, and then for
the sins of the people. He sacrificed for their
sins once for all when he offered himself. 28 For
the law appoints as high priests men who are
weak; but the oath, which came after the law,
appointed the Son, who has been made perfect
forever.

Hebrews 7:25

God Saves Completely

Therefore he is able to save completely those who come to God through him, because he always lives to intercede for them.

The High Priest of a New Covenant

8 The point of what we are saying is this: We
do have such a high priest, who sat down
at the right hand of the throne of the Majesty
in heaven, 2 and who serves in the sanctuary,
the true tabernacle set up by the Lord, not by
man.
3 Every high priest is appointed to offer both
gifts and sacrifices, and so it was necessary for
this one also to have something to offer. 4 If he
were on earth, he would not be a priest, for there
are already men who offer the gifts prescribed
by the law. 5 They serve at a sanctuary that is a
copy and shadow of what is in heaven. This is
why Moses was warned when he was about to
build the tabernacle: "See to it that you make
everything according to the pattern shown you
on the mountain."[c] 6 But the ministry Jesus has
received is as superior to theirs as the covenant
of which he is mediator is superior to the old
one, and it is founded on better promises.
7 For if there had been nothing wrong with
that first covenant, no place would have been
sought for another. 8 But God
found fault with the people
and said[d]:

"The time is coming,
declares the Lord,
when I will make a new
covenant
with the house of Israel
and with the house of
Judah.
9 It will not be like the
covenant
I made with their
forefathers
when I took them by the
hand
to lead them out of Egypt,
because they did not remain faithful to my
covenant,
and I turned away from them,
declares the Lord.
10 This is the covenant I will make with the
house of Israel
after that time, declares the Lord.
I will put my laws in their minds
and write them on their hearts.
I will be their God,
and they will be my people.
11 No longer will a man teach his
neighbor,
or a man his brother, saying, 'Know the
Lord,'
because they will all know me,
from the least of them to the
greatest.
12 For I will forgive their wickedness
and will remember their sins no
more."[e]

[a] 21 Psalm 110:4 [b] 25 Or *forever* [c] 5 Exodus 25:40 [d] 8 Some manuscripts may be translated *fault and said to the people.*
[e] 12 Jer. 31:31–34

Prayer From A–Z

Read: Hebrews 7:11–28

Hebrews 7:25

Therefore he is able to save completely those who come to God through him, because he always lives to intercede for them.

AN ELDERLY GENTLEMAN passed his granddaughter's room one night and listened in as she repeated the alphabet in an oddly reverent way. He peeked in and asked her, "What on earth are you up to?" She explained, "I'm saying my prayers, but I can't think of exactly the right words tonight, so I'm just saying all the letters. Jesus will put them together for me because he knows what I'm thinking."

We've all been there. Our thoughts grow so muddled or our situations have grown so complicated that we don't know how to pray. We know we ought to pray. We feel the need to pray. But when we get on our knees or sit on our beds with our Bibles open, our minds go blank. *Lord, I don't even know where to start.*

What do you do when you don't know what to pray, how to pray or where to begin? Do you start cleaning the house? Do you make a mental to-do list? Do you cry? Do you just give up? The answer is found in Hebrews 7:25: Come to God through Jesus and ask him to intercede for you—he "lives to intercede for [you]."

Maybe you could take a cue from the little girl in the story and start your prayer alphabetically. A—appointments; B—busyness; C—children; D—deadlines; E—empty-nest . . . you get the idea. You can fill in the blanks. More importantly, Jesus can fill in the blanks. He knows what you need before you even utter the words.

Prayer is simply a conversation between you and God. You don't have to bend your knees, although you can. You don't have to bow your head—you can look up to heaven. You can pray with closed eyes, open eyes, hands clasped or lifted in praise. You can pray as you drive your car, as you wash your dishes or as you take your daily walk. You can make your life a continual conversation with God. As you commune with God, Jesus will intercede for you. He'll cover all the things you need, from A–Z. It's what he lives to do.

reflection

1 How would you rate your prayer life on a scale of one to ten?

2 Do you talk to God as much as you talk to your best friend? Why or why not?

3 How does it make you feel to know that Jesus lives to intercede for *you*? Spend time with him now, asking him to intercede on your behalf. Go through the alphabet of your needs.

RELATED READINGS

Daniel 9:17–23;
Luke 11:1–13;
Romans 8:26–27

"Prayer enlarges the heart until it is capable of containing God's gift of himself."

Mother Teresa

Go to page 1483 for your next devotional reading.

[13]By calling this covenant "new," he has made the first one obsolete; and what is obsolete and aging will soon disappear.

Worship in the Earthly Tabernacle

9 Now the first covenant had regulations for worship and also an earthly sanctuary. [2]A tabernacle was set up. In its first room were the lampstand, the table and the consecrated bread; this was called the Holy Place. [3]Behind the second curtain was a room called the Most Holy Place, [4]which had the golden altar of incense and the gold-covered ark of the covenant. This ark contained the gold jar of manna, Aaron's staff that had budded, and the stone tablets of the covenant. [5]Above the ark were the cherubim of the Glory, overshadowing the atonement cover.[a] But we cannot discuss these things in detail now.

[6]When everything had been arranged like this, the priests entered regularly into the outer room to carry on their ministry. [7]But only the high priest entered the inner room, and that only once a year, and never without blood, which he offered for himself and for the sins the people had committed in ignorance. [8]The Holy Spirit was showing by this that the way into the Most Holy Place had not yet been disclosed as long as the first tabernacle was still standing. [9]This is an illustration for the present time, indicating that the gifts and sacrifices being offered were not able to clear the conscience of the worshiper. [10]They are only a matter of food and drink and various ceremonial washings—external regulations applying until the time of the new order.

The Blood of Christ

[11]When Christ came as high priest of the good things that are already here,[b] he went through the greater and more perfect tabernacle that is not man-made, that is to say, not a part of this creation. [12]He did not enter by means of the blood of goats and calves; but he entered the Most Holy Place once for all by his own blood, having obtained eternal redemption. [13]The blood of goats and bulls and the ashes of a heifer sprinkled on those who are ceremonially unclean sanctify them so that they are outwardly clean. [14]How much more, then, will the blood of Christ, who through the eternal Spirit offered himself unblemished to God, cleanse our consciences from acts that lead to death,[c] so that we may serve the living God!

[15]For this reason Christ is the mediator of a new covenant, that those who are called may receive the promised eternal inheritance—now that he has died as a ransom to set them free from the sins committed under the first covenant.

[16]In the case of a will,[d] it is necessary to prove the death of the one who made it, [17]because a will is in force only when somebody has died; it never takes effect while the one who made it is living. [18]This is why even the first covenant was not put into effect without blood. [19]When Moses had proclaimed every commandment of the law to all the people, he took the blood of calves, together with water, scarlet wool and branches of hyssop, and sprinkled the scroll and all the people. [20]He said, "This is the blood of the covenant, which God has commanded you to keep."[e] [21]In the same way, he sprinkled with the blood both the tabernacle and everything used in its ceremonies. [22]In fact, the law requires that nearly everything be cleansed with blood, and without the shedding of blood there is no forgiveness.

[23]It was necessary, then, for the copies of the heavenly things to be purified with these sacrifices, but the heavenly things themselves with better sacrifices than these. [24]For Christ did not enter a man-made sanctuary that was only a copy of the true one; he entered heaven itself, now to appear for us in God's presence. [25]Nor did he enter heaven to offer himself again and again, the way the high priest enters the Most Holy Place every year with blood that is not his own. [26]Then Christ would have had to suffer many times since the creation of the world. But now he has appeared once for all at the end of the ages to do away with sin by the sacrifice of himself. [27]Just as man is destined to die once, and after that to face judgment, [28]so Christ was sacrificed once to take away the sins of many people; and he will appear a second

[a]5 Traditionally *the mercy seat* [b]11 Some early manuscripts *are to come* [c]14 Or *from useless rituals* [d]16 Same Greek word as *covenant*; also in verse 17 [e]20 Exodus 24:8

time, not to bear sin, but to bring salvation to
those who are waiting for him.

Christ's Sacrifice Once for All

10 The law is only a shadow of the good
things that are coming—not the realities themselves. For this reason it can never, by
the same sacrifices repeated endlessly year after
year, make perfect those who draw near to worship. 2 If it could, would they not have stopped
being offered? For the worshipers would have
been cleansed once for all, and would no longer have felt guilty for their sins. 3 But those
sacrifices are an annual reminder of sins, 4 because it is impossible for the blood of bulls and
goats to take away sins.

5 Therefore, when Christ came into the
world, he said:

> "Sacrifice and offering you did not desire,
> but a body you prepared for me;
> 6 with burnt offerings and sin offerings
> you were not pleased.
> 7 Then I said, 'Here I am—it
> is written about me
> in the scroll—
> I have come to do your
> will, O God.' "[a]

8 First he said, "Sacrifices and
offerings, burnt offerings and
sin offerings you did not desire, nor were you pleased
with them" (although the law
required them to be made).
9 Then he said, "Here I am, I
have come to do your will."
He sets aside the first to establish the second.
10 And by that will, we have been made holy
through the sacrifice of the body of Jesus Christ
once for all.

11 Day after day every priest stands and performs his religious duties; again and again he
offers the same sacrifices, which can never take
away sins. 12 But when this priest had offered
for all time one sacrifice for sins, he sat down
at the right hand of God. 13 Since that time he
waits for his enemies to be made his footstool,
14 because by one sacrifice he has made perfect
forever those who are being made holy.

15 The Holy Spirit also testifies to us about
this. First he says:

> 16 "This is the covenant I will make with
> them
> after that time, says the Lord.
> I will put my laws in their hearts,
> and I will write them on their minds."[b]

17 Then he adds:

> "Their sins and lawless acts
> I will remember no more."[c]

18 And where these have been forgiven, there is
no longer any sacrifice for sin.

A Call to Persevere

19 Therefore, brothers, since we have confidence to enter the Most Holy Place by the
blood of Jesus, 20 by a new and living way
opened for us through the curtain, that is, his
body, 21 and since we have a great priest over
the house of God, 22 let us draw near to God
with a sincere heart in full assurance of faith,
having our hearts sprinkled to
cleanse us from a guilty conscience and having our bodies
washed with pure water. 23 Let
us hold unswervingly to the
hope we profess, for he who
promised is faithful. 24 And
let us consider how we may
spur one another on toward
love and good deeds. 25 Let us
not give up meeting together,
as some are in the habit of
doing, but let us encourage
one another—and all the more as you see the
Day approaching.

26 If we deliberately keep on sinning after
we have received the knowledge of the truth,
no sacrifice for sins is left, 27 but only a fearful
expectation of judgment and of raging fire
that will consume the enemies of God. 28 Anyone who rejected the law of Moses died without mercy on the testimony of two or three
witnesses. 29 How much more severely do you
think a man deserves to be punished who has
trampled the Son of God under foot, who has
treated as an unholy thing the blood of the cov-

Hebrews 10:23

God Is Faithful

Let us hold unswervingly
to the hope we profess,
for he who promised
is faithful.

[a] 7 Psalm 40:6–8 (see Septuagint) [b] 16 Jer. 31:33 [c] 17 Jer. 31:34

enant that sanctified him, and who has insulted
the Spirit of grace? 30For we know him who
said, "It is mine to avenge; I will repay,"[a] and
again, "The Lord will judge his people."[b] 31It
is a dreadful thing to fall into the hands of the
living God.

32Remember those earlier days after you
had received the light, when you stood your
ground in a great contest in the face of suffering. 33Sometimes you were publicly exposed
to insult and persecution; at other times you
stood side by side with those who were so
treated. 34You sympathized with those in
prison and joyfully accepted the confiscation
of your property, because you knew that you
yourselves had better and lasting possessions.

35So do not throw away your confidence;
it will be richly rewarded. 36You need to persevere so that when you have done the will of
God, you will receive what he has promised.
37For in just a very little while,

"He who is coming will come and will not
delay.
38 But my righteous one[c] will live by faith.
And if he shrinks back,
I will not be pleased with him."[d]

39But we are not of those who shrink back and
are destroyed, but of those who believe and
are saved.

By Faith

11 Now faith is being sure of what we
hope for and certain of what we do
not see. 2This is what the ancients were commended for.

3By faith we understand that the universe
was formed at God's command, so that what is
seen was not made out of what was visible.

4By faith Abel offered God a better sacrifice
than Cain did. By faith he was commended
as a righteous man, when God spoke well of
his offerings. And by faith he still speaks, even
though he is dead.

5By faith Enoch was taken from this life, so
that he did not experience death; he could not
be found, because God had taken him away.
For before he was taken, he was commended
as one who pleased God. 6And without faith
it is impossible to please God, because anyone who comes to him must believe that he
exists and that he rewards those who earnestly
seek him.

7By faith Noah, when warned about things
not yet seen, in holy fear built an ark to save his
family. By his faith he condemned the world
and became heir of the righteousness that
comes by faith.

8By faith Abraham, when called to go to a
place he would later receive as his inheritance,
obeyed and went, even though he did not
know where he was going. 9By faith he made
his home in the promised land like a stranger
in a foreign country; he lived in tents, as did
Isaac and Jacob, who were heirs with him of the
same promise. 10For he was looking forward to
the city with foundations, whose architect and
builder is God.

11By faith Abraham, even though he was
past age—and Sarah herself was barren—was
enabled to become a father because he[e] considered him faithful who had made the promise.
12And so from this one man, and he as good
as dead, came descendants as numerous as the
stars in the sky and as countless as the sand on
the seashore.

13All these people were still living by faith
when they died. They did not receive the things
promised; they only saw them and welcomed
them from a distance. And they admitted that
they were aliens and strangers on earth. 14Peo-
ple who say such things show that they are
looking for a country of their own. 15If they
had been thinking of the country they had
left, they would have had opportunity to return. 16Instead, they were longing for a better
country—a heavenly one. Therefore God is not
ashamed to be called their God, for he has prepared a city for them.

17By faith Abraham, when God tested him,
offered Isaac as a sacrifice. He who had received
the promises was about to sacrifice his one and
only son, 18even though God had said to him,
"It is through Isaac that your offspring[f] will
be reckoned."[g] 19Abraham reasoned that God
could raise the dead, and figuratively speaking,
he did receive Isaac back from death.

[a]30 Deut. 32:35 [b]30 Deut. 32:36; Psalm 135:14 [c]38 One early manuscript *But the righteous* [d]38 Hab. 2:3,4 [e]11 Or *By faith even Sarah, who was past age, was enabled to bear children because she* [f]18 Greek *seed* [g]18 Gen. 21:12

20 By faith Isaac blessed Jacob and Esau in regard to their future.

21 By faith Jacob, when he was dying, blessed each of Joseph's sons, and worshiped as he leaned on the top of his staff.

22 By faith Joseph, when his end was near, spoke about the exodus of the Israelites from Egypt and gave instructions about his bones.

23 By faith Moses' parents hid him for three months after he was born, because they saw he was no ordinary child, and they were not afraid of the king's edict.

24 By faith Moses, when he had grown up, refused to be known as the son of Pharaoh's daughter. 25 He chose to be mistreated along with the people of God rather than to enjoy the pleasures of sin for a short time. 26 He regarded disgrace for the sake of Christ as of greater value than the treasures of Egypt, because he was looking ahead to his reward. 27 By faith he left Egypt, not fearing the king's anger; he persevered because he saw him who is invisible. 28 By faith he kept the Passover and the sprinkling of blood, so that the destroyer of the firstborn would not touch the firstborn of Israel.

29 By faith the people passed through the Red Sea[a] as on dry land; but when the Egyptians tried to do so, they were drowned.

30 By faith the walls of Jericho fell, after the people had marched around them for seven days.

31 By faith the prostitute Rahab, because she welcomed the spies, was not killed with those who were disobedient.[b]

32 And what more shall I say? I do not have time to tell about Gideon, Barak, Samson, Jephthah, David, Samuel and the prophets, 33 who through faith conquered kingdoms, administered justice, and gained what was promised; who shut the mouths of lions, 34 quenched the fury of the flames, and escaped the edge of the sword; whose weakness was turned to strength; and who became powerful in battle and routed foreign armies. 35 Women received back their dead, raised to life again. Others were tortured and refused to be released, so that they might gain a better resurrection. 36 Some faced jeers and flogging, while still others were chained and put in prison. 37 They were stoned[c]; they were sawed in two; they were put to death by the sword. They went about in sheepskins and goatskins, destitute, persecuted and mistreated— 38 the world was not worthy of them. They wandered in deserts and mountains, and in caves and holes in the ground.

39 These were all commended for their faith, yet none of them received what had been promised. 40 God had planned something better for us so that only together with us would they be made perfect.

God Disciplines His Sons

12 Therefore, since we are surrounded by such a great cloud of witnesses, let us throw off everything that hinders and the sin that so easily entangles, and let us run with perseverance the race marked out for us. 2 Let us fix our eyes on Jesus, the author and perfecter of our faith, who for the joy set before him endured the cross, scorning its shame, and sat down at the right hand of the throne of God. 3 Consider him who endured such opposition from sinful men, so that you will not grow weary and lose heart.

4 In your struggle against sin, you have not yet resisted to the point of shedding your blood. 5 And you have forgotten that word of encouragement that addresses you as sons:

"My son, do not make light of the Lord's
discipline,
and do not lose heart when he rebukes
you,
6 because the Lord disciplines those he loves,
and he punishes everyone he accepts as
a son."[d]

Hebrews 12:2

God Perfects Our Faith

Let us fix our eyes on Jesus, the author and perfecter of our faith, who for the joy set before him endured the cross, scorning its shame, and sat down at the right hand of the throne of God.

[a]29 That is, Sea of Reeds [b]31 Or *unbelieving* [c]37 Some early manuscripts *stoned; they were put to the test;* [d]6 Prov. 3:11,12

Conviction

BERNICE

CASUALLY RAISING HER BEJEWELED HAND to her cheek, she felt her face flush with color.

Why are you blushing? Bernice silently chastised herself. She assuaged her worries by assuring herself that it was, indeed, rather warm in here. She *couldn't* let this man get to her, what with his wild tale of desert visions, voices and people being raised from the dead. He was crazy. A lunatic.

So, why, at the same time, did his words ring with authenticity? Why did they seem to pierce her very soul and sear her conscience as if with a white-hot rod of steel?

Bernice was used to these occasional waves of guilt that coursed through her from time to time. After stifling whatever conviction she may have felt over the years, the guilt became less and less frequent, and now it was almost entirely absent. She was a married woman and carrying on as someone's mistress, but it didn't bother her, per se. It didn't even really concern her that the man beside her listening to Paul's testimony, Herod Agrippa II, was her lover. Or that he was also her brother. In her mind, being her brother's mistress was nobody's business but their own.

At least she didn't *think* it bothered her. Until now. Listening to Paul explain his faith in God, she felt faint. She was light-headed and almost nauseated.

Outwardly, she sneered at his absurdity, but inside she was a royal mess. At the most dramatic points of Paul's testimony, she felt inexplicably drawn and completely repelled at the same time. Of course, she would never breathe a word of this to anyone. She had an image to uphold. So, when it came time to pronounce an opinion on the matter, she sided with her brother's nonchalance. But she never forgot that hour in Caesarea.

—Prayer—

Almighty God, give me courage to share with others your message of love. Like Paul, help me be a gracious witness for you.

Paul replied, "Short time or long—I pray God that not only you but all who are listening to me today may become what I am, except for these chains."

Acts 26:29

ASSIGNED READING:

Acts 25:13—26:32

Weekend

Go to page 1485 for your next devotional reading.

7 Endure hardship as discipline; God is treating you as sons. For what son is not disciplined by his father? 8 If you are not disciplined (and everyone undergoes discipline), then you are illegitimate children and not true sons. 9 Moreover, we have all had human fathers who disciplined us and we respected them for it. How much more should we submit to the Father of our spirits and live! 10 Our fathers disciplined us for a little while as they thought best; but God disciplines us for our good, that we may share in his holiness. 11 No discipline seems pleasant at the time, but painful. Later on, however, it produces a harvest of righteousness and peace for those who have been trained by it.

12 Therefore, strengthen your feeble arms and weak knees. 13 "Make level paths for your feet,"[a] so that the lame may not be disabled, but rather healed.

Warning Against Refusing God

14 Make every effort to live in peace with all men and to be holy; without holiness no one will see the Lord. 15 See to it that no one misses the grace of God and that no bitter root grows up to cause trouble and defile many. 16 See that no one is sexually immoral, or is godless like Esau, who for a single meal sold his inheritance rights as the oldest son. 17 Afterward, as you know, when he wanted to inherit this blessing, he was rejected. He could bring about no change of mind, though he sought the blessing with tears.

18 You have not come to a mountain that can be touched and that is burning with fire; to darkness, gloom and storm; 19 to a trumpet blast or to such a voice speaking words that those who heard it begged that no further word be spoken to them, 20 because they could not bear what was commanded: "If even an animal touches the mountain, it must be stoned."[b] 21 The sight was so terrifying that Moses said, "I am trembling with fear."[c]

22 But you have come to Mount Zion, to the heavenly Jerusalem, the city of the living God. You have come to thousands upon thousands of angels in joyful assembly, 23 to the church of the firstborn, whose names are written in heaven. You have come to God, the judge of all men, to the spirits of righteous men made perfect, 24 to Jesus the mediator of a new covenant, and to the sprinkled blood that speaks a better word than the blood of Abel.

25 See to it that you do not refuse him who speaks. If they did not escape when they refused him who warned them on earth, how much less will we, if we turn away from him who warns us from heaven? 26 At that time his voice shook the earth, but now he has promised, "Once more I will shake not only the earth but also the heavens."[d] 27 The words "once more" indicate the removing of what can be shaken—that is, created things—so that what cannot be shaken may remain.

28 Therefore, since we are receiving a kingdom that cannot be shaken, let us be thankful, and so worship God acceptably with reverence and awe, 29 for our "God is a consuming fire."[e]

Concluding Exhortations

13 Keep on loving each other as brothers. 2 Do not forget to entertain strangers, for by so doing some people have entertained angels without knowing it. 3 Remember those in prison as if you were their fellow prisoners, and those who are mistreated as if you yourselves were suffering.

4 Marriage should be honored by all, and the marriage bed kept pure, for God will judge the adulterer and all the sexually immoral. 5 Keep your lives free from the love of money and be content with what you have, because God has said,

"Never will I leave you;
never will I forsake you."[f]

6 So we say with confidence,

"The Lord is my helper; I will not be afraid.
What can man do to me?"[g]

7 Remember your leaders, who spoke the word of God to you. Consider the outcome of their way of life and imitate their faith. 8 Jesus Christ is the same yesterday and today and forever.

9 Do not be carried away by all kinds of strange teachings. It is good for our hearts to be strengthened by grace, not by ceremonial foods,

[a] 13 Prov. 4:26 [b] 20 Exodus 19:12,13 [c] 21 Deut. 9:19 [d] 26 Haggai 2:6 [e] 29 Deut. 4:24 [f] 5 Deut. 31:6 [g] 6 Psalm 118:6,7

The Meaning of Life

Read: Hebrews 13:1–21

AFTER DECADES OF RESEARCH, George Gallup Jr. listed the top spiritual needs of people today:

1. To believe that life is meaningful and has a purpose
2. To have a sense of community and deeper relationships
3. To be appreciated and respected
4. To be listened to
5. To feel they are growing in faith
6. To get practical help in developing a mature faith

Notice how many of the needs relate to relationships. That's because we are created to be relational people. God created us first to have a relationship with him and second to have relationships with one another. It is through our interactions with others that we find meaning in life. The Bible teaches that others will know whether our Christianity is genuine by looking at whether our love for each other is real (see John 13:35).

It's easy to love people who love us, but we are commanded to extend kindness and acts of service even to strangers. Doing so is a sign that our faith is dynamic and alive. God asks us to grow and mature by forgiving those who have wronged us. And Scripture instructs us to put others' needs ahead of our own, even if it's not convenient. That's how we show others we appreciate and respect them.

In Hebrews 13 the author instructs us concerning hospitality to strangers, marital relations and submission to authority—in essence, how to build relationships. But the whole catalog of interactions with others is rooted in, and gets its life source from, our relationship with Jesus. Our sacrifice of praise to God and our sacrifice of service to others are fundamentally linked to him. Our good works to others grow out of Christ's work *in* us, and that pleases him. None of our sacrifices for others are even comparable to the great sacrifice Jesus made in order to have a relationship with us. But the amazing thing is that when we offer the sacrifices of time, energy and good deeds to others, we not only grow closer to them, but we also grow closer to Jesus. In Christ, we find true meaning in our lives.

Monday

Go to page 1490 for your next devotional reading.

Hebrews 13:15–16

Through Jesus, therefore, let us continually offer to God a sacrifice of praise—the fruit of lips that confess his name. And do not forget to do good and to share with others, for with such sacrifices God is pleased.

reflection

1 Describe three incidents from Jesus' life on earth that depict how personal relationships were important to him.

2 In what ways have you put possessions, schedules or events ahead of people in your list of priorities?

3 Think of some practical ways you can show your family and friends this week that they are a priority to you.

RELATED READINGS

Job 29:11–17;
John 11:1–36;
3 John 1–4

which are of no value to those who eat them.
10 We have an altar from which those who minister at the tabernacle have no right to eat.
11 The high priest carries the blood of animals into the Most Holy Place as a sin offering,
but the bodies are burned outside the camp.
12 And so Jesus also suffered outside the city
gate to make the people holy through his own
blood. 13 Let us, then, go to him outside the
camp, bearing the disgrace he bore. 14 For here
we do not have an enduring city, but we are
looking for the city that is to come.
15 Through Jesus, therefore, let us continually
offer to God a sacrifice of praise—the fruit of
lips that confess his name. 16 And do not forget
to do good and to share with others, for with
such sacrifices God is pleased.
17 Obey your leaders and submit to their
authority. They keep watch over you as men
who must give an account. Obey them so that
their work will be a joy, not a burden, for that
would be of no advantage to you.
18 Pray for us. We are sure that we have a
clear conscience and desire to live honorably
in every way. 19 I particularly urge you to pray
so that I may be restored to you soon.
20 May the God of peace, who through the
blood of the eternal covenant brought back
from the dead our Lord Jesus, that great Shepherd of the sheep, 21 equip you with everything good for doing his will, and may he
work in us what is pleasing to him, through
Jesus Christ, to whom be glory for ever and
ever. Amen.

22 Brothers, I urge you to bear with my word
of exhortation, for I have written you only a
short letter.
23 I want you to know that our brother Timothy has been released. If he arrives soon, I will
come with him to see you.
24 Greet all your leaders and all God's people.
Those from Italy send you their greetings.
25 Grace be with you all.

James

Hypocrisy is one of the biggest blights on the Christian faith. We say one thing, but we act in an entirely different manner. It was a problem in James's day, and it's a problem for us today. James tackles this issue in his letter, challenging his readers to examine both their beliefs and their actions. He goes beyond telling them what a Christian should do, however. Instead he shows them, illustrating with verbal pictures and vivid details, what *a life transformed by Jesus* looks like. It was a transformation he knew firsthand. As Jesus' half brother, he spent many years as a skeptic. It was only after Jesus' death and resurrection that *he became a true believer.*

The book of James is often categorized as wisdom literature—the "Proverbs" of the New Testament. His advice is extremely practical. It's the kind of teaching we can read and then clearly see how it should play out in our own lives. But it is also difficult. Knowing what to do and doing it are two different things, and James clearly understands that. He comes alongside us as a brother, challenging and encouraging us to live what we believe, putting our faith into action so that when the world looks at us *they'll know by what they see,* not just what we say, that we belong to Jesus.

Author:
James, the brother of Jesus.

Audience:
Early Jewish Christians scattered because of persecution and all followers of Jesus.

Date:
About A.D. 49.

Setting:
James encouraged the former members of the Jerusalem church, now scattered to various places because of persecution.

Verse to Remember:
As the body without the spirit is dead, so faith without deeds is dead. (2:26)

1 James, a servant of God and of the Lord
Jesus Christ,

To the twelve tribes scattered among the nations:

Greetings.

Trials and Temptations

2 Consider it pure joy, my brothers, whenever
you face trials of many kinds, 3 because you
know that the testing of your faith develops
perseverance. 4 Perseverance must finish its
work so that you may be mature and complete,
not lacking anything. 5 If any of
you lacks wisdom, he should
ask God, who gives generously
to all without finding fault, and
it will be given to him. 6 But
when he asks, he must believe
and not doubt, because he who
doubts is like a wave of the sea,
blown and tossed by the wind.
7 That man should not think he
will receive anything from the
Lord; 8 he is a double-minded
man, unstable in all he does.
9 The brother in humble
circumstances ought to take
pride in his high position. 10 But
the one who is rich should take
pride in his low position, because he will pass
away like a wild flower. 11 For the sun rises
with scorching heat and withers the plant; its
blossom falls and its beauty is destroyed. In the
same way, the rich man will fade away even
while he goes about his business.
12 Blessed is the man who perseveres under
trial, because when he has stood the test, he will
receive the crown of life that God has promised
to those who love him.
13 When tempted, no one should say, "God
is tempting me." For God cannot be tempted
by evil, nor does he tempt anyone; 14 but each
one is tempted when, by his own evil desire, he
is dragged away and enticed. 15 Then, after desire has conceived, it gives birth to sin; and sin,
when it is full-grown, gives birth to death.
16 Don't be deceived, my dear brothers. 17 Every good and perfect gift is from above, coming
down from the Father of the heavenly lights,
who does not change like shifting shadows.
18 He chose to give us birth through the word
of truth, that we might be a kind of firstfruits
of all he created.

Listening and Doing

19 My dear brothers, take note of this: Everyone should be quick to listen, slow to speak
and slow to become angry, 20 for man's anger
does not bring about the righteous life that
God desires. 21 Therefore, get rid of all moral
filth and the evil that is so prevalent and humbly accept the word planted in you, which can
save you.
22 Do not merely listen to
the word, and so deceive yourselves. Do what it says. 23 Anyone who listens to the word
but does not do what it says is
like a man who looks at his face
in a mirror 24 and, after looking at himself, goes away and
immediately forgets what he
looks like. 25 But the man who
looks intently into the perfect
law that gives freedom, and
continues to do this, not forgetting what he has heard, but
doing it—he will be blessed in
what he does.
26 If anyone considers him-
self religious and yet does not keep a tight rein
on his tongue, he deceives himself and his religion is worthless. 27 Religion that God our
Father accepts as pure and faultless is this: to
look after orphans and widows in their distress
and to keep oneself from being polluted by
the world.

> **James 1:5**
>
> *God Gives Wisdom*
>
> If any of you lacks wisdom, he should ask God, who gives generously to all without finding fault, and it will be given to him.

Favoritism Forbidden

2 My brothers, as believers in our glorious
Lord Jesus Christ, don't show favoritism.
2 Suppose a man comes into your meeting wearing a gold ring and fine clothes, and a poor
man in shabby clothes also comes in. 3 If you
show special attention to the man wearing fine
clothes and say, "Here's a good seat for you,"
but say to the poor man, "You stand there"
or "Sit on the floor by my feet," 4 have you not
discriminated among yourselves and become
judges with evil thoughts?
5 Listen, my dear brothers: Has not God cho-

sen those who are poor in the eyes of the world
to be rich in faith and to inherit the kingdom
he promised those who love him? 6But you
have insulted the poor. Is it not the rich who
are exploiting you? Are they not the ones who
are dragging you into court? 7Are they not the
ones who are slandering the noble name of him
to whom you belong?

8If you really keep the royal law found in
Scripture, "Love your neighbor as yourself,"[a]
you are doing right. 9But if you show favoritism, you sin and are convicted by the law as
lawbreakers. 10For whoever keeps the whole
law and yet stumbles at just one point is guilty
of breaking all of it. 11For he who said, "Do not
commit adultery,"[b] also said, "Do not murder."[c]
If you do not commit adultery but do commit
murder, you have become a lawbreaker.

12Speak and act as those who are going to
be judged by the law that gives freedom, 13be-
cause judgment without mercy will be shown
to anyone who has not been merciful. Mercy
triumphs over judgment!

Faith and Deeds

14What good is it, my brothers, if a man
claims to have faith but has no deeds? Can such
faith save him? 15Suppose a brother or sister is
without clothes and daily food. 16If one of you
says to him, "Go, I wish you well; keep warm
and well fed," but does nothing about his physical needs, what good is it? 17In the same way,
faith by itself, if it is not accompanied by action,
is dead.

18But someone will say, "You have faith; I
have deeds."

Show me your faith without deeds, and I will
show you my faith by what I do. 19You believe
that there is one God. Good! Even the demons
believe that—and shudder.

20You foolish man, do you want evidence
that faith without deeds is useless[d]? 21Was not
our ancestor Abraham considered righteous
for what he did when he offered his son Isaac
on the altar? 22You see that his faith and his actions were working together, and his faith was
made complete by what he did. 23And the scripture was fulfilled that says, "Abraham believed
God, and it was credited to him as righteousness,"[e] and he was called God's friend. 24You
see that a person is justified by what he does
and not by faith alone.

25In the same way, was not even Rahab the
prostitute considered righteous for what she
did when she gave lodging to the spies and
sent them off in a different direction? 26As the
body without the spirit is dead, so faith without
deeds is dead.

Taming the Tongue

3 Not many of you should presume to be
teachers, my brothers, because you know
that we who teach will be judged more strictly.
2We all stumble in many ways. If anyone is
never at fault in what he says, he is a perfect
man, able to keep his whole body in check.

3When we put bits into the mouths of
horses to make them obey us, we can turn the
whole animal. 4Or take ships as an example.
Although they are so large and are driven by
strong winds, they are steered by a very small
rudder wherever the pilot wants to go. 5Like-
wise the tongue is a small part of the body, but
it makes great boasts. Consider what a great forest is set on fire by a small spark. 6The tongue
also is a fire, a world of evil among the parts of
the body. It corrupts the whole person, sets the
whole course of his life on fire, and is itself set
on fire by hell.

7All kinds of animals, birds, reptiles and
creatures of the sea are being tamed and have
been tamed by man, 8but no man can tame
the tongue. It is a restless evil, full of deadly
poison.

9With the tongue we praise our Lord and Father, and with it we curse men, who have been
made in God's likeness. 10Out of the same
mouth come praise and cursing. My brothers,
this should not be. 11Can both fresh water and
salt[f] water flow from the same spring? 12My
brothers, can a fig tree bear olives, or a grapevine bear figs? Neither can a salt spring produce fresh water.

Two Kinds of Wisdom

13Who is wise and understanding among
you? Let him show it by his good life, by deeds
done in the humility that comes from wisdom.

[a] 8 Lev. 19:18 [b] 11 Exodus 20:14; Deut. 5:18 [c] 11 Exodus 20:13; Deut. 5:17 [d] 20 Some early manuscripts *dead* [e] 23 Gen. 15:6
[f] 11 Greek *bitter* (see also verse 14)

Fire Control

James 3:5

The tongue is a small part of the body, but it makes great boasts. Consider what a great forest is set on fire by a small spark.

reflection

1 Do you know someone whose life has been burned by gossip or harsh words?

2 On a scale of one to ten, how hot are your words?

3 How will you begin to use your tongue for healing rather than harm?

RELATED READINGS

Psalm 52:1–5; Proverbs 11:11–13; 12:17–19; James 1:22–26

"Gossips and talebearers set on fire all the houses they enter."

Unknown

Read: James 3:1–18

IN 1944 THE NATIONAL FOREST SERVICE introduced the cartoon character Smokey Bear as the mascot for fire prevention. Soon afterward, a fire caused by human negligence ravaged 17,000 acres of forest in Capitan, New Mexico. During this fire, a tiny bear cub scampered up a tree. With badly burned paws and hind legs, the cub clung tenaciously to that pine tree until he was found by a firefighter. The cub was quickly dubbed Smokey Bear. School-age children were able to complete the phrase, "Only you . . ." with the concluding words ". . . can prevent forest fires." The phrase grew more popular than any other motto.

In the book of James we learn that our tongues can either be fire igniters or fire extinguishers. James pointed out that believers often engage in gossip, slander and backbiting. While working to build up the body of Christ with their actions, their tongues can insidiously cause fires throughout the church.

Lightning sometimes causes wildfires. But nine out of ten wildfires are caused by human negligence or arson. In the southwestern United States, a freight train threw sparks into ranch land, destroying 40,000 acres, along with an untold number of cattle. Word fires, like gossip, have split churches, ruined lives and can be just as scorching as forest fires. In California, landscape designers use ground cover as fire-retardant buffers around valuable property. Rather than using your words as combustible fodder, why not choose words that are fire resistant? Here are 12 words to quench a hot situation:

1: "Please" and **2, 3:** "Thank you:" Like water, these words refresh the listener.

4, 5: "I'm sorry." These two words quench the flames of heated arguments.

6, 7, 8: "I love you." These words carry tremendous power. They are the Niagara Falls of words.

9, 10, 11, 12: "I'm praying for you." These words let others know that you will ask God to give them the living water of Jesus and the Word. They will hydrate a dry and weary soul.

Go to page 1496 for your next devotional reading.

14 But if you harbor bitter envy and selfish
ambition in your hearts, do not boast about
it or deny the truth. 15 Such "wisdom" does
not come down from heaven but is earthly,
unspiritual, of the devil. 16 For where you have
envy and selfish ambition, there you find disorder and every evil practice.

17 But the wisdom that comes from heaven
is first of all pure; then peace-loving, considerate, submissive, full of mercy and good fruit,
impartial and sincere. 18 Peacemakers who sow
in peace raise a harvest of righteousness.

Submit Yourselves to God

4 What causes fights and quarrels among
you? Don't they come from your desires
that battle within you? 2 You want something
but don't get it. You kill and covet, but you cannot have what you want. You quarrel and fight.
You do not have, because you do not ask God.
3 When you ask, you do not receive, because
you ask with wrong motives, that you may
spend what you get on your pleasures.

4 You adulterous people, don't you know
that friendship with the world is hatred toward
God? Anyone who chooses to be a friend of the
world becomes an enemy of God. 5 Or do you
think Scripture says without reason that the
spirit he caused to live in us envies intensely?[a]
6 But he gives us more grace. That is why Scripture says:

> "God opposes the proud
> but gives grace to the
> humble."[b]

> **James 4:7**
>
> *God Looks for Submission*
>
> Submit yourselves, then, to God. Resist the devil, and he will flee from you.

7 Submit yourselves, then, to
God. Resist the devil, and he
will flee from you. 8 Come near
to God and he will come near
to you. Wash your hands, you
sinners, and purify your hearts,
you double-minded. 9 Grieve,
mourn and wail. Change your
laughter to mourning and your
joy to gloom. 10 Humble yourselves before the Lord, and he
will lift you up.

11 Brothers, do not slander one another. Anyone who speaks against his brother or judges
him speaks against the law and judges it. When
you judge the law, you are not keeping it, but
sitting in judgment on it. 12 There is only one
Lawgiver and Judge, the one who is able to save
and destroy. But you—who are you to judge
your neighbor?

Boasting About Tomorrow

13 Now listen, you who say, "Today or tomorrow we will go to this or that city, spend a year
there, carry on business and make money."
14 Why, you do not even know what will happen tomorrow. What is your life? You are a mist
that appears for a little while and then vanishes.
15 Instead, you ought to say, "If it is the Lord's
will, we will live and do this or that." 16 As it is,
you boast and brag. All such boasting is evil.
17 Anyone, then, who knows the good he ought
to do and doesn't do it, sins.

Warning to Rich Oppressors

5 Now listen, you rich people, weep and
wail because of the misery that is coming
upon you. 2 Your wealth has rotted, and moths
have eaten your clothes. 3 Your gold and silver are corroded. Their corrosion will testify
against you and eat your flesh like fire. You
have hoarded wealth in the last days. 4 Look!
The wages you failed to pay the workmen who
mowed your fields are crying out against you.
The cries of the harvesters have reached the
ears of the Lord Almighty. 5 You have lived on
earth in luxury and self-indul-
gence. You have fattened yourselves in the day of slaughter.[c]
6 You have condemned and
murdered innocent men, who
were not opposing you.

Patience in Suffering

7 Be patient, then, brothers,
until the Lord's coming. See
how the farmer waits for the
land to yield its valuable crop
and how patient he is for the
autumn and spring rains. 8 You
too, be patient and stand firm,
because the Lord's coming is near. 9 Don't grumble against each other, brothers, or you will be
judged. The Judge is standing at the door!

[a]5 Or *that God jealously longs for the spirit that he made to live in us*; or *that the Spirit he caused to live in us longs jealously*
[b]6 Prov. 3:34 [c]5 Or *yourselves as in a day of feasting*

10 Brothers, as an example of patience in the face of suffering, take the prophets who spoke in the name of the Lord. 11 As you know, we consider blessed those who have persevered. You have heard of Job's perseverance and have seen what the Lord finally brought about. The Lord is full of compassion and mercy.

12 Above all, my brothers, do not swear—not by heaven or by earth or by anything else. Let your "Yes" be yes, and your "No," no, or you will be condemned.

The Prayer of Faith

13 Is any one of you in trouble? He should pray. Is anyone happy? Let him sing songs of praise. 14 Is any one of you sick? He should call the elders of the church to pray over him and anoint him with oil in the name of the Lord. 15 And the prayer offered in faith will make the sick person well; the Lord will raise him up. If he has sinned, he will be forgiven. 16 Therefore confess your sins to each other and pray for each other so that you may be healed. The prayer of a righteous man is powerful and effective.

17 Elijah was a man just like us. He prayed earnestly that it would not rain, and it did not rain on the land for three and a half years. 18 Again he prayed, and the heavens gave rain, and the earth produced its crops.

19 My brothers, if one of you should wander from the truth and someone should bring him back, 20 remember this: Whoever turns a sinner from the error of his way will save him from death and cover over a multitude of sins.

James 5:16

God Hears Prayer

Therefore confess your sins to each other and pray for each other so that you may be healed. The prayer of a righteous man is powerful and effective.

1 Peter

Your attitude toward others *represents Christ to them.* Peter wants his readers to understand this point. Be as gentle as you can, especially when dealing with unbelievers. Forgive their harshness. Answer those in authority respectfully, even if they don't treat you well. Whether you're dealing with a hard boss, an unbelieving husband or someone else who sometimes makes life difficult, *live for Christ* and don't assert your own rights. Let the unbelievers see your good deeds and notice that you are different.

Peter's readers were suffering, and he wanted them to be able to accept that suffering and to let the suffering itself help them reflect the gospel. If they accepted the suffering as part of their Christian experience rather than fighting it, the world would have a chance *to see that Christ offers hope.*

Author:
The apostle Peter.

Audience:
Early Jewish Christians scattered because of persecution and all followers of Jesus.

Date:
About A.D. 62–64, possibly written from Rome.

Setting:
The Roman emperor Nero was leading severe persecution of Christians.

Verse to Remember:
It is better, if it is God's will, to suffer for doing good than for doing evil. (3:17)

1 Peter, an apostle of Jesus Christ,

To God's elect, strangers in the world, scattered throughout Pontus, Galatia, Cappadocia, Asia and Bithynia, 2who have been chosen according to the foreknowledge of God the Father, through the sanctifying work of the Spirit, for obedience to Jesus Christ and sprinkling by his blood:

Grace and peace be yours in abundance.

Praise to God for a Living Hope

3Praise be to the God and Father of our Lord Jesus Christ! In his great mercy he has given

us new birth into a living hope through the resurrection of Jesus Christ from the dead, 4and
into an inheritance that can never perish, spoil
or fade—kept in heaven for you, 5who through
faith are shielded by God's power until the coming of the salvation that is ready to be revealed
in the last time. 6In this you greatly rejoice,
though now for a little while you may have had
to suffer grief in all kinds of trials. 7These have
come so that your faith—of greater worth than
gold, which perishes even though refined by
fire—may be proved genuine and may result
in praise, glory and honor when Jesus Christ
is revealed. 8Though you have not seen him,
you love him; and even though you do not see
him now, you believe in him and are filled with
an inexpressible and glorious joy, 9for you are
receiving the goal of your faith, the salvation
of your souls.

10Concerning this salvation, the prophets,
who spoke of the grace that was to come to you,
searched intently and with the greatest care,
11trying to find out the time and circumstances
to which the Spirit of Christ in them was pointing when he predicted the sufferings of Christ
and the glories that would follow. 12It was revealed to them that they were not serving themselves but you, when they spoke of the things
that have now been told you by those who have
preached the gospel to you by the Holy Spirit
sent from heaven. Even angels long to look into
these things.

Be Holy

13Therefore, prepare your minds for action;
be self-controlled; set your hope fully on the
grace to be given you when Jesus Christ is
revealed. 14As obedient children, do not conform to the evil desires you had when you lived
in ignorance. 15But just as he who called you is
holy, so be holy in all you do; 16for it is written:
"Be holy, because I am holy."[a]

17Since you call on a Father who judges each
man's work impartially, live your lives as strangers here in reverent fear. 18For you know that it
was not with perishable things such as silver or
gold that you were redeemed from the empty
way of life handed down to you from your
forefathers, 19but with the precious blood of
Christ, a lamb without blemish or defect. 20He
was chosen before the creation of the world,
but was revealed in these last times for your
sake. 21Through him you believe in God, who
raised him from the dead and glorified him,
and so your faith and hope are in God.

22Now that you have purified yourselves
by obeying the truth so that you have sincere
love for your brothers, love one another deeply,
from the heart.[b] 23For you have been born
again, not of perishable seed, but of imperishable, through the living and enduring word of
God. 24For,

"All men are like grass,
and all their glory is like the flowers of
the field;
the grass withers and the flowers fall,
25 but the word of the Lord stands forever."[c]

And this is the word that was preached to you.

2 Therefore, rid yourselves of all malice and
all deceit, hypocrisy, envy, and slander of
every kind. 2Like newborn babies, crave pure
spiritual milk, so that by it you may grow up in
your salvation, 3now that you have tasted that
the Lord is good.

The Living Stone and a Chosen People

4As you come to him, the living Stone—
rejected by men but chosen by God and precious to him— 5you also, like living stones, are
being built into a spiritual house to be a holy
priesthood, offering spiritual sacrifices acceptable to God through Jesus Christ. 6For in Scripture it says:

"See, I lay a stone in Zion,
a chosen and precious cornerstone,
and the one who trusts in him
will never be put to shame."[d]

7Now to you who believe, this stone is precious.
But to those who do not believe,

"The stone the builders rejected
has become the capstone,[e]"[f]

8and,

"A stone that causes men to stumble
and a rock that makes them fall."[g]

[a]16 Lev. 11:44,45; 19:2 [b]22 Some early manuscripts *from a pure heart* [c]25 Isaiah 40:6–8 [d]6 Isaiah 28:16 [e]7 Or *cornerstone*
[f]7 Psalm 118:22 [g]8 Isaiah 8:14

They stumble because they disobey the message—which is also what they were destined for.

[9]But you are a chosen people, a royal priesthood, a holy nation, a people belonging to God, that you may declare the praises of him who called you out of darkness into his wonderful light. [10]Once you were not a people, but now you are the people of God; once you had not received mercy, but now you have received mercy.

[11]Dear friends, I urge you, as aliens and strangers in the world, to abstain from sinful desires, which war against your soul. [12]Live such good lives among the pagans that, though they accuse you of doing wrong, they may see your good deeds and glorify God on the day he visits us.

Submission to Rulers and Masters

[13]Submit yourselves for the Lord's sake to every authority instituted among men: whether to the king, as the supreme authority, [14]or to governors, who are sent by him to punish those who do wrong and to commend those who do right. [15]For it is God's will that by doing good you should silence the ignorant talk of foolish men. [16]Live as free men, but do not use your freedom as a cover-up for evil; live as servants of God. [17]Show proper respect to everyone: Love the brotherhood of believers, fear God, honor the king.

[18]Slaves, submit yourselves to your masters with all respect, not only to those who are good and considerate, but also to those who are harsh. [19]For it is commendable if a man bears up under the pain of unjust suffering because he is conscious of God. [20]But how is it to your credit if you receive a beating for doing wrong and endure it? But if you suffer for doing good and you endure it, this is commendable before God. [21]To this you were called, because Christ suffered for you, leaving you an example, that you should follow in his steps.

[22]"He committed no sin,
and no deceit was found in his mouth."[a]

[23]When they hurled their insults at him, he did not retaliate; when he suffered, he made no threats. Instead, he entrusted himself to him who judges justly. [24]He himself bore our sins in his body on the tree, so that we might die to sins and live for righteousness; by his wounds you have been healed. [25]For you were like sheep going astray, but now you have returned to the Shepherd and Overseer of your souls.

Wives and Husbands

3 Wives, in the same way be submissive to your husbands so that, if any of them do not believe the word, they may be won over without words by the behavior of their wives, [2]when they see the purity and reverence of your lives. [3]Your beauty should not come from outward adornment, such as braided hair and the wearing of gold jewelry and fine clothes. [4]Instead, it should be that of your inner self, the unfading beauty of a gentle and quiet spirit, which is of great worth in God's sight. [5]For this is the way the holy women of the past who put their hope in God used to make themselves beautiful. They were submissive to their own husbands, [6]like Sarah, who obeyed Abraham and called him her master. You are her daughters if you do what is right and do not give way to fear.

[7]Husbands, in the same way be considerate as you live with your wives, and treat them with respect as the weaker partner and as heirs with you of the gracious gift of life, so that nothing will hinder your prayers.

Suffering for Doing Good

[8]Finally, all of you, live in harmony with one another; be sympathetic, love as brothers, be compassionate and humble. [9]Do not repay evil with evil or insult with insult, but with blessing, because to this you were called so that you may inherit a blessing. [10]For,

"Whoever would love life
and see good days
must keep his tongue from evil
and his lips from deceitful speech.
[11]He must turn from evil and do good;
he must seek peace and pursue it.
[12]For the eyes of the Lord are on the righteous
and his ears are attentive to their prayer,
but the face of the Lord is against those who do evil."[b]

[a]22 Isaiah 53:9 [b]12 Psalm 34:12–16

Suffering Well

Read: 1 Peter 2:4–25

"WHAT GOOD IS SUFFERING?"

Have you ever asked that question? If so, you're not alone. The problem of pain and suffering in the world has turned many people away from faith in God and has inspired countless books and articles. Scholars and laypeople have tried for centuries to unravel the mystery of how God's plan can include evil in any form.

We live in a corrupt, fallen world in which illness occurs, violence happens and evil, for the time being, is allowed to run its course. Suffering is inevitable . . . our passage today even tells us we were "called" to suffer. It's not a matter of *if* we will suffer but *when* we will suffer. As believers in Jesus Christ, however, suffering offers the opportunity to display Christ's character and grace. For Christians, rather than asking, "Why does God allow suffering?" or even, "Why am *I* suffering?" we should ask, "How can I suffer *well*?"

Most of the early church leaders suffered violent deaths because of their outspoken and radical faith in Jesus. But every time one of them was martyred, the number of Christians grew. Why? Because people long to give themselves fully to a cause worth dying for. We all long for purpose and peace—and Jesus Christ offers both.

In his book *Velvet Elvis*, Bible teacher Rob Bell writes, "Ultimately our gift to the world around us is hope. Not blind hope that pretends everything is fine and refuses to acknowledge how things are. But the kind of hope that comes from staring pain and suffering right in the eyes and refusing to believe that this is all there is. It is what we all need—hope that comes not from going around suffering but from going through it."

Let's pray that God will allow us the privilege and strength of suffering well . . . for our sake, for his sake and for the sake of those who don't yet know him.

1 Peter 2:20

But if you suffer for doing good and you endure it, this is commendable before God.

reflection

1 Does the concept of "suffering well" resonate with you? Why or why not?

2 Can you think of a time when God used a period of suffering to help you comfort another person?

3 How do you think suffering can make you more Christlike?

RELATED READINGS

Psalm 107:1–43; Isaiah 53:1–12; Romans 5:1–5; Philippians 3:7–11

"The Bible is a Christian's guidebook, and I believe the knowledge it sheds on pain and suffering is the great antidote to fear for suffering people. Knowledge can dissolve fear as light destroys darkness."

Philip Yancey

Wednesday

Go to page 1502 for your next devotional reading.

13 Who is going to harm you if you are eager to do good? 14 But even if you should suffer for what is right, you are blessed. "Do not fear what they fear[a]; do not be frightened."[b] 15 But in your hearts set apart Christ as Lord. Always be prepared to give an answer to everyone who asks you to give the reason for the hope that you have. But do this with gentleness and respect, 16 keeping a clear conscience, so that those who speak maliciously against your good behavior in Christ may be ashamed of their slander. 17 It is better, if it is God's will, to suffer for doing good than for doing evil. 18 For Christ died for sins once for all, the righteous for the unrighteous, to bring you to God. He was put to death in the body but made alive by the Spirit, 19 through whom[c] also he went and preached to the spirits in prison 20 who disobeyed long ago when God waited patiently in the days of Noah while the ark was being built. In it only a few people, eight in all, were saved through water, 21 and this water symbolizes baptism that now saves you also—not the removal of dirt from the body but the pledge[d] of a good conscience toward God. It saves you by the resurrection of Jesus Christ, 22 who has gone into heaven and is at God's right hand—with angels, authorities and powers in submission to him.

> **1 Peter 3:17**
>
> *God Values Suffering*
>
> It is better, if it is God's will, to suffer for doing good than for doing evil.

Living for God

4 Therefore, since Christ suffered in his body, arm yourselves also with the same attitude, because he who has suffered in his body is done with sin. 2 As a result, he does not live the rest of his earthly life for evil human desires, but rather for the will of God. 3 For you have spent enough time in the past doing what pagans choose to do—living in debauchery, lust, drunkenness, orgies, carousing and detestable idolatry. 4 They think it strange that you do not plunge with them into the same flood of dissipation, and they heap abuse on you. 5 But they will have to give account to him who is ready to judge the living and the dead. 6 For this is the reason the gospel was preached even to those who are now dead, so that they might be judged according to men in regard to the body, but live according to God in regard to the spirit.

7 The end of all things is near. Therefore be clear minded and self-controlled so that you can pray. 8 Above all, love each other deeply, because love covers over a multitude of sins. 9 Offer hospitality to one another without grumbling. 10 Each one should use whatever gift he has received to serve others, faithfully administering God's grace in its various forms. 11 If anyone speaks, he should do it as one speaking the very words of God. If anyone serves, he should do it with the strength God provides, so that in all things God may be praised through Jesus Christ. To him be the glory and the power for ever and ever. Amen.

Suffering for Being a Christian

12 Dear friends, do not be surprised at the painful trial you are suffering, as though something strange were happening to you. 13 But rejoice that you participate in the sufferings of Christ, so that you may be overjoyed when his glory is revealed. 14 If you are insulted because of the name of Christ, you are blessed, for the Spirit of glory and of God rests on you. 15 If you suffer, it should not be as a murderer or thief or any other kind of criminal, or even as a meddler. 16 However, if you suffer as a Christian, do not be ashamed, but praise God that you bear that name. 17 For it is time for judgment to begin with the family of God; and if it begins with us, what will the outcome be for those who do not obey the gospel of God? 18 And,

"If it is hard for the righteous to be saved,
  what will become of the ungodly and the
    sinner?"[e]

19 So then, those who suffer according to God's will should commit themselves to their faithful Creator and continue to do good.

[a] 14 Or *not fear their threats* [b] 14 Isaiah 8:12 [c] 18,19 Or *alive in the spirit, 19 through which* [d] 21 Or *response* [e] 18 Prov. 11:31

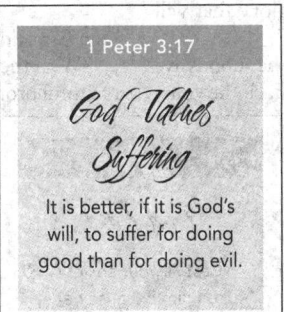

To Elders and Young Men

5 To the elders among you, I appeal as a fellow elder, a witness of Christ's sufferings and one who also will share in the glory to be revealed: 2Be shepherds of God's flock that is under your care, serving as overseers—not because you must, but because you are willing, as God wants you to be; not greedy for money, but eager to serve; 3not lording it over those entrusted to you, but being examples to the flock. 4And when the Chief Shepherd appears, you will receive the crown of glory that will never fade away.

5Young men, in the same way be submissive to those who are older. All of you, clothe yourselves with humility toward one another, because,

> "God opposes the proud
> but gives grace to the
> humble."[a]

6Humble yourselves, therefore, under God's mighty hand, that he may lift you up in due time. 7Cast all your anxiety on him because he cares for you.

> 1 Peter 5:7
>
> *God Cares*
>
> Cast all your anxiety on him because he cares for you.

8Be self-controlled and alert. Your enemy the devil prowls around like a roaring lion looking for someone to devour. 9Resist him, standing firm in the faith, because you know that your brothers throughout the world are undergoing the same kind of sufferings.

10And the God of all grace, who called you to his eternal glory in Christ, after you have suffered a little while, will himself restore you and make you strong, firm and steadfast. 11To him be the power for ever and ever. Amen.

Final Greetings

12With the help of Silas,[b] whom I regard as a faithful brother, I have written to you briefly, encouraging you and testifying that this is the true grace of God. Stand fast in it.

13She who is in Babylon, chosen together with you, sends you her greetings, and so does my son Mark. 14Greet one another with a kiss of love.

Peace to all of you who are in Christ.

[a]5 Prov. 3:34 [b]12 Greek *Silvanus*, a variant of *Silas*

2 Peter

When spiritual leaders begin to draw people away from Christ, confusion results. Peter saw this happening among people he cared about, and he wrote this letter to remind them *to look at the Lord Jesus Christ* and not at their leaders if their leaders failed to follow Christ. The apostle Peter, one of the closest disciples to Jesus, continues to refer to Jesus throughout the letter with *titles that speak of respect:* Jesus is "our Lord and Savior" and "our Lord Jesus Christ." He is the One to be followed, no matter what anyone else says.

Peter tells us that people who follow Jesus for a short while and then choose a life of sin instead, leading others astray in the process, are worse off than those who never followed Christ in the first place. He warns his readers not to follow such false prophets into condemnation. He lists the spiritual virtues that Christ's followers should be striving for, and he tells us *to look to Jesus*—not other people—for the rewards of faith.

Author:
The apostle Peter.

Audience:
All followers of Jesus.

Date:
About A.D. 67.

Setting:
Shortly before his death, Peter wrote this letter to warn believers about false teachers.

Verse to Remember:
The Lord knows how to rescue godly men from trials and to hold the unrighteous for the day of judgment, while continuing their punishment. (2:9)

1 Simon Peter, a servant and apostle of Jesus Christ,

To those who through the righteousness of our God and Savior Jesus Christ have received a faith as precious as ours:

2 Grace and peace be yours in abundance through the knowledge of God and of Jesus our Lord.

Making One's Calling and Election Sure

3 His divine power has given us everything we need for life and godliness through our knowledge of him who called us by his own
glory and goodness. 4 Through these he has
given us his very great and precious promises, so that through them you may participate in the divine nature and escape the corruption in the world caused by evil desires.

5For this very reason, make every effort to
add to your faith goodness; and to goodness,
knowledge; 6and to knowledge, self-control;
and to self-control, perseverance; and to perseverance, godliness; 7and to godliness, brotherly
kindness; and to brotherly kindness, love. 8For
if you possess these qualities in increasing measure, they will keep you from being ineffective
and unproductive in your knowledge of our
Lord Jesus Christ. 9But if anyone does not
have them, he is nearsighted and blind, and
has forgotten that he has been cleansed from
his past sins.
10Therefore, my brothers, be all the more eager to make your calling and election sure. For
if you do these things, you will never fall, 11and
you will receive a rich welcome into the eternal
kingdom of our Lord and Savior Jesus Christ.

Prophecy of Scripture

12So I will always remind you of these
things, even though you know them and are
firmly established in the truth you now have.
13I think it is right to refresh your memory as
long as I live in the tent of this body, 14because
I know that I will soon put it aside, as our Lord
Jesus Christ has made clear to me. 15And I will
make every effort to see that after my departure you will always be able to remember these
things.
16We did not follow cleverly
invented stories when we told
you about the power and coming of our Lord Jesus Christ,
but we were eyewitnesses of
his majesty. 17For he received
honor and glory from God
the Father when the voice
came to him from the Majestic
Glory, saying, "This is my Son,
whom I love; with him I am
well pleased."[a] 18We ourselves
heard this voice that came from
heaven when we were with him
on the sacred mountain.
19And we have the word of
the prophets made more cer-
tain, and you will do well to pay attention to
it, as to a light shining in a dark place, until the
day dawns and the morning star rises in your
hearts. 20Above all, you must understand that
no prophecy of Scripture came about by the
prophet's own interpretation. 21For prophecy
never had its origin in the will of man, but men
spoke from God as they were carried along by
the Holy Spirit.

False Teachers and Their Destruction

2 But there were also false prophets among
the people, just as there will be false teachers among you. They will secretly introduce
destructive heresies, even denying the sovereign Lord who bought them—bringing swift
destruction on themselves. 2Many will follow
their shameful ways and will bring the way
of truth into disrepute. 3In their greed these
teachers will exploit you with stories they have
made up. Their condemnation has long been
hanging over them, and their destruction has
not been sleeping.
4For if God did not spare angels when they
sinned, but sent them to hell,[b] putting them
into gloomy dungeons[c] to be held for judgment;
5if he did not spare the ancient world when he
brought the flood on its ungodly people, but
protected Noah, a preacher of righteousness,
and seven others; 6if he condemned the cities
of Sodom and Gomorrah by burning them to
ashes, and made them an example of what is going to happen to the ungodly;
7and if he rescued Lot, a righteous man, who was distressed
by the filthy lives of lawless
men 8(for that righteous man,
living among them day after
day, was tormented in his righteous soul by the lawless deeds
he saw and heard)— 9if this is
so, then the Lord knows how to
rescue godly men from trials
and to hold the unrighteous
for the day of judgment, while
continuing their punishment.[d]
10This is especially true of
those who follow the corrupt
desire of the sinful nature[e] and
despise authority.
Bold and arrogant, these men are not afraid

2 Peter 2:9

God Can Rescue Us

If this is so, then the Lord knows how to rescue godly men from trials and to hold the unrighteous for the day of judgment.

[a]17 Matt. 17:5; Mark 9:7; Luke 9:35 [b]4 Greek *Tartarus* [c]4 Some manuscripts *into chains of darkness* [d]9 Or *unrighteous for punishment until the day of judgment* [e]10 Or *the flesh*

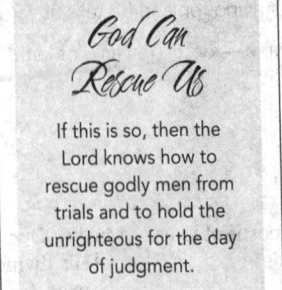

to slander celestial beings; 11yet even angels,
although they are stronger and more powerful, do not bring slanderous accusations
against such beings in the presence of the
Lord. 12But these men blaspheme in matters
they do not understand. They are like brute
beasts, creatures of instinct, born only to be
caught and destroyed, and like beasts they too
will perish.

13They will be paid back with harm for
the harm they have done. Their idea of pleasure is to carouse in broad daylight. They are
blots and blemishes, reveling in their pleasures
while they feast with you.[a] 14With eyes full of
adultery, they never stop sinning; they seduce
the unstable; they are experts in greed—an accursed brood! 15They have left the straight way
and wandered off to follow the way of Balaam
son of Beor, who loved the wages of wickedness. 16But he was rebuked for his wrongdoing
by a donkey—a beast without speech—who
spoke with a man's voice and restrained the
prophet's madness.

17These men are springs without water and
mists driven by a storm. Blackest darkness is
reserved for them. 18For they mouth empty,
boastful words and, by appealing to the lustful
desires of sinful human nature, they entice people who are just escaping from those who live
in error. 19They promise them freedom, while
they themselves are slaves of depravity—for a
man is a slave to whatever has mastered him.
20If they have escaped the corruption of the
world by knowing our Lord and Savior Jesus
Christ and are again entangled in it and overcome, they are worse off at the end than they
were at the beginning. 21It would have been better for them not to have known the way of righteousness, than to have known it and then to
turn their backs on the sacred command that
was passed on to them. 22Of them the proverbs
are true: "A dog returns to its vomit,"[b] and, "A
sow that is washed goes back to her wallowing
in the mud."

The Day of the Lord

3 Dear friends, this is now my second letter
to you. I have written both of them as reminders to stimulate you to wholesome thinking. 2I want you to recall the words spoken
in the past by the holy prophets and the command given by our Lord and Savior through
your apostles.

3First of all, you must understand that in
the last days scoffers will come, scoffing and
following their own evil desires. 4They will
say, "Where is this 'coming' he promised? Ever
since our fathers died, everything goes on as
it has since the beginning of creation." 5But
they deliberately forget that long ago by God's
word the heavens existed and the earth was
formed out of water and by water. 6By these
waters also the world of that time was deluged
and destroyed. 7By the same word the present
heavens and earth are reserved for fire, being
kept for the day of judgment and destruction
of ungodly men.

8But do not forget this one thing, dear
friends: With the Lord a day is like a thousand
years, and a thousand years are like a day. 9The
Lord is not slow in keeping his promise, as
some understand slowness. He is patient with
you, not wanting anyone to perish, but everyone to come to repentance.

10But the day of the Lord will come like a
thief. The heavens will disappear with a roar;
the elements will be destroyed by fire, and the
earth and everything in it will be laid bare.[c]

11Since everything will be destroyed in this
way, what kind of people ought you to be?
You ought to live holy and godly lives 12as
you look forward to the day of God and speed
its coming.[d] That day will bring about the destruction of the heavens by fire, and the elements will melt in the heat. 13But in keeping
with his promise we are looking forward to
a new heaven and a new earth, the home of
righteousness.

14So then, dear friends, since you are looking forward to this, make every effort to be
found spotless, blameless and at peace with
him. 15Bear in mind that our Lord's patience
means salvation, just as our dear brother Paul
also wrote you with the wisdom that God gave
him. 16He writes the same way in all his letters, speaking in them of these matters. His
letters contain some things that are hard to

[a]13 Some manuscripts *in their love feasts* [b]22 Prov. 26:11 [c]10 Some manuscripts *be burned up* [d]12 Or *as you wait eagerly for the day of God to come*

Eternal Perspective

Read: 2 Peter 3:8–14

2 Peter 3:11–12

Since everything will be destroyed in this way, what kind of people ought you to be? You ought to live holy and godly lives as you look forward to the day of God and speed its coming.

THESE VERSES FROM 2 PETER state clearly that earth's time clock is ticking. The world as we know it will come to an end one day. It may or may not occur in our lifetime, but it will occur one day because God has promised that it will. The important question is: How are you going to live until then? How will you spend your days?

Perhaps you or someone dear to you has been diagnosed with a life-threatening illness, and you know their life is winding down. Suddenly your perspective has shifted. What once seemed important no longer seems quite so important. We begin to ask the question Peter asked in verse 11: "What kind of people ought you to be?" We return to the realization that our relationships should come first—our relationship with God, our relationships with our family members and with fellow believers, friends and coworkers.

Thinking about the end of the world can seem frightening or depressing, especially when the signs can't be ignored: the deterioration of morality, growing violence and terrorism, unprecedented natural disasters, war, disease and famine throughout the earth. Watching the nightly news is enough to cause even the most optimistic woman to stay in bed and pull the covers over her head. The truth is that Peter is not asking us to dwell on end-time events but to consider how we will live our lives, right here, right now, while looking forward to a new heaven and a new earth.

How do we keep an eternal perspective while living on earth? Here are a few suggestions: Start each day by praying that God will use you for his purposes. Make it your ambition to please God in everything you do—whether you are packing your children's lunches, running a company or volunteering at church. Each night, thank God for the opportunities he's given you to serve him by serving others.

Living a holy and godly life not only ensures that you are at peace with God and with others, it also ensures that you are ready for whatever may come.

reflection

1. If you knew the world would end tomorrow, how would you reprioritize your life?
2. How do you keep a positive outlook during discouraging times?
3. How will you go about making your life more godly and holy as you look toward eternity?

RELATED READINGS

Philippians 1:27–30; 3:18–21; Titus 2:11–14

Go to page 1508 for your next devotional reading.

understand, which ignorant and unstable people distort, as they do the other Scriptures, to their own destruction.

17 Therefore, dear friends, since you already know this, be on your guard so that you may not be carried away by the error of lawless men and fall from your secure position. 18 But grow in the grace and knowledge of our Lord and Savior Jesus Christ. To him be glory both now and forever! Amen.

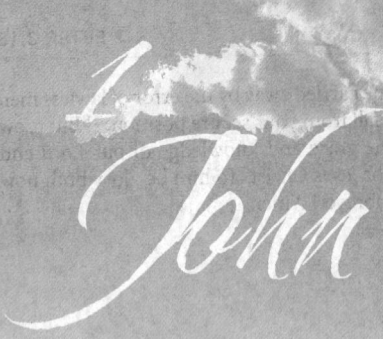

1 John

Author:
The apostle John.

Audience:
All the early churches and every follower of Jesus.

Date:
Between A.D. 85 and 95.

Setting:
Now an old man, this beloved disciple and close friend of Jesus writes to encourage the early churches.

Verse to Remember:
This is how we know what love is: Jesus Christ laid down his life for us. And we ought to lay down our lives for our brothers. (3:16)

We toss the word love around easily enough, but when it comes to defining it, to nailing down exactly what it means, we tend to stumble. We can come up with comparisons or things that it is like, but what is it really? When we strip away all the trappings, *what is love?*

That's the question the apostle John addresses in this letter. He wanted his readers to know beyond any doubt what love was. He wanted them to be secure in God's love, to know for certain where they stood with him. Through his words we again feel *the wonder of being loved by God.* John shows us that God's love is not a vague, intangible wisp we try to grasp, only to find it has slipped through our fingers yet again. *God's love is both solid and transforming.* We can look at our lives and see if we have God's love based on the tests he gives: how we handle sin, how we relate to others, what we do with false teaching and, above all else, what we believe about Jesus Christ. *It is through Jesus,* after all, that we are even able to know what love is.

The Word of Life

1 That which was from the beginning,
which we have heard, which we have seen
with our eyes, which we have looked at and
our hands have touched—this we proclaim
concerning the Word of life. 2 The life appeared;
we have seen it and testify to it, and we proclaim to you the eternal life, which was with
the Father and has appeared to us. 3 We proclaim to you what we have seen and heard, so

that you also may have fellowship with us. And
our fellowship is with the Father and with his
Son, Jesus Christ. 4We write this to make our[a]
joy complete.

Walking in the Light

5This is the message we have heard from
him and declare to you: God is light; in him
there is no darkness at all. 6If we claim to have
fellowship with him yet walk in the darkness,
we lie and do not live by the truth. 7But if we
walk in the light, as he is in the
light, we have fellowship with
one another, and the blood of
Jesus, his Son, purifies us from
all[b] sin.
8If we claim to be without
sin, we deceive ourselves and
the truth is not in us. 9If we
confess our sins, he is faithful
and just and will forgive us our
sins and purify us from all unrighteousness. 10If we claim we
have not sinned, we make him
out to be a liar and his word
has no place in our lives.

> **1 John 1:9**
>
> *God Purifies Us*
>
> If we confess our sins, he is faithful and just and will forgive us our sins and purify us from all unrighteousness.

2

My dear children, I write this to you so
that you will not sin. But if anybody does
sin, we have one who speaks to the Father in
our defense—Jesus Christ, the Righteous One.
2He is the atoning sacrifice for our sins, and
not only for ours but also for[c] the sins of the
whole world.
3We know that we have come to know him
if we obey his commands. 4The man who says,
"I know him," but does not do what he commands is a liar, and the truth is not in him. 5But
if anyone obeys his word, God's love[d] is truly
made complete in him. This is how we know
we are in him: 6Whoever claims to live in him
must walk as Jesus did.
7Dear friends, I am not writing you a new
command but an old one, which you have had
since the beginning. This old command is the
message you have heard. 8Yet I am writing you
a new command; its truth is seen in him and
you, because the darkness is passing and the
true light is already shining.
9Anyone who claims to be in the light
but hates his brother is still in the darkness.
10Whoever loves his brother lives in the light,
and there is nothing in him[e] to make him stumble. 11But whoever hates his brother is in the
darkness and walks around in the darkness; he
does not know where he is going, because the
darkness has blinded him.

12I write to you, dear children,
because your sins have been forgiven on
account of his name.
13I write to you, fathers,
because you have known
him who is from
the beginning.
I write to you, young men,
because you have
overcome the evil
one.
I write to you, dear
children,
because you have known
the Father.
14I write to you, fathers,
because you have known
him who is from
the beginning.
I write to you, young men,
because you are strong,
and the word of God lives in you,
and you have overcome the evil one.

Do Not Love the World

15Do not love the world or anything in the
world. If anyone loves the world, the love of the
Father is not in him. 16For everything in the
world—the cravings of sinful man, the lust of
his eyes and the boasting of what he has and
does—comes not from the Father but from
the world. 17The world and its desires pass
away, but the man who does the will of God
lives forever.

Warning Against Antichrists

18Dear children, this is the last hour; and as
you have heard that the antichrist is coming,
even now many antichrists have come. This is
how we know it is the last hour. 19They went
out from us, but they did not really belong to
us. For if they had belonged to us, they would

[a]4 Some manuscripts *your* [b]7 Or *every* [c]2 Or *He is the one who turns aside God's wrath, taking away our sins, and not only ours but also*
[d]5 Or *word, love for God* [e]10 Or *it*

have remained with us; but their going showed
that none of them belonged to us.
20But you have an anointing from the Holy
One, and all of you know the truth.[a] 21I do
not write to you because you do not know the
truth, but because you do know it and because
no lie comes from the truth. 22Who is the liar?
It is the man who denies that Jesus is the Christ.
Such a man is the antichrist—he denies the Father and the Son. 23No one who denies the Son
has the Father; whoever acknowledges the Son
has the Father also.
24See that what you have heard from the beginning remains in you. If it does, you also will
remain in the Son and in the Father. 25And this
is what he promised us—even eternal life.
26I am writing these things to you about
those who are trying to lead you astray. 27As
for you, the anointing you received from him
remains in you, and you do not need anyone
to teach you. But as his anointing teaches you
about all things and as that anointing is real,
not counterfeit—just as it has taught you, remain in him.

Children of God

28And now, dear children, continue in him,
so that when he appears we may be confident
and unashamed before him at his coming.
29If you know that he is righteous, you know that everyone
who does what is right has
been born of him.

3 How great is the love the
Father has lavished on
us, that we should be called
children of God! And that is
what we are! The reason the
world does not know us is that
it did not know him. 2Dear
friends, now we are children
of God, and what we will be
has not yet been made known.
But we know that when he appears,[b] we shall be like him,
for we shall see him as he is.
3Everyone who has this hope
in him purifies himself, just as
he is pure.
4Everyone who sins breaks the law; in fact,
sin is lawlessness. 5But you know that he appeared so that he might take away our sins.
And in him is no sin. 6No one who lives in him
keeps on sinning. No one who continues to sin
has either seen him or known him.
7Dear children, do not let anyone lead you
astray. He who does what is right is righteous,
just as he is righteous. 8He who does what is sinful is of the devil, because the devil has been sinning from the beginning. The reason the Son of
God appeared was to destroy the devil's work.
9No one who is born of God will continue to
sin, because God's seed remains in him; he cannot go on sinning, because he has been born of
God. 10This is how we know who the children
of God are and who the children of the devil
are: Anyone who does not do what is right is
not a child of God; nor is anyone who does not
love his brother.

Love One Another

11This is the message you heard from the beginning: We should love one another. 12Do not
be like Cain, who belonged to the evil one and
murdered his brother. And why did he murder
him? Because his own actions were evil and his
brother's were righteous. 13Do not be surprised,
my brothers, if the world hates you. 14We know
that we have passed from death to life, because
we love our brothers. Anyone
who does not love remains in
death. 15Anyone who hates his
brother is a murderer, and you
know that no murderer has
eternal life in him.
16This is how we know
what love is: Jesus Christ laid
down his life for us. And we
ought to lay down our lives for
our brothers. 17If anyone has
material possessions and sees
his brother in need but has no
pity on him, how can the love
of God be in him? 18Dear children, let us not love with words
or tongue but with actions and
in truth. 19This then is how
we know that we belong to
the truth, and how we set our hearts at rest in
his presence 20whenever our hearts condemn

> **1 John 3:2**
>
> *God Calls Us His Children*
>
> Dear friends, now we are children of God, and what we will be has not yet been made known. But we know that when he appears, we shall be like him, for we shall see him as he is.

[a]20 Some manuscripts *and you know all things* [b]2 Or *when it is made known*

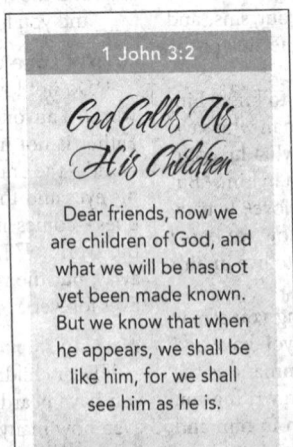

us. For God is greater than our hearts, and he
knows everything.
21 Dear friends, if our hearts do not condemn
us, we have confidence before God 22 and receive from him anything we ask, because we
obey his commands and do what pleases him.
23 And this is his command: to believe in the
name of his Son, Jesus Christ, and to love one
another as he commanded us. 24 Those who
obey his commands live in
him, and he in them. And this
is how we know that he lives in
us: We know it by the Spirit he
gave us.

Test the Spirits

4 Dear friends, do not believe every spirit, but test
the spirits to see whether they
are from God, because many
false prophets have gone out
into the world. 2 This is how you
can recognize the Spirit of God:
Every spirit that acknowledges
that Jesus Christ has come in the flesh is from
God, 3 but every spirit that does not acknowledge Jesus is not from God. This is the spirit of
the antichrist, which you have heard is coming
and even now is already in the world.
4 You, dear children, are from God and
have overcome them, because the one who
is in you is greater than the one who is in the
world. 5 They are from the world and therefore
speak from the viewpoint of the world, and the
world listens to them. 6 We are from God, and
whoever knows God listens to us; but whoever
is not from God does not listen to us. This is
how we recognize the Spirit[a] of truth and the
spirit of falsehood.

God's Love and Ours

7 Dear friends, let us love one another, for
love comes from God. Everyone who loves has
been born of God and knows God. 8 Whoever
does not love does not know God, because
God is love. 9 This is how God showed his love
among us: He sent his one and only Son[b] into
the world that we might live through him.
10 This is love: not that we loved God, but that
he loved us and sent his Son as an atoning sacrifice for[c] our sins. 11 Dear friends, since God
so loved us, we also ought to love one another.
12 No one has ever seen God; but if we love one
another, God lives in us and his love is made
complete in us.
13 We know that we live in him and he in us,
because he has given us of his Spirit. 14 And we
have seen and testify that the Father has sent
his Son to be the Savior of the world. 15 If anyone acknowledges that Jesus is
the Son of God, God lives in
him and he in God. 16 And so
we know and rely on the love
God has for us.
God is love. Whoever lives
in love lives in God, and God
in him. 17 In this way, love is
made complete among us so
that we will have confidence on
the day of judgment, because
in this world we are like him.
18 There is no fear in love. But
perfect love drives out fear, because fear has to do with punishment. The one
who fears is not made perfect in love.
19 We love because he first loved us. 20 If anyone says, "I love God," yet hates his brother,
he is a liar. For anyone who does not love his
brother, whom he has seen, cannot love God,
whom he has not seen. 21 And he has given us
this command: Whoever loves God must also
love his brother.

> 1 John 4:16
>
> *God Is Love*
>
> And so we know and rely on the love God has for us. God is love. Whoever lives in love lives in God, and God in him.

Faith in the Son of God

5 Everyone who believes that Jesus is the
Christ is born of God, and everyone who
loves the father loves his child as well. 2 This is
how we know that we love the children of God:
by loving God and carrying out his commands.
3 This is love for God: to obey his commands.
And his commands are not burdensome, 4 for
everyone born of God overcomes the world.
This is the victory that has overcome the world,
even our faith. 5 Who is it that overcomes the
world? Only he who believes that Jesus is the
Son of God.
6 This is the one who came by water and
blood—Jesus Christ. He did not come by water only, but by water and blood. And it is the

[a]6 Or *spirit* [b]9 Or *his only begotten Son* [c]10 Or *as the one who would turn aside his wrath, taking away*

A Love Like No Other

Read: 1 John 4:7–21

LOVE'S DEEPEST DEFINITION is found in the simple but profound words, "God is love." But how can we transfer this amazing truth to our daily lives? Our finite minds can't understand a love so infinite, so fathomless, so unconditional, so beyond our imagining.

Perhaps a few illustrations of God's love can help us grasp the profound concept that God *is* love. First, consider the story of a farmer who had an unusual weathervane on his barn. Inscribed on the arrow were the words "God is love." A passerby asked the farmer, "What do you mean by that? Do you think God's love is changeable, turning in the wind like the arrow?" "Oh, no," replied the farmer, "I mean that whichever way the wind blows, God is still love." Think about it—God's love is unchanging.

But there is so much more to God's love than its immutability. A little girl and her mother were reading the New Testament one morning when they read, "For God so loved the world that he gave his one and only Son" (John 3:16). The mother stopped and asked the girl, "Don't you think it's wonderful how giving God is?" The child shook her head and said, "Why, no, Mommy, it would be wonderful if it were anybody else, but it is just like God." She knew that it is completely within God's loving character to be sacrificial.

We've all heard about Helen Keller, who was blind, deaf and mute as a child. Her teacher, Annie Sullivan, was determined to teach her to communicate through the sense of touch. Annie decided to tell her the story of Jesus Christ, using sign language. Helen responded, "Oh, I knew he must exist, but I didn't know his name!" Helen Keller is an example of God's amazing love and desire to reveal himself to anyone and everyone.

Though we may not grasp the true depth of the phrase "God is love," we know that he is unchanging and sacrificial, and he desires for every person to know him. No human love can compare with God's love—it's a love like no other.

1 John 4:16

And so we know and rely on the love God has for us. God is love. Whoever lives in love lives in God, and God in him.

reflection

1 When was the last time you spent time dwelling on the truth that "God is love"? Prayerfully do so now.

2 What are some examples or stories from your life that are evidence of God's love for you?

3 Emphasize the words in the phrase "God is love" in different ways to help you grasp the significance: *God* is love. God *is* love. God is *love*.

RELATED READINGS

Psalm 107:1–43; John 15:9–13; Romans 5:6–8

Go to page 1516 for your next devotional reading.

Spirit who testifies, because the Spirit is the
truth. 7For there are three that testify: 8the[a]
Spirit, the water and the blood; and the three
are in agreement. 9We accept man's testimony,
but God's testimony is greater because it is the
testimony of God, which he has given about his
Son. 10Anyone who believes in the Son of God
has this testimony in his heart. Anyone who
does not believe God has made him out to be a
liar, because he has not believed the testimony
God has given about his Son. 11And this is the
testimony: God has given us eternal life, and
this life is in his Son. 12He who has the Son has
life; he who does not have the Son of God does
not have life.

Concluding Remarks

13I write these things to you who believe
in the name of the Son of God so that you
may know that you have eternal life. 14This is
the confidence we have in approaching God:
that if we ask anything according to his will,
he hears us. 15And if we know that he hears
us—whatever we ask—we know that we have
what we asked of him.

16If anyone sees his brother commit a sin
that does not lead to death, he should pray and
God will give him life. I refer to those whose
sin does not lead to death. There is a sin that
leads to death. I am not saying that he should
pray about that. 17All wrongdoing is sin, and
there is sin that does not lead to death.

18We know that anyone born of God does
not continue to sin; the one who was born of
God keeps him safe, and the evil one cannot
harm him. 19We know that we are children
of God, and that the whole world is under the
control of the evil one. 20We know also that
the Son of God has come and has given us understanding, so that we may know him who is
true. And we are in him who is true—even in
his Son Jesus Christ. He is the true God and
eternal life.

21Dear children, keep yourselves from
idols.

[a]7,8 Late manuscripts of the Vulgate *testify in heaven: the Father, the Word and the Holy Spirit, and these three are one. 8And there are three that testify on earth: the* (not found in any Greek manuscript before the fourteenth century)

2 John

Author:
The apostle John.

Audience:
All the early churches and every follower of Jesus.

Date:
Between A.D. 85 and 95.

Setting:
John addressed his letter to "the chosen lady and her children," who may have been a personal friend of John's or a metaphor for a church and its members.

Verse to Remember:
And this is love: that we walk in obedience to his commands. As you have heard from the beginning, his command is that you walk in love. (6)

Sometimes we are so intimately acquainted with someone that we don't have to identify ourselves before conversing. A child calls out across a busy store and the mother knows her child's voice. A friend calls on the phone and simply begins talking, with no need to identify herself. *That is the intimacy we see in this letter.* John addresses "the chosen lady and her children" without explaining who they are, implying a heart-to-heart relationship that the writer and recipient completely understand.

As in all of John's letters, there is heavy emphasis on "truth" and "love." Because we know the truth, Jesus Christ himself, we are recipients of God's love. And *because we know Jesus,* we are to be givers of God's love. As you read this short and intimate letter, see yourself as the "chosen lady" and allow John's words to wrap you in truth and love.

1 The elder,

To the chosen lady and her children, whom
I love in the truth—and not I only, but also all
who know the truth—
2 because of the truth,
which lives in us and will be with us forever:

3 Grace, mercy and peace from God the Father and from Jesus Christ, the Father's Son,
will be with us in truth and love.

4 It has given me great joy to find some of
your children walking in the truth, just as the
Father commanded us.
5 And now, dear lady, I
am not writing you a new command but one
we have had from the beginning. I ask that we
love one another.
6 And this is love: that we
walk in obedience to his commands. As you
have heard from the beginning, his command
is that you walk in love.

[7]Many deceivers, who do not acknowledge
Jesus Christ as coming in the flesh, have gone
out into the world. Any such person is the
deceiver and the antichrist. [8]Watch out that
you do not lose what you have worked for, but
that you may be rewarded fully. [9]Anyone who
runs ahead and does not continue in the teaching of Christ does not have God; whoever continues in the teaching has both the Father and
the Son. [10]If anyone comes to you and does
not bring this teaching, do not take him into
your house or welcome him. [11]Anyone who
welcomes him shares in his wicked work.

[12]I have much to write to you, but I do not
want to use paper and ink. Instead, I hope to
visit you and talk with you face to face, so that
our joy may be complete.

[13]The children of your chosen sister send
their greetings.

3 John

Author:
The apostle John.

Audience:
Members of all the early churches, specifically a friend named Gaius, and all followers of Jesus.

Date:
Between A.D. 85 and 95.

Setting:
Traveling pastors relied on church members' hospitality.

Verse to Remember:
I have no greater joy than to hear that my children are walking in the truth. (4)

This short letter to Gaius from John was a quick note of support. John had noted Gaius's faithfulness, and he encourages him to *continue to do what is good.* The letter is short because it brought good news: John was on his way and would soon be able to speak with Gaius in person.

Sometimes it gets discouraging to do the right thing when others around us do not. It can be easy to join others in gossip, complaining or small acts of dishonesty. Be encouraged that even if others do not see your faithfulness, *God does.* And if you are struggling to be faithful, pray and ask him to help you do so. *Look for others who can be an example* to you, and seek out those whom you can thank for their actions that please God.

1The elder,

To my dear friend Gaius, whom I love in
the truth.

2Dear friend, I pray that you may enjoy good
health and that all may go well with you, even
as your soul is getting along well. 3It gave me
great joy to have some brothers come and tell
about your faithfulness to the truth and how
you continue to walk in the truth. 4I have no
greater joy than to hear that my children are
walking in the truth.
5Dear friend, you are faithful in what you
are doing for the brothers, even though they
are strangers to you. 6They have told the

church about your love. You will do well to
send them on their way in a manner worthy
of God. 7It was for the sake of
the Name that they went out,
receiving no help from the pagans. 8We ought therefore to
show hospitality to such men
so that we may work together
for the truth.

9I wrote to the church, but
Diotrephes, who loves to be
first, will have nothing to do
with us. 10So if I come, I will
call attention to what he is
doing, gossiping maliciously
about us. Not satisfied with
that, he refuses to welcome the
brothers. He also stops those who want to do so
and puts them out of the church.

11Dear friend, do not imitate what is evil
but what is good. Anyone who does what is
good is from God. Anyone
who does what is evil has not
seen God. 12Demetrius is well
spoken of by everyone—and
even by the truth itself. We
also speak well of him, and
you know that our testimony
is true.

13I have much to write you,
but I do not want to do so with
pen and ink. 14I hope to see
you soon, and we will talk face
to face.

Peace to you. The friends
here send their greetings. Greet the friends
there by name.

3 John 4

God Causes Growth

I have no greater joy than to hear that my children are walking in the truth.

Jude

Author:
Jude, brother of James and Jesus.

Audience:
Jewish Christians and all followers of Jesus.

Date:
About A.D. 65.

Setting:
Jude issued a warning about false teachers who lead people astray.

Verse to Remember:
Dear friends, although I was very eager to write to you about the salvation we share, I felt I had to write and urge you to contend for the faith that was once for all entrusted to the saints. (3)

Sin is never a pleasant topic. There are many things Jude might have discussed, but he felt that dealing with false teachers was the utmost importance. He no longer saw Jesus as the fanatical brother who refused to quietly blend in. *He now saw Jesus as the Messiah.* And he wanted to share that knowledge.

But as he smoothed his parchment, his thoughts were pierced by the realization that there were enemies in their midst, infiltrating the ranks. And they needed to be dealt with—now!

Jude reminds us that *the Christian life is a battleground.* When we take up our cross, we're inviting attack. From the world, yes, but unfortunately, the attack often comes from within the church as well. Believers don't have the option of drifting along quietly, undisturbed. We're in enemy territory, and we need to know how to fight. There are times for peaceful words of encouragement, and there are times for sharp words of rebuke. Jude reminds us that *we need to be alert* to both.

1 Jude, a servant of Jesus Christ and a brother
of James,

To those who have been called, who are loved
by God the Father and kept by[a] Jesus Christ:

2 Mercy, peace and love be yours in abundance.

The Sin and Doom of Godless Men

3 Dear friends, although I was very eager
to write to you about the salvation we share,
I felt I had to write and urge you to contend
for the faith that was once for all entrusted to
the saints. 4 For certain men whose condemnation was written about[b] long ago have secretly

[a] 1 Or *for*; or *in* [b] 4 Or *men who were marked out for condemnation*

slipped in among you. They are godless men, who change the grace of our God into a license for immorality and deny Jesus Christ our only Sovereign and Lord.

5 Though you already know all this, I want to remind you that the Lord[a] delivered his people out of Egypt, but later destroyed those who did not believe. 6 And the angels who did not keep their positions of authority but abandoned their own home—these he has kept in darkness, bound with everlasting chains for judgment on the great Day. 7 In a similar way, Sodom and Gomorrah and the surrounding towns gave themselves up to sexual immorality and perversion. They serve as an example of those who suffer the punishment of eternal fire.

8 In the very same way, these dreamers pollute their own bodies, reject authority and slander celestial beings. 9 But even the archangel Michael, when he was disputing with the devil about the body of Moses, did not dare to bring a slanderous accusation against him, but said, "The Lord rebuke you!" 10 Yet these men speak abusively against whatever they do not understand; and what things they do understand by instinct, like unreasoning animals—these are the very things that destroy them.

11 Woe to them! They have taken the way of Cain; they have rushed for profit into Balaam's error; they have been destroyed in Korah's rebellion.

12 These men are blemishes at your love feasts, eating with you without the slightest qualm—shepherds who feed only themselves. They are clouds without rain, blown along by the wind; autumn trees, without fruit and uprooted—twice dead. 13 They are wild waves of the sea, foaming up their shame; wandering stars, for whom blackest darkness has been reserved forever.

14 Enoch, the seventh from Adam, prophesied about these men: "See, the Lord is coming with thousands upon thousands of his holy ones 15 to judge everyone, and to convict all the ungodly of all the ungodly acts they have done in the ungodly way, and of all the harsh words ungodly sinners have spoken against him." 16 These men are grumblers and faultfinders; they follow their own evil desires; they boast about themselves and flatter others for their own advantage.

A Call to Persevere

17 But, dear friends, remember what the apostles of our Lord Jesus Christ foretold. 18 They said to you, "In the last times there will be scoffers who will follow their own ungodly desires." 19 These are the men who divide you, who follow mere natural instincts and do not have the Spirit.

20 But you, dear friends, build yourselves up in your most holy faith and pray in the Holy Spirit. 21 Keep yourselves in God's love as you wait for the mercy of our Lord Jesus Christ to bring you to eternal life.

22 Be merciful to those who doubt; 23 snatch others from the fire and save them; to others show mercy, mixed with fear—hating even the clothing stained by corrupted flesh.

Doxology

24 To him who is able to keep you from falling and to present you before his glorious presence without fault and with great joy— 25 to the only God our Savior be glory, majesty, power and authority, through Jesus Christ our Lord, before all ages, now and forevermore! Amen.

Jude 21

God Brings Eternal Life

Keep yourselves in God's love as you wait for the mercy of our Lord Jesus Christ to bring you to eternal life.

[a] 5 Some early manuscripts *Jesus*

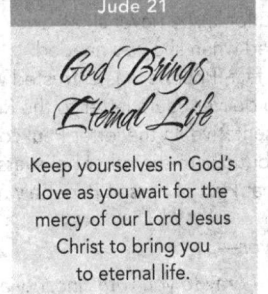

Working Hard

PHOEBE

I commend to you our sister Phoebe, a servant of the church in Cenchrea.

Romans 16:1

"YOU'RE GLOWING!" The older widow pointed out Phoebe's countenance.

"She is—look at her!" Now the other women in the church were pointing to her and smiling as she made her way past them. Wherever she went, Phoebe practically radiated Christ's love. It was in the way she greeted others on the street, in the way she took a hurting child in her arms, in the way she served food to the poor.

"She is never too busy to help . . ." one woman said.

". . . And never too preoccupied with her own life to see someone else's need," finished another. It was the way most people described Phoebe.

"You know, you can't love someone at arm's length," said another elderly woman, describing Phoebe's ability to embrace others. "That's what I learned from Phoebe."

"We've *all* learned from Phoebe," said another, and all agreed.

Phoebe had more than just a sunny disposition, as if all she did was delicately hover over life's circumstances—far removed from the grit and grime of tragedy and concern. Even with her positive outlook, she never shied away from the messiness of getting involved when she was needed.

In fact, Phoebe was entrusted with a difficult assignment: she was to deliver Paul's letter to the Roman church and serve as his representative. In the letter Paul commended her and noted her contributions to the other believers. Of course, they already could tell what kind of person Phoebe was. It was obvious.

ASSIGNED READING:

Romans 16:1–2

—Prayer—

Savior, I pray to you with sincerity and ask that you help me radiate your love wherever I go.

Weekend

Go to page 1519 for your next devotional reading.

Revelation

Visions of weird beasts. Candlesticks and sealed scrolls. Dragons and falling stars. Blood and violence. Glory. Majesty. Mystery. *The imagery of Revelation* can inspire and confuse. Interpreting it can stump the finest theologian or draw all-out theological warfare. *Revelation tells of the end times,* but exactly what it means has often been debated.

But one recurring image takes center stage. The risen Lord Jesus appears throughout the book. As a Lamb. As an awe-inspiring man. But always as the One who has conquered death and is now unquestionably the King. *Jesus Christ rules,* and he is in charge in these visions and letters of future battle and future triumph.

Look for Jesus in this book—for his words of exhortation and comfort, for his wrath against those who oppose him, but *especially for his promise* that he will soon return for his people and make all things new. That day is worth waiting for! Come, Lord Jesus.

Author:
The apostle John.

Audience:
Seven churches in Asia and all followers of Jesus.

Date:
About A.D. 95.

Setting:
John wrote about a vision he had while exiled on the island of Patmos near the end of his life.

Verse to Remember:
Then I heard every creature in heaven and on earth and under the earth and on the sea, and all that is in them, singing: "To him who sits on the throne and to the Lamb be praise and honor and glory and power, for ever and ever!" (5:13)

Prologue

1 The revelation of Jesus Christ, which God
gave him to show his servants what must
soon take place. He made it known by sending
his angel to his servant John, 2who testifies to
everything he saw—that is, the word of God
and the testimony of Jesus Christ. 3Blessed is
the one who reads the words of this prophecy,
and blessed are those who hear it and take to
heart what is written in it, because the time
is near.

Greetings and Doxology

4John,

To the seven churches in the province of
Asia:

Grace and peace to you from him who is,
and who was, and who is to come, and from
the seven spirits[a] before his throne, 5and from
Jesus Christ, who is the faithful witness, the
firstborn from the dead, and the ruler of the
kings of the earth.

To him who loves us and has freed us from
our sins by his blood, 6and has made us to be
a kingdom and priests to serve his God and Father—to him be glory and power for ever and
ever! Amen.

7 Look, he is coming with the clouds,
and every eye will see him,
even those who pierced him;
and all the peoples of the earth will
mourn because of him.
So shall it be! Amen.

8"I am the Alpha and the Omega," says the
Lord God, "who is, and who was, and who is to
come, the Almighty."

One Like a Son of Man

9I, John, your brother and companion in
the suffering and kingdom and patient endurance that are ours in Jesus, was on the island
of Patmos because of the word of God and the
testimony of Jesus. 10On the Lord's Day I was in
the Spirit, and I heard behind me a loud voice
like a trumpet, 11which said: "Write on a scroll
what you see and send it to the seven churches:
to Ephesus, Smyrna, Pergamum, Thyatira, Sardis, Philadelphia and Laodicea."
12I turned around to see the voice that was
speaking to me. And when I turned I saw
seven golden lampstands, 13and among the
lampstands was someone "like a son of man,"[b]
dressed in a robe reaching down to his feet and
with a golden sash around his chest. 14His head
and hair were white like wool, as white as snow,
and his eyes were like blazing fire. 15His feet
were like bronze glowing in a furnace, and his
voice was like the sound of rushing waters. 16In
his right hand he held seven stars, and out of
his mouth came a sharp double-edged sword.
His face was like the sun shining in all its brilliance.
17When I saw him, I fell at his feet as though
dead. Then he placed his right hand on me and
said: "Do not be afraid. I am the First and the
Last. 18I am the Living One; I was dead, and
behold I am alive for ever and ever! And I hold
the keys of death and Hades.
19"Write, therefore, what you have seen,
what is now and what will take place later.
20The mystery of the seven stars that you saw
in my right hand and of the seven golden lampstands is this: The seven stars are the angels[c] of
the seven churches, and the seven lampstands
are the seven churches.

To the Church in Ephesus

2 "To the angel[d] of the church in Ephesus
write:

These are the words of him who holds
the seven stars in his right hand and walks
among the seven golden lampstands: 2I
know your deeds, your hard work and
your perseverance. I know that you cannot
tolerate wicked men, that you have tested
those who claim to be apostles but are not,
and have found them false. 3You have persevered and have endured hardships for
my name, and have not grown weary.
4Yet I hold this against you: You have
forsaken your first love. 5Remember the
height from which you have fallen! Repent and do the things you did at first. If
you do not repent, I will come to you and
remove your lampstand from its place.
6But you have this in your favor: You hate
the practices of the Nicolaitans, which I
also hate.
7He who has an ear, let him hear what
the Spirit says to the churches. To him
who overcomes, I will give the right to eat
from the tree of life, which is in the paradise of God.

To the Church in Smyrna

8"To the angel of the church in Smyrna write:

These are the words of him who is the
First and the Last, who died and came to
life again. 9I know your afflictions and
your poverty—yet you are rich! I know
the slander of those who say they are Jews
and are not, but are a synagogue of Satan.

[a]4 Or *the sevenfold Spirit* [b]13 Daniel 7:13 [c]20 Or *messengers* [d]1 Or *messenger*; also in verses 8, 12 and 18

Never the Same?

Read: Revelation 1:1–8

DO YOU EVER WISH that things could simply stay the same? Just when you figure out how to deal with a temperamental two-year-old, she moves into the terrific threes, and you begin to wonder who this small person is wearing your child's clothes . . . and, by the way, why don't those clothes fit anymore? Just when you get settled into your new home and neighborhood, you get transferred and have to begin packing and looking for another new home, new church and new friends. Just when you're collecting the travel brochures, an aging parent goes into the hospital and needs your constant care.

Wearily, you lay your head on the pillow and lament, "Doesn't anything ever stay the same?" An ancient Greek philosopher said, "There is nothing permanent except change."

But amidst the changes of life, if you listen very carefully, you can hear the voice of God speaking comfort to your soul: "[I am] the same yesterday and today and forever" (Hebrews 13:8). Though our children may change, though our job situations may be in flux, though our parents may have failing health, though circumstances may be unsettled, we can trust in the truth that our everlasting God never changes.

John's final book of the Bible, Revelation, tells of the changes that lie ahead. But John is quick to remind us that we have one constant in our lives: God. He is, and he was, and he is to come. He is the Alpha and the Omega, the beginning and the end. He bookends time. He is able to provide stability amidst the transitions of life.

If your legs feel unsteady because of the changes you face, look to God. He started everything, and he will finish what he started. His character never changes, his love never fails and his power never wanes. Yes, it's good to know that some things never change.

Revelation 1:8

"I am the Alpha and the Omega," says the Lord God, "who is, and who was, and who is to come, the Almighty."

reflection

1. When have the changes in your life seemed overwhelming?
2. Who has been a constant source of encouragement during the changing seasons of your life?
3. How has Jesus helped you weather the changes you've experienced?

RELATED READINGS

Psalm 136:1–26; Hebrew 6:16–20; James 1:17

"In a threatened world, in the kaleidoscope whirl of our life patterns, it can be enormously reassuring to remind ourselves that God is unchanging."

Gini Andrews

Go to page 1523 for your next devotional reading.

[10]Do not be afraid of what you are about
to suffer. I tell you, the devil will put some
of you in prison to test you, and you will
suffer persecution for ten days. Be faithful, even to the point of death, and I will
give you the crown of life.
[11]He who has an ear, let him hear what
the Spirit says to the churches. He who
overcomes will not be hurt at all by the
second death.

To the Church in Pergamum

[12]"To the angel of the church in Pergamum
write:

These are the words of him who has
the sharp, double-edged sword. [13]I know
where you live—where Satan has his
throne. Yet you remain true to my name.
You did not renounce your faith in me,
even in the days of Antipas, my faithful
witness, who was put to death in your
city—where Satan lives.
[14]Nevertheless, I have a few things
against you: You have people there who
hold to the teaching of Balaam, who
taught Balak to entice the Israelites to sin
by eating food sacrificed to idols and by
committing sexual immorality. [15]Like-
wise you also have those who hold to
the teaching of the Nicolaitans. [16]Repent
therefore! Otherwise, I will soon come to
you and will fight against them with the
sword of my mouth.
[17]He who has an ear, let him hear
what the Spirit says to the churches. To
him who overcomes, I will give some of
the hidden manna. I will also give him a
white stone with a new name written on
it, known only to him who receives it.

To the Church in Thyatira

[18]"To the angel of the church in Thyatira
write:

These are the words of the Son of God,
whose eyes are like blazing fire and whose
feet are like burnished bronze. [19]I know
your deeds, your love and faith, your service and perseverance, and that you are
now doing more than you did at first.
[20]Nevertheless, I have this against you:
You tolerate that woman Jezebel, who
calls herself a prophetess. By her teaching she misleads my servants into sexual
immorality and the eating of food sacrificed to idols. [21]I have given her time to
repent of her immorality, but she is unwilling. [22]So I will cast her on a bed of suffering, and I will make those who commit
adultery with her suffer intensely, unless
they repent of her ways. [23]I will strike her
children dead. Then all the churches will
know that I am he who searches hearts
and minds, and I will repay each of you according to your deeds. [24]Now I say to the
rest of you in Thyatira, to you who do not
hold to her teaching and have not learned
Satan's so-called deep secrets (I will not
impose any other burden on you): [25]Only
hold on to what you have until I come.
[26]To him who overcomes and does my
will to the end, I will give authority over
the nations—

[27]'He will rule them with an iron
scepter;
he will dash them to pieces like
pottery'[a]—

just as I have received authority from my
Father. [28]I will also give him the morning
star. [29]He who has an ear, let him hear
what the Spirit says to the churches.

To the Church in Sardis

3 "To the angel[b] of the church in Sardis
write:

These are the words of him who holds
the seven spirits[c] of God and the seven
stars. I know your deeds; you have a reputation of being alive, but you are dead.
[2]Wake up! Strengthen what remains and
is about to die, for I have not found your
deeds complete in the sight of my God.
[3]Remember, therefore, what you have received and heard; obey it, and repent. But
if you do not wake up, I will come like a
thief, and you will not know at what time
I will come to you.
[4]Yet you have a few people in Sardis

[a]27 Psalm 2:9 [b]1 Or *messenger*; also in verses 7 and 14 [c]1 Or *the sevenfold Spirit*

who have not soiled their clothes. They
will walk with me, dressed in white, for
they are worthy. 5He who overcomes will,
like them, be dressed in white. I will never
blot out his name from the book of life,
but will acknowledge his name before my
Father and his angels. 6He who has an ear,
let him hear what the Spirit says to the
churches.

To the Church in Philadelphia

7"To the angel of the church in Philadelphia
write:

These are the words of him who is holy
and true, who holds the key of David.
What he opens no one can shut, and what
he shuts no one can open.
8I know your deeds. See, I
have placed before you an
open door that no one can
shut. I know that you have
little strength, yet you have
kept my word and have not
denied my name. 9I will
make those who are of the
synagogue of Satan, who
claim to be Jews though
they are not, but are liars—I
will make them come and
fall down at your feet and acknowledge that I have loved
you. 10Since you have kept
my command to endure patiently, I will
also keep you from the hour of trial that
is going to come upon the whole world to
test those who live on the earth.
11I am coming soon. Hold on to what
you have, so that no one will take your
crown. 12Him who overcomes I will make
a pillar in the temple of my God. Never
again will he leave it. I will write on him
the name of my God and the name of the
city of my God, the new Jerusalem, which
is coming down out of heaven from my
God; and I will also write on him my new
name. 13He who has an ear, let him hear
what the Spirit says to the churches.

To the Church in Laodicea

14"To the angel of the church in Laodicea
write:

These are the words of the Amen, the
faithful and true witness, the ruler of God's
creation. 15I know your deeds, that you
are neither cold nor hot. I wish you were
either one or the other! 16So, because you
are lukewarm—neither hot nor cold—I
am about to spit you out of my mouth.
17You say, 'I am rich; I have acquired
wealth and do not need a thing.' But you
do not realize that you are wretched, piti-
ful, poor, blind and naked. 18I counsel you
to buy from me gold refined in the fire, so
you can become rich; and white clothes
to wear, so you can cover your shameful
nakedness; and salve to put on your eyes,
so you can see.
19Those whom I love I re-
buke and discipline. So be
earnest, and repent. 20Here
I am! I stand at the door and
knock. If anyone hears my
voice and opens the door,
I will come in and eat with
him, and he with me.
21To him who over-
comes, I will give the right
to sit with me on my throne,
just as I overcame and sat
down with my Father on his
throne. 22He who has an ear,
let him hear what the Spirit
says to the churches."

> **Revelation 3:21**
>
> *God Grants Favor*
>
> To him who overcomes, I will give the right to sit with me on my throne, just as I overcame and sat down with my Father on his throne.

The Throne in Heaven

4 After this I looked, and there before me
was a door standing open in heaven.
And the voice I had first heard speaking to
me like a trumpet said, "Come up here, and
I will show you what must take place after
this." 2At once I was in the Spirit, and there
before me was a throne in heaven with someone sitting on it. 3And the one who sat there
had the appearance of jasper and carnelian. A
rainbow, resembling an emerald, encircled the
throne. 4Surrounding the throne were twenty-
four other thrones, and seated on them were
twenty-four elders. They were dressed in
white and had crowns of gold on their heads.
5From the throne came flashes of lightning,
rumblings and peals of thunder. Before the
throne, seven lamps were blazing. These are

the seven spirits[a] of God. 6Also before the
throne there was what looked like a sea of
glass, clear as crystal.

In the center, around the throne, were four
living creatures, and they were covered with
eyes, in front and in back. 7The first living
creature was like a lion, the second was like an
ox, the third had a face like a man, the fourth
was like a flying eagle. 8Each of the four living
creatures had six wings and was covered with
eyes all around, even under his wings. Day and
night they never stop saying:

"Holy, holy, holy
is the Lord God Almighty,
who was, and is, and is to come."

9Whenever the living creatures give glory,
honor and thanks to him who sits on the
throne and who lives for ever and ever, 10the
twenty-four elders fall down before him who
sits on the throne, and worship him who lives
for ever and ever. They lay their crowns before
the throne and say:

11"You are worthy, our Lord and God,
to receive glory and honor and power,
for you created all things,
and by your will they were created
and have their being."

The Scroll and the Lamb

5 Then I saw in the right hand of him who
sat on the throne a scroll with writing on
both sides and sealed with seven seals. 2And I
saw a mighty angel proclaiming in a loud voice,
"Who is worthy to break the seals and open the
scroll?" 3But no one in heaven or on earth or
under the earth could open the scroll or even
look inside it. 4I wept and wept because no one
was found who was worthy to open the scroll
or look inside. 5Then one of the elders said to
me, "Do not weep! See, the Lion of the tribe of
Judah, the Root of David, has triumphed. He is
able to open the scroll and its seven seals."

6Then I saw a Lamb, looking as if it had been
slain, standing in the center of the throne, encircled by the four living creatures and the elders.
He had seven horns and seven eyes, which are
the seven spirits[a] of God sent out into all the
earth. 7He came and took the scroll from the
right hand of him who sat on the throne. 8And
when he had taken it, the four living creatures
and the twenty-four elders fell down before
the Lamb. Each one had a harp and they were
holding golden bowls full of incense, which
are the prayers of the saints. 9And they sang
a new song:

"You are worthy to take the scroll
and to open its seals,
because you were slain,
and with your blood you purchased men
for God
from every tribe and language and
people and nation.
10You have made them to be a kingdom and
priests to serve our God,
and they will reign on the earth."

11Then I looked and heard the voice of many
angels, numbering thousands upon thousands,
and ten thousand times ten thousand. They encircled the throne and the living creatures and
the elders. 12In a loud voice they sang:

"Worthy is the Lamb, who was slain,
to receive power and wealth and wisdom
and strength
and honor and glory and praise!"

13Then I heard every creature in heaven and
on earth and under the earth and on the sea,
and all that is in them, singing:

"To him who sits on the throne and to the
Lamb
be praise and honor and glory and power,
for ever and ever!"

14The four living creatures said, "Amen," and
the elders fell down and worshiped.

The Seals

6 I watched as the Lamb opened the first of
the seven seals. Then I heard one of the
four living creatures say in a voice like thunder,
"Come!" 2I looked, and there before me was a
white horse! Its rider held a bow, and he was
given a crown, and he rode out as a conqueror
bent on conquest.

[a]5,6 Or *the sevenfold Spirit*

Once and for All

Read: Revelation 5:1–14

AT THE END OF THE DAY, how do you feel when you check off all the items on your to-do list? Great! What about the days you're only able to check off three out of ten? Ugh!

So much of our lives are spent trying to prove we are worthy—worthy of love, worthy of appreciation, worthy of value. The truth, especially for women, is that we battle feelings of unworthiness—as followers of Jesus, as leaders, as mothers, as students, as neighbors. No matter how hard we work at it, we never quite measure up to what we think we *should* be or do. We're all too aware of unmet goals, unmet expectations, shortcomings and failings. When we base our feelings of significance upon what we do, just a passing glance at our unfinished to-do list can depress us. Unworthy—that's how we often feel. Unworthy to receive God's love. Unworthy to be called righteous. Unworthy to be used by God.

The truth is that we can never prove we're worthy because in and of ourselves we're not. In Revelation 5 John cried out with great weeping at the realization that no one in heaven, on earth or under the earth was worthy to open the heavenly scroll.

Yet suddenly before John's eyes stood the only One worthy to open the scroll. "Worthy is the Lamb, who was slain, to receive power and wealth and wisdom and strength and honor and glory and praise!" (verse 12). By *his* blood—not by the blood, sweat and tears of our striving—we have been redeemed. We no longer have to prove our significance or earn our way. God has established our worth for all time.

In the light of eternity, it's good to know that your to-do list, the title on your business card, your clothing size, car or accomplishments have no bearing upon your worth. You have been made worthy not because of what you have or have not done, but because of what Jesus Christ has done on your behalf. Nothing you can do can make you any more or less loved, valued and precious to God. The sacrificial blood of Jesus, the only worthy One, has made you worthy.

Revelation 5:9

"You are worthy to take the scroll and to open its seals, because you were slain, and with your blood you purchased men for God from every tribe and language and people and nation."

reflection

1 In what situations do you most often feel unworthy?

2 How have you worked to "do a little more" to prove your worth?

3 Spend some time thanking Jesus for being the worthy One and for passing on his worth to you.

RELATED READINGS

Isaiah 43:2–4;
Romans 3:20–26; 5:1–2;
2 Corinthians 5:21

Go to page 1529 for your next devotional reading.

3When the Lamb opened the second seal, I
heard the second living creature say, "Come!"
4Then another horse came out, a fiery red one.
Its rider was given power to take peace from
the earth and to make men slay each other. To
him was given a large sword.
5When the Lamb opened the third seal, I
heard the third living creature say, "Come!"
I looked, and there before me was a black
horse! Its rider was holding a pair of scales in
his hand. 6Then I heard what sounded like a
voice among the four living creatures, saying,
"A quart[a] of wheat for a day's wages,[b] and three
quarts of barley for a day's wages,[b] and do not
damage the oil and the wine!"
7When the Lamb opened the fourth seal, I
heard the voice of the fourth living creature say,
"Come!" 8I looked, and there before me was a
pale horse! Its rider was named Death, and Hades was following close behind him. They were
given power over a fourth of the earth to kill
by sword, famine and plague, and by the wild
beasts of the earth.
9When he opened the fifth seal, I saw under
the altar the souls of those who had been slain
because of the word of God and the testimony
they had maintained. 10They called out in a
loud voice, "How long, Sovereign Lord, holy
and true, until you judge the inhabitants of the
earth and avenge our blood?" 11Then each of
them was given a white robe, and they were
told to wait a little longer, until the number of
their fellow servants and brothers who were to
be killed as they had been was completed.
12I watched as he opened the sixth seal.
There was a great earthquake. The sun turned
black like sackcloth made of goat hair, the
whole moon turned blood red, 13and the stars
in the sky fell to earth, as late figs drop from a
fig tree when shaken by a strong wind. 14The
sky receded like a scroll, rolling up, and every mountain and island was removed from
its place.
15Then the kings of the earth, the princes,
the generals, the rich, the mighty, and every
slave and every free man hid in caves and
among the rocks of the mountains. 16They
called to the mountains and the rocks, "Fall on
us and hide us from the face of him who sits
on the throne and from the wrath of the Lamb!
17For the great day of their wrath has come,
and who can stand?"

144,000 Sealed

7 After this I saw four angels standing at the
four corners of the earth, holding back the
four winds of the earth to prevent any wind
from blowing on the land or on the sea or on
any tree. 2Then I saw another angel coming up
from the east, having the seal of the living God.
He called out in a loud voice to the four angels
who had been given power to harm the land
and the sea: 3"Do not harm the land or the sea
or the trees until we put a seal on the foreheads
of the servants of our God." 4Then I heard the
number of those who were sealed: 144,000
from all the tribes of Israel.

5From the tribe of Judah 12,000 were
sealed,
from the tribe of Reuben 12,000,
from the tribe of Gad 12,000,
6from the tribe of Asher 12,000,
from the tribe of Naphtali 12,000,
from the tribe of Manasseh 12,000,
7from the tribe of Simeon 12,000,
from the tribe of Levi 12,000,
from the tribe of Issachar 12,000,
8from the tribe of Zebulun 12,000,
from the tribe of Joseph 12,000,
from the tribe of Benjamin 12,000.

The Great Multitude in White Robes

9After this I looked and there before me was
a great multitude that no one could count, from
every nation, tribe, people and language, standing before the throne and in front of the Lamb.
They were wearing white robes and were holding palm branches in their hands. 10And they
cried out in a loud voice:

"Salvation belongs to our God,
who sits on the throne,
and to the Lamb."

11All the angels were standing around the
throne and around the elders and the four living creatures. They fell down on their faces before the throne and worshiped God, 12saying:

"Amen!

[a]6 Greek *a choinix* (probably about a liter) [b]6 Greek *a denarius*

Praise and glory
and wisdom and thanks and honor
and power and strength
be to our God for ever and ever.
Amen!"

13 Then one of the elders
asked me, "These in white robes
—who are they, and where did
they come from?"
14 I answered, "Sir, you
know."
And he said, "These are they
who have come out of the great
tribulation; they have washed
their robes and made them
white in the blood of the Lamb.
15 Therefore,

"they are before the throne
of God
and serve him day and
night in his temple;
and he who sits on the throne will spread
his tent over them.
16 Never again will they hunger;
never again will they thirst.
The sun will not beat upon them,
nor any scorching heat.
17 For the Lamb at the center of the throne
will be their shepherd;
he will lead them to springs of living
water.
And God will wipe away every tear from
their eyes."

Revelation 7:12

God Deserves Praise

"Praise and glory and wisdom and thanks and honor and power and strength be to our God for ever and ever."

The Seventh Seal and the Golden Censer

8 When he opened the seventh seal, there
was silence in heaven for about half
an hour.
2 And I saw the seven angels who stand before
God, and to them were given seven trumpets.
3 Another angel, who had a golden censer,
came and stood at the altar. He was given much
incense to offer, with the prayers of all the
saints, on the golden altar before the throne.
4 The smoke of the incense, together with the
prayers of the saints, went up before God from
the angel's hand. 5 Then the angel took the
censer, filled it with fire from the altar, and
hurled it on the earth; and there came peals of
thunder, rumblings, flashes of lightning and
an earthquake.

The Trumpets

6 Then the seven angels who had the seven
trumpets prepared to sound them.
7 The first angel sounded his
trumpet, and there came hail
and fire mixed with blood, and
it was hurled down upon the
earth. A third of the earth was
burned up, a third of the trees
were burned up, and all the
green grass was burned up.
8 The second angel sounded
his trumpet, and something
like a huge mountain, all
ablaze, was thrown into the
sea. A third of the sea turned
into blood, 9 a third of the living creatures in the sea died,
and a third of the ships were
destroyed.
10 The third angel sounded his trumpet, and
a great star, blazing like a torch, fell from the
sky on a third of the rivers and on the springs
of water— 11 the name of the star is Wormwood.[a] A third of the waters turned bitter, and
many people died from the waters that had become bitter.
12 The fourth angel sounded his trumpet,
and a third of the sun was struck, a third of the
moon, and a third of the stars, so that a third of
them turned dark. A third of the day was without light, and also a third of the night.
13 As I watched, I heard an eagle that was flying in midair call out in a loud voice: "Woe!
Woe! Woe to the inhabitants of the earth, because of the trumpet blasts about to be sounded
by the other three angels!"
9 The fifth angel sounded his trumpet, and
I saw a star that had fallen from the sky
to the earth. The star was given the key to the
shaft of the Abyss. 2 When he opened the Abyss,
smoke rose from it like the smoke from a gigantic furnace. The sun and sky were darkened
by the smoke from the Abyss. 3 And out of the
smoke locusts came down upon the earth and
were given power like that of scorpions of the
earth. 4 They were told not to harm the grass of

[a] 11 That is, Bitterness

the earth or any plant or tree, but only those people who did not have the seal of God on their foreheads. 5They were not given power to kill them, but only to torture them for five months. And the agony they suffered was like that of the sting of a scorpion when it strikes a man. 6During those days men will seek death, but will not find it; they will long to die, but death will elude them.

7The locusts looked like horses prepared for battle. On their heads they wore something like crowns of gold, and their faces resembled human faces. 8Their hair was like women's hair, and their teeth were like lions' teeth. 9They had breastplates like breastplates of iron, and the sound of their wings was like the thundering of many horses and chariots rushing into battle. 10They had tails and stings like scorpions, and in their tails they had power to torment people for five months. 11They had as king over them the angel of the Abyss, whose name in Hebrew is Abaddon, and in Greek, Apollyon.[a]

12The first woe is past; two other woes are yet to come.

13The sixth angel sounded his trumpet, and I heard a voice coming from the horns[b] of the golden altar that is before God. 14It said to the sixth angel who had the trumpet, "Release the four angels who are bound at the great river Euphrates." 15And the four angels who had been kept ready for this very hour and day and month and year were released to kill a third of mankind. 16The number of the mounted troops was two hundred million. I heard their number.

17The horses and riders I saw in my vision looked like this: Their breastplates were fiery red, dark blue, and yellow as sulfur. The heads of the horses resembled the heads of lions, and out of their mouths came fire, smoke and sulfur. 18A third of mankind was killed by the three plagues of fire, smoke and sulfur that came out of their mouths. 19The power of the horses was in their mouths and in their tails; for their tails were like snakes, having heads with which they inflict injury.

20The rest of mankind that were not killed by these plagues still did not repent of the work of their hands; they did not stop worshiping demons, and idols of gold, silver, bronze, stone and wood—idols that cannot see or hear or walk. 21Nor did they repent of their murders, their magic arts, their sexual immorality or their thefts.

The Angel and the Little Scroll

10 Then I saw another mighty angel coming down from heaven. He was robed in a cloud, with a rainbow above his head; his face was like the sun, and his legs were like fiery pillars. 2He was holding a little scroll, which lay open in his hand. He planted his right foot on the sea and his left foot on the land, 3and he gave a loud shout like the roar of a lion. When he shouted, the voices of the seven thunders spoke. 4And when the seven thunders spoke, I was about to write; but I heard a voice from heaven say, "Seal up what the seven thunders have said and do not write it down."

5Then the angel I had seen standing on the sea and on the land raised his right hand to heaven. 6And he swore by him who lives for ever and ever, who created the heavens and all that is in them, the earth and all that is in it, and the sea and all that is in it, and said, "There will be no more delay! 7But in the days when the seventh angel is about to sound his trumpet, the mystery of God will be accomplished, just as he announced to his servants the prophets."

8Then the voice that I had heard from heaven spoke to me once more: "Go, take the scroll that lies open in the hand of the angel who is standing on the sea and on the land."

9So I went to the angel and asked him to give me the little scroll. He said to me, "Take it and eat it. It will turn your stomach sour, but in your mouth it will be as sweet as honey." 10I took the little scroll from the angel's hand and ate it. It tasted as sweet as honey in my mouth, but when I had eaten it, my stomach turned sour. 11Then I was told, "You must prophesy again about many peoples, nations, languages and kings."

The Two Witnesses

11 I was given a reed like a measuring rod and was told, "Go and measure the temple of God and the altar, and count the

[a]11 *Abaddon* and *Apollyon* mean *Destroyer.* [b]13 That is, projections

worshipers there. 2But exclude the outer court;
do not measure it, because it has been given to
the Gentiles. They will trample on the holy city
for 42 months. 3And I will give power to my
two witnesses, and they will prophesy for 1,260
days, clothed in sackcloth." 4These are the two
olive trees and the two lampstands that stand
before the Lord of the earth. 5If
anyone tries to harm them, fire
comes from their mouths and
devours their enemies. This
is how anyone who wants to
harm them must die. 6These
men have power to shut up
the sky so that it will not rain
during the time they are prophesying; and they have power
to turn the waters into blood
and to strike the earth with every kind of plague as often as
they want.
7Now when they have fin-
ished their testimony, the
beast that comes up from
the Abyss will attack them,
and overpower and kill them. 8Their bodies
will lie in the street of the great city, which is
figuratively called Sodom and Egypt, where
also their Lord was crucified. 9For three and
a half days men from every people, tribe, language and nation will gaze on their bodies and
refuse them burial. 10The inhabitants of the
earth will gloat over them and will celebrate
by sending each other gifts, because these two
prophets had tormented those who live on
the earth.
11But after the three and a half days a breath
of life from God entered them, and they stood
on their feet, and terror struck those who saw
them. 12Then they heard a loud voice from
heaven saying to them, "Come up here." And
they went up to heaven in a cloud, while their
enemies looked on.
13At that very hour there was a severe earthquake and a tenth of the city collapsed. Seven
thousand people were killed in the earthquake,
and the survivors were terrified and gave glory
to the God of heaven.
14The second woe has passed; the third woe
is coming soon.

> **Revelation 11:17**
>
> *God Reigns Over All*
>
> "We give thanks to you,
> Lord God Almighty,
> the One who is
> and who was,
> because you have taken
> your great power
> and have begun to reign."

The Seventh Trumpet

15The seventh angel sounded his trumpet, and there were loud voices in heaven,
which said:

"The kingdom of the world has become
the kingdom of our Lord and of his
Christ,
and he will reign for ever
and ever."

16And the twenty-four elders,
who were seated on their
thrones before God, fell on
their faces and worshiped God,
17saying:

"We give thanks to
you, Lord God
Almighty,
the One who is and who
was,
because you have taken
your great power
and have begun to reign.
18The nations were angry;
and your wrath has come.
The time has come for judging the dead,
and for rewarding your servants the
prophets
and your saints and those who reverence
your name,
both small and great—
and for destroying those who destroy the
earth."

19Then God's temple in heaven was opened,
and within his temple was seen the ark of his
covenant. And there came flashes of lightning,
rumblings, peals of thunder, an earthquake
and a great hailstorm.

The Woman and the Dragon

12 A great and wondrous sign appeared
in heaven: a woman clothed with the
sun, with the moon under her feet and a crown
of twelve stars on her head. 2She was pregnant
and cried out in pain as she was about to give
birth. 3Then another sign appeared in heaven:
an enormous red dragon with seven heads
and ten horns and seven crowns on his heads.
4His tail swept a third of the stars out of the

sky and flung them to the earth. The dragon
stood in front of the woman who was about to
give birth, so that he might devour her child
the moment it was born. 5She gave birth to
a son, a male child, who will rule all the nations with an iron scepter. And her child was
snatched up to God and to his throne. 6The
woman fled into the desert to a place prepared
for her by God, where she might be taken care
of for 1,260 days.
7And there was war in heaven. Michael and
his angels fought against the dragon, and the
dragon and his angels fought back. 8But he was
not strong enough, and they lost their place in
heaven. 9The great dragon was hurled down—
that ancient serpent called the devil, or Satan,
who leads the whole world astray. He was
hurled to the earth, and his angels with him.
10Then I heard a loud voice in heaven say:

"Now have come the salvation and the
power and the
kingdom of our
God,
and the authority of his
Christ.
For the accuser of our
brothers,
who accuses them
before our God day
and night,
has been hurled down.
11They overcame him
by the blood of the
Lamb
and by the word of their
testimony;
they did not love their lives
so much
as to shrink from death.
12Therefore rejoice, you heavens
and you who dwell in them!
But woe to the earth and the sea,
because the devil has gone down to you!
He is filled with fury,
because he knows that his time is short."

13When the dragon saw that he had been
hurled to the earth, he pursued the woman
who had given birth to the male child. 14The
woman was given the two wings of a great eagle, so that she might fly to the place prepared
for her in the desert, where she would be
taken care of for a time, times and half a time,
out of the serpent's reach. 15Then from his
mouth the serpent spewed water like a river,
to overtake the woman and sweep her away
with the torrent. 16But the earth helped the
woman by opening its mouth and swallowing
the river that the dragon had spewed out of his
mouth. 17Then the dragon was enraged at the
woman and went off to make war against the
rest of her offspring—those who obey God's
commandments and hold to the testimony
13 of Jesus. 1And the dragon[a] stood on
the shore of the sea.

The Beast out of the Sea

And I saw a beast coming out of the sea.
He had ten horns and seven heads, with ten
crowns on his horns, and on each head a blasphemous name. 2The beast I
saw resembled a leopard, but
had feet like those of a bear
and a mouth like that of a lion.
The dragon gave the beast his
power and his throne and great
authority. 3One of the heads
of the beast seemed to have
had a fatal wound, but the fatal
wound had been healed. The
whole world was astonished
and followed the beast. 4Men
worshiped the dragon because
he had given authority to the
beast, and they also worshiped
the beast and asked, "Who is
like the beast? Who can make
war against him?"
5The beast was given a mouth to utter proud
words and blasphemies and to exercise his
authority for forty-two months. 6He opened
his mouth to blaspheme God, and to slander
his name and his dwelling place and those who
live in heaven. 7He was given power to make
war against the saints and to conquer them.
And he was given authority over every tribe,
people, language and nation. 8All inhabitants
of the earth will worship the beast—all whose
names have not been written in the book of life

> **Revelation 12:11**
>
> *God Helps Us Overcome*
>
> "They overcame him
> by the blood of the Lamb
> and by the word of
> their testimony;
> they did not love their
> lives so much
> as to shrink from death."

[a]1 Some late manuscripts *And I*

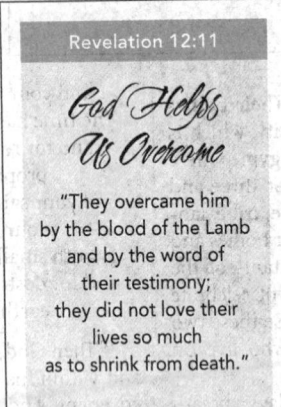

Imperfect Yet Forgiven

Read: Revelation 12:1–17

COMMON WISDOM HOLDS that we should never discuss two topics: religion and politics. Nevertheless, two travelers waiting for a delayed flight began a conversation about religion. One of them was a skeptic who was hostile to Christianity; the other was a timid girl who was undecided about her faith. The skeptic was trying to defend her lack of faith by exposing the evils historically afflicting Christendom: hypocrisy, covetousness, divisiveness and the corruption of well-known religious leaders.

Nearby, a Christian woman sat listening to the conversation. She knew the accusations were true—she had dealt with many of these issues in her own life. Soon, the skeptic loudly extended the circle of her audience and addressed the other travelers sitting nearby, including the Christian lady overhearing the exchange. "I can tell you are quick to condemn evil," the Christian lady replied. "You've just listed the things that make Christians human. I must tell you that I am a Christian and love Jesus. I won't speak a word in our defense since I have committed many of the sins you accuse us of. But I do challenge you to speak a word against Jesus Christ himself."

The skeptic was surprised. She seemed almost frightened as she sheepishly replied, "Well, no! I've read the Bible and I could not find fault with him. Even I know he was perfect." The timid girl looked at the Christian woman and smiled.

One of Satan's greatest tactics is to accuse believers. And most of his accusations are true. We *do* sin—we all fall short of the glory of God. The accuser of the Christian community doesn't have to look far to find accusations to hold against us.

Jesus overcame Satan at the cross and will one day hurl him into the lake of fire at the end of time. But today his accusations against believers carry no weight with God because our sins have been forgiven. As John tells us in the book of Revelation, the accuser was overcome by "the blood of the Lamb."

So the next time Satan or his minions accuse you of sin, don't grow defensive. Simply say, "You're right . . . but, hallelujah, I'm forgiven!"

Wednesday

Go to page 1535 for your next devotional reading.

Revelation 12:10–11

"For the accuser of our brothers, who accuses them before our God day and night, has been hurled down. They overcame him by the blood of the Lamb and by the word of their testimony; they did not love their lives so much as to shrink from death."

reflection

1 Do you grow defensive when someone accuses you of sin?

2 Based on your knowledge of Scripture, what tactics does Satan use to try to make you an ineffective Christian?

3 Spend some time thanking God for overcoming Satan. Ask him to give you strength to overcome and to be a good witness to those you encounter.

RELATED READINGS

Romans 16:20; James 4:7–10; 1 Peter 5:8–10

"Nothing in this world bears the impress of the Son of God so surely as forgiveness."

Alice Cary

belonging to the Lamb that was slain from the
creation of the world.[a]
9 He who has an ear, let him hear.

10 If anyone is to go into captivity,
into captivity he will go.
If anyone is to be killed[b] with the sword,
with the sword he will be killed.

This calls for patient endurance and faithfulness on the part of the saints.

The Beast out of the Earth

11 Then I saw another beast, coming out of
the earth. He had two horns like a lamb, but
he spoke like a dragon. 12 He exercised all the
authority of the first beast on his behalf, and
made the earth and its inhabitants worship the
first beast, whose fatal wound had been healed.
13 And he performed great and miraculous
signs, even causing fire to come down from
heaven to earth in full view of men. 14 Because
of the signs he was given power to do on behalf
of the first beast, he deceived the inhabitants of
the earth. He ordered them to set up an image
in honor of the beast who was wounded by the
sword and yet lived. 15 He was given power to
give breath to the image of the first beast, so
that it could speak and cause all who refused to
worship the image to be killed. 16 He also forced
everyone, small and great, rich and poor, free
and slave, to receive a mark on his right hand
or on his forehead, 17 so that no one could buy
or sell unless he had the mark, which is the
name of the beast or the number of his name.
18 This calls for wisdom. If anyone has insight, let him calculate the number of the beast,
for it is man's number. His number is 666.

The Lamb and the 144,000

14 Then I looked, and there before me
was the Lamb, standing on Mount
Zion, and with him 144,000 who had his name
and his Father's name written on their foreheads. 2 And I heard a sound from heaven like
the roar of rushing waters and like a loud peal
of thunder. The sound I heard was like that of
harpists playing their harps. 3 And they sang
a new song before the throne and before the
four living creatures and the elders. No one
could learn the song except the 144,000 who
had been redeemed from the earth. 4 These
are those who did not defile themselves with
women, for they kept themselves pure. They
follow the Lamb wherever he goes. They were
purchased from among men and offered as
firstfruits to God and the Lamb. 5 No lie was
found in their mouths; they are blameless.

The Three Angels

6 Then I saw another angel flying in midair,
and he had the eternal gospel to proclaim to
those who live on the earth—to every nation,
tribe, language and people. 7 He said in a loud
voice, "Fear God and give him glory, because
the hour of his judgment has come. Worship
him who made the heavens, the earth, the sea
and the springs of water."
8 A second angel followed and said, "Fallen!
Fallen is Babylon the Great, which made all the
nations drink the maddening wine of her adulteries."
9 A third angel followed them and said in a
loud voice: "If anyone worships the beast and
his image and receives his mark on the forehead or on the hand, 10 he, too, will drink of the
wine of God's fury, which has been poured full
strength into the cup of his wrath. He will be
tormented with burning sulfur in the presence
of the holy angels and of the Lamb. 11 And the
smoke of their torment rises for ever and ever.
There is no rest day or night for those who worship the beast and his image, or for anyone who
receives the mark of his name." 12 This calls for
patient endurance on the part of the saints who
obey God's commandments and remain faithful to Jesus.
13 Then I heard a voice from heaven say,
"Write: Blessed are the dead who die in the
Lord from now on."
"Yes," says the Spirit, "they will rest from
their labor, for their deeds will follow them."

The Harvest of the Earth

14 I looked, and there before me was a white
cloud, and seated on the cloud was one "like a
son of man"[c] with a crown of gold on his head
and a sharp sickle in his hand. 15 Then another
angel came out of the temple and called in a

[a] 8 Or *written from the creation of the world in the book of life belonging to the Lamb that was slain* [b] 10 Some manuscripts *anyone kills*
[c] 14 Daniel 7:13

loud voice to him who was sitting on the cloud,
"Take your sickle and reap, because the time
to reap has come, for the harvest of the earth
is ripe." [16]So he who was seated on the cloud
swung his sickle over the earth, and the earth
was harvested.
[17]Another angel came out of the temple in
heaven, and he too had a sharp sickle. [18]Still
another angel, who had charge of the fire, came
from the altar and called in a loud voice to him
who had the sharp sickle, "Take your sharp
sickle and gather the clusters of grapes from the
earth's vine, because its grapes are ripe." [19]The
angel swung his sickle on the earth, gathered its
grapes and threw them into the great winepress
of God's wrath. [20]They were trampled in the
winepress outside the city, and blood flowed
out of the press, rising as high as the horses'
bridles for a distance of 1,600 stadia.[a]

Seven Angels With Seven Plagues

15 I saw in heaven another great and marvelous sign: seven angels with the seven
last plagues—last, because with them God's
wrath is completed. [2]And I saw what looked
like a sea of glass mixed with fire and, standing
beside the sea, those who had been victorious
over the beast and his image and over the number of his name. They held harps given them by
God [3]and sang the song of Moses the servant
of God and the song of the Lamb:

"Great and marvelous are
your deeds,
Lord God Almighty.
Just and true are your ways,
King of the ages.
[4]Who will not fear you,
O Lord,
and bring glory to your
name?
For you alone are holy.
All nations will come
and worship before you,
for your righteous acts have
been revealed."

[5]After this I looked and in heaven the temple, that is, the tabernacle of the Testimony, was
opened. [6]Out of the temple came the seven angels with the seven plagues. They were dressed
in clean, shining linen and wore golden sashes
around their chests. [7]Then one of the four living creatures gave to the seven angels seven
golden bowls filled with the wrath of God, who
lives for ever and ever. [8]And the temple was
filled with smoke from the glory of God and
from his power, and no one could enter the temple until the seven plagues of the seven angels
were completed.

The Seven Bowls of God's Wrath

16 Then I heard a loud voice from the
temple saying to the seven angels,
"Go, pour out the seven bowls of God's wrath
on the earth."
[2]The first angel went and poured out his
bowl on the land, and ugly and painful sores
broke out on the people who had the mark of
the beast and worshiped his image.
[3]The second angel poured out his bowl on
the sea, and it turned into blood like that of
a dead man, and every living thing in the sea
died.
[4]The third angel poured out his bowl on the
rivers and springs of water, and they became
blood. [5]Then I heard the angel in charge of the
waters say:

"You are just in these judgments,
you who are and who were, the Holy
One,
because you have so judged;
[6]for they have shed the
blood of your saints
and prophets,
and you have given them
blood to drink as
they deserve."

[7]And I heard the altar respond:

"Yes, Lord God Almighty,
true and just are your
judgments."

[8]The fourth angel poured
out his bowl on the sun, and
the sun was given power to
scorch people with fire. [9]They were seared by
the intense heat and they cursed the name of
God, who had control over these plagues, but
they refused to repent and glorify him.

Revelation 15:4

God Is Holy

"Who will not fear you,
O Lord,
and bring glory
to your name?
For you alone are holy."

[a]20 That is, about 180 miles (about 300 kilometers)

10The fifth angel poured out his bowl on the throne of the beast, and his kingdom was plunged into darkness. Men gnawed their tongues in agony 11and cursed the God of heaven because of their pains and their sores, but they refused to repent of what they had done.

12The sixth angel poured out his bowl on the great river Euphrates, and its water was dried up to prepare the way for the kings from the East. 13Then I saw three evil[a] spirits that looked like frogs; they came out of the mouth of the dragon, out of the mouth of the beast and out of the mouth of the false prophet. 14They are spirits of demons performing miraculous signs, and they go out to the kings of the whole world, to gather them for the battle on the great day of God Almighty.

15"Behold, I come like a thief! Blessed is he who stays awake and keeps his clothes with him, so that he may not go naked and be shamefully exposed."

16Then they gathered the kings together to the place that in Hebrew is called Armageddon.

17The seventh angel poured out his bowl into the air, and out of the temple came a loud voice from the throne, saying, "It is done!" 18Then there came flashes of lightning, rumblings, peals of thunder and a severe earthquake. No earthquake like it has ever occurred since man has been on earth, so tremendous was the quake. 19The great city split into three parts, and the cities of the nations collapsed. God remembered Babylon the Great and gave her the cup filled with the wine of the fury of his wrath. 20Every island fled away and the mountains could not be found. 21From the sky huge hailstones of about a hundred pounds each fell upon men. And they cursed God on account of the plague of hail, because the plague was so terrible.

The Woman on the Beast

17 One of the seven angels who had the seven bowls came and said to me, "Come, I will show you the punishment of the great prostitute, who sits on many waters. 2With her the kings of the earth committed adultery and the inhabitants of the earth were intoxicated with the wine of her adulteries."

3Then the angel carried me away in the Spirit into a desert. There I saw a woman sitting on a scarlet beast that was covered with blasphemous names and had seven heads and ten horns. 4The woman was dressed in purple and scarlet, and was glittering with gold, precious stones and pearls. She held a golden cup in her hand, filled with abominable things and the filth of her adulteries. 5This title was written on her forehead:

MYSTERY
BABYLON THE GREAT
THE MOTHER OF PROSTITUTES
AND OF THE ABOMINATIONS OF THE EARTH.

6I saw that the woman was drunk with the blood of the saints, the blood of those who bore testimony to Jesus.

When I saw her, I was greatly astonished. 7Then the angel said to me: "Why are you astonished? I will explain to you the mystery of the woman and of the beast she rides, which has the seven heads and ten horns. 8The beast, which you saw, once was, now is not, and will come up out of the Abyss and go to his destruction. The inhabitants of the earth whose names have not been written in the book of life from the creation of the world will be astonished when they see the beast, because he once was, now is not, and yet will come.

9"This calls for a mind with wisdom. The seven heads are seven hills on which the woman sits. 10They are also seven kings. Five have fallen, one is, the other has not yet come; but when he does come, he must remain for a little while. 11The beast who once was, and now is not, is an eighth king. He belongs to the seven and is going to his destruction.

12"The ten horns you saw are ten kings who have not yet received a kingdom, but who for one hour will receive authority as kings along with the beast. 13They have one purpose and will give their power and authority to the beast. 14They will make war against the Lamb, but the Lamb will overcome them because he is Lord of lords and King of kings—and with him will be his called, chosen and faithful followers."

15Then the angel said to me, "The waters you saw, where the prostitute sits, are peoples,

[a]13 Greek *unclean*

multitudes, nations and languages. 16 The beast
and the ten horns you saw will hate the prostitute. They will bring her to ruin and leave her
naked; they will eat her flesh and burn her with
fire. 17 For God has put it into their hearts to
accomplish his purpose by agreeing to give the
beast their power to rule, until God's words are
fulfilled. 18 The woman you saw is the great city
that rules over the kings of the earth."

The Fall of Babylon

18 After this I saw another angel coming down from heaven. He had great
authority, and the earth was illuminated by his
splendor. 2 With a mighty voice he shouted:

"Fallen! Fallen is Babylon the Great!
She has become a home for demons
and a haunt for every evil[a] spirit,
a haunt for every unclean and detestable bird.
3 For all the nations have drunk
the maddening wine of her adulteries.
The kings of the earth committed adultery with her,
and the merchants of the earth grew rich from her excessive luxuries."

4 Then I heard another voice from heaven
say:

"Come out of her, my people,
so that you will not share in her sins,
so that you will not receive any of her plagues;
5 for her sins are piled up to heaven,
and God has remembered her crimes.
6 Give back to her as she has given;
pay her back double for what she has done.
Mix her a double portion from her own cup.
7 Give her as much torture and grief
as the glory and luxury she gave herself.
In her heart she boasts,
'I sit as queen; I am not a widow,
and I will never mourn.'
8 Therefore in one day her plagues will overtake her:
death, mourning and famine.
She will be consumed by fire,
for mighty is the Lord God who judges her.

9 "When the kings of the earth who committed adultery with her and shared her luxury see
the smoke of her burning, they will weep and
mourn over her. 10 Terrified at her torment,
they will stand far off and cry:

" 'Woe! Woe, O great city,
O Babylon, city of power!
In one hour your doom has come!'

11 "The merchants of the earth will weep
and mourn over her because no one buys their
cargoes any more— 12 cargoes of gold, silver,
precious stones and pearls; fine linen, purple,
silk and scarlet cloth; every sort of citron wood,
and articles of every kind made of ivory, costly
wood, bronze, iron and marble; 13 cargoes of
cinnamon and spice, of incense, myrrh and
frankincense, of wine and olive oil, of fine
flour and wheat; cattle and sheep; horses and
carriages; and bodies and souls of men.
14 "They will say, 'The fruit you longed for is
gone from you. All your riches and splendor
have vanished, never to be recovered.' 15 The
merchants who sold these things and gained
their wealth from her will stand far off, terrified at her torment. They will weep and mourn
16 and cry out:

" 'Woe! Woe, O great city,
dressed in fine linen, purple and scarlet,
and glittering with gold, precious stones and pearls!
17 In one hour such great wealth has been brought to ruin!'

"Every sea captain, and all who travel by ship,
the sailors, and all who earn their living from
the sea, will stand far off. 18 When they see the
smoke of her burning, they will exclaim, 'Was
there ever a city like this great city?' 19 They will
throw dust on their heads, and with weeping
and mourning cry out:

" 'Woe! Woe, O great city,
where all who had ships on the sea
became rich through her wealth!
In one hour she has been brought to ruin!
20 Rejoice over her, O heaven!

[a] 2 Greek *unclean*

Rejoice, saints and apostles and
prophets!
God has judged her for the way she treated
you.'"

21 Then a mighty angel picked up a boulder
the size of a large millstone and threw it into
the sea, and said:

"With such violence
the great city of Babylon will be thrown
down,
never to be found again.
22 The music of harpists and musicians, flute
players and trumpeters,
will never be heard in you again.
No workman of any trade
will ever be found in you again.
The sound of a millstone
will never be heard in you again.
23 The light of a lamp
will never shine in you again.
The voice of bridegroom and bride
will never be heard in you again.
Your merchants were the world's great
men.
By your magic spell all the nations were
led astray.
24 In her was found the blood of prophets and
of the saints,
and of all who have been killed on the
earth."

Hallelujah!

19 After this I heard what sounded like
the roar of a great multitude in heaven
shouting:

"Hallelujah!
Salvation and glory and power belong to
our God,
2 for true and just are his judgments.
He has condemned the great prostitute
who corrupted the earth by her
adulteries.
He has avenged on her the blood of his
servants."

3 And again they shouted:

"Hallelujah!
The smoke from her goes up for ever and
ever."

4 The twenty-four elders and the four living
creatures fell down and worshiped God, who
was seated on the throne. And they cried:

"Amen, Hallelujah!"

5 Then a voice came from the throne, saying:

"Praise our God,
all you his servants,
you who fear him,
both small and great!"

6 Then I heard what sounded like a great multitude, like the roar of rushing waters and like
loud peals of thunder, shouting:

"Hallelujah!
For our Lord God Almighty reigns.
7 Let us rejoice and be glad
and give him glory!
For the wedding of the Lamb has come,
and his bride has made herself ready.
8 Fine linen, bright and clean,
was given her to wear."
(Fine linen stands for the righteous acts of the
saints.)

9 Then the angel said to me, "Write: 'Blessed
are those who are invited to the wedding supper of the Lamb!'" And he added, "These are
the true words of God."
10 At this I fell at his feet to worship him.
But he said to me, "Do not do it! I am a fellow servant with you and with your brothers
who hold to the testimony of Jesus. Worship
God! For the testimony of Jesus is the spirit
of prophecy."

The Rider on the White Horse

11 I saw heaven standing open and there before me was a white horse, whose rider is called
Faithful and True. With justice he judges and
makes war.
12 His eyes are like blazing fire, and
on his head are many crowns. He has a name
written on him that no one knows but he himself.
13 He is dressed in a robe dipped in blood,
and his name is the Word of God.
14 The ar-
mies of heaven were following him, riding on
white horses and dressed in fine linen, white
and clean.
15 Out of his mouth comes a sharp
sword with which to strike down the nations.

The Book of Life

Read: Revelation 20:1–15

THE DAY OF CHRIST will be a great and terrible day. Great for the righteous and terrible for the unrighteous. "In the end that Face which is the delight or the terror of the universe must be turned upon each of us either with one expression or the other."

I'm just grateful that Scripture speaks of that time as only "a day." It may mean the Great Judgment will be swift. After all, there are only two kinds of people in the end: those who say to God, "Thy will be done," and those to whom God says, in the end, "*Thy* will be done." All that are in Hell, choose it.

For all the people who insisted "My will be done!" God will not dissuade. He will no longer strive with them, either by pointing to His glory in creation or by preaching to them from the Gospel. For those who turn their backs on Christ, there is no heaven.

Yes, there is a hell.

It's unthinkable to talk about heaven without at least mentioning hell. Please note I didn't refer to it as "heaven's counterpart." Heaven has no counterpart. It has no opposite. Just as Satan is not God's opposite (for the devil is merely a created being—and a fallen one, at that!), neither does heaven have an opposite. In the vastness of God's infinite as well as cleansed and purified universe, hell may end up being only a speck. A trash heap. A garbage heap . . .

Rather than debate the census figures of heaven and hell, it is simply sufficient to say that hell exists; it's horrible, you don't want to go there, and you want to do everything in your power to keep others from choosing it. Jesus' teaching about hell with its wormwood and gall is meant to strike terror in our hearts, warning us that if heaven is better than we could dream, so hell will be worse than we can imagine.

Hell warns us to seek heaven.
It is its own best deterrent.
— *Joni Eareckson Tada*

Go to page 1537 for your next devotional reading.

Revelation 20:12

And I saw the dead, great and small, standing before the throne, and books were opened. Another book was opened, which is the book of life. The dead were judged according to what they had done as recorded in the books.

reflection

1 How do you know that your name is written in the book of life? If you aren't sure, read Romans 10:9 and talk about it with your pastor.

2 Until the day of the Lord comes, there is time to tell others about Jesus. Who will you share the Good News of the gospel with?

3 Most people don't like to talk about hell. How did this devotional help you understand the warning that hell brings to an unbelieving world?

RELATED READINGS

Matthew 7:13–14;
Luke 16:22–31;
2 Peter 2:4–9; 3:10–17

"He will rule them with an iron scepter."[a] He treads the winepress of the fury of the wrath of God Almighty. 16On his robe and on his thigh he has this name written:

KING OF KINGS AND LORD OF LORDS.

17And I saw an angel standing in the sun, who cried in a loud voice to all the birds flying in midair, "Come, gather together for the great supper of God, 18so that you may eat the flesh of kings, generals, and mighty men, of horses and their riders, and the flesh of all people, free and slave, small and great."

19Then I saw the beast and the kings of the earth and their armies gathered together to make war against the rider on the horse and his army. 20But the beast was captured, and with him the false prophet who had performed the miraculous signs on his behalf. With these signs he had deluded those who had received the mark of the beast and worshiped his image. The two of them were thrown alive into the fiery lake of burning sulfur. 21The rest of them were killed with the sword that came out of the mouth of the rider on the horse, and all the birds gorged themselves on their flesh.

The Thousand Years

20 And I saw an angel coming down out of heaven, having the key to the Abyss and holding in his hand a great chain. 2He seized the dragon, that ancient serpent, who is the devil, or Satan, and bound him for a thousand years. 3He threw him into the Abyss, and locked and sealed it over him, to keep him from deceiving the nations anymore until the thousand years were ended. After that, he must be set free for a short time.

4I saw thrones on which were seated those who had been given authority to judge. And I saw the souls of those who had been beheaded because of their testimony for Jesus and because of the word of God. They had not worshiped the beast or his image and had not received his mark on their foreheads or their hands. They came to life and reigned with Christ a thousand years. 5(The rest of the dead did not come to life until the thousand years were ended.) This is the first resurrection. 6Blessed and holy are those who have part in the first resurrection. The second death has no power over them, but they will be priests of God and of Christ and will reign with him for a thousand years.

Satan's Doom

7When the thousand years are over, Satan will be released from his prison 8and will go out to deceive the nations in the four corners of the earth—Gog and Magog—to gather them for battle. In number they are like the sand on the seashore. 9They marched across the breadth of the earth and surrounded the camp of God's people, the city he loves. But fire came down from heaven and devoured them. 10And the devil, who deceived them, was thrown into the lake of burning sulfur, where the beast and the false prophet had been thrown. They will be tormented day and night for ever and ever.

The Dead Are Judged

11Then I saw a great white throne and him who was seated on it. Earth and sky fled from his presence, and there was no place for them. 12And I saw the dead, great and small, standing before the throne, and books were opened. Another book was opened, which is the book of life. The dead were judged according to what they had done as recorded in the books. 13The sea gave up the dead that were in it, and death and Hades gave up the dead that were in them, and each person was judged according to what he had done. 14Then death and Hades were thrown into the lake of fire. The lake of fire is the second death. 15If anyone's name was not found written in the book of life, he was thrown into the lake of fire.

The New Jerusalem

21 Then I saw a new heaven and a new earth, for the first heaven and the first earth had passed away, and there was no longer any sea. 2I saw the Holy City, the new Jerusalem, coming down out of heaven from God, prepared as a bride beautifully dressed for her husband. 3And I heard a loud voice from the throne saying, "Now the dwelling of God is with men, and he will live with them. They will be his people, and God himself will be with them and be their God. 4He will wipe

[a]15 Psalm 2:9

The Day Death Died

Read: Revelation 21:1–27

HAVE YOU READ the staggering statistics on death? One out of every one people dies! Yet despite the inevitability of death, people desperately try to avoid it. In fact, some are willing to pay a hefty price to prolong their life. Whether it's a year, a month or a day, those who attempt to cheat death go to great lengths. Some resort to cryonics, a technology in which ultra-cold temperatures are used to freeze their bodies so they can be restored at a later time. Celebrities seek the fountain of youth through vitamins, yoga and trendy diets. Yet every day, celebrities and ordinary citizens die. Health nuts and couch potatoes alike fall to the inevitability of death.

The good news is that there is a day coming when death will die. And death's companions—sorrow, tears and pain—will also meet their demise. The apostle John "heard a loud voice from the throne saying '. . . There will be no more death.' " What death did to Jesus is nothing compared to what Jesus did to death. His resurrection brought defeat to our enemies—the enemies of sadness, sin and death. In the future heavenly kingdom, they will have no hold over us.

Revelation 21 reveals that the true fountain of youth is Jesus. He said, "I am the Alpha and the Omega, the Beginning and the End. To him who is thirsty I will give to drink without cost from the spring of the water of life" (verse 6). If you want to cheat death, you must believe in Jesus, who promised, "I am the resurrection and the life. He who believes in me will live, even though he dies" (John 11:25). Knowing that death will die should affect the way you live. You don't need beauty products, exercise regimes or fad diets to add years to your life. Instead, Jesus adds life to your years.

For the believer, death holds no sting and the grave has no victory. Yes, we grieve when we're separated for a time from those we love. But in the face of death, we can be more hopeful than fearful, knowing that death isn't the end; it's the beginning of life ever more.

Revelation 21:4

"He will wipe every tear from their eyes. There will be no more death or mourning or crying or pain, for the old order of things has passed away."

reflection

1 How have you been more fearful than hopeful in the face of death?

2 How does the promise of death's demise give you hope for today?

3 How will you live differently based on the truths in this devotional?

RELATED READINGS

John 11:21–27;
Romans 6:8–10;
1 Corinthians 15:51–58

"In my end is my beginning."

Mary, Queen of Scots

Go to page 1539 for your next devotional reading.

every tear from their eyes. There will be no more death or mourning or crying or pain, for the old order of things has passed away."

5 He who was seated on the throne said, "I am making everything new!" Then he said, "Write this down, for these words are trustworthy and true."

6 He said to me: "It is done. I am the Alpha and the Omega, the Beginning and the End. To him who is thirsty I will give to drink without cost from the spring of the water of life. 7 He who overcomes will inherit all this, and I will be his God and he will be my son. 8 But the cowardly, the unbelieving, the vile, the murderers, the sexually immoral, those who practice magic arts, the idolaters and all liars—their place will be in the fiery lake of burning sulfur. This is the second death."

9 One of the seven angels who had the seven bowls full of the seven last plagues came and said to me, "Come, I will show you the bride, the wife of the Lamb." 10 And he carried me away in the Spirit to a mountain great and high, and showed me the Holy City, Jerusalem, coming down out of heaven from God. 11 It shone with the glory of God, and its brilliance was like that of a very precious jewel, like a jasper, clear as crystal. 12 It had a great, high wall with twelve gates, and with twelve angels at the gates. On the gates were written the names of the twelve tribes of Israel. 13 There were three gates on the east, three on the north, three on the south and three on the west. 14 The wall of the city had twelve foundations, and on them were the names of the twelve apostles of the Lamb.

15 The angel who talked with me had a measuring rod of gold to measure the city, its gates and its walls. 16 The city was laid out like a square, as long as it was wide. He measured the city with the rod and found it to be 12,000 stadia[a] in length, and as wide and high as it is long. 17 He measured its wall and it was 144 cubits[b] thick,[c] by man's measurement, which the angel was using. 18 The wall was made of jasper, and the city of pure gold, as pure as glass. 19 The foundations of the city walls were decorated with every kind of precious stone. The first foundation was jasper, the second sapphire, the third chalcedony, the fourth emerald, 20 the fifth sardonyx, the sixth carnelian, the seventh chrysolite, the eighth beryl, the ninth topaz, the tenth chrysoprase, the eleventh jacinth, and the twelfth amethyst.[d] 21 The twelve gates were twelve pearls, each gate made of a single pearl. The great street of the city was of pure gold, like transparent glass.

22 I did not see a temple in the city, because the Lord God Almighty and the Lamb are its temple. 23 The city does not need the sun or the moon to shine on it, for the glory of God gives it light, and the Lamb is its lamp. 24 The nations will walk by its light, and the kings of the earth will bring their splendor into it. 25 On no day will its gates ever be shut, for there will be no night there. 26 The glory and honor of the nations will be brought into it. 27 Nothing impure will ever enter it, nor will anyone who does what is shameful or deceitful, but only those whose names are written in the Lamb's book of life.

The River of Life

22 Then the angel showed me the river of the water of life, as clear as crystal, flowing from the throne of God and of the Lamb 2 down the middle of the great street of the city. On each side of the river stood the tree of life, bearing twelve crops of fruit, yielding its fruit every month. And the leaves of the tree are for the healing of the nations. 3 No longer will there be any curse. The throne of God and of the Lamb will be in the city, and his servants will serve him. 4 They will see his face, and his name will be on their foreheads. 5 There will be no more night. They will not need the light of a lamp or the light of the sun, for the Lord God will give them light. And they will reign for ever and ever.

6 The angel said to me, "These words are trustworthy and true. The Lord, the God of the spirits of the prophets, sent his angel to show his servants the things that must soon take place."

Jesus Is Coming

7 "Behold, I am coming soon! Blessed is he who keeps the words of the prophecy in this book."

[a] 16 That is, about 1,400 miles (about 2,200 kilometers) [b] 17 That is, about 200 feet (about 65 meters) [c] 17 Or *high* [d] 20 The precise identification of some of these precious stones is uncertain.

Generations

EUNICE

"YOU MUST BE SO PROUD of Timothy." Her neighbor smiled. People were always saying things like that to her. Eunice took the compliments in stride and considered them some of the perks of motherhood.

Yes, she was extremely proud of her son. So much so, she had willingly paid the price of God entrusting her with such a unique gift. How many sunrises had she witnessed after praying through the night for him? Too many to count. She prayed for his personal purity, for his walk with God, for his future ministry and even for his future spouse—as confidently as if she could call her by name.

Thinking back through the years reminded her of her own special times with her godly mother, Lois. "You come from a long line of strong women," she remembered saying to Timothy, as the newborn slept in her arms.

Later, when he was older, she shared with him stories about his grandmother's stalwart faith. His eyes would gleam at the prospect of growing up to be like his hero. He wanted to be just like his grandmother—which was the same wish Eunice had had when she was a young girl.

In the absence of a spiritually strong male figure in Timothy's life, she felt that one of the most important prayers she ever prayed was one for a godly man to intersect Timothy's life. And God did not disappoint. Although Timothy came from two generations of faithful women, Paul was the spiritual father Timothy never had. And with that, Timothy committed to make his mother proud. He would raise the next generation in likewise fashion. How could she be more proud of him?

Although she realized God had his hand on Timothy's life, she likely never expected that his name and example would be included in the history of the early church. To his mother, he was just her little boy.

—Prayer—

Thank you, generous God, for all the blessings of this life and allowing me to enjoy them.

I [Paul] have been reminded of your sincere faith, which first lived in your grandmother Lois and in your mother Eunice and, I am persuaded, now lives in you also.

2 Timothy 1:5

ASSIGNED READING:

Acts 16:1; 2 Timothy 1:5

Weekend

8 I, John, am the one who heard and saw
these things. And when I had heard and seen
them, I fell down to worship at the feet of the angel who had been showing them to me. 9 But he
said to me, "Do not do it! I am a fellow servant
with you and with your brothers the prophets
and of all who keep the words of this book.
Worship God!"
10 Then he told me, "Do not seal up the words
of the prophecy of this book, because the time
is near. 11 Let him who does wrong continue
to do wrong; let him who is
vile continue to be vile; let him
who does right continue to do
right; and let him who is holy
continue to be holy."

12 "Behold, I am coming
soon! My reward is with me,
and I will give to everyone according to what he has done.
13 I am the Alpha and the
Omega, the First and the Last,
the Beginning and the End.
14 "Blessed are those who
wash their robes, that they
may have the right to the tree
of life and may go through the gates into the
city. 15 Outside are the dogs, those who practice
magic arts, the sexually immoral, the murderers, the idolaters and everyone who loves and
practices falsehood.
16 "I, Jesus, have sent my angel to give you[a]
this testimony for the churches. I am the Root
and the Offspring of David, and the bright
Morning Star."

17 The Spirit and the bride say, "Come!" And
let him who hears say, "Come!" Whoever is
thirsty, let him come; and whoever wishes, let
him take the free gift of the water of life.

18 I warn everyone who hears
the words of the prophecy of
this book: If anyone adds anything to them, God will add
to him the plagues described
in this book. 19 And if anyone
takes words away from this
book of prophecy, God will
take away from him his share
in the tree of life and in the
holy city, which are described
in this book.
20 He who testifies to these
things says, "Yes, I am coming
soon."
Amen. Come, Lord Jesus.
21 The grace of the Lord Jesus be with God's
people. Amen.

> **Revelation 22:20**
>
> ***God Is Coming Soon***
>
> He who testifies to these things says, "Yes, I am coming soon." Amen. Come, Lord Jesus.

[a] 16 The Greek is plural.

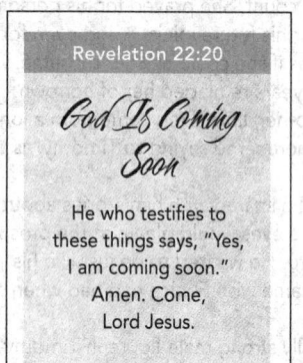

Contents

Table of Weights and Measures

	BIBLICAL UNIT	APPROXIMATE AMERICAN EQUIVALENT	APPROXIMATE METRIC EQUIVALENT
WEIGHTS	talent (60 minas)	75 pounds	34 kilograms
	mina (50 shekels)	1 1/4 pounds	0.6 kilogram
	shekel (2 bekas)	2/5 ounce	11.5 grams
	pim (2/3 shekel)	1/3 ounce	7.6 grams
	beka (10 gerahs)	1/5 ounce	5.5 grams
	gerah	1/50 ounce	0.6 gram
LENGTH	cubit	18 inches	0.5 meter
	span	9 inches	23 centimeters
	handbreadth	3 inches	8 centimeters
CAPACITY			
Dry Measure	cor [homer] (10 ephahs)	6 bushels	220 liters
	lethek (5 ephahs)	3 bushels	110 liters
	ephah (10 omers)	3/5 bushels	22 liters
	seah (1/3 ephah)	7 quarts	7.3 liters
	omer (1/10 ephah)	2 quarts	2 liters
	cab (1/18 ephah)	1 quart	1 liter
Liquid Measure	bath (1 ephah)	6 gallons	22 liters
	hin (1/6 bath)	4 quarts	4 liters
	log (1/72 bath)	1/3 quart	0.3 liter

The figures of the table are calculated on the basis of a shekel equaling 11.5 grams, a cubit equaling 18 inches and an ephah equaling 22 liters. The quart referred to is either a dry quart (slightly larger than a liter) or a liquid quart (slightly smaller than a liter), whichever is applicable. The ton referred to in the footnotes is the American ton of 2,000 pounds. Since most readers are more familiar with dry measures being given in weight rather than capacity (bushel, quart), dry measures have been converted in the footnotes to approximate weights.

This table is based upon the best available information, but it is not intended to be mathematically precise; like the measurement equivalents in the footnotes, it merely gives approximate amounts and distances. Weights and measures differed somewhat at various times and places in the ancient world. There is uncertainty particularly about the ephah and the bath; further discoveries may shed more light on these units of capacity.

One Year Through the Bible

DAY	PASSAGE
January 1	Genesis 1—4
January 2	Genesis 5—8
January 3	Genesis 9—12
January 4	Genesis 13—17
January 5	Genesis 18—20
January 6	Genesis 21—23
January 7	Genesis 24—25
January 8	Genesis 26—28
January 9	Genesis 29—31
January 10	Genesis 32—35
January 11	Genesis 36—38
January 12	Genesis 39—41
January 13	Genesis 42—43
January 14	Genesis 44—46
January 15	Genesis 47—50
January 16	Exodus 1—4
January 17	Exodus 5—7
January 18	Exodus 8—10
January 19	Exodus 11—13
January 20	Exodus 14—16
January 21	Exodus 17—20
January 22	Exodus 21—23
January 23	Exodus 24—27
January 24	Exodus 28—30
January 25	Exodus 31—34
January 26	Exodus 35—37
January 27	Exodus 38—40
January 28	Leviticus 1—4
January 29	Leviticus 5—7
January 30	Leviticus 8—10
January 31	Leviticus 11—13
February 1	Leviticus 14—15
February 2	Leviticus 16—18
February 3	Leviticus 19—21
February 4	Leviticus 22—23
February 5	Leviticus 24—25
February 6	Leviticus 26—27
February 7	Numbers 1—2
February 8	Numbers 3—4
February 9	Numbers 5—6
February 10	Numbers 7
February 11	Numbers 8—10
February 12	Numbers 11—13
February 13	Numbers 14—15
February 14	Numbers 16—18
February 15	Numbers 19—21

DAY	PASSAGE
February 16	Numbers 22—24
February 17	Numbers 25—26
February 18	Numbers 27—29
February 19	Numbers 30—32
February 20	Numbers 33—36
February 21	Deuteronomy 1—2
February 22	Deuteronomy 3—4
February 23......	Deuteronomy 5—8
February 24	Deuteronomy 9—11
February 25	Deuteronomy 12—15
February 26	Deuteronomy 16—19
February 27	Deuteronomy 20—23
February 28	Deuteronomy 24—27
March 1.........	Deuteronomy 28—29
March 2.........	Deuteronomy 30—32
March 3.........	Deuteronomy 33—34
March 4.........	Joshua 1—4
March 5.........	Joshua 5—7
March 6.........	Joshua 8—10
March 7.........	Joshua 11—13
March 8.........	Joshua 14—17
March 9.........	Joshua 18—20
March 10	Joshua 21—22
March 11	Joshua 23—24
March 12	Judges 1—3
March 13	Judges 4—5
March 14	Judges 6—8
March 15	Judges 9—10
March 16	Judges 11—13
March 17	Judges 14—16
March 18	Judges 17—19
March 19	Judges 20—21
March 20	Ruth 1—4
March 21	1 Samuel 1—3
March 22	1 Samuel 4—7
March 23	1 Samuel 8—12
March 24	1 Samuel 13—14
March 25	1 Samuel 15—16
March 26	1 Samuel 17—18
March 27	1 Samuel 19—21
March 28	1 Samuel 22—24
March 29	1 Samuel 25—27
March 30	1 Samuel 28—31
March 31	2 Samuel 1—3
April 1.........	2 Samuel 4—7
April 2.........	2 Samuel 8—11

DAY	PASSAGE
April 3	2 Samuel 12—13
April 4	2 Samuel 14—16
April 5	2 Samuel 17—19
April 6	2 Samuel 20—22
April 7	2 Samuel 23—24
April 8	1 Kings 1—2
April 9	1 Kings 3—5
April 10	1 Kings 6—7
April 11	1 Kings 8—9
April 12	1 Kings 10—12
April 13	1 Kings 13—15
April 14	1 Kings 16—18
April 15	1 Kings 19—20
April 16	1 Kings 21—22
April 17	2 Kings 1—3
April 18	2 Kings 4—5
April 19	2 Kings 6—8
April 20	2 Kings 9—10
April 21	2 Kings 11—13
April 22	2 Kings 14—16
April 23	2 Kings 17—18
April 24	2 Kings 19—21
April 25	2 Kings 22—23
April 26	2 Kings 24—25
April 27	1 Chronicles 1—2
April 28	1 Chronicles 3—4
April 29	1 Chronicles 5—6
April 30	1 Chronicles 7—9
May 1	1 Chronicles 10—12
May 2	1 Chronicles 13—16
May 3	1 Chronicles 17—19
May 4	1 Chronicles 20—23
May 5	1 Chronicles 24—26
May 6	1 Chronicles 27—29
May 7	2 Chronicles 1—4
May 8	2 Chronicles 5—7
May 9	2 Chronicles 8—11
May 10	2 Chronicles 12—16
May 11	2 Chronicles 17—20
May 12	2 Chronicles 21—24
May 13	2 Chronicles 25—28
May 14	2 Chronicles 29—31
May 15	2 Chronicles 32—34
May 16	2 Chronicles 35—36
May 17	Ezra 1—4
May 18	Ezra 5—7
May 19	Ezra 8—10
May 20	Nehemiah 1—3
May 21	Nehemiah 4—7

DAY	PASSAGE
May 22	Nehemiah 8—9
May 23	Nehemiah 10—11
May 24	Nehemiah 12—13
May 25	Esther 1—3
May 26	Esther 4—7
May 27	Esther 8—10
May 28	Job 1—4
May 29	Job 5—8
May 30	Job 9—12
May 31	Job 13—16
June 1	Job 17—20
June 2	Job 21—24
June 3	Job 25—30
June 4	Job 31—34
June 5	Job 35—38
June 6	Job 39—42
June 7	Psalms 1—8
June 8	Psalms 9—17
June 9	Psalms 18—21
June 10	Psalms 22—27
June 11	Psalms 28—33
June 12	Psalms 34—37
June 13	Psalms 38—42
June 14	Psalms 43—49
June 15	Psalms 50—55
June 16	Psalms 56—61
June 17	Psalms 62—68
June 18	Psalms 69—72
June 19	Psalms 73—77
June 20	Psalms 78—80
June 21	Psalms 81—88
June 22	Psalms 89—94
June 23	Psalms 95—103
June 24	Psalms 104—106
June 25	Psalms 107—111
June 26	Psalms 112—118
June 27	Psalm 119
June 28	Psalms 120—133
June 29	Psalms 134—140
June 30	Psalms 141—150
July 1	Proverbs 1—3
July 2	Proverbs 4—7
July 3	Proverbs 8—11
July 4	Proverbs 12—14
July 5	Proverbs 15—17
July 6	Proverbs 18—20
July 7	Proverbs 21—23
July 8	Proverbs 24—26
July 9	Proverbs 27—29

DAY	PASSAGE
July 10	Proverbs 30—31
July 11	Ecclesiastes 1—4
July 12	Ecclesiastes 5—8
July 13	Ecclesiastes 9—12
July 14	Song of Songs 1—4
July 15	Song of Songs 5—8
July 16	Isaiah 1—3
July 17	Isaiah 4—8
July 18	Isaiah 9—11
July 19	Isaiah 12—14
July 20	Isaiah 15—19
July 21	Isaiah 20—24
July 22	Isaiah 25—28
July 23	Isaiah 29—31
July 24	Isaiah 32—34
July 25	Isaiah 35—37
July 26	Isaiah 38—40
July 27	Isaiah 41—43
July 28	Isaiah 44—46
July 29	Isaiah 47—49
July 30	Isaiah 50—52
July 31	Isaiah 53—56
August 1	Isaiah 57—59
August 2	Isaiah 60—63
August 3	Isaiah 64—66
August 4	Jeremiah 1—3
August 5	Jeremiah 4—5
August 6	Jeremiah 6—8
August 7	Jeremiah 9—11
August 8	Jeremiah 12—14
August 9	Jeremiah 15—17
August 10	Jeremiah 18—21
August 11	Jeremiah 22—24
August 12	Jeremiah 25—27
August 13	Jeremiah 28—30
August 14	Jeremiah 31—33
August 15	Jeremiah 34—36
August 16	Jeremiah 37—39
August 17	Jeremiah 40—43
August 18	Jeremiah 44—46
August 19	Jeremiah 47—48
August 20	Jeremiah 49
August 21	Jeremiah 50
August 22	Jeremiah 51—52
August 23	Lamentations 1—2
August 24	Lamentations 3—5
August 25	Ezekiel 1—4
August 26	Ezekiel 5—8
August 27	Ezekiel 9—12

DAY	PASSAGE
August 28	Ezekiel 13—15
August 29	Ezekiel 16—17
August 30	Ezekiel 18—20
August 31	Ezekiel 21—22
September 1	Ezekiel 23—24
September 2	Ezekiel 25—27
September 3	Ezekiel 28—30
September 4	Ezekiel 31—32
September 5	Ezekiel 33—35
September 6	Ezekiel 36—38
September 7	Ezekiel 39—40
September 8	Ezekiel 41—43
September 9	Ezekiel 44—46
September 10	Ezekiel 47—48
September 11	Daniel 1—3
September 12	Daniel 4—5
September 13	Daniel 6—8
September 14	Daniel 9—12
September 15	Hosea 1—4
September 16	Hosea 5—9
September 17	Hosea 10—14
September 18	Joel 1—3
September 19	Amos 1—4
September 20	Amos 5—9
September 21	Obadiah and Jonah
September 22	Micah 1—4
September 23	Micah 5—7
September 24	Nahum 1—3
September 25	Habakkuk 1—3
September 26	Zephaniah 1—3
September 27	Haggai
September 28	Zechariah 1—5
September 29	Zechariah 6—10
September 30	Zechariah 11—14
October 1	Malachi 1—4
October 2	Matthew 1—4
October 3	Matthew 5—6
October 4	Matthew 7—9
October 5	Matthew 10—11
October 6	Matthew 12—13
October 7	Matthew 14—17
October 8	Matthew 18—20
October 9	Matthew 21—22
October 10	Matthew 23—24
October 11	Matthew 25—26
October 12	Matthew 27—28
October 13	Mark 1—3
October 14	Mark 4—5
October 15	Mark 6—7

DAY	PASSAGE
October 16	Mark 8—9
October 17	Mark 10—11
October 18	Mark 12—13
October 19	Mark 14
October 20	Mark 15—16
October 21	Luke 1—2
October 22	Luke 3—4
October 23	Luke 5—6
October 24	Luke 7—8
October 25	Luke 9—10
October 26	Luke 11—12
October 27	Luke 13—15
October 28	Luke 16—18
October 29	Luke 19—20
October 30	Luke 21—22
October 31	Luke 23—24
November 1	John 1—2
November 2	John 3—4
November 3	John 5—6
November 4	John 7—8
November 5	John 9—10
November 6	John 11—12
November 7	John 13—15
November 8	John 16—17
November 9	John 18—19
November 10	John 20—21
November 11	Acts 1—3
November 12	Acts 4—5
November 13	Acts 6—7
November 14	Acts 8—9
November 15	Acts 10—11
November 16	Acts 12—13
November 17	Acts 14—15
November 18	Acts 16—17
November 19	Acts 18—19
November 20	Acts 20—21
November 21	Acts 22—23
November 22	Acts 24—26
November 23	Acts 27—28

DAY	PASSAGE
November 24	Romans 1—3
November 25	Romans 4—7
November 26	Romans 8—10
November 27	Romans 11—14
November 28	Romans 15—16
November 29	1 Corinthians 1—4
November 30	1 Corinthians 5—9
December 1	1 Corinthians 10—13
December 2	1 Corinthians 14—16
December 3	2 Corinthians 1—4
December 4	2 Corinthians 5—9
December 5	2 Corinthians 10—13
December 6	Galatians 1—3
December 7	Galatians 4—6
December 8	Ephesians 1—6
December 9	Philippians 1—4
December 10	Colossians 1—4
December 11	1 Thessalonians 1—5
December 12	2 Thessalonians 1—3
December 13	1 Timothy 1—6
December 14	2 Timothy 1—4
December 15	Titus and Philemon
December 16	Hebrews 1—4
December 17	Hebrews 5—8
December 18	Hebrews 9—10
December 19	Hebrews 11—13
December 20	James 1—5
December 21	1 Peter 1—5
December 22	2 Peter 1—3
December 23	1 John 1—5
December 24	2, 3 John, Jude
December 25	Revelation 1—3
December 26	Revelation 4—7
December 27	Revelation 8—11
December 28	Revelation 12—14
December 29	Revelation 15—17
December 30	Revelation 18—19
December 31	Revelation 20—22

60-Day Overview of the Bible

DAY	THEME	PASSAGE
☐	In the Beginning	Genesis 1:1—2:25
☐	Sin Enters the Picture	Genesis 3:1–24
☐	Water, Water Everywhere	Genesis 6:1—9:29
☐	God's Promise to Abraham	Genesis 12:1—18:15; 20:1—22:19
☐	Goodbye, Sodom and Gomorrah	Genesis 18:16—19:29
☐	Isaac Loves Rebekah	Genesis 24:1–67
☐	Between Brothers	Genesis 25:19–34; 27:1—33:20
☐	Joseph's Egyptian Adventure	Genesis 37:1–36; 39:1—50:26
☐	A Man Named Moses	Exodus 1:1—7:7
☐	Escape From Egypt	Exodus 7:8—14:31
☐	Life in the Wilderness	Exodus 15:22—18:27
☐	Ten Commandments	Exodus 19:1–21
☐	Calf Worship	Exodus 32:1–35
☐	Assignment From God	Exodus 33:1—40:38
☐	Moses Loses His Cool—and a Lot More	Numbers 20:1–13
☐	Joshua Takes Command	Joshua 1:1—6:27
☐	Destination: Promised Land	Joshua 8:1—12:24
☐	Gideon, the Reluctant Leader	Judges 6:1—8:35
☐	The Weak Strong Man	Judges 13:1—16:31
☐	Calling Samuel	1 Samuel 1:1—3:21
☐	Israel Gets Its King	1 Samuel 8:1—11:15
☐	Rejected	1 Samuel 15:1—16:23
☐	David Versus Goliath	1 Samuel 17:1–58
☐	King David	2 Samuel 1:1—8:14
☐	Wise Guy	1 Kings 1:1—4:34
☐	Building the Temple	1 Kings 5:1—8:66
☐	Elijah and the Battle Royale	1 Kings 17:1—19:18
☐	The Exile of Israel	2 Kings 17:1–41
☐	The Fall of Jerusalem	2 Kings 25:1–30
☐	Return to Jerusalem	Ezra 1:1—8:36
☐	Rebuilding the Walls	Nehemiah 1:1—7:3
☐	Esther Saves Her People	Esther 2:1—8:17
☐	Job, the Noble Sufferer	Job 1:1—2:10; 42:1–17
☐	The Shepherd's Psalm	Psalm 23:1–6
☐	A Prayer of Forgiveness	Psalm 51:1–19
☐	The Coming Messiah	Isaiah 52:13—53:12
☐	A Night in the Lions' Den	Daniel 6:1–28
☐	The Ultimate Fish Story	Jonah 1:1—4:11
☐	The First Christmas	Matthew 1:18—2:23; Luke 2:1–52
☐	The Sermon on the Mount	Matthew 5:1—7:29
☐	Miracle After Miracle	Matthew 8:1—9:38; Mark 5:1—6:56
☐	Parable After Parable	Matthew 13:1–58; 18:1–35; 21:28—25:46
☐	The Lord's Prayer	Luke 11:1–13
☐	The Raising of Lazarus	John 11:1–44

DAY	THEME	PASSAGE
☐	The Passion of the Christ	John 18:1—19:42
☐	He Lives!	John 20:1—21:25
☐	Welcome, Holy Spirit	Acts 2:1–47
☐	The First Martyr	Acts 6:8—7:60
☐	Saul Sees the Light	Acts 9:1–31
☐	Good News for Gentiles	Acts 10:1—11:18
☐	Hit the Road, Paul	Acts 13:1—28:31
☐	Sin and Salvation	Romans 2:1—8:39
☐	Love Is	1 Corinthians 13:1–13
☐	Arm Yourself	Ephesians 6:10–20
☐	Jesus Is Coming	1 Thessalonians 4:13—5:11
☐	The Faith Hall of Fame	Hebrews 11:1–40
☐	Just Do It	James 1:2–27
☐	Love, Love, Love	1 John 3:11–24
☐	Judgment Day	Revelation 20:1–15
☐	Forever and Ever	Revelation 21:1—22:21

30 Days for Beginning Your Walk With Christ

DAY	DESCRIPTION	PASSAGE
☐	The Fall of Humanity	Genesis 3:1–19
☐	A People for God	Genesis 28:10–15; 32:22–28
☐	The Ten Commandments	Exodus 20:1–17
☐	Sacrifices Required Under Law	Leviticus 5:14–19
☐	Punishments for Sin Under Law	Leviticus 20:7–27
☐	Obedience From Love	Deuteronomy 11:13–21
☐	Cycles of Disobedience	Judges 2:10–19
☐	The People Demand a King	1 Samuel 8:1–22
☐	Saul Fails and Is Rejected	1 Samuel 15:17–23
☐	Many Kings Fail	Jeremiah 1—17
☐	The Sin of the People	Ezekiel 20:5–26
☐	An Eternal King Promised	Jeremiah 23:1–6; Isaiah 9:6–7; Zechariah 9:9–10
☐	The Promised King Is Born	Luke 2:1–20
☐	The Word Became Flesh	John 1:1–18
☐	Signs and Miracles of Authority	Matthew 9:1–8; Luke 13:10–17
☐	Jesus Fulfills the Law	Matthew 5:17–20; Romans 8:1–4
☐	Jesus Teaches About New Life	John 3:1–36
☐	Jesus Willingly Taken	John 18:1–11
☐	Jesus' Death and Resurrection	Luke 23:44—24:12
☐	Christ a Sacrifice for All	Hebrews
☐	God's Wrath Explained	Romans 1:18–32
☐	God's Judgment Explained	Romans 2:5–11
☐	Righteousness by Faith	Romans 3:9–26
☐	Life Through Christ	Romans 5:12–21
☐	Life by the Spirit	Romans 8:1–17; Galatians 5:16–26
☐	Living Sacrifices	Romans 12:1–21
☐	Walking in the Light	1 John 1—2
☐	Living for God	1 Peter 1–11
☐	Love for One Another	1 John 3:11–24
☐	Promise of Eternity	2 Corinthians 5:1–10; Revelation 21:1–4

30 Days With Jesus

DAY	DESCRIPTION	PASSAGE
☐	Jesus' coming is predicted.	Isaiah 7:14; 9:1–9; Luke 1:26–38
☐	Jesus is born.	Matthew 1:18—2:23; Luke 2:1–20
☐	Jesus is baptized by John the Baptist.	Matthew 3:1–17
☐	Jesus begins his public ministry.	Matthew 4:1–17; Luke 4:14–44
☐	Jesus calls his disciples.	Luke 5:1–11; 6:12–16; John 1:35–51
☐	Jesus talks to a Pharisee and a Samaritan.	John 3:1—4:42
☐	Jesus delivers the Sermon on the Mount.	Matthew 5:1—7:29
☐	Jesus heals people in need.	Matthew 8:1—9:8
☐	Jesus tangles with the Pharisees.	Matthew 12:1–45
☐	Jesus teaches his disciples using parables.	Matthew 13:1–52
☐	Jesus demonstrates his power over nature.	Mark 6:45–52; Luke 8:22–25
☐	Jesus heals many.	Mark 5:1–43
☐	Jesus feeds 5,000 followers.	John 6:1–15
☐	Jesus is identified as the Christ.	Matthew 16:13—17:13
☐	Jesus casts out an evil spirit.	Mark 9:14–32
☐	Jesus teaches on forgiveness.	Matthew 18:15–35
☐	Jesus teaches on the kingdom of heaven.	Matthew 13:24–52
☐	Jesus confronts the rich young man.	Mark 10:17–31
☐	Jesus sends out his disciples.	Luke 10:1–24
☐	Jesus teaches how to love and pray.	Luke 10:25—11:13
☐	Jesus teaches about himself.	John 10:1–42
☐	Jesus raises Lazarus from the dead.	John 11:1–44
☐	Jesus travels to Jerusalem.	Matthew 21:1–27
☐	Jesus eats the Last Supper.	Matthew 26:17–30; John 13:1–17
☐	Jesus comforts his disciples.	John 14:1—16:33
☐	Jesus is arrested.	Matthew 26:36–75
☐	Jesus is put on trial.	John 18:19—19:16
☐	Jesus is crucified and buried.	John 19:17–42
☐	Jesus rises from the dead.	John 20:1—21:25
☐	Jesus ascends to heaven.	Matthew 28:16–20; Luke 24:36–53

30 Days in the Psalms

DAY	DESCRIPTION	PASSAGE
☐	Blessing	Psalms 67, 72, 84, 128
☐	Calling to God	Psalms 4, 5, 22
☐	Confidence	Psalms 27, 36, 71, 125
☐	Deeds of God	Psalms 9, 18, 118
☐	Doubt	Psalms 42, 73, 77
☐	Faithfulness of God	Psalms 105, 119:137–144, 146
☐	Fear	Psalms 37, 49, 91
☐	Glory of God	Psalms 19, 24, 29
☐	God Is a Helper	Psalms 54, 115, 119:169–176
☐	Identity	Psalms 8, 139
☐	Justice of God	Psalms 7, 26, 82
☐	Meditation	Psalms 119:9–16, 41–48
☐	Mercy	Psalms 13, 28, 86
☐	Music	Psalms 6, 149, 150
☐	Nature	Psalms 50, 104, 147, 148
☐	Peace	Psalms 23, 133, 119:161–168
☐	Power of God	Psalms 68, 93, 135
☐	Praise	Psalms 65, 98, 138
☐	Prayer	Psalms 17, 20, 102
☐	Protection	Psalms 59, 62, 124
☐	Safety in God	Psalms 11, 16, 142, 46
☐	Rejoicing	Psalms 30, 47, 97
☐	Righteousness	Psalms 1, 15, 112
☐	Salvation	Psalms 3, 14, 121
☐	Sin and Repentance	Psalms 25, 32, 38, 51
☐	Thanksgiving	Psalms 75, 106, 136
☐	Trust	Psalms 31, 40, 56
☐	Victory	Psalms 21, 76, 144
☐	Wisdom	Psalms 90, 107, 111
☐	Worship	Psalms 33, 34, 145

30 Days in Proverbs

DAY	PASSAGE
☐	Proverbs 1
☐	Proverbs 2
☐	Proverbs 3
☐	Proverbs 4
☐	Proverbs 5
☐	Proverbs 6
☐	Proverbs 7
☐	Proverbs 8
☐	Proverbs 9
☐	Proverbs 10
☐	Proverbs 11
☐	Proverbs 12
☐	Proverbs 13
☐	Proverbs 14
☐	Proverbs 15
☐	Proverbs 16
☐	Proverbs 17
☐	Proverbs 18
☐	Proverbs 19
☐	Proverbs 20
☐	Proverbs 21
☐	Proverbs 22
☐	Proverbs 23
☐	Proverbs 24
☐	Proverbs 25
☐	Proverbs 26
☐	Proverbs 27
☐	Proverbs 28
☐	Proverbs 29
☐	Proverbs 30–31

20 Not-So-Famous Bible Stories

DAY	DESCRIPTION	PASSAGE
☐	Fire and Birds: God Lays Down the Law	Numbers 11
☐	Miriam: Leprous as Snow	Numbers 12
☐	Korah, Dathan and Abiran: Gulp!	Numbers 16
☐	Aaron: A Budding Leader	Numbers 17
☐	Moses Strikes Out	Numbers 20:1–13
☐	Afraid of Snakes?	Numbers 21:4–9
☐	Balaam's . . . er, Donkey	Numbers 22—24
☐	Laws for a Special People in a Special Time	Deuteronomy 21
☐	Moses: End of an Era	Deuteronomy 31; 32:44–52; 34
☐	Solar Stand Still	Joshua 10:1–15
☐	Ehud: Left Handed Wonder	Judges 3:12–30
☐	David and Abigail: Wisdom in a Tough Situation	1 Samuel 25
☐	Mephibosheth: Rags to Riches	2 Samuel 9
☐	Elisha: Miracle Man	2 Kings 2:23–25; 4:8–37; 6:1–23
☐	Asa: But if You Forsake Him	2 Chronicles 15; 16
☐	Joash: Kindness Forgotten	2 Chronicles 22:10—23:21; 24
☐	Josiah: Youthful Ruler	2 Chronicles 34—35
☐	Nehemiah: Homesickness	Nehemiah 1—2
☐	Jerusalem Falls: Judgment Arrives	Jeremiah 52
☐	The Writing on the Wall	Daniel 5

30 Days With Paul

DAY	THEME	PASSAGE
☐	Elusive righteousness	Romans 3:9–26
☐	Peace and joy	Romans 5:1–11
☐	Sin and death	Romans 5:12–21
☐	Alive in Christ	Romans 6:1–14
☐	Battle with sin	Romans 7:7–25
☐	Being a conqueror	Romans 8:28–39
☐	A living sacrifice	Romans 12:1–8
☐	Running the race	1 Corinthians 9:19–27
☐	One body	1 Corinthians 12:12–31
☐	Love	1 Corinthians 13:1–13
☐	Resurrection	1 Corinthians 15:12–34
☐	Longing for heaven	2 Corinthians 5:1–10
☐	Christian hardships	2 Corinthians 6:3–13
☐	Weakness	2 Corinthians 12:1–10
☐	Christian freedom	Galatians 5:1–15
☐	Fruit of the Spirit	Galatians 5:16–26
☐	Incomparable grace	Ephesians 2:1–10
☐	Christian unity	Ephesians 4:1–16
☐	People of light	Ephesians 4:17—5:21
☐	Family dynamics	Ephesians 5:22—6:4
☐	Armor of God	Ephesians 6:10–20
☐	Imitating Jesus	Philippians 2:1–11
☐	Reaching the ultimate goal	Philippians 3:12—4:1
☐	Christ the head	Colossians 1:15–23
☐	Pleasing God	1 Thessalonians 4:1–12
☐	Jesus is coming	1 Thessalonians 4:13—5:11
☐	Avoiding idleness	2 Thessalonians 3:6–18
☐	Instructions for a young believer	1 Timothy 4:1–16
☐	Money	1 Timothy 6:3–10
☐	Staying strong	2 Timothy 3:10—4:8

30 Days of Promises

DAY	THEME	PASSAGE
☐	When you're discouraged	Deuteronomy 31:1–8
☐	When you're looking for direction	Psalm 32:1–11
☐	When you're scared	Psalm 34:1–22
☐	When you're facing troubling circumstances	Psalm 49:1–20
☐	When you're tempted to cut corners	Proverbs 28:1–28
☐	When you need peace of mind	Isaiah 26:1–21
☐	When you're uncertain about the future	Jeremiah 29:4–14
☐	When you don't think you can change	Ezekiel 36:22–32
☐	When you can't let go of a grudge	Matthew 6:5–15
☐	When you've reached the end of your rope	Matthew 11:25–30
☐	When you're feeling cocky	Matthew 23:1–12
☐	When you're tempted to seek revenge	Luke 6:27–36
☐	When you need to reprioritize your life	Luke 12:22–34
☐	When a situation seems hopeless	Luke 18:18–30
☐	When you're facing persecution	Luke 21:8–19
☐	When you're tired of the way you're living	John 8:12–30
☐	When you're questioning your faith	John 10:22–42
☐	When you need a glimpse of eternity	John 14:1–7
☐	When you have a major request of God	John 14:8–14
☐	When you're memorizing Scripture	John 14:25–31
☐	When you're sharing your faith	Romans 10:1–13
☐	When temptation won't let go	1 Corinthians 10:1–13
☐	When you wonder whether you can trust God's promises	2 Corinthians 1:12–22
☐	When Satan targets you	2 Thessalonians 3:1–5
☐	When you're facing a tough decision	James 1:2–18
☐	When you're feeling distant from God	James 4:1–9
☐	When you're trying to get ahead	James 4:10–17
☐	When you need forgiveness	1 John 1:1–9
☐	When you're waiting for an answer to prayer	1 John 5:13–21
☐	When you're overwhelmed by death, sorrow or pain	Revelation 21:1–27

30 Days of Leadership

DAY	THEME	PASSAGE
☐	Responding to an unusual assignment	Genesis 6:1—7:24
☐	Relocating	Genesis 12:1–9
☐	Preparing for lean times	Genesis 41:41–57
☐	Leading an exodus	Exodus 13:17—14:31
☐	Delegating responsibility	Exodus 18:1–27
☐	Dealing with wrongdoers	Exodus 32:1–35
☐	Handling opposition	Numbers 12:1–16
☐	Facing down challengers	Numbers 16:1–50
☐	Motivating followers	Deuteronomy 11:1–32
☐	Appointing a successor	Deuteronomy 31:1–8
☐	Succeeding a legend	Joshua 1:1–18
☐	Identifying cause of failure	Joshua 7:1–26
☐	Saying goodbye	Joshua 23:1–16
☐	Recognizing a call	Judges 6:1–40
☐	Giving a necessary rebuke	1 Samuel 12:1–15
☐	Doing what no one else will	1 Samuel 17:1–54
☐	Mending fences	2 Samuel 9:1–13
☐	Accepting responsibility	2 Samuel 12:1–25
☐	Recognizing what's important	1 Kings 3:1–15
☐	Putting wisdom to use	1 Kings 3:16–28
☐	Tackling a huge project	1 Kings 6:1–14
☐	Avoiding critical mistakes	1 Kings 11:1–39
☐	Learning from the example of a predecessor	1 Kings 15:9–24
☐	Understanding what it means to be first and last	Matthew 19:16–30
☐	Dealing with ambitious subordinates	Mark 10:35–45
☐	Managing shrewdly	Luke 16:1–15
☐	Entering into partnerships	2 Corinthians 6:3–13
☐	Practicing generosity	2 Corinthians 9:6–15
☐	Living a holy life	Colossians 3:1–17
☐	Qualifying for leadership	1 Timothy 3:1–16

30 Days of Prayer

DAY	THEME	PASSAGE
☐	Abraham's plea for Sodom	Genesis 18:16–33
☐	A servant's plea for success	Genesis 24:12–27
☐	The song of Moses and Miriam	Exodus 15:1–18
☐	Moses' desperate request	Deuteronomy 3:23–29
☐	The song of Deborah	Judges 5:1–31
☐	Hannah's rejoicing	1 Samuel 2:1–10
☐	A king's prayer	2 Samuel 7:18–29
☐	David's song of praise	2 Samuel 22:1–51
☐	Solomon's prayer of dedication	1 Kings 8:22–53
☐	A nation's prayer promise	2 Chronicles 7:11–22
☐	Nehemiah's request	Nehemiah 1:5–11
☐	Appreciating God's majesty	Psalm 8:1–9
☐	David's plea for mercy	Psalm 51:1–19
☐	The God who answers prayer	Psalm 65:1–13
☐	A song of praise	Isaiah 26:1–21
☐	Words from a fish's belly	Jonah 2:1–10
☐	The Lord's prayer	Matthew 6:5–15
☐	Jesus' prayer in Gethsemane	Matthew 26:36–46
☐	Asking, seeking and knocking	Luke 11:7–13
☐	Jesus prays for himself	John 17:1–5
☐	Jesus prays for his disciples	John 17:6–19
☐	Jesus prays for all believers	John 17:20–26
☐	Help from the Holy Spirit	Romans 8:18–27
☐	Paul prays for the Ephesian believers	Ephesians 1:15–23
☐	Paul prays for the Colossian believers	Colossians 1:3–14
☐	Paul thanks God for the Thessalonian believers	1 Thessalonians 1:2–10
☐	Paul prays for the Thessalonian believers	2 Thessalonians 1:3–12
☐	Paul requests prayer for himself	2 Thessalonians 3:1–5
☐	Praying for others	1 Timothy 2:1–7
☐	Prayer of faith	James 5:13–20

30 Days of Knowing God

DAY	THEME	PASSAGE
☐	Maker of covenants	Genesis 9:8–17
☐	Thwarter of evil ambition	Genesis 11:1–8
☐	Wrestler	Genesis 32:22–32
☐	Bestower of talents	Genesis 41:1–39
☐	Master of the unexpected	Exodus 3:1–17
☐	Protector of the faithful	Exodus 12:1–30
☐	Caterer par excellence	Exodus 16:1–18
☐	Lawgiver	Exodus 20:1–21
☐	Punisher of rebellion	Numbers 14:1–45
☐	Opener of eyes	Numbers 22:21–41
☐	Initiator of vengeance	Numbers 31:1–24
☐	One and only	Deuteronomy 4:32–40
☐	Sole object of worship	Deuteronomy 13:1–18
☐	Offerer of proof	Judges 6:1–40
☐	Protector of widows	Ruth 4:1–12
☐	Hearer of prayers	1 Samuel 1:1–30
☐	Late night caller	1 Samuel 3:1–21
☐	Rejecter of the unfaithful	1 Samuel 15:1–29
☐	Supporter of the underdog	1 Samuel 17:1–54
☐	Provider of wisdom	1 Kings 3:1–15
☐	Sustainer	1 Kings 17:1–24
☐	Undefeated competitor	1 Kings 18:16–40
☐	Gentle whisperer	1 Kings 19:9–18
☐	Orchestrator of perfect justice	Esther 6:1—7:10
☐	Holder of Satan's reins	Job 1:1–12
☐	Rewarder of faithfulness	Job 42:7–17
☐	Refuge	Psalm 18:1–50
☐	Shepherd	Psalm 23:1–6
☐	Originator of prophecy	Isaiah 53:1–12
☐	Provider of salvation	John 3:1–21

30 Stories of Great Faith

DAY	THEME	PASSAGE
☐	Noah builds an ark.	Genesis 6:1—7:24
☐	Abram moves to a strange land.	Genesis 12:1–20
☐	Abram trusts God's promise.	Genesis 15:1–21
☐	Abraham offers Isaac.	Genesis 22:1–19
☐	Abraham's servant chooses a wife for Isaac.	Genesis 24:1–67
☐	Jacob works 14 years in order to marry Rachel.	Genesis 29:15–30
☐	Joseph flourishes in an Egyptian prison.	Genesis 39:20—40:16
☐	Joseph reveals God's plan to his brothers.	Genesis 45:1–20
☐	Moses' mother trusts God to take care of her baby.	Exodus 2:1–10
☐	Moses reveals himself as an Israelite.	Exodus 2:11–25
☐	Moses and Aaron confront Pharaoh.	Exodus 6:28—7:13
☐	Moses parts the Red Sea.	Exodus 14:5–31
☐	Moses coaxes water from a rock.	Exodus 17:1–7
☐	Caleb recommends invading the promised land.	Numbers 13:26–33
☐	Rahab hides Israelite spies.	Joshua 2:1–24
☐	Joshua defeats the Amorites.	Joshua 10:1–15
☐	Gideon leads his men against the Midianites.	Judges 7:1–25
☐	Ruth accompanies her mother-in-law.	Ruth 1:1–22
☐	Hannah dedicates her son to God's service.	1 Samuel 1:1–28
☐	David confronts Goliath.	1 Samuel 17:1–54
☐	Solomon asks for wisdom.	1 Kings 3:1–15
☐	Elijah challenges the prophets of Baal and Asherah.	1 Kings 18:16–40
☐	Job continues to trust God in the midst of tragedy.	Job 1:6–22
☐	Shadrach, Meshach and Abednego face death.	Daniel 3:1–30
☐	Daniel refuses to give up prayer.	Daniel 6:1–28
☐	Peter walks on water.	Matthew 14:22–36
☐	Mary trusts God.	Luke 1:26–56
☐	Zacchaeus changes his ways.	Luke 19:1–10
☐	Stephen loses his life.	Acts 6:8–15; 7:54–60
☐	Saul meets Christ.	Acts 9:1–31

Acknowledgments

RUTH HALEY BARTON

Devotion found on page 147

Taken from *Invitation to Solitude and Silence* © 2004 by Ruth Haley Barton. Used with permission of InterVarsity Press, PO Box 1400, Downers Grove, IL 60515. www.ivpress.com

KATIE BRAZELTON

Devotion found on page 326

Taken from *Pathway to Purpose for Women* © 2005 by Katherine F. Brazelton. Used by permission of The Zondervan Corporation.

SALLY BREEDLOVE

Devotion found on page 67

Taken from *Choosing Rest* © 2002 by Sally Breedlove. Used by permission of NavPress, Colorado Springs, CO. All rights reserved.

AMY CARMICHAEL

Devotion found on page 1092

Taken from *Thou Givest, They Gather* © 1958, pp 193–195. Used by permission of CLC Publications.

Devotion found on page 259

Taken from *Candles in the Dark* © 1982, pp 41, 43. Used by permission of CLC Publications.

JAN DRAVECKY

Devotion found on page 96

Taken from *Hope for Woman's Soul*, Grand Rapids, Inspiro, 2000, pp 11, 15.

ELISABETH ELLIOT

Devotion found on page 1276

Taken from *God's Guidance* © 1997 by Elisabeth Elliot. Used by permission of Fleming H. Revell, a division of Baker Publishing Group.

LISA HARPER

Devotion found on page 1140

Taken from *Every Woman's Hope: Defined by Grace, Beloved by God* © 2001 by Lisa Harper. Used by permission of Howard Books, a division of Simon & Schuster Adult Publishing Group.

LIZ CURTIS HIGGS

Devotion found on page 1328

Reprinted from *Rise and Shine* © 2002, 2004 by Liz Curtis Higgs. Used by permission of Waterbrook Press, Colorado Springs, CO. All rights reserved.

BARBARA HUGHES

Devotion found on page 1227

Taken from *Devotions for Ministry Wives* © 2002 by Barbara Hughes. Used by permission of The Zondervan Corporation.

CAROLYN CUSTIS JAMES

Devotion found on page 1255

Taken from *When Life and Beliefs Collide* © 2001 by Carolyn C. James. Used by permission of The Zondervan Corporation.

NANCY KENNEDY

Devotion found on page 1077

Taken from *Praying with Women of the Bible* © 2004 by Nancy Kennedy. Used by permission of The Zondervan Corporation.

CAROL KENT

Devotion found on page 1381

Taken from *Kisses of Sunshine for Sisters* © 2005 by Speak Up, Inc. Used by permission of The Zondervan Corporation.

ANNE GRAHAM LOTZ

Devotions found on pages 847, 1309

Taken from *I Saw the Lord* © 2006 by Anne Graham Lotz. Used by permission of The Zondervan Corporation.

PENNY PIERCE ROSE

Devotion found on page 292

Taken from *A Garden of Friends*, Ventura, Regal Books, pp 116–121.

EDITH SCHAEFFER

Devotion found on page 1000

Taken from *The Art of Life* © 1987 by Edith Schaeffer. Used by permission of Crossway Books.

PRISCILLA EVANS SHIRER

Devotion found on page 1394

Taken from *A Jewel in His Crown* © 1999 by Priscilla Evans. Used by permission of Moody Press.

HANNAH WHITALL SMITH

Devotion found on page 1447

Taken from *The God of All Comfort* © 1956 by Hannah Whitall Smith. Used by permission of Moody Press.

LUCI SWINDOLL

Devotion found on page 738

Taken from *The Best Devotions of Luci Swindoll* © 2001 by Women of Faith. Used by permission of The Zondervan Corporation.

JONI EARECKSON TADA

Devotion found on page 1535

Taken from *Heaven: Your Real Home* © 1995 by Joni Eareckson Tada. Used by permission of The Zondervan Corporation.

Devotion found on page 813

Taken from *The God I Love: A Memoir* © 2003 by Joni Eareckson Tada. Used by permission of The Zondervan Corporation.

MOTHER TERESA

Devotion found on page 231

Taken from *Mother Teresa, In the Heart of the World: Thoughts, Stories, & Prayers* © 1997. Used by permission of New World Library.

Additional benediction by Mother Teresa, original source unknown.

CYNTHIA ULRICH TOBIAS

Devotion found on page 1215

Taken from *Redefining the Strong-Willed Woman* © 2002 by Cynthia Ulrich Tobias. Used by permission of The Zondervan Corporation.

SHEILA WALSH

Devotion found on page 316

Taken from *Hope for a Woman's Soul: Meditations to Energize Your Spirit* © 2000 by New Life Clinics. Used by permission of The Zondervan Corporation.

Devotion found on page 379

Taken from *Honestly* © 1996 by Sheila Walsh. Used by permission of The Zondervan Corporation.

THELMA WELLS

Devotion found on page 1381

Taken from *Kisses of Sunshine for Sisters* © 2005 by Speak Up, Inc. Used by permission of The Zondervan Corporation.

CHRISTINE WYRTZEN

Devotion found on page 174

Taken from *Long Live the Child* © 2003 by Christine, Inc. Used by permission of The Zondervan Corporation.

Contributor Biographies

RUTH HALEY BARTON is a spiritual director, teacher and retreat leader. Ruth is co-founder of The Transforming Center providing leadership in the areas of vision, community building, teaching and content development. Ruth has served on the pastoral staff of several churches, including Willow Creek Community Church in South Barrington, Illinois, as associate director of spiritual formation.

SHARON BETTERS is executive director of MARK INC Ministries, a multimedia outreach designed to help turn broken people toward the heart of God. She has authored several books, including *Treasures of Encouragement, Treasures in Darkness, A Grieving Mother Shares Her Heart* and along with her husband, Chuck, *Treasures of Faith*.

JANET CHESTER BLY has authored 11 books and coauthored 18 with her husband, Stephen, both nonfiction and fiction. She writes and speaks on issues of a woman's heart. Her books include *Hope Lives Here* and *The Heart of a Runaway*.

KATIE BRAZELTON currently serves as Director of Women's Bible Studies at Saddleback Church. A licensed minister, Katie has earned a Ph.D. in Human Behavior/Leadership, an M.A. in Theology, an M.A. in Educational Administration, an M.A. in English, and is near completion of her Masters of Divinity. Katie has two adult children and one daughter-in-law.

SALLY BREEDLOVE is a frequent speaker at leadership conferences in North America and abroad. She has spoken to numerous groups, including Women Alive (Canada), Wycliffe Bible Translators (Asia), and Dixie Women (Alabama). Sally has been published in *Decision* magazine and written study notes for *The Women of Faith Study Bible* (Zondervan).

DIANNE E. BUTTS has written for over 50 Christian magazines and a dozen compilation books. Her writing has appeared in Great Britain, Bulgaria, Poland, Canada and Korea. She enjoys riding her motorcycle with her husband, Hal, and gardening with her cat, P. C. The trio lives in Colorado.

AMY CARMICHAEL (1867–1951) was born in Ireland, but spent her life serving the Lord as a missionary in India for 56 years, working with underprivileged children. She is the author of many books including, *God's Missionary* (CLC) and *You Are My Hiding Place* (Bethany House).

SUZIE CROSS markets books for a Christian publisher and has contributed writing for five devotional Bibles, including Zondervan's *True Images* teen Bible. Her writing reflects a mission and desire to help those experiencing pain find the hope and joy of Christ in and beyond their circumstances.

MARLENE DEPLER is a writer, inspirational speaker and "mentor" for young mothers. She has published numerous articles, devotionals, stories and poems in magazines such as *HomeLife, Woman's Touch, The Quiet Hour* and *Mature Living*. Marlene is the mother of three grown children and grandmother of six. She and her husband make their home in Colorado.

JENN DOUCETTE is a freelance writer and humorist who tries to find the funnies in the yuckies of life. She has authored *The Velveteen Mommy—Laughter and Tears from the Toy Box Years*, and coauthored *Live it Real—Devotions for Teens*. The Doucettes make their home in Snohomish, Washington.

JAN DRAVECKY co-founded Outreach of Hope Ministries with her husband, former baseball pitcher Dave Dravecky. She and Dave live in Colorado Springs. With Dave, she is the co-author of *Do Not Lose Heart* and *Stand by Me*.

PAIGE DRYGAS is a teacher, writer and editor who has helped develop Bible products including the *True Identity* and *True Images*. Paige lives outside Chicago with her husband.

CHERYL DUNLOP is the author of *Follow Me as I Follow Christ* and a freelance writer and editor. She loves to minister to children with troubled backgrounds and to explore God's creation.

DENA DYER is a wife, mom, writer and speaker from Texas. She loves to encourage women to find their hope, rest and joy in Jesus—our only true source of peace in the midst of a chaotic world. Her books include *Grace for the Race: Meditations for Busy Moms, The Groovy Chicks' Roadtrip to Peace* and The *Groovy Chicks' Roadtrip to Love.*

ELISABETH ELLIOT is best known for her classic book, *Through the Gates of Splendor* (Tyndale). She and her husband, Jim Elliot, served as missionaries in Ecuador, where Jim was killed by Auca Indians. She is a speaker and bestselling author of numerous other books, including *Passion and Purity* (Baker) and *A Chance to Die* (Baker). Elisabeth now lives with her husband, Lars Gren, in Magnolia, Massachusetts.

PAULA GAMBLE is an international worship leader, songwriter, author and intercultural training specialist with Campus Crusade for Christ, Intl. She is also the founder of *IseetheKing Productions*, which promotes enthusiasm for the King and world mission through Sojourney retreats and recordings.

STACY FRYE GRAVES is a freelance writer, corporate communications expert and former Bible Study Fellowship leader. She lives in Tyler, Texas, with her husband, Glen, and their two young sons, Landry and Luke.

GAYLE GRESHAM lives in Elbert, Colorado, with her husband and their two teenagers. Her articles have appeared in *Today's Christian Woman, The Lookout* and *Christian Standard.*

LISA HARPER was the creator and hostess of Renewing the Heart, Focus on the Family's conference series involving almost 200,000 women. She is the author of several books including *Relentless Love* and *Every Woman's Hope.*

RACHEL HAWKINS is employed at The Livingstone Corporation, located in Carol Stream, IL. She has contributed to the *New Women's Devotional Journal* (Zondervan).

LENYA HEITZIG is the author of *Holy Moments* and coauthor of the award-winning Bible study *Pathway to God's Treasure: Ephesians, Pathway to God's Plan: Ruth and Esther*, and *Pathway to Living Faith: James.* She founded Women at Calvary at Calvary Albuquerque Church and is currently the Women's Ministry Director at Ocean Hills Church in San Juan Capistrano where her husband, Skip Heitzig, is Senior Pastor. She has one son, Nathan.

LIZ CURTIS HIGGS is the author of 23 books, including her nonfiction bestseller *Bad Girls of the Bible* (Random House) and her fiction bestseller *Thorn in My Heart (Random House).* Her children's Parable Series was awarded the ECPA Gold Medallion for Excellence in 1998. Liz has also presented more than 1500 inspirational programs for audiences in all 50 United States and 8 foreign countries.

BARBARA HUGHES has many years of experience as a pastor's wife. Married to Kent Hughes, pastor of College Church in Wheaten, Illinois, she is the author of *Disciplines of a Godly Woman* and co-author with her husband of *Liberating Ministry from the Success Syndrome* and *Common Sense Parenting*. She is the mother of four children.

CAROLYN CUSTIS JAMES travels extensively as a popular speaker for women's conferences, churches, colleges, seminaries and other Christian organizations. Her ministry organization, Whitby Forum, promotes thoughtful Biblical discussion to help men and women join forces in serving God together. She is author of *When Life and Beliefs Collide* (Zondervan) and *Lost Women of the Bible* (Zondervan). Carolyn lives in Orlando, Florida, with her husband and daughter.

SHARON JAYNES is a popular speaker at women's events internationally. She is the author of ten books including *Becoming a Woman who Listens to God, Ultimate Makeover, Your Scars are Beautiful to God* and *Becoming the Woman of His Dreams*. Her joy is bringing God's truth to today's woman.

JOAN JONES has served as a freelance consultant with The Livingstone Corporation in Carol Stream, IL. She is active in her church's children's ministry and is the mother of four. Joan lives in the Midwest with her husband and youngest daughter.

DEB KALMBACH is the coauthor of *Because I Said Forever: Embracing Hope in a Not-So-Perfect Marriage* and the author of a children's book, *Corey's Dad Drinks Too Much*. She is a vibrant and engaging speaker who gives hope and practical solutions to those who struggle with difficult relationships. Deb and her husband, Randy, make their home in Winthrop, Washington.

NANCY KENNEDY is an editor, feature writer and columnist for the *Citrus County Chronicle*. Her features have won several first place Excellence in Religious Writing awards from the Florida Press Club. Her books include *Praying With Women of the Bible* (Zondervan), *Between Two Loves* (Zondervan) and *When Perfect Isn't Enough* (Random House). Nancy and her husband live in Florida.

CAROL KENT is a popular writer, highly requested speaker and the president of Speak Up Speaker Services, a Christian speakers' bureau. She has numerous books to her credit including *When I Lay My Isaac Down* (NavPress) and *Becoming a Women of Influence* (NavPress). Carol lives with her husband, Gene, in Port Huron, Michigan.

ROSALIE KRUSEMARK is a freelance editor based in Minnesota.

MARY ANN LACKLAND is the founder and CEO of Fluency, specializing in communications consulting and fulfillment for ministries and nonprofits. She is a contributing author/editor of more than 60 published titles.

ANNE GRAHAM LOTZ, daughter of Billy and Ruth Graham, is the president and executive director of AnGeL Ministries, a nonprofit organization offering Christian outreach. Anne has spoken on all seven continents in more than 20 foreign countries. She has written many books, including *Just Give Me Jesus (Thomas Nelson)*, and *I Saw the Lord* (Zondervan). Anne and her husband, Daniel, reside in Raleigh, North Carolina.

KATHI MACIAS is a former pastor and counselor. She is a full-time writer/editor who has authored 17 books, as well as numerous short stories and magazine articles. Kathi is a mother and a grandmother and lives in Southern California with her husband, Al.

MARTHA MANIKAS-FOSTER served as the acquisitions editor of the first *Women's Devotional Bible*, and her writing has appeared in several national magazines. A radio announcer for the *Family Life Network*, Martha lives in western New York State with her husband, David, and their children, Connie and Peter.

SALLY MARCEY, a licensed clinical professional counselor and a licensed marriage and family therapist, is the author of two children's books: *The Underground Railroad* and *The Silverlake*

Stranger. She has contributed to works such as the *Soul Care Bible* and the *True Identity Bible*. She has worked in church ministry for the past 30 years, has been married for 34 years and has two grown children.

JANET HOLM MCHENRY is the author of 19 books and speaks about developing a stronger life of prayer. She has helped thousands across the country begin the practice of devotional prayerwalking. Her books include *PrayerWalk, Prayer Changes Teens: How to Parent From Your Knees* and *PrayerStreaming: Staying in Touch With God All Day Long*.

JUDY GORDON (MORROW) employs her love of words as a writer, speaker and editor. She has written books ranging from the topic of pregnancy loss to the theme of "Life's too short . . ." She also writes poetry, song lyrics and children's books. Judy has three grown sons and lives in the charming mountain town of Quincy, California.

LINDA NATHAN is the president of Logos Word Designs, Inc., a Christian writing, editing and marketing service. She writes and teaches with her husband Richard in an apologetics ministry and is the author of *The Dark Side of Karate*.

SARAH OVERTURF lives in Longmont, Colorado, with her husband and three children. She enjoys hiking and camping with her family, getting lost in a good story and taking moonlit walks with her dog.

STACEY PADRICK is the author of *Living With Mystery: Finding God in the Midst of Unanswered Questions*. As a writer, speaker and spiritual director, she loves to encourage women in their faith. She's written numerous articles for *Discipleship Journal, PRAY!, Today's Christian Women, The Upper Room* and more. She and her husband are about to adopt their first child.

TABITHA PLUEDDEMANN writes for freelance, as well as for the mission organization, SIM International. She lives in Charlotte, North Carolina, with her husband, Danny, and their son.

WHITNEY PROSPERI has a heart for teen girls. She is the author of *Life Style: Real Perspectives from Radical Women in the Bible* and *Girls Ministry 101*.

AMBER RAE has contributed to many Bible projects including *True Images* and *True Identity*. She is the author of the *True Images Devotional*. Amber leads her church's ladies ministry and is the mother of three small children.

RHONDA RHEA is the author of *Who Put the Cat in the Fridge* and other insanely funny books, including *I'm Dreaming of Some White Chocolate*. She is a radio personality and humor columnist and speaks at conferences and events nationwide. Rhonda lives in the St. Louis area with her pastor/husband and their five children.

PENNY PIERCE ROSE loves to study and teach God's Word. She has authored *A Garden of Friends* and coauthored the award-winning Bible study *Pathway to God's Treasure: Ephesians, Pathway to God's Plan: Ruth and Esther*, and *Pathway to Living Faith: James*. She is at home in Albuquerque, New Mexico, with her husband and three teens.

MAGGIE WALLEM ROWE is a speaker, dramatist, communications instructor and freelance writer who has contributed to a number of devotional Bibles for women and families. Maggie and her husband, Mike, a pastor, make their home in Wheaton, Illinois, where they serve First Baptist Church.

EDITH SCHAEFFER is the widow of philosopher Dr. Francis Schaeffer. Together they founded L'Abri Fellowship, an international study center and Christian community in

Switzerland. She has written many books including *L'Abri* (Crossway), *The Hidden Art of Homemaking* (Tyndale) and *A Celebration of Children* (Tyndale).

BETSY SCHMITT has worked with The Livingstone Corporation since 1999. She is an editor and writer who also heads up the New Product Development team for Livingstone. She is author of *Sticky Situations, Sticky Situations 2, The Big Book of Bible Fun* and the recently released *Trivia Twist Devotions.*

PRISCILLA EVANS SHIRER is the daughter of noted pastor, speaker and author Dr. Tony Evans and Lois Evans. Priscilla has been featured on Focus on the Family and is a corporate trainer with the Zig Ziglar Corporation. She hosts television and radio programs across the nation and speaks for major corporations and Christian audiences. She and her husband, Jerry, live in Dallas, Texas, with their young son.

CAROL SMITH is a writer and songwriter living in Nashville. She's the author of *Stranger Online*, a teen novel for girls, and contributes regularly to Bibles and Bible study products.

HANNAH WHITALL SMITH (1832–1911) was born into a strict Quaker home in Philadelphia and became a major influence in the Holiness movement of the late nineteenth century. Besides *The Christian's Secret of a Happy Life* (Baker), Smith also wrote *The God of All Comfort* (Moody).

ELISA STANFORD works as a writer and editor with Edit Resource in Colorado. She is the author of *Ordinary Losses: Naming the Graces That Shape Us.*

KAY MARSHALL STROM is the author of 31 books. She is also a sought-after speaker for conferences, retreats and special events. More and more her writing and speaking are taking her to countries around the world.

LUCI SWINDOLL is author of *Celebrating Life* and a co-author of various Women of Faith devotionals. She has served as a business executive of Mobil Oil Corporation and as vice president with Insight for Living. She lives in Palm Desert, California.

JONI EARECKSON TADA is the founder of Joni and Friends, an organization accelerating Christian outreach in the disability community that numbers 610 million people worldwide. Joni is also an artist and the author of numerous best-selling books, including *Diamonds in the Dust, More Precious Than Silver*, the Platinum award-winning *Joni, Heaven: Your Real Home, When God Weeps* and *The God I Love.*

ASHLEY TAYLOR is an editor with The Livingstone Corporation based outside Chicago, IL. Ashley has contributed to Bible projects such as *The Serendipity Study Bible, True Images*, and *True Identity.*

MOTHER TERESA OF CALCUTTA (1910–1997) is known around the globe for her indefatigable work on behalf of the poor, the sick and the dying. She devoted her life to giving hope to the hopeless in more than 120 countries. In 1979 she was awarded the Nobel Peace Prize for her work, and she continued to work faithfully until her death in 1997.

LINDA TAYLOR is the editorial director for The Livingstone Corporation based outside Chicago, IL. Linda is the author of *Does God Care if I Can't Pay My Bills?* and was a contributing editor to *The Life Application Study Bible.*

JESSICA THOMAS is a writer and exiled Southerner living in the great industrial towns of the Northeast and Midwest. Her reviews have appeared in the *Yale Review of Books*, the *New York Times Book Review* and the *Chattanooga Pulse.*

NANETTE THORSEN-SNIPES is a Georgia-based freelance writer and editor. She's published articles in more than 50 print magazines, including *Home Life*, *Mature Living*, and Focus on the Family's *Clubhouse*. She has published stories in more than 30 compilation books, including *Soul Matters*, *God's Way* and *Stories for the Heart* series. She is a freelance editor with The Christian PEN.

CYNTHIA ULRICH TOBIAS is founder and CEO of AppLe St. (Applied Learning Styles) and coordinates education and commerce programs throughout North America and internationally. She is a speaker and the best-selling author of several books including *I Hate School: How to Help Your Child Love Learning* (Zondervan), *Every Child Can Succeed* (Tyndale) and *Redefining the Strong-Willed Woman* (Zondervan). She lives near Seattle, Washington.

SHEILA WALSH is a speaker, author, singer and television talk show host. She is the author or coauthor of several books including *Honestly* (Zondervan), *Living Fearlessly* (Zondervan) and *Extraordinary Faith: God's Perfect Gift for Every Woman's Heart* (Thomas Nelson). She is also the creator of Children of Faith and the *Gnoo Zoo* (Thomas Nelson), a ministry to children that communicates God's love for them.

KARLA WARKENTIN is the author of the *Time-Stone Travelers* series for children (Cook Communications) and a student at Providence Theological Seminary. She draws her mission statement from Psalm 71: to "declare his power to the next generation, his might to all who are to come." Karla lives in Manitoba, Canada, with her husband and three children.

THELMA WELLS, a college professor at Master's Divinity School and Graduate School, was the first black woman to become assistant vice president of a commercial bank. She organized her own international speaking and consulting company, receiving the Small Business Administration's Entrepreneur of the Year Award, and implemented a national mentoring program for women in ministry. Thelma wrote *Listen Up Honey: Good News for Your Soul* (Thomas Nelson) and *Girl, Have I Got Good News for You* (Thomas Nelson).

CHRISTINE WYRTZEN is the founder and director of Daughters of Promise. Christine has been in ministry 28 years, has released 15 albums, as well as two books. Her daily radio program Daughters of Promise, can be heard each weekday on over 500 stations.

Subject Index

THE NIV *Women's* DEVOTIONAL BIBLE

General Editor
Penny Pierce Rose

Managing Editor
Ashley Taylor

Project Management and Editorial
Shari Vanden Berg

Editorial Assistance
Amy Ballor
Elisabeth Banks
Natalie Block
Mary Horner Collins
Ruth DeJager
Donna Huisjen
Mary Larsen

Production Management
Jake Barton
Phil Herich
Will Reaves

Art Direction
Jamie DeBruyn
Ron Huizinga
Kirk Lutrell

Cover Design
Brand Navigation and Jamie DeBruyn

Interior Design
Kirk Lutrell

Proofreading
Peachtree Editorial and Proofreading Service, Peachtree, GA

Interior Typesetting
The Livingstone Corporation, Carol Stream, IL
Kathy Ristow and Tom Ristow

Guarantee

We want to make sure you're satisfied with the quality of your purchase, and we stand behind the quality of all Zondervan Bibles. That's why we guarantee them for a lifetime against manufacturing defects. For more information on our quality guarantee and product care instructions, visit us at www.zondervan.com.

Care

We suggest loosening the binding of your new Bible by gently pressing on a small section of pages at a time from the center. To ensure against breakage of the spine, it is best not to bend the cover backward around the spine or to carry study notes, church bulletins, pens, etc. inside the cover. Because a felt-tipped marker will "bleed" through the pages, we recommend use of a ballpoint pen or pencil to underline favorite passages. Your Bible should not be exposed to excessive heat, cold or humidity. Protecting the gold or silver edges of the paper from moisture will avoid spotting, streaking or fading.